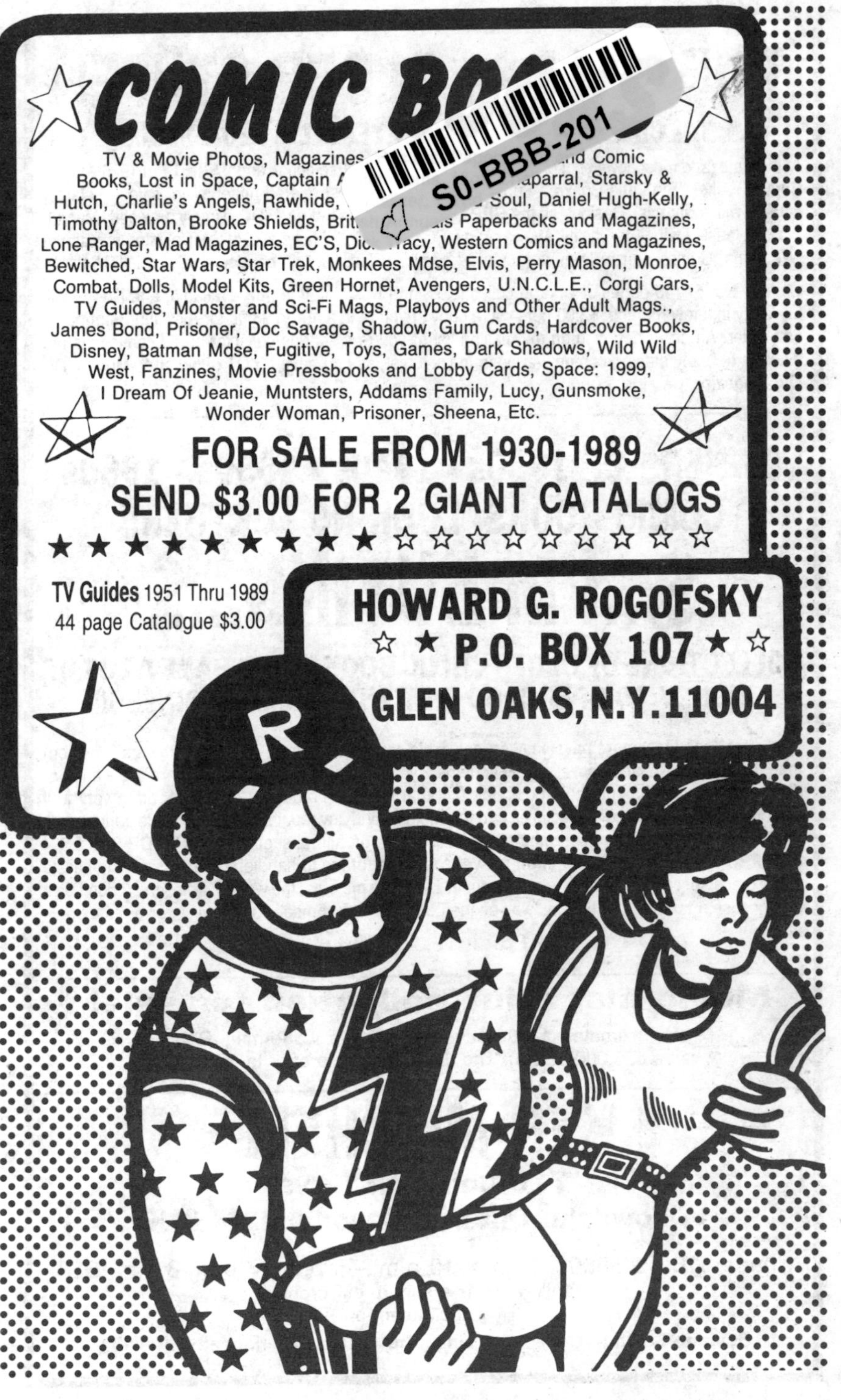
COMIC BOO
S0-BBB-201
TV & Movie Photos, Magazines ... and Comic
Books, Lost in Space, Captain ... aparral, Starsky &
Hutch, Charlie's Angels, Rawhide, ... Soul, Daniel Hugh-Kelly,
Timothy Dalton, Brooke Shields, Brit... Paperbacks and Magazines,
Lone Ranger, Mad Magazines, EC'S, Dic... racy, Western Comics and Magazines,
Bewitched, Star Wars, Star Trek, Monkees Mdse, Elvis, Perry Mason, Monroe,
Combat, Dolls, Model Kits, Green Hornet, Avengers, U.N.C.L.E., Corgi Cars,
TV Guides, Monster and Sci-Fi Mags, Playboys and Other Adult Mags.,
James Bond, Prisoner, Doc Savage, Shadow, Gum Cards, Hardcover Books,
Disney, Batman Mdse, Fugitive, Toys, Games, Dark Shadows, Wild Wild
West, Fanzines, Movie Pressbooks and Lobby Cards, Space: 1999,
I Dream Of Jeanie, Muntsters, Addams Family, Lucy, Gunsmoke,
Wonder Woman, Prisoner, Sheena, Etc.
FOR SALE FROM 1930-1989
SEND $3.00 FOR 2 GIANT CATALOGS
TV Guides 1951 Thru 1989
44 page Catalogue $3.00
HOWARD G. ROGOFSKY
P.O. BOX 107
GLEN OAKS, N.Y. 11004
R

# THE OFFICIAL® OVERSTREET Comic Book PRICE GUIDE 1991- 1992

**21st Edition**

**BOOKS FROM 1900—PRESENT INCLUDED**
**CATALOGUE & EVALUATION GUIDE—ILLUSTRATED**

**By**
**Robert M. Overstreet**

**SPECIAL CONTRIBUTORS TO THIS EDITION**

Harry Thomas, Bruce Hamilton, Tom Inge,
and Gary Carter

**SPECIAL ADVISORS TO THIS EDITION**

*Bruce Hamilton *Hugh O'Kennon *Ron Pussell *Gary M. Carter
*Walter Wang *John Snyder *Terry Stroud *Jon Warren
*Dan Malan *Steve Geppi *Gary Colabuono *Jay Maybruck
*Joe Vereneault *James Payette *Harry Matetsky *Harry Thomas
*Jerry Weist *John Verzyl *Joe Mannarino *Stephen Fishler

THE HOUSE OF COLLECTIBLES
NEW YORK, NEW YORK 10022

*Important Notice.* All of the information, including valuations, in this book has been compiled from the most reliable sources, and every effort has been made to eliminate errors and questionable data. Nevertheless, the possibility of error, in a work of such immense scope, always exists. The publisher will not be held responsible for losses which may occur in the purchase, sale, or other transaction of items because of information contained herein. Readers who feel they have discovered errors are invited to write and inform us, so they may be corrected in subsequent editions.



Published by the House of Collectibles and distributed to the book trade by Ballantine Books, a division of Random House, Inc., New York and simultaneously in Canada by Random House of Canada Limited, Toronto.

Published and distributed to the collectors' market by Overstreet Publications, Inc., 780 Hunt Cliff Dr. N.W., Cleveland, TN 37311.

Manufactured in the United States of America

Cover Illustration by Alex Schomburg.

ISBN 0-876-37859-9
ISSN 0891-8872
10 9 8 7 6 5 4 3 2 1

21st Edition

## TABLE OF CONTENTS

## ACKNOWLEDGEMENTS

Larry Bigman (Frazetta-Williamson data); Glenn Bray (Kurtzman data); Dan Malan & Charles Heffelfinger (Classic Comics data); Gary Carter (DC data); J. B. Clifford Jr. (E. C. data); Gary Coddington (Superman data); Wilt Conine (Fawcett data); Dr. S. M. Davidson (Cupples & Leon data); Al Dellinges (Kubert data); Kevin Hancer (Tarzan data); Charles Heffelfinger and Jim Ivey (March of Comics listing); R. C. Holland and Ron Pussell (Seduction and Parade of Pleasure data); Grant Irwin (Quality data); Richard Kravitz (Kelly data); Phil Levine (giveaway data); Fred Nardelli (Frazetta data); Michelle Nolan (love comics); Mike Nolan (MLJ, Timely, Nedor data); George Olshevsky (Timely data); Don Rosa (Late 1940s to 1950s data); Richard Olson (LOA & R. F. Outcault data); Scott Pell ('50s data); Greg Robertson (National data); Frank Scigliano (Little Lulu data); Gene Seger (Buck Rogers data); Rick Sloane (Archie data); David R. Smith, Archivist, Walt Disney Productions (Disney data); Don and Maggie Thompson (Four Color listing); Mike Tiefenbacher & Jerry Sinkovec (Atlas and National data); Raymond True (Classic Comics data); Jim Vadeboncoeur Jr. (Williamson and Atlas data); Kim Weston (Disney and Barks data); Cat Yronwode (Spirit data); Andrew Zerbe and Gary Behymer (M. E. data).

My appreciation must also be extended to Don Maris, John Snyder, Steve Geppi, Bruce Hamilton, Harry Thomas, Gary Carter, and especially to Hugh and Louise O'Kennon for their support and help. Special acknowledgement is also given to Ron Pussell, Ken Mitchell, Michelle Nolan, Garth Wood, Terry Stroud, and Jeremy Dollar for submitting corrective data; to Dr. Richard Olson for rewriting grading definitions; to Larry Breed for his suggestions on re-organizing the introductory section; to Dan Malan for revamping the Classics section; to Terry Stroud, Ron Pussell, Hugh O'Kennon, Jon Warren, Dave Smith, Rod Dyke, Jay Maybruck, Joe Vereneault, James Payette, John Snyder, Gary Carter, Rick Sloane, Stephen Fishler, Jerry Weist, Walter Wang, Steve Geppi, Harley Yee, Joe Mannarino, John Verzyl, Gary Colabuono, Dave Anderson (Okla.) and Dave Anderson (VA.)(pricing); to Tom Inge for his "Chronology of the American Comic Book;" to Harry Thomas and Gary Carter for their entertaining article; to Alex Schomburg for his inspired cover art; to Landon Chesney and Dave Noah for their work on the key comic book list; to L. B. Cole, Steve Saffel, and Jerry DeFuccio for their counsel and help; to Bill Spicer and Zetta DeVoe (Western Publishing Co.) for their contribution of data; and especially to Bill for his kind permission to reprint portions of his and Jerry Bails' **America's Four Color Pastime**; and to Walter Presswood, Dave Noah, and Jeff Overstreet for their help in editing this volume.

I will always be indebted to Jerry Bails, Landon Chesney, Bruce Hamilton and Larry Bigman whose advice and concern have helped in making **The Comic Book Price Guide** a reality; to my wife Martha for her encouragement and help in putting this reference work together; and to everyone who placed ads in this edition.

Acknowledgement is also due to the following people who have so generously contributed much needed data for this edition:

John Q. Adams
Dave Anderson (VA)
Dave Anderson (OK)
Stephen Baer
Tim Barnes
John Bayers
Lauren Becker
Jon S. Berk
John Binder, M.D.
Jeff Birkel
James A. Bowshier
Ron Briggs
John Brillhart
Shannon Burns
Bill Clark
Jeffrey Clark
Kurt Cooper
Bob Craig
Sterling Dashiell
Jeff Dicken
Larry Doucet
Clayton Emery
Bruce G. Fabian
Joe Frank
Phil Gaudino
Grant Geissman
Michael Goldstein
David S. Gordon
Michael J. Gronsky
Paul G. Hammond
Prentice Hammond
Leonora Harper
Anton Hermus
Fred Himes
Carl Horak
D. W. Howard

Paul Howley
Bill Hutchison
Ken Kaake
Gary Kirkland
Richard L. Kolkman, Jr.
A. M. J. Kristel
Dan Kurdilla
Grant Lambert
John Lemaire
James LeMay
Neil Lentz
Dan D. Long
Tom Mackie
Gregory Z. Manos
James P. McLoughlin
Karl Mehring
Jon Merrill
Bruce L. Miller
Harry Miller
Wayne Mills
Ken Mitchell
Bob Myers

John Newberry
Don Norrid
Emil J. Novak
Ben O'Callaghan, Jr.
Stephen O'Day
Hugh O'Kennon
Frank A. Paul
George Poulios
Brian Powell
Dave Puckett
Thomas F. Quirk
Julio F. Reis, Jr.
Sven Restel
Berkley M. Rice
Andrew Roazen
Charlie Roberts
Rafel Ruiz
William K. Schoch
George Schwartz
Randall W. Scott
Sergei S. Scurfield
Michael Secula

Paul Shedd
Eddie Shock
Robert J. Simpson
James Smith, Jr.
David Sorochty
(Dick Tracy data)
William Neal Stacy
Mark Steel
Brett Sterling-Greene
Ray Storch
Tom Struck
Marcus D. Swayze
Steve Thompson
Mike Tickal
Bill Tighe
Jim Valentino
John K. Vavra
Jerome Wenker
Randall Wiggins
Gary Woloszyn
Garth Wood

## PREFACE

Comic book values listed in this reference work were recorded from convention sales, dealers' lists, adzines, and by special contact with dealers and collectors from coast to coast. Prices paid for rare comics vary considerably from one locale to another. We have attempted to list a realistic average between the lowest and highest range observed. The reader should keep in mind that the prices listed only reflect the market just prior to publication. Any new trends that have developed since the preparation of this book would not be shown.

The values listed are based on reports where ever possible. Each new edition of the guide is actually an average report of sales that occurred during the year; not an estimate of what we feel the books will be bringing next year. Even though many prices listed will remain current throughout the year, the wise user of this book would keep abreast of current market trends to get the fullest potential out of his invested dollar.

By the same token, many of the scarcer books are seldom offered for sale in top condition. This makes it difficult to arrive at a realistic market value. Some of the issues in this category are: Action #1, All-American #16, Batman #1, Large Feature Comic #20, Captain America #1, Captain Marvel #1, Detective #27, Double Action #2, the No-# Feature Books, Green Giant #1, March of Comics #4, Marvel #1, More Fun #52, Famous Funnies #1s, Superman #1, Whiz #2 (#1), Amazing Man #5, New Fun #1, and Wow #1.

Some rare comics were published in a complete black and white format; i.e., All-New #15, Blood Is the Harvest, Boy Explorers #2, Eerie #1, If the Devil Would Talk, Is This Tomorrow, Flash #1, Thrill #1 and Stuntman #3. As we have learned in the case of Eerie #1, the collector or investor in these books would be well advised to give due consideration to the possibility of counterfeits before investing large sums of money.

This book is the most comprehensive listing of newsstand comic books ever attempted. Comic book titles, dates of first and last issues, publishing companies, origin and special issues are listed when known.

The Guide will be listing only American comic books due to space limitation. Some variations of the regular comic book format will be listed. These basically include those pre-1933 comic strip reprint books with varying size—usually with cardboard covers, but sometimes with hardback. As forerunners of the modern comic book format, they deserve to be listed despite their obvious differences in presentation. Other books that will be listed are key black and white comics of the 1980s, giveaway comics—but only those that contain known characters, work by known collectible artists, or those of special interest.

All titles are listed as if they were one word, ignoring spaces, hyphens and apostrophes. Page counts listed will always include covers.

IMPORTANT. Prices listed in this book are in U. S. currency and are for your reference only. This book is not a dealer's price list, although some dealers may base their prices on the values listed. The true value of any comic book is what you are willing to pay. Prices listed herein are an indication of what collectors (not dealers) would probably pay. For one reason or another, these collectors might want certain books badly, or else need specific issues to complete their runs and so are willing to pay more. Dealers are not in a position to pay the full prices listed, but work on a percentage depending largely on the amount of investment required and the quality of material offered. Usually they will pay from 20 to 70 percent of the list price depending on how long it will take them to sell the collection after making the investment; the higher the demand and better the condition, the more the percentage. Most dealers are faced with expenses such as advertising, travel, telephone and mailing, rent, employee salaries, plus convention costs. These costs all go in before the books are sold. The high demand books usually sell right away but there are many other titles that are difficult to sell due to low demand. Sometimes a dealer will have cost tied up in this type of material for several years before finally moving it. Remember, his position is that of handling, demand and overhead. Most dealers are victims of these economics.

**Black and White comics of the 1980s**: In recent years an explosion of new comic book titles has occurred in the direct market. Since many of these books are produced in an inexpensive black & white format, anyone today can become a publisher of comic books; the result has been dozens of new publishers and hundreds of new titles entering the market place. The quality of these publications vary from very poor to excellent. THE PRICE GUIDE'S POSITION: In the past, we have attempted to list all newsstand comic books that qualified for listing. Today, with the advent of the new formatted black and whites, consideration must be given for their inclusion, but obviously all cannot or should not be listed. Just because someone puts out a black and white comic out of their basement does not mean that we should acknowledge its existence in this book. However, there are many collectible and important titles that should and have been listed in this edition. The selection of titles to list was made by our panel of advisors who send in pricing information for the Updates. Of course a much better coverage of these books will be made in the bi-monthly Updates throughout the year.

## GRADING COMIC BOOKS

Before a comic book's true value can be assessed, its condition or state of preservation must be determined. In all comic books the better the condition the more desirable and valuable the book. Comic books in MINT condition will bring several times the price of the same book in POOR condition. Therefore it is very important to be able to properly grade your books. Comics should be graded from the inside out, so the following steps should be taken to properly grade a comic book:

**1. Check inside pages**. Gently open the comic to the centerfold (except for annuals) and let it lay in the cup of your hand. Check the condition of the paper for suppleness, whiteness/browning/brittleness. Smell paper for freshness/acidity. If the book is brittle or too brown, you may not want to go further; especially check along the spine and outer edges for browning/brittleness. If the paper looks o.k., then proceed and check the following: Centerfold for tightness and secured staples (centerfolds are sometimes replaced from other books—check for trimming and color variations from rest of book); tears or chunks missing from the inside pages; missing pages (count pages); edges for possible trimming (trimmed book edges appear whiter and flatter than normal); soiling, water marks, tape, crayoning, inking or pencilling; repairs, gluing and paper replacement; panels, coupons or pages cut out.

**2. Check inside covers**. Check the condition of the inside cover paper for suppleness, whiteness/browning/brittleness. Look for unusual whiteness compared to other pages in the book which may indicate the book has been bleached. Look for tears, chunks missing, paper replacement, tear repairs, tape, writing, dirt, water marks, soiling or any noticeable defect that would detract from the grading. Let light reflect off the surface of the cover and check cover edges for pieces replaced.

**3. Check inside spine**. Check the entire area along the spine, especially where the cover is attached. Look for spine splitting, loose staples that have pulled through the cover, cover & spine paper replacement, tear repairs, gluing, tape repairs, staple reinforcement, recoloring bleed-through from front, spine reinforcement, bleaching or any other noticeable defect.

**4. Check outside spine**. Check spine for tightness, proper folding (centering & rolled spine), proper stapling and condition of spine corners. Spine corners are easily damaged, so look for rubbing, pieces missing and splitting. Check spine for stress lines and determine the number of stress lines along the spine. Check staple areas for tear repair, recoloring, reinforcement and staple replacement (replaced staples should match the originals as closely as possible) (fraying around staple holes may indicate that the staples had been removed at one time). Look for splitting, paper replacement, recoloring, sewing holes, gluing, tape, soiling, pieces missing or any other defect that would detract from the grade.

**5. Check outside covers**. Here is where the slightest amount of wear and abuse really shows. The outside appearance of covers subjectively affects grading more than anything else, although inside condition must influence the final grade given a book. Remember, a mint cover with brittle insides is still a brittle book! Check for squareness of trim, sharpness of edges and corners, amount of gloss, color fading, centering and proper placement of staples and centering of cover art. Look for defects such as subscription creases, other creases, tears, corners missing, chips, color flakes, folds, holes, yellowing, soiling, rubbing, writing, color touch-up, paper replacement, tape, retrimming or anything else that would detract from the grade.

After all the above steps have been taken, then the reader can begin to consider an overall grade for his or her book. The grading of a comic book is done by simply looking at the book and describing its condition, which may range from absolutely perfect newsstand condition (MINT) to extremely worn, dirty, and torn (POOR).

**Note on understanding terminologies and descriptions:** A flaw that is permitted in a higher grade is also permitted in all lower grades, even though the flaw may not be mentioned again in lower grade descriptions. A flaw that is not permitted in a higher grade, but is not noted as being not permitted in the next lower grade, is permitted in that grade and all lower grades. For example, if VF cannot have yellowish pages, but FN does not exclude yellowish pages as a defect, then yellowish pages are allowed in that grade and all lower grades below it.

When a book is described as simply FVF condition, you can expect a book that does not fall abnormally outside of the FVF grade description. When a book is graded as FVF and described as having a 1'' spine split, this means that there is a defect which is not allowed in the FVF grade that is present in this copy, otherwise the appearance of the book is a standard FVF copy. In such case, the value of the book should be reduced to reflect the defect.

Numerous variables (as outlined above) influence the evaluation of a comic's condition and **all** must be considered in the final evaluation. As grading is the most subjective aspect of determining a comic's value, it is very important that the grader must be careful and not allow wishful thinking to influence what the eyes see. It is also very important to realize that older comics in MINT condition are extremely scarce and are rarely advertised for sale; most of the higher grade comics advertised range from VERY FINE to NEAR MINT. To the novice grading will appear difficult at first; but, as experience is gained accuracy will improve. Whenever in doubt, consult with a reputable dealer or experienced collector in your area. The following grading guide is given to aid the collector.

## RESTORED COMICS:

Many rare and expensive books are being restored by professionals and amateurs. After restoration, these books are not actually higher grades, but are altered lower grade books. It has been brought to our attention that some dealers have been selling these books to unsuspecting collectors/investors—without telling them of the restoration. In some cases these restored books are being priced the same as unrestored books. **Very Important:** Use the guidelines above to examine books very closely for repairing or restoration before purchase. The more expensive the book, the greater the likelihood of restoration. Major things to look for are: bleaching, whitening, trimming, interior spine and tear reinforcement, gluing, restapling, missing pieces replaced, wrinkles pressed out of covers, recoloring and reglossing covers. Dealers should state that a book has been restored and not expect to get as much as a book unrestored in that condition would bring. Any kind of restoration is considered a defect from the original condition of the book, and should affect value from slight to large depending on what is done. A minor ¼ inch tear on a book would not change the value whether it is mended or not.

## DETERMINING THE VALUE OF RESTORED/REPAIRED COMICS

Restored/repaired books do have a place in the market as well as a collector's value. The most important factor concerning value is the eye-appeal of the finished comic after the work has been done. **Professional** work (which is always reversible) obviously would be less damaging to a book than unskilled work, and would enhance the value somewhat over its unrestored value. **Minor restoration** or repair such as one or two tiny color specks added or a ¼ inch tear (mended or unmended) may reduce the grade by ¼. However, on rare books, the value may not necessarily be affected.

**General restoration**, such as roll spine removal, cover cleaning, staple mending, one inch or less tear reinforcement, etc. may drop the grade and value from ½ to a full grade if the book is otherwise in a high grade. If the book is in a good or very good grade, the value drop would be much less — zero to ¼.

**More serious defects** that are restored are bleaching, one inch and larger pieces replacement, complete spine mending & or recoloring, cover reglossing, cover recoloring, cover creases pressed out, etc. Otherwise higher grade books may drop by 2 - 4 grades where lower grades may drop by 1 - 2 grades. Remember, the lower the grade, the more defects are accepted.

## GRADING DEFINITIONS

The hardest part of evaluating a comic is being honest and objective with yourself, and knowing what characteristics to look for in making your assessment.

**VERY IMPORTANT:** A book must be graded in its entirety, considering all defects, fairly and honestly. Do not grade just the cover alone. A book in any of the grades listed must be in **ORIGINAL UNRESTORED** condition. **Restored books** must be described as such. The value of an extensively restored book may improve slightly from its original unrestored state. After examining these characteristics a comic may be assigned to one of the following grades:

**NOTE:** Tiny—1/16" or less; Small—1/8" or less; Minor—¼" or less; Light—½" or less.
**Eye-appeal:** The final grade given any book is determined by how appealing the book appears to the eye. Therefore, defects to the back cover affect the grade less than the same defects to the front cover. A final grade is the sum of all positive and negative aspects of a book. Since eye-appeal is subjective, grading is an art and not a science. Defects that disturb one collector may not be a factor to another. Use these grading guidelines as a general consensus of most knowledgable collectors and dealers.

**MINT (M):** Absolutely perfect in every way, regardless of age. No printing defects are allowed. The cover has full original gloss, is crisp, cut square with sharp corners and shows no imperfections of any sort. Minute color fading is allowed. The cover and all pages are creamy white and fresh; the spine is tight, flat, and clean with no stress lines; not even the slightest blemish can be detected around staples, along spine and edges or at corners. Arrival dates pencilled on the cover are usually acceptable so long as they are very small. When the surface of the front and back covers is held to the light, not the slightest wear, indentations, wrinkles or defects of any kind can be observed. As comics must be truly perfect to be in this grade, they are obviously extremely scarce and seldom are offered for sale. Books prior to 1970 in this grade can and usually do bring above guide prices.

**NEAR MINT (NM):** Nearly perfect. Upon close inspection, one or possibly two very tiny imperfections can be found. Often these imperfections are noticed only when holding the surface of the front and back covers under bright light. Possibly a tiny (1/16th inch) color flake missing at a staple, corner or edge. Or, a tiny (1/16th inch) spine tear is permitted if no other defects are observed. No crease of any kind. Near perfect cover gloss retained. Not more than three very tiny stress lines along the spine may be present. Pages and covers should be creamy to white, not yellow or brown. No color touch-up, repair or restoration of any kind is allowed in this grade. No printing defects are allowed. This grade is also very rare in books prior to 1970.

**VERY FINE-NEAR MINT (VFNM):** Beautiful, glossy and excellent in every way with only minor imperfections that keep it out of the higher grades. One tiny corner crease of less than 1/8th inch length is allowed. Up to 6 tiny (1/16th inch) stress lines along the spine are acceptable if the eye appeal of the book is not seriously affected. Pages should be creamy at least. A common defect in this grade is a tiny spine tear at the upper or lower spine not greater than 1/16th inch in length. One or no more than two tiny tears (1/16th inch) are permitted in this grade. An extremely tiny tear repair, microscopic dot color touch-up, unobtrusive arrival date erasure or other similar invisible alterations, on an otherwise perfect copy, is permitted in this grade.

**VERY FINE (VF):** An excellent copy with outstanding eye-appeal. Sharp, bright, clean and glossy with supple pages. Slight wear beginning to show; possibly 5 or 6 tiny wrinkles or stress lines at staples or along spine where cover has been opened a few times; still clean and flat with 80 per cent of cover gloss retained. Pages and covers can be yellowish/tannish (at the least) but not brown and will usually be creamy to white. 4 or 5 tiny color flakes are acceptable. One ¼ inch corner crease on an otherwise exceptional copy is permitted. Very minor restoration or repair is not allowed in this grade unless it is specifically noted and described. Comics in this grade are normally the highest grade offered for sale and often books graded higher are misgraded VFs.

**FINE—VERY FINE (FVF)**—Nearly Very Fine. A sharp, clean copy but without the crispness associated with Very Fine. Pages can be slightly tannish but not brown or brittle. Up to 8 tiny stress lines along the spine or covers can be expected. Several tiny color flakes are permitted. No subscription creases or spine roll allowed. A minor printing defect is allowed. Corners may be very slightly rounded. Exceptional cover gloss remains (60 per cent or more).

**FINE (FN):** An exceptional, above-average copy that shows minor wear, but still relatively flat, clean and glossy with no subscription crease, writing on cover (except an arrival date), brown margins or tape repairs. Typical defects include: Light spine wear, minor surface wear, a light crease (¼ inch in length), minor yellowing/tanning to interior pages. Still a bright copy with 50 per cent cover gloss. A few stress lines around staples and along spine to be expected, but not more than 1/8th inch in length. One small edge chip or several tiny chips are allowed. One minor tear is allowed when on an otherwise FVF copy. Very minor spine roll allowed on an otherwise clean and uncreased copy.

**VERY GOOD (VG):** The average used comic book most commonly found. Significant wear is obvious with original printing lustre and gloss almost gone; some discoloration or fading, but not soiled. One or two minor markings on covers is permitted as is a minor spine roll. Lightly creased along spine or extremities; a subscription crease is allowed. Cover could have a minor tear or crease where a corner was folded under or a loose centerfold. A minor chip or piece missing is allowed when noted. No chunks missing. Pages and inside covers may be brown but not brittle, but would usually be yellowish to creamy. One small tape repair permitted. Still enough eye-appeal to be collectable.

**GOOD-VERY GOOD (GVG)**—A worn copy without the extreme wear associated with the lower grades. Several significant defects such as tape repairs, minor tears or long creases may be present.

**GOOD (G):** A heavily worn copy but complete. Creased, scuffed, not glossy and soiled. Although a copy in this grade could have white pages and covers, the accumulation of defects such as creases, tears or chips and general wear prevent the book from a higher classification.

**FAIR (F):** Very heavily read and soiled, but still complete. Damaged beyond collectibility for most collectors, bringing 30-50 per cent of the Good price.

**POOR (p):** Damaged; heavily weathered; soiled; or otherwise unsuited for collection purposes. Possibly incomplete or coverless; pages may be missing, bringing 15 to 25 per cent of the Good price.

**COVERLESS (c):** Coverless comics are usually hard to sell and in many cases are worthless.

**IMPORTANT NOTE:** Exceptional cases in all grades exist. The following are some exceptions for the amateur to consider:

1. Comics in all grades with fresh extra white pages are more desirable. Thus, a VG copy with white pages is worth more than the same copy with browning pages.
2. A high grade comic with a major, unusual defect should be down graded two or more grades. An example would be a NM comic which has a half inch spine split or a VF comic with brownish pages or covers.
3. Corner creases are the most commonly disputed defects. A long corner crease on a high grade book should lower the grade at least two steps.
4. A comic which appears NM or M but has brittle or flaking pages should be dropped six or more steps. A VF or better comic with brown covers or pages should be dropped at least one or more steps.
5. Other exceptional defects such as books with panels missing, coupons cut, torn or taped covers and pages, brown or brittle pages, restapled, retrimmed, taped spines, pages or covers, water-marked, printing defects, rusted staples, stained, holed, or other imperfections should be taken into consideration by the grader and the grade should be lowered several steps according to the severity of the defect.
6. In no case is a restored book ever worth the same as a book that has no restoration.

**DUST JACKETS:** Many of the early strip reprint comics were printed in hardback with dust jackets. Books with dust jackets are worth more. The value can increase from 20 to 50 percent depending on the rarity of book. Usually, the earlier the book, the greater the percentage. Unless noted, prices listed are without dust jackets. The condition of the dust jacket should be graded independently of the book itself.

## SCARCITY OF COMIC BOOKS RELATED TO GRADE

**1900-1933 Comics:** Most of these books are bound with thick cardboard covers and are very rare to non-existent in fine or better condition. Due to their extreme age, paper browning is very common. Brittleness could be a problem.

**1933-1940 Comics:** There are many issues from this period that are very scarce in any condition, especially from the early to mid-1930s. Surviving copies of any particular issue range from a handful to several hundred. Near Mint to Mint copies are virtually non-existent. Known examples of this grade are five or less copies for any particular issue. Most surviving copies are in FVF or less condition. Brittleness or browning of paper is fairly common and could be a problem.

**1941-1952 Comics:** Surviving comic books would number from less than 100 to several thousand copies of each issue. Near Mint to Mint copies are a little more common but are still relatively scarce with only a dozen or so copies in this grade existing of any particular issue. Exceptions would be recent warehouse finds of most Dell comics (6-100 copies, but usually 30 or less), and Harvey comics (1950s-1970s) surfacing. Due to low paper quality of the late 1940s and 1950s, many comics from this period are rare in Near Mint to Mint condition. Most remaining copies are VF or less. Browning of paper could be a problem.

**1953-1959 Comics:** As comic book sales continued to drop during the 1950s, production values were lowered resulting in cheaply printed comics. For this reason, high grade copies are extremely rare. Many Atlas and Marvel comics have chipping along the trimmed edges (Marvel chipping) which reduces even more the number of surviving high grade copies.

**1960-1970 Comics:** Early 60s comics are rare in Near Mint to Mint condition. Most copies of early 60s Marvels and DCs grade no higher than VF. Many early keys in NM or M exist in numbers less than 10-20 of each. Mid to late 60s books in high grade are more common due to the hoarding of comics that began in the mid-60s.

**1970-Present:** Comics of today are common in high grade. NM to M is the standard rather than the exception.

When you consider how few Golden and Silver Age books exist compared to the current market, you will begin to appreciate the true rarity of these early books. In many cases less than 5-10 copies exist of a particular issue in Near Mint to Mint condition, while most of the 1930s books do not exist in this grade at all.

### TERMINOLOGY

Many of the following terms and abbreviations are used in the comic book market and are explained here:

**a**—Story art; **a(i)**—Story art inks; **a(p)**—Story art pencils; **a(r)**—Story art reprint.

**Annual**—A book that is published yearly.

**Arrival date**—Markings on a comic book cover (usually in pencil) made by either the newsstand dealer or the distributor. These markings denote the date the book was placed on the newsstand. Usually the arrival date is one to two months prior to the cover date.

**Ashcan**—A publisher's inhouse facsimile of a proposed new title. Most ashcans have black & white covers stapled to an existing coverless comic on the inside. Other ashcans are totally black and white.

**B&W**—Black and white art.

**Bi-monthly**—Published every two months.

**Bi-weekly**—Published every two weeks.

**Bondage cover**—Usually denotes a female in bondage.

**Brittleness**—The final stage of paper deterioration.

**c**—Cover art; **c(i)**—Cover inks; **c(p)**—Cover pencils; **c(r)**—Cover reprint.

**Cameo**—When a character appears briefly in one or two panels.

**CCA**—Comics Code Authority.

**CCA seal**—An emblem that was placed on the cover of all CCA approved comics beginning in April-May, 1955.

**Centerfold**—The two folded pages in the center of a comic at the terminal end of the staples.

**Church, Edgar collection**—A large high grade comic book collection discovered by Mile High Comics in Colorado (over 22,000 books).

**Colorist**—Artist that applies color to the black and white pen and ink art.

**Comic book repair**—When a tear, loose staple or centerfold has been mended without changing or adding to the original finish of the book. Repair may involve tape, glue or nylon gossamer and is easily detected. It is considered a defect.

**Comic book restoration**—Any attempt, whether professional or amateur, to enhance the appearance of a comic book. These procedures may include any or all of the following techniques: Recoloring, adding missing paper, stain, ink, dirt, tape removal, whitening, pressing out wrinkles, staple replacement, trimming, re-glossing, etc. Note: Unprofessional work can lower the value of a book. In all cases, a restored book can never be worth the same as an unrestored book in the same condition.

**Comics Code Authority**—In 1954 the major publishers joined together and formed a committee who set up guide lines for acceptable comic contents. It was their task to approve the contents of comics before publication.

**Con**—A Convention or public gathering of fans.

**Cosmic Aeroplane**—Refers to a large collection discovered by Cosmic Aeroplane Books.

**Debut**—The first time that a character appears anywhere.

**Double cover**—An error in the binding process which results in two or more covers being bound to a single book. Multiple covers are not considered a defect.

**Drug propaganda story**—Where comic makes an editorial stand about drug abuse.

**Drug use story**—Shows the actual use of drugs: shooting, taking a trip, harmful effects, etc.

**Fanzine**—An amateur fan publication.

**File Copy**—A high grade comic originating from the publisher's file. Not all file copies are in pristine condition. Note: An arrival date on the cover of a comic does not indicate that it is a file copy.

**First app.**—Same as debut.

**Flashback**—When a previous story is being recalled.

**Four color**—A printing process in which all primary colors plus black are used. Also refers to the Four Color series published by Dell.

**Foxing**—Tiny orange-brown spots on the cover or pages of a comic book.

**G. A.**—Golden Age.

**Golden Age (G.A.)**—The period beginning with Action #1 (June, 1938) and ending with World War II in 1945.

**Headlight**—Protruding breasts.

**i**—Art inks.

**Indicia**—Publishers title, issue number, date, copyright and general information statement usually located on the inside front cover, facing page or inside back cover.

**Infinity cover**—Shows a scene that repeats itself to infinity.

**Inker**—Artist that does the inking.

**Intro**—Same as debut.

**JLA**—Justice League of America.

**JLI**—Justice League International.

**JSA**—Justice Society of America.

**Lamont Larson**—Refers to a large high grade collection of comics. Many of the books have Lamont or Larson written on the cover.

**Logo**—The title of a strip or comic book as it appears on the cover or title page.

**LSH**—Legion of Super-Heroes.

**Marvel chipping**—A defect that occurred during the trimming process of 1950s & 1960s Marvels which produced a ragged edge around the comic cover. Usually takes the form of a tiny chip or chips along the right-hand edge of the cover.

**Mile High**—Refers to a large NM-Mint collection of comics originating from Denver, Colorado (Edgar Church collection).

**nd**—No date.

**nn**—No number.

**N. Y. Legis. Comm.**—New York Legislative Committee to Study the Publication of Comics (1951).

**One-shot**—When only one issue is published of a title, or when a series is published where each issue is a different title (i.e. Four Color).

**Origin**—When the story of the character's creation is given.

**Over guide**—When a comic book is priced at a value over guide list.

**p**—Art pencils.

**Pedigree**—A book from a famous collection, e.g. Allentown, Larson, Church/Mile High, Denver, San Francisco, Cosmic Aeroplane, etc. Note: Beware of non-pedigree collections being promoted as pedigree books. Only outstanding high grade collections similar to those listed qualify.

**Penciler**—Artist that does the pencils.

**POP—Parade of Pleasure**, book about the censorship of comics.
**Post-Code**—Comic books published with the CCA seal.
**Post-Golden Age**—Comic books published between 1945 and 1950.
**Post-Silver Age**—Comic books published from 1969 to present.
**Poughkeepsie**—Refers to a large collection of Dell Comics' "file copies" believed to have originated from the warehouse of Western Publishing in Poughkeepsie, N. Y.
**Pre-Code**—Comic books published before the CCA seal.
**Pre-Golden Age**—Comic books published prior to Action #1 (June, 1938).
**Pre-Silver Age**—Comic books published between 1950 and Showcase #4 (1956).
**Printing defect**—A defect caused by the printing process. Examples would include paper wrinkling, mis-cut edges, mis-folded spine, untrimmed pages, off-registered color, off-centered trimming, mis-folded and mis-bound pages. It should be noted that these are defects that lower the grade of the book.
**Provenance**—When the owner of a book is known and is stated for the purpose of authenticating and documenting the history of the book. Example: A book from the Stan Lee or Forrest Ackerman collection would be an example of a value-adding provenance.
**Quarterly**—Published every three months (four times a year).
**R or r**—Reprint.
**Rare**—10 to 20 copies estimated to exist.
**Reprint comics**—Comic books that contain newspaper strip reprints.
**Rice paper**—A thin, transparent paper commonly used by restorers to repair tears and replace small pieces on covers and pages of comic books.
**S. A.**—Silver Age.
**Scarce**—20 to 100 copies estimated to exist.
**Silver Age**—Officially begins with Showcase #4 in 1956 and ends in 1969.
**Silver proof**—A black & white actual size print on thick glossy paper given to the colorist to indicate colors to the engraver.
**S&K**—Simon and Kirby (artists).
**SOTI—Seduction of the Innocent**, book about the censorship of comics. Refer to listing in this guide.
**Spine**—The area representing the folded and stapled part of a comic book.
**Spine roll**—A defect caused by improper storage which results in uneven pages and the shifting or bowing of the spine.
**Splash panel**—A large panel that usually appears at the front of a comic story.
**Squarebound**—A comic book glue-bound with a square spined cover.
**Stress lines**—Light, tiny wrinkles occuring along the spine, projecting from the staples or appearing anywhere on the covers of a comic book.
**Subscription crease**—A center crease caused by the folding of comic books for mailing to subscribers. This is considered a defect.
**3-D comic**—Comic art that is drawn and printed in two-color layers, producing a true 3-D effect when viewed through special glasses.
**3-D Effect comic**—Comic art that is drawn to appear 3-D, but isn't.
**Under guide**—When a comic book is priced at a value less than guide list.
**Very rare**—1 to 10 copies estimated to exist.
**Warehouse copy**—Originating from a publisher's warehouse; similar to file copy.
**X-over**—When one character crosses over into another's strip.
**Zine**—See Fanzine.

Marvel comic books are cover coded for the direct sales (comic shop), newsstand, and foreign markets. They are all first printings, with the special coding being the only difference. The comics sold to the comic shops have to be coded differently, as they are sold on a no-return basis while newsstand comics are not. The Price Guide has not detected any price difference between these versions. Currently, the difference is easily detected by looking at the front cover bar code (a box located at the lower left). The bar code is filled in for newsstand sales and is left blank or contains a character for comic shop sales. The following emblems were used in the early 1980s.

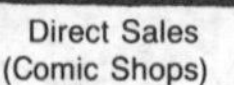

Direct Sales
(Comic Shops)

Newsstand

Newsstand
Overseas

**Marvel Reprints:** In recent years Marvel has reprinted some of their comics. There has been confusion in identifying the reprints from the originals. However, in 99 percent of the cases, the reprints have listed "reprint," or "2nd printing," etc. in the indicia, along with a later copyright date in some cases. The only known exceptions are a few of the movie books such as *Star Wars*, the *Marvel Treasury Editions*, and tie-in books such as *G. I. Joe*. These books were reprinted and not identified as reprints. The *Star Wars* reprints have a large diamond with no date and a blank UPC symbol on the cover. The other reprints had some cover variation such as a date missing, different colors, etc. Beginning in mid-1990, all Marvel 2nd printings will have a gold logo.

Gold Key and other comics were also sold with a Whitman label. There are collectors who prefer the regular labels to Whitman, although the Price Guide does not differentiate in the price. Beginning in 1980, all comics produced by Western carried the Whitman label.

Many of the better artists are pointed out. When more than one artist worked on a story, their names are separated by a (/). The first name did the pencil drawings and the second did the inks. When two or more artists work on a story, only the most prominent will be noted in some cases. We wish all good artists could be listed, but due to space limitation, only the most popular can. The following list of artists are considered to be either the most collected in the comic field or are historically significant and should be pointed out. Artists designated below with an (*) indicate that only their most noted work will be listed. The rest will eventually have all their work shown as the information becomes available. This list could change from year to year as new artists come into prominence.

Adams, Arthur
Adams, Neal
*Aparo, Jim
*Austin, Terry
Baker, Matt
Barks, Carl
Beck, C. C.
*Brunner, Frank
*Buscema, John
Byrne, John
*Check, Sid
Cole, Jack
Cole, L. B.
Craig, Johnny
Crandall, Reed
Davis, Jack
Disbrow, Jayson
*Ditko, Steve
Eisner, Will
*Elder, Bill
Evans, George
Everett, Bill
Feldstein, Al
Fine, Lou
Foster, Harold
Fox, Matt
Frazetta, Frank
*Giffen, Keith
Golden, Michael
Gottfredson, Floyd
*Guardineer, Fred
Gustavson, Paul
*Heath, Russ
Howard, Wayne
Ingels, Graham
Jones, Jeff
Kamen, Jack
Kane, Bob
*Kane, Gil
Kelly, Walt
Kinstler, E. R.
Kirby, Jack
Krenkel, Roy
Krigstein, Bernie
*Kubert, Joe
Kurtzman, Harvey
Manning, Russ
McFarland, Todd
McWilliams, Al
*Meskin, Mort
Miller, Frank
Moreira, Ruben
*Morisi, Pete
*Newton, Don
Nostrand, Howard
Orlando, Joe
Pakula, Mac
*Palais, Rudy
*Perez, George
Powell, Bob
Raboy, Mac
Raymond, Alex
Ravielli, Louis
*Redondo, Nestor
Rogers, Marshall
Schomburg, Alex
Siegel & Shuster
Simon & Kirby (S&K)
*Simonson, Walt
Smith, Barry
Smith, Paul
Stanley, John
*Starlin, Jim
Steranko, Jim
Stevens, Dave
Torres, Angelo
Toth, Alex
Tuska, George
Ward, Bill
Williamson, Al
Woggon, Bill
Wolverton, Basil
Wood, Wallace
Wrightson, Bernie

The following abbreviations are used with the cover reproductions throughout the book for copyright credit purposes. The companies they represent are listed here:

**AC**—AC Comics (Americomics)
**ACE**—Ace Periodicals
**ACG**—American Comics Group
**AJAX**—Ajax-Farrell
**AP**—Archie Publications
**ATLAS**—Atlas Comics (see below)
**AVON**—Avon Periodicals
**BP**—Better Publications
**C & L**—Cupples & Leon
**CC**—Charlton Comics
**CEN**—Centaur Publications
**CCG**—Columbia Comics Group
**CG**—Catechetical Guild
**CHES**—Harry 'A' Chesler
**CLDS**—Classic Det. Stories
**CM**—Comics Magazine
**DC**—DC Comics, Inc.
**DELL**—Dell Publishing Co.
**DH**—Dark Horse
**DMP**—David McKay Publishing
**DS**—D. S. Publishing Co.
**EAS**—Eastern Color Printing Co.
**EC**—E. C. Comics
**ECL**—Eclipse Comics
**ENWIL**—Enwil Associates
**EP**—Elliott Publications
**ERB**—Edgar Rice Burroughs
**FAW**—Fawcett Publications
**FC**—First Comics
**FF**—Famous Funnies
**FH**—Fiction House Magazines
**FOX**—Fox Features Syndicate
**GIL**—Gilberton
**GK**—Gold Key
**GP**—Great Publications
**HARV**—Harvey Publications
**HILL**—Hillman Periodicals
**HOKE**—Holyoke Publishing Co.
**KING**—King Features Syndicate
**LEV**—Lev Gleason Publications
**ME**—Magazine Enterprises
**MEG**—Marvel Ent. Group
**MLJ**—MLJ Magazines
**MS**—Mirage Studios
**NOVP**—Novelty Press
**PG**—Premier Group
**PINE**—Pines
**PMI**—Parents' Magazine Institute
**PRIZE**—Prize Publications
**QUA**—Quality Comics Group
**REAL**—Realistic Comics
**RH**—Rural Home
**S & S**—Street and Smith Publishers
**SKY**—Skywald Publications
**STAR**—Star Publications
**STD**—Standard Comics
**STJ**—St. John Publishing Co.
**SUPR**—Superior Comics
**TC**—Tower Comics
**TM**—Trojan Magazines
**TOBY**—Toby Press
**UFS**—United Features Syndicate
**VITL**—Vital Publications
**WDC**—The Walt Disney Company
**WEST**—Western Publishing Co.
**WHIT**—Whitman Publishing Co.
**WHW**—William H. Wise
**WMG**—William M. Gaines (E. C.)
**WP**—Warren Publishing Co.
**YM**—Youthful Magazines
**Z-D**—Ziff-Davis Publishing Co.

**TIMELY/MARVEL/ATLAS COMICS.** "A Marvel Magazine" and "Marvel Group" was the symbol used between December 1946 and May 1947 (not used on all titles/issues during period). The Timely Comics symbol was used between July 1942 and September 1942 (not on all titles/issues during period). The round "Marvel Comic" symbol was used between February 1949 and June 1950. Early comics code symbol (star and bar) was used between April 1952 and February 1955. The Atlas globe symbol was used between December 1951 and September 1957. The M over C symbol (beginning of Marvel Comics) was used between July 1961 until the price increased to 12 cents on February 1962.

**TIMELY/MARVEL/ATLAS Publishers' Abbreviation Codes:**

**ACI**—Animirth Comics, Inc.
**AMI**—Atlas Magazines, Inc.
**ANC**—Atlas News Co., Inc.
**BPC**—Bard Publishing Corp.
**BFP**—Broadcast Features Pubs.
**CBS**—Crime Bureau Stories
**CIDS**—Classic Detective Stories
**CCC**—Comic Combine Corp.
**CDS**—Current Detective Stories
**CFI**—Crime Files, Inc.
**CmPI**—Comedy Publications, Inc.
**CmPS**—Complete Photo Story
**CnPC**—Cornell Publishing Corp.
**CPC**—Chipiden Publishing Corp.
**CPI**—Crime Publications, Inc.
**CPS**—Canam Publishing Sales Corp.
**CSI**—Classics Syndicate, Inc.
**DCI**—Daring Comics, Inc.
**EPC**—Euclid Publishing Co.
**EPI**—Emgee Publications, Inc.
**FCI**—Fantasy Comics, Inc.
**FPI**—Foto Parade, Inc.
**GPI**—Gem Publishing, Inc.
**HPC**—Hercules Publishing Corp.
**IPS**—Interstate Publishing Corp.
**JPI**—Jaygee Publications, Inc.
**LBI**—Lion Books, Inc.
**LCC**—Leading Comic Corp.
**LMC**—Leading Magazine Corp.
**MALE**—Male Publishing Corp.
**MAP**—Miss America Publishing Corp.
**MCI**—Marvel Comics, Inc.
**MgPC**—Margood Publishing Corp.
**MjMC**—Marjean Magazine Corp.
**MMC**—Mutual Magazine Corp.
**MPC**—Medalion Publishing Corp.
**MPI**—Manvis Publications, Inc.
**NPI**—Newsstand Publications, Inc.
**NPP**—Non-Pareil Publishing Corp.
**OCI**—Official Comics, Inc.
**OMC**—Official Magazine Corp.
**OPI**—Olympia Publications, Inc.
**PPI**—Postal Publications, Inc.
**PrPI**—Prime Publications, Inc.
**RCM**—Red Circle Magazines, Inc.
**SAI**—Sports Actions, Inc.
**SePI**—Select Publications, Inc.
**SnPC**—Snap Publishing Co.
**SPC**—Select Publishing Co.
**SPI**—Sphere Publications, Inc.
**TCI**—Timely Comics, Inc.
**TP**—Timely Publications
**20 CC**—20th Century Comics Corp.
**USA**—U.S.A. Publications, Inc.
**VPI**—Vista Publications, Inc.
**WFP**—Western Fiction Publishing
**WPI**—Warwick Publications, Inc.
**YAI**—Young Allies, Inc.
**ZPC**—Zenith Publishing Co., Inc.

**YOUR INFORMATION IS NEEDED:** In order to make future Guides more accurate and complete, we are interested in any relevant information or facts that you might have. **Relevant and significant data includes:**

Works by the artists named elsewhere. **Caution:** Most artists did not sign their work and many were imitated by others. When submitting this data, advise whether the work was signed or not. In many cases, it takes an expert to identify certain artists—so extreme caution should be observed in submitting this data.

Issues mentioned by Wertham and others in **Seduction**, **Parade . . .**, origin issues, first and last appearances of strips or characters, title continuity information, beginning and ending numbers of runs, atomic bomb, Christmas, Flag and infinity covers, swipes and photo covers.

To record something in the Guide, **documented** facts are needed. Please send a photo copy of indicia or page in question if possible.

**Non-relevent data**—Most giveaway comics will not be listed. Literally thousands of titles came out, many of which have educational themes. We will only list significant collectible giveaways such as March of Comics, Disney items, communist books (but not civil defense educational comics), and books that contain illustrated stories by top artists or top collected characters.

Good Luck and Happy Hunting . . . Robert M. Overstreet

## STORAGE OF COMIC BOOKS

Acids left in comic book paper during manufacture are believed to be the primary cause of aging and yellowing, although exposure to atmospheric pollutants can be another factor. Improper storage can accelerate the aging process.

The importance of storage is proven when looking at the condition of books from large collections that have surfaced over the past few years. In some cases, an entire collection has brown or yellowed pages approaching brittleness. Collections of this type were probably stored in too much heat or moisture, or exposed to atmospheric pollution (sulfur dioxide) or light. On the other hand, other collections of considerable age (30 to 50 years) have emerged with creamy white, supple pages and little sign of aging. Thus we learn that proper storage is imperative to insure the long life of our comic book collections.

Store books in a dark, cool place with an ideal relative humidity of 50 percent and a temperature of 40 to 50 degrees or less. Air conditioning is recommended. Do not use regular cardboard boxes, since most contain harmful acids. Use acid-free boxes instead. Seal books in Mylar[1] or other suitable wrappings or bags and store them in the proper containers or cabinets, to protect them from heat, excessive dampness, ultraviolet light (use tungsten filament lights), polluted air, and dust.

Many collectors seal their books in plastic bags and store them in a cool dark room in cabinets or on shelving. Plastic bags should be changed every two to three years, since most contain harmful acids. Cedar chest storage is recommended, but the ideal method of storage is to stack your comics (preferably in Mylar[1] bags) vertically in acid-free boxes. The boxes can be arranged on shelving for easy access. Storage boxes, plastic bags, backing boards, Mylar[1] bags, archival supplies, etc. are available from dealers. (See ads in this edition.)

Some research has been done on deacidifying comic book paper, but no easy or inexpensive, clear-cut method is available to the average collector. The best and longest-lasting procedure involves soaking the paper in solutions or spraying each page with specially prepared solutions. These procedures should be left to experts. Covers of comics pose a special problem in deacidifying due to their varied composition of papers used.

Here is a list of persons who offer services in restoration or archival supplies:

—Bill Cole, P.O. Box 60, Randolph, MA 02368-0060. Archival supplies, storage protection, deacidification solutions.

—The Restoration Lab, Susan Cicconi, P.O. Box 632, New Town Branch, Boston, MA 02258.

—The Art Conservatory, Mark Wilson, P.O. Box 340, Castle Rock, WA 98611. Restoration.

—Comic Conservation Lab, Jef Hinds, P.O. Box 5L, Bakersfield, CA 93385. PH: (805) 872-8428. Restoration & preservation supplies.

—Lee Tennant Enterprises, P.O. Box 296, Worth, IL 60482. Preservation supplies.

[1]***Mylar is a registered trademark of the DuPont Company.***

## 1990 MARKET REPORT

### by Bob Overstreet[1]

Prices extended their steady upward trend during the first half of the year as the economy continued to expand. Led by huge increases in the Silver-Age area, sales remained at a brisk clip throughout the marketplace. as the second half of the year began, sales above the previously achieved highs became less frequent. With the onset of the Mideast crisis, prices began to firm up throughout the marketplace. Sell offers began to exceed want list requests for the first time in years as the economy slipped into recession.

Due to their overall scarcity, prime Silver-Age and Golden-Age books continued to show steady price increases. Since the prior year's increases were of a limited nature, one would expect little impact to prices in the event of a short recession. Rather one would expect a firming of prices in the short term with limited growth in the most popular areas. When the economy begins to rebound with a new expansion, prices in the comic marketplace should again resume their strong upward direction.

[1]*With helpful assistance from Steve Geppi, Hugh O'Kennon, Ron Pussell, Jay Maybruck, Joe Vereneault, Dan Malan, Rick Sloane, John Snyder, Terry Stroud, Gary Colabuono, Walter Wang, James Payette, Jon Warren, Stephen Fishler, Harry Thomas, Bruce Hamilton, John Verzyl, Gary Carter, Mark Wilson and Joe Mannarino.*

Collectables in general continued to appreciate despite a tightening economy at year's end. Toys, original art, autographs, baseball memorabilia, movie posters and pop culture were receiving heightened awareness. At Christie's vintage movie poster auction in December, astronomical prices were paid for key one sheets and lobby cards.

In recent years demand for the best condition copies of all the historic key comic books has increased tremendously. Whenever a high grade copy emerges, usually a new record price is paid. Since the guide has always shown average prices paid over a given period of time, prices for these exceptional copies has not been shown. As an experiment, beginning with this edition, we will be showing a fourth price for certain key books. This price correspondes to only the finest grade copies of that particular book. Books of this grade are very scarce and are seldom sold in any given year. Because of this, when actual sales prices are not available, the new listed fourth price is based on an educated estimate from a nationwide survey of top dealers. Of course, this price could change dramatically up or down when an actual copy sells.

While attending some of the major comic conventions last year, we could see that the new price adjustments in #20 price guide for *Batman* and *Detective* were holding very well. These books were still selling for slightly over guide, but not at the previous year's multiples. Everywhere we traveled, most Golden and Silver Age books were selling very well. We noticed the scarcity of high grade Silver Age DCs and Marvels and how fast they were moving when copies did appear.

Many large collections surfaced during the year. One of the most significant came out of central Tennessee. This collection consisted of runs of most titles from 1942 to 1950. They were stored in a small attic room for the past 45 to 50 years and totaled over 4,000 books. Another collection of Mickey Mouse Magazines surfaced, selling quickly for multiples of guide list. Late in the year a couple of large high grade western collections came out and sold rapidly to anxious buyers. Early in the year, a Silver Age collection numbering in the thousands of issues from the late 50s and 60s came out of central Tennessee, selling to local collectors.

The grading section has been updated again in this edition. As in last year's guide, the highest grade is now just Mint, which means a perfect copy. Terms such as Pristine Mint, Superb Mint, etc. are still being used in the market by some to describe the exceptional. However, no matter how it is described, a perfect book is still just Mint. Today's market has become stricter in grading Mint books, and in 99 per cent of the cases the highest grade observed in vintage books will only be NM, not Mint. In recent years, many dealers and collectors have learned that 1930s to early 1960s books in NM-Mint condition are extremely rare to non-existent. This is why, except for the keys, the highest grade listed is NM.

Of course, as we explained last year, true mint books from the 1970s and 1980s do exist, and the NM value listed should be interpreted as a Mint value for these books.

The comic book market enjoyed good growth in 1990 as the guide's circulation increased again over 1989. This increased exposure of the guide continued to cause collections to surface during the year. Note: We do know that the large Tenn. collection owner did buy his price guide at the local book store.

The San Diego Comic Con repeated its 1989 record breaking attendance. Comic books of all types, Golden and Silver Age, were selling very well. The dollar volume of sales at this convention was as good as the year before. We observed that pedigree books were selling extremely well and again, setting record prices. Hottest titles were DC, Fawcett and Timely with most DC Church copies selling for 4-5 times guide generally. Larson's, San Francisco, Denver, Pennsylvania, Allentown and other pedigree books were bringing 1.5 to 2 times guide list. We watched a small collection of NM Walt Disney's Comics and Stories sell at 1.5 times guide list. While at San Diego, Bob Overstreet, along with Bill Gaines and others were priviledged to receive the coveted Ink Pot award.

The July 4th Chicago Convention was a huge success attracting thousands of people. Silver Age was the hot ticket item here even though Golden Age always sells well. Collectors and dealers were looking for high grade copies of most Silver Age keys to buy, but few copies were for sale.

Late in the year, Bill Gaines' E.C.s went on the market for sale by Russ Cochran. They were priced at 3-5 times guide list and it is our understanding that many copies sold making the project a huge success. These were the incomplete runs of comics sold as individual issues. Next year, Cochran will be selling complete title sets of the remaining E.C.s.

**SILVER AGE**—Still one of the hottest areas in collecting. Prices for high grade material continued to set new records. During the year all pre-1970 super hero titles were in high demand selling for over guide list. The average NM copy of any Marvel super hero was bringing 1.5 times guide list. *Spider-Man, Iron Man, Captain America* and any *Punisher* appearance were very volatile. Late 50s DC's in high grade were very much in demand with *Batman* #100 in any grade selling at up to double guide. Other titles in demand were *Flash, Justice League, Showcase, Brave and the Bold, Green Lantern, The Atom, Hawkman and Superman.* TV titles such as *Star Trek, Dark Shadows*, etc. set record prices. However, due to large price increases in the market, the second half of the year saw a reduction in demand for the lesser condition books. Prices on these books were available at Update list by year's end.

**GOLDEN AGE**—The big news for 1990 was the sale of the Allentown *Detective* #27, NM-Mint for $80,000. Later in the year, the Church copy of *Whiz* #1, Mint sold for a staggering sum of $74,000 (cash/trade). During the year, 1930s and 1940s books showed solid demand with Fawcetts and Timelys coming on strong. All Atlas and E.C. titles sold extremely well. However, due to the slowing economy and the Gulf crisis late in the year, the market took a more conservative posture. Price increases in this edition reflect this more conservative attitude.

**1920s Titles**—These books are scarce, especially in Fine to Mint condition. All titles from *Bringing Up Father* to the more obscure were in high demand.

**1930s Titles**—Demand was still far greater than supply in this scarce area of collecting. These books sell in all grades. Early DCs are rarely offered for sale, and almost never at guide prices. Centaurs still remained scarce. The early historic books such as *Funnies On Parade, Century Of Comics, Famous Funnies Series 1, Famous Funnies #1, Famous Funnies, A Carnival Of Comics, New Fun, New Comics,* etc. showed increased interest selling for way over guide list. A few reported sales are: *Action* #1VF(r)—$18,500, VF(r)—$19,750, G(no cf)—$5,000, *Detective* #1VG(r)—$4900, #27(no fc)—$900, #27VG(r)—$11,000, #31VF—$5500, #31VF—$7100, #33FR—$1000, #37VF—$1900, *Funny Pages* #10VG —$400, #10VF(Cosmic Aeroplane)—$1400, *Funny Picture Stories* #2VG—$290, *Keen Detective Funnies* #19NM—$315, *More Fun* #38VF-$350, *New Adventure* #13VF—$625, *New Book Of Comics* #1VG—$2000, *Marvel Comics* #1NM (Allentown)—$25,000 (Cash/trade), #1FN—$13,500.

**1940s Titles**—All titles and issue numbers were strong. DCs remained very strong but were not selling for multiples of guide as a year before. Fawcetts and Timelys showed increased sales as well as key Disneys. There was special emphasis on cover theme (Hitler covers) and many titles from the late 40s sold well.

**DC**—Still the number one publisher in the hearts of collectors and difficult for dealers to restock due to the large demand. Hot in all grades. Batman and related titles are still number one. Flash has become number two (new TV series?) with Superman number three followed by Green Lantern. Wonder Woman and related titles are the slowest selling if you can say DCs sell slowly. Late 40s DCs remained scarce and sold extremely well. All the offbeat titles (war, romance, humor, horror, crime, etc.) also sell very well. Reported sales: *Action* #13VF(r)—$1200, *All-American* #16FN—$9000, #25VF(r)—$1150, #42FN+—$200, #61FA—$90, #65VG—$200, *All*

*Flash* #1FR—$300, *All Star* #48VF—$350, *Batman* #1NM—$22,000, #1VF+—$19,500, #1NM—$18,000, #5VF—$1600, #8FN+—$1200, #23VF(r)—$700, #23VF—$750, #23VG—$220, #66VF—$350, *Big All-American* VF—$2500, *Detective* #45VF—$1000, #56VF+—$750, #58FN+—$520, #65VG—$450, #69G—$120, #85VF—$475, #91FN(r)—$400, *Flash* #1FVF—$4600, #12NM—$750, #28FN+—$250, #56FN—$150, #58FR—$60, #92G+—$165, #92NM—$800, *Green Lantern* #1 (Church)—$25,000, #9NM—$550, #13VF—$450, *More Fun* #58VF—$600 cash, $400 trade, #57VF(r)—$950, #68VF—$700, #69FN+—$700, *Star Spangled* #7 (Church)—$5900 trade, $1000 cash, *Superman* #9VF—$750, #14VF(r)—$700, #14G—$140, #14G—$160,#18VF—$750, #76VF+—$750, #76FN—$262, *Superman Work Book* VF+—$2000.

**TIMELY**—After several years of relative inactivity, this company's titles have again become very popular. The hottest title is *Captain America*, especially #30 up, followed closely by his *USA* and *Marvel Mystery* appearances. *Captain America* was probably one of the hottest titles in 1990. Good solid gains for both *Human Torch* and *Sub-Mariner*. *Namora* showed increased interest as well as the All Winners Squad in *All Winners* #19 & #21. Early *Marvel Mystery* #1-10 were selling a bit slower due to the higher list prices. All late 40s offbeat titles (humor, romance, war, etc.) showed strong interest. Reported sales: *Captain America* #1VG—$12,750, #1NM (Allentown)—$16,500, #1VG—$3000, #11NM—$700, #16VF—$900.

**FAWCETT**—Strong demand for Captain Marvel and Captain Marvel Jr. related titles. Early *Master* was still hard to find. Raboy issues of this title remained popular. *Spy Smasher* was very hot. *Marvel Family* sold very well. *Mary Marvel* and *Wow* showed moderate sales. All sports titles had solid sales.

**CENTAUR**—Sales on most titles have peaked due to strong price increases over the past few years. Most issues still remained scarce in the market. *Amazing-Man* is the strongest title followed by *The Arrow*. The first Arrow in *Funny Pages* V2#10 is still highly sought after.

**FOX**—All books with Lou Fine covers and stories were still in high demand. *Wonderworld*, *Mysterymen*, and *Fantastic* were the hottest titles. Late 40s titles showed increased interest, especially the weird and jungle titles, *Blue Beetle* and *Phantom Lady*. Several Church copies of *Rulah, Jo-Jo*, etc. sold for 2x guide list.

**CLASSICS**—Strong sales at above guide list on all original editions #1-50, especially in higher grade. Good sales on issues #51 up. The first and second reprints of the early issues were also very strong. Many of the giveaways remained very scarce. A Saks 34th St. sold for $3150 and a Robin Hood Flour brought $1000.

**FICTION HOUSE**—Strong demand continued for *Jumbo, Jungle, Wings and Rangers. Planet* still remains the most popular title. Early issues of *Jumbo* were scarce and sold for over guide whenever copies turned up.

**QUALITY**—Slow growth, with the strongest demand for Lou Fine issues which were scarce. *Military, Modern* and *Blackhawk* still sold well at above guide list prices. Later 40s titles such as *Lady Luck* and *Buccaneers* were popular.

**MLJ**—Slow growth, demand with over guide prices primarily for keys and first issues. *Katy Keene* and *Archie* titles had slow to moderate sales. An *Archie* #1NM (Denver) sold for $4000. *Zip* and *Pep* had good sales. A *Zip* #1VG brought $200. Archie is celebrating their 50th anniversary in 1991.

**GLEASON**—Slow to moderated sales overall. Early crime titles were selling well.

**HARVEY**—Moderate sales for the super hero titles such as *Green Hornet, Speed* and *Black Cat*. There was increased interest in *Dick Tracy* due to the movie release in the Summer.

**DISNEY**—Market demand is primarily for key issues and high grade copies. High grade copies of *Four Color* #9 and #16 as well as *March of Comics* sold for over guide list. A set of Duck *March of Comics* #4(r), 20NM, & 41NM sold for $7000 as a set. A Mickey Mouse *Four Color* #16VF sold for $4000. The rare Bibo and Lang Mickey Mouse book was selling for double guide. Bibo & Lang #1VF+-$4000, #1FN—

$2500, #1VF—$3000, VG + —$3000. A file copy of *Mickey Mouse Magazine* Series 1 V1 sold for $3500 and a complete run of *Mickey Mouse Magazines* sold for 1.25x guide (avg. cond. f/f +). A series 3 #1FN sold for $2500, in GVG—$1500, another copy in VG—$1500, #3FN(r) sold for $750. A VG copy of a complete Waddle Book sold at Christie's on Oct. 20th, 1990 for $8500 + 10 per cent commission. Disney titles *Uncle Scrooge*, pre-Barks C&S, *Mickey Mouse Magazines* and *Four Color Donald* and Mickey sold well in high grade. NM Ducks and Mickey sold at over guide as well as *Mickey Mouse Magazines*. *Zorro* remained hot as well as *Large Feat. Book* #19 (Dumbo). Most Disney's in low grade (g-vg) sold slowly.

**FUNNY ANIMAL**—Most miscellaneous publishers had slowed sales with DC, Dell, ACG and Timely the most in demand. *Looney Tunes* showed increased demand for the early issues #1-20. Other Dell titles were slow except for the Giants and TV related titles such as *Deputy Dawg*. DC's *Funny Stuff* showed strong demand because of Dodo and the Frog as well as *Real Screen* due to the Fox and the Crow.

**MISCELLANEOUS**—The Shadow and Doc Savage by Street & Smith were very hot with subsequent price increases. Most super hero keys and first issues were in high demand. *Green Giant* remained rare and highly sought. Other titles such as *Big Shot, Sparkler* (Tarzan covers), and *Skyman* sold well.

**1950s TITLES**—E.C.s are very hot due to the hit Crypt Keeper HBO series. Late in the year Bill Gaines' file copies began to be sold at multiples of guide list. Three copies of *Mad* #1 sold for $2500 each. The horror titles were the most in demand followed by *Mad, Panic*, crime and science fiction titles. These books have also been bringing well over guide list in auctions for the past year. Most other company's books from this period sold extremely well, especially all the horror and love titles.

**ATLAS**—Strong sales on all titles. *Millie The Model* was very hot. Westerns such as *Kid Colt, Rawhide Kid* were very popular, but titles like *Black Rider, Blaze Carson* and *Whip Wilson* were very hot. The pre-super hero titles such as *Amazing Adult Fantasy, Strange Tales, Tales Of Suspense, Journey Into Mystery*, and *Tales To Astonish* were in high demand, especially in fine or better.

**TV/MOVIE TITLES**—Sales were solid at around guide list for most movie titles. Most TV titles enjoyed strong sales, especially those with photo covers. The Dell file copies continued to sell at over guide despite significant increases last year. Some of the best titles are *I Love Lucy, Star Trek, Flintstones, Jetsons, Andy Griffith, Munsters, Dark Shadows, Atom Ant, Jonny Quest, Mr. Ed*, etc. as well as all western titles. Some *Andy Griffith Four Colors* sold for $100 ea. A *Jetsons* #1NM brought $313 in an auction.

**WESTERNS**—Very strong sales were noted, especially in the midwest and southeastern states. In the Dell line the strongest titles were *Red Ryder* #1-50, *Roy Rogers* #1-25 and the TV photo cover titles such as the later Clayton Moore *Lone Rangers, Rin Tin Tin* and *Cisco Kid*. The early Four Color in condition sold very well. *John Wayne* movie books were in high demand, especially his own title. Most Fawcett and Charlton westerns remained scarce and recorded strong sales. *Smiley Burnette, Sunset Carson, Tim McCoy* and *Andy Devine* were the hottest titles followed by *Bob Steele, Ken Maynard, Lash LaRue*, Rocky Lane and others. All Atlas titles sold extremely well such as *Black Rider, Wild Western, Kid Colt, Rawhide Kid, Whip Wilson, Reno Browne*, etc. Other companies such as ME and ACG enjoyed average sales.

**EC**—The hottest area in the hobby! Fueled by the HBO series *Tales From The Crypt*, this entire publishing line has taken off. The horror titles are selling for anywhere from 25%-50% over guide. The Science Fiction titles are selling at over guide as well. *Mad* #1-30 sold very well along with *Psychoanalysis* and *Aces High*. The war titles are the slowest in the line. Late in the year Russ Cochran put on sale the Bill Gaines E.C. file copies. They were priced at several multiples of guide list and early reports indicate that many copies sold to anxious buyers. These books were sold on an individual issue basis. Remaining are five complete sets of all New Trend and New Direction titles which will be sold in 1991.

**GIANTS**—Due to their scarcity, most giants continued to sell well at or slightly over guide list. Collectors are beginning to realize the scarcity of these books in high grade.

**3-D COMICS**—Average sales, but the scarcer issues like *3-D Love* and *3-D Tales Of The West* were in high demand. *Batman 3-D* in both editions remained hot.

**ROMANCE COMICS**—Still very much gaining in popularity with collectors, especially the DC titles. Many bargains to be found here.

**ERB COMICS**—Early *Tarzans* enjoyed moderate sales, numbers 1-20.

**HUMOR COMICS**—Mad imitators, such as *Riot* and *Wild* were in high demand. *Dennis The Menace* and *Richie Rich* #1-20 had average sales. All DC titles were in high demand like *Advs. Of Bob Hope, Jerry Lewis, Scribbly, Sugar & Spike*, etc. Other titles that enjoyed good sales were *Humbug, Juke Box Comics, Abbott & Costello, Kilroy* and especially *The Three Stooges*.

**GOOD-GIRL-ART COMICS**—Renewed interest was evident, especially in the Fox titles *Rulah, Blue Beetle, Jo-Jo, All Top, Phantom Lady*, etc. Other titles that enjoyed good sales were *Brenda Starr, Cave Girl, Undercover Girl* and *Seven Seas* with art by Matt Baker. The more suggestive romance comics that fall into this category were selling at a premium.

**1950s DC**—One of the hottest, most explosive areas in comics. Collectors want these books in any condition, especially titles like *Adventures Of Alan Ladd, Advs. Of Ozzie and Harriet, Jimmy Wakely*, etc. All the war, science fiction and horror titles were selling very well, especially in high grade. The early Sgt. Rock *Our Army At War* were hot as well as the Dinosaur issues of *Star Spangled War*. Enemy Ace in these titles was also highly sought. All super hero titles of this period remained scarce and could not supply the demand. There was increased demand for *Tomahawk* as well as his appearances in the later *Star Spangleds*. The Ghost Breaker issues of this title were also hot.

**HORROR AND CRIME COMICS**—This was an explosive area in comics during the year. Led by the very popular EC titles, all other company's titles were highly collected. Many of the odd titles did well such as *Crimes By Women, Forbidden Worlds, Black Cat, Women Outlaws, Strange Suspense Stories, The Thing, This Is Suspense, Adventures Into The Unknown, Dark Mysteries*, and many more. Of course all Atlas and DC titles were hot and couldn't meet demand.

**SPORT COMICS**—Due to the high cross-over interest from those in the sports collectibles field, this area of collecting was very hot. All titles sold very well at premium prices. *Babe Ruth Sports, Joe Louis, Jackie Robinson, Sport Comics, Sports Action*, etc. were some of the hottest titles.

**ART COMICS**—Matt Baker romance comics had moderate sales. Interest in Frazetta books has waned while Kirby, Ditko and Wolverton comics are in high demand. Toth, Krigstein and Kurtzman books enjoyed moderate sales.

**ORIGINAL ART**—Many collectors are asking for Golden Age original covers. Lou Fine's better original covers have sold in the $5-6 thousand range, with average ones going for $3-5 thousand. An Early Batman cover was priced at the $5-10 thousand level. A Matt Baker Seven Seas #6 cover original sold for $2000-$2500.

**1960s-1970s TITLES**—This was an extremely explosive area of collecting throughout the year. **MARVEL:** Early issues of *Spider-Man* were very hot in the Fine-Mint grades. Other titles that exploded were early issues of *Fantastic Four, Tales Of Suspense* and *Astonish, Journey Into Mystery, Iron Man, Captain America, Sgt. Fury, Incredible Hulk, Sub-Mariner* and *Silver Surfer*. **DC:** All mid-1950s and 1960s titles were very volatile. *Showcase* #1-60 were very hot with the early issues remaining very scarce in any condition. The same applies to *Brave and the Bold* early issues. All Sgt. Rock issues in *Our Army At War* were hot, as well as all other DC war titles. Books like *Atom, Hawkman, Metal Men, Action, Batman, Doom Patrol, Teen Titans, Metamorpho*, etc. all enjoyed excellent sales. Reported sales: *Adventure* #247FN(r)—

$600, *Amazing Fantasy* #15VG—$1025, VF(r)—$2200, VF(r)—$2300, VG + —$1625, VG + —$1800, VF(r)—$2900, NM—$10,000, *Amazing Spider-Man* #1VF(r)—$2750, VF—$4500, VF + —$5200, VF(r)—$2300, #2M—$1200, #3FN + —$550, #5M—$550, #6VF—$500, #10VF—$265, #14VF + (r)—$425, #14VG—$125, *Avengers* #1FN—$500, #4VF(r)—$390, *Brave and the Bold* #28NM—$2000, *Daredevil* #1FN—$400, NM(r)—$650, *Fantastic Four* #1NM—$6000, VF(r)—$2700, VF + (r)—$3000, #2G—$225, #3VF—$600, #4VF(r)—$550, #11VF(r)—$175, #48NM—$125, *Flash* #105VF—$1200, *Incredible Hulk* #1NM(r)—$900, #2NM(r)—$425, #180NM—$100, #181NM—$425, *Iron Man* #1VF + —$260, *Journey Into Mystery* #83NM—$1400, *Justice League* #1VF—$1200, *Showcase* #4FN—$1800, FN(r)—$2900, #22VF—$1200, VF—$1250, VG—$750, #28FN + —$45, #57VF + —$15, #58NM—$10, *Tales Of Suspense* #39NM—$1500, NM—$1850, G—$265, FN—$550, #40NM—$480, *X-Men* #1VF + (r)—$1100.

**1980s TITLES-** After the incredible increase in comic book sales in 1989 due to the success of the Batman movie, most retailers thought 1990 would be a year to consolidate the gains of 1989. They were oh so wrong!!! *Spider-Man* #1 by Todd McFarlane was the single biggest seller of all time in terms of dollars generated by a comic book. The first printing was simultaneously released in four different formats, a direct sales version (silver), a newsstand version (yellow), a bagged limited edition direct sales version, and a bagged limited edition newsstand version. With total sales well over 3,000,000 copies and a total immediate sellout, what could Marvel do but immediately produce a fifth version, a second printing (gold) and late in 1990 through a direct solicitation to retail stores, there will be a sixth version released in 1991, a limited edition (platinum) version. And they all sold through!!! The interest, though reduced, was still very strong in subsequent issues as the title continued to sell over 500,000 copies per issue. The excitement caused by Spider-Man spilled over to the entire Marvel line and to DC and other publishers as well. As a Marvel spokesperson commented in 1989, ''The best thing to happen to Marvel this year (1989) was Batman,'' so all other publishers can say that in 1990 the best thing to happen to their business was Spider-Man.

Don't think DC was sitting on the sidelines watching Marvel grab the spotlight. The best planned promotion of the year was done for the five issue mini-series Robin. With a new Robin character introduced in *Batman* #457 and then developed in the mini-series DC promoted the character with posters, stickers, pins, and extensive advertising programs. The promotion was a huge success as *Batman* #457, *Robin* #1, and *Robin* #2 all sold out immediately and required 2nd and in the case of *Robin* #1, a third printing.

The biggest media event of the year was the attention generated by television, radio and newspaper interest in the proposal by Superman to Lois Lane in *Superman* #50. The media attention, while hoped for, caught all retailers, distributors and even DC totally by surprise as the book sold out within hours and the demand was overwhelming. DC quickly responded with a second printing to try to satisfy the demand of the reading public. As this report is going to press, a similar media blitz is developing for *Action* #662 and *Superman* #53 in which Superman reveals his Clark Kent alter ego to Lois. With sufficient time to plan for the anticipated demand, most retailers and distributors have ordered enough copies to satisfy the expected customers.

With the deluge of new titles, hot artists, crossovers, guest appearances and the like, retailers and distributors are constantly running short of quick selling issues. The publishers have responded by setting up efficient reorder systems managed by detail-oriented people like Felisa Garrido at Marvel and Ileana Jimenez at DC. Through their efforts, additional copies of hot selling books flow quickly to the distributors who then, through their own systems, get these books to the retail outlets. In the event of a complete sell- out, the publishers have set up quick decision making processes to decide on whether to do a second printing. At peak efficiency, additional copies and even second printings can be in local retail outlets the week following a sell out! These efforts have contributed to keeping interest at high levels and sales climbing, and are a clear indication that the growth of our hobby is through a great deal of effort at many levels.

Marvel's success was not only in the Spider-Man title and character. Other titles experiencing a jump in sales were Guardians of The Galaxy, Namor, Hulk, and the biggest surprise of all, Ghostrider. Ghostrider #1 was an instant sellout and a gold edition 2nd printing was immediately ordered. Sales were spiked again in issue #5 with a Punisher crossover and another gold 2nd printing was necessary to satisfy demand. Punisher, Wolverine, and all the Spider-Man titles remained strong sellers during 1990 and there appears to be no let up in sales in spite of the recession of 1990.

DC also had other big winners in 1990. Lobo was a highly promoted mini-series whose first issue sold well enough to justify a 2nd printing. The World's Finest mini-series was an up-priced format that sold extremely well. The whole group of Batman titles continued their strong sales figures established in 1989 with the Batman movie. Other strong selling DC titles included the Superman group, Sandman, Doom Patrol, the Green Lantern miniseries and Hellblazer. During 1990 DC experienced numerous delays in their announced shipping schedule. These delays had a very negative effect on sales as interest lost momentum and readers looked towards other titles to substitute for the delayed books. DC has acknowledged the problem and has made getting back on schedule their number one priority for 1991.

A growing area of importance to the comic book publishers is the graphic novel, trade paperback market. Included in this genre are both hardcover and softcover editions of new editorial material, and reprints of selected issues of titles or anthologies of stories from various titles. All have met with success and many have been kept in print as backlist titles available for many months if not years. This area represents a real dilemma for the collector in our hobby. On the one hand, these graphic novels, trade paperbacks, archives, and masterworks generally do not appreciate in value. On the other hand they are a relatively inexpensive way for a newer collector to obtain the earlier issues which he/she might not otherwise ever be able to enjoy.

The independent publishers also had their share of successes in 1990. A very notable success was the revival of the *Classics Illustrated* line of comics by First Comics. By year's end, there were over 20 issues available and all were well accepted by the comic book collecting audience but the more significant aspect was their wide acceptance by a new audience who were attracted by nostalgia, literacy benefits, high quality art, deluxe format, and the media attention the project received. Classics are being distributed to the book store trade by the Berkeley Publishing Group and are available in book stores as well as comic book specialty shops.

Dark Horse continued to shine among the independent publishers in 1990 with huge successes in the movie licensing area such as *Aliens: Earth War, Aliens vs Predator* and *Terminator*. Two Frank Miller projects, *Give Me Liberty* and *Hard Boiled* also sold extremely well. Like many of the other publishers, Dark Horse went to second printings to satisfy demand for their hot selling titles.

A new entry into the comic book marketplace was the Walt Disney Company who took back publishing of their own titles from Gladstone. With the resources of the Disney Company behind them and a new editorial policy of fewer reprints, more original stories, more emphasis on the animated television show titles (Duck Tales and Rescue Rangers), and more movie-related titles (Roger Rabbit, Little Mermaid, Dick Tracy), the Disney line made an immediate impact on the marketplace. Everyone is watching Disney and expecting even bigger things from the giant company in 1991.

Upon losing the Disney titles, Gladstone immediately switched gears and picked up the rights to reprint the EC line of the 50's. Originally experimenting with *Weird Science* and *Tales From the Crypt*, the sales on the horror title so far exceeded the science fiction that by late 1990, the line had switched over entirely to reprinting the three EC horror titles (*Tales From The Crypt, Vault of Horror* and *Haunt of Fear*).

Rock and Roll music made a bit of a splash in the comic book world in 1990 as Revolutionary Comics, Rock Fantasy and Harvey all introduced comics featuring current rock groups and individual singers. The Revolutionary and Rock Fantasy books were unlicensed and caused a stir while lawyers negotiated the legalities of the titles and some distributors carried the titles while others did not. In the end, a compromise was struck and with all distributors carrying the products, they sold very well again with 2nd printings of high demand books. Harvey introduced a line of New Kids on The Block titles. These were fully licensed and met with moderate success. The real benefit of the development of these titles is the new readers they will attract from the music audience and our industry gains breadth of product and readership.

A less positive area of growth in 1990 was the proliferation of Adults Only and Mature Readers titles coming from virtually all publishers other than Archie, Disney, and Harvey. While we certainly need to develop comics with adult themes there is little justification for some of the titles. The success of the first few novelty comics spawned a deluge of comics with an orientation towards sex and violence. While some of these titles sold well initially, even the best-selling titles are slowing down as the marketplace becomes flooded with similar titles.

The fourth quarter of 1990 brought us the recession caused by the Persian Gulf oil price increase. The recession hit the comic book industry as it had never before been hit by recession. This industry had changed dramatically during the past five years of economic prosperity. Many more projects were in upscale up-priced formats, many expensive hardcover books were published, expensive bisque statues and other collectibles were offered to the buying public. This shift away from the inexpensive entertainment which traditionally had made the comic book industry invulnerable to recession was the major cause for the impact the recession of 1990 had on our industry. True to form, however, the demand for the inexpensive books continued to grow while sales of many of the more expensive items slowed as the recession continued. Most economic forecasters are predicting an end to this recession in 1991 and the comic book industry as a whole hopes their predictions are true.

## INVESTOR'S DATA

The following table denotes the rate of appreciation of the top 50 most valuable Golden Age titles over the past year and the past five years (1986-1991). The retail value for a complete mint run of each title in 1991 is compared to its value in 1990 and 1986. The 1971 values are also included as an interesting point of reference. The rate of return for 1991 over 1990, and the yearly average rate of return for each year since 1986, is given. For example, a complete mint run of *Detective Comics* retails at $227,810 in 1991, $194,745 in 1990, and $83,497 in 1986. The rate of increase of 1991 over 1990 can be easily calculated at 17.0%, while the average yearly increase or rate of return over the past five years is 34.6%. This means that the mint value of this title has increased an average of 34.6% each year over the past five years.

The place in rank is given for each title by year, with its corresponding mint value. This table can be very useful in forecasting trends in the market place. For instance, the investor might want to know which title is yielding the best dividend from one year to the next, or one might just be interested in seeing how the popularity of titles changes from year to year. For instance, *Shadow Comics* was in 72nd place in 1971 and has advanced to 33rd place in 1991. *Donald Duck* was in 53rd place in 1971, in 14th place in 1990 and has currently dropped to 16th place in 1991.

*Batman* overtook *Four Color* for the number 6 spot, and *All American Comics* overtook *All Star Comics* for the number 10 spot this year. *Strange Adventures* entered the top 50 jumping from 62nd to 48th spot. *Green Lantern* increased by 20.8% from

1990, but shows a yearly average increase of 23.3%. *Captain America Comics* was up 27.8% and *Classic Comics* up 13.2%.

The following tables are meant as a guide to the investor and it is hoped that they might aid him in choosing titles in which to invest. However, it should be pointed out that trends may change at anytime and that some titles can meet market resistance with a slowdown in price increases, while others can develop into real comers from a presently dormant state. In the long run, if the investor sticks to the titles that are appreciating steadily each year, he shouldn't go very far wrong.

The Silver Age titles continued to show movement, especially early issues of Marvels and DCs in high grade. Golden & Silver Age titles are continuing to appreciate faster than economic inflationary values during the same period.

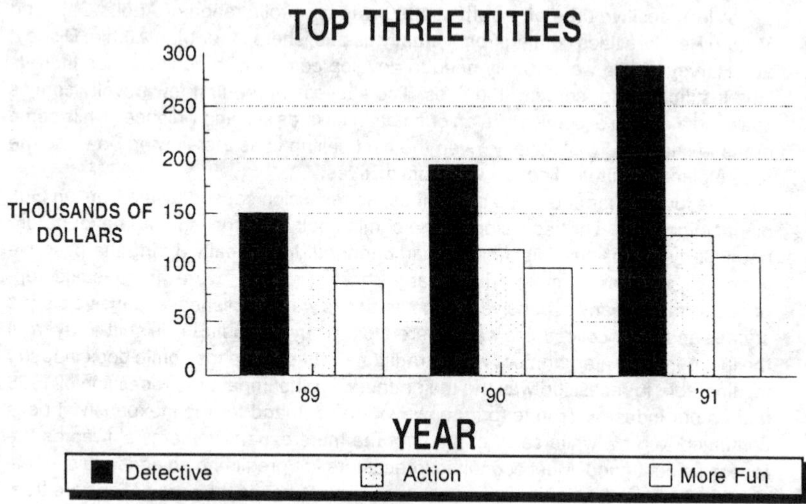


TOP 50 TITLES

TOP 50 TITLES & RATE OF INCREASE OVER 1990 AND 1986 GUIDE VALUES

| Title | 1991 Guide Rank | 1991 Guide Value | %Change From '90 Value | Avg.Yrly. Return '86-'91 | 1990 Guide Rank | 1990 Guide Value | 1986 Guide Rank | 1986 Guide Value | 1971 Guide Rank | 1971 Guide Value |
|---|---|---|---|---|---|---|---|---|---|---|
| Detective Comics | 1 | $227,810 | +17.0 | +34.6 | 1 | $194,745 | 1 | $83,497 | 4 | $2,747 |
| Action Comics | 2 | 130,489 | +10.6 | +11.9 | 2 | 117,999 | 2 | 81,788 | 7 | 2,354 |
| More Fun Comics | 3 | 110,270 | +10.3 | +24.1 | 3 | 100,015 | 5 | 50,004 | 3 | 2,816 |
| Adventure Comics | 4 | 104,948 | +11.9 | +25.4 | 5 | 93,768 | 7 | 46,210 | 2 | 3,066 |
| Marvel Mystery Comics | 5 | 88,806 | + 3.4 | + 6.7 | 5 | 79,135 | 3 | 66,414 | 5 | 2,584 |
| Batman | 6 | 85,564 | +15.1 | + 4.0 | 7 | 74,357 | 11 | 28,524 | 19 | 1,246 |
| Four Color | 7 | 83,781 | + 9.0 | +12.5 | 6 | 76,889 | 4 | 51,516 | 1 | 4,229 |
| Superman | 8 | 78,264 | +11.3 | +14.6 | 8 | 71,416 | 6 | 49,813 | 13 | 1,460 |
| Captain America | 9 | 63,975 | +27.8 | +18.1 | 9 | 50,045 | 8 | 33,624 | 17 | 1,303 |
| All American Comics | 10 | 55,550 | +14.8 | +25.0 | 11 | 48,405 | 14 | 24,685 | 24 | 1,189 |
| All Star Comics | 11 | $54,619 | + 9.3 | +16.9 | 10 | $49,975 | 10 | $29,585 | 10 | $1,657 |
| Flash Comics | 12 | 54,255 | +15.4 | +21.7 | 12 | 47,015 | 13 | 26,045 | 15 | 1,344 |
| Whiz Comics | 13 | 47,130 | +16.1 | + 8.7 | 13 | 40,578 | 9 | 32,865 | 14 | 1,357 |
| Planet Comics | 14 | 32,003 | + 9.7 | +13.7 | 16 | 29,162 | 17 | 18,988 | 50 | 613 |
| World's Fair & Finest | 15 | 30,988 | + 4.5 | +18.2 | 15 | 29,665 | 19 | 16,237 | 33 | 841 |
| Donald Duck | 16 | 30,853 | + 3.0 | + 3.6 | 14 | 29,946 | 12 | 26,155 | 53 | 604 |
| Walt Disney's C & S | 17 | 29,862 | + 4.9 | + 4.8 | 17 | 28,454 | 15 | 24,069 | 12 | 1,487 |
| Famous Funnies | 18 | 29,320 | +13.4 | +27.7 | 18 | 25,855 | 31 | 12,306 | 8 | 2,343 |
| Jumbo Comics | 19 | 29,265 | +13.2 | +20.4 | 19 | 25,850 | 22 | 14,496 | 16 | 1,320 |
| Mickey Mouse Magazine | 20 | 28,550 | +18.0 | +23.5 | 20 | 24,195 | 28 | 13,139 | 18 | 1,252 |
| Police Comics | 21 | $25,255 | + 6.3 | + 8.9 | 21 | $23,766 | 18 | $17,449 | 30 | $903 |
| Star Spangled Comics | 22 | 25,210 | +10.4 | +17.6 | 22 | 22,841 | 26 | 13,419 | 35 | 830 |
| Captain Marvel Advs. | 23 | 24,885 | +16.7 | +11.0 | 23 | 21,322 | 20 | 16,046 | 29 | 1,009 |
| Green Lantern | 24 | 24,180 | +20.8 | +23.3 | 25 | 20,015 | 32 | 11,160 | 87 | 390 |

## TOP 50 TITLES

### TOP 50 TITLES & RATE OF INCREASE OVER 1990 AND 1986 GUIDE VALUES

| Title | 1991 Guide Rank | 1991 Guide Value | %Change From '90 Value | Avg.Yrly. Return '86-'91 | 1990 Guide Rank | 1990 Guide Value | 1986 Guide Rank | 1986 Guide Value | 1971 Guide Rank | 1971 Guide Value |
|---|---|---|---|---|---|---|---|---|---|---|
| Master Comics | 25 | $23,243 | +11.1 | +12.3 | 24 | $20,922 | 23 | $14,394 | 28 | $1,021 |
| Classic Comics | 26 | 21,208 | +13.2 | +26.6 | 28 | 18,740 | 40 | 9,111 | 189 | 65 |
| Human Torch | 27 | 20,070 | +10.6 | + 6.3 | 31 | 18,140 | 21 | 15,255 | 46 | 632 |
| Dick Tracy | 28 | 20,062 | + 6.9 | + 9.5 | 27 | 18,769 | 24 | 13,618 | 25 | 1,116 |
| Sensation Comics | 29 | 19,600 | + 7.1 | +10.1 | 29 | 18,293 | 29 | 13,004 | 41 | 681 |
| Pep Comics | 30 | 19,457 | + 6.4 | + 9.4 | 30 | 18,279 | 27 | 13,220 | 31 | 880 |
| The Spirit | 31 | $19,327 | - 0 - | - 17.0 | 26 | $19,327 | 16 | $21,087 | 44 | $645 |
| Sub-Mariner | 32 | 18,100 | +11.5 | + 6.9 | 33 | 16,235 | 25 | 13,445 | 54 | 601 |
| Shadow Comics | 33 | 17,375 | +19.2 | +26.7 | 38 | 14,575 | 59 | 7,443 | 72 | 495 |
| Wonder Woman | 34 | 17,202 | +10.7 | +11.4 | 35 | 15,533 | 33 | 10,942 | 64 | 537 |
| King Comics | 35 | 16,943 | + 3.6 | +17.6 | 32 | 16,348 | 44 | 9,014 | 6 | 2,490 |
| Jungle Comics | 36 | 16,791 | +18.5 | +13.2 | 39 | 14,166 | 34 | 10,105 | 32 | 861 |
| Tip Top Comics | 37 | 16,695 | + 7.5 | +13.7 | 36 | 15,525 | 36 | 9,905 | 9 | 2,088 |
| Target | 38 | 16,450 | + 6.9 | +16.7 | 37 | 15,385 | 45 | 8,967 | 38 | 746 |
| Feature Books | 39 | 15,682 | - 0 - | + 5.5 | 34 | 15,682 | 30 | 12,323 | 26 | 1,069 |
| Popular Comics | 40 | 15,280 | + 8.8 | +17.7 | 41 | 14,040 | 54 | 8,116 | 11 | 1,598 |
| Military Comics | 41 | $15,265 | +12.0 | +13.9 | 42 | $13,630 | 43 | $9,015 | 68 | $520 |
| Amazing-Man Comics | 42 | 14,960 | + 5.8 | +13.0 | 40 | 14,145 | 41 | 9,055 | 108 | 314 |
| Feature & Feature Funnies | 43 | 14,392 | + 7.1 | +11.9 | 43 | 13,442 | 42 | 9,026 | 22 | 1,214 |
| Comic Cavalcade | 44 | 14,025 | +17.7 | +15.9 | 49 | 11,913 | 64 | 7,824 | 93 | 361 |
| Marge's Little Lulu | 45 | 14,011 | + 7.5 | + 9.6 | 45 | 13,028 | 37 | 9,468 | 135 | 219 |
| Silver Streak | 46 | 13,970 | + 6.0 | + 9.6 | 44 | 13,175 | 38 | 9,447 | 86 | 394 |
| Daredevil Comics | 47 | 13,354 | +10.5 | +12.6 | 47 | 12,090 | 52 | 8,202 | 45 | 639 |
| Strange Adventures | 48 | 13,066 | +27.3 | +27.7 | 62 | 10,260 | 77 | 5,482 | 114 | 292 |
| Hit Comics | 49 | 12,802 | + 5.3 | + 5.8 | 46 | 12,155 | 35 | 9,912 | 67 | 523 |
| Superboy | 50 | 12,768 | + 6.6 | + 8.8 | 48 | 11,978 | 47 | 8,876 | 94 | 360 |

## TREND ANALYSIS

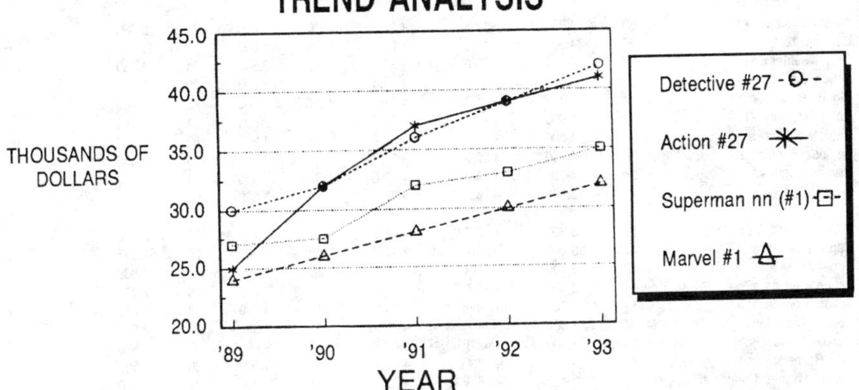


The above trend analysis based on prices form the 1986-1991 Overstreet Price Guide.

The following tables show the rate of return of the 50 most valuable Golden Age books, the 40 most valuable Silver Age titles and the 40 most valuable Silver Age books over the past year. It also shows the average yearly rate of return over the past five years (1990-1985). Comparisons can be made in the same way as in the previous table of the Top 50 titles. Ranking in many cases is relative since so many books have the same value. These books are listed alphabetically within the same value.

### 50 MOST VALUABLE GOLDEN AGE BOOKS AND RATE OF RETURN

| Issue | 1991 Guide Rank | 1991 Guide Value | %Change From '90 Value | Avg.Yrly. Return '86-'91 | 1990 Guide Rank | 1990 Guide Value | 1986 Guide Rank | 1986 Guide Value |
|---|---|---|---|---|---|---|---|---|
| Detective Comics #27 | 1 | $37,000 | +13.8 | +32.9 | 1 | $32,500 | 4 | $14,000 |
| Action Comics #1 | 2 | 36,000 | +10.9 | +13.3 | 1 | 32,500 | 2 | 21,600 |

## 50 MOST VALUABLE GOLDEN AGE BOOKS AND RATE OF RETURN

| Issue | 1991 Guide Rank & Value | | %Change From '90 Value | Avg.Yrly. Return '86-'91 | 1990 Guide Rank & Value | | 1986 Guide Rank & Value | |
|---|---|---|---|---|---|---|---|---|
| Marvel Comics #1 | 3 | $32,000 | +16.4 | + 7.8 | 3 | $27,500 | 1 | $23,000 |
| Superman #1 | 4 | 28,000 | + 7.7 | +12.0 | 4 | 26,000 | 3 | 17,500 |
| Whiz Comics #1 | 5 | 23,000 | +26.4 | +15.4 | 5 | 18,200 | 5 | 13,000 |
| Batman #1 | 6 | 18,000 | +24.1 | +35.4 | 6 | 14,500 | 6 | 6,500 |
| Captain America #1 | 7 | 14,000 | +55.6 | +32.8 | 10 | 9,000 | 10 | 5,300 |
| All American Comics #16 | 8 | 13,000 | +30.0 | +41.9 | 8 | 10,000 | 13 | 4,200 |
| Detective Comics #1 | 8 | 13,000 | +14.0 | +45.0 | 7 | 11,400 | 16 | 4,000 |
| More Fun Comics #52 | 10 | 11,000 | +14.6 | +14.9 | 9 | 9,600 | 7 | 6,300 |
| Flash #1 | 11 | $9,000 | +28.6 | +44.3 | 13 | $7,000 | 26 | $2,800 |
| All Star #3 | 12 | 8,500 | +13.3 | +24.2 | 11 | 7,500 | 18 | 3,850 |
| Detective Comics #31 | 13 | 8,200 | +64.0 | +71.9 | 20 | 5,000 | 53 | 1,785 |
| Captain Marvel Advs. #1 | 14 | 8,000 | +14.3 | + 9.6 | 13 | 7,000 | 9 | 5,400 |
| New Fun #1 | 14 | 8,000 | +11.1 | +77.3 | 12 | 7,200 | 60 | 1,645 |
| Detective Comics #38 | 16 | 7,800 | +11.4 | +32.0 | 13 | 7,000 | 22 | 3,000 |
| More Fun Comics #53 | 17 | 7,500 | +21.0 | +17.5 | 18 | 6,200 | 16 | 4,000 |
| Detective Comics #33 | 18 | 7,200 | +10.8 | +28.0 | 16 | 6,500 | 22 | 3,000 |
| Double Action Comics #2 | 19 | 6,500 | - 0 - | + 2.4 | 16 | 6,500 | 8 | 5,800 |
| Detective Comics #29 | 20 | 5,500 | +10.0 | +35.0 | 20 | 5,000 | 44 | 2,000 |
| New Fun Comics #2 | 20 | $5,500 | + 9.1 | +58.6 | 19 | $5,040 | 77 | $1,400 |
| Detective Comics #28 | 22 | 5,200 | +13.0 | + 9.7 | 25 | 4,600 | 19 | 3,500 |
| Wow Comics #1 | 22 | 5,200 | + 4.0 | + 3.1 | 20 | 5,000 | 12 | 4,500 |
| Action Comics #2 | 24 | 5,000 | + 4.2 | + 3.8 | 24 | 4,800 | 13 | 4,200 |
| Famous Funnies Series #1 | 24 | 5,000 | +19.0 | +69.3 | 27 | 4,200 | 110 | 1,120 |
| Motion Picture Funnies Weekly | 24 | 5,000 | - 0 - | - 0 - | 20 | 5,000 | 11 | 5,000 |
| Marvel Mystery Comics #2 | 27 | 4,900 | + 8.9 | + 4.0 | 26 | 4,500 | 15 | 4,085 |
| Adventure Comics #40 | 28 | 4,800 | +33.3 | +65.3 | 32 | 3,600 | 107 | 1,125 |
| Amazing-Man #5 | 28 | 4,800 | + 6.7 | +19.2 | 26 | 4,500 | 31 | 2,450 |
| Adventure Comics #48 | 30 | 4,500 | +32.4 | +60.0 | 38 | 3,400 | 107 | 1,125 |
| All-Star Comics #1 | 30 | 4,500 | +12.5 | +17.8 | 28 | 4,000 | 35 | 2,380 |
| Batman #2 | 30 | $4,500 | +12.5 | +26.8 | 28 | $4,000 | 47 | $1,925 |
| Green Lantern #1 | 30 | 4,500 | +28.6 | +31.4 | 33 | 3,500 | 54 | 1,750 |
| Action Comics #3 | 34 | 4,000 | + 5.3 | + 5.4 | 30 | 3,800 | 20 | 3,150 |
| Big Book Of Fun #1 | 34 | 4,000 | +14.3 | +37.1 | 33 | 3,500 | 77 | 1,400 |
| Daring Mystery #1 | 34 | 4,000 | +14.3 | +12.7 | 33 | 3,500 | 31 | 2,450 |
| Detective Comics #2 | 34 | 4,000 | +14.3 | +30.0 | 33 | 3,500 | 62 | 1,600 |
| Famous Funnies #1 | 34 | 4,000 | +27.0 | +56.2 | 46 | 3,150 | 119 | 1,050 |
| Human Torch #1 | 34 | 4,000 | +14.3 | + 7.6 | 33 | 3,500 | 24 | 2,900 |
| Jumbo Comics #1 | 40 | 3,800 | +15.2 | +38.5 | 40 | 3,300 | 91 | 1,300 |
| Walt Disney's C&S #1 | 40 | 3,800 | + 2.7 | + 6.2 | 31 | 3,700 | 24 | 2,900 |
| Captain America #2 | 42 | $3,600 | +24.1 | +10.7 | 49 | $2,900 | 36 | $2,345 |
| Superman #2 | 42 | 3,600 | + 5.9 | + 5.7 | 38 | 3,400 | 27 | 2,800 |
| Action Comics #7 | 44 | 3,500 | + 9.4 | +10.8 | 41 | 3,200 | 38 | 2,275 |
| Action Comics #10 | 44 | 3,500 | + 9.4 | +10.8 | 41 | 3,200 | 38 | 2,275 |
| Donald Duck March Of Comics #4 | 44 | 3,500 | +16.7 | + 6.9 | 47 | 3,000 | 28 | 2,600 |
| Mickey Mouse Book | 44 | 3,500 | +45.8 | +67.5 | 70 | 2,400 | — | 800 |
| Red Raven #1 | 49 | 3,500 | + 9.4 | + 8.0 | 41 | 3,200 | 30 | 2,500 |
| Marvel Mystery Comics #5 | 49 | 3,400 | + 6.3 | + 2.3 | 41 | 3,200 | 21 | 3,050 |
| Action #5 | 50 | 3,200 | - 0 - | + 4.6 | 41 | 3,200 | 28 | 2,600 |

## TOP TEN ISSUES

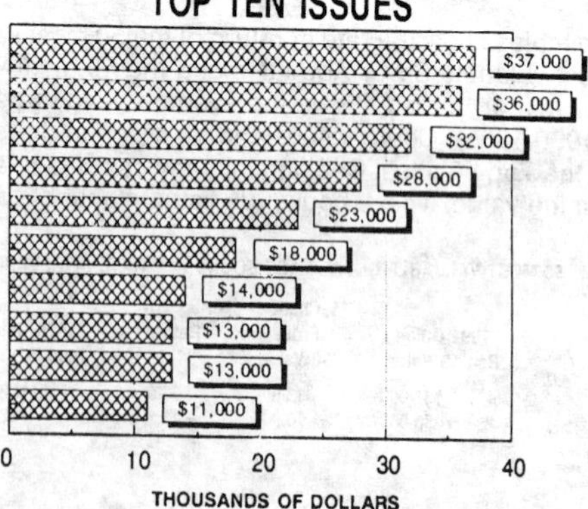

## 40 MOST VALUABLE SILVER AGE TITLES AND RATE OF INCREASE

| Issue | 1991 Guide Rank | & Value | %Change From '90 Value | Avg.Yrly. Return '86-'91 | 1990 Guide Rank | & Value | 1986 Guide Rank | & Value |
|---|---|---|---|---|---|---|---|---|
| Amaz. Spider-Man | 1 | $19,931 | + 52.0 | + 70.7 | 1 | $13,109 | 3 | $4,395 |
| Showcase | 2 | 17,917 | + 46.5 | + 41.9 | 2 | 12,232 | 1 | 5,787 |
| Fantastic Four | 3 | 13,651 | + 31.1 | + 36.9 | 3 | 10,412 | 2 | 4,797 |
| Strange Adventures | 4 | 13,066 | + 27.3 | + 27.7 | 4 | 10,260 | — | 5,482 |
| The Flash | 5 | 9,980 | + 10.8 | + 36.9 | 4 | 9,008 | 5 | 3,506 |
| Tales To Astonish/Inc. Hulk | 6 | 9,155 | + 39.4 | + 48.6 | 5 | 6,566 | 7 | 2,669 |
| Brave And The Bold | 7 | 7,821 | + 22.7 | + 24.6 | 6 | 6,375 | 4 | 3,508 |
| Green Lantern | 8 | 6,944 | + 30.1 | + 43.7 | 9 | 5,337 | 11 | 2,179 |
| Justice League | 9 | 6,703 | + 15.9 | + 38.6 | 8 | 5,781 | 10 | 2,288 |
| X-Men | 10 | 6,566 | + 9.8 | + 31.9 | 7 | 5,979 | 9 | 2,529 |
| Tales of Suspense/Capt. America | 11 | $6,036 | + 47.1 | + 91.5 | 15 | $4,104 | 21 | $1,083 |
| Sugar & Spike | 12 | 5,243 | + 10.8 | + 15.0 | 10 | 4,731 | 6 | 2,993 |
| Journey Into Mystery | 13 | 5,060 | + 34.3 | + 46.1 | 12 | 3,769 | 16 | 1,531 |
| Challengers Of The Unknown | 14 | 4,956 | + 33.7 | + 30.5 | 13 | 3,706 | 13 | 1,961 |
| Avengers | 15 | 4,365 | + 12.7 | + 26.2 | 11 | 3,873 | 14 | 1,889 |
| Daredevil | 16 | 4,275 | + 48.5 | + 62.4 | 16 | 2,879 | 23 | 1,037 |
| Superman's Pal J. Olson | 17 | 3,736 | + 18.8 | + 16.2 | 14 | 3,144 | 12 | 2,063 |
| Superman's Girlfriend L. Lane | 18 | 3,582 | + 36.7 | + 24.0 | 19 | 2,621 | 15 | 1,628 |
| Mystery In Space | 19 | 3,261 | + 15.7 | + 27.3 | 17 | 2,818 | 19 | 1,379 |
| Tales Of The Unexpected | 20 | 3,062 | + 28.4 | + 38.1 | 21 | 2,385 | 22 | 1,054 |
| Richie Rich | 21 | $2,751 | + 0.3 | + 0.7 | 18 | $2,744 | 8 | $2,664 |
| Strange Tales | 22 | 2,746 | + 14.1 | + 62.2 | 20 | 2,406 | 26 | $668 |
| Atom | 23 | 2,365 | + 67.3 | +151.4 | 26 | 1,414 | 35 | 276 |
| Our Army At War | 24 | 2,105 | + 39.7 | + 37.1 | 25 | 1,507 | — | 737 |
| Iron Man | 25 | 1,907 | + 24.6 | + 70.8 | 24 | 1,530 | 29 | 420 |
| Harvey Hits | 26 | 1,858 | + 5.4 | + 4.3 | 27 | 1,763 | 17 | 1,529 |
| Sgt. Fury | 27 | 1,849 | + 40.8 | +132.8 | 28 | 1,313 | 37 | 242 |
| Captain America | 28 | 1,735 | + 52.9 | +100.9 | 34 | 1,135 | — | 287 |
| Aquaman | 29 | 1,652 | + 36.6 | + 91.6 | 31 | 1,209 | 34 | 296 |
| Cerebus | 30 | 1,620 | − 13.6 | + 11.6 | 22 | 1,876 | 24 | 1,026 |
| Little Archie | 31 | $1,541 | + 11.3 | + 5.9 | 27 | $1,384 | 20 | $1,189 |
| Rip Hunter | 32 | 1,535 | + 38.9 | + 71.1 | 35 | 1,105 | 32 | 337 |
| Doom Patrol | 33 | 1,448 | + 22.6 | +126.3 | 32 | 1,181 | 41 | 198 |
| G. I. Combat | 34 | 1,310 | + 8.0 | + 21.7 | 30 | 1,213 | 27 | 629 |
| Advs. Of The Big Boy | 35 | 1,303 | + 0.4 | − 2.9 | 29 | 1,298 | 18 | 1,523 |
| Metal Men | 36 | 1,299 | + 11.0 | +147.6 | 33 | 1,170 | 45 | 155 |
| Hawkman | 37 | 1,292 | + 35.9 | +150.0 | 36 | 951 | 47 | 152 |
| Advs. Of The Fly | 38 | 1,177 | + 39.3 | + 42.3 | 38 | 845 | 30 | 378 |
| Sea Devils | 38 | 1,177 | + 52.5 | + 77.3 | 41 | 772 | 37 | 242 |
| Playful Little Audrey | 40 | 926 | + 3.2 | + 1.3 | 37 | 897 | 25 | 868 |

## 40 MOST VALUABLE SILVER AGE BOOKS AND RATE OF RETURN

| Issue | 1991 Guide Rank | & Value | %Change From '90 Value | Avg.Yrly. Return '86-'91 | 1990 Guide Rank | & Value | 1986 Guide Rank | & Value |
|---|---|---|---|---|---|---|---|---|
| Showcase #4 | 1 | $4,000 | +33.3 | +52.7 | 1 | $3,000 | 2 | $1,100 |
| Amazing Fantasy #15 | 2 | 3,500 | +25.0 | +43.6 | 2 | 2,800 | 2 | 1,100 |
| Fantastic Four #1 | 3 | 3,500 | +32.1 | +43.6 | 4 | 2,650 | 2 | 1,100 |
| Amaz. Spider-Man #1 | 4 | 3,400 | +23.6 | +65.0 | 3 | 2,750 | 5 | 800 |
| Adventure Comics #247 | 5 | 1,700 | + 6.3 | + 8.3 | 5 | 1,600 | 1 | 1,200 |
| Brave & The Bold #28 | 6 | 1,400 | +27.3 | +60.0 | 7 | 1,100 | 21 | 350 |
| Showcase #8 | 7 | 1,400 | +55.6 | +60.0 | 10 | 900 | 16 | 385 |
| Detective #225 | 8 | 1,350 | +17.4 | +38.1 | 8 | 1,150 | 7 | 465 |
| X-Men #1 | 9 | 1,260 | +27.3 | +43.0 | 8 | 990 | 13 | 400 |
| Incredible Hulk #1 | 10 | 1,250 | +31.6 | +23.1 | 9 | 950 | 6 | 580 |
| Tales of Suspense #39 | 11 | $1,150 | +31.4 | +45.7 | 12 | $875 | 21 | $350 |
| Showcase #22 | 12 | 1,050 | +44.8 | +40.0 | 17 | 725 | 21 | 350 |
| Adventure #210 | 13 | 1,000 | +25.0 | +51.4 | 14 | 800 | 34 | 280 |
| Amaz. Spider-Man #2 | 13 | 1,000 | +51.5 | +43.5 | 20 | 660 | 26 | 315 |
| Flash #105 | 13 | 1,000 | +25.0 | +37.1 | 14 | 800 | 21 | 350 |
| Justice League #1 | 13 | 1,000 | +11.1 | +25.5 | 10 | 900 | 10 | 440 |
| Journey Into Mystery #83 | 17 | 925 | +23.3 | +26.3 | 16 | 750 | 13 | 400 |
| Fantastic Four #2 | 18 | 900 | +28.6 | +19.1 | 19 | 700 | 8 | 460 |
| Tales To Astonish #27 | 18 | 900 | + 9.1 | +25.0 | 13 | 825 | 13 | 400 |
| Avengers #1 | 20 | 875 | +20.7 | +26.1 | 17 | 725 | 18 | 380 |

| Issue | 1991Guide Rank & Value | | %Change From '90 Value | Avg.Yrly. Return '86-'91 | 1990uide Rank & Value | | 1986Guide Rank & Value | |
|---|---|---|---|---|---|---|---|---|
| Showcase #13 | 21 | $820 | +36.7 | +38.6 | 23 | $600 | 29 | $280 |
| Showcase #14 | 21 | 820 | +36.7 | +43.1 | 23 | 600 | 29 | 260 |
| Green Lantern #1 | 23 | 780 | +18.2 | +32.0 | 20 | 660 | 28 | 300 |
| Fantastic Four #5 | 24 | 725 | +52.6 | +52.5 | 32 | 475 | 38 | 200 |
| Amaz. Spider-Man #3 | 25 | 700 | +59.1 | +60.0 | 33 | 440 | 44 | 175 |
| Fantastic Four #3 | 25 | 700 | +16.7 | +18.9 | 23 | 600 | 20 | 360 |
| Fantastic Four #4 | 25 | 700 | +33.3 | +31.9 | 27 | 525 | 31 | 270 |
| Showcase #6 | 25 | 700 | +40.0 | +24.4 | 29 | 500 | 26 | 315 |
| Superman's Pal J. Olson #1 | 29 | 680 | +11.5 | +12.4 | 22 | 610 | 12 | 420 |
| Daredevil #1 | 30 | 660 | +25.7 | +46.0 | 27 | 525 | 38 | 200 |
| Showcase #1 | 31 | 485 | + 7.8 | + 7.7 | 23 | 450 | 18 | 350 |
| Tales To Astonish #35 | 31 | 630 | +26.0 | +64.0 | 29 | 500 | 48 | 150 |
| Brave and the Bold #1 | 33 | 625 | + 8.7 | + 7.5 | 26 | 575 | 9 | 455 |
| Amaz. Spider-Man #14 | 34 | 620 | +175.6 | +186.7 | 78 | 225 | — | 60 |
| Brave And The Bold #29 | 35 | 550 | +25.0 | +64.6 | 33 | 440 | 61 | 130 |
| Brave And The Bold #30 | 35 | 550 | +25.0 | +64.6 | 33 | 440 | 61 | 130 |
| Showcase #1 | 35 | 550 | +13.4 | + 8.6 | 31 | 485 | 16 | 385 |
| Tales of Suspense #40 | 35 | 550 | +37.5 | +71.7 | 37 | 400 | 64 | 120 |
| Challengers of the Unknown #1 | 39 | 525 | +31.3 | +22.0 | 37 | 400 | 32 | 250 |
| Amaz. Spider-Man #4 | 40 | 500 | +38.9 | +51.4 | 42 | 360 | 54 | 140 |

## THE FIRST WAVE OF COMIC BOOKS 1933-1943 (Key books listed and ranked)

The first modern format comic book came out in 1933 and represents the beginning of comic books as we know them today. The impact of these early characters and ideas are today deeply engrained in American folklore and continue to feed and inspire this ever changing industry.

Over the years historians, collectors and bibliofiles have tried to make some sense out of this era. The question 'what are considered to be the most important books?' has been a topic of discussion and debate for many years. With certain criteria considered, how would the top key issues be ranked in order of importance? How would they relate to each other? In an attempt to answer some of these questions, the following list has been prepared. The books are grouped chronologically in the order they were published. The most important books are ranked into seven tiers, with the top six designated with stars. The more important the book is, the more stars it receives. The following criteria were used to determine the importance and placement of each book in each tier:

A. Durability of character(s)
b. Durability of title
c. Popularity of character(s)
d. First app. anywhere of a major character
e. First issue of a title
f. Originality of character (first of a type)
g. First or most significant work of a major artist
h. Starts a trend
i. First of a genre
j. Historical significance
k. First of a publisher
l. First appearance in comic books of a character from another medium

This list was compiled by several people* and represents a collective opinion of all. The list is not perfect, not by any means. Adjustments will be made over time as more input is received. The final ranking of a book depends greatly on the overall importance and impact of that book on the comic book market. Obviously, the further you get away from the top key books, the more difficult it becomes for proper ranking. For this reason, books ranked in the lower numbered tiers could change drastically. The final rating given a book is not based entirely on the quantity of points it receives, but rather the overall weight of the points it does receive. For example, the first appearance of *The Fighting Yank* is not as important as the first appearance of *Superman* who was a trend setting character and long lasting.

In the comics market there are several comics that have become high demand, valuable books due primarily to rarity. A list of the top key books ranked due to value, demand and rarity would look entirely different than what we have here. As we have learned in coins, stamps and other hobbies, rarity is an important factor that affects value and it is not our intention to demean the collectibility of any particular book that is rare. Quite the contrary. There are many rare books that would enhance anyone's collection. Consideration of rarity, for the ranking of books in this list has been kept at a minimum.

The following list covers the period 1933 through 1943 and includes **every** key book of this period of which we are currently aware. Any omissions will be added in future lists. It should be noted that many other issues, although highly collectible, were not considered important for the purpose of this list: i.e., origin issues, early issues in a run, special cover and story themes, etc.

**Special thanks is due* ***Landon Chesney*** *who contributed considerable energy and thought to the individual write-ups; to* ***David Noah*** *who polished and edited, and to the following people who contributed their time and ideas to the compilation of this list: Hugh O'Kennon, Steve Geppi, Richard Halegua, John Snyder, Joe Tricarichi, Walter Wang, Jon Warren, Bruce Hamilton, Ray Belden and Chuck Wooley*

***NOTE:*** *All* ***first issues*** *are included as well as books that introduce an important new character, or has key significance in some other way.*

# CHRONOLOGICAL LIST OF KEY COMIC BOOKS FOR PERIOD 1933 - 1943

### (All first issues listed)

### GENRE CODES (Main theme)

| | | | |
|---|---|---|---|
| **An** - Anthology (mixed) | **H** - Costumed/Superhero | **Mg** - Magic | **Sp** - Sport |
| **Av** - Aviation | **Hr** - Horror | **M** - Movie | **TA** - Teen-Age |
| **Cr** - Crime | **Hm** - Humor | **R** - Strip Reprints | **Tr** - True Fact |
| **D** - Detective | **J** - Jungle | **Re** - Religious | **W** - War |
| **F** - Funny Animal | **Lit** - Literature | **SF** - Science Fiction | **Ws** - Western |

**NOTE:** The stars signify the ranking of books into seven different tiers of importance. The top (most important) books receive six stars (1st tier), dropping to no star (7th tier) as their significance diminishes. The following information is provided for each comic: 1. Ranking, 2. Title, 3. Issue number, 4. Date, 5. Publisher, 6. Genre code, 7. Description. 8. Criteria codes.

## PRE-GOLDEN AGE PERIOD

## 1933 ■

★★★★ **FUNNIES ON PARADE** nn (1933, Eastern Color, R)-The very first comic book in the modern format reprinting popular strip characters. Given away to test the feasibility of demand for repackaged Sunday newspaper funnies. (An 8-page tabloid folded down to 32 pages).
(a,c,d,e,h,i,j,k,l)

★★★★ **FAMOUS FUNNIES, A CARNIVAL OF COMICS** nn (1933, Eastern Color, R)-The second comic book. Given away to test reader demand. Its success set up another test to come in the following year to see if the public would actually pay 10 cents for this type of product (an 8-page tabloid folded down to 32 pages). The first of three first issues for this title.
(a,b,c,e,f,h,j)

★ **CENTURY OF COMICS** nn (1933, Eastern Color, R)-The third comic book. A 100-pager given away with three times the contents of the previous two books.
(e,j)

## 1934 ■

★ **SKIPPY'S OWN BOOK OF COMICS** nn (1934, Eastern Color, R)-The fourth comic book. The first to feature a single character-this wasn't tried again until ***Superman*** No. 1.
(e,j)

★★★★ **FAMOUS FUNNIES, SERIES I** (1934, Eastern Color, R)-The first comic book sold to the general public (through chain stores). The acid test, its unprecedented success set up the beginning of the first continuous series (anthology reprint) title in comics, and started the chain reaction.
(a,b,c,e,f,h,j)

★★★★★ **FAMOUS FUNNIES** No. 1 (7/34, Eastern Color, R)-Satisfied with the public response, this issue began the series and was the first comic book sold to the general public through newsstand distribution.
(a,b,c,e,f,h,j)

★ **FAMOUS FUNNIES** No. 3 (9/34, Eastern Color, R)-This issue ushered in the famous and very popular *Buck Rogers* strip reprints. Not trend setting, but important for the survival of the run which lasted 22 years.
(a,b,c,f,i,j,l)

## 1935 ■

★★★★ **NEW FUN COMICS** No. 1 (2/35, DC, An)-The first prototype of the modern comic in that it featured an anthology format of continuing characters and original rather than reprinted material. First of the DC line and the first tabloid-size book (albeit short-lived), surviving 13 years as ***More Fun Comics***.
(b,e,h,i,j,k)

★ **MICKEY MOUSE MAGAZINE** No. 1 (Sum/35, K.K., F)-Magazine-size protocomic introducing the already legendary transfer characters to the fledgling comic book market. This title first appeared in 1933 as a black & white giveaway comic, and after going through format changes, eventually led to the ultimate "funny animal" comic, ***Walt Disney's Comics & Stories***, to come five years later.
(a,b,c,e,g,j,k)

★ **NEW COMICS** No. 1 (12/35, DC, An)-DC felt enough confidence in the market to issue a second anthology title featuring original, continuing characters. It was second only to ***New Fun*** of its kind. Evolved into ***Adventure Comics***, warhorse of the DC line. DC parlayed the second most perfect comic book title (the first is ***Action***) into a forty plus year run.
(b,e,h,j)

## 1936 ■

**MORE FUN COMICS** No. 7 (1/36, DC, An)-DC cancelled the title ***New Fun*** due to the appearance of ***New Comics***, continuing the series under this changed title.
(b,e,j)

★★★ **POPULAR COMICS** No. 1 (2/36, Dell, R)-The second anthology format title of continuing reprint strips. First of the Dell line, the third publisher to enter the field. Featuring the first comic book appearance of *Dick Tracy, Little Orphan Annie, Terry & the Pirates* and others, lasting 13 years.
(a,b,c,e,j,k,l)

**BIG BOOK OF FUN COMICS** (Spr/36, DC, An)-The first annual in comics (56 pages, large size; reprints from ***New Fun*** No. 1-5).
(e,h,i,j)

★★★ **KING COMICS** No. 1 (4/36, McKay, R)-Ties as the third continuous series reprint title. The first of a publisher (4th to enter the field). Showcase title of all the King Feature characters-the most popular and widely circulated in the world, featuring Segar's *Popeye* and Raymond's *Flash Gordon* series as the mainstay, lasting 16 years.
(a,b,c,e,j,k,l)

★★★ **TIP TOP COMICS** No. 1 (4/36, UFS, R)-Ties as the third continuous series reprint anthology title. The first of a publisher (5th to enter the field). Featuring the *Tarzan* and *Li'l Abner* series and surviving 25 years.
(a,b,c,e,j,k,l)

★ **COMICS MAGAZINE, THE** (Funny Pages) No. 1 (5/36, Comics Mag., An)-The third anthology format title of original material. The first of a publisher (6th to enter the field). This book is unique in that its cover and entire contents were purchased from DC. This material created gaps in the story line continuity of DC's titles ***More Fun*** and ***New Adventure*** from which it came.
(e,j,k)

**WOW COMICS** No. 1 (7/36, McKay, An)-The fourth anthology title of original material. McKay's second series (first with original contents), lasting only 4 issues to 11/36. The Unpublished inventory formed the basis of the Eisner/Iger shop.
(e)

**NEW BOOK OF COMICS** No. 1 (6-8/36, DC, An)-The second annual in comics; 100 pages, reprinting popular strips from ***More Fun*** and ***New Comics***. Second and last issue appeared in Spring of 1938.
(e)

**FUNNIES, THE** No. 1 (10/36, Dell, R)-Having published this title six years earlier as a tabloid, Dell brought it back as a regular comic book. Featuring more popular strip characters, this became Dell's second comic book title and ran for 6 years.
(b,e)

**FUNNY PAGES** No. 6 (11/36, Comics Mag., An)-Continued from ***The Comics Magazine****; introduced The Clock*(?), the first masked hero (detective type, transition hero) in a comic book.
(a,b,c,d,e,f,h,i,j)

**FUNNY PICTURE STORIES** No. 1 (11/36, Comics Mag., An)-Actually this company's second title, featuring their popular original character, *The Clock*, who appeared on the cover. Title continues for 3 years.
(e)

**DETECTIVE PICTURE STORIES** No. 1 (12/36, Comic Mag., D)-The first anthology comic title series devoted to a single theme and the first to focus on this subject. Popular in pulps, magazines and films of the time, lasted 7 issues.
(e,h,i,j)

## 1937 ■

**NEW ADVENTURE COMICS** No. 12 (1/37, DC, An)-Title change from ***New Comics***, continues series.
(e)

**STAR COMICS** No. 1 (2/37, Chesler, An)-Ties as first of a publisher. Anthology format of continuing original material, but short lived (2½ years). Large-size format.
(e,k)

**STAR RANGER** No. 1 (2/37, Chesler, Ws)-Ties as first of a publisher, and as the first continuous series western anthology title (see ***Western Picture Stories***). Large-size format of original material, lasting only 1 year.
(e,i,j,k)

**WESTERN PICTURE STORIES** No. 1 (2/37, Comics Mag, Ws)-Ties with ***Star Ranger*** as the first anthology comic title of original material to focus on this subject, the second of a single theme, not lasting out the year.
(e,i,j)

**COMICS, THE** No. 1 (3/37, Dell, R)-Dell's third anthology reprint title. The first comic book appearance of *Tom Mix*, lasting only one year.
(e,d)

★ ★ ★ **DETECTIVE COMICS** No. 1 (3/37, DC, D)-Inaugurated the longest run in comics. Initially a pulpy anthology of mystery men and private eyes, it emerged as the first important title on a single theme with the debut of the implacable *Batman* in '39 (Siegel and Shuster's *Slam Bradley* series is a flavorful example of title's '37-'38 period).
(a,b,c,e,f,h,i,j)

**ACE COMICS** No. 1 (4/37, McKay, R)-Due to the enormous success of McKay's first series, ***King Comics***, this companion title was published featuring, among others, Raymond's *Jungle Jim*, lasting 12 years.
(a,b,c,e,j,l)

**WESTERN ACTION THRILLERS** No. 1 (4/37, Dell, Ws)-The third title devoted to westerns. A one-shot of 100 pages.
(e)

**FEATURE BOOK** nn (Popeye)(1937, McKay, R)-A new concept. The first series of comic books representing a divergence from the normal anthology format. Each issue in the run is actually a one-shot devoted to a single character. More than one issue in the run can be devoted to the same character. These books began in a B&W, magazine-size format. Improvements on this concept came a year later with UFS's ***Single Series*** (in color, comic book size), and still a year later with Dell's ***Four Color*** series, the only one to last.
(a,b,c,e,h,i,j)

**FEATURE FUNNIES** No. 1 (10/37, Chesler, R)-Another reprint title to add to the list, surviving 13 years as ***Feature Comics***; carrying *Joe Palooka, Mickey Finn* and others.
(e)

**100 PAGES OF COMICS** No. 101 (1937, Dell, R)-Another 100-page reprint anthology book (Dell's 2nd) with a western cover. Only one issue.
(e)

## 1938 ■

**ACE COMICS** No. 11 (2/38, McKay, R)-First comic book appearance of *The Phantom*. Premiere mystery man and first costumed hero. The Ghost Who Walks never made the impact in comics that he enjoyed as a syndicated star.
(a,b,c,f,i,j,l)

**FUNNY PAGES** V2/6 (3/38, Centaur, An)-Ties with ***Funny Picture Stories***, ***Star Comics*** and ***Star Ranger*** as first of a publisher. Series picked up from Chesler, ending two years later.
(k)

**FUNNY PICTURE STORIES** V2/6 (3/38, Centaur, An)-Ties with ***Funny Pages***, ***Star Comics***, and ***Star Ranger*** as first of a publisher. Series picked up from Comics Magazine, ending one year later.
(k)

**STAR COMICS** No. 10 (3/38, Centaur, An)-Ties with ***Funny Pages***, ***Funny Picture Stories***, and ***Star Ranger*** as first of a publisher. Series picked up from Chesler, ending one year later.
(k)

**STAR RANGER** V2/10 (3/38, Centaur, Ws)-Ties with ***Funny Picture Stories***, ***Star Ranger***, and ***Funny Pages*** as first of a publisher. Series picked up from Chesler, lasting 2 more issues.
(k)

**COMICS ON PARADE** No. 1 (4/38, UFS, R)-The second title of this publisher, featuring much the same reprint strips as ***Tip Top***, their first. This series survived 17 years.
(a,b,c,e,j)

**MAMMOTH COMICS** No. 1 (1938, Whitman, R)-First of a publisher, in the same format as the McKay ***Feature Books***. Only one issue.
(e,k)

**SUPER COMICS** No. 1 (5/38, Dell, R)-A dynamic new title, Dell's fourth. Debuted with some of the heavy weights transferred from the already successful ***Popular Comics***. This new line-up of *Dick Tracy, Terry & The Pirates,* etc. proved to be a sound marketing strategy, lasting 11 years.
(a,b,c,e,j)

# GOLDEN AGE PERIOD

★ ★ ★ ★ ★ ★ **ACTION COMICS** No. 1 (6/38, DC, H)-The ultimate refinement of the anthology, continuing character title. The first appearance of *Superman*, the quintessential hero with extraordinary powers. Arguably the most imitated character in all of fiction. Standard bearer of the DC line.

The most important comic book ever published, and in tandem with ***Superman***, one of the most influential, prevailed beyond four decades.
(a,b,c,d,e,f,h,i,j)

**CIRCUS COMICS** No. 1 (6/38, Globe, An)-A unique short-lived title featuring a top artist line-up. Introduced Wolverton's *Spacehawks*, later to appear in ***Target Comics*** as *Spacehawk*. First of a publisher.
(d,e,f,j,k)

**CRACKAJACK FUNNIES** No. 1 (6/38, Dell, R)-A new Dell title, replacing the defunct ***The Comics*** with a similar but different mix of reprint strips. Lasted 4 years.
(e)

**COWBOY COMICS** No. 13 (7/38, Centaur, Ws)-Continued from ***Star Ranger*** and lasted only two issues. The fourth western anthology title.
(e)

**KEEN DETECTIVE FUNNIES** No. 8 (7/38, Centaur, An)-Continued from ***Detective Picture Stories***, this title became one of Centaur's mainstays introducing the *Masked Marvel* one year later, lasting 2 years.
(e)

**LITTLE GIANT COMICS** No. 1 (7/38, Centaur, An)-Small-size diversion from the regular format and short-lived (4 issues).
(e)

**AMAZING MYSTERY FUNNIES** No. 1 (8/38, Centaur, An)-Standard bearer of the Centaur line. Top artist line-up due to its production by the Everett shop. Ran for two years.
(e,g)

**LITTLE GIANT MOVIE FUNNIES** No. 1 (8/38, Centaur, An)-A miniature-sized format comic lasting two issues. A small cartoon panel appears on the right edge of each page giving the illusion of motion when riffled (a flip book) (the cover is set up to represent a movie theater).
(e,i)

★ **FUNNY PAGES** V2/10 (9/38, Centaur, H)-First appearance of *The Arrow* who is the very first costumed hero originating in the comic book (3 months after *Superman*). A primitive percursor of the more refined archers to come, *The Arrow* executed his adversaries with the medieval bluntness his uniform suggested.
(a,b,d,f,h,i,j)

★★★ **JUMBO COMICS** No. 1 (9/38, FH, J)-Publisher of the most perused, but least read, of Golden Age comics, Fiction House did not so much initiate a trend as continue the trusty formula that sustained their line of pulps, cheesecake cast against a variety of single theme adventurous backgrounds (aviation, s/f, jungle & war). ***Jumbo*** was the pilot model of the FH line and the first of the exploitation comics. The debut of *Sheena, Queen of the Jungle* heralded hordes of jungle goddesses to follow. The line overall is perhaps best remembered as a showcase for Matt Baker's patented 'calendar girl' art which, after Caniff and Raymond, was the most pervasive of Golden Age styles, enduring 15 years.
(a,b,c,e,f,h,i,j,k,l)

**DETECTIVE COMICS** No. 20 (10/38, DC, H)-First appearance of *The Crimson Avenger*, a *Shadow* look-a-like, who was the second comic book costumed hero (4 months after *Superman*).
(b,c,d,f,h,i,j)

**LITTLE GIANT DETECTIVE FUNNIES** No. 1 (10/38, Centaur, An)-Small-size format only lasting a few issues.
(e)

**STAR RANGER FUNNIES** No. 15 (10/38, Centaur, An)-Links to ***Star Ranger*** and ***Cowboy Comics***, only lasting a few months. (Packaged by the Iger Shop.)
(e)

★★★ **DONALD DUCK** nn (1938, Whitman, F)-The first *Donald Duck*, as well as the first Walt Disney comic book; in the format of McKay's ***Feature Book*** (B&W with color cover), reprinting 1936 & 1937 Sunday comics. The first funny animal comic devoted to a single character. Precursor to great things to come for this character.
(a,b,c,e,f,i,j,l)

★★ **SINGLE SERIES** nn (Captain & The Kids) (1938, UFS, R)-UFS refined McKay's one-shot ***Feature Book*** format by adding color and adopting the standard comic book size, resulting in a more marketable package. Dell adopted this format for their ***Four Color*** series, which started a year later. This is UFS' third continuous series title.
(e,f,h,i,j)

**COCOMALT BIG BOOK OF COMICS** No. 1 (1938, Chesler, An)-A one-shot mixed anthology Charles Biro creation, packaged by the Chesler shop (top-notch art).
(e)

**NICKEL COMICS** No. 1 (1938, Dell, An)-A small-size divergent format one-shot, lasting only one issue.
(e)

## 1939 ■

**ALL-AMERICAN COMICS** No. 1 (4/39, DC, R)-DC finally bends to the reprint anthology format, but includes some original material for flavor. *Scribbly* by Mayer begins; a ten-year run.
(a,b,c,d,e,j)

**NEW YORK WORLD'S FAIR** (3-5/39, DC, H)-The first newsstand comic with a commercial tie-in, capitalizing on the enormous publicity of a real life public event, featuring DC's top characters. The thick format, as well as the title segued into ***World's Finest Comics*** two years later.
(a,c,e,i,j)

★ **MOVIE COMICS** No. 1 (4/39, DC, M)-A unique but short-lived idea. The notion of adapting films to comics in fumetti form (the panels were half-tones of stills from the films) was a good one, but didn't work any better in '39 than it does today. (The first movie adaptation comic in standard comic book form and probably the first attempt at a fumetti continuity.)
(e,f,j,i)

★★★★★ **DETECTIVE COMICS** No. 27 (5/39, DC, H)-Reliable but predictable 'funny paper' cops 'n robbers anthology came into focus with the debut of *The Batman*. DC's second powerhouse set another standard for the industry to follow. The 'dynamic' hero—costumed athlete sans extraordinary powers—proved a viable alternative for the burgeoning competition to mimic, but Bob Kane broke the mold. The character's unique personna defied any but the most oblique imitation. ***Detective*** shared standard bearer honors with ***Action*** and provided the initials by which the company was known. One of the top four comics.
(a,b,c,d,f,h,j)

**KEEN KOMICS** V2/1 (5/39, Centaur, An)-A large size mixed anthology comic changing to regular size with number two. Packaged by the Everett shop and lasting only three issues.
(e)

★★ **WONDER COMICS** No. 1 (5/39, Fox, H)-Salutory effort of Fox (packaged by Eisner/Iger). First, and shortest-lived, of *Superman* imitations. Historically significant because the debut of Fox's *Wonder Man* prompted DC's first attempt to successfully defend their copyright on *Superman*. (A precedent that would prove decisive when the Man of Steel confronted a more formidable courtroom adversary a decade hence). Only one more issue followed.
(d,e,j,k)

★★★ **MOTION PICTURE FUNNIES WEEKLY** No.1 (5/39? Funnies, Inc., H)-Produced as a theatre giveaway, this title featured the first appearance of *Sub-Mariner*. His official

newsstand debut occurred later in the year in ***Marvel Comics*** No. 1. Only seven known copies exist.
(a,c,d,e,f,g,h,i,j,k)

**FEATURE COMICS** No. 21 (6/39, Quality, An)-Continues from ***Feature Funnies*** of two years earlier. A discreet title change, indicating that original adventure comics were becoming a significant alternative to the formerly dominant reprints.
(b,e,k)

★★ **ADVENTURE COMICS** No. 40 (7/39, DC, H)-The *Sandman*, a transition crime fighter who stuck tenaciously to the trusty regalia of the pulp heroes. Finally, the pressure to adopt modern togs was brought to bear. The original mystery man vanished into oblivion, replaced by a swashbuckling Kirby hero.
(a,b,c,d,j)

**AMAZING MYSTERY FUNNIES** V2/7 (7/39, Centaur, H)-Debut of *The Fantom of the Fair*, mystery man, whose headquarters were under the World's Fair (An unexpected attraction for Fair goers). Destined for extinction with the 1940 wind-up of the Fair. Top artist line-up and exciting cover concepts.
(c,d,j)

**COMIC PAGES** V3/4 (7/39, Centaur, An)-A mixed anthology series continuing from ***Funny Picture Stories*** of three years earlier, lasting 3 issues.
(e)

**KEEN DETECTIVE FUNNIES** V2/7 (7/39, Centaur, H)-*The Masked Marvel*, super sleuth, and his three confederates began a terror campaign against lawless gangs. His big amphibian plane, secret laboratory and projected red shadow were devices used in the strip, lasting one year.
(d,j)

★★★ **MUTT AND JEFF** nn (Sum/39, DC, R)-This one shot represented a significant departure for DC. Formerly they had avoided the reprint title, preferring to develop their own original characters. This title was obviously a test to see if the market would support an entire book devoted to a single character (or in this case characters). This book has the honor of being the very first *newsstand* comic devoted to a single reprint strip. After a very slow start (four issues in four years), ***Mutt And Jeff*** was made a quarterly and soon became a popular run lasting 26 astounding years. It was the only successful reprint series of a single character to enjoy a respectible run. The syndicated *Mutt and Jeff* strip was, after *The Katzenjammer Kids,* the oldest continuously published newspaper strip.
(a,b,c,e,j)

★★★★★ **SUPERMAN** No. 1 (Sum/39, DC, H)-This landmark issue signaled a major turning point for the industry. Arguably, the second most important comic ever published (***Action*** being the first), and possibly the most influential. *Superman* was the first original character promoted from headling an anthology title to starring in a book of his own. More importantly, this tandem exposure demonstrated to the industry that it could survive on its own original material, independent of the proven syndicated stars. As other publishers were attracted to the field in the months to come, they emulated not only *Superman*, but the tandem anthology/headline format that had contributed to his unprecedented success. A double trend setter. Contains reprint material from ***Action*** No. 1-4. Title has continued beyond four decades.
(a,b,c,e,h,i,j)

**WONDERWORLD COMICS** No. 3 (7/39, Fox, H)-After the *Wonder Man* debacle, Fox bounces back with a revised title and a new lead character (courtesy of the Iger shop). *The Flame* got off to a brilliant start, but was snuffed out when Iger and Fox parted company, lasting 3 years.
(a,c,d,e,j)

**MAGIC COMICS** No. 1 (8/39, McKay, R)-King Features' third reprint anthology (after ***King*** and ***Ace Comics***) featured such popular syndicated stars as *Mandrake, Henry,* and *Blondie*. By 1940 *Blondie* had become the most widely syndicated newspaper strip in the world, and became the prime cover feature for the balance of the run, title enduring 10½ years.
(a,b,c,e,j)

★ **MYSTERYMEN COMICS** No. 1 (8/39, Fox, H)-Fox was on firm ground with a trio of potential contenders: ***Wonderworld's*** *The Flame* and, debuting in this title, *The Blue Beetle* and *The Green Mask*. These early products of the Eisner/Iger shop are worth a second look. Potential glows from every page. Soon, due to the E/I and Fox break up, the characters sunk into hack oblivion.
(a,c,d,e,j)

**SMASH COMICS** No. 1 (8/39, Quality, An)-This is the first title that Quality developed entirely on their own, (previous titles having been purchased from other publishers). The series lacked originality until the debut of Lou Fine's *Ray* which began in issue No. 14.
(b,e,j)

**AMAZING MAN COMICS** No. 5 (9/39, Centaur, H)-Everett's *A-Man* was launched here, the first Centaur character to headline his own title. The first costumed hero to shrink (*Minimidget*) begins. (This concept was better used later in Quality's *Doll Man.*) Top artist line-up in this series which ended in early 1942. The standard bearer of the Centaur line.
(e,j)

**SPEED COMICS** No. 1 (10/39, Harvey, H)-First of a publisher. *Shock Gibson* is the main hero. The characters in this series lacked the charisma of the competition's best; had a few bright moments when top artists entered the line-up, surviving as an average run for 7 years.
(a,b,e,k)

**BEST COMICS** No. 1 (11/39, BP, H)-First of a publisher. Debut of the Red Mask. An experimental large format book that read sideways; it failed to find an audience after four issues and folded.
(e,j,k)

**BLUE RIBBON COMICS** No. 1 (11/39, MLJ, An)-First of a publisher. Contents unremarkable (*Rang-A-Tang, The Wonder Dog*, for example). An MLJ anthology that failed to survive beyond 1942 despite the influx of super heroes.
(e,j,k)

★★★★★ **MARVEL COMICS** No. 1 (11/39, Timely, H)-Timely, the first publisher to hit with a smash twin bill in their inaugural title (courtesy of the Everett shop). From the onset, the formula of iconoclast as hero would prove to be Timely's most successful newstand strategy. *The Human Torch* and *Sub-Mariner* won immediate reader approval, paving the way for more marvels to come from the pre-eminent Thrill Factory of comicdom. Possibly The most sought after of all Golden Age comics. Title lasted 10 years.
(a,b,c,d,e,f,g,h,i,j,k)

**CHAMPION COMICS** No. 2 (12/39, Harvey, An)-Early transitional anthology title with a sports theme, changing over to costumed heroes early on. None of the characters caught on enough to sustain the run for more than four years.
(e)

**FANTASTIC COMICS** No. 1 (12/39, Fox, H)-Biblical character *Samson* debuts. This series is more noted for the Lou Fine covers (Iger Shop). *Stardust* begins, one of the most bizarre super heroes in comics (Almost child-like, almost surrealistic art and plotting). He assassinated wrong doers regularly.
(e)

★★ **FEATURE COMICS** No. 27 (12/39, Quality, H)-Debut of the *Dollman* (Quality's first super hero), who was the second, but most significant, with the power to shrink (See

***Amazing Man***). The stories were generally undistinguished but Quality's high standards of illustration (Eisner in this case) lent the strip a credibility that would have been lacking in lesser hands. This title lasted 11 years.
(a,b,c,d,j)

★ **SILVER STREAK COMICS** No. 1 (12/39, Lev, An)-First of a publisher. Debut of *The Claw*, one of the most bizarre villains in the annals of comics. Standing 100 feet tall with claws and fangs was the ultimate refinement of the 'yellow peril' theme from the pulps. Such a formidable figure had to have an adversary to match (See ***Silver Streak*** No. 7). The first comic book to display a metallic silver logo to insure prominence on the stands.
(a,c,d,e,f,k)

**TOP-NOTCH COMICS** No. 1 (12/39, MLJ, H)-*The Wizard*, one of MLJ's top characters debuted. Their second anthology title, lasting 4½ years.
(a,b,c,d,e,j)

**LARGE FEATURE COMIC** nn (1939, Dell, R)-Black and white, magazine size, one-shot series with color covers (identical to Mckay ***Feature Books*** of two years earlier), lasting four years.
(a,c,e)

**CAPTAIN EASY** nn (1939, Hawley, R)-First of a publisher. A one-shot reprint comic devoted to a single character, already proven successful by other publishers.
(a,c,e,k)

★★ **FOUR COLOR** No. 1 (Dick Tracy)(1939, Dell, R)-Exact format of UFS's ***Single Series*** of one year earlier. The most successful of the one-shot continuity titles, lasting 23 years. This series also provided a testing arena for new characters and concepts.
(a,b,c,e,j)

**LONE RANGER COMICS, THE** nn (1939, giveaway, Ws)-Fifth western title, first of a major character. This one-shot may have had newsstand distribution as price (10 cents) was stamped on cover.
(a,c,e)

## 1940 ■

★★ **BLUE BEETLE, THE** No. 1 (Wint/39-40, Fox, H)-The star of the second continuous series title devoted to a single character exemplified the pioneer 'crime fighter' of the early comics. His uniform was as simple and direct as the four-color medium itself– unadorned, form-fitting chain mail. Disdaining cloak, cape and the cover of night, *Blue Beetle* trounced crime where he found it, usually in the street and in broad daylight. Striking figure made an indelible impression on readers and, had Fox been more committed to long term development, would have doubtless gone the distance. The series eventually succumbed to tepid scripts and lack-lustre art, but the character was of sufficient personal appeal to survive, in memory, not only the demise of his title but legions of better produced, longer tenured heroes.

★★★★★ **FLASH COMICS** No. 1 (1/40, DC, H)-DC reinforced its arsenal with two more dynamos: *The Flash* (first, and most significant hero with lightning speed), and *The Hawkman* (first and most significant winged hero). Both trend setters, with series lasting beyond 40 years.
(a,b,c,d,e,f,h,i,j)

★★ **FLASH COMICS** No. 1 (1/40, Faw, H)-An in-house b&w proof produced to secure pre-publication copyright. Important changes made before the book was officially released were, a title change from ***Flash*** to ***Whiz*** (DC had already gone to press with their ***Flash Comics***), and the name of the lead character was changed from *Captain Thunder* to *Captain Marvel*. (8 known copies exist.)
(e,f,g,j,k)

**THRILL COMICS** No. 1 (1/40, Faw, H)-Identical to ***Flash Comics*** listed above, only a different title. Only three known copies exist.
(e,f,g,j,k)

**JUNGLE COMICS** No. 1 (1/40, FH, J)-The second single theme anthology series of this subject (cloned from ***Jumbo***). The title more perfectly suggested the 'jungle' theme with format selling rather than strong characters. Third series of a publisher, lasting as long as its parent (14½ years), with no competition until six years later.
(a,b,c,d,e,j)

★★ **PEP COMICS** No. 1 (1/40, MLJ, H)-Debut of *The Shield*, the first patriotic hero, later eclipsed by Simon & Kirby's *Captain America*, the bombshell of 1941. MLJ's third and longest lasting (over 40 years) anthology title. Archie eventually takes over the series.
(a,b,c,d,e,f,h,i,j)

★★★★ **PLANET COMICS** No. 1 (1/40, FH, SF)-The publisher's fourth anthology title of continuing characters. The first and by far the most successful science fiction run in comics. As with ***Jumbo*** and ***Jungle***, this title had no competition for many years. Fiction House's style of action-packed covers and art made up for the routine plotting, lasting 14 years.
(a,b,c,e,f,h,i,j)

**MIRACLE COMICS** No. 1 (2/40, Hillman, H)-A mixed anthology series similar to ***Rocket Comics*** published a month later. First of a publisher. Covers have good eye-appeal, ending with the fourth issue.
(e,k)

★★★ **MORE FUN COMICS** No. 52,53 (2,3/40, DC, H)-DC modernizes its first anthology title, introducing the ominous *Spectre* in this two-part origin series. This frightening ethereal hero was too much a match for his adversaries, but gave DC an exciting alternative to their swelling ranks of wondermen. A trend setter, lasting 4 years in this title.
(a,b,c,d,f,h,i,j)

**SCIENCE COMICS** No. 1 (2/40, Fox, SF)-With qualifications, the second science fiction anthology title (very few of the stories dealt with outer space). Aside from the Lou Fine covers (No. 1 & 2), the artwork was not attractive and the series died after eight issues. First *Eagle* (the second winged hero).
(e)

**TARGET COMICS** No. 1 (2/40, Novelty, H)-First of a publisher. An early Everett shop super hero production. First *White Streak* by Burgos (the second android super hero). Top artist line-up featuring above average covers and stories, lasting 10 years.
(b,e,k)

**THRILLING COMICS** No. 1 (2/40, Better, H)-The first successful anthology title by this publisher (their second series). Debut of *Dr. Strange*. Logo carried over from the pulp. The Schomburg covers are the highlight of the run. The title lasted 11 years, switching to a jungle theme near the end.
(a,b,c,e,j)

★★★★★ **WHIZ COMICS** No. 2 (2/40, Faw, H)-After ***Action***, the most significant of all hero/adventure anthologies was this late entry from Fawcett. Origin, first appearance of *Captain Marvel*, humor hero par excellence. The most accessible of miracle men came from behind to eclipse the competition's best. He also founded the industry's first character dynasty (Marvel's *Junior, Mary* and even *Bunny*), a tactic that would prove as fundamental to comics' merchandising as DC's hero team concept. Landmark first issue also introduced such secondary stalwarts as *Sivana, Old Shazam, Spy Smasher* (the definitive aviator/mysteryman), and *Ibis the Invincible*, most memorable of comic book sorcerers. Flagship of the Fawcett line and a perennial favorite for 13 years.
(a,b,c,d,e,f,g,j,k)

**ZIP COMICS** No. 1 (2/40, MLJ, H)-MLJ's fourth anthology title (featuring *Steel Sterling*). Interesting stylized covers and

art. Series lasted four years. With the exception of *Wilbur* (an Archie clone), none of the characters reached their own titles.
(a,b,c,d,j)

★★ **ADVENTURE COMICS** No. 48 (3/40, DC, H)-Debut of *The Hourman*. A substantial secondary feature that sold a few books for DC, but never received adequate creative support. Interesting premise came to dominate all the stories resulting in monotonous repetition.
(a,b,c,d,e,j)

**COLOSSUS COMICS** No. 1 (3/40, Sun, H)-An early esoteric book which ties to the esoteric ***Green Giant*** comic.
(e)

★★★ **DONALD DUCK FOUR COLOR** No. 4 (3/40?, Dell, F)-The first comic book devoted to this important transfer character. Still confined to one page gag strips. Full potential not yet reached.
(a,b,c,j)

**MASTER COMICS** No. 1 (3/40, Faw, H)-An experimental format at first (magazine size, priced at 15¢ and 52 pages). Debut of *Master Man*, an imitation of *Superman*, killed by DC after six issues; just in time for *Bulletman* to become the lead figure with issue no. 7, transferred from the defunct ***Nickel Comics***.
(b,e,j,k)

**MYSTIC COMICS** No. 1 (3/40, Timely, H)-Unusual anthology title (their third) in that each issue featured a practically new line-up of costumed heroes. High impact covers and art, lasting only 10 issues.
(e)

**PRIZE COMICS** No. 1 (3/40, Prize, H)-High quality anthology series with the debut of *Power Nelson*. First of a publisher. Dick Briefer's unique *Frankenstein* was introduced in No. 7 as well as Simon & Kirby's *Black Owl*. The covers have tremendous eye-appeal.
(a,b,e,j,k)

**ROCKET COMICS** No. 1 (3/40, Hillman, H)-The title is misleading. This is actually a mixed anthology title with science fiction covers; short-lived with only three issues. Companion mag to ***Miracle Comics***. The second Hillman title.
(e)

★ **SHADOW COMICS** No. 1 (3/40, S&S, H)-The venerable pulp publisher tested the comic waters with a heavyweight who had dominated both the pulp and radio markets but never quite found his metier in a medium that relied on action over ethereal atmosphere. *Doc Savage*, another renowned pulp character, debuted in this issue. A respectable but undistinguished run (9 years) probably sustained by popularity of radio program.
(a,b,c,e,f,i,j,k,l)

**SLAM BANG COMICS** No. 1 (3/40, Faw, An)-Fawcett's third title was an ill conceived adventure anthology starring civilian heroes. This formula had gone out two years before with the appearance of *Superman*. The title was retired after 8 issues.
(e)

**SUN FUN KOMIKS** No. 1 (3/40, Sun, Hm)-An esoteric one-shot printed in black and red. A satire on comic books. The first of its kind not to be fully developed until ***Mad*** of 12 years hence.
(e,i,j)

★★★★ **DETECTIVE COMICS** No. 38 (4/40, DC, H)-DC initiates yet another breakthrough concept—the apprentice costumed hero. Origin, first appearance of *Robin*, the first and most enduring juvenile aide. For the first time in popular literature, the youthful apprentice was accepted as an equal by his partner. Bob Kane set another standard for the industry to mimic. The foreboding and enigmatic *Batman* was never the same after this issue.
(a,b,c,d,f,h,i,j)

**EXCITING COMICS** No. 1 (4/40, Better, H)-A sister anthology title to ***Thrilling***, becoming Better's second successful series. This title launched *The Black Terror* in No. 9, with Schomburg doing the covers early on (a poor man's Timely). Title lasted 9 years with jungle theme covers at the end.
(b,e,j)

★★ **NEW YORK WORLD'S FAIR** (3-5/40, DC, H)-The second comic book produced for a public event, ending the series. The first book to feature *Superman* and *Batman* together on a cover, as well as the first to showcase all of a company's stars, all in one book.
(a,c,j)

**SUPERWORLD COMICS** No. 1 (4/40, Gernsback, SF)-Following the success of ***Planet***, this title takes the honors as the third continuous series science fiction anthology. But Gernsback soon learned that 'raw' science fiction without a unique art style or gimmick (cheesecake) wouldn't sell. Disappeared after only three issues.
(e,k)

**WEIRD COMICS** No. 1 (4/40, Fox, H)-Another mixed anthology title with costumed heroes. The first to capitalize on this title, which became more common a decade later. Early issues by the Iger shop. First *Birdman* (the third winged hero). First *Thor*, from Greek mythology. Title lasted 2 years.
(e)

**BIG SHOT COMICS** No. 1 (5/40, CCG, Av)-First *Skyman*, the second aviation hero (noted for his flying wing)(See ***Whiz***). The first of a publisher. Mixed anthology series with original and reprint strips (*Joe Palooka*), lasting 9 years.
(a,b,c,d,e,j,k)

**CRACK COMICS** No. 1 (5/40, Quality, H)-Debut of Fine's *Black Condor* (the fourth winged hero). *Madame Fatal* begins, a bizarre hero who dresses as a woman to fight crime. A top quality series, lasting 9 years.
(a,b,c,d,e)

**CRASH COMICS** No. 1 (5/40, Tem/Holyoke, H)-The first Simon & Kirby art team-up, whose loose style of action reached maturity a year later with *Captain America*. Kirby was on his way to becoming one of the most influencial artists in comics. First of a publisher. A short lived mixed anthology series with costumed heroes, lasting 5 issues.
(e,g,k)

**DOC SAVAGE COMICS** No. 1 (5/40, S&S, H)-The legendary Man of Bronze headlined Street & Smith's second comic title. But it soon became evident that the original 'super man' was out of his depth. His prose adventures, which crackled with vitality in the pulps, seemed bland and derivative in the four-color medium. Outclassed by the characters he inspired, Doc and his title were retired after 3 years of so-so performance.
(c,e)

**HYPER MYSTERY COMICS** No. 1 (5/40, Hyper, H)-First of a publisher. A costumed hero anthology title which could not compete with the many heroes on the market at this time, lasting 2 issues.
(e,k)

★ **MORE FUN COMICS** No. 55 (5/40, DC, H)-First *Dr. Fate*, DC's second supernatural hero was given immediate cover exposure. Above average art and stories; colorful costume, lasting 3½ years and not achieving his own title.
(a,b,c,d,j)

★★★ **NICKEL COMICS** No. 1 (5/40, Faw, H)-Introduced *Bulletman*, Fawcett's third costumed hero. This book was experimental, selling for 5 cents, came out biweekly, and lasting only 8 issues. (After *Bulletman* was moved to ***Master Comics***, he won his own title in 1941.)
(a,c,d,e,j)

**WAR COMICS** No. 1 (5/40, Dell, W)-The first single theme

anthology series devoted to war. The combat genre did not find a significant market until the outbreak of the Korean conflict a decade later.
(e,i,j)

**AMAZING ADVENTURE FUNNIES** No. 1 (6/40, Centaur, H)-Outstanding collection of Centaur's best characters reprinted from earlier titles. Centaur was increasingly thrown back to all reprint books. Conjecture is that Timely's sudden success pre-empted all of the Everett shop's time.
(c,e)

★★★★ **BATMAN** No. 1 (Spr/40, DC, H)-Has arrival date of 4/25/40. DC's second strongest character achieved stardom and was given his own title. Assembled from ***Detective Comics***' inventory, containing the last solo appearance of *The Batman*. *The Joker* and *The Cat* debut. Title has run uninterrupted over four decades.
(a,b,c,e,j)

**BLUE BOLT** No. 1 (6/40, Novelty, H)-Second of a publisher. Costumed hero anthology title. Important early Simon & Kirby development began in No. 3. The heroes in this series could not be sustained, with *Dick Cole* eventually taking over, lasting 9 years.
(a,b,c,d,e,j)

**CYCLONE COMICS** No. 1 (6/40, Bilbara, An)-An anthology title with emphasis on subjects other than costumed hero. First of a publisher, expiring after 5 issues.
(e,j,k)

**FUTURE COMICS** No. 1 (6/40, McKay, R)-McKay's first new title in about a year. A reprint anthology with a science fiction theme (the fourth ever). This issue is noted for *The Phantom's* origin and science fiction cover. Went down for the count after 4 issues.
(e)

★★★**SPIRIT, THE** No. 1 (6/2/40, Eisner, D)-A weekly comic book (the only in comics) featuring the blockbuster strip distributed through newspapers. Notably, one of the best written and illustrated strips ever. A trend setter. Ingenious themes; capital atmospheric art with movie-like continuity and humorous plotting. Focus on special effects, lighting and unusual angles, lasting 12 years and endlessly revived.
(a,b,c,d,e,f,h,i,j)

**STARTLING COMICS** No. 1 (6/40, Better, H)-Better's third companion anthology series; *Wonder Man* and *Captain Future* begin. *The Fighting Yank* debuted in No. 10. Schomburg covers began early giving the books more impact. Cover theme changed to science fiction at the end.
(a,b,c,e,j)

**SURE-FIRE COMICS** No. 1 (6/40, Ace, H)-First of a publisher. A super hero anthology title of average quality lasting 4 issues before a title change.
(e,k)

**WHIRLWIND COMICS** No. 1 (6/40, Nita, H)-First of a publisher. A Three-issue run of mediocre quality with no sustaining characters.
(e,k)

★★★★ **ALL-AMERICAN COMICS** No. 16 (7/40, DC, H)-DC scored with another winning variation on the mystery man/adventure theme. Origin and first appearance of most enduring of DC's magic oriented heroes. The ancient fable of the magic lamp was transformed into a modern and more accessible, more mysterious form. *The Green Lantern's* chant became a staple of school boy mythology and another great career was launched. Series ended in 1949, although the name continued beyond 4 decades.
(a,b,c,d,j)

★★★ **ALL-STAR COMICS** No. 1 (Sum/40, DC, H)-The first continuous series showcase comic (see ***New York World's Fair***, 1940) for giving more exposure to top characters, who all headlined anthology series but as yet were not strong enough to have titles of their own. (This abundance of popular characters was unique to DC, forcing them to come up with this new format.)
(a,b,c,e)

**FLAME, THE** No. 1 (Sum/40, Fox, H)-One of Fox's top characters given prominence, reprinted from ***Wonderworld***. Lou Fine art in this issue, but the quality dropped early on, with the title lasting only 1½ years.
(c,e)

**GREEN MASK, THE** No. 1 (Sum/40, Fox, H)-Fox's emerald mystery man achieved stardom, but was squelched early on due to sub-standard art. An intriguing concept that was resurrected several times over the next 15 years, none of which were successful.
(c,e)

★ **MARVEL MYSTERY COMICS** No. 9 (7/40, Timely, H)-Epic battle issue. The first time in comics that two super heroes appeared together in one story. *Sub-Mariner* and *The Human Torch* each give up their usual space and battle for 22 pages. A coming together of the ancient basic elements, Water and Fire. Ignited newsstands everywhere.
(a,b,c,h,j)

**HIT COMICS** No. 1 (7/40, Quality, H)-Quality's fourth anthology title. Distinguished primarily by Iger shop graphics (Lou Fine). Non-memorable characters until *Kid Eternity* took over as main feature two years later. Series lasted 10 years.
(a,b,e,j)

**NATIONAL COMICS** No. 1 (7/40, Quality, H)-Of equal quality to ***Hit***, Lou Fine at his very best (covers and story art). Debut of *Uncle Sam*, Quality's top patriot. Legendary artist line-up with series lasting 9 years.
(a,b,c,d,e,f,j)

**OKAY COMICS** No. 1 (7/40, UFS, R)-Not having published a new title since 1938 (***Single Series***), United decides to make a comeback. Three new titles are released simultaneously with a fourth the following month. This one-shot issue features *The Captain and the Kids* and *Hawkshaw the Detective*.
(e)

**OK COMICS** No. 1 (7/40, UFS, H)-United tries their first super hero anthology title, but the characters were not strong enough to endure the stiff competition, lasting only two issues. Their second new title for the month.
(e)

**SHIELD-WIZARD COMICS** No. 1 (Sum/40, MLJ, H)-MLJ gave their top two characters joint stardom. A unique concept, titling a book after more than one character to insure its survival—a first in comics. The series lasted 4 years (the dual title wasn't enough).
(c,e)

**SPARKLER COMICS** No. 1 (7/40, UFS, R)-A two-issue reprint anthology series featuring *Jim Hardy* in No. 1 and *Frankie Doodle* in No. 2. United's third new title for the month.
(c,e)

**SUPER-MYSTERY COMICS** No. 1 (7/40, Ace, H)-Ace's second title, featuring more prominent characters and art, becoming their mainstay run. The series lasted 9 years, sustained by colorful covers and top artists.
(a,b,c,e)

**FANTOMAN** No. 2 (8/40, Centaur, H)-Centaur's second title reprinting their top characters and lasting three issues. Their second series of repackaged material.
(e)

**HEROIC COMICS** No. 1 (8/40, Eastern Color, H)-Seven years after introducing ***Famous Funnies***, Eastern came out with their second anthology title (their third ever). Original rather than reprinted material. *Hydroman*, a spin-off of the *Sub-Mariner* debuted. Eventually the format was changed to true stories of heroism, lasting 15 years. Top artists in-

cluded throughout the run.
(e)

**RED RAVEN COMICS** No. 1 (8/40, Timely, H)-A one-shot esoteric super hero book featuring Kirby art. Highly sought after due to its lineage and rarity. Timely's fourth title.
(e)

★★★★ **SPECIAL EDITION COMICS** No. 1 (8/40, Fawcett, H)-Due to the enormous popularity of ***Whiz's*** explosive character, a single theme (Fawcett's first) anthology one-shot of *Captain Marvel* was published. A few months later, he began his own series. Beck cover and story art—high quality throughout.
(a,c,e,j)

**UNITED COMICS** No. 1 (8/40, UFS, R)-The popular *Fritzi Ritz* strip was featured and sustained the run for 12½ years. United's fourth and only successful title in their recent comeback attempt beginning a month earlier. The first comic book series to focus on the career girl theme (proto-type of *Katy Keene*).
(a,b,c,e)

**CRASH COMICS** No. 4(9/40, Holyoke, H)-*Catman* debuted for two issues then stayed dormant for six months before appearing in his own title.
(a,c,d,j)

**MASKED MARVEL** No. 1 (9/40, Centaur, H)-After exposure in ***Keen Detective Funnies***, the crimson sleuth was given his own title, lasting only 3 issues.
(e)

★ **MICKEY MOUSE MAGAZINE** V5/12, (9/40, K.K. F)-This historically significant publication was one step removed from becoming the first official funny animal series. As a magazine, it had evolved through various sizes and formats to finally become a full-fledged comic book. The following month, a title change to ***Walt Disney's Comics & Stories*** completed the transition.
(a,c,h,j)

**PRIZE COMICS** No. 7 (9/40, Prize, H)-Debut of Dick Briefer's *Frankenstein* series, and *The Black Owl* by Simon & Kirby. Above average strips with eye-catching covers.
(a,b,c,d,j)

★ **RED RYDER COMICS** No. 1 (9/40, Hawley/Dell, Ws)-A one-shot devoted to the popular strip character by Fred Harman, not becoming a continuous series until Dell picked up the title a year later. Ties with ***Tom Mix*** as the second book devoted to a single western character, but the first to receive widespread newsstand distribution. Lasted 17 years due to popular movie series. The second title of a publisher.
(a,b,c,e,f,h,i,j,l)

★★★ **SILVER STREAK COMICS** No. 6 (9/40, Lev, H)-High impact cover of *The Claw* by Jack Cole. Debut of *Daredevil* with his unprecedented costume of dichromatic symmetry. (See ***Silver Streak*** no. 7.)
(a,b,c,d,f,j)

**SKY BLAZERS** No. 1 (9/40, Hawley, Av)-Ties with ***Red Ryder*** as 2nd of a publisher. Inspired by the radio show, not lasting beyond 2 issues.
(e)

★★ **TOM MIX** No. 1 (9/40, Ralston, Ws)-The first continuous series single theme western comic, but a giveaway by Ralston—not sold on the stands.
(a,b,c,e,j,k)

★ **WINGS COMICS** No. 1 (9/40, FH, Av)-The publisher's fifth single theme anthology title. The first to focus entirely on aviation (a subject of high appeal to boys of the era). With no competition, the series lasted 14 years.
(a,b,c,e,h,i,j)

**ALL-AMERICAN COMICS** No. 19 (10/40, DC, H)-Debut of *The Atom* (a hero for short people). Good filler material as a back-up to the main feature, who lasted 4½ years.
(a,b,c,d,f,h,j)

**ARROW, THE** No. 1 (10/40, Centaur, H)-The very first costume hero (pre-*Batman*) was given prominence after a two-year run in ***Funny Pages***. Folded after 3 issues (Centaur phasing out).
(e)

**BIG 3** No. 1 (Fall/40, Fox, H)-Fox's first showcase anthology title featuring their top characters together in one magazine. A good idea, but not surviving more than 7 issues.
(e)

**BILL BARNES COMICS** No. 1 (10/40, S&S, Av)-The celebrated pulp ace got his own comic title, but after three years failed to find an audience. Street & Smith's third title.
(c,e,l)

**CHAMP COMICS** No. 11 (10/40, Harvey, H)-Continued from ***Champion***, now featuring super heroes in full swing. Later on the popular and saleable Simon & Kirby art style was copied as an attempt to sustain the run. The title ended in 1944.
(e)

★★★ **HUMAN TORCH, THE** No. 2(Fall/40, Timely, H)-From the pages of ***Marvel Mystery***, the android flys into his own title. Inspired concept. High impact, eye-catching character, making appearances over the next 40 years.
(a,b,c,e,j)

**REX DEXTER OF MARS** No. 1 (Fall/40, Fox, SF)-A modest success in ***Mysterymen***, but not important enough to carry a title of his own. Expired after one issue.
(e)

**SAMSON** No. 1 (Fall/40, Fox, H)-One of Fox's top characters from ***Fantastic*** achieves stardom. Lack-luster art leads to the early death of the run the following year.
(e)

**SPORT COMICS** No. 1 (10/40, S&S, Sp)-A good idea 'real life' comic series featuring notable sport figures and lasting (through a title change) for 9 years. The first comic series devoted entirely to this theme (see ***Champion** and **Fight***).
(b,c,e,h,i,j)

**SUPER SPY** No. 1 (10/40, Centaur, H)-Late Centaur super hero anthology title, introducing *The Sparkler*. Interesting early vintage comic with only two issues published.
(e)

**TOP-NOTCH COMICS** No. 9 (10/40, MLJ, H)-Debut of *The Black Hood*, key MLJ hero. One of the few at MLJ to later star in his own title. The costume had eye-appeal which sustained the character, lasting 3 years.
(c,d,j)

★★★★★ **WALT DISNEY'S COMICS AND STORIES** No. 1 (10/40, Dell, F)-The first funny animal continuous series comic book title. Miscellaneous collection of proven Disney characters began to come into focus around consistently high quality strips by Taliaferro and Gottfredson, who consistently delivered the goods. The definitive funny animal anthology comic after which all others were modeled. A trend setter. Suspected to have achieved the highest circulation of any comic, lasting beyond 40 years.
(a,b,c,e,h,i,j)

**WESTERN DESPERADO COMICS** No. 8 (10/40, Fawcett, Ws)-Fawcett's first western theme anthology title, only one issue.
(e)

**DETECTIVE EYE** No. 1 (11/40, Centaur, H)-More exposure for characters from ***Keen Detective Funnies***, lasting 2 issues.
(e)

**HI-SPOT COMICS** No. 2 (11/40, Hawley, An)-A one-shot book featuring an Edgar Rice Burroughs strip, *David Innes of Pellucidar*.

(e)

**WHAM COMICS** No. 1 (11/40, Centaur, H)-Another short-lived anthology title, similar to ***Super Spy*** (reprinting earlier material).
(e)

★★ **GREEN HORNET COMICS** No. 1 (12/40, Harvey, H)-The respected radio and movie hero tried his wings in comics. Intriguing concept, with a few high points of good artists in the run. He never excelled in the medium, but did present a respectable run of 9 years—probably sustained by the popularity of the radio program.
(a,b,c,e,l)

**LIGHTNING COMICS** No. 4 (12/40, Ace, H)-Continued from ***Sure-Fire***, becoming Ace's third title. Colorful covers (some exceptional) could not sustain the run beyond 18 months.
(e)

**DOUBLE COMICS** (1940, Elliot, H)-The first attempt at repackaging (and remarketing) remaindered comics. First of a publisher. Elliot produced these unique books for four years, taking advantage of the insatiable public demand for comics.
(e,h,j,k)

**GREEN GIANT COMICS** No. 1 (1940, Funnies, Inc., H)-A very rare one-shot test comic. Conjecture is that its circulation was limited to the New York City area only.
(e,j)

## 1941 ■

★★★★★ **ALL-STAR COMICS** No. 3 (Wint/40-41, DC, H)-A breakthrough concept, second in importance only to the creation of the super hero. For the first time in comics, top characters come together in one book to form a crime fighting organization *The Justice Society*. A trend setter. Unprecedented in all of literature (the gods of Mt. Olympus weren't on speaking terms; the Knights of the Round Table didn't foregather to confront a common foe). Forerunner of *The Justice League*, and inspiration for many hero groups that followed.
(a,b,c,f,h,i,j)

**BUCK ROGERS** No. 1 (Wint/40-41, FF, R)-Due to the enormous popularity of the strip in ***Famous Funnies***, he earned his own title, which is the first continuous title devoted to a reprint character. Unfortunately, like many other transfer characters, the series didn't last, running only 6 issues.
(a,c,e)

**SILVER STREAK COMICS** No. 7 (1/41, Lev, H)-Epic clash between *Daredevil* and *The Claw* began in this issue. (Rivaled only by the *Torch-Sub-Mariner* brouhaha). Early enthusiastic work by Jack Cole. *DD's* costume colors change to red and blue, giving him a sinister, demonic appearance (unforgettable). Smash hit series launched *DD* to stardom with own title.
(a,c,f,j)

**WOW COMICS** No. 1 (Wint/40-41, Faw, H)-Featuring the costumed hero *Mr. Scarlet* (imitation of *Batman*), drawn by Kirby. Included other features with small impact to the comic scene. The major feature of this title was *Mary Marvel*, a *Captain Marvel* clone, who dominated from No. 9 on. This particular issue is highly prized due to its rarity and early Kirby art.
(b,e)

★★★★ **CAPTAIN MARVEL ADVENTURES** nn (1-2/41?, Faw, H)-Following the wake of ***Special Edition***, the celebrated character started his own series (this issue illustrated by Kirby), reaching a two-week publication frequency at one point, lasting 13 years.
(a,b,c,e,j)

**BLUE RIBBON COMICS** No. 9 (2/41, MLJ, H)-Inspired by DC's *The Spectre*, *Mr. Justice* began this issue and survived to the end of the run (1942).
(d)

★★★★★ **CAPTAIN AMERICA COMICS** No. 1 (3/41, Timely, H)-Simon & Kirby's most classic creation; a patriotic paragon (the second but foremost of patriotic heroes) that set the comics market reeling. A trend setter. One of the top ten most sought after books. With a few interruptions, the character has survived beyond 40 years.
(a,b,c,d,e,g,j)

**JACKPOT COMICS** No. 1 (Spr/41, MLJ, H)-MLJ's first showcase title to give more exposure to their top characters. The mediocre scripts and art could only keep the run alive for 2 years.
(c,e)

★★★ **SUB-MARINER COMICS** No. 1 (Spr/41, Timely, H)-The aquatic anti-hero is given prominence. The potential of the character was never fully realized. High impact covers, sustaining the run for 8 years.
(a,b,c,e,j)

★★★ **WORLD'S BEST COMICS** No. 1 (Spr/41, DC, H)-Using the successful format of ***The World's Fair*** books, DC created this title to feature their top two attractions, *Batman* and *Superman*. This was the first thick format continuous series comic (as ***World's Finest***). Series lasted beyond 40 years without interruption.
(a,b,c,e,h,j)

★★★ **MICKEY MOUSE FOUR COLOR** No. 16 (4/41?, Dell, F)-The first comic devoted to this world renowned character. The subject of this landmark issue was Gottfredson's classic, *The Phantom Blot*.
(a,b,c,j)

★★ **ADVENTURE COMICS** No. 61 (4/41, DC, H)-*Starman* was introduced as DC continued to create new characters. Visually, an intriguing alternative with enough appeal to last 3½ years in this run, but not quite strong enough to appear in his own title.
(a,b,c,d,j)

**TRUE COMICS** No. 1 (4/41, PM, TR)-The second anthology series based on true stories (see ***Sport Comics***). The first of a publisher, lasting 9 years.
(b,e,h,i,h,k)

**AMERICA'S GREATEST COMICS** No. 1 (5/41?, Faw, H)-Fawcett's first showcase anthology title (in thick format) featuring their top characters, lasting 8 issues.
(a,c,e)

**ARMY AND NAVY** No. 1 (5/41, S&S, W)-S&S's fifth anthology title, the second ever with a war theme, lasting 5 issues.
(e)

**CATMAN COMICS** No. 1 (5/41, Holyoke, H)-Continued from ***Crash***, *Catman* got his own series. Second of a publisher. Adequate, but unexceptional covers and stories. Expired after 5 years.
(a,b,c,e)

**EXCITING COMICS** No. 9 (5/41, BP, H)-Debut of *The Black Terror*, nemesis of crime. Editors never adequately capitalized on the tremendous eye-appeal of the character. Indifferent scripts, lack-luster art disappointed more often than not. The indomitable character endured despite lack of staff support. Logical yet striking appearance of costume sustained character.
(a,b,c,d,j)

**STARS AND STRIPES COMICS** No. 2 (5/41, Centaur, H)-After the failure of Centaur's last flurry of reprint books a year earlier, they tried to make a comeback. Following Timely's newsstand hit, Centaur picked up on the patriotic theme with the first of three books of this type, lasting only 5 issues.
(e)

**SUPER MAGIC** No. 1 (5/41, S&S, Mg)-A one-shot book featuring *Blackstone the Magician* and *Rex King*. The first

title to focus on magicians. The title was modified to ***Super Magician*** and the series lasted 6 years.
(b,e,i,j)

**LIBERTY SCOUTS** No. 2 (6/41, Centaur, H)-Centaur's second patriotic theme series lasted only two issues.
(e)

★ ★ ★ **ALL FLASH COMICS** No. 1 (Sum/41, DC, H)-The hero of speed achieved stardom and was given his own title. Momentarily retired after 6 years.
(a,b,c,e)

★ **ALL WINNERS COMICS** No. 1 (Sum/41, Timely, H)-First Timely showcase title to give more exposure to their top characters. High impact covers and characters sustained run for 5 years.
(a,c,e)

★ ★ **BULLETMAN** No. 1 (7/41, Faw, H)-The hit of ***Master Comics***, receives his own title, lasting 5 years. The Raboy cover and silver logo gets the series off to a good start.
(a,c,e)

**CAPTAIN BATTLE COMICS** No. 1 (Sum/41, Lev, H)-The third patriotic hero (see ***Pep Comics*** and ***Captain America***) from ***Silver Streak*** is given his own title. Lacked necessary distinctiveness to compete, folding with the second issue.
(e)

★ ★ **DAREDEVIL COMICS** No. 1 (7/41, Lev, H)-High impact cover, inspired costume design and massive support from Biro's strong, complex plotting sustained momentum of "The Greatest Name in Comics" splash debut. Immediately stood out from the hordes of rival strongmen glutting the stands. Series prevailed for 15 years.
(a,b,c,e,j)

**EAGLE, THE** No. 1 (7/41, Fox, H)-Another publisher on the patriotic band wagon. *The Eagle* only flew for four issues.
(e)

**FUNNIES, THE** No. 57 (7/41, Dell, H)-Debut of *Captain Midnight*, a patriotic aviation hero who was an established attraction on radio. He was also featured in Dell's ***Popular Comics*** before being picked up by Fawcett as a regular series.
(a,c,d,j)

**MINUTEMAN** No. 1 (7/41, Faw, H)-Fawcett's answer to a patriotic hero who began in ***Master Comics***. This less than distinguished hero only lasted three issues in his own title.
(e)

**PEP COMICS** No. 17 (7/41, MLJ, H)-Landmark issue. The first time in comics that a major character (*The Comet*) actually died, and a new character (*The Hangman*) was created in the same story.
(a,b,c,d,h)

**SPARKLER COMICS** No. 1 (7/41, UFS, R)-After three years of costumed heroes glutting the stands, UFS tries its second costumed hero series. Debut of *Sparkman*, a colorful character who eventually gave way to *Tarzan* and other reprint characters, title proved competitive through 14 years.
(a,b,c,e,j)

★ **YOUNG ALLIES** No. 1 (Sum/41, Timely, H)-The first sidekick group in comics. The *Red Skull* guest-starred to give the title a good send-off. Proto-type of the more successful *Teen Titans* of 25 years hence, it managed a respectable run of 5 years.
(e,f,h,i,j)

**CAPTAIN FEARLESS** No. 1 (8/41, Helnit, H)-Third of a publisher. An interesting mix of super patriots not lasting beyond the second issue.
(e)

★ ★ ★ ★ **MILITARY COMICS** No. 1 (8/41, Qua, Av)-Otherwise predictable war-theme anthology (the third of its kind) sparked by debut of aviation feature of geniune classic proportions. The crack *Blackhawk* team took command of the series and continued at the helm 9 years after a title change (to ***Modern Comics***) indicated the public had grown jaded with war-themes generally. Ace concept (air-borne privateers meet the axis on its own terms) backed by sterling Iger graphics (the shop's piece de resistance) and top-drawer scripting propelled feature into its own title and a phenomenal 40 year run (with interruptions). The introduction of *Blackhawk*, and *Plastic Man* later the same month, lifted Quality into the first rank of comics publishers. A masterpiece of collaborative art.
(a,b,c,d,e,f,h,i,j)

**OUR FLAG COMICS** No. 1 (8/41, Ace, H)-Ace joined the other publishers with a host of patriotic strongmen debuting in this book. High impact patriotic cover. Series lasted 5 issues.
(e,j)

**POCKET COMICS** No. 1 (8/41, Harv, H)-An experimental pocket size comic book series featuring Harvey's top characters. Most divergent forms didn't last long and this was no exception, expiring after 4 issues.
(e)

★ ★ ★ ★ **POLICE COMICS** No. 1 (8/41, Quality, H)-Debut of one of the most ingenious super heroes in comics, *Plastic Man*. An original concept, fully exploited by Jack Cole in the ensuing years. Sheer entertainment with the incomparable *Cole* at the top of his form. Shares standard bearer honors with ***Military***, lasting 12 years.
(a,b,c,d,e,f,i,j)

★ **RED RYDER COMICS** No. 3 (8/41, Hawley, Ws)-The first continuous series single theme western comic for newsstand sales. Ties back to a one-shot issue of a year earlier. Title lasted 16 years due to popular movie series.
(a,b,c,e,f,h,i,j)

**SPITFIRE COMICS** No. 1 (8/41, Harvey, Av)-An experimental aviation pocket size comic book, lasting 2 issues.
(e)

★ **UNCLE SAM QUARTERLY** No. 1 (8/41, Qua, H)-Eisner's version of a patriotic hero, the star of ***National Comics***, is given his own book, lasting 8 issues. Usual Iger shop excellence.
(e)

**USA COMICS** No. 1 (8/41, Timely, H)-Timely, extending the patriotic theme, created another showcase title for introducing new characters. After five issues, their trend setting *Captain America* was brought in to save the run and it endured 4 years.
(a,c,e)

**VICTORY COMICS** No. 1 (8/41, Hill, H)-Classic Everett Nazi war cover. Hillman tried their third title, this time with a patriotic costumed hero theme, again unsuccessfully. It lasted only 4 issues.
(e)

**BANNER COMICS** No. 3 (9/41, Ace, H)-Debut of *Captain Courageous*, a derivative patriotic hero—not prominent enough to survive more than 3 issues.
(e)

**CALLING ALL GIRLS** No. 1 (9/41, PMI, TR)-Second of a publisher. The true fact anthology, with biographies of famous persons and sketches of historic events (occassionally mixed with magazine-type photo features), was a comics format pioneered by Parent's Magazine Institute. Here the target audience was adolescent girls. Similar titles were cloned later on. Enjoyed a run of 7 years.
(b,e,f,h,i,j)

**FOUR FAVORITES** No. 1 (9/41, Ace, H)-Ace's first showcase title featuring their top characters together in one book, lasting 6 years.
(e)

**REAL HEROES COMICS** No. 1 (9/41, PMI, TR)-With the success of ***True Comics***, the publisher attempted another title based on true stories. Their third series, lasting 5 years. ***Heroic Comics*** was later converted to this theme.
(e)

**REAL LIFE COMICS** No. 1 (9/41, BP, TR)-Inspired by the newsstand success of PMI's ***True Comics***, this publisher came out with their version, lasting 11 years.
(b,e)

**STARTLING COMICS** No. 10 (9/41, BP, H)-Debut of *The Fighting Yank*, America's super patriot. Interesting variation on the patriotic theme in that he could call up heroes from the American revolution to assist in the modern fight against crime. Tremendous eye-appeal of character never fully realized due to low standard story art. High impact Schomburg covers sustained the run.
(a,b,c,d,j)

**SUPER MAGICIAN COMICS** No. 2 (9/41, S&S, Mg)-The first continuous series anthology title on the subject of magic, continuing from ***Super Magic*** and lasting 6 years.
(e,j)

**YANKEE COMICS** No. 1 (9/41, Chesler, H)-Chesler re-entered the comic market with this patriotic title. Debut of *Yankee Doodle Jones*. Sensational patriotic cover. Despite its visual appeal, it endured only 4 issues.
(e)

★★★★ **CLASSIC COMICS** No. 1 (10/41, Gil, Lit)-First and most enduring of 'educational' theme comics, Gilberton drew on works of great literature for their highly visible newsstand product. One of the few lines that could be endorsed without reservation by parents and educators, its marketing success was not tied to single-theme titles or continuing characters. Variable art quality somewhat diminished the overall impact of the line. The only comic publisher to place each issue into endless reprints while continuing to publish new titles on a monthly basis, lasting 30 years.
(a,b,c,e,f,h,i,j,k)

**DOLL MAN** No. 1 (Fall/41, Qua, H)-After a successful two-year run in ***Feature***, the mighty mite leaped into his own title, lasting 12 years. The proto-type of the Silver Age Atom.
(a,b,c,e,j)

**DYNAMIC COMICS** No. 1 (10/41, Chesler, H)-Chesler's second patriotic super hero series. Debut of *Major Victory*. Suspended after three issues and brought back with a format change in 1944, lasting four more years.
(e)

★★★ **GREEN LANTERN** No. 1 (Fall/41, DC, H)-Having headlined ***All-American*** for one year, one of DC's foremost heroes achieved the distinction of his own title. It ran for 8 years and went on to become one of the key revival characters of the Silver Age.
(a,b,c,e)

★★★★ **LOONEY TUNES & MERRY MELODIES** No. 1 (Fall/41, Dell, F)-The companion title to the enormously successful ***WDC&S***. Dell's second funny animal anthology featured *Bugs Bunny, Porky Pig* and *Elmer Fudd*. This was the first comic book appearance of Warner Brothers film characters. The series ran for 21 years.
(a,b,c,e,h,j,l)

**RANGERS COMICS** No. 1( 10/41, FH, W)-The publisher's sixth single theme anthology title (war theme). Standard FH style of cheesecake art and covers, lasting 11 years.
(a,b,c,e)

**SKYMAN** No. 1 (Fall/41, CCG, Av)-After a year's successful run in ***Big Shot***, he was given his own title. Second of a publisher, lasting only 4 issues. (He remained the main feature in ***Big Shot*** for 9 years.)
(a,c,e)

★★ **SPYSMASHER** No. 1 (Fall/41, Faw, Av)-Popular war hero graduating from ***Whiz*** into his own title, lasting 2 years. Maiden issue featured unusual logo printed in metallic silver.
(a,c,e)

**STAR SPANGLED COMICS** No. 1(10/41, DC, H)-DC's first patriotic theme title featuring the *Star Spangled Kid*. Due to the weak contents, the title had a dramatic format change with No. 7 when *The Guardian* and *The Newsboy Legion* were introduced.
(b,e)

**WORLD FAMOUS HEROES MAGAZINE** No. 1 (10/41, Comic Corp, TR)-Similar theme to PMI's ***Real Heroes***, and Eastern's ***Heroic***, with stories of famous people, lasting 4 issues.
(e)

**AIRFIGHTERS COMICS** No. 1 (11/41, Hill, Av)-An early attempt at an aviation theme comic (like ***Wings***), lasting only one issue. A year later the title was revived more successfully with a new 'dynamic' character in *Airboy*.
(e)

**GREAT COMICS** No. 1 (11/41, Great, H)-First of a publisher, featuring super heroes. The third and last issue is a classic: *Futuro* takes *Hitler* to hell.
(e,k)

**MAN OF WAR** No. 1 (11/41, Centaur, H)-Centaur's third and last patriotic theme title, lasting 2 issues. Conjecture is that Centaur itself expired with this book.
(e)

**SCOOP COMICS** No. 1 (11/41, Chesler, H)-Chesler's third attempt at a comeback with this anthology of super heroes. Debut of *Rocketman* and *Rocketgirl*, lasting 8 issues.
(e)

**U.S. JONES** No. 1 (11/41, Fox, H)-Fox's second patriotic theme title, lasting 2 issues.
(e)

★★★★ **ALL-STAR COMICS** No. 8 (11-12/41, DC, H)-*Wonder Woman*, the first super-heroine, created by Charles Moulton and drawn by H.G. Peter, debuted in this issue as an 8 page add-on. Her origin continued in ***Sensation*** No. 1, where she becomes the lead feature. A trend setter.
(a,b,c,d,f,h,i,j)

**BANG-UP COMICS** No. 1 (12/41, Progressive, H)-A new publisher entered the field. This series was mediocre in its content only surviving 3 issues.
(e,k)

**CAPTAIN AERO COMICS** No. 7 (12/41, Hoke, Av)-Cashing in on the popularity of *Spy Smasher* and *Captain Midnight*, this publisher began with another aviation hero. With strong, colorful covers, the series lasted 5 years.
(e)

**CHOICE COMICS** No. 1 (12/41, Great, H)-The publisher's second title. A mixed anthology, lasting 3 issues.
(e)

**MASTER COMICS** No. 21 (12/41, Faw, H)-*Captain Marvel* and *Bulletman* team-up to fight *Captain Nazi*. A classic battle sequence, rare in comics at this time. High impact (classic) Raboy cover and story art.
(a,b,c)

**PIONEER PICTURE STORIES** No. 1 (12/41, S&S, TR)-An anthology of true stories about heroes (ala ***Heroic Comics***), lasting 9 issues.
(e)

★★★★ **PEP COMICS** No. 22 (12/41, MLJ, TA)-The eternal sophomore and his friends began the first of over forty consecutive terms at Riverdale High. Never rose above pat formula, but survived vagaries of shifting market that did in a host of illustrious predecessors and glut of imitators (many of which originated at MLJ itself). Auxillary characters achieved stardom with their own titles. Trend setter, lasting

beyond 40 years.
(a,b,c,d,f,h,i,j)

**PUNCH COMICS** No. 1 (12/41, Chesler, H)-Chesler's fourth attempt to get back into the market. A mixed anthology series with a successful format, lasting 6 years.
(e)

★★★ **WHIZ COMICS** No. 25 (12/12/41, Faw, H)-*Captain Marvel* was cloned for the second time (see *Lt. Marvels*) into a junior size as *Captain Marvel Jr.* Classic art by Mac Raboy gave the character a slick streamlined 'Raymond' look. He was given immediate headlining in ***Master Comics***. This was the first significant character cloned.
(a,b,c,d,j)

**X-MAS COMICS** No. 1 (12/41, Faw, H)-A new concept. Earlier in the year, Fawcett began over-running certain selected comics with indicias, page numbers, etc. removed. These comics were then bound up into a thick book (324 pgs.) to be sold as a special comic for Christmas. This successful format evolved into several other titles and lasted for 11 years.
(a,b,c,e,f,h,j)

**CAPTAIN MARVEL THRILL BOOK** nn (1941, Faw, H)-A large-size black & white comic reprinting popular *Captain Marvel* stories, lasting one issue. (Half text, half illustration.)
(e)

**DICKIE DARE** No. 1 (1941, Eastern, R)-Another single theme anthology title of the popular strip, lasting 4 issues.
(e)

**DOUBLE UP** nn (1941, Elliott, H)-The same idea as ***Double***, except this was a one-shot remarketing of remaindered digest-sized issues of ***Speed, Spitfire*** and ***Pocket***. Probably a special deal to Elliott due to heavy returns?
(e)

**FACE, THE** No. 1 (1941, CCG, H)-The popular strip from ***Big Shot*** achieved brief stardom, lasting only two issues.
(e)

**KEY RING COMICS** (1941, Dell, An)-A special formated comic series of 16 pages each to put in a two-ring binder (sold as a set of five).
(e)

**TRAIL BLAZERS** No. 1 (1941, S&S, TR)-True fact anthology of heroic deeds, lasting 4 issues.
(e)

**USA IS READY** No. 1 (1941, Dell, W)-Dell's second war title lasting one issue.
(e)

★★★ **ANIMAL COMICS** No. 1 (12-1/41-42, Dell, F)-Debut of Walt Kelly's classic character, *Pogo*, which became syndicated in 1948. Dell's third funny animal single theme anthology title following the success of ***WDC&S*** and ***Looney Tunes***. The first funny animal comic with original characters at Dell.
(a,c,d,e,j)

## 1942 ■

**FOUR MOST** No. 1 (Wint/41-42, Novelty, H)-A showcase title featuring Novelty's best characters from ***Target*** and ***Blue Bolt***. Series taken over by *Dick Cole* with No. 3 on. Their third title.
(a,b,c,e)

★ **LEADING COMICS** No. 1 (Wint/41-42, DC, H)-Like ***All-Star***, this title provided a showcase for DC's secondary heroes (a poor man's ***All-Star***). Series ran 14 issues then changed to a funny animal format for the rest of its 7 year existance.
(e)

★★★★★ **SENSATION COMICS** No. 1 (1/42, DC, H)-*Wonder Woman's* origin continued from ***All-Star*** No. 8 (her first appearance). A very strong character from the onset, achieving stardom instantly as a headline feature of this series. She won her own title within a few months which has run uninterrupted for over 40 years. (One of the few characters to achieve this kind of exposure.)
(a,b,c,e,f,h,j)

**SPECIAL COMICS** No. 1 (Wint/41-42, MLJ, H)-A one-shot special featuring *The Hangman* from ***Pep Comics***. A hit on the stands, the character was launched into his own series with No. 2.
(c,e)

**V...- COMICS** No. 1 (1/42, Fox, H)-another short-lived title from Fox. His third patriotic theme comic. Introduced *V-Man*, lasted only two issues.
(e)

**AMERICA'S BEST COMICS** No. 1 (2/42, BP, H)-A showcase title to give more exposure to their top characters. The high impact covers (many by Schomburg) sustained the run, lasting 7 years.
(a,b,c,e)

**CAMP COMICS** No. 1 (2/42, Dell, Hm)-A mixed (humorous) anthology title with pretty girl photo covers. An unusual format slanted to the soldier boys at camp.
(e)

★★ **GENE AUTRY COMICS** No. 1 (2/42, Faw, Ws)-The second newsstand continuous series western title devoted to a single character. *Gene* ties with *Roy Rogers* as the most popular cowboy star of the sound era. Title survived 18 years.
(a,b,c,e,h,j,l)

**JINGLE JANGLE COMICS** No. 1 (2/42, Eastern Color, Hm)-A young children's comic, containing illustrations and script by George Carlson, a children's book heavyweight (*Uncle Wiggily*). Eastern's second anthology title of original material (see ***Heroic***), lasting 7 years.
(a,b,e,j)

**TRUE SPORT PICTURE STORIES** No. 5 (2/42, S&S, Sp)-Continued from ***Sport Comics***, lasting 7 years.
(e)

**CAPTAIN COURAGEOUS COMICS** No. 6 (3/42, Ace, H)-Introduced in ***Banner***, the character was given his own title but lasted only one issue.
(e)

**TOUGH KID SQUAD** No. 1 (3/42, Timely, H)-Timely's second series devoted to sidekicks (see ***Young Allies***). Highly prized due to its rarity.
(e)

★★ **BOY COMICS** No. 3 (4/42, Lev, H)-Gleason's second successful title, introducing *Crimebuster*. This series survived 14 years due to Biro's strong, complex plotting.
(a,b,c,d,e,j)

**COMEDY COMICS** No. 9 (4/42, Timely, H)-The title is misleading. A super hero anthology title changing to a humorous and funny animal format early on.
(e)

**HANGMAN COMICS** No. 2 (Spr/42, MLJ, H)-The smash hit of ***Pep Comics*** received his own series, but lasted only 7 issues.
(e)

★ **JOKER COMICS** No. 1 (4/42, Timely, Hm)-First *Powerhouse Pepper* by Wolverton. Wolverton, an original if there ever was one, stood totally aloof from the mainstream of comic art. His effect on later comics ranging from the original ***Mad*** to the sixties undergrounds, is incalculable. (He tried to fit in, but the effect of playing it straight made his work even more bizzarre.)
(a,b,c,d,e,f,g,j)

**SHEENA, QUEEN OF THE JUNGLE** No. 1 (Spr/42, FH, J)-

After three years exposure in ***Jumbo Comics***, *Sheena* finally graduated to her own title, lasting 18 issues spread over 11 years.
(a,b,c,e)

★ ★ **STAR SPANGLED COMICS** No. 7 (4/42, DC, H)-Debut of *The Guardian* and *The Newsboy Legion* by Simon and Kirby (vintage). Title lasted 11 years.
(a,b,c,d,j)

**WAMBI, JUNGLE BOY** No. 1 (Spr/42, FH, J)-From ***Jungle Comics***. Not strong enough to carry his own title which had erratic publishing (18 issues in 11 years).
(e)

★ ★ ★ ★ **CRIME DOES NOT PAY** No. 22 (6/42, Lev, C)-Aside from being the first crime comic, this title was the first of many to be deliberately targeted at the adult reader. Inspired by the widely read ***True Detective*** - style magazines of the time. Implicit and unsavory subject matter, in the context of what was popularly understood as publications for children, assured the attention and disapproval of Wertham and others. Established conventions of graphically depicted violence that would be exploited to the extreme in the horror comics of a decade later. Arguably the third most influential comic ever published (after ***Action*** and ***Superman***), ***CDNP*** was a belated trend setter. Gleason had the field all to himself for six years. Then, in 1948 the industry suffered a severe slump in sales. In desperation, publishers turned en masse to the formerly untapped 'crime' market. This move was abetted in part by Gleason himself. In mid-1947 he had begun publishing circulation figures on the covers of ***CDNP***, reporting sales of 5 million - 6 million copies (per issue?), an astounding record for a comics periodical and, an open invitation to imitation.
(a,b,c,e,f,h,i,j)

★ **DETECTIVE COMICS** No. 64 (6/42, DC, H)-Simon and Kirby introduce the *Boy Commandos*. A more timely version of the *Newsboy Legion*, this popular series found the Axis plagued with a platoon of wise-cracking juveniles. An immediate hit, the lads were rewarded with a quarterly of their own within a matter of months.
(a,c,d,j)

**FAIRY TALE PARADE** No. 1 (6-7/42, Dell, F)-Dell's second continuous series funny animal title with original characters. Its popularity was carried entirely by the imaginative illustrative genius of Walt Kelly.
(c,e)

**BIG CHIEF WAHOO** No. 1 (7/42, Eastern, R)-Popular transfer strip debuts in his own comic series, lasting 23 issues.
(c,e)

**DIXIE DUGAN** No. 1 (7/42, CCG, R)-Popular strip character given own title, lasting 7 years (13 issues).
(e)

**KRAZY KOMICS** No. 1 (7/42, Timely, F)-With four funny animal anthology titles on the stands (all by Dell), Timely entered this new developing field. This series had a humorous format with no strong characters, lasting 4 years. The second publisher in this genre.
(e)

**NAPOLEON AND UNCLE ELBY** No. 1 (7/42), Eastern Color, R)-A one-shot single theme anthology title of the popular transfer strip.
(e)

**NEW FUNNIES** No. 65 (7/42, Dell, F)-The funny animal fever was catching on as Dell gave stardom to their newly acquired characters, *Andy Panda* and *Woody Woodpecker*. Lantz created these characters who became an instant success for Dell's ***The Funnies***. This was Dell's fifth funny animal series (with only six on the stands).
(a,b,c,e,j)

**OAKY DOAKS** No. 1 (7/42, Eastern Color, R)-A one-shot strip reprint book which couldn't compete on the stands.
(e)

**STRICTLY PRIVATE** No. 1 (7/42), Eastern Color, R)-A two-issue run of the famous strip, not surviving as a comic book.
(e)

**WAR VICTORY ADVENTURES** No. 1 (Sum/42, Harv, W)-A unique super hero title produced to promote purchase of war savings bonds, lasting 3 issues.
(e)

★ ★ ★ ★ **WONDER WOMAN** No. 1 (Sum/42, DC, H)-One of the few characters in comics to make her own title just months from her debut in ***All-Star*** No. 8. The only mythological character to flourish in the comics format, her only concession to the present was adopting a modern costume. The amazing Amazon was a trend setter whose popularity has lasted beyond 40 years.
(a,b,c,e,j)

**WAR HEROES** No. 1 (7-9/42, Dell, W)-Dell's third war title, lasting 11 issues.
(e)

★ **CAPTAIN MIDNIGHT** No. 1 (9/42, Faw, Av)-This book heralds one of the most changed transfer characters adapted successfully to the comic book format. Fawcett's version of the character is the most memorable (see ***The Funnies*** No. 57), lasting 6 years. Kept alive by the long lasting radio series and a movie serial. A spin-off of *Spy Smasher*.
(a,b,c,e)

**FIGHTING YANK** No. 1 (9/42, BP, H)-After a year's exposure in ***Startling***, the colonial hero was given his own series. The outstanding Schomburg covers sustained the run, lasting 7 years.
(a,b,c,e,j)

**OUR GANG COMICS** No. 1 (9-10/42, Dell, F)-A strong early licensed group from MGM films who didn't quite come across as well in the comic medium due to necessary changes in the stereotyping of *Buckwheat* and others. The comic version is mainly collected due to the outstanding art by Walt Kelly and the back-up strips by Carl Barks.
(a,b,c,e,f,j,l)

★ **COO COO COMICS** No. 1 (10/42, BP, F)-Seeing the stands beginning to swell with Dell's funny animal titles (5), Better got on the band wagon. *Super Mouse* debuted, the first funny animal super hero (cloned from *Superman*). (7 funny animal titles now on the stands.)
(a,b,c,d,e,f,h,i,j)

★ ★ ★ ★ ★ **DONALD DUCK FOUR COLOR** No. 9 (10/42, Dell, F)-Debut of anonymous artist, who breathed life into the character and turned the strip into full-length adventure stories. Carl Barks' successful adaptation won him the position as *Donald Duck's* biographer for almost three decades beginning with ***Walt Disney's Comics and Stories*** No. 31.
(a,b,c,g,h,j)

★ **JUNGLE GIRL** No. 1 (Fall/42, Faw, J)-Inspired by the popular film serial, *Perils of Nyoka*, this one-shot introduced the jungle heroine to comics. The series was picked up again in 1945 (retitled ***Nyoka***), lasting 8 years.
(a,b,c,e,f,j,l)

**PICTURE STORIES FROM THE BIBLE** No. 1 (Fall/42, DC, TR)-The pilot model of M. C. Gaines' projected 'educational comics' line was laudable in concept but squelched at the stands by abysmal art, pedantic scripting and the normal resistance of kids to anything even remotely preachy. Sustained primarily by lot sales to educators and church groups. Ironically, the first comic ever to bear the EC seal.
(a,c,e,i,j,l)

**SUPERSNIPE COMICS** No. 6 (10/42, S&S, H)-Probably the best, and certainly the most original comic book character of this pulp publisher. A super hero parody lasting 7 years.
(a,b,c,e,f,j)

★ **TERRY-TOONS COMICS** No. 1 (10/42, Timely, F)-20th Century Fox's characters enter the comic field with this book. Timely's second funny animal anthology series (8 titles are now on the stands). 20th Century Fox's *Mighty Mouse* appeared in films the following year and entered this run with No. 38.
(a,b,c,e,j,l)

★ **AIR FIGHTERS** No. 2 (11/42, Hill, Av)-First appearance of one ot the top aviation features also marked Hillman's first successful title. Engaging origin featured air-minded monk who designed and built the premier imaginary aircraft in all of comics. At the controls of the unusual bat-winged orinthopter, dubbed *Birdie*, was the youth who would become known as *Airboy*. He managed to make the standard garb of the pilot—goggles, scarf, flight jacket, et al—look as if they were designed expressly for him. Thoughtful scripting and complimentary art (ala Caniff) propelled this feature through the war years and beyond. Duration 11 years. (*The Heap*, one of the most original characters in comics, began in the next issue.)
(a,b,c,d,j)

★ ★ **CAPTAIN MARVEL JR** No. 1 (11/42, Faw, H)-Fawcett's second most popular hero (from ***Master***) was given his own series. Raboy classic covers/story art sustained the run, lasting 11 years.
(a,b,c,e)

**MICKEY FINN** No. 1 (11/42, Eastern Color, R)-The popular transfer character tried his wings in a title of his own. Like *Sparky Watts*, only 17 issues came out in a 10 year period.
(a,c,e)

**SPARKY WATTS** No. 1 (11/42, CCG, R)-Humorous, off-beat character (proven in ***Big Shot***) is given own title, struggling through 10 issues in 7 years.
(a,c,e)

**TOPIX** No. 1 (11/42, CG, Re)-The first continuous series comic with a religious theme, lasting 10 years. First of a publisher.
(b,e,i,j,k)

★ **CAPTAIN MARVEL ADVENTURES** No. 18 (12/11/42, Faw, H)-*Captain Marvel* is cloned again. Debut of *Mary Marvel* and *The Marvel Family. Mary Marvel* was given instant stardom in ***Wow***.
(a,b,c,d,j)

**FAWCETT'S FUNNY ANIMAL COMICS** No. 1 (12/42, Faw, F)-The first appearance of *Hoppy The Marvel Bunny*, (cloned from *Captain Marvel*), lasting 13 years. The second funny animal super hero (see ***Coo Coo***). Fawcett joined Dell, Timely and Better entering the funny animal market (10 titles now on the stands). (*Captain Marvel* himself introduced *Hoppy* on the cover.)
(a,b,c,d,e,h,j)

**FUNNY BOOK** No. 1 (12/42, PMI, F)-Another publisher entered the funny animal market with this book. Weak concepts overall, the title lasting 9 issues over 4 years (10 titles now on the stands).
(e)

**GIFT COMICS** No. 1 (12/42, Faw, H)-Fawcett's second thick-format title containing original comics to be released at Christmas with ***Holiday*** and ***Xmas*** for 50¢.
(a,c,e)

**HIT COMICS** No. 25 (12/42, Qua, H)-*Kid Eternity* debuts. Recurring war-era theme of life after life was given novel twist in this long running series. Youthful hero, dying ahead of his appointed time, was not only miraculously restored to life but granted the ability to call on all the great heroes of the past for assistance in solving crimes (see *The Fighting Yank*). Intriguing concept was given usual stellar Iger shop treatment.
(a,b,c,d,j)

**HOLIDAY COMICS** No. 1 (12/42, Faw, H)-Fawcett's third thick-format title of original comics to be released at Christmas with ***Gift*** and ***Xmas*** for 25¢.
(a,c,e)

**SANTA CLAUS FUNNIES** No. 1 (12/42, Dell, F)-A special Christmas book illustrated by Kelly. A successful concept that was repeated annually for 20 years.
(a,b,c,e)

**AMERICA IN ACTION** nn (1942, Dell, W)-A one-shot war anthology book.
(e)

**FAMOUS STORIES** No. 1 (1942, Dell, Lit)-An educational theme comic, similar to ***Classic Comics***, not lasting beyond the 2nd issue.
(e)

**JOE PALOOKA** No. 1 (1942, CCG, R)-With proven success in ***Big Shot*** (not to mention syndication), the character became a star in his own title. Early issues boast "over 1,000,000 copies sold." The series lasted 19 years.
(a,b,c,e)

**WAR STORIES** No. 1 (1942, Dell, W)-Dell's fourth war theme anthology title, lasting 8 issues. *Night Devils*, a mysterious costumed war team debuted in No. 3.
(e)

## 1943 ■

**ALL NEW COMICS** No. 1 (1/43, Harv, H)-A super hero anthology title of mediocre quality, lasting 15 issues.
(e)

★ ★ ★ **ARCHIE COMICS** No. 1 (Wint/42-43, AP, TA)-Early stardom for a non-super hero theme. A successful formula with many spin-off characters, lasting beyond 40 years.
(a,b,c,d,e,h,i,j)

**BLACK TERROR** No. 1 (Wint/42-43, BP, H)-Fighting his way from ***Exciting***, the character begins his own series. Sterling costume. High impact Schomburg covers mislead the buyer as to the quality of the contents. Lasted 7 years.
(a,b,c,e,j)

**BOY COMMANDOS** No. 1 (Wint/42-43, DC, W)-After *Captain America*, this was the second title that Simon and Kirby had all to themselves. Pat variation of favorite S&K theme: Kid group with adult mentor. Seldom rose above the expected, but S&K were at their loosest and the strip conveys the sense of fun they probably had doing it. Earlier covers, sans redundant blurbs and intrusive dialogue balloons, are superb poster art.
(a,b,c,e,j)

**CAPTAIN BATTLE** No. 3 (Wint/42-43, Mag. Press, H)-After a year's delay, the character from ***Silver Streak*** was given another chance, only lasting 3 issues.
(e)

**CLUE COMICS** No. 1 (1/43, Hill, H)-Hillman's second most successful title. Unusual heroes and bizarre villains sustained run for four years.
(e)

**COMIC CAVALCADE** No. 1 (Wint/42-43, DC, H)-Following the success of ***World's Finest***, DC launched this companion book in thick format featuring their next tier of top characters, *Wonder Woman, The Flash* and *Green Lantern*.
(a,b,c,e)

**COMICS DIGEST** No. 1 (Wint/42-43, PMI, TR)-A one-shot war theme reprint anthology (pocket size) from ***True Comics***.
(e)

**FLYING CADET** No. 1 (1/43, Flying Cadet, Av)-A true theme World War II aviation anthology (with real photos), lasting 4 years.
(e)

**GOLDEN ARROW** No. 1 (Wint/42-43, Faw, Ws)-Fawcett's original western character from ***Whiz*** finally given own title, lasting 6 issues.
(a,e)

**HELLO PAL COMICS** No. 1 (1/43, Harv, An)-Unusual format featuring photographic covers of movie stars. *Rocketman* and *Rocketgirl* appear (see ***Scoop***), lasting 3 issues.
(e)

**MISS FURY COMICS** No. 1 (Wint/42-43, Timely, H)-A strong transfer character by Tarpe Mills. Noteworthy and unique in that she rarely appeared in costume.
(a,c,e,f,j)

**MAJOR HOOPLE COMICS** No. 1 (1/43, BP, R)-A one-shot comic of the famous strip character, as Better tried to enter the reprint market.
(e)

**REAL FUNNIES** No. 1 (1/43, Nedor, F)-The publisher's second funny animal title (11 titles now on stands), only lasting 3 issues. First appearance of *The Black Terrier* (cloned from *The Black Terror*), the third funny animal super hero.
(e)

**RED DRAGON COMICS** No. 5 (1/43, S&S, An)-Pulpy anthology series not strong enough to last over 5 issues.
(e)

**DON WINSLOW OF THE NAVY** No. 1 (2/43, Faw, W)-His comic book career was launched here with an introduction by *Captain Marvel* himself. Successful adaptation of this popular transfer character, lasting 12 years.
(a,b,c,e,j,l)

**HEADLINE COMICS** No. 1 (2/43, Prize, TR)-Taking up the "True" theme of PMI's ***True*** and ***Real Heroes*** and Better's ***Real Life***, Prize entered the field with this, their second title, which lasted 13 years.
(b,e)

**HOPALONG CASSIDY** No. 1 (2/43, Faw, Ws)-A one-shot issue continuing as a series three years later. The third continuous series newsstand western title, lasting 16 years. A transfer character kept alive by William Boyd's strong following in the movies and on TV.
(a,b,c,e)

**IBIS, THE INVINCIBLE** No. 1 (2/43, Faw, Mg)-As a solid back-up feature in ***Whiz***, he was invincible, but not invincible enough to support a title of his own. The title expired after 6 issues.
(e)

**KID KOMICS** No. 1 (2/43, Timely, H)-Timely's third series devoted to sidekicks. The Schomburg covers and guest appearances of secondary characters sustained the run through 10 issues.
(e)

**ALL HERO COMICS** No. 1 (3/43, Faw, H)-Fawcett's second title that showcased their top characters (see ***America's Greatest***). A thick format one-shot.
(a,c,e)

**CAPTAIN MARVEL ADVENTURES** No. 22 (3/43, Faw, H)-Begins the 25-issue *Mr. Mind* serial which captured nationwide attention at the time. Tremendous and brilliant marketing strategy by Fawcett. An epic by any standard, unmatched before or since.
(c,d,f,h,i,j)

**COMEDY COMICS** No. 14 (3/43, Timely, F)-The first *Super Rabbit* (the fourth funny animal super hero) (the 12th title on the stands). Given his own title the following year. (An imitation of *Hoppy The Marvel Bunny*.)
(a,c,d,e,j)

**FUNNY FUNNIES** No. 1 (4/43, BP, F)-A one-shot funny animal title (their third) (13 titles now on the stands). No enduring characters.
(e)

★ ★ ★ ★ **WALT DISNEY'S COMICS AND STORIES** No. 31 (4/43, Dell, F)-Anonymous staffer who defined what funny animal continuity is all about began this issue (2nd Barks *DD* story; see ***DD Four Color*** No. 9). Cinched long-term success of Disney anthology. One of a half-dozen absolute masters of the form, Carl Barks' achievement on individual stories is exceeded only by remarkable consistency of the series over the length of its run (over 40 years).
(a,b,c,j)

**GOOFY COMICS** No. 1 (6/43, Nedor, F)-Nedor's fourth funny animal title and one of the most enduring, lasting 10 years. No memorable characters. (13 funny animal titles on the stands.)
(b,e)

**JOLLY JINGLES** No. 10 (Sum/43, MLJ, F)-A new publisher tried their hand at funny animals, introducing *Super Duck* (the fifth funny animal super hero). (A hybrid of *Superman* and *Donald Duck*.) (14 titles on the stands.)
(a,c,d,e,j)

★ ★ **PLASTIC MAN** No. 1 (Sum/43, Qua, H)-After a slow start, this title outlasts ***Police Comics***, surviving 13 years. One of the top hero concepts carried by the exciting plotting/art of Jack Cole.
(a,b,c,e)

**HAPPY COMICS** No. 1 (8/43, Standard, F)-Their fifth funny animal title. No memorable characters, lasting 7 years (14 titles on the stands.)
(b,e)

**ALL-SELECT COMICS** No. 1 (Fall/43, Timely, H)-Timely's second showcase title featuring their top three characters (see ***All Winners***). Series carried by Schomburg covers (a proven sales feature), lasting 3 years.
(a,c,e)

**ALL SURPRISE** No. 1 (Fall/43, Timely, F)-Timely's fourth funny animal title, giving more exposure to their leading character, *Super Rabbit*, lasting 4 years. (15 titles on the stands.)
(e)

**SUPER RABBIT** No. 1 (Fall/43, Timely, F)-After his debut in ***Comedy Comics***, *Super Rabbit* is given his own title, lasting 5 years. (15 titles on the stands.)
(e)

**CAPTAIN BATTLE JR** No. 1 (Fall/43, Comic House, H)-Clone of *Captain Battle*. The *Claw* vs. *The Ghost*, lasting 2 issues.
(e)

**GIGGLE COMICS** No. 1 (10/43, ACG, F)-Ties as first title of a new publisher, reinforcing the trend to funny animals. The quality and style of ACG's whole line was heavily influenced by the mastery of the teacher-artist of Ken Hultgren, the series' artist (beginning in 1944). This title lasted 12 years. (17 titles on the stands.)
(a,b,c,e,j,k)

**HA HA COMICS** No. 1 (10/43, ACG, F)-Ties as first title of a new publisher, reinforcing the trend to funny animals. A double impact-with sister title on the stands. Ingenious plotting and art by Ken Hultgren begins the following year. This series lasted 12 years. (17 titles on the stands.)
(a,b,c,e,j,k)

**SUSPENSE COMICS** No. 1 (12/43, Continental, D)-Debut of *The Grey Mask* (imitation of *The Spirit*). Atmospheric radio drama in a comic book form, lasting 3 years.
(e)

**AVIATION CADETS** nn (1943, S&S, Av)-A World War II aviation anthology one-shot. Navy pre-flight training involving sports.
(e)

**COLUMBIA COMICS** No. 1 (1943, Wise, R)-More exposure for Columbia's reprint characters, *Joe Palooka, Dixie Duggan*, etc., lasting 4 issues.
(e)

**POWERHOUSE PEPPER** No. 1 (1943, Timely, Hm)-The protagonist of ***Joker Comics*** of a year earlier, Wolverton's humorous plotting made this character a memorable one. Popular enough to receive his own title.
(a,c,e,j)

**TINY TOTS COMICS** No. 1 (1943, Dell, F)-A one-shot anthology book of funny animals with Walt Kelly art.
(e)

**TREASURE COMICS** nn (1943, Prize, H)-Rebinding of coverless copies of ***Prize*** No. 7-11 from 1942. A very rare book with only one copy known to exist.
(e)

**UNITED STATES MARINES** nn (1943, Wise, W)-A documentary style war anthology series mixed with magazine-type photo features from the front, surviving one year. The title was resurrected for a brief period after the Korean conflict.
(e)

**ALL FUNNY COMICS** No. 1 (Wint/43-44, DC, Hm)-DC's first all funny anthology title. A popular series with the humorous plotting of *Genius Jones*, lasting 4½ years.
(e,j)

**BLACK HOOD COMICS** No. 9 (Wint/43-44, MLJ, H)-The Man of Mystery graduates from ***Top-Notch*** into his own title, lasting 11 issues.
(e)

# CHRONOLOGICAL LIST OF COMIC BOOK TITLES BY PUBLISHER FOR PERIOD 1933 - 1943

**(The indented titles are key books other than No. 1's)**

## ACE MAGAZINES

**Sure-Fire** No. 1, 6/40
**Super Mystery** No. 1, 7/40
**Lightning** No. 4, 12/40
**Our Flag** No. 1, 8/41
**Banner** No. 3, 9/41
**Four Favorites** No. 1, 9/41
**Captain Courageous** No. 6, 3/42

## AMERICAN COMICS GROUP

**Giggle** No. 1, 10/43
**Ha Ha** No. 1, 10/43

## BETTER PUBL. (Standard)

**Best** No. 1, 11/39
**Thrilling** No. 1, 2/40
**Exciting** No. 1, 4/40
  **Exciting** No. 9, 5/41
**Startling** No. 1, 6/40
**Real Life** No. 1, 9/41
  **Startling** No. 10, 9/41
**America's Best** No. 1, 2/42
**Fighting Yank** No. 1, 9/42
**Coo Coo** No. 1, 10/42
**Black Terror** No. 1, Wint/42-43
**Major Hoople** No. 1, 1/43
**Real Funnies** No. 1, 1/43
**Funny Funnies** No. 1, 4/43
**Goofy** No. 1, 6/43
**Happy** No. 1, 8/43

## BILBARA PUBLISHING CO.

**Cyclone** No. 1, 6/40

## CENTAUR PUBLICATIONS

**Funny Pages** V2/6, 3/38
**Funny Pic. Stories** V2/6, 3/38
**Star Comics** No. 10, 3/38
**Star Ranger** No. 10, 3/38
**Cowboy** No. 13, 7/38
**Keen Detective** No. 8, 7/38
**Little Giant** No. 1, 7/38
**Amazing Mystery Funnies** No. 1, 8/38
**Little Giant Movie** No. 1, 8/38
  **Funny Pages** V2/10, 9/38
**Star Ranger Funnies** No. 15, 10/38
**Little Giant Det.** No. 1, 10/38
**Keen Komics** V2/1, 5/39
  **Amazing Mystery Funnies** V2/7, 7/39
**Comic Pages** V3/4, 7/39
  **Keen Detective** V2/7, 7/39
**Amazing Man** No. 5, 9/39
**Amazing Adventure Funnies** No. 1, 6/40
**Fantoman** No. 2, 8/40
**Masked Marvel** No. 1, 9/40
**Arrow, The** No. 1, 10/40
**Super Spy** No. 1, 10/40
**Detective Eye** No. 1, 11/40
**Wham** No. 1, 11/40
**Stars and Stripes** No. 2, 5/41
**Liberty Scouts** No. 2, 6/41
**World Famous Heroes** No. 1, 10/41
**Man Of War** No. 1, 11/41

## CATECHETICAL GUILD

**Topix** No. 1, 11/42

## HARRY 'A' CHESLER

**Star** No. 1, 2/37
**Star Ranger** No. 1, 2/37
**Feature Funnies** No. 1, 10/37
**Cocomalt Big Book** No. 1, 1938
**Yankee** No. 1, 9/41
**Dynamic** No. 1, 10/41
**Scoop** No. 1, 11/41
**Punch** No. 1, 12/41

## COLUMBIA COMICS GROUP

**Big Shot** No. 1, 5/40
**Skyman** No. 1, Fall/41
**Face, The** No. 1, 1941
**Dixie Duggan** No. 1, 7/42
**Joe Palooka** No. 1, 1942
**Sparky Watts** No. 1, 11/42

## COMICS MAGAZINE

**Comics Magazine** No. 1, 5/36
**Funny Pages** No. 6, 11/36
**Funny Picture Stories** No. 1, 11/36
**Detective Picture Stories** No. 1, 12/36
**Western Picture Stories** No. 1, 2/37

## DC COMICS

**New Fun** No. 1, 2/35
**New Comics** No. 1, 12/35
**More Fun** No. 7, 1/36
**Big Book of Fun** No. 1, Spr/36
**New Book of Comics** No. 1, 6-8/36
**New Adventure** No. 12, 1/37
**Detective** No. 1, 3/37
**Action** No. 1, 6/38
  **Detective** No. 20, 10/38
**Adventure** No. 32, 11/38
**All-American** No. 1, 4/39
**New York World's Fair** 3-5/39
**Movie** No. 1, 4/39
  **Detective** No. 27, 5/39
  **Adventure** No. 40, 7/39
**Mutt and Jeff** No. 1, Sum/39
**Superman** No. 1, Sum/39
**Double Action** No. 2, 1/40
**Flash** No. 1, 1/40
  **More Fun** No. 52,53, 2,3/40
  **Adventure** No. 48, 3/40
**Batman** No. 1, Spr/40
**New York World's Fair** 3-5/40
  **More Fun** No. 55, 5/40
  **All-American** No. 16, 7/40
**All-Star** No. 1, Sum/40
  **All-American** No. 19, 10/40
  **All-Star** No. 3, Wint/40-41
  **Adventure** No. 61, 4/41
**World's Best** No. 1, Spr/41
**All Flash** No. 1, Sum/41
**World's Finest** No. 2, Sum/41
**Green Lantern** No. 1, Fall/41
**Star Spangled** No. 1, 10/41
  **All-Star** No. 8, 11-12/41
**Leading** No. 1, Wint/41-42
**Sensation** No. 1, 1/42
  **Star Spangled** No. 7, 4/42
  **Detective** No. 64, 6/42
**Wonder Woman** No. 1, Sum/42
**Pic. Stories/Bible** No. 1, Fall/42
**Boy Commandos** No. 1, Wint/42-43
**Comic Cavalcade** No. 1, Wint/42-43
**All Funny** No. 1, Wint/43-44

## DELL PUBLISHING CO.

**Popular** No. 1, 2/36
**Funnies** No. 1, 10/36
**Comics** No. 1, 3/37
**West. Action Thrillers** No. 1, 4/37
**100 Pages of Comics** No. 1, 1937
**Super** No. 1, 5/38
**Crackajack** No. 1, 6/38
**Nickel** No. 1, 1938
**Large Feature Comic** No. 1, 1939
**Four-Color** No. 1, 1939
**Donald Duck 4-Color** No. 4, 3/40?
**War** No. 1, 5/40
**W.D.'s Comics & Stories** No. 1, 10/40
**Mickey Mouse 4-Color** No. 16, 4/41
  **Funnies** No. 57, 7/41
**Red Ryder** No. 3, 8/41
**Looney Tunes** No. 1, Fall/41
**Key Ring** No. 1, 1941
**Large Feature** No. 1, 1941
**USA Is Ready** No. 1, 1941
**Animal** No. 1, 12-1/41-42
**Camp** No. 1, 2/42
**Fairy Tale Parade** No. 1, 6-7/42
**New Funnies** No. 65, 7/42
**War Heroes** No. 1, 7-9/42
**Our Gang** No. 1, 9-10/42
**Santa Claus Funnies** No. 1, 12/42
**America In Action** No. 1, 1942
**Donald Duck 4-Color** No. 9, 1942
**Famous Stories** No. 1, 1942
**War Stories** No. 1, 1942
  **W.D. Comics & Stories** No. 31, 4/43
**Tiny Tots** No. 1, 1943

## EASTERN COLOR

**Funnies On Parade** nn, 1933
**F. F., A Carnival--** nn, 1933
**Century Of Comics** nn, 1933
**Skippy's Own Book** nn, 1934

**Famous Funnies** Series 1, 1934
**Famous Funnies** No. 1, 7/34
**Heroic** No. 1, 8/40
**Buck Rogers** No. 1, Wint/40-41
**Dickie Dare** No. 1, 1941
**Big Chief Wahoo** No. 1, Wint/41-42
**Jingle Jangle** No. 1, 2/42
**Oaky Doaks** No. 1, 7/42
**Mickey Finn** No. 1, 11/42
**Napoleon & Uncle Elby** No. 1, 11/42
**Strictly Private** No. 1, 11/42
**Tiny Tots** No. 1, 1943

## WILL EISNER
**Spirit** No. 1, 6/2/40

## ELLIOT PUBLICATIONS
**Double** 1940
**Double Up** 1941

## FAWCETT PUBLICATIONS
**Flash** No. 1, 1/40
**Whiz** No. 2, 2/40
**Master** No. 1, 3/40
**Slam Bang** No. 1, 3/40
**Nickel** No. 1, 5/40
**Special Edition** No. 1, 8/40
**Western Desperado** No. 8, 10/40
**Wow** No. 1, Wint/40-41
**Captain Marvel** No. 1, 1-2/41
**America's Greatest** No. 1, 5/41
**Bulletman** No. 1, 7/41
**Minuteman** No. 1, 7/41
**Capt. Marvel Thrill Book** 1941
**Gene Autry** No. 1, Fall/41
**Spysmasher** No. 1, Fall/41
  **Master** No. 21, 12/41
  **Whiz** No. 25, 12/12/41
**Xmas** No. 1, 12/41
**Captain Midnight** No. 1, 9/42
**Jungle Girl** No. 1, Fall/42
**Captain Marvel Jr.** No. 1, 11/42
  **Captain Marvel** No. 18, 12/11/42
**Fawcett's Funny Animals** No. 1, 12/42
**Gift** No. 1, 12/42
**Holiday** No. 1, 12/42
**Golden Arrow** No. 1, Wint/42-43
**Don Winslow** No. 1, 2/43
**Hopalong Cassidy** No. 1, 2/43
**Ibis** No. 1, 2/43
**All Hero** No. 1, 3/43
  **Captain Marvel** No. 22, 3/43

## FICTION HOUSE
**Jumbo** No. 1, 9/38
**Fight** No. 1, 1/40
**Jungle** No. 1, 1/40
**Planet** No. 1, 1/40
**Wings** No. 1, 9/40
**Rangers** No. 1, 10/41
**Sheena** No. 1, Spr/42
**Wambi** No. 1, Spr/42

## FLYING CADET
**Flying Cadet** No. 1, 1/43

## FOX FEATURES SYNDICATE
**Wonder** No. 1, 5/39
**Wonderworld** No. 3, 7/39
**Mysterymen** No. 1, 8/39
**Fantastic** No. 1, 12/39
**Blue Beetle** No. 1, Wint/39-40
**Science** No. 1, 2/40
**Weird** No. 1, 4/40
**Flame, The** No. 1, Sum/40
**Green Mask** No. 1, Sum/40
**Big 3** No. 1, Fall/40
**Rex Dexter** No. 1, Fall/40
**Samson** No. 1, Fall/40
**Eagle, The** No. 1, 7/41
**U.S. Jones** No. 1, 11/41
**V-Comics** No. 1, 1/42

## FUNNIES, INC.
**Motion Pic. Funn. Weekly** No. 1, 5/39?
**Green Giant** No. 1, 1940

## LEV GLEASON
**Silver Streak** No. 1, 12/39
  **Silver Streak** No. 6, 9/40
  **Silver Streak** No. 7, 1/41
**Captain Battle** No. 1, Sum/41
**Daredevil** No. 1, 7/41
**Boy** No. 3, 4/42
**Crime Does Not Pay** No. 22, 6/42
**Captain Battle** No. 3, Wint/42-43
**Captain Battle Jr.** No. 1, Fall/43

## HUGO GERNSBACK
**Superworld** No. 1, 4/40

## GILBERTON PUBLICATIONS
**Classic** No. 1, 10/41

## GLOBE SYNDICATE
**Circus** No. 1, 6/38

## GREAT PUBLICATIONS
**Great** No. 1, 11/41
**Choice** No. 1, 12/41

## HARVEY PUBL. (Helnit)
**Speed** No. 1, 10/39
**Champion** No. 2, 12/39
**Champ** No. 11, 10/40
**Green Hornet** No. 1, 12/40
**Pocket** No. 1, 8/41
**War Victory** No. 1, Sum/42
**All New** No. 1, 1/43
**Hello Pal** No. 1, 1/43

## HAWLEY PUBLICATIONS
**Captain Easy** nn, 1939
**Red Ryder** No. 1, 9/40
**Sky Blazers** No. 1, 9/40
**Hi-Spot** No. 2, 11/40

## HILLMAN PERIODICALS
**Miracle** No. 1, 2/40
**Rocket** No. 1, 3/40
**Victory** No. 1, 8/41
**Air Fighters** No. 1, 11/41
  **Air Fighters** No. 2, 11/42
**Clue** No. 1, 1/43

## HOLYOKE (Continental)
**Crash** No. 1, 5/40
  **Crash** No. 4, 9/40
**Catman** No. 1, 5/41
**Captain Fearless** No. 1, 8/41
**Captain Aero** No. 7, 12/41
**Suspense** No. 1, 12/43

## HYPER PUBLICATIONS
**Hyper Mystery** No. 1, 5/40

## K.K. PUBLICATIONS
**Mickey Mouse Mag.** No. 1, Sum/35
**Mickey Mouse Mag.** V5/12, 9/40

## DAVID MCKAY PUBL.
**King** No. 1, 4/36
**Wow** No. 1, 5/36
**Ace** No. 1, 4/37
**Feature Book** nn, 1-4/37
**Magic** No. 1, 8/39
**Future** No. 1, 6/40

## MLJ MAGAZINES
**Blue Ribbon** No. 1, 11/39
**Top-Notch** No. 1, 12/39
**Pep** No. 1, 1/40
**Zip** No. 1, 2/40
**Shield-Wizard** No. 1, Sum/40
  **Top-Notch** No. 9, 10/40
  **Blue Ribbon** No. 9, 2/41
**Jackpot** No. 1, Spr/41
  **Pep** No. 17, 7/41
  **Pep** No. 22, 12/41
**Special** No. 1, Wint/41-42
**Hangman** No. 2, Spr/42
**Archie** No. 1, Wint/42-43
**Jolly Jingles** No. 10, Sum/43
**Black Hood** No. 9, Wint/43-44

## NITA PUBLICATIONS
**Whirlwind** No. 1, 6/40

## NOVELTY PUBLICATIONS
**Target** No. 1, 2/40
**Blue Bolt** No. 1, 6/40
**Four Most** No. 1, Wint/41-42

## PARENT'S MAGAZINE INST.
**True** No. 1, 4/41
**Calling All Girls** No. 1, 9/41
**Real Heroes** No. 1, 9/41
**Funny Book** No. 1, 12/42
**Comics Digest** No. 1, Wint/42-43

## PRIZE PUBLICATIONS
**Prize** No. 1, 3/40
  **Prize** No. 7, 9/40
**Headline** No. 1, 2/43
**Treasure** nn, 1943

## PROGRESSIVE PUBLISHERS
**Bang-Up** No. 1, 12/41

## QUALITY COMICS GROUP
**Feature** No. 21, 6/39
**Smash** No. 1, 8/39
  **Feature** No. 27, 12/39
**Crack** No. 1, 5/40
**Hit** No. 1, 7/40
**National** No. 1, 7/40
**Military** No. 1, 8/41
**Police** No. 1, 8/41
**Uncle Sam** No. 1, 8/41
**Doll Man** No. 1, Fall/41
  **Hit** No. 25, 12/42
**Plastic Man** No. 1, Sum/43

## RALSTON-PURINA CO.
**Tom Mix** No. 1, 9/40

## STREET AND SMITH PUBL.
**Shadow** No. 1, 3/40
**Doc Savage** No. 1, 5/40
**Bill Barnes** No. 1, 10/40
**Sport** No. 1, 10/40
**Army and Navy** No. 1, 5/41
**Super Magic** No. 1, 5/41
**Super Magician** No. 2, 9/41
**Pioneer Pic. Stories** No. 1, 12/41
**Trail Blazers** No. 1, 1941
**True Sport Pic. Stories** No. 5, 2/42
**Supersnipe** No. 6, 10/42
**Devil Dogs** No. 1, 1942
**Remember Pearl Harbor** nn, 1942
**Red Dragon** No. 5, 1/43
**Aviation Cadets** No. 1, 1943

## SUN PUBLICATIONS
**Colossus** No. 1, 3/40
**Sun Fun** No. 1, 3/40

## TIMELY COMICS (Marvel)
**Marvel** No. 1, 11/39
**Marvel Mystery** No. 2, 12/39
**Daring Mystery** No. 1, 1/40
**Mystic** No. 1, 3/40
  **Marvel Mystery** No. 9, 7/40
**Red Raven** No. 1, 8/40
**Human Torch** No. 2, Fall/40
**Captain America** No. 1, 3/41
**Sub-Mariner** No. 1, Spr/41
**All-Winners** No. 1, Sum/41
**Young Allies** No. 1, Sum/41
**USA** No. 1, 8/41
**Tough Kid Squad** No. 1, 3/42
**Comedy** No. 9, 4/42
**Joker** No. 1, 4/42
**Krazy** No. 1, 7/42
**Terry-Toons** No. 1, 10/42
**Miss Fury** No. 1, Wint/42-43
**Kid Komics** No. 1, 2/43
  **Comedy** No. 14, 3/43
**All-Select** No. 1, Fall/43
**All-Surprise** No. 1, Fall/43
**Super Rabbit** No. 1, Fall/43
**Powerhouse Pepper** No. 1, 1943

## UNITED FEATURES SYND.
**Tip Top** No. 1, 4/36
**Comics On Parade** No. 1, 4/38
**Single Series** No. 1, 1938
**Okay** No. 1, 7/40
**O.K.** No. 1, 7/40
**Sparkler** No. 1, 7/40
**United** No. 1, 8/40
**Sparkler** No. 1, 7/41

## WHITMAN PUBLISHING CO.
**Mammoth** No. 1, 1937
**Donald Duck** nn, 1938

## WILLIAM H. WISE
**Columbia Comics** No. 1, 1943
**United States Marines** No. 1, 1943

## COMICS WITH LITTLE IF ANY VALUE

There exists in the comic book market, as in all other collector's markets, items, usually of recent origin, that have relatively little if any value. Why even mention it? We wouldn't, except for one thing—this is where you could probably take your worst beating, investment-wise. Since these books are listed by dealers in such profusion, at prices which will vary up to 500 percent from one dealer's price list to another, determining a realistic "market" value is almost impossible. And since the same books are listed repeatedly, list after list, month after month, it is difficult to determine whether or not these books are selling. In some cases, it is doubtful that they are even being collected. Most dealers must get a minimum price for their books; otherwise, it would not be profitable to handle. This will sometimes force a value on an otherwise valueless item. Most dealers who handle new comics get a minimum price of at least 75 cents to $2.00 per copy. This is the **available** price to obtain a **reading** copy. However, this is not what dealers will pay to restock. Since many of these books are not yet collector's items, their salvage value would be very low. You may not get more than 5 cents to 10 cents per copy selling them back to a dealer. This type of material, from an investment point of view, would be of maximum risk since the salvage value is so low. For this reason, recent comics should be bought for enjoyment as reading copies and if they go up in value, consider it a bonus.

## COLLECTING FOREIGN COMICS AND AMERICAN REPRINTS

One extremely interesting source of comics of early vintage—one which does not necessarily have to be expensive—is the foreign market. Many American strips, from both newspapers and magazines, are reprinted abroad (both in English and in other languages) months and even years after they appear in the states. By working out trade agreements with foreign collectors, one can obtain, for practically the cover price, substantial runs of a number of newspaper strips and reprints of American comic books dating back five, ten, or occasionally even twenty or more years. These reprints are often in black and white, and sometimes the reproduction is poor, but this is not always the case. In any event, this is a source of material that every serious collector should look into.

Once the collector discovers comics published in foreign lands, he often becomes fascinated with the original strips produced in these countries. Many are excellent, and have a broader range of appeal than those of American comic books.

## CANADIAN REPRINTS (E.C.s: by J. B. Clifford)

Several E.C. titles were published in Canada by Superior Comics from 1949 to at least 1953. Canadian editions of the following E.C. titles are known: (Pre-Trend) *Saddle Romances, Moon Girl, A Moon A Girl. . . Romance, Modern Love, Saddle Justice;* (New-Trend) *Crypt of Terror—Tales From the Crypt, Haunt of Fear, Vault of Horror, Weird Science, Weird Fantasy, Two-Fisted Tales, Frontline Combat,* and *Mad. Crime SuspenStories* was also published in Canada under the title *Weird SuspenStories* (Nos. 1-3 known). No reprints of *Shock SuspenStories* by Superior are known, nor have any "New Direction" reprints ever been reported. No reprints later than January 1954 are known. Canadian reprints sometimes exchanged cover and contents with adjacent numbers (e.g., a *Frontline Combat* 12 with a *Frontline Combat* No. 11 cover). They are distinguished both in cover and contents. As the interior pages are always reprinted poorly, these comics are of less value (about ½) than the U.S. editions; they were printed from asbestos plates made from the original plates. On some reprints, the Superior seal replaces the E.C. seal. Superior publishers took over Dynamic in 1947.

## CANADIAN REPRINTS (Dells: by Ronald J. Ard)

Canadian editions of Dell comics, and presumably other lines, began in March-

April, 1948 and lasted until February-March, 1951. They were a response to the great Canadian dollar crisis of 1947. Intensive development of the post-war Canadian economy was financed almost entirely by American capital. This massive import or money reached such a level that Canada was in danger of having grossly disproportionate balance of payments which could drive it into technical bankruptcy in the midst of the biggest boom in its history. The Canadian government responded by banning a long list of imports. Almost 500 separate items were involved. Alas, the consumers of approximately 499 of them were politically more formidable than the consumers of comic books.

Dell responded by publishing its titles in Canada, through an arrangement with Wilson Publishing Company of Toronto. This company had not existed for a number of years and it is reasonable to assume that its sole business was the production and distribution of Dell titles in Canada. There is no doubt that they had a captive market. If you check the publication data on the U. S. editions of the period you will see the sentence "Not for sale in Canada." Canada was thus the only area of the Free World in those days technically beyond the reach of the American comic book industry.

We do not know whether French editions existed of the Dell titles put out by Wilson. The English editions were available nationwide. They were priced at 10 cents and were all 36 pages in length, at a time when their American parents were 52 pages. The covers were made of coarser paper, similar to that used in the Dell Four Color series in 1946 and 1947 and were abandoned as the more glossy cover paper became more economical. There was also a time lag of from six to eight weeks between, say, the date an American comic appeared and the date that the Canadian edition appeared.

Many Dell covers had seasonal themes and by the time the Canadian edition came out (two months later) the season was over. Wilson solved this problem by switching covers around so that the appropriate season would be reflected when the books hit the stands. Most Dell titles were published in Canada during this period including the popular Atom Bomb giveaway, *Walt Disney Comics and Stories* and the *Donald Duck* and *Mickey Mouse* Four Color one-shots. The quality of the Duck one-shots is equal to that of their American counterparts and generally bring about 30 percent less.

By 1951 the Korean War had so stimulated Canadian exports that the restrictions on comic book importation, which in any case were an offense against free trade principle, could be lifted without danger of economic collapse. Since this time Dell, as well as other companies, have been shipping direct into Canada.

**CANADIAN REPRINTS (DCs: by Doug A. England)**

Many DC comics were reprinted in Canada by National Comics Publications Limited and Simcoe Publishing and Distributing Co., both of Toronto, for years 1948-1950 at least. Like the Dells, these issues were 36 pages rather than the 52 pages offered in the U.S. editions, and the inscription "Published in Canada" would appear in place of "A 52 Page Magazine" or "52 Big Pages" appearing on U.S. editions. These issues contained no advertisements and some had no issue numbers.

**HOW TO START COLLECTING**

Most collectors of comic books begin by buying new issues in mint condition directly off the newsstand or from their local comic store. (Subscription copies are available from several mail-order services.) Each week new comics appear on the stands that are destined to become true collectors items. The trick is to locate a store that carries a complete line of comics. In several localities this may be difficult. Most panelologists frequent several magazine stands in order not to miss something they want. Even then, it pays to keep in close contact with collectors in other areas. Sooner or later, nearly every collector has to rely upon a friend in Fandom to obtain for him an item that is unavailable locally.

Before you buy any comic to add to your collection, you should carefully inspect its condition. Unlike stamps and coins, defective comics are generally not highly prized. The cover should be properly cut and printed. Remember that every blemish or sign of wear depreciates the beauty and value of your comics.

The serious panelologist usually purchases extra copies of popular titles. He may trade these multiples for items unavailable locally (for example, foreign comics), or he may store the multiples for resale at some future date. Such speculation is, of course, a gamble, but unless collecting trends change radically in the future, the value of certain comics in mint condition should appreciate greatly, as new generations of readers become interested in collecting.

## COLLECTING BACK ISSUES

In addition to current issues, most panelologists want to locate back issues. Some energetic collectors have had great success in running down large hoards of rare comics in their home towns. Occasionally, rare items can be located through agencies that collect old papers and magazines, such as the Salvation Army. The lucky collector can often buy these items for much less than their current market value. Placing advertisements in trade journals, newspapers, etc., can also produce good results. However, don't be discouraged if you are neither energetic nor lucky. Most panelologists build their collections slowly but systematically by placing mail orders with dealers and other collectors.

Comics of early vintage are extremely expensive if they are purchased through a regular dealer or collector, and unless you have unlimited funds to invest in your hobby, you will find it necessary to restrict your collecting in certain ways. However you define your collection, you should be careful to set your goals well within your means.

## PROPER HANDLING OF COMIC BOOKS

Before picking up an old rare comic book, caution should be exercised to handle it properly. Old comic books are very fragile and can be easily damaged. Because of this, many dealers hesitate to let customers personally handle their rare comics. They would prefer to remove the comic from its bag and show it to the customer themselves. In this way, if the book is damaged, it would be the dealer's responsibility—not the customer's. Remember, the slightest crease or chip could render an otherwise Mint book to Near Mint or even Very Fine. The following steps are provided to aid the novice in the proper handling of comic books: 1. Remove the comic from its protective sleeve or bag very carefully. 2. Gently lay the comic (un-opened) in the palm of your hand so that it will stay relatively flat and secure. 3. You can now leaf through the book by carefully rolling or flipping the pages with the thumb and forefinger of your other hand. Caution: Be sure the book always remains relatively flat or slightly rolled. Avoid creating stress points on the covers with your fingers and be particularly cautious in bending covers back too far on Mint books. 4. After examining the book, carefully insert it back into the bag or protective sleeve. Watch corners and edges for folds or tears as you replace the book.

## HOW TO SELL YOUR COMICS

If you have a collection of comics for sale, large or small, the following steps should be taken. (1) Make a detailed list of the books for sale, being careful to grade them accurately, showing any noticeable defects; i.e., torn or missing pages, centerfolds, etc. (2) Decide whether to sell or trade wholesale to a dealer all in one lump or to go through the long laborious process of advertising and selling piece by piece to collectors. Both have their advantages and disadvantages.

# Your Comics Ar

**Beware of False Promises!** Even though you honestly believe you have properly stored your valuable comic collection in protective sleeves made of polyethylene or polypropylene, all you have really done is speed up the deterioration process that makes them lose their value!

**Get the true answers** to your preservation questions once and for all. We at Bill Cole Enterprises have built our reputation as "The Preservation Professionals"℠ by making sure we manufacture and sell only the highest quality preservation products at the most affordable prices. We stand behind our products with a 100% satisfaction guarantee.

**The professionals rely on products from Bill Cole Enterprises. Shouldn't you?**

***Susan Cicconi, Conservator and Owner of The Restoration Lab in Boston, Massachusetts*** *says, "I can always count on Bill Cole for the highest quality products and a trusting and professional relationship."*

***Craig Miller of Lone Star Comics & Science Fiction in Arlington, Texas*** *writes, "...our eight stores are selling your Mylar® and Mylite™ products faster than ever before! Of course, the quality of your merchandise makes our job that much easier."*

## Turn to Bill Cole Enterprises for these fine products:

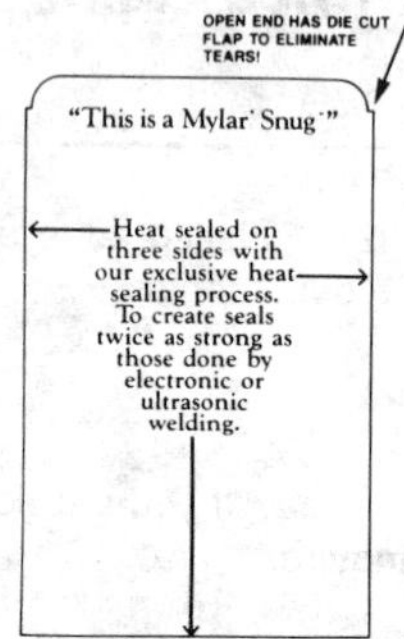


**Mylar® Snugs™ --** Bill Cole's exclusive 4-mil thick protective sleeves have the strongest heat-sealed seams available, plus our exclusive rounded corner-cut openings. Don't be fooled by cheap imitations! Only Snugs™ give you the archival-quality protection you want for your valuable comic collection.

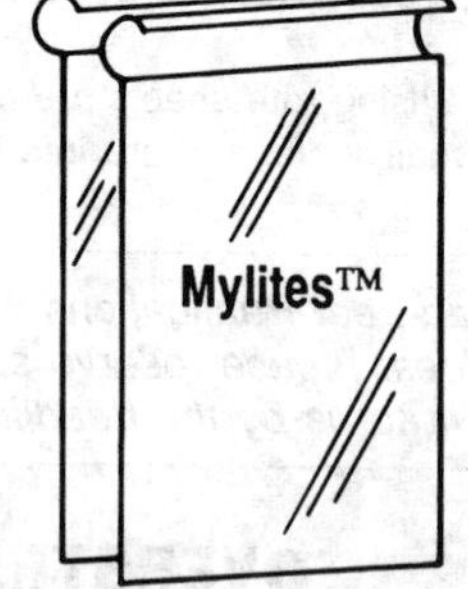


**Mylites™ --** These 1 mil-thick Mylar® sleeves from Bill Cole Enterprises, Inc. are the only safe archival atlernative to polyethylene or polypropylene bags for your more common collectibles!

Mylites™ and Snugs™ are trademarks of E. Gerber Products, Inc. with exclusive rights to Bill Cole Enterprises, Inc. Time-Loks® is a registered trademark of Bill Cole Enterprises, Inc. Time-X-Tenders™ and Ultra-Weld™ are trademarks of Bill Cole Enterprises, Inc. The Preservation Professionals℠ is a service mark of Bill Cole Enterprises, Inc. All references to Mylar® refer to archival quality polyester film such as Mylar® type D by du Pont Co., or equivalent material such as Melinex® 516 by ICI Corp.

# WE BUY IT ALL

© DC Comics

- COMIC BOOKS

© The Disney Co.

- CARTOON POSTERS

© John F. Dille

- BIG LITTLE BOOKS

- ORIGINAL ART

© DC Comics

- ANIMATION CELS

**WORLD'S FINEST COMICS & COLLECTIBLES**

(800) 225-4189 or (206) 274-9163

⑤ P.O. Box 340 Castle Rock, WA 98611

# BUYING CARTOON POSTERS

## ORIGINALS ONLY

© The Disney Co.

© The Disney Co.

- **Highest Prices Paid**
- **Immediate Payment**
- **Free Appraisal**

We are actively seeking **All** Cartoon character Movie Posters from 1920 through 1956.

© The Disney Co.

**Including:**
All Disney Full Feature Cartoons & Shorts
All Fleisher Cartoons
All Super hero Cartoons & Serials
All Warner Brothers Cartoons
All MGM, Universal & Columbia Cartoons

© The Disney Co.

© The Disney Co.

If you have a Cartoon Poster—**We'll buy it!** Lobby Cards too!

Give us a call today at (206) 274-9163 or write:

**WORLD'S FINEST COMICS & COLLECTIBLES**
**P.O. Box 340**
**Castle Rock, WA 98611**

Have any Old Movie Posters with Real People? We buy those too

6

NEW
Records were made to be broken.
MARVEL COMICS '91

ITEM ISSUE!
THE LEGEND
OF THE
ARACHKNIGHT

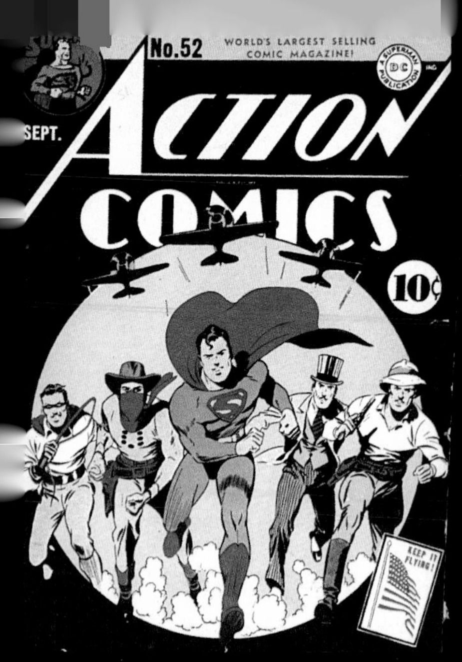


**Action Comics** #52, 1942 © DC.
The Ameri-commandos begin.

**Action Comics** #55, 1942, © DC.

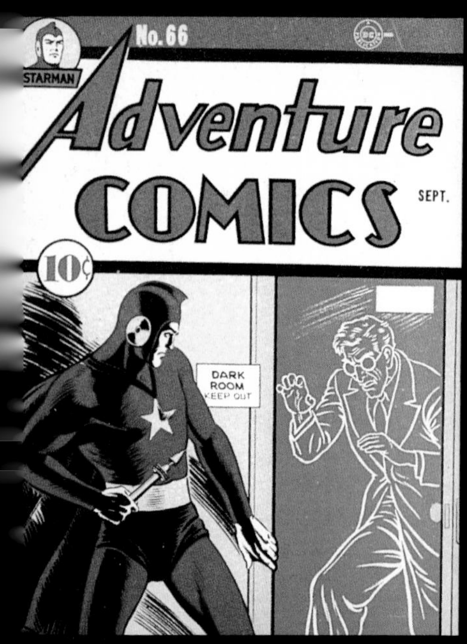


**Adventure Comics** #66, 1941, © DC.

**Adventures Of The Jaguar** #2, 1961

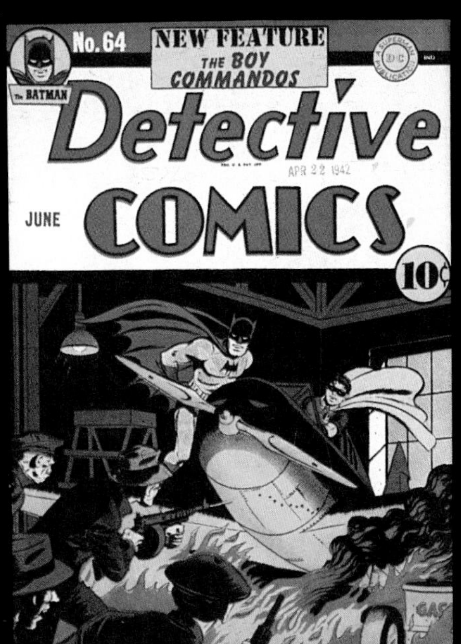


**Detective Comics** #64, 1942, © DC.
First Boy Commandos.

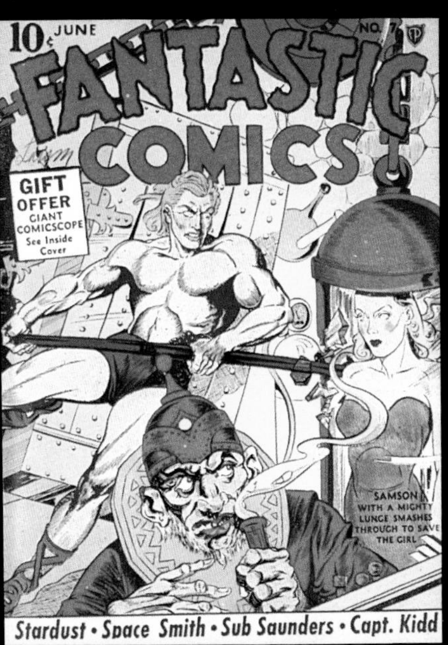


**Fantastic Comics** #7, 1940, © FOX.

**The Flash** #106, 1959, © DC. Grodd,
the Super Gorilla trilogy begins.

**Flash Comics** #33, 1942, © DC.
Shelly Moldoff cover art.

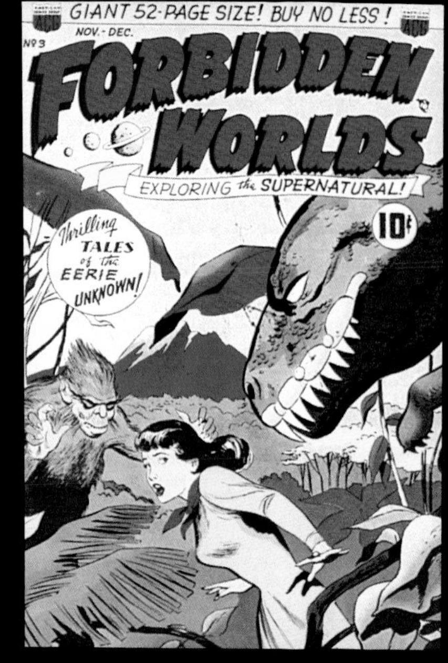


**Forbidden Worlds** #3, 1951, © ACG.

**Frankenstein** #4, 1946, © PRIZE.
Dick Briefer cover art.

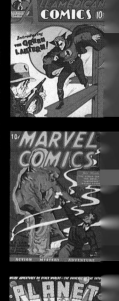

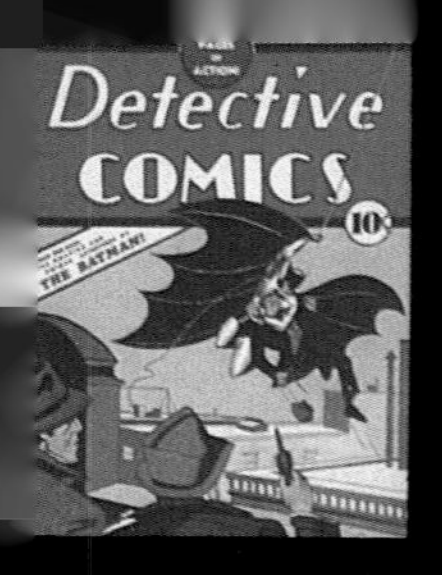

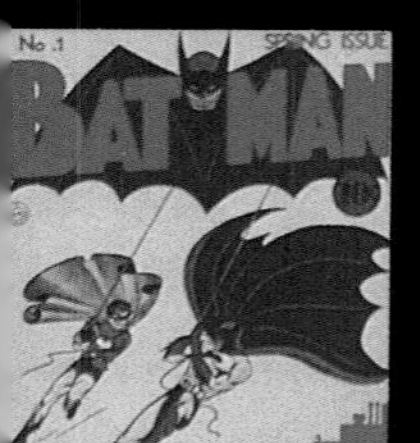


# WANTED

# OLD COMICS!!

## $CASH REWARD$

FOR THESE AND MANY OTHER ELUSIVE COMIC BOOKS FROM THE GOLDEN AGE. SEEKING WHITE PAGE COLLECTIBLE COPIES IN VG OR BETTER CONDITION. ALSO GOLDEN AGE **BOUND VOLUMES** WANTED.

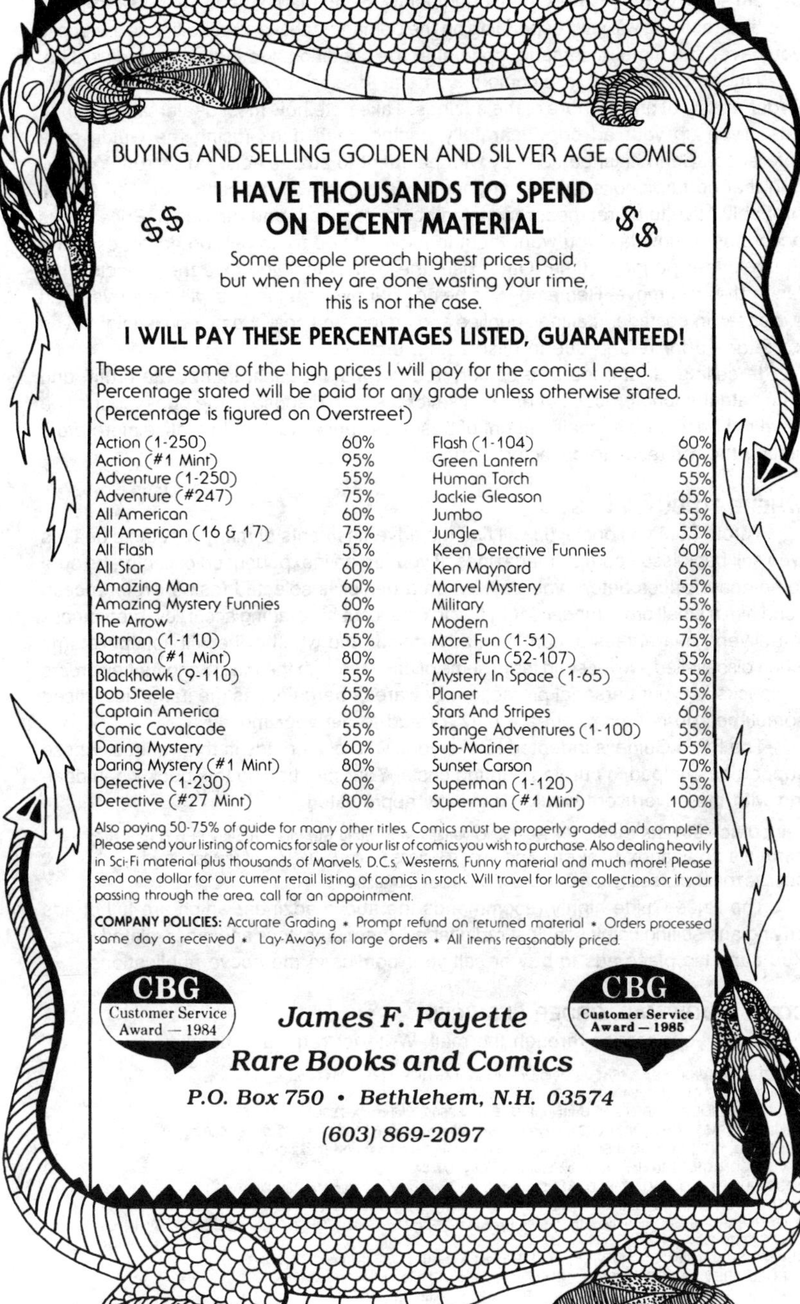
BUYING AND SELLING GOLDEN AND SILVER AGE COMICS
I HAVE THOUSANDS TO SPEND ON DECENT MATERIAL
$$
$$
Some people preach highest prices paid, but when they are done wasting your time, this is not the case.
I WILL PAY THESE PERCENTAGES LISTED, GUARANTEED!
These are some of the high prices I will pay for the comics I need. Percentage stated will be paid for any grade unless otherwise stated. (Percentage is figured on Overstreet)
Action (1-250) 60%
Action (#1 Mint) 95%
Adventure (1-250) 55%
Adventure (#247) 75%
All American 60%
All American (16 & 17) 75%
All Flash 55%
All Star 60%
Amazing Man 60%
Amazing Mystery Funnies 60%
The Arrow 70%
Batman (1-110) 55%
Batman (#1 Mint) 80%
Blackhawk (9-110) 55%
Bob Steele 65%
Captain America 60%
Comic Cavalcade 55%
Daring Mystery 60%
Daring Mystery (#1 Mint) 80%
Detective (1-230) 60%
Detective (#27 Mint) 80%
Flash (1-104) 60%
Green Lantern 60%
Human Torch 55%
Jackie Gleason 65%
Jumbo 55%
Jungle 55%
Keen Detective Funnies 60%
Ken Maynard 65%
Marvel Mystery 55%
Military 55%
Modern 55%
More Fun (1-51) 75%
More Fun (52-107) 55%
Mystery In Space (1-65) 55%
Planet 55%
Stars And Stripes 60%
Strange Adventures (1-100) 55%
Sub-Mariner 55%
Sunset Carson 70%
Superman (1-120) 55%
Superman (#1 Mint) 100%
Also paying 50-75% of guide for many other titles. Comics must be properly graded and complete. Please send your listing of comics for sale or your list of comics you wish to purchase. Also dealing heavily in Sci-Fi material plus thousands of Marvels, D.C.s, Westerns, Funny material and much more! Please send one dollar for our current retail listing of comics in stock. Will travel for large collections or if your passing through the area, call for an appointment.
COMPANY POLICIES: Accurate Grading • Prompt refund on returned material • Orders processed same day as received • Lay-Aways for large orders • All items reasonably priced.
CBG Customer Service Award — 1984
CBG Customer Service Award — 1985
James F. Payette
Rare Books and Comics
P.O. Box 750 • Bethlehem, N.H. 03574
(603) 869-2097

In selling to dealers, you will get the best price by letting everything go at once—the good with the bad—all for one price. Simply select names either from ads in this book or from some of the adzines mentioned below. Send them your list and ask for bids. The bids received will vary depending on the demand, rarity and condition of the books you have. The more in demand, and better the condition, the higher the bids will be.

On the other hand, you could become a "dealer" and sell the books yourself. Order a copy of one or more of the adzines. Take note how most dealers lay out their ads. Type up your ad copy, carefully pricing each book (using the Guide as a reference). Send finished ad copy with payment to adzine editor to be run. You will find that certain books will sell at once while others will not sell at all. The ad will probably have to be retyped, remaining books repriced, and run again. Price books according to how fast you want them to move. If you try to get top dollar, expect a much longer period of time. Otherwise, the better deal you give the collector, the faster they will move. Remember, in being your own dealer, you will have overhead expenses in postage, mailing supplies and advertising cost. Some books might even be returned for refund due to misgrading, etc.

In selling all at once to a dealer, you get instant cash, immediate profit, and eliminate the long process of running several ads to dispose of the books; but if you have patience, and a small amount of business sense, you could realize more profit selling them directly to collectors yourself.

## WHERE TO BUY AND SELL

Throughout this book you will find the advertisements of many reputable dealers who sell back-issue comics magazines. If you are an inexperienced collector, be sure to compare prices before you buy. When a dealer is selected (ask for references), send him a small order (under $100) first to check out his grading accuracy, promptness in delivery, guarantees of condition advertised, and whether he will accept returns when dissatisfied. Never send large sums of cash through the mail. Send money orders or checks for your personal protection. Beware of bargains, as the items advertised sometimes do not exist, but are only a fraud to get your money.

The Price Guide is indebted to everyone who placed ads in this volume, whose support has helped in curbing printing costs. Your mentioning this book when dealing with the advertisers would be greatly appreciated.

**THE COMICS BUYERS GUIDE**, Krause Publications, 700 E. State St., Iola, WI 54990 PH:(715) 445-2214.
**CARTER'S COMICBOOK MARKETPLACE**, P.O. Box 180534, Coronado, CA 92178-0534.
**COLLECTORS' CLASSIFIED**, P.O. Box 347, Holbrook, MA 02343.

The Price Guide highly recommends the above adzines, which are full of ads buying and selling comics, pulps, radio tapes, premiums, toys and other related items. You can also place ads to buy or sell your comics in the above publications.

## COMIC BOOK MAIL ORDER SERVICES

Order your comics through the mail. Write for rates and details:

AT YOUR SERVICE SUB., 4524 Jenning Dr., Plano, TX. 75093, (214) 964-0766
COLLECTOR'S CHOICE, 3405 Keith St., Cleveland, TN 37312. (615) 476-2501
THE COMIC SOURCE, Bruce B. Brittain, P.O. Box 863605, Plano, TX 75086-3605
COMICS TO ASTONISH, 4001-C Country Club Rd., Winston-Salem, NC 27104 (919) 765-0400
COMIX 4-U, INC., 1121 State St., 2nd Floor, Schenectady, NY 12304 (518) 372-6612
DAVE'S COMICS, 1240 Harvard Ave., Salt Lake City, UT 84105
DOUG SULIPA'S COMIC WORLD, 374 Donald St., Winnipeg, Man., Canada R3B 2J2
FANTACO ENTERPRISES, INC., 21 Central Ave., Albany, NY 12210-1391. PH: (518) 463-1400
FRIENDLY FRANK'S Distribution, Inc., 3990 Broadway, Gary IN 46408-2705 (219)884-5052 or 884-5053
1025 North Vigo, Gary, IN 46403
GEPPI'S SUBSCRIPTION SERVICE, 1720 Belmont Ave., Bay-C, Baltimore, MD 21207
HEROES AREN'T HARD TO FIND, 1214 Thomas Ave., Charlotte, NC 28205
M&M, P.O. Box 6, Orland Park, IL 60462. PH: 312-349-2486
MEMBERS ONLY COMIC SERVICE, 6257 Yale St., Halifax, Nova Scotia, CA, B3L 1C9, PH:902-423-MOCS
MR. MONSTERS COMIC CRYPT, 1805 Wash. Blvd, Easton, PA 18042
PRESIDENTIAL COMIC BOOK SERVICE, P. O. Box 41, Scarsdale, NY 10583
STYX COMIC SERVICE, 605 Roseberry St., Winnipeg, Manitoba Canada R3H 0T3
LEE TENNANT, THE COMIC SHOP, P.O. Box 296, Worth, IL 60482-(312) 448-2937
THE WESTFIELD COMPANY, 8608 University Green, P.O. Box 470, Middleton, WI 53562 (608)836-1945

## COMIC BOOK CONVENTIONS

As is the case with most other aspects of comic collecting, comic book conventions, or cons as they are referred to, were originally conceived as the comic-book counterpart to science-fiction fandom conventions. There were many attempts to form successful national cons prior to the time of the first one that materialized, but they were all stillborn. It is interesting that after only three relatively organized years of existence, the first comic con was held. Of course, its magnitude was nowhere near as large as most established cons held today.

What is a comic con? As might be expected, there are comic books to be found at these gatherings. Dealers, collectors, fans, whatever they call themselves can be found trading, selling, and buying the adventures of their favorite characters for hours on end. Additionally if at all possible, cons have guests of honor, usually professionals in the field of comic art, either writers, artists, or editors. The committees put together panels for the con attendees where the assembled pros talk about certain areas of comics, most of the time fielding questions from the assembled audience. At cons one can usually find displays of various and sundry things, usually original art. There might be radio listening rooms; there is most certainly a daily showing of different movies, usually science-fiction or horror type. Of course there is always the chance to get together with friends at cons and just talk about comics; one also has a good opportunity to make new friends who have similar interests and with whom one can correspond after the con.

It is difficult to describe accurately what goes on at a con. The best way to find out is to go to one or more if you can.

The addresses below are those currently available for conventions to be held in the upcoming year. Unfortunately, addresses for certain major conventions are unavailable as this list is being compiled. Once again, the best way to keep abreast of conventions is through the various adzines. Please remember when writing for convention information to include a self-addressed, stamped envelope for reply. Most conventions are non-profit, so they appreciate the help. Here is the list:

### COMIC BOOK CONVENTIONS FOR 1991

(**Note:** All convention listings must be submitted to us by December 15th of each year)

AMERICON - March 9, 1991, Florrie Chappell Gym, Georgia Southwestern College, Americus, GA. Contact Elwyn Hightower, GSW Box 813, Georgia Southwestern College, Americus, GA 31709.

ATLANTA FANTASY FAIR XVII, Jul. 26-28, 1991, Atlanta Hilton & Towers, Atlanta, GA. Info: Atlanta Fantasy Fair, 4175 Eliza Ct., Lithonia, GA 30058. PH: (404) 985-1230.

BIG-D Super Comic & Collectibles Show (Formally CHILDHOOD TREASURES) July, 1991-Dallas Sheraton Park Central Hotel, Hwy 635 & Coit Rd. Write Don Maris, Box 111266 Arlington, TX 76007. (817)-261-8745

CAROLINA COMIC BOOK FAIR—For info contact New Dimension Comics, 2609 Central Ave., Charlotte, NC 28205. PH: (704) 372-4376.

CAROLINA CON X—Sept, 1991, Sponsored by The Carolina Pictorial Fiction Assn. Send SASE to Steve Harris, 100 E. Augusta Place, Greenville, SC 29605.

CENTRAL NEW JERSEY COMIC BOOK SHOW—Held monthly on Sundays at the Washington Twp. Volunteer Fire Dept., Rt. 130, Robbinsville. Contact Michael Chaudhuri of EMCEE Conventions, P.O. Box 151, Hightstown, NJ 08520. PH: (609) 448-7585.

CHICAGO - Baseball Card & Comic Book Show. Held monthly at University of Illinois at Chicago. For more info call Rich at (312) 733-2266.

CHICAGO COMICON—Larry Charet, 1219-A West Devon Ave., Chicago, IL 60660. Phone (312) 274-1832.

CREATION CON—249-04 Hillside Ave., Bellerose, N.Y. 11426. Phone (718) 343-0202. Holds major conventions in the following cities: Atlanta, Boston, Cincinnati, Cleveland, Detroit, London, Los Angeles, Philadelphia, Rochester, San Francisco, and Washington, D.C. Write or call for details.

CROWN POINT'S PREMIERE MONTHLY CARD AND COMIC SHOW—Crown Point, IN, Knight's of Columbus, 700 Merrillville Rd. Contact Marilyn Hall, P.O. Box 507, Crown Point, IN. 46307. PH: 219-663-8561.

DALLAS FANTASY FAIR, A Bulldog Prod. Convention. For info: Lary Lankford, P.O. Box 820488, Dallas, TX 75382, PH: (214) 349-3367.

DETROIT AREA COMIC BOOK/BASEBALL CARD SHOWS. Held every 2-3 weeks in Royal Oak and Livonia Mich., write: Michael Goldman, Suite 231, 19785 W. 12 Mile Rd., Southfield, MI 48076. PH: (313) 350-2633.

EL PASO FANTASY FESTIVAL—c/o Rita's Fantasy Shop, No. 34 Sunrise Center, El Paso, TX 79904. PH: (915) 757-1143. Late July-Early August.

GREAT EASTERN CONVENTIONS, 225 Everitts Road, Ringoes, NJ 08551, PH: (201) 788-6845. Holds cons in the following cities: Atlanta, Boston, Chicago, Los Angeles, New York and San Francisco.

HEROES CONVENTION '91—June 14-16, 1991. H. Shelton Drum, P. O. Box 9181, Charlotte, NC 28299, PH: (704) 376-5766 or 1-800-321-4370.

ILLINOIS/INDIANA—Pinsky Baseball Card & Comic Book Supershow, c/o Louis Pinsky, P.O. Box 1072, Lombard, IL 60148-8072, PH: (708) 620-0865. Holds conventions in these cities: Illinois: Alsip, Carol Stream, Countryside/LaGrange, Crystal Lake, Downers Grove, Elgin, Glen Ellyn/Lombard, Itasca, Oakbrook Terrace, Willowbrook/Hinsdale. Indiana: Merrillville.

ISLAND NOSTALGIA COMIC BOOK/BASEBALL CARD SHOWS, Hauppauge, N.Y.-Holiday Inn off L.I.E. exit 55, 10a.m.-4p.m. 1740 Express Drive South, Hauppauge, N.Y., For more info call Dennis (516) 724-7422 or Day of Shows only (516) 234-3030, ext 450.

KANSAS CITY COMIC CONVENTION (Formally MO-KAN COMICS FESTIVAL)—c/o Kansas City Comic Book Club, 734 North 78th St., Kansas City, KS 66112.

LONG ISLAND COMIC BOOK & COLLECTOR'S CONVENTION—(Held monthly). Rockville Centre, Holiday Inn, 173 Sunrise Hwy, Long Island, NY.For info: Cosmic Comics & Books of Rockville Centre, 139 N. Park Ave., Rockville Centre, NY 11570. (516) 763-1133.

LOS ANGELES COMIC BOOK & SCIENCE FICTION CONVENTION, held monthly. For information contact: Bruce Schwartz, 1802 West Olive Ave., Burbank, CA 91506. PH: (818) 954-8432.

MICHIANA COMICON: April 20, Oct. 19, 1991, South Bend, IN. Contact Jim Rossow, 53100 Poppy Rd., South Bend, IN 46628. PH: (219) 232-8129.

MOBI-CON 91, June 7-9, 1991, The Days Inn (Airport & I-65), Mobile, AL 36608. For more info: Mobi-Con, P.O. Box 161257, Mobile, AL 36608.

MOTOR CITY COMIC CON, Dearborn, MI. Held March & Oct. 1991 at the Dearborn Civic Center, 15801 Michigan Ave. Contact Michael Goldman, Suite 231, 19785 W. 12 Mile Rd., Southfield, MI 48076. PH: (313) 350-2633.

NOSTALIGA CON—Held in Elizabeth, NJ, Lyndhurst, NJ, Hempstead, NY. Contact George Downes, G.A. Corp., Box 572, Nutley, NJ 07110. PH: (201) 661-3358.

THE ORIGINAL LONG ISLAND MONTHLY COMIC BOOK & BASEBALL CARD SHOW, Held 1st Sunday each month at the Coliseum Motor Inn, 1650 Hempstead Turnpike, East Meadow, Long Island, NY. Contact: Perry Albert, P.O. Box 66, Fredonia, NY 14063. PH: (716) 672-2913.

ORLANDO CON, Sept. 21, 22, 1991, International Inn, Orlando, FL. Info: Jim Ivey, 4300 S. Semoran, Suite 109, Orlando, FL 32822-2453, PH: (407) 273-0141.

SAN DIEGO COMIC-CON—Box 17066, San Diego, CA 92117. July 4th week, 1991, San Diego Convention Center.

THE SCENIC CITY COMICS & COLLECTIBLES FAIR, April, 1991, Chattanooga at Eastgate Mall, Mark Derrick, 3244 Castle Ave., Chattanooga, TN 37412. PH: (615) 624-3704.

Schenectady, New York, THE CAPITAL DISTRICT ANNUAL SHOW, S.A.S.E. with inquiry or call Jared Nathanson at 518-372-6612 or write: Comix 4-U, Inc., 1121 State St., 2nd Floor, Schenectady, NY 12304.

SEATTLE CENTER CON, Apr, July, Oct, 1991, Box 2043, Kirkland, Wash, 98033. Phone (206) 822-5709 or 827-5129.

SEATTLE QUEST NORTHWEST, Seattle, Wash. Write: Ron Church or Steve Sibra, P.O. Box 82676, Kenmore, WA 98028.

WESTERN NEW YORK COMIC BOOK BASEBALL CARD & COLLECTIBLES SHOW—(held monthly), Masonic Lodge, 321 E. Main St., Fredonia, NY. Contact: Perry Albert, P.O. Box 66, Fredonia, NY 14063. PH: (716) 672-2913.

## COMIC BOOK CLUBS

ALABAMA—The Mobile Panelology Assoc. Meets 1st Monday of each month at 2301 Airport Blvd. (Back Bldg. Mobile Recreation Dept.), Mobile, Ala.; 7:00 p.m. to 9:00 p.m. Club business address: 161 West Grant St., Chickasaw, AL 36611. (205) 456-4514. Founded 1973.

CALIFORNIA—The California Comic Book Collectors Club, c/o Matt Ornbaun, 23601 Hwy. 128, Yorkville, CA 95494. Send 50 cents and SASE for information and enrollment.

Alpha Omega, c/o Donald Ensign, 6011 Agnes Ave., Temple City, CA 91780. Puts out bi-monthly pub.

USC Comics Club, University of Southern California Intramural Recreation Dept., Heritage Hall 103, University Park, Los Angeles, CA 90089-0601. PH 213-743-5127.

West Coast Comic Club, c/o Frank Como, 2536 Terrace, Anaheim, CA 92806-1656. Meets the second Saturday of the month at the community meeting hall in the City Mall at 7:00 p.m.

CONNETICUT—Collectors' Club, c/o Susan Dorne, President, 551 Park Ave., Windsor, CT 06095. Publishes a bi-monthly newsletter.

GEORGIA—The Defenders of Dreams, Inc., World Headquarters, c/o Will Rose, Chairman of the Board, 3121 Shady Grove Rd., Carrollton, GA 30117. (Publishes own fanzine *Just Imagine*. . . bi-monthly and a pulpzine *Pulp Adventures* quarterly.) Please send business size SASE for details.

IDAHO—Mr. O's Comic Book Collectors Club, S. 1200 Agate Rd., Coeur D'Alene, Idaho 83814.

MASSACHUSETTS—The Gloo Club, c/o Ron Holmes, 140 Summit St., New Bedford, Mass. 02740. Write for details and send SASE. (This club is both national and international.)

MINNESOTA—The Pogo Fan Club. A mail club dedicated to Walt Kelly's career. Puts out a bi-monthly 'The Fort Mudge Most.'' Write: Steve Thompson, 6908 Wentworth Ave. So., Richfield, MN 55423.

OHIO—International Comics Club, meets monthly at Cleveland Hts., University Hts. Library, 2345 Lee Rd., Cleveland Hts., Ohio on 1st Monday of each month, 7p.m. Contact: Richard Bennett, 6204 Fullerton Ave., Apt. 3, Cleveland, OH 44105.

OKLAHOMA—Fandom International. For information, write to: Dan DePalma, 5823 E. 22 St., Tulsa, OK 74114. Phone 834-8035.

TEXAS—The Gulf Coast Comic Collectors' Society (GCCCS). Write to GCCCS Headquarters, c/o Mike Mills, 4318 Iroquois St., Houston, TX 77504.

CANADA—The Collectors' Club. Write: T.M. Maple, Box 1272, Station B., Weston, Ontario M9L 2R9 Canada. Bimonthly newsletter.

## THE HISTORY OF COMICS FANDOM

At this time it is possible to discern two distinct and largely unrelated movements in the history of Comics Fandom. The first of these movements began about 1953 as a response to the then-popular, trend-setting EC lines of comics. The first true comics fanzines of this movement were short-lived. Bhob Stewart's EC FAN BULLETIN was a hectographed newsletter that ran two issues about six months apart; and Jimmy Taurasi's FANTASY COMICS, a newsletter devoted to all science-fiction comics of the period, was a monthly that ran for about six months. These were followed by other newsletters, such as Mike May's EC FAN JOURNAL, and George Jennings' EC WORLD PRESS. EC fanzines of a wider and more critical scope appeared somewhat later. Two of the finest were POTRZEBIE, the product of a number of fans, and Ron Parker's HOOHAH. Gauging from the response that POTRZEBIE received from a plug in an EC letter column, Ted White estimated the average age of EC fans to lie in the range of 9 to 13, while many EC fans were in their mid-teens. This fact was taken as discouraging to many of the faneds, who had hoped to reach an older audience. Consequently, many of them gave up their efforts in behalf of Comics Fandom, especially with the demise of the EC groups, and turned their attention to science-fiction fandom with its longer tradition and older membership. While the flourish of fan activity in response to the EC comics was certainly noteworthy, it is fair to say that it never developed into a full-fledged, independent, and self-sustaining movement.

The second comics fan movement began in 1960. It was largely a response to (though it later became a stimulus for) the Second Heroic Age of Comics. Most fan historians date the Second Heroic Age from the appearance of the new FLASH comics magazine (numbered 105 and dated February 1959). The letter departments of Julius Schwartz (editor at National Periodicals), and later those of Stan Lee (Marvel Group) and Bill Harris (Gold Key) were most influential in bringing comics readers into Fandom. Beyond question, it was the reappearance of the costumed hero that sparked the comics fan movement of the sixties. Sparks were lit among some science-fiction fans first, when experienced fan writers, who were part of an established tradition, produced the first in a series of articles on the comics of the forties—ALL IN COLOR FOR A DIME. The series was introduced in XERO No. 1 (September 1960), a general fanzine for science-fiction fandom edited and published by Dick Lupoff.

Meanwhile, outside science-fiction fandom, Jerry Bails and Roy Thomas, two strictly comics fans of long-standing, conceived the first true comics fanzine in response to the Second Heroic Age. The fanzine, ALTER EGO, appeared in March 1961. The first several issues were widely circulated among comics fans, and were to influence profoundly the comics fan movement to follow. Unlike the earlier EC fan movement, this new movement attracted many fans in their twenties and thirties. A number of these older fans had been active collectors for years but had been largely unknown to each other. Joined by scores of new, younger fans, this group formed the nucleus of a new movement that is still growing and shows every indication of being self-sustaining. Although it has borrowed a few of the more appropriate terms coined by science-fiction fans, Comics Fandom of the Sixties was an independent if fledging movement, without, in most cases, the advantages and disadvantages of a longer tradition. What Comics Fandom did derive from science-fiction fandom it did so thanks largely to the fanzines produced by so-called double fans. The most notable of this type is COMIC ART, edited and published by Don and Maggie Thompson.

## HOW TO SELECT FANZINES

In the early 1960s, only a few comic fanzines were being published. A fan could easily afford to subscribe to them all. Today, the situation has radically changed, and it has become something of a problem to decide which fanzines to order.

Fanzines are not all of equal quality or general interest. Even different issues of the same fanzine may vary significantly. To locate issues that will be of interest to you, learn to look for the names of outstanding amatuer artists, writers, and editors and consult fanzine review columns. Although you may not always agree with the judgements of the reviewers, you will find these reviews to be a valuable source of information about the content and quality of the current fanzines.

When ordering a fanzine, remember that print runs are small and the issue you may want may be out of print (OP). Ordinarily in this case, you will receive the next issue. Because of irregular publishing schedules that nearly all fanzines must, of necessity, observe, allow up to 90 days or more for your copy to reach you. It is common courtesy when addressing an inquiry to an ama-publisher to enclose a self-addressed, stamped envelope.

### FAN PUBLICATIONS OF INTEREST

**NOTE:** We must be notified each year by December 1 for listing to be included, due to changes of address, etc. Please send sample copy.

ANNIE PEOPLE—Jon Merrill, P.O. Box 431, Cedar Knolls, NJ 07927. Bi-monthly Little Orphan Annie newsletter.

THE ARCHIE FANZINE—Mary Smith, 185 Ashland St., Holliston, MA 01746. Monthly fanzine about Archie and the people behind the books plus news and opinions. Sample copy: $3.00. 6 issue subscription: $15.00.

CANIFFITES—Carl Horak, 1319 108th Ave. S.W., Calgary, Alberta, Canada T2W 0C6. Fanzine devoted to the art of Milton Caniff. Sample copy of newsletter: $1.50. 6 issue subscription: $6.00.

COMIC ART AND FANTASY—Stephen Barrington, 161 West Grant Street, Chickasaw, AL 36611. Published quarterly for comics, gaming & sf fans. $1.00 for two issues.

THE COMICOL MONTHLY—Todd Estes, Rt. 1, Box 22, Brilliant, AL 35548. Features news and reviews on everything; the big two, the independents and the small press. Either a stamp or SASE gets you complete info.

COMICS CAREER NEWSLETTER, 601 Clinkscales, Columbia, MO 65203. Information and advice for amateur comics writers and artists who wish to become professionals. Sample copy: $3.00. 12-issue subs.: $24.

COMICS INTERVIEW—c/o Fictioneer Books Ltd., #1 Screamer Mtn., Clayton, GA 30525.

THE COMPLETE EC LIBRARY—Russ Cochran, P. O. Box 437, West Plains, MO 65775. (A must for all EC collectors. Reprinting of the complete EC line is planned. Write for details.)

DITKOMANIA—A quarterly, digest devoted to Steve Ditko's work. Now in its 7th year of continuous publication. $1 per issue. Write: Bill Hall, 556 Main St., Cromwell, CT 05416.

THE DUCKBURG TIMES—Barks/Disney fanzine. Sample copy $1.50, Subscription $6 (Foreign rates double). Dana Gabbard, 3010 Wilshire Blvd., #362, Los Angeles, CA 90010.

FANTACO NOOZ—FantaCo. Enterprises Inc., 21 Central Ave., Albany, NY 12210. Free with SASE.

FCA & ME TOO!—Bill & Teresa Harper, 301 E. Buena Vista Ave., North Augusta, SC 29841. Covers Golden Age Fawcett and Magazine Enterprises. Sample $1.00. 4 issue subscription, $5. Now in it's 15th year.

FORT MUDGE MOST—Bi-monthly magazine of the Pogo Fan Club. Subscription: $15/yr. Sample $3. Spring Hollow Books, 6908 Wentworth Ave. So., Richfield, MN 55423.

THE HARVEYVILLE FUN TIMES!—Mark Arnold, 1464 La Playa #105, San Francisco, CA 94122. Fanzine dedicated to the Harvey World. Published quarterly. Subscriptions are $6.00 for 4 issues and $11.00 for 8. Sample: $2.00

INSIDE REVIEW on comics—J.E. Essick, Rt. 10, Box 369D, Winston-Salem, NC 27127. Monthly current comics newsletter. Sample 90 cents, 1 year subs-$9. Checks only.

IT'S A FANZINE—Gene Kehoe, 2424 Adams Ave., Des Moines, IA 50310. Lively '60s style comic fanzine now in it's 11th year. Sample copy: $1.50 ppd. Subscription: 4 issues for $5.00.

THE MAD PANIC—Ed Norris, 91 Kelly Dr., Lancaster, MA 01523. Fanzine for Mad/Panic/Alfred E. Neuman fans. Sample issue: $1.00. 6 issue subscription is $5.00

OM MANI PADME HUM—Rogers O. Cadenhead, 1510-B McCormick, Denton, TX 76205. The fanzine of forgotten and obscure comics. Sample copy: $1.75. 4 issue subscription: $5.50.

POW-POW—Bill & Teresa Harper, 301 E. Buena Vista Ave., North Augusta, SC 29841. Fanzine covering the Straight Arrow radio show, comics & strip reprints. Sample copy: $1.00. 4 issue subscription: $5.00.

VERTICAL HOLD, 85 Burnie St., Lyons, ACT Australia 2606. Fanzine mainly about cult television series, also covering comic books.

THE YELLOW KID NOTES—The Yellow Kid Society, 103 Doubloon Dr., Slidell, LA 70461. PH: 504-641-5173.

## COLLECTING STRIPS

Collecting newspaper comic strips is somewhat different than collecting magazines, although it can be equally satisfying.

Obviously, most strip collectors begin by clipping strips from their local paper, but many soon branch out to strips carried in out-of-town papers. Naturally this can become more expensive and it is often frustrating, because it is easy to miss editions of out-of-town papers. Consequently, most strip collectors work out trade agreements with collectors in other cities in order to get an uninterrupted supply of the strips they want. This usually necessitates saving local strips to be used for trade purposes only.

Back issues of strips dating back several decades are also available from time to time from dealers. The prices per panel vary greatly depending on the age, condition, and demand for the strip. When the original strips are unavailable, it is sometimes possible to get photostatic copies from collectors, libraries, or newspaper morgues.

## COLLECTING ORIGINAL ART

In addition to magazines and strips, some enthusiasts also collect the original art for the comics. These black and white, inked drawings are usually done on illustration paper at about 30 percent up (i.e., 30 percent larger than the original printed panels). Because original art is a one-of-a-kind article, it is highly prized and often difficult to obtain.

Interest in original comic art has increased tremendously in the past several years. Many companies now return the originals to the artists who have in turn offered them for sale, usually at cons but sometimes through agents and dealers. As with any other area of collecting, rarity and demand governs value. Although the masters' works bring fine art prices, most art is available at moderate prices. Comic strips are the most popular facet with collectors, followed by comic book art. Once scarce, current and older comic book art has surfaced within the last few years. In 1974 several original painted covers of vintage comic books and coloring books turned up from Dell, Gold Key, Whitman, and Classic Comics.

The following are sources for original art:

Abraxas Graphix, 9847 Belair Rd., Perry Hall, MD 21128.
Artman, Bruce Bergstrom, 1620 Valley St., Fort Lee, NJ 07024.
Cartoon Carnival, 408 Bickmore Dr., Wallingford, PA 19086, PH: (215) 566-1292.
The Cartoon Museum, Jim Ivey, 4300 S. Semoran, Suite 109, Orlando, FL 32822-2453. PH: (407) 273-0141.
Russ Cochran, P.O. Box 437, West Plains, MO 65775.
Collectors Paradise Gallery, Harry Kleinman, P.O. Box 1540, Studio City, CA 91604.
The Comic Character Shop, Old Firehouse Antiques, 110 Alaskan Way S., Seattle, WA 98104. (206) 283-0532.
Tony Dispoto, Comic Art Showcase, P. O. Box 425, Lodi, NJ 07644.
Scott Dunbier, P.O. Box 1446, Gracie Station, New York, NY, 10028. PH: (212) 666-0982, FAX: (212) 662-8732.
Graphic Collectibles, Mitch Itkowitz, P.O. Box 683, Staten Island, NY 10302. PH: (718) 273-3685.
Richard Halegua, Comic Art & Graffix Gallery, 2033 Madison Rd., Cincinnati, OH 45208. PH: (513) 321-4208.
Steve Herrington, 30 W. 70th St., New York, NY 10023.
Carsten Lagua, Havensteinstr. 54, 1000 Berlin 46, West Germany, Tel. 030/7734665.
Museum Graphics, Jerome K. Muller, Box 743, Costa Mesa, CA 92627.
Original Artwork, Martin Hilland, AM Josefshaus 6, 4040 Neuss 21, West Germany.
San Mateo Comic Books/Original art, 306 Baldwin Ave. San Mateo, CA 94401. PH: (415) 344-1536.
TRH Gallery (Tom Horvitz), 255 N. Cielo #601, Palm Springs, CA 92263. PH: (619) 341-8592.

## A Chronology of the Development of THE AMERICAN COMIC BOOK

**By**
**M. Thomas Inge***

**Precursors:** The facsimile newspaper strip reprint collections constitute the earliest "comic books." The first of these was a collection of Richard Outcault's **Yellow Kid** from the Hearst **New York American** in March 1897. Commercial and promotional reprint collections, usually in cardboard covers, appeared through the 1920s and featured such newspaper strips as **Mutt and Jeff, Foxy Grandpa, Buster Brown,** and **Barney Google**. During 1922 a reprint magazine, **Comic Monthly**, appeared with each issue devoted to a separate strip, and from 1929 to 1930 George Delacorte published 36 issues of **The Funnies** in tabloid format with original comic pages in color, becoming the first four-color comic newsstand publication.

**1933:** The Ledger syndicate published a small broadside of their Sunday comics on 7" by 9" plates. Employees of Eastern Color Printing Company in New York, sales manager Harry I. Wildenberg and salesman Max C. Gaines, saw it and figured that two such plates would fit a tabloid page, which would produce a book about 7½" x 10" when folded. Thus 10,000 copies of **Funnies on Parade**, containing 32 pages of Sunday newspaper reprints, was published for Proctor and Gamble to be given away as premiums. Some of the strips included were: **Joe Palooka, Mutt and Jeff, Hairbreadth Harry,** and **Reg'lar Fellas**. M. C. Gaines was very impressed with this book and convinced Eastern Color that he could sell a lot of them to such big advertisers as Milk-O-Malt, Wheatena, Kinney Shoe Stores, and others to be used as premiums and radio give-aways. So, Eastern Color printed **Famous Funnies: A Carnival of Comics**, and then **Century of Comics**, both as before, containing Sunday newspaper reprints. Mr. Gaines sold these books in quantities of 100,000 to 250,000.

**1934:** The give-away comics were so successful that Mr. Gaines believed that youngsters would buy comic books for ten cents like the "Big Little Books" coming out at that time. So, early in 1934, Eastern Color ran off 35,000 copies of **Famous Funnies, Series 1**, 64 pages of reprints for Dell Publishing Company to be sold for ten cents in chain stores. Since it sold out promptly on the stands, Eastern Color, in May 1934, issued **Famous Funnies** No. 1 (dated July 1934) which became, with issue No. 2 in July, the first monthly comic magazine. The title continued for over 20 years through 218 issues, reaching a circulation peak of over 400,000 copies a month. At the same time, Mr. Gaines went to the sponsors of Percy Crosby's **Skippy**, who was on the radio, and convinced them to put out a Skippy book, advertise it on the air, and give away a free copy to anyone who bought a tube of Phillip's toothpaste. Thus 500,000 copies of **Skippy's Own Book of Comics** was run off and distributed through drug stores everywhere. This was the first four-color comic book of reprints devoted to a single character.

**1935:** Major Malcolm Wheeler-Nicholson's National Periodical Publications issued in February a tabloid-sized comic publication called **New Fun**, which became **More Fun** after the sixth issue and converted to the normal comic-book size after issue eight. **More Fun** was the first comic book of a standard size to publish original material and continued publication until 1949. **Mickey Mouse Magazine** began in the summer, to become **Walt Disney's Comics and Stories** in 1940, and combined original material with reprinted newspaper strips in most issues.

**1936:** In the wake of the success of **Famous Funnies**, other publishers, in conjunction with the major newspaper strip syndicates, inaugurated more reprint comic books: **Popular Comics** (News-Tribune, February), **Tip Top Comics** (United Features, April), **King Comics** (King Features, April), and **The Funnies** (new series, NEA, October). Four issues of **Wow Comics**, from David McKay and Henle Publications, appeared, edited by S. M. Iger and including early art by Will Eisner, Bob Kane, and Alex Raymond. The first non-reprint comic book devoted to a single theme was **Detective Picture Stories** issued in December by The Comics Magazine Company.

**1937:** The second single-theme title, **Western Picture Stories**, came in February from The Comics Magazine Company, and the third was **Detective Comics**, an offshoot of **More Fun**, which began in March to be published to the present. The book's initials, "D.C.," have long served to refer to National Periodical Publications, which was purchased from Major Nicholson by Harry Donenfeld late this year.

**1938:** "DC" copped a lion's share of the comic book market with the publication of **Action Comics** No. 1 in June which contained the first appearance of Superman by writer Jerry Siegel and artist Joe Shuster, a discovery of Max C. Gaines. The "man of steel" inaugurated the "Golden Era" in comic book history. Fiction House, a pulp publisher, entered the comic book field in September with **Jumbo Comics**, featuring Sheena, Queen of the Jungle, and appearing in over-sized format for the first eight issues.

**1939:** The continued success of "DC" was assured in May with the publication of **Detective Comics** No. 27 containing the first episode of Batman by artist Bob Kane and writer Bill Finger. **Superman Comics** appeared in the summer. Also, during the summer, a black and white premium comic titled **Motion Picture Funnies Weekly** was published to be given away at motion picture theatres. The plan was to issue it weekly and to have continued stories so that the kids would come back week after week not to miss an episode. Four issues were planned but only one came out. This book contains the first appearance and origin of the Sub-Mariner by Bill Everett (8 pages) which was later reprinted in **Marvel Comics**. In November, the first issue of **Marvel Comics** came out, featuring the Human Torch by Carl Burgos and the Sub-Mariner reprint with color added.

**1940:** The April issue of **Detective Comics** No. 38 introduced Robin the Boy Wonder as a sidekick to Batman, thus establishing the "Dynamic Duo" and a major precedent for later costume heroes who would also have boy companions. **Batman Comics** began in the spring. Over 60 different comic book titles were being issued, including **Whiz Comics** begun in February by Fawcett Publications. A creation of writer Bill Parker and artist C. C. Beck, **Whiz's** Captain Marvel was the only superhero ever to surpass Superman in comic book sales. Drawing on their own popular pulp magazine heroes, Street and Smith Publications introduced **Shadow Comics** in March and **Doc Savage Comics** in May. A second trend was established with the summer appearance of the first issue of **All-Star Comics**, which brought several superheroes together in one story and in its third issue that winter would announce the establishment of the Justice Society of America.

**1941:** Wonder Woman was introduced in the spring issue of **All-Star Comics** No. 8, the creation of psychologist William Moulton Marston and artist Harry Peter. **Captain Marvel Adventures** began this year. By the end of 1941, over 160 titles were being published, including **Captain America** by Jack Kirby and Joe Simon, **Police Comics** with Jack Cole's Plastic Man and later Will Eisner's Spirit, **Military Comics** with Blackhawk by Eisner and Charles Cuidera, **Daredevil Comics** with the original character by Charles Biro, **Air Fighters** with Airboy also by Biro, and **Looney Tunes & Merrie Melodies** with Porky Pig, Bugs Bunny, and Elmer Fudd, reportedly created by Bob Clampett for the Leon Schlesinger Productions animated films and drawn for the comics by Chase Craig. Also, Albert Kanter's Gilberton Company initiated the **Classics Illustrated** series with **The Three Musketeers**.

**1942: Crime Does Not Pay** by editor Charles Biro and publisher Lev Gleason, devoted to factual accounts of criminals' lives, began a different trend in realistic crime stories. **Wonder Woman** appeared in the summer. John Goldwater's character Archie, drawn by Bob Montana, first published in **Pep Comics**, was given his own magazine **Archie Comics**, which has remained popular over 40 years. The first issue of **Animal Comics** contained Walt Kelly's "Albert Takes the Cake," featuring the new character of Pogo. In mid-1942, the undated Dell Four Color title, No. 9, **Donald Duck Finds Pirate Gold**, appeared with art by Carl Barks and Jack Hannah. Barks, also featured in **Walt Disney's Comics and Stories**, remained the most popular delineator of Donald Duck and later introduced his greatest creation, Uncle Scrooge, in **Christmas on Bear Mountain** (Dell Four Color No. 178). The fantasy work of George Carlson appeared in the first issue of **Jingle Jangle Comics**, one of the most imaginative titles for children ever to be published.

**1945:** The first issue of **Real Screen Comics** introduced the Fox and the Crow by James F. Davis, and John Stanley began drawing the **Little Lulu** comic book based on a popular feature in the **Saturday Evening Post** by Marjorie Henderson Buell from 1935 to 1944. Bill Woggon's Katy Keene appears in issue No. 5 of **Wilbur Comics** to be followed by appearances in **Laugh, Pep, Suzie** and her own comic book in 1950. The popularity of Dick Briefer's satiric version of the Frankenstein monster, originally drawn for **Prize Comics** in 1941, led to the publication of **Frankenstein** by Prize publications.

**1950:** The son of Max C. Gaines, William M. Gaines, who earlier had inherited his father's firm Educational Comics (later Entertaining Comics), began publication of a series of well-written and masterfully drawn titles which would establish a "New Trend" in comics magazines: **Crypt of Terror** (later **Tales from the Crypt**, April), **The Vault of Horror** (April), **The Haunt of Fear** (May), **Weird Science** (May), **Weird Fantasy** (May), **Crime SuspenStories** (October), and **Two-Fisted Tales** (November), the latter stunningly edited by Harvey Kurtzman.

**1952:** In October "E.C." published the first number of **Mad** under Kurtzman's creative editorship, thus establishing a style of humor which would inspire other publications and powerfully influence the underground comic book movement of the 1960s.

**1953:** All Fawcett titles featuring Captain Marvel were ceased after many years of litigation in the courts during which National Periodical Publications claimed that the super-hero was an infringement on the copyrighted Superman.

**1954:** The appearance of Fredric Wertham's book **Seduction of the Innocent** in the spring was the culmination of a continuing war against comic books fought by those who believed they corrupted youth and debased culture. The U. S. Senate Subcommittee on Juvenile Delinquency investigated comic books and in response the major publishers banded together in October to create the Comics Code Authority and adopted, in their own words, "the most stringent code in existence for any communications media." Before the Code took effect, more than 1,000,000,000 issues of comic books were being sold annually.

**1955:** In an effort to avoid the Code, "E.C." launched a "New Direction" series of titles, such as **Impact, Valor, Aces High, Extra, M.D.**, and **Psychoanalysis**, none of which lasted beyond the year. **Mad** was changed into a larger magazine format with issue No. 24 in July to escape the Comics Code entirely, and "E.C." closed down its line of comic books altogether.

**1956:** Beginning with the Flash in **Showcase** No. 4, Julius Schwartz began a popular revival of "DC" superheroes which would lead to the "Silver Age" in comic book history.

**1957:** Atlas reduced the number of titles published by two-thirds, with **Journey into Mystery** and **Strange Tales** surviving, while other publishers did the same or went out of business. Atlas would survive as a part of the Marvel Comics Group.

**1960:** After several efforts at new satire magazines (**Trump** and **Humbug**), Harvey Kurtzman, no longer with Gaines, issued in August the first number of another abortive effort, **Help!**, where the early work of underground cartoonists Jay Lynch, Skip Williamson, Gilbert Shelton, and Robert Crumb appeared.

**1961:** Stan Lee edited in November the first **Fantastic Four**, featuring Mr. Fantastic, the Human Torch, the Thing, and the Invisible Girl, and inaugurated an enormously popular line of titles from Marvel Comics featuring a more contemporary style of superhero.

**1962:** Lee introduced **The Amazing Spider-Man** in August, with art by Steve Ditko, **The Hulk** in May and **Thor** in August, the last two produced by Dick Ayers and Jack Kirby.

**1963:** Marvel's **The X-Men**, with art by Jack Kirby, began a successful run in November, but the title would experience a revival and have an even more popular reception in the 1980s.

**1965:** James Warren issued **Creepy**, a larger black and white comic book, outside Comics Code's control, which emulated the "E.C." horror comic line. Warren's **Eerie** began in September and **Vampirella** in September 1969.

**1967:** Robert Crumb's **Zap** No. 1 appeared, the first popular underground comic book to achieve wide popularity, although the undergrounds had began in 1962 with **Adventures of Jesus** by Foolbert Sturgeon (Frank Stack) and 1964 with **God**

**Nose** by Jack Jackson.

**1970:** Editor Roy Thomas at Marvel begins **Conan the Barbarian** based on fiction by Robert E. Howard with art by Barry Smith, and Neal Adams began to draw for "DC" a series of **Green Lantern/Green Arrow** stories which would deal with relevant social issues such as racism, urban poverty, and drugs.

**1972: The Swamp Thing** by Berni Wrightson begins in November from "DC."

**1973:** In February, "DC" revived the original Captain Marvel with new art by C. C. Beck and reprints in the first issue of **Shazam** and in October **The Shadow** with scripts by Denny O'Neil and art by Mike Kaluta.

**1974:** "DC" began publication in the spring of a series of over-sized facsimile reprints of the most valued comic books of the past under the general title of "Famous First Editions," beginning with a reprint of **Action** No. 1 and including afterwards **Detective Comics** No. 27, **Sensation Comics** No. 1, **Whiz Comics** No. 2, **Batman** No. 1, **Wonder Woman** No. 1, **All-Star Comics** No. 3, **Flash Comics** No. 1, and **Superman** No. 1. Mike Friedrich, an independent publisher, released **Star★Reach** with work by Jim Starlin, Neal Adams, and Dick Giordano, with ownership of the characters and stories invested in the creators themselves.

**1975:** In the first collaborative effort between the two major comic book publishers of the previous decade, Marvel and "DC" produced together an over-sized comic-book version of **MGM's Marvelous Wizard of Oz** in the fall, and then the following year in an unprecedented cross-over produced **Superman vs. the Amazing Spider-Man**, written by Gerry Conway, drawn by Ross Andru, and inked by Dick Giordano.

**1976:** Frank Brunner's Howard the Duck, who had appeared earlier in Marvel's **Fear** and **Man-Thing**, was given his own book in January, which because of distribution problems became an over-night collector's item. After decades of litigation, Jerry Siegel and Joe Shuster were given financial recompense and recognition by National Periodical Publications for their creation of Superman, after several friends of the team made a public issue of the case.

**1977:** Stan Lee's **Spider-Man** was given a second birth, fifteen years after his first, through a highly successful newspaper comic strip, which began syndication on January 3 with art by John Romita. This invasion of the comic strip by comic book characters continued with the appearance on June 6 of Marvel's **Howard the Duck**, with story by Steve Gerber and visuals by Gene Colan. In an unusually successful collaborative effort, Marvel began publication of the comic book adaption of the George Lucas film **Star Wars**, with script by Roy Thomas and art by Howard Chaykin, at least three months before the film was released nationally on May 25. The demand was so great that all six issues of **Star Wars** were reprinted at least seven times, and the installments were reprinted in two volumes of an over-sized Marvel Special Edition and a single paperback volume for the book trade. Dave Sim, with an issue dated December, began self-publication of his **Cerebus the Aardvark**, the success of which would help establish the independent market for non-traditional black-and-white comics.

**1978:** In an effort to halt declining sales, Warner Communications drastically cut back on the number of "DC" titles and overhauled its distribution process in June. The interest of the visual media in comic book characters reached a new high with the Hulk, Spider-Man, and Doctor Strange, the subjects of television shows; with various projects begun to produce film versions of Flash Gordon, Dick Tracy, Popeye, Conan, The Phantom, and Buck Rogers; and with the movement reaching an outlandish peak of publicity with the release of **Superman** in December. Two significant applications of the comic book format to traditional fiction appeared this year: **A Contract with God and Other Tenement Stories** by Will Eisner and **The Silver Surfer** by Stan Lee and Jack Kirby. Eclipse Enterprises published Don McGregor and Paul Gulacy's **Sabre**, the first graphic album produced for the direct sales market, and initiated a policy of paying royalties and granting copyrights to comic book creators. Wendy and Richard Pini's **Elfquest**, a self-publishing project begun this year, eventually became so popular that it achieved bookstore distribution. The magazine **Heavy Metal** brought to American attention the avant-garde comic book work of European artists.

**1980:** Publication of the November premier issue of **The New Teen Titans**, with art by George Perez and story by Marv Wolfman, brought back to widespread popularity a title originally published by "DC" in 1966.

**1981:** The distributor Pacific Comics began publishing titles for direct sales through comic shops with the inaugural issue of Jack Kirby's **Captain Victory and the Galactic Rangers** and offered royalties to artists and writers on the basis of sales. "DC" would do the same for regular newsstand comics in November (with payments retroactive to July 1981), and Marvel followed suit by the end of the year. The first issue of **Raw**, irregularly published by Art Spiegelman and Francoise Mouly, carried comic book art into new extremes of experimentation and innovation with work by European and American artists. With issue No. 158, Frank Miller began to write and draw Marvel's **Daredevil** and brought a vigorous style of violent action to comic book pages.

**1982:** The first slick format comic book in regular size appeared, **Marvel Fanfare** No. 1, with a March date. Fantagraphics Books began publication in July of **Love and Rockets** by Mario, Gilbert, and Jaime Hernandez and brought a new ethnic sensibility and sophistication in style and content to comic book narratives for adults.

**1983:** This year saw more comic book publishers, aside from Marvel and DC, issuing more titles than had existed in the past 40 years, most small independent publishers relying on direct sales, such as Americomics, Capital, Eagle, Eclipse, First, Pacific, and Red Circle, and with Archie, Charlton, and Whitman publishing on a limited scale. Frank Miller's mini-series **Ronin** demonstrated a striking use of sword-play and martial arts typical of Japanese comic book art, and Howard Chaykin's stylish but controversial **American Flagg** appeared with an October date on its first issue.

**1984:** A publishing, media, film, and merchandising phenomenon began with the first issue of **Teenage Mutant Ninja Turtles** from Mirage Studios by Kevin Eastman and Peter Laird.

**1985:** Ohio State University's Library of Communication and Graphic Arts hosted the first major exhibition devoted to the comic book May 19 through August 2. In what was billed as an irreversible decision, the silver age superheroine Supergirl was killed in the seventh (October) issue of **Crisis on Infinite Earths**, a limited series intended to reorganize and simplify the DC universe on the occasion of the publisher's 50th anniversary.

**1986:** In recognition of its twenty-fifth anniversary, Marvel began publication of several new ongoing titles comprising Marvel's "New Universe," a self-contained fictional world. DC attracted extensive publicity and media coverage with its revisions of the character of **Superman** by John Byrne and of **Batman** in the **Dark Knight** series by Frank Miller. **Watchmen**, a limited-series graphic novel by Alan Moore and artist Dave Gibbons, began publication with a September issue from DC and Marvel's **The 'Nam**, written by Vietnam veteran Doug Murray and penciled by Michael Golden, began with its December issue. DC issued guidelines in December for labelling their titles as either for mature readers or for readers of all ages; in response, many artists and writers publicly objected or threatened to resign.

**1987:** Art Spiegelman's **Maus: A Survivor's Tale** was nominated for the National Book Critics Circle Award in biography, the first comic book to be so honored. A celebration of Superman's fiftieth Birthday began with the opening of an exhibition on his history at the Smithsonian's Museum of American History in Washington, D.C., in June and a symposium on "The Superhero in America" in October.

**1988:** Superman's birthday celebration continued with a public party in New York and a CBS television special in February, a cover story in **Time** magazine in March (the first comic book character to appear on the cover), and an international exposition in Cleveland in June. With issue number 601 for May 24, **Action Comics** became the first modern weekly comic book, which ceased publication after 42 issues with the December 13 number. In August, DC initiated a new policy of allowing creators of new characters to retain ownership of them rather than rely solely on work-for-hire.

**1989:** The fiftieth anniversary of Batman was marked by the release of the film **Batman**, starring Michael Keaton as Bruce Wayne and Jack Nicholson as the Joker; it grossed more money in the weekend it opened than any other motion picture in film history to that time.

**1990:** The publication of a new **Classics Illustrated** series began in January from Berkley/First with adaptations of Poe's **The Raven and Other Poems** by Gahan Wilson, Dickens' **Great Expectations** by Rick Geary, Carroll's **Through the Looking Glass** by Kyle Baker, and Melville's **Moby Dick** by Bill Sienkiewicz, with extensive media attention. The adaptation of characters to film continued with the most successful in terms of popularity and box-office receipts being **Teenage Mutant Ninja Turtles** and Warren Beatty's **Dick Tracy**. In November, the engagement of Clark Kent and Lois Lane was announced in **Superman** No. 50 which brought public fanfare about the planned marriage.

**Note:** A special word of thanks is due Gerard Jones for his suggestions and contributions to the above chronology.

# ARCHIE COMIC PUBLICATIONS: THE MIRTH OF A LEGEND

by Scott D. Fulop

The catch phrase the mirth of a nation adorned his comic books in the 1940s. He's been called everything from America's teen sensation, laugh sensation, and top teenager to America's typical teenager but mostly, everyone knows him as America's #1 teenager, Archie Andrews.

Archie and his friends originally appeared in the pages of *Pep Comics* published by MLJ Magazines (whose initials stood for its three partners Maurice Coyne, Louis Siblerkleit, and John Goldwater). MLJ had entered the growing comic book market place in 1939 with *Blue Ribbon Comics*, and shortly thereafter introduced the aforementioned *Pep* as well as other titles that were dominated by hero/adventure stories. To this day, *Pep Comics* #1 still stands out in the minds of most comic book aficionados since it introduced the industry's first patriotic superhero, the Shield. While MLJ's hero titles and yarns were successful in their own right, publisher John Goldwater reasoned that the timing was right for something other than costumed mysterymen.

John Goldwater was inspired by the Andy Hardy movies of that era and decided to put that inspiration to good use. John was determined to develop an everyman, a normal man, who, like Andy Hardy, the reader could identify with and who would entertain the public with his arresting mishaps and astounding mayhem. John related his ideas to partner and co-publisher Louis Silberkleit who gave John's concept an overwhelming seal of approval.

In December, 1941, with the aid of writer Vic Bloom, and artist Bob Montana, MLJ magazines released the first appearance of America's newest boy friend in the pages of *Pep Comics* #22. Christened Archibald, and requesting that you call him Chick, Archie, his girl-hating, unusually named friend Jughead, and the new girl next door, Betty Cooper, embarked upon a series of adventures which marked the dawn of a legend. Soon after, a whole host of new characters were introduced including rich and gorgeous Veronica Lodge, arch-rival Reggie Mantle, and Principal Weatherbee. New Archie dominated titles were also introduced (sans the superheroes) including *Archie Comics* #1, from 1942. Eventually, the company adopted the name of its flagship character and the letters MLJ gave way to Archie Publications.

Fifty years after his inception, the classic perennial love triangle between Archie, Betty, and Veronica still exists, the meaning of the 'S' on Jughead's shirt still remains a secret, and Archie is still running afoul of Mr. Lodge. Yes, the Archie tradition does indeed continue as the sons and grandchildren of Louis Silberkleit and John Goldwater proudly carry on that tradition and move forward with an American institution. The third largest comic book company in the country, Archie Comic Publications publishes over 40 different titles per year which translates into sales of over 16 million copies annually. Archie Comics are printed in seven different languages and distrubuted worldwide. Archie merchandise, everything from dolls to watches, grace the shelves of stores everywhere. A radio show running from the '40s through the '50s, numerous live action and highly rated animated television productions from the '60s to the present, a band with #1 chart-busting hits and Gold Records, (is there anyone out there who doesn't remember "Sugar, Sugar" and "Jingle, Jangle"?), and a nationally syndicated newspaper strip running continuously for the past 40 years are just a handful of reasons why Archie has always been a household word.

Archie owes his success to more than just licensed merchandise and television. Archie's popularity and uniqueness stems from the,fact that although the times changed, Archie changed with them. Archie and his peers have always remained contemporary to the times in which their stories were published, always sporting the latest fashions, verbalizing with the most current slang, and participating in the trendiest pastimes. And although Archie did indeed change, his hilarious misadventures always contained the essence of the original concept. The situations he and his pals faced (and still face today) were those that the reader himself could identify with, those adversities of adolescence that the reader, like Archie had to meet and conquer.

1991 will be a year well remembered by Archie fans and the general public as this is the year that Archie Comics celebrates its 50th anniversary. Celebratory events will include a revival and national tour of the Archies band, a live-action major motion picture from Warner Brothers, specialized children's museum tours, and creation of hundreds of licensed consumer products just to name a few. In addition, Archie Comics will publish scores of commemorative publications including a five volume series of trade paperback books entitled the *Archie Americana Series* which will showcase a half-century of Archie's most memorable stories.

Archie and his friends have thrilled millions of readers for years. Those eternal high school students from the fabled town of Riverdale have become an American institution. 50 years from now Archie Comics will have another anniversary celebration and another writer will be detailing Archie's history. Archie Andrews and his pals are, and always will be, America's number one teenagers.

*(Scott D. Fulop is the Editorial Director of New Product Development for Archie Comics.)*

# 1941: COMIC BOOKS GO TO WAR!
## *Those fabulous comics of World War II*

by

**HARRY B. THOMAS**
**and**
**GARY M. CARTER**

**Action Comics**, **Superman** covers © DC Comics; **Captain Marvel**, **Captain Midnight**, **Whiz Comics**, **Master Comics** covers © FAW; **Black Terror** cover © Nedor.

Dateline 1939...... The Wizard Of Oz and Gone With The Wind......Jack Benny and Fred Allen.......Batman and the Human Torch......The New York World's Fair and The World Of Tomorrow......and regrettably, for the millions of wounded and dead, the War in Europe and Adolf Hitler. The well-worn quote was never more applicable; "it was the best of times, it was the worst of times." It was a time in our history when the drums of war began to echo across America...and as the national anti-axis sentiment began to gel, the comic book industry jumped on the bandwagon. For several truly historic years, World War II and the Golden Age of Comics walked hand in hand, as it were, down the path of history.

Nationalism was at an all time high, and with it came a veritable litany of media, fueling the fires of patriotism from Maine to California. One Hollywood film after another played out the horrors of the Nazi war machine in Europe. Movie stars with ties to Great Britain began to volunteer for military service. Newspaper editorials warned that the occupation of Manchuria was only the precursor of further Japanese Imperialism in the Pacific theater. Newsreel footage graphically depicted the agony of thousands of innocent Chinese refugees. *Life* and other magazines published pictorial evidence of Germany's savage and ruthless blitzkrieg. Radio programs satirized the leaders of the Axis powers in a steady stream of skits and monologues while others used villains with obvious German and Oriental accents. Sunday comic strips had a field day with a seemingly endless parade of military protagonists. Pulp magazines chronicled spies plotting to undermine the American military establishment and steal the latest secret weapon (right out from under the collective noses of the defense industry). Highway billboards and storefront recruiting posters pleaded, cajoled, ordered, and inspired young men and women to rush to the aid of their country.

But what of America's new entry into the mass media community? As 1939 marched on and the full extent of Hitler's evil became known to the public, the seven-year-old comic book industry quickly established itself as one of the most stalwart defenders of truth, justice, and the American way....

In late 1939 and early 1940, the comic book industry began using more and more war theme covers. This early cover art was basically generic in nature, in that there were no indications that soldiers or weaponry belonged to any specific country. No swastikas, iron crosses, or rising suns overtly labeled the enemy, but the readers knew...they knew!

Classic examples of these war covers can be found on DC's *Action Comics* #10, #11, #15, #17, #19, and #21. These covers all feature non-identifiable soldiers and/or weapons. And all these issues are from 1939 and early 1940! America may not have been officially at war, but (as illustrated by the covers of *Action* #10, #17, #19, and #21) it's famous son from the planet Krypton was getting things started on his own! One of the most poignant covers from this pre-World War II era is the cover of *Action Comics* #31 (December 1940). In what appears to be a European country overrun by the Germans, Superman flies in at the last moment to protect the victim of a firing squad from a hail of deadly bullets. Like the rest of the first 84 *Action* covers, there is no speech balloon to explain. The interpretation of the cover is dependent on the nonverbal emblems of helmets, fixed bayonets and the Europeanesque buildings in the background. Also important to the interpretation of the cover of *Action* #31 is Superman's clinched fist and facial expression. It's clear that ole Sup' is about to clobber these guys...and what kind of guys does he usually clobber? BADGUYS, that's who! If we can depend on anything, it's that Superman knows who the bad guys are. This is very important because this cover was published more than one year before Pearl Harbor!!! To lend further credence to Superman's ability to identify the enemy far ahead of the Government, note the covers of *Action Comics* #35 and #39

**Action Comics** #17, © DC. Generic Superman war cover.

**Action Comics** #31, © DC. Generic Superman war cover.

**Marvel Mystery Comics** #4, © MCG. Sub-Mariner battles Germans. Note Nazi flag.

**Pep Comics** #1, © MLJ. Introduces The Shield, America's first patriotic hero.

(obvious German helmet), #40 (German cross on tank), #43 (German paratrooper with swastika arm band, first swastika used on an *Action* cover), and #44 (German helmets and swastika), all on the stands before Pearl Harbor.

When it came to identifying the bad guys early, Superman was in good company. In February of 1940, (nearly two years before Pearl Harbor) Timely published the cover of *Marvel Mystery Comics* #4. This amazing cover depicted one of Timely's most popular heroes, the Submariner, punching it out with a submarine crew somewhere on the Atlantic. The Death Raider submarine is clearly emblazoned with a German swastika and flies the black and red German battle flag with a large swastika as its central design element! The covers of *Marvel Mystery Comics* continued to dish out punishment for the Third Reich on 13 more covers that hit the stands before Pearl Harbor.

By 1940, the youth of America were scouring the newsstands, not only for Superman, Batman, Submariner, and the Human Torch...but for any new hero who might be making a first appearance. There didn't seem to be enough of these new costumed heroes to appease the comic book buying public! To fill this demand, hundreds of new comic book titles would appear on the stands before the close of 1940.

As the war in Europe edged ever closer to America, established costumed heroes began to do their part against the Axis. Another group of comic book heroes were created expressly for this task. These champions of liberty are often defined as patriotic heroes. The Shield, first of these red, white, and blue heroes, was created by MLJ Publishing (now Archie) and appeared in *Pep Comics* #1, January, 1940. The front of his costume was made to resemble a shield (which, in actuality, it was) adorned with bars and stars borrowed from Old Glory. Couple this with leggings, boots, and a mask and America's first patriotic hero was born!

The Shield was billed as the G-Man EXTRAORDINARY and as such, most of his early adventures were centered around home-grown criminals. He was later cast in stories of intrigue and espionage. The Shield would remain MLJ'S premier character through the early years and *Pep Comics* their flagship publication. The only other MLJ character to get much attention was the Hangman, whose adventures would also be associated with the war.

Covers are, and always have been, one of the most important aspects of comic books. Editors and retailers still argue that the cover sells the comic. Many enthusiasts collect old comics based entirely on their covers. The war years produced an incredible number of wonderful covers, that can be loosely classified into two categories, the war cover and the patriotic cover. The war cover usually depicts the hero(s) in pitched battle against the enemy. The "patriotic cover" was much more symbolic in nature, and often employed the use of flags, eagles, swastikas, the rising sun, etc.

MLJ Comics mostly featured war covers; however, special notice should be given to the cover to *Pep* #20, one of the top patriotic covers published during the war. *Pep* #20 featured a giant swastika that takes up two thirds of the cover, with flames and hands coming up through it. In the background, rushing to help free the oppressed people trapped by the giant swastika, are the Shield, Dusty (his boy companion), and the Hangman. This cover ranks as one of the finest covers using the swastika as its central theme.

In March of 1941, Timely's Captain America, the greatest of all the patriotic comic book heroes, stormed onto America's newsstand. To help launch the new title, the cover featured an appearance by der Fuhrer himself!

No hero of the patriotic genre would create such excitement in comic books. The creative team of Joe Simon and Jack Kirby, considered by most as the best creative masters of the Golden Age of comics, would share the credit for the creation of America's hero. With the introduction of Captain America, all patriotic heroes, before and after, would pale by comparison.

Cap, as Captain America is fondly referred to by collectors, had a true All-American origin. After failing his army physical, a weak and skinny American youth Steve Rogers volunteers to be the test subject of a top secret experiment. An army research scientist injects Steve with a serum that instantly transforms him into a muscular, athletic, and superior human specimen—the perfect warrior! Somewhat predictably, the scientist is assassinated by Nazi spies, the secret formula is lost forever, and Steve Rogers assumes the guise of Captain America!

Many have argued that Cap's costume ranks as one of the top, if not the top, costumes of the Golden Age. It was artistically original, and visually stunning! The blue hood, the wings on either side of the large white 'A' emblazoned on the forehead, the blue chain mail jersey with a white star on the chest, the vertical red and white stripes around the waist, the blue tights and red seven-league boots, the red gloves, and of course, the symbolic circular red white and blue shield, make Simon and Kirby's creation America personified!

Although there were none, the character would have been a perfect medium for patriotic covers. Instead, most issues sported an incredible action cover with a tantalizing caption calculated to entice a young reader to plunk down a dime!

**Captain America Comics** #1, © MCG. One of the top costumes of the Golden Age.

**Captain America Comics** #2, © MCG. Hitler appears on cover.

**Captain America Comics** #3, © MCG. The Red Skull's first cover appearance.

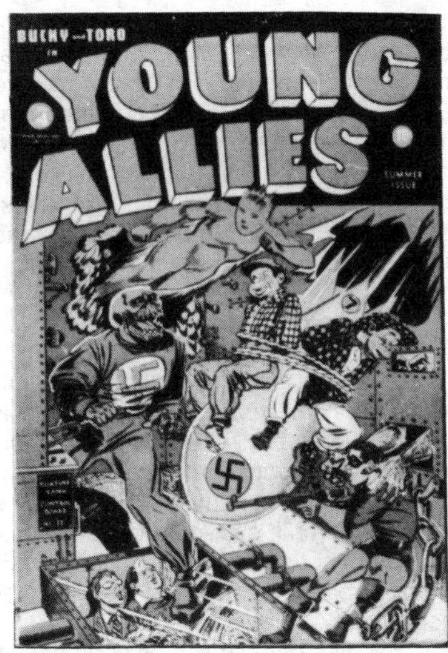


**Young Allies** #4, © MCG. The Red Skull appears on cover.

Consider these examples of intriguing cover captions and note how well they illustrate Cap's penchant for the melodramatic. "WAS BUCKY TO BE THE NEXT VICTIM OF THE HORROR HOSPITAL?" "WAS THE SENATOR TO BE THE NEXT VICTIM OF THE RINGMASTER'S WHEEL OF DEATH?" "WOULD BUCKY'S BE ANOTHER TERRIBLE DEATH IN THE CHAMBER OF HORRORS, OR WOULD CAPTAIN AMERICA BE THERE IN TIME?" "CAN THE MIGHTY CAPTAIN AMERICA BE IN TIME TO SAVE BUCKY FROM THE HORROR OF THE FEUDING MOUNTAINEERS?" "ARE CAPTAIN AMERICA AND BUCKY DOOMED TO BECOME PYGMIES FOR ALL TIME?" In every case, these compelling questions could be answered by simply buying the comic book or, better yet, sneaking a peek at the end of the story before the newsstand owner spotted you. In either situation, no fan could resist.

Whether by Simon and Kirby, Al Avison, Sid Shores, Alex Schomburg, or their successors, each cover stands as a monument to the American ideal of helping the underdog and taking the bad guys to task with no quarter asked....and no quarter given.

Captain America spawned one of the most memorable villains of WWII......the Red Skull! An awesome sight to behold, the horrible blood-red skull sat atop a figure attired in a one-piece coverall outfit with a giant swastika on the chest. As villains go, the Red Skull was really not that different from other Timely antagonists of the period. He was just another crazed German agent, totally devoted to Hitler, world conquest, and the superiority of the German race. Even though his appearance made the Red Skull a pretty scary proposition, little was done to develop him into the potentially world class villain he might have become. Though he was written into numerous war era stories, the editors seemed to communicate a similar lack of confidence in the Red Skull, allotting him but a single cover appearance during the war years (issue #3). He would also make a cover appearance on *Young Allies* #4 which featured Cap's sidekick Bucky along with the Human Torch's sidekick Toro. Even though his potential may not have been fully realized, the Red Skull remains one of the most recognizable World War II villains ever created. This fact can be supported by the many Golden Age collectors who prize Red Skull issues above all others.

Captain America was Timely's most acclaimed character, but Timely had others that were almost as popular with the comic book buying public. Two of these other heroes appeared in the monthly anthology that served as the flagship of Timely Publications......*MARVEL MYSTERY*!

With the publication of *Marvel Com-*

*ics* #1 in November of 1939 (it would not be *Marvel Mystery Comics* until the second issue), the Human Torch and the Submariner began their long careers at Timely. The Torch and Submariner would alternate cover duties (along with five appearances by the Angel) during the first two years. The Human Torch was featured on nearly all the remaining covers.

As noted earlier, the Submariner was already at war with the Germans by the fourth issue, but that should have come as no great surprise. Submariner was at war with everybody! As a matter of fact, Subby even fought against a fellow hero, the Human Torch, both in *Marvel Mystery* and the Torch's own magazine. It's important to note that (at least conceptually) the Submariner was most likely the first comic book anti-hero.

By mid-1940, the story content of *Marvel Mystery* had taken on the same characteristics found in all the Timely publications during the war years. They dealt entirely with their costumed heroes battling the cruel German minions or the crafty, demon-like Japanese.

The covers for the entire run of *Marvel Mystery* are so similar (especially after Alex Schomburg took over the artistic chores) that young readers had no difficulty spotting the distinctive look of their favorite title, even at some distance from the display rack. Schomburg covers, even though similar, are distinctive and fantastic beauties to behold. Schomburg could literally cram a cover full of heroes, Germans, Japanese, ships, bombs, planes, artillery, explosions, and of course, an obligatory torture machine or two, to round out the scene. Something thrilling was happening in every inch of a Schomburg cover! Most comic book collectors and historians alike credit him as the best war genre cover artist of the Golden Age and certainly one of the most prolific. Not only did he draw practically every cover for every title at Timely during the '40s, he was also producing a massive amount of covers for Nedor/Standard! It has been suggested on more than one occasion that no collection of Golden Age books would be complete without one of Schomburg's graphic gems.

While nearly all of Timely's covers were war covers, they did produce a smattering of patriotic and symbolic pieces. The cover of *All Winners* #4 ranks among the very best of the entire war! The first issue of *All Winners* was dated Summer 1941 and was likely published as Timely's answer to DC's very popular *All Star Comics*. Like *All Star's* format, Timely placed their most popular characters (Captain America, Human Torch, Submariner, the Whizzer, the Destroyer, etc.)

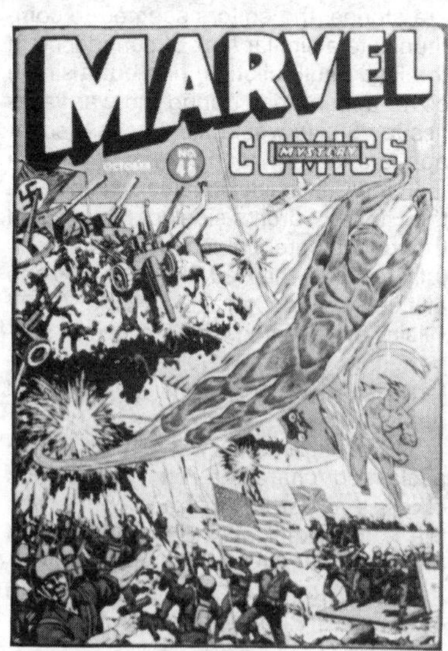


**Marvey Mystery Comics** #48, © MCG. One of the many classic Schomburg war covers.

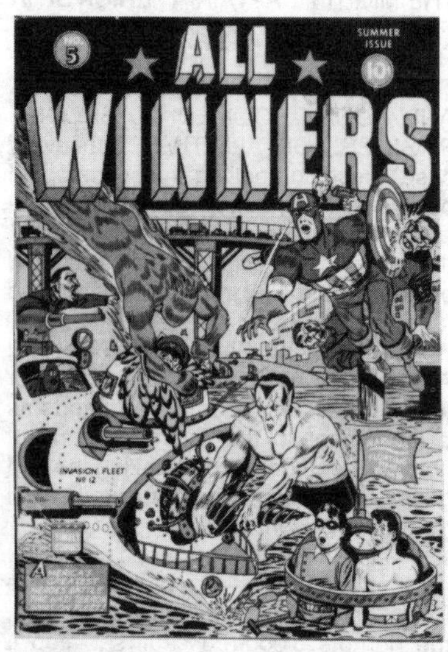


**All Winners Comics** #5, © MCG. America's heroes stop the Nazi invasion fleet.

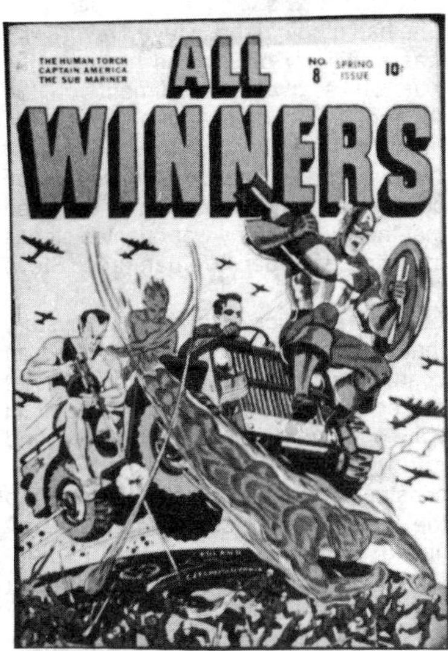


**All Winners Comics** #8, © MCG. American heroes attack German troops.

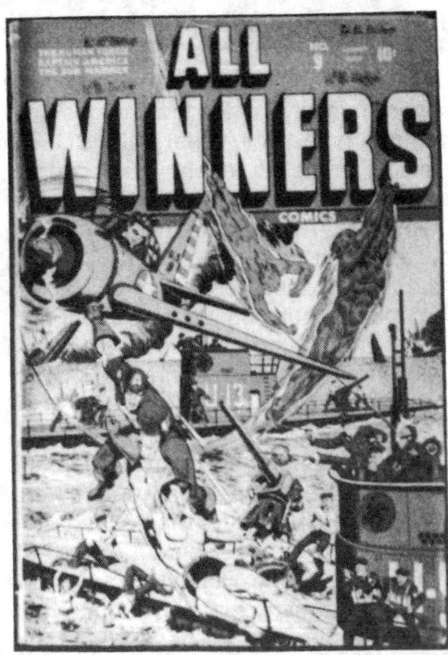


**All Winners Comics** #9, © MCG. German U-boat war cover.

into one regularly published magazine. The important fundamental difference between the two titles was that DC's heroes banded together as a team (starting with the now famous third issue) for a book-length adventure. *All Winners* was an anthology book, segregating its heroes in separate, individual adventures (like *All Stars* 1 and 2). Just imagine a Justice Society of Timely super stars . . . wow . . . that would have really scorched the newsstand!

The covers of the first eight issues of *All Winners* are truly outstanding and make this title a particular favorite with collectors. The first three covers are more or less war themes but are rendered with a touch of symbolism. And then came issue #4. All the heroes appearing in that issue are seen rising like giants of freedom over a world aflame and overrun by mad Germans. No better cover produced during the war years can be found at Timely! Other particularly nice patriotic covers were #6—a flag cover which also featured Hitler, Mussolini, and Hirohito—and issue #8 featuring the heroes in a jeep mowing down terrorized German troups.

This leads us to an important question. If Timely characters and titles were so popular, why did the company nearly die out so quickly after the war? This can at least be partly answered by reviewing just a few factors. First, *All Winners* and the other Timely action titles were all war-oriented. If there is no war then it is easy to see how quickly the interest of the "fickle public" will be focused elsewhere. Even the very existence of the characters becomes hard to justify. This sudden lack of social relevance at wars-end would lead directly to the failure of many of their titles.

Secondly, Timely used what at best could be described as skimpy plot development and, with the notable exception of the Submariner, character development was virtually non-existent. While other major comic book publishers such as DC and Fawcett were building enduring characters, intricate plots, and essential supporting casts, Timely seemed to manufacture a nearly continuous stream of the standard anti-German/Japanese stories. One notable comic book researcher described Timely as the absolute master of the all-action, no-brains story.

When the war ended, Timely was left with no continuity to build on......there were no recurring villains (to speak of) such as the Joker, Penguin, Luthor, or Sivana......nothing to keep people coming back for more. After the war, Timely's heroes were basically left in a vacuum.

Timely's six year reign as the number one publisher of war theme comics would cost them dearly in popularity when the war ended, but those astonishingly beautiful issues from 1940 to

1945 will always be considered classics by historians and collectors alike!

Over at DC, possibly the number one comics publisher of the time, things were being handled very differently. DC was building for the future. They balanced war stories and covers with a mixture of other themes, including crime, horror, murder, comedy, and even holidays. DC also established good secondary characters to populate their comics. This continuing line of character actors would develop a following that would continue long after the war.

For instance, such characters as Doiby Dickles and his taxi Goitrude, the 3 Dimwits, Lois Lane, Jimmy Olsen, Perry White, Lex Luthor, the Joker, the Penguin, Two-Face, Shierra, Alfred, Etta Candy and the Holiday Girls, Steve Trevor, and many more, were introduced in various titles. These characters came to play an essential role in the legends of the main characters. Consider the fact that most comic fans can readily name the strips each of the above second bananas appeared in! In contrast, Timely had their heroes so involved with Hitler, Hirohito, Mussolini and their assorted henchmen, that when the war ended, there was no cast of secondary characters or villains to build on.

DC also had its own red, white and blue clad character—Wonder Woman. She had a boy friend (Steve Trevor) who was a military officer and her costume was DC's own embodiment of the American flag motif. Even though the number of war theme covers on *Wonder Woman* and *Sensation Comics* can be counted on both hands, it must be noted that there were many war-oriented stories involving Wonder Woman and Steve Trevor.

On reflection, it is really a mystery that Wonder Woman in her All American costume was not used on the covers of her books in a more patriotic effect. In spite of all her exploits, moral fiber, and nationalistic spirit, her "gender-constricted" readers persistently clung to the idea that Wonder Woman was afflicted with an overwhelming and incurable genetic handicap. She was a woman!

While the lack of exploitation of Wonder Woman as a patriotic symbol is a bit of a puzzle, there is little mystery as to why Superman was chosen to carry the flag (both figuratively and literally). In 1941 Superman was DC's most popular character and considered by many to be the most popular character in comic books.

Superman war stories had to be tough to write. Even the youngest of readers were asking the obvious question—why doesn't Superman just fly

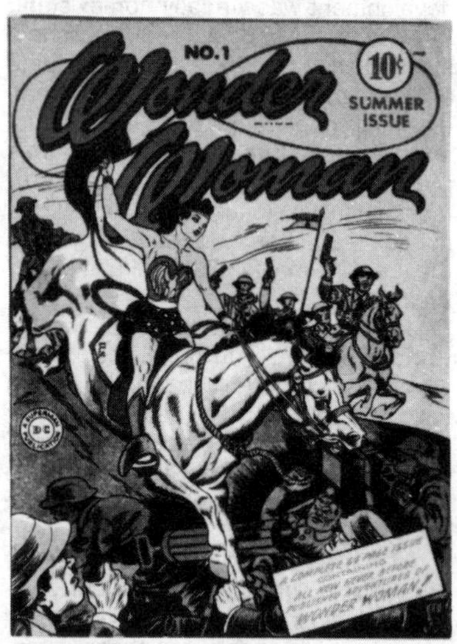


**Wonder Woman** #1, © DC. DC never fully exploited Wonder Woman on patriotic covers.

**Superman** #18, © DC. Superman bombs the Japanazis!

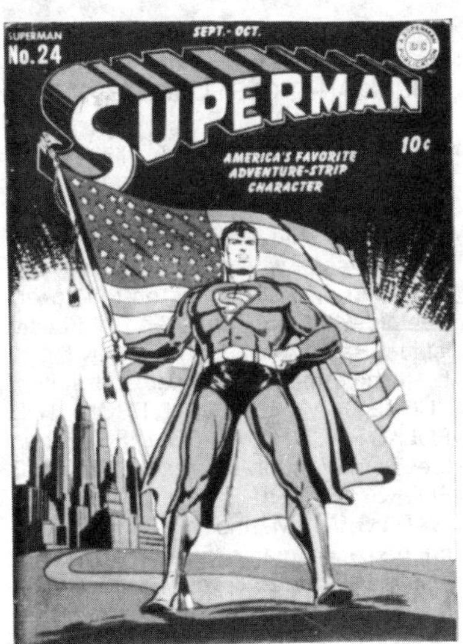


**Superman** #24, © DC. Classic flag cover.

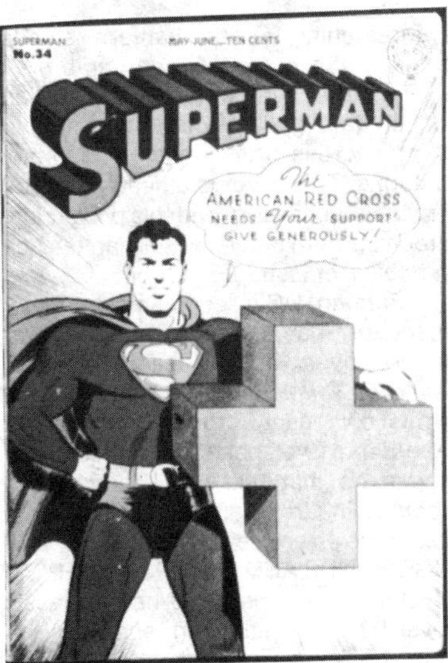


**Superman** #34, © DC. American Red Cross cover.

over to Berlin and knock the stuffin's out of the whole darned German army? Even the most ergonomically deficient first graders figured out that Superman, all by himself, could easily win the war in no time at all.

To overcome this thematic "catch 22" DC kept the Superman stories self-contained and on an adventure-by-adventure basis, not worrying much about philosophy and continuity. When they did feature a war story, it would be treated as any other tale and kept within the context of that individual story. The writers never gave the reader paradoxes to ponder or plots that required excessive thought. And why should they? After all, the explosive sales of *Superman* and *Action Comics* communicated to the publishers that the strip had all the literary excellence that it required.

It would be on the covers, though, that Superman would really let his colors show. Nothing was held back! *Action Comics* and *Superman Comics* from 1941 through 1944 featured more of the war and patriotic/symbolic genre covers than any other of DC's major publications. Two of the covers of *Superman Comics* during this period are true classics of the patriotic/symbolic genre. On the cover of *Superman* #14, he is seen standing, full-bodied, in front of a red, white and blue shield. His arm is raised and on it is perched an eagle. The background is solid black, giving the whole cover a fantastic, almost surreal, three-dimensional effect.

The second exceptional cover is similar to #14 in that it also employs the same black background. *Superman* #24 boasts the famous American flag cover and is a classic of American symbolism. Longtime followers of *The Official Overstreet Comic Book Price Guide* may remember way back to the 1972 (#2) issue where many a collector was first mesmerized by the cover of *Superman* #24. Both covers are truly breathtaking and once they find their way into someone's collection rarely find themselves back in the hobby marketplace.

The last Superman war cover appeared on *Action Comics* #86. It depicts Superman inundating a high-ranking Japanese officer with a huge pile of war-bonds. Superman's disclaimer is simply stated in his speech balloon—"AND IT ISN'T SUPERMAN WHO'S DOING THIS—IT'S THE AMERICAN PEOPLE!"

Though *Action Comics* was doing its patriotic duty, some of the other publications at DC had amazingly few (if any) covers that were directly war-related. Notable exceptions to this general lack of patriotic fervor were the covers of their single character books *Superman, Batman,* and *Green Lantern*, which were more likely to feature war theme covers.

*Green Lantern*, for instance, had some outstanding war-related covers (and stories). Issue #3 featured the world covered with flames and swastikas while a threatening Green Lantern stands gigantic above it all. *Green Lantern* #4 shows the Green Lantern in his civilian identity (along with Doiby Dickles) marching across the cover in military uniforms. This cover is a dead ringer for a recruitment poster. With his power ring, Green Lantern battles a German tank on the cover of issue #5.

Batman, DC's second most popular character, may not have had many war theme covers as the lead feature of *Detective Comics*, but he made up for it in his own title. *Batman Comics* #12 (Aug/Sept, 1942) began the series of war covers on that title with Batman and Robin riding in an army jeep. Batman's first words on any cover were "WAR SAVINGS BONDS AND STAMPS—KEEP'EM ROLLING!" *Batman* #13 had a classic cover by Jerry Robinson, showing Batman and Robin descending from a solid black night sky with billowing white parachutes. High grade copies of this cover are enough to give you collecting shivers! Another well-loved Batman cover was done for issue #15 and shows Batman firing a water-cooled machine gun complete with tripod. Robin is expertly feeding belts of cartridges into the side of the weapon with the look of someone who is having a great time. Issue #17 depicts the dynamic duo astride the back of a giant eagle while giving the victory sign. Robin speaks up for the first time on a cover with the words "KEEP THE AMERICAN EAGLE FLYING! BUY WAR BONDS AND STAMPS!."

Other more "cartoony" examples of Batman and Robin at war can be found on the cover of #18 (featuring caricatures of Hitler, Hirohito, and Mussolini) and #30, the first issue where both Gotham City crusaders actually speak on the cover. Set on what appears to be a Pacific island, Batman hands over a new M1 rifle to an American soldier and states, "HERE'S A NEW GUN FROM THE FOLKS BACK HOME, SOLDIER!" Then the Boy Wonder chimes "YEP! THE FOLKS THAT'RE BACKING THE 7TH WAR LOAN!" Marines all over the world cringed at Batman's faux pas. They had just spent agonizing weeks in boot camp learning never to call a rifle a gun!!

Very few Batman stories would take the hero to the actual warfront. Instead, he would confront home-grown menaces, expose espionage agents, promote patriotism, and support the sale of war bonds and stamps. Keeping its heroes off the front lines would be the common policy in most of DC's titles.

By 1941 Simon and Kirby had left Timely (a whole article in itself) and were busy at DC. It was here that their artistic talents matured to a high level of excellence rarely matched in the world of

**Green Lantern** #3, © DC. One of the top most collected war covers.

**Batman** #18, © DC. Hitler, Hirohito, Mussolini cover.

**Star Spangled Comics** #7, © DC. First appearance of the Guardian and the Newsboy Legion.

**Boy Commandos** #2, © DC. Simon & Kirby at their best.

comic books, even to this day!

Simon and Kirby had experimented with kid groups at Timely, but it was at DC that Jack and Joe would really perfect this unusual genre. Two of the most popular strips at DC during the years 1941 through 1945 would be kid groups originated by these two comic book geniuses.

In the summer of 1941 issue #7 of *Star Spangled Comics* hit the stands. Taking over the cover spot (previously occupied by a distinctly patriotic hero, the Star Spangled Kid and his sidekick Stripesy) was S & K's newest smash feature, the Guardian and the Newsboy Legion! The first story disclosed that the Newsboy Legion was made up of four New York slum kids with very different personalities. The Guardian was the costumed alter ego of a New York cop who took the kids under his protective wing. The Newsboy Legion proved to be one of the most popular features ever produced by DC and was not only strong enough to survive the departure of Simon and Kirby, but even survived past the end of the war.

The art work by Simon and Kirby is among the best ever done in the super hero genre and the covers they created for this series are absolutely stunning! It is amazing that this superb title remains so low in value when compared to other DC publications of the same time period. Like Batman, there were numerous stories of the Guardian and his pals foiling the un-American antics of villain after villain.

The other (and apparently more popular) "kid" group created by the Simon and Kirby team was another assemblage of preteens, this time with an international flavor. The Boy Commandos had their origin and first appearance in issue #64 of *Detective Comics* and their only cover appearance in *Detective* #65.

This "two-fisted" group's protective adult was army Capt. Rip Carter whose only costume was his military uniform. One major difference between this group of heroes and most of the other strips at DC during this period was that their adventures would take place at the front rather than in the U.S.A. The Boy Commandos proved so popular that in the winter of 1942 they were given their own magazine and the Simon and Kirby covers on the first few issues are again shining examples of the team's classic talents. Simon and Kirby's wonderful cover to *Boy Commandos* #2 is an enduring classic. It features the boys giving the bum's rush to no less than Hitler himself! Rip and the four boys would continue to battle with the Axis on the first 13 of their 36 covers.

In one of their most flavorful and famous stories (published in *Detective Comics* #106, December 1945) the Boy Commandos "MEET THE COMMANDOS FROM NIPPON!" They are Bugi

(World's Greatest Acrobat), Fugi (World's Greatest Jiujitsu Expert), Mugi (World's Greatest Sniper), and, last but not least, Yugi (World's Greatest Knife Thrower). In typical Boy Commandos fashion, Alfy, Andre, Jan, and Brooklyn swiftly dispatch (as in kill) the rival Commandos one by one. In the last panel of the story, the four dead Nipponese commandos, standing on clouds, argue with each other about the failure of their mission while a sign in the foreground reads "BROKEN-DOWN LAND OF HONORABLE ANCESTORS OVERCROWDED!" This attempted insult of something very sacred to the Japanese may have backfired. Perplexed readers across the country now had graphic proof that, contrary to popular opinion, "Japs" went to heaven too!!!

While the idea of kid groups might seem silly to the more cynical readers of today, the concept was incredibly successful. The Newsboy Legion and the Boy Commandos were among the most popular wartime features at DC.

DC did not relegate Simon and Kirby to drawing and writing only kid groups. They were also responsible for the (new) Sandman and Manhunter strips in *Adventure Comics* during this same time period. Their work on these two strips, however, did not seem to reveal the same enthusiasm as the kid heroes. Some notable *Adventure Comics* covers with war themes (some by S & K, some S & K look-alikes) are issues #78, #79, #82, #86, #88, #91, #95, and #96.

With the exception of the Boy Commandos, DC utilized war stories and covers on a more or less intermittent basis. Their costumed heroes seemed to take on their war duties as a somewhat lower priority than the standard fare offered by ordinary adventures. *All Star* #4 (the first bimonthly issue, Mar/Apr, 1941) introduced an important change in this editorial policy.

On the last page of *All Star* #3, below a drawing of the eight heroes shown on the cover, the editors announce two things. First, that *All Star* will be published every two months instead of every three months. And secondly, that "IN THE NEXT ISSUE OF ALL STAR COMICS—YOU WILL FOLLOW THE ADVENTURES OF ALL YOUR FAVORITE CHARACTERS, PICTURED ON THIS PAGE, IN ONE BIG EPISODE IN WHICH THEY WORK HAND-IN-HAND WITH THE CHIEF OF THE F.B.I. IN WASHINGTON, AND WE KNOW YOU WILL GET EVEN A GREATER KICK OUT OF THE NEXT ISSUE THAN YOU GOT OUT OF THIS ONE!"

Issue #4 begins at that Washington meeting where the FBI director (J. Edgar Hoover, no less) proceeds to enlist the members of the JSA (Justice Society Of

**Adventure Comics** #79, © DC. Manhunter stalks a German U-boat.

**All Star Comics** #4, © DC. The Justice Society goes to Washington.

**All Star Comics** #11, © DC. Hawkman battles a Japanese soldier.

**All Star Comics** #12, © DC. "V" for victory cover.

America) to fight national internal espionage which is threatening to undermine freedom and democracy in America. This incredible issue has one of the most beautiful patriotic covers of the entire 57-issue run. Beginning with issue #4, *All Star* would be DC's most war-oriented costumed hero title.

*All Star's* war theme cover "hall of fame" continued with issue #7 (members raising money to help feed war orphans in Europe), issue #9 (symbolic eagle and shield), issue #11 (which featured Hawkman in a man-to-man duel with a Japanese soldier). Issue #11 also stated that the JSA was being disbanded so the various team members could join the armed services in their civilian identities and "properly serve their country in time of need." All the current JSA membership (Hawkman, Dr. Fate, Sandman, the Atom, Dr. Mid-Nite, Starman, and Johnny Thunder) proceeded to join the armed forces. Only the Spectre, as a bonafide ghost, was unable to pass the physical. In spite of this minor setback, he declared he would continue the fight on the home front while the other members went off to Europe.

After arriving at the front, it didn't take long for the heroes to don their costumes and help the troops. It soon became obvious to the military hierarchy that the JSA had secretly enlisted. This news resulted in the disruption of normal military procedures and the commanding officer persuaded the JSA to form an elite and exclusive fighting group called the Justice Batallion to remain in effect til war's end.

The distinctive and beautiful cover of *All Star* #12 depicts the JSA team members in a full cover "V" for victory. Wonder Woman, now a full-fledged member, forms the base of the "V." *All Star* #14 made a rare wartime statement with the cover blurb "FOOD FOR STARVING PATRIOTS." This subdued and historically significant "Horn of Plenty" cover is still relevant, considering the present state of world hunger. *All Star* #16 featured a symbolic cover with the JSA members surrounded by Americans of all walks of life and a banner along the cover bottom reading, "The Justice Society For A United America!" Issue #22 is the famous American flag cover, with renderings of Washington and Lincoln in the background in case the flag alone did not stir you to patriotic feelings. Issue #24 ranks as one of the most unusual covers and stories of the series. Rarely, if ever, would DC make such a blatantly propagandistic, distorted, and racist statement as in the story "THIS IS OUR ENEMY." In contrast, issue #27 suggests love, care and understanding, and explores the tragedy of disabled veterans returning home from war.

Only one other company would so effectively exploit the notion of America at war. That company started with a single word. . . . . . "SHAZAM!"

From the stand point of pure physical attractiveness, the Fawcett comic books published in the early '40s were a real class act. This was because Fawcett covers were printed on higher quality, heavier paper stock than any other company's. Many collectors have noted that the spines of DC and Timely comics from the '40s tend to flake easily when opened. The spines of Fawcett books seem to resist this defect to a much higher degree. Also, due to the better paper stock, the colors of Fawcett covers seem a bit brighter and seldom have serious browning so common in the majority of other contemporaneous comics. Fawcett could also claim the most popular costumed hero of the 1940's—Captain Marvel!

Considered by many comic book researchers and collectors to be the best super hero origin story ever published, Captain Marvel and *Whiz Comics* seemed destined for success right from the beginning.

Billy Batson, a young boy who looked to be somewhere between 11 and 13 years of age, was given the power to become the adult Captain Marvel by saying the magic word, Shazam! Actually, Billy did not become Captain Marvel. He and the "Big Red Cheese" merely exchanged places when the magic word was spoken. Readers were never given an explanation of where Captain Marvel came from (or who he was), or where Billy would disappear to. No one seemed to mind because the popularity of C. C. Beck's wonderful hero spread like lightning all across the country.

Captain Marvel's adventures only got better and better as each story was published. His tales were always just slightly "off center"—never quite planting the reader in reality. In fact, this surreal quality seemed to actually advance the popularity of Captain Marvel stories.

Captain Marvel was portrayed as shy, not overly smart, impetuous, laughable (his #1 nemesis, Dr. Sivana, invented the humorously derogatory term "the big red cheese"), dedicated, heroic......in other words, one of the few really interesting personalities in a world populated by bland, two-dimensional heroes.

C.C. Beck was the genius behind the good Captain throughout most of his long career, including a great deal of input into the stories. C.C. Beck was an innovative master of comic book illustration and one of the few to seriously challenge the team of Simon and Kirby!

Beck's style was deceptively cartoonish but upon closer inspection reveals a stylistic intricacy and has yet to be equaled. He was one of the few illustrators to make a comic book hero ac-

**All Star Comics** #24, © DC. "This is our enemy" issue.

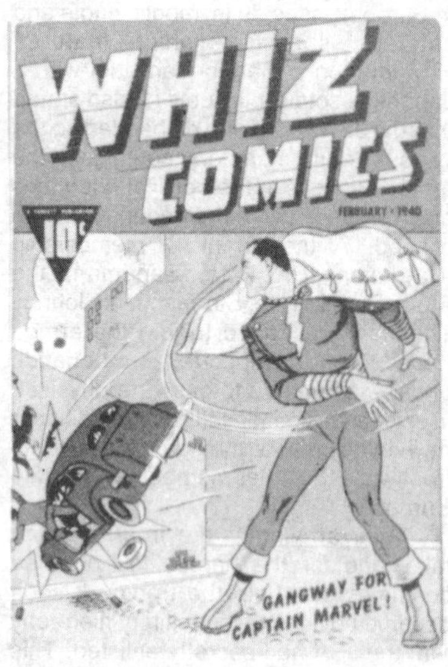


**Whiz Comics** #1, © FAW. First Captain Marvel, the most popular hero of the 1940s.

**Captain Marvel Adventures** #12, © FAW. Captain Marvel joins the Army.

**Captain Marvel Adventures** #14, © FAW. Captain Marvel swats the Japs.

tually appear to have weight and substance. Captain Marvel was rounded, making the costume appear full. This contrasted greatly with the more common illustrative method of sharp angles and costumes which looked as though they were part of the hero.

Billy Batson and Captain Marvel were both dedicated to goodness and fair play, so when Hitler and his cohorts started the nasty business of world conquest, they both stepped forward to do their patriotic duty.

In issue #12 of *Captain Marvel Adventures*, Billy Batson's attempted enlistment in the Army failed because he was underage. Billy walked out of the recruiting office, spoke the magic word "Shazam," re-entered and signed up as Captain Marvel.

The Army was ecstatic to get so perfect a specimen! They appeared to have never heard of Captain Marvel (again, that hint of being slightly beyond the accepted bounds of reality) and treated him as just another recruit. (...Almost sounds like Elvis.)

At the story's end, old Shazam, who had granted Billy Batson the power to become Captain Marvel, appeared as an army officer (he had joined due to his belief that America would need him to defeat the evil of Hitler), and told Captain Marvel he could best serve the world by remaining free and independent of the Army. Sadly, Captain Marvel agreed and his stint in the U.S. Army came to an abrupt end.

Later in issue #12, Captain Marvel, now a civilian, would have one of his many confrontations with Hitler himself. The two foes would meet many times during the course of the war, supplying Captain Marvel with many opportunities to totally embarrass the German leader. In all of Hitler's many appearances in Fawcett comics, he was always depicted as a jumping, screaming, mad clown, with a severe case of spoiled brat syndrome.

*Whiz Comics*, of which Captain Marvel was the cover and lead feature, and *Captain Marvel Adventures* would both feature loads of patriotic/war covers. Fawcett excelled in cover art and almost any cover on any of their titles during the early '40s could have been used for poster art!

The main villains in *Captain Marvel Adventures*, Dr. Sivana (a mad scientist) and Mr. Mind (a worm from outer space bent on world conquest) gave outstanding performances over the years and were examples of genuine unique literary creations.

At different times, and independent of one another, the two villains joined forces with Hitler (as well as with Hirohito and Stalin) in their drive for world conquest, but with a twist—Sivana and Mr. Mind both planned to betray the Axis powers at the earliest opportunity and to take over the world themselves. However, both Sivana and Mr. Mind soon withdrew their aid from Hitler and his gang, determining that they (the Nazis) were too stupid to be of much use to them. How embarrassing—even the villains at Fawcett had no use for the Axis!

Some outstanding examples of Captain Marvel World War II covers can be found on *Captain Marvel Adventures* #12 (Captain Marvel leading an Army troop through barbed wire and shell bursts), #14 (Swats the Japs), #15 (Paste the Axis), #16 (Marvel and Uncle Sam side by side, rolling up their sleeves to take on the enemy), #17 (fantastic and rarely done painted cover of Captain Marvel in an aerial dog fight with enemy planes), #21 (swastika cover), #26 (flag cover), #27 (Captain Marvel joins the Navy), #28 (Uncle Sam pins medal on Captain Marvel) and #37 (Buy War Stamps).

*Whiz Comics* also had many, many war-related covers, two of the very best being issue #31 which featured Captain Marvel posing beside a poster of General MacArthur and the visually stunning issue #44 with Captain Marvel leading our troops onto an enemy beachhead while carrying an American flag!

While Captain Marvel was the mainstay at Fawcett, his protege', Captain Marvel Jr., was also very popular and was possibly the most successful boy hero of the '40s. Captain Marvel Jr. was driven with avengence against the Hun, and with good reason. Hitler and the war were directly responsible for the creation of Captain Marvel Jr., and his origin trilogy of stories in *Master Comics* #21, *Whiz Comics* #25, and *Master Comics* #22 form one of the best character introductions in the history of comic books! Not only did the trilogy introduce the very successful Captain Marvel Jr.—it also introduced another of the major WWII comic book villains, Captain Nazi!

Captain Nazi was a unique stroke of genius for Fawcett in that unlike the more commonly done villains that were parodies of German, Japanese, and Italian foes, Captain Nazi was the personification of German aggrandizement and Aryan perfection. He was tall, muscular, movie star handsome, blond, and totally dedicated to Hitler's warped ideals and goals.

Captain Nazi made his first appearance in *Master* #21, with a cover featuring Captain Marvel and Bulletman standing on either side of a grinning, arrogant, green-clad Captain Nazi. Readers knew this issue contained something very special—and they were right!

As the story began, Hitler introduced (to a gathering of his generals and allies) his latest and greatest secret weapon, Captain Nazi. Hitler proudly announced that this new German superman

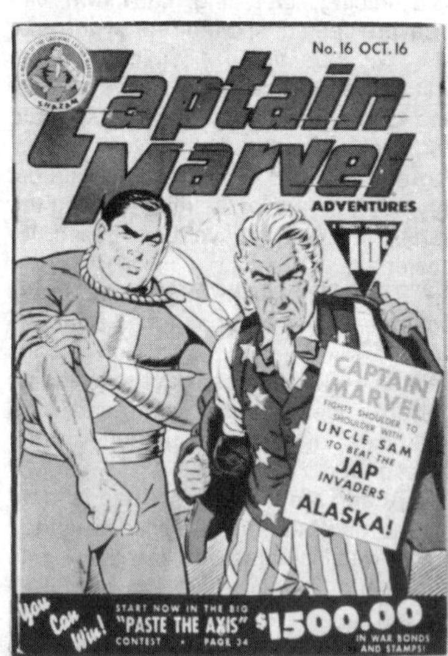


**Captain Marvel Adventures** #16, © FAW. Patriotic Uncle Sam cover.

**Master Comics** #21, © FAW. Captain Nazi's first appearance and part I of Captain Marvel Jr. trilogy origin.

**Whiz Comics** #25, © FAW. Part II of Captain Marvel Jr.'s origin.

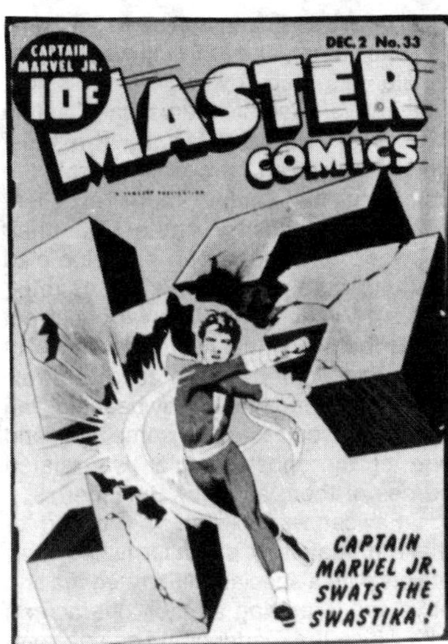


**Master Comics** #33, © FAW. One of the best swastika covers.

would defeat any super hero that America might send against him.

Captain Nazi possessed super powers except for the ability to fly (and he would acquire that power a little later in his career). Where he attained those powers was never revealed.

Captain Nazi's first stop in America was in *Master Comics* #21 where he began making a shambles of Bulletman's territory. However, Billy Batson just happened to be visiting the area, and one Shazam later, Captain Marvel himself joined Bulletman. The team proved too much for the super German agent and, as Captain Nazi fled, he threw out a challenge to Captain Marvel—"I'm headed for *Whiz Comics*. If you (C.M.) are brave enough, I'll be waiting."

Nazi arrived at *Whiz* just in time for the 25th issue (December 1941). Captain Marvel immediately proceeded to give him a good thrashing, the last blow of which sent the evil German far out and into a giant lake. An old man and his grandson in a fishing boat watched Captain Nazi hit the water, rushed to his aid, and dragged the villain into their small boat. As a reward for this kind act, Captain Nazi beat the old man to death with a boat oar and swatted the young boy into the lake. Captain Marvel spied the drowning lad and rushed him to a hospital, where he was informed that the boy, Freddy Freeman (a name symbolic for the times), had been mortally injured. Blaming himself, Captain Marvel took Freddy to his mentor, Old Shazam, and asked him to save the boy. Old Shazam not only saved Freddy, but gave him super powers similar to those of Captain Marvel.

The artist of Captain Marvel Jr. was Mac Raboy. Raboy was more of an illustrator rather than a strip artist, taking his inspiration from the likes of Alex Raymond whose comic strip, Flash Gordon, he would one day draw. Each panel of a Raboy comic strip was lovingly rendered in a posed format, making it stand out individually much like an illustration in a novel. Raboy's art is nothing short of breathtaking and is often reminiscent of near-photographic accuracy. Raboy's skill as a cover illustrator was rarely equaled.

The highly symbolic and colorful covers of *Master Comics* from the war years are the epitome of comic book patriotic/war covers. The most outstanding of these covers appeared on the following issues: #27 (V For Victory), #28 (Liberty Bell), #29 (Hitler and Hirohito), #30 (stunning flag cover), #32 (American eagle), #33 (the very best cover ever done using the swastika as a symbol), #34 (Captain Nazi), #36 (absolutely breathtaking Statue of Liberty cover), #40 (another fabulous flag cover), and #41 (tribute to the armed forces). Raboy covers on Captain Marvel Jr. are also worthy of note, including #4 (Jr. standing in front of a fiery shell burst), #11 (war theme), #13 (Hitler's football game), and #25 (with yet another outstanding flag cover).

Though Captain Marvel and Captain Marvel Jr. were by far the two most popular war years heroes at Fawcett, the company had many more excellent characters such as Minute Man (their answer to the red, white, and blue clad patriotic hero), Bulletman, Mr. Scarlet, Captain Midnight, Mary Marvel (check out her tribute to the wartime effort of American women on the cover to *Wow Comics* #11 and the equally beautiful flag cover on issue #15 of the same title), and one of the most popular war-related heroes of them all—Spy Smasher.

Fawcett was so filled with support for the war that they even furnished their buyers with a specially illustrated mailing envelope (featuring all their characters) with which the reader could supply comics to the troops overseas. Fawcett expended a great deal of patriotic effort yet established a line of strong titles and characters that would be successful long after the war.

Other companies that enjoyed various degrees of success during the war years were Holyoke, Prize, Harvey (the Green Hornet), Hillman (Airboy), Centaur, Ace, and Nedor/Better (the Black Terror, Fighting Yank). Fiction House, with their two publications *Wings* and *Fight*, proved that cheesecake could sell war comics. Actually, they proved that cheesecake could sell any title! Dell Comics, publisher of primarily comic strip reprint titles (such as *Popular, Super, Crackajack Funnies, Walt Disney Comics and Stories*) had its fair share of war theme covers.

During the early part of the war years, Dell even introduced two of the earliest war comics, both featuring original stories. *War Comics* had a four-issue run starting with #1 in May of 1940 and *War Heroes*, which appeared in 1942 and lasted 11 issues. Neither title was that successful, supporting evidence for the theory that war theme comics needed the pizazz of a costumed hero to be really successful. Dell did have some outstanding patriotic covers on their books, the best of which, surprisingly, appeared on their two funny animal titles, *Walt Disney's Comics & Stories* and *Looney Tunes*.

Quality Comics—and they were quality—introduced two extremely popular strips to comic book fans in the early '40s—Blackhawk in *Military Comics* and Plastic Man in *Police Comics*. When introduced in *Military* #1 in August of 1941, before America's official entry into the war, Blackhawk was a Polish freedom fighter. As a result of Hitler's atrocities to his country and family, he

**Captain Marvel Jr.** #4, © FAW. Classic Raboy cover art.

**Wow Comics** #15, © FAW. Patriotic flag cover.

**Military Comics** #21, © QUA. Crandall art in these issues are unbeatable.

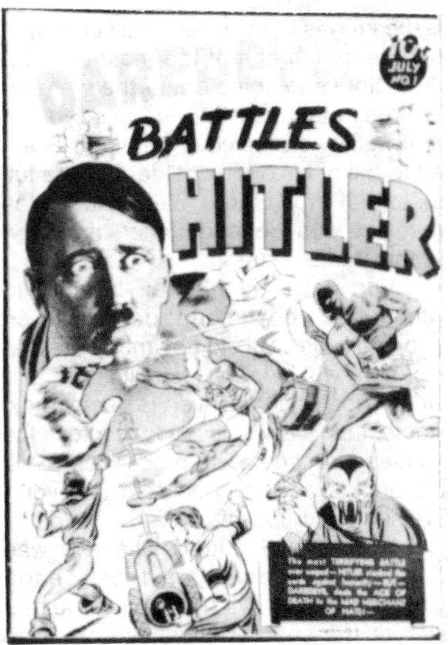


**Daredevil Battles Hitler** #1, © LEV. One of the best Hitler covers.

formed a band of international airfighters from various countries who were also victims of Nazi aggression. At a later date, Blackhawk's origin would be revised, giving him an American nationality. The exact number of team members that made up the early Blackhawks was not clear in the first few issues of *Military*, but soon stabilized at seven. The earliest adventures were drawn by Charles Cuidera, with inspiration and guidance from the great Will Eisner.

With issue #12, Reed Crandall took over and delivered some of the very best work done during the war. Crandall was a fantastic talent and his work on issues #12 through #22 of *Military Comics* are unbeatable! His attention to detail is amazing and his ability to illustrate women was unequaled during the war years.

The Lev Gleason Company published relatively few titles, but those they did publish were among the very best of the era. Their two most popular titles from the war years were *Daredevil* and *Boy Comics*. Daredevil's first issue was titled *Daredevil Battles Hitler* starring, once again, the mad man of Germany. After that first issue, *Daredevil Comics* was more like DC and Fawcett titles in that the character would do a mix of stories—some involving the war and some with other themes.

Daredevil, as well as Crime Buster (the lead feature in *Boy Comics*) tended to be a little more realistic and adult-oriented than their contemporaries. Even though the stories could, at times, prove to be extremely gruesome, they are still among the most original ever published.

Couple these beautifully crafted stories with the artistic virtuosity of Charles Biro, and the result was great reading! Biro was a premier Golden Age artist and very prolific, not only doing the work at Lev Gleason, but also doing covers and lead features at MLJ Comics.

As inspired as Biro's work may have been on the Daredevil stories, it paled when compared to his efforts on the Crimebuster strip in *Boy Comics*! *Boy Comics* started with issue #3 (the first two issues of the book had been called *Captain Battle*) dated April of 1942. It not only introduced Crimebuster and his pet monkey Winks, but also the most sinister and cruel World War II villain of all, Iron Jaw!

In issue #3, teenager Chuck Chandler's mother and father are destroyed by Hitler's ace agent, Iron Jaw. Iron Jaw was a fearful sight to behold. Crew-cut hair, snub nose, and a lower jaw replaced with a massive cast iron piece with two sets of serrated teeth. These DEADLY DENTURES were used primarily to tear out the throats of his enemies.

Hitler himself would be considered the only war villain more evil than Iron Jaw, and that would be questionable as issue #6 of *Boy Comics* would prove.

Issue #6 was the best single issue of that title, featuring one of the most outstanding stories to come out of the war era. The book featured the first appearance of Iron Jaw on the cover, then proceeded to tell of his origin inside. But the full extent of Iron Jaw's evil nature was revealed with the introduction of his son in this same issue.

Iron Jaw had his son brought to America to serve alongside him as an agent of Hitler. He did not anticipate that his son would soon forsake his and Hitler's ideals and convert to democracy. Rather than see his offspring embrace the causes of freedom, he proceeded to kill his own son! Strong content for World War II comic books!

Even though Chuck Chandler was the title character of those early Crimebuster tales, Iron Jaw was the real star of the show. Never, even in *Dick Tracy*, was there ever a villain more vile and contemptable! Fans and historians of the comic book's Golden Age suggest that he is second in villainy only to Batman's foe, the Joker. All the Crimebuster stories in *Boy Comics* #3 thru #15 were of above-average fare. #15 is worthy of special note because it contains the death (he came back) of Iron Jaw. Some of the truly graphic covers that should be noted in this same period are #5 (great war cover), #7 (flag and Hitler), #9 (classic Statue of Liberty/Iron Jaw piece), #10 (equally classic swastika/Iron Jaw cover), #12 (Japanese torturing American soldier) and #17 (a beautiful flag cover).

It would take a book rather than an article, to completely chronicle all the notable comic books published during World War II. Although this effort just begins to scratch the surface of this fascinating topic, it does permit a number of interesting conclusions to be drawn. First, nearly every comic book company of the time produced war covers and stories. Second, no other thematic idea was so readily embraced and so universally exploited by the comic book industry. Third, the nationalistic and patriotic effect of war theme comics, although inferred by many, will be a great challenge to future historians to conclusively prove. And fourth, although war comics were produced in conjunction with other wars, they never attained the extreme popularity of those published during World War II.

When comic books went to war half a century ago, they did so in a grand and glorious manner. How much patriotic fervor they developed among their young readers may never be accurately measured. What can be qualified, however, is the intense interest of collectors who will always strive to obtain these fascinating, gorgeous, and rare artifacts of the past—the comic books that went to war........!

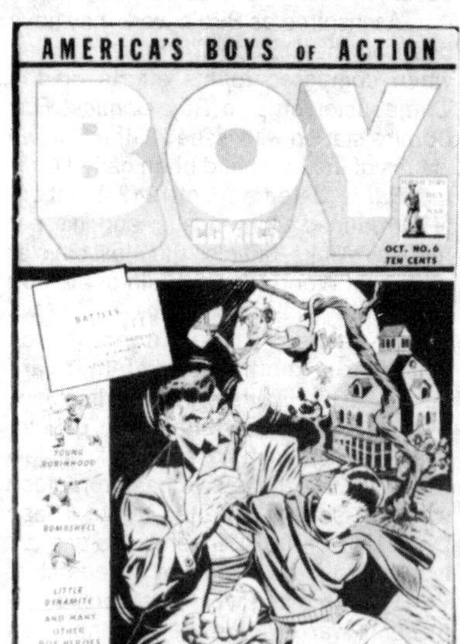


**Boy Comics** #6, © LEV. Origin and first appearance of Iron Jaw. Iron Jaw kills his son.

**Boy Comics** #11, © LEV. Classic Iron Jaw cover.

# DIRECTORY OF COMIC AND NOSTALGIA SHOPS

This is a current up-to-date list, but is not all-inclusive. We cannot assume any responsibility in your dealings with these shops. This list is provided for your information only. When planning your trips, it would be advisable to make appointments in advance. To get your shop included in the next edition, write for rates. Items stocked by these shops are listed just after the telephone numbers and are coded as follows:

(a) Golden Age comics
(b) Silver Age comics
(c) New comics, magazines
(d) Pulps
(e) Paperbacks
(f) Big Little Books
(g) Magazines (old)
(h) Books (old)
(i) Movie posters, lobby cards
(j) Original art
(k) Toys (old)
(l) Records (old)
(m) Gum trading cards
(n) Underground comics
(o) Video tapes
(p) Premiums
(q) Comic related posters
(r) Comic supplies
(s) Role playing games
(t) Star Trek items
(u) Dr. Who items
(v) Japanese animation items

## ALABAMA:

**Camelot Books**
2201 Quintard Avenue
Anniston, AL 36201
PH:205-236-3474 (a-v)

**Discount Comic Book Shop**
1301 Noble Street
Anniston, AL 36201
PH:205-238-8373 (a-c,e,m,q,r)

**Wizard's Comics & Cards**
324 N. Court Street
Florence, AL 35630
PH:205-236-3474
(a-c,e,g-k,m,n,q-v)

**Sincere Comics**
3738 Airport Blvd.
Mobile, AL 36608
PH:205-342-2603 (a-c,e,q-u)

## ARIZONA:

**FantaCity**
1600 McCulloch Blvd., Unit #4-1B
Lake Havasu City, AZ 86403
PH:602-680-4004 (a-c,g,j,p-s)

**Atomic Comics**
1318 West Southern #9
Mesa, AZ 85202
PH:602-649-0807
(a-g,i-k,m-o,q-v)

**Ed Kalb - Buy + Sell**
(Mail Order Only)
1353 S. Los Alamos
Mesa, AZ 85204
(a-g,m)

**AAA Best Comics, Etc.**
8336 N. Seventh St. Suite #B-C
Phoenix, AZ 85020
PH:602-997-4012 (b,c,m,q-s,v)

**Lost Dutchman Comics**
5805 N. 7th St.
Phoenix, AZ 85014
PH:602-263-5249 (a-c,e,g,i-n,q-u)

**All About Books & Comics**
517 E. Camelback
Phoenix, AZ 85012
PH:602-277-0757 (a-i,k,m-o,q-v)

**All About Books & Comics West**
4208 W. Dunlap
Phoenix, AZ 85051
PH:602-435-0410
(a-c,e,g,m,n,q-v)

**All About Books & Comics III**
4000 N. Scottsdale Rd. #102
Scottsdale, AZ 85251
PH:602-994-1812 (a-c,q-v)

**Planet Comics**
10219 N. Scottsdale Rd.
Scottsdale, AZ 85254
PH:602-991-1972
(a-c,g,i-k,m,n,q-v)

**The ONE Book Shop**
120-A East University Drive
Tempe, AZ 85281
PH:602-967-3551 (c,e,i,n,o,q-v)

## ARKANSAS:

**Paperbacks Plus**
2207 Rogers Avenue
Fort Smith, AR 72901
PH:501-785-5642 (a-c,e,h,m,q-s)

**The Comic Book Store**
9307 Treasure Hill
Little Rock, AR 72207
PH:501-227-9777 (a-c,e,o,q-v)

**Pie-Eyes**
5223 W. 65th St.
Little Rock, AR 72209
PH:501-568-1414 (a-u)

**Collector's Edition Comics**
5310 MacArthur Drive
North Little Rock, AR 72118
PH:501-753-2586 (a-c,e,o,q-v)

**TNT Collectors Hut**
503 W. Hale Ave.
Osceola, AR 72370
PH:501-563-5760 (c,m,r)

## CALIFORNIA:

**Comic Heaven**
24 W. Main Street
Alhambra, CA 91801
PH:818-289-3945 (a-c,g,j,q-t)

**Comic Relief**
2138 University Ave.
Berkeley, CA 94704
PH:415-843-5002 (a-d,f-h,j,n,q,r,v)

**Comics & Comix, Inc.**
2461 Telegraph Ave.
Berkeley, CA 94704
PH:415-845-4091

**Fantasy Kingdom**
1802 W. Olive Ave.
Burbank, CA 91506
PH:818-954-8432 (a-c,i,m,n,q,r,t-v)

**Book Castle**
200 N. San Fernando Blvd.
Burbank, CA 91502
PH:818-845-1563 (a,b,d,f-h,n)

**Movie World**
212 N. San Fernando Blvd.
Burbank, CA 91502
PH:818-846-0459 (i,o,t)

**Crush Comics & Cards**
2785 Castro Valley Blvd.
Castro Valley, CA 94546
PH:415-581-4779 (a-c,g,k,m,n,q,r)

**Collectors Ink**
932 W. 8th Ave.
Chico, CA 95926
PH:916-345-0958 (a-c,g,m,o,q,r,t)

**New Age Comics**
225 Main St.
Chico, CA 95928
PH:916-898-0550 (c,m-s,v)

**Comics & Comix, Inc.**
6135 Sunrise Blvd.
Citrus Heights, CA 95610
PH:916-969-0717

**Superior Comics**
1630 Superior Ave.
Costa Mesa, CA 92627
PH:714-631-3933 (a-k,m-o,q-t,v)

**Graphitti Comics & Games**
4325 Overland Ave.
Culver City, CA 90230
PH:213-559-2058 (b,c,n,q-s)

**Comic Quest**
24344 Muirlands Blvd.
El Toro, CA 92630
PH:714-951-9668 (a-c,m-o,q-s,v)

**Comic Gallery**
675 N. Broadway
Escondido, CA 92025
PH:619-745-5660 (a-c,j,m,n,q-t,v)

**The Comic Castle**
330 - 5th Street
Eureka, CA 95501
PH:707-444-2665 (c,n,q)

**Comics & Comix, Inc**
1350 Travis Blvd.
Fairfield, CA 94533
PH:707-427-1202

**Adventureland Comics**
106 N. Harbor Blvd.
Fullerton, CA 92632
PH:714-738-3698 (a-c,q,r,t,v)

**Fantasy Illustrated**
12553 Harbor Blvd.
Garden Grove, CA 92640
PH:714-537-0087 (a-g,j,r)

**Geoffrey's Comics**
15530 Crenshaw Blvd.
Gardena, CA 90249
PH:213-538-3198
(a,c,g,j,m-o,q-s,v)

**Bud Plant Comic Art**
13393 Grass Valley Ave. #7
P. O. Box 1689
Grass Valley, CA 95945
PH:916-273-2166 (c,h,n,o,q,r,v)

**Comic Grapevine**
22 W. Lodi Ave.
Lodi, CA 95240
PH:209-368-1096 (a-c,m,n,q-t,v)

**The American Comic Book Co.**
3972 Atlantic Ave.
Long Beach, CA 90807
PH:213-426-0393 (a-f,j,m,n)

**Cheap Comics - 2**
7779 Melrose Ave.
Los Angeles, CA 90046
PH:213-655-9323 (a-d,g,i,k,m-v)

**Golden Apple Comics**
7711 Melrose Ave.
Los Angeles, CA 90046
PH:213-658-6047 (a-c,e,m-o,q,r,u)

**Golden Apple Comics**
8934 West Pico Blvd.
Los Angeles, CA 90034
PH:213-274-2008 (c,m-o,q-s,v)

**Graphitti-Westwood—UCLA**
960 Gayley Ave.
Los Angeles, CA 90024
PH:213-824-3656 (a-c,g-i,m,n,q-t)

**Pacific Comic Exchange, Inc.**
(By Appointment Only)
P. O. Box 34849
Los Angeles, CA 90034
PH:213-836-PCEI (a,b)

**WonderWorld Comic Books + Baseball Cards**
1579 El Camino
Millbrae, CA 94030
PH:415-871-2674 (a-c,g,j,m,n,q,r)

**Comic Pendragon**
73 N. Milpitas Blvd.
Milpitas, CA 95035
PH:408-942-6903 (a-h,m,q,r)

**Bonanza Books & Comics**
Roseburg Square Center
813 W. Roseburg Avenue
Modesto, CA 95350-5058
PH:209-529-0415 (a-e,h,i,m,q-u)

**Ninth Nebula: The Comic Book Store**
11517 Burbank Blvd.
North Hollywood, CA 91601
PH:818-509-2901 (a-v)

**Golden Apple Comics**
8962 Reseda Blvd.
Northridge, CA 91324
PH:818-993-7804 (a-c,e,l-o,q,r,v)

**Freedonia Funnyworks**
350 S. Tustin Ave.
Orange, CA 92666
PH:714-639-5830 (a-c,e-j,m-t,v)

**Desert Comics**
406 N. Palm Canyon Dr.
Palm Springs, CA 92262
PH:619-325-5805 (c,m,r-t)

**Comics & Comix, Inc.**
405 California Ave.
Palo Alto, CA 94306
PH:415-328-8100

**Lee's Comics**
3783 El Camino Real
Palo Alto, CA 94306
PH:415-493-3957 (a-g,m-o,q-v)

**Bud Plant Illustrated Books**
c/o Jim Vadeboncoeur, Jr.
3809 Laguna Ave.
Palo Alto, CA 94306
PH:415-493-1191 (evenings, weekends) (g,h)

**Galaxy Comics & Cards**
1503 Aviation Blvd.
Redondo Beach, CA 90278
PH:213-374-7440 (a,m,o,v)

**Comics & Comix, Inc.**
921 K Street
Sacramento, CA 95814
PH:916-442-5142

**Comic Gallery**
4224 Balboa Ave.
San Diego, CA 92117
PH:619-483-4853 (a-c,j,m,n,q-t,v)

**Comics & Comix, Inc.**
650 Irving
San Francisco, CA 94122
PH:415-665-5888

**Comics & Comix, Inc.**
700 Lombard Street
San Francisco, CA 94133
PH:415-982-3511

**Comics and Da-Kind**
1643 Noriega St.
San Francisco, CA 94122
PH:415-753-9678 (a-c,m,q,r)

**The Funny Papers**
7253 Geary Blvd.
San Francisco, CA 94121
PH:415-752-1914
(a-d,f,g,j,k,m,o,q-t)

**Gary's Corner Bookstore**
1051 San Gabriel Blvd.
San Gabriel, CA 91776
PH:818-285-7575 (b,c,e,m,q,r,t,v)

**Comics Pendragon I**
1189 Branham Lane
San Jose, CA 95118
PH:408-265-3233 (a-c,e-g,m-v)

**Bob Sidebottom's Comic Collector Shop**
73 E. San Fernando
San Jose, CA 95113
PH:408-287-2254 (a-g,i,l,n,o,r)

**The Comic Shop**
2164 E. 14th Street
San Leandro, CA 94577
PH:415-483-0205 (a-c,g,m,q-s)

**Lee's Comics**
2222 El Camino Real
San Mateo, CA 94003
PH:415-571-1489 (a-g,m-o,q-v)

**San Mateo Comic Books, Baseball Cards, & Original Art**
106 South B Street
San Mateo, CA 94401
PH:415-344-1536 (a-c,g,j,m,n,q,r)

**Brian's Books**
2767 El Camino
Santa Clara, CA 95051
PH:408-985-7481 (a-h,m,n,q,r)

**R & K Comics**
3153 El Camino Real
Santa Clara, CA 95051
PH:408-554-6512 (a-c,g,k,n,o,q-v)

**Atlantis Fantasyworld**
610 F Cedar Street
Santa Cruz, CA 95060
PH:408-426-0158 (a-c,g,n,q-t)

**Hi De Ho Comics & Fantasy**
525 Santa Monica Blvd.
Santa Monica, CA 90401
PH:213-394-2820 (a-j,m-o,q-v)

**Superior Comics**
220 Pier Ave.
Santa Monica, CA 90405
PH:213-396-7005 (a-c,g,j,m,n,q,t)

**Forbidden Planet**
14513 Ventura Blvd.
Sherman Oaks, CA 91403
PH:818-995-0151 (a-c,e,g,i-k,n-v)

**Superhero Universe VIII**
Sycamore Plaza
2955-A5 Cochran St.
Simi Valley, CA 93065
PH:805-583-3027 & 800-252-9997
(a-c,e-v)

**Cheap Comics - 1**
12123 Garfield Ave.
South Gate, CA 90280
PH:213-408-0900 (a-d,g,i,k,m-v)

**Altered Images**
12661 Beach Blvd.
Stanton, CA 90680
PH:714-373-9922 (c,q,r)

**Grapevine Comics & Cards**
9321-C N. Thornton Rd.
Stockton, CA 95209
PH:209-952-9303 (a-c,m,n,q-t,v)

**Graphitti Studio City**
12080 Ventura Pl., No. 3
Studio City, CA 91604
PH:818-980-4976 (a-h,i-n,q-t,v)

**Superhero Universe IV**
18722 Ventura Blvd.
Tarzana, CA 93156
PH:818-774-0969 (a-c,e-v)

**Pantechnicon**
1165 E. Thousand Oaks Blvd.
Thousand Oaks, CA 91360
PH:805-495-0299 (a-j,m,n,q-v)

**J & K Comics and Toys**
3535 Torrance Blvd., Suite 9
Torrance, CA 90503
PH:213-540-9685 (a-h,k-m,o-v)

**Roleplayers**
5933 Adobe Rd.
29 Palms, CA 92277
PH:619-367-6282 (c,m-o,q-t,v)

**Hi De Ho Comics & Fantasy**
64 Windward Ave.
Venice, CA 90291
PH:213-399-6206 (a-j,m-o,q-v)

**Ralph's Comic Corner**
2377 E. Main St.
Ventura, CA 93003
PH:805-653-2732 (a-f,m,n,q-t)

**The Second Time Around**
391 E. Main St.
Ventura, CA 93003
PH:805-643-3154 (a,b,d,e,g,i,r,t)

**Graphitti - South Bay!**
Airport/Marina Hotel (Rear)
8639 Lincoln Blvd., No. 102
Westchester, L. A., CA 90045
PH:213-641-8661
(b,c,e,g,h,m,n,q-s)

## COLORADO:

**Colorado Comic Book Co.**
220 N. Tejon St.
Colorado Springs, CO 80903
PH:719-635-2516
(a-c,e,n,q-u)

**Heroes & Dragons**
The Citadel #2158
Colorado Springs, CO 80909
PH:719-550-9570 (b,c,e,o,q-v)

## CONNECTICUT:

**A Timeless Journey**
402 Elm Street
Stamford, CT 06902
PH:203-353-1720 (a-h,j,k,m-r,t-v)

## FLORIDA:

**Phil's Comic Shoppe**
7778 Wiles Rd.
Coral Springs, FL 33067
PH:305-752-4514 (b,c,m,q,r)

**Cliff's Books**
209 N. Woodland Blvd. (17-92)
De Land, FL 32720
PH:904-734-6963 (a-f,h,j-v)

**Family Book Shop**
1301 N Woodland Blvd.
De Land, FL 32720
PH:904-736-6501 (b,c,e,g,h,m,r)

**Novel Ideas**
804 West University Ave.
Gainesville, FL 32601
PH:904-374-8593 (b,c,e,n,q-s)

**Novel Ideas**
3206 S.W. 35th Blvd.
Butler Plaza
Gainesville, FL 32608
PH:904-377-2694 (c,e,r,s)

**Comics U.S.A.**
5883 Lake Worth Rd.
Greenacres City, FL 33463
PH:407-433-9111 (a-g,j,k,m,q-t)

**Charlie's Comics & Games**
1255 West 46th Street #26
Hialeah, FL 33012
PH:305-557-5994 (a-c,n,q-s,u,v)

**Mark's Comics/Louie's Baseball Cards**
1678 B Ridgewood Ave.
Holly Hills, FL 32117
PH:904-676-7464 (a-u)

**Adventure Into Comics**
3863 Lake Emma Rd.
Lake Mary, FL 32746
PH:407-333-9353 (a-c,e,g,i,k,m-u)

**Past—Present—Future Comics**
6186 S. Congress Ave., Suite A4
Lantana, FL 33462
PH:407-433-3068 (b,c,q-s,v)

**Phil's Comic Shoppe**
614 S. State Rd. 7
Margate, FL 33068
PH:305-977-6947 (b-d,m,n,q,r)

**Comic Warehouse, Inc.**
1029 Airport Rd. N., #B-6
Naples, FL 33942
PH:813-643-1020 (b,c,e,j,m,o,q-v)

**Tropic Comics South, Inc.**
742 N.E. 167th St.
N. Miami Beach, FL 33162
PH:305-940-8700 (a-d,j,n,r,v)

**Adventure Into Comics**
841 Bennett Rd.
Orlando, FL 32803
PH:407-896-4047 (a-c,e,g,i,k,m-u)

**Cartoon Museum**
4300 S. Semoran, Suite 109
Orlando, FL 32822
PH:407-273-0141 (a-k,m,n,p-r)

**Enterprise 1701**
2814 Corrine Drive
Orlando, FL 32803
PH:407-896-1701 (c,e,g,j,n,o,q-v)

**Past—Present—Future Comics North**
4270 Northlake Blvd.
Palm Beach Gardens, FL 33410
PH:407-775-2141 (b,c,q-s)

**Sincere Comics**
3300 N. Pace Blvd.
Pensacola, FL 32505
PH:904-432-1352 (a-c,e,q-u)

**Tropic Comics**
313 S. State Road 7
Plantation, FL 33317
PH:305-587-8878 (a-d,j,n,q,r,v)

**Comics U.S.A.**
3231 N. Federal Highway
Pompano Beach, FL 33064
PH:305-942-1455 (a-g,j,k,m,q-t)

**New England Comics**
Northdale Court
15836 N. Dale Mabry Highway
Tampa, FL 33618
PH:813-264-1848 (a-c,m,q-v)

**Tropic Comics North, Inc.**
1018 - 21st St. (U.S. 1)
Vero Beach, FL 32960
PH:407-562-8501 (a-c,j,n,q-s)

## GEORGIA:

**Titan Games & Comics, Inc.**
5439 Riverdale Rd.
College Park, GA 30349
PH:404-996-9129 (a-c,g,n,o,q-u)

**Titan Games & Comics IV**
2131 Pleasant Hill Rd.
Duluth, GA 30136
PH:404-497-0202 (a-c,g,n,o,q-u)

**The Comic Company, Ltd.**
3320 D Thompson Bridge Rd. NE
Gainesville, GA 30506
PH:404-536-4340 (a-c,m,n,p-s)

**Showcase Collectibles**
(By Appointment)
P. O. Box 921185
Norcross, GA 30092
PH:404-594-0074 (a,b,i,j)

**Fischer's Book Store**
6569 Riverdale Road
Riverdale, GA 30274
PH:404-997-7323 (b,c,e,q,r)

**Titan Games & Comics III**
2585 Spring Rd.
Smyrna, GA 30080
PH:404-433-8226 (a-c,g,n,o,q-u)

**Titan Games & Comics II**
3853C Lawrenceville Hwy.
Tucker, GA 30084
PH:404-491-8067 (a-c,g,n,o,q-u)

## HAWAII:

**Compleat Comics Company**
1728 Kaahumanu Avenue
Wailuku, Maui, HI 96793
PH:808-242-5875 (b,c,n,q-s)

## IDAHO:

**King's Komix Kastle**
1706 N. 18th St. (appointments)
Boise, ID 83702
PH:208-343-7142 (a-i,m,n,q,r)

**King's Komix Kastle II**
2560 Leadville (drop in)
Mail: 1706 N. 18th
Boise, ID 83702
PH:208-343-7055 (a-i,m,n,q,r)

**New Mythology Comics & Science Fiction**
1725 Broadway
Boise, ID 83706
PH:208-344-6744 (a-c,e,n,q-t)

## ILLINOIS:

**Friendly Frank's Distribution**
(Wholesale Only)
727 Factory Rd.
Addison, IL 60101

**Friendly Frank's Comics**
11941 S Cicero
Alsip, IL 60658
PH:312-371-6760 (a-d,f,g,i,j,n,q,r)

**All-American Comic Shops 3**
9118 Ogden Ave.
Brookfield, IL 60513
PH:708-387-9588 (a-c,e,j,m,q,r)

**Moondog's Comicland**
1231 W. Dundee Rd.
Plaza Verde
Buffalo Grove, IL 60090
PH:708-259-6060 (a-c,e,m,o,q-v)

**AF Books**
1856 Sibley Blvd.
Calumet City, IL 60409
PH:708-891-2260 (a-c,e,q-s)

**All-American Comic Shops 6**
6457 W. Archer Ave.
Chicago, IL 60638
PH:312-586-5090 (a-c,e,j,m,q,r)

**Comics for Heroes**
1702 W. Foster
Chicago, IL 60640
PH:312-769-4745 (a-c,m,n,q-v)

**Larry's Comic Book Store**
1219 W. Devon Ave.
Chicago, IL 60660
PH:312-274-1832 (a-c,r,u,v)

**Larry Laws** (by appointment only)
(Call First)
831 Cornelia
Chicago, IL 60657
PH:312-477-9247 (e,g,h,m,o)

**Mikes on Mars**
(An All-American Affiliate 7)
1753 W. 69th St.
Chicago, IL 60637
PH:312-778-6990 (a-c,e,j,m,q,r)

**Moondog's Comicland**
2301 N. Clark St.
Chicago, IL 60614
PH:312-248-6060 (a-c,e,m,o,q-v)

**Joe Sarno's Comic Kingdom**
5941 W. Irving Park Rd.
Chicago, IL 60634
PH:312-545-2231 (a-d,j,m,r)

**Yesterday**
1143 W. Addison St.
Chicago, IL 60613
PH:312-248-8087 (a,b,d-g,i-n,r,t)

**All-American Comic Shops 5**
1701 N. Larkin Ave.
Hillcrest Shopping Center
Crest Hill, IL 60435
PH:815-744-2094 (a-c,e,j,m,q,r)

**Moondog's Comicland**
114 S. Waukegan Rd.
Deerbrook Mall
Deerfield, IL 60015
PH:708-272-6080 (a-c,e,m,o,q-v)

**The Paper Escape**
205 W. First Street
Dixon, IL 61021
PH:815-284-7567 (b,c,e,g,m,q-t)

**Graham Crackers Comics**
5228 S. Main St.
Downers Grove, IL 60515
PH:708-852-1810 (c,q-s,v)

**GEM Comics**
156 N. York Rd.
Elmhurst, IL 60126
PH:708-833-8787 (b,c,q-s)

**All-American Comic Shops, Ltd.**
3514 W. 95th St.
Evergreen Park, IL 60642
PH:708-425-7555 (a-c,e,j,m,q,r)

**Galaxy of Books**
Rt 137 & Sheridan
CNW Great Lakes Train Station
Great Lakes, IL 60064
PH:708-473-1099 (b,c,e,q-s)

**Moondog's Comicland**
139 W. Prospect Ave.
Mt. Prospect, IL 60056
PH:708-398-6060 (a-c,e,m,o,q-v)

**Moondog's Comicland**
Randhurst Shopping Center
Mt. Prospect, IL 60056
PH:708-577-8668 (c,e,m,o,q-v)

**Graham Cracker Comics**
5 E. Chicago Ave.
Naperville, IL 60540
PH:708-355-4310 (b,c,n,o,q-s,v)

**All-American Comic Shops 2**
14620 S. LaGrange Rd.
Orland Park, IL 60462
PH:708-460-5556 (a-c,e,j,m,q,r)

**All-American Comic Shops 4**
22305 S. Central Park Ave.
Park Forest, IL 60466
PH:708-748-2509 (a-c,e,j,m,q,r)

**Tomorrow Is Yesterday**
5600 N. 2nd St.
Rockford, IL 61111
PH:815-633-0330 (a-j,m-o,q-v)

**Moondog's Comicland**
1455 W. Schaumburg Rd.
Schaumburg Plaza
Schaumburg, IL 60194
PH:708-529-6060 (a-c,e,m,o,q-v)

**Family Book**
3123 S. Dirksen Pkwy
Springfield, IL 62703
PH:217-529-1709 (a-c,e,r,s)

**Unicorn Comics & Cards**
216 S. Villa Ave.
Villa Park, IL 60181
PH:708-279-5777
(a-c,e,g,h,j,l-n,q-s)

**Kane's Comics & Collectibles**
749 W. Dundee Rd.
Wheeling, IL 60090
PH:708-808-8877 (b-g,j,m-o,q,r,v)

**Heroland Comics**
6963 W. 11th St.
Worth, IL 60482
PH:708-448-2937 (a-e,i-s)

**Galaxy of Books**
1908 Sheridan Rd.
Zion, IL 60099
PH:708-872-3313 (b,c,e,f,h,i,q,r)

## INDIANA:

**Pen Comics & Entertainment Store**
501 Main St.
Beech Grove, IN 46107
PH:317-782-3450 (a-d,f,i,j,k,n,q-v)

**Comics Cave**
1089 North National Rd.
Columbus, IN 47201
PH:812-372-8430 (a-d,f,i,j,k,n,q-v)

**The Bookstack**
112 W. Lexington Ave.
Elkhart, IN 46516
PH:219-293-3815 (a-c,e,h,k,l,r,s,t)

**The Book Broker**
2127 S. Weinbach (Fairlawn Ctr.)
Evansville, IN 47714
PH:812-479-5647 (a-c,e-h,l-o,q-t)

**Broadway Comics**
2423 Broadway
Fort Wayne, IN 46807
PH:219-744-1456 (a-c,f,g,m,n,q-u)

**Friendly Frank's Distr., Inc.**
(Wholesale Only)
3990 Broadway
Gary, IN 46408
PH:219-884-5052 (c,g,n,r,s)

**Friendly Frank's Comics**
220 Main Street
Hobart, IN 46342
PH:219-942-6020 (a-d,f,g,i,j,n,q,r)

**Blue Moon Comics & Games**
8336 E. West 10th St.
Indianapolis, IN 46234
PH:317-271-1479 (b,c,g,m,n,q-v)

**Cartoon Carnival & Nostalgia Emporium**
7311 U.S. 31 South
Indianapolis, IN 46227
PH:317-889-8899 (a-j,m-u)

**Comic Carnival & Nostalgia Emporium**
6265 N. Carrollton Ave.
Indianapolis, IN 46220
PH:317-253-8882 (a-j,m-u)

**Comic Carnival & Nostalgia Emporium**
5002 S. Madison Ave.
Indianapolis, IN 46227
PH:317-787-3773 (a-j,m-u)

**Comic Carnival & Nostalgia Emporium**
982 N. Mitthoeffer Rd.
Indianapolis, IN 46229
PH:317-898-5010 (a-j,m-u)

**Comic Carnival & Nostalgia Emporium**
3837 N. High School Rd.
Indianapolis, IN 46254
PH:317-293-4386 (a-j,m-u)

**John's Comic Closet**
4610 East 10th Street
Indianapolis, IN 46201
PH:317-357-6611
(b,c,g,i,j,m,n,q-v)

**Galactic Greg's**
1407 Lincolnway
Valparaiso, IN 46383
PH:219-464-0119 (a-c,e,m,n,q-s)

## IOWA:

**Mayhem Collectibles**
2532 Lincoln Way
Ames, IA 50010
PH:515-292-3510 (a-c,i,j,m,o,q-v)

**Oak Leaf Comics**
5219 University Ave.
Cedar Falls, IA 50428
PH:319-277-1835 (b,c,k,m,n,q-v)

**Comic World & Baseball Cards**
1626 Central Ave.
Dubuque, IA 52001
PH:319-557-1897
(a-c,g,h,m,n,q-u)

**Oak Leaf Comics**
23 - 5th S.W.
Mason City, IA 50401
PH:515-424-0333 (a-c,f,i-v)

**The Comiclogue**
520 Elm St.
P.O. Box 65304 (mail only)
West Des Moines, IA 50265
PH:515-279-9006 (a-c,n-r,u)

## KANSAS:

**Kwality Books, Comics, & Games**
1111 Massachusetts Street
Lawrence, KS 66044
PH:913-843-7239 (a-c,e,i,q,u)

**1,000,000 Comix Inc.**
5332 West 95th St.
Prairie Village, KS 66207
PH:913-383-1777
(a-d,f-h,j,m,n,p-v)

**Air Capital Comics & Games**
954 S. Oliver
Wichita, KS 67218
PH:316-681-0219 (a-h,j,k,m-v)

**Air Capital Comics & Games**
601 N West St. Suite #202
Wichita, KS 67203
PH:316-942-6642 (a-h,j,k,m-v)

**Prairie Dog Comics East**
Oxford Square Mall
6100 E. 21st St., Suite 190
Wichita, KS 67208
PH:316-688-5576 (a-n,p-s)

**Prairie Dog Comics West**
Maple Ridge Mall
7130 W Maple Suite 240
Wichita, KS 67209
PH:316-942-3456 (a-v)

## KENTUCKY:

**Pac-Rat's, Inc.**
1051 Bryant Way
Greenwood Station S/C
Bowling Green, KY 42103
PH:502-782-8092 (a-d,l,n,o,q-v)

**Comic Book World**
7130 Turfway Road
Florence, KY 41042
PH:606-371-9562 (a-c,m,o,q-v)

**The Great Escape**
2433 Bardstown Road
Louisville, KY 40205
PH:502-456-2216 (a-c,e,i,j,l-o,q-v)

## LOUISIANA:

**B.T. & W.D. Giles**
P. O. Box 271
Keithville, LA 71047
PH:318-925-6654 (a,b,d-f,h)

**Bookworm of N.O.E.**
7011 Read Blvd.
New Orleans, LA 70127
PH:504-242-7608 (a-c,e,g,m,q,r)

## MAINE:

**Lippincott Books**
624 Hammond St.
Bangor, ME 04401
PH:207-942-4398
(a,b,d-h,n,p,r,t,u)

**Moonshadow Comics**
357 Maine Mall Road
South Portland, ME 04106
PH:207-772-4605
(a-c,e,g,i,m-o,q-u)

**Book Barn**
U.S. Rt 1, P. O. Box 557
Wells, ME 04090
PH:207-646-4926 (a,b,e,h,m,r)

## MARYLAND:

**Universal Comics**
5300 East Dr.
Arbutus, MD 21227
PH:301-242-4578
(a-c,e,g,k,m,n,q,r,t)

**Comic Book Kingdom, Inc.**
4307 Harford Road
Baltimore, MD 21214
PH:301-426-4529 (a-h,i,k,m,q,r,t)

**Geppi's Comic World**
7019 Security Blvd.
Hechinger's Square at Security Mall
Baltimore, MD 21207
PH:301-298-1758 (a-c,f)

**Geppi's Comic World**
Upper Level, Light St. Pavillion
301 Light Street
Baltimore, MD 21202
PH:301-547-0910 (a-c,f)

**Big Planet Comics**
4865 Cordell Ave.
Bethesda, MD 20814
PH:301-654-6856 (c,j,n,q,r)

**The Magic Page**
7416 Laurel-Bowie Rd. (Rt. 197)
Bowie, MD 20715
PH:301-262-4735 (b,c,e,m,q,s-v)

**Alternate Worlds**
9924 York Road
Cockeysville, MD 21030
PH:301-667-0440
(b,c,e,g,k,m-o,q-v)

**The Closet of Comics**
7319 Baltimore Ave. (U.S. 1)
College Park, MD 20740
PH:301-699-0498 (a-c,e,g,i,m,n,r)

**Comic Classics**
203 E. Main St.
Frostburg, MD 21532
PH:301-689-1823 (a-c,e,m-o,q-v)

**Comic Classics**
365 Main Street
Laurel, MD 20707
PH:301-792-4744, 490-9811
(a-c,e,m-o,q-v)

**Zenith Comics & Collectibles**
18200 Georgia Ave.
Olney, MD 20832
PH:301-774-1345 (b,c,m,q-u)

**The Closet of Comics**
Calvert Village Shopping Center
Prince Frederick, MD 20678
PH:301-535-4731 (b-d,e,g,i,m,n,r)

**Geppi's Comic World**
8317 Fenton St.
Silver Spring, MD 20910
PH:301-588-2546 (a-c,e,f)

**Barbarian Bookshop**
11254 Triangle Lane
Wheaton, MD 20902
PH:301-946-4184
(a-c,e,f,h,m-o,q-v)

## MASSACHUSETTS:

**New England Comics**
168 Harvard Ave.
Allston (Boston), MA 02134
PH:617-783-1848 (a-c,m,n,q-v)

**Comically Speaking**
1322 Mass. Ave.
Arlington, MA 02174
PH:617-643-XMEN
(a-c,f,m,n,q-t,v)

**Bargain Books and Collectibles**
247 So. Main St.
Attleboro, MA 02703
PH:508-226-1668 (b,c,k,m,q,r)

**Superhero Universe III**
41 West Street
Boston, MA 02111
PH:617-423-6676 (a-c,e-v)

**New England Comics**
748 Crescent Street
East Crossing Plaza
Brockton, MA 02402
PH:508-559-5068 (a-c,m,q-v)

**New England Comics**
316 Harvard St.
Brookline, MA 02146
PH:617-566-0115 (a-c,m,n,q-v)

**Superhero Universe I**
1105 Massachusetts Ave.
Cambridge, MA 02138
PH:617-354-5344 (a-c,e-v)

**World of Fantasy**
529 Broadway
Everett, MA 02149
PH:617-381-0411
(a-c,e,g-k,m-o,q-v)

**That's Entertainment**
387 Main St.
Fitchburg, MA 01420
PH:508-342-8607 (a-h,j-o,q-v)

**Bop City Comics**
80 Worcester Road
Marshalls Mall
Framingham, MA 01701
PH:508-872-2317

**Ernie's Bookland**
143 Central St. Downtown Lowell
Lowell, MA 01854
PH:508-453-0445 (c,e,g,h,i)

**New England Comics**
12A Pleasant St.
Malden, MA 02148
PH:617-322-2404 (a-c,m,q-v)

**Buddy's**
(Wholesale, Subscription Service)
P. O. Box 4
Medford, MA 02155
PH:617-322-5731 (b,c)

**New England Comics**
732 Washington Street
Norwood, MA 02062
PH:617-769-4552 (a-c,m,q-v)

**Imagine That Bookstore**
58 Dalton Ave.
Pittsfield, MA 01201
PH:413-445-5934 (a-i,l-o,q-u)

**New England Comics**
11 Court Street
Plymouth, MA 02360
PH:508-746-8797 (a-c,m,q-v)

**New England Comics**
1350 Hancock Street
Quincy, MA 02169
PH:617-770-1848 (a-c,m,q-v)

**Park Nostalgia**
1242 Wilbur Avenue
Somerset, MA 02725
PH:508-673-0303 (b,c,g,m,r)

**The Outer Limits**
457 Moody St.
Waltham, MA 02154
PH:617-891-0444 (a-h,k,m-o,q-v)

**Mayo Beach Bookstore**
Kendrick Ave., Mayo Beach
Wellfleet, MA 02667
PH:508-349-3154 (a-i)

**Fabulous Fiction Book Store**
984 Main St.
Worcester, MA 01603
PH:508-754-8826 (a-h,o,q-v)

**That's Entertainment**
151 Chandler Street
Worcester, MA 01609
PH:508-755-4207 (a-h,j-o,q-v)

## MICHIGAN

**Tom & Terry Comics**
508 Layfayette Ave.
Bay City, MI 48708
PH:517-895-5525 (b,c,e,m,o,q,r,t)

**Curious Book Shop**
307 E Grand River Ave.
East Lansing, MI 48823
PH:517-332-0112 (a-k,m-p)

**Amazing Book Store, Inc.**
3718 Richfield Rd.
Flint, MI 48506
PH:313-736-3025 (a-c,r)

**Argos Book Shop**
1405 Robinson Rd. SE
Grand Rapids, MI 49506
PH:616-454-0111 (a-h,m,n)

**Tardy's Collectors Corner, Inc.**
2009 Eastern Ave. SE
Grand Rapids, MI 49507
PH:616-247-7828 (a-c,f,g,m,n,q,r)

**Book Stop**
1160 Chicago Drive SW
Wyoming, MI 49509-1004
PH:616-245-0090
(a-c,e,g,m-o,q,r,t)

## MINNESOTA:

**Collector's Connection**
21 East Superior Street
Duluth, MN 55802-2088
PH:218-722-9551 (b,c,m,r,s)

**College of Comic Book Knowledge**
3151 Hennepin Ave. S.
Minneapolis, MN 55408
PH:612-822-2309
(a-c,e-i,k-n,p-r,t-v)

**Midway Book & Comic**
1579 University Ave.
St. Paul, MN 55104
PH:612-644-7605 (a-h,n,o,q-u)

## MISSISSIPI:

**Diversions**
1670K Pass Rd.
Biloxi, MS 39531
PH:601-374-6632
(a-c,e,g-i,k-o,q-v)

**Star Store**
4212 N. State Street
Jackson, MS 39206
PH:601-362-8001 (a-v)

**Spanish Trail Books**
1006 Thorn Ave.
Ocean Springs, MS 39564
PH:601-875-1144 (a,b,d-h)

## MISSOURI:

**B & R Comix Center**
4747 Morganford
St. Louis, MO 63116
PH:314-353-4013 (a-c,g,j,n,q,r)

**Mo's Comics and Stories**
4530 Gravois
St. Louis, MO 63116
PH:314-353-9500 (a-d,f,p-r)

**The Book Rack**
300 W. Olive
Springfield, MO 65806
PH:417-865-4945 (b-e,h,q-s)

## MONTANA:

**The Book Exchange**
2335 Brooks
Trempers Shopping Center
Missoula, MT 59801
PH:406-728-6342 (a-h,n,q-t)

## NEBRASKA:

**Star Realm**
7305 South 85th St.
Omaha, NE 68128
PH:402-331-4844 (c,e,i,m,o,q-u)

## NEVADA:

**Fandom's Comicworld of Reno**
2001 East Second St.
Reno, NV 89502
PH:702-786-6663 (a-c,j,q,r)

## NEW HAMPSHIRE:

**James F. Payette**
P. O. Box 750
Bethlehem, NH 03574
PH:603-869-2097 (a,b,d-h)

## NEW JERSEY:

**A & S Comics & Cards III**
67 South Washington Ave.
Bergenfield, NJ 07621
PH:201-384-2307 (b,m,q-s)

**The Comic Zone**
71 Rt. 73 & Day Ave.
Berlin, NJ 08009
PH:609-768-8186 (b,c,g,h,m,n,q-s)

**Fantasy Factory Comics**
Harbortowne Plaza
Tilton Rd. & Black Horse Pike
Cardiff, NJ 08232
PH:609-641-0025 (b,c,o,q-s)

**Time Warp Comics & Games**
584 Pompton Ave.
Cedar Grove, NJ 07009
PH:201-857-9788 (b,c,m-o,q-s,u,v)

**Rainbow Comics**
Laurel Hill Plaza
Clementon, NJ 08021
PH:609-627-1711 (a-c,f,g,m,r)

**1,000,000 Comix, Inc.**
629 Palisade Ave.
Cliffside Park, NJ 07010
PH:201-313-0373
(a-d,f-h,j,m,n,p-v)

**Steve's Comic Relief**
1555 St. George Ave.
Colonia, NJ 07067
PH:908-382-3736 (a-c,j,n,q,r,t-v)

**Steve's Comic Relief**
24 Mill Run Plaza
Delran, NJ 08075
PH:609-461-1770 (a-c,j,n,q,r,t-v)

**Ron's Gallery of Collectibles**
2177 Woodbridge Ave.
Edison, NJ 08817
PH:201-985-9210 (a-c,g,k-m,r,s)

**Collector's Center, Inc.**
729 Edgar Rd.
Elizabeth, NJ 07202
PH:908-355-7942 (a-c,g,r)

**Thunder Road Comics & Cards**
Parkway Plaza
831 Parkway Ave.
Ewing Township, NJ 08618
PH:609-771-1055 (a-c,m,q,r)

**Star Spangled Comics**
353 Route 22
King George Plaza
Green Brook, NJ 08812
PH:908-356-8338 (a-c,g,h,m,q-s)

**Dreamer's Comics**
103 Church St.
Hackettstown, NJ 07840
PH:908-850-5255 (a-c,g,h,k,m,q,r)

**Thunder Road Comics & Cards**
3694 Nottingham Way
Hamilton Square, NJ 08690
PH:609-587-5353 (a-c,m,q,r)

**Steve's Comic Relief**
106 Clifton Ave.
Lakewood, NJ 08701
PH:908-363-3899 (a-c,j,n,q,r,t-v)

**Steve's Comic Relief**
156A Mercer Mall
Lawrenceville, NJ 08648
PH:609-452-7548 (a-c,j,n,q,r,t-v)

**Comics Plus**
1300 Highway 35
Middletown, NJ 07748
PH:908-706-0102 (a-c,g,h,k,m,q,r)

**Comic Museum**
434 Pine Street
Mount Holly, NJ 08060
PH:609-261-0996 (a-c,g,n,q,r,u,v)

**A & S Comics & Cards I**
7113 Bergenline Ave.
North Bergen, NJ 07047
PH:201-869-0280 (b,m,q-s)

**Comicrypt**
521 White Horse Pike
Oaklyn, NJ 08107
PH:609-858-3877
(b-e,g,i,j,k,m,n,q-s,u)

**Sparkle City** (appointment only)
P. O. Box 67
Sewell, NJ 08080
PH:609-881-1174 (a,b,d,f)

**A & S Comics & Cards II**
396 Cedar Lane
Teaneck, NJ 07666
PH:201-801-0500 (b,m,q-s)

**Steve's Comic Relief**
635 Bay Avenue
Toms River, NJ 08753
PH:908-244-5003 (a-c,j,n,q,r,t-v)

**Mr. Collector**
327 Union Blvd.
Totowa, NJ 07512
PH:201-595-0900 (b,c,g,m,r,t)

**Comics Plus**
Ocean Plaza
Hwy. 35 & Sunset Ave.
Wanamassa, NJ 07712
PH:908-922-3308 (a-c,g,h,k,m,q,r)

**1,000,000 Comix Inc.**
875 Mantua Pike
Southwood Shopping Centre
Woodbury Heights, NJ 08096
PH:609-384-8844
(a-d,f-h,j,m,n,p-v)

## NEW MEXICO:

**The Comic Warehouse**
9617 Menaul Blvd. NE
Albuquerque, NM 87112
PH:505-293-3065 (b,c,g,m,n,q,r)

**Captain Comic's Specialty Shop**
109 W. 4th Street
Clovis, NM 88101
PH:505-769-1543 (a-c,q,r)

## NEW YORK:

**Earthworld Comics**
327 Central Ave.
Albany, NY 12206
PH:518-465-5495 (b,c,n,q,r)

**FantaCo Enterprises Inc.**
21 Central Avenue - Level Two
Albany, NY 12210
PH:518-463-3667 (c,e,g,h,m,o)

**FantaCo Archival Research Center**
21 Central Ave. - Sublevel One
Albany, NY 12210
PH:518-463-3667 (c,e,g-j,m-o)

**FantaCo Comic Shop**
21Central Ave. - Level 2
Albany, NY 12210
PH:518-463-1400
(a-c,e,g,j,m-o,q-v)

**FantaCon Organization Offices**
21 Central Ave. - Level3
Albany, NY 12210
PH:518-463-1400 (a-v)

**FantaCo Publications**
21 Central Ave. - Level 3
Albany, NY 12210
PH:518-463-3667 (c,e,q)

**Official Night Of The Living Dead Comic Headquarters**
21 Central Ave. - Level 2
Albany, NY 12210
PH:518-463-3667 (c,e)

**Long Island Comics**
1670-D Sunrise Hwy.
Bay Shore, NY 11706
PH:516-665-4342 (a-c,g,j,q-t)

**Fordham Comics**
390 East Fordham Rd.
Bronx, NY 10458
PH:212-933-9245 (a-c,h,i,m,q-s)

**Brain Damage Comics**
1301 Prospect Ave.
Brooklyn, NY 11218
PH:718-438-1335
(a-c,e,g,i,k,m,n,q-u)

**Memory Lane**
1301 Prospect Ave.
Brooklyn, NY 11218
PH:718-438-1335
(a-c,e,g,i,k,m,n,q-u)

**Pinocchio Comic Shop**
1814 McDonald Ave. near Ave. P
Brooklyn, NY 11223
PH:718-645-2573 (a,c,g,m,t)

**Dimension Comics**
R#1 Box 204-A
Cold Spring, NY 10516
PH:914-265-2649 (a-c,g,i,j,m,r)

**Comics for Collectors**
211 West Water St.
Elmira, NY 14901
PH:607-732-2299 (a-c,m,n,q-v)

**Comics For Collectors**
148 The Commons
Ithaca, NY 14850
PH:607-272-3007 (a-c,j,m,n,q-v)

**Long Beach Books, Inc.**
17 E. Park Ave.
Long Beach, NY 11561
PH:516-432-2265 & 432-0063
(a-h,n,r-u)

**Port Comics & Cards**
3120 Rt. 112
Medford, NY 11763
PH:516-732-9143 (a-c,g,m,q,r,t)

**Alex's MVP Comics & Cards**
256 E. 89th Street
New York, NY 10128
PH:212-831-2273

**Big Apple Comics**
2489 Broadway (92 - 93 St.)
New York, NY 10025
PH:212-724-0085 (a-d,j,m,n,r)

**Funny Business**
656 Amsterdam Ave.
(Corner 92nd St.)
New York, NY 10025
PH:212-799-9477 (a-c,g,n,o,q,r)

**Golden Age Express**
2489 Broadway (92-93)
New York, NY 10025
PH:212-769-9570 (a,b,j,r)

**Jim Hanley's Universe**
At A&S Plaza, 6th Floor
901 Ave. of Americas (at 33rd)
New York, NY 10001
PH:212-268-7088 (a-c,e,g,m,q-v)

**Metropolis Collectibles**
(by appointment)
7 West 18th St.
New York, NY 10011
PH:212-627-9691
(a,b,d,g,h,j,k,m,p)

**West Side Comics**
107 West 86 St.
New York, NY 10024
PH:212-724-0432 (a-c,n,r)

**L & S Comix**
1379 Jerusalem Ave.
N. Merrick, NY 11566
PH:516-489-XMEN, 489-9311
(b,c,e,j,k,m,n,q-u)

**Fantastic Planet**
24 Oak Street
Plattsburgh, NY 12901
PH:518-563-2946 (b-e,g,m,q,r,t-v)

**Iron Vic Comics**
1 Raymond Ave.
Poughkeepsie, NY 12603
PH:914-473-8365 (a-d,g,j,m,n,r)

**Alien World, Inc.**
322 Sunrise Hwy.
Rockville Center, NY 11570
PH:516-536-8151 (a-c,h,i,m,q-s)

**Amazing Comics**
12 Gillette Ave.
Sayville, NY 11782
PH:516-567-8069 (a-c,j,q-s)

**Electric City Comics**
1704 Van Vranken Ave.
Schenectady, NY 12308
PH:518-377-1500 (a-c,g,j,n,q,r,u)

**Jim Hanley's Universe**
350 New Dorp Lane
Staten Island, NY 10306
PH:718-351-6299 (a-c,e,g,m,q-v)

**Comic Book Heaven**
48-14 Skillman Avenue
Sunnyside, Queens, NY 11104
PH:718-899-4175 (a-c,e,g,k,m,q-s)

**Dream Days Comic Book Shop**
312 South Clinton St.
Syracuse, NY 13202
PH:315-475-3995 (a-d,f-h,j,n,q,r)

**Michael Sagert**
P. O. Box 456 - Downtown
Syracuse, NY 13201
PH:315-475-3995 (a,b,d,f,h,j)

**Twilight Book & Game Emporium, Inc.**
1401 North Salina Street
Syracuse, NY 13208
PH:315-471-3139 (a-c,e,n,q-v)

**Aquilonia Comics**
412 Fulton St.
Troy, NY 12180
PH:518-271-1069 (a-c,g,q-s)

**Ravenswood, Inc.**
263 Genesee Street
Utica, NY 13501
PH:315-735-3699 (a-c,g,i,k,m,q-u)

**Iron Vic Comics II**
420 Windsor Hwy.
Vail's Gate, NY 12584
PH:914-565-6525 (a-d,g,j,m,n,r)

**Collector's Comics**
3247 Sunrise Highway
Wantagh, NY 11793
PH:516-783-8700 (a-c,e,g,m,n,q-v)

**The Dragon's Den**
2614 Central Park Ave.
Yonkers, NY 10710
PH:914-793-4630 (a-c,g,m,q-t,v)

## NORTH CAROLINA:

**Super Giant Books & Comics**
344 Merrimon Ave.
Asheville, NC 28801
PH:803-576-4990 (a-e,h,j,l,r)

**Heroes Aren't Hard to Find**
Corner Central Ave. & The Plaza
P. O. Box 9181
Charlotte, NC 28299
PH:704-375-7462
(a-c,g,j,k,m,n,q-t,v)

**Heroes Aren't Hard to Find**
(Mail Order Subscriptions & Wholesale)
P. O. Box 9181
Charlotte, NC 28299
PH:704-376-5766, 800-321-4370
(a-c,g,j,k,m,n,q-t,v)

**Heroes Are Here**
208 South Berkeley Blvd.
Goldsboro, NC 27530
PH:919-751-3131 (a-c,m,q,r)

**Parts Unknown—The Comic Book Store**
The Cotton Mill Square
801 Merritt Dr./Spring Garden St.
Greensboro, NC 27407
PH:919-294-0091 (a-c,g,i,n,q,r)

**Heroes Are Here, Too**
116 E. Fifth St.
Greenville, NC 27584
PH:919-757-0948 (a-c,m,q,r)

**The Nostalgia Newsstand**
919 Dickinson Ave.
Greenville, NC 27834
PH:919-758-6909 (b,c,e,n,q,r)

**Tales Resold**
3936 Atlantic Ave.
Raleigh, NC 27604
PH:919-878-8551 (a-c,e,g,h,j,l,q,r)

**The Booktrader**
121 Country Club Rd.
Rocky Mount, NC 27801
PH:919-443-3993 (b,c,e,r)

**Bargain Books, Comics, & Music**
Main Street
Downtowner Office Bldg.
Sylva, NC
No Phone (b,c,e,m,r,s)

**Bargain Bookstore II**
Delwood Rd.
Waynesville, NC 28786
PH:704-452-2539 (b,c,e,m,r,s)

**Heroes Aren't Hard to Find**
Silas Creek Crossing Shop. Ctr.
3234 Silas Creek Parkway
Winston-Salem, NC 27103
PH:919-765-4370
(a-c,g,j,k,m,n,q-t,v)

## NORTH DAKOTA:

**Collector's Corner**
City Center Mall
Grand Forks, ND 58201
PH:701-772-2518 (a-c,f,g,j,l-n,q-t)

**Tom's Coin, Stamp, Gem, Baseball, & Comic Shop**
#2 1st SW
Minot, ND 58701
PH:701-852-4522
(a-c,e,g,i-k,m,n,p-r)

## OHIO:

**Trade Those Tunes®**
1320 Whipple NW
Meyers Lake Plaza
Canton, OH 44708
PH:216-477-5535 (a-c,l,m,r)

**Collectors Warehouse Inc.**
5437 Pearl Road
Cleveland, OH 44129
PH:216-842-2896 (a-i,k-n,q-t)

**Dark Star II**
1410 West Dorothy Lane
Dayton, OH 45409
PH:513-293-7307
(a-c,e-h,m,n,q-v)

**Troll and Unicorn**
5460 Brandt Pike
Huber Heights, OH 45424
PH:513-233-6535
(a-c,e,g,i,k,n,q-t,v)

**Bookie Parlor**
2778 Wilmington Pike
Kettering, OH 45419
PH:513-293-2243 (a-c,q,r)

**Don Parker's Records & Comics**
122 W. Loveland Ave.
Loveland, OH 45140
PH:513-677-3140 (a-c,g,l,q-u)

**Rich's Comic Shoppe**
2441 N. Verity Parkway
Middletown, OH 45042
PH:513-424-1095 (a-c,k,m,q,r,t,u)

**Monarch Cards & Comics**
2620 Airport Hwy.
Toledo, OH 43609
PH:419-382-1451 (b,c,g,m,q,r)

**Funnie Farm Bookstore**
328 N. Dixie Drive
Vandalia, OH 45377
PH:513-898-2794 (a-c,m,q-t)

**Dark Star Books**
231 Xenia Ave.
Yellow Springs, OH 45387
PH:513-767-9400 (a-c,e-h,m,n,q-v)

## OKLAHOMA:

**New World Comics & Games**
2203 W. Main
Norman, OK 73069
PH:405-321-7445 (a-j,m,n,q-v)

**Planet Comics #1**
918 W. Main
Norman, OK 73069
PH:405-329-9695 (a-j,n,o,q-v)

**New World Comics & Games**
6219 N. Meridian Avenue
Oklahoma City, OK 73112
PH:405-721-7634 (a-j,m,n,q-v)

**New World Comics & Games**
4420 S.E. 44th St.
Oklahoma City, OK 73135
PH:405-677-2559 (a-j,m,n,q-v)

**Planet Comics #2**
2136 S.W. 74th
Oklahoma City, OK 73159
PH:405-682-9144 (a-j,n,o,q-v)

**Comic Empire of Tulsa**
3122 S. Mingo Rd.
Tulsa, OK 74146
PH:918-664-5808 (a-c,n,q,r,t,u)

**Comics, Cards & Collectibles**
4618 East 31st Street
Tulsa, OK 74135
PH:918-749-8500 (a-v)

**Starbase 21**
2130 S. Sheridan Rd.
Tulsa, OK 74129
PH:918-838-3388
(a-c,e,g,i,k,m,q-v)

## OREGON:

**More Fun**
102 Will Dodge Way
Ashland, OR 97520
PH:503-488-1978 (b,c,m,n,r,s)

**Pegasus Books**
4390 S.W. Lloyd
Beaverton, OR 97005
PH:503-643-4222 (a-c,m,q-t,v)

**Emerald City Comics**
770 E. 13th
Eugene, OR 97401
PH:503-345-2568 (b,c,g,m-o,q-s)

**Nostalgia Collectibles**
527 Williamette St.
Eugene, OR 97401
PH:503-484-9202 (a-i,k-n,q-s)

**House of Fantasy**
2005 E. Burnside
P. O. Box 472
Gresham, OR 97030
PH:503-661-1815 (a-c,e,g,q-s)

**It Came From Outer Space**
10812 S.E. Oak St.
Milwaukie, OR 97222
PH:503-786-0865 (a-c,m,q-t,v)

**Pegasus Books**
10902 SE Main
Milwaukie, OR 97222
PH:503-652-2752 (a-c,m,q-t,v)

**It Came From Outer Space**
Plaza 205 Ste. 'P'
9738 SE Washington
Portland, OR 97216
PH:503-275-2701 (a-c,m,q-t,v)

**Pegasus Books**
1401 SE Division Street
Portland, OR 97214
PH:503-233-0768 (a-c,m,q-t,v)

**Pegasus Books**
5015 NE Sandy
Portland, OR 97218
PH:503-284-4693 (a-c,m,q-t,v)

## PENNSYLVANIA:

**Cap's Comic Cavalcade**
1980 Catasauqua Rd.
Allentown, PA 18103
PH:215-264-5540 (a-c,e,g,j,k,m-v)

**Cap's Comic Cavalcade**
Tilghman Square Shopping Center
Allentown, PA 18104
PH:215-395-0979 (a-c,e,g,j,k,m-v)

**Dreamscape Comics**
404 West Broad St.
Bethlehem, PA 18018
PH:215-867-1178 (a-c,m,q-s)

**Dreamscape Comics**
9 East Third St.
Bethlehem, PA 18015
PH:215-865-4636 (b,c,m,q-s)

**Time Tunnel Collectibles**
1001 Castle Shannon Blvd.
Castle Shannon, PA 15234
PH:412-531-8833 (a-c,g,j,m,q-s)

**Comic Universe**
Bazaar of All Nations, Store 228
Clifton Heights, PA 19018
PH:215-259-9943 (a-f,m,n,q-u)

**Dreamscape Comics**
25th St. Shopping Center
Easton, PA 18042
PH:215-250-9818 (a-c,m,q-s)

**Comic Universe**
446 MacDade Blvd.
Folsom, PA 19033
PH:215-461-7960 (a-f,m,n,q-u)

**Comic Universe**
395 Lancaster Avenue
Frazer, PA 19355
PH:215-889-3320 (a-f,m,n,q-u)

**Comics & Collectibles, Inc.**
983 W. County Line Rd.
Rosemore Shopping Center
Hatboro, PA 19040
PH:215-675-8708 (a-i,l,m,o-t)

**Golden Unicorn Comics**
860 Alter St.
Hazleton, PA 18201
PH:717-455-4645 (b,c,n,q-s)

**Ott's Trading Post**
201 Allegheny Street
Hollidaysburg, PA 16648
PH:814-696-3494 (a-d,f,g,l,r)

**Charlie's Collectors Corner**
100-D West Second St.
Hummelstown, PA 17036
PH:717-566-7216 (b,c,m,r)

**The Comic Store**
Station Square 28 McGovern Ave.
Lancaster, PA 17602
PH:717-397-8737
(a-c,e,g,j,m,n,q-v)

**Steve's Comic Relief**
4153 Woerner Ave.
Levittown, PA 19057
PH:215-945-7954 (a-c,j,n,q,r,t-v)

**Fat Jack's Comicrypt I**
2006 Sansom Street
Philadelphia, PA 19103
PH:215-963-0788
(a-c,e,g,j,n,q,r,u,v)

**Fat Jack's Comicrypt II**
7598 Haverford Ave.
Philadelphia, PA 19151
PH:215-473-6333 (b,c,g,n,q,r,u)

**Fat Jack's Comicrypt III**
5736 North 5th Street
Philadelphia, PA 19120
PH:215-924-8210 (b,c,g,o,r,t,u)

**Sparkle City Comics**
Philadelphia, PA
(Philly area by appointment)
PH:609-881-1174 (a,b,d,f)

**Steve's Comic Relief**
1244 Franklin Mills Circle
Philadelphia, PA 19154
PH:215-281-3730 (a-c,j,n,q,r,t-v)

**Adventure in Comics**
1368 Illinois Ave.
Pittsburgh, PA 15216
PH:412-531-5644 (a-c,j,k,m,o,q-u)

**BEM: The Store**
622 South Ave.
Pittsburgh, PA 15221
PH:412-243-2736
(a-e,g,h,j,m-o,q,r,v)

**Eide's Entertainment**
1111 Penn Ave.
Pittsburgh, PA 15222
PH:412-261-0900 (a-j,l-v)

**The Comic Store - West**
Northwest Plaza
915 Loucks Road
York, PA 17404 (b,c,m,n,q-v)

## RHODE ISLAND:

**Starship Excalibur**
Lincoln Mall
Rt. 116 Washington Hwy.
Lincoln, RI 02864
PH:401-334-3883 (b,c,m,q-v)

**The Annex**
314 Broadway
Newport, RI 02840
PH:401-847-4607 (b,c,g,m,r)

**Starship Excalibur**
60 Washington St.
Providence, RI 02903
PH:401-273-8390 (a-c,m-o,q-v)

**Starship Excalibur**
834 Hope St.
Providence, RI 02906
PH:401-861-1177 (b,c,m,n,q,r,u,v)

**Starship Excalibur**
830-832 Post Rd., Warwick Plaza
Warwick, RI 02888
PH:401-941-8890 (b,c,m,n,q-t)

## SOUTH CAROLINA:

**Super Giant Comics & Records**
Market Place/Cinema Center
3466 Clemson Blvd.
Anderson, SC 29621
PH:803-225-9024 (a-c,j,l,m,q,r)

**Book Exchange**
1219 Savannah Hwy.
Charleston, SC 29407
PH:803-556-5051 (a-c,e,g,r)

**Heroes Aren't Hard to Find**
1415-A Laurens Rd.
Greenville, SC 29607
PH:803-235-3488
(a-c,g,j,k,m,n,q-t,v)

**Grand Slam Baseball Cards & Comics**
2349-41 Cherry Rd.
Rock Hill, SC 29732
PH:803-327-4414
(a-c,e,g,i,k,l-n,q,r)

**Super Giant Comics**
Wal-Mart Plaza
7500 Greenville Hwy.
Spartanburg, SC 29301
PH:803-576-4990 (a-c,e,j,m,q-u)

**Haven For Heroes**
1131 Dick Pond Road
Surfside Beach, SC
PH:803-238-9975
(a-c,e,g,i-k,m,n,q-t,v)

## TENNESSEE:

**Comics and Curios #1**
3472 Brainerd Rd.
Chattanooga, TN 37411
PH:615-698-1710 (a-c,m,n,q-v)

**Comics and Curios #2**
629 Signal Mountain Rd.
Chattanooga, TN 37405
PH:615-266-4315 (a-c,m,q-v)

**Collector's Choice**
3405 Keith St., Shoney's Plaza
Cleveland, TN 37311
PH:615-472-6649 (c,i,m,q-t)

**Gotham City Comics**
2075 Exeter #10
Germantown, TN 38138
PH:901-757-9665
(b,c,e,g,k,m,n,q-s)

**Comics and Curios #3**
5131-B Hixson Pike
Hixson, TN
(a-c,m,q-v)

**Collector's Choice**
2104 Cumberland Ave.
Knoxville, TN 37916
PH:615-546-2665 (c,i,m,q-t)

**Comics Universe**
1869 Hwy. 45 By-Pass North
Jackson, TN 38305
PH:901-664-9131 (a-c,j,p,q-s)

**Mountain Empire Books, Comics & Games III**
1210 N. Roan St.
Johnson City, TN 37602
PH:615-929-8245 (a-c,e,h,i,m,q-t)

**Mountain Empire Books, Comics & Games II**
1451 E. Center St.
Kingsport, TN 37664
PH:615-245-0364 (a-c,e,h,i,m,q-t)

**The Great Escape**
Gallatin Rd. at Old Hickory Blvd.
Madison, TN 37115
PH:615-865-8052 (a-v)

**Comics And Collectibles**
4730 Poplar Ave. #2
Memphis, TN 38117
PH:901-683-7171 (a-e,g,i,m,n,q-v)

**Memphis Comics & Records**
665 So. Highland
Memphis, TN 38111
PH:901-452-1304 (a-v)

**Collector's World**
1511 East Main St.
Murfreesboro, TN 37130
PH:615-895-1120 (a-g,i-m,o-v)

**Collector's World**
5751 Nolensville Rd.
Nashville, TN 37211
PH:615-333-9458 (a-g,i-m,o-v)

**The Great Escape**
1925 Broadway
Nashville, TN 37203
PH:615-327-0646 (a-v)

**Walt's Paperback Books**
2604 Franklin Rd.
Nashville, TN 37204
PH:615-298-2506 (b,c,e,o,r)

## TEXAS:

**Lone Star Comics Books & Games**
511 East Abram Street
Arlington, TX 76010
PH:817-Metro 265-0491
(a-c,e,g,h,m,q-s)

**Lone Star Comics Books & Games**
5721 W. I-20 at Green Oaks Blvd.
Arlington, TX 76016
PH:817-478-5405 (b,c,e,g,h,m,q-s)

**Mighty Comics**
(Mail Order)
P. O. Box 110194
Carrollton, TX 75011-0194
PH:214-245-3474 & 466-1359
TDD (b,c,e,g,i,k,m-o,q-v)

**Lone Star Comics Books & Games**
11661 Preston Forest Village
Dallas, TX 75230
PH:214-373-0934 (a-c,e,h,m,n,q-s)

**Remember When**
2431 Valwood Parkway
Dallas, TX 75234
PH:214-243-3439
(a-c,e,g,i,j,m,n,q,r,t,u)

**Lone Star Comics Books & Games**
3014 West 7th St.
Fort Worth, TX 76107
PH:817-654-0333 (a-c,e,g,h,m,q-s)

**B & D Trophy Shop**
4404 N. Shepherd
Houston, TX 77018
PH:713-694-8436 (a-c,i,r)

**Bedrock City Comic Co.**
6521 Westheimer
Houston, TX 77057
PH:713-780-0675
(a-g,i-k,m,n,p-r,t-v)

**Houston's Favorite Game & Comic Emporium**
2007 Southwest Freeway at Shepherd
Houston, TX 77098
PH:713-520-8700
(a-c,e,g,h,m-o,q-v)

**Nan's Games and Comics, Too!**
2011 Southwest Freeway (US 59 at Shepherd)
Houston, TX 77098-4805
PH:713-520-8700
(a-c,e,g,h,m-o,q-v)

**Third Planet Books**
2439 Bissonnet
Houston, TX 77005
PH:713-528-1067 (a-k,m-v)

**Lone Star Comics, Books & Games**
807 Melbourne
Hurst, TX 76053
PH:817-595-4375 (a-c,e,g,h,m,q-s)

**Lone Star Comics, Books & Games**
2550 N. Beltline Road
Irving, TX 75062
PH:214-659-0317 (a-c,e,g,h,m,q-s)

**Lone Star Comics, Books & Games**
3600 Gus Thomasson, Suite 107
Mesquite, TX 75150
PH:214-681-2040 (b,c,e,m,q-s)

**Lone Star Comics, Books & Games**
1900 Preston Rd. #345
Plano, TX 75093
PH:214-985-1953 (a-c,e,g,h,m,q-s)

**Comics (& Records) Unlimited**
6858 Ingram Road
San Antonio, TX 78238
PH:512-522-9063
(a-c,e,f,i,k-m,q-u)

**Comics Unlimited**
2359 Austin Hwy.
San Antonio, TX 78218
PH:512-653-6588
(a-c,e,f,i,k,m,q-u)

**Comics Unlimited**
226 Bitters Rd., Suite 102
San Antonio, TX 78216
PH:512-545-9063
(a-c,e,f,i,k,m,q-u)

**Comics Unlimited**
7101 Blanco Rd.
San Antonio, TX 78216
PH:512-340-0074
(a-c,e,f,i,k,m,q-u)

**Heroes & Fantasies**
#114 North Star Mall
San Antonio, TX 78216
PH:512-366-2273 (c,e,m,q-u)

## UTAH:

**The Bookshelf**
2456 Washington Blvd.
Ogden, UT 84401
PH:801-621-4752 (b-e,g,h,l,o,q-t,v)

**Comics Utah**
1956 S. 1100 East
Salt Lake City, UT 84105
PH:801-487-5390 (b,c,e,n,q-t)

**Comics Utah**
2985 W. 3500 South
Salt Lake City, UT 84119
PH:801-966-8581 (b,c,e,n,q-t)

## VERMONT:

**Comics Outpost**
27 Granite St.
Barre, VT 05641
PH:802-476-4553 or 800-564-4553 in state (a-c,f,q-s)

**Comics City, Inc.**
6 No. Winooski Ave.
Burlington, VT 05401
PH:802-865-3828
(b,c,e,j,m,n,q,r,t-v)

**Earth Prime Comics**
154 Church St.
Burlington, VT 05401
PH:802-863-3666 (a-c,e,f,m,n,q-s)

## VIRGINIA:

**Capital Comics Center Storyland, U.S.A.**
2008 Mt. Vernon Ave.
Alexandria, VA 22301 (D.C. area)
PH:703-548-3466 (a-c,e,f,m,o,q-u)

**Geppi's Crystal City Comics**
1675 Crystal Square Arcade
Arlington, VA 22202
PH:703-521-4618 (a-c,f)

**Mountain Empire Books, Comics + Games I**
509 State Street
Bristol, VA 24201
PH:703-466-6337 (a-c,e,h,i,m,q-t)

**Burke Centre Books**
5741 Burke Centre Pkwy.
Burke, VA 22015
PH:703-250-5114 (b-h,m,q-v)

**Fantasia Comics and Records**
1419½ University Ave.
Charlottesville, VA 22903
PH:804-971-1029 (b,c,e,h,i,l,n,q-u)

**Fantasia Comics and Records**
1861 Seminole Trail (29 North)
Charlottesville, VA 22901
PH:804-974-7512 (b,c,e,k,l,n,q-u)

**Trilogy Shop #3**
3580-F Forest Haven Ln.
Chesapeake, VA 23321
PH:804-483-4173 (a-c,e,m,q-v)

**Hole in the Wall Books**
905 West Broad St.
Falls Church, VA 22046
PH:703-536-2511
(b,c,e,g-i,n,o,q-v)

**Marie's Books and Things**
1701 Princess Anne St.
Fredericksburg, VA 22401
PH:703-373-5196 (a-c,e,h,l,r)

**Franklin Farm Books**
13320-I Franklin Farm Rd.
Herndon, VA 22071
PH:703-437-9530 (b-h,m,q-v)

**Trilogy Shop #2**
700 E. Little Creek Rd.
Norfolk, VA 23518
PH:804-587-2540 (a-c,e,m,q-v)

**Trilogy Shop #5**
3535 Airline Blvd.
Portsmouth, VA 23701
(c,m,q,r)

**Dave's Comics**
7019-F Three Chopt Rd.
Richmond, VA 23226
PH:804-282-1211 (b,c,m,q-v)

**Nostalgia Plus**
601 Willow Lawn Drive
Richmond, VA 23230
PH:804-282-5532 (a-c,m,n,q,r)

**B & D Comic Shop**
3514 Williamson Rd. N.W.
Roanoke, VA 24012
PH:703-563-4161 (b,c,e,m-o,q-t)

**Trilogy Shop #1**
5773 Princess Anne Rd.
Virginia Beach, VA 23462
PH:804-490-2205 (a-c,e,m,q-v)

**Trilogy Shop #4**
857 S. Lynnhaven Rd.
Virginia Beach, VA 23452
PH:804-468-0412 (a-c,e,m,q-v)

## WASHINGTON:

**Paperback Exchange Yardbirds**
2100 N. National Ave. (upstairs)
Chehalis, WA 98532
PH:206-748-4792
(a-c,e-g,i,k,m,n,q-t)

**Everett Comics & Cards**
2934½ Colby Ave.
Everett, WA 98201
PH:206-252-8181 (a-c,k,m,n,q-u)

**Olympic Cards & Comics**
311 S. Sound Ctr.
Lacey, WA 98503
PH:206-459-7721
(a-c,e-g,i,k,m,n,q-t)

**Paperback Exchange**
909 Sleater Kinney
Lacey, WA 98503
PH:206-456-8170 (e,g)

**The Comic Character Shop**
Old Firehouse Antique Mall
110 Alaskan Way South
Seattle, WA 98104
PH:206-283-0532 (a,b,h-k,q)

**Corner Comics**
6565 N.E. 181st
Seattle, WA 98155
PH:206-486-XMEN (a-c,q-s)

**Corner Comics II**
5226 University Way N.E.
Seattle, WA 98105
PH:206-525-9394 (b,c,q,r)

**Gemini Book Exchange and Comic Center**
9614 - 16th Ave. S.W.
Seattle, WA 98106
PH:206-762-5543 (b,c,e,g,m,r)

**Golden Age Collectables, Ltd.**
1501 Pike Place Market
401 Lower Level
Seattle, WA 98101
PH:206-622-9799 (a-g,i-k,m-o,q-v)

**Zanadu Comics**
1923 3rd Ave.
Seattle, WA 98101
PH:206-443-1316
(a-c,e-g,j,n,o,q,r,v)

**Zanadu Comics**
4518 University Way N.E.
2nd Floor Arcade Bldg.
Seattle, WA 98105
PH:206-632-0989 (b,c,n,o,q,r,v)

**The Book Exchange**
N. 6504 Division
Spokane, WA 99208
PH:509-489-2053 (a-h,n,q-t)

**The Book Exchange**
University City East
E. 10812 Sprague
Spokane, WA 99206
PH:509-928-4073 (a-h,n,q-t)

**Lady Jayne's Comics & Books**
5969 - 6th Ave.
Tacoma, WA 98406
PH:206-564-6168 (c,e,q-u)

**Ron's Coin & Book Center II**
Valley Mall
Union Gap, WA 98907
PH:509-575-1180
(a-c,e-g,i,k,m,o,q,r)

**Pegasus Books**
813 Grand Blvd.
Vancouver, WA 98661
PH:206-693-1240 (a-c,m,q-t,v)

**Galaxy Comics**
1720 - 5th St., Suite D
Wenatchee, WA 98801
PH:509-663-4330 (b,c,g,q-t)

**Ron's Coin & Book Center**
6 N. 3rd St.
Yakima, WA 98901
PH:509-248-1117
(a-c,e-g,i,k,m,o,q,r)

## WEST VIRGINIA:

**Cheryl's Comics & Toys**
5216½ MacCorkle Ave. S.E.
Charleston, WV 25304
PH:304-925-7269 (a-c,g,i,k,q-u)

**Comic World**
613 West Lee St.
Charleston, WV 25302
PH:304-343-3874
(a-c,g,k,m,q,r,t,v)

**Comic World**
1204 - 4th Avenue
Huntington, WV 25701
PH:304-522-3923 (a-c,g,m,q,r,t-v)

**Triple Play Cards, Comics, & Collectibles**
6A Bank St.
Nitro, WV 25143
PH:304-755-5529 (a-c,m,q-s)

**Books & Things**
2506 Pike Street
Parkersburg, WV 26101
PH:304-422-0666 (b,c,e,g-i,m,q-u]

**Triple Play Cards, Comics & Collectibles**
335 - 4th Avenue
South Charleston, WV 25303
PH:304-744-2602 (a-c,m,q-s)

## WISCONSIN:

**Westfield's Comics, Etc.**
17125E W. Bluemound Rd.
Loehmann's Plaza
Brookfield (Milwaukee), WI
53005-9998
PH:414-821-0242 (a-c,e,m-o,q-v)

**River City Cards & Comics**
512 Cass Street
La Crosse, WI 54601
PH:608-782-5540 (b,c,m,q-v)

**Capital City Comics**
1910 Monroe St.
Madison, WI 53711
PH:608-251-8445 (a-c,f,n,q,r,v)

**Capital City Comics**
6640 Odana Road
in Market Square
Madison, WI 53711
PH:608-833-6964 (a-c,f,n,q,r,v)

**20th Century Books**
108 King Street
Madison, WI 53703
PH:608-251-6226 (a-h,m,n,q-v)

**Westfield's Comics, Etc.**
Whitney Square Mall
676 S. Whitney Way
Madison, WI 53711
PH:608-277-1280 (a-c,e,m-o,q-v)

**The Westfield Company of Wisconsin, Inc.**
(Comic Subscription Service)
8608 University Green
P. O. Box 470
Middleton, WI 53562
PH:608-836-1945 (c,o,q-s)

**Capital City Comics**
2565 North Downer St.
Milwaukee, WI 53210
PH:414-332-8199 (a-c,f,n,q,r,v)

## CANADA:

### ALBERTA:

**Comic Legends** - Head Office
#205, 908 17th Ave. S.W.
Calgary, Alberta, Can. T2T 0A3
PH:403-245-5884
(a-c,g,m,n,q,r,t,u)

**Comic Legends**
Bay #8, 10015 Oakfield Dr. SW
Calgary, Alberta, Can.
PH:403-251-5964
(a-c,g,m,n,q,r,t,u)

**Scorpio Comics, Books, & Sports Cards**
7640 Fairmount Dr. SE
Calgary, Alberta, Can. T2H 0X8
PH:403-258-0035 (a-c,e-i,k,m,r,t,u)

**Comic Legends**
1275 3rd Ave., South
Lethbridge, Alberta, Can.
PH:403-327-8558
(a-c,g,m,n,q,r,t,u)

### BRITISH COLUMBIA:

**L.A. Comics & Books**
371 Victoria St.
Kamloops, B.C., Can. V2C 2A3
PH:604-828-1995 (c,e,m,n,q-s)

**Page After Page**
1763 Harvey Ave.
Kelowna, B.C., Can. V1Y 6G4
PH:604-860-6554 (a,c,e,h,q,r)

**Ted's Paperback & Comics**
269 Leon Ave.
Kelowna, B.C., Can. V1Y 6J1
PH:604-763-1258 (b,c,e,r)

**The Comic Guard Co.**
190 East 11th Ave.
Prince Rupert, B.C.,
Can. V8J 4B9
PH:604-627-7106 (r)

**Island Fantasy**
#29 Market Square
560 Johnson St.
Victoria, B.C., Can. V8W 3C6
PH:604-381-1134 (a-c,f-j,m,n,q-v)

### MANITOBA:

**International Comic Book Co.**
**Calvin Slobodian**
859 - 4th Avenue
Rivers, Man., Can. R0K 1X0
PH:204-328-7846 (a,b,d,f-j,r)

**Collector's Slave**
156 Imperial Avenue
Winnipeg, Man., Can. R2M 0K8
PH:204-237-4428
(a-g,i,j,l-n,q,r,t,u)

**Comic Factory II**
380 Donald St.
Winnipeg, Man., Can. R3B 2J2
PH:204-957-1978 (a-c,g,j,n,q,r,t)

**Doug Sulipa's Comic World**
374 Donald St.
Winnipeg, Man., Can. R3B 2J2
PH:204-943-3642

### NEW BRUNSWICK:

**1,000,000 Comix, Inc.**
345 Mountain Rd.
Moncton, N.B., Can. E1C 2M4
PH:506-855-0056
(a-d,f-h,j,m,n,p-v)

### NOVA SCOTIA:

**Members Only Comic Service**
(Mail Order Service Only)
6257 Yale St.
Halifax, N.S., Can. B3L 1C9
PH:902-423-MOCS (c-g,i-k,o,q-v)

**1,000,000 Comix, Inc.**
6251 Quinpool Rd.
Halifax, N.S., Can. B3L 1A4
PH:902-425-5594
(a-d,f-h,j,m,n,p-v)

### ONTARIO:

**1,000,000 Comix, Inc.**
2400 Guelph Line
Burlington, Ont., Can. L7P 4M7
PH:416-332-5600
(a-d,f-h,j,m,n,p-v)

**Starlite Comics and Books**
132 Westminster Drive South
Cambridge, Ont., Can. N3H 1S8
PH:519-653-6571 (a-h,m,q,r,t,u)

**Lookin' For Heroes**
93 Ontario St. S.
Kitchener, Ont., Can. N2G 1X5
PH:519-570-0873 (a-c,m,n,q,r)

**1,000,000 Comix, Inc.**
2150 Burnhamthorpe Rd.
South Common Mall
Mississauga, Ont., Can. L5L 3A2
PH:416-828-8208
(a-d,f-h,j,m,n,p-v)

**1,000,000 Comix, Inc.**
513B Yonge St.
Toronto, Ont., Can
PH:416-944-3016
(a-d,f-h,j,m,n,p-v)

**Ken Mitchell Comics**
(by appointment only)
710 Conacher Drive
Willowdale, Ont., Can. M2M 3N6
PH:416-222-5808 (a,b,f,g,h)

### QUEBEC:

**Capitaine Quebec - Dollard**
4305 Blvd. St. Jean
D.D.O., Que., Can. H9H 2A4
PH:514-620-1866 (a-c,e,g,m,n,q-v)

**Capitaine Quebec - Snowdon**
5108 Decarie
Montreal, Que., Can. H3X 2H9
PH:514-487-0970 (a-c,e,g,m,n,q-v)

**Capitaine Quebec - Centre-Ville**
1837 St. Catherine O.
Montreal, Que., Can. H3H 1M2
PH:514-939-9970 (a-c,e,g,m,n,q-v)

**Cosmix**
931 Decarie
Montreal, Que., Can. H4L 3M3
PH:514-744-9494 (a-c,e,m-o,q-t,v)

**Multinational Comics/Cards**
8918A Lajeunesse
Montreal, Que., Can. H2M 1R9
PH: 514-385-6273
(a-c,e,f,i-k,m-v)

**1,000,000 Comix, Inc.**
315 Dorval Ave.
Montreal, Que., Can
PH:514-636-8016
(a-d,f-h,j,m,n,p-v)

**1,000,000 Comix, Inc.**
Corporate Headquarters
5164 Queen Mary Rd.
Montreal, Que., Can. H3W 1X5
PH:514-486-1175

**1,000,000 Comix, Inc.**
372 Sherbrooke St. West
Montreal, Que., Can.
PH:514-844-9313
(a-d,f-h,j,m,n,p-v)

**1,000,000 Comix, Inc.**
1260 Dollard St., LaSalle
Montreal, Que., Can. H8N 2P2
PH:514-486-1175
(a-d,f-h,j,m,n,p-v)

**1,000,000 Comix, Inc.**
1539 Van Horne
Montreal, Que., Can.
PH:514-486-1175
(a-d,f-h,j,m,n,p-v)

**1,000,000 Comix, Inc.**
3846 Jean-Talon
Montreal, Que., Can.
PH:514-725-1355
(a-d,f-h,j,m,n,p-v)

**Premiere Issue**
27 'A' D'Auteuil
Quebec City, (Vieux - Quebec)
Canada G1R 4B9
PH:418-692-3985 (a-c,e,i,m,q-u)

**Comix Plus** (1,000,000 Comix affil.)
1475 McDonald
St. Laurent, Que., Can.
PH:514-334-0732
(a-d,f-h,j,m,n,p-v)

**Capitaine Quebec - Verdun**
4422 Wellington
Verdun, Que., Can. H4G 1W5
PH:514-768-1351 (a-c,e,g,m,n,q-v)

## AUSTRALIA

**Australian Comics Trader**
P. O. Box 786
Penrith, NSW 2751, Australia
PH: (047) 36-2095 (c,s)

## ENGLAND

**Stateside Comics PLC**
125 East Barnet Road
Barnet, London EN4 8RF, England
PH:(01144) 81 449 5535 10 Lines
(a-c,e,i-k,o,q-u)

**Adventure Into Comics**
P. O. Box 606
London, England SE 24 9NP
(a-c,f,k,t,u)

## DIRECTORY OF ADVERTISERS (Cl = Classified, c = color)

## DIRECTORY OF ADVERTISERS (continued)

Hake's
P.O. BOX 1444G
YORK, PA 17405
(717) 848-1333
ILLUSTRATION BY BILL NELSON

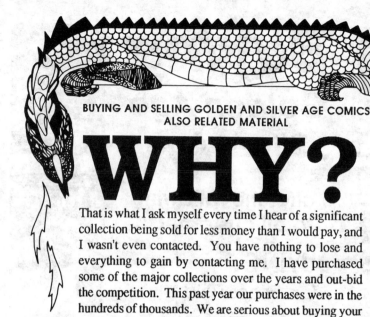

## We are paying 60% of guide for the following:

- Adventure (32-267)
- Adv. of Bob Hope (1-50)
- Adv. of Jerry Lewis (1-50)
- Adv. of Ozzie & Harriet
- All American
- All Flash
- All New
- All Top (8-18)
- Blackhawk (9-110)
- Blue Beetle (47-57)
- Captain America (1st)
- Flash (1st)
- Hit (1-20)
- House of Mystery (1-50)
- House of Secrets (1-25)
- Leading (1-14)
- Legend of Dan'l Boone
- Mary Marvel
- Military
- Movie Comics (D.C.)
- My Greatest Adventure (1-50)
- Mystery Men
- National (1-23)
- New Book of Comics
- Phantom Stranger
- Science (Fox)
- Shadow (Fox)
- Showcase (1-30)
- Speed (1-20)
- Superman (1-125)
- Superman's Pal (1-30)

## We are paying 55% of guide for the following:

- Airboy
- Air Fighters
- All Select
- All Star
- All Winners
- Amazing Spiderman (1-20)
- America's Greatest
- Blonde Phamtom
- Brave & the Bold (1-30)
- Brenda Starr (1-12)
- Bulletman
- Captain Marvel
- Captain Marvel Jr.
- Captain Midnight
- Catman
- Challengers of the Unknown (1-10)
- Classics Comics (1st 1-20)
- Comic Cavalcade (1-29)
- Crash
- Daredevil (1st 1-20)
- Daring Mystery
- Dollman
- Fantastic
- Fantastic Four (1-20)
- Frontier Fighters
- Green Hornet (1-20)
- Human Torch
- Ibis
- John Wayne
- JO-JO (7-29)
- Journey into Mystery (1-85)
- Jungle (1-10)
- Kid Komics
- Lash Larue (1-46)
- Marvel Family
- Marvel Mystery
- Master
- Miss Fury
- Modern
- More Fun (52-107)
- Mystery In Space (1-90)
- Mystic (1st)
- Nickel
- Pep (1-40)
- Phamtom Lady
- Planet
- Pogo Possum
- Police (1-20)
- Rangers (1-20)
- Rulah
- Saint
- Sensation
- Shield Wizard
- Silver Streak (1-17)
- Smash
- Spy Smasher
- Star Spangled
- Strange Adventure (1-120)
- Strange Tales (1-100)
- Sub-Mariner (1st)
- Superboy (1-50)
- Tomahawk (1-30)
- Top-Notch
- U.S.A.
- W.D. Comics & Stories (1-40)
- Weird Comics
- Whiz
- World's Finest (1-110)
- Young Allies
- Zip (1-39)
- Zoot (7-16)

We are also paying 50-75% of guide for many other titles. Comics must be properly graded and complete. Please send your listing of comics for sale or your list of comics you wish to purchase. We are also dealing heavily in Sci-Fi material plus thousands of Marvels, D.C.'s Western, Funny Material and Much More! Please Send one dollar for our current retail listing of comics in stock. Will Travel for Large Collections or if you're passing through the area call for an appointment.

**JAMES F. PAYETTE**
**RARE BOOKS AND COMICS**
**P.O. BOX 750, BETHLEHEM, NH 03574**
**(603) 869-2097**

©DC

# COMIC BOOKS WANTED

©MCG

## NO COLLECTION TOO LARGE OR TOO SMALL

## NO ONE PAYS MORE!

©MCG

IF YOU HAVE ANY COMIC BOOKS TO SELL

CONTACT US!

WE WILL TRAVEL TO VIEW LARGE COLLECTIONS

©CEN

7 W. 18TH STREET
NEW YORK, N.Y. 10011
(212) 627-9691 FAX: (212) 627-5947

(BY APPOINTMENT ONLY)

©MCG

©DC

## METROPOLIS COMICS

★ Accurate Grading ★ Competitive Pricing ★ Large Selection Of Golden And Silver Age ★ Complete Want List Service ★ New Approval Policy (Available To Want List Customers Only) Will Ship All Books Under $5000 To Any Want List Customer Without Pre-Payment. Payment Due Within 7 Days Unless Other Arrangements Are Made ★ Time Payments Possible

©MCG

©DC

7 W. 18TH STREET
NEW YORK, N.Y. 10011
(212) 627-9691 FAX: (212) 627-5947

(BY APPOINTMENT ONLY)

©FAW

©DIS

**CLASSICS *Illustrated***

**CLASSIC COMICS**
**CLASSICS ILLUSTRATED**

Originals, reprints, juniors, special issues, WAU's, foreign editions, artwork and more! All priced to sell! Send SASE for catalog:

**BOB LEVY**

2456 East 18th Street, Brooklyn, New York 11235

Selling your "CLASSICS"? Please write.

# PUT ON YOUR OWN MONEY-MAKING COMIC CONVENTION$

**Learn the secrets of staging your own money-making conventions with only a small investment. Anyone can earn $600-$2000 every single show. New book tells how to draw dealers, collectors , buyers & celebrities to your show, outdraw other shows, promote & advertise your convention at rock bottom prices, get free advertising, and build/expand into your own business. Results guaranteed! Full refund if not satisfied! Send $20 postpaid to: Collins Publishing, Box 803-L Glenwood, Illinois 60425**

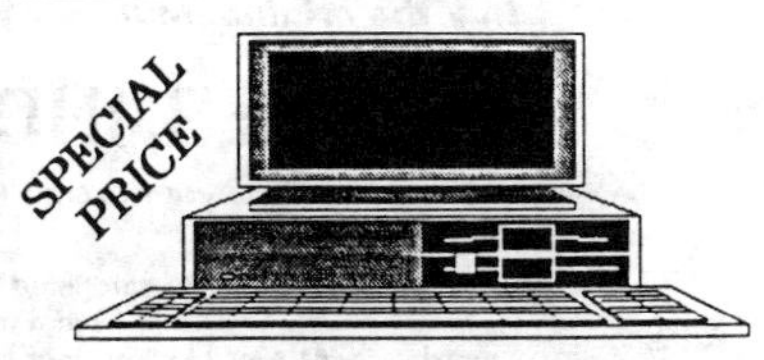

SPECIAL PRICE

# COMPUTERIZED

COMIC BOOK INVENTORY SYSTEM FOR IBM & IBM COMPATIBLES (512K)

PROGRAM FEATURES:

$25

- Keep track of all your comics
- Add/Change/Delete comic records
- Produce screen and printer reports
- Determine percentage increase over purchase price
- Easy to use menu system and documentation

AVAILABLE IN 3 1/2 & 5 1/4 INCH DISKS

CANADIAN RESIDENTS PAY IN CANADIAN FUNDS

U.S AND OTHERS PAY IN U.S. FUNDS TO COVER SHIPPING

CONTACT: ROGER GOODEN

1892 PINE CREEK CRT.
PICKERING, ONTARIO
CANADA L1V 3R4
(416) 839-7251

**HAL FOSTER**(TARZAN, PRINCE VALIANT, MEDIEVAL CASTLE, SONG OF BERNADETTE) **PERCY CROSBY**(SKIPPY)**FRANK GODWIN**(CONNIE, RUSTY RILEY)**WALT KELLY** (POGO) **CHARLES SCHULTZ** (PEANUTS) **JOSE SALINAS** (CISCO KID) **RUSS MANNING**(STRIP ART ONLY) **FRANK KING**(GASOLINE ALLEY) **AL WILLIAMSON** (STRIP ART) **HERRIMAN** (KRAZY KAT)

**ALEX RAYMOND** (X-9,JUNGLE JIM/FLASH GORDON,RIP KIRBY) **FRAZETTA** (JOHNNY COMET/ACE MCCOY; ILLUSTRATIONS) **MCMANUS** (BRINGING UP FATHER) **MCBRIDE** (NAPOLEON) **MCCAY** (LITTLE NEMO)

**CLASSIC STRIP ART COLLECTOR**

ORIGINAL ART BY CLASSIC ARTISTS SOUGHT.
PREFER SUNDAY PAGE FORMAT.
PRIVATE AND DISCREET
COLLECTOR HAS AVID INTEREST IN ARCHIVAL AND HISTORIC ASPECTS OF ALL SIGNIFICANT ORIGINAL NEWSPAPER STRIP ART
COLLECTOR CORRESPONDENCE WELCOMED

© K.F.S.

© K.F.S.

**JACK GILBERT**
**PO BOX 122 VILLAGE STATION**
**NYC, NY 10014**

**212.242 5535**
**212.627 7943 FAX**

© K.F.S

"Reprinted with special permission of King Features Syndicate"

***Buy the original multi-purpose comic divider and index***

# DIVIDER INDEX SYSTEMS

©1985 DIVIDER INDEX SYSTEMS

Our heavy-duty cardboard dividers are reasonably priced and have a multitude of uses. Left or right tabs are available.

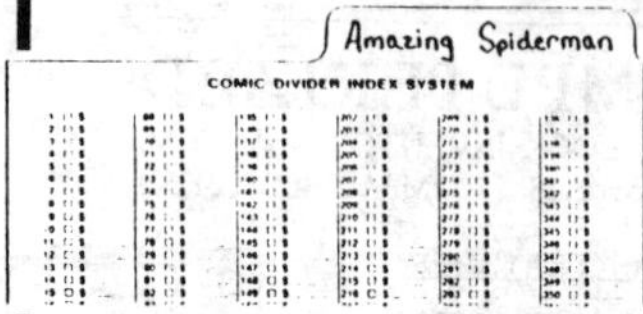

Amazing Spiderman

COMIC DIVIDER INDEX SYSTEM

*To order write or call –*

**DIVIDER INDEX SYSTEMS**
**P.O. Box 917**
**Marshfield, WI 54449**
**1-715-384-4941**

**FREE STAND-UP SALES CARD WITH EACH BOX OF 500**

Index Man presents the

# "BAG TAG"

**Give your business and/or collection the professional look. Instantly display the PRICE and CONDITION of each comic for the buyer & seller.**

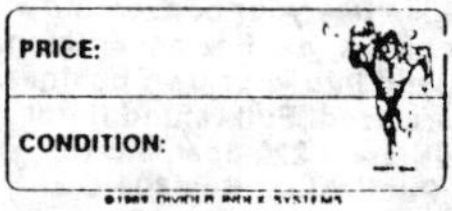

**PRICE:**

**CONDITION:**

**YOUR BAGGED COMIC BOOK**

**A Professional Look!**

INDEX MAN

Adhesive backing will attach to any comic bag protector.

# COMICS BY MAIL

1,000,000 INVENTORY
COMICS PRE-1970

*Phone Credit Cards Accepted*

*Books Shipped Immediately!*

**SPARKLE CITY COMICS**
P.O. Box 67 Sewell, NJ 08080
Toll Free 800-284-6555 To Buy Comics
609-881-1174 For Free Catalog Info

**NOW!**

There are 2

# CHEAP! COMICS T.M. STORES

**SPECIALIZING IN**

**COMICS · BASEBALL CARDS · VIDEOS · MOVIE MEMORABILIA · TOYS**

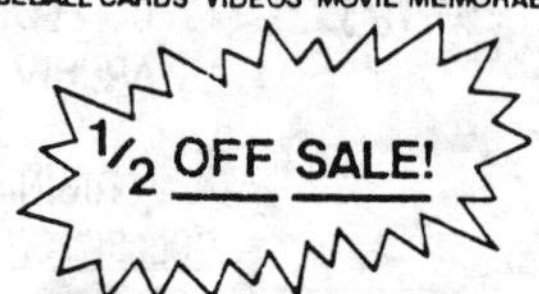


**ON ALL BACK ISSUE COMICS & BASEBALL CARDS**
**2nd. SAT. OF EACH MONTH at CHEAP COMICS–1**
**2nd. SUN. OF EACH MONTH at CHEAP COMICS–2**

**10% TO 40% OFF THE REST!**

| CHEAP COMICS–1 | CHEAP COMICS–2 |
|---|---|
| 12123 GARFIELD AVE. | 7779 MELROSE AVE. |
| SOUTH GATE, CA. 90280 | LOS ANGELES, CA. 90046 |
| 213-408-0900 | 213-655-9323 |
| MON.–SAT. 12-7 PM | MON.–SAT. 12-8 PM |
| SUN. 12-5 PM | SUN. 12-6 PM |

**'WE WORK WITH YOU!'**

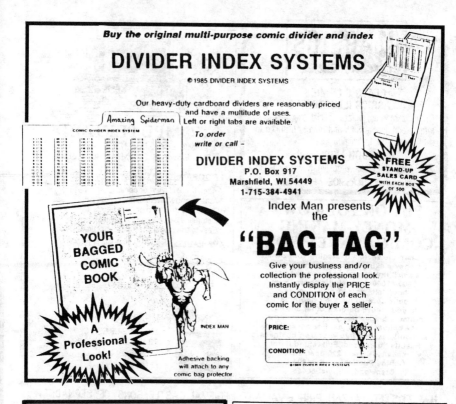

# WALL STREET MOVE OVER!!

ANNOUNCING

# PACIFIC COMIC EXCHANGE, INC.

The Pacific Comic Exchange, Inc. ("PCE") is the first computerized on-line comic book trading company specializing in Golden and Silver Age comics from 1933-1969. All comics listed on the exchange have been graded and certified by the Comic Grading Service of America ("CGSA"), which has developed a new standardized numerical grading system that ensures an unprecedented degree of accuracy and consistency.

## LIQUIDITY

- ❖ International network of dealers, collectors, and retailers
- ❖ Excellent selection of Golden and Silver Age comics
- ❖ Negotiable prices, prompt payment to Sellers
- ❖ Sellers enjoy the lowest commissions in the industry

## ACCESS

- ❖ The Exchange is accessible via phone, computer or mail

## CONFIDENCE AND PROTECTION

- ❖ Books CGSA certified and guaranteed to be in stated condition
- ❖ Full disclosure of any restoration, certified by such respected experts as **Susan Cicconi of Restoration Lab**
- ❖ All books uniquely identified and catalogued - Buyer and Seller protected from fraudulent substitutions and damage

## MEMBERSHIP BENEFITS

- ❖ Reduced commissions and lower fees for special PCE services
- ❖ Free access to all on-line services
- ❖ Detailed monthly reports of sales data, updated listings, special market analyses, etc.
- ❖ Limited Charter Memberships now available

## COMPREHENSIVE ON-LINE SERVICE

- ❖ All statistics available on-line: prices, market trends, grading, restoration information, etc.
- ❖ "Want Lists" link Sellers with interested Buyers
- ❖ Buyers and Sellers can utilize extended "after hours" trading
- ❖ Reduced commissions on all computer on-line transactions

Copyright © 1991 by PACIFIC COMIC EXCHANGE, INC. All Rights Reserved

| Item# | Publ | Title | Symbol | No | Year | P | R | CGSA | Grade | Bid Price | Ask Price | Status |
|---|---|---|---|---|---|---|---|---|---|---|---|---|
| S552 | MVL | AMAZING ADULT FANTASY | AMZ | 13 | 1962 | | | FN/VFN | 50 | 50.00 | 75.00 | AVL |
| S097 | MVL | AMAZING SPIDER-MAN | SPD | 8 | 1964 | | | VFN | 55 | 225.00 | 300.00 | AVL |
| S104 | MVL | AMAZING SPIDER-MAN | SPD | 20 | 1965 | | | NM | 85 | 150.00 | 175.00 | AVL |
| S282 | MVL | AVENGERS, THE | AV | 5 | 1964 | | | VFN/NM | 70 | 110.00 | 150.00 | AVL |
| S458 | DC | BATMAN | B | 6 | 1941 | | | VFN | 65 | 1200.00 | 1600.00 | AVL |
| S547 | DC | BATMAN | B | 27 | 1945 | | | NM | 85 | 1000.00 | 1300.00 | AVL |
| S169 | DC | BATMAN | B | 28 | 1945 | P | | NM/M | 90 | 2200.00 | 2200.00 | SLD |
| S489 | DC | BATMAN | B | 35 | 1949 | | | NM | 80 | 900.00 | 900.00 | SLD |
| S001 | EC | CRIME SUSPENSTORIES | CRMSS | 5 | 1951 | | | VFN | 90 | 250.00 | 320.00 | AVL |
| S005 | EC | CRYPT OF TERROR | CRYPT | 18 | 1950 | | | NM/M | 90 | 0.00 | 800.00 | AVL |
| S501 | MVL | DAREDEVIL | DD | 1 | 1964 | | | VG/FN | 30 | 275.00 | 300.00 | AVL |
| S556 | DC | DETECTIVE COMICS | DET | 28 | 1939 | | R | FN | 35 | 0.00 | 4000.00 | AVL |
| S549 | DC | DETECTIVE COMICS | DET | 56 | 1941 | | | NM | 85 | 1000.00 | 1400.00 | AVL |
| S239 | DC | DETECTIVE COMICS | DET | 180 | 1952 | | | NM | 85 | 500.00 | 500.00 | SLD |
| S302 | MVL | FANTASTIC FOUR | FF | 13 | 1963 | | R | VG | 20 | 55.00 | 75.00 | AVL |
| S545 | DC | FLASH COMICS | F | 104 | 1949 | | | G | 10 | 225.00 | 300.00 | AVL |
| S553 | DC | FLASH, THE | F | 111 | 1960 | | | VFN | 60 | 75.00 | 90.00 | AVL |
| S112 | DC | GREEN LANTERN | GLA | 59 | 1968 | | | FN | 40 | 50.00 | 65.00 | AVL |
| S546 | DC | JUSTICE LEAGUE OF AMERICA | JLA | 1 | 1960 | | | VG | 25 | 275.00 | 350.00 | AVL |
| S499 | DC | RIP HUNTER TIME MASTER | RHTM | 2 | 1961 | | | FN | 45 | 0.00 | 65.00 | AVL |
| S554 | DC | SHOWCASE | SHO | 14 | 1958 | | | FN | 35 | 350.00 | 400.00 | AVL |
| S028 | DC | SUPERMAN | S | 4 | 1940 | | | VFN | 60 | 2000.00 | 2000.00 | SLD |
| S250 | EC | TALES FROM THE CRYPT | CRYPT | 33 | 1953 | | | VFN | 50 | 0.00 | 300.00 | AVL |
| S160 | MVL | TALES OF SUSPENSE | TOS | 40 | 1963 | | | VFN/NM | 70 | 425.00 | 525.00 | AVL |

--hit any key to continue--

## TRADE WITH CONFIDENCE, TRADE WITH PCE

Call or write for a catalogue of books currently listed on The Exchange and for more information on how to become a member or open a trading account. You can also register to receive this information and view an on-line demo by calling our modem line (parity: N, data bits: 8, stop bits: 1, duplex: full). Meetings and consultations by appointment only.

**Pacific Comic Exchange, Inc.**
P.O. Box 34849 ❖ Los Angeles, CA ❖ 90034
Tel: (213) 836-PCEI Fax: (213) 836-7127 Modem: (213) 836-3076

DET27 90$90000 JLA1 25$350 S4 60$2000 B28 90$2200 FF1 95$7000 SHO14 35$400 SPD1 96$5000

MasterCard

*ATTENTION!*

# LONG ISLAND, BROOKLYN, QUEENS, MANHATTAN

## The Nation's Foremost Comic Dealers are Right in Your Backyard

See
Next
Page!

# Collecting Supplies

**Next day shipping available!**

## Comic Storage Bags

- High clarity polypropylene
- 2″ flap
- More acid-resistant than polyethylene
- Labeled outer bag
- Bagged in 100's

***Bags as low as $18.50 per 1000!***
***See details below!***

| NAME | SIZE | QUANTITY | PRICE | CASE PRICE • 2000 per case unless noted: UNIT PRICE | TOTAL | WEIGHT |
|---|---|---|---|---|---|---|
| **Current** Fits new comics nice and tight. | 6⅞″ x 10¼″ | 1000-1900 | $2.75/100 | Current and Regular Bags: $22/1000 | $44 | 24 lbs |
| **Regular** Fits normal size comics published after 1965. | 7⅛″ x 10¼″ | 1000-1900 | $2.75/100 | (see Discount Quantities below) | | |
| **Silver Age** Fits Giants, Annuals, DC's 1951-1965, and 50's Dells. | 7⅜″ x 10¼″ | 200-400<br>500-1900 | $4.50/100<br>$3.50/100 | $26/1000 | $52 | 25 lbs |
| **Golden Age** Fits comics 1944 and later. | 7⅝″ x 10¼″ | 200-400<br>500-1900 | $4.50/100<br>$3.50/100 | $26/1000 | $52 | 26 lbs |
| **Magazine** Fits Marvel, Warren and many common magazines. | 8½″ x 11″ | 500-1900 | $3.75/100 | $30/1000 | $60 | 31 lbs |
| **Thick Magazine** Fits Playboy,Dragon, most standard mags & music books. Use with our PEARL WHITE magazine boards. | 8¾″ x 11″ | 200-400<br>500-1900 | $5.00/100<br>$3.95/100 | $30/1000 | $60 | 33 lbs |
| **Treasury** Fits Treasury comics and folded movie posters. | 10½″ x 13½″ | 200-400<br>500-1900 | $10.00/100<br>$ 8.00/100 | $55/1000 | $110 | 46 lbs |
| **Life Magazine** | 11¼″ x 14¼″ | 100-400<br>500-900 | $12.50/100<br>$ 9.50/100 | $70/1000 (1000 Life bags per case) | $70 | 28 lbs |
| **Paperback Book** | 5″ x 7⅜″ | 200-400<br>500-1900 | $5.00/100<br>$3.95/100 | $30/1000 (4,000 Paperback Book bags per case) | $120 | 13 lbs |

**DISCOUNT QUANTITIES**

| Cases | No. Bags | Weight | Unit Price | Price |
|---|---|---|---|---|
| 1 Case | 2.000 | 24 lbs | $22.00/1000 | $ 44.00 |
| 5 Cases | 10.000 | 120 lbs | $20.00/1000 | $200.00 |
| 13 Cases | 26.000 | 312 lbs | $19.50/1000 | $507.00 |
| 25 Cases | 50.000 | 600 lbs | $18.50/1000 | $925.00 |

## ComiCovers

- Virgin polyethylene
- Labeled outer bag
- 1½″ flap
- Bagged in 100's
- Free display upon request

• 2000 per case

| NAME | SIZE | QUANTITY | PRICE | UNIT PRICE | TOTAL |
|---|---|---|---|---|---|
| **Modern** | 6⅞″ x 10½″ | 1000-1900 | $2.95/100 | $24/1,000 | $48.00 |
| **Regular** | 7⅛″ x 10½″ | 1000-1900 | $2.95/100 | $24/1,000 | $48.00 |

# Friendly Frank's DISTRIBUTION, INC.

HEADQUARTERS: 3990 Broadway, Gary, IN 46408 • 219/884-5052/3 • FAX:887-2205
CHICAGO: 727 Factory Rd., Addison, IL 60101 • 708/543-6262 • FAX:543-6263
DETROIT: 976 E. 10 Mile Rd., Hazel Park, MI 48030 • 313/542-2525 • FAX:542-2526

ORIGINAL COMIC ART
©1990 S. McMANUS
BUY
TRADE
SELL
SCOTT DUNBIER
P.O. BOX 1446 GRACIE STATION NYC, NY 10028
212 666 0982 (TEL) 212 662 8732 (FAX)

THE UNDISPUTED WORLD LEADERS IN MARVEL BACK ISSUES!!!

GERRY ROSS present ROBERT CRESTOHL

**THE COMPLETE MARVEL COLLECTION AT SPECIAL DISCOUNT PRICES!!!**

**20 YRS EXPERIENC**
**HONEST GRADING**
**LARGE STOCK**

**HOW TO ORDER: 1)** Comics listed by price/condition. GD / VG = good to very good; VG / F = very good to fine; F / VF = fine to very fine; VF / NM = ve fine to near mint; M = mint. Note that our pricing scale is based + / − 5% (approx.) on a percentage of the mint price, i.e. mint = 100%; nm / m = 85 vf / nm = 65%; f / vf = 50%; vg / f = 30%; and g / vg = 15%. **2)** Prices listed are for each comic, ex.: Conan #82-99; 1.50 (each issue). **3)** Payment; in U. funds by check, money order, MasterCard or Visa (Canadian residents add 15% to Canadian funds. **4)** LIST ALTERNATE CHOICES, and receive a **10** discount!!! **5)** Please try to list a RANGE OF CONDITIONS when ordering; ex.: Conan #1 in condition from fine to mint. List lowest and highest possib condition acceptable, to insure that your order will be fully processed. (We will upgrade or downgrade to fill if no instructions given). Print clearly. **6)** Prices c hot books subject to change, so call if in doubt. POSTAGE and HANDLING; add $3.00 if up to 10 comics; $6.00 if more than 11 comics. Overseas orde multiply postage by 3. **7)** Customer responsible for maintaining condition on all returns (15% restocking fee). PLEASE INCLUDE YOUR AREA CODE AN PHONE NUMBERS WITH ALL ORDERS!!! Catalog FREE with all orders. **8) WE TAKE PHONE MASTERCARD AND VISA. HAVE YOUR CARD IN FRON OF YOU WHEN ORDERING, CALL (514) 630-4518. SPECIAL PHONE DISCOUNT 5% OFF!!! TAKE 15% OFF ALL ORDERS OVER $2000.00** (so lor as no two books make up half). **10% DISCOUNT OFF ALL ORDERS WITH ALTERNATE CHOICES** (equal in value to first choices)**!!! We grade accurate Not responsible for typos. SEND FOR GIANT MARVEL CATALOG $1.00!!! (FREE WITH ORDER) Collectors note. This marks our 20th year of helpir collectors fill out their runs. In this time period prices have skyrocketted! Comics (believe it or not!) have outperformed almost every other type investment! This company has the largest selection of early, middle, and later Marvels in the world (20-50 copies of each number of each title!), ar is usually the sole company listing the complete run of all Marvel titles from 1960 on. You should receive all (or most) of your order, especially you have followed directions as per above. If you are looking for titles not listed here send a want list with phone number, $5.00 and detailed info capital to invest in purchases, etc. and we will call you. Titles, companies we have include D.C., Gold Key, Dell, Classics, Big little Books, Pulp with special emphasis on golden age DC, and Timely; see Overstreet guide for more ad info.**

VISA MasterCard

MAIL ALL ORDERS/PAYMENT/QUERIES TO:

**(514) 630-4518**

**CRESTOHL / ROSS**
**4732 Circle Road, Dept. IM**
**Montreal, Quebec, Canada H3W 1Z1**

| | gd/vg | vg/f | f/vf | vf/nm | nm/m | mint |
|---|---|---|---|---|---|---|
| **AMAZING SPIDERMAN** | | | | | | |
| AF #15 (origin) | 500.00 | 1200.00 | 2500.00 | 5600.00 | 7200.00 | 8000.00 |
| #1 | 500.00 | 1200.00 | 2500.00 | 5600.00 | 7200.00 | 8000.00 |
| 2 | 135.00 | 270.00 | 540.00 | 840.00 | 1100.00 | 1500.00 |
| 3, 14 | 120.00 | 265.00 | 450.00 | 625.00 | 800.00 | 1000.00 |
| 4-6 | 90.00 | 160.00 | 275.00 | 400.00 | 500.00 | 600.00 |
| 7-10; 129 | 60.00 | 105.00 | 175.00 | 240.00 | 350.00 | 400.00 |
| 11-13; 15, 17, 20, 50 | | 75.00 | 115.00 | 160.00 | 220.00 | 265.00 |
| 16, 18, 19 | 22.00 | 45.00 | 75.00 | 90.00 | 135.00 | 150.00 |
| 21-30; 39, 40, 42, 100 | | 29.00 | 55.00 | 75.00 | 100.00 | 120.00 |
| 31-38 | 6.00 | 15.00 | 30.00 | 42.00 | 60.00 | 70.00 |
| 41, 43-49; 51, 96-98; 101, 102 | | 9.00 | 15.00 | 20.00 | 27.00 | 30.00 |
| 52-60; 90, 94 | | 8.00 | 12.00 | 15.00 | 21.00 | 25.00 |
| 61-89; 91-93; 95, 99 | | 6.00 | 8.00 | 12.00 | 15.00 | 19.00 |
| 103-120; 123, 124 (Hulk X-Over) | | 4.00 | 6.00 | 8.00 | 12.00 | 15.00 |
| 121, 122 (Death issues) | | 20.00 | 40.00 | 50.00 | 75.00 | 95.00 |
| 125-128; 130-133; 136-140 | | 3.00 | 6.00 | 8.00 | 12.00 | 15.00 |
| 129 (1st Punisher) | 40.00 | 90.00 | 150.00 | 200.00 | 250.00 | 300.00 |
| 134, 135, 161, 162 | 6.00 | 15.00 | 20.00 | 30.00 | 40.00 | 50.00 |
| 141-160; 189, 190 (Byrne), 200 | | | 4.00 | 6.00 | 7.00 | 8.00 |
| 163-173; 176-188; 191-199; 203 | | | 4.00 | 6.00 | 7.00 | 8.00 |
| 174-175, gs #4 (Punisher) | | 10.00 | 20.00 | 25.00 | 30.00 | 35.00 |
| 201, 202 (Punisher), 300 | | 6.00 | 8.00 | 10.00 | 15.00 | 20.00 |
| 204-237; 255-283 | | | | | 4.00 | 5.00 |
| 290-292 | | | | | 3.00 | 4.00 |
| 238 (1st hobg) | | | | | 25.00 | 30.00 |
| 239 | | | | | 10.00 | 12.00 |
| 240-251; 254 | | | | | | 3.00 |
| 252, 285 (new uni, punisher) | | | | | 8.00 | 10.00 |
| 253, 284, 286-289; 293-296 | | | | | | 4.00 |
| 297 | | | | | | 2.00 |
| 298 (1st McFarlane) | | | | | | 50.00 |
| 299, 301 (scarce) | | | | | | 20.00 |
| 300 | | | | | | 30.00 |
| 302-315 | | | | | | 12.00 |
| 316-320 | | | | | | 8.00 |
| 321-326, 328 (Last McFarlane) | | | | | | 6.00 |
| 327, 329 | | | | | | 2.00 |
| 330, 331 (Punisher) | | | | | | 3.00 |
| 332 up | | | | | | 2.00 |
| Annual 1 | 35.00 | 75.00 | 140.00 | 180.00 | 270.00 | 300.00 |
| 2 | 10.00 | 20.00 | 30.00 | 36.00 | 60.00 | 70.00 |
| 3, 4 | 5.00 | 10.00 | 15.00 | 18.00 | 25.00 | 30.00 |
| 5-9, 14 (Miller), 15 (Punisher) | | | 10.00 | 12.00 | 16.00 | 20.00 |
| 10-13 (Byrne) | | | 5.00 | 6.00 | 8.00 | 10.00 |
| 16-20 | | | | | 3.00 | 4.00 |
| 21 (Wedding Peter Parker cover) | | | | | | 10.00 |
| 21 (Wedding Spiderman cover) | | | | | | 5.00 |
| 22, 23 (Evolutionary war) | | | | | | 4.00 |
| Marvel Superaction #2 punisher | | | | | 150.00 | 200.00 |
| Marvel Preview punisher | | | | | 150.00 | 200.00 |
| Giant Size 1 | | | | | 10.00 | 12.00 |
| 2, 3, 5, 6 | | | | | 8.00 | 10.00 |
| 4 (3rd Punisher app.) | | | | | 50.00 | 60.00 |
| **AVENGERS** | | | | | | |
| #1 | 125.00 | 250.00 | 400.00 | 750.00 | 820.00 | 1200.00 |
| 2 | 50.00 | 95.00 | 170.00 | 230.00 | 300.00 | 380.00 |
| 3 | 35.00 | 70.00 | 120.00 | 150.00 | 190.00 | 260.00 |
| 4 (1st Silver app.) | 75.00 | 150.00 | 250.00 | 380.00 | 450.00 | 600.00 |
| 5 | 25.00 | 50.00 | 75.00 | 95.00 | 130.00 | 160.00 |
| 6-11; 16 | 20.00 | 40.00 | 55.00 | 75.00 | 90.00 | 130.00 |
| 12-15 | 15.00 | 25.00 | 40.00 | 48.00 | 60.00 | 85.00 |
| 17-19; 57 | 9.00 | 15.00 | 25.00 | 30.00 | 42.00 | 50.00 |
| 20-22; 58 | | 12.00 | 19.00 | 24.00 | 32.00 | 40.00 |
| 23-30; 28, 50, 71 (1st Invaders) | | | 13.00 | 16.00 | 20.00 | 27.00 |
| 31-47; 51-56; 59-65 | | 5.00 | 7.00 | 9.00 | 12.00 | 15.00 |
| 48 (1st Black Knight) | | 9.00 | 14.00 | 18.00 | 24.00 | 30.00 |
| 66, 67, 110, 111 (X-Men) | | 6.00 | 9.00 | 12.00 | 14.00 | 18.00 |
| 68-70; 72-92; 116-118 | | 4.00 | 6.00 | 7.00 | 8.00 | 11.00 |
| 93, 100 (Adams, Smith art) | | 14.00 | 21.00 | 28.00 | 35.00 | 43.00 |
| 94-96 | | 8.00 | 12.00 | 15.00 | 20.00 | 25.00 |
| 97-99 | | 6.00 | 9.00 | 12.00 | 15.00 | 19.00 |
| 101-109; 112-115 | | 4.00 | 5.00 | 6.00 | 7.00 | 9.00 |
| 119-140 | | 3.00 | 4.00 | 5.00 | 6.00 | 8.00 |
| 141-163; 167-191 (Byrne) | | | 2.00 | 3.00 | 4.00 | 5.00 |
| 164-166 (Byrne art) | | | 4.00 | 5.00 | 6.00 | 8.00 |
| 192-199; 201, 202, 272 | | | | 2.00 | 3.00 | 4.00 |
| 200, 263 (1st X-Factor), 300 | | | | 2.00 | 3.00 | 4.00 |
| 203-262; 264-271; 273-299, 301 up | | | | | 2.00 | 3.00 |
| Annual 1 | | 13.00 | 20.00 | 24.00 | 30.00 | 40.00 |
| 2, 3, 7 (Starlin) | | | 6.00 | 12.00 | 15.00 | 20.00 |
| 4-6 | | | 4.00 | 5.00 | 6.00 | 9.00 |
| 8 up | | | | 3.00 | 4.00 | 6.00 |
| Giant Size 1-5 | | | | 4.00 | 5.00 | 8.00 |
| **CAPTAIN AMERICA (See also Tales of Suspense 58-99)** | | | | | | |
| #100 (origin) | 35.00 | 75.00 | 150.00 | 200.00 | 250.00 | 300.00 |
| 101, 109 (Origin Retold) | | 20.00 | 30.00 | 36.00 | 45.00 | 55.00 |
| 241 (Punisher app. scarce) | | | 30.00 | 35.00 | 50.00 | 60.00 |
| 102-108, 117 (1st Falcon) | | 7.00 | 15.00 | 18.00 | 24.00 | 30.00 |
| 110, 111, 113 (Steranko) | | 15.00 | 22.00 | 25.00 | 35.00 | 45.00 |
| 112, 114-116; 118-136; 139, 140 | | 4.00 | 5.00 | 6.00 | 8.00 | 10.00 |
| 137, 138 (Spiderman) | | 5.00 | 7.00 | 9.00 | 12.00 | 15.00 |
| 141-171; 176-179; 200 | | | 2.00 | 3.00 | 4.00 | 5.00 |
| 172-175 (All X-Men) | | | 4.00 | 5.00 | 7.00 | 9.00 |
| 180-199 | | | 1.00 | 2.00 | 3.00 | 4.00 |
| 201-240; 242-246; 256-331; 341 up | | | | | 2.00 | 3.00 |
| 332, 333 (Cap resigns, New Cap) | | | | | | 10.00 |
| 247-255 (Byrne issues) | | | | | | 4.00 |
| 334-349 | | | | | | 3.00 |
| 350 | | | | | | 5.00 |
| Annual 1, 2 | | | 12.00 | 15.00 | 20.00 | 25.00 |
| 3-7; 9 | | | | 3.00 | 4.00 | 6.00 |
| 8 (Wolverine) | | | | | | 20.00 |
| Giant Size 1 | | | | 7.00 | 10.00 | 12.00 |
| **CONAN** | | | | | | |
| #1 | 25.00 | 45.00 | 75.00 | 90.00 | 125.00 | 160.00 |
| 2 | | 18.00 | 30.00 | 36.00 | 48.00 | 60.00 |
| 3 (Scarce) | | 22.00 | 30.00 | 36.00 | 65.00 | 75.00 |
| 4, 5, 14, 15 | | | 15.00 | 18.00 | 25.00 | 30.00 |
| 6-10 | | | 12.00 | 14.00 | 18.00 | 23.00 |
| 11-13; 16, 23, 24 | | | 9.00 | 11.00 | 15.00 | 18.00 |
| 17-22 | | | 7.00 | 8.00 | 11.00 | 14.00 |
| 25, 37 (Adams) | | | 4.00 | 5.00 | 7.00 | 9.00 |
| 26-30 | | | 3.00 | 4.00 | 6.00 | 7.00 |
| 31-36; 38-40 | | | | 4.00 | 6.00 | 7.00 |
| 41-60; 100 | | | | 3.00 | 4.00 | 5.00 |
| 61-99; 115, 200 | | | | 2.00 | 3.00 | 4.00 |
| 101-114; 116 up | | | | | 1.00 | 2.00 |
| Annual 1 (King Size) | | | 3.00 | 4.00 | 6.00 | 8.00 |
| Annual 2-11 and up | | | | 2.00 | 3.00 | 4.00 |
| Giant Size 1-5 | | | | 3.00 | 4.00 | 5.00 |

| | gd/vg | vg/f | f/vf | vf/nm | nm/m | mint |
|---|---|---|---|---|---|---|
| **DAREDEVIL** | | | | | | |
| #1 | 120.00 | 250.00 | 450.00 | 650.00 | 900.00 | 1400.00 |
| 2 | 40.00 | 95.00 | 150.00 | 200.00 | 290.00 | 350.00 |
| 3 | 30.00 | 60.00 | 90.00 | 120.00 | 150.00 | 190.00 |
| 4, 5, 7 (costume) | 20.00 | 35.00 | 50.00 | 65.00 | 85.00 | 110.00 |
| 6, 8-10 | 17.00 | 30.00 | 45.00 | 60.00 | 70.00 | 90.00 |
| 11-17 | 12.00 | 20.00 | 30.00 | 36.00 | 45.00 | 60.00 |
| 18-20; 100 | 6.00 | 13.00 | 17.00 | 21.00 | 25.00 | 34.00 |
| 21-30 | 4.00 | 8.00 | 14.00 | 16.00 | 23.00 | 28.00 |
| 31-40; 50, 52, 57 | 3.00 | 7.00 | 11.00 | 14.00 | 17.00 | 23.00 |
| 41-49; 53 | | 5.00 | 7.00 | 9.00 | 10.00 | 15.00 |
| 54-60; 81, 138 | | 4.00 | 5.00 | 6.00 | 7.00 | 9.00 |
| 61-80; 82-99 | | | 3.00 | 4.00 | 5.00 | 7.00 |
| 101-120; 162 | | | 3.00 | 4.00 | 5.00 | 6.00 |
| 121-130; 132-137; 139-157 | | | 2.00 | 3.00 | 4.00 | 5.00 |
| 131 (1st Bullseye) | | | 10.00 | 15.00 | 20.00 | 25.00 |
| 158 (1st Miller) | | 18.00 | 30.00 | 36.00 | 55.00 | 60.00 |
| 159 | | | 10.00 | 12.00 | 16.00 | 20.00 |
| 160, 161, 163, 164 | | | 8.00 | 10.00 | 13.00 | 16.00 |
| 165-167; 169, 170 | | | 6.00 | 8.00 | 10.00 | 12.00 |
| 168 (1st Electra) | | 12.00 | 16.00 | 22.00 | 30.00 | 35.00 |
| 171-181; 226, 229-233 | | | 3.00 | 4.00 | 5.00 | 6.00 |
| 227, 228, 248, 249 | | | | | 5.00 | 6.00 |
| 182-184; 196, 257 (Punisher) | | | | 5.00 | 6.00 | 7.00 |
| 185-195; 197-225 | | | | | | 3.00 |
| 254-256 (Typhoid Mary) | | | | | | 6.00 |
| 234-247; 250, 251, 253, 258 up | | | | | | 2.00 |
| Annual 1 | | 12.00 | 18.00 | 24.00 | 35.00 | 40.00 |
| 2-4 | | 7.00 | 10.00 | 13.00 | 16.00 | 20.00 |
| Giant Size 1 | | | | 5.00 | 6.00 | 8.00 |
| **DEFENDERS** | | | | | | |
| #1 | | | 12.00 | 17.00 | 25.00 | 30.00 |
| 2-10 | | | 6.00 | 8.00 | 10.00 | 13.00 |
| 11-20 | | | 2.00 | 3.00 | 4.00 | 6.00 |
| 21-151 | | | 1.00 | 2.00 | 2.50 | 3.00 |
| 152 last issue (scarce, X-Factor app.) | | | | | 4.00 | 5.00 |
| Giant Size 1-5 | | | 4.00 | 5.00 | 8.00 | 10.00 |
| **DOCTOR STRANGE** | | | | | | |
| #169 (origin) | | 45.00 | 55.00 | 75.00 | 85.00 | 100.00 |
| 170-183 | | | 12.00 | 17.00 | 20.00 | 25.00 |
| 1 (1974) | | | 13.00 | 17.00 | 25.00 | 30.00 |
| 2-81 | | | 2.00 | 3.00 | 4.00 | 5.00 |
| Annual 1 | | | | | 4.00 | 5.00 |
| Giant Size 1 | | | | | 4.00 | 5.00 |
| Special Edition 1 | | | | | | 2.00 |
| **FANTASTIC FOUR** | | | | | | |
| #1 | 650.00 | 1450.00 | 2700.00 | 4600.00 | 7200.00 | 8000.00 |
| 2 | 125.00 | 290.00 | 500.00 | 660.00 | 860.00 | 1100.00 |
| 3-5 | 100.00 | 210.00 | 350.00 | 420.00 | 650.00 | 750.00 |
| 6 (Dr. Doom/Submariner) | | 150.00 | 300.00 | 400.00 | 550.00 | 600.00 |
| 7-10; 12 | 50.00 | 90.00 | 140.00 | 210.00 | 310.00 | 420.00 |
| 11, 13 | 45.00 | 80.00 | 140.00 | 180.00 | 220.00 | 300.00 |
| 14-20; 25, 26, 48 | 30.00 | 45.00 | 75.00 | 90.00 | 120.00 | 150.00 |
| 21-24; 27, 28 | 15.00 | 25.00 | 45.00 | 50.00 | 75.00 | 85.00 |
| 29-40; 49, 50, 100 | 9.00 | 15.00 | 25.00 | 30.00 | 40.00 | 50.00 |
| 41-47 (45 - 1st Inhumans) | | 11.00 | 16.00 | 20.00 | 25.00 | 32.00 |
| 51-60; 66, 67 | 5.00 | 9.00 | 15.00 | 18.00 | 24.00 | 30.00 |
| 61-65; 68-70; 72-77; 112,116 | | 6.00 | 9.00 | 12.00 | 15.00 | 17.00 |
| 71, 73, 78-99 | 2.00 | 4.00 | 6.00 | 8.00 | 10.00 | 12.00 |
| 101-111; 113-115; 117-120 | | | 3.00 | 4.00 | 5.00 | 7.00 |
| 121-123; 155-157 (all Surfer) | | | | 5.00 | 6.00 | 8.00 |
| 124-149; 150-154; 158-160 | | | | 2.00 | 3.00 | 4.00 |
| 161-180 | | | | 1.50 | 2.50 | 3.50 |
| 181-199; 201-208 | | | | 1.00 | 2.00 | 3.00 |
| 209 up | | | | 1.00 | 2.00 | 3.00 |
| Annual 1 | | 25.00 | 45.00 | 90.00 | 120.00 | 150.00 |
| 2 | | 13.50 | 27.50 | 50.50 | 68.00 | 85.00 |
| 3 | | 10.00 | 22.00 | 27.00 | 36.00 | 45.00 |
| 4-6 | | 7.00 | 8.00 | 9.00 | 12.00 | 15.00 |
| 7-10 | | 3.50 | 4.00 | 5.00 | 7.00 | 9.00 |
| 11 up | | | | | 3.00 | 4.00 |
| Giant Size 1-6 | | | 4.00 | 5.00 | 6.00 | 8.00 |
| **INCREDIBLE HULK** | | | | | | |
| #1 | 200.00 | 350.00 | 650.00 | 950.00 | 1200.00 | 1500.00 |
| 2 | 80.00 | 135.00 | 225.00 | 280.00 | 420.00 | 450.00 |
| 3 | 50.00 | 95.00 | 170.00 | 210.00 | 315.00 | 350.00 |
| 4-6 | 45.00 | 80.00 | 145.00 | 175.00 | 260.00 | 290.00 |
| 102 | 30.00 | 60.00 | 80.00 | 120.00 | 150.00 | 200.00 |
| 103-110 | | 10.00 | 15.00 | 20.00 | 27.00 | 35.00 |
| 111-117; 176-178 | | 6.00 | 8.00 | 10.00 | 12.00 | 15.00 |
| 162, 172, 200, 314 | | | 5.00 | 6.00 | 8.00 | 10.00 |
| 330, 331, 340 (McFarlane, Wolverine) | | | | | | 20.00 |
| 118-125; 272, 324, 332-346 | | | 5.00 | 6.00 | 8.00 | 10.00 |
| 126-161; 300, 315-319 | | | 3.00 | 4.00 | 5.00 | 7.00 |
| 183-199, 250 | | | 2.00 | 3.00 | 4.00 | 6.00 |
| 163-171; 173-175; 179, 324 | | | 2.00 | 3.00 | 4.00 | 6.00 |
| 180, 182 | | | 30.00 | 40.00 | 50.00 | 70.00 |
| 181 | 40.00 | 70.00 | 150.00 | 200.00 | 250.00 | 300.00 |
| 201-249; 251-271; 273-299; 301-313; 320-323; 325-329; 347 up | | | | | 1.00 | 2.00 |
| Annual 1 (Steranko cvr) | | 14.00 | 17.00 | 25.00 | 30.00 | 35.00 |
| 2, 3, 7 (Byrne) | | | 9.00 | 12.00 | 15.00 | 20.00 |
| 4, 5, 6, 8 | | | | 4.00 | 5.00 | 6.00 |
| 9 up | | | | | | 3.00 |
| Giant Size 1 | | | | | 6.00 | 8.00 |
| **IRONMAN** | | | | | | |
| #1 (origin) | 45.00 | 85.00 | 195.00 | 300.00 | 395.00 | 475.00 |
| 2 | 15.00 | 30.00 | 50.00 | 60.00 | 80.00 | 100.00 |
| 3, 4, 5 | 12.00 | 30.00 | 42.00 | 50.00 | 55.00 | 85.00 |
| 6-10 | 6.00 | 13.00 | 17.00 | 20.00 | 27.00 | 35.50 |
| 11-15, 47 (origin retold), 50 | | 8.00 | 13.00 | 16.00 | 22.00 | 27.00 |
| 16-40; 53, 55, 56, 100, 118 (Byrne) | | | 7.50 | 9.00 | 13.00 | 15.00 |
| 41-46; 48-52; 54, 57-70 | | 4.00 | 5.00 | 6.00 | 8.00 | 9.00 |
| 169 (New Ironman) | | | | | 9.00 | 11.00 |
| 71-99; 170 | | | 3.00 | 4.00 | 5.00 | 6.00 |
| 101-117; 119-130; 171 | | | 2.00 | 3.00 | 4.00 | 5.00 |
| 131-168; 172 up | | | | 2.00 | 3.00 | 3.50 |
| Annual 1 | | | 25.00 | 35.00 | 45.00 | 50.00 |
| 2 | | | | 15.00 | 20.00 | 25.00 |
| 3, 4 | | | | 14.00 | 16.00 | 20.50 |
| 5 up | | | | | 6.00 | 8.00 |
| Giant Size 1 | | | | | 16.00 | 20.00 |
| Crash Graphic Novel | | | | | | 13.00 |
| Iron Man & Submariner (1968) 1 | | | | 50.00 | 60.00 | 75.00 |
| **PETER PARKER (Spectacular Spiderman)** | | | | | | |
| #1, 27, 28, 64 | | | | 20.00 | 28.00 | 35.00 |
| 2-5; 69, 70, 131 | | | | 5.00 | 6.00 | 8.00 |
| 6-10; 22, 23, 90, 91 | | | | 4.00 | 5.00 | 6.00 |
| 11-21; 24-26; 58, 100, 140, 141 | | | | 3.00 | 4.00 | 5.00 |

| | gd/vg | vg/f | f/vf | vf/nm | nm/m | m |
|---|---|---|---|---|---|---|
| **PETER PARKER (cont.)** | | | | | | |
| #29-40; 60, 75 | | | | 2.00 | 3.00 | 4. |
| 41-57; 59, 132-139 | | | | | 2.00 | 3. |
| 61-63; 65-68; 71-74; 76-80; 84-89 | | | | | 2.00 | 3. |
| 92-99; 101-130; 142 up | | | | | | 2. |
| 81-83 (Punisher) | | | | | 8.00 | 10. |
| **PUNISHER** | | | | | | |
| Marvel preview #2 (origin Punisher) scarce | | | | | 95.00 | 125. |
| Marvel super action #1 (1976, Punisher) scarce | | | | | 75.00 | 95. |
| Miniseries #1 | | | | | 40.00 | 45. |
| 2 | | | | | 20.00 | 25. |
| 3-5 | | | | | 13.00 | 15. |
| Regular series #1, 10 | | | | | | 15. |
| 2-5 | | | | | | 7. |
| 6-9 | | | | | | 10. |
| 11-15 | | | | | | 5. |
| 16-25 | | | | | | 3. |
| 25 up | | | | | | 2. |
| Annual 1, 2 | | | | | | 5. |
| **SILVER SURFER** | | | | | | |
| #1, 4 | 50.00 | 75.00 | 125.00 | 150.00 | 200.00 | 250. |
| 2, 3 | | 25.00 | 30.00 | 40.00 | 50.00 | 75. |
| 5-7 | | 15.00 | 20.00 | 25.00 | 35.00 | 50. |
| 8-10; 14 | | 12.00 | 15.00 | 20.00 | 27.00 | 40. |
| 11-13; 15-18 | | 10.00 | 15.00 | 18.00 | 24.00 | 30. |
| **STRANGE TALES** | | | | | | |
| #101 | 50.00 | 110.00 | 190.00 | 240.00 | 270.00 | 400. |
| 102, 114, 115 | | 45.00 | 75.00 | 90.00 | 110.00 | 150. |
| 103-105; 107 | 20.00 | 35.00 | 60.00 | 84.00 | 95.00 | 120. |
| 106, 108, 109, 111 | 15.00 | 25.00 | 45.00 | 55.00 | 65.00 | 90. |
| 110 (1st Dr. Strange) | | 90.00 | 150.00 | 180.00 | 270.00 | 300. |
| 112, 113, 135 | | 20.00 | 30.00 | 36.00 | 45.00 | 60. |
| 116-120; 130 | 6.00 | 10.00 | 15.00 | 18.00 | 24.00 | 30. |
| 121-129; 131-134 | | 6.00 | 9.00 | 11.00 | 14.00 | 18. |
| 136-147; 149, 150, 152-158; 160-166, 168 | | | | 9.00 | 12.00 | 15. |
| 148, 151, 159, 167 | | 7.00 | 9.00 | 11.00 | 15.00 | 18. |
| 169-177 | | | | | 2.00 | 3. |
| 178 (Origin Warlock) | | | | | 10.00 | 14. |
| 179-181 (all Warlock) | | | | | 5.00 | 6. |
| Annual 1, 2 scarce | | 45.00 | 75.00 | 90.00 | 120.00 | 150. |
| **TALES OF SUSPENSE** | | | | | | |
| #39 (1st Ironman) | 150.00 | 380.00 | 575.00 | 730.00 | 1080.00 | 1350. |
| 40 | 60.00 | 130.00 | 225.00 | 360.00 | 500.00 | 600. |
| 41 | 40.00 | 60.00 | 135.00 | 225.00 | 275.00 | 300. |
| 42-45 | 22.00 | 36.00 | 60.00 | 92.00 | 115.00 | 120. |
| 46, 47, 52 | 9.00 | 20.00 | 30.00 | 36.00 | 65.00 | 75. |
| 58 | 20.00 | 35.00 | 60.00 | 75.00 | 90.00 | 120. |
| 48, 57 (1st Hawkeye), 63 (1st Silver C. Amer.) | | 30.00 | 45.00 | 60.00 | 80.00 | 100. |
| 49, 50, 51, 53 | | 20.00 | 30.00 | 36.00 | 48.00 | 60. |
| 59 (Cap beg.) | | 40.00 | 60.00 | 70.00 | 80.00 | 90. |
| 65, 66 | | 15.00 | 20.00 | 25.00 | 35.00 | 50. |
| 54-56 | 6.00 | 13.00 | 17.00 | 20.00 | 25.00 | 35. |
| 60-62; 64, 67-99 | | 7.00 | 10.00 | 12.00 | 15.00 | 20. |
| **TALES TO ASTONISH** | | | | | | |
| #27 (1st Antman) | 150.00 | 250.00 | 400.00 | 600.00 | 875.00 | 1200. |
| 35 | 90.00 | 180.00 | 300.00 | 450.00 | 600.00 | 700. |
| 36 | 35.00 | 70.00 | 95.00 | 150.00 | 235.00 | 250. |
| 37-40; 44, 49 | 20.00 | 35.00 | 65.00 | 75.00 | 105.00 | 130. |
| 41-43; 59, 60 | | 20.00 | 30.00 | 36.00 | 65.00 | 75. |
| 45-48; 57 (Spiderman) | | 15.00 | 24.00 | 29.00 | 45.00 | 50. |
| 50-56; 58, 70, 92, 93 | | 9.00 | 15.00 | 20.00 | 25.00 | 30. |
| 61-69; 100 | 5.00 | 7.00 | 14.00 | 20.00 | 23.00 | 28. |
| 70 | | | 30.00 | 40.00 | 50.00 | 60. |
| 71-91; 94-99; 101 | | 7.00 | 13.00 | 16.00 | 20.00 | 25. |
| **THOR (JOURNEY INTO MYSTERY)** | | | | | | |
| #83 | 165.00 | 275.00 | 450.00 | 675.00 | 965.00 | 1350.0 |
| 84 | 50.00 | 90.00 | 150.00 | 180.00 | 240.00 | 300.0 |
| 85 | 36.00 | 70.00 | 110.00 | 135.00 | 180.00 | 225.0 |
| 86 | 25.00 | 45.00 | 75.00 | 90.00 | 120.00 | 150.0 |
| 87-89 | 20.00 | 40.00 | 65.00 | 75.00 | 95.00 | 135.0 |
| 90-100; 112, 126 | | 23.00 | 37.00 | 45.00 | 59.00 | 75.0 |
| 101-110; 115 | 7.00 | 12.00 | 17.00 | 22.00 | 28.00 | 35.0 |
| 111, 113, 114, 116-125; 158, 193 | | | 10.00 | 15.00 | 20.00 | 25.0 |
| 134, 135 | | 8.00 | 10.00 | 15.00 | 20.00 | 25.0 |
| 127-133; 136-140 | | 7.00 | 9.00 | 12.00 | 16.00 | 20.0 |
| 141-157; 159, 160, 162, 168, 169 | | | 7.00 | 8.00 | 12.00 | 15.0 |
| 161, 163, 164, 167, 170-179; 200 | | | 3.00 | 4.00 | 5.00 | 6.0 |
| 165, 166, 180, 181 | | 5.00 | 6.00 | 7.00 | 10.00 | 12.0 |
| 182, 192, 194-199; 300, 400 | | | 2.00 | 3.00 | 4.00 | 5.0 |
| 201-299 | | | 1.00 | 2.00 | 3.00 | 4.0 |
| 301-336; 341-373; 375-381; 383, 385-389; 401 up | | | | | 1.00 | 2.0 |
| 337 | | | | | 5.00 | 6.0 |
| 338, 374 | | | | | | 4.0 |
| 339, 340, 382, 384 | | | | | | 2.0 |
| Annual 1 | 15.00 | 25.00 | 35.00 | 55.00 | 65.00 | 90.0 |
| 2-4 | 8.00 | 12.00 | 18.00 | 27.00 | 35.00 | 40.0 |
| 5 up | | | 3.00 | 4.00 | 5.00 | 6.0 |
| Giant Size 1 | | | 4.00 | 6.00 | 8.00 | 10.0 |
| Special Edition 1-4 | | 5.00 | 8.00 | 12.00 | 15.00 | 25.0 |
| Tales of Asgarrd 1 | | 4.00 | 6.00 | 12.00 | 15.00 | 25.0 |
| **X-MEN** | | | | | | |
| #1 | 190.00 | 350.00 | 600.00 | 850.00 | 1400.00 | 1800.0 |
| 2 | 80.00 | 120.00 | 180.00 | 275.00 | 380.00 | 540.0 |
| 3 | 50.00 | 70.00 | 100.00 | 150.00 | 200.00 | 300.0 |
| 4 | 40.00 | 55.00 | 80.00 | 120.00 | 160.00 | 240.0 |
| 5 | 35.00 | 50.00 | 70.00 | 105.00 | 140.00 | 210.0 |
| 6-10 | 30.00 | 40.00 | 50.00 | 75.00 | 100.00 | 150.0 |
| 11-15 | | 25.00 | 35.00 | 50.00 | 75.00 | 100.0 |
| 16-20; 28 | | 15.00 | 20.00 | 30.00 | 40.00 | 60.0 |
| 12-27; 29, 30 | | 15.00 | 20.00 | 25.00 | 35.00 | 50.0 |
| 31-40 | | 10.00 | 12.00 | 16.00 | 22.00 | 33.0 |
| 41-49; 52 | | 8.00 | 10.00 | 12.00 | 16.00 | 24.0 |
| 50, 51, 53 (Steranko, Smith) | | 11.00 | 14.00 | 18.00 | 24.00 | 36.0 |
| 54, 55 | | 10.00 | 12.00 | 15.00 | 20.00 | 30.0 |
| 56-65 (Adams art) | | 12.00 | 15.00 | 20.00 | 27.00 | 40.0 |
| 66-93 | | 6.00 | 7.00 | 8.00 | 10.00 | 15.0 |
| 94 | 40.00 | 60.00 | 80.00 | 100.00 | 150.00 | 175.0 |
| 95 | 8.00 | 20.00 | 30.00 | 35.00 | 45.00 | 55.0 |
| 96-99; 100, 101, 108, 109 | | 12.00 | 18.00 | 23.00 | 28.00 | 35.0 |
| 102-107; 110, 111 | | 6.00 | 9.00 | 11.00 | 14.00 | 18.0 |
| 112-119 | | 5.00 | 7.00 | 9.00 | 12.00 | 15.0 |
| 120, 121 | | 12.00 | 17.00 | 20.00 | 28.00 | 35.0 |
| 122-130; 139 | | 6.00 | 8.00 | 11.00 | 13.00 | 17.0 |
| 131-138; 171 (1st Rouge) | | | 6.00 | 8.00 | 10.00 | 13.0 |
| 140-142 | | | 10.00 | 12.00 | 16.00 | 20.0 |
| 143-150; 158, 175, 193, 195, 200 | | | | 4.00 | 5.00 | 6.0 |
| 151-164; 167-170; 173, 205 (Wolverine) | | | | 3.00 | 4.00 | 5.0 |
| 172, 174, 176-192; 194, 196-199; 201-208 | | | | | | 2.5 |
| 209-213; 224-227 | | | | | | 4.0 |
| 214-223; 228 up | | | | | | 2.0 |

ADVANCE COMICS
More Advance Listings!
#24 $1
ADVANCE COMICS
ELEKTRA LIVES AGAIN!
Plan what you want to buy!
Know the hot books to watch for!
Full-color covers preview upcoming releases!
More listings over 1000 releases each month.

# COMIC BOOK II

The finest full-featured and professionally written Comic software package that is easy to use.

FEATURES

- MENU DRIVEN
- QUICK ENTRY
- ON LINE HELP
- MOUSE OPTION
- BASIC DATA TRACKING
  ·TITLE, ISSUE#, CONDITION AND QUANTITY
- DETAILED DATA TRACKING
  ·VOLUME, PUBLISHER, DATE PURCHASED, DATE SOLD, PRICE SOLD, COVER PRICE, VALUE, TYPE, DATE PUBLISHED, AND COMMENTS
- USER'S MANUAL
- REPORTS PRINTOUT TO SCREEN OR PRINTER
  ·TOTAL QUANTITIES, VALUES, MISSING ISSUES, AND ETC

Send $35.00 and $1.95 for shipping and handling to:

Data Loggers
P.O. BOX 434
Burlington, IA
52601

---

Will run on IBM and compatibles with at lest 512K of memory and a hard drive. Specify 3 1/2" or 5 1/4" floppy Drives.

---

# Quite Simply the Best in Brooklyn for your Golden and Silver Age "HARD TO FIND" COMICS

**We sell Marvel, D.C., and Independent comics, which come in every Thursday. Magazine bags, comic bags, mylars, paperbacks, backboards, posters, comic and magazine boxes, rollplaying games, baseball cards (old & new), football cards etc.**

**We have spent $250,000 this year in comics and collections. Make us even happier by spending double this year or more.**

**We are located at: 1301 Prospect Ave. Brooklyn, NY 11218. Easy to get to by train or bus. Take F train to the Ft. Hamilton Parkway Station or buses #33 to Prospect Ave. or the #68 to Greenwood Ave.**

**OPEN MON. THRU SAT.**
**FROM 12 NOON TO 7:30PM**
**TEL. (718) 438-1335.**
**FAX. (718) 871-6948**

**We are always interested in early Golden Age & Silver Age books, Marvel's & D.C's, etc. for immediate cash.**

# BUYING COMICS!

**J&S COMICS**
**98 MADISON AVE.**
**RED BANK, NJ 07701**

**908-747-2322**
**(11 A.M.-8P.M. EST.**
**No Collect Calls)**

At J&S Comics, we buy **all** comics from 1933-1966. We also buy better comics from 1967-present, entire collections of **any** size, quantities of key recent issues, warehouses, inventories, estates, and sport cards. There are many "TOP PRICES PAID" ads in this Price Guide, but how many are willing to list the prices they'll pay? Few, if any. We have listed, on these 2 pages, the prices we'll pay for top Silver Age issues in a **full** range of conditions, from GOOD to MINT. Just grade your comics strictly, or save the work and let us grade them, ship the comics to us, and you will be paid these prices promptly, with your shipping expenses reimbursed. You may also send us **any** comics from 1933-1966, valuable issues from 1967-present, or sport card stars, packs, and sets before 1986. If you are not COMPLETELY SATISFIED with our payment for anything you send, we will immediately return your shipment at our expense. You can be assured of fairness and honesty when dealing with us. We have had 2 page ads in this price guide for the last 14 years and have purchased well over 1000 collections from satisfied sellers.

Of course we will be glad to travel to you to view and purchase large or valuable collections in person. You may also bring your comics and cards to one of our two COMICS PLUS stores in central New Jersey: 1300 Hwy. 35 Middletown, and Hwy. 35 and Sunset Ave. Wanamassa (Ocean Plaza). We'll give you an immediate appraisal and offer. These 2 stores are also the place to go if you are interested in buying the comics listed on these 2 page or thousands of others form the 30's through the 90's. A complete selection of new comics is available at each store every Friday. We also have an extensive mail order business and will be glad to quote prices for items on your want list by phone. Major credit cards accepted.

***NUMBERS LISTED BELOW ARE THE AMOUNT IN DOLLARS WE PAY FOR CONDITION LISTED***

| Title/Issue # | Good | V/Good | Fine | F/VF | V/Fine | VF/NM | N/Mint | NM/M | Mint |
|---|---|---|---|---|---|---|---|---|---|
| Amazing Fantasy 15 | 300 | 600 | 1000 | 1250 | 1700 | 2000 | 2500 | 2900 | 3600 |
| Amaz. Spider-Man 1 | 280 | 565 | 950 | 1200 | 1625 | 1925 | 2400 | 2800 | 3500 |
| 2 | 100 | 210 | 375 | 450 | 600 | 720 | 900 | 1000 | 1300 |
| 3 | 75 | 150 | 250 | 315 | 425 | 500 | 625 | 700 | 850 |
| 4-6,14 | 40 | 80 | 140 | 170 | 240 | 300 | 400 | 450 | 575 |
| 7-10 | 25 | 50 | 90 | 110 | 170 | 205 | 270 | 310 | 375 |
| 11-13,15,17,129,ann.1 | 16 | 32 | 55 | 68 | 95 | 110 | 150 | 165 | 200 |
| Avengers 1 | 75 | 160 | 275 | 325 | 425 | 525 | 675 | 750 | 900 |
| 2 | 27 | 55 | 90 | 115 | 160 | 190 | 250 | 280 | 340 |
| 3 | 17 | 35 | 60 | 72 | 95 | 115 | 150 | 175 | 225 |
| 4 | 37 | 80 | 140 | 170 | 235 | 275 | 350 | 390 | 475 |
| Batman 101-110 | 13 | 26 | 42 | 52 | 70 | 85 | 110 | 125 | 150 |
| 111-130,155 | 6 | 13 | 22 | 27 | 38 | 45 | 60 | 67 | 80 |
| 131-145,148 | 5 | 11 | 17 | 20 | 28 | 34 | 45 | 50 | 60 |
| Brave & Bold 28 | 80 | 180 | 340 | 450 | 625 | 750 | 1000 | 1175 | 1500 |
| 29, 30 | 37 | 80 | 145 | 170 | 240 | 295 | 385 | 435 | 525 |
| 34 | 16 | 33 | 55 | 67 | 95 | 110 | 150 | 175 | 220 |
| Capt America 100 | 12 | 32 | 53 | 64 | 90 | 110 | 155 | 175 | 215 |
| Daredevil 1 | 50 | 105 | 185 | 235 | 330 | 410 | 535 | 615 | 775 |
| 2 | 20 | 42 | 67 | 80 | 120 | 145 | 205 | 235 | 300 |
| Detective 225 | 115 | 250 | 405 | 490 | 675 | 835 | 1050 | 1225 | 1550 |

| Title/Issue # | Good | V/Good | Fine | F/VF | V/Fine | VF/NM | N/Mint | NM/M | Mint |
|---|---|---|---|---|---|---|---|---|---|
| 226-240 | 11 | 23 | 38 | 46 | 60 | 75 | 100 | 115 | 140 |
| 241-260 | 7 | 16 | 27 | 33 | 47 | 57 | 75 | 85 | 105 |
| 261-280 | 4 | 9 | 15 | 18 | 25 | 31 | 40 | 45 | 55 |
| Fantastic Four 1 | 300 | 580 | 1050 | 1300 | 1765 | 2075 | 2600 | 3000 | 3700 |
| 2 | 85 | 170 | 280 | 345 | 460 | 560 | 715 | 820 | 1025 |
| 3-5 | 55 | 115 | 200 | 240 | 330 | 410 | 535 | 600 | 725 |
| 6-10 | 24 | 50 | 90 | 115 | 155 | 190 | 255 | 285 | 340 |
| 11-20,25,26,48,ann.1 | 13 | 26 | 42 | 52 | 68 | 80 | 110 | 125 | 150 |
| Flash 105 | 77 | 155 | 275 | 350 | 520 | 635 | 850 | 950 | 1125 |
| 106,123 | 30 | 65 | 110 | 135 | 180 | 215 | 290 | 330 | 400 |
| 107-110 | 15 | 32 | 55 | 70 | 955 | 115 | 145 | 165 | 200 |
| 111-120,129,137 | 6 | 13 | 20 | 25 | 33 | 41 | 52 | 58 | 70 |
| Green Lantern 1 | 70 | 140 | 245 | 310 | 430 | 540 | 700 | 775 | 925 |
| 2 | 28 | 60 | 105 | 125 | 175 | 210 | 280 | 310 | 375 |
| 3-5, 40 | 12 | 25 | 41 | 52 | 75 | 100 | 125 | 140 | 175 |
| Hulk 1 | 85 | 175 | 310 | 390 | 575 | 740 | 950 | 1050 | 1275 |
| 2 | 33 | 72 | 125 | 155 | 225 | 280 | 375 | 415 | 500 |
| 3-6 | 19 | 41 | 72 | 88 | 130 | 170 | 225 | 250 | 305 |
| Iron Man 1 | 19 | 40 | 70 | 85 | 120 | 145 | 200 | 220 | 275 |
| Journey into Mystery 83 | 80 | 160 | 275 | 340 | 465 | 590 | 775 | 875 | 1025 |
| 84 | 19 | 42 | 75 | 100 | 150 | 185 | 235 | 260 | 325 |
| 85-90 | 10 | 19 | 29 | 36 | 50 | 62 | 85 | 95 | 115 |
| Justice League 1 | 82 | 165 | 290 | 360 | 515 | 640 | 825 | 950 | 1150 |
| 2 | 21 | 45 | 75 | 90 | 135 | 170 | 225 | 250 | 300 |
| 3,4,9 | 14 | 28 | 48 | 57 | 80 | 100 | 135 | 150 | 180 |
| 5-8,10,21,22 | 8 | 16 | 27 | 33 | 45 | 56 | 78 | 85 | 105 |
| Showcase 1,6 | 50 | 100 | 170 | 215 | 290 | 355 | 485 | 540 | 650 |
| 2,3,5,15,20,27,30,37,43 | 15 | 32 | 53 | 65 | 85 | 105 | 140 | 160 | 190 |
| 4 | 325 | 650 | 1200 | 1450 | 2100 | 2900 | 3650 | 4150 | 5200 |
| 7,9,10,17,23,24,34 | 30 | 65 | 110 | 145 | 190 | 235 | 315 | 370 | 450 |
| 11,12,18,19 | 19 | 39 | 67 | 80 | 110 | 135 | 185 | 205 | 250 |
| 13,14 | 60 | 130 | 215 | 280 | 390 | 500 | 660 | 735 | 890 |
| 8,22 | 75 | 160 | 280 | 360 | 510 | 675 | 900 | 1005 | 1225 |
| 21,25-29,31-33,36-40 | 6 | 12 | 19 | 25 | 33 | 40 | 55 | 62 | 75 |
| Strange Tales 101,110 | 25 | 52 | 85 | 105 | 140 | 180 | 235 | 270 | 325 |
| 102-105,114,115 | 10 | 19 | 31 | 40 | 52 | 65 | 85 | 94 | 112 |
| Superman 101-120 | 8 | 16 | 24 | 30 | 41 | 51 | 68 | 77 | 92 |
| 121-140,146,147,149 | 5 | 10 | 16 | 20 | 27 | 33 | 43 | 48 | 60 |
| Tales of Suspense 39 | 90 | 180 | 310 | 410 | 595 | 745 | 1025 | 1150 | 1400 |
| 40 | 45 | 95 | 160 | 200 | 290 | 370 | 480 | 540 | 650 |
| 1,41 | 25 | 50 | 90 | 115 | 155 | 190 | 250 | 280 | 335 |
| 2-4,42-45 | 10 | 20 | 36 | 46 | 62 | 79 | 103 | 115 | 140 |
| Tales to Astonish 27 | 73 | 150 | 250 | 325 | 455 | 570 | 735 | 815 | 1000 |
| 35 | 48 | 100 | 175 | 215 | 305 | 380 | 510 | 575 | 690 |
| 2-5,36-40 | 10 | 21 | 37 | 46 | 63 | 80 | 105 | 115 | 140 |
| X-Men 1 | 95 | 200 | 355 | 450 | 610 | 815 | 1120 | 1270 | 1525 |
| 2 | 36 | 75 | 130 | 160 | 215 | 270 | 370 | 410 | 500 |
| 3,4 | 14 | 28 | 47 | 57 | 80 | 100 | 140 | 155 | 190 |
| 5-10,94 | 8 | 17 | 30 | 37 | 52 | 64 | 80 | 87 | 105 |

GOLDEN AGE

© MCG

SILVER AGE

© DC

# WANT LIST COMICS

## *WE FILL WANT LISTS*

### ATTENTION: INVESTORS AND COLLECTORS

**Can't** find those missing comic books **yet**? Are these books priced **TOO high** or are they just **IMPOSSIBLE** to find? Have local stores and conventions **not** produced what you want? **(Have you sent us a want list yet?)**

### WHAT ARE YOU WAITING FOR?

"The **Batman #1** you sold me was in the **nicest, unrestored condition** I've seen!", **Bob Overstreet, author "The Official Overstreet Comic Book Price Guide".**

"I **loved** the **Showcase #4** you sold me this year. Your **grading, price** and **time payment plan** were very **fair!**", **John Seiple, Dallas, TX.**

These are just two of the **many** satisfied customers that have bought books from us in the past. Over the years, we have developed a **very strong return customer base** because we **accurately** price, grade and describe books (in detail if needed) over the phone and through the mail. **Customer references are always available upon request.** If a book is restored, we will tell you **up front** so you won't be **UNpleasantly** surprised or deceived. As each year goes by, we complete more and more of our customers' comic want lists. For example, **in 1990 alone**, we acquired Golden Age treasures for our clients like **Detective 27, Famous Funnies (1933),** and **Marvel Comics 1. Because of the high demand for Silver Age books,** we purchased **multiple copies of nearly all** "key" issues like Showcase 4, 22, 34, Amazing Fantasy 15, FF1, Hulk 1, Xmen 1, J.I.M. 83, Tales of Suspense 39, Green Lantern 1, and Brave and the Bold 28. We **SPECIALIZE** in **Golden Age and Silver Age books (1933-1969),** but we also have some later issues.

We don't claim that we can fill every list all the time, but if any company can accomplish this, it **would certainly** be us! We can say this with **much confidence** because we travel to the **majority** of the 50 states and Canada plus attend **all** the major comic book conventions (San Diego, Chicago, New York, Mid-Ohio, Dallas, etc.) to uncover books **you would not** have the opportunity to find. When we are not on the road we spend **MANY** hours on the phone locating books from our **long** list of past and present comic sources we've developed over the **19 years** we have been dealing in comic books. When sending your want list, **please** include an SASE if possible, **your phone number,** and a good time to reach you. We **don't** send out catalogs, so **please** ask us for **specific** books and **conditions** desired. We will contact you **when** we find the items you've requested. **FAXes and phone calls are also welcomed. WE WILL GLADLY SUGGEST AND PERSONALLY PUT TOGETHER COMIC BOOK INVESTMENT PORTFOLIOS FOR BIG AND SMALL INVESTORS. OUR ADVICE IS ALWAYS FREE!**

**SAVE YOURSELF ALL THE HASSLE AND LET US DO THE LOOKING FOR YOU**
**CALL, MAIL OR FAX US YOUR WANT LIST**
***YOU HAVE NOTHING TO LOSE AND EVERYTHING ON YOUR WANT LIST TO GAIN!!!***

**Competitive pricing always. Accurate** grading. Friendly, courteous service. **Interest free time payments/layaways possible.** Visa, Mastercard and American Express accepted for total payment **OR** down payment on books. No collect calls. Books shipped within 48 hours of payment.

## Our NEW office/warehouse # is:
## 1-918-299-0440
### FAX# 918-299-0440

## *WANT LIST COMICS*
## *BOX 701932*
## *TULSA, OK 74170-1932*

*** Advisor to the Overstreet Price Guide ***
**References gladly provided!**

Sleuthing done dirt cheap!

Can't find that number one (or origin issue)? Then why not try me?

**Yes,** I have **all** of the **No. 1** issues shown above and other **hard-to-find** comics especially those much sought after **early Marvels** (there is always a near-complete set of all Marvel titles available in stock).

And besides this I also have the following:

**(A) WALT DISNEY COMICS** - All titles: Mickey Mouse, Donald Duck, Uncle Scrooge, and Disney Collectibles.

**(B) DC COMICS** - Golden Age, Silver Age up to the present—old Flash, Green Lantern, Superman, Batman, and other Super Heroes.

**(C) GOLDEN AGE & SILVER AGE COMICS** - These include Quality, Timely, Fox, Avon, Fiction House, Fawcett, Motion Picture Comics, Dell, Westerns, Funny Animal Comics, Classics, etc.

**(D) MAD COMICS** - Panic, Humbug, Trump, Help & Horror, Crime and **EC** comics.

**(E) BIG LITTLE BOOKS** - All major and minor titles. Also available—the **original** Cupples & Leon comic "books".

**(F) RARE PULPS** - Science fiction and pulp hero titles.

**(G) ORIGINAL ART** - Including fine classic as well as modern artists.

**(H) SUNDAY COMIC PAGES** - Just about every major and minor comic strip character from the early **1900's** to the **1950's.** Strips include: **Little Nemo, Krazy Kat, Mickey Mouse, Donald Duck, Popeye, Tarzan, Flash Gordon, Prince Valiant, Terry & The Pirates, Dick Tracy, Superman,** and many, many more too numerous to list here.

I also **BUY & TRADE,** so let me know what you have. For my latest **GIANT** 1991 catalog "Number One Plus", write to the address below enclosing $1.00 in cash (or stamps). Hurry now or you could miss out on getting that issue you've been looking for!

## *SPECIAL* MOVIE SALE *SPECIAL*

**A ONCE IN A LIFETIME OFFER!** Huge Catalog listing hundreds and hundreds of rare (and **ORIGINAL**) movie posters, lobby cards, autographed photos from the 1930's to the 1980's. You'll find your favorite movie stars: Bogart, Gable, Garbo, Garland, Laurel & Hardy, Presley, Disney Titles and many, many more. Wide selection from B-Westerns, Horror, Science-Fiction, Comedy, Musicals, etc. Act **NOW** to receive my **"1991 MOVIE CATALOG".**

(NOTE: Those wishing to receive **ONLY** the Movie Catalog **MUST** enclose 50 cents and a self-addressed stamped envelope. Want lists also welcomed. If you wish to receive **BOTH** the Comic and the Movie Catalogs, send $1.50).

**Write: HAL VERB**
**P.O. BOX 1815**
**SAN FRANCISCO, CA 94101**

If you're vacationing in New York or if you're just escaping the city, then **THE DRAGON'S DEN** is the place to visit. Located in the heart of Westchesters' finest shopping area, **THE DRAGON'S DEN** is only thirty minutes from midtown Manhattan and easily accessible to all major New York roadways.

Check out our enormous inventory of collectibles, including:

- **Over 1,000,000 Back Issue Marvel, D.C. & Alternate Comics**
- **All New Comic Releases**
- **Comic Bags, Boxes and Mylars**
- **Baseball, Football, Basketball & Hockey stars, sets & unopened material from 1909 to the present**
- **Plastic sheets, binders, lucites, card cases & boxes**
- **Fantasy Role Playing Games and Figures**
- **Role Playing Accessories & Dice**
- **Posters & Models**

Along with our impressive inventory, we have a veteran staff that will be happy to assist you in your selection. We accept all major credit cards and we're even open every day. What more could you ask for? Convenient parking? We have that too!

**Call (914) 793-4630 for easy directions.**

**THE DRAGON'S DEN**

**(914) 793-4630**

**2614 CENTRAL AVENUE, YONKERS, NY 10710**

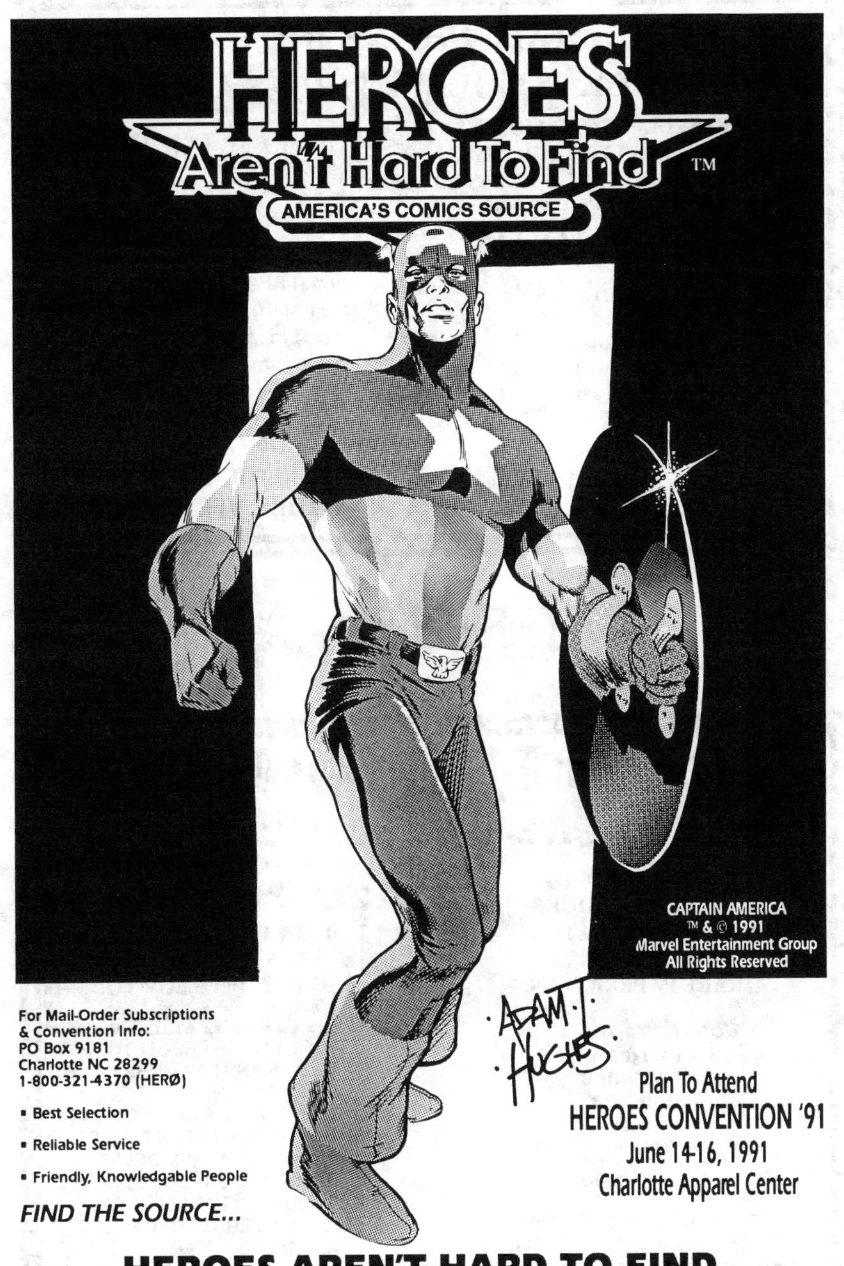
HEROES
Aren't Hard To Find ™
AMERICA'S COMICS SOURCE
CAPTAIN AMERICA
™ & © 1991
Marvel Entertainment Group
All Rights Reserved
ADAM
HUGHES

We Mail Order Anywhere!

West Coast's Largest Selection of Gold and Silver-Age Collectibles!

Over 7,000 Graphic Novels, Art Books, and Movie/TV Books in Stock!

Computerized Want-list Service!

**COMIC RELIEF**

2138 University Ave.
Berkeley, CA. 94704
(415) 843-5002

COMIC RELIEF™

# SHOWCASE COLLECTIBLES

## BUYING/SELLING

LARGE SELECTION OF
HIGH QUALITY GOLDEN
AND SILVER AGE COMICS
ALL:

ACCURATELY GRADED
COMPETETIVELY PRICED
AND OFFERED WITH A 100%
BUYBACK GUARANTEE

---

TIME PAYMENTS AND WANT LIST
SERVICES AVAILABLE

---

SELLING COMICS?
CALL EVERYONE ELSE, **THEN**
CALL US FOR YOUR BEST OFFER

**SHOWCASE COLLECTIBLES**
**P.O. BOX 921185**
**NORCROSS, GEORGIA 30092**
**(404) 594-0074**
**FAX: (404) 518-9113**

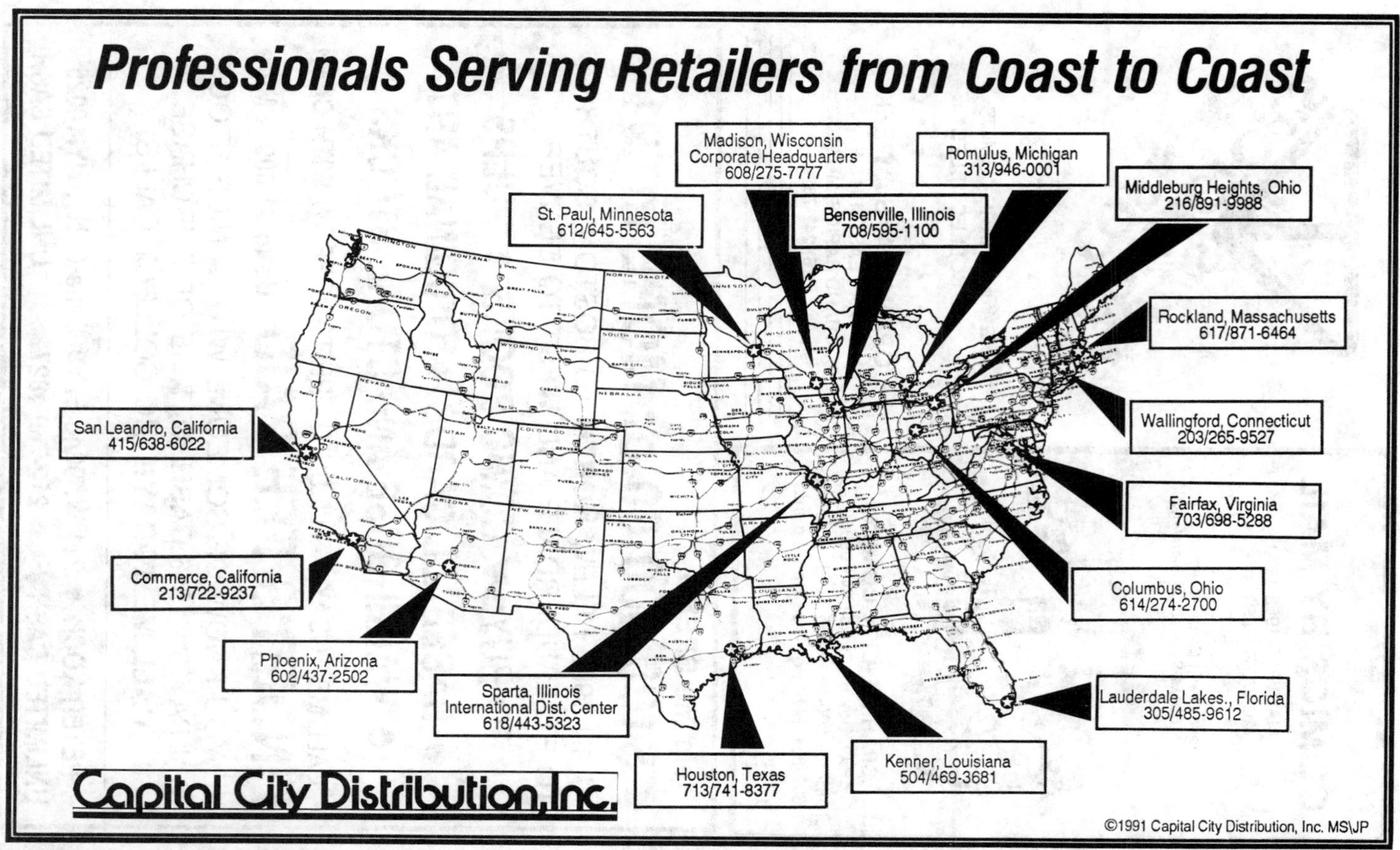
Professionals Serving Retailers from Coast to Coast
Madison, Wisconsin
Corporate Headquarters
608/275-7777
Romulus, Michigan
313/946-0001
Middleburg Heights, Ohio
216/891-9988
St. Paul, Minnesota
612/645-5563
Bensenville, Illinois
708/595-1100
Rockland, Massachusetts
617/871-6464
Wallingford, Connecticut
203/265-9527
San Leandro, California
415/638-6022
Fairfax, Virginia
703/698-5288
Commerce, California
213/722-9237
Columbus, Ohio
614/274-2700
Phoenix, Arizona
602/437-2502
Sparta, Illinois
International Dist. Center
618/443-5323
Lauderdale Lakes., Florida
305/485-9612
Houston, Texas
713/741-8377
Kenner, Louisiana
504/469-3681
Capital City Distribution, Inc.
©1991 Capital City Distribution, Inc. MS\JP

RARE COMIC ART IS MY BAG
. . .and I love to trade bags of money, or other art for items of special interest to me.
I'll pay top dollar for original artwork by Carl Barks, E.C. Segar, and other classic cartoonists, as well as paintings, cartoon movie posters from the '30s and '40s, and other rare comic oriented esoterica.
If you have rare material for sale **contact me first**. If you don't, you may be selling your collection short.
Bruce Hamilton
P.O. Box 4235
Prescott, AZ 86302
(602)776-1300

YOU WANT RARE "GOLDEN AGE" COMICS?.
ARE YOU FOR REAL?!
THOSE OLD COMICS HAVE ALL GONE TO HEAVEN!!
?!
KOOK'S COMICS
THOR
HULK

SORRY-- CAN'T HELP YOU!
IF YOU WANT QUALITY GOLDEN AGE BOOKS, YOU'LL HAVE TO CLIMB!!
US LOCAL CONVENTIONS CAN'T HELP YOU!!
SALE!
3 FOR $1.00
HALF OFF
20¢
10¢

**COMIC HEAVEN** 24 W. MAIN STREET
ALHAMBRA, CALIFORNIA 91801 **(818) 289-3945**

GULP! -- ALMOST THERE!
DON'T LOOK DOWN!!

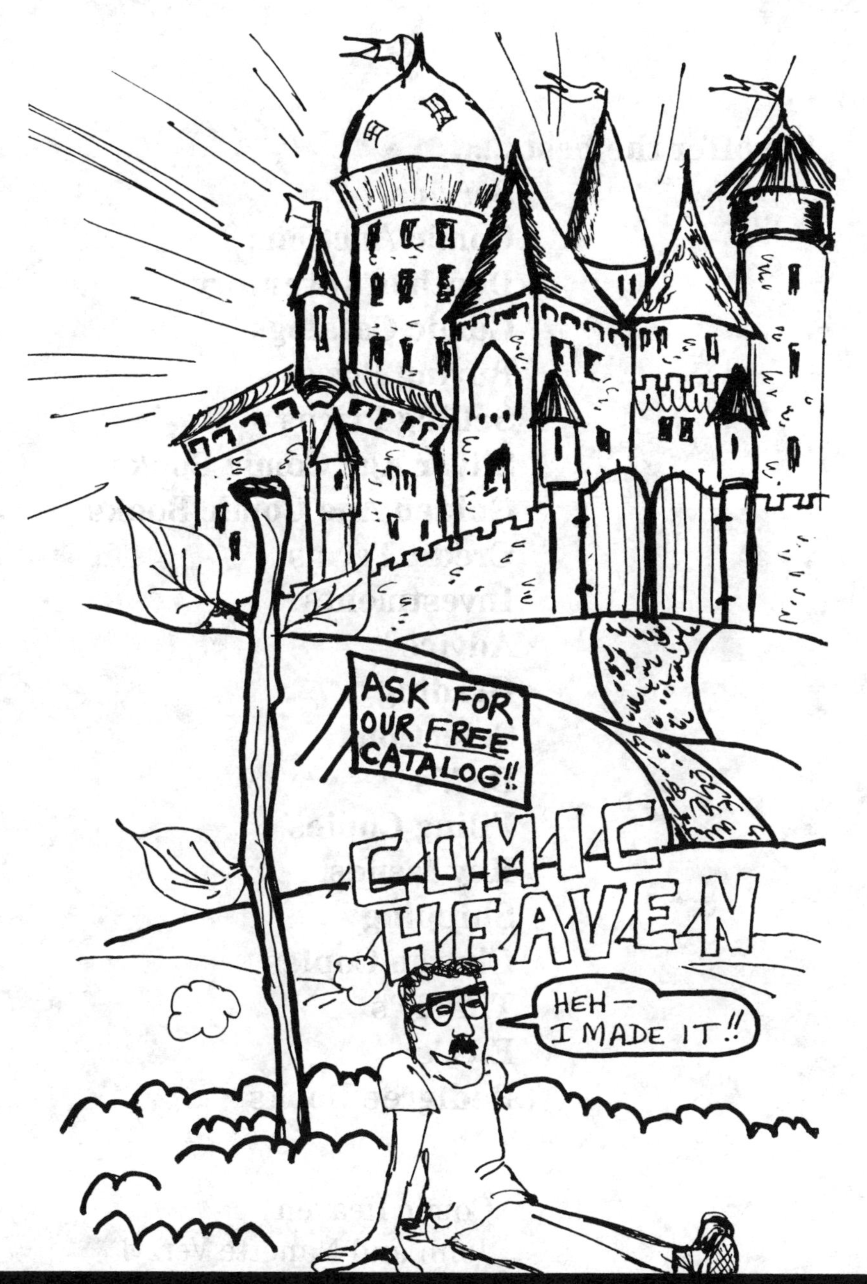
ASK FOR OUR FREE CATALOG!!
COMIC HEAVEN
HEH — I MADE IT!!

# SATISFACTION GUARANTEED

All Comic purchased from COMIC HEAVEN may be returned (within 14 days) for a full refund if for any reason you are not satisified.*

Here is what a few happy COMIC HEAVEN customers have to say about us.

M. Steel says - "I buy all of my pedigree comic books from COMIC HEAVEN."

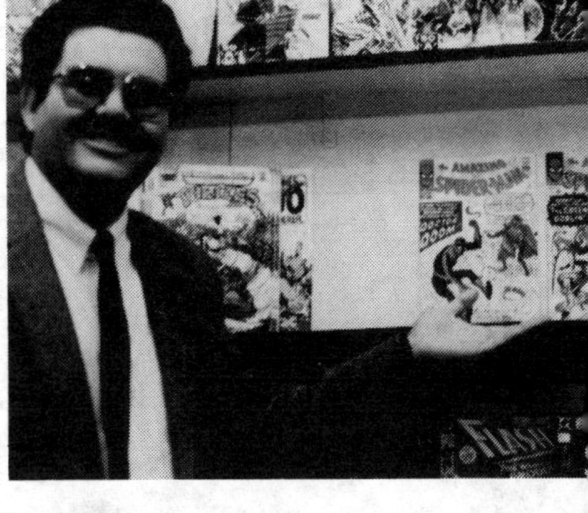


P. Gama Says - "For the Last 7 years I've gotten really great deals from Comic Heaven."

Comic Heaven
John and Nanette Verzyl
24 W. Main Street
Alhambra, CA 91801
**1-818-289-3945**

* Books must be securely wrapped and returned to us in the same condition as they were sent.

A BRIEF HISTORICAL NOTE ABOUT "COMIC HEAVEN"

John Verzyl starte l collecting comic books in 1965, and within ten years, he had amassed thousands of Golden and Silver Age comic books. In 1979, with his wife Nanette, he opened "COMIC HEAVEN", a retail store devoted entirely to the buying and selling of comic books.

Over the years, John Verzyl has come to be recognized as an authority in the field of comic books,. He has served as an advisor to the "Overstreet Price Guide". Thousands of his "mint" comics were photographed for Ernst Gerbers newly-released "Photo-Journal Guide To Comic Books". His tables and displays at the annual San Diego Comic Convention draw customers from all over the country.

The first COMIC HEAVEN AUCTION was held in 1987, and today his Auction Catalogs are mailed out to more then ten thousand interested collectors (and dealers).

E. Gerber Products
We Buy & Sell
We Specialize in
"Mile High" comics*
and other
High Grade
Comics 1933-'65
3/4 mile
1/2 mile
1/4 mile
Write or Call for FREE
Catalog or Buy Quote!
E. Gerber Products, Inc.
P.O. Box 906 (m)
Minden, Nevada 89423
(702) 883-4100 (9-1, M-S)
CONSIGNMENT SERVICE: We can sell your comics for you. Clients have received more than 90% of 'GUIDE' for their share!! CALL for info., pre 1968 collections only.
Nevada
Sea Level
*The Edgar Church Collection

Abbott and Costello #10, © STJ

Ace Comics #76, © ACE

Action Comics #1, © DC

The correct title listing for each comic book can be determined by consulting the indicia (publication data) on the beginning interior pages of the comic. The official title is determined by those words of the title in capital letters only, and not by what is on the cover.

Titles are listed in this book as if they were one word, ignoring spaces, hyphens, and apostrophes, to make finding titles easier.

Comic publishers are invited to send us sample copies for possible inclusion in future guides.

Near Mint is the highest grade listed in this price guide. True mint books from the 1970s and 1980s do exist, so the Near Mint value listed should be interpreted as a Mint value for these books.

**IMPORTANT NOTICE**

Throughout the listings in this book, you will find that certain key issues have four prices instead of the usual three. The fourth price represents a value for that issue in a high investment grade. This price represents, usually a small number of high grade copies, but not necessarily the best known copy. Since books in this grade are so rare that they are seldom offered for sale, this price is based on an educated estimate from a canvas of the top dealers across the country and is provided for your information. **Caution!** When actual sales occur, prices realized could vary from the list price. Other non-key issues are not necessarily worth the same multiple as the key issues.

**A-1** (See A-One)

**ABBIE AN' SLATS** (...With Becky No. 1-4) (See Comics On Parade, Fight for Love, Giant Comics Edition 2, Sparkler Comics, Tip Topper, Treasury of Comics, & United Comics)
1940; March, 1948 - No. 4, Aug, 1948 (Reprints)
United Features Syndicate

| | Good | Fine | N-Mint |
|---|---|---|---|
| Single Series 25 ('40) | 20.00 | 60.00 | 140.00 |
| Single Series 28 | 18.00 | 54.00 | 125.00 |
| 1 (1948) | 9.30 | 28.00 | 65.00 |
| 2-4: 3 r-/Sparkler #68-72 | 4.50 | 14.00 | 32.00 |

**ABBOTT AND COSTELLO** (...Comics)(See Treasury of Comics)
Feb, 1948 - No. 40, Sept, 1956 (Mort Drucker art in most issues)
St. John Publishing Co.

| | | | |
|---|---|---|---|
| 1 | 24.00 | 73.00 | 170.00 |
| 2 | 12.00 | 36.00 | 84.00 |
| 3-9 (#8, 8/49; #9, 2/50) | 7.00 | 21.00 | 50.00 |
| 10-Son of Sinbad story by Kubert (new) | 13.00 | 40.00 | 90.00 |
| 11,13-20 (#11, 10/50; #13, 8/51; #15, 12/52) | 4.50 | 14.00 | 32.00 |
| 12-Movie issue | 6.00 | 18.00 | 42.00 |
| 21-30: 28 r-#8. 30-Painted-c | 4.00 | 12.00 | 28.00 |
| 31-40: #33, 38-r | 3.00 | 9.00 | 21.00 |
| 3-D #1 (11/53)-Infinity-c | 20.00 | 60.00 | 140.00 |

**ABBOTT AND COSTELLO** (TV)
Feb, 1968 - No. 22, Aug, 1971 (Hanna-Barbera)
Charlton Comics

| | | | |
|---|---|---|---|
| 1 | 2.65 | 8.00 | 18.00 |
| 2-10 | 1.35 | 4.00 | 8.00 |
| 11-22 | .75 | 2.25 | 4.50 |

**ABC** (See America's Best TV Comics)

**ABRAHAM LINCOLN LIFE STORY** (See Dell Giants)

**ABSENT-MINDED PROFESSOR, THE** (See 4-Color Comics No. 1199)

**ABYSS, THE**
June, 1989 - No. 2, July, 1989 ($2.25, color, 2 issue series)
Dark Horse Comics

| | Good | Fine | N-Mint |
|---|---|---|---|
| 1,2-Movie adaptation; Kaluta, Moebius-a | .40 | 1.15 | 2.30 |

**ACE COMICS**
April, 1937 - No. 151, Oct-Nov, 1949
David McKay Publications

| | | | |
|---|---|---|---|
| 1-Jungle Jim by Alex Raymond, Blondie, Ripley's Believe It Or Not, Krazy Kat begin | 165.00 | 415.00 | 1000.00 |
| 2 | 53.00 | 160.00 | 370.00 |
| 3-5 | 37.00 | 110.00 | 260.00 |
| 6-10 | 27.00 | 81.00 | 190.00 |
| 11-The Phantom begins(In brown costume, 2/38) | 34.00 | 100.00 | 235.00 |
| 12-20 | 20.00 | 60.00 | 140.00 |
| 21-25,27-30 | 16.50 | 50.00 | 115.00 |
| 26-Origin Prince Valiant (begins series?) | 46.00 | 140.00 | 325.00 |
| 31-40: 37-Krazy Kat ends | 12.00 | 36.00 | 84.00 |
| 41-60 | 10.00 | 30.00 | 70.00 |
| 61-64,66-76-(7/43; last 68pgs.) | 8.50 | 25.50 | 60.00 |
| 65-(8/42; Flag-c) | 9.00 | 27.00 | 63.00 |
| 77-84 (3/44; all 60pgs.) | 7.00 | 21.00 | 50.00 |
| 85-99 (52 pgs.) | 6.00 | 18.00 | 42.00 |
| 100 (7/45; last 52 pgs.) | 7.00 | 21.00 | 50.00 |
| 101-134: 128-11/47; Brick Bradford begins. 134-Last Prince Valiant (All 36 pgs.) | 5.00 | 15.00 | 35.00 |
| 135-151: 135-6/48; Lone Ranger begins | 4.00 | 12.00 | 28.00 |

**ACE KELLY** (See Tops Comics & Tops In Humor)

**ACE KING** (See Adventures of the Detective)

**ACES**
Apr, 1988 - No. 5, Dec, 1988 ($2.95, B&W, Magazine)
Acme Press (Eclipse Comics)

| | | | |
|---|---|---|---|
| 1-5 | .50 | 1.50 | 3.00 |

**ACES HIGH**
Mar-Apr, 1955 - No. 5, Nov-Dec, 1955
E.C. Comics

| | | | |
|---|---|---|---|
| 1-Not approved by code | 10.00 | 30.00 | 70.00 |
| 2 | 7.00 | 21.00 | 50.00 |
| 3-5 | 5.70 | 17.00 | 40.00 |

NOTE: *All have stories by* ***Davis, Evans, Krigstein,*** *and* ***Wood; Evans*** *c-1-5.*

**ACTION ADVENTURE** (War) (Formerly Real Adventure)
V1#2, June, 1955 - No. 4, Oct, 1955
Gillmor Magazines

| | | | |
|---|---|---|---|
| V1#2-4 | 1.50 | 4.50 | 10.00 |

**ACTION COMICS** (See Special Ed.; ...Weekly No. 601 -642)
6/38 - No. 583, 9/86; No. 584, 1/87 - Present
National Periodical Publ./Detective Comics/DC Comics

1-Origin & 1st app. Superman by Siegel & Shuster, Marco Polo, Tex Thompson, Pep Morgan, Chuck Dawson & Scoop Scanlon; 1st app. Zatara & Lois Lane; Superman story missing 4 pgs. which were included when reprinted in Superman #1.

| Good | Fine | Vf-NM | N-Mint |
|---|---|---|---|
| 6,600.00 | 16,500.00 | 36,000.00 | 55,000.00 |

(Estimated up to 100 total copies exist, 4 in NM/Mint)
(Issues 1 - 10 are all scarce to rare)

1-Reprint, Oversize 13½"x10." **WARNING:** This comic is an exact reprint of the original except for its size. DC published it in 1974 with a second cover titling it as a **Famous First Edition**. There have been many reported cases of the outer cover being removed and the interior sold as the original edition. The reprint with the new outer cover removed is practically worthless.

| | Good | Fine | N-Mint |
|---|---|---|---|
| 1(1976,1983)-Giveaway; paper cover, 16pgs. in color; reprints complete Superman story from #1 ('38) | .70 | 2.00 | 4.00 |
| 1(1987 Nestle Quik giveaway; 1988, 50 cent-c) | | .25 | .50 |
| 2 | 835.00 | 2100.00 | 5000.00 |
| 3 (Scarce) | 670.00 | 1675.00 | 4000.00 |
| 4 | 450.00 | 1125.00 | 2700.00 |
| 5 (Rare) | 535.00 | 1340.00 | 3200.00 |
| 6-1st Jimmy Olsen (called office boy) | 450.00 | 1125.00 | 2700.00 |
| 7,10-Superman covers | 585.00 | 1460.00 | 3500.00 |
| 8,9 | 385.00 | 960.00 | 2300.00 |
| 11,12,14: 14-Clip Carson begins, ends #41 | 200.00 | 500.00 | 1200.00 |
| 13-Superman cover; last Scoop Scanlon | 292.00 | 730.00 | 1750.00 |
| 15-Superman cover | 292.00 | 730.00 | 1750.00 |
| 16 | 165.00 | 410.00 | 980.00 |
| 17-Superman cover; last Marco Polo | 220.00 | 550.00 | 1320.00 |
| 18-Origin 3 Aces; 1st X-Ray Vision? | 155.00 | 385.00 | 925.00 |
| 19-Superman covers begin | 200.00 | 500.00 | 1200.00 |
| 20-'S' left off Superman's chest; Clark Kent works at 'Daily Star' | 185.00 | 460.00 | 1100.00 |
| 21,22,24,25: 24-Kent at Daily Planet. 25-Last app. Gargantua T. Potts, Tex Thompson's sidekick | 115.00 | 290.00 | 700.00 |
| 23-1st app. Luthor & Black Pirate; Black Pirate by Moldoff; 1st mention of The Daily Planet? (4/40) | 168.00 | 415.00 | 1000.00 |
| 26-30 | 90.00 | 225.00 | 540.00 |
| 31,32 | 68.00 | 170.00 | 410.00 |
| 33-Origin Mr. America | 80.00 | 200.00 | 480.00 |
| 34-40: 37-Origin Congo Bill. 40-Intro/1st app. Star Spangled Kid & Stripesy | 68.00 | 170.00 | 410.00 |
| 41 | 63.00 | 158.00 | 380.00 |
| 42-1st app./origin Vigilante; Bob Daley becomes Fat Man; origin Mr. America's magic flying carpet; The Queen Bee & Luthor app; Black Pirate ends; not in #41 | 92.00 | 230.00 | 550.00 |
| 43-46,48-50: 44-Fat Man's i.d. revealed to Mr. America. 45-1st app. Stuff | 63.00 | 158.00 | 380.00 |
| 47-1st Luthor cover | 75.00 | 188.00 | 450.00 |
| 51-1st app. The Prankster | 58.00 | 146.00 | 350.00 |
| 52-Fat Man & Mr. America become the Ameri-commandos; origin Vigilante retold | 63.00 | 158.00 | 380.00 |
| 53-60: 56-Last Fat Man. 59-Kubert Vigilante begins?, ends #70. 60-First app. Lois Lane as Superwoman | 47.00 | 115.00 | 280.00 |
| 61-63,65-70: 63-Last 3 Aces | 42.00 | 105.00 | 255.00 |
| 64-Intro Toyman | 47.00 | 115.00 | 280.00 |
| 71-79: 74-Last Mr. America | 37.00 | 92.00 | 220.00 |
| 80-2nd app. & 1st Mr. Mxyztplk-c (1/45) | 60.00 | 150.00 | 360.00 |
| 81-90: 83-Intro Hocus & Pocus | 37.00 | 92.00 | 220.00 |
| 91-99: 93-X-Mas-c. 99-1st small logo (7/46) | 32.00 | 81.00 | 195.00 |
| 100 | 75.00 | 188.00 | 450.00 |
| 101-Nuclear explosion-c | 43.00 | 108.00 | 260.00 |
| 102-120: 105,117-X-Mas-c | 33.00 | 83.00 | 200.00 |
| 121-126,128-140: 135,136,138-Zatara by Kubert | 32.00 | 80.00 | 190.00 |
| 127-Vigilante by Kubert; Tommy Tomorrow begins | 43.00 | 110.00 | 260.00 |
| 141-157,159-161: 156-Lois Lane as Super Woman. 160-Last 52 pgs. | 32.00 | 80.00 | 190.00 |
| 158-Origin Superman | 40.00 | 100.00 | 240.00 |
| 162-180: 168,176-Used in **POP**, pg. 90 | 19.00 | 56.00 | 130.00 |
| 181-201: 191-Intro. Janu in Congo Bill. 198-Last Vigilante. 201-Last pre-code issue | 17.00 | 51.00 | 120.00 |
| 202-220 | 14.00 | 43.00 | 100.00 |
| 221-240: 224-1st Golden Gorilla story | 11.50 | 34.00 | 80.00 |
| 241,243-251: 248-Congo Bill becomes Congorilla. 251-Last Tommy Tomorrow | 8.50 | 25.50 | 60.00 |
| 242-Origin & 1st app. Brainiac (7/58); 1st mention of Shrunken City of Kandor | 46.00 | 138.00 | 320.00 |
| 252-Origin & 1st app. Supergirl (5/59); Re-intro Metallo (see Superboy #49 for 1st app.) | 66.00 | 200.00 | 460.00 |

| | Good | Fine | N-Mint |
|---|---|---|---|
| 253-2nd app. Supergirl | 11.50 | 34.00 | 80.00 |
| 254-1st meeting of Bizarro & Superman | 12.00 | 36.00 | 85.00 |
| 255-1st Bizarro Lois & both Bizarros leave Earth to make Bizarro World | 9.30 | 28.00 | 65.00 |
| 256-261: 259-Red Kryptonite used. 261-1st X-Kryptonite which gave Streaky his powers; last Congorilla in Action; origin & 1st app. Streaky the Super Cat | 5.70 | 17.00 | 40.00 |
| 262-266,268-270: 263-Origin Bizarro World | 4.30 | 13.00 | 30.00 |
| 267(8/60)-3rd Legion app; 1st app. Chameleon Boy, Colossal Boy, & Invisible Kid | 31.50 | 95.00 | 220.00 |
| 271-275,277-282: Last 10 cent issue | 4.00 | 12.00 | 28.00 |
| 276(5/61)-6th Legion app; 1st app. Brainiac 5, Phantom Girl, Triplicate Girl, Bouncing Boy, Sun Boy, & Shrinking Violet; Supergirl joins Legion | 11.50 | 34.00 | 80.00 |
| 283(12/61)-Legion of Super-Villains app | 5.00 | 15.00 | 35.00 |
| 284(1/62)-Mon-el app. | 5.00 | 15.00 | 35.00 |
| 285(2/62)-12th Legion app; Brainiac 5 cameo; Supergirl's existance revealed to world | 5.00 | 15.00 | 35.00 |
| 286(3/62)-Legion of Super Villains app. | 2.65 | 8.00 | 18.00 |
| 287(4/62)-14th Legion app.(cameo) | 2.65 | 8.00 | 18.00 |
| 288-Mon-el app.; r-origin Supergirl | 2.65 | 8.00 | 18.00 |
| 289(6/62)-16th Legion app.(Adult); Lightning Man & Saturn Woman's marriage 1st revealed | 2.65 | 8.00 | 18.00 |
| 290(7/62)-17th Legion app; Phantom Girl app. | 2.65 | 8.00 | 18.00 |
| 291,292,294-299: 292-2nd app. Superhorse (see Adv. 293). 297-Mon-el app; 298-Legion app. | 1.70 | 5.00 | 12.00 |
| 293-Origin Comet(Superhorse) | 3.70 | 11.00 | 26.00 |
| 300 | 2.00 | 6.00 | 14.00 |
| 301-303,305-308,310-320: 306-Brainiac 5, Mon-el app. 307-Saturn Girl app. 314-r-origin Supergirl; J.L.A. x-over. 317-Death of Nor-Kan of Kandor. 319-Shrinking Violet app. | 1.15 | 3.50 | 7.00 |
| 304-Origin & 1st app. Black Flame | 1.15 | 3.50 | 7.00 |
| 309-Legion app. | 1.15 | 3.50 | 8.00 |
| 321-333,335-340: 336-Origin Akvar(Flamebird). 340-Origin, 1st app. Parasite | .85 | 2.50 | 5.00 |
| 334-Giant G-20; origin Supergirl, Streaky, Superhorse & Legion (all-r) | 1.50 | 4.50 | 10.00 |
| 341-346,348-359 | .70 | 2.00 | 4.00 |
| 347,360-Gnt. Supergirl G-33,G-45; 347-Origin Comet-r. 360-Legion-r; r-origin Supergirl | 1.00 | 3.00 | 7.00 |
| 361-372,374-380: 365-Legion app. 370-New facts about Superman's origin. 376-Last Supergirl in Action. 377-Legion begins | .35 | 1.00 | 2.00 |
| 373-Giant Supergirl G-57; Legion-r | .85 | 2.50 | 5.00 |
| 381-402: 392-Last Legion in Action. Saturn Girl gets new costume. 393-402-All Superman issues | .25 | .75 | 1.50 |
| 403-413: All 52pg. issues; 411-Origin Eclipso-(r). 413-Metamorpho begins, ends #418 | .25 | .75 | 1.50 |
| 414-424: 419-Intro. Human Target. 421-Intro Capt. Strong; Green Arrow begins. 422,423-Origin Human Target | .25 | .75 | 1.50 |
| 425-Neal Adams-a; The Atom begins | .35 | 1.00 | 2.00 |
| 426-436,438,439,442,444-450 | .25 | .75 | 1.50 |
| 437,443-100pg. giants | .35 | 1.00 | 2.00 |
| 440-1st Grell-a on Green Arrow | .70 | 2.00 | 4.00 |
| 441-Grell-a on Green Arrow continues | .40 | 1.25 | 2.50 |
| 451-499: 454-Last Atom. 458-Last Green Arrow. 487-488, 44pgs. 487-1st app. Microwave Man; origin Atom retold. 488-Earth II Superman & Lois Lane wed | .25 | .75 | 1.50 |
| 500-($1.00, 68 pgs.)-Infinity-c; Superman life story; shows Legion statues in museum | | .60 | 1.20 |
| 501-551,554-582: 511-514-New Airwave. 513-The Atom begins. 517-Aquaman begins; ends #541. 521-1st app. The Vixen. 532-New Teen Titans cameo. 535,536-Omega Men app.; 536-New Teen Titans cameo. 544-(Mando paper, 68pgs.)-Origins New Luthor & Brainiac; Omega Men cameo. 546-J.L.A. & New Teen Titans app. 551-Starfire becomes Red-Star | | .50 | 1.00 |

*Action Comics #20, © DC*

*Action Comics #74, © DC*

*Action Comics #487, © DC*

Action Comics #553, © DC

Adam-12 #7, © Adam-12 Productions

Adventure Comics #67, © DC

Good Fine N-Mint
552,553-Animal Man-c & app. (2/84 & 3/84) 2.00 6.00 12.00
583-Alan Moore scripts 2.00 6.00 12.00
584-Byrne-a begins; New Teen Titans app. .25 .75 1.50
585-597,599: 586-Legends x-over. 596-Millennium x-over .50 1.00
598-1st app. Checkmate .50 1.50 3.00
600-($2.50, 84 pgs., 5/88) .70 2.00 4.00
601-642-Weekly issues ($1.50, 52 pgs.); 601-Re-intro The Secret Six. 611-614: Catwoman (new costume in #611). 613-618: Nightwing .25 .75 1.50
643-Superman & monthly issues begin again; Perez-c/a/scripts begin; Cover swipe Superman #1 .25 .75 1.50
644-649,651-660: 654-Part 3 of Batman storyline. 655-Free extra 8 pgs. 660-Death of Lex Luthor .40 .80
650-$1.50, 52 pgs. .25 .75 1.50
Annual 1 (10/87)-Art Adams-c/a(p) 1.00 3.00 6.00
Annual 2 (7/89, $1.75, 68 pgs.)-Perez-c/a(i) .35 1.00 2.00
Theater Giveaway (1947, 32 pgs., 6½x8¼", nn)-Vigilante story based on Vigilante Columbia serial 43.00 110.00 300.00

NOTE: ***Supergirl's*** *origin in 262, 280, 285, 291, 305, 309.* ***N. Adams*** *c-356, 358, 359, 361-364, 366, 367, 370-374, 377-379i, 398-400, 402, 404-406, 419p, 466, 468, 473i, 485.* ***Bailey*** *a-24, 25.* ***Byrne*** *a-584-588p, 589i, 594-598p, 599i, 600p; c-596-600.* ***Grell*** *a-440-442, 444-446, 450-452, 456-458; c-456.* ***Guardineer*** *a-24, 25; c-8, 11, 12, 14-16, 18. 25.* ***Bob Kane's*** *Clip Carson-14-41.* ***Gil Kane*** *a-493r, 539-541, 544-546, 551-554; c-535p, 540, 541, 544p, 545-549, 551-554.* ***Meskin*** *a-42-121(most).* ***Moldoff*** *a-23-25.* ***Perez*** *a-600i, 643-652p; c-529p, 643-651.* ***Starlin*** *a-509.* ***Leonard Starr*** *a-597i(part),* ***Staton*** *a-525p, 526p, 531p, 535p, 536p.* ***Toth*** *a-406, 407, 413, 418, 419, 425, 431.* ***Tuska*** *a-486p, 550.* ***Williamson*** *a-568i.*

**ACTION FORCE** (Also see G.I. Joe European Missions)
Mar, 1987 - No. 40?, 1988 (Magazine size, $1.00, color, weekly)
Marvel Comics Ltd. (British)

1-40: British G.I. Joe series. 3-w/poster insert .50 1.00

**ACTUAL CONFESSIONS** (Formerly Love Adventures)
No. 13, October, 1952 - No. 14, December, 1952
Atlas Comics (MPI)

13,14 1.50 4.50 10.00

**ACTUAL ROMANCES**
October, 1949 - No. 2, Jan, 1950 (52 pgs.)
Marvel Comics (IPS)

1 3.50 10.50 24.00
2-Photo-c 2.00 6.00 14.00

**ADAM AND EVE**
1975, 1978 (35-49 cents)
Spire Christian Comics (Fleming H. Revell Co.)

nn-By Al Hartley .25 .50

**ADAM STRANGE** (See Mystery in Space #53 & Showcase #17)
1990 - No. 3, 1990 ($3.95, 52 pgs., mini-series, squarebound)
DC Comics

Book One - Three: Andy & Adam Kubert-c/a .70 2.00 4.00

**ADAM-12** (TV)
Dec, 1973 - No. 10, Feb, 1976 (photo covers)
Gold Key

1 1.70 5.00 12.00
2-10 .85 2.60 6.00

**ADDAMS FAMILY** (TV)
Oct, 1974 - No. 3, Apr, 1975 (Hanna-Barbera)
Gold Key

1 2.00 6.00 14.00
2,3 1.15 3.50 8.00

**ADLAI STEVENSON**
December, 1966
Dell Publishing Co.

Good Fine N-Mint
12-007-612-Life story; photo-c 2.35 7.00 16.00

**ADOLESCENT RADIOACTIVE BLACK BELT HAMSTERS** (See Clint)
1986 - No. 9, Jan, 1988 ($1.50, B&W)
Comic Castle/Eclipse Comics

1-9: 1-1st & 2nd printings exist .25 .75 1.50
3-D 1(7/86) - 4 .30 .90 1.80
2-D 1(Limited edition, not in 3-D) .75 2.25 4.50
2-D 2-4 ($2.50) .35 1.25 2.50
...Massacre The Japanese Invasion #1 (8/89, $2.00) .35 1.00 2.00

**ADULT TALES OF TERROR ILLUSTRATED** (See Terror Illustrated)

**ADVANCED DUNGEONS & DRAGONS** (Also see TSR Worlds)
Dec, 1988 - Present ($1.25, color) (Newsstand #1 is Holiday, 1988-89)
DC Comics

1-Based on TSR role playing game 1.85 5.50 11.00
2 1.35 4.00 8.00
3 .85 2.50 5.00
4-10: Later issues $1.50 cover .50 1.50 3.00
11-15 .35 1.00 2.00
16-24 .25 .75 1.50
24-28: 24-Begin $1.75-c .30 .90 1.80
Annual 1 (1990, $3.95, 68 pgs.) .70 2.00 4.00

**ADVENTURE BOUND** (See 4-Color Comics No. 239)

**ADVENTURE COMICS** (Formerly New Adventure)(...Presents Dial H For Hero #479-490)
No. 32, 11/38 - No. 490, 2/82; No. 491, 9/82 - No. 503, 9/83
National Periodical Publications/DC Comics

32-Anchors Aweigh (ends #52), Barry O'Neil (ends #60, not in #33), Captain Desmo (ends #47), Dale Daring (ends #47), Federal Men (ends #70), The Golden Dragon (ends #36), Rusty & His Pals (ends #52) by Bob Kane, Todd Hunter (ends #38) and Tom Brent (ends #39) begin 108.00 270.00 650.00
33-38: 37-Cover used on Double Action #2 63.00 160.00 380.00
39(1/39)-Jack Wood begins, ends #42: 1st mention of Marijuana in comics 70.00 175.00 420.00
40-(Rare, 7/39, on stands 6/10/39)-The Sandman begins; believed to be 1st conceived story (see N.Y. World's Fair '39 for 1st published app.); Socko Strong begins, ends #54

Good Fine VF-NM NM/Mint
800.00 2000.00 4800.00 7000.00
(Estimated up to 70 total copies exist, 3 in NM/Mint)

Good Fine N-Mint
41 167.00 417.00 1000.00
42,44,46,47: All Sandman covers. 47-Steve Conrad Adventurer begins, ends #76 125.00 312.00 750.00
43,45 112.00 280.00 675.00
48-Intro. & 1st app. The Hourman by Bernard Baily

Good Fine VF-NM NM/Mint
750.00 1875.00 4500.00 5200.00
(Estimated up to 100 total copies exist, 5 in NM/Mint)

Good Fine N-Mint
49,50: 50-Cotton Carver by Jack Lehti begins, ends #59? 107.00 265.00 640.00
51-60: 53-1st app. Jimmy "Minuteman" Martin & the Minutemen of America in Hourman; ends #78. 58-Paul Kirk Manhunter begins (1st app.), ends #72 100.00 250.00 600.00
61-1st app. Starman by Jack Burnley

Good Fine VF-NM NM/Mint
417.00 1040.00 2500.00 3600.00
(Estimated up to 110 total copies exist, 7 in NM/Mint)

Good Fine N-Mint
62-65,67,68,70: 67-Origin The Mist. 70-Last Federal Men 87.00 215.00 520.00

Good Fine N-Mint
66-Origin/1st app. Shining Knight 117.00 290.00 700.00
69-1st app. Sandy the Golden Boy (Sandman's sidekick) by Bob Kane; Sandman dons new costume 108.00 270.00 650.00
71-Jimmy Martin becomes costume aide to the Hourman; 1st app. Hourman's Miracle Ray machine 87.00 215.00 520.00
72-1st Simon & Kirby Sandman Good Fine VF-NM NM/Mint
368.00 915.00 2200.00 2800.00
(Estimated up to 165 total copies exist, 8 in NM/Mint)
73-(Scarce)-Origin Manhunter by Simon & Kirby; begin new series
Good Fine VF-NM NM/Mint
400.00 1000.00 2400.00 3300.00
(Estimated up to 160 total copies exist, 7 in NM/Mint)
74-80: 74-Thorndyke replaces Jimmy, Hourman's assistant. 77-Origin Genius Jones; Mist story. 80-Last Simon & Kirby Manhunter & Burnley Starman
Good Fine N-Mint
108.00 270.00 650.00
81-90: 83-Last Hourman. 84-Mike Gibbs begins, ends #102
70.00 175.00 420.00
91-Last Simon & Kirby Sandman 60.00 150.00 360.00
92-99,101,102: 92-Last Manhunter. 102-Last Starman, Sandman, & Genius Jones. Most-S&K-c 46.00 115.00 275.00
100 75.00 185.00 450.00
103-Aquaman, Green Arrow, Johnny Quick, Superboy begin; 1st small logo (4/46) 183.00 460.00 1100.00
104 58.00 145.00 350.00
105-110 48.00 120.00 290.00
111-120: 113-X-Mas-c 42.00 105.00 250.00
121-126,128-130: 128-1st meeting Superboy & Lois Lane
33.00 85.00 200.00
127-Brief origin Shining Knight retold 38.00 95.00 225.00
131-141,143-149: 132-Shining Knight 1st return to King Arthur time; origin aide Sir Butch 29.00 73.00 175.00
142-Origin Shining Knight & Johnny Quick retold
33.00 85.00 200.00
150,151,153,155,157,159,161,163-All have 6 pg. Shining Knight stories by Frank Frazetta. 159-Origin Johnny Quick 43.00 110.00 260.00
152,154,156,158,160,162,164-169: 166-Last Shining Knight. 168-Last 52 pgs. 23.00 70.00 160.00
170-180 21.00 62.00 145.00
181-199: 189-B&W and color illo in **POP** 19.00 56.00 130.00
200 26.00 78.00 180.00
201-209: 207-Last Johnny Quick (not in 205). 209-Last Pre-code issue; origin Speedy 19.00 57.00 130.00
210-1st app. Krypto (Superdog) 143.00 430.00 1000.00
211-220: 214,220-Krypto app. 16.00 48.00 110.00
221-246: 237-1st Intergalactic Vigilante Squadron (Legion tryout)
13.50 41.00 95.00
247(4/58)-1st Legion of Super Heroes app.; 1st app. Cosmic Boy, Lightning Boy (later Lightning Lad in #267), & Saturn Girl (origin)
Good Fine N-Mint Mint
240.00 720.00 1700.00 2500.00
(Estimated up to 500 total copies exist, 9 in Mint)
Good Fine N-Mint
248-252,254,255: All Kirby Green Arrow. 255-Intro. Red Kryptonite in Superboy (used in #252 but with no effect) 8.50 25.50 60.00
253-1st meeting of Superboy & Robin; Green Arrow by Kirby
11.00 32.50 75.00
256-Origin Green Arrow by Kirby 32.00 96.00 225.00
257-259 8.50 25.50 60.00
260-1st S.A. Aquaman; origin retold 27.00 81.00 190.00
261-266,268,270: 262-Origin Speedy in Green Arrow. 270-Congorilla begins, ends #281,283 6.50 19.50 45.00
267(12/59)-2nd Legion of Super Heroes; Lightning Boy now called Lightning Lad; new costumes for Legion 61.00 183.00 425.00
269-Intro. Aqualad; last Green Arrow (not in #206)
11.50 34.00 80.00

Good Fine N-Mint
271-Origin Luthor 13.50 41.00 95.00
272-274,277-280: 279-Intro White Kryptonite in Superboy. 280-1st meeting Superboy-Lori Lemaris 4.50 14.00 32.00
275-Origin Superman-Batman team retold (see World's Finest #94)
7.00 21.00 50.00
276-(9/60) Re-intro Metallo (3rd app?); story similar to Superboy #49
4.50 14.00 32.00
281,284,287-289: 281-Last Congorilla. 284-Last Aquaman in Adv. 287,288-Intro. Dev-Em, the Knave from Krypton. 287-1st Bizarro Perry White & J. Olsen. 289-Legion cameo (statues)
4.00 12.00 28.00
282(3/61)-5th Legion app; intro/origin Star Boy 10.00 30.00 70.00
283-Intro. The Phantom Zone 6.00 18.00 42.00
285-1st Bizarro World story (ends #299) in Adv. (See Action #255)
7.00 21.00 50.00
286-1st Bizarro Mxyzptlk 5.70 17.00 40.00
290(11/61)-8th Legion app; origin Sunboy in Legion (last 10 cent issue)
9.30 28.00 65.00
291,292,295-298: 292-1st Bizarro Lana Lang & Lucy Lane. 295-1st Bizarro Titano 3.50 10.50 24.00
293(2/62)-13th Legion app; Mon-el & Legion Super Pets (1st app. & origin) app. (1st Superhorse). 1st Bizarro Luthor & Kandor
6.85 20.50 48.00
294-1st Bizarro M. Monroe, Pres. Kennedy 6.50 19.50 45.00
299-1st Gold Kryptonite (8/62) 3.60 11.00 25.00
300-Legion series begins; Mon-el leaves Phantom Zone (temporarily), joins Legion 29.00 86.00 200.00
301-Origin Bouncing Boy 9.30 28.00 65.00
302-305: 303-1st app. Matter Eater Lad. 304-Death of Lightning Lad in Legion 5.15 15.50 36.00
306-310: 306-Intro. Legion of Substitute Heroes. 307-1st app. Element Lad in Legion. 308-1st app. Lightning Lass in Legion
4.00 12.00 28.00
311-320: 312-Lightning Lad back in Legion. 315-Last new Superboy story; Colossal Boy app. 316-Origins & powers of Legion given. 317-Intro. Dream Girl in Legion; Lightning Lass becomes Light Lass; Hall of Fame series begins. 320-Dev-Em 2nd app.
2.85 8.50 20.00
321-Intro Time Trapper 2.15 6.50 15.00
322-330: 327-Intro Timber Wolf in Legion. 329-Intro Legion of Super Bizarros 1.85 5.50 13.00
331-340: 337-Chlorophyll Kid & Night Girl app. 340-Intro Computo in Legion 1.70 5.00 12.00
341-Triplicate Girl becomes Duo Damsel 1.15 3.50 8.00
342-345,347,350,351: 345-Last Hall of Fame; returns in 356,371. 351-1st app. White Witch 1.00 3.00 7.00
346,348,349: 346-1st app. Karate Kid, Princess Projectra, Ferro Lad, & Nemesis Kid. 348-Origin Sunboy; intro Dr. Regulus in Legion. 349-Intro Universo & Rond Vidar 1.15 3.50 8.00
352,354-360: 355-Insect Queen joins Legion (4/67)
1.00 3.00 6.00
353-Death of Ferro Lad in Legion 1.50 4.50 10.00
361-364,366,368-370: 369-Intro Mordru in Legion .75 2.25 4.50
365,367,371,372: 365-Intro Shadow Lass; lists origins & powers of L.S.H. 367-New Legion headquarters. 371-Intro. Chemical King. 372-Timber Wolf & Chemical King join .90 2.75 5.50
373,374,376-380: Last Legion in Adv. .75 2.25 4.50
375-Intro Quantum Queen & The Wanderers .90 2.75 5.50
381-389,391-400: 381-Supergirl begins. 399-Unpubbed G.A. Black Canary story. 400-New costume for Supergirl .60 1.20
390-Giant Supergirl G-69 .70 2.00 4.00
401,402,404-410: 409-420-52pg. issues .60 1.20
403-68pg. Giant G-81 .70 2.00 4.00
411,413,414: 413-Hawkman by Kubert; G.A. Robotman-r/Det. #178; Zatanna begins, ends #421 .40 .80
412-Reprints origin Animal Man/Str. Advs. #180 1.00 3.00 6.00

*Adventure Comics #132, © DC*

*Adventure Comics #340, © DC*

*Adventure Comics #413, © DC*

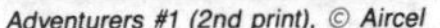
Adventurers #1 (2nd print), © Aircel

Adventures Into Darkness #12, © STD

Adventures Into Terror #7, © MEG

| | Good | Fine | N-Mint |
|---|---|---|---|
| 415,420,421-Animal Man reprints | .35 | 1.00 | 2.00 |
| 416-Giant DC-100 Pg. Super Spect. #10; GA-r | | .60 | 1.20 |
| 417-Morrow Vigilante; Frazetta Shining Knight r-/Adv. #161; origin The Enchantress | | .60 | 1.20 |
| 418,419,422-424: Last Supergirl in Adv. | | .40 | .80 |
| 425-New look, content change to adventure; Toth-a, origin Capt. Fear | .25 | .75 | 1.50 |
| 426-458: 427-Last Vigilante. 428-430-Black Orchid app. 431-440-Spectre app. 433-437-Cover title is Weird Adv. Comics. 435-Mike Grell's 1st comic work ('74). 440-New Spectre origin. 441-452-Aquaman app. 445-447-The Creeper app. 449-451-Martian Manhunter app. 453-458-Superboy app; intro Mighty Girl No. 453. 457, 458-Eclipso app. | | .40 | .80 |
| 459-466($1.00 size, 68pgs.): 459-Flash (ends 466), Deadman (ends 466), Wonder Woman (ends 464), Gr. Lantern (ends 460), New Gods begin (ends 460). 460-Aquaman begins; ends 478. 461-Justice Society begins; ends 466; death Earth II Batman (also #462) | | .45 | .90 |
| 467-490: 467-Starman by Ditko, Plastic Man begin, end 478. 469,470-Origin Starman. 479-Dial 'H' For Hero begins, ends 490 | | .40 | .80 |
| 491-499: 491-100pg. Digest size begins; r-Legion of Super Heroes/Adv. 247 & 267; Spectre, Aquaman, Superboy, S&K Sandman, Bl. Canary-r & new Shazam by Newton begin. 493-Challengers of the Unknown begins by Tuska w/brief origin. 492,495,496,499-S&K Sandman-r/Adventure in all; 494-499-Spectre-r/Spectre 1-3, 5-7. 493-495,497-499-G.A. Captain Marvel-r. 498-Plastic Man-r begin; origin Bouncing Boy-r/#301 | | .60 | 1.20 |
| 500-All Legion-r (Digest size, 148 pgs.) | .25 | .80 | 1.60 |
| 501-503-G.A.-r | | .60 | 1.20 |

NOTE: *Bizarro covers-285, 286, 288, 294, 295. Vigilante app.-420, 426, 427.* ***N. Adams*** *a(r)-495i-498i; c-365-369, 371-373, 375-379, 381-383.* ***Austin*** *a-449i-451i.* ***Bernard Baily*** *c-50, 52-57, 59.* ***Ditko*** *a-467p-478p; c-467p.* ***Giffen*** *c-491p-494p, 500p.* ***Grell*** *a-435-437, 440.* ***Guardineer*** *c-34, 45.* ***Kaluta*** *c-425.* ***G. Kane*** *a-414r, 425; c-496-499, 537.* ***Kirby*** *a-250-256.* ***Kubert*** *a-413.* ***Meskin*** *a-81, 127.* ***Moldoff*** *a-494i; c-49.* ***Morrow*** *a-413-415, 417, 422, 502r, 503r.* ***Newton*** *a-459-461, 464-466, 491p, 492p.* ***Orlando*** *a-457p, 458p.* ***Perez*** *c-484-486, 490p.* ***Simon/Kirby*** *c-73-97, 101, 102.* ***Starlin*** *c-471.* ***Staton*** *a-445-447i, 456-458p, 459, 460, 461p-465p, 466, 467p-478p, 502p(r); c-458, 461(back).* ***Toth*** *a-418, 419, 425, 431, 495p-497p.* ***Tuska*** *a-494p.*

**ADVENTURE COMICS**
No date (early 1940s) Paper cover, 32 pgs.
IGA

| | Good | Fine | N-Mint |
|---|---|---|---|
| Two different issues; Super-Mystery reprints from 1941 | 14.00 | 43.00 | 100.00 |

**ADVENTURE IN DISNEYLAND** (Giveaway)
May, 1955 (16 pgs., soft-c) (Dist. by Richfield Oil)
Walt Disney Productions

| | Good | Fine | N-Mint |
|---|---|---|---|
| nn | 3.00 | 9.00 | 21.00 |

**ADVENTURE INTO FEAR**
1951
Superior Publ. Ltd.

| | Good | Fine | N-Mint |
|---|---|---|---|
| 1-Exist? | 7.00 | 21.00 | 50.00 |

**ADVENTURE INTO MYSTERY**
May, 1956 - No. 8, July, 1957
Atlas Comics (BFP No. 1/OPI No. 2-8)

| | Good | Fine | N-Mint |
|---|---|---|---|
| 1-Everett-c | 11.50 | 34.00 | 80.00 |
| 2-Flying Saucer story | 5.40 | 16.00 | 38.00 |
| 3,6,8: 3,6-Everett-c | 4.50 | 14.00 | 32.00 |
| 4-Williamson-a, 4 pgs; Powell-a | 5.70 | 17.00 | 40.00 |
| 5-Everett-c/a, Orlando-a | 4.50 | 14.00 | 32.00 |
| 7-Torres-a; Everett-c | 4.50 | 14.00 | 32.00 |

**ADVENTURE IS MY CAREER**
1945 (44 pgs.)
U.S. Coast Guard Academy/Street & Smith

| | Good | Fine | N-Mint |
|---|---|---|---|
| nn-Simon, Milt Gross-a | 7.00 | 21.00 | 50.00 |

**ADVENTURERS, THE**
Aug, 1986 - No. 10, 1987? ($1.50, B&W)
V2#1, 1987? - V2#9, 1988; V3#1, Oct, 1989 - No. V3#6, 1990
Aircel Comics/Adventure Publ.

| | Good | Fine | N-Mint |
|---|---|---|---|
| 1-Peter Hsu-a | .85 | 2.50 | 5.00 |
| 1-Cover variant, limited ed. | 1.70 | 5.00 | 10.00 |
| 1-2nd print (1986); 1st app. Elf Warrior | .50 | 1.50 | 3.00 |
| 2,3 | .40 | 1.25 | 2.50 |
| 0 (#4, 12/86)-Origin | .35 | 1.00 | 2.00 |
| 4-10 | .25 | .80 | 1.60 |
| Book II, regular & limited ed. #1 | .25 | .80 | 1.60 |
| Book II, #2,3,0,4-9 | .25 | .80 | 1.60 |
| Book III, #1 (10/89, $2.25)-Regular & limited-c | .40 | 1.15 | 2.25 |
| Book III, #2-6 | .40 | 1.15 | 2.25 |

**ADVENTURES** (No. 2 Spectacular. . . on cover)
Nov, 1949 - No. 2, Feb, 1950 (No. 1 . . .in Romance on cover)
St. John Publishing Co. (Slightly large size)

| | Good | Fine | N-Mint |
|---|---|---|---|
| 1(Scarce); Bolle, Starr-a(2) | 12.00 | 36.00 | 84.00 |
| 2(Scarce)-Slave Girl; China Bombshell app.; Bolle, L. Starr-a | 18.50 | 56.00 | 130.00 |

**ADVENTURES FOR BOYS**
December, 1954
Bailey Enterprises

| | Good | Fine | N-Mint |
|---|---|---|---|
| nn-Comics, text, & photos | 2.15 | 6.50 | 15.00 |

**ADVENTURES IN PARADISE** (See 4-Color No. 1301)

**ADVENTURES IN ROMANCE** (See Adventures)

**ADVENTURES IN SCIENCE** (See Classics Illustrated Special Issue)

**ADVENTURES IN 3-D**
Nov, 1953 - No. 2, Jan, 1954
Harvey Publications

| | Good | Fine | N-Mint |
|---|---|---|---|
| 1-Nostrand, Powell-a, 2-Powell-a | 10.00 | 30.00 | 70.00 |

**ADVENTURES INTO DARKNESS** (See Seduction of/Innocent 3-D)
No. 5, Aug, 1952 - No. 14, 1954
Better-Standard Publications/Visual Editions

| | Good | Fine | N-Mint |
|---|---|---|---|
| 5-Katz-c/a; Toth-a(p) | 9.30 | 28.00 | 65.00 |
| 6-Tuska, Katz-a | 6.00 | 18.00 | 42.00 |
| 7-Katz-c/a | 6.50 | 19.50 | 45.00 |
| 8,9-Toth-a(p) | 7.00 | 21.00 | 50.00 |
| 10,11-Jack Katz-a | 5.00 | 15.00 | 35.00 |
| 12-Toth-a?; lingerie panels | 5.30 | 16.00 | 38.00 |
| 13-Toth-a(p); Cannibalism story cited by T. E. Murphy articles | 7.00 | 21.00 | 50.00 |
| 14 | 4.00 | 12.00 | 28.00 |

NOTE: ***Fawcette*** *a-13.* ***Moriera*** *a-5.* ***Sekowsky*** *a-10, 11, 13(2).*

**ADVENTURES INTO TERROR** (Formerly Joker Comics)
No. 43, Nov, 1950 - No. 31, May, 1954
Marvel/Atlas Comics (CDS)

| | Good | Fine | N-Mint |
|---|---|---|---|
| 43(#1) | 13.00 | 40.00 | 90.00 |
| 44(#2, 2/51) | 10.00 | 30.00 | 70.00 |
| 3(4/51), 4 | 7.00 | 21.00 | 50.00 |
| 5-Wolverton-c panel/Mystic #6. Atom Bomb story | 8.00 | 24.00 | 55.00 |
| 6,8: 8-Wolverton text illo r-/Marvel Tales #104 | 5.70 | 17.00 | 40.00 |
| 7-Wolverton-a "Where Monsters Dwell", 6 pgs.; Tuska-c | 20.00 | 60.00 | 140.00 |
| 9,10,12-Krigstein-a. 9-Decapitation panels | 7.00 | 21.00 | 50.00 |
| 11,13-20 | 4.30 | 13.00 | 30.00 |
| 21-24,26-31 | 3.50 | 10.50 | 24.00 |
| 25-Matt Fox-a | 5.70 | 17.00 | 40.00 |

NOTE: ***Ayers*** *a-21.* ***Colan*** *a-3, 5, 14, 21, 24, 25, 28, 29; c-27.* ***Colletta*** *a-30.* ***Everett*** *c-13,*

*21, 25.* ***Fass*** *a-28, 29.* ***Forte*** *a-28.* ***Heath*** *a-43, 44, 4-6, 22, 24, 26; c-43, 9, 11.* ***Lazarus*** *a-7.* ***Maneely*** *a-7, 10, 11, 21. c-15, 29.* ***Don Rico*** *a-4, 5.* ***Sekowsky*** *a-43, 3, 4.* ***Sinnott*** *a-8, 9, 11, 28.* ***Tuska*** *a-14.*

**ADVENTURES INTO THE UNKNOWN**
Fall, 1948 - No. 174, Aug, 1967 (No. 1-33: 52 pgs.)
American Comics Group

(1st continuous series horror comic; see Eerie #1)

| | Good | Fine | N-Mint |
|---|---|---|---|
| 1-Guardineer-a; adapt. of 'Castle of Otranto' by Horace Walpole | 55.00 | 165.00 | 385.00 |
| 2 | 27.00 | 81.00 | 190.00 |
| 3-Feldstein-a, 9 pgs. | 28.00 | 86.00 | 200.00 |
| 4,5 | 16.00 | 48.00 | 110.00 |
| 6-10 | 12.00 | 36.00 | 84.00 |
| 11-16,18-20: 13-Starr-a | 8.50 | 25.50 | 60.00 |
| 17-Story similar to movie 'The Thing' | 12.00 | 36.00 | 84.00 |
| 21-26,28-30 | 7.00 | 21.00 | 50.00 |
| 27-Williamson/Krenkel-a, 8 pgs. | 14.00 | 42.00 | 100.00 |
| 31-50: 38-Atom bomb panels | 5.00 | 15.00 | 35.00 |
| 51(1/54) - 58 (3-D effect-c/stories). 52-E.C. swipe/Haunt Of Fear 14 | 11.50 | 34.00 | 80.00 |
| 59-3-D effect story only | 7.00 | 21.00 | 50.00 |
| 60-Woodesque-a by Landau | 4.00 | 12.00 | 28.00 |
| 61-Last pre-code issue (1-2/55) | 3.50 | 10.50 | 24.00 |
| 62-70 | 2.65 | 8.00 | 18.00 |
| 71-90 | 1.70 | 5.00 | 12.00 |
| 91,96(#95 on inside),107,116-All contain Williamson-a | 2.85 | 8.50 | 20.00 |
| 92-95,97-99,101-106,108-115,117-127: 109-113,118-Whitney painted-c | 1.50 | 4.50 | 10.00 |
| 100 | 2.00 | 6.00 | 14.00 |
| 128-Williamson/Krenkel/Torres-a(r)/Forbidden Worlds #63; last 10 cent issue | 1.70 | 5.00 | 12.00 |
| 129-150 | 1.15 | 3.50 | 8.00 |
| 151-153: 153-Magic Agent app. | .70 | 2.00 | 5.00 |
| 154-Nemesis series begins (origin), ends #170 | 1.15 | 3.50 | 8.00 |
| 155-167,169-174: 157-Magic Agent app. | .70 | 2.00 | 5.00 |
| 168-Ditko-a(p) | 1.15 | 3.50 | 8.00 |

NOTE: *"Spirit of Frankenstein" series in 5, 6, 8-10, 12, 16.* ***Buscema*** *a-100, 106, 108-110, 158r, 165r.* ***Craig*** *a-152, 160.* ***Goode*** *a-45, 47, 60.* ***Landau*** *a-51, 59-63.* ***Lazarus*** *a-48, 51, 52, 58, 79, 87; c-51, 52, 58.* ***Reinman*** *a-102, 111, 112, 115-118, 124, 130, 137, 141, 145, 164.* ***Whitney*** *c-most.* ***Torres/Williamson*** *a-116.*

**ADVENTURES INTO WEIRD WORLDS**
Jan, 1952 - No. 30, June, 1954
Marvel/Atlas Comics (ACI)

| | Good | Fine | N-Mint |
|---|---|---|---|
| 1-Atom bomb panels | 14.30 | 43.00 | 100.00 |
| 2-Sci/fic stories (2) | 8.50 | 25.50 | 60.00 |
| 3-9: 7-Tongue ripped out | 6.00 | 18.00 | 42.00 |
| 10-Krigstein, Everett-a | 6.00 | 18.00 | 42.00 |
| 11-21: 21-Hitler in Hell story | 4.50 | 14.00 | 32.00 |
| 22-26: 24-Man holds hypo & splits in two | 3.50 | 10.50 | 24.00 |
| 27-Matt Fox end of world story-a; severed head cover | 10.00 | 30.00 | 70.00 |
| 28-Atom bomb story; decapitation panels | 4.50 | 14.00 | 32.00 |
| 29,30 | 3.00 | 9.00 | 21.00 |

NOTE: ***Ayers*** *a-8, 26.* ***Everett*** *a-4, 5; c-6, 8, 10-13, 18, 19, 22, 24; a-4, 25.* ***Fass*** *a-7.* ***Forte*** *a-21, 24.* ***Heath*** *a-1, 4, 17, 22; c-7.* ***Rico*** *a-13.* ***Maneely*** *a-3, 11, 20, 22, 23, 25; c-3, 25-27, 29.* ***Reinman*** *a-24, 28.* ***Robinson*** *a-13.* ***Sinnott*** *a-25, 30.* ***Tuska*** *a-1, 12, 15.* ***Whitney*** *a-7.* ***Wildey*** *a-28. Bondage c-22.*

**ADVENTURES IN WONDERLAND**
April, 1955 - No. 5, Feb, 1956 (Jr. Readers Guild)
Lev Gleason Publications

| | Good | Fine | N-Mint |
|---|---|---|---|
| 1-Maurer-a | 3.70 | 11.00 | 26.00 |
| 2-4 | 2.30 | 7.00 | 16.00 |
| 5-Christmas issue | 2.65 | 8.00 | 18.00 |

**ADVENTURES OF ALAN LADD, THE**
Oct-Nov, 1949 - No. 9, Feb-Mar, 1951 (All 52 pgs.)
National Periodical Publications

| | Good | Fine | N-Mint |
|---|---|---|---|
| 1-Photo-c | 41.00 | 122.00 | 285.00 |
| 2-Photo-c | 26.00 | 77.00 | 180.00 |
| 3-6: Last photo-c | 20.00 | 60.00 | 140.00 |
| 7-9 | 16.50 | 50.00 | 115.00 |

NOTE: ***Dan Barry*** *a-1.* ***Moreira*** *a-3-7.*

**ADVENTURES OF ALICE**
1945 (Also see Alice in Wonderland & . . . at Monkey Island)
Civil Service Publ./Pentagon Publishing Co.

| | Good | Fine | N-Mint |
|---|---|---|---|
| 1 | 6.00 | 18.00 | 42.00 |
| 2-Through the Magic Looking Glass | 4.50 | 14.00 | 32.00 |

**ADVENTURES OF BARON MUNCHAUSEN, THE**
July, 1989 - No. 4, Oct, 1989 ($1.75, color, mini-series)
Now Comics

| | Good | Fine | N-Mint |
|---|---|---|---|
| 1-4: Movie adaptation | .30 | .90 | 1.80 |

**ADVENTURES OF BAYOU BILLY, THE**
Sept, 1989 - No. 5, June, 1990 ($1.00, color)
Archie Comics

| | Good | Fine | N-Mint |
|---|---|---|---|
| 1-5: Esposito-c/a(i). 5-Kelley Jones-c | | .50 | 1.00 |

**ADVENTURES OF BOB HOPE, THE** (Also see True Comics 59)
Feb-Mar, 1950 - No. 109, Feb-Mar, 1968 (#1-10: 52pgs.)
National Periodical Publications

| | Good | Fine | N-Mint |
|---|---|---|---|
| 1-Photo-c | 57.00 | 171.00 | 400.00 |
| 2-Photo-c | 29.00 | 85.00 | 200.00 |
| 3,4-Photo-c | 19.00 | 56.00 | 130.00 |
| 5-10 | 14.30 | 43.00 | 100.00 |
| 11-20 | 8.50 | 25.50 | 60.00 |
| 21-31 (2-3/55; last precode) | 5.70 | 17.00 | 40.00 |
| 32-40 | 4.50 | 14.00 | 32.00 |
| 41-50 | 3.50 | 10.50 | 24.00 |
| 51-70 | 2.30 | 7.00 | 16.00 |
| 71-93,95-105 | 1.15 | 3.50 | 8.00 |
| 94-Aquaman cameo | 1.50 | 4.50 | 10.00 |
| 106-109-Neal Adams-c/a | 2.85 | 8.50 | 20.00 |

NOTE: *Kitty Karr of Hollywood in #17-20, 22, 28. Liz in #26, 109. Miss Beverly Hills of Hollywood in #7, 10, 13, 14. Miss Melody Lane of Broadway in #15. Rusty in #23, 25. Tommy in #24. No 2nd feature in #2-4, 6, 8, 11, 12, 28-108.*

**ADVENTURES OF DEAN MARTIN AND JERRY LEWIS, THE**
(The Adventures of Jerry Lewis No. 41 on)
July-Aug, 1952 - No. 40, Oct, 1957
National Periodical Publications

| | Good | Fine | N-Mint |
|---|---|---|---|
| 1 | 41.00 | 122.00 | 285.00 |
| 2 | 20.00 | 60.00 | 140.00 |
| 3-10 | 11.00 | 32.00 | 75.00 |
| 11-19: Last precode (2/55) | 5.70 | 17.00 | 40.00 |
| 20-30 | 4.30 | 13.00 | 30.00 |
| 31-40 | 3.15 | 9.50 | 22.00 |

**ADVENTURES OF FORD FAIRLANE, THE**
May, 1990 - No. 4, Aug, 1990 ($1.50, mini-series, mature readers)
DC Comics

| | Good | Fine | N-Mint |
|---|---|---|---|
| 1-4: Movie tie-in; Don Heck inks | .25 | .75 | 1.50 |

**ADVENTURES OF G. I. JOE**
1969 (3¼"x7") (20 & 16 pgs.)
Giveaways

**First Series:** 1-Danger of the Depths. 2-Perilous Rescue. 3-Secret Mission to Spy Island. 4-Mysterious Explosion. 5-Fantastic Free Fall. 6-Eight Ropes of Danger. 7-Mouth of Doom. 8-Hidden Missile Discovery. 9-Space Walk Mystery. 10-Fight for Survival. 11-The Shark's Surprise. **Second Series:** 2-Flying Space Adventure. 4-White Tiger Hunt. 7-Capture of the Pygmy Gorilla. 12-Secret of the Mummy's Tomb. **Third Series:** Reprinted surviving titles of First Series. **Fourth Series:** 13-Adventure Team Head

*Adventures Into the Unknown #38, © ACG*

*Adventures Into Weird Worlds #27, © MEG*

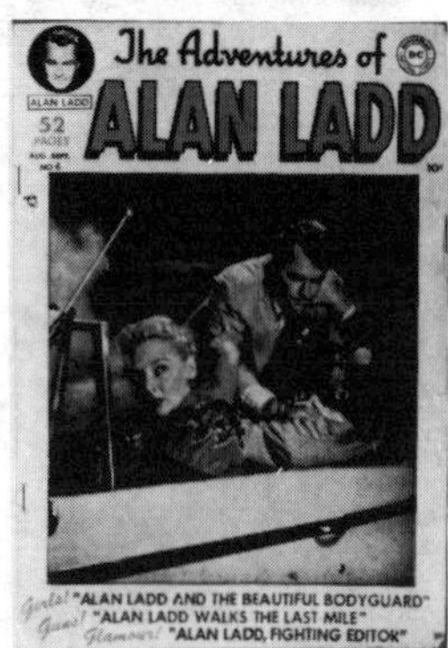

*The Adventures of Alan Ladd #6, © DC*

The Adventures of Jerry Lewis #103, © DC

Adventures of Mighty Mouse #10, © Viacom Int.

Adventures of Rex the Wonder Dog #3, © DC

| | Good | Fine | N-Mint |
|---|---|---|---|
| quarters. 14-Search For the Stolen Idol. each.... | | .30 | .60 |

**ADVENTURES OF HAWKSHAW** (See Hawkshaw The Detective)
1917 (9-3/4 x 13½", 48 pgs., Color & two-tone)
The Saalfield Publishing Co.

| | Good | Fine | N-Mint |
|---|---|---|---|
| By Gus Mager (only 24 pgs. of strips, reverse of each page is blank) | 17.00 | 51.00 | 120.00 |

**ADVENTURES OF HOMER COBB, THE**
September, 1947 (Oversized)
Say/Bart Prod. (Canadian)

| | Good | Fine | N-Mint |
|---|---|---|---|
| 1-(Scarce)-Feldstein-a | 17.00 | 50.00 | 120.00 |

**ADVENTURES OF HOMER GHOST** (See Homer The Happy Ghost)
June, 1957 - No. 2, August, 1957
Atlas Comics

| | Good | Fine | N-Mint |
|---|---|---|---|
| V1#1, 2 | 1.70 | 5.00 | 12.00 |

**ADVENTURES OF JERRY LEWIS, THE** (Advs. of Dean Martin & Jerry Lewis No. 1-40)(See Super DC Giant)
No. 41, Nov, 1957 - No. 124, May-June, 1971
National Periodical Publications

| | Good | Fine | N-Mint |
|---|---|---|---|
| 41-60 | 2.65 | 8.00 | 18.00 |
| 61-80: 68,74-Photo-c | 2.00 | 6.00 | 14.00 |
| 81-91,93-96,98-100: 89-Bob Hope app. | 1.15 | 3.50 | 8.00 |
| 92-Superman cameo | 1.50 | 4.50 | 10.00 |
| 97-Batman/Robin x-over; Joker-c/story | 2.65 | 8.00 | 18.00 |
| 101-104-Neal Adams-c/a; 102-Beatles app. | 2.65 | 8.00 | 18.00 |
| 105-Superman x-over | 1.50 | 4.50 | 10.00 |
| 106-111,113-116 | .70 | 2.00 | 4.00 |
| 112-Flash x-over | 1.50 | 4.50 | 10.00 |
| 117-Wonder Woman x-over | .85 | 2.50 | 5.00 |
| 118-124 | .50 | 1.50 | 3.00 |

**ADVENTURES OF LUTHER ARKWRIGHT, THE**
Oct, 1987 - No. 9, Jan, 1989 ($2.00, B&W)
Mar, 1990 - No. 9, 1990? ($1.95, B&W)
Valkyrie Press/Dark Horse Comics

| | Good | Fine | N-Mint |
|---|---|---|---|
| 1-9: 1-Alan Moore intro | .35 | 1.00 | 2.00 |
| V2#1-9: (Dark Horse)-reprints 1st series; new-c | .35 | 1.00 | 2.00 |

**ADVENTURES OF MARGARET O'BRIEN, THE**
1947 (20 pgs. in color; slick cover; regular size) (Premium)
Bambury Fashions (Clothes)

| | Good | Fine | N-Mint |
|---|---|---|---|
| In "The Big City"-movie adaptation (Scarce) | 13.00 | 40.00 | 90.00 |

**ADVENTURES OF MIGHTY MOUSE** (Mighty Mouse Advs. No. 1)
No. 2, Jan, 1952 - No. 18, May, 1955
St. John Publishing Co.

| | Good | Fine | N-Mint |
|---|---|---|---|
| 2 | 10.00 | 30.00 | 70.00 |
| 3-5 | 6.00 | 18.00 | 42.00 |
| 6-18 | 4.00 | 12.00 | 28.00 |

**ADVENTURES OF MIGHTY MOUSE** (2nd Series)
(Two No. 144's; formerly Paul Terry's Comics; No. 129-137 have nn's)(Becomes Mighty Mouse No. 161 on)
No. 126, Aug, 1955 - No. 160, Oct, 1963
St. John/Pines/Dell/Gold Key

| | Good | Fine | N-Mint |
|---|---|---|---|
| 126(8/55), 127(10/55), 128(11/55)-St. John | 2.30 | 7.00 | 16.00 |
| nn(129, 4/56)-144(8/59)-Pines | 1.70 | 5.00 | 12.00 |
| 144(10-12/59)-155(7-9/62) Dell | 1.50 | 4.50 | 10.00 |
| 156(10/62)-160(10/63) Gold Key | 1.50 | 4.50 | 10.00 |

NOTE: *Early issues titled "Paul Terry's Adventures of . . . ."*

**ADVENTURES OF MIGHTY MOUSE** (Formerly Mighty Mouse)
No. 166, Mar, 1979 - No. 172, Jan, 1980
Gold Key

| | Good | Fine | N-Mint |
|---|---|---|---|
| 166-172 | .50 | 1.50 | 3.00 |

**ADVS. OF MR. FROG & MISS MOUSE** (See Dell Junior Treasury No. 4)

**ADVENTURES OF OZZIE AND HARRIET, THE** (Radio)
Oct-Nov, 1949 - No. 5, June-July, 1950
National Periodical Publications

| | Good | Fine | N-Mint |
|---|---|---|---|
| 1-Photo-c | 37.00 | 110.00 | 250.00 |
| 2 | 23.00 | 70.00 | 160.00 |
| 3-5 | 20.00 | 60.00 | 140.00 |

**ADVENTURES OF PATORUZU**
Aug, 1946 - Winter, 1946
Green Publishing Co.

| | Good | Fine | N-Mint |
|---|---|---|---|
| nn's-Contains Animal Crackers reprints | 2.00 | 6.00 | 14.00 |

**ADVENTURES OF PINKY LEE, THE** (TV)
July, 1955 - No. 5, Dec, 1955
Atlas Comics

| | Good | Fine | N-Mint |
|---|---|---|---|
| 1 | 11.50 | 34.00 | 80.00 |
| 2-5 | 6.50 | 19.00 | 45.00 |

**ADVENTURES OF PIPSQUEAK, THE** (Formerly Pat the Brat)
No. 34, Sept, 1959 - No. 39, July, 1960
Archie Publications (Radio Comics)

| | Good | Fine | N-Mint |
|---|---|---|---|
| 34 | 2.65 | 8.00 | 18.00 |
| 35-39 | 1.70 | 5.00 | 12.00 |

**ADVENTURES OF QUAKE & QUISP, THE** (See Quaker Oats "Plenty of Glutton")

**ADVENTURES OF REX THE WONDER DOG, THE** (Rex. . . No. 1)
Jan-Feb, 1952 - No. 45, May-June, 1959; No. 46, Nov-Dec, 1959
National Periodical Publications

| | Good | Fine | N-Mint |
|---|---|---|---|
| 1-(Scarce)-Toth-a | 55.00 | 165.00 | 385.00 |
| 2-(Scarce)-Toth-a | 27.00 | 81.00 | 190.00 |
| 3-(Scarce)-Toth-a | 21.50 | 64.00 | 150.00 |
| 4,5 | 14.00 | 43.00 | 100.00 |
| 6-10 | 10.00 | 30.00 | 70.00 |
| 11-Atom bomb c/story | 11.00 | 32.00 | 75.00 |
| 12-19: Last precode (1-2/55) | 5.70 | 17.00 | 40.00 |
| 20-46 | 3.70 | 11.00 | 26.00 |

NOTE: ***Infantino, Gil Kane** art in most issues.*

**ADVENTURES OF ROBIN HOOD, THE** (Formerly Robin Hood)
No. 7, 9/57 - No. 8, 11/57 (Based on Richard Greene TV Show)
Magazine Enterprises (Sussex Publ. Co.)

| | Good | Fine | N-Mint |
|---|---|---|---|
| 7,8-Richard Greene photo-c. 7-Powell-a | 5.00 | 15.00 | 35.00 |

**ADVENTURES OF ROBIN HOOD, THE**
March, 1974 - No. 7, Jan, 1975 (Disney Cartoon) (36 pgs.)
Gold Key

| | Good | Fine | N-Mint |
|---|---|---|---|
| 1(90291-403)-Part-r of $1.50 editions | .70 | 2.00 | 4.00 |
| 2-7: 1-7 are part-r | .45 | 1.25 | 2.50 |

**ADVENTURES OF SLIM AND SPUD, THE**
1924 (3¾"x9¾")(104 pg. B&W strip reprints)
Prairie Farmer Publ. Co.

| | Good | Fine | N-Mint |
|---|---|---|---|
| nn | 10.00 | 30.00 | 70.00 |

**ADVENTURES OF STUBBY, SANTA'S SMALLEST REINDEER, THE**
nd (early 1940s) 12 pgs.
W. T. Grant Co. (Giveaway)

| | Good | Fine | N-Mint |
|---|---|---|---|
| nn | 2.00 | 6.00 | 14.00 |

**ADVENTURES OF SUPERMAN** (Formerly Superman)
No. 424, Jan, 1987 - Present
DC Comics

| | Good | Fine | N-Mint |
|---|---|---|---|
| 424 | .35 | 1.00 | 2.00 |
| 425-449: 426-Legends x-over. 432-1st app. Jose Delgado who becomes Gangbuster in #434. 436-Byrne scripts begin. 436,437-Millennium x-over. 438-New Brainiac app. 440-Batman app. | | .50 | 1.00 |

450-476: 457-Perez plots. 463-Superman/Flash race. 467-Part 2 of Bat-

| | Good | Fine | N-Mint |
|---|---|---|---|
| man story. 473-Hal Jordan, Guy Gardner x-over | | .40 | .80 |
| Annual 1 (9/87)-Starlin-c | .25 | .70 | 1.40 |
| Annual 2 (1990, $2.00, 68 pgs.)-Byrne-c/a(i) | .25 | .70 | 1.40 |

**ADVENTURES OF THE BIG BOY**
1956 - Present (Giveaway)(East & West editions of early issues)
Timely Comics/Webs Adv. Corp./Illus. Features

| | Good | Fine | N-Mint |
|---|---|---|---|
| 1-Everett-a | 45.00 | 135.00 | 315.00 |
| 2-Everett-a | 22.00 | 65.00 | 154.00 |
| 3-5 | 7.00 | 21.00 | 50.00 |
| 6-10: 6-Sci/fic issue | 4.50 | 13.50 | 30.00 |
| 11-20 | 2.35 | 7.00 | 15.00 |
| 21-30 | 1.35 | 4.00 | 8.00 |
| 31-50 | .70 | 2.00 | 4.00 |
| 51-100 | .35 | 1.00 | 2.00 |
| 101-150 | | .50 | 1.00 |
| 151-240 | | .20 | .40 |
| 241-376: 266-Superman x-over | | | .10 |
| 1-50 ('76-'84,Paragon Prod.) | | .10 | .20 |
| Summer, 1959 issue, large size | 2.50 | 7.50 | 15.00 |

**ADVENTURES OF THE DETECTIVE**
No date (1930's) 36 pgs.; 9½x12"; B&W (paper cover)
Humor Publ. Co.

| | Good | Fine | N-Mint |
|---|---|---|---|
| nn-Not reprints; Ace King by Martin Nadle | 6.50 | 19.50 | 45.00 |
| 2nd version (printed in red & blue) | 6.50 | 19.50 | 45.00 |

**ADVENTURES OF THE DOVER BOYS**
September, 1950 - No. 2, 1950 (No month given)
Archie Comics (Close-up)

| | Good | Fine | N-Mint |
|---|---|---|---|
| 1,2 | 4.00 | 12.00 | 28.00 |

**ADVENTURES OF THE FLY** (The Fly, No. 2; Fly Man No. 32-39; See The Double Life of Private Strong & Laugh Comics)
Aug, 1959 - No. 30, Oct, 1964; No. 31, May, 1965
Archie Publications/Radio Comics

| | Good | Fine | N-Mint |
|---|---|---|---|
| 1-Shield app.; origin The Fly; S&K-c/a | 37.00 | 112.00 | 260.00 |
| 2-Williamson, S&K, Powell-a | 21.00 | 63.00 | 145.00 |
| 3-Origin retold; Davis, Powell-a | 13.50 | 41.00 | 95.00 |
| 4-Neal Adams-a(p)(1 panel); S&K-c; Powell-a; Shield x-over | 9.30 | 28.00 | 65.00 |
| 5-10: 7-Black Hood app. 8,9-Shield x-over. 9-1st app. Cat Girl. 10-Black Hood app. | 5.70 | 17.00 | 40.00 |
| 11-13,15-20: 16-Last 10 cent issue. 20-Origin Fly Girl retold | 3.15 | 9.50 | 22.00 |
| 14-Intro. & origin Fly Girl | 4.85 | 14.50 | 34.00 |
| 21-30: 23-Jaguar cameo. 29-Black Hood cameo. 30-Comet x-over in Fly Girl | 2.30 | 7.00 | 16.00 |
| 31-Black Hood, Shield, Comet app. | 2.85 | 8.50 | 20.00 |

NOTE: ***Tuska** a-1. **Simon** c-2-4.*

**ADVENTURES OF THE JAGUAR, THE** (See Blue Ribbon Comics, Laugh Comics & Mighty Crusaders)
Sept, 1961 - No. 15, Nov, 1963
Archie Publications (Radio Comics)

| | Good | Fine | N-Mint |
|---|---|---|---|
| 1-Origin Jaguar(1st app?); by J. Rosenberger | 11.50 | 34.00 | 80.00 |
| 2,3: 3-Last 10 cent issue | 5.70 | 17.00 | 40.00 |
| 4,5-Catgirl app. | 4.00 | 12.00 | 28.00 |
| 6-10: 6-Catgirl app. | 3.15 | 9.50 | 22.00 |
| 11-15: 13,14-Catgirl, Black Hood app. in both | 2.30 | 7.00 | 16.00 |

**ADVENTURES OF THE OUTSIDERS, THE** (Formerly Batman & The Outsiders; also see The Outsiders)
No. 33, May, 1986 - No. 46, June, 1987
DC Comics

| | Good | Fine | N-Mint |
|---|---|---|---|
| 33-46 | | .35 | .70 |

**ADVENTURES OF TINKER BELL** (See 4-Color No. 982)

**ADVENTURES OF TOM SAWYER** (See Dell Junior Treasury No. 10)

**ADVENTURES OF WILLIE GREEN, THE**
1915 (8½X16, 50 cents, B&W, soft-c)
Frank M. Acton Co.

| | Good | Fine | N-Mint |
|---|---|---|---|
| Book 1-By Harris Brown; strip-r | 11.00 | 32.00 | 75.00 |

**ADVENTURES OF YOUNG DR. MASTERS, THE**
Aug, 1964 - No. 2, Nov, 1964
Archie Comics (Radio Comics)

| | Good | Fine | N-Mint |
|---|---|---|---|
| 1,2 | .85 | 2.50 | 5.00 |

**ADVENTURES OF ZOT! IN DIMENSION 10 ½**
Sept, 1987 (One shot, $2.00, B&W)
Eclipse Comics

| | Good | Fine | N-Mint |
|---|---|---|---|
| 14 ½ | .35 | 1.00 | 2.00 |

**ADVENTURES ON OTHER WORLDS** (See Showcase #17 & 18)

**ADVENTURES ON THE PLANET OF THE APES**
Oct, 1975 - No. 11, Dec, 1976
Marvel Comics Group

| | Good | Fine | N-Mint |
|---|---|---|---|
| 1-Planet of the Apes-r in color; Starlin-c | | .50 | 1.00 |
| 2-11 | | .30 | .60 |

NOTE: ***Alcala** a-6-11r. **Buckler** c-2p. **Nasser** c-7. **Starlin** c-6. **Tuska** a-1-5r.*

**ADVENTURES WITH SANTA CLAUS**
No date (early 50's) (24 pgs.; 9¾x6¾"; paper cover) (Giveaway)
Promotional Publ. Co. (Murphy's Store)

| | Good | Fine | N-Mint |
|---|---|---|---|
| nn-Contains 8 pgs. ads | 3.00 | 9.00 | 21.00 |
| 16 page version | 3.00 | 9.00 | 21.00 |

**AFRICA**
1955
Magazine Enterprises

| | Good | Fine | N-Mint |
|---|---|---|---|
| 1(A-1 #137)-Cave Girl, Thun'da; Powell-c/a(4) | 11.50 | 34.00 | 80.00 |

**AFRICAN LION** (See 4-Color No. 665)

**AFTER DARK**
No. 6, May, 1955 - No. 8, Sept, 1955
Sterling Comics

| | Good | Fine | N-Mint |
|---|---|---|---|
| 6-8-Sekowsky-a in all | 2.85 | 8.50 | 20.00 |

**AGAINST BLACKSHARD 3-D** (Also see SoulQuest)
August, 1986 ($2.25)
Sirius Comics

| | Good | Fine | N-Mint |
|---|---|---|---|
| 1 | .40 | 1.15 | 2.30 |

**AGGIE MACK**
Jan, 1948 - No. 8, Aug, 1949
Four Star Comics Corp./Superior Comics Ltd.

| | Good | Fine | N-Mint |
|---|---|---|---|
| 1-Feldstein-a, "Johnny Prep" | 11.50 | 34.00 | 80.00 |
| 2,3-Kamen-c | 5.70 | 17.00 | 40.00 |
| 4-Feldstein "Johnny Prep;" Kamen-c | 7.00 | 21.00 | 50.00 |
| 5-8-Kamen-c/a | 5.15 | 15.50 | 36.00 |

**AGGIE MACK** (See 4-Color Comics No. 1335)

**AIDA-ZEE**
1990 ($1,50, color, Baxter paper, adults)
The Nate Butler Studio

| | Good | Fine | N-Mint |
|---|---|---|---|
| 1-Disbrow-a, N. Redondo-i, M. Anderson-c(p) | .25 | .75 | 1.50 |

**AIN'T IT A GRAND & GLORIOUS FEELING?**
1922 (52 pgs.; 9x9¾"; stiff cardboard cover)
Whitman Publishing Co.

| | Good | Fine | N-Mint |
|---|---|---|---|
| nn-1921 daily strip-r; B&W, color-c; Briggs-a | 11.00 | 32.00 | 75.00 |

**AIR ACE** (Formerly Bill Barnes No. 1-12)
V2#1, Jan, 1944 - V3#8(No. 20), Feb-Mar, 1947
Street & Smith Publications

*Adventures of the Big Boy #7, © Illus. Feat.*

*Adventures of the Fly #16, © AP*

*The Adventures of the Jaguar #8, © AP*

Air Ace V3#6, © S&S

Airboy Comics V9#2, © HILL

Air Fighters Comics V2#7, © HILL

| | Good | Fine | N-Mint |
|---|---|---|---|
| V2#1 | 8.50 | 25.50 | 60.00 |
| V2#2-12: 7-Powell-a | 4.30 | 13.00 | 30.00 |
| V3#1-6 | 2.65 | 8.00 | 18.00 |
| V3#7-Powell bondage-c/a; all atomic issue | 7.00 | 21.00 | 50.00 |
| V3#8 (V5#8 on-c)-Powell-c/a | 3.00 | 9.00 | 21.00 |

**AIRBOY** (Also see Airmaidens, Skywolf, Target: Airboy & Valkyrie)
July, 1986 - No. 50, Oct, 1989 (#1-8, 50 cents, 20pgs., bi-weekly; #9-on, 36pgs; #34 on published monthly)(9-32: $1.25; 33-41: $1.75-c)
Eclipse Comics

| | Good | Fine | N-Mint |
|---|---|---|---|
| 1 | .50 | 1.50 | 3.00 |
| 2-4,6-8: 2-1st Marisa; Skywolf gets new costume. 3-The Heap begins | .35 | 1.00 | 2.00 |
| 5-Valkyrie returns; Dave Stevens-c | .50 | 1.50 | 3.00 |
| 9-49: 9-Skywolf begins. 11-Origin of G.A. Airboy & his plane Birdie. 28-Mr. Monster vs. The Heap. 41-r/1st app. Valkyrie from Air Fighters. 38-40-The Heap-r by Infantino. 46,47-part-r/Air Fighters. 42-Begins $1.95-c. 48-Black Angel-r/A.F. | .25 | .80 | 1.60 |
| 50 ($4.95, 52 pgs.)-Kubert-c | .70 | 2.00 | 4.95 |
| . . . Meets The Prowler 1 (12/87, $1.95, one-shot) | .35 | 1.00 | 2.00 |
| . . . - Mr. Monster Special 1 (8/87, $1.75) | .35 | 1.00 | 2.00 |
| . . . Versus The Air Maidens 1 (7/88, $1.95) | .35 | 1.00 | 2.00 |

NOTE: ***Evans** c-21. **Gulacy** c-20. **Spiegle** a-34, 35, 37. **Ken Steacy** painted c-17, 33.*

**AIRBOY COMICS** (Air Fighters Comics No. 1-22)
V2#11, Dec, 1945 - V10#4, May, 1953 (No V3#3)
Hillman Periodicals

| | Good | Fine | N-Mint |
|---|---|---|---|
| V2#11 | 30.00 | 90.00 | 210.00 |
| 12-Valkyrie app. | 20.00 | 60.00 | 140.00 |
| V3#1,2(no #3) | 17.00 | 51.00 | 120.00 |
| 4-The Heap app. in Skywolf | 14.00 | 43.00 | 100.00 |
| 5-8,10,11: 6-Valkyrie app. | 12.00 | 36.00 | 85.00 |
| 9-Origin The Heap | 14.00 | 43.00 | 100.00 |
| 12-Skywolf & Airboy x-over; Valkyrie app. | 16.00 | 48.00 | 110.00 |
| V4#1-Iron Lady app. | 14.00 | 43.00 | 100.00 |
| 2,3,12: 2-Rackman begins | 8.50 | 25.50 | 60.00 |
| 4-Simon & Kirby-c | 10.00 | 30.00 | 70.00 |
| 5-11-All S&K-a | 12.00 | 36.00 | 85.00 |
| V5#1-9: 4-Infantino Heap. 5-Skull-c | 6.00 | 18.00 | 42.00 |
| 10,11: 10-Origin The Heap | 6.00 | 18.00 | 42.00 |
| 12-Krigstein-a(p) | 8.00 | 24.00 | 55.00 |
| V6#1-3,5-12: 6,8-Origin The Heap | 6.00 | 18.00 | 42.00 |
| 4-Origin retold | 7.00 | 21.00 | 50.00 |
| V7#1-12: 7,8,10-Origin The Heap | 6.00 | 18.00 | 42.00 |
| V8#1-3,6-12 | 5.00 | 15.00 | 35.00 |
| 4-Krigstein-a | 7.00 | 21.00 | 50.00 |
| 5(#100) | 6.00 | 18.00 | 42.00 |
| V9#1-12: 2-Valkyrie app. 7-One pg. Frazetta ad | 5.00 | 15.00 | 35.00 |
| V10#1-4 | 5.00 | 15.00 | 35.00 |

NOTE: ***Barry** a-V2#3, 7. **Bolle** a-V4#12. **McWilliams** a-V3#7, 9. **Powell** a-V7#2, 3, V8#1, 6. **Starr** a-V5#1, 12. **Dick Wood** a-V4#12. Bondage-c V5#8.*

**AIR FIGHTERS CLASSICS**
Nov, 1987 - No. 6, May, 1989 ($3.95, B&W, 68 pgs.)
Eclipse Comics

| | Good | Fine | N-Mint |
|---|---|---|---|
| 1-6: r/G.A. Air Fighters #2-7. 1-Origin Airboy | .70 | 2.00 | 4.00 |

**AIR FIGHTERS COMICS** (Airboy Comics #23 (V2#11) on)
Nov, 1941; No. 2, Nov, 1942 - V2#10, Fall, 1945
Hillman Periodicals

| | Good | Fine | N-Mint |
|---|---|---|---|
| V1#1-(Produced by Funnies, Inc.); Black Commander only app. | 100.00 | 300.00 | 700.00 |
| 2(11/42)-(Produced by Quality artists & Biro for Hillman); Origin Airboy & Iron Ace; Black Angel, Flying Dutchman & Skywolf begin; Fuje-a; Biro-c/a | 150.00 | 450.00 | 1050.00 |
| 3-Origin The Heap & Skywolf | 78.00 | 235.00 | 550.00 |
| 4 | 53.00 | 160.00 | 375.00 |
| 5,6 | 39.00 | 118.00 | 275.00 |
| 7-12 | 32.00 | 96.00 | 225.00 |
| V2#1,3-9: 5-Flag-c; Fuje-a. 7-Valkyrie app. | 28.50 | 86.00 | 200.00 |
| 2-Skywolf by Giunta; Flying Dutchman by Fuje; 1st meeting Valkyrie & Airboy (She worked for the Nazis in beginning) | 36.00 | 107.00 | 250.00 |
| 10-Origin The Heap & Skywolf | 36.00 | 107.00 | 250.00 |

NOTE: ***Fuje** a-V1#2, 5, 7, V2#2, 3, 5, 7-9. **Giunta** a-V2#2, 3, 7, 9.*

**AIRFIGHTERS MEET SGT. STRIKE SPECIAL, THE**
Jan, 1988 ($1.95, color, one-shot, stiff-c)
Eclipse Comics

| | Good | Fine | N-Mint |
|---|---|---|---|
| 1-Airboy, Valkyrie, Skywolf app. | .35 | 1.00 | 2.00 |

**AIR FORCES** (See American Air Forces)

**AIRMAIDENS SPECIAL**
August, 1987 ($1.75, color)(Baxter, One-shot)
Eclipse Comics

| | Good | Fine | N-Mint |
|---|---|---|---|
| 1-Marisa becomes La Lupina (origin) | .30 | .90 | 1.80 |

**AIR POWER** (CBS TV & the U.S. Air Force Presents)
1956 (32pgs, 5¼x7¼", soft-c)
Prudential Insurance Co. giveaway

| | Good | Fine | N-Mint |
|---|---|---|---|
| nn-Toth-a? Based on 'You Are There' TV program by Walter Cronkite | 5.00 | 15.00 | 30.00 |

**AIR RAIDERS**
Nov, 1987 - No. 5, Mar, 1988 ($1.00, color)
Star Comics/Marvel #3 on

| | Good | Fine | N-Mint |
|---|---|---|---|
| 1-5 | | .50 | 1.00 |

**AIR WAR STORIES**
Sept-Nov, 1964 - No. 8, Aug, 1966
Dell Publishing Co.

| | Good | Fine | N-Mint |
|---|---|---|---|
| 1-Painted-c; Glanzman-c/a begins | 1.50 | 4.50 | 10.00 |
| 2-8 | .85 | 2.60 | 6.00 |

**AKIRA**
Sept, 1988 - Present ($3.50, color, deluxe, 68pgs.)
Epic Comics (Marvel)

| | Good | Fine | N-Mint |
|---|---|---|---|
| 1 | 1.35 | 4.00 | 8.00 |
| 1,2-2nd printings ('89, $3.95) | .70 | 2.00 | 4.00 |
| 2 | 1.00 | 3.00 | 6.00 |
| 3-28: Later issues are $3.95 | .65 | 1.90 | 3.75 |

**ALADDIN** (See Dell Junior Treasury No. 2)

**ALAN LADD** (See The Adventures of . . .)

**ALARMING ADVENTURES**
Oct, 1962 - No. 3, Feb, 1963
Harvey Publications

| | Good | Fine | N-Mint |
|---|---|---|---|
| 1 | 3.50 | 10.50 | 24.00 |
| 2,3 | 2.30 | 7.00 | 16.00 |

NOTE: ***Bailey** a-1, 3. **Crandall** a-1, 2. **Powell** a-2(2). **Severin** c-1-3. **Torres** a-2? **Tuska** a-1. **Williamson** a-1i, 2i, 3.*

**ALARMING TALES**
Sept, 1957 - No. 6, Nov, 1958
Harvey Publications (Western Tales)

| | Good | Fine | N-Mint |
|---|---|---|---|
| 1-Kirby-c/a(4) | 5.70 | 17.00 | 40.00 |
| 2-Kirby-a(4) | 5.70 | 17.00 | 40.00 |
| 3,4-Kirby-a | 4.00 | 12.00 | 28.00 |
| 5-Kirby/Williamson-a | 4.50 | 14.00 | 32.00 |
| 6-Williamson-a? | 3.50 | 10.50 | 24.00 |

**ALBEDO**
April, 1985 - No. 14, Spring, 1989 (B&W)
Thoughts And Images

| | Good | Fine | N-Mint |
|---|---|---|---|
| 0-Yellow cover; 50 copies | 15.00 | 45.00 | 90.00 |

| | Good | Fine | N-Mint |
|---|---|---|---|
| 0-White cover, 450 copies | 11.60 | 35.00 | 70.00 |
| 0-Blue, 1st printing, 500 copies | 6.70 | 20.00 | 40.00 |
| 0-Blue, 2nd printing, 1000 copies | 4.15 | 12.50 | 25.00 |
| 0-3rd printing | .70 | 2.00 | 4.00 |
| 0-4th printing | .25 | .80 | 1.60 |
| 1-Dark red; 1st app. Usagi Yojimbo | 6.70 | 20.00 | 40.00 |
| 1-Bright red | 5.00 | 15.00 | 30.00 |
| 2 | 5.00 | 15.00 | 30.00 |
| 3 | 1.00 | 3.00 | 6.00 |
| 4 | 1.70 | 5.00 | 10.00 |
| 5 | .85 | 2.50 | 5.00 |
| 6 | 1.15 | 3.50 | 7.00 |
| 7-14 | .35 | 1.00 | 2.00 |

(Prices vary widely on this series)

**ALBERTO** (See The Crusaders)

**ALBERT THE ALLIGATOR & POGO POSSUM** (See Four Color Comics #105, 148)

**ALBUM OF CRIME** (See Fox Giants)

**ALBUM OF LOVE** (See Fox Giants)

**AL CAPP'S DOGPATCH** (Also see Mammy Yokum)
No. 71, June, 1949 - No. 4, Dec, 1949
Toby Press

| | | | |
|---|---|---|---|
| 71(#1)-R-/from Tip Top #112-114 | 16.00 | 48.00 | 110.00 |
| 2-4: 4-R-/from Li'l Abner #73 | 11.00 | 32.00 | 75.00 |

**AL CAPP'S SHMOO** (Also see Oxydol-Dreft)
July, 1949 - No. 5, April, 1950 (None by Al Capp)
Toby Press

| | | | |
|---|---|---|---|
| 1 | 22.00 | 65.00 | 155.00 |
| 2-5: 3-Sci-fi trip to moon. 4-X-Mas-c; origin/1st app. Super-Shmoo | 17.00 | 51.00 | 120.00 |

**AL CAPP'S WOLF GAL**
1951 - No. 2, 1952
Toby Press

| | | | |
|---|---|---|---|
| 1,2-Edited-r from Li'l Abner #63,64 | 21.50 | 64.00 | 150.00 |

**ALEXANDER THE GREAT** (See 4-Color No. 688)

**ALF** (TV) (See Star Comics Digest)
Mar, 1988 - Present ($1.00, color)
Marvel Comics

| | | | |
|---|---|---|---|
| 1-Post-a; photo-c | 1.00 | 3.00 | 6.00 |
| 2-Post-a | .55 | 1.60 | 3.20 |
| 3-5 | .25 | .80 | 1.60 |
| 6-40: 6-Photo-c. 26-Infinity-c | | .50 | 1.00 |
| Annual 1 ($1.75, 68 pgs.)-Evolutionary War | .60 | 1.75 | 3.50 |
| Annual 2 (1989, $2.00, 68 pgs.)-Sienkiewicz-c | .35 | 1.00 | 2.00 |
| Annual 3 (1990, $2.00, 68 pgs.)-TMNT parody | .35 | 1.00 | 2.00 |
| ...Comics Digest 1 (1988)-Reprints Alf #1,2 | .25 | .75 | 1.50 |
| Holiday Special 1 ($1.75, 1988, 68 pgs.) | .30 | .90 | 1.75 |
| Holiday Special 2 ($2.00, Winter, 1989, 68 pgs.) | .35 | 1.00 | 2.00 |
| Spring Special 1 (Spr/89, $1.75, 68 pgs.) | .30 | .90 | 1.75 |

**ALGIE**
Dec, 1953 - No. 3, 1954
Timor Publ. Co.

| | | | |
|---|---|---|---|
| 1-Teenage | 1.70 | 5.00 | 12.00 |
| 2,3 | 1.15 | 3.50 | 8.00 |
| Accepted Reprint #2(nd) | .70 | 2.00 | 5.00 |
| Super Reprint 15 | .60 | 1.80 | 4.00 |

**ALIAS:**
July, 1990 - No. 5, Nov, 1990 ($1.75, color)
Now Comics

| | | | |
|---|---|---|---|
| 1-5: 1-Sienkiewicz-c | .30 | .90 | 1.80 |

**ALICE** (New Adventures in Wonderland)
No. 10, 7-8/51 - No. 2, 11-12/51
Ziff-Davis Publ. Co.

| | Good | Fine | N-Mint |
|---|---|---|---|
| 10-Painted-c (spanking scene); Berg-a | 11.50 | 34.00 | 80.00 |
| 11-Dave Berg-a | 5.70 | 17.00 | 40.00 |
| 2-Dave Berg-a | 4.30 | 13.00 | 30.00 |

**ALICE AT MONKEY ISLAND** (See The Adventures of Alice)
No. 3, 1946
Pentagon Publ. Co. (Civil Service)

| | | | |
|---|---|---|---|
| 3 | 4.00 | 12.00 | 28.00 |

**ALICE IN BLUNDERLAND**
1952 (Paper cover, 16 pages in color)
Industrial Services

| | | | |
|---|---|---|---|
| nn-Facts about big government waste and inefficiency | 12.00 | 36.00 | 84.00 |

**ALICE IN WONDERLAND** (See Advs. of Alice, 4-Color No. 331,341, Dell Jr. Treasury No. 1, The Dreamery, Movie Comics, Single Series No. 24, Walt Disney Showcase No. 22, and World's Greatest Stories)

**ALICE IN WONDERLAND**
1965; 1982
Western Printing Company/Whitman Publ. Co.

| | | | |
|---|---|---|---|
| ...Meets Santa Claus(1950s), nd, 16pgs | 2.75 | 8.00 | 16.00 |
| Rexall Giveaway(1965, 16 pgs., 5x7¼") Western Printing (TV-Hanna-Barbera) | 2.00 | 6.00 | 12.00 |
| Wonder Bakery Giveaway(16 pgs, color, nn, nd) (Continental Baking Co. (1969) | 2.00 | 6.00 | 12.00 |
| 1-(Whitman; 1982)-r/4-Color #331 | | .40 | .80 |

**ALICE IN WONDERLAND MEETS SANTA**
nd (16 pgs., 6-5/8x9-11/16", paper cover)
No publisher (Giveaway)

| | | | |
|---|---|---|---|
| nn | 10.00 | 30.00 | 60.00 |

**ALIEN ENCOUNTERS** (Replaces Alien Worlds)
June, 1985 - No. 14, Aug, 1987 ($1.75; Baxter, mature readers)
Eclipse Comics

| | | | |
|---|---|---|---|
| 1-14: Nudity, strong language | .35 | 1.00 | 2.00 |

**ALIEN FIRE**
1987 - No. 3, 1987? ($2.00, B&W)
Kitchen Sink Press

| | | | |
|---|---|---|---|
| 1-3 | .40 | 1.25 | 2.50 |

**ALIEN LEGION** (See Marvel Graphic Novel #25)
April, 1984 - No. 20, Sept, 1987
Epic Comics (Marvel)

| | | | |
|---|---|---|---|
| 1-$2.00 cover, high quality paper | .50 | 1.50 | 3.00 |
| 2-5 | .35 | 1.00 | 2.00 |
| 6-20 | .25 | .75 | 1.50 |

NOTE: *Austin a-1i, 4i; c-3i-5i.*

**ALIEN LEGION** (2nd series)
Aug, 1987 (indicia) (10/87 on-c) - No. 18, Aug, 1990 ($1.25, color)
Epic Comics (Marvel)

| | | | |
|---|---|---|---|
| V2#1 | .35 | 1.00 | 2.00 |
| V2#2-18: 7-Begin $1.50 cover | .25 | .75 | 1.50 |

**ALIEN NATION**
Dec, 1988 ($2.50; 68 pgs.)
DC Comics

| | | | |
|---|---|---|---|
| 1-Adapts movie; painted-c | .40 | 1.25 | 2.50 |

**ALIENS, THE** (Captain Johner and...)(Also see Magnus Robot...)
Sept-Dec, 1967; No. 2, May, 1982
Gold Key

| | | | |
|---|---|---|---|
| 1-Reprints from Magnus #1,3,4,6-10, all by Russ Manning | 1.15 | 3.50 | 8.00 |

*Al Capp's Shmoo #5, © UFS*

*Alien Encounters #3, © Eclipse*

*Alien Legion #14 (2nd series), © MEG*

All-American Comics #16, © DC

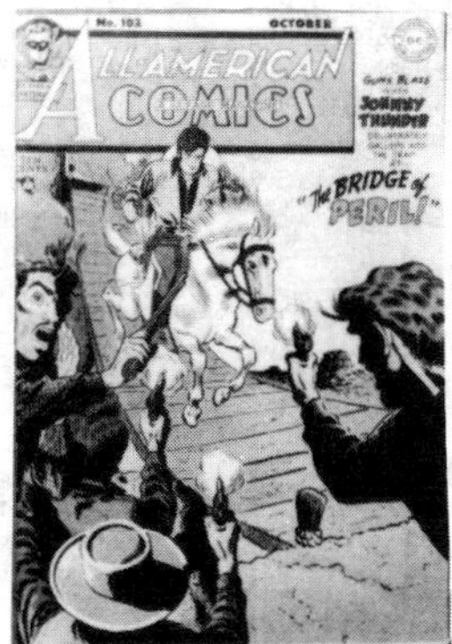

All-American Comics #102, © DC

All-American Men of War #128 (#2), © DC

| | Good | Fine | N-Mint |
|---|---|---|---|
| 2-Magnus-r/#1 by Manning | .40 | 1.25 | 2.50 |

**ALIENS** (See Alien: The Illustrated . . . & Dark Horse Presents #24)
1988 - No. 6, 1989 ($1.95, B&W, mini-series)
V2#1, Aug, 1989 - No. 4, 1990 ($2.25, color, mini-series)
Dark Horse Comics

| | Good | Fine | N-Mint |
|---|---|---|---|
| 1-Based on movie sequel | 3.70 | 11.00 | 22.00 |
| 1-2nd printing | .85 | 2.50 | 5.00 |
| 1-3rd & 4th printings; 4th w/new inside front-c | .35 | 1.00 | 2.00 |
| 2 | 2.50 | 7.50 | 15.00 |
| 2-2nd printing | .50 | 1.50 | 3.00 |
| 2-3rd printing w/new inside f/c | .35 | 1.00 | 2.00 |
| 3-6 | .70 | 2.00 | 4.00 |
| 3-6-2nd printings | .35 | 1.00 | 2.00 |
| . . . Collection 1 ($10.95,)-r/1-6 plus Dark Horse Presents #24 plus new-a | 1.85 | 5.50 | 11.00 |
| Hardcover ('90, $24.95, B&W)-r/1-6, DHP #24 | 4.15 | 12.50 | 25.00 |
| V2#1 ($2.25, color)-Adapts sequel | 1.00 | 3.00 | 6.00 |
| 1-2nd printing ($2.25) | .40 | 1.15 | 2.25 |
| 2-4 | .70 | 2.00 | 4.00 |

**ALIENS: EARTH WARS**
June, 1990 - No. 4, Oct, 1990 ($2.50, color, mini-series)
Dark Horse Comics

| | Good | Fine | N-Mint |
|---|---|---|---|
| 1-Bolton painted-c on all | 1.15 | 3.50 | 7.00 |
| 1-2nd printing | .40 | 1.25 | 2.50 |
| 2 | .85 | 2.50 | 5.00 |
| 3,4 | .70 | 2.00 | 4.00 |

**ALIENS VS. PREDATOR** (See Dark Horse Presents #36)
June, 1990 - No. 4, Dec, 1990 ($2.50, color, mini-series)
Dark Horse Comics

| | Good | Fine | N-Mint |
|---|---|---|---|
| 1-Painted-c | .85 | 2.50 | 5.00 |
| 1-2nd printing | .40 | 1.25 | 2.50 |
| 0-(7/90, $1.95, B&W)-r/Dark Horse Pres. #34-36 | .60 | 1.75 | 3.50 |
| 2,3 | .60 | 1.75 | 3.50 |
| 4-Dave Dorman painted-c | .40 | 1.25 | 2.50 |

**ALIEN TERROR** (See 3-D Alien Terror)

**ALIEN: THE ILLUSTRATED STORY** (Also see Aliens)
1980 ($3.95, color, soft-c, 8X11")
Heavy Metal Books

| | Good | Fine | N-Mint |
|---|---|---|---|
| nn-Movie adaptation; Simonson-a | .70 | 2.00 | 4.00 |

**ALIEN WORLDS** (Also see Three Dimensional Alien Worlds)
12/82; No. 2, 6/83 - No. 7, 4/84; No. 8, 11/84 - No. 9, 1/85
(Baxter paper, $1.50, mature readers on-c)
Pacific Comics No. 1-7/Eclipse No. 8, 9

| | Good | Fine | N-Mint |
|---|---|---|---|
| 1-Williamson, Redondo-a; nudity | .60 | 1.75 | 3.50 |
| 2-7: 4-Nudity scenes | .50 | 1.50 | 3.00 |
| 8-Williamson-a | .30 | .85 | 1.70 |
| 9 | .35 | 1.00 | 2.00 |

NOTE: ***Bolton** c-5, 9. **Brunner** a-6p, 9; c-6. **Conrad** a-1. **Corben** a-7. **Jeff Jones** a-4p (2pgs.). **Krenkel** a-6. **Morrow** a-7. **Perez** a-7. **Stevens** a-2, 4i; c-2, 4. **Williamson/Frazetta** a-4r/Witzend No. 1.*

**ALIEN WORLDS** (See Eclipse Graphic Album Series #22)

**ALL-AMERICAN COMICS** (. . . Western #103-126, . . . Men of War #127 on; Also see The Big All-American Comic Book)
April, 1939 - No. 102, Oct, 1948
National Periodical Publications/All-American

| | Good | Fine | N-Mint |
|---|---|---|---|
| 1-Hop Harrigan, Scribbly, Toonerville Folks, Ben Webster, Spot Savage, Mutt & Jeff, Red White & Blue, Adv. in the Unknown, Tippie, Reg'lar Fellers, Skippy, Bobby Thatcher, Mystery Men of Mars, Daiseybelle, & Wiley of West Point begin | 250.00 | 625.00 | 1500.00 |
| 2-Ripley's Believe It or Not begins, ends #24 | 92.00 | 230.00 | 550.00 |
| 3-5: 5-The American Way begins, ends #10 | 64.00 | 160.00 | 385.00 |
| 6,7: 6-Last Spot Savage; Popsicle Pete begins, ends #26, 28. 7-Last Bobby Thatcher | 50.00 | 150.00 | 300.00 |
| 8-The Ultra Man begins | 83.00 | 208.00 | 500.00 |
| 9,10: 10-X-Mas-c | 57.00 | 144.00 | 345.00 |
| 11-15: 12-Last Toonerville Folks. 15-Last Tippie & Reg'lar Fellars | 47.00 | 118.00 | 285.00 |

16-(Rare)-Origin/1st app. Green Lantern (7/40) & begin series; created by Martin Nodell. Inspired by Aladdin's Lamp; the suggested alter ego name Alan Ladd, was never capitalized on. It was changed to Alan Scott before Alan Ladd became a major film star (he was in two films before this issue)

| Good | Fine | VF-NM | NM/Mint |
|---|---|---|---|
| 2,165.00 | 5,420.00 | 13,000.00 | 20,000.00 |

(Estimated up to 50 total copies exist, 3 in NM/Mint)

| | Good | Fine | N-Mint |
|---|---|---|---|
| 17-(Scarce)-2nd Green Lantern | 500.00 | 1250.00 | 3000.00 |
| 18-N.Y. World's Fair-c/story | 350.00 | 875.00 | 2100.00 |

19-Origin/1st app. The Atom (10/40); Last Ultra Man

| Good | Fine | VF-NM | NM/Mint |
|---|---|---|---|
| 400.00 | 1000.00 | 2400.00 | 3400.00 |

(Estimated up to 80 total copies exist, 5 in NM/Mint)

| | Good | Fine | N-Mint |
|---|---|---|---|
| 20-Atom dons costume; Hunkle becomes Red Tornado; Rescue on Mars begins, ends #25; 1 pg. origin Green Lantern | 175.00 | 438.00 | 1050.00 |
| 21-23: 21-Last Wiley of West Point & Skippy. 23-Last Daiseybelle; 3 Idiots begin, end #82 | 117.00 | 291.00 | 700.00 |
| 24-Sisty & Dinky become the Cyclone Kids; Ben Webster ends. Origin Dr. Mid-Nite & Sargon, The Sorcerer in text with app. | 125.00 | 312.00 | 750.00 |

25-Origin & 1st story app. Dr. Mid-Nite by Stan Asch; Hop Harrigan becomes Guardian Angel; last Adventure in the Unknown

| Good | Fine | VF-NM | NM/Mint |
|---|---|---|---|
| 283.00 | 710.00 | 1700.00 | 2400.00 |

(Estimated up to 120 total copies exist, 6 in NM/Mint)

| | Good | Fine | N-Mint |
|---|---|---|---|
| 26-Origin/1st story app. Sargon, the Sorcerer | 142.00 | 354.00 | 850.00 |
| 27: #27-32 are misnumbered in indicia with correct No. appearing on cover. Intro. Doiby Dickles, Green Lantern's sidekick | 183.00 | 460.00 | 1100.00 |
| 28-Hop Harrigan gives up costumed i.d. | 83.00 | 208.00 | 500.00 |
| 29,30 | 83.00 | 208.00 | 500.00 |
| 31-40: 35-Doiby learns Green Lantern's i.d. | 62.00 | 154.00 | 370.00 |
| 41-50: 50-Sargon ends | 54.00 | 135.00 | 325.00 |
| 51-60: 59-Scribbly & the Red Tornado ends | 46.00 | 115.00 | 275.00 |
| 61-Origin/1st app. Solomon Grundy | 158.00 | 395.00 | 950.00 |
| 62-70: 70-Kubert Sargon; intro Sargon's helper, Maximillian O'Leary | 40.00 | 100.00 | 240.00 |
| 71-88,90-99: 71-Last Red White & Blue. 72-Black Pirate begins (not in #74-82); last Atom. 73-Winky, Blinky & Noddy begins, ends #82. 90-Origin Icicle. 99-Last Hop Harrigan | 33.00 | 83.00 | 200.00 |
| 89-Origin Harlequin | 42.00 | 105.00 | 250.00 |
| 100-1st app. Johnny Thunder by Alex Toth | 67.00 | 167.00 | 400.00 |
| 101-Last Mutt & Jeff | 53.00 | 135.00 | 320.00 |
| 102-Last Green Lantern, Black Pirate & Dr. Mid-Nite | 67.00 | 165.00 | 400.00 |

NOTE: *No Atom in 47, 62-69. **Kinstler** Black Pirate-89. **Stan Aschmeier** a-25, 40, 55, 70; c-7. **Moldoff** c-16-23. **Paul Reinman** a-55, 70; c-55, 70, 75, 78, 80. **Toth** a-88, 92, 96, 98-102; c-92, 96-102.*

**ALL-AMERICAN MEN OF WAR** (Previously All-American Western)
No. 127, Aug-Sept, 1952 - No. 117, Sept-Oct, 1966
National Periodical Publications

| | Good | Fine | N-Mint |
|---|---|---|---|
| 127 (1952) | 34.00 | 102.00 | 240.00 |
| 128 (1952) | 21.50 | 65.00 | 150.00 |

| | Good | Fine | N-Mint |
|---|---|---|---|
| 2(12-1/'52-53)-5 | 19.00 | 58.00 | 135.00 |
| 6-10 | 11.50 | 34.00 | 80.00 |
| 11-18: Last precode (2/55) | 10.00 | 30.00 | 70.00 |
| 19-28 | 7.00 | 21.00 | 50.00 |
| 29,30,32-Wood-a | 7.85 | 23.50 | 55.00 |
| 31,33-40 | 5.00 | 15.00 | 35.00 |
| 41-50 | 3.60 | 11.00 | 25.00 |
| 51-66 | 2.65 | 8.00 | 18.00 |
| 67-1st Gunner & Sarge by Andru | 3.60 | 11.00 | 25.00 |
| 68-80 | 1.50 | 4.50 | 10.00 |
| 81-100: 82-Johnny Cloud begins, ends #111,114,115 | 1.00 | 3.00 | 6.00 |
| 101-117: 112-Balloon Buster series begins, ends #114,116; 115-Johnny Cloud app. | .85 | 2.50 | 5.00 |

NOTE: *Colan a-112.* ***Drucker*** *a-47, 65, 71, 74, 77.* ***Heath*** *a-27, 32, 47, 71, 95, 111, 112; c-95, 100, 112.* ***Krigstein*** *a-128('52), 2, 3, 5.* ***Kirby*** *a-29.* ***Kubert*** *a-29, 36, 38, 41, 43, 47, 49, 50, 52, 53, 55, 56, 60, 63, 65, 69, 71-73, 103, 114; c-41, 77, 114. Tank Killer in 69, 71, 76 by* ***Kubert. P. Reinman*** *c-55, 57, 61, 62, 71, 72, 74-76, 80.*

**ALL-AMERICAN SPORTS**
October, 1967
Charlton Comics

| | Good | Fine | N-Mint |
|---|---|---|---|
| 1 | .50 | 1.50 | 3.00 |

**ALL-AMERICAN WESTERN** (Formerly All-American Comics; Becomes All-American Men of War)
No. 103, Nov, 1948 - No. 126, June-July, 1952 (103-121: 52 pgs.)
National Periodical Publications

| | Good | Fine | N-Mint |
|---|---|---|---|
| 103-Johnny Thunder & his horse Black Lightning continues by Toth, ends #126; Foley of The Fighting 5th, Minstrel Maverick, & Overland Coach begin; Captain Tootsie by Beck; mentioned in **Love and Death** | 26.00 | 77.00 | 180.00 |
| 104-Kubert-a | 17.00 | 51.00 | 120.00 |
| 105,107-Kubert-a | 14.00 | 43.00 | 100.00 |
| 106,108-110,112: 112-Kurtzman "Pot-Shot Pete," (1 pg.) | 11.00 | 32.00 | 75.00 |
| 111,114-116-Kubert-a | 11.50 | 34.00 | 80.00 |
| 113-Intro. Swift Deer, J. Thunder's new sidekick; classic Toth-c; Kubert-a | 13.00 | 40.00 | 90.00 |
| 117-126: 121-Kubert-a | 9.30 | 28.00 | 65.00 |

NOTE: ***Kubert*** *a-103-105, 107, 111, 112(1 pg.), 113-116, 121.* ***Toth*** *c/a 103-126.*

**ALL COMICS**
1945
Chicago Nite Life News

| | Good | Fine | N-Mint |
|---|---|---|---|
| 1 | 6.00 | 18.00 | 42.00 |

**ALLEY OOP** (See The Comics, 4-Color No. 3, The Funnies, Red Ryder and Super Book No. 9)

**ALLEY OOP**
No. 10, 1947 - No. 18, Oct, 1949
Standard Comics

| | Good | Fine | N-Mint |
|---|---|---|---|
| 10 | 13.00 | 40.00 | 90.00 |
| 11-18: 17,18-Schomburg-c | 9.30 | 28.00 | 65.00 |

**ALLEY OOP**
Nov, 1955 - No. 3, March, 1956 (Newspaper reprints)
Argo Publ.

| | Good | Fine | N-Mint |
|---|---|---|---|
| 1 | 9.30 | 28.00 | 65.00 |
| 2,3 | 6.50 | 19.00 | 45.00 |

**ALLEY OOP**
12-2/62-63 - No. 2, 9-11/63
Dell Publishing Co.

| | Good | Fine | N-Mint |
|---|---|---|---|
| 1,2 | 4.30 | 13.00 | 30.00 |

**ALL-FAMOUS CRIME** (Becomes All-Famous Police Cases #6 on)
No. 8, 5/51 - No. 10, 11/51; No. 4, 2/52 - No. 5, 5/52
Star Publications

| | Good | Fine | N-Mint |
|---|---|---|---|
| 8 (#1) | 5.00 | 15.00 | 35.00 |
| 9-Used in **SOTI**, illo-"The wish to hurt or kill couples in lovers' lanes is not uncommon perversion;" L.B. Cole-c/a(r)/Law-Crime #3 | 9.30 | 28.00 | 65.00 |
| 10,4,5 | 2.65 | 8.00 | 18.00 |

NOTE: *All have* ***L.B. Cole*** *covers.*

**ALL FAMOUS CRIME STORIES** (See Fox Giants)

**ALL-FAMOUS POLICE CASES** (Formerly All Famous Crime #5?)
No. 6, Feb, 1952 - No. 16, Sept, 1954
Star Publications

| | Good | Fine | N-Mint |
|---|---|---|---|
| 6 | 5.00 | 15.00 | 30.00 |
| 7,8: 7-Kubert-a. 8-Marijuana story | 3.50 | 10.50 | 24.00 |
| 9-16 | 2.65 | 8.00 | 18.00 |

NOTE: ***L. B. Cole*** *c-all; a-15, 1pg.* ***Hollingsworth*** *a-15.*

**ALL-FLASH** (. . .Quarterly No. 1-5)
Summer, 1941 - No. 32, Dec-Jan, 1947-48
National Periodical Publications/All-American

| | Good | Fine | VF-NM | NM/Mint |
|---|---|---|---|---|
| 1-Origin The Flash retold by E. Hibbard | 400.00 | 1000.00 | 2400.00 | 3600.00 |

(Estimated up to 200 total copies exist, 11 in NM/Mint)

| | Good | Fine | N-Mint |
|---|---|---|---|
| 2-Origin recap | 125.00 | 312.00 | 750.00 |
| 3,4 | 83.00 | 210.00 | 500.00 |
| 5-Winky, Blinky & Noddy begins, ends #32 | 62.00 | 156.00 | 375.00 |
| 6-10 | 54.00 | 135.00 | 325.00 |
| 11-13: 12-Origin The Thinker. 13-The King app. | 46.00 | 115.00 | 275.00 |
| 14-Green Lantern cameo | 50.00 | 125.00 | 300.00 |
| 15-20: 18-Mutt & Jeff begins, ends #22 | 40.00 | 100.00 | 240.00 |
| 21-31 | 35.00 | 87.00 | 210.00 |
| 32-Origin The Fiddler; 1st Star Sapphire | 42.00 | 105.00 | 250.00 |

NOTE: *Book length stories in 2-13, 16. Bondage c-31, 32.*

**ALL FOR LOVE** (Young Love V3/5-on)
Apr-May, 1957 - V3#4, Dec-Jan, 1959-60
Prize Publications

| | Good | Fine | N-Mint |
|---|---|---|---|
| V1#1 | 3.00 | 9.00 | 21.00 |
| 2-6: 5-Orlando-c | 1.70 | 5.00 | 12.00 |
| V2#1-5(1/59), 5(3/59) | 1.15 | 3.50 | 8.00 |
| V3#1(5/59), 1(7/59)-4: 2-Powell-a | .85 | 2.50 | 5.00 |

**ALL FUNNY COMICS**
Winter, 1943-44 - No. 23, May-June, 1948
Tilsam Publ./National Periodical Publications (Detective)

| | Good | Fine | N-Mint |
|---|---|---|---|
| 1-Genius Jones, Buzzy (ends #4), Dover & Clover begin; Bailey-a | 26.00 | 77.00 | 180.00 |
| 2 | 11.50 | 34.00 | 80.00 |
| 3-10 | 7.00 | 21.00 | 50.00 |
| 11-13,15,18,19-Genius Jones app. | 5.50 | 16.50 | 38.00 |
| 14,17,20-23 | 4.00 | 12.00 | 28.00 |
| 16-DC Super Heroes app. | 13.00 | 40.00 | 90.00 |

**ALL GOOD**
Oct, 1949 (260 pgs., 50 cents)
St. John Publishing Co.

| | Good | Fine | N-Mint |
|---|---|---|---|
| (8 St. John comics bound together) | 45.00 | 135.00 | 315.00 |

NOTE: *Also see Li'l Audrey Yearbook & Treasury of Comics.*

**ALL GOOD COMICS** (See Fox Giants)
Spring, 1946 (36 pgs.)
Fox Features Syndicate

| | Good | Fine | N-Mint |
|---|---|---|---|
| 1-Joy Family, Dick Transom, Rick Evans, One Round Hogan | 8.50 | 25.50 | 60.00 |

*All-American Western #116, © DC*

*All-Flash #18, © DC*

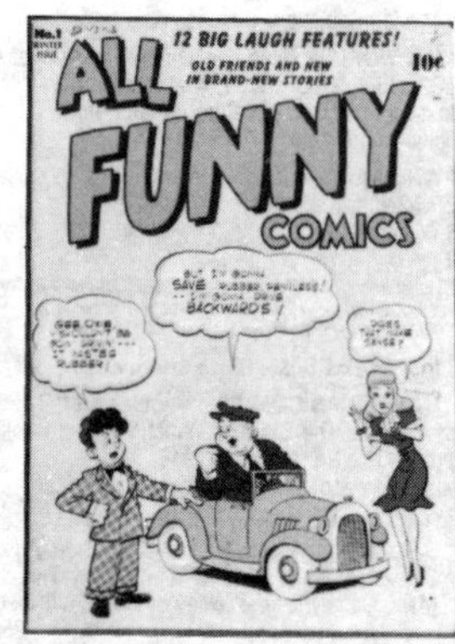

*All Funny Comics #1, © DC*

*All Humor Comics #7, © QUA*

*All Picture Adventure Magazine #1, © STJ*

*All-Select Comics #10, © MEG*

**ALL GREAT** (See Fox Giants)
1946 (36 pgs.)
Fox Feature Syndicate

| | Good | Fine | N-Mint |
|---|---|---|---|
| 1-Crazy House, Bertie Benson Boy Detective, Gussie the Gob | 7.00 | 21.00 | 50.00 |

**ALL GREAT**
nd (1945?) (132 pgs.)
William H. Wise & Co.

| | | | |
|---|---|---|---|
| nn-Capt. Jack Terry, Joan Mason, Girl Reporter, Baron Doomsday; Torture scenes | 20.00 | 60.00 | 140.00 |

**ALL GREAT COMICS** (Dagar, Desert Hawk No. 14 on)
No. 14, Oct, 1947 - No. 13, Dec, 1947
Fox Features Syndicate

| | | | |
|---|---|---|---|
| 14-Brenda Starr-r (Scarce) | 17.00 | 51.00 | 120.00 |
| 13-Origin Dagar, Desert Hawk; Brenda Starr (all-r); Kamen-c | 16.00 | 47.00 | 110.00 |

**ALL-GREAT CONFESSIONS** (See Fox Giants)

**ALL GREAT CRIME STORIES** (See Fox Giants)

**ALL GREAT JUNGLE ADVENTURES** (See Fox Giants)

**ALL HALLOWS EVE**
1991 ($4.95, color, 52 pgs.)
Innovation Publishing

| | | | |
|---|---|---|---|
| 1-Painted-c/a | .85 | 2.50 | 5.00 |

**ALL HERO COMICS**
March, 1943 (100 pgs.) (Cardboard cover)
Fawcett Publications

| | | | |
|---|---|---|---|
| 1-Captain Marvel Jr., Capt. Midnight, Golden Arrow, Ibis the Invincible, Spy Smasher, & Lance O'Casey | 71.00 | 215.00 | 500.00 |

**ALL HUMOR COMICS**
Spring, 1946 - No. 17, December, 1949
Quality Comics Group

| | | | |
|---|---|---|---|
| 1 | 7.00 | 21.00 | 50.00 |
| 2-Atomic Tot story; Gustavson-a | 3.60 | 11.00 | 25.00 |
| 3-9: 5-1st app. Hickory? 8-Gustavson-a | 2.30 | 7.00 | 16.00 |
| 10-17 | 1.50 | 4.50 | 10.00 |

**ALL LOVE** (. . . Romances No. 26)(Formerly Ernie Comics)
No. 26, May, 1949 - No. 32, May, 1950
Ace Periodicals (Current Books)

| | | | |
|---|---|---|---|
| 26(No. 1)-Ernie, Lily Belle app. | 3.00 | 9.00 | 21.00 |
| 27-L. B. Cole-a | 3.50 | 10.50 | 24.00 |
| 28-32 | 1.70 | 5.00 | 12.00 |

**ALL-NEGRO COMICS**
June, 1947 (15 cents)
All-Negro Comics

| | | | |
|---|---|---|---|
| 1 (Rare) | 79.00 | 235.00 | 550.00 |

NOTE: *Seldom found in fine or mint condition; many copies have brown pages.*

**ALL-NEW COLLECTORS' EDITION** (Formerly Limited . . .)
Jan, 1978 - No. C-62, 1979 (No. 54-58: 76 pgs.)
DC Comics, Inc.

| | | | |
|---|---|---|---|
| C-53-Rudolph the Red-Nosed Reindeer | | .50 | 1.00 |
| C-54-Superman Vs. Wonder Woman | .25 | .75 | 1.50 |
| C-55-Superboy & the Legion of Super-Heroes | .70 | 2.00 | 4.00 |
| C-56-Superman Vs. Muhammad Ali: story & wraparound N. Adams-c | .35 | 1.00 | 2.00 |
| C-58-Superman Vs. Shazam | | .60 | 1.20 |
| C-60-Rudolph's Summer Fun(8/78) | | .60 | 1.20 |
| C-62-Superman the Movie (68 pgs.; 1979) | | .60 | 1.20 |

**ALL-NEW COMICS** (. . . Short Story Comics No. 1-3)
Jan, 1943 - No. 14, Nov, 1946; No. 15, Mar-Apr, 1947
Family Comics (Harvey Publications)

| | Good | Fine | N-Mint |
|---|---|---|---|
| 1-Steve Case, Crime Rover, Johnny Rebel, Kayo Kane, The Echo, Night Hawk, Ray O'Light, Detective Shane begin; Red Blazer on cover only; Sultan-a | 64.00 | 193.00 | 450.00 |
| 2-Origin Scarlet Phantom by Kubert | 28.00 | 86.00 | 200.00 |
| 3 | 24.00 | 73.00 | 170.00 |
| 4,5 | 21.00 | 64.00 | 150.00 |
| 6-The Boy Heroes & Red Blazer (text story) begin, end #12; Black Cat app.; intro. Sparky in Red Blazer | 24.00 | 72.00 | 165.00 |
| 7-Kubert, Powell-a; Black Cat & Zebra app. | 24.00 | 72.00 | 165.00 |
| 8,9: 8-Shock Gibson app.; Kubert, Powell-a; Schomburg bondage-c. 9-Black Cat app.; Kubert-a | 24.00 | 72.00 | 165.00 |
| 10-12: 10-The Zebra app.; Kubert-a(3). 11-Girl Commandos, Man In Black app. 12-Kubert-a | 21.00 | 62.00 | 145.00 |
| 13-Stuntman by Simon & Kirby; Green Hornet, Joe Palooka, Flying Fool app. | 24.00 | 72.00 | 165.00 |
| 14-The Green Hornet & The Man in Black Called Fate by Powell, Joe Palooka app. | 21.00 | 62.00 | 145.00 |

15-(Rare)-Small size (5½x8½"; B&W; 32 pgs.). Distributed to mail subscribers only. Black Cat and Joe Palooka app.
Estimated value....$200-250

NOTE: *Also see Boy Explorers No. 2, Flash Gordon No. 5, and Stuntman No. 3.* ***Powell*** *a-11.* ***Schomburg*** *c-7, 8, 10, 11.*

**ALL-OUT WAR**
Sept-Oct, 1979 - No. 6, Aug, 1980 ($1.00, 68 pgs.)
DC Comics

| | | | |
|---|---|---|---|
| 1-6: 1-The Viking Commando(origin), Force Three(origin), & Black Eagle Squadron begin | | .25 | .50 |

NOTE: ***Ayers*** *a(p)-1-6.* ***Elias*** *r-2.* ***Evans*** *a-1-6.* ***Kubert*** *c-1-6.*

**ALL PICTURE ADVENTURE MAGAZINE**
Oct, 1952 - No. 2, Nov, 1952 (100 pg. Giants, 25 cents, squarebound)
St. John Publishing Co.

| | | | |
|---|---|---|---|
| 1-War comics | 13.00 | 40.00 | 90.00 |
| 2-Horror-crime comics | 18.50 | 56.00 | 130.00 |

NOTE: *Above books contain three St. John comics rebound; variations possible.* ***Baker*** *art known in both.*

**ALL PICTURE ALL TRUE LOVE STORY**
October, 1952 (100 pages)
St. John Publishing Co.

| | | | |
|---|---|---|---|
| 1-Canteen Kate by Matt Baker | 25.00 | 75.00 | 175.00 |

**ALL-PICTURE COMEDY CARNIVAL**
October, 1952 (100 pages, 25 cents)(Contains 4 rebound comics)
St. John Publishing Co.

| | | | |
|---|---|---|---|
| 1-Contents can vary; Baker-a | 25.00 | 75.00 | 175.00 |

**ALL REAL CONFESSION MAGAZINE** (See Fox Giants)

**ALL ROMANCES** (Mr. Risk No. 7 on)
Aug, 1949 - No. 6, June, 1950
A. A. Wyn (Ace Periodicals)

| | | | |
|---|---|---|---|
| 1 | 3.70 | 11.00 | 26.00 |
| 2 | 1.70 | 5.00 | 12.00 |
| 3-6 | 1.50 | 4.50 | 10.00 |

**ALL-SELECT COMICS** (Blonde Phantom No. 12 on)
Fall, 1943 - No. 11, Fall, 1946
Timely Comics (Daring Comics)

| | | | |
|---|---|---|---|
| 1-Capt. America, Human Torch, Sub-Mariner begin; Black Widow app. | 229.00 | 573.00 | 1375.00 |
| 2-Red Skull app. | 110.00 | 270.00 | 650.00 |
| 3-The Whizzer begins | 67.00 | 167.00 | 400.00 |
| 4,5-Last Sub-Mariner | 54.00 | 135.00 | 325.00 |
| 6-9: 6-The Destroyer app. 8-No Whizzer | 46.00 | 115.00 | 275.00 |
| 10-The Destroyer & Sub-Mariner app.; last Capt. America & Human Torch issue | 46.00 | 115.00 | 275.00 |

11-1st app. Blonde Phantom; Miss America app.; all Blonde

Good Fine N-Mint

Phantom-c by Shores 75.00 188.00 450.00

NOTE: *Schomburg c-1-10. No. 7 & 8 show 1944 in indicia, but should be 1945.*

**ALL SPORTS COMICS** (Formerly Real Sports Comics; becomes All Time Sports Comics No. 4 on)
No. 2, Dec-Jan, 1948-49; No. 3, Feb-Mar, 1949
Hillman Periodicals

2-Krigstein-a(p), Powell, Starr-a 11.50 34.00 80.00
3-Mort Lawrence-a 8.50 25.50 60.00

**ALL STAR COMICS** (All Star Western No. 58 on)
Summer, 1940 - No. 57, Feb-Mar, 1951; No. 58, Jan-Feb, 1976 - No. 74, Sept-Oct, 1978
National Periodical Publ./All-American/DC Comics

1-The Flash(No.1 by Harry Lampert), Hawkman(by Shelly), Hourman, The Sandman, The Spectre, Biff Bronson, Red White & Blue begin; Ultra Man's only app.

| Good | Fine | VF-NM | NM/Mint |
|---|---|---|---|
| 750.00 | 1875.00 | 4500.00 | 5700.00 |

(Estimated up to 200 total copies exist, 6 in NM/Mint)

Good Fine N-Mint

2-Green Lantern, Johnny Thunder begin 350.00 875.00 2100.00

3-Origin Justice Society of America; Dr. Fate & The Atom begin, Red Tornado cameo; last Red White & Blue; reprinted in Famous First Edition

| Good | Fine | VF-NM | NM/Mint |
|---|---|---|---|
| 1415.00 | 3540.00 | 8500.00 | 12,000.00 |

(Estimated up to 150 total copies exist, 6 in NM/Mint)

Good Fine N-Mint

4 383.00 960.00 2300.00
5-1st app. Shiera Sanders as Hawkgirl 400.00 1000.00 2400.00
6-Johnny Thunder joins JSA 267.00 670.00 1600.00
7-Batman, Superman, Flash cameo; last Hourman; Doiby Dickles app. 267.00 670.00 1600.00

8-Origin & 1st app. Wonder Woman (added as 8pgs. making book 76 pgs.; origin cont'd in Sensation #1); Dr. Fate dons new helmet; Dr.Mid-Nite, Hop Harrigan text stories & Starman begin; Shiera app.; Hop Harrigan JSA guest

| Good | Fine | VF-NM | NM/Mint |
|---|---|---|---|
| 533.00 | 1335.00 | 3200.00 | 4700.00 |

(Estimated up to 150 total copies exist, 6 in NM/Mint)

Good Fine N-Mint

9,10: 9-Shiera app. 10-Flash, Green Lantern cameo, Sandman new costume 208.00 520.00 1250.00
11,12: 11-Wonder Woman begins; Spectre cameo; Shiera app. 12-Wonder Woman becomes JSA Secretary 183.00 460.00 1100.00
13-15: Sandman w/Sandy in #14 & 15; 15-Origin Brain Wave; Shiera app. 175.00 438.00 1050.00
16-19: 19-Sandman w/Sandy 130.00 325.00 780.00
20-Dr. Fate & Sandman cameo 130.00 325.00 780.00
21-23: 21-Spectre & Atom cameo; Dr. Fate by Kubert; Dr. Fate, Sandman end. 22-Last Hop Harrigan; Flag-c. 23-Origin Psycho Pirate; last Spectre & Starman 113.00 285.00 680.00
24-Flash & Green Lantern cameo; Mr. Terrific only app.; Wildcat, JSA guest; Kubert Hawkman begins 113.00 285.00 680.00
25-27: 25-The Flash & Green Lantern start again. 27-Wildcat, JSA guest 104.00 260.00 625.00
28-32 87.00 220.00 525.00
33-Solomon Grundy, Hawkman, Doiby Dickles app. 175.00 440.00 1050.00
34,35-Johnny Thunder cameo in both 80.00 240.00 480.00
36-Batman & Superman JSA guests 175.00 525.00 1050.00
37-Johnny Thunder cameo; origin Injustice Society; last Kubert Hawkman 89.00 223.00 535.00
38-Black Canary begins; JSA Death issue 104.00 260.00 625.00
39,40: 39-Last Johnny Thunder 64.00 160.00 385.00
41-Black Canary joins JSA; Injustice Society app. 62.00 156.00 375.00

Good Fine N-Mint

42-Atom & the Hawkman don new costumes 62.00 156.00 375.00
43-49,51-56: 55-Sci/Fi story 62.00 156.00 375.00
50-Frazetta art, 3 pgs. 71.00 177.00 425.00
57-Kubert-a, 6 pgs. (Scarce) 80.00 200.00 480.00
V12#58-74(1976-78)-Flash, Hawkman, Dr. Mid-Nite, Wildcat, Dr. Fate, Green Lantern, Star Spangled Kid, & Robin app.; intro Power Girl. 58-JSA app. 69-1st app. Huntress .25 .50

NOTE: *No Atom-27, 36; no Dr. Fate-13; no Flash-8, 9, 11-23; no Green Lantern-8, 9, 11-23; no Johnny Thunder-5, 36; no Wonder Woman-9, 10, 23. Book length stories in 4-9, 11-14, 18-22, 25, 26, 29, 30, 32-36, 42, 43. Johnny Peril in #42-46, 48, 49, 51, 52, 54-57.* ***Baily*** *a-1-10, 12, 13, 14i, 15-20.* ***Burnley*** *Starman-8-13; c-12, 13.* ***Grell*** *c-58.* ***Kubert*** *Hawkman-24-30, 33-37.* ***Moldoff*** *Hawkman-3-23; c-11.* ***Simon & Kirby*** *Sandman -14-17, 19.* ***Staton*** *a-66-74p. c-74p.* ***Toth*** *a-37(2), 38(2), 40, 41; c-38, 41.* ***Wood*** *a-58i-63i, 64, 65; c-63i, 64, 65.*

**ALL STAR INDEX, THE**
Feb, 1987 ($2.00, Baxter)
Independent Comics Group (Eclipse)

1 .35 1.00 2.00

**ALL-STAR SQUADRON** (See Justice League of America #193)
Sept, 1981 - No. 67, March, 1987
DC Comics

1-Original Atom, Hawkman, Dr. Mid-Nite, Robotman (origin), Plastic Man, Johnny Quick, Liberty Belle, Shining Knight begin .25 .75 1.50
2-24: 5-Danette Reilly becomes new Firebrand. 8-Re-intro Steel, the Indestructable Man. 12-Origin G.A. Hawkman retold. 23-Origin/1st app. The Amazing Man. 24-Batman app. .40 .80
25-1st Infinity, Inc. (9/83) .50 1.50 3.00
26-Origin Infinity, Inc. (2nd app.); Robin app. .40 1.25 2.50
27-46,48,49: 33-Origin Freedom Fighters of Earth-X. 41-Origin Starman .40 .80
47-Origin Dr. Fate; McFarlane-a (1st full story)/part-c (7/85) .60 1.75 3.50
50-Double size; Crisis x-over .25 .75 1.50
51-56-Crisis x-over .50 1.00
57-67: 61-Origin Liberty Belle. 62-Origin The Shining Knight. 63-Origin Robotman. 65-Origin Johnny Quick. 66-Origin Tarantula .40 .80
Annual 1-3: 1(11/82)-Retells origin of G.A. Atom, Guardian & Wildcat. 2(11/83)-Infinity, Inc. app. 3(9/84) .50 1.00

NOTE: ***Kubert*** *c-2, 7-18. JLA app. in 14, 15. JSA app. in 4, 14, 15, 19, 27, 28.*

**ALL-STAR STORY OF THE DODGERS, THE**
April, 1979 (Full Color) ($1.00)
Stadium Communications

1 .50 1.00

**ALL STAR WESTERN** (Formerly All Star Comics No. 1-57)
No. 58, Apr-May, 1951 - No. 119, June-July, 1961
National Periodical Publications

58-Trigger Twins (ends #116), Strong Bow, The Roving Ranger & Don Caballero begin 23.00 70.00 160.00
59,60: Last 52 pgs. 11.00 32.00 75.00
61-66: 61,64-Toth-a 9.00 27.00 62.00
67-Johnny Thunder begins; Gil Kane-a 11.00 32.00 75.00
68-81: Last precode (2-3/55) 5.00 15.00 35.00
82-98 4.00 12.00 28.00
99-Frazetta-a r-/Jimmy Wakely #4 5.50 16.00 38.00
100 5.00 15.00 35.00
101-107,109-116,118,119 3.00 9.00 21.00
108-Origin Johnny Thunder 7.00 21.00 50.00
117-Origin Super Chief 5.00 15.00 35.00

NOTE: ***Infantino*** *art in most issues. Madame .44 app.-#117-119.*

**ALL-STAR WESTERN** (Weird Western Tales No. 12 on)
Aug-Sept, 1970 - No. 11, Apr-May, 1972
National Periodical Publications

*All Star Comics #33, © DC*

*All-Star Squadron #47, © DC*

*All Star Western #81, © DC*

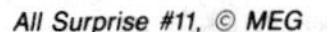
All Surprise #11, © MEG

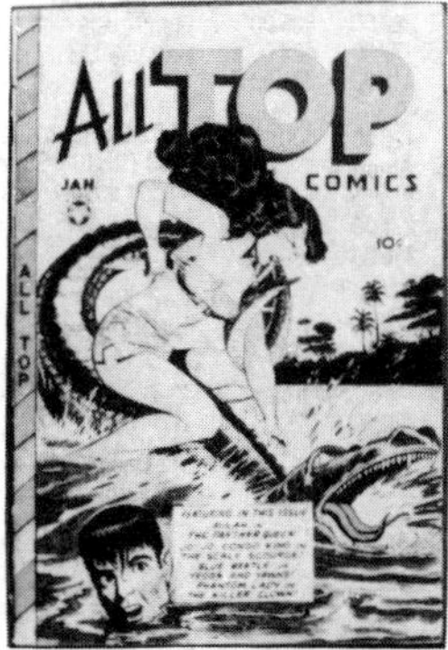

All Top Comics #9, © FOX

All True Romance #1, © AJAX

| | Good | Fine | N-Mint |
|---|---|---|---|
| 1-Pow-Wow Smith-r; Infantino-a | .70 | 2.00 | 4.00 |
| 2-8: 2-Outlaw begins; El Diablo by Morrow begins; has cameos by Williamson, Torres, Gil Kane, Giordano & Phil Seuling. 3-Origin El Diablo. 5-Last Outlaw issue. 6-Billy the Kid begins, ends #8 | .40 | 1.25 | 2.50 |
| 9-Frazetta-a, 3pgs.(r) | .70 | 2.00 | 4.00 |
| 10-Jonah Hex begins (1st app.) | 2.65 | 8.00 | 18.00 |
| 11 | 1.15 | 3.50 | 7.00 |

NOTE: ***Neal Adams** c-1-5; **Aparo** a-5. **G. Kane** a-3, 4, 6, 8. **Kubert** a-4r, 7-9r. **Morrow** a-2-4, 10, 11. No. 7-11 have 52 pages.*

**ALL SURPRISE** (Becomes Jeanie #13 on)
Fall, 1943 - No. 12, Winter, 1946-47
Timely/Marvel (CPC)

| | Good | Fine | N-Mint |
|---|---|---|---|
| 1-Super Rabbit & Gandy & Sourpuss | 12.00 | 36.00 | 80.00 |
| 2 | 5.00 | 15.00 | 35.00 |
| 3-10,12 | 3.60 | 11.00 | 25.00 |
| 11-Kurtzman "Pigtales" art | 5.30 | 16.00 | 38.00 |

**ALL TEEN** (Formerly All Winners; Teen Comics No. 21 on)
No. 20, January, 1947
Marvel Comics (WFP)

| | Good | Fine | N-Mint |
|---|---|---|---|
| 20-Georgie, Mitzi, Patsy Walker, Willie app. | 3.70 | 11.00 | 26.00 |

**ALL THE FUNNY FOLKS**
1926 (hardcover, 112 pgs., 11½x3½") (Full color)
World Press Today, Inc.

| | Good | Fine | N-Mint |
|---|---|---|---|
| nn-Barney Google, Spark Plug, Jiggs & Maggie, Tillie The Toiler, Happy Hooligan, Hans & Fritz, Toots & Casper, etc. | 20.00 | 60.00 | 140.00 |

**ALL-TIME SPORTS COMICS** (Formerly All Sports Comics)
V2No. 4, Apr-May, 1949 - V2No. 7, Oct-Nov, 1949
Hillman Periodicals

| | Good | Fine | N-Mint |
|---|---|---|---|
| V2#4 | 8.00 | 24.00 | 56.00 |
| 5-7: 5-Powell-a. 7-Krigstein-a(p) | 5.70 | 17.00 | 40.00 |

**ALL TOP**
1944 (132 pages)
William H. Wise Co.

| | Good | Fine | N-Mint |
|---|---|---|---|
| Capt. V, Merciless the Sorceress, Red Robbins, One Round Hogan, Mike the M.P., Snooky, Pussy Katnip app. | 14.00 | 43.00 | 100.00 |

**ALL TOP COMICS** (My Experience No. 19 on)
1945; No. 2, Sum, 1946 - No. 18, Mar, 1949; 1957 - 1959
Fox Features Synd./Green Publ./Norlen Mag.

| | Good | Fine | N-Mint |
|---|---|---|---|
| 1-Cosmo Cat & Flash Rabbit begin | 11.00 | 32.00 | 75.00 |
| 2 | 5.30 | 16.00 | 38.00 |
| 3-7 | 4.00 | 12.00 | 28.00 |
| 8-Blue Beetle, Phantom Lady, & Rulah, Jungle Goddess begin (11/47); Kamen-c | 64.00 | 193.00 | 450.00 |
| 9-Kamen-c | 39.00 | 118.00 | 275.00 |
| 10-Kamen bondage-c | 41.00 | 123.00 | 285.00 |
| 11-13,15-17: 15-No Blue Beetle | 30.00 | 90.00 | 210.00 |
| 14-No Blue Beetle; used in **SOTI**, illo-"Corpses of colored people strung up by their wrists" | 37.00 | 110.00 | 260.00 |
| 18-Dagar, Jo-Jo app; no Phantom Lady or Blue Beetle | 24.00 | 73.00 | 170.00 |
| 6(1957-Green Publ.)-Patoruzu the Indian; Cosmo Cat on cover only | 1.50 | 4.50 | 10.00 |
| 6(1958-Literary Ent.)-Muggy Doo; Cosmo Cat on cover only | 1.50 | 4.50 | 10.00 |
| 6(1959-Norlen)-Atomic Mouse; Cosmo Cat on cover only | 1.50 | 4.50 | 10.00 |
| 6(1959)-Little Eva | 1.50 | 4.50 | 10.00 |
| 6(Cornell)-Supermouse on-c | 1.50 | 4.50 | 10.00 |

NOTE: *Jo-Jo by **Kamen**-12,18.*

**ALL TRUE ALL PICTURE POLICE CASES**
Oct, 1952 - No. 2, Nov, 1952 (100 pages)
St. John Publishing Co.

| | Good | Fine | N-Mint |
|---|---|---|---|
| 1-Three rebound St. John crime comics | 21.50 | 64.00 | 150.00 |
| 2-Three comics rebound | 18.50 | 56.00 | 130.00 |

NOTE: *Contents may vary.*

**ALL-TRUE CRIME** (. . .Cases No. 26-35; formerly Official True Crime Cases)
No. 26, Feb, 1948 - No. 52, Sept, 1952
Marvel/Atlas Comics(OFI No. 26,27/CFI No. 28,29/LCC No. 30-46/LMC No. 47-52)

| | Good | Fine | N-Mint |
|---|---|---|---|
| 26(#1) | 7.00 | 21.00 | 50.00 |
| 27(4/48)-Electric chair-c | 6.00 | 18.00 | 42.00 |
| 28-41,43-48,50-52: 36-Photo-c | 2.30 | 7.00 | 16.00 |
| 42-Krigstein-a | 3.60 | 11.00 | 25.00 |
| 49-Used in **POP**, Pg. 79; Krigstein-a | 3.60 | 11.00 | 25.00 |

NOTE: ***Robinson** a-47. **Shores** c-26. **Tuska** a-48(3).*

**ALL-TRUE DETECTIVE CASES** (Kit Carson No. 5 on)
Feb-Mar, 1954 - No. 4, Aug-Sept, 1954
Avon Periodicals

| | Good | Fine | N-Mint |
|---|---|---|---|
| 1 | 11.00 | 32.00 | 75.00 |
| 2-Wood-a | 9.30 | 28.00 | 65.00 |
| 3-Kinstler-c | 4.00 | 12.00 | 28.00 |
| 4-Wood(?), Kamen-a | 8.00 | 24.00 | 56.00 |
| nn(100 pgs.)-7 pg. Kubert-a, Kinstler back-c | 21.50 | 65.00 | 150.00 |

**ALL TRUE ROMANCE** (. . . Illustrated No. 3)
3/51 - No. 20, 12/54; No. 22, 3/55 - No. 30?, 7/57; No. 3(#31), 9/57 - No. 4(#32), 11/57; No. 33, 2/58 - No. 34, 3/58
Artful Publ. #1-3/Harwell(Comic Media) #4-20?/Ajax-Farrell(Excellent Publ.) No. 22 on/Four Star Comic Corp.

| | Good | Fine | N-Mint |
|---|---|---|---|
| 1 (3/51) | 7.00 | 21.00 | 50.00 |
| 2 (10/51; 11/51 on-c) | 4.00 | 12.00 | 28.00 |
| 3(12/51) - #5(5/52) | 3.50 | 10.50 | 24.00 |
| 6-Wood-a, 9 pgs. (exceptional) | 10.00 | 30.00 | 70.00 |
| 7-10 | 2.65 | 8.00 | 18.00 |
| 11-13,16-19 (2/54) | 2.00 | 6.00 | 14.00 |
| 14-Marijuana story | 2.65 | 8.00 | 18.00 |
| 20,22: Last precode issue (Ajax, 3/55) | 1.70 | 5.00 | 12.00 |
| 23-27,29,30 | 1.50 | 4.50 | 10.00 |
| 28 (9/56)-L. B. Cole, Disbrow-a | 3.00 | 9.00 | 21.00 |
| 3,4,33,34 (Farrell, '57-'58) | .85 | 2.60 | 6.00 |

**ALL WESTERN WINNERS** (Formerly All Winners; becomes Western Winners with No. 5; see Two-Gun Kid No. 5)
No. 2, Winter, 1948-49 - No. 4, April, 1949
Marvel Comics(CDS)

| | Good | Fine | N-Mint |
|---|---|---|---|
| 2-Black Rider (Origin & 1st app.) & his horse Satan, Kid Colt & his horse Steel, & Two-Gun Kid & his horse Cyclone begin | 21.50 | 65.00 | 150.00 |
| 3-Anti-Wertham editorial | 15.00 | 45.00 | 105.00 |
| 4-Black Rider i.d. revealed | 15.00 | 45.00 | 105.00 |

**ALL WINNERS COMICS** (All Teen #20)
Summer, 1941 - No. 19, Fall, 1946; No. 21, Winter, 1946-47
(no No. 20) (No. 21 continued from Young Allies No. 20)
USA No. 1-7/WFP No. 10-19/YAI No. 21

| | Good | Fine | VF-NM | NM/Mint |
|---|---|---|---|---|
| 1-The Angel & Black Marvel only app.; Capt. America by Simon & Kirby, Human Torch & Sub-Mariner begin (#1 was advertised as All Aces) | 350.00 | 875.00 | 2100.00 | 2900.00 |

| | Good | Fine | N-Mint |
|---|---|---|---|
| 2-The Destroyer & The Whizzer begin; Simon & Kirby Captain America | 167.00 | 415.00 | 1000.00 |
| 3,4 | 129.00 | 323.00 | 775.00 |
| 5,6: 6-The Black Avenger only app.; no Whizzer story | | | |

| | Good | Fine | N-Mint |
|---|---|---|---|
| | 88.00 | 220.00 | 525.00 |
| 7-10 | 71.00 | 177.00 | 425.00 |
| 11,13-18: 14-16-No Human Torch | 46.00 | 115.00 | 275.00 |
| 12-Red Skull story; last Destroyer; no Whizzer story | 50.00 | 125.00 | 300.00 |
| 19-(Scarce)-1st app. & origin All Winners Squad (Capt. America & Bucky, Human Torch & Toro, Sub-Mariner, Whizzer, & Miss America; r-in Fantasy Masterpieces #10 | 108.00 | 271.00 | 650.00 |
| 21-(Scarce)-All Winners Squad; bondage-c | 100.00 | 250.00 | 600.00 |

NOTE: ***Everett** Sub-Mariner-1, 3, 4; **Burgos** Torch-1, 3, 4. **Schomburg** c-1, 7-18.*

(2nd Series - August, 1948, Marvel Comics (CDS))
(Becomes All Western Winners with No. 2)

| | Good | Fine | N-Mint |
|---|---|---|---|
| 1-The Blonde Phantom, Capt. America, Human Torch, & Sub-Mariner app. | 88.00 | 220.00 | 525.00 |

**ALL YOUR COMICS** (See Fox Giants)
Spring, 1946 (36 pages)
Fox Feature Syndicate (R. W. Voight)

| | Good | Fine | N-Mint |
|---|---|---|---|
| 1-Red Robbins, Merciless the Sorceress app. | 6.85 | 20.50 | 48.00 |

**ALMANAC OF CRIME** (See Fox Giants)

**AL OF FBI** (See Little Al of the FBI)

**ALONG THE FIRING LINE WITH ROGER BEAN**
1916 (Hardcover, B&W) (6x17") (66 pages)
Chas. B. Jackson

| | Good | Fine | N-Mint |
|---|---|---|---|
| 3-by Chic Jackson (1915 daily strips) | 10.00 | 30.00 | 70.00 |

**ALPHA AND OMEGA**
1978 (49 cents)
Spire Christian Comics (Fleming H. Revell)

| | Good | Fine | N-Mint |
|---|---|---|---|
| nn | | .30 | .60 |

**ALPHA FLIGHT** (See X-Men #120,121)
Aug, 1983 - Present (#52-on are direct sale only)
Marvel Comics Group

| | Good | Fine | N-Mint |
|---|---|---|---|
| 1-Byrne-a begins (52pgs.)-Wolverine & Nightcrawler cameo | .85 | 2.50 | 5.00 |
| 2-Vindicator becomes Guardian; origin Marrina & Alpha Flight | .40 | 1.25 | 2.50 |
| 3-11: 3-Concludes origin Alpha Flight. 6-Origin Shaman. 7-Origin Snowbird. 10,11-Origin Sasquatch | .35 | 1.00 | 2.00 |
| 12-Double size; death of Guardian | .40 | 1.25 | 2.50 |
| 13-Wolverine app. | 1.35 | 4.00 | 8.00 |
| 14-16: 16-Wolverine app? | .25 | .75 | 1.50 |
| 17-X-Men x-over; Wolverine cameo | .85 | 2.50 | 5.00 |
| 18-28: 20-New headquarters. 25-Return of Guardian. 28-Last Byrne issue | .25 | .75 | 1.50 |
| 29-32,35-49,51,54-64 | | .65 | 1.30 |
| 33,34: 33-X-Men (Wolverine) app. 34-Origin Wolverine | .85 | 2.50 | 5.00 |
| 50-Double size | .25 | .75 | 1.50 |
| 52,53-Wolverine app. | .70 | 2.00 | 4.00 |
| 65-74,76-86,91-95: 65-Begin $1.50-c. 71-Intro The Sorcerer (villian). 74-Wolverine, Spider-Man & The Avengers app. 89-Original Guardian returns. 91-Dr. Doom app. | .25 | .75 | 1.50 |
| 75-Double size ($1.95, 52 pgs.) | .35 | 1.00 | 1.95 |
| 87-90-Wolverine 4 part story w/Jim Lee covers | .25 | .75 | 1.50 |
| Annual 1 (9/86, $1.25) | .30 | .90 | 1.80 |
| Annual 2(12/87, $1.25) | | .65 | 1.30 |

NOTE: ***Austin** c-1i, 2i, 53i. **Byrne** c-81, 82. **Guice** c-85, 91, 92.*

**ALPHA TRACK**
Feb, 1986 - No. 2, 1986? ($1.75 cover)
Fantasy General Comics

| | Good | Fine | N-Mint |
|---|---|---|---|
| 1,2 | .25 | .75 | 1.50 |

**ALPHA WAVE**
March, 1987 ($1.75, color, 36 pgs.)
Darkline Comics

| | Good | Fine | N-Mint |
|---|---|---|---|
| 1 | .25 | .75 | 1.50 |

**ALPHONSE & GASTON & LEON**
1903 (15x10" Sunday strip reprints in color)
Hearst's New York American & Journal

| | Good | Fine | N-Mint |
|---|---|---|---|
| nn-by Fred Opper | 32.00 | 96.00 | 225.00 |

**ALTER EGO**
May, 1986 - No. 4, Nov, 1986 (Mini-series)
First Comics

| | Good | Fine | N-Mint |
|---|---|---|---|
| 1 | .30 | .90 | 1.80 |
| 2-4 | .20 | .70 | 1.40 |

**ALVIN** (TV) (See 4-Color Comics No. 1042)
Oct-Dec, 1962 - No. 28, Oct, 1973
Dell Publishing Co.

| | Good | Fine | N-Mint |
|---|---|---|---|
| 12-021-212 (#1) | 5.00 | 15.00 | 35.00 |
| 2 | 3.00 | 9.00 | 21.00 |
| 3-10 | 2.00 | 6.00 | 14.00 |
| 11-28 | 1.30 | 4.00 | 9.00 |
| Alvin For President (10/64) | 1.15 | 3.50 | 8.00 |
| ...& His Pals in Merry Christmas with Clyde Crashcup & Leonardo 1(02-120-402)-12-2/64, reprinted in 1966 (12-023-604) | 2.30 | 7.00 | 16.00 |

**AMAZING ADULT FANTASY** (Formerly Amazing Adventures #1-6; Becomes Amazing Fantasy #15)
No. 7, Dec, 1961 - No. 14, July, 1962
Marvel Comics Group (AMI)

| | Good | Fine | N-Mint |
|---|---|---|---|
| 7: 7-Ditko-c/a begins, ends #14 | 18.00 | 54.00 | 125.00 |
| 8-Last 10 cent issue | 16.00 | 48.00 | 110.00 |
| 9-14: 12-1st app. Mailbag. 13-Anti-communist story | 13.00 | 40.00 | 90.00 |

**AMAZING ADVENTURE FUNNIES** (Fantoman No. 2 on)
June, 1940 - No. 2, Sept. 1940
Centaur Publications

| | Good | Fine | N-Mint |
|---|---|---|---|
| 1-The Fantom of the Fair by Gustavson (r-/Amaz. Mystery Funnies V2/7, V2/8), The Arrow, Skyrocket Steele From the Year X by Everett (r-/AMF 2); Burgos-a | 107.00 | 320.00 | 750.00 |
| 2-Reprints; Published after Fantoman #2 | 71.00 | 215.00 | 500.00 |

NOTE: ***Burgos** a-1(2). **Everett** a-1(3). **Gustavson** a-1(5), 2(3). **Pinajian** a-2.*

**AMAZING ADVENTURES** (Also see Science Comics)
1950 - No. 6, Fall, 1952 (Painted covers)
Ziff-Davis Publ. Co.

1950 (no month given) (8½x11") (8 pgs.) Has the front & back cover plus Schomburg story used in Amazing Advs. #1 (Sent to subscribers of Z-D s/f magazines & ordered through mail for 10 cents. Used to test market) Estimated value....190.00

| | Good | Fine | N-Mint |
|---|---|---|---|
| 1-Wood, Schomburg, Anderson, Whitney-a | 32.00 | 92.00 | 225.00 |
| 2-5-Anderson-a. 3,5-Starr-a | 12.00 | 36.00 | 84.00 |
| 6-Krigstein-a | 17.00 | 51.00 | 120.00 |

**AMAZING ADVENTURES** (Becomes Amazing Adult Fantasy #7 on)
June, 1961 - No. 6, Nov, 1961
Atlas Comics (AMI)/Marvel Comics No. 3 on

| | Good | Fine | N-Mint |
|---|---|---|---|
| 1-Origin Dr. Droom (1st Marvel-Age Superhero) by Kirby; Ditko & Kirby-a in all; Kirby c-1-6 | 43.00 | 130.00 | 300.00 |
| 2 | 26.00 | 78.00 | 185.00 |
| 3-6: 6-Last Dr. Droom | 19.00 | 58.00 | 135.00 |

**AMAZING ADVENTURES**
Aug, 1970 - No. 39, Nov, 1976
Marvel Comics Group

1-Inhumans by Kirby(p) & Black Widow (1st app. in Tales of

*All Winners Comics #10, © MEG*

*Alpha Flight #2, © MEG*

*Amazing Adult Fantasy #10, © MEG*

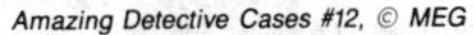
Amazing Detective Cases #12, © MEG

Amazing Ghost Stories #15, © STJ

Amazing-Man Comics #7, © CEN

Good Fine N-Mint

Suspense #52) begin .85 2.50 5.00
2-4: Last Kirby Inhumans .60 1.75 3.50
5-8-Neal Adams-a; 8-Last Black Widow .85 2.50 5.00
9,10: 10-Last Inhumans (origin-r by Kirby) .50 1.50 3.00
11-New Beast begins(origin in flashback); X-Men cameo in flashback (11-17 are all X-Men tie-ins) 1.00 3.00 6.00
12-17: 13-Brotherhood of Evil Mutants x-over from X-Men. 15-X-Men app. 17-Last Beast (origin); X-Men app. .70 2.00 4.00
18-War of the Worlds begins; 1st app. Killraven; Neal Adams-a(p) .85 2.50 5.00
19-39: 35-Giffen's first story-art, along with Deadly Hands of Kung-Fu #22 (3/76) .35 1.00 2.00

NOTE: ***N. Adams*** *c-6-8.* ***Buscema*** *a-1p, 2p.* ***Colan*** *a-3-5p, 26p.* ***Ditko*** *a-24r.* ***Everett*** *inks-3-5, 7-9.* ***Giffen*** *a-35i, 38p.* ***G. Kane*** *c-11, 25p, 29p.* ***Ploog*** *a-12i.* ***Russell*** *c-28, 34, 37.* ***Starlin*** *a-17; c-15p, 16, 17, 27.* ***Sutton*** *a-11-15p.*

**AMAZING ADVENTURES**
December, 1979 - No. 14, January, 1981
Marvel Comics Group

V2#1-r story/X-Men #1 & 38 (origins) .50 1.50 3.00
2-14: 2-6-Early X-Men-r. 7,8-Origin Iceman .35 1.00 2.00

NOTE: ***Byrne*** *c-6p, 9p.* ***Kirby*** *a-1-14r; c-7, 9.* ***Steranko*** *a-12r.* ***Tuska*** *a-7-9.*

**AMAZING ADVENTURES**
July, 1988 ($4.95, One-shot, color, squarebound, 80 pgs.)
Marvel Comics

1-Anthology; Austin, Golden-a .85 2.50 5.00

**AMAZING ADVENTURES OF CAPTAIN CARVEL AND HIS CARVEL CRUSADERS, THE** (See Carvel Comics)

**AMAZING CHAN & THE CHAN CLAN, THE** (TV)
May, 1973 - No. 4, Feb, 1974 (Hanna-Barbera)
Gold Key

1 .70 2.00 4.00
2-4 .50 1.50 3.00

**AMAZING COMICS** (Complete Comics No. 2)
Fall, 1944
Timely Comics (EPC)

1-The Destroyer, The Whizzer, The Young Allies, Sergeant Dix; Schomburg-c 72.00 215.00 500.00

**AMAZING CYNICALMAN, THE**
June, 1987 ($1.50, B&W)
Eclipse Comics

1 .25 .75 1.50

**AMAZING DETECTIVE CASES** (Formerly Suspense No. 2?)
No. 3, Nov, 1950 - No. 14, Sept, 1952
Marvel/Atlas Comics (CCC)

3 8.00 24.00 56.00
4-6 4.00 12.00 28.00
7-10 3.00 9.00 21.00
11,14: 11-(3/52)-change to horror 4.00 12.00 28.00
12-Krigstein-a 4.30 13.00 30.00
13-Everett-a; electrocution-c/story 5.70 17.00 40.00

NOTE: ***Colan*** *a-9.* ***Maneely*** *c-13.* ***Sekowsky*** *a-12.* ***Sinnott*** *a-13.* ***Tuska*** *a-10.*

**AMAZING FANTASY** (Formerly Amazing Adult Fantasy #7-14)
No. 15, Aug, 1962 (Sept, 1962 shown in indicia)
Marvel Comics Group (AMI)

15-Origin & 1st app. of Spider-Man by Ditko; Kirby/Ditko-c

| Good | Fine | N-Mint | Mint |
|---|---|---|---|
| 350.00 | 1400.00 | 3500.00 | 6100.00 |

(Estimated up to 1400 total copies exist, 45 in Mint)

**AMAZING GHOST STORIES** (Formerly Nightmare)
No. 14, Oct, 1954 - No. 16, Feb, 1955
St. John Publishing Co.

Good Fine N-Mint

14-Pit & the Pendulum story by Kinstler; Baker-c 11.00 32.00 75.00
15-R/Weird Thrillers #5; Baker-c, Powell-a 7.00 21.00 50.00
16-Kubert reprints of Weird Thrillers #4; Baker-c; Roussos, Tuska, Kinstler-a 8.00 24.00 56.00

**AMAZING HIGH ADVENTURE**
8/84; No. 2, 10/85; No. 3, 10/86 - No. 5, 1987 (Baxter No. 3,4)($2.00)
Marvel Comics

1-5 .35 1.00 2.00

NOTE: ***Bissette*** *a-5.* ***Bolton*** *c/a-4, 5.* ***Severin*** *a-1, 3.* ***P. Smith*** *a-2.* ***Williamson*** *a-2i.*

**AMAZING-MAN COMICS** (Formerly Motion Picture Funnies Wkly?)
(Also see Stars And Stripes Comics)
No. 5, Sept, 1939 - No. 27, Feb, 1942
Centaur Publications

5(No.1)(Rare)-Origin/1st app. A-Man the Amazing Man by Bill Everett; The Cat-Man by Tarpe Mills (also #8), Mighty Man by Filchock, Minimidget & sidekick Ritty, & The Iron Skull by Burgos begins

| Good | Fine | VF-NM | NM/Mint |
|---|---|---|---|
| 800.00 | 2000.00 | 4800.00 | 6800.00 |

(Estimated up to 60 total copies exist, 3 in NM/Mint)

6-Origin The Amazing Man retold; The Shark begins; Ivy Menace by Tarpe Mills app.

Good Fine N-Mint

233.00 585.00 1400.00

7-Magician From Mars begins; ends #11 142.00 426.00 850.00
8-Cat-Man dresses as woman 86.00 257.00 600.00
9-Magician From Mars battles the 'Elemental Monster,' swiped into The Spectre in More Fun #54 & 55 84.00 252.00 590.00
10,11: 11-Zardi, the Eternal Man begins; ends #16; Amazing Man dons costume; last Everett issue 72.00 215.00 500.00
12,13 70.00 210.00 490.00
14-Reef Kinkaid, Rocke Wayburn (ends #20), & Dr. Hypno (ends #21) begin; no Zardi or Chuck Hardy 56.00 167.00 390.00
15,17-20: 15-Zardi returns; no Rocke Wayburn. 17-Dr. Hypno returns; no Zardi 43.00 130.00 300.00
16-Mighty Man's powers of super strength & ability to shrink & grow explained; Rocke Wayburn returns; no Dr. Hypno; Al Avison (a character) begins, ends #18 (a tribute to the famed artist) 46.00 137.00 320.00
21-Origin Dash Dartwell (drug-use story); origin & only app. T.N.T. 43.00 130.00 300.00
22-Dash Dartwell, the Human Meteor & The Voice app; last Iron Skull & The Shark; Silver Streak app. 43.00 130.00 300.00
23-Two Amazing Man stories; intro/origin Tommy the Amazing Kid; The Marksman only app. 46.00 137.00 320.00
24,27: 24-King of Darkness, Nightshade, & Blue Lady begin; end #26; 1st App. Super-Ann 43.00 130.00 300.00
25,26 (Scarce)-Meteor Martin by Wolverton in both; 26-Electric Ray app. 72.00 215.00 505.00

NOTE: ***Everett*** *a-5-11; c-5-11.* ***Gilman*** *a-14-20.* ***Giunta/Mirando*** *a-7-10.* ***Sam Glanzman*** *a-14-16, 18-21, 23.* ***Louis Glanzman*** *a-6, 9-11, 14-21; c-13-19, 21.* ***Robert Golden*** *a-9.* ***Gustavson*** *a-6; c-22, 23.* ***Lubbers*** *a-14-21.* ***Simon*** *a-10.* ***Frank Thomas*** *a-6, 9-11, 14, 15, 17-21.*

**AMAZING MYSTERIES** (Formerly Sub-Mariner No. 31)
No. 32, May, 1949 - No. 35, Jan, 1950
Marvel Comics (CCC)

32-The Witness app; 1st Marvel horror comic 29.00 86.00 200.00
33-Horror format 9.00 27.00 62.00
34,35-Change to Crime. 35-Photo-c 5.70 17.00 40.00

**AMAZING MYSTERY FUNNIES**
Aug, 1938 - No. 24, Sept, 1940 (All 52 pgs.)
Centaur Publications

V1#1-Everett-c(1st); Dick Kent Adv. story; Skyrocket Steele in the Year X on cover only 233.00 583.00 1400.00

| | Good | Fine | N-Mint |
|---|---|---|---|
| 2-Everett 1st-a (Skyrocket Steele) | 108.00 | 270.00 | 650.00 |
| 3 | 54.00 | 160.00 | 375.00 |
| 3(#4, 12/38)-nn on cover, #3 on inside; bondage-c | 43.00 | 130.00 | 300.00 |
| V2#1-4,6: 2-Drug use story. 3-Air-Sub DX begins by Burgos. 4-Dan Hastings, Sand Hog begins (ends #5). 6-Last Skyrocket Steele | 39.00 | 118.00 | 275.00 |
| 5-Classic Everett-c | 43.00 | 130.00 | 300.00 |
| 7 (Scarce)-Intro. The Fantom of the Fair; Everett, Gustavson, Burgos-a | 185.00 | 560.00 | 1300.00 |
| 8-Origin & 1st app. Speed Centaur | 82.00 | 245.00 | 575.00 |
| 9-11: 11-Self portrait and biog. of Everett; Jon Linton begins | 43.00 | 130.00 | 300.00 |
| 12 (Scarce)-Wolverton Space Patrol-a (12/39) | 92.00 | 275.00 | 645.00 |
| V3#1(#17, 1/40)-Intro. Bullet; Tippy Taylor serial begins, ends #24 (continued in The Arrow #2) | 43.00 | 130.00 | 300.00 |
| 18,20: 18-Fantom of the Fair by Gustavson | 36.00 | 107.00 | 275.00 |
| 19,21-24-Space Patrol by Wolverton in all | 65.00 | 195.00 | 455.00 |

NOTE: ***Burgos** a-V2#3-9. **Eisner** a-V1#2, 3(2). **Everett** a-V1#2-4, V2#1, 3-6; c-V1#1-4, V2#3, 5, 18. **Filchock** a-V2#9. **Flessel** a-V2#6. **Guardineer** a-V1#4, V2#4-6; **Gustavson** a-V2#4, 5, 9-12, V3#1, 18, 19; c-V2#7, 9, 12, V3#1, 21, 22; **McWilliams** a-V2#9, 10. **Tarpe Mills** a-V2#2, 4-6, 9-12, V3#1. **Leo Morey**(Pulp artist) c-V2#10; text illo-V2#11. **Frank Thomas** c-V2/11. **Webster** a-V2#4.*

**AMAZING SAINTS**
1974 (39 cents)
Logos International

| | Good | Fine | N-Mint |
|---|---|---|---|
| nn-True story of Phil Saint | | .20 | .40 |

**AMAZING SPIDER-MAN, THE** (See All Detergent Comics, Amazing Fantasy, America's Best TV Comics, Aurora, Giant-Size Spider-Man, Giant Size Super-Heroes Feat. . . ., Marvel Coll. Item Classics, Marvel Fanfare, Marvel Graphic Novel, Marvel Spec. Ed., Marvel Tales, Marvel Team-Up, Marvel Treasury Ed., Nothing Can Stop the Juggernaut, Official Marvel Index To. . ., Power Record Comics, Spectacular. . ., Spider-Man, Spider-Man Digest, Spider-Man Vs. Wolverine, Spidey Super Stories, Strange Tales Annual #2, Superman Vs. . . ., Try-Out Winner Book & Web of Spider-man)

**AMAZING SPIDER-MAN, THE**
March, 1963 - Present
Marvel Comics Group

| | Good | Fine | N-Mint | Mint |
|---|---|---|---|---|
| 1-Retells origin by Steve Ditko; 1st Fantastic Four x-over; intro. John Jameson & The Chameleon; Kirby-c | 340.00 | 1360.00 | 3400.00 | 5600.00 |

(Estimated up to 1700 total copies exist, 70 in Mint)

| | Good | Fine | N-Mint |
|---|---|---|---|
| 1-Reprint from the Golden Record Comic set | 8.50 | 25.50 | 60.00 |
| with record (still sealed) | 17.00 | 51.00 | 120.00 |
| 2-1st app. the Vulture & the Terrible Tinkerer | 143.00 | 430.00 | 1000.00 |
| 3-Human Torch cameo; intro. & 1st app. Doc Octopus; Dr. Doom & Ant-Man app. | 100.00 | 300.00 | 700.00 |
| 4-Origin & 1st app. The Sandman; Intro. Betty Brant & Liz Allen | 71.00 | 213.00 | 500.00 |
| 5-Dr. Doom app. | 66.00 | 198.00 | 460.00 |
| 6-1st app. Lizard | 71.00 | 213.00 | 500.00 |
| 7,8,10: 8-Fantastic Four app. 10-1st app. Big Man & Enforcers | 47.00 | 141.00 | 330.00 |
| 9-1st app. Electro (origin) | 51.00 | 153.00 | 360.00 |
| 11,12: 11-1st app. Bennett Brant | 29.00 | 86.00 | 200.00 |
| 13-1st app. Mysterio | 36.00 | 108.00 | 250.00 |
| 14-1st app. The Green Goblin; Hulk x-over | 89.00 | 267.00 | 620.00 |
| 15-1st app. Kraven the Hunter | 31.00 | 93.00 | 220.00 |
| 16,18,19: 16-1st Daredevil x-over. 18-Fant.-4 app; 18-1st app. Ned Leeds | 23.00 | 70.00 | 160.00 |
| 17-2nd app. Green Goblin | 40.00 | 120.00 | 280.00 |
| 20-Origin & 1st app. The Scorpion | 22.00 | 66.00 | 155.00 |
| 21,22: 22-1st app. Princess Python | 16.00 | 48.00 | 110.00 |
| 23-3rd app. The Green Goblin (c/story) | 23.50 | 71.00 | 165.00 |
| 24 | 14.00 | 43.00 | 100.00 |
| 25-(6/65)-1st app. Mary Jane Watson (cameo; face not shown); 1st app. Spencer Smythe | 16.00 | 48.00 | 110.00 |
| 26-4th app. The Green Goblin; 1st app. Crime Master; dies in #27 | 19.00 | 58.00 | 135.00 |
| 27-5th app. The Green Goblin | 18.00 | 54.00 | 125.00 |
| 28-Origin & 1st app. Molten Man | 18.50 | 56.00 | 130.00 |
| 29,30 | 13.50 | 41.00 | 95.00 |
| 31-38: 31-1st app. Harry Osborn, Gwen Stacy & Prof. Warren. 36-1st app. Looter. 37-Intro. Norman Osborn. 38-Last Ditko issue | 9.30 | 28.00 | 65.00 |
| 39-The Green Goblin-c/story; Green Goblin's i.d. revealed as Norman Osborn | 11.00 | 32.00 | 75.00 |
| 40-Origin The Green Goblin (1st told origin) | 14.00 | 43.00 | 100.00 |
| 41,43-49: 41-1st app. Rhino. 46-Intro. Shocker | 5.70 | 17.00 | 40.00 |
| 42-2nd app. Mary Jane Watson (cameo in last 2 panels); 1st time face is shown | 7.85 | 23.50 | 55.00 |
| 50-1st app. Kingpin | 21.00 | 63.00 | 145.00 |
| 51-2nd app. Kingpin | 7.00 | 21.00 | 50.00 |
| 52-60: 52-1st app. Joe Robertson. 56-1st app. Capt. George Stacy. 57,58-Ka-Zar app. 59-1st app. Brainwasher (alias Kingpin) | 3.60 | 11.00 | 25.00 |
| 61-80: 67-1st app. Randy Robertson. 73-1st app. Silvermane. 78-1st app. Prowler | 2.30 | 7.00 | 16.00 |
| 81-89,91-93,95,99: 83-1st app. Schemer & Vanessa (Kingpin's wife). 93-1st app. Arthur Stacy | 2.15 | 6.50 | 15.00 |
| 90-Death of Capt. Stacey | 2.85 | 8.50 | 20.00 |
| 94-Origin retold | 4.30 | 13.00 | 30.00 |
| 96-98-Drug books not approved by CCA | 4.50 | 14.00 | 32.00 |
| 100-Anniversary issue | 11.00 | 32.00 | 75.00 |
| 101-1st app. Morbius the Living Vampire | 3.00 | 9.00 | 21.00 |
| 102-Origin Morbius (52 pgs.) | 3.60 | 11.00 | 25.00 |
| 103-120: 108-1st app. Sha-Shan. 110-1st app. Gibbon. 111-Kraven the Hunter app. 113-1st app. Hammerhead | 1.85 | 5.50 | 13.00 |
| 121-Death of Gwen Stacy (r-/in Marv. Tales 98) | 7.85 | 23.50 | 55.00 |
| 122-Death of The Green Goblin (r-/in Marvel Tales #99) | 12.00 | 36.00 | 85.00 |
| 123-128: 124-1st app. Man Wolf, origin in #125 | 1.70 | 5.00 | 12.00 |
| 129-1st app. The Punisher (2/74) | 39.00 | 117.00 | 275.00 |
| 130-133,137-160: 139-1st app. Grizzly. 140-1st app. Glory Grant. 143-1st app. Cyclone | 1.30 | 4.00 | 9.00 |
| 134-Punisher cameo (7/74); 1st app. Tarantula | 2.85 | 8.50 | 20.00 |
| 135-Punisher app. (8/75) | 7.85 | 23.50 | 55.00 |
| 136-Reappearance of The Green Goblin | 2.85 | 8.50 | 20.00 |
| 161-Nightcrawler app. from X-Men; Punisher cameo | 1.60 | 4.80 | 11.00 |
| 162-Punisher, Nightcrawler app. | 3.15 | 9.50 | 22.00 |
| 163-173,176,181-188: 167-1st app. Will O' The Wisp. 171-Nova app. 181-Origin retold; gives life history of Spider-Man | .85 | 2.50 | 5.00 |
| 174,175-Punisher app. | 2.30 | 7.00 | 16.00 |
| 177-180-Green Goblin app. | 1.35 | 4.00 | 8.00 |
| 189-193,195-199,203-219: 189,190-Byrne-a(p). 196-Faked death of Aunt May. 203-2nd app. Dazzler. 210-1st app. Madame Web. 212-1st app. Hydro Man | .85 | 2.50 | 5.00 |
| 194-1st app. Black Cat | 1.15 | 3.50 | 7.00 |
| 200-Giant origin issue | 2.30 | 7.00 | 14.00 |
| 201,202-Punisher app. | 3.35 | 10.00 | 20.00 |
| 220-224,226-237: 226,227-Black Cat returns. 236-Tarantula dies. 234-Free 16 pg. insert "Marvel Guide to Collecting Comics." 235-Origin Will-'O-The-Wisp | .85 | 2.50 | 5.00 |
| 225-Foolkiller app. | .85 | 2.50 | 5.00 |
| 238-1st app. Hobgoblin; came with skin "Tatooz" decal | 5.00 | 15.00 | 35.00 |
| 239-2nd app. Hobgoblin | 2.65 | 8.00 | 18.00 |
| 240-250: 241-Origin The Vulture | .85 | 2.50 | 5.00 |
| 251-Last old costume | 1.15 | 3.50 | 7.00 |

*Amazing Mystery Funnies V2#7, © CEN*

*The Amazing Spider-Man #14, © MEG*

*The Amazing Spider-Man #162, © MEG*

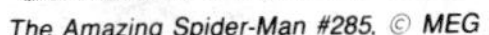

The Amazing Spider-Man #285, © MEG

The Amazing Spider-Man Annual #1, © MEG

America in Action #1 (1945), © Mayflower H.

| | Good | Fine | N-Mint |
|---|---|---|---|
| 252-Spider-Man dons new costume (5/84); ties with Spectacular Spider-Man #90 for 1st new costume | 1.70 | 5.00 | 10.00 |
| 253-1st app. The Rose | 1.00 | 3.00 | 6.00 |
| 254 | .70 | 2.00 | 4.00 |
| 255-260: 259-Spidey back to old costume | .50 | 1.50 | 3.00 |
| 261-Hobgoblin app. | 1.00 | 3.00 | 6.00 |
| 262-274,276-283 | .50 | 1.50 | 3.00 |
| 275-Origin-r by Ditko ($1.25, double-size) | 1.00 | 3.00 | 6.00 |
| 284-Punisher cameo; Gang War story begins | .85 | 2.50 | 5.00 |
| 285-Punisher app. | 2.50 | 7.50 | 15.00 |
| 286-288: 288-Last Gang War | .85 | 2.50 | 5.00 |
| 289-(52 pgs.)-Hobgoblin's i.d. revealed | 3.00 | 9.00 | 18.00 |
| 290-292 | .70 | 2.00 | 4.00 |
| 293,294-Part 2 & 5 of Kraven story from Web of Spider-Man. 294-Death of Kraven | 1.15 | 3.50 | 7.00 |
| 295-297 | .85 | 2.50 | 5.00 |
| 298-Todd McFarlane-c/a begins; 1st Venom | 5.30 | 16.00 | 32.00 |
| 299-McFarlane-a | 2.65 | 8.00 | 16.00 |
| 300 ($1.50, 52 pgs.; 25th Anniversary)-Last black costume | 5.30 | 16.00 | 32.00 |
| 301-305: 301 ($1.00 issues begin). 304-1st bi-weekly issue | 2.65 | 8.00 | 16.00 |
| 306-315: 306-Cover swipe from Action #1. 312-Hobgoblin app. | 2.00 | 6.00 | 12.00 |
| 316-,323,325: 319-Bi-weekly begins again | 1.15 | 3.50 | 7.00 |
| 324-Sabertooth app.; McFarlane cover only | .50 | 1.50 | 3.00 |
| 326,327,329: 327-Cosmic Spidey continues from Spect. Spider-Man. (no McFarlane-c/a) | .35 | 1.00 | 2.00 |
| 328-Hulk x-over; last McFarlane issue | 1.15 | 3.50 | 7.00 |
| 330,331-Punisher app. | .50 | 1.50 | 3.00 |
| 332-346: 341-Tarantula app. | | .50 | 1.00 |
| Annual 1 (1964)-Origin Spider-Man; 1st app. Sinister Six; Kraven the Hunter app. | 24.00 | 72.00 | 170.00 |
| Annual 2 | 10.00 | 30.00 | 70.00 |
| Special 3,4 | 4.30 | 13.00 | 30.00 |
| Special 5-8 (12/71) | 2.15 | 6.50 | 15.00 |
| King Size 9 ('73)-Green Goblin app. | 1.50 | 4.50 | 10.00 |
| Annual 10(6/76)-Old Human Fly app. | 1.00 | 3.00 | 6.00 |
| Annual 11(9/77), 12(8/78) | 1.00 | 3.00 | 6.00 |
| Annual 13(11/79)-Byrne-a | 1.15 | 3.50 | 7.00 |
| Annual 14(12/80)-Miller-c/a(p), 40pgs. | 1.35 | 4.00 | 8.00 |
| Annual 15(1981)-Miller-c/a(p); Punisher app. | 3.35 | 10.00 | 20.00 |
| Annual 16-20: 16(12/82)-Origin/1st app. new Capt. Marvel (female heroine). 17(12/83). 18 ('84). 19(11/85). 20(11/86)-Origin Iron Man of 2020 | .85 | 2.50 | 5.00 |
| Annual 21('87)-Special wedding issue | 1.15 | 3.50 | 7.00 |
| Annual 22('88, $1.75, 68 pgs.)-1st app. Speedball; Evolutionary War x-over | 1.15 | 3.50 | 7.00 |
| Annual 23 ('89, $2.00, 68 pgs.)-Atlantis Attacks; origin Spider-Man retold; She-Hulk app.; Byrne-c | .85 | 2.50 | 5.00 |
| Annual 24 ('90, $2.00, 68 pgs.)-Ant-Man app. | .50 | 1.50 | 3.00 |
| Parallel Lives (graphic novel, '90, $8.95, 68pgs.) | 1.50 | 4.50 | 9.00 |
| Aim Toothpaste giveaway(36pgs., reg. size)-Green Goblin app. | .35 | 1.00 | 2.00 |
| Aim Toothpaste giveaway (16pgs., reg. size)-Dr. Octopus app. | | .50 | 1.00 |
| All Detergent Giveaway ('79, 36 pgs.), nn-Origin-r | .85 | 2.50 | 5.00 |
| Giveaway-Acme & Dingo Children's Boots(1980)-Spider-Woman app. | | .50 | 1.00 |
| . . .& Power Pack ('84, nn)(Nat'l Committee for Prevention of Child Abuse. (two versions, mail offer & store giveaway)-Mooney-a; Byrne-c | | .30 | .60 |
| . . .& The Hulk (Special Edition)(6/8/80; 20 pgs.; Chicago Tribune giveaway) | .70 | 2.00 | 4.00 |
| . . .& The Incredible Hulk (1981, 1982; 36 pgs.), Sanger Harris, Dallas Times, Denver Post, Kansas City Star, The Jones Store-giveaway; 16 pgs. (1983) | 1.00 | 3.00 | 6.00 |
| . . ., Captain America, The Incredible Hulk, & Spider-Woman ('81) (7-11 Stores giveaway; 36 pgs.) | | .30 | .60 |
| . . .: Christmas In Dallas (1983) (Supplement to Dallas Times Herald) giveaway | | .30 | .60 |
| . . ., Fire-Star, and Iceman At the Dallas Ballet Nutcracker (1983; supplement to Dallas Times Herald)-Mooney-p | | .30 | .60 |
| Giveaway-Esquire & Eye Magazines(2/69)-Miniature-Still attached | 5.00 | 15.00 | 35.00 |
| . . ., Storm & Powerman ('82; 20 pgs.)(American Cancer Society)-giveaway | | .30 | .60 |
| . . .Vs. The Hulk (Special Edition; 1979)(Supplement to Columbus Dispatch)-Giveaway | .50 | 1.50 | 3.00 |
| . . .vs. the Prodigy Giveaway, 16 pgs. in color ('76)-5x6½"-Sex education; (1 million printed; 35-50 cents) | | .25 | .50 |

NOTE: ***Austin*** *a(i)-248, 335, 337, Annual 13; c(i)-188, 241, 242, 248, 331, 334, 343.* ***J. Buscema*** *a(p)-72, 73, 76-81, 84, 85.* ***Byrne*** *a-189p, 190p, 206p, Annual 3r, 6r, 7r, 13p; c-189p, 268, 296, Annual 12.* ***Ditko*** *a-1-38, Annual 1, 2, 24(2); c-1-38.* ***Gil Kane*** *a(p)-89-105, 120-124, 150, Annual 10, 12i, 24p; c-90p, 96, 98, 99, 101-105p, 129p, 131p, 132p, 137-140p, 143p, 148p, 149p, 151p, 153p, 160p, 161p, Annual 10p, 24.* ***Kirby*** *a-8.* ***McFarlane*** *a-298p, 299p, 300-303, 304-323p, 325p, 328; c-298-325, 328.* ***Miller*** *c-218, 219.* ***Mooney*** *a-65i, 67-82i, 84-88i, 173i, 178i, 189i, 190i, 192i, 193i, 196-202i, 207i, 211-219i, 221i, 222i, 226i, 227i, 229-233i, Annual 11i, 17i.* ***Nasser*** *c-228p.* ***Nebres*** *a-Annual 24i.* ***Simonson*** *c-222, 337i.* ***Starlin*** *a-113i, 114i, 187p.*

**AMAZING WILLIE MAYS, THE**
No date (Sept, 1954)
Famous Funnies Publ.

| | Good | Fine | N-Mint |
|---|---|---|---|
| nn | 37.00 | 110.00 | 260.00 |

**AMAZING WORLD OF SUPERMAN** (See Superman)

**AMAZON, THE**
Mar, 1989 - No. 3, May, 1989 ($1.95, color, mini-series)
Comico

| | Good | Fine | N-Mint |
|---|---|---|---|
| 1-3: Ecological theme | .35 | 1.00 | 2.00 |

**AMAZON ATTACK 3-D**
Sept, 1990 ($3.95, 28 pgs.)
The 3-D Zone

| | Good | Fine | N-Mint |
|---|---|---|---|
| 1-Chaykin-a | .70 | 2.00 | 4.00 |

**AMBUSH** (See 4-Color Comics No. 314)

**AMBUSH BUG** (Also see Son of. . .)
June, 1985 - No. 4, Sept, 1985 (75 cents, mini-series)
DC Comics

| | Good | Fine | N-Mint |
|---|---|---|---|
| 1-4: Giffen-c/a in all | | .40 | .70 |
| . . .Stocking Stuffer (2/86, $1.25)-Giffen-c/a | | .65 | 1.30 |

**AMERICA IN ACTION**
1942; Winter, 1945 (36 pages)
Dell(Imp. Publ. Co.)/Mayflower House Publ.

| | Good | Fine | N-Mint |
|---|---|---|---|
| 1942-Dell-(68 pages) | 9.30 | 28.00 | 65.00 |
| 1(1945)-Has 3 adaptations from American history; Kiefer, Schrotter & Webb-a | 6.00 | 18.00 | 42.00 |

**AMERICA MENACED!**
1950 (Paper cover)
Vital Publications

| | Good | Fine | N-Mint |
|---|---|---|---|
| nn-Anti-communism estimated value. . . . | | | 125.00 |

**AMERICAN, THE**
July, 1987 - No. 8, 1989 ($1.50-$1.75, B&W)
Dark Horse Comics

| | Good | Fine | N-Mint |
|---|---|---|---|
| 1 ($1.50) | 1.10 | 3.25 | 6.50 |
| 2 | .75 | 2.20 | 4.40 |
| 3-5 | .50 | 1.50 | 3.00 |
| 6-8 | .30 | .90 | 1.75 |
| . . .Collection ($5.95, B&W)-reprints | 1.00 | 3.00 | 5.95 |

| | Good | Fine | N-Mint |
|---|---|---|---|
| Special 1 (1990, $2.25, B&W) | .40 | 1.15 | 2.30 |

**AMERICAN AIR FORCES, THE** (See A-1 Comics)
Sept-Oct, 1944 - No. 4, 1945; No. 5, 1951 - No. 12, 1954
William H. Wise(Flying Cadet Publ. Co./Hasan(No.1)/Life's Romances/Magazine Ent. No. 5 on)

| | Good | Fine | N-Mint |
|---|---|---|---|
| 1-Article by Zack Mosley, creator of Smilin' Jack | 5.70 | 17.00 | 40.00 |
| 2-4 | 4.00 | 12.00 | 28.00 |

NOTE: *All part comic, part magazine. Art by* ***Whitney, Chas. Quinlan, H. C. Kiefer,*** *and* ***Tony Dipreta.***

| | Good | Fine | N-Mint |
|---|---|---|---|
| 5(A-1 45)(Formerly Jet Powers), 6(A-1 54),7(A-1 58),8(A-1 65) 9(A-1 67),10(A-1 74),11(A-1 79),12(A-1 91) | 2.15 | 6.50 | 15.00 |

NOTE: ***Powell*** *c/a-5-12.*

**AMERICAN COMICS**
1940's
Theatre Giveaways (Liberty Theatre, Grand Rapids, Mich. known)

Many possible combinations. "Golden Age" superhero comics with new cover added and given away at theaters. Following known: Superman #59, Capt. Marvel #20, Capt. Marvel Jr. #5, Action #33, Classics Comics #8, Whiz #39. Value would vary with book and should be 70-80 percent of the original.

**AMERICAN FLAGG!** (Also see First Comics Graphic Novel 3, 9, 12, 21 and Howard Chaykin's. . .)
Oct, 1983 - No. 50, Mar, 1988
First Comics

| | Good | Fine | N-Mint |
|---|---|---|---|
| 1-Chaykin-c/a begins | .50 | 1.50 | 3.00 |
| 2-50: 21-27-Alan Moore scripts. 31-Origin Bob Violence | | .50 | 1.00 |
| Special 1 (11/86) | .25 | .75 | 1.50 |

**AMERICAN GRAPHICS**
No. 1, 1954; No. 2, 1957 (25 cents)
Henry Stewart

| | Good | Fine | N-Mint |
|---|---|---|---|
| 1-The Maid of the Mist, The Last of the Eries (Indian Legends of Niagara) (Sold at Niagara Falls) | 4.00 | 12.00 | 28.00 |
| 2-Victory at Niagara & Laura Secord (Heroine of the War of 1812) | 2.85 | 8.50 | 20.00 |

**AMERICAN INDIAN, THE** (See Picture Progress)

**AMERICAN LIBRARY**
No. 3, 1944 - No. 6, 1944 (68 pages) (15 cents, B&W, text & pictures)
David McKay Publications

| | Good | Fine | N-Mint |
|---|---|---|---|
| 3-6: 3-Look to the Mountain. 4-Case of the Crooked Candle (Perry Mason). 5-Duel in the Sun. 6-Wingate's Raiders | 7.00 | 21.00 | 50.00 |

NOTE: *Also see Guadalcanal Diary & Thirty Seconds Over Tokyo (part of series?).*

**AMERICA'S BEST COMICS**
Feb, 1942 - No. 31, July, 1949
Nedor/Better/Standard Publications

| | Good | Fine | N-Mint |
|---|---|---|---|
| 1-The Woman in Red, Black Terror, Captain Future, Doc Strange, The Liberator, & Don Davis, Secret Ace begin | 62.00 | 185.00 | 435.00 |
| 2-Origin The American Eagle; The Woman in Red ends | 34.00 | 100.00 | 235.00 |
| 3-Pyroman begins | 25.00 | 75.00 | 175.00 |
| 4 | 21.50 | 64.00 | 150.00 |
| 5-Last Captain Future (not in #4); Lone Eagle app. | 18.50 | 56.00 | 130.00 |
| 6,7: 6-American Crusader app. 7-Hitler, Mussolini & Hirohito-c | 16.50 | 49.00 | 115.00 |
| 8-Last Liberator | 13.00 | 40.00 | 90.00 |
| 9-The Fighting Yank begins; The Ghost app. | 13.00 | 40.00 | 90.00 |
| 10-14: 10-Flag-c. 14-American Eagle ends | 11.50 | 34.00 | 80.00 |
| 15-20 | 11.00 | 32.00 | 75.00 |
| 21,22: 21-Infinity-c. 22-Capt. Future app. | 9.30 | 28.00 | 65.00 |
| 23-Miss Masque begins; last Doc Strange | 12.00 | 36.00 | 84.00 |
| 24-Miss Masque bondage-c | 11.00 | 32.00 | 75.00 |
| 25-Last Fighting Yank; Sea Eagle app. | 9.30 | 28.00 | 65.00 |
| 26-The Phantom Detective & The Silver Knight app.; Frazetta text illo & some panels in Miss Masque | 12.00 | 36.00 | 84.00 |
| 27-31: 27,28-Commando Cubs. 27-Doc Strange. 28-Tuska Black Terror. 29-Last Pyroman | 9.30 | 28.00 | 65.00 |

NOTE: *American Eagle not in 3, 8, 9, 13. Fighting Yank not in 10, 12. Liberator not in 2, 6, 7. Pyroman not in 9, 11, 14-16, 23, 25-27.* ***Schomburg (Xela)*** *c-5, 7-31. Bondage c-18, 24.*

**AMERICA'S BEST TV COMICS** (TV)
1967 (Produced by Marvel Comics) (25 cents, 68 pgs.)
American Broadcasting Company

| | Good | Fine | N-Mint |
|---|---|---|---|
| 1-Spider-Man, Fantastic Four (by Kirby/Ayers), Casper, King Kong, George of the Jungle, Journey to the Center of the Earth app. (Promotes new TV cartoon show) | 3.15 | 9.50 | 22.00 |

**AMERICA'S BIGGEST COMICS BOOK**
1944 (196 pages) (One Shot)
William H. Wise

| | Good | Fine | N-Mint |
|---|---|---|---|
| 1-The Grim Reaper, The Silver Knight, Zudo, the Jungle Boy, Commando Cubs, Thunderhoof app. | 25.00 | 75.00 | 175.00 |

**AMERICA'S FUNNIEST COMICS**
1944 - No. 2, 1944 (80 pages) (15 cents)
William H. Wise

| | Good | Fine | N-Mint |
|---|---|---|---|
| nn(#1), 2 | 13.00 | 40.00 | 90.00 |

**AMERICA'S GREATEST COMICS**
May?/1941 - No. 8, Summer, 1943 (100 pgs.) (Soft cardboard covers)
Fawcett Publications (15 cents)

| | Good | Fine | N-Mint |
|---|---|---|---|
| 1-Bulletman, Spy Smasher, Capt. Marvel, Minute Man & Mr. Scarlet begin; Mac Raboy-c | 140.00 | 420.00 | 980.00 |
| 2 | 68.00 | 205.00 | 475.00 |
| 3 | 46.00 | 137.00 | 320.00 |
| 4,5: 4-Commando Yank begins; Golden Arrow, Ibis the Invincible & Spy Smasher cameo in Captain Marvel | 38.00 | 115.00 | 270.00 |
| 6,7: 7-Balbo the Boy Magician app.; Captain Marvel, Bulletman cameo in Mr. Scarlet | 30.00 | 90.00 | 210.00 |
| 8-Capt. Marvel Jr. & Golden Arrow app.; Spy Smasher x-over in Capt. Midnight; no Minute Man or Commando Yank | 30.00 | 90.00 | 210.00 |

**AMERICA'S SWEETHEART SUNNY** (See Sunny, . . .)

**AMERICA VS. THE JUSTICE SOCIETY**
Jan, 1985 - No. 4, Apr, 1985 ($1.00, mini-series)
DC Comics

| | Good | Fine | N-Mint |
|---|---|---|---|
| 1-Double size; Alcala-a in all | .25 | .75 | 1.50 |
| 2-4 | | .50 | 1.00 |

**AMERICOMICS**
April, 1983 - No. 6, Mar, 1984 ($2.00, color, Baxter paper, slick paper)
Americomics

| | Good | Fine | N-Mint |
|---|---|---|---|
| 1-Intro/origin The Shade; Intro. The Slayer, Captain Freedom and The Liberty Corps; Perez-c | .40 | 1.25 | 2.50 |
| 1,2-2nd printings ($2.00) | .35 | 1.00 | 2.00 |
| 2-6: 2-Messenger app., & 1st app. Tara on Jungle Island 3-New & old Blue Beetle battle. 4-Origin Dragonfly & Shade. 5-Origin Commando D. 6-Origin the Scarlet Scorpion | .40 | 1.25 | 2.50 |
| Special 1(8/83, $2.00)-Sentinels of Justice (Blue Beetle, Captain Atom Nightshade, & The Question) | .40 | 1.20 | 2.50 |

**AMETHYST**
Jan, 1985 - No. 16, Aug, 1986 (75 cents)
DC Comics

| | Good | Fine | N-Mint |
|---|---|---|---|
| 1-16: 8-Fire Jade's i.d. revealed | | .40 | .80 |
| Special 1 (10/86, $1.25) | | .65 | 1.30 |

*The American Air Forces #2, © ME*

*America's Best Comics #21, © STD*

*America's Greatest Comics #1, © FAW*

*Anchors Andrews #1, © STJ*

*Animal Adventures #1, © Timor Publ.*

*Animal Comics #4, © DELL*

**AMETHYST**
Nov, 1987 - No. 4, Feb, 1988 ($1.25, color, mini-series)
DC Comics

| | Good | Fine | N-Mint |
|---|---|---|---|
| 1-4 | | .60 | 1.25 |

**AMETHYST, PRINCESS OF GEMWORLD**
May, 1983 - No. 12, April, 1984 (12 issue maxi-series)
DC Comics

| | Good | Fine | N-Mint |
|---|---|---|---|
| 1-60 cent cover | | .30 | .60 |
| 1,2-35 cent-tested in Austin & Kansas City | | .30 | .60 |
| 2-12: Perez-c(p) #6-11 | | .30 | .60 |
| Annual 1(9/84) | | .65 | 1.30 |

**ANARCHO DICTATOR OF DEATH** (See Comics Novel)

**ANCHORS ANDREWS** (The Saltwater Daffy)
Jan, 1953 - No. 4, July, 1953 (Anchors the Saltwater... No. 4)
St. John Publishing Co.

| | Good | Fine | N-Mint |
|---|---|---|---|
| 1-Canteen Kate by Matt Baker (9 pgs.) | 9.30 | 28.00 | 65.00 |
| 2-4 | 2.65 | 8.00 | 18.00 |

**ANDY & WOODY** (See March of Comics No. 40, 55, 76)

**ANDY BURNETT** (See 4-Color Comics No. 865)

**ANDY COMICS** (Formerly Scream Comics; becomes Ernie Comics)
No. 20, June, 1948 - No. 21, Aug, 1948
Current Publications (Ace Magazines)

| | Good | Fine | N-Mint |
|---|---|---|---|
| 20,21-Archie-type comic | 2.65 | 8.00 | 18.00 |

**ANDY DEVINE WESTERN**
Dec, 1950 - No. 2, 1951
Fawcett Publications

| | Good | Fine | N-Mint |
|---|---|---|---|
| 1 | 29.00 | 85.00 | 200.00 |
| 2 | 20.00 | 60.00 | 140.00 |

**ANDY GRIFFITH SHOW, THE** (See 4-Color No. 1252, 1341)

**ANDY HARDY COMICS** (See Movie Comics No. 3 by Fiction House)
April, 1952 - No. 6, Sept-Nov, 1954
Dell Publishing Co.

| | Good | Fine | N-Mint |
|---|---|---|---|
| 4-Color 389 (#1) | 2.00 | 6.00 | 14.00 |
| 4-Color 447,480,515,5,6 | 1.15 | 3.50 | 8.00 |
| ...& the New Automatic Gas Clothes Dryer ('52, 16 pgs., 5x7¼") Bendix Giveaway (soft-c) | 2.00 | 6.00 | 14.00 |

**ANDY PANDA** (Also see Crackajack Funnies #39, The Funnies, New Funnies & Walter Lantz ...)
1943 - No. 56, Nov-Jan, 1961-62 (Walter Lantz)
Dell Publishing Co.

| | Good | Fine | N-Mint |
|---|---|---|---|
| 4-Color 25(#1, 1943) | 27.00 | 80.00 | 190.00 |
| 4-Color 54('44) | 17.00 | 51.00 | 120.00 |
| 4-Color 85('45) | 11.00 | 32.00 | 75.00 |
| 4-Color 130('46),154,198 | 5.30 | 16.00 | 38.00 |
| 4-Color 216,240,258,280,297 | 3.00 | 9.00 | 21.00 |
| 4-Color 326,345,358 | 2.00 | 6.00 | 14.00 |
| 4-Color 383,409 | 1.30 | 4.00 | 9.00 |
| 16(11-1/52-53) - 30 | .85 | 2.60 | 6.00 |
| 31-56 | .55 | 1.80 | 4.00 |

(See March of Comics #5, 22, 79, & Super Book #4, 15, 27.)

**ANGEL**
Aug, 1954 - No. 16, Nov-Jan, 1958-59
Dell Publishing Co.

| | Good | Fine | N-Mint |
|---|---|---|---|
| 4-Color 576(#1, 8/54) | 1.15 | 3.50 | 8.00 |
| 2(5-7/55) - 16 | .70 | 2.00 | 5.00 |

**ANGEL AND THE APE** (Meet Angel No. 7) (See Limited Collector's Edition C-34 & Showcase No. 77)
Nov-Dec, 1968 - No. 6, Sept-Oct, 1969
National Periodical Publications

| | Good | Fine | N-Mint |
|---|---|---|---|
| 1-Not Wood-a | 1.70 | 5.00 | 12.00 |
| 2-6-Wood inks in all | 1.30 | 4.00 | 9.00 |

**ANGELIC ANGELINA**
1909 (11½x17"; 30 pgs.; 2 colors)
Cupples & Leon Company

| | Good | Fine | N-Mint |
|---|---|---|---|
| nn-By Munson Paddock | 14.00 | 42.00 | 100.00 |

**ANGEL LOVE**
Aug, 1986 - No. 8, Mar, 1987 (75 cents, mini-series)
DC Comics

| | Good | Fine | N-Mint |
|---|---|---|---|
| 1-8 | | .40 | .80 |
| Special 1 (1987, $1.25, 52 pgs.) | | .65 | 1.30 |

**ANGEL OF LIGHT, THE** (See The Crusaders)

**ANIMAL ADVENTURES**
Dec, 1953 - No. 3, Apr?, 1954
Timor Publications/Accepted Publications (reprints)

| | Good | Fine | N-Mint |
|---|---|---|---|
| 1 | 1.70 | 5.00 | 12.00 |
| 2,3 | 1.15 | 3.50 | 8.00 |
| 1-3 (reprints, nd) | .85 | 2.60 | 6.00 |

**ANIMAL ANTICS** (Movie Town... No. 24 on)
Mar-Apr, 1946 - No. 23, Nov-Dec, 1949 (All 52 pgs.?)
National Periodical Publications

| | Good | Fine | N-Mint |
|---|---|---|---|
| 1-Raccoon Kids begins by Otto Feur; some-c by Grossman | 25.00 | 75.00 | 175.00 |
| 2 | 12.00 | 36.00 | 85.00 |
| 3-10: 10-Post-c/a | 8.00 | 24.00 | 56.00 |
| 11-23: 14,15,18,19-Post-a | 4.50 | 14.00 | 32.00 |

**ANIMAL COMICS**
Dec-Jan, 1941-42 - No. 30, Dec-Jan, 1947-48
Dell Publishing Co.

| | Good | Fine | N-Mint |
|---|---|---|---|
| 1-1st Pogo app. by Walt Kelly (Dan Noonan art in most issues) | 86.00 | 257.00 | 600.00 |
| 2-Uncle Wiggily begins | 36.00 | 107.00 | 250.00 |
| 3,5 | 25.00 | 75.00 | 175.00 |
| 4,6,7-No Pogo | 14.00 | 42.00 | 100.00 |
| 8-10 | 17.00 | 51.00 | 120.00 |
| 11-15 | 11.00 | 32.00 | 75.00 |
| 16-20 | 7.00 | 21.00 | 50.00 |
| 21-30: 25-30-"Jigger" by John Stanley | 5.00 | 15.00 | 35.00 |

NOTE: ***Dan Noonan** a-18-30. **Gollub** art in most later issues.*

**ANIMAL CRACKERS** (Also see Adventures of Patoruzu)
1946; No. 31, July, 1950; 1959
Green Publ. Co./Norlen/Fox Feat.(Hero Books)

| | Good | Fine | N-Mint |
|---|---|---|---|
| 1-Super Cat begins | 5.70 | 17.00 | 40.00 |
| 2 | 2.65 | 8.00 | 18.00 |
| 3-10 (Exist?) | 1.30 | 4.00 | 9.00 |
| 31(Fox)-Formerly My Love Secret | 2.30 | 7.00 | 16.00 |
| 9(1959-Norlen) | .85 | 2.60 | 6.00 |
| nn, nd ('50s), no publ.; infinity-c | .85 | 2.60 | 6.00 |

**ANIMAL FABLES**
July-Aug, 1946 - No. 7, Nov-Dec, 1947
E. C. Comics(Fables Publ. Co.)

| | Good | Fine | N-Mint |
|---|---|---|---|
| 1-Freddy Firefly (clone of Human Torch), Korky Kangaroo, Petey Pig, Danny Demon begin | 26.00 | 77.00 | 180.00 |
| 2-Aesop Fables begin | 16.00 | 48.00 | 110.00 |
| 3-6 | 13.00 | 40.00 | 90.00 |
| 7-Origin Moon Girl | 43.00 | 130.00 | 300.00 |

**ANIMAL FAIR** (Fawcett's...)
March, 1946 - No. 11, Feb, 1947
Fawcett Publications

| | Good | Fine | N-Mint |
|---|---|---|---|
| 1 | 11.00 | 32.00 | 75.00 |
| 2 | 5.00 | 15.00 | 35.00 |

| | Good | Fine | N-Mint |
|---|---|---|---|
| 3-6 | 3.60 | 11.00 | 25.00 |
| 7-11 | 2.65 | 8.00 | 18.00 |

**ANIMAL FUN**
1953
Premier Magazines

| | Good | Fine | N-Mint |
|---|---|---|---|
| 1-(3-D) | 23.00 | 70.00 | 160.00 |

**ANIMAL MAN** (Also see Action Comics #552, 553, DC Comics Presents #77, 78, Secret Origins #39, Strange Adventures #180 & Wonder Woman #267, 268)
Sept, 1988 - Present ($1.25-$1.50, color)
DC Comics

| | Good | Fine | N-Mint |
|---|---|---|---|
| 1-Bolland c-1-28; Grant Morrison scripts begin | 4.15 | 12.50 | 25.00 |
| 2 | 2.00 | 6.00 | 12.00 |
| 3,4 | 1.15 | 3.50 | 7.00 |
| 5-10: 6-Invasion tie-in | .85 | 2.50 | 5.00 |
| 11-15 | .70 | 2.00 | 4.00 |
| 16-20 | .50 | 1.50 | 3.00 |
| 21-26: 24-Arkham Asylum story. 25-Inferior Five app. 26-Last Grant Morrison scripts; part photo-c | .40 | 1.25 | 2.50 |
| 27-34 | .25 | .75 | 1.50 |

**ANIMAL WORLD, THE** (See 4-Color Comics No. 713)

**ANIMATED COMICS**
No date given (Summer, 1947?)
E. C. Comics

| | Good | Fine | N-Mint |
|---|---|---|---|
| 1 (Rare) | 57.00 | 171.00 | 400.00 |

**ANIMATED FUNNY COMIC TUNES** (See Funny Tunes)

**ANIMATED MOVIE-TUNES** (Movie Tunes No. 3)
Fall, 1945 - No. 2, Sum, 1946
Margood Publishing Corp. (Timely)

| | Good | Fine | N-Mint |
|---|---|---|---|
| 1,2-Super Rabbit, Ziggy Pig & Silly Seal | 8.00 | 24.00 | 56.00 |

**ANIMAX**
Dec, 1986 - No. 4, June, 1987
Star Comics (Marvel)

| | Good | Fine | N-Mint |
|---|---|---|---|
| 1-4: Based on toys | | .40 | .80 |

**ANNETTE** (See 4-Color Comics No. 905)

**ANNETTE'S LIFE STORY** (See 4-Color No. 1100)

**ANNIE**
Oct, 1982 - No. 2, Nov, 1982 (60 cents)
Marvel Comics Group

| | Good | Fine | N-Mint |
|---|---|---|---|
| 1,2-Movie adaptation | | .30 | .60 |
| Treasury Edition (Tabloid size) | .35 | 1.00 | 2.00 |

**ANNIE OAKLEY** (Also see Tessie The Typist #19, Two-Gun Kid & Wild Western)
Spring, 1948 - No. 4, 11/48; No. 5, 6/55 - No. 11, 6/56
Marvel/Atlas Comics(MPI No. 1-4/CDS No. 5 on)

| | Good | Fine | N-Mint |
|---|---|---|---|
| 1 (1st Series, '48)-Hedy Devine app. | 18.50 | 56.00 | 130.00 |
| 2 (7/48, 52 pgs.)-Kurtzman-a, "Hey Look," 1 pg; Intro. Lana; Hedy Devine app; Captain Tootsie by Beck | 13.00 | 40.00 | 90.00 |
| 3,4 | 10.00 | 30.00 | 70.00 |
| 5 (2nd Series)(1955)-Reinman-a | 6.50 | 19.00 | 45.00 |
| 6-9: 6,8-Woodbridge-a. 9-Williamson-a (4 pgs.) | 5.00 | 15.00 | 35.00 |
| 10,11: 11-Severin-c | 4.30 | 13.00 | 30.00 |

**ANNIE OAKLEY AND TAGG** (TV)
1953 - No. 18, Jan-Mar, 1959; July, 1965 (all photo-c)
Dell Publishing Co./Gold Key

| | Good | Fine | N-Mint |
|---|---|---|---|
| 4-Color 438 (#1) | 8.50 | 25.50 | 60.00 |
| 4-Color 481,575 | 5.30 | 16.00 | 38.00 |
| 4(7-9/55)-10 | 4.30 | 13.00 | 30.00 |
| 11-18(1-3/59) | 3.60 | 11.00 | 25.00 |
| 1(7/65-Gold Key)-Photo-c | 3.00 | 9.00 | 21.00 |

NOTE: ***Manning** a-13. Photo back c-4, 9, 11.*

**ANOTHER WORLD** (See Strange Stories From . . .)

**ANTHRO** (See Showcase #74)
July-Aug, 1968 - No. 6, July-Aug, 1969
National Periodical Publications

| | Good | Fine | N-Mint |
|---|---|---|---|
| 1-Howie Post-a in all | 2.15 | 6.50 | 15.00 |
| 2-6: 6-Wood-c/a (inks) | 1.50 | 4.50 | 10.00 |

**ANTONY AND CLEOPATRA** (See Ideal, a Classical Comic)

**ANYTHING GOES**
Oct, 1986 - No. 6, 1987 ($2.00, mini-series, mature readers)
Fantagraphics Books (#1-5: color & B&W; #6: B&W)

| | Good | Fine | N-Mint |
|---|---|---|---|
| 1-Flaming Carrot app. (1st in color?) | .60 | 1.75 | 3.50 |
| 2-4,6: 2-Miller-c(p); Alan Moore scripts. 3-Capt. Jack, Cerebus app.; Cerebus-c by N. Adams. 4-Perez-c | .35 | 1.00 | 2.00 |
| 5-1st color Teenage Mutant Ninja Turtles app. | .60 | 1.75 | 3.50 |

**A-1 COMICS** (A-1 appears on covers No. 1-17 only)(See individual title listings. 1st two issues not numbered.)
1944 - No. 139, Sept-Oct, 1955 (No #2)
Life's Romances Publ.-No. 1/Compix/Magazine Ent.

| | Good | Fine | N-Mint |
|---|---|---|---|
| nn-Kerry Drake, Johnny Devildog, Rocky, Streamer Kelly (Slightly large size) | 13.00 | 40.00 | 90.00 |
| 1-Dotty Dripple (1 pg.), Mr. Ex, Bush Berry, Rocky, Lew Loyal (20 pgs.) | 5.00 | 15.00 | 35.00 |
| 3-8,10-Texas Slim & Dirty Dalton, The Corsair, Teddy Rich, Dotty Dripple, Inca Dinca, Tommy Tinker, Little Mexico & Tugboat Tim, The Masquerader & others. 8-Intro. Rodeo Ryan | 2.30 | 7.00 | 16.00 |
| 9-Texas Slim (all) | 2.30 | 7.00 | 16.00 |
| 11-Teena | 3.00 | 9.00 | 21.00 |
| 12,15-Teena | 2.30 | 7.00 | 16.00 |
| 13-Guns of Fact & Fiction (1948). Used in **SOTI**, pg. 19; Ingels & Johnny Craig-a | 13.00 | 40.00 | 90.00 |
| 14-Tim Holt Western Adventures #1 (1948) | 38.00 | 115.00 | 265.00 |
| 16-Vacation Comics | 1.70 | 5.00 | 12.00 |
| 17-Tim Holt #2. Last issue to carry A-1 on cover (9-10/48) | 24.00 | 72.00 | 165.00 |
| 18,20-Jimmy Durante; photo covers | 17.00 | 51.00 | 120.00 |
| 19-Tim Holt #3 | 16.00 | 48.00 | 110.00 |
| 21-Joan of Arc(1949)-Movie adaptation; Ingrid Bergman photo-covers & interior photos; Whitney-a | 14.00 | 43.00 | 100.00 |
| 22-Dick Powell(1949) | 10.00 | 30.00 | 70.00 |
| 23-Cowboys 'N' Indians #6 | 3.00 | 9.00 | 21.00 |
| 24-Trail Colt #1-Frazetta, r-in Manhunt #13; Ingels-c; L. B. Cole-a | 29.00 | 85.00 | 200.00 |
| 25-Fibber McGee & Molly(1949) (Radio) | 4.00 | 12.00 | 28.00 |
| 26-Trail Colt #2-Ingels-c | 23.00 | 70.00 | 160.00 |
| 27-Ghost Rider #1(1950)-Origin Ghost Rider | 36.00 | 107.00 | 250.00 |
| 28-Christmas-(Koko & Kola #6)(1950) | 1.70 | 5.00 | 12.00 |
| 29-Ghost Rider #2-Frazetta-c (1950) | 36.00 | 107.00 | 250.00 |
| 30-Jet Powers #1-Powell-a | 17.00 | 51.00 | 120.00 |
| 31-Ghost Rider #3-Frazetta-c & origin ('51) | 36.00 | 107.00 | 250.00 |
| 32-Jet Powers #2 | 12.00 | 36.00 | 84.00 |
| 33-Muggsy Mouse #1('51) | 2.30 | 7.00 | 16.00 |
| 34-Ghost Rider #4-Frazetta-c (1951) | 36.00 | 107.00 | 250.00 |
| 35-Jet Powers #3-Williamson/Evans-a | 21.50 | 64.00 | 150.00 |
| 36-Muggsy Mouse #2; Racist-c | 4.30 | 13.00 | 30.00 |
| 37-Ghost Rider #5-Frazetta-c (1951) | 36.00 | 107.00 | 250.00 |
| 38-Jet Powers #4-Williamson & Wood-a | 21.50 | 64.00 | 150.00 |
| 39-Muggsy Mouse #3 | 1.30 | 4.00 | 9.00 |
| 40-Dogface Dooley #1('51) | 2.65 | 8.00 | 18.00 |
| 41-Cowboys 'N' Indians #7 | 2.15 | 6.50 | 15.00 |
| 42-Best of the West #1-Powell-a | 23.00 | 70.00 | 160.00 |

*Animal Man #1, © DC*

*A-1 Comics #1, © ME*

*A-1 Comics #25, © ME*

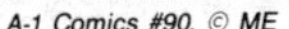
A-1 Comics #90, © ME

A-1 Comics #123, © ME

Apache #1, © FH

| | Good | Fine | N-Mint |
|---|---|---|---|
| 43-Dogface Dooley #2 | 1.70 | 5.00 | 12.00 |
| 44-Ghost Rider #6 | 13.00 | 40.00 | 90.00 |
| 45-American Air Forces #5-Powell-c/a | 2.15 | 6.50 | 15.00 |
| 46-Best of the West #2 | 11.50 | 34.00 | 80.00 |
| 47-Thun'da, King of the Congo #1-Frazetta-c/a('52) | 83.00 | 250.00 | 580.00 |
| 48-Cowboys 'N' Indians #8 | 2.15 | 6.50 | 15.00 |
| 49-Dogface Dooley #3 | 1.70 | 5.00 | 12.00 |
| 50-Danger Is Their Business #11 (1952)-Powell-a | 5.70 | 17.00 | 40.00 |
| 51-Ghost Rider #7 ('52) | 13.00 | 40.00 | 90.00 |
| 52-Best of the West #3 | 10.00 | 30.00 | 70.00 |
| 53-Dogface Dooley #4 | 1.70 | 5.00 | 12.00 |
| 54-American Air Forces #6(8/52)-Powell-a | 2.15 | 6.50 | 15.00 |
| 55-U.S. Marines #5-Powell-a | 2.65 | 8.00 | 18.00 |
| 56-Thun'da #2-Powell-c/a | 12.00 | 36.00 | 84.00 |
| 57-Ghost Rider #8 | 11.00 | 32.00 | 75.00 |
| 58-American Air Forces #7-Powell-a | 2.15 | 6.50 | 15.00 |
| 59-Best of the West #4 | 10.00 | 30.00 | 70.00 |
| 60-The U.S. Marines #6-Powell-a | 2.65 | 8.00 | 18.00 |
| 61-Space Ace #5(1953)-Guardineer-a | 19.00 | 56.00 | 130.00 |
| 62-Starr Flagg, Undercover Girl #5 (#1) | 22.00 | 65.00 | 155.00 |
| 63-Manhunt #13-Frazetta reprinted from A-1 #24 | 17.00 | 51.00 | 120.00 |
| 64-Dogface Dooley #5 | 1.70 | 5.00 | 12.00 |
| 65-American Air Forces #8-Powell-a | 2.15 | 6.50 | 15.00 |
| 66-Best of the West #5 | 10.00 | 30.00 | 70.00 |
| 67-American Air Forces #9-Powell-a | 2.15 | 6.50 | 15.00 |
| 68-U.S. Marines #7-Powell-a | 2.65 | 8.00 | 18.00 |
| 69-Ghost Rider #9(10/52) | 11.00 | 32.00 | 75.00 |
| 70-Best of the West #6 | 7.00 | 21.00 | 50.00 |
| 71-Ghost Rider #10(12/52) | 11.00 | 32.00 | 75.00 |
| 72-U.S. Marines #8-Powell-a(3) | 2.65 | 8.00 | 18.00 |
| 73-Thun'da #3-Powell-c/a | 9.00 | 27.00 | 62.00 |
| 74-American Air Forces #10-Powell-a | 2.15 | 6.50 | 15.00 |
| 75-Ghost Rider #11(3/52) | 8.50 | 25.50 | 60.00 |
| 76-Best of the West #7 | 7.00 | 21.00 | 50.00 |
| 77-Manhunt #14 | 11.50 | 34.00 | 80.00 |
| 78-Thun'da #4-Powell-c/a | 9.00 | 27.00 | 62.00 |
| 79-American Air Forces #11-Powell-a | 2.15 | 6.50 | 15.00 |
| 80-Ghost Rider #12(6/52) | 8.50 | 25.50 | 60.00 |
| 81-Best of the West #8 | 7.00 | 21.00 | 50.00 |
| 82-Cave Girl #11(1953)-Powell-c/a; origin (#1) | 23.00 | 70.00 | 160.00 |
| 83-Thun'da #5-Powell-c/a | 8.00 | 24.00 | 56.00 |
| 84-Ghost Rider #13(7-8/53) | 8.50 | 25.50 | 60.00 |
| 85-Best of the West #9 | 7.00 | 21.00 | 50.00 |
| 86-Thun'da #6-Powell-c/a | 8.00 | 24.00 | 56.00 |
| 87-Best of the West #10(9-10/53) | 7.00 | 21.00 | 50.00 |
| 88-Bobby Benson's B-Bar-B Riders #20 | 4.00 | 12.00 | 28.00 |
| 89-Home Run #3-Powell-a; Stan Musial photo-c | 10.00 | 30.00 | 70.00 |
| 90-Red Hawk #11(1953)-Powell-c/a | 5.00 | 15.00 | 35.00 |
| 91-American Air Forces #12-Powell-a | 2.15 | 6.50 | 15.00 |
| 92-Dream Book of Romance #5-photo-c; Guardineer-a | 3.00 | 9.00 | 21.00 |
| 93-Great Western #8('54)-Origin The Ghost Rider; Powell-a | 11.00 | 32.00 | 75.00 |
| 94-White Indian #11-Frazetta-a(r); Powell-c | 16.00 | 48.00 | 110.00 |
| 95-Muggsy Mouse #4 | 1.30 | 4.00 | 9.00 |
| 96-Cave Girl #12, with Thun'da; Powell-c/a | 17.00 | 51.00 | 120.00 |
| 97-Best of the West #11 | 7.00 | 21.00 | 50.00 |
| 98-Undercover Girl #6-Powell-c | 20.00 | 60.00 | 140.00 |
| 99-Muggsy Mouse #5 | 1.30 | 4.00 | 9.00 |
| 100-Badmen of the West #1-Meskin-a(?) | 12.00 | 36.00 | 85.00 |
| 101-White Indian #12-Frazetta-a(r) | 16.00 | 48.00 | 110.00 |
| 101-Dream Book of Romance #6 (4-6/54); Marlon Brando photo-c; Powell, Bolle, Guardineer-a | 7.00 | 21.00 | 50.00 |
| 103-Best of the West #12-Powell-a | 7.00 | 21.00 | 50.00 |
| 104-White Indian #13-Frazetta-a(r)('54) | 16.00 | 48.00 | 110.00 |
| 105-Great Western #9-Ghost Rider app.; Powell-a, 6 pgs.; Bolle-c | 5.00 | 15.00 | 35.00 |
| 106-Dream Book of Love #1 (6-7/54)-Powell, Bolle-a; Montgomery Clift, Donna Reed photo-c | 4.50 | 14.00 | 32.00 |
| 107-Hot Dog #1 | 3.00 | 9.00 | 21.00 |
| 108-Red Fox #15 (1954)-L.B. Cole c/a; Powell-a | 9.00 | 27.00 | 62.00 |
| 109-Dream Book of Romance #7 (7-8/54). Powell-a; photo-c | 3.00 | 9.00 | 21.00 |
| 110-Dream Book of Romance #8 (10/54) | 3.00 | 9.00 | 21.00 |
| 111-I'm a Cop #1 ('54); drug mention story; Powell-a | 6.00 | 18.00 | 42.00 |
| 112-Ghost Rider #14 ('54) | 8.50 | 25.50 | 60.00 |
| 113-Great Western #10; Powell-a | 5.00 | 15.00 | 35.00 |
| 114-Dream Book of Love #2-Guardineer, Bolle-a; Peter Lorre, Victor Mature photo-c | 3.50 | 10.50 | 24.00 |
| 115-Hot Dog #3 | 1.70 | 5.00 | 12.00 |
| 116-Cave Girl #13-Powell-c/a | 17.00 | 51.00 | 120.00 |
| 117-White Indian #14 | 6.50 | 19.50 | 45.00 |
| 118-Undercover Girl #7-Powell-c | 20.00 | 60.00 | 140.00 |
| 119-Straight Arrow's Fury #1 (origin); Fred Meagher-c/a | 6.00 | 18.00 | 42.00 |
| 120-Badmen of the West #2 | 7.00 | 21.00 | 50.00 |
| 121-Mysteries of Scotland Yard #1; reprinted from Manhunt (5 stories) | 6.50 | 19.00 | 45.00 |
| 122-Black Phantom #1(11/54) | 17.00 | 51.00 | 120.00 |
| 123-Dream Book of Love #3(10-11/54) | 3.00 | 9.00 | 21.00 |
| 124-Dream Book of Romance #8(10-11/54) | 3.00 | 9.00 | 21.00 |
| 125-Cave Girl #14-Powell-c/a | 17.00 | 51.00 | 120.00 |
| 126-I'm a Cop #2-Powell-a | 3.15 | 9.50 | 22.00 |
| 127-Great Western #11('54)-Powell-a | 5.00 | 15.00 | 35.00 |
| 128-I'm a Cop #3-Powell-a | 3.15 | 9.50 | 22.00 |
| 129-The Avenger #1('55)-Powell-c | 17.00 | 51.00 | 120.00 |
| 130-Strongman #1-Powell-a | 10.00 | 30.00 | 70.00 |
| 131-The Avenger #2('55)-Powell-c/a | 10.00 | 30.00 | 70.00 |
| 132-Strongman #2 | 9.00 | 27.00 | 62.00 |
| 133-The Avenger #3-Powell-c/a | 10.00 | 30.00 | 70.00 |
| 134-Strongman #3 | 9.00 | 27.00 | 62.00 |
| 135-White Indian #15 | 6.50 | 19.50 | 45.00 |
| 136-Hot Dog #4 | 1.70 | 5.00 | 12.00 |
| 137-Africa #1-Powell-c/a(4) | 11.50 | 34.00 | 80.00 |
| 138-The Avenger #4-Powell-c/a | 10.00 | 30.00 | 70.00 |
| 139-Strongman #4-Powell-a | 9.00 | 27.00 | 62.00 |

NOTE: *Bolle a-110. Photo-c-110.*

**APACHE**

1951

Fiction House Magazines

| | Good | Fine | N-Mint |
|---|---|---|---|
| 1-Baker-c | 9.00 | 27.00 | 62.00 |
| I.W. Reprint No. 1 | 1.00 | 3.00 | 6.00 |

**APACHE HUNTER**

1954 (18 pgs. in color) (promo copy) (saddle stitched)

Creative Pictorials

| | Good | Fine | N-Mint |
|---|---|---|---|
| nn-Severin, Heath stories | 13.00 | 39.00 | 90.00 |

**APACHE KID** (Formerly Reno Browne; Western Gunfighters #20 on)
(Also see Two-Gun Western & Wild Western)

No. 53, 12/50 - No. 10, 1/52; No. 11, 12/54 - No. 19, 4/56

Marvel/Atlas Comics(MPC No. 53-10/CPS No. 11 on)

| | Good | Fine | N-Mint |
|---|---|---|---|
| 53(#1)-Apache Kid & his horse Nightwind (origin), Red Hawkins by Syd Shores begins | 10.00 | 30.00 | 70.00 |
| 2(2/51) | 5.30 | 16.00 | 38.00 |
| 3-5 | 3.60 | 11.00 | 25.00 |
| 6-10 (1951-52) | 2.85 | 8.50 | 20.00 |

| | Good | Fine | N-Mint |
|---|---|---|---|
| 11-19 (1954-56) | 2.30 | 7.00 | 16.00 |

NOTE: ***Heath** c-11, 13. **Maneely** a-53; c-53(#1), 12, 14-16. **Powell** a-14. **Severin** c-17.*

**APACHE MASSACRE** (See Chief Victorio's. . .)

**APACHE TRAIL**
Sept, 1957 - No. 4, June, 1958
Steinway/America's Best

| | Good | Fine | N-Mint |
|---|---|---|---|
| 1 | 3.70 | 11.00 | 26.00 |
| 2-4: 2-Tuska-a | 2.00 | 6.00 | 14.00 |

**APPLESEED**
Sept, 1988 - Book 3, Vol. 5, Mar, 1990 (B&W, $2.50-$2.75, 52pgs)
Eclipse Comics

| | Good | Fine | N-Mint |
|---|---|---|---|
| Book One, Volume 1 ($2.50) | 2.00 | 6.00 | 12.00 |
| Book One, Volume 2-5: 5-(1/89, $2.75 cover) | .50 | 1.50 | 3.00 |
| Book Two, Vol. 1(2/89) -5(7/89): Art Adams-c | .45 | 1.40 | 2.75 |
| Book Three, Volume 1(8/89)-4 ($2.75) | .45 | 1.40 | 2.75 |
| Book Three, Volume 5 ($3.50) | .60 | 1.75 | 3.50 |

**APPROVED COMICS**
March, 1954 - No. 12, Aug, 1954 (All painted-c)
St. John Publishing Co. (Most have no c-price)

| | Good | Fine | N-Mint |
|---|---|---|---|
| 1-The Hawk #5-r | 4.00 | 12.00 | 28.00 |
| 2-Invisible Boy-r(3/54)-Origin; Saunders-c | 8.00 | 24.00 | 56.00 |
| 3-Wild Boy of the Congo #11-r(4/54) | 4.00 | 12.00 | 28.00 |
| 4,5: 4-Kid Cowboy-r. 5-Fly Boy-r | 4.00 | 12.00 | 28.00 |
| 6-Daring Adv.-r(5/54); Krigstein-a(2); Baker-c | 5.70 | 17.00 | 40.00 |
| 7-The Hawk #6-r | 4.00 | 12.00 | 28.00 |
| 8-Crime on the Run; Powell-a; Saunders-c | 4.00 | 12.00 | 28.00 |
| 9-Western Bandit Trails #3-r, with new-c; Baker-c/a | 5.30 | 16.00 | 38.00 |
| 11-Fightin' Marines #3-r; Canteen Kate app; Baker-c/a | 5.70 | 17.00 | 40.00 |
| 12-North West Mounties #4-r(8/54); new Baker-c | 6.00 | 18.00 | 42.00 |

**AQUAMAN** (See Adventure #260, Brave & the Bold, DC Comics Presents #5, DC Special #28, DC Special Series #1, DC Super Stars #7, Detective, Justice League of America, More Fun #73, Showcase #30-33, Super DC Giant, Super Friends, and World's Finest Comics)

**AQUAMAN**
Jan-Feb, 1962 - No. 56, Mar-Apr, 1971; No. 57, Aug-Sept, 1977 - No. 63, Aug-Sept, 1978
National Periodical Publications/DC Comics

| | Good | Fine | N-Mint |
|---|---|---|---|
| 1-Intro. Quisp | 26.00 | 78.00 | 180.00 |
| 2 | 11.50 | 34.00 | 80.00 |
| 3-5 | 7.85 | 23.50 | 55.00 |
| 6-10 | 5.00 | 15.00 | 35.00 |
| 11-20: 11-1st app. Mera. 18-Aquaman weds Mera; JLA cameo | 3.60 | 11.00 | 25.00 |
| 21-32,34-40: 23-Birth of Aquababy. 26-Huntress app.(3-4/66). 29-1st app. Ocean Master, Aquaman's step-brother | 2.15 | 6.50 | 15.00 |
| 33-1st app. Aqua-Girl | 2.65 | 8.00 | 18.00 |
| 41-47,49 | 1.00 | 3.00 | 6.00 |
| 48-Origin reprinted | 1.15 | 3.50 | 7.00 |
| 50-52-Deadman by Neal Adams | 1.70 | 5.00 | 12.00 |
| 53-56('71): 56-1st app. Crusader | .85 | 2.50 | 5.00 |
| 57('77)-63: 58-Origin retold | .50 | 1.50 | 3.00 |

NOTE: ***Aparo** a-40-59; c-57-60, 63. **Newton** a-60-63.*

**AQUAMAN**
Feb, 1986 - No. 4, May, 1986 (Mini-series)
DC Comics

| | Good | Fine | N-Mint |
|---|---|---|---|
| 1-New costume | .85 | 2.50 | 5.00 |
| 2-4 | .50 | 1.50 | 3.00 |
| Special 1 ('88, $1.50, 52 pgs.) | .35 | 1.00 | 2.00 |

**AQUAMAN**
June, 1989 - No. 5, Oct, 1989 ($1.00, mini-series)
DC Comics

| | Good | Fine | N-Mint |
|---|---|---|---|
| 1-5: Giffen plots/breakdowns; Swan-p | | .50 | 1.00 |
| Special 1 (Legend of. . ., $2.00, 1989, 52 pgs.)-Giffen plots/breakdowns; Swan-p | .35 | 1.00 | 2.00 |

**AQUANAUTS** (See 4-Color No. 1197)

**ARABIAN NIGHTS** (See Cinema Comics Herald)

**ARACHNOPHOBIA**
1990 ($5.95, color. 68 pg. graphic novel)
Hollywood Comics (Disney Comics)

| | Good | Fine | N-Mint |
|---|---|---|---|
| nn-Movie adaptation; Spiegle-a | 1.00 | 3.00 | 6.00 |
| Comic edition ($2.95, 68 pgs.) | .50 | 1.50 | 3.00 |

**ARAK/SON OF THUNDER** (See Warlord #48)
Sept, 1981 - No. 50, Nov, 1985
DC Comics

| | Good | Fine | N-Mint |
|---|---|---|---|
| 1-Origin; 1st app. Angelica, Princess of White Cathay | | .50 | 1.00 |
| 2-50: 3-Intro Valda, The Iron Maiden. 12-Origin Valda. 20-Origin Angelica. 24-$1.00 size. 50-double size | | .50 | 1.00 |
| Annual 1(10/84) | | .50 | 1.00 |

**ARCHIE AND BIG ETHEL**
1982 (69 cents)
Spire Christian Comics (Fleming H. Revell Co.)

| | Good | Fine | N-Mint |
|---|---|---|---|
| nn | | .30 | .60 |

**ARCHIE AND ME** (See Archie Giant Series Mag. 578, 591, 603, 616)
Oct, 1964 - No. 162, 1987
Archie Publications

| | Good | Fine | N-Mint |
|---|---|---|---|
| 1 | 10.00 | 30.00 | 70.00 |
| 2 | 4.50 | 14.00 | 32.00 |
| 3-5 | 2.30 | 7.00 | 16.00 |
| 6-10 | 1.15 | 3.50 | 8.00 |
| 11-20 | .70 | 2.00 | 4.00 |
| 21-30: 26-X-Mas-c | .50 | 1.50 | 3.00 |
| 31-63: 43-63-(All Giants) | | .60 | 1.20 |
| 64-162-(Regular size) | | .30 | .60 |

**ARCHIE AND MR. WEATHERBEE**
1980 (59 cents)
Spire Christian Comics (Fleming H. Revell Co.)

| | Good | Fine | N-Mint |
|---|---|---|---|
| nn | | .30 | .60 |

**ARCHIE. . .ARCHIE ANDREWS, WHERE ARE YOU?** (. . .Comics Digest No. 9, 10; . . .Comics Digest Mag. No. 11 on)
Feb, 1977 - Present (Digest size, 160-128 pages)
Archie Publications

| | Good | Fine | N-Mint |
|---|---|---|---|
| 1 | .35 | 1.00 | 2.00 |
| 2,3,5,7-9-N. Adams-a; 8-r-/origin The Fly by S&K. 9-Steel Sterling-r | .50 | 1.50 | 3.00 |
| 4,6,10-72 ($1.00-$1.50): 17-Katy Keene story | | .50 | 1.00 |

**ARCHIE AS PUREHEART THE POWERFUL**
Sept, 1966 - No. 6, Nov, 1967
Archie Publications (Radio Comics)

| | Good | Fine | N-Mint |
|---|---|---|---|
| 1 | 5.00 | 15.00 | 35.00 |
| 2 | 3.00 | 9.00 | 21.00 |
| 3-6 | 1.70 | 5.00 | 12.00 |

NOTE: *Evilheart cameos in all. Title: . . .As Capt. Pureheart the Powerful-No. 4, 6; . . .As Capt. Pureheart-No. 5.*

**ARCHIE AT RIVERDALE HIGH** (See Archie Giant Series Magazine 573, 586, 604 & Riverdale High)
Aug, 1972 - No. 114, 1987
Archie Publications

*Appleseed Book 1, Vol. 4, © Eclipse*

*Approved Comics #6, © STJ*

*Aquaman #3 (5-6/62), © DC*

Archie Comics #1, © AP

Archie Comics #78, © AP

Archie Comics #132, © AP

| | Good | Fine | N-Mint |
|---|---|---|---|
| 1 | 3.00 | 9.00 | 21.00 |
| 2 | 1.30 | 4.00 | 9.00 |
| 3-5 | .70 | 2.00 | 4.00 |
| 6-10 | .35 | 1.00 | 2.00 |
| 11-30 | | .50 | 1.00 |
| 31-114: 96-Anti-smoking issue | | .30 | .60 |

**ARCHIE COMICS** (Archie No. 158 on)(See Christmas & Archie, Everything's. . ., Explorers of the Unknown, Jackpot, Little. . ., Oxydol-Dreft, Pep & Riverdale High)
(First Teen-age comic)(Radio show 1st aired 6/2/45, by NBC)
Winter, 1942-43 - No. 19, 3-4/46; No. 20, 5-6/46 - Present
MLJ Magazines No. 1-19/Archie Publ.No. 20 on

| | Good | Fine | VF-NM | NM/Mint |
|---|---|---|---|---|
| 1 (Scarce)-Jughead, Veronica app. | 367.00 | 920.00 | 2200.00 | 4000.00 |

(Estimated up to 90 total copies exist, 5 in NM/Mint)

| | Good | Fine | N-Mint |
|---|---|---|---|
| 2 | 118.00 | 354.00 | 825.00 |
| 3 (60 pgs.) | 86.00 | 260.00 | 600.00 |
| 4,5 | 59.00 | 178.00 | 415.00 |
| 6-10 | 41.00 | 122.00 | 285.00 |
| 11-20: 15,17,18-Dotty & Ditto by Woggon. 16-Woggon-a | 25.00 | 75.00 | 175.00 |
| 21-30: 23-Betty & Veronica by Woggon. 25-Woggon-a | 17.00 | 51.00 | 120.00 |
| 31-40 | 11.00 | 32.00 | 75.00 |
| 41-50 | 7.00 | 21.00 | 50.00 |
| 51-70 (1954): 51,65-70-Katy Keene app. | 4.00 | 12.00 | 28.00 |
| 71-99: 72-74-Katy Keene app. | 2.35 | 7.00 | 16.00 |
| 100 | 2.65 | 8.00 | 18.00 |
| 101-130 (1962) | 1.15 | 3.50 | 8.00 |
| 131-160 | .70 | 2.00 | 4.00 |
| 161-200 | .40 | 1.25 | 2.50 |
| 201-240 | | .60 | 1.20 |
| 241-282 | | .50 | 1.00 |
| 283-Cover/story plugs "International Children's Appeal" which was a fraudulent charity, according to TV's 20/20 news program broadcast July 20, 1979 | | .60 | 1.25 |
| 284-388: 300-Anniversary issue | | .50 | 1.00 |
| Annual 1('50)-116 pgs. (Scarce) | 86.00 | 257.00 | 600.00 |
| Annual 2('51) | 43.00 | 130.00 | 300.00 |
| Annual 3('52) | 25.00 | 75.00 | 175.00 |
| Annual 4,5(1953-54) | 18.00 | 54.00 | 125.00 |
| Annual 6-10(1955-59) | 10.00 | 30.00 | 70.00 |
| Annual 11-15(1960-65) | 4.30 | 13.00 | 30.00 |
| Annual 16-20(1966-70) | 1.50 | 4.50 | 10.00 |
| Annual 21-26(1971-75) | .60 | 1.75 | 3.50 |
| Annual Digest 27('75)-58('83-'90)(. . .Magazine #35 on) | | .60 | 1.20 |
| . . .All-Star Specials(Winter '75)-$1.25; 6 remaindered Archie comics rebound in each; titles: "The World of Giant Comics," "Giant Grab Bag of Comics," "Triple Giant Comics," and "Giant Spec. Comics" | .70 | 2.00 | 4.00 |
| Mini-Comics (1970-Fairmont Potato Chips Giveaway-Miniature)(8 issues-nn's., 8 pgs. each) | 1.00 | 3.00 | 7.00 |
| Official Boy Scout Outfitter(1946)-9½x6½", 16 pgs., B. R. Baker Co. (Scarce) | 25.00 | 75.00 | 175.00 |
| Shoe Store giveaway (1948, Feb?) | 8.50 | 25.50 | 60.00 |

**ARCHIE COMICS DIGEST** (. . .Magazine No. 37-95)
Aug, 1973 - Present (Small size, 160-128 pages)
Archie Publications

| | Good | Fine | N-Mint |
|---|---|---|---|
| 1 | 2.50 | 7.50 | 15.00 |
| 2 | 1.35 | 4.00 | 8.00 |
| 3-5 | .70 | 2.00 | 4.00 |
| 6-10 | .25 | .75 | 1.50 |
| 11-33: 32,33-The Fly-r by S&K | | .50 | 1.00 |
| 34-106: 36-Katy Keene story; 88,94,100,106-Xmas-c | | .40 | .80 |

NOTE: ***Neal Adams*** *a-1, 2, 4, 5, 19-21, 24, 25, 27, 29, 31, 33.*

**ARCHIE GETS A JOB**
1977
Spire Christian Comics (Fleming H. Revell Co.)

| | Good | Fine | N-Mint |
|---|---|---|---|
| nn | | .30 | .60 |

**ARCHIE GIANT SERIES MAGAZINE**
1954 - Present (No No. 36-135, no No. 252-451)
Archie Publications

| | Good | Fine | N-Mint |
|---|---|---|---|
| 1-Archie's Christmas Stocking | 54.00 | 160.00 | 375.00 |
| 2-Archie's Christmas Stocking('55) | 29.00 | 85.00 | 200.00 |
| 3-6-Archie's Christmas Stocking('56-'59) | 17.00 | 51.00 | 120.00 |
| 7-10: 7-Katy Keene Holiday Fun(9/60). 8-Betty & Veronica Summer Fun (10/60). 9-The World of Jughead (12/60). 10-Archie's Christmas Stocking (1/61) | 12.00 | 36.00 | 84.00 |
| 11-20: 11-Betty & Veronica Spectacular (6/61). 12-Katy Keene Holiday Fun (9/61). 13-Betty & Veronica Summer Fun (10/61). 14-The World of Jughead (12/61). 15-Archie's Christmas Stocking (1/62). 16-Betty & Veronica Spectacular (6/62). 17-Archie's Jokes (9/62); Katy Keene app. 18-Betty & Veronica Summer Fun (10/62). 19-The World of Jughead (12/62). 20-Archie's Christmas Stocking (1/63) | 8.50 | 25.50 | 60.00 |
| 21-30: 21-Betty & Veronica Spectacular (6/63). 22-Archie's Jokes (9/63). 23-Betty & Veronica Summer Fun (10/63). 24-The World of Jughead (12/63). 25-Archie's Christmas Stocking (1/64). 26-Betty & Veronica Spectacular (6/64). 27-Archie's Jokes (8/64). 28-Betty & Veronica Summer Fun (9/64). 29-Around the World with Archie (10/64). 30-The World of Jughead (12/64) | 4.30 | 13.00 | 30.00 |
| 31-35,136-141: 31-Archie's Christmas Stocking (1/65). 32-Betty & Veronica Spectacular (6/65). 33-Archie's Jokes (8/65). 34-Betty & Veronica Summer Fun (9/65). 35-Around the World with Archie (10/65). 136-The World of Jughead (12/65). 137-Archie's Christmas Stocking (1/66). 138-Betty & Veronica Spectacular (6/66). 139-Archie's Jokes (6/66). 140-Betty & Veronica Summer Fun (8/66). 141-Around the World with Archie (9/66) | 2.85 | 8.50 | 20.00 |
| 142-Archie's Super-Hero Special (10/66)-Origin Capt. Pureheart, Capt. Hero, and Evilheart | 3.50 | 10.50 | 24.00 |
| 143-160: 143-The World of Jughead (12/66). 144-Archie's Christmas Stocking (1/67). 145-Betty & Veronica Spectacular (6/67). 146-Archie's Jokes (6/67). 147-Betty & Veronica Summer Fun (8/67) 148-World of Archie (9/67). 149-World of Jughead (10/67). 150-Archie's Christmas Stocking (1/68). 151-World of Archie (2/68) 152-World of Jughead (2/68). 153-Betty & Veronica Spectacular (6/68). 154-Archie Jokes (6/68). 155-Betty & Veronica Summer Fun (8/68). 156-World of Archie (10/68). 157-World of Jughead (12/68). 158-Archie's Christmas Stocking (1/69). 159-Betty & Veronica Christmas Spect. (1/69). 160-World of Archie (2/69) | 1.35 | 4.00 | 8.00 |

161-200: 161-World of Jughead (2/69). 162-Betty & Veronica Spectacular (6/69). 163-Archie's Jokes (8/69). 164-Betty & Veronica Summer Fun (9/69). 165-World of Archie (9/69). 166-World of Jughead (9/69). 167-Archie's Christmas Stocking (1/70). 168-Betty & Veronica Christmas Spect. (1/70). 169-Archie's Christmas Love-In (1/70). 170-Jughead's Eat-Out Comic Book Mag. (12/69) 171-World of Archie (2/70). 172-World of Jughead (2/70). 173-Betty & Veronica Spectacular (6/70). 174-Archie's Jokes (8/70) 175-Betty & Veronica Summer Fun (9/70). 176-Li'l Jinx Giant Laugh-Out (8/70). 177-World of Archie (9/70). 178-World of Jughead (9/70). 179-Archie's Christmas Stocking (1/71). 180-Betty & Veronica Christmas Spect. (1/71). 181-Archie's Christmas Love-In (1/71). 182-World of Archie (2/71). 183-World of Jughead (2/71). 184-Betty & Veronica Spectacular (6/71). 185-Li'l Jinx

| | Good | Fine | N-Mint |
|---|---|---|---|

Giant Laugh-Out (6/71). 186-Archie's Jokes (8/71). 187-Betty & Veronica Summer Fun (9/71). 188-World of Archie (9/71). 189-World of Jughead (9/71). 190-Archie's Christmas Stocking (12/71). 191-Betty & Veronica Christmas Spectacular (2/72). 192-Archie's Christmas Love-In (1/72). 193-World of Archie (3/72). 194-World of Jughead (4/72). 195-Li'l Jinx Christmas Bag (1/72). 196-Sabrina's Christmas Magic (1/72). 197-Betty & Veronica Spectacular (6/72). 198-Archie's Jokes (8/72). 199-Betty & Veronica Summer Fun (9/72). 200-World of Archie (10/72) .50 1.50 3.00

201-251: 201-Betty & Veronica Spectacular (10/72). 202-World of Jughead (11/72). 203-Archie's Christmas Stocking (12/72). 204-Betty & Veronica Christmas Spectacular (2/73). 205-Archie's Christmas Love-In (1/73). 206-Li'l Jinx Christmas Bag (12/72). 207-Sabrina's Christmas Magic (12/72). 208-World of Archie (3/73). 209-World of Jughead (4/73). 210-Betty & Veronica Spectacular (6/73). 211-Archie's Jokes (8/73). 212-Betty & Veronica Summer Fun (9/73). 213-World of Archie (10/73). 214-Betty & Veronica Spectacular (10/73). 215-World of Jughead (11/73). 216-Archie's Christmas Stocking (12/73). 217-Betty & Veronica Christmas Spectacular (2/74). 218-Archie's Christmas Love-In (1/74). 219-Li'l Jinx Christmas Bag (12/73). 220-Sabrina's Christmas Magic (12/73). 221-Betty & Veronica Spectacular (Advertised as World of Archie) (6/74). 222-Archie's Jokes (Advertised as World of Jughead)(8/74). 223-Li'l Jinx (8/74). 224-Betty & Veronica Summer Fun (9/74). 225-World of Archie (9/74). 226-Betty & Veronica Spectacular (10/74). 227-World of Jughead (10/74). 228-Archie's Christmas Stocking (12/74). 229-Betty & Veronica Christmas Spectacular (12/74). 230-Archie's Christmas Love-In (1/75). 231-Sabrina's Christmas Magic (1/75). 232-World of Archie (3/75). 233-World of Jughead (4/75). 234-Betty & Veronica Spectacular (6/75). 235-Archie's Jokes (8/75). 236-Betty & Veronica Summer Fun (9/75). 237-World of Archie (9/75) 238-Betty & Veronica Spectacular (10/75). 239-World of Jughead (10/75). 240-Archie's Christmas Stocking (12/75). 241-Betty & Veronica Christmas Spectacular (12/75). 242-Archie's Christmas Love-In (1/76). 243-Sabrina's Christmas Magic (1/76). 244-World of Archie (3/76). 245-World of Jughead (4/76). 246-Betty & Veronica Spectacular (6/76). 247-Archie's Jokes (8/76). 248-Betty & Veronica Summer Fun (9/76). 249-World of Archie (9/76). 250-Betty & Veronica Spectacular (10/76). 251-World of Jughead .70 1.40

452-500: 452-Archie's Christmas Stocking (12/76). 453-Betty & Veronica Christmas Spectacular (12/76). 454-Archie's Christmas Love-In (1/77). 455-Sabrina's Christmas Magic (1/77). 456-World of Archie (3/77). 457-World of Jughead (4/77). 458-Betty & Veronica Spectacular (6/77). 459-Archie's Jokes (8/77)-Shows 8/76 in error. 460-Betty & Veronica Summer Fun (9/77). 461-World of Archie (9/77). 462-Betty & Veronica Spectacular (10/77) 463-World of Jughead (10/77). 464-Archie's Christmas Stocking (12/77). 465-Betty & Veronica Christmas Spectacular (12/77). 466-Archie's Christmas Love-In (1/78). 467-Sabrina's Christmas Magic (1/78). 468-World of Archie (2/78). 469-World of Jughead (2/78). 470-Betty & Veronica Spectacular (6/78). 471-Archie's Jokes (8/78). 472-Betty & Veronica Summer Fun (9/78). 473-World of Archie (9/78). 474-Betty & Veronica Spectacular (10/78) 475-World of Jughead (10/78). 476-Archie's Christmas Stocking (12/78). 477-Betty & Veronica Christmas Spectacular (12/78). 478-Archie's Christmas Love-In (1/79). 479-Sabrina Christmas Magic (1/79). 480-The World of Archie (3/79). 481-World of Jughead (4/79). 482-Betty & Veronica Spectacular (6/79). 483-Archie's Jokes (8/79). 484-Betty & Veronica Summer Fun (9/79). 485-The World of Archie (9/79). 486-Betty & Veronica Spectacular (10/79). 487-The World of Jughead (10/79). 488-Archie's Christmas Stocking (12/79). 489-Betty & Veronica Christmas Spectacular (1/80) 490-Archie's Christmas Love-in (1/80). 491-Sabrina's Christmas Magic (1/80). 492-The World of Archie (2/80). 493-The World of Jughead (4/80). 494-Betty & Veronica Spectacular (6/80). 495-Archie's Jokes (8/80). 496-Betty & Veronica Summer Fun (9/80) 497-The World of Archie (9/80). 498-Betty & Veronica Spectacular (10/80). 499-The World of Jughead (10/80). 500-Archie's Christmas Stocking (12/80) each.... .40 .80

501-550: 501-Betty & Veronica Christmas Spectacular (12/80). 502-Archie's Christmas Love-in (1/81). 503-Sabrina Christmas Magic (1/81). 504-The World of Archie (3/81). 505-The World of Jughead (4/81). 506-Betty & Veronica Spectacular (6/81). 507-Archie's Jokes (8/81). 508-Betty & Veronica Summer Fun (9/81). 509-The World of Archie (9/81). 510-Betty & Vernonica Spectacular (9/81) 511-The World of Jughead (10/81). 512-Archie's Christmas Stocking (12/81). 513-Betty & Veronica Christmas Spectacular (12/81) 514-Archie's Christmas Love-in (1/82). 515-Sabrina's Christmas Magic (1/82). 516-The World of Archie (3/82). 517-The World of Jughead (4/82). 518-Betty & Veronica Spectacular (6/82). 519-Archie's Jokes (8/82). 520-Betty & Veronica Summer Fun (9/82) 521-The World of Archie (9/82). 522-Betty & Veronica Spectacular (10/82). 523-The World of Jughead (10/82). 524-Archie's Christmas Stocking (1/83). 525-Betty and Veronica Christmas Spectacular (1/83). 526-Betty and Veronica Spectacular (5/83) 527-Little Archie (8/83). 528-Josie and the Pussycats (8/83) 529-Betty and Veronica Summer Fun (8/83). 530-Betty and Veronica Spectacular (9/83). 531-The World of Jughead (9/83) 532-The World of Archie (10/83). 533-Space Pirates by Frank Bolling (10/83). 534-Little Archie (1/84). 535-Archie's Christmas Stocking (1/84). 536-Betty and Veronica Christmas Spectacular (1/84). 537-Betty and Veronica Spectacular (6/84). 538-Little Archie (8/84). 539-Betty and Veronica Summer Fun 8/84). 540-Josie and the Pussycats (8/84). 541-Betty and Veronica Spectacular (9/84). 542-The World of Jughead (9/84). 543-The World of Archie (10/84). 544-Sabrina the Teen-Age Witch (10/84). 545-Little Archie (12/84). 546-Archie's Christmas Stocking (12/84) 547-Betty and Veronica Christmas Spectacular (12/84). 548-? 549-Little Archie. 550-Betty and Veronica Summer Fun each.... .40 .80

551-600: 551-Josie and the Pussycats. 552-Betty and Veronica Spectacular. 553-The World of Jughead. 554-The World of Archie 555-Betty's Diary. 556-Little Archie (1/86). 557-Archie's Christmas Stocking (1/86). 558-Betty & Veronica Christmas Spectacular (1/86). 559-Betty & Veronica Spectacular. 560-Little Archie. 561-Betty & Veronica Summer Fun. 562-Josie and the Pussycats. 563-Betty & Veronica Spectacular. 564-World of Jughead. 565-World of Archie. 566-Little Archie. 567-Archie's Christmas Stocking. 568-Betty & Veronica Christmas Spectacular. 569-Betty & Veronica Spring Spectacular. 570-Little Archie. 571-Josie & The Pussycats. 572-Betty & Veronica Summer Fun. 573-Archie At Riverdale High. 574-World of Archie. 575-Betty & Veronica Spectacular. 576-Pep. 577-World of Jughead. 578-Archie And Me. 579-Archie's Christmas Stocking. 580-Betty and Veronica Christmas Spectacular. 581-Little Archie Christmas Special. 582-Betty & Veronica Spring Spectacular. 583-Little Archie. 584-Josie and The Pussycats. 585-Betty & Veronica Summer Fun. 586-Archie At Riverdale High. 587-The World of Archie (10/88); 1st app. Explorers of the Unknown. 588-Betty & Veronica Spectacular. 589-Pep (10/88). 590-The World of Jughead. 591-Archie & Me. 592-Archie's Christmas Stocking. 593-Betty & Veronica Christmas Spectacular. 594-Little Archie. 595-Betty & Veronica Spring Spectacular. 596-Little Archie. 597-Josie and the Pussycats. 598-Betty & Veronica Summer Fun. 599-The World of Archie (10/89); 2nd app. Explorers/Unknown. 600-Betty and Veronica Spectacular each.... .40 .80

601-619: 601-Pep. 602-The World of Jughead. 603-Archie and Me. 604-Archie at Riverdale High. 605-Archie's Christmas Stocking. 606-Betty and Veronica Christmas Spectacular. 607-Little Archie. 608-

Archie Giant Series #587, © AP

Archie Giant Series #601, © AP

Archie's Girls, Betty & Veronica #70, © AP

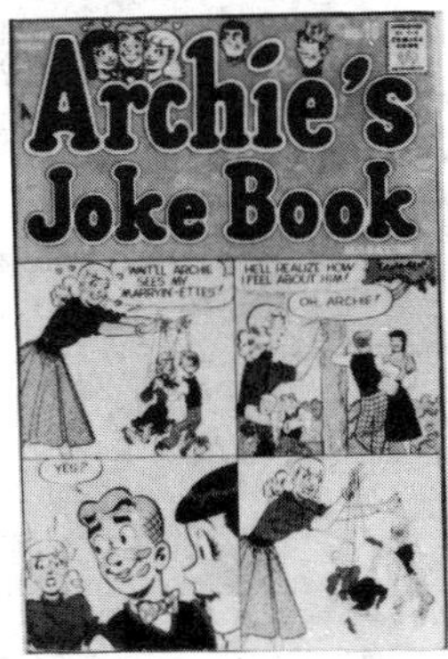

Archie's Joke Book Magazine #16, © AP

Archie's Joke Book Magazine #67, © AP

Archie's Madhouse #1, © AP

| | Good | Fine | N-Mint |
|---|---|---|---|
| Betty and Veronica Spectacular. 609-Little Archie. 610-Josie and the Pussycats. 611-Betty and Veronica Summer Fun. 612-The World of Archie. 613-Betty and Veronica Spectacular. 614-Pep (10/90). 615-Veronica's Summer Special. 616-Archie and Me. 617-Archie's Christmas Stocking. 618-Betty & Veronica Christmas Spectacular. 619-Little Archie | | | |
| each.... | | .40 | .80 |

**ARCHIE'S ACTIVITY COMICS DIGEST MAGAZINE**
1985 - Present? (Annual, 128 pgs.; digest size)
Archie Enterprises

| | Good | Fine | N-Mint |
|---|---|---|---|
| 1-4 | | .50 | 1.00 |

**ARCHIE'S CAR**
1979 (49 cents)
Spire Christian Comics (Fleming H. Revell Co.)

| | Good | Fine | N-Mint |
|---|---|---|---|
| nn | | .30 | .60 |

**ARCHIE'S CHRISTMAS LOVE-IN** (See Archie Giant Series Mag. No. 169, 181, 192, 205, 218, 230, 242, 454, 466, 478, 490, 502, 514)

**ARCHIE'S CHRISTMAS STOCKING** (See Archie Giant Series Mag. No. 1-6, 10, 15, 20, 25, 31, 137, 144, 150, 158, 167, 179, 190, 203, 216, 228, 240, 452, 464, 476, 488, 500, 512, 524, 535, 546, 557, 567, 579, 592, 605, 617)

**ARCHIE'S CLEAN SLATE**
1973 (35-49 cents)
Spire Christian Comics (Fleming H. Revell Co.)

| | Good | Fine | N-Mint |
|---|---|---|---|
| 1(Some issues have nn) | .35 | 1.00 | 2.00 |

**ARCHIE'S DATE BOOK**
1981
Spire Christian Comics (Fleming H. Revell Co.)

| | Good | Fine | N-Mint |
|---|---|---|---|
| nn | | .30 | .60 |

**ARCHIE'S DOUBLE DIGEST QUARTERLY MAGAZINE**
1981 - Present ($1.95-$2.25, 256pgs.) (A.D.D. Magazine No. 10 on)
Archie Comics

| | Good | Fine | N-Mint |
|---|---|---|---|
| 1-52: 6-Katy Keene story. 29-Pureheart story | .35 | 1.10 | 2.25 |

**ARCHIE'S FAMILY ALBUM**
1978 (36 pages) (39 cents)
Spire Christian Comics (Fleming H. Revell Co.)

| | Good | Fine | N-Mint |
|---|---|---|---|
| nn | | .30 | .60 |

**ARCHIE'S FESTIVAL**
1980 (49 cents)
Spire Christian Comics (Fleming H. Revell Co.)

| | Good | Fine | N-Mint |
|---|---|---|---|
| nn | | .30 | .60 |

**ARCHIE'S GIRLS, BETTY AND VERONICA** (Becomes Betty & Veronica)(Also see Veronica)
1950 - No. 347, 1987
Archie Publications (Close-Up)

| | Good | Fine | N-Mint |
|---|---|---|---|
| 1 | 71.00 | 215.00 | 500.00 |
| 2 | 36.00 | 107.00 | 250.00 |
| 3-5 | 19.00 | 58.00 | 135.00 |
| 6-10: 10-2pg. Katy Keene app. | 16.00 | 48.00 | 110.00 |
| 11-20: 11,13,14,17-19-Katy Keene app. 20-Debbie's Diary, 2 pgs. | 10.00 | 30.00 | 70.00 |
| 21-30: 27-Katy Keene app. | 8.00 | 24.00 | 56.00 |
| 31-50 | 5.30 | 16.00 | 38.00 |
| 51-74 | 3.50 | 10.50 | 24.00 |
| 75-Betty & Veronica sell souls to Devil | 7.00 | 21.00 | 50.00 |
| 76-99 | 2.00 | 6.00 | 14.00 |
| 100 | 2.65 | 8.00 | 18.00 |
| 101-140: 118-Origin Superteen. 119-Last Superteen story | 1.00 | 3.00 | 7.00 |
| 141-180 | .50 | 1.50 | 3.00 |
| 181-220 | | .60 | 1.20 |
| 221-347: 300-Anniversary issue | | .35 | .70 |

| | Good | Fine | N-Mint |
|---|---|---|---|
| Annual 1 (1953) | 43.00 | 130.00 | 300.00 |
| Annual 2(1954) | 20.00 | 60.00 | 140.00 |
| Annual 3-5 ('55-'57) | 14.00 | 43.00 | 100.00 |
| Annual 6-8 ('58-'60) | 10.00 | 30.00 | 70.00 |

**ARCHIE SHOE-STORE GIVEAWAY**
1944-49 (12-15 pgs. of games, puzzles, stories like Superman-Tim books, No nos. - came out monthly)
Archie Publications

| | Good | Fine | N-Mint |
|---|---|---|---|
| (1944-47)-issues | 9.00 | 27.00 | 62.00 |
| 2/48-Peggy Lee photo-c | 6.00 | 18.00 | 42.00 |
| 3/48-Marylee Robb photo-c | 6.00 | 18.00 | 42.00 |
| 4/48-Gloria De Haven photo-c | 6.00 | 18.00 | 42.00 |
| 5/48,6/48,7/48 | 6.00 | 18.00 | 42.00 |
| 8/48-Story on Shirley Temple | 6.00 | 18.00 | 42.00 |
| 10/48-Archie as Wolf on cover | 6.00 | 18.00 | 42.00 |
| 5/49-Kathleen Hughes photo-c | 4.50 | 13.50 | 32.00 |
| 7/49 | 4.50 | 13.50 | 32.00 |
| 8/49-Archie photo-c from radio show | 6.00 | 18.00 | 42.00 |
| 10/49-Gloria Mann photo-c from radio show | 5.50 | 16.50 | 38.00 |
| 11/49,12/49 | 4.50 | 13.50 | 32.00 |

**ARCHIE'S JOKEBOOK COMICS DIGEST ANNUAL** (See Jokebook...)

**ARCHIE'S JOKE BOOK MAGAZINE** (See Joke Book . . .)
1953 - No. 3, Sum, 1954; No. 15, Fall, 1954 - No. 288, 11/82
Archie Publications

| | Good | Fine | N-Mint |
|---|---|---|---|
| 1953-One Shot (#1) | 45.00 | 135.00 | 315.00 |
| 2 | 26.00 | 77.00 | 180.00 |
| 3 (no #4-14) | 17.00 | 51.00 | 120.00 |
| 15-20: (Formerly Archie's Rival Reggie #14). 15-17-Katy Keene app. | 13.00 | 40.00 | 90.00 |
| 21-30 | 8.50 | 25.50 | 60.00 |
| 31-40,42,43 | 4.30 | 13.00 | 30.00 |
| 41-1st professional comic work by Neal Adams ('59), 1 pg. | 13.00 | 40.00 | 90.00 |
| 44-47-N. Adams-a in all, 1-2 pgs. | 7.00 | 21.00 | 50.00 |
| 48-Four pgs. N. Adams-a | 7.00 | 21.00 | 50.00 |
| 49-60 (1962) | 2.00 | 6.00 | 14.00 |
| 61-80 | 1.30 | 4.00 | 8.00 |
| 81-100 | .70 | 2.00 | 4.00 |
| 101-140 | .35 | 1.00 | 2.00 |
| 141-200 | | .60 | 1.20 |
| 201-288 | | .35 | .70 |
| Drug Store Giveaway (No. 39 w/new-c) | 2.00 | 6.00 | 14.00 |

**ARCHIE'S JOKES** (See Archie Giant Series Mag. No. 17, 22, 27, 33, 139, 146, 154, 163, 174, 186, 198, 211, 222, 235, 247, 459, 471, 483, 495, 519)

**ARCHIE'S LOVE SCENE**
1973 (35-49 cents)
Spire Christian Comics (Fleming H. Revell Co.)

| | Good | Fine | N-Mint |
|---|---|---|---|
| 1(Some issues have nn) | .35 | 1.00 | 2.00 |

**ARCHIE'S MADHOUSE** (Madhouse Ma-ad No. 67 on)
Sept, 1959 - No. 66, Feb, 1969
Archie Publications

| | Good | Fine | N-Mint |
|---|---|---|---|
| 1-Archie begins | 17.00 | 51.00 | 120.00 |
| 2 | 8.50 | 25.50 | 60.00 |
| 3-5 | 6.50 | 19.00 | 45.00 |
| 6-10 | 4.30 | 13.00 | 30.00 |
| 11-16 (Last w/regular characters) | 3.00 | 9.00 | 21.00 |
| 17-21,23-30 (New format) | 1.15 | 3.50 | 7.00 |
| 22-1st app. Sabrina, the Teen-age Witch (10/62) | 4.30 | 13.00 | 30.00 |
| 31-40 | .50 | 1.50 | 3.00 |
| 41-66: 43-Mighty Crusaders cameo. 44-Swipes Mad #4 (Super-Duper-man) in "Bird Monsters From Outer Space" | | .60 | 1.20 |

| | Good | Fine | N-Mint |
|---|---|---|---|
| Annual 1 (1962-63) | 3.60 | 11.00 | 25.00 |
| Annual 2 (1964) | 2.00 | 6.00 | 14.00 |
| Annual 3 (1965)-Origin Sabrina The Teen-Age Witch | 1.00 | 3.00 | 7.00 |
| Annual 4-6('66-69)(Becomes Madhouse Ma-ad Annual #7 on) | .70 | 2.00 | 4.00 |

NOTE: *Cover title to 61-65 is "Madhouse" and to 66 is "Madhouse Ma-ad Jokes."*

**ARCHIE'S MECHANICS**
Sept, 1954 - No. 3, 1955
Archie Publications

| | Good | Fine | N-Mint |
|---|---|---|---|
| 1-(15 cents; 52 pgs.) | 64.00 | 193.00 | 450.00 |
| 2-(10 cents) | 37.00 | 110.00 | 260.00 |
| 3-(10 cents) | 32.00 | 96.00 | 225.00 |

**ARCHIE'S ONE WAY**
1972 (35 cents, 39 cents, 49 cents) (36 pages)
Spire Christian Comics (Fleming H. Revell Co.)

| | Good | Fine | N-Mint |
|---|---|---|---|
| nn | .35 | 1.00 | 2.00 |

**ARCHIE'S PAL, JUGHEAD** (Jughead No. 122 on)
1949 - No. 126, Nov, 1965
Archie Publications

| | Good | Fine | N-Mint |
|---|---|---|---|
| 1 (1949) | 69.00 | 205.00 | 480.00 |
| 2 (1950) | 34.00 | 103.00 | 240.00 |
| 3-5 | 22.00 | 65.00 | 155.00 |
| 6-10: 7-Suzie app. | 13.00 | 40.00 | 90.00 |
| 11-20 | 10.00 | 30.00 | 70.00 |
| 21-30: 23-25,28-30-Katy Keene app. 28-Debbie's Diary app. | 6.50 | 19.00 | 45.00 |
| 31-50 | 3.70 | 11.00 | 26.00 |
| 51-70 | 2.65 | 8.00 | 18.00 |
| 71-100 | 1.50 | 4.50 | 9.00 |
| 101-126 | 1.00 | 3.00 | 6.00 |
| Annual 1 (1953) | 32.00 | 96.00 | 225.00 |
| Annual 2 (1954) | 19.00 | 58.00 | 135.00 |
| Annual 3-5 (1955-57) | 13.00 | 40.00 | 90.00 |
| Annual 6-8 (1958-60) | 9.00 | 27.00 | 62.00 |

**ARCHIE'S PALS 'N' GALS**
1952-53 - No. 6, 1957-58; No. 7, 1958 - Present
Archie Publications

| | Good | Fine | N-Mint |
|---|---|---|---|
| 1-(116 pages) | 39.00 | 118.00 | 275.00 |
| 2(Annual)('53-'54) | 22.00 | 65.00 | 154.00 |
| 3-5(Annual, '54-57) | 14.00 | 42.00 | 100.00 |
| 6-10('58-'60) | 8.00 | 24.00 | 56.00 |
| 11-20 | 3.70 | 11.00 | 26.00 |
| 21-40: 29-Beatles satire | 2.00 | 6.00 | 14.00 |
| 41-60 | .85 | 2.60 | 6.00 |
| 61-80 | .50 | 1.50 | 3.00 |
| 81-110 | .25 | .75 | 1.50 |
| 111-224: Later issues $1.00 cover | | .40 | .80 |

**ARCHIE'S PARABLES**
1973, 1975 (36 pages, 39-49 cents)
Spire Christian Comics (Fleming H. Revell Co.)

| | Good | Fine | N-Mint |
|---|---|---|---|
| nn-By Al Hartley | | .40 | .80 |

**ARCHIE'S R/C RACERS**
Sept, 1989 - No. 10, Mar?, 1991 (95 cents, $1.00, color)
Archie Comics

| | Good | Fine | N-Mint |
|---|---|---|---|
| 1-10: Radio control cars | | .50 | 1.00 |

**ARCHIE'S RIVAL REGGIE** (Reggie & Archie's Joke Book #15 on)
1950 - No. 14, Aug, 1954
Archie Publications

| | Good | Fine | N-Mint |
|---|---|---|---|
| 1 | 48.00 | 145.00 | 335.00 |
| 2 | 25.00 | 75.00 | 175.00 |
| 3-5 | 17.00 | 51.00 | 120.00 |
| 6-10 | 11.00 | 32.00 | 75.00 |
| 11-14: Katy Keene in No. 10-14, 1-2pgs. | 8.00 | 24.00 | 56.00 |

**ARCHIE'S ROLLER COASTER**
1981 (69 cents)
Spire Christian Comics (Fleming H. Revell Co.)

| | Good | Fine | N-Mint |
|---|---|---|---|
| nn | | .40 | .80 |

**ARCHIE'S SOMETHING ELSE**
1975 (36 pages, 39-49 cents)
Spire Christian Comics (Fleming H. Revell Co.)

| | Good | Fine | N-Mint |
|---|---|---|---|
| nn | | .40 | .80 |

**ARCHIE'S SONSHINE**
1973, 1974 (36 pages, 39-49 cents)
Spire Christian Comics (Fleming H. Revell Co.)

| | Good | Fine | N-Mint |
|---|---|---|---|
| nn | .35 | 1.00 | 2.00 |

**ARCHIE'S SPORTS SCENE**
1983
Spire Christian Comics (Fleming H. Revell Co.)

| | Good | Fine | N-Mint |
|---|---|---|---|
| nn | | .40 | .80 |

**ARCHIE'S STORY & GAME COMICS DIGEST MAGAZINE**
Nov, 1986 - Present (Digest size, $1.25, $1.35, $1.50, 128 pgs.)
Archie Enterprises

| | Good | Fine | N-Mint |
|---|---|---|---|
| 1-18 | .25 | .75 | 1.50 |

**ARCHIE'S SUPER HERO SPECIAL** (See Archie Giant Series Mag. No. 142)

**ARCHIE'S SUPER HERO SPECIAL** (. . .Comics Digest Mag. 2)
Jan, 1979 - No. 2, Aug, 1979 (148 pages, 95 cents)
Archie Publications (Red Circle)

| | Good | Fine | N-Mint |
|---|---|---|---|
| 1-Simon & Kirby r-/Double Life of Pvt. Strong #1,2; Black Hood, The Fly, Jaguar, The Web app. | | .40 | .80 |
| 2-Contains contents to the never published Black Hood #1; origin Black Hood; N. Adams, Wood, McWilliams, Morrow, S&K-a(r); N. Adams-c. The Shield, The Fly, Jaguar, Hangman, Steel Sterling, The Web, The Fox-r | | .40 | .80 |

**ARCHIE'S TV LAUGH-OUT**
Dec, 1969 - No. 106, 1986
Archie Publications

| | Good | Fine | N-Mint |
|---|---|---|---|
| 1 | 4.00 | 12.00 | 28.00 |
| 2 | 1.70 | 5.00 | 10.00 |
| 3-5 | .85 | 2.50 | 5.00 |
| 6-10 | .35 | 1.00 | 2.00 |
| 11-20 | | .50 | 1.00 |
| 21-106 | | .30 | .60 |

**ARCHIE'S WORLD**
1973, 1976 (39-49 cents)
Spire Christian Comics (Fleming H. Revell Co.)

| | Good | Fine | N-Mint |
|---|---|---|---|
| nn | | .40 | .80 |

**ARCHIE 3000**
May, 1989 - Present (75 & 95 cents, $1.00, color)
Archie Comics

| | Good | Fine | N-Mint |
|---|---|---|---|
| 1-14: 6-X-Mas-c | | .50 | 1.00 |

**AREA 88**
May 26, 1987 - No. 42, 1989 ($1.50-$1.75, B&W)
Eclipse Comics/VIZ Comics #37 on

| | Good | Fine | N-Mint |
|---|---|---|---|
| 1-36: 1,2-2nd printings exist | .25 | .75 | 1.50 |
| 37-42: 37-Begin $1.75-c | .30 | .90 | 1.80 |

**ARENA** (Also see Marvel Graphic Novel)
Jan, 1990 ($1.50, color, 20 pgs., 7X10-1/8")
Alchemy Studios

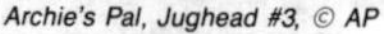

*Archie's Pal, Jughead #3, © AP*

*Archie's Pals 'N' Gals #9, © AP*

*Archie 3000 #5, © AP*

*Army and Navy #3, © S&S*

*The Arrow #3, © CEN*

*Arrowhead #2, © MEG*

| | Good | Fine | N-Mint |
|---|---|---|---|
| 1-Science fiction | .25 | .75 | 1.50 |
| 1-Signed & numbered edition (500 copies) | .50 | 1.50 | 2.95 |

**ARIANE AND BLUEBEARD**
1989 ($3.95, color, 52 pgs.)
Eclipse Books

| | Good | Fine | N-Mint |
|---|---|---|---|
| nn-P. Craig Russell-c/a | .70 | 2.00 | 4.00 |

**ARION, LORD OF ATLANTIS** (Also see Warlord #55)
Nov, 1982 - No. 35, Sept, 1985
DC Comics

| | Good | Fine | N-Mint |
|---|---|---|---|
| 1-35: 1-Story cont'd from Warlord #62 | | .50 | 1.00 |
| Special #1 (11/85) | | .50 | 1.00 |

**ARISTOCATS** (See Movie Comics & Walt Disney Showcase No. 16)

**ARISTOCRATIC X-TRATERRESTRIAL TIME-TRAVELING THIEVES**
Aug, 1986; Feb, 1987 - No. 6, 1988? ($1.75, B&W, 28 pgs.)
Fictioneer Books, Ltd.

| | Good | Fine | N-Mint |
|---|---|---|---|
| 1-One shot (8/86) | .30 | .90 | 1.75 |
| 1-2nd print (12/86) | .30 | .90 | 1.75 |
| 1-6: 1-Begin new series (2/87) | .30 | .90 | 1.75 |

**ARISTOKITTENS, THE** (. . . Meet Jiminy Cricket No. 1)(Disney)
Oct, 1971 - No. 9, Oct, 1975 (No. 6: 52 pages)
Gold Key

| | Good | Fine | N-Mint |
|---|---|---|---|
| 1 | 1.15 | 3.50 | 8.00 |
| 2-9 | .70 | 2.00 | 5.00 |

**ARIZONA KID, THE** (Also see The Comics & Wild Western)
March, 1951 - No. 6, Jan, 1952
Marvel/Atlas Comics(CSI)

| | Good | Fine | N-Mint |
|---|---|---|---|
| 1 | 8.50 | 25.50 | 60.00 |
| 2-4: 2-Heath-a(3) | 5.00 | 15.00 | 30.00 |
| 5,6 | 4.00 | 12.00 | 28.00 |

NOTE: ***Heath** a-1-3; c-1-3. **Maneely** c-4-6. **Morisi** a-4-6.*

**ARK, THE** (See The Crusaders)

**ARKHAM ASYLUM** (Also see Animal Man #24, Black Orchid #2 & The Saga of Swamp Thing #52, 53)
1989 ($24.95, hard-c, mature readers, 132 pgs.)
DC Comics

| | Good | Fine | N-Mint |
|---|---|---|---|
| nn-Joker-c/story; Grant Morrison scripts | 5.00 | 15.00 | 30.00 |
| nn-Soft cover reprint ($14.95) | 2.50 | 7.50 | 15.00 |

**ARMAGEDDON FACTOR, THE**
1987 - No. 2, 1987?; No. 3, 1990 ($1.95, color)
AC Comics

| | Good | Fine | N-Mint |
|---|---|---|---|
| 1,2: Sentinels of Justice, Dragonfly, Femforce | .35 | 1.00 | 2.00 |
| 3-($3.95, color)-Almost all AC characters app. | .70 | 2.00 | 4.00 |

**ARMOR** (AND THE SILVER STREAK)
Sept, 1985 - Present ($2.00, color)
Continuity Comics

| | Good | Fine | N-Mint |
|---|---|---|---|
| 1-7: 1-Intro/origin Armor & the Silver Streak; Neal Adams-c/a. 7-Origin Armor; Nebres-i | .35 | 1.00 | 2.00 |

**ARMY AND NAVY COMICS** (Supersnipe No. 6 on)
May, 1941 - No. 5, July, 1942
Street & Smith Publications

| | Good | Fine | N-Mint |
|---|---|---|---|
| 1-Cap Fury & Nick Carter | 25.00 | 75.00 | 175.00 |
| 2-Cap Fury & Nick Carter | 12.00 | 36.00 | 85.00 |
| 3,4 | 9.00 | 27.00 | 62.00 |
| 5-Supersnipe app.; see Shadow V2#3 for 1st app.; Story of Douglas MacArthur | 23.00 | 70.00 | 160.00 |

**ARMY ATTACK**
July, 1964 - No. 4, Feb, 1965; V2#38, July, 1965 - No. 47, Feb, 1967
Charlton Comics

| | Good | Fine | N-Mint |
|---|---|---|---|
| V1#1 | 1.00 | 3.00 | 6.00 |
| 2-4(2/65) | .50 | 1.50 | 3.00 |
| V2#38(7/65)-47 (formerly U.S. Air Force #1-37) | .50 | 1.50 | 3.00 |

NOTE: ***Glanzman** a-1-3. **Montes/Bache** a-44.*

**ARMY AT WAR** (Also see Our Army at War & Cancelled Comic Cavalcade)
Oct-Nov, 1978
DC Comics

| | Good | Fine | N-Mint |
|---|---|---|---|
| 1-Kubert-c | | .30 | .60 |

**ARMY SURPLUS KOMIKZ FEATURING CUTEY BUNNY**
1982 - No. 5, 1985 ($1.50, B&W)
Army Surplus Komikz/Eclipse Comics No. 5

| | Good | Fine | N-Mint |
|---|---|---|---|
| 1-Cutey Bunny begins | 1.00 | 3.00 | 6.00 |
| 2-5: 5-JLA/X-Men/Batman parody | .50 | 1.50 | 3.00 |

**ARMY WAR HEROES** (Also see Iron Corporal)
Dec, 1963 - No. 38, June, 1970
Charlton Comics

| | Good | Fine | N-Mint |
|---|---|---|---|
| 1 | 1.00 | 3.00 | 6.00 |
| 2-38: 22-Origin & 1st app. Iron Corporal series by Glanzman. 24-Intro. Archer & Corp. Jack series | .35 | 1.00 | 2.00 |
| Modern Comics Reprint 36 ('78) | | .30 | .60 |

NOTE: ***Montes/Bache** a-1, 16, 17, 21, 23-25, 27-30.*

**AROUND THE BLOCK WITH DUNC & LOO** (See Dunc and Loo)

**AROUND THE WORLD IN 80 DAYS** (See Four Color Comics #784 and A Golden Picture Classic)

**AROUND THE WORLD UNDER THE SEA** (See Movie Classics)

**AROUND THE WORLD WITH ARCHIE** (See Archie Giant Series Magazine No. 29, 35, 141)

**AROUND THE WORLD WITH HUCKLEBERRY & HIS FRIENDS** (See Dell Giant No. 44)

**ARRGH!** (Satire)
Dec, 1974 - No. 5, Sept, 1975
Marvel Comics Group

| | Good | Fine | N-Mint |
|---|---|---|---|
| 1 | | .60 | 1.20 |
| 2-5 | | .40 | .80 |

NOTE: ***Alcala** a-2; c-3. **Everett** a-1r, 2r. **Maneely** a-4r. **Sekowsky** a-1p. **Sutton** a-1, 2.*

**ARROW, THE** (See Funny Pages)
Oct, 1940 - No. 2, Nov, 1940; No. 3, Oct, 1941
Centaur Publications

| | Good | Fine | N-Mint |
|---|---|---|---|
| 1-The Arrow begins(r/Funny Pages) | 125.00 | 320.00 | 750.00 |
| 2-Tippy Taylor serial continues from Amazing Mystery Funnies 24 | 64.00 | 193.00 | 450.00 |
| 3-Origin Dash Dartwell, the Human Meteor; origin The Rainbow-r; bondage-c | 64.00 | 193.00 | 450.00 |

NOTE: ***Gustavson** a-1, 2; c-3.*

**ARROWHEAD** (See Black Rider and Wild Western)
April, 1954 - No. 4, Nov, 1954
Atlas Comics (CPS)

| | Good | Fine | N-Mint |
|---|---|---|---|
| 1-Arrowhead & his horse Eagle begin | 6.00 | 18.00 | 42.00 |
| 2-4: 4-Forte-a | 3.60 | 11.00 | 25.00 |

NOTE: ***Heath** c-3. **Jack Katz** a-3. **Maneely** c-2. **Pakula** a-2. **Sinnott** a-1-4; c-1.*

**ASSASSINS, INC.**
1987 - No. 2, 1987?($1.95, color)
Silverline Comics

| | Good | Fine | N-Mint |
|---|---|---|---|
| 1,2 | .35 | 1.00 | 2.00 |

**ASTONISHING** (Marvel Boy No. 1,2)
No. 3, April, 1951 - No. 63, Aug, 1957
Marvel/Atlas Comics(20CC)

| | Good | Fine | N-Mint |
|---|---|---|---|
| 3-Marvel Boy continues | 32.00 | 95.00 | 225.00 |

| | Good | Fine | N-Mint |
|---|---|---|---|
| 4-6-Last Marvel Boy; 4-Stan Lee app. | 25.00 | 75.00 | 175.00 |
| 7-10 | 7.00 | 21.00 | 50.00 |
| 11,12,15,17,20 | 5.70 | 17.00 | 40.00 |
| 13,14,16,19-Krigstein-a | 6.50 | 19.00 | 45.00 |
| 18-Jack The Ripper story | 6.50 | 19.00 | 45.00 |
| 21,22,24 | 4.50 | 14.00 | 32.00 |
| 23-E.C. swipe-'The Hole In The Wall' from Vault Of Horror #16 | 5.70 | 17.00 | 40.00 |
| 25-Crandall-a | 5.70 | 17.00 | 40.00 |
| 26-29: 29-Decapitation-c | 4.00 | 12.00 | 28.00 |
| 30-Tentacled eyeball story | 6.50 | 19.00 | 45.00 |
| 31-37-Last pre-code issue | 3.50 | 10.50 | 24.00 |
| 38-43,46,48-52,56,58,59,61 | 2.65 | 8.00 | 18.00 |
| 44-Crandall swipe/Weird Fantasy #22 | 4.00 | 12.00 | 28.00 |
| 45,47-Krigstein-a | 4.00 | 12.00 | 28.00 |
| 53,54: 53-Crandall, Ditko-a. 54-Torres-a | 3.50 | 10.50 | 24.00 |
| 55-Crandall, Torres-a | 4.00 | 12.00 | 28.00 |
| 57-Williamson/Krenkel-a (4 pgs.) | 5.00 | 15.00 | 35.00 |
| 60-Williamson/Mayo-a (4 pgs.) | 5.00 | 15.00 | 35.00 |
| 62-Torres, Powell -a | 2.85 | 8.50 | 20.00 |
| 63-Last issue; Woodbridge-a | 2.85 | 8.50 | 20.00 |

NOTE: ***Ayers*** *a-16.* ***Berg*** *a-36, 53, 56.* ***Cameron*** *a-50.* ***Gene Colan*** *a-12, 20, 29, 56.* ***Ditko*** *a-50, 53.* ***Drucker*** *a-41, 62.* ***Everett*** *a-3-5(3), 6, 10, 12, 37, 47, 48, 58, 61; c-3-5, 13, 15, 16, 18, 29, 47, 49, 51, 53-55, 57, 59-63.* ***Fass*** *a-11, 34.* ***Forte*** *a-53, 58.* ***Fuje*** *a-11.* ***Heath*** *c/a-8; c-9, 26.* ***Kirby*** *a-56.* ***Lawrence*** *a-28, 37, 38, 42.* ***Maneely*** *c-31, 33, 34, 56.* ***Moldoff*** *a-33.* ***Morisi*** *a-10?* ***Morrow*** *a-52, 61.* ***Orlando*** *a-47, 58, 61.* ***Powell*** *a-43, 44, 48.* ***Ravielli*** *a-28.* ***Reinman*** *a-32, 34, 38.* ***Robinson*** *a-20.* ***J. Romita*** *a-7, 18, 24, 43, 57, 61.* ***Roussos*** *a-55.* ***Sale*** *a-28, 38, 59.* ***Sekowsky*** *a-13.* ***Severin*** *c-46.* ***Shores*** *a-16.* ***Sinnott*** *a-11, 30.* ***Ed Win*** *a-20. Canadian reprints exist.*

**ASTONISHING TALES** (See Ka-Zar)
Aug, 1970 - No. 36, July, 1976 (#1-7: 15 cents; #8: 25 cents)
Marvel Comics Group

| | Good | Fine | N-Mint |
|---|---|---|---|
| 1-Ka-Zar by Kirby(p) & Dr. Doom by Wood begin; Kraven the Hunter-c/story | 1.30 | 4.00 | 9.00 |
| 2-Kraven the Hunter-c/story; Kirby, Wood-a | 1.00 | 3.00 | 6.00 |
| 3-6: Smith-p; Wood-a-#3,4. 5-Red Skull app. | 1.15 | 3.50 | 8.00 |
| 7,8: 8-(52 pgs.)-Last Dr. Doom & Kirby-a | 1.00 | 3.00 | 6.00 |
| 9-Lorna-r | .40 | 1.25 | 2.50 |
| 10-Barry Smith-a(p) | .60 | 1.75 | 3.50 |
| 11-Origin Ka-Zar & Zabu | .50 | 1.50 | 3.00 |
| 12-Man-Thing by Neal Adams (apps. #13 also) | .70 | 2.00 | 4.00 |
| 13-24: 20-Last Ka-Zar. 21-It! the Living Colossus begins, ends #24 | .25 | .75 | 1.50 |
| 25-Deathlok the Demolisher begins (1st app.); Perez 1st work, 2pgs. (8/74) | 1.35 | 4.00 | 8.00 |
| 26-28,30 | .70 | 2.00 | 4.00 |
| 29-Origin Guardians of the Galaxy | 1.35 | 4.00 | 8.00 |
| 31-36 | .50 | 1.50 | 3.00 |

NOTE: ***Buckler*** *a-13i, 16p, 25, 26p, 27p, 28, 29p-36p; c-13, 25p, 26-30, 32-35p, 36.* ***John Buscema*** *a-9, 12p-14p, 16p; c-4-6p, 12p.* ***Colan*** *a-7p, 8p.* ***Ditko*** *a-21r.* ***Everett*** *a-6i.* ***G. Kane*** *a-11p, 15p; c-10p, 11p, 14, 15p, 21p.* ***McWilliams*** *a-30i.* ***Starlin*** *a-19p; c-16p.* ***Sutton & Trimpe*** *a-8.* ***Tuska*** *a-5p, 6p, 8p.* ***Wood*** *a-1-4.* ***Wrightson*** *c-31i.*

**ASTRO BOY** (TV) (See March of Comics #285 & The Original . . .)
August, 1965 (12 cents)
Gold Key

| | Good | Fine | N-Mint |
|---|---|---|---|
| 1(10151-508) | 18.50 | 56.00 | 130.00 |

**ASTRO COMICS**
1969 - 1979 (Giveaway)
American Airlines (Harvey)

| | Good | Fine | N-Mint |
|---|---|---|---|
| nn-Harvey's Casper, Spooky, Hot Stuff, Stumbo the Giant, Little Audrey, Little Lotta, & Richie Rich reprints | .70 | 2.00 | 4.00 |

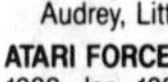

**ATARI FORCE**
1982; Jan, 1984 - No. 20, Aug, 1985 (Mando paper)
DC Comics

| | Good | Fine | N-Mint |
|---|---|---|---|
| 1-3 (1982, color, 52 pgs., 5X7")-Given away with Atari games | | .50 | 1.00 |
| 1-20: 1-(1/84)-1st app. Tempest, Packrat, Babe, Morphea, & Dart | | .50 | 1.00 |
| Special 1 (4/86) | | .50 | 1.00 |

NOTE: ***Byrne*** *c-Special 1i.* ***Giffen*** *a-12p, 13i.* ***Rogers*** *a-18p, Special 1p.*

**A-TEAM, THE** (TV)
March, 1984 - No. 3, May, 1984
Marvel Comics Group

| | Good | Fine | N-Mint |
|---|---|---|---|
| 1-3 | | .30 | .60 |

**ATLANTIS CHRONICLES, THE**
Mar, 1990 - No. 7, Sept, 1990 ($2.95, mini-series, 52 pgs.)
DC Comics

| | Good | Fine | N-Mint |
|---|---|---|---|
| 1-7: 7-Nudity panels | .50 | 1.50 | 3.00 |

**ATLANTIS, THE LOST CONTINENT** (See 4-Color No. 1188)

**ATLAS** (See First Issue Special)

**ATOM, THE** (See Action, All-American #19, Brave & the Bold, D.C. Special Series #1, Detective, Flash Comics #80, Power Of The Atom, Showcase #34, Super Friends, Sword Of The Atom & World's Finest)

**ATOM, THE** (. . . & the Hawkman No. 39 on)
June-July, 1962 - No. 38, Aug-Sept, 1968
National Periodical Publications

| | Good | Fine | N-Mint |
|---|---|---|---|
| 1-Intro Plant-Master; 1st app. Maya | 57.00 | 171.00 | 400.00 |
| 2 | 19.00 | 58.00 | 135.00 |
| 3-1st Time Pool story; 1st app. Chronos (origin) | 12.00 | 36.00 | 85.00 |
| 4,5: 4-Snapper Carr x-over | 9.30 | 28.00 | 65.00 |
| 6-10: 7-Hawkman x-over (1st Atom & Hawkman team-up). 8-Justice League, Dr. Light app. | 7.00 | 21.00 | 50.00 |
| 11-15 | 5.00 | 15.00 | 35.00 |
| 16-20: 19-Zatanna x-over | 3.60 | 11.00 | 25.00 |
| 21-28,30 | 2.15 | 6.50 | 15.00 |
| 29-Golden Age Atom x-over (1st S.A. app.) | 5.70 | 17.00 | 40.00 |
| 31-38: 31-Hawkman x-over. 36-G.A. Atom x-over. 37-Intro. Major Mynah; Hawkman cameo | 2.15 | 6.50 | 15.00 |

NOTE: ***Anderson*** *a-1-11i, 13i; c-inks-1-25, 31-35, 37.* ***Sid Greene*** *a-8i-38i.* ***Gil Kane*** *a-1p-38p; c-1p-28p, 29, 33p, 34. Time Pool stories also in 6, 9,12, 17, 21, 27, 35.*

**ATOM AGE** (See Classics Illustrated Special Issue)

**ATOM-AGE COMBAT**
June, 1952 - No. 5, April, 1953; Feb, 1958
St. John Publishing Co.

| | Good | Fine | N-Mint |
|---|---|---|---|
| 1 | 20.00 | 60.00 | 140.00 |
| 2 | 12.00 | 36.00 | 84.00 |
| 3,5: 3-Mayo-a (6 pgs.) | 9.30 | 28.00 | 65.00 |
| 4 (Scarce) | 11.00 | 32.00 | 75.00 |
| 1(2/58-St. John) | 7.00 | 21.00 | 50.00 |

**ATOM-AGE COMBAT**
Nov, 1958 - No. 3, March, 1959
Fago Magazines

| | Good | Fine | N-Mint |
|---|---|---|---|
| 1 | 11.00 | 32.00 | 75.00 |
| 2,3 | 7.00 | 21.00 | 50.00 |

**ATOMAN**
Feb, 1946 - No. 2, April, 1946
Spark Publications

| | Good | Fine | N-Mint |
|---|---|---|---|
| 1-Origin Atoman; Robinson/Meskin-a; Kidcrusaders, Wild Bill Hickok, Marvin the Great app. | 24.00 | 70.00 | 165.00 |
| 2: Robinson/Meskin-a; Robinson c-1,2 | 17.00 | 51.00 | 120.00 |

**ATOM & HAWKMAN, THE** (Formerly The Atom)
No. 39, Oct-Nov, 1968 - No. 45, Oct-Nov, 1969
National Periodical Publications

| | Good | Fine | N-Mint |
|---|---|---|---|
| 39-45: 43-1st app. Gentlemen Ghost, origin-44 | 1.50 | 4.50 | 10.00 |

*Astonishing #23,* © *MEG*

*Astonishing Tales #5,* © *MEG*

*The Atom #1,* © *DC*

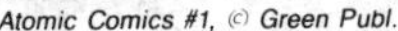

Atomic Comics #1, © Green Publ.

The Atomic Thunderbolt #1, © Regor Co.

Attack #4, © YM

NOTE: ***M. Anderson** a-39, 40i, 41i, 43, 44. **Sid Greene** a-40i-45i. **Kubert** a-40p, 41p; c-39-45.*

**ATOM ANT** (TV)
January, 1966 (Hanna-Barbera)
Gold Key

| | Good | Fine | N-Mint |
|---|---|---|---|
| 1(10170-601) | 7.00 | 21.00 | 50.00 |

**ATOMIC AGE**
Nov, 1990 - No. 4, Feb, 1991 ($4.50, mini-series, squarebound, 52pgs.)
Epic Comics (Marvel)

| | | | |
|---|---|---|---|
| 1-4: 1-Williamson-a(i) | .75 | 2.25 | 4.50 |

**ATOMIC ATTACK** (Formerly Attack, first series)
No. 5, Jan, 1953 - No. 8, Oct, 1953
Youthful Magazines

| | | | |
|---|---|---|---|
| 5-Atomic bomb-c | 14.00 | 42.00 | 100.00 |
| 6-8 | 7.00 | 21.00 | 50.00 |

**ATOMIC BOMB**
1945 (36 pgs.)
Jay Burtis Publications

| | | | |
|---|---|---|---|
| 1-Airmale & Stampy | 16.00 | 48.00 | 110.00 |

**ATOMIC BUNNY** (Formerly Atomic Rabbit)
No. 12, Aug, 1958 - No. 19, Dec, 1959
Charlton Comics

| | | | |
|---|---|---|---|
| 12 | 5.00 | 15.00 | 35.00 |
| 13-19 | 2.85 | 8.50 | 20.00 |

**ATOMIC COMICS**
1946 - No. 4, 1946 (Reprints)
Daniels Publications (Canadian)

| | | | |
|---|---|---|---|
| 1-Rocketman, Yankee Boy, Master Key; bondage-c | 9.30 | 28.00 | 65.00 |
| 2-4 | 6.00 | 18.00 | 42.00 |

**ATOMIC COMICS**
Jan, 1946 - No. 4, July-Aug, 1946
Green Publishing Co.

| | | | |
|---|---|---|---|
| 1-Radio Squad by Siegel & Shuster; Barry O'Neal app.; Fang Gow cover-r/Det. Comics | 34.00 | 103.00 | 240.00 |
| 2-Inspector Dayton; Kid Kane by Matt Baker; Lucky Wings, Congo King, Prop Powers (only app.) begin | 19.00 | 56.00 | 130.00 |
| 3,4: 3-Zero Ghost Detective app.; Baker-a(2) each; 4-Baker-c | 11.50 | 34.00 | 80.00 |

**ATOMIC MOUSE** (TV, Movies) (See Blue Bird, Funny Animals, Giant Comics & Wotalife Comics)
3/53 - No. 54, 6/63; No. 1, 12/84; V2/10, 9/85 - No. 13, ?/86
Capitol Stories/Charlton Comics

| | | | |
|---|---|---|---|
| 1-Origin; Al Fago c/a | 10.00 | 30.00 | 70.00 |
| 2 | 4.50 | 14.00 | 32.00 |
| 3-10: 5-Timmy The Timid Ghost app.; see Zoo Funnies | 3.70 | 11.00 | 26.00 |
| 11-13,16-25 | 2.00 | 6.00 | 14.00 |
| 14,15-Hoppy The Marvel Bunny app. | 2.85 | 8.50 | 20.00 |
| 26-(68 pages) | 4.00 | 12.00 | 28.00 |
| 27-40: 36,37-Atom The Cat app. | 1.30 | 4.00 | 9.00 |
| 41-54 | .70 | 2.00 | 4.00 |
| 1 (1984) | | .40 | .80 |
| V2#10 (10/85) -13-Fago-r. #12(1/86) | | .40 | .80 |

**ATOMIC RABBIT** (Atomic Bunny No. 12 on; see Wotalife Comics)
August, 1955 - No. 11, March, 1958
Charlton Comics

| | | | |
|---|---|---|---|
| 1-Origin; Al Fago-a | 9.30 | 28.00 | 65.00 |
| 2 | 4.30 | 13.00 | 30.00 |
| 3-10-Fago-a in most | 2.85 | 8.50 | 20.00 |
| 11-(68 pages) | 4.00 | 12.00 | 28.00 |

**ATOMIC SPY CASES**
Mar-Apr, 1950 (Painted-c)
Avon Periodicals

| | Good | Fine | N-Mint |
|---|---|---|---|
| 1-No Wood-a; A-bomb blast panels; Fass-a | 14.00 | 43.00 | 100.00 |

**ATOMIC THUNDERBOLT, THE**
Feb, 1946 (One shot)
Regor Company

| | | | |
|---|---|---|---|
| 1-Intro. Atomic Thunderbolt & Mr. Murdo | 16.00 | 48.00 | 110.00 |

**ATOMIC WAR!**
Nov, 1952 - No. 4, April, 1953
Ace Periodicals (Junior Books)

| | | | |
|---|---|---|---|
| 1-Atomic bomb-c | 36.00 | 107.00 | 250.00 |
| 2,3: 3-Atomic bomb-c | 25.00 | 75.00 | 175.00 |
| 4-Used in **POP**, pg. 96 & illo. | 26.00 | 77.00 | 180.00 |

**ATOM THE CAT** (Formerly Tom Cat)
No. 9, Oct, 1957 - No. 17, Aug, 1959
Charlton Comics

| | | | |
|---|---|---|---|
| 9 | 3.00 | 9.00 | 21.00 |
| 10,13-17 | 1.70 | 5.00 | 12.00 |
| 11-(64pgs)-Atomic Mouse app., 12(100pgs) | 4.00 | 12.00 | 28.00 |

**ATTACK**
May, 1952 - No. 4, Nov, 1952; No. 5, Jan, 1953 - No. 5, Sept, 1953
Youthful Mag./Trojan No. 5 on

| | | | |
|---|---|---|---|
| 1-(1st series)-Extreme violence | 7.00 | 21.00 | 50.00 |
| 2,3: 3-Harrison-c/a | 3.70 | 11.00 | 26.00 |
| 4-Krenkel-a (7 pgs.); Harrison-a (becomes Atomic Attack #5 on) | 4.30 | 13.00 | 30.00 |
| 5-(#1, Trojan, 2nd series) | 3.50 | 10.50 | 24.00 |
| 6-8 (#2-4), 5 | 2.30 | 7.00 | 16.00 |

**ATTACK**
No. 54, 1958 - No. 60, Nov, 1959
Charlton Comics

| | | | |
|---|---|---|---|
| 54(100 pages) | 3.50 | 10.50 | 24.00 |
| 55-60 | .70 | 2.00 | 5.00 |

**ATTACK!**
1962 - No. 15, 3/75; No. 16, 8/79 - No. 48, 10/84
Charlton Comics

| | | | |
|---|---|---|---|
| nn(#1)-('62) Special Edition | 1.15 | 3.50 | 8.00 |
| 2('63), 3(Fall, '64) | .70 | 2.00 | 5.00 |
| V4#3(10/66), 4(10/67)-(Formerly Special War Series #2; becomes Attack At Sea V4#5) | .50 | 1.50 | 3.00 |
| 1(9/71) | .35 | 1.00 | 2.00 |
| 2-15(3/75): 4-American Eagle app. | .25 | .75 | 1.50 |
| 16(8/79) - 47 | | .50 | 1.00 |
| 48(10/84)-Wood-r; S&K-c | | .60 | 1.20 |
| Modern Comics 13('78)-r | | .30 | .60 |

**ATTACK!**
1975 (39, 49 cents) (36 pages)
Spire Christian Comics (Fleming H. Revell Co.)

| | | | |
|---|---|---|---|
| nn | | .40 | .80 |

**ATTACK AT SEA** (Formerly Attack!, 1967)
V4#5, October, 1968
Charlton Comics

| | | | |
|---|---|---|---|
| V4#5 | .50 | 1.50 | 3.00 |

**ATTACK ON PLANET MARS** (See Strange Worlds #18)
1951
Avon Periodicals

| | | | |
|---|---|---|---|
| nn-Infantino, Fawcette, Kubert & Wood-a; adaptation of Tarrano the Conqueror by Ray Cummings | 45.00 | 135.00 | 315.00 |

**AUDREY & MELVIN** (Formerly Little. . .)
No. 62, September, 1974
Harvey Publications

| | Good | Fine | N-Mint |
|---|---|---|---|
| 62 | | .50 | 1.00 |

**AUGIE DOGGIE** (TV) (See Spotlight #2 & Whitman Comic Books)
October, 1963 (Hanna-Barbera)
Gold Key

| | Good | Fine | N-Mint |
|---|---|---|---|
| 1 | 5.00 | 15.00 | 35.00 |

**AURORA COMIC SCENES INSTRUCTION BOOKLET**
1974 (Slick paper, 8 pgs.)(6¼x9¾")(in full color)
(Included with superhero model kits)
Aurora Plastics Co.

| | Good | Fine | N-Mint |
|---|---|---|---|
| 181-140-Tarzan; Neal Adams-a | .35 | 1.00 | 2.00 |
| 182-140-Spider-Man. 183-140-Tonto(Gil Kane art). 184-140-Hulk. 185-140-Superman. 186-140-Superboy. 187-140-Batman. 188-140-The Lone Ranger(1974-by Gil Kane). 192-140-Captain America(1975). 193-140-Robin each.... | | .50 | 1.00 |

**AUTHENTIC POLICE CASES**
2/48 - No. 6, 11/48; No. 7, 5/50 - No. 38, 3/55
St. John Publishing Co.

| | Good | Fine | N-Mint |
|---|---|---|---|
| 1-Hale the Magician by Tuska begins | 13.00 | 40.00 | 90.00 |
| 2-Lady Satan, Johnny Rebel app. | 9.00 | 27.00 | 62.00 |
| 3-Veiled Avenger app.; blood drainage story plus 2 Lucky Coyne stories; used in **SOTI**, illo. from Red Seal #16 | 19.00 | 56.00 | 130.00 |
| 4,5: 4-Masked Black Jack app. 5-Late 1930s Jack Cole-a(r); transvestism story | 8.00 | 24.00 | 56.00 |
| 6-Matt Baker-c; used in **SOTI**, illo-"An invitation to learning", r-in Fugitives From Justice #3; Jack Cole-a; also used by the N.Y. Legis. Comm. | 19.00 | 56.00 | 130.00 |
| 7,8,10-14: 7-Jack Cole-a; Matt Baker art begins #8; Vic Flint in #10-14 | 8.00 | 24.00 | 56.00 |
| 9-No Vic Flint | 6.50 | 19.00 | 45.00 |
| 15-Drug-c/story; Vic Flint app.; Baker-c | 8.00 | 24.00 | 56.00 |
| 16,18,20,21,23 | 4.00 | 12.00 | 28.00 |
| 17,19,22-Baker-c | 4.30 | 13.00 | 30.00 |
| 24-28 (All 100 pages): 26-Transvestism | 11.00 | 32.00 | 75.00 |
| 29,30 | 2.65 | 8.00 | 18.00 |
| 31,32,37-Baker-c | 3.00 | 9.00 | 21.00 |
| 33-Transvestism; Baker-c | 3.70 | 11.00 | 26.00 |
| 34-Drug-c by Baker | 3.70 | 11.00 | 26.00 |
| 35-Baker-c/a(2) | 3.50 | 10.50 | 24.00 |
| 36-Vic Flint strip-r; Baker-c | 2.65 | 8.00 | 18.00 |
| 38-Baker-c/a | 3.70 | 11.00 | 26.00 |

NOTE: ***Matt Baker*** *c-6-16, 17, 19, 22, 27, 29, 31-38; a-13, 16. Bondage c-1, 3.*

**AUTUMN ADVENTURES** (Walt Disney's)
Autumn, 1990 - Present ($2.95, color, quarterly, 68 pgs.)
Disney Comics

| | Good | Fine | N-Mint |
|---|---|---|---|
| 1-Donald Duck-r(2) by Barks, Pluto-r, & new-a | .50 | 1.50 | 3.00 |

**AVENGER, THE** (See A-1 Comics)
1955 - No. 4, Aug-Sept, 1955
Magazine Enterprises

| | Good | Fine | N-Mint |
|---|---|---|---|
| 1(A-1 #129)-Origin | 17.00 | 51.00 | 120.00 |
| 2(A-1 #131), 3(A-1 #133), 4(A-1 #138) | 10.00 | 30.00 | 70.00 |
| IW Reprint #9('64)-Reprints #1 (new cover) | 1.30 | 4.00 | 9.00 |

NOTE: ***Powell*** *a-2-4; c-1-4.*

**AVENGERS, THE** (See Giant-Size. . ., Kree/Skrull War Starring. . ., Marvel Graphic Novel #27, Marvel Super Action, Marvel Super Heroes('66), Marvel Treasury Ed., Marvel Triple Action, Solo Avengers, Tales Of Suspense, West Coast Avengers & X-Men Vs. . . .)

**AVENGERS, THE**
Sept, 1963 - Present
Marvel Comics Group

| | Good | Fine | N-Mint |
|---|---|---|---|
| 1-Origin & 1st app. The Avengers (Thor, Iron Man, Hulk, Ant-Man, Wasp) | 125.00 | 375.00 | 875.00 |
| 2 | 46.00 | 138.00 | 325.00 |
| 3-1st Sub-Mariner x-over (outside the F.F.) | 28.50 | 86.00 | 200.00 |
| 4-Revival of Captain America who joins the Avengers; 1st Silver Age app. of Captain America (3/64) | 64.00 | 192.00 | 450.00 |
| 4-Reprint from the Golden Record Comic set | 7.00 | 21.00 | 50.00 |
| With Record (still sealed) | 13.00 | 40.00 | 90.00 |
| 5-Hulk leaves | 18.00 | 54.00 | 125.00 |
| 6-10: 6-Intro The Masters of Evil. 8-Intro Kang. 9-Intro Wonder Man who dies in same story | 14.00 | 43.00 | 100.00 |
| 11-Spider-Man-c & x-over | 13.50 | 41.00 | 95.00 |
| 12-16: 15-Death of Zemo. 16-New Avengers line-up (Hawkeye, Quicksilver, Scarlet Witch join; Thor, Iron Man, Giant-Man, Wasp leave.) | 9.30 | 28.00 | 65.00 |
| 17-19: 19-Intro. Swordsman; origin Hawkeye | 6.50 | 19.00 | 45.00 |
| 20-22: Wood inks | 4.50 | 14.00 | 32.00 |
| 23-30: 28-Giant-Man becomes Goliath | 3.15 | 9.50 | 22.00 |
| 31-40 | 2.15 | 6.50 | 15.00 |
| 41-52,54-56: 48-Origin/1st app. new Black Knight. 52-Black Panther joins; 1st app. The Grim Reaper. 54-1st app. new Masters of Evil | 1.50 | 4.50 | 10.00 |
| 53-X-Men app. | 1.70 | 5.00 | 12.00 |
| 57-1st app. The Vision | 4.30 | 13.00 | 30.00 |
| 58-Origin The Vision | 2.85 | 8.50 | 20.00 |
| 59-67: 59-Intro. Yellowjacket. 60-Wasp & Yellowjacket wed. 63-Goliath becomes Yellowjacket; Hawkeye becomes the new Goliath. 65-Last 12 cent issue. 66,67: B. Smith-a | 1.70 | 5.00 | 12.00 |
| 68-70 | 1.35 | 4.00 | 8.00 |
| 71-1st app. The Invaders; Black Knight joins | 1.35 | 4.00 | 8.00 |
| 72-82,84-91: 80-Intro. Red Wolf. 87-Origin The Black Panther. 88-Written by Harlan Ellison | 1.15 | 3.50 | 7.00 |
| 83-Intro. The Liberators (Wasp, Valkyrie, Scarlet Witch, Medusa & the Black Widow) | 1.35 | 4.00 | 8.00 |
| 92-Neal Adams-c | 1.35 | 4.00 | 8.00 |
| 93-(52 pgs.)-Neal Adams-c/a | 5.00 | 15.00 | 35.00 |
| 94-96-Neal Adams-c/a | 3.15 | 9.50 | 22.00 |
| 97-G.A. Capt. America, Sub-Mariner, Human Torch, Patriot, Vision, Blazing Skull, Fin, Angel, & new Capt. Marvel x-over | 1.50 | 4.50 | 9.00 |
| 98-Goliath becomes Hawkeye; Smith c/a(i) | 2.30 | 7.00 | 16.00 |
| 99-Smith/Sutton-a | 2.30 | 7.00 | 16.00 |
| 100-Smith-c/a; featuring everyone who was an Avenger | 4.30 | 13.00 | 30.00 |
| 101-106,108,109: 101-Harlan Ellison scripts | 1.00 | 3.00 | 6.00 |
| 107-Starlin-a(p) | 1.15 | 3.50 | 7.00 |
| 110,111-X-Men app. | 1.70 | 5.00 | 10.00 |
| 112-1st app. Mantis | 1.35 | 4.00 | 8.00 |
| 113-120: 116-118-Defenders/Silver Surfer app. | .85 | 2.50 | 5.00 |
| 121-130: 123-Origin Mantis | .85 | 2.50 | 5.00 |
| 131-140: 136-Ploog-r/Amaz. Advs. #12 | .70 | 2.00 | 4.00 |
| 141-149: 144-Origin & 1st app. Hellcat | .50 | 1.50 | 3.00 |
| 150-Kirby-a(r); new line-up: Capt. America, Scarlet Witch, Iron Man, Wasp, Yellowjacket, Vision & The Beast | .50 | 1.50 | 3.00 |
| 151-163: 151-Wonderman returns with new costume | .50 | 1.50 | 3.00 |
| 164-166-Byrne-a | .75 | 2.25 | 4.50 |
| 167-180 | .40 | 1.25 | 2.50 |
| 181-191-Byrne-a. 181-New line-up: Capt. America, Scarlet Witch, Iron Man, Wasp, Vision, Beast & The Falcon. 183-Ms. Marvel joins. 185-Origin Quicksilver & Scarlet Witch | .40 | 1.25 | 2.50 |
| 192-202: Perez-a. 195-1st Taskmaster. 200-Double size; Ms. Marvel leaves | .35 | 1.00 | 2.00 |

203-262,264-271,273: 211-New line-up: Capt. America, Iron Man, Tigra, Thor, Wasp & Yellowjacket. 213-Yellowjacket leaves. 214-Ghost Rider app. 215,216-Silver Surfer app. 216-Tigra leaves. 217-Yellowjacket & Wasp return. 221-Hawkeye & She-Hulk join. 227-Capt.

*Authentic Police Cases #6, © STJ*

*The Avengers #4, © MEG*

*The Avengers #100, © MEG*

*The Avengers #1, © ABC Television*

*A-V in 3-D #1, © A-V*

*Babe Ruth Sports Comics #5, © HARV*

| | Good | Fine | N-Mint |
|---|---|---|---|
| Marvel (female) joins; origins of Ant-Man, Wasp, Giant-Man, Goliath, Yellowjacket, & Avengers. 230-Yellowjacket quits. 231-Ironman leaves. 232-Starfox (Eros) joins. 234-Origin Quicksilver, Scarlet Witch. 236-New logo. 238-Origin Blackout. 240-Spider-Woman revived. 250-($1.00, 52 pgs.) | | .60 | 1.20 |
| 263-1st app. X-Factor (1/86)(story continues in Fantastic Four #286) | .70 | 2.00 | 4.00 |
| 272-Alpha Flight guest star | .35 | 1.00 | 2.00 |
| 274-299: 291-$1.00 issues begin. 297-Black Knight, She-Hulk & Thor resign. 298-Inferno tie-in | | .60 | 1.20 |
| 300 ($1.75, 68 pgs.)-Thor joins | .30 | .90 | 1.80 |
| 301-304,306-332: 302-Re-intro Quasar. 314-318-Spider-Man x-over. 320-324-Alpha Flight app. (320-cameo) | | .50 | 1.00 |
| 305-Byrne scripts begin | .35 | 1.00 | 2.00 |
| Annual 6(11/76) | .70 | 2.00 | 4.00 |
| Annual 7(11/77)-Starlin-c/a; Warlock dies | 1.15 | 3.50 | 7.00 |
| Annual 8(10/78) | .60 | 1.75 | 3.50 |
| Annual 9(10/79)-Newton-a | .40 | 1.25 | 2.50 |
| Annual 10(10/81)-Golden-p; X-Men cameo; 1st app. Rogue & Madelyne Pryor | .85 | 2.50 | 5.00 |
| Annual 11-16: 11(12/82), 12(1/84), 13(11/84), 14(11/85), 15(10/86), 16(10/87) | .40 | 1.25 | 2.50 |
| Annual 17(11/88)-Evolutionary War x-over | .50 | 1.50 | 3.00 |
| Annual 18(1989, $2.00, 68 pgs.)-Atlantis Attacks | .40 | 1.25 | 2.50 |
| Annual 19(1990, $2.00, 68 pgs.) | .35 | 1.00 | 2.00 |
| Special 1(9/67, 25 cents, 68 pgs.)-New-a | 4.30 | 13.00 | 30.00 |
| Special 2(9/68, 25 cents, 68 pgs.)-New-a | 1.50 | 4.50 | 10.00 |
| Special 3(9/69, 25 cents, 68 pgs.)-r/Avengers #4 plus new Kirby-a(3); Origin Red Skull | 1.50 | 4.50 | 10.00 |
| Special 4(1/71, 25 cents, 68 pgs.), 5(1/72) | .85 | 2.50 | 5.00 |

NOTE: ***Austin** c(i)-157, 167, 168, 170-177, 181, 183-188, 198-201, Annual 8. **John Buscema** a-41-44p, 46p, 47p, 49, 50, 51-62p, 68-71, 74-77, 79-85, 87-91, 97, 105p, 121p, 124p, 125p, 152, 153p, 255-279p, 281-302p; c-41-66, 68-71, 73-91, 97-99, 178, 256-259p, 261-279p, 281-302p. **Byrne** a-164-166p, 181-191p, 233p, Annual 13, 14p; c-186-190p, 233p, 260, 305p; scripts-305-312. **Colan** c/a(p)-63-65, 111, 206-208, 210, 211. **Guice** a-Annual 12p. **Kane** c-37p, 159p. **Kane/ Everett** c-97. **Kirby** a-1-8p, Special 3r, 4r(p); c-1-30, 148, 151-158; layouts-14-16. **Miller** c-193p. **Mooney** a-86i, 179p, 180p. **Nebres** a-178i; c-179i. **Newton** a-204p, Annual 9p. **Perez** a(p)-141, 143, 144, 148, 154p, 155p, 160p, 161, 162, 167, 168, 170, 171, 194, 195, 196p, 198-202, Annual 6(p), 8; c-160-162p, 164-166p, 170-174p, 181p, 183-185p, 191p, 192p, 194-201p, Annual 8p. **Starlin** c-121, 135. **Staton** a-127-134i. **Tuska** a-47i, 48i, 51i, 53i, 54i, 106p, 107p, 135p, 137-140p, 163p.*

**AVENGERS, THE** (TV)
Nov, 1968 ("John Steed & Emma Peel" cover title) (15 cents)
Gold Key

| | Good | Fine | N-Mint |
|---|---|---|---|
| 1-Photo-c | 14.00 | 42.00 | 100.00 |

**AVENGERS SPOTLIGHT** (Formerly Solo Avengers #1-20)
No. 21, Aug, 1989 - No. 40, Jan, 1991 (.75-$1.00, color)
Marvel Comics

| | Good | Fine | N-Mint |
|---|---|---|---|
| 21 (75 cents)-Byrne-c/a | | .50 | 1.00 |
| 22-40 ($1.00): 26-Acts of Vengeance story. 31-34-U.S. Agent series. 36-Heck-i. 37-Mortimer-i. 40-The Black Knight app. | | .50 | 1.00 |

**AVENGERS WEST COAST** (Formerly West Coast Avengers)
No. 48, Sept, 1989 - Present ($1.00, color)
Marvel Comics

| | Good | Fine | N-Mint |
|---|---|---|---|
| 48-70: Byrne-c/a & scripts continue thru #57. 50-Re-intro original Human Torch. 54-Cover swipe/F.F. #1 | | .50 | 1.00 |

**AVIATION ADVENTURES AND MODEL BUILDING**
No. 16, Dec, 1946 - No. 17, Feb, 1947 (True Aviation Adv. . .No. 15)
Parents' Magazine Institute

| | Good | Fine | N-Mint |
|---|---|---|---|
| 16,17-Half comics and half pictures | 3.50 | 10.50 | 24.00 |

**AVIATION CADETS**
1943
Street & Smith Publications

| | Good | Fine | N-Mint |
|---|---|---|---|
| nn | 7.00 | 21.00 | 50.00 |

**A-V IN 3-D**
Dec, 1984 (28 pgs. w/glasses)
Aardvark-Vanaheim

| | Good | Fine | N-Mint |
|---|---|---|---|
| 1-Cerebus, Flaming Carrot, Normalman & Ms. Tree | .75 | 2.25 | 4.50 |

**AWFUL OSCAR** (Formerly & becomes Oscar Comics with No. 13)
No. 11, June, 1949 - No. 12, Aug, 1949
Marvel Comics

| | Good | Fine | N-Mint |
|---|---|---|---|
| 11,12 | 3.00 | 9.00 | 21.00 |

**AXA**
Apr, 1987 - No. 2, Aug, 1987 ($1.75, color)
Eclipse Comics

| | Good | Fine | N-Mint |
|---|---|---|---|
| 1,2 | .30 | .90 | 1.80 |

**AXEL PRESSBUTTON** (Pressbutton No. 5; see Laser Eraser & Pressbutton)
Nov, 1984 - No. 6, July, 1985 ($1.50-$1.75, Baxter paper)
Eclipse Comics

| | Good | Fine | N-Mint |
|---|---|---|---|
| 1-6: r/Warrior (British mag.); 1-Bolland-c; origin Laser Eraser & Pressbutton | .30 | .90 | 1.75 |

**AZTEC ACE**
Mar, 1984 - No. 15, Sept, 1985 (Baxter paper, 36 pgs. No. 2 on)
Eclipse Comics

| | Good | Fine | N-Mint |
|---|---|---|---|
| 1-$2.25 cover (52 pgs.) | .40 | 1.15 | 2.30 |
| 2,3-$1.50 cover | .25 | .75 | 1.50 |
| 4-15-$1.75-$1.50 cover | .30 | .90 | 1.80 |

NOTE: ***N. Redondo** a-1i-8i, 10i; c-6-8i.*

**BABE** (. . .Darling of the Hills, later issues)(Also see Big Shot and Sparky Watts)
June-July, 1948 - No. 11, Apr-May, 1950
Prize/Headline/Feature

| | Good | Fine | N-Mint |
|---|---|---|---|
| 1-Boody Rogers-a | 9.00 | 27.00 | 62.00 |
| 2-Boody Rogers-a | 5.70 | 17.00 | 40.00 |
| 3-11-All by Boody Rogers | 4.30 | 13.00 | 30.00 |

**BABE AMAZON OF OZARKS**
No. 5, 1948
Standard Comics

| | Good | Fine | N-Mint |
|---|---|---|---|
| 5-Exist? | 3.50 | 10.50 | 24.00 |

**BABE RUTH SPORTS COMICS**
April, 1949 - No. 11, Feb, 1951
Harvey Publications

| | Good | Fine | N-Mint |
|---|---|---|---|
| 1-Powell-a | 14.00 | 42.00 | 100.00 |
| 2-Powell-a | 11.50 | 34.00 | 80.00 |
| 3-11: Powell-a in most | 10.00 | 30.00 | 70.00 |

**BABES IN TOYLAND** (See 4-Color No. 1282 & Golden Pix Story Book ST-3)

**BABY HUEY AND PAPA** (See Paramount Animated. . .)
May, 1962 - No. 33, Jan, 1968 (Also see Casper The Friendly. . .)
Harvey Publications

| | Good | Fine | N-Mint |
|---|---|---|---|
| 1 | 8.00 | 24.00 | 56.00 |
| 2 | 3.70 | 11.00 | 26.00 |
| 3-5 | 2.00 | 6.00 | 14.00 |
| 6-10 | 1.50 | 4.50 | 9.00 |
| 11-20 | .85 | 2.50 | 5.00 |
| 21-33 | .70 | 2.00 | 4.00 |

**BABY HUEY DUCKLAND**
Nov, 1962 - No. 15, Nov, 1966 (25 cent Giants) (all 68 pgs.)
Harvey Publications

| | Good | Fine | N-Mint |
|---|---|---|---|
| 1 | 5.00 | 15.00 | 35.00 |
| 2-5 | 1.85 | 5.50 | 12.00 |
| 6-15 | 1.00 | 3.00 | 6.00 |

**BABY HUEY, THE BABY GIANT** (Also see Blackthorne 3-D Series #58, Casper, Harvey Hits #22, Harvey Comics Hits #60, & Paramount Animated Comics)
9/56 - #97, 10/71; #98, 10/72; #99, 10/80; #100, 10/90 -Present
Harvey Publications

| | Good | Fine | N-Mint |
|---|---|---|---|
| 1-Infinity-c | 22.00 | 65.00 | 150.00 |
| 2 | 11.00 | 32.00 | 75.00 |
| 3-Baby Huey takes anti-pep pills | 6.50 | 19.00 | 45.00 |
| 4,5 | 4.35 | 13.00 | 30.00 |
| 6-10 | 2.15 | 6.50 | 15.00 |
| 11-20 | 1.35 | 4.00 | 9.00 |
| 21-40 | 1.00 | 3.00 | 7.00 |
| 41-60 | .85 | 2.50 | 5.00 |
| 61-79(12/67) | .50 | 1.50 | 3.00 |
| 80(12/68) - 95-All 68 pg. Giants | .70 | 2.00 | 4.00 |
| 96,97-Both 52 pg. Giants | .60 | 1.75 | 3.50 |
| 98-99: Regular size | .25 | .75 | 1.50 |
| 100-102 ($1.00) | | .50 | 1.00 |

**BABY SNOOTS** (Also see March of Comics No. 359, 371, 396, 401, 419, 431, 443, 450, 462, 474, 485)
Aug, 1970 - No. 22, Nov, 1975
Gold Key

| | Good | Fine | N-Mint |
|---|---|---|---|
| 1 | 1.00 | 3.00 | 6.00 |
| 2 | .35 | 1.00 | 2.00 |
| 3-22: 22-Titled Snoots, the Forgetful Elefink | | .60 | 1.20 |

**BACHELOR FATHER** (TV)
No. 1332, 4-6/62 - No. 2, 1962
Dell Publishing Co.

| | Good | Fine | N-Mint |
|---|---|---|---|
| 4-Color 1332 (#1) | 4.50 | 14.00 | 32.00 |
| 2-Written by Stanley | 4.50 | 14.00 | 32.00 |

**BACHELOR'S DIARY**
1949
Avon Periodicals

| | Good | Fine | N-Mint |
|---|---|---|---|
| 1(Scarce)-King Features panel cartoons & text-r; pin-up, girl wrestling photos | 19.00 | 57.00 | 135.00 |

**BAD COMPANY**
Aug, 1988 - Present ($1.50-$1.75, color, high quality paper)
Quality Comics/Fleetway Quality #15 on

| | Good | Fine | N-Mint |
|---|---|---|---|
| 1-15: 5,6-Guice-c | .25 | .75 | 1.50 |
| 16-18: ($1.75-c) | .30 | .90 | 1.80 |

**BADGE OF JUSTICE**
No. 22, 1/55 - No. 23, 3/55; 4/55 - No. 4, 10/55
Charlton Comics

| | Good | Fine | N-Mint |
|---|---|---|---|
| 22(1/55) | 3.15 | 9.00 | 22.00 |
| 23(3/55), 1 | 2.15 | 6.50 | 15.00 |
| 2-4 | 1.50 | 4.50 | 10.00 |

**BADGER, THE** (Also see Coyote #14 & First Comics Graphic N. #15)
10/83 - No. 4, 4/84; No. 5, 5/85 - Present (Baxter paper)
Capital Comics/First Comics No. 5 on

| | Good | Fine | N-Mint |
|---|---|---|---|
| 1-Badger, Ham the Weather Wizard begin | 1.00 | 3.00 | 6.00 |
| 2-4 | .75 | 2.25 | 4.50 |
| 5(5/85) | .70 | 2.00 | 4.00 |
| 6 | .60 | 1.75 | 3.50 |
| 7-10 | .55 | 1.60 | 3.20 |
| 11-20 | .45 | 1.30 | 2.60 |
| 21-30 | .35 | 1.10 | 2.20 |
| 31-49,51,55-63: 32-Steve Rude-c | .30 | 1.00 | 2.00 |
| 50-($3.95, 52 pgs.) | .70 | 2.00 | 3.95 |
| 52-54-Tim Vigil-c/a | .75 | 2.25 | 4.50 |
| 64-72: 64-Begin $2.25-c | .40 | 1.15 | 2.30 |

**BADGER GOES BERSERK**
Sept, 1989 - No. 4, Dec, 1989 ($1.95, color, mini-series, Baxter)
First Comics

| | Good | Fine | N-Mint |
|---|---|---|---|
| 1-4: 2-Paul Chadwick-c/a(2 pgs.) | .35 | 1.00 | 2.00 |

**BADMEN OF THE WEST**
1951 (Giant - 132 pages)(Painted-c)
Avon Periodicals

| | Good | Fine | N-Mint |
|---|---|---|---|
| 1-Contains rebound copies of Jesse James, King of the Bad Men of Deadwood, Badmen of Tombstone; other combinations possible. Issues with Kubert-a. . . . | 19.00 | 57.00 | 135.00 |

**BADMEN OF THE WEST!** (See A-1 Comics)
1953 - No. 3, 1954
Magazine Enterprises

| | Good | Fine | N-Mint |
|---|---|---|---|
| 1(A-1 100)-Meskin-a? | 12.00 | 36.00 | 85.00 |
| 2(A-1 120), 3: 2-Larsen-a | 7.00 | 21.00 | 50.00 |

**BADMEN OF TOMBSTONE**
1950
Avon Periodicals

| | Good | Fine | N-Mint |
|---|---|---|---|
| nn | 6.50 | 19.00 | 45.00 |

**BAFFLING MYSTERIES** (Formerly Indian Braves No. 1-4; Heroes of the Wild Frontier No. 26-on)
No. 5, Nov, 1951 - No. 26, Oct, 1955
Periodical House (Ace Magazines)

| | Good | Fine | N-Mint |
|---|---|---|---|
| 5 | 10.00 | 30.00 | 70.00 |
| 6,7,9,10: 10-E.C. Crypt Keeper swipe on-c | 6.50 | 19.00 | 45.00 |
| 8-Woodish-a by Cameron | 6.50 | 19.00 | 45.00 |
| 11-24: 24-Last pre-code issue | 6.50 | 19.00 | 45.00 |
| 25-Reprints; surrealistic-c | 4.50 | 13.50 | 32.00 |
| 26-Reprints | 2.85 | 8.50 | 22.00 |

NOTE: ***Cameron*** *a-8, 16-18, 20-22.* ***Colan*** *a-5, 11, 25r/5.* ***Sekowsky*** *a-5, 6, 22. Bondage c-20. Reprints in 18(1), 19(1), 24(3).*

**BALBO** (See Master Comics #33 & Mighty Midget Comics)

**BALDER THE BRAVE**
Nov, 1985 - No. 4, 1986 (Mini-series)
Marvel Comics Group

| | Good | Fine | N-Mint |
|---|---|---|---|
| 1-4: Simonson-c/a; character from Thor | | .50 | 1.00 |

**BALLAD OF HALO JONES, THE**
Sept, 1987 - No. 12, Aug, 1988 ($1.25-$1.50, color)
Quality Comics

| | Good | Fine | N-Mint |
|---|---|---|---|
| 1-12: Alan Moore scripts in all | .25 | .75 | 1.50 |

**BALOO & LITTLE BRITCHES**
April, 1968 (Walt Disney)
Gold Key

| | Good | Fine | N-Mint |
|---|---|---|---|
| 1-From the Jungle Book | 1.70 | 5.00 | 10.00 |

**BALTIMORE COLTS**
1950 (Giveaway)
American Visuals Corp.

| | Good | Fine | N-Mint |
|---|---|---|---|
| nn-Eisner-c | 31.00 | 94.00 | 220.00 |

**BAMBI** (See 4-Color No. 12,30,186, Movie Classics, Movie Comics, and Walt Disney Showcase No. 31)

**BAMBI** (Disney)
1941, 1942, 1984
K. K. Publications (Giveaways)/Whitman Publ. Co.

| | Good | Fine | N-Mint |
|---|---|---|---|
| 1941-Horlick's Malted Milk & various toy stores - text & pictures; most copies mailed out with store stickers on cover | 13.00 | 40.00 | 90.00 |
| 1942-Same as 4-Color 12, but no price (Same as '41 issue?) (Scarce) | 20.00 | 60.00 | 140.00 |
| 1-(Whitman, 1984; 60 cents)-r/4-Color 186 | | .30 | .60 |

**BAMM BAMM & PEBBLES FLINTSTONE** (TV)
Oct, 1964 (Hanna-Barbera)
Gold Key

*The Badger #54, © First Comics*

*Badmen of Tombstone nn, © AVON*

*Baffling Mysteries #10, © ACE*

Bang-Up Comics #2, © Prog. Publ.

Banner Comics #5, © ACE

Baoh #1, © Shueisha, Inc. & Viz

| | Good | Fine | N-Mint |
|---|---|---|---|
| 1 | 2.65 | 8.00 | 18.00 |

**BANANA OIL**
1924 (52 pages)(Black & White)
MS Publ. Co.

| | | | |
|---|---|---|---|
| nn-Milt Gross-a; not reprints | 14.00 | 42.00 | 100.00 |

**BANANA SPLITS, THE** (TV) (See March of Comics No. 364)
June, 1969 - No. 8, Oct, 1971 (Hanna-Barbera)
Gold Key

| | | | |
|---|---|---|---|
| 1 | 1.50 | 4.50 | 10.00 |
| 2-8 | .85 | 2.50 | 5.00 |

**BAND WAGON** (See Hanna-Barbera Band Wagon)

**BANG-UP COMICS**
Dec, 1941 - No. 3, June, 1942
Progressive Publishers

| | | | |
|---|---|---|---|
| 1-Cosmo Mann & Lady Fairplay begin; Buzz Balmer by Rick Yager in all (origin #1) | 43.00 | 130.00 | 300.00 |
| 2,3 | 25.00 | 75.00 | 175.00 |

**BANNER COMICS** (Captain Courageous No. 6)
No. 3, Sept, 1941 - No. 5, Jan, 1942
Ace Magazines

| | | | |
|---|---|---|---|
| 3-Captain Courageous & Lone Warrior & Sidekick Dicky begin | 54.00 | 161.00 | 375.00 |
| 4,5: 4-Flag-c | 36.00 | 107.00 | 250.00 |

**BAOH**
1990 - No. 8, 1990 ($2.95, B&W, limited series, 52 pgs.)
Viz Select Comics

| | | | |
|---|---|---|---|
| 1-8: Japanese manga adapted to English | .50 | 1.50 | 3.00 |

**BARBARIANS, THE**
June, 1975
Atlas Comics/Seaboard Periodicals

| | | | |
|---|---|---|---|
| 1-Origin, only app. Andrax; Iron Jaw app. | | .50 | 1.00 |

**BARBIE**
Jan, 1991 - Present ($1.00, color)
Marvel Comics

| | | | |
|---|---|---|---|
| 1-4: 1-Sealed in plastic bag w/Barbie Pink Card; Romita-c | | .50 | 1.00 |

**BARBIE & KEN**
May-July, 1962 - No. 5, Nov-Jan, 1963-64
Dell Publishing Co.

| | | | |
|---|---|---|---|
| 01-053-207(#1)-Based on toy dolls | 13.00 | 40.00 | 90.00 |
| 2-5 | 10.00 | 30.00 | 70.00 |

**BARBIE FASHION**
Jan, 1991 - Present ($1.00, color)
Marvel Comics

| | | | |
|---|---|---|---|
| 1-4: 1-Sealed in plastic bag w/doorknob hanger | | .50 | 1.00 |

**BARKER, THE** (Also see National Comics #42)
Autumn, 1946 - No. 15, Dec, 1949
Quality Comics Group/Comic Magazine

| | | | |
|---|---|---|---|
| 1 | 8.00 | 24.00 | 56.00 |
| 2 | 3.70 | 11.00 | 26.00 |
| 3-10 | 2.65 | 8.00 | 18.00 |
| 11-14 | 2.00 | 6.00 | 14.00 |
| 15-Jack Cole-a(p) | 2.85 | 8.50 | 20.00 |

NOTE: ***Jack Cole** art in some issues.*

**BARNEY AND BETTY RUBBLE** (TV) (Flintstones' Neighbors)
Jan, 1973 - No. 23, Dec, 1976 (Hanna-Barbera)
Charlton Comics

| | Good | Fine | N-Mint |
|---|---|---|---|
| 1 | 1.70 | 5.00 | 12.00 |
| 2-10 | .85 | 2.60 | 6.00 |
| 11-23 | .50 | 1.50 | 3.00 |

**BARNEY BAXTER** (Also see Magic Comics)
1938 - No. 2, 1956
David McKay/Dell Publishing Co./Argo

| | | | |
|---|---|---|---|
| Feature Books 15(McKay-1938) | 19.00 | 56.00 | 130.00 |
| 4-Color 20(1942) | 17.00 | 51.00 | 120.00 |
| 4,5 | 8.50 | 25.50 | 60.00 |
| 1,2(1956-Argo) | 3.60 | 11.00 | 25.00 |

**BARNEY BEAR . . .**
1977 - 1981
Spire Christian Comics (Fleming H. Revell Co.)

| | | | |
|---|---|---|---|
| . . .Home Plate nn-(1979, 49 cents) | | .30 | .60 |
| . . .Lost and Found nn-(1979, 49 cents) | | .30 | .60 |
| . . .Out of The Woods nn-(1980, 49 cents) | | .30 | .60 |
| . . .Sunday School Picnic nn-(1981, 69 cents) | | .30 | .60 |
| . . .The Swamp Gang! nn-(1980, 59 cents) | | .30 | .60 |
| . . .Wakes Up nn-(1977, 39 cents) | | .30 | .60 |

**BARNEY GOOGLE AND SPARK PLUG** (See Comic Monthly & Giant Comic Album)
1923 - No. 6, 1928 (Daily strip reprints; B&W) (52 pages)
Cupples & Leon Co.

| | | | |
|---|---|---|---|
| 1-By Billy DeBeck | 17.00 | 51.00 | 120.00 |
| 2-6 | 11.00 | 32.00 | 75.00 |

NOTE: *Started in 1918 as newspaper strip; Spark Plug began 1922, 1923.*

**BARNEY GOOGLE & SNUFFY SMITH**
1942 - April, 1964
Dell Publishing Co./Gold Key

| | | | |
|---|---|---|---|
| 4-Color 19('42) | 27.00 | 80.00 | 185.00 |
| 4-Color 40('44) | 14.00 | 42.00 | 100.00 |
| Large Feature Comic 11(1943) | 14.00 | 42.00 | 100.00 |
| 1(10113-404)-Gold Key (4/64) | 1.70 | 5.00 | 12.00 |

**BARNEY GOOGLE & SNUFFY SMITH**
June, 1951 - No. 4, Feb, 1952 (Reprints)
Toby Press

| | | | |
|---|---|---|---|
| 1 | 6.50 | 19.00 | 45.00 |
| 2,3 | 3.70 | 11.00 | 26.00 |
| 4-Kurtzman-a "Pot Shot Pete," 5 pgs.; reprints/John Wayne #5 | 4.50 | 14.00 | 32.00 |

**BARNEY GOOGLE AND SNUFFY SMITH**
March, 1970 - No. 6, Jan, 1971
Charlton Comics

| | | | |
|---|---|---|---|
| 1 | 1.15 | 3.50 | 8.00 |
| 2-6 | .70 | 2.00 | 5.00 |

**BARNYARD COMICS** (Dizzy Duck No. 32 on)
June, 1944 - No. 31, Sept, 1950; No. 10, 1957
Nedor/Polo Mag./Standard(Animated Cartoons)

| | | | |
|---|---|---|---|
| 1(nn, 52 pgs.) | 10.00 | 30.00 | 70.00 |
| 2 (52 pgs.) | 4.50 | 14.00 | 32.00 |
| 3-5 | 3.00 | 9.00 | 21.00 |
| 6-12,16 | 2.30 | 7.00 | 16.00 |
| 13-15,17,21,23,26,27,29-All contain Frazetta text illos | 3.00 | 9.00 | 21.00 |
| 18-20,22,24,25-All contain Frazetta-a & text illos | 8.00 | 24.00 | 56.00 |
| 28,30,31 | 1.50 | 4.50 | 10.00 |
| 10(1957)(Exist?) | .70 | 2.00 | 5.00 |

**BARRY M. GOLDWATER**
March, 1965 (Complete life story)
Dell Publishing Co.

| | Good | Fine | N-Mint |
|---|---|---|---|
| 12-055-503: Photo-c | 2.30 | 7.00 | 16.00 |

**BASEBALL COMICS**
Spring, 1949 (Reprinted later as a Spirit section)
Will Eisner Productions

| | | | |
|---|---|---|---|
| 1-Will Eisner-c/a | 43.00 | 130.00 | 300.00 |

**BASEBALL HEROES**
1952 (One Shot)
Fawcett Publications

| | | | |
|---|---|---|---|
| nn (Scarce)-Babe Ruth photo-c; baseball's Hall of Fame briographies | 41.00 | 122.00 | 285.00 |

**BASEBALL THRILLS**
No. 10, Sum, 1951 - No. 3, Sum, 1952 (Saunders painted-c No.1,2)
Ziff-Davis Publ. Co.

| | | | |
|---|---|---|---|
| 10(#1) | 20.00 | 60.00 | 140.00 |
| 2-Powell-a(2)(Late Sum, '51) | 12.00 | 36.00 | 85.00 |
| 3-Kinstler-c/a | 12.00 | 36.00 | 85.00 |

**BASEBALL THRILLS 3-D**
May, 1990 ($2.95, w/glasses)
The 3-D Zone

| | | | |
|---|---|---|---|
| 1-New L. B. Cole-c; life stories of Ty Cobb & Ted Williams | .50 | 1.50 | 3.00 |

**BASICALLY STRANGE** (Magazine)
December, 1982 (B&W, $1.95)
John C. Comics (Archie Comics Group)

| | | | |
|---|---|---|---|
| 1-(21,000 printed; all but 1,000 destroyed—pages out of sequence) | .30 | 1.00 | 2.00 |
| 1-Wood, Toth-a; Corben-c. Reprints & new art | .30 | 1.00 | 2.00 |

**BASIC HISTORY OF AMERICA ILLUSTRATED**
1976 (B&W)
Pendulum Press

07-1999 America Becomes a World Power 1890-1920. 07-2251 The Industrial Era 1865-1915. 07-226x Before the Civil War 1830-1860. 07-2278 Americans Move Westward 1800-1850. 07-2286 The Civil War 1850-1876 - Redondo-a. 07-2294 The Fight for Freedom 1750-1783. 07-2308 The New World 1500-1750. 07-2316 Problems of the New Nation 1800-1830. 07-2324 Roaring Twenties and the Great Depression 1920-1940. 07-2332 The United States Emerges 1783-1800. 07-2340 America Today 1945-1976. 07-2359 World War II 1940-1945

| | | | |
|---|---|---|---|
| Softcover | | | 1.50 |
| Hardcover | | | 4.50 |

**BASIL** (. . .the Royal Cat)
Jan, 1953 - No. 4, Sept, 1953
St. John Publishing Co.

| | | | |
|---|---|---|---|
| 1 | 2.00 | 6.00 | 14.00 |
| 2-4 | 1.00 | 3.00 | 7.00 |
| I.W. Reprint 1 | .35 | 1.00 | 2.00 |

**BASIL WOLVERTON'S GATEWARY TO HORROR**
June, 1988 (One-shot, $1.75, B&W)
Dark Horse Comics

| | | | |
|---|---|---|---|
| 1-Wolverton-r | .30 | .90 | 1.80 |

**BASIL WOLVERTON'S PLANET OF TERROR**
Oct, 1987 (One-shot, $1.75, B&W)
Dark Horse Comics

| | | | |
|---|---|---|---|
| 1-Wolverton-r | .30 | .90 | 1.80 |

**BATGIRL SPECIAL** (See Teen Titans #50)
1988 (One shot, color, $1.50, 52pgs)
DC Comics

| | | | |
|---|---|---|---|
| 1 | 1.35 | 4.00 | 8.00 |

**BAT LASH** (See DC Special Series #16, Showcase #76 & Weird Western Tales)
Oct-Nov, 1968 - No. 7, Oct-Nov, 1969
National Periodical Publications

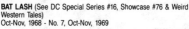

| | Good | Fine | N-Mint |
|---|---|---|---|
| 1 | 1.00 | 3.00 | 6.00 |
| 2-7 | .50 | 1.50 | 3.00 |

**BATMAN** (See Arkham Asylum, Aurora, The Best of DC #2, Blind Justice, The Brave & the Bold, Cosmic Odyssey, DC 100-Page Super Spec. #14,20, DC Special, DC Special Series, Detective, Dynamic Classics, 80-Page Giants, Gotham By Gaslight, Greatest Batman Stories Ever Told, Greatest Joker Stories Ever Told, Heroes Against Hunger, The Joker, Justice League of America #250, Justice League Int., Legends of the Dark Knight, Limited Coll. Ed., Man-Bat, Power Record Comics, Real Fact #5, Saga of Ra's Al Ghul, Shadow of the. . ., Star Spangled, Super Friends, 3-D Batman, Untold Legend of. . ., Wanted. . . & World's Finest)

**BATMAN**
Spring, 1940 - Present
National Periodical Publ./Detective Comics/DC Comics

1-Origin The Batman retold by Bob Kane; see Detective #33 for 1st origin; 1st app. Joker & The Cat (Catwoman); has Batman story without Robin originally planned for Detective #38. This book was created entirely from the inventory of Detective Comics

| Good | Fine | VF-NM | NM/Mint |
|---|---|---|---|
| 3,000.00 | 7,500.00 | 18,000.00 | 27,000.00 |

(Estimated up to 300 total copies exist, 16 in NM/Mint)

1-Reprint, oversize 13½"x10." **WARNING**: This comic is an exact duplicate reprint of the original except for its size. DC published it in 1974 with a second cover titling it as a **Famous First Edition**. There have been many reported cases of the outer cover being removed and the interior sold as the original edition. The reprint with the new outer cover removed is practically worthless.

| | Good | Fine | N-Mint |
|---|---|---|---|
| 2 | 760.00 | 1875.00 | 4500.00 |
| 3-1st Catwoman in costume; 1st Puppetmaster app. | 550.00 | 1250.00 | 3000.00 |
| 4 | 417.00 | 1040.00 | 2500.00 |
| 5-1st app. of the Batmobile with its bat-head front | 308.00 | 770.00 | 1850.00 |
| 6-10: 8-Infinity-c | 225.00 | 562.00 | 1350.00 |
| 11-Classic Joker-c (2nd Joker-c, 6-7/42) | 250.00 | 620.00 | 1500.00 |
| 12-15: 13-Jerry Siegel, creator of Superman appears in a Batman story. 14-2nd Penguin-c (12-1/42-43) | 183.00 | 460.00 | 1100.00 |

| | Good | Fine | VF-NM | NM/Mint |
|---|---|---|---|---|
| 16-Intro Alfred (4-5/43) | 258.00 | 645.00 | 1550.00 | 2300.00 |

(Estimated up to 300 total copies exist, 16 in NM/Mint)

| | Good | Fine | N-Mint |
|---|---|---|---|
| 17-20: 18-Hitler, Hirohito, Mussolini-c | 117.00 | 292.00 | 700.00 |
| 21,22,24,26,28-30: 22-1st Alfred solo | 108.00 | 270.00 | 650.00 |
| 23-Joker-c/story | 142.00 | 355.00 | 850.00 |
| 25-Only Joker/Penguin team-up | 133.00 | 335.00 | 800.00 |
| 27-Christmas-c | 108.00 | 270.00 | 650.00 |
| 31,32,34-36,38,39: 31-Infinity logo-c. 32-Origin Robin retold. 38-Penguin-c | 67.00 | 167.00 | 400.00 |
| 33-Christmas-c | 83.00 | 210.00 | 500.00 |
| 37,40,44-Joker-c/stories | 92.00 | 230.00 | 550.00 |
| 41-43,45,46: 42-2nd Catwoman-c (8-9/47). 43-Penguin-c. 45-Christmas cover | 58.00 | 146.00 | 350.00 |
| 47-1st detailed origin The Batman (6-7/48) | 183.00 | 460.00 | 1100.00 |
| 48-1000 Secrets of Batcave; r-in #203 | 63.00 | 156.00 | 375.00 |
| 49-Joker-c/story; 1st Vicki Vale & Mad Hatter | 92.00 | 230.00 | 550.00 |
| 50-Two-Face impostor app. | 58.00 | 146.00 | 350.00 |
| 51,53,54,56-61: 57-Centerfold is a 1950 calendar. 58-Penguin-c. 161-Origin Batman Plane II | 52.00 | 131.00 | 315.00 |
| 52,55-Joker-c/stories | 71.00 | 178.00 | 425.00 |
| 62-Origin Catwoman; Catwoman-c | 64.00 | 160.00 | 385.00 |
| 63-65,67-72,74-77,79,80: 65,69-Catwoman-c. 68-Two-Face app. 72-Last 52 pgs. 74-Used in **POP**, Pg. 90 | 42.00 | 105.00 | 250.00 |
| 66,73-Joker-c/stories | 56.00 | 140.00 | 335.00 |
| 78-(8-9/53)-Roh Kar, The Man Hunter from Mars story-the 1st lawman of Mars to come to Earth (green skinned) | 52.00 | 130.00 | 310.00 |
| 81-89: 84-Catwoman-c; Two-Face app. 86-Intro Batmarine (Batman's submarine). 89-Last Pre-Code issue | 42.00 | 105.00 | 250.00 |
| 90,91,93-99: 97-2nd app. Bat-Hound | 27.00 | 70.00 | 165.00 |

*Baseball Comics #1, © Will Eisner*

*Batman #1, © DC*

*Batman #13, © DC*

*Batman #105, © DC*

*Batman #366, © DC*

*Batman #436, © DC*

| | Good | Fine | N-Mint |
|---|---|---|---|
| 92-1st app. Bat-Hound | 35.00 | 87.00 | 210.00 |
| 100 | 120.00 | 300.00 | 720.00 |
| 101-104,106-109 | 22.00 | 66.00 | 155.00 |
| 105-1st Batwoman in Batman | 28.50 | 86.00 | 200.00 |
| 110-Joker story | 28.00 | 84.00 | 195.00 |
| 111-120: 113-1st app. Fatman | 16.00 | 48.00 | 110.00 |
| 121,122,124-126,128-130: 129-Origin Robin retold; Bondage-c | 13.00 | 40.00 | 90.00 |
| 123-Joker story; 2nd app. Bat-Hound | 16.00 | 48.00 | 110.00 |
| 127-Joker story; Superman cameo | 16.00 | 48.00 | 110.00 |
| 131-135,137-139,141-143: Last 10 cent issue. 131-Intro 2nd Batman & Robin series. 133-1st Bat-Mite in Batman. 134-Origin The Dummy. 139-Intro old Bat-Girl | 9.30 | 28.00 | 65.00 |
| 136-Joker-c/story | 14.00 | 43.00 | 100.00 |
| 140,144-Joker stories | 10.00 | 30.00 | 70.00 |
| 145,148-Joker-c/stories | 11.50 | 34.00 | 80.00 |
| 146,147,149,150 | 7.00 | 21.00 | 50.00 |
| 151,153,154,156-158,160-162,164-170: 164-New Batmobile; New look & Mystery Analysts series begins | 5.00 | 15.00 | 35.00 |
| 152-Joker story | 5.70 | 17.00 | 40.00 |
| 155-1st S.A. app. The Penguin | 12.00 | 36.00 | 85.00 |
| 159,163-Joker-c/stories | 7.00 | 21.00 | 50.00 |
| 171-Riddler app.(5/65), 1st since 12/48 | 36.00 | 108.00 | 250.00 |
| 172-175,177,178,180,181,183,184: 181-Batman & Robin poster insert; intro. Poison Ivy | 3.50 | 10.50 | 24.00 |
| 176-80-Pg. Giant G-17; Joker-c/story | 4.50 | 14.00 | 32.00 |
| 179-2nd app. Silver Age Riddler | 7.85 | 23.50 | 55.00 |
| 182,187-80 Pg. Giants G-24, G-30; Joker-c/stories | 4.30 | 13.00 | 30.00 |
| 185-80 Pg. Giant G-27 | 3.70 | 11.00 | 36.00 |
| 186-Joker-c/story | 2.65 | 8.00 | 18.00 |
| 188-192,194-197,199: 197-New Bat-Girl app. | 2.00 | 6.00 | 14.00 |
| 193-80-Pg. Giant G-37 | 2.30 | 7.00 | 16.00 |
| 198-80-Pg. Giant G-43; Joker story; Origin-r | 2.65 | 8.00 | 18.00 |
| 200-Joker-story; retells origin of Batman & Robin | 14.00 | 43.00 | 100.00 |
| 201-Joker story | 2.30 | 7.00 | 16.00 |
| 202,204-207,209,210 | 1.50 | 4.50 | 9.00 |
| 203-80 Pg. Giant G-49; r/#48, 61, & Det. 185; Batcave Blueprints | 1.70 | 5.00 | 12.00 |
| 208-80 Pg. Giant G-55; New origin Batman by Gil Kane | 1.70 | 5.00 | 12.00 |
| 211,212,214-217: 216-Alfred given a new last name-"Pennyworth." (see Detective #96) | 1.50 | 4.50 | 9.00 |
| 213-80-Pg. Giant G-61; origin Alfred, Joker(r/Det. 168), Clayface; new origin Robin | 4.30 | 13.00 | 30.00 |
| 218-80-Pg. Giant G-67 | 1.70 | 5.00 | 12.00 |
| 219-Neal Adams-a | 2.65 | 8.00 | 18.00 |
| 220,221,224-227,229-231 | 1.35 | 4.00 | 8.00 |
| 222-Beatles take-off | 2.30 | 7.00 | 16.00 |
| 223,228,233-80-Pg. Giants G-73,G-79,G-85 | 1.70 | 5.00 | 10.00 |
| 232,237-N. Adams-a. 232-Intro/1st app. Ras Al Ghul. 237-G.A. Batman-r/Det. #37; Wrightson/Ellison plots | 2.85 | 8.50 | 20.00 |
| 234-1st S.A. app. Two-Face; N. Adams-a; 52 pg. issues begin, end #242 | 4.30 | 13.00 | 30.00 |
| 235,236,239-242: 239-XMas-c. 241-Reprint/#5 | 1.15 | 3.50 | 7.00 |
| 238-DC-8 100 pg. Super Spec.; unpubbed G.A. Atom, Sargon, Plastic Man stories; Doom Patrol origin-r; Batman, Legion, Aquaman-r; N. Adams-c | 1.35 | 4.00 | 8.00 |
| 243-245-Neal Adams-a | 2.15 | 6.50 | 15.00 |
| 246-250,252,253: 253-Shadow app. | 1.15 | 3.50 | 7.00 |
| 251-N. Adams-c/a; Joker-c/story | 4.30 | 13.00 | 30.00 |
| 254,256-259,261-All 100 pg. editions; part-r | 1.35 | 4.00 | 8.00 |
| 255-N. Adams-c/a; tells of Bruce Wayne's father who wore bat costume & fought crime (100 pgs.) | 1.70 | 5.00 | 12.00 |
| 260-Joker-c/story (100pgs.) | 2.85 | 8.50 | 20.00 |

| | Good | Fine | N-Mint |
|---|---|---|---|
| 262-285,287-290,292,293,295-299: 262-68pgs. 266-Catwoman back to old costume | .70 | 2.00 | 4.00 |
| 286,291,294-Joker-c/stories | 1.00 | 3.00 | 6.00 |
| 300-Double-size | 1.00 | 3.00 | 6.00 |
| 301-320,322-352,354-356,358,360-365,367,369,370: 304-(44 pgs.). 311-Batgirl reteams w/Batman. 316-Robin returns. 323,324-Catman & Catwoman app. 332-Catwoman's 1st solo. 325-Death of Comm. Gordon. 345-New Dr. Death app. 361-1st app. Harvey Bullock | .70 | 2.00 | 4.00 |
| 321,353,359-Joker-c/stories | 1.00 | 3.00 | 6.00 |
| 357-1st app. Jason Todd (3/83); see Det. 524 | 1.35 | 4.00 | 8.00 |
| 366-Jason Todd 1st in Robin costume; Joker-c/story | 4.15 | 12.50 | 25.00 |
| 368-1st new Robin in costume (Jason Todd) | 3.35 | 10.00 | 20.00 |
| 371-399,401-403: 386,387-Intro Black Mask (villain). 401-2nd app. Magpie | .50 | 1.50 | 3.00 |
| NOTE: *Most issues between 397 & 432 were reprinted in 1989 and sold in multi-packs. Some are not identified as reprints but have newer ads copyrighted after cover dates. 2nd and 3rd printings exist.* | | | |
| 400 ($1.50, 64pgs.)-Dark Knight special; intro by Steven King; Art Adams/Austin-a | 3.00 | 9.00 | 18.00 |
| 404-Miller scripts begin (end 407); Year 1 | 1.70 | 5.00 | 10.00 |
| 405-407: 407-Year 1 ends (See Det. for Year 2) | 1.00 | 3.00 | 6.00 |
| 408-410: New Origin Jason Todd (Robin) | 1.00 | 3.00 | 6.00 |
| 411-416,421-425: 412-Origin/1st app. Mime. 415,416-Millennium tie-ins. 416-Nightwing-c/story | .50 | 1.50 | 3.00 |
| 417-420: "Ten Nights of the Beast" storyline | 2.50 | 7.50 | 15.00 |
| 426-($1.50, 52 pgs.)-"A Death In The Family" storyline begins, ends #429 | 4.15 | 12.50 | 25.00 |
| 427,428: 428-Death of Robin (Jason Todd) | 3.00 | 9.00 | 18.00 |
| 429-Joker-c/story; Superman app. | 1.35 | 4.00 | 8.00 |
| 430-432 | .30 | .90 | 1.80 |
| 433-435-"Many Deaths of the Batman" story by John Byrne-c/scripts | .50 | 1.50 | 3.00 |
| 436-Year 3 begins (ends #439); origin original Robin retold by Nightwing (Dick Grayson) | .85 | 2.50 | 5.00 |
| 436-2nd print | | .50 | 1.00 |
| 437-439: 437-Origin Robin continued | .50 | 1.50 | 3.00 |
| 440,441: "A Lonely Place of Dying" Parts 1 & 3; 440-1st app. Timothy Drake | .25 | .70 | 1.40 |
| 442-1st app. New Robin (Timothy Drake) | .85 | 2.50 | 5.00 |
| 443-456,458-462: 445-447-Batman goes to Russia. 448,449-"The Penguin Affair" parts 1 & 3. 450,451-Joker-c/stories. 452-454-"Dark Knight Dark City" storyline | | .50 | 1.00 |
| 457-Timothy Drake officially becomes Robin | 1.35 | 4.00 | 8.00 |
| 457-2nd printing | | .50 | 1.00 |
| Annual 1(8-10/61)-Swan-c | 28.50 | 86.00 | 200.00 |
| Annual 2 | 12.00 | 36.00 | 85.00 |
| Annual 3(Summer, '62)-Joker-c/story | 13.50 | 41.00 | 95.00 |
| Annual 4,5 | 5.70 | 17.00 | 40.00 |
| Annual 6,7(7/64) | 4.30 | 13.00 | 30.00 |
| Annual 8(10/82) | .85 | 2.50 | 5.00 |
| Annual 9(7/85), 10(8/86), 12('88, $1.50) | .55 | 1.65 | 3.30 |
| Annual 11('87, $1.25)-Alan Moore scripts | .85 | 2.50 | 5.00 |
| Annual 13('89, $1.75, 68 pgs.)-Gives history of Bruce Wayne, Dick Grayson, Jason Todd, Alfred, Comm. Gordon, Barbara Gordon (Batgirl) & Vicki Vale; Morrow-i | .35 | 1.10 | 2.20 |
| Annual 14('90, $2.00, 68 pgs.)-Origin Two-Face | .35 | 1.00 | 2.00 |
| Death In The Family trade paperback (1988, $3.95)-r/Batman #426-429 by Aparo | 1.35 | 4.00 | 8.00 |
| Death In The Family: 2nd - 5th printings | .70 | 2.00 | 4.00 |
| Lonely Place of Dying (1990, $3.95, 132 pgs.)-r/Batman #440-442 & New Titans #60,61; Perez-c | .70 | 2.00 | 4.00 |
| Year One Hardcover (1988, $12.95) | 2.50 | 7.50 | 15.00 |
| Year One trade paperback (1988, $9.95)-r/Batman #404-407 by Miller; introduction by Miller | 3.00 | 9.00 | 18.00 |

| | Good | Fine | N-Mint |
|---|---|---|---|
| Year One trade paperback: 2nd & 3rd prints | 1.70 | 5.00 | 10.00 |
| Year Two trade paperback (1990, $9.95)-r/Det. 575-578 by McFarlane; wraparound-c | 1.70 | 5.00 | 10.00 |
| Pizza Hut giveaway(12/77)-exact r-/of #122,123; Joker-c/story | .35 | 1.00 | 2.00 |
| Prell Shampoo giveaway('66)-16 pgs. "The Joker's Practical Jokes" (6-7/8"x3-3/8") | 2.00 | 6.00 | 14.00 |
| Special 1(4/84)-Golden c/a(p) | .85 | 2.50 | 5.00 |

NOTE: ***Art Adams*** *a-400p.* ***Neal Adams*** *c-200, 203, 210, 217, 219-222, 224-227, 229, 230, 232, 234, 236-241, 243-246, 251, 255, Annual 14.* ***Bolland*** *c-445-447.* ***Burnley*** *a-10, 12-18, 20, 25, 27; c-28.* ***Byrne*** *c-401, 433-435, 533-535, Annual 11i.* ***Colan*** *a-340p, 343-345p, 348-351p, 373p, 383p; c-343p, 345p, 350p.* ***J. Cole*** *a-238r.* ***Golden*** *a-295, 303p.* ***Grell*** *a-287, 288p, 289p, 290; c-287-290.* ***Kaluta*** *c-242, 248, 253, Annual 12.* ***Bob Kane*** *a-1, 2; c-1-5, 7.* ***G. Kane*** *a-(r)-254, 255, 259, 261, 353i.* ***Kubert*** *a-238r, 400; c-310, 319p, 327, 328, 344.* ***McFarlane*** *c-423.* ***Mooney*** *a-255r.* ***Newton*** *a-305, 306, 328p, 331p, 332p, 337p, 338p, 346p, 352-357p, 360-372p, 374-378p; c-374p, 378p.* ***Nino*** *a-Annual 9.* ***Perez*** *a-400; c-436-442.* ***Robinson/Roussos*** *a-12-17, 20, 22, 24, 25, 27, 28, 31, 33, 37.* ***Robinson*** *a-12, 14, 18, 22-32, 34, 36, 37, 255r, 260r, 261r; c-6, 8-10, 12-15, 18, 21, 24, 26, 27, 30, 37, 39.* ***Simonson*** *a-300p, 312p, 321p; c-300p, 312p, 366, 413i.* ***P. Smith*** *a-Annual 9.* ***Starlin*** *c/a-402.* ***Staton*** *a-334.* ***Wrightson*** *a-265i, 400; c-320r. Catwoman back-ups in 332, 345, 346, 348-351. Robin solo back-up stories in 337-339, 341-343.*

**BATMAN** (Kellogg's Poptarts comics)
1966 (set of 6) (16 pages)
National Periodical Publications

| | | | |
|---|---|---|---|
| "The Man in the Iron Mask," "The Penguin's Fowl Play," "The Joker's Happy Victims," "The Catwoman's Catnapping Caper," "The Mad Hatter's Hat Crimes," "The Case of the Batman II" each.... | 1.70 | 5.00 | 10.00 |

NOTE: *All above were folded and placed in Poptarts boxes.* ***Infantino*** *art on Catwoman and Joker issues.*

**BATMAN AND OTHER DC CLASSICS**
1989 (Giveaway)
DC Comics/Diamond Comic Distributors

| | | | |
|---|---|---|---|
| 1-Batman origin-r/Batman #47, Camelot 3000-r by Bolland, Justice League-r('87), New Teen Titans-r by Perez | | .50 | 1.00 |

**BATMAN AND THE OUTSIDERS** (The Adventures of the Outsiders #33 on)(Also see Brave & The Bold #200 & The Outsiders)
Aug, 1983 - No. 32, Apr, 1986 (Mando paper No. 5 on)
DC Comics

| | | | |
|---|---|---|---|
| 1-32: 1-Batman, Halo, Geo-Force, Katana, Metamorpho & Black Lightning begin. 5-New Teen Titans x-over. 9-Halo begins. 11,12-Origin Katana. 18-More facts about Metamorpho's origin. 28-31-Lookers origin. 32-Team disbands | | .55 | 1.10 |
| Annual 1,2: 1(9/84)-Miller/Aparo-c; Aparo-i. 2(9/85)-Metamorpho & Sapphire Stagg wed; Aparo-c | .25 | .80 | 1.60 |

NOTE: ***Aparo*** *a-1-9, 11, 12p, 16-20; c-1-4, 5i, 6-21.* ***B. Kane*** *a-3r.* ***Layton*** *a-19i, 20i.* ***Lopez*** *a-3p.* ***Perez*** *c-5p.* ***B. Willingham*** *a-14p.*

**BATMAN: DIGITAL JUSTICE**
1990 ($24.95, hardcover)
DC Comics

| | | | |
|---|---|---|---|
| nn-Computer generated art | 4.15 | 12.50 | 25.00 |

**BATMAN FAMILY, THE**
Sept-Oct, 1975 - No. 20, Oct-Nov, 1978 (No.1-4, 17-on: 68 pages)
(Combined with Detective Comics with No. 481)
National Periodical Publications/DC Comics

| | | | |
|---|---|---|---|
| 1-Origin Batgirl-Robin team-up (The Dynamite Duo); reprints plus one new story begins; N. Adams-a(r) | .85 | 2.50 | 5.00 |
| 2-5: 3-Batgirl & Robin learn each's i.d. | .50 | 1.50 | 3.00 |
| 6,9-Joker's daughter on cover | .85 | 2.50 | 5.00 |
| 7,8,10,14-16: 10-1st revival Batwoman | .50 | 1.50 | 3.00 |
| 11-13: Rogers-p. 11-New stories begin; Man-Bat begins | .85 | 2.50 | 5.00 |
| 17-($1.00 size)-Batman, Huntress begin | .50 | 1.50 | 3.00 |
| 18-20: Huntress by Staton in all. 20-Origin Ragman retold | .30 | .90 | 1.75 |

NOTE: ***Aparo*** *a-17; c-11-16.* ***Austin*** *a-12i.* ***Chaykin*** *a-14p.* ***Michael Golden*** *a-15-17, 18-20p.* ***Grell*** *a-1; c-1.* ***Gil Kane*** *a-2r.* ***Kaluta*** *c-17, 19.* ***Newton*** *a-13.* ***Robinson*** *a-1r, 3i(r), 9r.* ***Russell*** *a-18i, 19i.* ***Starlin*** *a-17; c-18, 20.*

**BATMAN MINIATURE** (See Batman Kellogg's)

**BATMAN RECORD COMIC**
1966 (One Shot)
National Periodical Publications

| | Good | Fine | N-Mint |
|---|---|---|---|
| 1-With record (still sealed) | 8.50 | 25.50 | 60.00 |
| Comic only | 1.50 | 4.50 | 10.00 |

**BATMAN: SON OF THE DEMON**
Sept, 1987 (80 pgs., hardcover, $14.95)
DC Comics

| | | | |
|---|---|---|---|
| 1-Hardcover | 10.00 | 30.00 | 60.00 |
| Limited signed & numbered hard-c (1,700) | 15.00 | 45.00 | 90.00 |
| Softcover w/new-c ($8.95) | 2.50 | 7.50 | 15.00 |
| Softcover, 2nd print (1989, $9.95)-4th print | 1.70 | 5.00 | 10.00 |

**BATMAN SPECTACULAR** (See DC Special Series No. 15)

**BATMAN: THE CULT**
1988 - No. 4, Nov, 1988 ($3.50, color, deluxe mini-series)
DC Comics

| | | | |
|---|---|---|---|
| 1-Wrightson-a/painted-c in all | 3.00 | 9.00 | 18.00 |
| 2 | 2.30 | 7.00 | 14.00 |
| 3,4 | 2.00 | 6.00 | 12.00 |

**BATMAN: THE DARK KNIGHT RETURNS**
March, 1986 - No. 4, 1986
DC Comics

| | | | |
|---|---|---|---|
| 1-Miller story & a(p); set in the future | 8.35 | 25.00 | 50.00 |
| 1-2nd printing | 1.70 | 5.00 | 10.00 |
| 1-3rd printing | .70 | 2.00 | 4.00 |
| 2-Carrie Kelly becomes Robin (female) | 4.70 | 14.00 | 28.00 |
| 2-2nd printing | 1.00 | 3.00 | 6.00 |
| 2-3rd printing | .60 | 1.80 | 3.60 |
| 3-Death of Joker | 2.00 | 6.00 | 12.00 |
| 3-2nd printing | .70 | 2.00 | 4.00 |
| 4-Death of Alfred | 1.35 | 4.00 | 8.00 |
| Hardcover, signed & numbered edition ($40.00)(4000 copies) | 50.00 | 150.00 | 300.00 |
| Hardcover, trade edition | 10.85 | 32.50 | 65.00 |
| Softcover, trade edition (1st thru 8th printings) | 2.85 | 8.50 | 17.00 |

NOTE: *The #2 second printings can be identified by matching the grey background colors on the inside front cover and facing page. The inside front cover of the second printing has a dark grey background which does not match the lighter grey of the facing page. On the true 1st printings, the backgrounds are both light grey. All other issues are clearly marked.*

**BATMAN: THE KILLING JOKE**
1988 ($3.50, 52pgs. color, deluxe, adults)
DC Comics

| | | | |
|---|---|---|---|
| 1-Bolland-c/a; Alan Moore scripts | 5.00 | 15.00 | 30.00 |
| 1-2nd thru 8th printings | .85 | 2.50 | 5.00 |

**BATMAN: THE OFFICIAL COMIC ADAPTATION OF THE WARNER BROS. MOTION PICTURE**
1989 ($2.50, $4.95, 68 pgs.) (Movie adaptation)
DC Comics

| | | | |
|---|---|---|---|
| 1-Regular format ($2.50)-Ordway-c/a | .70 | 2.00 | 4.00 |
| 1-Prestige format ($4.95)-Diff.-c, same insides | 1.00 | 3.00 | 6.00 |

**BATMAN VS. THE INCREDIBLE HULK** (See DC Special Series No. 27)

**BAT MASTERSON** (TV)
Aug-Oct, 1959; Feb-Apr, 1960 - No. 9, Nov-Jan, 1961-62
Dell Publishing Co.

| | | | |
|---|---|---|---|
| 4-Color 1013 (8-10/59) | 5.70 | 17.00 | 40.00 |
| 2-9: Gene Barry photo-c on all | 3.60 | 11.00 | 25.00 |

**BATS** (See Tales Calculated to Drive You Bats)

*Batman: Son of the Demon soft-c, © DC*

*Batman: The Cult #1, © DC*

*Batman: The Dark Knight Returns #1, © DC*

Battle #41, © MEG

Battle Attack #3, © Stanmor Publ.

Battlefront #3, © MEG

**BATS, CATS & CADILLACS**
Oct, 1990 - No. 2, Nov, 1990 ($1.75, color)
Now Comics

| | Good | Fine | N-Mint |
|---|---|---|---|
| 1,2: 1-Gustovich-a(i) | .30 | .90 | 1.80 |

**BATTLE**
March, 1951 - No. 70, June, 1960
Marvel/Atlas Comics(FPI No. 1-62/Male No. 63 on)

| | Good | Fine | N-Mint |
|---|---|---|---|
| 1 | 7.00 | 21.00 | 50.00 |
| 2 | 3.00 | 9.00 | 21.00 |
| 3-10: 4-1st Buck Pvt. O'Toole. 10-Pakula-a | 2.30 | 7.00 | 16.00 |
| 11-20: 11-Check-a | 1.70 | 5.00 | 12.00 |
| 21,23-Krigstein-a | 2.65 | 8.00 | 18.00 |
| 22,24-36: 36-Everett-a | 1.50 | 4.50 | 10.00 |
| 37-Kubert-a (Last precode, 2/55) | 1.70 | 5.00 | 12.00 |
| 38-40,42-48 | 1.00 | 3.00 | 7.00 |
| 41-Kubert/Moskowitz-a | 1.70 | 5.00 | 12.00 |
| 49-Davis-a | 2.00 | 6.00 | 14.00 |
| 50-54,56-58 | .85 | 2.60 | 6.00 |
| 55-Williamson-a (5 pgs.) | 3.00 | 9.00 | 21.00 |
| 59-Torres-a | 1.50 | 4.50 | 10.00 |
| 60-62: Combat Kelly app.-#60,62; Combat Casey app.-#61 | .70 | 2.00 | 5.00 |
| 63-65: 63-Ditko-a. 64,65-Kirby-a | 2.30 | 7.00 | 16.00 |
| 66-Kirby, Davis-a | 2.65 | 8.00 | 18.00 |
| 67,68: 67-Williamson/Crandall-a (4 pgs.); Kirby, Davis-a. 68-Kirby/Williamson-a (4 pgs.); Kirby/Ditko-a | 3.00 | 9.00 | 21.00 |
| 69-Kirby-a | 1.70 | 5.00 | 12.00 |
| 70-Kirby/Ditko-a | 2.00 | 6.00 | 14.00 |

NOTE: ***Andru** a-37. **Berg** a-8, 14, 60-62. **Colan** a-33, 55. **Everett** a-36, 50, 70; c-56, 57. **Heath** a-6, 9, 13, 31, 69; c-6, 9, 26, 35, 37. **Kirby** c-64-69. **Maneely** a-4, 31; c-4, 59, 61. **Orlando** a-47. **Powell** a-53, 55. **Reinman** a-8, 9, 26, 32. **Robinson** a-9, 39. **Romita** a-26. **Severin** a-28, 32-34, 66-69; c-36, 55. **Sinnott** a-33, 37. **Tuska** a-32. **Woodbridge** a-52, 55.*

**BATTLE ACTION**
Feb, 1952 - No. 12, 5/53; No. 13, 11/54 - No. 30, 8/57
Atlas Comics (NPI)

| | Good | Fine | N-Mint |
|---|---|---|---|
| 1-Pakula-a | 7.00 | 21.00 | 50.00 |
| 2 | 3.00 | 9.00 | 21.00 |
| 3,4,6,7,9,10: 6-Robinson c/a. 7-partial nudity | 2.00 | 6.00 | 14.00 |
| 5-Used in **POP**, pg. 93,94 | 1.70 | 5.00 | 12.00 |
| 8-Krigstein-a | 2.65 | 8.00 | 18.00 |
| 11-15 (Last precode, 2/55) | 1.70 | 5.00 | 12.00 |
| 16-26,28,29 | 1.15 | 3.50 | 8.00 |
| 27,30-Torres-a | 1.70 | 5.00 | 12.00 |

NOTE: *Battle Brady app. 5-7, 10-12. **Check** a-11. **Everett** a-7; c-13, 25. **Heath** a-8; c-3, 15, 21. **Maneely** a-1. **Reinman** a-1. **Robinson** a-6, 7; c-6. **Shores** a-7. **Woodbridge** a-28, 30.*

**BATTLE ATTACK**
Oct, 1952 - No. 8, Dec, 1955
Stanmor Publications

| | Good | Fine | N-Mint |
|---|---|---|---|
| 1 | 3.60 | 11.00 | 25.00 |
| 2 | 1.70 | 5.00 | 12.00 |
| 3-8: 3-Hollingsworth-a | 1.15 | 3.50 | 8.00 |

**BATTLE BEASTS**
Feb, 1988 - No. 4, 1988 ($1.50, B&W, 4: $1.75, color)
Blackthorne Publishing

| | Good | Fine | N-Mint |
|---|---|---|---|
| 1-3 (B&W)-Based on Hasbro toys | .25 | .75 | 1.50 |
| 4 (Color) | .30 | .90 | 1.80 |

**BATTLE BRADY** (Formerly Men in Action No. 1-9; see 3-D Action)
No. 10, Jan, 1953 - No. 14, June, 1953
Atlas Comics (IPC)

| | Good | Fine | N-Mint |
|---|---|---|---|
| 10 | 4.00 | 12.00 | 28.00 |
| 11-Used in **POP**, pg. 95 plus B&W & color illos. | 2.65 | 8.00 | 18.00 |
| 12-14 | 1.70 | 5.00 | 12.00 |

**BATTLE CLASSICS** (See Cancelled Comic Cavalcade)
Sept-Oct, 1978 (44 pages)
DC Comics

| | Good | Fine | N-Mint |
|---|---|---|---|
| 1-Kubert-r; new Kubert-c | | .40 | .80 |

**BATTLE CRY**
1952(May) - No. 20, Sept, 1955
Stanmor Publications

| | Good | Fine | N-Mint |
|---|---|---|---|
| 1 | 4.00 | 12.00 | 28.00 |
| 2,4: 4-Classic E.C. swipe | 2.00 | 6.00 | 14.00 |
| 3,5-10: 8-Pvt. Ike begins, ends #13,17 | 1.30 | 4.00 | 9.00 |
| 11-20 | 1.00 | 3.00 | 7.00 |

NOTE: ***Hollingsworth** a-9; c-20.*

**BATTLEFIELD** (War Adventures on the...)
April, 1952 - No. 11, May, 1953
Atlas Comics (ACI)

| | Good | Fine | N-Mint |
|---|---|---|---|
| 1-Pakula, Reinman-a | 5.70 | 17.00 | 40.00 |
| 2-5 | 2.30 | 7.00 | 16.00 |
| 6-11 | 1.30 | 4.00 | 9.00 |

NOTE: ***Colan** a-11. **Everett** c-8. **Heath** a-1, 5p; c-2, 9, 11. **Ravielli** a-11.*

**BATTLEFIELD ACTION** (Formerly Foreign Intrigues)
No. 16, Nov, 1957 - No. 62, 2-3/66; No. 63, 7/80 - No. 89, 11/84
Charlton Comics

| | Good | Fine | N-Mint |
|---|---|---|---|
| V2#16 | 1.30 | 4.00 | 9.00 |
| 17,20-30 | .70 | 2.00 | 4.00 |
| 18,19-Check-a (2 stories in #18) | .85 | 2.50 | 5.00 |
| 31-62(1966) | .40 | 1.25 | 2.50 |
| 63-89(1983-'84) | | .30 | .60 |

NOTE: ***Montes/Bache** a-43, 55, 62. **Glanzman** a-87r.*

**BATTLE FIRE**
April, 1955 - No. 7, 1955
Aragon Magazine/Stanmor Publications

| | Good | Fine | N-Mint |
|---|---|---|---|
| 1 | 2.00 | 6.00 | 14.00 |
| 2 | 1.30 | 4.00 | 9.00 |
| 3-7 | .85 | 2.60 | 6.00 |

**BATTLE FOR A THREE DIMENSIONAL WORLD**
May, 1983 (20 pgs., slick paper w/stiff covers, $3.00)
3D Cosmic Publications

| | Good | Fine | N-Mint |
|---|---|---|---|
| nn-Kirby c/a in 3-D; shows history of 3-D | .50 | 1.50 | 3.00 |

**BATTLEFORCE**
Nov, 1987 - No. 2?, 1988 ($1.75) (#1: color; #2: B&W)
Blackthorne Publishing

| | Good | Fine | N-Mint |
|---|---|---|---|
| 1,2-Based on game | .30 | .90 | 1.80 |

**BATTLE FOR THE PLANET OF THE APES** (See Power Record Comics)

**BATTLEFRONT**
June, 1952 - No. 48, Aug, 1957
Atlas Comics (PPI)

| | Good | Fine | N-Mint |
|---|---|---|---|
| 1-Heath-c | 8.00 | 24.00 | 56.00 |
| 2-Robinson-a(4) | 3.60 | 11.00 | 25.00 |
| 3-5-Robinson-a(4) in each | 2.85 | 8.50 | 20.00 |
| 6-10: Combat Kelly in No. 6-10 | 2.30 | 7.00 | 16.00 |
| 11-22,24-28: 22-Teddy Roosevelt & His Rough Riders story. 28-Last precode (2/55). Battle Brady in #14,16 | 1.50 | 4.50 | 10.00 |
| 23-Check-a | 1.70 | 5.00 | 12.00 |
| 29-39 | 1.15 | 3.50 | 8.00 |
| 40,42-Williamson-a | 2.85 | 8.50 | 20.00 |
| 41,44-47 | .85 | 2.60 | 6.00 |
| 43-Check-a | 1.50 | 4.50 | 10.00 |
| 48-Crandall-a | 1.70 | 5.00 | 12.00 |

NOTE: ***Ayers** a-19. **Berg** a-44. **Colan** a-21, 22, 33. **Drucker** a-28, 29. **Everett** a-44.*

*Heath c-23, 26, 27, 29.* ***Maneely*** *c/a-22, c-13, 35.* ***Morisi*** *a-42.* ***Morrow*** *a-41.* ***Orlando*** *a-47.* ***Powell*** *a-19, 21, 25, 29, 47.* ***Robinson*** *a-1-5; c-4, 5.* ***Robert Sale*** *a-19.* ***Severin*** *c-40.* ***Woodbridge*** *a-45, 46.*

**BATTLEFRONT**
No. 5, June, 1952
Standard Comics

| | Good | Fine | N-Mint |
|---|---|---|---|
| 5-Toth-a | 5.70 | 17.00 | 40.00 |

**BATTLE GROUND**
Sept, 1954 - No. 20, Aug, 1957
Atlas Comics (OMC)

| | Good | Fine | N-Mint |
|---|---|---|---|
| 1 | 6.50 | 19.00 | 45.00 |
| 2-Jack Katz-a | 3.15 | 9.50 | 22.00 |
| 3,4-Last precode (3/55) | 2.00 | 6.00 | 14.00 |
| 5-8,10 | 1.70 | 5.00 | 12.00 |
| 9-Krigstein-a | 2.65 | 8.00 | 18.00 |
| 11,13,18-Williamson-a in each | 2.85 | 8.50 | 20.00 |
| 12,15-17,19,20 | 1.50 | 4.50 | 10.00 |
| 14-Kirby-a | 1.70 | 5.00 | 12.00 |

NOTE: ***Colan*** *a-11.* ***Drucker*** *a-7, 12, 13, 20.* ***Heath*** *c-5.* ***Orlando*** *a-17.* ***Pakula*** *a-11.* ***Severin*** *a-5, 12, 19. c-20.* ***Tuska*** *a-11.*

**BATTLE HEROES**
Sept, 1966 - No. 2, Nov, 1966 (25 cents)
Stanley Publications

| | Good | Fine | N-Mint |
|---|---|---|---|
| 1,2 | .70 | 2.00 | 4.00 |

**BATTLE OF THE BULGE** (See Movie Classics)

**BATTLE OF THE PLANETS** (TV)
6/79 - No. 10, 12/80 (Based on syndicated cartoon by Sandy Frank)
Gold Key/Whitman No. 6 on

| | Good | Fine | N-Mint |
|---|---|---|---|
| 1 | | .40 | .80 |
| 2-10: Mortimer a-1-4,7-10 | | .30 | .60 |

**BATTLE REPORT**
Aug, 1952 - No. 6, June, 1953
Ajax/Farrell Publications

| | Good | Fine | N-Mint |
|---|---|---|---|
| 1 | 2.65 | 8.00 | 18.00 |
| 2-6 | 1.50 | 4.50 | 10.00 |

**BATTLE SQUADRON**
April, 1955 - No. 5, Dec, 1955
Stanmor Publications

| | Good | Fine | N-Mint |
|---|---|---|---|
| 1 | 2.15 | 6.50 | 15.00 |
| 2-5: 3-Iwo Jima & flag-c | 1.15 | 3.50 | 8.00 |

**BATTLESTAR GALACTICA** (TV)(Also see Marvel Super Special #8)
March, 1979 - No. 23, January, 1981
Marvel Comics Group

| | Good | Fine | N-Mint |
|---|---|---|---|
| 1: 1-5 adapt TV episodes | | .35 | .70 |
| 2-23: 1-3-Partial-r | | .25 | .50 |

NOTE: ***Austin*** *c-9i, 10i.* ***Golden*** *c-18.* ***Simonson*** *a(p)-4, 5, 11-13, 15-20, 22, 23; c(p)-4, 5, 11-15.*

**BATTLE STORIES** (See XMas Comics)
Jan, 1952 - No. 11, Sept, 1953
Fawcett Publications

| | Good | Fine | N-Mint |
|---|---|---|---|
| 1-Evans-a | 5.70 | 17.00 | 40.00 |
| 2 | 2.65 | 8.00 | 18.00 |
| 3-11 | 1.70 | 5.00 | 12.00 |

**BATTLE STORIES**
1963 - 1964
Super Comics

| | Good | Fine | N-Mint |
|---|---|---|---|
| Reprints #10-12,15-18; 15-r-/American Air Forces by Powell | .35 | 1.00 | 2.00 |

**BATTLETECH** (See Blackthorne 3-D Series #41 for 3-D issue)
Oct, 1987 - No. 6? ($1.75-2.00; #1-color, #2 on-B&W)
Blackthorne Publishing

| | Good | Fine | N-Mint |
|---|---|---|---|
| 1-6: Based on game | .30 | .90 | 1.75 |
| Annual 1 ($4.50, B&W) | .75 | 2.25 | 4.50 |

**BEACH BLANKET BINGO** (See Movie Classics)

**BEAGLE BOYS, THE** (Walt Disney)(See The Phantom Blot)
11/64; No. 2, 11/65; No. 3, 8/66 - No. 47, 2/79 (See WDC&S #134)
Gold Key

| | Good | Fine | N-Mint |
|---|---|---|---|
| 1 | 2.35 | 7.00 | 14.00 |
| 2-5 | 1.35 | 4.00 | 8.00 |
| 6-10 | .85 | 2.50 | 5.00 |
| 11-20: 11,14,19-r | .50 | 1.50 | 3.00 |
| 21-47: 27-r | .25 | .75 | 1.50 |

**BEAGLE BOYS VERSUS UNCLE SCROOGE**
March, 1979 - No. 12, Feb, 1980
Gold Key

| | Good | Fine | N-Mint |
|---|---|---|---|
| 1 | .25 | .80 | 1.60 |
| 2-12: 9-r | | .40 | .80 |

**BEANBAGS**
Winter, 1951 - No. 2, Spring, 1952
Ziff-Davis Publ. Co. (Approved Comics)

| | Good | Fine | N-Mint |
|---|---|---|---|
| 1,2 | 4.00 | 12.00 | 28.00 |

**BEANIE THE MEANIE**
1958 - No. 3, May, 1959
Fago Publications

| | Good | Fine | N-Mint |
|---|---|---|---|
| 1-3 | 1.50 | 4.50 | 10.00 |

**BEANY AND CECIL** (TV) (Bob Clampett's. . .)
Jan, 1952 - 1955; July-Sept, 1962 - No. 5, July-Sept, 1963
Dell Publishing Co.

| | Good | Fine | N-Mint |
|---|---|---|---|
| 4-Color 368 | 13.00 | 40.00 | 90.00 |
| 4-Color 414,448,477,530,570,635(1/55) | 10.00 | 30.00 | 70.00 |
| 01-057-209 (#1) | 10.00 | 30.00 | 70.00 |
| 2-5 | 7.00 | 21.00 | 50.00 |

**BEAR COUNTRY** (Disney) (See 4-Color No. 758)

**BEATLES, THE** (See Girls' Romances #109, Go-Go, Heart Throbs #101, Herbie #5, Howard the Duck Mag. #4, Laugh #166, Marvel Comics Super Special 4, My Little Margie 54, Not Brand Echh, Strange Tales 130, Summer Love, Superman's Pal Jimmy Olsen #79, Teen Confessions 37, Tippy's Friends & Tippy Teen)

**BEATLES, THE** (Life Story)
Sept-Nov, 1964 (35 cents)
Dell Publishing Co.

| | Good | Fine | N-Mint |
|---|---|---|---|
| 1-(Scarce)-Stories with color photo pin-ups | 35.00 | 105.00 | 245.00 |

**BEATLES YELLOW SUBMARINE** (See Movie Comics under Yellow. . .)

**BEAUTIFUL STORIES FOR UGLY CHILDREN**
1989 - Present ($2.00-$2.50, B&W, mature readers)
Piranha Press (DC Comics)

| | Good | Fine | N-Mint |
|---|---|---|---|
| Vol. 1-11 ($2.00) | .35 | 1.00 | 2.00 |
| 12-18 ($2.50) | .40 | 1.25 | 2.50 |

**BEAUTY AND THE BEAST, THE**
Jan, 1985 - No. 4, Apr, 1985 (Mini-series)
Marvel Comics Group

| | Good | Fine | N-Mint |
|---|---|---|---|
| 1-4: Dazzler & the Beast | .25 | .75 | 1.50 |

**BEAUTY AND THE BEAST: PORTRAIT OF LOVE** (TV)
May, 1989 ($5.95, 60 pgs., color, squarebound)
First Comics

| | Good | Fine | N-Mint |
|---|---|---|---|
| 1-Based on TV show, Wendy Pini-a/scripts | 1.35 | 4.00 | 8.00 |
| 2-. . .: Night of Beauty; by Wendy Pini | 1.00 | 3.00 | 6.00 |

**BEAVER VALLEY** (See 4-Color No. 625)

**BEDKNOBS AND BROOMSTICKS** (See Walt Disney Showcase No. 6 & 50)

*Battle Squadron #3, © Stanmor Publ.*

*Battle Stories #4, © FAW*

*Beautiful Stories For Ugly Children #1, © DC*

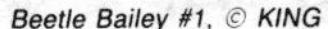

*Beetle Bailey #1, © KING*

*Ben Casey #8, © Bing Crosby Prod.*

*The Best From Boys' Life #1, © GIL*

**BEDLAM!**
Sept, 1985 - No. 2, Sept, 1985 (B&W-r in color)
Eclipse Comics

| | Good | Fine | N-Mint |
|---|---|---|---|
| 1,2-Bissette-a | .30 | .90 | 1.80 |

**BEDTIME STORY** (See Cinema Comics Herald)

**BEEP BEEP, THE ROAD RUNNER** (TV)(Also see Daffy)
July, 1958 - No. 14, Aug-Oct, 1962; Oct, 1966 - No. 105, 1983
Dell Publishing Co./Gold Key No. 1-88/Whitman No. 89 on

| | Good | Fine | N-Mint |
|---|---|---|---|
| 4-Color 918 (#1, 7/58) | 4.50 | 14.00 | 32.00 |
| 4-Color 1008,1046 (11-1/59-60) | 2.30 | 7.00 | 16.00 |
| 4(2-4/60)-14(Dell) | 1.70 | 5.00 | 12.00 |
| 1(10/66, Gold Key) | 2.00 | 6.00 | 14.00 |
| 2-5 | 1.00 | 3.00 | 7.00 |
| 6-14 (1962) | .70 | 2.00 | 5.00 |
| 15-18,20-40 | .50 | 1.50 | 3.00 |
| 19-w/pull-out poster | 1.35 | 4.00 | 8.00 |
| 41-60 | | .60 | 1.20 |
| 61-105 | | .40 | .80 |
| Kite Fun Book-Giveaway ('67,'71), 16pgs., soft-c, 5x7¼" | .70 | 2.00 | 5.00 |

NOTE: See March of Comics #351, 353, 375, 387, 397, 416, 430, 442, 455. #5, 8-10, 35, 53, 59-62, 68-r; 96-102, 104 ⅓-r.

**BEETLE BAILEY** (See Comics Reading Library, Giant Comic Album & Sarge Snorkel)
#459, 5/53 - #38, 5-7/62; #39, 11/62 - #53, 5/66; #54, 8/66 - #65, 12/67; #67, 2/69 - #119, 11/76; #120, 4/78 - #132, 4/80
Dell Publishing Co./Gold Key No. 39-53/King No. 54-66/Charlton No. 67-119/Gold Key No. 120-131/Whitman No. 132

| | Good | Fine | N-Mint |
|---|---|---|---|
| 4-Color 469 (#1)-By Mort Walker | 5.70 | 17.00 | 40.00 |
| 4-Color 521,552,622 | 2.85 | 8.50 | 20.00 |
| 5(2-4/56)-10(5-7/57) | 2.30 | 7.00 | 16.00 |
| 11-20(4-5/59) | 1.50 | 4.50 | 10.00 |
| 21-38(5-7/62) | 1.00 | 3.00 | 7.00 |
| 39-53(5/66) | .70 | 2.00 | 4.00 |
| 54-119 (No. 66 publ. overseas only?) | .35 | 1.00 | 2.00 |
| 120-132 | | .50 | 1.00 |
| Bold Detergent Giveaway('69)-same as regular issue (#67) minus price | | .50 | 1.00 |
| Cerebral Palsy Assn. Giveaway V2#71('69)-V2#73; (#1), 1/70, Charlton | | .50 | 1.00 |
| Red Cross Giveaway, 16pp, 5x7", 1969, paper-c | | .40 | .80 |

**BEE 29, THE BOMBARDIER**
Feb, 1945
Neal Publications

| | Good | Fine | N-Mint |
|---|---|---|---|
| 1-(Funny animal) | 8.50 | 25.50 | 60.00 |

**BEHIND PRISON BARS**
1952
Realistic Comics (Avon)

| | Good | Fine | N-Mint |
|---|---|---|---|
| 1-Kinstler-c | 14.00 | 42.00 | 100.00 |

**BEHOLD THE HANDMAID**
1954 (Religious) (25 cents with a 20 cent sticker price)
George Pflaum

| | Good | Fine | N-Mint |
|---|---|---|---|
| nn | 2.30 | 7.00 | 16.00 |

**BELIEVE IT OR NOT** (See Ripley's . . .)

**BEN AND ME** (See 4-Color No. 539)

**BEN BOWIE AND HIS MOUNTAIN MEN**
1952 - No. 17, Nov-Jan, 1958-59
Dell Publishing Co.

| | Good | Fine | N-Mint |
|---|---|---|---|
| 4-Color 443 (#1) | 4.00 | 12.00 | 28.00 |
| 4-Color 513,557,599,626,657 | 2.30 | 7.00 | 16.00 |
| 7(5-7/56)-11: 11-Intro/origin Yellow Hair | 1.70 | 5.00 | 12.00 |
| 12-17 | 1.15 | 3.50 | 8.00 |

**BEN CASEY** (TV)
June-July, 1962 - No. 10, June-Aug, 1965 (Photo-c)
Dell Publishing Co.

| | Good | Fine | N-Mint |
|---|---|---|---|
| 12-063-207 (#1) | 3.00 | 9.00 | 21.00 |
| 2(10/62)-10: 4-Marijuana & heroin use story | 1.70 | 5.00 | 12.00 |

**BEN CASEY FILM STORY** (TV)
November, 1962 (25 cents) (Photo-c)
Gold Key

| | Good | Fine | N-Mint |
|---|---|---|---|
| 30009-211-All photos | 5.00 | 15.00 | 35.00 |

**BENEATH THE PLANET OF THE APES** (See Movie Comics & Power Record Comics)

**BEN FRANKLIN KITE FUN BOOK**
1975, 1977 (16 pages; 5-1/8"x6-5/8")
Southern Calif. Edison Co./PG&E('77)

| | Good | Fine | N-Mint |
|---|---|---|---|
| nn | .50 | 1.50 | 3.00 |

**BEN HUR** (See 4-Color No. 1052)

**BEN ISRAEL**
1974 (39 cents)
Logos International

| | Good | Fine | N-Mint |
|---|---|---|---|
| nn | | .50 | 1.00 |

**BEOWULF** (See First Comics Graphic Novel #1)
April-May, 1975 - No. 6, Feb-Mar, 1976
National Periodical Publications

| | Good | Fine | N-Mint |
|---|---|---|---|
| 1 | | .45 | .90 |
| 2-6: 5-Flying saucer-c/story | | .25 | .50 |

**BERNI WRIGHTSON, MASTER OF THE MACABRE**
July, 1983 - No. 5, Nov, 1984 ($1.50; Baxter paper)
Pacific Comics/Eclipse Comics No. 5

| | Good | Fine | N-Mint |
|---|---|---|---|
| 1-Wrightson c/a-r in all | .40 | 1.25 | 2.50 |
| 2-5: 4-Jeff Jones-r (11 pgs.) | .35 | 1.00 | 2.00 |

**BERRYS, THE** (Also see Funny World)
May, 1956
Argo Publ.

| | Good | Fine | N-Mint |
|---|---|---|---|
| 1-Reprints daily & Sunday strips & daily Animal Antics by Ed Nofziger | 2.65 | 8.00 | 18.00 |

**BEST COMICS**
Nov, 1939 - No. 4, Feb, 1940 (large size, reads sideways)
Better Publications

| | Good | Fine | N-Mint |
|---|---|---|---|
| 1-(Scarce)-Red Mask begins | 32.00 | 95.00 | 225.00 |
| 2-4: 4-Cannibalism story | 20.00 | 60.00 | 140.00 |

**BEST FROM BOY'S LIFE, THE**
Oct, 1957 - No. 5, Oct, 1958 (35 cents)
Gilberton Company

| | Good | Fine | N-Mint |
|---|---|---|---|
| 1-Space Conquerors & Kam of the Ancient Ones begin, end #5 | 3.70 | 11.00 | 26.00 |
| 2,3,5 | 1.70 | 5.00 | 12.00 |
| 4-L.B. Cole-a | 2.30 | 7.00 | 16.00 |

**BEST LOVE** (Formerly Sub-Mariner No. 32)
No. 33, Aug, 1949 - No. 36, April, 1950 (Photo-c 33-36)
Marvel Comics (MPI)

| | Good | Fine | N-Mint |
|---|---|---|---|
| 33-Kubert-a | 4.50 | 14.00 | 32.00 |
| 34 | 2.00 | 6.00 | 14.00 |
| 35,36-Everett-a | 3.00 | 9.00 | 21.00 |

**BEST OF BUGS BUNNY, THE**
Oct, 1966 - No. 2, Oct, 1968
Gold Key

| | Good | Fine | N-Mint |
|---|---|---|---|
| 1,2-Giants | 2.00 | 6.00 | 16.00 |

**BEST OF DC, THE** (Blue Ribbon Digest) (See Limited Coll. Ed. C-52)
Sept-Oct, 1979 - No. 71, Apr, 1986 (100-148 pgs; all reprints)
DC Comics

| | Good | Fine | N-Mint |
|---|---|---|---|
| 1-17,19-34,36-71: 34-Has #497 on-c from Adv. | | .40 | .80 |
| 18-The New Teen Titans | .25 | .80 | 1.60 |
| 35-The Year's Best Comics Stories(148pgs.) | | .60 | 1.20 |

NOTE: ***N. Adams*** *a-26, 51.* ***Aparo*** *a-9, 14, 26, 30; c-9, 14, 26.* ***Austin*** *a-51i.* ***Buckler*** *a-40p; c-22.* ***Giffen*** *a-50, 52; c-33p.* ***Grell*** *a-33p.* ***Grossman*** *a-37.* ***Heath*** *a-26.* ***Kaluta*** *a-40.* ***G. Kane*** *c-40, 44.* ***Kubert*** *a-21, 26.* ***Layton*** *a-21.* ***S. Mayer*** *c-29, 37, 41, 43, 47; a-28, 29, 37, 41, 43, 47, 58, 65, 68.* ***Moldoff*** *c-64p.* ***Morrow*** *a-40; c-40.* ***W. Mortimer*** *a-39p.* ***Newton*** *a-5, 51.* ***Perez*** *a-24, 50p; c-18, 21, 23.* ***Rogers*** *a-14, 51p.* ***Spiegle*** *a-52.* ***Starlin*** *a-51.* ***Staton*** *a-5, 21.* ***Tuska*** *a-24.* ***Wolverton*** *a-60.* ***Wood*** *a-60, 63; c-60, 63.* ***Wrightson*** *a-60. New art in No. 14, 18, 24.*

**BEST OF DENNIS THE MENACE, THE**
Summer, 1959 - No. 5, Spring, 1961 (100 pages)
Hallden/Fawcett Publications

| | Good | Fine | N-Mint |
|---|---|---|---|
| 1-All reprints; Wiseman-a | 3.00 | 9.00 | 21.00 |
| 2-5 | 2.00 | 6.00 | 14.00 |

**BEST OF DONALD DUCK, THE**
Nov, 1965 (36 pages)
Gold Key

| | Good | Fine | N-Mint |
|---|---|---|---|
| 1-Reprints 4-Color #223 by Barks | 5.00 | 15.00 | 30.00 |

**BEST OF DONALD DUCK & UNCLE SCROOGE, THE**
Nov, 1964 - No. 2, Sept, 1967 (25 cent giant)
Gold Key

| | Good | Fine | N-Mint |
|---|---|---|---|
| 1(30022-411)('64)-Reprints 4-Color #189 & 408 by Carl Barks; No. 189-c redrawn by Barks | 4.50 | 14.00 | 32.00 |
| 2(30022-709)('67)-Reprints 4-Color #256 & "Seven Cities of Cibola" & U.S. #8 by Barks | 3.70 | 11.00 | 26.00 |

**BEST OF HORROR AND SCIENCE FICTION COMICS**
1987 ($2.00, color)
Bruce Webster

| | Good | Fine | N-Mint |
|---|---|---|---|
| 1-Wolverton, Frazetta, Powell, Ditko-r | .35 | 1.00 | 2.00 |

**BEST OF MARMADUKE, THE**
1960 (a dog)
Charlton Comics

| | Good | Fine | N-Mint |
|---|---|---|---|
| 1-Brad Anderson's strip reprints | 1.15 | 3.50 | 8.00 |

**BEST OF MS. TREE, THE**
1987 - No. 4, 1988 ($2.00, B&W, mini-series)
Pyramid Comics

| | Good | Fine | N-Mint |
|---|---|---|---|
| 1-4 | .35 | 1.00 | 2.00 |

**BEST OF THE BRAVE AND THE BOLD, THE** (See Super DC Giant)
Oct, 1988 - No. 6, Jan, 1989 ($2.50, color, mini-series)
DC Comics

| | Good | Fine | N-Mint |
|---|---|---|---|
| 1-6: Neal Adams-r in all | .40 | 1.25 | 2.50 |

**BEST OF THE WEST** (See A-1 Comics)
1951 - No. 12, April-June, 1954
Magazine Enterprises

| | Good | Fine | N-Mint |
|---|---|---|---|
| 1(A-1 42)-Ghost Rider, Durango Kid, Straight Arrow, Bobby Benson begin | 23.00 | 70.00 | 160.00 |
| 2(A-1 46) | 11.50 | 34.00 | 80.00 |
| 3(A-1 52), 4(A-1 59), 5(A-1 66) | 10.00 | 30.00 | 70.00 |
| 6(A-1 70), 7(A-1 76), 8(A-1 81), 9(A-1 85), 10(A-1 87), 11(A-1 97), 12(A-1 103) | 7.00 | 21.00 | 50.00 |

NOTE: ***Bolle*** *a-9.* ***Borth*** *a-12.* ***Guardineer*** *a-5, 12.* ***Powell*** *a-1, 12.*

**BEST OF UNCLE SCROOGE & DONALD DUCK, THE**
November, 1966 (25 cents)
Gold Key

| | Good | Fine | N-Mint |
|---|---|---|---|
| 1(30030-611)-Reprints part 4-Color 159 & 456 & Uncle Scrooge 6,7 by Carl Barks | 4.00 | 12.00 | 28.00 |

**BEST OF WALT DISNEY COMICS, THE**
1974 (In color; $1.50; 52 pages) (Walt Disney)
8½x11" cardboard covers; 32,000 printed of each
Western Publishing Co.

| | Good | Fine | N-Mint |
|---|---|---|---|
| 96170-Reprints 1st two stories less 1 pg. each from 4-Color #62 | 1.00 | 3.00 | 7.00 |
| 96171-Reprints Mickey Mouse and the Bat Bandit of Inferno Gulch from 1934 (strips) by Gottfredson | 1.00 | 3.00 | 7.00 |
| 96172-Reprints Uncle Scrooge #386 & two other stories | 1.00 | 3.00 | 7.00 |
| 96173-Reprints "Ghost of the Grotto" (from 4-Color #159) & "Christmas on Bear Mtn." (from 4-Color #178) | 1.00 | 3.00 | 7.00 |

**BEST ROMANCE**
No. 5, Feb-Mar, 1952 - No. 7, Aug, 1952
Standard Comics (Visual Editions)

| | Good | Fine | N-Mint |
|---|---|---|---|
| 5-Toth-a; photo-c | 5.70 | 17.00 | 40.00 |
| 6,7-Photo-c | 1.70 | 5.00 | 12.00 |

**BEST SELLER COMICS** (See Tailspin Tommy)

**BEST WESTERN** (Formerly Terry Toons?) (Western Outlaws & Sheriffs No. 60 on)
No. 58, June, 1949 - No. 59, Aug, 1949
Marvel Comics (IPC)

| | Good | Fine | N-Mint |
|---|---|---|---|
| 58,59-Black Rider, Kid Colt, Two-Gun Kid app. | 7.00 | 21.00 | 50.00 |

**BETTY AND HER STEADY** (Going Steady with Betty No. 1)
No. 2, Mar-Apr, 1950
Avon Periodicals

| | Good | Fine | N-Mint |
|---|---|---|---|
| 2 | 5.00 | 15.00 | 35.00 |

**BETTY AND ME**
Aug, 1965 - Present
Archie Publications

| | Good | Fine | N-Mint |
|---|---|---|---|
| 1 | 8.00 | 24.00 | 55.00 |
| 2 | 4.00 | 12.00 | 28.00 |
| 3-5: 3-Origin Superteen. Superteen in new costume #4-7; dons new helmet #5, ends #8 | 2.30 | 7.00 | 16.00 |
| 6-10 | 1.00 | 3.00 | 6.00 |
| 11-30 | .40 | 1.20 | 2.40 |
| 31-55 (52 pages #36-55) | | .60 | 1.20 |
| 56-194: Later issues $1.00 cover | | .50 | 1.00 |

**BETTY AND VERONICA** (Also see Archie's Girls. . .)
June, 1987 - Present (75 & 95 cents)
Archie Enterprises

| | Good | Fine | N-Mint |
|---|---|---|---|
| 1-42 | | .40 | .75 |

**BETTY & VERONICA ANNUAL DIGEST** (. . .Digest Mag. #2-4, 44 on; . . .Comics Digest Mag. #5-43)
November, 1980 - Present ($1.00 - 1.50)
Archie Publications

| | Good | Fine | N-Mint |
|---|---|---|---|
| 1, 2(11/81-Katy Keene story), 3(8/82) - 48('91) | | .40 | .80 |

**BETTY & VERONICA ANNUAL DIGEST** (. . . Magazine #3 on)
Aug?, 1989 - Present ($1.50, 128 pgs.)
Archie Comics

| | Good | Fine | N-Mint |
|---|---|---|---|
| 1-4 | .25 | .75 | 1.50 |

**BETTY & VERONICA CHRISTMAS SPECTACULAR** (See Archie Giant Series Mag. #159, 168, 180, 191, 204, 217, 229, 241, 453, 465, 477, 489, 501, 513, 525, 536, 547, 558, 568, 580, 593, 606, 618)

**BETTY & VERONICA DOUBLE DIGEST MAGAZINE**
1987 - Present (Digest size, 256 pgs., $2.25)(. . .Digest #12 on)
Archie Enterprises

| | Good | Fine | N-Mint |
|---|---|---|---|
| 1-23: 5,17-Xmas-c. 16-Capt. Hero story | .35 | 1.10 | 2.25 |

**BETTY & VERONICA SPECTACULAR** (See Archie Giant Series Mag. #11, 16, 21, 26, 32, 138, 145, 153, 162, 173, 184, 197, 201, 210, 214, 221, 226, 234, 238, 246, 250, 458, 462, 470, 482, 486, 494, 498, 506, 510, 518, 522, 526, 530, 537, 552, 559, 563, 569,

*The Best of Dennis the Menace #1, © FAW*

GOLD KEY
WALT DISNEY'S
25¢
THE BEST OF
DONALD DUCK and
UNCLE SCROOGE
Two famous Disney Classics
THE OLD CASTLE'S SECRET—THE GOLDEN HELMET

*Best of Donald Duck & U. S. #1, © Disney Co.*

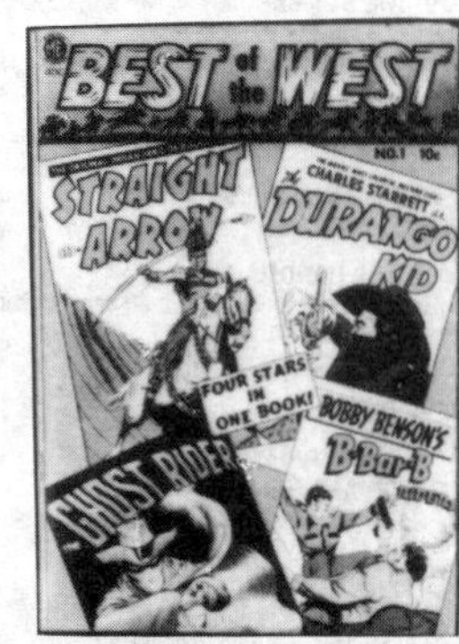

*Best of the West #1, © ME*

*The Beverly Hillbillies #16, © Filmways TV Prod.* *Beware #10, © TM* *The Beyond #18, © ACE*

575, 582, 588, 600, 608, 613)

**BETTY & VERONICA SPRING SPECTACULAR** (See Archie Giant Series Magazine #569, 582, 595)

**BETTY & VERONICA SUMMER FUN** (See Archie Giant Series Mag. #8, 13, 18, 23, 28, 34, 140, 147, 155, 164, 175, 187, 199, 212, 224, 236, 248, 460, 484, 496, 508, 520, 529, 539, 550, 561, 572, 585, 598, 611)

**BETTY BOOP IN 3-D** (See Blackthorne 3-D series #11)

**BETTY BOOP'S BIG BREAK**
1990 ($5.95 color, 52 pgs.)
First Publishing

| | Good | Fine | N-Mint |
|---|---|---|---|
| nn-By Joshua Quaqmire; 60th anniversary ish. | 1.00 | 3.00 | 6.00 |

**BETTY'S DIARY** (See Archie Giant Series Mag. No. 555)
April, 1986 - Present (75 & 95 cents)
Archie Enterprises

| | Good | Fine | N-Mint |
|---|---|---|---|
| 1-40 | | .40 | .75 |

**BEVERLY HILLBILLIES** (TV)
4-6/63 - No. 18, 8/67; No. 19, 10/69; No. 20, 10/70; No. 21, Oct, 1971
Dell Publishing Co.

| | Good | Fine | N-Mint |
|---|---|---|---|
| 1 | 7.00 | 21.00 | 50.00 |
| 2 | 3.50 | 10.50 | 24.00 |
| 3-10 | 2.65 | 8.00 | 18.00 |
| 11-21 | 2.15 | 6.50 | 15.00 |

NOTE: *#1-3, 5, 8-14, 17-21 are photo covers. #19 reprints #1.*

**BEWARE** (Formerly Fantastic; Chilling Tales No. 13 on)
No. 10, June, 1952 - No. 12, Oct, 1952
Youthful Magazines

| | Good | Fine | N-Mint |
|---|---|---|---|
| 10-Pit & the Pendulum adaptation; Wildey, Harrison-a; atom bomb-c | 14.00 | 43.00 | 100.00 |
| 11-Harrison-a; Ambrose Bierce adapt. | 10.00 | 30.00 | 70.00 |
| 12-Used in **SOTI**, pg. 388; Harrison-a | 10.00 | 30.00 | 70.00 |

**BEWARE**
No. 13, 1/53 - No. 13, 1/55; No. 14, 3/55, No. 15, 5/55
Trojan Magazines/Merit Publ. No. ?

| | Good | Fine | N-Mint |
|---|---|---|---|
| 13(#1)-Harrison-a | 11.50 | 34.00 | 80.00 |
| 14(#2)-Krenkel/Harrison-c; dismemberment, severed head panels | 8.50 | 24.50 | 60.00 |
| 15,16(#3,4)-Harrison-a | 6.00 | 18.00 | 42.00 |
| 5,9,12,13 | 6.00 | 18.00 | 42.00 |
| 6-Ill. in **SOTI**-"Children are first shocked and then desensitized by all this brutality." Corpse on cover swipe/V.O.H. #26; girl on cover swipe/Advs. Into Darkness #10 | 16.00 | 48.00 | 110.00 |
| 7,8-Check-a | 9.30 | 28.00 | 65.00 |
| 10-Frazetta/Check-c; Disbrow, Check-a | 30.00 | 90.00 | 210.00 |
| 11-Disbrow-a; heart torn out, blood drainage | 10.00 | 30.00 | 70.00 |
| 14,15: 14-Fass-c. 15-Harrison-a | 8.00 | 24.00 | 56.00 |

NOTE: ***Fass** a-5, 6; c-6, 11, 14. **Hollingsworth** a-15(3), 16(4), 9; c-16(4), 8, 9. **Kiefer** a-5, 6, 10.*

**BEWARE** (Tomb of Darkness No. 9 on)
March, 1973 - No. 8, May, 1974 (All reprints)
Marvel Comics Group

| | Good | Fine | N-Mint |
|---|---|---|---|
| 1-Everett-c; Sinnott-r ('54) | .35 | 1.00 | 2.00 |
| 2-8: 2-Forte, Colan-r. 6-Tuska-a. 7-Torres r-/Mystical Tales #7 | | .50 | 1.00 |

**BEWARE TERROR TALES**
May, 1952 - No. 8, July, 1953
Fawcett Publications

| | Good | Fine | N-Mint |
|---|---|---|---|
| 1-E.C. art swipe/Haunt of Fear #5 & Vault of Horror #26 | 11.50 | 34.00 | 80.00 |
| 2 | 7.00 | 21.00 | 50.00 |
| 3-8: 8-Tothish-a | 5.70 | 17.00 | 40.00 |

NOTE: ***Andru** a-2. **Bernard Bailey** a-1; c-1-5. **Powell** a-1, 2, 8. **Sekowsky** a-2.*

**BEWARE THE CREEPER** (See Adventure, Best of the Brave & the Bold, Brave & the Bold, First Issue Special, Flash #318-323, Showcase, and World's Finest #249)
May-June, 1968 - No. 6, March-April, 1969
National Periodical Publications

| | Good | Fine | N-Mint |
|---|---|---|---|
| 1-Ditko-a in all; c-1-5 | 3.50 | 10.50 | 24.00 |
| 2-6: 6-G. Kane-c | 2.15 | 6.50 | 15.00 |

**BEWITCHED** (TV)
4-6/65 - No. 11, 10/67; No. 12, 10/68 - No. 13, 1/69; No. 14, 10/69
Dell Publishing Co.

| | Good | Fine | N-Mint |
|---|---|---|---|
| 1 | 7.00 | 21.00 | 50.00 |
| 2 | 4.00 | 12.00 | 28.00 |
| 3-14: Photo-c #3-13 | 3.00 | 9.00 | 21.00 |

**BEYOND, THE**
Nov, 1950 - No. 30, Jan, 1955
Ace Magazines

| | Good | Fine | N-Mint |
|---|---|---|---|
| 1-Bakerish-a(p) | 16.00 | 48.00 | 110.00 |
| 2-Bakerish-a(p) | 8.50 | 25.50 | 60.00 |
| 3-10: 10-Woodish-a by Cameron | 5.70 | 17.00 | 40.00 |
| 11-20: 18-Used in **POP**, pgs. 81,82 | 4.00 | 12.00 | 28.00 |
| 21-26,28-30 | 3.70 | 11.00 | 26.00 |
| 27-Used in **SOTI**, pg. 111 | 4.00 | 12.00 | 28.00 |

NOTE: ***Cameron** a-10, 11p, 12p, 15, 20-27, 30; c-20. **Colan** a-6, 13, 17. **Sekowsky** a-2, 3, 5, 7, 11, 14, 27r. No. 1 was to appear as Challenge of the Unknown No. 7.*

**BEYOND THE GRAVE**
July, 1975 - No. 6, June, 1976; No. 7, Jan, 1983 - No. 17, Oct, 1984
Charlton Comics

| | Good | Fine | N-Mint |
|---|---|---|---|
| 1-Ditko-a (6 pgs.); Sutton painted-c | .35 | 1.00 | 2.00 |
| 2-6-Ditko-a (Ditko c-2,3,6) | | .60 | 1.20 |
| 7-17: ('83-'84) Reprints. 15-Sutton-c | | .30 | .60 |
| Modern Comics Reprint 2('78) | | .20 | .40 |

**BIBLE TALES FOR YOUNG FOLK** (. . .Young People No. 3-5)
Aug, 1953 - No. 5, Mar, 1954
Atlas Comics (OMC)

| | Good | Fine | N-Mint |
|---|---|---|---|
| 1 | 8.50 | 25.50 | 60.00 |
| 2-Everett, Krigstein-a | 7.00 | 21.00 | 50.00 |
| 3-5: 4-Robinson-c | 5.00 | 15.00 | 35.00 |

**BIG**
March, 1989 ($2.00, color)
Hit Comics (Dark Horse)

| | Good | Fine | N-Mint |
|---|---|---|---|
| 1-Paul Chadwick-c; movie adaptation | .35 | 1.00 | 2.00 |

**BIG ALL-AMERICAN COMIC BOOK, THE**
1944 (One Shot) (132 pages)
All-American/National Periodical Publ.

1-Wonder Woman, Green Lantern, Flash, The Atom, Wildcat, Scribbly, The Whip, Ghost Patrol, Hawkman by Kubert (1st on Hawkman), Hop Harrigan, Johnny Thunder, Little Boy Blue, Mr. Terrific, Mutt & Jeff app.; Sargon on cover only

| Good | Fine | VF-NM | NM/Mint |
|---|---|---|---|
| 367.00 | 915.00 | 2200.00 | 3400.00 |

(Estimated up to 120 total copies exist, 6 in NM/Mint)

**BIG BLACK KISS**
Sept, 1989 - No, 3, Nov, 1989 ($3.75, B&W, adults, 52 pgs.)
Vortex Comics

| | Good | Fine | N-Mint |
|---|---|---|---|
| 1-r/Black Kiss #1-4 w/new Chaykin-c | .85 | 2.50 | 5.00 |
| 2,3-r/Black Kiss #5-12 w/new Chaykin-c | .70 | 2.00 | 4.00 |

**BIG BOOK OF FUN COMICS** (1st DC Annual)
Spring, 1936 (52 pages, large size) (1st comic book annual)
National Periodical Publications

| | Good | Fine | VF-NM | Mint |
|---|---|---|---|---|
| 1 (Very rare)-r-/New Fun #1-5 | 667.00 | 1670.00 | 4000.00 | 5600.00 |

(Estimated up to 23 total copies exist, 1 in NM/Mint)

**BIG BOOK ROMANCES**
February, 1950(no date given) (148 pages)
Fawcett Publication

| | Good | Fine | N-Mint |
|---|---|---|---|
| 1-Contains remaindered Fawcett romance comics - several combinations possible | 16.00 | 48.00 | 110.00 |

**BIG BOY** (See Adventures of the Big Boy)

**BIG CHIEF WAHOO**
July, 1942 - No. 23, 1945?
Eastern Color Printing/George Dougherty

| | Good | Fine | N-Mint |
|---|---|---|---|
| 1-Newspaper-r (on sale 6/15/42) | 21.50 | 65.00 | 150.00 |
| 2-Steve Roper app. | 11.00 | 32.00 | 75.00 |
| 3-5 | 7.50 | 22.00 | 52.00 |
| 6-10 | 5.30 | 16.00 | 38.00 |
| 11-23 | 4.00 | 12.00 | 28.00 |

NOTE: *Kerry Drake in some issues.*

**BIG CIRCUS, THE** (See 4-Color No. 1036)

**BIG COUNTRY, THE** (See 4-Color No. 946)

**BIG DADDY ROTH**
Oct-Nov, 1964 - No. 4, Apr-May, 1965 (Magazine; 35 cents)
Millar Publications

| | Good | Fine | N-Mint |
|---|---|---|---|
| 1-Toth-a | 10.00 | 30.00 | 70.00 |
| 2-4-Toth-a | 7.00 | 21.00 | 50.00 |

**BIG HERO ADVENTURES** (See Jigsaw)

**BIG JIM'S P.A.C.K.**
No date (16 pages)
Mattel, Inc. (Marvel Comics)

| | Good | Fine | N-Mint |
|---|---|---|---|
| nn-Giveaway with Big Jim doll | | .15 | .30 |

**BIG JON & SPARKIE** (Radio)(Formerly Sparkie, Radio Pixie)
No. 4, Sept-Oct, 1952 (Painted-c)
Ziff-Davis Publ. Co.

| | Good | Fine | N-Mint |
|---|---|---|---|
| 4-Based on children's radio program | 7.00 | 21.00 | 50.00 |

**BIG LAND, THE** (See 4-Color No. 812)

**BIG RED** (See Movie Comics)

**BIG SHOT COMICS**
May, 1940 - No. 104, Aug, 1949
Columbia Comics Group

| | Good | Fine | N-Mint |
|---|---|---|---|
| 1-Intro. Skyman; The Face (Tony Trent), The Cloak (Spy Master), Marvelo, Monarch of Magicians, Joe Palooka, Charlie Chan, Tom Kerry, Dixie Dugan, Rocky Ryan begin | 71.00 | 215.00 | 500.00 |
| 2 | 32.00 | 95.00 | 225.00 |
| 3-The Cloak called Spy Chief; Skyman-c | 27.00 | 81.00 | 190.00 |
| 4,5 | 24.00 | 73.00 | 170.00 |
| 6-10 | 20.00 | 60.00 | 140.00 |
| 11-14: 14-Origin Sparky Watts | 17.00 | 51.00 | 120.00 |
| 15-Origin The Cloak | 20.00 | 60.00 | 140.00 |
| 16-20 | 12.00 | 36.00 | 85.00 |
| 21-30: 24-Tojo-c. 29-Intro. Capt. Yank; Bo (a dog) newspaper strip reprints by Frank Beck begin, ends #104 | 9.30 | 28.00 | 65.00 |
| 31-40: 32-Vic Jordan newspaper strip reprints begin, ends #52; 32-Hitler, Tojo, Musselini-c | 8.00 | 24.00 | 56.00 |
| 41-50: 42-No Skyman. 43-Hitler-c. 50-Origin The Face retold | 6.50 | 19.00 | 45.00 |
| 51-60 | 5.00 | 15.00 | 35.00 |
| 61-70: 63 on-Tony Trent, the Face | 4.00 | 12.00 | 28.00 |
| 71-80: 73-The Face cameo. 74-(2/47)-Mickey Finn begins. 74,80-The Face app. in Tony Trent. 78-Last Charlie Chan strip reprints | 3.70 | 11.00 | 26.00 |
| 81-90: 85-Tony Trent marries Babs Walsh. 86-Valentines-c | 3.00 | 9.00 | 21.00 |
| 91-99,101-104: 69-94-Skyman in Outer Space. 96-Xmas-c | 2.65 | 8.00 | 18.00 |
| 100 | 3.60 | 11.00 | 25.00 |

NOTE: ***Mart Bailey** art on "The Face"-No. 1-104. **Guardineer** a-5. Sparky Watts by **Boody Rogers**-No. 14-42, 77-104, (by others No. 43-76). Others than Tony Trent wear "The Face" mask in No. 46-63, 93. Skyman by **Ogden Whitney**-No. 1, 2, 4, 12-37, 49, 70-101. Skyman covers-No. 1, 6, 10, 11, 14, 16, 20, 27, 89, 95, 100.*

**BIG TEX**
June, 1953
Toby Press

| | Good | Fine | N-Mint |
|---|---|---|---|
| 1-Contains (3) John Wayne stories-r with name changed to Big Tex | 4.00 | 12.00 | 28.00 |

**BIG-3**
Fall, 1940 - No. 7, Jan, 1942
Fox Features Syndicate

| | Good | Fine | N-Mint |
|---|---|---|---|
| 1-Blue Beetle, The Flame, & Samson begin | 82.00 | 245.00 | 575.00 |
| 2 | 36.00 | 107.00 | 250.00 |
| 3-5 | 29.00 | 85.00 | 200.00 |
| 6-Last Samson; bondage-c | 24.00 | 73.00 | 170.00 |
| 7-V-Man app. | 24.00 | 73.00 | 170.00 |

**BIG TOP COMICS, THE** (TV's Great Circus Show)
1951 - No. 2, 1951 (no month)
Toby Press

| | Good | Fine | N-Mint |
|---|---|---|---|
| 1,2 | 3.00 | 9.00 | 21.00 |

**BIG TOWN** (Radio/TV)
Jan, 1951 - No. 50, Mar-Apr, 1958 (No. 1-9: 52pgs.)
National Periodical Publications

| | Good | Fine | N-Mint |
|---|---|---|---|
| 1-Dan Barry-a begins | 26.00 | 78.00 | 180.00 |
| 2 | 13.00 | 40.00 | 90.00 |
| 3-10 | 8.00 | 24.00 | 56.00 |
| 11-20 | 5.00 | 15.00 | 35.00 |
| 21-31: Last pre-code (1-2/55) | 3.50 | 10.50 | 24.00 |
| 32-50 | 2.65 | 8.00 | 18.00 |

**BIG VALLEY, THE** (TV)
June, 1966 - No. 5, Oct, 1967; No. 6, Oct, 1969
Dell Publishing Co.

| | Good | Fine | N-Mint |
|---|---|---|---|
| 1: Photo-c #1-5 | 2.85 | 8.50 | 20.00 |
| 2-6: 6 r-/#1 | 1.50 | 4.50 | 10.00 |

**"BILL AND TED'S EXCELLENT ADVENTURE" MOVIE ADAPTATION**
1989 (No cover price, color)
DC Comics

| | Good | Fine | N-Mint |
|---|---|---|---|
| nn-Torres-a | | .50 | 1.00 |

**BILL BARNES COMICS** (. . . America's Air Ace Comics No. 2 on)
(Becomes Air Ace V2#1 on; also see Shadow Comics)
Oct, 1940(No. month given) - No. 12, Oct, 1943
Street & Smith Publications

| | Good | Fine | N-Mint |
|---|---|---|---|
| 1-23 pgs.-comics; Rocket Rooney begins | 39.00 | 118.00 | 275.00 |
| 2-Barnes as The Phantom Flyer app.; Tuska-a | 23.00 | 70.00 | 160.00 |
| 3-5 | 18.00 | 56.00 | 130.00 |
| 6-12 | 14.00 | 43.00 | 100.00 |

**BILL BATTLE, THE ONE MAN ARMY** (Also see Master No. 133)
Oct, 1952 - No. 4, Apr, 1953 (All photo-c)
Fawcett Publications

| | Good | Fine | N-Mint |
|---|---|---|---|
| 1 | 3.15 | 9.50 | 22.00 |
| 2 | 1.70 | 5.00 | 12.00 |
| 3,4 | 1.30 | 4.00 | 9.00 |

**BILL BLACK'S FUN COMICS**
Dec, 1982 - No. 4, March, 1983 ($1.75, Baxter paper)
Paragon #1-3/Americomics #4

| | Good | Fine | N-Mint |
|---|---|---|---|
| 1-Intro. Capt. Paragon, Phantom Lady & Commando D (#1-3 are B&W fanzines; 8½ x 11") | .40 | 1.25 | 2.50 |

*Big Chief Wahoo #3, © EAS*

*Big Shot Comics #32, © CCG*

*Bill Barnes Comics #8, © S&S*

*Bill Boyd Western #1, © FAW*

*Billy Buckskin Western #1, © MEG*

*Billy the Kid Adventure Magazine #13, © TOBY*

| | Good | Fine | N-Mint |
|---|---|---|---|
| 2-4: 4-($2.00, color); origin Nightfall (Formerly Phantom Lady); Nightveil app. | .35 | 1.00 | 2.00 |

**BILL BOYD WESTERN** (Movie star; see Hopalong Cassidy & Western Hero)
Feb, 1950 - No. 23, June, 1952 (1-3,7,11,14-on: 36 pgs.)
Fawcett Publications

| | Good | Fine | N-Mint |
|---|---|---|---|
| 1-Bill Boyd & his horse Midnite begin; photo front/back-c | 25.00 | 75.00 | 175.00 |
| 2-Painted-c | 15.00 | 45.00 | 105.00 |
| 3-Photo-c begin, end #23; last photo back-c | 13.50 | 41.00 | 95.00 |
| 4-6(52pgs.) | 11.00 | 32.00 | 75.00 |
| 7,11(36pgs.) | 8.50 | 25.50 | 60.00 |
| 8-10,12,13(52pgs.) | 9.30 | 28.00 | 65.00 |
| 14-22 | 8.00 | 24.00 | 55.00 |
| 23-Last issue | 8.50 | 25.50 | 60.00 |

**BILL BUMLIN** (See Treasury of Comics No. 3)

**BILL ELLIOTT** (See Wild Bill Elliott)

**BILL STERN'S SPORTS BOOK**
Spring-Summer, 1951 - V2#2, Winter, 1952
Ziff-Davis Publ. Co.(Approved Comics)

| | Good | Fine | N-Mint |
|---|---|---|---|
| V1#10(1951) | 8.50 | 25.50 | 60.00 |
| 2(Sum'52-reg. size) | 7.00 | 21.00 | 50.00 |
| V2#2(1952,96 pgs.)-Krigstein, Kinstler-a | 9.30 | 28.00 | 65.00 |

**BILLY AND BUGGY BEAR**
1958; 1964
I.W. Enterprises/Super

| | Good | Fine | N-Mint |
|---|---|---|---|
| I.W. Reprint #1(early Timely funny animal-r), #7(1958) | .50 | 1.50 | 3.00 |
| Super Reprint #10(1964) | .50 | 1.50 | 3.00 |

**BILLY BUCKSKIN WESTERN** (2-Gun Western No. 4)
Nov, 1955 - No. 3, March, 1956
Atlas Comics (IMC No. 1/MgPC No. 2,3)

| | Good | Fine | N-Mint |
|---|---|---|---|
| 1-Mort Drucker-a; Maneely-c/a | 7.00 | 21.00 | 50.00 |
| 2-Mort Drucker-a | 4.30 | 13.00 | 30.00 |
| 3-Williamson, Drucker-a | 5.00 | 15.00 | 35.00 |

**BILLY BUNNY** (Black Cobra No. 6 on)
Feb-Mar, 1954 - No. 5, Oct-Nov, 1954
Excellent Publications

| | Good | Fine | N-Mint |
|---|---|---|---|
| 1 | 2.85 | 8.50 | 20.00 |
| 2 | 1.70 | 5.00 | 12.00 |
| 3-5 | 1.15 | 3.50 | 8.00 |

**BILLY BUNNY'S CHRISTMAS FROLICS**
1952 (100 pages, 25 cent giant)
Farrell Publications

| | Good | Fine | N-Mint |
|---|---|---|---|
| 1 | 6.50 | 19.00 | 45.00 |

**BILLY MAKE BELIEVE** (See Single Series No. 14)

**BILLY THE KID** (Formerly Masked Raider; see Doc Savage Comics & Return of the Outlaw)
No. 9, Nov, 1957 - No. 121, Dec, 1976; No. 122, Sept, 1977 - No. 123, Oct, 1977; No. 124, Feb, 1978 - No. 153, Mar, 1983
Charlton Publ. Co.

| | Good | Fine | N-Mint |
|---|---|---|---|
| 9 | 4.00 | 12.00 | 28.00 |
| 10,12,14,17-19 | 2.30 | 7.00 | 16.00 |
| 11-(68 pgs., origin, 1st app. The Ghost Train) | 3.00 | 9.00 | 21.00 |
| 13-Williamson/Torres-a | 3.60 | 11.00 | 25.00 |
| 15-Origin; 2pgs. Williamson-a | 3.60 | 11.00 | 25.00 |
| 16-Two pgs. Williamson | 3.60 | 11.00 | 25.00 |
| 20-22,24-26-Severin-a(3-4) | 3.60 | 11.00 | 25.00 |
| 23,27-30 | 1.70 | 5.00 | 12.00 |
| 31-40 | 1.00 | 3.00 | 7.00 |
| 41-60 | .70 | 2.00 | 4.00 |
| 61-80: 66-Bounty Hunter series begins. Not in #79,82,84-86 | .35 | 1.00 | 2.00 |
| 81-99,101-123: 87-Last Bounty Hunter. 111-Origin The Ghost Train; 117-Gunsmith & Co., The Cheyenne Kid app. | | .50 | 1.00 |
| 100 | | .60 | 1.25 |
| 124(2/78)-153 | | .30 | .60 |
| Modern Comics 109 (1977 reprint) | | .15 | .30 |

NOTE: ***Severin** a(r)-121-129, 134; c-25. **Sutton** a-111.*

**BILLY THE KID ADVENTURE MAGAZINE**
Oct, 1950 - No. 30, 1955
Toby Press

| | Good | Fine | N-Mint |
|---|---|---|---|
| 1-Williamson/Frazetta, 4 pgs; photo-c | 16.00 | 48.00 | 110.00 |
| 2-Photo-c | 4.00 | 12.00 | 28.00 |
| 3-Williamson/Frazetta "The Claws of Death," 4 pgs. plus Williamson art | 17.00 | 51.00 | 120.00 |
| 4,5,7,8,10: 7-Photo-c | 2.65 | 8.00 | 18.00 |
| 6-Frazetta story assist on "Nightmare;" photo-c | 7.00 | 21.00 | 50.00 |
| 9-Kurtzman Pot-Shot Pete; photo-c | 6.00 | 18.00 | 42.00 |
| 11,12,15-20: 11-Photo-c | 2.30 | 7.00 | 16.00 |
| 13-Kurtzman r-/John Wayne 12 (Genius) | 2.65 | 8.00 | 18.00 |
| 14-Williamson/Frazetta; r-of #1, 2 pgs. | 5.00 | 15.00 | 35.00 |
| 21,23-30 | 1.70 | 5.00 | 12.00 |
| 22-Williamson/Frazetta r(1pg.)-/#1; photo-c | 1.85 | 8.00 | 18.00 |

**BILLY THE KID AND OSCAR** (Also see Fawcett's Funny Animals)
Winter, 1945 - No. 3, Summer, 1946 (funny animal)
Fawcett Publications

| | Good | Fine | N-Mint |
|---|---|---|---|
| 1 | 5.70 | 17.00 | 40.00 |
| 2,3 | 3.50 | 10.50 | 24.00 |

**BILLY WEST** (Bill West No. 9,10)
1949 - No. 9, Feb, 1951; No. 10, Feb, 1952
Standard Comics (Visual Editions)

| | Good | Fine | N-Mint |
|---|---|---|---|
| 1 | 4.50 | 13.50 | 32.00 |
| 2 | 2.35 | 7.00 | 16.00 |
| 3-10: 7,8-Schomburg-c | 1.70 | 5.00 | 12.00 |

NOTE: ***Celardo** a-1-6, 9; c-1-3. **Moreira** a-3. **Roussos** a-2.*

**BING CROSBY** (See Feature Films)

**BINGO** (. . .Comics) (H. C. Blackerby)
1945 (Reprints National material)
Howard Publ.

| | Good | Fine | N-Mint |
|---|---|---|---|
| 1-L. B. Cole opium-c | 12.00 | 36.00 | 85.00 |

**BINGO, THE MONKEY DOODLE BOY**
Aug, 1951; Oct, 1953
St. John Publishing Co.

| | Good | Fine | N-Mint |
|---|---|---|---|
| 1(8/51)-by Eric Peters | 2.85 | 8.50 | 20.00 |
| 1(10/53) | 2.00 | 6.00 | 14.00 |

**BINKY** (Formerly Leave It to. . .)
No. 72, 4-5/70 - No. 81, 10-11/71; No. 82, Summer/77
National Periodical Publ./DC Comics

| | Good | Fine | N-Mint |
|---|---|---|---|
| 72-81 | .50 | 1.50 | 3.00 |
| 82('77)-(One Shot) | .25 | .75 | 1.50 |

**BINKY'S BUDDIES**
Jan-Feb, 1969 - No. 12, Nov-Dec, 1970
National Periodical Publications

| | Good | Fine | N-Mint |
|---|---|---|---|
| 1 | .85 | 2.60 | 6.00 |
| 2-12 | .50 | 1.50 | 3.00 |

**BIONIC WOMAN, THE** (TV)
October, 1977 - No. 5, June, 1978
Charlton Publications

| | Good | Fine | N-Mint |
|---|---|---|---|
| 1-5 | | .50 | 1.00 |

**BIZARRE ADVENTURES** (Formerly Marvel Preview)
No. 25, 3/81 - No. 34, 2/83 (#25-33: Magazine-$1.50)
Marvel Comics Group

| | Good | Fine | N-Mint |
|---|---|---|---|
| 25-Lethal Ladies. 26-King Kull | | .60 | 1.20 |
| 27-Phoenix, Iceman & Nightcrawler app. 28-The Unlikely Heroes; Elektra by Miller; Neal Adams-a | .25 | .75 | 1.50 |
| 29-Horror. 30-Tomorrow. 31-After The Violence Stops; new Hangman story; Miller-a. 32-Gods. 33-Horror; photo-c | | .60 | 1.20 |
| 34 ($2.00, Baxter paper, comic size)-Son of Santa; Christmas spec.; Howard the Duck by P. Smith | .25 | .75 | 1.50 |

NOTE: ***Alcala*** *a-27i.* ***Austin*** *a-25i, 28i.* ***J. Buscema*** *a-27p, 29, 30p; c-26.* ***Byrne*** *a-31(2pgs.).* ***Golden*** *a-25p, 28p.* ***Perez*** *a-27p.* ***Reese*** *a-31i.* ***Rogers*** *a-25p.* ***Simonson*** *a-29; c-29.* ***Paul Smith*** *a-34.*

**BIZARRE 3-D ZONE** (See Blackthorne 3-D Series No. 5)

**BLACK AND WHITE** (See Large Feature Comic, Series I)

**BLACKBEARD'S GHOST** (See Movie Comics)

**BLACK BEAUTY** (See 4-Color No. 440)

**BLACK CAT COMICS** (. . .Western #16-19; . . .Mystery #30 on)
(See All-New #7,9, The Original Black Cat, Pocket & Speed Comics)
June-July, 1946 - No. 29, June, 1951
Harvey Publications (Home Comics)

| | Good | Fine | N-Mint |
|---|---|---|---|
| 1-Kubert-a | 28.00 | 86.00 | 200.00 |
| 2-Kubert-a | 16.00 | 48.00 | 110.00 |
| 3,4: 4-The Red Demons begin (The Demon #4 & 5) | 11.50 | 34.00 | 80.00 |
| 5,6-The Scarlet Arrow app. in ea. by Powell; S&K-a in both. 6-Origin Red Demon | 14.00 | 43.00 | 100.00 |
| 7-Vagabond Prince by S&K plus 1 more story | 14.00 | 43.00 | 100.00 |
| 8-S&K-a; Kerry Drake begins, ends #13 | 13.00 | 40.00 | 90.00 |
| 9-Origin Stuntman (r-/Stuntman #1) | 16.00 | 48.00 | 110.00 |
| 10-20: 14,15,17-Mary Worth app. plus Invisible Scarlet O'Neil-#15,20, 24 | 10.00 | 30.00 | 70.00 |
| 21-26 | 8.50 | 25.50 | 60.00 |
| 27-Used in **SOTI**, pg. 193; X-Mas-c; 2 pg. John Wayne story | 10.00 | 30.00 | 70.00 |
| 28-Intro. Kit, Black Cat's new sidekick | 10.00 | 30.00 | 70.00 |
| 29-Black Cat bondage-c; Black Cat stories | 9.30 | 28.00 | 65.00 |

**BLACK CAT MYSTERY** (Formerly Black Cat; . . .Western Mystery #54; . . .Western #55,56; . . .Mystery #57; . . .Mystic #58-62; Black Cat #63-65)
No. 30, Aug, 1951 - No. 65, April, 1963
Harvey Publications

| | Good | Fine | N-Mint |
|---|---|---|---|
| 30-Black Cat on cover only | 8.00 | 24.00 | 55.00 |
| 31,32,34,37,38,40 | 5.00 | 15.00 | 35.00 |
| 33-Used in **POP**, pg. 89; electrocution-c | 5.70 | 17.00 | 40.00 |
| 35-Atomic disaster cover/story | 6.50 | 19.00 | 45.00 |
| 36,39-Used in **SOTI**: #36-Pgs. 270,271; #39-Pgs. 386-388 | 8.50 | 25.50 | 60.00 |
| 41-43 | 4.50 | 14.00 | 32.00 |
| 44-Eyes, ears, tongue cut out; Nostrand-a | 5.30 | 16.00 | 38.00 |
| 45-Classic "Colorama" by Powell; Nostrand-a | 9.30 | 28.00 | 65.00 |
| 46-49,51-Nostrand-a in all | 6.00 | 18.00 | 42.00 |
| 50-Check-a; Warren Kremer?-c showing a man's face burning away | 9.30 | 28.00 | 65.00 |
| 52,53 (r-#34 & 35) | 3.70 | 11.00 | 26.00 |
| 54-Two Black Cat stories (2/55, last pre-code) | 6.00 | 18.00 | 42.00 |
| 55,56-Black Cat app. | 4.00 | 12.00 | 28.00 |
| 57(7/56)-Simon?-c | 2.85 | 8.50 | 20.00 |
| 58-60-Kirby-a(4) | 5.30 | 16.00 | 38.00 |
| 61-Nostrand-a; "Colorama" r-/45 | 4.30 | 13.00 | 30.00 |
| 62(3/58)-E.C. story swipe | 3.15 | 9.50 | 22.00 |
| 63-Giant(10/62); Reprints; Black Cat app.; origin Black Kitten | 4.50 | 14.00 | 32.00 |
| 64-Giant(1/63); Reprints; Black Cat app. | 4.50 | 14.00 | 32.00 |
| 65-Giant(4/63); Reprints; Black Cat app. | 4.50 | 14.00 | 32.00 |

NOTE: ***Kremer*** *a-37, 39, 43; c-36, 37, 47.* ***Meskin*** *a-51.* ***Palais*** *a-30, 31(2), 32(2), 33-35, 37-40.* ***Powell*** *a-32-35, 36(2), 40, 41, 43-53, 57.* ***Simon*** *c-63-65.* ***Sparling*** *a-44. Bondage-c No. 32, 34, 43.*

**BLACK COBRA** (Bride's Diary No. 4 on)
No. 1, 10-11/54; No. 6(No. 2), 12-1/54-55; No. 3, 2-3/55
Ajax/Farrell Publications

| | Good | Fine | N-Mint |
|---|---|---|---|
| 1 | 11.50 | 34.00 | 80.00 |
| 6(No. 2)-Formerly Billy Bunny | 7.00 | 21.00 | 50.00 |
| 3-(pre-code)-Torpedoman app. | 7.00 | 21.00 | 50.00 |

**BLACK CROSS SPECIAL** (See Dark Horse Presents)
Jan, 1988 ($1.75, B&W, One shot)(Reprints & new-a)
Dark Horse Comics

| | Good | Fine | N-Mint |
|---|---|---|---|
| 1-1st and 2nd printings; 2nd has 2 pgs. new-a | .30 | .90 | 1.80 |

**BLACK DIAMOND**
May, 1983 - No. 5, 1984 (no month) ($2.00-$1.75, color, Baxter)
Americomics

| | Good | Fine | N-Mint |
|---|---|---|---|
| 1-3-Movie adaptation; 1-Colt back up begins | .50 | 1.50 | 3.00 |
| 4,5 | .25 | .75 | 1.50 |

NOTE: ***Bill Black*** *a-1i; c-1.* ***Gulacy*** *c-2-5. Sybil Danning photo back-c 1.*

**BLACK DIAMOND WESTERN** (Formerly Desperado No. 1-8)
No. 9, Mar, 1949 - No. 60, Feb, 1956 (No. 9-28: 52 pgs.)
Lev Gleason Publications

| | Good | Fine | N-Mint |
|---|---|---|---|
| 9-Origin | 9.30 | 28.00 | 65.00 |
| 10 | 5.00 | 15.00 | 35.00 |
| 11-15 | 3.70 | 11.00 | 26.00 |
| 16-28-Wolverton's Bing Bang Buster | 5.00 | 15.00 | 35.00 |
| 29,30,32-40 | 2.30 | 7.00 | 16.00 |
| 31-One pg. Frazetta-a | 2.30 | 7.00 | 16.00 |
| 41-50,53-59 | 2.00 | 6.00 | 14.00 |
| 51-3-D effect-c/story | 6.00 | 18.00 | 42.00 |
| 52-3-D effect story | 5.00 | 15.00 | 35.00 |
| 60-Last issue | 2.30 | 7.00 | 16.00 |

NOTE: ***Biro*** *c-9-24?.* ***Fass*** *a-58, c-54-56, 58.* ***Guardineer*** *a-9, 18.* ***Kida*** *a-9.* ***Maurer*** *a-10.* ***Morisi*** *a-55.* ***Tuska*** *a-10, 48.*

**BLACK DRAGON, THE**
5/85 - No. 6, 10/85 (Baxter paper; mini-series; adults only)
Epic Comics (Marvel)

| | Good | Fine | N-Mint |
|---|---|---|---|
| 1-Bolton-c/a in all | .50 | 1.50 | 3.00 |
| 2-6 | .30 | .90 | 1.80 |

**BLACK FURY** (Becomes Wild West No. 58) (See Blue Bird)
May, 1955 - No. 57, Mar-Apr, 1966 (Horse stories)
Charlton Comics Group

| | Good | Fine | N-Mint |
|---|---|---|---|
| 1 | 2.65 | 8.00 | 18.00 |
| 2 | 1.30 | 4.00 | 9.00 |
| 3-10 | .85 | 2.60 | 6.00 |
| 11-15,19,20 | .70 | 2.00 | 4.00 |
| 16-18-Ditko-a | 3.00 | 9.00 | 21.00 |
| 21-30 | .45 | 1.35 | 3.00 |
| 31-57 | .35 | 1.00 | 2.00 |

**BLACK GOLD**
1945? (8 pgs. in color)
Esso Service Station (Giveaway)

| | Good | Fine | N-Mint |
|---|---|---|---|
| Reprints from True Comics | 3.00 | 9.00 | 21.00 |

**BLACK GOLIATH**
Feb, 1976 - No. 5, Nov, 1976
Marvel Comics Group

| | Good | Fine | N-Mint |
|---|---|---|---|
| 1: 1-3-Tuska-a(p) | .60 | 1.75 | 3.50 |

*Black Cat Comics #8, © HARV*

*Black Cat Mystery #50, © HARV*

*Black Diamond Western #51, © LEV*

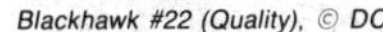
Blackhawk #22 (Quality), © DC

Black Hood Comics #19, © AP

The Black Knight #4 (1956), © MEG

| | Good | Fine | N-Mint |
|---|---|---|---|
| 2-5 | .35 | 1.00 | 2.00 |

**BLACKHAWK** (Formerly Uncle Sam #1-8; Also see Military Comics & Modern Comics)
No. 9, Winter, 1944 - No. 243, 10-11/68; No. 244, 1-2/76 - No. 250, 1-2/77; No. 251, 10/82 - No. 273, 11/84
Comic Magazines(Quality)No. 9-107(12/56); National Periodical Publ. No. 108(1/57)-250; DC Comics No. 251 on

| | Good | Fine | N-Mint |
|---|---|---|---|
| 9 (1944) | 115.00 | 345.00 | 800.00 |
| 10 (1946) | 50.00 | 150.00 | 350.00 |
| 11-15: 14-Ward-a; 13,14-Fear app. | 38.00 | 114.00 | 265.00 |
| 16-20: 20-Ward Blackhawk | 32.00 | 95.00 | 225.00 |
| 21-30 | 24.00 | 72.00 | 165.00 |
| 31-40: 31-Chop Chop by Jack Cole | 17.00 | 51.00 | 120.00 |
| 41-49,51-60 | 12.00 | 36.00 | 84.00 |
| 50-1st Killer Shark; origin in text | 15.00 | 45.00 | 105.00 |
| 61-Used in **POP**, pg. 91 | 11.00 | 32.00 | 75.00 |
| 62-Used in **POP**, pg. 92 & color illo | 11.00 | 32.00 | 75.00 |
| 63-65,67-70,72-80: 70-Return of Killer Shark. 75-Intro. Blackie the Hawk | 10.00 | 30.00 | 70.00 |
| 66-B&W and color illos in **POP** | 10.00 | 30.00 | 70.00 |
| 71-Origin retold; flying saucer-c; A-Bomb panels | 13.00 | 40.00 | 90.00 |
| 81-86: Last precode (3/55) | 9.30 | 28.00 | 65.00 |
| 87-92,94-99,101-107 | 6.50 | 19.00 | 45.00 |
| 93-Origin in text | 8.00 | 24.00 | 56.00 |
| 100 | 8.50 | 25.50 | 60.00 |
| 108-Re-intro. Blackie, the Hawk, their mascot; not in #115 | 24.00 | 72.00 | 165.00 |
| 109-117 | 5.70 | 17.00 | 40.00 |
| 118-Frazetta r-/Jimmy Wakely #4 (3 pgs.) | 7.00 | 21.00 | 50.00 |
| 119-130 | 2.85 | 8.50 | 20.00 |
| 131-163,165,166: 133-Intro. Lady Blackhawk. 143-Kurtzman r-/Jimmy Wakely #4. 166-Last 10 cent issue | 2.15 | 6.50 | 15.00 |
| 164-Origin retold | 2.30 | 7.00 | 16.00 |
| 167-180 | 1.00 | 3.00 | 6.00 |
| 181-190 | .85 | 2.50 | 5.00 |
| 191-197,199-202,204-210: Combat Diary series begins. 197-New look for Blackhawks | .70 | 2.00 | 4.00 |
| 198-Origin retold | 1.00 | 3.00 | 6.00 |
| 203-Origin Chop Chop (12/64) | .85 | 2.50 | 5.00 |
| 211-243(1968): 228-Batman, Green Lantern, Superman, The Flash cameos. 230-Blackhawks become superheroes. 242-Return to old costumes | .70 | 2.00 | 4.00 |
| 244 ('76) -250: 250-Chuck dies | .35 | 1.00 | 2.00 |
| 251-264: 251-Origin retold; Black Knights return. 252-Intro Domino. 253-Part origin Hendrickson. 258-Blackhawk's Island destroyed. 259-Part origin Chop-Chop | | .50 | 1.00 |
| 265-273 (75 cent cover price) | | .50 | 1.00 |

NOTE: **Chaykin** a-260; c-257-260, 262. **Crandall** a-10, 11, 13, 16, 18-20, 22-26, 30-33, 36(2), 37, 39-44, 46-50, 52-58, 60, 63, 64, 66, 67; c-18-20, 22-on(most). **Evans** a-244, 245, 246i, 248-250i. **G. Kane** c-263, 264. **Kubert** c-244, 245. **Newton** a-266p. **Severin** a-257. **Spiegle** a-261-267, 269-273; c-265-272. **Toth** a-260p. **Ward** a-16-27(Chop Chop, 8pgs. ea.); pencilled stories-No. 17-63(approx.). **Wildey** a-268.

**BLACKHAWK**
Mar, 1988 - No. 3, May, 1988 ($2.95, mini-series)
DC Comics

| | Good | Fine | N-Mint |
|---|---|---|---|
| 1-3: Chaykin painted-c/a | .50 | 1.50 | 3.00 |

**BLACKHAWK**
March, 1989 - No. 16, Aug, 1990 ($1.50, color, mature readers)
DC Comics

| | Good | Fine | N-Mint |
|---|---|---|---|
| 1-6,8-16: 16-Reed Crandall-c(p) | .25 | .75 | 1.50 |
| 7-($2.50, 52 pgs.)-story-r/Military #1 | .40 | 1.25 | 2.50 |
| Annual 1 (1989, $2.95, 68 pgs.)-Recaps origin of Blackhawk, Lady Blackhawk, and others | .50 | 1.50 | 3.00 |

**BLACKHAWK INDIAN TOMAHAWK WAR, THE**
1951
Avon Periodicals

| | Good | Fine | N-Mint |
|---|---|---|---|
| nn-Kinstler-c; Kit West story | 8.00 | 24.00 | 56.00 |

**BLACK HOLE** (See Walt Disney Showcase #54)
March, 1980 - No. 4, September, 1980 (Disney movie)
Whitman Publishing Co.

| | Good | Fine | N-Mint |
|---|---|---|---|
| 11295(#1)-Photo-c; Spiegle-a | | .50 | 1.00 |
| 2,3-Spiegle-a; 3-McWilliams-a; photo-c | | .50 | 1.00 |
| 4-Spiegle-a | | .40 | .80 |

**BLACK HOOD, THE** (See Blue Ribbon, Flyman & Mighty Comics)
Jun, 1983 - No. 3, Oct, 1983 (Printed on Mandell paper)
Red Circle Comics (Archie)

| | Good | Fine | N-Mint |
|---|---|---|---|
| 1-Morrow, McWilliams, Wildey-a; Toth-c | | .60 | 1.20 |
| 2,3: MLJ's The Fox by Toth, c/a | | .50 | 1.00 |

*(Also see Archie's Super-Hero Special Digest #2)*

**BLACK HOOD COMICS** (Formerly Hangman #2-8; Laugh Comics #20 on; also see Black Swan, Jackpot, Roly Poly & Top-Notch #9)
No. 9, Winter, 1943-44 - No. 19, Summer, 1946 (on radio in 1943)
MLJ Magazines

| | Good | Fine | N-Mint |
|---|---|---|---|
| 9-The Hangman & The Boy Buddies cont'd | 36.00 | 107.00 | 250.00 |
| 10-The Hangman & Dusty, the Boy Detective app. | 16.00 | 48.00 | 110.00 |
| 11-Dusty app.; no Hangman | 13.00 | 40.00 | 90.00 |
| 12-18: 14-Kinstler blood-c | 13.00 | 40.00 | 90.00 |
| 19-I.D. exposed | 16.00 | 48.00 | 110.00 |

NOTE: *Hangman by* **Fuje** *in 9, 10.* **Kinstler** *a-15, c-14-16.*

**BLACK JACK** (Rocky Lane's. . ., formerly Jim Bowie)
No. 20, Nov, 1957 - No. 30, Nov, 1959
Charlton Comics

| | Good | Fine | N-Mint |
|---|---|---|---|
| 20 | 3.00 | 9.00 | 21.00 |
| 21,27,29,30 | 1.50 | 4.50 | 10.00 |
| 22-(68 pages) | 2.65 | 8.00 | 18.00 |
| 23-Williamson/Torres-a | 3.50 | 10.50 | 24.00 |
| 24-26,28-Ditko-a | 3.00 | 9.00 | 21.00 |

**BLACK KISS** (See Big Black Kiss)
June, 1988 - No. 12, July, 1989 ($1.25-1.50, B&W, 16 pgs., adults)
Vortex Comics

| | Good | Fine | N-Mint |
|---|---|---|---|
| 1-By Howard Chaykin | 1.50 | 4.50 | 9.00 |
| 1-2nd, 3rd print | | .60 | 1.25 |
| 2 | .60 | 1.75 | 3.50 |
| 2-2nd print | | .60 | 1.25 |
| 3 | .35 | 1.00 | 2.00 |
| 4-6 | .30 | .90 | 1.80 |
| 7-12: 10-on are $1.50 | | .60 | 1.25 |

**BLACK KNIGHT, THE**
May, 1953; 1963
Toby Press

| | Good | Fine | N-Mint |
|---|---|---|---|
| 1-Bondage-c | 8.50 | 25.50 | 60.00 |
| Super Reprint No. 11 (1963) | 1.15 | 3.50 | 8.00 |

**BLACK KNIGHT, THE** (Also see The Avengers #48, Marvel Super Heroes & Tales To Astonish #52)
May, 1955 - No. 5, April, 1956
Atlas Comics (MgPC)

| | Good | Fine | N-Mint |
|---|---|---|---|
| 1-Origin Crusader; Maneely-c/a | 45.00 | 135.00 | 315.00 |
| 2 | 30.00 | 90.00 | 210.00 |
| 3-5: 4-Maneely-c/a. 5-Maneely-c, Shores-a | 24.00 | 72.00 | 165.00 |

**BLACK KNIGHT**
June, 1990 - No. 4, Sept, 1990 ($1.50, mini-series)
Marvel Comics

| | Good | Fine | N-Mint |
|---|---|---|---|
| 1-4: 1-Original Black Knight returns | .25 | .75 | 1.50 |

**BLACK LIGHTNING** (See Brave & The Bold, Cancelled Comic Cavalcade, DC Comics Presents #16, Detective #490 and World's Finest)
April, 1977 - No. 11, Sept-Oct, 1978
National Periodical Publications/DC Comics

| | Good | Fine | N-Mint |
|---|---|---|---|
| 1 | | .40 | .80 |
| 2-11: 4-Intro Cyclotronic Man. 11-The Ray app. | | .25 | .50 |

NOTE: ***Buckler*** *c-1-3p, 6-11p. #11 is 44 pgs.*

**BLACK MAGIC** (. . . Magazine) (Becomes Cool Cat V8#6 on)
10-11/50 - V4#1, 6-7/53: V4#2, 9-10/53 - V5#3, 11-12/54; V6#1, 9-10/57 - V7#2, 11-12/58: V7#3, 7-8/60 - V8#5, 11-12/61
(V1#1-5, 52pgs.; V1#6-V3#3, 44pgs.)
Crestwood Publ. V1#1-4,V6#1-V7#5/Headline V1#5-V5#3,V7#6-V8#5

| | Good | Fine | N-Mint |
|---|---|---|---|
| V1#1-S&K-a, 10 pgs.; Meskin-a(2) | 29.00 | 85.00 | 200.00 |
| 2-S&K-a, 17 pgs.; Meskin-a | 14.00 | 43.00 | 100.00 |
| 3-6(8-9/51)-S&K, Roussos, Meskin-a | 11.50 | 34.00 | 80.00 |
| V2#1(10-11/51),4,5,7(#13),9(#15),12(#18)-S&K-a | 8.00 | 24.00 | 55.00 |
| 2,3,6,8,10,11(#17) | 5.00 | 15.00 | 35.00 |
| V3#1(#19, 12/52) - 6(#24, 5/53)-S&K-a | 6.50 | 19.00 | 45.00 |
| V4#1(#25, 6-7/53), 2(#26, 9-10/53)-S&K-a(3-4) | 7.00 | 21.00 | 50.00 |
| 3(#27, 11-12/53)-S&K-a; Ditko-a(1st in comics) | 14.00 | 43.00 | 100.00 |
| 4(#28)-Eyes ripped out/story-S&K, Ditko-a | 11.00 | 32.00 | 75.00 |
| 5(#29, 3-4/54)-S&K, Ditko-a | 8.50 | 25.50 | 60.00 |
| 6(#30, 5-6/54)-S&K, Powell?-a | 4.30 | 13.00 | 30.00 |
| V5#1(#31, 7-8/54 - 3(#33, 11-12/54)-S&K-a | 4.00 | 12.00 | 28.00 |
| V6#1(#34, 9-10/57), 2(#35, 11-12/57) | 2.00 | 6.00 | 14.00 |
| 3(1-2/58) - 6(7-8/58) | 2.00 | 6.00 | 14.00 |
| V7#1(9-10/58) - 3(7-8/60) | 1.70 | 5.00 | 12.00 |
| 4(9-10/60), 5(11-12/60)-Torres-a | 2.15 | 6.50 | 15.00 |
| 6(1-2/61)-Powell-a(2) | 1.70 | 5.00 | 12.00 |
| V8#1(3-4/61)-Powell-c/a | 1.70 | 5.00 | 12.00 |
| 2(5-6/61)-E.C. story swipe/W.F. #22; Ditko, Powell-a | 2.15 | 6.50 | 15.00 |
| 3(7-8/61)-E.C. story swipe/W.F. #22; Powell-a(2) | 2.00 | 6.00 | 14.00 |
| 4(9-10/61)-Powell-a(5) | 1.70 | 5.00 | 12.00 |
| 5-E.C. story swipe/W.S.F. #28; Powell-a(3) | 2.00 | 6.00 | 14.00 |

NOTE: ***Bernard Baily*** *a-V4#6?, V5#3(2).* ***Grandenetti*** *a-V2#3, 11.* ***Kirby*** *c-V1#1-6, V2#1-12, V3#1-6, V4#1, 2, 4-6, V5#1-3.* ***McWilliams*** *a-V3#2i.* ***Meskin*** *a-V1#1(2), 2, 3, 4(2), 5(2), 6, V2/1, 2, 3(2), 4(3), 5, 6(2), 7-9, 11, 12i, V3#1(2), 5, 6, V5#1(2), 2.* ***Orlando*** *a-V6#1, 4, V7#2; c-V6/1-6.* ***Powell*** *a-V5#1?.* ***Roussos*** *a-V1#3-5, 6(2), V2#3(2), 4, 5(2), 6, 8, 9, 10(2), 11, 12p, V3#1(2), 2i, 5, V5#2.* ***Simon*** *a-V2#12, V3#2, V7#5? c-V4#3?, V7#3?, 4, 5?, 6?, V8#1-5.* ***Simon & Kirby*** *a-V1#1, 2(2), 3-6, V2#1, 4, 5, 7, 9, 12, V3#1-6, V4#1(3), 2(4), 3(2), 4(2), 5, 6, V5#1-3; c-V2#1.* ***Leonard Starr*** *a-V1#1.* ***Tuska*** *a-V6#3, 4.* ***Woodbridge*** *a-V7#4.*

**BLACK MAGIC**
Oct-Nov, 1973 - No. 9, Apr-May, 1975
National Periodical Publications

| | Good | Fine | N-Mint |
|---|---|---|---|
| 1-S&K reprints | | .30 | .60 |
| 2-9-S&K reprints | | .20 | .40 |

**BLACK MAGIC**
Apr, 1990 - No. 4, Oct, 1990 ($2.75, B&W, mini-series, 52 pgs.)
Eclipse International

| | Good | Fine | N-Mint |
|---|---|---|---|
| 1-($3.50, 68 pgs.)-Japanese manga | .60 | 1.75 | 3.50 |
| 2-4 ($2.75) | .45 | 1.40 | 2.80 |

**BLACKMAIL TERROR** (See Harvey Comics Library)

**BLACKMAN**
No Date (1981, no cover price)
Leader Comics Group

| | Good | Fine | N-Mint |
|---|---|---|---|
| V1#1 | | .30 | .60 |

**BLACK ORCHID** (See Adventure Comics #428 & Phantom Stranger)
Holiday, 1988-'89 - No. 3, 1989 ($3.50, mini-series, prestige format)
DC Comics

| | Good | Fine | N-Mint |
|---|---|---|---|
| Book 1,3 | .60 | 1.75 | 3.50 |
| Book 2-Arkham Asylum story; Batman app. | .85 | 2.50 | 5.00 |

**BLACKOUTS** (See Broadway Hollywood . . .)

**BLACK PANTHER, THE** (Also see Avengers #52, Fantastic Four #52 & Jungle Action)
Jan, 1977 - No. 15, May, 1979
Marvel Comics Group

| | Good | Fine | N-Mint |
|---|---|---|---|
| 1 | .60 | 1.75 | 3.50 |
| 2-15: 14,15-Avengers x-over | .35 | 1.00 | 2.00 |

NOTE: ***J. Buscema*** *c-15p.* ***Kirby*** *c/a-1-14.* ***Layton*** *c-13i.*

**BLACK PANTHER**
July, 1988 - No. 4, Oct, 1988 ($1.25, color)
Marvel Comics Group

| | Good | Fine | N-Mint |
|---|---|---|---|
| 1-4 | .25 | .75 | 1.50 |

**BLACK PHANTOM** (See Tim Holt #25, 38)
Nov, 1954 (One shot) (Female outlaw)
Magazine Enterprises

| | Good | Fine | N-Mint |
|---|---|---|---|
| 1 (A-1 122)-The Ghost Rider story plus 3 Black Phantom stories; Headlight-c/a | 17.00 | 51.00 | 120.00 |

**BLACK PHANTOM**
1989 - Present ($2.50, B&W; #2 on: color)(Reprint & new-a)
AC Comics

| | Good | Fine | N-Mint |
|---|---|---|---|
| 1,2: 1-Ayers-r, Bolle-r/B.P. #1. 2-Redmask-r | .40 | 1.25 | 2.50 |
| 3 ($2.75, color)-B.P., Redmask-r & new-a | .45 | 1.40 | 2.80 |

**BLACK PHANTOM, RETURN OF THE** (See Wisco)

**BLACK RIDER** (Formerly Western Winners; Western Tales of Black Rider #28-31; Gunsmoke Western #32 on)(Also see All Western Winners, Best Western, Kid Colt, Outlaw Kid, Rex Hart, Two-Gun Kid, Two-Gun Western, Western Gunfighters, Western Winners, & Wild Western)
No. 8, 3/50 - No. 18, 1/52; No. 19, 11/53 - No. 27, 3/55
Marvel/Atlas Comics(CDS No. 8-17/CPS No. 19 on)

| | Good | Fine | N-Mint |
|---|---|---|---|
| 8 (#1)-Black Rider & his horse Satan begin; 36pgs; photo-c | 20.00 | 60.00 | 140.00 |
| 9-52 pgs. begin, end #14 | 10.00 | 30.00 | 70.00 |
| 10-Origin Black Rider | 12.00 | 36.00 | 85.00 |
| 11-14(Last 52pgs.) | 7.00 | 21.00 | 50.00 |
| 15-19: 19-Two-Gun Kid app. | 6.50 | 19.50 | 45.00 |
| 20-Classic-c; Two-Gun Kid app. | 7.00 | 21.00 | 50.00 |
| 21-26: 21-23-Two-Gun Kid app. 24,25-Arrowhead app. 26-Kid Colt app. | 5.00 | 15.00 | 35.00 |
| 27-Last issue; last precode. Kid Colt app. The Spider (a villain) burns to death | 5.30 | 16.00 | 38.00 |

NOTE: ***Ayers*** *c-22.* ***Jack Keller*** *a-15, 26, 27.* ***Maneely*** *a-14; c-16, 17, 25, 27.* ***Syd Shores*** *a-19, 21, 22, 23(3), 24(3), 25-27; c-19, 21, 23.* ***Sinnott*** *a-24, 25.* ***Tuska*** *a-12, 19-21.*

**BLACK RIDER RIDES AGAIN!, THE**
September, 1957
Atlas Comics (CPS)

| | Good | Fine | N-Mint |
|---|---|---|---|
| 1-Kirby-a(3); Powell-a; Severin-c | 11.00 | 32.00 | 75.00 |

**BLACKSTONE** (See Super Magician Comics & Wisco Giveaways)

**BLACKSTONE, MASTER MAGICIAN COMICS**
Mar-Apr, 1946 - No. 3, July-Aug, 1946
Vital Publications/Street & Smith Publ.

| | Good | Fine | N-Mint |
|---|---|---|---|
| 1 | 12.00 | 36.00 | 85.00 |
| 2,3 | 8.50 | 25.50 | 60.00 |

**BLACKSTONE, THE MAGICIAN**
No. 2, May, 1948 - No. 4, Sept, 1948 (No #1)
Marvel Comics (CnPC)

| | Good | Fine | N-Mint |
|---|---|---|---|
| 2-The Blonde Phantom begins | 26.00 | 77.00 | 180.00 |

3,4-(. . .Detective on cover only). 3,4-Bondage-c

*Black Magic V8#3, © PRIZE*

*Black Orchid #2, © DC*

*The Black Rider #25, © MEG*

Black Swan Comics #1, © AP

The Black Terror #21, © STD

Blackthorne 3-D Series #13, © Winsor McCay

Good Fine N-Mint
17.00 51.00 120.00

**BLACKSTONE, THE MAGICIAN DETECTIVE FIGHTS CRIME**
Fall, 1947
E. C. Comics
1-1st app. Happy Houlihans 27.00 80.00 185.00

**BLACK SWAN COMICS**
1945
MLJ Magazines (Pershing Square Publ. Co.)
1-The Black Hood reprints from Black Hood No. 14; Bill Woggon-a; Suzie app. 9.30 28.00 65.00

**BLACK TARANTULA** (See Feature Presentations No. 5)

**BLACK TERROR** (See America's Best & Exciting Comics)
Wint, 1942-43 - No. 27, June, 1949
Better Publications/Standard

| | Good | Fine | N-Mint |
|---|---|---|---|
| 1-Black Terror, Crime Crusader begin | 68.00 | 205.00 | 475.00 |
| 2 | 32.00 | 96.00 | 225.00 |
| 3 | 24.00 | 72.00 | 165.00 |
| 4,5 | 19.00 | 56.00 | 130.00 |
| 6-10: 7-The Ghost app. | 14.00 | 43.00 | 100.00 |
| 11-20: 20-The Scarab app. | 12.00 | 36.00 | 85.00 |
| 21-Miss Masque app. | 13.00 | 40.00 | 90.00 |
| 22-Part Frazetta-a on one Black Terror story | 13.50 | 41.00 | 95.00 |
| 23,25-27 | 11.50 | 34.00 | 80.00 |
| 24-¼ pg. Frazetta-a | 12.00 | 36.00 | 85.00 |

NOTE: ***Schomburg (Xela)*** *c-2-27; bondage c-2, 17, 24.* ***Meskin*** *a-27.* ***Moreira*** *a-27.* ***Robinson/Meskin*** *a-23, 24(3), 25, 26.* ***Roussos/Mayo*** *a-24.* ***Tuska*** *a-26, 27.*

**BLACK TERROR, THE** (Also see Total Eclipse)
10/89 - No. 3, 6/90 ($4.95, color, squarebound, mini-series, 52 pgs.)
Eclipse Comics
1-3: Painted-c/a .85 2.50 5.00

**BLACKTHORNE 3-D SERIES**
May, 1985 - No. 80?, 1989 ($2.25-2.50)
Blackthorne Publishing Co.
1-Sheena In 3-D #1; D. Stevens-c/retouched-a .40 1.25 2.50
2-10: 2-MerlinRealm In 3-D #1. 3-3-D Heroes #1. Goldyn In 3-D #1. 5-Bizarre 3-D Zone #1. 6-Salimba In 3-D #1. 7-Twisted Tales In 3-D #1. 8-Dick Tracy In 3-D #1. 9-Salimba In 3-D #2. 10-Gumby In 3-D #1 .40 1.25 2.50
11-20: 11-Betty Boop In 3-D #1. 12-Hamster Vice In 3-D #1. 13-Little Nemo In 3-D #1. 14-Gumby In 3-D #2. 15-Hamster Vice #6 In 3-D. 16-Laffin' Gas #6 In 3-D. 17-Gumby In 3-D #3. 18-Bullwinkle and Rocky In 3-D #1. 19-The Flintstones In 3-D #1. 20-G.I. Joe In 3-D #1 .40 1.25 2.50
21-30: 21-Gumby In 3-D #4. 22-The Flintstones In 3-D #2. 23-Laurel & Hardy In 3-D #1. 24-Bozo the Clown In 3-D #1. 25-The Transformers In 3-D #1. 26-G.I.Joe In 3-D #2. 27-Bravestarr In 3-D #1. 28-Gumby In 3-D #5. 29-The Transformers In 3-D #2. 30-Star Wars In 3-D #1 .40 1.25 2.50
31-40: 31-The California Raisins In 3-D #1. 32-Richie Rich & Casper In 3-D #1. 33-Gumby In 3-D #6. 34-Laurel & Hardy In 3-D #2. 35-G.I. Joe In 3-D #3. 36-The Flintstones In 3-D #3. 37-The Transformers In 3-D #3. 38-Gumby In 3-D #7. 39-G.I. Joe In 3-D #4. 40-Bravestarr In 3-D #2 .40 1.25 2.50
41-50: 41-Battletech In 3-D #1. 42-The Flintstones In 3-D #4. 43-Underdog In 3-D #1. 44-The California Raisins In 3-D #2. 45-Red Heat In 3-D #1 (movie adapt.). 46-The California Raisins In 3-D #3. 47, 48-Star Wars In 3-D #2,3. 49-Rambo In 3-D #1. 49-Sad Sack In 3-D #1. 50-Bullwinkle For President In 3-D #1 .40 1.25 2.50
51-60: 51-Kull In 3-D #1. 52-G.I. Joe in 3-D #5. 53-Red Sonja in 3-D #1. 54-Bozo in 3-D #2. 55-Waxwork In 3-D #1 (movie adapt.). 56-? 57-Casper In 3-D #1. 58-Baby Huey In 3-D #1. 59-Little Dot In 3-D #1. 60-Solomon Kane In 3-D #1 .40 1.25 2.50

Good Fine N-Mint
61-70: 61-Werewolf In 3-D #1. 62-G.I. Joe In 3-D Annual #1. 63-The California Raisins in 3-D #4. 64-To Die For In 3-D #1. 65-Capt. Holo In 3-D #1. 66-Playful Little Audrey In 3-D #1. 67-Kull in 3-D #2. 68-? 69-The California Raisins in 3-D #5. 70-Wendy In 3-D #1 .40 1.25 2.50
71-80: 71-? 72-Sports Hall of Shame #1. 73? 74-The Noid In 3-D #1. 75-Moonwalker In 3-D #1 (Michael Jackson Movie adapt.). 76-? 77-? 78-? 79? 80-The Noid in 3-D #2 .40 1.25 2.50

**BLACK ZEPPELIN** (See Gene Day's...)

**BLADE RUNNER**
Oct, 1982 - No. 2, Nov, 1982 (Movie adaptation)
Marvel Comics Group
1,2-r/Marvel Super Special #22; 1-Williamson-c/a. 2-Williamson-a .30 .60

**BLAKE HARPER** (See City Surgeon...)

**BLAST** (Satire Magazine)
Feb, 1971 - No. 2, May, 1971
G & D Publications
1-Wrightson & Kaluta-a 1.70 5.00 10.00
2-Kaluta-a 1.20 3.50 7.00

**BLASTERS SPECIAL**
1989 ($2.00, one-shot)
DC Comics
1-Invasion spin-off .35 1.00 2.00

**BLAST-OFF** (Three Rocketeers)
October, 1965
Harvey Publications (Fun Day Funnies)
1-Kirby/Williamson-a(2); Williamson/Crandall-a; Williamson/Torres/Krenkel-a; Kirby/Simon-c 2.30 7.00 16.00

**BLAZE CARSON** (Rex Hart No. 6 on)
(See Kid Colt, Tex Taylor, Wild Western, Wisco)
Sept, 1948 - No. 5, June, 1949
Marvel Comics (USA)
1-Shores-c 11.00 32.00 75.00
2 7.00 21.00 50.00
3-Used by N.Y. State Legis. Comm.(Injury to eye splash); Tex Morgan app. 8.50 25.50 60.00
4,5: 4-Two-Gun Kid app. 5-Tex Taylor app. 7.00 21.00 50.00

**BLAZE THE WONDER COLLIE**
No. 2, Oct, 1949 - No. 3, Feb, 1950 (Both have photo covers)
Marvel Comics(SePI)
2(#1), 3-(Scarce) 10.00 30.00 70.00

**BLAZING BATTLE TALES**
July, 1975
Seaboard Periodicals (Atlas)
1-Intro. Sgt. Hawk & the Sky Demon; Severin; McWilliams, Sparling-a; Thorne-c .30 .60

**BLAZING COMBAT** (Magazine)
Oct, 1965 - No. 4, July, 1966 (Black & White, 35 cents)
Warren Publishing Co.
1-Frazetta painted-c on all 8.00 24.00 56.00
2 2.50 7.50 15.00
3,4: 4-Frazetta ½ pg. ad 1.70 5.00 10.00
...Anthology (reprints from No. 1-4) .70 2.00 4.00

NOTE: *Above has art by* ***Colan, Crandall, Evans, Morrow, Orlando, Severin, Torres, Toth, Williamson,*** *and* ***Wood.***

**BLAZING COMICS**
6/44 - #3, 9/44; #4, 2/45; #5, 3/45; #5(V2#2), 3/55 - #6(V2#3), 1955?
Enwil Associates/Rural Home

| | Good | Fine | N-Mint |
|---|---|---|---|
| 1-The Green Turtle, Red Hawk, Black Buccaneer begin; origin Jun-Gal | 23.00 | 70.00 | 160.00 |
| 2-5: 3-Briefer-a. 5-(V2#2 inside) | 13.00 | 40.00 | 90.00 |
| 5(3/55, V2#2-inside)-Black Buccaneer-c, 6(V2#3-inside, 1955)-Indian/Jap-c | 4.30 | 13.00 | 30.00 |

NOTE: *No. 5 & 6 contain remaindered comics rebound and the contents can vary. Cloak & Daggar, Will Rogers, Superman 64, Star Spangled 130, Kaanga known. Value would be half of contents.*

**BLAZING SIXGUNS**
December, 1952
Avon Periodicals

| | Good | Fine | N-Mint |
|---|---|---|---|
| 1-Kinstler-c/a; Larsen/Alascia-a(2), Tuska?-a; Jesse James, Kit Carson, Wild Bill Hickok app. | 7.00 | 21.00 | 50.00 |

**BLAZING SIXGUNS**
1964
I.W./Super Comics

| | Good | Fine | N-Mint |
|---|---|---|---|
| I.W. Reprint #1,8,9: 8-Kinstler-c; 9-Ditko-a | .85 | 2.50 | 5.00 |
| Super Reprint #10,11,15,16(Buffalo Bill, Swift Deer),17(1964) | .70 | 2.00 | 4.00 |
| 12-Reprints Bullseye #3; S&K-a | 2.00 | 6.00 | 12.00 |
| 18-Powell's Straight Arrow | .85 | 2.60 | 6.00 |

**BLAZING SIX-GUNS** (Also see Sundance Kid)
Feb, 1971 - No. 2, April, 1971 (52 pages)
Skywald Comics

| | Good | Fine | N-Mint |
|---|---|---|---|
| 1-The Red Mask, Sundance Kid begin, Avon's Geronimo reprint by Kinstler; Wyatt Earp app. | .35 | 1.00 | 2.00 |
| 2-Wild Bill Hickok, Jesse James, Kit Carson-r | | .50 | 1.00 |

**BLAZING WEST** (Also see The Hooded Horseman)
Fall, 1948 - No. 22, Mar-Apr, 1952
American Comics Group(B&I Publ./Michel Publ.)

| | Good | Fine | N-Mint |
|---|---|---|---|
| 1-Origin & 1st app. Injun Jones, Tenderfoot & Buffalo Belle; Texas Tim & Ranger begins, ends #13 | 8.50 | 25.50 | 60.00 |
| 2,3 | 4.30 | 13.00 | 30.00 |
| 4-Origin & 1st app. Little Lobo; Starr-a | 3.00 | 9.00 | 21.00 |
| 5-10: 5-Starr-a | 2.65 | 8.00 | 18.00 |
| 11-13 | 2.00 | 6.00 | 14.00 |
| 14-Origin & 1st app. The Hooded Horseman | 4.50 | 14.00 | 32.00 |
| 15-22: 15,16,19-Starr-a | 2.65 | 8.00 | 18.00 |

**BLAZING WESTERN**
Jan, 1954 - No. 5, Sept, 1954
Timor Publications

| | Good | Fine | N-Mint |
|---|---|---|---|
| 1-Ditko-a; Text story by Bruce Hamilton | 6.00 | 18.00 | 42.00 |
| 2-4 | 2.65 | 8.00 | 18.00 |
| 5-Disbrow-a | 3.00 | 9.00 | 21.00 |

**BLESSED PIUS X**
No date (32 pages; ½ text, ½ comics) (Paper cover)
Catechetical Guild (Giveaway)

| | Good | Fine | N-Mint |
|---|---|---|---|
| nn | 2.30 | 7.00 | 16.00 |

**BLIND JUSTICE**
1989 (Giveaway, squarebound)
DC Comics/Diamond Comic Distributors

| | Good | Fine | N-Mint |
|---|---|---|---|
| nn-Contains Detective #598-600 by Batman movie writer Sam Hamm, w/covers; published same time as originals? | .35 | 1.00 | 2.00 |

**BLITZKRIEG**
Jan-Feb, 1976 - No. 5, Sept-Oct, 1976
National Periodical Publications

| | Good | Fine | N-Mint |
|---|---|---|---|
| 1-Kubert-c on all | | .50 | 1.00 |
| 2-5 | | .30 | .60 |

**BLONDE PHANTOM** (Formerly All-Select #1-11; Lovers #23 on) (Also see Blackstone, Marvel Mystery, Millie The Model #2, Sub-Mariner Comics #25 & Sun Girl)
No. 12, Winter, 1946-47 - No. 22, March, 1949
Marvel Comics (MPC)

| | Good | Fine | N-Mint |
|---|---|---|---|
| 12-Miss America begins, ends #14 | 54.00 | 161.00 | 375.00 |
| 13-Sub-Mariner begins | 36.00 | 107.00 | 250.00 |
| 14,15; 14-Male Bondage-c; Namora app. 15-Kurtzman's 'Hey Look' | 30.00 | 90.00 | 210.00 |
| 16-Captain America with Bucky app.; Kurtzman's "Hey Look" | 39.00 | 118.00 | 275.00 |
| 17-22: 22-Anti Wertham editorial | 29.00 | 86.00 | 200.00 |

NOTE: ***Shores*** *c-12-18.*

**BLONDIE** (See Ace Comics, Comics Reading Libraries, Dagwood, Daisy & Her Pups, Eat Right to Work . . ., King & Magic Comics)
1942 - 1946
David McKay Publications

| | Good | Fine | N-Mint |
|---|---|---|---|
| Feature Books 12 (Rare) | 40.00 | 120.00 | 280.00 |
| Feature Books 27-29,31,34(1940) | 9.30 | 28.00 | 65.00 |
| Feature Books 36,38,40,42,43,45,47 | 8.50 | 25.50 | 60.00 |
| . . .1944, hard-c, 1938-'44 daily strip-r, B&W, 128 pgs. | 8.50 | 25.50 | 60.00 |

**BLONDIE & DAGWOOD FAMILY**
Oct, 1963 - No. 4, Dec, 1965 (68 pages)
Harvey Publications (King Features Synd.)

| | Good | Fine | N-Mint |
|---|---|---|---|
| 1 | 1.70 | 5.00 | 12.00 |
| 2-4 | 1.00 | 3.00 | 7.00 |

**BLONDIE COMICS** (. . . Monthly No. 16-141)
Spring, 1947 - No. 163, Nov, 1965; No. 164, Aug, 1966 - No. 175, Dec, 1967; No. 177, Feb, 1969 - No. 222, Nov, 1976
David McKay #1-15/Harvey #16-163/King #164-175/Charlton #177 on

| | Good | Fine | N-Mint |
|---|---|---|---|
| 1 | 11.00 | 32.00 | 75.00 |
| 2 | 5.00 | 15.00 | 35.00 |
| 3-5 | 3.70 | 11.00 | 26.00 |
| 6-10 | 2.85 | 8.50 | 20.00 |
| 11-15 | 2.00 | 6.00 | 14.00 |
| 16-(3/50; 1st Harvey issue) | 2.30 | 7.00 | 16.00 |
| 17-20 | 1.70 | 5.00 | 12.00 |
| 21-30 | 1.30 | 4.00 | 9.00 |
| 31-50 | 1.00 | 3.00 | 7.00 |
| 51-80 | .85 | 2.60 | 6.00 |
| 81-124,126-130 | .85 | 2.50 | 5.00 |
| 125 (80 pgs.) | 1.00 | 3.00 | 7.00 |
| 131-136,138,139 | .70 | 2.00 | 4.00 |
| 137,140-(80 pages) | .85 | 2.60 | 6.00 |
| 141-166(#148,155,157-159,161-163 are 68 pgs.) | .85 | 2.60 | 6.00 |
| 167-One pg. Williamson ad | .35 | 1.00 | 2.00 |
| 168-175,177-222 (no #176) | .25 | .75 | 1.50 |
| Blondie, Dagwood & Daisy 1(100 pgs., 1953) | 9.30 | 28.00 | 65.00 |
| 1950 Giveaway | 1.70 | 5.00 | 12.00 |
| 1962,1964 Giveaway | .50 | 1.50 | 3.00 |
| N. Y. State Dept. of Mental Hygiene Giveaway-('50,'56,'61) Regular size (Diff. issues) 16 pages; no # | 1.00 | 3.00 | 6.00 |

**BLOOD**
Feb, 1988 - No. 4, Apr, 1988 ($3.25, adults)
Epic Comics (Marvel)

| | Good | Fine | N-Mint |
|---|---|---|---|
| 1-4 | .55 | 1.65 | 3.30 |

**BLOOD IS THE HARVEST**
1950 (32 pages) (paper cover)
Catechetical Guild

| | Good | Fine | N-Mint |
|---|---|---|---|
| (Scarce)-Anti-communism(13 known copies) | 64.00 | 190.00 | 450.00 |
| Black & white version (5 known copies), saddle stitched | 30.00 | 90.00 | 200.00 |

Untrimmed version (only one known copy); estimated value-$600

NOTE: *In 1979 nine copies of the color version surfaced from the old Guild's files plus*

*Blazing Comics #1, © RH*

*Blazing West #14, © ACG*

*Blondie Comics #12, © KING*

Blood of Dracula #8, © Apple Comics

The Blue Beetle #32, © FOX

Blue Beetle #3 (Charlton, 1967), © DC

*the five black & white copies.*

**BLOOD OF DRACULA**
Nov, 1987 - Present ($1.75-$1.95, B&W)($2.25 #14,16 on)
Apple Comics

| | Good | Fine | N-Mint |
|---|---|---|---|
| 1-13: 6-Begin $1.95-c. 10-Chadwick-c | .35 | 1.00 | 2.00 |
| 14,16-20 ($2.25): 14,19-Lost Frankenstein pgs. by Wrightson | .40 | 1.15 | 2.30 |
| 15-Contains stereo flexidisc ($3.75) | .65 | 1.90 | 3.80 |

**BLOOD OF THE INNOCENT** (See Warp Graphics Annual)
1/7/86 - No. 4, 1/28/86 (Weekly mini-series; color, adults only)
WaRP Graphics

| | | | |
|---|---|---|---|
| 1-4 | .50 | 1.50 | 3.00 |
| Bound Volume | 1.30 | 4.00 | 7.95 |

**BLOODSCENT**
Oct, 1988 (One-shot, color, $2.00, Baxter paper)
Comico

| | | | |
|---|---|---|---|
| 1-Colan-p | .35 | 1.00 | 2.00 |

**BLOOD SWORD, THE**
Aug, 1988 - Present ($1.50-1.95, color, 68 pgs.)
Jademan Comics

| | | | |
|---|---|---|---|
| 1-8 ($1.50)-Kung Fu stories | .25 | .75 | 1.50 |
| 9-28: ($1.95) | .35 | 1.00 | 2.00 |

**BLOOD SWORD DYNASTY**
1989 - Present ($1.25, color, 36 pgs.)
Jademan Comics

| | | | |
|---|---|---|---|
| 1-14: Ties into Blood Sword | | .65 | 1.30 |

**BLUE BEETLE, THE** (Also see All Top, Big-3, Mystery Men & Weekly Comic Magazine)
Winter, 1939-40 - No. 60, Aug, 1950
Fox Publ. No. 1-11, 31-60; Holyoke No. 12-30

| | Good | Fine | N-Mint |
|---|---|---|---|
| 1-Reprints from Mystery Men 1-5; Blue Beetle origin; Yarko the Great-r/from Wonder/Wonderworld 2-5 all by Eisner; Master Magician app.; (Blue Beetle in 4 different costumes) | 158.00 | 400.00 | 950.00 |
| 2-K-51-r by Powell/Wonderworld 8,9 | 61.00 | 182.00 | 425.00 |
| 3-Simon-c | 43.00 | 130.00 | 300.00 |
| 4-Marijuana drug mention story | 30.00 | 90.00 | 210.00 |
| 5-Zanzibar The Magician by Tuska | 25.00 | 75.00 | 175.00 |
| 6-Dynamite Thor begins; origin Blue Beetle | 24.00 | 72.00 | 165.00 |
| 7,8-Dynamo app. in both. 8-Last Thor | 22.00 | 65.00 | 150.00 |
| 9,10-The Blackbird & The Gorilla app. in both. 10-Bondage/hypo-c | 19.00 | 58.00 | 135.00 |
| 11(2/42)-The Gladiator app. | 19.00 | 58.00 | 135.00 |
| 12(6/42)-The Black Fury app. | 19.00 | 58.00 | 135.00 |
| 13-V-Man begins, ends #18; Kubert-a | 22.00 | 66.00 | 155.00 |
| 14,15-Kubert-a in both. 14-Intro. side-kick (c/text only), Sparky (called Spunky #17-19) | 22.00 | 65.00 | 150.00 |
| 16-18 | 17.00 | 50.00 | 115.00 |
| 19-Kubert-a | 19.00 | 58.00 | 135.00 |
| 20-Origin/1st app. Tiger Squadron; Arabian Nights begin | 19.00 | 58.00 | 135.00 |
| 21-26: 24-Intro. & only app. The Halo. 26-General Patton story & photo | 13.00 | 40.00 | 90.00 |
| 27-Tamaa, Jungle Prince app. | 11.00 | 32.00 | 75.00 |
| 28-30(2/44) | 9.30 | 28.00 | 65.00 |
| 31(6/44), 33-40: "The Threat from Saturn" serial in #34-38 | 7.00 | 21.00 | 50.00 |
| 32-Hitler-c | 10.00 | 30.00 | 60.00 |
| 41-45 | 6.00 | 18.00 | 42.00 |
| 46-The Puppeteer app. | 6.50 | 19.00 | 45.00 |
| 47-Kamen & Baker-a begin | 38.00 | 115.00 | 265.00 |
| 48-50 | 30.00 | 90.00 | 210.00 |
| 51,53 | 27.00 | 81.00 | 190.00 |
| 52-Kamen bondage-c | 38.00 | 115.00 | 265.00 |
| 54-Used in **SOTI**. Illo-"Children call these "headlights' comics" | 57.00 | 171.00 | 400.00 |
| 55,57(7/48)-Last Kamen issue | 27.00 | 81.00 | 190.00 |
| 56-Used in **SOTI**, pg. 145 | 27.00 | 81.00 | 190.00 |
| 58(4/50)-60-No Kamen-a | 4.50 | 14.00 | 32.00 |

NOTE: ***Kamen** a-47-51, 53, 55-57; c-47, 49-52. **Powell** a-4(2). Bondage-c 9-12, 46, 52.*

**BLUE BEETLE** (Formerly The Thing; becomes Mr. Muscles No. 22 on) (See Charlton Bullseye & Space Adventures)
No. 18, Feb, 1955 - No. 21, Aug, 1955
Charlton Comics

| | | | |
|---|---|---|---|
| 18,19-(Pre-1944-r). 19-Bouncer, Rocket Kelly-r | 6.50 | 19.00 | 45.00 |
| 20-Joan Mason by Kamen | 7.00 | 21.00 | 50.00 |
| 21-New material | 5.30 | 16.00 | 38.00 |

**BLUE BEETLE** (Unusual Tales #1-49; Ghostly Tales #55 on)(Also see Charlton Bullseye)
V2No. 1, 6/64 - V2No. 5, 3-4/65; V3No. 50, 7/65 - V3No. 54, 2-3/66; No. 1, 6/67 - No. 5, 11/68
Charlton Comics

| | | | |
|---|---|---|---|
| V2#1-Origin Dan Garrett-Blue Beetle | 4.30 | 13.00 | 30.00 |
| 2-5, V3#50-54 | 2.85 | 8.50 | 20.00 |
| 1(1967)-Question series begins by Ditko | 7.00 | 21.00 | 50.00 |
| 2-Origin Ted Kord-Blue Beetle; Dan Garrett x-over | 2.65 | 8.00 | 18.00 |
| 3-5 (All Ditko-c/a in #1-5) | 2.00 | 6.00 | 14.00 |
| 1,3(Modern Comics-1977)-Reprints | | .15 | .30 |

NOTE: *#6 only appeared in the fanzine 'The Charlton Portfolio.'*

**BLUE BEETLE** (Also see Americomics & Crisis On Infinite Earths)
June, 1986 - No. 24, May, 1988 (Also see Capt. Atom #83-86)
DC Comics

| | | | |
|---|---|---|---|
| 1-Origin retold; intro. Firefist | .25 | .75 | 1.50 |
| 2-24: 2-Origin Firefist. 5-7-The Question app. 11-14-New Teen Titans x-over. 18-Begin $1.00-c. 20-Justice League app. 20,21-Millennium tie-ins | | .50 | 1.00 |

**BLUE BIRD COMICS**
Late 1940's - 1964 (Giveaway)
Various Shoe Stores/Charlton Comics

| | | | |
|---|---|---|---|
| nn(1947-50)(36 pgs.)-Several issues; Human Torch, Sub-Mariner app. in some | 3.60 | 11.00 | 25.00 |
| 1959-Li'l Genius, Timmy the Timid Ghost, Wild Bill Hickok (All #1) | .85 | 2.50 | 5.00 |
| 1959-(6 titles; all #2) Black Fury #1,4,5, Freddy #4, Li'l Genius, Timmy the Timid Ghost #4, Masked Raider #4, Wild Bill Hickok (Charlton) | .85 | 2.50 | 5.00 |
| 1959-(#5) Masked Raider #21 | .85 | 2.50 | 5.00 |
| 1960-(6 titles)(All #4) Black Fury #8,9, Masked Raider, Freddy #8,9, Timmy the Timid Ghost #9, Li'l Genius #7,9 (Charlton) | .85 | 2.50 | 5.00 |
| 1961,1962-(All #10's) Atomic Mouse #12,13,16, Black Fury #11,12, Freddy, Li'l Genius, Masked Raider, Six Gun Heroes, Texas Rangers in Action, Timmy the Ghost, Wild Bill Hickok, Wyatt Earp #3,11-13,16-18 (Charlton) | .70 | 2.00 | 4.00 |
| 1963-Texas Rangers #17 (Charlton) | .35 | 1.00 | 2.00 |
| 1964-Mysteries of Unexplored Worlds #18, Teenage Hotrodders #18, War Heroes #18 (Charlton) | .35 | 1.00 | 2.00 |
| 1965-War Heroes #18 | | .60 | 1.20 |

NOTE: *More than one issue of each character could have been published each year. Numbering is sporadic.*

**BLUE BIRD CHILDREN'S MAGAZINE, THE**
1957 - No. 9? 1958 (16 pages; soft cover; regular size)
Graphic Information Service

| | | | |
|---|---|---|---|
| V1#2-9: Pat, Pete & Blue Bird app. | .40 | 1.20 | 2.40 |

**BLUE BOLT**
June, 1940 - No. 101 (V10No.2), Sept-Oct, 1949
Funnies, Inc. No. 1/Novelty Press/Premium Group of Comics

| | Good | Fine | N-Mint |
|---|---|---|---|
| V1#1-Origin Blue Bolt by Joe Simon, Sub-Zero, White Rider & Super Horse, Dick Cole, Wonder Boy & Sgt. Spook | 121.00 | 365.00 | 850.00 |
| 2-Simon-a | 65.00 | 195.00 | 455.00 |
| 3-1 pg. Space Hawk by Wolverton; S&K-a | 50.00 | 150.00 | 350.00 |
| 4,5-S&K-a in each; 5-Everett-a begins on Sub-Zero | 46.00 | 140.00 | 325.00 |
| 6,8-10-S&K-a | 41.00 | 125.00 | 290.00 |
| 7-S&K-c/a | 43.00 | 130.00 | 300.00 |
| 11,12 | 19.00 | 58.00 | 135.00 |
| V2#1-Origin Dick Cole & The Twister; Twister x-over in Dick Cole, Sub-Zero, & Blue Bolt. Origin Simba Karno who battles Dick Cole through V2#5 & becomes main supporting character V2#6 on; battle-c | 13.00 | 40.00 | 90.00 |
| 2-Origin The Twister retold in text | 10.00 | 30.00 | 70.00 |
| 3-5: 5-Intro. Freezum | 8.00 | 24.00 | 56.00 |
| 6-Origin Sgt. Spook retold | 7.00 | 21.00 | 50.00 |
| 7-12: 7-Lois Blake becomes Blue Bolt's costume aide; last Twister | 5.70 | 17.00 | 40.00 |
| V3#1-3 | 4.50 | 14.00 | 32.00 |
| 4-12: 4-Blue Bolt abandons costume | 3.70 | 11.00 | 26.00 |
| V4#1-Hitler, Tojo, Mussolini-c | 4.50 | 14.00 | 32.00 |
| V4#2-12: 3-Shows V4#3 on-c, V4#4 inside (9-10/43). 5-Infinity-c. 8-Last Sub-Zero | 3.00 | 9.00 | 21.00 |
| V5#1-8, V6#1-3,5-10, V7#1-12 | 2.00 | 6.00 | 14.00 |
| V6#4-Racist cover | 3.00 | 9.00 | 21.00 |
| V8#1-6,8-12, V9#1-5,7,8 | 1.70 | 5.00 | 12.00 |
| V8#7,V9#6,9-L. B. Cole-c | 2.30 | 7.00 | 16.00 |
| V10#1(#100) | 2.00 | 6.00 | 14.00 |
| V10#2(#101)-Last Dick Cole, Blue Bolt | 2.00 | 6.00 | 14.00 |

NOTE: ***Everett** c-V1#4, 11, V2#1, 2. **Gustavson** a-V1#1-12, V2#1-7. **Kiefer** c-V3#1. **Rico** a-V6#10, V7#4. Blue Bolt not in V9#8.*

**BLUE BOLT** (Becomes Ghostly Weird Stories #120 on; continuation of Novelty Blue Bolt) (. . .Weird Tales #112-119)
No. 102, Nov-Dec, 1949 - No. 119, May-June, 1953
Star Publications

| | Good | Fine | N-Mint |
|---|---|---|---|
| 102-The Chameleon, & Target app. | 11.00 | 32.00 | 75.00 |
| 103,104-The Chameleon app.; last Target-#104 | 10.00 | 30.00 | 70.00 |
| 105-Origin Blue Bolt (from #1) retold by Simon; Chameleon & Target app.; opium den story | 24.00 | 72.00 | 165.00 |
| 106-Blue Bolt by S&K begins; Spacehawk reprints from Target by Wolverton begins, ends #110; Sub-Zero begins; ends #109 | 19.00 | 58.00 | 130.00 |
| 107-110: 108-Last S&K Blue Bolt reprint. 109-Wolverton-c(r)/inside Spacehawk splash. 110-Target app. | 19.00 | 58.00 | 130.00 |
| 111-Red Rocket & The Mask-r; last Blue Bolt; 1pg. L. B. Cole-a | 19.00 | 57.00 | 130.00 |
| 112-Last Torpedo Man app. | 17.00 | 50.00 | 115.00 |
| 113-Wolverton's Spacehawk r-/Target V3#7 | 18.00 | 54.00 | 125.00 |
| 114,116: 116-Jungle Jo-r | 17.00 | 50.00 | 115.00 |
| 115-Sgt. Spook app. | 19.00 | 57.00 | 130.00 |
| 117-Jo-Jo & Blue Bolt-r | 17.00 | 50.00 | 115.00 |
| 118-"White Spirit" by Wood | 19.00 | 57.00 | 130.00 |
| 119-Disbrow/Cole-c; Jungle Jo-r | 17.00 | 50.00 | 115.00 |
| Accepted Reprint #103(1957?, nd) | 3.50 | 10.50 | 24.00 |

NOTE: ***L. B. Cole** c-102-108, 110 on. **Disbrow** a-112(2), 113(3), 114(2), 115(2), 116-118. **Hollingsworth** a-117. **Palais** a-112r. Sci/Fi c-105-110. Horror c-111.*

**BLUE BULLETEER, THE** (Also see Femforce Special)
1989 ($2.25, B&W, one-shot)
AC Comics

| | Good | Fine | N-Mint |
|---|---|---|---|
| 1-Origin by Bill Black; Bill Ward-a | .40 | 1.25 | 2.50 |

**BLUE CIRCLE COMICS** (Also see Roly Poly Comic Book)
June, 1944 - No. 5, Mar, 1945
Enwil Associates/Rural Home

| | Good | Fine | N-Mint |
|---|---|---|---|
| 1-The Blue Circle begins; origin Steel Fist | 10.00 | 30.00 | 70.00 |
| 2,3: 3-Hitler parody-c | 5.70 | 17.00 | 40.00 |
| 4,5: 5-Last Steel Fist | 4.00 | 12.00 | 28.00 |
| 6-(1950s)-Colossal Features-r | 4.00 | 12.00 | 28.00 |

**BLUE DEVIL** (See Fury of Firestorm #24)
June, 1984 - No. 31, Dec, 1986 (75 cents)
DC Comics

| | Good | Fine | N-Mint |
|---|---|---|---|
| 1-30: 4-Origin Nebiros. 17-19: Crisis x-over | | .40 | .80 |
| 31-($1.25, 52 pgs.) | | .65 | 1.30 |
| Annual 1 (11/85)-Team-ups w/Black Orchid, Creeper, Demon, Madame Xanadu, Man-Bat & Phantom Stranger | | .65 | 1.30 |

**BLUE PHANTOM, THE**
June-Aug, 1962
Dell Publishing Co.

| | Good | Fine | N-Mint |
|---|---|---|---|
| 1(01-066-208)-by Fred Fredericks | 2.00 | 6.00 | 14.00 |

**BLUE RIBBON COMICS** (. . .Mystery Comics No. 9-18)
Nov, 1939 - No. 22, March, 1942 (1st MLJ series)
MLJ Magazines

| | Good | Fine | N-Mint |
|---|---|---|---|
| 1-Dan Hastings, Richy the Amazing Boy, Rang-A-Tang the Wonder Dog begin; Little Nemo app. (not by W. McCay); Jack Cole-a(3) | 129.00 | 385.00 | 900.00 |
| 2-Bob Phantom, Silver Fox (both in #3), Rang-A-Tang Club & Cpl. Collins begin; Jack Cole-a | 54.00 | 160.00 | 375.00 |
| 3-J. Cole-a | 36.00 | 107.00 | 250.00 |
| 4-Doc Strong, The Green Falcon, & Hercules begin; origin & 1st app. The Fox & Ty-Gor, Son of the Tiger | 41.00 | 122.00 | 285.00 |
| 5-8: 8-Last Hercules; 6,7-Biro, Meskin-a. 7-Fox app. on-c | 25.00 | 75.00 | 175.00 |
| 9-(Scarce)-Origin & 1st app. Mr. Justice | 107.00 | 320.00 | 750.00 |
| 10-13: 12-Last Doc Strong. 13-Inferno, the Flame Breather begins, ends #19; Devil-c | 46.00 | 140.00 | 325.00 |
| 14,15,17,18: 15-Last Green Falcon | 41.00 | 122.00 | 285.00 |
| 16-Origin & 1st app. Captain Flag | 79.00 | 235.00 | 550.00 |
| 19-22: 20-Last Ty-Gor. 22-Origin Mr. Justice retold | 36.00 | 107.00 | 250.00 |

NOTE: ***Biro** c-3-5.*

**BLUE RIBBON COMICS** (Becomes Teen-Age Diary Secrets #4)
Feb, 1949 - No. 6, Aug, 1949 (See Heckle & Jeckle)
Blue Ribbon (St. John)

| | Good | Fine | N-Mint |
|---|---|---|---|
| 1,3-Heckle & Jeckle | 3.50 | 10.50 | 24.00 |
| 2(4/49)-Diary Secrets; Baker-c | 5.30 | 16.00 | 38.00 |
| 4(6/49)-Teen-Age Diary Secrets; Baker c/a(2) | 6.50 | 19.00 | 45.00 |
| 5(8/49)-Teen-Age Diary Secrets; Oversize; photo-c; Baker-a(2)- Continues as Teen-Age Diary Secrets | 8.00 | 24.00 | 56.00 |
| 6-Dinky Duck(8/49) | 1.30 | 4.00 | 9.00 |

**BLUE-RIBBON COMICS**
Nov, 1983 - No. 14, Dec, 1984
Red Circle Prod./Archie Ent. No. 5 on

| | Good | Fine | N-Mint |
|---|---|---|---|
| 1-S&K-r/Advs. of the Fly #1,2; Williamson/Torres-r/Fly #2; Ditko-c | | .50 | 1.00 |
| 2-14: 3-Origin Steel Sterling. 5-S&K Shield-r. 6,7-The Fox app. 8,11-Black Hood. 12-Thunder Agents. 13-Thunder Bunny. 14-Web & Jaguar | | .50 | 1.00 |

NOTE: ***N. Adams** a(r)-8. **Buckler** a-4i. **Nino** a-2i. **McWilliams** a-8. **Morrow** a-8.*

**BLUE STREAK** (See Holyoke One-Shot No. 8)

**BLYTHE** (See 4-Color No. 1072)

**B-MAN** (See Double-Dare Adventures)

**BO** (Also see Big Shot No. 29 & Dixie Dugan; Tom Cat No. 4 on)
June, 1955 - No. 3, Oct, 1955 (a dog)

*Blue Bolt #1, © NOVP*

*Blue Bolt Weird Tales #115, © STAR*

*Blue Ribbon Comics #9, © AP*

*Bobby Benson's B-Bar-B Riders #14, © ME*

*Bob Steele Western #10, © FAW*

*Bonanza #11, © NBC*

Charlton Comics Group

| | Good | Fine | N-Mint |
|---|---|---|---|
| 1-3-Newspaper reprints by Frank Beck | 4.00 | 12.00 | 28.00 |

**BOATNIKS, THE** (See Walt Disney Showcase No. 1)

**BOB & BETTY & SANTA'S WISHING WELL**
1941 (12 pages) (Christmas giveaway)
Sears Roebuck & Co.
nn 6.00 18.00 42.00

**BOBBY BENSON'S B-BAR-B RIDERS** (Radio) (See Best of The West, The Lemonade Kid & Model Fun)
May-June, 1950 - No. 20, May-June, 1953
Magazine Enterprises
1-Powell-a 14.00 43.00 100.00
2 7.00 21.00 50.00
3-5: 4-Lemonade Kid-c 5.70 17.00 40.00
6-8,10 4.50 14.00 32.00
9,11,13-Frazetta-c; Ghost Rider in #13-15 by Ayers-a. 13-Ghost Rider-c 14.00 42.00 100.00
12,17-20: 20-(A-1 #88) 4.00 12.00 28.00
14-Decapitation/Bondage-c & story; horror-c 6.00 18.00 42.00
15-Ghost Rider-c 6.50 19.00 45.00
16-Photo-c 5.70 17.00 40.00
...in the Tunnel of Gold-(1936, 5¼x8"; 100 pgs.) Radio giveaway by Hecker-H.O. Company(H.O. Oats); contains 22 color pages of comics, rest in novel form 5.30 16.00 38.00
...And The Lost Herd-same as above 5.30 16.00 38.00
NOTE: ***Ayers*** *a-13-15, 20.* ***Powell*** *a-1-12(4 ea.), 13(3), 14-16(Red Hawk only); c-1-8,10,12. Lemonade Kid in most 1-13.*

**BOBBY COMICS**
May, 1946
Universal Phoenix Features
1-by S. M. Iger 4.00 12.00 28.00

**BOBBY SHELBY COMICS**
1949
Shelby Cycle Co./Harvey Publications
nn 1.85 5.50 13.00

**BOBBY SHERMAN** (TV)
Feb, 1972 - No. 7, Oct, 1972 (Photo-c, 4)
Charlton Comics
1-7-Based on TV show "Getting Together" 1.20 3.50 7.00

**BOBBY THATCHER & TREASURE CAVE**
1932 (86 pages; B&W; hardcover; 7x9")
Altemus Co.
nn-Reprints; Storm-a 6.00 18.00 42.00

**BOBBY THATCHER'S ROMANCE**
1931 (7x8¾")
The Bell Syndicate/Henry Altemus Co.
nn-By Storm 6.00 18.00 42.00

**BOB COLT** (Movie star)(See XMas Comics)
Nov, 1950 - No. 10, May, 1952
Fawcett Publications
1-Bob Colt, his horse Buckskin & sidekick Pablo begin; photo front/back-c begin 25.00 75.00 175.00
2 16.50 50.00 115.00
3-5 14.00 43.00 100.00
6-Flying Saucer story 12.00 36.00 85.00
7-10: 9-Last photo back-c 11.00 32.00 75.00

**BOB HOPE** (See Adventures of...)

**BOB POWELL'S TIMELESS TALES**
March, 1989 ($2.00, B&W)
Eclipse Comics

| | Good | Fine | N-Mint |
|---|---|---|---|
| 1-Powell-r/Black Cat #5 (Scarlet Arrow), 9 & Race for the Moon #1 | .35 | 1.00 | 2.00 |

**BOB SCULLY, TWO-FISTED HICK DETECTIVE**
No date (1930's) (36 pages; 9½x12"; B&W; paper cover)
Humor Publ. Co.
nn-By Howard Dell; not reprints 5.00 15.00 35.00

**BOB SON OF BATTLE** (See 4-Color No. 729)

**BOB STEELE WESTERN** (Movie star)
Dec, 1950 - No. 10, June, 1952
Fawcett Publications
1-Bob Steele & his horse Bullet begin; photo front/back-c begin 25.00 75.00 175.00
2 16.50 50.00 115.00
3-5: 4-Last photo back-c 14.00 43.00 100.00
6-10: 10-Last photo-c 11.00 32.00 75.00

**BOB SWIFT** (Boy Sportsman)
May, 1951 - No. 5, Jan, 1952
Fawcett Publications
1 3.15 9.50 22.00
2-5: Saunders painted-c #1-5 2.00 6.00 14.00

**BOLD ADVENTURES**
Oct, 1983 - No. 3, June, 1984
Pacific Comics
1-Time Force, Anaconda, The Weirdling begin .25 .75 1.50
2,3: 2-Soldiers of Fortune begins. 3-Spitfire .25 .75 1.50
NOTE: ***Kaluta*** *c-3.* ***Nebres*** *a-3.* ***Nino*** *a-2, 3.* ***Severin*** *a-3.*

**BOLD STORIES** (Also see Candid Tales & It Rhymes With Lust)
Mar, 1950 - July, 1950 (Digest size; 144 pgs.; full color)
Kirby Publishing Co.
March issue (Very Rare) - Contains "The Ogre of Paris" by Wood 36.00 107.00 250.00
May issue (Very Rare) - Contains "The Cobra's Kiss" by Graham Ingels (21 pgs.) 27.00 81.00 190.00
July issue (Very Rare) - Contains "The Ogre of Paris" by Wood 30.00 90.00 210.00

**BOMBARDIER** (See Bee 29, the Bombardier & Cinema Comics Herald)

**BOMBA THE JUNGLE BOY** (TV)
Sept-Oct, 1967 - No. 7, Sept-Oct, 1968 (12 cents)
National Periodical Publications
1-Intro. Bomba; Infantino/Anderson-c 1.15 3.50 8.00
2-7 .85 2.50 5.00

**BOMBER COMICS**
March, 1944 - No. 4, Winter, 1944-45
Elliot Publ. Co./Melverne Herald/Farrell/Sunrise Times
1-Wonder Boy, & Kismet, Man of Fate begin 19.00 58.00 135.00
2-4: 2-4-Have Classics Comics ad to HRN 20 13.00 40.00 90.00

**BONANZA** (TV)
June-Aug, 1960 - No. 37, Aug, 1970 (All Photo-c)
Dell/Gold Key
4-Color 1110 (6-8/60) 8.50 25.50 60.00
4-Color 1221,1283, & #01070-207, 01070-210 7.00 21.00 50.00
1(12/62-Gold Key) 7.00 21.00 50.00
2 4.00 12.00 28.00
3-10 3.00 9.00 21.00
11-20 2.30 7.00 16.00
21-37: 29-Reprints 1.50 4.50 10.00

**BONGO** (See Story Hour Series)

**BONGO & LUMPJAW** (See 4-Color #706,886, & Walt Disney Showcase #3)

**BON VOYAGE** (See Movie Classics)

**BOOK AND RECORD SET** (See Power Record Comics)

**BOOK OF ALL COMICS**
1945 (196 pages)
William H. Wise

| | Good | Fine | N-Mint |
|---|---|---|---|
| nn-Green Mask, Puppeteer | 22.00 | 65.00 | 155.00 |

**BOOK OF COMICS, THE**
No date (1944) (132 pages) (25 cents)
William H. Wise

| | | | |
|---|---|---|---|
| nn-Captain V app. | 22.00 | 65.00 | 155.00 |

**BOOK OF LOVE** (See Fox Giants)

**BOOK OF NIGHT, THE**
July, 1987 - No. 3, 1987 ($1.75, B&W)
Dark Horse Comics

| | | | |
|---|---|---|---|
| 1-3: Reprints from Epic Illustrated | .30 | .90 | 1.80 |

**BOOSTER GOLD** (See Justice League #4)
Feb, 1986 - No. 25, Feb, 1988 (75 cents)
DC Comics

| | | | |
|---|---|---|---|
| 1-25: 4-Rose & Thorn app. 6-Origin. 6,7,23-Superman app. 8,9-LSH app. 22-JLI app. 24,25-Millennium tie-ins | | .40 | .80 |

NOTE: ***Austin** c-22i. **Byrne** c-23i.*

**BOOTS AND HER BUDDIES**
No. 5, 9/48 - No. 9, 9/49; 12/55 - No. 3, 1956
Standard Comics/Visual Editions/Argo (NEA Service)

| | | | |
|---|---|---|---|
| 5-Strip-r | 8.00 | 24.00 | 56.00 |
| 6,8 | 5.00 | 15.00 | 35.00 |
| 7-(Scarce)-Spanking panels(3) | 7.00 | 21.00 | 50.00 |
| 9-(Scarce)-Frazetta-a (2 pgs.) | 17.00 | 51.00 | 120.00 |
| 1-3(Argo-1955-56)-Reprints | 2.00 | 6.00 | 14.00 |

**BOOTS & SADDLES** (See 4-Color No. 919, 1029, 1116)

**BORDER PATROL**
May-June, 1951 - No. 3, Sept-Oct, 1951
P. L. Publishing Co.

| | | | |
|---|---|---|---|
| 1 | 4.30 | 13.00 | 30.00 |
| 2,3 | 2.65 | 8.00 | 18.00 |

**BORDER WORLDS** (Also see Megaton Man)
7/86 - #7, 1987; V2#1, 1990 - No. 4?, 1990 ($1.95-$2.00, B&W, adults)
Kitchen Sink Press

| | | | |
|---|---|---|---|
| 1-7: ($1.95)-By Donald Simpson | .35 | 1.00 | 2.00 |
| V2#1-4 ($2.00)-By Donald Simpson | .35 | 1.00 | 2.00 |

**BORIS KARLOFF TALES OF MYSTERY** (TV) (. . .Thriller No. 1,2)
No. 3, April, 1963 - No. 97, Feb, 1980
Gold Key

| | | | |
|---|---|---|---|
| 3-8,10-(Two #5's, 10/63,11/63) | 1.30 | 4.00 | 9.00 |
| 9-Wood-a | 1.70 | 5.00 | 12.00 |
| 11-Williamson-a, Orlando-a, 8 pgs. | 1.70 | 5.00 | 12.00 |
| 12-Torres, McWilliams-a; Orlando-a(2) | 1.15 | 3.50 | 8.00 |
| 13,14,16-20 | .85 | 2.60 | 6.00 |
| 15-Crandall,Evans-a | 1.00 | 3.00 | 7.00 |
| 21-Jeff Jones-a(3 pgs.) "The Screaming Skull" | 1.00 | 3.00 | 7.00 |
| 22-30: 23-Reprint; photo-c | .70 | 2.00 | 4.00 |
| 31-50 | .40 | 1.25 | 2.50 |
| 51-74: 74-Origin & 1st app. Taurus | | .60 | 1.20 |
| 75-97: 80-86-(52 pages) | | .40 | .80 |
| Story Digest 1(7/70-Gold Key)-All text | .70 | 2.00 | 4.00 |

(See Mystery Comics Digest No. 2, 5, 8, 11, 14, 17, 20, 23, 26)

NOTE: ***Bolle** a-51-54, 56, 58, 59. **McWilliams** a-12, 14, 18, 19, 80, 81, 93. **Orlando** a-11-15, 21. Reprints: 78, 81-86, 88, 90, 92, 95, 97.*

**BORIS KARLOFF THRILLER** (TV) (Becomes Boris Karloff Tales. . .)
Oct, 1962 - No. 2, Jan, 1963 (80 pages)
Gold Key

| | Good | Fine | N-Mint |
|---|---|---|---|
| 1-Photo-c | 3.00 | 9.00 | 24.00 |
| 2 | 2.75 | 8.25 | 22.00 |

**BORIS THE BEAR INSTANT COLOR CLASSICS**
July, 1987 - No. 3?, 1987 ($1.75-$1.95, color)
Dark Horse Comics

| | | | |
|---|---|---|---|
| 1-3 | .30 | .90 | 1.80 |

**BORN AGAIN**
1978 (39 cents)
Spire Christian Comics (Fleming H. Revell Co.)

| | | | |
|---|---|---|---|
| nn-Watergate, Nixon, etc. | | .50 | 1.00 |

**BOUNCER, THE** (Formerly Green Mask?)
1944 - No. 14, Jan, 1945
Fox Features Syndicate

| | | | |
|---|---|---|---|
| nn(1944)-Same as #14 | 9.30 | 28.00 | 65.00 |
| 11(#1)(9/44)-Origin; Rocket Kelly, One Round Hogan app. | 9.30 | 28.00 | 65.00 |
| 12-14 | 6.50 | 19.00 | 45.00 |

**BOUNTY GUNS** (See 4-Color No. 739)

**BOY AND HIS 'BOT, A**
Jan, 1987 ($1.95, color)
Now Comics

| | | | |
|---|---|---|---|
| 1-A Holiday Special | .35 | 1.00 | 2.00 |

**BOY AND THE PIRATES, THE** (See 4-Color No. 1117)

**BOY COMICS** (Captain Battle No. 1 & 2; Boy Illustories No. 43-108)
(Stories by Charles Biro)
No. 3, April, 1942 - No. 119, March, 1956
Lev Gleason Publications (Comic House)

| | | | |
|---|---|---|---|
| 3(No.1)-Origin Crimebuster, Bombshell & Young Robin Hood; Yankee Longago, Case 1001-1008, Swoop Storm, & Boy Movies begin; 1st app. Iron Jaw | 112.00 | 335.00 | 780.00 |
| 4-Hitler, Tojo, Mussolini-c | 49.00 | 145.00 | 340.00 |
| 5 | 39.00 | 118.00 | 275.00 |
| 6-Origin Iron Jaw; origin & death of Iron Jaw's son; Little Dynamite begins, ends #39 | 82.00 | 245.00 | 575.00 |
| 7,9: 7-Flag & Hitler, Tojo, Mussolini-c | 32.00 | 95.00 | 225.00 |
| 8-Death of Iron Jaw | 36.00 | 107.00 | 250.00 |
| 10-Return of Iron Jaw; classic Biro-c | 46.00 | 140.00 | 325.00 |
| 11-14 | 21.00 | 64.00 | 150.00 |
| 15-Death of Iron Jaw | 26.00 | 77.00 | 180.00 |
| 16,18-20 | 14.00 | 43.00 | 100.00 |
| 17-Flag-c | 16.00 | 48.00 | 110.00 |
| 21-26 | 9.30 | 28.00 | 65.00 |
| 27-29,31,32-(All 68 pages). 28-Yankee Longago ends. 32-Swoop Storm & Young Robin Hood end | 10.00 | 30.00 | 70.00 |
| 30-(68 pgs.)-Origin Crimebuster retold | 12.00 | 36.00 | 85.00 |
| 33-40: 34-Crimebuster story(2); suicide-c/story | 5.00 | 15.00 | 35.00 |
| 41-50 | 3.50 | 10.50 | 24.00 |
| 51-59: 57-Dilly Duncan begins, ends #71 | 2.30 | 7.00 | 16.00 |
| 60-Iron Jaw returns | 3.00 | 9.00 | 21.00 |
| 61-Origin Crimebuster & Iron Jaw retold | 4.00 | 12.00 | 28.00 |
| 62-Death of Iron Jaw explained | 4.00 | 12.00 | 28.00 |
| 63-73: 73-Frazetta 1-pg. ad | 2.00 | 6.00 | 14.00 |
| 74-88: 80-1st app. Rocky X of the Rocketeers; becomes "Rocky X" #101; Iron Jaw, Sniffer & the Deadly Dozen begins, ends #118 | 1.70 | 5.00 | 12.00 |
| 89-92-The Claw serial app. in all | 2.15 | 6.50 | 15.00 |
| 93-Claw cameo; Check-a(Rocky X) | 2.85 | 8.50 | 20.00 |
| 94-97,99 | 1.70 | 5.00 | 12.00 |
| 98-Rocky X by Sid Check | 3.15 | 9.50 | 22.00 |
| 100 | 2.65 | 8.00 | 18.00 |

101-107,109,111,119: 111-Crimebuster becomes Chuck Chandler.

*The Book of Comics nn, © WHW*

*Boris Karloff Tales of Mys. #9, © Estate of B.K.*

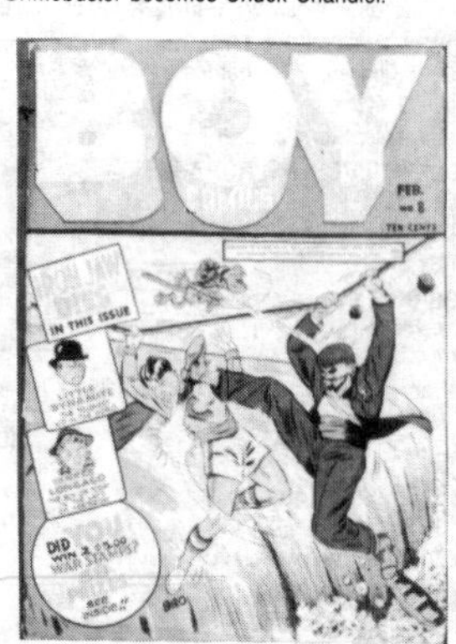


*Boy Comics #8, © LEV*

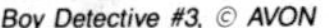
Boy Detective #3, © AVON

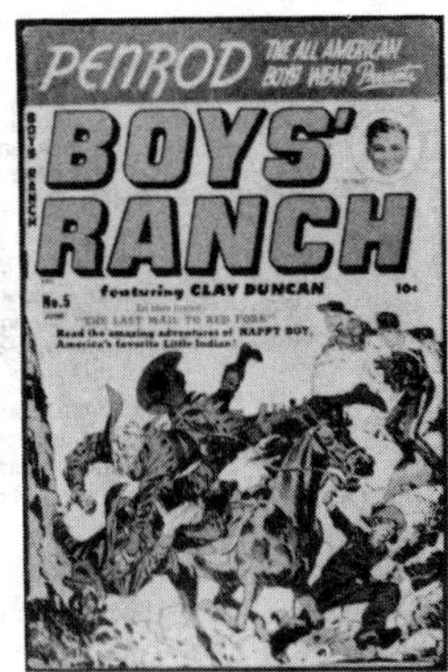

Boys' Ranch #5, © HARV

The Brain #1, © ME

| | Good | Fine | N-Mint |
|---|---|---|---|
| 119-Last Crimebuster | 1.70 | 5.00 | 12.00 |
| 108,110,112-118-Kubert-a | 2.65 | 8.00 | 18.00 |

(See Giant Boy Book of Comics)

NOTE: Boy Movies in 3-5,40,41. Iron Jaw app.-3, 4, 6, 8, 10, 11, 13-15; returns-60-62, 68, 69, 72-79, 81-118. **Biro** c-all. **Briefer** a-5, 13, 14, 16-20 among others. **Fuje** a-55, 18 pgs. **Palais** a-14, 16, 17, 19, 20 among others.

**BOY COMMANDOS** (See Detective #64 & World's Finest Comics #8)
Winter, 1942-43 - No. 36, Nov-Dec, 1949
National Periodical Publications

| | Good | Fine | N-Mint |
|---|---|---|---|
| 1-Origin Liberty Belle; The Sandman & The Newsboy Legion x-over in Boy Commandos; S&K-a, 48 pgs. | 175.00 | 438.00 | 1050.00 |
| 2-Last Liberty Belle; S&K-a, 46 pgs. | 71.00 | 215.00 | 500.00 |
| 3-S&K-a, 45 pgs. | 50.00 | 150.00 | 350.00 |
| 4,5 | 29.00 | 86.00 | 200.00 |
| 6-8,10: 6-S&K-a | 21.00 | 62.00 | 145.00 |
| 9-No S&K-a | 14.00 | 43.00 | 100.00 |
| 11-Infinity-c | 14.00 | 43.00 | 100.00 |
| 12-16,18-20 | 11.50 | 34.00 | 80.00 |
| 17-Sci/fi-c/story | 12.00 | 36.00 | 85.00 |
| 21,22,24,25: 22-Judy Canova x-over | 8.50 | 25.50 | 60.00 |
| 23-S&K-c/a(all) | 10.00 | 30.00 | 70.00 |
| 26-Flying Saucer story (3-4/48)-4th of this theme | 9.30 | 28.00 | 65.00 |
| 27,28,30: 30-Cleveland Indians story | 8.50 | 25.50 | 60.00 |
| 29-S&K story (1) | 9.30 | 28.00 | 65.00 |
| 31-35: 32-Dale Evans app. on-c & story. 34-Intro. Wolf, their mascot | 8.50 | 25.50 | 60.00 |
| 36-Intro The Atomobile c/sci-fi story | 11.00 | 32.00 | 75.00 |

NOTE: Most issues signed by **Simon & Kirby** are not by them. **S&K** c-1-9. **Feller** c-30.

**BOY COMMANDOS**
Sept-Oct, 1973 - No. 2, Nov-Dec, 1973 (G.A. S&K reprints)
National Periodical Publications

| | Good | Fine | N-Mint |
|---|---|---|---|
| 1,2: 1-Reprints story from Boy Commandos #1 & Detective #66 by S&K. 2-Infantino/Orlando-c | | .50 | 1.00 |

**BOY DETECTIVE**
May-June, 1951 - No. 4, May, 1952
Avon Periodicals

| | Good | Fine | N-Mint |
|---|---|---|---|
| 1 | 10.00 | 30.00 | 70.00 |
| 2,3: 3-Kinstler-c | 5.50 | 16.50 | 38.00 |
| 4-Kinstler-c/a | 8.50 | 25.50 | 60.00 |

**BOY EXPLORERS COMICS** (Terry and The Pirates No. 3 on)
May-June, 1946 - No. 2, Sept-Oct, 1946
Family Comics (Harvey Publications)

| | Good | Fine | N-Mint |
|---|---|---|---|
| 1-Intro The Explorers, Duke of Broadway, Calamity Jane & Danny Dixon . . . Cadet; S&K-c/a, 24 pgs | 40.00 | 120.00 | 280.00 |

2-(Scarce)-Small size (5½x8½''; B&W; 32 pgs.) Distributed to mail subscribers only; S&K-a. Estimated value $250-$400

(Also see All New No. 15, Flash Gordon No. 5, and Stuntman No. 3)

**BOY ILLUSTORIES** (See Boy Comics)

**BOY LOVES GIRL** (Boy Meets Girl No. 1-24)
No. 25, July, 1952 - No. 57, June, 1956
Lev Gleason Publications

| | Good | Fine | N-Mint |
|---|---|---|---|
| 25(#1) | 3.50 | 10.50 | 24.00 |
| 26,27,29-42: 30-33-Serial, 'Loves of My Life.' 39-Lingerie panels | 1.70 | 5.00 | 12.00 |
| 28-Drug propaganda story | 2.35 | 7.00 | 16.00 |
| 43-Toth-a | 3.70 | 11.00 | 26.00 |
| 44-50: 50-Last pre-code (2/55) | 1.30 | 4.00 | 9.00 |
| 51-57: 57-Ann Brewster-a | 1.00 | 3.00 | 7.00 |

**BOY MEETS GIRL** (Boy Loves Girl No. 25 on)
Feb, 1950 - No. 24, June, 1952 (No. 1-17: 52 pgs.)
Lev Gleason Publications

| | Good | Fine | N-Mint |
|---|---|---|---|
| 1-Guardineer-a | 3.50 | 10.50 | 24.00 |
| 2 | 1.70 | 5.00 | 12.00 |
| 3-10 | 1.35 | 4.00 | 9.00 |
| 11-24 | 1.15 | 3.50 | 8.00 |

NOTE: **Briefer** a-24. **Fuje** c-3,7. Painted-c 1-17. Photo-c 19-21, 23.

**BOYS' AND GIRLS' MARCH OF COMICS** (See March of Comics)

**BOYS' RANCH** (Also see Western Tales & Witches' Western Tales)
Oct, 1950 - No. 6, Aug, 1951 (No.1-3, 52 pgs.; No. 4-6, 36 pgs.)
Harvey Publications

| | Good | Fine | N-Mint |
|---|---|---|---|
| 1-S&K-a(3) | 36.00 | 107.00 | 250.00 |
| 2-S&K-a(3) | 27.00 | 81.00 | 190.00 |
| 3-S&K-a(2); Meskin-a | 24.00 | 73.00 | 170.00 |
| 4-S&K-c/a, 5pgs. | 19.00 | 58.00 | 135.00 |
| 5,6-S&K splashes & centerspread only; Meskin-a | 11.50 | 34.00 | 80.00 |
| Shoe Store Giveaway #5,6 (Identical to regular issues except S&K centerfold replaced with ad) | 9.30 | 28.00 | 65.00 |

NOTE: **Simon & Kirby** c-1-6.

**BOZO THE CLOWN** (TV) (Bozo No. 7 on)
July, 1950 - No. 4, Oct-Dec, 1963
Dell Publishing Co.

| | Good | Fine | N-Mint |
|---|---|---|---|
| 4-Color 285(#1) | 8.50 | 25.50 | 60.00 |
| 2(7-9/51)-7(10-12/52) | 5.70 | 17.00 | 40.00 |
| 4-Color 464,508,551,594(10/54) | 5.70 | 17.00 | 40.00 |
| 1(nn, 5-7/62) - 4(1963) | 2.65 | 8.00 | 18.00 |
| Giveaway-1961, 16 pgs., 3½x7¼'', Apsco Products | 1.70 | 5.00 | 12.00 |

**BOZO THE CLOWN IN 3-D** (See Blackthorne 3-D Series #24 & 54)

**BOZZ CHRONICLES, THE**
Dec, 1985 - No. 6, 1986 (Adults only)(Mini-series)
Epic Comics (Marvel)

| | Good | Fine | N-Mint |
|---|---|---|---|
| 1-6 | .25 | .75 | 1.50 |

**BRADY BUNCH, THE** (TV)
Feb, 1970 - No. 2, May, 1970
Dell Publishing Co.

| | Good | Fine | N-Mint |
|---|---|---|---|
| 1,2 | 2.85 | 8.50 | 20.00 |
| Kite Fun Book (PG&E, 1976) | 1.00 | 3.00 | 7.00 |

**BRAIN, THE**
Sept, 1956 - No. 7, 1958
Sussex Publ. Co./Magazine Enterprises

| | Good | Fine | N-Mint |
|---|---|---|---|
| 1 | 3.00 | 9.00 | 21.00 |
| 2,3 | 1.50 | 4.50 | 10.00 |
| 4-7 | 1.00 | 3.00 | 7.00 |
| I.W. Reprints #1-4,8-10('63),14: 2-Reprints Sussex #2 with new cover added | .50 | 1.50 | 3.00 |
| Super Reprint #17,18(nd) | .50 | 1.50 | 3.00 |

**BRAIN BOY**
April-June, 1962 - No. 6, Sept-Nov, 1963 (Painted c-5,6)
Dell Publishing Co.

| | Good | Fine | N-Mint |
|---|---|---|---|
| 4-Color 1330(#1)-Gil Kane-a; origin | 4.00 | 12.00 | 28.00 |
| 2(7-9/62),3-6: 4-origin retold | 2.30 | 7.00 | 16.00 |

**BRAND ECHH** (See Not Brand Echh)

**BRAND OF EMPIRE** (See 4-Color No. 771)

**BRAVADOS, THE** (See Wild Western Action)
August, 1971 (52 pages) (One-Shot)
Skywald Publ. Corp.

| | Good | Fine | N-Mint |
|---|---|---|---|
| 1-Red Mask, The Durango Kid, Billy Nevada-r | | .40 | .80 |

**BRAVE AND THE BOLD, THE** (See Best Of . . . & Super DC Giant)
Aug-Sept, 1955 - No. 200, July, 1983

National Periodical Publications/DC Comics

| | Good | Fine | N-Mint |
|---|---|---|---|
| 1-Viking Prince by Kubert, Silent Knight, Golden Gladiator begin | 90.00 | 270.00 | 625.00 |
| 2 | 39.00 | 117.00 | 275.00 |
| 3,4 | 22.00 | 66.00 | 155.00 |
| 5-Robin Hood begins | 16.50 | 50.00 | 115.00 |
| 6-10: 6-Robin Hood by Kubert; Golden Gladiator last app.; Silent Knight; no Viking Prince | 17.00 | 51.00 | 120.00 |
| 11-22: 22-Last Silent Knight | 13.00 | 40.00 | 90.00 |
| 23-Viking Prince origin by Kubert | 16.00 | 48.00 | 110.00 |
| 24-Last Viking Prince by Kubert | 16.00 | 48.00 | 110.00 |
| 25-27-Suicide Squad | 7.00 | 21.00 | 50.00 |

28-(2-3/60)-Justice League intro./1st app.; origin Snapper Carr

| Good | Fine | N-Mint | Mint |
|---|---|---|---|
| 200.00 | 600.00 | 1400.00 | 2200.00 |

(Estimated up to 530 total copies exist, 23 in Mint)

| | Good | Fine | N-Mint |
|---|---|---|---|
| 29,30-Justice League | 78.00 | 234.00 | 550.00 |
| 31-33-Cave Carson | 7.00 | 21.00 | 50.00 |
| 34-Origin/1st app. Silver-Age Hawkman & Byth by Kubert | 32.00 | 66.00 | 220.00 |
| 35,36-Hawkman by Kubert; origin Shadow Thief #36 | 11.00 | 32.00 | 75.00 |
| 37-39-Suicide Squad. 38-Last 10 cent issue | 5.70 | 17.00 | 40.00 |
| 40,41-Cave Carson Inside Earth; #40 has Kubert art | 5.70 | 17.00 | 40.00 |
| 42,44-Hawkman by Kubert | 7.85 | 23.50 | 55.00 |
| 43-Origin Hawkman by Kubert retold | 11.00 | 32.00 | 75.00 |
| 45-49-Strange Sports Stories by Infantino | 1.50 | 4.50 | 10.00 |
| 50-The Green Arrow & Manhunter From Mars; team-ups begin | 7.85 | 23.50 | 55.00 |
| 51-Aquaman & Hawkman | 1.70 | 5.00 | 12.00 |
| 52-Sgt. Rock by Kubert, Haunted Tank, Johnny Cloud, & Mlle. Marie | 1.70 | 5.00 | 12.00 |
| 53-Atom & The Flash by Toth | 2.15 | 6.50 | 15.00 |
| 54-Kid Flash, Robin & Aqualad; 1st app./origin Teen Titans (6-7/64) | 16.00 | 48.00 | 110.00 |
| 55-Metal Men & The Atom | 1.00 | 3.00 | 7.00 |
| 56-The Flash & Manhunter From Mars | 1.00 | 3.00 | 7.00 |
| 57-Origin & 1st app. Metamorpho | 7.85 | 23.50 | 55.00 |
| 58-Metamorpho by Fradon | 1.70 | 5.00 | 12.00 |
| 59-Batman & Green Lantern; 1st Batman team-up in Brave and the Bold | 4.50 | 14.00 | 32.00 |
| 60-Teen Titans (2nd app.)-1st app. new Wonder Girl (Donna Troy), who joins Titans (6-7/65) | 5.70 | 17.00 | 40.00 |
| 61,62-Origin Starman & Black Canary by Anderson. 62-Huntress app. | 1.50 | 4.50 | 10.00 |
| 63-Supergirl & Wonder Woman | 1.00 | 3.00 | 6.00 |
| 64-Batman Versus Eclipso | 2.65 | 8.00 | 18.00 |
| 65-Flash & Doom Patrol | 1.00 | 3.00 | 6.00 |
| 66-Metamorpho & Metal Men | 1.00 | 3.00 | 6.00 |
| 67-Batman & The Flash by Infantino; Batman team-ups begin, end #200 | 1.15 | 3.50 | 8.00 |
| 68-Batman/Joker/Riddler/Penguin-c/story | 2.30 | 7.00 | 16.00 |
| 69-78: Batman team-ups | 1.15 | 3.50 | 8.00 |
| 79-Batman-Deadman by Neal Adams | 2.85 | 8.50 | 18.00 |
| 80-Batman-Creeper; N. Adams-a | 2.15 | 6.50 | 15.00 |
| 81-Batman-Flash; N. Adams-a | 2.15 | 6.50 | 15.00 |
| 82-Batman-Aquaman; N. Adams-a; origin Ocean Master retold | 2.15 | 6.50 | 15.00 |
| 83-Batman-Teen Titans; N. Adams-a | 3.60 | 11.00 | 25.00 |
| 84-Batman(GA)-Sgt. Rock; N. Adams-a | 2.30 | 7.00 | 16.00 |
| 85-Batman-Green Arrow; 1st new costume for Green Arrow by Neal Adams | 2.30 | 7.00 | 16.00 |
| 86-Batman-Deadman; N. Adams-a | 2.30 | 7.00 | 16.00 |
| 87-92: Batman team-ups | 1.00 | 3.00 | 6.00 |
| 93-Batman-House of Mystery; N. Adams-a | 2.15 | 6.50 | 15.00 |
| 94-Batman-Teen Titans | 1.00 | 3.00 | 6.00 |
| 95-99: 97-Origin Deadman-r | .85 | 2.50 | 5.00 |
| 100-Batman-Green Lantern-Gr. Arrow-Black Canary-Robin; Deadman by N. Adams (52 pgs., 25 cents) | 2.15 | 6.50 | 15.00 |
| 101-Batman-Metamorpho; Kubert Viking Prince | .50 | 1.50 | 3.00 |
| 102-Batman-Teen Titans; N. Adams-a(p) | .85 | 2.50 | 5.00 |
| 103-110: Batman team-ups | .50 | 1.50 | 3.00 |
| 111-Batman/Joker-c/story | 1.35 | 4.00 | 8.00 |
| 112-117: All 100 pgs.; Batman team-ups | .70 | 2.00 | 4.00 |
| 118-Batman/Wildcat/Joker-c/story | 1.15 | 3.50 | 7.00 |
| 119-128,131-140: Batman team-ups | .40 | 1.25 | 2.50 |
| 129,130-Batman/Joker-c/stories | 1.35 | 4.00 | 8.00 |
| 141-Batman vs. Joker-c/story | 1.15 | 3.50 | 7.00 |
| 142-190,192-199: 148-XMas-c. 149-Batman-Teen Titans. 150-Anniversary issue; Superman. 179-LSH. 182-Batman/Robin. 181-Hawk & Dove. 183-Riddler. 187-Metal Men. 196-Origin Ragman retold. 197-Earth II Batman & Catwoman marry | .35 | 1.00 | 2.00 |
| 191-Batman/Joker-c/story | .85 | 2.50 | 5.00 |
| 200-Double-sized (64 pgs.); printed on Mando paper; Earth One & Earth Two Batman team-up; Intro/1st app. Batman & The Outsiders | 1.00 | 3.00 | 6.00 |

NOTE: ***Neal Adams*** *a-79-86, 93, 100r, 102; c-75, 76, 79-86, 88-90, 93, 95, 99, 100r.* ***Anderson*** *a-115r; c-72i, 96i.* ***Aparo*** *a-98, 100-102, 104-125, 126i, 127-136, 138-145, 147, 148i, 149-152, 154, 155, 157-162, 168-170, 173-178, 180-182, 184, 186i-189i, 191i-193i, 195, 196, 200; c-105-109, 111-136, 137i, 138-175, 177, 180-184, 186-200.* ***Austin*** *a-166i.* ***Buckler*** *a-185, 186p; c-137, 178p, 185p, 186p.* ***Giordano*** *a-143, 144.* ***Infantino*** *a-67p, 72p, 97r, 98r, 172p, 183p, 190p, 194p; c-45-49, 67p, 69p, 70p, 72p, 96p, 98r.* ***Kaluta*** *c-176.* ***Kane*** *a-115r.* ***Kubert &/or Heath*** *a-1-24; reprints-101, 113, 115, 117.* ***Kubert*** *c-22-24, 34-36, 40, 42-44, 52.* ***Mooney*** *a-114r.* ***Newton*** *a-153p, 156p, 165p.* ***Roussos*** *a-114r.* ***Staton*** *148p. 52 pgs.-97, 100; 64 pgs.-120; 100 pgs.-112-117.*

**BRAVE AND THE BOLD SPECIAL, THE** (See DC Special Series No. 8)

**BRAVE EAGLE** (See 4-Color No. 705, 770, 816, 879, 929)

**BRAVE ONE, THE** (See 4-Color No. 773)

**BRAVESTARR IN 3-D** (See Blackthorne 3-D Series #27, 40)

**BREATHTAKER**
1990 - No. 4, 1990 ($4.95, prestige format, mature readers, 52 pgs.)
DC Comics

| | Good | Fine | N-Mint |
|---|---|---|---|
| Book 1-By Hempel & Wheatley painted-c/a | .90 | 2.75 | 5.50 |
| Book 2-4 | .85 | 2.50 | 5.00 |

**BREEZE LAWSON, SKY SHERIFF** (See Sky Sheriff)

**BRENDA LEE STORY, THE**
September, 1962
Dell Publishing Co.

| | Good | Fine | N-Mint |
|---|---|---|---|
| 01-078-209 | 5.70 | 17.00 | 40.00 |

**BRENDA STARR** (Also see All Great)
No. 13, 9/47; No. 14, 3/48; V2No.3, 6/48 - V2#12, 12/49
Four Star Comics Corp./Superior Comics Ltd.

| | Good | Fine | N-Mint |
|---|---|---|---|
| V1#13-By Dale Messick | 36.00 | 107.00 | 250.00 |
| 14-Kamen bondage-c | 36.00 | 107.00 | 250.00 |
| V2#3-Baker-a? | 29.00 | 86.00 | 200.00 |
| 4-Used in **SOTI**, pg. 21; Kamen bondage-c | 32.00 | 95.00 | 225.00 |
| 5-10 | 25.00 | 75.00 | 175.00 |
| 11,12 (Scarce) | 30.00 | 90.00 | 210.00 |

NOTE: *Newspaper reprints plus original material through #6. All original #7 on.*

**BRENDA STARR** (. . . Reporter)(Young Lovers No. 16 on?)
No. 13, June, 1955 - No. 15, Oct, 1955
Charlton Comics

| | Good | Fine | N-Mint |
|---|---|---|---|
| 13-15-Newspaper-r | 17.00 | 51.00 | 120.00 |

*The Brave and the Bold #34, © DC*

*The Brave and the Bold #141, © DC*

*Brenda Starr #14, © SUPR*

Brick Bradford #6, © KING

Bringing Up Father #14, © C&L

Brother Power, the Geek #2, © DC

**BRENDA STARR REPORTER**
October, 1963
Dell Publishing Co.

| | Good | Fine | N-Mint |
|---|---|---|---|
| 1 | 13.00 | 40.00 | 90.00 |

**BRER RABBIT** (See 4-Color No. 129,208,693, Walt Disney Showcase No. 28, and Wheaties)

**BRER RABBIT IN "A KITE TAIL"**
1955 (16 pages, 5x7¼", soft-c) (Walt Disney) (Premium)
Pacific Gas & Electric Co./Southern Calif. Edison

| | Good | Fine | N-Mint |
|---|---|---|---|
| nn-(Rare)-Kite fun book | 16.00 | 48.00 | 110.00 |

**BRER RABBIT IN "ICE CREAM FOR THE PARTY"**
1955 (16 pages, 5x7¼", soft-c) (Walt Disney) (Premium)
American Dairy Association

| | Good | Fine | N-Mint |
|---|---|---|---|
| nn-(Rare) | 8.50 | 25.50 | 60.00 |

**BRIAN BOLLAND'S BLACK BOOK**
July, 1985 (One-shot)
Eclipse Comics

| | Good | Fine | N-Mint |
|---|---|---|---|
| 1-British B&W-r in color | .25 | .75 | 1.50 |

**BRICK BRADFORD** (Also see Ace Comics & King Comics)
No. 5, July, 1948 - No. 8, 1949 (Ritt & Grey reprints)
King Features Syndicate/Standard

| | Good | Fine | N-Mint |
|---|---|---|---|
| 5 | 8.50 | 25.50 | 60.00 |
| 6-8: 7-Schomburg-c | 6.50 | 19.50 | 45.00 |

**BRIDE'S DIARY** (Formerly Black Cobra No. 3)
No. 4, May, 1955 - No. 10, Aug, 1956
Ajax/Farrell Publ.

| | Good | Fine | N-Mint |
|---|---|---|---|
| 4 (#1) | 3.00 | 9.00 | 21.00 |
| 5-8 | 2.00 | 6.00 | 14.00 |
| 9,10-Disbrow-a | 3.00 | 9.00 | 21.00 |

**BRIDES IN LOVE** (Hollywood Romances & Summer Love No. 46 on)
Aug, 1956 - No. 45, Feb, 1965
Charlton Comics

| | Good | Fine | N-Mint |
|---|---|---|---|
| 1 | 2.65 | 8.00 | 18.00 |
| 2 | 1.30 | 4.00 | 9.00 |
| 3-10 | .85 | 2.50 | 6.00 |
| 11-20 | .50 | 1.50 | 3.00 |
| 21-45 | .35 | 1.00 | 2.00 |

**BRIDES ROMANCES**
Nov, 1953 - No. 23, Dec, 1956
Quality Comics Group

| | Good | Fine | N-Mint |
|---|---|---|---|
| 1 | 5.00 | 15.00 | 35.00 |
| 2 | 2.65 | 8.00 | 18.00 |
| 3-10: Last precode (3/55) | 1.70 | 5.00 | 12.00 |
| 11-14,16,17,19-22 | 1.15 | 3.50 | 8.00 |
| 15-Baker-a(p); Colan-a | 1.30 | 4.00 | 9.00 |
| 18-Baker-a | 1.85 | 5.50 | 13.00 |
| 23-Baker-c/a | 2.85 | 8.50 | 20.00 |

**BRIDE'S SECRETS**
Apr-May, 1954 - No. 19, May, 1958
Ajax/Farrell(Excellent Publ.)/Four-Star Comic

| | Good | Fine | N-Mint |
|---|---|---|---|
| 1 | 5.00 | 15.00 | 35.00 |
| 2 | 2.65 | 8.00 | 18.00 |
| 3-6: Last precode (3/55) | 1.70 | 5.00 | 12.00 |
| 7-19: 12-Disbrow-a. 18-Hollingsworth-a | 1.30 | 4.00 | 9.00 |

**BRIDE-TO-BE ROMANCES** (See True. . .)

**BRIGAND, THE** (See Fawcett Movie Comics No. 18)

**BRINGING UP FATHER** (See 4-Color #37 & Large Feature Comic #9)

**BRINGING UP FATHER**
1917 (16½x5½"; cardboard cover; 100 pages; B&W)
Star Co. (King Features)

| | Good | Fine | N-Mint |
|---|---|---|---|
| nn-(Rare) Daily strip reprints by George McManus (no price on-c) | 32.00 | 95.00 | 225.00 |

**BRINGING UP FATHER**
1919 - 1934 (by George McManus)(No. 22 is 9¼x9½")
(10x10"; stiff cardboard covers; B&W; daily strip reprints; 52 pgs.)
Cupples & Leon Co.

| | Good | Fine | N-Mint |
|---|---|---|---|
| 1 | 25.00 | 75.00 | 175.00 |
| 2-10 | 13.00 | 40.00 | 90.00 |
| 11-26 (Scarcer) | 19.00 | 58.00 | 135.00 |
| The Big Book 1(1926)-Thick book (hardcover); 10¼x10¼", 142pgs. | 32.00 | 95.00 | 225.00 |
| The Big Book 2(1929) | 25.00 | 75.00 | 175.00 |

NOTE: *The Big Books contain 3 regular issues rebound and probably w/dust jackets.*

**BRINGING UP FATHER, THE TROUBLE OF**
1921 (9x15") (Sunday reprints in color)
Embee Publ. Co.

| | Good | Fine | N-Mint |
|---|---|---|---|
| nn-(Rare) | 32.00 | 95.00 | 225.00 |

**BROADWAY HOLLYWOOD BLACKOUTS**
Mar-Apr, 1954 - No. 3, July-Aug, 1954
Stanhall

| | Good | Fine | N-Mint |
|---|---|---|---|
| 1 | 5.00 | 15.00 | 35.00 |
| 2,3 | 3.50 | 10.50 | 24.00 |

**BROADWAY ROMANCES**
January, 1950 - No. 5, Sept, 1950
Quality Comics Group

| | Good | Fine | N-Mint |
|---|---|---|---|
| 1-Ward-c/a (9pgs.); Gustavson-a | 14.00 | 42.00 | 100.00 |
| 2-Ward-a (9pgs.); photo-c | 9.30 | 28.00 | 65.00 |
| 3-5: 4,5-Photo-c | 4.00 | 12.00 | 28.00 |

**BROKEN ARROW** (See 4-Color No. 855,947)

**BROKEN CROSS, THE** (See The Crusaders)

**BRONCHO BILL** (See Comics On Parade, Sparkler & Tip Top Comics)
1939 - 1940; No. 5, 1?/48 - No. 16, 8?/50
United Features Syndicate/Standard(Visual Editions) No. 5-on

| | Good | Fine | N-Mint |
|---|---|---|---|
| Single Series 2 ('39) | 26.00 | 77.00 | 180.00 |
| Single Series 19 ('40)(#2 on cvr) | 22.00 | 65.00 | 150.00 |
| 5 | 5.00 | 15.00 | 35.00 |
| 6(4/48)-10(4/49) | 3.00 | 9.00 | 21.00 |
| 11(6/49)-16 | 2.30 | 7.00 | 16.00 |

NOTE: ***Schomburg*** *c-6, 7, 9-13, 16.*

**BROTHER POWER, THE GEEK** (See Saga of Swamp Thing Annual)
Sept-Oct, 1968 - No. 2, Nov-Dec, 1968
National Periodical Publications

| | Good | Fine | N-Mint |
|---|---|---|---|
| 1-Origin; Simon-c(i?) | 2.85 | 8.50 | 20.00 |
| 2 | 2.00 | 6.00 | 14.00 |

**BROTHERS, HANG IN THERE, THE**
1979 (49 cents)
Spire Christian Comics (Fleming H. Revell Co.)

| | Good | Fine | N-Mint |
|---|---|---|---|
| nn | | .30 | .60 |

**BROTHERS OF THE SPEAR** (Also see Tarzan)
June, 1972 - No. 17, Feb, 1976; No. 18, May, 1982
Gold Key/Whitman No. 18 on

| | Good | Fine | N-Mint |
|---|---|---|---|
| 1 | 1.15 | 3.50 | 8.00 |
| 2 | .85 | 2.60 | 6.00 |
| 3-10 | .70 | 2.00 | 4.00 |
| 11-17 | .35 | 1.00 | 2.00 |
| 18-Manning-r/No. 2; Leopard Girl-r | | .50 | 1.00 |

NOTE: *Painted-c No. 2-17.* ***Spiegle*** *a-13-17.*

**BROTHERS, THE CULT ESCAPE, THE**
1980 (49 Cents)
Spire Christian Comics (Fleming H. Revell Co.)

| | Good | Fine | N-Mint |
|---|---|---|---|
| nn | | .30 | .60 |

**BROWNIES** (See 4-Color No. 192, 244, 293, 337, 365, 398, 436, 482, 522, 605 & New Funnies)

**BRUCE GENTRY**
Jan, 1948 - No. 2, Nov, 1948; No. 3, Jan, 1949 - No. 8, July, 1949
Better/Standard/Four Star Publ./Superior No. 3

| | Good | Fine | N-Mint |
|---|---|---|---|
| 1-Ray Bailey strip reprints begin, end #3; E. C. emblem appears as a monogram on stationery in story; negligee panels | 22.00 | 65.00 | 150.00 |
| 2,3 | 14.00 | 43.00 | 100.00 |
| 4-8 | 11.00 | 32.00 | 75.00 |

NOTE: ***Kamenish** a-2-7; c-1-8.*

**BRUTE, THE**
Feb, 1975 - No. 3, July, 1975
Seaboard Publ. (Atlas)

| | Good | Fine | N-Mint |
|---|---|---|---|
| 1-Origin & 1st app; Sekowsky-a(p) | | .40 | .80 |
| 2,3: 2-Sekowsky-a(p) | | .25 | .50 |

**BRUTE FORCE**
Aug, 1990 - No. 4, Nov, 1990 ($1.00, color, limited series)
Marvel Comics

| | Good | Fine | N-Mint |
|---|---|---|---|
| 1-4: Animal super-heroes | | .50 | 1.00 |

**BUCCANEER**
No date (1963)
I. W. Enterprises

| | Good | Fine | N-Mint |
|---|---|---|---|
| I.W. Reprint #1(r-/Quality #20), #8(r-/#23): Crandall-a in each | 1.30 | 4.00 | 9.00 |
| Super Reprint #12('64, r-/#21)-Crandall-a | 1.30 | 4.00 | 9.00 |

**BUCCANEERS** (Formerly Kid Eternity)
No. 19, Jan, 1950 - No. 27, May, 1951 (No. 24-27: 52 pages)
Quality Comics Group

| | Good | Fine | N-Mint |
|---|---|---|---|
| 19-Captain Daring, Black Roger, Eric Falcon & Spanish Main begin; Crandall-a | 24.00 | 73.00 | 170.00 |
| 20,23-Crandall-a | 18.00 | 54.00 | 125.00 |
| 21-Crandall-c/a | 22.00 | 65.00 | 150.00 |
| 22-Bondage-c | 13.00 | 40.00 | 90.00 |
| 24-26: 24-Adam Peril, U.S.N. begins. 25-Origin & 1st app. Corsair Queen. 26-last Spanish Main | 11.00 | 32.00 | 75.00 |
| 27-Crandall-c/a | 19.00 | 56.00 | 130.00 |

**BUCCANEERS, THE** (See 4-Color No. 800)

**BUCKAROO BANZAI**
Dec, 1984 - No. 2, Feb, 1985 (Movie adaptation)
Marvel Comics Group

| | Good | Fine | N-Mint |
|---|---|---|---|
| 1,2-r/Marvel Super Special #33 | | .40 | .80 |

**BUCK DUCK**
June, 1953 - No. 4, Dec, 1953
Atlas Comics (ANC)

| | Good | Fine | N-Mint |
|---|---|---|---|
| 1-Funny animal stories in all | 3.50 | 10.50 | 24.00 |
| 2-4: 2-Ed Win-a(5) | 2.00 | 6.00 | 14.00 |

**BUCK JONES** (Also see Crackajack Funnies, Famous Feature Stories & Master Comics #7)
No. 299, Oct, 1950 - No. 850, Oct, 1957 (All Painted-c)
Dell Publishing Co.

| | Good | Fine | N-Mint |
|---|---|---|---|
| 4-Color 299(#1)-Buck Jones & his horse Silver-B begin; painted back-c begins, ends #5 | 10.00 | 30.00 | 70.00 |
| 2(4-6/51) | 5.00 | 15.00 | 35.00 |
| 3-8(10-12/52) | 3.70 | 11.00 | 26.00 |
| 4-Color 460,500,546,589 | 3.50 | 10.50 | 24.00 |
| 4-Color 652,733,850 | 2.30 | 7.00 | 16.00 |

**BUCK ROGERS** (In the 25th Century)
1933 (36 pages in color) (6x8")
Kelloggs Corn Flakes Giveaway

| | Good | Fine | N-Mint |
|---|---|---|---|
| 370A-By Phil Nowlan & Dick Calkins; 1st Buck Rogers radio premium (tells origin) | 25.00 | 75.00 | 175.00 |

**BUCK ROGERS** (Also see Famous Funnies, Pure Oil Comics, Salerno Carnival of Comics, 24 Pages of Comics, & Vicks Comics)
Winter, 1940-41 - No. 6, Sept, 1943
Famous Funnies

| | Good | Fine | N-Mint |
|---|---|---|---|
| 1-Sunday strip reprints by Rick Yager; begins with strip #190; Calkins-c | 125.00 | 375.00 | 875.00 |
| 2 (7/41)-Calkins-c | 75.00 | 225.00 | 525.00 |
| 3 (12/41), 4 (7/42) | 61.00 | 182.00 | 425.00 |
| 5-Story continues with Famous Funnies No. 80; ½ Buck Rogers, ½ Sky Roads | 54.00 | 161.00 | 375.00 |
| 6-Reprints of 1939 dailies; contains B.R. story "Crater of Doom" (2 pgs.) by Calkins not reprinted from Famous Funnies | 54.00 | 161.00 | 375.00 |

**BUCK ROGERS**
No. 100, Jan, 1951 - No. 9, May-June, 1951
Toby Press

| | Good | Fine | N-Mint |
|---|---|---|---|
| 100(7) | 16.00 | 48.00 | 110.00 |
| 101(8), 9-All Anderson-a('47-'49-r/dailies) | 12.00 | 36.00 | 85.00 |

**BUCK ROGERS** (. . . in the 25th Century No. 5 on) (TV)
Oct, 1964; No. 2, July, 1979 - No. 16, May, 1982 (No #10)
Gold Key/Whitman No. 7 on

| | Good | Fine | N-Mint |
|---|---|---|---|
| 1(10128-410)-Painted-c; 12 cents | 2.85 | 8.50 | 20.00 |
| 2(8/79)-Movie adaptation | .35 | 1.00 | 2.00 |
| 3-9,11-16: 3,4-Movie adaptation; 5-new stories | | .50 | 1.00 |
| Giant Movie Edition 11296(64pp, Whitman, $1.50), reprints GK #2-4 minus cover; tabloid size | .35 | 1.00 | 2.00 |
| Giant Movie Edition 02489(Western/Marvel, $1.50), reprints GK #2-4 minus cover | .35 | 1.00 | 2.00 |

NOTE: ***Bolle** a-2p-4p, Movie Ed.(p). **McWilliams** a-2i-4i, 5-11, Movie Ed.(i). Painted-c No. 1-9, 11-13.*

**BUCK ROGERS**
1990 - Present ($2.95, color)
TSR, Inc.

| | Good | Fine | N-Mint |
|---|---|---|---|
| 1-8: 1-Painted-c; 48 pgs. plus fold-out | .50 | 1.50 | 3.00 |

**BUCKSKIN** (Movie) (See 4-Color No. 1011,1107)

**BUCKY O'HARE** (Graphic Novel)
1988 ($5.95, color)(Reprints serial from Echo of Futurepast)
Continuity Comics

| | Good | Fine | N-Mint |
|---|---|---|---|
| 1-Michael Golden-c/a(r); funny animal | 1.00 | 3.00 | 6.00 |
| Deluxe Hardcover ($40.00, 52 pgs., 8X11") | 7.00 | 20.00 | 40.00 |

**BUDDIES IN THE U.S. ARMY**
Nov, 1952 - No. 2, 1953
Avon Periodicals

| | Good | Fine | N-Mint |
|---|---|---|---|
| 1-Lawrence-c | 6.50 | 19.50 | 45.00 |
| 2-Mort Lawrence-c/a | 4.60 | 14.00 | 32.00 |

**BUDDY TUCKER & HIS FRIENDS** (Also see Buster Brown)
1906 (11x17") (In color)
Cupples & Leon Co.

| | Good | Fine | N-Mint |
|---|---|---|---|
| 1905 Sunday strip reprints by R. F. Outcault | 22.00 | 65.00 | 150.00 |

**BUFFALO BEE** (See 4-Color No. 957,1002,1061)

**BUFFALO BILL** (Also see Frontier Fighters, Super Western Comics & Western Action Thrillers)
No. 2, Oct, 1950 - No. 9, Dec, 1951
Youthful Magazines

| | Good | Fine | N-Mint |
|---|---|---|---|
| 2 | 4.00 | 12.00 | 28.00 |

*Bruce Gentry #1, © STD*

*Buccaneers #24, © QUA*

*Buck Rogers #6 (9/43), © KING*

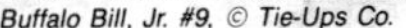
Buffalo Bill, Jr. #9, © Tie-Ups Co.

Bugs Bunny #1 (6/90), © Warner Bros.

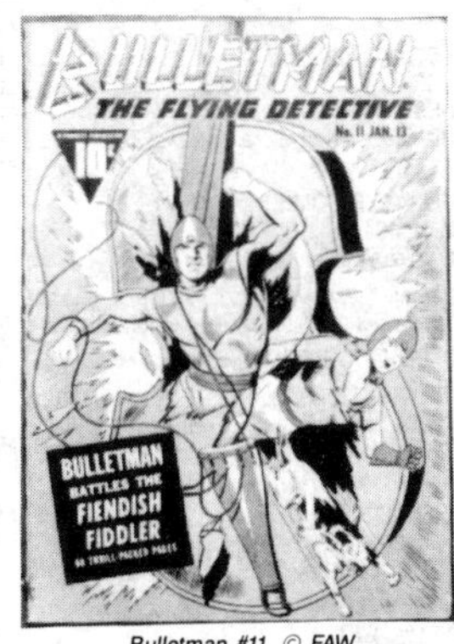

Bulletman #11, © FAW

| | Good | Fine | N-Mint |
|---|---|---|---|
| 3-9: 3,4-Walter Johnson-c/a | 2.00 | 6.00 | 14.00 |

**BUFFALO BILL CODY** (See Cody of the Pony Express)

**BUFFALO BILL, JR.** (TV) (See Western Roundup under Dell Giants)
Jan, 1956 - No. 13, Aug-Oct, 1959; 1965 (All photo-c)
Dell Publishing Co./Gold Key

| | Good | Fine | N-Mint |
|---|---|---|---|
| 4-Color 673 (#1) | 4.30 | 13.00 | 30.00 |
| 4-Color 742,766,798,828,856(11/57) | 3.00 | 9.00 | 21.00 |
| 7(2-4/58)-13 | 2.30 | 7.00 | 16.00 |
| 1(6/65-Gold Key) | 1.50 | 4.50 | 10.00 |

**BUFFALO BILL PICTURE STORIES**
June-July, 1949 - No. 2, Aug-Sept, 1949
Street & Smith Publications

| | Good | Fine | N-Mint |
|---|---|---|---|
| 1,2-Wildey, Powell-a in each | 5.30 | 16.00 | 38.00 |

**BUFFALO BILL'S PICTURE STORIES**
1909 (Soft cardboard cover)
Street & Smith Publications

| | Good | Fine | N-Mint |
|---|---|---|---|
| nn | 11.50 | 34.00 | 80.00 |

**BUGALOOS** (TV)
Sept, 1971 - No. 4, Feb, 1972
Charlton Comics

| | Good | Fine | N-Mint |
|---|---|---|---|
| 1-4 | .35 | 1.00 | 2.00 |

NOTE: *No. 3(1/72) went on sale late in 1972 (after No. 4) with the 1/73 issues.*

**BUGHOUSE** (Satire)
Mar-Apr, 1954 - No. 4, Sept-Oct, 1954
Ajax/Farrell (Excellent Publ.)

| | Good | Fine | N-Mint |
|---|---|---|---|
| V1#1 | 7.00 | 21.00 | 50.00 |
| 2-4 | 4.30 | 13.00 | 30.00 |

**BUGHOUSE FABLES**
1921 (48 pgs.) (4x4½") (10 cents)
Embee Distributing Co. (King Features)

| | Good | Fine | N-Mint |
|---|---|---|---|
| 1-Barney Google | 9.30 | 28.00 | 65.00 |

**BUG MOVIES**
1931 (52 pages) (B&W)
Dell Publishing Co.

| | Good | Fine | N-Mint |
|---|---|---|---|
| nn-Not reprints; Stookie Allen-a | 8.50 | 25.50 | 60.00 |

**BUGS BUNNY** (See The Best of..., Camp Comics, Comic Album #2, 6, 10, 14, Dell Giant #28, 32, 46, Dynabrite, Golden Comics Digest #1, 3, 5, 6, 8, 10, 14, 15, 17, 21, 26, 30, 34, 39, 42, 47, Large Feature Comic #8, Looney Tunes and Merry Melodies, March of Comics #44, 59, 75, 83, 97, 115, 132, 149, 160, 179, 188, 201, 220, 231, 245, 259, 273, 287, 301, 315, 329, 343, 363, 367, 380, 392, 403, 415, 428, 440, 452, 464, 476, 487, Porky Pig, Puffed Wheat, Story Hour Series #802, Super Book #14, 26 and Whitman Comic Books)

**BUGS BUNNY** (See Dell Giants for annuals)
1942 - No. 245, 1983
Dell Publishing Co./Gold Key No. 86-218/Whitman No. 219 on

| | Good | Fine | N-Mint |
|---|---|---|---|
| Large Feature Comic 8(1942)-(Rarely found in fine-mint condition) | 59.00 | 175.00 | 410.00 |
| 4-Color 33 ('43) | 35.00 | 105.00 | 245.00 |
| 4-Color 51 | 20.00 | 60.00 | 140.00 |
| 4-Color 88 | 12.00 | 36.00 | 85.00 |
| 4-Color 123('46),142,164 | 7.00 | 21.00 | 50.00 |
| 4-Color 187,200,217,233 | 6.00 | 18.00 | 42.00 |
| 4-Color 250-Used in **SOTI**, pg. 309 | 6.00 | 18.00 | 42.00 |
| 4-Color 266,274,281,289,298('50) | 4.50 | 14.00 | 32.00 |
| 4-Color 307,317(#1),327(#2),338,347,355,366,376,393 | 3.70 | 11.00 | 26.00 |
| 4-Color 407,420,432 | 2.65 | 8.00 | 18.00 |
| 28(12-1/52-53)-30 | 1.50 | 4.50 | 10.00 |
| 31-50 | .85 | 2.60 | 6.00 |
| 51-85(7-9/62) | .75 | 2.25 | 5.00 |
| 86(10/62)-88-Bugs Bunny's Showtime-(80 pgs.)(25 cents) | 2.25 | 6.75 | 18.00 |
| 89-100 | .70 | 2.00 | 4.00 |
| 101-120 | .40 | 1.25 | 2.50 |
| 121-140 | .35 | 1.00 | 2.00 |
| 141-170 | | .60 | 1.20 |
| 171-228,230-245 | | .35 | .70 |
| 229-Swipe of Barks story/WDC&S 223 | | .40 | .80 |

NOTE: *Reprints-100, 102, 104, 123, 143, 144, 147, 167, 173, 175-177, 179-185, 187, 190.*

| | Good | Fine | N-Mint |
|---|---|---|---|
| ...Comic-Go-Round 11196-(224 pgs.)($1.95)(Golden Press, 1979) | .40 | 1.20 | 2.40 |
| Kite Fun Book ('60,'68)-Giveaway, 16 pgs., 5x7¼" | 1.15 | 3.50 | 8.00 |
| Winter Fun 1(12/67-Gold Key)-Giant | 1.75 | 5.25 | 14.00 |

**BUGS BUNNY** (Puffed Rice Giveaway)
1949 (32 pages each, 3-1/8x6-7/8")
Quaker Cereals

A1-Traps the Counterfeiters, A2-Aboard Mystery Submarine, A3- Rocket to the Moon, A4-Lion Tamer, A5-Rescues the Beautiful Princess, B1-Buried Treasure, B2-Outwits the Smugglers, B3-Joins the Marines, B4-Meets the Dwarf Ghost, B5-Finds Aladdin's Lamp, C1-Lost in the Frozen North, C2-Secret Agent, C3-Captured by Cannibals, C4-Fights the Man from Mars, C5-And the Haunted Cave

| | Good | Fine | N-Mint |
|---|---|---|---|
| each.... | 1.70 | 5.00 | 10.00 |

**BUGS BUNNY** (3-D)
1953 (Pocket size) (15 titles)
Cheerios Giveaway

| | Good | Fine | N-Mint |
|---|---|---|---|
| each.... | 5.00 | 15.00 | 35.00 |

**BUGS BUNNY**
June, 1990 - No. 3, Aug, 1990 ($1.00, color, mini-series)
DC Comics

| | Good | Fine | N-Mint |
|---|---|---|---|
| 1-Daffy Duck, Elmer Fudd, others app. | .25 | .75 | 1.50 |
| 2,3 | | .50 | 1.00 |

**BUGS BUNNY & PORKY PIG**
Sept, 1965 (100 pages; paper cover; giant)
Gold Key

| | Good | Fine | N-Mint |
|---|---|---|---|
| 1(30025-509) | 2.85 | 8.50 | 20.00 |

**BUGS BUNNY'S ALBUM** (See 4-Color No. 498,585,647,724)

**BUGS BUNNY LIFE STORY ALBUM** (See 4-Color No. 838)

**BUGS BUNNY MERRY CHRISTMAS** (See 4-Color No. 1064)

**BULLET CROW, FOWL OF FORTUNE**
Mar, 1987 - No. 2, Apr, 1987 ($2.00, B&W, mini-series)
Eclipse Comics

| | Good | Fine | N-Mint |
|---|---|---|---|
| 1,2-Reprints from The Comic Reader & new-a | .35 | 1.00 | 2.00 |

**BULLETMAN** (See Fawcett Miniatures, Master Comics, Mighty Midget Comics, Nickel Comics & XMas Comics)
Sum, 1941 - #12, 2/12/43; #14, Spr, 1946 - #16, Fall, 1946 (nn 13)
Fawcett Publications

| | Good | Fine | N-Mint |
|---|---|---|---|
| 1 | 167.00 | 420.00 | 1000.00 |
| 2 | 76.00 | 230.00 | 535.00 |
| 3 | 54.00 | 160.00 | 375.00 |
| 4,5 | 46.00 | 140.00 | 325.00 |
| 6-10: 7-Ghost Stories as told by the night watchman of the cemetery begins; Eisnerish-a | 39.00 | 118.00 | 275.00 |
| 11,12,14-16 (nn 13) | 34.00 | 100.00 | 235.00 |
| ...Well Known Comics (1942)-Paper-c, glued binding; printed in red (Bestmaid/Samuel Lowe giveaway) | 12.00 | 36.00 | 72.00 |

NOTE: ***Mac Raboy*** *c-1-3, 5, 6, 10.*

**BULLS-EYE** (Cody of The Pony Express No. 8 on)
7-8/54 - No. 5, 3-4/55; No. 6, 6/55; No. 7, 8/55
Mainline No. 1-5/Charlton No. 6,7

| | Good | Fine | N-Mint |
|---|---|---|---|
| 1-S&K-c, 2 pages-a | 26.00 | 77.00 | 180.00 |
| 2-S&K-c/a | 24.00 | 73.00 | 170.00 |

| | Good | Fine | N-Mint |
|---|---|---|---|
| 3-5-S&K-c/a(2 each) | 17.00 | 51.00 | 120.00 |
| 6-S&K-c/a | 13.00 | 40.00 | 90.00 |
| 7-S&K-c/a(3) | 17.00 | 51.00 | 120.00 |
| Great Scott Shoe Store giveaway-Reprints #2 with new cover | 9.30 | 28.00 | 65.00 |

**BULLS-EYE COMICS**
No. 11, 1944
Harry 'A' Chesler

| | | | |
|---|---|---|---|
| 11-Origin K-9, Green Knight's sidekick, Lance; The Green Knight, Lady Satan, Yankee Doodle Jones app. | 14.00 | 43.00 | 100.00 |

**BULLWHIP GRIFFIN** (See Movie Comics)

**BULLWINKLE** (TV) (. . .and Rocky No. 20 on; See March of Comics No. 233, and Rocky & Bullwinkle) (Jay Ward)
3-5/62 - #11, 4/74; #12, 6/76 - #19, 3/78; #20, 4/79 - #25, 2/80
Dell/Gold Key

| | | | |
|---|---|---|---|
| 4-Color 1270 (3-5/62) | 8.50 | 25.50 | 60.00 |
| 01-090-209 (Dell, 7-9/62) | 8.50 | 25.50 | 60.00 |
| 1(11/62, Gold Key) | 5.70 | 17.00 | 40.00 |
| 2(2/63) | 5.00 | 15.00 | 35.00 |
| 3(4/72)-11(4/74-Gold Key) | 1.50 | 4.50 | 10.00 |
| 12(6/76)-reprints | .85 | 2.50 | 5.00 |
| 13(9/76), 14-new stories | 1.00 | 3.00 | 7.00 |
| 15-25 | .85 | 2.50 | 5.00 |
| Mother Moose Nursery Pomes 01-530-207 (5-7/62-Dell) | 5.70 | 17.00 | 40.00 |

NOTE: *Reprints: 6, 7, 20-24.*

**BULLWINKLE** (. . .& Rocky No. 2 on)(TV)
July, 1970 - No. 7, July, 1971
Charlton Comics

| | | | |
|---|---|---|---|
| 1 | 1.70 | 5.00 | 12.00 |
| 2-7 | 1.15 | 3.50 | 8.00 |

**BULLWINKLE AND ROCKY**
Nov, 1987 - No. 9, Mar, 1989
Star Comics/Marvel Comics No. 3 on

| | | | |
|---|---|---|---|
| 1-9 | | .50 | 1.00 |

**BULLWINKLE AND ROCKY IN 3-D** (See Blackthorne 3-D Series #18)

**BULLWINKLE FOR PRESIDENT IN 3-D** (See Blackthorne 3-D Series #50)

**BUNNY** (Also see Rock Happening)
Dec, 1966 - No. 20, Dec, 1971; No. 21, Nov, 1976
Harvey Publications

| | | | |
|---|---|---|---|
| 1: 68 pg. Giant | 1.50 | 4.50 | 10.00 |
| 2-18: 68 pg. Giants | 1.15 | 3.50 | 8.00 |
| 19-21: 52 pg. Giants | 1.00 | 3.00 | 7.00 |

**BURKE'S LAW** (TV)
1-3/64; No. 2, 5-7/64; No. 3, 3-5/65 (Gene Barry photo-c, all)
Dell Publishing Co.

| | | | |
|---|---|---|---|
| 1-Photo-c | 2.65 | 8.00 | 18.00 |
| 2,3-Photo-c | 1.70 | 5.00 | 12.00 |

**BURNING ROMANCES** (See Fox Giants)

**BUSTER BEAR**
Dec, 1953 - No. 10, June, 1955
Quality Comics Group (Arnold Publ.)

| | | | |
|---|---|---|---|
| 1-Funny animal | 2.65 | 8.00 | 18.00 |
| 2 | 1.50 | 4.50 | 10.00 |
| 3-10 | 1.00 | 3.00 | 7.00 |
| I.W. Reprint #9,10 (Super on inside) | .50 | 1.50 | 3.00 |

**BUSTER BROWN** (Also see Buddy Tucker & His Friends)
1903 - 1916 (11x17" strip reprints in color)
Frederick A. Stokes Co.

| | Good | Fine | VF |
|---|---|---|---|
| . . .& His Resolutions (1903) by R. F. Outcault | 50.00 | 150.00 | 350.00 |
| . . .Abroad (1904)-86 pgs.; hardback; 8x10¼"; B&W; by R. F. Outcault(76pgs.) | 40.00 | 120.00 | 280.00 |
| . . .His Dog Tige & Their Troubles (1904) | 40.00 | 120.00 | 280.00 |
| . . .Pranks (1905) | 40.00 | 120.00 | 280.00 |
| . . .Antics (1906)-11x17", 66p | 40.00 | 120.00 | 280.00 |
| . . .And Company (1906)-11x17" in color | 40.00 | 120.00 | 280.00 |
| . . .Mary Jane & Tige (1906) | 40.00 | 120.00 | 280.00 |
| . . .My Resolutions (1906)-68 pgs.; B&W; hardcover; Sunday panel reprints | 40.00 | 120.00 | 280.00 |
| Collection of Buster Brown Comics (1908) | 40.00 | 120.00 | 280.00 |
| Buster Brown Up to Date (1910) | 40.00 | 120.00 | 280.00 |
| . . .The Fun Maker (1912) | 40.00 | 120.00 | 280.00 |
| . . .The Little Rogue (1916)(10x15¾," 62pp, in color) | 29.00 | 86.00 | 200.00 |

NOTE: *Rarely found in fine or mint condition.*

**BUSTER BROWN**
1906 - 1917 (11x17" strip reprints in color)
Cupples & Leon Co./N. Y. Herald Co.

| (By R. F. Outcault) | Good | Fine | VF |
|---|---|---|---|
| . . .His Dog Tige & Their Jolly Times (1906), 58p | 36.00 | 107.00 | 250.00 |
| . . .Latest Frolics (1906), 58 pgs. | 32.00 | 95.00 | 225.00 |
| . . .Amusing Capers (1908), 46p | 32.00 | 95.00 | 225.00 |
| . . .And His Pets (1909) | 32.00 | 95.00 | 225.00 |
| . . .On His Travels (1910) | 32.00 | 95.00 | 225.00 |
| . . .Happy Days (1911) | 32.00 | 95.00 | 225.00 |
| . . .In Foreign Lands (1912) | 29.00 | 86.00 | 200.00 |
| . . .And the Cat (1917) | 29.00 | 86.00 | 200.00 |

NOTE: *Rarely found in fine or mint condition.*

**BUSTER BROWN COMICS** (Also see My Dog Tige)
1945 - No. 43, 1959 (No. 5: paper cover)
Brown Shoe Co.

| | Good | Fine | N-Mint |
|---|---|---|---|
| nn, nd (#1) | 11.50 | 34.00 | 80.00 |
| 2 | 5.00 | 15.00 | 35.00 |
| 3-10 | 2.65 | 8.00 | 18.00 |
| 11-20 | 1.85 | 5.50 | 13.00 |
| 21-24,26-28 | 1.50 | 4.50 | 10.00 |
| 25,31,33-37,40-43-Crandall-a in all | 3.65 | 11.00 | 25.00 |
| 29,30,32-"Interplanetary Police Vs. the Space Siren" by Crandall | 3.65 | 11.00 | 25.00 |
| 38,39 | 1.15 | 3.50 | 8.00 |
| . . .Goes to Mars (2/58-Western Printing), slick-c, 20 pgs., reg. size | 2.30 | 7.00 | 16.00 |
| . . .In "Buster Makes the Team!" (1959-Custom Comics) | 1.15 | 3.50 | 8.00 |
| . . .In The Jet Age ('50s), slick-c, 20 pgs., 5x7¼" | 2.00 | 6.00 | 14.00 |
| . . .Of the Safety Patrol ('60-Custom Comics) | 1.15 | 3.50 | 8.00 |
| . . .Out of This World ('59-Custom Comics) | 1.15 | 3.50 | 8.00 |
| . . .Safety Coloring Book (1958)-Slick paper, 16 pages | 1.15 | 3.50 | 8.00 |

**BUSTER BUNNY**
Nov, 1949 - No. 16, Oct, 1953
Standard Comics(Animated Cartoons)/Pines

| | | | |
|---|---|---|---|
| 1-Frazetta 1 pg. text illo. | 3.70 | 11.00 | 26.00 |
| 2 | 1.85 | 5.50 | 13.00 |
| 3-16: 15-Racist-c | 1.15 | 3.50 | 8.00 |

**BUSTER CRABBE** (TV)
Nov, 1951 - No. 12, 1953
Famous Funnies

| | | | |
|---|---|---|---|
| 1-Frazetta back-c | 18.00 | 54.00 | 125.00 |

*Bulls-Eye #7, © CC*

*Burke's Law #2, © Four Star*

*Buster Brown Comics #10, © Buster Brown*

Buzzy #17, © DC

Caliber Presents #1, © Caliber Press

Camera Comics #3, © U.S. Camera Publ.

| | Good | Fine | N-Mint |
|---|---|---|---|
| 2,3-Toth-a | 11.50 | 34.00 | 80.00 |

**BUTCH CASSIDY**
June, 1971 - No. 3, Oct, 1971 (52 pages)
Skywald Comics

| | Good | Fine | N-Mint |
|---|---|---|---|
| 1-Red Mask reprint, retitled Maverick; Bolle-a | | .60 | 1.20 |
| 2,3: 2-Whip Wilson-r. 3-Dead Canyon Days reprint/Crack Western No. 63; Sundance Kid app.; Crandall-a | | .40 | .80 |

**BUTCH CASSIDY** (. . .& the Wild Bunch)
1951
Avon Periodicals

| | Good | Fine | N-Mint |
|---|---|---|---|
| 1-Kinstler-c/a | 9.30 | 28.00 | 65.00 |

NOTE: ***Reinman** story; Issue No. on inside spine.*

**BUTCH CASSIDY** (See Fun-In No. 11 & Western Adventure Comics)

**BUTCHER, THE**
May, 1990 - No. 5, Sept, 1990 ($1.50, color, mature readers)
DC Comics

| | Good | Fine | N-Mint |
|---|---|---|---|
| 1-5: 1-No indicia inside | .25 | .75 | 1.50 |

**BUZ SAWYER** (Sweeney No. 4 on)
June, 1948 - No. 3, 1949
Standard Comics

| | Good | Fine | N-Mint |
|---|---|---|---|
| 1-Roy Crane-a | 10.00 | 30.00 | 70.00 |
| 2-Intro his pal Sweeney | 6.00 | 18.00 | 42.00 |
| 3 | 4.50 | 14.00 | 32.00 |

**BUZ SAWYER'S PAL, ROSCOE SWEENEY** (See Sweeney)

**BUZZY** (See All Funny Comics)
Winter, 1944-45 - No. 75, 1-2/57; No. 76, 10/57; No. 77, 10/58
National Periodical Publications/Detective Comics

| | Good | Fine | N-Mint |
|---|---|---|---|
| 1 (52 pgs. begin) | 16.00 | 48.00 | 110.00 |
| 2 | 8.00 | 24.00 | 55.00 |
| 3-5 | 4.50 | 14.00 | 32.00 |
| 6-10 | 3.15 | 9.50 | 22.00 |
| 11-20 | 2.30 | 7.00 | 16.00 |
| 21-30 | 1.85 | 5.50 | 13.00 |
| 31,35-38 | 1.50 | 4.50 | 10.00 |
| 32-34,39-Last 52 pgs. Scribbly by Mayer in all (These four stories were done for Scribbly #14 which was delayed for a year) | 1.70 | 5.00 | 12.00 |
| 40-77: 62-Last precode (2/55) | 1.15 | 3.50 | 8.00 |

**BUZZY THE CROW** (See Harvey Hits #18 & Paramount Animated Comics #1)

**CADET GRAY OF WEST POINT** (See Dell Giants)

**CADILLACS & DINOSAURS**
Nov, 1990 - No. 6, Apr, 1991 ($2.50, color, limited series, coated paper)
Epic Comics (Marvel)

| | Good | Fine | N-Mint |
|---|---|---|---|
| 1-6: r/Xenozoic Tales in color w/new-c | .40 | 1.25 | 2.50 |

**CAIN'S HUNDRED** (TV)
May-July, 1962 - No. 2, Sept-Nov, 1962
Dell Publishing Co.

| | Good | Fine | N-Mint |
|---|---|---|---|
| nn(01-094-207) | 1.70 | 5.00 | 12.00 |
| 2 | 1.15 | 3.50 | 8.00 |

**CALIBER PRESENTS**
Jan, 1989 - Present ($1.95-$2.50, B&W, 52 pgs.)
Caliber Press

| | Good | Fine | N-Mint |
|---|---|---|---|
| 1-Anthology; The Crow, others; Tim Vigil-c/a | 1.00 | 3.00 | 6.00 |
| 2-Deadworld story; Tim Vigil-a | .70 | 2.00 | 4.00 |
| 3-14: 9-Begin $2.50-c | .50 | 1.50 | 3.00 |
| 15-18-($3.50, 68 pgs.) | .60 | 1.75 | 3.50 |

**CALIFORNIA GIRLS**
June, 1987 - No. 8, May, 1988 ($2.00, B&W, 40pgs)
Eclipse Comics

| | Good | Fine | N-Mint |
|---|---|---|---|
| 1-8: All contain color paper dolls | .35 | 1.00 | 2.00 |

**CALIFORNIA RAISINS IN 3-D, THE** (See Blackthorne 3-D Series #31, 44, 46, 63, 69)

**CALL FROM CHRIST**
1952 (36 pages) (Giveaway)
Catechetical Educational Society

| | Good | Fine | N-Mint |
|---|---|---|---|
| nn | 1.50 | 4.50 | 10.00 |

**CALLING ALL BOYS** (Tex Granger No. 18 on)
Jan, 1946 - No. 17, May, 1948
Parents' Magazine Institute

| | Good | Fine | N-Mint |
|---|---|---|---|
| 1 | 4.00 | 12.00 | 28.00 |
| 2 | 2.00 | 6.00 | 14.00 |
| 3-7,9,11,14-17: 11-Rin Tin Tin photo-c. 14-J. Edgar Hoover photo-c | 1.50 | 4.50 | 10.00 |
| 8-Milton Caniff story | 2.30 | 7.00 | 16.00 |
| 10-Gary Cooper photo-c | 2.65 | 8.00 | 18.00 |
| 12-Bob Hope photo-c | 3.00 | 9.00 | 21.00 |
| 13-Bing Crosby photo-c | 2.65 | 8.00 | 18.00 |

**CALLING ALL GIRLS**
Sept, 1941 - No. 89, Sept, 1949 (Part magazine, part comic)
Parents' Magazine Institute

| | Good | Fine | N-Mint |
|---|---|---|---|
| 1 | 5.70 | 17.00 | 40.00 |
| 2 | 2.85 | 8.50 | 20.00 |
| 3-Shirley Temple photo-c | 4.00 | 12.00 | 28.00 |
| 4-10: 9-Flag-c | 1.70 | 5.00 | 12.00 |
| 11-20: 11-Photo-c | 1.30 | 4.00 | 9.00 |
| 21-39,41-43(10-11/45)-Last issue with comics | .85 | 2.60 | 6.00 |
| 40-Liz Taylor photo-c | 3.00 | 9.00 | 21.00 |
| 44-51(7/46)-Last comic book size issue | .70 | 2.00 | 4.00 |
| 52-89 | .50 | 1.50 | 3.00 |

NOTE: ***Jack Sparling** art in many issues. Becomes a girls' magazine "Senior Prom" with #90.*

**CALLING ALL KIDS** (Also see True Comics)
Dec-Jan, 1945-46 - No. 26, Aug, 1949
Parents' Magazine Institute

| | Good | Fine | N-Mint |
|---|---|---|---|
| 1-Funny animal | 3.50 | 10.50 | 24.00 |
| 2 | 1.70 | 5.00 | 12.00 |
| 3-10 | 1.00 | 3.00 | 7.00 |
| 11-26 | .55 | 1.65 | 4.00 |

**CALVIN** (See Li'l Kids)

**CALVIN & THE COLONEL** (TV)
No. 1354, Apr-June, 1962 - No. 2, July-Sept, 1962
Dell Publishing Co.

| | Good | Fine | N-Mint |
|---|---|---|---|
| 4-Color 1354(#1) | 4.00 | 12.00 | 28.00 |
| 2 | 3.00 | 9.00 | 21.00 |

**CAMELOT 3000**
12/82 - No. 11, 7/84; No. 12, 4/85 (Direct Sale; Mando paper)
DC Comics (Maxi-series)

| | Good | Fine | N-Mint |
|---|---|---|---|
| 1-12: 5-Intro Knights of New Camelot | .35 | 1.00 | 2.00 |

NOTE: ***Austin** a-7i-12i. **Bolland** a-1-12p; c-1-12.*

**CAMERA COMICS**
July, 1944 - No. 9, Summer, 1946
U.S. Camera Publishing Corp./ME

| | Good | Fine | N-Mint |
|---|---|---|---|
| nn (7/44) | 11.00 | 32.00 | 75.00 |
| nn (9/44) | 8.00 | 24.00 | 56.00 |
| 1(10/44)-The Grey Comet | 8.00 | 24.00 | 56.00 |
| 2 | 5.70 | 17.00 | 40.00 |
| 3-Nazi WW II-c; ½ photos | 5.00 | 15.00 | 35.00 |
| 4-9: All ½ photos | 4.00 | 12.00 | 28.00 |

**CAMP CANDY** (TV)
May, 1990 - No. 6, Oct, 1990 ($1.00, color)
Marvel Comics

| | Good | Fine | N-Mint |
|---|---|---|---|
| 1-6: Post-c/a(p); featuring John Candy | | .50 | 1.00 |

**CAMP COMICS**
Feb, 1942 - No. 3, April, 1942 (All have photo-c)
Dell Publishing Co.

| | Good | Fine | N-Mint |
|---|---|---|---|
| 1-"Seaman Sy Wheeler" by Kelly, 7 pgs.; Bugs Bunny app. | 34.00 | 100.00 | 235.00 |
| 2-Kelly-a, 12 pgs.; Bugs Bunny app. | 25.00 | 75.00 | 175.00 |
| 3-(Scarce)-Kelly-a | 34.00 | 100.00 | 235.00 |

**CAMP RUNAMUCK** (TV)
April, 1966
Dell Publishing Co.

| | Good | Fine | N-Mint |
|---|---|---|---|
| 1-Photo-c | 1.50 | 4.50 | 10.00 |

**CAMPUS LOVES**
Dec, 1949 - No. 5, Aug, 1950
Quality Comics Group (Comic Magazines)

| | Good | Fine | N-Mint |
|---|---|---|---|
| 1-Ward-c/a, 9 pgs. | 15.00 | 45.00 | 105.00 |
| 2-Ward-c/a | 11.00 | 32.00 | 75.00 |
| 3-5: 5-Spanking panels (2) | 5.00 | 15.00 | 35.00 |

NOTE: ***Gustavson** a-1-5. Photo-c-3-5.*

**CAMPUS ROMANCE** (. . . Romances on cover)
Sept-Oct, 1949 - No. 3, Feb-Mar, 1950
Avon Periodicals/Realistic

| | Good | Fine | N-Mint |
|---|---|---|---|
| 1-Walter Johnson-a; c-/Avon paperback 348 | 11.00 | 32.00 | 75.00 |
| 2-Grandenetti-a; c-/Avon paperback 151 | 8.50 | 25.50 | 60.00 |
| 3-c-/Avon paperback 201 | 8.50 | 25.50 | 60.00 |
| Realistic reprint | 3.50 | 10.50 | 24.00 |

**CANADA DRY PREMIUMS** (See Swamp Fox, The & Terry & The Pirates)

**CANCELLED COMIC CAVALCADE**
Summer, 1978 - No. 2, Fall, 1978 (8½x11"; B&W)
(Xeroxed pages on one side only w/blue cover and taped spine)
DC Comics, Inc.

1-(412 pages) Contains xeroxed copies of art for: Black Lightning #12, cover to #13; Claw #13,14; The Deserter #1; Doorway to Nightmare #6; Firestorm #6; The Green Team #2,3.

2-(532 pages) Contains xeroxed copies of art for: Kamandi #60 (including Omac), #61; Prez #5; Shade #9 (including The Odd Man); Showcase #105 (Deadman), 106 (The Creeper); The Vixen #1; and covers to Army at War #2, Battle Classics #3, Demand Classics #1 & 2, Dynamic Classics #3, Mr. Miracle #26, Ragman #6, Weird Mystery #25 & 26, & Western Classics #1 & 2. (Rare)

(One set sold in 1989 for $1,200.00)

NOTE: In June, 1978, DC cancelled several of their titles. For copyright purposes, the unpublished original art for these titles was xeroxed, bound in the above books, published and distributed. Only 35 copies were made.

**CANDID TALES** (Also see Bold Stories & It Rhymes With Lust)
April, 1950; June, 1950 (Digest size) (144 pages) (Full color)
Kirby Publishing Co.

| | Good | Fine | N-Mint |
|---|---|---|---|
| nn-(Scarce) Contains Wood female pirate story, 15 pgs., and 14 pgs. in June issue; Powell-a | 43.00 | 130.00 | 300.00 |

NOTE: *Another version exists with Dr. Kilmore by Wood; no female pirate story.*

**CANDY**
Fall, 1944 - No. 3, Spring, 1945
William H. Wise & Co.

| | Good | Fine | N-Mint |
|---|---|---|---|
| 1-Two Scoop Scuttle stories by Wolverton | 14.00 | 43.00 | 100.00 |
| 2,3-Scoop Scuttle by Wolverton, 2-4 pgs. | 11.00 | 32.00 | 75.00 |

**CANDY** (Teen-age)
Autumn, 1947 - No. 64, July, 1956
Quality Comics Group (Comic Magazines)

| | Good | Fine | N-Mint |
|---|---|---|---|
| 1-Gustavson-a | 7.00 | 21.00 | 50.00 |
| 2-Gustavson-a | 3.70 | 11.00 | 26.00 |
| 3-10 | 2.30 | 7.00 | 16.00 |
| 11-30 | 1.50 | 4.50 | 10.00 |
| 31-63 | 1.15 | 3.50 | 8.00 |
| 64-Ward-c(p)? | 1.65 | 5.00 | 11.50 |
| Super Reprint No. 2,10,12,16,17,18('63-'64) | .70 | 2.00 | 4.00 |

NOTE: ***Jack Cole** 1-2 pg. art in many issues.*

**CANNONBALL COMICS**
Feb, 1945 - No. 2, Mar, 1945
Rural Home Publishing Co.

| | Good | Fine | N-Mint |
|---|---|---|---|
| 1-The Crash Kid, Thunderbrand, The Captive Prince & Crime Crusader begin | 25.00 | 75.00 | 175.00 |
| 2 | 17.00 | 51.00 | 120.00 |

**CANTEEN KATE** (Also see All Picture All True Love Story & Fightin' Marines)
June, 1952 - No. 3, Nov, 1952
St. John Publishing Co.

| | Good | Fine | N-Mint |
|---|---|---|---|
| 1-Matt Baker-c/a | 24.00 | 72.00 | 170.00 |
| 2-Matt Baker-c/a | 20.00 | 60.00 | 140.00 |
| 3-(Rare)-Used in **POP**, pg. 75; Baker-c/a | 26.00 | 77.00 | 180.00 |

**CAP'N CRUNCH COMICS** (See Quaker Oats)
1963; 1965 (16 pgs.; miniature giveaways; 2½x6½")
Quaker Oats Co.

| | Good | Fine | N-Mint |
|---|---|---|---|
| (1963 titles)-"The Picture Pirates," "The Fountain of Youth," "I'm Dreaming of a Wide Isthmus." (1965 titles)-"Bewitched, Betwitched, & Betweaked," Seadog Meets the Witch Doctor" (another 1965 title suspected) | 1.30 | 4.00 | 9.00 |

**CAP'N QUICK & A FOOZLE**
July, 1985 - No. 3, Nov, 1985 ($1.50; Baxter paper)
Eclipse Comics

| | Good | Fine | N-Mint |
|---|---|---|---|
| 1-3-Rogers-c/a | .25 | .75 | 1.50 |

**CAPTAIN ACTION**
Oct-Nov, 1968 - No. 5, June-July, 1969 (Based on Ideal toy)
National Periodical Publications

| | Good | Fine | N-Mint |
|---|---|---|---|
| 1-Origin; Wood-a; Superman-c app. | 3.15 | 9.50 | 22.00 |
| 2,3,5-Kane/Wood-a | 2.15 | 6.50 | 15.00 |
| 4 | 1.70 | 5.00 | 12.00 |
| . . . & Action Boy('67)-Ideal Toy Co. giveaway | 3.60 | 11.00 | 25.00 |

**CAPTAIN AERO COMICS** (Samson No. 1-6; also see Veri Best Sure Fire & Veri Best Sure Shot Comics)
V1#7(#1), Dec, 1941 - V2#4(#10), Jan, 1943; V3#9(#11), Sept, 1943 - V4#3(#17), Oct, 1944; #21, Dec, 1944 - #26, Aug, 1946 (No #18-20)
Holyoke Publishing Co.

| | Good | Fine | N-Mint |
|---|---|---|---|
| V1#7(#1)-Flag-Man & Solar, Master of Magic, Captain Aero, Cap Stone, Adventurer begin | 54.00 | 160.00 | 375.00 |
| 8(#2)-Pals of Freedom app. | 30.00 | 90.00 | 210.00 |
| 9(#3)-Alias X begins; Pals of Freedom app. | 30.00 | 90.00 | 210.00 |
| 10(#4)-Origin The Gargoyle; Kubert-a | 30.00 | 90.00 | 210.00 |
| 11,12(#5,6)-Kubert-a; Miss Victory in #6 | 25.00 | 75.00 | 175.00 |
| V2#1,2(#7,8): 8-Origin The Red Cross; Miss Victory app. | 14.00 | 43.00 | 100.00 |
| 3(#9)-Miss Victory app. | 11.00 | 32.00 | 75.00 |
| 4(#10)-Miss Victory app. | 8.50 | 25.50 | 60.00 |
| V3#9 - V3#13(#11-15): 11,15-Miss Victory app. | 6.50 | 19.00 | 45.00 |
| V4#2, V4#3(#16,17) | 5.30 | 16.00 | 38.00 |
| 21-24,26-L. B. Cole covers. 22-Intro/origin Mighty Mite | 8.00 | 24.00 | 56.00 |
| 25-L. B. Cole S/F-c | 10.00 | 30.00 | 70.00 |

NOTE: ***Hollingsworth** a-23. **Infantino** a-23.*

**CAPTAIN AMERICA** (See All-Select, All Winners, Aurora, Avengers #4, Giant-Size. . ., The Invaders, Marvel Double Feature, Marvel Fanfare, Marvel Mystery, Marvel Super-Action, Marvel Super Heroes, Marvel Team-Up, Marvel Treasury Special, Power

*Candy #1 (1944), © WHW*

*Captain Action #2, © DC*

*Captain Aero #5, © HOKE*

*Captain America #111, © MEG*

*Captain America Special #2, © MEG*

*Captain America Comics #16, © MEG*

Record Comics, USA Comics, Young Allies & Young Men)

**CAPTAIN AMERICA** (Formerly Tales of Suspense #1-99; Captain America and the Falcon #134-223)
No. 100, April, 1968 - Present
Marvel Comics Group

| | Good | Fine | N-Mint |
|---|---|---|---|
| 100-Flashback on Cap's revival with Avengers & Sub-Mariner | 31.00 | 93.00 | 220.00 |
| 101 | 7.00 | 21.00 | 50.00 |
| 102-108 | 4.30 | 13.00 | 30.00 |
| 109-Origin Capt. America | 5.00 | 15.00 | 35.00 |
| 110,111,113-Steranko-c/a. 110-Rick becomes Cap's partner. 110-Hulk x-over. 111-Death of Steve Rogers. 113-Cap's funeral | 5.70 | 17.00 | 40.00 |
| 112-Origin retold | 2.15 | 6.50 | 15.00 |
| 114-116,118-120 | 1.70 | 5.00 | 12.00 |
| 117-1st app. The Falcon | 2.00 | 6.00 | 14.00 |
| 121-140: 121-Retells origin. 133-The Falcon becomes Cap's partner; origin Modok. 137,138-Spider-Man x-over. 140-Origin Grey Gargoyle retold | 1.15 | 3.50 | 8.00 |
| 141-171,176-179: 143-(52 pgs.). 155-Origin; redrawn with Falcon added. 164-1st app. Nightshade. 176-End of Capt. America | .85 | 2.50 | 5.00 |
| 172-175-X-Men x-over | 1.50 | 4.50 | 10.00 |
| 180-200: 180-Intro/origin of Nomad; Steve Rogers becomes Nomad. 181-Intro & origin of new Capt. America. 183-Death of New Cap; Nomad becomes Cap. 186-True origin The Falcon | .70 | 2.00 | 4.00 |
| 201-240,242-246: 233-Death of Sharon Carter. 235-Daredevil x-over; (7/79)-Miller involved? 244,245-Miller-c | .50 | 1.50 | 3.00 |
| 241-Punisher app.; Miller-c | 7.85 | 23.50 | 55.00 |
| 247-255-Byrne-a. 255-Origin; Miller-c | .60 | 1.75 | 3.50 |
| 256-323,325-327,329-331: 265-Nick Fury app. 266-Spider-Man app. 267-1st app. Everyman. 269-1st Team America. 281-'50s Bucky returns. 282-Bucky becomes Nomad. 284-Patriot (Jack Mace) app. 285-Death of Patriot. 298-Origin Red Skull | .35 | 1.00 | 2.00 |
| 324-1st app. Super Patriot | .70 | 2.00 | 4.00 |
| 328-Origin & 1st app. D-Man | .50 | 1.50 | 3.00 |
| 332-Old Cap resigns | 1.70 | 5.00 | 10.00 |
| 333-Intro new Captain (Super Patriot) | 1.15 | 3.50 | 7.00 |
| 334 | .90 | 2.75 | 5.50 |
| 335-340: 339-Fall of the Mutants tie-in | .85 | 2.50 | 5.00 |
| 341-343,345-349 | .30 | .85 | 1.70 |
| 344-Double size, $1.50 | .35 | 1.10 | 2.20 |
| 350-($1.75, 68 pgs.)-Return of Steve Rogers (original Cap) to original costume | .75 | 2.25 | 4.50 |
| 351-354: 351-Nick Fury app. 354-1st app. U.S. Agent (see Avengers West Coast) | .30 | .85 | 1.70 |
| 355-382,384: 373-Bullseye app. 375-Daredevil app. | | .50 | 1.00 |
| 383-($2.00, 68 pgs.)-50th anniversary issue | .35 | 1.00 | 2.00 |
| . . .& The Campbell Kids (1980, 36pg. giveaway, Campbell's Soup/U.S. Dept. of Energy) | .35 | 1.00 | 2.00 |
| . . .Meets the Asthma Monster (No #, 1987, giveaway, Your Physician and Glaxo, Inc.) | | .30 | .60 |
| Special 1(1/71) | 1.70 | 5.00 | 12.00 |
| Special 2(1/72)-Colan-r/Not Brand Echh | 1.30 | 4.00 | 9.00 |
| Annual 3-7: 3(4/76), 4(1977, 52 pgs.)-Kirby-c/a, 5(1981, 52 pgs.), 6 (11/82, 52 pgs.), 7('83, 52 pgs.) | .40 | 1.25 | 2.50 |
| Annual 8(9/86)-Wolverine featured | 3.70 | 11.00 | 22.00 |
| Annual 9(1990, $2.00, 68 pgs.)-Nomad back-up | .35 | 1.00 | 2.00 |

NOTE: ***Austin*** *c-225i, 239i, 246i.* ***Buscema*** *a-115p, 217p; c-136p, 217.* ***Byrne*** *part c-223, 238, 239, 247p-254p, 290, 291, 313; a-247-254p, 255, 313p.* ***Colan*** *a(p)-116-137, 256, Annual 5; c(p)-116-123, 126, 129.* ***Everett*** *a-136i, 137i; c-126i.* ***Gil Kane*** *a-145p; c-147p, 149p, 150p, 170p, 172-174, 180, 181p, 183-190p, 215, 216, 220, 221.* ***Kirby*** *a(p)-100-109, 112, 193-214, 216, Special 1, 2(layouts), Annual 3, 4; c-100-109, 112, 126p, 193-214.* ***Miller*** *c-241p, 244p, 245p, 255p, Annual 5.* ***Mooney*** *a-149i.* ***Morrow*** *a-144.* ***Perez*** *c-243p, 246p.* ***Roussos*** *a-140i, 168i.* ***Starlin/Sinnott*** *c-162.* ***Sutton*** *a-244i.* ***Tuska*** *a-112i, 215p, Special 2.* ***Williamson*** *a-313i.* ***Wood*** *a-127i.*

**CAPTAIN AMERICA COMICS**
Mar, 1941 - No. 75, Jan, 1950; No. 76, 5/54 - No. 78, 9/54
(No. 74 & 75 titled Capt. America's Weird Tales)
Timely/Marvel Comics (TCI 1-20/CmPS 21-68/MjMC 69-75/Atlas Comics (PrPI 76-78)

1-Origin & 1st app. Captain America & Bucky by S&K; Hurricane, Tuk the Caveboy begin by S&K; Red Skull app. Hitler-c

| Good | Fine | VF-NM | NM/Mint |
|---|---|---|---|
| 2,335.00 | 5,835.00 | 14,000.00 | 21,000.00 |

(Estimated up to 180 total copies exist, 8 in NM/Mint)

| | Good | Fine | N-Mint |
|---|---|---|---|
| 2-S&K Hurricane; Tuk by Avison (Kirby splash) | 600.00 | 1500.00 | 3600.00 |
| 3-Red Skull app; Stan Lee's 1st text | 435.00 | 1085.00 | 2600.00 |
| 4-1st full page panel in comics | 285.00 | 710.00 | 1700.00 |
| 5 | 267.00 | 665.00 | 1600.00 |
| 6-Origin Father Time; Tuk the Caveboy ends | 217.00 | 540.00 | 1300.00 |
| 7-Red Skull app | 217.00 | 540.00 | 1300.00 |
| 8-10-Last S&K issue, (S&K centerfold #6-10) | 183.00 | 460.00 | 1100.00 |
| 11-Last Hurricane, Headline Hunter; Al Avison Captain America begins, ends #20 | 142.00 | 355.00 | 850.00 |
| 12-The Imp begins, ends #16; Last Father Time | 139.00 | 350.00 | 835.00 |
| 13-Origin The Secret Stamp; classic-c | 150.00 | 375.00 | 900.00 |
| 14,15 | 139.00 | 348.00 | 835.00 |
| 16-Red Skull unmasks Cap | 158.00 | 395.00 | 950.00 |
| 17-The Fighting Fool only app. | 125.00 | 312.00 | 750.00 |
| 18,19-Human Torch begins #19 | 108.00 | 270.00 | 650.00 |
| 20-Sub-Mariner app.; no H. Torch | 108.00 | 270.00 | 650.00 |
| 21-25: 25-Cap drinks liquid opium | 100.00 | 250.00 | 600.00 |
| 26-30: 27-Last Secret Stamp; last 68 pg. issue? 28-60 pg. issues begin? | 89.00 | 223.00 | 535.00 |
| 31-36,38-40 | 80.00 | 200.00 | 480.00 |
| 37-Red Skull app. | 87.00 | 217.00 | 520.00 |
| 41-47: 41-Last Jap War-c. 46-German Holocaust-c. 47-Last German War-c | 67.00 | 167.00 | 400.00 |
| 48-58,60 | 63.00 | 156.00 | 375.00 |
| 59-Origin retold | 90.00 | 225.00 | 540.00 |
| 61-Red Skull-c/story | 80.00 | 200.00 | 480.00 |
| 62,64,65: 65-"Hey Look" by Kurtzman | 63.00 | 156.00 | 375.00 |
| 63-Intro/origin Asbestos Lady | 67.00 | 167.00 | 400.00 |
| 66-Bucky is shot; Golden Girl teams up with Captain America & learns his i.d; origin Golden Girl | 76.00 | 190.00 | 455.00 |
| 67-Captain America/Golden Girl team-up; Mxyztplk swipe; last Toro in Human Torch | 63.00 | 156.00 | 375.00 |
| 68,70-Sub-Mariner/Namora, and Captain America/Golden Girl team-up in each. 70-Science fiction- c/story | 63.00 | 156.00 | 375.00 |
| 69,71-73: 69-Human Torch/Sun Girl team-up. 71-Anti Wertham editorial; The Witness, Bucky app. | 63.00 | 156.00 | 375.00 |
| 74-(Scarce)(1949)-Titled "C.A.'s Weird Tales;" Red Skull app. | 98.00 | 245.00 | 585.00 |
| 75(2/50)-Titled "C.A.'s Weird Tales;" no C.A. app.; horror cover/stories | 66.00 | 165.00 | 395.00 |
| 76-78(1954): Human Torch/Toro stories | 42.00 | 105.00 | 250.00 |
| 132-Pg. Issue (B&W-1942)(Canadian)-Has blank inside-c and back-c | 250.00 | 625.00 | 1500.00 |
| Shoestore Giveaway #77 | 23.00 | 56.00 | 135.00 |

NOTE: *Bondage c-3, 7, 15, 16, 34, 38.* ***Crandall*** *a-2i, 3i, 9i, 10i.* ***Kirby*** *c-8p.* ***Rico*** *c-70, 71.* ***Romita*** *c-77, 78.* ***Schomburg*** *c-26-29, 31, 33, 37-39, 41-43, 45-54, 58.* ***Shores*** *c-20-25, 30, 32, 34-36, 40, 59, 61-63.* ***S&K*** *c-1, 2, 5-7, 9, 10.*

**CAPTAIN AMERICA SPECIAL EDITION**
Feb, 1984 - No. 2, Mar, 1984 ($2.00, Baxter paper)
Marvel Comics Group

| | Good | Fine | N-Mint |
|---|---|---|---|
| 1,2-Steranko-c/a(r) | .40 | 1.25 | 2.50 |

**CAPTAIN AND THE KIDS, THE** (See Famous Comics Cartoon Books)

**CAPTAIN AND THE KIDS, THE** (See Comics on Parade, Okay Comics & Sparkler Comics)
1938 -12/39; Sum, 1947 - No. 32, 1955; 4-Color No. 881, Feb, 1958
United Features Syndicate/Dell Publ. Co.

| | Good | Fine | N-Mint |
|---|---|---|---|
| Single Series 1('38) | 43.00 | 130.00 | 300.00 |
| Single Series 1(Reprint)(12/39-"Reprint" on cover) | 24.00 | 73.00 | 170.00 |
| 1(Summer, 1947-UFS) | 6.50 | 19.00 | 45.00 |
| 2 | 3.70 | 11.00 | 26.00 |
| 3-10 | 2.30 | 7.00 | 16.00 |
| 11-20 | 1.70 | 5.00 | 12.00 |
| 21-32(1955) | 1.30 | 4.00 | 9.00 |
| 50th Anniversary issue('48)-Contains a 2 page history of the strip, including an account of the famous Supreme Court decision allowing both Pulitzer & Hearst to run the same strip under different names | 3.50 | 10.50 | 24.00 |
| Special Summer issue, Fall issue (1948) | 2.65 | 8.00 | 18.00 |
| 4-Color 881 (Dell) | 1.70 | 5.00 | 12.00 |

**CAPTAIN ATOM**
1950 - No. 7, 1951 (5x7¼") (5 cents, 52 pgs.)
Nationwide Publishers

| | Good | Fine | N-Mint |
|---|---|---|---|
| 1-Sci/fic | 8.50 | 25.50 | 60.00 |
| 2-7 | 5.00 | 15.00 | 35.00 |
| ...- Secret of the Columbian Jungle (16 pgs. in color, paper-c, 3¾x 5-1/8")-Fireside Marshmallow giveaway | 1.70 | 5.00 | 12.00 |

**CAPTAIN ATOM** (Formerly Strange Suspense Stories No. 77)
V2#78, Dec, 1965 - V2#89, Dec, 1967 (Also see Space Adventures)
Charlton Comics

| | Good | Fine | N-Mint |
|---|---|---|---|
| 78-Origin retold | 5.00 | 15.00 | 35.00 |
| 79-82: 82-Intro. Nightshade | 3.15 | 9.50 | 22.00 |
| 83-86: Ted Kord Blue Beetle in all | 2.65 | 8.00 | 18.00 |
| 87-89-Nightshade by Aparo in all | 2.65 | 8.00 | 18.00 |
| 83-85(Modern Comics-1977)-reprints | | .15 | .30 |

NOTE: ***Aparo** a-87-89. **Ditko** c/a(p) 78-89. #90 only published in fanzine 'The Charlton Bullseye' #1, 2.*

**CAPTAIN ATOM** (Also see Americomics & Crisis On Infinite Earths)
March, 1987 - Present (Direct sale only #35 on)
DC Comics

| | Good | Fine | N-Mint |
|---|---|---|---|
| 1-(44 pgs., $1.00)-Origin/1st app. with new costume | .35 | 1.00 | 2.00 |
| 2-49: 5-Firestorm x-over. 6-Intro. new Dr. Spectro. 11-Millennium tie-in. 14-Nightshade app. 16-Justice League app. 17-$1.00-c begins; Swamp Thing app. 20-Blue Beetle x-over | | .60 | 1.20 |
| 50-($2.00, 52 pgs.) | .35 | 1.00 | 2.00 |
| Annual 1 (3/88, $1.25)-Intro Major Force | .25 | .75 | 1.50 |
| Annual 2 (12/88, $1.50) | .25 | .75 | 1.50 |

**CAPTAIN BATTLE** (Boy Comics #3 on) (See Silver Streak Comics)
Summer, 1941 - No. 2, Fall, 1941
New Friday Publ./Comic House

| | Good | Fine | N-Mint |
|---|---|---|---|
| 1-Origin Blackout by Rico; Captain Battle begins | 54.00 | 160.00 | 375.00 |
| 2 | 36.00 | 108.00 | 250.00 |

**CAPTAIN BATTLE** (2nd Series)
No. 3, Wint, 1942-43 - No. 5, Sum, 1943 (#3: 52pgs., nd)(#5: 68pgs.)
Magazine Press/Picture Scoop No. 5

| | Good | Fine | N-Mint |
|---|---|---|---|
| 3-Origin Silver Streak-r/SS#3; Origin Lance Hale-r/Silver Streak; Simon-a(r) | 30.00 | 90.00 | 210.00 |
| 4,5: 5-Origin Blackout retold | 20.00 | 60.00 | 140.00 |

**CAPTAIN BATTLE, JR.**
Fall, 1943 - No. 2, Winter, 1943-44
Comic House (Lev Gleason)

| | Good | Fine | N-Mint |
|---|---|---|---|
| 1-The Claw vs. The Ghost | 43.00 | 130.00 | 300.00 |
| 2-Wolverton's Scoop Scuttle; Don Rico-c/a; The Green Claw story | 36.00 | 108.00 | 250.00 |

**CAPTAIN BRITAIN** (Also see Marvel Team-Up No. 65,66)
Oct. 13, 1976 - No. 39, July 6, 1977 (Weekly)
Marvel Comics International

| | Good | Fine | N-Mint |
|---|---|---|---|
| 1-Origin; with Capt. Britain's face mask inside | .85 | 2.50 | 5.00 |
| 2-Origin, conclusion; Capt. Britain's Boomerang inside | .60 | 1.80 | 3.60 |
| 3-8: 3,8-Vs. Bank Robbers. 4-7-Vs. Hurricane | .35 | 1.00 | 2.00 |
| 9-15: 9-13-Vs. Dr. Synne. 14,15-Vs. Mastermind | .30 | .90 | 1.80 |
| 16-20-With Capt. America; 17 misprinted & color section reprinted in No. 18 | .30 | .90 | 1.80 |
| 21-23,25,26-With Capt. America | .30 | .90 | 1.80 |
| 24-With C.B.'s Jet Plane inside | .60 | 1.80 | 3.60 |
| 27,33-35: 27-Origin retold. 33-35-More on origin | .30 | .90 | 1.80 |
| 28-32,36-39: 28-32-Vs. Lord Hawk. 36-Star Sceptre. 37-39-Vs. Highwayman & Munipulator | .25 | .75 | 1.50 |
| Annual(1978,Hardback,64pgs.)-Reprints No. 1-7 with pin-ups of Marvel characters | 1.35 | 4.00 | 8.00 |
| Summer Special (1980, 52pp)-Reprints | .35 | 1.00 | 2.00 |

NOTE: *No. 1, 2, & 24 are rarer in mint due to inserts. Distributed in Great Britain only. Nick Fury-r by Steranko in 1-20, 24-31, 35-37. Fantastic Four-r by J. Buscema in all. New Buscema-a in 24-30. Story from No. 39 continues in Super Spider-Man (British weekly) No. 231-247. Following cancellation of his series, new Captain Britain stories appeared in "Super Spider-Man" (British weekly) No. 231-247. Captain Britain stories which appear in Super-Spider-Man No. 248-253 are reprints of Marvel Team-Up No. 65&66. Capt. Britain strips also appeared in Hulk Comic (weekly) 1, 3-30, 42-55, 57-60, in Marvel Superheroes (monthly) 377-388, in Daredevils (monthly) 1-11, Mighty World of Marvel (monthly) 7-16 & Captain Britain (monthly) 1-present.*

**CAPTAIN CANUCK**
7/75 - No. 4, 7/77; No. 4, 7-8/79 - No. 14, 3-4/81
Comely Comix (Canada) (All distr. in U. S.)

| | Good | Fine | N-Mint |
|---|---|---|---|
| 1-1st app. Bluefox | .40 | 1.25 | 2.50 |
| 2-1st app. Dr. Walker, Redcoat & Kebec | .30 | .90 | 1.80 |
| 3(5-7/76)-1st app. Heather | .30 | .90 | 1.80 |
| 4(1st printing-2/77)-10x14½"; (5.00); B&W; 300 copies serially numbered and signed with one certificate of authenticity | 5.00 | 15.00 | 30.00 |
| 4(2nd printing-7/77)-11x17", B&W; only 15 copies printed; signed by creator Richard Comely, serially #'d and two certificates of authenticity inserted; orange cardboard covers (Very Rare) | 8.00 | 25.00 | 50.00 |
| 4(7-8/79)-1st app. Tom Evans & Mr. Gold; origin The Catman | | .40 | .80 |
| 5-14: 5-Origin Capt. Canuck's powers; 1st app. Earth Patrol & Chaos Corps. 8-Jonn 'The Final Chapter'. 9-1st World Beyond. 11-1st 'Chariots of Fire' story | | .40 | .80 |
| Summer Special 1(7-9/80, 95 cents, 64pgs.) | | .50 | 1.00 |

NOTE: *30,000 copies of No. 2 were destroyed in Winnipeg.*

**CAPTAIN CARROT AND HIS AMAZING ZOO CREW**
March, 1982 - No. 20, Nov, 1983 (Also see New Teen Titans)
DC Comics

| | Good | Fine | N-Mint |
|---|---|---|---|
| 1-20: 1-Superman app. 3-Re-intro Dodo & The Frog. 9-Re-intro Three Mouseketeers, the Terrific Whatzit. 10,11- Pig Iron reverts back to Peter Porkchops. 20-The Changeling app. | | .30 | .60 |

**CAPTAIN CARVEL AND HIS CARVEL CRUSADERS** (See Carvel Comics)

**CAPTAIN COURAGEOUS COMICS** (Banner No. 3-5)
No. 6, March, 1942
Periodical House (Ace Magazines)

| | Good | Fine | N-Mint |
|---|---|---|---|
| 6-Origin & 1st app. The Sword; Lone Warrior, Capt. Courageous app. | 40.00 | 120.00 | 280.00 |

**CAPT'N CRUNCH COMICS** (See Cap'n...)

*Captain Atom #88 (Charlton), © DC*

*Captain Battle #1, © LEV*

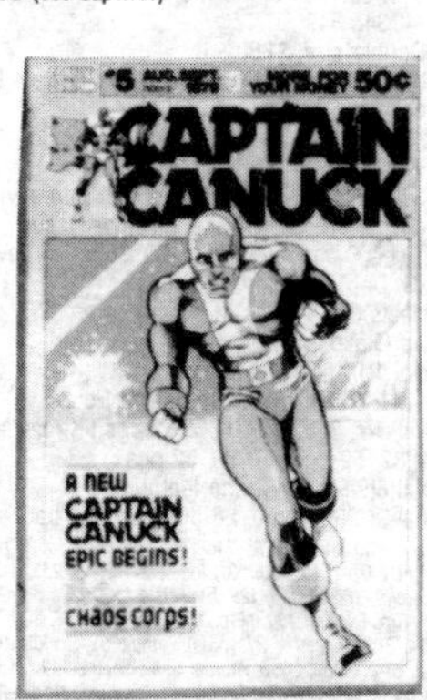

*Captain Canuck #5, © Comely Comics*

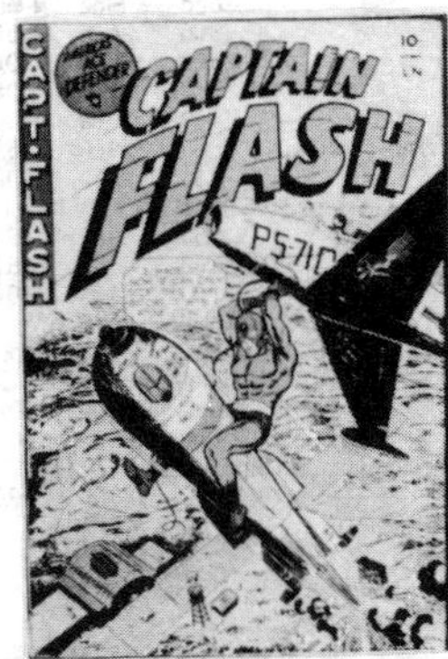

Captain Flash #1, © Sterling Comics

Captain Jet #1, © AJAX

Captain Marvel #2, © MEG

**CAPTAIN DAVY JONES** (See 4-Color No. 598)

**CAPTAIN EASY** (See The Funnies & Red Ryder #3-32)
1939 - No. 17, Sept, 1949; April, 1956
Hawley/Dell Publ./Standard(Visual Editions)/Argo

| | Good | Fine | N-Mint |
|---|---|---|---|
| Hawley(1939)-Contains reprints from The Funnies & 1938 Sunday strips by Roy Crane | 36.00 | 108.00 | 250.00 |
| 4-Color 24 (1943) | 23.00 | 70.00 | 160.00 |
| 4-Color 111(6/46) | 9.30 | 28.00 | 65.00 |
| 10(Standard-10/47) | 4.30 | 13.00 | 30.00 |
| 11-17: All contain 1930's & '40's strip-r | 3.15 | 9.50 | 22.00 |
| Argo 1(4/56)-(r) | 3.00 | 9.00 | 21.00 |

NOTE: *Schomburg c-13, 16.*

**CAPTAIN EASY & WASH TUBBS** (See Famous Comics Cartoon Books)

**CAPTAIN ELECTRON**
Aug, 1986 ($2.25, color)
Brick Computer Science Institute

| | | | |
|---|---|---|---|
| 1-Disbrow-a | .35 | 1.10 | 2.25 |

**CAPTAIN EO 3-D** (Disney)
July, 1987 (Eclipse 3-D Special #18, $3.50, Baxter)
Eclipse Comics

| | | | |
|---|---|---|---|
| 1-Adapts 3-D movie | .60 | 1.75 | 3.50 |
| 1-2-D limited edition | .85 | 2.50 | 5.00 |
| 1-Large size (11x17", 8/87)-Sold only at Disney Theme parks ($6.95) | 1.20 | 3.50 | 7.00 |

**CAPTAIN FEARLESS COMICS** (Also see Holyoke One-Shot #6, Old Glory Comics & Silver Streak #1)
August, 1941 - No. 2, Sept, 1941
Helnit Publishing Co. (Holyoke Publishing Co.)

| | | | |
|---|---|---|---|
| 1-Origin Mr. Miracle, Alias X, Captain Fearless, Citizen Smith Son of the Unknown Soldier; Miss Victory begins | 34.00 | 103.00 | 240.00 |
| 2-Grit Grady, Captain Stone app. | 22.00 | 65.00 | 150.00 |

**CAPTAIN FLASH**
Nov, 1954 - No. 4, July, 1955
Sterling Comics

| | | | |
|---|---|---|---|
| 1-Origin; Sekowsky-a; Tomboy (female super hero) begins; Last pre-code issue | 13.00 | 40.00 | 90.00 |
| 2-4 | 7.00 | 21.00 | 50.00 |

**CAPTAIN FLEET**
Fall, 1952
Ziff-Davis Publishing Co.

| | | | |
|---|---|---|---|
| 1-Painted-c | 7.00 | 21.00 | 50.00 |

**CAPTAIN FLIGHT COMICS**
Mar, 1944 - No. 10, Dec, 1945; No. 11, Feb-Mar, 1947
Four Star Publications

| | | | |
|---|---|---|---|
| nn | 11.50 | 34.00 | 80.00 |
| 2 | 6.00 | 18.00 | 42.00 |
| 3,4: 4-Rock Raymond begins, ends #7 | 5.00 | 15.00 | 35.00 |
| 5-Bondage, torture-c; Red Rocket begins; the Grenade app. | 7.00 | 21.00 | 50.00 |
| 6,7 | 6.00 | 18.00 | 42.00 |
| 8,9: 8-Yankee Girl, Black Cobra begin; intro. Cobra Kid. 9-Torpedoman app.; last Yankee Girl; Kinstler-a | 9.30 | 28.00 | 65.00 |
| 10-Deep Sea Dawson, Zoom of the Jungle, Rock Raymond, Red Rocket, & Black Cobra app; L. B. Cole bondage-c | 9.30 | 28.00 | 65.00 |
| 11-Torpedoman, Blue Flame app.; last Black Cobra, Red Rocket; L. B. Cole-c | 9.30 | 28.00 | 65.00 |

NOTE: *L. B. Cole c-7-11.*

**CAPTAIN FORTUNE PRESENTS**
1955 - 1959 (16 pages; 3¼x6-7/8") (Giveaway)
Vital Publications

| | Good | Fine | N-Mint |
|---|---|---|---|
| "Davy Crockett in Episodes of the Creek War," "Davy Crockett at the Alamo," "In Sherwood Forest Tells Strange Tales of Robin Hood" ('57), "Meets Bolivar the Liberator" ('59), "Tells How Buffalo Bill Fights the Dog Soldiers"('57), "Young Davy Crockett" | .85 | 2.50 | 5.00 |

**CAPTAIN GALLANT** (...of the Foreign Legion) (TV)
(Texas Rangers in Action No. 5 on?)
1955: No. 2, Jan, 1956 - No. 4, Sept, 1956
Charlton Comics

| | | | |
|---|---|---|---|
| Heinz Foods Premium (#1?)(1955; regular size)-U.S. Pictorial; contains Buster Crabbe photos; Don Heck-a | 4.00 | 12.00 | 28.00 |
| Non-Heinz version (same as above except pictures of show replaces ads) (#1)-Buster Crabbe photo on-c | 4.00 | 12.00 | 28.00 |
| 2-4: Buster Crabbe in all | 3.50 | 10.50 | 24.00 |

**CAPTAIN HERO** (See Jughead as...)

**CAPTAIN HERO COMICS DIGEST MAGAZINE**
Sept, 1981
Archie Publications

| | | | |
|---|---|---|---|
| 1-Reprints of Jughead as Super-Guy | | .30 | .60 |

**CAPTAIN HOBBY COMICS**
Feb, 1948 (Canadian)
Export Publication Ent. Ltd. (Dist. in U.S. by Kable News Co.)

| | | | |
|---|---|---|---|
| 1 | 3.00 | 9.00 | 21.00 |

**CAPT. HOLO IN 3-D** (See Blackthorne 3-D Series #65)

**CAPTAIN HOOK & PETER PAN** (See 4-Color No. 446 and Peter Pan)

**CAPTAIN JET** (Fantastic Fears No. 7 on)
May, 1952 - No. 5, Jan, 1953
Four Star Publ./Farrell/Comic Media

| | | | |
|---|---|---|---|
| 1-Bakerish-a | 7.00 | 21.00 | 50.00 |
| 2 | 5.00 | 15.00 | 35.00 |
| 3-5,6(?) | 3.00 | 9.00 | 21.00 |

**CAPTAIN JUSTICE**
March, 1988 - No. 2, April, 1988
Marvel Comics

| | | | |
|---|---|---|---|
| 1,2-Based on TV series, True Colors | | .65 | 1.30 |

**CAPTAIN KANGAROO** (See 4-Color No. 721,780,872)

**CAPTAIN KIDD** (Formerly Dagar; My Secret Story #26 on)(Also see Comic Comics & Fantastic Comics)
No. 24, June, 1949 - No. 25, Aug, 1949
Fox Feature Syndicate

| | | | |
|---|---|---|---|
| 24,25 | 7.00 | 21.00 | 50.00 |

**CAPTAIN MARVEL** (See All Hero, All-New Collectors' Ed., America's Greatest, Fawcett Min., Gift, Legends, Limited Collectors' Ed., Marvel Family, Master No. 21, Mighty Midget Comics, Shazam, Special Edition Comics, Whiz, Wisco, and XMas)

**CAPTAIN MARVEL** (Becomes ...Presents the Terrible 5 No. 5)
April, 1966 - No. 4, Nov, 1966 (25 cent Giants)
M. F. Enterprises

| | | | |
|---|---|---|---|
| nn-(#1 on pg. 5)-Origin; created by Carl Burgos | .85 | 2.50 | 5.00 |
| 2,4 | .50 | 1.50 | 3.00 |
| 3-(#3 on page 4)-Fights the Bat | .50 | 1.50 | 3.00 |

**CAPTAIN MARVEL** (See Giant-Size..., Life Of..., Marvel Graphic Novel, Marvel Spotlight & Marvel Super-Heroes #12)
May, 1968 - No. 19, Dec, 1969; No. 20, June, 1970 - No. 21, Aug, 1970; No. 22, Sept, 1972 - No. 62, May, 1979
Marvel Comics Group

| | | | |
|---|---|---|---|
| 1 | 9.30 | 28.00 | 65.00 |
| 2 | 2.15 | 6.50 | 15.00 |
| 3-5 | 1.70 | 5.00 | 12.00 |
| 6-11: 11-Smith/Trimpe-c; Death of Una | 1.15 | 3.50 | 8.00 |
| 12-24: 17-New costume | 1.00 | 3.00 | 6.00 |

Good Fine N-Mint
25-Starlin-c/a 1.50 4.50 10.00
26-Starlin-c/a 1.15 3.50 8.00
27-34-Starlin-c/a. 29-C.M. gains more powers. 34-C.M. contracts cancer which eventually kills him 1.00 3.00 6.00
35-62: 36-Origin recap; Starlin-a (3 pgs.). 39-Origin Watcher. 41,43-Wrightson part inks; #43-c(i) .25 .75 1.50

NOTE: ***Alcala** a-35. **Austin** a-46i, 49-53i; c-52i. **Buscema** a-18p-21p. **Colan** a(p)-1-4; c(p)-1-4, 8, 9. **Heck** a-5p-10p, 16p. **Gil Kane** a-17-21p; c-17-24p, 37p, 53. **McWilliams** a-40i.*

**CAPTAIN MARVEL**
Nov, 1989 ($1.50, color, one-shot, 52 pgs.)
Marvel Comics

1-Super-hero from Avengers; new powers .25 .75 1.50

**CAPTAIN MARVEL ADVENTURES** (See Special Edition Comics for pre-No. 1)
1941 (March) - No. 150, Nov, 1953 (#1 on stands 1/16/41)
Fawcett Publications

Good Fine VF-NM NM/Mint
nn(#1)-Captain Marvel & Sivana by Jack Kirby. The cover was printed on unstable paper stock and is rarely found in Fine or Mint condition; blank inside-c 1334.00 3335.00 8000.00 12,000.00
(Estimated up to 140 total copies exist, 3 in NM/Mint)

Good Fine N-Mint
2-(Advertised as #3, which was counting Special Edition Comics as the real #1); Tuska-a 186.00 560.00 1300.00
3-Metallic silver-c 100.00 300.00 700.00
4-Three Lt. Marvels app. 71.00 215.00 500.00
5 57.00 171.00 400.00
6-10 45.00 135.00 315.00
11-15: 13-Two-pg. Capt. Marvel pin-up. 15-Comic cards on back-c begin, end #26 36.00 107.00 250.00
16,17: 17-Painted-c 32.00 95.00 225.00
18-Origin & 1st app. Mary Marvel & Marvel Family (12/11/42); painted-c; Mary Marvel by Marcus Swayze 46.00 140.00 325.00
19-Mary Marvel x-over; Christmas-c 30.00 90.00 210.00
20,21-Attached to the cover, each has a miniature comic just like the Mighty Midget Comics #11, except that each has a full color promo ad on the back cover. Most copies were circulated without the miniature comic. These issues with miniatures attached are very rare, and should not be mistaken for copies with the similar Mighty Midget glued in its place. The Mighty Midgets had blank back covers except for a small victory stamp seal. Only the Capt. Marvel and Captain Marvel Jr. No. 11 miniatures have been positively documented as having been affixed to these covers. Each miniature was only partially glued by its back cover to the Captain Marvel comic making it easy to see if it's the genuine miniature rather than a Mighty Midget.
with comic attached.... 86.00 260.00 600.00
20,21-Without miniature 26.00 77.00 180.00
22-Mr. Mind serial begins 43.00 130.00 300.00
23-25 24.00 73.00 170.00
26-30: 26-Flag-c 20.00 60.00 140.00
31-35: 35-Origin Radar 19.00 56.00 130.00
36-40: 37-Mary Marvel x-over 16.00 48.00 110.00
41-46: 42-Christmas-c. 43-Capt. Marvel 1st meets Uncle Marvel; Mary Batson cameo. 46-Mr. Mind serial ends 13.00 40.00 90.00
47-50 11.50 34.00 80.00
51-53,55-60: 52-Origin & 1st app. Sivana Jr.; Capt. Marvel Jr. x-over 10.00 30.00 70.00
54-Special oversize 68-pg. issue 11.00 32.00 75.00
61-The Cult of the Curse serial begins 11.50 34.00 80.00
62-66-Serial ends; Mary Marvel x-over in #65. 66-Atomic War-c 9.30 28.00 65.00
67-77,79: 69-Billy Batson's Christmas; Uncle Marvel, Mary Marvel, Capt. Marvel Jr. x-over. 71-Three Lt. Marvels app. 79-Origin Mr. Tawny 8.50 25.50 60.00
78-Origin Mr. Atom 10.00 30.00 70.00
80-Origin Capt. Marvel retold 15.00 45.00 105.00
81-84,86-90: 81,90-Mr. Atom app. 82-Infinity-c. 86-Mr. Tawny app.

Good Fine N-Mint
8.00 24.00 55.00
85-Freedom Train issue 10.00 30.00 70.00
91-99: 96-Mr. Tawny app. 7.00 21.00 50.00
100-Origin retold 14.00 43.00 100.00
101-120: 116-Flying Saucer issue (1/51) 6.50 19.00 45.00
121-Origin retold 8.50 25.50 60.00
122-141,143-149: 138-Flying Saucer issue (11/52). 141-Pre-code horror story "The Hideous Head-Hunter" 6.50 19.00 45.00
142-Used in **POP**, pgs. 92,96 6.50 19.00 45.00
150-(Low distribution) 11.50 34.00 80.00
Bond Bread Giveaways-(24 pgs.; pocket size-7¼x3½"; paper cover): "...& the Stolen City ('48)," "The Boy Who Never Heard of Capt. Marvel," "Meets the Weatherman"-(1950)(reprint)
each.... 13.00 40.00 80.00
...Well Known Comics (1944; 12 pgs.; 8½x10½")-printed in red & in blue; soft-c; glued binding)-Bestmaid/Samuel Lowe Co. giveaway 16.00 48.00 96.00

NOTE: ***Swayze** a-12, 14, 15, 18, 19, 40; c-12, 15, 19.*

**CAPTAIN MARVEL ADVENTURES**
1945 (6x8") (Full color, paper cover)
Fawcett Publications (Wheaties Giveaway)

"Captain Marvel & the Threads of Life" plus 2 other stories (32pgs.) 17.00 51.00 120.00

NOTE: *All copies were taped at each corner to a box of Wheaties and are never found in Fine or Mint condition.*

**CAPTAIN MARVEL AND THE GOOD HUMOR MAN** (Movie)
1950
Fawcett Publications

nn-Partial photo-c w/Jack Carson & the Captain Marvel Club Boys 22.00 65.00 150.00

**CAPTAIN MARVEL AND THE LTS. OF SAFETY**
1950 - 1951 (3 issues - no No.'s)
Ebasco Services/Fawcett Publications

"Danger Flies a Kite"('50)," "Danger Takes to Climbing"('50), "Danger Smashes Street Lights"('51) 13.00 40.00 90.00

**CAPTAIN MARVEL COMIC STORY PAINT BOOK** (See Comic Story....)

**CAPTAIN MARVEL, JR.** (See Fawcett Miniatures, Marvel Family, Master Comics, Mighty Midget Comics, Shazam & Whiz Comics)

**CAPTAIN MARVEL, JR.**
Nov, 1942 - No. 119, June, 1953 (nn 34)
Fawcett Publications

1-Origin Capt. Marvel Jr. retold (Whiz No. 25); Capt. Nazi app. 129.00 385.00 900.00
2-Vs. Capt. Nazi; origin Capt. Nippon 64.00 193.00 450.00
3,4 47.00 140.00 325.00
5-Vs. Capt. Nazi 36.00 107.00 250.00
6-10: 8-Vs. Capt. Nazi. 9-Flag-c. 10-Hitler-c 29.00 86.00 200.00
11,12,15-Capt. Nazi app. 24.00 72.00 165.00
13,14,16-20: 14-X-Mas-c. 16-Capt. Marvel & Sivana x-over. 19-Capt. Nazi & Capt. Nippon app. 18.00 54.00 125.00
21-30: 25-Flag-c 11.50 34.00 80.00
31-33,36-40: 37-Infinity-c 7.00 21.00 54.00
35-#34 on inside; cover shows origin of Sivana Jr. which is not on inside. Evidently the cover to #35 was printed out of sequence and bound with contents to #34 7.00 21.00 50.00
41-50 5.00 15.00 35.00
51-70: 53-Atomic Bomb story 4.30 13.00 30.00
71-99,101-104: 104-Used in **POP**, pg. 89 3.60 11.00 25.00
100 4.30 13.00 30.00
105-114,116-119: 119-Electric chair-c 3.60 11.00 25.00
115-Injury to eye-c; Eyeball story w/injury-to-eye panels 5.70 17.00 40.00
...Well Known Comics (1944; 12 pgs.; 8½x10½")(Printed in blue;

*Captain Marvel Adventures #19, © FAW*

*Captain Marvel Adventures #142, © FAW*

*Captain Marvel, Jr. #53, © FAW*

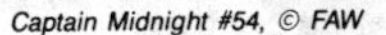
Captain Midnight #54, © FAW

Captain Savage #1, © MEG

Captain Science #5, © YM

| | Good | Fine | N-Mint |
|---|---|---|---|
| paper-c, glued binding)-Bestmaid/Samuel Lowe Co. giveaway | 12.00 | 36.00 | 72.00 |

NOTE: ***Mac Raboy*** *c-1-10, 12-14, 16, 19, 21, 22, 25, 27, 28, 30-33, 57 among others.*

**CAPTAIN MARVEL PRESENTS THE TERRIBLE FIVE**
Aug, 1966; V2#5, Sept, 1967 (No #2-4) (25 cents)
M. F. Enterprises

| | | | |
|---|---|---|---|
| 1 | 1.00 | 3.00 | 6.00 |
| V2#5-(Formerly Capt. Marvel) | .50 | 1.50 | 3.00 |

**CAPTAIN MARVEL'S FUN BOOK**
1944 (½" thick) (cardboard covers)
Samuel Lowe Co.

| | | | |
|---|---|---|---|
| nn-Puzzles, games, magic, etc.; infinity-c | 14.00 | 43.00 | 100.00 |

**CAPTAIN MARVEL SPECIAL EDITION** (See Special Edition)

**CAPTAIN MARVEL STORY BOOK**
Summer, 1946 - No. 4, Summer?, 1948
Fawcett Publications

| | | | |
|---|---|---|---|
| 1-½ text | 29.00 | 86.00 | 200.00 |
| 2-4 | 20.00 | 60.00 | 140.00 |

**CAPTAIN MARVEL THRILL BOOK** (Large-Size)
1941 (Black & White; color cover)
Fawcett Publications

| | Good | Fine | VF-NM |
|---|---|---|---|
| 1-Reprints from Whiz #8,10, & Special Edition #1 (Rare) | 135.00 | 405.00 | 950.00 |

NOTE: *Rarely found in Fine or Mint condition.*

**CAPTAIN MIDNIGHT** (Radio, films, TV) (See The Funnies & Popular Comics) (Becomes Sweethearts No. 68 on)
Sept, 1942 - No. 67, Fall, 1948 (#1-14: 68 pgs.)
Fawcett Publications

| | Good | Fine | N-Mint |
|---|---|---|---|
| 1-Origin Captain Midnight; Captain Marvel cameo on cover | 125.00 | 315.00 | 750.00 |
| 2 | 50.00 | 150.00 | 350.00 |
| 3-5 | 36.00 | 107.00 | 250.00 |
| 6-10: 9-Raboy-c. 10-Raboy Flag-c | 25.00 | 75.00 | 175.00 |
| 11-20: 11,17-Raboy-c | 16.50 | 50.00 | 115.00 |
| 21-30 | 13.00 | 40.00 | 90.00 |
| 31-40 | 10.00 | 30.00 | 70.00 |
| 41-59,61-67: 54-Sci/fi theme begins? | 7.00 | 21.00 | 50.00 |
| 60-Flying Saucer issue (2/48)-3rd of this theme; see Shadow Comics V7#10 & Boy Commandos #26 | 11.50 | 34.00 | 80.00 |

**CAPTAIN NICE** (TV)
Nov, 1967 (One Shot)
Gold Key

| | | | |
|---|---|---|---|
| 1(10211-711)-Photo-c | 3.00 | 9.00 | 21.00 |

**CAPTAIN N: THE GAME MASTER** (TV)
1990 - Present ($1.95, color, thick stock, coated-c)
Valiant Comics

| | | | |
|---|---|---|---|
| 1-6: 4,5,6-Layton-c | .35 | 1.00 | 2.00 |

**CAPTAIN PARAGON** (See Bill Black's Fun Comics)
Dec, 1983 - No. 4, 1985? (#2-4 are in color)
Americomics

| | | | |
|---|---|---|---|
| 1-4: 1-Ms. Victory begins (Intro/1st app.) | .25 | .75 | 1.50 |

**CAPTAIN PARAGON AND THE SENTINELS OF JUSTICE**
April, 1985 - No. 6, 1986? ($1.75, color)
AC Comics

| | | | |
|---|---|---|---|
| 1-6: 1-Capt. Paragon, Commando D., Nightveil, Scarlet Scorpion, Stardust & Atoman begin | .30 | .90 | 1.80 |

**CAPTAIN POWER AND THE SOLDIERS OF THE FUTURE** (TV)
Aug, 1988 - No. 2? ($2.00, color)
Continuity Comics

| | Good | Fine | N-Mint |
|---|---|---|---|
| 1,2: 1-Neal Adams-c/layouts/inks | .35 | 1.00 | 2.00 |

**CAPTAIN PUREHEART** (See Archie as. . .)

**CAPTAIN ROCKET**
November, 1951
P. L. Publ. (Canada)

| | | | |
|---|---|---|---|
| 1 | 17.00 | 51.00 | 120.00 |

**CAPT. SAVAGE AND HIS LEATHERNECK RAIDERS**
Jan, 1968 - No. 19, Mar, 1970 (See Sgt. Fury No. 10)
Marvel Comics Group (Animated Timely Features)

| | | | |
|---|---|---|---|
| 1-Sgt. Fury & Howlers cameo | 1.00 | 3.00 | 6.00 |
| 2-10: 2-Origin Hydra. 1-5,7-Ayers/Shores-a | .50 | 1.50 | 3.00 |
| 11-19 | .40 | 1.25 | 2.50 |

**CAPTAIN SCIENCE** (Fantastic No. 8 on)
Nov, 1950 - No. 7, Dec, 1951
Youthful Magazines

| | | | |
|---|---|---|---|
| 1-Wood-a; origin | 45.00 | 135.00 | 315.00 |
| 2 | 21.00 | 62.00 | 145.00 |
| 3,6,7; 3-Bondage c-swipe/Wings #94 | 17.00 | 51.00 | 120.00 |
| 4,5-Wood/Orlando-c/a(2) each | 39.00 | 118.00 | 275.00 |

NOTE: ***Fass*** *a-4. Bondage c-3, 6, 7.*

**CAPTAIN SILVER'S LOG OF SEA HOUND** (See Sea Hound)

**CAPTAIN SINDBAD** (Movie Adaptation) (See Movie Comics)

**CAPTAIN STEVE SAVAGE** (. . .& His Jet Fighters, No. 2-13)
1950 - No. 8, 1/53; No. 5, 9-10/54 - No. 13, 5-6/56
Avon Periodicals

| | | | |
|---|---|---|---|
| nn(1st series)-Wood art, 22 pgs. (titled ". . .Over Korea") | 22.00 | 65.00 | 150.00 |
| 1(4/51)-Reprints nn issue (Canadian) | 9.30 | 28.00 | 65.00 |
| 2-Kamen-a | 5.30 | 16.00 | 38.00 |
| 3-11 (#6, 9-10/54, last precode) | 3.15 | 9.50 | 22.00 |
| 12-Wood-a (6pgs.) | 6.50 | 19.00 | 45.00 |
| 13-Check, Lawrence-a | 4.30 | 13.00 | 30.00 |

NOTE: ***Kinstler*** *c-2-5, 7-9, 11.* ***Lawrence*** *a-8.* ***Ravielli*** *a-5, 9.*

| | | | |
|---|---|---|---|
| 5(9-10/54-2nd series)(Formerly Sensational Police Cases) | 3.50 | 10.50 | 24.00 |
| 6-Reprints nn issue; Wood-a | 5.30 | 16.00 | 38.00 |
| 7-13: 13 reprints cover to #8 (1st series) | 1.85 | 5.50 | 13.00 |

**CAPTAIN STONE** (See Holyoke One-Shot No. 10)

**CAPT. STORM** (Also see G. I. Combat #138)
May-June, 1964 - No. 18, Mar-Apr, 1967
National Periodical Publications

| | | | |
|---|---|---|---|
| 1-Origin | 1.15 | 3.50 | 8.00 |
| 2-18: 3,6,13-Kubert-a. 12-Kubert-c | .85 | 2.50 | 5.00 |

**CAPTAIN 3-D**
December, 1953
Harvey Publications

| | | | |
|---|---|---|---|
| 1-Kirby/Ditko-a | 4.00 | 12.00 | 28.00 |

**CAPTAIN THUNDER AND BLUE BOLT**
Sept, 1987 - No. 10, 1988 ($1.95, color)
Hero Comics

| | | | |
|---|---|---|---|
| 1-10: 1-Origin Blue Bolt. 3-Origin Capt. Thunder. 6-1st app. Wicket 8-Champions x-over | .35 | 1.00 | 2.00 |

**CAPTAIN TOOTSIE & THE SECRET LEGION** (Advs. of. .)(Also see Monte Hale #30,39 & Real Western Hero)
Oct, 1950 - No. 2, Dec, 1950
Toby Press

| | | | |
|---|---|---|---|
| 1-Not Beck-a | 12.00 | 36.00 | 85.00 |
| 2-The Rocketeer Patrol app.; not Beck-a | 7.00 | 21.00 | 50.00 |

**CAPTAIN VENTURE & THE LAND BENEATH THE SEA**
Oct, 1968 - No. 2, Oct, 1969 (See Space Family Robinson)
Gold Key

| | Good | Fine | N-Mint |
|---|---|---|---|
| 1,2: 1-r/Space Family Robinson serial; Spiegle-a in both | 2.65 | 8.00 | 18.00 |

**CAPTAIN VICTORY AND THE GALACTIC RANGERS**
Nov, 1981 - No. 13, Jan, 1984 ($1.00) (36-48 pgs.)
Pacific Comics (Sold only through comic shops)

| | Good | Fine | N-Mint |
|---|---|---|---|
| 1-13: 1-1st app. Mr. Mind. 3-N. Adams-a | | .50 | 1.00 |
| Special Issue #1(10/83)-Kirby c/a(p) | | .50 | 1.00 |

NOTE: *Conrad a-10, 11. **Ditko** a-6. **Kirby** a-1-13p; c-1-13.*

**CAPTAIN VIDEO** (TV) (See XMas Comics)
Feb, 1951 - No. 6, Dec, 1951 (No. 1,5,6-36pgs.; 2-4, 52pgs.)
Fawcett Publications

| | Good | Fine | N-Mint |
|---|---|---|---|
| 1-George Evans-a(2) | 40.00 | 120.00 | 280.00 |
| 2-Used in **SOTI**, pg. 382 | 30.00 | 90.00 | 210.00 |
| 3-6-All Evans-a | 25.00 | 75.00 | 175.00 |

NOTE: *Minor **Williamson** assist on most issues. Photo c-1, 5, 6; painted c-2-4.*

**CAPTAIN WILLIE SCHULTZ** (Also see Fightin' Army)
No. 76, Oct, 1985 - No. 77, Jan, 1986
Charlton Comics

| | Good | Fine | N-Mint |
|---|---|---|---|
| 76,77 | | .40 | .75 |

**CAPTAIN WIZARD COMICS** (Also see Meteor)
1946
Rural Home

| | Good | Fine | N-Mint |
|---|---|---|---|
| 1-Capt. Wizard dons new costume; Impossible Man, Race Wilkins app. | 10.00 | 30.00 | 70.00 |

**CARDINAL MINDSZENTY** (The Truth Behind the Trial of. . .)
1949 (24 pages; paper cover, in color)
Catechetical Guild Education Society

| | Good | Fine | N-Mint |
|---|---|---|---|
| nn-Anti-communism | 4.30 | 13.00 | 30.00 |
| Press Proof-(Very Rare)-(Full color, 7½x11¾", untrimmed) Only two known copies | | | 120.00 |
| Preview Copy (B&W, stapled), 18 pgs.; contains first 13 pgs. of Cardinal Mindszenty and was sent out as an advance promotion. Only one known copy | | | $150.00 - $200.00 |

NOTE: *Regular edition also printed in French. There was also a movie released in 1949 called "Guilty of Treason" which is a fact-based account of the trial and imprisonment of Cardinal Mindszenty by the Communist regime in Hungary.*

**CARE BEARS** (TV, Movie)(See Star Comics Magazine)
Nov, 1985 - No. 20, Jan, 1989 ($1.00 #11 on)
Star Comics/Marvel Comics No. 15 on

| | Good | Fine | N-Mint |
|---|---|---|---|
| 1-20: Post-a begins | | .40 | .80 |

**CAREER GIRL ROMANCES** (Formerly Three Nurses)
June, 1964 - No. 78, Dec, 1973
Charlton Comics

| | Good | Fine | N-Mint |
|---|---|---|---|
| V4#24-31,33-50 | .35 | 1.00 | 2.00 |
| 32-Elvis Presley, Hermans Hermits, Johnny Rivers line drawn-c | 2.15 | 6.50 | 15.00 |
| 51-78 | | .40 | .80 |

**CAR 54, WHERE ARE YOU?** (TV)
Mar-May, 1962 - No. 7, Sept-Nov, 1963; 1964 - 1965 (All photo-c)
Dell Publishing Co.

| | Good | Fine | N-Mint |
|---|---|---|---|
| 4-Color 1257(#1, 3-5/62) | 4.00 | 12.00 | 28.00 |
| 2(6-8/62)-7 | 2.30 | 7.00 | 16.00 |
| 2,3(10-12/64), 4(1-3/65)-Reprints #2,3,&4 of 1st series | 1.70 | 5.00 | 12.00 |

**CARNATION MALTED MILK GIVEAWAYS** (See Wisco)

**CARNIVAL COMICS**
1945
Harry 'A' Chesler/Pershing Square Publ. Co.

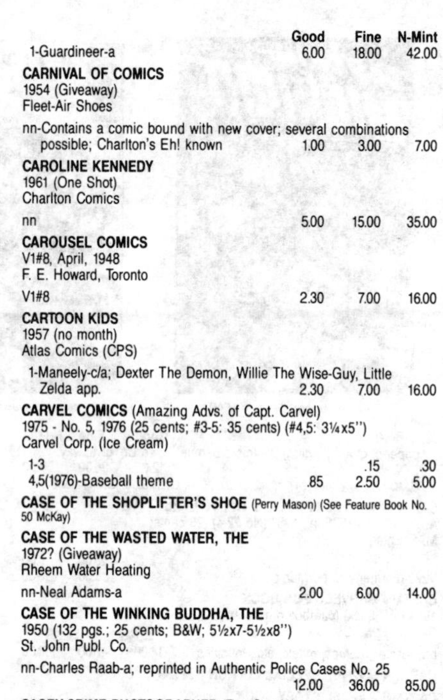

| | Good | Fine | N-Mint |
|---|---|---|---|
| 1-Guardineer-a | 6.00 | 18.00 | 42.00 |

**CARNIVAL OF COMICS**
1954 (Giveaway)
Fleet-Air Shoes

| | Good | Fine | N-Mint |
|---|---|---|---|
| nn-Contains a comic bound with new cover; several combinations possible; Charlton's Eh! known | 1.00 | 3.00 | 7.00 |

**CAROLINE KENNEDY**
1961 (One Shot)
Charlton Comics

| | Good | Fine | N-Mint |
|---|---|---|---|
| nn | 5.00 | 15.00 | 35.00 |

**CAROUSEL COMICS**
V1#8, April, 1948
F. E. Howard, Toronto

| | Good | Fine | N-Mint |
|---|---|---|---|
| V1#8 | 2.30 | 7.00 | 16.00 |

**CARTOON KIDS**
1957 (no month)
Atlas Comics (CPS)

| | Good | Fine | N-Mint |
|---|---|---|---|
| 1-Maneely-c/a; Dexter The Demon, Willie The Wise-Guy, Little Zelda app. | 2.30 | 7.00 | 16.00 |

**CARVEL COMICS** (Amazing Advs. of Capt. Carvel)
1975 - No. 5, 1976 (25 cents; #3-5: 35 cents) (#4,5: 3¼x5")
Carvel Corp. (Ice Cream)

| | Good | Fine | N-Mint |
|---|---|---|---|
| 1-3 | | .15 | .30 |
| 4,5(1976)-Baseball theme | .85 | 2.50 | 5.00 |

**CASE OF THE SHOPLIFTER'S SHOE** (Perry Mason) (See Feature Book No. 50 McKay)

**CASE OF THE WASTED WATER, THE**
1972? (Giveaway)
Rheem Water Heating

| | Good | Fine | N-Mint |
|---|---|---|---|
| nn-Neal Adams-a | 2.00 | 6.00 | 14.00 |

**CASE OF THE WINKING BUDDHA, THE**
1950 (132 pgs.; 25 cents; B&W; 5½x7-5½x8")
St. John Publ. Co.

| | Good | Fine | N-Mint |
|---|---|---|---|
| nn-Charles Raab-a; reprinted in Authentic Police Cases No. 25 | 12.00 | 36.00 | 85.00 |

**CASEY-CRIME PHOTOGRAPHER** (Two-Gun Western No. 5 on)
Aug, 1949 - No. 4, Feb, 1950 (Radio)
Marvel Comics (BFP)

| | Good | Fine | N-Mint |
|---|---|---|---|
| 1-Photo-c; 52 pgs. | 7.00 | 21.00 | 50.00 |
| 2-4: Photo-c | 5.00 | 15.00 | 35.00 |

**CASEY JONES** (See 4-Color No. 915)

**CASPER AND. . .**
1987 - Present (.75-$1.00, all reprints)
Harvey Comics

| | Good | Fine | N-Mint |
|---|---|---|---|
| 1-10: 1-Ghostly Trio. 2-Spooky; begin $1.00-c. 3-Wendy. 4-Nightmare. 5-Ghostly Trio. 6-Spooky. 7-Wendy. (titles rotate) | | .50 | 1.00 |

**CASPER AND NIGHTMARE** (See Harvey Hits No. 37, 45, 52, 56, 59, 62, 65, 68, 71, 75)

**CASPER AND NIGHTMARE** (Nightmare & Casper No. 1-5) (25 cents)
No. 6, 11/64 - No. 44, 10/73; No. 45, 6/74 - No. 46, 8/74
Harvey Publications

| | Good | Fine | N-Mint |
|---|---|---|---|
| 6: 68 pg. Giants begin, ends #32 | 2.00 | 6.00 | 12.00 |
| 7-10 | 1.00 | 3.00 | 6.00 |
| 11-20 | .50 | 1.50 | 3.00 |
| 21-32 | .35 | 1.00 | 2.00 |
| 33-37: 52 pg. Giants | .35 | 1.00 | 2.00 |
| 38-46: regular size | .35 | 1.00 | 2.00 |

NOTE: *Many issues contain reprints.*

*Capt. Victory & the Galactic Rangers #1, © PC*

*Cartoon Kids #1, © MEG*

*Casey-Crime Photographer #4, © MEG*

*Casper, the Friendly. . . #1 ('49), © Paramount*

*Casper, the Friendly Ghost #13, © Paramount*

*The Cat #1, © MEG*

**CASPER AND SPOOKY** (See Harvey Hits No. 20)
Oct, 1972 - No. 7, Oct, 1973
Harvey Publications

| | Good | Fine | N-Mint |
|---|---|---|---|
| 1 | .85 | 2.50 | 5.00 |
| 2-7 | .35 | 1.00 | 2.00 |

**CASPER AND THE GHOSTLY TRIO**
Nov, 1972 - No. 7, Nov, 1973
Harvey Publications

| | Good | Fine | N-Mint |
|---|---|---|---|
| 1 | .85 | 2.50 | 5.00 |
| 2-7 | .35 | 1.00 | 2.00 |

**CASPER AND WENDY**
Sept, 1972 - No. 8, Nov, 1973
Harvey Publications

| | Good | Fine | N-Mint |
|---|---|---|---|
| 1: 52 pg. Giant | .85 | 2.50 | 5.00 |
| 2-8 | .35 | 1.00 | 2.00 |

**CASPER CAT** (See Dopey Duck)
1958; 1963
I. W. Enterprises/Super

| | Good | Fine | N-Mint |
|---|---|---|---|
| 1,7-Reprint, Super No. 14('63) | .50 | 1.50 | 3.00 |

**CASPER DIGEST** (. . . Magazine #?; . . .Halloween Digest #8, 10)
Oct, 1986 - Present ($1.25-$1.75, digest-size)
Harvey Publications

| | Good | Fine | N-Mint |
|---|---|---|---|
| 1-20: 8,10-. . .Halloween Digest | .25 | .75 | 1.50 |

**CASPER DIGEST STORIES**
Feb, 1980 - No. 4, Nov, 1980 (95 cents; 132 pgs.; digest size)
Harvey Publications

| | Good | Fine | N-Mint |
|---|---|---|---|
| 1 | .50 | 1.50 | 3.00 |
| 2-4 | .35 | 1.00 | 2.00 |

**CASPER DIGEST WINNERS**
April, 1980 - No. 3, Sept, 1980 (95 cents; 132 pgs.; digest size)
Harvey Publications

| | Good | Fine | N-Mint |
|---|---|---|---|
| 1 | .35 | 1.00 | 2.00 |
| 2,3 | .25 | .75 | 1.50 |

**CASPER HALLOWEEN TRICK OR TREAT**
January, 1976 (52 pgs.)
Harvey Publications

| | Good | Fine | N-Mint |
|---|---|---|---|
| 1 | .35 | 1.00 | 2.00 |

**CASPER IN SPACE** (Formerly Casper Spaceship)
No. 6, June, 1973 - No. 8, Oct, 1973
Harvey Publications

| | Good | Fine | N-Mint |
|---|---|---|---|
| 6-8 | .35 | 1.00 | 2.00 |

**CASPER IN 3-D** (See Blackthorne 3-D Series #57)

**CASPER'S GHOSTLAND**
Winter, 1958-59 - No. 97, 12/77; No. 98, 12/79 (25 cents)
Harvey Publications

| | Good | Fine | N-Mint |
|---|---|---|---|
| 1: 68 pgs. begin, ends #61 | 8.50 | 25.50 | 60.00 |
| 2 | 4.30 | 13.00 | 30.00 |
| 3-10 | 2.85 | 8.50 | 20.00 |
| 11-20: 13-X-Mas-c | 1.70 | 5.00 | 12.00 |
| 21-40 | 1.15 | 3.50 | 8.00 |
| 41-61: Last 68 pg. issue | .85 | 2.60 | 6.00 |
| 62-77: All 52 pgs. | .50 | 1.50 | 3.00 |
| 78-98: 94-X-Mas-c | .35 | 1.00 | 2.00 |

NOTE: *Most issues contain reprints.*

**CASPER SPACESHIP** (Casper in Space No. 6 on)
Aug, 1972 - No. 5, April, 1973
Harvey Publications

| | Good | Fine | N-Mint |
|---|---|---|---|
| 1: 52 pg. Giant | .85 | 2.50 | 5.00 |
| 2-5 | .35 | 1.00 | 2.00 |

**CASPER STRANGE GHOST STORIES**
October, 1974 - No. 14, Jan, 1977 (All 52 pgs.)
Harvey Publications

| | Good | Fine | N-Mint |
|---|---|---|---|
| 1 | .70 | 2.00 | 4.00 |
| 2-14 | .35 | 1.00 | 2.00 |

**CASPER, THE FRIENDLY GHOST** (See America's Best TV Comics, Famous TV Funday Funnies, The Friendly Ghost. . ., Nightmare &. . ., Richie Rich, Tastee-Freez & Treasury of Comics)

**CASPER, THE FRIENDLY GHOST** (Becomes Harvey Comics Hits No. 61 (No. 6), and then continued with Harvey issue No. 7)
9/49 - No. 3, 8/50; 9/50 - No. 5, 5/51
St. John Publishing Co.

| | Good | Fine | N-Mint |
|---|---|---|---|
| 1(1949)-Origin & 1st app. Baby Huey | 54.00 | 160.00 | 375.00 |
| 2,3 | 30.00 | 90.00 | 210.00 |
| 1(9/50) | 37.00 | 110.00 | 260.00 |
| 2-5 | 24.00 | 70.00 | 165.00 |

**CASPER, THE FRIENDLY GHOST** (Paramount Picture Star. . .)
No. 7, Dec, 1952 - No 70, July, 1958
Harvey Publications (Family Comics)

Note: No. 6 is Harvey Comics Hits No. 61 (10/52)

| | Good | Fine | N-Mint |
|---|---|---|---|
| 7-Baby Huey begins, ends #9 | 17.00 | 51.00 | 120.00 |
| 8-10: 10-Spooky begins(1st app.), ends #70? | 8.50 | 25.50 | 60.00 |
| 11-19: 19-1st app. Nightmare (4/54) | 5.70 | 17.00 | 40.00 |
| 20-Wendy the Witch begins (1st app., 5/54) | 6.50 | 19.50 | 45.00 |
| 21-30: 24-Infinity-c | 4.50 | 14.00 | 32.00 |
| 31-40 | 3.75 | 11.25 | 26.00 |
| 41-50 | 3.00 | 9.00 | 21.00 |
| 51-70 | 2.30 | 7.00 | 16.00 |
| American Dental Association (Giveaways): | | | |
| . . .'s Dental Health Activity Book-1977 | .30 | .80 | 1.60 |
| . . .Presents Space Age Dentistry-1972 | .40 | 1.20 | 2.40 |
| . . ., His Den, & Their Dentist Fight the Tooth Demons-1974 | .40 | 1.20 | 2.40 |

**CASPER THE FRIENDLY GHOST** (Formerly The Friendly Ghost. . .)
No. 254, July, 1990 - No. 260, Jan, 1991 ($1.00, color)
Harvey Comics

| | Good | Fine | N-Mint |
|---|---|---|---|
| 254-260 | | .50 | 1.00 |

**CASPER T.V. SHOWTIME**
Jan, 1980 - No. 5, Oct, 1980
Harvey Comics

| | Good | Fine | N-Mint |
|---|---|---|---|
| 1 | .35 | 1.00 | 2.00 |
| 2-5 | | .50 | 1.00 |

**CASSETTE BOOKS**
(Classics Illustrated)
1984 (48 pgs, b&w comic with cassette tape)
Cassette Book Co./I.P.S. Publ.

Note: This series was illegal. The artwork was illegally obtained, and the Classics Illustrated copyright owner, Twin Circle Publ. sued to get an injunction to prevent the continued sale of this series. Many C.I. collectors obtained copies before the 1987 injunction, but now they are already scarce. Here again the market is just developing, but sealed mint copies of comic and tape should be worth at least $25.

1001 (Cl#1-A2)New-PC 1002(Cl#3-A2)Cl-PC 1003(Cl#13-A2)Cl-PC
1004(Cl#25)Cl-LDC 1005(Cl#10-A2)New-PC 1006(Cl#64)Cl-LDC

**CASTILIAN** (See Movie Classics)

**CAT, T.H.E.** (TV) (See T.H.E. Cat)

**CAT, THE** (See Movie Classics)

**CAT, THE**
Nov, 1972 - No. 4, June, 1973
Marvel Comics Group

| | Good | Fine | N-Mint |
|---|---|---|---|
| 1-Origin The Cat; Mooney-a(i); Wood-c(i)/a(i) | 1.00 | 3.00 | 7.00 |
| 2,3: 2-Mooney-a(i). 3-Everett inks | .85 | 2.50 | 5.00 |
| 4-Starlin/Weiss-a(p) | .85 | 2.50 | 5.00 |

**CAT & MOUSE**
Dec, 1988 ($1.75, color w/part B&W)
EF Graphics (Silverline)

| | Good | Fine | N-Mint |
|---|---|---|---|
| 1-1st printing (12/88, 32 pgs.) | .30 | .90 | 1.75 |
| 1-2nd printing (5/89, 36 pgs.) | .30 | .90 | 1.75 |

**CAT FROM OUTER SPACE** (See Walt Disney Showcase #46)

**CATHOLIC COMICS** (See Heroes All Catholic . . .)
June, 1946 - V3No.10, July, 1949
Catholic Publications

| | Good | Fine | N-Mint |
|---|---|---|---|
| 1 | 10.00 | 30.00 | 70.00 |
| 2 | 5.00 | 15.00 | 35.00 |
| 3-13(7/47) | 3.60 | 11.00 | 25.00 |
| V2#1-10 | 2.00 | 6.00 | 14.00 |
| V3#1-10: Reprints 10-part Treasure Island serial from Target V2#2-11 (See Key Comics #5) | 2.65 | 8.00 | 18.00 |

**CATHOLIC PICTORIAL**
1947
Catholic Guild

| | Good | Fine | N-Mint |
|---|---|---|---|
| 1-Toth-a(2) (Rare) | 17.00 | 51.00 | 120.00 |

**CATMAN COMICS** (Crash No. 1-5)
5/41 - No. 17, 1/43; No. 18, 7/43 - No. 22, 12/43; No. 23, 3/44 - No. 26, 11/44; No. 27, 4/45 - No. 30, 12/45; No. 31, 6/46 - No. 32, 8/46
Holyoke Publishing Co./Continental Magazines V2#12, 7/44 on

| | Good | Fine | N-Mint |
|---|---|---|---|
| 1(V1#6)-Origin The Deacon & Sidekick Mickey, Dr. Diamond & Rag-Man; The Black Widow app.; The Catman by Chas. Quinlan & Blaze Baylor begin | 71.00 | 215.00 | 500.00 |
| 2(V1#7) | 34.00 | 100.00 | 235.00 |
| 3(V1#8), 4(V1#9): 3-The Pied Piper begins | 27.00 | 80.00 | 185.00 |
| 5(V2#10)-Origin Kitten; The Hood begins (c-redated), 6,7(V2#11,12) | 22.00 | 65.00 | 150.00 |
| 8(V2#13,3/42)-Origin Little Leaders; Volton by Kubert begins (his 1st comic book work) | 29.00 | 88.00 | 205.00 |
| 9(V2#14) | 19.00 | 58.00 | 135.00 |
| 10(V2#15)-Origin Blackout; Phantom Falcon begins | 19.00 | 58.00 | 135.00 |
| 11(V3#1)-Kubert-a | 19.00 | 58.00 | 135.00 |
| 12(V3#2) - 15, 17, 18(V3#8, 7/43) | 14.00 | 43.00 | 100.00 |
| 16 (V3#5)-Hitler, Tojo, Mussolini, Stalin-c | 17.00 | 51.00 | 120.00 |
| 19 (V2#6)-Hitler, Tojo, Mussolini-c | 17.00 | 51.00 | 120.00 |
| 20(V2#7) - 23(V2#10, 3/44) | 14.00 | 43.00 | 100.00 |
| nn(V3#13, 5/44)-Rico-a; Schomburg bondage-c | 13.00 | 40.00 | 90.00 |
| nn(V2#12, 7/44) | 13.00 | 40.00 | 90.00 |
| nn(V3#1, 9/44)-Origin The Golden Archer; Leatherface app.; | 13.00 | 40.00 | 90.00 |
| nn(V3#2, 11/44)-L. B. Cole-c | 18.00 | 54.00 | 125.00 |
| 27-Origin Kitten retold; L. B. Cole Flag-c | 19.00 | 58.00 | 135.00 |
| 28-Catman learns Kitten's I.D.; Dr. Macabre, Deacon app.; L. B. Cole-c/a | 22.00 | 65.00 | 150.00 |
| 29-32-L. B. Cole-c; bondage-#30 | 18.00 | 54.00 | 125.00 |

NOTE: ***Fuje*** *a-11, 29(3), 30.* ***Palais*** *a-11, 29(2), 30.* ***Rico*** *a-11(2).*

**CAT TALES** (3-D)
April, 1989 ($2.95)
Eternity Comics

| | Good | Fine | N-Mint |
|---|---|---|---|
| 1-Felix the Cat-r in 3-D | .50 | 1.50 | 3.00 |

**CATWOMAN** (Also see Action Comics Weekly #611-614 & Batman)
Feb, 1989 - No. 4, May, 1989 ($1.50, mini-series, mature readers)
DC Comics

| | Good | Fine | N-Mint |
|---|---|---|---|
| 1 | 2.50 | 7.50 | 15.00 |
| 2 | 1.50 | 4.50 | 9.00 |
| 3,4: 3-Batman cameo. 4-Batman app. | .85 | 2.50 | 5.00 |

**CAUGHT**
Aug, 1956 - No. 5, April, 1957
Atlas Comics (VPI)

| | Good | Fine | N-Mint |
|---|---|---|---|
| 1 | 5.70 | 17.00 | 40.00 |
| 2,4: 4-Severin-c; Maneely-a | 2.65 | 8.00 | 18.00 |
| 3-Maneely, Pakula, Torres-a | 3.15 | 9.50 | 22.00 |
| 5-Crandall, Krigstein-a; Severin-c | 4.00 | 12.00 | 28.00 |

**CAVALIER COMICS**
1945; 1952 (Early DC reprints)
A. W. Nugent Publ. Co.

| | Good | Fine | N-Mint |
|---|---|---|---|
| 2(1945)-Speed Saunders, Fang Gow | 8.00 | 24.00 | 56.00 |
| 2(1952) | 3.70 | 11.00 | 26.00 |

**CAVE GIRL** (Also see Africa)
No. 11, 1953 - No. 14, 1954
Magazine Enterprises

| | Good | Fine | N-Mint |
|---|---|---|---|
| 11(A-1 82)-Origin; all Cave Girl stories | 23.00 | 70.00 | 160.00 |
| 12(A-1 96), 13(A-1 116), 14(A-1 125)-Thunda by Powell in each | 17.00 | 51.00 | 120.00 |

NOTE: ***Powell*** *c/a in all.*

**CAVE GIRL**
1988 ($2.95, 44 pgs., 16 pgs. of color, rest B&W)
AC Comics

| | Good | Fine | N-Mint |
|---|---|---|---|
| 1-Powell-r/Cave Girl #11; Nyoka photo back-c from movie; Powell/Bill Black-c; Special Limited Edition on-c | .50 | 1.50 | 3.00 |

**CAVE KIDS** (TV)
Feb, 1963 - No. 16, Mar, 1967 (Hanna-Barbera)
Gold Key

| | Good | Fine | N-Mint |
|---|---|---|---|
| 1 | 1.70 | 5.00 | 12.00 |
| 2-5 | 1.15 | 3.50 | 8.00 |
| 6-16: 7-Pebbles & Bamm Bamm app. | .70 | 2.00 | 5.00 |

**CENTURION OF ANCIENT ROME, THE**
1958 (no month listed) (36 pages) (B&W)
Zondervan Publishing House

| | Good | Fine | N-Mint |
|---|---|---|---|
| (Rare) All by Jay Disbrow Estimated Value. . . . | | | 200.00 |

**CENTURIONS**
June, 1987 - No. 4, Sept, 1987 (75 cents, mini-series)
DC Comics

| | Good | Fine | N-Mint |
|---|---|---|---|
| 1-4 | | .40 | .80 |

**CENTURY OF COMICS**
1933 (100 pages) (Probably the 3rd comic book)
Eastern Color Printing Co.

Bought by Wheatena, Milk-O-Malt, John Wanamaker, Kinney Shoe Stores, & others to be used as premiums and radio giveaways. No publisher listed.

| | Good | Fine | N-Mint |
|---|---|---|---|
| nn-Mutt & Jeff, Joe Palooka, etc. reprints | 500.00 | 1250.00 | 3000.00 |

**CEREBUS BI-WEEKLY**
Dec. 2, 1988 - No. 26, Nov. 11, 1989 ($1.25, B&W)
Aardvark-Vanaheim

| | Good | Fine | N-Mint |
|---|---|---|---|
| 1-26: Reprints Cerebus #1-26 | | .60 | 1.30 |

**CEREBUS: HIGH SOCIETY**
Jan?, 1990 - No. 25 ($1.70, B&W)
Aardvark-Vanaheim

| | Good | Fine | N-Mint |
|---|---|---|---|
| 1-20: r/Cerebus #26-45 | .30 | .85 | 1.70 |

**CEREBUS JAM**
Apr, 1985
Aardvark-Vanaheim

| | Good | Fine | N-Mint |
|---|---|---|---|
| 1-Eisner, Austin-a | .60 | 1.75 | 3.50 |

**CEREBUS THE AARDVARK** (See A-V in 3-D & Nucleus)
Dec, 1977 - Present ($1.70-$2.00, B&W)
Aardvark-Vanaheim

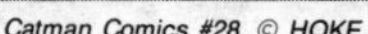
*Catman Comics #28, © HOKE*

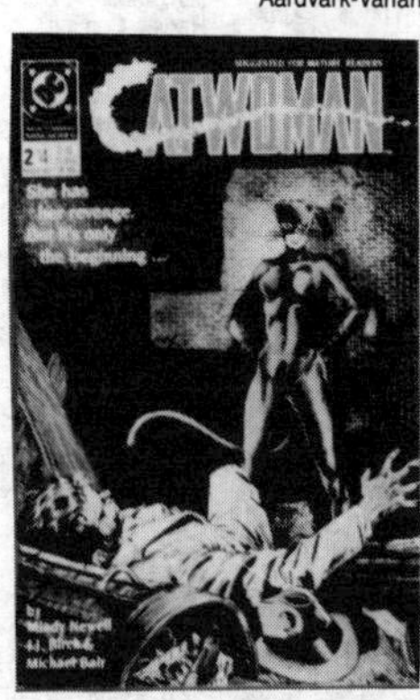

*Catwoman #2, © DC*

*Centurion of Ancient Rome nn, © Zondervan*

*Cerebus the Aardvark #3, © A-V*

*Challengers of the Unknown #43, © DC*

*Chamber of Chills #7, © HARV*

| | Good | Fine | N-Mint |
|---|---|---|---|
| 1-2000 print run; most copies poorly printed | 50.00 | 150.00 | 300.00 |

**Note:** There is a counterfeit version known to exist. It can be distinguished from the original in the following ways: inside cover is glossy instead of flat, black background on the front cover is blotted or spotty.

| | Good | Fine | N-Mint |
|---|---|---|---|
| 2-Dave Sim art in all | 22.50 | 67.50 | 135.00 |
| 3-Origin Red Sophia | 18.30 | 55.00 | 110.00 |
| 4-Origin Elrod the Albino | 12.50 | 37.50 | 75.00 |
| 5,6 | 10.00 | 30.00 | 60.00 |
| 7-10 | 6.70 | 20.00 | 40.00 |
| 11,12: 11-Origin Capt. Coachroach | 7.50 | 22.50 | 45.00 |
| 13-15: 14-Origin Lord Julius | 4.15 | 12.50 | 25.00 |
| 16-20 | 2.50 | 7.50 | 15.00 |
| 21-Scarcer | 11.70 | 35.00 | 70.00 |
| 22-Low distribution; no cover price | 3.35 | 10.00 | 20.00 |
| 23-28: 26-High Society storyline begins | 1.85 | 5.50 | 11.00 |
| 29,30 | 2.15 | 6.50 | 13.00 |
| 31-Origin Moonroach | 2.50 | 7.50 | 15.00 |
| 32-40 | 1.00 | 3.00 | 6.00 |
| 41-50,52: 52-Cutey Bunny app. | .85 | 2.50 | 5.00 |
| 51-Not reprinted; Cutey Bunny app. | 3.00 | 9.00 | 18.00 |
| 53-Intro. Wolveroach (cameo) | 1.15 | 3.50 | 7.00 |
| 54-Wolveroach 1st full story | 1.70 | 5.00 | 10.00 |
| 55,56-Wolveroach app. | 1.15 | 3.50 | 7.00 |
| 57-60 | .60 | 1.75 | 3.50 |
| 61,62: Flaming Carrot app. | .85 | 2.50 | 5.00 |
| 63-68 | .70 | 2.00 | 4.00 |
| 69-75 | .55 | 1.60 | 3.20 |
| 76-79 | .50 | 1.50 | 3.00 |
| 80-85 | .45 | 1.25 | 2.50 |
| 86-136: 104-Flaming Carrot app. 112/113-Double issue | .35 | 1.00 | 2.00 |
| 137-142: 137-Begin $2.25-c | .40 | 1.15 | 2.30 |

**CHALLENGE OF THE UNKNOWN** (Formerly Love Experiences)
No. 6, Sept, 1950 (See Web Of Mystery No. 19)
Ace Magazines

| | Good | Fine | N-Mint |
|---|---|---|---|
| 6-'Villa of the Vampire' used in N.Y. Joint Legislative Comm. Publ; Sekowsky-a | 9.00 | 27.00 | 62.00 |

**CHALLENGER, THE**
1945 - No. 4, Oct-Dec, 1946
Interfaith Publications/T.C. Comics

| | Good | Fine | N-Mint |
|---|---|---|---|
| nn; nd; 32 pgs.; Origin the Challenger Club; Anti-Fascist with funny animal filler | 14.00 | 43.00 | 100.00 |
| 2-4-Kubert-a; 4-Fuje-a | 13.00 | 40.00 | 90.00 |

**CHALLENGERS OF THE UNKNOWN** (See Showcase #6, 7, 11, 12, Super DC Giant, and Super Team Family)
4-5/58 - No. 77, 12-1/70-71; No. 78, 2/73 - No. 80, 6-7/73;
No. 81, 6-7/77 - No. 87, 6-7/78
National Periodical Publications/DC Comics

| | Good | Fine | N-Mint |
|---|---|---|---|
| 1-Kirby/Stein-a(2) | 75.00 | 225.00 | 525.00 |
| 2-Kirby/Stein-a(2) | 43.00 | 130.00 | 300.00 |
| 3-Kirby/Stein-a(2) | 33.00 | 100.00 | 230.00 |
| 4-8-Kirby/Wood-a plus c-#8 | 27.00 | 81.00 | 190.00 |
| 9,10 | 13.50 | 41.00 | 95.00 |
| 11-15: 14-Origin Multi-Man | 8.50 | 25.50 | 60.00 |
| 16-22: 18-Intro. Cosmo, the Challengers Spacepet. 22-Last 10 cent issue | 6.50 | 19.00 | 45.00 |
| 23-30 | 3.60 | 11.00 | 25.00 |
| 31-Retells origin of the Challengers | 2.85 | 8.50 | 20.00 |
| 32-40 | 1.70 | 5.00 | 12.00 |
| 41-60: 43-New look begins. 48-Doom Patrol app. 49-Intro. Challenger Corps. 51-Sea Devils app. 55-Death of Red Ryan. 60-Red Ryan returns | 1.00 | 3.00 | 6.00 |
| 61-73,75-77: 64,65-Kirby origin-r, parts 1 & 2. 69-1st app. Corinna | .50 | 1.50 | 3.00 |
| 74-Deadman by Tuska/N. Adams | 1.30 | 4.00 | 8.00 |
| 78-87: 82-Swamp Thing begins | .35 | 1.00 | 2.00 |

NOTE: ***N. Adams** c-67, 68, 70, 72, 74i, 81i. **Buckler** c-83-86p. **Giffen** a-83-87p. **Kirby** a-75-80r; c-75, 77, 78. **Kubert** c-64, 66, 69, 76, 79. **Nasser** c/a-81p, 82p. **Tuska** a-73. **Wood** r-76.*

**CHALLENGE TO THE WORLD**
1951 (36 pages) (10 cents)
Catechetical Guild

| | Good | Fine | N-Mint |
|---|---|---|---|
| nn | 2.30 | 7.00 | 16.00 |

**CHAMBER OF CHILLS** (. . .of Clues No. 27 on)
No. 21, June, 1951 - No. 26, Dec, 1954
Harvey Publications/Witches Tales

| | Good | Fine | N-Mint |
|---|---|---|---|
| 21 (#1) | 11.50 | 34.00 | 80.00 |
| 22,24 | 6.00 | 18.00 | 42.00 |
| 23-Excessive violence; eyes torn out | 8.00 | 24.00 | 56.00 |
| 5(2/52)-Decapitation, acid in face scene | 8.00 | 24.00 | 56.00 |
| 6-Woman melted alive | 7.00 | 21.00 | 50.00 |
| 7-Used in **SOTI**, pg. 389; decapitation/severed head panels | 5.70 | 17.00 | 40.00 |
| 8-10: 8-Decapitation panels | 5.00 | 15.00 | 35.00 |
| 11,12,14 | 3.70 | 11.00 | 26.00 |
| 13,15-24-Nostrand-a in all; c-#20. 13,21-Decapitation panels. 18-Atom bomb panels | 6.50 | 19.00 | 45.00 |
| 25,26 | 3.15 | 9.50 | 22.00 |

NOTE: *About half the issues contain bondage, torture, sadism, perversion, gore, cannabalism, eyes ripped out, acid in face, etc. **Kremer** a-12, 17. **Palais** a-21(1), 23. **Nostrand/Powell** a-13, 15, 16. **Powell** a-21, 23, 24('51), 5-8, 11, 13, 18-21, 23-25. Bondage-c-21, 24('51), 7. 25 r-No. 5; 26 r-No. 9.*

**CHAMBER OF CHILLS**
Nov, 1972 - No. 25, Nov, 1976
Marvel Comics Group

| | Good | Fine | N-Mint |
|---|---|---|---|
| 1-Harlan Ellison adaptation | .35 | 1.00 | 2.00 |
| 2-25 | | .50 | 1.00 |

NOTE: ***Adkins** a-1i, 2i. **Brunner** a-2-4; c-4. **Ditko** r-14, 16, 19, 23, 24. **Everett** a-3i, 11r, 21r. **Heath** a-1r. **Gil Kane** c-2p. **Powell** a-13r. **Russell** a-1p, 2p. **Williamson/Mayo** a-13r. **Robert E. Howard** horror story adaptation-2, 3.*

**CHAMBER OF CLUES** (Formerly Chamber of Chills)
No. 27, Feb, 1955 - No. 28, April, 1955
Harvey Publications

| | Good | Fine | N-Mint |
|---|---|---|---|
| 27-Kerry Drake r-/#19; Powell-a; last pre-code | 4.50 | 14.00 | 32.00 |
| 28-Kerry Drake | 2.65 | 8.00 | 18.00 |

**CHAMBER OF DARKNESS** (Monsters on the Prowl #9 on)
Oct, 1969 - No. 8, Dec, 1970
Marvel Comics Group

| | Good | Fine | N-Mint |
|---|---|---|---|
| 1-Buscema-a(p) | 1.50 | 4.50 | 10.00 |
| 2-Neal Adams script | .70 | 2.00 | 4.00 |
| 3-Smith, Buscema-a | .85 | 2.50 | 5.00 |
| 4-A Conanesque tryout by Smith; reprinted in Conan #16 | 2.85 | 8.50 | 20.00 |
| 5,6,8: 5-H.P. Lovecraft adaptation | .50 | 1.50 | 3.00 |
| 7-Wrightson-c/a, 7pgs. (his 1st work at Marvel); Wrightson draws himself in 1st & last panels | 1.15 | 3.50 | 8.00 |
| 1-(1/72; 25 cent Special) | .85 | 2.50 | 5.00 |

NOTE: ***Adkins/Everett** a-8. **Craig** a-5. **Ditko** a-6-8r. **Kirby** a(p)-4, 5, 7. **Kirby/Everett** c-5. **Severin/Everett** c-6. **Wrightson** c-7, 8.*

**CHAMP COMICS** (Formerly Champion No. 1-10)
No. 11, Oct, 1940 - No. 29, March, 1944
Worth Publ. Co./Champ Publ./Family Comics(Harvey Publ.)

| | Good | Fine | N-Mint |
|---|---|---|---|
| 11-Human Meteor cont'd. | 36.00 | 107.00 | 250.00 |
| 12-20: 14,15-Crandall-c. 19-The Wasp app. 20-The Green Ghost app. | 27.00 | 81.00 | 190.00 |
| 21-29: 22-The White Mask app. 23-Flag-c | 23.00 | 70.00 | 160.00 |

**CHAMPION** (See Gene Autry's. . .)

**CHAMPION COMICS** (Champ No. 11 on)
No. 2, Dec, 1939 - No. 10, Aug, 1940 (no No.1)
Worth Publ. Co.(Harvey Publications)

| | Good | Fine | N-Mint |
|---|---|---|---|
| 2-The Champ, The Blazing Scarab, Neptina, Liberty Lads, Jungle-man, Bill Handy, Swingtime Sweetie begin | 54.00 | 160.00 | 375.00 |
| 3-7: 7-The Human Meteor begins? | 27.00 | 81.00 | 190.00 |
| 8-10-Kirbyish-c; bondage #10 | 31.00 | 92.00 | 215.00 |

**CHAMPIONS, THE**
October, 1975 - No. 17, Jan, 1978
Marvel Comics Group

| | | | |
|---|---|---|---|
| 1-The Angel, Black Widow, Ghost Rider, Hercules, Ice Man (The Champions) begin w/origin; Kane/Adkins-c; Venus x-over | 1.00 | 3.00 | 7.00 |
| 2-10,16: 2,3-Venus x-over | .50 | 1.50 | 3.00 |
| 11-15,17-Byrne-a | .85 | 2.50 | 5.00 |

NOTE: *Buckler/Adkins c-3. Kane/Layton c-11. Tuska a-3p, 4p, 6p.*

**CHAMPIONS**
June, 1986 - No. 6, Feb, 1987 (Limited series)(Based on game)
Eclipse Comics

| | | | |
|---|---|---|---|
| 1-6: 1-Intro Flare (origin #5) | .25 | .75 | 1.50 |

**CHAMPIONS** (Also see The League of Champions)
Sept, 1987 - No. 12, 1989? ($1.95, color)
Hero Comics

| | | | |
|---|---|---|---|
| 1-12: 1-Intro The Marksman & The Rose. 14-Origin Malice | .35 | 1.00 | 2.00 |
| Annual 1(1988, $2.75, 52 pgs.)-Origin of Giant | .45 | 1.40 | 2.75 |

**CHAMPION SPORTS**
Oct-Nov, 1973 - No. 3, Feb-Mar, 1974
National Periodical Publications

| | | | |
|---|---|---|---|
| 1-3 | | .40 | .80 |

**CHAOS** (See The Crusaders)

**CHARLIE CHAN** (See Columbia Comics, Feature Comics & The New Advs. of...)

**CHARLIE CHAN** (The Adventures of...) (Zaza The Mystic No. 10 on)
6-7/48 - No.5, 2-3/49; No.6, 6/55 - No.9, 3/56
Crestwood(Prize) No. 1-5; Charlton No. 6(6/55) on

| | | | |
|---|---|---|---|
| 1-S&K-c, 2 pages; Infantino-a | 25.00 | 75.00 | 175.00 |
| 2-S&K-c | 15.00 | 45.00 | 105.00 |
| 3-5-All S&K-c (#3-S&K-c/a) | 14.00 | 43.00 | 100.00 |
| 6(6/55-Charlton)-S&K-c | 10.00 | 30.00 | 70.00 |
| 7-9 | 5.70 | 17.00 | 40.00 |

**CHARLIE CHAN**
Oct-Dec, 1965 - No. 2, Mar, 1966
Dell Publishing Co.

| | | | |
|---|---|---|---|
| 1-Springer-a | 1.70 | 5.00 | 12.00 |
| 2 | 1.00 | 3.00 | 7.00 |

**CHARLIE CHAPLIN**
1917 (9x16"; large size; softcover; B&W)
Essanay/M. A. Donohue & Co.

| | | | |
|---|---|---|---|
| Series 1, #315-Comic Capers (9¾x15¾")-18pp by Segar, Series 1, #316-In the Movies | 50.00 | 150.00 | 350.00 |
| Series 1, #317-Up in the Air. 318-In the Army | 50.00 | 150.00 | 350.00 |
| ...Funny Stunts-(12½x16-3/8") in color | 39.00 | 118.00 | 275.00 |

NOTE: *All contain Segar -a; pre-Thimble Theatre.*

**CHARLIE McCARTHY** (See Edgar Bergen Presents...)
No. 171, Nov, 1947 - No. 571, July, 1954 (See True Comics #14)
Dell Publishing Co.

| | Good | Fine | N-Mint |
|---|---|---|---|
| 4-Color 171 | 10.00 | 30.00 | 70.00 |
| 4-Color 196-Part photo-c; photo back-c | 8.50 | 25.50 | 60.00 |
| 1(3-5/49)-Part photo-c; photo back-c | 8.50 | 25.50 | 60.00 |
| 2-9(7/52; #5,6-52 pgs.) | 3.50 | 10.50 | 24.00 |
| 4-Color 445,478,527,571 | 2.65 | 8.00 | 18.00 |

**CHARLTON BULLSEYE**
1975 - No. 5, 1976 (B&W, bi-monthly, magazine format)
CPL/Gang Publications

| | | | |
|---|---|---|---|
| 1-Jeff Jones, Byrne, Ditko-a; 1st app. new Capt. Atom by Ditko | .85 | 2.50 | 5.00 |
| 2-Capt. Atom by Ditko; Byrne-a | .85 | 2.50 | 5.00 |
| 3-Wrong Country by Sanho Kim | .50 | 1.50 | 3.00 |
| 4-Doomsday + 1 by John Byrne | .85 | 2.50 | 5.00 |
| 5-Doomsday + 1 by Byrne, The Question by Ditko; Neal Adams back-c | .85 | 2.50 | 5.00 |

**CHARLTON BULLSEYE**
June, 1981 - No. 10, Dec, 1982; Nov, 1986
Charlton Publications

| | | | |
|---|---|---|---|
| 1-Blue Beetle, The Question | | .40 | .80 |
| 2-10: 2-1st app. Neil The Horse. 6-Origin & 1st app. Thunderbunny | | .30 | .60 |
| Special 1(11/86)(½-in B&W) | .35 | 1.00 | 2.00 |
| Special 2-Atomic Mouse app. ('87) | .25 | .75 | 1.50 |

**CHARLTON CLASSICS**
April, 1980 - No. 9, Aug, 1981
Charlton Comics

| | | | |
|---|---|---|---|
| 1 | | .30 | .60 |
| 2-9 | | .25 | .50 |

**CHARLTON CLASSICS LIBRARY** (1776)
V10No.1, March, 1973 (One Shot)
Charlton Comics

| | | | |
|---|---|---|---|
| 1776 (title) - Adaptation of the film musical "1776"; given away at movie theatres | .35 | 1.00 | 2.00 |

**CHARLTON PREMIERE** (Formerly Marine War Heroes)
V1No.19, July, 1967; V2No.1, Sept, 1967 - No. 4, May, 1968
Charlton Comics

| | | | |
|---|---|---|---|
| V1#19-Marine War Heroes, V2#1-Trio; intro. Shape, Tyro Team, & Spookman, 2-Children of Doom, 3-Sinistro Boy Fiend; Blue Beetle Peacemaker x-over, 4-Unlikely Tales; Ditko-a | .35 | 1.00 | 2.00 |

**CHARLTON SPORT LIBRARY - PROFESSIONAL FOOTBALL**
Winter, 1969-70 (Jan. on cover) (68 pages)
Charlton Comics

| | | | |
|---|---|---|---|
| 1 | 1.00 | 3.00 | 6.00 |

**CHASING THE BLUES**
1912 (52 pages) (7½x10"; B&W; hardcover)
Doubleday Page

| | | | |
|---|---|---|---|
| nn-by Rube Goldberg | 30.00 | 90.00 | 210.00 |

**CHECKMATE** (TV)
Oct, 1962 - No. 2, Dec, 1962
Gold Key

| | | | |
|---|---|---|---|
| 1,2-Photo-c | 2.65 | 8.00 | 18.00 |

**CHECKMATE** (See Action Comics #598)
April, 1988 - No. 33, Jan, 1991 ($1.25)
DC Comics

| | | | |
|---|---|---|---|
| 1 | .60 | 1.75 | 3.50 |
| 2 | .40 | 1.25 | 2.50 |
| 3-5 | .30 | .90 | 1.75 |
| 6-20: 13-30 are $1.50, new format | .25 | .75 | 1.50 |
| 21-30 | | .65 | 1.30 |
| 31-33 ($2.00-c) | .35 | 1.00 | 2.00 |

NOTE: *Gil Kane c-2, 4, 7, 8, 10, 11, 15-19.*

*The Champions #1 (10/75), © MEG*

*Charlie McCarthy #2, © Edgar Bergen*

*Checkmate #4, © DC*

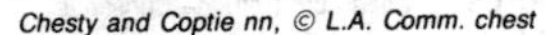

Chesty and Coptie nn, © L.A. Comm. chest

Cheyenne #12, © Warner Bros.

The Chief #2, © DELL

**CHEERIOS PREMIUMS** (Disney)
1947 (32 pages) (Pocket size; 16 titles)
Walt Disney Productions

| | Good | Fine | N-Mint |
|---|---|---|---|
| Set "W"-Donald Duck & the Pirates | 2.65 | 8.00 | 18.00 |
| Bucky Bug & the Cannibal King | 1.50 | 4.50 | 10.00 |
| Pluto Joins the F.B.I. | 1.50 | 4.50 | 10.00 |
| Mickey Mouse & the Haunted House | 2.30 | 7.00 | 16.00 |
| Set "X"-Donald Duck, Counter Spy | 2.00 | 6.00 | 14.00 |
| Goofy Lost in the Desert | 1.50 | 4.50 | 10.00 |
| Br'er Rabbit Outwits Br'er Fox | 1.50 | 4.50 | 10.00 |
| Mickey Mouse at the Rodeo | 2.30 | 7.00 | 16.00 |
| Set "Y"-Donald Duck's Atom Bomb by Carl Barks | 40.00 | 120.00 | 280.00 |
| Br'er Rabbit's Secret | 1.50 | 4.50 | 10.00 |
| Dumbo & the Circus Mystery | 2.00 | 6.00 | 14.00 |
| Mickey Mouse Meets the Wizard | 2.30 | 7.00 | 16.00 |
| Set "Z"-Donald Duck Pilots a Jet Plane (not by Barks) | 2.00 | 6.00 | 14.00 |
| Pluto Turns Sleuth Hound | 1.50 | 4.50 | 10.00 |
| The Seven Dwarfs & the Enchanted Mtn. | 2.00 | 6.00 | 14.00 |
| Mickey Mouse's Secret Room | 2.30 | 7.00 | 16.00 |

**CHEERIOS 3-D GIVEAWAYS** (Disney)
1954 (Pocket size) (24 titles)
Walt Disney Productions

(Glasses were cut-outs on boxes)

| | | | |
|---|---|---|---|
| Glasses only.... | 4.00 | 12.00 | 28.00 |

(Set 1)
1-Donald Duck & Uncle Scrooge, the Firefighters
2-Mickey Mouse & Goofy, Pirate Plunder
3-Donald Duck's Nephews, the Fabulous Inventors
4-Mickey Mouse, Secret of the Ming Vase
5-Donald Duck with Huey, Dewey, & Louie; ...the Seafarers (title on 2nd page)
6-Mickey Mouse, Moaning Mountain
7-Donald Duck, Apache Gold
8-Mickey Mouse, Flight to Nowhere

| | | | |
|---|---|---|---|
| (per book).... | 5.00 | 15.00 | 35.00 |

(Set 2)
1-Donald Duck, Treasure of Timbuktu
2-Mickey Mouse & Pluto, Operation China
3-Donald Duck in the Magic Cows
4-Mickey Mouse & Goofy, Kid Kokonut
5-Donald Duck, Mystery Ship
6-Mickey Mouse, Phantom Sheriff
7-Donald Duck, Circus Adventures
8-Mickey Mouse, Arctic Explorers

| | | | |
|---|---|---|---|
| (per book).... | 5.00 | 15.00 | 35.00 |

(Set 3)
1-Donald Duck & Witch Hazel
2-Mickey Mouse in Darkest Africa
3-Donald Duck & Uncle Scrooge, Timber Trouble
4-Mickey Mouse, Rajah's Rescue
5-Donald Duck in Robot Reporter
6-Mickey Mouse, Slumbering Sleuth
7-Donald Duck in the Foreign Legion
8-Mickey Mouse, Airwalking Wonder

| | | | |
|---|---|---|---|
| (per book).... | 5.00 | 15.00 | 35.00 |

**CHESTY AND COPTIE**
1946 (4 pages) (Giveaway) (Disney)
Los Angeles Community Chest

| | | | |
|---|---|---|---|
| nn-(Very Rare) by Floyd Gottfredson | 20.00 | 60.00 | 140.00 |

**CHESTY AND HIS HELPERS**
1943 (12 pgs., Disney giveaway, 5½x7¼")
Los Angeles War Chest

| | Good | Fine | N-Mint |
|---|---|---|---|
| nn-Chesty & Coptie | 22.00 | 65.00 | 150.00 |

**CHEVAL NOIR**
1989 - Present ($3.50, B&W, 68 pgs.)
Dark Horse Comics

| | | | |
|---|---|---|---|
| 1-8,10: 6-Moebius poster insert | .60 | 1.75 | 3.50 |
| 9,11,13 ($4.50, 84 pgs.) | .75 | 2.25 | 4.50 |
| 12 ($3.95)-Geary-a; Mignola-c | .70 | 2.00 | 4.00 |
| 14 ($4.95, 76 pgs.)(8 pgs. color) | .85 | 2.50 | 5.00 |

NOTE: ***Bolland** a-2, 13, 14. **Bolton** a-2, 4; c-4. **Chadwick** c-13. **Geary** a-13, 14. **Kaluta** c/a-6. **Moebius** c-5, 9. **Dave Stevens** c-1, 7.*

**CHEYENNE** (TV)
No. 734, Oct, 1956 - No. 25, Dec-Jan, 1961-62
Dell Publishing Co.

| | | | |
|---|---|---|---|
| 4-Color 734(#1)-Clint Walker photo-c | 7.00 | 21.00 | 50.00 |
| 4-Color 772,803: 772-Ty Hardin photo-c begin | 4.30 | 13.00 | 30.00 |
| 4(8-10/57) - 12-Last Ty Hardin photo-c | 3.50 | 10.50 | 24.00 |
| 13-25 (All Clint Walker photo-c) | 3.00 | 9.00 | 21.00 |

**CHEYENNE AUTUMN** (See Movie Classics)

**CHEYENNE KID** (Formerly Wild Frontier No. 1-7)
No. 8, July, 1957 - No. 99, Nov, 1973
Charlton Comics

| | | | |
|---|---|---|---|
| 8 (#1) | 3.00 | 9.00 | 21.00 |
| 9,15-17,19 | 1.50 | 4.50 | 10.00 |
| 10-Williamson/Torres-a(3); Ditko-c | 5.50 | 16.50 | 38.00 |
| 11,12-Williamson/Torres-a(2) ea.; 11-(68 pgs.)-Cheyenne Kid meets Geronimo | 5.50 | 16.50 | 38.00 |
| 13-Williamson/Torres-a, 5 pgs. | 3.50 | 10.50 | 24.00 |
| 14,18-Williamson-a, 5 pgs.? | 3.50 | 10.50 | 24.00 |
| 20-22,25-Severin c/a(3) each | 1.70 | 5.00 | 12.00 |
| 23,24,27-29 | .85 | 2.60 | 6.00 |
| 26,30-Severin-a | 1.00 | 3.00 | 7.00 |
| 31-59 | .50 | 1.50 | 3.00 |
| 60-99: 66-Wander by Aparo begins, ends #87. Apache Red begins #88, origin #89 | | .50 | 1.00 |
| Modern Comics Reprint 87,89('78) | | .20 | .40 |

**CHICAGO MAIL ORDER** (See C-M-O Comics)

**CHIEF, THE** (Indian Chief No. 3 on)
No. 290, Aug, 1950 - No. 2, Apr-June, 1951
Dell Publishing Co.

| | | | |
|---|---|---|---|
| 4-Color 290(#1), 2 | 3.50 | 10.50 | 24.00 |

**CHIEF CRAZY HORSE** (See Wild Bill Hockok #21)
1950
Avon Periodicals

| | | | |
|---|---|---|---|
| nn-Fawcette-c | 11.50 | 34.00 | 80.00 |

**CHIEF VICTORIO'S APACHE MASSACRE**
1951
Avon Periodicals

| | | | |
|---|---|---|---|
| nn-Williamson/Frazetta-a, 7 pgs.; Larsen-a; Kinstler-c | 25.00 | 75.00 | 175.00 |

**CHILDREN OF FIRE**
Nov, 1987 - No. 3, 1988 ($2.00, color, mini-series)
Fantagor Press

| | | | |
|---|---|---|---|
| 1-3: by Richard Corben | .35 | 1.00 | 2.00 |

**CHILDREN'S BIG BOOK**
1945 (68 pages; stiff covers) (25 cents)
Dorene Publ. Co.

| | | | |
|---|---|---|---|
| nn-Comics & fairy tales; David Icove-a | 6.00 | 18.00 | 42.00 |

**CHILI** (Millie's Rival)
5/69 - No. 17, 9/70; No. 18, 8/72 - No. 26, 12/73

Marvel Comics Group

| | Good | Fine | N-Mint |
|---|---|---|---|
| 1 | 1.50 | 4.50 | 10.00 |
| 2-5 | .85 | 2.50 | 5.00 |
| 6-17 | .70 | 2.00 | 4.00 |
| 18-26 | .50 | 1.50 | 3.00 |
| Special 1(12/71) | .85 | 2.50 | 5.00 |

**CHILLING ADVENTURES IN SORCERY** (. . .as Told by Sabrina #1, 2) (Red Circle Sorcery No. 6 on)
9/72 - No. 2, 10/72; No. 3, 10/73 - No. 5, 2/74
Archie Publications (Red Circle Prod.)

| | | | |
|---|---|---|---|
| 1,2-Sabrina cameo in both | .70 | 2.00 | 4.00 |
| 3-Morrow-c/a, all | .40 | 1.25 | 2.50 |
| 4,5-Morrow-c/a, 5,6 pgs. | .40 | 1.25 | 2.50 |

**CHILLING TALES** (Formerly Beware)
No. 13, Dec, 1952 - No. 17, Oct, 1953
Youthful Magazines

| | | | |
|---|---|---|---|
| 13(No.1)-Harrison-a; Matt Fox-c/a | 17.00 | 50.00 | 115.00 |
| 14-Harrison-a | 9.00 | 27.00 | 62.00 |
| 15-Has #14 on-c; Matt Fox-c; Harrison-a | 11.50 | 34.00 | 80.00 |
| 16-Poe adapt.-'Metzengerstein'; Rudyard Kipling adapt.-'Mark of the Beast,' by Kiefer; bondage-c | 9.00 | 27.00 | 62.00 |
| 17-Matt Fox-c; Sir Walter Scott & Poe adapt. | 11.50 | 34.00 | 80.00 |

**CHILLING TALES OF HORROR** (Magazine)
V1#1, 6/69 - V1#7, 12/70; V2#2, 2/71 - V2#5, 10/71
(52 pages; black & white) (50 cents)
Stanley Publications

| | | | |
|---|---|---|---|
| V1#1 | 1.15 | 3.50 | 8.00 |
| 2-7: 7-Cameron-a | .70 | 2.00 | 4.00 |
| V2#2,3,5: 2-Spirit of Frankenstein r-/Adventures into the Unknown #16 | .70 | 2.00 | 4.00 |
| V2#4-r-9 pg. Feldstein-a from Adventures into the Unknown #3 | .85 | 2.50 | 5.00 |

NOTE: *Two issues of V2No.2 exist, Feb, 1971 and April, 1971.*

**CHILLY WILLY** (See 4-Color #740, 852, 967, 1017, 1074, 1122, 1177, 1212, 1281)

**CHINA BOY** (See Wisco)

**CHIP 'N' DALE** (Walt Disney)(See Walt Disney's C&S #204)
Nov, 1953 - No. 30, June-Aug, 1962; Sept, 1967 - No. 83, 1982
Dell Publishing Co./Gold Key/Whitman No. 65 on

| | | | |
|---|---|---|---|
| 4-Color 517(#1) | 2.00 | 6.00 | 14.00 |
| 4-Color 581,636 | 1.30 | 4.00 | 9.00 |
| 4(12/55-2/56)-10 | .75 | 2.25 | 5.00 |
| 11-30 | .55 | 1.65 | 4.00 |
| 1(Gold Key reprints, 1967) | .85 | 2.50 | 5.00 |
| 2-10 | .35 | 1.00 | 2.00 |
| 11-20 | | .60 | 1.20 |
| 21-83 | | .40 | .80 |

NOTE: *All Gold Key/Whitman issues have reprints except No. 32-35, 38-41, 45-47. No. 23-28, 30-42, 45-47, 49 have new covers.*

**CHIP 'N DALE RESCUE RANGERS**
June, 1990 - Present ($1.50, color)
Disney Comics

| | | | |
|---|---|---|---|
| 1-12: New stories; 1,2-Origin | .25 | .75 | 1.50 |

**CHITTY CHITTY BANG BANG** (See Movie Comics)

**CHOICE COMICS**
Dec, 1941 - No. 3, Feb, 1942
Great Publications

| | | | |
|---|---|---|---|
| 1-Origin Secret Circle; Atlas the Mighty app.; Zomba, Jungle Fight, Kangaroo Man, & Fire Eater begin | 50.00 | 150.00 | 350.00 |
| 2 | 34.00 | 100.00 | 235.00 |
| 3-Double feature; Features movie "The Lost City" (classic cover); continued from Great Comics #3 | 46.00 | 137.00 | 320.00 |

**CHOO CHOO CHARLIE**
Dec, 1969
Gold Key

| | Good | Fine | N-Mint |
|---|---|---|---|
| 1-John Stanley-a (scarce) | 5.70 | 17.00 | 40.00 |

**CHRISTIAN HEROES OF TODAY**
1964 (36 pages)
David C. Cook

| | | | |
|---|---|---|---|
| nn | .70 | 2.00 | 4.00 |

**CHRISTMAS** (See A-1 No. 28)

**CHRISTMAS ADVENTURE, A** (See Classics Comics Giveaways, 12/69)

**CHRISTMAS ADVENTURE, THE**
1963 (16 pages)
S. Rose (H. L. Green Giveaway)

| | | | |
|---|---|---|---|
| nn | .85 | 2.50 | 5.00 |

**CHRISTMAS ALBUM** (See March of Comics No. 312)

**CHRISTMAS & ARCHIE** ($1.00)
Jan, 1975 (68 pages) (10¼x13¼")
Archie Comics

| | | | |
|---|---|---|---|
| 1 | 1.70 | 5.00 | 10.00 |

**CHRISTMAS AT THE ROTUNDA** (Titled Ford Rotunda Christmas Book 1957 on) (Regular size)
Given away every Christmas at one location
1954 - 1961
Ford Motor Co. (Western Printing)

| | | | |
|---|---|---|---|
| 1954-56 issues (nn's) | 2.00 | 6.00 | 14.00 |
| 1957-61 issues (nn's) | 1.50 | 4.50 | 10.00 |

**CHRISTMAS BELLS** (See March of Comics No. 297)

**CHRISTMAS CARNIVAL**
1952 (100 pages, 25 cents) (One Shot)
Ziff-Davis Publ. Co./St. John Publ. Co. No. 2

| | | | |
|---|---|---|---|
| nn | 10.00 | 30.00 | 70.00 |
| 2-Reprints Ziff-Davis issue plus-c | 7.00 | 21.00 | 50.00 |

**CHRISTMAS CAROL, A** (See March of Comics No. 33)

**CHRISTMAS CAROL, A**
No date (1942-43) (32 pgs.; 8¼x10¾"; paper cover)
Sears Roebuck & Co. (Giveaway)

| | | | |
|---|---|---|---|
| nn-Comics & coloring book | 5.00 | 15.00 | 30.00 |

**CHRISTMAS CAROL, A**
1940s ? (20 pgs.)
Sears Roebuck & Co. (Christmas giveaway)

| | | | |
|---|---|---|---|
| nn-Comic book & animated coloring book | 4.00 | 12.00 | 24.00 |

**CHRISTMAS CAROLS**
1959 ? (16 pgs.)
Hot Shoppes Giveaway

| | | | |
|---|---|---|---|
| nn | 1.20 | 3.50 | 7.00 |

**CHRISTMAS COLORING FUN**
1964 (20 pgs.; slick cover; B&W inside)
H. Burnside

| | | | |
|---|---|---|---|
| nn | .70 | 2.00 | 4.00 |

**CHRISTMAS DREAM, A**
1950 (16 pages) (Kinney Shoe Store Giveaway)
Promotional Publishing Co.

| | | | |
|---|---|---|---|
| nn | 1.35 | 4.00 | 8.00 |

**CHRISTMAS DREAM, A**
1952? (16 pgs.; paper cover)
J. J. Newberry Co. (Giveaway)

| | | | |
|---|---|---|---|
| nn | 1.35 | 4.00 | 8.00 |

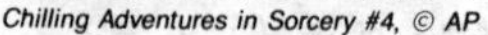
*Chilling Adventures in Sorcery #4, © AP*

*Chip 'N Dale Rescue Rangers #1, © Disney*

*Choice Comics #1, © GP*

*Christmas Parade #5, © The Disney Co.*

*Christmas With the Super-Heroes #2, © DC*

*The Christophers nn, © CG*

**CHRISTMAS DREAM, A**
1952 (16 pgs.; paper cover)
Promotional Publ. Co. (Giveaway)

| | Good | Fine | N-Mint |
|---|---|---|---|
| nn | 1.35 | 4.00 | 8.00 |

**CHRISTMAS EVE, A** (See March of Comics No. 212)

**CHRISTMAS FUN AROUND THE WORLD**
No date (early 50's) (16 pages; paper cover)
No publisher

| | | | |
|---|---|---|---|
| nn | 2.00 | 6.00 | 12.00 |

**CHRISTMAS IN DISNEYLAND** (See Dell Giants)

**CHRISTMAS JOURNEY THROUGH SPACE**
1960
Promotional Publishing Co.

| | | | |
|---|---|---|---|
| nn-Reprints 1954 issue Jolly Christmas Book with new slick cover | 1.50 | 4.50 | 10.00 |

**CHRISTMAS ON THE MOON**
1958 (20 pgs.; slick cover)
W. T. Grant Co. (Giveaway)

| | | | |
|---|---|---|---|
| nn | 1.75 | 5.25 | 12.00 |

**CHRISTMAS PARADE** (See Dell Giant No. 26, Dell Giants, March of Comics No. 284, Walt Disney Christmas Parade & Walt Disney's. . .)

**CHRISTMAS PARADE** (Walt Disney's)
1/63 (no month) - No. 9, 1/72; Wint/88 (#1,5: 80pgs.; #2-4,7-9: 36pgs.)
Gold Key

| | | | |
|---|---|---|---|
| 1 (30018-301)-Giant | 3.75 | 11.00 | 26.00 |
| 2-6: 2-R/F.C. #367 by Barks. 3-R/F.C. #178 by Barks. 4-R/F.C. #203 by Barks. 5-R/Christ. Parade #1 (Dell) by Barks; giant. 6-R/Christmas Parade #2 (Dell) by Barks (64pgs.); giant | 4.00 | 12.00 | 28.00 |
| 7,9: 7-Pull-out poster | 2.00 | 6.00 | 14.00 |
| 8-R/F.C. #367 by Barks; pull-out poster | 4.00 | 12.00 | 28.00 |

**CHRISTMAS PARTY** (See March of Comics No. 256)

**CHRISTMAS PLAY BOOK**
1946 (16 pgs.; paper cover)
Gould-Stoner Co. (Giveaway)

| | | | |
|---|---|---|---|
| nn | 2.75 | 8.00 | 16.00 |

**CHRISTMAS ROUNDUP**
1960
Promotional Publishing Co.

| | | | |
|---|---|---|---|
| nn-Marv Levy-c/a | 1.00 | 3.00 | 7.00 |

**CHRISTMAS STORIES** (See 4-Color No. 959,1062)

**CHRISTMAS STORY** (See March of Comics No. 326)

**CHRISTMAS STORY BOOK** (See Woolworth's Christmas Story Book)

**CHRISTMAS STORY CUT-OUT BOOK, THE**
1951 (36 pages) (15 cents)
Catechetical Guild

| | | | |
|---|---|---|---|
| 393-½ text, ½ comics | 2.75 | 8.00 | 16.00 |

**CHRISTMAS TREASURY, A** (See Dell Giants & March of Comics No. 227)

**CHRISTMAS USA** (Through 300 Years) (Also see Uncle Sam's. . .)
1956
Promotional Publ. Co. (Giveaway)

| | | | |
|---|---|---|---|
| nn-Marv Levy c/a | 1.00 | 3.00 | 6.00 |

**CHRISTMAS WITH ARCHIE**
1973, 1974 (52 pages) (49 cents)
Spire Christian Comics (Fleming H. Revell Co.)

| | | | |
|---|---|---|---|
| nn | | .60 | 1.20 |

**CHRISTMAS WITH MOTHER GOOSE** (See 4-Color No. 90,126,172,201,253)

**CHRISTMAS WITH SANTA** (See March of Comics No. 92)

**CHRISTMAS WITH SNOW WHITE AND THE SEVEN DWARFS**
1953 (16 pages, paper cover)
Kobackers Giftstore of Buffalo, N.Y.

| | Good | Fine | N-Mint |
|---|---|---|---|
| nn | 3.00 | 9.00 | 18.00 |

**CHRISTMAS WITH THE SUPER-HEROES** (See Limited Coll. Ed.)
1988; No. 2, 1989 ($2.95, all reprints)(#2-68 pgs.)
DC Comics

| | | | |
|---|---|---|---|
| 1-(100 pgs.)-N. Adams-r, Byrne-c; Batman, Superman, JLA, LSH Christmas stories; r-Miller's 1st Batman/DC Special Series #21 | .50 | 1.50 | 3.00 |
| 2-Superman by Chadwick, Batman, Wonder Woman, Deadman, Gr. Lantern, Flash app.; Enemy Ace by Byrne | .50 | 1.50 | 3.00 |

**CHRISTOPHERS, THE**
1951 (36 pages) (Some copies have 15 cent sticker)
Catechetical Guild (Giveaway)

| | | | |
|---|---|---|---|
| nn-Hammer & sickle dripping blood-c; Stalin as Satan in Hell | 17.00 | 51.00 | 120.00 |

**CHROME**
1986 - No. 3, 1986? ($1.50, color)
Hot Comics

| | | | |
|---|---|---|---|
| 1-3 | .25 | .75 | 1.50 |

**CHRONICLES OF CORUM, THE** (Also see Corum. . .)
Jan, 1987 - No. 12, Nov, 1988 ($1.75-$1.95, deluxe series)
First Comics

| | | | |
|---|---|---|---|
| 1-12: Adapts Michael Moorcock's novel | .35 | 1.00 | 2.00 |

**CHUCKLE, THE GIGGLY BOOK OF COMIC ANIMALS**
1945 (132 pages) (One Shot)
R. B. Leffingwell Co.

| | | | |
|---|---|---|---|
| 1-Funny animal | 11.00 | 32.00 | 75.00 |

**CHUCK NORRIS** (TV)
Jan, 1987 - No. 5, Sept, 1987
Star Comics (Marvel)

| | | | |
|---|---|---|---|
| 1-5: 1-Ditko-a | | .40 | .80 |

**CHUCK WAGON** (See Sheriff Bob Dixon's. . .)

**CICERO'S CAT**
July-Aug, 1959 - No. 2, Sept-Oct, 1959
Dell Publishing Co.

| | | | |
|---|---|---|---|
| 1,2 | 1.70 | 5.00 | 12.00 |

**CIMARRON STRIP** (TV)
January, 1968
Dell Publishing Co.

| | | | |
|---|---|---|---|
| 1 | 2.30 | 7.00 | 16.00 |

**CINDER AND ASHE**
May, 1988 - No. 4, Aug, 1988 ($1.75, mini-series)
DC Comics

| | | | |
|---|---|---|---|
| 1-4: Mature readers | .30 | .90 | 1.80 |

**CINDERELLA** (See 4-Color No. 272, 786, & Movie Comics)

**CINDERELLA**
April, 1982
Whitman Publishing Co.

| | | | |
|---|---|---|---|
| nn-Reprints 4-Color #272 | | .30 | .60 |

**CINDERELLA IN "FAIREST OF THE FAIR"**
1955 (16 pages, 5x7¼", soft-c) (Walt Disney)
American Dairy Association (Premium)

| | | | |
|---|---|---|---|
| nn | 5.00 | 15.00 | 35.00 |

**CINDERELLA LOVE**
No. 10, 1950; No. 11, 4/51; No. 12, 9/51; No. 4, 10-11/51 - No. 11, Fall, 1952; No. 12, 10/53 - No. 15, 8/54; No.25, 12/54 -No.29, 10/55

(No #16-24)
Ziff-Davis/St. John Publ. Co. No. 12 on

| | Good | Fine | N-Mint |
|---|---|---|---|
| 10 (#1)(1st Series, 1950) | 5.00 | 15.00 | 35.00 |
| 11(4/51), 12(9/51) | 2.15 | 6.50 | 15.00 |
| 4-8: 4,7-Photo-c | 1.85 | 5.50 | 13.00 |
| 9-Kinstler-a; photo-c | 3.00 | 9.00 | 21.00 |
| 10-Whitney painted-c | 2.30 | 7.00 | 16.00 |
| 11(Fall/'52)-Crandall-a; Saunders painted-c | 3.70 | 11.00 | 26.00 |
| 12(St. John-10/53) - #14: 13-Painted-c | 1.70 | 5.00 | 12.00 |
| 15 (8/54)-Matt Baker-c | 2.85 | 8.50 | 20.00 |
| 25(2nd Series)(Formerly Romantic Marriage) | 1.70 | 5.00 | 12.00 |
| 26-Baker-c; last precode (2/55) | 3.00 | 9.00 | 21.00 |
| 27,28 | 1.30 | 4.00 | 9.00 |
| 29-Matt Baker-c | 3.00 | 9.00 | 21.00 |

**CINDY COMICS** (. . .Smith No. 39,40; Crime Can't Win No. 41 on) (Formerly Krazy Komics)(See Teen Comics)
No. 27, Fall, 1947 - No. 40, July, 1950
Timely Comics

| | Good | Fine | N-Mint |
|---|---|---|---|
| 27-Kurtzman-a, 3 pgs: Margie, Oscar begin | 7.00 | 21.00 | 50.00 |
| 28-31-Kurtzman-a | 4.00 | 12.00 | 28.00 |
| 32-40: 33-Georgie story; anti-Wertham edit. | 2.85 | 8.50 | 20.00 |

NOTE: ***Kurtzman's** "Hey Look"-#27(3), 29(2), 30(2), 31; "Giggles 'N' Grins"- #28.*

**CINEMA COMICS HERALD**
1941 - 1943 (4-pg. movie "trailers," paper-c, 7½x10½")
Paramount Pictures/Universal/RKO/20th Century Fox/Republic (Giveaway)

| | Good | Fine | N-Mint |
|---|---|---|---|
| "Mr. Bug Goes to Town"-(1941) | 3.35 | 10.00 | 20.00 |
| "Bedtime Story" | 3.35 | 10.00 | 20.00 |
| "Lady For A Night," John Wayne, Joan Blondell (1942) | 4.30 | 13.00 | 30.00 |
| "Reap The Wild Wind"-(1942) | 3.35 | 10.00 | 20.00 |
| "Thunder Birds"-(1942) | 3.35 | 10.00 | 20.00 |
| "They All Kissed the Bride" | 3.35 | 10.00 | 20.00 |
| "Arabian Nights," nd | 3.35 | 10.00 | 20.00 |
| "Bombardier"-(1943) | 3.35 | 10.00 | 20.00 |
| "Crash Dive"-(1943)-Tyrone Power | 3.35 | 10.00 | 20.00 |

NOTE: *The 1941-42 issues contain line art with color photos. 1943 issues are line art.*

**CIRCUS** (. . .the Comic Riot)
June, 1938 - No. 3, Aug, 1938
Globe Syndicate

| | Good | Fine | N-Mint |
|---|---|---|---|
| 1-(Scarce)-Spacehawks (2 pgs.), & Disk Eyes by Wolverton (2 pgs.), Pewee Throttle by Cole (2nd comic book work; see Star Comics V1#11), Beau Gus, Ken Craig & The Lords of Crillon, Jack Hinton by Eisner, Van Bragger by Kane | 215.00 | 640.00 | 1500.00 |
| 2,3-(Scarce)-Eisner, Cole, Wolverton, Bob Kane-a in each | 107.00 | 321.00 | 750.00 |

**CIRCUS BOY** (See 4-Color No. 759,785,813)

**CIRCUS COMICS**
1945 - No. 2, June, 1945; Winter, 1948-49
Farm Women's Publishing Co./D. S. Publ.

| | Good | Fine | N-Mint |
|---|---|---|---|
| 1-Funny animal | 4.50 | 14.00 | 32.00 |
| 2 | 3.50 | 10.50 | 24.00 |
| 1(1948)-D.S. Publ.; 2 pgs. Frazetta | 13.50 | 41.00 | 95.00 |

**CIRCUS OF FUN COMICS**
1945 - No. 3, Dec, 1947 (a book of games & puzzles)
A. W. Nugent Publishing Co.

| | Good | Fine | N-Mint |
|---|---|---|---|
| 1 | 5.70 | 17.00 | 40.00 |
| 2,3 | 3.60 | 11.00 | 25.00 |

**CIRCUS WORLD** (See Movie Classics)

**CISCO KID, THE** (TV)
July, 1950 - No. 41, Oct-Dec, 1958
Dell Publishing Co.

| | Good | Fine | N-Mint |
|---|---|---|---|
| 4-Color 292(#1)-Cisco Kid, his horse Diablo, & sidekick Pancho & his horse Loco begin; painted-c begin | 11.00 | 32.00 | 75.00 |
| 2(1/51)-5 | 5.00 | 15.00 | 35.00 |
| 6-10 | 4.30 | 13.00 | 30.00 |
| 11-20 | 3.15 | 9.50 | 22.00 |
| 21-36-Last painted-c | 2.65 | 8.00 | 18.00 |
| 37-41: All photo-c | 6.00 | 18.00 | 42.00 |

NOTE: ***Buscema** a-40. **Ernest Nordli** painted-c-5-16, 20, 35.*

**CISCO KID COMICS**
Winter, 1944 - No. 3?, 1945
Bernard Bailey/Swappers Quarterly

| | Good | Fine | N-Mint |
|---|---|---|---|
| 1-Illustrated Stories of the Operas: Faust; Funnyman by Giunta; Cisco Kid begins | 22.00 | 65.00 | 150.00 |
| 2,3 (Exist?) | 16.00 | 48.00 | 110.00 |

**CITIZEN SMITH** (See Holyoke One-Shot No. 9)

**CITY OF THE LIVING DEAD** (See Fantastic Tales No. 1)
1952
Avon Periodicals

| | Good | Fine | N-Mint |
|---|---|---|---|
| nn-Hollingsworth-c/a | 19.00 | 58.00 | 135.00 |

**CITY SURGEON** (Blake Harper. . .)
August, 1963
Gold Key

| | Good | Fine | N-Mint |
|---|---|---|---|
| 1(10075-308)-Painted-c | 1.15 | 3.50 | 8.00 |

**CIVIL WAR MUSKET, THE** (Kadets of America Handbook)
1960 (36 pages) (Half-size; 25 cents)
Custom Comics, Inc.

| | Good | Fine | N-Mint |
|---|---|---|---|
| nn | 1.50 | 4.50 | 10.00 |

**CLAIRE VOYANT** (Also see Keen Teens)
1946 - No. 4, 1947 (Sparling strip reprints)
Leader Publ./Standard/Pentagon Publ.

| | Good | Fine | N-Mint |
|---|---|---|---|
| nn | 27.00 | 81.00 | 190.00 |
| 2,4: 2-Kamen-c. 4-Kamen bondage-c | 22.00 | 65.00 | 150.00 |
| 3-Kamen bridal-c; contents mentioned in **Love and Death**, a book by Gershom Legman('49) referenced by Dr. Wertham | 24.00 | 73.00 | 170.00 |

**CLANCY THE COP**
1930 - No. 2, 1931 (52 pages; B&W) (not reprints) (10"x10")
Dell Publishing Co. (Soft cover)

| | Good | Fine | N-Mint |
|---|---|---|---|
| 1,2-Vep-a | 8.00 | 24.00 | 56.00 |

**CLASSIC COMICS/ILLUSTRATED - INTRODUCTION**
**by Dan Malan**

Further revisions have been made to help in understanding the **Classics** section. **Classics** reprint editions prior to 1963 had either incorrect dates or no dates listed. Those reprint editions should be identified only by the highest number on the reorder list (HRN). Past price guides listed what were calculated to be approximately correct dates, but many people found it confusing for the price guide to list a date not listed in the comic itself.

We have also attempted to clear up confusion about edition variations, such as color, printer, etc. Such variations will be identified by letters. Editions will now be determined by three categories. Original edition variations will be Edition 1A, 1B, etc. All reprint editions prior to 1963 will be identified by HRN only. All reprint editions from 9/63 on will be identified by the correct date listed in the comic.

We have also included new information on four recent reprintings of **Classics** not previously listed. From 1968-1976 Twin Circle, the Catholic newspaper, serialized over 100 **Classics** titles. That list can be found under non-series items at the end of this section. In 1972 twelve **Classics** were reissued as **Now Age Books Illustrated**. They are listed under **Pendulum Illustrated Classics**. In 1982, 20 Classics were reissued, adapted for teaching English as a second language. They are listed under **Regents Illustrated Classics**. Then in 1984, six Classics were reissued with cassette

*Cindy #38, © MEG*

*The Cisco Kid #36, © DELL*

*Claire Voyant #3, © STD*

tapes. See the listing under **Cassette Books**.

## UNDERSTANDING CLASSICS ILLUSTRATED

**by Dan Malan**

Since **Classics Illustrated** is the most complicated comic book series, with all its reprint editions and variations, with changes in covers and artwork, with a variety of means of identifying editions, and with the most extensive worldwide distribution of any comic-book series; therefore this introductory section is provided to assist you in gaining expertise about this series.

### THE HISTORY OF CLASSICS

The **Classics** series was the brain child of Albert L. Kanter, who saw in the new comic-book medium a means of introducing children to the great classics of literature. In October of 1941 his Gilberton Co. began the **Classic Comics** series with **The Three Musketeers**, with 64 pages of storyline. In those early years, the struggling series saw irregular schedules and numerous printers, not to mention variable art quality and liberal story adaptations. With No.13 the page total was reduced to 56 (except for No. 33, originally scheduled to be No. 9), and with No. 15 the coming-next ad on the outside back cover moved inside. In 1945 the Jerry Iger Shop began producing all new CC titles, beginning with No. 23. In 1947 the search for a classier logo resulted in **Classics Illustrated**, beginning with No. 35, **The Last Days of Pompeii**. With No. 45 the page total dropped again to 48, which was to become the standard.

Two new developments in 1951 had a profound effect upon the success of the series. One was the introduction of painted covers, instead of the old line drawn covers, beginning with No. 81, **The Odyssey**. The second was the switch to the major national distributor — Curtis. They raised the cover price from 10 to 15 cents, making it the highest priced comic-book, but it did not slow the growth of the series, because they were marketed as books, not comics. Because of this higher quality image, **Classics** flourished during the fifties while other comic series were reeling from outside attacks. They diversified with their new **Juniors**, **Specials**, and **World Around Us** series.

**Classics** artwork can be divided into three distinct periods. The pre-Iger era (1941-44) was mentioned above for its variable art quality. The Iger era (1945-53) was a major improvement in art quality and adaptations. It came to be dominated by artists Henry Kiefer and Alex Blum, together accounting for some 50 titles. Their styles gave the first real personality to the series. The EC era (1954-62) resulted from the demise of the EC horror series, when many of their artists made the major switch to classical art.

But several factors brought the production of new CI titles to a complete halt in 1962. Gilberton lost its 2nd class mailing permit. External factors like television, cheap paperback books, and Cliff Notes were all eating away at their market. Production halted with No.167, **Faust**, even though many more titles were already in the works. Many of those found their way into foreign series, and are very desirable to collectors. In 1967, **Classics Illustrated** was sold to Patrick Frawley and his Catholic publication, Twin Circle. They issued two new titles in 1969 as part of an attempted revival, but succumbed to major distribution problems in 1971. In 1988, the trio: First Publishing, Berkley Press, and Classics Media Group acquired the use rights for the old CI series art, logo, and name from the Frawley Group. So far they have used only the name in the new series, but do have plans to reprint the old CI.

One of the unique aspects of the **Classics Illustrated** (CI) series was the proliferation of reprint variations. Some titles had as many as 25 editions. Reprinting began in 1943. Some **Classic Comics** (CC) reprints (r) had the logo format revised to a banner logo, and added a motto under the banner. In 1947 CC titles changed to the CI logo, but kept their line drawn covers (LDC). In 1948, Nos. 13, 18, 29 and 41 received second covers (LDC2), replacing covers considered too violent, and reprints of Nos. 13-44 had pages reduced to 48, except for No. 26, which had 48 pages to begin with.

Starting in the mid-1950s, 70 of the 80 LDC titles were reissued with new painted covers (PC). Thirty of them also received new interior artwork (A2). The new artwork was generally higher quality with larger art panels and more faithful but abbreviated storylines. Later on, there were 29 second painted covers (PC2), mostly by Twin Circle. Altogether there were 199 interior art variations (169 (O)s and 30 A2 editions) and 272 different covers (169 (O)s, four LDC2s, 70 new PCs of LDC (O)s, and 29 PC2s). It is mildly astounding to realize that there are nearly 1400 different editions in the U.S. CI series.

### FOREIGN CLASSICS ILLUSTRATED

If U.S. **Classics** variations are mildly astounding, the veritable plethora of foreign CI variations will boggle your imagination. While we still anticipate additional discoveries, we presently know about series in 25 languages and 27 countries. There were 250 new CI titles in foreign series, and nearly 400 new foreign covers of U.S. titles. The 1400 U.S. CI editions pale in comparison to the 4000+ foreign editions. The very nature of CI lent itself to flourishing as an international series. Worldwide, they published over one billion copies! The first foreign CI series consisted of six Canadian **Classic Comic** reprints in 1946.

Here is a chart showing when CI series first began in each country:

1946: Canada. 1947: Australia. 1948: Brazil/The Netherlands. 1950: Italy. 1951: Greece/Japan/Hong Kong(?)/England/Argentina/Mexico. 1952: West Germany. 1954: Norway. 1955: New Zealand/South Africa. 1956: Denmark/Sweden/Iceland. 1957: Finland/France. 1962: Singapore(?). 1964: India (8 languages). 1971: Ireland (Gaelic). 1973: Belgium(?)/Philippines(?)/Malaysia(?).

Significant among the early series were Brazil and Greece. In 1950, Brazil was the first country to begin doing its own new titles. They issued nearly 80 new CI titles by Brazilian authors. In Greece in 1951 they actually had debates in parliament about the effects of **Classics Illustrated** on Greek culture, leading to the inclusion of 88 new Greek History & Mythology titles in the CI series.

But by far the most important foreign CI development was the joint European series which began in 1956 in 10 countries simultaneously. By 1960, CI had the largest European distribution of any American publication, not just comics! So when all the problems came up with U.S. distribution, they literally moved the CI operation to Europe in 1962, and continued producing new titles in all four CI series. Many of them were adapted and drawn in the U.S., the most famous of which was the British CI #158A. **Dr. No**, drawn by Norman Nodel. Unfortunately, the British CI series ended in late 1963, which limited the European CI titles available in English to 15. Altogether there were 82 new CI art titles in the joint European series, which ran until 1976.

### CLASSICS REFERENCE INFORMATION

**The Classics Collector Magazine** (formerly **Worldwide Classics Newsletter**) (1987-1991) Dan Malan, Editor/Publisher. This magazine is the nerve center of the classics-collecting hobby, with subscribers in 22 countries. It covers the official CI series (old and new), related classical comic-book series, foreign series, various memorabilia collectibles, and even illustrated books. Features include new discoveries, market analysis, interviews, pictorials, artist info, and classical ads. It is available by subscription directly from the publisher at 7519 Lindbergh Dr., St. Louis, MO 63117, or at local comic specialty shops.

(Note: CI reference works such as **The Classics Handbook** are now out of print, and the anticipated **Complete Guide to Classics Collectibles** has been delayed. For current info on CI reference books, refer to TCC magazine)

### IDENTIFYING CLASSICS EDITIONS

**HRN**: This is the highest number on the reorder list. It should be listed in ( ) after the title number. It is crucial to understanding various CI editions.

**ORIGINALS (O)**: This is the all-important First Edition. To determine (O)s, there is one primary rule and two secondary rules (with exceptions):

**Rule No. 1**: All (O)s and only (O)s have coming-next ads for the next number. **Exceptions**: No. 14(15) (reprint) has an ad on the last inside text page only. No. 14(0) also has a full-page outside back cover ad (also rule 2). Nos.55(75) and 57(75) have coming-next ads. (Rules 2 and 3 apply here). Nos. 168(0) and 169(0) do not have coming-next ads. No.168 was never reprinted; No. 169(0) has HRN (166). No. 169(169) is the only reprint.

**Rule No. 2**: On nos.1-80, all (O)s and only (O)s list 10c on the front cover. **Exceptions**: Reprint variations of Nos. 37(62), 39(71), and 46(62) list 10c on the front cover. (Rules 1 and 3 apply here.)

**Rule No. 3**: All (O)s have HRN close to that title No. **Exceptions**: Some reprints also have HRNs close to that title number: a few CC(r)s, 58(62), 60(62), 149(149), 152(149) 153(149), and title nos. in the 160's. (Rules 1 and 2 apply here.)

**DATES**: Many reprint editions list either an incorrect date or no date. Since Gilberton apparently kept track of CI editions by HRN, they often left the (O) date on reprints. Often, someone with a CI collection for sale will swear that all their copies are originals. That is why we are so detailed in pointing out how to identify original editions. Except for original editions, which should have a coming-next ad, etc., all CI dates prior to 1963 are incorrect! So you want to go by HRN only if it is (165) or below, and go by listed date if it is 1963 or later. There are a few (167) editions with incorrect dates. They could be listed either as (167) or (62/3), which is meant to indicate that they were issued sometime between late 1962 and early 1963.

**COVERS**: A change from CC to LDC indicates a logo change, not a cover change; while a change from LDC to LDC2, LDC to PC, or from PC to PC2 does indicate a new cover. New PCs can be identified by HRN, and PC2s can be identified by HRN and date. Several covers had color changes, particularly from purple to blue.

**Notes**: If you see 15c in Canada on a front cover, it does not necessarily indicate a Canadian edition. Check the publisher's address. An HRN listing two numbers with a / between them indicates that there are two different reorder lists in the front and back covers. Official Twin Circle editions have a full-page back cover ad for their TC magazine, with no CI reorder list. Any CI with just a Twin Circle sticker on the front is not an official TC edition.

### TIPS ON LISTING CLASSICS FOR SALE

It may be easy to just list Edition 17, but **Classics** collectors keep track of CI editions in terms of HRN and/or date, (O) or (r), CC or LDC, PC or PC2, A1 or A2, soft or stiff cover, etc. Try to help them out. For originals, just list (0), unless there are variations such as color (Nos. 10 and 61), printer (Nos. 18-22), HRN (Nos. 95, 108, 160), etc. For reprints, just list HRN if its (165) or below. Above that, list HRN and date. Also, please list type of logo/cover/art for the convenience of buyers. They will appreciate it.

**CLASSIC COMICS** (Also see Best from Boys Life, Cassette Books, Famous Stories, Fast Fiction, Golden Picture Classics, King Classics, Marvel Classics Comics, Pendulum Illustrated Classics, Picture Parade, Picture Progress, Regents Ill. Classics, Stories by Famous Authors, Superior Stories, and World Around Us.)

**CLASSIC COMICS** (Classics Illustrated No. 35 on)
10/41 - No. 34, 2/47; No. 35, 3/47 - No. 169, Spring 1969
(Reprint Editions of almost all titles 5/43 - Spring 1971)
(Painted Covers (0)s No. 81 on, and (r)s of most Nos. 1-80)
Elliot Publishing #1-3 (1941-1942)/Gilberton Publications #4-167 (1942-1967)/Twin Circle Pub. (Frawley) #168-169 (1968-1971)

**Abbreviations:**

A-Art; C or c—Cover; CC—Classic Comics; CI—Classics Ill.; Ed—Edition; LDC—Line Drawn Cover; PC—Painted Cover; r—Reprint

**1. The Three Musketeers**

| Ed | HRN | Date | Details | A | C | Good | Fine | N-Mint |
|---|---|---|---|---|---|---|---|---|
| 1 | — | 10/41 | Date listed-1941; Elliot Pub; 68 pgs. | 1 | 1 | 285.00 | 857.00 | 2000.00 |
| 2 | 10 | — | 10¢ price removed on all (r)s; Elliot Pub; CC-r | 1 | 1 | 20.00 | 60.00 | 140.00 |
| 3 | 15 | — | Long Isl. Ind. Ed.; CC-r | 1 | 1 | 15.00 | 45.00 | 105.00 |
| 4 | 18/20 | — | Sunrise Times Ed.; CC-r | 1 | 1 | 11.50 | 34.00 | 80.00 |
| 5 | 21 | — | Richmond Courier Ed.; CC-r | 1 | 1 | 10.00 | 30.00 | 70.00 |
| 6 | 28 | 1946 | CC-r | 1 | 1 | 8.00 | 24.00 | 56.00 |
| 7 | 36 | — | LDC-r | 1 | 1 | 4.00 | 12.00 | 28.00 |
| 8 | 60 | — | LDC-r | 1 | 1 | 2.65 | 8.00 | 18.00 |
| 9 | 64 | — | LDC-r | 1 | 1 | 2.15 | 6.50 | 15.00 |
| 10 | 78 | — | C-price 15¢; LDC-r | 1 | 1 | 1.70 | 5.00 | 12.00 |
| 11 | 93 | — | LDC-r | 1 | 1 | 1.70 | 5.00 | 12.00 |
| 12 | 114 | — | Last LDC-r | 1 | 1 | 1.70 | 5.00 | 10.00 |
| 13 | 134 | — | New-c; old-a; 64 pg. PC-r | 1 | 2 | 1.70 | 5.00 | 10.00 |
| 14 | 143 | — | Old-a; PC-r; 64 pg. | 1 | 2 | 1.30 | 4.00 | 8.00 |
| 15 | 150 | — | New-a; PC-r; Evans/Crandall-a | 2 | 2 | 1.50 | 4.50 | 10.00 |
| 16 | 149 | — | PC-r | 2 | 2 | 1.25 | 2.50 | 5.00 |
| 17 | 167 | — | PC-r | 2 | 2 | 1.25 | 2.50 | 5.00 |
| 18 | 167 | 4/64 | PC-r | 2 | 2 | 1.25 | 2.50 | 5.00 |
| 19 | 167 | 1/65 | PC-r | 2 | 2 | 1.25 | 2.50 | 5.00 |
| 20 | 167 | 3/66 | PC-r | 2 | 2 | 1.25 | 2.50 | 5.00 |
| 21 | 166 | 11/67 | PC-r | 2 | 2 | 1.25 | 2.50 | 5.00 |
| 22 | 166 | Spr/69 | C-price 25 ¢; stiff-c; PC-r | 2 | 2 | 1.25 | 2.50 | 5.00 |
| 23 | 169 | Spr/71 | PC-r; stiff-c | 2 | 2 | 1.25 | 2.50 | 5.00 |

**2. Ivanhoe**

| Ed | HRN | Date | Details | A | C | Good | Fine | N-Mint |
|---|---|---|---|---|---|---|---|---|
| 1 | (O) | 12/41? | Date listed-1941; Elliot Pub; 68 pgs. | 1 | 1 | 129.00 | 385.00 | 900.00 |
| 2 | 10 | — | Price & 'Presents' removd; Elliot Pub; CC-r | 1 | 1 | 17.00 | 50.00 | 115.00 |
| 3 | 15 | — | Long Isl. Ind. ed.; CC-r | 1 | 1 | 12.00 | 36.00 | 85.00 |
| 4 | 18/20 | — | Sunrise Times ed.; CC-r | 1 | 1 | 11.00 | 32.00 | 75.00 |
| 5 | 21 | — | Richmond Courier ed.; CC-r | 1 | 1 | 9.30 | 28.00 | 65.00 |
| 6 | 28 | 1946 | Last 'Comics'-r | 1 | 1 | 8.00 | 24.00 | 56.00 |
| 7 | 36 | — | 1st LDC-r | 1 | 1 | 4.00 | 12.00 | 28.00 |
| 8 | 60 | — | LDC-r | 1 | 1 | 2.65 | 8.00 | 18.00 |
| 9 | 64 | — | LDC-r | 1 | 1 | 2.30 | 7.00 | 16.00 |
| 10 | 78 | — | C-price 15¢; LDC-r | 1 | 1 | 2.00 | 6.00 | 14.00 |
| 11 | 89 | — | LDC-r | 1 | 1 | 1.70 | 5.00 | 12.00 |
| 12 | 106 | — | LDC-r | 1 | 1 | 1.70 | 5.00 | 10.00 |
| 13 | 121 | — | Last LDC-r | 1 | 1 | 1.50 | 4.50 | 9.00 |
| 14 | 136 | — | New-c&a; PC-r | 2 | 2 | 1.70 | 5.00 | 12.00 |
| 15 | 142 | — | PC-r | 2 | 2 | 1.25 | 2.50 | 5.00 |
| 16 | 153 | — | PC-r | 2 | 2 | 1.25 | 2.50 | 5.00 |
| 17 | 149 | — | PC-r | 2 | 2 | 1.25 | 2.50 | 5.00 |
| 18 | 167 | — | PC-r | 2 | 2 | 1.25 | 2.50 | 5.00 |
| 19 | 167 | 5/64 | PC-r | 2 | 2 | 1.25 | 2.50 | 5.00 |
| 20 | 167 | 1/65 | PC-r | 2 | 2 | 1.25 | 2.50 | 5.00 |
| 21 | 167 | 3/66 | PC-r | 2 | 2 | 1.25 | 2.50 | 5.00 |
| 22A | 166 | 9/67 | PC-r | 2 | 2 | 1.25 | 2.50 | 5.00 |
| 22B | 166 | — | Center ad for Children's Digest & Young Miss; rare; PC-r | 2 | 2 | 1.70 | 5.00 | 12.00 |
| 23 | 166 | R/1968 | C-Price 25¢; PC-r | 2 | 2 | 1.25 | 2.50 | 5.00 |
| 24 | 169 | Win/69 | Stiff-c | 2 | 2 | 1.25 | 2.50 | 5.00 |
| 25 | 169 | Win/71 | PC-r; stiff-c | 2 | 2 | 1.25 | 2.50 | 5.00 |

**3. The Count of Monte Cristo**

| Ed | HRN | Date | Details | A | C | Good | Fine | N-Mint |
|---|---|---|---|---|---|---|---|---|
| 1 | (O) | 3/42 | Elliot Pub; 68 pgs. | 1 | 1 | 93.00 | 280.00 | 650.00 |
| 2 | 10 | — | Conray Prods; CC-r | 1 | 1 | 17.00 | 50.00 | 115.00 |
| 3 | 15 | — | Long Isl. Ind. ed.; CC-r | 1 | 1 | 12.00 | 36.00 | 85.00 |
| 4 | 18/20 | — | Sunrise Times ed.; CC-r | 1 | 1 | 11.00 | 32.00 | 75.00 |
| 5 | 20 | — | Sunrise Times ed.; CC-r | 1 | 1 | 10.00 | 30.00 | 70.00 |
| 6 | 21 | — | Richmond Courier ed.; CC-r | 1 | 1 | 9.30 | 28.00 | 65.00 |
| 7 | 28 | 1946 | CC-r; new Banner logo | 1 | 1 | 8.00 | 24.00 | 56.00 |
| 8 | 36 | — | 1st LDC-r | 1 | 1 | 4.00 | 12.00 | 28.00 |
| 9 | 60 | — | LDC-r | 1 | 1 | 2.65 | 8.00 | 18.00 |
| 10 | 62 | — | LDC-r | 1 | 1 | 3.50 | 10.50 | 24.00 |
| 11 | 71 | — | LDC-r | 1 | 1 | 2.00 | 6.00 | 14.00 |
| 12 | 87 | — | C-price 15¢; LDC-r | 1 | 1 | 1.70 | 5.00 | 12.00 |
| 13 | 113 | — | LDC-r | 1 | 1 | 1.70 | 5.00 | 10.00 |
| 14 | 135 | — | New-c&a; PC-r | 2 | 2 | 1.70 | 5.00 | 10.00 |
| 15 | 143 | — | PC-r | 2 | 2 | 1.25 | 2.50 | 5.00 |
| 16 | 153 | — | PC-r | 2 | 2 | 1.25 | 2.50 | 5.00 |
| 17 | 161 | — | PC-r | 2 | 2 | 1.25 | 2.50 | 5.00 |
| 18 | 167 | — | PC-r | 2 | 2 | 1.25 | 2.50 | 5.00 |
| 19 | 167 | 7/64 | PC-r | 2 | 2 | 1.25 | 2.50 | 5.00 |
| 20 | 167 | 7/65 | PC-r | 2 | 2 | 1.25 | 2.50 | 5.00 |
| 21 | 167 | 7/66 | PC-r | 2 | 2 | 1.25 | 2.50 | 5.00 |
| 22 | 166 | R/1968 | C-price 25¢;; PC-r | 2 | 2 | 1.25 | 2.50 | 5.00 |
| 23 | 169 | Win/69 | Stiff-c; PC-r | 2 | 2 | 1.25 | 2.50 | 5.00 |

**4. The Last of the Mohicans**

| Ed | HRN | Date | Details | A | C | Good | Fine | N-Mint |
|---|---|---|---|---|---|---|---|---|
| 1 | (O) | 8/42? | Date listed-1942; Gilberton #4(0) on; 68 pgs. | 1 | 1 | 75.00 | 225.00 | 525.00 |
| 2 | 12 | — | Elliot Pub; CC-r | 1 | 1 | 15.00 | 45.00 | 105.00 |
| 3 | 15 | — | Long Isl. Ind. ed.; CC-r | 1 | 1 | 13.00 | 40.00 | 90.00 |
| 4 | 20 | — | Long Isl. Ind. ed.; CC-r; banner logo | 1 | 1 | 11.50 | 34.00 | 80.00 |
| 5 | 21 | — | Queens Home News ed.; CC-r | 1 | 1 | 10.00 | 30.00 | 70.00 |
| 6 | 28 | 1946 | Last CC-r; new | 1 | 1 | 8.00 | 24.00 | 56.00 |
| 7 | 36 | — | 1st LDC-r | 1 | 1 | 4.00 | 12.00 | 28.00 |
| 8 | 60 | — | LDC-r | 1 | 1 | 2.65 | 8.00 | 18.00 |
| 9 | 64 | — | LDC-r | 1 | 1 | 2.15 | 6.50 | 15.00 |
| 10 | 78 | — | C-price 15¢; LDC-r | 1 | 1 | 2.00 | 6.00 | 14.00 |
| 11 | 89 | — | LDC-r | 1 | 1 | 1.70 | 5.00 | 12.00 |
| 12 | 117 | — | Last LDC-r | 1 | 1 | 1.70 | 5.00 | 10.00 |

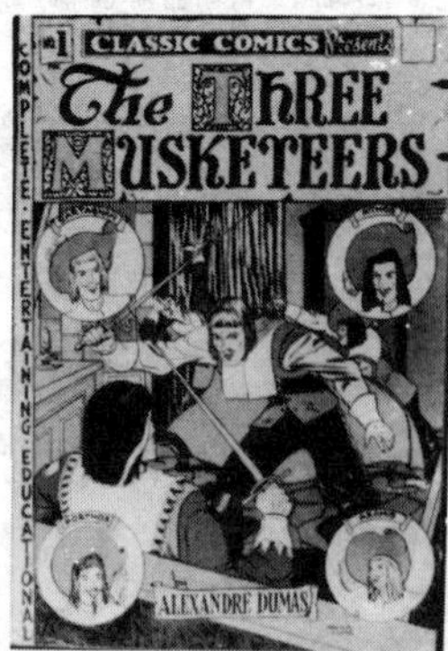

Classic Comics #1 (Orig.), © GIL

Classic Comics #3 (HRN-20), © GIL

Classic Comics #4 (Orig?), © GIL

Classic Comics #5 (HRN-36), © GIL

Classic Comics #6 (HRN-20), © GIL

Classic Comics #8 (HRN-20), © GIL

| Ed | HRN | Date | Details | A C | Good | Fine | N-Mint |
|---|---|---|---|---|---|---|---|
| 13 | 135 | — | New-c; PC-r | 1 2 | 1.70 | 5.00 | 10.00 |
| 14 | 141 | — | PC-r | 1 2 | 1.50 | 4.50 | 9.00 |
| 15 | 150 | — | New-a; PC-r; Sev-erin, L.B. Cole-a | 2 2 | 1.70 | 5.00 | 10.00 |
| 16 | 161 | — | PC-r | 2 2 | 1.25 | 2.50 | 5.00 |
| 17 | 167 | — | PC-r | 2 2 | 1.25 | 2.50 | 5.00 |
| 18 | 167 | 6/64 | PC-r | 2 2 | 1.25 | 2.50 | 5.00 |
| 19 | 167 | 8/65 | PC-r | 2 2 | 1.25 | 2.50 | 5.00 |
| 20 | 167 | 8/66 | PC-r | 2 2 | 1.25 | 2.50 | 5.00 |
| 21 | 166 | R/1967 | C-price 25¢; PC-r | 2 2 | 1.25 | 2.50 | 5.00 |
| 22 | 169 | Spr/69 | Stiff-c; PC-r | 2 2 | 1.25 | 2.50 | 5.00 |

**5. Moby Dick**

| Ed | HRN | Date | Details | A C | Good | Fine | N-Mint |
|---|---|---|---|---|---|---|---|
| 1 | (O) | 9/42? | Date listed-1942; Gilberton; 68 pgs. | 1 1 | 93.00 | 280.00 | 650.00 |
| 2 | 10 | — | Conray Prods; Pg. 64 changed from 105 title list to letter from Editor; CC-r | 1 1 | 17.00 | 50.00 | 115.00 |
| 3 | 15 | — | Long Isl. Ind. ed.; Pg. 64 changed from Letter to the Editor to Ill. poem-Concord Hymn; CC-r | 1 1 | 13.00 | 40.00 | 90.00 |
| 4 | 18/20 | — | Sunrise Times ed.; CC-r | 1 1 | 13.00 | 40.00 | 90.00 |
| 5 | 20 | — | Sunrise Times ed.; CC-r | 1 1 | 11.50 | 34.00 | 80.00 |
| 6 | 21 | — | Sunrise Times ed.; CC-r | 1 1 | 10.00 | 30.00 | 70.00 |
| 7 | 28 | 1946 | CC-r; new banner logo | 1 1 | 8.00 | 24.00 | 56.00 |
| 8 | 36 | — | 1st LDC-r | 1 1 | 4.00 | 12.00 | 28.00 |
| 9 | 60 | — | LDC-r | 1 1 | 2.65 | 8.00 | 18.00 |
| 10 | 62 | — | LDC-r | 1 1 | 3.50 | 10.50 | 24.00 |
| 11 | 71 | — | LDC-r | 1 1 | 2.00 | 6.00 | 14.00 |
| 12 | 87 | — | C-price 15¢; LDC-r | 1 1 | 1.70 | 5.00 | 12.00 |
| 13 | 118 | — | LDC-r | 1 1 | 1.70 | 5.00 | 10.00 |
| 14 | 131 | — | New c&a; PC-r | 2 2 | 1.70 | 5.00 | 10.00 |
| 15 | 138 | — | PC-r | 2 2 | 1.25 | 2.50 | 5.00 |
| 16 | 148 | — | PC-r | 2 2 | 1.25 | 2.50 | 5.00 |
| 17 | 158 | — | PC-r | 2 2 | 1.25 | 2.50 | 5.00 |
| 18 | 167 | — | PC-r | 2 2 | 1.25 | 2.50 | 5.00 |
| 19 | 167 | 6/64 | PC-r | 2 2 | 1.25 | 2.50 | 5.00 |
| 20 | 167 | 7/65 | PC-r | 2 2 | 1.25 | 2.50 | 5.00 |
| 21 | 167 | 3/66 | PC-r | 2 2 | 1.25 | 2.50 | 5.00 |
| 22 | 166 | 9/67 | PC-r | 2 2 | 1.25 | 2.50 | 5.00 |
| 23 | 166 | Win/69 | New-c & c-price 25¢; Stiff-c; PC-r | 2 3 | 1.70 | 5.00 | 10.00 |
| 24 | 169 | Win/71 | PC-r | 2 3 | 1.70 | 5.00 | 10.00 |

**6. A Tale of Two Cities**

| Ed | HRN | Date | Details | A C | Good | Fine | N-Mint |
|---|---|---|---|---|---|---|---|
| 1 | (O) | 10/42 | Date listed-1942; 68 pgs. Zeckerberg c/a | 1 1 | 77.00 | 230.00 | 540.00 |
| 2 | 14 | — | Elliot Pub; CC-r | 1 1 | 15.00 | 45.00 | 105.00 |
| 3 | 18 | — | Long Isl. Ind. ed.; CC-r | 1 1 | 13.00 | 40.00 | 90.00 |
| 4 | 20 | — | Sunrise Times ed.; CC-r | 1 1 | 11.50 | 34.00 | 80.00 |
| 5 | 28 | 1946 | Last CC-r; new banner logo | 1 1 | 8.00 | 24.00 | 56.00 |
| 6 | 51 | — | 1st LDC-r | 1 1 | 3.50 | 10.50 | 24.00 |
| 7 | 64 | — | LDC-r | 1 1 | 2.30 | 7.00 | 16.00 |
| 8 | 78 | — | C-price 15¢; LDC-r | 1 1 | 1.70 | 5.00 | 12.00 |
| 9 | 89 | — | LDC-r | 1 1 | 1.70 | 5.00 | 10.00 |
| 10 | 117 | — | LDC-r | 1 1 | 1.50 | 4.50 | 9.00 |
| 11 | 132 | — | New-c&a; PC-r; Joe Orlando-a | 2 2 | 1.70 | 5.00 | 12.00 |
| 12 | 140 | — | PC-r | 2 2 | 1.25 | 2.50 | 5.00 |
| 13 | 147 | — | PC-r | 2 2 | 1.25 | 2.50 | 5.00 |
| 14 | 152 | — | PC-r; very rare | 2 2 | 8.50 | 25.50 | 60.00 |
| 15 | 153 | — | PC-r | 2 2 | 1.25 | 2.50 | 5.00 |
| 16 | 149 | — | PC-r | 2 2 | 1.25 | 2.50 | 5.00 |
| 17 | 167 | — | PC-r | 2 2 | 1.25 | 2.50 | 5.00 |
| 18 | 167 | 6/64 | PC-r | 2 2 | 1.25 | 2.50 | 5.00 |
| 19 | 167 | 8/65 | PC-r | 2 2 | 1.25 | 2.50 | 5.00 |
| 20 | 166 | 5/67 | PC-r | 2 2 | 1.25 | 2.50 | 5.00 |
| 21 | 166 | Fall/68 | New-c & 25¢-c; PC-r | 2 3 | 1.70 | 5.00 | 10.00 |
| 22 | 169 | Sum-70 | Stiff-c; PC-r | 2 3 | 1.70 | 5.00 | 10.00 |

**7. Robin Hood**

| Ed | HRN | Date | Details | A C | Good | Fine | N-Mint |
|---|---|---|---|---|---|---|---|
| 1 | (O) | 12/42 | Date listed-1942; first Gift Box ad-bc; 68 pgs. | 1 1 | 65.00 | 193.00 | 450.00 |
| 2 | 12 | — | Elliot Pub; CC-r | 1 1 | 15.00 | 45.00 | 105.00 |
| 3 | 18 | — | Long Isl. Ind. ed.; CC-r | 1 1 | 12.00 | 36.00 | 85.00 |
| 4 | 20 | — | Nassau Bulletin ed.; CC-r | 1 1 | 11.50 | 34.00 | 80.00 |
| 5 | 22 | — | Queens Cty. Times ed.; CC-r | 1 1 | 10.00 | 30.00 | 70.00 |
| 6 | 28 | — | CC-r | 1 | 8.00 | 24.00 | 56.00 |
| 7 | 51 | — | LDC-r | 1 1 | 3.50 | 10.50 | 24.00 |
| 8 | 64 | — | LDC-r | 1 1 | 2.30 | 7.00 | 16.00 |
| 9 | 78 | — | LDC-r | 1 1 | 1.70 | 5.00 | 12.00 |
| 10 | 97 | — | LDC-r | 1 1 | 1.70 | 5.00 | 12.00 |
| 11 | 106 | — | LDC-r | 1 1 | 1.70 | 5.00 | 10.00 |
| 12 | 121 | — | LDC-r | 1 1 | 1.50 | 4.50 | 9.00 |
| 13 | 129 | — | New-c; PC-r | 1 2 | 1.70 | 5.00 | 10.00 |
| 14 | 136 | — | New-a; PC-r | 2 2 | 1.70 | 5.00 | 10.00 |
| 15 | 143 | — | PC-r | 2 2 | 1.25 | 2.50 | 5.00 |
| 16 | 153 | — | PC-r | 2 2 | 1.25 | 2.50 | 5.00 |
| 17 | 164 | — | PC-r | 2 2 | 1.25 | 2.50 | 5.00 |
| 18 | 167 | — | PC-r | 2 2 | 1.25 | 2.50 | 5.00 |
| 19 | 167 | 6/64 | PC-r | 2 2 | 1.50 | 3.00 | 6.00 |
| 20 | 167 | 5/65 | PC-r | 2 2 | 1.25 | 2.50 | 5.00 |
| 21 | 167 | 7/66 | PC-r | 2 2 | 1.25 | 2.50 | 5.00 |
| 22 | 166 | 12/67 | PC-r | 2 2 | 1.50 | 3.00 | 6.00 |
| 23 | 169 | Sum-69 | Stiff-c; c-price 25¢; PC-r | 2 2 | 1.25 | 2.50 | 5.00 |

**8. Arabian Nights**

| Ed | HRN | Date | Details | A C | Good | Fine | N-Mint |
|---|---|---|---|---|---|---|---|
| 1 | (O) | 2/43 | Original; 68 pgs. Lilian Chestney-c/a | 1 1 | 143.00 | 430.00 | 1000.00 |
| 2 | 17 | — | Long Isl. ed.; pg. 64 changed from Gift Box ad to Letter from British Medical Worker; CC-r | 1 1 | 68.00 | 205.00 | 475.00 |
| 3 | 20 | — | Nassau Bulletin; Pg. 64 changed from letter to article-Three Men Named Smith; CC-r | 1 1 | 50.00 | 150.00 | 350.00 |
| 4 | 28 | 1946 | CC-r; new banner logo | 1 1 | 37.00 | 112.00 | 260.00 |
| 5 | 51 | — | LDC-r | 1 1 | 22.00 | 65.00 | 150.00 |

| Ed | HRN | Date | Details | A | C | Good | Fine | N-Mint |
|---|---|---|---|---|---|---|---|---|
| 6 | 64 | — | LDC-r | 1 | 1 | 17.00 | 51.00 | 120.00 |
| 7 | 78 | — | LDC-r | 1 | 1 | 15.00 | 45.00 | 105.00 |
| 8 | 164 | — | New-c&a; PC-r | 2 | 2 | 13.00 | 40.00 | 90.00 |

**9. Les Miserables**

| Ed | HRN | Date | Details | A | C | Good | Fine | N-Mint |
|---|---|---|---|---|---|---|---|---|
| 1A | (O) | 3/43 | Original; slick paper cover; 68 pgs. | 1 | 1 | 54.00 | 160.00 | 375.00 |
| 1B | (O) | 3/43 | Original; rough, pulp type-c; 68 pgs. | 1 | 1 | 57.00 | 170.00 | 400.00 |
| 2 | 14 | — | Elliot Pub; CC-r | 1 | 1 | 17.00 | 50.00 | 115.00 |
| 3 | 18 | 3/44 | Nassau Bul. Pg. 64 changed from Gift Box ad to Bill of Rights article; CC-r | 1 | 1 | 14.00 | 43.00 | 100.00 |
| 4 | 20 | — | Richmond Courier ed.; CC-r | 1 | 1 | 11.50 | 34.00 | 80.00 |
| 5 | 28 | 1946 | Gilberton; pgs. 60-64 rearranged/illos added; CC-r | 1 | 1 | 8.50 | 25.50 | 60.00 |
| 6 | 51 | — | LDC-r | 1 | 1 | 4.00 | 12.00 | 28.00 |
| 7 | 71 | — | LDC-r | 1 | 1 | 3.00 | 9.00 | 21.00 |
| 8 | 87 | — | C-price 15¢; LDC-r | 1 | 1 | 2.30 | 7.00 | 16.00 |
| 9 | 161 | — | New-c&a; PC-r | 2 | 2 | 2.30 | 7.00 | 16.00 |
| 10 | 167 | 9/63 | PC-r | 2 | 2 | 1.70 | 5.00 | 12.00 |
| 11 | 167 | 12/65 | PC-r | 2 | 2 | 1.70 | 5.00 | 12.00 |
| 12 | 166 | R/1968 | New-c & price 25¢; PC-r | 2 | 3 | 2.00 | 6.00 | 14.00 |

**10. Robinson Crusoe** (Used in **SOTI**, pg. 142)

| Ed | HRN | Date | Details | A | C | Good | Fine | N-Mint |
|---|---|---|---|---|---|---|---|---|
| 1A | (O) | 4/43 | Original; Violet-c; 68 pgs; Zuckerberg c/a | 1 | 1 | 54.00 | 160.00 | 375.00 |
| 1B | (O) | 4/43 | Original; blue-grey -c, 68 pgs. | 1 | 1 | 57.00 | 170.00 | 400.00 |
| 2A | 14 | — | Elliot Pub; violet-c; 68 pgs; CC-r | 1 | 1 | 14.00 | 43.00 | 100.00 |
| 2B | 14 | — | Elliot Pub; blue-grey -c; CC-r | 1 | 1 | 17.00 | 50.00 | 115.00 |
| 3 | 18 | — | Nassau Bul. Pg. 64 changed from Gift Box ad to Bill of Rights article; CC-r | 1 | 1 | 12.00 | 36.00 | 85.00 |
| 4 | 20 | — | Queens Home News ed.; CC-r | 1 | 1 | 11.00 | 32.00 | 75.00 |
| 5 | 28 | 1946 | Gilberton; pg. 64 changes from Bill-Rights to WWII article-One Leg Shot Away; last CC-r | 1 | 1 | 8.00 | 24.00 | 56.00 |
| 6 | 51 | — | LDC-r | 1 | 1 | 3.50 | 10.50 | 24.00 |
| 7 | 64 | — | LDC-r | 1 | 1 | 2.30 | 7.00 | 16.00 |
| 8 | 78 | — | C-price 15¢; LDC-r | 1 | 1 | 1.70 | 5.00 | 12.00 |
| 9 | 97 | — | LDC-r | 1 | 1 | 1.70 | 5.00 | 10.00 |
| 10 | 114 | — | LDC-r | 1 | 1 | 1.50 | 4.50 | 9.00 |
| 11 | 130 | — | New-c; PC-r | 1 | 2 | 1.70 | 5.00 | 10.00 |
| 12 | 140 | — | New-a; PC-r | 2 | 2 | 1.70 | 5.00 | 10.00 |
| 13 | 153 | — | PC-r | 2 | 2 | 1.25 | 2.50 | 5.00 |
| 14 | 164 | — | PC-r | 2 | 2 | 1.25 | 2.50 | 5.00 |
| 15 | 167 | — | PC-r | 2 | 2 | 1.25 | 2.50 | 5.00 |
| 16 | 167 | 7/64 | PC-r | 2 | 2 | 1.25 | 2.50 | 5.00 |
| 17 | 167 | 5/65 | PC-r | 2 | 2 | 1.50 | 4.50 | 9.00 |
| 18 | 167 | 6/66 | PC-r | 2 | 2 | 1.25 | 2.50 | 5.00 |
| 19 | 166 | Fall/68 | C-price 25¢; PC-r | 2 | 2 | 1.25 | 2.50 | 5.00 |
| 20 | 166 | R/68 | (No Twin Circle ad) | 2 | 2 | 1.50 | 3.00 | 6.00 |
| 21 | 169 | Sm/70 | Stiff-c; PC-r | 2 | 2 | 1.50 | 3.00 | 6.00 |

**11. Don Quixote**

| Ed | HRN | Date | Details | A | C | Good | Fine | N-Mint |
|---|---|---|---|---|---|---|---|---|
| 1 | 10 | 5/43 | First (O) with HRN list; 68 pgs. | 1 | 1 | 57.00 | 170.00 | 400.00 |
| 2 | 18 | — | Nassau Bulletin ed.; CC-r | 1 | 1 | 14.00 | 43.00 | 100.00 |
| 3 | 21 | — | Queens Home News ed.; CC-r | 1 | 1 | 11.50 | 34.00 | 80.00 |
| 4 | 28 | — | CC-r | 1 | 1 | 8.00 | 24.00 | 56.00 |
| 5 | 110 | — | New-PC; PC-r | 1 | 2 | 2.65 | 8.00 | 18.00 |
| 6 | 156 | — | Pgs. reduced 68 to 52; PC-r | 1 | 2 | 1.70 | 5.00 | 12.00 |
| 7 | 165 | — | PC-r | 1 | 2 | 1.75 | 3.50 | 7.00 |
| 8 | 167 | 1/64 | PC-r | 1 | 2 | 1.75 | 3.50 | 7.00 |
| 9 | 167 | 11/65 | PC-r | 1 | 2 | 1.75 | 3.50 | 7.00 |
| 10 | 166 | R/1968 | New-c & price 25¢; PC-r | 1 | 3 | 1.70 | 5.00 | 12.00 |

**12. Rip Van Winkle and the Headless Horseman**

| Ed | HRN | Date | Details | A | C | Good | Fine | N-Mint |
|---|---|---|---|---|---|---|---|---|
| 1 | 11 | 6/43 | Original; 68 pgs. | 1 | 1 | 59.00 | 176.00 | 410.00 |
| 2 | 15 | — | Long Isl. Ind. ed.; CC-r | 1 | 1 | 17.00 | 51.00 | 115.00 |
| 3 | 20 | — | Long Isl. Ind. ed.; | 1 | 1 | 12.00 | 36.00 | 85.00 |
| 4 | 22 | — | Queens Cty. Times ed.; CC-r | 1 | 1 | 11.00 | 32.00 | 75.00 |
| 5 | 28 | — | CC-r | 1 | 1 | 8.00 | 24.00 | 56.00 |
| 6 | 60 | — | 1st LDC-r. | 1 | 1 | 2.65 | 8.00 | 18.00 |
| 7 | 62 | — | LDC-r | 1 | 1 | 2.65 | 8.00 | 18.00 |
| 8 | 71 | — | LDC-r | 1 | 1 | 1.70 | 5.00 | 10.00 |
| 9 | 89 | — | C-price 15¢; LDC-r | 1 | 1 | 1.50 | 4.50 | 9.00 |
| 10 | 118 | — | LDC-r | 1 | 1 | 1.50 | 4.50 | 9.00 |
| 11 | 132 | — | New-c; PC-r | 1 | 2 | 1.70 | 5.00 | 10.00 |
| 12 | 150 | — | New-a; PC-r | 2 | 2 | 1.70 | 5.00 | 10.00 |
| 13 | 158 | — | PC-r | 2 | 2 | 1.25 | 2.50 | 5.00 |
| 14 | 167 | — | PC-r | 2 | 2 | 1.25 | 2.50 | 5.00 |
| 15 | 167 | 12/63 | PC-r | 2 | 2 | 1.25 | 2.50 | 5.00 |
| 16 | 167 | 4/65 | PC-r | 2 | 2 | 1.50 | 3.00 | 6.00 |
| 17 | 167 | 4/66 | PC-r | 2 | 2 | 1.25 | 2.50 | 5.00 |
| 18 | 166 | R/1968 | New-c&price 25¢; PC-r; stiff-c | 2 | 3 | 1.70 | 5.00 | 10.00 |
| 19 | 169 | Sm/70 | PC-r; stiff-c | 2 | 3 | 1.70 | 5.00 | 10.00 |

**13. Dr. Jekyll and Mr. Hyde** (Used in **SOTI**, pg. 143)

| Ed | HRN | Date | Details | A | C | Good | Fine | N-Mint |
|---|---|---|---|---|---|---|---|---|
| 1 | 12 | 8/43 | Original 60 pgs. | 1 | 1 | 66.00 | 200.00 | 465.00 |
| 2 | 15 | — | Long Isl. Ind. ed.; CC-r | 1 | 1 | 17.00 | 51.00 | 115.00 |
| 3 | 20 | — | Long Isl. Ind. ed.; CC-r | 1 | 1 | 12.00 | 36.00 | 85.00 |
| 4 | 28 | — | No c-price; CC-r | 1 | 1 | 10.00 | 30.00 | 70.00 |
| 5 | 60 | — | New-c; Pgs. reduced from 60 to 52; H.C. Kiefer-c; LDC-r | 1 | 2 | 3.50 | 10.50 | 24.00 |
| 6 | 62 | — | LDC-r | 1 | 2 | 3.00 | 9.00 | 21.00 |
| 7 | 71 | — | LDC-r | 1 | 2 | 2.00 | 6.00 | 14.00 |
| 8 | 87 | — | Date returns (erroneous); LDC-r | 1 | 2 | 1.70 | 5.00 | 12.00 |
| 9 | 112 | — | New-c&a; PC-r | 2 | 3 | 1.70 | 5.00 | 12.00 |
| 10 | 153 | — | PC-r | 2 | 3 | 1.25 | 2.50 | 5.00 |
| 11 | 161 | — | PC-r | 2 | 3 | 1.25 | 2.50 | 5.00 |
| 12 | 167 | — | PC-r | 2 | 3 | 1.25 | 2.50 | 5.00 |
| 13 | 167 | 8/64 | PC-r | 2 | 3 | 1.25 | 2.50 | 5.00 |
| 14 | 167 | 11/65 | PC-r | 2 | 3 | 1.25 | 2.50 | 5.00 |
| 15 | 166 | R/1968 | C-price 25¢; PC-r | 2 | 3 | 1.50 | 3.00 | 6.00 |
| 16 | 169 | Wn/69 | PC-r; stiff-c | 2 | 3 | 1.25 | 2.50 | 5.00 |

*Classic Comics #9 (Orig?),* © *GIL*

*Classic Comics #11 (Orig.),* © *GIL*

*Classic Comics #12 (HRN-20),* © *GIL*

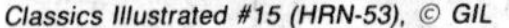
Classics Illustrated #15 (HRN-53), © GIL

Classic Comics #16, © GIL

Classic Comics #17, © GIL

**14. Westward Ho!**

| Ed | HRN | Date | Details | A | C | Good | Fine | N-Mint |
|---|---|---|---|---|---|---|---|---|
| 1 | 13 | 9/43 | Original; last outside bc coming-next ad; 60 pgs. | 1 | 1 | 121.00 | 365.00 | 850.00 |
| 2 | 15 | — | Long Isl. Ind. ed.; CC-r | 1 | 1 | 57.00 | 170.00 | 400.00 |
| 3 | 21 | — | Queens Home News; Pg. 56 changed from coming-next ad to Three Men Named Smith; CC-r | 1 | 1 | 43.00 | 130.00 | 300.00 |
| 4 | 28 | 1946 | Gilberton; Pg. 56 changed again to WWII article-Speaking for America; last CC-r | 1 | 1 | 34.00 | 103.00 | 240.00 |
| 5 | 53 | — | Pgs. reduced from 60 to 52; LDC-r | 1 | 1 | 26.00 | 77.00 | 180.00 |

**15. Uncle Tom's Cabin** (Used in **SOTI**, pgs. 102, 103)

| Ed | HRN | Date | Details | A | C | Good | Fine | N-Mint |
|---|---|---|---|---|---|---|---|---|
| 1 | 14 | 11/43 | Original; Outside-bc ad: 2 Gift Boxes; 60 pgs. | 1 | 1 | 50.00 | 150.00 | 350.00 |
| 2 | 15 | — | Long Isl. Ind. listed-bottom inside-fc; also Gilberton listed bottom-pg. 1; CC-r | 1 | 1 | 19.00 | 56.00 | 130.00 |
| 3 | 21 | — | Nassau Bulletin ed.; CC-r | 1 | 1 | 16.00 | 48.00 | 110.00 |
| 4 | 28 | — | No c-price; CC-r | 1 | 1 | 9.30 | 28.00 | 65.00 |
| 5 | 53 | — | Pgs. reduced 60 to 52; LDC-r | 1 | 1 | 3.70 | 11.00 | 26.00 |
| 6 | 71 | — | LDC-r | 1 | 1 | 2.65 | 8.00 | 18.00 |
| 7 | 89 | — | C-price 15¢; LDC-r | 1 | 1 | 2.30 | 7.00 | 16.00 |
| 8 | 117 | — | New-c/lettering changes; PC-r | 1 | 2 | 1.70 | 5.00 | 10.00 |
| 9 | 128 | — | 'Picture Progress' promo; PC-r | 1 | 2 | 1.75 | 3.50 | 8.00 |
| 10 | 137 | — | PC-r | 1 | 2 | 1.25 | 2.50 | 5.00 |
| 11 | 146 | — | PC-r | 1 | 2 | 1.25 | 2.50 | 5.00 |
| 12 | 154 | — | PC-r | 1 | 2 | 1.25 | 2.50 | 5.00 |
| 13 | 161 | — | PC-r | 1 | 2 | 1.25 | 2.50 | 5.00 |
| 14 | 167 | — | PC-r | 1 | 2 | 1.25 | 2.50 | 5.00 |
| 15 | 167 | 6/64 | PC-r | 1 | 2 | 1.25 | 2.50 | 5.00 |
| 16 | 167 | 5/65 | PC-r | 1 | 2 | 1.25 | 2.50 | 5.00 |
| 17 | 166 | 5/67 | PC-r | 1 | 2 | 1.25 | 2.50 | 5.00 |
| 18 | 166 | Wn/69 | New-stiff-c; PC-r | 1 | 3 | 1.70 | 5.00 | 10.00 |
| 19 | 169 | Sm/70 | PC-r; stiff-c | 1 | 3 | 1.70 | 5.00 | 10.00 |

**16. Gullivers Travels**

| Ed | HRN | Date | Details | A | C | Good | Fine | N-Mint |
|---|---|---|---|---|---|---|---|---|
| 1 | 15 | 12/43 | Original-Lilian Chestney c/a; 60 pgs. | 1 | 1 | 43.00 | 130.00 | 300.00 |
| 2 | 18/20 | — | Price deleted; Queens Home News ed; CC-r | 1 | 1 | 14.00 | 43.00 | 100.00 |
| 3 | 22 | — | Queens Cty. Times ed.; CC-r | 1 | 1 | 11.50 | 34.00 | 80.00 |
| 4 | 28 | — | CC-r | 1 | 1 | 8.00 | 24.00 | 56.00 |
| 5 | 60 | — | Pgs. reduced to 48; LDC-r | 1 | 1 | 2.65 | 8.00 | 18.00 |
| 6 | 62 | — | LDC-r | 1 | 1 | 2.30 | 7.00 | 16.00 |
| 7 | 78 | — | C-price 15¢; LDC-r | 1 | 1 | 1.70 | 5.00 | 12.00 |
| 8 | 89 | — | LDC-r | 1 | 1 | 1.70 | 5.00 | 10.00 |
| 9 | 155 | — | New-c; PC-r | 1 | 2 | 1.70 | 5.00 | 10.00 |
| 10 | 165 | — | PC-r | 1 | 2 | 1.25 | 2.50 | 5.00 |
| 11 | 167 | 5/64 | PC-r | 1 | 2 | 1.25 | 2.50 | 5.00 |
| 12 | 167 | 11/65 | PC-r | 1 | 2 | 1.25 | 2.50 | 5.00 |
| 13 | 166 | R/1968 | C-price 25¢; PC-r | 1 | 2 | 1.25 | 2.50 | 5.00 |
| 14 | 169 | Wn/69 | PC-r; stiff-c | 1 | 2 | 1.25 | 2.50 | 5.00 |

**17. The Deerslayer**

| Ed | HRN | Date | Details | A | C | Good | Fine | N-Mint |
|---|---|---|---|---|---|---|---|---|
| 1 | 16 | 1/44 | Original; Outside-bc ad: 3 Gift Boxes; 60 pgs. | 1 | 1 | 41.00 | 122.00 | 285.00 |
| 2A | 18 | — | Queens Cty Times (inside-fc); CC-r | 1 | 1 | 14.00 | 43.00 | 100.00 |
| 2B | 18 | — | Gilberton (bottom-pg. 1); CC-r; Scarce | 1 | 1 | 19.00 | 58.00 | 135.00 |
| 3 | 22 | — | Queens Cty. Times ed.; CC-r | 1 | 1 | 12.00 | 36.00 | 84.00 |
| 4 | 28 | — | CC-r | 1 | 1 | 7.00 | 21.00 | 56.00 |
| 5 | 60 | — | Pgs.reduced to 52; LDC-r | 1 | 1 | 2.65 | 8.00 | 18.00 |
| 6 | 64 | — | LDC-r | 1 | 1 | 2.00 | 6.00 | 14.00 |
| 7 | 85 | — | C-price 15¢; LDC-r | 1 | 1 | 1.70 | 5.00 | 12.00 |
| 8 | 118 | — | LDC-r | 1 | 1 | 1.70 | 5.00 | 10.00 |
| 9 | 132 | — | LDC-r | 1 | 1 | 1.50 | 4.50 | 9.00 |
| 10 | 167 | 11/66 | Last LDC-r | 1 | 1 | 1.50 | 4.50 | 9.00 |
| 11 | 166 | R/1968 | New-c & price 25¢; PC-r | 1 | 2 | 1.70 | 5.00 | 12.00 |
| 12 | 169 | Spr/71 | Stiff-c; letters from parents & educators; PC-r | 1 | 2 | 1.70 | 5.00 | 10.00 |

**18. The Hunchback of Notre Dame**

| Ed | HRN | Date | Details | A | C | Good | Fine | N-Mint |
|---|---|---|---|---|---|---|---|---|
| 1A | 17 | 3/44 | Orig.; Gilberton ed; 60 pgs. | 1 | 1 | 52.00 | 156.00 | 365.00 |
| 1B | 17 | 3/44 | Orig.; Island Pub. Ed.; 60 pgs. | 1 | 1 | 49.00 | 145.00 | 340.00 |
| 2 | 18/20 | — | Queens Home News ed.; CC-r | 1 | 1 | 15.00 | 45.00 | 105.00 |
| 3 | 22 | — | Queens Cty. Times ed.; CC-r | 1 | 1 | 11.50 | 34.00 | 80.00 |
| 4 | 28 | — | CC-r | 1 | 1 | 8.50 | 25.50 | 60.00 |
| 5 | 60 | — | New-c; 8pgs. deleted; Kiefer-c; LDC-r | 1 | 2 | 2.65 | 8.00 | 18.00 |
| 6 | 62 | — | LDC-r | 1 | 2 | 2.00 | 6.00 | 14.00 |
| 7 | 78 | — | C-price 15¢; LDC-r | 1 | 2 | 1.70 | 5.00 | 12.00 |
| 8A | 89 | — | H.C.Kiefer on bottom right-fc; LDC-r | 1 | 2 | 1.70 | 5.00 | 10.00 |
| 8B | 89 | — | Name omitted; LDC-r | 1 | 2 | 2.30 | 7.00 | 16.00 |
| 9 | 118 | — | LDC-r | 1 | 2 | 1.70 | 5.00 | 10.00 |
| 10 | 140 | — | New-c; PC-r | 1 | 3 | 2.65 | 8.00 | 18.00 |
| 11 | 146 | — | PC-r | 1 | 3 | 2.00 | 6.00 | 14.00 |
| 12 | 158 | — | New-c&a; PC-r; Evans/Crandall-a | 2 | 4 | 2.00 | 6.00 | 14.00 |
| 13 | 165 | — | PC-r | 2 | 4 | 1.50 | 3.00 | 6.00 |
| 14 | 167 | 9/63 | PC-r | 2 | 4 | 1.50 | 3.00 | 6.00 |
| 15 | 167 | 10/64 | PC-r | 2 | 4 | 1.50 | 3.00 | 6.00 |
| 16 | 167 | 4/66 | PC-r | 2 | 4 | 1.25 | 2.50 | 5.00 |
| 17 | 166 | R/1968 | New price 25¢; PC-r | 2 | 4 | 1.25 | 2.50 | 5.00 |
| 18 | 169 | Sp/70 | Stiff-c; PC-r | 2 | 4 | 1.25 | 2.50 | 5.00 |

**19. Huckleberry Finn**

| Ed | HRN | Date | Details | A | C | Good | Fine | N-Mint |
|---|---|---|---|---|---|---|---|---|
| 1A | 18 | 4/44 | Orig.; Gilberton ed.; | 1 | 1 | 35.00 | 105.00 | 245.00 |

| Ed | HRN | Date | Details | A C | Good | Fine | N-Mint |
|---|---|---|---|---|---|---|---|
| | | | 60 pgs. | | | | |
| 1B | 18 | 4/44 | Orig.; Island Pub.; 60 pgs. | 1 1 | 40.00 | 120.00 | 280.00 |
| 2 | 18 | — | Nassau Bulletin ed.; fc-price 15¢-Canada; no coming-next ad; CC-r | 1 1 | 14.00 | 43.00 | 100.00 |
| 3 | 22 | — | Queens Cty. Times ed.; CC-r | 1 1 | 12.00 | 36.00 | 84.00 |
| 4 | 28 | — | CC-r | 1 1 | 8.00 | 24.00 | 56.00 |
| 5 | 60 | — | Pgs. reduced to 48; LDC-r | 1 1 | 2.65 | 8.00 | 18.00 |
| 6 | 62 | — | LDC-r | 1 1 | 2.30 | 7.00 | 16.00 |
| 7 | 78 | — | LDC-r | 1 1 | 2.00 | 6.00 | 14.00 |
| 8 | 89 | — | LDC-r | 1 1 | 1.70 | 5.00 | 12.00 |
| 9 | 117 | — | LDC-r | 1 1 | 1.70 | 5.00 | 10.00 |
| 10 | 131 | — | New-c&a; PC-r | 2 2 | 1.70 | 5.00 | 10.00 |
| 11 | 140 | — | PC-r | 2 2 | 1.25 | 2.50 | 5.00 |
| 12 | 150 | — | PC-r | 2 2 | 1.25 | 2.50 | 5.00 |
| 13 | 158 | — | PC-r | 2 2 | 1.25 | 2.50 | 5.00 |
| 14 | 165 | — | PC-r | 2 2 | 1.25 | 2.50 | 5.00 |
| 15 | 167 | — | PC-r | 2 2 | 1.25 | 2.50 | 5.00 |
| 16 | 167 | 6/64 | PC-r | 2 2 | 1.25 | 2.50 | 5.00 |
| 17 | 167 | 6/65 | PC-r | 2 2 | 1.25 | 2.50 | 5.00 |
| 18 | 167 | 10/65 | PC-r | 2 2 | 1.25 | 2.50 | 5.00 |
| 19 | 166 | 9/67 | PC-r | 2 2 | 1.25 | 2.50 | 5.00 |
| 20 | 166 | Win/69 | C-price 25¢; PC-r; stiff-c | 2 2 | 1.25 | 2.50 | 5.00 |
| 21 | 169 | Sm/70 | PC-r; stiff-c | 2 2 | 1.25 | 2.50 | 5.00 |

**20. The Corsican Brothers**

| Ed | HRN | Date | Details | A C | Good | Fine | N-Mint |
|---|---|---|---|---|---|---|---|
| 1A | 20 | 6/44 | Orig.; Gilberton ed.; bc-ad: 4 Gift Boxes; 60 pgs. | 1 1 | 40.00 | 120.00 | 280.00 |
| 1B | 20 | 6/44 | Orig.; Courier ed.; 60 pgs. | 1 1 | 37.00 | 110.00 | 260.00 |
| 1C | 20 | 6/44 | Orig.; Long Island Ind. ed.; 60 pgs. | 1 1 | 37.00 | 110.00 | 260.00 |
| 1D | 20 | 6/44 | Orig.; Both Gilberton & Long Isl. Ind.; 60 pgs.(rare) | 1 1 | 49.00 | 145.00 | 340.00 |
| 2 | 22 | — | Queens Cty. Times ed.; white logo banner; CC-r | 1 1 | 17.00 | 51.00 | 120.00 |
| 3 | 28 | — | CC-r | 1 1 | 15.00 | 45.00 | 105.00 |
| 4 | 60 | — | CI logo; no price; 48 pgs.; LDC-r | 1 1 | 12.00 | 36.00 | 84.00 |
| 5 | 62 | — | LDC-r | 1 1 | 10.00 | 30.00 | 70.00 |
| 6 | 78 | — | C-price 15¢; LDC-r | 1 1 | 10.00 | 30.00 | 70.00 |
| 7 | 97 | — | LDC-r | 1 1 | 8.50 | 25.50 | 60.00 |

**21. 3 Famous Mysteries** ("The Sign of the 4," "The Murders in the Rue Morgue," "The Flayed Hand")

| Ed | HRN | Date | Details | A C | Good | Fine | N-Mint |
|---|---|---|---|---|---|---|---|
| 1A | 21 | 7/44 | Orig.; Gilberton ed.; 60 pgs. | 1 1 | 65.00 | 195.00 | 455.00 |
| 1B | 21 | 7/44 | Orig. Island Pub. Co.; 60 pgs. | 1 1 | 69.00 | 205.00 | 480.00 |
| 1C | 21 | 7/44 | Original; Courier Ed.; 60 pgs. | 1 1 | 59.00 | 175.00 | 410.00 |
| 2 | 22 | — | Nassau Bulletin ed.; CC-r | 1 1 | 29.00 | 85.00 | 200.00 |
| 3 | 30 | — | CC-r | 1 1 | 23.00 | 70.00 | 160.00 |
| 4 | 62 | — | LDC-r; 8 pgs. deleted; LDC-r | 1 1 | 17.00 | 50.00 | 115.00 |
| 5 | 70 | — | LDC-r | 1 1 | 14.00 | 43.00 | 100.00 |
| 6 | 85 | — | C-price 15¢; LDC-r | 1 1 | 12.00 | 36.00 | 85.00 |
| 7 | 114 | — | New-c; PC-r | 1 2 | 12.00 | 36.00 | 85.00 |

**22. The Pathfinder**

| Ed | HRN | Date | Details | A C | Good | Fine | N-Mint |
|---|---|---|---|---|---|---|---|
| 1A | 22 | 10/44 | Orig.; No printer listed; ownership statement inside fc lists Gilberton & date; 60 pgs. | 1 1 | 32.00 | 95.00 | 225.00 |
| 1B | 22 | 10/44 | Orig.; Island Pub. ed.; 60 pgs. | 1 1 | 26.00 | 77.00 | 180.00 |
| 1C | 22 | 10/44 | Orig.; Queens Cty Times ed. 60 pgs. | 1 1 | 26.00 | 77.00 | 180.00 |
| 2 | 30 | — | C-price removed; CC-r | 1 1 | 8.00 | 24.00 | 56.00 |
| 3 | 60 | — | Pgs. reduced to 52; LDC-r | 1 1 | 2.65 | 8.00 | 18.00 |
| 4 | 70 | — | LDC-r | 1 1 | 2.30 | 7.00 | 16.00 |
| 5 | 85 | — | C-price 15¢; LDC-r | 1 1 | 2.00 | 6.00 | 14.00 |
| 6 | 118 | — | LDC-r | 1 1 | 1.70 | 5.00 | 12.00 |
| 7 | 132 | — | LDC-r | 1 1 | 1.70 | 5.00 | 10.00 |
| 8 | 146 | — | LDC-r | 1 1 | 2.25 | 4.50 | 9.00 |
| 9 | 167 | 11/63 | New-c; PC-r | 1 2 | 2.65 | 8.00 | 18.00 |
| 10 | 167 | 12/65 | PC-r | 1 2 | 2.00 | 6.00 | 14.00 |
| 11 | 166 | 8/67 | PC-r | 1 2 | 2.00 | 6.00 | 14.00 |

**23. Oliver Twist** (1st Classic produced by the Iger Shop)

| Ed | HRN | Date | Details | A C | Good | Fine | N-Mint |
|---|---|---|---|---|---|---|---|
| 1 | 23 | 7/45 | Original; 60 pgs. | 1 1 | 24.00 | 73.00 | 170.00 |
| 2A | 30 | — | Printers Union logo on bottom left-fc—same as 23(Orig.) (very rare); CC-r | 1 1 | 17.00 | 51.00 | 120.00 |
| 2B | 30 | — | Union logo omitted; CC-r | 1 1 | 8.50 | 25.50 | 60.00 |
| 3 | 60 | — | Pgs. reduced to 48; LDC-r | 1 1 | 2.65 | 8.00 | 18.00 |
| 4 | 62 | — | LDC-r | 1 1 | 2.30 | 7.00 | 16.00 |
| 5 | 71 | — | LDC-r | 1 1 | 2.00 | 6.00 | 14.00 |
| 6 | 85 | — | C-price 15¢; LDC-r | 1 1 | 1.70 | 5.00 | 12.00 |
| 7 | 94 | — | LDC-r | 1 1 | 1.70 | 5.00 | 10.00 |
| 8 | 118 | — | LDC-r | 1 1 | 2.25 | 4.50 | 9.00 |
| 9 | 136 | — | New-PC, old-a; PC-r | 1 2 | 1.50 | 4.50 | 10.00 |
| 10 | 150 | — | Old-a; PC-r | 1 2 | 1.30 | 4.00 | 8.00 |
| 11 | 164 | — | Old-a; PC-r | 1 2 | 1.30 | 4.00 | 8.00 |
| 12 | 164 | — | New-a; PC-r; Evans/Crandall-a | 2 2 | 2.00 | 6.00 | 14.00 |
| 13 | 167 | — | PC-r | 2 2 | 1.50 | 4.50 | 9.00 |
| 14 | 167 | 8/64 | PC-r | 2 2 | 1.25 | 2.50 | 5.00 |
| 15 | 167 | 12/65 | PC-r | 2 2 | 1.25 | 2.50 | 5.00 |
| 16 | 166 | R/1968 | New 25¢-c; PC-r | 2 2 | 1.00 | 2.00 | 5.00 |
| 17 | 169 | Win/69 | Stiff-c; PC-r | 2 2 | 1.25 | 2.50 | 5.00 |

**24. A Connecticut Yankee in King Arthur's Court**

| Ed | HRN | Date | Details | A C | Good | Fine | N-Mint |
|---|---|---|---|---|---|---|---|
| 1 | — | 9/45 | Original | 1 1 | 25.00 | 75.00 | 175.00 |
| 2 | 30 | — | Price circle blank; CC-r | 1 1 | 8.00 | 24.00 | 56.00 |
| 3 | 60 | — | 8 pgs. deleted; LDC-r | 1 1 | 2.65 | 8.00 | 18.00 |
| 4 | 62 | — | LDC-r | 1 1 | 2.30 | 7.00 | 16.00 |
| 5 | 71 | — | LDC-r | 1 1 | 1.70 | 5.00 | 12.00 |
| 6 | 87 | — | C-price 15¢; LDC-r | 1 1 | 1.70 | 5.00 | 10.00 |
| 7 | 121 | — | LDC-r | 1 1 | 1.50 | 4.50 | 9.00 |
| 8 | 140 | — | New-c&a; PC-r | 2 2 | 1.50 | 4.50 | 9.00 |

*Classic Comics #20, © GIL*

*Classic Comics #21, © GIL*

*Classics Illustrated #23 (HRN-85?), © GIL*

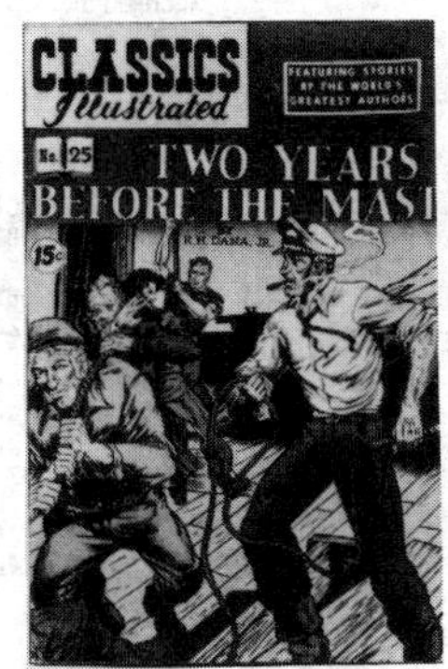

Classics Illustrated #25 (HRN-85?), © GIL

Classics Illustrated #26 (HRN-167), © GIL

Classics Illustrated #30 (HRN-167), © GIL

| | | | | | | Good | Fine | N-Mint |
|---|---|---|---|---|---|---|---|---|
| 9 | 153 | — | PC-r | 2 | 2 | 1.25 | 2.50 | 5.00 |
| 10 | 164 | — | PC-r | 2 | 2 | 1.25 | 2.50 | 5.00 |
| 11 | 167 | — | PC-r | 2 | 2 | 1.25 | 2.50 | 5.00 |
| 12 | 167 | 7/64 | PC-r | 2 | 2 | 1.25 | 2.50 | 5.00 |
| 13 | 167 | 6/66 | PC-r | 2 | 2 | 1.25 | 2.50 | 5.00 |
| 14 | 166 | R/1968 | C-price 25¢; PC-r | 2 | 2 | 1.25 | 2.50 | 5.00 |
| 15 | 169 | Spr/71 | PC-r; stiff-c | 2 | 2 | 1.25 | 2.50 | 5.00 |

**25. Two Years Before the Mast**

| Ed | HRN | Date | Details | A | C | Good | Fine | N-Mint |
|---|---|---|---|---|---|---|---|---|
| 1 | — | 10/45 | Original; Webb/Heames-a&c | 1 | 1 | 25.00 | 75.00 | 175.00 |
| 2 | 30 | — | Price circle blank; CC-r | 1 | 1 | 8.50 | 25.50 | 60.00 |
| 3 | 60 | — | 8 pgs. deleted; LDC-r | 1 | 1 | 2.65 | 8.00 | 18.00 |
| 4 | 62 | — | LDC-r | 1 | 1 | 2.30 | 7.00 | 16.00 |
| 5 | 71 | — | LDC-r | 1 | 1 | 1.70 | 5.00 | 12.00 |
| 6 | 85 | — | C-price 15¢; LDC-r | 1 | 1 | 1.70 | 5.00 | 10.00 |
| 7 | 114 | — | LDC-r | 1 | 1 | 1.50 | 4.50 | 9.00 |
| 8 | 156 | — | 3 pgs. replaced by fillers; new-c; PC-r | 1 | 2 | 1.50 | 4.50 | 9.00 |
| 9 | 167 | 12/63 | PC-r | 1 | 2 | 1.25 | 2.50 | 5.00 |
| 10 | 167 | 12/65 | PC-r | 1 | 2 | 1.25 | 2.50 | 5.00 |
| 11 | 166 | 9/67 | PC-r | 1 | 2 | 1.25 | 2.50 | 5.00 |
| 12 | 169 | Win/69 | C-price 25¢; stiff-c PC-r | 1 | 2 | 1.25 | 2.50 | 5.00 |

**26. Frankenstein**

| Ed | HRN | Date | Details | A | C | Good | Fine | N-Mint |
|---|---|---|---|---|---|---|---|---|
| 1 | 26 | 12/45 | Orig.; Webb/Brewster a&c; 52 pgs. | 1 | 1 | 59.00 | 175.00 | 410.00 |
| 2A | 30 | — | Price circle blank; no indicia; CC-r | 1 | 1 | 19.00 | 58.00 | 135.00 |
| 2B | 30 | — | With indicia; scarce; CC-r | 1 | 1 | 21.50 | 64.00 | 150.00 |
| 3 | 60 | — | LDC-r | 1 | 1 | 5.00 | 15.00 | 35.00 |
| 4 | 62 | — | LDC-r | 1 | 1 | 8.00 | 24.00 | 56.00 |
| 5 | 71 | — | LDC-r | 1 | 1 | 3.00 | 9.00 | 21.00 |
| 6A | 82 | — | C-price 15¢; soft-c LDC-r | 1 | 1 | 2.65 | 8.00 | 18.00 |
| 6B | 82 | — | Stiff-c; LDC-r | 1 | 1 | 1.35 | 4.00 | 8.00 |
| 7 | 117 | — | LDC-r | 1 | 1 | 1.70 | 5.00 | 12.00 |
| 8 | 146 | — | New Saunders-c PC-r | 1 | 2 | 1.70 | 5.00 | 12.00 |
| 9 | 152 | — | Scarce; PC-r | 1 | 2 | 2.65 | 8.00 | 18.00 |
| 10 | 153 | — | PC-r | 1 | 2 | 1.25 | 2.50 | 5.00 |
| 11 | 160 | — | PC-r | 1 | 2 | 1.25 | 2.50 | 5.00 |
| 12 | 165 | — | PC-r | 1 | 2 | 1.25 | 2.50 | 5.00 |
| 13 | 167 | — | PC-r | 1 | 2 | 1.25 | 2.50 | 5.00 |
| 14 | 167 | 6/64 | PC-r | 1 | 2 | 1.25 | 2.50 | 5.00 |
| 15 | 167 | 6/65 | PC-r | 1 | 2 | 1.25 | 2.50 | 5.00 |
| 16 | 167 | 10/65 | PC-r | 1 | 2 | 1.25 | 2.50 | 5.00 |
| 17 | 166 | 9/67 | PC-r | 1 | 2 | 1.25 | 2.50 | 5.00 |
| 18 | 169 | Fall/69 | C-price 25¢; stiff-c PC-r | 1 | 2 | 1.25 | 2.50 | 5.00 |
| 19 | 169 | Spr/71 | PC-r; stiff-c | 1 | 2 | 1.25 | 2.50 | 5.00 |

**27. The Adventures of Marco Polo**

| Ed | HRN | Date | Details | A | C | Good | Fine | N-Mint |
|---|---|---|---|---|---|---|---|---|
| 1 | — | 4/46 | Original | 1 | 1 | 25.00 | 75.00 | 175.00 |
| 2 | 30 | — | Last 'Comics' reprint; CC-r | 1 | 1 | 8.00 | 24.00 | 56.00 |
| 3 | 70 | — | 8 pgs. deleted; no c-price; LDC-r | 1 | 1 | 2.30 | 7.00 | 16.00 |
| 4 | 87 | — | C-price 15¢; LDC-r | 1 | 1 | 1.70 | 5.00 | 12.00 |
| 5 | 117 | — | LDC-r | 1 | 1 | 1.70 | 5.00 | 10.00 |
| 6 | 154 | — | New-c; PC-r | 1 | 2 | 1.50 | 4.50 | 9.00 |
| 7 | 165 | — | PC-r | 1 | 2 | 1.25 | 2.50 | 5.00 |
| 8 | 167 | 4/64 | PC-r | 1 | 2 | 1.25 | 2.50 | 5.00 |
| 9 | 167 | 6/66 | PC-r | 1 | 2 | 1.25 | 2.50 | 5.00 |
| 10 | 169 | Spr/69 | New price 25¢; stiff-c; PC-r | 1 | 2 | 1.25 | 2.50 | 5.00 |

**28. Michael Strogoff**

| Ed | HRN | Date | Details | A | C | Good | Fine | N-Mint |
|---|---|---|---|---|---|---|---|---|
| 1 | — | 6/46 | Original | 1 | 1 | 25.00 | 75.00 | 175.00 |
| 2 | 51 | — | 8 pgs. cut; LDC-r | 1 | 1 | 7.00 | 21.00 | 50.00 |
| 3 | 115 | — | New-c; PC-r | 1 | 2 | 1.70 | 5.00 | 12.00 |
| 4 | 155 | — | PC-r | 1 | 2 | 1.75 | 3.50 | 7.00 |
| 5 | 167 | 11/63 | PC-r | 1 | 2 | 1.75 | 3.50 | 7.00 |
| 6 | 167 | 7/66 | PC-r | 1 | 2 | 1.75 | 3.50 | 7.00 |
| 7 | 169 | Sm/69 | C-price 25¢; stiff-c PC-r | 1 | 3 | 1.70 | 5.00 | 10.00 |

**29. The Prince and the Pauper**

| Ed | HRN | Date | Details | A | C | Good | Fine | N-Mint |
|---|---|---|---|---|---|---|---|---|
| 1 | — | 7/46 | Orig.; "Horror"-c | 1 | 1 | 46.00 | 140.00 | 325.00 |
| 2 | 60 | — | 8 pgs. cut; new-c by Kiefer; LDC-r | 1 | 2 | 2.65 | 8.00 | 18.00 |
| 3 | 62 | — | LDC-r | 1 | 2 | 2.65 | 8.00 | 18.00 |
| 4 | 71 | — | LDC-r | 1 | 2 | 1.70 | 5.00 | 12.00 |
| 5 | 93 | — | LDC-r | 1 | 2 | 1.70 | 5.00 | 10.00 |
| 6 | 114 | — | LDC-r | 1 | 2 | 1.50 | 4.50 | 9.00 |
| 7 | 128 | — | New-c; PC-r | 1 | 3 | 1.50 | 4.50 | 9.00 |
| 8 | 138 | — | PC-r | 1 | 3 | 1.25 | 2.50 | 5.00 |
| 9 | 150 | — | PC-r | 1 | 3 | 1.25 | 2.50 | 5.00 |
| 10 | 164 | — | PC-r | 1 | 3 | 1.25 | 2.50 | 5.00 |
| 11 | 167 | — | PC-r | 1 | 3 | 1.25 | 2.50 | 5.00 |
| 12 | 167 | 7/64 | PC-r | 1 | 3 | 1.25 | 2.50 | 5.00 |
| 13 | 167 | 11/65 | PC-r | 1 | 3 | 1.25 | 2.50 | 5.00 |
| 14 | 166 | R/1968 | C-price 25¢; PC-r | 1 | 3 | 1.25 | 2.50 | 5.00 |
| 15 | 169 | Sm/70 | PC-r; stiff-c | 1 | 3 | 1.25 | 2.50 | 5.00 |

**30. The Moonstone**

| Ed | HRN | Date | Details | A | C | Good | Fine | N-Mint |
|---|---|---|---|---|---|---|---|---|
| 1 | — | 9/46 | Original; Rico-c/a | 1 | 1 | 25.00 | 75.00 | 175.00 |
| 2 | 60 | — | LDC-r; 8pgs. cut | 1 | 1 | 3.50 | 10.50 | 24.00 |
| 3 | 70 | — | LDC-r | 1 | 1 | 2.30 | 7.00 | 16.00 |
| 4 | 155 | — | New L.B. Cole-c; PC-r | 1 | 2 | 5.00 | 15.00 | 35.00 |
| 5 | 165 | — | PC-r; L.B. Cole-c | 1 | 2 | 2.00 | 6.00 | 14.00 |
| 6 | 167 | 1/64 | PC-r; L.B. Cole-c | 1 | 2 | 2.00 | 4.00 | 8.00 |
| 7 | 167 | 9/65 | PC-r; L.B. Cole-c | 1 | 2 | 1.50 | 3.00 | 6.00 |
| 8 | 166 | R/1968 | C-price 25¢; PC-r | 1 | 2 | 1.25 | 2.50 | 5.00 |

**31. The Black Arrow**

| Ed | HRN | Date | Details | A | C | Good | Fine | N-Mint |
|---|---|---|---|---|---|---|---|---|
| 1 | — | 10/46 | Original | 1 | 1 | 23.00 | 70.00 | 160.00 |
| 2 | 51 | — | CI logo; LDC-r 8pgs. deleted | 1 | 1 | 3.00 | 9.00 | 21.00 |
| 3 | 64 | — | LDC-r | 1 | 1 | 2.00 | 6.00 | 14.00 |
| 4 | 87 | — | C-price 15¢; LDC-r | 1 | 1 | 1.70 | 5.00 | 12.00 |
| 5 | 108 | — | LDC-r | 1 | 1 | 1.70 | 5.00 | 10.00 |
| 6 | 125 | — | LDC-r | 1 | 1 | 1.50 | 4.50 | 9.00 |
| 7 | 131 | — | New-c; PC-r | 1 | 2 | 1.50 | 3.50 | 7.00 |
| 8 | 140 | — | PC-r | 1 | 2 | 1.25 | 2.50 | 5.00 |
| 9 | 148 | — | PC-r | 1 | 2 | 1.25 | 2.50 | 5.00 |
| 10 | 161 | — | PC-r | 1 | 2 | 1.25 | 2.50 | 5.00 |
| 11 | 167 | — | PC-r | 1 | 2 | 1.25 | 2.50 | 5.00 |
| 12 | 167 | 7/64 | PC-r | 1 | 2 | 1.25 | 2.50 | 5.00 |
| 13 | 167 | 11/65 | PC-r | 1 | 2 | 1.25 | 2.50 | 5.00 |
| 14 | 166 | R/1968 | C-price 25¢; PC-r | 1 | 2 | 1.25 | 2.50 | 5.00 |

**32. Lorna Doone**

| Ed | HRN | Date | Details | A | C | Good | Fine | N-Mint |
|---|---|---|---|---|---|---|---|---|
| 1 | — | 12/46 | Original; Matt Baker c&a | 1 | 1 | 23.00 | 70.00 | 160.00 |
| 2 | 53/64 | — | 8 pgs. deleted; LDC-r | 1 | 1 | 3.65 | 11.00 | 25.00 |
| 3 | 85 | — | C-price 15¢; LDC-r; Baker c&a | 1 | 1 | 3.00 | 9.00 | 21.00 |
| 4 | 118 | — | LDC-r | 1 | 1 | 2.00 | 6.00 | 14.00 |
| 5 | 138 | — | New-c; old-c becomes new title pg.; PC-r | 1 | 2 | 1.50 | 4.50 | 9.00 |
| 6 | 150 | — | PC-r | 1 | 2 | 1.25 | 2.50 | 5.00 |
| 7 | 165 | — | PC-r | 1 | 2 | 1.25 | 2.50 | 5.00 |
| 8 | 167 | 1/64 | PC-r | 1 | 2 | 1.25 | 2.50 | 5.00 |
| 9 | 167 | 11/65 | PC-r | 1 | 2 | 1.25 | 2.50 | 5.00 |
| 10 | 166 | R/1968 | New-c; PC-r | 1 | 3 | 1.70 | 5.00 | 12.00 |

**33. The Adventures of Sherlock Holmes**

| Ed | HRN | Date | Details | A | C | Good | Fine | N-Mint |
|---|---|---|---|---|---|---|---|---|
| 1 | 33 | 1/47 | Original; Kiefer-c; contains Study in Scarlet & Hound of the Baskervilles; 68 pgs. | 1 | 1 | 75.00 | 225.00 | 525.00 |
| 2 | 53 | — | 'A Study in Scarlet' (17 pgs.) deleted; LDC-r | 1 | 1 | 34.00 | 100.00 | 240.00 |
| 3 | 71 | — | LDC-r | 1 | 1 | 26.00 | 77.00 | 180.00 |
| 4 | 89 | — | C-price 15¢; LDC-r | 1 | 1 | 21.00 | 62.00 | 145.00 |

**34. Mysterious Island** (Last 'Classic Comic')

| Ed | HRN | Date | Details | A | C | Good | Fine | N-Mint |
|---|---|---|---|---|---|---|---|---|
| 1 | — | 2/47 | Original; Webb/Heames-c/a | 1 | 1 | 25.00 | 75.00 | 175.00 |
| 2 | 60 | — | 8 pgs. deleted; LDC-r | 1 | 1 | 2.65 | 8.00 | 18.00 |
| 3 | 62 | — | LDC-r | 1 | 1 | 2.30 | 7.00 | 16.00 |
| 4 | 71 | — | LDC-r | 1 | 1 | 3.50 | 10.50 | 24.00 |
| 5 | 78 | — | C-price 15¢ in circle; LDC-r | 1 | 1 | 1.70 | 5.00 | 12.00 |
| 6 | 92 | — | LDC-r | 1 | 1 | 1.70 | 5.00 | 10.00 |
| 7 | 117 | — | LDC-r | 1 | 1 | 1.50 | 4.50 | 9.00 |
| 8 | 140 | — | New-c; PC-r | 1 | 2 | 1.50 | 4.50 | 9.00 |
| 9 | 156 | — | PC-r | 1 | 2 | 1.25 | 2.50 | 5.00 |
| 10 | 167 | 10/63 | PC-r | 1 | 2 | 1.25 | 2.50 | 5.00 |
| 11 | 167 | 5/64 | PC-r | 1 | 2 | 1.25 | 2.50 | 5.00 |
| 12 | 167 | 6/66 | PC-r | 1 | 2 | 1.25 | 2.50 | 5.00 |
| 13 | 166 | R/1968 | C-price 25¢; PC-r | 1 | 2 | 1.25 | 2.50 | 5.00 |

**35. Last Days of Pompeii** (First 'Classics Illustrated')

| Ed | HRN | Date | Details | A | C | Good | Fine | N-Mint |
|---|---|---|---|---|---|---|---|---|
| 1 | — | 3/47 | Original; LDC; Kiefer-c/a | 1 | 1 | 25.00 | 75.00 | 175.00 |
| 2 | 161 | — | New c&a; 15¢; PC-r; Jack Kirby-a | 2 | 2 | 2.30 | 7.00 | 16.00 |
| 3 | 167 | 1/64 | PC-r | 2 | 2 | 1.50 | 3.00 | 6.00 |
| 4 | 167 | 7/66 | PC-r | 2 | 2 | 1.50 | 3.00 | 6.00 |
| 5 | 169 | Spr/70 | New price 25¢; stiff-c; PC-r | 2 | 2 | 2.00 | 4.00 | 8.00 |

**36. Typee**

| Ed | HRN | Date | Details | A | C | Good | Fine | N-Mint |
|---|---|---|---|---|---|---|---|---|
| 1 | — | 4/47 | Original | 1 | 1 | 11.50 | 34.00 | 80.00 |
| 2 | 64 | — | No c-price; 8 pg. ed.; LDC-r | 1 | 1 | 3.00 | 9.00 | 21.00 |
| 3 | 155 | — | New-c; PC-r | 1 | 2 | 1.50 | 4.50 | 9.00 |
| 4 | 167 | 9/63 | PC-r | 1 | 2 | 1.50 | 3.50 | 7.00 |
| 5 | 167 | 7/65 | PC-r | 1 | 2 | 1.50 | 3.50 | 7.00 |
| 6 | 169 | Sm/69 | C-price 25¢; stiff-c PC-r | 1 | 2 | 1.50 | 3.00 | 6.00 |

**37. The Pioneers**

| Ed | HRN | Date | Details | A | C | Good | Fine | N-Mint |
|---|---|---|---|---|---|---|---|---|
| 1 | 37 | 5/47 | Original; Palais-c/a | 1 | 1 | 11.50 | 34.00 | 80.00 |
| 2A | 62 | — | 8 pgs. cut; LDC-r; price circle blank | 1 | 1 | 2.65 | 8.00 | 18.00 |
| 2B | 62 | — | 10 cent-c; LDC-r; | 1 | 1 | 8.00 | 24.00 | 56.00 |
| 3 | 70 | — | LDC-r | 1 | 1 | 1.70 | 5.00 | 12.00 |
| 4 | 92 | — | 15 cent-c; LDC-r | 1 | 1 | 1.70 | 5.00 | 10.00 |
| 5 | 118 | — | LDC-r | 1 | 1 | 1.50 | 4.50 | 9.00 |
| 6 | 131 | — | LDC-r | 1 | 1 | 1.50 | 4.50 | 9.00 |
| 7 | 132 | — | LDC-r | 1 | 1 | 1.50 | 4.50 | 9.00 |
| 8 | 153 | — | LDC-r | 1 | 1 | 1.50 | 3.50 | 7.00 |
| 9 | 167 | 5/64 | LDC-r | 1 | 1 | 1.50 | 3.50 | 7.00 |
| 10 | 167 | 6/66 | LDC-r | 1 | 1 | 1.50 | 3.50 | 7.00 |
| 11 | 166 | R/1968 | New-c; 15 cent-c; PC-r | 1 | 2 | 2.00 | 6.00 | 14.00 |

**38. Adventures of Cellini**

| Ed | HRN | Date | Details | A | C | Good | Fine | N-Mint |
|---|---|---|---|---|---|---|---|---|
| 1 | — | 6/47 | Original; Froehlich c/a | 1 | 1 | 22.00 | 65.00 | 150.00 |
| 2 | 164 | — | New-c&a; PC-r | 2 | 2 | 1.70 | 5.00 | 10.00 |
| 3 | 167 | 12/63 | PC-r | 2 | 2 | 1.50 | 3.00 | 6.00 |
| 4 | 167 | 7/66 | PC-r | 2 | 2 | 1.50 | 3.00 | 6.00 |
| 5 | 169 | Spr/70 | Stiff-c; new price 25¢; PC-r | 2 | 2 | 2.00 | 4.00 | 8.00 |

**39. Jane Eyre**

| Ed | HRN | Date | Details | A | C | Good | Fine | N-Mint |
|---|---|---|---|---|---|---|---|---|
| 1 | — | 7/47 | Original | 1 | 1 | 17.00 | 51.00 | 120.00 |
| 2 | 60 | — | No c-price; 8 pgs. cut; LDC-r | 1 | 1 | 3.00 | 9.00 | 21.00 |
| 3 | 62 | — | LDC-r | 1 | 1 | 3.00 | 9.00 | 21.00 |
| 4 | 71 | — | LDC-r; c-price 10¢ | 1 | 1 | 2.65 | 8.00 | 18.00 |
| 5 | 92 | — | C-price 15¢; LDC-r | 1 | 1 | 1.70 | 5.00 | 12.00 |
| 6 | 118 | — | LDC-r | 1 | 1 | 1.70 | 5.00 | 12.00 |
| 7 | 142 | — | New-c; old-a; PC-r | 1 | 2 | 2.00 | 6.00 | 14.00 |
| 8 | 154 | — | Old-a; PC-r | 1 | 2 | 1.70 | 5.00 | 12.00 |
| 9 | 165 | — | New-a; PC-r | 2 | 2 | 2.00 | 6.00 | 14.00 |
| 10 | 167 | 12/63 | PC-r | 2 | 2 | 2.00 | 6.00 | 14.00 |
| 11 | 167 | 4/65 | PC-r | 2 | 2 | 1.70 | 5.00 | 12.00 |
| 12 | 167 | 8/66 | PC-r | 2 | 2 | 1.70 | 5.00 | 12.00 |
| 13 | 166 | R/1968 | New-c; PC-r | 2 | 3 | 4.00 | 12.00 | 28.00 |

**40. Mysteries** (''The Pit and the Pendulum,'' ''The Advs. of Hans Pfall,'' ''The Fall of the House of Usher'')

| Ed | HRN | Date | Details | A | C | Good | Fine | N-Mint |
|---|---|---|---|---|---|---|---|---|
| 1 | — | 8/47 | Original; Kiefer-c/a, Froehlich, Griffiths-a | 1 | 1 | 52.00 | 156.00 | 365.00 |
| 2 | 62 | — | LDC-r; 8pgs cut | 1 | 1 | 20.00 | 60.00 | 140.00 |
| 3 | 75 | — | LDC-r | 1 | 1 | 17.00 | 51.00 | 120.00 |
| 4 | 92 | — | C-price 15¢; LDC-r | 1 | 1 | 11.50 | 34.00 | 80.00 |

**41. Twenty Years After**

| Ed | HRN | Date | Details | A | C | Good | Fine | N-Mint |
|---|---|---|---|---|---|---|---|---|
| 1 | — | 9/47 | Original; 'horror'-c | 1 | 1 | 36.00 | 107.00 | 250.00 |
| 2 | 62 | — | New-c; no c-price 8 pgs. cut; LDC-r; Kiefer-c | 1 | 2 | 2.65 | 8.00 | 18.00 |
| 3 | 78 | — | C-price 15¢; LDC-r | 1 | 2 | 2.00 | 6.00 | 14.00 |
| 4 | 156 | — | New-c; PC-r | 1 | 3 | 1.50 | 4.50 | 9.00 |
| 5 | 167 | 12/63 | PC-r | 1 | 3 | 1.25 | 2.50 | 5.00 |

*Classic Comics #33 (Orig.), © GIL*

*Classics Illustrated #35 (Orig?), © GIL*

*Classics Illustrated #37, © GIL*

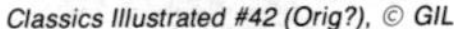
Classics Illustrated #42 (Orig?), © GIL

Classics Illustrated #45 (Orig.), © GIL

Classics Illustrated #49 (Orig.), © GIL

| Ed | HRN | Date | Details | A | C | Good | Fine | N-Mint |
|---|---|---|---|---|---|---|---|---|
| 6 | 167 | 11/66 | PC-r | 1 | 3 | 1.25 | 2.50 | 5.00 |
| 7 | 169 | Spr/70 | New price 25¢; stiff-c; PC-r | 1 | 3 | 1.25 | 2.50 | 5.00 |

**42. Swiss Family Robinson**

| Ed | HRN | Date | Details | A | C | Good | Fine | N-Mint |
|---|---|---|---|---|---|---|---|---|
| 1 | 42 | 10/47 | Orig.; Kiefer-c&a | 1 | 1 | 11.50 | 34.00 | 80.00 |
| 2A | 62 | — | 8 pgs. cut; outside-bc: Gift Box ad; LDC-r | 1 | 1 | 2.65 | 8.00 | 18.00 |
| 2B | 62 | — | 8 pgs. cut; outside-bc: Reorder list; scarce; LDC-r | 1 | 1 | 5.00 | 15.00 | 35.00 |
| 3 | 75 | — | LDC-r | 1 | 1 | 2.00 | 6.00 | 14.00 |
| 4 | 93 | — | LDC-r | 1 | 1 | 1.70 | 5.00 | 12.00 |
| 5 | 117 | — | LDC-r | 1 | 1 | 1.70 | 5.00 | 10.00 |
| 6 | 131 | — | New-c; old-a; PC-r | 1 | 2 | 1.70 | 5.00 | 10.00 |
| 7 | 137 | — | Old-a; PC-r | 1 | 2 | 1.50 | 4.50 | 9.00 |
| 8 | 141 | — | Old-a; PC-r | 1 | 2 | 1.50 | 4.50 | 9.00 |
| 9 | 152 | — | New-a; PC-r | 2 | 2 | 1.50 | 4.50 | 9.00 |
| 10 | 158 | — | PC-r | 2 | 2 | 1.25 | 2.50 | 5.00 |
| 11 | 165 | | PC-r | 2 | 2 | 1.50 | 4.50 | 9.00 |
| 12 | 167 | 12/63 | PC-r | 2 | 2 | 1.50 | 3.00 | 6.00 |
| 13 | 167 | 4/65 | PC-r | 2 | 2 | 1.50 | 3.00 | 6.00 |
| 14 | 167 | 5/66 | PC-r | 2 | 2 | 1.50 | 3.00 | 6.00 |
| 15 | 166 | 11/67 | PC-r | 2 | 2 | 1.25 | 2.50 | 5.00 |
| 16 | 169 | Spr/69 | PC-r; stiff-c | 2 | 2 | 1.25 | 2.50 | 5.00 |

**43. Great Expectations** (Used in **SOTI**, pg. 311)

| Ed | HRN | Date | Details | A | C | Good | Fine | N-Mint |
|---|---|---|---|---|---|---|---|---|
| 1 | — | 11/47 | Original; Kiefer-a/c | 1 | 1 | 57.00 | 170.00 | 400.00 |
| 2 | 62 | — | No c-price; 8 pgs. cut; LDC-r | 1 | 1 | 36.00 | 107.00 | 250.00 |

**44. Mysteries of Paris** (Used in **SOTI**, pg. 323)

| Ed | HRN | Date | Details | A | C | Good | Fine | N-Mint |
|---|---|---|---|---|---|---|---|---|
| 1A | 44 | 12/47 | Original; 56 pgs.; Kiefer-c/a | 1 | 1 | 44.00 | 133.00 | 310.00 |
| 1B | 44 | 12/47 | Orig.; printed on white/heavier paper; rare | 1 | 1 | 46.00 | 140.00 | 320.00 |
| 2A | 62 | — | 8 pgs. cut; outside-bc: Gift Box ad; LDC-r | 1 | 1 | 20.00 | 60.00 | 140.00 |
| 2B | 62 | — | 8 pgs. cut; outside-bc: reorder list; LDC-r | 1 | 1 | 20.00 | 60.00 | 140.00 |
| 3 | 78 | — | C-price 15¢; LDC-r | 1 | 1 | 17.00 | 51.00 | 120.00 |

**45. Tom Brown's School Days**

| Ed | HRN | Date | Details | A | C | Good | Fine | N-Mint |
|---|---|---|---|---|---|---|---|---|
| 1 | 44 | 1/48 | Original; 1st 48pg. issue | 1 | 1 | 8.50 | 25.50 | 60.00 |
| 2 | 64 | — | No c-price; LDC-r | 1 | 1 | 3.50 | 10.50 | 24.00 |
| 3 | 161 | — | New-c&a; PC-r | 2 | 2 | 1.70 | 5.00 | 10.00 |
| 4 | 167 | 2/64 | PC-r | 2 | 2 | 1.50 | 3.50 | 7.00 |
| 5 | 167 | 8/66 | PC-r | 2 | 2 | 1.50 | 3.50 | 7.00 |
| 6 | 166 | R/1968 | C-price 25¢; PC-r | 2 | 2 | 1.50 | 3.50 | 7.00 |

**46. Kidnapped**

| Ed | HRN | Date | Details | A | C | Good | Fine | N-Mint |
|---|---|---|---|---|---|---|---|---|
| 1 | 47 | 4/48 | Original; Webb-c/a | 1 | 1 | 8.00 | 24.00 | 56.00 |
| 2A | 62 | — | Price circle blank; LDC-r | 1 | 1 | 2.65 | 8.00 | 18.00 |
| 2B | 62 | — | C-price 10¢; rare; LDC-r | 1 | 1 | 8.00 | 24.00 | 56.00 |
| 3 | 78 | — | C-price 15¢; LDC-r | 1 | 1 | 2.00 | 6.00 | 14.00 |
| 4 | 87 | — | LDC-r | 1 | 1 | 1.70 | 5.00 | 12.00 |
| 5 | 118 | — | LDC-r | 1 | 1 | 1.70 | 5.00 | 10.00 |
| 6 | 131 | — | New-c; PC-r | 1 | 2 | 1.50 | 4.50 | 9.00 |
| 7 | 140 | — | PC-r | 1 | 2 | 1.25 | 2.50 | 5.00 |
| 8 | 150 | — | PC-r | 1 | 2 | 1.25 | 2.50 | 5.00 |
| 9 | 164 | — | Reduced pg.width; PC-r | 1 | 2 | 1.25 | 2.50 | 5.00 |
| 10 | 167 | — | PC-r | 1 | 2 | 1.25 | 2.50 | 5.00 |
| 11 | 67 | 3/64 | PC-r | 1 | 2 | 1.25 | 2.50 | 5.00 |
| 12 | 167 | 6/65 | PC-r | 1 | 2 | 1.25 | 2.50 | 5.00 |
| 13 | 167 | 12/65 | PC-r | 1 | 2 | 1.25 | 2.50 | 5.00 |
| 14 | 166 | 9/67 | PC-r | 1 | 2 | 1.25 | 2.50 | 5.00 |
| 15 | 166 | Win/69 | New price 25¢; PC-r; stiff-c | 1 | 2 | 1.25 | 2.50 | 5.00 |
| 16 | 169 | Sm/70 | PC-r; stiff-c | 1 | 2 | 1.25 | 2.50 | 5.00 |

**47. Twenty Thousand Leagues Under the Sea**

| Ed | HRN | Date | Details | A | C | Good | Fine | N-Mint |
|---|---|---|---|---|---|---|---|---|
| 1 | 47 | 5/48 | Orig.; Kiefer-a&c | 1 | 1 | 9.00 | 27.00 | 62.00 |
| 2 | 64 | — | No c-price; LDC-r | 1 | 1 | 2.65 | 8.00 | 18.00 |
| 3 | 78 | — | C-price 15¢; LDC-r | 1 | 1 | 2.00 | 6.00 | 14.00 |
| 4 | 94 | — | LDC-r | 1 | 1 | 1.70 | 5.00 | 12.00 |
| 5 | 118 | — | LDC-r | 1 | 1 | 1.70 | 5.00 | 10.00 |
| 6 | 128 | — | New-c; PC-r | 1 | 2 | 1.50 | 4.50 | 9.00 |
| 7 | 133 | — | PC-r | 1 | 2 | 1.50 | 4.50 | 9.00 |
| 8 | 140 | — | PC-r | 1 | 2 | 1.25 | 2.50 | 5.00 |
| 9 | 148 | — | PC-r | 1 | 2 | 1.25 | 2.50 | 5.00 |
| 10 | 156 | — | PC-r | 1 | 2 | 1.25 | 2.50 | 5.00 |
| 11 | 165 | — | PC-r | 1 | 2 | 1.25 | 2.50 | 5.00 |
| 12 | 167 | — | PC-r | 1 | 2 | 1.25 | 2.50 | 5.00 |
| 13 | 167 | 3/64 | PC-r | 1 | 2 | 1.25 | 2.50 | 5.00 |
| 14 | 167 | 8/65 | PC-r | 1 | 2 | 1.25 | 2.50 | 5.00 |
| 15 | 167 | 10/66 | PC-r | 1 | 2 | 1.25 | 2.50 | 5.00 |
| 16 | 166 | R/1968 | C-price 25¢; new-c PC-r | 1 | 3 | 1.70 | 5.00 | 10.00 |
| 17 | 169 | Spr/70 | Stiff-c; PC-r | 1 | 3 | 1.70 | 5.00 | 10.00 |

**48. David Copperfield**

| Ed | HRN | Date | Details | A | C | Good | Fine | N-Mint |
|---|---|---|---|---|---|---|---|---|
| 1 | 47 | 6/48 | Original; Kiefer-c/a | 1 | 1 | 8.50 | 25.50 | 60.00 |
| 2 | 64 | — | Price circle replaced by motif of boy reading; LDC-r | 1 | 1 | 2.65 | 8.00 | 18.00 |
| 3 | 87 | — | C-price 15¢; LDC-r | 1 | 1 | 1.70 | 5.00 | 12.00 |
| 4 | 121 | — | New-c; PC-r | 1 | 2 | 1.50 | 4.50 | 9.00 |
| 5 | 130 | — | PC-r | 1 | 2 | 1.50 | 3.00 | 6.00 |
| 6 | 140 | — | PC-r | 1 | 2 | 1.50 | 3.00 | 6.00 |
| 7 | 148 | — | PC-r | 1 | 2 | 1.50 | 3.00 | 6.00 |
| 8 | 156 | — | PC-r | 1 | 2 | 1.50 | 3.00 | 6.00 |
| 9 | 167 | — | PC-r | 1 | 2 | 1.25 | 2.50 | 5.00 |
| 10 | 167 | 4/64 | PC-r | 1 | 2 | 1.25 | 2.50 | 5.00 |
| 11 | 167 | 6/65 | PC-r | 1 | 2 | 1.25 | 2.50 | 5.00 |
| 12 | 166 | 5/67 | PC-r | 1 | 2 | 1.25 | 2.50 | 5.00 |
| 13 | 166 | R/67 | PC-r; C-price 25¢ | 1 | 2 | 1.50 | 4.50 | 9.00 |
| 14 | 166 | Spr/69 | C-price 25¢; stiff-c PC-r | 1 | 2 | 1.25 | 2.50 | 5.00 |
| 15 | 169 | Win/69 | Stiff-c; PC-r | 1 | 2 | 1.25 | 2.50 | 5.00 |

**49. Alice in Wonderland**

| Ed | HRN | Date | Details | A | C | Good | Fine | N-Mint |
|---|---|---|---|---|---|---|---|---|
| 1 | 47 | 7/48 | Original; 1st Blum a & c | 1 | 1 | 12.00 | 36.00 | 84.00 |
| 2 | 64 | — | No c-price; LDC-r | 1 | 1 | 3.00 | 9.00 | 21.00 |
| 3A | 85 | — | C-price 15¢; soft-c LDC-r | 1 | 1 | 2.30 | 7.00 | 16.00 |
| 3B | 85 | — | Stiff-c; LDC-r | 1 | 1 | .85 | 2.50 | 5.00 |
| 4 | 155 | — | New PC, similar to | 1 | 2 | 2.30 | 7.00 | 16.00 |

| Ed | HRN | Date | Details | A | C | Good | Fine | N-Mint |
|---|---|---|---|---|---|---|---|---|
| | | | orig.; PC-r | | | | | |
| 5 | 165 | — | PC-r | 1 | 2 | 1.70 | 5.00 | 12.00 |
| 6 | 167 | 3/64 | PC-r | 1 | 2 | 1.70 | 5.00 | 10.00 |
| 7 | 167 | 6/66 | PC-r | 1 | 2 | 1.70 | 5.00 | 10.00 |
| 8A | 166 | Fall/68 | New-c; soft-c; 25¢ c-price; PC-r | 1 | 3 | 2.30 | 7.00 | 18.00 |
| 8B | 166 | Fall/68 | New-c; stiff-c; 25¢ c-price; PC-r | 1 | 3 | 5.00 | 15.00 | 35.00 |

**50. Adventures of Tom Sawyer** (Used in **SOTI**, pg. 37)

| Ed | HRN | Date | Details | A | C | Good | Fine | N-Mint |
|---|---|---|---|---|---|---|---|---|
| 1A | 51 | 8/48 | Orig.; Aldo Rubano a&c | 1 | 1 | 9.30 | 28.00 | 65.00 |
| 1B | 51 | 9/48 | Orig.; Rubano c&a | 1 | 1 | 10.00 | 30.00 | 70.00 |
| 1C | 51 | 9/48 | Orig.; outside-bc: blue & yellow only; rare | 1 | 1 | 11.50 | 34.00 | 80.00 |
| 2 | 64 | — | No c-price; LDC-r | 1 | 1 | 2.65 | 8.00 | 18.00 |
| 3 | 78 | — | C-price 15¢; LDC-r | 1 | 1 | 2.00 | 6.00 | 14.00 |
| 4 | 94 | — | LDC-r | 1 | 1 | 1.70 | 5.00 | 12.00 |
| 5 | 117 | — | LDC-r | 1 | 1 | 1.70 | 5.00 | 10.00 |
| 6 | 132 | — | LDC-r | 1 | 1 | 1.50 | 4.50 | 9.00 |
| 7 | 140 | — | New-c; PC-r | 1 | 2 | 1.50 | 4.50 | 9.00 |
| 8 | 150 | — | PC-r | 1 | 2 | 1.30 | 4.00 | 8.00 |
| 9 | 164 | — | New-a; PC-r | 2 | 2 | 1.50 | 4.50 | 9.00 |
| 10 | 167 | — | PC-r | 2 | 2 | 1.25 | 2.50 | 5.00 |
| 11 | 167 | 1/65 | PC-r | 2 | 2 | 1.25 | 2.50 | 5.00 |
| 12 | 167 | 5/66 | PC-r | 2 | 2 | 1.25 | 2.50 | 5.00 |
| 13 | 166 | 12/67 | PC-r | 2 | 2 | 1.25 | 2.50 | 5.00 |
| 14 | 169 | Fall/69 | C-price 25¢; stiff-c PC-r | 2 | 2 | 1.25 | 2.50 | 5.00 |
| 15 | 169 | Win/71 | PC-r | 2 | 2 | 1.25 | 2.50 | 5.00 |

**51. The Spy**

| Ed | HRN | Date | Details | A | C | Good | Fine | N-Mint |
|---|---|---|---|---|---|---|---|---|
| 1A | 51 | 9/48 | Original; inside-bc illo: Christmas Carol | 1 | 1 | 8.00 | 24.00 | 56.00 |
| 1B | 51 | 9/48 | Original; inside-bc illo: Man in Iron Mask | 1 | 1 | 8.50 | 25.50 | 60.00 |
| 1C | 51 | 8/48 | Original; outside-bc: full color | 1 | 1 | 8.50 | 25.50 | 60.00 |
| 1D | 51 | 8/48 | Original; outside-bc: blue & yellow only; scarce | 1 | 1 | 12.00 | 36.00 | 84.00 |
| 2 | 89 | — | C-price 15¢; LDC-r | 1 | 1 | 2.00 | 6.00 | 14.00 |
| 3 | 121 | — | LDC-r | 1 | 1 | 1.70 | 5.00 | 12.00 |
| 4 | 139 | — | New-c; PC-r | 1 | 2 | 1.50 | 4.50 | 9.00 |
| 5 | 156 | — | PC-r | 1 | 2 | 1.25 | 2.50 | 5.00 |
| 6 | 167 | 11/63 | PC-r | 1 | 2 | 1.25 | 2.50 | 5.00 |
| 7 | 167 | 7/66 | PC-r | 1 | 2 | 1.25 | 2.50 | 5.00 |
| 8A | 166 | Win/69 | C-price 25¢; soft-c; scarce; PC-r | 1 | 2 | 1.70 | 5.00 | 12.00 |
| 8B | 166 | Win/69 | C-price 25¢; stiff-c; PC-r | 1 | 2 | 1.25 | 2.50 | 5.00 |

**52. The House of the Seven Gables**

| Ed | HRN | Date | Details | A | C | Good | Fine | N-Mint |
|---|---|---|---|---|---|---|---|---|
| 1 | 53 | 10/48 | Orig.; Griffiths a&c | 1 | 1 | 8.00 | 24.00 | 56.00 |
| 2 | 89 | — | C-price 15¢; LDC-r | 1 | 1 | 2.00 | 6.00 | 14.00 |
| 3 | 121 | — | LDC-r | 1 | 1 | 1.70 | 5.00 | 12.00 |
| 4 | 142 | — | New-c&a; PC-r Woodbridge-a | 2 | 2 | 1.50 | 4.50 | 9.00 |
| 5 | 156 | — | PC-r | 2 | 2 | 1.25 | 2.50 | 5.00 |
| 6 | 165 | — | PC-r | 2 | 2 | 1.25 | 2.50 | 5.00 |
| 7 | 167 | 5/64 | PC-r | 2 | 2 | 1.25 | 2.50 | 5.00 |
| 8 | 167 | 3/66 | PC-r | 2 | 2 | 1.25 | 2.50 | 5.00 |
| 9 | 166 | R/1968 | C-price 25¢; PC-r | 2 | 2 | 1.25 | 2.50 | 5.00 |
| 10 | 169 | Spr/70 | Stiff-c; PC-r | 2 | 2 | 1.25 | 2.50 | 5.00 |

**53. A Christmas Carol**

| Ed | HRN | Date | Details | A | C | Good | Fine | N-Mint |
|---|---|---|---|---|---|---|---|---|
| 1 | 53 | 11/48 | Original & only ed; Kiefer-a,c | 1 | 1 | 10.00 | 30.00 | 70.00 |

**54. Man in the Iron Mask**

| Ed | HRN | Date | Details | A | C | Good | Fine | N-Mint |
|---|---|---|---|---|---|---|---|---|
| 1 | 55 | 12/48 | Original; Froehlich-a, Kiefer-c | 1 | 1 | 8.00 | 24.00 | 56.00 |
| 2 | 93 | — | C-price 15¢; LDC-r | 1 | 1 | 2.00 | 6.00 | 14.00 |
| 3A | 111 | — | (O) logo lettering; scarce; LDC-r | 1 | 1 | 3.00 | 9.00 | 21.00 |
| 3B | 111 | — | New logo as PC; LDC-r | 1 | 1 | 2.00 | 6.00 | 14.00 |
| 4 | 142 | — | New-c&a; PC-r | 2 | 2 | 1.50 | 4.50 | 9.00 |
| 5 | 154 | — | PC-r | 2 | 2 | 1.25 | 2.50 | 5.00 |
| 6 | 165 | — | PC-r | 2 | 2 | 1.25 | 2.50 | 5.00 |
| 7 | 167 | 5/64 | PC-r | 2 | 2 | 1.25 | 2.50 | 5.00 |
| 8 | 167 | 4/66 | PC-r | 2 | 2 | 1.25 | 2.50 | 5.00 |
| 9A | 166 | Win/69 | C-price 25¢; soft-c PC-r | 2 | 2 | 2.00 | 6.00 | 14.00 |
| 9B | 166 | Win/69 | Stiff-c | 2 | 2 | 1.25 | 2.50 | 5.00 |

**55. Silas Marner** (Used in **SOTI**, pgs. 311, 312)

| Ed | HRN | Date | Details | A | C | Good | Fine | N-Mint |
|---|---|---|---|---|---|---|---|---|
| 1 | 55 | 1/49 | Original-Kiefer-c | 1 | 1 | 8.00 | 24.00 | 56.00 |
| 2 | 75 | — | Price circle blank; 'Coming Next' ad; LDC-r | 1 | 1 | 2.65 | 8.00 | 18.00 |
| 3 | 97 | — | LDC-r | 1 | 1 | 1.70 | 5.00 | 12.00 |
| 4 | 121 | — | New-c; PC-r | 1 | 2 | 1.50 | 4.50 | 9.00 |
| 5 | 130 | — | PC-r | 1 | 2 | 1.25 | 2.50 | 5.00 |
| 6 | 140 | — | PC-r | 1 | 2 | 1.25 | 2.50 | 5.00 |
| 7 | 154 | — | PC-r | 1 | 2 | 1.25 | 2.50 | 5.00 |
| 8 | 165 | — | PC-r | 1 | 2 | 1.25 | 2.50 | 5.00 |
| 9 | 167 | 2/64 | PC-r | 1 | 2 | 1.25 | 2.50 | 5.00 |
| 10 | 167 | 6/65 | PC-r | 1 | 2 | 1.25 | 2.50 | 5.00 |
| 11 | 166 | 5/67 | PC-r | 1 | 2 | 1.25 | 2.50 | 5.00 |
| 12A | 166 | Win/69 | C-price 25¢; soft-c PC-r | 1 | 2 | 2.00 | 6.00 | 14.00 |
| 12B | 166 | Win/69 | C-price 25¢; stiff-c PC-r | 1 | 2 | 1.25 | 2.50 | 5.00 |

**56. The Toilers of the Sea**

| Ed | HRN | Date | Details | A | C | Good | Fine | N-Mint |
|---|---|---|---|---|---|---|---|---|
| 1 | 55 | 2/49 | Original; A.M. Froehlich-c/a | 1 | 1 | 12.00 | 36.00 | 85.00 |
| 2 | 165 | — | New-c&a; PC-r; Angelo Torres-a | 2 | 2 | 3.00 | 9.00 | 21.00 |
| 3 | 167 | 3/64 | PC-r | 2 | 2 | 2.00 | 6.00 | 14.00 |
| 4 | 167 | 10/66 | PC-r | 2 | 2 | 2.00 | 6.00 | 14.00 |

**57. The Song of Hiawatha**

| Ed | HRN | Date | Details | A | C | Good | Fine | N-Mint |
|---|---|---|---|---|---|---|---|---|
| 1 | 55 | 3/49 | Original; Alex Blum a&c | 1 | 1 | 7.00 | 21.00 | 50.00 |
| 2 | 75 | — | No c-price; 'Coming Next'ad; LDC-r | 1 | 1 | 2.65 | 8.00 | 18.00 |
| 3 | 94 | — | C-price 15¢; LDC-r | 1 | 1 | 1.70 | 5.00 | 12.00 |
| 4 | 118 | — | LDC-r | 1 | 1 | 1.70 | 5.00 | 10.00 |
| 5 | 134 | — | New-c; PC-r | 1 | 2 | 1.50 | 4.50 | 9.00 |
| 6 | 139 | — | PC-r | 1 | 2 | 1.25 | 2.50 | 5.00 |
| 7 | 154 | — | PC-r | 1 | 2 | 1.25 | 2.50 | 5.00 |
| 8 | 167 | — | Has orig.date; PC-r | 1 | 2 | 1.25 | 2.50 | 5.00 |
| 9 | 167 | 9/64 | PC-r | 1 | 2 | 1.25 | 2.50 | 5.00 |

*Classics Illustrated #51 (Orig.), © GIL*

*Classics Illustrated #53 (Orig.), © GIL*

*Classics Illustrated #57 (Orig.), © GIL*

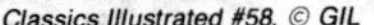
Classics Illustrated #58, © GIL

Classics Illustrated #64 (Orig.), © GIL

Classics Illustrated #67 (Orig.), © GIL

| | | | | | Good | Fine | N-Mint |
|---|---|---|---|---|---|---|---|
| 10 | 167 | 10/65 | PC-r | 1 2 | 1.25 | 2.50 | 5.00 |
| 11 | 166 | F/1968 | C-price 25¢; PC-r | 1 2 | 1.25 | 2.50 | 5.00 |

**58. The Prairie**

| Ed | HRN | Date | Details | A C | Good | Fine | N-Mint |
|---|---|---|---|---|---|---|---|
| 1 | 60 | 4/49 | Original; Palais c/a | 1 1 | 7.00 | 21.00 | 50.00 |
| 2 | 62 | — | No c-price; no coming-next ad; LDC-r | 1 1 | 4.00 | 12.00 | 28.00 |
| 3 | 78 | — | C-price 15¢ in dbl circle; LDC-r | 1 1 | 2.30 | 7.00 | 16.00 |
| 4 | 114 | — | LDC-r | 1 1 | 1.70 | 5.00 | 12.00 |
| 5 | 131 | — | LDC-r | 1 1 | 1.70 | 5.00 | 10.00 |
| 6 | 132 | — | LDC-r | 1 1 | 1.70 | 5.00 | 10.00 |
| 7 | 146 | — | New-c; PC-r | 1 2 | 1.50 | 4.50 | 9.00 |
| 8 | 155 | — | PC-r | 1 2 | 1.25 | 2.50 | 5.00 |
| 9 | 167 | 5/64 | PC-r | 1 2 | 1.25 | 2.50 | 5.00 |
| 10 | 167 | 4/66 | PC-r | 1 2 | 1.25 | 2.50 | 5.00 |
| 11 | 169 | Sm/69 | New price 25¢; stiff-c; PC-r | 1 2 | 1.25 | 2.50 | 5.00 |

**59. Wuthering Heights**

| Ed | HRN | Date | Details | A C | Good | Fine | N-Mint |
|---|---|---|---|---|---|---|---|
| 1 | 60 | 5/49 | Original; Kiefer a/c | 1 1 | 8.50 | 25.50 | 60.00 |
| 2 | 85 | — | C-price 15¢; LDC-r | 1 1 | 3.00 | 9.00 | 21.00 |
| 3 | 156 | — | New-c; PC-r | 1 2 | 1.70 | 5.00 | 10.00 |
| 4 | 167 | 1/64 | PC-r | 1 2 | 1.50 | 3.00 | 6.00 |
| 5 | 167 | 10/66 | PC-r | 1 2 | 1.50 | 3.00 | 6.00 |
| 6 | 169 | Sm/69 | C-price 25¢; stiff-c; PC-r | 1 2 | 1.25 | 2.50 | 5.00 |

**60. Black Beauty**

| Ed | HRN | Date | Details | A C | Good | Fine | N-Mint |
|---|---|---|---|---|---|---|---|
| 1 | 62 | 6/49 | Original; Froehlich c/a | 1 1 | 7.00 | 21.00 | 50.00 |
| 2 | 62 | — | No c-price; no coming-next ad; LDC-r (rare) | 1 1 | 8.00 | 24.00 | 56.00 |
| 3 | 85 | — | C-price 15¢; LDC-r | 1 1 | 2.65 | 8.00 | 18.00 |
| 4 | 158 | — | New L.B. Cole-c&a; PC-r | 2 2 | 2.65 | 8.00 | 18.00 |
| 5 | 167 | 2/64 | PC-r | 2 2 | 1.70 | 5.00 | 12.00 |
| 6 | 167 | 3/66 | PC-r | 2 2 | 1.70 | 5.00 | 12.00 |
| 7 | 166 | R/1968 | New-c&price, 25¢; PC-r | 2 3 | 5.00 | 15.00 | 35.00 |

**61. The Woman in White**

| Ed | HRN | Date | Details | A C | Good | Fine | N-Mint |
|---|---|---|---|---|---|---|---|
| 1A | 62 | 7/49 | Original; Blum-c/a fc-purple; bc: top illos light blue | 1 1 | 7.00 | 21.00 | 50.00 |
| 1B | 62 | 7/49 | Original; Blum-c/a fc-pink; bc: top illos light violet | 1 1 | 7.00 | 21.00 | 50.00 |
| 2 | 156 | — | New-c; PC-r | 1 2 | 2.00 | 6.00 | 14.00 |
| 3 | 167 | 1/64 | PC-r | 1 2 | 1.70 | 5.00 | 12.00 |
| 4 | 166 | R/1968 | C-price 25¢; PC-r | 1 2 | 1.70 | 5.00 | 12.00 |

**62. Western Stories** ("The Luck of Roaring Camp" and "The Outcasts of Poker Flat")

| Ed | HRN | Date | Details | A C | Good | Fine | N-Mint |
|---|---|---|---|---|---|---|---|
| 1 | 62 | 8/49 | Original; Kiefer-c/a | 1 1 | 7.00 | 21.00 | 50.00 |
| 2 | 89 | — | C-price 15¢; LDC-r | 1 1 | 2.30 | 7.00 | 16.00 |
| 3 | 121 | — | LDC-r | 1 1 | 1.70 | 5.00 | 12.00 |
| 4 | 137 | — | New-c; PC-r | 1 2 | 1.50 | 4.50 | 9.00 |
| 5 | 152 | — | PC-r | 1 2 | 1.50 | 3.00 | 6.00 |
| 6 | 167 | 10/63 | PC-r | 1 2 | 1.50 | 3.00 | 6.00 |
| 7 | 167 | 6/64 | PC-r | 1 2 | 1.25 | 2.50 | 5.00 |
| 8 | 167 | 11/66 | PC-r | 1 2 | 1.25 | 2.50 | 5.00 |
| 9 | 166 | R/1968 | New-c&price 25¢; PC-r | 1 3 | 1.70 | 5.00 | 12.00 |

**63. The Man Without a Country**

| Ed | HRN | Date | Details | A C | Good | Fine | N-Mint |
|---|---|---|---|---|---|---|---|
| 1 | 62 | 9/49 | Original; Kiefer-a,c | 1 1 | 7.00 | 21.00 | 50.00 |
| 2 | 78 | — | C-price 15¢ in double circle; LDC-r | 1 1 | 2.65 | 8.00 | 18.00 |
| 3 | 156 | — | New-c, old-a; PC-r | 1 2 | 2.30 | 7.00 | 16.00 |
| 4 | 165 | — | New-a & text pgs.; PC-r; A. Torres-a | 2 2 | 1.70 | 5.00 | 10.00 |
| 5 | 167 | 3/64 | PC-r | 2 2 | 1.25 | 2.50 | 5.00 |
| 6 | 167 | 8/66 | PC-r | 2 2 | 1.25 | 2.50 | 5.00 |
| 7 | 169 | Sm/69 | New price 25¢; stiff-c; PC-r | 2 2 | 1.25 | 2.50 | 5.00 |

**64. Treasure Island**

| Ed | HRN | Date | Details | A C | Good | Fine | N-Mint |
|---|---|---|---|---|---|---|---|
| 1 | 62 | 10/49 | Original; Blum-a,c | 1 1 | 7.00 | 21.00 | 50.00 |
| 2A | 82 | — | C-price 15¢; soft-c LDC-r | 1 1 | 2.30 | 7.00 | 16.00 |
| 2B | 82 | — | Stiff-c; LDC-r | 1 1 | .85 | 2.50 | 5.00 |
| 3 | 117 | — | LDC-r | 1 1 | 1.70 | 5.00 | 12.00 |
| 4 | 131 | — | New-c; PC-r | 1 2 | 1.50 | 4.50 | 9.00 |
| 5 | 138 | — | PC-r | 1 2 | 1.25 | 2.50 | 5.00 |
| 6 | 146 | — | PC-r | 1 2 | 1.25 | 2.50 | 5.00 |
| 7 | 158 | — | PC-r | 1 2 | 1.25 | 2.50 | 5.00 |
| 8 | 165 | — | PC-r | 1 2 | 1.25 | 2.50 | 5.00 |
| 9 | 167 | — | PC-r | 1 2 | 1.25 | 2.50 | 5.00 |
| 10 | 167 | 6/64 | PC-r | 1 2 | 1.25 | 2.50 | 5.00 |
| 11 | 167 | 12/65 | PC-r | 1 2 | 1.25 | 2.50 | 5.00 |
| 12A | 166 | 10/67 | PC-r | 1 2 | 1.50 | 4.50 | 9.00 |
| 12B | 166 | 10/67 | w/Grit ad stapled in book | 1 2 | 7.00 | 21.00 | 50.00 |
| 13 | 169 | Spr/69 | New price 25¢; stiff-c; PC-r | 1 2 | 1.25 | 2.50 | 5.00 |

**65. Benjamin Franklin**

| Ed | HRN | Date | Details | A C | Good | Fine | N-Mint |
|---|---|---|---|---|---|---|---|
| 1 | 64 | 11/49 | Original; Kiefer-c Iger Shop-a | 1 1 | 7.00 | 21.00 | 50.00 |
| 2 | 131 | — | New-c; PC-r | 1 2 | 1.70 | 5.00 | 10.00 |
| 3 | 154 | — | PC-r | 1 2 | 1.25 | 2.50 | 5.00 |
| 4 | 167 | 2/64 | PC-r | 1 2 | 1.25 | 2.50 | 5.00 |
| 5 | 167 | 4/66 | PC-r | 1 2 | 1.25 | 2.50 | 5.00 |
| 6 | 169 | Fall/69 | New price 25¢; stiff-c; PC-r | 1 2 | 1.00 | 2.00 | 4.00 |

**66. The Cloister and the Hearth**

| Ed | HRN | Date | Details | A C | Good | Fine | N-Mint |
|---|---|---|---|---|---|---|---|
| 1 | 67 | 12/49 | Original & only ed; Kiefer-a & c | 1 1 | 17.00 | 50.00 | 115.00 |

**67. The Scottish Chiefs**

| Ed | HRN | Date | Details | A C | Good | Fine | N-Mint |
|---|---|---|---|---|---|---|---|
| 1 | 67 | 1/50 | Original; Blum-a&c | 1 1 | 6.50 | 19.00 | 45.00 |
| 2 | 85 | — | C-price 15¢; LDC-r | 1 1 | 2.30 | 7.00 | 16.00 |
| 3 | 118 | — | LDC-r | 1 1 | 1.70 | 5.00 | 12.00 |
| 4 | 136 | — | New-c; PC-r | 1 2 | 1.50 | 4.50 | 9.00 |
| 5 | 154 | — | PC-r | 1 2 | 1.50 | 3.50 | 7.00 |
| 6 | 167 | 11/63 | PC-r | 1 2 | 1.50 | 3.50 | 7.00 |
| 7 | 167 | 8/65 | PC-r | 1 2 | 1.50 | 3.50 | 7.00 |

**68. Julius Caesar** (Used in **SOTI**, pgs. 36, 37)

| Ed | HRN | Date | Details | A | C | Good | Fine | N-Mint |
|---|---|---|---|---|---|---|---|---|
| 1 | 70 | 2/50 | Original; Kiefer-a,c | 1 | 1 | 7.00 | 21.00 | 50.00 |
| 2 | 85 | — | C-price 15¢; LDC-r | 1 | 1 | 2.30 | 7.00 | 16.00 |
| 3 | 108 | — | LDC-r | 1 | 1 | 1.70 | 5.00 | 12.00 |
| 4 | 156 | — | New L.B. Cole-c; PC-r | 1 | 2 | 2.30 | 7.00 | 16.00 |
| 5 | 165 | — | New-a by Evans, Crandall; PC-r | 2 | 2 | 2.30 | 7.00 | 16.00 |
| 6 | 167 | 2/64 | PC-r | 2 | 2 | 1.25 | 2.50 | 5.00 |
| 7 | 167 | 10/65 | Tarzan books inside cover; PC-r | 2 | 2 | 1.25 | 2.50 | 5.00 |
| 8 | 166 | R/1967 | PC-r | 2 | 2 | 1.25 | 2.50 | 5.00 |
| 9 | 169 | Win/69 | PC-r; stiff-c | 2 | 2 | 1.25 | 2.50 | 5.00 |

**69. Around the World in 80 Days**

| Ed | HRN | Date | Details | A | C | Good | Fine | N-Mint |
|---|---|---|---|---|---|---|---|---|
| 1 | 70 | 3/50 | Original; Kiefer-a/c | 1 | 1 | 7.00 | 21.00 | 50.00 |
| 2 | 87 | — | C-price 15¢; LDC-r | 1 | 1 | 2.30 | 7.00 | 16.00 |
| 3 | 125 | — | LDC-r | 1 | 1 | 1.70 | 5.00 | 12.00 |
| 4 | 136 | — | New-c; PC-r | 1 | 2 | 1.50 | 4.50 | 9.00 |
| 5 | 146 | — | PC-r | 1 | 2 | 1.25 | 2.50 | 5.00 |
| 6 | 152 | — | PC-r | 1 | 2 | 1.25 | 2.50 | 5.00 |
| 7 | 164 | — | PC-r | 1 | 2 | 1.25 | 2.50 | 5.00 |
| 8 | 167 | — | PC-r | 1 | 2 | 1.25 | 2.50 | 5.00 |
| 9 | 167 | 7/64 | PC-r | 1 | 2 | 1.25 | 2.50 | 5.00 |
| 10 | 167 | 11/65 | PC-r | 1 | 2 | 1.25 | 2.50 | 5.00 |
| 11 | 166 | 7/67 | PC-r | 1 | 2 | 1.25 | 2.50 | 5.00 |
| 12 | 169 | Spr/69 | C-price 25¢; stiff-c; PC-r | 1 | 2 | 1.25 | 2.50 | 5.00 |

**70. The Pilot**

| Ed | HRN | Date | Details | A | C | Good | Fine | N-Mint |
|---|---|---|---|---|---|---|---|---|
| 1 | 71 | 4/50 | Original; Blum-c/a | 1 | 1 | 5.70 | 17.00 | 40.00 |
| 2 | 92 | — | C-price 15¢; LDC-r | 1 | 1 | 2.30 | 7.00 | 16.00 |
| 3 | 125 | — | LDC-r | 1 | 1 | 1.70 | 5.00 | 12.00 |
| 4 | 156 | — | New-c; PC-r | 1 | 2 | 1.70 | 5.00 | 10.00 |
| 5 | 167 | 2/64 | PC-r | 1 | 2 | 1.50 | 3.50 | 7.00 |
| 6 | 167 | 5/66 | PC-r | 1 | 2 | 1.50 | 3.50 | 7.00 |

**71. The Man Who Laughs**

| Ed | HRN | Date | Details | A | C | Good | Fine | N-Mint |
|---|---|---|---|---|---|---|---|---|
| 1 | 71 | 5/50 | Original; Blum-a,c | 1 | 1 | 10.00 | 30.00 | 70.00 |
| 2 | 165 | — | New-c&a; PC-r | 2 | 2 | 6.50 | 19.50 | 45.00 |
| 3 | 167 | 4/64 | PC-r | 2 | 2 | 5.70 | 17.00 | 40.00 |

**72. The Oregon Trail**

| Ed | HRN | Date | Details | A | C | Good | Fine | N-Mint |
|---|---|---|---|---|---|---|---|---|
| 1 | 73 | 6/50 | Original; Kiefer-a,c | 1 | 1 | 5.70 | 17.00 | 40.00 |
| 2 | 89 | — | C-price 15¢; LDC-r | 1 | 1 | 2.30 | 7.00 | 16.00 |
| 3 | 121 | — | LDC-r | 1 | 1 | 1.70 | 5.00 | 12.00 |
| 4 | 131 | — | New-c; PC-r | 1 | 2 | 1.50 | 4.50 | 9.00 |
| 5 | 140 | — | PC-r | 1 | 2 | 1.50 | 3.00 | 6.00 |
| 6 | 150 | — | PC-r | 1 | 2 | 1.25 | 2.50 | 5.00 |
| 7 | 164 | — | PC-r | 1 | 2 | 1.25 | 2.50 | 5.00 |
| 8 | 167 | — | PC-r | 1 | 2 | 1.25 | 2.50 | 5.00 |
| 9 | 167 | 8/64 | PC-r | 1 | 2 | 1.25 | 2.50 | 5.00 |
| 10 | 167 | 10/65 | PC-r | 1 | 2 | 1.25 | 2.50 | 5.00 |
| 11 | 166 | R/1968 | C-price 25¢; PC-r | 1 | 2 | 1.25 | 2.50 | 5.00 |

**73. The Black Tulip**

| Ed | HRN | Date | Details | A | C | Good | Fine | N-Mint |
|---|---|---|---|---|---|---|---|---|
| 1 | 75 | 7/50 | 1st & only ed.; Alex Blum-a & c | 1 | 1 | 20.00 | 60.00 | 140.00 |

**74. Mr. Midshipman Easy**

| Ed | HRN | Date | Details | A | C | Good | Fine | N-Mint |
|---|---|---|---|---|---|---|---|---|
| 1 | 75 | 8/50 | 1st & only edition | 1 | 1 | 20.00 | 60.00 | 140.00 |

**75. The Lady of the Lake**

| Ed | HRN | Date | Details | A | C | Good | Fine | N-Mint |
|---|---|---|---|---|---|---|---|---|
| 1 | 75 | 9/50 | Original; Kiefer-a/c | 1 | 1 | 5.30 | 16.00 | 38.00 |
| 2 | 85 | — | C-price 15¢; LDC-r | 1 | 1 | 2.30 | 7.00 | 16.00 |
| 3 | 118 | — | LDC-r | 1 | 1 | 1.70 | 5.00 | 12.00 |
| 4 | 139 | — | New-c; PC-r | 1 | 2 | 1.50 | 4.50 | 9.00 |
| 5 | 154 | — | PC-r | 1 | 2 | 1.25 | 2.50 | 5.00 |
| 6 | 165 | — | PC-r | 1 | 2 | 1.25 | 2.50 | 5.00 |
| 7 | 167 | 4/64 | PC-r | 1 | 2 | 1.25 | 2.50 | 5.00 |
| 8 | 167 | 5/66 | PC-r | 1 | 2 | 1.25 | 2.50 | 5.00 |
| 9 | 169 | Spr/69 | New price 25¢; stiff-c; PC-r | 1 | 2 | 1.25 | 2.50 | 5.00 |

**76. The Prisoner of Zenda**

| Ed | HRN | Date | Details | A | C | Good | Fine | N-Mint |
|---|---|---|---|---|---|---|---|---|
| 1 | 75 | 10/50 | Original; Kiefer-a,c | 1 | 1 | 5.00 | 15.00 | 35.00 |
| 2 | 85 | — | C-price 15¢; LDC-r | 1 | 1 | 2.30 | 7.00 | 16.00 |
| 3 | 111 | — | LDC-r | 1 | 1 | 1.70 | 5.00 | 12.00 |
| 4 | 128 | — | New-c; PC-r | 1 | 2 | 1.50 | 4.50 | 9.00 |
| 5 | 152 | — | PC-r | 1 | 2 | 1.25 | 2.50 | 5.00 |
| 6 | 165 | — | PC-r | 1 | 2 | 1.25 | 2.50 | 5.00 |
| 7 | 167 | 4/64 | PC-r | 1 | 2 | 1.25 | 2.50 | 5.00 |
| 8 | 167 | 9/66 | PC-r | 1 | 2 | 1.25 | 2.50 | 5.00 |
| 9 | 169 | Fall/69 | New price 25¢; stiff-c; PC-r | 1 | 2 | 1.25 | 2.50 | 5.00 |

**77. The Iliad**

| Ed | HRN | Date | Details | A | C | Good | Fine | N-Mint |
|---|---|---|---|---|---|---|---|---|
| 1 | 78 | 11/50 | Original; Blum-a,c | 1 | 1 | 5.00 | 15.00 | 35.00 |
| 2 | 87 | — | C-price 15¢; LDC-r | 1 | 1 | 2.30 | 7.00 | 16.00 |
| 3 | 121 | — | LDC-r | 1 | 1 | 1.70 | 5.00 | 12.00 |
| 4 | 139 | — | New-c; PC-r | 1 | 2 | 1.50 | 4.50 | 9.00 |
| 5 | 150 | — | PC-r | 1 | 2 | 1.25 | 2.50 | 5.00 |
| 6 | 165 | — | PC-r | 1 | 2 | 1.25 | 2.50 | 5.00 |
| 7 | 167 | 10/63 | PC-r | 1 | 2 | 1.25 | 2.50 | 5.00 |
| 8 | 167 | 7/64 | PC-r | 1 | 2 | 1.25 | 2.50 | 5.00 |
| 9 | 167 | 5/66 | PC-r | 1 | 2 | 1.25 | 2.50 | 5.00 |
| 10 | 166 | R/1968 | C-price 25¢; PC-r | 1 | 2 | 1.25 | 2.50 | 5.00 |

**78. Joan of Arc**

| Ed | HRN | Date | Details | A | C | Good | Fine | N-Mint |
|---|---|---|---|---|---|---|---|---|
| 1 | 78 | 12/50 | Original; Kiefer-a,c | 1 | 1 | 5.00 | 15.00 | 35.00 |
| 2 | 87 | — | C-price 15¢; LDC-r | 1 | 1 | 2.30 | 7.00 | 16.00 |
| 3 | 113 | — | LDC-r | 1 | 1 | 1.70 | 5.00 | 12.00 |
| 4 | 128 | — | New-c; PC-r | 1 | 2 | 1.50 | 4.50 | 9.00 |
| 5 | 140 | — | PC-r | 1 | 2 | 1.25 | 2.50 | 5.00 |
| 6 | 150 | — | PC-r | 1 | 2 | 1.25 | 2.50 | 5.00 |
| 7 | 159 | — | PC-r | 1 | 2 | 1.25 | 2.50 | 5.00 |
| 8 | 167 | — | PC-r | 1 | 2 | 1.25 | 2.50 | 5.00 |
| 9 | 167 | 12/63 | PC-r | 1 | 2 | 1.25 | 2.50 | 5.00 |
| 10 | 167 | 6/65 | PC-r | 1 | 2 | 1.25 | 2.50 | 5.00 |
| 11 | 166 | 6/67 | PC-r | 1 | 2 | 1.25 | 2.50 | 5.00 |
| 12 | 166 | Win/69 | New-c&price, 25¢; PC-r; stiff-c | 1 | 3 | 1.70 | 5.00 | 12.00 |

**79. Cyrano de Bergerac**

| Ed | HRN | Date | Details | A | C | Good | Fine | N-Mint |
|---|---|---|---|---|---|---|---|---|
| 1 | 78 | 1/51 | Orig.; movie promo inside front-c; Blum-a & c | 1 | 1 | 5.00 | 15.00 | 35.00 |
| 2 | 85 | — | C-price 15¢; LDC-r | 1 | 1 | 2.30 | 7.00 | 16.00 |
| 3 | 118 | — | LDC-r | 1 | 1 | 1.70 | 5.00 | 12.00 |
| 4 | 133 | — | New-c; PC-r | 1 | 2 | 1.70 | 5.00 | 12.00 |
| 5 | 156 | — | PC-r | 1 | 2 | 1.50 | 4.50 | 9.00 |
| 6 | 167 | 8/64 | PC-r | 1 | 2 | 1.50 | 4.50 | 9.00 |

*Classics Illustrated #72 (Orig.), © GIL*

*Classics Illustrated #74 (Orig.), © GIL*

*Classics Illustrated #78 (HRN-128), © GIL*

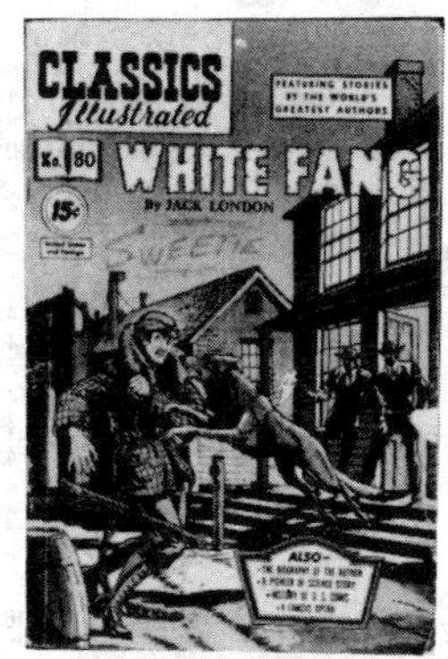

*Classics Illustrated #80, © GIL*

*Classics Illustrated #84 (HRN-167), © GIL*

*Classics Illustrated #88, © GIL*

**80. White Fang** (Last line drawn cover)

| Ed | HRN | Date | Details | A | C | Good | Fine | N-Mint |
|---|---|---|---|---|---|---|---|---|
| 1 | 79 | 2/51 | Orig.; Blum-a&c | 1 | 1 | 5.00 | 15.00 | 35.00 |
| 2 | 87 | — | C-price 15¢; LDC-r | 1 | 1 | 2.30 | 7.00 | 16.00 |
| 3 | 125 | — | LDC-r | 1 | 1 | 1.70 | 5.00 | 12.00 |
| 4 | 132 | — | New-c; PC-r | 1 | 2 | 1.50 | 4.50 | 9.00 |
| 5 | 140 | — | PC-r | 1 | 2 | 1.25 | 2.50 | 5.00 |
| 6 | 153 | — | PC-r | 1 | 2 | 1.25 | 2.50 | 5.00 |
| 7 | 167 | — | PC-r | 1 | 2 | 1.25 | 2.50 | 5.00 |
| 8 | 167 | 9/64 | PC-r | 1 | 2 | 1.25 | 2.50 | 5.00 |
| 9 | 167 | 7/65 | PC-r | 1 | 2 | 1.25 | 2.50 | 5.00 |
| 10 | 166 | 6/67 | PC-r | 1 | 2 | 1.25 | 2.50 | 5.00 |
| 11 | 169 | Fall/69 | New price 25¢; PC-r; stiff-c | 1 | 2 | 1.25 | 2.50 | 5.00 |

**81. The Odyssey** (1st painted cover)

| Ed | HRN | Date | Details | A | C | Good | Fine | N-Mint |
|---|---|---|---|---|---|---|---|---|
| 1 | 82 | 3/51 | First 15¢ Original; Blum-c | 1 | 1 | 3.50 | 10.50 | 24.00 |
| 2 | 167 | 8/64 | PC-r | 1 | 1 | 1.70 | 5.00 | 10.00 |
| 3 | 167 | 10/66 | PC-r | 1 | 1 | 1.70 | 5.00 | 10.00 |
| 4 | 169 | Spr/69 | New, stiff-c; PC-r | 1 | 2 | 1.70 | 5.00 | 10.00 |

**82. The Master of Ballantrae**

| Ed | HRN | Date | Details | A | C | Good | Fine | N-Mint |
|---|---|---|---|---|---|---|---|---|
| 1 | 82 | 4/51 | Original; Blum-c | 1 | 1 | 3.50 | 10.50 | 24.00 |
| 2 | 167 | 8/64 | PC-r | 1 | 1 | 1.70 | 5.00 | 12.00 |
| 3 | 166 | Fall/68 | New, stiff-c; PC-r | 1 | 2 | 1.70 | 5.00 | 12.00 |

**83. The Jungle Book**

| Ed | HRN | Date | Details | A | C | Good | Fine | N-Mint |
|---|---|---|---|---|---|---|---|---|
| 1 | 85 | 5/51 | Original; Blum-c Bossert/Blum-a | 1 | 1 | 3.50 | 10.50 | 24.00 |
| 2 | 110 | — | PC-r | 1 | 1 | 1.25 | 2.50 | 5.00 |
| 3 | 125 | — | PC-r | 1 | 1 | 1.25 | 2.50 | 5.00 |
| 4 | 134 | — | PC-r | 1 | 1 | 1.25 | 2.50 | 5.00 |
| 5 | 142 | — | PC-r | 1 | 1 | 1.25 | 2.50 | 5.00 |
| 6 | 150 | — | PC-r | 1 | 1 | 1.25 | 2.50 | 5.00 |
| 7 | 159 | — | PC-r | 1 | 1 | 1.25 | 2.50 | 5.00 |
| 8 | 167 | — | PC-r | 1 | 1 | 1.25 | 2.50 | 5.00 |
| 9 | 167 | 3/65 | PC-r | 1 | 1 | 1.25 | 2.50 | 5.00 |
| 10 | 167 | 11/65 | PC-r | 1 | 1 | 1.25 | 2.50 | 5.00 |
| 11 | 167 | 5/66 | PC-r | 1 | 1 | 1.25 | 2.50 | 5.00 |
| 12 | 166 | R/1968 | New c&a; stiff-c; PC-r | 2 | 2 | 1.50 | 4.50 | 10.00 |

**84. The Gold Bug and Other Stories** ("The Gold Bug," "The Tell-Tale Heart," "The Cask of Amontillado")

| Ed | HRN | Date | Details | A | C | Good | Fine | N-Mint |
|---|---|---|---|---|---|---|---|---|
| 1 | 85 | 6/51 | Original; Blum-c/a Palais, Laverly-a | 1 | 1 | 10.00 | 30.00 | 70.00 |
| 2 | 167 | 7/64 | PC-r | 1 | 1 | 5.30 | 16.00 | 38.00 |

**85. The Sea Wolf**

| Ed | HRN | Date | Details | A | C | Good | Fine | N-Mint |
|---|---|---|---|---|---|---|---|---|
| 1 | 85 | 7/51 | Original; Blum-a&c | 1 | 1 | 2.65 | 8.00 | 18.00 |
| 2 | 121 | — | PC-r | 1 | 1 | 1.00 | 2.00 | 4.00 |
| 3 | 132 | — | PC-r | 1 | 1 | 1.00 | 2.00 | 4.00 |
| 4 | 141 | — | PC-r | 1 | 1 | 1.00 | 2.00 | 4.00 |
| 5 | 161 | — | PC-r | 1 | 1 | 1.00 | 2.00 | 4.00 |
| 6 | 167 | 2/64 | PC-r | 1 | 1 | 1.00 | 2.00 | 4.00 |
| 7 | 167 | 11/65 | PC-r | 1 | 1 | 1.00 | 2.00 | 4.00 |
| 8 | 169 | Fall/69 | New price 25¢; stiff-c; PC-r | 1 | 1 | 1.00 | 2.00 | 4.00 |

**86. Under Two Flags**

| Ed | HRN | Date | Details | A | C | Good | Fine | N-Mint |
|---|---|---|---|---|---|---|---|---|
| 1 | 87 | 8/51 | Original; first delBourgo-a | 1 | 1 | 2.65 | 8.00 | 18.00 |
| 2 | 117 | — | PC-r | 1 | 1 | 1.00 | 2.00 | 4.00 |
| 3 | 139 | — | PC-r | 1 | 1 | 1.00 | 2.00 | 4.00 |
| 4 | 158 | — | PC-r | 1 | 1 | 1.00 | 2.00 | 4.00 |
| 5 | 167 | 2/64 | PC-r | 1 | 1 | 1.00 | 2.00 | 4.00 |
| 6 | 167 | 8/66 | PC-r | 1 | 1 | 1.00 | 2.00 | 4.00 |
| 7 | 169 | Sm/69 | New price 25¢; stiff-c; PC-r | 1 | 1 | 1.00 | 2.00 | 4.00 |

**87. A Midsummer Nights Dream**

| Ed | HRN | Date | Details | A | C | Good | Fine | N-Mint |
|---|---|---|---|---|---|---|---|---|
| 1 | 87 | 9/51 | Original; Blum c/a | 1 | 1 | 2.65 | 8.00 | 18.00 |
| 2 | 161 | — | PC-r | 1 | 1 | 1.25 | 2.50 | 5.00 |
| 3 | 167 | 4/64 | PC-r | 1 | 1 | 1.00 | 2.00 | 4.00 |
| 4 | 167 | 5/66 | PC-r | 1 | 1 | 1.00 | 2.00 | 4.00 |
| 5 | 169 | Sm/69 | New price 25¢; stiff-c; PC-r | 1 | 1 | 1.00 | 2.00 | 4.00 |

**88. Men of Iron**

| Ed | HRN | Date | Details | A | C | Good | Fine | N-Mint |
|---|---|---|---|---|---|---|---|---|
| 1 | 89 | 10/51 | Original | 1 | 1 | 3.00 | 9.00 | 21.00 |
| 2 | 154 | — | PC-r | 1 | 1 | 1.00 | 2.00 | 4.00 |
| 3 | 167 | 1/64 | PC-r | 1 | 1 | 1.00 | 2.00 | 4.00 |
| 4 | 166 | R/1968 | C-price 25¢; PC-r | 1 | 1 | 1.00 | 2.00 | 4.00 |

**89. Crime and Punishment** (Cover illo. in **POP**)

| Ed | HRN | Date | Details | A | C | Good | Fine | N-Mint |
|---|---|---|---|---|---|---|---|---|
| 1 | 89 | 11/51 | Original; Palais-a | 1 | 1 | 3.00 | 9.00 | 21.00 |
| 2 | 152 | — | PC-r | 1 | 1 | 1.00 | 2.00 | 4.00 |
| 3 | 167 | 4/64 | PC-r | 1 | 1 | 1.00 | 2.00 | 4.00 |
| 4 | 167 | 5/66 | PC-r | 1 | 1 | 1.00 | 2.00 | 4.00 |
| 5 | 169 | Fall/69 | New price 25¢ stiff-c; PC-r | 1 | 1 | 1.00 | 2.00 | 4.00 |

**90. Green Mansions**

| Ed | HRN | Date | Details | A | C | Good | Fine | N-Mint |
|---|---|---|---|---|---|---|---|---|
| 1 | 89 | 12/51 | Original; Blum-a&c | 1 | 1 | 3.50 | 10.50 | 24.00 |
| 2 | 148 | — | New L.B. Cole -c; PC-r | 1 | 2 | 2.00 | 4.00 | 8.00 |
| 3 | 165 | — | PC-r | 1 | 2 | 1.00 | 2.00 | 4.00 |
| 4 | 167 | 4/64 | PC-r | 1 | 2 | 1.00 | 2.00 | 4.00 |
| 5 | 167 | 9/66 | PC-r | 1 | 2 | 1.00 | 2.00 | 4.00 |
| 6 | 169 | Sm/69 | New price 25¢; stiff-c; PC-r | 1 | 2 | 1.00 | 2.00 | 4.00 |

**91. The Call of the Wild**

| Ed | HRN | Date | Details | A | C | Good | Fine | N-Mint |
|---|---|---|---|---|---|---|---|---|
| 1 | 92 | 1/52 | Orig.; delBourgo-a | 1 | 1 | 2.65 | 8.00 | 18.00 |
| 2 | 112 | — | PC-r | 1 | 1 | 1.25 | 2.50 | 5.00 |
| 3 | 125 | — | 'Picture Progress' on back-c; PC-r | 1 | 1 | 1.00 | 2.00 | 4.00 |
| 4 | 134 | — | PC-r | 1 | 1 | 1.00 | 2.00 | 4.00 |
| 5 | 143 | — | PC-r | 1 | 1 | 1.00 | 2.00 | 4.00 |
| 6 | 165 | — | PC-r | 1 | 1 | 1.00 | 2.00 | 4.00 |
| 7 | 167 | — | PC-r | 1 | 1 | 1.00 | 2.00 | 4.00 |
| 8 | 167 | 4/65 | PC-r | 1 | 1 | 1.00 | 2.00 | 4.00 |
| 9 | 167 | 3/66 | PC-r | 1 | 1 | 1.00 | 2.00 | 4.00 |
| 10 | 166 | 11/67 | PC-r | 1 | 1 | 1.00 | 2.00 | 4.00 |
| 11 | 169 | Spr/70 | New price 25¢; stiff-c; PC-r | 1 | 1 | 1.00 | 2.00 | 4.00 |

**92. The Courtship of Miles Standish**

| Ed | HRN | Date | Details | A | C | Good | Fine | N-Mint |
|---|---|---|---|---|---|---|---|---|
| 1 | 92 | 2/52 | Original; Blum-a&c | 1 | 1 | 2.65 | 8.00 | 18.00 |
| 2 | 165 | — | PC-r | 1 | 1 | 1.00 | 2.00 | 4.00 |
| 3 | 167 | 3/64 | PC-r | 1 | 1 | 1.00 | 2.00 | 4.00 |
| 4 | 166 | 5/67 | PC-r | 1 | 1 | 1.00 | 2.00 | 4.00 |
| 5 | 169 | Win/69 | New price 25¢ stiff-c; PC-r | 1 | 1 | 1.00 | 2.00 | 4.00 |

### 93. Pudd'nhead Wilson

| Ed | HRN | Date | Details | A | C | Good | Fine | N-Mint |
|---|---|---|---|---|---|---|---|---|
| 1 | 94 | 3/52 | Orig.; Kiefer-a&c; | 1 | 1 | 3.50 | 10.50 | 24.00 |
| 2 | 165 | — | New-c; PC-r | 1 | 2 | 1.50 | 3.50 | 7.00 |
| 3 | 167 | 3/64 | PC-r | 1 | 2 | 1.50 | 3.50 | 5.00 |
| 4 | 166 | R/1968 | New price 25¢; soft-c; PC-r | 1 | 2 | 1.50 | 3.50 | 7.00 |

### 94. David Balfour

| Ed | HRN | Date | Details | A | C | Good | Fine | N-Mint |
|---|---|---|---|---|---|---|---|---|
| 1 | 94 | 4/52 | Original; Palais-a | 1 | 1 | 3.50 | 10.50 | 24.00 |
| 2 | 167 | 5/64 | PC-r | 1 | 1 | 2.00 | 4.00 | 9.00 |
| 3 | 166 | R/1968 | C-price 25¢; PC-r | 1 | 1 | 2.00 | 4.00 | 9.00 |

### 95. All Quiet on the Western Front

| Ed | HRN | Date | Details | A | C | Good | Fine | N-Mint |
|---|---|---|---|---|---|---|---|---|
| 1A | 96 | 5/52 | Orig.; del Bourgo-a | 1 | 1 | 7.00 | 21.00 | 50.00 |
| 1B | 99 | 5/52 | Orig.; del Bourgo-a | 1 | 1 | 6.50 | 19.00 | 45.00 |
| 2 | 167 | 10/64 | PC-r | 1 | 1 | 2.00 | 6.00 | 14.00 |
| 3 | 167 | 11/66 | PC-r | 1 | 1 | 2.00 | 6.00 | 14.00 |

### 96. Daniel Boone

| Ed | HRN | Date | Details | A | C | Good | Fine | N-Mint |
|---|---|---|---|---|---|---|---|---|
| 1 | 97 | 6/52 | Original; Blum-a | 1 | 1 | 2.65 | 8.00 | 18.00 |
| 2 | 117 | — | PC-r | 1 | 1 | 1.00 | 2.00 | 4.00 |
| 3 | 128 | — | PC-r | 1 | 1 | 1.00 | 2.00 | 4.00 |
| 4 | 132 | — | PC-r | 1 | 1 | 1.00 | 2.00 | 4.00 |
| 5 | 134 | — | 'Story of Jesus' on back-c; PC-r | 1 | 1 | 1.00 | 2.00 | 4.00 |
| 6 | 158 | — | PC-r | 1 | 1 | 1.00 | 2.00 | 4.00 |
| 7 | 167 | 1/64 | PC-r | 1 | 1 | 1.00 | 2.00 | 4.00 |
| 8 | 167 | 5/65 | PC-r | 1 | 1 | 1.00 | 2.00 | 4.00 |
| 9 | 167 | 11/66 | PC-r | 1 | 1 | 1.00 | 2.00 | 4.00 |
| 10 | 166 | Win/69 | New-c; price 25¢; PC-r; stiff-c | 1 | 2 | 1.50 | 4.50 | 10.00 |

### 97. King Solomon's Mines

| Ed | HRN | Date | Details | A | C | Good | Fine | N-Mint |
|---|---|---|---|---|---|---|---|---|
| 1 | 96 | 7/52 | Orig.; Kiefer-a | 1 | 1 | 2.65 | 8.00 | 18.00 |
| 2 | 118 | — | PC-r | 1 | 1 | 1.50 | 3.50 | 7.00 |
| 3 | 131 | — | PC-r | 1 | 1 | 1.00 | 2.00 | 4.00 |
| 4 | 141 | — | PC-r | 1 | 1 | 1.00 | 2.00 | 4.00 |
| 5 | 158 | — | PC-r | 1 | 1 | 1.00 | 2.00 | 4.00 |
| 6 | 167 | 2/64 | PC-r | 1 | 1 | 1.00 | 2.00 | 4.00 |
| 7 | 167 | 9/65 | PC-r | 1 | 1 | 1.00 | 2.00 | 4.00 |
| 8 | 169 | Sm/69 | New price 25¢; stiff-c; PC-r | 1 | 1 | 1.25 | 2.50 | 5.00 |

### 98. The Red Badge of Courage

| Ed | HRN | Date | Details | A | C | Good | Fine | N-Mint |
|---|---|---|---|---|---|---|---|---|
| 1 | 98 | 8/52 | Original | 1 | 1 | 2.65 | 8.00 | 18.00 |
| 2 | 118 | — | PC-r | 1 | 1 | 1.00 | 2.00 | 4.00 |
| 3 | 132 | — | PC-r | 1 | 1 | 1.00 | 2.00 | 4.00 |
| 4 | 142 | — | PC-r | 1 | 1 | 1.00 | 2.00 | 4.00 |
| 5 | 152 | — | PC-r | 1 | 1 | 1.00 | 2.00 | 4.00 |
| 6 | 161 | — | PC-r | 1 | 1 | 1.00 | 2.00 | 4.00 |
| 7 | 167 | — | Has orig.date; PC-r | 1 | 1 | 1.00 | 2.00 | 4.00 |
| 8 | 167 | 9/64 | PC-r | 1 | 1 | 1.00 | 2.00 | 4.00 |
| 9 | 167 | 10/65 | PC-r | 1 | 1 | 1.00 | 2.00 | 4.00 |
| 10 | 166 | R/1968 | New-c&price 25¢; PC-r; stiff-c | 1 | 2 | 1.70 | 5.00 | 12.00 |

### 99. Hamlet (Used in **POP**, pg. 102)

| Ed | HRN | Date | Details | A | C | Good | Fine | N-Mint |
|---|---|---|---|---|---|---|---|---|
| 1 | 98 | 9/52 | Original; Blum-a | 1 | 1 | 3.00 | 9.00 | 21.00 |
| 2 | 121 | — | PC-r | 1 | 1 | 1.00 | 2.00 | 4.00 |
| 3 | 141 | — | PC-r | 1 | 1 | 1.00 | 2.00 | 4.00 |
| 4 | 158 | — | PC-r | 1 | 1 | 1.00 | 2.00 | 4.00 |
| 5 | 167 | — | Has orig.date; PC-r | 1 | 1 | 1.00 | 2.00 | 4.00 |
| 6 | 167 | 7/65 | PC-r | 1 | 1 | 1.00 | 2.00 | 4.00 |
| 7 | 166 | 4/67 | PC-r | 1 | 1 | 1.00 | 2.00 | 4.00 |
| 8 | 169 | Spr/69 | New-c&price 25¢; PC-r; stiff-c | 1 | 2 | 1.70 | 5.00 | 10.00 |

### 100. Mutiny on the Bounty

| Ed | HRN | Date | Details | A | C | Good | Fine | N-Mint |
|---|---|---|---|---|---|---|---|---|
| 1 | 100 | 10/52 | Original | 1 | 1 | 2.30 | 7.00 | 16.00 |
| 2 | 117 | — | PC-r | 1 | 1 | 1.00 | 2.00 | 4.00 |
| 3 | 132 | — | PC-r | 1 | 1 | 1.00 | 2.00 | 4.00 |
| 4 | 142 | — | PC-r | 1 | 1 | 1.00 | 2.00 | 4.00 |
| 5 | 155 | — | PC-r | 1 | 1 | 1.00 | 2.00 | 4.00 |
| 6 | 167 | — | Has orig. date; PC-r | 1 | 1 | 1.00 | 2.00 | 4.00 |
| 7 | 167 | 5/64 | PC-r | 1 | 1 | 1.00 | 2.00 | 4.00 |
| 8 | 167 | 3/66 | PC-r | 1 | 1 | 1.00 | 2.00 | 4.00 |
| 9 | 169 | Spr/70 | PC-r; stiff-c | 1 | 1 | 1.00 | 2.00 | 4.00 |

### 101. William Tell

| Ed | HRN | Date | Details | A | C | Good | Fine | N-Mint |
|---|---|---|---|---|---|---|---|---|
| 1 | 101 | 11/52 | Original; Kiefer-c delBourgo-a | 1 | 1 | 2.30 | 7.00 | 16.00 |
| 2 | 118 | — | PC-r | 1 | 1 | 1.00 | 2.00 | 4.00 |
| 3 | 141 | — | PC-r | 1 | 1 | 1.00 | 2.00 | 4.00 |
| 4 | 158 | — | PC-r | 1 | 1 | 1.00 | 2.00 | 4.00 |
| 5 | 167 | — | Has orig.date; PC-r | 1 | 1 | 1.00 | 2.00 | 4.00 |
| 6 | 167 | 11/64 | PC-r | 1 | 1 | 1.00 | 2.00 | 4.00 |
| 7 | 166 | 4/67 | PC-r | 1 | 1 | 1.00 | 2.00 | 4.00 |
| 8 | 169 | Win/69 | New price 25¢; stiff-c; PC-r | 1 | 1 | 1.00 | 2.00 | 4.00 |

### 102. The White Company

| Ed | HRN | Date | Details | A | C | Good | Fine | N-Mint |
|---|---|---|---|---|---|---|---|---|
| 1 | 101 | 12/52 | Original; Blum-a | 1 | 1 | 4.50 | 14.00 | 32.00 |
| 2 | 165 | — | PC-r | 1 | 1 | 2.65 | 8.00 | 18.00 |
| 3 | 167 | 4/64 | PC-r | 1 | 1 | 2.65 | 8.00 | 18.00 |

### 103. Men Against the Sea

| Ed | HRN | Date | Details | A | C | Good | Fine | N-Mint |
|---|---|---|---|---|---|---|---|---|
| 1 | 104 | 1/53 | Original; Kiefer-c, Palais-a | 1 | 1 | 3.00 | 9.00 | 21.00 |
| 2 | 114 | — | PC-r | 1 | 1 | 2.00 | 6.00 | 14.00 |
| 3 | 131 | — | New-c; PC-r | 1 | 2 | 1.70 | 5.00 | 10.00 |
| 4 | 158 | — | PC-r | 1 | 2 | 1.70 | 5.00 | 10.00 |
| 5 | 149 | — | White reorder list; came after HRN-158; PC-r | 1 | 2 | 2.65 | 8.00 | 18.00 |
| 6 | 167 | 3/64 | PC-r | 1 | 2 | 1.50 | 3.50 | 7.00 |

### 104. Bring 'Em Back Alive

| Ed | HRN | Date | Details | A | C | Good | Fine | N-Mint |
|---|---|---|---|---|---|---|---|---|
| 1 | 105 | 2/53 | Original; Kiefer c/a | 1 | 1 | 2.30 | 7.00 | 16.00 |
| 2 | 118 | — | PC-r | 1 | 1 | 1.00 | 2.00 | 4.00 |
| 3 | 133 | — | PC-r | 1 | 1 | 1.00 | 2.00 | 4.00 |
| 4 | 150 | — | PC-r | 1 | 1 | 1.00 | 2.00 | 4.00 |
| 5 | 158 | — | PC-r | 1 | 1 | 1.00 | 2.00 | 4.00 |
| 6 | 167 | 10/63 | PC-r | 1 | 1 | 1.00 | 2.00 | 4.00 |
| 7 | 167 | 9/65 | PC-r | 1 | 1 | 1.00 | 2.00 | 4.00 |
| 8 | 169 | Win/69 | New price 25¢; stiff-c; PC-r | 1 | 1 | 1.00 | 2.00 | 4.00 |

### 105. From the Earth to the Moon

| Ed | HRN | Date | Details | A | C | Good | Fine | N-Mint |
|---|---|---|---|---|---|---|---|---|
| 1 | 106 | 3/53 | Original; Blum-a | 1 | 1 | 2.30 | 7.00 | 16.00 |
| 2 | 118 | — | PC-r | 1 | 1 | 1.00 | 2.00 | 4.00 |
| 3 | 132 | — | PC-r | 1 | 1 | 1.00 | 2.00 | 4.00 |
| 4 | 141 | — | PC-r | 1 | 1 | 1.00 | 2.00 | 4.00 |
| 5 | 146 | — | PC-r | 1 | 1 | 1.00 | 2.00 | 4.00 |

*Classics Illustrated #94, © GIL*

*Classics Illustrated #97 (HRN-167), © GIL*

*Classics Illustrated #99, © GIL*

Classics Illustrated #107 (HRN-167), © GIL

Classics Illustrated #109, © GIL

Classics Illustrated #115 (Orig.), © GIL

| Ed | HRN | Date | Details | A C | Good | Fine | N-Mint |
|---|---|---|---|---|---|---|---|
| 6 | 156 | — | PC-r | 1 1 | 1.00 | 2.00 | 4.00 |
| 7 | 167 | — | Has orig. date; PC-r | 1 1 | 1.00 | 2.00 | 4.00 |
| 8 | 167 | 5/64 | PC-r | 1 1 | 1.00 | 2.00 | 4.00 |
| 9 | 167 | 5/65 | PC-r | 1 1 | 1.00 | 2.00 | 4.00 |
| 10A | 166 | 10/67 | PC-r | 1 1 | 1.00 | 2.00 | 4.00 |
| 10B | 166 | 10/67 | w/Grit ad | 1 1 | 8.00 | 24.00 | 56.00 |
| 11 | 169 | Sm/69 | New price 25¢; stiff-c; PC-r | 1 1 | 1.00 | 2.00 | 4.00 |
| 12 | 169 | Spr/71 | PC-r | 1 1 | 1.00 | 2.00 | 4.00 |

**106. Buffalo Bill**

| Ed | HRN | Date | Details | A C | Good | Fine | N-Mint |
|---|---|---|---|---|---|---|---|
| 1 | 107 | 4/53 | Orig.; delBourgo-a | 1 1 | 2.30 | 7.00 | 16.00 |
| 2 | 118 | — | PC-r | 1 1 | 1.00 | 2.00 | 4.00 |
| 3 | 132 | — | PC-r | 1 1 | 1.00 | 2.00 | 4.00 |
| 4 | 142 | — | PC-r | 1 1 | 1.00 | 2.00 | 4.00 |
| 5 | 161 | — | PC-r | 1 1 | 1.00 | 2.00 | 4.00 |
| 6 | 167 | 3/64 | PC-r | 1 1 | 1.00 | 2.00 | 4.00 |
| 7 | 166 | 7/67 | PC-r | 1 1 | 1.00 | 2.00 | 4.00 |
| 8 | 169 | Fall/69 | PC-r; stiff-c | 1 1 | 1.00 | 2.00 | 4.00 |

**107. King of the Khyber Rifles**

| Ed | HRN | Date | Details | A C | Good | Fine | N-Mint |
|---|---|---|---|---|---|---|---|
| 1 | 108 | 5/53 | Original | 1 1 | 2.65 | 8.00 | 18.00 |
| 2 | 118 | — | PC-r | 1 1 | 1.00 | 2.00 | 4.00 |
| 3 | 146 | — | PC-r | 1 1 | 1.00 | 2.00 | 4.00 |
| 4 | 158 | — | PC-r | 1 1 | 1.00 | 2.00 | 4.00 |
| 5 | 167 | — | Has orig.date; PC-r | 1 1 | 1.00 | 2.00 | 4.00 |
| 6 | 167 | — | PC-r | 1 1 | 1.00 | 2.00 | 4.00 |
| 7 | 167 | 10/66 | PC-r | 1 1 | 1.00 | 2.00 | 4.00 |

**108. Knights of the Round Table**

| Ed | HRN | Date | Details | A C | Good | Fine | N-Mint |
|---|---|---|---|---|---|---|---|
| 1A | 108 | 6/53 | Original; Blum-a | 1 1 | 2.65 | 8.00 | 18.00 |
| 1B | 109 | 6/53 | Original; scarce | 1 1 | 4.30 | 13.00 | 30.00 |
| 2 | 117 | — | PC-r | 1 1 | 1.00 | 2.00 | 4.00 |
| 3 | 165 | — | PC-r | 1 1 | 1.00 | 2.00 | 4.00 |
| 4 | 167 | 4/64 | PC-r | 1 1 | 1.00 | 2.00 | 4.00 |
| 5 | 166 | 4/67 | PC-r | 1 1 | 1.00 | 2.00 | 4.00 |
| 6 | 169 | Sm/69 | New price 25¢; stiff-c; PC-r | 1 1 | 1.00 | 2.00 | 4.00 |

**109. Pitcairn's Island**

| Ed | HRN | Date | Details | A C | Good | Fine | N-Mint |
|---|---|---|---|---|---|---|---|
| | | | | | 3.00 | 9.00 | 21.00 |
| | | | | | 1.50 | 3.50 | 7.00 |
| | | | | | 1.50 | 3.50 | 7.00 |
| | | | | | 1.50 | 3.50 | 7.00 |

| Ed | HRN | Date | Details | A C | Good | Fine | N-Mint |
|---|---|---|---|---|---|---|---|
| | | | | | 9.30 | 28.00 | 65.00 |
| | | | | | 6.00 | 18.00 | 42.00 |

| Ed | HRN | Date | Details | A C | Good | Fine | N-Mint |
|---|---|---|---|---|---|---|---|
| 1 | | | | | 4.30 | 13.00 | 30.00 |
| 2 | | | | | 1.25 | 2.50 | 5.00 |
| 3 | | | | | 1.25 | 2.50 | 5.00 |
| | | | | | 1.25 | 2.50 | 5.00 |

| Ed | HRN | Date | Details | A C | Good | Fine | N-Mint |
|---|---|---|---|---|---|---|---|
| | | | | | 4.30 | 13.00 | 30.00 |
| | | | | | 1.00 | 2.00 | 4.00 |
| | | | | | 1.00 | 2.00 | 4.00 |
| | | | | | 1.00 | 2.00 | 4.00 |

| Ed | HRN | Date | Details | A C | Good | Fine | N-Mint |
|---|---|---|---|---|---|---|---|
| 5 | 161 | — | PC-r | 1 1 | 1.00 | 2.00 | 4.00 |
| 6 | 167 | — | PC-r | 1 1 | 1.00 | 2.00 | 4.00 |
| 7 | 167 | 2/65 | PC-r | 1 1 | 1.00 | 2.00 | 4.00 |
| 8 | 167 | 5/66 | PC-r | 1 1 | 1.00 | 2.00 | 4.00 |
| 9 | 166 | Win/69 | New-c&price 25¢; PC-r; stiff-c | 1 2 | 1.70 | 5.00 | 10.00 |

**113. The Forty-Five Guardsmen**

| Ed | HRN | Date | Details | A C | Good | Fine | N-Mint |
|---|---|---|---|---|---|---|---|
| 1 | 114 | 11/53 | Orig.; delBourgo-a | 1 1 | 5.70 | 17.00 | 40.00 |
| 2 | 166 | 7/67 | PC-r | 1 1 | 2.65 | 8.00 | 18.00 |

**114. The Red Rover**

| Ed | HRN | Date | Details | A C | Good | Fine | N-Mint |
|---|---|---|---|---|---|---|---|
| 1 | 115 | 12/53 | Original | 1 1 | 5.70 | 17.00 | 40.00 |
| 2 | 166 | 7/67 | PC-r | 1 1 | 2.65 | 8.00 | 18.00 |

**115. How I Found Livingstone**

| Ed | HRN | Date | Details | A C | Good | Fine | N-Mint |
|---|---|---|---|---|---|---|---|
| 1 | 116 | 1/54 | Original | 1 1 | 5.00 | 15.00 | 35.00 |
| 2 | 167 | 1/67 | PC-r | 1 1 | 2.65 | 8.00 | 18.00 |

**116. The Bottle Imp**

| Ed | HRN | Date | Details | A C | Good | Fine | N-Mint |
|---|---|---|---|---|---|---|---|
| 1 | 117 | 2/54 | Orig.; Cameron-a | 1 1 | 6.00 | 18.00 | 42.00 |
| 2 | 167 | 1/67 | PC-r | 1 1 | 2.65 | 8.00 | 18.00 |

**117. Captains Courageous**

| Ed | HRN | Date | Details | A C | Good | Fine | N-Mint |
|---|---|---|---|---|---|---|---|
| 1 | 118 | 3/54 | Orig.; Costanza-a | 1 1 | 4.50 | 14.00 | 32.00 |
| 2 | 167 | 2/67 | PC-r | 1 1 | 1.70 | 5.00 | 10.00 |
| 3 | 169 | Fall/69 | New price 25¢; stiff-c; PC-r | 1 1 | 1.70 | 5.00 | 10.00 |

**118. Rob Roy**

| Ed | HRN | Date | Details | A C | Good | Fine | N-Mint |
|---|---|---|---|---|---|---|---|
| 1 | 119 | 4/54 | Original; Rudy & Walter Palais-a | 1 1 | 5.30 | 16.00 | 38.00 |
| 2 | 167 | 2/67 | PC-r | 1 1 | 2.65 | 8.00 | 18.00 |

**119. Soldiers of Fortune**

| Ed | HRN | Date | Details | A C | Good | Fine | N-Mint |
|---|---|---|---|---|---|---|---|
| 1 | 120 | 5/54 | Original Shaffenberger-a | 1 1 | 5.30 | 16.00 | 38.00 |
| 2 | 166 | 3/67 | PC-r | 1 1 | 1.70 | 5.00 | 12.00 |
| 3 | 169 | Spr/70 | New price 25¢; stiff-c; PC-r | 1 1 | 1.70 | 5.00 | 10.00 |

**120. The Hurricane**

| Ed | HRN | Date | Details | A C | Good | Fine | N-Mint |
|---|---|---|---|---|---|---|---|
| 1 | 121 | 6/54 | Orig.; Cameron-a | 1 1 | 5.30 | 16.00 | 38.00 |
| 2 | 166 | 3/67 | PC-r | 1 1 | 3.50 | 10.50 | 24.00 |

**121. Wild Bill Hickok**

| Ed | HRN | Date | Details | A C | Good | Fine | N-Mint |
|---|---|---|---|---|---|---|---|
| 1 | 122 | 7/54 | Original | 1 1 | 2.65 | 8.00 | 18.00 |
| 2 | 132 | — | PC-r | 1 1 | 1.00 | 2.00 | 4.00 |
| 3 | 141 | — | PC-r | 1 1 | 1.00 | 2.00 | 4.00 |
| 4 | 154 | — | PC-r | 1 1 | 1.00 | 2.00 | 4.00 |
| 5 | 167 | — | PC-r | 1 1 | 1.00 | 2.00 | 4.00 |
| 6 | 167 | 8/64 | PC-r | 1 1 | 1.00 | 2.00 | 4.00 |
| 7 | 166 | 4/67 | PC-r | 1 1 | 1.00 | 2.00 | 4.00 |
| 8 | 169 | Win/69 | PC-r; stiff-c | 1 1 | 1.00 | 2.00 | 4.00 |

**122. The Mutineers**

| Ed | HRN | Date | Details | A C | Good | Fine | N-Mint |
|---|---|---|---|---|---|---|---|
| 1 | 123 | 9/54 | Original | 1 1 | 2.65 | 8.00 | 18.00 |
| 2 | 136 | — | PC-r | 1 1 | 1.00 | 2.00 | 4.00 |
| 3 | 146 | — | PC-r | 1 1 | 1.00 | 2.00 | 4.00 |

| Ed | HRN | Date | Details | A C | Good | Fine | N-Mint |
|---|---|---|---|---|---|---|---|
| 4 | 158 | — | PC-r | 1 1 | 1.00 | 2.00 | 4.00 |
| 5 | 167 | 11/63 | PC-r | 1 1 | 1.00 | 2.00 | 4.00 |
| 6 | 167 | 3/65 | PC-r | 1 1 | 1.00 | 2.00 | 4.00 |
| 7 | 166 | 8/67 | PC-r | 1 1 | 1.00 | 2.00 | 4.00 |

**123. Fang and Claw**

| Ed | HRN | Date | Details | A C | Good | Fine | N-Mint |
|---|---|---|---|---|---|---|---|
| 1 | 124 | 11/54 | Original | 1 1 | 2.65 | 8.00 | 18.00 |
| 2 | 133 | — | PC-r | 1 1 | 1.00 | 2.00 | 4.00 |
| 3 | 143 | — | PC-r | 1 1 | 1.00 | 2.00 | 4.00 |
| 4 | 154 | — | PC-r | 1 1 | 1.00 | 2.00 | 4.00 |
| 5 | 167 | — | Has orig.date; PC-r | 1 1 | 1.00 | 2.00 | 4.00 |
| 6 | 167 | 9/65 | PC-r | 1 1 | 1.00 | 2.00 | 4.00 |

**124. The War of the Worlds**

| Ed | HRN | Date | Details | A C | Good | Fine | N-Mint |
|---|---|---|---|---|---|---|---|
| 1 | 125 | 1/55 | Orig.; Cameron c/a | 1 1 | 3.50 | 10.50 | 24.00 |
| 2 | 131 | — | PC-r | 1 1 | 1.25 | 2.50 | 5.00 |
| 3 | 141 | — | PC-r | 1 1 | 1.25 | 2.50 | 5.00 |
| 4 | 148 | — | PC-r | 1 1 | 1.25 | 2.50 | 5.00 |
| 5 | 156 | — | PC-r | 1 1 | 1.25 | 2.50 | 5.00 |
| 6 | 165 | — | PC-r | 1 1 | 1.25 | 2.50 | 5.00 |
| 7 | 167 | — | PC-r | 1 1 | 1.25 | 2.50 | 5.00 |
| 8 | 167 | 11/64 | PC-r | 1 1 | 1.25 | 2.50 | 5.00 |
| 9 | 167 | 11/65 | PC-r | 1 1 | 1.25 | 2.50 | 5.00 |
| 10 | 166 | R/1968 | C-price 25¢; PC-r | 1 1 | 1.25 | 2.50 | 5.00 |
| 11 | 169 | Sm/70 | PC-r; stiff-c | 1 1 | 1.25 | 2.50 | 5.00 |

**125. The Ox Bow Incident**

| Ed | HRN | Date | Details | A C | Good | Fine | N-Mint |
|---|---|---|---|---|---|---|---|
| 1 | — | 3/55 | Original; Picture Progress replaces reorder list | 1 1 | 2.65 | 8.00 | 18.00 |
| 2 | 143 | — | PC-r | 1 1 | 1.00 | 2.00 | 4.00 |
| 3 | 152 | — | PC-r | 1 1 | 1.00 | 2.00 | 4.00 |
| 4 | 149 | — | PC-r | 1 1 | 1.00 | 2.00 | 4.00 |
| 5 | 167 | — | PC-r | 1 1 | 1.00 | 2.00 | 4.00 |
| 6 | 167 | 11/64 | PC-r | 1 1 | 1.00 | 2.00 | 4.00 |
| 7 | 166 | 4/67 | PC-r | 1 1 | 1.00 | 2.00 | 4.00 |
| 8 | 169 | Win/69 | New price 25¢; stiff-c; PC-r | 1 1 | 1.00 | 2.00 | 4.00 |

**126. The Downfall**

| Ed | HRN | Date | Details | A C | Good | Fine | N-Mint |
|---|---|---|---|---|---|---|---|
| 1 | — | 5/55 | Orig.; 'Picture Progress' replaces reorder list; Cameron c/a | 1 1 | 2.65 | 8.00 | 18.00 |
| 2 | 167 | 8/64 | PC-r | 1 1 | 1.50 | 3.50 | 5.00 |
| 3 | 166 | R/1968 | C-price 25¢; PC-r | 1 1 | 1.50 | 3.50 | 7.00 |

**127. The King of the Mountains**

| Ed | HRN | Date | Details | A C | Good | Fine | N-Mint |
|---|---|---|---|---|---|---|---|
| 1 | 128 | 7/55 | Original | 1 1 | 2.65 | 8.00 | 18.00 |
| 2 | 167 | 6/64 | PC-r | 1 1 | 1.50 | 3.50 | 7.00 |
| 3 | 166 | F/1968 | C-price 25¢; PC-r | 1 1 | 1.50 | 3.50 | 7.00 |

**128. Macbeth** (Used in **POP**, pg. 102)

| Ed | HRN | Date | Details | A C | Good | Fine | N-Mint |
|---|---|---|---|---|---|---|---|
| 1 | 128 | 9/55 | Orig.; last Blum-a | 1 1 | 3.00 | 9.00 | 20.00 |
| 2 | 143 | — | PC-r | 1 1 | 1.00 | 2.00 | 4.00 |
| 3 | 158 | — | PC-r | 1 1 | 1.00 | 2.00 | 4.00 |
| 4 | 167 | — | PC-r | 1 1 | 1.00 | 2.00 | 4.00 |
| 5 | 167 | 6/64 | PC-r | 1 1 | 1.00 | 2.00 | 4.00 |
| 6 | 166 | 4/67 | PC-r | 1 1 | 1.00 | 2.00 | 4.00 |
| 7 | 166 | R/1968 | C-Price 25¢; PC-r | 1 1 | 1.00 | 2.00 | 4.00 |
| 8 | 169 | Spr/70 | Stiff-c; PC-r | 1 1 | 1.00 | 2.00 | 4.00 |

**129. Davy Crockett**

| Ed | HRN | Date | Details | A C | Good | Fine | N-Mint |
|---|---|---|---|---|---|---|---|
| 1 | 129 | 11/55 | Orig.; Cameron-a | 1 1 | 6.50 | 19.00 | 45.00 |
| 2 | 167 | 9/66 | PC-r | 1 1 | 4.00 | 12.00 | 28.00 |

**130. Caesar's Conquests**

| Ed | HRN | Date | Details | A C | Good | Fine | N-Mint |
|---|---|---|---|---|---|---|---|
| 1 | 130 | 1/56 | Original; Orlando-a | 1 1 | 2.65 | 8.00 | 18.00 |
| 2 | 142 | — | PC-r | 1 1 | 1.00 | 2.00 | 4.00 |
| 3 | 152 | — | PC-r | 1 1 | 1.00 | 2.00 | 4.00 |
| 4 | 149 | — | PC-r | 1 1 | 1.00 | 2.00 | 4.00 |
| 5 | 167 | — | PC-r | 1 1 | 1.00 | 2.00 | 4.00 |
| 6 | 167 | 10/64 | PC-r | 1 1 | 1.00 | 2.00 | 4.00 |
| 7 | 167 | 4/66 | PC-r | 1 1 | 1.00 | 2.00 | 4.00 |

**131. The Covered Wagon**

| Ed | HRN | Date | Details | A C | Good | Fine | N-Mint |
|---|---|---|---|---|---|---|---|
| 1 | 131 | 3/56 | Original | 1 1 | 2.65 | 8.00 | 18.00 |
| 2 | 143 | — | PC-r | 1 1 | 1.00 | 2.00 | 4.00 |
| 3 | 152 | — | PC-r | 1 1 | 1.00 | 2.00 | 4.00 |
| 4 | 158 | — | PC-r | 1 1 | 1.00 | 2.00 | 4.00 |
| 5 | 167 | — | PC-r | 1 1 | 1.00 | 2.00 | 4.00 |
| 6 | 167 | 11/64 | PC-r | 1 1 | 1.00 | 2.00 | 4.00 |
| 7 | 167 | 4/66 | PC-r | 1 1 | 1.00 | 2.00 | 4.00 |
| 8 | 169 | Win/69 | New price 25 cents; stiff-c; PC-r | 1 1 | 1.00 | 2.00 | 4.00 |

**132. The Dark Frigate**

| Ed | HRN | Date | Details | A C | Good | Fine | N-Mint |
|---|---|---|---|---|---|---|---|
| 1 | 132 | 5/56 | Original | 1 1 | 2.65 | 8.00 | 18.00 |
| 2 | 150 | — | PC-r | 1 1 | 1.50 | 3.50 | 7.00 |
| 3 | 167 | 1/64 | PC-r | 1 1 | 1.50 | 3.50 | 7.00 |
| 4 | 166 | 5/67 | PC-r | 1 1 | 1.50 | 3.50 | 7.00 |

**133. The Time Machine**

| Ed | HRN | Date | Details | A C | Good | Fine | N-Mint |
|---|---|---|---|---|---|---|---|
| 1 | 132 | 7/56 | Orig.; Cameron-a | 1 1 | 3.50 | 10.50 | 24.00 |
| 2 | 142 | — | PC-r | 1 1 | 1.25 | 2.50 | 5.00 |
| 3 | 152 | — | PC-r | 1 1 | 1.25 | 2.50 | 5.00 |
| 4 | 158 | — | PC-r | 1 1 | 1.25 | 2.50 | 5.00 |
| 5 | 167 | — | PC-r | 1 1 | 1.25 | 2.50 | 5.00 |
| 6 | 167 | 6/64 | PC-r | 1 1 | 1.25 | 2.50 | 5.00 |
| 7 | 167 | 3/66 | PC-r | 1 1 | 1.25 | 2.50 | 5.00 |
| 8 | 166 | 12/67 | PC-r | 1 1 | 1.25 | 2.50 | 5.00 |
| 9 | 169 | Win/71 | New price 25 cents; stiff-c; PC-r | 1 1 | 1.50 | 3.00 | 6.00 |

**134. Romeo and Juliet**

| Ed | HRN | Date | Details | A C | Good | Fine | N-Mint |
|---|---|---|---|---|---|---|---|
| 1 | 134 | 9/56 | Original; Evans-a | 1 1 | 2.65 | 8.00 | 18.00 |
| 2 | 161 | — | PC-r | 1 1 | 1.00 | 2.00 | 4.00 |
| 3 | 167 | 9/63 | PC-r | 1 1 | 1.00 | 2.00 | 4.00 |
| 4 | 167 | 5/65 | PC-r | 1 1 | 1.00 | 2.00 | 4.00 |
| 5 | 166 | 6/67 | PC-r | 1 1 | 1.00 | 2.00 | 4.00 |
| 6 | 166 | Win/69 | New c&price 25¢; stiff-c; PC-r | 1 2 | 2.65 | 8.00 | 18.00 |

**135. Waterloo**

| Ed | HRN | Date | Details | A C | Good | Fine | N-Mint |
|---|---|---|---|---|---|---|---|
| 1 | 135 | 11/56 | Orig.; G. Ingels-a | 1 1 | 2.65 | 8.00 | 18.00 |
| 2 | 153 | — | PC-r | 1 1 | 1.00 | 2.00 | 4.00 |
| 3 | 167 | — | PC-r | 1 1 | 1.00 | 2.00 | 4.00 |
| 4 | 167 | 9/64 | PC-r | 1 1 | 1.00 | 2.00 | 4.00 |
| 5 | 166 | R/1968 | C-price 25 cents; PC-r | 1 1 | 1.00 | 2.00 | 4.00 |

**136. Lord Jim**

| Ed | HRN | Date | Details | A C | Good | Fine | N-Mint |
|---|---|---|---|---|---|---|---|
| 1 | 136 | 1/57 | [illegible] | [illegible] | 2.65 | 8.00 | 18.00 |

*Classics Illustrated #124 (HRN-167), © GIL*

*Classics Illustrated #130 (Orig.), © GIL*

Classics Illustrated #138, © GIL

Classics Illustrated #140 (HRN-160), © GIL

Classics Illustrated #149 (Orig?), © GIL

| Ed | HRN | Date | Details | A C | Good | Fine | N-Mint |
|---|---|---|---|---|---|---|---|
| 2 | 165 | — | PC-r | 1 1 | 1.00 | 2.00 | 4.00 |
| 3 | 167 | 3/64 | PC-r | 1 1 | 1.00 | 2.00 | 4.00 |
| 4 | 167 | 9/66 | PC-r | 1 1 | 1.00 | 2.00 | 4.00 |
| 5 | 169 | Sm/69 | New price 25 cents; stiff-c; PC-r | 1 1 | 1.00 | 2.00 | 4.00 |

**137. The Little Savage**

| Ed | HRN | Date | Details | A C | Good | Fine | N-Mint |
|---|---|---|---|---|---|---|---|
| 1 | 136 | 3/57 | Original; Evans-a | 1 1 | 2.65 | 8.00 | 18.00 |
| 2 | 148 | — | PC-r | 1 1 | 1.00 | 2.00 | 4.00 |
| 3 | 156 | — | PC-r | 1 1 | 1.00 | 2.00 | 4.00 |
| 4 | 167 | — | PC-r | 1 1 | 1.00 | 2.00 | 4.00 |
| 5 | 167 | 10/64 | PC-r | 1 1 | 1.00 | 2.00 | 4.00 |
| 6 | 166 | 8/67 | PC-r | 1 1 | 1.00 | 2.00 | 4.00 |
| 7 | 169 | Spr/70 | New price 25 cents; stiff-c; PC-r | 1 1 | 1.00 | 2.00 | 4.00 |

**138. A Journey to the Center of the Earth**

| Ed | HRN | Date | Details | A C | Good | Fine | N-Mint |
|---|---|---|---|---|---|---|---|
| 1 | 136 | 5/57 | Original | 1 1 | 3.00 | 9.00 | 21.00 |
| 2 | 146 | — | PC-r | 1 1 | 1.00 | 2.00 | 4.00 |
| 3 | 156 | — | PC-r | 1 1 | 1.00 | 2.00 | 4.00 |
| 4 | 158 | — | PC-r | 1 1 | 1.00 | 2.00 | 4.00 |
| 5 | 167 | — | PC-r | 1 1 | 1.00 | 2.00 | 4.00 |
| 6 | 167 | 6/64 | PC-r | 1 1 | 1.00 | 2.00 | 4.00 |
| 7 | 167 | 4/66 | PC-r | 1 1 | 1.00 | 2.00 | 4.00 |
| 8 | 166 | R/1968 | C-price 25 cents; PC-r | 1 1 | 1.00 | 2.00 | 4.00 |

**139. In the Reign of Terror**

| Ed | HRN | Date | Details | A C | Good | Fine | N-Mint |
|---|---|---|---|---|---|---|---|
| 1 | 139 | 7/57 | Original; Evans-a | 1 1 | 2.65 | 8.00 | 18.00 |
| 2 | 154 | — | PC-r | 1 1 | 1.00 | 2.00 | 4.00 |
| 3 | 167 | — | Has orig.date; PC-r | 1 1 | 1.00 | 2.00 | 4.00 |
| 4 | 167 | 7/64 | PC-r | 1 1 | 1.00 | 2.00 | 4.00 |
| 5 | 166 | R/1968 | C-price 25 cents; PC-r | 1 1 | 1.00 | 2.00 | 4.00 |

**140. On Jungle Trails**

| Ed | HRN | Date | Details | A C | Good | Fine | N-Mint |
|---|---|---|---|---|---|---|---|
| 1 | 140 | 9/57 | Original | 1 1 | 2.65 | 8.00 | 18.00 |
| 2 | 150 | — | PC-r | 1 1 | 1.00 | 2.00 | 4.00 |
| 3 | 160 | — | PC-r | 1 1 | 1.00 | 2.00 | 4.00 |
| 4 | 167 | 9/63 | PC-r | 1 1 | 1.00 | 2.00 | 4.00 |
| 5 | 167 | 9/65 | PC-r | 1 1 | 1.00 | 2.00 | 4.00 |

**141. Castle Dangerous**

| Ed | HRN | Date | Details | A C | Good | Fine | N-Mint |
|---|---|---|---|---|---|---|---|
| 1 | 141 | 11/57 | Original | 1 1 | 2.65 | 8.00 | 18.00 |
| 2 | 152 | — | PC-r | 1 1 | 1.00 | 2.00 | 4.00 |
| 3 | 167 | — | PC-r | 1 1 | 1.00 | 2.00 | 4.00 |
| 4 | 166 | 7/67 | PC-r | 1 1 | 1.00 | 2.00 | 4.00 |

**142. Abraham Lincoln**

| Ed | HRN | Date | Details | A C | Good | Fine | N-Mint |
|---|---|---|---|---|---|---|---|
| 1 | 142 | 1/58 | Original | 1 1 | 2.65 | 8.00 | 18.00 |
| 2 | 154 | — | PC-r | 1 1 | 1.00 | 2.00 | 4.00 |
| 3 | 158 | — | PC-r | 1 1 | 1.00 | 2.00 | 4.00 |
| 4 | 167 | 10/63 | PC-r | 1 1 | 1.00 | 2.00 | 4.00 |
| 5 | 167 | 7/65 | PC-r | 1 1 | 1.00 | 2.00 | 4.00 |
| 6 | 166 | 11/67 | PC-r | 1 1 | 1.00 | 2.00 | 4.00 |
| 7 | 169 | Fall/69 | New price 25 cents; stiff-c; PC-r | 1 1 | 1.00 | 2.00 | 4.00 |

**143. Kim**

| Ed | HRN | Date | Details | A C | Good | Fine | N-Mint |
|---|---|---|---|---|---|---|---|
| 1 | 143 | 3/58 | Original; Orlando-a | 1 1 | 2.65 | 8.00 | 18.00 |
| 2 | 165 | — | PC-r | 1 1 | 1.00 | 2.00 | 4.00 |
| 3 | 167 | 11/63 | PC-r | 1 1 | 1.00 | 2.00 | 4.00 |
| 4 | 167 | 8/65 | PC-r | 1 1 | 1.00 | 2.00 | 4.00 |
| 5 | 169 | Win/69 | New price 25 cents; stiff-c; PC-r | 1 1 | 1.00 | 2.00 | 4.00 |

**144. The First Men in the Moon**

| Ed | HRN | Date | Details | A C | Good | Fine | N-Mint |
|---|---|---|---|---|---|---|---|
| 1 | 143 | 5/58 | Original; Woodbridge/Williamson/Torres-a | 1 1 | 3.00 | 9.00 | 21.00 |
| 2 | 153 | — | PC-r | 1 1 | 1.00 | 2.00 | 4.00 |
| 3 | 161 | — | PC-r | 1 1 | 1.00 | 2.00 | 4.00 |
| 4 | 167 | — | PC-r | 1 1 | 1.00 | 2.00 | 4.00 |
| 5 | 167 | 12/65 | PC-r | 1 1 | 1.00 | 2.00 | 4.00 |
| 6 | 166 | Fall/68 | New-c&price 25¢; PC-r; stiff-c | 1 2 | 1.50 | 3.50 | 7.00 |
| 7 | 169 | Win/69 | Stiff-c; PC-r | 1 2 | 1.50 | 3.50 | 7.00 |

**145. The Crisis**

| Ed | HRN | Date | Details | A C | Good | Fine | N-Mint |
|---|---|---|---|---|---|---|---|
| 1 | 143 | 7/58 | Original; Evans-a | 1 1 | 2.65 | 8.00 | 18.00 |
| 2 | 156 | — | PC-r | 1 1 | 1.00 | 2.00 | 4.00 |
| 3 | 167 | 10/63 | PC-r | 1 1 | 1.00 | 2.00 | 4.00 |
| 4 | 167 | 3/65 | PC-r | 1 1 | 1.00 | 2.00 | 4.00 |
| 5 | 166 | R/1968 | C-price 25¢; PC-r | 1 1 | 1.00 | 2.00 | 4.00 |

**146. With Fire and Sword**

| Ed | HRN | Date | Details | A C | Good | Fine | N-Mint |
|---|---|---|---|---|---|---|---|
| 1 | 143 | 9/58 | Original; Woodbridge-a | 1 1 | 2.65 | 8.00 | 18.00 |
| 2 | 156 | — | PC-r | 1 1 | 1.50 | 3.50 | 7.00 |
| 3 | 167 | 11/63 | PC-r | 1 1 | 1.50 | 3.50 | 7.00 |
| 4 | 167 | 3/65 | PC-r | 1 1 | 1.50 | 3.50 | 7.00 |

**147. Ben-Hur**

| Ed | HRN | Date | Details | A C | Good | Fine | N-Mint |
|---|---|---|---|---|---|---|---|
| 1 | 147 | 11/58 | Original; Orlando-a | 1 1 | 2.65 | 8.00 | 18.00 |
| 2 | 152 | — | Scarce; PC-r | 1 1 | 3.00 | 9.00 | 21.00 |
| 3 | 153 | — | PC-r | 1 1 | 1.00 | 2.00 | 4.00 |
| 4 | 158 | — | PC-r | 1 1 | 1.00 | 2.00 | 4.00 |
| 5 | 167 | — | Orig.date; but PC-r | 1 1 | 1.00 | 2.00 | 4.00 |
| 6 | 167 | 2/65 | PC-r | 1 1 | 1.00 | 2.00 | 4.00 |
| 7 | 167 | 9/66 | PC-r | 1 1 | 1.00 | 2.00 | 4.00 |
| 8A | 166 | Fall/68 | New-c&price 25¢; PC-r; soft-c | 1 2 | 1.70 | 5.00 | 12.00 |
| 8B | 166 | Fall/68 | New-c&price 25¢; PCpr; stiff-c; scarce | 1 2 | 3.50 | 10.50 | 24.00 |

**148. The Buccaneer**

| Ed | HRN | Date | Details | A C | Good | Fine | N-Mint |
|---|---|---|---|---|---|---|---|
| 1 | 148 | 1/59 | Orig.; Evans/Jenny-a; Saunders-c | 1 1 | 2.65 | 8.00 | 18.00 |
| 2 | 568 | — | Juniors list only PC-r | 1 1 | 1.50 | 3.50 | 7.00 |
| 3 | 167 | — | PC-r | 1 1 | 1.00 | 2.00 | 4.00 |
| 4 | 167 | 9/65 | PC-r | 1 1 | 1.00 | 2.00 | 4.00 |
| 5 | 169 | Sm/69 | New price 25¢; PC-r; stiff-c | 1 1 | 1.00 | 2.00 | 4.00 |

**149. Off on a Comet**

| Ed | HRN | Date | Details | A C | Good | Fine | N-Mint |
|---|---|---|---|---|---|---|---|
| 1 | 149 | 3/59 | Orig.; G.McCann-a; blue reorder list | 1 1 | 2.65 | 8.00 | 18.00 |
| 2 | 155 | — | PC-r | 1 1 | 1.00 | 2.00 | 4.00 |
| 3 | 149 | — | PC-r; white reorder list; no coming-next ad | 1 1 | 1.00 | 2.00 | 4.00 |
| 4 | 167 | 12/63 | PC-r | 1 1 | 1.00 | 2.00 | 4.00 |

| Ed | HRN | Date | Details | A C | Good | Fine | N-Mint |
|---|---|---|---|---|---|---|---|
| 5 | 167 | 2/65 | PC-r | 1 1 | 1.00 | 2.00 | 4.00 |
| 6 | 167 | 10/66 | PC-r | 1 1 | 1.00 | 2.00 | 4.00 |
| 7 | 166 | Fall/68 | New-c&price 25¢; PC-r | 1 2 | 1.70 | 5.00 | 12.00 |

**150. The Virginian**

| Ed | HRN | Date | Details | A C | Good | Fine | N-Mint |
|---|---|---|---|---|---|---|---|
| 1 | 150 | 5/59 | Original | 1 1 | 3.50 | 10.50 | 24.00 |
| 2 | 164 | — | PC-r | 1 1 | 1.70 | 5.00 | 10.00 |
| 3 | 167 | 10/63 | PC-r | 1 1 | 1.50 | 4.50 | 9.00 |
| 4 | 167 | 12/65 | PC-r | 1 1 | 1.50 | 4.50 | 9.00 |

**151. Won By the Sword**

| Ed | HRN | Date | Details | A C | Good | Fine | N-Mint |
|---|---|---|---|---|---|---|---|
| 1 | 150 | 7/59 | Original | 1 1 | 3.70 | 11.00 | 26.00 |
| 2 | 164 | — | PC-r | 1 1 | 1.50 | 4.50 | 9.00 |
| 3 | 167 | 10/63 | PC-r | 1 1 | 1.50 | 4.50 | 9.00 |
| 4 | 166 | 7/67 | PC-r | 1 1 | 1.50 | 4.50 | 9.00 |

**152. Wild Animals I Have Known**

| Ed | HRN | Date | Details | A C | Good | Fine | N-Mint |
|---|---|---|---|---|---|---|---|
| 1 | 152 | 9/59 | Orig.; L.B. Cole c/a | 1 1 | 3.50 | 10.50 | 24.00 |
| 2A | 149 | — | PC-r; white reorder list; no coming-next ad; IBC: Jr. list #572 | 1 1 | 1.25 | 2.50 | 5.00 |
| 2B | 149 | — | PC-r; inside-bc: Jr. list to #555 | 1 1 | 1.50 | 3.50 | 7.00 |
| 2C | 149 | — | PC-r; inside-bc: has World Around Us ad; scarce | 1 1 | 2.00 | 6.00 | 14.00 |
| 3 | 167 | 9/63 | PC-r | 1 1 | 1.00 | 2.00 | 4.00 |
| 4 | 167 | 8/65 | PC-r | 1 1 | 1.00 | 2.00 | 4.00 |
| 5 | 169 | Fall/69 | New price 25¢; stiff-c; PC-r | 1 1 | 1.00 | 2.00 | 4.00 |

**153. The Invisible Man**

| Ed | HRN | Date | Details | A C | Good | Fine | N-Mint |
|---|---|---|---|---|---|---|---|
| 1 | 153 | 11/59 | Original | 1 1 | 3.50 | 10.50 | 24.00 |
| 2A | 149 | — | PC-r; white reorder list; no coming-next ad; inside-bc: Jr. list to #572 | 1 1 | 1.25 | 2.50 | 5.00 |
| 2B | 149 | — | PC-r; inside-bc: Jr. | 1 1 | 1.50 | 3.50 | 7.00 |
| 3 | 167 | — | PC-r | 1 1 | 1.00 | 2.00 | 4.00 |
| 4 | 167 | 2/65 | PC-r | 1 1 | 1.00 | 2.00 | 4.00 |
| 5 | 167 | 9/66 | PC-r | 1 1 | 1.00 | 2.00 | 4.00 |
| 6 | 166 | Win/69 | New price 25¢; PC-r; stiff-c | 1 1 | 1.00 | 2.00 | 4.00 |
| 7 | 169 | Spr/71 | Stiff-c; letters spelling 'Invisible Man' are 'solid' not'invisible;' PC-r | 1 1 | 1.00 | 2.00 | 4.00 |

**154. The Conspiracy of Pontiac**

| Ed | HRN | Date | Details | A C | Good | Fine | N-Mint |
|---|---|---|---|---|---|---|---|
| 1 | 154 | 1/60 | Original | 1 1 | 3.50 | 10.50 | 24.00 |
| 2 | 167 | 11/63 | PC-r | 1 1 | 1.70 | 5.00 | 12.00 |
| 3 | 167 | 7/64 | PC-r | 1 1 | 1.70 | 5.00 | 12.00 |
| 4 | 166 | 12/67 | PC-r | 1 1 | 1.70 | 5.00 | 12.00 |

**155. The Lion of the North**

| Ed | HRN | Date | Details | A C | Good | Fine | N-Mint |
|---|---|---|---|---|---|---|---|
| 1 | 154 | 3/60 | Original | 1 1 | 3.00 | 9.00 | 21.00 |
| 2 | 167 | 1/64 | PC-r | 1 1 | 1.50 | 4.50 | 9.00 |
| 3 | 166 | R/1967 | C-price 25¢; PC-r | 1 1 | 1.50 | 4.50 | 9.00 |

**156. The Conquest of Mexico**

| Ed | HRN | Date | Details | A C | Good | Fine | N-Mint |
|---|---|---|---|---|---|---|---|
| 1 | 156 | 5/60 | Orig.; Bruno Premiani-a&c | 1 1 | 3.00 | 9.00 | 21.00 |
| 2 | 167 | 1/64 | PC-r | 1 1 | 1.50 | 3.00 | 6.00 |
| 3 | 166 | 8/67 | PC-r | 1 1 | 1.50 | 3.00 | 6.00 |
| 4 | 169 | Spr/70 | New price 25¢; stiff-c; PC-r | 1 1 | 1.25 | 2.50 | 5.00 |

**157. Lives of the Hunted**

| Ed | HRN | Date | Details | A C | Good | Fine | N-Mint |
|---|---|---|---|---|---|---|---|
| 1 | 156 | 7/60 | Orig.; L.B. Cole-c | 1 1 | 3.50 | 10.50 | 24.00 |
| 2 | 167 | 2/64 | PC-r | 1 1 | 1.70 | 5.00 | 12.00 |
| 3 | 166 | 10/67 | PC-r | 1 1 | 1.70 | 5.00 | 12.00 |

**158. The Conspirators**

| Ed | HRN | Date | Details | A C | Good | Fine | N-Mint |
|---|---|---|---|---|---|---|---|
| 1 | 156 | 9/60 | Original | 1 1 | 3.50 | 10.50 | 24.00 |
| 2 | 167 | 7/64 | PC-r | 1 1 | 1.70 | 5.00 | 12.00 |
| 3 | 166 | 10/67 | PC-r | 1 1 | 1.70 | 5.00 | 12.00 |

**159. The Octopus**

| Ed | HRN | Date | Details | A C | Good | Fine | N-Mint |
|---|---|---|---|---|---|---|---|
| 1 | 159 | 11/60 | Orig.; Gray Morrow & Evans-a; L.B. Cole-c | 1 1 | 3.00 | 9.00 | 21.00 |
| 2 | 167 | 2/64 | PC-r | 1 1 | 1.70 | 5.00 | 10.00 |
| 3 | 166 | R/1967 | C-price 25¢; PC-r | 1 1 | 1.70 | 5.00 | 10.00 |

**160. The Food of the Gods**

| Ed | HRN | Date | Details | A C | Good | Fine | N-Mint |
|---|---|---|---|---|---|---|---|
| 1A | 159 | 1/61 | Original | 1 1 | 3.00 | 9.00 | 21.00 |
| 1B | 160 | 1/61 | Original; same, except for HRN | 1 1 | 3.00 | 9.00 | 21.00 |
| 2 | 167 | 1/64 | PC-r | 1 1 | 1.70 | 5.00 | 10.00 |
| 3 | 166 | 6/67 | PC-r | 1 1 | 1.70 | 5.00 | 10.00 |

**161. Cleopatra**

| Ed | HRN | Date | Details | A C | Good | Fine | N-Mint |
|---|---|---|---|---|---|---|---|
| 1 | 161 | 3/61 | Original | 1 1 | 4.00 | 12.00 | 28.00 |
| 2 | 167 | 1/64 | PC-r | 1 1 | 2.00 | 6.00 | 14.00 |
| 3 | 166 | 8/67 | PC-r | 1 1 | 2.00 | 6.00 | 14.00 |

**162. Robur the Conqueror**

| Ed | HRN | Date | Details | A C | Good | Fine | N-Mint |
|---|---|---|---|---|---|---|---|
| 1 | 162 | 5/61 | Original | 1 1 | 3.00 | 9.00 | 21.00 |
| 2 | 167 | 7/64 | PC-r | 1 1 | 1.70 | 5.00 | 10.00 |
| 3 | 166 | 8/67 | PC-r | 1 1 | 1.70 | 5.00 | 10.00 |

**163. Master of the World**

| Ed | HRN | Date | Details | A C | Good | Fine | N-Mint |
|---|---|---|---|---|---|---|---|
| 1 | 163 | 7/61 | Original; Gray Morrow-a | 1 1 | 3.00 | 9.00 | 21.00 |
| 2 | 167 | 1/65 | PC-r | 1 1 | 1.70 | 5.00 | 10.00 |
| 3 | 166 | R/1968 | C-price 25¢; PC-r | 1 1 | 1.70 | 5.00 | 10.00 |

**164. The Cossack Chief**

| Ed | HRN | Date | Details | A C | Good | Fine | N-Mint |
|---|---|---|---|---|---|---|---|
| 1 | 164 | (1961) | Original; nd (10/61?) | 1 1 | 3.50 | 10.50 | 24.00 |
| 2 | 167 | 4/65 | PC-r | 1 1 | 1.70 | 5.00 | 10.00 |
| 3 | 166 | Fall/68 | C-price 25¢; PC-r | 1 1 | 1.70 | 5.00 | 10.00 |

**165. The Queen's Necklace**

| Ed | HRN | Date | Details | A C | Good | Fine | N-Mint |
|---|---|---|---|---|---|---|---|
| 1 | 164 | 1/62 | Original; Morrow-a | 1 1 | 3.50 | 10.50 | 24.00 |
| 2 | 167 | 4/65 | PC-r | 1 1 | 1.70 | 5.00 | 10.00 |
| 3 | 166 | Fall/68 | C-price 25¢; PC-r | 1 1 | 1.70 | 5.00 | 10.00 |

*Classics Illustrated #160 (HRN-160), © GIL*

*Classics Illustrated #161 (HRN-167), © GIL*

*Classics Illustrated #161 (HRN-167), © GIL*

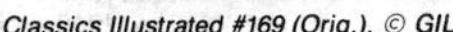

Classics Illustrated #169 (Orig.), © GIL

Classics Giveaway 1956 B.F. 5&10, © GIL

Classics Illustrated Giants (Exciting. . .), © GIL

**166. Tigers and Traitors**

| Ed | HRN | Date | Details | A C | Good | Fine | N-Mint |
|---|---|---|---|---|---|---|---|
| 1 | 165 | 5/62 | Original | 1 1 | 5.00 | 15.00 | 35.00 |
| 2 | 167 | 2/64 | PC-r | 1 1 | 2.00 | 6.00 | 14.00 |
| 3 | 167 | 11/66 | PC-r | 1 1 | 2.00 | 6.00 | 14.00 |

**167. Faust**

| Ed | HRN | Date | Details | A C | Good | Fine | N-Mint |
|---|---|---|---|---|---|---|---|
| 1 | 165 | 8/62 | Original | 1 1 | 9.00 | 27.00 | 62.00 |
| 2 | 167 | 2/64 | PC-r | 1 1 | 4.30 | 13.00 | 30.00 |
| 3 | 166 | 6/67 | PC-r | 1 1 | 4.30 | 13.00 | 30.00 |

**168. In Freedom's Cause**

| Ed | HRN | Date | Details | A C | Good | Fine | N-Mint |
|---|---|---|---|---|---|---|---|
| 1 | 169 | Win/69 | Original; Evans/Crandall-a; stiff-c; 25¢; no coming-next ad; | 1 1 | 8.00 | 24.00 | 56.00 |

**169. Negro Americans—The Early Years**

| Ed | HRN | Date | Details | A C | Good | Fine | N-Mint |
|---|---|---|---|---|---|---|---|
| 1 | 166 | Spr/69 | Orig. & last issue; 25¢; Stiff-c; no coming-next ad; other sources indicate pub. date of 5/69. | 1 1 | 8.00 | 24.00 | 56.00 |
| 2 | 169 | Spr/69 | Stiff-c | 1 1 | 5.00 | 15.00 | 35.00 |

NOTE: *Many other titles were prepared or planned but were only issued in British/European series.*

**CLASSICS GIVEAWAYS** (Arranged in chronological order)

1942—Double Comics containing CC#1 (orig.) (diff. cover) (not actually a giveaway) (very rare) (also see Double Comics); (only one known copy) 150.00 450.00 1050.00

12/42—Saks 34th St. Giveaway containing CC#7 (orig.) (diff. cover) (very rare; only 6 known copies) 345.00 1030.00 2400.00

2/43—American Comics containing CC#8 (orig.) (Liberty Theatre Giveaway) (diff. cover) (only one known copy) (see American Comics) 86.00 260.00 600.00

12/44—Robin Hood Flour Co. Giveaway - #7-CC(R) (diff. cover) (rare) (edition probably 5 [22]) 143.00 430.00 1000.00

NOTE: *How are above editions determined without CC covers? 1942 is dated 1942, and CC#1-first reprint did not come out until 5/43. 12/42 and 2/43 are determined by blue note at bottom of first text page only in original edition. 12/44 is estimate from page width—each reprint edition had progressively slightly smaller page width.*

1951—Shelter Thru the Ages (C.I. Educational Series) (actually Giveaway by the Ruberoid Co.) (16 pgs.) (contains original artwork by H. C. Kiefer) (there are back cover ad variations) (scarce) 54.00 160.00 375.00

1952—George Daynor Biography Giveaway (CC logo) (partly comic book/pictures/newspaper articles) (story of man who built Palace Depression out of junkyard swamp in NJ) (64 pgs.) (very rare; only 2 known copies, one missing-bc) 300.00 900.00 2100.00

1953—Westinghouse/Dreams of a Man (C.I. Educational Series) (Westinghouse bio./Westinghouse Co. giveaway) (contains original artwork by H. C. Kiefer) (16 pgs.) (also French/Spanish/Italian versions) (scarce) 47.00 170.00 400.00

NOTE: *Reproductions of 1951, 1952, and 1953 exist — color photocopy covers and black & white photocopy interior ("W.C.N. Reprint")* 1.50 4.50 10.00

1951-53—Coward Shoe Giveaways (all editions very rare) (two variations of back cover Coward Shoe ads) 5 (87), 12 (89), 22 (85), 49 (85), 69 (87), 72 (no HRN), 80 (0), 91 (0), 92 (0), 96 (0), 98 (0), 100 (0), 101 (0), 103-109 (all 0s), 110 (111), 112 (0). (some above editions recently discovered—some only one copy currently known to exist)

| | Good | Fine | N-Mint |
|---|---|---|---|
| | 34.00 | 103.00 | 240.00 |

1956—Ben Franklin 5-10 Store Giveaway (#65-PC with back cover ad) (scarce) 22.00 65.00 150.00

1956—Ben Franklin Insurance Co. Giveaway (#65-PC with diff. back cover ad) (very rare) 50.00 150.00 350.00

11/56—Sealtest Co. Edition - #4 (135) (identical to regular edition except for Sealtest logo printed, not stamped, on front cover) (only one copy known to exist) 26.00 77.00 180.00

1958—Get-Well Giveaway containing #15-CI (new cartoon-type cover) (Pressman Pharmacy) (only one copy known to exist) 21.50 64.00 150.00

67-68—Twin Circle Giveaway Editions - all HRN 166, with back cover ad for National Catholic Press.

| | Good | Fine | N-Mint |
|---|---|---|---|
| 2(R68), 4(R67), 10(R68), 13(R68) | 2.65 | 8.00 | 18.00 |
| 48(R67), 128(R68), 535(576-R68) | 3.50 | 10.50 | 24.00 |
| 16(R68), 68(R67) | 4.50 | 14.00 | 32.00 |

12/69—Christmas Giveaway ("A Christmas Adventure") (reprints Picture Parade #4-1953, new cover) (4 ad variations)

| | Good | Fine | N-Mint |
|---|---|---|---|
| Stacy's Dept. Store | 2.00 | 6.00 | 14.00 |
| Anne & Hope Store | 5.70 | 17.00 | 40.00 |
| Gibson's Dept. Store (rare) | 5.70 | 17.00 | 40.00 |
| "Merry Christmas" & blank ad space | 2.30 | 7.00 | 16.00 |

**CLASSICS ILLUSTRATED GIANTS**
October, 1949 (One-Shots - "OS")
Gilberton Publications

These Giant Editions, all with new Kiefer front and back covers, were advertised from 10/49 to 2/52. They were 50 cents on the newsstand and 60 cents by mail. They are actually four classics in one volume. All the stories are reprints of the Classics Illustrated Series. NOTE: *There were also British hardback Adventure & Indian Giants in 1952, with the same covers but different contents: Adventure - 2, 7, 10; Indian - 17, 22, 37, 58. They are also rare.*

"An Illustrated Library of Great Adventure Stories" - reprints of No. 6,7,8,10 (Rare); Kiefer-c 86.00 260.00 600.00

"An Illustrated Library of Exciting Mystery Stories" - reprints of No. 30,21,40,13 (Rare) 89.00 265.00 620.00

"An Illustrated Library of Great Indian Stories" - reprints of No. 4,17, 22,37 (Rare) 77.00 230.00 540.00

**INTRODUCTION TO CLASSICS ILLUSTRATED JUNIOR**

Collectors of Juniors can be put into one of two categories — those who want any copy of each title, and those who want all the originals. Those seeking every original and reprint edition are a limited group, primarily because Juniors have no changes in art or covers to spark interest, and because reprints are so low in value it is difficult to get dealers to look for specific reprint editions. Anyone interested in information about the full scope of Junior editions should write to **Jim McLoughlin, 28 Mercury Ave., East Patchogue, NY 11772.** He has been doing research in this area for several years.

In recent years it has become apparent that most serious Classics collectors seek Junior originals. Those seeking reprints seek them for low cost. This has made the previous note about the comparative market value of reprints inadequate. Most dealers report difficulty in moving reprints for more than $2-$4 for mint copies. Some may be worth $5-$7, just because of the popularity of the title, such as Snow White, Sleeping Beauty, and Wizard of Oz. Others may be worth $5-$7, because of the scarcity of particular title nos., such as 514, 560, 562, 575 & 576. Three particular reprint editions are worth even more. For the 535-Twin Circle edition, see Giveaways. There are also reprint editions of 501 and 503 which have a full-page bc ad for the very rare Junior record. Those may sell as high as $10-$15 in mint. Original editions of 557 and 558 also have that ad.

There are no reprint editions of 577. The only edition, from 1969, is a 25 cent stiff-cover edition with no ad for the next issue. All other original editions have coming-next ad. But 577, like C.I. #168, was prepared in 1962 but not issued. Copies of 577 can be found in 1963 British/European series, which then continued with dozens of additional new Junior titles.

**PRICES LISTED BELOW ARE FOR ORIGINAL EDITIONS, WHICH HAVE AN AD FOR THE NEXT ISSUE.**

**CLASSICS ILLUSTRATED JUNIOR**
Oct, 1953 - Spring, 1971
Famous Authors Ltd. (Gilberton Publications) — Good / Fine / N-Mint

501-Snow White & the Seven Dwarfs; Alex Blum-a 8.00 24.00 56.00
502-The Ugly Duckling 5.00 15.00 35.00
503-Cinderella 3.00 9.00 21.00
504-512: 504-The Pied Piper. 505-The Sleeping Beauty. 506-The Three Little Pigs. 507-Jack & the Beanstalk. 508-Goldilocks & the Three Bears. 509-Beauty and the Beast. 510-Little Red Riding Hood. 511-Puss-N-Boots. 512-Rumpel Stiltskin 2.00 6.00 14.00
513-Pinocchio 3.00 9.00 21.00
514-The Steadfast Tin Soldier 4.00 12.00 28.00
515-Johnny Appleseed 2.00 6.00 14.00
516-Aladdin and His Lamp 3.00 9.00 21.00
517-519: 517-The Emperor's New Clothes. 518-The Golden Goose. 519-Paul Bunyan 2.00 6.00 14.00
520-Thumbelina 3.00 9.00 21.00
521-King of the Golden River 2.00 6.00 14.00
522-530: 522-The Nightingale. 523-The Gallant Tailor. 524-The Wild Swans. 525-The Little Mermaid. 526-The Frog Prince. 527-The Golden-Haired Giant. 528-The Penny Prince. 529-The Magic Servants. 530-The Golden Bird 1.50 4.50 10.00
531-Rapunzel 2.00 6.00 14.00
532-534: 532-The Dancing Princesses. 533-The Magic Fountain. 534-The Golden Touch 1.50 4.50 10.00
535-The Wizard of Oz 4.00 12.00 28.00
536-538: 536-The Chimney Sweep. 537-The Three Fairies. 538-Silly Hans 1.50 4.50 10.00
539-The Enchanted Fish 3.00 9.00 21.00
540-The Tinder-Box 3.00 9.00 21.00
541-Snow White & Rose Red 2.00 6.00 14.00
542-The Donkey's Tale 2.00 6.00 14.00
543-The House in the Woods 1.50 4.50 10.00
544-The Golden Fleece 4.00 12.00 28.00
545-The Glass Mountain 2.00 6.00 14.00
546-The Elves & the Shoemaker 2.00 6.00 14.00
547-551: 547-The Wishing Table. 548-The Magic Pitcher. 549-Simple Kate. 550-The Singing Donkey. 551-The Queen Bee 1.50 4.50 10.00
552-The Three Little Dwarfs 2.00 6.00 14.00
553-556: 553-King Thrushbeard. 554-The Enchanted Deer. 555-The Three Golden Apples. 556-The Elf Mound 1.50 4.50 10.00
557-Silly Willy 3.00 9.00 21.00
558-The Magic Dish; L.B. Cole-c; soft and stiff-c exist on (O) 3.00 9.00 21.00
559-The Japanese Lantern; 1 pg. Ingels-a; L.B. Cole-c 3.00 9.00 21.00
560-The Doll Princess; L.B. Cole-c 3.00 9.00 21.00
561-Hans Humdrum; L.B. Cole-c 1.50 4.50 10.00
562-The Enchanted Pony; L.B. Cole-c 3.00 9.00 21.00
563-570: 563-The Wishing Well; L.B. Cole-c. 564-The Salt Mountain; L.B. Cole-c. 565-The Silly Princess; L.B. Cole-c. 566-Clumsy Hans; L.B. Cole-c. 567-The Bearskin Soldier; L.B. Cole-c. 568-The Happy Hedgehog; L.B. Cole-c. 569-The Three Giants. 570-The Pearl Princess 1.50 4.50 10.00
571-574: 571-How Fire Came to the Indians. 572-The Drummer Boy. 573-The Crystal Ball. 574-Brightboots 1.70 5.00 12.00
575-The Fearless Prince 2.00 6.00 14.00
576-The Princess Who Saw Everything 3.00 9.00 21.00
577-The Runaway Dumpling 4.00 12.00 28.00

NOTE: *Last reprint - Spring, 1971.* ***Costanza & Shaffenberger*** *art in many issues.*

**CLASSICS ILLUSTRATED SPECIAL ISSUE**
Dec, 1955 - July, 1962 (100 pages) (35 cents)
Gilberton Co. (Came out semi-annually) — Good / Fine / N-Mint

129-The Story of Jesus (titled ...Special Edition) "Jesus on Mountain" cover 3.70 11.00 26.00
"Three Camels" cover(12/58) 5.70 17.00 40.00
"Mountain" cover (1968 re-issue; has black 50 cent circle) 2.30 7.00 16.00
132A-The Story of America (6/56) 3.15 9.50 22.00
135A-The Ten Commandments(12/56) 4.00 12.00 28.00
138A-Adventures in Science(6/57) 3.15 9.50 22.00
141A-The Rough Rider (Teddy Roosevelt)(12/57); Evans-a 3.00 9.00 21.00
144A-Blazing the Trails West(6/58)- 73 pages of Crandall/Evans plus Severin-a 3.00 9.00 21.00
147A-Crossing the Rockies(12/58)-Crandall/Evans-a 4.30 13.00 30.00
150A-Royal Canadian Police(6/59)-Ingels, Sid Check-a 4.30 13.00 30.00
153A-Men, Guns & Cattle(12/59)-Evans-a, 26 pgs.; Kinstler-a 4.30 13.00 30.00
156A-The Atomic Age(6/60)-Crandall/Evans, Torres-a 3.15 9.50 22.00
159A-Rockets, Jets and Missiles(12/60)-Evans, Morrow-a 3.15 9.50 22.00
162A-War Between the States(6/61)-Kirby & Crandall/Evans-a; Ingels-a 6.50 19.00 45.00
165A-To the Stars(12/61)-Torres, Crandall/Evans, Kirby-a 3.15 9.50 22.00
166A-World War II('62)-Torres, Crandall/Evans, Kirby-a 4.30 13.00 30.00
167A-Prehistoric World(7/62)-Torres & Crandall/Evans-a 4.50 14.00 32.00
nn Special Issue-The United Nations (1964; 50 cents; scarce); This is actually part of the European Special Series, which continued on after the U.S. series stopped issuing new titles in 1962. This English edition was prepared specifically for sale at the U.N. It was printed in Norway. 24.00 73.00 170.00

NOTE: *There was another U.S. Special Issue prepared in 1962 with artwork by Kirby, Crandall & Evans, entitled* ***World War I****. Unfortunately, it was never issued in any English-language edition. It was issued in 1964 in West Germany, The Netherlands, and some Scandanavian countries, with another edition in 1974 with a new cover.*

**CLASSIC PUNISHER** (Also see Punisher)
Dec, 1989 ($4.95, B&W, deluxe format, 68 pgs.)
Marvel Comics

1-R/Marvel Super Action #1 & Marvel Preview #2 plus new story .85 2.50 5.00

**CLASSICS ILLUSTRATED**
Feb, 1990 - Present ($3.75-$3.95, color, 52 pgs.)
First Comics

1-21: 1-The Raven and Other Poems; Gahan Wilson-c/a. 2-Great Expectations. 3-Through the Looking-Glass. 4-Moby Dick; painted-c/a by Sienkiewicz. 5-Hamlet. 6-The Scarlet Letter; Russell scripts/layouts. 7-The Count of Monte Cristo; Spiegle-a. 8-Dr. Jekyll and Mr. Hyde. 9-The Advs. of Tom Sawyer; Ploog-c/a. 10-The Call of the Wild. 11-Rip Van Winkle. 12-The Island of Dr. Moreau. 13-Wuthering Heights. 14-The Fall of the House of Usher. 15-The Gift of the Magi & Other Stories. 16-A Christmas Carol; Staton-a. 17-Treasure Island .65 1.90 3.80
18-21: 18-The Devil's Dictionary; Gahan Wilson-c/a; begin $3.95-c. 19-The Secret Agent. 20-The Invisible Man; Geary-a. 21-Ivanhoe .70 2.00 4.00

**CLASSICS LIBRARY** (See King Classics)

**CLASSIC X-MEN** (Becomes X-Men Classic #46 on)
Sept, 1986 - No. 45, Mar, 1990 (#27 on: $1.25)
Marvel Comics Group

1-Begins-r of New X-Men 1.35 4.00 8.00
2-4 .85 2.50 5.00

*Classics Illustrated Junior #512, © GIL*

*Classics Illustrated Junior #562, © GIL*

*Classics Illustrated Special Issue #150A, © GIL*

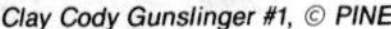
*Clay Cody Gunslinger #1, © PINE*

*Clive Barker's Hellraiser #1, © MEG*

*Clue Comics #7, © HILL*

| | Good | Fine | N-Mint |
|---|---|---|---|
| 5-10 | .70 | 2.00 | 4.00 |
| 11-15 | .50 | 1.50 | 3.00 |
| 16,18-20 | .40 | 1.25 | 2.50 |
| 17-Wolverine-c | 1.00 | 3.00 | 6.00 |
| 21-25,27-30: 27-r/X-Men #121 | .35 | 1.00 | 2.00 |
| 26-r/X-Men #120; Wolverine-c/app. | .50 | 1.50 | 3.00 |
| 31-42,44,45: 35-r/X-Men #129 (1st Kitty Pryde) | .30 | .90 | 1.80 |
| 43-Byrne-c/a(r); $1.75, double-size | .40 | 1.25 | 2.50 |

NOTE: ***Art Adams** c(p)-1-10, 12-16, 18, 19, 25. **Austin** c-19i. **Bolton** back up stories in many issues. **Williamson** c-12i, 13i.*

**CLAW THE UNCONQUERED** (See Cancelled Comic Cavalcade)
5-6/75 - No. 9, 9-10/76; No. 10, 4-5/78 - No. 12, 8-9/78
National Periodical Publications/DC Comics

| | Good | Fine | N-Mint |
|---|---|---|---|
| 1 | .25 | .75 | 1.50 |
| 2,3: 3-Nudity panel | | .50 | 1.00 |
| 4-12: 9-Origin | | .40 | .80 |

NOTE: ***Giffen** a-8-12p. **Kubert** c-10-12. **Layton** a-9i, 12i.*

**CLAY CODY, GUNSLINGER**
Fall, 1957
Pines Comics

| | Good | Fine | N-Mint |
|---|---|---|---|
| 1-Painted-c | 2.00 | 6.00 | 14.00 |

**CLEAN FUN, STARRING "SHOOGAFOOTS JONES"**
1944 (24 pgs.; B&W; oversized covers) (10 cents)
Specialty Book Co.

nn-Humorous situations involving Negroes in the Deep South

| | Good | Fine | N-Mint |
|---|---|---|---|
| White cover issue.... | 2.75 | 8.00 | 16.00 |
| Dark grey cover issue.... | 3.00 | 9.00 | 18.00 |

**CLEMENTINA THE FLYING PIG** (See Dell Jr. Treasury)

**CLEOPATRA** (See Ideal, a Classical Comic No. 1)

**CLIFF MERRITT SETS THE RECORD STRAIGHT**
Giveaway (2 different issues)
Brotherhood of Railroad Trainsmen

| | Good | Fine | N-Mint |
|---|---|---|---|
| ...and the Very Candid Candidate by Al Williamson | .40 | 1.20 | 2.40 |
| ...Sets the Record Straight by Al Williamson (2 different-c: one by Williamson, the other by McWilliams) | .40 | 1.20 | 2.40 |

**CLIFFORD McBRIDE'S IMMORTAL NAPOLEON & UNCLE ELBY**
1932 (12x17"; softcover cartoon book)
The Castle Press

| | Good | Fine | N-Mint |
|---|---|---|---|
| nn-Intro. by Don Herod | 8.00 | 24.00 | 56.00 |

**CLIMAX!**
July, 1955 - No. 2, Sept, 1955
Gillmor Magazines

| | Good | Fine | N-Mint |
|---|---|---|---|
| 1,2 (Mystery) | 5.30 | 16.00 | 38.00 |

**CLINT** (Also see Adolescent Radioactive Black Belt Hamsters)
Sept, 1986 - No. 2, Jan, 1987 ($1.50, B&W)
Eclipse Comics

| | Good | Fine | N-Mint |
|---|---|---|---|
| 1,2 | .25 | .75 | 1.50 |

**CLINT & MAC** (See 4-Color No. 889)

**CLIVE BARKER'S HELLRAISER** (Also see Tapping the Vein)
1989 - Present ($4.95, color, mature readers, quarterly, 68 pgs.)
Epic Comics (Marvel)

| | Good | Fine | N-Mint |
|---|---|---|---|
| Book 1-4: Based on Hellraiser & Hellbound movies; 1-Bolton-c/a; Spiegle & Wrightson-a (graphic album) | .85 | 2.50 | 5.00 |

**CLIVE BARKER'S NIGHTBREED**
Apr, 1990 - Present ($1.95-$2.25, color, adults)
Epic Comics (Marvel)

| | Good | Fine | N-Mint |
|---|---|---|---|
| 1: 1-4-Adapt horror movie | .50 | 1.50 | 3.00 |
| 2-4 | .35 | 1.00 | 2.00 |

| | Good | Fine | N-Mint |
|---|---|---|---|
| 5-8: 5-New stories begin; Guice-a(p) | .40 | 1.15 | 2.30 |

**CLOAK AND DAGGER**
Fall, 1952
Ziff-Davis Publishing Co.

| | Good | Fine | N-Mint |
|---|---|---|---|
| 1-Saunders painted-c | 11.50 | 34.00 | 80.00 |

**CLOAK AND DAGGER** (Also see Marvel Fanfare)
Oct, 1983 - No. 4, Jan, 1984 (Mini-series)(See Spect. Spider-Man #64)
Marvel Comics Group

| | Good | Fine | N-Mint |
|---|---|---|---|
| 1-4-Austin-c/a(i) in all. 4-Origin | .25 | .75 | 1.50 |

**CLOAK AND DAGGER** (Also see Marvel Graphic Novel #34, Mutant Misadventures Of... & Strange Tales, 2nd series)
July, 1985 - No. 11, Jan, 1987
Marvel Comics Group

| | Good | Fine | N-Mint |
|---|---|---|---|
| 1 | .25 | .75 | 1.50 |
| 2-8,10,11 | | .50 | 1.00 |
| 9-Art Adams-p | .50 | 1.50 | 3.00 |
| ...And Power Pack (1990, $7.95, 68 pgs.) | 1.35 | 4.00 | 8.00 |

**CLONEZONE SPECIAL**
1989 ($2.00, B&W)
Dark Horse Comics/First Comics

| | Good | Fine | N-Mint |
|---|---|---|---|
| 1-Back-up series from Badger & Nexus | .35 | 1.00 | 2.00 |

**CLOSE ENCOUNTERS** (See Marvel Comics Super Spec. & Marvel Special Ed.)

**CLOSE SHAVES OF PAULINE PERIL, THE** (TV?)
June, 1970 - No. 4, March, 1971 (Jay Ward?)
Gold Key

| | Good | Fine | N-Mint |
|---|---|---|---|
| 1 | 1.00 | 3.00 | 6.00 |
| 2-4 | .70 | 2.00 | 4.00 |

**CLOWN COMICS** (No. 1 titled Clown Comic Book)
1945 - No. 3, Wint, 1946
Clown Comics/Home Comics/Harvey Publ.

| | Good | Fine | N-Mint |
|---|---|---|---|
| nn | 4.00 | 12.00 | 28.00 |
| 2,3 | 2.30 | 7.00 | 16.00 |

**CLUBHOUSE RASCALS** (#1 titled ... Presents?)
June, 1956 - No. 2, Oct, 1956 (Also see Three Rascals)
Sussex Publ. Co. (Magazine Enterprises)

| | Good | Fine | N-Mint |
|---|---|---|---|
| 1,2: The Brain app. | 2.00 | 6.00 | 14.00 |

**CLUB "16"**
June, 1948 - No. 4, Dec, 1948
Famous Funnies

| | Good | Fine | N-Mint |
|---|---|---|---|
| 1-Teen-age humor | 5.00 | 15.00 | 35.00 |
| 2-4 | 2.65 | 8.00 | 18.00 |

**CLUE COMICS** (Real Clue Crime V2#4 on)
Jan, 1943 - No. 15(V2#3), May, 1947
Hillman Periodicals

| | Good | Fine | N-Mint |
|---|---|---|---|
| 1-Origin The Boy King, Nightmare, Micro-Face, Twilight, & Zippo | 47.00 | 140.00 | 325.00 |
| 2 | 24.00 | 73.00 | 170.00 |
| 3 | 19.00 | 58.00 | 135.00 |
| 4 | 16.00 | 48.00 | 110.00 |
| 5 | 13.00 | 40.00 | 90.00 |
| 6,8,9: 8-Palais-c/a(2) | 10.00 | 30.00 | 70.00 |
| 7-Classic torture-c | 14.00 | 43.00 | 100.00 |
| 10-Origin The Gun Master | 11.00 | 32.00 | 75.00 |
| 11 | 7.00 | 21.00 | 50.00 |
| 12-Origin Rackman; McWilliams-a, Guardineer-a(2) | 10.00 | 30.00 | 70.00 |
| V2#1-Nightro new origin; Iron Lady app.; Simon & Kirby-a | 14.00 | 43.00 | 100.00 |

V2#2-S&K-a(2)-Bondage/torture-c; man attacks & kills people with

| | Good | Fine | N-Mint |
|---|---|---|---|
| electric iron. Infantino-a | 14.00 | 43.00 | 100.00 |
| V2#3-S&K-a(3) | 14.00 | 43.00 | 100.00 |

**CLUTCHING HAND, THE**
July-Aug, 1954
American Comics Group

| | | | |
|---|---|---|---|
| 1 | 11.00 | 32.00 | 75.00 |

**CLYDE BEATTY COMICS** (Also see Crackajack Funnies)
October, 1953 (84 pages)
Commodore Productions & Artists, Inc.

| | | | |
|---|---|---|---|
| 1-Photo front/back-c; includes movie scenes and comics | 14.00 | 43.00 | 100.00 |
| . . . African Jungle Book('56)-Richfield Oil Co. 16 pg. giveaway, soft-c | 5.00 | 15.00 | 35.00 |

**CLYDE CRASHCUP** (TV)
Aug-Oct, 1963 - No. 5, Sept-Nov, 1964
Dell Publishing Co.

| | | | |
|---|---|---|---|
| 1-All written by John Stanley | 5.00 | 15.00 | 35.00 |
| 2-5 | 3.60 | 11.00 | 25.00 |

**C-M-O COMICS**
1942 - No. 2, 1942 (68 pages, full color)
Chicago Mail Order Co.(Centaur)

| | | | |
|---|---|---|---|
| 1-Invisible Terror, Super Ann, & Plymo the Rubber Man app. (All Centaur costume heroes) | 40.00 | 120.00 | 280.00 |
| 2-Invisible Terror, Super Ann app. | 27.00 | 81.00 | 190.00 |

**COBALT BLUE** (Also see Power Comics)
Sept, 1989 - No. 2, Oct?, 1989 ($1.95, color, mini-series, 28 pgs.)
Innovation Publishing

| | | | |
|---|---|---|---|
| 1,2-Gustovich-c/a/scripts | .35 | 1.00 | 2.00 |
| The Graphic Novel ($6.95, color, 52 pgs.)-r/1,2 | 1.15 | 3.50 | 7.00 |

**COBRA**
1990 - No. 12 ($2.95-$3.25, B&W, 52 pgs.)
Viz Select Comics

| | | | |
|---|---|---|---|
| 1-6: Japanese manga translated to English | .50 | 1.50 | 3.00 |
| 7-12: 7-Begin $3.25-c | .55 | 1.65 | 3.30 |

**COCOMALT BIG BOOK OF COMICS**
1938 (Regular size; full color; 52 pgs.)
Harry 'A' Chesler (Cocomalt Premium)

| | | | |
|---|---|---|---|
| 1-(Scarce)-Biro-c/a; Little Nemo by Winsor McCay Jr., Dan Hastings; Guardineer, Jack Cole, Gustavson, Bob Wood-a | 80.00 | 240.00 | 560.00 |

**CODE NAME: ASSASSIN** ( See First Issue Special)

**CODENAME: DANGER**
Aug, 1985 - No. 4, May, 1986 ($1.50 cover)
Lodestone Publishing

| | | | |
|---|---|---|---|
| 1-4 | .25 | .75 | 1.50 |

**CODENAME SPITFIRE** (Formerly Spitfire And The Troubleshooters)
No. 10, July, 1987 - No. 13, Oct, 1987
Marvel Comics Group

| | | | |
|---|---|---|---|
| 10-13: 10-Rogers-c/a | | .50 | 1.00 |

**CODE NAME: TOMAHAWK**
Sept, 1986 ($1.75, color, high quality paper)
Fantasy General Comics

| | | | |
|---|---|---|---|
| 1-Sci/fi | .30 | .90 | 1.80 |

**CODY OF THE PONY EXPRESS** (See Colossal Features Magazine)
Sept, 1950 - No. 3, Jan, 1951 (See Women Outlaws)
Fox Features Syndicate

| | | | |
|---|---|---|---|
| 1-3 (actually #3-5). 1-Painted-c | 5.30 | 16.00 | 38.00 |

**CODY OF THE PONY EXPRESS** (Buffalo Bill . . .) (Outlaws of the West #11 on; Formerly Bullseye)
No. 8, Oct, 1955; No. 9, Jan, 1956; No. 10, June, 1956
Charlton Comics

| | Good | Fine | N-Mint |
|---|---|---|---|
| 8-Bullseye on splash pg; not S&K-a | 3.00 | 9.00 | 21.00 |
| 9,10: 10-Buffalo Bill app. | 2.00 | 6.00 | 14.00 |

**CO-ED ROMANCES**
November, 1951
P. L. Publishing Co.

| | | | |
|---|---|---|---|
| 1 | 2.65 | 8.00 | 18.00 |

**COLLECTORS ITEM CLASSICS** (See Marvel Collectors Item Classics)

**COLOSSAL FEATURES MAGAZINE** (Formerly I Loved) (See Cody of the Pony Express)
No. 33, May, 1950 - No. 34, July, 1950; No. 3, Sept, 1950
Fox Features Syndicate

| | | | |
|---|---|---|---|
| 33,34-Cody of the Pony Express begins (based on Columbia serial). 33-Painted-c; 34-Photo-c | 5.00 | 15.00 | 35.00 |
| 3-Authentic criminal cases | 5.00 | 15.00 | 35.00 |

**COLOSSAL SHOW, THE** (TV)
October, 1969
Gold Key

| | | | |
|---|---|---|---|
| 1 | 2.00 | 6.00 | 14.00 |

**COLOSSUS COMICS** (See Green Giant & Motion Picture Fun. Wkly.)
March, 1940
Sun Publications (Funnies, Inc.?)

| | | | |
|---|---|---|---|
| 1-(Scarce)-Tulpa of Tsang (hero); Colossus app. | 100.00 | 300.00 | 700.00 |

NOTE: *Cover by artist that drew Colossus in Green Giant Comics.*

**COLT .45** (TV)
No. 924, 8/58 - No. 1058, 11-1/59-60; No. 4, 2-4/60 - No. 9, 5-7/61
Dell Publishing Co.

| | | | |
|---|---|---|---|
| 4-Color 924(#1)-Wayde Preston photo-c on all | 6.00 | 18.00 | 42.00 |
| 4-Color 1004,1058; #4,5,7-9 | 4.00 | 12.00 | 28.00 |
| 6-Toth-a | 5.70 | 17.00 | 40.00 |

**COLUMBIA COMICS**
1943
William H. Wise Co.

| | | | |
|---|---|---|---|
| 1-Joe Palooka, Charlie Chan, Capt. Yank, Sparky Watts, Dixie Dugan app. | 14.00 | 43.00 | 100.00 |

**COMANCHE** (See 4-Color No. 1350)

**COMANCHEROS, THE** (See 4-Color No. 1300)

**COMBAT**
June, 1952 - No. 11, April, 1953
Atlas Comics (ANC)

| | | | |
|---|---|---|---|
| 1 | 5.70 | 17.00 | 40.00 |
| 2 | 2.65 | 8.00 | 18.00 |
| 3,5-9,11: 9-Robert Q. Sale-a | 1.70 | 5.00 | 12.00 |
| 4-Krigstein-a | 2.65 | 8.00 | 18.00 |
| 10-B&W and color illos. in **POP** | 2.00 | 6.00 | 14.00 |

NOTE: *Combat Casey in 7-11.* ***Heath*** *c-1, 9.* ***Maneely*** *a-1.* ***Pakula*** *a-1.* ***Reinman*** *a-1.*

**COMBAT**
Oct-Nov, 1961 - No. 40, Oct, 1973 (No #9)
Dell Publishing Co.

| | | | |
|---|---|---|---|
| 1 | 2.30 | 7.00 | 16.00 |
| 2-5: 4-John F. Kennedy c/story (P.T. 109) | 1.50 | 4.50 | 10.00 |
| 6,7,8(4-6/63), 8(7-9/63) | 1.00 | 3.00 | 6.00 |
| 10-27 | .85 | 2.50 | 5.00 |
| 28-40(reprints #1-14). 30-r/#4 | .70 | 2.00 | 4.00 |

NOTE: ***Glanzman*** *c/a-1-27, 28-40r.*

*Cobra #1, © Viz Communications*

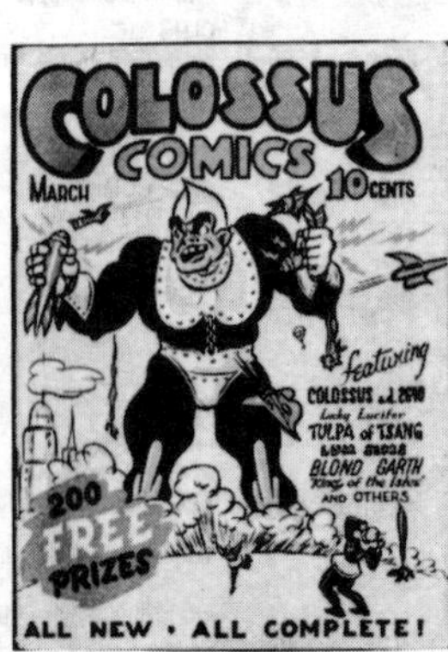

*Colossus Comics #1, © Sun Publ.*

*Colt .45 #6, © Warner Bros.*

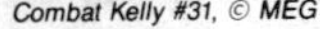
Combat Kelly #31, © MEG

Comedy Comics #2, © MEG

Comic Album #8, © M.G.M.

**COMBAT CASEY** (Formerly War Combat)
No. 6, Jan, 1953 - No. 34, July, 1957
Atlas Comics (SAI)

| | Good | Fine | N-Mint |
|---|---|---|---|
| 6 (Indicia shows 1/52 in error) | 4.00 | 12.00 | 28.00 |
| 7-Spanking panel | 2.65 | 8.00 | 18.00 |
| 8-Used in **POP**, pg. 94 | 2.00 | 6.00 | 14.00 |
| 9 | 1.70 | 5.00 | 12.00 |
| 10,13-19-Violent art by R. Q. Sale; Battle Brady x-over #10 | 2.30 | 7.00 | 16.00 |
| 11,12,20-Last Precode (2/55) | 1.30 | 4.00 | 9.00 |
| 21-34 | 1.00 | 3.00 | 7.00 |

NOTE: *Everett a-6. Heath c-10, 17, 19, 30. Powell a-29(5), 30(5), 34. Severin c-26, 33.*

**COMBAT KELLY**
Nov, 1951 - No. 44, Aug, 1957
Atlas Comics (SPI)

| | Good | Fine | N-Mint |
|---|---|---|---|
| 1-Heath-a | 8.00 | 24.00 | 56.00 |
| 2 | 3.00 | 9.00 | 21.00 |
| 3-10 | 2.00 | 6.00 | 14.00 |
| 11-Used in **POP**, pages 94,95 plus color illo. | 1.70 | 5.00 | 12.00 |
| 12-Color illo. in **POP** | 1.70 | 5.00 | 12.00 |
| 13-16 | 1.15 | 3.50 | 8.00 |
| 17-Violent art by R. Q. Sale; Combat Casey app. | 3.00 | 9.00 | 21.00 |
| 18-20,22-44: 18-Battle Brady app. 28-Last precode (1/55). 38-Green Berets story(8/56) | 1.15 | 3.50 | 8.00 |
| 21-Transvestism-c | 2.00 | 6.00 | 14.00 |

NOTE: *Berg a-8, 12-14, 16, 17, 19-23, 25, 26, 28, 31-36, 42-44. Colan a-42. Heath a-4; c-31. Lawrence a-23. Maneely a-4(2), 6, 7(3), 8; c-7, 8, 25. R.Q. Sale a-17, 25. Severin c-41, 42. Whitney a-5.*

**COMBAT KELLY** (. . . and the Deadly Dozen)
June, 1972 - No. 9, Oct, 1973
Marvel Comics Group

| | Good | Fine | N-Mint |
|---|---|---|---|
| 1-Intro. Combat Kelly; Ayers/Mooney-a; Severin-c | | .50 | 1.00 |
| 2-9 | | .40 | .80 |

**COMBINED OPERATIONS** (See The Story of the Commandos)

**COMEDY CARNIVAL**
no date (1950's) (100 pages)
St. John Publishing Co.

| | Good | Fine | N-Mint |
|---|---|---|---|
| nn-Contains rebound St. John comics | 16.00 | 48.00 | 110.00 |

**COMEDY COMICS** (1st Series) (Formerly Daring Mystery No. 1-8)
(Becomes Margie Comics No. 35 on)
No. 9, April, 1942 - No. 34, Fall, 1946
Timely Comics (TCI 9,10)

| | Good | Fine | N-Mint |
|---|---|---|---|
| 9-(Scarce)-The Fin by Everett, Capt. Dash, Citizen V, & The Silver Scorpion app.; Wolverton-a; 1st app. Comedy Kid; satire on Hitler & Stalin | 112.00 | 281.00 | 675.00 |
| 10-(Scarce)-Origin The Fourth Musketeer, Victory Boys; Monstro, the Mighty app. | 69.00 | 205.00 | 480.00 |
| 11-Vagabond, Stuporman app. | 22.00 | 65.00 | 150.00 |
| 12,13 | 6.00 | 18.00 | 42.00 |
| 14-Origin & 1st app. Super Rabbit | 24.00 | 73.00 | 170.00 |
| 15-20 | 5.00 | 15.00 | 35.00 |
| 21-32 | 3.70 | 11.00 | 26.00 |
| 33-Kurtzman-a, 5 pgs. | 5.00 | 15.00 | 35.00 |
| 34-Intro Margie; Wolverton-a, 5 pgs. | 7.00 | 21.00 | 50.00 |

**COMEDY COMICS** (2nd Series)
May, 1948 - No. 10, Jan, 1950
Marvel Comics (ACI)

| | Good | Fine | N-Mint |
|---|---|---|---|
| 1-Hedy, Tessie, Millie begin; Kurtzman's "Hey Look" (he draws himself) | 14.00 | 43.00 | 100.00 |
| 2 | 5.00 | 15.00 | 35.00 |
| 3,4-Kurtzman's "Hey Look"(?&3) | 7.00 | 21.00 | 50.00 |
| 5-10 | 2.65 | 8.00 | 18.00 |

**COMET, THE** (See The Mighty Crusaders & Pep Comics #1)
Oct, 1983 - No. 2, Dec, 1983
Red Circle Comics

| | Good | Fine | N-Mint |
|---|---|---|---|
| 1,2: 1-Re-intro & origin The Comet; The American Shield begins; 2-Origin continues | | .50 | 1.00 |

**COMET MAN, THE**
Feb, 1987 - No. 6, July, 1987 (Mini-series)
Marvel Comics Group

| | Good | Fine | N-Mint |
|---|---|---|---|
| 1-6 | | .50 | 1.00 |

**COMIC ALBUM** (Also see Disney Comic Album)
Mar-May, 1958 - No. 18, June-Aug, 1962
Dell Publishing Co.

| | Good | Fine | N-Mint |
|---|---|---|---|
| 1-Donald Duck | 3.50 | 10.50 | 24.00 |
| 2-Bugs Bunny | 1.50 | 4.50 | 10.00 |
| 3-Donald Duck | 2.85 | 8.50 | 20.00 |
| 4-6,8-10: 4-Tom & Jerry. 5-Woody Woodpecker. 6,10-Bugs Bunny. 8-Tom & Jerry. 9-Woody Woodpecker | 1.30 | 4.00 | 9.00 |
| 7-Popeye (9-11/59) | 2.30 | 7.00 | 16.00 |
| 11-Popeye (9-11/60) | 2.30 | 7.00 | 16.00 |
| 12-14: 12-Tom & Jerry. 13-Woody Woodpecker. 14-Bugs Bunny | 1.30 | 4.00 | 9.00 |
| 15-Popeye | 2.30 | 7.00 | 16.00 |
| 16-Flintstones (12-2/61-62)-3rd app. | 3.00 | 9.00 | 21.00 |
| 17-Space Mouse (3rd app.) | 1.70 | 5.00 | 12.00 |
| 18-Three Stooges; photo-c | 6.00 | 18.00 | 42.00 |

**COMIC BOOK** (Also see Comics From Weatherbird)
1954 (Giveaway)
American Juniors Shoe

Contains a comic rebound with new cover. Several combinations possible. Contents determines price.

**COMIC BOOK MAGAZINE**
1940 - 1943 (Similar to Spirit Sections)
(7¾x10¾"; full color; 16-24 pages each)
Chicago Tribune & other newspapers

| | Good | Fine | N-Mint |
|---|---|---|---|
| 1940 issues | 5.00 | 15.00 | 35.00 |
| 1941, 1942 issues | 4.00 | 12.00 | 28.00 |
| 1943 issues | 3.35 | 10.00 | 23.00 |

NOTE: *Published weekly. Texas Slim, Kit Carson, Spooky, Josie, Nuts & Jolts, Lew Loyal, Brenda Starr, Daniel Boone, Captain Storm, Rocky, Smokey Stover, Tiny Tim, Little Joe, Fu Manchu appear among others. Early issues had photo stories with pictures from the movies; later issues had comic art.*

**COMIC BOOKS** (Series 1)
1950 (16 pgs.; 5¼x8½"; full color; bound at top; paper cover)
Metropolitan Printing Co. (Giveaway)

| | Good | Fine | N-Mint |
|---|---|---|---|
| 1-Boots and Saddles; intro. The Masked Marshal | 3.35 | 10.00 | 23.00 |
| 1-The Green Jet; Green Lama by Raboy | 20.00 | 60.00 | 140.00 |
| 1-My Pal Dizzy (Teen-age) | 1.70 | 5.00 | 12.00 |
| 1-New World; origin Atomaster (costumed hero) | 5.00 | 15.00 | 35.00 |
| 1-Talullah (Teen-age) | 1.70 | 5.00 | 12.00 |

**COMIC CAPERS**
Fall, 1944 - No. 6, Summer, 1946
Red Circle Mag./Marvel Comics

| | Good | Fine | N-Mint |
|---|---|---|---|
| 1-Super Rabbit, The Creeper, Silly Seal, Ziggy Pig, Sharpy Fox begin | 11.00 | 32.00 | 75.00 |
| 2 | 5.00 | 15.00 | 35.00 |
| 3-6 | 3.60 | 11.00 | 25.00 |

**COMIC CAVALCADE**
Winter, 1942-43 - No. 63, June-July, 1954
(Contents change with No. 30, Dec-Jan, 1948-49 on)
All-American/National Periodical Publications

1-The Flash, Green Lantern, Wonder Woman, Wildcat, The Black

Good Fine N-Mint

Pirate by Moldoff (also #2), Ghost Patrol, and Red White & Blue begin; Scribbly app., Minute Movies

| Good | Fine | VF-NM | NM/Mint |
|---|---|---|---|
| 267.00 | 665.00 | 1600.00 | 2600.00 |

(Estimated up to 175 total copies exist, 6 in NM/Mint)

2-Mutt & Jeff begin; last Ghost Patrol & Black Pirate; Minute Movies

| Good | Fine | N-Mint |
|---|---|---|
| 125.00 | 312.00 | 750.00 |

3-Hop Harrigan & Sargon, the Sorcerer begin; The King app. 92.00 230.00 550.00

4,5: 4-The Gay Ghost, The King, Scribbly, & Red Tornado app. 5-Christmas-c 80.00 240.00 480.00

6-10: 7-Red Tornado & Black Pirate app.; last Scribbly. 9-X-mas-c 60.00 150.00 360.00

11,12,14-20: 12-Last Red White & Blue. 15-Johnny Peril begins, ends #29. 19-Christmas-c 49.00 123.00 295.00

13-Solomon Grundy app.; X-mas-c 83.00 210.00 500.00

21-23 49.00 123.00 295.00

24-Solomon Grundy x-over in Green Lantern 60.00 150.00 360.00

25-29: 25-Black Canary app.; X-mas-c. 26-28-Johnny Peril app. 28-Last Mutt & Jeff. 29-(10-11/48)-Last Flash, Wonder Woman, Green Lantern & Johnny Peril; Wonder Woman invents "Thinking Machine;" 1st computer in comics? 38.00 95.00 230.00

30-(12-1/48-49)-The Fox & the Crow, Dodo & the Frog & Nutsy Squirrel begin 23.00 70.00 160.00

31-35 10.00 30.00 70.00

36-49 8.00 24.00 55.00

50-62(Scarce) 10.00 30.00 70.00

63(Rare) 17.00 51.00 120.00

Giveaway (1944, 8 pgs., paper-c, in color)-One Hundred Years of Co-operation-r/Comic Cavalcade #9 21.50 64.00 150.00

Giveaway (1945, 16 pages, paper-c, in color)-Movie "Tomorrow The World" (Nazi theme) 39.00 118.00 275.00

Giveaway (c. 1944-45; 8 pgs, paper-c, in color)-The Twain Shall Meet-r/C. Cavalcade 29.00 85.00 200.00

NOTE: ***Grossman*** *a-30-63.* ***Sheldon Mayer*** *a(2-3)-40-63.* ***Post*** *a-31, 36.* ***Reinman*** *a-15, 20.* ***Toth*** *a-26-28(Green Lantern); c-23, 27. Atom app.-22, 23.*

**COMIC COMICS**
April, 1946 - No. 10, Feb, 1947
Fawcett Publications

1-Captain Kidd 5.00 15.00 35.00

2-10-Wolverton-a, 4 pgs. each. 5-Captain Kidd app. 6.00 18.00 42.00

**COMIC CUTS** (Also see The Funnies)
5/19/34 - 7/28/34 (5 cents; 24 pages) (Tabloid size in full color)
(Not reprints; published weekly; created for newsstand sale)
H. L. Baker Co., Inc.

V1#1 - V1#7(6/30/34), V1#8(7/14/34), V1#9(7/28/34)-Idle Jack strips 7.00 21.00 50.00

**COMIC LAND**
March, 1946
Fact and Fiction Publ.

1-Sandusky & the Senator, Sam Stupor, Sleuth, Marvin the Great, Sir Passer, Phineas Gruff app.; Irv Tirman & Perry Williams art 5.70 17.00 40.00

**COMIC MONTHLY**
Jan, 1922 - No. 12, Dec, 1922 (32 pgs.)(8½x9")(10 cents)
(1st monthly newsstand comic publication) (Reprints 1921 B&W dailies)
Embee Dist. Co.

1-Polly & Her Pals 33.00 100.00 230.00

2-Mike & Ike 7.00 21.00 50.00

3-S'Matter, Pop? 7.00 21.00 50.00

Good Fine N-Mint

4-Barney Google 14.00 42.00 100.00

5-Tillie the Toiler 10.00 30.00 70.00

6-12: 6-Indoor Sports. 7-Little Jimmy. 8-Toots and Casper. 9,10-Foolish Questions. 11-Barney Google & Spark Plug in the Abadaba Handicap. 12-Polly & Her Pals 6.00 18.00 42.00

**COMICO CHRISTMAS SPECIAL**
Dec, 1988 ($2.50, 44pgs, color)
Comico

1-Rude/Williamson-a; Stevens-c .40 1.25 2.50

**COMICO PRIMER** (See Primer)

**COMIC PAGES** (Formerly Funny Picture Stories)
V3#4, July, 1939 - V3#6, Dec, 1939
Centaur Publications

V3#4-Bob Wood-a 29.00 85.00 200.00

5,6 19.00 58.00 135.00

**COMIC PAINTING AND CRAYONING BOOK**
1917 (32 pages)(10x13½")(No price on cover)
Saalfield Publ. Co.

nn-Tidy Teddy by F. M. Follett, Clarence the Cop, Mr. & Mrs. Butt-In. Regular comic stories to read or color 8.50 25.50 60.00

**COMICS** (See All Good)

**COMICS, THE**
March, 1937 - No. 11, Nov, 1938 (Newspaper strip-r; bi-monthly)
Dell Publishing Co.

1-1st Tom Mix in comics; Wash Tubbs, Tom Beatty, Myra North, Arizona Kid, Erik Noble & International Spy w/Doctor Doom begin 71.00 215.00 500.00

2 34.00 103.00 270.00

3-11: 3-Alley Oop begins 28.00 85.00 225.00

**COMICS AND STORIES** (See Walt Disney's...)

**COMICS CALENDAR, THE** (The 1946...)
1946 (116 pgs.; 25 cents)(Stapled at top)
True Comics Press (ordered through the mail)

nn-(Rare) Has a "strip" story for every day of the year in color 20.00 60.00 140.00

**COMICS DIGEST** (Pocket size)
Winter, 1942-43 (100 pages) (Black & White)
Parents' Magazine Institute

1-Reprints from True Comics (non-fiction World War II stories) 5.00 15.00 35.00

**COMIC SELECTIONS** (Shoe store giveaway)
1944-46 (Reprints from Calling All Girls, True Comics, True Aviation, & Real Heroes)
Parents' Magazine Press

1 1.70 5.00 12.00

2-5 1.30 4.00 9.00

**COMICS EXPRESS**
Nov, 1989 - Present? ($2.95, B&W, 68 pgs.)
Eclipse Comics

1,2: Collection of strip-r; 2(12/89-c, 1/90 inside) .50 1.50 3.00

**COMICS FOR KIDS**
1945 (no month); No. 2, Sum, 1945 (Funny animal)
London Publishing Co./Timely

1,2-Puffy Pig, Sharpy Fox 6.00 18.00 42.00

**COMICS FROM WEATHER BIRD** (Also see Comic Book, Edward's Shoes, Free Comics to You & Weather Bird)
1954 - 1957 (Giveaway)
Weather Bird Shoes

*Comic Cavalcade #15, © DC*

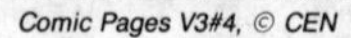

*Comic Pages V3#4, © CEN*

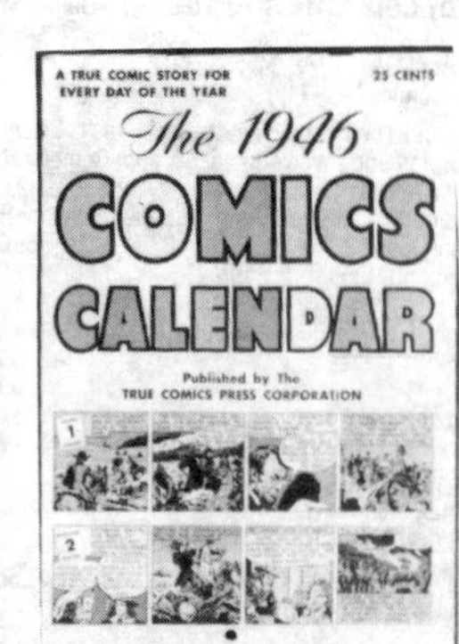


*The Comics Calendar nn, © PMI*

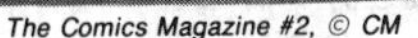
*The Comics Magazine #2, © CM*

*Comics on Parade #18, © UFS*

*Comics Revue #2, © UFS*

Contains a comic bound with new cover. Many combinations possible. Contents would determine price. Some issues do not contain complete comics, but only parts of comics. Value equals 40 to 60 percent of contents.

**COMICS HITS** (See Harvey Comics Hits)

**COMICS MAGAZINE, THE** (. . .Funny Pages #3)(Funny Pages #6 on)
May, 1936 - No. 5, Sept, 1936 (Paper covers)
Comics Magazine Co.

| | Good | Fine | N-Mint |
|---|---|---|---|
| 1: Dr. Mystic, The Occult Detective by Siegel & Shuster (1st episode continues in More Fun #14); 1pg. Kelly-a; Sheldon Mayer-a | 225.00 | 562.00 | 1350.00 |
| 2: Federal Agent by Siegel & Shuster; 1pg. Kelly-a | 96.00 | 290.00 | 675.00 |
| 3-5 | 82.00 | 245.00 | 575.00 |

**COMICS NOVEL** (Anarcho, Dictator of Death)
1947
Fawcett Publications

| | Good | Fine | N-Mint |
|---|---|---|---|
| 1-All Radar | 17.00 | 51.00 | 120.00 |

**COMICS ON PARADE** (No. 30 on, continuation of Single Series)
April, 1938 - No. 104, Feb, 1955
United Features Syndicate

| | Good | Fine | N-Mint |
|---|---|---|---|
| 1-Tarzan by Foster; Captain & the Kids, Little Mary Mixup, Abbie & Slats, Ella Cinders, Broncho Bill, Li'l Abner begin | 150.00 | 375.00 | 900.00 |
| 2 | 61.00 | 182.00 | 425.00 |
| 3 | 49.00 | 145.00 | 340.00 |
| 4,5 | 37.00 | 110.00 | 260.00 |
| 6-10 | 27.00 | 80.00 | 185.00 |
| 11-20 | 22.00 | 65.00 | 150.00 |
| 21-29: 22-Son of Tarzan begins. 29-Last Tarzan issue | 19.00 | 56.00 | 130.00 |
| 30-Li'l Abner | 13.00 | 40.00 | 90.00 |
| 31-The Captain & the Kids | 9.30 | 28.00 | 65.00 |
| 32-Nancy & Fritzi Ritz | 7.50 | 22.50 | 52.00 |
| 33-Li'l Abner | 11.00 | 32.00 | 75.00 |
| 34-The Captain & the Kids (10/41) | 8.50 | 25.50 | 60.00 |
| 35-Nancy & Fritzi Ritz | 7.50 | 22.50 | 52.00 |
| 36-Li'l Abner | 11.00 | 32.00 | 75.00 |
| 37-The Captain & the Kids (6/42) | 8.50 | 25.50 | 60.00 |
| 38-Nancy & Fritzi Ritz; infinity-c | 7.50 | 22.50 | 52.00 |
| 39-Li'l Abner | 11.00 | 32.00 | 75.00 |
| 40-The Captain & the Kids (3/43) | 8.50 | 25.50 | 60.00 |
| 41-Nancy & Fritzi Ritz | 5.70 | 17.00 | 40.00 |
| 42-Li'l Abner | 11.00 | 32.00 | 75.00 |
| 43-The Captain & the Kids | 8.50 | 25.50 | 60.00 |
| 44-Nancy & Fritzi Ritz (3/44) | 5.70 | 17.00 | 40.00 |
| 45-Li'l Abner | 9.00 | 27.00 | 62.00 |
| 46-The Captain & the Kids | 7.50 | 22.50 | 52.00 |
| 47-Nancy & Fritzi Ritz | 5.70 | 17.00 | 40.00 |
| 48-Li'l Abner (3/45) | 9.00 | 27.00 | 62.00 |
| 49-The Captain & the Kids | 7.50 | 22.50 | 52.00 |
| 50-Nancy & Fritzi Ritz | 5.70 | 17.00 | 40.00 |
| 51-Li'l Abner | 7.50 | 22.50 | 52.00 |
| 52-The Captain & the Kids (3/46) | 5.00 | 15.00 | 35.00 |
| 53-Nancy & Fritzi Ritz | 5.00 | 15.00 | 35.00 |
| 54-Li'l Abner | 7.50 | 22.50 | 52.00 |
| 55-Nancy & Fritzi Ritz | 5.00 | 15.00 | 35.00 |
| 56-The Captain & the Kids (r-/Sparkler) | 5.00 | 15.00 | 35.00 |
| 57-Nancy & Fritzi Ritz | 5.00 | 15.00 | 35.00 |
| 58-Li'l Abner | 7.50 | 22.50 | 52.00 |
| 59-The Captain & the Kids | 4.30 | 13.00 | 30.00 |
| 60-70-Nancy & Fritzi Ritz | 4.30 | 13.00 | 30.00 |
| 71-76-Nancy only | 3.00 | 9.00 | 21.00 |
| 77-99,101-104-Nancy & Sluggo | 3.00 | 9.00 | 21.00 |
| 100-Nancy & Sluggo | 4.00 | 12.00 | 28.00 |
| Special Issue, 7/46; Summer, 1948 - The Captain & the Kids app. | 3.00 | 9.00 | 21.00 |

NOTE: Bound Volume (Very Rare) includes No. 1-12; bound by publisher in pictorial comic boards & distributed at the 1939 World's Fair and through mail order from ads in comic books (Also see Tip Top) 160.00 480.00 1120.00

NOTE: *Li'l Abner reprinted from Tip Top.*

**COMICS READING LIBRARIES** (Educational Series)
1973, 1977, 1979 (36 pages in color) (Giveaways)
King Features (Charlton Publ.)

| | Good | Fine | N-Mint |
|---|---|---|---|
| R-01-Tiger, Quincy | | .15 | .30 |
| R-02-Beetle Bailey, Blondie & Popeye | | .15 | .30 |
| R-03-Blondie, Beetle Bailey | | .30 | .60 |
| R-04-Tim Tyler's Luck, Felix the Cat | 1.30 | 4.00 | 8.00 |
| R-05-Quincy, Henry | | .15 | .30 |
| R-06-The Phantom, Mandrake | 2.30 | 7.00 | 14.00 |
| 1977 reprint(R-04) | .85 | 2.50 | 5.00 |
| R-07-Popeye, Little King | .85 | 2.50 | 5.00 |
| R-08-Prince Valiant(Foster), Flash Gordon | 4.00 | 12.00 | 24.00 |
| 1977 reprint | 1.35 | 4.00 | 8.00 |
| R-09-Hagar the Horrible, Boner's Ark | | .15 | .30 |
| R-10-Redeye, Tiger | | .15 | .30 |
| R-11-Blondie, Hi & Lois | | .25 | .50 |
| R-12-Popeye-Swee'pea, Brutus | .85 | 2.50 | 5.00 |
| R-13-Beetle Bailey, Little King | | .15 | .30 |
| R-14-Quincy-Hamlet | | .15 | .30 |
| R-15-The Phantom, The Genius | 2.30 | 7.00 | 14.00 |
| R-16-Flash Gordon, Mandrake | 4.00 | 12.00 | 24.00 |
| 1977 reprint | 1.35 | 4.00 | 8.00 |
| Other 1977 editions.... | | .15 | .30 |
| 1979 editions(68pgs.) | | .20 | .40 |

NOTE: *Above giveaways available with purchase of $45.00 in merchandise. Used as a reading skills aid for small children.*

**COMICS REVUE**
June, 1947 - No. 5, Jan, 1948
St. John Publ. Co. (United Features Synd.)

| | Good | Fine | N-Mint |
|---|---|---|---|
| 1-Ella Cinders & Blackie | 5.70 | 17.00 | 40.00 |
| 2-Hap Hopper (7/47) | 3.70 | 11.00 | 26.00 |
| 3-Iron Vic (8/47) | 3.00 | 9.00 | 21.00 |
| 4-Ella Cinders (9/47) | 3.70 | 11.00 | 26.00 |
| 5-Gordo No. 1 (1/48) | 3.00 | 9.00 | 21.00 |

**COMIC STORY PAINT BOOK**
1943 (68 pages) (Large size)
Samuel Lowe Co.

| | Good | Fine | N-Mint |
|---|---|---|---|
| 1055-Captain Marvel & a Captain Marvel Jr. story to read & color; 3 panels in color per page (reprints) | 31.00 | 92.00 | 215.00 |

**COMIX BOOK** (B&W Magazine - $1.00)
1974 - No. 5, 1976
Marvel Comics Group/Krupp Comics Works No. 4,5

| | Good | Fine | N-Mint |
|---|---|---|---|
| 1-Underground comic artists; 2 pgs. Wolverton-a | .70 | 2.00 | 4.00 |
| 2-Wolverton-a (1 pg.) | .40 | 1.20 | 2.40 |
| 3-Low distribution (3/75) | .50 | 1.50 | 3.00 |
| 4(2/76), 4(5/76), 5 | .40 | 1.20 | 2.40 |

NOTE: *Print run No. 1-3: 200-250M; No. 4&5: 10M each.*

**COMIX INTERNATIONAL**
July, 1974 - No. 5, Spring, 1977 (Full color)
Warren Magazines

| | Good | Fine | N-Mint |
|---|---|---|---|
| 1-Low distribution; all Corben remainders from Warren | 4.00 | 12.00 | 24.00 |
| 2-Wood, Wrightson-r | 1.20 | 3.50 | 7.00 |
| 3-5: 4-Crandall-a | .70 | 2.00 | 4.00 |

NOTE: *No. 4 had two printings with extra* ***Corben*** *story in one.*

**COMMANDER BATTLE AND THE ATOMIC SUB**
July-Aug, 1954 - No. 7, Aug-Sept, 1955
American Comics Group (Titan Publ. Co.)

| | Good | Fine | N-Mint |
|---|---|---|---|
| 1 (3-D effect) | 20.00 | 60.00 | 140.00 |
| 2,4-7: 4-(1-2/55)-Last pre-code; Landau-a. 5-3-D effect story (2 pgs.). 6,7-Landau-a | 8.00 | 24.00 | 56.00 |
| 3-H-Bomb-c; Atomic Sub becomes Atomic Spaceship | 11.00 | 32.00 | 75.00 |

**COMMANDMENTS OF GOD**
1954, 1958
Catechetical Guild

| | | | |
|---|---|---|---|
| 300-Same contents in both editions; diff-c | 1.70 | 5.00 | 10.00 |

**COMMANDO ADVENTURES**
June, 1957 - No. 2, Aug, 1957
Atlas Comics (MMC)

| | | | |
|---|---|---|---|
| 1,2-Severin-c; 2-Drucker-a | 2.00 | 6.00 | 14.00 |

**COMMANDO YANK** (See Mighty Midget & Wow Comics)

**COMPLETE BOOK OF COMICS AND FUNNIES**
1944 (196 pages) (One Shot) (25 cents)
William H. Wise & Co.

| | | | |
|---|---|---|---|
| 1-Origin Brad Spencer, Wonderman; The Magnet, The Silver Knight by Kinstler, & Zudo the Jungle Boy app. | 23.00 | 70.00 | 160.00 |

**COMPLETE BOOK OF TRUE CRIME COMICS**
No date (Mid 1940's) (132 pages) (25 cents)
William H. Wise & Co.

| | | | |
|---|---|---|---|
| nn-Contains Crime Does Not Pay rebound (includes #22) | 53.00 | 160.00 | 370.00 |

**COMPLETE COMICS** (Formerly Amazing Comics No. 1)
No. 2, Winter, 1944-45
Timely Comics (EPC)

| | | | |
|---|---|---|---|
| 2-The Destroyer, The Whizzer, The Young Allies & Sergeant Dix; Schomburg-c | 57.00 | 171.00 | 400.00 |

**COMPLETE LOVE MAGAZINE** (Formerly a pulp with same title)
V26#2, May-June, 1951 - V32#4(#191), Sept, 1956
Ace Periodicals (Periodical House)

| | | | |
|---|---|---|---|
| V26#2-Painted-c (52 pgs.) | 2.65 | 8.00 | 18.00 |
| V26#3-6(2/52), V27#1(4/52)-6(1/53) | 1.70 | 5.00 | 12.00 |
| V28#1(3/53), V28#2(5/53), V29#3(7/53)-6(12/53) | 1.50 | 4.50 | 10.00 |
| V30#1(2/54), V30#1(#176, 4/54)-6(#181, 1/55): 178-Rock Hudson photo-c | 1.50 | 4.50 | 10.00 |
| V31#1(#182, 3/55)-Last precode | 1.30 | 4.00 | 9.00 |
| V31#2(5/55)-6(#187, 1/56) | 1.00 | 3.00 | 7.00 |
| V32#1(#188, 3/56)-4(#191, 9/56) | 1.00 | 3.00 | 7.00 |

NOTE: *(34 total issues). Photo-c V27#5-on. Painted-c V26#3.*

**COMPLETE MYSTERY** (True Complete Mystery No. 5 on)
Aug, 1948 - No. 4, Feb, 1949 (Full length stories)
Marvel Comics (PrPI)

| | | | |
|---|---|---|---|
| 1-Seven Dead Men | 16.00 | 48.00 | 110.00 |
| 2-Jigsaw of Doom! | 11.00 | 32.00 | 75.00 |
| 3-Fear in the Night; Burgos-a | 11.00 | 32.00 | 75.00 |
| 4-A Squealer Dies Fast | 11.00 | 32.00 | 75.00 |

**COMPLETE ROMANCE**
1949
Avon Periodicals

| | | | |
|---|---|---|---|
| 1-(Scarce)-Reprinted as Women to Love | 22.00 | 65.00 | 154.00 |

**COMPLIMENTARY COMICS**
No date (1950's)
Sales Promotion Publ. (Giveaway)

| | | | |
|---|---|---|---|
| 1-Strongman by Powell, 3 stories | 4.00 | 12.00 | 28.00 |

**CONAN** (See Chamber of Darkness #4, Giant-Size..., Handbook of..., King Conan, Marvel Graphic Novel #19, 28, Marvel Treasury Ed., Power Record Comics, Robert E. Howard's..., Savage Sword of Conan, and Savage Tales)

**CONAN SAGA, THE**
June, 1987 - Present ($2.00-$2.25, B&W magazine)
Marvel Comics

| | Good | Fine | N-Mint |
|---|---|---|---|
| 1-Barry Smith-r begin | .35 | 1.00 | 2.00 |
| 2-27: 13,15-Boris-c. 22-r/Giant-Size Conan 1,2 | .35 | 1.00 | 2.00 |
| 28-48 ($2.25): 31-Red Sonja-r by N. Adams/SSOC #1. 32-Newspaper strip-r begin by Buscema. 33-Smith/Conrad-a. 34-Chaykin-a, Starlin-c. 37-Nino-a. 39-r/Kull #1('71) by Andru/Wood. 44-Cover swipe/Savage Tales #1 | .40 | 1.15 | 2.30 |

**CONAN, THE BARBARIAN**
Oct, 1970 - Present
Marvel Comics Group

| | | | |
|---|---|---|---|
| 1-Origin/1st app. Conan by Barry Smith; Kull app. | 17.00 | 51.00 | 120.00 |
| 2 | 6.50 | 19.00 | 45.00 |
| 3-(low distribution in some areas) | 10.00 | 30.00 | 70.00 |
| 4,5 | 5.00 | 15.00 | 35.00 |
| 6-10: 8-Hidden panel message, pg. 14. 10-52 pgs.; Black Knight-r; Kull story by Severin | 3.50 | 10.50 | 24.00 |
| 11-13: 11-(52 pgs.). 12-Wrightson-c(i) | 2.65 | 8.00 | 18.00 |
| 14,15-Elric app. | 3.70 | 11.00 | 26.00 |
| 16,19,20: 16-Conan-r/Savage Tales #1 | 2.00 | 6.00 | 14.00 |
| 17,18-No Barry Smith-a | 1.35 | 4.00 | 8.00 |
| 21,22: 22-has r-from #1 | 1.70 | 5.00 | 12.00 |
| 23-1st app. Red Sonja | 2.30 | 7.00 | 16.00 |
| 24-1st full story Red Sonja; last Smith-a | 2.30 | 7.00 | 16.00 |
| 25-John Buscema-c/a begins | 1.35 | 4.00 | 8.00 |
| 26-30 | .70 | 2.00 | 4.00 |
| 31-36,38-40 | .40 | 1.25 | 2.50 |
| 37-Neal Adams-c/a | .85 | 2.50 | 5.00 |
| 41-43,46-49: 48-Origin retold | .30 | .85 | 1.70 |
| 44,45-N. Adams-i(Crusty Bunkers). 45-Adams-c | .35 | 1.00 | 2.00 |
| 50-57,59,60: 59-Origin Belit | .30 | .85 | 1.70 |
| 58-2nd Belit app. (see Giant-Size Conan #1) | .50 | 1.50 | 3.00 |
| 61-99: 68-Red Sonja story cont'd from Marvel Feature #7. 84-Intro. Zula. 85-Origin Zula. 87-R/Savage Sword of Conan #3 in color | | .60 | 1.20 |
| 100-(52 pg. Giant)-Death of Belit | .40 | 1.25 | 2.50 |
| 101-114,116-193 | | .50 | 1.00 |
| 115-Double size | | .60 | 1.20 |
| 194-199,201-242: 196-200,204,241-Red Sonja app. 232-Young Conan storyline begins; Conan is born | | .50 | 1.00 |
| 200-Double size ($1.50) | .25 | .75 | 1.50 |
| King Size 1(9/73, 35 cents)-Smith-r/#2,4; Smith-c | 1.00 | 3.00 | 6.00 |
| Annual 2(6/76, 50 cents)-New stories | .40 | 1.25 | 2.50 |
| Annual 3(2/78)-Reprints | .35 | 1.00 | 2.00 |
| Annual 4(10/78), 5(12/79)-Buscema-a/part-c | .25 | .75 | 1.50 |
| Annual 6(10/81)-Kane-c/a | .25 | .75 | 1.50 |
| Annual 7(11/82), 8(2/84), 9(12/84) | | .60 | 1.25 |
| Annual 10(2/85), 11(2/86), 12(2/87) | | .60 | 1.25 |
| Special Edition 1 (Red Nails) | .60 | 1.75 | 3.50 |

NOTE: ***Neal Adams** a-116r(i); c-49i. **Austin** a-125, 126; c-125i, 126i. **Brunner** c-17i. c-40. **Buscema** a-25-36p, 38, 39, 41-56p, 58-63p, 65-67p, 68, 70-78p, 84-86p, 88-91p, 93-126p, 136p, 140, 141-144p, 146-158p, 159, 161, 162, 163p, 165p-185p, 187p-190p, Annual 2-5p, 7p; c(p)-26, 36, 44, 46, 52, 56, 58, 59, 64, 65, 72, 78-80, 83-91, 93-103, 105-126, 136-151, 155-159, 161, 162, 168, 169, 171, 172, 174, 175, 178-185, 188, 189. **Chaykin** a-79-83. **Golden** c-152. **Kaluta** c-167. **Gil Kane** a-12p, 17p, 18p, 127-130, 131-134p; c-12p, 17p, 18p, 23, 25, 27-32, 34, 35, 38, 39, 41-43, 45-51, 53-55, 57, 60-63, 65-71, 73p, 76p, 127-134. **McFarlane** c-241. **Ploog** a-57. **Russell** a-21. **Simonson** c-135. **B. Smith** a-1-11p, 12, 13-15p, 16, 19-21, 23, 24; c-1-11, 13-16, 19-24p. **Starlin** a-64. **Wood** a-47r. Issue Nos. 3-5, 7-9, 11, 16-18, 21, 23, 25, 27-30, 35, 37, 38, 42, 45, 52, 57, 58, 65, 69-71, 73, 79-83, 99, 100, 104, 114, Annual 2 have original Robert E. Howard stories adapted. Issues #32-34 adapted from Norvell Page's novel **Flame Winds.***

*Commando Adventures #1, © MEG*

*Conan, the Barbarian #2, © MEG*

*Conan, the Barbarian #24, © MEG*

Confessions of Love #13, © STAR

Congo Bill #1, © DC

Contact Comics #1, © Aviation Press

**CONAN THE BARBARIAN MOVIE SPECIAL**
Oct, 1982 - No. 2, Nov, 1982
Marvel Comics Group

| | Good | Fine | N-Mint |
|---|---|---|---|
| 1,2-Movie adaptation; Buscema-a | | .25 | .50 |

**CONAN THE DESTROYER**
Jan, 1985 - No. 2, Mar, 1985 (Movie adaptation)
Marvel Comics Group

| | Good | Fine | N-Mint |
|---|---|---|---|
| 1,2-r/Marvel Super Special | | .40 | .80 |

**CONAN THE KING** (Formerly King Conan)
No. 20, Jan, 1984 - No. 55, Nov, 1989
Marvel Comics Group

| | Good | Fine | N-Mint |
|---|---|---|---|
| 20-55: 48-55 ($1.50) | .25 | .75 | 1.50 |

NOTE: ***Kaluta*** *c-20-23, 24i, 26, 27, 50, 52.* ***Williamson*** *a-37i; c-37i, 38i.*

**CONCRETE** (Also see Dark Horse Presents)
March, 1987 - No. 10, 1989 ($1.50, B&W)
Dark Horse Comics

| | Good | Fine | N-Mint |
|---|---|---|---|
| 1-Paul Chadwick-c/a in all | 1.85 | 5.50 | 11.00 |
| 1-2nd print | .45 | 1.40 | 2.80 |
| 2 | 1.00 | 3.00 | 6.00 |
| 3-Origin | .55 | 1.65 | 3.30 |
| 4 | .45 | 1.40 | 2.80 |
| 5-10 | .35 | 1.10 | 2.20 |
| . . .: A New Life 1 ('89, $2.95, B&W)-r/#3,4 plus new-a (11 pgs.) | .50 | 1.50 | 3.00 |
| . . .: Land And Sea 1 ('89, $2.95, B&W)-r/#1,2 | .50 | 1.50 | 3.00 |
| . . .Color Special 1 (2/89, $2.95, 44 pgs.)-r/1st two Conrete app. from Dark Horse Presents #1,2 plus new-a | .55 | 1.65 | 3.30 |
| . . .Celebrates Earth Day 1990 ($3.50, color, 52 pgs.)-Moebius, Vess & Chadwick-a | .60 | 1.75 | 3.50 |

**CONDORMAN** (Walt Disney)
Oct, 1981 - No. 3, Jan, 1982
Whitman Publishing

| | Good | Fine | N-Mint |
|---|---|---|---|
| 1-3: 1,2-Movie adaptation; photo-c | | .30 | .60 |

**CONFESSIONS ILLUSTRATED** (Magazine)
Jan-Feb, 1956 - No. 2, Spring, 1956
E. C. Comics

| | Good | Fine | N-Mint |
|---|---|---|---|
| 1-Craig, Kamen, Wood, Orlando-a | 8.50 | 25.50 | 60.00 |
| 2-Craig, Crandall, Kamen, Orlando-a | 7.00 | 21.00 | 50.00 |

**CONFESSIONS OF LOVE**
Apr, 1950 - No. 2, July, 1950 (25 cents; 132 pgs. in color)(7¼x5¼")
Artful Publ.

| | Good | Fine | N-Mint |
|---|---|---|---|
| 1-Bakerish-a | 17.00 | 51.00 | 120.00 |
| 2-Art & text; Bakerish-a | 10.00 | 30.00 | 70.00 |

**CONFESSIONS OF LOVE** (Confessions of Romance No. 7 on)
No. 11, July, 1952 - No. 6, Aug, 1953
Star Publications

| | Good | Fine | N-Mint |
|---|---|---|---|
| 11-13: 12,13-Disbrow-a | 4.00 | 12.00 | 28.00 |
| 14,5,6 | 2.65 | 8.00 | 18.00 |
| 4-Disbrow-a | 3.00 | 9.00 | 21.00 |

NOTE: *All have* ***L. B. Cole*** *covers.*

**CONFESSIONS OF ROMANCE** (Formerly Confessions of Love)
No. 7, Nov, 1953 - No. 11, Nov, 1954
Star Publications

| | Good | Fine | N-Mint |
|---|---|---|---|
| 7 | 4.00 | 12.00 | 28.00 |
| 8 | 2.65 | 8.00 | 18.00 |
| 9-Wood-a | 6.50 | 19.50 | 45.00 |
| 10,11-Disbrow-a | 3.15 | 9.50 | 22.00 |

NOTE: *All have* ***L. B. Cole*** *covers.*

**CONFESSIONS OF THE LOVELORN** (Formerly Lovelorn)
No. 52, Aug, 1954 - No. 114, June-July, 1960
American Comics Group (Regis Publ./Best Synd. Features)

| | Good | Fine | N-Mint |
|---|---|---|---|
| 52 (3-D effect) | 11.00 | 32.00 | 75.00 |
| 53,55 | 2.15 | 6.50 | 15.00 |
| 54 (3-D effect) | 10.00 | 30.00 | 70.00 |
| 56-Communist propaganda story, 10 pgs; last pre-code (2/55) | 2.85 | 8.50 | 20.00 |
| 57-90 | 1.30 | 4.00 | 9.00 |
| 91-Williamson-a | 4.00 | 12.00 | 28.00 |
| 92-99,101-114 | 1.00 | 3.00 | 7.00 |
| 100 | 1.30 | 4.00 | 9.00 |

NOTE: ***Whitney*** *a-most issues. Painted c-106, 107.*

**CONFIDENTIAL DIARY** (Formerly High School Confidential Diary; Three Nurses No. 18 on)
No. 12, May, 1962 - No. 17, March, 1963
Charlton Comics

| | Good | Fine | N-Mint |
|---|---|---|---|
| 12-17 | .50 | 1.50 | 3.00 |

**CONGO BILL** (See Action Comics & More Fun Comics #56)
Aug-Sept, 1954 - No. 7, Aug-Sept, 1955
National Periodical Publications

| | Good | Fine | VF-NM |
|---|---|---|---|
| 1-(Scarce) | 37.00 | 112.00 | 260.00 |
| 2-(Scarce) | 30.00 | 90.00 | 210.00 |
| 3-7 (Scarce), 4-Last precode issue | 25.00 | 75.00 | 175.00 |

NOTE: *(Rarely found in fine to mint condition.)*

**CONNECTICUT YANKEE, A** (See King Classics)

**CONQUEROR, THE** (See 4-Color No. 690)

**CONQUEROR COMICS**
Winter, 1945
Albrecht Publishing Co.

| | Good | Fine | N-Mint |
|---|---|---|---|
| nn | 7.00 | 21.00 | 50.00 |

**CONQUEROR OF THE BARREN EARTH**
Feb, 1985 - No. 4, May, 1985 (Mini-series)
DC Comics

| | Good | Fine | N-Mint |
|---|---|---|---|
| 1-4: Back-up series from Warlord | | .50 | 1.00 |

**CONQUEST**
1953 (6 cents)
Store Comics

| | Good | Fine | N-Mint |
|---|---|---|---|
| 1-Richard the Lion Hearted, Beowulf, Swamp Fox | 2.85 | 8.50 | 20.00 |

**CONQUEST**
Spring, 1955
Famous Funnies

| | Good | Fine | N-Mint |
|---|---|---|---|
| 1-Crandall-a, 1 pg.; contains contents of 1953 issue | 2.15 | 6.50 | 15.00 |

**CONTACT COMICS**
July, 1944 - No. 12, May, 1946
Aviation Press

| | Good | Fine | N-Mint |
|---|---|---|---|
| nn-Black Venus, Flamingo, Golden Eagle, Tommy Tomahawk begin | 14.00 | 43.00 | 100.00 |
| 2-5: 3-Last Flamingo. 3,4-Black Venus by L. B. Cole. 5-The Phantom Flyer app. | 10.00 | 30.00 | 70.00 |
| 6,11-Kurtzman's Black Venus; 11-Last Golden Eagle, last Tommy Tomahawk; Feldstein-a | 13.00 | 40.00 | 90.00 |
| 7-10,12: 12-Sky Rangers, Air Kids, Ace Diamond app. | 8.50 | 25.50 | 60.00 |

NOTE: ***L. B. Cole*** *a-9; c-1-12.* ***Giunta*** *a-3.* ***Hollingsworth*** *a-5, 7, 10.* ***Palais*** *a-11, 12.*

**CONTEMPORARY MOTIVATORS**
1977 - 1978 (5-3/8x8")(31 pgs., B&W, $1.45)
Pendelum Press

14-3002 The Caine Mutiny; 14-3010 Banner in the Sky; 14-3029 God Is My Co-Pilot; 14-3037 Guadalcanal Diary; 14-3045 Hiroshima; 14-3053 Hot Rod; 14-3061 Just Dial a

| | Good | Fine | N-Mint |
|---|---|---|---|
| Number; 14-307x Star Wars; 14-3088 The Diary of Anne Frank; 14-3096 Lost Horizon | | | 1.50 |

NOTE: *Also see Now Age Illustrated. Above may have been distributed the same.*

**CONTEST OF CHAMPIONS** (See Marvel Super-Hero. . .)

**CONTRACTORS**
June, 1987 ($2.00, B&W, one-shot)
Eclipse Comics

| | Good | Fine | N-Mint |
|---|---|---|---|
| 1-Funny animal | .35 | 1.00 | 2.00 |

**COO COO COMICS** (. . . the Bird Brain No. 57 on)
Oct, 1942 - No. 62, April, 1952
Nedor Publ. Co./Standard (Animated Cartoons)

| | Good | Fine | N-Mint |
|---|---|---|---|
| 1-Origin/1st app. Super Mouse & begin series (cloned from Superman)-The first funny animal super hero | 11.50 | 34.00 | 80.00 |
| 2 | 5.00 | 15.00 | 35.00 |
| 3-10 (3/44) | 3.15 | 9.50 | 22.00 |
| 11-33: 33-1pg. Ingels-a | 2.30 | 7.00 | 16.00 |
| 34-40,43-46,48-50-Text illos by Frazetta in all | 4.00 | 12.00 | 28.00 |
| 41-Frazetta-a(2) | 8.50 | 25.50 | 60.00 |
| 42,47-Frazetta-a & text illos. | 6.00 | 18.00 | 42.00 |
| 51-62: 56-Last Super Mouse? | 1.70 | 5.00 | 12.00 |

**"COOKIE"** (Also see Topsy-Turvy)
April, 1946 - No. 55, Aug-Sept, 1955
Michel Publ./American Comics Group(Regis Publ.)

| | Good | Fine | N-Mint |
|---|---|---|---|
| 1-Teen-age humor | 9.30 | 28.00 | 65.00 |
| 2 | 4.50 | 14.00 | 32.00 |
| 3-10 | 3.00 | 9.00 | 21.00 |
| 11-20 | 2.30 | 7.00 | 16.00 |
| 21-23,25-30 | 1.70 | 5.00 | 12.00 |
| 24-Starlet O'Hara app. | 2.00 | 6.00 | 14.00 |
| 31-34,37-55 | 1.30 | 4.00 | 9.00 |
| 35,36-Starlett O'Hara story | 1.70 | 5.00 | 12.00 |

**COOL CAT** (Formerly Black Magic)
V8#6, Mar-Apr, 1962 - V9#2, July-Aug, 1962
Prize Publications

| | Good | Fine | N-Mint |
|---|---|---|---|
| V8#6, nn(V9#1), V9#2 | 1.70 | 5.00 | 12.00 |

**COPPER CANYON** (See Fawcett Movie Comics)

**COPS** (TV)
Aug, 1988 - No. 15, Aug, 1989 ($1.00, color)
DC Comics

| | Good | Fine | N-Mint |
|---|---|---|---|
| 1 ($1.50, 52 pgs.)-Based on Hasbro Toys | .25 | .75 | 1.50 |
| 2-15: 14-Orlando-c(p) | | .50 | 1.00 |

**CORBEN SPECIAL, A**
May, 1984 (One-shot)
Pacific Comics

| | Good | Fine | N-Mint |
|---|---|---|---|
| 1-Corben-c/a; E.A. Poe Adaptation | .35 | 1.00 | 2.00 |

**CORKY & WHITE SHADOW** (See 4-Color No. 707)

**CORLISS ARCHER** (See Meet Corliss Archer)

**CORMAC MAC ART** (Robert E. Howard's. . .)
1990 - No. 4, 1990 ($1.95, B&W, mini-series)
Dark Horse Comics

| | Good | Fine | N-Mint |
|---|---|---|---|
| 1-4: All have Bolton painted-c; Howard adapts. | .35 | 1.00 | 2.00 |

**CORPORAL RUSTY DUGAN** (See Holyoke One-Shot #2)

**CORPSES OF DR. SACOTTI, THE** (See Ideal a Classical Comic)

**CORSAIR, THE** (See A-1 Comics No. 5, 7, 10)

**CORUM: THE BULL AND THE SPEAR** (See Chronicles Of Corum)
Jan, 1989 - No. 4, July, 1989 ($1.95, color, limited series)
First Comics

| | Good | Fine | N-Mint |
|---|---|---|---|
| 1-4: Adapts Michael Moorcock's novel | .35 | 1.00 | 2.00 |

**COSMIC BOOK, THE**
Dec, 1986 - No. 2?, 1987 ($1.95, color)
Ace Comics

| | Good | Fine | N-Mint |
|---|---|---|---|
| 1-(44 pgs.)-Wood, Toth-r | .35 | 1.00 | 2.00 |
| 2-(B&W) | .25 | .80 | 1.60 |

**COSMIC BOY** (See The Legion of Super-Heroes)
Dec, 1986 - No. 4, Mar, 1987 (Mini-series)
DC Comics

| | Good | Fine | N-Mint |
|---|---|---|---|
| 1-Legends tie-in, all issues | .25 | .75 | 1.50 |
| 2-4 | | .50 | 1.00 |

**COSMIC ODYSSEY**
1988 - No. 4, 1988 ($3.50, color, squarebound)
DC Comics

| | Good | Fine | N-Mint |
|---|---|---|---|
| 1-4: Superman, Batman, Green Lantern app. | .70 | 2.00 | 4.00 |

**COSMO CAT** (Also see Wotalife Comics)
July-Aug, 1946 - No. 10, Oct, 1947; 1957; 1959
Fox Publications/Green Publ. Co./Norlen Mag.

| | Good | Fine | N-Mint |
|---|---|---|---|
| 1 | 8.00 | 24.00 | 56.00 |
| 2 | 4.00 | 12.00 | 28.00 |
| 3-Origin (11-12/46) | 4.30 | 13.00 | 30.00 |
| 4-10 | 3.00 | 9.00 | 21.00 |
| 2-4(1957-Green Publ. Co.) | 1.15 | 3.50 | 8.00 |
| 2-4(1959-Norlen Mag.) | .85 | 2.60 | 6.00 |
| I.W. Reprint #1 | .50 | 1.50 | 3.00 |

**COSMO THE MERRY MARTIAN**
Sept, 1958 - No. 6, Oct, 1959
Archie Publications (Radio Comics)

| | Good | Fine | N-Mint |
|---|---|---|---|
| 1-Bob White-a in all | 7.00 | 21.00 | 50.00 |
| 2-6 | 4.50 | 14.00 | 32.00 |

**COTTON WOODS** (See 4-Color No. 837)

**COUGAR, THE** (Cougar No. 2)
April, 1975 - No. 2, July, 1975
Seaboard Periodicals (Atlas)

| | Good | Fine | N-Mint |
|---|---|---|---|
| 1-Adkins-a(p) | | .40 | .80 |
| 2-Origin; Buckler-c(p) | | .25 | .50 |

**COUNTDOWN** (See Movie Classics)

**COUNT DUCKULA** (TV)
Nov, 1988 - No. 15, Jan, 1991 ($1.00, color)
Marvel Comics

| | Good | Fine | N-Mint |
|---|---|---|---|
| 1-15: Dangermouse back-ups. 8-Geraldo Rivera photo-c | | .50 | 1.00 |

**COUNT OF MONTE CRISTO, THE** (See 4-Color No. 794)

**COURAGE COMICS**
1945
J. Edward Slavin

| | Good | Fine | N-Mint |
|---|---|---|---|
| 1,2,77 | 4.00 | 12.00 | 28.00 |

**COURTSHIP OF EDDIE'S FATHER** (TV)
Jan, 1970 - No. 2, May, 1970
Dell Publishing Co.

| | Good | Fine | N-Mint |
|---|---|---|---|
| 1,2-Bill Bixby photo-c | 2.00 | 6.00 | 14.00 |

**COVERED WAGONS, HO** (See 4-Color No. 814)

**COWBOY ACTION** (Formerly Western Thrillers No. 1-4; Becomes Quick Trigger Western No. 12 on)
No. 5, March, 1955 - No. 11, March, 1956
Atlas Comics (ACI)

| | Good | Fine | N-Mint |
|---|---|---|---|
| 5 | 4.30 | 13.00 | 30.00 |
| 6-10: 6-8-Heath-c | 2.65 | 8.00 | 18.00 |
| 11-Williamson-a, 4 pgs., Baker-a | 4.00 | 12.00 | 28.00 |

NOTE: ***Ayers** a-8. **Drucker** a-6. **Maneely** c/a-5, 6. **Severin** c-10. **Shores** a-7.*

*Coo Coo Comics #31, © STD*

*Cormac Mac Art #1, © Dark Horse*

*Count Duckula #8, © Cosgrove-Hall Prod.*

Cowboy Romances #1, © MEG

Cow Puncher #7, © AVON

Crackajack Funnies #7, © DELL

**COWBOY COMICS** (...Stories No. 14; formerly Star Ranger)
(Star Ranger Funnies No. 15 on)
No. 13, July, 1938 - No. 14, Aug, 1938
Centaur Publishing Co.

| | Good | Fine | N-Mint |
|---|---|---|---|
| 13-(Rare)-Ace and Deuce, Lyin Lou, Air Patrol, Aces High, Lee Trent, Trouble Hunters begin | 54.00 | 160.00 | 375.00 |
| 14 | 37.00 | 112.00 | 260.00 |

NOTE: *Guardineer a-13, 14. Gustavson a-13, 14.*

**COWBOY IN AFRICA** (TV)
March, 1968
Gold Key

| | | | |
|---|---|---|---|
| 1(10219-803)-Chuck Connors photo-c | 2.00 | 6.00 | 14.00 |

**COWBOY LOVE** (Becomes Range Busters?)
7/49 - V2#10, 6/50; No. 11, 1951; No. 28, 2/55 - No. 31, 8/55
Fawcett Publications/Charlton Comics No. 28 on

| | | | |
|---|---|---|---|
| V1#1-Rocky Lane photo back-c | 7.00 | 21.00 | 50.00 |
| 2 | 2.30 | 7.00 | 16.00 |
| V1#3,4,6 (12/49) | 2.00 | 6.00 | 14.00 |
| 5-Bill Boyd photo back-c (11/49) | 3.50 | 10.50 | 24.00 |
| V2#7-Williamson/Evans-a | 4.50 | 14.00 | 32.00 |
| V2#8-11 | 1.70 | 5.00 | 12.00 |
| V1#28 (Charlton)-Last precode (2/55) (Formerly Romantic Story?) | 1.50 | 4.50 | 10.00 |
| V1#29-31 (Charlton; becomes Sweetheart Diary #32 on) | 1.15 | 3.50 | 8.00 |

NOTE: *Powell a-10. Photo c-1-11. No. 1-3, 5-7, 9, 10 are 52 pgs.*

**COWBOY ROMANCES** (Young Men No. 4 on)
Oct, 1949 - No. 3, Mar, 1950
Marvel Comics (IPC)

| | | | |
|---|---|---|---|
| 1-Photo-c | 9.30 | 28.00 | 65.00 |
| 2-William Holden, Mona Freeman 'Streets of Laredo' photo-c | 7.00 | 21.00 | 50.00 |
| 3 | 5.00 | 15.00 | 35.00 |

**COWBOYS 'N' INJUNS** (...'N' Indians No. 6 on)
1946 - No. 5, 1947; No. 6, 1949 - No. 8, 1952
Compix No. 1-5/Magazine Enterprises No. 6 on

| | | | |
|---|---|---|---|
| 1 | 3.70 | 11.00 | 26.00 |
| 2-5-All funny animal western | 2.15 | 6.50 | 15.00 |
| 6(A-1 23)-half violent, half funny | 3.00 | 9.00 | 21.00 |
| 7(A-1 41, 1950), 8(A-1 48)-All funny | 2.15 | 6.50 | 15.00 |
| I.W. Reprint No. 1,7 (reprinted in Canada by Superior, No. 7) | .70 | 2.00 | 4.00 |
| Super Reprint #10 (1963) | .70 | 2.00 | 4.00 |

**COWBOY WESTERN COMICS** (Formerly Jack In The Box; Becomes Space Western No. 40-45 & Wild Bill Hickok & Jingles No. 68 on; title: ...Heroes No. 47 & 48; Cowboy Western No. 49 on (TV))
No. 17, 7/48 - No. 39, 8/52; No. 46, 10/53; No. 47, 12/53; No. 48 Spr, '54; No. 49, 5-6/54 - No. 67, 3/58 (nn 40-45)
Charlton(Capitol Stories)

| | | | |
|---|---|---|---|
| 17-Jesse James, Annie Oakley, Wild Bill Hickok & Texas Rangers app. | 7.00 | 21.00 | 50.00 |
| 18,19-Orlando-c/a | 4.30 | 13.00 | 30.00 |
| 20-25 | 2.65 | 8.00 | 18.00 |
| 26-George Montgomery photo-c | 4.50 | 14.00 | 32.00 |
| 27,30-Sunset Carson photo-c | 32.00 | 95.00 | 220.00 |
| 28,29-Sunset Carson app. | 13.00 | 40.00 | 90.00 |
| 31-39,47-50 (no #40-45) | 2.30 | 7.00 | 16.00 |
| 46-(Formerly Space Western)-Space western story | 7.00 | 21.00 | 50.00 |
| 51-57,59-66 | 1.70 | 5.00 | 12.00 |
| 58 (68 pgs.)-Wild Bill Hickok & Jingles | 2.30 | 7.00 | 16.00 |
| 67-Williamson/Torres-a, 5 pgs. | 5.00 | 15.00 | 35.00 |

NOTE: *Many issues trimmed 1" shorter.*

**COWGIRL ROMANCES** (Formerly Jeanie Comics)
No. 28, Jan, 1950 (52 pgs.)
Marvel Comics (CCC)

| | Good | Fine | N-Mint |
|---|---|---|---|
| 28(#1)-Photo-c | 10.00 | 30.00 | 70.00 |

**COWGIRL ROMANCES**
1950 - No. 12, Winter, 1952-53 (No. 1-3: 52 pgs.)
Fiction House Magazines

| | | | |
|---|---|---|---|
| 1-Kamen-a | 16.00 | 48.00 | 110.00 |
| 2 | 8.00 | 24.00 | 56.00 |
| 3-5 | 6.50 | 19.00 | 45.00 |
| 6-9,11,12 | 5.00 | 15.00 | 35.00 |
| 10-Frazetta?/Williamson-a; Kamen/Baker-a | 16.00 | 48.00 | 110.00 |

**COW PUNCHER** (...Comics)
Jan, 1947; No. 2, Sept, 1947 - No. 7, 1949
Avon Periodicals

| | | | |
|---|---|---|---|
| 1-Clint Cortland, Texas Ranger, Kit West, Pioneer Queen begin; Kubert-a; Alabam stories begin | 19.00 | 58.00 | 135.00 |
| 2-Kubert, Kamen/Feldstein-a; Kamen bondage-c | 16.00 | 48.00 | 110.00 |
| 3-5,7: 3-Kiefer story | 10.00 | 30.00 | 70.00 |
| 6-Opium drug mention story; bondage, headlight-c; Reinman-a | 12.00 | 36.00 | 85.00 |

**COWPUNCHER**
1953 (nn) (Reprints Avon's No. 2)
Realistic Publications

| | | | |
|---|---|---|---|
| nn-Kubert-a | 5.70 | 17.00 | 40.00 |

**COWSILLS, THE** (See Harvey Pop Comics)

**COYOTE**
June, 1983 - No. 16, Mar, 1986 ($1.50, adults only)
Epic Comics (Marvel)

| | | | |
|---|---|---|---|
| 1-10,15,16: 1,2-Origin issues. 7,9-Ditko-p | .25 | .75 | 1.50 |
| 11-14-1st Todd McFarlane-a | .50 | 1.50 | 3.00 |

**CRACKAJACK FUNNIES** (Giveaway)
1937 (32 pgs.; full size; soft cover; full color)(Before No. 1?)
Malto-Meal

| | | | |
|---|---|---|---|
| nn-Features Dan Dunn, G-Man, Speed Bolton, Freckles, Buck Jones, Clyde Beatty, The Nebbs, Major Hoople, Wash Tubbs | 43.00 | 130.00 | 300.00 |

**CRACKAJACK FUNNIES**
June, 1938 - No. 43, Jan, 1942
Dell Publishing Co.

| | | | |
|---|---|---|---|
| 1-Dan Dunn, Freckles, Myra North, Wash Tubbs, Apple Mary, The Nebbs, Don Winslow, Tom Mix, Buck Jones, Major Hoople, Clyde Beatty, Boots begin | 91.00 | 272.00 | 635.00 |
| 2 | 43.00 | 130.00 | 300.00 |
| 3 | 29.00 | 88.00 | 205.00 |
| 4,5: 5-Nude woman on cover | 24.00 | 72.00 | 165.00 |
| 6-8,10 | 19.00 | 56.00 | 130.00 |
| 9-(3/39)-Red Ryder strip-r begin by Harman; 1st app. in comics & 1st cover app. | 27.00 | 80.00 | 185.00 |
| 11-14 | 17.00 | 51.00 | 120.00 |
| 15-Tarzan text feature begins by Burroughs (9/39); not in #26,35 | 19.00 | 56.00 | 130.00 |
| 16-24 | 13.00 | 40.00 | 90.00 |
| 25-The Owl begins; in new costume #26 by Frank Thomas | 30.00 | 90.00 | 210.00 |
| 26-30: 28-Owl-c. 29-Ellery Queen begins | 23.00 | 70.00 | 160.00 |
| 31-Owl covers begin | 20.00 | 60.00 | 140.00 |
| 32-Origin Owl Girl | 23.00 | 70.00 | 160.00 |
| 33-38: 36-Last Tarzan issue | 16.00 | 48.00 | 110.00 |
| 39-Andy Panda begins (intro/1st app.) | 17.00 | 51.00 | 120.00 |
| 40-43: 42-Last Owl cover | 14.00 | 43.00 | 100.00 |

NOTE: ***McWilliams** art in most issues.*

**CRACK COMICS** (. . .Western No. 63 on)
May, 1940 - No. 62, Sept, 1949
Quality Comics Group

| | Good | Fine | N-Mint |
|---|---|---|---|
| 1-Origin The Black Condor by Lou Fine, Madame Fatal, Red Torpedo, Rock Bradden & The Space Legion; The Clock, Alias the Spider, Wizard Wells, & Ned Brant begin; Powell-a; Note: Madame Fatal is a man dressed up as a woman | 185.00 | 560.00 | 1300.00 |
| 2 | 90.00 | 270.00 | 630.00 |
| 3 | 66.00 | 200.00 | 465.00 |
| 4 | 57.00 | 171.00 | 400.00 |
| 5-10: 5-Molly The Model begins. 10-Tor, the Magic Master begins | 45.00 | 135.00 | 315.00 |
| 11-20: 18-1st app. Spitfire? | 39.00 | 118.00 | 275.00 |
| 21-24-Last Fine Black Condor | 30.00 | 90.00 | 210.00 |
| 25,26 | 20.00 | 60.00 | 140.00 |
| 27-Intro & origin Captain Triumph by Alfred Andriola (Kerry Drake artist) | 43.00 | 130.00 | 300.00 |
| 28-30 | 17.00 | 51.00 | 120.00 |
| 31-39: 31-Last Black Condor | 10.00 | 30.00 | 70.00 |
| 40-46 | 7.00 | 21.00 | 50.00 |
| 47-57,59,60-Capt. Triumph by Crandall | 8.00 | 24.00 | 56.00 |
| 58,61,62-Last Captain Triumph | 6.00 | 18.00 | 42.00 |

NOTE: *Black Condor by **Fine**: No. 1, 2, 4-6, 8, 10-24; by **Sultan**: No. 3, 7; by **Fugitani**: No. 9. **Cole** a-34. **Crandall** c-55, 59, 60. **Guardineer** a-17. **Gustavson** a-17. **McWilliams** a-15-21, 23-27.*

**CRACKED** (Magazine) (Satire) (Also see The 3-D Zone #19)
Feb-Mar, 1958 - Present
Major Magazines

| | Good | Fine | N-Mint |
|---|---|---|---|
| 1-One pg. Williamson-a | 7.00 | 21.00 | 50.00 |
| 2-1st Shut-Ups & Bonus Cut-Outs | 3.00 | 9.00 | 21.00 |
| 3-6 | 1.70 | 5.00 | 12.00 |
| 7-10: 7-Reprints 1st 6 covers on-c | 1.50 | 4.50 | 10.00 |
| 11-12, 13(nn,3/60), 14-17, 18(nn,2/61), 19,20 | 1.00 | 3.00 | 7.00 |
| 21-27(11/62), 27(No.28, 2/63; mis-#d), 29(5/63) | 1.00 | 3.00 | 6.00 |
| 31-60 | .70 | 2.00 | 4.00 |
| 61-100: 99-Alfred E. Neuman on-c | .40 | 1.25 | 2.50 |
| 101-257: 234-Don Martin-a begins ($1.75 #? on) | .30 | .90 | 1.80 |
| Biggest. . .(Winter, 1977) | .50 | 1.50 | 3.00 |
| Biggest, Greatest. . .nn('65) | 1.50 | 4.50 | 10.00 |
| Biggest, Greatest. . .2('66) - #12('76) | 1.00 | 3.00 | 6.00 |
| . . .Blockbuster 1,2('88) | .45 | 1.40 | 2.75 |
| . . .Digest 1(Fall, '86, 148p) - #5 | .35 | 1.00 | 2.00 |
| . . .Collectors' Edition ('73; formerly . . .Special) 4 | .70 | 2.00 | 4.00 |
| 5-70 | .25 | .75 | 1.50 |
| 71-84: 83-Elvis, Batman parodies | .45 | 1.40 | 2.75 |
| . . .Party Pack 1,2('88) | .45 | 1.40 | 2.75 |
| . . .Shut-Ups (2/72-'72; Cracked Spec. #3) 1,2 | .70 | 2.00 | 4.00 |
| . . .Special 3('73; formerly Cracked Shut-Ups; . . .Collectors' Edition #4 on) | .70 | 2.00 | 4.00 |
| Extra Special. . .1('76), 2('76) | | .60 | 1.20 |
| Giant. . .nn('65) | 1.15 | 3.50 | 8.00 |
| Giant. . .2('66)-12('76), nn(9/77)-48('87) | 1.00 | 3.00 | 6.00 |
| King Sized. . .1('67) | 2.15 | 6.50 | 15.00 |
| King Sized. . .2('68)-11('77) | 1.15 | 3.50 | 8.00 |
| King Sized. . .12-22 (Sum/'86) | .35 | 1.00 | 2.00 |
| Super. . .1('68) | 1.70 | 5.00 | 12.00 |
| Super. . .2('69)-24('88) | 1.00 | 3.00 | 6.00 |
| Super. . .1('87, 100p)-Severin & Elder-a | .45 | 1.40 | 2.75 |

NOTE: ***Burgos** a-1-10. **Colan** a-257. **Davis** a-5, 11-17, 24, 40, 80; c-12-14, 16. **Elder** a-5, 6, 10-13; c-10. **Everett** a-1-10, 23-25, 61; c-1. **Heath** a-1-3, 6, 13, 14, 17, 110; c-6. **Jaffee** a-5, 6. **Morrow** a-8-10. **Reinman** a-1-4. **Severin** a-in most all issues. **Shores** a-3-7. **Torres** a-7-10. **Ward** a-22-24, 143, 144, 149, 150, 152, 153, 156. **Williamson** a-1 (1 pg.). **Wolverton** a-10 (2 pgs.), Giant nn('65). **Wood** a-27, 35, 40.*

**CRACK WESTERN** (Formerly Crack Comics; Jonesy No. 85 on)
No. 63, Nov, 1949 - No. 84, May, 1953 (36pgs., 63-68,74-on)
Quality Comics Group

| | Good | Fine | N-Mint |
|---|---|---|---|
| 63(#1)-Two-Gun Lil (origin & 1st app.)(ends #84), Arizona Ames, his horse Thunder (sidekick Spurs & his horse Calico), Frontier Marshal (ends #70), & Dead Canyon Days (ends #69) begin; Crandall-a | 10.00 | 30.00 | 70.00 |
| 64,65-Crandall-a | 8.00 | 24.00 | 56.00 |
| 66,68-Photo-c. 66-Arizona Ames becomes A. Raines (ends #84) | 7.00 | 21.00 | 50.00 |
| 67-Randolph Scott photo-c; Crandall-a | 8.50 | 25.50 | 60.00 |
| 69(52pgs.)-Crandall-a | 7.00 | 21.00 | 50.00 |
| 70(52pgs.)-The Whip (origin & 1st app.) & his horse Diablo begin (ends #84); Crandall-a | 7.00 | 21.00 | 50.00 |
| 71(52pgs.)-Frontier Marshal becomes Bob Allen F. Marshal (ends #84); Crandall-c/a | 8.50 | 25.50 | 60.00 |
| 72(52pgs.)-Tim Holt photo-c | 7.00 | 21.00 | 50.00 |
| 73(52pgs.)-Photo-c | 5.00 | 15.00 | 35.00 |
| 74,77,79,80,82 | 3.50 | 10.50 | 24.00 |
| 75,76,78,81,83-Crandall-c | 5.70 | 17.00 | 40.00 |
| 84-Crandall-c/a | 8.00 | 24.00 | 55.00 |

**CRASH COMICS** (Catman Comics No. 6 on)
May, 1940 - No. 5, Nov, 1940
Tem Publishing Co.

| | Good | Fine | N-Mint |
|---|---|---|---|
| 1-The Blue Streak, Strongman (origin), The Perfect Human, Shangra begin; Kirby-a | 100.00 | 300.00 | 700.00 |
| 2-Simon & Kirby-a | 50.00 | 150.00 | 350.00 |
| 3-Simon & Kirby-a | 40.00 | 120.00 | 280.00 |
| 4-Origin & 1st app. The Catman; S&K-a | 65.00 | 195.00 | 455.00 |
| 5-S&K-a | 40.00 | 120.00 | 280.00 |

NOTE: *Solar Legion by **Kirby** No. 1-5 (5 pgs. each).*

**CRASH DIVE** (See Cinema Comics Herald)

**CRASH RYAN** (Also see Dark Horse Presents #44)
Oct, 1984 - No. 4, Jan, 1985 (Baxter paper, limited series)
Epic Comics (Marvel)

| | Good | Fine | N-Mint |
|---|---|---|---|
| 1-4 | .25 | .75 | 1.50 |

**CRAZY**
Dec, 1953 - No. 7, July, 1954
Atlas Comics (CSI)

| | Good | Fine | N-Mint |
|---|---|---|---|
| 1-Everett-c/a | 8.50 | 25.50 | 60.00 |
| 2 | 7.00 | 21.00 | 50.00 |
| 3-7: 4-I Love Lucy satire. 5-Satire on censorship | 5.70 | 17.00 | 40.00 |

NOTE: ***Ayers** a-5. **Berg** a-1, 2. **Burgos** c-5, 6. **Drucker** a-6. **Everett** a-1-4. **Heath** a-3, 7; c-7. **Maneely** a-1-7; c-3, 4. **Post** a-3-6.*

**CRAZY** (People Who Buy This Magazine Is. . .) (Formerly This Magazine Is. . .)
V3#3, Nov, 1957 - V4#8, Feb, 1959 (Magazine) (Satire)
Charlton Publications

| | Good | Fine | N-Mint |
|---|---|---|---|
| V3#3 - V4#7 | 1.15 | 3.50 | 8.00 |
| V4#8-Davis-a, 8 pgs. | 1.70 | 5.00 | 12.00 |

**CRAZY** (Satire)
Feb, 1973 - No. 3, June, 1973
Marvel Comics Group

| | Good | Fine | N-Mint |
|---|---|---|---|
| 1-3-Not Brand Echh-r. 1-Beatles cameo (r) | | .40 | .80 |

**CRAZY** (. . .Magazine #? on) (Satire)
Oct, 1973 - No. 94, Apr, 1983 (40-90 cents, B&W magazine)
Marvel Comics Group

| | Good | Fine | N-Mint |
|---|---|---|---|
| 1-Wolverton(1 pg.), Ploog, Bode-a; 3 pg. photo story of Neal Adams & Dick Giordano | .35 | 1.00 | 2.00 |
| 2-N. Adams-a; Kurtzman's "Hey Look" reprint, 2 pgs.; Buscema-a | | .60 | 1.20 |

*Crack Comics #32, © QUA*

*Crack Western #78, © QUA*

*Crazy #6 (1954), © MEG*

Creatures on the Loose #10, © MEG

Crime and Punishment #3, © LEV

Crime Clinic #10(#1), © Z-D

| | Good | Fine | N-Mint |
|---|---|---|---|
| 3-16: 3-Drucker-a. 4,7-Ploog-a. 9-16-Eisner-a | | .40 | .80 |
| 17-41,43-48,50,51,53-57,59-81,83-90: 41-Kiss-c. 43-E.C. swipe from Mad #131. 60,92-Star Trek parodies. 62-Kiss-c & 2pg. story. 76-Best of . . .Super Special. 81-Wolverine/Hulk parody | | .30 | .60 |
| 42,49,52: Specials ($1.00) | | .50 | 1.00 |
| 58-Super Special ($1.25); contains free Crazy #1 (2/73) comic reprint | | .65 | 1.30 |
| 82: Super Special issue($1.25); X-Men on-c | | .65 | 1.30 |
| 91-94: ($1.25) 91-Super Special; Black Knight by Maneely. 94-Avengers parody | | .65 | 1.30 |
| Super Special 1(Summer, 1975, 100pgs.)-Ploog, Neal Adams-r | .25 | .80 | 1.60 |

NOTE: ***N. Adams*** *a-94p.* ***Austin*** *a-82i.* ***Buscema*** *a-82.* ***Byrne*** *c-82p.* ***Cardy*** *c-7, 8.* ***Freas*** *c-1, 2, 4, 6; a-7.* ***Rogers*** *a-82.* ***Sparling*** *a-92.*

**CRAZY, MAN, CRAZY** (Magazine) (Satire)
V2#2, June, 1956
Humor Magazines

| | Good | Fine | N-Mint |
|---|---|---|---|
| V2#2-Wolverton-a, 3 pgs. | 5.00 | 15.00 | 35.00 |

**CREATURE, THE** (See Movie Classics)

**CREATURES ON THE LOOSE** (Tower of Shadows No. 1-9)
No. 10, March, 1971 - No. 37, Sept, 1975
Marvel Comics Group

| | Good | Fine | N-Mint |
|---|---|---|---|
| 10-First King Kull story; Wrightson-a | 2.65 | 8.00 | 18.00 |
| 11-37: 13-Crandall-a. 16-Origin Warrior of Mars. 21,22-Steranko-c. 22-29-Thongor app. 30-Manwolf begins | .25 | .75 | 1.50 |

NOTE: ***Ditko*** *r-15, 17, 18, 20, 22, 24, 27, 28.* ***Everett*** *r-16i.* ***Gil Kane*** *r-16p, 17p; c-16, 20, 25, 29, 33p, 35p, 36p.* ***Morrow*** *a-20, 21.* ***Perez*** *a-33-37; c-34p.* ***Tuska*** *a-31p, 32p.*

**CREEPER, THE** (See Beware. . . & First Issue Special)

**CREEPY** (Magazine)(See Warren Presents)
1964 - No. 145, Feb, 1983; No. 146, 1985 (B&W)
Warren Publishing Co./Harris Publ. #146

| | Good | Fine | N-Mint |
|---|---|---|---|
| 1-Frazetta-a; Jack Davis-c; 1st Warren mag? | 2.65 | 8.00 | 18.00 |
| 2 | 1.30 | 4.00 | 9.00 |
| 3-13: 7,10-Frazetta-c. 10-Wrightson sketch | .85 | 2.50 | 5.00 |
| 14-Neal Adams 1st Warren work | 1.15 | 3.50 | 7.00 |
| 15-25 | 1.00 | 3.00 | 6.00 |
| 26-40: 32-Harlan Ellison story | .85 | 2.50 | 5.00 |
| 41-47,49-54,56-61: 61-Wertham parody | .70 | 2.00 | 4.00 |
| 48,55,65-(1973, 1974, 1975 Annuals) | 1.00 | 3.00 | 6.00 |
| 62-64,66-145: 144-Giant, $2.25; Frazetta-c | .70 | 2.00 | 4.00 |
| 146 ($2.95) | 1.00 | 3.00 | 6.00 |
| Year Book 1968, 1969 | 1.00 | 3.00 | 6.00 |
| Year Book 1970-Neal Adams, Ditko-a(r) | 1.00 | 3.00 | 6.00 |
| Annual 1971,1972 | 1.00 | 3.00 | 6.00 |

NOTE: *All issues contain many good artists works:* ***Neal Adams, Brunner, Corben, Craig (Taycee), Crandall, Ditko, Evans, Frazetta, Heath, Jeff Jones, Krenkel, McWilliams, Morrow, Nino, Orlando, Ploog, Severin, Torres, Toth, Williamson, Wood, & Wrightson;*** *covers by* ***Crandall, Davis, Frazetta, Morrow, San Julian, Todd/Bode;*** *Otto Binder's "Adam Link" stories in No. 2, 4, 6, 8, 9, 12, 13, 15 with* ***Orlando*** *art.*

**CREEPY THINGS**
July, 1975 - No. 6, June, 1976
Charlton Comics

| | Good | Fine | N-Mint |
|---|---|---|---|
| 1 | | .50 | 1.00 |
| 2-6: Ditko-a in 3,5. Sutton c-3,4 | | .40 | .80 |
| Modern Comics Reprint 2-6('77) | | .25 | .50 |

**CRIME AND JUSTICE** (Rookie Cop? No. 27 on)
March, 1951 - No. 26, Sept, 1955
Capitol Stories/Charlton Comics

| | Good | Fine | N-Mint |
|---|---|---|---|
| 1-Spanking panel | 13.00 | 40.00 | 90.00 |
| 2 | 3.15 | 9.50 | 22.00 |
| 3-8,10,11,13: 6-Negligee panels | 2.85 | 8.50 | 20.00 |
| 9-Classic story "Comics Vs. Crime" | 7.00 | 21.00 | 50.00 |
| 12-Bondage-c | 4.00 | 12.00 | 28.00 |
| 14-Color illos in **POP**; gory story of man who beheads women | 4.50 | 14.00 | 32.00 |
| 15-17,19-26 | 2.00 | 6.00 | 14.00 |
| 18-Ditko-a | 10.00 | 30.00 | 70.00 |

NOTE: ***Alascia*** *c-20.* ***Ayers*** *a-17.* ***Shuster*** *a-19-21; c-19. Bondage c-11, 12.*

**CRIME AND PUNISHMENT** (Title inspired by 1935 film)
April, 1948 - No. 74, Aug, 1955
Lev Gleason Publications

| | Good | Fine | N-Mint |
|---|---|---|---|
| 1-Mr. Crime app. on-c | 10.00 | 30.00 | 70.00 |
| 2 | 4.50 | 14.00 | 32.00 |
| 3-Used in **SOTI**, pg. 112; injury-to-eye panel; Fuje-a | 5.70 | 17.00 | 40.00 |
| 4,5 | 3.60 | 11.00 | 25.00 |
| 6-10 | 2.85 | 8.50 | 20.00 |
| 11-20 | 2.65 | 8.00 | 18.00 |
| 21-30 | 2.00 | 6.00 | 14.00 |
| 31-38,40-44,46: 46-One page Frazetta-a | 1.70 | 5.00 | 12.00 |
| 39-Drug mention story "The 5 Dopes" | 3.15 | 9.50 | 22.00 |
| 45-"Hophead Killer" drug story | 3.25 | 9.75 | 22.00 |
| 47-58,60-65,70-74: 58-Used in **POP**, pg. 79 | 1.50 | 4.50 | 10.00 |
| 59-Used in **SOTI**, illo-"What comic-book America stands for" | 11.50 | 34.00 | 80.00 |
| 66-Toth-c/a(4); 3-D effect issue(3/54) | 16.00 | 48.00 | 110.00 |
| 67-"Monkey on His Back"-heroin story; 3-D effect issue | 12.00 | 36.00 | 84.00 |
| 68-3-D effect issue; Toth-c (7/54) | 11.00 | 32.00 | 75.00 |
| 69-"The Hot Rod Gang"-dope crazy kids | 3.00 | 9.00 | 21.00 |

NOTE: ***Biro*** *c-most.* ***Everett*** *a-31.* ***Fuje*** *a-3, 4, 12, 13, 17, 18, 20, 26, 27.* ***Guardineer*** *a-2-4, 10, 14, 17, 18, 20, 26-28, 32, 38-44.* ***Kinstler*** *c-69.* ***McWilliams*** *a-41, 48, 49.* ***Tuska*** *a-28, 30, 64.*

**CRIME AND PUNISHMENT: MARSHALL LAW TAKES MANHATTAN**
1989 ($4.95, color, 52 pgs., direct sale only, mature readers)
Epic Comics (Marvel)

| | Good | Fine | N-Mint |
|---|---|---|---|
| nn-Graphic album featuring Marshall Law | .85 | 2.50 | 5.00 |

**CRIME CAN'T WIN** (Formerly Cindy Smith)
No. 41, 9/50 - No. 43, 2/51; No. 4, 4/51 - No. 12, 9/53
Marvel/Atlas Comics (TCI 41/CCC 42,43,4-12)

| | Good | Fine | N-Mint |
|---|---|---|---|
| 41(#1) | 8.50 | 25.50 | 60.00 |
| 42 | 4.30 | 13.00 | 30.00 |
| 43-Horror story | 5.00 | 15.00 | 35.00 |
| 4(4/51),5-12: 10-Possible use in **SOTI**, pg. 161 | 3.50 | 10.50 | 24.00 |

NOTE: ***Robinson*** *a-9-11.* ***Tuska*** *a-43.*

**CRIME CASES COMICS** (Formerly Willie Comics)
No. 24, 8/50 - No. 27, 3/51; No. 5, 5/51 - No. 12, 7/52
Marvel/Atlas Comics(CnPC No.24-8/MJMC No.9-12)

| | Good | Fine | N-Mint |
|---|---|---|---|
| 24 (#1, 52 pgs.) | 5.00 | 15.00 | 35.00 |
| 25-27: 27-Morisi-a | 3.00 | 9.00 | 21.00 |
| 5-12: 11-Robinson-a, 12-Tuska-a | 2.65 | 8.00 | 18.00 |

**CRIME CLINIC**
No. 10, July-Aug, 1951 - No. 5, Summer, 1952
Ziff-Davis Publishing Co.

| | Good | Fine | N-Mint |
|---|---|---|---|
| 10(#1)-Painted-c; origin Dr. Tom Rogers | 11.00 | 32.00 | 75.00 |
| 11,3-5: 3-Used in **SOTI**, pg. 18. 4,5-Painted-c | 6.85 | 21.00 | 48.00 |

NOTE: *Painted covers by* ***Saunders. Starr*** *a-10.*

**CRIME DETECTIVE COMICS**
Mar-Apr, 1948 - V3#8, May-June, 1953
Hillman Periodicals

| | Good | Fine | N-Mint |
|---|---|---|---|
| V1#1-The Invisible 6, costumed villains app; Fuje-c | 8.50 | 25.50 | 60.00 |
| 2 | 3.50 | 10.50 | 24.00 |
| 3,4,6,7,10-12: 6-McWilliams-a | 2.65 | 8.00 | 18.00 |

| | Good | Fine | N-Mint |
|---|---|---|---|
| 5-Krigstein-a | 3.70 | 11.00 | 26.00 |
| 8-Kirbyish-a by McCann | 3.15 | 9.50 | 22.00 |
| 9-Used in **SOTI**, pg. 16 & "Caricature of the author in a position comic book publishers wish he were in permanently" illo. | 11.50 | 34.00 | 80.00 |
| V2#1,4,7-Krigstein-a | 3.15 | 9.50 | 22.00 |
| 2,3,5,6,8-12 (1-2/52) | 2.00 | 6.00 | 14.00 |
| V3#1-Drug use-c | 2.00 | 6.00 | 14.00 |
| 2-8 | 1.70 | 5.00 | 12.00 |

NOTE: ***Briefer** a-V3#1. **Kinstlerish** -a by **McCann**-V2#7, V3#2. **Powell** a-11.*

**CRIME DETECTOR**
Jan, 1954 - No. 5, Sept, 1954
Timor Publications

| | Good | Fine | N-Mint |
|---|---|---|---|
| 1 | 6.50 | 19.00 | 45.00 |
| 2 | 3.00 | 9.00 | 21.00 |
| 3,4 | 2.65 | 8.00 | 18.00 |
| 5-Disbrow-a (classic) | 8.00 | 24.00 | 56.00 |

**CRIME DOES NOT PAY** (Formerly Silver Streak Comics No. 1-21)
No. 22, June, 1942 - No. 147, July, 1955 (1st crime comic)
Comic House/Lev Gleason/Golfing (Title inspired by film)

| | Good | Fine | N-Mint |
|---|---|---|---|
| 22(23 on cover, 22 on indicia)-Origin The War Eagle & only app.; Chip Gardner begins; #22 was rebound in Complete Book of True Crime (Scarce) | 90.00 | 270.00 | 630.00 |
| 23 (Scarce) | 50.00 | 150.00 | 350.00 |
| 24-Intro. & 1st app. Mr. Crime (Scarce) | 43.00 | 130.00 | 300.00 |
| 25-30 | 23.00 | 70.00 | 160.00 |
| 31-40 | 13.00 | 40.00 | 90.00 |
| 41-Origin & 1st app. Officer Common Sense | 9.30 | 28.00 | 65.00 |
| 42-Electrocution-c | 11.00 | 32.00 | 75.00 |
| 43-46,48-50: 44,45,50 are 68 pg. issues | 7.00 | 21.00 | 50.00 |
| 47-Electric chair-c | 11.00 | 32.00 | 75.00 |
| 51-62,65-70 | 4.00 | 12.00 | 28.00 |
| 63,64-Possible use in **SOTI**, pg. 306. #63-Contains Biro-Gleason's self censorship code of 12 listed restrictions (5/48) | 4.00 | 12.00 | 28.00 |
| 71-99: 87-Chip Gardner begins, ends #99 | 2.65 | 8.00 | 18.00 |
| 100 | 3.00 | 9.00 | 21.00 |
| 101-104,107-110: 102-Chip Gardner app. | 2.00 | 6.00 | 14.00 |
| 105-Used in **POP**, pg. 84 | 2.00 | 6.00 | 14.00 |
| 106,114-Frazetta, 1 pg. | 2.00 | 6.00 | 14.00 |
| 111-Used in **POP**, pgs. 80 & 81; injury-to-eye story illo | 1.70 | 5.00 | 12.00 |
| 112,113,115-130 | 1.30 | 4.00 | 9.00 |
| 131-140 | 1.15 | 3.50 | 8.00 |
| 141,142-Last pre-code issue; Kubert-a(1) | 2.30 | 7.00 | 16.00 |
| 143,147-Kubert-a, one each | 2.30 | 7.00 | 16.00 |
| 144-146 | 1.00 | 3.00 | 7.00 |
| 1(Golfing-1945) | 1.70 | 5.00 | 12.00 |
| The Best of...(1944, 128 pgs.)-Series contains 4 rebound issues | 32.00 | 96.00 | 225.00 |
| ...1945 issue | 29.00 | 86.00 | 200.00 |
| ...1946-48 issues | 23.00 | 70.00 | 160.00 |
| ...1949-50 issues | 17.00 | 51.00 | 120.00 |
| ...1951-53 issues | 14.00 | 43.00 | 100.00 |

NOTE: *Many issues contain violent covers and stories. Who Dunnit by **Guardineer**-39-42, 44-105, 108-110; Chip Gardner by **Bob Fujitani (Fuje)**-88-103. **Alderman** a-29, 41-44, 49. **Dan Barry** a-75. **Biro** c-1-76, 122, 142. **Briefer** a-29(2), 30, 31, 33, 37, 39. **Fuje** c-88, 89, 91-94, 96, 98, 99, 102, 103. **Guardineer** a-57, 71. **Kubert** c-143. **Landau** a-118. **Maurer** a-29, 39, 41, 42. **McWilliams** a-91, 93, 95, 100-103. **Palais** a-30, 33, 37, 39, 41-43, 44(2), 46, 49. **Powell** a-146, 147. **Tuska** a-48, 50(2), 51, 52, 56, 57(2), 60-64, 66, 67, 71. Painted c-87-102. Bondage c-43, 62, 98.*

**CRIME EXPOSED**
June, 1948; Dec, 1950 - No. 14, June, 1952
Marvel Comics (PPI)/Marvel Atlas Comics (PrPI)

| | Good | Fine | N-Mint |
|---|---|---|---|
| 1(6/48) | 10.00 | 30.00 | 70.00 |
| 1(12/50) | 6.00 | 18.00 | 42.00 |
| 2 | 3.60 | 11.00 | 25.00 |
| 3-11,14: 10-Used in **POP**, pg. 81 | 2.65 | 8.00 | 18.00 |
| 12-Krigstein & Robinson-a | 3.00 | 9.00 | 21.00 |
| 13-Used in **POP**, pg. 81; Krigstein-a | 3.50 | 10.50 | 24.00 |

NOTE: ***Maneely** c-8. **Robinson** a-11, 12. **Tuska** a-3, 4.*

**CRIMEFIGHTERS**
April, 1948 - No. 10, Nov, 1949
Marvel Comics (CmPS 1-3/CCC 4-10)

| | Good | Fine | N-Mint |
|---|---|---|---|
| 1-Some copies are undated & could be reprints | 8.50 | 25.50 | 60.00 |
| 2,3: 3-Morphine addict story | 3.60 | 11.00 | 25.00 |
| 4-10: 6-Anti-Wertham editorial. 9,10-Photo-c | 3.00 | 9.00 | 21.00 |

**CRIME FIGHTERS** (...Always Win)
No. 11, Sept, 1954 - No. 13, Jan, 1955
Atlas Comics (CnPC)

| | Good | Fine | N-Mint |
|---|---|---|---|
| 11,12: 11-Maneely-a | 3.15 | 9.50 | 22.00 |
| 13-Pakula, Reinman, Severin-a | 3.60 | 11.00 | 25.00 |

**CRIME FIGHTING DETECTIVE** (Shock Detective Cases No. 20 on; formerly Criminals on the Run)
No. 11, Apr-May, 1950 - No. 19, June, 1952
Star Publications

| | Good | Fine | N-Mint |
|---|---|---|---|
| 11-L. B. Cole-c/a, 2pgs. | 4.00 | 12.00 | 28.00 |
| 12,13,15-19: 17-Young King Cole & Dr. Doom app.; L. B. Cole-c on all | 2.85 | 8.50 | 20.00 |
| 14-L. B. Cole-c/a, r-/Law-Crime No. 2 | 3.70 | 11.00 | 26.00 |

**CRIME FILES**
No. 5, Sept, 1952 - No. 6, Nov, 1952
Standard Comics

| | Good | Fine | N-Mint |
|---|---|---|---|
| 5-Alex Toth-a; used in **SOTI**, pg. 4 (text) | 11.00 | 32.00 | 75.00 |
| 6-Sekowsky-a | 4.50 | 14.00 | 32.00 |

**CRIME ILLUSTRATED** (Magazine, 25 cents)
Nov-Dec, 1955 - No. 2, Spring, 1956 (Adult Suspense Stories on-c)
E. C. Comics

| | Good | Fine | N-Mint |
|---|---|---|---|
| 1-Ingels & Crandall-a | 7.00 | 21.00 | 50.00 |
| 2-Ingels & Crandall-a | 5.70 | 17.00 | 40.00 |

NOTE: ***Craig** a-2. **Crandall** a-1, 2; c-2. **Evans** a-1. **Davis** a-2. **Ingels** a-1, 2. **Krigstein/Crandall** a-1. **Orlando** a-1, 2; c-1.*

**CRIME INCORPORATED** (Formerly Crimes Incorporated)
No. 2, Aug, 1950; No. 3, Aug, 1951
Fox Features Syndicate

| | Good | Fine | N-Mint |
|---|---|---|---|
| 2 | 8.50 | 25.50 | 60.00 |
| 3(1951)-Hollingsworth-a | 5.70 | 17.00 | 40.00 |

**CRIME MACHINE** (Magazine)
Feb, 1971 - No. 2, May, 1971 (B&W)
Skywald Publications

| | Good | Fine | N-Mint |
|---|---|---|---|
| 1-Kubert-a(2)(r)(Avon) | 1.15 | 3.50 | 8.00 |
| 2-Torres, Wildey-a; violent-c/a | 1.15 | 3.50 | 8.00 |

**CRIME MUST LOSE!** (Formerly Sports Action?)
No. 4, Oct, 1950 - No. 12, April, 1952
Sports Action (Atlas Comics)

| | Good | Fine | N-Mint |
|---|---|---|---|
| 4-Ann Brewster-a in all; c-used in N.Y. Legis. Comm. documents | 5.70 | 17.00 | 40.00 |
| 5-12: 9-Robinson-a. 11-Used in **POP**, pg. 89 | 2.85 | 8.50 | 20.00 |

**CRIME MUST PAY THE PENALTY** (Formerly Four Favorites; Penalty No. 47,48)
No. 33, Feb, 1948; No. 2, June, 1948 - No. 48, Jan, 1956
Ace Magazines (Current Books)

| | Good | Fine | N-Mint |
|---|---|---|---|
| 33(#1, 2/48)-Becomes Four Teeners #34? | 11.00 | 32.00 | 75.00 |
| 2(6/48)-Extreme violence; Palais-a? | 7.00 | 21.00 | 50.00 |

*Crime Does Not Pay #87, © LEV*

*Crime Fighting Detective #14, © STAR*

*Crime Must Lose! #12, © MEG*

*Crime Mysteries #4, © TM*

*Crime Reporter #3, © STJ*

*Crime SuspenStories #11, © WMG*

| | Good | Fine | N-Mint |
|---|---|---|---|
| 3-'Frisco Mary' story used in Senate Investigation report, pg. 7 | 3.60 | 11.00 | 25.00 |
| 4,8-Transvestism stories | 5.00 | 15.00 | 35.00 |
| 5-7,9,10 | 2.65 | 8.00 | 18.00 |
| 11-20 | 2.00 | 6.00 | 14.00 |
| 21-32,34-40,42-48 | 1.70 | 5.00 | 12.00 |
| 33(7/53)-"Dell Fabry-Junk King"-drug story; mentioned in **Love and Death** | 3.15 | 9.50 | 22.00 |
| 41-Drug story-"Dealers in White Death" | 3.15 | 9.50 | 22.00 |

NOTE: ***Cameron*** *a-30-32, 34, 39-41.* ***Colan*** *a-20, 31.* ***Kremer*** *a-3, 37r.* ***Palais*** *a-5?, 37.*

**CRIME MUST STOP**
October, 1952 (52 pgs.)
Hillman Periodicals

| | Good | Fine | N-Mint |
|---|---|---|---|
| V1#1(Scarce)-Similar to Monster Crime; Mort Lawrence-a | 29.00 | 86.00 | 200.00 |

**CRIME MYSTERIES** (Secret Mysteries No. 16 on; combined with Crime Smashers No. 7 on)
May, 1952 - No. 15, Sept, 1954
Ribage Publishing Corp. (Trojan Magazines)

| | Good | Fine | N-Mint |
|---|---|---|---|
| 1-Transvestism story | 22.00 | 65.00 | 150.00 |
| 2-Marijuana story (7/52) | 13.00 | 40.00 | 90.00 |
| 3-One pg. Frazetta | 10.00 | 30.00 | 70.00 |
| 4-Cover shows girl in bondage having her blood drained; 1 pg. Frazetta | 18.00 | 54.00 | 125.00 |
| 5-10 | 8.50 | 25.50 | 60.00 |
| 11,12,14 | 7.00 | 21.00 | 50.00 |
| 13-Angelo Torres 1st comic work; Check-a | 11.50 | 34.00 | 80.00 |
| 15-Acid in face-c | 13.00 | 40.00 | 90.00 |

NOTE: ***Fass*** *c-4.* ***Hollingsworth*** *a-10-12, 15; c-12, 15.* ***Kiefer*** *a-4.* ***Woodbridge*** *a-13. Bondage-c-1, 8, 12.*

**CRIME ON THE RUN** (See Approved Comics)
No. 8, 1949
St. John Publishing Co.

| | Good | Fine | N-Mint |
|---|---|---|---|
| 8 (Exist?) | 3.00 | 9.00 | 21.00 |

**CRIME ON THE WATERFRONT** (Formerly Famous Gangsters)
No. 4, May, 1952 (Painted cover)
Realistic Publications

| | Good | Fine | N-Mint |
|---|---|---|---|
| 4 | 13.00 | 40.00 | 90.00 |

**CRIME PATROL** (International #1-5; International Crime Patrol #6, becomes Crypt of Terror #17 on)
No. 7, Summer, 1948 - No. 16, Feb-Mar, 1950
E. C. Comics

| | Good | Fine | N-Mint |
|---|---|---|---|
| 7-Intro. Captain Crime | 35.00 | 105.00 | 245.00 |
| 8-14: 12-Ingels-a | 30.00 | 90.00 | 210.00 |
| 15-Intro. of Crypt Keeper (inspired by Witches Tales radio show) & Crypt of Terror; used by N.Y. Legis. Comm.-last pg. Feldstein-a | 82.00 | 245.00 | 575.00 |
| 16-2nd Crypt Keeper app. | 68.00 | 205.00 | 475.00 |

NOTE: ***Craig*** *c/a in most issues.*

**CRIME PHOTOGRAPHER** (See Casey. . .)

**CRIME REPORTER**
Aug, 1948 - No. 3, Dec, 1948 (Shows Oct.)
St. John Publ. Co.

| | Good | Fine | N-Mint |
|---|---|---|---|
| 1-Drug club story | 19.00 | 56.00 | 130.00 |
| 2-Used in **SOTI**: illo-"Children told me what the man was going to do with the red-hot poker;" r-/Dynamic #17 with editing; Baker-c; Tuska-a | 34.00 | 103.00 | 240.00 |
| 3-Baker-c; Tuska-a | 14.00 | 43.00 | 100.00 |

**CRIMES BY WOMEN**
June, 1948 - No. 15, Aug, 1951; 1954
Fox Features Syndicate

| | Good | Fine | N-Mint |
|---|---|---|---|
| 1 | 50.00 | 150.00 | 350.00 |
| 2,3: 3-Used in **SOTI**, pg. 234 | 24.00 | 73.00 | 170.00 |
| 4,5,7-9,11-15: 8-Used in **POP** | 22.00 | 65.00 | 154.00 |
| 6-Classic girl fight-c; acid-in-face panel | 25.00 | 75.00 | 175.00 |
| 10-Used in **SOTI**, pg. 72 | 22.00 | 65.00 | 154.00 |
| 54(M.S. Publ.-'54)-Reprint; (formerly My Love Secret) | 10.00 | 30.00 | 70.00 |

**CRIMES INCORPORATED** (Formerly My Past)
No. 12, June, 1950 (Crime Incorporated No. 2 on)
Fox Features Syndicate

| | Good | Fine | N-Mint |
|---|---|---|---|
| 12 | 4.50 | 14.00 | 32.00 |

**CRIMES INCORPORATED** (See Fox Giants)

**CRIME SMASHER**
Summer, 1948 (One Shot)
Fawcett Publications

| | Good | Fine | N-Mint |
|---|---|---|---|
| 1-Formerly Spy Smasher; see Whiz #76 | 18.00 | 54.00 | 125.00 |

**CRIME SMASHERS** (Secret Mysteries No. 16 on)
Oct, 1950 - No. 15, Mar, 1953
Ribage Publishing Corp.(Trojan Magazines)

| | Good | Fine | N-Mint |
|---|---|---|---|
| 1-Used in **SOTI**, pg. 19,20, & illo-"A girl raped and murdered;" Sally the Sleuth begins | 32.00 | 95.00 | 225.00 |
| 2-Kubert-c | 16.00 | 48.00 | 110.00 |
| 3,4 | 12.00 | 36.00 | 84.00 |
| 5-Wood-a | 19.00 | 56.00 | 130.00 |
| 6,8-11 | 10.00 | 30.00 | 70.00 |
| 7-Female heroin junkie story | 11.00 | 32.00 | 75.00 |
| 12-Injury to eye panel; 1 pg. Frazetta-a | 11.50 | 34.00 | 80.00 |
| 13-Used in **POP**, pgs. 79,80; 1 pg. Frazetta-a | 10.00 | 30.00 | 70.00 |
| 14,15 | 10.00 | 30.00 | 70.00 |

NOTE: ***Hollingsworth*** *a-14.* ***Kiefer*** *a-15. Bondage c-7, 9.*

**CRIME SUSPENSTORIES** (Formerly Vault of Horror No. 12-14)
No. 15, Oct-Nov, 1950 - No. 27, Feb-Mar, 1955
E. C. Comics

15-Identical to #1 in content; #1 printed on outside front cover. #15 (formerly "The Vault of Horror") printed and blackened out on inside front cover with Vol. 1, No. 1 printed over it. Evidently, several of No. 15 were printed before a decision was made not to drop the Vault of Horror and Haunt of Fear series. The print run was stopped on No. 15 and continued on No. 1. All of No. 15 were changed as described above.

| | Good | Fine | N-Mint |
|---|---|---|---|
| 15 | 82.00 | 245.00 | 575.00 |
| 1 | 64.00 | 193.00 | 450.00 |
| 2 | 38.00 | 115.00 | 265.00 |
| 3-5 | 25.00 | 75.00 | 175.00 |
| 6-10 | 19.00 | 58.00 | 135.00 |
| 11,12,14,15 | 13.50 | 41.00 | 95.00 |
| 13,16-Williamson-a | 17.00 | 50.00 | 115.00 |
| 17-Williamson/Frazetta-a, 6 pgs. | 19.00 | 56.00 | 130.00 |
| 18,19: 19-Used in **SOTI**, pg. 235 | 11.50 | 34.00 | 80.00 |
| 20-Cover used in **SOTI**, illo-"Cover of a children's comic book" | 15.00 | 45.00 | 105.00 |
| 21,25-27 | 8.50 | 25.50 | 60.00 |
| 22,23-Used in Senate investigation on juvenile delinquency. 22-Ax decapitation-c | 12.00 | 36.00 | 85.00 |
| 24-'Food For Thought' similar to 'Cave In' in Amazing Detective Cases #13 ('52) | 8.50 | 25.50 | 60.00 |

NOTE: ***Craig*** *a-1-21; c-1-18, 20-22.* ***Crandall*** *a-18-26.* ***Davis*** *a-4, 5, 7, 9-12, 20.* ***Elder*** *a-17, 18.* ***Evans*** *a-15, 19, 21, 23, 25, 27; c-23, 24.* ***Feldstein*** *c-19.* ***Ingels*** *a-1-12, 14, 15, 27.* ***Kamen*** *a-2, 4-18, 20-27; c-25-27.* ***Krigstein*** *a-22, 24, 25, 27.* ***Kurtzman*** *a-1, 3.* ***Orlando*** *a-16, 22, 24, 26.* ***Wood*** *a-1, 3. Issues No. 11-15 have E. C. "quickie" stories. No. 25 contains the famous "Are You a Red Dupe?" editorial.*

**CRIMINALS ON THE RUN** (Formerly Young King Cole)
(Crime Fighting Detective No. 11 on)
V4#1, Aug-Sept, 1948 - #10, Dec-Jan, 1949-50
Premium Group (Novelty Press)

| | Good | Fine | N-Mint |
|---|---|---|---|
| V4#1-Young King Cole continues | 8.00 | 24.00 | 56.00 |
| 2-6: 6-Dr. Doom app. | 6.00 | 18.00 | 42.00 |
| 7-Classic "Fish in the Face" cover by L. B. Cole | 15.00 | 45.00 | 105.00 |
| V5#1,2 (#8,9) | 6.00 | 18.00 | 42.00 |
| 10-L. B. Cole-c | 6.00 | 18.00 | 42.00 |

NOTE: *Most issues have* ***L. B. Cole*** *covers.* ***McWilliams*** *a-V4#6, 7, V5#2; c-V4#5.*

**CRIMSON AVENGER, THE** (See Detective Comics #20 for 1st app.) (Also see Leading Comics #1 & World's Best/Finest Comics)
June, 1988 - No. 4, Sept, 1988 ($1.00, color, limited series)
DC Comics

| | Good | Fine | N-Mint |
|---|---|---|---|
| 1-4 | | .50 | 1.00 |

**CRISIS ON INFINITE EARTHS** (Also see Official...Index)
Apr, 1985 - No. 12, Mar, 1986 (12 issue maxi-series)
DC Comics

| | Good | Fine | N-Mint |
|---|---|---|---|
| 1-1st DC app. Blue Beetle & Detective Karp from Charlton; Perez-c on all | .70 | 2.00 | 4.00 |
| 2 | .50 | 1.50 | 3.00 |
| 3 | .40 | 1.25 | 2.50 |
| 4-6: 6-Intro Charlton's Capt. Atom, Nightshade, Question, Judomaster, Peacemaker & Thunderbolt | .35 | 1.00 | 2.00 |
| 7-Double size; death of Supergirl | .70 | 2.00 | 4.00 |
| 8-Death of Flash | .70 | 2.00 | 4.00 |
| 9-11: 9-Intro. Charlton's Ghost. 10-Intro. Charlton's Banshee, Dr. Spectro, Image, Punch & Jewellee | .35 | 1.00 | 2.00 |
| 12-Double size; deaths of Dove, Kole, Lori Lemaris, Sunburst, G.A. Robin & Huntress; Kid Flash becomes new Flash | .50 | 1.50 | 3.00 |

**CRITICAL MASS** (See A Shadowline Saga: Critical Mass)

**CRITTERS** (Also see Usagi Yojimbo Summer Special)
1986 - No. 50, 1990 ($1.70/$2.00, B&W)
Fantagraphics Books

| | Good | Fine | N-Mint |
|---|---|---|---|
| 1-Cutey Bunny, Usagi Yojimbo app. | 1.15 | 3.50 | 7.00 |
| 2 | .70 | 2.00 | 4.00 |
| 3-Usagi Yojimbo app. | .50 | 1.50 | 3.00 |
| 4-10: 10-Usagi Yojimbo app. | .40 | 1.25 | 2.50 |
| 11-Christmas Special (68 pgs.); Usagi Yojimbo | .60 | 1.75 | 3.50 |
| 12-22,24-49: 14,38-Usagi Yojimbo app. 22-Watchmen parody; two diff. covers exist | .35 | 1.00 | 2.00 |
| 23-With Alan Moore Flexi-disc ($3.95) | .70 | 2.00 | 4.00 |
| 50 ($4.95, 84 pgs.)-Neil the Horse, Capt. Jack, Sam & Max & Usagi Yojimbo app. | .85 | 2.50 | 5.00 |
| Special 1 (1/88, $2.00) | .35 | 1.00 | 2.00 |

**CROSLEY'S HOUSE OF FUN** (Also see Tee and Vee Crosley...)
1950 (32 pgs.; full color; paper cover)
Crosley Div. AVCO Mfg. Corp. (Giveaway)

| | Good | Fine | N-Mint |
|---|---|---|---|
| nn-Strips revolve around Crosley appliances | 1.70 | 5.00 | 12.00 |

**CROSS AND THE SWITCHBLADE, THE**
1972 (35-49 cents)
Spire Christian Comics/Fleming H. Revell Co.

| | Good | Fine | N-Mint |
|---|---|---|---|
| 1(Some issues have nn) | | .40 | .80 |

**CROSSFIRE**
1973 (39,49cents)
Spire Christian Comics (Fleming H. Revell Co.)

| | Good | Fine | N-Mint |
|---|---|---|---|
| nn | | .40 | .80 |

**CROSSFIRE**
5/84 - No. 17, 3/86; No. 18, 1/87 - No. 26, 2/88 ($1.50, Baxter paper)
Eclipse Comics

| | Good | Fine | N-Mint |
|---|---|---|---|
| 1-17: 1-DNAgents x-over; Spiegle-c/a begins. 12,13-Death of Marilyn Monroe; 12-Stevens-c | .25 | .75 | 1.50 |
| 18-26 (B&W) | .30 | .90 | 1.80 |

**CROSSFIRE AND RAINBOW**
June, 1986 - No. 4, Sept, 1986 ($1.25, mini-series)
Eclipse Comics

| | Good | Fine | N-Mint |
|---|---|---|---|
| 1-3: Spiegle-a | | .65 | 1.30 |
| 4-Dave Stevens-c | .35 | 1.00 | 2.00 |

**CROSSING THE ROCKIES** (See Classics Illustrated Special Issue)

**CROSSROADS**
July, 1988 - No. 5, Nov, 1988 ($3.25, color, deluxe)
First Comics

| | Good | Fine | N-Mint |
|---|---|---|---|
| 1-5 | .55 | 1.60 | 3.25 |

**CROWN COMICS**
Winter, 1944-45 - No. 19, July, 1949
Golfing/McCombs Publ.

| | Good | Fine | N-Mint |
|---|---|---|---|
| 1-"The Oblong Box"-Poe adaptation | 17.00 | 51.00 | 120.00 |
| 2,3-Baker-a | 9.30 | 28.00 | 65.00 |
| 4-6-Baker-c/a; Voodah app. #4,5 | 10.00 | 30.00 | 70.00 |
| 7-Feldstein, Baker, Kamen-a; Baker-c | 9.30 | 28.00 | 65.00 |
| 8-Baker-a; Voodah app. | 8.50 | 25.50 | 60.00 |
| 9-11,13-19: Voodah in #10-19 | 4.30 | 13.00 | 30.00 |
| 12-Feldstein?, Starr-a | 5.00 | 15.00 | 35.00 |

NOTE: ***Bolle*** *a-11, 13-16, 18, 19; c-11p, 15.* ***Powell*** *a-19.* ***Starr*** *a-11-13; c-11i.*

**CRUSADER FROM MARS** (See Tops in Adventure)
Jan-Mar, 1952 - No. 2, Fall, 1952
Ziff-Davis Publ. Co.

| | Good | Fine | N-Mint |
|---|---|---|---|
| 1 | 36.00 | 107.00 | 250.00 |
| 2-Bondage-c | 27.00 | 80.00 | 185.00 |

**CRUSADER RABBIT** (See 4-Color No. 735,805)

**CRUSADERS, THE**
1974 - Vol. 16, 1985 (36 pg.) (39-69 cents) (Religious)
Chick Publications

| | Good | Fine | N-Mint |
|---|---|---|---|
| Vol. 1-Operation Bucharest('74). Vol. 2-The Broken Cross('74). Vol. 3-Scarface('74). Vol. 4-Exorcists('75). Vol. 5-Chaos('75). each.... | | .40 | .80 |
| Vol. 6-Primal Man?('76)-(Disputes evolution theory). Vol. 7-The Ark-(Claims proof of existence, destroyed by Bolsheviks). Vol. 8-The Gift-(Life story of Christ). Vol. 9-Angel of Light-(Story of the Devil). Vol. 10-Spellbound?-(Tells how rock music is Satanical & produced by witches). 11-Sabotage?. 12-Alberto. 13-Double-Cross 14-The Godfathers. (No. 6-14 low in distribution; Loaded in religious propaganda.). 15-The Force. 16-The Four Horsemen | | .40 | .80 |

**CRUSADERS** (Southern Knights No. 2 on)
1982 (Magazine size, B&W)
Guild Publications

| | Good | Fine | N-Mint |
|---|---|---|---|
| 1-1st app. Southern Knights | 1.70 | 5.00 | 10.00 |

**CRYING FREEMAN**
1989 - No. 8, 1990; V2#1, 1990 - No. 9, 1991 ($3.50, B&W, 68 pgs.)
Viz Premiere Comics

| | Good | Fine | N-Mint |
|---|---|---|---|
| 1-8: Japanese manga; mature readers | .60 | 1.75 | 3.50 |
| Part 2, #1-9 | .60 | 1.75 | 3.50 |

**CRYIN' LION COMICS**
Fall, 1944 - No. 3, Spring, 1945
William H. Wise Co.

| | Good | Fine | N-Mint |
|---|---|---|---|
| 1-Funny animal | 7.00 | 21.00 | 50.00 |
| 2,3 | 4.00 | 12.00 | 28.00 |

**CRYPT OF SHADOWS**
Jan, 1973 - No. 21, Nov, 1975
Marvel Comics Group

| | Good | Fine | N-Mint |
|---|---|---|---|
| 1-Wolverton-r/Advs. Into Terror No. 7 | | .60 | 1.20 |
| 2-21 | | .40 | .80 |

NOTE: ***Briefer*** *a-2r.* ***Ditko*** *a-13r, 18-20r.* ***Everett*** *a-6, 14r; c-2i.* ***Heath*** *a-1r.* ***Mort Lawrence*** *a-1r.* ***Maneely*** *a-2r.* ***Moldoff*** *a-8.* ***Powell*** *a-12r, 14r.*

*Crisis on Infinite Earths #8, © DC*

*Crossfire #12, © Eclipse*

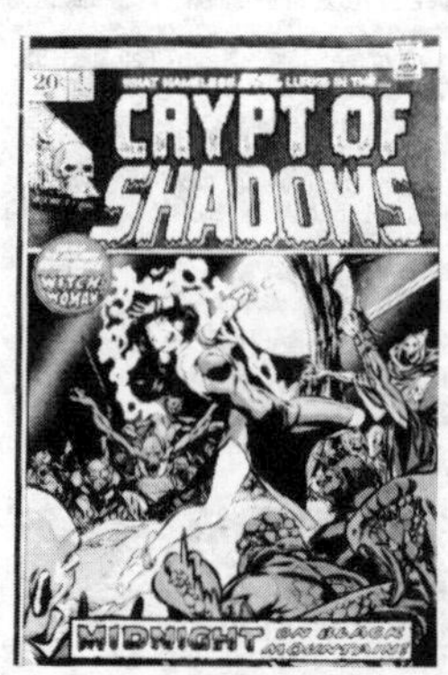

*Crypt of Shadows #1, © MEG*

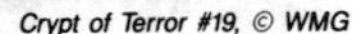
*Crypt of Terror #19, © WMG*

*Curly Kayoe Comics #1, © UFS*

*Daffy Duck #18, © Warner Bros.*

**CRYPT OF TERROR** (Tales From the Crypt No. 20 on; formerly Crime Patrol)
No. 17, Apr-May, 1950 - No. 19, Aug-Sept, 1950
E. C. Comics

| | Good | Fine | N-Mint |
|---|---|---|---|
| 17-1st New Trend to hit stands | 97.00 | 290.00 | 675.00 |
| 18,19 | 71.00 | 215.00 | 500.00 |

NOTE: ***Craig** c/a-17-19. **Feldstein** a-17-19. **Ingels** a-19. **Kurtzman** a-18. **Wood** a-18. Canadian reprints known; see Table of Contents.*

**CUPID**
Dec, 1949 - No. 2, Mar, 1950
Marvel Comics (U.S.A.)

| | Good | Fine | N-Mint |
|---|---|---|---|
| 1-Photo-c | 5.70 | 17.00 | 40.00 |
| 2-Betty Page ('50s pin-up queen) photo-c; Powell-a (see My Love #4, Miss America #4) | 9.30 | 28.00 | 65.00 |

**CURIO**
1930's(?) (Tabloid size, 16-20 pages)
Harry 'A' Chesler

| | Good | Fine | N-Mint |
|---|---|---|---|
| nn | 7.00 | 21.00 | 50.00 |

**CURLY KAYOE COMICS** (Boxing)
1946 - No. 8, 1950; Jan, 1958
United Features Syndicate/Dell Publ. Co.

| | Good | Fine | N-Mint |
|---|---|---|---|
| 1 (1946)-Strip-r (Fritzi Ritz); biography of Sam Leff, Kayoe's artist | 7.00 | 21.00 | 50.00 |
| 2 | 3.60 | 11.00 | 25.00 |
| 3-8 | 2.65 | 8.00 | 18.00 |
| United Presents. . . (Fall, 1948) | 2.65 | 8.00 | 18.00 |
| 4-Color 871 (Dell, 1/58) | 2.00 | 6.00 | 14.00 |

**CUSTER'S LAST FIGHT**
1950
Avon Periodicals

| | Good | Fine | N-Mint |
|---|---|---|---|
| nn-Partial reprint of Cowpuncher #1 | 9.30 | 28.00 | 65.00 |

**CUTEY BUNNY** (See Army Surplus Komikz Featuring. . .)

**CUTIE PIE**
May, 1955 - No. 3, Dec, 1955; No. 4, Feb, 1956; No. 5, Aug, 1956
Junior Reader's Guild (Lev Gleason)

| | Good | Fine | N-Mint |
|---|---|---|---|
| 1 | 2.65 | 8.00 | 18.00 |
| 2-5: 4-Misdated 2/55 | 1.50 | 4.50 | 10.00 |

**CYBERPUNK**
Sept, 1989 - No. 2, Oct?, 1989 ($1.95, color, mini-series, 28 pgs.)
Book 2, #1, May, 1990 - No. 2, 1990 ($2.25, color, 28 pgs.)
Innovation Publishing

| | Good | Fine | N-Mint |
|---|---|---|---|
| 1,2-Both have Ken Steacy painted-c (Adults) | .35 | 1.00 | 2.00 |
| Book 2, #1,2 | .40 | 1.15 | 2.30 |

**CYBERPUNK: THE SERAPHIM FILES**
Nov, 1990 - No. 2, Dec?, 1990 ($2.50, color, mature readers, 28 pgs.)
Innovation Publishing

| | Good | Fine | N-Mint |
|---|---|---|---|
| 1,2: 1-Painted-c; story con'd from Seraphim | .40 | 1.25 | 2.50 |

**CYBER 7**
Mar, 1989 - #7, Sept, 1989; V2#1, Oct, 1989 - Present ($2.00, B&W)
Eclipse Comics

| | Good | Fine | N-Mint |
|---|---|---|---|
| 1-7: Stories translated from Japanese | .35 | 1.00 | 2.00 |
| Book Two, #1-10 | .35 | 1.00 | 2.00 |

**CYCLONE COMICS** (Also see Whirlwind Comics)
June, 1940 - No. 5, Nov, 1940
Bilbara Publishing Co.

| | Good | Fine | N-Mint |
|---|---|---|---|
| 1-Origin Tornado Tom; Volton begins, Mister Q app. | 47.00 | 140.00 | 325.00 |
| 2 | 24.00 | 73.00 | 170.00 |
| 3-5: 4,5-Mr. Q app. | 20.00 | 60.00 | 140.00 |

**CYNTHIA DOYLE, NURSE IN LOVE** (Formerly Sweetheart Diary)
No. 66, Oct, 1962 - No. 74, Feb, 1964
Charlton Publications

| | Good | Fine | N-Mint |
|---|---|---|---|
| 66-74 (#74, exist?) | .60 | 1.75 | 3.50 |

**DAFFY** (. . . Duck No. 18 on)(See Looney Tunes)
#457, 3/53 - #30, 7-9/62; #31, 10-12/62 - #145, 1983 (No #132,133)
Dell Publishing Co./Gold Key No. 31-127/Whitman No. 128 on

| | Good | Fine | N-Mint |
|---|---|---|---|
| 4-Color 457(#1)-Elmer Fudd x-overs begin | 2.65 | 8.00 | 18.00 |
| 4-Color 536,615('55) | 1.70 | 5.00 | 12.00 |
| 4(1-3/56)-11('57) | 1.30 | 4.00 | 9.00 |
| 12-19(1958-59) | 1.00 | 3.00 | 7.00 |
| 20-40(1960-64) | .70 | 2.00 | 4.00 |
| 41-60(1964-68) | .40 | 1.25 | 2.50 |
| 61-90(1969-73)-Road Runner in most | | .60 | 1.20 |
| 91-131,134-145(1974-83) | | .40 | .80 |
| Mini-Comic 1 (1976; 3¼x6½") | | .25 | .50 |

NOTE: *Reprint issues-No.41-46, 48, 50, 53-55, 58, 59, 65, 67, 69, 73, 81, 96, 103-108; 136-142, 144, 145(⅓-⅔-r). (See March of Comics No. 277, 288, 313, 331, 347, 357, 375, 387, 397, 402, 413, 425, 437, 460).*

**DAFFYDILS**
1911 (52 pgs.; 6x8"; B&W; hardcover)
Cupples & Leon Co.

| | Good | Fine | N-Mint |
|---|---|---|---|
| nn-by Tad | 10.00 | 30.00 | 70.00 |

**DAFFY TUNES COMICS**
June, 1947 - No. 2, Aug, 1947
Four Star Publications

| | Good | Fine | N-Mint |
|---|---|---|---|
| nn | 3.70 | 11.00 | 26.00 |
| 2-Al Fago-c/a | 3.15 | 9.50 | 22.00 |

**DAGAR, DESERT HAWK** (Capt. Kidd No. 24-on; formerly All Great)
No. 14, Feb, 1948 - No. 23, Apr, 1949 (No #17,18)
Fox Features Syndicate

| | Good | Fine | N-Mint |
|---|---|---|---|
| 14-Tangi & Safari Cary begin; Edmond Good bondage-c/a | 28.00 | 84.00 | 195.00 |
| 15,16-E. Good-a; 15-Bondage-c | 17.00 | 50.00 | 115.00 |
| 19,20,22: 19-Used in **SOTI**, pg. 180 (Tangi) | 14.00 | 43.00 | 100.00 |
| 21-'Bombs & Bums Away' panel in 'Flood of Death' story used in **SOTI** | 18.00 | 54.00 | 125.00 |
| 23-Bondage-c | 17.00 | 50.00 | 115.00 |

NOTE: *Tangi by **Kamen**-14-16, 19, 20; c-20, 21.*

**DAGAR THE INVINCIBLE** (Tales of Sword & Sorcery. . .) (Also see Dan Curtis & Gold Key Spotlight)
Oct, 1972 - No. 18, Dec, 1976; No. 19, Apr, 1982
Gold Key

| | Good | Fine | N-Mint |
|---|---|---|---|
| 1-Origin; intro. Villains Olstellon & Scorpio | 1.15 | 3.50 | 8.00 |
| 2-5: 3-Intro. Graylin, Dagar's woman; Jarn x-over | .70 | 2.00 | 4.00 |
| 6-1st Dark Gods story | .50 | 1.50 | 3.00 |
| 7-10: 9-Intro. Torgus. 10-1st Three Witches story | .50 | 1.50 | 3.00 |
| 11-18: 13-Durak & Torgus x-over; story continues in Dr. Spektor #15. 14-Dagar's origin retold. 18-Origin retold | .25 | .75 | 1.50 |
| 19-Origin-r/#18 | | .40 | .80 |

NOTE: *Durak app.-7, 12, 13. Tragg app.-5, 11.*

**DAGWOOD** (Chic Young's) (Also see Blondie Comics)
Sept, 1950 - No. 140, Nov, 1965
Harvey Publications

| | Good | Fine | N-Mint |
|---|---|---|---|
| 1 | 7.00 | 21.00 | 50.00 |
| 2 | 3.50 | 10.50 | 25.00 |
| 3-10 | 3.00 | 9.00 | 21.00 |
| 11-30 | 1.70 | 5.00 | 12.00 |
| 31-70 | 1.00 | 3.00 | 6.00 |
| 71-100 | .85 | 2.50 | 5.00 |
| 101-128,130,135 | .70 | 2.00 | 4.00 |
| 129,131-134,136-140-All are 68-pg. issues | 1.00 | 3.00 | 6.00 |

NOTE: *Popeye and other one page strips appeared in early issues.*

**DAGWOOD SPLITS THE ATOM** (Also see Topix V8No.4)
1949 (Science comic with King Features characters) (Giveaway)
King Features Syndicate

| | Good | Fine | N-Mint |
|---|---|---|---|
| nn-½ comic, ½ text; Popeye, Olive Oyl, Henry, Mandrake, Little King, Katzenjammer Kids app. | 3.00 | 9.00 | 21.00 |

**DAI KAMIKAZE!**
June, 1987 - No. 12, Aug, 1988 ($1.75, color)
Now Comics

1-12: 1-1st app. Speed Racer; 2nd print exists .30 .90 1.80

**DAISY AND DONALD** (See Walt Disney Showcase No. 8)
May, 1973 - No. 59, 1984 (no No. 48)
Gold Key/Whitman No. 42 on

| | Good | Fine | N-Mint |
|---|---|---|---|
| 1-Barks r-/WDC&S #280,308 | .50 | 1.50 | 3.00 |
| 2-5: 4-Barks r-/WDC&S #224 | .35 | 1.00 | 2.00 |
| 6-10 | .25 | .75 | 1.50 |
| 11-20 | | .50 | 1.00 |
| 21-47,49,50: 32-r-/WDC&S #308. 50-r-/#3 | | .40 | .80 |
| 51-Barks r-/4-Color #1150 | | .50 | 1.00 |
| 52-59: 52-r-/#2. 55-r-/#5 | | .35 | .70 |

**DAISY & HER PUPS** (Blondie's Dogs)
No. 21, 7/51 - No. 27, 7/52; No. 8, 9/52 - No. 25, 7/55
Harvey Publications

| | Good | Fine | N-Mint |
|---|---|---|---|
| 21-27 (#1-7): 26,27 have No. 6 & 7 on cover but No. 26 & 27 on inside | 1.00 | 3.00 | 6.00 |
| 8-25: 19-25-Exist? | .85 | 2.50 | 5.00 |

**DAISY COMICS**
Dec, 1936 (Small size: 5¼x7½")
Eastern Color Printing Co.

Joe Palooka, Buck Rogers (2 pgs. from Famous Funnies No. 18), Napoleon Flying to Fame, Butty & Fally 17.00 50.00 115.00

**DAISY DUCK & UNCLE SCROOGE PICNIC TIME** (See Dell Giant #33)

**DAISY DUCK & UNCLE SCROOGE SHOW BOAT** (See Dell Giant #55)

**DAISY DUCK'S DIARY** (See Dynabrite Comics, Four Color No. 600,659,743, 858,948,1055,1150,1247 & Walt Disney's Comics & Stories #298)

**DAISY HANDBOOK**
1946; No. 2, 1948 (132 pgs.)(10 cents)(Pocket-size)
Daisy Manufacturing Co.

| | Good | Fine | N-Mint |
|---|---|---|---|
| 1-Buck Rogers, Red Ryder | 19.00 | 56.00 | 130.00 |
| 2-Captain Marvel & Ibis the Invincible, Red Ryder, Boy Commandos & Robotman; 2 pgs. Wolverton-a; contains 8pg. color catalog | 19.00 | 56.00 | 130.00 |

**DAISY LOW OF THE GIRL SCOUTS**
1954, 1965 (16 pgs.; paper cover)
Girl Scouts of America

| | Good | Fine | N-Mint |
|---|---|---|---|
| 1954-Story of Juliette Gordon Low | 2.15 | 6.50 | 15.00 |
| 1965 | .85 | 2.50 | 5.00 |

**DAISY MAE** (See Oxydol-Dreft)

**DAISY'S RED RYDER GUN BOOK**
1955 (132 pages)(25 cents)(Pocket-size)
Daisy Manufacturing Co.

nn-Boy Commandos, Red Ryder, 1 pg. Wolverton-a 12.00 36.00 85.00

**DAKOTA LIL** (See Fawcett Movie Comics)

**DAKOTA NORTH**
1986 - No. 5, Feb, 1987
Marvel Comics Group

1-5 .40 .80

**DAKTARI** (Ivan Tors) (TV)
July, 1967 - No. 3, Oct, 1968; No. 4, Sept, 1969 (Photo-c)
Dell Publishing Co.

| | Good | Fine | N-Mint |
|---|---|---|---|
| 1 | 2.00 | 6.00 | 14.00 |
| 2-4 | 1.30 | 4.00 | 9.00 |

**DALE EVANS COMICS** (Also see Queen of the West . . .)
Sept-Oct, 1948 - No. 24, July-Aug, 1952 (No. 1-19: 52 pgs.)
National Periodical Publications

| | Good | Fine | N-Mint |
|---|---|---|---|
| 1-Dale Evans & her horse Buttermilk begin; Sierra Smith begins by Alex Toth | 26.00 | 77.00 | 180.00 |
| 2-Alex Toth-a | 17.00 | 50.00 | 115.00 |
| 3-11-Alex Toth-a | 13.50 | 41.00 | 95.00 |
| 12-24 | 7.00 | 21.00 | 50.00 |

NOTE: *Photo-c-1, 2, 4-14.*

**DALGODA**
Aug, 1984 - No. 8, Feb, 1986 (Color, high quality paper)
Fantagraphics Books

| | Good | Fine | N-Mint |
|---|---|---|---|
| 1-($2.25 cover price). Fujitake-c/a in all | .50 | 1.50 | 3.00 |
| 2-8-($1.50). 2,3-Debut Grimwood's Daughter. 8-Alan Moore story | .35 | 1.00 | 2.00 |

**DALTON BOYS, THE**
1951
Avon Periodicals

1-(No. on spine)-Kinstler-c 8.50 25.50 60.00

**DAMAGE CONTROL**
5/89 - #4, 8/89; V2#1, 12/89 - #4, 2/90 ($1.00, color, both mini-series)
Marvel Comics

| | Good | Fine | N-Mint |
|---|---|---|---|
| 1-4: 4-Wolverine app. | | .60 | 1.20 |
| V2#1-4: 2,4-Punisher app. | .25 | .75 | 1.50 |

**DAN CURTIS GIVEAWAYS**
1974 (24 pages) (3x6") (in color, all reprints)
Western Publishing Co.

1-Dark Shadows, 2-Star Trek, 3-The Twilight Zone, 4-Ripley's Believe It or Not!, 5-Turok, Son of Stone, 6-Star Trek, 7-The Occult Files of Dr. Spektor, 8-Dagar the Invincible, 9-Grimm's Ghost Stories Set . . . .50 1.50 3.00

**DANDEE**
1947
Four Star Publications

nn 2.65 8.00 18.00

**DAN DUNN** (See Crackajack Funnies, Detective Dan, Famous Feature Stories & Red Ryder)

**DANDY COMICS** (Also see Happy Jack Howard)
Spring, 1947 - No. 7, Spring, 1948
E. C. Comics

| | Good | Fine | N-Mint |
|---|---|---|---|
| 1-Vince Fago-a in all | 18.00 | 54.00 | 125.00 |
| 2 | 13.00 | 40.00 | 90.00 |
| 3-7 | 11.00 | 32.00 | 75.00 |

**DANGER**
January, 1953 - No. 11, Aug, 1954
Comic Media/Allen Hardy Assoc.

| | Good | Fine | N-Mint |
|---|---|---|---|
| 1-Heck-c/a | 5.70 | 17.00 | 40.00 |
| 2,3,5-7,9-11 | 2.15 | 6.50 | 15.00 |
| 4-Marijuana cover/story | 5.00 | 15.00 | 35.00 |
| 8-Bondage/torture/headlights panels | 5.50 | 16.50 | 38.00 |

NOTE: ***Morisi** a-2, 5, 6(3); c-2. Contains some-r from Danger & Dynamite.*

**DANGER** (Jim Bowie No. 15 on; formerly Comic Media title)
No. 12, June, 1955 - No. 14, Oct, 1955
Charlton Comics Group

| | Good | Fine | N-Mint |
|---|---|---|---|
| 12(#1) | 3.70 | 11.00 | 26.00 |
| 13,14: 14 r-/#12 | 2.30 | 7.00 | 16.00 |

*Daktari #2, © Ivan Tors Films, Inc.*

*Dale Evans Comics #7, © Roy Rogers*

*Danger #1. © ME*

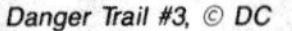
*Danger Trail #3, © DC*

*Daredevil #10, © MEG*

*Daredevil #248, © MEG*

**DANGER**
1964
Super Comics

| | Good | Fine | N-Mint |
|---|---|---|---|
| Super Reprint #10-12 (Black Dwarf; #11-r-/from Johnny Danger), #15,16 (Yankee Girl & Johnny Rebel), #17 (Capt. Courage & Enchanted Dagger), #18(nd) (Gun-Master, Annie Oakley, The Chameleon; L.B. Cole-a) | .85 | 2.50 | 5.00 |

**DANGER AND ADVENTURE** (Formerly This Magazine Is Haunted; Robin Hood and His Merry Men No. 28 on)
No. 22, Feb, 1955 - No. 27, Feb, 1956
Charlton Comics

| | | | |
|---|---|---|---|
| 22-Ibis the Invincible, Nyoka app. | 4.50 | 14.00 | 32.00 |
| 23-Nyoka, Lance O'Casey app. | 4.50 | 14.00 | 32.00 |
| 24-27: 24-Mike Danger & Johnny Adventure begin | 2.85 | 8.50 | 20.00 |

**DANGER IS OUR BUSINESS!**
1953(Dec.) - No. 10, June, 1955
Toby Press

| | | | |
|---|---|---|---|
| 1-Captain Comet by Williamson/Frazetta-a, 6 pgs. (Science Fiction) | 29.00 | 85.00 | 200.00 |
| 2 | 3.70 | 11.00 | 26.00 |
| 3-10 | 3.00 | 9.00 | 21.00 |
| I.W. Reprint #9('64)-Williamson/Frazetta-a r-/#1; Kinstler-c | 6.50 | 19.50 | 45.00 |

**DANGER IS THEIR BUSINESS** (See A-1 Comics No. 50)

**DANGER MAN** (See 4-Color No. 1231)

**DANGER TRAIL** (Also see Showcase #50, 51)
July-Aug, 1950 - No. 5, Mar-Apr, 1951 (52 pgs.)
National Periodical Publications

| | | | |
|---|---|---|---|
| 1-King Farrady begins, ends #4; Toth-a | 43.00 | 130.00 | 300.00 |
| 2-Toth-a | 33.00 | 100.00 | 230.00 |
| 3-5-Toth-a in all; Johnny Peril app. #5 | 29.00 | 85.00 | 200.00 |

**DANIEL BOONE** (See The Exploits of..., Fighting..., 4-Color No. 1163, Frontier Scout..., The Legends of... & March of Comics No. 306)

**DAN'L BOONE**
Sept, 1955 - No. 8, Sept, 1957
Magazine Enterprises/Sussex Publ. Co. No. 2 on

| | | | |
|---|---|---|---|
| 1 | 5.30 | 16.00 | 38.00 |
| 2 | 3.50 | 10.50 | 24.00 |
| 3-8 | 2.65 | 8.00 | 18.00 |

**DANIEL BOONE** (TV) (See March of Comics No. 306)
Jan, 1965 - No. 15, Apr, 1969
Gold Key

| | | | |
|---|---|---|---|
| 1 | 1.70 | 5.00 | 12.00 |
| 2-5 | .85 | 2.60 | 6.00 |
| 6-15: 4,6-Fess Parker photo-c | .70 | 2.00 | 4.00 |

**DANNY BLAZE** (Nature Boy No. 3 on)
Aug, 1955 - No. 2, Oct, 1955
Charlton Comics

| | | | |
|---|---|---|---|
| 1,2 | 3.15 | 9.50 | 22.00 |

**DANNY DINGLE** (See Single Series #17 & Sparkler Comics)

**DANNY KAYE'S BAND FUN BOOK**
1959
H & A Selmer (Giveaway)

| | | | |
|---|---|---|---|
| nn | 2.30 | 7.00 | 16.00 |

**DANNY THOMAS SHOW, THE** (See 4-Color No. 1180,1249)

**DARBY O'GILL & THE LITTLE PEOPLE** (See 4-Color No. 1024 & Movie Comics)

**DAREDEVIL** (...& the Black Widow #92-107 on-c only; see Giant-Size..., Marvel Advs., Marvel Graphic Novel #24, Marvel Super Heroes, '66 & Spider-Man and...)
April, 1964 - Present
Marvel Comics Group

| | Good | Fine | N-Mint |
|---|---|---|---|
| 1-Origin & 1st app. Daredevil; r-/in Marvel Super Heroes #1, 1966. Death of Battling Murdock; intro Foggy Nelson & Karen Page | 95.00 | 285.00 | 660.00 |
| 2-Fantastic Four cameo | 38.00 | 114.00 | 265.00 |
| 3-Origin & 1st app. The Owl | 23.00 | 70.00 | 160.00 |
| 4,5: 5-New Costume; Wood-a begins | 13.50 | 41.00 | 95.00 |
| 6,8-10: 8-Origin/1st app. Stilt-Man | 10.00 | 30.00 | 70.00 |
| 7-Dons new red costume | 12.00 | 36.00 | 85.00 |
| 11-15: 12-Romita's 1st work at Marvel. 13-Facts about Ka-Zar's origin; Kirby-a | 6.50 | 19.00 | 45.00 |
| 16,17-Spider-Man x-over | 7.85 | 23.50 | 55.00 |
| 18-20: 18-Origin & 1st app. Gladiator | 5.00 | 15.00 | 35.00 |
| 21-30: 24-Ka-Zar app. | 3.15 | 9.50 | 22.00 |
| 31-40 | 2.30 | 7.00 | 18.00 |
| 41-49: 41-Death Mike Murdock. 43-Vs. Capt. America | 1.70 | 5.00 | 12.00 |
| 50-53: 50-52-Smith-a. 53-Origin retold | 2.00 | 6.00 | 14.00 |
| 54-56,58-60 | 1.00 | 3.00 | 7.00 |
| 57-Reveals i.d. to Karen Page | 1.15 | 3.50 | 8.00 |
| 61-99: 62-1st app. Nighthawk. 81-Oversize issue; Black Widow begins | 1.00 | 3.00 | 6.00 |
| 100-Origin retold | 1.70 | 5.00 | 12.00 |
| 101-106,108-113,115-120 | .40 | 1.25 | 2.50 |
| 107-Starlin-c | .50 | 1.50 | 3.00 |
| 114-1st app. Deathstalker | .70 | 2.00 | 4.00 |
| 121-130,132-137: 124-1st app. Copperhead; Black Widow leaves. 126-1st New Torpedo | .35 | 1.00 | 2.00 |
| 131-Origin Bullseye (1st app. in Nick Fury #15) | 1.70 | 5.00 | 12.00 |
| 138-Ghost Rider-c/story; Byrne-a | 1.00 | 3.00 | 6.00 |
| 139-157: 142-Nova cameo. 148-30 & 35 cent issues exist. 150-1st app. Paladin. 151-Reveals i.d. to Heather Glenn. 155-Black Widow returns. 156-1960s Daredevil app. | .35 | 1.00 | 2.00 |
| 158-Frank Miller art begins (5/79); origin/death of Deathstalker (See Spect. Spider-Man for Miller's 1st D.D. | 5.70 | 17.00 | 40.00 |
| 159 | 2.65 | 8.00 | 18.00 |
| 160,161 | 1.50 | 4.50 | 9.00 |
| 162-Ditko-a, no Miller-a | .40 | 1.25 | 2.50 |
| 163,164: 163-Hulk cameo. 164-Origin | 1.35 | 4.00 | 8.00 |
| 165-167,170 | 1.00 | 3.00 | 6.00 |
| 168-Origin/1st app. Elektra | 2.85 | 8.50 | 20.00 |
| 169-Elektra app. | 1.35 | 4.00 | 8.00 |
| 171-175: 174,175-Elektra app. | .70 | 2.00 | 4.00 |
| 176-180-Elektra app. 179-Anti-smoking issue mentioned in the Congressional Record | .50 | 1.50 | 3.00 |
| 181-Double size; death of Elektra; Punisher cameo out of costume | .60 | 1.75 | 3.50 |
| 182-184-Punisher app. by Miller | 1.35 | 4.00 | 8.00 |
| 185-191: 187-New Black Widow. 189-Death of Stick. 190-Double size; Elektra returns, part origin. 191-Last Miller Daredevil | .25 | .75 | 1.50 |
| 192-195,197-210: 208-Harlan Ellison scripts | | .60 | 1.20 |
| 196-Wolverine app. | 1.15 | 3.50 | 7.00 |
| 211-225: 219-Miller scripts | | .50 | 1.00 |
| 226-Frank Miller plots begin | .25 | .75 | 1.50 |
| 227-Miller scripts begin | .70 | 2.00 | 4.00 |
| 228-233-Last Miller scripts | .35 | 1.00 | 2.00 |
| 234-237,239,240,242-247 | | .50 | 1.00 |
| 238-Mutant Massacre | .35 | 1.00 | 2.00 |
| 241-Todd McFarlane-a(p) | .50 | 1.50 | 3.00 |
| 248,249-Wolverine app. | .70 | 2.00 | 4.00 |
| 250,251,253,255,256,258,259 | | .50 | 1.00 |
| 252-Double size, 52 pgs. Fall of the Mutants | .40 | 1.25 | 2.50 |
| 254-Origin Typhoid Mary | .85 | 2.50 | 5.00 |
| 257-Punisher app. | .70 | 2.00 | 4.00 |

Good Fine N-Mint

260-Double size .35 1.00 2.00

261-292: 272-Intro Shotgun (villain). 282-Silver Surfer app. (cameo in #281). 283-Capt. America app. .50 1.00

Special 1(9/67, 25 cents, 68 pgs.)-new art 2.15 6.50 15.00

Special 2,3: 2(2/71, 25 cents, 52 pgs.)-Entire book has Powell/Wood-r; Wood-c. 3(1/72)-reprints 1.15 3.50 8.00

Annual 4(10/76) .70 2.00 4.00

Annual 4(1989, $2.00, 68 pgs.)-Atlantis Attacks .40 1.25 2.50

Annual 6(1990, $2.00, 68 pgs.)-Sutton-a .35 1.00 2.00

NOTE: ***Art Adams** c-238p, 239. **Austin** a-191i; c-151i, 200i. **John Buscema** a-136, 137p, 234p, 235p; c-86p, 136i, 137p, 142, 219. **Byrne** c-200p, 201, 203, 223. **Colan** a(p)-20-49, 53-82, 84-98, 100, 110, 112, 124, 153, 154, 156, 157, Spec. 1p; c(p)-20-42, 44-49, 53-60, 71, 92, 98, 138, 153, 154, 156, 157, Annual 1. **Craig** a-50i, 52i. **Ditko** a-162, 234p, 235p, 264p; c-162. **Everett** c/a-1; inks-21, 83. **Gil Kane** a-141p, 146-148p, 151p; c(p)-85, 90, 91, 93, 94, 115, 116, 119, 120, 125-128, 133, 139, 147, 152. **Kirby** c-2-4, 5p, 12p, 13p, 136p. **Layton** c-202. **Miller** scripts-168-182, 183(part), 184-191, 219, 227-233; a-158-161p, 163-184p, 191p; c-158-161p, 163-184p, 185-189, 190p, 191. **Orlando** a-2-4p. **Powell** a-9p, 11p, Special 1r, 2r. **B. Smith** a-83p, 236p. **Smith** c-51p, 52p. **Simonson** c-199. **Starlin** a-105p. **Steranko** c-44i. **Tuska** a-39i, 145p. **Williamson** a(i)-237, 239, 240, 243, 248-257, 259-282, 283(part), 284, 285, 287, 288; c(i)-237, 243, 244, 248-257, 259-263, 265-278, 280-288. **Wood** a-5-9i, 10, 11i, Spec. 2i; c-5i, 6-11, 164i.*

**DAREDEVIL AND THE PUNISHER** (Child's Play trade paperback)
1988 ($4.95, color, squarebound, one-shot; 2nd & 3rd printings exist)
Marvel Comics

1-r/Daredevil #182-184 by Miller 1.35 4.00 8.00

**DAREDEVIL COMICS** (See Silver Streak Comics)
July, 1941 - No. 134, Sept, 1956 (Charles Biro stories)
Lev Gleason Publications (Funnies, Inc. No. 1)

1-No. 1 titled "Daredevil Battles Hitler;" The Silver Streak, Lance Hale, Cloud Curtis, Dickey Dean, Pirate Prince team up w/Daredevil and battle Hitler; Daredevil battles the Claw; Origin of Hitler feature story. Hitler photo app. on-c

| Good | Fine | VF-NM | NM/Mint |
|---|---|---|---|
| 335.00 | 835.00 | 2000.00 | 2600.00 |

(Estimated up to 215 total copies exist, 12 in NM/Mint)

2-London, Pat Patriot, Nightro, Real American No. 1, Dickie Dean, Pirate Prince, & Times Square begin; intro. & only app. The Pioneer, Champion of America

Good Fine N-Mint

143.00 430.00 1000.00

3-Origin of 13 85.00 260.00 600.00

4 71.00 215.00 500.00

5-Intro. Sniffer & Jinx; Ghost vs. Claw begins by Bob Wood, ends #20 65.00 195.00 450.00

6-(#7 on indicia) 54.00 160.00 375.00

7-10: 8-Nightro ends 45.00 140.00 325.00

11-London, Pat Patriot end; bondage/torture-c 41.00 125.00 290.00

12-Origin of The Claw; Scoop Scuttle by Wolverton begins (2-4 pgs.), ends #22, not in #21 63.00 190.00 440.00

13-Intro. of Little Wise Guys 63.00 190.00 440.00

14 32.00 95.00 225.00

15-Death of Meatball 48.00 145.00 335.00

16,17 29.00 85.00 200.00

18-New origin of Daredevil-Not same as Silver Streak #6 63.00 190.00 440.00

19,20 25.00 75.00 175.00

21-Reprints cover of Silver Streak #6(on inside) plus intro. of The Claw from Silver Streak #1 38.00 115.00 265.00

22-30 16.00 48.00 110.00

31-Death of The Claw 29.00 85.00 200.00

32-37: 35-Two Daredevil stories begin, end #68 (35-40 are 64 pgs.) 11.00 32.00 75.00

38-Origin Daredevil retold from #18 22.00 65.00 150.00

39,40 11.00 32.00 75.00

41-50: 42-Intro. Kilroy in Daredevil 7.00 21.00 50.00

51-69-Last Daredevil issue (12/50) 5.00 15.00 35.00

Good Fine N-Mint

70-Little Wise Guys take over book; McWilliams-a; Hot Rock Flanagan begins, ends #80 2.85 8.50 20.00

71-79,81: 79-Daredevil returns 2.15 6.50 15.00

80-Daredevil x-over 2.30 7.00 16.00

82,90-One page Frazetta ad in both 2.30 7.00 16.00

83-89,91-99,101-134 1.70 5.00 12.00

100 3.00 9.00 21.00

NOTE: ***Wolverton's** Scoop Scuttle-12-20, 22. **Biro** c/a-all?. **Bolle** a-125. **Maurer** a-75. **McWilliams** a-73, 75, 79, 80.*

**DARING ADVENTURES** (Also see Approved Comics)
Nov, 1953 (3-D)
St. John Publishing Co.

1 (3-D)-Reprints lead story/Son of Sinbad #1 by Kubert 21.50 65.00 150.00

**DARING ADVENTURES**
1963 - 1964
I.W. Enterprises/Super Comics

I.W. Reprint #9-Disbrow-a(3) 2.00 6.00 14.00

Super Reprint #10,11('63)-r/Dynamic #24,16; 11-Marijuana story; Yankee Boy app. 1.15 3.50 8.00

Super Reprint #12('64)-Phantom Lady from Fox(r/#14,15) 8.00 24.00 56.00

Super Reprint #15('64)-Hooded Menace 5.00 15.00 35.00

Super Reprint #16('64)-r/Dynamic #12 1.00 3.00 7.00

Super Reprint #17('64)-Green Lama by Raboy from Green Lama #3 2.00 6.00 14.00

Super Reprint #18-Origin Atlas 1.00 3.00 7.00

**DARING COMICS** (Formerly Daring Mystery) (Jeanie No. 13 on)
No. 9, Fall, 1944 - No. 12, Fall, 1945
Timely Comics (HPC)

9-Human Torch & Sub-Mariner begin 41.00 122.00 285.00

10-The Angel only app. 35.00 105.00 245.00

11,12-The Destroyer app. 35.00 105.00 245.00

NOTE: ***Schomburg** c-9-11.*

**DARING CONFESSIONS** (Formerly Youthful Hearts)
No. 4, 11/52 - No. 7, 5/53; No. 8, 10/53
Youthful Magazines

4-Doug Wildey-a 4.50 14.00 32.00

5-8: 6,8-Wildey-a 3.00 9.00 21.00

**DARING LOVE** (Radiant Love No. 2 on)
Sept-Oct, 1953
Gilmor Magazines

1 3.00 9.00 21.00

**DARING LOVE** (Formerly Youthful Romances)
No. 15, 12/52; No. 16, 2/53-c, 4/53-Indicia; No. 17-4/53-c & indicia
Ribage/Pix

15 3.70 11.00 26.00

16,17: 17-Photo-c 3.00 9.00 21.00

NOTE: ***Colletta** a-15. **Wildey** a-17.*

**DARING LOVE STORIES** (See Fox Giants)

**DARING MYSTERY COMICS** (Comedy Comics No. 9 on; title changed to Daring Comics with No. 9)
1/40 - No. 5, 6/40; No. 6, 9/40; No. 7, 4/41 - No. 8, 1/42
Timely Comics (TPI 1-6/TCI 7,8)

1-Origin The Fiery Mask by Joe Simon; Monako, Prince of Magic, John Steele, Soldier of Fortune, Doc Doyle begin; Flash Foster & Barney Mullen, Sea Rover only app; bondage-c

| Good | Fine | VF-NM | NM/Mint |
|---|---|---|---|
| 670.00 | 1670.00 | 4000.00 | 5200.00 |

(Estimated up to 125 total copies exist, 5 in NM/Mint)

2-(Rare)-Origin The Phantom Bullet & only app.; The Laughing Mask

*Daredevil Special #1, © MEG*

*Daredevil Comics #3, © LEV*

*Daredevil Comics #32, © LEV*

*Daring Mystery Comics #3, © MEG*

*Dark Mysteries #3, © Merit Publ.*

*Dark Shadows #3, © AJAX*

| | Good | Fine | N-Mint |
|---|---|---|---|
| & Mr. E only app.; Trojak the Tiger Man begins, ends #6; Zephyr Jones & K-4 & His Sky Devils app., also #4 | 335.00 | 835.00 | 2000.00 |
| 3-The Phantom Reporter, Dale of FBI, Breeze Barton, Captain Strong & Marvex the Super-Robot only app.; The Purple Mask begins | 235.00 | 585.00 | 1400.00 |
| 4-Last Purple Mask; Whirlwind Carter begins; Dan Gorman, G-Man app. | 150.00 | 375.00 | 900.00 |
| 5-The Falcon begins; The Fiery Mask, Little Hercules app. by Sagendorf in the Segar style; bondage-c | 150.00 | 375.00 | 900.00 |
| 6-Origin & only app. Marvel Boy by S&K; Flying Flame, Dynaman, & Stuporman only app.; The Fiery Mask by S&K; S&K-c | 191.00 | 480.00 | 1150.00 |
| 7-Origin The Blue Diamond, Captain Daring by S&K, The Fin by Everett, The Challenger, The Silver Scorpion & The Thunderer by Burgos; Mr. Millions app. | 170.00 | 415.00 | 1000.00 |
| 8-Origin Citizen V; Last Fin, Silver Scorpion, Capt. Daring by Borth, Blue Diamond & The Thunderer; S&K-c; Rudy the Robot only app. | 140.00 | 355.00 | 850.00 |

NOTE: ***Schomburg*** *c-1-4, 7.* ***Simon*** *a-2, 3, 5.*

**DARING NEW ADVENTURES OF SUPERGIRL, THE**
Nov, 1982 - No. 13, Nov, 1983 (Supergirl No. 14-on)
DC Comics

| | Good | Fine | N-Mint |
|---|---|---|---|
| 1-Origin retold; Lois Lane back-ups in #2-12 | | .40 | .80 |
| 2-13: 8,9-Doom Patrol app. 13-New costume; flag-c | | .25 | .50 |

NOTE: ***Buckler*** *c-1p, 2p.* ***Giffen*** *c-3p, 4p.* ***Gil Kane*** *c-6, 8, 9, 11-13.*

**DARK CRYSTAL, THE**
April, 1983 - No. 2, May, 1983
Marvel Comics Group

| | Good | Fine | N-Mint |
|---|---|---|---|
| 1,2-Movie adaptation, part 1&2 | | .25 | .50 |

**DARKEWOOD**
1987 - No. 5, 1988 ($2.00, color, 28 pgs., mini-series)
Aircel Publishing

| | Good | Fine | N-Mint |
|---|---|---|---|
| 1-5 | .35 | 1.00 | 2.00 |

**DARK HORSE PRESENTS**
July, 1986 - Present ($1.50, $1.75, $1.95, B&W)
Dark Horse Comics

| | Good | Fine | N-Mint |
|---|---|---|---|
| 1-1st app. Concrete by Paul Chadwick | 2.50 | 7.50 | 15.00 |
| 1-2nd print | .50 | 1.50 | 3.00 |
| 2-Concrete app. | 1.70 | 5.00 | 10.00 |
| 3-Concrete app. | 1.35 | 4.00 | 8.00 |
| 4,5-Concrete app. | 1.00 | 3.00 | 6.00 |
| 6,8,10-Concrete app. | .75 | 2.25 | 4.50 |
| 7,9 | .60 | 1.75 | 3.50 |
| 11-19,21-23: 12,14,16,18,22-Concrete app. | .40 | 1.25 | 2.50 |
| 20-($2.95, 68 pgs.)-Concrete & Flaming Carrot | .70 | 2.00 | 4.00 |
| 24-1st app. Aliens; Concrete, Mr. Monster app. | 4.15 | 12.50 | 25.00 |
| 25-31,33: 33-($2.25, 44 pgs.). 28-($2.95, 52 pgs.)-Concrete app. | .50 | 1.50 | 3.00 |
| 32-($3.50, 68 pgs.)-Annual; Concrete, American | .70 | 2.00 | 4.00 |
| 34-Aliens story | 1.70 | 5.00 | 10.00 |
| 35-Predator story; begin $1.95-c | 1.70 | 5.00 | 10.00 |
| 36-1st Aliens Vs. Predator story | 2.50 | 7.50 | 15.00 |
| 37-39,41,44,45: 38-Concrete. 44-Crash Ryan | .35 | 1.00 | 2.00 |
| 40-($2.95, 52 pgs.)-1st Argosy story | .50 | 1.50 | 3.00 |
| 42,43-Aliens-c/stories | .70 | 2.00 | 4.00 |
| 46-Prequel to new Predator mini-series | .50 | 1.50 | 3.00 |

**DARK KNIGHT** (See Batman: The Dark Knight Returns)

**DARKLON THE MYSTIC** (Also see Eerie Magazine #79, 80)
Oct, 1983 (One shot)
Pacific Comics

| | Good | Fine | N-Mint |
|---|---|---|---|
| 1-Starlin-c/a(r) | .35 | 1.00 | 2.00 |

**DARKMAN**
Sept, 1990; Oct, 1990 - No. 3, Nov, 1990 ($1.50, color, movie adapt.)
Marvel Comics

| | Good | Fine | N-Mint |
|---|---|---|---|
| 1 (9/90, $2.25, B&W mag., 68 pgs.) | .40 | 1.15 | 2.30 |
| 1-3: Reprints B&W magazine | .25 | .75 | 1.50 |

**DARK MANSION OF FORBIDDEN LOVE, THE** (Becomes Forbidden Tales of Dark Mansion No. 5 on)
Sept-Oct, 1971 - No. 4, Mar-Apr, 1972
National Periodical Publications

| | Good | Fine | N-Mint |
|---|---|---|---|
| 1 | .25 | .75 | 1.50 |
| 2-4: 2-Adams-c. 3-Jeff Jones-c | | .50 | 1.00 |

**DARK MYSTERIES**
June-July, 1951 - No. 25?, 1955
"Master"-"Merit" Publications

| | Good | Fine | N-Mint |
|---|---|---|---|
| 1-Wood-c/a, 8 pgs. | 30.00 | 90.00 | 210.00 |
| 2-Wood/Harrison-c/a, 8 pgs. | 24.00 | 70.00 | 165.00 |
| 3-9: 7-Dismemberment, hypo blood drainage stories | 8.50 | 25.50 | 60.00 |
| 10-Cannibalism story | 10.00 | 30.00 | 70.00 |
| 11-13,15-18: 11-Severed head panels. 13-Dismemberment-c/story | 7.00 | 21.00 | 50.00 |
| 14-Several E.C. Craig swipes | 8.00 | 24.00 | 55.00 |
| 19-Injury-to-eye panel | 10.00 | 30.00 | 70.00 |
| 20-Female bondage, blood drainage story | 8.50 | 25.50 | 60.00 |
| 21,22-Last pre-code issue, mis-dated 3/54 instead of 3/55 | 5.70 | 17.00 | 40.00 |
| 23-25 (#25-Exist?) | 4.00 | 12.00 | 28.00 |

NOTE: ***Cameron*** *a-1, 2.* ***Myron Fass*** *c/a-21.* ***Harrison*** *a-3, 7; c-3.* ***Hollingsworth*** *a-7-17, 20, 21, 23.* ***Wildey*** *a-5.* ***Woodish*** *art by* ***Fleishman****-9; c-10. Bondage-c, 10, 18, 19.*

**DARK SHADOWS**
October, 1957 - No. 3, May, 1958
Steinway Comic Publications (Ajax)(America's Best)

| | Good | Fine | N-Mint |
|---|---|---|---|
| 1 | 5.00 | 15.00 | 35.00 |
| 2,3 | 3.50 | 10.50 | 24.00 |

**DARK SHADOWS** (TV) (See Dan Curtis)
March, 1969 - No. 35, Feb, 1976 (Photo-c: 2-7)
Gold Key

| | Good | Fine | N-Mint |
|---|---|---|---|
| 1(30039-903)-With pull-out poster (25 cents) | 14.00 | 43.00 | 100.00 |
| 1-Without poster | 7.00 | 21.00 | 50.00 |
| 2 | 6.50 | 19.00 | 45.00 |
| 3-With pull-out poster | 8.50 | 25.50 | 60.00 |
| 3-Without poster | 5.70 | 17.00 | 40.00 |
| 4-7: Last photo-c | 5.70 | 17.00 | 40.00 |
| 8-10 | 4.00 | 12.00 | 28.00 |
| 11-20 | 3.00 | 9.00 | 21.00 |
| 21-35: 30-last painted-c | 2.15 | 6.50 | 15.00 |
| Story Digest 1 (6/70)-Photo-c | 3.15 | 9.50 | 22.00 |

**DARLING LOVE**
Oct-Nov, 1949 - No. 11, 1952 (no month) (52 pgs.)
Close Up/Archie Publ. (A Darling Magazine)

| | Good | Fine | N-Mint |
|---|---|---|---|
| 1-Photo-c | 5.70 | 17.00 | 40.00 |
| 2 | 3.15 | 9.50 | 22.00 |
| 3-8,10,11: 5,6-photo-c | 2.30 | 7.00 | 16.00 |
| 9-Krigstein-a | 3.70 | 11.00 | 26.00 |

**DARLING ROMANCE**
Sept-Oct, 1949 - No. 7, 1951 (All photo-c)
Close Up (MLJ Publications)

| | Good | Fine | N-Mint |
|---|---|---|---|
| 1-(52 pgs.)-Betty Page photo-c? | 5.70 | 17.00 | 40.00 |
| 2 | 3.15 | 9.50 | 22.00 |
| 3-7 | 2.30 | 7.00 | 16.00 |

**DASTARDLY & MUTTLEY IN THEIR FLYING MACHINES** (See Fun-In No. 1-4, 6)

**DASTARDLY & MUTTLEY KITE FUN BOOK** (Giveaway)
1969 (16 pages) (5x7", soft-c) (Hanna-Barbera's)
Florida Power & Light Co./Sou. Calif. Edison/Pacific Gas & Electric

| | Good | Fine | N-Mint |
|---|---|---|---|
| nn | 1.15 | 3.50 | 8.00 |

**DATE WITH DANGER**
No. 5, Dec, 1952 - No. 6, Feb, 1953
Standard Comics

| | | | |
|---|---|---|---|
| 5,6 | 3.00 | 9.00 | 21.00 |

**DATE WITH DEBBI** (Also see Debbi's Dates)
Jan-Feb, 1969 - No. 17, Sept-Oct, 1971; No. 18, Oct-Nov, 1972
National Periodical Publications

| | | | |
|---|---|---|---|
| 1 | 1.15 | 3.50 | 8.00 |
| 2-5 | .85 | 2.50 | 5.00 |
| 6-18 | .60 | 1.75 | 3.50 |

**DATE WITH JUDY, A** (Radio/TV, and 1948 movie)
Oct-Nov, 1947 - No. 79, Oct-Nov, 1960 (No. 1-25: 52 pgs.)
National Periodical Publications

| | | | |
|---|---|---|---|
| 1-Teenage | 13.00 | 40.00 | 90.00 |
| 2 | 6.50 | 19.00 | 45.00 |
| 3-10 | 4.50 | 14.00 | 32.00 |
| 11-20 | 2.85 | 8.50 | 20.00 |
| 21-40 | 2.15 | 6.50 | 15.00 |
| 41-45: 45-Last pre-code (2-3/55) | 1.70 | 5.00 | 12.00 |
| 46-79: 79-Drucker-c/a | 1.30 | 4.00 | 9.00 |

**DATE WITH MILLIE, A** (Life With Millie No. 8 on)
Oct, 1956 - No. 7, Aug, 1957; Oct, 1959 - No. 7, Oct, 1960
Atlas/Marvel Comics (MPC)

| | | | |
|---|---|---|---|
| 1(10/56)-(1st Series) | 8.50 | 25.50 | 60.00 |
| 2 | 4.30 | 13.00 | 30.00 |
| 3-7 | 3.50 | 10.50 | 24.00 |
| 1(10/59)-(2nd Series) | 5.00 | 15.00 | 35.00 |
| 2-7 | 2.65 | 8.00 | 18.00 |

**DATE WITH PATSY, A** (Also see Patsy Walker)
September, 1957
Atlas Comics

| | | | |
|---|---|---|---|
| 1-Starring Patsy Walker | 4.00 | 12.00 | 28.00 |

**DAVID AND GOLIATH** (See 4-Color No. 1205)

**DAVID CASSIDY** (TV?)(See Swing With Scooter #33)
Feb, 1972 - No. 14, Sept, 1973
Charlton Comics

| | | | |
|---|---|---|---|
| 1 | 1.00 | 3.00 | 6.00 |
| 2-14: 5,7,9,14-Photo-c | .70 | 2.00 | 4.00 |

**DAVID LADD'S LIFE STORY** (See Movie Classics)

**DAVY CROCKETT** (See Dell Giants, Fightin..., Frontier Fighters, It's Game Time, Power Record Comics, Western Tales & Wild Frontier)

**DAVY CROCKETT**
1951
Avon Periodicals

| | | | |
|---|---|---|---|
| nn-Tuska?, Reinman-a; Fawcette-c | 8.50 | 25.50 | 60.00 |

**DAVY CROCKETT** (...King of the Wild Frontier No. 1,2)(TV)
5/55 - No. 671, 12/55; No. 1, 12/63; No. 2, 11/69 (Walt Disney)
Dell Publishing Co./Gold Key

| | Good | Fine | N-Mint |
|---|---|---|---|
| 4-Color 631(#1)-Fess Parker photo-c | 4.30 | 13.00 | 30.00 |
| 4-Color 639-Photo-c | 4.00 | 12.00 | 28.00 |
| 4-Color 664,671(Marsh-a)-Photo-c | 4.50 | 14.00 | 32.00 |
| 1(12/63-Gold Key)-r; Fess Parker photo-c | 2.00 | 6.00 | 14.00 |
| 2(11/69)-r; Fess Parker photo-c | 1.15 | 3.50 | 8.00 |
| ..Christmas Book (no date, 16pgs, paper-c) Sears giveaway | 1.70 | 5.00 | 12.00 |
| ..In the Raid at Piney Creek (1955, 16pgs, 5x7¼")American Motors giveaway; slick, photo-c | 3.50 | 10.50 | 24.00 |
| ..Safety Trails (1955, 16pgs, 3¼x7") Cities Service giveaway | 3.00 | 9.00 | 21.00 |

**DAVY CROCKETT** (...Frontier Fighter #1,2; Kid Montana #9 on)
Aug, 1955 - No. 8, Jan, 1957
Charlton Comics

| | | | |
|---|---|---|---|
| 1 | 3.70 | 11.00 | 26.00 |
| 2 | 2.00 | 6.00 | 14.00 |
| 3-8 | 1.30 | 4.00 | 9.00 |
| Hunting With...('55, 16 pgs.)-Ben Franklin Store giveaway (Publ.-S. Rose) | 1.30 | 4.00 | 9.00 |

**DAYS OF THE MOB** (See In the Days of the Mob)

**DAZEY'S DIARY**
June-Aug, 1962
Dell Publishing Co.

| | | | |
|---|---|---|---|
| 01-174-208: Bill Woggon-c/a | 2.30 | 7.00 | 16.00 |

**DAZZLER, THE** (Also see Marvel Graphic Novel & X-Men #130)
March, 1981 - No. 42, Mar, 1986
Marvel Comics Group

| | | | |
|---|---|---|---|
| 1,2-X-Men app. | .35 | 1.00 | 2.00 |
| 3-37,39-42: 10,11-Galactus app. 21-Double size; photo-c. 42-The Beast app. | | .50 | 1.00 |
| 38-Wolverine-c/app.; X-Men app. | .70 | 2.00 | 4.00 |

NOTE: *No. 1 distributed only through comic shops.* ***Alcala*** *a-1i, 2i.* ***Chadwick*** *a-38-42p; c(p)-39, 41, 42.* ***Guice*** *a-38i, 42i; c-38, 40.*

**DC CHALLENGE**
Nov, 1985 - No. 12, Oct, 1986 ($1.25-$2.00; 12 issue maxi-series)
DC Comics

| | | | |
|---|---|---|---|
| 1-11: 1-Colan-a. 4-Gil Kane-c/a | .25 | .75 | 1.50 |
| 12($2.00)-Perez/Austin-c | .25 | .75 | 1.50 |

NOTE: *Batman app. in 1-4, 6-12. Joker app. in 7.* ***Giffen*** *c-11.* ***Swan/Austin*** *c-10.*

**DC COMICS PRESENTS**
July-Aug, 1978 - No. 97, Sept, 1986 (Superman team-ups in all)
DC Comics

| | | | |
|---|---|---|---|
| 1-12,14-25: 19-Batgirl | .25 | .75 | 1.50 |
| 13-Legion of Super Heroes (also in #43 & 80) | .40 | 1.25 | 2.50 |
| 26-(10/80)-Green Lantern; intro Cyborg, Starfire, Raven, New Teen Titans; Starlin-c/a; Sargon the Sorcerer back-up; 16 pgs. preview of the New Teen Titans | 1.15 | 3.50 | 7.00 |
| 27-40,42-71,73-76,79-84,86-97: 31,58-Robin. 35-Man-Bat. 52-Doom Patrol. 82-Adam Strange. 83-Batman & Outsiders. 86-88-Crisis x-over. 88-Creeper | .25 | .75 | 1.50 |
| 41-Superman/Joker-c/story | .50 | 1.50 | 3.00 |
| 72-Joker/Phantom Stranger-c/story | .50 | 1.50 | 3.00 |
| 77,78-Animal Man app. (77-cover app. also) | 1.00 | 3.00 | 6.00 |
| 85-Swamp Thing; Alan Moore scripts | .35 | 1.00 | 2.00 |
| Annual 1-4: 1(9/82)-G.A. Superman. 2(7/83)-Intro/origin Superwoman. 3(9/84)-Shazam. 4(10/85)-Superwoman | | .60 | 1.20 |

NOTE: ***Adkins*** *a-2, 54; c-2.* ***Gil Kane*** *a-28, 35, Annual 3; c-48p, 56, 58, 60, 62, 64, 68, Annual 2, 3.* ***Kirby*** *c/a-84.* ***Kubert*** *c/a-66.* ***Morrow*** *c/a-65.* ***Newton*** *c/a-54p.* ***Orlando*** *c-53i.* ***Perez*** *a-26p, 61p; c-38, 61, 94.* ***Starlin*** *a-26-29p, 36p, 37p; c-26-29, 36, 37, 93.* ***Toth*** *a-84.* ***Williamson*** *i-79, 85, 87.*

**DC GRAPHIC NOVEL** (Also see DC Science Fiction...)
Nov, 1983 - No. 7, 1986 ($5.95, 68 pgs.)
DC Comics

| | | | |
|---|---|---|---|
| 1-5,7: 1-Star Raiders. 2-Warlords; not from regular Warlord series. 3-The Medusa Chain; Ernie Colon story/a. 4-The Hunger Dogs; Kirby-c/a. 5-Me And Joe Priest. 7-Space Clusters | 1.00 | 3.00 | 6.00 |
| 6-Metalzoic | 1.20 | 3.50 | 7.00 |

**DC 100 PAGE SUPER SPECTACULAR**
(Title is 100 Page...No. 14 on)(Square bound) (Reprints, 50 cents)

*A Date With Patsy #1, © MEG*

*Davy Crockett #3, © CC*

*DC Comics Presents #77, © DC*

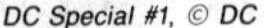
DC Special #1, © DC

DC Super-Stars #1, © DC

Dead-Eye Western Comics V2#6, © HILL

No. 4, 1971 - No. 13, 6/72; No. 14, 2/73 - No. 22, 11/73 (No #1-3)
National Periodical Publications

| | Good | Fine | N-Mint |
|---|---|---|---|
| 4,5: 4-Weird Mystery Tales; Johnny Peril & Phantom Stranger; cover & splashes by Wrightson; origin Jungle Boy of Jupiter. 5-Love Stories; Wood inks, 7pgs. | .35 | 1.00 | 2.00 |
| 6-"World's Greatest Super-Heroes"-JLA, JSA, Spectre, Johnny Quick, Vigilante, Wildcat & Hawkman; N. Adams wrap-around-c | .40 | 1.25 | 2.50 |
| 7-13: 7-(See Superman #245). 8-(See Batman #238). 9-(See Our Army at War #242). 10-(See Adventure #416). 11-(See Flash #214). 12-(See Superboy #185). 13-(See Superman #252) | | | |
| 14-Batman-r/Detective #31,32 | .85 | 2.50 | 5.00 |
| 15-22: 20-Batman-r/Det. #66,68 & others; origin Two-Face. 21-r/Brave & Bold #54. 22-r/All-Flash #13 | | .50 | 1.00 |

NOTE: ***Anderson** r-11, 14, 18i, 22. **B. Baily** r-18, 20. **Burnley** r-18, 20. **Crandall** r-14p, 20. **Drucker** r-4. **Infantino** r-17, 20, 22. **G. Kane** r-18. **Kubert** r-6, 7, 16, 17; c-16, 19. **Meskin** r-4, 22. **Mooney** r-15, 21. **Toth** r-17, 20.*

**DC SCIENCE FICTION GRAPHIC NOVEL**
1985 - No. 7, 1987 ($5.95)
DC Comics

| | Good | Fine | N-Mint |
|---|---|---|---|
| SF1-SF7: SF1-Hell on Earth by Robert Bloch. SF2-Nightwings by Robert Silverberg. SF3-Frost & Fire by Bradbury. SF4-Merchants of Venus. SF5-Demon With A Glass Hand by Ellison; M. Rogers-a. SF6-The Magic Goes Away by Niven. SF7-Sandkings by George R.R. Martin | 1.00 | 3.00 | 6.00 |

**DC SPECIAL** (Also see Super DC. . .)
10-12/68 - No. 15, 11-12/71; No. 16, Spr/75 - No. 29, 8-9/77
National Periodical Publications

| | Good | Fine | N-Mint |
|---|---|---|---|
| 1-All Infantino issue; Flash, Batman, Adam Strange-r (Begin 68 pg., 25 cent issues, ends ?) | .85 | 2.50 | 5.00 |
| 2-29: 5-All Kubert issue; Viking Prince, Sgt. Rock-r. 12-Viking Prince; Kubert-c/a. 15-G.A. Plastic Man origin r/Police #1; origin Woozy by Cole; Last 68 pg. issue. 16-Super Heroes Battle Super Gorillas. 22-Origin Robin Hood. 28-Earth Shattering Disaster Stories; Legion of Super-Heroes story. 29-Secret Origin of the Justice Society | .35 | 1.00 | 2.00 |

NOTE: ***N. Adams** c-3, 4, 6, 11, 29. **Grell** a-20; c-17. **Heath** a-12r. **G. Kane** a-6p, 13r, 17r, 19-21r. **Kubert** a-6r, 12r, 22. **Meskin** a-10. **Moreira** a-10. **Staton** a-29p. **Toth** a-13, 20r.*

**DC SPECIAL BLUE-RIBBON DIGEST**
Mar-Apr, 1980 - No. 24, Aug, 1982
DC Comics

| | Good | Fine | N-Mint |
|---|---|---|---|
| 1-24: All reprints? | | .50 | 1.00 |

NOTE: ***N. Adams** a-16(6)r, 17r, 23r; c-16. **Aparo** a-6r, 24r; c-23. **Grell** a-8, 10; c-10. **Heath** a-14. **Kaluta** a-17r. **Gil Kane** a-22r. **Kirby** a-23r. **Kubert** a-3, 18r, 21r; c-7, 12, 14, 17, 18, 21, 24. **Morrow** a-24r. **Orlando** a-17r, 22r; c-1, 20. **Perez** c-19p. **Toth** a-21r, 24r. **Wood** a-3, 17r, 24r. **Wrightson** a-16r, 17r, 24r.*

**DC SPECIAL SERIES**
9/77 - No. 16, Fall, 1978; No. 17, 8/79 - No. 27, Fall, 1981
(No. 23 & 24 - digest size; No. 25-27 - over-sized)
National Periodical Publications/DC Comics

| | Good | Fine | N-Mint |
|---|---|---|---|
| 1-Five-Star Super-Hero Spectacular; Atom, Flash, Green Lantern, Aquaman, Batman, Kobra app.; N. Adams-c; Staton, Nasser-a | .40 | 1.25 | 2.50 |
| 2(#1)-Original Swamp Thing Saga, The(1977)-r/Swamp Thing #1&2 by Wrightson; Wrightson wrap-around-c | .35 | 1.00 | 2.00 |
| 3-20,22-24: 6-Jones-a. 10-Origin Dr. Fate, Lightray & Black Canary. 14,17,20-Original Swamp Thing Saga; r/Swamp Thing #3-10 by Wrightson (52-68 pgs.); 22-G.I. Combat | .25 | .75 | 1.50 |
| 21-Miller-a (1st on Batman) | 2.00 | 6.00 | 12.00 |
| 25-($2.95, Sum, '81)-Superman II The Adventure Continues; photos from movie (Same as All-New Coll. Ed. C-64?) | .40 | 1.25 | 2.50 |
| 26-($2.95, Sum, '81)-Superman and His Incredible Fortress of Solitude (Same as All-New Co.. Ed. C-63?) | .40 | 1.25 | 2.50 |
| 27-($2.50)-Batman vs. The Incredible Hulk | .40 | 1.25 | 2.50 |

NOTE: ***Golden** a-15. **Heath** a-12i, 16. **Kubert** c-13. **Rogers** c/a-15. **Starlin** c-12.*

**DC SPOTLIGHT**
1985 (50th anniversary special)
DC Comics (giveaway)

| | Good | Fine | N-Mint |
|---|---|---|---|
| 1 | | .40 | .80 |

**DC SUPER-STARS**
March, 1976 - No. 18, Winter, 1978 (No.3-18: 52 pgs.)
National Periodical Publications/DC Comics

| | Good | Fine | N-Mint |
|---|---|---|---|
| 1-Re-intro Teen Titans (68 pgs.) | .25 | .75 | 1.50 |
| 2-9,11-16,18: 2-6,8-Adam Strange; 2-(68 pgs.). 8-r-1st Space Ranger/ Showcase #15. 13-Sergio Aragones Special | | .50 | 1.00 |
| 10-Batman/Joker-c/story | .70 | 2.00 | 4.00 |
| 17-Secret Origins of Super-Heroes(origin of The Huntress); origin Green Arrow by Grell; Legion app.; Earth II Batman & Catwoman marry (1st revealed; also see B&B #197) | | .60 | 1.20 |

NOTE: ***M. Anderson** r-2, 4, 6. **Aparo** c-7, 14, 17, 18. **Austin** a-11i. **Buckler** a-14p; c-10. **Grell** a-17. **G. Kane** a-1r, 10r. **Kubert** c-15. **Layton** c/a-16i, 17i. **Mooney** a-4r, 6r. **Morrow** c/a-11r. **Nasser** a-11. **Newton** c/a-16p. **Staton** a-17; c-17. No. 10, 12-18 contain all new material; the rest are reprints.*

**D-DAY** (Also see Special War Series)
Sum/63; No. 2, Fall/64; No. 4, 9/66; No. 5, 10/67; No. 6, 11/68
Charlton Comics (no No. 3)

| | Good | Fine | N-Mint |
|---|---|---|---|
| 1(1963)-Montes/Bache-c | 1.15 | 3.50 | 8.00 |
| 2(Fall,'64)-Wood-a(3) | 1.50 | 4.50 | 10.00 |
| 4-6('66-'68)-Montes/Bache-a #5 | .85 | 2.60 | 6.00 |

**DEAD END CRIME STORIES**
April, 1949 (52 pages)
Kirby Publishing Co.

| | Good | Fine | N-Mint |
|---|---|---|---|
| nn-(Scarce)-Powell, Roussos-a | 24.00 | 73.00 | 170.00 |

**DEAD-EYE WESTERN COMICS**
Nov-Dec, 1948 - V3#1, Apr-May, 1953
Hillman Periodicals

| | Good | Fine | N-Mint |
|---|---|---|---|
| V1#1-(52 pgs.)-Krigstein, Roussos-a | 7.00 | 21.00 | 50.00 |
| V1#2,3-(52 pgs.) | 3.70 | 11.00 | 26.00 |
| V1#4-12 | 2.30 | 7.00 | 16.00 |
| V2#1,2,5-8,10-12: 6,7-(52 pgs.) | 1.70 | 5.00 | 12.00 |
| 3,4-Krigstein-a (52 pgs.) | 3.50 | 10.50 | 24.00 |
| 9-One pg. Frazetta ad | 1.70 | 5.00 | 12.00 |
| V3#1 | 1.50 | 4.50 | 10.00 |

NOTE: ***Briefer** a-V1#8. Kinstleresque stories by **McCann**-12, V2#1, 2, V3#1.*

**DEADLIEST HEROES OF KUNG FU**
Summer, 1975 (Magazine)
Marvel Comics Group

| | Good | Fine | N-Mint |
|---|---|---|---|
| 1 | .30 | .90 | 1.80 |

**DEADLY HANDS OF KUNG FU, THE** (See Master of Kung Fu)
April, 1974 - No. 33, Feb, 1977 (75 cents) (B&W - Magazine)
Marvel Comics Group

| | Good | Fine | N-Mint |
|---|---|---|---|
| 1(V1#4 listed in error)-Origin Sons of the Tiger; Shang-Chi, Master of Kung Fu begins; Bruce Lee photo pin-up | .40 | 1.25 | 2.50 |
| 2,3,5 | .30 | .90 | 1.80 |
| 4-Bruce Lee painted-c by Neal Adams; 8 pg. biog of Bruce Lee | .40 | 1.25 | 2.50 |
| 6-15: 15-(Annual 1, Summer '75) | .30 | .90 | 1.80 |
| 16-19,21-27,29-33: 17-1st Giffen-a (1 pg.; 11/75). 19-1st White Tiger. 22-1st Giffen story-a | | .60 | 1.20 |
| 20-Origin The White Tiger; Perez-a | .30 | .90 | 1.80 |
| 28-Origin Jack of Hearts; Bruce Lee life story | .40 | 1.25 | 2.50 |
| Special Album Edition 1(Summer, '74)-Adams-i | .30 | .90 | 1.80 |

NOTE: ***N. Adams** c-1, 2-4, 11, 12, 14, 17. **Giffen** a-22p, 24p. **G. Kane** a-23p. **Kirby** a-5r. **Perez** a(p)-6-14, 16, 17, 19, 21. **Rogers** a-32, 33. **Starlin** a-1, 2r, 15r. **Staton** a-28p, 31, 32. Sons of the Tiger in 1, 3, 4, 6-14, 16-19.*

**DEADMAN** (See The Brave and the Bold & Phantom Stranger #39)
May, 1985 - No. 7, Nov, 1985 ($1.75, Baxter paper)

DC Comics

| | Good | Fine | N-Mint |
|---|---|---|---|
| 1-Deadman-r by Infantino, N. Adams in all | .30 | .90 | 1.80 |
| 2-7: 5-Batman-c/story-r/Str. Advs. 7-Batman-r | .30 | .90 | 1.80 |

**DEADMAN**
Mar, 1986 - No. 4, June, 1986 (75 cents, mini-series)
DC Comics

| | Good | Fine | N-Mint |
|---|---|---|---|
| 1-4: Lopez-c/a. 4-Byrne-c(p) | | .40 | .80 |

**DEADMAN: LOVE AFTER DEATH**
1989 - No. 2, 1990 ($3.95, 2 issue series, mature readers, 52 pgs.)
DC Comics

| | Good | Fine | N-Mint |
|---|---|---|---|
| Book One, Two: 1-Contains nudity | .70 | 2.00 | 4.00 |

**DEAD OF NIGHT**
Dec, 1973 - No. 11, Aug, 1975
Marvel Comics Group

| | Good | Fine | N-Mint |
|---|---|---|---|
| 1-Horror reprints | | .60 | 1.20 |
| 2-11: 11-Intro Scarecrow; Kane/Wrightson-c | | .40 | .80 |

NOTE: ***Ditko** r-7, 10. **Everett** c-2. **Sinnott** r-1.*

**DEADSHOT** (See Detective Comics #518)
Nov, 1988 - No. 4, Feb, 1989 ($1.00, color, mini-series)
DC Comics

| | Good | Fine | N-Mint |
|---|---|---|---|
| 1-4: Deadshot is a Batman villain | | .50 | 1.00 |

**DEAD WHO WALK, THE** (Also see Strange Myst., Super-r #15,16)
1952 (One Shot)
Realistic Comics

| | Good | Fine | N-Mint |
|---|---|---|---|
| nn | 24.00 | 70.00 | 165.00 |

**DEADWOOD GULCH**
1931 (52 pages) (B&W)
Dell Publishing Co.

| | Good | Fine | N-Mint |
|---|---|---|---|
| nn-By Gordon Rogers | 8.50 | 25.50 | 60.00 |

**DEADWORLD** (Also see The Realm)
Dec, 1986 - Present ($1.50-$1.95, B&W, adults)($2.50 #15 on)
Arrow Comics/Caliber Comics

| | Good | Fine | N-Mint |
|---|---|---|---|
| 1 | 1.00 | 3.00 | 6.00 |
| 2 | .60 | 1.75 | 3.50 |
| 3,4 | .50 | 1.50 | 3.00 |
| 5-11: Graphic covers | .50 | 1.50 | 3.00 |
| 5-11: Tame covers | .35 | 1.00 | 2.00 |
| 12-18: Graphic covers | .40 | 1.25 | 2.50 |
| 12-18: Tame covers | .35 | 1.00 | 2.00 |

**DEAN MARTIN & JERRY LEWIS** (See Adventures of. . .)

**DEAR BEATRICE FAIRFAX**
No. 5, Nov, 1950 - No. 9, Sept, 1951 (Vern Greene art)
Best/Standard Comics(King Features)

| | Good | Fine | N-Mint |
|---|---|---|---|
| 5 | 3.50 | 10.50 | 24.00 |
| 6-9 | 2.00 | 6.00 | 14.00 |

NOTE: ***Schomburg** air brush c-5-9.*

**DEAR HEART** (Formerly Lonely Heart)
No. 15, July, 1956 - No. 16, Sept, 1956
Ajax

| | Good | Fine | N-Mint |
|---|---|---|---|
| 15,16 | 2.00 | 6.00 | 14.00 |

**DEAR LONELY HEART** (. . . Illustrated No. 1-6)
Mar, 1951; No. 2, Oct, 1951 - No. 8, Oct, 1952
Artful Publications

| | Good | Fine | N-Mint |
|---|---|---|---|
| 1 | 8.50 | 25.50 | 60.00 |
| 2 | 4.00 | 12.00 | 28.00 |
| 3-Matt Baker Jungle Girl story | 8.50 | 25.50 | 60.00 |
| 4-8 | 3.50 | 10.50 | 24.00 |

**DEAR LONELY HEARTS** (Lonely Heart #9 on)
Aug, 1953 - No. 8, Oct, 1954
Harwell Publ./Mystery Publ. Co. (Comic Media)

| | Good | Fine | N-Mint |
|---|---|---|---|
| 1 | 3.50 | 10.50 | 24.00 |
| 2-8 | 2.00 | 6.00 | 14.00 |

**DEARLY BELOVED**
Fall, 1952
Ziff-Davis Publishing Co.

| | Good | Fine | N-Mint |
|---|---|---|---|
| 1-Photo-c | 8.00 | 24.00 | 56.00 |

**DEAR NANCY PARKER**
June, 1963 - No. 2, Sept, 1963
Gold Key

| | Good | Fine | N-Mint |
|---|---|---|---|
| 1,2-Painted-c | 1.70 | 5.00 | 12.00 |

**DEATHLOK** (Also see Astonishing Tales #25)
July, 1990 - No. 4, Oct, 1990 ($3.95, limited series, 52 pgs.)
Marvel Comics

| | Good | Fine | N-Mint |
|---|---|---|---|
| 1-Guice-a(p) | .75 | 2.25 | 4.50 |
| 2-4: 2-Guice-a(p). 3,4-Denys Cowan-a, c-4 | .70 | 2.00 | 4.00 |

**DEATH OF CAPTAIN MARVEL** (See Marvel Graphic Novel #1)

**DEATH RATTLE** (Formerly an Underground)
V2#1, 10/85 - No. 18, 1988 ($1.95, Baxter)(Mature readers)
Kitchen Sink Press

| | Good | Fine | N-Mint |
|---|---|---|---|
| V2#1-18: 1-Corben-c. 2-Unpubbed Spirit story by Eisner. 5-Robot Woman-r by Wolverton. 6-B&W issues begin. 16-Wolverton Spacehawk-r | .35 | 1.00 | 2.00 |

**DEATH'S HEAD**
Dec, 1988 - No. 10, Dec, 1989 ($1.75, color)(Dragon's Claws spin-off)
Marvel Comics

| | Good | Fine | N-Mint |
|---|---|---|---|
| 1-10: 9-Simonson-c(p) | .30 | .90 | 1.80 |

**DEATH VALLEY**
Oct, 1953 - No. 6, Aug, 1954?
Comic Media

| | Good | Fine | N-Mint |
|---|---|---|---|
| 1-Old Scout; Morisi-a | 4.50 | 14.00 | 32.00 |
| 2 | 2.65 | 8.00 | 18.00 |
| 3-6: 3,5-Morisi-a. 5-Discount-a | 2.00 | 6.00 | 14.00 |

**DEATH VALLEY** (Becomes Frontier Scout, Daniel Boone No.10-13)
No. 7, 6/55 - No. 9, 10/55 (Cont. from Comic Media series)
Charlton Comics

| | Good | Fine | N-Mint |
|---|---|---|---|
| 7-9: 8-Wolverton-a (½ pg.) | 2.00 | 6.00 | 14.00 |

**DEBBIE DEAN, CAREER GIRL**
April, 1945 - No. 2, July, 1945
Civil Service Publ.

| | Good | Fine | N-Mint |
|---|---|---|---|
| 1,2-Newspaper reprints by Bert Whitman | 8.00 | 24.00 | 56.00 |

**DEBBI'S DATES** (Also see Date With Debbi)
Apr-May, 1969 - No. 11, Dec-Jan, 1970-71
National Periodical Publications

| | Good | Fine | N-Mint |
|---|---|---|---|
| 1 | 1.15 | 3.50 | 8.00 |
| 2-11: 4-Neal Adams text illo. | .70 | 2.00 | 4.00 |

**DEEP, THE** (Movie)
November, 1977
Marvel Comics Group

| | Good | Fine | N-Mint |
|---|---|---|---|
| 1-Infantino-c/a | | .50 | 1.00 |

**DEFENDERS, THE** (TV)
Sept-Nov, 1962 - No. 2, Feb-Apr, 1963
Dell Publishing Co.

| | Good | Fine | N-Mint |
|---|---|---|---|
| 12-176-211(#1), 12-176-304(#2) | 1.70 | 5.00 | 12.00 |

**DEFENDERS, THE** (Also see Giant-Size. . ., Marvel Feature & Marvel Treasury Edition; The New. . .#140-on)
Aug, 1972 - No. 152, Feb, 1986

*Dead of Night #1, © MEG*

*Deadworld #1, © Caliber Comics*

*Death Valley #4, © Comic Media*

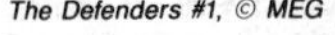


*The Defenders #1, © MEG*

*Dell Giant Comics #24, © Walter Lantz Prod.*

*Dell Giant Comics #55, © The Disney Co.*

Marvel Comics Group — Good / Fine / N-Mint

1-The Hulk, Doctor Strange, & Sub-Mariner begin — 3.60 / 11.00 / 25.00
2-9: 4-Valkyrie joins. 9,10-Avengers app. — 1.15 / 3.50 / 8.00
10-Thor battles Hulk — 1.50 / 4.50 / 10.00
11-25,30-50: 15,16-Magneto & Brotherhood of Evil Mutants app. from X-Men. 31,32-Origin Nighthawk. 35-Intro. New Red Guardian. 44-Hellcat joins. 45-Dr. Strange leaves — .50 / 1.50 / 3.00
26-29-Guardians of the Galaxy app. — .85 / 2.50 / 5.00
51-72,76-151: 53-1st app. Lunatik in cameo(Lobo lookalike). 55-Origin Red Guardian; Lunatik cameo. 56-1st full Lunatik story. 61-Lunatik & Spider-Man app. 70-73-Lunatik app.(origin #71). 77-Origin Omega. 78-Original Defenders return thru #101. 96-Ghost Rider app. 100-Double size. 104-The Beast joins. 106-Death of Nighthawk. 125-Double size; 1st app. Mad Dog; intro. new Defenders. 129-New Mutants cameo. 150-Dbl. size; origin Cloud — .25 / .75 / 1.50
73-75-Foolkiller II app. (Greg Salinger). 74-Nighthawk resigns — .70 / 2.00 / 4.00
152-Double size; ties in with X-Factor & Secret Wars II — .35 / 1.00 / 2.00
Annual 1 (11/76, 52 pgs.)-All new-a — .50 / 1.50 / 3.00

NOTE: ***Art Adams** c-142p. **Austin** a-53i; c-65i, 119i, 145i. **Frank Bolle** a-7i, 10i, 11i. **Buckler** c(p)-34, 38, 76, 77, 79-86, 90, 91. **J. Buscema** c-66. **Giffen** a-42-49p, 50, 51-54p. **Golden** a-53p, 54p; c-94, 96. **Guice** c-129. **G. Kane** c(p)-13, 16, 18, 19, 21-26, 31-33, 35-37, 40, 41, 52, 55. **Kirby** c-42-45. **Mooney** a-3i, 31-34i, 62i, 63i, 85i. **Nasser** c-88p. **Perez** c(p)-51, 53, 54. **Rogers** c-98. **Starlin** c-110. **Tuska** a-57p. Silver Surfer in No. 2, 3, 6, 8-11, 92, 98-101, 107, 112-115, 122-125.*

**DEFENDERS OF THE EARTH** (TV)
Jan, 1987 - No. 5, Sept, 1987
Star Comics (Marvel)

1-5: The Phantom, Mandrake The Magician, Flash Gordon begin — .40 / .80

**THE DEFINITIVE DIRECTORY OF THE DC UNIVERSE** (See Who's Who. . .)

**DELECTA OF THE PLANETS** (See Don Fortune & Fawcett Miniatures)

**DELLA VISION** (Patty Powers #4 on)
April, 1955 - No. 3, Aug, 1955
Atlas Comics

1 — 7.00 / 21.00 / 50.00
2,3 — 5.00 / 15.00 / 35.00

**DELL GIANT COMICS**
No. 21, Sept, 1959 - No. 55, Sept, 1961 (Most 84 pages, 25 cents)
Dell Publishing Co.

21-M.G.M.'s Tom & Jerry Picnic Time (84pp, stapled binding) — 5.00 / 15.00 / 35.00
22-Huey, Dewey & Louie Back to School(10/59, 84pp, square binding begins) — 3.50 / 14.00 / 35.00
23-Marge's Little Lulu & Tubby Halloween Fun (10/59)-Tripp-a — 7.00 / 28.00 / 70.00
24-Woody Woodpecker's Family Fun (11/59) — 3.00 / 12.00 / 30.00
25-Tarzan's Jungle World(11/59)-Marsh-a — 5.00 / 20.00 / 50.00
26-Christmas Parade-Barks-a, 16pgs.(Disney; 12/59)-Barks draws himself on wanted poster pg. 13 — 8.00 / 32.00 / 80.00
27-Man in Space r-/4-Color 716,866, & 954 (100 pages, 35 cents) (Disney)(TV) — 3.50 / 14.00 / 35.00
28-Bugs Bunny's Winter Fun (2/60) — 3.00 / 12.00 / 30.00
29-Marge's Little Lulu & Tubby in Hawaii (4/60)-Tripp-a — 7.00 / 28.00 / 70.00
30-Disneyland USA(6/60)-Reprinted in Vacation in Disneyland — 4.50 / 18.00 / 45.00
31-Huckleberry Hound Summer Fun (7/60)(TV) — 7.00 / 28.00 / 70.00
32-Bugs Bunny Beach Party — 2.50 / 10.00 / 25.00
33-Daisy Duck & Uncle Scrooge Picnic Time (9/60) — 4.00 / 16.00 / 40.00
34-Nancy & Sluggo Summer Camp (8/60) — 3.00 / 12.00 / 30.00

Good / Fine / N-Mint

35-Huey, Dewey & Louie Back to School (10/60) — 3.50 / 14.00 / 35.00
36-Marge's Little Lulu & Witch Hazel Halloween Fun(10/60)-Tripp-a — 7.00 / 28.00 / 70.00
37-Tarzan, King of the Jungle(11/60)-Marsh-a — 4.50 / 18.00 / 45.00
38-Uncle Donald & His Nephews Family Fun (11/60) — 3.50 / 14.00 / 35.00
39-Walt Disney's Merry Christmas(12/60) — 3.50 / 14.00 / 35.00
40-Woody Woodpecker Christmas Parade(12/60) — 2.50 / 10.00 / 25.00
41-Yogi Bear's Winter Sports (12/60)(TV) — 5.50 / 22.00 / 55.00
42-Marge's Little Lulu & Tubby in Australia (4/61) — 7.00 / 28.00 / 70.00
43-Mighty Mouse in Outer Space (5/61) — 8.00 / 32.00 / 80.00
44-Around the World with Huckleberry & His Friends (7/61)(TV) — 6.00 / 24.00 / 60.00
45-Nancy & Sluggo Summer Camp (8/61) — 3.00 / 12.00 / 30.00
46-Bugs Bunny Beach Party (8/61) — 2.50 / 10.00 / 25.00
47-Mickey & Donald in Vacationland (8/61) — 3.50 / 14.00 / 35.00
48-The Flintstones (No. 1)(Bedrock Bedlam)(7/61)(TV) — 8.00 / 32.00 / 80.00
49-Huey, Dewey & Louie Back to School (9/61) — 3.50 / 14.00 / 35.00
50-Marge's Little Lulu & Witch Hazel Trick 'N' Treat (10/61) — 7.00 / 28.00 / 70.00
51-Tarzan, King of the Jungle by Jesse Marsh (11/61) — 4.50 / 18.00 / 45.00
52-Uncle Donald & His Nephews Dude Ranch (11/61) — 3.50 / 14.00 / 35.00
53-Donald Duck Merry Christmas(12/61)-Not by Barks — 3.50 / 14.00 / 35.00
54-Woody Woodpecker Christmas Party(12/61)-issued after No. 55 — 2.50 / 10.00 / 25.00
55-Daisy Duck & Uncle Scrooge Showboat (9/61)-1st app. Daisy Duck's nieces, April, May & June — 5.00 / 20.00 / 50.00

NOTE: *All issues printed with & without ad on back cover.*

### (OTHER DELL GIANT EDITIONS)

**Abraham Lincoln Life Story** 1(3/58, 100p) — 3.00 / 12.00 / 30.00
**Bugs Bunny Christmas Funnies** 1(11/50, 116p) — 8.00 / 32.00 / 80.00
. . .**Christmas Funnies** 2(11/51, 116p) — 5.00 / 20.00 / 50.00
. . .**Christmas Funnies** 3-5(11/52-11/54, 100p)-Becomes Christmas Party No. 6 — 3.50 / 14.00 / 35.00
. . .**Christmas Funnies** 7-9(12/56-12/58, 100p) — 3.00 / 12.00 / 30.00
. . .**Christmas Party** 6(11/55, 100p)-Formerly Bugs Bunny Christmas Funnies #5 — 3.50 / 14.00 / 35.00
. . .**County Fair** 1(9/57, 100p) — 3.50 / 14.00 / 35.00
. . .**Halloween Parade** 1(10/53, 100p) — 6.00 / 24.00 / 60.00
. . .**Halloween Parade** 2(10/54, 100p)-Trick 'N' Treat Halloween Fun No. 3-on — 5.00 / 20.00 / 50.00
. . .**Trick 'N' Treat Halloween Fun** 3,4(10/55-10/56, 100p)-Formerly Halloween Parade #2 — 4.00 / 16.00 / 40.00
. . .**Vacation Funnies** 1(7/51, 112p) — 8.00 / 32.00 / 80.00
. . .**Vacation Funnies** 2('52, 100p) — 5.00 / 20.00 / 50.00
. . .**Vacation Funnies** 3-5('53-'55, 100p) — 3.50 / 14.00 / 35.00
. . .**Vacation Funnies** 6-9('54-6/59, 100p) — 3.00 / 12.00 / 30.00
**Cadet Gray of West Point** 1(4/58, 100p)-Williamson-a, 10pgs.; Buscema-a, photo-c — 4.00 / 16.00 / 40.00
**Christmas In Disneyland** 1(12/57, 100p)-Barks-a, 18pgs. — 8.00 / 32.00 / 80.00
**Christmas Parade** 1(11/49)-Barks-a, 25pgs; r-in G.K. Christmas Parade #5 — 33.00 / 130.00 / 325.00
**Christmas Parade** 2('50)-Barks-a, 25pgs; r-in G.K. Christmas Parade #6 — 19.00 / 76.00 / 190.00
**Christmas Parade** 3-7('51-'55, 116-100p) — 4.00 / 16.00 / 40.00
**Christmas Parade** 8(12/56, 100p)-Barks-a, 8pgs.

Good Fine N-Mint

8.00 32.00 80.00

**Christmas Parade** 9(12/58, 100p)-Barks-a, 20pgs. 10.00 40.00 100.00

**Christmas Treasury, A** 1(11/54, 100p) 5.00 20.00 50.00

**Davy Crockett, King Of The Wild Frontier** 1(9/55, 100p)-Photo-c; Marsh-a 11.00 44.00 110.00

**Disneyland Birthday Party** 1(10/58, 100p)-Barks-a, 16pgs. 7.00 28.00 70.00

**Donald and Mickey In Disneyland** 1(5/58, 100p) 3.50 14.00 35.00

**Donald Duck Beach Party** 1(7/54, 100p) 6.00 24.00 60.00

...**Beach Party** 2('55, 100p) 4.00 16.00 40.00

...**Beach Party** 3-5('56-'58, 100p) 3.50 14.00 35.00

...**Beach Party** 6(8/59, 84p)-Stapled 2.50 10.00 25.00

**Donald Duck Fun Book** 1,2('53-10/54, 100p)-Games, puzzles, comics & cut-outs (Rare) 14.00 56.00 140.00

**Donald Duck In Disneyland** 1(9/55, 100p) 3.50 14.00 35.00

**Golden West Rodeo Treasury** 1(10/57, 100p) 4.50 18.00 45.00

**Huey, Dewey and Louie Back To School** 1(9/58, 100p) 4.00 16.00 40.00

**Lady and The Tramp** 1(6/55, 100p) 5.00 20.00 50.00

**Life Stories of American Presidents** 1(11/57, 100p)-Buscema-a 3.00 12.00 30.00

**Lone Ranger Golden West** 3(8/55, 100p)-Formerly Lone Ranger Western Treasury 7.50 30.00 75.00

**Lone Ranger Movie Story** nn(3/56, 100p)-Origin Lone Ranger in text; Clayton Moore photo-c 18.00 72.00 180.00

...**Western Treasury** 1(9/53, 100p)-Origin Lone Ranger, Silver, & Tonto 12.50 50.00 125.00

...**Western Treasury** 2(8/54, 100p)-Becomes Lone Ranger Golden West #3 7.00 28.00 70.00

**Marge's Little Lulu & Alvin Story Telling Time** 1(3/59)-r/#2,5,3,11, 30,10,21,17,8,14,16; Stanley-a 8.00 32.00 80.00

...**& Her Friends** 4(3/56, 100p)-Tripp-a 6.50 26.00 65.00

...**& Her Special Friends** 3(3/55, 100p)-Tripp-a 6.50 26.00 65.00

...**& Tubby At Summer Camp** 5(10/57, 100p)-Tripp-a 6.50 26.00 65.00

...**& Tubby At Summer Camp** 2(10/58, 100p)-Tripp-a 6.50 26.00 65.00

...**& Tubby Halloween Fun** 6(10/57, 100p)-Tripp-a 6.50 26.00 65.00

...**& Tubby Halloween Fun** 2(10/58, 100p)-Tripp-a 7.00 30.00 75.00

...**& Tubby In Alaska** 1(7/59, 100p)-Tripp-a 7.00 30.00 75.00

...**On Vacation** 1(7/54, 100p)-r/4C-110,14,4C-146,5,4C-97,4,4C-158,3,1; Stanley-a 11.00 44.00 110.00

...**& Tubby Annual** 1(3/53, 100p)-r/4C-165,4C-74,4C-146,4C-97,4C-158, 4C-139,4C-131; Stanley-a 16.00 64.00 160.00

...**& Tubby Annual** 2('54, 100p)-r/4C-139,6,4C-115,4C-74,5,4C-97,3, 4C-146,18; Stanley-a 14.00 56.00 140.00

**Marge's Tubby & His Clubhouse Pals** 1(10/56, 100p)-1st app. Gran'pa Feeb, written by Stanley; 1st app. Janie; Tripp-a 9.00 36.00 90.00

**Mickey Mouse Almanac** 1(12/57, 100p)-Barks-a, 8pgs. 10.00 40.00 100.00

...**Birthday Party** 1(9/53, 100p)-r-/entire 48pgs. of Gottfredson's "Mickey Mouse in Love Trouble" from WDC&S 36-39. Quality equal to original. Also reprints one story each from 4-Color 27, 29, & 181 plus 6 panels of highlights in the career of Mickey Mouse 15.00 60.00 150.00

...**Club Parade** 1(12/55, 100p)-R-/4-Color 16 with some art redrawn by Paul Murry & recolored with night scenes turned into day; quality much poorer than original 12.00 48.00 120.00

...**In Fantasy Land** 1(5/57, 100p) 6.00 24.00 60.00

...**In Frontier Land** 1(5/56, 100p)-Mickey Mouse Club issue

Good Fine N-Mint

6.00 24.00 60.00

...**Summer Fun** 1(8/58, 100p)-Mobile cut-outs on back-c; becomes Summer Fun #2 5.00 20.00 50.00

**Moses & The Ten Commandments** 1(8/57, 100p)-Not based on movie; Dell's adaptation; Sekowsky-a 3.00 12.00 30.00

**Nancy & Sluggo Travel Time** 1(9/58, 100p) 3.50 14.00 35.00

**Peter Pan Treasure Chest** 1(1/53, 212p)-Disney; contains movie adaptation plus other stories 30.00 120.00 300.00

**Picnic Party** 6,7(7/55-6/56, 100p)(Formerly Vacation Parade)-Uncle Scrooge, Mickey & Donald 3.50 14.00 35.00

**Picnic Party** 8(7/57, 100p)-Barks-a, 6pgs. 6.00 24.00 60.00

**Pogo Parade** 1(9/53, 100p)-Kelly-a(r-/Pogo from Animal Comics in this order: #11,13,21,14,27,16,23,9,18,15,17) 20.00 80.00 200.00

**Raggedy Ann & Andy** 1(2/55, 100p) 5.50 22.00 55.00

**Santa Claus Funnies** 1(11/52, 100p)-Dan Noonan -**A Christmas Carol** adaptation 5.00 20.00 50.00

**Silly Symphonies** 1(9/52, 100p)-r/Chicken Little, M. Mouse "The Brave Little Tailor," Mother Pluto, Three Little Pigs, Lady, Bucky Bug, Wise Little Hen, Little Hiawatha, Pedro, The Grasshopper & The Ants 11.00 44.00 110.00

**Silly Symphonies** 2(9/53, 100p)-r/M. Mouse-"The Sorcerer's Apprentice," Little Hiawatha, Peculiar Penguins, Lambert The Sheepish Lion, Pluto, Spotty Pig, The Golden Touch, Elmer Elephant, The Pelican & The Snipe 7.00 28.00 70.00

**Silly Symphonies** 3(2/54, 100p)-r/Mickey & The Beanstalk (4-Color #157), Little Minnehaha, Pablo, The Flying Gauchito, Pluto, & Bongo 6.50 26.00 65.00

**Silly Symphonies** 4(8/54, 100p)-r/Dumbo (4-Color 234), Morris The Midget Moose, The Country Cousin, Bongo, & Clara Cluck 5.50 22.00 55.00

**Silly Symphonies** 5(2/55, 100p)-r/Cinderella (4-Color 272), Bucky Bug, Pluto, Little Hiawatha, The 7 Dwarfs & Dumbo, Pinocchio 5.50 22.00 55.00

**Silly Symphonies** 6(8/55, 100p)-r/Pinocchio(WDC&S 63), The 7 Dwarfs & Thumper (WDC&S 45), M. Mouse-"Adventures With Robin Hood," Johnny Appleseed, Pluto & Peter Pan, & Bucky Bug; Cut-out on back-c 5.50 22.00 55.00

**Silly Symphonies** 7(2/57, 100p)-r/Reluctant Dragon (4-Color 13), Ugly Duckling, M. Mouse & Peter Pan, Jiminy Cricket, Peter & The Wolf, Brer Rabbit, Bucky Bug; Cut-out on back-c 6.00 24.00 60.00

**Silly Symphonies** 8(2/58, 100p)-r/Thumper Meets The 7 Dwarfs (4-Color 19), Jiminy Cricket, Niok, Brer Rabbit; Cut-out on back-c 5.00 20.00 50.00

**Silly Symphonies** 9(2/59, 100p)-r/Paul Bunyan, Humphrey Bear, Jiminy Cricket, The Social Lion, Goliath II; Cut-out on back-c 5.00 20.00 50.00

**Sleeping Beauty** 1(4/59, 100p) 9.00 36.00 90.00

**Summer Fun** 2(8/59, 100p)(Formerly Mickey Mouse...)-Barks-a(2), 24 pgs. 6.00 24.00 60.00

**Tales From The Tomb** (See Tales From The Tomb)

**Tarzan's Jungle Annual** 1(8/52, 100p) 6.50 26.00 65.00

...**Annual** 2(8/53, 100p) 5.50 22.00 55.00

...**Annual** 3-7('54-9/58, 100p)(two No. 5s)-Manning-a-No. 3,5-7; Marsh-a in No. 1-7 4.50 18.00 45.00

**Tom And Jerry Back To School** 1(9/56, 100p) 3.50 14.00 35.00

...**Picnic Time** 1(7/58, 100p) 3.00 12.00 30.00

...**Summer Fun** 1(7/54, 100p)-Droopy written by Barks 7.00 28.00 70.00

...**Summer Fun** 2-4(7/55-7/57, 100p) 3.00 12.00 30.00

...**Toy Fair** 1(6/58, 100p) 3.50 14.00 35.00

...**Winter Carnival** 1(12/52, 100p)-Droopy written by Barks 9.00 36.00 90.00

...**Winter Carnival** 2(12/53, 100p)-Droopy written by Barks 5.00 20.00 50.00

...**Winter Fun** 3(12/54, 100p) 3.50 14.00 35.00

...**Winter Fun** 4-7(12/55-11/58, 100p) 3.00 12.00 30.00

*Davy Crockett King... #1, © The Disney Co.*

*Lone Ranger Western Treasury #2, © L. Ranger*

*Mickey Mouse Summer Fun #1, © Disney Co.*

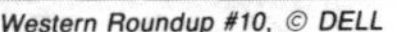
Western Roundup #10, © DELL

Dell Junior Treasury #8, © DELL

The Demon #1 (8-9/72), © DC

| | Good | Fine | N-Mint |
|---|---|---|---|
| **Treasury of Dogs, A** 1(10/56, 100p) | 2.50 | 10.00 | 25.00 |
| **Treasury of Horses, A** 1(9/55, 100p) | 2.50 | 10.00 | 25.00 |
| **Uncle Scrooge Goes To Disneyland** 1(8/57, 100p)-Barks-a, 20pgs. | 8.00 | 32.00 | 80.00 |
| **Universal Presents-Dracula-The Mummy & Other Stories** 02-530-311 (9-11/63, 84p)-R-/Dracula 12-231-212, The Mummy 12-437-211 & part of Ghost Stories No. 1 | 4.00 | 16.00 | 40.00 |
| **Vacation In Disneyland** 1(8/58, 100p) | 4.00 | 16.00 | 40.00 |
| **Vacation Parade** 1(7/50, 130p)-Donald Duck & Mickey Mouse; Barks-a, 55 pgs. | 50.00 | 200.00 | 500.00 |
| **Vacation Parade** 2(7/51, 100p) | 8.00 | 32.00 | 80.00 |
| **Vacation Parade** 3-5(7/52-7/54, 100p)-Picnic Party No. 6 on | 4.00 | 16.00 | 40.00 |
| **Western Roundup** 1(6/52, 100p)-Photo-c; Gene Autry, Roy Rogers, Johnny Mack Brown, Rex Allen, & Bill Elliott begin; photo back-c begin, end No. 14,16,18 | 11.00 | 44.00 | 110.00 |
| **Western Roundup** 2(2/53, 100p)-Photo-c | 7.00 | 28.00 | 70.00 |
| **Western Roundup** 3-5(7-9/53 - 1-3/54)-Photo-c | 6.00 | 24.00 | 60.00 |
| **Western Roundup** 6-10(4-6/54 - 4-6/55)-Photo-c | 5.50 | 22.00 | 55.00 |
| **Western Roundup** 11-13,16,17(100p)-Photo-c; Manning-a. 11-Flying A's Range Rider, Dale Evans begin | 4.50 | 18.00 | 45.00 |
| **Western Roundup** 14,15,25(1-3/59; 100p)-Photo-c | 4.50 | 18.00 | 45.00 |
| **Western Roundup** 18(100p)-Toth-a; last photo-c; Gene Autry ends | 5.00 | 20.00 | 50.00 |
| **Western Roundup** 19-24(100p)-Manning-a; 19-Buffalo Bill Jr. begins. 21-Rex Allen, Johnny Mack Brown end. 22-Jace Pearson's... Texas Rangers, Rin Tin Tin, Tales of Wells Fargo & Wagon Train begin | 4.00 | 16.00 | 40.00 |
| **Woody Woodpecker Back To School** 1(10/52, 100p) | 4.00 | 16.00 | 40.00 |
| **...Back To School** 2-4,6('53-10/57, 100p)-County Fair No. 5 | 2.50 | 10.00 | 25.00 |
| **...County Fair** 5(9/56, 100p)-Formerly Back To School | 2.50 | 10.00 | 25.00 |
| **...County Fair** 2(11/58, 100p) | 2.50 | 10.00 | 25.00 |

**DELL JUNIOR TREASURY** (15 cents)
June, 1955 - No. 10, Oct, 1957 (All painted-c)
Dell Publishing Co.

| | Good | Fine | N-Mint |
|---|---|---|---|
| 1-Alice in Wonderland; reprints 4-Color #331 (52 pgs.) | 7.00 | 21.00 | 50.00 |
| 2-Aladdin & the Wonderful Lamp | 5.00 | 15.00 | 35.00 |
| 3-Gulliver's Travels(1/56) | 3.70 | 11.00 | 26.00 |
| 4-Adventures of Mr. Frog & Miss Mouse | 4.50 | 14.00 | 32.00 |
| 5-The Wizard of Oz(7/56) | 5.00 | 15.00 | 35.00 |
| 6-Heidi (10/56) | 3.70 | 11.00 | 26.00 |
| 7-Santa and the Angel | 3.70 | 11.00 | 26.00 |
| 8-Raggedy Ann and the Camel with the Wrinkled Knees | 3.70 | 11.00 | 26.00 |
| 9-Clementina the Flying Pig | 4.00 | 12.00 | 28.00 |
| 10-Adventures of Tom Sawyer | 4.50 | 14.00 | 32.00 |

**DEMON, THE** (See Detective Comics No. 482-485)
Aug-Sept, 1972 - V3#16, Jan, 1974
National Periodical Publications

| | Good | Fine | N-Mint |
|---|---|---|---|
| 1-Origin; Kirby-c/a in 1-16 | .85 | 2.50 | 5.00 |
| 2-16 | .50 | 1.50 | 3.00 |

**DEMON, THE** (2nd series)
Jan, 1987 - No. 4, Apr, 1987 (75 cents)
DC Comics

| | Good | Fine | N-Mint |
|---|---|---|---|
| 1-4 (1987, mini-series); 2-Has #4 of 4 on-c | | .40 | .80 |

**DEMON, THE** (3rd series)
July, 1990 - Present ($1.50, color)
DC Comics

| | Good | Fine | N-Mint |
|---|---|---|---|
| 1: 1-4-Painted-c | .30 | .90 | 1.80 |
| 3-10: 3-Batman app. (cameo #4) | .25 | .75 | 1.50 |

**DEMON DREAMS**
Feb, 1984 - No. 2, May, 1984
Pacific Comics

| | Good | Fine | N-Mint |
|---|---|---|---|
| 1,2-Mostly r-/Heavy Metal | .25 | .75 | 1.50 |

**DEMON-HUNTER**
September, 1975
Seaboard Periodicals (Atlas)

| | Good | Fine | N-Mint |
|---|---|---|---|
| 1-Origin; Buckler-c/a | | .30 | .60 |

**DEMON KNIGHT: A GRIMJACK GRAPHIC NOVEL**
1990 ($8.95, color, 52 pgs.)
First Publishing

| | Good | Fine | N-Mint |
|---|---|---|---|
| nn-Flint Henry-a | 1.50 | 4.50 | 9.00 |

**DEN**
1988 - No. 10, Dec?, 1989 ($2.00, color)
Fantagor Press

| | Good | Fine | N-Mint |
|---|---|---|---|
| 1-10: Corben-c/a. 9,10-Alex Nino-a | .35 | 1.00 | 2.00 |

**DENNIS THE MENACE** (Becomes ...Fun Fest Series; See The Best of... & The Very Best of...)
8/53 - #14, 1/56; #15, 3/56 - #31, 11/58; #32, 1/59 - #166, 11/79
Standard Comics/Pines No.15-31/Hallden (Fawcett) No.32 on

| | Good | Fine | N-Mint |
|---|---|---|---|
| 1-1st app. Mr. & Mrs. Wilson, Ruff & Dennis' mom & dad; Wiseman-a, written by Fred Toole-most issues | 23.00 | 70.00 | 160.00 |
| 2 | 11.50 | 34.00 | 80.00 |
| 3-10 | 6.50 | 19.00 | 45.00 |
| 11-20 | 4.00 | 12.00 | 28.00 |
| 21-30: 22-1st app. Margaret w/blonde hair | 2.15 | 6.50 | 15.00 |
| 31-40: 31-1st app. Joey | 1.50 | 4.50 | 10.00 |
| 41-60 | 1.00 | 3.00 | 7.00 |
| 61-90 | .70 | 2.00 | 4.00 |
| 91-166 | .30 | 1.00 | 2.00 |
| ...& Dirt('59,'68)-Soil Conservation giveaway; r-No. 36; Wiseman-c/a | .35 | 1.00 | 2.00 |
| ...Away We Go('70)-Caladayl giveaway | .35 | 1.00 | 2.00 |
| ...Coping with Family Stress-giveaway | | .50 | 1.00 |
| ...Takes a Poke at Poison('61)-Food & Drug Assn. giveaway; Wiseman-c/a | .35 | 1.00 | 2.00 |
| ...Takes a Poke at Poison-Revised 1/66, 11/70, 1972, 1974, 1977, 1981 | | .50 | 1.00 |

NOTE: *Wiseman c/a-1-46, 53, 68, 69.*

**DENNIS THE MENACE** (Giants) (No. 1 titled Giant Vacation Special; becomes Dennis the Menace Bonus Magazine No. 76 on)
(#1-8,18,23,25,30,38: 100 pgs.; rest to #41: 84 pgs.; #42-75: 68 pgs.)
Summer, 1955 - No. 75, Dec, 1969
Standard/Pines/Hallden(Fawcett)

| | Good | Fine | N-Mint |
|---|---|---|---|
| nn-Giant Vacation Special(Summ/55-Standard) | 6.50 | 19.00 | 45.00 |
| nn-Christmas issue (Winter '55) | 5.00 | 15.00 | 35.00 |
| 2-Giant Vacation Special (Summer '56-Pines)<br>3-Giant Christmas issue (Winter '56-Pines)<br>4-Giant Vacation Special (Summer '57-Pines)<br>5-Giant Christmas issue (Winter '57-Pines)<br>6-In Hawaii (Giant Vacation Special)(Summer '58-Pines)-Reprinted Summer '59 plus 3 more times<br>6-Giant Christmas issue (Winter '58)<br>each.... | 4.00 | 12.00 | 28.00 |
| 7-In Hollywood (Winter '59-Hallden) | | | |
| 8-In Mexico (Winter '60, 100 pgs.-Hallden/Fawcett) | | | |
| 8-In Mexico (Summer '62, 2nd printing) | | | |

| | Good | Fine | N-Mint |
|---|---|---|---|
| 9-Goes to Camp (Summer '61, 84 pgs., 2nd printing-Summer '62)-1st CCA approved issue | | | |
| 10-X-Mas issue (Winter '61) | | | |
| 11-Giant Christmas issue (Winter '62) | | | |
| 12-Triple Feature (Winter '62) each.... | 3.50 | 10.50 | 24.00 |
| 13-Best of Dennis the Menace (Spring '63)-Reprints | | | |
| 14-And His Dog Ruff (Summer '63) | | | |
| 15-In Washington, D.C. (Summer '63) | | | |
| 16-Goes to Camp (Summer '63)-Reprints No. 9 | | | |
| 17-& His Pal Joey (Winter '63) | | | |
| 18-In Hawaii (Reprints No. 6) | | | |
| 19-Giant Christmas issue (Winter '63) | | | |
| 20-Spring Special (Spring '64) each.... | 1.50 | 4.50 | 12.00 |
| 21-40 | 1.00 | 3.00 | 7.00 |
| 41-75 | .70 | 2.00 | 4.00 |

NOTE: ***Wiseman*** *c/a-1-8, 12, 14, 15, 17, 20, 22, 27, 28, 31, 35, 36, 41, 49.*

**DENNIS THE MENACE**
Nov, 1981 - No. 13, Nov, 1982
Marvel Comics Group

| | Good | Fine | N-Mint |
|---|---|---|---|
| 1-13: 1,2-New art. 3-Part-r. 4,5-r. 5-X-Mas-c | | .25 | .50 |

NOTE: ***Hank Ketcham*** *c-most; a-3, 12.* ***Wiseman*** *a-4, 5.*

**DENNIS THE MENACE AND HIS DOG RUFF**
Summer, 1961
Hallden/Fawcett

| | Good | Fine | N-Mint |
|---|---|---|---|
| 1-Wiseman-c/a | 3.50 | 10.50 | 24.00 |

**DENNIS THE MENACE AND HIS FRIENDS**
1969; No. 5, Jan, 1970 - No. 46, April, 1980 (All reprints)
Fawcett Publications

| | Good | Fine | N-Mint |
|---|---|---|---|
| Dennis the Menace & Joey No. 2 (7/69) | 1.35 | 4.00 | 8.00 |
| Dennis the Menace & Ruff No. 2 (9/69) | 1.00 | 3.00 | 6.00 |
| Dennis the Menace & Mr. Wilson No. 1 (10/69) | 1.00 | 3.00 | 6.00 |
| Dennis & Margaret No. 1 (Winter '69) | .50 | 1.50 | 3.00 |
| 5-20: 5-Dennis the Menace & Margaret. 6-...& Joey. 7-...& Ruff. 8-...& Mr. Wilson | .25 | .70 | 1.40 |
| 21-37 | | .60 | 1.20 |
| 38(begin digest size, 148 pgs., 4/78, 95 cents) - 46 | | .60 | 1.20 |

NOTE: *Titles rotate every four issues, beginning with No. 5.*

**DENNIS THE MENACE AND HIS PAL JOEY**
Summer, 1961 (10 cents) (See Dennis the Menace Giants No. 45)
Fawcett Publications

| | Good | Fine | N-Mint |
|---|---|---|---|
| 1-Wiseman-c/a | 3.50 | 10.50 | 24.00 |

**DENNIS THE MENACE AND THE BIBLE KIDS**
1977 (36 pages)
Word Books

| | Good | Fine | N-Mint |
|---|---|---|---|
| 1-Jesus. 2-Joseph. 3-David. 4-The Bible Girls. 5-Moses. 6-More About Jesus. 7-The Lord's Prayer. 8-Stories Jesus told. 9-Paul, God's Traveller. 10-In the Beginning each.... | | .30 | .60 |

NOTE: ***Ketcham*** *c/a in all.*

**DENNIS THE MENACE BIG BONUS SERIES**
No. 10, 1980 - No. 11, 1980
Fawcett Publications

| | Good | Fine | N-Mint |
|---|---|---|---|
| 10,11 | | .50 | 1.00 |

**DENNIS THE MENACE BONUS MAGAZINE** (Formerly Dennis the Menace Giants Nos. 1-75)
No. 76, 1/70 - No. 194, 10/79; (No. 76-124: 68 pgs.; No. 125-163: 52 pgs.; No. 164 on: 36 pgs.)
Fawcett Publications

| | Good | Fine | N-Mint |
|---|---|---|---|
| 76-90 | .35 | 1.00 | 2.00 |
| 91-110 | .25 | .75 | 1.50 |
| 111-194 | | .40 | .80 |

**DENNIS THE MENACE COMICS DIGEST**
April, 1982 - No. 3, Aug, 1982 (Digest Size, $1.25)
Marvel Comics Group

| | Good | Fine | N-Mint |
|---|---|---|---|
| 1-3-Reprints | .20 | .60 | 1.25 |

NOTE: ***Hank Ketcham*** *c-all.* ***Wiseman*** *a-all. A few thousand No. 1's were published with a DC emblem on cover.*

**DENNIS THE MENACE FUN BOOK**
1960 (100 pages)
Fawcett Publications/Standard Comics

| | Good | Fine | N-Mint |
|---|---|---|---|
| 1-Part Wiseman-a | 3.70 | 11.00 | 26.00 |

**DENNIS THE MENACE FUN FEST SERIES** (Formerly Dennis The Menace #166)
No. 16, Jan, 1980 - No. 17, Mar, 1980 (40 cents)
Hallden (Fawcett)

| | Good | Fine | N-Mint |
|---|---|---|---|
| 16,17-By Hank Ketcham | | .20 | .40 |

**DENNIS THE MENACE POCKET FULL OF FUN!**
Spring, 1969 - No. 50, March, 1980 (196 pages) (Digest size)
Fawcett Publications (Hallden)

| | Good | Fine | N-Mint |
|---|---|---|---|
| 1-Reprints in all issues | .85 | 2.50 | 5.00 |
| 2-10 | .40 | 1.25 | 2.50 |
| 11-28 | | .50 | 1.00 |
| 29-50: 35,40,46-Sunday strip-r | | .40 | .80 |

NOTE: *No. 1-28 are 196 pgs.; No. 29-36: 164 pgs.; No. 37: 148 pgs.; No. 38 on: 132 pgs. No. 8, 11, 15, 21, 25, 29 all contain strip reprints.*

**DENNIS THE MENACE TELEVISION SPECIAL**
Summer, 1961 - No. 2, Spring, 1962 (Giant)
Fawcett Publications (Hallden Div.)

| | Good | Fine | N-Mint |
|---|---|---|---|
| 1 | 3.50 | 10.50 | 24.00 |
| 2 | 2.00 | 6.00 | 14.00 |

**DENNIS THE MENACE TRIPLE FEATURE**
Winter, 1961 (Giant)
Fawcett Publications

| | Good | Fine | N-Mint |
|---|---|---|---|
| 1-Wiseman-c/a | 3.00 | 9.00 | 21.00 |

**DEPUTY, THE** (See 4-Color No. 1077,1130,1225)

**DEPUTY DAWG** (TV) (Also see New Terrytoons)
Oct-Dec, 1961 - No. 1299, 1962; No. 1, Aug, 1965
Dell Publishing Co./Gold Key

| | Good | Fine | N-Mint |
|---|---|---|---|
| 4-Color 1238,1299 | 5.70 | 17.00 | 40.00 |
| 1(10164-508)(8/65) | 4.50 | 14.00 | 32.00 |

**DEPUTY DAWG PRESENTS DINKY DUCK AND HASHIMOTO-SAN**
August, 1965 (TV)
Gold Key

| | Good | Fine | N-Mint |
|---|---|---|---|
| 1(10159-508) | 4.50 | 14.00 | 32.00 |

**DESIGN FOR SURVIVAL** (Gen. Thomas S. Power's...)
1968 (36 pages in color) (25 cents)
American Security Council Press

| | Good | Fine | N-Mint |
|---|---|---|---|
| nn-Propaganda against the Threat of Communism-Aircraft cover | 3.00 | 9.00 | 18.00 |
| Twin Circle edition-cover shows panels from inside | 1.70 | 5.00 | 10.00 |

**DESPERADO** (Black Diamond Western No. 9 on)
June, 1948 - No. 8, Feb, 1949
Lev Gleason Publications

| | Good | Fine | N-Mint |
|---|---|---|---|
| 1-Biro-c | 6.50 | 19.00 | 45.00 |
| 2 | 3.15 | 9.50 | 22.00 |
| 3-Story with over 20 killings | 2.85 | 8.50 | 20.00 |
| 4-8 | 2.30 | 7.00 | 16.00 |

NOTE: ***Barry*** *a-2.* ***Kida*** *a-3-7.* ***Fuje*** *a-4, 8.* ***Guardineer*** *a-6, 7.* ***Ed Moore*** *a-4, 6.*

*Dennis the Menace Giant #40, © FAW*

*Deputy Dawg Presents... #1, © Terrytoons*

*Design For Survival, © Amer. Security Council*

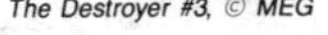

*The Destroyer #3, © MEG* *Detective Comics #27, © DC* *Detective Comics #85, © DC*

**DESTINATION MOON** (See Fawcett Movie Comics, Space Adventures #20, 23, & Strange Adventures #1)

**DESTROY!!**
1986 (One shot, B&W, Magazine size, $4.95)
Eclipse Comics

| | Good | Fine | N-Mint |
|---|---|---|---|
| 1 | .85 | 2.50 | 5.00 |
| 3-D Special 1-r-/#1 ($2.50) | .40 | 1.25 | 2.50 |

**DESTROYER, THE**
Nov, 1989 - No. 9, June, 1990 ($2.25, B&W, magazine, 52 pgs.)
Marvel Comics

| | | | |
|---|---|---|---|
| 1-Based on Remo Williams movie, paperbacks | .40 | 1.15 | 2.30 |
| 2-9: 2-Williamson part inks. 4-Ditko-a | .40 | 1.15 | 2.30 |

**DESTROYER DUCK**
1982 (no month) - No. 7, 5/84 (2-7: Baxter paper) ($1.50)
Eclipse Comics

| | | | |
|---|---|---|---|
| 1-Origin Destroyer Duck; 1st app. Groo | .85 | 2.50 | 5.00 |
| 2-7: 2-Starling back-up begins | .25 | .75 | 1.50 |

NOTE: ***Neal Adams*** *c-1i.* ***Kirby*** *c/a-1-5p.* ***Miller*** *c-7.*

**DESTRUCTOR, THE**
February, 1975 - No. 4, Aug, 1975
Atlas/Seaboard

| | | | |
|---|---|---|---|
| 1-Origin; Ditko/Wood-a; Wood-c(i) | | .60 | 1.20 |
| 2-4: 2-Ditko/Wood-a. 3,4-Ditko-a(p) | | .40 | .80 |

**DETECTIVE COMICS** (Also see Special Edition)
March, 1937 - Present
National Periodical Publications/DC Comics

| | Good | Fine | Vf-NM | NM/Mint |
|---|---|---|---|---|
| 1-(Scarce)-Slam Bradley & Spy by Siegel & Shuster, Speed Saunders by Guardineer, Flat Foot Flannigan by Gustavson, Cosmo, the Phantom of Disguise, Buck Marshall, Bruce Nelson begin; Chin Lung-c from 'Claws of the Red Dragon' serial; Flessel-c (1st?) | 2165.00 | 5400.00 | 13,000.00 | 22,000.00 |

(Estimated up to 35 total copies exist, 1 in NM/Mint)

| | Good | Fine | VF-NM |
|---|---|---|---|
| 2 (Rare) | 670.00 | 1670.00 | 4000.00 |
| 3 (Rare) | 535.00 | 1335.00 | 3200.00 |

| | Good | Fine | N-Mint |
|---|---|---|---|
| 4,5: 5-Larry Steele begins | 300.00 | 750.00 | 1800.00 |
| 6,7,9,10 | 192.00 | 480.00 | 1150.00 |
| 8-Mister Chang-c | 250.00 | 625.00 | 1500.00 |
| 11-17,19: 17-1st app. Fu Manchu in Det. | 167.00 | 420.00 | 1000.00 |
| 18-Fu Manchu-c | 225.00 | 560.00 | 1350.00 |
| 20-The Crimson Avenger begins (1st app.) | 250.00 | 625.00 | 1500.00 |
| 21,23-25 | 120.00 | 300.00 | 725.00 |
| 22-1st Crimson Avenger-c (12/38) | 175.00 | 440.00 | 1050.00 |
| 26 | 138.00 | 345.00 | 825.00 |

| | Good | Fine | VF-NM | NM/Mint |
|---|---|---|---|---|
| 27-The Batman & Commissioner Gordon begin (1st app.) by Bob Kane (5/39); Batman-c (1st) | 6,800.00 | 17,000.00 | 37,000.00 | 56,000.00 |

(Estimated up to 100 total copies exist, 3 in NM/Mint)

27-Reprint, Oversize 13½"x10." **WARNING**: This comic is an exact duplicate reprint of the original except for its size. DC published it in 1974 with a second cover titling it as Famous First Edition. There have been many reported cases of the outer cover being removed and the interior sold as the original edition. The reprint with the new outer cover removed is practically worthless.

| | Good | Fine | N-Mint |
|---|---|---|---|
| 27(1984)-Oreo Cookies giveaway (32 pgs., paper-c, r-/Det. 27, 38 & Batman No. 1 (1st Joker) | 1.15 | 3.50 | 7.00 |
| 28 | 870.00 | 2200.00 | 5200.00 |

| | Good | Fine | VF-NM | NM/Mint |
|---|---|---|---|---|
| 29-Batman-c; Doctor Death app. | 915.00 | 2300.00 | 5500.00 | 8200.00 |

(Estimated up to 140 total copies exist, 6 in NM/Mint)

| | Good | Fine | N-Mint |
|---|---|---|---|
| 30,32: 30-Dr. Death app. 32-Batman uses gun | 380.00 | 950.00 | 2300.00 |

| | Good | Fine | VF-NM | NM/Mint |
|---|---|---|---|---|
| 31-Classic Batman-c; 1st Julie Madison, Bat Plane (Bat-Gyro) & Batarang | 915.00 | 2300.00 | 5500.00 | 8200.00 |

(Estimated up to 140 total copies exist, 6 in NM/Mint)

| | Good | Fine | VF-NM | NM/Mint |
|---|---|---|---|---|
| 33-Origin The Batman; Batman gunholster-c | 1200.00 | 3000.00 | 7200.00 | 12,000.00 |

(Estimated up to 145 total copies exist, 7 in NM/Mint)

| | Good | Fine | N-Mint |
|---|---|---|---|
| 34-Steve Malone begins; 2nd Crimson Avenger-c | 335.00 | 835.00 | 2000.00 |
| 35-Batman-c begin; hypo-c | 500.00 | 1250.00 | 3000.00 |
| 36,37: 36-Origin Hugo Strange. 37-Cliff Crosby begins; last Batman solo story | 370.00 | 915.00 | 2200.00 |

| | Good | Fine | VF-NM | NM/Mint |
|---|---|---|---|---|
| 38-Origin/1st app. Robin the Boy Wonder (4/40) | 1300.00 | 3250.00 | 7800.00 | 11,000.00 |

(Estimated up to 165 total copies exist, 9 in NM/Mint)

| | Good | Fine | N-Mint |
|---|---|---|---|
| 39 | 315.00 | 790.00 | 1900.00 |
| 40-Origin & 1st app. Clay Face (Basil Karlo); 1st Clay Face cover app. (6/40) | 315.00 | 790.00 | 1900.00 |
| 41-Robin's 1st solo | 200.00 | 500.00 | 1200.00 |
| 42-44: 44-Crimson Avenger-new costume | 150.00 | 375.00 | 900.00 |
| 45-1st Joker story in Det. (3rd app.) | 225.00 | 560.00 | 1350.00 |
| 46-50: 48-1st time car called Batmobile; Gotham City 1st mention. 49-Last Clay Face | 135.00 | 340.00 | 810.00 |
| 51-57,59: 59-Last Steve Malone; 2nd Penguin; Wing becomes Crimson Avenger's aide | 108.00 | 270.00 | 650.00 |
| 58-1st Penguin app.; last Speed Saunders | 200.00 | 500.00 | 1200.00 |
| 60-Intro. Air Wave | 117.00 | 290.00 | 700.00 |
| 61,63: 63-Last Cliff Crosby; 1st app. Mr. Baffle | 100.00 | 250.00 | 600.00 |
| 62-Joker-c/story (1st Joker-c, 4/42) | 138.00 | 345.00 | 825.00 |
| 64-Origin & 1st app. Boy Commandos by Simon & Kirby (6/42); Joker app. | 267.00 | 665.00 | 1600.00 |
| 65-Boy Commandos-c | 132.00 | 335.00 | 800.00 |
| 66-Origin & 1st app. Two-Face | 183.00 | 460.00 | 1100.00 |
| 67,70: 67-1st Penguin-c (9/42) | 87.00 | 215.00 | 520.00 |
| 68-Two-Face-c/story | 92.00 | 230.00 | 550.00 |
| 69-Joker-c/story | 117.00 | 290.00 | 700.00 |
| 71-Joker-c/story | 105.00 | 260.00 | 625.00 |
| 72-75: 73-Scarecrow-c/story. 74-1st Tweedledum & Tweedledee; S&K-a | 80.00 | 200.00 | 480.00 |
| 76-Newsboy Legion & The Sandman x-over in Boy Commandos; S&K-a; Joker-c/story | 121.00 | 302.00 | 725.00 |
| 77-79: All S&K-a | 80.00 | 200.00 | 480.00 |
| 80-Two-Face app.; S&K-a | 83.00 | 210.00 | 500.00 |
| 81,82,84,86-90: 81-1st Cavalier app. 89-Last Crimson Avenger | 71.00 | 178.00 | 425.00 |
| 83-1st "Skinny" Alfred; last S&K Boy Commandos? Most issues #84 on signed S&K are not by them | 80.00 | 200.00 | 480.00 |
| 85-Joker-c/story; Last Spy | 93.00 | 235.00 | 560.00 |
| 91,102-Joker-c/story | 87.00 | 215.00 | 520.00 |
| 92-99: 96-Alfred's last name 'Beagle' revealed, later changed to 'Pennyworth'-214. 99-Penguin-c | 64.00 | 160.00 | 385.00 |
| 100 (6/45) | 96.00 | 240.00 | 575.00 |
| 101,103-108,110-113,115-117,119,120: 114-1st small logo (8/46). 120-Penguin-c | 58.00 | 145.00 | 350.00 |
| 109,114,118-Joker-c/stories | 80.00 | 200.00 | 480.00 |
| 121-123,125-127,129,130: 122-1st Catwoman-c (4/47). 126-Penguin-c | 56.00 | 140.00 | 335.00 |
| 124,128-Joker-c/stories | 73.00 | 185.00 | 440.00 |
| 131-136,139: 137-Last Air Wave | 48.00 | 120.00 | 285.00 |
| 137-Joker-c/story | 64.00 | 160.00 | 385.00 |

138-Origin Robotman (See Star Spangled No. 7, 1st app.); series

| | Good | Fine | N-Mint | Mint |
|---|---|---|---|---|
| ends No. 202 | 83.00 | 210.00 | 500.00 | |
| 140-The Riddler-c/story (1st app., 10/48) | 150.00 | 375.00 | 900.00 | 1400.00 |
| (Estimated up to 240 total copies exist, 18 in Mint) | | | | |
| 141,143-148,150: 150-Last Boy Commandos | 48.00 | 120.00 | 285.00 | |
| 142-2nd Riddler-c/story | 75.00 | 190.00 | 450.00 | |
| 149-Joker-c/story | 63.00 | 155.00 | 375.00 | |
| 151-Origin & 1st app. Pow Wow Smith | 50.00 | 125.00 | 300.00 | |
| 152,154,155,157-160: 152-Last Slam Bradley | 48.00 | 120.00 | 285.00 | |
| 153-1st Roy Raymond app.; origin The Human Fly | 50.00 | 125.00 | 300.00 | |
| 156(2/50)-The new classic Batmobile | 58.00 | 145.00 | 350.00 | |
| 161-167,169-176: Last 52 pgs. | 50.00 | 125.00 | 300.00 | |
| 168-Origin the Joker | 183.00 | 460.00 | 1100.00 | 1900.00 |
| (Estimated up to 250 total copies exist, 14 in Mint) | | | | |
| 177-189,191-199,201-204,206-212,214-216: 185-Secret of Batman's utility belt. 187-Two-Face app. 202-Last Robotman & Pow Wow Smith. 216-Last precode (2/55) | 33.00 | 84.00 | 200.00 | |
| 190-Origin Batman retold | 50.00 | 125.00 | 300.00 | |
| 200 | 48.00 | 120.00 | 285.00 | |
| 205-Origin Batcave | 50.00 | 125.00 | 300.00 | |
| 213-Origin Mirror Man | 46.00 | 115.00 | 275.00 | |
| 217-224 | 32.00 | 80.00 | 190.00 | |
| 225-(11/55)-1st app. Martian Manhunter-John Jones, later changed to J'onn J'onzz; also see Batman #78 | 193.00 | 580.00 | 1350.00 | 2300.00 |
| (Estimated up to 400 total copies exist, 21 in Mint) | | | | |
| 226-Origin Martian Manhunter continued | 48.00 | 144.00 | 340.00 | |
| 227-229 | 30.00 | 90.00 | 210.00 | |
| 230-1st app. Mad Hatter | 36.00 | 108.00 | 250.00 | |
| 231-Origin Martian Manhunter retold | 23.00 | 70.00 | 160.00 | |
| 232,234,236-240 | 20.00 | 60.00 | 140.00 | |
| 233-Origin & 1st app. Batwoman | 61.00 | 183.00 | 425.00 | |
| 235-Origin Batman & his costume | 30.00 | 90.00 | 210.00 | |
| 241-260: 246-Intro. Diane Meade, J. Jones' girl. 257-Intro. & 1st app. Whirly Bats | 15.00 | 45.00 | 105.00 | |
| 261-264,266,268-270: 261-1st app. Dr. Double X. 262-Origin Jackal | 11.50 | 34.00 | 80.00 | |
| 265-Batman's origin retold with new facts | 16.50 | 50.00 | 115.00 | |
| 267-Origin & 1st app. Bat-Mite | 12.00 | 36.00 | 85.00 | |
| 271,272,274-280: 276-2nd Bat-Mite | 9.00 | 27.00 | 62.00 | |
| 272-J'onn J'onzz i.d. revealed for 1st time | 10.00 | 30.00 | 70.00 | |
| 281-297: 287-Origin J'onn J'onzz retold. 292-Last Roy Raymond. 293-Aquaman begins, ends #300. 297-Last 10 cent issue (11/61) | 6.50 | 19.00 | 45.00 | |
| 298-1st modern Clayface (Matt Hagen) | 11.50 | 34.00 | 80.00 | |
| 299-326,329,330: 311-Intro. Zook in John Jones; 1st app. Catman. 322-Bat-Girl's 1st app. in Det. 326-Last J'onn J'onzz, story cont'd in H.O.M. #143; intro. Idol-Head of Diabolu | 3.60 | 11.00 | 25.00 | |
| 327-Elongated Man begins, ends #383; 1st new look Batman with new costume | 4.00 | 12.00 | 28.00 | |
| 328-Death of Alfred | 6.50 | 19.00 | 45.00 | |
| 331,333-340,342-358,360-364,366-368,370: 345-Intro Block Buster. 351-Elongated Man new costume. 355-Zatanna x-over in Elongated Man. 356-Alfred brought back in Batman | 2.15 | 6.50 | 15.00 | |
| 332,341,365-Joker-c/stories | 3.15 | 9.50 | 22.00 | |
| 359-Intro/origin new Batgirl | 3.15 | 9.50 | 22.00 | |
| 369-Neal Adams-a | 3.50 | 10.50 | 24.00 | |
| 371-386,389,390 | 1.50 | 4.50 | 10.00 | |
| 387-R/1st Batman story from #27; Joker-c | 3.15 | 9.50 | 22.00 | |

| | Good | Fine | N-Mint |
|---|---|---|---|
| 388-Joker-c/story | 2.30 | 7.00 | 16.00 |
| 391-394,396,398,399,401,403,405,406,409: 392-1st app. Jason Bard. 401-2nd Batgirl/Robin team-up | 1.35 | 4.00 | 8.00 |
| 395,397,402,404,407,408,410-Neal Adams-a | 2.00 | 6.00 | 14.00 |
| 400-Origin & 1st app. Man-Bat; 1st Batgirl/Robin team-up; Neal Adams-a | 2.85 | 8.50 | 20.00 |
| 411-420: 414-52 pgs. begin, end #424. 418-Creeper x-over | 1.35 | 4.00 | 8.00 |
| 421-436: 424-Last Batgirl; 1st She-Bat. 426-436-Elongated Man app. 428,434-Hawkman begins, ends #467 | 1.15 | 3.50 | 7.00 |
| 437-New Manhunter begins by Simonson, ends #443 | 1.50 | 4.50 | 9.00 |
| 438-445 (All 100 pgs.): 439-Origin Manhunter. 440-G.A. Manhunter, Hawkman, Dollman, Gr. Lantern; Toth-a. 441-G.A. Plastic Man, Batman, Ibis-r. 442-G.A. Newsboy Legion, Bl. Canary, Elongated Man, Dr. Fate-r. 443-Origin The Creeper-r; death of Manhunter; G.A. Green Lantern, Spectre-r. 444-G.A. Kid Eternity-r. 445-G.A. Dr. Midnite-r | 1.35 | 4.00 | 8.00 |
| 446-465,469,470,480: 457-Origin retold & updated. 480-(44 pgs.) | 1.00 | 3.00 | 6.00 |
| 466-468,471-474,478,479-Rogers-a; 478-1st app. 3rd Clayface (Preston Payne). 479-(44 pgs.) | 1.70 | 5.00 | 10.00 |
| 475,476-Joker-c/stories; Rogers-a | 3.00 | 9.00 | 18.00 |
| 477-Neal Adams-a(r); Rogers-a, 3pgs. | 2.00 | 6.00 | 12.00 |
| 481-(Combined with Batman Family, 12/78-1/79)(Begin $1.00, 68 pg. issues, ends #495); 481-495-Batgirl, Robin solo stories. | 1.50 | 4.50 | 9.00 |
| 482-Starlin/Russell, Golden-a; The Demon begins (origin-r), ends #485 (by Ditko #483-485) | 1.00 | 3.00 | 6.00 |
| 483-40th Anniversary issue; origin retold; Newton Batman begins | 1.15 | 3.50 | 7.00 |
| 484-499,501-503,505-523: 484-Origin Robin. 485-Death of Batwoman. 487-The Odd Man by Ditko. 489-Robin/Batgirl team-up. 490-Black Lightning begins. 491(492 on inside). 518-1st app. Deadshot? 519-Last Batgirl. 521-Green Arrow series begins. 523-Solomon Grundy app. | .70 | 2.00 | 4.00 |
| 500-($1.50)-Batman/Deadman team-up | 1.35 | 4.00 | 8.00 |
| 504-Joker-c/story | 1.15 | 3.50 | 7.00 |
| 524-2nd app. Jason Todd (cameo)(3/83) | .85 | 2.50 | 5.00 |
| 525-3rd app. Jason Todd (See Batman #357) | .70 | 2.00 | 4.00 |
| 526-Batman's 500th app. in Detective Comics (68 pgs., $1.50); contains 55 pg. Joker story | 2.00 | 6.00 | 12.00 |
| 527-531,533,534,536-568,571: 536-2nd Deadshot? 542-Jason Todd quits as Robin (becomes Robin again #547). 549,550-Alan Moore scripts(Gr. Arrow). 554-1st new Black Canary. 566-Batman villains profiled. 567-Harlan Ellison scripts | .50 | 1.50 | 3.00 |
| 532,569,570-Joker-c/stories | 1.00 | 3.00 | 6.00 |
| 535-Intro new Robin (Jason Todd)-1st appeared in Batman | 1.00 | 3.00 | 6.00 |
| 572 (60 pgs., $1.25)-50th Anniversary | .70 | 2.00 | 4.00 |
| 573 | .50 | 1.50 | 3.00 |
| 574-Origin Batman & Jason Todd retold | .85 | 2.50 | 5.00 |
| 575-Year 2 begins, ends #578 | 2.50 | 7.50 | 15.00 |
| 576-578: McFarlane-c/a | 2.00 | 6.00 | 12.00 |
| 579-597,601-610: 579-New bat wing logo. 589-595-(52 pgs.)-Each contain free 16 pg. Batman stories. 604-607-Mudpack storyline; 604, 607-Contain Batman mini-posters. 610-Faked death of Penguin | .25 | .75 | 1.50 |
| 598-($2.95, 84 pgs.)-"Blind Justice" storyline begins by Batman movie writer Sam Hamm, ends #600 | 2.00 | 6.00 | 12.00 |
| 599 | 1.35 | 2.00 | 4.00 |
| 600-($2.95, 84 pgs.)-50th Anniversary issue; 1 pg. N. Adams pin-up, among other artists | 1.00 | 3.00 | 6.00 |
| 611-630: 615-"The Penguin Affair" part 2 (See Batman #448,449). 617-Joker-c/story | | .50 | 1.00 |
| Annual 1(1988, $1.50) | .85 | 2.50 | 5.00 |

*Detective Comics #310, © DC*

*Detective Comics #387, © DC*

*Detective Comics #600, © DC*

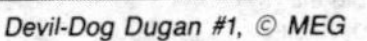

Devil-Dog Dugan #1, © MEG

Devil Kids Starring Hot Stuff #45, © HARV

Diary Loves #5, © QUA

| | Good | Fine | N-Mint |
|---|---|---|---|
| Annual 2(1989, $2.00, 68 pgs.) | .70 | 2.00 | 4.00 |
| Annual 3(1990, $2.00, 68 pgs.) | .35 | 1.00 | 2.00 |

NOTE: ***Neal Adams** c-369, 370, 372, 383, 385, 389, 391, 392, 394-422, 439. **Aparo** a-437, 438, 444-446, 500; c-430, 437, 440-446, 448, 468-470, 480, 484(back), 492-502, 508, 509, 515, 518-522. **Austin** a-450i, 451i, 463i-468i, 471-476i; c-474-476i, 478i. **Baily** a-443r. **Buckler** a-434, 446p, 479p; c-467p, 482p, 505p, 506p, 511p, 513-516p, 518p. **Colan** a(p)-510, 512, 517, 523, 528-538, 540-546, 555-567; c(p)-510, 512, 528, 530-535, 537, 538, 540, 541, 543-545, 556-558, 560-564. **J. Craig** a-488. **Ditko** a-443r, 483-485, 487. **Golden** a-482p. **Grell** a-445, 455, 463p, 464p; c-455. **Gustavson** a-441r. **Kaluta** c-423, 424, 426-428, 431, 434, 438, 484, 486, 572. **Bob Kane** a-Most early ish. #27 on, 297r, 438-440r, 442r, 443r. **Gil Kane** a(p)-368, 370-374, 384, 385, 388-407, 438r, 439r, 520. **Kubert** a-438r, 439r, 500; c-348-500. **McFarlane** c/a(p) 576-578. **Meskin** a-420r. **Mooney** a-444r. **Moreira** a-153-300, 419r, 444r, 445r. **Newton** a(p)-480, 481, 483-499, 501-509, 511, 513-516, 518-520, 524, 526, 539; c-526p. **Robinson** a-part: 66, 68, 71-73; all: 74-76, 79, 80; c-62, 64, 66, 68-74, 76, 79, 82, 86, 88, 442r, 443r. **Rogers** a-467, 478p, 479p, 481p; c-471p, 472p, 473, 474-479p. **Roussos** Airwave-76-105(most). **Russell** a-481i, 482i. **Simon/Kirby** a-440r, 442r. **Simonson** a-437-443, 450, 469, 470, 500. **Starlin** a-481p, 482p; c-503, 504, 567p. **Dick Sprang** c-622-624. **Starr** a-444r. **Toth** r-414, 416, 418, 424, 440-444. **Tuska** a-486p, 490p. **Wrightson** c-425.*

**DETECTIVE DAN, SECRET OP. 48**
1933 (36 pgs.; 9½x12") (B&W; Softcover)
Humor Publ. Co.

| | Good | Fine | N-Mint |
|---|---|---|---|
| nn-By Norman Marsh; forerunner of Dan Dunn | 8.50 | 25.50 | 60.00 |

**DETECTIVE EYE** (See Keen Detective Funnies)
Nov, 1940 - No. 2, Dec, 1940
Centaur Publications

| | Good | Fine | N-Mint |
|---|---|---|---|
| 1-Air Man & The Eye Sees begins; The Masked Marvel app. | 93.00 | 280.00 | 650.00 |
| 2-Origin Don Rance and the Mysticape; Binder-a; Frank Thomas-c | 70.00 | 210.00 | 485.00 |

**DETECTIVE PICTURE STORIES** (Keen Detective Funnies No. 8 on?)
Dec, 1936 - No. 7, 1937 (1st comic of a single theme)
Comics Magazine Company

| | Good | Fine | N-Mint |
|---|---|---|---|
| 1 | 132.00 | 395.00 | 925.00 |
| 2-The Clock app. | 63.00 | 190.00 | 440.00 |
| 3,4: 4-Eisner-a | 56.00 | 167.00 | 390.00 |
| 5-7: 5-Kane-a; 6,7 (Exist)? | 50.00 | 150.00 | 350.00 |

**DETECTIVES, THE** (See 4-Color No. 1168,1219,1240)

**DETECTIVES, INC.** (See Eclipse Graphic Album Series)
April, 1985 - No. 2, April, 1985 ($1.75, color; both have April dates)
Eclipse Comics

| | Good | Fine | N-Mint |
|---|---|---|---|
| 1,2: 2-Nudity | .30 | .90 | 1.80 |

**DETECTIVES, INC.: A TERROR OF DYING DREAMS**
June, 1987 - No. 3, Dec, 1987 ($1.75, duo-tone, mini-series)
Eclipse Comics

| | Good | Fine | N-Mint |
|---|---|---|---|
| 1-3: Adapts movie; Colan-c/a | .30 | .90 | 1.80 |

**DEVIL DINOSAUR**
April, 1978 - No. 9, Dec, 1978
Marvel Comics Group

| | Good | Fine | N-Mint |
|---|---|---|---|
| 1-9: Kirby/Royer-a in all; all have Kirby-c | | .25 | .50 |

**DEVIL-DOG DUGAN** (Tales of the Marines No. 4 on)
July, 1956 - No. 3, Nov, 1956
Atlas Comics (OPI)

| | Good | Fine | N-Mint |
|---|---|---|---|
| 1-Severin-c | 3.50 | 10.50 | 24.00 |
| 2-Iron Mike McGraw x-over; Severin-c | 2.30 | 7.00 | 16.00 |
| 3 | 1.70 | 5.00 | 12.00 |

**DEVIL DOGS**
1942
Street & Smith Publishers

| | Good | Fine | N-Mint |
|---|---|---|---|
| 1-Boy Rangers, U.S. Marines | 11.50 | 34.00 | 80.00 |

**DEVILINA**
Feb, 1975 - No. 2, May, 1975 (Magazine) (B&W)
Atlas/Seaboard

| | Good | Fine | N-Mint |
|---|---|---|---|
| 1,2: 1-Reese-a | .50 | 1.50 | 3.00 |

**DEVIL KIDS STARRING HOT STUFF**
July, 1962 - No. 107, Oct, 1981 (Giant-Size #41-55)
Harvey Publications (Illustrated Humor)

| | Good | Fine | N-Mint |
|---|---|---|---|
| 1 | 7.00 | 21.00 | 50.00 |
| 2 | 3.60 | 11.00 | 25.00 |
| 3-10 (1/64) | 2.35 | 7.00 | 16.00 |
| 11-20 | 1.35 | 4.00 | 8.00 |
| 21-30 | 1.00 | 3.00 | 6.00 |
| 31-40 ('71) | .70 | 2.00 | 4.00 |
| 41-50: All 68 pg. Giants | .85 | 2.50 | 5.00 |
| 51-55: All 52 pg. Giants | .70 | 2.00 | 4.00 |
| 56-70 | .40 | 1.20 | 2.40 |
| 71-90 | .25 | .80 | 1.60 |
| 91-107 | | .30 | .60 |

**DEXTER COMICS**
Summer, 1948 - No. 5, July, 1949
Dearfield Publ.

| | Good | Fine | N-Mint |
|---|---|---|---|
| 1-Teen-age humor | 3.50 | 10.50 | 24.00 |
| 2-Junie Prom app. | 2.30 | 7.00 | 16.00 |
| 3-5 | 1.50 | 4.50 | 10.00 |

**DEXTER THE DEMON** (Formerly Melvin The Monster)
No. 7, Sept, 1957 (Also see Cartoon Kids & Peter the Little Pest)
Atlas Comics (HPC)

| | Good | Fine | N-Mint |
|---|---|---|---|
| 7 | 1.70 | 5.00 | 12.00 |

**DIARY CONFESSIONS** (Formerly Ideal Romance)
No. 9, May, 1955 - No. 14, April, 1955
Stanmor/Key Publ.

| | Good | Fine | N-Mint |
|---|---|---|---|
| 9 | 2.85 | 8.50 | 20.00 |
| 10-14 (#11-13, Exist?) | 1.70 | 5.00 | 12.00 |

**DIARY LOVES** (Formerly Love Diary #1; G. I. Sweethearts #32 on)
No. 2, Nov, 1949 - No. 31, April, 1953
Quality Comics Group

| | Good | Fine | N-Mint |
|---|---|---|---|
| 2-Ward-c/a, 9 pgs. | 8.50 | 25.00 | 60.00 |
| 3 (1/50) | 3.00 | 9.00 | 21.00 |
| 4-Crandall-a | 4.85 | 14.50 | 34.00 |
| 5-7,10 | 2.15 | 6.50 | 15.00 |
| 8,9-Ward-a 6,8 pgs. plus Gustavson-#8 | 5.70 | 17.00 | 40.00 |
| 11,13,14,17-20 | 1.70 | 5.00 | 12.00 |
| 12,15,16-Ward-a 9,7,8 pgs. | 4.85 | 14.50 | 34.00 |
| 21-Ward-a, 7 pgs. | 4.00 | 12.00 | 28.00 |
| 22-31: 31-Whitney-a | 1.30 | 4.00 | 9.00 |

NOTE: *Photo c-3-5, 8, 12-27.*

**DIARY OF HORROR**
December, 1952
Avon Periodicals

| | Good | Fine | N-Mint |
|---|---|---|---|
| 1-Hollingsworth-c/a; bondage-c | 17.00 | 51.00 | 120.00 |

**DIARY SECRETS** (Formerly Teen-Age Diary Secrets)
No. 10, Feb, 1952 - No. 30, Sept, 1955
St. John Publishing Co.

| | Good | Fine | N-Mint |
|---|---|---|---|
| 10 | 6.50 | 19.50 | 45.00 |
| 11-16,18,19: 11-Spanking panel | 5.00 | 15.00 | 35.00 |
| 17,20-Kubert-a | 5.70 | 17.00 | 40.00 |
| 21-30: 28-Last precode (3/55) | 3.00 | 9.00 | 21.00 |

(See Giant Comics Ed. for Annual)

NOTE: ***Baker** c/a most issues.*

**DICK COLE** (Sport Thrills No. 11 on)(See Blue Bolt & Four Most #1)
Dec-Jan, 1948-49 - No. 10, June-July, 1950
Curtis Publ./Star Publications

| | Good | Fine | N-Mint |
|---|---|---|---|
| 1-Sgt. Spook; L. B. Cole-c; McWilliams-a; Curt Swan's 1st work | 8.00 | 24.00 | 56.00 |
| 2 | 4.50 | 14.00 | 32.00 |
| 3-10 | 4.00 | 12.00 | 28.00 |
| Accepted Reprint #7(V1#6 on-c)(1950's)-Reprints #7 L.B. Cole-c | 2.30 | 7.00 | 16.00 |
| Accepted Reprint #9(nd)-(Reprints #9 & #8-c) | 2.30 | 7.00 | 16.00 |

NOTE: ***L. B. Cole** a-all; c-1, 3, 4, 6-10. Dick Cole in 1-9.*

**DICKIE DARE**
1941 - No. 4, 1942 (#3 on sale 6/15/42)
Eastern Color Printing Co.

| | Good | Fine | N-Mint |
|---|---|---|---|
| 1-Caniff-a, Everett-c | 20.00 | 60.00 | 140.00 |
| 2 | 11.50 | 34.00 | 80.00 |
| 3,4-Half Scorchy Smith by Noel Sickles who was very influential in Milton Caniff's development | 12.00 | 36.00 | 85.00 |

**DICK POWELL** (See A-1 Comics No. 22)

**DICK QUICK, ACE REPORTER** (See Picture News #10)

**DICK'S ADVENTURES IN DREAMLAND** (See 4-Color No. 245)

**DICK TRACY** (See Blackthorne 3-D Series #8, Famous Feature Stories, Harvey Comics Library, Limited Collectors' Ed., Mammoth Comics, Merry Christmas, The Original . . ., Popular Comics, Super Book No. 1, 7, 13, 25, Super Comics & Tastee-Freez)

**DICK TRACY**
May, 1937 - Jan, 1938
David McKay Publications

| | Good | Fine | N-Mint |
|---|---|---|---|
| Feature Books nn - 100 pgs., part reprinted as 4-Color No. 1 (appeared before Large Feat. Comics, 1st Dick Tracy comic book) (Very Rare-three known copies) Estimated Value. . . . | 500.00 | 1400.00 | 3000.00 |
| Feature Books 4 - Reprints nn issue but with new cover added | 80.00 | 240.00 | 560.00 |
| Feature Books 6,9 | 65.00 | 195.00 | 455.00 |

**DICK TRACY** (. . . Monthly #1-24)
1939 - No. 24, Dec, 1949
Dell Publishing Co.

| | Good | Fine | N-Mint |
|---|---|---|---|
| Large Feature Comic 1(1939) | 93.00 | 280.00 | 650.00 |
| Large Feature Comic 4 | 50.00 | 150.00 | 350.00 |
| Large Feature Comic 8,11,13,15 | 46.00 | 140.00 | 325.00 |

| | Good | Fine | VF-NM | NM/Mint |
|---|---|---|---|---|
| 4-Color 1(1939)('35-r) | 171.00 | 515.00 | 1200.00 | 2000.00 |

(Estimated up to 115 total exist, 5 in NM/Mint)

| | Good | Fine | N-Mint |
|---|---|---|---|
| 4-Color 6(1940)('37-r)-(Scarce) | 86.00 | 255.00 | 600.00 |
| 4-Color 8(1940)('38-'39-r) | 57.00 | 171.00 | 400.00 |
| Large Feature Comic 3(1941, Series II) | 43.00 | 130.00 | 300.00 |
| 4-Color 21('41)('38-r) | 49.00 | 145.00 | 340.00 |
| 4-Color 34('43)('39-'40-r) | 35.00 | 105.00 | 245.00 |
| 4-Color 56('44)('40-r) | 26.00 | 77.00 | 180.00 |
| 4-Color 96('46)('40-r) | 19.00 | 58.00 | 135.00 |
| 4-Color 133('47)('40-'41-r) | 17.00 | 51.00 | 115.00 |
| 4-Color 163('47)('41-r) | 13.00 | 40.00 | 90.00 |
| 4-Color 215('48)-Titled "Sparkle Plenty," Tracy-r | 8.00 | 24.00 | 55.00 |
| 1(1/48)('34-r) | 40.00 | 120.00 | 280.00 |
| 2,3 | 22.00 | 65.00 | 150.00 |
| 4-10 | 19.00 | 56.00 | 130.00 |
| 11-18: 13-Bondage-c | 14.00 | 43.00 | 100.00 |
| 19-1st app. Sparkle Plenty, B.O. Plenty & Gravel Gertie in a 3-pg. strip not by Gould | 16.00 | 48.00 | 110.00 |
| 20-1st app. Sam Catchem; c/a not by Gould | 12.00 | 36.00 | 85.00 |
| 21-24-Only 2 pg. Gould-a in each | 12.00 | 36.00 | 85.00 |

NOTE: *No. 19-24 have a 2 pg. biography of a famous villain illustrated by Gould: 19-Little Face; 20-Flattop; 21-Breathless Mahoney; 22-Measles; 23-Itchy; 24-The Brow.*

**DICK TRACY** (Cont'd from Dell series)(. . . Comics Monthly #25-140)
No. 25, Mar, 1950 - No. 145, April, 1961
Harvey Publications

| | Good | Fine | N-Mint |
|---|---|---|---|
| 25 | 16.00 | 48.00 | 110.00 |
| 26-28,30: 28-Bondage-c | 12.00 | 36.00 | 85.00 |
| 29-1st app. Gravel Gertie in a Gould-r | 16.00 | 48.00 | 110.00 |
| 31,32,34,35,37-40: 40-Intro/origin 2-way wrist radio | 11.00 | 32.00 | 75.00 |
| 33-"Measles the Teen-Age Dope Pusher" | 12.00 | 36.00 | 85.00 |
| 36-1st app. B.O. Plenty in a Gould-r | 12.00 | 36.00 | 85.00 |
| 41-50 | 9.30 | 28.00 | 65.00 |
| 51-56,58-80: 51-2pgs Powell-a | 8.50 | 25.50 | 60.00 |
| 57-1st app. Sam Catchem, Gould-r | 11.00 | 32.00 | 75.00 |
| 81-99,101-140 | 6.50 | 19.00 | 45.00 |
| 100 | 7.00 | 21.00 | 50.00 |
| 141-145 (25 cents)(titled "Dick Tracy") | 6.00 | 18.00 | 42.00 |

NOTE: ***Powell** a(1-2pgs.)-43, 44, 104, 108, 109, 145. No. 110-120, 141-145 are all reprints from earlier issues.*

**DICK TRACY** (Reuben Award Winner Series)
12/84 - No. 24, 6/89 (1-12: $5.95; 13-24: $6.95, B&W, 76 pgs.)
Blackthorne Publishing

| | Good | Fine | N-Mint |
|---|---|---|---|
| 1-3-1st printings; hardcover editions ($14.95) | 2.50 | 7.50 | 15.00 |
| 1-3-1st printings; squarebound, thick-c | 1.00 | 3.00 | 6.00 |
| 1-3-2nd printings, 1986; hard cover editions | 2.50 | 7.50 | 15.00 |
| 1-3-2nd printings, 1986; squarebound, thick-c | 1.00 | 3.00 | 6.00 |
| 4-8-Hardcover editions ($14.95) | 2.50 | 7.50 | 15.00 |
| 4-12: Squarebound, thick-c | 1.00 | 3.00 | 6.00 |
| 13-24 ($6.95): 21,22-Regular-c & stapled | 1.15 | 3.50 | 7.00 |

NOTE: ***Gould** daily & Sunday strip-r in all: 1-12 r-12/31/45-4/5/49; 13-24 r-7/13/41-2/20/44.*

**DICK TRACY**
1990 - No. 3, 1990 (Color)(Book Three adapts 1990 movie)
WD Publications (Disney)

| | Good | Fine | N-Mint |
|---|---|---|---|
| Book One ($3.95, 52 pgs.)-Kyle Baker-c/a | .70 | 2.00 | 4.00 |
| Book Two, Three ($5.95, 68 pgs.)-Direct sale | 1.00 | 3.00 | 6.00 |
| Book Two, Three ($2.95, 68 pgs.)-Newsstand | .50 | 1.50 | 3.00 |

**DICK TRACY & DICK TRACY JR. CAUGHT THE RACKETEERS, HOW**
1933 (88 pages) (7x8½") (Hardcover)
Cupples & Leon Co.

| | Good | Fine | N-Mint |
|---|---|---|---|
| 2-(numbered on pg. 84)-Continuation of Stooge Viller book (daily strip reprints from 8/3/33 thru 11/8/33) (Rarer than No. 1) | 38.00 | 115.00 | 265.00 |
| with dust jacket. . . . | 60.00 | 180.00 | 420.00 |
| Book 2 (32 pgs.; soft-c; has strips 9/18/33-11/8/33) | 19.00 | 57.00 | 132.00 |

**DICK TRACY & DICK TRACY JR. AND HOW THEY CAPTURED "STOOGE" VILLER** (See Treasure Box of Famous Comics)
1933 (7x8½") (Hard cover; One Shot; 100 pgs.)
Reprints 1932 & 1933 Dick Tracy daily strips
Cupples & Leon Co.

| | Good | Fine | N-Mint |
|---|---|---|---|
| nn(No.1)-1st app. of "Stooge" Viller | 27.00 | 81.00 | 190.00 |
| with dust jacket. . . . | 42.00 | 125.00 | 295.00 |

**DICK TRACY, EXPLOITS OF**
1946 (Strip reprints) (Hardcover) ($1.00)
Rosdon Books, Inc.

| | Good | Fine | N-Mint |
|---|---|---|---|
| 1-Reprints the near complete case of "The Brow" from 6/12/44 to 9/24/44 (story starts a few weeks late) | 19.00 | 57.00 | 132.00 |
| with dust jacket. . . . | 32.00 | 95.00 | 225.00 |

**DICK TRACY GIVEAWAYS**
1939 - 1958; 1990

| | Good | Fine | N-Mint |
|---|---|---|---|
| Buster Brown Shoes Giveaway (1940s?, 36 pgs. in color); 1938-39-r by Gould | 25.00 | 75.00 | 175.00 |

*Dick Cole #4, © STAR*

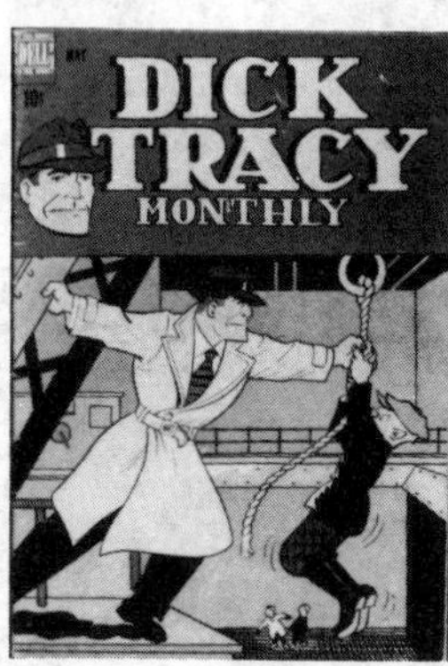

*Dick Tracy #5, © N.Y. News Syndicate*

*Dick Tracy, Book One ('90), © The Disney Co.*

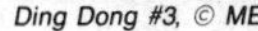
*Ding Dong #3, © ME*

*Dinosaur Rex #1, © Fantagraphics Books*

*Dinosaurs For Hire 3-D #1, © Eternity Comics*

Gillmore Giveaway (See Superbook) — Good / Fine / N-Mint

. . . Hatful of Fun (No date, 1950-52)-32 pgs.; 8½x10;'' Dick Tracy hat promotion; Dick Tracy games, magic tricks. Miller Bros. premium — 6.50 19.00 45.00

Motorola Giveaway (1953)-Reprints Harvey Comics Library #2 — 3.50 10.50 24.00

Original Dick Tracy by Chester Gould, The (Aug, 1990, 16 pgs., 5½x 8½'')-Gladstone Publ.; Bread Giveaway — .25 .50

Popped Wheat Giveaway (1947, 16 pgs. in color)-'40-r; Sig Feuchtwanger Publ.; Gould-a — .85 2.50 5.00

. . . Presents the Family Fun Book; Tip Top Bread Giveaway, no date or number (1940, Fawcett Publ., 16 pgs. in color)-Spy Smasher, Ibis, Lance O'Casey app. — 27.00 81.00 190.00

Same as above but without app. of heroes & Dick Tracy on cover only — 8.00 24.00 55.00

Service Station Giveaway (1958, 16 pgs. in color)(regular size, slick cover)-Harvey Info. Press — 2.00 6.00 14.00

Shoe Store Giveaway (Weatherbird)(1939, 16 pgs.)-Gould-a — 11.00 32.00 75.00

**DICK TRACY MONTHLY/WEEKLY**
May, 1986 - No. 99, 1989 ($2.00, B&W) (Becomes Weekly #26 on)
Blackthorne Publishing

1-99: Gould-r. 30,31-Mr. Crime app. — .35 1.00 2.00

NOTE: *#1-10 reprint strips 3/10/40-7/13/41; #10(pg.8)-51 reprint strips 4/6/49-12/31/55; #52-99 reprint strips 12/26/56-1964?*

**DICK TRACY SHEDS LIGHT ON THE MOLE**
1949 (16 pgs.) (Ray-O-Vac Flashlights giveaway)
Western Printing Co.

nn-Not by Gould — 5.00 15.00 35.00

**DICK TRACY SPECIAL**
Jan, 1988 - No. 3, Aug(no month), 1989 ($2.95, B&W)
Blackthorne Publishing

1-3: 1-Origin D. Tracy; r/strips 10/12/31-3/30/32 — .50 1.50 3.00

**DICK TRACY: THE EARLY YEARS**
Aug, 1987 - No. 4, Aug(no month), 1989 ($6.95, B&W, 76 pgs.)
Blackthorne Publishing

1-3: 1-4-r/strips 10/12/31(1st daily)-8/31/32 & Sunday strips 6/12/32-8/28/32; Big Boy apps. in #1-3 — 1.15 3.50 7.00
4 ($2.95, 52 pgs.) — .50 1.50 3.00

**DICK TRACY UNPRINTED STORIES**
Sept, 1987 - No. 4, June, 1988 ($2.95, B&W)
Blackthorne Publishing

1-4: Reprints strips 1/1/56-12/25/56 — .50 1.50 3.00

**DICK TURPIN** (See Legend of Young. . .)

**DICK WINGATE OF THE U.S. NAVY**
1951; 1953 (no month)
Superior Publ./Toby Press

nn-U.S. Navy giveaway — 1.30 4.00 9.00
1(1953, Toby) — 2.00 6.00 14.00

**DIE, MONSTER, DIE** (See Movie Classics)

**DIG 'EM**
1973 (16 pgs.) ( 2-3/8x6'')
Kellogg's Sugar Smacks Giveaway

4 different issues — .50 1.00

**DILLY** (Dilly Duncan from Daredevil Comics; see Boy Comics #57)
May, 1953 - No. 3, Sept, 1953
Lev Gleason Publications

1-Biro-c — 2.65 8.00 18.00
2,3-Biro-c — 1.50 4.50 10.00

**DILTON'S STRANGE SCIENCE**
May, 1989 - No. 5, May, 1990 (.75-$1.00, color)
Archie Comics — Good / Fine / N-Mint

1-5 — .50 1.00

**DIME COMICS**
1945; 1951
Newsbook Publ. Corp.

1-Silver Streak app.; L. B. Cole-c — 13.00 40.00 90.00
1(1951), 5 — 2.00 6.00 14.00

**DINGBATS** (See First Issue Special)

**DING DONG**
Summer?, 1946 - No. 5, 1947 (52 pgs.)
Compix/Magazine Enterprises

1-Funny animal — 5.00 15.00 35.00
2 (11/46) — 2.65 8.00 18.00
3 (Wint '46-'47) - 5 — 2.00 6.00 14.00

**DINKY DUCK** (Paul Terry's. . .) (See Blue Ribbon & New Terrytoons)
Nov, 1951 - No. 16, Sept, 1955; No. 16, Fall, 1956; No. 17, May, 1957 - No. 19, Summer, 1958
St. John Publishing Co./Pines No. 16 on

1 — 3.70 11.00 26.00
2 — 2.00 6.00 14.00
3-10 — 1.30 4.00 9.00
11-16(9/55) — 1.00 3.00 7.00
16(Fall,'56) - 19 — .70 2.00 5.00

**DINKY DUCK & HASHIMOTO-SAN** (See Deputy Dawg Presents. . .)

**DINO** (TV)(The Flintstones)
Aug, 1973 - No. 20, Jan, 1977
Charlton Publications

1 — .70 2.00 4.00
2-20 — .25 .75 1.50

**DINO RIDERS**
Feb, 1989 - No. 3, 1989 ($1.00, color)
Marvel Comics

1-3: Based on toys — .50 1.00

**DINOSAUR REX**
1986 - No. 3, 1986 ($2.00, mini-series)
Upshot Graphics (Fantagraphics Books)

1-3 — .35 1.00 2.00

**DINOSAURS FOR HIRE**
Mar, 1988 - No. 9?, 1989 ($1.95, B&W)
Eternity Comics

1-9: 1-1st & 2nd printings — .35 1.00 2.00
. . . Fall Classic 1 (11/88, $2.25, B&W, 52 pgs.) — .40 1.15 2.30
. . . 3-D 1 (10/88, $2.95) — .50 1.50 3.00

**DINOSAURUS** (See 4-Color No. 1120)

**DIPPY DUCK**
October, 1957
Atlas Comics (OPI)

1-Maneely-a — 2.65 8.00 18.00

**DIRECTORY TO A NONEXISTENT UNIVERSE**
Dec, 1987 ($2.00, B&W)
Eclipse Comics

1 — .35 1.00 2.00

**DIRTY DOZEN** (See Movie Classics)

**DIRTY PAIR**
Dec, 1988 - No. 4, April, 1989 ($2.00, B&W, mini-series)
Eclipse Comics

1-4: Japanese manga with original stories — .35 1.00 2.00

**DIRTY PAIR II**
June, 1989 - No. 5, Mar, 1990 ($2.00, B&W, mini-series)
Eclipse Comics

| | Good | Fine | N-Mint |
|---|---|---|---|
| 1-5: 3-Cover is misnumbered as #1 | .35 | 1.00 | 2.00 |

**DIRTY PAIR III, THE**
Aug, 1990 - No. 5, 1991 ($2.00, B&W, mini-series)
Eclipse Comics

| | | | |
|---|---|---|---|
| 1-5 | .35 | 1.00 | 2.00 |

**DISHMAN**
Sept, 1988 ($2.50, B&W, 52pgs)
Eclipse Comics

| | | | |
|---|---|---|---|
| 1 | .40 | 1.25 | 2.50 |

**DISNEY COMIC ALBUM**
1990(no month, year) - Present ($6.95-$7.95, color)
Disney Comics

| | | | |
|---|---|---|---|
| 1,2 ($6.95): 1-Donald Duck and Gyro Gearloose by Barks(r). 2-Uncle Scrooge by Barks(r); Jr. Woodchucks app. | 1.15 | 3.50 | 7.00 |
| 3-7: 3-Donald Duck-r/F.C. 308 by Barks; begin $7.95-c. 4-Mickey Mouse Meets the Phantom Blot; strip-r. 5-Chip 'n' Dale Rescue Rangers; new-a. 6-Uncle Scrooge. 7-Donald Duck in Too Many Pets; Barks-r(4) | 1.35 | 4.00 | 8.00 |
| Special 1 (1990, $7.95)-Super Goof Adventures; r/Super Goof #1, Donald Duck #102 & others | 1.35 | 4.00 | 8.00 |

**DISNEYLAND BIRTHDAY PARTY** (Also see Dell Giants)
Aug, 1985 ($2.50)
Gladstone Publishing Co.

| | | | |
|---|---|---|---|
| 1-R-/Dell Giant with new-photo-c | .40 | 1.25 | 2.50 |
| . . . Comics Digest #1-(Digest) | | .60 | 1.25 |

**DISNEYLAND, USA** (See Dell Giant No. 30)

**DISNEY'S DUCKTALES** (TV) (Also see Ducktales)
Oct, 1988 - No. 13, May, 1990 (1,2,9-11: $1.50; 3-8: 95 cents, color)
Gladstone Publishing

| | | | |
|---|---|---|---|
| 1-Barks-r | .60 | 1.75 | 3.50 |
| 2-5: 2,4,5-Barks-r | .35 | 1.00 | 2.00 |
| 6-11: 6,9-11-Barks-r. 7-Barks-r(1 pg.) | | .55 | 1.10 |
| 12,13 ($1.95, 68 pgs.)-Barks-r; 12-r/F.C. #495 | .35 | 1.10 | 2.20 |

**DISNEY'S TALESPIN LIMITED SERIES: "TAKE OFF"**
Jan, 1991 - No. 4, Apr, 1991 ($1.50, color, mini-series, 52 pgs.)
W. D. Publications (Disney Comics)

| | | | |
|---|---|---|---|
| 1-4: Based on animated series; 4 part origin | .25 | .75 | 1.50 |

**DIVER DAN** (TV)
Feb-Apr, 1962 - No. 2, June-Aug, 1962
Dell Publishing Co.

| | | | |
|---|---|---|---|
| 4-Color 1254(#1), 2 | 3.50 | 10.50 | 24.00 |

**DIXIE DUGAN** (See Big Shot, Columbia Comics & Feature Funnies)
July, 1942 - No. 13, 1949 (Strip reprints in all)
McNaught Syndicate/Columbia/Publication Ent.

| | | | |
|---|---|---|---|
| 1-Joe Palooka x-over by Ham Fisher | 14.00 | 43.00 | 100.00 |
| 2 | 7.00 | 21.00 | 50.00 |
| 3 | 5.70 | 17.00 | 40.00 |
| 4,5(1945-46)-Bo strip-r | 3.70 | 11.00 | 26.00 |
| 6-13(1/47-49): 6-Paperdoll cut-outs | 2.65 | 8.00 | 18.00 |

**DIXIE DUGAN**
V3#1, Nov, 1951 - V4#4, Feb, 1954
Prize Publications (Headline)

| | | | |
|---|---|---|---|
| V3#1 | 3.70 | 11.00 | 26.00 |
| 2-4 | 2.30 | 7.00 | 16.00 |
| V4#1-4(#5-8) | 1.70 | 5.00 | 12.00 |

**DIZZY DAMES**
Sept-Oct, 1952 - No. 6, July-Aug, 1953
American Comics Group (B&M Distr. Co.)

| | Good | Fine | N-Mint |
|---|---|---|---|
| 1 | 4.00 | 12.00 | 28.00 |
| 2 | 2.65 | 8.00 | 18.00 |
| 3-6 | 1.70 | 5.00 | 12.00 |

**DIZZY DON COMICS**
1942 - No. 22, Oct, 1946; No. 3, Apr, 1947 (B&W)
F. E. Howard Publications/Dizzy Don Ent. Ltd (Canada)

| | | | |
|---|---|---|---|
| 1 | 3.00 | 9.00 | 21.00 |
| 2 | 1.50 | 4.50 | 10.00 |
| 4-21 | 1.15 | 3.50 | 8.00 |
| 22-Full color, 52 pgs. | 2.65 | 8.00 | 18.00 |
| 3 (4/47)-Full color, 52 pgs. | 2.00 | 6.00 | 14.00 |

**DIZZY DUCK** (Formerly Barnyard Comics)
No. 32, Nov, 1950 - No. 39, Mar, 1952
Standard Comics

| | | | |
|---|---|---|---|
| 32 | 3.70 | 11.00 | 26.00 |
| 33-39 | 2.00 | 6.00 | 14.00 |

**DNAGENTS** (The New DNAgents V2/1 on)(Also see Surge)
March, 1983 - No. 24, July, 1985 ($1.50, Baxter paper)
Eclipse Comics

| | | | |
|---|---|---|---|
| 1-Origin | .50 | 1.50 | 3.00 |
| 2-10: 4-Amber app. 9-Spiegle-a | .40 | 1.25 | 2.50 |
| 11-24: 18-Infinity-c. 24-Dave Stevens-c | .35 | 1.00 | 2.00 |

**DOBERMAN** (See Sgt. Bilko's Private . . .)

**DOBIE GILLIS** (See The Many Loves of . . .)

**DOC CARTER VD COMICS**
1949 (16 pages in color) (Paper cover)
Health Publications Institute, Raleigh, N. C. (Giveaway)

| | | | |
|---|---|---|---|
| nn | 13.00 | 40.00 | 90.00 |

**DOC CHAOS: THE STRANGE ATTRACTOR**
Apr, 1990 - Present ($3.00, color, 32 pgs.)
Vortex Comics

| | | | |
|---|---|---|---|
| 1-3: The Lust For Order | .50 | 1.50 | 3.00 |

**DOC SAVAGE**
November, 1966
Gold Key

| | | | |
|---|---|---|---|
| 1-Adaptation of the Thousand-Headed Man; James Bama-c r-/'64 Doc Savage paperback | 4.30 | 13.00 | 30.00 |

**DOC SAVAGE**
Oct, 1972 - No. 8, Jan, 1974
Marvel Comics Group

| | | | |
|---|---|---|---|
| 1 | .85 | 2.50 | 5.00 |
| 2-8: 2,3-Steranko-c | .35 | 1.00 | 2.00 |
| Giant-Size 1(1975)-Reprints No. 1 & 2 | .35 | 1.00 | 2.00 |

NOTE: *Gil Kane c-5, 6. **Mooney** a-1i, Gnt-Size 1r. No. 1, 2 adapts pulp story "The Man of Bronze," No. 3, 4 adapts "Death in Silver," No. 5, 6 adapts "The Monsters," No. 7, 8 adapts "The Brand of The Werewolf."*

**DOC SAVAGE** (Magazine)
Aug, 1975 - No. 8, Spr, 1977 ($1.00, Black & White)
Marvel Comics Group

| | | | |
|---|---|---|---|
| 1-Cover from movie poster; Ron Ely photo-c | .50 | 1.50 | 3.00 |
| 2-8: Buscema-a in 1,3 | .25 | .75 | 1.50 |

**DOC SAVAGE**
Nov, 1987 - No. 4, Feb, 1988 ($1.75, mini-series)
DC Comics

| | | | |
|---|---|---|---|
| 1-4: Adam & Andy Kubert-c/a | .35 | 1.00 | 2.00 |

**DOC SAVAGE**
Nov, 1988 - No. 24, Oct, 1990 ($1.75-$2.00 #13 on, color)
DC Comics

| | | | |
|---|---|---|---|
| 1-Painted-c | .35 | 1.00 | 2.00 |

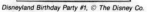

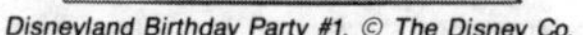
*Disneyland Birthday Party #1, © The Disney Co.*

*Dixie Dugan #6, © McNaught Synd.*

*Doc Savage #2 (12/72), © MEG*

Doc Savage Comics #1, © S&S

Doctor Strange #177, © MEG

Doctor Strange, Sorcerer Supreme #15, © MEG

Good Fine N-Mint

2-24: 2-Adam & Andy Kubert-c/a begins .35 1.00 2.00
Annual 1 (1989, $3.50, 68 pgs.) .60 1.75 3.50

**DOC SAVAGE COMICS** (Also see Shadow Comics)
May, 1940 - No. 20, Oct, 1943 (1st app. in Doc Savage pulp, 3/33)
Street & Smith Publications

1-Doc Savage, Cap Fury, Danny Garrett, Mark Mallory, The Whisperer, Captain Death, Billy the Kid, Sheriff Pete & Treasure Island begin; Norgil, the Magician app. 150.00 375.00 900.00
2-Origin & 1st app. Ajax, the Sun Man; Danny Garrett, The Whisperer end 68.00 205.00 475.00
3 54.00 160.00 375.00
4-Treasure Island ends; Tuska-a 40.00 120.00 280.00
5-Origin & 1st app. Astron, the Crocodile Queen, not in #9 & 11; Norgil the Magician app. 32.00 95.00 225.00
6-9: 6-Cap Fury ends; origin & only app. Red Falcon in Astron story. 8-Mark Mallory ends; Charlie McCarthy app. on cover. 9-Supersnipe app. 26.00 77.00 180.00
10-Origin & only app. The Thunderbolt 26.00 77.00 180.00
11,12 20.00 60.00 140.00
V2#1-8(#13-20): 16-The Pulp Hero, The Avenger app. 17-Sun Man ends; Nick Carter begins 20.00 60.00 140.00

**DOC STEARN . . . MR. MONSTER** (See Mr. Monster)

**DR. ANTHONY KING, HOLLYWOOD LOVE DOCTOR**
1952(Jan.) - No. 3, May, 1953; No. 4, May, 1954
Minoan Publishing Corp./Harvey Publications No. 4

1 5.00 15.00 35.00
2-4: 4-Powell-a 3.50 10.50 24.00

**DR. ANTHONY'S LOVE CLINIC** (See Mr. Anthony's . . .)

**DR. BOBBS** (See 4-Color No. 212)

**DOCTOR BOOGIE**
1987 ($1.75, color)
Media Arts Publishing

1-Airbrush wraparound-c; Nick Cuti-i .30 .90 1.75

**DR. FATE** (See First Issue Special, The Immortal . . ., Justice League, More Fun #55, & Showcase)

**DOCTOR FATE**
July, 1987 - No. 4, Oct, 1987 ($1.50, mini-series, Baxter)
DC Comics

1-4: Giffen-c/a in all .25 .75 1.50

**DOCTOR FATE**
Winter, 1988-'89 - Present ($1.25-$1.50 #5 on, color)
DC Comics

1-26: 15-Justice League app. .25 .75 1.50
Annual 1(1989, $2.95, 68 pgs.)-Sutton-a .50 1.50 3.00

**DR. FU MANCHU** (See The Mask of . . .)
1964
I.W. Enterprises

1-Reprints Avon's "Mask of Dr. Fu Manchu;" Wood-a 5.70 17.00 40.00

**DOCTOR GRAVES** (Formerly The Many Ghosts of . . .)
No. 73, Sept, 1985 - No. 75, Jan, 1986
Charlton Comics

73-75 .40 .75

**DR. JEKYLL AND MR. HYDE** (See A Star Presentation & Supernatural Thrillers #4)

**DR. KILDARE** (TV)
No. 1337, 4-6/62 - No. 9, 4-6/65 (All Richard Chamberlain photo-c)
Dell Publishing Co.

4-Color 1337(#1, 1962) 3.70 11.00 26.00

Good Fine N-Mint

2-9 2.65 8.00 18.00

**DR. MASTERS** (See The Adventures of Young . . .)

**DOCTOR SOLAR, MAN OF THE ATOM**
10/62 - No. 27, 4/69; No. 28, 4/81 - No. 31, 3/82
Gold Key/Whitman No. 28 on (Painted-c No. 1-27)

1-Origin/1st app. Dr. Solar (1st Gold Key comic-No. 10000-210) 5.00 15.00 35.00
2-Prof. Harbinger begins 2.65 8.00 18.00
3-5: 5-Intro. Man of the Atom in costume 2.00 6.00 14.00
6-10,15: 15-Origin retold 1.50 4.50 10.00
11-14,16-20 1.15 3.50 8.00
21-27 1.00 3.00 6.00
28-31: 29-Magnus Robot Fighter begins. 31-The Sentinel app. .50 1.00

NOTE: ***Frank Bolle*** *a-6-19, 29-31; c-29i, 30i.* ***Bob Fugitani*** *a-1-5.* ***Spiegle*** *a-29-31.* ***Al McWilliams*** *a-20-23.*

**DOCTOR SOLAR, MAN OF THE ATOM**
1990 - No. 10, 1991 ($7.95, color, card stock-c, high quality, 96 pgs.)
Valiant Comics

1-10: Reprints Gold Key series 1.35 4.00 8.00

**DOCTOR SPEKTOR** (See The Occult Files of . . .)

**DOCTOR STRANGE** (Formerly Strange Tales #1-168) (Also see The Defenders, Giant-Size . . ., Marvel Fanfare, Marvel Graphic Novel, Marvel Premiere, Marvel Treasury Ed. & Strange Tales, 2nd Series)
No. 169, 6/68 - No. 183, 11/69; 6/74 - No. 81, 2/87
Marvel Comics Group

169(#1)-Origin; panel swipe/M.D. #1-c 8.50 25.50 60.00
170-183: 177-New costume 2.85 8.50 20.00
1(6/74)-Brunner-c/a 2.85 8.50 20.00
2 1.50 4.50 10.00
3-5 1.00 3.00 6.00
6-26: 21-Origin-r/Doctor Strange #169 .50 1.50 3.00
27-81: 56-Origin retold. 78-New Costume .60 1.20
Annual 1 (1976)-New Russell-a .50 1.50 3.00

NOTE: ***Adkins*** *a-169, 170, 171i; c-169-171, 172i, 173.* ***Adams*** *a-4i.* ***Austin*** *a-48-60i, 66i, 68i, 70i; c-38i, 47-53i, 55i, 58-60i, 70i.* ***Brunner*** *a-1-5p; c-1-6, 22, 28-30, 33.* ***Colan*** *a(p)-172-178, 180-183, 6-18, 36-45, 47; c(p)-172, 174-183, 11-21, 23, 27, 35, 36, 47.* ***Ditko*** *a-179r, 3r.* ***Everett*** *c-183i.* ***Golden*** *a-46p, 55p; c-42-44, 46, 55p.* ***G. Kane*** *c(p)-8-10.* ***Miller*** *c-46p.* ***Nebres*** *a-20, 22, 23, 24i, 26i, 32i; c-32i, 34.* ***Rogers*** *a-48-53p; c-47p-53p.* ***Russell*** *a-34i, 46i, Annual 1.* ***B. Smith*** *c-179.* ***Paul Smith*** *a-54p, 56p, 65, 66p, 68p, 69, 71-73; c-56, 65, 66, 68, 71.* ***Starlin*** *a-23p, 26; c-25, 26.* ***Sutton*** *a-27-29p, 34p. Painted c-62, 63.*

**DOCTOR STRANGE CLASSICS**
Mar, 1984 - No. 4, June, 1984 ($1.50 cover price; Baxter paper)
Marvel Comics Group

1-4: Ditko-r; Byrne-c. 4-New Golden pin-up .30 .90 1.80

**DOCTOR STRANGE/SILVER DAGGER** (Special Edition)
Mar, 1983 ($2.50, Baxter paper)
Marvel Comics

1-r/Dr. Strange #1,2,4,5; Wrightson-c .35 1.00 2.00

**DOCTOR STRANGE, SORCERER SUPREME**
Nov, 1988 - Present (Mando paper, $1.25-1.50, direct sales only)
Marvel Comics

1 ($1.25) .85 2.50 5.00
2-14,16-28: ($1.50): 3-New Defenders app. 5-Guice-c/a begins. 11-Hobgoblin app. 26-Werewolf by Night app. .25 .75 1.50
15-Unauthorized Amy Grant photo-c 1.10 3.25 6.50

NOTE: ***Colan*** *c/a-19.* ***Guice*** *a-5-16, 18, 20-24; c-5-12, 20-24.*

**DR. TOM BRENT, YOUNG INTERN**
Feb, 1963 - No. 5, Oct, 1963
Charlton Publications

1 1.00 3.00 6.00

| | Good | Fine | N-Mint |
|---|---|---|---|
| 2-5 | .60 | 1.75 | 3.50 |

**DR. VOLTZ** (See Mighty Midget Comics)

**DOCTOR WHO** (Also see Marvel Premiere #57-60)
Oct, 1984 - No. 23, Aug, 1986 ($1.50, Direct sales, Baxter paper)
Marvel Comics Group

| | Good | Fine | N-Mint |
|---|---|---|---|
| 1-($1.50 cover)-British-r | .35 | 1.00 | 2.00 |
| 2-23 | | .50 | 1.00 |

**DR. WHO & THE DALEKS** (See Movie Classics)

**DOCTOR ZERO**
April, 1988 - No. 8, Aug, 1989 ($1.25/$1.50, color)
Epic Comics (Marvel)

| | Good | Fine | N-Mint |
|---|---|---|---|
| 1-8: 1-Sienkiewicz-c. 6,7-Spiegle-a | .25 | .75 | 1.50 |

**DO-DO**
1950 - No. 7, 1951 (5x7¼" Miniature) (5 cents)
Nation Wide Publishers

| | Good | Fine | N-Mint |
|---|---|---|---|
| 1 (52 pgs.); funny animal | 4.50 | 14.00 | 32.00 |
| 2-7 | 2.65 | 8.00 | 18.00 |

**DODO & THE FROG, THE** (Formerly Funny Stuff)
No. 80, 9-10/54 - No. 88, 1-2/56; No. 89, 8-9/56; No. 90, 10-11/56; No. 91, 9/57; No. 92, 11/57 (See Comic Cavalcade)
National Periodical Publications

| | Good | Fine | N-Mint |
|---|---|---|---|
| 80-Doodles Duck by Sheldon Mayer | 7.00 | 21.00 | 50.00 |
| 81-91: Doodles Duck by Sheldon Mayer in #81,83-90 | 4.00 | 12.00 | 28.00 |
| 92-(Scarce)-Doodles Duck by S. Mayer | 5.70 | 17.00 | 40.00 |

**DOGFACE DOOLEY**
1951 - No. 5, 1953
Magazine Enterprises

| | Good | Fine | N-Mint |
|---|---|---|---|
| 1(A-1 40) | 2.65 | 8.00 | 18.00 |
| 2(A-1 43), 3(A-1 49), 4(A-1 53), 5(A-1 64) | 1.70 | 5.00 | 12.00 |
| I.W. Reprint #1('64), Super Reprint #17 | .70 | 2.00 | 4.00 |

**DOG OF FLANDERS, A** (See 4-Color No. 1088)

**DOGPATCH** (See Al Capp's . . . & Mammy Yokum)

**DOINGS OF THE DOO DADS, THE**
1922 (34 pgs.; 7¾x7¾"; B&W) (50 cents)
(Red & White cover; square binding)
Detroit News (Universal Feat. & Specialty Co.)

| | Good | Fine | N-Mint |
|---|---|---|---|
| nn-Reprints 1921 newspaper strip "Text & Pictures" given away as prize in the Detroit News Doo Dads contest; by Arch Dale | 8.50 | 25.50 | 60.00 |

**DOLLFACE & HER GANG** (See 4-Color No. 309)

**DOLL MAN** (Also see Feature Comics #27 & Freedom Fighters)
Fall, 1941 - No. 7, Fall, '43; No. 8, Spring, '46 - No. 47, Oct, 1953
Quality Comics Group

| | Good | Fine | N-Mint |
|---|---|---|---|
| 1-Dollman (by Cassone) & Justin Wright begin | 107.00 | 320.00 | 750.00 |
| 2-The Dragon begins; Crandall-a(5) | 55.00 | 165.00 | 385.00 |
| 3,4 | 40.00 | 120.00 | 280.00 |
| 5-Crandall-a | 29.00 | 86.00 | 200.00 |
| 6,7(1943) | 21.00 | 62.00 | 145.00 |
| 8(1946)-1st app. Torchy by Bill Ward | 23.00 | 70.00 | 160.00 |
| 9 | 18.00 | 54.00 | 125.00 |
| 10-20 | 14.00 | 43.00 | 100.00 |
| 21-30 | 12.00 | 36.00 | 85.00 |
| 31-36,38,40: Jeb Rivers app. #32-34 | 10.00 | 30.00 | 75.00 |
| 37-Origin Dollgirl; Dollgirl bondage-c | 13.00 | 40.00 | 90.00 |
| 39-"Narcotics. . .the Death Drug"-c-/story | 10.00 | 30.00 | 70.00 |
| 41-47 | 7.00 | 21.00 | 50.00 |
| Super Reprint #11('64, r-#20),15(r-#23),17(r-#28): Torchy app.-#15,17 | 1.35 | 4.00 | 8.00 |

NOTE: *Ward Torchy in 8, 9, 11, 12, 14-24, 27; by Fox-#30, 35-47. Crandall a-2, 5, 10, 13 & Super #11, 17, 18. Guardineer a-3. Bondage c-27, 37, 38, 39.*

**DOLLY**
No. 10, 1951 (Funny animal)
Ziff-Davis Publ. Co.

| | Good | Fine | N-Mint |
|---|---|---|---|
| 10 | 2.00 | 6.00 | 14.00 |

**DOLLY DILL**
1945
Marvel Comics/Newsstand Publ.

| | Good | Fine | N-Mint |
|---|---|---|---|
| 1 | 8.00 | 24.00 | 56.00 |

**DOLLY DIMPLES & BOBBY BOONCE'**
1933
Cupples & Leon Co.

| | Good | Fine | N-Mint |
|---|---|---|---|
| nn | 8.00 | 24.00 | 56.00 |

**DOMINION**
Dec, 1990 - No. 6, July, 1990 ($2.00, B&W, mini-series)
Eclipse Comics

| | Good | Fine | N-Mint |
|---|---|---|---|
| 1-6: Japanese comics translated to English | .35 | 1.00 | 2.00 |

**DOMINO CHANCE**
May-June, 1982 - No. 9, May, 1985 (B&W)
Chance Enterprises

| | Good | Fine | N-Mint |
|---|---|---|---|
| 1 | 1.35 | 4.00 | 8.00 |
| 1-Reprint, May 1985 | .50 | 1.50 | 3.00 |
| 2-6,9 | | .50 | 1.00 |
| 7-1st app. Gizmo, 2 pgs. | 1.15 | 3.50 | 7.00 |
| 8-1st full Gizmo story | 1.70 | 5.00 | 10.00 |

**DONALD AND MICKEY IN DISNEYLAND** (See Dell Giants)

**DONALD AND MICKEY MERRY CHRISTMAS** (Formerly Famous Gang Book Of Comics)
1943 - 1949 (20 pgs.)(Giveaway) Put out each Christmas; 1943 issue titled "Firestone Presents Comics" (Disney)
K. K. Publ./Firestone Tire & Rubber Co.

| | Good | Fine | N-Mint |
|---|---|---|---|
| 1943-Donald Duck reprint from WDC&S #32 by Carl Barks | 50.00 | 150.00 | 350.00 |
| 1944-Donald Duck reprint from WDC&S #35 by Barks | 48.00 | 144.00 | 335.00 |
| 1945-"Donald Duck's Best Christmas," 8 pgs. Carl Barks; intro. & 1st app. Grandma Duck in comic books | 61.00 | 184.00 | 430.00 |
| 1946-Donald Duck in "Santa's Stormy Visit," 8 pgs. Carl Barks | 46.00 | 137.00 | 320.00 |
| 1947-Donald Duck in "Three Good Little Ducks," 8 pgs. Carl Barks | 38.00 | 115.00 | 265.00 |
| 1948-Donald Duck in "Toyland," 8 pgs. Carl Barks | 36.00 | 107.00 | 250.00 |
| 1949-Donald Duck in "New Toys," 8 pgs. Carl Barks | 43.00 | 130.00 | 305.00 |

**DONALD AND THE WHEEL** (See 4-Color No. 1190)

**DONALD DUCK** (See Cheerios, Disney's Ducktales, Ducktales, Dynabrite Comics, Gladstone Comic Album, Mickey & Donald, Mickey Mouse Mag., Story Hour Series, Uncle Scrooge, Walt Disney's Comics & Stories, Wheaties & Whitman Comic Books)

**DONALD DUCK**
1935, 1936 (Linen-like text & color pictures; 1st book ever devoted to Donald Duck; see The Wise Little Hen for earlier app.) (9½x13")
Whitman Publishing Co./Grosset & Dunlap/K.K.

| | Good | Fine | N-Mint |
|---|---|---|---|
| 978(1935)-16 pgs.; story book | 85.00 | 260.00 | 600.00 |
| nn(1936)-36 pgs.; reprints '35 edition with expanded ill. & text | 55.00 | 165.00 | 385.00 |
| with dust jacket . . . . | 70.00 | 210.00 | 490.00 |

Doll Man #13, © QUA

Dominion #1, © Masamune Shirow

Donald & Mickey Merry . . ., 1946, © Disney Co.

*Donald Duck nn (1938), © The Disney Co.*

*Donald Duck Four Color #4, © The Disney Co.*

*Donald Duck #257, © The Disney Co.*

**DONALD DUCK** (Walt Disney's) (10 cents)
1938 (B&W) (8½x11½") (Cardboard covers)
Whitman/K.K. Publications

(Has Donald Duck with bubble pipe on front cover)

| | Good | Fine | VF-NM |
|---|---|---|---|
| nn-The first Donald Duck & Walt Disney comic book; 1936 & 1937 Sunday strip-r(in B&W); same format as the Feature Books; 1st strips with Huey, Dewey & Louie from 10/17/37 | 110.00 | 335.00 | 780.00 |

(Prices vary widely on this book)

**DONALD DUCK** (Walt Disney's. . .#262 on; see 4-Color listings for titles & 4-Color No. 1109 for origin story)
1940 - #84, 9-11/62; #85, 12/62 - #245, 1984; #246, 10/86 - #279, 5/90
Dell Publishing Co./Gold Key No. 85-216/Whitman No. 217-245/
Gladstone Publishing No. 246 on

| | Good | Fine | VF-NM | NM/Mint |
|---|---|---|---|---|
| 4-Color 4(1940)-Daily 1939 strip-r by Al Taliaferro | 357.00 | 1070.00 | 2500.00 | 3900.00 |

(Estimated up to 175 total copies exist, 9 in NM/Mint)

| | Good | Fine | N-Mint |
|---|---|---|---|
| (Large Feature Comic 16(1/41?)-1940 Sunday strips-r in B&W | 170.00 | 515.00 | 1200.00 |
| Large Feature Comic 20('41)-Comic Paint Book, r-single panels from Large Feature #16 at top of each page to color; daily strip-r across bottom of each page | 230.00 | 685.00 | 1600.00 |

| | Good | Fine | VF-NM | NM/Mint |
|---|---|---|---|---|
| 4-Color 9('42)-"Finds Pirate Gold;"-64 pgs. by Carl Barks & Jack Hannah (pgs. 1,2,5,12-40 are by Barks, his 1st comic book work; © 8/17/42) | 370.00 | 1115.00 | 2800.00 | 3700.00 |

(Estimated up to 270 total copies exist, 18 in NM/Mint)

| | Good | Fine | VF-NM | NM/Mint |
|---|---|---|---|---|
| 4-Color 29(9/43)-"Mummy's Ring" by Carl Barks; reprinted in Uncle Scrooge & Donald Duck #1('65), W. D. Comics Digest #44('73) & Donald Duck Advs. #14 | 243.00 | 730.00 | 1850.00 | 2800.00 |

(Estimated up to 300 total copies exist, 14 in NM/Mint)

| | Good | Fine | N-Mint |
|---|---|---|---|
| 4-Color 62(1/45)-"Frozen Gold;" 52 pgs. by Carl Barks, reprinted in The Best of W.D. Comics & Donald Duck Advs. #4 | 120.00 | 360.00 | 910.00 |
| 4-Color 108(1946)-"Terror of the River;" 52 pgs. by Carl Barks; reprinted in Gladstone Comic Album #2 | 90.00 | 270.00 | 680.00 |
| 4-Color 147(5/47)-in "Volcano Valley" by Carl Barks | 60.00 | 180.00 | 455.00 |
| 4-Color 159(8/47)-in "The Ghost of the Grotto;" 52 pgs. by Carl Barks-reprinted in Best of Uncle Scrooge & Donald Duck #1 ('66) & The Best of W.D. Comics & D.D. Advs. #9; two Barks stories | 54.00 | 160.00 | 410.00 |
| 4-Color 178(12/47)-1st Uncle Scrooge by Carl Barks; reprinted in Gold Key Christmas Parade No. 3 & The Best of W.D. Comics | 64.00 | 192.00 | 485.00 |
| 4-Color 189(6/48)-by Carl Barks; reprinted in Best of Donald Duck & Uncle Scrooge #1('64) & D.D. Advs. #19 | 54.00 | 160.00 | 410.00 |
| 4-Color 199(10/48)-by Carl Barks; mentioned in **Love and Death**; r/in Gladstone Comic Album #5 | 54.00 | 160.00 | 410.00 |
| 4-Color 203(12/48)-by Barks; reprinted as Gold Key Christmas Parade #4 | 36.00 | 108.00 | 270.00 |
| 4-Color 223(4/49)-by Barks; reprinted as Best of Donald Duck #1 & Donald Duck Advs. #3 | 50.00 | 150.00 | 380.00 |
| 4-Color 238(8/49), 256(12/49)-by Barks; No. 256-reprinted in Best of Donald Duck & Uncle Scrooge #2('67), Gladstone Comic Album #16 & W.D. Comics Digest #44('73) | 27.00 | 81.00 | 205.00 |
| 4-Color 263(2/50)-Two Barks stories; r-in D.D. #278 | 27.00 | 81.00 | 205.00 |
| 4-Color 275(5/50), 282(7/50), 291(9/50), 300(11/50)-All by Carl Barks; #275,282 reprinted in W.D. Comics Digest #44('73). #275 r/in Gladstone Comic Album #10. #291 r/in Donald Duck Advs. #16 | 25.00 | 75.00 | 190.00 |
| 4-Color 308(1/51), 318(3/51)-by Barks; #318-reprinted in W.D. Comics Digest #34 & D.D. Advs. #2,19 | 21.00 | 63.00 | 160.00 |
| 4-Color 328(5/51)-by Carl Barks | 23.00 | 70.00 | 175.00 |
| 4-Color 339(7-8/51), 379-not by Barks | 4.35 | 13.00 | 30.00 |
| 4-Color 348(9-10/51), 356,394-Barks-c only | 6.50 | 19.00 | 45.00 |
| 4-Color 367(1-2/52)-by Barks; reprinted as Gold Key Christmas Parade #2 & #8 | 20.00 | 60.00 | 150.00 |
| 4-Color 408(7-8/52), 422(9-10/52)-All by Carl Barks. #408-R/in Best of Donald Duck & Uncle Scrooge #1('64) & Gladstone Comic Album #13 | 20.00 | 60.00 | 150.00 |
| 26(11-12/52)-In "Trick or Treat"(Barks-a, 36pgs.) 1st story r-/Walt Disney Digest #16 & Gladstone C.A. #23 | 22.00 | 65.00 | 165.00 |
| 27-30-Barks-c only | 4.30 | 13.00 | 30.00 |
| 31-40 | 2.65 | 8.00 | 18.00 |
| 41-44,47-50 | 2.00 | 6.00 | 14.00 |
| 45-Barks-a, 6 pgs. | 7.00 | 21.00 | 55.00 |
| 46-"Secret of Hondorica" by Barks, 24 pgs.; reprinted in Donald Duck #98 & 154 | 8.00 | 24.00 | 60.00 |
| 51-Barks, ½ pg. | 1.70 | 5.00 | 12.00 |
| 52-"Lost Peg-Leg Mine" by Barks, 10 pgs. | 6.50 | 19.50 | 50.00 |
| 53,55-59 | 1.60 | 4.80 | 11.00 |
| 54-"Forbidden Valley" by Barks, 26 pgs. | 7.50 | 22.00 | 58.00 |
| 60-"Donald Duck & the Titanic Ants" by Barks, 20 pgs. plus 6 more pages | 6.50 | 19.50 | 50.00 |
| 61-67,69,70 | 1.30 | 4.00 | 9.00 |
| 68-Barks-a, 5 pgs. | 3.75 | 11.25 | 26.00 |
| 71-Barks-r, ½ pg. | 1.50 | 4.50 | 10.00 |
| 72-78,80,82-97,99,100: 96-Donald Duck Album | 1.15 | 3.50 | 8.00 |
| 79,81-Barks-a, 1pg. | 1.50 | 4.50 | 10.00 |
| 98-Reprints #46 (Barks) | 2.15 | 6.50 | 15.00 |
| 101-133: 102-Super Goof. 112-1st Moby Duck | .85 | 2.50 | 6.00 |
| 134-Barks-r/#52 & WDC&S 194 | 1.00 | 3.00 | 7.00 |
| 135-Barks-r/WDC&S 198, 19 pgs. | .70 | 2.00 | 5.00 |
| 136-153,155,156,158 | .50 | 1.50 | 3.00 |
| 154-Barks-r(#46) | .70 | 2.00 | 5.00 |
| 157,159,160,164: 157-Barks-r(#45). 159-Reprints/WDC&S #192 (10 pgs.). 160-Barks-r(#26). 164-Barks-r(#79) | .40 | 1.25 | 2.50 |
| 161-163,165-170 | .25 | .75 | 1.50 |
| 171-173,175-187,189-191 | | .60 | 1.20 |
| 174,188: 174-R/4-Color #394. 188-Barks-r/#68 | .35 | 1.00 | 2.00 |
| 192-Barks-r(40 pgs.) from Donald Duck #60 & WDC&S #226,234 (52 pgs.) | .40 | 1.25 | 2.50 |
| 193-200,202-207,209-211,213-218: 217 has 216 on-c | | .50 | 1.00 |
| 201,208,212: 201-Barks-r/Christmas Parade #26, 16pgs. 208-Barks-r/#60 (6 pgs.). 212-Barks-r/WDC&S #130 | .35 | 1.00 | 2.00 |
| 219-Barks-r/WDC&S #106,107, 10 pgs. ea. | | .60 | 1.20 |
| 220-227,231-245 | | .35 | .70 |
| 228-230: 228-Barks-r/F.C. #275. 229-Barks-r/F.C. #282. 230-Barks-r/#52 & WDC&S #194 | .25 | .75 | 1.50 |
| 246-(1st Gladstone issue)-Barks-r/FC #422 | 1.50 | 4.50 | 9.00 |
| 247-249: 248-Barks-r/DD #54. 249-Barks-r/DD #26 | .70 | 2.00 | 4.00 |
| 250-($1.50, 68 pgs.)-Barks-r/4-Color #9 | 2.50 | 7.50 | 15.00 |
| 251-256: 251-Barks-r/'45 Firestone. 254-Barks-r/FC #328. 256-Barks-r/FC #147 | .50 | 1.50 | 3.50 |
| 257-($1.50, 52 pgs.)-Barks-r/Vac. Parade #1 | .70 | 2.00 | 4.00 |
| 258-260 | .40 | 1.25 | 2.50 |
| 261-277: 261-Barks-r/FC #300. 275-Kelly-r/FC #92 | .25 | .75 | 1.50 |
| 278-($1.95, 68 pgs.)-Rosa-a; Barks-r/FC #263 | .40 | 1.25 | 2.50 |
| 279-($1.95, 68 pgs.)-Rosa-c; Barks-r/MOC #4 | .40 | 1.25 | 2.50 |
| Mini-Comic #1(1976)-(3¼x6½"); R/D.D. #150 | | | .10 |

NOTE: ***Carl Barks** wrote all issues he illustrated, but #117, 126, 138 contain his script only. Issues 4-Color #189, 199, 203, 223, 238, 256, 263, 275, 282, 308, 348, 356, 367, 394, 408, 422, 26-30, 35, 44, 46, 52, 55, 57, 60, 65, 70-73, 77-80, 83, 101, 103, 105, 106, 111, 126, 246r, 266r, 268r, 271r, 275r, 278r(F.C. 263) all have **Barks** covers. **Barks*** *r-263-267, 269-278. #96 titled "Comic Album," #99-"Christmas Album." New art issues (not reprints)-106-46, 148-63, 167, 169, 170, 172, 173, 175, 178, 179, 196, 209, 223, 225, 236.*

**DONALD DUCK**
1944 (16 pg. Christmas giveaway)(paper cover)(2 versions)
K. K. Publications

| | Good | Fine | N-Mint |
|---|---|---|---|
| nn-Kelly cover reprint | 39.00 | 115.00 | 270.00 |

**DONALD DUCK ADVENTURES** (Walt Disney's. . .#4 on)
Nov, 1987 - No. 20, Apr, 1990
Gladstone Publishing

| | | | |
|---|---|---|---|
| 1 | .55 | 1.65 | 3.30 |
| 2-r/F.C. #308 | .35 | 1.10 | 2.20 |
| 3,4,6,7,9-11,13,15-18: 3-r/F.C. #223. 4-r/F.C. #62. 9-r/F.C. #159. 16-r/F.C. #291; Rosa-c. 18-r/F.C. #318; Rosa-c | .30 | .85 | 1.70 |
| 5,8-Don Rosa-a | .35 | 1.10 | 2.20 |
| 12($1.50, 52pgs)-Rosa-c/a w/Barks poster | .35 | 1.10 | 2.20 |
| 14-r/F.C. #29, "Mummy's Ring" | .40 | 1.25 | 2.50 |
| 19 ($1.95, 68 pgs.)-Barks-r/F.C. #199 | .35 | 1.00 | 2.00 |
| 20 ($1.95, 68 pgs.)-Barks-r/F.C. #189 & cover-r | .35 | 1.00 | 2.00 |

NOTE: ***Barks** a-1-19r; c-10r, 14r. **Rosa** a-5, 8, 12; c-13, 16-18.*

**DONALD DUCK ADVENTURES** (2nd series)
June, 1990 - Present ($1.50, color)
Disney Comics

| | | | |
|---|---|---|---|
| 1-12: 1-Rosa-a & scripts. 2,3-Barks-r & new-a. 4,5-New-a? 9-r/F.C. #178 by Barks | .25 | .75 | 1.50 |

**DONALD DUCK ALBUM** (See Comic Album No. 1,3 & Duck Album)
5-7/59 - F.C. No. 1239, 10-12/61; 1962; 8/63 - No. 2, Oct, 1963
Dell Publishing Co./Gold Key

| | | | |
|---|---|---|---|
| 4-Color 995,1182, 01204-207 (1962-Dell) | 2.00 | 6.00 | 14.00 |
| 4-Color 1099,1140,1239-Barks-c | 2.30 | 7.00 | 16.00 |
| 1(8/63-Gold Key)-Barks-c | 2.00 | 6.00 | 14.00 |
| 2(10/63) | 1.00 | 3.00 | 7.00 |

**DONALD DUCK AND THE BOYS** (Also see Story Hour Series)
1948 (Hardcover book; 5¼x5½") 100pgs., ½art, ½text
Whitman Publishing Co.

| | | | |
|---|---|---|---|
| 845-Partial r-/WDC&S No. 74 by Barks | 17.00 | 51.00 | 120.00 |

(Prices vary widely on this book)

**DONALD DUCK AND THE RED FEATHER**
1948 (4 pages) (8½x11") (Black & White)
Red Feather Giveaway

| | | | |
|---|---|---|---|
| nn | 5.70 | 17.00 | 40.00 |

**DONALD DUCK BEACH PARTY** (Also see Dell Giants)
Sept, 1965 (25 cents)
Gold Key

| | | | |
|---|---|---|---|
| 1(#10158-509)-Barks-r/WDC&S #45 | 3.00 | 9.00 | 21.00 |

**DONALD DUCK BOOK** (See Story Hour Series)

**DONALD DUCK COMIC PAINT BOOK** (See Large Feature Comic No. 20)

**DONALD DUCK COMICS DIGEST**
Nov, 1986 - No. 5, July, 1987 ($1.25-$1.50, 96 pgs.)
Gladstone Publishing

| | | | |
|---|---|---|---|
| 1-3: 1-Barks c/a-r | | .60 | 1.25 |
| 4,5 | .25 | .75 | 1.50 |

**DONALD DUCK FUN BOOK** (See Dell Giants)

**DONALD DUCK IN DISNEYLAND** (See Dell Giants)

**DONALD DUCK IN "THE LITTERBUG"**
1963 (16 pgs., 5x7¼", soft-c) (Disney giveaway)
Keep America Beautiful

| | | | |
|---|---|---|---|
| nn | 2.65 | 8.00 | 18.00 |

**DONALD DUCK MARCH OF COMICS**
No. 4, 1947 - No. 69, 1951; No. 263, 1964 (Giveaway) (Disney)
K. K. Publications

| | Good | Fine | N-Mint |
|---|---|---|---|
| nn(No.4)-"Maharajah Donald;" 30 pgs. by Carl Barks-(1947) | 500.00 | 1500.00 | 3500.00 |
| 20-"Darkest Africa" by Carl Barks-(1948); 22 pgs. | 271.00 | 815.00 | 1900.00 |
| 41-"Race to South Seas" by Carl Barks-(1949); 22 pgs.(On Disney's banned list) | 200.00 | 600.00 | 1400.00 |
| 56-(1950)-Barks-a on back-c | 22.00 | 65.00 | 140.00 |
| 69-(1951)-Not by Barks; Barks-a on back-c | 19.00 | 57.00 | 125.00 |
| 263-Not by Barks | 6.00 | 18.00 | 36.00 |

**DONALD DUCK MERRY CHRISTMAS** (See Dell Giant No. 53)

**DONALD DUCK PICNIC PARTY** (See Picnic Party under Dell Giants)

**DONALD DUCK "PLOTTING PICNICKERS"**
1962 (16 pgs., 3¼x7", soft-c) (Disney)(Also see Ludwig Von Drake & Mickey Mouse)
Fritos Giveaway

| | | | |
|---|---|---|---|
| nn | 3.00 | 9.00 | 21.00 |

**DONALD DUCK'S SURPRISE PARTY**
1948 (16 pgs.) (Giveaway for Icy Frost Twins Ice Cream Bars)
Walt Disney Productions

| | | | |
|---|---|---|---|
| nn-(Rare)-Kelly-c/a | 107.00 | 320.00 | 750.00 |

**DONALD DUCK TELLS ABOUT KITES**
Nov, 1954 (Giveaway) (8 pgs. - no cover) (Disney)
Southern California Edison Co./Pacific Gas & Electric Co./Florida Power & Light Co.

| | | | |
|---|---|---|---|
| Fla. Power, S.C.E. & version with blank label issues-Barks pencils-8 pgs.; inks-7 pgs. (Rare) | 285.00 | 850.00 | 1800.00 |
| P.G.&E. issue-7th page redrawn changing middle 3 panels to show P.G.&E. in story line; (All Barks; last page Barks pencils only) (Scarce) | 250.00 | 750.00 | 1600.00 |

(Prices vary widely on above books)

NOTE: *These books appeared one month apart in the Fall and were distributed on the West and East Coasts.*

**DONALD DUCK, THIS IS YOUR LIFE** (See 4-Color No. 1109)

**DONALD DUCK XMAS ALBUM** (See regular Donald Duck No. 99)

**DONALD IN MATHMAGIC LAND** (See 4-Color No. 1051, 1198)

**DONATELLO, TEENAGE MUTANT NINJA TURTLE**
Aug, 1986 (One-shot, $1.50, B&W, 44 pgs.)
Mirage Studios

| | | | |
|---|---|---|---|
| 1 | 1.70 | 5.00 | 10.00 |

**DONDI** (See 4-Color No. 1176,1276)

**DON FORTUNE MAGAZINE**
Aug, 1946 - No. 6, Feb, 1947
Don Fortune Publishing Co.

| | | | |
|---|---|---|---|
| 1-Delecta of the Planets by C. C. Beck in all | 9.30 | 28.00 | 65.00 |
| 2 | 5.70 | 17.00 | 40.00 |
| 3-6: 3-Bondage-c | 3.70 | 11.00 | 26.00 |

**DON NEWCOMBE**
1950 (Baseball)
Fawcett Publications

| | | | |
|---|---|---|---|
| nn | 20.00 | 60.00 | 140.00 |

**DON'T GIVE UP THE SHIP** (See 4-Color #1049)

**DON WINSLOW OF THE NAVY** (See Crackajack Funnies, Famous Feature Stories, Four Color #2, 22, Popular Comics & Super Book #5,6)

**DON WINSLOW OF THE NAVY** (See TV Teens; Movie, Radio, TV)
2/43 - #64, 12/48; #65, 1/51 - #69, 9/51; #70, 3/55 - #73, 9/55
(Fightin' Navy No. 74 on)
Fawcett Publications/Charlton No. 70 on

*Donald Duck Adventures #14, © The Disney Co.*

*Donatello, Teenage Mutant. . . #1, © Mirage*

*Don Fortune Magazine #2, © Don Fortune*

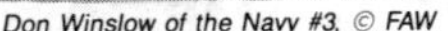
Don Winslow of the Navy #3, © FAW

The Doom Patrol #86, © DC

Doom Patrol #29, © DC

| | Good | Fine | N-Mint |
|---|---|---|---|
| 1-(68 pgs.)-Captain Marvel on cover | 47.00 | 140.00 | 325.00 |
| 2 | 23.00 | 70.00 | 160.00 |
| 3 | 16.00 | 48.00 | 110.00 |
| 4-6: 6-Flag-c | 12.00 | 36.00 | 84.00 |
| 7-10: 8-Last 68pg. issue? | 8.50 | 25.50 | 60.00 |
| 11-20 | 5.70 | 17.00 | 40.00 |
| 21-40 | 4.00 | 12.00 | 28.00 |
| 41-63 | 2.85 | 8.50 | 20.00 |
| 64(12/48)-Matt Baker-a | 3.15 | 9.50 | 22.00 |
| 65(1/51) - 69(9/51): All photo-c. 65-Flying Saucer attack | 4.00 | 12.00 | 28.00 |
| 70(3/55)-73: 70-73 r-/#26,58 & 59 | 2.65 | 8.00 | 18.00 |

**DOOM PATROL, THE** (My Greatest Adv. No. 1-85; see Brave and the Bold, DC Special Blue Ribbon Digest 19, Official . . . Index & Showcase No. 94-96)
No. 86, 3/64 - No. 121, 9-10/68; No. 122, 2/73 - No. 124, 6-7/73
National Periodical Publications

| | Good | Fine | N-Mint |
|---|---|---|---|
| 86-1pg. origin | 7.00 | 21.00 | 50.00 |
| 87-99: 88-Origin The Chief. 91-Intro. Mento. 99-Intro. Beast Boy who later became the Changeling in the New Teen Titans | 5.00 | 15.00 | 35.00 |
| 100-Origin Beast Boy; Robot-Maniac series begins | 6.00 | 18.00 | 42.00 |
| 101-110: 102-Challengers/Unknown app. 105-Robot-Maniac series ends. 106-Negative Man begins (origin) | 2.85 | 8.50 | 20.00 |
| 111-120 | 2.30 | 7.00 | 16.00 |
| 121-Death of Doom Patrol; Orlando-c | 7.00 | 21.00 | 50.00 |
| 122-124(reprints) | .35 | 1.00 | 2.00 |

**DOOM PATROL**
Oct, 1987 - Present (New format, direct sale, $1.50 #19 on)
DC Comics

| | Good | Fine | N-Mint |
|---|---|---|---|
| 1 | .40 | 1.25 | 2.50 |
| 2-18: 3-1st app. Lodestone. 4-1st app. Karma. 8,15,16-Art Adams-c(i). 18-Invasion | | .50 | 1.00 |
| 19-New format & Grant Morrison scripts begin | 3.35 | 10.00 | 20.00 |
| 20-25 | 1.70 | 5.00 | 10.00 |
| 26-30: 29-Superman app. | 1.00 | 3.00 | 6.00 |
| 31-36 | .50 | 1.50 | 3.00 |
| 37-44 | .25 | .75 | 1.50 |
| . . . And Suicide Squad Special 1($1.50,3/88) | .25 | .75 | 1.50 |
| Annual 1 ('88, $1.50) | .25 | .75 | 1.50 |

**DOOMSDAY + 1**
July, 1975 - No. 6, June, 1976; No. 7, June, 1978 - No. 12, May, 1979
Charlton Comics

| | Good | Fine | N-Mint |
|---|---|---|---|
| 1 | 1.00 | 3.00 | 6.00 |
| 2 | .75 | 2.25 | 4.50 |
| 3-6: 4-Intro Lor | .70 | 2.00 | 4.00 |
| V3#7-12 (reprints #1-6) | .30 | .80 | 1.60 |
| 5 (Modern Comics reprint, 1977) | | .20 | .40 |

NOTE: *Byrne c/a-1-12; Painted covers-2-7.*

**DOOMSDAY SQUAD, THE**
Aug, 1986 - No. 7, Feb, 1987 ($2.00, color)
Fantagraphics Books

| | Good | Fine | N-Mint |
|---|---|---|---|
| 1-7: Byrne-a in all. 1-3-New Byrne-c. 3-Usagi Yojimbo app. (1st in color). 4-N. Adams-c. 5-7-Gil Kane-c | .35 | 1.00 | 2.00 |

**DOORWAY TO NIGHTMARE** (See Cancelled Comic Cavalcade)
Jan-Feb, 1978 - No. 5, Sept-Oct, 1978
DC Comics

| | Good | Fine | N-Mint |
|---|---|---|---|
| 1-5-Madame Xanadu in all. 4-Craig-a | | .30 | .60 |

NOTE: *Kaluta covers on all. Merged into The Unexpected with No. 190.*

**DOPEY DUCK COMICS** (Wacky Duck No. 3) (See Super Funnies)
Fall, 1945 - No. 2, April, 1946
Timely Comics (NPP)

| | Good | Fine | N-Mint |
|---|---|---|---|
| 1,2-Casper Cat, Krazy Krow | 9.00 | 27.00 | 62.00 |

**DOROTHY LAMOUR** (Formerly Jungle Lil)(Stage, screen, radio)
No. 2, June, 1950 - No. 3, Aug, 1950
Fox Features Syndicate

| | Good | Fine | N-Mint |
|---|---|---|---|
| 2,3-Wood-a(3) each, photo-c | 11.00 | 32.00 | 75.00 |

**DOT AND DASH AND THE LUCKY JINGLE PIGGIE**
1942 (12 pages)
Sears Roebuck Christmas giveaway

| | Good | Fine | N-Mint |
|---|---|---|---|
| nn-Contains a war stamp album and a punch out Jingle Piggie bank | 4.00 | 12.00 | 28.00 |

**DOT DOTLAND** (Formerly Little Dot Dotland)
No. 62, Sept, 1974 - No. 63, November, 1974
Harvey Publications

| | Good | Fine | N-Mint |
|---|---|---|---|
| 62,63 | | .60 | 1.20 |

**DOTTY** (. . . & Her Boy Friends) (Formerly Four Teeners; Glamorous Romances No. 41 on)
No. 35, July, 1948 - No. 40, May, 1949
Ace Magazines (A. A. Wyn)

| | Good | Fine | N-Mint |
|---|---|---|---|
| 35 | 3.70 | 11.00 | 26.00 |
| 36,38-40 | 2.00 | 6.00 | 14.00 |
| 37-Transvestism story | 2.30 | 7.00 | 16.00 |

**DOTTY DRIPPLE** (Horace & Dotty Dripple No. 25 on)
1946 - No. 24, June, 1952 (See A-1 No. 1-8, 10)
Magazine Ent.(Life's Romances)/Harvey No. 3 on

| | Good | Fine | N-Mint |
|---|---|---|---|
| nn (nd) (10 cent) | 3.00 | 9.00 | 21.00 |
| 2 | 1.50 | 4.50 | 10.00 |
| 3-10: 3,4-Powell-a | 1.00 | 3.00 | 7.00 |
| 11-24 | .75 | 2.25 | 5.00 |

**DOTTY DRIPPLE AND TAFFY**
No. 646, Sept, 1955 - No. 903, May, 1958
Dell Publishing Co.

| | Good | Fine | N-Mint |
|---|---|---|---|
| 4-Color 646 | 1.70 | 5.00 | 12.00 |
| 4-Color 691,718,746,801,903 | 1.30 | 4.00 | 9.00 |

**DOUBLE ACTION COMICS**
No. 2, Jan, 1940 (Regular size; 68 pgs.; B&W, color cover)
National Periodical Publications

2-Contains original stories(?); pre-hero DC contents; same cover as Adventure No. 37. (Five known copies) (not an ashcan)
Estimated value. . . . 6500.00

NOTE: *The cover to this book was probably reprinted from Adventure #37. #1 exists as an ash can copy with B&W cover; contains a coverless comic on inside with 1st & last page missing.*

**DOUBLE COMICS**
1940 - 1944 (132 pages)
Elliot Publications

| | Good | Fine | N-Mint |
|---|---|---|---|
| 1940 issues; Masked Marvel-c & The Mad Mong vs. The White Flash covers known | 125.00 | 312.00 | 750.00 |
| 1941 issues; Tornado Tim-c, Nordac-c, & Green Light covers known | 79.00 | 235.00 | 550.00 |
| 1942 issues | 64.00 | 193.00 | 450.00 |
| 1943,1944 issues | 50.00 | 150.00 | 350.00 |

NOTE: *Double Comics consisted of an almost endless combination of pairs of remaindered, unsold issues of comics representing most publishers and usually mixed publishers in the same book; e.g., a Captain America with a Silver Streak, or a Feature with a Detective, etc., could appear inside the same cover. The actual contents would have to determine its price. Prices listed are for average contents. Any containing rare origin or first issues are worth much more. Covers also vary in same year. Value would be approximately 50 percent of contents.*

**DOUBLE-CROSS** (See The Crusaders)

**DOUBLE-DARE ADVENTURES**
Dec, 1966 - No. 2, March, 1967 (35-25 cents, 68 pgs.)

Harvey Publications

| | Good | Fine | N-Mint |
|---|---|---|---|
| 1-Origin Bee-Man, Glowing Gladiator, & Magic-Master; Simon/Kirby-a (last S&K art as a team?) | 1.30 | 4.00 | 9.00 |
| 2-Williamson/Crandall-a; r-/Alarming Adv. #3('63) | 1.70 | 5.00 | 12.00 |

NOTE: ***Powell** a-1. **Simon/Sparling** c-1, 2.*

**DOUBLE LIFE OF PRIVATE STRONG, THE**
June, 1959 - No. 2, Aug, 1959
Archie Publications/Radio Comics

| | Good | Fine | N-Mint |
|---|---|---|---|
| 1-Origin The Shield; Simon & Kirby-c/a; intro./1st app. The Fly | 36.00 | 108.00 | 250.00 |
| 2-S&K-c/a; Tuska-a; The Fly app. | 26.00 | 78.00 | 180.00 |

**DOUBLE TALK** (Also see Two-Faces)
No date (1962?) (32 pgs.; full color; slick cover)
Christian Anti-Communism Crusade (Giveaway)
Feature Publications

| | Good | Fine | N-Mint |
|---|---|---|---|
| nn | 8.50 | 25.50 | 60.00 |

**DOUBLE TROUBLE**
Nov, 1957 - No. 2, Jan-Feb, 1958
St. John Publishing Co.

| | Good | Fine | N-Mint |
|---|---|---|---|
| 1,2 | 2.00 | 6.00 | 14.00 |

**DOUBLE TROUBLE WITH GOOBER**
No. 417, Aug, 1952 - No. 556, May, 1954
Dell Publishing Co.

| | Good | Fine | N-Mint |
|---|---|---|---|
| 4-Color 417 | 1.50 | 4.50 | 10.00 |
| 4-Color 471,516,556 | 1.00 | 3.00 | 7.00 |

**DOUBLE UP**
1941 (200 pages) (Pocket size)
Elliott Publications

| | Good | Fine | N-Mint |
|---|---|---|---|
| 1-Contains rebound copies of digest sized issues of Pocket Comics, Speed Comics, & Spitfire Comics | 47.00 | 140.00 | 325.00 |

**DOVER BOYS** (See Adventures of the. . .)

**DOVER THE BIRD**
Spring, 1955
Famous Funnies Publishing Co.

| | Good | Fine | N-Mint |
|---|---|---|---|
| 1 | 2.00 | 6.00 | 14.00 |

**DOWN WITH CRIME**
Nov, 1952 - No. 7, Nov, 1953
Fawcett Publications

| | Good | Fine | N-Mint |
|---|---|---|---|
| 1 | 10.00 | 30.00 | 70.00 |
| 2,4-Powell-a each | 5.70 | 17.00 | 40.00 |
| 3,5: 3-Used in **POP**, pg. 106. 5-Bondage-c | 5.70 | 17.00 | 40.00 |
| 6,7: 6-Used in **POP**, pg. 80 | 4.00 | 12.00 | 28.00 |

**DO YOU BELIEVE IN NIGHTMARES?**
Nov, 1957 - No. 2, Jan, 1958
St. John Publishing Co.

| | Good | Fine | N-Mint |
|---|---|---|---|
| 1-Ditko-c/a(most) | 14.00 | 43.00 | 100.00 |
| 2-Ayers-a | 7.00 | 21.00 | 50.00 |

**D.P. 7**
Nov, 1986 - No. 32, June, 1989 (26 on: $1.50)
Marvel Comics Group

| | Good | Fine | N-Mint |
|---|---|---|---|
| 1-32 | | .60 | 1.20 |
| Annual #1 (11/87)-Intro. The Witness | | .65 | 1.30 |

NOTE: ***Williamson** a-9i, 11i; c-9i.*

**DRACULA** (See Giant-Size. . ., Marvel Graphic Novel & Tomb of. . .; also see Movie Classics under Universal Presents as well as Dracula)

**DRACULA** (See Movie Classics for No. 1)
No. 2, 11/66 - No. 4, 3/67; No. 6, 7/72 - No. 8, 7/73 (No #5)
Dell Publishing Co.

| | Good | Fine | N-Mint |
|---|---|---|---|
| 2-Origin Dracula (11/66) | 1.15 | 3.50 | 8.00 |
| 3,4-Intro. Fleeta #4('67) | .85 | 2.50 | 5.00 |
| 6-('72)-r-/#2 w/origin | .50 | 1.50 | 3.00 |
| 7,8: 7 r-/#3, 8-r/#4 | .35 | 1.00 | 2.00 |

**DRACULA** (Magazine)
1979 (120 pages, full color)
Warren Publishing Co.

| | Good | Fine | N-Mint |
|---|---|---|---|
| Book 1-Maroto art; Spanish material translated into English | 1.00 | 3.00 | 6.00 |

**DRACULA LIVES!** (Magazine)
1973(no month) - No. 13, July, 1975 (B&W) (75 cents)
Marvel Comics Group

| | Good | Fine | N-Mint |
|---|---|---|---|
| 1-3: 2-Origin | .50 | 1.50 | 3.00 |
| 4-Ploog-a | .45 | 1.25 | 2.50 |
| 5(V2#1)-13: 5-Dracula series begins | .35 | 1.00 | 2.00 |
| Annual 1('75, $1.25)-Morrow-c | .35 | 1.00 | 2.00 |

NOTE: ***N. Adams** a-2, 3i, 10i, Annual 1r(2, 3i). **Alcala** a-9. **Buscema** a-3p, 6p, Annual 1. **Colan** a(p)-1, 2, 5, 6, 8. **Evans** a-7. **Heath** a-1r, 13. **Pakula** a-6r. **Starlin** a-2.*

**DRAFT, THE**
1988 (One shot, $3.50, color, squarebound)
Marvel Comics

| | Good | Fine | N-Mint |
|---|---|---|---|
| 1-Sequel to "The Pitt" | .60 | 1.75 | 3.50 |

**DRAG 'N' WHEELS** (Formerly Top Eliminator)
No. 30, Sept, 1968 - No. 59, May, 1973
Charlton Comics

| | Good | Fine | N-Mint |
|---|---|---|---|
| 30-40-Scot Jackson begins | .50 | 1.50 | 3.00 |
| 41-50 | .35 | 1.00 | 2.00 |
| 51-59: Scot Jackson | .25 | .75 | 1.50 |
| Modern Comics Reprint 58('78) | | .40 | .80 |

**DRAGONFLY** (See Americomics #4)
Sum, 1985 - No. 8? ($1.75, $195)(#1, 3-8: color)
Americomics

| | Good | Fine | N-Mint |
|---|---|---|---|
| 1 | .85 | 2.50 | 5.00 |
| 2-8 | .40 | 1.25 | 2.50 |

**DRAGONFORCE**
1988 - No. 13, 1989 ($2.00, color)
Aircel Publishing

| | Good | Fine | N-Mint |
|---|---|---|---|
| 1-13 | .35 | 1.00 | 2.00 |
| . . .Chronicles Book 1-5 ($2.95, B&W, 60 pgs.): r/Dragonforce & Dragonring | .50 | 1.50 | 3.00 |

**DRAGONLANCE** (Also see TSR Worlds)
Dec, 1988 - Present ($1.25-$1.50, color, Mando paper)
DC Comics

| | Good | Fine | N-Mint |
|---|---|---|---|
| 1-Based on TSR game | 1.00 | 3.00 | 6.00 |
| 2 | .70 | 2.00 | 4.00 |
| 3-5 | .60 | 1.75 | 3.50 |
| 6-10: 6-Begin $1.50-c | .50 | 1.50 | 3.00 |
| 11-15 | .35 | 1.00 | 2.00 |
| 16-24 | .25 | .75 | 1.50 |
| 25-28: 25-Begin $1.75-c | .30 | .90 | 1.80 |
| Annual 1 (1990, $2.95, 68 pgs.) | .50 | 1.50 | 3.00 |

**DRAGONQUEST**
Dec, 1986 - No. 3, 1987 ($1.50, B&W, 28 pgs.)
Silverwolf Comics

| | Good | Fine | N-Mint |
|---|---|---|---|
| 1-Tim Vigil-c/a in all | 1.70 | 5.00 | 10.00 |
| 2,3 | 1.00 | 3.00 | 6.00 |

**DRAGONRING**
1986 - V2#15, 1988 ($1.70, B&W)
Aircel Publishing

| | Good | Fine | N-Mint |
|---|---|---|---|
| 1 | .60 | 1.75 | 3.50 |

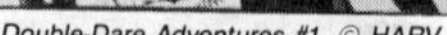
*Double-Dare Adventures #1, © HARV*

*Dragonlance #3, © TSR*

*Dragonquest #1, © Silverwolf Comics*

Dragonring #6, © Aircel Publ.

Dreadstar #28, © First Comics

Duck Album #531, © The Disney Co.

| | Good | Fine | N-Mint |
|---|---|---|---|
| 2-6: 6-Last B&W issue | .35 | 1.10 | 2.20 |
| V2#1 ($2.00, color) | .35 | 1.00 | 2.00 |
| 2-15 | .30 | .90 | 1.80 |

**DRAGON'S CLAWS**
July, 1988 - No. 12, June?, 1989 ($1.25-$1.75, color, British)
Marvel Comics Ltd.

| | Good | Fine | N-Mint |
|---|---|---|---|
| 1-4: 2-Begin $1.50-c | .25 | .75 | 1.50 |
| 5-12: 5-Begin $1.75-c | 30 | .90 | 1.80 |

**DRAGONSLAYER**
October, 1981 - No. 2, Nov, 1981
Marvel Comics Group

| | Good | Fine | N-Mint |
|---|---|---|---|
| 1,2-Paramount Disney movie adaptation | | .25 | .50 |

**DRAGOON WELLS MASSACRE** (See 4-Color No. 815)

**DRAGSTRIP HOTRODDERS** (World of Wheels No. 17 on)
Sum, 1963; No. 2, Jan, 1965 - No. 16, Aug, 1967
Charlton Comics

| | Good | Fine | N-Mint |
|---|---|---|---|
| 1 | 1.50 | 4.50 | 10.00 |
| 2-5 | .85 | 2.60 | 6.00 |
| 6-16 | .70 | 2.00 | 4.00 |

**DRAMA OF AMERICA, THE**
1973 (224 pages) ($1.95)
Action Text

| | Good | Fine | N-Mint |
|---|---|---|---|
| 1-"Students' Supplement to History" | .50 | 1.50 | 3.00 |

**DREADSTAR** (Also see Epic Ill. & Marvel Graphic Novel)
Nov, 1982 - Present ($1.50, Direct sale, Baxter paper)
Epic Comics (Marvel)/First Comics No. 27 on

| | Good | Fine | N-Mint |
|---|---|---|---|
| 1-Story continued from Epic Illustrated #15 | .55 | 1.60 | 3.20 |
| 2 | .40 | 1.25 | 2.50 |
| 3-5 | .35 | 1.00 | 2.00 |
| 6-26: 12-New costume. 16-New powers | .25 | .80 | 1.60 |
| 27-First Comics; new look | .25 | .80 | 1.60 |
| 28-38: New look | .25 | .70 | 1.40 |
| 39-49,51-65 ($1.95/$2.25) | .25 | .80 | 1.60 |
| 50 ($3.95, 52 pgs.)-Anniversary issue | .70 | 2.00 | 4.00 |
| Annual 1 (12/83)-Reprints The Price | .30 | .90 | 1.80 |

NOTE: ***Starlin** a-1-23, 25-32; c-1-32, Annual 1.* ***Wrightson** a-6, 7.*

**DREADSTAR AND COMPANY**
July, 1985 - No. 6, Dec, 1985
Epic Comics (Marvel)

| | Good | Fine | N-Mint |
|---|---|---|---|
| 1-6: Reprints of Dreadstar series | | .50 | 1.00 |

**DREAM BOOK OF LOVE** (See A-1 Comics No. 106,114,123)

**DREAM BOOK OF ROMANCE** (See A-1 No. 92,101,109,110,124)

**DREAMERY, THE**
Dec, 1986 - No. 14, Feb, 1989 ($2.00, B&W, Baxter)
Eclipse Comics

| | Good | Fine | N-Mint |
|---|---|---|---|
| 1-14: 2-7-Alice in Wonderland adaptation | .35 | 1.00 | 2.00 |

**DREAM OF LOVE**
1958 (Reprints)
I. W. Enterprises

| | Good | Fine | N-Mint |
|---|---|---|---|
| 1,2,8: 1-Powell-a. 8-Kinstler-c | .50 | 1.50 | 3.00 |
| 9-Kinstler-c; 1pg. John Wayne interview | .50 | 1.50 | 3.00 |

**DREAMS OF THE RAREBIT FIEND**
1905
Doffield & Co.?

nn-By Winsor McCay (Very Rare) (Three copies known to exist)
Estimated value.... $600.00—$1200.00

**DRIFT MARLO**
May-July, 1962 - No. 2, Oct-Dec, 1962
Dell Publishing Co.

| | Good | Fine | N-Mint |
|---|---|---|---|
| 01-232-207(#1), 2(12-232-212) | 1.50 | 4.50 | 10.00 |

**DRISCOLL'S BOOK OF PIRATES**
1934 (124 pgs.) (B&W; hardcover; 7x9")
David McKay Publ. (Not reprints)

| | Good | Fine | N-Mint |
|---|---|---|---|
| nn-By Montford Amory | 8.50 | 25.50 | 60.00 |

**DROIDS**
April, 1986 - No. 8, June, 1987 (Based on Sat. morning cartoon)
Star Comics (Marvel)

| | Good | Fine | N-Mint |
|---|---|---|---|
| 1-R2D2, C-3PO from Star Wars | | .40 | .80 |
| 2-8: 3-Romita/Williamson-a | | .40 | .80 |

NOTE: ***Williamson** a-2i, 3i, 5i, 7i, 8i.*

**DROWNED GIRL, THE**
1990 ($5.95, color, mature readers, 52 pgs.)
Piranha Press (DC)

| | Good | Fine | N-Mint |
|---|---|---|---|
| nn | 1.00 | 3.00 | 6.00 |

**DRUG WARS**
1989 ($1.95, color)
Pioneer Comics

| | Good | Fine | N-Mint |
|---|---|---|---|
| 1-Grell-c | .35 | 1.00 | 2.00 |

**DRUM BEAT** (See 4-Color No. 610)

**DRUNKEN FIST**
Aug, 1988 - Present ($1.50-1.95, color, 68 pgs.)
Jademan Comics

| | Good | Fine | N-Mint |
|---|---|---|---|
| 1-8 ($1.50) | .25 | .75 | 1.50 |
| 9-28 ($1.95) | .35 | 1.00 | 2.00 |

**DUCK ALBUM** (See Donald Duck Album)
No. 353, Oct, 1951 - No. 840, Sept, 1957
Dell Publishing Co.

| | Good | Fine | N-Mint |
|---|---|---|---|
| 4-Color 353-Barks-c | 3.00 | 9.00 | 21.00 |
| 4-Color 450-Barks-c | 2.65 | 8.00 | 18.00 |
| 4-Color 492,531,560,586,611,649,686 | 2.00 | 6.00 | 14.00 |
| 4-Color 726,782,840 | 1.70 | 5.00 | 12.00 |

**DUCKTALES** (Also see Disney's Ducktales)
June, 1990 - Present ($1.50, color)
Disney Comics

| | Good | Fine | N-Mint |
|---|---|---|---|
| 1-12: All new stories | .25 | .75 | 1.50 |
| ...: The Movie nn (1990, 7.95, 68 pgs.)-Graphic novel adapting animated movie | 1.35 | 4.00 | 8.00 |

**DUDLEY** (Teen-age)
Nov-Dec, 1949 - No. 3, Mar-Apr, 1950
Feature/Prize Publications

| | Good | Fine | N-Mint |
|---|---|---|---|
| 1-By Boody Rogers | 7.00 | 21.00 | 50.00 |
| 2,3 | 3.50 | 10.50 | 24.00 |

**DUDLEY DO-RIGHT** (TV)
Aug, 1970 - No. 7, Aug, 1971 (Jay Ward)
Charlton Comics

| | Good | Fine | N-Mint |
|---|---|---|---|
| 1 | 2.85 | 8.50 | 20.00 |
| 2-7 | 2.00 | 6.00 | 14.00 |

**DUKE OF THE K-9 PATROL**
April, 1963
Gold Key

| | Good | Fine | N-Mint |
|---|---|---|---|
| 1 (10052-304) | 1.75 | 5.25 | 12.00 |

**DUMBO** (See 4-Color #17,234,668, Movie Comics, & Walt Disney Showcase #12)

**DUMBO** (Walt Disney's...)
1941 (K.K. Publ. Giveaway)
Weatherbird Shoes/Ernest Kern Co.(Detroit)

| | Good | Fine | N-Mint |
|---|---|---|---|
| nn-16 pgs., 9x10" (Rare) | 22.00 | 65.00 | 154.00 |

Good Fine N-Mint

nn-52 pgs., 5½x8½", slick cover in color; B&W interior; half text, half reprints/4-Color No. 17 13.00 40.00 90.00

**DUMBO COMIC PAINT BOOK** (See Large Feature Comic No. 19)

**DUMBO WEEKLY**
1942 (Premium supplied by Diamond D-X Gas Stations)
Walt Disney Productions

1 10.00 30.00 60.00
2-16 5.00 15.00 30.00

NOTE: *A cover and binder came separate at gas stations. Came with membership card.*

**DUNC AND LOO** (1-3 titled "Around the Block with Dunc and Loo")
Oct-Dec, 1961 - No. 8, Oct-Dec, 1963
Dell Publishing Co.

1 5.00 15.00 35.00
2 3.50 10.50 24.00
3-8 2.30 7.00 16.00

NOTE: *Written by **John Stanley**; **Bill Williams** art.*

**DUNE**
April, 1985 - No. 3, June, 1985
Marvel Comics

1-3-r/Marvel Super Special; movie adaptation .40 .80

**DURANGO KID, THE** (Also see Best of the West, Great Western & White Indian) (Charles Starrett starred in Columbia's Durango Kid movies)
Oct-Nov, 1949 - No. 41, Oct-Nov, 1955 (All 36pgs.)
Magazine Enterprises

1-Charles Starrett photo-c; Durango Kid & his horse Raider begin; Dan Brand & Tipi (origin) begin by Frazetta & continue through #16 39.00 118.00 275.00
2(Starrett photo-c) 25.00 75.00 175.00
3-5(All-Starrett photo-c) 21.50 64.00 150.00
6-10: 7-Atomic weapon-c/story 11.00 32.00 75.00
11-16-Last Frazetta issue 8.00 24.00 55.00
17-Origin Durango Kid 10.00 30.00 70.00
18-Fred Meagher-a on Dan Brand begins 5.50 16.50 38.00
19-30: 19-Guardineer-c/a(3) begin, end #41. 23-Intro. The Red Scorpion 5.50 16.50 38.00
31-Red Scorpion returns 4.50 14.00 32.00
32-41-Bolle/Frazetta-a (Dan Brand) 6.00 18.00 42.00

NOTE: *#6, 8, 14, 15 contain **Frazetta** art not reprinted in White Indian. **Ayers** c-18. **Guardineer** a(3)-19-41; c-19-41. **Fred Meagher** a-18-29 at least.*

**DURANGO KID, THE**
1990 - Present ($2.50, ½ color, ½ B&W)
AC Comics

1-Starrett photo front/back-c; Guardineer-r .40 1.25 2.50
2-($2.75, B&W)-Starrett photo-c; White Indian-r by Frazetta; Guardineer-r (50th anniversary of films) .45 2.40 2.75

**DWIGHT D. EISENHOWER**
December, 1969
Dell Publishing Co.

01-237-912 - Life story 2.00 6.00 14.00

**DYNABRITE COMICS**
1978 - 1979 (69 cents; 48 pgs.)(10x7-1/8"; cardboard covers)
(Blank inside covers)
Whitman Publishing Co.

11350 - Walt Disney's Mickey Mouse & the Beanstalk (4-C 157). 11350-1 - Mickey Mouse Album (4-C 1057,1151,1246). 11351 - Mickey Mouse & His Sky Adventure (4-C 214,343). 11352 - Donald Duck (4-C 408, Donald Duck 45,52)-Barks-a. 11352-1 - Donald Duck (4-C 318, 10 pg. Barks/WDC&S 125,128)-Barks-c(r). 11353 - Daisy Ducks Diary (4-C 1055,1150) - Barks-a. 11354 - Goofy: A Gaggle of Giggles. 11354-1 - Super Goof Meets Super Thief. 11355 - Uncle Scrooge (Barks-a/U.S. 12, 33). 11355-1 - Uncle Scrooge (Barks-a/U.S. 13,16) - Barks-c(r). 11356 - Bugs Bunny(?). 11357 - Star Trek (r-Star Trek 33 & 41). 11358 - Star Trek (r-Star Trek 34, 36). 11359 - Bugs Bunny-r. 11360 - Winnie the Pooh Fun and Fantasy (Disney-r). 11361 - Gyro Gearloose & the Disney Ducks (4-C 1047,1184)-Barks-c(r)
each.... .50 1.00

**DYNAMIC ADVENTURES**
No. 8, 1964 - No. 9, 1964
I. W. Enterprises

8-Kayo Kirby by Baker? 1.20 3.50 7.00
9-Reprints Avon's "Escape From Devil's Island"-Kinstler-c 1.35 4.00 8.00
nn(no date)-Reprints Risks Unlimited with Rip Carson, Senorita Rio 1.20 3.50 7.00

**DYNAMIC CLASSICS** (See Cancelled Comic Cavalcade)
Sept-Oct, 1978 (44 pgs.)
DC Comics

1-Neal Adams Batman, Simonson Manhunter-r .40 1.25 2.50

**DYNAMIC COMICS** (No #4-7)
Oct, 1941 - No. 3, Feb, 1942; No. 8, 1944 - No. 25, May, 1948
Harry 'A' Chesler

1-Origin Major Victory by Charles Sultan (reprinted in Major Victory #1), Dynamic Man & Hale the Magician; The Black Cobra only app. 65.00 195.00 455.00
2-Origin Dynamic Boy & Lady Satan; intro. The Green Knight & sidekick Lance Cooper 32.00 95.00 220.00
3 26.00 77.00 180.00
8-Dan Hastings, The Echo, The Master Key, Yankee Boy begin; Yankee Doodle Jones app.; hypo story 26.00 77.00 180.00
9-Mr. E begins; Mac Raboy-c 27.00 81.00 190.00
10 22.00 65.00 150.00
11-15: 15-The Sky Chief app. 16.00 48.00 110.00
16-Marijuana story 17.00 51.00 120.00
17(1/46)-Illustrated in **SOTI**, "The children told me what the man was going to do with the hot poker," but Wertham saw this in Crime Reporter #2 24.00 70.00 165.00
18,19,21,22,24,25 10.00 30.00 70.00
20-Bare-breasted woman-c 14.00 43.00 100.00
23-Yankee Girl app. 11.00 32.00 75.00
I.W. Reprint #1,8('64): 1-r/#23 .85 2.50 5.00

NOTE: ***Kinstler** c-IW #1. **Tuska** art in many issues, #3, 9, 11, 12, 16, 19. Bondage c-16.*

**DYNAMITE** (Johnny Dynamite No. 10 on)
May, 1953 - No. 9, Sept, 1954
Comic Media/Allen Hardy Publ.

1-Pete Morisi-a; r-as Danger #6 8.00 24.00 56.00
2 4.30 13.00 30.00
3-Marijuana story; Johnny Dynamite begins by Pete Morisi 5.70 17.00 40.00
4-Injury-to-eye, prostitution; Morisi-a 6.50 19.00 45.00
5-9-Morisi-a in all. 6-Morisi-c 3.70 11.00 26.00

**DYNAMO** (Also see Tales of Thunder & T.H.U.N.D.E.R. Agents)
Aug, 1966 - No. 4, June, 1967 (25 cents)
Tower Comics

1-Crandall/Wood, Ditko/Wood-a; Weed series begins; NoMan & Lightning cameos; Wood-c/a 3.60 11.00 25.00
2-4: Wood-c/a in all 2.30 7.00 16.00

NOTE: ***Adkins/Wood** a-2. **Ditko** a-4. **Tuska** a-2, 3.*

**DYNAMO JOE** (Also see First Adventures & Mars)
May, 1986 - No. 15, Jan, 1988 (#12-15: $1.75)
First Comics

1-15: 4-Cargonauts begin .25 .75 1.50
Special 1(1/87)-Mostly-r/Mars .25 .75 1.50

**DYNOMUTT** (TV)(See Scooby-Doo, 3rd series)
Nov, 1977 - No. 6, Sept, 1978 (Hanna-Barbera)
Marvel Comics Group

*The Durango Kid #8, © ME*

*Dynamic Classics #1, © DC*

*Dynamic Comics #11, © CHES*

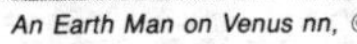
An Earth Man on Venus nn, © AVON

Eb'nn the Raven #3, © Now Comics

Eclipse Graphic Album Series #22, © Eclipse

| | Good | Fine | N-Mint |
|---|---|---|---|
| 1-6: 3-Scooby Doo story | | .50 | 1.00 |

**EAGLE, THE** (1st Series) (See Science Comics & Weird Comics #8)
July, 1941 - No. 4, Jan, 1942
Fox Features Syndicate

| | Good | Fine | N-Mint |
|---|---|---|---|
| 1-The Eagle begins; Rex Dexter of Mars app. by Briefer | 68.00 | 205.00 | 475.00 |
| 2-The Spider Queen begins (origin) | 39.00 | 118.00 | 275.00 |
| 3,4: 3-Joe Spook begins (origin) | 30.00 | 90.00 | 210.00 |

**EAGLE** (2nd Series)
Feb-Mar, 1945 - No. 2, Apr-May, 1945
Rural Home Publ.

| | Good | Fine | N-Mint |
|---|---|---|---|
| 1-Aviation stories | 9.00 | 27.00 | 62.00 |
| 2-Lucky Aces | 8.00 | 24.00 | 55.00 |

NOTE: *L. B. Cole c/a in each.*

**EAGLE**
Sept, 1986 - No. 26?, 1989 ($1.50/1.75/1.95, B&W)
Crystal Comics/Apple Comics #17 on

| | Good | Fine | N-Mint |
|---|---|---|---|
| 1 | .70 | 2.00 | 4.00 |
| 1-Signed and limited | .85 | 2.50 | 5.00 |
| 2-11,13-26 | .35 | 1.00 | 2.00 |
| 12-Origin issue ($2.50) | .40 | 1.25 | 2.50 |

**EARTH MAN ON VENUS (An . . .)** (Also see Strange Planets)
1951
Avon Periodicals

| | Good | Fine | N-Mint |
|---|---|---|---|
| nn-Wood-a, 26 pgs.; Fawcette-c | 71.00 | 215.00 | 500.00 |

**EASTER BONNET SHOP** (See March of Comics No. 29)

**EASTER WITH MOTHER GOOSE** (See 4-Color No. 103,140,185,220)

**EAST MEETS WEST**
Apr, 1990 - No. 2, 1990 ($2.50, color, adults, mini-series)
Innovation Publishing

| | Good | Fine | N-Mint |
|---|---|---|---|
| 1,2: 1-Stevens part-i; Redondo-c(i). 2-Stevens-c(i); 1st app. Cheech & Chong in comics | .40 | 1.25 | 2.50 |

**EAT RIGHT TO WORK AND WIN**
1942 (16 pages) (Giveaway)
Swift & Company

| | Good | Fine | N-Mint |
|---|---|---|---|
| Blondie, Henry, Flash Gordon by Alex Raymond, Toots & Casper, Thimble Threatre (Popeye), Tillie the Toiler, The Phantom, The Little King, & Bringing Up Father - original strips just for this book - (in daily strip form which shows what foods we should eat and why) | 18.00 | 54.00 | 125.00 |

**EB'NN THE RAVEN**
Oct, 1985 - No. 10, 1987 ($1.50, B&W)
Crowquill Comics/Now Comics #3 on

| | Good | Fine | N-Mint |
|---|---|---|---|
| 1-10: 1,2-(44 pgs.). 3-(52 pgs.). 10-Full color | .25 | .75 | 1.50 |

**E. C. CLASSIC REPRINTS**
May, 1973 - No. 12, 1976 (E. C. Comics reprinted in color minus ads)
East Coast Comix Co.

| | Good | Fine | N-Mint |
|---|---|---|---|
| 1-The Crypt of Terror #1 (Tales From the Crypt #46) | 1.00 | 3.00 | 6.00 |
| 2-Weird Science #15('52) | .70 | 2.00 | 4.00 |
| 3-12: 3-Shock SuspenStories #12. 4-Haunt of Fear #12. 5-Weird Fantasy #13('52). 6-Crime SuspenStories #25. 7-Vault of Horror #26. 8-Shock SuspenStories #6. 9-Two-Fisted Tales #34. 10-Haunt of Fear #23. 11-Weird Science #12(#1). 12-Shock SuspenStories #2 | .50 | 1.50 | 3.00 |

**EC CLASSICS**
1985 - No. 12, 1986? (High quality paper; each r-/8 stories in color)
Russ Cochran (#2-12 were resolicited in 1990)($4.95, 56 pgs., 8X11")

| | Good | Fine | N-Mint |
|---|---|---|---|
| 1-12: 1-Shock SuspenStories. 2-Weird Science. 3-Two-Fisted Tales. 4-Shock SuspenStories. 5-Weird Fantasy. 6-Vault of Horror. 7-Weird Science-Fantasy (r/23,24). 8-Crime SuspensStories. 9-Haunt of Fear. 10-Panic (r/1,2). 11-Tales From the Crypt (r/23,24). 12-Weird Science (r/20,22) | .85 | 2.50 | 5.00 |

**ECHO OF FUTUREPAST**
May, 1984 - No. 9, Jan, 1986 ($2.95, color, 52 pgs.)
Pacific Comics/Continuity Comics

| | Good | Fine | N-Mint |
|---|---|---|---|
| 1-9: Neal Adams-c/a in all | .50 | 1.50 | 3.00 |

NOTE: ***N. Adams*** *a-1-6; c-1-3, 5p, 8.* ***Golden*** *a-1-6(Bucky O'Hare); c-6.* ***Toth*** *a-6, 7.*

**ECLIPSE GRAPHIC ALBUM SERIES**
Oct, 1978 - Present (8½x11") (B&W #1-5)
Eclipse Comics

| | Good | Fine | N-Mint |
|---|---|---|---|
| 1-Sabre (10/78, B&W, 1st print.) | 1.35 | 4.00 | 8.00 |
| 1-Sabre (2nd printing, 1/79) | 1.35 | 4.00 | 8.00 |
| 1-Sabre (3rd printing) | 1.00 | 3.00 | 5.95 |
| 2-Night Music (11/79, B&W)-Russell-a | .85 | 2.50 | 5.00 |
| 3-Detectives, Inc. (5/80, B&W)-Rogers-a | 1.15 | 3.50 | 7.00 |
| 4-Stewart The Rat ('80, B&W)-G. Colan-a | 1.15 | 3.50 | 7.00 |
| 5-The Price (10/81, B&W)-Starlin-a | 2.00 | 6.00 | 12.00 |
| 6-I Am Coyote (11/84, color)-Rogers c/a | 1.35 | 4.00 | 8.00 |
| 7-The Rocketeer (9/85, color)-Dave Stevens-a | 1.70 | 5.00 | 10.00 |
| 7-The Rocketeer (2nd print, $7.95) | 1.35 | 4.00 | 8.00 |
| 7-The Rocketeer, signed & limited hardcover | 10.00 | 30.00 | 60.00 |
| 8-Zorro In Old California ('86, color) | 1.35 | 4.00 | 8.00 |
| 8-Hard cover | 2.00 | 6.00 | 11.95 |
| 9-Sacred And The Profane ('86)-Steacy-a | 2.70 | 8.00 | 16.00 |
| 9-Hard cover | 4.00 | 12.50 | 24.95 |
| 10-Somerset Holmes ('86, color)-Adults, soft-c | 2.70 | 8.00 | 16.00 |
| 10-Hard cover | 4.00 | 12.50 | 24.95 |
| 11-Floyd Farland, Citizen of the Future ('87, B&W) | .70 | 2.00 | 4.00 |
| 12-Silverheels ('87, color) | 1.50 | 4.50 | 9.00 |
| 12-Hard cover | 2.50 | 7.50 | 14.95 |
| 12-Hard cover, signed & #'d | 4.00 | 12.50 | 24.95 |
| 13-The Sisterhood of Steel ('87, color) | 1.70 | 5.00 | 10.00 |
| 14-Samurai, Son of Death ('87, B&W) | .85 | 2.50 | 5.00 |
| 14-Samurai, Son of Death (2nd print.) | .70 | 2.00 | 3.95 |
| 15-Twisted Tales (11/87, color)-Dave Stevens-c | .70 | 2.00 | 3.95 |
| 16-See Airfighters Classics #1 | | | |
| 17-Valkyrie, Prisoner of the Past ('88, color) | .70 | 2.00 | 3.95 |
| 18-See Airfighters Classics #2 | | | |
| 19-Scout: The Four Monsters ('88, color)-r/Scouts #1-7; soft-c | 2.50 | 7.50 | 14.95 |
| 20-See Airfighters Classics #3 | | | |
| 21-XYR-Multiple ending comic ('88, B&W) | .70 | 2.00 | 3.95 |
| 22-Alien Worlds #1 (5/88, $3.95, 52 pgs.)-Nudity | .70 | 2.00 | 3.95 |
| 23-See Airfighters Classics #4 | | | |
| 24-Heartbreak ($4.95, B&W) | .85 | 2.50 | 4.95 |
| 25-Alex Toth's Zorro Vol. 1 ($10.95, B&W) | 1.85 | 5.50 | 10.95 |
| 26-Alex Toth's Zorro Vol. 2 ($10.95, B&W) | 1.85 | 5.50 | 10.95 |
| 27-Fast Fiction (She) ($5.95, B&W) | 1.00 | 3.00 | 5.95 |
| 28-Miracleman Book I ($5.95) | 1.00 | 3.00 | 5.95 |
| 29-Real Love: The Best of the Simon and Kirby Romance Comics ($12.95) | 2.15 | 6.50 | 12.95 |
| 30-Brought To Light; Alan Moore scripts | 1.85 | 5.50 | 10.95 |
| 30-Limited hardcover ed. ($29.95) | 5.00 | 15.00 | 29.95 |
| 31-Pigeons From Hell by Robert E. Howard | 1.35 | 4.00 | 7.95 |
| 31-Signed & Limited Edition ($29.95) | 5.00 | 15.00 | 30.00 |

**ECLIPSE MONTHLY**
Aug, 1983 - No. 10, July, 1984 (Baxter paper; 1-3: 52 pgs., $2.00)
Eclipse Comics

| | Good | Fine | N-Mint |
|---|---|---|---|
| 1-3: ($2.00)-Cap'n Quick and a Foozle by Rogers, Static by Ditko, Dope by Trina Robbins, Rio by Doug Wildey, The Masked Man by Boyer begin. 3-Ragamuffins begins | .35 | 1.00 | 2.00 |
| 4-10: 4-10-$1.50-c. 9,10-$1.75-c | .30 | .90 | 1.80 |

NOTE: ***Boyer*** *c-6.* ***Ditko*** *a-1-3.* ***Rogers*** *a-1-4; c-2, 4.* ***Wildey*** *a-1, 2, 5, 9, 10; c-5, 10.*

**E. C. 3-D CLASSICS** (See Three Dimensional. . .)

**EDDIE STANKY** (Baseball Hero)
1951 (New York Giants)
Fawcett Publications

| | Good | Fine | N-Mint |
|---|---|---|---|
| nn-Photo-c | 11.50 | 34.00 | 80.00 |

**EDGAR BERGEN PRESENTS CHARLIE McCARTHY**
No. 764, 1938 (36 pgs.; 15x10½"; in color)
Whitman Publishing Co. (Charlie McCarthy Co.)

| | | | |
|---|---|---|---|
| 764 (Scarce) | 45.00 | 135.00 | 315.00 |

**EDGE OF CHAOS**
July, 1983 - No. 3, Jan, 1984
Pacific Comics

| | | | |
|---|---|---|---|
| 1-3-Morrow-c/a; all contain nudity | .35 | 1.00 | 2.00 |

**EDWARD'S SHOES GIVEAWAY**
1954 (Has clown on cover)
Edward's Shoe Store

Contains comic with new cover. Many combinations possible. Contents determines price, 50-60 percent of original. (Similar to Comics From Weatherbird & Free Comics to You)

**ED WHEELAN'S JOKE BOOK STARRING FAT & SLAT** (See Fat & Slat)

**EERIE** (Strange Worlds No. 18 on)
No. 1, Jan, 1947; No. 1, May-June, 1951 - No. 17, Aug-Sept, 1954
Avon Periodicals

| | | | |
|---|---|---|---|
| 1(1947)-1st horror comic; Kubert, Fugitani-a; bondage-c | 43.00 | 130.00 | 300.00 |
| 1(1951)-Reprints story/'47 No. 1 | 24.00 | 70.00 | 165.00 |
| 2-Wood-c/a; bondage-c | 26.00 | 77.00 | 180.00 |
| 3-Wood-c; Kubert, Wood/Orlando-a | 26.00 | 77.00 | 180.00 |
| 4,5-Wood-c | 24.00 | 70.00 | 165.00 |
| 6,13,14 | 9.30 | 28.00 | 65.00 |
| 7-Wood/Orlando-c; Kubert-a | 16.00 | 48.00 | 110.00 |
| 8-Kinstler-a; bondage-c; Phantom Witch Doctor story | 9.30 | 28.00 | 65.00 |
| 9-Kubert-a; Check-c | 11.00 | 32.00 | 75.00 |
| 10,11-Kinstler-a | 8.50 | 25.50 | 60.00 |
| 12-Dracula story from novel, 25 pgs. | 11.50 | 34.00 | 80.00 |
| 15-Reprints No. 1('51)minus-c(bondage) | 5.70 | 17.00 | 40.00 |
| 16-Wood-a r-/No. 2 | 7.00 | 21.00 | 50.00 |
| 17-Wood/Orlando & Kubert-a; reprints #3 minus inside & outside Wood-c | 9.30 | 28.00 | 65.00 |

NOTE: ***Hollingsworth*** *a-9-11; c-10, 11.*

**EERIE**
1964
I. W. Enterprises

| | | | |
|---|---|---|---|
| I.W. Reprint #1(1964)-Wood-c(r) | 1.50 | 4.50 | 10.00 |
| I.W. Reprint #2,6,8: 8-Dr. Drew by Grandenetti from Ghost #9 | .85 | 2.50 | 5.00 |
| I.W. Reprint #9-From Eerie #2(Avon); Wood-c | 1.50 | 4.50 | 10.00 |

**EERIE** (Magazine)(See Warren Presents)
No. 1, Sept, 1965; No. 2, Mar, 1966 - No. 139, Feb, 1983
Warren Publishing Co.

1-24 pgs., black & white, small size (5¼x7¼"), low distribution; cover from inside back cover of Creepy No. 2; stories reprinted from Creepy No. 7, 8. At least three different versions exist.

**First Printing** - B&W, 5¼" wide x 7¼" high, evenly trimmed. On page 18, panel 5, in the upper left-hand corner, the large rear view of a bald headed man blends into solid black and is unrecognizable. Overall printing quality is poor. 14.00 42.00 100.00

**Second Printing** - B&W, 5¼x7¼", with uneven, untrimmed edges (if one of these were trimmed evenly, the size would be less than as indicated). The figure of the bald headed man on page 18, panel 5 is clear and discernible. The staples have a ¼" blue stripe. 7.00 21.00 50.00

Other unauthorized reproductions for comparison's sake would be practically worthless. One known version was probably shot off a first printing copy with some loss of detail; the finer lines tend to disappear in this version which can be determined by looking at the lower right-hand corner of page one, first story. The roof of the house is shaded with straight lines. These lines are sharp and distinct on original, but broken on this version.

NOTE: ***The Official Overstreet Comic Book Price Guide*** *recommends that, before buying a 1st issue, you consult an expert.*

| | Good | Fine | N-Mint |
|---|---|---|---|
| 2-Frazetta-c | 1.70 | 5.00 | 12.00 |
| 3-Frazetta-c, 1 pg. art | 1.00 | 3.00 | 7.00 |
| 4-10: 4-Frazetta-a (½ pg.). 9-Headlight-c | 1.00 | 3.00 | 6.00 |
| 11-41,43-45 | .85 | 2.50 | 5.00 |
| 42,51-(1973 & 1974 Annuals) | 1.00 | 3.00 | 6.00 |
| 46-50,52,53,56-59,61-78: 78-The Mummy-r | .50 | 1.50 | 3.00 |
| 54,55-Color Spirit story by Eisner, 12/21/47 & 6/16/46 | .70 | 2.00 | 4.00 |
| 60-Summer Giant ($1.25) | .70 | 2.00 | 4.00 |
| 79,80-Origin Darklon the Mystic by Starlin | .50 | 1.50 | 3.00 |
| 81-139 | .35 | 1.00 | 2.00 |
| Year Book 1970, 1971-Reprints in both | 1.15 | 3.50 | 8.00 |
| Year Book 1972-Reprints | 1.00 | 3.00 | 6.00 |

NOTE: *The above books contain art by many good artists:* ***N. Adams, Brunner, Corben, Craig (Taycee), Crandall, Ditko, Eisner, Evans, Jeff Jones, Kinstler, Krenkel, McWilliams, Morrow, Orlando, Ploog, Severin, Starlin, Torres, Toth, Williamson, Wood,*** *and* ***Wrightson;*** *covers by* ***Bode', Corben, Davis, Frazetta, Morrow,*** *and* ***Orlando.*** *Annuals from 1973-on are included in regular numbering. 1970-74 Annuals are complete reprints. Annuals from 1975-on are in the format of the regular issues.*

**EERIE ADVENTURES** (Also see Weird Adventures)
Winter, 1951
Ziff-Davis Publ. Co.

| | | | |
|---|---|---|---|
| 1-Powell-a(2), Kinstler-a; used in **SOTI**; bondage-c; Krigstein back-c | 12.00 | 36.00 | 85.00 |

NOTE: *Title dropped due to similarity to Avon's Eerie & legal action.*

**EERIE TALES** (Magazine)
1959 (Black & White)
Hastings Associates

| | | | |
|---|---|---|---|
| 1-Williamson, Torres, Tuska-a, Powell(2), & Morrow(2)-a | 4.50 | 14.00 | 32.00 |

**EERIE TALES**
1964
Super Comics

| | | | |
|---|---|---|---|
| Super Reprint No. 10,11,12,18: Purple Claw in #11,12; #12 reprints Avon's Eerie #1('51) | .70 | 2.00 | 4.00 |
| 15-Wolverton-a, Spacehawk-r/Blue Bolt Weird Tales #113; Disbrow-a | 2.30 | 7.00 | 16.00 |

**EGBERT**
Spring, 1946 - No. 20, 1950
Arnold Publications/Quality Comics Group

| | | | |
|---|---|---|---|
| 1-Funny animal; intro Egbert & The Count | 10.00 | 30.00 | 70.00 |
| 2 | 5.00 | 15.00 | 35.00 |
| 3-10 | 3.00 | 9.00 | 21.00 |
| 11-20 | 2.00 | 6.00 | 14.00 |

**EH!** (. . . Dig This Crazy Comic) (From Here to Insanity No. 8 on)
Dec, 1953 - No. 7, Nov-Dec, 1954 (Satire)
Charlton Comics

| | | | |
|---|---|---|---|
| 1-Davisish-c/a by Ayers, Woodish-a by Giordano; Atomic Mouse app. | 11.00 | 32.00 | 75.00 |
| 2-Ayers-c/a | 8.00 | 24.00 | 55.00 |
| 3-7: 4,6-Sexual innuendo-c. 6-Ayers-a | 7.00 | 21.00 | 50.00 |

**EIGHT IS ENOUGH KITE FUN BOOK** (TV)
1979 (Paper-c, giveaway, 5X7¼")
Pacific Gas & Electric Co.

| | | | |
|---|---|---|---|
| nn | .50 | 1.50 | 3.00 |

*Eerie #5, © AVON*

*Egbert #12, © QUA*

*Eh! #1, © CC*

80 Page Giant #6, © DC

Electric Warrior #3, © DC

The Elementals #10, © Comico

**80 PAGE GIANT** (. . . Magazine No. 1-15) (25 cents)
8/64 - No. 15, 10/65; No. 16, 11/65 - No. 89, 7/71 (All reprints)
National Periodical Publications (#1-56: 84 pgs.; #57-89: 68 pages)

| | Good | Fine | N-Mint |
|---|---|---|---|
| 1-Superman Annual | 10.00 | 40.00 | 80.00 |
| 2-Jimmy Olsen | 5.00 | 15.00 | 35.00 |
| 3,4: 3-Lois Lane. 4-Flash-G.A.-r; Infantino-a | 3.00 | 9.00 | 21.00 |
| 5-Batman; has Sunday newspaper strip; Catwoman-r; Batman's Life Story-r (25th anniversary special) | 4.30 | 13.00 | 30.00 |
| 6-Superman | 3.00 | 9.00 | 21.00 |
| 7-Sgt. Rock's Prize Battle Tales; Kubert-c/a | 3.00 | 9.00 | 21.00 |
| 8-More Secret Origins-origins of JLA, Aquaman, Robin, Atom, & Superman; Infantino-a | 11.00 | 32.00 | 75.00 |
| 9-11: 9-Flash(r/Flash #123); Infantino-a. 10-Superboy. 11-Superman; All Luthor issue | 3.00 | 9.00 | 21.00 |
| 12-Batman; has Sunday newspaper strip | 3.60 | 11.00 | 25.00 |
| 13,14: 13-Jimmy Olsen. 14-Lois Lane | 3.00 | 9.00 | 21.00 |
| 15-Superman and Batman; Joker-c/story | 4.30 | 13.00 | 30.00 |

Continued as part of regular series under each title in which that particular book came out, a Giant being published instead of the regular size. Issues No. 16 to No. 89 are listed for your information. See individual titles for prices.

16-JLA #39 (11/65), 17-Batman #176, 18-Superman #183, 19-Our Army at War #164, 20-Action #334, 21-Flash #160, 22-Superboy #129, 23-Superman #187, 24-Batman #182, 25-Jimmy Olsen #95, 26-Lois Lane #68, 27-Batman #185, 28-World's Finest #161, 29-JLA #48, 30-Batman #187, 31-Superman #193, 32-Our Army at War #177, 33-Action #347, 34-Flash #169, 35-Superboy #138, 36-Superman #197, 37-Batman #193, 38-Jimmy Olsen #104, 39-Lois Lane #77, 40-World's Finest #170, 41-JLA #58, 42-Superman #202, 43-Batman #198, 44-Our Army at War #190, 45-Action #360, 46-Flash #178, 47-Superboy #147, 48-Superman #207, 49-Batman #203, 50-Jimmy Olsen #113, 51-Lois Lane #86, 52-World's Finest #179, 53-JLA #67, 54-Superman #212, 55-Batman #208, 56-Our Army at War #203, 57-Action #373, 58-Flash #187, 59-Superboy #156, 60-Superman #217, 61-Batman #213, 62-Jimmy Olsen #122, 63-Lois Lane #95, 64-World's Finest #188, 65-JLA #76, 66-Superman #222, 67-Batman #218, 68-Our Army at War #216, 69-Adventure #390, 70-Flash #196, 71-Superboy #165, 72-Superman #227, 73-Batman #223, 74-Jimmy Olsen #131, 75-Lois Lane #104, 76-World's Finest #197, 77-JLA #85, 78-Superman #232, 79-Batman #228, 80-Our Army at War #229, 81-Adventure #403, 82-Flash #205, 83-Superboy #174, 84-Superman #239, 85-Batman #233, 86-Jimmy Olsen #140, 87-Lois Lane #113, 88-World's Finest #206, 89-JLA #93

**87TH PRECINCT** (TV)
Apr-June, 1962 - No. 2, July-Sept, 1962
Dell Publishing Co.

| | Good | Fine | N-Mint |
|---|---|---|---|
| 4-Color 1309(#1); Krigstein-a | 6.50 | 19.00 | 45.00 |
| 2 | 5.00 | 15.00 | 35.00 |

**EINHERIAR: THE CHOSEN**
1987 (Color, $1.50)
Vanguard Graphics (Canadian)

| | Good | Fine | N-Mint |
|---|---|---|---|
| 1 | .25 | .75 | 1.50 |

**EL BOMBO COMICS**
1946
Standard Comics/Frances M. McQueeny

| | Good | Fine | N-Mint |
|---|---|---|---|
| nn(1946) | 5.70 | 17.00 | 40.00 |
| 1(no date) | 5.70 | 17.00 | 40.00 |

**EL CID** (See 4-Color No. 1259)

**EL DIABLO** (See All-Star Western #2 & Weird Western Tales #12)
Aug, 1989 - No. 16, Jan, 1991 ($1.50-$1.75, color)
DC Comics

| | Good | Fine | N-Mint |
|---|---|---|---|
| 1 ($2.50, 52 pgs.)-Masked hero | .40 | 1.25 | 2.50 |
| 2-6 ($1.50) | .25 | .75 | 1.50 |
| 7-11: 7-Begin $1.75-c | .30 | .90 | 1.80 |
| 12-16: 12-Begin $2.00-c | .35 | 1.00 | 2.00 |

**EL DORADO** (See Movie Classics)

**ELECTRIC UNDERTOW** (See Strikeforce Morituri: Electric Undertow)

**ELECTRIC WARRIOR**
May, 1986 - No. 18, Oct, 1987 ($1.50, Baxter paper)
DC Comics

| | Good | Fine | N-Mint |
|---|---|---|---|
| 1-18 | .25 | .75 | 1.50 |

**ELEKTRA: ASSASSIN**
Aug, 1986 - No. 8, Mar, 1987 (Limited series)(Adults)
Epic Comics (Marvel)

| | Good | Fine | N-Mint |
|---|---|---|---|
| 1-Miller scripts in all | .90 | 2.75 | 5.50 |
| 2 | .70 | 2.00 | 4.00 |
| 3-7 | .50 | 1.50 | 3.00 |
| 8 | .75 | 2.25 | 4.50 |
| Signed & numbered hardcover (Graphitti Designs, $39.95, 2000 print run)-reprints 1-8 | 6.75 | 20.00 | 40.00 |

**ELEKTRA SAGA, THE**
Feb, 1984 - No. 4, June, 1984 ($2.00, Baxter paper)
Marvel Comics Group

| | Good | Fine | N-Mint |
|---|---|---|---|
| 1-4-r/Daredevil 168-190; Miller-c/a | 1.00 | 3.00 | 6.00 |

**ELEMENTALS, THE** (See The Justice Machine & Morningstar Spec.)
June, 1984 - No. 29, Sept, 1988; V2#1, Mar, 1989 - Present
Comico The Comic Co. ($1.50, Baxter paper)

| | Good | Fine | N-Mint |
|---|---|---|---|
| 1-Willingham-c/a, 1-8 | 1.35 | 4.00 | 8.00 |
| 2 | .70 | 2.00 | 4.00 |
| 3 | .50 | 1.50 | 3.00 |
| 4-7 | .45 | 1.35 | 2.70 |
| 8-10: 9-Bissette-a(p). 10-Photo-c | .30 | .90 | 1.80 |
| 11-29 | .25 | .80 | 1.60 |
| V2#1-3 ($1.95) | .35 | 1.00 | 1.95 |
| V2#4-15 ($2.50) | .40 | 1.25 | 2.50 |
| Special 1 (3/86)-Willingham-a(p) | .30 | .90 | 1.80 |
| Special 2 (1/89, $1.95) | .35 | 1.00 | 1.95 |

**ELFLORD**
1986 - No. 30?, 1989 ($1.70, B&W, V2#1 on are $2.00 & color)
Aircel Publishing

| | Good | Fine | N-Mint |
|---|---|---|---|
| 1 | 1.00 | 3.00 | 6.00 |
| 1,2-2nd printings | .25 | .75 | 1.50 |
| 2 | .40 | 1.25 | 2.50 |
| 3 | .45 | 1.35 | 2.70 |
| 4-6: Last B&W issue | .25 | .80 | 1.60 |
| V2#1-(color begins) | .40 | 1.25 | 2.50 |
| 2-20 | .25 | .80 | 1.60 |
| 21-Double size, $4.95 | .75 | 2.25 | 4.50 |
| 22-30: 22-New cast; 25-Begin B&W, $1.95-c | .30 | .90 | 1.80 |

**ELFQUEST** (Also see Fantasy Quarterly & Warp Graphics Annual)
No. 2, Aug, 1978 - No. 21, Feb, 1985 (All magazine size)
No. 1, April, 1979
WaRP Graphics, Inc.

NOTE: ***Elfquest*** was originally published as one of the stories in **Fantasy Quarterly** #1. When the publisher went out of business, the creative team, Wendy and Richard Pini, formed WaRP Graphics and continued the series, beginning with **Elfquest** #2. **Elfquest** #1, which reprinted the story from **Fantasy Quarterly,** was published about the same time **Elfquest** #4 was released. Thereafter, most issues were reprinted as demand warranted, until Marvel announced it would reprint the entire series under its Epic imprint (Aug., 1985).

| | Good | Fine | N-Mint |
|---|---|---|---|
| 1(4/79)-Reprints Elfquest story from Fantasy Quarterly No. 1 | | | |
| 1st printing ($1.00 cover) | 5.50 | 16.50 | 33.00 |
| 2nd printing ($1.25 cover) | 1.70 | 5.00 | 10.00 |
| 3rd printing ($1.50 cover) | .85 | 2.50 | 5.00 |
| 2(8/78)-5: 1st printings ($1.00 cover) | 3.35 | 10.00 | 20.00 |
| 2nd printings ($1.25 cover) | .85 | 2.50 | 5.00 |
| 3rd printings ($1.50 cover) | .50 | 1.50 | 3.00 |
| 6-9: 1st printings ($1.25 cover) | 1.50 | 4.50 | 9.00 |
| 2nd printings ($1.50 cover) | .70 | 2.00 | 4.00 |
| 3rd printings ($1.50 cover) | .35 | 1.00 | 2.00 |
| 10-21: ($1.50 cover); 16-8pg. preview of A Distant Soil | 1.00 | 3.00 | 6.00 |

**ELFQUEST**
Aug, 1985 - No. 32, Mar, 1988

Epic Comics (Marvel)

| | Good | Fine | N-Mint |
|---|---|---|---|
| 1-Reprints in color the Elfquest epic by WaRP Graphics | .85 | 2.50 | 5.00 |
| 2-5 | .50 | 1.50 | 3.00 |
| 6-10 | .40 | 1.15 | 2.25 |
| 11-20 | .30 | .90 | 1.80 |
| 21-32 | .25 | .75 | 1.50 |

**ELFQUEST**
1989 - No. 4, 1989 ($1.50, B&W)
WaRP Graphics

| | Good | Fine | N-Mint |
|---|---|---|---|
| 1-4: Reprints original Elfquest series | .25 | .75 | 1.50 |

**ELFQUEST: KINGS OF THE BROKEN WHEEL**
June, 1990 - Present ($2.00, B&W)
WaRP Graphics

| | Good | Fine | N-Mint |
|---|---|---|---|
| 1-4: By Richard & Wendy Pini; 1-Color insert | .35 | 1.00 | 2.00 |

**ELFQUEST: SIEGE AT BLUE MOUNTAIN**
Mar, 1987 - No. 8, Dec, 1988 ($1.75/$1.95, B&W, mini-series)
WaRP Graphics/Apple Comics

| | Good | Fine | N-Mint |
|---|---|---|---|
| 1-Staton-a(i) in all | 1.35 | 4.00 | 8.00 |
| 1-2nd printing | .35 | 1.00 | 2.00 |
| 2 | .70 | 2.00 | 4.00 |
| 2-2nd printing | .30 | .90 | 1.80 |
| 3-8 | .40 | 1.25 | 2.50 |

**ELF-THING**
March, 1987 ($1.50, B&W, one-shot)
Eclipse Comics

| | Good | Fine | N-Mint |
|---|---|---|---|
| 1 | .25 | .75 | 1.50 |

**ELF WARRIOR** (See Adventurers)
1987 - No. 4, 1988 ($1.95, B&W)
Adventure Publications

| | Good | Fine | N-Mint |
|---|---|---|---|
| 1-4 | .35 | 1.00 | 2.00 |

**ELLA CINDERS** (See Comics On Parade, Comics Revue #1,4, Famous Comics Cartoon Book, Sparkler Comics, Tip Top & Treasury of Comics)

**ELLA CINDERS**
1938 - 1940
United Features Syndicate

| | Good | Fine | N-Mint |
|---|---|---|---|
| Single Series 3(1938) | 24.00 | 71.00 | 165.00 |
| Single Series 21(#2 on-c, #21 on inside), 28('40) | 20.00 | 60.00 | 140.00 |

**ELLA CINDERS**
March, 1948 - No. 5, March, 1949
United Features Syndicate

| | Good | Fine | N-Mint |
|---|---|---|---|
| 1-(#2 on cover) | 8.50 | 25.50 | 60.00 |
| 2 | 4.30 | 13.00 | 30.00 |
| 3-5 | 3.00 | 9.00 | 21.00 |

**ELLERY QUEEN**
May, 1949 - No. 4, Nov, 1949
Superior Comics Ltd.

| | Good | Fine | N-Mint |
|---|---|---|---|
| 1-Kamen-c; L.B. Cole-a; r-in Haunted Thrills | 22.00 | 65.00 | 150.00 |
| 2-4: 3-Drug use stories(2) | 13.00 | 40.00 | 90.00 |

NOTE: *Iger shop art in all issues.*

**ELLERY QUEEN** (TV)
1-3/52 - No. 2, Summer/52 (Saunders painted covers)
Ziff-Davis Publishing Co.

| | Good | Fine | N-Mint |
|---|---|---|---|
| 1-Saunders-c | 22.00 | 65.00 | 150.00 |
| 2-Saunders bondage, torture-c | 19.00 | 56.00 | 130.00 |

**ELLERY QUEEN** (See 4-Color No. 1165,1243,1289)

**ELMER FUDD** (Also see Camp Comics, Daffy & Super Book #10, 22)
No. 470, May, 1953 - No. 1293, Mar-May, 1962
Dell Publishing Co.

| | Good | Fine | N-Mint |
|---|---|---|---|
| 4-Color 470,558,628,689('56) | 1.15 | 3.50 | 8.00 |
| 4-Color 725,783,841,888,938,977,1032,1081,1131,1171,1222,1293('62) | .85 | 2.50 | 6.00 |

**ELMO COMICS**
January, 1948 (Daily strip-r)
St. John Publishing Co.

| | Good | Fine | N-Mint |
|---|---|---|---|
| 1-By Cecil Jensen | 7.00 | 17.00 | 40.00 |

**ELRIC** (Of Melnibone) (See First Comics Graphic Novel #6 & Marvel Graphic Novel #2)
Apr, 1983 - No. 6, Apr, 1984 ($1.50, Baxter paper)
Pacific Comics

| | Good | Fine | N-Mint |
|---|---|---|---|
| 1-6: Russell-c/a(i) in all | .25 | .75 | 1.50 |

**ELRIC: SAILOR ON THE SEAS OF FATE**
June, 1985 - No. 7, June, 1986 ($1.75, color, limited series)
First Comics

| | Good | Fine | N-Mint |
|---|---|---|---|
| 1-7: Adapts Michael Moorcock's novel | .30 | .90 | 1.80 |

**ELRIC: THE BANE OF THE BLACK SWORD**
Aug, 1988 - No. 6, June, 1989 ($1.75-$1.95, color, limited series)
First Comics

| | Good | Fine | N-Mint |
|---|---|---|---|
| 1-4: Adapts Michael Moorcock's novel | .35 | 1.00 | 2.00 |

**ELRIC: THE VANISHING TOWER**
Aug, 1987 - No. 6, June, 1988 ($1.75, color, limited series)
First Comics

| | Good | Fine | N-Mint |
|---|---|---|---|
| 1-6: Adapts Michael Moorcock's novel | .30 | .90 | 1.80 |

**ELRIC: WEIRD OF THE WHITE WOLF**
Oct, 1986 - No. 5, June, 1987 ($1.75, color, limited series)
First Comics

| | Good | Fine | N-Mint |
|---|---|---|---|
| 1-5: Adapts Michael Moorcock's novel | .30 | .90 | 1.80 |

**EL SALVADOR - A HOUSE DIVIDED**
March, 1989 ($2.50, B&W, Baxter paper, stiff-c, 52 pgs.)
Eclipse Comics

| | Good | Fine | N-Mint |
|---|---|---|---|
| 1-Gives history of El Salvador | .40 | 1.25 | 2.50 |

**ELSEWHERE PRINCE, THE**
May, 1990 - No. 6, Oct, 1990 ($1.95, color, limited series)
Epic Comics (Marvel)

| | Good | Fine | N-Mint |
|---|---|---|---|
| 1-6: Moebius scripts & back-up-a in all | .35 | 1.00 | 2.00 |

**ELSIE THE COW**
Oct-Nov, 1949 - No. 3, July-Aug, 1950
D. S. Publishing Co.

| | Good | Fine | N-Mint |
|---|---|---|---|
| 1-(36 pages) | 13.00 | 40.00 | 90.00 |
| 2,3 | 10.00 | 30.00 | 70.00 |
| Borden Milk Giveaway-(16 pgs., nn) (3 issues, 1957) | 4.30 | 13.00 | 30.00 |
| Elsie's Fun Book(1950; Borden Milk) | 5.00 | 15.00 | 35.00 |
| Everyday Birthday Fun With . . .(1957; 20 pgs.)(100th Anniversary); Kubert-a | 4.30 | 13.00 | 30.00 |

**ELSON'S PRESENTS**
1981 (100 pgs., no cover price)
DC Comics

| | Good | Fine | N-Mint |
|---|---|---|---|
| Series 1-6: Repackaged 1981 DC comics; Superman, Action, Flash DC Comics Presents & Batman known. Series I has a Batman/Joker-c. Series 3-New Teen Titans #3('81) | .85 | 2.50 | 5.00 |

**ELVIRA'S HOUSE OF MYSTERY**
Jan, 1986 - No. 11, Jan, 1987
DC Comics

| | Good | Fine | N-Mint |
|---|---|---|---|
| 1 ($1.50, 68pgs.)-Photo back-c | .50 | 1.50 | 3.00 |
| 2-11: 6-Reads sideways. 7-Sci/fic issue. 9-Photo-c. 11-Double-size Halloween issue | .25 | .80 | 1.60 |

*Ellery Queen #3, © SUPR*

*The Elsewhere Prince #1, © MEG*

*Elson's Presents #1, © DC Comics*

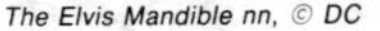
The Elvis Mandible nn, © DC

E-Man #5 (1st series), © CC

E-Man V4#1 (1/90), © Comico

| | Good | Fine | N-Mint |
|---|---|---|---|
| Special #1 (3/87, $1.25)-Haunted Holidays | .25 | .75 | 1.50 |

NOTE: ***Ayers/DeZuniga** a-5. **Bolland** c-1. **Orlando** c-10. **Spiegel** a-1. **Stevens** c-11.*

**ELVIRA'S MISTRESS OF THE DARK**
Oct, 1988 ($2.00, B&W, magazine size)
Marvel Comics

| | | | |
|---|---|---|---|
| 1-Movie adaptation | .35 | 1.10 | 2.20 |

**ELVIS MANDIBLE, THE**
1990 ($3.50, B&W, mature readers, 52 pgs.)
Piranha Press (DC)

| | | | |
|---|---|---|---|
| nn | .60 | 1.75 | 3.50 |

**ELVIS PRESLEY** (See Career Girl Romances #32, Go-Go, Howard Chaykin's American Flagg #10, Humbug #8, I Love You #60 & Young Lovers #18)

**E-MAN**
Oct, 1973 - No. 10, Sept, 1975 (Painted-c No. 7-10)
Charlton Comics

| | | | |
|---|---|---|---|
| 1-Origin E-Man; Staton c/a in all | 1.50 | 4.50 | 10.00 |
| 2-4: 2,4-Ditko-a. 3-Howard-a | .85 | 2.50 | 5.00 |
| 5-Miss Liberty Belle app. by Ditko | .70 | 2.00 | 4.00 |
| 6,7,9,10-Byrne-a in all | .85 | 2.50 | 5.00 |
| 8-Full-length story; Nova begins as E-Man's partner | .85 | 2.60 | 6.00 |
| 1-4,9,10(Modern Comics reprints, '77) | | .15 | .30 |

NOTE: *Killjoy app.-No. 2, 4. Liberty Belle app.-No. 5. Rog 2000 app.-No. 6, 7, 9, 10. Travis app.-No. 3. **Tom Sutton** a-1.*

**E-MAN** (Also see Michael Mauser & The Original E-Man)
Apr, 1983 - No. 25, Aug, 1985 (Direct Sale only, $1.00-$1.25)
First Comics

| | | | |
|---|---|---|---|
| 1-25: 2-X-Men satire. 3-X-Men/Phoenix satire. 6-Origin retold. 8-Cutey Bunny app. 10-Origin Nova Kane. 24-Origin Michael Mauser | | .50 | 1.00 |

NOTE: ***Staton** a-1-5, 6-25p; c-1-25.*

**E-MAN**
Sept, 1989 ($2.75, color, one-shot, no ads, high quality paper)
Comico

| | | | |
|---|---|---|---|
| 1-Staton-c/a; Michael Mauser story | .45 | 1.40 | 2.80 |

**E-MAN**
V4#1, Jan, 1990 - No. 3, Mar?, 1990 ($2.50, color, mini-series)
Comico

| | | | |
|---|---|---|---|
| 1-3: Staton-c/a | .40 | 1.25 | 2.50 |

**EMERGENCY** (Magazine)
June, 1976 - No. 4, Jan, 1977 (B&W)
Charlton Comics

| | | | |
|---|---|---|---|
| 1-Neal Adams-c/a; Heath, Austin-a | .50 | 1.50 | 3.00 |
| 2,4: 2-N. Adams-c. 4-Alcala-a | .25 | .80 | 1.60 |
| 3-N. Adams-a | .35 | 1.00 | 2.00 |

**EMERGENCY** (TV)
June, 1976 - No. 4, Dec, 1976
Charlton Comics

| | | | |
|---|---|---|---|
| 1-Staton-c; Byrne-a | .50 | 1.50 | 3.00 |
| 2-4: 2-Staton-c | .25 | .75 | 1.50 |

**EMERGENCY DOCTOR**
Summer, 1963 (One Shot)
Charlton Comics

| | | | |
|---|---|---|---|
| 1 | .70 | 2.00 | 4.00 |

**EMIL & THE DETECTIVES** (See Movie Comics)

**EMMA PEEL & JOHN STEED** (See The Avengers)

**EMPIRE STRIKES BACK, THE** (See Marvel Comics Super Special #16 & Marvel Special Edition)

**ENCHANTED APPLES OF OZ, THE** (See First Comics Graphic Novel #5)

**ENCHANTER**
Apr, 1987 - No. 3, Aug, 1987 ($2.00, B&W, mini-series)
Eclipse Comics

| | Good | Fine | N-Mint |
|---|---|---|---|
| 1-3 | .35 | 1.00 | 2.00 |

**ENCHANTING LOVE**
Oct, 1949 - No. 6, July, 1950 (All, 52 pgs.)
Kirby Publishing Co.

| | | | |
|---|---|---|---|
| 1-Photo-c | 5.00 | 15.00 | 35.00 |
| 2-Photo-c; Powell-a | 3.00 | 9.00 | 21.00 |
| 3,4,6: 3-Jimmy Stewart photo-c | 2.30 | 7.00 | 16.00 |
| 5-Ingels-a, 9 pgs.; photo-c | 9.00 | 27.00 | 62.00 |

**ENCHANTMENT VISUALETTES** (Magazine)
Dec, 1949 - No. 5, April, 1950
World Editions

| | | | |
|---|---|---|---|
| 1-Contains two romance comic strips each; painted-c | 8.00 | 24.00 | 55.00 |
| 2 | 6.50 | 19.00 | 45.00 |
| 3-5 | 5.00 | 15.00 | 35.00 |

**ENEMY ACE SPECIAL** (Also see Our Army at War #151, Showcase #57, 58 & Star Spangled War Stories #138)
1990 ($1.00, color)
DC Comics

| | | | |
|---|---|---|---|
| 1-Kubert-r/Our Army #151,153; c-r/Showcase 57 | | .50 | 1.00 |

**ENSIGN O'TOOLE** (TV)
Aug-Oct, 1963 - No. 2, 1964
Dell Publishing Co.

| | | | |
|---|---|---|---|
| 1,2 | 1.30 | 4.00 | 9.00 |

**ENSIGN PULVER** (See Movie Classics)

**EPIC ILLUSTRATED** (Magazine)
Spring, 1980 - No. 34, Mar, 1986 ($2.00-$2.50, B&W/Color, adults)
Marvel Comics Group

| | | | |
|---|---|---|---|
| 1-Frazetta-c | .35 | 1.00 | 2.00 |
| 2-26: 12-Wolverton Spacehawk-r edited & recolored w/article on him. 13-Bladerunner preview by Williamson. 14-Elric of Melnibone by Russell; Revenge of the Jedi preview. 15-Vallejo-c & interview; 1st Dreadstar story (cont'd in Dreadstar #1). 16-B. Smith-c/a(2). 20-The Sacred & the Profane begins by Ken Steacy. 26-Galactus series begins, ends #34; Cerebus the Aardvark story by Dave Sim | .25 | .75 | 1.50 |
| 27-34: ($2.50): 28-Cerebus app. | .40 | 1.25 | 2.50 |

NOTE: ***N. Adams** a-7; c-6. **Austin** a-15-20i. **Bode** a-19, 23, 27r. **Bolton** a-7, 10-12, 15, 18, 22-25; c-10, 18, 22, 23. **Boris** c/a-15. **Brunner** c-12. **Buscema** a-1p, 9p, 11p-13p. **Byrne/Austin** a-26-34. **Chaykin** a-2; c-8. **Conrad** a-2-5, 7-9, 25-34; c-17. **Corben** a-15; c-2. **Frazetta** c-1. **Golden** a-3. **Gulacy** c/a-3. **Jeff Jones** c-25. **Kaluta** a-17r, 21, 24r, 26; c-4, 28. **Nebres** a-1. **Reese** a-12. **Russell** a-2-4, 9, 14, 33; c-14. **Simonson** a-17. **B. Smith** c/a-7, 16. **Starlin** a-1-9, 14, 15, 34. **Steranko** c-19. **Williamson** a-13, 27, 34. **Wrightson** a-13p, 22, 25, 27, 34; c-30.*

**EPSILON WAVE**
Oct, 1985 - V2#2, 1987 (Color, #1-3: $1.50, #4: $1.25, #5-8: $1.75)
Independent Comics/Elite Comics No. 5 on

| | | | |
|---|---|---|---|
| 1-4: 1-3-Seadragon app. | .25 | .75 | 1.50 |
| 5-8: 6-Seadragon app. | .30 | .90 | 1.75 |
| V2#1,2 (B&W) | .30 | .80 | 1.60 |

**ERNIE COMICS** (Formerly Andy Comics No. 21; All Love Romances No. 26 on)
No. 22, Sept, 1948 - No. 25, Mar, 1949
Current Books/Ace Periodicals

| | | | |
|---|---|---|---|
| nn(9/48,11/48; #22,23) | 3.70 | 11.00 | 26.00 |
| 24,25 | 2.30 | 7.00 | 16.00 |

**ESCAPADE IN FLORENCE** (See Movie Comics)

**ESCAPE FROM DEVIL'S ISLAND**
1952

Avon Periodicals

| | Good | Fine | N-Mint |
|---|---|---|---|
| 1-Kinstler-c; r/as Dynamic Adventures #9 | 17.00 | 51.00 | 120.00 |

**ESCAPE FROM FEAR**
1956, 1962, 1969 (8 pages full color) (On birth control)
Planned Parenthood of America (Giveaway)

| | Good | Fine | N-Mint |
|---|---|---|---|
| 1956 edition | 10.00 | 30.00 | 70.00 |
| 1962 edition | 7.00 | 21.00 | 50.00 |
| 1969 edition | 3.50 | 10.50 | 24.00 |

**ESCAPE FROM THE PLANET OF THE APES** (See Power Record Comics)

**ESCAPE TO WITCH MOUNTAIN** (See Walt Disney Showcase No. 29)

**ESPERS**
July, 1986 - No. 5, April, 1987 ($1.25-$1.75, color, Mando paper, color)
Eclipse Comics

| | Good | Fine | N-Mint |
|---|---|---|---|
| 1-3 ($1.25) | | .65 | 1.30 |
| 4,5 ($1.75) | .30 | .90 | 1.80 |

**ESPIONAGE** (TV)
May-July, 1964 - No. 2, Aug-Oct, 1964
Dell Publishing Co.

| | Good | Fine | N-Mint |
|---|---|---|---|
| 1,2 | 1.50 | 4.50 | 10.00 |

**ETC**
1989 - No. 5, 1990 ($4.50, color, mini-series, adults, 60 pgs.)
Piranha Press (DC Comics)

| | Good | Fine | N-Mint |
|---|---|---|---|
| Book 1-5: Conrad scripts/layouts in all | .75 | 2.25 | 4.50 |

**ETERNAL BIBLE, THE**
1946 (Large size) (16 pages in color)
Authentic Publications

| | Good | Fine | N-Mint |
|---|---|---|---|
| 1 | 6.50 | 19.00 | 45.00 |

**ETERNALS, THE**
July, 1976 - No. 19, Jan, 1978
Marvel Comics Group

| | Good | Fine | N-Mint |
|---|---|---|---|
| 1-Origin | .35 | 1.00 | 2.00 |
| 2-19: 2-1st app. Ajak & The Celestials | .25 | .75 | 1.50 |
| Annual 1(10/77) | .25 | .75 | 1.50 |

NOTE: ***Kirby*** *c/a(p) in all. Price changed from 25 cents to 30 cents during run of #1.*

**ETERNALS, THE**
Oct, 1985 - No. 12, Sept, 1986 (Maxi-series, mando paper)
Marvel Comics Group

| | Good | Fine | N-Mint |
|---|---|---|---|
| 1,12 ($1.25, 52 pgs.): 12-Williamson-a(i) | | .65 | 1.30 |
| 2-11-(75 cents) | | .40 | .80 |

**ETERNITY SMITH**
Sept, 1986 - No. 5, May, 1987 (Color, 36 pgs.)
Renegade Press

| | Good | Fine | N-Mint |
|---|---|---|---|
| 1 ($1.25)-1st app. Eternity Smith | | .65 | 1.30 |
| 2-5 ($1.50): 5-Death of Jasmine | .25 | .75 | 1.50 |

**ETERNITY SMITH**
Sept, 1987 - No. 9?, 1988 ($1.95, color)
Hero Comics

| | Good | Fine | N-Mint |
|---|---|---|---|
| V2#1-9: 8-Indigo begins | .35 | 1.00 | 2.00 |

**ETTA KETT**
No. 11, Dec, 1948 - No. 14, Sept, 1949
King Features Syndicate/Standard

| | Good | Fine | N-Mint |
|---|---|---|---|
| 11 | 5.00 | 15.00 | 35.00 |
| 12-14 | 3.50 | 10.50 | 24.00 |

**EVANGELINE** (Also see Primer)
1984 - #2, 6/84; V2#1, 5/87 - V2#12, Mar, 1989 (Color; Baxter paper)
Comico/First Comics V2#1 on/Lodestone Publ.

| | Good | Fine | N-Mint |
|---|---|---|---|
| 1 | .85 | 2.50 | 5.00 |
| 2 | .40 | 1.25 | 2.50 |
| V2#1 (5/87) - 12 | .35 | 1.00 | 2.00 |
| Special #1 ('86, $2.00, color)-Lodestone Publ. | .35 | 1.00 | 2.00 |

**EVA THE IMP**
1957 - No. 2, Nov, 1957
Red Top Comic/Decker

| | Good | Fine | N-Mint |
|---|---|---|---|
| 1,2 | 1.30 | 4.00 | 9.00 |

**EVEL KNIEVEL**
1974 (20 pages) (Giveaway)
Marvel Comics Group (Ideal Toy Corp.)

| | Good | Fine | N-Mint |
|---|---|---|---|
| nn-Contains photo on inside back-c | | .40 | .80 |

**EVERYBODY'S COMICS** (See Fox Giants)

**EVERYTHING HAPPENS TO HARVEY**
Sept-Oct, 1953 - No. 7, Sept-Oct, 1954
National Periodical Publications

| | Good | Fine | N-Mint |
|---|---|---|---|
| 1 | 11.50 | 34.00 | 80.00 |
| 2 | 6.50 | 19.00 | 45.00 |
| 3-7 | 5.00 | 15.00 | 35.00 |

**EVERYTHING'S ARCHIE**
May, 1969 - Present (Giant issues No. 1-20)
Archie Publications

| | Good | Fine | N-Mint |
|---|---|---|---|
| 1 | 4.65 | 14.00 | 32.00 |
| 2 | 2.30 | 7.00 | 16.00 |
| 3-5 | 1.30 | 4.00 | 9.00 |
| 6-10 | .85 | 2.50 | 5.00 |
| 11-20 | .35 | 1.00 | 2.00 |
| 21-156 | | .50 | 1.00 |

**EVERYTHING'S DUCKY** (See 4-Color No. 1251)

**EWOKS** (TV) (See Star Comics Magazine)
June, 1985 - No. 15, Sept, 1987 (75 cents)
Star Comics (Marvel)

| | Good | Fine | N-Mint |
|---|---|---|---|
| 1-13 (From Star Wars): 10-Williamson-a | | .35 | .70 |
| 14,15($1.00) | | .50 | 1.00 |

**EXCALIBUR** (Also see Marvel Comics Presents #31)
Apr, 1988; Oct, 1988 - Present ($1.50, Baxter)($1.75 #? on)
Marvel Comics

| | Good | Fine | N-Mint |
|---|---|---|---|
| Special Edition nn (The Sword is Drawn)(1987, $3.25)-This is the 1st Excalibur comic | 2.50 | 7.50 | 15.00 |
| Special Edition nn (2nd print, 10/88, $3.50) | 1.00 | 3.00 | 6.00 |
| Special Edition nn (3rd print, 12/89, 4.50) | .75 | 2.25 | 4.50 |
| 1($1.50)-X-Men spin-of; Nightcrawler, Shadowcat(Kitty Pryde), Capt. Britain, Phoenix & Meggan begin | 1.70 | 5.00 | 10.00 |
| 2 | 1.00 | 3.00 | 6.00 |
| 3,4 | .70 | 2.00 | 4.00 |
| 5-10 | .50 | 1.50 | 3.00 |
| 11-15: 10,11-Rogers/Austin-a | .35 | 1.00 | 2.00 |
| 16-36: 19-Austin-i. 21-Intro Crusader X. 22-Iron Man x-over. 24-John Byrne app. in story. 27-B. Smith-a(p) | .25 | .75 | 1.50 |
| ...Mojo Mayhem nn ($4.50, 12/89)-Art Adams/Austin-c/a | .85 | 2.50 | 5.00 |

**EXCITING COMICS**
April, 1940 - No. 69, Sept, 1949
Nedor/Better Publications/Standard Comics

| | Good | Fine | N-Mint |
|---|---|---|---|
| 1-Origin The Mask, Jim Hatfield, Sgt. Bill King, Dan Williams begin | 68.00 | 205.00 | 475.00 |
| 2-The Sphinx begins; The Masked Rider app. | 30.00 | 90.00 | 210.00 |
| 3 | 26.00 | 77.00 | 180.00 |
| 4 | 20.00 | 60.00 | 140.00 |
| 5 | 16.00 | 48.00 | 110.00 |
| 6-8 | 13.00 | 40.00 | 90.00 |

*ESPers #1, © Eclipse Comics*

*Eternity Smith #1 (9/86), © Renegade Press*

*Excalibur #20, © MEG*

Exciting Comics #62, © STD

Exploits of Daniel Boone #5, © QUA

Explorers of the Unknown #1, © AP

| | Good | Fine | N-Mint |
|---|---|---|---|
| 9-Origin/1st app. of The Black Terror & sidekick Tim, begin series | 68.00 | 205.00 | 475.00 |
| 10-13 | 29.00 | 86.00 | 200.00 |
| 14-Last Sphinx, Dan Williams | 19.00 | 58.00 | 135.00 |
| 15-The Liberator begins (origin) | 24.00 | 71.00 | 165.00 |
| 16-20: 20-The Mask ends | 13.00 | 40.00 | 90.00 |
| 21,23-30: 28-Crime Crusader begins, ends #58 | 12.00 | 36.00 | 85.00 |
| 22-Origin The Eaglet; The American Eagle begins | 13.00 | 40.00 | 90.00 |
| 31-38: 35-Liberator ends, not in 31-33 | 11.50 | 34.00 | 80.00 |
| 39-Origin Kara, Jungle Princess | 17.00 | 51.00 | 120.00 |
| 40-50: 42-The Scarab begins. 49-Last Kara, Jungle Princess. 50-Last American Eagle | 14.00 | 43.00 | 100.00 |
| 51-Miss Masque begins | 19.00 | 58.00 | 135.00 |
| 52-54: Miss Masque ends | 14.00 | 43.00 | 100.00 |
| 55-Judy of the Jungle begins(origin), ends #69; 1 pg. Ingels-a | 19.00 | 58.00 | 135.00 |
| 56-58: All airbrush-c | 17.00 | 51.00 | 120.00 |
| 59-Frazetta art in Caniff style; signed Frank Frazeta (one t), 9 pgs. | 21.50 | 64.00 | 150.00 |
| 60-66: 60-Rick Howard, the Mystery Rider begins. 66-Robinson/Meskin-a | 13.00 | 40.00 | 90.00 |
| 67-69 | 8.50 | 25.50 | 60.00 |

NOTE: ***Schomburg (Xela)*** *c-28-68; airbrush c-57-66. Black Terror by* ***R. Moreira****-#65.* ***Roussos*** *a-62. Bondage-c 9, 12, 13, 20, 23, 25, 30, 59.*

**EXCITING ROMANCES**
1949 (nd); No. 2, Spring, 1950 - No. 5, 10/50; No. 6 (1951, nd), No. 7, 9/51 - No. 14, 1/53
Fawcett Publications

| | Good | Fine | N-Mint |
|---|---|---|---|
| 1(1949)-Photo-c | 4.50 | 14.00 | 32.00 |
| 2-5-(1950): 4-Photo-c | 3.15 | 9.50 | 22.00 |
| 6-14 | 2.00 | 6.00 | 14.00 |

NOTE: ***Powell*** *a-8-10. Photo c-1, 4-7, 11, 12.*

**EXCITING ROMANCE STORIES** (See Fox Giants)

**EXCITING WAR** (Korean war)
No. 5, Sept, 1952 - No. 8, May, 1953; No. 9, Nov, 1953
Standard Comics (Better Publ.)

| | Good | Fine | N-Mint |
|---|---|---|---|
| 5 | 3.00 | 9.00 | 21.00 |
| 6,7,9 | 1.70 | 5.00 | 12.00 |
| 8-Toth-a | 3.70 | 11.00 | 26.00 |

**EX-MUTANTS** (Also see Solo Ex-Mutants)
Aug, 1986 - No. 15? ($1.80-1.95, B&W)
Eternity Comics/Amazing Comics/Eternity Comics

| | Good | Fine | N-Mint |
|---|---|---|---|
| 1-15: 5-1st app. the New Humans | .35 | 1.00 | 2.00 |
| Special 1 | .30 | .90 | 1.80 |
| Graphic Novel 1 ($5.95) | 1.00 | 3.00 | 6.00 |
| Graphic Novel 1-2nd & 3rd print w/new text | 1.15 | 3.50 | 7.00 |
| Graphic Novel 2 ('88, $7.95) | 1.35 | 4.00 | 8.00 |
| Pin-Up Book ($1.95, color) | .35 | 1.00 | 2.00 |
| Winter Special 1 (2/89, $1.95) | .35 | 1.00 | 2.00 |

**EX-MUTANTS: THE SHATTERED EARTH CHRONICLES**
Apr, 1988 - No. 7?, ($1.95, B&W)
Eternity Comics

| | Good | Fine | N-Mint |
|---|---|---|---|
| 1-7 | .35 | 1.00 | 2.00 |

**EXORCISTS** (See The Crusaders)

**EXOTIC ROMANCES** (Formerly True War Romances)
No. 22, Oct, 1955 - No. 31, Nov, 1956
Quality Comics Group (Comic Magazines)

| | Good | Fine | N-Mint |
|---|---|---|---|
| 22 | 4.30 | 13.00 | 30.00 |
| 23-26,29 | 2.30 | 7.00 | 16.00 |
| 27,31-Baker-c/a | 4.30 | 13.00 | 30.00 |
| 28,30-Baker-a | 4.00 | 12.00 | 28.00 |

**EXPLOITS OF DANIEL BOONE**
Nov, 1955 - No. 6, Sept, 1956
Quality Comics Group

| | Good | Fine | N-Mint |
|---|---|---|---|
| 1 | 8.50 | 25.50 | 60.00 |
| 2 | 4.30 | 13.00 | 30.00 |
| 3-6 | 4.00 | 12.00 | 28.00 |

**EXPLOITS OF DICK TRACY** (See Dick Tracy)

**EXPLORER JOE**
Winter, 1951 - No. 2, Oct-Nov, 1952
Ziff-Davis Comic Group (Approved Comics)

| | Good | Fine | N-Mint |
|---|---|---|---|
| 1-Saunders painted-c | 6.00 | 18.00 | 42.00 |
| 2-Krigstein-a | 7.00 | 21.00 | 50.00 |

**EXPLORERS OF THE UNKNOWN** (See Archie Giant Series 587, 599)
June, 1990 - Present ($1.00, color)
Archie Comics

| | Good | Fine | N-Mint |
|---|---|---|---|
| 1-6: Featuring Archie and the gang | | .50 | 1.00 |

**EXPOSED** (. . .True Crime Cases)
Mar-Apr, 1948 - No. 9, July-Aug, 1949
D. S. Publishing Co.

| | Good | Fine | N-Mint |
|---|---|---|---|
| 1 | 8.00 | 24.00 | 55.00 |
| 2-Giggling killer story with excessive blood; two eye injury panels | 8.50 | 25.50 | 60.00 |
| 3,8,9 | 4.00 | 12.00 | 28.00 |
| 4-Orlando-a | 4.30 | 13.00 | 30.00 |
| 5-Breeze Lawson, Sky Sheriff by E. Good | 4.30 | 13.00 | 30.00 |
| 6-Ingels-a; used in **SOTI**, illo.-"How to prepare an alibi" | 17.00 | 51.00 | 120.00 |
| 7-Illo. in **SOTI**, "Diagram for housebreakers"; used by N.Y. Legis. Committee | 15.00 | 45.00 | 105.00 |

**EXTRA!**
Mar-Apr, 1955 - No. 5, Nov-Dec, 1955
E. C. Comics

| | Good | Fine | N-Mint |
|---|---|---|---|
| 1 | 8.50 | 25.50 | 60.00 |
| 2-5 | 6.00 | 18.00 | 42.00 |

NOTE: ***Craig, Crandall, Severin*** *art in all.*

**EXTRA COMICS**
1948
Magazine Enterprises

| | Good | Fine | N-Mint |
|---|---|---|---|
| 1-Giant; consisting of rebound ME comics. Two versions known; (1)-Funnyman by Siegel & Shuster, Space Ace, Undercover Girl, Red Fox by L.B. Cole, Trail Colt & (2)-All Funnyman | 24.00 | 73.00 | 170.00 |

**FACE, THE** (Tony Trent, the Face No. 3 on)
1941 - No. 2, 1941? (See Big Shot Comics)
Columbia Comics Group

| | Good | Fine | N-Mint |
|---|---|---|---|
| 1-The Face; Mart Bailey-c | 34.00 | 100.00 | 235.00 |
| 2-Bailey-c | 22.00 | 65.00 | 150.00 |

**FACULTY FUNNIES**
June, 1989 - No. 5, May, 1990 (75 cents, color; 95 cents #2 on)
Archie Comics

| | Good | Fine | N-Mint |
|---|---|---|---|
| 1-5: 1,2-The Awesome Four app. | | .50 | 1.00 |

**FAFHRD AND THE GREY MOUSER** (Also see Wonder Woman #202)
Oct, 1990 - No. 4, 1991 ($4.50, color, 52 pgs.)
Marvel Comics

| | Good | Fine | N-Mint |
|---|---|---|---|
| 1-4: Mignola/Williamson-a; Chaykin scripts | .75 | 2.25 | 4.50 |

**FAIRY TALE PARADE** (See Famous Fairy Tales)
June-July, 1942 - No. 121, Oct, 1946 (Most all by Walt Kelly)
Dell Publishing Co.

| | Good | Fine | N-Mint |
|---|---|---|---|
| 1-Kelly-a begins | 86.00 | 257.00 | 600.00 |
| 2(8-9/42) | 48.00 | 145.00 | 335.00 |
| 3-5 (10-11/42 - 2-4/43) | 31.00 | 92.00 | 215.00 |
| 6-9 (5-7/43 - 11-1/43-44) | 24.00 | 72.00 | 170.00 |
| 4-Color 50('44) | 23.00 | 70.00 | 160.00 |
| 4-Color 69('45) | 20.00 | 60.00 | 140.00 |
| 4-Color 87('45) | 17.00 | 51.00 | 120.00 |
| 4-Color 104,114('46)-Last Kelly issue | 15.00 | 45.00 | 105.00 |
| 4-Color 121('46)-Not by Kelly | 9.30 | 28.00 | 65.00 |

NOTE: *#1-9, 4-Color #50, 69 have **Kelly** c/a; 4-Color #87, 104, 114-**Kelly** art only. #9 has a redrawn version of The Reluctant Dragon. This series contains all the classic fairy tales from Jack In The Beanstalk to Cinderella.*

**FAIRY TALES**
No. 10, 1951 - No. 11, June-July, 1951
Ziff-Davis Publ. Co. (Approved Comics)

| | Good | Fine | N-Mint |
|---|---|---|---|
| 10,11-Painted-c | 8.00 | 24.00 | 55.00 |

**FAITHFUL**
November, 1949 - No. 2, Feb, 1950 (52 pgs.)
Marvel Comics/Lovers' Magazine

| | Good | Fine | N-Mint |
|---|---|---|---|
| 1,2-Photo-c | 3.15 | 9.50 | 22.00 |

**FALCON** (Also see Avengers #181 & Captain America #117 & 133)
Nov, 1983 - No. 4, Feb, 1984 (Mini-series)(See Marvel Premiere #49)
Marvel Comics Group

| | Good | Fine | N-Mint |
|---|---|---|---|
| 1-4: 1-Paul Smith-c/a(p). 2-P. Smith-c | | .50 | 1.00 |

**FALLEN ANGELS**
April, 1987 - No. 8, Nov, 1987 (Mini-series)
Marvel Comics Group

| | Good | Fine | N-Mint |
|---|---|---|---|
| 1 | .35 | 1.10 | 2.20 |
| 2-8 | .25 | .70 | 1.40 |

**FALLING IN LOVE**
Sept-Oct, 1955 - No. 143, Oct-Nov, 1973
Arleigh Publ. Co./National Periodical Publications

| | Good | Fine | N-Mint |
|---|---|---|---|
| 1 | 14.00 | 43.00 | 100.00 |
| 2 | 7.00 | 21.00 | 50.00 |
| 3-10 | 4.30 | 13.00 | 30.00 |
| 11-20 | 2.65 | 8.00 | 18.00 |
| 21-40 | 1.70 | 5.00 | 12.00 |
| 41-46: 46-Last 10 cent issue | 1.30 | 4.00 | 9.00 |
| 47-100,108: 108-Wood-a (4 pgs., 7/69) | .85 | 2.50 | 5.00 |
| 101-107,109-143 | .70 | 2.00 | 4.00 |

NOTE: *Colan c/a-75, 81. 52 pgs.-#125-133.*

**FALL OF THE HOUSE OF USHER, THE** (See A Corben Special & Spirit section 8/22/48)

**FALL OF THE ROMAN EMPIRE** (See Movie Comics)

**FAMILY AFFAIR** (TV)
Feb, 1970 - No. 4, Oct, 1970 (25 cents)
Gold Key

| | Good | Fine | N-Mint |
|---|---|---|---|
| 1-With pull-out poster; photo-c | 2.65 | 8.00 | 18.00 |
| 2-4: 3,4-Photo-c | 1.70 | 5.00 | 12.00 |

**FAMILY FUNNIES**
No. 9, Aug-Sept, 1946
Parents' Magazine Institute

| | Good | Fine | N-Mint |
|---|---|---|---|
| 9 | 2.30 | 7.00 | 16.00 |

**FAMILY FUNNIES** (Tiny Tot Funnies No. 9 on)
Sept, 1950 - No. 8, April?, 1951
Harvey Publications

| | Good | Fine | N-Mint |
|---|---|---|---|
| 1-Mandrake (has over 30 King Feature strips) | 3.50 | 10.50 | 24.00 |
| 2-Flash Gordon, 1 pg. | 2.35 | 7.00 | 16.00 |
| 3-8: 4,5,7-Flash Gordon, 1 pg. | 2.00 | 6.00 | 14.00 |
| 1(black & white) | 1.20 | 3.50 | 8.00 |

**FAMOUS AUTHORS ILLUSTRATED** (See Stories by . . .)

**FAMOUS COMICS** (Also see Favorite Comics)
No date; Mid 1930's (24 pages) (paper cover)
Zain-Eppy/United Features Syndicate

| | Good | Fine | N-Mint |
|---|---|---|---|
| nn-Reprinted from 1933 & 1934 newspaper strips in color; Joe Palooka, Hairbreadth Harry, Napoleon, The Nebbs, etc. (Nine different versions known) | 20.00 | 60.00 | 140.00 |

**FAMOUS COMICS**
1934 (100 pgs., daily newspaper reprints)
(3½x8½"; paper cover) (came in a box)
King Features Syndicate (Whitman Publ. Co.)

| | Good | Fine | N-Mint |
|---|---|---|---|
| 684(#1)-Little Jimmy, Katzenjammer Kids, & Barney Google | 16.00 | 48.00 | 110.00 |
| 684(#2)-Polly, Little Jimmy, Katzenjammer Kids | 16.00 | 48.00 | 110.00 |
| 684(#3)-Little Annie Rooney, Polly, Katzenjammer Kids | 16.00 | 48.00 | 110.00 |
| . . . . Box price. . . . | 7.00 | 28.00 | 70.00 |

**FAMOUS COMICS CARTOON BOOKS**
1934 (72 pgs.; 8x7¼"; daily strip reprints)
Whitman Publishing Co. (B&W; hardbacks)

| | Good | Fine | N-Mint |
|---|---|---|---|
| 1200-The Captain & the Kids (1st app?); Dirks reprints credited to Bernard Dibble | 11.50 | 34.00 | 80.00 |
| 1202-Captain Easy (1st app?) & Wash Tubbs by Roy Crane | 16.00 | 48.00 | 110.00 |
| 1203-Ella Cinders (1st app?) | 11.50 | 34.00 | 80.00 |
| 1204-Freckles & His Friends (1st app?) | 9.30 | 28.00 | 65.00 |

NOTE: *Called Famous Funnies Cartoon Books inside.*

**FAMOUS CRIMES**
June, 1948 - No. 19, Sept, 1950; No. 20, Aug, 1951; No. 51, 52, 1953
Fox Features Syndicate/M.S. Dist. No. 51,52

| | Good | Fine | N-Mint |
|---|---|---|---|
| 1-Blue Beetle app. & crime story r-/Phantom Lady #16; Hollingsworth-a | 16.00 | 48.00 | 110.00 |
| 2-Shows woman dissolved in acid; lingerie-c/panels | 13.00 | 40.00 | 90.00 |
| 3-Injury-to-eye story used in **SOTI**, pg. 112; has two electrocution stories | 16.00 | 48.00 | 110.00 |
| 4-6 | 6.50 | 19.00 | 45.00 |
| 7-"Tarzan, the Wyoming Killer" used in **SOTI**, pg. 44; drug trial/possession story | 13.00 | 40.00 | 90.00 |
| 8-20: 17-Morisi-a | 4.50 | 14.00 | 32.00 |
| 51(nd, 1953) | 5.00 | 15.00 | 35.00 |
| 52 | 2.85 | 8.50 | 20.00 |

**FAMOUS FAIRY TALES**
1943 (32 pgs.); 1944 (16 pgs.) (Soft covers)
K. K. Publ. Co. (Giveaway)

| | Good | Fine | N-Mint |
|---|---|---|---|
| 1943-Reprints from Fairy Tale Parade No. 2,3; Kelly inside art | 40.00 | 120.00 | 260.00 |
| 1944-Kelly inside art | 28.00 | 85.00 | 180.00 |

**FAMOUS FEATURE STORIES**
1938 (68 pgs., 7½x11")
Dell Publishing Co.

| | Good | Fine | N-Mint |
|---|---|---|---|
| 1-Tarzan, Terry & the Pirates, King of the Royal Mtd., Buck Jones, Dick Tracy, Smilin' Jack, Dan Dunn, Don Winslow, G-Man, Tailspin Tommy, Mutt & Jeff, & Little Orphan Annie reprints - all illustrated text | 43.00 | 130.00 | 300.00 |

**FAMOUS FIRST EDITION** (See Limited Collectors' Edition)
($1.00; 10x13½"-Giant Size)(72pgs.; No.6-8, 68 pgs.)
1974 - No. 8, Aug-Sept, 1975; C-61, Sept, 1978
National Periodical Publications/DC Comics

| | Good | Fine | N-Mint |
|---|---|---|---|
| C-26-Action No. 1 | 1.00 | 3.00 | 7.00 |
| C-28-Detective No. 27 | 5.00 | 15.00 | 30.00 |

*Fairy Tale Parade #7, © DELL*

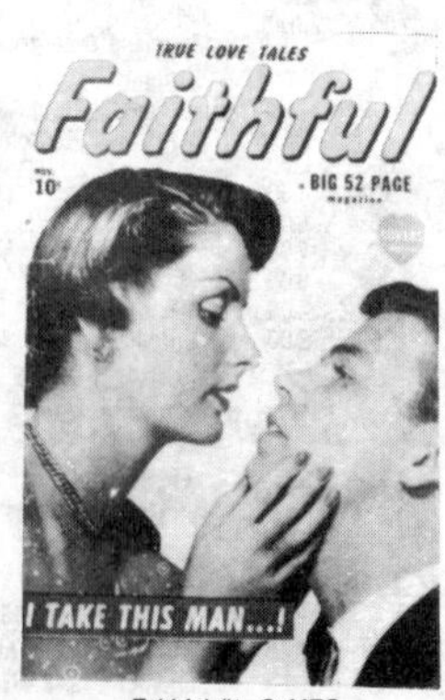

*Faithful #1, © MEG*

*Famous Crimes #1, © FOX*

Famous Funnies #6, © EAS

Famous Funnies #135, © EAS

Famous Funnies #215, © EAS

| | Good | Fine | N-Mint |
|---|---|---|---|
| C-28-Hardbound edition | 7.00 | 21.00 | 50.00 |
| C-30-Sensation No. 1(1974) | 1.00 | 3.00 | 7.00 |
| F-4-Whiz No. 2(No.1)(10-11/74)-Cover not identical to original | 1.00 | 3.00 | 7.00 |
| F-5-Batman No. 1(F-6 on inside) | 5.00 | 15.00 | 30.00 |
| F-6-Wonder Woman No. 1 | .85 | 2.50 | 6.00 |
| F-7-All-Star Comics No. 3 | 1.00 | 3.00 | 7.00 |
| F-8-Flash No. 1(8-9/75) | .85 | 2.50 | 6.00 |
| C-61-Superman No. 1(9/78) | 1.35 | 4.00 | 8.00 |
| Hardbound editions (w/dust jackets $5.00 extra) (Lyle Stuart, Inc.) C-26,C-30,F-4,F-6 known | 1.75 | 5.25 | 12.00 |

**Warning:** The above books are almost **exact** reprints of the originals that they represent except for the Giant-Size format. None of the originals are Giant-Size. The first five issues and C-61 were printed with two covers. Reprint information can be found on the outside cover, but not on the inside cover which was reprinted exactly like the original (inside and out).

**FAMOUS FUNNIES**
1933 - No. 218, July, 1955
Eastern Color

| | Good | Fine | Vf-NM | NM/Mint |
|---|---|---|---|---|
| **A Carnival of Comics** (probably the second comic book), 36 pgs., no date given, no publisher, no number; contains strip reprints of The Bungle Family, Dixie Dugan, Hairbreadth Harry, Joe Palooka, Keeping Up With the Jones, Mutt & Jeff, Reg'lar Fellers, S'Matter Pop, Strange As It Seems, and others. This book was sold by M. C. Gaines to Wheatena, Milk-O-Malt, John Wanamaker, Kinney Shoe Stores, & others to be given away as premiums and radio giveaways (1933). | 400.00 | 1000.00 | 2400.00 | 3700.00 |

(Estimated up to 50 total copies exist, 2 in NM/Mint)

| | Good | Fine | Vf-NM | NM/Mint |
|---|---|---|---|---|
| **Series 1**-(Very rare)(nd-early 1934)(68 pgs.) No publisher given (Eastern Color Printing Co.); sold in chain stores for 10 cents. 35,000 print run. Contains Sunday strip reprints of Mutt & Jeff, Reg'lar Fellers, Nipper, Hairbreadth Harry, Strange As It Seems, Joe Palooka, Dixie Dugan, The Nebbs, Keeping Up With the Jones, and others. Inside front and back covers and pages 1-16 of Famous Funnies Series 1, #s 49-64 reprinted from **Famous Funnies, A Carnival of Comics,** and most of pages 17-48 reprinted from **Funnies on Parade.** This was the first comic book sold. | 835.00 | 2100.00 | 5000.00 | 8000.00 |

(Estimated up to 12 copies exist, 1 in NM/Mint)

| | Good | Fine | Vf-NM | NM/Mint |
|---|---|---|---|---|
| **No. 1** (Rare)(7/34-on stands 5/34) - Eastern Color Printing Co. First monthly newsstand comic book. Contains Sunday strip reprints of Toonerville Folks, Mutt & Jeff, Hairbreadth Harry, S'Matter Pop, Nipper, Dixie Dugan, The Bungle Family, Connie, Ben Webster, Tailspin Tommy, The Nebbs, Joe Palooka, & others. | 670.00 | 1670.00 | 4000.00 | 5700.00 |

(Estimated up to 30 total copies exist, 2 in NM/Mint)

| | Good | Fine | VF-NM |
|---|---|---|---|
| 2 (Rare) | 167.00 | 415.00 | 1000.00 |
| 3-Buck Rogers Sunday strip reprints by Rick Yager begins, ends #218; not in #191-208; the number of the 1st strip reprinted is pg. 190, Series No. 1 | 235.00 | 585.00 | 1400.00 |
| 4 | 78.00 | 235.00 | 550.00 |
| 5 | 63.00 | 190.00 | 440.00 |
| 6-10 | 50.00 | 150.00 | 350.00 |

| | Good | Fine | N-Mint |
|---|---|---|---|
| 11,12,18-Four pgs. of Buck Rogers in each issue, completes stories in Buck Rogers #1 which lacks these pages; #18-Two pgs. of Buck Rogers reprinted in Daisy Comics #1 | 43.00 | 130.00 | 300.00 |
| 13-17,19,20: 14-Has two Buck Rogers panels missing. 17-1st Christmas-c on a newsstand comic | 32.00 | 95.00 | 225.00 |
| 21,23-30: 27-War on Crime begins; part photo-c. 29-X-Mas-c | 23.00 | 70.00 | 160.00 |
| 22-Four pgs. of Buck Rogers needed to complete stories in Buck Rogers #1 | 25.00 | 75.00 | 175.00 |
| 31-34,36,37,39,40: 33-Careers of Baby Face Nelson & John Dillinger traced | 17.00 | 51.00 | 120.00 |
| 35-Two pgs. Buck Rogers omitted in Buck Rogers #2 | 19.00 | 56.00 | 130.00 |
| 38-Full color portrait of Buck Rogers | 17.00 | 51.00 | 120.00 |
| 41-60: 41,53-X-Mas-c. 55-Last bottom panel, pg. 4 in Buck Rogers redrawn in Buck Rogers #3 | 12.00 | 36.00 | 85.00 |
| 61-64,66,67,69,70 | 10.00 | 30.00 | 70.00 |
| 65,68-Two pgs. Kirby-a-"Lightnin & the Lone Rider" | 11.00 | 32.00 | 75.00 |
| 71,73,77-80: 80-Buck Rogers story continues from Buck Rogers #5 | 8.50 | 25.50 | 60.00 |
| 72-Speed Spaulding begins by Marvin Bradley (artist), ends #88. This series was written by Edwin Balmer & Philip Wylie and later appeared as film & book "When Worlds Collide" | 9.30 | 28.00 | 65.00 |
| 74-76-Two pgs. Kirby-a in all | 8.00 | 24.00 | 55.00 |
| 81-Origin Invisible Scarlet O'Neil; strip begins #82, ends #167 | 6.50 | 19.00 | 45.00 |
| 82-Buck Rogers-c | 8.00 | 24.00 | 55.00 |
| 83-87,90: 87 has last Buck Rogers full page-r. 90-Bondage-c | 6.50 | 19.00 | 45.00 |
| 88-Buck Rogers in "Moon's End" by Calkins, 2 pgs.(not reprints). Beginning with #88, all Buck Rogers pages have rearranged panels | 7.00 | 21.00 | 50.00 |
| 89-Origin Fearless Flint, the Flint Man | 7.00 | 21.00 | 50.00 |
| 91-93,95,96,98-99,101-110: 105-Series 2 begins (Strip Page #1) | 5.00 | 15.00 | 35.00 |
| 94-Buck Rogers in "Solar Holocaust" by Calkins, 3 pgs.(not reprints) | 6.00 | 18.00 | 42.00 |
| 97-War Bond promotion, Buck Rogers by Calkins, 2 pgs.(not reprints) | 6.00 | 18.00 | 42.00 |
| 100 | 6.00 | 18.00 | 42.00 |
| 111-130 | 4.00 | 12.00 | 28.00 |
| 131-150: 137-Strip page No. 110½ omitted | 2.85 | 8.50 | 20.00 |
| 151-162,164-168 | 2.30 | 7.00 | 16.00 |
| 163-St. Valentine's Day-c | 2.85 | 8.50 | 20.00 |
| 169,170-Two text illos. by Williamson, his 1st comic book work | 5.50 | 16.50 | 38.00 |
| 171-180: 171-Strip pgs. 227,229,230, Series 2 omitted. 172-Strip Pg. 232 omitted | 2.30 | 7.00 | 16.00 |
| 181-190: Buck Rogers ends with start of strip pg. 302, Series 2 | 1.85 | 5.50 | 13.00 |
| 191-197,199,201,203,206-208: No Buck Rogers | 1.60 | 4.70 | 11.00 |
| 198,202,205-One pg. Frazetta ads; no Buck Rogers | 2.00 | 6.00 | 14.00 |
| 200-Frazetta 1 pg. ad | 2.15 | 6.50 | 15.00 |
| 204-Used in **POP**, pgs. 79,99 | 2.15 | 6.50 | 15.00 |
| 209-Buck Rogers begins with strip pg. 480, Series 2; Frazetta-c | 26.00 | 77.00 | 180.00 |
| 210-216: Frazetta-c. 211-Buck Rogers ads by Anderson begins, ends #217. #215-Contains B. Rogers strip pg. 515-518, series 2 followed by pgs. 179-181, Series 3 | 26.00 | 77.00 | 180.00 |
| 217,218-Buck Rogers ends with pg. 199, Series 3 | 2.30 | 7.00 | 16.00 |

NOTE: ***Rick Yager*** *did the Buck Rogers Sunday strips reprinted in Famous Funnies. The Sundays were formerly done by Russ Keaton and Lt. Dick Calkins did the dailies, but would sometimes assist Yager on a panel or two from time to time. Strip No. 169 is Yager's first full Buck Rogers page. Yager did the strip until 1958 when* ***Murphy Anderson*** *took over.* ***Tuska*** *art from 4/26/59 - 1965. Virtually every panel was rewritten for Famous Funnies. Not identical to the original Sunday page. The Buck Rogers reprints run continuously through Famous Funnies issue No. 190 (Strip No. 302) with no break in story line. The story line has no continuity after No. 190. The Buck Rogers newspaper strips came out in four series: Series 1, 3/30/30 - 9/21/41 (No. 1 - 600); Series 2, 9/28/41 -10/21/51 (No. 1 -525)(Strip No. 110½ (½ pg.) published in only a few newspapers); Series 3, 10/28/51 -2/9/58 (No. 100-428)(No No. 1-99); Series 4, 2/16/58 - 6/13/65 (No numbers, dates only).* ***Everett*** *c-86.* ***Moulton*** *a-100.*

**FAMOUS FUNNIES**
1964
Super Comics

| | Good | Fine | N-Mint |
|---|---|---|---|
| Super Reprint Nos. 15-18 | .50 | 1.50 | 3.00 |

**FAMOUS GANG BOOK OF COMICS** (Becomes Donald & Mickey Merry Christmas 1943 on)
Dec, 1942 (32 pgs.; paper cover) (Christmas giveaway)
Firestone Tire & Rubber Co.

| | Good | Fine | N-Mint |
|---|---|---|---|
| nn-(Rare)-Porky Pig, Bugs Bunny, Sniffles; r-/Looney Tunes | 67.00 | 200.00 | 500.00 |

**FAMOUS GANGSTERS** (Crime on the Waterfront No. 4)
April, 1951 - No. 3, Feb, 1952
Avon Periodicals/Realistic

| | Good | Fine | N-Mint |
|---|---|---|---|
| 1-Capone, Dillinger; c-/Avon paperback 329 | 14.00 | 42.00 | 100.00 |
| 2-Wood-c/a (1 pg.); r-/Saint #7 & retitled "Mike Strong" | 15.00 | 45.00 | 105.00 |
| 3-Lucky Luciano & Murder, Inc; c-/Avon paperback #66 | 15.00 | 45.00 | 105.00 |

**FAMOUS INDIAN TRIBES**
July-Sept, 1962; No. 2, July, 1972
Dell Publishing Co.

| | Good | Fine | N-Mint |
|---|---|---|---|
| 12-264-209(#1) (The Sioux) | 1.00 | 3.00 | 7.00 |
| 2(7/72)-Reprints above | .25 | .75 | 1.50 |

**FAMOUS STARS**
Nov-Dec, 1950 - No. 6, Spring, 1952 (All photo covers)
Ziff-Davis Publ. Co.

| | Good | Fine | N-Mint |
|---|---|---|---|
| 1-Shelley Winters, Susan Peters, Ava Gardner, Shirley Temple | 14.00 | 43.00 | 100.00 |
| 2-Betty Hutton, Bing Crosby, Colleen Townsend, Gloria Swanson; Everett-a(2) | 10.00 | 30.00 | 70.00 |
| 3-Farley Granger, Judy Garland's ordeal, Alan Ladd | 9.30 | 28.00 | 65.00 |
| 4-Al Jolson, Bob Mitchum, Ella Raines, Richard Conte, Vic Damone; Crandall-a, 6pgs. | 8.50 | 25.50 | 60.00 |
| 5-Liz Taylor, Betty Grable, Esther Williams, George Brent; Krigstein-a | 11.50 | 34.00 | 80.00 |
| 6-Gene Kelly, Hedy Lamarr, June Allyson, William Boyd, Janet Leigh, Gary Cooper | 8.50 | 25.50 | 60.00 |

NOTE: ***Whitney*** *a-1, 3.*

**FAMOUS STORIES** (. . .Book No. 2)
1942 - No. 2, 1942
Dell Publishing Co.

| | Good | Fine | N-Mint |
|---|---|---|---|
| 1,2: 1-Treasure Island. 2-Tom Sawyer | 16.00 | 48.00 | 110.00 |

**FAMOUS TV FUNDAY FUNNIES**
Sept, 1961
Harvey Publications

| | Good | Fine | N-Mint |
|---|---|---|---|
| 1-Casper the Ghost | 3.00 | 9.00 | 21.00 |

**FAMOUS WESTERN BADMEN** (Formerly Redskin)
No. 13, Dec, 1952 - No. 15, 1953
Youthful Magazines

| | Good | Fine | N-Mint |
|---|---|---|---|
| 13 | 4.50 | 14.00 | 32.00 |
| 14,15 | 3.00 | 9.00 | 21.00 |

**FANTASTIC** (Formerly Captain Science; Beware No. 10 on)
No. 8, Feb, 1952 - No. 9, April, 1952
Youthful Magazines

| | Good | Fine | N-Mint |
|---|---|---|---|
| 8-Capt. Science by Harrison; decapitation, shrunken head panels | 13.00 | 40.00 | 90.00 |
| 9-Harrison-a | 8.00 | 24.00 | 55.00 |

**FANTASTIC ADVENTURES**
1963 - 1964 (Reprints)
Super Comics

| | Good | Fine | N-Mint |
|---|---|---|---|
| 9,10,12,15,16,18: 16-Briefer-a. 18-r/Superior Stories #1 | 1.15 | 3.50 | 8.00 |
| 11-Wood-a; r/Blue Bolt #118 | 1.70 | 5.00 | 12.00 |
| 17-Baker-a(2) r-/Seven Seas #6 | 1.50 | 4.50 | 10.00 |

**FANTASTIC COMICS**
Dec, 1939 - No. 23, Nov, 1941
Fox Features Syndicate

| | Good | Fine | N-Mint |
|---|---|---|---|
| 1-Intro/Origin Samson; Stardust, The Super Wizard, Space Smith, Sub Saunders (by Kiefer), Capt. Kidd begin | 130.00 | 390.00 | 915.00 |
| 2-Powell text illos | 65.00 | 195.00 | 455.00 |
| 3-5: 3-Powell text illos | 54.00 | 160.00 | 375.00 |
| 6-9: 6,7-Simon-c | 43.00 | 130.00 | 300.00 |
| 10-Intro/origin David, Samson's aide | 32.00 | 95.00 | 225.00 |
| 11-17,19,20,22: 16-Stardust ends | 25.00 | 75.00 | 175.00 |
| 18-1st app. Black Fury & sidekick Chuck; ends #23 | 29.00 | 86.00 | 200.00 |
| 21,23: 21-The Banshee begins(origin); ends #23; Hitler-c. 23-Origin The Gladiator | 29.00 | 86.00 | 200.00 |

NOTE: ***Lou Fine*** *c-1-5.* ***Tuska*** *a-3-5, 8. Bondage c-6, 8, 9.*

**FANTASTIC COMICS** (Fantastic Fears #1-9; Becomes Samson #12)
No. 10, Nov-Dec, 1954 - No. 11, Jan-Feb, 1955
Ajax/Farrell Publ.

| | Good | Fine | N-Mint |
|---|---|---|---|
| 10,11 | 5.00 | 15.00 | 35.00 |

**FANTASTIC FABLES**
Feb, 1987 ($1.50, B&W, 28 pgs.)
Silverwolf Comics

| | Good | Fine | N-Mint |
|---|---|---|---|
| 1-Tim Vigil-a (6 pgs.) | .50 | 1.50 | 3.00 |

**FANTASTIC FEARS** (Formerly Captain Jet) (Fantastic Comics #10 on)
No. 7, May, 1953 - No. 9, Sept-Oct, 1954
Ajax/Farrell Publ.

| | Good | Fine | N-Mint |
|---|---|---|---|
| 7(#1, 5/53) | 11.50 | 34.00 | 80.00 |
| 8(#2, 7/53) | 7.00 | 21.00 | 50.00 |
| 3,4 | 5.70 | 17.00 | 40.00 |
| 5-1st Ditko story is written by Bruce Hamilton reprinted in Weird V2#8 | 23.00 | 70.00 | 160.00 |
| 6-Decapitation of girl's head with paper cutter (classic) | 14.00 | 43.00 | 100.00 |
| 7(5-6/54), 9(9-10/54) | 5.00 | 15.00 | 35.00 |
| 8(7-8/54)-Contains story intended for Jo-Jo; name changed to Kaza; decapitation story | 7.00 | 21.00 | 50.00 |

**FANTASTIC FOUR** (See America's Best TV. . ., Giant-Size. . ., Giant Size Super-Stars, Marvel Collectors Item Classics, Marvel's Greatest, Marvel Treasury Edition, Marvel Triple Action, Official Marvel Index to. . . & Power Record Comics)

**FANTASTIC FOUR**
Nov, 1961 - Present
Marvel Comics Group

| | Good | Fine | N-Mint | Mint |
|---|---|---|---|---|
| 1-Origin/1st app. The Fantastic Four (Reed Richards: Mr. Fantastic, Johnny Storm: The Human Torch, Sue Storm: The Invisible Girl, & Ben Grimm: The Thing); origin The Mole Man (Marvel's 1st super-hero group since the G.A.) | 350.00 | 1400.00 | 3500.00 | 7000.00 |

(Estimated up to 1400 total copies exist, 65 in Mint)

| | Good | Fine | N-Mint |
|---|---|---|---|
| 1-Golden Record Comic Set-r | 11.00 | 32.00 | 75.00 |
| with record (still sealed) | 21.50 | 65.00 | 150.00 |
| 2-Vs. The Skrulls (last 10 cent issue) | 129.00 | 388.00 | 900.00 |
| 3-Fantastic Four don costumes & establish Headquarters; brief 1pg. origin; intro The Fantasticar; Human Torch drawn w/two left hands on-c | 100.00 | 300.00 | 700.00 |
| 4-1st Silver Age Sub-Mariner app. | 100.00 | 300.00 | 700.00 |
| 5-Origin & 1st app. Doctor Doom | 104.00 | 312.00 | 725.00 |
| 6-Sub-Mariner, Dr. Doom team up; 1st Marvel villain team-up | 66.00 | 198.00 | 460.00 |
| 7-10: 7-1st app. Kurrgo. 8-1st app. Puppet-Master & Alicia Masters | 49.00 | 147.00 | 340.00 |
| 11-Origin The Impossible Man | 33.00 | 100.00 | 230.00 |
| 12-Fantastic Four Vs. The Hulk (1st x-over) | 37.00 | 111.00 | 260.00 |
| 13-Intro. The Watcher; 1st app. The Red Ghost | 29.00 | 88.00 | 200.00 |

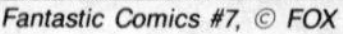

*Fantastic Comics #7, © FOX*

*Fantastic Comics #10, © AJAX*

*Fantastic Four #6, MEG*

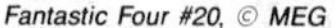
*Fantastic Four #20, © MEG*

*Fantastic Four #55, © MEG*

*Fantastic Four #164, © MEG*

| | Good | Fine | N-Mint |
|---|---|---|---|
| 14-19: 16-1st Ant-Man x-over (7/63). 18-Origin The Super Skrull. 19-Intro. Rama-Tut | 20.00 | 60.00 | 140.00 |
| 20-Origin The Molecule Man | 21.50 | 65.00 | 150.00 |
| 21-24,27: 21-Intro. The Hate Monger; 1st Sgt. Fury x-over (11/63). 27-1st Doctor Strange x-over (6/64) | 11.00 | 32.00 | 75.00 |
| 25,26-The Thing vs. The Hulk. 26-1st Avengers x-over (5/64) | 21.00 | 63.00 | 145.00 |
| 28-1st X-Men x-over | 13.00 | 40.00 | 90.00 |
| 29,30: 30-Intro. Diablo | 8.00 | 24.00 | 55.00 |
| 31-40: 31-Early Avengers x-over. 33-1st app. Attuma; part photo-c. 35-Intro/1st app. Dragon Man. 36-Intro/1st app. Madam Medusa & the Frightful Four (Sandman, Wizard, Paste Pot Pete). 39-Wood inks on Daredevil (early x-over) | 5.70 | 17.00 | 40.00 |
| 41-47: 41-43-Frightful Four app. 44-Intro. Gorgan. 45-Intro. The Inhumans | 4.00 | 12.00 | 28.00 |
| 48-Origin/1st app. The Silver Surfer & Galactus (3/66); Galactus app. in last panel (cameo); 1st of 3 part story | 29.00 | 88.00 | 200.00 |
| 49-2nd app. Silver Surfer & Galactus | 8.50 | 25.50 | 60.00 |
| 50-Silver Surfer battles Galactus | 13.00 | 40.00 | 90.00 |
| 51,53,54: 53-Origin The Black Panther. 54-Inhumans cameo | 3.15 | 9.50 | 22.00 |
| 52-1st app. The Black Panther | 4.30 | 13.00 | 30.00 |
| 55-60: Silver Surfer x-over. 59,60-Inhumans cameo | 4.00 | 12.00 | 28.00 |
| 61-65,68-70: 61-Silver Surfer cameo | 3.00 | 9.00 | 21.00 |
| 66,67-1st app. & origin Him (Warlock) | 3.15 | 9.50 | 22.00 |
| 71,73,78-80 | 1.70 | 5.00 | 12.00 |
| 72,74-77: Silver Surfer app. in all | 2.30 | 7.00 | 16.00 |
| 81-88: 81-Crystal joins & dons costume. 82,83-Inhumans app. 84-87-Dr. Doom app. 88-Last 12 cent issue | 1.50 | 4.50 | 10.00 |
| 89-99,101,102: 94-Intro. Agatha Harkness | 1.15 | 3.50 | 8.00 |
| 100 | 3.15 | 9.50 | 22.00 |
| 103-111: 108-Last Kirby issue (not in #103-107) | 1.00 | 3.00 | 7.00 |
| 112-Hulk Vs. Thing | 2.65 | 8.00 | 18.00 |
| 113-120: 115-Last I5 cent issue? 116-(52 pgs.) | 1.00 | 3.00 | 6.00 |
| 121-123-Silver Surfer x-over | 1.00 | 3.00 | 7.00 |
| 124-127,129-149,151-154,158-160: 126-Origin F.F. retold; cover swipe of F.F. #1. 129-Intro. Thundra. 130-Sue leaves F.F. 131-Quicksilver app. 132-Medusa joins. 133-Thundra Vs. Thing. 142-Kirbyish-a by Buckler begins. 143-Dr. Doom app. 151-Origin Thundra. 159-Medusa leaves, Sue rejoins | .70 | 2.00 | 4.00 |
| 128-Four pg. insert of F.F. Friends & Fiends | .85 | 2.50 | 5.00 |
| 150-Crystal & Quicksilver's wedding | .85 | 2.50 | 5.00 |
| 155-157: Silver Surfer in all | .85 | 2.50 | 5.00 |
| 161-180: 164-The Crusader (old Marvel Boy) revived(origin #165). 176-Re-intro Impossible Man; Marvel artists app. | .35 | 1.05 | 2.10 |
| 181-199: 190-191-Fantastic Four break up | .25 | .80 | 1.60 |
| 200-Giant size; F.F. re-united | .70 | 2.00 | 4.00 |
| 201-208,219 | | .65 | 1.30 |
| 209-216,218,220,221-Byrne-a. 209-1st Herbie the Robot. 220-Brief origin | .25 | .80 | 1.60 |
| 217-Dazzler app. by Byrne | .45 | 1.35 | 2.70 |
| 222-231 | | .65 | 1.30 |
| 232-Byrne-a begins | .50 | 1.55 | 3.10 |
| 233-235,237-249: All Byrne-a. 238-Origin Frankie Ray | .40 | 1.25 | 2.50 |
| 236-20th Anniversary issue(11/81, 64pgs., $1.00)-Brief origin F.F. | .50 | 1.55 | 3.10 |
| 250,260: 250-Double size; Byrne-a; Skrulls impersonate New X-Men. 260-Alpha Flight app. | .50 | 1.55 | 3.10 |
| 251-259: Byrne-c/a. 252-Reads sideways; Annihilus app. 254-Contains skin "Tatooz" decals | .40 | 1.15 | 2.30 |
| 261-285: 261-Silver Surfer. 262-Origin Galactus; Byrne writes & draws himself into story. 264-Swipes-c of F.F. #1 | .35 | 1.05 | 2.10 |
| 286-2nd app. X-Factor cont./Avengers #263 | .60 | 1.80 | 3.60 |
| 287-295,297-305,307-318,320-330: 292-Nick Fury app. 300-Johnny Storm & Alicia Masters wed. 312-X-Factor x-over. 327-Mr. Fantastic & Invisible Girl return | | .50 | 1.00 |
| 296-($1.50)-Barry Smith-c/a; Thing rejoins | .35 | 1.05 | 2.10 |
| 306-New team begins | .25 | .75 | 1.50 |
| 319-Double size | .35 | 1.00 | 2.00 |
| 331-346,350-352: 334-Simonson-c/scripts begin. 337-Simonson-a begins. 342-Spider-Man cameo | | .50 | 1.00 |
| 347-349-Ghost Rider, Wolverine, Spider-Man & Hulk-c/stories; Arthur Adams-c/a(p) | .35 | 1.00 | 2.00 |
| Annual 1('63)-Origin F.F.; Ditko-i | 27.00 | 81.00 | 190.00 |
| Annual 2('64)-Dr. Doom origin & x-over | 20.00 | 60.00 | 140.00 |
| Annual 3('65)-Reed & Sue wed | 9.30 | 28.00 | 65.00 |
| Special 4(11/66)-G.A. Torch x-over & origin retold | 4.30 | 13.00 | 30.00 |
| Special 5(11/67)-New art; Intro. Psycho-Man; early Black Panther, Inhumans & Silver Surfer app. | 2.15 | 6.50 | 15.00 |
| Special 6(11/68)-Intro. Annihilus; no reprints; birth of Franklin Richards | 2.30 | 6.50 | 15.00 |
| Special 7(11/69)-All reprints | 2.30 | 7.00 | 15.00 |
| Special 8(12/70), 9(12/71), 10('73)-All reprints | 1.35 | 4.00 | 8.00 |
| Annual 11-14: 11(6/76), 12(2/78), 13(10/78), 14(1/80) | .85 | 2.50 | 5.00 |
| Annual 15-20: 15(10/80), 16(10/81), 17(9/83), 18(11/84), 19(11/85), 20(9/87) | .50 | 1.50 | 3.00 |
| Annual 21(9/88)-Evolutionary War x-over | .55 | 1.70 | 3.40 |
| Annual 22(1989, $2.00, 64pg.)-Atlantis Attacks x-over; Sub-Mariner & The Avengers app. Buckler-a | .35 | 1.00 | 2.00 |
| Annual 23('90, $2.00, 68 pgs.)-Byrne-c, Guice-p | .35 | 1.00 | 2.00 |
| Special Edition 1 (5/84)-r/Annual #1; Byrne-c/a | .35 | 1.05 | 2.10 |
| Giveaway (nn, 1981, 32pgs., Young Model Builders Club) | .25 | .80 | 1.60 |

NOTE: ***Arthur Adams*** *c/a-347-349p.* ***Austin*** *c(i)-232-236, 238, 240-242, 250i, 286i.* ***John Buscema*** *a(p)-107, 108(w/****Kirby & Romita****),109-130, 132, 134-141, 160, 173-175, 202, 296p-309p, Annual 11, 13; c(p)-107-122, 124-129, 133-139, 202, Annual 12p, Special 10.* ***Byrne*** *a-209-218p, 220p, 221p, 232-265, 266i, 267-273, 274-293p, Annual 17, 19; c-211-214p, 220p, 232-236p, 237, 238p, 239, 240-242p, 243-249, 250p, 251-267, 269-277, 278-281p, 283p, 284, 285, 286p, 288-293, Annual, 17.* ***Ditko*** *a-13i, Annual 16.* ***G. Kane*** *c-150p, 160p.* ***Kirby*** *a-1-102p, 108, 180r, 189r, 236p, Special 1-10; c-1-101, 164, 167, 171-177, 180, 181, 190, 200, Annual 11, Special 1-7, 9.* ***Marcos*** *a-Annual 14i.* ***Mooney*** *a-118i, 152i.* ***Perez*** *a-164-167, 170-172, 176-178, 184-188, 191p, 192p. Annual 14p, 15p; c(p)-183-188, 191, 192, 194-197.* ***Simonson*** *a-337-341, 343, 344p, 345p, 346; c-212, 334-341, 342p, 343-346.* ***Steranko*** *c-130-132p.*

**FANTASTIC FOUR INDEX** (See Official . . .)

**FANTASTIC FOUR ROAST**
May, 1982 (One Shot, Direct Sale)
Marvel Comics Group

| | Good | Fine | N-Mint |
|---|---|---|---|
| 1-Celebrates 20th anniversary of F.F.#1; Golden, Miller, Buscema, Rogers, Byrne, Anderson, Austin-c(i) | .60 | 1.80 | 3.60 |

**FANTASTIC FOUR VS. X-MEN**
Feb, 1987 - No. 4, Jun, 1987 (Mini-series)
Marvel Comics

| | Good | Fine | N-Mint |
|---|---|---|---|
| 1 | .60 | 1.75 | 3.50 |
| 2-4: 4-Austin-a(i) | .40 | 1.25 | 2.50 |

**FANTASTIC GIANTS** (Konga No. 1-23)
V2#24, September, 1966 (25 cents, 68 pgs.)
Charlton Comics

| | Good | Fine | N-Mint |
|---|---|---|---|
| V2#24-Origin Konga & Gorgo reprinted; two new Ditko stories | 3.00 | 9.00 | 21.00 |

**FANTASTIC TALES**
1958 (no date) (Reprint)
I. W. Enterprises

| | Good | Fine | N-Mint |
|---|---|---|---|
| 1-Reprints Avon's "City of the Living Dead" | 1.35 | 4.00 | 9.00 |

**FANTASTIC VOYAGE** (See Movie Comics)
Aug, 1969 - No. 2, Dec, 1969

Gold Key

| | Good | Fine | N-Mint |
|---|---|---|---|
| 1,2 (TV) | 1.70 | 5.00 | 12.00 |

**FANTASTIC VOYAGES OF SINDBAD, THE**
Oct, 1965 - No. 2, June, 1967
Gold Key

| | Good | Fine | N-Mint |
|---|---|---|---|
| 1,2-Painted-c | 2.30 | 7.00 | 16.00 |

**FANTASTIC WORLDS**
No. 5, Sept, 1952 - No. 7, Jan, 1953
Standard Comics

| | Good | Fine | N-Mint |
|---|---|---|---|
| 5-Toth, Anderson-a | 13.00 | 40.00 | 90.00 |
| 6-Toth story | 11.50 | 34.00 | 80.00 |
| 7 | 6.50 | 19.50 | 45.00 |

**FANTASY FEATURES**
1987 - No. 2, 1987 ($1.75, color)
Americomics

| | Good | Fine | N-Mint |
|---|---|---|---|
| 1,2 | .30 | .90 | 1.80 |

**FANTASY MASTERPIECES** (Marvel Super Heroes No. 12 on)
Feb, 1966 - No. 11, Oct, 1967; Dec, 1979 - No. 14, Jan, 1981
Marvel Comics Group

| | Good | Fine | N-Mint |
|---|---|---|---|
| 1-Photo of Stan Lee (12 cent-c #1,2) | 3.15 | 9.50 | 22.00 |
| 2 | 1.00 | 3.00 | 7.00 |
| 3-8: 3-G.A. Capt. America-r begin, end #6; 1st 25 cent Giant; Colan reprint. 7-Begin G.A. Sub-Mariner, Torch-r/M. Mystery. 8-Torch battles the Sub-Mariner r-/Marvel Mystery #9 | 1.50 | 4.50 | 10.00 |
| 9-Origin Human Torch r-/Marvel Comics #1 | 1.70 | 5.00 | 12.00 |
| 10,11: 10-R/origin & 1st app. All Winners Squad from All Winners #19. 11-R/origin of Toro(H.T. #1) & Black Knight | 1.15 | 3.50 | 8.00 |
| V2#1(12/79)-52 pgs.; 75 cents; r-/origin Silver Surfer from S. Surfer #1 with editing; J. Buscema-a | .70 | 2.00 | 4.00 |
| 2-14-Silver Surfer-r | .40 | 1.25 | 2.50 |

NOTE: ***Buscema** c-V2#7-9(in part). **Ditko** r-1-3, 7, 9. **Everett** r-9. **Matt Fox** r-9i. **Kirby** r-1-11. **Starlin** r-8-13. Some direct sale V2#14's had a 50 cent cover price.*

**FANTASY QUARTERLY** (Also see Elfquest)
Spring, 1978 (B&W)
Independent Publishers Syndicate

| | Good | Fine | N-Mint |
|---|---|---|---|
| 1-1st app. Elfquest (2nd printing exist?) | 8.35 | 25.00 | 50.00 |

**FANTOMAN** (Formerly Amazing Adventure Funnies)
No. 2, Aug, 1940 - No. 4, Dec, 1940
Centaur Publications

| | Good | Fine | N-Mint |
|---|---|---|---|
| 2-The Fantom of the Fair, The Arrow, Little Dynamite-r begin; origin The Ermine by Filchock; Burgos, J. Cole, Ernst, Gustavson-a | 75.00 | 225.00 | 525.00 |
| 3,4: Gustavson-a(r). 4-Bondage-c | 55.00 | 165.00 | 385.00 |

**FARGO KID** (Formerly Justice Traps the Guilty)
V11#3(#1), June-July, 1958 - V11#5, Oct-Nov, 1958
Prize Publications

| | Good | Fine | N-Mint |
|---|---|---|---|
| V11#3(#1)-Origin Fargo Kid, Severin-c/a; Williamson-a(2) | 9.00 | 27.00 | 62.00 |
| V11#4,5-Severin-c/a | 5.00 | 15.00 | 35.00 |

**FARMER'S DAUGHTER, THE**
Feb-Mar, 1954 - No. 3, June-July, 1954; No. 4, Oct, 1954
Stanhall Publ./Trojan Magazines

| | Good | Fine | N-Mint |
|---|---|---|---|
| 1-Lingerie, nudity panel | 8.00 | 24.00 | 56.00 |
| 2-4(Stanhall) | 4.30 | 13.00 | 30.00 |

**FASHION IN ACTION**
Aug, 1986 - Feb, 1987 (Color, Baxter paper)
Eclipse Comics

| | Good | Fine | N-Mint |
|---|---|---|---|
| . . . Summer Special 1 ($1.75) | .30 | .90 | 1.80 |
| . . . Winter Special 1(2/87, $2.00) | .35 | 1.00 | 2.00 |

**FASTEST GUN ALIVE, THE** (See 4-Color No. 741)

**FAST FICTION** (. . . Action) (Stories by Famous Authors Ill. #6 on)
Oct, 1949 - No. 5, Mar, 1950 (All have Kiefer-c)(48 pgs.)
Seaboard Publ./Famous Authors Ill.

| | Good | Fine | N-Mint |
|---|---|---|---|
| 1-Scarlet Pimpernel; Jim Lavery-a | 22.00 | 65.00 | 155.00 |
| 2-Captain Blood; H. C. Kiefer-a | 20.00 | 60.00 | 140.00 |
| 3-She, by Rider Haggard; Vincent Napoli-a | 25.00 | 75.00 | 175.00 |
| 4-(1/50, 52 pgs.)-The 39 Steps; Lavery-a | 16.00 | 48.00 | 110.00 |
| 5-Beau Geste; Kiefer-a | 16.00 | 48.00 | 110.00 |

NOTE: ***Kiefer** a-2, 5; c-2, 3, 5. **Lavery** c/a-1, 4. **Napoli** a-3.*

**FAST WILLIE JACKSON**
October, 1976 - No. 7, 1977
Fitzgerald Periodicals, Inc.

| | Good | Fine | N-Mint |
|---|---|---|---|
| 1-7 | | .50 | 1.00 |

**FAT ALBERT** (. . .& the Cosby Kids) (TV)
March, 1974 - No. 29, Feb, 1979
Gold Key

| | Good | Fine | N-Mint |
|---|---|---|---|
| 1 | .35 | 1.00 | 2.00 |
| 2-29 | | .40 | .80 |

**FAT AND SLAT** (Ed Wheelan) (Gunfighter No. 5 on)
Summer, 1947 - No. 4, Spring, 1948
E. C. Comics

| | Good | Fine | N-Mint |
|---|---|---|---|
| 1-Intro/origin Voltage, Man of Lightning | 18.00 | 54.00 | 125.00 |
| 2,4 | 13.00 | 40.00 | 90.00 |
| 3 | 11.50 | 34.00 | 80.00 |

**FAT AND SLAT JOKE BOOK**
Summer, 1944 (One Shot, 52 pages)
All-American Comics (William H. Wise)

| | Good | Fine | N-Mint |
|---|---|---|---|
| nn-by Ed Wheelan | 13.00 | 40.00 | 90.00 |

**FATE** (See Hand of Fate, & Thrill-O-Rama)

**FATHER OF CHARITY**
No date (32 pgs.; paper cover)
Catechetical Guild Giveaway

| | Good | Fine | N-Mint |
|---|---|---|---|
| nn | 1.50 | 4.50 | 10.00 |

**FATHOM**
May, 1987 - No. 3, July, 1987 ($1.50, color, mini-series)
Comico

| | Good | Fine | N-Mint |
|---|---|---|---|
| 1-3 | .25 | .75 | 1.50 |

**FATIMA. . .CHALLENGE TO THE WORLD**
1951, 36 pgs. (15 cent cover)
Catechetical Guild

| | Good | Fine | N-Mint |
|---|---|---|---|
| nn (not same as 'Challenge to the World') | 1.70 | 5.00 | 12.00 |

**FATMAN, THE HUMAN FLYING SAUCER**
April, 1967 - No. 3, Aug-Sept, 1967 (68 pgs.)
Lightning Comics(Milson Publ. Co.) (Written by Otto Binder)

| | Good | Fine | N-Mint |
|---|---|---|---|
| 1-Origin Fatman & Tinman by C. C. Beck | 4.30 | 13.00 | 30.00 |
| 2-Beck-a | 2.85 | 8.50 | 20.00 |
| 3-(Scarce)-Beck-a | 5.00 | 15.00 | 35.00 |

**FAUNTLEROY COMICS** (Superduck Presents. . .)
1950 - No. 3, 1952
Close-Up/Archie Publications

| | Good | Fine | N-Mint |
|---|---|---|---|
| 1 | 4.30 | 13.00 | 30.00 |
| 2,3 | 2.65 | 8.00 | 18.00 |

**FAUST**
1989?(nd) - No. 4(B&W; 1,2: $2.00, 3-on: $2.25; adults, violent)
Northstar Publishing

| | Good | Fine | N-Mint |
|---|---|---|---|
| 1-Decapitation-c; Tim Vigil-c/a in all | 3.60 | 11.00 | 22.00 |
| 1-2nd printing | 1.70 | 5.00 | 10.00 |
| 1-3rd printing | .40 | 1.25 | 2.50 |
| 2 | 3.60 | 11.00 | 22.00 |

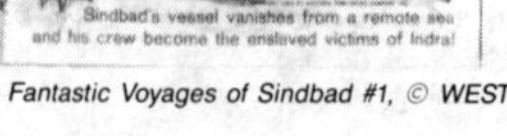


*The Fantastic Voyages of Sindbad #1, © WEST*

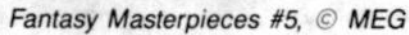

*Fantasy Masterpieces #5, © MEG*

*Fat and Slat #1, © WMG*

Fawcett Movie Comic #14, © Paramount

Fawcett's Funny Animals #8, © FAW

Fear #10, © MEG

Good Fine N-Mint
2-2nd & 3rd printings .40 1.25 2.50
3-Begin $2.25-c 2.00 6.00 12.00
3-2nd printing .40 1.25 2.50
4 1.15 3.50 7.00

**FAVORITE COMICS** (Also see Famous Comics)
1934 (36 pgs.)
Grocery Store Giveaway (Dif Corp.) (detergent)
Book #1-The Nebbs, Strange As It Seems, Napoleon, Dixie Dugan, Joe Palooka, S'Matter Pop, Hairbreadth Harry, etc. reprints
25.00 75.00 175.00
Book #2,3 22.00 65.00 150.00

**FAWCETT MINIATURES** (See Mighty Midget)
1946 (12-24 pgs.; 3¾x5") (Wheaties giveaways)
Fawcett Publications
Captain Marvel-"And the Horn of Plenty;" Bulletman story
3.00 9.00 21.00
Captain Marvel-"& the Raiders From Space;" Golden Arrow story
3.00 9.00 21.00
Captain Marvel Jr.-"The Case of the Poison Press!" Bulletman story
3.00 9.00 21.00
Delecta of the Planets-C. C. Beck art; B&W inside; 12 pgs.; 3 printing variations (coloring) exist 10.00 30.00 70.00

**FAWCETT MOTION PICTURE COMICS** (See Motion Picture Comics)

**FAWCETT MOVIE COMIC**
1949 - No. 20, Dec, 1952 (All photo-c)
Fawcett Publications
nn-"Dakota Lil"-George Montgomery & Rod Cameron('49)
23.00 70.00 160.00
nn-"Copper Canyon"-Ray Milland & Hedy Lamarr('50)
17.00 51.00 120.00
nn-"Destination Moon"-(1950) 50.00 150.00 350.00
nn-"Montana"-Errol Flynn & Alexis Smith('50) 17.00 51.00 120.00
nn-"Pioneer Marshal"-Monte Hale(1950) 17.00 51.00 120.00
nn-"Powder River Rustlers"-Rocky Lane(1950) 18.50 55.00 130.00
nn-"Singing Guns"-Vaughn Monroe & Ella Raines(1950)
16.00 48.00 110.00
7-"Gunmen of Abilene"-Rocky Lane; Bob Powell-a(1950)
18.50 55.00 130.00
8-"King of the Bullwhip"-Lash LaRue; Bob Powell-a(1950)
32.00 95.00 225.00
9-"The Old Frontier"-Monte Hale; Bob Powell-a(2/51; mis-dated 2/50)
17.00 51.00 120.00
10-"The Missourians"-Monte Hale(4/51) 17.00 51.00 120.00
11-"The Thundering Trail"-Lash LaRue(6/51) 24.00 73.00 170.00
12-"Rustlers on Horseback"-Rocky Lane(8/51) 18.50 55.00 130.00
13-"Warpath"-Edmond O'Brien & Forrest Tucker(10/51)
13.00 40.00 90.00
14-"Last Outpost"-Ronald Reagan(12/51) 35.00 105.00 245.00
15-(Scarce)-"The Man From Planet X"-Robert Clark; Shaffenberger-a (2/52) 150.00 450.00 1050.00
16-"10 Tall Men"-Burt Lancaster 10.00 30.00 70.00
17-"Rose of Cimarron"-Jack Buetel & Mala Powers
6.50 19.50 45.00
18-"The Brigand"-Anthony Dexter; Shaffenberger-a
7.00 21.00 50.00
19-"Carbine Williams"-James Stewart; Costanza-a
9.00 27.00 62.00
20-"Ivanhoe"-Liz Taylor 13.00 40.00 90.00

**FAWCETT'S FUNNY ANIMALS** (No. 1-26, 80-on titled "Funny Animals;" Li'l Tomboy No. 92 on?)
12/42 - #79, 4/53; #80, 6/53 - #83, 12?/53; #84, 4/54 - #91, 2/56
Fawcett Publications/Charlton Comics No. 84 on
1-Capt. Marvel on cover; intro. Hoppy The Captain Marvel Bunny, cloned from Capt. Marvel; Billy the Kid & Willie the Worm begin
Good Fine N-Mint
29.00 85.00 200.00
2-Xmas-c 14.00 43.00 100.00
3-5 10.00 30.00 70.00
6,7,9,10 6.50 19.00 45.00
8-Flag-c 7.00 21.00 50.00
11-20 4.30 13.00 30.00
21-40: 25-Xmas-c. 26-St. Valentines Day-c 2.65 8.00 18.00
41-88,90,91 2.00 6.00 14.00
89-(2/55)-Merry Mailman ish (TV)-part photo-c 2.30 7.00 16.00
NOTE: *Marvel Bunny in all issues to at least No. 68 (not in 49-54).*

**FAZE ONE FAZERS**
1986 - No. 4, Sept, 1986 (Color, mini-series)
Americomics (AC Comics)
1-4 .25 .75 1.50

**F.B.I., THE**
April-June, 1965
Dell Publishing Co.
1-Sinnott-a 1.30 4.00 9.00

**F.B.I. STORY, THE** (See 4-Color No. 1069)

**FEAR** (Adventure into. . .)
Nov, 1970 - No. 31, Dec, 1975 (No.1-6: Giant Size)
Marvel Comics Group
1-Fantasy & Sci-Fi reprints in early issues .70 2.00 4.00
2-6 .40 1.25 2.50
7-9,11,12: 11-N. Adams-c. 12-Starlin/Buckler-a .35 1.00 2.00
10-Man-Thing begins, ends #19; Morrow/Chaykin-c/a
.85 2.50 5.00
13,14,16-18,20-31: 17-Origin/1st app. Wundarr. 20-Morbius, the Living Vampire begins, ends #31; Gulacy-a(p) .25 .75 1.50
15-1st full-length Man-Thing story .50 1.50 3.00
19-Intro. Howard the Duck; Val Mayerik-a 1.70 5.00 12.00
NOTE: ***Bolle** a-13i. **Brunner** c-15-17. **Buckler** a-11p. **Chaykin** a-10i. **Colan** a-23r. **Craig** a-10p. **Ditko** a-6-8r. **Evans** a-30. **Everett** a-9, 10i, 21r. **Gil Kane** a-21p; c(p)-20, 21, 23-28, 31. **Kirby** a-8r, 9r. **Maneely** a-24r. **Mooney** a-11i, 26r. **Morrow** a-11i. **Paul Reinman** a-14r. **Russell** a-23p, 24p. **Severin** c-8. **Starlin** c-12p.*

**FEARBOOK**
April, 1986 (One shot) ($1.75, color, adults)
Eclipse Comics
1-Scholastic Mag.-r; Bissette-a .30 .90 1.80

**FEAR IN THE NIGHT** (See Complete Mystery No. 3)

**FEARLESS FAGAN** (See 4-Color No. 441)

**FEATURE BOOK** (Dell) (See Large Feature Comic)

**FEATURE BOOKS** (Newspaper-r, early issues)
May, 1937 - No. 57, 1948 (B&W; Full color, 68 pgs. begin #26 on)
David McKay Publications
nn-Popeye & the Jeep (#1, 100 pgs.); reprinted as Feature Books #3 (Very Rare; only 3 known copies, 1-vf, 2-in low grade)
Estimated value. . . . 467.00 1400.00 2800.00
nn-Dick Tracy (#1)-Reprinted as Feature Book #4 (100 pgs.) & in part as 4-Color #1 (Rare, less than 10 known copies)
Estimated value. . . . 467.00 1400.00 2800.00
NOTE: *Above books were advertised together with different covers from Feature Books No. 3 & 4.*
1-King of the Royal Mtd. (#1) 41.00 122.00 285.00
2-Popeye(6/37) by Segar 54.00 160.00 375.00
3-Popeye(7/37) by Segar; same as nn issue but a new cover added
45.00 135.00 315.00
4-Dick Tracy(8/37)-Same as nn issue but a new cover added
72.00 215.00 500.00
5-Popeye(9/37) by Segar 37.00 110.00 260.00

| | Good | Fine | N-Mint |
|---|---|---|---|
| 6-Dick Tracy(10/37) | 60.00 | 180.00 | 420.00 |
| 7-Little Orphan Annie (#1) (Rare)-Reprints strips from 12/31/34 to 7/17/35 | 75.00 | 225.00 | 525.00 |
| 8-Secret Agent X-9-Not by Raymond | 28.00 | 85.00 | 170.00 |
| 9-Dick Tracy(1/38) | 60.00 | 180.00 | 420.00 |
| 10-Popeye(2/38) | 37.00 | 110.00 | 260.00 |
| 11-Little Annie Rooney (#1) | 19.00 | 57.00 | 135.00 |
| 12-Blondie (#1) (4/38) (Rare) | 39.00 | 118.00 | 275.00 |
| 13-Inspector Wade | 11.50 | 34.00 | 80.00 |
| 14-Popeye(6/38) by Segar (Scarce) | 50.00 | 150.00 | 350.00 |
| 15-Barney Baxter (#1) (7/38) | 17.00 | 51.00 | 120.00 |
| 16-Red Eagle | 11.00 | 32.00 | 75.00 |
| 17-Gangbusters (#1) | 24.00 | 73.00 | 170.00 |
| 18,19-Mandrake | 24.00 | 73.00 | 170.00 |
| 20-Phantom (#1) | 43.00 | 130.00 | 300.00 |
| 21-Lone Ranger | 43.00 | 130.00 | 300.00 |
| 22-Phantom | 36.00 | 107.00 | 250.00 |
| 23-Mandrake | 24.00 | 73.00 | 170.00 |
| 24-Lone Ranger(1941) | 43.00 | 130.00 | 300.00 |
| 25-Flash Gordon (#1)-Reprints not by Raymond | 54.00 | 163.00 | 380.00 |
| 26-Prince Valiant(1941)-Harold Foster-a; newspaper strips reprinted, pgs. 1-28,30-63. Color, 68 pg. issues begin | 73.00 | 218.00 | 510.00 |
| 27-29,31,34-Blondie | 8.50 | 25.50 | 60.00 |
| 30-Katzenjammer Kids (#1) | 9.30 | 28.00 | 65.00 |
| 32,35,41,44-Katzenjammer Kids | 7.00 | 21.00 | 50.00 |
| 33(nn)-Romance of Flying-World War II photos | 7.00 | 21.00 | 50.00 |
| 36('43),38,40('44),42,43,45,47-Blondie | 8.00 | 24.00 | 56.00 |
| 37-Katzenjammer Kids; has photo & biog of Harold H. Knerr(1883-1949) who took over strip from Rudolph Dirks in 1914 | 8.50 | 25.50 | 60.00 |
| 39-Phantom | 26.00 | 77.00 | 180.00 |
| 46-Mandrake in the Fire World-(58 pgs.) | 20.00 | 60.00 | 140.00 |
| 48-Maltese Falcon by Dashiell Hammett('46) | 41.00 | 124.00 | 290.00 |
| 49,50-Perry Mason | 13.00 | 40.00 | 90.00 |
| 51,54-Rip Kirby c/a by Raymond; origin-#51 | 20.00 | 60.00 | 140.00 |
| 52,55-Mandrake | 17.00 | 51.00 | 120.00 |
| 53,56,57-Phantom | 20.00 | 60.00 | 140.00 |

NOTE: *All Feature Books through #25 are over-sized 8½x11-3/8" comics with color covers and black and white interiors. The covers are rough, heavy stock. The page counts, including covers, are as follows: nn, #3, 4-100 pgs.; #1, 2-52 pgs.; #5-25 are all 76 pgs. #33 was found in bound set from publisher.*

**FEATURE COMICS** (Formerly Feature Funnies)
No. 21, June, 1939 - No. 144, May, 1950
Quality Comics Group

| | Good | Fine | N-Mint |
|---|---|---|---|
| 21-Strips continue from Feature Funnies | 25.00 | 75.00 | 175.00 |
| 22-26: 23-Charlie Chan begins | 19.00 | 58.00 | 135.00 |
| 26-(nn, nd)-c-in one color, (10 cents, 36pgs.; issue No. blanked out. 2 variations exist, each contain half of the regular #26) | 5.50 | 16.50 | 38.00 |
| 27-(Rare)-Origin/1st app. Dollman by Eisner | 150.00 | 450.00 | 1050.00 |
| 28-1st Lou Fine Dollman | 70.00 | 210.00 | 490.00 |
| 29,30 | 43.00 | 130.00 | 300.00 |
| 31-Last Clock & Charlie Chan issue | 34.00 | 103.00 | 240.00 |
| 32-37: 32-Rusty Ryan & Samar begin. 34-Captain Fortune app. 37-Last Fine Dollman | 27.00 | 80.00 | 185.00 |
| 38-41: 38-Origin the Ace of Space. 39-Origin The Destroying Demon, ends #40. 40-Bruce Blackburn in costume | 19.00 | 58.00 | 135.00 |
| 42,43,45-50: 42-USA, the Spirit of Old Glory begins. 46-Intro. Boyville Brigadiers in Rusty Ryan. 48-USA ends | 13.00 | 40.00 | 90.00 |
| 44-Dollman by Crandall begins, ends #63; Crandall-a(2) | 18.50 | 56.00 | 130.00 |
| 51-60: 56-Marijuana story in "Swing Session." 57-Spider Widow begins. 60-Raven begins, ends #71 | 11.00 | 32.00 | 75.00 |
| 61-68 (5/43) | 10.00 | 30.00 | 70.00 |
| 69,70-Phantom Lady x-over in Spider Widow | 11.00 | 32.00 | 75.00 |
| 71-80,100: 71-Phantom Lady x-over. 72-Spider Widow ends | 7.00 | 21.00 | 50.00 |
| 81-99 | 6.00 | 18.00 | 42.00 |
| 101-144: 139-Last Dollman. 140-Intro. Stuntman Stetson | 4.50 | 14.00 | 32.00 |

NOTE: ***Celardo** a-37-43. **Crandall** a-44-60, 62, 63-on(most). **Gustavson** a-(Rusty Ryan) -32-134. **Powell** a-34, 64-73.*

**FEATURE FILMS**
Mar-Apr, 1950 - No. 4, Sept-Oct, 1950 (1-3: photo-c)
National Periodical Publications

| | Good | Fine | N-Mint |
|---|---|---|---|
| 1-"Captain China" with John Payne, Gail Russell, Lon Chaney & Edgar Bergen | 35.00 | 105.00 | 245.00 |
| 2-"Riding High" with Bing Crosby | 27.00 | 81.00 | 190.00 |
| 3-"The Eagle & the Hawk" with John Payne, Rhonda Fleming & D. O'Keefe | 27.00 | 81.00 | 190.00 |
| 4-"Fancy Pants"-Bob Hope & Lucille Ball | 30.00 | 90.00 | 210.00 |

**FEATURE FUNNIES** (Feature Comics No. 21 on)
Oct, 1937 - No. 20, May, 1939
Harry 'A' Chesler

| | Good | Fine | N-Mint |
|---|---|---|---|
| 1(V9#1-indicia)-Joe Palooka, Mickey Finn, The Bungles, Jane Arden, Dixie Dugan, Big Top, Ned Brant, Strange As It Seems, & Off the Record strip reprints begin | 148.00 | 445.00 | 890.00 |
| 2-The Hawk app. (11/37); Goldberg-c | 62.00 | 185.00 | 435.00 |
| 3-Hawks of Seas begins by Eisner, ends #12; The Clock begins; Christmas-c | 43.00 | 130.00 | 300.00 |
| 4,5 | 31.00 | 92.00 | 215.00 |
| 6-12: 11-Archie O'Toole by Bud Thomas begins, ends #22 | 25.00 | 75.00 | 175.00 |
| 13-Espionage, Starring Black X begins by Eisner, ends #20 | 27.00 | 81.00 | 190.00 |
| 14-20 | 22.00 | 65.00 | 150.00 |

**FEATURE PRESENTATION, A** (Feature Presentations Mag. #6)
(Formerly Women in Love) (Also see Startling Terror Tales #11)
No. 5, April, 1950
Fox Features Syndicate

| | Good | Fine | N-Mint |
|---|---|---|---|
| 5-Black Tarantula | 17.00 | 50.00 | 115.00 |

**FEATURE PRESENTATIONS MAGAZINE** (Formerly A Feature Presentation #5; becomes Feature Stories Magazine #3 on)
No. 6, July, 1950
Fox Features Syndicate

| | Good | Fine | N-Mint |
|---|---|---|---|
| 6-Moby Dick; Wood-c | 14.00 | 43.00 | 100.00 |

**FEATURE STORIES MAGAZINE** (Formerly Feat. Present. Mag. #6)
No. 3, Aug, 1950 - No. 4, Oct, 1950
Fox Features Syndicate

| | Good | Fine | N-Mint |
|---|---|---|---|
| 3-Jungle Lil, Zegra stories; bondage-c | 11.50 | 34.00 | 80.00 |
| 4 | 8.50 | 25.50 | 60.00 |

**FEDERAL MEN COMICS** (See Adventure Comics #32, The Comics Magazine, New Adv. Comics, New Book of Comics & New Comics)
No. 2, 1945 (DC reprints from 1930's)
Gerard Publ. Co.

| | Good | Fine | N-Mint |
|---|---|---|---|
| 2-Siegel & Shuster-a; cover redrawn from Detective #9; spanking panel | 12.00 | 36.00 | 85.00 |

**FELIX'S NEPHEWS INKY & DINKY**
Sept, 1957 - No. 7, Oct, 1958
Harvey Publications

| | Good | Fine | N-Mint |
|---|---|---|---|
| 1-Cover shows Inky's left eye with 2 pupils | 4.30 | 13.00 | 30.00 |
| 2-7 | 2.00 | 6.00 | 14.00 |

NOTE: *Contains no **Messmer** art.*

**FELIX THE CAT**
1931 (24 pgs.; 8x10¼")(1926,'27 color strip reprints)
McLoughlin Bros.

*Feature Books #27, © KING*

*Feature Films #1, © Paramount*

*Feature Funnies #19, © CHES*

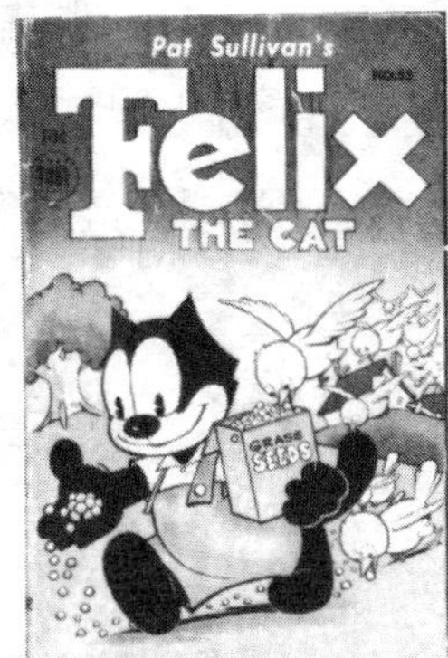

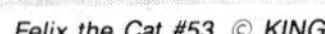
Felix the Cat #53, © KING

Fight Against Crime #1, © Story Comics

Fight Comics #42, © FH

| | Good | Fine | N-Mint |
|---|---|---|---|
| 260-(Rare)-by Otto Messmer | 71.00 | 215.00 | 500.00 |

**FELIX THE CAT** (See Cat Tales 3-D, The Funnies, March of Comics #24,36,51, New Funnies & Popular Comics)
1943 - No. 118, Nov, 1961; Sept-Nov, 1962 - No. 12, July-Sept, 1965
Dell Publ. No. 1-19/Toby No. 20-61/Harvey No. 62-118/Dell

| | Good | Fine | N-Mint |
|---|---|---|---|
| 4-Color 15 | 43.00 | 130.00 | 300.00 |
| 4-Color 46('44) | 31.00 | 92.00 | 215.00 |
| 4-Color 77('45) | 26.00 | 78.00 | 185.00 |
| 4-Color 119('46) | 20.00 | 60.00 | 140.00 |
| 4-Color 135('46) | 16.00 | 48.00 | 110.00 |
| 4-Color 162(9/47) | 11.50 | 34.00 | 80.00 |
| 1(2-3/48)(Dell) | 16.00 | 48.00 | 110.00 |
| 2 | 8.00 | 24.00 | 55.00 |
| 3-5 | 6.00 | 18.00 | 42.00 |
| 6-19(2-3/51-Dell) | 4.30 | 13.00 | 30.00 |
| 20-30(Toby): 28-(2/52)-Some copies have #29 on cover, #28 on inside | 3.70 | 11.00 | 26.00 |
| 31,34,35-No Messmer-a | 2.00 | 6.00 | 14.00 |
| 32,33,36-61(6/55-Toby)-Last Messmer issue | 2.65 | 8.00 | 18.00 |
| 62(8/55)-100 (Harvey) | 1.15 | 3.50 | 8.00 |
| 101-118(11/61) | 1.00 | 3.00 | 7.00 |
| 12-269-211(#1, 9-11/62)(Dell) | 1.70 | 5.00 | 12.00 |
| 2-12(7-9/65)(Dell, TV) | .85 | 2.60 | 6.00 |
| 3-D Comic Book 1(1953-One Shot) | 22.00 | 65.00 | 150.00 |
| Summer Annual 2('52)-Early 1930s Sunday strip-r (Exist?) | 19.00 | 56.00 | 130.00 |
| Summer Annual nn('53, 100 pgs., Toby)-1930s daily & Sunday-r | 19.00 | 56.00 | 130.00 |
| Winter Annual 2('54, 100 pgs., Toby)-1930s daily & Sunday-r | 12.00 | 36.00 | 85.00 |
| Summer Annual 3('55) (Exist?) | 11.00 | 32.00 | 75.00 |

NOTE: *4-Color No. 15, 46, 77 and the Toby Annuals are all daily or Sunday newspaper reprints from the 1930's drawn by Otto Messmer, who created Felix in 1915 for the Sullivan animation studio. He drew Felix from the beginning under contract to Pat Sullivan. In 1946 he went to work for Dell and wrote and pencilled most of the stories and inked some of them through the Toby Press issues. No. 107 reprints No. 71 interior; No. 110 reprints No. 56 interior.*

**FELIX THE CAT & HIS FRIENDS**
Dec, 1953 - No. 4, 1954
Toby Press

| | Good | Fine | N-Mint |
|---|---|---|---|
| 1 | 4.00 | 12.00 | 28.00 |
| 2-4 | 2.65 | 8.00 | 18.00 |

**FEM FANTASTIQUE**
Aug, 1988 ($1.95, B&W)
AC Comics

| | Good | Fine | N-Mint |
|---|---|---|---|
| V2#1-By Bill Black; Betty Page pin-up | .45 | 1.40 | 2.75 |

**FEMFORCE** (Also see Untold Origin of the Femforce)
Apr, 1985 - Present ($1.75/1.95/2.25; in color; B&W #12? on)
Americomics

| | Good | Fine | N-Mint |
|---|---|---|---|
| 1-Black-a in most; Nightveil, Ms. Victory begin | .85 | 2.50 | 5.00 |
| 2 | .50 | 1.50 | 3.00 |
| 3-30: 12-15-$1.95-c. 16-19-$2.25-c. 20-Begin $2.50-c, 44 pgs. 25-1st app. new Ms. Victory. 28-Colt leaves | .40 | 1.25 | 2.50 |
| 31-34: 31-Begin $2.75-c | .45 | 1.40 | 2.80 |
| Special 1 (Fall, '84)(B&W, 52pgs.)-1st app. Ms. Victory, She-Cat, Blue Bulleteer, Rio Rita & Lady Luger | .35 | 1.00 | 2.00 |
| In the House of Horror 1 ('89, $2.50, B&W) | .40 | 1.25 | 2.50 |
| Night of the Demon 1 ('90, $2.75, B&W) | .45 | 1.40 | 2.80 |
| Out of the Asylum Special 1 ('87, B&W, $1.95) | .35 | 1.00 | 2.00 |

**FERDINAND THE BULL** (See Mickey Mouse Magazine V4/3)
1938 (10 cents)(Large size; some color, rest B&W)
Dell Publishing Co.

| | Good | Fine | N-Mint |
|---|---|---|---|
| nn | 9.30 | 28.00 | 65.00 |

**FIBBER McGEE & MOLLY** (See A-1 Comics No. 25)

**55 DAYS AT PEKING** (See Movie Comics)

**FIGHT AGAINST CRIME** (Fight Against the Guilty #22,23)
May, 1951 - No. 21, Sept, 1954
Story Comics

| | Good | Fine | N-Mint |
|---|---|---|---|
| 1 | 11.00 | 32.00 | 75.00 |
| 2 | 5.00 | 15.00 | 35.00 |
| 3,5: 5-Frazetta-a, 1 pg. | 4.00 | 12.00 | 28.00 |
| 4-Drug story-"Hopped Up Killers" | 6.50 | 19.00 | 45.00 |
| 6,7: 6-Used in **POP**, pgs. 83,84 | 4.00 | 12.00 | 28.00 |
| 8-Last crime format issue | 4.00 | 12.00 | 28.00 |

NOTE: *No. 9-21 contain violent, gruesome stories with blood, dismemberment, decapitation, E.C. style plot twists and several E.C. swipes. Bondage c-4, 6, 18, 19.*

| | Good | Fine | N-Mint |
|---|---|---|---|
| 9-11,13 | 8.00 | 24.00 | 56.00 |
| 12-Morphine drug story-"The Big Dope" | 10.00 | 30.00 | 70.00 |
| 14-Tothish art by Ross Andru; electrocution-c | 8.00 | 24.00 | 56.00 |
| 15-B&W & color illos in **POP** | 8.00 | 24.00 | 56.00 |
| 16-E.C. story swipe/Haunt of Fear No. 19; Tothish-a by Ross Andru; bondage-c | 10.00 | 30.00 | 70.00 |
| 17-Wildey E.C. swipe/Shock SuspenStories No. 9; knife through neck-c (1/54) | 10.00 | 30.00 | 70.00 |
| 18,19: 19-Bondage/torture-c | 7.00 | 21.00 | 50.00 |
| 20-Decapitation cover; contains hanging, ax murder, blood & violence | 16.00 | 48.00 | 120.00 |
| 21-E.C. swipe | 8.50 | 25.50 | 60.00 |

NOTE: ***Cameron** a-4, 5. **Hollingsworth** a-3, 4, 9, 10, 13. **Wildey** a-15, 16.*

**FIGHT AGAINST THE GUILTY** (Formerly Fight Against Crime)
No. 22, Dec, 1954 - No. 23, Mar, 1955
Story Comics

| | Good | Fine | N-Mint |
|---|---|---|---|
| 22-Tothish-a by Ross Andru; Ditko-a; E.C. story swipe; electrocution-c | 8.00 | 24.00 | 56.00 |
| 23 (Last pre-code)-Hollingsworth-a | 5.00 | 15.00 | 35.00 |

**FIGHT COMICS**
Jan, 1940 - No. 83, 11/52; No. 84, Wint, 1952-53; No. 85, Spring, 1953; No. 86, Summer, 1954
Fiction House Magazines

| | Good | Fine | N-Mint |
|---|---|---|---|
| 1-Origin Spy Fighter, Starring Saber; Fine/Eisner-c; Eisner-a | 100.00 | 300.00 | 700.00 |
| 2-Joe Louis life story | 43.00 | 130.00 | 300.00 |
| 3-Rip Regan, the Power Man begins | 40.00 | 120.00 | 280.00 |
| 4,5: 4-Fine-c | 30.00 | 90.00 | 210.00 |
| 6-10: 6,7-Powell-c | 25.00 | 75.00 | 175.00 |
| 11-14: Rip Regan ends | 22.00 | 65.00 | 150.00 |
| 15-1st Super American | 29.00 | 86.00 | 200.00 |
| 16-Captain Fight begins; Spy Fighter ends | 29.00 | 86.00 | 200.00 |
| 17,18: Super American ends | 25.00 | 75.00 | 175.00 |
| 19-Captain Fight ends; Senorita Rio begins (origin & 1st app.); Rip Carson, Chute Trooper begins | 25.00 | 75.00 | 175.00 |
| 20 | 19.00 | 56.00 | 130.00 |
| 21-30 | 12.00 | 36.00 | 85.00 |
| 31,33-50: 31-Decapitation-c. 44-Capt. Flight returns. 48-Used in **Love and Death** by Legman | 11.00 | 32.00 | 75.00 |
| 32-Tiger Girl begins | 11.50 | 34.00 | 80.00 |
| 51-Origin Tiger Girl; Patsy Pin-Up app. | 17.00 | 51.00 | 120.00 |
| 52-60 | 8.50 | 25.50 | 60.00 |
| 61-Origin Tiger Girl retold | 11.00 | 32.00 | 75.00 |
| 62-65-Last Baker issue | 8.50 | 25.50 | 60.00 |
| 66-78: 78-Used in **POP**, pg. 99 | 7.00 | 21.00 | 50.00 |
| 79-The Space Rangers app. | 7.00 | 21.00 | 50.00 |
| 80-85 | 6.00 | 18.00 | 42.00 |
| 86-Two Tigerman stories by Evans; Moreira-a | 7.00 | 21.00 | 50.00 |

NOTE: *Bondage covers, Lingerie, headlights panels are common. Tiger Girl by **Baker**-#36-60, 62-65; Kayo Kirby by **Baker**-#52-64, 67. **Eisner** c-1-3, 5, 10, 11. **Kamen** a-54?, 57?. **Tuska** a-1, 5, 8, 10, 21, 29.*

**FIGHT FOR FREEDOM**
1949, 1951 (16 pgs.) (Giveaway)
National Association of Mfgrs./General Comics

| | Good | Fine | N-Mint |
|---|---|---|---|
| nn-Dan Barry-c/a; used in **POP**, pg. 102 | 5.00 | 15.00 | 30.00 |

**FIGHT FOR LOVE**
1952 (no month)
United Features Syndicate

| | Good | Fine | N-Mint |
|---|---|---|---|
| nn-Abbie & Slats newspaper-r | 6.50 | 19.50 | 45.00 |

**FIGHTING AIR FORCE** (See United States Fighting Air Force)

**FIGHTIN' AIR FORCE** (Formerly Sherlock Holmes?; Never Again? War and Attack #54 on)
No. 3, Feb, 1956 - No. 53, Feb-Mar, 1966
Charlton Comics

| | Good | Fine | N-Mint |
|---|---|---|---|
| V1#3 | 1.70 | 5.00 | 12.00 |
| 4-10 | .85 | 2.60 | 6.00 |
| 11(3/58, 68 pgs.) | 1.15 | 3.50 | 8.00 |
| 12 (100 pgs.) | 1.70 | 5.00 | 12.00 |
| 13-30: 13,24-Glanzman-a. 24-Glanzman-c | .70 | 2.00 | 4.00 |
| 31-50: 50-American Eagle begins | .50 | 1.50 | 3.00 |
| 51-53 | .25 | .75 | 1.50 |

**FIGHTING AMERICAN**
Apr-May, 1954 - No. 7, Apr-May, 1955
Headline Publications/Prize

| | Good | Fine | N-Mint |
|---|---|---|---|
| 1-Origin Fighting American & Speedboy; S&K-c/a(3) | 80.00 | 240.00 | 560.00 |
| 2-S&K-a(3) | 39.00 | 116.00 | 270.00 |
| 3,4-S&K-a(3) | 34.00 | 100.00 | 235.00 |
| 5-S&K-a(2); Kirby/?-a | 34.00 | 100.00 | 235.00 |
| 6-Origin-r (4 pgs.) plus 2 pgs. by S&K | 31.00 | 92.00 | 215.00 |
| 7-Kirby-a | 29.00 | 86.00 | 200.00 |

NOTE: ***Simon & Kirby*** *covers on all.*

**FIGHTING AMERICAN**
October, 1966 (25 cents)
Harvey Publications

| | Good | Fine | N-Mint |
|---|---|---|---|
| 1-Origin Fighting American & Speedboy by S&K-r; S&K-c/a(3); 1 pg. Neal Adams ad | 1.70 | 5.00 | 12.00 |

**FIGHTIN' ARMY** (Formerly Soldier and Marine Comics; see Captain Willy Schultz)
No. 16, 1/56 - No. 127, 12/76; No. 128, 9/77 - No. 172, 11/84
Charlton Comics

| | Good | Fine | N-Mint |
|---|---|---|---|
| 16 | 1.50 | 4.50 | 10.00 |
| 17-19,21-23,25-30 | .70 | 2.00 | 4.00 |
| 20-Ditko-a | 1.15 | 3.50 | 8.00 |
| 24 (68 pgs., 3/58) | 1.15 | 3.50 | 8.00 |
| 31-45 | .50 | 1.50 | 3.00 |
| 46-60 | | .60 | 1.20 |
| 61-80: 75-The Lonely War of Willy Schultz begins, ends #92 | | .50 | 1.00 |
| 81-172: 89,90,92-Ditko-a; Devil Brigade in #79,82,83 | | .30 | .60 |
| 108(Modern Comics-1977)-Reprint | | .15 | .30 |

NOTE: ***Aparo*** *c-154.* ***Montes/Bache*** *a-48, 49, 51, 69, 75, 76, 170r.*

**FIGHTING DANIEL BOONE**
1953
Avon Periodicals

| | Good | Fine | N-Mint |
|---|---|---|---|
| nn-Kinstler c/a, 22 pgs. | 8.50 | 25.50 | 60.00 |
| I.W. Reprint #1-Kinstler c/a; Lawrence/Alascia-a | 1.00 | 3.00 | 6.00 |

**FIGHTING DAVY CROCKETT** (Formerly Kit Carson)
No. 9, Oct-Nov, 1955
Avon Periodicals

| | Good | Fine | N-Mint |
|---|---|---|---|
| 9-Kinstler-c | 3.50 | 10.50 | 24.00 |

**FIGHTIN' 5, THE** (Formerly Space War; also see The Peacemaker)
July, 1964 - No. 41, Jan, 1967; No. 42, Oct, 1981 - No. 49, Dec, 1982
Charlton Comics

| | Good | Fine | N-Mint |
|---|---|---|---|
| V2#28-Origin Fightin' Five | .85 | 2.60 | 6.00 |
| 29-39,41 | .70 | 2.00 | 4.00 |
| 40-Peacemaker begins | .85 | 2.60 | 6.00 |
| 42-49: Reprints | | .40 | .80 |

**FIGHTING FRONTS!**
Aug, 1952 - No. 5, Jan, 1953
Harvey Publications

| | Good | Fine | N-Mint |
|---|---|---|---|
| 1 | 2.00 | 6.00 | 14.00 |
| 2-Extreme violence; Nostrand/Powell-a | 2.65 | 8.00 | 18.00 |
| 3-5: 3-Powell-a | 1.30 | 4.00 | 9.00 |

**FIGHTING INDIAN STORIES** (See Midget Comics)

**FIGHTING INDIANS OF THE WILD WEST!**
Mar, 1952 - No. 2, Nov, 1952
Avon Periodicals

| | Good | Fine | N-Mint |
|---|---|---|---|
| 1-Kinstler, Larsen-a | 7.00 | 21.00 | 50.00 |
| 2-Kinstler-a | 4.60 | 14.00 | 32.00 |
| 100 Pg. Annual(1952, 25 cents)-Contains three comics rebound | 15.00 | 45.00 | 105.00 |

**FIGHTING LEATHERNECKS**
Feb, 1952 - No. 6, Dec, 1952
Toby Press

| | Good | Fine | N-Mint |
|---|---|---|---|
| 1-"Duke's Diary"-full pg. pin-ups by Sparling | 6.50 | 19.00 | 45.00 |
| 2-"Duke's Diary" | 4.30 | 13.00 | 30.00 |
| 3-5-"Gil's Gals"-full pg. pin-ups | 4.30 | 13.00 | 30.00 |
| 6-(Same as No. 3-5?) | 2.85 | 8.50 | 20.00 |

**FIGHTING MAN, THE** (War)
May, 1952 - No. 8, July, 1953
Ajax/Farrell Publications(Excellent Publ.)

| | Good | Fine | N-Mint |
|---|---|---|---|
| 1 | 3.50 | 10.50 | 24.00 |
| 2 | 1.70 | 5.00 | 12.00 |
| 3-8 | 1.50 | 4.50 | 10.00 |
| Annual 1 (100 pgs, 1952) | 12.00 | 36.00 | 84.00 |

**FIGHTIN' MARINES** (Formerly The Texan; see Approved Comics)
No. 15, 8/51 - No. 12, 3/53; No. 14, 5/55 - No. 132, 11/76;
No. 133, 10/77 - No. 176, 9/84 (No #13?)
St. John(Approved Comics)/Charlton Comics No. 14 on

| | Good | Fine | N-Mint |
|---|---|---|---|
| 15(No.1)-Matt Baker c/a "Leatherneck Jack;" slightly large size; Fightin' Texan No. 16 & 17? | 11.00 | 32.00 | 75.00 |
| 2-1st Canteen Kate by Baker; slightly large size | 13.00 | 40.00 | 90.00 |
| 3-9,11-Canteen Kate by Matt Baker; Baker c-#2,3,5-11 | 7.00 | 21.00 | 50.00 |
| 10-Baker-c | 2.00 | 6.00 | 14.00 |
| 12-No Baker; last St. John issue? | 1.30 | 4.00 | 9.00 |
| 14 (5/55; 1st Charlton issue; formerly?)-Canteen Kate by Baker | 5.70 | 17.00 | 40.00 |
| 15-Baker-c | 2.00 | 6.00 | 14.00 |
| 16,18-20-Not Baker-c | 1.15 | 3.50 | 8.00 |
| 17-Canteen Kate by Baker | 5.00 | 15.00 | 35.00 |
| 21-24 | .85 | 2.60 | 6.00 |
| 25-(68 pgs.)(3/58)-Check-a? | 1.70 | 5.00 | 12.00 |
| 26-(100 pgs.)(8/58)-Check-a(5) | 3.00 | 9.00 | 21.00 |
| 27-50 | .70 | 2.00 | 4.00 |
| 51-81,83-100: 78-Shotgun Harker & the Chicken series begin | .40 | 1.25 | 2.50 |
| 82-(100 pgs.) | .70 | 2.00 | 5.00 |

101-122: 122-Pilot issue for "War" title (Fightin' Marines Presents

*Fighting American #1, © HARV*

*Fighting Leathernecks #6, © TOBY*

*Fightin' Marines #4, © STJ*

Fightin' Navy #84, © CC

Fighting Yank #20, © STD

Firestorm #4 (9/78), © DC

| | Good | Fine | N-Mint |
|---|---|---|---|
| War) | | .50 | 1.00 |
| 123-176 | | .35 | .70 |
| 120(Modern Comics reprint, 1977) | | .25 | .50 |

NOTE: *No. 14 & 16 (CC) reprint St. John issues; No. 16 reprints St. John insignia on cover.* ***Colan*** *a-3, 7.* ***Glanzman*** *c/a-92, 94.* ***Montes/Bache*** *a-48, 53, 55, 64, 65, 72-74, 77-83, 176r.*

**FIGHTING MARSHAL OF THE WILD WEST** (See The Hawk)

**FIGHTIN' NAVY** (Formerly Don Winslow)
No. 74, 1/56 - No. 125, 4-5/66; No. 126, 8/83 - No. 133, 10/84
Charlton Comics

| | Good | Fine | N-Mint |
|---|---|---|---|
| 74 | 1.50 | 4.50 | 10.00 |
| 75-81 | .85 | 2.60 | 6.00 |
| 82-Sam Glanzman-a | .85 | 2.50 | 5.00 |
| 83-99,101-105,106-125('66) | .50 | 1.50 | 3.00 |
| 100 | .60 | 1.75 | 3.50 |
| 126-133('84) | | .35 | .70 |

NOTE: ***Montes/Bache*** *a-109.* ***Glanzman*** *a-131r.*

**FIGHTING PRINCE OF DONEGAL, THE** (See Movie Comics)

**FIGHTIN' TEXAN** (Formerly The Texan & Fightin' Marines?)
No. 16, Oct, 1952 - No. 17, Dec, 1952
St. John Publishing Co.

| | Good | Fine | N-Mint |
|---|---|---|---|
| 16,17-Tuska-a each. 17-Cameron-c/a | 3.15 | 9.50 | 22.00 |

**FIGHTING UNDERSEA COMMANDOS** (See Undersea Fighting . . .)
1952 - No. 5, April, 1953
Avon Periodicals

| | Good | Fine | N-Mint |
|---|---|---|---|
| 1 | 5.00 | 15.00 | 35.00 |
| 2 | 3.50 | 10.50 | 24.00 |
| 3-5: 3-Ravielli-c. 4-Kinstler-c | 3.00 | 9.00 | 21.00 |

**FIGHTING WAR STORIES**
Aug, 1952 - No. 5, 1953
Men's Publications/Story Comics

| | Good | Fine | N-Mint |
|---|---|---|---|
| 1 | 2.65 | 8.00 | 18.00 |
| 2-5 | 1.50 | 4.50 | 10.00 |

**FIGHTING YANK** (See America's Best & Startling Comics)
Sept, 1942 - No. 29, Aug, 1949
Nedor/Better Publ./Standard

| | Good | Fine | N-Mint |
|---|---|---|---|
| 1-The Fighting Yank begins; Mystico, the Wonder Man app; bondage-c | 68.00 | 205.00 | 475.00 |
| 2 | 32.00 | 95.00 | 225.00 |
| 3 | 22.00 | 65.00 | 150.00 |
| 4 | 17.00 | 51.00 | 120.00 |
| 5-10: 7-The Grim Reaper app. | 13.00 | 40.00 | 90.00 |
| 11-20: 11-The Oracle app. 12-Hirohito bondage-c. 18-The American Eagle app. | 11.50 | 34.00 | 80.00 |
| 21,23,24: 21-Kara, Jungle Princess app. 24-Miss Masque app. | 13.00 | 40.00 | 90.00 |
| 22-Miss Masque-c/story | 16.00 | 48.00 | 110.00 |
| 25-Robinson/Meskin-a; strangulation, lingerie panel; The Cavalier app. | 16.00 | 48.00 | 110.00 |
| 26-29: All-Robinson/Meskin-a. 28-One pg. Williamson-a | 12.00 | 36.00 | 85.00 |

NOTE: ***Schomburg (Xela)*** *c-4-29; airbrush-c 28, 29. Bondage c-4, 8, 11, 15, 17.*

**FIGHT THE ENEMY**
Aug, 1966 - No. 3, Mar, 1967 (25 cents, 68 pgs.)
Tower Comics

| | Good | Fine | N-Mint |
|---|---|---|---|
| 1-Lucky 7 & Mike Manly begin | 1.70 | 5.00 | 12.00 |
| 2-Boris Vallejo, McWilliams-a | 2.00 | 6.00 | 14.00 |
| 3-Wood-a ½pg; McWilliams, Bolle-a | 1.50 | 4.50 | 10.00 |

**FILM FUNNIES**
Nov, 1949 - No. 2, Feb, 1950 (52 pgs.)
Marvel Comics (CPC)

| | Good | Fine | N-Mint |
|---|---|---|---|
| 1-Krazy Krow | 8.00 | 24.00 | 56.00 |
| 2 | 6.00 | 18.00 | 42.00 |

**FILM STARS ROMANCES**
Jan-Feb, 1950 - No. 3, May-June, 1950
Star Publications

| | Good | Fine | N-Mint |
|---|---|---|---|
| 1-Rudy Valentino story; L. B. Cole-c; lingerie panels | 16.00 | 48.00 | 110.00 |
| 2-Liz Taylor/Robert Taylor photo-c | 17.00 | 51.00 | 120.00 |
| 3-Photo-c | 13.00 | 40.00 | 90.00 |

**FINAL CYCLE, THE**
July, 1987 - No. 4, 1988 (Mini-series, color)
Dragon's Teeth Productions

| | Good | Fine | N-Mint |
|---|---|---|---|
| 1-4 | .35 | 1.00 | 2.00 |

**FIRE AND BLAST**
1952 (16 pgs.; paper cover) (Giveaway)
National Fire Protection Assoc.

| | Good | Fine | N-Mint |
|---|---|---|---|
| nn-Mart Baily A-Bomb-c; about fire prevention | 12.00 | 35.00 | 80.00 |

**FIRE BALL XL5** (See Steve Zodiac & The . . .)

**FIRE CHIEF AND THE SAFE OL' FIREFLY, THE**
1952 (16 pgs.) (Safety brochure given away at schools)
National Board of Fire Underwriters (produced by American Visuals Corp.) (Eisner)

| | Good | Fine | N-Mint |
|---|---|---|---|
| nn-(Rare) Eisner-c/a | 35.00 | 105.00 | 245.00 |

**FIREHAIR COMICS** (Pioneer West Romances #3-6; also see Rangers Comics)
Winter/48-49 - No. 2, Wint/49-50; No. 7, Spr/51 - No. 11, Spr/52
Fiction House Magazines (Flying Stories)

| | Good | Fine | N-Mint |
|---|---|---|---|
| 1 | 22.00 | 65.00 | 150.00 |
| 2 | 11.00 | 32.00 | 75.00 |
| 7-11 | 8.00 | 24.00 | 56.00 |
| I.W. Reprint 8-Kinstler-c; reprints Rangers #57; Dr. Drew story by Grandenetti (nd) | .85 | 2.60 | 6.00 |

**FIRESTAR**
March, 1986 - No. 4, June, 1986 (From Spider-Man TV series)
Marvel Comics Group

| | Good | Fine | N-Mint |
|---|---|---|---|
| 1-X-Men & New Mutants app. | .35 | 1.00 | 2.00 |
| 2-Wolverine-c by Art Adams (p) | .85 | 2.50 | 5.00 |
| 3,4 | .25 | .75 | 1.50 |

**FIRESTONE** (See Donald And Mickey Merry Christmas)

**FIRESTORM** (See Cancelled Comic Cavalcade, DC Comics Presents, Flash #289, The Fury of . . . & Justice League of America #179)
March, 1978 - No. 5, Oct-Nov, 1978
DC Comics

| | Good | Fine | N-Mint |
|---|---|---|---|
| 1-Origin & 1st app. | .50 | 1.50 | 3.00 |
| 2-5: 2-Origin Multiplex. 3-Origin Killer Frost. 4-1st app. Hyena | .35 | 1.00 | 2.00 |

**FIRESTORM, THE NUCLEAR MAN** (Formerly Fury of Firestorm)
No. 65, Nov, 1987 - No. 100, Aug, 1990
DC Comics

| | Good | Fine | N-Mint |
|---|---|---|---|
| 65-99: 66-1st app. Zuggernaut; Green Lantern app. 71-Death of Capt. X. 67,68-Millennium tie-ins. 83-1st new look | | .50 | 1.00 |
| 100-($2.95, 68 pgs.) | .50 | 1.50 | 3.00 |
| Annual 5 (10/87)-1st app. new Firestorm | | .65 | 1.30 |

**FIRST ADVENTURES**
Dec, 1985 - No. 5, Apr, 1986 ($1.25, color)
First Comics

| | Good | Fine | N-Mint |
|---|---|---|---|
| 1-5: Blaze Barlow, Whisper & Dynamo Joe in all | | .65 | 1.30 |

**FIRST AMERICANS, THE** (See 4-Color No. 843)

**FIRST CHRISTMAS, THE** (3-D)
1953 (25 cents) (Oversized - 8¼x10¼")
Fiction House Magazines (Real Adv. Publ. Co.)

| | Good | Fine | N-Mint |
|---|---|---|---|
| nn-(Scarce)-Kelly Freas-c; Biblical theme, birth of Christ; Nativity-c | 29.00 | 85.00 | 200.00 |

**FIRST COMICS GRAPHIC NOVEL**
Jan, 1984 - No. 20? (52-176 pgs, high quality paper)
First Comics

| | Good | Fine | N-Mint |
|---|---|---|---|
| 1-Beowulf ($5.95) | 1.00 | 3.00 | 6.00 |
| 1-2nd printing | 1.15 | 3.50 | 7.00 |
| 2-Time Beavers ($5.95) | 1.00 | 3.00 | 6.00 |
| 3($11.95, 100 pgs.)-American Flagg! Hard Times. (2 printings) | 2.00 | 6.00 | 12.00 |
| 4-Nexus ($6.95)-r/B&W 1-3 | 1.30 | 4.00 | 8.00 |
| 5-The Enchanted Apples of Oz ($7.95, 52pp)-Intro by Harlan Ellison (1986) | 1.35 | 4.00 | 8.00 |
| 6-Elric of Melnibone ($14.95, 176pp)-r with new color | 2.50 | 7.50 | 15.00 |
| 7-The Secret Island Of Oz ($7.95) | 1.35 | 4.00 | 8.00 |
| 8-Teenage Mutant Ninja Turtles Book I(132 pgs., r-/TMNT #1-3 in color w/12 pgs. new-a ($9.95)-Origin | 2.50 | 7.50 | 15.00 |
| 9-Time 2: The Epiphany by Chaykin, 52 pgs. ($7.95) | 1.35 | 4.00 | 8.00 |
| 10-Teenage Mutant Ninja Turtles Book II ($9.95)-r/TMNT #4-6 in color | 2.50 | 7.50 | 15.00 |
| 11-Sailor On The Sea of Fate | 2.50 | 7.50 | 15.00 |
| 12-American Flagg! Southern Comfort ($11.95) | 2.00 | 6.00 | 12.00 |
| 13-The Ice King Of Oz | 1.35 | 4.00 | 8.00 |
| 14-Teenage Mutant Ninja Turtles Book III ($9.95)-r/TMNT #7,8 in color plus new 12 pg. story | 2.50 | 7.50 | 15.00 |
| 15-Hex Breaker: Badger (64 pgs., $7.95) | 1.35 | 4.00 | 8.00 |
| 16-The Forgotten Forest of Oz ($8.95) | 1.50 | 4.50 | 9.00 |
| 17-Mazinger (64pgs., $8.95) | 1.50 | 4.50 | 9.00 |
| 18-Teenage Mutant Ninja Turtles Book IV ($9.95)-r/TMNT #10,11 plus 3 pg. fold-out | 1.70 | 5.00 | 10.00 |
| 19-The Original Nexus Graphic Novel ($7.95, 104pgs)-Reprints First Comics Graphic Novel #4 ($7.95) | 1.35 | 4.00 | 8.00 |
| 20-American Flagg!: State of the Union; r/A.F. 7-9 ($11.95, 96 pgs.) | 2.00 | 6.00 | 12.00 |

NOTE: *Most or all issues have been reprinted.*

**1ST FOLIO** (The Joe Kubert School Presents. . .)
March, 1984 ($1.50, color)
Pacific Comics

| | Good | Fine | N-Mint |
|---|---|---|---|
| 1-Kubert-c/a(2pgs.); Adam & Andy Kubert-a | .25 | .75 | 1.50 |

**1ST ISSUE SPECIAL**
April, 1975 - No. 13, April, 1976
National Periodical Publications

| | Good | Fine | N-Mint |
|---|---|---|---|
| 1-7,9-13: 1-Intro. Atlas; Kirby-c/a. 2-Green Team (see Cancelled Comic Cavalcade). 3-Metamorpho by Ramona Fraden. 4-Lady Cop. 5-Manhunter; Kirby-c/a. 6-Dingbats; Kirby-c/a. 7-The Creeper by Ditko(c/a). 9-Dr. Fate; Kubert-c; Simonson-a. 10-The Outsiders. 11-Code Name: Assassin; Grell-c. 12-Origin/1st app. new Starman; Kubert-c. 13-Return of the New Gods | | .50 | 1.00 |
| 8-Origin/1st app. The Warlord; Grell-c/a | 1.70 | 5.00 | 10.00 |

**FIRST KISS**
Dec, 1957 - No. 40, Jan, 1965
Charlton Comics

| | Good | Fine | N-Mint |
|---|---|---|---|
| V1#1 | 1.15 | 3.50 | 8.00 |
| V1#2-10 | .70 | 2.00 | 4.00 |
| 11-40 | .35 | 1.00 | 2.00 |

**FIRST LOVE ILLUSTRATED**
2/49 - No. 9, 6/50; No. 10, 1/51 - No. 86, 3/58; No. 87, 9/58 - No. 88, 11/58; No. 89, 11/62, No. 90, 2/63
Harvey Publications(Home Comics)(True Love)

| | Good | Fine | N-Mint |
|---|---|---|---|
| 1-Powell-a(2) | 5.00 | 15.00 | 35.00 |
| 2-Powell-a | 2.65 | 8.00 | 18.00 |
| 3-"Was I Too Fat To Be Loved" story | 2.30 | 7.00 | 16.00 |
| 4-10 | 2.00 | 6.00 | 14.00 |
| 11-30: 30-Lingerie panel | 1.15 | 3.50 | 8.00 |
| 31-34,37,39-49: 49-Last pre-code (2/55) | 1.00 | 3.00 | 7.00 |
| 35-Used in **SOTI**, illo-"The title of this comic book is First Love" | 4.30 | 13.00 | 30.00 |
| 36-Communism story, "Love Slaves" | 1.30 | 4.00 | 9.00 |
| 38-Nostrand-a | 2.30 | 7.00 | 16.00 |
| 50-90 | .75 | 2.25 | 4.50 |

NOTE: ***Disbrow** a-13. **Orlando** c-87. **Powell** a-1, 3-5, 7, 10, 11, 13-17, 19-24, 26-29, 33, 35-41, 43, 45, 46, 50, 54, 55, 57, 58, 61-63, 65, 71-73, 76, 79r, 82, 84, 88.*

**FIRST MEN IN THE MOON** (See Movie Comics)

**FIRST ROMANCE MAGAZINE**
8/49 - #6, 6/50; #7, 6/51 - #50, 2/58; #51, 9/58 - #52, 11/58
Home Comics(Harvey Publ.)/True Love

| | Good | Fine | N-Mint |
|---|---|---|---|
| 1 | 5.00 | 15.00 | 35.00 |
| 2 | 2.65 | 8.00 | 18.00 |
| 3-5 | 2.30 | 7.00 | 16.00 |
| 6-10 | 1.70 | 5.00 | 12.00 |
| 11-20 | 1.30 | 4.00 | 9.00 |
| 21-27,29-32: 32-Last pre-code issue (2/55) | 1.00 | 3.00 | 7.00 |
| 28-Nostrand-a(Powell swipe) | 2.00 | 6.00 | 14.00 |
| 33-52 | .75 | 2.25 | 4.50 |

NOTE: ***Powell** a-1-5, 8-10, 14, 18, 20-22, 24, 25, 28, 36, 46, 48, 51.*

**FIRST TRIP TO THE MOON** (See Space Adventures No. 20)

**FISH POLICE** (Inspector Gill of the. . . #2, 3)
Dec, 1985 - No. 11, Nov, 1987 ($1.50, B&W)
V2#5, April, 1988 - V2#17, May, 1989 ($1.75, color)
No. 18, Aug, 1989 - No. 26, 1990 ($2.25, B&W)
Fishwrap Productions/Comico V2#5-17/Apple Comics #18 on

| | Good | Fine | N-Mint |
|---|---|---|---|
| 1 | .70 | 2.00 | 4.00 |
| 1-2nd print (5/86) | .30 | .90 | 1.80 |
| 2 | .30 | 1.00 | 2.00 |
| 2-2nd print | .25 | 75 | 1.50 |
| 3-11 | .25 | .75 | 1.50 |
| V2#5-17(Color): V2#5-11-r/V1#5-11. 12-17, new-a | .40 | 1.25 | 2.50 |
| 18-26 ($2.25-c, B&W) 18-Origin Inspector Gill | .35 | 1.00 | 2.00 |
| Special 1 ($2.50, 7/87, Comico) | .40 | 1.25 | 2.50 |
| Graphic Novel: The Hairball Saga (r/1-4, color) | 1.35 | 4.00 | 8.00 |

**FIST OF THE NORTH STAR, THE**
1989 - No. 8, 1989 ($2.95, B&W, mini-series, 52 pgs.)
Viz Comics

| | Good | Fine | N-Mint |
|---|---|---|---|
| 1-8: Martial arts super-hero | .50 | 1.50 | 3.00 |

**5-STAR SUPER-HERO SPEC.** (See DC Special Series No. 1)

**FLAME, THE** (See Big 3 & Wonderworld Comics)
Summer, 1940 - No. 8, Jan, 1942 (#1,2: 68 pgs; #3-8: 44 pgs.)
Fox Features Syndicate

| | Good | Fine | N-Mint |
|---|---|---|---|
| 1-Flame stories from Wonderworld #5-9; origin The Flame; Lou Fine-a, 36 pgs., r-/Wonderworld 3,10 | 150.00 | 450.00 | 900.00 |
| 2-Fine-a(2). Wing Turner by Tuska | 61.00 | 182.00 | 425.00 |
| 3-8: 3-Powell-a | 35.00 | 105.00 | 245.00 |

**FLAME, THE** (Formerly Lone Eagle)
No. 5, Dec-Jan, 1954-55 - No. 3, April-May, 1955
Ajax/Farrell Publications (Excellent Publ.)

| | Good | Fine | N-Mint |
|---|---|---|---|
| 5(#1) | 13.00 | 40.00 | 90.00 |
| 2,3 | 10.00 | 30.00 | 70.00 |

**FLAMING CARROT** (Also see Anything Goes, Cerebus & Visions)
5/84 - No. 5, 1/85; No. 6, 3/85 - Present ($1.70-$2.00, B&W)

*1st Issue Special #2, © DC*

*First Kiss #1, © CC*

*The Flame #3 (4-5/55), © AJAX*

*Flaming Carrot #2, © Bob Burden*

*The Flash #123, © DC*

*The Flash #215, © DC*

Aardvark-Vanaheim/Renegade Press #6-17/Dark Horse #18 on

| | Good | Fine | N-Mint |
|---|---|---|---|
| 1-Bob Burden story/art | 8.00 | 24.00 | 55.00 |
| 2 | 5.00 | 15.00 | 35.00 |
| 3 | 4.15 | 12.50 | 25.00 |
| 4-6 | 3.00 | 9.00 | 18.00 |
| 7-9 | 2.00 | 6.00 | 12.00 |
| 10-12 | 1.00 | 3.00 | 6.00 |
| 13-15 | .70 | 2.00 | 4.00 |
| 15-Variant without cover price | 1.85 | 5.50 | 11.00 |
| 16-23,25: 18-1st Dark Horse issue | .50 | 1.50 | 3.00 |
| 24-($2.50, 52 pgs.)-10th anniversary issue | .50 | 1.50 | 3.00 |

**FLAMING CARROT COMICS** (Also see Junior Carrot Patrol)
Summer-Fall, 1981 ($1.95, One Shot) (Large size, 8½x11)
Killian Barracks Press

| | Good | Fine | N-Mint |
|---|---|---|---|
| 1-By Bob Burden | 13.00 | 40.00 | 90.00 |

**FLAMING LOVE**
Dec, 1949 - No. 6, Oct, 1950 (Photo covers No. 2-6)
Quality Comics Group (Comic Magazines)

| | Good | Fine | N-Mint |
|---|---|---|---|
| 1-Ward-c/a (9 pgs.) | 17.00 | 51.00 | 120.00 |
| 2 | 8.00 | 24.00 | 56.00 |
| 3-Ward-a (9 pgs.); Crandall-a | 12.00 | 36.00 | 84.00 |
| 4-6: 4-Gustavson-a | 6.00 | 18.00 | 42.00 |

**FLAMING WESTERN ROMANCES**
Nov-Dec, 1949 - No. 3, Mar-Apr, 1950
Star Publications

| | Good | Fine | N-Mint |
|---|---|---|---|
| 1-L. B. Cole-c | 14.00 | 43.00 | 100.00 |
| 2-L. B. Cole-c | 10.00 | 30.00 | 70.00 |
| 3-Robert Taylor, Arlene Dahl photo-c with biographies inside; L. B. Cole-c | 16.00 | 48.00 | 110.00 |

**FLARE** (Also see Champions for 1st app. & League of Champions)
Nov, 1988 - No. 3?, 1989 ($2.75, color, 52 pgs)
V2#1, Nov, 1990 - Present ($2.95, color, mature readers, 52 pgs.)
Hero Comics/Hero Graphics Vol. 2 on

| | Good | Fine | N-Mint |
|---|---|---|---|
| 1-3 | .60 | 1.75 | 3.50 |
| V2#1-4-Beachum-c/a | .50 | 1.50 | 3.00 |

**FLASH, THE** (See Adventure, The Brave and the Bold, Crisis On Infinite Earths, DC Comics Presents, DC Special, DC Special Series, DC Super-Stars, Green Lantern, Justice League of America, Showcase, Super Team Family, & World's Finest)

**FLASH, THE** (Formerly Flash Comics)
No. 105, Feb-Mar, 1959 - No. 350, Oct, 1985
National Periodical Publ./DC Comics

| | Good | Fine | N-Mint | Mint |
|---|---|---|---|---|
| 105-Origin Flash(retold), & Mirror Master | 143.00 | 430.00 | 1000.00 | 2300.00 |

(Estimated up to 800 total copies exist, 21 in NM/Mint)

| | Good | Fine | N-Mint |
|---|---|---|---|
| 106-Origin Grodd & Pied Piper; Flash's 1st visit to Gorilla City; begin Grodd the Super Gorilla trilogy, ends #108 | 60.00 | 180.00 | 420.00 |
| 107 | 31.00 | 93.00 | 220.00 |
| 108,109 | 26.00 | 78.00 | 180.00 |
| 110-Intro/origin The Weather Wizard & Kid Flash who later becomes Flash in Crisis On Infinite Earths #12 | 46.00 | 138.00 | 320.00 |
| 111 | 14.00 | 43.00 | 100.00 |
| 112-Origin & 1st app. Elongated Man | 16.00 | 48.00 | 110.00 |
| 113-Origin Trickster | 14.00 | 43.00 | 100.00 |
| 114-Captain Cold app. | 13.00 | 40.00 | 90.00 |
| 115-120: 117-Origin Capt. Boomerang. 119-Elongated Man marries Sue Dearborn | 11.00 | 32.00 | 75.00 |
| 121,122: 122-Origin & 1st app. The Top | 8.00 | 24.00 | 55.00 |
| 123-Re-intro. Golden Age Flash; origins of both Flashes; 1st mention of an Earth II where DC Golden Age heroes live | 47.00 | 141.00 | 330.00 |
| 124-Last 10 cent issue | 7.00 | 21.00 | 50.00 |
| 125-128,130: 128-Origin Abra Kadabra | 5.00 | 15.00 | 35.00 |
| 129-G.A. Flash x-over; J.S.A. cameo in flashback | 13.00 | 40.00 | 90.00 |
| 131-136,138-140: 136-1st Dexter Miles. 139-Origin Prof. Zoom. 140-Origin & 1st app. Heat Wave | 5.00 | 15.00 | 35.00 |
| 137-G.A. Flash x-over; J.S.A. cameo (1st real app. since 2-3/51); 1st Silver Age app. Vandall Savage | 14.00 | 43.00 | 100.00 |
| 141-150 | 2.65 | 8.00 | 18.00 |
| 151-159: 151-G.A. Flash x-over | 1.70 | 5.00 | 12.00 |
| 160-80-Pg. Giant G-21-G.A.-r Flash & Johnny Quick | 2.85 | 8.50 | 20.00 |
| 161-168,170: 165-Silver Age Flash weds Iris West. 167-New facts about Flash's origin. 170-Dr. Mid-Nite, Dr. Fate, G.A. Flash x-over | 1.50 | 4.50 | 10.00 |
| 169-80-Pg. Giant G-34 | 2.85 | 8.50 | 20.00 |
| 171-177,179,180: 171-JLA, Green Lantern, Atom flashbacks. 173-G.A. Flash x-over. 174-Barry Allen reveals I.D. to wife. 175-2nd Superman/Flash race; JLA cameo | 1.15 | 3.50 | 8.00 |
| 178-80-Pg. Giant G-46 | 2.00 | 6.00 | 14.00 |
| 181-186,188-195,197-200: 186-Re-intro. Sargon | .85 | 2.50 | 5.00 |
| 187,196: 68-Pg. Giants G-58, G-70 | 1.30 | 4.00 | 9.00 |
| 201-204,206-210: 201-New G.A. Flash story. 208-52 pg. begin, end #213,215,216. 206-Elongated Man begins | .50 | 1.50 | 3.00 |
| 205-68-Pg. Giant G-82 | 1.00 | 3.00 | 7.00 |
| 211-213,216,220: 211-G.A. Flash origin-r/#104. 213-Reprints #137 | .50 | 1.50 | 3.00 |
| 214-DC 100 Page Super Spectacluar DC-11; origin Metal Men-r/Showcase #37; never before pubbed G.A. Flash story | .85 | 2.50 | 5.00 |
| 215 (52 pgs.)-Flash-r/Showcase #4; G.A. Flash x-over, r-in #216 | .50 | 1.50 | 3.00 |
| 217-219: Neal Adams-a in all. 217-Green Lantern/Green Arrow series begins. 219-Last Green Arrow | 1.00 | 3.00 | 7.00 |
| 221-225,227,228,230,231 | .50 | 1.50 | 3.00 |
| 226-Neal Adams-a | .75 | 2.25 | 4.50 |
| 229,232,233-(All 100pgs.)-G.A. Flash-r & new-a | .60 | 1.75 | 3.50 |
| 234-274,277-288,290: 243-Death of The Top. 246-Last Green Lantern. 256-Death of The Top retold. 265-267-(44 pgs.). 267-Origin of Flash's uniform. 270-Intro The Clown. 286-Intro/origin Rainbow Raider | .35 | 1.00 | 2.00 |
| 275,276-Iris West Allen dies | .40 | 1.25 | 2.50 |
| 289-Perez 1st DC art; new Firestorm series begins, ends #304 | .50 | 1.50 | 3.00 |
| 291-299,301-305: 291-Intro/origin Colonel Computron. 298-Intro/origin Shade. 301-Atomic Bomb-c. 303-The Top returns. 305-G.A. Flash x-over | .35 | 1.00 | 2.00 |
| 300-(52pgs.)-Origin Flash retold; 25th ann. ish | .50 | 1.50 | 3.00 |
| 306-Dr. Fate by Giffen begins, ends #313 | .40 | 1.25 | 2.50 |
| 307-313-Giffen-a. 309-Origin Flash retold | .35 | 1.00 | 2.00 |
| 314-349: 318-323-Creeper back-ups. 323,324-Two part Flash vs. Flash story. 324-Death of Reverse Flash (Prof. Zoom). 328-Iris West Allen's death retold. 344-Origin Kid Flash | .35 | 1.00 | 2.00 |
| 350-Double size ($1.25) | .75 | 2.25 | 4.50 |
| Annual 1(10-12/63, 84pgs.)-Origin Elongated Man & Kid Flash-r; origin Grodd, G.A. Flash-r | 26.00 | 78.00 | 185.00 |

*NOTE: **N. Adams** c-194, 195, 203, 204, 206-208, 211, 213, 215, 246. **M. Anderson** a-202i. **Austin** a-233i, 234i, 246i. **Buckler** a-271p, 272p; c(p)-247-250, 252, 253p, 255, 256p, 258, 262, 265-267, 269-271. **Giffen** a-306-313p; c-310p, 315. **Sid Greene** a-167-174i, 229i(r). **Grell** a-237p, 238p, 240-243p; c-236. **G. Kane** a-195p, 197-199p, 229r, 232r; c-197-199, 312p. **Kubert** a-108p, 215i(r); c-189-191. **Lopez** c-272. **Meskin** a-229r, 232r. **Perez** a-289-293p; c-293. **Starlin** a-294-296p. **Staton** c-263p, 264p. Green Lantern x-over-131, 143, 168, 171, 191.*

**FLASH**
June, 1987 - Present (75 cents, $1.00 #17 on)
DC Comics

| | Good | Fine | N-Mint |
|---|---|---|---|
| 1-Guice-c/a begins; New Teen Titans app. | 1.50 | 4.50 | 9.00 |
| 2 | 1.00 | 3.00 | 6.00 |
| 3-Intro. Kilgore | .70 | 2.00 | 4.00 |
| 4-6: 5-Intro. Speed McGee | .50 | 1.50 | 3.00 |
| 7-10: 7-1st app. Blue Trinity. 8,9-Millennium tie-ins. 9-1st app. The Chunk | .40 | 1.25 | 2.50 |
| 11-20: 12-Free extra 16 pg. Dr. Light story. 19-Free extra 16 pg. Flash story | .35 | 1.00 | 2.00 |
| 21-30: 28-Capt. Cold app. 29-New Phantom Lady app. | .25 | .75 | 1.50 |
| 31-49: 40-Dr. Alchemy app. | | .50 | 1.00 |
| Annual 1 (9/87, $1.25) | .60 | 1.75 | 3.50 |
| Annual 2 (10/88, $1.50) | .50 | 1.50 | 3.00 |
| Annual 3 (7/89, $1.75, 68 pgs.)-Gives history of G.A., Silver Age, & new Flash in text | .40 | 1.25 | 2.50 |
| Special 1 (1990, $2.95, 84 pgs.)-50th anniversary issue; Kubert-c | .60 | 1.75 | 3.50 |

NOTE: ***Guice** a-1-9p, 11p, Annual 1p; c-1-9p, Annual 1p. **Perez** c-15-17, Annual 2i.*

**FLASH COMICS** (Whiz Comics No. 2 on)
Jan, 1940 (12 pgs., B&W, regular size)
(Not distributed to newsstands; printed for in-house use)
Fawcett Publications

NOTE: **Whiz Comics** #2 was preceded by two books, **Flash Comics** and **Thrill Comics**, both dated Jan, 1940, (12 pgs, B&W, regular size) and were not distributed. These two books are identical except for the title, and were sent out to major distributors as ad copies to promote sales. It is believed that the complete 68 page issue of Fawcett's **Flash** and **Thrill Comics** #1 was finished and ready for publication with the January date. Since D.C. Comics was also about to publish a book with the same date and title, Fawcett hurriedly printed up the black and white version of **Flash Comics** to secure copyright before D.C. The inside covers are blank, with the covers and inside pages printed on a high quality uncoated paper stock. The eight page origin story of Captain Thunder is composed of pages 1-7 and 13 of the Captain Marvel story essentially as they appeared in the first issue of **Whiz Comics**. The balloon dialogue on page thirteen was relettered to tie the story into the end of page seven in **Flash** and **Thrill Comics** to produce a shorter version of the origin story for copyright purposes. Obviously, D.C. acquired the copyright and Fawcett dropped **Flash** as well as **Thrill** and came out with **Whiz Comics** a month later. Fawcett never used the cover to **Flash** and **Thrill** #1, designing a new cover for **Whiz Comics**. Fawcett also must have discovered that Captain Thunder had already been used by another publisher (Captain Terry Thunder by Fiction House). All references to Captain Thunder were relettered to Captain Marvel before appearing in **Whiz**.

1 (nn on-c, #1 on inside)-Origin & 1st app. Captain Thunder. Eight copies of **Flash** and three copies of **Thrill** exist. All 3 copies of Thrill sold in 1986 for between $4,000-$10,000 each. A NM copy of Thrill sold in 1987 for $12,000. A vg copy of Thrill sold in 1987 for $9000 cash; another copy sold in 1987 for $2000 cash, $10,000 trade.

**FLASH COMICS** (The Flash No. 105 on) (Also see All-Flash)
Jan, 1940 - No. 104, Feb, 1949
National Periodical Publications/All-American

| | Good | Fine | VF-NM | NM/Mint |
|---|---|---|---|---|
| 1-Origin The Flash by Harry Lampert, Hawkman by Gardner Fox, The Whip, & Johnny Thunder by Stan Asch; Cliff Cornwall by Moldoff, Minute Movies begin; Moldoff (Shelly) cover; 1st app. Shiera Sanders who later becomes Hawkgirl, #24; reprinted in Famous First Edition (on sale 11/10/39) | 1500.00 | 3750.00 | 9000.00 | 15,000.00 |

(Estimated up to 150 total exist, 7 in NM/Mint)

| | Good | Fine | N-Mint |
|---|---|---|---|
| 2-Rod Rian begins, ends #11 | 335.00 | 835.00 | 2000.00 |
| 3-The King begins, ends #41 | 258.00 | 645.00 | 1550.00 |
| 4-Moldoff (Shelly) Hawkman begins | 225.00 | 560.00 | 1350.00 |
| 5 | 200.00 | 500.00 | 1200.00 |
| 6,7 | 158.00 | 395.00 | 950.00 |
| 8-10 | 120.00 | 302.00 | 725.00 |
| 11-20: 12-Les Watts begins; "Sparks" #16 on. 17-Last Cliff Cornwall | 92.00 | 230.00 | 550.00 |
| 21-23 | 79.00 | 200.00 | 475.00 |
| 24-Shiera becomes Hawkgirl | 92.00 | 230.00 | 550.00 |
| 25-30: 28-Last Les Sparks. 29-Ghost Patrol begins(origin, 1st app.), ends #104 | 67.00 | 167.00 | 400.00 |
| 31-40: 35-Origin Shade | 58.00 | 145.00 | 350.00 |
| 41-50 | 54.00 | 135.00 | 325.00 |
| 51-61: 59-Last Minute Movies. 61-Last Moldoff Hawkman | 45.00 | 112.00 | 270.00 |
| 62-Hawkman by Kubert begins | 57.00 | 142.00 | 340.00 |
| 63-70: 66-68-Hop Harrigan in all | 45.00 | 112.00 | 270.00 |
| 71-85: 80-Atom begins, ends #104 | 45.00 | 112.00 | 270.00 |
| 86-Intro. The Black Canary in Johnny Thunder; rare in Mint due to black ink smearing on white cover | 117.00 | 291.00 | 700.00 |
| 87-90: 88-Origin Ghost. 89-Intro villain Thorn | 57.00 | 141.00 | 340.00 |
| 91,93-99: 98-Atom dons new costume | 71.00 | 177.00 | 425.00 |
| 92-1st solo Black Canary | 103.00 | 255.00 | 615.00 |
| 100 (10/48),103(Scarce)-52 pgs. each | 117.00 | 291.00 | 700.00 |
| 101,102(Scarce) | 92.00 | 230.00 | 550.00 |
| 104-Origin The Flash retold (Scarce) | 217.00 | 541.00 | 1300.00 |
| Wheaties Giveaway (1946, 32 pgs., 6½x8¼")-Johnny Thunder, Ghost Patrol, The Flash & Kubert Hawkman app. NOTE: All known copies were taped to Wheaties boxes and are never found in mint condition. Copies with light tape residue bring the listed prices in all grades | 50.00 | 125.00 | 300.00 |

NOTE: ***Infantino** a-86p, 90, 93-95, 99-104. **Kinstler** a-87, 89(Hawkman). **Chet Kozlak** c-77, 79, 81. **Krigstein** a-94. **Kubert** a-62-76, 83, 85, 86, 88-104; c-63, 65, 67, 70, 71, 73, 75, 83, 85, 86, 88, 89, 91, 94, 96, 98, 100, 104. **Moldoff** a-3; c-3, 7, 9, 17, 21, 23, 25, 27, 29, 31, 33, 37, 43, 55, 57. #8-Male bondage-c.*

**FLASH DIGEST, THE** (See DC Special Series #24)

**FLASH GORDON** (See Defenders Of The Earth, Eat Right to Work..., Feature Book #25 (McKay), Giant Comic Album, King Classics, King Comics, March of Comics #118, 133, 142, The Phantom #18, Street Comix & Wow Comics, 1st series)

**FLASH GORDON**
No. 10, 1943 - No. 512, Nov, 1953
Dell Publishing Co.

| | Good | Fine | N-Mint |
|---|---|---|---|
| 4-Color 10(1943)-by Alex Raymond; reprints/"The Ice Kingdom" | 50.00 | 150.00 | 350.00 |
| 4-Color 84(1945)-by Alex Raymond; reprints/"The Fiery Desert" | 33.00 | 100.00 | 230.00 |
| 4-Color 173,190: 190-Bondage-c | 11.50 | 34.00 | 80.00 |
| 4-Color 204,247 | 9.00 | 27.00 | 62.00 |
| 4-Color 424 | 6.50 | 19.50 | 45.00 |
| 2(5-7/53-Dell)-Evans-a | 3.50 | 10.50 | 24.00 |
| 4-Color 512 | 3.50 | 10.50 | 24.00 |
| Macy's Giveaway(1943)-(Rare)-20 pgs.; not by Raymond | 60.00 | 160.00 | 320.00 |

**FLASH GORDON** (See Tiny Tot Funnies)
Oct, 1950 - No. 4, April, 1951
Harvey Publications

| | Good | Fine | N-Mint |
|---|---|---|---|
| 1-Alex Raymond-a; bondage-c; reprints strips from 7/14/40 to 12/8/40 | 17.00 | 51.00 | 120.00 |
| 2-Alex Raymond-a; r/strips 12/15/40-4/27/41 | 13.00 | 40.00 | 90.00 |
| 3,4-Alex Raymond-a; 3-bondage-c. 4-r/strips 10/24/37-3/27/38 | 12.00 | 36.00 | 80.00 |

5-(Rare)-Small size-5½x8½"; B&W; 32 pgs.; Distributed to some mail subscribers only Estimated value.... $200.00—$300.00

(Also see All-New No. 15, Boy Explorers No. 2, and Stuntman No. 3)

**FLASH GORDON**
1951 (Paper cover; 16 pgs. in color; regular size)
Harvey Comics (Gordon Bread giveaway)

| | Good | Fine | N-Mint |
|---|---|---|---|
| 1,2: 1-r/strips 10/24/37 - 2/6/38. 2-r/strips 7/14/40 - 10/6/40; Reprints by Raymond each.... | 1.50 | 4.50 | 10.00 |

NOTE: *Most copies have brittle edges.*

*Flash #4 (4/87), © DC*

*Flash Comics #1, © DC*

*Flash Comics #104, © DC*

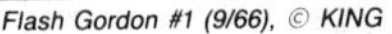
*Flash Gordon #1 (9/66), © KING*

*The Flintstones #2 (Dell), © Hanna-Barbera*

*Flip #2, © HARV*

**FLASH GORDON**
June, 1965
Gold Key

| | Good | Fine | N-Mint |
|---|---|---|---|
| 1 (1947 reprint)-Painted-c | 2.30 | 7.00 | 16.00 |

**FLASH GORDON** (Also see Comics Reading Libraries)
9/66 - #11, 12/67; #12, 2/69 - #18, 1/70; #19, 10-11/78 - #37, 3/82
(Painted covers No. 19-30, 34)
King #1-11/Charlton #12-18/Gold Key #19-23/Whitman #24 on

| | Good | Fine | N-Mint |
|---|---|---|---|
| 1-Army giveaway(1968)("Complimentary" on cover)(Same as regular #1 minus Mandrake story & back-c) | 1.50 | 4.50 | 10.00 |
| 1-Williamson c/a(2); E.C. swipe/Incredible S.F. #32. Mandrake story | 2.00 | 6.00 | 14.00 |
| 2-Bolle, Gil Kane-c; Mandrake story | 1.50 | 4.50 | 10.00 |
| 3-Williamson-c | 1.70 | 5.00 | 12.00 |
| 4-Secret Agent X-9 begins, Williamson-c/a(3) | 1.70 | 5.00 | 12.00 |
| 5-Williamson-c/a(2) | 1.70 | 5.00 | 12.00 |
| 6,8-Crandall-a. 8-Secret Agent X-9-r | 2.30 | 7.00 | 16.00 |
| 7-Raboy-a | 1.70 | 5.00 | 12.00 |
| 9,10-Raymond-r. 10-Buckler's 1st pro work (11/67); Briggs-c | 2.00 | 6.00 | 14.00 |
| 11-Crandall-a | 1.50 | 4.50 | 10.00 |
| 12-Crandall-c/a | 1.70 | 5.00 | 12.00 |
| 13-Jeff Jones-a (15 pgs.) | 1.70 | 5.00 | 12.00 |
| 14-17: 17-Brick Bradford story | .85 | 2.60 | 6.00 |
| 18-Kaluta-a (1st pro work?) | 1.00 | 3.00 | 7.00 |
| 19(9/78, G.K.), 20-30(10/80) | .35 | 1.00 | 2.00 |
| 30 (7/81; re-issue) | | .30 | .60 |
| 31-33: Movie adaptation; Williamson-a | | .50 | 1.00 |
| 34-37: Movie adaptation | | .40 | .80 |

NOTE: *Aparo a-8.* ***Bolle*** *a-21, 22.* ***Boyette*** *a-14-18.* ***Buckler*** *a-10.* ***Crandall*** *c-6.* ***Estrada*** *a-3.* ***Gene Fawcette*** *a-29, 30, 34, 37.* ***McWilliams*** *a-31-33, 36.*

**FLASH GORDON**
June, 1988 - No. 9, Holiday, 1988-'89 ($1.25, color, mini-series)
DC Comics

| | Good | Fine | N-Mint |
|---|---|---|---|
| 1-Painted-c | .35 | 1.00 | 2.00 |
| 2-9: 5-Painted-c | .25 | .75 | 1.50 |

**FLASH GORDON THE MOVIE**
1980 ($1.95. color, 68pgs)
Western Publishing Co.

| | Good | Fine | N-Mint |
|---|---|---|---|
| 11294-Williamson-c/a; adapts movie | .35 | 1.00 | 2.00 |

**FLASH SPECTACULAR, THE** (See DC Special Series No. 11)

**FLAT-TOP**
11/53 - No. 3, 5/54; No. 4, 3/55 - No. 6, 7/55
Mazie Comics/Harvey Publ.(Magazine Publ.) No. 4 on

| | Good | Fine | N-Mint |
|---|---|---|---|
| 1-Teenage | 2.00 | 6.00 | 14.00 |
| 2,3 | 1.15 | 3.50 | 8.00 |
| 4-6 | .85 | 2.60 | 6.00 |

**FLESH AND BONES**
June, 1986 - No. 4, Dec, 1986 (Color, mini-series)
Upshot Graphics (Fantagraphics Books)

| | Good | Fine | N-Mint |
|---|---|---|---|
| 1-Dalgoda by Fujitake-r; Alan Moore scripts | .40 | 1.25 | 2.50 |
| 2-4: Alan Moore scripts | .35 | 1.00 | 2.00 |

**FLINTSTONE KIDS, THE** (TV; See Star Comics Digest)
Aug, 1987 - No. 11, April, 1989
Star Comics/Marvel Comics #5 on

| | Good | Fine | N-Mint |
|---|---|---|---|
| 1-11 | | .50 | 1.00 |

**FLINTSTONES, THE** (TV)(See Dell Giant #48 for No. 1)
No. 2, Nov-Dec, 1961 - No. 60, Sept, 1970 (Hanna-Barbera)
Dell Publ. Co./Gold Key No. 7 (10/62) on

| | Good | Fine | N-Mint |
|---|---|---|---|
| 2 | 4.50 | 14.00 | 32.00 |
| 3-6(7-8/62) | 3.00 | 9.00 | 21.00 |
| 7 (10/62; 1st GK) | 3.00 | 9.00 | 21.00 |
| 8-10: Mr. & Mrs. J. Evil Scientist begin? | 2.65 | 8.00 | 18.00 |
| 11-1st app. Pebbles (6/63) | 3.50 | 10.50 | 24.00 |
| 12-15,17-20 | 2.30 | 7.00 | 16.00 |
| 16-1st app. Bamm-Bamm (1/64) | 2.65 | 8.00 | 18.00 |
| 21-30: 24-1st app. The Grusomes app. | 2.00 | 6.00 | 14.00 |
| 31-33,35-40: 31-Xmas-c. 33-Meet Frankenstein & Dracula. 39-Reprints | 1.70 | 5.00 | 12.00 |
| 34-1st app. The Great Gazoo | 2.30 | 7.00 | 16.00 |
| 41-60: 45-Last 12 cent issue | 1.50 | 4.50 | 10.00 |
| At N. Y. World's Fair('64)-J.W. Books(25 cents)-1st printing; no date on-c (29 cent version exists, 2nd print?) | 2.65 | 8.00 | 18.00 |
| At N. Y. World's Fair (1965 on-c; re-issue). NOTE: Warehouse find in 1984 | .70 | 2.00 | 4.00 |
| Bigger & Boulder 1(#30013-211) (Gold Key Giant, 11/62, 25 cents, 84 pgs.) | 4.30 | 13.00 | 30.00 |
| Bigger & Boulder 2-(25 cents)(1966)-reprints B&B No. 1 | 3.60 | 11.00 | 25.00 |
| ...With Pebbles & Bamm Bamm(100 pgs., G.K.)-30028-511 (paper-c, 25 cents)(11/65) | 3.60 | 11.00 | 25.00 |

NOTE: *(See Comic Album #16, Bamm-Bamm & Pebbles Flintstone, Dell Giant 48, March of Comics #229, 243, 271, 289, 299, 317, 327, 341, Pebbles Flintstone, and Whitman Comic Books.)*

**FLINTSTONES, THE** (TV)(...& Pebbles)
Nov, 1970 - No. 50, Feb, 1977 (Hanna-Barbera)
Charlton Comics

| | Good | Fine | N-Mint |
|---|---|---|---|
| 1 | 2.15 | 6.50 | 15.00 |
| 2 | 1.15 | 3.50 | 8.00 |
| 3-7,9,10 | .85 | 2.60 | 6.00 |
| 8-"Flintstones Summer Vacation," 52 pgs. (Summer, 1971) | 1.00 | 3.00 | 7.00 |
| 11-20 | .70 | 2.00 | 5.00 |
| 21-50: 37-Byrne text illos (1st work). 42-Byrne-a, 2pgs. | .70 | 2.00 | 4.00 |

(Also see Barney & Betty Rubble, Dino, The Great Gazoo, & Pebbles & Bamm-Bamm)

**FLINTSTONES, THE** (TV)(See Yogi Bear, 3rd series)
October, 1977 - No. 9, Feb, 1979 (Hanna-Barbera)
Marvel Comics Group

| | Good | Fine | N-Mint |
|---|---|---|---|
| 1-9: Yogi Bear app. 4-The Jetsons app. | | .50 | 1.00 |

**FLINTSTONES CHRISTMAS PARTY, THE** (See The Funtastic World of Hanna-Barbera No. 1)

**FLINTSTONES IN 3-D, THE** (See Blackthorne 3-D Series #19, 22, 36, 42)

**FLIP**
April, 1954 - No. 2, June, 1954 (Satire)
Harvey Publications

| | Good | Fine | N-Mint |
|---|---|---|---|
| 1,2-Nostrand-a each. 2-Powell-a | 9.30 | 28.00 | 65.00 |

**FLIPPER** (TV)
April, 1966 - No. 3, Nov, 1967 (Photo-c)
Gold Key

| | Good | Fine | N-Mint |
|---|---|---|---|
| 1 | 3.00 | 9.00 | 21.00 |
| 2,3 | 2.00 | 6.00 | 14.00 |

**FLIPPITY & FLOP**
12-1/51-52 - No. 46, 8-10/59; No. 47, 9-11/60
National Periodical Publ. (Signal Publ. Co.)

| | Good | Fine | N-Mint |
|---|---|---|---|
| 1 | 13.00 | 40.00 | 90.00 |
| 2 | 7.00 | 21.00 | 50.00 |
| 3-5 | 5.00 | 15.00 | 35.00 |
| 6-10 | 4.30 | 13.00 | 30.00 |
| 11-20: 20-Last precode (3/55) | 3.00 | 9.00 | 21.00 |
| 21-47 | 2.00 | 6.00 | 14.00 |

**FLOYD FARLAND** (See Eclipse Graphic Album Series #11)

**FLY, THE** (Also see Adventures of . . ., Blue Ribbon Comics & Flyman)
May, 1983 - No. 9, Oct, 1984 (See The Advs. of . . .)
Archie Enterprises, Inc.

| | Good | Fine | N-Mint |
|---|---|---|---|
| 1-Mr. Justice app; origin Shield | | .50 | 1.00 |
| 2-9: 2-Flygirl app. | | .40 | .80 |

NOTE: ***Buckler** a-1, 2. **Ditko** a-2-9; c-4-8p. **Nebres** c-3, 4, 5i, 6, 7i. **Steranko** c-1, 2.*

**FLY BOY** (Also see Approved Comics)
Spring, 1952 - No. 4, 1953
Ziff-Davis Publ. Co. (Approved)

| | Good | Fine | N-Mint |
|---|---|---|---|
| 1-Saunders painted-c | 6.50 | 19.00 | 45.00 |
| 2-Saunders painted-c | 4.00 | 12.00 | 28.00 |
| 3,4-Saunders painted-c | 3.00 | 9.00 | 21.00 |

**FLYING ACES**
July, 1955 - No. 5, March, 1956
Key Publications

| | Good | Fine | N-Mint |
|---|---|---|---|
| 1 | 2.00 | 6.00 | 14.00 |
| 2-5: 2-Trapani-a | 1.15 | 3.50 | 8.00 |

**FLYING A'S RANGE RIDER, THE** (TV) (See Western Roundup under Dell Giants)
#404, 6-7/52; #2, June-Aug, 1953 - #24, Aug, 1959 (All photo-c)
Dell Publishing Co.

| | Good | Fine | N-Mint |
|---|---|---|---|
| 4-Color 404(#1)-Titled "The Range Rider" | 6.50 | 19.00 | 45.00 |
| 2 | 4.00 | 12.00 | 28.00 |
| 3-10 | 3.50 | 10.50 | 24.00 |
| 11-16,18-24 | 3.00 | 9.00 | 21.00 |
| 17-Toth-a | 4.00 | 12.00 | 28.00 |

**FLYING CADET** (WW II Plane Photos)
Jan, 1943 - V2#8, 1947 (½ photos, ½ comics)
Flying Cadet Publishing Co.

| | Good | Fine | N-Mint |
|---|---|---|---|
| V1#1 | 6.50 | 19.00 | 45.00 |
| 2 | 3.15 | 9.50 | 22.00 |
| 3-9 (Two #6's, Sept. & Oct.) | 2.65 | 8.00 | 18.00 |
| V2#1-7(#10-16) | 2.00 | 6.00 | 14.00 |
| 8(#17)-Bare-breasted woman-c | 7.00 | 21.00 | 50.00 |

**FLYIN' JENNY**
1946 - No. 2, 1947 (1945 strip reprints)
Pentagon Publ. Co./Leader Enterprises #2

| | Good | Fine | N-Mint |
|---|---|---|---|
| nn-Marcus Swayze strip-r (entire insides) | 5.50 | 16.50 | 40.00 |
| 2-Baker-c; Swayze strip reprints | 6.50 | 19.50 | 45.00 |

**FLYING MODELS**
V61#3, May, 1954 (16 pgs.) (5 cents)
H-K Publ. (Health-Knowledge Publs.)

| | Good | Fine | N-Mint |
|---|---|---|---|
| V61#3 (Rare) | 3.50 | 10.50 | 24.00 |

**FLYING NUN** (TV)
Feb, 1968 - No. 4, Nov, 1968
Dell Publishing Co.

| | Good | Fine | N-Mint |
|---|---|---|---|
| 1 | 2.00 | 6.00 | 14.00 |
| 2-4: 2-Sally Field photo-c | 1.15 | 3.50 | 8.00 |

**FLYING NURSES** (See Sue & Sally Smith . . .)

**FLYING SAUCERS**
1950; 1952; 1953
Avon Periodicals/Realistic

| | Good | Fine | N-Mint |
|---|---|---|---|
| 1(1950)-Wood-a, 21 pgs.; Fawcette-c | 38.00 | 114.00 | 265.00 |
| nn(1952)-Cover altered plus 2 pgs. of Wood-a not in original | 35.00 | 105.00 | 245.00 |
| nn(1953)-Reprints above | 20.00 | 60.00 | 140.00 |

**FLYING SAUCERS** (Comics)
April, 1967 - No. 4, Nov, 1967; No. 5, Oct, 1969
Dell Publishing Co.

| | Good | Fine | N-Mint |
|---|---|---|---|
| 1 | 1.00 | 3.00 | 7.00 |
| 2-5 | .70 | 2.00 | 4.00 |

**FLY MAN** (Formerly Adventures of The Fly; Mighty Comics #40 on)
No. 32, July, 1965 - No. 39, Sept, 1966 (Also see Mighty Crusaders)
Mighty Comics Group (Radio Comics) (Archie)

| | Good | Fine | N-Mint |
|---|---|---|---|
| 32,33-Comet, Shield, Black Hood, The Fly & Flygirl x-over; re-intro. Wizard, Hangman #33 | 2.30 | 7.00 | 16.00 |
| 34-36: 34-Shield begins. 35-Origin Black Hood. 36-Hangman x-over in Shield; re-intro. & origin of Web | 1.70 | 5.00 | 12.00 |
| 37-39: 37-Hangman, Wizard x-over in Flyman; last Shield issue. 38-Web story. 39-Steel Sterling story | 1.70 | 5.00 | 12.00 |

**FOES**
1989 - No. 3? ($1.95, color, mini-series)
Ram Comics

| | Good | Fine | N-Mint |
|---|---|---|---|
| 1-3 | .35 | 1.00 | 2.00 |

**FOLLOW THE SUN** (TV)
May-July, 1962 - No. 2, Sept-Nov, 1962 (Photo-c)
Dell Publishing Co.

| | Good | Fine | N-Mint |
|---|---|---|---|
| 01-280-207(No.1), 12-280-211(No.2) | 2.30 | 7.00 | 16.00 |

**FOODINI** (TV)(The Great . . .; see Jingle Dingle & Pinhead & . . .)
March, 1950 - No. 5, 1950
Continental Publications (Holyoke)

| | Good | Fine | N-Mint |
|---|---|---|---|
| 1 (52 pgs.) | 7.00 | 21.00 | 50.00 |
| 2 | 3.60 | 11.00 | 25.00 |
| 3-5 | 2.65 | 8.00 | 18.00 |

**FOOEY** (Magazine) (Satire)
Feb, 1961 - No. 4, May, 1961
Scoff Publishing Co.

| | Good | Fine | N-Mint |
|---|---|---|---|
| 1 | 1.70 | 5.00 | 12.00 |
| 2-4 | 1.15 | 3.50 | 8.00 |

**FOOFUR** (TV)
Aug, 1987 - No. 6, June, 1988
Star Comics/Marvel Comics No. 5 on

| | Good | Fine | N-Mint |
|---|---|---|---|
| 1-6 | | .50 | 1.00 |

**FOOLKILLER** (Also see The Defenders #73, Man-Thing #3 & Omega the Unknown #8)
Oct, 1990 - No. 10, July, 1991 ($1.75, color, limited series)
Marvel Comics

| | Good | Fine | N-Mint |
|---|---|---|---|
| 1-Origin 3rd Foolkiller; Greg Salinger app. | .35 | 1.00 | 2.00 |
| 2-10: DeZuniga-a(i) in 1-4 | .30 | .90 | 1.80 |

**FOOTBALL THRILLS** (See Tops In Adventure)
Fall-Winter, 1951-52 - No. 2, Fall, 1952
Ziff-Davis Publ. Co.

| | Good | Fine | N-Mint |
|---|---|---|---|
| 1-Powell a(2); Saunders painted-c. Red Grange, Jim Thorpe app. | 11.50 | 34.00 | 80.00 |
| 2-Saunders painted-c | 7.00 | 21.00 | 50.00 |

**FOR A NIGHT OF LOVE**
1951
Avon Periodicals

| | Good | Fine | N-Mint |
|---|---|---|---|
| nn-Two stories adapted from the works of Emile Zola; Astarita, Ravielli-a; Kinstler-c | 16.00 | 48.00 | 110.00 |

**FORBIDDEN LOVE**
Mar, 1950 - No. 4, Sept, 1950
Quality Comics Group

| | Good | Fine | N-Mint |
|---|---|---|---|
| 1-(Scarce)Classic photo-c; Crandall-a | 50.00 | 150.00 | 350.00 |
| 2,3(Scarce)-Photo-c | 22.00 | 65.00 | 150.00 |
| 4-(Scarce)Ward/Cuidera-a; photo-c | 24.00 | 72.00 | 170.00 |

**FORBIDDEN LOVE** (See Dark Mansion of . . .)

*Flying Aces #3, © Key Publ.*

*The Flying A's Range Rider #5, © Tie-Ups*

*Flying Saucers #1, © AVON*

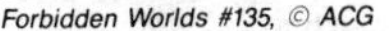
Forbidden Worlds #135, © ACG

Forever People #5 (10-11/71), © DC

Forgotten Realms #1, © TSR

**FORBIDDEN TALES OF DARK MANSION** (Dark Mansion of Forbidden Love #1-4)
No. 5, May-June, 1972 - No. 15, Feb-Mar, 1974
National Periodical Publications

| | Good | Fine | N-Mint |
|---|---|---|---|
| 5-15: 13-Kane/Howard-a | | .50 | 1.00 |

NOTE: ***N. Adams*** *c-9.* ***Alcala*** *a-9-11, 13.* ***Chaykin*** *a-7,15.* ***Evans*** *a-14.* ***Kaluta*** *c-7-11, 13.* ***G. Kane*** *a-13.* ***Kirby*** *a-6.* ***Nino*** *a-8, 12, 15.* ***Redondo*** *a-14.*

**FORBIDDEN WORLDS**
7-8/51 - No. 34, 10-11/54; No. 35, 8/55 - No. 145, 8/67
(No. 1-5: 52 pgs.; No. 6-8: 44 pgs.)
American Comics Group

| | Good | Fine | N-Mint |
|---|---|---|---|
| 1-Williamson/Frazetta-a (10 pgs.) | 64.00 | 193.00 | 450.00 |
| 2 | 29.00 | 85.00 | 200.00 |
| 3-Williamson/Wood/Orlando-a (7 pgs.) | 31.00 | 92.00 | 215.00 |
| 4 | 14.00 | 43.00 | 100.00 |
| 5-Williamson/Krenkel-a (8 pgs.) | 25.00 | 75.00 | 175.00 |
| 6-Harrison/Williamson-a (8 pgs.) | 22.00 | 65.00 | 155.00 |
| 7,8,10 | 11.00 | 32.00 | 75.00 |
| 9-A-Bomb explosion story | 11.50 | 34.00 | 80.00 |
| 11-20 | 7.00 | 21.00 | 50.00 |
| 21-33: 24-E.C. swipe by Landau | 5.00 | 15.00 | 35.00 |
| 34(10-11/54)(Becomes Young Heroes #35 on)-Last pre-code issue; A-Bomb explosion story | 5.00 | 15.00 | 35.00 |
| 35(8/55)-62 | 2.85 | 8.50 | 20.00 |
| 63,69,76,78-Williamson-a in all; w/Krenkel #69 | 4.30 | 13.00 | 30.00 |
| 64,66-68,70-72,74,75,77,79-90: 86-Flying saucer-c | 2.15 | 6.50 | 15.00 |
| 65-"There's a New Moon Tonight" listed in #114 as holding 1st record fan mail response | 2.15 | 6.50 | 15.00 |
| 73-1st app. Herbie by Ogden Whitney | 17.00 | 51.00 | 120.00 |
| 91-93,95-100 | 1.50 | 4.50 | 10.00 |
| 94-Herbie app. | 4.30 | 13.00 | 30.00 |
| 101-109,111-113,115,117-120 | 1.15 | 3.50 | 8.00 |
| 110,114,116-Herbie app. 114-1st Herbie-c; contains list of editor's top 20 ACG stories. 116-Herbie goes to Hell | 2.65 | 8.00 | 18.00 |
| 121-124: 124-Magic Agent app. | 1.15 | 3.50 | 8.00 |
| 125-Magic Agent app.; intro. & origin Magicman series, ends #141 | 1.30 | 4.00 | 9.00 |
| 126-130 | 1.00 | 3.00 | 7.00 |
| 131-141: 133-Origin/1st app. Dragonia in Magicman (1-2/66); returns in #138. 136-Nemesis x-over in Magicman. 140-Mark Midnight app. by Ditko | .85 | 2.60 | 6.00 |
| 142-145 | .70 | 2.00 | 5.00 |

NOTE: ***Buscema*** *a-75, 79, 81, 82, 140r.* ***Disbrow*** *a-10.* ***Ditko*** *a-137p, 138, 140.* ***Landau*** *a-24, 27-29, 31-34, 48, 86r, 96, 143-45.* ***Lazarus*** *a-18, 23, 24, 57.* ***Moldoff*** *a-27, 31, 139r.* ***Reinman*** *a-93.* ***Whitney*** *a-115, 116, 137; c-40, 46, 57, 60, 68, 78, 79, 90, 93, 94, 100, 102, 103, 106-108, 114, 129.*

**FORCE, THE** (See The Crusaders)

**FORCE OF BUDDHA'S PALM THE**
Aug, 1988 - Present ($1.50-$1.95, color, 68 pgs.)
Jademan Comics

| | Good | Fine | N-Mint |
|---|---|---|---|
| 1-8 ($1.50)-Kung Fu stories | .25 | .75 | 1.50 |
| 9-28 ($1.95) | .35 | 1.00 | 2.00 |

**FORD ROTUNDA CHRISTMAS BOOK** (See Christmas at the Rotunda)

**FOREIGN INTRIGUES** (Formerly Johnny Dynamite; Battlefield Action No. 16 on)
No. 13, 1956 - No. 15, Aug, 1956
Charlton Comics

| | Good | Fine | N-Mint |
|---|---|---|---|
| 13-15-Johnny Dynamite continues | 2.15 | 6.50 | 15.00 |

**FOREMOST BOYS** (See Four Most)

**FOREST FIRE** (Also see Smokey The Bear)
1949 (dated-1950) (16 pgs., paper-c)
American Forestry Assn.(Commerical Comics)

| | Good | Fine | N-Mint |
|---|---|---|---|
| nn-Intro/1st app. Smokey The Forest Fire Preventing Bear; created by Rudy Wendelein; Wendelein/Sparling-a; 'Carter Oil Co.' on back-c of original | 11.00 | 32.00 | 75.00 |

**FOREVER, DARLING** (See 4-Color No. 681)

**FOREVER PEOPLE, THE**
Feb-Mar, 1971 - No. 11, Oct-Nov, 1972
National Periodical Publications

| | Good | Fine | N-Mint |
|---|---|---|---|
| 1-Superman x-over; Kirby-c/a begins | 1.50 | 4.50 | 10.00 |
| 2-5: 4-G.A. reprints begin, end #9 | 1.00 | 3.00 | 6.00 |
| 6-11: 9,10-Deadman app. | .75 | 2.25 | 4.50 |

NOTE: ***Kirby*** *c/a(p)-1-11; #4-9 contain Sandman reprints from Adventure #85, 84, 75, 80, 77, 74 in that order. #1-3, 10-11 are 36pgs; #4-9 are 52pgs.*

**FOREVER PEOPLE**
Feb, 1988 - No. 6, July, 1988 ($1.25, mini-series)
DC Comics

| | Good | Fine | N-Mint |
|---|---|---|---|
| 1-6 | | .60 | 1.25 |

**FOR GIRLS ONLY**
Nov, 1953 (Digest size, 100 pgs.)
Bernard Bailey Enterprises

| | Good | Fine | N-Mint |
|---|---|---|---|
| 1-½ comic book, ½ magazine | 6.00 | 18.00 | 42.00 |

**FORGOTTEN FOREST OF OZ, THE** (See First Comics Graphic Novel #16)

**FORGOTTEN REALMS** (Also see TSR Worlds)
Sept, 1989 - Present ($1.50-$1.75, color)
DC Comics

| | Good | Fine | N-Mint |
|---|---|---|---|
| 1-Based on TSR role-playing game | .40 | 1.25 | 2.50 |
| 2,3 | .35 | 1.00 | 2.00 |
| 4-10 | .30 | .90 | 1.80 |
| 11-15 | .25 | .75 | 1.50 |
| 16-20: 16-Begin $1.75-c | .30 | .90 | 1.80 |

**FORGOTTEN STORY BEHIND NORTH BEACH, THE**
No date (8 pgs.; paper cover)
Catechetical Guild

| | Good | Fine | N-Mint |
|---|---|---|---|
| nn | 1.50 | 4.50 | 10.00 |

**FOR LOVERS ONLY** (Formerly Hollywood Romances)
No. 60, Aug, 1971 - No. 87, Nov, 1976
Charlton Comics

| | Good | Fine | N-Mint |
|---|---|---|---|
| 60-87: 73-Spanking scene-c/story | | .30 | .60 |

**40 BIG PAGES OF MICKEY MOUSE**
No. 945, 1936 (44 pgs.; 10¼x12½"; cardboard cover)
Whitman Publishing Co.

| | Good | Fine | N-Mint |
|---|---|---|---|
| 945-Reprints Mickey Mouse Magazine #1, but with a different cover. Ads were eliminated and some illustrated stories had expanded text. The book is ¾" shorter than Mickey Mouse Mag. #1, but the reprints are the same size. (Rare) | 55.00 | 165.00 | 385.00 |

**48 FAMOUS AMERICANS**
1947 (Giveaway) (Half-size in color)
J. C. Penney Co. (Cpr. Edwin H. Stroh)

| | Good | Fine | N-Mint |
|---|---|---|---|
| nn-Simon & Kirby-a | 6.75 | 20.00 | 40.00 |

**FOR YOUR EYES ONLY** (See James Bond . . .)

**FOUR COLOR**
Sept?, 1939 - No. 1354, Apr-June, 1962
Dell Publishing Co.

NOTE: *Four Color only appears on issues #19-25, 1-99,101. Dell Publishing Co. filed these as Series I, #1-25, and Series II, #1-1354. Issues beginning with #710? were printed with and without ads on back cover. Issues without ads are worth more.*

| SERIES I: | Good | Fine | VF-NM | NM/Mint |
|---|---|---|---|---|
| 1(nn)-Dick Tracy | 171.00 | 515.00 | 1200.00 | 2000.00 |

(Estimated up to 115 total copies exist, 5 in NM/Mint)

| | Good | Fine | N-Mint |
|---|---|---|---|
| 2(nn)-Don Winslow of the Navy (#1) (Rare) (11/39?) | 79.00 | 235.00 | 550.00 |
| 3(nn)-Myra North (1/40?) | 39.00 | 118.00 | 275.00 |
| 4-Donald Duck by Al Taliaferro('40)(Disney) (3/40?) | 357.00 | 1070.00 | 2500.00 |
| *(Prices vary widely on this book)* | | | |
| 5-Smilin' Jack (#1) (5/40?) | 45.00 | 135.00 | 315.00 |
| 6-Dick Tracy (Scarce) | 86.00 | 255.00 | 600.00 |
| 7-Gang Busters | 24.00 | 72.00 | 165.00 |
| 8-Dick Tracy | 57.00 | 171.00 | 400.00 |
| 9-Terry and the Pirates-r/Super #9-29 | 48.00 | 145.00 | 335.00 |
| 10-Smilin' Jack | 43.00 | 130.00 | 300.00 |
| 11-Smitty (#1) | 26.00 | 77.00 | 180.00 |
| 12-Little Orphan Annie; reprints strips from 12/19/37 to 6/4/38 | 37.00 | 110.00 | 260.00 |
| 13-Walt Disney's Reluctant Dragon('41)-Contains 2 pages of photos from film; 2 pg. foreword to Fantasia by Leopold Stokowski; Donald Duck, Goofy, Baby Weems & Mickey Mouse (as the Sorcerer's Apprentice) app. (Disney) | 89.00 | 268.00 | 625.00 |
| 14-Moon Mullins (#1) | 24.00 | 72.00 | 165.00 |
| 15-Tillie the Toiler (#1) | 24.00 | 72.00 | 165.00 |
| | **Good** | **Fine** | **VF-NM** |
| 16-Mickey Mouse (#1) (Disney) by Gottfredson | 371.00 | 1115.00 | 2600.00 |
| *(Prices vary widely on this book)* | | | |
| | **Good** | **Fine** | **N-Mint** |
| 17-Walt Disney's Dumbo, the Flying Elephant (#1)(1941)-Mickey Mouse, Donald Duck, & Pluto app. (Disney) | 89.00 | 268.00 | 625.00 |
| 18-Jiggs and Maggie (#1)(1936-'38-r) | 24.00 | 73.00 | 170.00 |
| 19-Barney Google and Snuffy Smith (#1)-(1st issue with Four Color on the cover) | 27.00 | 80.00 | 185.00 |
| 20-Tiny Tim | 23.00 | 70.00 | 160.00 |
| 21-Dick Tracy | 49.00 | 145.00 | 340.00 |
| 22-Don Winslow | 19.00 | 57.00 | 135.00 |
| 23-Gang Busters | 18.00 | 54.00 | 125.00 |
| 24-Captain Easy | 23.00 | 70.00 | 160.00 |
| 25-Popeye | 43.00 | 130.00 | 300.00 |
| SERIES II: | | | |
| 1-Little Joe | 32.00 | 95.00 | 225.00 |
| 2-Harold Teen | 18.00 | 54.00 | 125.00 |
| 3-Alley Oop (#1) | 37.00 | 111.00 | 260.00 |
| 4-Smilin' Jack | 34.00 | 103.00 | 240.00 |
| 5-Raggedy Ann and Andy (#1) | 36.50 | 110.00 | 255.00 |
| 6-Smitty | 14.00 | 43.00 | 100.00 |
| 7-Smokey Stover (#1) | 24.00 | 72.00 | 165.00 |
| 8-Tillie the Toiler | 14.00 | 43.00 | 100.00 |
| 9-Donald Duck Finds Pirate Gold, by Carl Barks & Jack Hannah (Disney) (c. 8/17/42) | 370.00 | 1115.00 | 2800.00 |
| *(Prices vary widely on this book)* | | | |
| 10-Flash Gordon by Alex Raymond; r-/from "The Ice Kingdom" | 50.00 | 150.00 | 350.00 |
| 11-Wash Tubbs | 22.00 | 65.00 | 150.00 |
| 12-Walt Disney's Bambi (#1); reprinted in Gladstone Comic Album #9 | 38.00 | 115.00 | 265.00 |
| 13-Mr. District Attorney (#1)-See The Funnies #35 for 1st app. | 18.00 | 54.00 | 125.00 |
| 14-Smilin' Jack | 27.00 | 81.00 | 190.00 |
| 15-Felix the Cat (#1) | 43.00 | 130.00 | 300.00 |
| 16-Porky Pig (#1)(1942)-"Secret of the Haunted House" | 40.00 | 120.00 | 280.00 |
| 17-Popeye | 36.00 | 107.00 | 250.00 |
| 18-Little Orphan Annie's Junior Commandos; Flag-c; reprints strips from 6/14/42 to 11/21/42 | 29.00 | 86.00 | 200.00 |
| 19-Walt Disney's Thumper Meets the Seven Dwarfs (Disney); r-in Silly Symphonies | 37.00 | 110.00 | 260.00 |

| | Good | Fine | N-Mint |
|---|---|---|---|
| 20-Barney Baxter | 17.00 | 51.00 | 120.00 |
| 21-Oswald the Rabbit (#1)(1943) | 24.00 | 73.00 | 170.00 |
| 22-Tillie the Toiler | 11.00 | 32.00 | 75.00 |
| 23-Raggedy Ann and Andy | 26.50 | 80.00 | 185.00 |
| 24-Gang Busters | 18.00 | 54.00 | 125.00 |
| 25-Andy Panda (#1) (Walter Lantz) | 27.00 | 81.00 | 190.00 |
| 26-Popeye | 34.00 | 100.00 | 235.00 |
| 27-Walt Disney's Mickey Mouse and the Seven Colored Terror | 50.00 | 150.00 | 350.00 |
| 28-Wash Tubbs | 16.00 | 48.00 | 110.00 |
| 29-Donald Duck and the Mummy's Ring, by Carl Barks (Disney) (9/43) | 243.00 | 730.00 | 1850.00 |
| *(Prices vary widely on this book)* | | | |
| 30-Bambi's Children(1943)-Disney | 36.00 | 110.00 | 255.00 |
| 31-Moon Mullins | 13.00 | 40.00 | 90.00 |
| 32-Smitty | 11.50 | 34.00 | 80.00 |
| 33-Bugs Bunny "Public Nuisance #1" | 35.00 | 105.00 | 245.00 |
| 34-Dick Tracy | 35.00 | 105.00 | 245.00 |
| 35-Smokey Stover | 12.00 | 36.00 | 84.00 |
| 36-Smilin' Jack | 16.00 | 48.00 | 110.00 |
| 37-Bringing Up Father | 13.00 | 40.00 | 90.00 |
| 38-Roy Rogers (#1, c. 4/44)-1st western comic with photo-c | 55.00 | 165.00 | 385.00 |
| 39-Oswald the Rabbit('44) | 17.00 | 51.00 | 120.00 |
| 40-Barney Google and Snuffy Smith | 14.00 | 42.00 | 100.00 |
| 41-Mother Goose and Nursery Rhyme Comics (#1)-All by Walt Kelly | 19.00 | 57.00 | 135.00 |
| 42-Tiny Tim (1934-r) | 12.00 | 36.00 | 85.00 |
| 43-Popeye (1938-'42-r) | 23.00 | 70.00 | 160.00 |
| 44-Terry and the Pirates ('38-r) | 29.00 | 85.00 | 200.00 |
| 45-Raggedy Ann | 22.00 | 65.00 | 155.00 |
| 46-Felix the Cat and the Haunted Castle | 31.00 | 92.00 | 215.00 |
| 47-Gene Autry (© 6/16/44) | 36.00 | 107.00 | 250.00 |
| 48-Porky Pig of the Mounties by Carl Barks (7/44) | 70.00 | 210.00 | 490.00 |
| 49-Snow White and the Seven Dwarfs (Disney) | 30.00 | 90.00 | 210.00 |
| 50-Fairy Tale Parade-Walt Kelly art (1944) | 23.00 | 70.00 | 160.00 |
| 51-Bugs Bunny Finds the Lost Treasure | 20.00 | 60.00 | 140.00 |
| 52-Little Orphan Annie; reprints strips from 6/18/38 to 11/19/38 | 22.00 | 65.00 | 150.00 |
| 53-Wash Tubbs | 11.50 | 34.00 | 80.00 |
| 54-Andy Panda | 17.00 | 51.00 | 120.00 |
| 55-Tillie the Toiler | 8.50 | 25.50 | 60.00 |
| 56-Dick Tracy | 26.00 | 77.00 | 180.00 |
| 57-Gene Autry | 31.00 | 92.00 | 215.00 |
| 58-Smilin' Jack | 16.00 | 48.00 | 110.00 |
| 59-Mother Goose and Nursery Rhyme Comics-Kelly-c/a | 17.00 | 51.00 | 120.00 |
| 60-Tiny Folks Funnies | 11.00 | 32.00 | 75.00 |
| 61-Santa Claus Funnies(11/44)-Kelly art | 22.00 | 65.00 | 150.00 |
| 62-Donald Duck in Frozen Gold, by Carl Barks (Disney) (1/45) | 120.00 | 360.00 | 910.00 |
| 63-Roy Rogers-Photo-c | 37.00 | 110.00 | 250.00 |
| 64-Smokey Stover | 9.30 | 28.00 | 65.00 |
| 65-Smitty | 9.30 | 28.00 | 65.00 |
| 66-Gene Autry | 31.00 | 92.00 | 215.00 |
| 67-Oswald the Rabbit | 11.50 | 34.00 | 80.00 |
| 68-Mother Goose and Nursery Rhyme Comics, by Walt Kelly | 17.00 | 51.00 | 120.00 |
| 69-Fairy Tale Parade, by Walt Kelly | 20.00 | 60.00 | 140.00 |
| 70-Popeye and Wimpy | 19.00 | 58.00 | 135.00 |
| 71-Walt Disney's Three Caballeros, by Walt Kelly(c. 4/45)-(Disney) | 60.00 | 180.00 | 420.00 |
| 72-Raggedy Ann | 18.00 | 54.00 | 125.00 |

*Four Color #12 (Series I), © News Synd.*

*Four Color #29, © The Disney Co.*

*Four Color #57, © Gene Autry*

Four Color #78, © Warner Bros.

Four Color #101, © News Syndicate

Four Color #164, © Warner Bros.

| | Good | Fine | N-Mint |
|---|---|---|---|
| 73-The Gumps (No.1) | 7.00 | 21.00 | 50.00 |
| 74-Marge's Little Lulu (No.1) | 90.00 | 270.00 | 630.00 |
| 75-Gene Autry and the Wildcat | 25.00 | 75.00 | 175.00 |
| 76-Little Orphan Annie; reprints strips from 2/28/40 to 6/24/40 | 17.00 | 51.00 | 120.00 |
| 77-Felix the Cat | 26.00 | 78.00 | 185.00 |
| 78-Porky Pig and the Bandit Twins | 16.00 | 48.00 | 110.00 |
| 79-Walt Disney's Mickey Mouse in The Riddle of the Red Hat by Carl Barks (8/45) | 64.00 | 193.00 | 450.00 |
| 80-Smilin' Jack | 12.00 | 36.00 | 85.00 |
| 81-Moon Mullins | 7.00 | 21.00 | 50.00 |
| 82-Lone Ranger | 32.00 | 95.00 | 225.00 |
| 83-Gene Autry in Outlaw Trail | 25.00 | 75.00 | 175.00 |
| 84-Flash Gordon by Alex Raymond-Reprints from "The Fiery Desert" | 33.00 | 100.00 | 230.00 |
| 85-Andy Panda and the Mad Dog Mystery | 11.00 | 32.00 | 75.00 |
| 86-Roy Rogers-Photo-c | 29.00 | 85.00 | 200.00 |
| 87-Fairy Tale Parade by Walt Kelly; Dan Noonan cover | 17.00 | 51.00 | 120.00 |
| 88-Bugs Bunny's Great Adventure | 12.00 | 36.00 | 85.00 |
| 89-Tillie the Toiler | 8.00 | 24.00 | 55.00 |
| 90-Christmas with Mother Goose by Walt Kelly (11/45) | 16.50 | 50.00 | 115.00 |
| 91-Santa Claus Funnies by Walt Kelly (11/45) | 16.00 | 48.00 | 110.00 |
| 92-Walt Disney's The Wonderful Adventures Of Pinocchio(1945); Donald Duck by Kelly, 16 pgs. (Disney) | 27.00 | 80.00 | 185.00 |
| 93-Gene Autry in The Bandit of Black Rock | 21.00 | 62.00 | 145.00 |
| 94-Winnie Winkle (1945) | 9.30 | 28.00 | 65.00 |
| 95-Roy Rogers Comics-Photo-c | 29.00 | 85.00 | 200.00 |
| 96-Dick Tracy | 19.00 | 58.00 | 135.00 |
| 97-Marge's Little Lulu (1946) | 47.00 | 140.00 | 330.00 |
| 98-Lone Ranger, The | 26.00 | 77.00 | 180.00 |
| 99-Smitty | 8.00 | 24.00 | 55.00 |
| 100-Gene Autry Comics-Photo-c | 21.00 | 62.00 | 145.00 |
| 101-Terry and the Pirates | 19.00 | 57.00 | 130.00 |

*NOTE: No. 101 is last issue to carry "Four Color" logo on cover; all issues beginning with No. 100 are marked ". . .O. S." (One Shot) which can be found in the bottom left-hand panel on the first page; the numbers following "O. S." relate to the year/month issued.*

| | Good | Fine | N-Mint |
|---|---|---|---|
| 102-Oswald the Rabbit-Walt Kelly art, 1 pg. | 10.00 | 30.00 | 70.00 |
| 103-Easter with Mother Goose by Walt Kelly | 16.00 | 48.00 | 110.00 |
| 104-Fairy Tale Parade by Walt Kelly | 15.00 | 45.00 | 105.00 |
| 105-Albert the Alligator and Pogo Possum (No.1) by Kelly (4/46) | 60.00 | 180.00 | 420.00 |
| 106-Tillie the Toiler | 6.50 | 19.00 | 45.00 |
| 107-Little Orphan Annie; reprints strips from 11/16/42 to 3/24/43 | 14.00 | 43.00 | 100.00 |
| 108-Donald Duck in The Terror of the River, by Carl Barks (Disney) (c. 4/16/46) | 90.00 | 270.00 | 680.00 |
| 109-Roy Rogers Comics | 22.00 | 65.00 | 150.00 |
| 110-Marge's Little Lulu | 33.00 | 100.00 | 230.00 |
| 111-Captain Easy | 9.30 | 28.00 | 65.00 |
| 112-Porky Pig's Adventure in Gopher Gulch | 8.50 | 25.50 | 60.00 |
| 113-Popeye | 10.00 | 30.00 | 70.00 |
| 114-Fairy Tale Parade by Walt Kelly | 15.00 | 45.00 | 105.00 |
| 115-Marge's Little Lulu | 33.00 | 100.00 | 230.00 |
| 116-Mickey Mouse and the House of Many Mysteries (Disney) | 17.00 | 51.00 | 120.00 |
| 117-Roy Rogers Comics-Photo-c | 16.00 | 48.00 | 110.00 |
| 118-Lone Ranger, The | 26.00 | 77.00 | 180.00 |
| 119-Felix the Cat | 20.00 | 60.00 | 140.00 |
| 120-Marge's Little Lulu | 30.00 | 90.00 | 210.00 |
| 121-Fairy Tale Parade-(not Kelly) | 9.30 | 28.00 | 65.00 |
| 122-Henry (No.1)(10/46) | 6.50 | 19.00 | 45.00 |
| 123-Bugs Bunny's Dangerous Venture | 7.00 | 21.00 | 50.00 |
| 124-Roy Rogers Comics-Photo-c | 16.00 | 48.00 | 110.00 |
| 125-Lone Ranger, The | 19.00 | 57.00 | 130.00 |

| | Good | Fine | N-Mint |
|---|---|---|---|
| 126-Christmas with Mother Goose by Walt Kelly (1946) | 13.00 | 40.00 | 90.00 |
| 127-Popeye | 10.00 | 30.00 | 70.00 |
| 128-Santa Claus Funnies-"Santa & the Angel" by Gollub; "A Mouse in the House" by Kelly | 12.00 | 36.00 | 84.00 |
| 129-Walt Disney's Uncle Remus and His Tales of Brer Rabbit (No.1) (1946) | 13.00 | 40.00 | 90.00 |
| 130-Andy Panda (Walter Lantz) | 5.30 | 16.00 | 38.00 |
| 131-Marge's Little Lulu | 30.00 | 90.00 | 210.00 |
| 132-Tillie the Toiler('47) | 6.50 | 19.00 | 45.00 |
| 133-Dick Tracy | 16.50 | 50.00 | 115.00 |
| 134-Tarzan and the Devil Ogre | 45.00 | 135.00 | 315.00 |
| 135-Felix the Cat | 16.00 | 48.00 | 110.00 |
| 136-Lone Ranger, The | 19.00 | 57.00 | 130.00 |
| 137-Roy Rogers Comics-Photo-c | 16.00 | 48.00 | 110.00 |
| 138-Smitty | 6.50 | 19.50 | 45.00 |
| 139-Marge's Little Lulu (1947) | 27.00 | 81.00 | 190.00 |
| 140-Easter with Mother Goose by Walt Kelly | 13.00 | 40.00 | 90.00 |
| 141-Mickey Mouse and the Submarine Pirates (Disney) | 16.00 | 48.00 | 110.00 |
| 142-Bugs Bunny and the Haunted Mountain | 7.00 | 21.00 | 50.00 |
| 143-Oswald the Rabbit & the Prehistoric Egg | 5.00 | 15.00 | 35.00 |
| 144-Roy Rogers Comics ('47)-Photo-c | 16.00 | 48.00 | 110.00 |
| 145-Popeye | 10.00 | 30.00 | 70.00 |
| 146-Marge's Little Lulu | 27.00 | 81.00 | 190.00 |
| 147-Donald Duck in Volcano Valley, by Carl Barks (Disney)(5/47) | 60.00 | 180.00 | 455.00 |
| 148-Albert the Alligator and Pogo Possum by Walt Kelly (5/47) | 50.00 | 150.00 | 350.00 |
| 149-Smilin' Jack | 8.50 | 25.50 | 60.00 |
| 150-Tillie the Toiler (6/47) | 5.00 | 15.00 | 35.00 |
| 151-Lone Ranger, The | 16.00 | 48.00 | 110.00 |
| 152-Little Orphan Annie; reprints strips from 1/2/44 to 5/6/44 | 10.00 | 30.00 | 70.00 |
| 153-Roy Rogers Comics-Photo-c | 12.00 | 36.00 | 85.00 |
| 154-Walter Lantz Andy Panda | 5.30 | 16.00 | 38.00 |
| 155-Henry (7/47) | 4.50 | 14.00 | 32.00 |
| 156-Porky Pig and the Phantom | 6.50 | 19.50 | 45.00 |
| 157-Mickey Mouse & the Beanstalk (Disney) | 16.00 | 48.00 | 110.00 |
| 158-Marge's Little Lulu | 27.00 | 81.00 | 190.00 |
| 159-Donald Duck in the Ghost of the Grotto, by Carl Barks (Disney) (8/47) | 54.00 | 160.00 | 410.00 |
| 160-Roy Rogers Comics-Photo-c | 12.00 | 36.00 | 85.00 |
| 161-Tarzan and the Fires Of Tohr | 40.00 | 120.00 | 280.00 |
| 162-Felix the Cat (9/47) | 11.50 | 34.00 | 80.00 |
| 163-Dick Tracy | 13.00 | 40.00 | 90.00 |
| 164-Bugs Bunny Finds the Frozen Kingdom | 7.00 | 21.00 | 50.00 |
| 165-Marge's Little Lulu | 27.00 | 81.00 | 190.00 |
| 166-Roy Rogers Comics-52 pgs.,Photo-c | 12.00 | 36.00 | 85.00 |
| 167-Lone Ranger, The | 16.00 | 48.00 | 110.00 |
| 168-Popeye (10/47) | 10.00 | 30.00 | 70.00 |
| 169-Woody Woodpecker (No.1)-"Manhunter in the North"; drug use story | 8.50 | 25.50 | 60.00 |
| 170-Mickey Mouse on Spook's Island (11/47)(Disney)-reprinted in Mickey Mouse No. 103 | 13.00 | 40.00 | 90.00 |
| 171-Charlie McCarthy (No.1) and the Twenty Thieves | 10.00 | 30.00 | 70.00 |
| 172-Christmas with Mother Goose by Walt Kelly (11/47) | 13.00 | 40.00 | 90.00 |
| 173-Flash Gordon | 11.50 | 34.00 | 80.00 |
| 174-Winnie Winkle | 5.00 | 15.00 | 35.00 |
| 175-Santa Claus Funnies by Walt Kelly ('47) | 12.00 | 36.00 | 84.00 |
| 176-Tillie the Toiler (12/47) | 5.00 | 15.00 | 35.00 |
| 177-Roy Rogers Comics-36 pgs, Photo-c | 12.00 | 36.00 | 85.00 |
| 178-Donald Duck "Christmas on Bear Mountain" by Carl Barks; 1st app. Uncle Scrooge (Disney)(12/47) | 64.00 | 192.00 | 485.00 |

| | Good | Fine | N-Mint |
|---|---|---|---|
| 179-Uncle Wiggily (No.1)-Walt Kelly-c | 10.00 | 30.00 | 70.00 |
| 180-Ozark Ike (No.1) | 6.00 | 18.00 | 42.00 |
| 181-Walt Disney's Mickey Mouse in Jungle Magic | 13.00 | 40.00 | 90.00 |
| 182-Porky Pig in Never-Never Land (2/48) | 6.50 | 19.50 | 45.00 |
| 183-Oswald the Rabbit (Lantz) | 5.00 | 15.00 | 35.00 |
| 184-Tillie the Toiler | 5.00 | 15.00 | 35.00 |
| 185-Easter with Mother Goose by Walt Kelly (1948) | 12.00 | 36.00 | 85.00 |
| 186-Walt Disney's Bambi (4/48)-Reprinted as Movie Classic Bambi #3('56) | 8.00 | 24.00 | 56.00 |
| 187-Bugs Bunny and the Dreadful Dragon | 6.00 | 18.00 | 42.00 |
| 188-Woody Woodpecker (Lantz, 5/48) | 5.70 | 17.00 | 40.00 |
| 189-Donald Duck in The Old Castle's Secret, by Carl Barks (Disney) (6/48) | 54.00 | 160.00 | 410.00 |
| 190-Flash Gordon ('48) | 11.50 | 34.00 | 80.00 |
| 191-Porky Pig to the Rescue | 6.50 | 19.50 | 45.00 |
| 192-The Brownies (No.1)-by Walt Kelly (7/48) | 11.50 | 34.00 | 80.00 |
| 193-M.G.M. Presents Tom and Jerry (No.1)(1948) | 9.00 | 27.00 | 62.00 |
| 194-Mickey Mouse in The World Under the Sea (Disney)-Reprinted in Mickey Mouse No. 101 | 13.00 | 40.00 | 90.00 |
| 195-Tillie the Toiler | 3.70 | 11.00 | 26.00 |
| 196-Charlie McCarthy in The Haunted Hide-Out | 8.50 | 25.50 | 60.00 |
| 197-Spirit of the Border (No.1) (Zane Grey) (1948) | 7.00 | 21.00 | 50.00 |
| 198-Andy Panda | 5.30 | 16.00 | 38.00 |
| 199-Donald Duck in Sheriff of Bullet Valley, by Carl Barks; Barks draws himself on wanted poster, last page; used in **Love & Death** (Disney) (10/48) | 54.00 | 160.00 | 410.00 |
| 200-Bugs Bunny, Super Sleuth (10/48) | 6.00 | 18.00 | 42.00 |
| 201-Christmas with Mother Goose by W. Kelly | 11.50 | 34.00 | 80.00 |
| 202-Woody Woodpecker | 3.50 | 10.50 | 24.00 |
| 203-Donald Duck in the Golden Christmas Tree, by Carl Barks (Disney) (12/48) | 36.00 | 108.00 | 270.00 |
| 204-Flash Gordon (12/48) | 9.00 | 27.00 | 62.00 |
| 205-Santa Claus Funnies by Walt Kelly | 11.00 | 32.00 | 76.00 |
| 206-Little Orphan Annie; reprints strips from 11/10/40 to 1/11/41 | 5.70 | 17.00 | 40.00 |
| 207-King of the Royal Mounted (#1) (12/48) | 11.50 | 34.00 | 80.00 |
| 208-Brer Rabbit Does It Again (Disney)(1/49) | 8.00 | 24.00 | 55.00 |
| 209-Harold Teen | 2.30 | 7.00 | 16.00 |
| 210-Tippie and Cap Stubbs | 2.30 | 7.00 | 16.00 |
| 211-Little Beaver (No. 1) | 3.50 | 10.50 | 24.00 |
| 212-Dr. Bobbs | 2.30 | 7.00 | 16.00 |
| 213-Tillie the Toiler | 3.70 | 11.00 | 26.00 |
| 214-Mickey Mouse and His Sky Adventure (2/49)(Disney)-Reprinted in Mickey Mouse No. 105 | 10.00 | 30.00 | 70.00 |
| 215-Sparkle Plenty (Dick Tracy-r by Gould) | 8.00 | 24.00 | 55.00 |
| 216-Andy Panda and the Police Pup (Lantz) | 3.00 | 9.00 | 21.00 |
| 217-Bugs Bunny in Court Jester | 6.00 | 18.00 | 42.00 |
| 218-3 Little Pigs and the Wonderful Magic Lamp (Disney)(3/49) | 6.50 | 19.50 | 45.00 |
| 219-Swee'pea | 6.50 | 19.50 | 45.00 |
| 220-Easter with Mother Goose by Walt Kelly | 11.50 | 34.00 | 80.00 |
| 221-Uncle Wiggily-Walt Kelly cover in part | 7.00 | 21.00 | 50.00 |
| 222-West of the Pecos (Zane Grey) | 5.00 | 15.00 | 35.00 |
| 223-Donald Duck "Lost in the Andes" by Carl Barks (Disney-4/49) (square egg story) | 50.00 | 150.00 | 380.00 |
| 224-Little Iodine (No. 1), by Hatlo (4/49) | 5.00 | 15.00 | 35.00 |
| 225-Oswald the Rabbit (Lantz) | 3.00 | 9.00 | 21.00 |
| 226-Porky Pig and Spoofy, the Spook | 4.30 | 13.00 | 30.00 |
| 227-Seven Dwarfs (Disney) | 8.00 | 24.00 | 55.00 |
| 228-Mark of Zorro, The (No. 1) ('49) | 18.00 | 54.00 | 125.00 |
| 229-Smokey Stover | 3.00 | 9.00 | 21.00 |

| | Good | Fine | N-Mint |
|---|---|---|---|
| 230-Sunset Pass (Zane Grey) | 5.00 | 15.00 | 35.00 |
| 231-Mickey Mouse and the Rajah's Treasure (Disney) | 10.00 | 30.00 | 70.00 |
| 232-Woody Woodpecker (Lantz, 6/49) | 3.50 | 10.50 | 24.00 |
| 233-Bugs Bunny, Sleepwalking Sleuth | 6.00 | 18.00 | 42.00 |
| 234-Dumbo in Sky Voyage (Disney) | 5.70 | 17.00 | 40.00 |
| 235-Tiny Tim | 3.70 | 11.00 | 26.00 |
| 236-Heritage of the Desert (Zane Grey)('49) | 5.00 | 15.00 | 35.00 |
| 237-Tillie the Toiler | 3.70 | 11.00 | 26.00 |
| 238-Donald Duck in Voodoo Hoodoo, by Carl Barks (Disney) (8/49) | 27.00 | 81.00 | 205.00 |
| 239-Adventure Bound (8/49) | 2.65 | 8.00 | 18.00 |
| 240-Andy Panda (Lantz) | 3.00 | 9.00 | 21.00 |
| 241-Porky Pig, Mighty Hunter | 4.30 | 13.00 | 30.00 |
| 242-Tippie and Cap Stubbs | 2.00 | 6.00 | 14.00 |
| 243-Thumper Follows His Nose (Disney) | 5.70 | 17.00 | 40.00 |
| 244-The Brownies by Walt Kelly | 10.00 | 30.00 | 70.00 |
| 245-Dick's Adventures in Dreamland (9/49) | 3.00 | 9.00 | 21.00 |
| 246-Thunder Mountain (Zane Grey) | 3.70 | 11.00 | 26.00 |
| 247-Flash Gordon | 9.00 | 27.00 | 62.00 |
| 248-Mickey Mouse and the Black Sorcerer (Disney) | 10.00 | 30.00 | 70.00 |
| 249-Woody Woodpecker in the "Globetrotter" (10/49) | 3.50 | 10.50 | 24.00 |
| 250-Bugs Bunny in Diamond Daze-Used in **SOTI**, pg. 309 | 6.00 | 18.00 | 42.00 |
| 251-Hubert at Camp Moonbeam | 2.65 | 8.00 | 18.00 |
| 252-Pinocchio (Disney)-not by Kelly; origin | 7.00 | 21.00 | 50.00 |
| 253-Christmas with Mother Goose by W. Kelly | 10.00 | 30.00 | 70.00 |
| 254-Santa Claus Funnies by Walt Kelly; Pogo & Albert story by Kelly (11/49) | 11.00 | 32.00 | 76.00 |
| 255-The Ranger (Zane Grey) (1949) | 3.70 | 11.00 | 26.00 |
| 256-Donald Duck in "Luck of the North" by Carl Barks (Disney) (12/49)-Shows No. 257 on inside | 27.00 | 81.00 | 205.00 |
| 257-Little Iodine | 3.70 | 11.00 | 26.00 |
| 258-Andy Panda and the Balloon Race (Lantz) | 3.00 | 9.00 | 21.00 |
| 259-Santa and the Angel (Gollub art-condensed from No. 128) & Santa at the Zoo (12/49)-two books in one | 3.50 | 10.50 | 24.00 |
| 260-Porky Pig, Hero of the Wild West(12/49) | 4.30 | 13.00 | 30.00 |
| 261-Mickey Mouse and the Missing Key (Disney) | 10.00 | 30.00 | 70.00 |
| 262-Raggedy Ann and Andy | 4.00 | 12.00 | 28.00 |
| 263-Donald Duck in "Land of the Totem Poles" by Carl Barks (Disney)(2/50)-has two Barks stories | 27.00 | 81.00 | 205.00 |
| 264-Woody Woodpecker in the Magic Lantern (Lantz) | 3.50 | 10.50 | 24.00 |
| 265-King of the Royal Mounted (Zane Grey) | 8.00 | 24.00 | 56.00 |
| 266-Bugs Bunny on the Isle of Hercules"(2/50)-Reprinted in Best of Bugs Bunny No. 1 | 4.50 | 14.00 | 32.00 |
| 267-Little Beaver-Harmon-c/a | 2.30 | 7.00 | 16.00 |
| 268-Mickey Mouse's Surprise Visitor (1950) (Disney) | 10.00 | 30.00 | 70.00 |
| 269-Johnny Mack Brown (No. 1)-Photo-c | 13.00 | 40.00 | 90.00 |
| 270-Drift Fence (Zane Grey) (3/50) | 3.70 | 11.00 | 26.00 |
| 271-Porky Pig in Phantom of the Plains | 4.30 | 13.00 | 30.00 |
| 272-Cinderella (Disney)(4/50) | 5.00 | 15.00 | 35.00 |
| 273-Oswald the Rabbit (Lantz) | 3.00 | 9.00 | 21.00 |
| 274-Bugs Bunny, Hare-brained Reporter | 4.50 | 14.00 | 32.00 |
| 275-Donald Duck in "Ancient Persia" by Carl Barks (Disney) (5/50) | 25.00 | 75.00 | 190.00 |
| 276-Uncle Wiggily | 4.00 | 12.00 | 28.00 |
| 277-Porky Pig in Desert Adventure (5/50) | 4.30 | 13.00 | 30.00 |
| 278-Bill Elliott Comics (No. 1)-Photo-c | 11.50 | 34.00 | 80.00 |
| 279-Mickey Mouse and Pluto Battle the Giant Ants (Disney); r-/in Mickey Mouse No. 102 & 245 | 8.50 | 25.50 | 60.00 |
| 280-Andy Panda in The Isle Of Mechanical Men (Lantz) | | | |

Four Color #193, © M.G.M.

Four Color #204, © KING

Four Color #252, © The Disney Co.

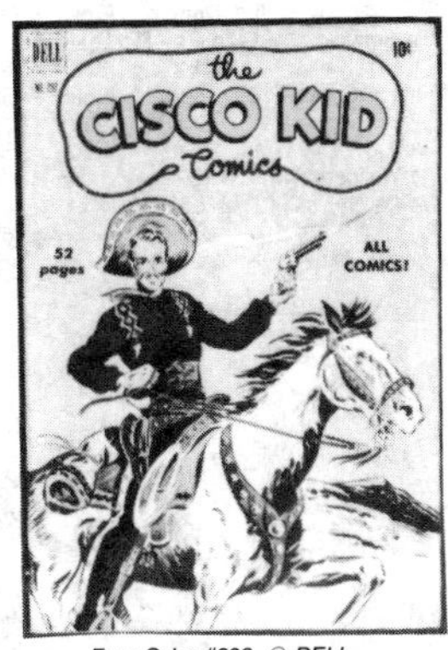

Four Color #292, © DELL

Four Color #325, © The Disney Co.

Four Color #359, © DELL

| | Good | Fine | N-Mint |
|---|---|---|---|
| | 3.00 | 9.00 | 21.00 |
| 281-Bugs Bunny in The Great Circus Mystery | 4.50 | 14.00 | 32.00 |
| 282-Donald Duck and the Pixilated Parrot by Carl Barks (Disney) (c. 5/23/50) | 25.00 | 75.00 | 190.00 |
| 283-King of the Royal Mounted (7/50) | 8.00 | 24.00 | 56.00 |
| 284-Porky Pig in The Kingdom of Nowhere | 4.30 | 13.00 | 30.00 |
| 285-Bozo the Clown and His Minikin Circus (No. 1)(TV) | 8.50 | 25.50 | 60.00 |
| 286-Mickey Mouse in The Uninvited Guest (Disney) | 8.50 | 25.50 | 60.00 |
| 287-Gene Autry's Champion in The Ghost Of Black Mountain (No. 1)-Photo-c | 6.50 | 19.00 | 45.00 |
| 288-Woody Woodpecker in Klondike Gold (Lantz) | 3.50 | 10.50 | 24.00 |
| 289-Bugs Bunny in "Indian Trouble" | 4.50 | 14.00 | 32.00 |
| 290-The Chief (No. 1) | 3.50 | 10.50 | 24.00 |
| 291-Donald Duck in "The Magic Hourglass" by Carl Barks (Disney) (9/50) | 25.00 | 75.00 | 190.00 |
| 292-The Cisco Kid Comics (No. 1) | 11.00 | 32.00 | 75.00 |
| 293-The Brownies-Kelly-c/a | 9.50 | 28.50 | 65.00 |
| 294-Little Beaver | 2.30 | 7.00 | 16.00 |
| 295-Porky Pig in President Porky (9/50) | 4.30 | 13.00 | 30.00 |
| 296-Mickey Mouse in Private Eye for Hire (Disney) | 8.50 | 25.50 | 60.00 |
| 297-Andy Panda in The Haunted Inn (Lantz, 10/50) | 3.00 | 9.00 | 21.00 |
| 298-Bugs Bunny in Sheik for a Day | 4.50 | 14.00 | 32.00 |
| 299-Buck Jones & the Iron Horse Trail (No. 1) | 10.00 | 30.00 | 70.00 |
| 300-Donald Duck in "Big-Top Bedlam" by Carl Barks (Disney) (11/50) | 25.00 | 75.00 | 190.00 |
| 301-The Mysterious Rider (Zane Grey) | 3.70 | 11.00 | 26.00 |
| 302-Santa Claus Funnies (11/50) | 2.30 | 7.00 | 16.00 |
| 303-Porky Pig in The Land of the Monstrous Flies | 3.00 | 9.00 | 21.00 |
| 304-Mickey Mouse in Tom-Tom Island (Disney) (12/50) | 5.70 | 17.00 | 40.00 |
| 305-Woody Woodpecker (Lantz) | 2.30 | 7.00 | 16.00 |
| 306-Raggedy Ann | 3.00 | 9.00 | 21.00 |
| 307-Bugs Bunny in Lumber Jack Rabbit | 3.70 | 11.00 | 26.00 |
| 308-Donald Duck in "Dangerous Disguise" by Carl Barks (Disney) (1/51) | 21.00 | 63.00 | 160.00 |
| 309-Betty Betz' Dollface and Her Gang ('51) | 2.65 | 8.00 | 18.00 |
| 310-King of the Royal Mounted (1/51) | 5.00 | 15.00 | 35.00 |
| 311-Porky Pig in Midget Horses of Hidden Valley | 3.00 | 9.00 | 21.00 |
| 312-Tonto (No. 1) | 10.00 | 30.00 | 70.00 |
| 313-Mickey Mouse in The Mystery of the Double-Cross Ranch (No. 1) (Disney) (2/51) | 5.70 | 17.00 | 40.00 |
| 314-Ambush (Zane Grey) | 3.70 | 11.00 | 26.00 |
| 315-Oswald the Rabbit (Lantz) | 2.00 | 6.00 | 14.00 |
| 316-Rex Allen (No. 1)-Photo-c; Marsh-a | 12.00 | 36.00 | 85.00 |
| 317-Bugs Bunny in Hair Today Gone Tomorrow (No. 1) | 3.70 | 11.00 | 26.00 |
| 318-Donald Duck in "No Such Varmint" by Carl Barks (No. 1) Indicia shows #317 (Disney, c. 1/23/51) | 21.00 | 63.00 | 160.00 |
| 319-Gene Autry's Champion | 3.00 | 9.00 | 21.00 |
| 320-Uncle Wiggily (No. 1) | 3.00 | 9.00 | 21.00 |
| 321-Little Scouts (No. 1) | 1.70 | 4.00 | 9.00 |
| 322-Porky Pig in Roaring Rockets (No. 1) | 3.00 | 9.00 | 21.00 |
| 323-Susie Q. Smith (3/51) | 1.50 | 4.50 | 10.00 |
| 324-I Met a Handsome Cowboy (3/51) | 5.00 | 15.00 | 35.00 |
| 325-Mickey Mouse in The Haunted Castle (No. 2)(Disney)(4/51) | 5.70 | 17.00 | 40.00 |
| 326-Andy Panda (No. 1, Lantz) | 2.00 | 6.00 | 14.00 |
| 327-Bugs Bunny and the Rajah's Treasure (No. 2) | 3.70 | 11.00 | 26.00 |

| | Good | Fine | N-Mint |
|---|---|---|---|
| 328-Donald Duck in Old California (No. 2) by Carl Barks-Peyote drug use issue (Disney) (5/51) | 23.00 | 70.00 | 175.00 |
| 329-Roy Roger's Trigger (No. 1)(5/51)-Photo-c | 8.00 | 24.00 | 55.00 |
| 330-Porky Pig Meets the Bristled Bruiser (No. 2) | 3.00 | 9.00 | 21.00 |
| 331-Alice in Wonderland (Disney) (1951) | 8.50 | 25.50 | 60.00 |
| 332-Little Beaver | 2.30 | 7.00 | 16.00 |
| 333-Wilderness Trek (Zane Grey) (5/51) | 3.70 | 11.00 | 26.00 |
| 334-Mickey Mouse and Yukon Gold (Disney) (6/51) | 5.70 | 17.00 | 40.00 |
| 335-Francis the Famous Talking Mule (No. 1) | 2.00 | 6.00 | 14.00 |
| 336-Woody Woodpecker (Lantz) | 2.30 | 7.00 | 16.00 |
| 337-The Brownies-not by Walt Kelly | 2.65 | 8.00 | 18.00 |
| 338-Bugs Bunny and the Rocking Horse Thieves | 3.70 | 11.00 | 26.00 |
| 339-Donald Duck and the Magic Fountain-not by Carl Barks (Disney) (7-8/51) | 4.35 | 13.00 | 30.00 |
| 340-King of the Royal Mounted (7/51) | 5.00 | 15.00 | 35.00 |
| 341-Unbirthday Party with Alice in Wonderland (Disney) (7/51) | 8.50 | 25.50 | 60.00 |
| 342-Porky Pig the Lucky Peppermint Mine | 2.30 | 7.00 | 16.00 |
| 343-Mickey Mouse in The Ruby Eye of Homar-Guy-Am (Disney)-Reprinted in Mickey Mouse No. 104 | 4.30 | 13.00 | 30.00 |
| 344-Sergeant Preston from Challenge of The Yukon (No. 1)(TV) | 6.50 | 19.00 | 45.00 |
| 345-Andy Panda in Scotland Yard (8-10/51)(Lantz) | 2.00 | 6.00 | 14.00 |
| 346-Hideout (Zane Grey) | 3.70 | 11.00 | 26.00 |
| 347-Bugs Bunny the Frigid Hare (8-9/51) | 3.70 | 11.00 | 26.00 |
| 348-Donald Duck "The Crocodile Collector"-Barks-c only (Disney) (9-10/51) | 6.50 | 19.00 | 45.00 |
| 349-Uncle Wiggily | 3.00 | 9.00 | 21.00 |
| 350-Woody Woodpecker (Lantz) | 2.30 | 7.00 | 16.00 |
| 351-Porky Pig and the Grand Canyon Giant (9-10/51) | 2.30 | 7.00 | 16.00 |
| 352-Mickey Mouse in The Mystery of Painted Valley (Disney) | 4.30 | 13.00 | 30.00 |
| 353-Duck Album (No.1)-Barks-c (Disney) | 3.00 | 9.00 | 21.00 |
| 354-Raggedy Ann & Andy | 3.00 | 9.00 | 21.00 |
| 355-Bugs Bunny Hot-Rod Hare | 3.70 | 11.00 | 26.00 |
| 356-Donald Duck in "Rags to Riches"-Barks-c only (Disney) | 6.50 | 19.00 | 45.00 |
| 357-Comeback (Zane Grey) | 3.00 | 9.00 | 21.00 |
| 358-Andy Panda (Lantz)(11-1/52) | 2.00 | 6.00 | 14.00 |
| 359-Frosty the Snowman (No.1) | 3.00 | 9.00 | 21.00 |
| 360-Porky Pig in Tree of Fortune (11-12/51) | 2.30 | 7.00 | 16.00 |
| 361-Santa Claus Funnies | 2.30 | 7.00 | 16.00 |
| 362-Mickey Mouse and the Smuggled Diamonds (Disney) | 4.30 | 13.00 | 30.00 |
| 363-King of the Royal Mounted | 4.00 | 12.00 | 28.00 |
| 364-Woody Woodpecker (Lantz) | 1.70 | 5.00 | 12.00 |
| 365-The Brownies-not by Kelly | 2.65 | 8.00 | 18.00 |
| 366-Bugs Bunny Uncle Buckskin Comes to Town (12-1/52) | 3.70 | 11.00 | 26.00 |
| 367-Donald Duck in "A Christmas for Shacktown" by Carl Barks (Disney) (1-2/52) | 20.00 | 60.00 | 150.00 |
| 368-Bob Clampett's Beany and Cecil (No.1) | 13.00 | 40.00 | 90.00 |
| 369-The Lone Ranger's Famous Horse Hi-Yo Silver (No.1); Silver's origin | 6.50 | 19.00 | 45.00 |
| 370-Porky Pig in Trouble in the Big Trees | 2.30 | 7.00 | 16.00 |
| 371-Mickey Mouse in The Inca Idol Case ('52) (Disney) | 4.30 | 13.00 | 30.00 |
| 372-Riders of the Purple Sage (Zane Grey) | 3.00 | 9.00 | 21.00 |
| 373-Sergeant Preston (TV) | 4.00 | 12.00 | 28.00 |
| 374-Woody Woodpecker (Lantz) | 1.70 | 5.00 | 12.00 |
| 375-John Carter of Mars (E. R. Burroughs)-Jesse Marsh-a; origin | | | |

| | Good | Fine | N-Mint |
|---|---|---|---|
| | 14.00 | 43.00 | 100.00 |
| 376-Bugs Bunny, "The Magic Sneeze" | 3.70 | 11.00 | 26.00 |
| 377-Susie Q. Smith | 1.50 | 4.50 | 10.00 |
| 378-Tom Corbett, Space Cadet (No.1)(TV)-McWilliams-a | 8.50 | 25.50 | 60.00 |
| 379-Donald Duck in "Southern Hospitality"-not by Barks (Disney) | 4.35 | 13.00 | 30.00 |
| 380-Raggedy Ann & Andy | 3.00 | 9.00 | 21.00 |
| 381-Marge's Tubby (No.1) | 11.00 | 36.00 | 84.00 |
| 382-Snow White and the Seven Dwarfs (Disney)-origin; partial reprint of 4-Color No. 49 (Movie) | 5.00 | 15.00 | 35.00 |
| 383-Andy Panda (Lantz) | 1.30 | 4.00 | 9.00 |
| 384-King of the Royal Mounted (3/52)(Zane Grey) | 4.00 | 12.00 | 28.00 |
| 385-Porky Pig in The Isle of Missing Ships (3-4/52) | 2.30 | 7.00 | 16.00 |
| 386-Uncle Scrooge No. 1 by Carl Barks (Disney) in "Only a Poor Old Man" (3/52) | 60.00 | 180.00 | 450.00 |
| 387-Mickey Mouse in High Tibet (Disney) (4-5/52) | 4.30 | 13.00 | 30.00 |
| 388-Oswald the Rabbit (Lantz) | 2.00 | 6.00 | 14.00 |
| 389-Andy Hardy Comics (No.1) | 2.00 | 6.00 | 14.00 |
| 390-Woody Woodpecker (Lantz) | 1.70 | 5.00 | 12.00 |
| 391-Uncle Wiggily | 2.65 | 8.00 | 18.00 |
| 392-Hi-Yo Silver | 3.00 | 9.00 | 21.00 |
| 393-Bugs Bunny | 3.70 | 11.00 | 26.00 |
| 394-Donald Duck in Malayalaya-Barks-c only (Disney) | 6.50 | 19.00 | 45.00 |
| 395-Forlorn River (Zane Grey) (1952)-First Nevada (5/52) | 3.00 | 9.00 | 21.00 |
| 396-Tales of the Texas Rangers (No.1)(TV)-Photo-c | 6.00 | 18.00 | 42.00 |
| 397-Sergeant Preston of the Yukon (TV)(5/52) | 4.00 | 12.00 | 28.00 |
| 398-The Brownies-not by Kelly | 2.65 | 8.00 | 18.00 |
| 399-Porky Pig in The Lost Gold Mine | 2.30 | 7.00 | 16.00 |
| 400-Tom Corbett, Space Cadet (TV)-McWilliams-c/a | 6.50 | 19.00 | 45.00 |
| 401-Mickey Mouse and Goofy's Mechanical Wizard (Disney) (6-7/52) | 3.50 | 10.50 | 24.00 |
| 402-Mary Jane and Sniffles | 7.00 | 21.00 | 50.00 |
| 403-Li'l Bad Wolf (Disney) (6/52) | 2.30 | 7.00 | 16.00 |
| 404-The Range Rider (No.1)(TV)-Photo-c | 6.50 | 19.00 | 45.00 |
| 405-Woody Woodpecker (Lantz) (6-7/52) | 1.70 | 5.00 | 12.00 |
| 406-Tweety and Sylvester (No.1) | 2.00 | 6.00 | 14.00 |
| 407-Bugs Bunny, Foreign-Legion Hare | 2.65 | 8.00 | 18.00 |
| 408-Donald Duck and the Golden Helmet by Carl Barks (Disney) (7-8/52) | 20.00 | 60.00 | 150.00 |
| 409-Andy Panda (7-9/52) | 1.30 | 4.00 | 9.00 |
| 410-Porky Pig in The Water Wizard (7/52) | 2.30 | 7.00 | 16.00 |
| 411-Mickey Mouse and the Old Sea Dog (Disney) (8-9/52) | 3.50 | 10.50 | 24.00 |
| 412-Nevada (Zane Grey) | 3.00 | 9.00 | 21.00 |
| 413-Robin Hood (Disney-Movie) (8/52)-Photo-c | 3.50 | 10.50 | 24.00 |
| 414-Bob Clampett's Beany and Cecil (TV) | 10.00 | 30.00 | 70.00 |
| 415-Rootie Kazootie (No. 1)(TV) | 5.00 | 15.00 | 35.00 |
| 416-Woody Woodpecker (Lantz) | 1.70 | 5.00 | 12.00 |
| 417-Double Trouble with Goober (No. 1; 8/52) | 1.50 | 4.50 | 10.00 |
| 418-Rusty Riley, a Boy, a Horse, and a Dog (No. 1)-Frank Godwin-a (strip reprints) (8/52) | 2.00 | 6.00 | 14.00 |
| 419-Sergeant Preston (TV) | 4.00 | 12.00 | 28.00 |
| 420-Bugs Bunny in The Mysterious Buckaroo (8-9/52) | 2.65 | 8.00 | 18.00 |
| 421-Tom Corbett, Space Cadet (TV)-McWilliams-a | 6.50 | 19.00 | 45.00 |
| 422-Donald Duck and the Gilded Man, by Carl Barks (Disney) (9-10/52) (No.423 on inside) | 20.00 | 60.00 | 150.00 |

| | Good | Fine | N-Mint |
|---|---|---|---|
| 423-Rhubarb, Owner of the Brooklyn Ball Club (The Millionaire Cat) (No. 1) | 1.15 | 3.50 | 8.00 |
| 424-Flash Gordon-Test Flight in Space (9/52) | 6.50 | 19.50 | 45.00 |
| 425-Zorro, the Return of | 10.00 | 30.00 | 70.00 |
| 426-Porky Pig in The Scalawag Leprechaun | 2.30 | 7.00 | 16.00 |
| 427-Mickey Mouse and the Wonderful Whizzix (Disney) (10-11/52)-reprinted in Mickey Mouse No. 100 | 3.50 | 10.50 | 24.00 |
| 428-Uncle Wiggily | 2.30 | 7.00 | 16.00 |
| 429-Pluto in "Why Dogs Leave Home" (Disney)(10/52) | 3.50 | 10.50 | 24.00 |
| 430-Marge's Tubby, the Shadow of a Man-Eater | 7.00 | 21.00 | 50.00 |
| 431-Woody Woodpecker (10/52)(Lantz) | 1.70 | 5.00 | 12.00 |
| 432-Bugs Bunny and the Rabbit Olympics | 2.65 | 8.00 | 18.00 |
| 433-Wildfire (Zane Grey) | 3.00 | 9.00 | 21.00 |
| 434-Rin Tin Tin-"In Dark Danger" (No. 1)(TV)(11/52)-Photo-c | 6.00 | 18.00 | 42.00 |
| 435-Frosty the Snowman | 2.30 | 7.00 | 16.00 |
| 436-The Brownies-not by Kelly (11/52) | 2.30 | 7.00 | 16.00 |
| 437-John Carter of Mars (E. R. Burroughs)-Marsh-a | 12.00 | 36.00 | 85.00 |
| 438-Annie Oakley (No. 1) (TV) | 8.50 | 25.50 | 60.00 |
| 439-Little Hiawatha (Disney) (12/52) | 2.30 | 7.00 | 16.00 |
| 440-Black Beauty (12/52) | 1.70 | 5.00 | 12.00 |
| 441-Fearless Fagan | 1.15 | 3.50 | 8.00 |
| 442-Peter Pan (Disney) (Movie) | 5.00 | 15.00 | 35.00 |
| 443-Ben Bowie and His Mountain Men (No.1) | 4.00 | 12.00 | 28.00 |
| 444-Marge's Tubby | 7.00 | 21.00 | 50.00 |
| 445-Charlie McCarthy | 2.65 | 8.00 | 18.00 |
| 446-Captain Hook and Peter Pan (Disney) (Movie) (1/53) | 5.00 | 15.00 | 35.00 |
| 447-Andy Hardy Comics | 1.15 | 3.50 | 8.00 |
| 448-Bob Clampett's Beany and Cecil (TV) | 10.00 | 30.00 | 70.00 |
| 449-Tappan's Burro (Zane Grey) (2-4/53) | 3.00 | 9.00 | 21.00 |
| 450-Duck Album-Barks-c (Disney) | 2.65 | 8.00 | 18.00 |
| 451-Rusty Riley-Frank Godwin-a (strip reprints) (2/53) | 1.70 | 5.00 | 12.00 |
| 452-Raggedy Ann & Andy ('53) | 3.00 | 9.00 | 21.00 |
| 453-Susie Q. Smith (2/53) | 1.30 | 4.00 | 9.00 |
| 454-Krazy Kat Comics-not by Herriman | 2.30 | 7.00 | 16.00 |
| 455-Johnny Mack Brown Comics(3/53)-Photo-c | 3.50 | 10.50 | 24.00 |
| 456-Uncle Scrooge Back to the Klondike (No. 2) by Barks (3/53) (Disney) | 29.00 | 86.00 | 215.00 |
| 457-Daffy (No. 1) | 2.65 | 8.00 | 18.00 |
| 458-Oswald the Rabbit (Lantz) | 1.30 | 4.00 | 9.00 |
| 459-Rootie Kazootie (TV) | 4.00 | 12.00 | 28.00 |
| 460-Buck Jones (4/53) | 3.50 | 10.50 | 24.00 |
| 461-Marge's Tubby | 6.50 | 19.50 | 45.00 |
| 462-Little Scouts | .85 | 2.50 | 6.00 |
| 463-Petunia (4/53) | 1.30 | 4.00 | 9.00 |
| 464-Bozo (4/53) | 5.70 | 17.00 | 40.00 |
| 465-Francis the Famous Talking Mule | 1.15 | 3.50 | 8.00 |
| 466-Rhubarb, the Millionaire Cat | .85 | 2.50 | 6.00 |
| 467-Desert Gold (Zane Grey) (5-7/53) | 3.00 | 9.00 | 21.00 |
| 468-Goofy (No. 1) (Disney) | 3.00 | 9.00 | 21.00 |
| 469-Beetle Bailey (No. 1)(5/53) | 5.70 | 17.00 | 40.00 |
| 470-Elmer Fudd | 1.15 | 3.50 | 8.00 |
| 471-Double Trouble with Goober | 1.00 | 3.00 | 7.00 |
| 472-Wild Bill Elliott (6/53)-Photo-c | 4.50 | 14.00 | 32.00 |
| 473-Li'l Bad Wolf (Disney)(6/53) | 2.00 | 6.00 | 14.00 |
| 474-Mary Jane and Sniffles | 6.00 | 18.00 | 42.00 |
| 475-M.G.M.'s The Two Mouseketeers (No. 1) | 1.50 | 4.50 | 10.00 |
| 476-Rin Tin Tin (TV)-Photo-c | 4.30 | 13.00 | 30.00 |
| 477-Bob Clampett's Beany and Cecil (TV) | 10.00 | 30.00 | 70.00 |
| 478-Charlie McCarthy | 2.65 | 8.00 | 18.00 |

*Four Color #379, © The Disney Co.*

*Four Color #445, © Edgar Bergen*

*Four Color #469, © KING*

Four Color #499, © M.G.M.

Four Color #551, © Capitol Records

Four Color #570, © Bob Clampett

| | Good | Fine | N-Mint |
|---|---|---|---|
| 479-Queen of the West Dale Evans (No. 1) | 8.00 | 24.00 | 56.00 |
| 480-Andy Hardy Comics | 1.15 | 3.50 | 8.00 |
| 481-Annie Oakley And Tagg (TV) | 5.30 | 16.00 | 38.00 |
| 482-Brownies-not by Kelly | 2.30 | 7.00 | 16.00 |
| 483-Little Beaver (7/53) | 2.00 | 6.00 | 14.00 |
| 484-River Feud (Zane Grey) (8-10/53) | 3.00 | 9.00 | 21.00 |
| 485-The Little People-Walt Scott (No. 1) | 2.65 | 8.00 | 18.00 |
| 486-Rusty Riley-Frank Godwin strip-r | 1.70 | 5.00 | 12.00 |
| 487-Mowgli, the Jungle Book (Rudyard Kipling's) | 2.65 | 8.00 | 18.00 |
| 488-John Carter of Mars (Burroughs)-Marsh-a | 12.00 | 36.00 | 85.00 |
| 489-Tweety and Sylvester | 1.15 | 3.50 | 8.00 |
| 490-Jungle Jim (No. 1) | 2.65 | 8.00 | 18.00 |
| 491-Silvertip (#1) (Max Brand)-Kinstler-a (8/53) | 4.00 | 12.00 | 28.00 |
| 492-Duck Album (Disney) | 2.00 | 6.00 | 14.00 |
| 493-Johnny Mack Brown-Photo-c | 3.50 | 10.50 | 24.00 |
| 494-The Little King (No. 1) | 5.00 | 15.00 | 35.00 |
| 495-Uncle Scrooge (No. 3)(Disney)-by Carl Barks (9/53) | 26.00 | 77.00 | 215.00 |
| 496-The Green Hornet | 11.50 | 34.00 | 80.00 |
| 497-Zorro (Sword of. . .) | 10.00 | 30.00 | 70.00 |
| 498-Bugs Bunny's Album (9/53) | 1.70 | 5.00 | 12.00 |
| 499-M.G.M.'s Spike and Tyke (No. 1)(9/53) | 1.30 | 4.00 | 9.00 |
| 500-Buck Jones | 3.50 | 10.50 | 24.00 |
| 501-Francis the Famous Talking Mule | 1.15 | 3.50 | 8.00 |
| 502-Rootie Kazootie (TV) | 4.00 | 12.00 | 28.00 |
| 503-Uncle Wiggily (10/53) | 2.30 | 7.00 | 16.00 |
| 504-Krazy Kat-not by Herriman | 2.30 | 7.00 | 16.00 |
| 505-The Sword and the Rose (Disney) (10/53) (TV)-Photo-c | 3.50 | 10.50 | 24.00 |
| 506-The Little Scouts | .85 | 2.50 | 6.00 |
| 507-Oswald the Rabbit (Lantz) | 1.30 | 4.00 | 9.00 |
| 508-Bozo (10/53) | 5.70 | 17.00 | 40.00 |
| 509-Pluto (Disney) (10/53) | 3.50 | 10.50 | 24.00 |
| 510-Son of Black Beauty | 1.70 | 5.00 | 12.00 |
| 511-Outlaw Trail (Zane Grey)-Kinstler-a | 3.50 | 10.50 | 24.00 |
| 512-Flash Gordon (11/53) | 3.50 | 10.50 | 24.00 |
| 513-Ben Bowie and His Mountain Men | 2.30 | 7.00 | 16.00 |
| 514-Frosty the Snowman (11/53) | 2.00 | 6.00 | 14.00 |
| 515-Andy Hardy | 1.15 | 3.50 | 8.00 |
| 516-Double Trouble With Goober | 1.00 | 3.00 | 7.00 |
| 517-Chip 'N' Dale (No.1)(Disney) | 2.00 | 6.00 | 14.00 |
| 518-Rivets (11/53) | 1.15 | 3.50 | 8.00 |
| 519-Steve Canyon (No.1)-not by Milton Caniff | 4.00 | 12.00 | 28.00 |
| 520-Wild Bill Elliott-Photo-c | 4.50 | 14.00 | 32.00 |
| 521-Beetle Bailey (12/53) | 2.85 | 8.50 | 20.00 |
| 522-The Brownies | 2.30 | 7.00 | 16.00 |
| 523-Rin Tin Tin (TV)-Photo-c (12/53) | 4.30 | 13.00 | 30.00 |
| 524-Tweety and Sylvester | 1.15 | 3.50 | 8.00 |
| 525-Santa Claus Funnies | 1.70 | 5.00 | 12.00 |
| 526-Napoleon | 1.15 | 3.50 | 8.00 |
| 527-Charlie McCarthy | 2.65 | 8.00 | 18.00 |
| 528-Queen of the West Dale Evans-Photo-c | 5.70 | 17.00 | 40.00 |
| 529-Little Beaver | 2.00 | 6.00 | 14.00 |
| 530-Bob Clampett's Beany and Cecil (TV) (1/54) | 10.00 | 30.00 | 70.00 |
| 531-Duck Album (Disney) | 2.00 | 6.00 | 14.00 |
| 532-The Rustlers (Zane Grey) (2-4/54) | 3.00 | 9.00 | 21.00 |
| 533-Raggedy Ann and Andy | 3.00 | 9.00 | 21.00 |
| 534-Western Marshal (Ernest Haycox's)-Kinstler-a | 3.50 | 10.50 | 24.00 |
| 535-I Love Lucy (No. 1)(TV) (2/54)-photo-c | 18.00 | 54.00 | 125.00 |
| 536-Daffy (3/54) | 1.70 | 5.00 | 12.00 |
| 537-Stormy, the Thoroughbred . . . (Disney-Movie) on top ⅔ of each page; Pluto story on bottom ⅓ of each page (2/54) | 2.30 | 7.00 | 16.00 |

| | Good | Fine | N-Mint |
|---|---|---|---|
| 538-The Mask of Zorro-Kinstler-a | 11.00 | 32.00 | 75.00 |
| 539-Ben and Me (Disney) (3/54) | 1.50 | 4.50 | 10.00 |
| 540-Knights of the Round Table (3/54) (Movie)-Photo-c | 3.70 | 11.00 | 26.00 |
| 541-Johnny Mack Brown-Photo-c | 3.50 | 10.50 | 24.00 |
| 542-Super Circus Featuring Mary Hartline (TV) (3/54) | 3.00 | 9.00 | 21.00 |
| 543-Uncle Wiggily (3/54) | 2.30 | 7.00 | 16.00 |
| 544-Rob Roy (Disney-Movie)-Manning-a; photo-c | 5.70 | 17.00 | 40.00 |
| 545-The Wonderful Adventures of Pinocchio-Partial reprint of 4-Color #92 (Disney-Movie) | 3.00 | 9.00 | 21.00 |
| 546-Buck Jones | 3.50 | 10.50 | 24.00 |
| 547-Francis the Famous Talking Mule | 1.15 | 3.50 | 8.00 |
| 548-Krazy Kat-not by Herriman (4/54) | 2.00 | 6.00 | 14.00 |
| 549-Oswald the Rabbit (Lantz) | 1.30 | 4.00 | 9.00 |
| 550-The Little Scouts | .85 | 2.50 | 6.00 |
| 551-Bozo (4/54) | 5.70 | 17.00 | 40.00 |
| 552-Beetle Bailey | 2.85 | 8.50 | 20.00 |
| 553-Susie Q. Smith | 1.30 | 4.00 | 9.00 |
| 554-Rusty Riley (Frank Godwin strip-r) | 1.75 | 5.25 | 12.00 |
| 555-Range War (Zane Grey) | 3.00 | 9.00 | 21.00 |
| 556-Double Trouble With Goober (5/54) | 1.00 | 3.00 | 7.00 |
| 557-Ben Bowie and His Mountain Men | 2.30 | 7.00 | 16.00 |
| 558-Elmer Fudd (5/54) | 1.15 | 3.50 | 8.00 |
| 559-I Love Lucy (No. 2)(TV)-Photo-c | 13.00 | 40.00 | 90.00 |
| 560-Duck Album (Disney)(5/54) | 2.00 | 6.00 | 14.00 |
| 561-Mr. Magoo (5/54) | 5.00 | 15.00 | 35.00 |
| 562-Goofy (Disney) | 2.30 | 7.00 | 16.00 |
| 563-Rhubarb, the Millionaire Cat (6/54) | .85 | 2.50 | 6.00 |
| 564-Li'l Bad Wolf (Disney) | 1.70 | 5.00 | 12.00 |
| 565-Jungle Jim | 2.00 | 6.00 | 14.00 |
| 566-Son of Black Beauty | 1.75 | 5.25 | 12.00 |
| 567-Prince Valiant (No.1)-by Bob Fuje (Movie)-Photo-c | 5.70 | 17.00 | 40.00 |
| 568-Gypsy Colt (Movie) | 2.65 | 8.00 | 18.00 |
| 569-Priscilla's Pop | 1.50 | 4.50 | 10.00 |
| 570-Bob Clampett's Beany and Cecil (TV) | 10.00 | 30.00 | 70.00 |
| 571-Charlie McCarthy | 2.65 | 8.00 | 18.00 |
| 572-Silvertip (Max Brand)(7/54); Kinstler-a | 3.50 | 10.50 | 24.00 |
| 573-The Little People by Walt Scott | 2.00 | 6.00 | 14.00 |
| 574-The Hand of Zorro | 10.00 | 30.00 | 70.00 |
| 575-Annie Oakley and Tagg(TV)-Photo-c | 5.30 | 16.00 | 38.00 |
| 576-Angel (No.1) (8/54) | 1.15 | 3.50 | 8.00 |
| 577-M.G.M.'s Spike and Tyke | 1.00 | 3.00 | 7.00 |
| 578-Steve Canyon (8/54) | 3.50 | 10.50 | 24.00 |
| 579-Francis the Famous Talking Mule | 1.15 | 3.50 | 8.00 |
| 580-Six Gun Ranch (Luke Short-8/54) | 2.30 | 7.00 | 16.00 |
| 581-Chip 'N' Dale (Disney) | 1.30 | 4.00 | 9.00 |
| 582-Mowgli Jungle Book (Kipling)(8/54) | 2.30 | 7.00 | 16.00 |
| 583-The Lost Wagon Train (Zane Grey) | 3.00 | 9.00 | 21.00 |
| 584-Johnny Mack Brown-Photo-c | 3.50 | 10.50 | 24.00 |
| 585-Bugs Bunny's Album | 1.70 | 5.00 | 12.00 |
| 586-Duck Album (Disney) | 2.00 | 6.00 | 14.00 |
| 587-The Little Scouts | .85 | 2.50 | 6.00 |
| 588-King Richard and the Crusaders (Movie) (10/54) Matt Baker-a; photo-c | 8.00 | 24.00 | 56.00 |
| 589-Buck Jones | 3.50 | 10.50 | 24.00 |
| 590-Hansel and Gretel; partial photo-c | 3.70 | 11.00 | 26.00 |
| 591-Western Marshal (Ernest Haycox's)-Kinstler-a | 3.50 | 10.50 | 24.00 |
| 592-Super Circus (TV) | 3.00 | 9.00 | 21.00 |
| 593-Oswald the Rabbit (Lantz) | 1.30 | 4.00 | 9.00 |
| 594-Bozo (10/54) | 5.70 | 17.00 | 40.00 |
| 595-Pluto (Disney) | 2.30 | 7.00 | 16.00 |
| 596-Turok, Son of Stone (No.1) | 27.00 | 81.00 | 190.00 |

| | Good | Fine | N-Mint |
|---|---|---|---|
| 597-The Little King | 3.50 | 10.50 | 24.00 |
| 598-Captain Davy Jones | 1.70 | 5.00 | 12.00 |
| 599-Ben Bowie and His Mountain Men | 2.30 | 7.00 | 16.00 |
| 600-Daisy Duck's Diary (No.1)(Disney)(11/54) | 2.00 | 6.00 | 14.00 |
| 601-Frosty the Snowman | 2.00 | 6.00 | 14.00 |
| 602-Mr. Magoo and Gerald McBoing-Boing | 5.00 | 15.00 | 35.00 |
| 603-M.G.M.'s The Two Mouseketeers | 1.00 | 3.00 | 7.00 |
| 604-Shadow on the Trail (Zane Grey) | 3.00 | 9.00 | 21.00 |
| 605-The Brownies-not by Kelly (12/54) | 2.30 | 7.00 | 16.00 |
| 606-Sir Lancelot (not TV) | 6.50 | 19.50 | 45.00 |
| 607-Santa Claus Funnies | 1.70 | 5.00 | 12.00 |
| 608-Silvertip-"Valley of Vanishing Men" (Max Brand)-Kinstler-a | 3.50 | 10.50 | 24.00 |
| 609-The Littlest Outlaw (Disney-Movie) (1/55)-Photo-c | 3.00 | 9.00 | 21.00 |
| 610-Drum Beat (Movie); Alan Ladd photo-c | 8.00 | 24.00 | 55.00 |
| 611-Duck Album (Disney) | 2.00 | 6.00 | 14.00 |
| 612-Little Beaver (1/55) | 1.50 | 4.50 | 10.00 |
| 613-Western Marshal (Ernest Haycox's) (2/55)-Kinstler-a | 3.50 | 10.50 | 24.00 |
| 614-20,000 Leagues Under the Sea (Disney) (Movie) (2/55) | 3.50 | 10.50 | 24.00 |
| 615-Daffy | 1.70 | 5.00 | 12.00 |
| 616-To the Last Man (Zane Grey) | 3.00 | 9.00 | 21.00 |
| 617-The Quest of Zorro | 10.00 | 30.00 | 70.00 |
| 618-Johnny Mack Brown-Photo-c | 3.50 | 10.50 | 24.00 |
| 619-Krazy Kat-not by Herriman | 2.00 | 6.00 | 14.00 |
| 620-Mowgli Jungle Book (Kipling) | 2.30 | 7.00 | 16.00 |
| 621-Francis the Famous Talking Mule | 1.00 | 3.00 | 7.00 |
| 622-Beetle Bailey | 2.85 | 8.50 | 20.00 |
| 623-Oswald the Rabbit (Lantz) | .85 | 2.50 | 6.00 |
| 624-Treasure Island (Disney-Movie) (4/55)-Photo-c | 3.00 | 9.00 | 21.00 |
| 625-Beaver Valley (Disney-Movie) | 2.00 | 6.00 | 14.00 |
| 626-Ben Bowie and His Mountain Men | 2.30 | 7.00 | 16.00 |
| 627-Goofy (Disney) (5/55) | 2.30 | 7.00 | 16.00 |
| 628-Elmer Fudd | 1.15 | 3.50 | 8.00 |
| 629-Lady and the Tramp with Jock (Disney) | 2.00 | 6.00 | 14.00 |
| 630-Priscilla's Pop | 1.15 | 3.50 | 8.00 |
| 631-Davy Crockett, Indian Fighter (No.1)(Disney)(5/55)(TV)-Fess Parker photo-c | 4.30 | 13.00 | 30.00 |
| 632-Fighting Caravans (Zane Grey) | 3.00 | 9.00 | 21.00 |
| 633-The Little People by Walt Scott (6/55) | 2.00 | 6.00 | 14.00 |
| 634-Lady and the Tramp Album (Disney) (6/55) | 1.70 | 5.00 | 12.00 |
| 635-Bob Clampett's Beany and Cecil (TV) | 10.00 | 30.00 | 70.00 |
| 636-Chip 'N' Dale (Disney) | 1.30 | 4.00 | 9.00 |
| 637-Silvertip (Max Brand)-Kinstler-a | 3.50 | 10.50 | 24.00 |
| 638-M.G.M.'s Spike and Tyke (8/55) | 1.00 | 3.00 | 7.00 |
| 639-Davy Crockett at the Alamo (Disney) (7/55)(TV)-Fess Parker photo-c | 4.00 | 12.00 | 28.00 |
| 640-Western Marshal (Ernest Haycox's)-Kinstler-a | 3.50 | 10.50 | 24.00 |
| 641-Steve Canyon ('55)-by Caniff | 3.50 | 10.50 | 24.00 |
| 642-M.G.M.'s The Two Mouseketeers | 1.00 | 3.00 | 7.00 |
| 643-Wild Bill Elliott-Photo-c | 3.70 | 11.00 | 26.00 |
| 644-Sir Walter Raleigh (5/55)-Based on movie "The Virgin Queen;" photo-c | 4.50 | 14.00 | 32.00 |
| 645-Johnny Mack Brown-Photo-c | 3.50 | 10.50 | 24.00 |
| 646-Dotty Dripple and Taffy (No.1) | 1.70 | 5.00 | 12.00 |
| 647-Bugs Bunny's Album (9/55) | 1.70 | 5.00 | 12.00 |
| 648-Jace Pearson of the Texas Rangers (TV)-Photo-c | 4.00 | 12.00 | 28.00 |
| 649-Duck Album (Disney) | 2.00 | 6.00 | 14.00 |
| 650-Prince Valiant - by Bob Fuje | 3.50 | 10.50 | 24.00 |
| 651-King Colt (Luke Short)(9/55)-Kinstler-a | 3.00 | 9.00 | 21.00 |
| 652-Buck Jones | 2.30 | 7.00 | 16.00 |

| | Good | Fine | N-Mint |
|---|---|---|---|
| 653-Smokey the Bear (No.1) (10/55) | 3.00 | 9.00 | 21.00 |
| 654-Pluto (Disney) | 2.30 | 7.00 | 16.00 |
| 655-Francis the Famous Talking Mule | 1.00 | 3.00 | 7.00 |
| 656-Turok, Son of Stone (No.2) (10/55) | 19.00 | 58.00 | 135.00 |
| 657-Ben Bowie and His Mountain Men | 2.30 | 7.00 | 16.00 |
| 658-Goofy (Disney) | 2.30 | 7.00 | 16.00 |
| 659-Daisy Duck's Diary (Disney) | 1.70 | 5.00 | 12.00 |
| 660-Little Beaver | 1.50 | 4.50 | 10.00 |
| 661-Frosty the Snowman | 2.00 | 6.00 | 14.00 |
| 662-Zoo Parade (TV)-Marlin Perkins (11/55) | 3.00 | 9.00 | 21.00 |
| 663-Winky Dink (TV) | 4.00 | 12.00 | 28.00 |
| 664-Davy Crockett in the Great Keelboat Race (TV) (Disney)(11/55)-Fess Parker photo-c | 4.50 | 14.00 | 32.00 |
| 665-The African Lion (Disney-Movie) (11/55) | 2.30 | 7.00 | 16.00 |
| 666-Santa Claus Funnies | 1.70 | 5.00 | 12.00 |
| 667-Silvertip and the Stolen Stallion (Max Brand) (12/55)-Kinstler-a | 3.50 | 10.50 | 24.00 |
| 668-Dumbo (Disney) (12/55) | 3.50 | 10.50 | 24.00 |
| 668-Dumbo (Disney) (1/58) different cover, same contents | 3.50 | 10.50 | 24.00 |
| 669-Robin Hood (Disney-Movie) (12/55)-reprint of No. 413-Photo-c | 2.30 | 7.00 | 16.00 |
| 670-M.G.M's Mouse Musketeers (No.1)(1/56)-Formerly the Two Mouseketeers | 1.00 | 3.00 | 7.00 |
| 671-Davy Crockett and the River Pirates (TV) (Disney) (12/55)-Jesse Marsh-a; Fess Parker photo-c | 4.50 | 14.00 | 32.00 |
| 672-Quentin Durward (1/56)(Movie)-Photo-c | 3.70 | 11.00 | 26.00 |
| 673-Buffalo Bill, Jr. (No.1)(TV)-Photo-c | 4.30 | 13.00 | 30.00 |
| 674-The Little Rascals (No.1) (TV) | 2.30 | 7.00 | 16.00 |
| 675-Steve Donovan, Western Marshal (No.1)(TV)-Kinstler-a; photo-c | 5.00 | 15.00 | 35.00 |
| 676-Will-Yum! | 1.50 | 4.50 | 10.00 |
| 677-Little King | 3.00 | 9.00 | 21.00 |
| 678-The Last Hunt (Movie)-Photo-c | 3.70 | 11.00 | 26.00 |
| 679-Gunsmoke (No.1) (TV) | 7.00 | 21.00 | 50.00 |
| 680-Out Our Way with the Worry Wart (2/56) | 1.50 | 4.50 | 10.00 |
| 681-Forever, Darling (Movie) with Lucille Ball & Desi Arnaz (2/56)-Photo-c | 7.00 | 21.00 | 50.00 |
| 682-When Knighthood Was in Flower (Disney-Movie)-Reprint of No. 505-Photo-c | 2.85 | 8.50 | 20.00 |
| 683-Hi and Lois (3/56) | 1.00 | 3.00 | 7.00 |
| 684-Helen of Troy (Movie)-Buscema-a; photo-c | 8.00 | 24.00 | 55.00 |
| 685-Johnny Mack Brown-Photo-c | 3.50 | 10.50 | 24.00 |
| 686-Duck Album (Disney) | 2.00 | 6.00 | 14.00 |
| 687-The Indian Fighter (Movie)-Kirk Douglas Photo-c | 3.50 | 10.50 | 24.00 |
| 688-Alexander the Great (Movie) (5/56) Buscema-a; photo-c | 4.00 | 12.00 | 28.00 |
| 689-Elmer Fudd (3/56) | 1.15 | 3.50 | 8.00 |
| 690-The Conqueror (Movie) - John Wayne photo-c | 11.50 | 34.00 | 80.00 |
| 691-Dotty Dripple and Taffy | 1.30 | 4.00 | 9.00 |
| 692-The Little People-Walt Scott | 1.70 | 5.00 | 12.00 |
| 693-Song of the South (Disney)(1956)-Partial reprint of No. 129 | 2.00 | 6.00 | 14.00 |
| 694-Super Circus (TV)-Photo-c | 3.00 | 9.00 | 21.00 |
| 695-Little Beaver | 1.50 | 4.50 | 10.00 |
| 696-Krazy Kat-not by Herriman (4/56) | 2.00 | 6.00 | 14.00 |
| 697-Oswald the Rabbit (Lantz) | .85 | 2.50 | 6.00 |
| 698-Francis the Famous Talking Mule (4/56) | 1.00 | 3.00 | 7.00 |
| 699-Prince Valiant-by Bob Fuje | 3.50 | 10.50 | 24.00 |
| 700-Water Birds and the Olympic Elk (Disney-Movie)(4/56) | 2.65 | 8.00 | 18.00 |
| 701-Jiminy Cricket (No.1)(Disney)(5/56) | 2.65 | 8.00 | 18.00 |
| 702-The Goofy Success Story (Disney) | 2.00 | 6.00 | 14.00 |
| 703-Scamp (No.1) (Disney) | 1.70 | 5.00 | 12.00 |

*Four Color #618, © DELL*

*Four Color #652, © DELL*

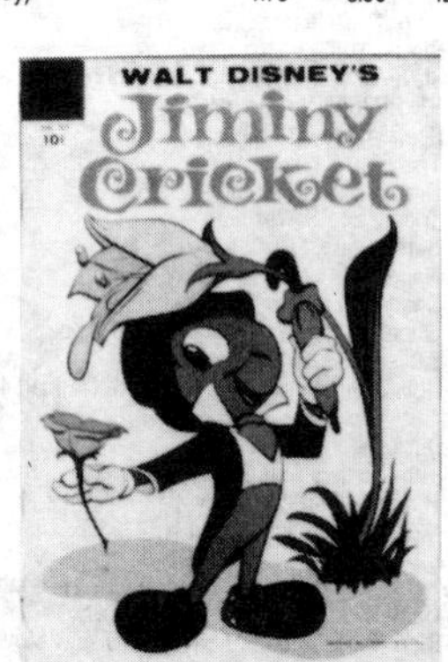

*Four Color #701, © The Disney Co.*

Four Color #732, © DELL

Four Color #768, © DELL

Four Color #805, © DELL

| | Good | Fine | N-Mint |
|---|---|---|---|
| 704-Priscilla's Pop (5/56) | 1.15 | 3.50 | 8.00 |
| 705-Brave Eagle (No.1) (TV)-Photo-c | 2.65 | 8.00 | 18.00 |
| 706-Bongo and Lumpjaw (Disney)(6/56) | 1.50 | 4.50 | 10.00 |
| 707-Corky and White Shadow (Disney)(5/56)-Mickey Mouse Club (TV)-Photo-c | 2.30 | 7.00 | 16.00 |
| 708-Smokey the Bear | 2.00 | 6.00 | 14.00 |
| 709-The Searchers (Movie) - John Wayne photo-c | 17.00 | 51.00 | 120.00 |
| 710-Francis the Famous Talking Mule | 1.00 | 3.00 | 7.00 |
| 711-M.G.M's Mouse Musketeers | .85 | 2.50 | 6.00 |
| 712-The Great Locomotive Chase (Disney-Movie) (9/56)-Photo-c | 3.50 | 10.50 | 24.00 |
| 713-The Animal World (Movie) (8/56) | 3.00 | 9.00 | 21.00 |
| 714-Spin and Marty (No.1)(TV)(Disney)-Mickey Mouse Club (6/56)-Photo-c | 4.50 | 14.00 | 32.00 |
| 715-Timmy (8/56) | 1.50 | 4.50 | 10.00 |
| 716-Man in Space (Disney-Movie) | 2.65 | 8.00 | 18.00 |
| 717-Moby Dick (Movie)-Photo-c | 5.00 | 15.00 | 35.00 |
| 718-Dotty Dripple and Taffy | 1.30 | 4.00 | 9.00 |
| 719-Prince Valiant - by Bob Fuje (8/56) | 3.50 | 10.50 | 24.00 |
| 720-Gunsmoke (TV)-Photo-c | 4.50 | 14.00 | 32.00 |
| 721-Captain Kangaroo (TV)-Photo-c | 9.30 | 28.00 | 65.00 |
| 722-Johnny Mack Brown-Photo-c | 3.50 | 10.50 | 24.00 |
| 723-Santiago (Movie)-Kinstler-a(9/56); Alan Ladd photo-c | 8.00 | 24.00 | 55.00 |
| 724-Bugs Bunny's Album | 1.70 | 5.00 | 12.00 |
| 725-Elmer Fudd (9/56) | .85 | 2.50 | 6.00 |
| 726-Duck Album (Disney) (9/56) | 1.70 | 5.00 | 12.00 |
| 727-The Nature of Things (TV) (Disney)-Jesse Marsh-a | 2.65 | 8.00 | 18.00 |
| 728-M.G.M's Mouse Musketeers | .85 | 2.50 | 6.00 |
| 729-Bob Son of Battle (11/56) | 1.70 | 5.00 | 12.00 |
| 730-Smokey Stover | 1.70 | 5.00 | 12.00 |
| 731-Silvertip and The Fighting Four (Max Brand)-Kinstler-a | 3.50 | 10.50 | 24.00 |
| 732-Zorro, the Challenge of (10/56) | 10.00 | 30.00 | 70.00 |
| 733-Buck Jones | 2.30 | 7.00 | 16.00 |
| 734-Cheyenne (No.1)(TV)(10/56)-Photo-c | 7.00 | 21.00 | 50.00 |
| 735-Crusader Rabbit (No. 1) (TV) | 8.00 | 24.00 | 55.00 |
| 736-Pluto (Disney) | 1.70 | 5.00 | 12.00 |
| 737-Steve Canyon-Caniff-a | 3.50 | 10.50 | 24.00 |
| 738-Westward Ho, the Wagons (Disney-Movie)-Fess Parker photo-c | 3.00 | 9.00 | 21.00 |
| 739-Bounty Guns (Luke Short)-Drucker-a | 2.30 | 7.00 | 16.00 |
| 740-Chilly Willy (No.1)(Walter Lantz) | 1.50 | 4.50 | 10.00 |
| 741-The Fastest Gun Alive (Movie) (9/56)-Photo-c | 4.00 | 12.00 | 28.00 |
| 742-Buffalo Bill, Jr. (TV)-Photo-c | 3.00 | 9.00 | 21.00 |
| 743-Daisy Duck's Diary (Disney) (11/56) | 1.70 | 5.00 | 12.00 |
| 744-Little Beaver | 1.50 | 4.50 | 10.00 |
| 745-Francis the Famous Talking Mule | 1.00 | 3.00 | 7.00 |
| 746-Dotty Dripple and Taffy | 1.30 | 4.00 | 9.00 |
| 747-Goofy (Disney) | 2.30 | 7.00 | 16.00 |
| 748-Frosty the Snowman (11/56) | 1.70 | 5.00 | 12.00 |
| 749-Secrets of Life (Disney-Movie)-Photo-c | 2.65 | 8.00 | 18.00 |
| 750-The Great Cat Family (Disney-Movie) | 3.00 | 9.00 | 21.00 |
| 751-Our Miss Brooks (TV)-Photo-c | 4.50 | 14.00 | 32.00 |
| 752-Mandrake, the Magician | 5.00 | 15.00 | 35.00 |
| 753-Walt Scott's Little People (11/56) | 1.70 | 5.00 | 12.00 |
| 754-Smokey the Bear | 2.00 | 6.00 | 14.00 |
| 755-The Littlest Snowman (12/56) | 2.15 | 6.50 | 16.00 |
| 756-Santa Claus Funnies | 1.70 | 5.00 | 12.00 |
| 757-The True Story of Jesse James (Movie)-Photo-c | 5.70 | 17.00 | 40.00 |
| 758-Bear Country (Disney-Movie) | 2.65 | 7.00 | 18.00 |
| 759-Circus Boy (TV)-The Monkees' Mickey Dolenz photo-c (12/56) | 7.00 | 21.00 | 50.00 |
| 760-The Hardy Boys (No. 1) (TV) (Disney)-Mickey Mouse Club-Photo-c | 5.70 | 17.00 | 40.00 |
| 761-Howdy Doody (TV) (1/57) | 5.70 | 17.00 | 40.00 |
| 762-The Sharkfighters (Movie)(1/57)(Scarce); Buscema-a; photo-c | 9.30 | 28.00 | 65.00 |
| 763-Grandma Duck's Farm Friends (No. 1) (Disney) | 2.30 | 7.00 | 16.00 |
| 764-M.G.M's Mouse Musketeers | .85 | 2.50 | 6.00 |
| 765-Will-Yum! | 1.15 | 3.50 | 8.00 |
| 766-Buffalo Bill, Jr. (TV)-Photo-c | 3.00 | 9.00 | 21.00 |
| 767-Spin and Marty (TV)(Disney)-Mickey Mouse Club (2/57) | 4.00 | 12.00 | 28.00 |
| 768-Steve Donovan, Western Marshal (TV)-Kinstler-a; photo-c | 4.00 | 12.00 | 28.00 |
| 769-Gunsmoke (TV) | 4.50 | 14.00 | 32.00 |
| 770-Brave Eagle (TV)-Photo-c | 1.70 | 5.00 | 12.00 |
| 771-Brand of Empire (Luke Short)(3/57)-Drucker-a | 2.30 | 7.00 | 16.00 |
| 772-Cheyenne (TV)-Photo-c | 4.30 | 13.00 | 30.00 |
| 773-The Brave One (Movie)-Photo-c | 2.65 | 8.00 | 18.00 |
| 774-Hi and Lois (3/57) | 1.00 | 3.00 | 7.00 |
| 775-Sir Lancelot and Brian (TV)-Buscema-a; photo-c | 7.00 | 21.00 | 50.00 |
| 776-Johnny Mack Brown-Photo-c | 3.50 | 10.50 | 24.00 |
| 777-Scamp (Disney)(3/57) | 1.15 | 3.50 | 8.00 |
| 778-The Little Rascals (TV) | 1.70 | 5.00 | 12.00 |
| 779-Lee Hunter, Indian Fighter (3/57) | 3.00 | 9.00 | 21.00 |
| 780-Captain Kangaroo (TV)-Photo-c | 8.50 | 25.50 | 60.00 |
| 781-Fury (No.1)(TV)(3/57)-Photo-c | 5.70 | 17.00 | 40.00 |
| 782-Duck Album (Disney) | 1.70 | 5.00 | 12.00 |
| 783-Elmer Fudd | .85 | 2.50 | 6.00 |
| 784-Around the World in 80 Days (Movie) (2/57)-Photo-c | 3.70 | 11.00 | 26.00 |
| 785-Circus Boy (TV) (4/57)-The Monkees' Mickey Dolenz photo-c | 7.00 | 21.00 | 50.00 |
| 786-Cinderella (Disney) (3/57)-Partial reprint of No. 272 | 2.00 | 6.00 | 14.00 |
| 787-Little Hiawatha (Disney) (4/57) | 1.70 | 5.00 | 12.00 |
| 788-Prince Valiant - by Bob Fuje | 3.50 | 10.50 | 24.00 |
| 789-Silvertip-Valley Thieves (Max Brand) (4/57)-Kinstler-a | 3.50 | 10.50 | 24.00 |
| 790-The Wings of Eagles (Movie) (John Wayne)-Toth-a; John Wayne photo-c; 10 & 15 cent editions exist | 13.50 | 41.00 | 95.00 |
| 791-The 77th Bengal Lancers (TV)-Photo-c | 4.00 | 12.00 | 28.00 |
| 792-Oswald the Rabbit (Lantz) | .85 | 2.50 | 6.00 |
| 793-Morty Meekle | 1.50 | 4.50 | 10.00 |
| 794-The Count of Monte Cristo (5/57) (Movie)-Buscema-a | 6.50 | 19.00 | 45.00 |
| 795-Jiminy Cricket (Disney) | 2.00 | 6.00 | 14.00 |
| 796-Ludwig Bemelman's Madeleine and Genevieve | 2.30 | 7.00 | 16.00 |
| 797-Gunsmoke (TV)-Photo-c | 4.50 | 14.00 | 32.00 |
| 798-Buffalo Bill, Jr. (TV)-Photo-c | 3.00 | 9.00 | 21.00 |
| 799-Priscilla's Pop | 1.15 | 3.50 | 8.00 |
| 800-The Buccaneers (TV)-Photo-c | 4.30 | 13.00 | 30.00 |
| 801-Dotty Dripple and Taffy | 1.30 | 4.00 | 9.00 |
| 802-Goofy (Disney) (5/57) | 2.30 | 7.00 | 16.00 |
| 803-Cheyenne (TV)-Photo-c | 4.30 | 13.00 | 30.00 |
| 804-Steve Canyon-Caniff-a (1957) | 3.50 | 10.50 | 24.00 |
| 805-Crusader Rabbit (TV) | 7.00 | 21.00 | 50.00 |
| 806-Scamp (Disney) (6/57) | 1.15 | 3.50 | 8.00 |
| 807-Savage Range (Luke Short)-Drucker-a | 2.30 | 7.00 | 16.00 |
| 808-Spin and Marty (TV)(Disney)-Mickey Mouse Club-Photo-c | 4.00 | 12.00 | 28.00 |
| 809-The Little People-Walt Scott | 1.70 | 5.00 | 12.00 |

| | Good | Fine | N-Mint |
|---|---|---|---|
| 810-Francis the Famous Talking Mule | 1.00 | 3.00 | 7.00 |
| 811-Howdy Doody (TV) (7/57) | 5.70 | 17.00 | 40.00 |
| 812-The Big Land(Movie); Alan Ladd photo-c | 8.00 | 24.00 | 55.00 |
| 813-Circus Boy (TV)-The Monkees' Mickey Dolenz photo-c | 7.00 | 21.00 | 50.00 |
| 814-Covered Wagons, Ho! (Disney)-Donald Duck (TV)(6/57); Mickey Mouse app. | 2.00 | 6.00 | 14.00 |
| 815-Dragoon Wells Massacre (Movie)-photo-c | 5.00 | 15.00 | 35.00 |
| 816-Brave Eagle (TV)-photo-c | 1.70 | 5.00 | 12.00 |
| 817-Little Beaver | 1.50 | 4.50 | 10.00 |
| 818-Smokey the Bear (6/57) | 2.00 | 6.00 | 14.00 |
| 819-Mickey Mouse in Magicland (Disney) (7/57) | 2.00 | 6.00 | 14.00 |
| 820-The Oklahoman (Movie)-Photo-c | 5.70 | 17.00 | 40.00 |
| 821-Wringle Wrangle (Disney)-Based on movie "Westward Ho, the Wagons"-Marsh-a; Fess Parker photo-c | 4.30 | 13.00 | 30.00 |
| 822-Paul Revere's Ride with Johnny Tremain (TV)(Disney)-Toth-a | 7.00 | 21.00 | 50.00 |
| 823-Timmy | 1.15 | 3.50 | 8.00 |
| 824-The Pride and the Passion (Movie)(8/57)-Frank Sinatra & Cary Grant photo-c | 5.00 | 15.00 | 35.00 |
| 825-The Little Rascals (TV) | 1.70 | 5.00 | 12.00 |
| 826-Spin and Marty and Annette (TV)(Disney)-Mickey Mouse Club-Annette Funicello photo-c | 10.00 | 30.00 | 70.00 |
| 827-Smokey Stover (8/57) | 1.70 | 5.00 | 12.00 |
| 828-Buffalo Bill, Jr. (TV)-Photo-c | 3.00 | 9.00 | 21.00 |
| 829-Tales of the Pony Express (TV) (8/57)-Painted-c | 2.30 | 7.00 | 16.00 |
| 830-The Hardy Boys (TV)(Disney)-Mickey Mouse Club (8/57)-Photo-c | 5.00 | 15.00 | 35.00 |
| 831-No Sleep 'Til Dawn (Movie)-Carl Malden photo-c | 3.70 | 11.00 | 26.00 |
| 832-Lolly and Pepper (No.1) | 1.70 | 5.00 | 12.00 |
| 833-Scamp (Disney) (9/57) | 1.15 | 3.50 | 8.00 |
| 834-Johnny Mack Brown-Photo-c | 3.50 | 10.50 | 24.00 |
| 835-Silvertip-The Fake Rider (Max Brand) | 2.65 | 8.00 | 18.00 |
| 836-Man in Flight (Disney) (TV)(9/57) | 2.65 | 8.00 | 18.00 |
| 837-All-American Athlete Cotton Woods | 2.65 | 8.00 | 18.00 |
| 838-Bugs Bunny's Life Story Album (9/57) | 2.00 | 6.00 | 14.00 |
| 839-The Vigilantes (Movie) | 4.00 | 12.00 | 28.00 |
| 840-Duck Album (Disney)(9/57) | 1.70 | 5.00 | 12.00 |
| 841-Elmer Fudd | .85 | 2.50 | 6.00 |
| 842-The Nature of Things (Disney-Movie)('57)-Jesse Marsh-a (TV series) | 3.00 | 9.00 | 21.00 |
| 843-The First Americans (Disney)(TV)-Marsh-a | 3.00 | 9.00 | 21.00 |
| 844-Gunsmoke (TV)-Photo-c | 4.50 | 14.00 | 32.00 |
| 845-The Land Unknown (Movie)-Alex Toth-a | 11.00 | 32.00 | 75.00 |
| 846-Gun Glory (Movie)-by Alex Toth-photo-c | 10.00 | 30.00 | 70.00 |
| 847-Perri (squirrels) (Disney-Movie)-Two different covers published | 1.50 | 4.50 | 10.00 |
| 848-Marauder's Moon | 3.50 | 10.50 | 24.00 |
| 849-Prince Valiant-by Bob Fuje | 3.50 | 10.50 | 24.00 |
| 850-Buck Jones | 2.30 | 7.00 | 16.00 |
| 851-The Story of Mankind (Movie) (1/58)-Hedy Lamarr & Vincent Price photo-c | 3.70 | 11.00 | 26.00 |
| 852-Chilly Willy (2/58)(Lantz) | 1.00 | 3.00 | 7.00 |
| 853-Pluto (Disney) (10/57) | 1.70 | 5.00 | 12.00 |
| 854-The Hunchback of Notre Dame (Movie)-Photo-c | 8.50 | 25.50 | 60.00 |
| 855-Broken Arrow (TV)-Photo-c | 3.00 | 9.00 | 21.00 |
| 856-Buffalo Bill, Jr. (TV)-Photo-c | 3.00 | 9.00 | 21.00 |
| 857-The Goofy Adventure Story (Disney) (11/57) | 2.00 | 6.00 | 14.00 |
| 858-Daisy Duck's Diary (Disney) (11/57) | 1.70 | 5.00 | 12.00 |
| 859-Topper and Neil (TV)(11/57) | 1.50 | 4.40 | 10.00 |
| 860-Wyatt Earp (No.1)(TV)-Manning-a; photo-c | 8.00 | 24.00 | 55.00 |

| | Good | Fine | N-Mint |
|---|---|---|---|
| 861-Frosty the Snowman | 1.70 | 5.00 | 12.00 |
| 862-The Truth About Mother Goose (Disney-Movie) (11/57) | 3.50 | 10.50 | 24.00 |
| 863-Francis the Famous Talking Mule | 1.00 | 3.00 | 7.00 |
| 864-The Littlest Snowman | 2.15 | 6.50 | 16.00 |
| 865-Andy Burnett (TV) (Disney) (12/57)-Photo-c | 5.00 | 15.00 | 35.00 |
| 866-Mars and Beyond (Disney-Movie) | 2.65 | 8.00 | 18.00 |
| 867-Santa Claus Funnies | 1.70 | 5.00 | 12.00 |
| 868-The Little People (12/57) | 1.70 | 5.00 | 12.00 |
| 869-Old Yeller (Disney-Movie)-Photo-c | 2.65 | 8.00 | 18.00 |
| 870-Little Beaver (1/58) | 1.50 | 4.50 | 10.00 |
| 871-Curly Kayoe | 2.00 | 6.00 | 14.00 |
| 872-Captain Kangaroo (TV)-Photo-c | 8.50 | 25.50 | 60.00 |
| 873-Grandma Duck's Farm Friends (Disney) | 2.00 | 6.00 | 14.00 |
| 874-Old Ironsides (Disney-Movie with Johnny Tremain) (1/58) | 2.65 | 8.00 | 18.00 |
| 875-Trumpets West (Luke Short) (2/58) | 2.30 | 7.00 | 16.00 |
| 876-Tales of Wells Fargo (No.1) (TV) (2/58)-Photo-c | 5.70 | 17.00 | 40.00 |
| 877-Frontier Doctor with Rex Allen (TV)-Alex Toth-a; photo-c | 8.50 | 25.50 | 60.00 |
| 878-Peanuts (No.1)-Schulz-c only (2/58) | 7.00 | 21.00 | 50.00 |
| 879-Brave Eagle (TV)(2/58)-Photo-c | 1.70 | 5.00 | 12.00 |
| 880-Steve Donovan, Western Marshal-Drucker-a (TV)-Photo-c | 2.65 | 8.00 | 18.00 |
| 881-The Captain and the Kids (2/58) | 1.70 | 5.00 | 12.00 |
| 882-Zorro (Disney)-1st Disney issue by Alex Toth (TV) (2/58)-Photo-c | 8.50 | 25.50 | 60.00 |
| 883-The Little Rascals (TV) | 1.70 | 5.00 | 12.00 |
| 884-Hawkeye and the Last of the Mohicans (TV)-Photo-c (3/58) | 3.70 | 11.00 | 26.00 |
| 885-Fury (TV) (3/58)-Photo-c | 4.00 | 12.00 | 28.00 |
| 886-Bongo and Lumpjaw (Disney, 3/58) | 1.30 | 4.00 | 9.00 |
| 887-The Hardy Boys (Disney)(TV)-Mickey Mouse Club (1/58)-Photo-c | 5.00 | 15.00 | 35.00 |
| 888-Elmer Fudd (3/58) | .85 | 2.50 | 6.00 |
| 889-Clint and Mac (Disney)(TV)-Alex Toth-a (3/58)-Photo-c | 7.00 | 21.00 | 50.00 |
| 890-Wyatt Earp (TV)-by Russ Manning; photo-c | 4.50 | 14.00 | 32.00 |
| 891-Light in the Forest (Disney-Movie) (3/58)-Fess Parker photo-c | 3.00 | 9.00 | 21.00 |
| 892-Maverick (No.1) (TV) (4/58)-James Garner/Jack Kelly photo-c | 8.00 | 24.00 | 55.00 |
| 893-Jim Bowie (TV)-Photo-c | 3.50 | 10.50 | 24.00 |
| 894-Oswald the Rabbit (Lantz) | .85 | 2.50 | 6.00 |
| 895-Wagon Train (No.1)(TV)(3/58)-Photo-c | 5.70 | 17.00 | 40.00 |
| 896-The Adventures of Tinker Bell (Disney) | 3.00 | 9.00 | 21.00 |
| 897-Jiminy Cricket (Disney) | 2.00 | 6.00 | 14.00 |
| 898-Silvertip (Max Brand)-Kinstler-a (5/58) | 3.50 | 10.50 | 24.00 |
| 899-Goofy (Disney)(5/58) | 2.00 | 6.00 | 14.00 |
| 900-Prince Valiant-by Bob Fuje | 3.50 | 10.50 | 24.00 |
| 901-Little Hiawatha (Disney) | 1.70 | 5.00 | 12.00 |
| 902-Will-Yum! | 1.15 | 3.50 | 8.00 |
| 903-Dotty Dripple and Taffy | 1.30 | 4.00 | 9.00 |
| 904-Lee Hunter, Indian Fighter | 2.30 | 7.00 | 16.00 |
| 905-Annette (Disney,TV, 5/58)-Mickey Mouse Club; Annette Funicello photo-c | 13.00 | 40.00 | 90.00 |
| 906-Francis the Famous Talking Mule | 1.00 | 3.00 | 7.00 |
| 907-Sugarfoot (No.1)(TV)Toth-a; photo-c | 10.00 | 30.00 | 70.00 |
| 908-The Little People and the Giant-Walt Scott (5/58) | 1.70 | 5.00 | 12.00 |
| 909-Smitty | 1.70 | 5.00 | 12.00 |
| 910-The Vikings (Movie)-Buscema-a; Kirk Douglas photo-c | 7.00 | 21.00 | 50.00 |
| 911-The Gray Ghost (TV)(Movie)-Photo-c | 5.00 | 15.00 | 35.00 |

*Four Color #814, © The Disney Co.*

*Four Color #846, © M.G.M.*

*Four Color #900, © DELL*

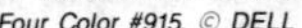
Four Color #915, © DELL

Four Color #945, © Warner Bros.

Four Color #981, © Hanna-Barbera

| | Good | Fine | N-Mint |
|---|---|---|---|
| 912-Leave It to Beaver (No.1)(TV)-Photo-c | 14.00 | 43.00 | 100.00 |
| 913-The Left-Handed Gun (Movie) (7/58); Paul Newman photo-c | 8.00 | 24.00 | 55.00 |
| 914-No Time for Sergeants (Movie)-Photo-c; Toth-a | 6.50 | 19.00 | 45.00 |
| 915-Casey Jones (TV)-Alan Hale photo-c | 3.50 | 10.50 | 24.00 |
| 916-Red Ryder Ranch Comics | 1.70 | 5.00 | 12.00 |
| 917-The Life of Riley (TV)-Photo-c | 8.50 | 25.50 | 60.00 |
| 918-Beep Beep, the Roadrunner (No.1)(7/58)-Two different back covers published | 4.50 | 14.00 | 32.00 |
| 919-Boots and Saddles (No.1)(TV)-Photo-c | 5.00 | 15.00 | 35.00 |
| 920-Zorro (Disney-TV)(6/58)Toth-a; photo-c | 8.50 | 25.50 | 60.00 |
| 921-Wyatt Earp (TV)-Manning-a; photo-c | 4.50 | 14.00 | 32.00 |
| 922-Johnny Mack Brown by Russ Manning-Photo-c | 4.00 | 12.00 | 28.00 |
| 923-Timmy | 1.15 | 3.50 | 8.00 |
| 924-Colt .45 (No.1)(TV)(8/58)-Photo-c | 6.00 | 18.00 | 42.00 |
| 925-Last of the Fast Guns (Movie) (8/58)-Photo-c | 4.00 | 12.00 | 28.00 |
| 926-Peter Pan (Disney)-Reprint of No. 442 | 2.00 | 6.00 | 14.00 |
| 927-Top Gun (Luke Short) Buscema-a | 2.30 | 7.00 | 16.00 |
| 928-Sea Hunt (No.1, 9/58) (TV)-Lloyd Bridges photo-c | 6.50 | 19.00 | 45.00 |
| 929-Brave Eagle (TV)-Photo-c | 1.70 | 5.00 | 12.00 |
| 930-Maverick (TV) (7/58)-James Garner/Jack Kelly photo-c | 5.70 | 17.00 | 40.00 |
| 931-Have Gun, Will Travel (No.1) (TV)-Photo-c | 7.00 | 21.00 | 50.00 |
| 932-Smokey the Bear (His Life Story) | 2.00 | 6.00 | 14.00 |
| 933-Zorro (Disney)-by Alex Toth (TV)(9/58) | 8.50 | 25.50 | 60.00 |
| 934-Restless Gun (No.1)(TV)-Photo-c | 7.00 | 21.00 | 50.00 |
| 935-King of the Royal Mounted | 3.00 | 9.00 | 21.00 |
| 936-The Little Rascals (TV) | 1.70 | 5.00 | 12.00 |
| 937-Ruff and Reddy (No.1, 9/58)(TV)(1st Hanna-Barbera comic book) | 3.50 | 10.50 | 24.00 |
| 938-Elmer Fudd (9/58) | .85 | 2.50 | 6.00 |
| 939-Steve Canyon - not by Caniff | 3.00 | 9.00 | 21.00 |
| 940-Lolly and Pepper (10/58) | 1.30 | 4.00 | 9.00 |
| 941-Pluto (Disney) (10/58) | 1.70 | 5.00 | 12.00 |
| 942-Pony Express (TV) | 2.30 | 7.00 | 16.00 |
| 943-White Wilderness (Disney-Movie) (10/58) | 3.00 | 9.00 | 21.00 |
| 944-The 7th Voyage of Sindbad (Movie) (9/58)-Buscema-a | 11.00 | 32.00 | 75.00 |
| 945-Maverick (TV)-James Garner/Jack Kelly photo-c | 5.70 | 17.00 | 40.00 |
| 946-The Big Country (Movie)-Photo-c | 3.70 | 11.00 | 26.00 |
| 947-Broken Arrow (TV)-Photo-c (11/58) | 3.00 | 9.00 | 21.00 |
| 948-Daisy Duck's Diary (Disney) (11/58) | 1.70 | 5.00 | 12.00 |
| 949-High Adventure (Lowell Thomas')(TV)-Photo-c | 3.00 | 9.00 | 21.00 |
| 950-Frosty the Snowman | 1.70 | 5.00 | 12.00 |
| 951-The Lennon Sisters Life Story (TV)-Toth-a, 32pgs.-Photo-c | 10.00 | 30.00 | 70.00 |
| 952-Goofy (Disney) (11/58) | 2.00 | 6.00 | 14.00 |
| 953-Francis the Famous Talking Mule | 1.00 | 3.00 | 7.00 |
| 954-Man in Space-Satellites (Disney-Movie) | 2.65 | 8.00 | 18.00 |
| 955-Hi and Lois (11/58) | 1.00 | 3.00 | 7.00 |
| 956-Ricky Nelson (No.1)(TV)-Photo-c | 14.00 | 43.00 | 100.00 |
| 957-Buffalo Bee (No.1)(TV) | 4.30 | 13.00 | 30.00 |
| 958-Santa Claus Funnies | 1.50 | 4.50 | 10.00 |
| 959-Christmas Stories-(Walt Scott's Little People)(1951-56 strip reprints) | 1.70 | 5.00 | 12.00 |
| 960-Zorro (Disney)(TV)(12/58)-Toth art | 8.50 | 25.50 | 60.00 |
| 961-Jace Pearson's Tales of the Texas Rangers (TV)-Spiegle-a; photo-c | 3.50 | 10.50 | 24.00 |
| 962-Maverick (TV) (1/59)-James Garner/Jack Kelly photo-c | 5.70 | 17.00 | 40.00 |

| | Good | Fine | N-Mint |
|---|---|---|---|
| 963-Johnny Mack Brown-Photo-c | 3.50 | 10.50 | 24.00 |
| 964-The Hardy Boys (TV)(Disney)-Mickey Mouse Club (1/59)-Photo-c | 5.00 | 15.00 | 35.00 |
| 965-Grandma Duck's Farm Friends (Disney) (1/59) | 2.00 | 6.00 | 14.00 |
| 966-Tonka (starring Sal Mineo; Disney-Movie)-Photo-c | 3.70 | 11.00 | 26.00 |
| 967-Chilly Willy (2/59)(Lantz) | 1.00 | 3.00 | 7.00 |
| 968-Tales of Wells Fargo (TV)-Photo-c | 5.00 | 15.00 | 35.00 |
| 969-Peanuts (2/59) | 5.70 | 17.00 | 40.00 |
| 970-Lawman (No.1)(TV)-Photo-c | 7.00 | 21.00 | 50.00 |
| 971-Wagon Train (TV)-Photo-c | 3.70 | 11.00 | 26.00 |
| 972-Tom Thumb (Movie)-George Pal (1/59) | 8.00 | 24.00 | 55.00 |
| 973-Sleeping Beauty and the Prince (Disney) (5/59) | 4.00 | 12.00 | 28.00 |
| 974-The Little Rascals (TV)(3/59) | 1.70 | 5.00 | 12.00 |
| 975-Fury (TV)-Photo-c | 4.00 | 12.00 | 28.00 |
| 976-Zorro (Disney)(TV)-Toth-a; photo-c | 8.50 | 25.50 | 60.00 |
| 977-Elmer Fudd (3/59) | .85 | 2.50 | 6.00 |
| 978-Lolly and Pepper | 1.30 | 4.00 | 9.00 |
| 979-Oswald the Rabbit (Lantz) | .85 | 2.50 | 6.00 |
| 980-Maverick (TV) (4-6/59)-James Garner/Jack Kelly photo-c | 5.70 | 17.00 | 40.00 |
| 981-Ruff and Reddy (TV)(Hanna-Barbera) | 2.30 | 7.00 | 16.00 |
| 982-The New Adventures of Tinker Bell (TV-Disney) | 3.00 | 9.00 | 21.00 |
| 983-Have Gun, Will Travel (TV) (4-6/59)-Photo-c | 4.50 | 14.00 | 32.00 |
| 984-Sleeping Beauty's Fairy Godmothers (Disney) | 4.00 | 12.00 | 28.00 |
| 985-Shaggy Dog (Disney-Movie)-Photo-c | 3.00 | 9.00 | 21.00 |
| 986-Restless Gun (TV)-Photo-c | 5.00 | 15.00 | 35.00 |
| 987-Goofy (Disney) (7/59) | 2.00 | 6.00 | 14.00 |
| 988-Little Hiawatha (Disney) | 1.70 | 5.00 | 12.00 |
| 989-Jiminy Cricket (Disney) (5-7/59) | 2.00 | 6.00 | 14.00 |
| 990-Huckleberry Hound (No.1) (TV) (Hanna-Barbera) | 4.00 | 12.00 | 28.00 |
| 991-Francis the Famous Talking Mule | 1.00 | 3.00 | 7.00 |
| 992-Sugarfoot (TV)-Toth-a; photo-c | 10.00 | 30.00 | 70.00 |
| 993-Jim Bowie (TV)-Photo-c | 3.50 | 10.50 | 24.00 |
| 994-Sea Hunt (TV)-Lloyd Bridges photo-c | 5.00 | 15.00 | 35.00 |
| 995-Donald Duck Album (Disney) (5-7/59) | 2.00 | 6.00 | 14.00 |
| 996-Nevada (Zane Grey) | 2.30 | 7.00 | 16.00 |
| 997-Walt Disney Presents-Tales of Texas John Slaughter (No. 1) (TV-Disney)-Photo-c | 3.50 | 10.50 | 24.00 |
| 998-Ricky Nelson (TV)-Photo-c | 14.00 | 43.00 | 100.00 |
| 999-Leave It to Beaver (TV)-Photo-c | 13.00 | 40.00 | 90.00 |
| 1000-The Gray Ghost (Movie) (6-8/59)-Photo-c | 5.00 | 15.00 | 35.00 |
| 1001-Lowell Thomas' High Adventure (TV) (8-10/59)-Photo-c | 3.00 | 9.00 | 21.00 |
| 1002-Buffalo Bee (TV) | 3.50 | 10.50 | 24.00 |
| 1003-Zorro (TV) (Disney)-Photo-c | 7.00 | 21.00 | 50.00 |
| 1004-Colt .45 (TV) (6-8/59)-Photo-c | 4.00 | 12.00 | 28.00 |
| 1005-Maverick (TV)-James Garner/Jack Kelly photo-c | 5.70 | 17.00 | 40.00 |
| 1006-Hercules (Movie)-Buscema-a | 8.00 | 24.00 | 55.00 |
| 1007-John Paul Jones (Movie)-Robert Stack photo-c | 3.00 | 9.00 | 21.00 |
| 1008-Beep Beep, the Road Runner (7-9/59) | 2.30 | 7.00 | 16.00 |
| 1009-The Rifleman (No.1) (TV)-Photo-c | 10.00 | 30.00 | 70.00 |
| 1010-Grandma Duck's Farm Friends (Disney)-by Carl Barks | 6.00 | 18.00 | 42.00 |
| 1011-Buckskin (No.1)(TV)-Photo-c | 5.70 | 17.00 | 40.00 |
| 1012-Last Train from Gun Hill (Movie) (7/59)-Photo-c | 5.00 | 15.00 | 35.00 |
| 1013-Bat Masterson (No.1) (TV) (8/59)-Gene Barry photo-c | | | |

| | Good | Fine | N-Mint |
|---|---|---|---|
| | 5.70 | 17.00 | 40.00 |
| 1014-The Lennon Sisters (TV)-Toth-a; photo-c | 9.30 | 28.00 | 65.00 |
| 1015-Peanuts-Schulz-c | 5.70 | 17.00 | 40.00 |
| 1016-Smokey the Bear Nature Stories | 1.30 | 4.50 | 10.00 |
| 1017-Chilly Willy (Lantz) | 1.00 | 3.00 | 7.00 |
| 1018-Rio Bravo (Movie)(6/59)-John Wayne; Toth-a; John Wayne, Dean Martin & Ricky Nelson photo-c | 18.00 | 54.00 | 125.00 |
| 1019-Wagon Train (TV)-Photo-c | 3.70 | 11.00 | 26.00 |
| 1020-Jungle Jim-McWilliams-a | 1.70 | 5.00 | 12.00 |
| 1021-Jace Pearson's Tales of the Texas Rangers (TV)-Photo-c | 3.00 | 9.00 | 21.00 |
| 1022-Timmy | 1.15 | 3.50 | 8.00 |
| 1023-Tales of Wells Fargo (TV)-Photo-c | 5.00 | 15.00 | 35.00 |
| 1024-Darby O'Gill and the Little People (Disney-Movie)-Toth-a; photo-c | 6.50 | 19.00 | 45.00 |
| 1025-Vacation in Disneyland (8-10/59)-Carl Barks-a (Disney) | 6.00 | 18.00 | 42.00 |
| 1026-Spin and Marty (TV)(Disney)-Mickey Mouse Club (9-11/59)-Photo-c | 4.00 | 12.00 | 28.00 |
| 1027-The Texan (TV)-Photo-c | 4.30 | 13.00 | 30.00 |
| 1028-Rawhide (No.1, 9-11/59)(TV)-Clint Eastwood photo-c; Tufts-a | 17.00 | 51.00 | 120.00 |
| 1029-Boots and Saddles (9/59, TV)-Photo-c | 3.50 | 10.50 | 24.00 |
| 1030-Spanky and Alfalfa, the Little Rascals (TV) | 1.50 | 4.50 | 10.00 |
| 1031-Fury (TV)-Photo-c | 4.00 | 12.00 | 28.00 |
| 1032-Elmer Fudd | .85 | 2.50 | 6.00 |
| 1033-Steve Canyon-not by Caniff; photo-c | 3.00 | 9.00 | 21.00 |
| 1034-Nancy and Sluggo Summer Camp (9-11/59) | 1.70 | 5.00 | 12.00 |
| 1035-Lawman (TV)-Photo-c | 4.30 | 13.00 | 30.00 |
| 1036-The Big Circus (Movie)-Photo-c | 3.00 | 9.00 | 21.00 |
| 1037-Zorro (Disney)(TV)-Tufts-a; Annette Funicello photo-c | 9.30 | 28.00 | 65.00 |
| 1038-Ruff and Reddy (TV)(Hanna-Barbera)('59) | 2.30 | 7.00 | 16.00 |
| 1039-Pluto (Disney) (11-1/60) | 1.70 | 5.00 | 12.00 |
| 1040-Quick Draw McGraw (No.1)(TV)(Hanna-Barbera)(12-2/60) | 4.30 | 13.00 | 30.00 |
| 1041-Sea Hunt (10-12/59)(TV)-Toth-a; Lloyd Bridges photo-c | 7.00 | 21.00 | 50.00 |
| 1042-The Three Chipmunks (Alvin, Simon & Theodore) (No.1)(TV) (10-12/59) | 1.00 | 3.00 | 7.00 |
| 1043-The Three Stooges (No.1)-Photo-c | 8.50 | 25.50 | 60.00 |
| 1044-Have Gun, Will Travel (TV)-Photo-c | 4.50 | 14.00 | 32.00 |
| 1045-Restless Gun (TV)-Photo-c | 5.00 | 15.00 | 35.00 |
| 1046-Beep Beep, the Road Runner (11-1/60) | 2.30 | 7.00 | 16.00 |
| 1047-Gyro Gearloose (No.1)(Disney)-Barks-c/a | 6.50 | 19.50 | 45.00 |
| 1048-The Horse Soldiers (Movie) (John Wayne)-Sekowsky-a | 14.00 | 43.00 | 100.00 |
| 1049-Don't Give Up the Ship (Movie) (8/59)-Jerry Lewis photo-c | 4.00 | 12.00 | 28.00 |
| 1050-Huckleberry Hound (TV)(Hanna-Barbera)(10-12/59) | 2.65 | 8.00 | 18.00 |
| 1051-Donald in Mathmagic Land (Disney-Movie) | 4.00 | 12.00 | 28.00 |
| 1052-Ben-Hur (Movie) (11/59)-Manning-a | 6.50 | 19.00 | 45.00 |
| 1053-Goofy (Disney) (11-1/60) | 2.00 | 6.00 | 14.00 |
| 1054-Huckleberry Hound Winter Fun (TV)(Hanna-Barbera)(12/59) | 2.65 | 8.00 | 18.00 |
| 1055-Daisy Duck's Diary (Disney)-by Carl Barks (11-1/60) | 5.00 | 15.00 | 35.00 |
| 1056-Yellowstone Kelly (Movie)-Clint Walker photo-c | 3.00 | 9.00 | 21.00 |
| 1057-Mickey Mouse Album (Disney) | 1.70 | 5.00 | 12.00 |
| 1058-Colt .45 (TV)-Photo-c | 4.00 | 12.00 | 28.00 |
| 1059-Sugarfoot (TV)-Photo-c | 5.70 | 17.00 | 40.00 |

| | Good | Fine | N-Mint |
|---|---|---|---|
| 1060-Journey to the Center of the Earth (Movie)-Photo-c | 9.30 | 28.00 | 65.00 |
| 1061-Buffalo Bee (TV) | 3.50 | 10.50 | 24.00 |
| 1062-Christmas Stories-(Walt Scott's Little People strip-r) | 1.50 | 4.50 | 10.00 |
| 1063-Santa Claus Funnies | 1.50 | 4.50 | 10.00 |
| 1064-Bugs Bunny's Merry Christmas (12/59) | 1.70 | 5.00 | 12.00 |
| 1065-Frosty the Snowman | 1.70 | 5.00 | 12.00 |
| 1066-77 Sunset Strip (No.1)(TV)-Toth-a (1-3/60)-Photo-c | 8.00 | 24.00 | 55.00 |
| 1067-Yogi Bear (No.1)(TV)(Hanna-Barbera) | 5.00 | 15.00 | 35.00 |
| 1068-Francis the Famous Talking Mule | 1.00 | 3.00 | 7.00 |
| 1069-The FBI Story (Movie)-Toth-a; James Stewart photo-c | 8.00 | 24.00 | 55.00 |
| 1070-Solomon and Sheba (Movie)-Sekowsky-a; photo-c | 6.50 | 19.00 | 45.00 |
| 1071-The Real McCoys (#1, 1-3/60)(TV)-Toth-a; photo-c | 8.00 | 24.00 | 55.00 |
| 1072-Blythe (Marge's) | 2.30 | 7.00 | 16.00 |
| 1073-Grandma Duck's Farm Friends-Barks-c/a (Disney) | 6.00 | 18.00 | 42.00 |
| 1074-Chilly Willy (Lantz) | 1.00 | 3.00 | 7.00 |
| 1075-Tales of Wells Fargo (TV)-Photo-c | 5.00 | 15.00 | 35.00 |
| 1076-The Rebel (#1)(TV)-Sekowsky-a; photo-c | 8.00 | 24.00 | 55.00 |
| 1077-The Deputy (No.1)(TV)-Buscema-a; Henry Fonda photo-c | 8.50 | 25.50 | 60.00 |
| 1078-The Three Stooges (2-4/60)-Photo-c | 5.70 | 17.00 | 40.00 |
| 1079-The Little Rascals (TV)(Spanky & Alfalfa) | 1.50 | 4.50 | 10.00 |
| 1080-Fury (TV) (2-4/60)-Photo-c | 4.00 | 12.00 | 28.00 |
| 1081-Elmer Fudd | .85 | 2.50 | 6.00 |
| 1082-Spin and Marty (Disney)(TV)-Photo-c | 4.00 | 12.00 | 28.00 |
| 1083-Men into Space (TV)-Anderson-a; photo-c | 3.50 | 10.50 | 24.00 |
| 1084-Speedy Gonzales | 1.50 | 4.50 | 10.00 |
| 1085-The Time Machine (H.G. Wells) (Movie) (3/60)-Alex Toth-a | 10.00 | 30.00 | 70.00 |
| 1086-Lolly and Pepper | 1.30 | 4.00 | 9.00 |
| 1087-Peter Gunn (TV)-Photo-c | 5.70 | 17.00 | 40.00 |
| 1088-A Dog of Flanders (Movie)-Photo-c | 2.65 | 8.00 | 18.00 |
| 1089-Restless Gun (TV)-Photo-c | 5.00 | 15.00 | 35.00 |
| 1090-Francis the Famous Talking Mule | 1.00 | 3.00 | 7.00 |
| 1091-Jacky's Diary (4-6/60) | 3.00 | 9.00 | 21.00 |
| 1092-Toby Tyler (Disney-Movie)-Photo-c | 2.65 | 8.00 | 18.00 |
| 1093-MacKenzie's Raiders (Movie)-Photo-c | 4.00 | 12.00 | 28.00 |
| 1094-Goofy (Disney) | 2.00 | 6.00 | 14.00 |
| 1095-Gyro Gearloose (Disney)-Barks-c/a | 5.50 | 16.50 | 38.00 |
| 1096-The Texan (TV)-Rory Calhoun photo-c | 4.30 | 13.00 | 30.00 |
| 1097-Rawhide (TV)-Manning-a; Clint Eastwood photo-c | 13.00 | 40.00 | 90.00 |
| 1098-Sugarfoot (TV)-Photo-c | 5.70 | 17.00 | 40.00 |
| 1099-Donald Duck Album (Disney) (5-7/60) - Barks-c | 2.30 | 7.00 | 16.00 |
| 1100-Annette's Life Story (Disney-Movie)(5/60)-Annette Funicello photo-c | 14.00 | 43.00 | 100.00 |
| 1101-Robert Louis Stevenson's Kidnapped (Disney-Movie) (5/60); photo-c | 3.70 | 11.00 | 26.00 |
| 1102-Wanted: Dead or Alive (No.1)(TV) (5-7/60); Steve McQueen photo-c | 8.50 | 25.50 | 60.00 |
| 1103-Leave It to Beaver (TV)-Photo-c | 13.00 | 40.00 | 90.00 |
| 1104-Yogi Bear Goes to College (TV)(Hanna-Barbera)(6-8/60) | 3.50 | 10.50 | 24.00 |
| 1105-Gale Storm (Oh! Susanna) (TV)-Toth-a; photo-c | 9.00 | 27.00 | 62.00 |
| 1106-77 Sunset Strip (TV)(6-8/60)-Toth-a; photo-c | 6.50 | 19.00 | 45.00 |
| 1107-Buckskin (TV)-Photo-c | 4.00 | 12.00 | 28.00 |
| 1108-The Troubleshooters (TV)-Keenan Wynn photo-c | | | |

Four Color #1023, © Overland Prod.

Four Color #1051, © The Disney Co.

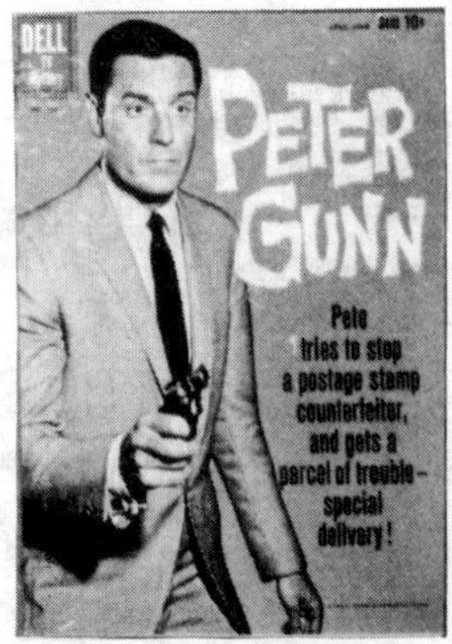

Four Color #1087, © Spartan Prod.

Four Color #1115, © Ozzie Nelson

Four Color #1142, © Four Star

Four Color #1196, © Hanna-Barbera

| | Good | Fine | N-Mint |
|---|---|---|---|
| | 3.70 | 11.00 | 26.00 |
| 1109-This Is Your Life, Donald Duck (Disney)(TV)(8-10/60)-Gyro flash-back to WDC&S #141. Origin Donald Duck (1st told) | 7.00 | 21.00 | 50.00 |
| 1110-Bonanza (No.1) (TV) (6-8/60)-Photo-c | 8.50 | 25.50 | 60.00 |
| 1111-Shotgun Slade (TV) | 4.00 | 12.00 | 28.00 |
| 1112-Pixie and Dixie and Mr. Jinks (No.1) (TV) (Hanna-Barbera) (7-9/60) | 3.50 | 10.50 | 24.00 |
| 1113-Tales of Wells Fargo (TV)-Photo-c | 5.00 | 15.00 | 35.00 |
| 1114-Huckleberry Finn (Movie) (7/60)-Photo-c | 3.00 | 9.00 | 21.00 |
| 1115-Ricky Nelson (TV)-Manning-a; photo-c | 14.00 | 43.00 | 100.00 |
| 1116-Boots and Saddles (TV)(8/60)-Photo-c | 3.50 | 10.50 | 24.00 |
| 1117-Boy and the Pirates (Movie)-Photo-c | 4.00 | 12.00 | 28.00 |
| 1118-The Sword and the Dragon (Movie) (6/60)-Photo-c | 5.00 | 15.00 | 35.00 |
| 1119-Smokey the Bear Nature Stories | 1.50 | 4.50 | 10.00 |
| 1120-Dinosaurus (Movie)-Painted-c | 3.50 | 10.50 | 24.00 |
| 1121-Hercules Unchained (Movie)(8/60)-Crandall/Evans-a | 6.50 | 19.00 | 45.00 |
| 1122-Chilly Willy (Lantz) | 1.00 | 3.00 | 7.00 |
| 1123-Tombstone Territory (TV)-Photo-c | 5.70 | 17.00 | 40.00 |
| 1124-Whirlybirds (No.1) (TV)-Photo-c | 5.70 | 17.00 | 40.00 |
| 1125-Laramie (No. 1)(TV)-Photo-c; G. Kane/Heath-a | 6.00 | 18.00 | 42.00 |
| 1126-Sundance (TV) (8-10/60)-Earl Holliman photo-c | 6.50 | 19.00 | 45.00 |
| 1127-The Three Stooges-Photo-c | 5.70 | 17.00 | 40.00 |
| 1128-Rocky and His Friends (No.1)(TV) (Jay Ward) (8-10/60) | 11.50 | 34.00 | 80.00 |
| 1129-Pollyanna (Disney-Movie)-Hayley Mills photo-c | 7.00 | 21.00 | 50.00 |
| 1130-The Deputy (TV)-Buscema-a; Henry Fonda photo-c | 6.50 | 19.00 | 45.00 |
| 1131-Elmer Fudd (9-11/60) | .85 | 2.50 | 6.00 |
| 1132-Space Mouse (Lantz)(8-10/60) | 1.70 | 5.00 | 12.00 |
| 1133-Fury (TV)-Photo-c | 4.00 | 12.00 | 28.00 |
| 1134-Real McCoys (TV)-Toth-a; photo-c | 8.00 | 24.00 | 55.00 |
| 1135-M.G.M.'s Mouse Musketeers (9-11/60) | .85 | 2.50 | 6.00 |
| 1136-Jungle Cat (Disney-Movie)-Photo-c | 3.70 | 11.00 | 26.00 |
| 1137-The Little Rascals (TV) | 1.50 | 4.50 | 10.00 |
| 1138-The Rebel (TV)-Photo-c | 6.50 | 19.00 | 45.00 |
| 1139-Spartacus (Movie) (11/60)-Buscema-a; photo-c | 8.50 | 25.50 | 60.00 |
| 1140-Donald Duck Album (Disney) | 2.30 | 7.00 | 16.00 |
| 1141-Huckleberry Hound for President (TV)(Hanna-Barbera)(10/60) | 2.30 | 7.00 | 16.00 |
| 1142-Johnny Ringo (TV)-Photo-c | 5.00 | 15.00 | 35.00 |
| 1143-Pluto (Disney) (11-1/61) | 1.70 | 5.00 | 12.00 |
| 1144-The Story of Ruth (Movie)-Photo-c | 8.00 | 24.00 | 55.00 |
| 1145-The Lost World (Movie)-Gil Kane-a; photo-c | 8.00 | 24.00 | 55.00 |
| 1146-Restless Gun (TV)-Photo-c; Wildey-a | 5.00 | 15.00 | 35.00 |
| 1147-Sugarfoot (TV)-Photo-c | 5.70 | 17.00 | 40.00 |
| 1148-I Aim at the Stars-the Wernher Von Braun Story (Movie) (11-1/61)-Photo-c | 3.50 | 10.50 | 24.00 |
| 1149-Goofy (Disney) (11-1/61) | 2.00 | 6.00 | 14.00 |
| 1150-Daisy Duck's Diary (Disney) (12-1/61) by Carl Barks | 5.00 | 15.00 | 35.00 |
| 1151-Mickey Mouse Album (Disney) (11-1/61) | 1.70 | 5.00 | 12.00 |
| 1152-Rocky and His Friends (Jay Ward) (TV) (12-2/61) | 10.00 | 30.00 | 70.00 |
| 1153-Frosty the Snowman | 1.50 | 4.50 | 10.00 |
| 1154-Santa Claus Funnies | 1.50 | 4.50 | 10.00 |
| 1155-North to Alaska (Movie) - John Wayne-Photo-c | 12.00 | 36.00 | 85.00 |
| 1156-Walt Disney Swiss Family Robinson (Movie) (12/60)-Photo-c | | | |

| | Good | Fine | N-Mint |
|---|---|---|---|
| | 3.70 | 11.00 | 26.00 |
| 1157-Master of the World (Movie) (7/61) | 3.70 | 11.00 | 26.00 |
| 1158-Three Worlds of Gulliver (2 issues with different covers) (Movie)-Photo-c | 3.70 | 11.00 | 26.00 |
| 1159-77 Sunset Strip (TV)-Toth-a; photo-c | 6.50 | 19.00 | 45.00 |
| 1160-Rawhide (TV)-Clint Eastwood photo-c | 13.00 | 40.00 | 90.00 |
| 1161-Grandma Duck's Farm Friends (Disney) by Carl Barks (2-4/61) | 6.00 | 18.00 | 42.00 |
| 1162-Yogi Bear Joins the Marines (TV)(Hanna-Barbera)(5-7/61) | 3.50 | 10.50 | 24.00 |
| 1163-Daniel Boone (3-5/61); Marsh-a | 3.00 | 9.00 | 21.00 |
| 1164-Wanted: Dead or Alive (TV); Steve McQueen photo-c | 7.00 | 21.00 | 50.00 |
| 1165-Ellery Queen (No.1)(3-5/61) | 7.00 | 21.00 | 50.00 |
| 1166-Rocky and His Friends (Jay Ward) (TV) | 10.00 | 30.00 | 70.00 |
| 1167-Tales of Wells Fargo (TV)-Photo-c | 4.50 | 14.00 | 32.00 |
| 1168-The Detectives (TV)-Robert Taylor photo-c | 5.00 | 15.00 | 35.00 |
| 1169-New Adventures of Sherlock Holmes | 12.00 | 36.00 | 85.00 |
| 1170-The Three Stooges-Photo-c (3-5/61) | 5.70 | 17.00 | 40.00 |
| 1171-Elmer Fudd | .85 | 2.50 | 6.00 |
| 1172-Fury (TV)-Photo-c | 4.00 | 12.00 | 28.00 |
| 1173-The Twilight Zone (No.1)-Crandall/Evans-c/a (TV) (5/61) | 7.00 | 21.00 | 50.00 |
| 1174-The Little Rascals (TV) | 1.50 | 4.50 | 10.00 |
| 1175-M.G.M.'s Mouse Musketeers (3-5/61) | .85 | 2.50 | 6.00 |
| 1176-Dondi (Movie)-Origin; photo-c | 2.30 | 7.00 | 16.00 |
| 1177-Chilly Willy (Lantz)(4-6/61) | 1.00 | 3.00 | 7.00 |
| 1178-Ten Who Dared (Disney-Movie) (12/60) | 3.00 | 9.00 | 21.00 |
| 1179-The Swamp Fox (TV)(Disney)-Leslie Nielson photo-c | 3.70 | 11.00 | 26.00 |
| 1180-The Danny Thomas Show (TV)-Toth-a; photo-c | 11.50 | 34.00 | 80.00 |
| 1181-Texas John Slaughter (TV)(Disney)(4-6/61)-Photo-c | 2.65 | 8.00 | 18.00 |
| 1182-Donald Duck Album (Disney) (5-7/61) | 2.00 | 6.00 | 14.00 |
| 1183-101 Dalmatians (Disney-Movie) (3/61) | 3.50 | 10.50 | 24.00 |
| 1184-Gyro Gearloose; Barks-c/a (Disney) (5-7/61) Two variations exist | 5.50 | 16.50 | 38.00 |
| 1185-Sweetie Pie | 1.70 | 5.00 | 12.00 |
| 1186-Yak Yak (No.1) by Jack Davis (2 versions - one minus 3-pg. Davis-c/a) | 5.00 | 15.00 | 35.00 |
| 1187-The Three Stooges (6-8/61)-Photo-c | 5.70 | 17.00 | 40.00 |
| 1188-Atlantis, the Lost Continent (Movie) (5/61)-Photo-c | 8.00 | 24.00 | 55.00 |
| 1189-Greyfriars Bobby (Disney-Movie, 11/61)-Photo-c | 3.50 | 10.50 | 24.00 |
| 1190-Donald and the Wheel (Disney-Movie) (11/61); Barks-c | 3.70 | 11.00 | 26.00 |
| 1191-Leave It to Beaver (TV)-Photo-c | 13.00 | 40.00 | 90.00 |
| 1192-Ricky Nelson (TV)-Manning-a; photo-c | 14.00 | 43.00 | 100.00 |
| 1193-The Real McCoys (TV)(6-8/61)-Photo-c | 6.50 | 19.00 | 45.00 |
| 1194-Pepe (Movie) (4/61)-Photo-c | 2.30 | 7.00 | 16.00 |
| 1195-National Velvet (No.1)(TV)-Photo-c | 2.65 | 8.00 | 18.00 |
| 1196-Pixie and Dixie and Mr. Jinks (TV) (Hanna-Barbera) (7-9/61) | 2.30 | 7.00 | 16.00 |
| 1197-The Aquanauts (TV) (5-7/61)-Photo-c | 3.70 | 11.00 | 26.00 |
| 1198-Donald in Mathmagic Land - reprint of No. 1051 (Disney-Movie) | 4.00 | 12.00 | 28.00 |
| 1199-The Absent-Minded Professor (Disney-Movie) (4/61)-Photo-c | 3.70 | 11.00 | 26.00 |
| 1200-Hennessey (TV) (8-10/61)-Gil Kane-a; photo-c | 4.00 | 12.00 | 28.00 |
| 1201-Goofy (Disney) (8-10/61) | 2.00 | 6.00 | 14.00 |
| 1202-Rawhide (TV)-Clint Eastwood photo-c | 13.00 | 40.00 | 90.00 |
| 1203-Pinocchio (Disney) (3/62) | 2.00 | 6.00 | 14.00 |
| 1204-Scamp (Disney) | .85 | 2.50 | 6.00 |

| | Good | Fine | N-Mint |
|---|---|---|---|
| 1205-David and Goliath (Movie) (7/61)-Photo-c | 3.50 | 10.50 | 24.00 |
| 1206-Lolly and Pepper (9-11/61) | 1.30 | 4.00 | 9.00 |
| 1207-The Rebel (TV)-Sekowsky-a; photo-c | 6.50 | 19.00 | 45.00 |
| 1208-Rocky and His Friends (Jay Ward) (TV) | 10.00 | 30.00 | 70.00 |
| 1209-Sugarfoot (TV)-Photo-c (10-12/61) | 5.70 | 17.00 | 40.00 |
| 1210-The Parent Trap (Disney-Movie)(8/61)-Hayley Mills photo-c | 8.00 | 24.00 | 55.00 |
| 1211-77 Sunset Strip (TV)-Manning-a; photo-c | 5.30 | 16.00 | 38.00 |
| 1212-Chilly Willy (Lantz)(7-9/61) | 1.00 | 3.00 | 7.00 |
| 1213-Mysterious Island (Movie)-Photo-c | 5.00 | 15.00 | 35.00 |
| 1214-Smokey the Bear | 1.50 | 4.50 | 10.00 |
| 1215-Tales of Wells Fargo (TV) (10-12/61)-Photo-c | 4.50 | 14.00 | 32.00 |
| 1216-Whirlybirds (TV)-Photo-c | 5.00 | 15.00 | 35.00 |
| 1218-Fury (TV)-Photo-c | 4.00 | 12.00 | 28.00 |
| 1219-The Detectives (TV)-Robert Taylor & Adam West photo-c | 4.30 | 13.00 | 30.00 |
| 1220-Gunslinger (TV)-Photo-c | 4.50 | 14.00 | 32.00 |
| 1221-Bonanza (TV) (9-11/61)-Photo-c | 7.00 | 21.00 | 50.00 |
| 1222-Elmer Fudd (9-11/61) | .85 | 2.50 | 6.00 |
| 1223-Laramie (TV)-Gil Kane-a; photo-c | 4.30 | 13.00 | 30.00 |
| 1224-The Little Rascals (TV)(10-12/61) | 1.50 | 4.50 | 10.00 |
| 1225-The Deputy (TV)-Henry Fonda photo-c | 6.50 | 19.00 | 45.00 |
| 1226-Nikki, Wild Dog of the North (Disney-Movie) (9/61)-Photo-c | 2.00 | 6.00 | 14.00 |
| 1227-Morgan the Pirate (Movie)-Photo-c | 6.50 | 19.00 | 45.00 |
| 1229-Thief of Baghdad (Movie)-Evans-a; photo-c | 8.00 | 24.00 | 55.00 |
| 1230-Voyage to the Bottom of the Sea (#1) (Movie)-Photo insert on-c | 4.50 | 14.00 | 32.00 |
| 1231-Danger Man (TV) (9-11/61); Patrick McGoohan photo-c | 5.00 | 15.00 | 35.00 |
| 1232-On the Double (Movie) | 2.65 | 8.00 | 18.00 |
| 1233-Tammy Tell Me True (Movie) (1961) | 4.00 | 12.00 | 28.00 |
| 1234-The Phantom Planet (Movie) (1961) | 3.70 | 11.00 | 26.00 |
| 1235-Mister Magoo (12-2/62) | 4.00 | 12.00 | 28.00 |
| 1235-Mister Magoo (3-5/65) 2nd printing - reprint of 12-2/62 issue | 2.35 | 7.00 | 16.00 |
| 1236-King of Kings (Movie)-Photo-c | 5.00 | 15.00 | 35.00 |
| 1237-The Untouchables (No.1)(TV)-not by Toth; photo-c | 6.50 | 19.00 | 45.00 |
| 1238-Deputy Dawg (TV) | 5.70 | 17.00 | 40.00 |
| 1239-Donald Duck Album (Disney) (10-12/61)-Barks-c | 2.30 | 7.00 | 16.00 |
| 1240-The Detectives (TV)-Tufts-a; Robert Taylor photo-c | 4.00 | 12.00 | 28.00 |
| 1241-Sweetie Pie | 1.70 | 5.00 | 12.00 |
| 1242-King Leonardo and His Short Subjects (No.1) (TV) (11-1/62) | 5.70 | 17.00 | 40.00 |
| 1243-Ellery Queen | 5.00 | 15.00 | 35.00 |
| 1244-Space Mouse (Lantz) (11-1/62) | 1.70 | 5.00 | 12.00 |
| 1245-New Adventures of Sherlock Holmes | 12.00 | 36.00 | 85.00 |
| 1246-Mickey Mouse Album (Disney) | 1.70 | 5.00 | 12.00 |
| 1247-Daisy Duck's Diary (Disney) (12-2/62) | 1.70 | 5.00 | 12.00 |
| 1248-Pluto (Disney) | 1.70 | 5.00 | 12.00 |
| 1249-The Danny Thomas Show (TV)-Manning-a; photo-c | 11.00 | 32.00 | 75.00 |
| 1250-The Four Horsemen of the Apocalypse (Movie)-Photo-c | 4.00 | 12.00 | 28.00 |
| 1251-Everything's Ducky (Movie) (1961) | 3.00 | 9.00 | 21.00 |
| 1252-The Andy Griffith Show (TV)-Photo-c; 1st show aired 10/3/60 | 14.00 | 43.00 | 100.00 |
| 1253-Space Man (No.1) (1-3/62) | 4.00 | 12.00 | 28.00 |
| 1254-"Diver Dan" (No.1)(TV) (2-4/62)-Photo-c | 3.50 | 10.50 | 24.00 |
| 1255-The Wonders of Aladdin (Movie) (1961) | 3.70 | 11.00 | 26.00 |
| 1256-Kona, Monarch of Monster Isle (No.1) (2-4/62)-Glanzman-a | 3.50 | 10.50 | 24.00 |
| 1257-Car 54, Where Are You? (No.1) (TV) (3-5/62)-Photo-c | 4.00 | 12.00 | 28.00 |
| 1258-The Frogmen (No.1)-Evans-a | 4.00 | 12.00 | 28.00 |
| 1259-El Cid (Movie) (1961)-Photo-c | 3.70 | 11.00 | 26.00 |
| 1260-The Horsemasters (TV, Movie - Disney) (12-2/62)-Annette Funicello photo-c | 5.70 | 17.00 | 40.00 |
| 1261-Rawhide (TV)-Clint Eastwood photo-c | 13.00 | 40.00 | 90.00 |
| 1262-The Rebel (TV)-Photo-c | 6.50 | 19.00 | 45.00 |
| 1263-77 Sunset Strip (TV) (12-2/62)-Manning-a; photo-c | 5.30 | 16.00 | 38.00 |
| 1264-Pixie and Dixie and Mr. Jinks (TV) (Hanna-Barbera) | 2.30 | 7.00 | 16.00 |
| 1265-The Real McCoys (TV)-Photo-c | 6.50 | 19.00 | 45.00 |
| 1266-M.G.M.'s Spike and Tyke (12-2/62) | .85 | 2.50 | 6.00 |
| 1267-Gyro Gearloose; Barks c/a, 4 pgs. (Disney) (12-2/62) | 4.00 | 12.00 | 28.00 |
| 1268-Oswald the Rabbit (Lantz) | .85 | 2.50 | 6.00 |
| 1269-Rawhide (TV)-Clint Eastwood photo-c | 13.00 | 40.00 | 90.00 |
| 1270-Bullwinkle and Rocky (No.1) (Jay Ward) (TV) (3-5/62) | 8.50 | 25.50 | 60.00 |
| 1271-Yogi Bear Birthday Party (TV) (Hanna-Barbera) (11/61) | 2.65 | 8.00 | 18.00 |
| 1272-Frosty the Snowman | 1.50 | 4.50 | 10.00 |
| 1273-Hans Brinker (Disney-Movie)-Photo-c | 3.50 | 10.50 | 24.00 |
| 1274-Santa Claus Funnies (12/61) | 1.50 | 4.50 | 10.00 |
| 1275-Rocky and His Friends (Jay Ward) (TV) | 10.00 | 30.00 | 70.00 |
| 1276-Dondi | 1.70 | 5.00 | 12.00 |
| 1278-King Leonardo and His Short Subjects (TV) | 5.70 | 17.00 | 40.00 |
| 1279-Grandma Duck's Farm Friends (Disney) | 2.00 | 6.00 | 14.00 |
| 1280-Hennessey (TV)-Photo-c | 4.00 | 12.00 | 28.00 |
| 1281-Chilly Willy (Lantz) (4-6/62) | 1.00 | 3.00 | 7.00 |
| 1282-Babes in Toyland (Disney-Movie) (1/62); Annette Funicello photo-c | 7.00 | 21.00 | 50.00 |
| 1283-Bonanza (TV) (2-4/62)-Photo-c | 7.00 | 21.00 | 50.00 |
| 1284-Laramie (TV)-Heath-a; photo-c | 4.30 | 13.00 | 30.00 |
| 1285-Leave It to Beaver (TV)-Photo-c | 13.00 | 40.00 | 90.00 |
| 1286-The Untouchables (TV)-Photo-c | 6.50 | 19.00 | 45.00 |
| 1287-Man from Wells Fargo (TV)-Photo-c | 3.70 | 11.00 | 26.00 |
| 1288-The Twilight Zone (TV) (4/62)-Crandall/Evans-c/a | 5.70 | 17.00 | 40.00 |
| 1289-Ellery Queen | 5.00 | 15.00 | 35.00 |
| 1290-M.G.M.'s Mouse Musketeers | .85 | 2.50 | 6.00 |
| 1291-77 Sunset Strip (TV)-Manning-a; photo-c | 5.30 | 16.00 | 38.00 |
| 1293-Elmer Fudd (3-5/62) | .85 | 2.50 | 6.00 |
| 1294-Ripcord (TV) | 4.00 | 12.00 | 28.00 |
| 1295-Mister Ed, the Talking Horse (No.1) (TV) (3-5/62)-Photo-c | 6.50 | 19.00 | 45.00 |
| 1296-Fury (TV) (3-5/62)-Photo-c | 4.00 | 12.00 | 28.00 |
| 1297-Spanky, Alfalfa and the Little Rascals (TV) | 1.50 | 4.50 | 10.00 |
| 1298-The Hathaways (TV)-Photo-c | 3.00 | 9.00 | 21.00 |
| 1299-Deputy Dawg (TV) | 5.70 | 17.00 | 40.00 |
| 1300-The Comancheros (Movie) (1961)-John Wayne | 12.00 | 36.00 | 85.00 |
| 1301-Adventures in Paradise (TV) (2-4/62) | 2.65 | 8.00 | 18.00 |
| 1302-Johnny Jason, Teen Reporter (2-4/62) | 1.50 | 4.50 | 10.00 |
| 1303-Lad: A Dog (Movie)-Photo-c | 2.65 | 8.00 | 18.00 |
| 1304-Nellie the Nurse (3-5/62)-Stanley-a | 5.70 | 17.00 | 40.00 |
| 1305-Mister Magoo (3-5/62) | 4.00 | 12.00 | 28.00 |
| 1306-Target: The Corruptors (No. 1) (TV) (3-5/62)-Photo-c | 2.30 | 7.00 | 16.00 |
| 1307-Margie (TV) (3-5/62) | 2.30 | 7.00 | 16.00 |
| 1308-Tales of the Wizard of Oz (TV) (3-5/62) | 8.00 | 24.00 | 55.00 |
| 1309-87th Precinct (No. 1) (TV) (4-6/62)-Krigstein-a; photo-c | | | |

Four Color #1208, © Jay Ward Prod.

Four Color #1271, © Hanna-Barbera

Four Color #1285, © Gomalco Prod.

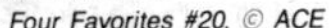
Four Favorites #20, © ACE

Four Most V2#1, © NOVP

Fox and the Crow #2, © DC

| | Good | Fine | N-Mint |
|---|---|---|---|
| | 6.50 | 19.00 | 45.00 |
| 1310-Huck and Yogi Winter Sports (TV) (Hanna-Barbera) (3/62) | 2.65 | 8.00 | 18.00 |
| 1311-Rocky and His Friends (Jay Ward) (TV) | 10.00 | 30.00 | 70.00 |
| 1312-National Velvet (TV)-Photo-c | 2.30 | 7.00 | 16.00 |
| 1313-Moon Pilot (Disney-Movie)-Photo-c | 3.00 | 9.00 | 21.00 |
| 1328-The Underwater City (Movie)-Evans-a (1961)-Photo-c | 4.50 | 14.00 | 32.00 |
| 1330-Brain Boy (No.1)-Gil Kane-a | 4.00 | 12.00 | 28.00 |
| 1332-Bachelor Father (TV) | 4.50 | 14.00 | 32.00 |
| 1333-Short Ribs (4-6/62) | 3.00 | 9.00 | 21.00 |
| 1335-Aggie Mack (4-6/62) | 2.30 | 7.00 | 16.00 |
| 1336-On Stage - not by Leonard Starr | 3.00 | 9.00 | 21.00 |
| 1337-Dr. Kildare (No.1) (TV) (4-6/62)-Photo-c | 3.50 | 10.50 | 24.00 |
| 1341-The Andy Griffith Show (TV) (4-6/62)-Photo-c | 14.00 | 43.00 | 100.00 |
| 1348-Yak Yak (No.2)-Jack Davis-c/a | 5.00 | 15.00 | 35.00 |
| 1349-Yogi Bear Visits the U.N. (TV) (Hanna-Barbera) (1/62)-Photo-c | 2.65 | 8.00 | 18.00 |
| 1350-Comanche (Disney-Movie)(1962)-Reprints 4-Color 966 (title change from "Tonka" to "Comanche") (4-6/62)-Sal Mineo photo-c | 2.65 | 8.00 | 18.00 |
| 1354-Calvin & the Colonel (No. 1) (TV) (4-6/62) | 4.00 | 12.00 | 28.00 |

NOTE: *Missing numbers probably do not exist.*

**4-D MONKEY, THE** (Adventures of... #? on)
1988 - No. 11?, 1990 ($1.80-$2.00, color, 52 pgs.)
Leung's Publications

| | | | |
|---|---|---|---|
| 1-Karate Pig, Ninja Flounder & 4-D Monkey (48 pgs., centerfold is a Christmas card | .30 | .90 | 1.80 |
| 2-4 (52 pgs.) | .30 | .90 | 1.80 |
| 5-11 ($2.00-c) | .35 | 1.00 | 2.00 |

**FOUR FAVORITES** (Crime Must Pay the Penalty No. 33 on)
Sept, 1941 - No. 32, Dec, 1947
Ace Magazines

| | | | |
|---|---|---|---|
| 1-Vulcan, Lash Lightning, Magno the Magnetic Man & The Raven begin; flag-c | 50.00 | 150.00 | 350.00 |
| 2-The Black Ace only app. | 25.00 | 75.00 | 175.00 |
| 3-Last Vulcan | 20.00 | 60.00 | 140.00 |
| 4,5: 4-The Raven & Vulcan end; Unknown Soldier begins, ends #28. 5-Captain Courageous begins, ends #28; not in #6 | 19.00 | 58.00 | 135.00 |
| 6-8: 6-The Flag app.; Mr. Risk begins | 16.00 | 48.00 | 110.00 |
| 9,11-Kurtzman-a; 11-Hitler, Mussolini, Hirohito-c; L.B. Cole-a | 22.00 | 65.00 | 150.00 |
| 10-Classic Kurtzman-c/a | 24.00 | 72.00 | 165.00 |
| 12-L.B. Cole-a | 11.50 | 34.00 | 80.00 |
| 13-20: 18,20-Palais-c/a | 10.00 | 30.00 | 70.00 |
| 21-No Unknown Soldier; The Unknown app. | 7.00 | 21.00 | 50.00 |
| 22-26: 22-Captain Courageous drops costume. 23-Unknown Soldier drops costume. 26-Last Magno | 7.00 | 21.00 | 50.00 |
| 27-32: 29-Hap Hazard app. | 6.00 | 18.00 | 42.00 |

NOTE: ***Jim Mooney** c-3. **Palais** c-18, 20, 24, 25.*

**FOUR HORSEMEN, THE** (See The Crusaders)

**FOUR HORSEMEN OF THE APOCALYPSE, THE** (See 4-Color No. 1250)

**FOUR MOST** (... Boys No. 32-41)
Winter, 1941-42 - V8#5(#36), 9-10/49; #37, 11-12/49 - #41, 6-7/50
Novelty Publications/Star Publications No. 37-on

| | | | |
|---|---|---|---|
| V1#1-The Target by Sid Greene, The Cadet & Dick Cole begin with origins retold; produced by Funnies Inc. | 50.00 | 150.00 | 350.00 |
| 2-Last Target | 24.00 | 72.00 | 165.00 |
| 3-Flag-c | 21.00 | 62.00 | 145.00 |
| 4-1pg. Dr. Seuss(signed) | 16.00 | 48.00 | 110.00 |
| V2#1-4, V3#1-4 | 4.00 | 12.00 | 28.00 |
| V4#1-4 | 3.00 | 9.00 | 21.00 |
| V5#1-5: 1-The Target & Targeteers app. | 2.65 | 8.00 | 18.00 |
| V6#1-4,6: 1-White Rider & Super Horse begin | 2.65 | 8.00 | 18.00 |
| 5-L. B. Cole-c | 4.00 | 12.00 | 28.00 |
| V7#1,3,5, V8#1 | 2.65 | 8.00 | 18.00 |
| 2,4,6-L. B. Cole-c. 6-Last Dick Cole | 4.00 | 12.00 | 28.00 |
| V8#2,3,5-L. B. Cole-c/a | 5.30 | 16.00 | 38.00 |
| 4-L. B. Cole-a | 3.50 | 10.50 | 24.00 |
| 37-41: 38,39-L.B. Cole-c. 38-Johnny Weismuller life story. 41-Exist? | 3.50 | 10.50 | 24.00 |
| Accepted Reprint 38-40 (nd); L.B. Cole-c | 2.30 | 7.00 | 16.00 |

**FOUR-STAR BATTLE TALES**
Feb-Mar, 1973 - No. 5, Nov-Dec, 1973
National Periodical Publications

| | | | |
|---|---|---|---|
| 1-5: All reprints. 5-Krigstein-a(r) | | .30 | .60 |

NOTE: ***Drucker** r-1, 3-5. **Heath** r-2, 5; c-1. **Kubert** r-4; c-2.*

**FOUR STAR SPECTACULAR**
Mar-Apr, 1976 - No. 6, Jan-Feb, 1977
National Periodical Publications

| | | | |
|---|---|---|---|
| 1-6: Reprints in all. 2-Infinity cover | | .30 | .60 |

NOTE: *All contain DC Superhero reprints. #1 has 68 pages; #2-6, 52 pages. #1, 4-Hawkman app.; #2-Kid Flash app.; #3-Green Lantern app; #2, 4, 5-Wonder Woman, Superboy app; #5-Gr. Arrow, Vigilante app; #6-Blackhawk G.A.-r.*

**FOUR TEENERS** (Formerly Crime Must Pay The Penalty?; Dotty No. 35 on)
No. 34, April, 1948 (Teen-age comic)
A. A. Wyn

| | | | |
|---|---|---|---|
| 34 | 2.15 | 6.50 | 15.00 |

**FOX AND THE CROW** (Stanley & His Monster No. 109 on)
(See Comic Cavalcade & Real Screen Comics)
Dec-Jan, 1951-52 - No. 108, Feb-Mar, 1968
National Periodical Publications

| | | | |
|---|---|---|---|
| 1 | 54.00 | 160.00 | 375.00 |
| 2(Scarce) | 27.00 | 80.00 | 185.00 |
| 3-5 | 16.00 | 48.00 | 110.00 |
| 6-10 | 11.00 | 32.00 | 75.00 |
| 11-20 | 7.00 | 21.00 | 50.00 |
| 21-40: 22-Last precode (2/55) | 4.30 | 13.00 | 30.00 |
| 41-60 | 3.00 | 9.00 | 21.00 |
| 61-80 | 2.00 | 6.00 | 14.00 |
| 81-94 | 1.30 | 4.00 | 9.00 |
| 95-Stanley & His Monster begins (origin) | 2.00 | 6.00 | 14.00 |
| 96-99,101-108 | 1.00 | 3.00 | 7.00 |
| 100 | 1.30 | 4.00 | 9.00 |

NOTE: *Many covers by **Mort Drucker.***

**FOX AND THE HOUND, THE** (Disney)
Aug, 1981 - No. 3, Oct, 1981
Whitman Publishing Co.

| | | | |
|---|---|---|---|
| 11292 ('81)-Based on animated movie | | .30 | .60 |
| 2,3 | | .30 | .60 |

**FOX GIANTS**
1944 - 1950 (132 - 196 pgs.)
Fox Features Syndicate

| | | | |
|---|---|---|---|
| Album of Crime nn(1949, 132p) | 27.00 | 81.00 | 190.00 |
| Album of Love nn(1949, 132p) | 22.00 | 65.00 | 150.00 |
| All Famous Crime Stories nn('49, 132p) | 27.00 | 81.00 | 190.00 |
| All Good Comics 1(1944, 132p)(R.W. Voigt)-The Bouncer, Purple Tigress, Puppeteer, Green Mask; Infinity-c | 20.00 | 60.00 | 140.00 |
| All Great nn(1944, 132p)-Capt. Jack Terry, Rick Evans, Jaguar Man | 20.00 | 60.00 | 140.00 |
| All Great nn(Chicago Nite Life News)(1945, 132p)-Green Mask, Bouncer, Puppeteer, Rick Evans, Rocket Kelly | 25.00 | 75.00 | 175.00 |

| | Good | Fine | N-Mint |
|---|---|---|---|
| All-Great Confessions nn(1949, 132p) | 22.00 | 65.00 | 150.00 |
| All Great Crime Stories nn('49, 132p) | 27.00 | 81.00 | 190.00 |
| All Great Jungle Adventures nn('49, 132p) | 29.00 | 86.00 | 200.00 |
| All Real Confession Magazine 3 (3/49, 132p) | 21.00 | 62.00 | 145.00 |
| All Real Confession Magazine 4 (4/49, 132p) | 21.00 | 62.00 | 145.00 |
| All Your Comics 1(1944, 132p)-The Puppeteer, Red Robbins, & Merciless the Sorcerer | 21.00 | 62.00 | 145.00 |
| Almanac Of Crime nn(1948, 148p) | 27.00 | 81.00 | 190.00 |
| Almanac Of Crime 1(1950, 132p) | 27.00 | 81.00 | 190.00 |
| Book Of Love nn(1950, 132p) | 21.00 | 62.00 | 145.00 |
| Burning Romances 1(1949, 132p) | 25.00 | 75.00 | 175.00 |
| Crimes Incorporated nn(1950, 132p) | 25.00 | 77.00 | 175.00 |
| Daring Love Stories nn(1950, 132p) | 21.00 | 62.00 | 145.00 |
| Everybody's Comics 1(1944, 196p)-The Green Mask, The Puppeteer, The Bouncer; (50 cents) | 23.00 | 70.00 | 160.00 |
| Everybody's Comics 1(1946, 196p)-Green Lama, The Puppeteer | 19.00 | 58.00 | 135.00 |
| Everybody's Comics 1(1946, 196p)-Same as '45 Ribtickler | 16.00 | 48.00 | 110.00 |
| Everybody's Comics nn(1947, 132p)-Jo-Jo, Purple Tigress, Cosmo Cat, Bronze Man | 19.00 | 58.00 | 135.00 |
| Exciting Romance Stories nn('49, 132p | 21.00 | 62.00 | 145.00 |
| Intimate Confessions nn(1950, 132p) | 21.00 | 62.00 | 145.00 |
| Journal Of Crime nn(1949, 132p) | 25.00 | 75.00 | 175.00 |
| Love Problems nn(1949, 132p) | 21.00 | 62.00 | 145.00 |
| Love Thrills nn(1950, 132p) | 21.00 | 62.00 | 145.00 |
| March of Crime nn('48, 132p)-Female w/rifle-c | 25.00 | 75.00 | 175.00 |
| March of Crime nn('49, 132p)-Cop w/pistol-c | 25.00 | 75.00 | 175.00 |
| March of Crime nn(1949, 132p)-Coffin & man w/machine-gun-c | 25.00 | 75.00 | 175.00 |
| Revealing Love Stories nn(1950, 132p) | 21.00 | 62.00 | 145.00 |
| Ribtickler nn(1945, 196p, 50¢)-Chicago Nite Life News; Marvel Mutt, Cosmo Cat, Flash Rabbit, The Nebbs app. | 19.00 | 58.00 | 135.00 |
| Romantic Thrills nn(1950, 132p) | 21.00 | 62.00 | 145.00 |
| Secret Love nn(1949, 132p) | 21.00 | 62.00 | 145.00 |
| Secret Love Stories nn(1949, 132p) | 21.00 | 62.00 | 145.00 |
| Strange Love nn(1950, 132p)-Photo-c | 25.00 | 75.00 | 175.00 |
| Sweetheart Scandals nn(1950, 132p) | 21.00 | 62.00 | 145.00 |
| Teen-Age Love nn(1950, 132p) | 21.00 | 62.00 | 145.00 |
| Throbbing Love nn(1950, 132p)-Photo-c | 25.00 | 75.00 | 175.00 |
| Truth About Crime nn(1949, 132p) | 25.00 | 75.00 | 175.00 |
| Variety Comics 1(1946, 132p)-Blue Beetle, Jungle Jo | 21.00 | 62.00 | 145.00 |
| Variety Comics nn(1950, 132p) | 19.00 | 58.00 | 135.00 |
| Western Roundup nn(1950, 132p)-Hoot Gibson | 22.00 | 65.00 | 150.00 |

NOTE: Each of the above usually contain four remaindered Fox books minus covers. Since these missing covers often had the first page of the first story, most Giants therefore are incomplete. Approximate values are listed. Books with appearances of Phantom Lady, Rulah, Jo-Jo, etc. could bring more.

**FOXHOLE** (Becomes Never Again #8?)
9-10/54 - No. 4, 3-4/55; No. 5, 7/55 - No. 7, 3/56
Mainline/Charlton Comics No. 5 on

| | Good | Fine | N-Mint |
|---|---|---|---|
| 1,2: 1-Kirby-c. 2-Kirby-c/a(2) | 7.00 | 21.00 | 50.00 |
| 3,5-Kirby-c only | 3.50 | 10.50 | 24.00 |
| 4,7 | 1.15 | 3.50 | 8.00 |
| 6-Kirby-c/a(2) | 5.70 | 17.00 | 40.00 |
| Super Reprints #10-12,15-18 | .35 | 1.00 | 2.00 |

NOTE: ***Kirby** a(r)-Super #11, 12.* ***Powell** a(r)-Super #15, 16.*

**FOXY FAGAN COMICS**
Dec, 1946 - No. 7, Summer, 1948
Dearfield Publishing Co.

| | Good | Fine | N-Mint |
|---|---|---|---|
| 1-Foxy Fagan & Little Buck begin | 6.50 | 19.00 | 45.00 |
| 2 | 3.00 | 9.00 | 21.00 |
| 3-7 | 2.30 | 7.00 | 16.00 |

**FOXY GRANDPA** (Also see The Funnies, 1st series)
1901 - 1916 (Hardcover; strip reprints)
N. Y. Herald/Frederick A. Stokes Co./M. A. Donahue & Co./Bunny Publ.(L. R. Hammersly Co.)

| | Good | Fine | VF-NM |
|---|---|---|---|
| 1901-9x15" in color-N. Y. Herald | 35.00 | 105.00 | 245.00 |
| 1902-"Latest Larks of . . . ," 32 pgs. in color, 9½x15½" | 35.00 | 105.00 | 245.00 |
| 1902-"The Many Advs. of . . . ," 9x15", 148 pgs. in color (Hammersly) | 43.00 | 130.00 | 300.00 |
| 1903-"Latest Advs.," 9x15", 24 pgs. in color, Hammersly Co. | 35.00 | 105.00 | 245.00 |
| 1903-". . .'s New Advs.," 10x15, 32 pgs. in color, Stokes | 35.00 | 105.00 | 245.00 |
| 1904-"Up to Date," 10x15", 28 pgs. in color, Stokes | 35.00 | 105.00 | 245.00 |
| 1905-"& Flip Flaps," 9½x15½", 52 pgs., in color | 35.00 | 105.00 | 245.00 |
| 1905-"The Latest Advs. of," 9x15", 28, 52, & 66 pgs, in color, M.A. Donohue Co.; re-issue of 1902 issue | 24.00 | 70.00 | 165.00 |
| 1905-"Merry Pranks of," 9½x15½", 52 pgs. in color, Donahue | 24.00 | 70.00 | 165.00 |
| 1905-"Latest Larks of," 9½x15½", 52 pgs. in color, Donahue; re-issue of 1902 issue | 24.00 | 70.00 | 165.00 |
| 1905-"Latest Larks of," 9½x15½", 24 pg. edition in color, Donahue; re-issue of 1902 issue | 24.00 | 70.00 | 165.00 |
| 1906-"Frolics," 10x15", 30 pgs. in color, Stokes | 24.00 | 70.00 | 165.00 |
| 1907 | 22.00 | 65.00 | 150.00 |
| 1908?-"Triumphs," 10x15" | 22.00 | 65.00 | 150.00 |
| 1908?-"& Little Brother," 10x15" | 22.00 | 65.00 | 150.00 |
| 1911-"Latest Tricks," r-1910,1911 Sundays in color-Stokes Co. | 22.00 | 65.00 | 150.00 |
| 1914-9½x15½", 24 pgs., 6 color cartoons/page, Bunny Publ. | 18.00 | 54.00 | 125.00 |
| 1916-"Merry Book," 10x15", 30 pgs. in color, Stokes | 18.00 | 54.00 | 125.00 |

**FOXY GRANDPA SPARKLETS SERIES**
1908 (6½x7¾"; 24 pgs. in color)
M. A. Donahue & Co.

| | Good | Fine | VF-NM |
|---|---|---|---|
| ". . . Rides the Goat," ". . .& His Boys," ". . .Playing Ball," ". . .Fun on the Farm," ". . .Fancy Shooting," ". . .Show the Boys Up Sports," ". . .Plays Santa Claus" each. . . . | 22.00 | 65.00 | 150.00 |
| 900-. . .Playing Ball; Bunny illos; 8 pgs., linen like pgs., no date | 14.00 | 43.00 | 100.00 |

**FRACTURED FAIRY TALES** (TV)
October, 1962 (Jay Ward)
Gold Key

| | Good | Fine | N-Mint |
|---|---|---|---|
| 1 (10022-210) | 5.70 | 17.00 | 40.00 |

**FRAGGLE ROCK** (TV)
Apr, 1985 - No. 8, Sept, 1986; V2#1, Apr, 1988 - No. 6, Sept, 1988
Star Comics (Marvel)/Marvel V2#1 on

| | Good | Fine | N-Mint |
|---|---|---|---|
| 1-8 | | .40 | .80 |
| V2#1-6($1.00): Reprints 1st series | | .50 | 1.00 |

**FRANCIS, BROTHER OF THE UNIVERSE**
1980 (75 cents) (52 pgs.) (One Shot)
Marvel Comics Group

| | Good | Fine | N-Mint |
|---|---|---|---|
| nn-Buscema/Marie Severin-a; story of Francis Bernadone celebrating his 800th birthday in 1982 | | .30 | .60 |

**FRANCIS THE FAMOUS TALKING MULE** (All based on movie) (See 4-Color No. 335, 465, 501, 547, 579, 621, 655, 698, 710, 745, 810, 863, 906, 953, 991, 1068, 1090)

**FRANK BUCK** (Formerly My True Love)
No. 70, May, 1950 - No. 3, Sept, 1950

*Fox Giants (All Your Comics), © FOX*

*Fox Giants (Romantic Thrills), © FOX*

*Foxy Fagan Comics #1, © Dearfield Publ.*

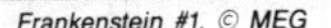
*Frankenstein #1, © MEG*

*Frankenstein Comics #9, © PRIZE*

*Frankie Comics #7, © MEG*

Fox Features Syndicate

| | Good | Fine | N-Mint |
|---|---|---|---|
| 70-Wood a(p)(3 stories)-Photo-c | 9.30 | 28.00 | 65.00 |
| 71-Wood a? (9 pgs.), 3-Painted-c | 5.70 | 17.00 | 40.00 |

**FRANKENSTEIN** (See Movie Classics)
Aug-Oct, 1964; No. 2, Sept, 1966 - No. 4, Mar, 1967
Dell Publishing Co.

| | Good | Fine | N-Mint |
|---|---|---|---|
| 1(12-283-410)(1964) | 1.50 | 4.50 | 10.00 |
| 2-Intro. & origin super-hero character (9/66) | .85 | 2.60 | 6.00 |
| 3,4 | .70 | 2.00 | 4.00 |

**FRANKENSTEIN** (The Monster of. . .; also see Monsters Unleased #2, Power Record Comics & Psycho)
Jan, 1973 - No. 18, Sept, 1975
Marvel Comics Group

| | Good | Fine | N-Mint |
|---|---|---|---|
| 1-Ploog-c/a begins, ends #6 | .50 | 1.50 | 3.00 |
| 2-18: 8,9-Dracula app. | .25 | .75 | 1.50 |

NOTE: ***Adkins*** *c-17i.* ***Buscema*** *a-7-10p.* ***Ditko*** *a-12r.* ***G. Kane*** *c-15p.* ***Orlando*** *a-8r.* ***Ploog*** *a-1-3, 4p, 5p, 6; c-1-6.* ***Wrightson*** *c-18i.*

**FRANKENSTEIN COMICS** (Also See Prize Comics)
Sum, 1945 - V5#5(#33), Oct-Nov, 1954
Prize Publications (Crestwood/Feature)

| | Good | Fine | N-Mint |
|---|---|---|---|
| 1-Frankenstein begins by Dick Briefer (origin); Frank Sinatra parody | 40.00 | 120.00 | 280.00 |
| 2 | 18.00 | 54.00 | 125.00 |
| 3-5 | 14.00 | 43.00 | 100.00 |
| 6-10: 7-S&K a(r)/Headline Comics. 8(7-8/47)-Superman satire | 13.00 | 40.00 | 90.00 |
| 11-17(1-2/49)-11-Boris Karloff parody-c/story. 17-Last humor issue | 10.00 | 30.00 | 70.00 |
| 18(3/52)-New origin, horror series begins | 13.00 | 40.00 | 90.00 |
| 19,20(V3#4, 8-9/52) | 7.00 | 21.00 | 50.00 |
| 21(V3#5), 22(V3#6) | 7.00 | 21.00 | 50.00 |
| 23(V4#1) - #28(V4#6) | 6.50 | 19.00 | 45.00 |
| 29(V5#1) - #33(V5#5) | 6.50 | 19.00 | 45.00 |

NOTE: ***Briefer*** *c/a-all.* ***Meskin*** *a-21, 29.*

**FRANKENSTEIN, JR.** (. . .& the Impossibles) (TV)
January, 1967 (Hanna-Barbera)
Gold Key

| | Good | Fine | N-Mint |
|---|---|---|---|
| 1 | 1.50 | 4.50 | 10.00 |

**FRANK FRAZETTA'S THUNDA TALES**
1987 ($2.00, color, one shot)
Fantagraphics Books

| | Good | Fine | N-Mint |
|---|---|---|---|
| 1-Frazetta-r | .35 | 1.00 | 2.00 |

**FRANK FRAZETTA'S UNTAMED LOVE** (Also see Untamed Love)
Nov, 1987 ($2.00, color, one shot)
Fantagraphics Books

| | Good | Fine | N-Mint |
|---|---|---|---|
| 1-Frazetta-r from 1950s romance comics | .35 | 1.00 | 2.00 |

**FRANKIE COMICS** (. . .& Lana No. 13-15) (Formerly Movie Tunes; becomes Frankie Fuddle No. 16 on)
No. 4, Wint, 1946-47 - No. 15, June, 1949
Marvel Comics (MgPC)

| | Good | Fine | N-Mint |
|---|---|---|---|
| 4-Mitzi, Margie, Daisy app. | 6.00 | 18.00 | 42.00 |
| 5-9 | 3.00 | 9.00 | 21.00 |
| 10-15: 13-Anti-Wertham editorial | 2.30 | 7.00 | 16.00 |

**FRANKIE DOODLE** (See Single Series #7 and Sparkler, both series)

**FRANKIE FUDDLE** (Formerly Frankie & Lana)
No. 16, Aug, 1949 - No. 17, Nov, 1949
Marvel Comics

| | Good | Fine | N-Mint |
|---|---|---|---|
| 16,17 | 2.65 | 8.00 | 18.00 |

**FRANK LUTHER'S SILLY PILLY COMICS** (See Jingle Dingle. . .)
1950 (10 cents)
Children's Comics

| | Good | Fine | N-Mint |
|---|---|---|---|
| 1-Characters from radio, records, & TV | 2.65 | 8.00 | 18.00 |

**FRANK MERRIWELL AT YALE** (Speed Demons No. 5 on?)
June, 1955 - No. 4, Jan, 1956 (Also see Shadow Comics)
Charlton Comics

| | Good | Fine | N-Mint |
|---|---|---|---|
| 1 | 2.15 | 6.50 | 15.00 |
| 2-4 | 1.30 | 4.00 | 9.00 |

**FRANTIC** (Magazine) (See Ratfink & Zany)
Oct, 1958 - V2#2, April, 1959 (Satire)
Pierce Publishing Co.

| | Good | Fine | N-Mint |
|---|---|---|---|
| V1#1,2 | 1.15 | 3.50 | 8.00 |
| V2#1,2: 1-Burgos-a, Severin-c/a | .70 | 2.00 | 5.00 |

**FRECKLES AND HIS FRIENDS** (See Crackajack Funnies, Famous Comics Cartoon Book, Honeybee Birdwhistle. . . & Red Ryder)

**FRECKLES AND HIS FRIENDS**
No. 5, 11/47 - No. 12, 8/49; 11/55 - No. 4, 6/56
Standard Comics/Argo

| | Good | Fine | N-Mint |
|---|---|---|---|
| 5-Reprints | 4.00 | 12.00 | 28.00 |
| 6-12-Reprints; 11-Lingerie panels | 2.00 | 6.00 | 14.00 |

NOTE: *Some copies of No. 8 & 9 contain a printing oddity. The negatives were elongated in the engraving process, probably to conform to page dimensions on the filler pages. Those pages only look normal when viewed at a 45 degree angle.*

| | Good | Fine | N-Mint |
|---|---|---|---|
| 1(Argo,'55)-Reprints (NEA Service) | 2.30 | 7.00 | 16.00 |
| 2-4 | 1.30 | 4.00 | 9.00 |

**FREDDY** (Formerly My Little Margie's Boy Friends)
V2#12, June, 1958 - No. 47, Feb, 1965 (Also see Blue Bird)
Charlton Comics

| | Good | Fine | N-Mint |
|---|---|---|---|
| V2#12 | .85 | 2.50 | 6.00 |
| 13-15 | .50 | 1.50 | 3.00 |
| 16-47 | .35 | 1.00 | 2.00 |
| Schiff's Shoes Presents. . . No. 1(1959)-Giveaway | .35 | 1.00 | 2.00 |

**FREDDY**
May-July, 1963 - No. 3, Oct-Dec, 1964
Dell Publishing Co.

| | Good | Fine | N-Mint |
|---|---|---|---|
| 1-3 | .55 | 1.65 | 4.00 |

**FRED HEMBECK DESTROYS THE MARVEL UNIVERSE**
July, 1989 ($1.50, One-shot)
Marvel Comics

| | Good | Fine | N-Mint |
|---|---|---|---|
| 1-Punisher app.; Staton-i (5 pgs.) | .25 | .75 | 1.50 |

**FRED HEMBECK SELLS THE MARVEL UNIVERSE**
Oct, 1990 ($1.25, color, one-shot)
Marvel Comics

| | Good | Fine | N-Mint |
|---|---|---|---|
| 1-Punisher, Wolverine parodies; Hembeck/Austin-c | | .65 | 1.30 |

**FREE COMICS TO YOU FROM. . . (name of shoe store)** (Has clown on cover & another with a rabbit) (Like comics from Weather Bird & Edward's Shoes)
Circa 1956, 1960-61
Shoe Store Giveaway

Contains a comic bound with new cover - several combinations possible; Some Harvey titles known. contents determines price.

**FREEDOM AGENT** (Also see John Steele)
April, 1963
Gold Key

| | Good | Fine | N-Mint |
|---|---|---|---|
| 1 (10054-304)-Painted-c | 1.00 | 3.00 | 7.00 |

**FREEDOM FIGHTERS** (See Justice League of America No. 107,108)
Mar-Apr, 1976 - No. 15, July-Aug, 1978
National Periodical Publications/DC Comics

| | Good | Fine | N-Mint |
|---|---|---|---|
| 1-Uncle Sam, The Ray, Black Condor, Doll Man, Human Bomb, & Phantom Lady begin | | .35 | .70 |

| | Good | Fine | N-Mint |
|---|---|---|---|
| 2-15: 7-1st app. Crusaders. 10-Origin Doll Man. 11-Origin The Ray. 12-Origin Firebrand. 13-Origin Black Condor. 14,15-Batgirl & Batwoman app. 15-Origin Phantom Lady | | .25 | .50 |

NOTE: ***Buckler** c-5-11p, 13p, 14p. Cat-Man app. in #10.*

**FREEDOM TRAIN**
1948 (Giveaway)
Street & Smith Publications

| | Good | Fine | N-Mint |
|---|---|---|---|
| nn-Powell-c | 1.70 | 5.00 | 10.00 |

**FRENZY** (Magazine) (Satire)
April, 1958 - No. 6, March, 1959
Picture Magazine

| | Good | Fine | N-Mint |
|---|---|---|---|
| 1 | .85 | 2.50 | 5.00 |
| 2-6 | .50 | 1.50 | 3.00 |

**FRIDAY FOSTER**
October, 1972
Dell Publishing Co.

| | Good | Fine | N-Mint |
|---|---|---|---|
| 1 | 1.00 | 3.00 | 6.00 |

**FRIENDLY GHOST, CASPER, THE** (Becomes Casper. . . #254 on)
Aug, 1958 - No. 224, Oct, 1982; No. 225, Oct, 1986 - No. 253, 1989
Harvey Publications

| | Good | Fine | N-Mint |
|---|---|---|---|
| 1-Infinity-c | 14.00 | 42.00 | 100.00 |
| 2 | 7.00 | 21.00 | 50.00 |
| 3-10: 6-X-Mas-c | 4.00 | 12.00 | 28.00 |
| 11-20: 18-X-Mas-c | 2.65 | 8.00 | 18.00 |
| 21-30 | 1.20 | 3.50 | 8.00 |
| 31-50 | .70 | 2.00 | 5.00 |
| 51-100: 54-X-Mas-c | .55 | 1.60 | 3.20 |
| 101-159 | | .60 | 1.20 |
| 160-163: All 52 pg. Giants | .25 | .75 | 1.50 |
| 164-238: 173,179,185-Cub Scout Specials. 238-on $1.00 issues | | .35 | .70 |
| 239-253 ($1.00) | | .50 | 1.00 |
| American Dental Assoc. giveaway-Small size (1967, 16 pgs.) | .50 | 1.50 | 3.00 |

**FRIGHT**
June, 1975 (August on inside)
Atlas/Seaboard Periodicals

| | Good | Fine | N-Mint |
|---|---|---|---|
| 1-Origin The Son of Dracula; Frank Thorne-c/a | | .40 | .80 |

**FRIGHT NIGHT**
Oct, 1988 - No. 22, 1990 ($1.75, color)
Now Comics

| | Good | Fine | N-Mint |
|---|---|---|---|
| 1-22: 1-3-Adapts movie. 8,9-Evil Ed horror photo-c from movie | .30 | .90 | 1.80 |

**FRIGHT NIGHT II**
1989 ($3.95, color, 52 pgs.)
Now Comics

| | Good | Fine | N-Mint |
|---|---|---|---|
| 1-Adapts movie sequel | .70 | 2.00 | 4.00 |

**FRISKY ANIMALS** (Formerly Frisky Fables; Super Cat #56 on)
No. 44, Jan, 1951 - No. 55, Sept, 1953
Star Publications

| | Good | Fine | N-Mint |
|---|---|---|---|
| 44-Super Cat | 7.00 | 21.00 | 50.00 |
| 45-Classic L. B. Cole-c | 11.00 | 32.00 | 75.00 |
| 46-51,53-55-Super Cat | 5.70 | 17.00 | 40.00 |
| 52-L. B. Cole-c/a, 3 pgs. | 7.00 | 21.00 | 50.00 |

NOTE: *All have **L. B. Cole**-c. No. 47-No Super Cat. **Disbrow** a-49, 52. **Fago** a-51.*

**FRISKY ANIMALS ON PARADE** (Formerly Parade Comics; becomes Superspook)
Sept, 1957 - No. 3, Dec-Jan, 1957-1958
Ajax-Farrell Publ. (Four Star Comic Corp.)

| | Good | Fine | N-Mint |
|---|---|---|---|
| 1-L. B. Cole-c | 5.00 | 15.00 | 35.00 |
| 2-No L. B. Cole-c | 2.65 | 8.00 | 18.00 |
| 3-L. B. Cole-c | 3.60 | 11.00 | 25.00 |

**FRISKY FABLES** (Frisky Animals No. 44 on)
Spring, 1945 - No. 44, Oct-Nov, 1949
Premium Group/Novelty Publ.

| | Good | Fine | N-Mint |
|---|---|---|---|
| V1#1-Al Fago-c/a | 7.00 | 21.00 | 50.00 |
| 2,3(1945) | 3.60 | 11.00 | 25.00 |
| 4-7(1946) | 2.65 | 8.00 | 18.00 |
| V2#1-9,11,12(1947) | 1.70 | 5.00 | 12.00 |
| 10-Christmas-c | 2.00 | 6.00 | 14.00 |
| V3#1-12(1948): 4-Flag-c. 9-Infinity-c | 1.50 | 4.50 | 10.00 |
| V4#1-7 | 1.50 | 4.50 | 10.00 |
| 36-44(V4#8-12, V5#1-4)-L. B. Cole-c; 40-X-mas-c | 5.70 | 17.00 | 40.00 |
| Accepted Reprint No. 43 (nd); L.B. Cole-c | 2.30 | 7.00 | 16.00 |

**FRITZI RITZ** (See Comics On Parade, Single Series #5,1(reprint), Tip Top & United Comics)

**FRITZI RITZ** (United Comics No. 8-26)
Fall/48 - No. 7, 1949; No. 27, 3-4/53 - No. 36, 9-10/54; No. 42, 1/55; No. 43, 6/56 - No. 55, 9-11/57; No. 56, 12-2/57-58 - No. 59, 9-11/58
United Features Synd./St. John No. 37?-55/Dell No. 56 on

| | Good | Fine | N-Mint |
|---|---|---|---|
| nn(1948)-Special Fall issue | 7.00 | 21.00 | 50.00 |
| 2 | 3.60 | 11.00 | 25.00 |
| 3-7(1949): 6-Abbie & Slats app. | 2.65 | 8.00 | 18.00 |
| 27-29(1953): 29-Five pg. Abbie & Slats; 1 pg. Mamie by Russell Patterson | 1.70 | 5.00 | 12.00 |
| 30-59: 36-1 pg. Mamie by Patterson. 43-Peanuts by Schulz | 1.15 | 3.50 | 8.00 |

NOTE: *Abbie & Slats in #6,7, 27-31. Li'l Abner in #33, 35, 36. Peanuts in #31, 43, 58, 59.*

**FROGMAN COMICS**
Jan-Feb, 1952 - No. 11, May, 1953
Hillman Periodicals

| | Good | Fine | N-Mint |
|---|---|---|---|
| 1 | 5.00 | 15.00 | 35.00 |
| 2 | 2.65 | 8.00 | 18.00 |
| 3,4,6-11: 4-Meskin-a | 2.00 | 6.00 | 14.00 |
| 5-Krigstein, Torres-a | 3.70 | 11.00 | 26.00 |

**FROGMEN, THE**
No. 1258, Feb-Apr, 1962 - No. 11, Nov-Jan, 1964-65 (Painted-c)
Dell Publishing Co.

| | Good | Fine | N-Mint |
|---|---|---|---|
| 4-Color 1258(#1)-Evans-a | 3.70 | 11.00 | 26.00 |
| 2,3-Evans-a; part Frazetta inks in #2,3 | 4.50 | 14.00 | 32.00 |
| 4,6-11 | 1.70 | 5.00 | 12.00 |
| 5-Toth-a | 3.00 | 9.00 | 21.00 |

**FROM BEYOND THE UNKNOWN**
10-11/69 - No. 25, 11-12/73 (No. 7-11: 64 pgs.; No. 12-17: 52 pgs.)
National Periodical Publications

| | Good | Fine | N-Mint |
|---|---|---|---|
| 1 | .50 | 1.50 | 3.00 |
| 2-10: 7-Intro. Col. Glenn Merrit | .25 | .75 | 1.50 |
| 11-25: Star Rovers-r begin #18,19. Space Museum in #23-25 | | .50 | 1.00 |

NOTE: ***N. Adams** c-3, 6, 8, 9. **Anderson** c-2, 4, 5, 10, 11i, 15-17, 22; reprints-3, 4, 6-8, 10, 11, 13-16, 24, 25. **Infantino** r-1-5, 7-19, 23-25; c-11p. **Kaluta** c-18, 19. **Kubert** c-1, 7, 12-14. **Toth** a-2r. **Wood** a-13i. Photo c-22.*

**FROM HERE TO INSANITY** (Satire) (Formerly Eh! No. 1-7)
(See Frantic & Frenzy)
No. 8, Feb, 1955 - V3#1, 1956
Charlton Comics

| | Good | Fine | N-Mint |
|---|---|---|---|
| 8 | 4.50 | 14.00 | 32.00 |
| 9 | 3.50 | 10.50 | 24.00 |
| 10-Ditko-c/a (3 pgs.) | 7.00 | 21.00 | 50.00 |
| 11,12-All Kirby except 4 pgs. | 8.00 | 24.00 | 56.00 |

V3#1(1956)-Ward-c/a(2)(signed McCartney); 5 pgs. Wolverton; 3 pgs.

Frisky Animals #53, © STAR

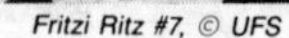
Fritzi Ritz #7, © UFS

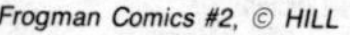
Frogman Comics #2, © HILL

Frontier Fighters #7, © DC

Frontline Combat #1, © WMG

Fun Comics #10, © STAR

| | Good | Fine | N-Mint |
|---|---|---|---|
| Ditko; magazine format | 16.00 | 48.00 | 110.00 |

**FRONTIER DAYS**
1956 (Giveaway)
Robin Hood Shoe Store (Brown Shoe)

| | Good | Fine | N-Mint |
|---|---|---|---|
| 1 | 1.35 | 4.00 | 8.00 |

**FRONTIER DOCTOR** (See 4-Color No. 877)

**FRONTIER FIGHTERS**
Sept-Oct, 1955 - No. 8, Nov-Dec, 1956
National Periodical Publications

| | Good | Fine | N-Mint |
|---|---|---|---|
| 1-Davy Crockett, Buffalo Bill by Kubert, Kit Carson begin (Scarce) | 27.00 | 80.00 | 185.00 |
| 2 | 18.00 | 54.00 | 125.00 |
| 3-8 | 14.00 | 43.00 | 100.00 |

NOTE: *Buffalo Bill by **Kubert** in all.*

**FRONTIER ROMANCES**
Nov-Dec, 1949 - No. 2, Feb-Mar, 1950 (Painted-c)
Avon Periodicals/I. W.

| | Good | Fine | N-Mint |
|---|---|---|---|
| 1-Used in **SOTI**, pg. 180(General reference) & illo. "Erotic spanking in a western comic book" | 28.00 | 85.00 | 200.00 |
| 2 (Scarce) | 17.00 | 51.00 | 120.00 |
| 1-I.W.(reprints Avon's #1) | 2.75 | 8.00 | 16.00 |
| I.W. Reprint #9 | 1.35 | 4.00 | 8.00 |

**FRONTIER SCOUT: DAN'L BOONE** (Formerly Death Valley; The Masked Raider No. 14 on)
No. 10, Jan, 1956 - No. 13, Aug, 1956; V2#14, March, 1965
Charlton Comics

| | Good | Fine | N-Mint |
|---|---|---|---|
| 10 | 3.00 | 9.00 | 21.00 |
| 11-13(1956) | 1.70 | 5.00 | 12.00 |
| V2#14(3/65) | .70 | 2.00 | 5.00 |

**FRONTIER TRAIL** (The Rider No. 1-5)
No. 6, May, 1958
Ajax/Farrell Publ.

| | Good | Fine | N-Mint |
|---|---|---|---|
| 6 | 1.70 | 5.00 | 12.00 |

**FRONTIER WESTERN**
Feb, 1956 - No. 10, Aug, 1957
Atlas Comics (PrPI)

| | Good | Fine | N-Mint |
|---|---|---|---|
| 1 | 7.00 | 21.00 | 50.00 |
| 2,3,6-Williamson-a, 4 pgs. each | 5.70 | 17.00 | 40.00 |
| 4,7,9,10: 10-Check-a | 2.65 | 8.00 | 18.00 |
| 5-Crandall, Baker, Wildey, Davis-a; Williamson text illos | 4.00 | 12.00 | 28.00 |
| 8-Crandall, Morrow, & Wildey-a | 2.65 | 8.00 | 18.00 |

NOTE: ***Colan** a-2. **Drucker** a-3, 4. **Heath** c-5. **Maneely** a-2, 7. c-2. **Romita** a-7. **Severin** c-6, 8, 10. **Tuska** a-2. Ringo Kid in No. 4.*

**FRONTLINE COMBAT**
July-Aug, 1951 - No. 15, Jan, 1954
E. C. Comics

| | Good | Fine | N-Mint |
|---|---|---|---|
| 1 | 39.00 | 118.00 | 275.00 |
| 2 | 26.00 | 79.00 | 185.00 |
| 3 | 19.00 | 58.00 | 135.00 |
| 4-Used in **SOTI**, pg. 257; contains "Airburst" by Kurtzman which is his personal all-time favorite story | 16.00 | 48.00 | 115.00 |
| 5 | 14.00 | 43.00 | 100.00 |
| 6-10 | 11.50 | 34.00 | 80.00 |
| 11-15 | 9.30 | 28.00 | 65.00 |

NOTE: ***Davis** a-in all; c-11, 12. **Evans** a-10-15. **Heath** a-1. **Kubert** a-14. **Kurtzman** a-1-5; c-1-9. **Severin** a-5-7, 9, 13, 15. **Severin/Elder** a-2-11; c-10. **Toth** a-8, 12. **Wood** a-1-4, 6-10, 12-15; c-13-15. Special issues: No. 7 (Iwo Jima), No. 9 (Civil War), No. 12 (Air Force). (Canadian reprints known; see Table of Contents.)*

**FRONT PAGE COMIC BOOK**
1945
Front Page Comics (Harvey)

| | Good | Fine | N-Mint |
|---|---|---|---|
| 1-Kubert-a; intro. & 1st app. Man in Black by Powell; Fuje-c | 17.00 | 51.00 | 120.00 |

**FROST AND FIRE** (See DC Science Fiction Graphic Novel)

**FROSTY THE SNOWMAN**
No. 359, Nov, 1951 - No. 1272, Dec-Feb?/1961-62
Dell Publishing Co.

| | Good | Fine | N-Mint |
|---|---|---|---|
| 4-Color 359 | 3.00 | 9.00 | 21.00 |
| 4-Color 435 | 2.30 | 7.00 | 16.00 |
| 4-Color 514,601,661 | 2.00 | 6.00 | 14.00 |
| 4-Color 748,861,950,1065 | 1.70 | 5.00 | 12.00 |
| 4-Color 1153,1272 | 1.50 | 4.50 | 10.00 |

**FRUITMAN SPECIAL**
Dec, 1969 (68 pages)
Harvey Publications

| | Good | Fine | N-Mint |
|---|---|---|---|
| 1-Funny super hero | 1.00 | 3.00 | 6.00 |

**F-TROOP** (TV)
Aug, 1966 - No. 7, Aug, 1967 (All have photo-c)
Dell Publishing Co.

| | Good | Fine | N-Mint |
|---|---|---|---|
| 1 | 4.00 | 12.00 | 28.00 |
| 2-7 | 2.00 | 6.00 | 14.00 |

**FUGITIVES FROM JUSTICE**
Feb, 1952 - No. 5, Oct, 1952
St. John Publishing Co.

| | Good | Fine | N-Mint |
|---|---|---|---|
| 1 | 7.00 | 21.00 | 50.00 |
| 2-Matt Baker-a; Vic Flint strip reprints begin | 7.00 | 21.00 | 50.00 |
| 3-Reprints panel from Authentic Police Cases that was used in **SOTI** with changes; Tuska-a | 7.00 | 21.00 | 50.00 |
| 4 | 3.50 | 10.50 | 24.00 |
| 5-Last Vic Flint-r; bondage-c | 4.30 | 13.00 | 30.00 |

**FUGITOID**
1985 (One shot, B&W, magazine size)
Mirage Studios

| | Good | Fine | N-Mint |
|---|---|---|---|
| 1-Ties into Teenage Mutant Ninja Turtles #5 | 1.85 | 5.50 | 11.00 |

**FULL COLOR COMICS**
1946
Fox Features Syndicate

| | Good | Fine | N-Mint |
|---|---|---|---|
| nn | 6.00 | 18.00 | 42.00 |

**FULL OF FUN**
Aug, 1957 - No. 2, Nov, 1957; 1964
Red Top (Decker Publ.)(Farrell)/I. W. Enterprises

| | Good | Fine | N-Mint |
|---|---|---|---|
| 1(1957)-Dave Berg-a | 2.30 | 7.00 | 16.00 |
| 2-Reprints Bingo, the Monkey Doodle Boy | 1.50 | 4.50 | 10.00 |
| 8-I.W. Reprint('64) | .35 | 1.00 | 2.00 |

**FUN AT CHRISTMAS** (See March of Comics No. 138)

**FUN CLUB COMICS** (See Interstate Theatres . . .)

**FUN COMICS** (Mighty Bear No. 13 on)
No. 9, Jan, 1953 - No. 12, Oct, 1953
Star Publications

| | Good | Fine | N-Mint |
|---|---|---|---|
| 9(Giant)-L. B. Cole-c | 7.00 | 21.00 | 50.00 |
| 10-12-L. B. Cole-c | 4.50 | 14.00 | 32.00 |

**FUNDAY FUNNIES** (See Famous TV . . ., and Harvey Hits No. 35,40)

**FUN-IN** (TV)(Hanna-Barbera)
Feb, 1970 - No. 10, Jan, 1972; No. 11, 4/74 - No. 15, 12/74
Gold Key

| | Good | Fine | N-Mint |
|---|---|---|---|
| 1-Dastardly & Muttley in Their Flying Machines; Perils of Penelope Pitstop in 1-4; It's the Wolf in all | .85 | 2.60 | 6.00 |

| | Good | Fine | N-Mint |
|---|---|---|---|
| 2-4,6-Cattanooga Cats in 2-4 | .60 | 1.75 | 3.50 |
| 5,7-Motormouse & Autocat, Dastardly & Muttley in both; It's the Wolf in #7 | .50 | 1.50 | 3.00 |
| 8,10-The Harlem Globetrotters, Dastardly & Muttley in #10 | .50 | 1.50 | 3.00 |
| 9-Where's Huddles?, Dastardly & Muttley, Motormouse & Autocat app. | .50 | 1.50 | 3.00 |
| 11-15: 11-Butch Cassidy. 12,15-Speed Buggy. 13-Hair Bear Bunch. 14-Inch High Private Eye | .35 | 1.00 | 2.00 |

**FUNKY PHANTOM, THE** (TV)
Mar, 1972 - No. 13, Mar, 1975 (Hanna-Barbera)
Gold Key

| | Good | Fine | N-Mint |
|---|---|---|---|
| 1 | 1.00 | 3.00 | 7.00 |
| 2-5 | .70 | 2.00 | 4.00 |
| 6-13 | .50 | 1.50 | 3.00 |

**FUNLAND**
No date (25 cents)
Ziff-Davis (Approved Comics)

| | Good | Fine | N-Mint |
|---|---|---|---|
| nn-Contains games, puzzles, etc. | 7.00 | 21.00 | 50.00 |

**FUNLAND COMICS**
1945
Croyden Publishers

| | Good | Fine | N-Mint |
|---|---|---|---|
| 1 | 7.00 | 21.00 | 50.00 |

**FUNNIES, THE** (Also see Comic Cuts)
1929 - No. 36, 10/18/30 (10 cents; 5 cents No. 22 on) (16 pgs.)
Full tabloid size in color; not reprints; published every Saturday
Dell Publishing Co.

| | Good | Fine | N-Mint |
|---|---|---|---|
| 1-My Big Brudder, Johnathan, Jazzbo & Jim, Foxy Grandpa, Sniffy, Jimmy Jams & other strips begin; first four-color comic newsstand publication; also contains magic, puzzles & stories | 27.00 | 81.00 | 190.00 |
| 2-21 (1930, 30 cents) | 10.00 | 30.00 | 70.00 |
| 22(nn-7/12/30-5 cents) | 7.00 | 21.00 | 50.00 |
| 23(nn-7/19/30-5 cents), 24(nn-7/26/30-5 cents), 25(nn-8/2/30), 26(nn-8/9/30), 27(nn-8/16/30), 28(nn-8/23/30), 29(nn-8/30/30), 30(nn-9/6/30), 31(nn-9/13/30), 32(nn-9/20/30), 33(nn-9/27/30), 34(nn-10/4/30), 35(nn-10/11/30), 36(nn, no date-10/18/30) each.... | 7.00 | 21.00 | 50.00 |

**FUNNIES, THE** (New Funnies No. 65 on)
Oct, 1936 - No. 64, May, 1942
Dell Publishing Co.

| | Good | Fine | N-Mint |
|---|---|---|---|
| 1-Tailspin Tommy, Mutt & Jeff, Alley Oop (1st app?), Capt. Easy, Don Dixon begin | 100.00 | 250.00 | 600.00 |
| 2-Scribbly by Mayer begins | 43.00 | 130.00 | 300.00 |
| 3 | 38.00 | 115.00 | 265.00 |
| 4,5: 4-Christmas-c | 31.00 | 92.00 | 215.00 |
| 6-10 | 24.00 | 73.00 | 170.00 |
| 11-20: 16-Christmas-c | 22.00 | 65.00 | 150.00 |
| 21-29 | 18.00 | 54.00 | 125.00 |
| 30-John Carter of Mars (origin) begins by Edgar Rice Burroughs | 54.00 | 160.00 | 375.00 |
| 31-44: 33-John Coleman Burroughs art begins on John Carter. 35-(9/39)-Mr. District Attorney begins-based on radio show | 31.00 | 92.00 | 215.00 |
| 45-Origin/1st app. Phantasmo, the Master of the World (Dell's 1st super-hero) & his sidekick Whizzer McGee | 24.00 | 73.00 | 170.00 |
| 46-50: 46-The Black Knight begins, ends #62 | 22.00 | 65.00 | 150.00 |
| 51-56-Last ERB John Carter of Mars | 22.00 | 65.00 | 150.00 |
| 57-Intro. & origin Captain Midnight | 54.00 | 160.00 | 375.00 |
| 58-60 | 22.00 | 65.00 | 150.00 |
| 61-Andy Panda begins by Walter Lantz | 24.00 | 70.00 | 165.00 |
| 62,63: 63-Last Captain Midnight-c; bondage-c | 22.00 | 65.00 | 150.00 |
| 64-Format change; Oswald the Rabbit, Felix the Cat, Li'l Eight Ball app.; origin & 1st app. Woody Woodpecker in Oswald; last Capt. Midnight | 45.00 | 135.00 | 315.00 |

NOTE: ***Mayer*** *c-26, 48.* ***McWilliams*** *art in many issues on "Rex King of the Deep."*

**FUNNIES ANNUAL, THE**
1959 ($1.00)(B&W; tabloid-size, approx. 7x10")
Avon Periodicals

| | Good | Fine | N-Mint |
|---|---|---|---|
| 1-(Rare)-Features the best newspaper comic strips of the year: Archie, Snuffy Smith, Beetle Bailey, Henry, Blondie, Steve Canyon, Buz Sawyer, The Little King, Hi & Lois, Popeye, & others. Also has a chronological history of the comics from 2000 B.C. to 1959. | 26.00 | 77.00 | 180.00 |

**FUNNIES ON PARADE** (Premium)
1933 (Probably the 1st comic book) (36 pgs.; slick cover)
No date or publisher listed
Eastern Color Printing Co.

| | Good | Fine | VF-NM | NM/Mint |
|---|---|---|---|---|
| nn-Contains Sunday page reprints of Mutt & Jeff, Joe Palooka, Hairbreadth Harry, Reg'lar Fellers, Skippy, & others (10,000 print run). This book was printed for Proctor & Gamble to be given away & came out before Famous Funnies or Century of Comics. | 415.00 | 1040.00 | 2500.00 | 3500.00 |

(Estimated up to 50 total copies exist, 3 in NM/Mint)

**FUNNY ANIMALS** (See Fawcett's Funny Animals)
Sept, 1984 - No. 2, Nov, 1984
Charlton Comics

| | Good | Fine | N-Mint |
|---|---|---|---|
| 1,2-Atomic Mouse-r | | .30 | .60 |

**FUNNYBONE**
1944 (132 pages)
La Salle Publishing Co.

| | Good | Fine | N-Mint |
|---|---|---|---|
| nn | 12.00 | 36.00 | 85.00 |

**FUNNY BOOK** (. . . Magazine) (Hocus Pocus No. 9)
Dec, 1942 - No. 9, Aug-Sept, 1946
Parents' Magazine Press (Funny Book Publishing Corp.)

| | Good | Fine | N-Mint |
|---|---|---|---|
| 1-Funny animal; Alice In Wonderland app. | 8.00 | 24.00 | 56.00 |
| 2 | 3.70 | 11.00 | 26.00 |
| 3-9: 9-Hocus-Pocus strip | 2.65 | 8.00 | 18.00 |

**FUNNY COMICS** (7 cents)
1955 (36 pgs.; 5x7"; in color)
Modern Store Publ.

| | Good | Fine | N-Mint |
|---|---|---|---|
| 1-Funny animal | .80 | 2.25 | 4.50 |

**FUNNY COMIC TUNES** (See Funny Tunes)

**FUNNY FABLES**
Aug, 1957 - V2#2, Nov, 1957
Decker Publications (Red Top Comics)

| | Good | Fine | N-Mint |
|---|---|---|---|
| V1#1 | 1.70 | 5.00 | 12.00 |
| V2#1,2 | 1.15 | 3.50 | 8.00 |

**FUNNY FILMS**
Sept-Oct, 1949 - No. 29, May-June, 1954 (No. 1-4: 52 pgs.)
American Comics Group(Michel Publ./Titan Publ.)

| | Good | Fine | N-Mint |
|---|---|---|---|
| 1-Puss An' Boots, Blunderbunny begin | 8.50 | 25.50 | 60.00 |
| 2 | 4.00 | 12.00 | 28.00 |
| 3-10 | 2.65 | 8.00 | 18.00 |
| 11-20 | 2.00 | 6.00 | 14.00 |
| 21-29 | 1.50 | 4.50 | 10.00 |

**FUNNY FOLKS** (Hollywood . . . on cover only No. 16-26; becomes Hollywood Funny Folks No. 27 on)
April-May, 1946 - No. 26, June-July, 1950 (52 pgs., #16 on)
National Periodical Publications

| | Good | Fine | N-Mint |
|---|---|---|---|
| 1-Nutsy Squirrel begins (1st app.) by Rube Grossman | 22.00 | 65.00 | 150.00 |
| 2 | 10.00 | 30.00 | 70.00 |
| 3-5 | 7.00 | 21.00 | 50.00 |

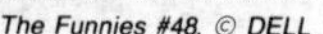
*The Funnies #48, © DELL*

*Funnies on Parade nn, © EAS*

*Funny Folks #5, © DC*

Funnyman #1, © ME

Funny Picture Stories V1#1, © CM

Funny Stuff #47, © DC

| | Good | Fine | N-Mint |
|---|---|---|---|
| 6-10 | 5.00 | 15.00 | 35.00 |
| 11-26: 16-Begin 52 pg. issues (10-11/48) | 3.60 | 11.00 | 25.00 |

NOTE: ***Sheldon Mayer*** *a-in some issues.* ***Post*** *a-18.*

**FUNNY FROLICS**
Summer, 1945 - No. 5, Dec, 1946
Timely/Marvel Comics (SPI)

| | Good | Fine | N-Mint |
|---|---|---|---|
| 1-Sharpy Fox, Puffy Pig, Krazy Krow | 9.30 | 28.00 | 65.00 |
| 2 | 5.00 | 15.00 | 35.00 |
| 3,4 | 4.00 | 12.00 | 28.00 |
| 5-Kurtzman-a | 5.00 | 15.00 | 35.00 |

**FUNNY FUNNIES**
April, 1943 (68 pages)
Nedor Publishing Co.

| | Good | Fine | N-Mint |
|---|---|---|---|
| 1 (Funny animals) | 11.00 | 32.00 | 75.00 |

**FUNNYMAN** (Also see Extra Comics)
Dec, 1947; No. 1, Jan, 1948 - No. 6, Aug, 1948
Magazine Enterprises

nn(12/47)-Prepublication B&W undistributed copy by Siegel & Shuster-(5¾x8"), 16 pgs.; Sold in San Francisco in 1976 for $300.00

| | Good | Fine | N-Mint |
|---|---|---|---|
| 1-Siegel & Shuster-a in all | 16.00 | 48.00 | 115.00 |
| 2 | 12.00 | 36.00 | 85.00 |
| 3-6 | 10.00 | 30.00 | 70.00 |

**FUNNY MOVIES** (See 3-D Funny Movies)

**FUNNY PAGES** (Formerly The Comics Magazine)
No. 6, Nov, 1936 - No. 42, Oct, 1940
Comics Magazine Co./Ultem Publ.(Chesler)/Centaur Publications

| | Good | Fine | N-Mint |
|---|---|---|---|
| V1#6 (nn, nd)-The Clock begins (2 pgs., 1st app.), ends #11 | 50.00 | 150.00 | 350.00 |
| 7-11 | 32.00 | 95.00 | 225.00 |
| V2#1 (9/37)(V2#2 on-c; V2#1 in indicia) | 25.00 | 75.00 | 175.00 |
| V2#2 (10/37)(V2#3 on-c; V2#2 in indicia) | 25.00 | 75.00 | 175.00 |
| 3(11/37)-5 | 25.00 | 75.00 | 175.00 |
| 6(1st Centaur, 3/38) | 39.00 | 118.00 | 275.00 |
| 7-9 | 29.00 | 85.00 | 200.00 |
| 10(Scarce)-1st app. of The Arrow by Gustavson (Blue costume) | 125.00 | 310.00 | 750.00 |
| 11,12 | 54.00 | 160.00 | 375.00 |
| V3#1-6 | 54.00 | 160.00 | 375.00 |
| 7-1st Arrow-c (9/39) | 68.00 | 205.00 | 475.00 |
| 8,9: 9-Tarpe Mills jungle-c | 54.00 | 160.00 | 375.00 |
| 10-2nd Arrow-c | 59.00 | 178.00 | 415.00 |
| V4#1(1/40, Arrow-c)-(Rare)-The Owl & The Phantom Rider app.; origin Mantoka, Maker of Magic by Jack Cole. Mad Ming begins, ends #42. Tarpe Mills-a | 64.00 | 193.00 | 450.00 |
| 35-38: 35-Arrow-c. 36-38-Mad Ming-c | 47.00 | 140.00 | 325.00 |
| 39-42-Arrow-c. 42-Last Arrow | 47.00 | 140.00 | 325.00 |

NOTE: ***Burgos*** *c-V3#10.* ***Jack Cole*** *a-V2#3, 7, 8, 10, 11, V3#2, 6, 9, 10, V4#1, 37.* ***Eisner*** *a-V1#7, 8, 10.* ***Ken Ernst*** *a-#7.* ***Everett*** *a-V2#11 (illos).* ***Gill Fox*** *a-V2#11.* ***Sid Greene*** *a-39.* ***Guardineer*** *a-V2#2, 3, 5.* ***Gustavson*** *a-V2#5, 11, 12, V3#1-10, 35, 38-42; c-V3#7, 35, 39-42.* ***Bob Kane*** *a-V3#1.* ***McWilliams*** *a-V2#12, V3#1, 3-6.* ***Tarpe Mills*** *a-V3#8-10, V4#1; c-V3#9.* ***Ed Moore Jr.*** *a-V2#12.* ***Bob Wood*** *a-V2#2, 3, 8, 11, V3#6, 9, 10; c-V2#6, 7.*

**FUNNY PICTURE STORIES** (Comic Pages V3#4 on)
Nov, 1936 - V3#3, May, 1939
Comics Magazine Co./Centaur Publications

| | Good | Fine | N-Mint |
|---|---|---|---|
| V1#1-The Clock begins (c-feature)(See Funny Pages for 1st app.) | 117.00 | 290.00 | 700.00 |
| 2 | 45.00 | 135.00 | 315.00 |
| 3-9: 4-Eisner-a; Christmas-c | 31.00 | 92.00 | 215.00 |
| V2#1 (9/37; V1#10 on-c; V2#1 in indicia)-Jack Strand begins | 24.00 | 73.00 | 170.00 |
| 2 (10/37; V1#11 on-c; V2#2 in indicia) | 24.00 | 73.00 | 170.00 |
| 3-5: 4-Xmas-c | 22.00 | 65.00 | 150.00 |
| 6-(1st Centaur, 3/38) | 36.00 | 107.00 | 250.00 |
| 7-11 | 23.00 | 70.00 | 160.00 |
| V3#1-3 | 20.00 | 60.00 | 140.00 |
| Laundry giveaway (16-20 pgs., 1930s)-slick-c | 10.00 | 30.00 | 70.00 |

NOTE: ***Biro*** *c-V2#1.* ***Guardineer*** *a-V1#11.* ***Bob Wood*** *c/a-V1#11, V2#2.*

**FUNNY STUFF** (Becomes The Dodo & the Frog No. 80)
Summer, 1944 - No. 79, July-Aug, 1954
All-American/National Periodical Publications No. 7 on

| | Good | Fine | N-Mint |
|---|---|---|---|
| 1-The Three Mouseketeers & The "Terrific Whatzit" begin-Sheldon Mayer-a | 54.00 | 160.00 | 375.00 |
| 2-Sheldon Mayer-a | 27.00 | 80.00 | 185.00 |
| 3-5 | 16.00 | 48.00 | 110.00 |
| 6-10 (6/46) | 10.00 | 30.00 | 70.00 |
| 11-20: 18-The Dodo & the Frog begin? | 7.00 | 21.00 | 50.00 |
| 21,23-30: 24-Infinity-c | 5.00 | 15.00 | 35.00 |
| 22-Superman cameo | 16.50 | 50.00 | 115.00 |
| 31-79: 75-Bo Bunny by Mayer | 3.15 | 9.50 | 22.00 |
| Wheaties Giveaway(1946, 6½x8¼") (Scarce) | 11.50 | 34.00 | 80.00 |

NOTE: ***Mayer*** *a-1-8, 55, ,57, 58, 61, 62, 64, 65, 68, 70, 72, 74-79; c-2, 5, 6, 8.*

**FUNNY STUFF STOCKING STUFFER**
March, 1985 (52 pgs.)
DC Comics

| | Good | Fine | N-Mint |
|---|---|---|---|
| 1-Almost every DC funny animal featured | | .60 | 1.25 |

**FUNNY 3-D**
December, 1953
Harvey Publications

| | Good | Fine | N-Mint |
|---|---|---|---|
| 1 | 7.00 | 21.00 | 50.00 |

**FUNNY TUNES** (Animated Funny Comic Tunes No. 16-22; Funny Comic Tunes No. 23, on covers only; formerly Krazy Komics #15; Oscar No. 24 on)
No. 16, Summer, 1944 - No. 23, Fall, 1946
U.S.A. Comics Magazine Corp. (Timely)

| | Good | Fine | N-Mint |
|---|---|---|---|
| 16-Silly, Ziggy, Krazy Krow begin | 6.00 | 18.00 | 42.00 |
| 17 (Fall/'44)-Becomes Gay Comics #18 on? | 4.00 | 12.00 | 28.00 |
| 18-22: 21-Super Rabbit app. | 3.50 | 10.50 | 24.00 |
| 23-Kurtzman-a | 4.30 | 13.00 | 30.00 |

**FUNNY TUNES** (Becomes Space Comics #4 on)
July, 1953 - No. 3, Dec-Jan, 1953-54
Avon Periodicals

| | Good | Fine | N-Mint |
|---|---|---|---|
| 1-Space Mouse begins | 3.70 | 11.00 | 26.00 |
| 2,3 | 2.65 | 8.00 | 18.00 |

**FUNNY WORLD**
1947 - No. 3, 1948
Marbak Press

| | Good | Fine | N-Mint |
|---|---|---|---|
| 1-The Berrys, The Toodles & other strip reprints begin | 4.30 | 13.00 | 30.00 |
| 2,3 | 3.00 | 9.00 | 21.00 |

**FUNTASTIC WORLD OF HANNA-BARBERA, THE** (TV)
Dec, 1977 - No. 3, June, 1978 ($1.25) (Oversized)
Marvel Comics Group

| | Good | Fine | N-Mint |
|---|---|---|---|
| 1-3: 1-The Flintstones Christmas Party(12/77). 2-Yogi Bear's Easter Parade(3/78). 3-Laff-a-lympics(6/78) | .35 | 1.00 | 2.00 |

**FUN TIME**
1953; No. 2, Spr, 1953; No. 3(nn), Sum, 1953; No. 4, Wint, 1953-54
Ace Periodicals

| | Good | Fine | N-Mint |
|---|---|---|---|
| 1 | 1.70 | 5.00 | 12.00 |
| 2-4 (100 pgs. each) | 5.00 | 15.00 | 35.00 |

**FUN WITH SANTA CLAUS** (See March of Comics No. 11, 108, 325)

**FURTHER ADVENTURES OF INDIANA JONES, THE** (Also see Indiana Jones and the Temple of Doom)
Jan, 1983 - No. 34, Mar, 1986
Marvel Comics Group

| | Good | Fine | N-Mint |
|---|---|---|---|
| 1-34: 1-Byrne/Austin-a. 2-Byrne/Austin-c/a | | .55 | 1.10 |

NOTE: ***Austin*** *a-6i, 9i; c-1i, 2i, 6i, 9i.* ***Chaykin*** *a-6p; c-6p, 8p-10p.* ***Ditko*** *a-21p, 25, 26, 34.* ***Simonson*** *c-9. Painted c-14.*

**FURTHER ADVENTURES OF NYOKA, THE JUNGLE GIRL, THE**
1988 - No. 5?, 1989 ($1.95, color; $2.25-$2.50, B&W)(See Nyoka)
AC Comics

| | Good | Fine | N-Mint |
|---|---|---|---|
| 1,2 ($1.95, color)-Bill Black-a plus reprints | .35 | 1.00 | 2.00 |
| 3,4 ($2.25, B&W) 3-Photo-c. 4-Krigstein-r | .40 | 1.15 | 2.30 |
| 5 ($2.50, B&W)-Reprints plus movie photos | .40 | 1.25 | 2.50 |

**FURY** (Straight Arrow's Horse. . .) (See A-1 No. 119)

**FURY** (TV) (See March Of Comics #200)
No. 781, Mar, 1957 - Nov, 1962 (All photo-c)
Dell Publishing Co./Gold Key

| | Good | Fine | N-Mint |
|---|---|---|---|
| 4-Color 781 | 5.70 | 17.00 | 40.00 |
| 4-Color 885,975,1031,1080,1133,1172,1218,1296, 01292-208(#1-'62) | 4.00 | 12.00 | 28.00 |
| 10020-211(11/62-G.K.)-Crandall-a | 4.00 | 12.00 | 28.00 |

**FURY OF FIRESTORM, THE** (Becomes Firestorm The Nuclear Man #65 on; also see Firestorm)
June, 1982 - No. 64, Oct, 1987 (#19-on: 75 cents)
DC Comics

| | Good | Fine | N-Mint |
|---|---|---|---|
| 1-Intro The Black Bison; brief origin | .40 | 1.25 | 2.50 |
| 2 | .25 | .80 | 1.60 |
| 3-18: 4-JLA x-over. 17-1st app. Firehawk | | .65 | 1.30 |
| 19-40: 21-Death of Killer Frost. 22-Origin. 23-Intro. Byte. 24-1st app. Blue Devil & Bug (origin); origin Byte. 34-1st app./origin Killer Frost II. 39-Weasel's i.d. revealed | | .50 | 1.00 |
| 41,42-Crisis x-over | | .60 | 1.20 |
| 43-64: 48-Intro. Moonbow. 53-Origin/1st app. Silver Shade. 55,56-Legends x-over. 58-1st app./origin Parasite | | .45 | .90 |
| 61-Test cover; Superman logo | 10.85 | 32.50 | 65.00 |
| Annual 1(11/83)-1st app. new Firehawk | | .65 | 1.30 |
| Annual 2-4: 2(11/84), 3(11/85), 4(10/86) | | .65 | 1.30 |

NOTE: ***Colan*** *a-19p, Annual 4p.* ***Giffen*** *a-Annual 4p.* ***Gil Kane*** *c-30.* ***Nino*** *a-37.* ***Tuska*** *a-17p, 18p, 32p, 45p.*

**FUSION**
Jan, 1987 - No. 17, Oct, 1989 ($2.00, B&W, Baxter paper)
Eclipse Comics

| | Good | Fine | N-Mint |
|---|---|---|---|
| 1 | .40 | 1.25 | 2.50 |
| 2-17: 11-The Weasel Patrol begins (1st app?) | .35 | 1.00 | 2.00 |

**FUTURE COMICS**
June, 1940 - No. 4, Sept, 1940
David McKay Publications

| | Good | Fine | N-Mint |
|---|---|---|---|
| 1-Origin The Phantom; The Lone Ranger, & Saturn Against the Earth begin | 115.00 | 345.00 | 800.00 |
| 2 | 60.00 | 180.00 | 420.00 |
| 3,4 | 50.00 | 150.00 | 350.00 |

**FUTURE WORLD COMICS**
Summer, 1946 - No. 2, Fall, 1946
George W. Dougherty

| | Good | Fine | N-Mint |
|---|---|---|---|
| 1,2 | 11.50 | 34.00 | 80.00 |

**FUTURE WORLD COMIX** (Warren Presents. . . on cover)
September, 1978
Warren Publications

| | Good | Fine | N-Mint |
|---|---|---|---|
| 1 | | .50 | 1.00 |

**FUTURIANS, THE** (See Marvel Graphic Novel #9)
Sept, 1985 - No. 3, 1985 ($1.50, color)
Lodestone Publishing/Eternity Comics

| | Good | Fine | N-Mint |
|---|---|---|---|
| 1-3: Indicia title "Dave Cockrum's. . ." | .25 | .75 | 1.50 |
| Graphic Novel 1 ($9.95, Eternity)-r/#1-3, plus never published #4 issue | 1.70 | 5.00 | 10.00 |

**G-8** (See G-Eight)

**GABBY** (Formerly Ken Shannon) (Teen humor)
No. 11, July, 1953; No. 2, Sept, 1953 - No. 9, Sept, 1954
Quality Comics Group

| | Good | Fine | N-Mint |
|---|---|---|---|
| 11(#1)(7/53) | 3.00 | 9.00 | 21.00 |
| 2 | 1.70 | 5.00 | 12.00 |
| 3-9 | 1.15 | 3.50 | 8.00 |

**GABBY GOB** (See Harvey Hits No. 85, 90, 94, 97, 100, 103, 106, 109)

**GABBY HAYES ADVENTURE COMICS**
Dec, 1953
Toby Press

| | Good | Fine | N-Mint |
|---|---|---|---|
| 1-Photo-c | 7.00 | 21.00 | 50.00 |

**GABBY HAYES WESTERN** (Movie star) (See Monte Hale, Real Western Hero & Western Hero)
Nov, 1948 - No. 50, Jan, 1953; No. 51, Dec, 1954 - No. 59, Jan, 1957
Fawcett/Toby Press/Charlton Comics No. 51 on

| | Good | Fine | N-Mint |
|---|---|---|---|
| 1-Gabby & his horse Corker begin; Photo front/back-c begin | 27.00 | 80.00 | 185.00 |
| 2 | 12.00 | 36.00 | 85.00 |
| 3-5 | 9.30 | 28.00 | 65.00 |
| 6-10 | 8.00 | 24.00 | 56.00 |
| 11-20: 19-Last photo back-c? | 5.70 | 17.00 | 40.00 |
| 21-49 | 3.70 | 11.00 | 26.00 |
| 50-(1/53)-Last Fawcett issue; last photo-c? | 4.00 | 12.00 | 28.00 |
| 51-(12/54)-1st Charlton issue; photo-c | 4.00 | 12.00 | 28.00 |
| 52-59(Charlton '55-57): 53,55-Photo-c | 2.30 | 7.00 | 16.00 |
| Quaker Oats Giveaway nn(#1-5, 1951) (Dell?) | 2.65 | 8.00 | 18.00 |

**GAGS**
July, 1937 - V3#10, Oct, 1944 (13¾x10¾")
United Features Synd./Triangle Publ. No. 9 on

| | Good | Fine | N-Mint |
|---|---|---|---|
| 1(7/37)-52 pgs.; 20 pgs. Grin & Bear It, Fellow Citizen | 4.00 | 12.00 | 28.00 |
| V1#9 (36 pgs.) (7/42) | 2.30 | 7.00 | 16.00 |
| V3#10 | 1.70 | 5.00 | 12.00 |

**GALACTIC WAR COMIX** (Warren Presents. . . on cover)
December, 1978
Warren Publications

| | Good | Fine | N-Mint |
|---|---|---|---|
| nn-Wood, Williamson-r | .25 | .75 | 1.50 |

**GALLANT MEN, THE** (TV)
October, 1963 (Photo-c)
Gold Key

| | Good | Fine | N-Mint |
|---|---|---|---|
| 1(10085-310)-Manning-a | 1.15 | 3.50 | 8.00 |

**GALLEGHER, BOY REPORTER** (TV)
May, 1965 (Disney)
Gold Key

| | Good | Fine | N-Mint |
|---|---|---|---|
| 1(10149-505)-Photo-c | 1.15 | 3.50 | 8.00 |

**GAMEBOY**
1990 - Present ($1.95, color, coated-c)
Valiant Comics

| | Good | Fine | N-Mint |
|---|---|---|---|
| 1-6: 3,4,6-Layton-c. 5-Layton-c(i) | .35 | 1.00 | 2.00 |

**GAMMARAUDERS**
Jan, 1989 - No. 10, Dec, 1989 ($1.25, $1.50, $2.00, color)
DC Comics

| | Good | Fine | N-Mint |
|---|---|---|---|
| 1-Based on TSR game | .40 | 1.25 | 2.50 |
| 2-10 | .35 | 1.00 | 2.00 |

*The Fury of Firestorm #42, © DC*

*Gabby Hayes Western #19, © FAW*

*Gammarauders #1, © TSR*

# WANTED

## OLD COMICS!!

## $CASH REWARD$

FOR THESE AND MANY OTHER ELUSIVE COMIC BOOKS FROM THE GOLDEN AGE. SEEKING WHITE PAGE COLLECTIBLE COPIES IN VG OR BETTER CONDITION. ALSO GOLDEN AGE **BOUND VOLUMES** WANTED.

## ◄ COMIC BOOKS GO TO WAR ►
## *A GALLERY OF PATRIOTIC COVERS*

**Ace Comics** #65, 1942, © DMP.

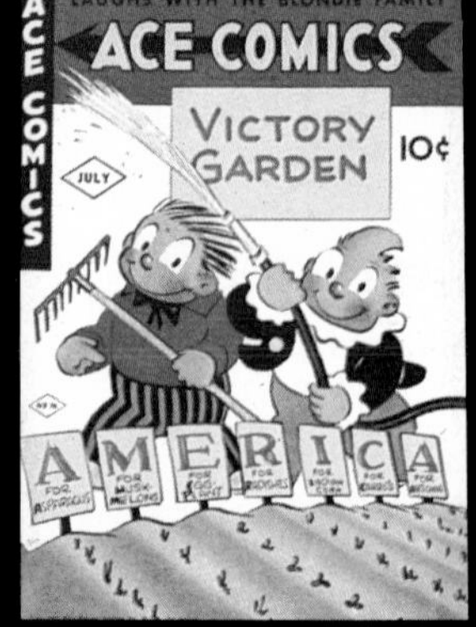


**Ace Comics** #76, 1943, © DMP.

**Action Comics** #86, 1945, © DC.

**All Star Comics** #22, 1944, © DC.

**The American Air Forces** #2, 1944, © WHW.

**Batman** #17, 1943, © DC.

**Big Shot** #46, 1944, © CCG.

**Boy Comics** #7, 1942,

**Captain Marvel Adventures**

**Captain Marvel JR.** #9, 1943,
© FAW.

**Comic Cavalcade** #6, 1944,
© DC.

© FAW.

**4 Most** #3, 1942, © NOVP.

**Green Lama** #6, 1945,
© Spark Publ.

**Looney Tunes** #10, 1942,
© Leon Schlesinger.

**Master Comics** #36, 1943,
© FAW. Raboy cover art.

**Master Comics** #40, 1943,
© FAW. Raboy cover art.

**Military Comics** #11, 1942,
© QUA.

**Pep Comics** #20, 1941,
© AP.

**Pep Comics** #26, 1942,
© AP.

**Power Comics** #2, 1944,
© Narrative Publ.

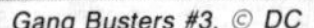

Gang Busters #3, © DC

Gangsters Can't Win #2, © DS

Gene Autry Comics #4 (Faw.), © Gene Autry

**GANDY GOOSE** (See All Surprise, Paul Terry's & Terry-Toons)
Mar, 1953 - No. 5, Nov, 1953; No. 5, Fall, 1956 - No. 6, Sum/58
St. John Publ. Co./Pines No. 5,6

| | Good | Fine | N-Mint |
|---|---|---|---|
| 1 | 3.50 | 10.50 | 24.00 |
| 2 | 1.70 | 5.00 | 12.00 |
| 3-5(1953)(St. John) | 1.50 | 4.50 | 10.00 |
| 5,6(1956-58)(Pines) | 1.00 | 3.00 | 7.00 |

**GANG BUSTERS** (See Popular Comics #38)
1938 - 1943
David McKay/Dell Publishing Co.

| | | | |
|---|---|---|---|
| Feature Books 17(McKay)('38) | 26.00 | 77.00 | 180.00 |
| Large Feature Comic 10('39)-(Scarce) | 32.00 | 95.00 | 225.00 |
| Large Feature Comic 17('41) | 20.00 | 60.00 | 140.00 |
| 4-Color 7(1940) | 24.00 | 72.00 | 165.00 |
| 4-Color 23,24('42-43) | 18.00 | 54.00 | 125.00 |

**GANG BUSTERS** (Radio/TV)
Dec-Jan, 1947-48 - No. 67, Dec-Jan, 1958-59 (No. 1-23: 52 pgs.)
National Periodical Publications

| | | | |
|---|---|---|---|
| 1 | 36.00 | 107.00 | 250.00 |
| 2 | 16.00 | 48.00 | 110.00 |
| 3-8 | 9.30 | 28.00 | 65.00 |
| 9,10-Photo-c | 11.00 | 32.00 | 75.00 |
| 11-13-Photo-c | 8.50 | 25.50 | 60.00 |
| 14,17-Frazetta-a, 8 pgs. each. 14-Photo-c | 18.00 | 54.00 | 125.00 |
| 15,16,18-20 | 5.70 | 17.00 | 40.00 |
| 21-30: 26-Kirby-a | 4.30 | 13.00 | 30.00 |
| 31-44: 44-Last Pre-code (2-3/55) | 3.60 | 11.00 | 25.00 |
| 45-67 | 2.65 | 8.00 | 18.00 |

NOTE: ***Barry** a-6, 8, 10. **Drucker** a-51. **Moreira** a-48, 50, 59. **Roussos** a-8.*

**GANGSTERS AND GUN MOLLS**
Sept, 1951 - No. 4, June, 1952 (Painted-c)
Avon Periodical/Realistic Comics

| | | | |
|---|---|---|---|
| 1-Wood-a, 1 pg; c-/Avon paperback #292 | 22.00 | 65.00 | 150.00 |
| 2-Check-a, 8 pgs.; Kamen-a | 16.00 | 48.00 | 110.00 |
| 3-Marijuana mention story; used in **POP**, pg. 84-85 | 14.00 | 43.00 | 100.00 |
| 4 | 11.50 | 34.00 | 80.00 |

**GANGSTERS CAN'T WIN**
Feb-Mar, 1948 - No. 9, June-July, 1949
D. S. Publishing Co.

| | | | |
|---|---|---|---|
| 1 | 12.00 | 36.00 | 85.00 |
| 2 | 6.00 | 18.00 | 42.00 |
| 3-6: 4-Acid in face story | 7.00 | 21.00 | 50.00 |
| 7-9 | 3.50 | 10.50 | 24.00 |

NOTE: ***Ingles** a-5, 6. **McWilliams** a-5, 7. **Reinman** c-6.*

**GANG WORLD**
No. 5, Nov, 1952 - No. 6, Jan, 1953
Standard Comics

| | | | |
|---|---|---|---|
| 5-Bondage-c | 7.00 | 21.00 | 50.00 |
| 6 | 4.50 | 14.00 | 32.00 |

**GARGOYLE**
June, 1985 - No. 4, Sept, 1985 (75 cents, limited series)
Marvel Comics Group

| | | | |
|---|---|---|---|
| 1-4: 1-Wrightson-c; character from Defenders | | .40 | .80 |

**GARRISON'S GORILLAS** (TV)
Jan, 1968 - No. 4, Oct, 1968; No. 5, Oct, 1969 (Photo-c)
Dell Publishing Co.

| | | | |
|---|---|---|---|
| 1 | 2.15 | 6.50 | 15.00 |
| 2-5: 5-Reprints #1 | 1.50 | 4.50 | 10.00 |

**GASOLINE ALLEY** (Also see Popular & Super Comics)
1929 (B&W daily strip reprints)(7x8¾"; hardcover)
Reilly & Lee Publishers

| | Good | Fine | N-Mint |
|---|---|---|---|
| nn-By King (96 pgs.) | 10.00 | 30.00 | 70.00 |

**GASOLINE ALLEY** (Top Love Stories No. 3 on?)
Sept-Oct, 1950 - No. 2, Dec, 1950 (Newspaper reprints)
Star Publications

| | | | |
|---|---|---|---|
| 1-Contains 1 pg. intro. history of the strip (The Life of Skeezix); reprints 15 scenes of highlights from 1921-1935, plus an adventure from 1935 and 1936 strips; a 2-pg. filler is included on the life of the creator Frank King, with photo of the cartoonist. | 10.00 | 30.00 | 70.00 |
| 2-(1936-37 reprints)-L. B. Cole-c | 11.00 | 32.00 | 75.00 |

(See Super Book No. 21)

**GASP!**
March, 1967 - No. 4, Aug, 1967 (12 cents)
American Comics Group

| | | | |
|---|---|---|---|
| 1-L.S.D. drug mention | 1.70 | 5.00 | 12.00 |
| 2-4 | 1.15 | 3.50 | 8.00 |

**GAY COMICS** (Honeymoon No. 41)
Mar, 1944 (no month); No. 18, Fall, 1944 - No. 40, Oct, 1949
Timely Comics/USA Comic Mag. Co. No. 18-24

| | | | |
|---|---|---|---|
| 1-Wolverton's Powerhouse Pepper; Tessie the Typist begins; Millie The Model & Willie app. (One Shot) | 22.00 | 65.00 | 150.00 |
| 18-(Formerly Funny Tunes #17?)-Wolverton-a | 11.50 | 34.00 | 80.00 |
| 19-29-Wolverton-a in all. 24,29-Kurtzman-a | 9.30 | 28.00 | 65.00 |
| 30,33,36,37-Kurtzman's "Hey Look" | 3.50 | 10.50 | 24.00 |
| 31-Kurtzman's "Hey Look"(1), Giggles 'N' Grins (1½) | 3.50 | 10.50 | 24.00 |
| 32,35,38-40: 35-Nellie The Nurse begins? | 2.65 | 8.00 | 18.00 |
| 34-Three Kurtzman's "Hey Look" | 4.00 | 12.00 | 28.00 |

**GAY COMICS** (Also see Smile, Tickle, & Whee Comics)
1955 (52 pgs.; 5x7¼"; 7 cents)
Modern Store Publ.

| | | | |
|---|---|---|---|
| 1 | .50 | 1.50 | 3.00 |

**GAY PURR-EE** (See Movie Comics)

**GEEK, THE** (See Brother Power . . .)

**G-8 AND HIS BATTLE ACES**
October, 1966
Gold Key

| | | | |
|---|---|---|---|
| 1 (10184-610)-Painted-c | 1.75 | 5.25 | 12.00 |

**GEM COMICS**
April, 1945 (52 pgs.) (Bondage-c)
Spotlight Publishers

| | | | |
|---|---|---|---|
| 1-Little Mohee, Steve Strong app. | 10.00 | 30.00 | 70.00 |

**GENE AUTRY** (See March of Comics No. 25, 28, 39, 54, 78, 90, 104, 120, 135, 150 & Western Roundup under Dell Giants)

**GENE AUTRY COMICS** (Movie, Radio star; singing cowboy)
(Dell takes over with No. 11)
1941 (On sale 12/31/41) - No. 10, 1943 (68 pgs.)
Fawcett Publications

| | | | |
|---|---|---|---|
| 1 (Rare)-Gene Autry & his horse Champion begin | 156.00 | 390.00 | 935.00 |
| 2 | 52.00 | 156.00 | 365.00 |
| 3-5 | 40.00 | 120.00 | 280.00 |
| 6-10 | 35.00 | 105.00 | 245.00 |

**GENE AUTRY COMICS** (. . .& Champion No. 102 on)
No. 11, 1943 - No. 121, Jan-Mar, 1959 (TV - later issues)
Dell Publishing Co.

| | | | |
|---|---|---|---|
| 11 (1943, 60 pgs.)-Continuation of Fawcett series; photo back-c | 39.00 | 118.00 | 270.00 |
| 12 (2/44, 60 pgs.) | 37.00 | 110.00 | 260.00 |
| 4-Color 47(1944, 60 pgs.) | 36.00 | 107.00 | 250.00 |
| 4-Color 57(11/44),66('45)(52 pgs. each) | 31.00 | 92.00 | 215.00 |

| | Good | Fine | N-Mint |
|---|---|---|---|
| 4-Color 75,83('45, 36 pgs. each) | 25.00 | 75.00 | 175.00 |
| 4-Color 93,100('45-46, 36 pgs. each) | 21.00 | 62.00 | 145.00 |
| 1(5-6/46, 52 pgs.) | 36.00 | 107.00 | 250.00 |
| 2(7-8/46)-Photo-c begin, end #111 | 18.00 | 54.00 | 125.00 |
| 3-5: 4-Intro Flapjack Hobbs | 14.00 | 43.00 | 100.00 |
| 6-10 | 10.00 | 30.00 | 70.00 |
| 11-20: 12-Line drawn-c. 20-Panhandle Pete begins | 7.00 | 21.00 | 50.00 |
| 21-29(36pgs.) | 5.70 | 17.00 | 40.00 |
| 30-40(52pgs.) | 5.70 | 17.00 | 40.00 |
| 41-56(52pgs.) | 4.30 | 13.00 | 30.00 |
| 57-66(36pgs.): 58-X-mas-c | 2.85 | 8.50 | 20.00 |
| 67-80(52pgs.) | 3.50 | 10.50 | 24.00 |
| 81-90(52pgs.): 82-X-mas-c. 87-Blank inside-c | 2.65 | 8.00 | 18.00 |
| 91-99(36pgs. No. 91-on). 94-X-mas-c | 1.70 | 5.00 | 12.00 |
| 100 | 2.65 | 8.00 | 18.00 |
| 101-111-Last Gene Autry photo-c | 1.70 | 5.00 | 12.00 |
| 112-121-All Champion painted-c | 1.15 | 3.50 | 8.00 |
| . . . Adventure Comics And Play-Fun Book ('40s)-36 pgs., 8x6½"; games, comics, magic | 13.00 | 40.00 | 90.00 |
| Pillsbury Premium('47)-36 pgs., 6½x7½"; games, comics, puzzles | 12.00 | 36.00 | 84.00 |
| Quaker Oats Giveaway(1950)-2½x6¾"; 5 different versions; "Death Card Gang, Phantom of the Cave, Riddle of Laughing Mtn., Secret of Lost Valley, Bond of Broken Arrow" (came in wrapper) each . . . | 5.50 | 16.50 | 38.00 |
| 3-D Giveaway(1953)-Pocket-size; 5 different | 5.50 | 16.50 | 38.00 |

NOTE: *Photo back-c, 4-18, 20-45, 48-65.* ***Manning*** *a-118.* ***Jesse Marsh*** *art: 4-Color No. 66, 75, 93, 100, No. 1-25, 27-37, 39, 40.*

**GENE AUTRY'S CHAMPION** (TV)
No. 287, 8/50; No. 319, 2/51; No. 3, 8-10/51 - No. 19, 8-10/55
Dell Publishing Co.

| | Good | Fine | N-Mint |
|---|---|---|---|
| 4-Color 287(#1)('50, 52pgs.)-Photo-c | 6.50 | 19.00 | 45.00 |
| 4-Color 319(#2, '51), 3-(Painted-c begin) | 3.00 | 9.00 | 21.00 |
| 4-19: 19-Last painted-c | 1.30 | 4.00 | 9.00 |

**GENE AUTRY TIM** (Formerly Tim) (Becomes Tim in Space)
1950 (Half-size) (Black & White Giveaway)
Tim Stores

| | Good | Fine | N-Mint |
|---|---|---|---|
| nn-Several issues (All Scarce) | 5.00 | 15.00 | 35.00 |

**GENE DAY'S BLACK ZEPPELIN**
April, 1985 - No. 5, Oct, 1986 ($1.70, B&W)
Renegade Press

| | Good | Fine | N-Mint |
|---|---|---|---|
| 1-5 | .30 | .85 | 1.70 |

**GENERAL DOUGLAS MACARTHUR**
1951
Fox Features Syndicate

| | Good | Fine | N-Mint |
|---|---|---|---|
| nn | 10.00 | 30.00 | 70.00 |

**GENERIC COMIC, THE**
April, 1984 (One-shot)
Marvel Comics Group

| | Good | Fine | N-Mint |
|---|---|---|---|
| 1 | | .30 | .60 |

**GENTLE BEN** (TV)
Feb, 1968 - No. 5, Oct, 1969 (All photo-c)
Dell Publishing Co.

| | Good | Fine | N-Mint |
|---|---|---|---|
| 1 | 1.70 | 5.00 | 12.00 |
| 2-5: 5-Reprints #1 | 1.00 | 3.00 | 7.00 |

**GEORGE OF THE JUNGLE** (TV)(See America's Best TV Comics)
Feb, 1969 - No. 2, Oct, 1969 (Jay Ward)
Gold Key

| | Good | Fine | N-Mint |
|---|---|---|---|
| 1,2 | 3.00 | 9.00 | 21.00 |

**GEORGE PAL'S PUPPETOONS**
Dec, 1945 - No. 18, Dec, 1947; No. 19, 1950
Fawcett Publications

| | Good | Fine | N-Mint |
|---|---|---|---|
| 1-Captain Marvel on cover | 23.00 | 70.00 | 160.00 |
| 2 | 11.50 | 34.00 | 80.00 |
| 3-10 | 7.00 | 21.00 | 50.00 |
| 11-19 | 5.00 | 15.00 | 35.00 |

**GEORGIE COMICS** (. . . & Judy Comics #20-35?; see All Teen & Teen Comics)
Spring, 1945 - No. 39, Oct, 1952
Timely Comics/GPI No. 1-34

| | Good | Fine | N-Mint |
|---|---|---|---|
| 1-Dave Berg-a | 9.30 | 28.00 | 65.00 |
| 2 | 4.50 | 14.00 | 32.00 |
| 3-5,7,8 | 3.00 | 9.00 | 21.00 |
| 6-Georgie visits Timely Comics | 4.00 | 12.00 | 28.00 |
| 9,10-Kurtzman's "Hey Look" (1 & ?); Margie app. | 4.00 | 12.00 | 28.00 |
| 11,12: 11-Margie, Millie app. | 2.65 | 8.00 | 18.00 |
| 13-Kurtzman's "Hey Look," 3 pgs. | 3.70 | 11.00 | 26.00 |
| 14-Wolverton art, 1 pg. & Kurtzman's "Hey Look" | 4.00 | 12.00 | 28.00 |
| 15,16,18-20 | 2.00 | 6.00 | 14.00 |
| 17,29-Kurtzman's "Hey Look," 1 pg. | 2.85 | 8.50 | 20.00 |
| 21-24,27,28,30-39: 21-Anti-Wertham editorial | 1.50 | 4.50 | 10.00 |
| 25-Painted cover by classic pin-up artist Peter Driben | 3.50 | 10.50 | 24.00 |
| 26-Logo design swipe from Archie Comics | 1.50 | 4.50 | 10.00 |

**GERALD McBOING-BOING AND THE NEARSIGHTED MR. MAGOO** (TV)(Mr. Magoo No. 6 on)
Aug-Oct, 1952 - No. 5, Aug-Oct, 1953
Dell Publishing Co.

| | Good | Fine | N-Mint |
|---|---|---|---|
| 1 | 5.00 | 15.00 | 35.00 |
| 2-5 | 4.00 | 12.00 | 28.00 |

**GERONIMO**
1950 - No. 4, Feb, 1952
Avon Periodicals

| | Good | Fine | N-Mint |
|---|---|---|---|
| 1-Indian Fighter; Maneely-a; Texas Rangers r-/Cowpuncher No. 1; Fawcette-c | 9.00 | 27.00 | 62.00 |
| 2-On the Warpath; Kit West app.; Kinstler c/a | 5.50 | 16.50 | 38.00 |
| 3-And His Apache Murderers; Kinstler c/a(2); Kit West, r-Cowpuncher #6 | 5.50 | 16.50 | 38.00 |
| 4-Savage Raids of; Kinstler c/a(3) | 4.30 | 13.00 | 30.00 |

**GERONIMO JONES**
Sept, 1971 - No. 9, Jan, 1973
Charlton Comics

| | Good | Fine | N-Mint |
|---|---|---|---|
| 1 | | .50 | 1.00 |
| 2-9 | | .30 | .60 |
| Modern Comics Reprint #7('78) | | .20 | .40 |

**GETALONG GANG, THE** (TV)
May, 1985 - No. 6, March, 1986
Star Comics (Marvel)

| | Good | Fine | N-Mint |
|---|---|---|---|
| 1-6: Saturday morning TV stars | | .35 | .70 |

**GET LOST**
Feb-Mar, 1954 - No. 3, June-July, 1954 (Satire)
Mikeross Publications

| | Good | Fine | N-Mint |
|---|---|---|---|
| 1 | 9.30 | 28.00 | 65.00 |
| 2-Has 4 pg. E.C. parody featuring "the Sewer Keeper" | 6.50 | 19.00 | 45.00 |
| 3-John Wayne 'Hondo' parody | 5.00 | 15.00 | 35.00 |

**GET SMART** (TV)
June, 1966 - No. 8, Sept, 1967 (All have Don Adams photo-c)
Dell Publishing Co.

*Gene Autry's Champion #19, © Gene Autry*

*Georgie #4, © MEG*

*Geronimo #1, © AVON*

Ghost Rider #6 (1951), © ME

Ghost Rider #3 (10/73), © MEG

Ghost Rider #1 (5/90), © MEG

| | Good | Fine | N-Mint |
|---|---|---|---|
| 1 | 5.70 | 17.00 | 40.00 |
| 2-Ditko-a | 4.00 | 12.00 | 28.00 |
| 3-8: 3-Ditko-a(p) | 3.50 | 10.50 | 24.00 |

**GHOST** (. . . Comics #9)
1951(Winter) - No. 11, Summer, 1954
Fiction House Magazines

| | | | |
|---|---|---|---|
| 1 | 31.00 | 92.00 | 215.00 |
| 2 | 14.00 | 43.00 | 100.00 |
| 3-9: 3,6,7,9-Bondage-c | 12.00 | 36.00 | 85.00 |
| 10,11-Dr. Drew by Grandenetti in each, reprinted from Rangers; 11-Evans-a | 14.00 | 43.00 | 100.00 |

**GHOST BREAKERS** (Also see Racket Squad in Action, Red Dragon & (CC) Sherlock Holmes Comics)
Sept, 1948 - No. 2, Dec, 1948 (52 pages)
Street & Smith Publications

| | | | |
|---|---|---|---|
| 1-Powell-c/a(3); Dr. Neff (magician) app. | 17.00 | 51.00 | 120.00 |
| 2-Powell-c/a(2); Maneely-a | 13.00 | 40.00 | 90.00 |

**GHOSTBUSTERS** (TV)(Also see Real . . . and Slimer)
Feb, 1987 - No. 6, Aug, 1987 ($1.25, color)
First Comics

| | | | |
|---|---|---|---|
| 1-6: Based on new animated TV series | | .65 | 1.30 |

**GHOSTBUSTERS II**
Oct, 1989 - No. 3, Dec, 1989 ($1.95, color, mini-series)
Now Comics

| | | | |
|---|---|---|---|
| 1-3: Movie adaptation | .35 | 1.00 | 2.00 |

**GHOST CASTLE** (See Tales of . . .)

**GHOSTLY HAUNTS** (Formerly Ghost Manor)
#20, 9/71 - #53, 12/76; #54, 9/77 - #55, 10/77; #56, 1/78 - #58, 4/78
Charlton Comics

| | | | |
|---|---|---|---|
| 20-58: 27-Dr. Graves x-over. 39-Origin & 1st app. Destiny Fox. 42-Newton-c/a | | .60 | 1.20 |
| 40,41(Modern Comics-r, 1977, 1978) | | .20 | .40 |

NOTE: ***Ditko*** *a-22-28, 31-34, 36-41, 43-48, 50, 52, 54, 56r; c-22-27, 30, 33-37, 47, 54, 56.* ***Glanzman*** *a-20.* ***Howard*** *a-27, 30, 35, 42.* ***Staton*** *a-35; c-46.* ***Sutton*** *c-33, 39.*

**GHOSTLY TALES** (Blue Beetle No. 50-54)
No. 55, 4-5/66 - No. 124, 12/76; No. 125, 9/77 - No. 169, 10/84
Charlton Comics

| | | | |
|---|---|---|---|
| 55-Intro. & origin Dr. Graves | .70 | 2.00 | 4.00 |
| 56-70-Dr. Graves ends | .35 | 1.00 | 2.00 |
| 71-169: 107-Sutton, Wood-a. 114-Newton-a | .25 | .75 | 1.50 |

NOTE: ***Ditko*** *a-55-58, 60, 61, 67, 69-73, 75-90, 92-97, 99-118, 120-122, 125r, 126r, 131-133r, 136-141r, 143r, 144r, 152, 155, 161, 163; c-67, 69, 73, 77, 78, 83, 84, 86-90, 92-97, 99, 102, 109, 111, 118, 120-122, 125, 131-133, 163.* ***Glanzman*** *a-167.* ***Howard*** *a-95, 98, 99, 117; c-98, 107, 120, 121, 161.* ***Morisi*** *a-83, 84, 86.* ***Newton*** *a-114; c-115.* ***Staton*** *a-161; c-117.* ***Sutton*** *a-107, 112-114.* ***Wood*** *a-107.*

**GHOSTLY WEIRD STORIES** (Formerly Blue Bolt Weird)
No. 120, Sept, 1953 - No. 124, Sept, 1954
Star Publications

| | | | |
|---|---|---|---|
| 120-Jo-Jo-r | 12.00 | 36.00 | 85.00 |
| 121-Jo-Jo-r | 9.00 | 27.00 | 62.00 |
| 122-The Mask-r/Capt. Flight #5; Rulah-r; has 1pg. story 'Death and the Devil Pills'-r/Western Outlaws #17 | 9.00 | 27.00 | 62.00 |
| 123-Jo-Jo; Disbrow-a(2) | 9.00 | 27.00 | 62.00 |
| 124-Torpedo Man | 9.00 | 27.00 | 62.00 |

NOTE: ***Disbrow*** *a-120-124.* ***L. B. Cole*** *covers-all issues (#122 is a sci-fi cover).*

**GHOST MANOR** (Ghostly Haunts No. 20 on)
July, 1968 - No. 19, July, 1971
Charlton Comics

| | | | |
|---|---|---|---|
| 1 | .70 | 2.00 | 4.00 |
| 2-5 | .35 | 1.00 | 2.00 |
| 6-12,17: 17-Morisi-a | .25 | .75 | 1.50 |

| | Good | Fine | N-Mint |
|---|---|---|---|
| 13-16,18,19-Ditko-a; c-15,18,19 | .35 | 1.00 | 2.00 |

**GHOST MANOR** (2nd Series)
Oct, 1971 - No. 32, Dec, 1976; No. 33, Sept, 1977 - No. 77, 11/84
Charlton Comics

| | | | |
|---|---|---|---|
| 1 | .50 | 1.50 | 3.00 |
| 2-7,9,10 | .35 | 1.00 | 2.00 |
| 8-Wood-a | .40 | 1.25 | 2.50 |
| 11-56,58-77: 18-20-Newton-a. 22-Newton-c/a. 21-E-Man, Blue Beetle, Capt. Atom cameos. 28-Nudity panels. 40-Torture & drug use | | .50 | 1.00 |
| 57-Wood, Ditko, Howard-a | | .60 | 1.20 |
| 19(Modern Comics reprint, 1977) | | .20 | .40 |

NOTE: ***Ditko*** *a-4, 8, 10, 11(2), 13, 14, 18, 20-22, 24-26, 28, 29, 31, 37r, 38r, 40r, 42-44r, 46r, 47, 51r, 52r, 54r, 57, 60, 62(4), 64r, 71; c-2-7, 9-11, 14-16, 28, 31, 37, 38, 42, 43, 46, 47, 51, 52, 60, 62, 64.* ***Howard*** *a-4, 8, 19-21, 57.* ***Newton*** *a-18-20, 22, 64.* ***Sutton*** *a-19; c-8.*

**GHOST RIDER** (See A-1 Comics, Best of the West, Black Phantom, Bobby Benson, Great Western, Red Mask & Tim Holt)
1950 - No. 14, 1954
Magazine Enterprises

NOTE: The character was inspired by Vaughn Monroe's "Ghost Riders in the Sky," and Disney's movie "The Headless Horseman."

| | | | |
|---|---|---|---|
| 1(A-1 #27)-Origin Ghost Rider | 36.00 | 107.00 | 250.00 |
| 2-5: 2(A-1 #29), 3(A-1 #31), 4(A-1 #34), 5(A-1 #37)-All Frazetta-c only | 36.00 | 107.00 | 250.00 |
| 6,7: 6(A-1 #44), 7(A-1 #51) | 13.00 | 40.00 | 90.00 |
| 8,9: 8(A-1 #57)-Drug use story, 9(A-1 #69)-L.S.D. story | 11.00 | 32.00 | 75.00 |
| 10(A-1 #71)-vs. Frankenstein | 11.00 | 32.00 | 75.00 |
| 11-14: 11(A-1 #75), 12(A-1 #80, bondage-c), 13(A-1 #84), 14(A-1 #112) | 8.50 | 25.50 | 60.00 |

NOTE: ***Dick Ayers*** *art in all; c-1, 6-14.*

**GHOST RIDER, THE** (See Night Rider & Western Gunfighters)
Feb, 1967 - No. 7, Nov, 1967 (Western hero)(All 12 cent-c)
Marvel Comics Group

| | | | |
|---|---|---|---|
| 1-Origin Ghost Rider; Kid Colt-r begin | 3.50 | 10.50 | 24.00 |
| 2-7: 6-Last Kid Colt-r; All Ayers-c/a(p) | 1.30 | 4.00 | 9.00 |

**GHOST RIDER** (See The Champions, Marvel Spotlight #5, Marvel Team-Up #15, 58 & Marvel Treasury Edition #18)
Sept, 1973 - No. 81, June, 1983 (Super-hero)
Marvel Comics Group

| | | | |
|---|---|---|---|
| 1 | 4.00 | 12.00 | 28.00 |
| 2 | 2.15 | 6.50 | 15.00 |
| 3-5: 3-Ghost Rider gets new cycle; Son of Satan app. | 1.70 | 5.00 | 12.00 |
| 6-10: 10-Reprints origin/1st app. from Marvel Spotlight #5; Ploog-a | 1.15 | 3.50 | 8.00 |
| 11-19 | 1.00 | 3.00 | 7.00 |
| 20-Byrne-a | 1.30 | 4.00 | 9.00 |
| 21-30 | .70 | 2.00 | 4.00 |
| 31-50: 50-Double size | .50 | 1.50 | 3.00 |
| 51-81: 68-Origin | .35 | 1.00 | 2.00 |

NOTE: ***Anderson*** *c-64p.* ***Infantino*** *a(p)-43, 44, 51.* ***G. Kane*** *a-21p; c(p)-1, 2, 4, 5, 8, 9, 11-13, 19, 20, 24, 25.* ***Kirby*** *c-21-23.* ***Mooney*** *a-2-9p, 30i.* ***Nebres*** *c-26i.* ***Newton*** *a-23i.* ***Perez*** *c-26p.* ***Shores*** *a-2i.* ***J. Sparling*** *a-62p, 64p, 65p.* ***Starlin*** *a(p)-35.* ***Sutton*** *a-1p, 44i, 64i, 65i, 66, 67i.* ***Tuska*** *a-13p, 14p, 16p.*

**GHOST RIDER**
V2#1, May, 1990 - Present ($1.00, color)
Marvel Comics

| | | | |
|---|---|---|---|
| V2#1-($1.95, 52 pgs.)-Origin; Kingpin app. | 2.50 | 7.50 | 15.00 |
| 2 | 1.50 | 4.50 | 9.00 |
| 3,4: 3-Kingpin app. | 1.00 | 3.00 | 6.00 |
| 5-Punisher app. | 1.70 | 5.00 | 10.00 |

| | Good | Fine | N-Mint |
|---|---|---|---|
| 5-Gold 2nd printing | 1.00 | 3.00 | 6.00 |
| 6-Punisher app. | 1.00 | 3.00 | 6.00 |
| 7-9: 9-X-Factor app. | .50 | 1.50 | 3.00 |
| 10-12 | .25 | .75 | 1.50 |

**GHOSTS** (Ghost No. 1)
Sept-Oct, 1971 - No. 112, May, 1982 (No. 1-5: 52 pgs.)
National Periodical Publications/DC Comics

| | | | |
|---|---|---|---|
| 1,2: 2-Wood-a | .35 | 1.00 | 2.00 |
| 3-10 | | .50 | 1.00 |
| 11-112: 97-99-The Spectre app. 100-Infinity-c | | .25 | .50 |

NOTE: ***B. Baily** a-77. **J. Craig** a-108. **Ditko** a-77, 111. **Giffen** a-104p, 106p, 111p. **Golden** a-88. **Kaluta** c-7, 93, 101. **Kubert** c-89, 105-108, 111. **Mayer** a-111. **McWilliams** a-99. **Win Mortimer** a-89, 91, 94. **Newton** a-92p, 94p. **Nino** a-35, 37, 57. **Orlando** a-74i; c-80. **Redondo** a-8, 13, 45. **Sparling** a(p)-90, 93, 94. **Spiegle** a-103, 105.*

**GHOSTS SPECIAL** (See DC Special Series No. 7)

**GHOST STORIES** (See Amazing Ghost Stories)

**GHOST STORIES**
Sept-Nov, 1962; No. 2, Apr-June, 1963 - No. 37, Oct, 1973
Dell Publishing Co.

| | | | |
|---|---|---|---|
| 12-295-211(#1)-Written by John Stanley | 2.65 | 8.00 | 18.00 |
| 2 | 1.50 | 4.50 | 10.00 |
| 3-10: Two No. 6's exist with different c/a(12-295-406,12-295-503) | .85 | 2.60 | 6.00 |
| 11-20 | .70 | 2.00 | 4.00 |
| 21-37 | .50 | 1.50 | 3.00 |

NOTE: *#21-34, 36, 37 all reprint earlier issues.*

**GHOUL TALES** (Magazine)
Nov, 1970 - No. 5, July, 1971 (52 pages) (B&W)
Stanley Publications

| | | | |
|---|---|---|---|
| 1-Aragon pre-code reprints; Mr. Mystery as host; bondage-c | 1.15 | 3.50 | 8.00 |
| 2,3: 2-(1/71)Reprint/Climax #1. 3-(3/71) | .70 | 2.00 | 5.00 |
| 4-(5/71)Reprints story "The Way to a Man's Heart" used in **SOTI** | 1.70 | 5.00 | 12.00 |
| 5-ACG reprints | .70 | 2.00 | 5.00 |

NOTE: *No. 1-4 contain pre-code Aragon reprints.*

**GIANT BOY BOOK OF COMICS** (See Boy)
1945 (Hardcover) (240 pages)
Newsbook Publications (Gleason)

| | | | |
|---|---|---|---|
| 1-Crimebuster & Young Robin Hood | 50.00 | 150.00 | 350.00 |

**GIANT COMIC ALBUM**
1972 (52 pgs., 11x14", B&W, 59 cents, cardboard-c)
King Features Syndicate

| | | | |
|---|---|---|---|
| Newspaper reprints: Little Iodine, Katzenjammer Kids, Henry, Mandrake the Magician ('59 Falk), Popeye, Beetle Bailey, Barney Google, Blondie, Flash Gordon ('68-69 Dan Barry), & Snuffy Smith each... | 1.00 | 3.00 | 6.00 |

**GIANT COMICS**
Summer, 1957 - No. 3, Winter, 1957 (100 pgs.) (25 cents)
Charlton Comics

| | | | |
|---|---|---|---|
| 1-Atomic Mouse, Hoppy app. | 9.00 | 27.00 | 62.00 |
| 2,3-Atomic Mouse, Rabbit, Christmas Book, Romance stories known | 7.00 | 21.00 | 50.00 |

NOTE: *The above may be rebound comics; contents could vary.*

**GIANT COMICS** (See Wham-O Giant Comics)

**GIANT COMICS EDITION** (See Terry-Toons)
1947 - No. 17, 1950 (All 100-164 pgs.) (25 cents)
St. John Publishing Co.

| | Good | Fine | N-Mint |
|---|---|---|---|
| 1-Mighty Mouse | 25.00 | 75.00 | 175.00 |
| 2-Abbie & Slats | 11.50 | 34.00 | 80.00 |
| 3-Terry-Toons Album; 100 pgs. | 17.00 | 51.00 | 120.00 |
| 4-Crime comics; contains Red Seal No. 16, used & illo. in **SOTI** | 29.00 | 85.00 | 200.00 |
| 5-Police Case Book(4/49)-Contents varies; contains remaindered St. John books - some volumes contain 5 copies rather than 4, with 160 pages; Matt Baker-c | 27.00 | 80.00 | 185.00 |
| 5A-Terry-Toons Album, 132 pgs. | 17.00 | 51.00 | 120.00 |
| 6-Western Picture Stories; Baker-c/a(3); Tuska-a; The Sky Chief, Blue Monk, Ventrilo app., 132 pgs. | 25.00 | 75.00 | 175.00 |
| 7-Contains a teen-age romance plus 3 Mopsy comics | 16.50 | 50.00 | 115.00 |
| 8-The Adventures of Mighty Mouse (10/49) | 16.50 | 50.00 | 115.00 |
| 9-Romance and Confession Stories; Kubert-a(4); Baker-a; photo-c | 25.00 | 75.00 | 175.00 |
| 10-Terry-Toons | 16.50 | 50.00 | 115.00 |
| 11-Western Picture Stories-Baker-c/a(4); The Sky Chief, Desperado, & Blue Monk app.; another version with Son of Sinbad by Kubert | 23.00 | 70.00 | 160.00 |
| 12-Diary Secrets; Baker prostitute-c; 4 St. John romance comics; Baker-a | 40.00 | 120.00 | 280.00 |
| 13-Romances; Baker, Kubert-a | 22.00 | 65.00 | 154.00 |
| 14-Mighty Mouse Album | 16.50 | 50.00 | 115.00 |
| 15-Romances (4 love comics)-Baker-c | 23.00 | 70.00 | 165.00 |
| 16-Little Audrey, Abbott & Costello, Casper | 16.50 | 50.00 | 115.00 |
| 17(nn)-Mighty Mouse Album (nn, no date, but did follow No. 16); 100 pgs. on cover but has 148 pgs. | 16.50 | 50.00 | 115.00 |

NOTE: *The above books contain remaindered comics and contents could vary with each issue. No. 11, 12 have part photo magazine insides.*

**GIANT COMICS EDITIONS**
1940's (132 pages)
United Features Syndicate

| | | | |
|---|---|---|---|
| 1-Abbie & Slats, Abbott & Costello, Jim Hardy, Ella Cinders, Iron Vic | 22.00 | 65.00 | 150.00 |
| 2-Jim Hardy & Gordo | 16.00 | 48.00 | 110.00 |

NOTE: *Above books contain rebound copies; contents can vary.*

**GIANT GRAB BAG OF COMICS** (See Archie All-Star Specials under Archie Comics)

**GIANTS** (See Thrilling True Stories of...)

**GIANT-SIZE...**
May, 1974 - Dec, 1975 (35-50 cents, 52-68 pgs.)(Some titles quarterly)
Marvel Comics Group

| | | | |
|---|---|---|---|
| **Avengers** 1(8/74)-New-a plus G.A. H. Torch-r | .75 | 2.25 | 4.50 |
| **Avengers** 2,3: 2(11/74)-Death of the Swordsman. 3(2/75) | .60 | 1.75 | 3.50 |
| **Avengers** 4,5: 4(6/75)-Vision marries Scarlet Witch. 5(12/75)-Reprints Special #1 | .40 | 1.25 | 2.50 |
| **Captain America** 1(12/75)-r/stories T.O.S. 59-63 by Kirby | 1.00 | 3.00 | 7.00 |
| **Captain Marvel** 1(12/75)-r/Capt. Marvel #17, 20 by Gil Kane (p) | .85 | 2.50 | 5.00 |
| **Chillers** 1(6/74, 52 pgs)-Curse of Dracula; origin/1st app. Lilith, Dracula's daughter; Heath-r, Colan-c/a(p); becomes Giant-Size Dracula #2 on | | .60 | 1.20 |
| **Chillers** 1(2/75, 50 cents, 68 pgs.)-Alacala-a | | .50 | 1.00 |
| **Chillers** 2(5/75)-All-r; Everett-r/Advs./Weird Worlds | | .40 | .80 |
| **Chillers** 3(8/75)-Wrightson-c/a; Smith-r | | .60 | 1.20 |
| **Conan** 1(9/74)-B. Smith-r/#3; start adaptation of Howard's "Hour of the Dragon;" 1st app. Belit; new-a begins | .85 | 2.50 | 5.00 |
| **Conan** 2(12/74)-B. Smith-r/#5; Sutton-a(i)( #1 also); Buscema-c | .70 | 2.00 | 4.00 |
| **Conan** 3-5: 3(4/75)-B. Smith-r/#6; Sutton-a(i). 4(6/75)-B. Smith-r/#7. 5(1975)-B. Smith-r/#14,15; Kirby-c | .35 | 1.00 | 2.00 |
| **Creatures** 1(5/74, 52 pgs.)-Werewolf, Tigra app.; Crandall-r; becomes Giant-Size Werewolf #2 on | | .40 | .80 |
| **Daredevil** 1(1975) | .85 | 2.50 | 5.00 |

*Giant Comics Edition #5, © STJ*

*Giant-Size Avengers #1, © MEG*

*Giant-Size Captain Marvel #1, © MEG*

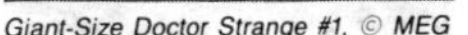
*Giant-Size Doctor Strange #1, © MEG*

*Giant-Size Fantastic Four #2, © MEG*

*Giant-Size X-Men #1, © MEG*

| | Good | Fine | N-Mint |
|---|---|---|---|
| **Defenders** 1(7/74)-Silver Surfer app.; Starlin-a; Ditko, Everett & Kirby reprints | .85 | 2.50 | 5.00 |
| **Defenders** 2(10/74, 68 pgs.)-New G. Kane-c/a(p); Everett-r; Ditko-r/Strange Tales #119 | .35 | 1.00 | 2.00 |
| **Defenders** 3-5: 3(1/75)-Newton, Starlin-a; Ditko, Everett-r. 4(4/75)-Ditko, Everett-r; G. Kane-c. 5-(7/75)-Guardians app. | .35 | 1.00 | 2.00 |
| **Doctor Strange** 1(11/75)-Reprints stories from Strange Tales #164-168; Lawrence, Tuska-r | .50 | 1.50 | 3.00 |
| **Dracula** 2(9/74, 50 cents)-Formerly Giant-Size Chillers | | .60 | 1.20 |
| **Dracula** 3(12/74)-Fox-r/Uncanny Tales #6 | | .50 | 1.00 |
| **Dracula** 4(3/75)-Ditko-r(2) | | .40 | .80 |
| **Dracula** 5(6/75)-1st Byrne art at Marvel | .70 | 2.00 | 4.00 |
| **Fantastic Four** 2-4: 2(8/74)-Formerly Giant-Size Super-Stars; Ditko-r. 3(11/74). 4(2/75); 2-4-All have Buscema-a | 1.00 | 3.00 | 6.00 |
| **Fantastic Four** 5,6: 5(5/75)-All-r; Kirby, G. Kane-r. 6(8/75)-All-r; Kirby-r | .70 | 2.00 | 4.00 |
| **Hulk** 1(1975) | .70 | 2.00 | 4.00 |
| **Invaders** 1(6/75, 50 cents, 68 pgs.)-Origin; G.A. Sub-Mariner-r/Sub-Mariner #1; intro Master Man | .70 | 2.00 | 4.00 |
| **Iron Man** 1(1975)-Ditko reprint | .85 | 2.50 | 5.00 |
| **Kid Colt** 1-3: 1(1/75). 2(4/75). 3(7/75) | .25 | .75 | 1.50 |
| **Man-Thing** 1(8/74)-New Ploog-c/a; Ditko, Kirby-r (#1-5 all have new Man-Thing stories, pre-hero-r & are 68 pgs.) | .50 | 1.50 | 3.00 |
| **Man-Thing** 2,3: 2(11/74)-Buscema-c/a(p); Kirby, Powell-r. 3(2/75)-Alcala-a; Ditko, Kirby, Sutton-r; Gil Kane-c | .25 | .75 | 1.50 |
| **Man-Thing** 4,5: 4(5/75)-Howard the Duck by Brunner-c/a; Ditko-r. 5 (8/75)-Howard the Duck by Brunner (p); Buscema-a(p); Sutton-a(i); G. Kane-c | .85 | 2.50 | 5.00 |
| **Marvel Triple Action** 1,2: 1(5/75). 2(7/75) | | .50 | 1.00 |
| **Master of Kung Fu** 1(9/74)-Russell-a; Yellow Claw-r; Gulacy-a in #1,2 | .50 | 1.50 | 3.00 |
| **Master of Kung Fu** 2(12/74)-r/Yellow Claw #1 | .35 | 1.00 | 2.00 |
| **Master of Kung Fu** 3(3/75) | .25 | .75 | 1.50 |
| **Master of Kung Fu** 4(6/75)-r/Yellow Claw | .25 | .75 | 1.50 |
| **Power Man** 1(1975) | .50 | 1.50 | 3.00 |
| **Spider-Man** 1(7/74)-Kirby/Ditko, Byrne-r plus new-a | 1.70 | 5.00 | 10.00 |
| **Spider-Man** 2,3: 2(10/74). 3(1/75)-Byrne-r | .85 | 2.50 | 5.00 |
| **Spider-Man** 4(4/75)-3rd Punisher app.; Byrne, Ditko-r | 7.00 | 21.00 | 50.00 |
| **Spider-Man** 5,6: 5(7/75)-Byrne-r. 6(9/75) | .85 | 2.50 | 5.00 |
| **Super-Heroes Featuring Spider-Man** 1(6/74, 35 cents, 52 pgs.)-Spider-Man vs. Man-Wolf; Morbius, the Living Vampire app.; Ditko-r; G. Kane-a(p); Spidey villains app. | 2.15 | 6.50 | 15.00 |
| **Super-Stars** 1(5/74, 35 cents, 52 pgs.)-Fantastic Four; Thing vs. Hulk; Kirbyish-c/a by Buckler/Sinnott; F.F. villains profiled; becomes Giant-Size Fantastic Four #2 on | 1.15 | 3.50 | 8.00 |
| **Super-Villain Team-Up** 1(3/75, 68 pgs.)-Craig-r(i) (Also see Fantastic Four #6 for 1st super-villain team-up) | .50 | 1.50 | 3.00 |
| **Super-Villain Team-Up** 2(6/75, 68 pgs.)-Dr. Doom, Sub-Mariner app.; Spider-Man-r/Amazing Spider-Man #8 by Ditko; Sekowsky-a(p) | 50 | 1.50 | 3.00 |
| **Thor** 1(7/75) | .50 | 1.50 | 3.00 |
| **Werewolf** 2(10/74, 68 pgs.)-Formerly Giant-Size Creatures; Ditko-r; Frankenstein app. | .35 | 1.00 | 2.00 |
| **Werewolf** 3-5: 3(1/75, 68 pgs.). 4(4/75, 68 pgs.)-Morbius the Living Vampire app. 5(7/75, 68 pgs.) | .35 | 1.00 | 2.00 |
| **X-Men** 1(Summer, 1975. 50 cents)-1st app. new X-Men; intro Nightcrawler, Storm, Colossus & Thunderbird; Wolverine app. | 15.00 | 45.00 | 105.00 |
| **X-Men** 2(11/75)-N. Adams-r(51 pgs) | 3.15 | 9.50 | 22.00 |

**GIANT SPECTACULAR COMICS** (See Archie All-Star Special under Archie Comics)

**GIANT SUMMER FUN BOOK** (See Terry-Toons...)

**G. I. COMBAT**
Oct, 1952 - No. 43, Dec, 1956
Quality Comics Group

| | Good | Fine | N-Mint |
|---|---|---|---|
| 1-Crandall-c | 18.00 | 54.00 | 125.00 |
| 2 | 6.50 | 19.00 | 45.00 |
| 3-5,10-Crandall-c/a | 6.50 | 19.00 | 45.00 |
| 6-Crandall-a | 5.70 | 17.00 | 40.00 |
| 7-9 | 4.00 | 12.00 | 28.00 |
| 11-20 | 2.65 | 8.00 | 18.00 |
| 21-31,33,35-43 | 2.30 | 7.00 | 16.00 |
| 32-Nuclear attack-c | 4.50 | 14.00 | 32.00 |
| 34-Crandall-a | 4.00 | 12.00 | 28.00 |

**G. I. COMBAT** (See DC Special Series #22)
No. 44, Jan, 1957 - No. 288, Mar, 1987
National Periodical Publications/DC Comics

| | Good | Fine | N-Mint |
|---|---|---|---|
| 44 | 16.50 | 50.00 | 115.00 |
| 45 | 8.50 | 25.50 | 60.00 |
| 46-50 | 5.70 | 17.00 | 40.00 |
| 51-60 | 4.00 | 12.00 | 28.00 |
| 61-66,68-80 | 2.85 | 8.50 | 20.00 |
| 67-1st Tank Killer | 5.00 | 15.00 | 35.00 |
| 81,82,84-86 | 1.50 | 4.50 | 10.00 |
| 83-1st Big Al, Little Al, & Charlie Cigar | 2.65 | 8.00 | 18.00 |
| 87-1st Haunted Tank | 5.00 | 15.00 | 35.00 |
| 88-90: Last 10 cent issue | 1.15 | 3.50 | 8.00 |
| 91-113,115-120 | 1.00 | 3.00 | 6.00 |
| 114-Origin Haunted Tank | 1.70 | 5.00 | 12.00 |
| 121-137,139,140 | .50 | 1.50 | 3.00 |
| 138-Intro. The Losers (Capt. Storm, Gunner/Sarge, Johnny Cloud) in Haunted Tank (10-11/69) | .70 | 2.00 | 4.00 |
| 141-200: 151,153-Medal of Honor series by Maurer | .35 | 1.00 | 2.00 |
| 201-281: 201-245,247-259 are $1.00 size. 232-Origin Kana the Ninja. 244-Death of Slim Stryker; 1st app. The Mercenaries. 246-(76pgs., $1.50)-30th Anniversary issue. 257-Intro. Stuart's Raiders. 260-Begin $1.25, 52 pg. issues, end #281. 264-Intro Sgt. Bullet; origin Kana. 269-Intro. The Bravos of Vietnam | .30 | .85 | 1.70 |
| 282-288 (75 cents): 282-New advs. begin | .30 | .85 | 1.70 |

NOTE: ***N. Adams*** *c-168, 201, 202.* ***Check*** *a-168, 173.* ***Drucker*** *a-48, 61, 63, 66, 71, 72, 76, 134, 140, 141, 144, 147, 148, 153.* ***Evans*** *a-135, 138, 158, 164, 166, 201, 202, 204, 205, 215, 256.* ***Giffen*** *a-267.* ***Glanzman*** *a-most issues.* ***Kubert/Heath*** *a-most issues;* ***Kubert*** *covers most issues.* ***Morrow*** *a-159-161(2 pgs.).* ***Redondo*** *a-189, 240i, 243i.* ***Sekowsky*** *a-162p.* ***Severin*** *a-147, 152.* ***Simonson*** *c-169.* ***Thorne*** *a-152, 156.* ***Wildey*** *a-153. Johnny Cloud app.-No. 112, 115, 120. Mlle. Marie app.-No. 123, 132, 200. Sgt. Rock app.-#111-113, 115, 120, 125, 141, 146, 147, 149, 200. USS Stevens by* ***Glanzman****-#145, 150-153, 157.*

**G. I. COMICS** (Also see Jeep & Overseas Comics)
1945 (Distributed to U. S. armed forces)
Giveaways

| | Good | Fine | N-Mint |
|---|---|---|---|
| 1-49-Contains Prince Valiant by Foster, Blondie, Smilin' Jack, Mickey Finn, Terry & the Pirates, Donald Duck, Alley Oop, Moon Mullins & Capt. Easy strip reprints | 4.00 | 12.00 | 28.00 |

**GIDGET** (TV)
April, 1966 - No. 2, Dec, 1966
Dell Publishing Co.

| | Good | Fine | N-Mint |
|---|---|---|---|
| 1,2: 1-Sally Field photo-c | 3.50 | 10.50 | 24.00 |

**GIFT** (See The Crusaders)

**GIFT COMICS** (50 cents)
1942 - No. 4, 1949 (No. 1-3: 324 pgs.; No. 4: 152 pgs.)
Fawcett Publications

| | Good | Fine | N-Mint |
|---|---|---|---|
| 1-Captain Marvel, Bulletman, Golden Arrow, Ibis the Invincible, Mr. Scarlet, & Spy Smasher app. Not rebound, remaindered comics, printed at same time as originals | 129.00 | 385.00 | 900.00 |
| 2 | 93.00 | 280.00 | 650.00 |

| | Good | Fine | N-Mint |
|---|---|---|---|
| 3 | 66.00 | 197.00 | 460.00 |
| 4-The Marvel Family, Captain Marvel, etc.; each issue can vary in contents | 44.00 | 133.00 | 310.00 |

**GIFTS FROM SANTA** (See March of Comics No. 137)

**GIGGLE COMICS** (Spencer Spook No. 100) (Also see Ha Ha)
Oct, 1943 - No. 99, Jan-Feb, 1955
Creston No.1-63/American Comics Group No. 64 on

| | Good | Fine | N-Mint |
|---|---|---|---|
| 1 | 17.00 | 50.00 | 115.00 |
| 2 | 7.00 | 21.00 | 50.00 |
| 3-5: Ken Hultgren-a begins? | 5.00 | 15.00 | 35.00 |
| 6-10: 9-1st Superkatt | 4.00 | 12.00 | 28.00 |
| 11-20 | 2.65 | 8.00 | 18.00 |
| 21-40: 32-Patriotic-c. 39-St. Valentine's Day-c | 2.15 | 6.50 | 15.00 |
| 41-54,56-59,61-99: 95-Spencer Spook app. | 1.70 | 5.00 | 12.00 |
| 55,60-Milt Gross-a | 2.15 | 6.50 | 15.00 |

**G-I IN BATTLE** (G-I No. 1 only)
Aug, 1952 - No. 9, July, 1953; Mar, 1957 - No. 6, May, 1958
Ajax-Farrell Publ./Four Star

| | Good | Fine | N-Mint |
|---|---|---|---|
| 1 | 3.00 | 9.00 | 21.00 |
| 2 | 1.50 | 4.50 | 10.00 |
| 3-9 | 1.15 | 3.50 | 8.00 |
| Annual 1(1952, 100 pgs.) | 13.00 | 40.00 | 90.00 |
| 1(1957-Ajax) | 2.00 | 6.00 | 14.00 |
| 2-6 | 1.00 | 3.00 | 7.00 |

**G. I. JANE**
May, 1953 - No. 11, Mar, 1955 (Misdated 3/54)
Stanhall/Merit No. 11

| | Good | Fine | N-Mint |
|---|---|---|---|
| 1 | 4.50 | 14.00 | 32.00 |
| 2-7(5/54) | 2.30 | 7.00 | 16.00 |
| 8-10(12/54, Stanhall) | 1.85 | 5.50 | 13.00 |
| 11 (3/55, Merit) | 1.70 | 5.00 | 12.00 |

**G. I. JOE** (Also see Advs. of . . ., Showcase #53,54 & The Yardbirds)
No. 10, 1950; No. 11, 4-5/51 - No. 51, 6/57 (52pgs.: 10-14,6-17?)
Ziff-Davis Publ. Co. (Korean War)

| | Good | Fine | N-Mint |
|---|---|---|---|
| 10(#1, 1950)-Saunders painted-c begin | 5.00 | 15.00 | 35.00 |
| 11-14(#2-5, 10/51) | 2.85 | 8.50 | 20.00 |
| V2#6(12/51)-17-(Last 52pgs.?) | 2.65 | 8.00 | 18.00 |
| 18-(100 pg. Giant-'52) | 8.50 | 25.50 | 60.00 |
| 19-30: 21-The Yardbirds app. | 2.30 | 7.00 | 16.00 |
| 31-47,49-51 | 2.00 | 6.00 | 14.00 |
| 48-Atom bomb story | 2.30 | 7.00 | 16.00 |

NOTE: ***Powell** a-V2#7, 8, 11. **Norman Saunders** painted c-10-14, V2#6-14, 26, 30, 31, 35, 38, 39. **Tuska** a-7. Bondage c-29, 35, 38.*

**G. I. JOE** (America's Movable Fighting Man)
1967 (36 pages) (5-1/8''x8-3/8'')
Custom Comics

| | Good | Fine | N-Mint |
|---|---|---|---|
| nn-Schaffenberger-a | | .40 | .80 |

**G. I. JOE AND THE TRANSFORMERS**
Jan, 1987 - No. 4, Apr, 1987 (Mini-series)
Marvel Comics Group

| | Good | Fine | N-Mint |
|---|---|---|---|
| 1 | .35 | 1.00 | 2.00 |
| 2-4 | .25 | .75 | 1.50 |

**G. I. JOE, A REAL AMERICAN HERO**
June, 1982 - Present
Marvel Comics Group

| | Good | Fine | N-Mint |
|---|---|---|---|
| 1-Printed on Baxter paper | 3.00 | 9.00 | 18.00 |
| 2-Printed on reg. paper | 4.15 | 12.50 | 25.00 |
| 2-10 (2nd printings) | .30 | .90 | 1.80 |
| 3-5 | 1.80 | 5.40 | 10.80 |
| 6,8 | 1.95 | 5.85 | 11.70 |
| 7,9,10 | 1.65 | 4.95 | 9.90 |
| 11-Intro Airborne | 1.20 | 3.60 | 7.20 |
| 12 | 1.80 | 5.40 | 10.80 |
| 13-15 | 1.50 | 4.50 | 9.00 |
| 14 (2nd printing) | .30 | .90 | 1.80 |
| 16 | 1.35 | 4.05 | 8.10 |
| 17-20 | .90 | 2.70 | 5.40 |
| 17-19 (2nd printings) | .25 | .70 | 1.40 |
| 21,22 | 1.15 | 3.40 | 6.80 |
| 23-25 | .60 | 1.80 | 3.60 |
| 21,23,25 (2nd printings) | .25 | .70 | 1.40 |
| 26,27-Origin Snake-Eyes parts 1 & 2 | .90 | 2.70 | 5.40 |
| 26,27 (2nd printings) | | .45 | .90 |
| 28-30 | .60 | 1.80 | 3.60 |
| 29,30 (2nd printings) | | .45 | .90 |
| 31-35: 33-New headquarters | .50 | 1.55 | 3.10 |
| 34-37 (2nd printings) | | .45 | .90 |
| 36-40 | .40 | 1.25 | 2.50 |
| 41-49 | .30 | .95 | 1.90 |
| 50-Double size; intro Special Missions | .55 | 1.70 | 3.40 |
| 51-59: 59-$1.00 issues begin | .25 | .75 | 1.50 |
| 51 (2nd printing) | | .35 | .70 |
| 60-Todd McFarlane-a | .30 | .90 | 1.80 |
| 61-99,101-112: 94-96,103-Snake-Eyes app. | | .45 | .90 |
| 100 ($1.50, 52 pgs.) | .25 | .75 | 1.50 |
| Special Treasury Edition (1982)-r/#1 | 1.20 | 3.60 | 7.20 |
| . . .Yearbook 1 ('84)-r/#1 | 1.05 | 3.15 | 6.30 |
| . . .Yearbook 2 ('85) | .60 | 1.80 | 3.60 |
| . . .Yearbook 3 ('86, 68 pgs.) | .45 | 1.35 | 2.70 |
| . . .Yearbook 4 (2/88) | .25 | .80 | 1.60 |

NOTE: ***Golden** c-23. **Heath** a-24. **Rogers** a-75p, 77-84p, 86p.*

**G. I. JOE COMICS MAGAZINE**
Dec, 1986 - No. 13, 1988 ($1.50, digest-size)
Marvel Comics Group

| | Good | Fine | N-Mint |
|---|---|---|---|
| 1-13: G.I. Joe-r | .25 | .75 | 1.50 |

**G.I. JOE EUROPEAN MISSIONS** (Action Force in indicia)
June, 1988 - No. 15, Dec, 1989 ($1.50/$1.75 #12 on, color)
Marvel Comics Ltd. (British)

| | Good | Fine | N-Mint |
|---|---|---|---|
| 1-15: Reprints Action Force | .25 | .75 | 1.50 |

**G.I. JOE IN 3-D** (See Blackthorne 3-D Series #20, 26, 35, 39, 52, 62)

**G. I. JOE ORDER OF BATTLE, THE**
Dec, 1986 - No. 4, Mar, 1987 (Mini-series)
Marvel Comics Group

| | Good | Fine | N-Mint |
|---|---|---|---|
| 1 | .55 | 1.60 | 3.20 |
| 2-4 | .30 | .90 | 1.80 |

**G. I. JOE SPECIAL MISSIONS** (Indicia title: Special Missions)
Oct, 1986 - No. 28, Dec, 1989 ($1.00, color)
Marvel Comics Group

| | Good | Fine | N-Mint |
|---|---|---|---|
| 1 | .50 | 1.50 | 3.00 |
| 2 | .30 | .90 | 1.80 |
| 3-10 | .25 | .75 | 1.50 |
| 11-28 | | .50 | 1.00 |

**G. I. JUNIORS** (See Harvey Hits No. 86, 91, 95, 98, 101, 104, 107, 110, 112, 114, 116, 118, 120, 122)

**GILGAMESH II**
1989 - No. 4, 1989 ($3.95, mini-series, prestige format)
DC Comics

| | Good | Fine | N-Mint |
|---|---|---|---|
| 1-4: Starlin-c/a, scripts; mature readers | .70 | 2.00 | 4.00 |

**GIL THORP**
May-July, 1963
Dell Publishing Co.

| | Good | Fine | N-Mint |
|---|---|---|---|
| 1-Caniffish-a | 2.00 | 6.00 | 14.00 |

*G.I. Joe V2#11, © Z-D*

*G.I. Joe Special Missions #1, © MEG*

*Gilgamesh II #1, © DC*

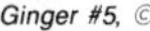
Ginger #5, © AP

Girls' Romances #15, © DC

G.I. War Brides #5, © SUPR

**GINGER** (Li'l Jinx No. 11 on?)
1951 - No. 10, Summer, 1954
Archie Publications

| | Good | Fine | N-Mint |
|---|---|---|---|
| 1 | 7.00 | 21.00 | 50.00 |
| 2 | 3.70 | 11.00 | 26.00 |
| 3-6 | 2.65 | 8.00 | 18.00 |
| 7-10-Katy Keene app. | 4.30 | 13.00 | 30.00 |

**GINGER FOX** (Also see The World of Ginger Fox)
Sept, 1988 - No. 4, Dec, 1988 ($1.75, color, mini-series)
Comico

| | Good | Fine | N-Mint |
|---|---|---|---|
| 1-4: 1-4-part photo-c | .30 | .90 | 1.80 |

**G.I. R.A.M.B.O.T.**
April, 1987 - No. 2? ($1.95, color)
Wonder Color Comics/Pied Piper #2

| | Good | Fine | N-Mint |
|---|---|---|---|
| 1,2: 2-Exist? | .35 | 1.00 | 2.00 |

**GIRL COMICS** (Girl Confessions No. 13 on)
Nov, 1949 - No. 12, Jan, 1952 (Photo-c 1-4)
Marvel/Atlas Comics(CnPC)

| | Good | Fine | N-Mint |
|---|---|---|---|
| 1 (52 pgs.) | 8.00 | 24.00 | 56.00 |
| 2-Kubert-a | 4.00 | 12.00 | 28.00 |
| 3-Everett-a; Liz Taylor photo-c | 5.30 | 16.00 | 38.00 |
| 4-11 | 2.30 | 7.00 | 16.00 |
| 12-Krigstein-a | 3.70 | 11.00 | 26.00 |

**GIRL CONFESSIONS** (Formerly Girl Comics)
No. 13, Mar, 1952 - No. 35, Aug, 1954
Atlas Comics (CnPC/ZPC)

| | Good | Fine | N-Mint |
|---|---|---|---|
| 13-Everett-a | 4.00 | 12.00 | 28.00 |
| 14,15,19,20 | 2.30 | 7.00 | 16.00 |
| 16-18-Everett-a | 2.85 | 8.50 | 20.00 |
| 21-35 | 1.70 | 5.00 | 12.00 |

**GIRL FROM U.N.C.L.E., THE** (TV) (Also see The Man From . . .)
Jan, 1967 - No. 5, Oct, 1967
Gold Key

| | Good | Fine | N-Mint |
|---|---|---|---|
| 1-McWilliams-a; Stephanie Powers photo front/back-c & pin-ups (no ads, 12 cents) | 4.00 | 12.00 | 28.00 |
| 2-5-Leonard Swift-Courier No. 5 | 2.65 | 8.00 | 18.00 |

**GIRLS' FUN & FASHION MAGAZINE** (Formerly Polly Pigtails)
V5#44, Jan, 1950 - V5#47, July, 1950
Parents' Magazine Institute

| | Good | Fine | N-Mint |
|---|---|---|---|
| V5#44 | 2.15 | 6.50 | 15.00 |
| 45-47 | 1.15 | 3.50 | 8.00 |

**GIRLS IN LOVE**
May, 1950 - No. 2, July, 1950
Fawcett Publications

| | Good | Fine | N-Mint |
|---|---|---|---|
| 1,2-Photo-c | 4.35 | 13.00 | 30.00 |

**GIRLS IN LOVE** (Formerly G. I. Sweethearts No. 45)
No. 46, Sept, 1955 - No. 57, Dec, 1956
Quality Comics Group

| | Good | Fine | N-Mint |
|---|---|---|---|
| 46 | 3.00 | 9.00 | 21.00 |
| 47-56: 54-'Commie' story | 1.70 | 5.00 | 12.00 |
| 57-Matt Baker-c/a | 3.50 | 10.50 | 24.00 |

**GIRLS IN WHITE** (See Harvey Comics Hits No. 58)

**GIRLS' LIFE**
Jan, 1954 - No. 6, Nov, 1954
Atlas Comics (BFP)

| | Good | Fine | N-Mint |
|---|---|---|---|
| 1-Patsy Walker | 4.00 | 12.00 | 28.00 |
| 2 | 2.30 | 7.00 | 16.00 |
| 3-6 | 1.50 | 4.50 | 10.00 |

**GIRLS' LOVE STORIES**
Aug-Sept, 1949 - No. 180, Nov-Dec, 1973 (No. 1-13: 52 pgs.)
National Comics(Signal Publ. No. 9-65/Arleigh No. 83-117)

| | Good | Fine | N-Mint |
|---|---|---|---|
| 1-Toth, Kinstler-a, 8 pgs. each; photo-c | 22.00 | 65.00 | 150.00 |
| 2-Kinstler-a? | 11.00 | 32.00 | 75.00 |
| 3-10: 1-9-Photo-c | 6.50 | 19.00 | 45.00 |
| 11-20 | 4.30 | 13.00 | 30.00 |
| 21-33: 21-Kinstler-a. 33-Last pre-code (1-2/55) | 2.85 | 8.50 | 20.00 |
| 34-50 | 2.30 | 7.00 | 16.00 |
| 51-99: 83-Last 10 cent issue | 1.30 | 4.00 | 9.00 |
| 100 | 1.50 | 4.50 | 10.00 |
| 101-146: 113-117-April O'Day app. | .70 | 2.00 | 5.00 |
| 147-151-"Confessions" serial | .50 | 1.50 | 3.00 |
| 152-180: 161-170, 52 pgs. | .35 | 1.00 | 2.00 |

**GIRLS' ROMANCES**
Feb-Mar, 1950 - No. 160, Oct, 1971 (No. 1-11: 52 pgs.)
National Periodical Publ.(Signal Publ. No. 7-79/Arleigh No. 84)

| | Good | Fine | N-Mint |
|---|---|---|---|
| 1-Photo-c | 22.00 | 65.00 | 150.00 |
| 2-Photo-c; Toth-a | 11.00 | 32.00 | 75.00 |
| 3-10: 3-6-Photo-c | 6.50 | 19.00 | 45.00 |
| 11,12,14-20 | 4.30 | 13.00 | 30.00 |
| 13-Toth-c | 5.00 | 15.00 | 35.00 |
| 21-31: 31-Last pre-code (2-3/55) | 2.85 | 8.50 | 20.00 |
| 32-50 | 2.30 | 7.00 | 16.00 |
| 51-99: 80-Last 10 cent issue | 1.30 | 4.00 | 9.00 |
| 100 | 1.50 | 4.50 | 10.00 |
| 101-108,110-120 | .85 | 2.60 | 6.00 |
| 109-Beatles-c/story | 3.00 | 9.00 | 21.00 |
| 121-133,135-140 | .70 | 2.00 | 4.00 |
| 134-Neal Adams-c | .85 | 2.60 | 6.00 |
| 141-160: 159,160-52 pgs. | .35 | 1.00 | 2.00 |

**G. I. SWEETHEARTS** (Formerly Diary Loves; Girls In Love #46 on)
No. 32, June, 1953 - No. 45, May, 1955
Quality Comics Group

| | Good | Fine | N-Mint |
|---|---|---|---|
| 32 | 3.00 | 9.00 | 21.00 |
| 33-45: 44-Last pre-code (3/55) | 1.70 | 5.00 | 12.00 |

**G. I. TALES** (Sgt. Barney Barker No. 1-3)
No. 4, Feb, 1957 - No. 6, July, 1957
Atlas Comics (MCI)

| | Good | Fine | N-Mint |
|---|---|---|---|
| 4-Severin-a(4) | 2.65 | 8.00 | 18.00 |
| 5 | 1.70 | 5.00 | 12.00 |
| 6-Orlando, Powell, & Woodbridge-a | 2.00 | 6.00 | 14.00 |

**GIVE ME LIBERTY**
June, 1990 - No. 4, 1991 ($4.95, color, mini-series, 52 pgs.)
Dark Horse Comics

| | Good | Fine | N-Mint |
|---|---|---|---|
| 1-4: Miller scripts, Dave Gibbons-a | .85 | 2.50 | 5.00 |

**G. I. WAR BRIDES**
April, 1954 - No. 8, June, 1955
Superior Publishers Ltd.

| | Good | Fine | N-Mint |
|---|---|---|---|
| 1 | 3.00 | 9.00 | 21.00 |
| 2 | 1.50 | 4.50 | 10.00 |
| 3-8: 4-Kamenesque-a; lingerie panels | 1.15 | 3.50 | 8.00 |

**G. I. WAR TALES**
Mar-Apr, 1973 - No. 4, Oct-Nov, 1973
National Periodical Publications

| | Good | Fine | N-Mint |
|---|---|---|---|
| 1-4: Reprints. 2-N. Adams-a(r), 4-Krigstein-a(r) | | .25 | .50 |

NOTE: ***Drucker** a-3r, 4r. **Heath** a-4r. **Kubert** a-2, 3; c-4r.*

**GIZMO** (Also see Domino Chance)
May-June, 1985 (B&W, one shot)
Chance Ent.

| | Good | Fine | N-Mint |
|---|---|---|---|
| 1 | 1.35 | 4.00 | 8.00 |

**GIZMO**
1986 - No. 6, July, 1987 ($1.50, B&W)

Mirage Studios

| | Good | Fine | N-Mint |
|---|---|---|---|
| 1 | .70 | 2.00 | 4.00 |
| 2-6 | .30 | .90 | 1.80 |

**GLADSTONE COMIC ALBUM**
1987 - No. 28, 1990 (8½x11")($5.95)(#26-28: $9.95)
Gladstone Publishing

| | Good | Fine | N-Mint |
|---|---|---|---|
| 1-10: 1-Uncle Scrooge; Barks-r; Beck-c. 2-Donald Duck; r/F.C. #108 by Barks. 3-Mickey Mouse-r by Gottfredson. 4-Uncle Scrooge; r/F.C. #456 by Barks. 5-Donald Duck Advs.; r/F.C. #199. 6-Uncle Scrooge-r by Barks. 7-Donald Duck-r by Barks. 8-Mickey Mouse-r. 9-Bambi; r/F.C. #12. 10-Donald Duck Advs.; r/F.C. #275 | 1.00 | 3.00 | 6.00 |
| 11-20: 11-Uncle Scrooge; r/U.S. #4. 12-Donald And Daisy; r/F.C. #1055, WDC&S. 13-Donald Duck Advs.; r/F.C. #408. 14-Uncle Scrooge; Barks-r/U.S #21. 15-Donald And Gladstone; Barks-r. 16-Donald Duck Advs.; r/F.C. #238. 17-Mickey Mouse strip-r (The World of Tomorrow, The Pirate Ghost Ship). 18-Donald Duck and the Junior Woodchucks; Barks-r. 19-Uncle Scrooge; r/U.S. #12; Rosa-c. 20-Uncle Scrooge; r/F.C. #386; Barks-c/a(r) | 1.00 | 3.00 | 6.00 |
| 21-25: 21-Donald Duck Family; Barks-c/a(r). 22-Mickey Mouse strip-r. 23-Donald Duck; Barks-r/D.D. #26. 24-Uncle Scrooge; Barks-r; Rosa-c. 25-D. Duck; Barks-c/a-r/F.C. #367 | 1.00 | 3.00 | 6.00 |
| 26-28: 26-Mickey and Donald; Gottfredson-c/a(r). 27-Donald Duck; r/WDC&S by Barks; Barks painted-c. 28-Uncle Scrooge & Donald Duck; Rosa-c/a (4 stories) | 1.70 | 5.00 | 10.00 |
| Special 1 (1989, $9.95)-Donald Duck Finds Pirate Gold; r/F.C. #9 | 1.70 | 5.00 | 10.00 |
| Special 2 (1989, $8.95)-Uncle Scrooge and Donald Duck; Barks-r/Uncle Scrooge #5; Rosa-c | 1.50 | 4.50 | 9.00 |
| Special 3 (1989, $8.95)-Mickey Mouse strip-r | 1.50 | 4.50 | 9.00 |
| Special 4 (1989, $11.95)-Uncle Scrooge; Rosa-c/a-r/Son of the Sun from U.S. #219 plus Barks-r/U.S. | 2.00 | 6.00 | 12.00 |
| Special 5 (1990, $11.95)-Donald Duck Advs.; Barks-r/F.C. #282 & 422 plus Barks painted-c | 2.00 | 6.00 | 12.00 |
| Special 6 (1990, $12.95)-Uncle Scrooge; Barks-c/a-r/Uncle Scrooge | 2.15 | 6.50 | 13.00 |
| Special 7 (1990, $13.95)-Mickey Mouse; Gottfredson strip-r | 2.35 | 7.00 | 14.00 |

**GLADSTONE COMIC ALBUM** (2nd series)
1990 - Present ($5.95, color, 8½X11," stiff-c, 52 pgs.)
Gladstone Publishing

| | Good | Fine | N-Mint |
|---|---|---|---|
| 1-The Original Dick Tracy | 1.00 | 3.00 | 6.00 |

**GLAMOROUS ROMANCES** (Formerly Dotty)
No. 41, Sept, 1949 - No. 90, Oct, 1956 (Photo-c 68-90)
Ace Magazines (A. A. Wyn)

| | Good | Fine | N-Mint |
|---|---|---|---|
| 41-Dotty app. | 3.00 | 9.00 | 21.00 |
| 42-72,74-80: 50-61-Painted-c. 80-Last pre-code (2/55) | 1.50 | 4.50 | 10.00 |
| 73-L.B. Cole-a(r)-/All Love #27 | 2.00 | 6.00 | 14.00 |
| 81-90 | 1.30 | 4.00 | 9.00 |

**GLOBAL FORCE**
1987 - No. 2? ($1.95, color)
Silverline Comics

| | Good | Fine | N-Mint |
|---|---|---|---|
| 1,2 | .35 | 1.00 | 2.00 |

**GNOME MOBILE, THE** (See Movie Comics)

**GOBBLEDYGOOK**
1984 - No. 2, 1984 (B&W)(1st Mirage comic, both pubbed same time)
Mirage Studios

| | Good | Fine | N-Mint |
|---|---|---|---|
| 1,2-24 pgs., early TMNT | 40.00 | 125.00 | 250.00 |

**GOBBLEDYGOOK**
Dec, 1986 (One shot, $3.50, B&W, 100 pgs.)
Mirage Studios

| | Good | Fine | N-Mint |
|---|---|---|---|
| 1-New 10 pg. TMNT story | 1.35 | 4.00 | 8.00 |

**GOBLIN, THE**
June, 1982 - No. 4, Dec, 1982 (Magazine, $2.25)
Warren Publishing Co.

| | Good | Fine | N-Mint |
|---|---|---|---|
| 1-The Gremlin app; Golden-a(p) | .35 | 1.10 | 2.25 |
| 2-4: 2-1st Hobgoblin | .35 | 1.10 | 2.25 |

**GODFATHERS, THE** (See The Crusaders)

**GOD IS**
1973, 1975 (35-49 Cents)
Spire Christian Comics (Fleming H. Revell Co.)

| | Good | Fine | N-Mint |
|---|---|---|---|
| nn-By Al Hartley | | .40 | .80 |

**GODS FOR HIRE**
Dec, 1986 - No. 3? ($1.50, color)
Hot Comics

| | Good | Fine | N-Mint |
|---|---|---|---|
| 1-3: 1-Barry Crain-c/a(p) | .25 | .75 | 1.50 |

**GOD'S HEROES IN AMERICA**
1956 (nn) (68 pgs.) (25-35 cents)
Catechetical Guild Educational Society

| | Good | Fine | N-Mint |
|---|---|---|---|
| 307 | 1.15 | 3.50 | 8.00 |

**GOD'S SMUGGLER** (Religious)
1972 (39 & 49 cents)
Spire Christian Comics/Fleming H. Revell Co.

| | Good | Fine | N-Mint |
|---|---|---|---|
| 1-Two variations exist | | .40 | .80 |

**GODZILLA**
August, 1977 - No. 24, July, 1979 (Based on movie series)
Marvel Comics Group

| | Good | Fine | N-Mint |
|---|---|---|---|
| 1-Mooney-i | .70 | 2.00 | 4.00 |
| 2-10: 2-Tuska-i. 3-Champions app. 4,5-Sutton-a | .50 | 1.50 | 3.00 |
| 11-24: 20-F.F. app. 21,22-Devil Dinosaur app. | .35 | 1.00 | 2.00 |

**GODZILLA**
May, 1988 - No. 6, 1988 ($1.95, B&W, mini-series)
Dark Horse Comics

| | Good | Fine | N-Mint |
|---|---|---|---|
| 1 | 1.00 | 3.00 | 6.00 |
| 2-6 | .50 | 1.50 | 3.00 |
| ...Collection (1990, $10.95)-r/1-6 with new-c | 1.85 | 5.50 | 11.00 |
| King Of The Monsters Special (8/87, $1.50)-Origin; Bissette-c/a | .50 | 1.50 | 3.00 |

**GO-GO**
June, 1966 - No. 9, Oct, 1967
Charlton Comics

| | Good | Fine | N-Mint |
|---|---|---|---|
| 1-Miss Bikini Luv begins; Rolling Stones, Beatles, Elvis, Sonny & Cher, Sinatra, Bob Dylan parody; Herman's Hermits pin-ups | 3.00 | 9.00 | 21.00 |
| 2-Ringo Starr, David McCallum, Beatles photo cover; Beatles story and photos | 3.00 | 9.00 | 21.00 |
| 3,4: 3-Blooperman begins, ends No. 6 | 1.50 | 4.50 | 10.00 |
| 5-9: 5-Super Hero & TV satire by Jim Aparo & Grass Green begins. 6-8-Aparo-a. 6-Petula Clark photo-c | 1.50 | 4.50 | 10.00 |

**GO-GO AND ANIMAL** (See Tippy's Friends...)

**GOING STEADY** (Formerly Teen-Age Temptations)
No. 10, Dec, 1954 - No. 13, June, 1955; No. 14, Oct, 1955
St. John Publishing Co.

| | Good | Fine | N-Mint |
|---|---|---|---|
| 10(1954)-Matt Baker-c/a | 7.00 | 21.00 | 50.00 |
| 11(2/55, last precode), 12(4/55)-Baker-c | 3.60 | 11.00 | 25.00 |
| 13(6/55)-Baker-c/a | 5.00 | 15.00 | 35.00 |
| 14(10/55)-Matt Baker-c/a, 25 pgs. | 5.30 | 16.00 | 38.00 |

**GOING STEADY** (Formerly Personal Love)
V3#3, Feb, 1960 - V3#6, Aug, 1960; V4#1, Sept-Oct, 1960
Prize Publications/Headline

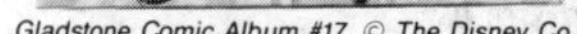
*Gladstone Comic Album #17, © The Disney Co.*

*Gobbledygook #1 (12/86), © Mirage Studios*

*Godzilla #23, © MEG*

Golden Arrow Western #6, © FAW

Golden Lad #2, © Spark Publ.

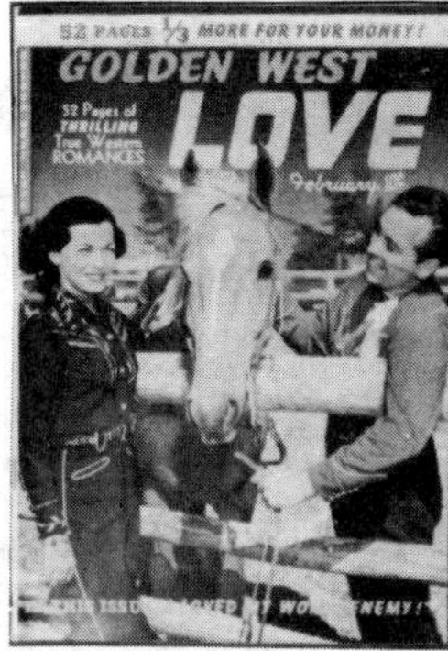

Golden West Love #3, © Kirby Publ.

| | Good | Fine | N-Mint |
|---|---|---|---|
| V3#3-6, V4#1 | .70 | 2.00 | 5.00 |

**GOING STEADY WITH BETTY** (Betty & Her Steady No. 2)
Nov-Dec, 1949
Avon Periodicals

| | Good | Fine | N-Mint |
|---|---|---|---|
| 1 | 6.50 | 19.00 | 45.00 |

**GOLDEN ARROW** (See Fawcett Miniatures, Mighty Midget & Whiz Comics)

**GOLDEN ARROW** (. . .Western No. 6)
Wint, 1942-43 - No. 6, Spring, 1947
Fawcett Publications

| | Good | Fine | N-Mint |
|---|---|---|---|
| 1-Golden Arrow begins | 18.00 | 54.00 | 125.00 |
| 2 | 8.00 | 24.00 | 56.00 |
| 3-5 | 5.70 | 17.00 | 40.00 |
| 6-Krigstein-a | 6.50 | 19.00 | 45.00 |
| . . .Well Known Comics (1944; 12 pgs.; 8½x10½"; paper-c; glued binding)-Bestmaid/Samuel Lowe giveaway; printed in green | 6.00 | 18.00 | 42.00 |

**GOLDEN COMICS DIGEST**
May, 1969 - No. 48, Jan, 1976
Gold Key

NOTE: *Whitman editions exist of many titles and are generally valued less.*

| | Good | Fine | N-Mint |
|---|---|---|---|
| 1-Tom & Jerry, Woody Woodpecker, Bugs Bunny | 1.15 | 3.50 | 8.00 |
| 2-Hanna-Barbera TV Fun Favorites; Space Ghost app. | .85 | 2.50 | 5.00 |
| 3-Tom & Jerry, Woody Woodpecker | .50 | 1.50 | 3.00 |
| 4-Tarzan; Manning & Marsh-a | 1.70 | 5.00 | 12.00 |
| 5,8-Tom & Jerry, W. Woodpecker, Bugs Bunny | .35 | 1.00 | 2.00 |
| 6-Bugs Bunny | .35 | 1.00 | 2.00 |
| 7-Hanna-Barbera TV Fun Favorites | .70 | 2.00 | 4.00 |
| 9-Tarzan | 1.50 | 4.50 | 10.00 |
| 10-17: 10-Bugs Bunny. 11-Hanna-Barbera TV Fun Favorites. 12-Tom & Jerry, Bugs Bunny, W. Woodpecker Journey to the Sun. 13-Tom & Jerry. 14-Bugs Bunny Fun Packed Funnies. 15-Tom & Jerry, Woody Woodpecker, Bugs Bunny. 16-Woody Woodpecker Cartoon Special. 17-Bugs Bunny | .50 | 1.50 | 3.00 |
| 18-Tom & Jerry; Barney Bear-r by Barks | .70 | 2.00 | 4.00 |
| 19-Little Lulu | 1.70 | 5.00 | 12.00 |
| 20-22: 20-Woody Woodpecker Falltime Funtime. 21-Bugs Bunny Showtime. 22-Tom & Jerry Winter Wingding | .50 | 1.50 | 3.00 |
| 23-Little Lulu & Tubby Fun Fling | 1.70 | 5.00 | 12.00 |
| 24-26,28: 24-Woody Woodpecker Fun Festival. 25-Tom & Jerry. 26-Bugs Bunny Halloween Hulla-Boo-Loo; Dr. Spektor article, also #25. 28-Tom & Jerry | .50 | 1.50 | 3.00 |
| 27-Little Lulu & Tubby in Hawaii | 1.50 | 4.50 | 10.00 |
| 29-Little Lulu & Tubby | 1.50 | 4.50 | 10.00 |
| 30-Bugs Bunny Vacation Funnies | .50 | 1.50 | 3.00 |
| 31-Turok, Son of Stone; r/4-Color #596,656 | 1.15 | 3.50 | 8.00 |
| 32-Woody Woodpecker Summer Fun | .50 | 1.50 | 3.00 |
| 33,36: 33-Little Lulu & Tubby Halloween Fun; Dr. Spektor app. 36-Little Lulu & Her Friends | 1.70 | 5.00 | 12.00 |
| 34,35,37-39: 34-Bugs Bunny Winter Funnies. 35-Tom & Jerry Snowtime Funtime. 37-Woody Woodpecker County Fair. 38-The Pink Panther. 39-Bugs Bunny Summer Fun | .50 | 1.50 | 3.00 |
| 40,43: 40-Little Lulu & Tubby Trick or Treat; all by Stanley. 43-Little Lulu in Paris | 1.70 | 5.00 | 12.00 |
| 41,42,44,45,47: 41-Tom & Jerry Winter Carnival. 42-Bugs Bunny. 44-Woody Woodpecker Family Fun Festival. 45-The Pink Panther. 47-Bugs Bunny | .35 | 1.00 | 2.00 |
| 46-Little Lulu & Tubby | 1.50 | 4.50 | 10.00 |
| 48-The Lone Ranger | .70 | 2.00 | 4.00 |

NOTE: *#1-30, 164 pages; #31 on, 132 pages.*

**GOLDEN LAD**
July, 1945 - No. 5, June, 1946
Spark Publications

| | Good | Fine | N-Mint |
|---|---|---|---|
| 1-Origin Golden Lad & Swift Arrow | 30.00 | 90.00 | 210.00 |
| 2-Mort Meskin-c/a | 14.00 | 43.00 | 100.00 |
| 3,4-Mort Meskin-c/a | 13.00 | 40.00 | 90.00 |
| 5-Origin Golden Girl; Shaman & Flame app. | 14.00 | 43.00 | 100.00 |

NOTE: *All have **Robinson**, and **Roussos** art plus **Meskin** covers and art. #5 is 52pgs.*

**GOLDEN LEGACY**
1966 - 1972 (Black History) (25 cents)
Fitzgerald Publishing Co.

| | Good | Fine | N-Mint |
|---|---|---|---|
| 1-Toussaint L'Ouverture (1966), 2-Harriet Tubman (1967), 3-Crispus Attucks & the Minutemen (1967), 4-Benjamin Banneker (1968), 5-Matthew Henson (1969), 6-Alexander Dumas & Family (1969), 7-Frederick Douglass, Part 1 (1969), 8-Frederick Douglass, Part 2 (1970), 9-Robert Smalls (1970), 10-J. Cinque & the Amistad Mutiny (1970), 11-Men in Action: White, Marshall J. Wilkins (1970), 12-Black Cowboys (1972), 13-The Life of Martin Luther King, Jr. (1972), 14-The Life of Alexander Pushkin (1971), 15-Ancient African Kingdoms (1972), 16-Black Inventors (1972) each. . . . | .25 | .75 | 1.50 |
| 1-10,12,13,15,16(1976)-Reprints | | .25 | .50 |

**GOLDEN LOVE STORIES** (Formerly Golden West Love)
No. 4, April, 1950
Kirby Publishing Co.

| | Good | Fine | N-Mint |
|---|---|---|---|
| 4-Powell-a; Glenn Ford/Janet Leigh photo-c | 7.00 | 21.00 | 50.00 |

**GOLDEN PICTURE CLASSIC, A**
1956-1957 (Text stories w/illustrations in color; 100 pgs. each)
Western Printing Co. (Simon & Shuster)

| | Good | Fine | N-Mint |
|---|---|---|---|
| CL-401: Treasure Island | 7.00 | 21.00 | 50.00 |
| CL-402: Tom Sawyer | 6.00 | 18.00 | 42.00 |
| CL-403: Black Beauty | 6.00 | 18.00 | 42.00 |
| CL-404: Little Women | 6.00 | 18.00 | 42.00 |
| CL-405: Heidi | 6.00 | 18.00 | 42.00 |
| CL-406: Ben Hur | 4.00 | 12.00 | 28.00 |
| CL-407: Around the World in 80 Days | 4.00 | 12.00 | 28.00 |
| CL-408: Sherlock Holmes | 5.00 | 15.00 | 35.00 |
| CL-409: The Three Musketeers | 4.00 | 12.00 | 28.00 |
| CL-410: The Merry Advs. of Robin Hood | 4.00 | 12.00 | 28.00 |
| CL-411: Hans Brinker | 5.00 | 15.00 | 35.00 |
| CL-412: The Count of Monte Cristo | 5.00 | 15.00 | 35.00 |

(Both soft & hardcover editions are valued the same)

NOTE: *Recent research has uncovered new information. Apparently #s 1-6 were issued in 1956 and #7-12 in 1957. But they can be found in five different series listings: CL-1 to CL-12 (softbound); CL-401 to CL-412 (also softbound); CL-101 to CL-112 (hardbound); plus two new series discoveries: **A Golden Reading Adventure**, publ. by Golden Press; edited down to 60 pages and reduced in size to 6"x9"; only #s discovered so far are #381 (CL-4), #382 (CL-6) & #387 (CL-3). They have no reorder list and some have covers different from GPC. There have also been found British hardbound editions of GPC with dust jackets. Copies of all five listed series vary from scarce to very rare. Some editions of some series have not yet been found at all.*

**GOLDEN PICTURE STORY BOOK**
Dec, 1961 (52 pgs.; 50 cents; large size)
Racine Press (Western)

| | Good | Fine | N-Mint |
|---|---|---|---|
| ST-1-Huckleberry Hound (TV) | 4.30 | 13.00 | 30.00 |
| ST-2-Yogi Bear (TV) | 4.30 | 13.00 | 30.00 |
| ST-3-Babes in Toyland (Walt Disney's. . .)-Annette Funicello photo-c | 4.30 | 13.00 | 30.00 |
| ST-4-(. . .of Disney Ducks)-Walt Disney's Wonderful World of Ducks (Donald Duck, Uncle Scrooge, Donald's Nephews, Grandma Duck, Ludwig Von Drake, & Gyro Gearloose stories) | 4.30 | 13.00 | 30.00 |

**GOLDEN RECORD COMIC** (See Amazing Spider-Man #1, Avengers #1, Fantastic Four #1, Journey Into Mystery #83)

**GOLDEN WEST LOVE** (Golden Love Stories No. 4)
Sept-Oct, 1949 - No. 3, Feb, 1950 (All 52 pgs.)
Kirby Publishing Co.

| | Good | Fine | N-Mint |
|---|---|---|---|
| 1-Powell-a in all; Roussos-a; painted-c | 8.00 | 24.00 | 55.00 |
| 2,3: 3-Photo-c | 6.00 | 18.00 | 42.00 |

**GOLDEN WEST RODEO TREASURY** (See Dell Giants)

**GOLDILOCKS** (See March of Comics No. 1)

**GOLDILOCKS & THE THREE BEARS**
1943 (Giveaway)
K. K. Publications

| | Good | Fine | N-Mint |
|---|---|---|---|
| nn | 6.75 | 20.00 | 40.00 |

**GOLD KEY CHAMPION**
Mar, 1978 - No. 2, May, 1978 (52 pages) (50 cents)
Gold Key

| | Good | Fine | N-Mint |
|---|---|---|---|
| 1-Space Family Robinson; ½-r | | .40 | .80 |
| 2-Mighty Samson; ½-r | | .40 | .80 |

**GOLD KEY SPOTLIGHT**
May, 1976 - No. 11, Feb, 1978
Gold Key

| | Good | Fine | N-Mint |
|---|---|---|---|
| 1-Tom, Dick & Harriet | | .60 | 1.20 |
| 2-5,7,10,11: 2-Wacky Advs. of Cracky. 3-Wacky Witch. 4-Tom, Dick & Harriet. 5-Wacky Advs. of Cracky. 7-Wacky Witch & Greta Ghost 10-O. G. Whiz. 11-Tom, Dick & Harriet | | .50 | 1.00 |
| 6,8,9: 6-Dagar the Invincible; Santos-a; origin Demonomicon. 8-The Occult Files of Dr. Spektor, Simbar, Lu-sai; Santos-a. 9-Tragg | .50 | 1.50 | 3.00 |

**GOLD MEDAL COMICS**
1945 (132 pages) (One shot)
Cambridge House

| | Good | Fine | N-Mint |
|---|---|---|---|
| nn-Captain Truth by Fugitani, Crime Detector, The Witch of Salem, Luckyman, others app. | 11.50 | 34.00 | 80.00 |

**GOLDYN IN 3-D** (See Blackthorne 3-D Series No. 4)

**GOMER PYLE** (TV)
July, 1966 - No. 3, Jan, 1967
Gold Key

| | Good | Fine | N-Mint |
|---|---|---|---|
| 1-Photo front/back-c | 4.00 | 12.00 | 28.00 |
| 2,3 | 3.00 | 9.00 | 21.00 |

**GOODBYE, MR. CHIPS** (See Movie Comics)

**GOOD GIRL ART QUARTERLY**
Fall, 1990 - Present ($3.95, B&W & color, 52 pgs.)
AC Comics

| | Good | Fine | N-Mint |
|---|---|---|---|
| 1-New 10 pg. Femforce story plus Phantom Lady-r(2) by Baker, & Skygirl-r by Baker | .70 | 2.00 | 4.00 |

**GOOFY** (Disney)(See Dynabrite Comics, Mickey Mouse Magazine V4/7, Walt Disney Showcase #35 & Wheaties)
No. 468, May, 1953 - Sept-Nov, 1962
Dell Publishing Co.

| | Good | Fine | N-Mint |
|---|---|---|---|
| 4-Color 468 | 3.00 | 9.00 | 21.00 |
| 4-Color 562,627,658,747,802 | 2.30 | 7.00 | 16.00 |
| 4-Color 899,952,987,1053,1094,1149,1201 | 2.00 | 6.00 | 14.00 |
| 12-308-211(Dell, 9-11/62) | 2.00 | 6.00 | 14.00 |

**GOOFY ADVENTURES**
June, 1990 - Present ($1.50, color)
Disney Comics

| | Good | Fine | N-Mint |
|---|---|---|---|
| 1-12: All new stories. 2-Joshua Quagmire-a w/free poster. 7-WDC&S-r plus new-a | .25 | .75 | 1.50 |

**GOOFY ADVENTURE STORY** (See 4-Color No. 857)

**GOOFY COMICS** (Companion to Happy Comics)
June, 1943 - No. 48, 1953
Nedor Publ. Co. No. 1-14/Standard No. 14-48(Animated Cartoons)

| | Good | Fine | N-Mint |
|---|---|---|---|
| 1 | 12.00 | 36.00 | 85.00 |
| 2 | 6.00 | 18.00 | 42.00 |
| 3-10 | 4.00 | 12.00 | 28.00 |
| 11-19 | 3.15 | 9.50 | 22.00 |
| 20-35-Frazetta text illos in all | 4.30 | 13.00 | 30.00 |
| 36-48 | 2.30 | 7.00 | 16.00 |

**GOOFY SUCCESS STORY** (See 4-Color No. 702)

**GOOSE** (Humor magazine)
Sept, 1976 - No. 3, 1976 (52 pgs.) (75 cents)
Cousins Publ. (Fawcett)

| | Good | Fine | N-Mint |
|---|---|---|---|
| 1-3 | | .50 | 1.00 |

**GORDO** (See Comics Revue No. 5)

**GORGO** (Based on movie) (See Return of. . .)
May, 1961 - No. 23, Sept, 1965
Charlton Comics

| | Good | Fine | N-Mint |
|---|---|---|---|
| 1-Ditko-a, 22 pgs. | 16.00 | 48.00 | 110.00 |
| 2,3-Ditko-c/a | 8.00 | 24.00 | 55.00 |
| 4-10: 4-Ditko-c | 5.00 | 15.00 | 35.00 |
| 11,13-16-Ditko-a | 4.00 | 12.00 | 28.00 |
| 12,17-23: 12-Reptisaurus x-over; Montes/Bache-a-No. 17-23. 20-Giordano-c | 1.70 | 5.00 | 12.00 |
| Gorgo's Revenge('62)-Becomes Return of. . . | 3.00 | 9.00 | 21.00 |

**GOSPEL BLIMP, THE**
1973, 1974 (36 pgs.) (35, 39 cents)
Spire Christian Comics (Fleming H. Revell Co.)

| | Good | Fine | N-Mint |
|---|---|---|---|
| nn | | .50 | 1.00 |

**GOTHAM BY GASLIGHT** (A Tale of the Batman)
1989 ($3.95, one-shot, squarebound, 52 pgs.)
DC Comics

| | Good | Fine | N-Mint |
|---|---|---|---|
| nn-Mignola/Russell-a; intro by Robert Bloch | .70 | 2.10 | 4.20 |

**GOTHIC ROMANCES**
January, 1975 (B&W Magazine) (75 cents)
Atlas/Seaboard Publ.

| | Good | Fine | N-Mint |
|---|---|---|---|
| 1-Neal Adams-a | .30 | .90 | 1.80 |

**GOVERNOR & J. J., THE** (TV)
Feb, 1970 - No. 3, Aug, 1970 (Photo-c)
Gold Key

| | Good | Fine | N-Mint |
|---|---|---|---|
| 1 | 2.30 | 7.00 | 16.00 |
| 2,3 | 1.70 | 5.00 | 12.00 |

**GRANDMA DUCK'S FARM FRIENDS** (See 4-Color #763, 873, 965, 1010, 1073, 1161, 1279, Walt Disney's Comics & Stories #293 & Wheaties)

**GRAND PRIX** (Formerly Hot Rod Racers)
No. 16, Sept, 1967 - No. 31, May, 1970
Charlton Comics

| | Good | Fine | N-Mint |
|---|---|---|---|
| 16: Features Rick Roberts | .85 | 2.60 | 6.00 |
| 17-20 | .70 | 2.00 | 4.00 |
| 21-31 | .50 | 1.50 | 3.00 |

**GRAY GHOST, THE** (See 4-Color No. 911, 1000)

**GREAT ACTION COMICS**
1958 (Reprints)
I. W. Enterprises

| | Good | Fine | N-Mint |
|---|---|---|---|
| 1-Captain Truth | 1.00 | 3.00 | 6.00 |
| 8,9-Phantom Lady No. 15 & 23 | 6.00 | 18.00 | 42.00 |

**GREAT AMERICAN COMICS PRESENTS - THE SECRET VOICE**
1945 (10 cents)
Peter George 4-Star Publ./American Features Syndicate

| | Good | Fine | N-Mint |
|---|---|---|---|
| 1-All anti-Nazi | 8.00 | 24.00 | 56.00 |

**GREAT AMERICAN WESTERN, THE**
1987 - No. 4? ($1.75-$2.95-$3.50, B&W with some color)
AC Comics

| | Good | Fine | N-Mint |
|---|---|---|---|
| 1 ($1.75)-Western-r plus Bill Black-a | .30 | .90 | 1.80 |
| 2,3 ($2.95) 2-Tribute to ME comics; Durango Kid photo-c. 3-Tribute to Tom Mix plus Roy Rogers, Durango Kid; Billy the Kid-r by Severin; photo-c | .50 | 1.50 | 3.00 |

4 ($3.50, 52 pgs., 16 pgs. color)-Tribute to Lash LaRue; photo-c &

*Goofy Adventures #1, © The Disney Co.*

*Gorgo #2, © CC*

*Great American Comics Presents. . . #1, © AFS*

Great Exploits #1, © Decker Publ.

Great Lover Romances #1, © TOBY

Green Arrow #1 (2/88), © DC

| | Good | Fine | N-Mint |
|---|---|---|---|
| interior photos; Fawcett-r | .60 | 1.75 | 3.50 |

**GREAT CAT FAMILY, THE** (See 4-Color No. 750)

**GREAT COMICS**
Nov, 1941 - No. 3, Jan, 1942
Great Comics Publications

| | Good | Fine | N-Mint |
|---|---|---|---|
| 1-Origin The Great Zarro; Madame Strange begins | 50.00 | 150.00 | 350.00 |
| 2 | 29.00 | 85.00 | 200.00 |
| 3-Futuro Takes Hitler to Hell; "The Lost City" movie story (starring William Boyd); continues in Choice Comics #3 | 52.00 | 156.00 | 365.00 |

**GREAT COMICS**
1945
Novack Publishing Co./Jubilee Comics

| | Good | Fine | N-Mint |
|---|---|---|---|
| 1-The Defenders, Capt. Power app.; L. B. Cole-c | 10.00 | 30.00 | 70.00 |
| 1-Same cover; Boogey Man, Satanas, & The Sorcerer & His Apprentice | 8.00 | 24.00 | 56.00 |

**GREAT DOGPATCH MYSTERY** (See Mammy Yokum & the. . .)

**GREATEST BATMAN STORIES EVER TOLD, THE**
1988 (Color reprints) (Greatest Stories Vol. 2)
DC Comics

| | Good | Fine | N-Mint |
|---|---|---|---|
| Softcover ($15.95)-Simonson-c | 3.00 | 9.00 | 18.00 |
| Hardcover ($24.95) with dust jacket | 8.35 | 25.00 | 50.00 |

**GREATEST JOKER STORIES EVER TOLD, THE**
1988 (Color reprints) (Greatest Stories Vol. 3)
DC Comics

| | Good | Fine | N-Mint |
|---|---|---|---|
| Softcover ($14.95)-Brian Bolland Joker-c | 2.70 | 8.00 | 16.00 |
| Hardcover ($19.95) with dust jacket | 6.70 | 20.00 | 40.00 |

**GREAT EXPLOITS**
October, 1957
Decker Publ./Red Top

| | Good | Fine | N-Mint |
|---|---|---|---|
| 1-Krigstein-a(2) (re-issue on cover); reprints/Daring Advs. #6 (Approved Comics) | 3.70 | 11.00 | 26.00 |

**GREAT FOODINI, THE** (See Foodini)

**GREAT GAZOO, THE** (The Flintstones)(TV)
Aug, 1973 - No. 20, Jan, 1977 (Hanna-Barbera)
Charlton Comics

| | Good | Fine | N-Mint |
|---|---|---|---|
| 1 | .50 | 1.50 | 3.00 |
| 2-20 | | .50 | 1.00 |

**GREAT GRAPE APE, THE** (TV)(See TV Stars #1)
Sept, 1976 - No. 2, Nov, 1976 (Hanna-Barbera)
Charlton Comics

| | Good | Fine | N-Mint |
|---|---|---|---|
| 1,2 | .35 | 1.00 | 2.00 |

**GREAT LOCOMOTIVE CHASE, THE** (See 4-Color No. 712)

**GREAT LOVER ROMANCES** (Young Lover Romances #4,5)
3/51; #2, 1951(nd); #3, 1952 (nd); #6, Oct?, 1952 - No. 22, May, 1955
Toby Press (Photo-c #1-3,13,17)

| | Good | Fine | N-Mint |
|---|---|---|---|
| 1-Jon Juan story-r/J.J. #1 by Schomburg; Dr. Anthony King app. | 6.50 | 19.00 | 45.00 |
| 2-Jon Juan, Dr. Anthony King app. | 3.15 | 9.50 | 22.00 |
| 3,7,9-14,16-22 (no #4,5) | 1.50 | 4.50 | 10.00 |
| 6-Kurtzman-a (10/52) | 3.50 | 10.50 | 24.00 |
| 8-Five pgs. of "Pin-Up Pete" by Sparling | 4.00 | 12.00 | 28.00 |
| 15-Liz Taylor photo-c | 3.50 | 10.50 | 24.00 |

**GREAT PEOPLE OF GENESIS, THE**
No date (64 pgs.) (Religious giveaway)
David C. Cook Publ. Co.

| | Good | Fine | N-Mint |
|---|---|---|---|
| nn-Reprint/Sunday Pix Weekly | 1.50 | 4.50 | 10.00 |

**GREAT RACE, THE** (See Movie Classics)

**GREAT SACRAMENT, THE**
1953 (36 pages, giveaway)
Catechetical Guild

| | Good | Fine | N-Mint |
|---|---|---|---|
| nn | 1.50 | 4.50 | 10.00 |

**GREAT SCOTT SHOE STORE** (See Bulls-Eye)

**GREAT WEST** (Magazine)
1969 (52 pages) (Black & White)
M. F. Enterprises

| | Good | Fine | N-Mint |
|---|---|---|---|
| V1#1 | .25 | .75 | 1.50 |

**GREAT WESTERN**
No. 8, Jan-Mar, 1954 - No. 11, Oct-Dec, 1954
Magazine Enterprises

| | Good | Fine | N-Mint |
|---|---|---|---|
| 8(A-1 93)-Trail Colt by Guardineer; Powell Red Hawk-r/Straight Arrow begins, ends #11; Durango Kid story | 11.00 | 32.00 | 75.00 |
| 9(A-1 105), 11(A-1 127)-Ghost Rider, Durango Kid app. in each. 9-Red Mask-c, but no app. | 5.00 | 15.00 | 35.00 |
| 10(A-1 113)-The Calico Kid by Guardineer-r/Tim Holt #8; Straight Arrow, Durango Kid app. | 5.00 | 15.00 | 35.00 |
| I.W. Reprint #1,2 9: Straight Arrow in #1,2 | .85 | 2.50 | 5.00 |
| I.W. Reprint #8-Origin Ghost Rider(Tim Holt #11); Tim Holt app.; Bolle-a | 1.20 | 3.50 | 8.00 |

NOTE: *Guardineer c-8. Powell a(r)-8-11 (from Straight Arrow).*

**GREEN ARROW** (See Action #440, Adventure, Brave & the Bold, DC Super Stars #17, Detective #521, Flash #217, Green Lantern #76, Justice League of America #4, Leading, More Fun #73 (1st app.) and World's Finest Comics)

**GREEN ARROW**
May, 1983 - No. 4, Aug, 1983 (Mini-series)
DC Comics

| | Good | Fine | N-Mint |
|---|---|---|---|
| 1-Origin; Speedy cameo | .70 | 2.00 | 4.00 |
| 2-4 | .50 | 1.50 | 3.00 |

**GREEN ARROW**
Feb, 1988 - Present ($1.00, mature readers)(Painted-c #1-3)
DC Comics

| | Good | Fine | N-Mint |
|---|---|---|---|
| 1-Mike Grell scripts in all | 1.35 | 4.00 | 8.00 |
| 2 | .70 | 2.00 | 4.00 |
| 3 | .50 | 1.50 | 3.00 |
| 4,5 | .40 | 1.25 | 2.50 |
| 6-12 | .35 | 1.00 | 2.00 |
| 13-20 | .25 | .75 | 1.50 |
| 21-44: 27,28-Warlord app. 35-38-Co-stars Black Canary (bi-weekly); Bill Wray-i. 40-Grell-a | | .60 | 1.25 |
| Annual 1 ('88)-No Grell scripts | .35 | 1.00 | 2.00 |
| Annual 2 ('89, $2.50, 68 pgs.)-No Grell scripts; recaps origin Green Arrow, Speedy, Black Canary & others | .40 | 1.25 | 2.50 |
| Annual 3 ('90, $2.50, 68 pgs.)-Bill wray-a | .40 | 1.25 | 2.50 |

NOTE: *Denys Cowan a(p)-39, 41, 42; c(p)-41, 42. Mike Grell c-1-4, 10p, 39.*

**GREEN ARROW: THE LONG BOW HUNTERS**
Aug, 1987 - No. 3, Oct, 1987 ($2.95, color, mature readers)
DC Comics

| | Good | Fine | N-Mint |
|---|---|---|---|
| 1-Grell c/a | 2.50 | 7.50 | 15.00 |
| 1,2-2nd printings | .50 | 1.50 | 3.00 |
| 2 | 1.35 | 4.00 | 8.00 |
| 3 | .85 | 2.50 | 5.00 |
| Trade paperback (1989, $12.95) reprints #1-3 | 2.15 | 6.50 | 12.95 |

**GREEN BERET, THE** (See Tales of. . .)

**GREEN GIANT COMICS** (Also see Colossus Comics)
1940 (no price on cover)
Pelican Publ. (Funnies, Inc.)

1-Dr. Nerod, Green Giant, Black Arrow, Mundoo & Master Mystic

| | Good | Fine | VF-NM | NM/Mint |
|---|---|---|---|---|
| app; origin Colossus. (Rare, only 10-20 copies exist) | 386.00 | 1160.00 | 2700.00 | 3750.00 |

(Estimated up to 17 copies exist, 3 in NM/Mint)

NOTE: *The idea for this book came about by a stroll through a grocery store. Printed by Moreau Publ. of Orange, N.J. as an experiment to see if they could profitably use the idle time of their 40-page Hoe color press. The experiment failed due to the difficulty of obtaining good quality color registration and Mr. Moreau believes the book never reached the stands. The book has no price or date which lends credence to this. Contains five pages reprinted from Motion Picture Funnies Weekly.*

**GREEN-GREY SPONGE-SUIT SUSHI TURTLES**
1990 ($3.33, color, 52 pgs.)
Mirage Studios

| | Good | Fine | N-Mint |
|---|---|---|---|
| nn-Parody of TMNT movie; painted-c/a | .55 | 1.65 | 3.33 |

**GREENHAVEN**
1988 - No. 3, 1988 ($2.00, color, mini-series, 28 pgs.)
Aircel Publishing

| | Good | Fine | N-Mint |
|---|---|---|---|
| 1-3 | .35 | 1.00 | 2.00 |

**GREEN HORNET, THE** (TV)(See Four Color 496)
Feb, 1967 - No. 3, Aug, 1967 (All have photo-c)
Gold Key

| | Good | Fine | N-Mint |
|---|---|---|---|
| 1-All have Bruce Lee photo-c | 11.00 | 32.00 | 75.00 |
| 2,3 | 8.00 | 24.00 | 55.00 |

**GREEN HORNET, THE** (Also see Tales of the Green Hornet)
Nov, 1989 - Present ($1.75-$1.95, color)
Now Comics

| | Good | Fine | N-Mint |
|---|---|---|---|
| 1 ($2.95, double-size)-Steranko painted-c; G.A. Green Hornet | 4.15 | 12.50 | 25.00 |
| 1-2nd printing ('90, $3.95)-New Butler-c | .70 | 2.00 | 4.00 |
| 2 | 2.00 | 6.00 | 12.00 |
| 3,4 | 1.00 | 3.00 | 6.00 |
| 5-Death of original (1930s) Green Hornet | .85 | 2.50 | 5.00 |
| 6-8 | .50 | 1.50 | 3.00 |
| 9-18: 16-Begin $1.95-c | .35 | 1.00 | 2.00 |

**GREEN HORNET COMICS** (. . . Racket Buster #44) (Radio, movies)
Dec, 1940 - No. 47, Sept, 1949 (See All New #13,14)
Helnit Publ. Co.(Holyoke) No. 1-6/Family Comics(Harvey) No. 7-on

| | Good | Fine | N-Mint |
|---|---|---|---|
| 1-Green Hornet begins(1st app.); painted-c | 140.00 | 420.00 | 980.00 |
| 2 | 64.00 | 193.00 | 420.00 |
| 3 | 50.00 | 150.00 | 350.00 |
| 4-6 (8/41) | 39.00 | 118.00 | 275.00 |
| 7 (6/42)-Origin The Zebra; Robin Hood & Spirit of 76 begin | 36.00 | 107.00 | 250.00 |
| 8-10 | 29.00 | 86.00 | 200.00 |
| 11,12-Mr. Q in both | 25.00 | 75.00 | 175.00 |
| 13-20 | 22.00 | 65.00 | 150.00 |
| 21-30: 24-Sci-Fi-c | 19.00 | 58.00 | 135.00 |
| 31-The Man in Black Called Fate begins | 20.00 | 60.00 | 140.00 |
| 32-36: 36-Spanking panel | 17.00 | 51.00 | 120.00 |
| 37-Shock Gibson app. by Powell; S&K Kid Adonis reprinted from Stuntman #3 | 19.00 | 56.00 | 130.00 |
| 38-Shock Gibson, Kid Adonis app. | 17.00 | 51.00 | 120.00 |
| 39-Stuntman story by S&K | 22.00 | 65.00 | 150.00 |
| 40,41 | 11.50 | 34.00 | 80.00 |
| 42-45,47-Kerry Drake in all. 45-Boy Explorers on cover only | 11.50 | 34.00 | 80.00 |
| 46-"Case of the Marijuana Racket" cover/story; Kerry Drake app. | 11.50 | 34.00 | 80.00 |

NOTE: ***Fuje** a-23, 24, 26. **Kubert** a-20, 30. **Powell** a-7-10, 12, 14, 16-21, 30, 31(2), 32(3), 33, 34(3), 35, 36, 37(2), 38. **Robinson** a-27. **Schomburg** c-15, 17-23. Kirbyish c-7, 9, 15. Bondage c-8, 14, 18, 26, 36.*

**GREEN JET COMICS, THE** (See Comic Books, Series 1)

**GREEN LAMA** (Also see Comic Books, Series 1, Daring Adventures #17 & Prize Comics #7)
Dec, 1944 - No. 8, March, 1946
Spark Publications/Prize No. 7 on

| | Good | Fine | N-Mint |
|---|---|---|---|
| 1-Intro. The Green Lama, Lt. Hercules & The Boy Champions; Mac Raboy-c/a #1-8 | 61.00 | 182.00 | 425.00 |
| 2-Lt. Hercules borrows the Human Torch's powers for one panel | 43.00 | 130.00 | 300.00 |
| 3,6-8: 7-X-mas-c; Raboy craft tint art | 31.00 | 92.00 | 215.00 |
| 4-Dick Tracy take-off in Lt. Hercules story by H. L. Gold (sci-fiction writer) | 31.00 | 92.00 | 215.00 |
| 5-Lt. Hercules story; Little Orphan Annie, Smilin' Jack & Snuffy Smith take-off (5/45) | 31.00 | 92.00 | 215.00 |

NOTE: ***Robinson** a-3-5. Formerly a pulp hero who began in 1940.*

**GREEN LANTERN** (1st Series) (See All-American, All Flash Quarterly, All Star Comics, The Big All-American & Comic Cavalcade)
Fall, 1941 - No. 38, May-June, 1949
National Periodical Publications/All-American

| | Good | Fine | VF-NM | NM/Mint |
|---|---|---|---|---|
| 1-Origin retold | 750.00 | 1875.00 | 4500.00 | 7000.00 |

(Estimated up to 200 total copies exist, 8 in NM/Mint)

| | Good | Fine | N-Mint |
|---|---|---|---|
| 2-1st book-length story | 300.00 | 750.00 | 1800.00 |
| 3 | 235.00 | 585.00 | 1400.00 |
| 4 | 158.00 | 395.00 | 950.00 |
| 5 | 125.00 | 312.00 | 750.00 |
| 6-8: 8-Hop Harrigan begins | 108.00 | 270.00 | 650.00 |
| 9,10: 10-Origin Vandal Savage | 95.00 | 240.00 | 570.00 |
| 11-17,19,20: 12-Origin Gambler | 79.00 | 200.00 | 475.00 |
| 18-Christmas-c | 90.00 | 225.00 | 540.00 |
| 21-30: 27-Origin Sky Pirate. 30-Origin/1st app. Streak the Wonder Dog by Toth | 67.00 | 170.00 | 400.00 |
| 31-35 | 56.00 | 140.00 | 335.00 |
| 36-38: 37-Sargon the Sorcerer app. | 67.00 | 170.00 | 400.00 |

NOTE: *Book-length stories #2-8. **Paul Reinman** c-11, 12, 15, 16, 18, 19, 22. **Toth** a-28, 30, 31, 34-38; c-28, 30, 34, 36-38.*

**GREEN LANTERN** (See Action Comics Weekly, Adventure Comics, Brave & the Bold, DC Special, DC Special Series, Flash, Justice League of America, Showcase & Tales of The. . . Corps)

**GREEN LANTERN** (2nd series)(Green Lantern Corps #206 on)
7-8/60 - No. 89, 4-5/72; No. 90, 8-9/76 - No. 205, 10/86
National Periodical Publications/DC Comics

| | Good | Fine | N-Mint |
|---|---|---|---|
| 1-Origin retold; Gil Kane-a begins | 112.00 | 336.00 | 780.00 |
| 2-1st Pieface | 50.00 | 150.00 | 350.00 |
| 3 | 30.00 | 90.00 | 210.00 |
| 4,5: 5-Origin & 1st app. Hector Hammond; 1st 5700 A.D. story | 24.00 | 72.00 | 170.00 |
| 6-10: 6-Intro Tomar-re the alien G.L. 7-Origin Sinestro. 9-1st Jordan Brothers; last 10 cent issue | 14.00 | 43.00 | 100.00 |
| 11-15: 13-Flash x-over. 14-Origin Sonar | 11.00 | 32.00 | 75.00 |
| 16-20: 16-Origin Star Sapphire. 20-Flash x-over | 9.30 | 28.00 | 65.00 |
| 21-30: 21-Origin Dr. Polaris. 23-1st Tattooed Man. 24-Origin Shark. 29-JLA cameo; 1st Blackhand | 8.00 | 24.00 | 55.00 |
| 31-39 | 5.70 | 17.00 | 40.00 |
| 40-1st app. Crisis (10/65); 1st solo G.A. Green Lantern in Silver Age; origin The Guardians; Doiby Dickles app. | 36.00 | 108.00 | 250.00 |
| 41-44,46-50: 42-Zatanna x-over. 43-Flash x-over | 3.50 | 10.50 | 24.00 |
| 45-G.A. Green Lantern x-over (2nd S.A. app.) | 4.50 | 14.00 | 32.00 |
| 51,53-58 | 2.00 | 6.00 | 14.00 |
| 52-G.A. Green Lantern x-over | 2.85 | 8.50 | 20.00 |
| 59-1st app. Guy Gardner (3/68) | 14.00 | 43.00 | 100.00 |
| 60,62-75: 69-Wood inks | 1.50 | 4.50 | 10.00 |
| 61-G.A. Green Lantern x-over | 2.00 | 6.00 | 14.00 |
| 76-Begin Green Lantern/Green Arrow series by Neal Adams, ends #122 | 8.50 | 25.50 | 60.00 |
| 77 | 3.15 | 9.50 | 22.00 |
| 78-80 | 2.65 | 8.00 | 18.00 |

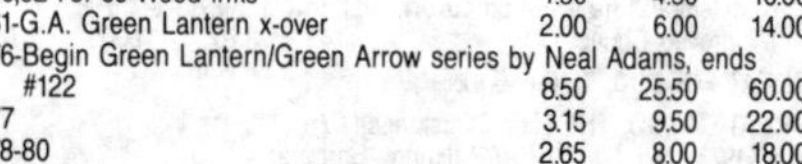

*Green Hornet Comics #11, © HARV*

*Green Lantern #1 (1941), © DC*

*Green Lantern #2 (9-10/60), © DC*

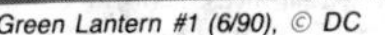
Green Lantern #1 (6/90), © DC

The Green Mask #1, © FOX

Grendel #1 (10/86), © Comico

Good Fine N-Mint

81-84: 82-One pg. Wrightson inks. 83-G.L. reveals i.d. to Carol Ferris. 84-N. Adams/Wrightson-a, 22pgs. 2.00 6.00 14.00
85,86(52 pgs.)-Drug propaganda books. 86-G.A. Green Lantern-r; Toth-a 2.85 8.50 20.00
87(52 pgs.): 2nd app. Guy Gardner (cameo); 1st app. John Stewart (becomes Green Lantern in #182) 1.70 5.00 12.00
88(52 pgs.,'72)-Unpubbed G.A. Green Lantern story; Green Lantern-r/ Showcase #23. N. Adams-a(1 pg.) .50 1.50 3.00
89(52 pgs.)-G.A. Green Lantern-r 1.15 3.50 7.00
90('76)-99 .35 1.00 2.00
100-(Giant)-1st app. new Air Wave .50 1.50 3.00
101-111,113-115,117-119: 107-1st Tales of the G.L. Corps story. 108-110-(44pgs)-G.A. Green Lantern. 111-Origin retold; G.A. Green Lantern app. .35 1.00 2.00
112-G.A. Green Lantern origin retold .60 1.75 3.50
116-1st app. Guy Gardner as a Green Lantern 1.50 4.50 10.00
120-135,138-140,144-149: 122-Last Gr. Arrow. 123-Gr. Lantern back to solo action. 130-132-Tales of the G.L. Corps. 132-Adam Strange begins new series, ends 147. 144-Omega Men cameo. 148-Tales of the G.L. Corps begins, ends #173 .60 1.20
136,137-1st app. Citadel; Space Ranger app. .35 1.00 2.00
141-1st app. Omega Men .50 1.50 3.00
142,143-The Omega Men app.; Perez-c .35 1.00 2.00
150-Anniversary issue, 52 pgs.; no G.L. Corps .35 1.00 2.00
151-170: 159-Origin Evil Star. 160,161-Omega Men app. 181-Hal Jordan resigns as G.L. 182-John Stewart becomes new G.L.; origin recap of Hal Jordan as G.L. .50 1.00
171-194,196-199,201-205: (75 cent cover). 185-Origin new G.L. (John Stewart). 188-I.D. revealed; Alan Moore back-up scripts. 191-1st app. Star Sapphire. 194,198-Crisis x-over. 194-Guardians choose Guy Gardner to become new G.L. 199-Hal Jordan returns as a member of G.L. Corps (3 G.L.s now). 201-Green Lantern Corps begins (is cover title & says premiere issue) .50 1.00
195-Guy Gardner becomes Green Lantern; Crisis x-over 1.00 3.00 6.00
200-Double-size .35 1.00 2.00
Annual 1 (See Tales Of The. . .)
Special 1 (1988), 2 (1989)-(Both $1.50, 52 pgs.) .35 1.00 2.00

NOTE: ***N. Adams*** *a-76, 77-87p, 89; c-63, 76-89.* ***M. Anderson*** *a-137i.* ***Austin*** *a-93i, 94i, 171i.* ***Greene*** *a-39-49i, 58-63i; c-54-58i.* ***Grell*** *a-90, 91, 92-100p, 106p, 108-110p; c-90, 93-100, 101p, 102-106, 108-112.* ***Gil Kane*** *a-1-49p, 50-57, 58-61p, 68-75p, 85p(r), 87p(r), 88p(r), 156, 177, 184p; c-1-52, 54-61p, 67-75, 123, 154, 156, 165-171, 177, 184.* ***Newton*** *a-148p, 149p, 181.* ***Perez*** *c-132p, 141-144.* ***Sekowsky*** *a-65p, 170p.* ***Sparling*** *a-63p.* ***Starlin*** *c-129, 133.* ***Staton*** *a-117p, 123-127p, 128, 129-131p, 132-139, 140p, 141-146, 147p, 148-150, 151-155p; c-107p, 117p, 135(i), 136p, 145p, 146, 147, 148-152p, 155p.* ***Toth*** *a-86r, 171p.* ***Tuska*** *a-166-168p, 170p.*

**GREEN LANTERN**
June, 1990 - Present ($1.00, color)
DC Comics

1-Hal Jordan, John Stewart & Guy Gardner return; Batman app. .50 1.50 3.00
2,3 .25 .75 1.50
4-12 .50 1.00

**GREEN LANTERN CORPS, THE** (Formerly Green Lantern)
No. 206, Nov, 1986 - No. 224, May, 1988
DC Comics

206-223: 220,221-Millennium tie-ins .50 1.00
224-Double size last issue .25 .75 1.50
..Corps Annual 2 (12/86)-Alan Moore scripts .25 .75 1.50
..Corps Annual 3 (8/87)-Moore scripts; Byrne-a .25 .75 1.50

NOTE: ***Austin*** *a-Annual 31.* ***Gil Kane*** *a-223, 224p; c-223, 224.* ***Staton*** *a-207-213p, 217p, 221p, 222p, Annual #3; c-207-213p, 217p, 221p, 222p.* ***Willingham*** *a-213p, 219p, 220p, 218p, 219p, Annual 2, 3p; c-218p, 219p.*

**GREEN LANTERN: EMERALD DAWN**
Dec, 1989 - No. 6, May, 1990 ($1.00, color, mini-series)
DC Comics

Good Fine N-Mint

1-Origin retold; Giffen plots in all 2.00 6.00 12.00
2 1.00 3.00 6.00
3,4 .50 1.50 3.00
5,6 .35 1.00 2.00

**GREEN LANTERN/GREEN ARROW** (Also see The Flash #217)
Oct, 1983 - No. 7, April, 1984 (52-60 pgs.)
DC Comics

1-7: Reprints Green Lantern #76-89 .50 1.50 3.00

NOTE: ***Neal Adams*** *r-1-7; c-1-4.* ***Wrightson*** *r-4, 5.*

**GREEN MASK, THE** (The Bouncer No. 11 on? See Mystery Men)
Summer, 1940 - No. 9, 2/42; No. 10, 8/44 - No. 11, 11/44;
V2#1, Spring, 1945 - No. 6, 10-11/46
Fox Features Syndicate

V1#1-Origin The Green Mask & Domino; reprints/Mystery Men No. 1-3,5-7; Lou Fine-c 100.00 300.00 700.00
2-Zanzibar The Magician by Tuska 49.00 145.00 340.00
3-Powell-a; Marijuana story 30.00 90.00 210.00
4-Navy Jones begins, ends No. 6 24.00 72.00 165.00
5 21.00 62.00 145.00
6-The Nightbird begins, ends No. 9; bondage/torture-c 18.00 54.00 125.00
7-9 14.00 43.00 100.00
10,11: 10-Origin One Round Hogan & Rocket Kelly 12.00 36.00 85.00
V2#1 9.30 28.00 65.00
2-6 7.00 21.00 50.00

**GREEN PLANET, THE**
1962 (One Shot)
Charlton Comics

nn 3.00 9.00 21.00

**GREEN TEAM** (See Cancelled Comic Cavalcade & First Issue Special)

**GREETINGS FROM SANTA** (See March of Comics No. 48)

**GRENDEL** (Also see Primer No. 2 and Mage)
Mar, 1983 - No. 3, Feb, 1984 (B&W)(#1 has indicia to Skrog #1)
Comico

1-Origin Hunter Rose 8.35 25.00 50.00
2,3: 2-Origin Argent 6.35 19.00 38.00

**GRENDEL**
Oct, 1986 - Present ($1.50-$1.95-$2.50, color) (Mature readers)
Comico

1 .70 2.00 4.00
1,2-2nd printings .25 .75 1.50
2 .45 1.30 2.60
3-5: 4-Dave Stevens-c(i) .35 1.10 2.20
6-10 .35 1.00 2.00
11-15: 13-15-Ken Steacy-c .30 .90 1.80
16-Re-intro Mage (series begins, ends #19) .70 2.00 4.00
17-32: 18-26-$1.75-c; 27-32-$1.95-c .35 1.00 2.00
33-($2.75, 44 pgs.) .45 1.40 2.75
34-41: 34-Begin $2.50 cover price .40 1.25 2.50
Devil by the Deed (Graphic Novel, 10/86, $5.95, 52 pgs.)-r/Grendel back-ups/Mage 6-14; Alan Moore intro. 1.15 3.50 7.00
Devil's Legacy ($14.95, 1988, Graphic Novel) 2.50 7.50 15.00
Devil's Vagary (10/87, B&W & red)-No price; included in Comico Collection 2.00 6.00 12.00

**GREY**
Oct, 1988 - No. 9, June?, 1989 ($2.95, B&W, mini-series, 72 pgs.)
Viz Comics

1-7: Japanese manga set in future .50 1.50 3.00
8,9 ($3.25) .55 1.65 3.30

**GREYFRIARS BOBBY** (See 4-Color No. 1189)

**GREYLORE**
12/85 - No. 5, Sept, 1986 ($1.50-$1.75, full color, high quality paper)
Sirius Comics

| | Good | Fine | N-Mint |
|---|---|---|---|
| 1-5: Bo Hampton-a in all | .25 | .75 | 1.50 |

**GRIM GHOST, THE**
Jan, 1975 - No. 3, July, 1975
Atlas/Seaboard Publ.

| | | | |
|---|---|---|---|
| 1-Origin | | .40 | .80 |
| 2,3: 3-Heath-c | | .30 | .60 |

**GRIMJACK** (Also see Demon Knight & Starslayer)
Aug, 1984 - Present
First Comics

| | | | |
|---|---|---|---|
| 1 | .40 | 1.20 | 2.40 |
| 2-10 | .25 | .80 | 1.60 |
| 11-25: 20-Sutton-c/a begins | | .70 | 1.40 |
| 26-2nd color Teenage Mutant Ninja Turtles | 1.00 | 3.00 | 6.00 |
| 27-38: 30-Dynamo Joe x-over; 31-Mandrake-c/a begins | | .65 | 1.30 |
| 39-74,76-82 (Later issues $1.95, $2.25-c) | .35 | 1.00 | 2.00 |
| 75-($5.95, 52 pgs.)-Fold-out map; coated stock | 1.00 | 3.00 | 6.00 |

**GRIMJACK CASEFILES**
Nov, 1990 - Present ($1.95, color)
First Comics

| | | | |
|---|---|---|---|
| 1-6: Reprints 1st stories from Starslayer #10 on | .35 | 1.00 | 2.00 |

**GRIMM'S GHOST STORIES** (See Dan Curtis)
Jan, 1972 - No. 60, June, 1982 (Painted-c No. 1-56)
Gold Key/Whitman No. 55 on

| | | | |
|---|---|---|---|
| 1 | .50 | 1.50 | 3.00 |
| 2-4,6,7,9,10 | .25 | .75 | 1.50 |
| 5,8-Williamson-a | .40 | 1.25 | 2.50 |
| 11-16,18-35: 32,34-Reprints | | .50 | 1.00 |
| 17-Crandall-a | .35 | 1.00 | 2.00 |
| 36-55,57-60: 43,44-(52 pgs.) | | .40 | .80 |
| 56-Williamson-a | | .50 | 1.00 |
| Mini-Comic No. 1 (3¼x6½", 1976) | | .30 | .60 |

NOTE: *Reprints-#32?, 34?, 39, 43, 44, 47?, 53; 56-60(⅓).* ***Bolle*** *a-23-25, 27, 29(2), 33, 35, 43r, 45(2), 48(2), 50, 52.* ***Lopez*** *a-24, 25.* ***McWilliams*** *a-33, 44r, 48, 58.* ***Win Mortimer*** *a-31, 33, 49, 51, 55, 56, 58(2), 59, 60.* ***Roussos*** *a-25, 30.* ***Sparling*** *a-23, 24, 28, 30, 31, 33, 43r, 45, 51(2), 52, 56, 58, 59(2), 60.*

**GRIN** (The American Funny Book) (Magazine)
Nov, 1972 - No. 3, April, 1973 (52 pgs.) (Satire)
APAG House Pubs

| | | | |
|---|---|---|---|
| 1 | | .60 | 1.20 |
| 2,3 | | .40 | .80 |

**GRIN & BEAR IT** (See Gags & Large Feature Comic No. 28)

**GRIPS** (Extreme violence)
Sept, 1986 - No. 4, Dec, 1986 ($1.50, B&W, adults)
Silverwolf Comics

| | | | |
|---|---|---|---|
| 1-Tim Vigil-c/a in all | 4.15 | 12.50 | 25.00 |
| 2 | 2.50 | 7.50 | 15.00 |
| 3 | 2.00 | 6.00 | 12.00 |
| 4 | 1.70 | 5.00 | 10.00 |

**GRIT GRADY** (See Holyoke One-Shot No. 1)

**GROO CHRONICLES, THE**
1989 - No. 6, Feb, 1990 ($3.50, color, squarebound, 52 pgs.)
Epic Comics (Marvel)

| | | | |
|---|---|---|---|
| Book 1-r/all Pacific issues & Eclipse one-shot w/new Aragones' covers (front & back) & some new-a | .70 | 2.00 | 4.00 |
| Book 2-6 | .60 | 1.75 | 3.50 |

**GROO SPECIAL**
Oct, 1984 ($2.00, 52 pgs., Baxter paper)
Eclipse Comics

| | | | |
|---|---|---|---|
| 1 | 7.50 | 22.50 | 45.00 |

**GROO THE WANDERER** (See Destroyer Duck, Marvel Graphic Novel #32, Sergio Aragones' Groo... & Starslayer)
Dec, 1982 - No. 8, March, 1984
Pacific Comics

| | | | |
|---|---|---|---|
| 1-Aragones-c/a(p) in all | 4.30 | 13.00 | 30.00 |
| 2 | 2.85 | 8.50 | 20.00 |
| 3-7 | 2.30 | 7.00 | 16.00 |
| 8 | 2.65 | 8.00 | 18.00 |

**GROOVY** (Cartoon Comics - not CCA approved)
March, 1968 - No. 3, July, 1968
Marvel Comics Group

| | | | |
|---|---|---|---|
| 1-Monkees, Ringo Starr photos | 2.15 | 6.50 | 15.00 |
| 2,3 | 1.50 | 4.50 | 10.00 |

**GROUP LARUE, THE**
1989 - No. 4, 1990 ($1.95, color, mini-series)
Innovation Publishing

| | | | |
|---|---|---|---|
| 1-4: By Mike Baron; 4-Exist? | .35 | 1.00 | 2.00 |

**GUADALCANAL DIARY** (Also see American Library)
1945 (One Shot) (See Thirty Seconds Over Tokyo)
David McKay Publishing Co.

| | | | |
|---|---|---|---|
| nn-B&W text & pictures; painted-c | 16.00 | 48.00 | 110.00 |

**GUARDIANS OF JUSTICE & THE O-FORCE**
1990 (no date) ($1.50, color, 7½x10¼)
Shadow Comics

| | | | |
|---|---|---|---|
| 1-Super-hero group | .25 | .75 | 1.50 |

**GUARDIANS OF THE GALAXY** (Also see Marvel Presents #3, Marvel Super-Heroes #18, Marvel Two-In-One #5)
June, 1990 - Present ($1.00, color)
Marvel Comics

| | | | |
|---|---|---|---|
| 1-Valentino-c/a(p); painted-c | .50 | 1.50 | 3.00 |
| 2-5: 5-McFarlane-c(i) | .25 | .75 | 1.50 |
| 6-12: 7-Perez-c(i) | | .50 | 1.00 |

**GUERRILLA WAR** (Formerly Jungle War Stories)
No. 12, July-Sept, 1965 - No. 14, Mar, 1966
Dell Publishing Co.

| | | | |
|---|---|---|---|
| 12-14 | .70 | 2.00 | 5.00 |

**GUILTY** (See Justice Traps the Guilty)

**GULF FUNNY WEEKLY** (Gulf Comic Weekly No. 1-4)
1933 - No. 422, 5/23/41 (in full color; 4 pgs.; tabloid size to 2/3/39; 2/10/39 on, regular comic book size)(early issues undated)
Gulf Oil Company (Giveaway)

| | | | |
|---|---|---|---|
| 1 | 10.00 | 30.00 | 60.00 |
| 2-30 | 4.00 | 12.00 | 24.00 |
| 31-100 | 3.00 | 9.00 | 18.00 |
| 101-196 | 2.00 | 6.00 | 12.00 |
| 197-Wings Winfair begins(1/29/37); by Fred Meagher beginning in 1938 | 15.00 | 45.00 | 90.00 |
| 198-300 (Last tabloid size) | 7.00 | 20.00 | 40.00 |
| 301-350 (Regular size) | 3.35 | 10.00 | 20.00 |
| 351-422 | 2.35 | 7.00 | 14.00 |

**GULLIVER'S TRAVELS** (See Dell Jr. Treasury No. 3)
Sept-Nov, 1965 - No. 3, May, 1966
Dell Publishing Co.

| | | | |
|---|---|---|---|
| 1 | 1.70 | 5.00 | 12.00 |
| 2,3 | 1.15 | 3.50 | 8.00 |

**GUMBY IN 3-D** (See Blackthorne 3-D Series #10, 14, 17, 21, 28, 33, 38)

*Grimjack #1, © First Comics*

*The Groo Chronicles #6, © MEG*

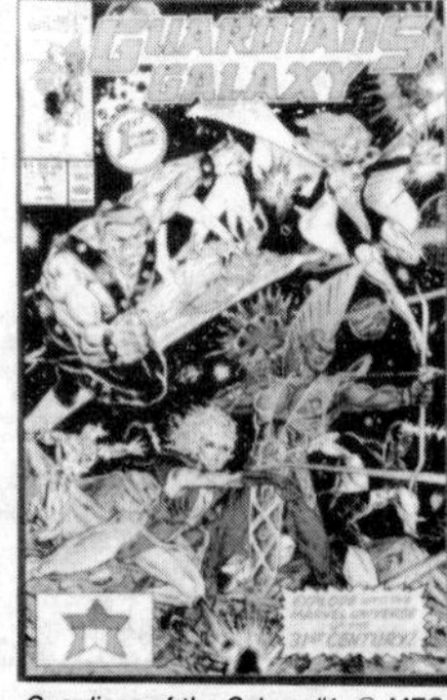

*Guardians of the Galaxy #1, © MEG*

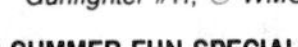
Gunfighter #11, © WMG

Gunsmoke #6, © YM

Gunsmoke Western #43, © MEG

**GUMBY'S SUMMER FUN SPECIAL**
July, 1987 ($2.50, color)
Comico

| | Good | Fine | N-Mint |
|---|---|---|---|
| 1-Art Adams-c/a, B. Burden story | .75 | 2.25 | 4.50 |

**GUMBY'S WINTER FUN SPECIAL**
Dec, 1988 ($2.50, 44pgs.)
Comico

| | Good | Fine | N-Mint |
|---|---|---|---|
| 1-Art Adams-c/a | 40 | 1.25 | 2.50 |

**GUMPS, THE**
No. 2, 1918; 1924 - No. 8, 1931 (10x10")(52 pgs.; black & white)
Landfield-Kupfer/Cupples & Leon No. 2

| | Good | Fine | N-Mint |
|---|---|---|---|
| Book No.2(1918)-(Rare); 5¼x13⅓"; paper cover; 36 pgs. daily strip reprints by Sidney Smith | 20.00 | 60.00 | 140.00 |
| nn(1924)-by Sidney Smith | 12.00 | 36.00 | 85.00 |
| 2,3 | 10.00 | 30.00 | 70.00 |
| 4-7 | 9.30 | 28.00 | 65.00 |
| 8-(10x14"); 36 pgs.; B&W; National Arts Co. | 9.30 | 28.00 | 65.00 |

**GUMPS, THE** (See Merry Christmas. . ., Popular & Super Comics)
No. 73, 1945; Mar-Apr, 1947 - No. 5, Nov-Dec, 1947
Dell Publ. Co./Bridgeport Herald Corp.

| | Good | Fine | N-Mint |
|---|---|---|---|
| 4-Color 73 (Dell)(1945) | 7.00 | 21.00 | 50.00 |
| 1 (3-4/47) | 7.00 | 21.00 | 50.00 |
| 2-5 | 4.30 | 13.00 | 30.00 |

**GUNFIGHTER** (Fat & Slat #1-4) (Becomes Haunt of Fear #15 on)
No. 5, Summer, 1948 - No. 14, Mar-Apr, 1950
E. C. Comics (Fables Publ. Co.)

| | Good | Fine | N-Mint |
|---|---|---|---|
| 5,6-Moon Girl in each | 35.00 | 105.00 | 245.00 |
| 7-14: 14-Bondage-c | 23.00 | 70.00 | 160.00 |

NOTE: ***Craig*** & ***H. C. Kiefer*** *art in most issues.* ***Craig*** *c-5, 6, 13, 14.* ***Feldstein/Craig*** *a-10.* ***Feldstein*** *a-7-11.* ***Harrison/Wood*** *a-13, 14.* ***Ingels*** *a-5-14; c-7-12.*

**GUNFIGHTERS, THE**
1963 - 1964
Super Comics (Reprints)

| | Good | Fine | N-Mint |
|---|---|---|---|
| 10,11(Billy the Kid), 12(Swift Arrow), 15(Straight Arrow-Powell-a), 16,18-All reprints | .50 | 1.50 | 3.00 |

**GUNFIGHTERS, THE** (Formerly Kid Montana)
No. 51, 10/66 - No. 52, 10/67; No. 53, 6/79 - No. 85, 7/84
Charlton Comics

| | Good | Fine | N-Mint |
|---|---|---|---|
| 51,52 | .40 | 1.25 | 2.50 |
| 53-85: 53,54-Williamson-r/Wild Bill Hickok. 56-Williamson/Severin-c/a; r-Sheriff of Tombstone. 85-S&K-r/1955 Bullseye | | .40 | .80 |

**GUN GLORY** (See 4-Color No. 846)

**GUNHAWK, THE** (Formerly Whip Wilson )(See Wild Western)
No. 12, Nov, 1950 - No. 18, Dec, 1951
Marvel Comics/Atlas (MCI)

| | Good | Fine | N-Mint |
|---|---|---|---|
| 12 | 7.00 | 21.00 | 50.00 |
| 13-18: 13-Tuska-a. 18-Maneely-c | 5.70 | 17.00 | 40.00 |

**GUNHAWKS** (Gunhawk No. 7)
October, 1972 - No. 7, October, 1973
Marvel Comics Group

| | Good | Fine | N-Mint |
|---|---|---|---|
| 1-Reno Jones, Kid Cassidy; Shores-c/a(p) | .25 | .75 | 1.50 |
| 2-7: 6-Kid Cassidy dies. 7-Reno Jones solo | | .50 | 1.00 |

**GUNMASTER** (Judo Master No. 89 on; formerly Six-Gun Heroes)
9/64 - No. 4, 1965; No. 84, 7/65 - No. 88, 3-4/66; No. 89, 10/67
Charlton Comics

| | Good | Fine | N-Mint |
|---|---|---|---|
| V1#1 | .85 | 2.60 | 6.00 |
| 2-4,V5#84-86: 4-Blank inside-c | .70 | 2.00 | 4.00 |
| V5#87-89 | .50 | 1.50 | 3.00 |

NOTE: *Vol. 5 was originally cancelled with #88 (3-4/66). #89 on, became Judo Master, then later in 1967, Charlton issued #89 as a Gunmaster one-shot.*

**GUNS AGAINST GANGSTERS** (True-To-Life Romances #8 on)
Sept-Oct, 1948 - V2#1, Sept-Oct, 1949
Curtis Publications/Novelty Press

| | Good | Fine | N-Mint |
|---|---|---|---|
| 1-Toni Gayle begins by Schomburg | 11.50 | 34.00 | 80.00 |
| 2 | 7.00 | 21.00 | 50.00 |
| 3-6, V2#1,2: 6-Toni Gayle-c | 6.50 | 19.00 | 45.00 |

NOTE: ***L. B. Cole*** *c-1-6, V2#1, 2; a-1, 2, 3(2), 4-6.*

**GUNSLINGER** (See 4-Color No. 1220)

**GUNSLINGER** (Formerly Tex Dawson. . .)
No. 2, April, 1973 - No. 3, June, 1973
Marvel Comics Group

| | Good | Fine | N-Mint |
|---|---|---|---|
| 2,3 | | .40 | .80 |

**GUNSMOKE**
Apr-May, 1949 - No. 16, Jan, 1952
Youthful Magazines

| | Good | Fine | N-Mint |
|---|---|---|---|
| 1-Gunsmoke & Masked Marvel begin by Ingels; Ingels bondage-c | 20.00 | 60.00 | 140.00 |
| 2-Ingels-c/a(2) | 11.00 | 32.00 | 75.00 |
| 3-Ingels bondage-c/a | 9.30 | 28.00 | 65.00 |
| 4-6: Ingels-c | 7.00 | 21.00 | 50.00 |
| 7-10 | 4.30 | 13.00 | 30.00 |
| 11-16 | 3.00 | 9.00 | 21.00 |

**GUNSMOKE** (TV)
No. 679, 2/56 - No. 27, 6-7/61; 2/69 - No. 6, 2/70
Dell Publishing Co./Gold Key (All have James Arness photo-c)

| | Good | Fine | N-Mint |
|---|---|---|---|
| 4-Color 679(No. 1) | 7.00 | 21.00 | 50.00 |
| 4-Color 720,769,797,844 | 4.50 | 14.00 | 32.00 |
| 6(11-1/57-58), 7 | 4.50 | 14.00 | 32.00 |
| 8,9,11,12-Williamson-a in all, 4 pgs. each | 5.70 | 17.00 | 40.00 |
| 10-Williamson/Crandall-a, 4 pgs. | 5.70 | 17.00 | 40.00 |
| 13-27 | 4.00 | 12.00 | 28.00 |
| Gunsmoke Film Story (11/62-G.K. Giant) No. 30008-211 | 4.50 | 14.00 | 32.00 |
| 1 (Gold Key) | 2.30 | 7.00 | 16.00 |
| 2-6('69-70) | 1.30 | 4.00 | 9.00 |

**GUNSMOKE TRAIL**
June, 1957 - No. 4, Dec, 1957
Ajax-Farrell Publ./Four Star Comic Corp.

| | Good | Fine | N-Mint |
|---|---|---|---|
| 1 | 5.00 | 15.00 | 35.00 |
| 2-4 | 2.65 | 8.00 | 18.00 |

**GUNSMOKE WESTERN** (Formerly Western Tales of Black Rider)
No. 32, Dec, 1955 - No. 77, July, 1963
Atlas Comics No. 32-35(CPS/NPI); Marvel No. 36 on

| | Good | Fine | N-Mint |
|---|---|---|---|
| 32 | 5.70 | 17.00 | 40.00 |
| 33,35,36-Williamson-a in each: 5,6 & 4 pgs. plus Drucker No. 33 | 6.50 | 19.00 | 45.00 |
| 34-Baker-a, 3 pgs. | 2.85 | 8.50 | 20.00 |
| 37-Davis-a(2); Williamson text illo | 3.15 | 9.50 | 22.00 |
| 38,39 | 2.15 | 6.50 | 15.00 |
| 40-Williamson/Mayo-a, 4 pgs. | 4.30 | 13.00 | 30.00 |
| 41,42,45-49,51-55,57-60: 49,52-Kid From Texas story. 57-1st Two Gun Kid by Severin. 60-Sam Hawk app. in Kid Colt | 1.50 | 4.50 | 10.00 |
| 43,44-Torres-a | 2.15 | 6.50 | 15.00 |
| 50,61-Crandall-a | 2.30 | 7.00 | 16.00 |
| 56-Matt Baker-a | 2.00 | 6.00 | 14.00 |
| 62-77: 72-Origin Kid Colt | 1.30 | 4.00 | 9.00 |

NOTE: ***Colan*** *a-36, 37, 72, 76.* ***Davis*** *a-37, 52, 54, 55; c-50, 54.* ***Ditko*** *a-56, 66.* ***Jack Keller*** *a-40, 60, 72; c-72.* ***Kirby*** *a-47, 50, 51, 59, 62(3), 63-67, 69, 71, 73, 77; c-56(w/* ***Ditko****),57, 58, 60, 61(w/****Ayers****), 62, 63, 66, 68, 69, 71-77.* ***Severin*** *a-60, 61; c-42, 43.* ***Wildey*** *a-10, 37, 42, 57. Kid Colt in all. Two-Gun Kid in No. 57, 59, 60-63. Wyatt Earp in No. 45, 48, 49, 52, 54, 55, 58.*

**GUNS OF FACT & FICTION** (See A-1 Comics No. 13)

**GUN THAT WON THE WEST, THE**
1956 (24 pgs.; regular size) (Giveaway)
Winchester-Western Division & Olin Mathieson Chemical Corp.

| | Good | Fine | N-Mint |
|---|---|---|---|
| nn-Painted-c | 2.65 | 8.00 | 18.00 |

**GYPSY COLT** (See 4-Color No. 568)

**GYRO GEARLOOSE** (See Dynabrite Comics, Walt Disney's C&S #140 & Walt Disney Showcase #18)
No. 1047, Nov-Jan/1959-60 - May-July, 1962 (Disney)
Dell Publishing Co.

| | Good | Fine | N-Mint |
|---|---|---|---|
| 4-Color 1047 (No. 1)-Barks-c/a | 6.50 | 19.50 | 45.00 |
| 4-Color 1095,1184-All by Carl Barks | 5.50 | 16.50 | 38.00 |
| 4-Color 1267-Barks c/a, 4 pgs. | 4.00 | 12.00 | 28.00 |
| No. 01-329-207 (5-7/62)-Barks-c only | 2.65 | 8.00 | 18.00 |

**HAGAR THE HORRIBLE** (See Comics Reading Libraries)

**HA HA COMICS** (Teepee Tim No. 100 on) (Also see Giggle)
Oct, 1943 - No. 99, Jan, 1955
Scope Mag.(Creston Publ.) No. 1-80/American Comics Group

| | Good | Fine | N-Mint |
|---|---|---|---|
| 1 | 17.00 | 50.00 | 115.00 |
| 2 | 7.00 | 21.00 | 50.00 |
| 3-5: Ken Hultgren-a begins? | 5.00 | 15.00 | 35.00 |
| 6-10 | 4.00 | 12.00 | 28.00 |
| 11-20: 14-Infinity-c | 2.65 | 8.00 | 18.00 |
| 21-40 | 2.15 | 6.50 | 15.00 |
| 41-94,96-99: 49-XMas-c | 1.70 | 5.00 | 12.00 |
| 95-3-D effect-c | 6.50 | 19.00 | 45.00 |

**HAIR BEAR BUNCH, THE** (TV) (See Fun-In No. 13)
Feb, 1972 - No. 9, Feb, 1974 (Hanna-Barbera)
Gold Key

| | Good | Fine | N-Mint |
|---|---|---|---|
| 1 | .85 | 2.50 | 5.00 |
| 2-9 | .50 | 1.50 | 3.00 |

**HALLELUJAH TRAIL, THE** (See Movie Classics)

**HALL OF FAME FEATURING THE T.H.U.N.D.E.R. AGENTS**
May, 1983 - No. 3, Dec, 1983
JC Productions(Archie Comics Group)

| | Good | Fine | N-Mint |
|---|---|---|---|
| 1-3: T.H.U.N.D.E.R. Agents-r | | .45 | .90 |

**HALLOWEEN HORROR**
Oct, 1987 (Seduction of the Innocent #7)($1.75, color)
Eclipse Comics

| | Good | Fine | N-Mint |
|---|---|---|---|
| 1-Pre-code horror-r | .30 | .90 | 1.80 |

**HALO JONES** (See The Ballad of...)

**HAMMER OF GOD**
Feb, 1990 - No. 4, May, 1990 ($1.95, color, limited series)
First Comics

| | Good | Fine | N-Mint |
|---|---|---|---|
| 1-4 | .35 | 1.00 | 2.00 |

**HAMSTER VICE IN 3-D** (See Blackthorne 3-D Series #12 & 15)

**HANDBOOK OF THE CONAN UNIVERSE, THE**
June, 1985 ($1.25, color, one-shot)
Marvel Comics

| | Good | Fine | N-Mint |
|---|---|---|---|
| 1 | | .65 | 1.30 |

**HAND OF FATE** (Formerly Men Against Crime)
No. 8, Dec, 1951 - No. 26, March, 1955
Ace Magazines

| | Good | Fine | N-Mint |
|---|---|---|---|
| 8: Surrealistic text story | 13.00 | 40.00 | 90.00 |
| 9,10 | 7.00 | 21.00 | 50.00 |
| 11-18,20,22,23 | 5.00 | 15.00 | 35.00 |
| 19-Bondage, hypo needle scenes | 6.50 | 19.00 | 45.00 |
| 21-Necronomicon story; drug belladonna used | 7.00 | 21.00 | 50.00 |
| 24-Electric chair-c | 8.50 | 25.50 | 60.00 |
| 25(11/54), 25(12/54) | 4.50 | 14.00 | 32.00 |
| 26-Nostrand-a | 5.70 | 17.00 | 40.00 |

NOTE: ***Cameron*** *art-No. 9, 10, 18-25; c-13.* ***Sekowsky*** *a-8, 9, 13, 14.*

**HAND OF FATE**
Feb, 1988 - No. 3, Apr, 1988 ($1.75, color, Baxter paper)
Eclipse Comics

| | Good | Fine | N-Mint |
|---|---|---|---|
| 1,2 (color, $1.75) | .30 | .90 | 1.75 |
| 3 (B&W, $2.00) | .35 | 1.00 | 2.00 |

**HANDS OF THE DRAGON**
June, 1975
Seaboard Periodicals (Atlas)

| | Good | Fine | N-Mint |
|---|---|---|---|
| 1-Origin; Mooney inks | | .50 | 1.00 |

**HANGMAN COMICS** (Special Comics No. 1; Black Hood No. 9 on) (Also see Flyman, Mighty Comics, Mighty Crusaders & Pep Comics)
No. 2, Spring, 1942 - No. 8, Fall, 1943
MLJ Magazines

| | Good | Fine | N-Mint |
|---|---|---|---|
| 2-The Hangman, Boy Buddies begin | 79.00 | 235.00 | 550.00 |
| 3-8 | 39.00 | 118.00 | 275.00 |

NOTE: ***Fuje*** *a-7(3), 8(3); c-3.* ***Reinman*** *c-3. Bondage c-3.*

**HANK**
1946
Pentagon Publishing Co.

| | Good | Fine | N-Mint |
|---|---|---|---|
| nn-Coulton Waugh's newspaper reprint | 4.30 | 13.00 | 30.00 |

**HANNA-BARBERA** (See Golden Comics Digest No. 2, 7, 11)

**HANNA-BARBERA BAND WAGON** (TV)
Oct, 1962 - No. 3, April, 1963
Gold Key

| | Good | Fine | N-Mint |
|---|---|---|---|
| 1,2-Giants, 84 pgs. | 3.50 | 10.50 | 28.00 |
| 3-Regular size | 2.00 | 6.00 | 14.00 |

**HANNA-BARBERA HI-ADVENTURE HEROES** (See Hi-Adventure...)

**HANNA-BARBERA PARADE** (TV)
Sept, 1971 - No. 10, Dec, 1972
Charlton Comics

| | Good | Fine | N-Mint |
|---|---|---|---|
| 1 | 1.70 | 5.00 | 12.00 |
| 2-10: 7-"Summer Picnic"-52 pgs. | .85 | 2.60 | 6.00 |

NOTE: *No. 4 (1/72) went on sale late in 1972 with the January 1973 issues.*

**HANNA-BARBERA SPOTLIGHT** (See Spotlight)

**HANNA-BARBERA SUPER TV HEROES** (TV)
April, 1968 - No. 7, Oct, 1969 (Hanna-Barbera)
Gold Key

| | Good | Fine | N-Mint |
|---|---|---|---|
| 1-The Birdman, The Herculoids(ends #2), Moby Dick, Young Samson & Goliath(ends #2,4), and The Mighty Mightor begin; Spiegle-a in all | 6.50 | 19.00 | 45.00 |
| 2-The Galaxy Trio app.; Shazzan begins | 4.50 | 14.00 | 32.00 |
| 3-7: The Space Ghost app. in #3,5-7 | 4.00 | 12.00 | 28.00 |

**HANNA-BARBERA (TV STARS)** (See TV Stars)

**HANS BRINKER** (See 4-Color No. 1273)

**HANS CHRISTIAN ANDERSEN**
1953 (100 pgs. - Special Issue)
Ziff-Davis Publ. Co.

| | Good | Fine | N-Mint |
|---|---|---|---|
| nn-Danny Kaye (movie)-Photo-c | 9.30 | 28.00 | 65.00 |

**HANSEL & GRETEL** (See 4-Color No. 590)

**HANSI, THE GIRL WHO LOVED THE SWASTIKA**
1973, 1976 (39-49 cents)
Spire Christian Comics (Fleming H. Revell Co.)

| | Good | Fine | N-Mint |
|---|---|---|---|
| nn | .35 | 1.00 | 2.00 |

**HANS UND FRITZ**
1917 (10x13½"; 1916 strip-r in B&W); 1929 (28 pgs.; 10x13½")

*Ha Ha Comics #74, © ACG*

*Hand of Fate #25 (12/54), © ACE*

*Hangman Comics #8, © AP*

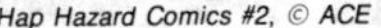
Hap Hazard Comics #2, © ACE

Happy Comics #21, © STD

Happy Houlihans #1, © WMG

The Saalfield Publishing Co.

| | Good | Fine | N-Mint |
|---|---|---|---|
| nn-by R. Dirks | 30.00 | 90.00 | 210.00 |
| 193-(Very Rare)-By R. Dirks; contains B&W Sunday strip reprints of Katzenjammer Kids & Hawkshaw the Detective from 1916 | 30.00 | 90.00 | 210.00 |
| . . .The Funny Larks Of 2(1929) | 30.00 | 90.00 | 210.00 |

**HAP HAZARD COMICS** (Real Love No. 25 on)
1944 - No. 24, Feb, 1949
Ace Magazines (Readers' Research)

| | | | |
|---|---|---|---|
| 1 | 6.00 | 18.00 | 42.00 |
| 2 | 3.00 | 9.00 | 21.00 |
| 3-10 | 2.00 | 6.00 | 14.00 |
| 11-13,15-24 | 1.50 | 4.50 | 10.00 |
| 14-Feldstein-c (4/47) | 4.00 | 12.00 | 28.00 |

**HAP HOPPER** (See Comics Revue No. 2)

**HAPPIEST MILLIONAIRE, THE** (See Movie Comics)

**HAPPINESS AND HEALING FOR YOU** (Also see Oral Roberts'. . .)
1955 (36 pgs.; slick cover) (Oral Roberts Giveaway)
Commercial Comics

| | | | |
|---|---|---|---|
| nn | 7.00 | 20.00 | 40.00 |

NOTE: *The success of this book prompted Oral Roberts to go into the publishing business himself to produce his own material.*

**HAPPI TIM** (See March of Comics No. 182)

**HAPPY COMICS** (Happy Rabbit No. 41 on)
Aug, 1943 - No. 40, Dec, 1950 (Companion to Goofy Comics)
Nedor Publ./Standard Comics (Animated Cartoons)

| | | | |
|---|---|---|---|
| 1 | 13.00 | 40.00 | 90.00 |
| 2 | 6.00 | 18.00 | 42.00 |
| 3-10 | 4.00 | 12.00 | 28.00 |
| 11-19 | 2.65 | 8.00 | 18.00 |
| 20-31,34-37-Frazetta text illos in all; 2 in #34&35, 3 in #27,28,30 | 3.50 | 10.50 | 24.00 |
| 32-Frazetta-a, 7 pgs. plus two text illos; Roussos-a | 10.00 | 30.00 | 70.00 |
| 33-Frazetta-a(2), 6 pgs. each (Scarce) | 16.00 | 48.00 | 110.00 |
| 38-40 | 1.70 | 5.00 | 12.00 |

NOTE: *Al Fago a-27.*

**HAPPY DAYS** (TV)
March, 1979 - No. 6, Feb, 1980
Gold Key

| | | | |
|---|---|---|---|
| 1 | .35 | 1.00 | 2.00 |
| 2-6 | | .50 | 1.00 |
| . . .With the Fonz Kite Fun Book(6¾x5¼'',78)-PG&E | .35 | 1.00 | 2.00 |

**HAPPY HOLIDAY** (See March of Comics No. 181)

**HAPPY HOOLIGAN** (See Alphonse. . .)
1903 (18 pgs.) (Sunday strip reprints in color)
Hearst's New York American-Journal

| | | | |
|---|---|---|---|
| Book 1-by Fred Opper | 32.00 | 95.00 | 225.00 |
| 50 Pg. Edition(1903)-10x15'' in color | 38.00 | 114.00 | 265.00 |

**HAPPY HOOLIGAN** (Handy. . .) (See The Travels of. . .)
1908 (32 pgs. in color) (10x15''; cardboard covers)
Frederick A. Stokes Co.

| | | | |
|---|---|---|---|
| nn | 27.00 | 81.00 | 190.00 |

**HAPPY HOOLIGAN** (Story of. . .)
No. 281, 1932 (16 pgs.; 9½x12''; softcover)
McLoughlin Bros.

| | | | |
|---|---|---|---|
| 281-Three-color text, pictures on heavy paper | 8.50 | 25.50 | 60.00 |

**HAPPY HOULIHANS** (Saddle Justice No. 3 on; see Blackstone, The Magician Detective)
Fall, 1947 - No. 2, Winter, 1947-48
E. C. Comics

| | Good | Fine | N-Mint |
|---|---|---|---|
| 1-Origin Moon Girl | 28.00 | 84.00 | 195.00 |
| 2 | 13.50 | 91.00 | 95.00 |

**HAPPY JACK**
August, 1957 - No. 2, Nov, 1957
Red Top (Decker)

| | | | |
|---|---|---|---|
| V1#1,2 | 1.70 | 5.00 | 12.00 |

**HAPPY JACK HOWARD**
1957
Red Top (Farrell)/Decker

| | | | |
|---|---|---|---|
| nn-Reprints Handy Andy story from E. C. Dandy Comics No. 5, renamed "Happy Jack" | 2.00 | 6.00 | 14.00 |

**HAPPY RABBIT** (Formerly Happy Comics)
No. 41, Feb, 1951 - No. 48, April, 1952
Standard Comics (Animated Cartoons)

| | | | |
|---|---|---|---|
| 41 | 2.85 | 8.50 | 20.00 |
| 42-48 | 1.50 | 4.50 | 10.00 |

**HARD BOILED**
Sept, 1990 - No. 3, 1991 ($4.95-$5.95, color, mini-series, 8½x11'')
Dark Horse Comics

| | | | |
|---|---|---|---|
| 1-3: Miller scripts; sexually explicit, violence | .85 | 2.50 | 5.00 |

**HARDY BOYS, THE** (Disney)(See 4-Color No. 760, 830, 887, 964)

**HARDY BOYS, THE** (TV)
April, 1970 - No. 4, Jan, 1971
Gold Key

| | | | |
|---|---|---|---|
| 1 | .85 | 2.60 | 6.00 |
| 2-4 | .50 | 1.50 | 3.00 |

**HARLEM GLOBETROTTERS** (TV) (See Fun-In No. 8,10)
April, 1972 - No. 12, Jan, 1975 (Hanna-Barbera)
Gold Key

| | | | |
|---|---|---|---|
| 1 | .50 | 1.50 | 3.00 |
| 2-12 | .25 | .75 | 1.50 |

NOTE: *#4, 8, and 12 contain 16 extra pages of advertising.*

**HAROLD TEEN** (See 4-Color #2, 209, Popular Comics, Super Comics & Treasure Box of Famous Comics)

**HAROLD TEEN** (Adv. of. . .)
1929-31 (36-52 pgs.) (Paper covers)
Cupples & Leon Co.

| | | | |
|---|---|---|---|
| nn-B&W daily strip reprints by Carl Ed | 9.00 | 27.00 | 62.00 |

**HARVEY**
Oct, 1970; No. 2, 12/70; No. 3, 6/72 - No. 6, 12/72
Marvel Comics Group

| | | | |
|---|---|---|---|
| 1 | .70 | 2.00 | 4.00 |
| 2-6 | .35 | 1.00 | 2.00 |

**HARVEY COLLECTORS COMICS** (Richie Rich Collectors Comics #10 on, cover title only)
Sept, 1975 - No. 15, Jan, 1978; No. 16, Oct, 1979 (52 pgs.)
Harvey Publications

| | | | |
|---|---|---|---|
| 1-Reprints Richie Rich #1,2 | .70 | 2.00 | 4.00 |
| 2-10 | .40 | 1.20 | 2.40 |
| 11-16: 16-Sad Sack-r | | .50 | 1.00 |

NOTE: *All reprints: Casper-#2, 7, Richie Rich-#1, 3, 5, 6, 8-15, Wendy-#4. #6 titled 'Richie Rich. . .'on inside.*

**HARVEY COMICS HITS**
No. 51, Oct, 1951 - No. 62, Dec, 1952
Harvey Publications

| | | | |
|---|---|---|---|
| 51-The Phantom | 12.00 | 36.00 | 84.00 |
| 52-Steve Canyon | 6.35 | 19.00 | 44.00 |

| | Good | Fine | N-Mint |
|---|---|---|---|
| 53-Mandrake the Magician | 11.00 | 32.00 | 75.00 |
| 54-Tim Tyler's Tales of Jungle Terror | 6.50 | 19.50 | 45.00 |
| 55-Mary Worth | 3.35 | 10.00 | 23.00 |
| 56-The Phantom; bondage-c | 11.00 | 32.00 | 75.00 |
| 57-Rip Kirby-"Kidnap Racket;" entire book by Alex Raymond | 9.25 | 28.00 | 65.00 |
| 58-Girls in White | 3.00 | 9.00 | 21.00 |
| 59-Tales of the Invisible Scarlet O'Neil | 6.50 | 20.00 | 45.00 |
| 60-Paramount Animated Comics No.1(2nd app. Baby Huey); 1st Harvey app. Baby Huey | 19.00 | 57.00 | 130.00 |
| 61-Casper the Friendly Ghost; 1st Harvey Casper | 19.00 | 57.00 | 130.00 |
| 62-Paramount Animated Comics | 7.00 | 21.00 | 50.00 |

**HARVEY COMICS LIBRARY**
April, 1952 - No. 2, 1952
Harvey Publications

| | Good | Fine | N-Mint |
|---|---|---|---|
| 1-Teen-Age Dope Slaves as exposed by Rex Morgan, M.D.; drug propaganda story; used in **SOTI**, pg. 27 | 45.00 | 135.00 | 315.00 |
| (Prices vary widely on this book) | | | |
| 2-Sparkle Plenty (Dick Tracy in "Blackmail Terror") | 11.50 | 34.50 | 80.00 |

**HARVEY COMICS SPOTLIGHT**
Sept, 1987 - No. 4? (#1-3: 75 cents, #4: $1.00)
Harvey Comics

| | Good | Fine | N-Mint |
|---|---|---|---|
| 1-3: 1-Sad Sack, 2-Baby Huey, 3-Little Dot | | .40 | .75 |
| 4-Little Audrey | | .50 | 1.00 |

**HARVEY DIGEST SPORTS**
1977 - No. 6, 1978 (Digest size)(Each issue features different sport)
Harvey Publications

| | Good | Fine | N-Mint |
|---|---|---|---|
| 1-6: Baseball, Basketball, Football, Hockey, etc. | | .50 | 1.00 |

**HARVEY HITS**
Sept, 1957 - No. 122, Nov, 1967
Harvey Publications

| | Good | Fine | N-Mint |
|---|---|---|---|
| 1-The Phantom | 14.00 | 43.00 | 100.00 |
| 2-Rags Rabbit (10/57) | 1.35 | 4.00 | 9.00 |
| 3-Richie Rich (11/57)-r/Little Dot; 1st book devoted to Richie Rich; see Little Dot for 1st app. | 54.00 | 160.00 | 350.00 |
| 4-Little Dot's Uncles (12/57) | 8.00 | 24.00 | 52.00 |
| 5-Stevie Mazie's Boy Friend | 1.35 | 4.00 | 9.00 |
| 6-The Phantom (2/58); Kirby-c; 2pg. Powell-a | 7.00 | 21.00 | 50.00 |
| 7-Wendy the Witch | 8.00 | 24.00 | 52.00 |
| 8-Sad Sack's Army Life | 2.75 | 8.00 | 18.00 |
| 9-Richie Rich's Golden Deeds-r (2nd book devoted to Richie Rich) | 29.00 | 85.00 | 200.00 |
| 10-Little Lotta | 5.70 | 17.00 | 40.00 |
| 11-Little Audrey Summer Fun (7/58) | 4.00 | 12.00 | 28.00 |
| 12-The Phantom; Kirby-c; 2pg. Powell-a (8/58) | 4.50 | 14.00 | 32.00 |
| 13-Little Dot's Uncles (9/58); Richie Rich 1pg. | 5.50 | 16.50 | 38.00 |
| 14-Herman & Katnip (10/58) | 1.35 | 4.00 | 9.00 |
| 15-The Phantom (12/58)-1 pg. origin | 5.00 | 15.00 | 35.00 |
| 16-Wendy the Witch (1/59) | 4.00 | 12.00 | 26.00 |
| 17-Sad Sack's Army Life (2/59) | 1.35 | 4.00 | 9.00 |
| 18-Buzzy & the Crow | 1.35 | 4.00 | 9.00 |
| 19-Little Audrey (4/59) | 2.75 | 8.00 | 18.00 |
| 20-Casper & Spooky | 4.00 | 12.00 | 26.00 |
| 21-Wendy the Witch | 3.00 | 9.00 | 20.00 |
| 22-Sad Sack's Army Life | 1.00 | 3.00 | 7.00 |
| 23-Wendy the Witch (8/59) | 3.00 | 9.00 | 20.00 |
| 24-Little Dot's Uncles (9/59); Richie Rich 1pg. | 4.00 | 12.00 | 26.00 |
| 25-Herman & Katnip (10/59) | 1.00 | 3.00 | 7.00 |
| 26-The Phantom (11/59) | 5.00 | 15.00 | 35.00 |
| 27-Wendy the Good Little Witch | 3.00 | 9.00 | 20.00 |
| 28-Sad Sack's Army Life | .50 | 1.50 | 3.00 |

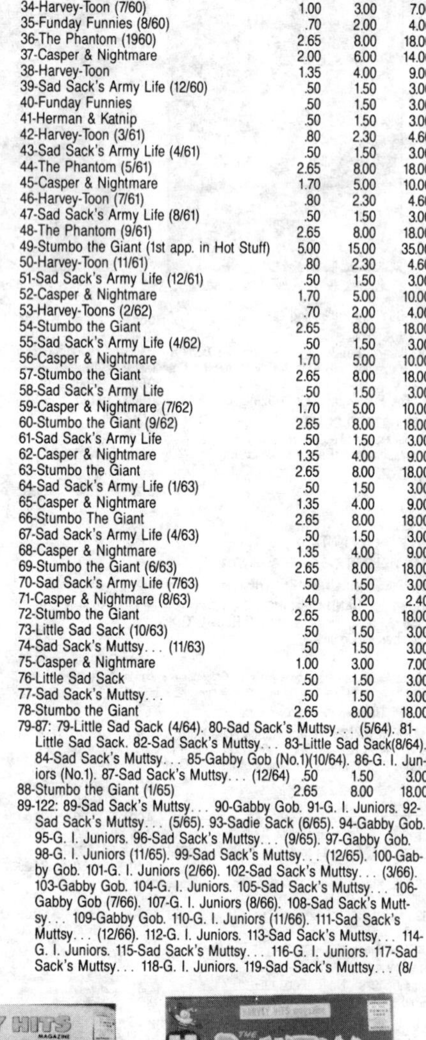

| | Good | Fine | N-Mint |
|---|---|---|---|
| 29-Harvey-Toon (No.1)('60); Casper, Buzzy | 2.00 | 6.00 | 14.00 |
| 30-Wendy the Witch (3/60) | 2.75 | 8.00 | 18.00 |
| 31-Herman & Katnip (4/60) | .70 | 2.00 | 4.00 |
| 32-Sad Sack's Army Life (5/60) | .50 | 1.50 | 3.00 |
| 33-Wendy the Witch (6/60) | 2.75 | 8.00 | 18.00 |
| 34-Harvey-Toon (7/60) | 1.00 | 3.00 | 7.00 |
| 35-Funday Funnies (8/60) | .70 | 2.00 | 4.00 |
| 36-The Phantom (1960) | 2.65 | 8.00 | 18.00 |
| 37-Casper & Nightmare | 2.00 | 6.00 | 14.00 |
| 38-Harvey-Toon | 1.35 | 4.00 | 9.00 |
| 39-Sad Sack's Army Life (12/60) | .50 | 1.50 | 3.00 |
| 40-Funday Funnies | .50 | 1.50 | 3.00 |
| 41-Herman & Katnip | .50 | 1.50 | 3.00 |
| 42-Harvey-Toon (3/61) | .80 | 2.30 | 4.60 |
| 43-Sad Sack's Army Life (4/61) | .50 | 1.50 | 3.00 |
| 44-The Phantom (5/61) | 2.65 | 8.00 | 18.00 |
| 45-Casper & Nightmare | 1.70 | 5.00 | 10.00 |
| 46-Harvey-Toon (7/61) | .80 | 2.30 | 4.60 |
| 47-Sad Sack's Army Life (8/61) | .50 | 1.50 | 3.00 |
| 48-The Phantom (9/61) | 2.65 | 8.00 | 18.00 |
| 49-Stumbo the Giant (1st app. in Hot Stuff) | 5.00 | 15.00 | 35.00 |
| 50-Harvey-Toon (11/61) | .80 | 2.30 | 4.60 |
| 51-Sad Sack's Army Life (12/61) | .50 | 1.50 | 3.00 |
| 52-Casper & Nightmare | 1.70 | 5.00 | 10.00 |
| 53-Harvey-Toons (2/62) | .70 | 2.00 | 4.00 |
| 54-Stumbo the Giant | 2.65 | 8.00 | 18.00 |
| 55-Sad Sack's Army Life (4/62) | .50 | 1.50 | 3.00 |
| 56-Casper & Nightmare | 1.70 | 5.00 | 10.00 |
| 57-Stumbo the Giant | 2.65 | 8.00 | 18.00 |
| 58-Sad Sack's Army Life | .50 | 1.50 | 3.00 |
| 59-Casper & Nightmare (7/62) | 1.70 | 5.00 | 10.00 |
| 60-Stumbo the Giant (9/62) | 2.65 | 8.00 | 18.00 |
| 61-Sad Sack's Army Life | .50 | 1.50 | 3.00 |
| 62-Casper & Nightmare | 1.35 | 4.00 | 9.00 |
| 63-Stumbo the Giant | 2.65 | 8.00 | 18.00 |
| 64-Sad Sack's Army Life (1/63) | .50 | 1.50 | 3.00 |
| 65-Casper & Nightmare | 1.35 | 4.00 | 9.00 |
| 66-Stumbo The Giant | 2.65 | 8.00 | 18.00 |
| 67-Sad Sack's Army Life (4/63) | .50 | 1.50 | 3.00 |
| 68-Casper & Nightmare | 1.35 | 4.00 | 9.00 |
| 69-Stumbo the Giant (6/63) | 2.65 | 8.00 | 18.00 |
| 70-Sad Sack's Army Life (7/63) | .50 | 1.50 | 3.00 |
| 71-Casper & Nightmare (8/63) | .40 | 1.20 | 2.40 |
| 72-Stumbo the Giant | 2.65 | 8.00 | 18.00 |
| 73-Little Sad Sack (10/63) | .50 | 1.50 | 3.00 |
| 74-Sad Sack's Muttsy. . . (11/63) | .50 | 1.50 | 3.00 |
| 75-Casper & Nightmare | 1.00 | 3.00 | 7.00 |
| 76-Little Sad Sack | .50 | 1.50 | 3.00 |
| 77-Sad Sack's Muttsy. . . | .50 | 1.50 | 3.00 |
| 78-Stumbo the Giant | 2.65 | 8.00 | 18.00 |
| 79-87: 79-Little Sad Sack (4/64). 80-Sad Sack's Muttsy. . . (5/64). 81-Little Sad Sack. 82-Sad Sack's Muttsy. . . 83-Little Sad Sack(8/64). 84-Sad Sack's Muttsy. . . 85-Gabby Gob (No.1)(10/64). 86-G. I. Juniors (No.1). 87-Sad Sack's Muttsy. . . (12/64) | .50 | 1.50 | 3.00 |
| 88-Stumbo the Giant (1/65) | 2.65 | 8.00 | 18.00 |
| 89-122: 89-Sad Sack's Muttsy. . . 90-Gabby Gob. 91-G. I. Juniors. 92-Sad Sack's Muttsy. . . (5/65). 93-Sadie Sack (6/65). 94-Gabby Gob. 95-G. I. Juniors. 96-Sad Sack's Muttsy. . . (9/65). 97-Gabby Gob. 98-G. I. Juniors (11/65). 99-Sad Sack's Muttsy. . . (12/65). 100-Gabby Gob. 101-G. I. Juniors (2/66). 102-Sad Sack's Muttsy. . . (3/66). 103-Gabby Gob. 104-G. I. Juniors. 105-Sad Sack's Muttsy. . . 106-Gabby Gob (7/66). 107-G. I. Juniors (8/66). 108-Sad Sack's Muttsy. . . 109-Gabby Gob. 110-G. I. Juniors (11/66). 111-Sad Sack's Muttsy. . . (12/66). 112-G. I. Juniors. 113-Sad Sack's Muttsy. . . 114-G. I. Juniors. 115-Sad Sack's Muttsy. . . 116-G. I. Juniors. 117-Sad Sack's Muttsy. . . 118-G. I. Juniors. 119-Sad Sack's Muttsy. . . (8/ | | | |

*Harvey Comics Hits #54, © HARV*

*Harvey Hits #2, © HARV*

*Harvey Hits #36, © KING*

Haunt of Fear #6, © WMG

Have Gun, Will Travel #7, © DELL

The Hawk #7, © STJ

| | Good | Fine | N-Mint |
|---|---|---|---|
| 67). 120-G. I. Juniors (9/67). 121-Sad Sack's Muttsy. . . (10/67). 122-G. I. Juniors | .50 | 1.50 | 3.00 |

**HARVEY HITS COMICS**
Nov, 1986 - No. 6, Oct, 1987
Harvey Publications

1-6: Little Lotta, Little Dot, Wendy, & Baby Huey app. .40 .75

**HARVEY POP COMICS** (Teen Humor)
Oct, 1968 - No. 2, Nov, 1969 (Both are 68 pg. Giants)
Harvey Publications

1,2-The Cowsills 1.00 3.00 7.00

**HARVEY 3-D HITS** (See Sad Sack)

**HARVEY-TOON (. . . S)** (See Harvey Hits No. 29, 34, 38, 42, 46, 50, 53)

**HARVEY WISEGUYS** (. . . Digest #? on)
Nov, 1987 - Present (98 pgs., digest-size, $1.25-$1.75)
Harvey Comics

1-Hot Stuff, Spooky, etc. .60 1.25
2 (11/88, 68 pgs.) .60 1.25
3 (4/89, $1.75) - 6 (3/90) .30 .90 1.75

**HATARI** (See Movie Classics)

**HATHAWAYS, THE** (See 4-Color No. 1298)

**HAUNTED** (See This Magazine Is Haunted)

**HAUNTED**
9/71 - No. 30, 11/76; No. 31, 9/77 - No. 75, 9/84
Charlton Comics

1 .50 1.50 3.00
2-5 .25 .75 1.50
6-21 .50 1.00
22-75: 64,75-r .30 .60

NOTE: *Aparo c-45.* ***Ditko*** *a-1-8, 11-16, 18, 23, 24, 28, 30, 34r, 36r, 39-42r, 47r, 49-51r, 57, 60. c-1-7, 11, 13, 14, 16, 30, 41, 47, 49-51.* ***Howard*** *a-18, 22, 32.* ***Morisi*** *a-13.* ***Newton*** *a-17, 21, 59r; c-21, 22(painted).* ***Staton*** *a-18, 21, 22, 30, 33; c-18, 33.* ***Sutton*** *a-21, 22, 38; c-17, 64r. #51 reprints #1; #49 reprints Tales of the Myst. Traveler #4.*

**HAUNTED LOVE**
April, 1973 - No. 11, Sept, 1975
Charlton Comics

1-Tom Sutton-a, 16 pgs. .60 1.20
2,3,6-11 .40 .80
4,5-Ditko-a .50 1.00
Modern Comics #1(1978) .20 .40

NOTE: ***Howard*** *a-8i.* ***Newton*** *c-8, 9.* ***Staton*** *a-5.*

**HAUNTED THRILLS**
June, 1952 - No. 18, Nov-Dec, 1954
Ajax/Farrell Publications

1-r/Ellery Queen #1 13.00 40.00 90.00
2-L. B. Cole-a r-/Ellery Queen #1 8.00 24.00 56.00
3-5: 3-Drug use story 6.50 19.00 45.00
6-12: 12-Webb-a 5.00 15.00 35.00
13,16-18: 18-Lingerie panels 4.00 12.00 28.00
14-Jesus Christ apps. in story by Webb 4.00 12.00 28.00
15-Jo-Jo-r 4.50 14.00 32.00

NOTE: *Kamenish art in most issues.*

**HAUNT OF FEAR** (Formerly Gunfighter)
No. 15, May-June, 1950 - No. 28, Nov-Dec, 1954
E. C. Comics

15(#1, 1950) 135.00 405.00 950.00
16 68.00 205.00 475.00
17-Origin of Crypt of Terror, Vault of Horror, & Haunt of Fear; used in **SOTI**, pg. 43; last pg. Ingels-a used by N.Y. Legis. Comm. 68.00 205.00 475.00

| | Good | Fine | N-Mint |
|---|---|---|---|
| 4 | 50.00 | 150.00 | 350.00 |
| 5-Injury-to-eye panel, pg. 4 | 38.00 | 114.00 | 265.00 |
| 6-10: 8-Shrunken head cover | 26.00 | 79.00 | 185.00 |
| 11-13,15-18 | 19.00 | 56.00 | 130.00 |
| 14-Origin Old Witch by Ingels | 26.00 | 79.00 | 185.00 |
| 19-Used in **SOTI**, ill.-"A comic book baseball game" & Senate investigation on juvenile delinq. bondage/decapitation-c | 25.00 | 75.00 | 175.00 |
| 20-Feldstein-r/Vault of Horror #12 | 17.00 | 51.00 | 120.00 |
| 21,22,25,27: 27-Cannibalism story | 11.00 | 32.00 | 75.00 |
| 23-Used in **SOTI**, pg. 241 | 12.00 | 36.00 | 85.00 |
| 24-Used in Senate Investigative Report, pg.8 | 11.50 | 34.00 | 80.00 |
| 26-Contains anti-censorship editorial, 'Are you a Red Dupe?' | 11.50 | 34.00 | 80.00 |
| 28-Low distribution | 13.00 | 40.00 | 90.00 |

NOTE: *(Canadian reprints known; see Table of Contents).* ***Craig*** *a-15-17, 5, 7, 10, 12, 13; c-15-17, 5-7.* ***Crandall*** *a-20, 21, 26, 27.* ***Davis*** *a-4-26, 28.* ***Evans*** *a-15-19, 22-25, 27.* ***Feldstein*** *a-15-17, 20; c-4, 8-10.* ***Ingels*** *a-16, 17, 4-28; c-11-28.* ***Kamen*** *a-16, 4, 6, 7, 9-11, 13-19, 21-28.* ***Krigstein*** *a-28.* ***Kurtzman*** *a-15(#1), 17(#3).* ***Orlando*** *a-9, 12.* ***Wood*** *a-15, 16, 4-6.*

**HAUNT OF HORROR, THE** (Magazine)
May, 1974 - No. 5, Jan, 1975 (75 cents) (B&W)
Cadence Comics Publ. (Marvel)

1 .85 2.50 5.00
2,4: 2-Origin & 1st app. Gabriel the Devil Hunter; Satana begins. 4-Neal Adams-a .70 2.00 4.00
3,5: 5-Evans-a(2) .50 1.50 3.00

NOTE: ***Alcala*** *a-2.* ***Colan*** *a-2p.* ***Heath*** *r-1.* ***Krigstein*** *r-3.* ***Reese*** *a-1.* ***Simonson*** *a-1.*

**HAVE GUN, WILL TRAVEL** (TV)
No. 931, 8/58 - No. 14, 7-9/62 (All Richard Boone photo-c)
Dell Publishing Co.

4-Color 931 (#1) 7.00 21.00 50.00
4-Color 983,1044 4.50 14.00 32.00
4 (1-3/60) - 14 3.70 11.00 26.00

**HAVOK AND WOLVERINE - MELTDOWN**
Mar, 1989 - No. 4, Oct, 1989 ($3.50, mini-series, squarebound)
Epic Comics (Marvel)

1-Mature readers, violent .85 2.50 5.00
2-4 .60 1.75 3.50

**HAWAIIAN EYE** (TV)
July, 1963 (Troy Donahue, Connie Stevens photo-c)
Gold Key

1 (10073-307) 3.00 9.00 21.00

**HAWAIIAN ILLUSTRATED LEGENDS SERIES**
1975 (B&W)(Cover printed w/blue, yellow, and green)
Hogarth Press

1-Kalelealuaka, the Mysterious Warrior .60 1.20
2,3(Exist?) .40 .80

**HAWK, THE** (Also see Approved Comics #1, 7 & Tops In Adventure)
Wint/51 - No. 3, 11-12/52; No. 4, 1953 - No. 12, 5/55
Ziff-Davis/St. John Publ. Co. No. 4 on

1-Anderson-a 9.30 28.00 65.00
2-Kubert, Infantino-a; painted-c 5.70 17.00 40.00
3-8,10-11: 8-Reprints #3 with diff.-c. 10-Reprints one story/#2. 11-Buckskin Belle & The Texan app. 4.00 12.00 28.00
9-Baker-c/a; Kubert-a(r)/#2 4.50 14.00 32.00
12-Baker-c/a; Buckskin Belle app. 4.50 14.00 32.00
3-D 1(11/53)-Baker-c 19.00 57.00 135.00

NOTE: ***Baker*** *c-8, 9, 11.* ***Tuska*** *a-1, 9, 12. Painted c-1, 7.*

**HAWK AND DOVE**
Oct, 1988 - No. 5, Feb, 1989 ($1.00, color, mini-series)
DC Comics

1 .75 2.25 4.50

| | Good | Fine | N-Mint |
|---|---|---|---|
| 2 | .50 | 1.50 | 3.00 |
| 3-5 | .35 | 1.00 | 2.00 |

**HAWK AND DOVE**
June, 1989 - Present ($1.00, color)
DC Comics

| | Good | Fine | N-Mint |
|---|---|---|---|
| 1 | .25 | .75 | 1.50 |
| 2-24: 9-Copperhead app. 12-New Titans app. 18,19-The Creeper app. | | .50 | 1.00 |

**HAWK AND THE DOVE, THE** (See Showcase #75 & Teen Titans)
Aug-Sept, 1968 - No. 6, June-July, 1969
National Periodical Publications

| | Good | Fine | N-Mint |
|---|---|---|---|
| 1-Ditko-c/a | 3.50 | 10.50 | 24.00 |
| 2-6: 5-Teen Titans cameo | 2.30 | 7.00 | 16.00 |

NOTE: ***Ditko** c/a-1, 2. **Gil Kane** a-3p, 4p, 5, 6p; c-3-6.*

**HAWKEYE** (See The Avengers #16 & Tales Of Suspense #57)
Sept, 1983 - No. 4, Dec, 1983 (Mini-series)
Marvel Comics Group

| | Good | Fine | N-Mint |
|---|---|---|---|
| 1-4: 1-Origin Hawkeye. 3-Origin Mockingbird | .35 | 1.00 | 2.00 |

**HAWKEYE & THE LAST OF THE MOHICANS** (See 4-Color No. 884)

**HAWKMAN** (See Atom & Hawkman, The Brave & the Bold, DC Comics Presents, Detective, Flash Comics, Hawkworld, Justice League of America 31, Mystery in Space, Shadow War Of. . ., Showcase, & World's Finest)

**HAWKMAN**
Apr-May, 1964 - No. 27, Aug-Sept, 1968
National Periodical Publications

| | Good | Fine | N-Mint |
|---|---|---|---|
| 1 | 25.00 | 75.00 | 175.00 |
| 2 | 9.30 | 28.00 | 65.00 |
| 3-5: 4-Zatanna x-over(origin & 1st app.) | 6.50 | 19.00 | 45.00 |
| 6-10: 9-Atom cameo; Hawkman & Atom learn each other's I.D.; 2nd app. Shadow Thief | 4.30 | 13.00 | 30.00 |
| 11-15 | 2.85 | 8.50 | 20.00 |
| 16-27: Adam Strange x-over #18, cameo #19. 25-G.A. Hawkman-r | 1.70 | 5.00 | 12.00 |

NOTE: ***Anderson** c/a-1-21. **Kubert** c-27. **Moldoff** a-25r.*

**HAWKMAN**
Aug, 1986 - No. 17, Dec, 1987
DC Comics

| | Good | Fine | N-Mint |
|---|---|---|---|
| 1 | .30 | .90 | 1.75 |
| 2-17: 10-Byrne-c | | .50 | 1.00 |
| Special #1 ('86, $1.25) | .25 | .75 | 1.50 |
| Trade paperback (1989, $19.95)-r/Brave and the Bold #34-36,42-44 by Kubert; Kubert-c | 3.35 | 10.00 | 20.00 |

**HAWKMOON: COUNT BRASS**
Feb, 1989 - No. 4, Aug, 1989 ($1.95, limited series, color, Baxter)
First Comics

| | Good | Fine | N-Mint |
|---|---|---|---|
| 1-4: Adapts novel by Michael Moorcock | .35 | 1.00 | 2.00 |

**HAWKMOON: THE JEWEL IN THE SKULL**
May, 1986 - No. 4, Nov, 1986 ($1.75, limited series, Baxter)
First Comics

| | Good | Fine | N-Mint |
|---|---|---|---|
| 1-4: Adapts novel by Michael Moorcock | .30 | .90 | 1.80 |

**HAWKMOON: THE MAD GOD'S AMULET**
Jan, 1987 - No. 4, July, 1987 ($1.75, limited series, Baxter)
First Comics

| | Good | Fine | N-Mint |
|---|---|---|---|
| 1-4: Adapts novel by Michael Moorcock | .30 | .90 | 1.80 |

**HAWKMOON: THE RUNESTAFF**
June, 1988 - No. 4, Dec, 1988 ($1.75-1.95, limited series, Baxter)
First Comics

| | Good | Fine | N-Mint |
|---|---|---|---|
| 1,2: ($1.75) Adapts novel by Michael Moorcock | .30 | .90 | 1.80 |
| 3,4 ($1.95) | .35 | 1.00 | 2.00 |

**HAWKMOON: THE SWORD OF DAWN**
Sept, 1987 - No. 4, Mar, 1988 ($1.75, limited series, Baxter)
First Comics

| | Good | Fine | N-Mint |
|---|---|---|---|
| 1-4: Adapts novel by Michael Moorcock | .30 | .90 | 1.80 |

**HAWKSHAW THE DETECTIVE** (See Advs. of. . ., Hans Und Fritz & Okay)
1917 (24 pgs.; B&W; 10½x13½") (Sunday strip reprints)
The Saalfield Publishing Co.

| | Good | Fine | N-Mint |
|---|---|---|---|
| nn-By Gus Mager | 10.00 | 30.00 | 70.00 |

**HAWKWORLD**
1989 - No. 3, 1989 ($3.95, prestige format, mini-series)
DC Comics

| | Good | Fine | N-Mint |
|---|---|---|---|
| Book 1-3: Truman-c/a/scripts; 1-New costume for Hawkman | .75 | 2.25 | 4.50 |

**HAWKWORLD**
June, 1990 - Present ($1.50, on-going series)
DC Comics

| | Good | Fine | N-Mint |
|---|---|---|---|
| 1-Hawkman spin-off | .35 | 1.00 | 2.00 |
| 2-10 | .25 | .75 | 1.50 |
| Annual 1 (1990, $2.95, 68 pgs.)-Flash app. | .50 | 1.50 | 3.00 |

**HAWTHORN-MELODY FARMS DAIRY COMICS**
No date (1950's) (Giveaway)
Everybody's Publishing Co.

| | Good | Fine | N-Mint |
|---|---|---|---|
| nn-Cheerie Chick, Tuffy Turtle, Robin Koo Koo, Donald & Longhorn Legends | .85 | 2.50 | 5.00 |

**HAYWIRE**
Oct, 1988 - No. 13, Sept, 1989 ($1.25, color, mature readers)
DC Comics

| | Good | Fine | N-Mint |
|---|---|---|---|
| 1-13 | | .65 | 1.30 |

**HEADLINE COMICS** (. . .Crime No. 32-39)
Feb, 1943 - No. 22, Nov-Dec, 1946; No. 23, 1947 - No. 77, Oct, 1956
Prize Publications

| | Good | Fine | N-Mint |
|---|---|---|---|
| 1-Yank & Doodle x-over in Junior Rangers | 20.00 | 60.00 | 140.00 |
| 2 | 8.50 | 25.50 | 60.00 |
| 3-Used in **POP**, pg. 84 | 7.00 | 21.00 | 50.00 |
| 4-7,9,10: 4,9,10-Hitler stories in each | 5.70 | 17.00 | 50.00 |
| 8-Classic Hitler-c | 10.00 | 30.00 | 70.00 |
| 11,12 | 4.00 | 12.00 | 28.00 |
| 13-15-Blue Streak in all | 4.30 | 13.00 | 30.00 |
| 16-Origin Atomic Man | 9.30 | 28.00 | 65.00 |
| 17,18,20,21: 21-Atomic Man ends (9-10/46) | 5.00 | 15.00 | 35.00 |
| 19-S&K-a | 11.00 | 32.00 | 75.00 |
| 22-Kiefer-c | 2.65 | 8.00 | 18.00 |
| 23,24: (All S&K-a). 24-Dope-crazy killer story | 11.00 | 32.00 | 75.00 |
| 25-35-S&K-c/a. 25-Powell-a | 7.00 | 21.00 | 50.00 |
| 36-S&K-a | 5.70 | 17.00 | 40.00 |
| 37-One pg. S&K, Severin-a | 2.85 | 8.50 | 20.00 |
| 38,40-Meskin-a | 2.30 | 7.00 | 16.00 |
| 39,41,42,45-48,50-55: 51-Kirby-c. 45-Kirby-a | 1.50 | 4.50 | 10.00 |
| 43,49-Meskin-a | 1.70 | 5.00 | 12.00 |
| 44-S&K-c; Severin/Elder, Meskin-a | 3.50 | 10.50 | 24.00 |
| 56-S&K-a | 2.85 | 8.50 | 20.00 |
| 57-77: 72-Meskin-c/a(i) | 1.50 | 4.50 | 10.00 |

NOTE: ***Hollingsworth** a-30. Photo c-38, 42, 43.*

**HEADMAN**
1990 ($2.50, color, mature readers)
Innovation Publishing

| | Good | Fine | N-Mint |
|---|---|---|---|
| 1-Sci/fi | .40 | 1.25 | 2.50 |

**HEAP, THE**
Sept, 1971 (52 pages)
Skywald Publications

| | Good | Fine | N-Mint |
|---|---|---|---|
| 1-Kinstler-r/Strange Worlds No. 8 | .50 | 1.50 | 3.00 |

*The Hawk and the Dove #2 (10-11/68), © DC*

*Hawkman #26 (6-7/68), © DC*

*Headline Comics #34, © PRIZE*

Heathcliff #47, © McNaught Synd.

Hedy Devine Comics #23, © MEG

Hellblazer #2, © DC

**HEART AND SOUL**
April-May, 1954 - No. 2, June-July, 1954
Mikeross Publications

| | Good | Fine | N-Mint |
|---|---|---|---|
| 1,2 | 2.65 | 8.00 | 18.00 |

**HEART THROBS** (Love Stories No. 147 on)
8/49 - No. 8, 10/50; No. 9, 3/52 - No. 146, Oct, 1972
Quality/National No. 47(4-5/57) on (Arleigh No. 48-101)

| | Good | Fine | N-Mint |
|---|---|---|---|
| 1-Classic Ward-c, Gustavson-a, 9 pgs. | 20.00 | 60.00 | 140.00 |
| 2-Ward-c/a (9 pgs); Gustavson-a | 11.50 | 34.00 | 80.00 |
| 3-Gustavson-a | 4.30 | 13.00 | 30.00 |
| 4,6,8-Ward-a, 8-9 pgs. | 6.50 | 19.50 | 45.00 |
| 5,7 | 2.30 | 7.00 | 16.00 |
| 9-Robert Mitchum, Jane Russell photo-c | 3.50 | 10.50 | 24.00 |
| 10,15-Ward-a | 4.65 | 14.00 | 32.00 |
| 11-14,16-20: 12 (7/52) | 1.70 | 5.00 | 12.00 |
| 21-Ward-c | 3.65 | 11.00 | 25.00 |
| 22,23-Ward-a(p) | 2.65 | 8.00 | 18.00 |
| 24-33: 33-Last pre-code (3/55) | 1.50 | 4.50 | 10.00 |
| 34-39,41-46 (12/56; last Quality issue) | 1.15 | 3.50 | 8.00 |
| 40-Ward-a; r-7 pgs./#21 | 2.15 | 6.50 | 15.00 |
| 47-(4-5/57; 1st DC issue) | 5.70 | 17.00 | 40.00 |
| 48-60 | 2.65 | 8.00 | 18.00 |
| 61-70 | 1.70 | 5.00 | 12.00 |
| 71-100: 74-Last 10 cent issue | 1.15 | 3.50 | 8.00 |
| 101-The Beatles app. on-c | 2.60 | 11.00 | 25.00 |
| 102-120: 102-123-(Serial)-Three Girls, Their Lives, Their Loves. 120-Neal Adams-c | .70 | 2.00 | 4.00 |
| 121-146: #133-142, 52 pgs. | .50 | 1.50 | 3.00 |

NOTE: ***Gustavson** a-8. **Tuska** a-128. Photo c-4, 8-10, 15, 17.*

**HEATHCLIFF** (See Star Comics Mag.)
Apr, 1985 - Present (#16-on, $1.00)
Star Comics/Marvel Comics No. 23 on

| | Good | Fine | N-Mint |
|---|---|---|---|
| 1-49,51-58: Post-a most issues. 43-X-Mas issue. 47-Batman parody (Catman vs. the Soaker) | | .50 | 1.00 |
| 50-($1.50, 52 pgs.) | .25 | .75 | 1.50 |
| Annual 1 ('87) | | .60 | 1.20 |

**HEATHCLIFF'S FUNHOUSE**
May, 1987 - No. 10, 1988
Star Comics/Marvel Comics No. 6 on

| | Good | Fine | N-Mint |
|---|---|---|---|
| 1-10 | | .50 | 1.00 |

**HECKLE AND JECKLE** (See Blue Ribbon, Paul Terry's & Terry-Toons Comics)
10/51 - No. 24, 10/55; No. 25, Fall/56 - No. 34, 6/59
St. John Publ. Co. No. 1-24/Pines No. 25 on

| | Good | Fine | N-Mint |
|---|---|---|---|
| 1 | 18.00 | 54.00 | 125.00 |
| 2 | 8.50 | 25.50 | 60.00 |
| 3-5 | 6.00 | 18.00 | 42.00 |
| 6-10 | 4.30 | 13.00 | 30.00 |
| 11-20 | 2.85 | 8.50 | 20.00 |
| 21-34 | 2.00 | 6.00 | 14.00 |

**HECKLE AND JECKLE** (TV) (See New Terrytoons)
11/62 - No. 4, 8/63; 5/66; No. 2, 10/66; No. 3, 8/67
Gold Key/Dell Publishing Co.

| | Good | Fine | N-Mint |
|---|---|---|---|
| 1 (11/62; Gold Key) | 2.65 | 8.00 | 18.00 |
| 2-4 | 1.50 | 4.50 | 10.00 |
| 1 (5/66; Dell) | 1.70 | 5.00 | 12.00 |
| 2,3 | 1.30 | 4.00 | 9.00 |

(See March of Comics No. 379, 472, 484)

**HECKLE AND JECKLE 3-D**
1987 - No. 2? ($2.50; color)
Spotlight Comics

| | Good | Fine | N-Mint |
|---|---|---|---|
| 1,2 | .40 | 1.25 | 2.50 |

**HECTOR COMICS**
Nov, 1953 - No. 3, 1954
Key Publications

| | Good | Fine | N-Mint |
|---|---|---|---|
| 1 | 2.35 | 7.00 | 16.00 |
| 2,3 | 1.50 | 4.50 | 10.00 |

**HECTOR HEATHCOTE** (TV)
March, 1964
Gold Key

| | Good | Fine | N-Mint |
|---|---|---|---|
| 1 (10111-403) | 2.35 | 7.00 | 16.00 |

**HEDY DEVINE COMICS** (Formerly All Winners #21?; Hedy of Hollywood #36 on; also see Annie Oakley, Comedy & Venus)
No. 22, Aug, 1947 - No. 50, Sept, 1952
Marvel Comics (RCM)/Atlas #50

| | Good | Fine | N-Mint |
|---|---|---|---|
| 22-1st app. Hedy Devine | 5.00 | 15.00 | 35.00 |
| 23,24,27-30: 23-Wolverton-a, 1 pg; Kurtzman's "Hey Look," 2 pgs. 24,27-30-"Hey Look" by Kurtzman, 1-3 pgs. | 6.00 | 18.00 | 42.00 |
| 25-Classic "Hey Look" by Kurtzman-"Optical Illusion" | 6.50 | 19.00 | 45.00 |
| 26-"Giggles & Grins" by Kurtzman | 4.30 | 13.00 | 30.00 |
| 31-34,36-50: 32-Anti-Wertham editorial | 2.30 | 7.00 | 16.00 |
| 35-Four pgs. "Rusty" by Kurtzman | 4.50 | 14.00 | 32.00 |

**HEDY-MILLIE-TESSIE COMEDY** (See Comedy)

**HEDY WOLFE** (Also see Patsy & Hedy)
August, 1957
Atlas Publishing Co. (Emgee)

| | Good | Fine | N-Mint |
|---|---|---|---|
| 1 | 3.50 | 10.50 | 24.00 |

**HEE HAW** (TV)
July, 1970 - No. 7, Aug, 1971
Charlton Press

| | Good | Fine | N-Mint |
|---|---|---|---|
| 1 | .85 | 2.60 | 6.00 |
| 2-7 | .70 | 2.00 | 4.00 |

**HEIDI** (See Dell Jr. Treasury No. 6)

**HELEN OF TROY** (See 4-Color No. 684)

**HELLBLAZER** (John Constantine) (See Saga of Swamp Thing #37)
Jan, 1988 - Present ($1.25-1.50, Adults)
DC Comics

| | Good | Fine | N-Mint |
|---|---|---|---|
| 1 | 1.35 | 4.00 | 8.00 |
| 2-5 | .85 | 2.50 | 5.00 |
| 6-10 | .60 | 1.75 | 3.50 |
| 11-20 | .40 | 1.25 | 2.50 |
| 21-30 | .35 | 1.00 | 2.00 |
| 31-42 | .25 | .75 | 1.50 |
| Annual 1 ('89, $2.95, 68 pgs.) | .70 | 2.00 | 4.00 |

**HELLO, I'M JOHNNY CASH**
1976 (39-49 cents)
Spire Christian Comics (Fleming H. Revell Co.)

| | Good | Fine | N-Mint |
|---|---|---|---|
| nn | | .40 | .80 |

**HELL ON EARTH** (See DC Science Fiction Graphic Novel)

**HELLO PAL COMICS** (Short Story Comics)
Jan, 1943 - No. 3, May, 1943 (Photo-c)
Harvey Publications

| | Good | Fine | N-Mint |
|---|---|---|---|
| 1-Rocketman & Rocketgirl begin; Yankee Doodle Jones app.; Mickey Rooney photo-c | 32.00 | 95.00 | 225.00 |
| 2-Charlie McCarthy photo-c | 22.00 | 65.00 | 150.00 |
| 3-Bob Hope photo-c | 23.00 | 70.00 | 160.00 |

**HELLRAISER** (See Clive Barker's . . .)

**HELL-RIDER** (Magazine)
Aug, 1971 - No. 2, Oct, 1971 (B&W)
Skywald Publications

| | Good | Fine | N-Mint |
|---|---|---|---|
| 1,2: 1-Origin & 1st app.; Butterfly & Wildbunch begins | .85 | 2.50 | 5.00 |

NOTE: *#3 advertised in Psycho #5 but did not come out.* ***Buckler*** *a-1, 2.* ***Morrow*** *c-3.*

**HE-MAN** (See Masters Of The Universe)

**HE-MAN** (Also see Tops In Adventure)
Fall, 1952
Ziff-Davis Publ. Co. (Approved Comics)

| | Good | Fine | N-Mint |
|---|---|---|---|
| 1-Kinstler-c; Powell-a | 6.00 | 18.00 | 42.00 |

**HE-MAN**
May, 1954 - No. 2, July, 1954 (Painted-c)
Toby Press

| | Good | Fine | N-Mint |
|---|---|---|---|
| 1 | 6.00 | 18.00 | 42.00 |
| 2 | 4.50 | 14.00 | 32.00 |

**HENNESSEY** (See 4-Color No. 1200, 1280)

**HENRY**
1935 (52 pages) (Daily B&W strip reprints)
David McKay Publications

| | Good | Fine | N-Mint |
|---|---|---|---|
| 1-By Carl Anderson | 8.00 | 24.00 | 56.00 |

**HENRY** (See King Comics & Magic Comics)
No. 122, Oct, 1946 - No. 65, Apr-June, 1961
Dell Publishing Co.

| | Good | Fine | N-Mint |
|---|---|---|---|
| 4-Color 122 | 6.50 | 19.00 | 45.00 |
| 4-Color 155 (7/47) | 4.50 | 14.00 | 32.00 |
| 1 (1-3/48) | 5.70 | 17.00 | 40.00 |
| 2 | 2.30 | 7.00 | 16.00 |
| 3-10 | 1.70 | 5.00 | 12.00 |
| 11-20: 20-Infinity-c | 1.30 | 4.00 | 9.00 |
| 21-30 | 1.00 | 3.00 | 7.00 |
| 31-40 | .85 | 2.50 | 5.00 |
| 41-65 | .70 | 2.00 | 4.00 |

**HENRY** (See Giant Comic Album and March of Comics No. 43, 58, 84, 101, 112, 129, 147, 162, 178, 189)

**HENRY ALDRICH COMICS** (TV)
Aug-Sept, 1950 - No. 22, Sept-Nov, 1954
Dell Publishing Co.

| | Good | Fine | N-Mint |
|---|---|---|---|
| 1-Part series written by John Stanley; Bill Williams-a | 5.00 | 15.00 | 35.00 |
| 2 | 2.65 | 8.00 | 18.00 |
| 3-5 | 2.30 | 7.00 | 16.00 |
| 6-10 | 2.00 | 6.00 | 14.00 |
| 11-22 | 1.50 | 4.50 | 10.00 |
| Giveaway (16p, soft-c, 1951)-Capehart radio | 2.30 | 7.00 | 16.00 |

**HENRY BREWSTER**
Feb, 1966 - V2#7, Sept, 1967 (All Giants)
Country Wide (M.F. Ent.)

| | Good | Fine | N-Mint |
|---|---|---|---|
| 1 | .70 | 2.00 | 4.00 |
| 2-6(12/66)-Powell-a in most | .50 | 1.50 | 3.00 |
| V2#7 | .35 | 1.00 | 2.00 |

**HERBIE** (See Forbidden Worlds & Unknown Worlds)
April-May, 1964 - No. 23, Feb, 1967 (All 12 cents)
American Comics Group

| | Good | Fine | N-Mint |
|---|---|---|---|
| 1-Whitney-c/a in most issues | 10.00 | 30.00 | 70.00 |
| 2-4 | 5.00 | 15.00 | 35.00 |
| 5-Beatles, Dean Martin, F. Sinatra app. | 6.00 | 18.00 | 42.00 |
| 6,7,9,10 | 3.50 | 10.50 | 24.00 |
| 8-Origin The Fat Fury | 5.00 | 15.00 | 35.00 |
| 11-23: 14-Nemesis & Magicman app. 17-R-2nd Herbie/Forbidden Worlds #94. 23-R-1st Herbie/F.W. #73 | 2.65 | 8.00 | 18.00 |

**HERBIE GOES TO MONTE CARLO, HERBIE RIDES AGAIN** (See Walt Disney Showcase No. 24, 41)

**HERCULES** (See Hit Comics #1-21, Journey Into Mystery Annual, Marvel Graphic Novel #37, Marvel Premiere #26 & The Mighty. . .)

**HERCULES**
Oct, 1967 - No. 13, Sept, 1969; Dec, 1968
Charlton Comics

| | Good | Fine | N-Mint |
|---|---|---|---|
| 1-Thane of Bagarth series begins; Glanzman, Aparo-a | .85 | 2.60 | 6.00 |
| 2-13: 3-5,7,9,10-Aparo-a | .70 | 2.00 | 4.00 |
| 8-(Low distribution)(12/68, 35 cents, B&W); magazine format; new Hercules story plus-r story/#1; Thane-r/#1-3 | 2.50 | 7.50 | 17.50 |
| Modern Comics reprint 10('77), 11('78) | | .20 | .40 |

**HERCULES** (Prince of Power) (Also see The Champions)
Sept, 1982 - No. 4, Dec, 1982; Mar, 1984 - No. 4, June, 1984
Marvel Comics Group

| | Good | Fine | N-Mint |
|---|---|---|---|
| 1-4 | .25 | .75 | 1.50 |
| V2#1-4 (Mini-series) | | .50 | 1.00 |

NOTE: ***Layton*** *a-1, 2, 3p, 4p, V2#1-4; c-1-4, V2#1-4.*

**HERCULES UNBOUND**
Oct-Nov, 1975 - No. 12, Aug-Sept, 1977
National Periodical Publications

| | Good | Fine | N-Mint |
|---|---|---|---|
| 1-Wood inks begin | | .40 | .80 |
| 2-12: 10-Atomic Knights x-over | | .30 | .60 |

NOTE: ***Buckler*** *c-7p.* ***Layton*** *inks-No. 9, 10.* ***Simonson*** *a-7-10p, 11, 12; c- 8p, 9-12.* ***Wood*** *inks-1-8; c-7i, 8i.*

**HERCULES UNCHAINED** (See 4-Color No. 1006, 1121)

**HERE COMES SANTA** (See March of Comics No. 30, 213, 340)

**HERE IS SANTA CLAUS**
1930s (16 pgs., 8 in color) (stiff paper covers)
Goldsmith Publishing Co. (Kann's in Washington, D.C.)

| | Good | Fine | N-Mint |
|---|---|---|---|
| nn | 4.00 | 12.00 | 28.00 |

**HERE'S HOW AMERICA'S CARTOONISTS HELP TO SELL U.S. SAVINGS BONDS**
1950? (16 pgs.; paper cover)
Harvey Comics giveaway

| | Good | Fine | N-Mint |
|---|---|---|---|
| Contains: Joe Palooka, Donald Duck, Archie, Kerry Drake, Red Ryder, Blondie & Steve Canyon | 8.50 | 25.50 | 60.00 |

**HERE'S HOWIE COMICS**
Jan-Feb, 1952 - No. 18, Nov-Dec, 1954
National Periodical Publications

| | Good | Fine | N-Mint |
|---|---|---|---|
| 1 | 12.00 | 36.00 | 85.00 |
| 2 | 6.00 | 18.00 | 42.00 |
| 3-5 | 4.50 | 14.00 | 32.00 |
| 6-10 | 3.50 | 10.50 | 24.00 |
| 11-18 | 2.65 | 8.00 | 18.00 |

**HERMAN & KATNIP** (See Harvey Hits #14,25,31,41 & Paramount Animated Comics #1)

**HERO** (Warrior of the Mystic Realms)
May, 1990 - No. 6, Oct, 1990 ($1.50, limited series)
Marvel Comics

| | Good | Fine | N-Mint |
|---|---|---|---|
| 1-6 | .25 | .75 | 1.50 |

**HERO ALLIANCE, THE**
Dec, 1985 - No. 2, Sept, 1986 (No. 2, $1.50)
Sirius Comics

| | Good | Fine | N-Mint |
|---|---|---|---|
| 1,2 | .25 | .75 | 1.50 |
| The Special Edition 1 (7/86)-Full color | .25 | .75 | 1.50 |

**HERO ALLIANCE**
May, 1987 ($1.95, color)
Wonder Color Comics

| | Good | Fine | N-Mint |
|---|---|---|---|
| 1 | .35 | 1.00 | 2.00 |

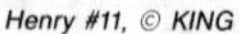
*Henry #11, © KING*

*Herbie #11, © ACG*

*Here's Howie #6, © DC*

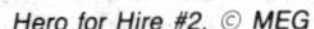
*Hero for Hire #2, © MEG*

*Heroic Comics #2, © EAS*

*Hex #13, © DC*

**HERO ALLIANCE**
Sept, 1989 - Present ($1.95, color, 28 pgs.)
Innovation Publishing

| | Good | Fine | N-Mint |
|---|---|---|---|
| V2#1-14: 1,2-Ron Lim-a | .35 | 1.00 | 2.00 |
| Annual 1 (1990, $2.75, 36 pgs.)-Paul Smith-c/a | .45 | 1.40 | 2.80 |

**HERO ALLIANCE: END OF THE GOLDEN AGE**
July, 1989 - No. 3, Aug, 1989 ($1.75, bi-weekly mini-series, color)
Innovation Publishing

| | Good | Fine | N-Mint |
|---|---|---|---|
| 1-3: By Bart Sears & Ron Lim-r & new-a | .30 | .90 | 1.80 |

**HEROES AGAINST HUNGER**
1986 (One shot) ($1.50) (For famine relief)
DC Comics

| | Good | Fine | N-Mint |
|---|---|---|---|
| 1-Superman, Batman app.; Neal Adams-c(p); includes many artists work; J. Jones assist(2pg.) on B. Smith-a | .25 | .75 | 1.50 |

**HEROES ALL CATHOLIC ACTION ILLUSTRATED**
1943 - V6#5, March 10, 1948 (paper covers)
Heroes All Co.

| | Good | Fine | N-Mint |
|---|---|---|---|
| V1#1,2-(16 pgs., 8x11") | 5.00 | 15.00 | 35.00 |
| V2#1(1/44)-3(3/44)-(16 pgs., 8x11") | 3.00 | 9.00 | 21.00 |
| V3#1(1/45)-10(10/45)-(16 pgs., 8x11") | 2.30 | 7.00 | 16.00 |
| V4#1-35 (12/20/46)-(16 pgs.) | 1.70 | 5.00 | 12.00 |
| V5#1(1/10/47)-8(2/28/47)-(16 pgs.) | 1.50 | 4.50 | 10.00 |
| V5#9(3/7/47)-20(11/25/47)-(32 pgs.) | 1.50 | 4.50 | 10.00 |
| V6#1(1/10/48)-5(3/10/48)-(32 pgs.) | 1.50 | 4.50 | 10.00 |

**HEROES FOR HOPE STARRING THE X-MEN**
Dec, 1985 ($1.50, One Shot, 52 pgs.)
Marvel Comics Group

| | Good | Fine | N-Mint |
|---|---|---|---|
| 1-Proceeds donated to famine relief; Stephen King scripts; Byrne, Miller, Corben-a; Wrightson/J. Jones-a(3pgs.); Art Adams-c | .60 | 1.75 | 3.50 |

**HEROES, INC. PRESENTS CANNON**
1969 - No. 2, 1976 (Sold at Army PX's)
Wally Wood/CPL/Gang Publ. No. 2

| | Good | Fine | N-Mint |
|---|---|---|---|
| nn-Ditko, Wood-a; Wood-c, Reese-a(i) | 1.35 | 4.00 | 8.00 |
| 2-Wood-c; Ditko, Byrne, Wood-a; 8½x10½"; B&W; $2.00 | .70 | 2.00 | 4.00 |

NOTE: *First issue not distributed by publisher; 1,800 copies were stored and 900 copies were stolen from warehouse. Many copies have surfaced in recent years.*

**HEROES OF THE WILD FRONTIER** (Formerly Baffling Mysteries)
No. 27, 1/56 - No. 2, 4/56
Ace Periodicals

| | Good | Fine | N-Mint |
|---|---|---|---|
| 27(No.1),2 | 1.70 | 5.00 | 12.00 |

**HERO FOR HIRE** (Power Man No. 17 on)
June, 1972 - No. 16, Dec, 1973
Marvel Comics Group

| | Good | Fine | N-Mint |
|---|---|---|---|
| 1-Origin Luke Cage retold; Tuska-a(p) | 1.50 | 4.50 | 10.00 |
| 2-10: 2,3-Tuska-a(p). 3-1st app. Mace. 4-1st app. Phil Fox of the Bugle | .70 | 2.00 | 4.00 |
| 11-16: 14-Origin retold. 15-Everett Subby-r('53). 16-Origin Stilletto; death of Rackham | .50 | 1.50 | 3.00 |

**HERO HOTLINE** (1st app. in Action Comics Weekly #637)
April, 1989 - No. 6, Sept, 1989 ($1.75, mini-series)
DC Comics

| | Good | Fine | N-Mint |
|---|---|---|---|
| 1-6: Super-hero humor; Schaffenberger-i | .30 | .90 | 1.80 |

**HEROIC ADVENTURES** (See Adventures)

**HEROIC COMICS** (Reg'lar Fellers. . .#1-15; New Heroic #41 on)
Aug, 1940 - No. 97, June, 1955
Eastern Color Printing Co./Famous Funnies(Funnies, Inc. No. 1)

| | Good | Fine | N-Mint |
|---|---|---|---|
| 1-Hydroman(origin) by Bill Everett, The Purple Zombie(origin) & Mann of India by Tarpe Mills begins | 57.00 | 171.00 | 400.00 |
| 2 | 29.00 | 85.00 | 200.00 |
| 3,4 | 25.00 | 75.00 | 175.00 |
| 5,6 | 18.00 | 54.00 | 125.00 |
| 7-Origin Man O'Metal, 1 pg. | 22.00 | 65.00 | 150.00 |
| 8-10: 10-Lingerie panels | 12.00 | 36.00 | 85.00 |
| 11,13: 13-Crandall/Fine-a | 11.00 | 32.00 | 75.00 |
| 12-Music Master(origin) begins by Everett, ends No. 31; last Purple Zombie & Mann of India | 12.00 | 36.00 | 85.00 |
| 14,15-Hydroman x-over in Rainbow Boy. 14-Origin Rainbow Boy. 15-1st app. Downbeat | 12.00 | 36.00 | 85.00 |
| 16-20: 17-Rainbow Boy x-over in Hydroman. 19-Rainbow Boy x-over in Hydroman & vice versa | 8.50 | 25.50 | 60.00 |
| 21-30:25-Rainbow Boy x-over in Hydroman. 28-Last Man O'Metal. 29-Last Hydroman | 5.70 | 17.00 | 40.00 |
| 31,34,38 | 1.70 | 5.00 | 12.00 |
| 32,36,37-Toth-a, 3-4 pgs. | 3.15 | 9.50 | 22.00 |
| 33,35-Toth-a, 8 & 9 pgs. | 3.50 | 10.50 | 24.00 |
| 39-42-Toth, Ingels-a | 3.50 | 10.50 | 24.00 |
| 43,46,47,49-Toth-a, 2-4 pgs. 47-Ingels-a | 2.30 | 7.00 | 16.00 |
| 44,45,50-Toth-a, 6-9 pgs. | 2.85 | 8.50 | 20.00 |
| 48,53,54 | 1.30 | 4.00 | 9.00 |
| 51-Williamson-a | 3.50 | 10.50 | 24.00 |
| 52-Williamson-a (3 pg. story) | 2.00 | 6.00 | 14.00 |
| 55-Toth-c/a | 2.65 | 8.00 | 18.00 |
| 56-60-Toth-c. 60-Everett-a | 2.30 | 7.00 | 16.00 |
| 61-Everett-a | 1.50 | 4.50 | 10.00 |
| 62,64-Everett-c/a | 1.70 | 5.00 | 12.00 |
| 63-Everett-c | 1.15 | 3.50 | 8.00 |
| 65-Williamson/Frazetta-a; Evans-a, 2 pgs. | 5.00 | 15.00 | 35.00 |
| 66,75,94-Frazetta-a, 2 pgs. each | 2.00 | 6.00 | 14.00 |
| 67,73-Frazetta-a, 4 pgs. each | 2.85 | 8.50 | 20.00 |
| 68,74,76-80,84,85,88-93,95-97 | 1.00 | 3.00 | 7.00 |
| 69,72-Frazetta-a (6 & 8 pgs. each) | 5.00 | 15.00 | 35.00 |
| 70,71,86,87-Frazetta, 3-4 pgs. each; 1 pg. ad by Frazetta in #70 | 2.65 | 8.00 | 18.00 |
| 81,82-One pg. Frazetta art | 1.30 | 4.00 | 9.00 |
| 83-Frazetta-a, ½ pg. | 1.30 | 4.00 | 9.00 |

NOTE: ***Evans** a-64, 65. **Everett** a-(Hydroman-c/a-No. 1-9), 44, 60-64; c-1-9, 62-64. **Sid Greene** a-38-43, 46. **Guardineer** a-42(3), 43, 44, 45(2), 49(3), 50, 60, 61(2), 65, 67(2), 70-72. **Ingels** c-41. **Kiefer** a-46, 48; c-19-22, 24, 44, 46, 48, 51-53, 65, 67-69, 71-74, 76, 77, 79, 80, 82, 85, 88, 89. **Mort Lawrence** a-45. **Tarpe Mills** a-2(2), 3(2), 10. **Ed Moore** a-49, 52-54, 56-63, 65-69, 72-74, 76, 77. **H.G. Peter** a-58-74, 76, 77, 87. **Paul Reinman** a-49. **Rico** a-31. Captain Tootsie by **Beck**-31, 32. Painted-c #16 on.*

**HEX** (Replaces Jonah Hex)
Sept, 1985 - No. 18, Feb, 1987 (Story continues from Jonah Hex 92)
DC Comics

| | Good | Fine | N-Mint |
|---|---|---|---|
| 1-Hex in post-atomic war world; origin | .25 | .75 | 1.50 |
| 2-10,14-18: 6-Origin Stiletta | | .50 | 1.00 |
| 11-13: All contain future Batman storyline. 13-Intro The Dogs of War (Origin #15) | .35 | 1.00 | 2.00 |

**HEXBREAKER** (See First Comics Graphic Novel #15)

**HEY THERE, IT'S YOGI BEAR** (See Movie Comics)

**HI-ADVENTURE HEROES** (TV)
May, 1969 - No. 2, Aug, 1969 (Hanna-Barbera)
Gold Key

| | Good | Fine | N-Mint |
|---|---|---|---|
| 1-Three Musketeers, Gulliver, Arabian Knights stories | 1.50 | 4.50 | 10.00 |
| 2-Three Musketeers, Micro-Venture, Arabian Knights | 1.15 | 3.50 | 8.00 |

**HI AND LOIS** (See 4-Color No. 683, 774, 955)

**HI AND LOIS**
Nov, 1969 - No. 11, July, 1971
Charlton Comics

| | Good | Fine | N-Mint |
|---|---|---|---|
| 1 | .85 | 2.60 | 6.00 |

| | Good | Fine | N-Mint |
|---|---|---|---|
| 2-11 | .70 | 2.00 | 4.00 |

**HICKORY** (See All Humor Comics)
Oct, 1949 - No. 6, Aug, 1950
Quality Comics Group

| | Good | Fine | N-Mint |
|---|---|---|---|
| 1-Sahl-c/a in all; Feldstein?-a | 7.00 | 21.00 | 50.00 |
| 2 | 3.50 | 10.50 | 24.00 |
| 3-6 | 2.65 | 8.00 | 18.00 |

**HIDDEN CREW, THE** (See The United States Air Force Presents: . . .)

**HIDE-OUT** (See 4-Color No. 346)

**HIDING PLACE, THE**
1973 (35-49 cents)
Spire Christian Comics/Fleming H. Revell Co.

| | Good | Fine | N-Mint |
|---|---|---|---|
| nn | | .40 | .80 |

**HIGH ADVENTURE**
October, 1957
Red Top(Decker) Comics (Farrell)

| | Good | Fine | N-Mint |
|---|---|---|---|
| 1-Krigstein-r from Explorer Joe (re-issue on cover) | 2.00 | 6.00 | 14.00 |

**HIGH ADVENTURE** (See 4-Color No. 949, 1001)

**HIGH CHAPPARAL** (TV)
August, 1968 (Photo-c)
Gold Key

| | Good | Fine | N-Mint |
|---|---|---|---|
| 1 (10226-808)-Tufts-a | 3.00 | 9.00 | 21.00 |

**HIGH SCHOOL CONFIDENTIAL DIARY** (Confidential Diary #12 on)
June, 1960 - No. 11, March, 1962
Charlton Comics

| | Good | Fine | N-Mint |
|---|---|---|---|
| 1 | 1.30 | 4.00 | 9.00 |
| 2-11 | .70 | 2.00 | 5.00 |

**HI-HO COMICS**
nd (2/46?) - No. 3, 1946
Four Star Publications

| | Good | Fine | N-Mint |
|---|---|---|---|
| 1-Funny Animal; L. B. Cole-c | 8.50 | 25.50 | 60.00 |
| 2,3: 2-L. B. Cole-c | 5.70 | 17.00 | 40.00 |

**HI-JINX** (See Teen-age Animal Funnies)
July-Aug, 1947 - No. 7, July-Aug, 1948
B&I Publ. Co.(American Comics Group)/Creston/LaSalle Publ. Co.

| | Good | Fine | N-Mint |
|---|---|---|---|
| 1-Teen-age, funny animal | 7.00 | 21.00 | 50.00 |
| 2,3 | 4.00 | 12.00 | 28.00 |
| 4-7-Milt Gross | 4.50 | 14.00 | 32.00 |
| 132 Pg. issue, nn, nd ('40s)(LaSalle) | 8.50 | 25.50 | 60.00 |

**HI-LITE COMICS**
Fall, 1945
E. R. Ross Publishing Co.

| | Good | Fine | N-Mint |
|---|---|---|---|
| 1-Miss Shady | 6.50 | 19.00 | 45.00 |

**HILLBILLY COMICS**
Aug, 1955 - No. 4, July, 1956 (Satire)
Charlton Comics

| | Good | Fine | N-Mint |
|---|---|---|---|
| 1 | 3.15 | 9.50 | 22.00 |
| 2-4 | 1.70 | 5.00 | 12.00 |

**HIP-IT-TY HOP** (See March of Comics No. 15)

**HI-SCHOOL ROMANCE** (. . . Romances No. 41 on)
Oct, 1949 - No. 5, June, 1950; No. 6, Dec, 1950 - No. 73, Mar, 1958;
No. 74, Sept, 1958 - No. 75, Nov, 1958
Harvey Publications/True Love(Home Comics)

| | Good | Fine | N-Mint |
|---|---|---|---|
| 1-Photo-c | 4.30 | 13.00 | 30.00 |
| 2 | 2.30 | 7.00 | 16.00 |
| 3-9: 5-Photo-c | 1.70 | 5.00 | 12.00 |
| 10-Rape story | 2.30 | 7.00 | 16.00 |
| 11-20 | 1.30 | 4.00 | 9.00 |
| 21-31 | 1.15 | 3.50 | 8.00 |
| 32-"Unholy passion" story | 1.70 | 5.00 | 12.00 |
| 33-36: 36-Last pre-code (2/55) | 1.00 | 3.00 | 7.00 |
| 37-75 | .85 | 2.60 | 6.00 |

NOTE: ***Powell*** *a-1-3, 5, 8, 12-14, 16, 18, 21-23, 25-27, 30-34, 36, 37, 39, 45-48, 50-52, 57, 58, 60, 64, 65, 67, 69.*

**HI-SCHOOL ROMANCE DATE BOOK**
Nov, 1962 - No. 3, Mar, 1963 (25 cent Giant)
Harvey Publications

| | Good | Fine | N-Mint |
|---|---|---|---|
| 1-Powell, Baker-a | 2.00 | 6.00 | 14.00 |
| 2,3 | 1.00 | 3.00 | 6.00 |

**HIS NAME IS SAVAGE** (Magazine format)
June, 1968 (35 cents, one shot, 52 pgs.)
Adventure House Press

| | Good | Fine | N-Mint |
|---|---|---|---|
| 1-Gil Kane-a | 2.00 | 6.00 | 14.00 |

**HI-SPOT COMICS** (Red Ryder No. 1 & No. 3 on)
No. 2, Nov, 1940
Hawley Publications

| | Good | Fine | N-Mint |
|---|---|---|---|
| 2-David Innes of Pellucidar; art by J. C. Burroughs; written by Edgar R. Burroughs | 64.00 | 193.00 | 450.00 |

**HISTORY OF THE DC UNIVERSE**
Sept, 1986 - No. 2, Nov, 1986 ($2.95)
DC Comics

| | Good | Fine | N-Mint |
|---|---|---|---|
| 1-Perez-c/a | .75 | 2.25 | 4.50 |
| 2 | .70 | 2.00 | 4.00 |
| Limited Edition hardcover | 7.50 | 22.50 | 45.00 |

**HIT COMICS**
July, 1940 - No. 65, July, 1950
Quality Comics Group

| | Good | Fine | N-Mint |
|---|---|---|---|
| 1-Origin Neon, the Unknown & Hercules; intro. The Red Bee; Bob & Swab, Blaze Barton, the Strange Twins, X-5 Super Agent, Casey Jones & Jack & Jill (ends #7) begin | 185.00 | 557.00 | 1300.00 |
| 2-The Old Witch begins, ends #14 | 87.00 | 261.00 | 610.00 |
| 3-Casey Jones ends; transvestism story-'Jack & Jill' | 71.00 | 215.00 | 500.00 |
| 4-Super Agent (ends #17), & Betty Bates (ends #65) begin; X-5 ends | 60.00 | 180.00 | 420.00 |
| 5-Classic cover | 89.00 | 270.00 | 625.00 |
| 6-10: 10-Old Witch by Crandall, 4 pgs.-1st work in comics | 50.00 | 150.00 | 350.00 |
| 11-17: 13-Blaze Barton ends. 17-Last Neon; Crandall Hercules in all | 47.00 | 140.00 | 325.00 |
| 18-Origin Stormy Foster, the Great Defender; The Ghost of Flanders begins; Crandall-c | 50.00 | 150.00 | 350.00 |
| 19,20 | 47.00 | 140.00 | 325.00 |
| 21-24: 21-Last Hercules. 24-Last Red Bee & Strange Twins | 40.00 | 140.00 | 280.00 |
| 25-Origin Kid Eternity and begins by Moldoff | 52.00 | 156.00 | 365.00 |
| 26-Blackhawk x-over in Kid Eternity | 41.00 | 124.00 | 290.00 |
| 27-29 | 24.00 | 72.00 | 165.00 |
| 30,31-"Bill the Magnificent" by Kurtzman, 11 pgs. in each | 20.00 | 60.00 | 140.00 |
| 32-40: 32-Plastic Man x-over. 34-Last Stormy Foster | 10.00 | 30.00 | 70.00 |
| 41-50 | 7.00 | 21.00 | 50.00 |
| 51-60-Last Kid Eternity | 6.00 | 18.00 | 42.00 |
| 61,63-Crandall-c/a; Jeb Rivers begins #61 | 7.00 | 21.00 | 50.00 |
| 62 | 5.30 | 16.00 | 38.00 |
| 64,65-Crandall-a | 6.00 | 18.00 | 42.00 |

NOTE: ***Crandall*** *a-11-17(Hercules), 23, 24(Stormy Foster); c-18-20, 23, 24.* ***Fine*** *c-1-14, 16, 17(most).* ***Ward*** *c-33. Bondage c-7, 64.*

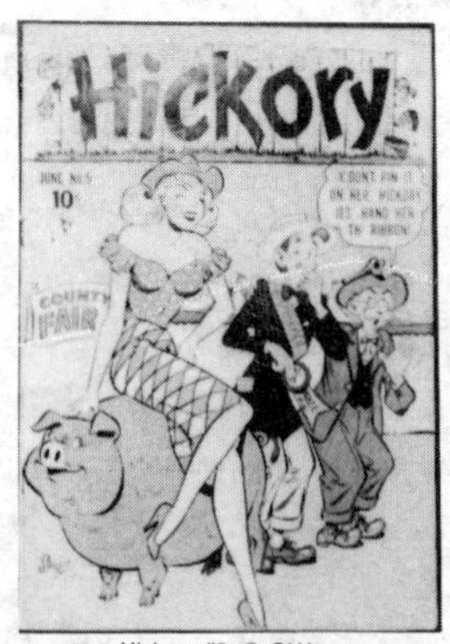

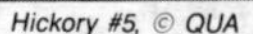
*Hickory #5, © QUA*

*Hi-Lite Comics #1, © E.R. Ross Publ.*

*Hit Comics #20, © QUA*

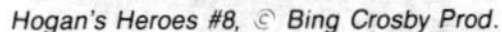

Hogan's Heroes #8, © Bing Crosby Prod.

Hollywood Diary #3, © QUA

Holyoke One-Shot #5, © HOKE

**HI-YO SILVER** (See Lone Ranger's Famous Horse... Also see The Lone Ranger and March of Comics No. 215)

**HOBBIT, THE**
1989 - No. 3, 1990 ($4.95, color, squarebound, 52 pgs.)
Eclipse Comics

| | Good | Fine | N-Mint |
|---|---|---|---|
| Book 1-3: Adapts novel (#1 has a 2nd printing) | .85 | 2.50 | 5.00 |

**HOCUS POCUS** (Formerly Funny Book)
No. 9, Aug-Sept, 1946
Parents' Magazine Press

| | | | |
|---|---|---|---|
| 9 | 2.35 | 7.00 | 16.00 |

**HOGAN'S HEROES** (TV) (No. 1-7 have photo-c)
June, 1966 - No. 8, Sept, 1967; No. 9, Oct, 1969
Dell Publishing Co.

| | | | |
|---|---|---|---|
| 1 | 3.50 | 10.50 | 24.00 |
| 2,3-Ditko-a(p) | 2.30 | 7.00 | 16.00 |
| 4-9: 9-Reprints #1 | 1.60 | 4.80 | 11.00 |

**HOLIDAY COMICS**
1942 (196 pages) (25 cents)
Fawcett Publications

| | | | |
|---|---|---|---|
| 1-Contains three Fawcett comics; Capt. Marvel, Nyoka #1, & Whiz. Not rebound, remaindered comics—printed at the same time as originals | 86.00 | 257.00 | 600.00 |

**HOLIDAY COMICS**
January, 1951 - No. 8, Oct, 1952
Star Publications

| | | | |
|---|---|---|---|
| 1-Funny animal contents (Frisky Fables) in all; L. B. Cole-c | 11.50 | 34.00 | 80.00 |
| 2-Classic L. B. Cole-c | 12.00 | 36.00 | 85.00 |
| 3-8: 5,8-X-Mas-c; all L.B. Cole-c | 8.00 | 24.00 | 56.00 |
| Accepted Reprint 4 (nd)-L.B. Cole-c | 3.70 | 11.00 | 26.00 |

**HOLIDAY DIGEST**
1988 ($1.25, digest-size)
Harvey Comics

| | | | |
|---|---|---|---|
| 1 | | .60 | 1.25 |

**HOLI-DAY SURPRISE** (Formerly Summer Fun)
V2#55, Mar, 1967 (25 cents)
Charlton Comics

| | | | |
|---|---|---|---|
| V2#55-Giant | .50 | 1.50 | 3.00 |

**HOLLYWOOD COMICS**
Winter, 1944 (52 pgs.)
New Age Publishers

| | | | |
|---|---|---|---|
| 1-Funny animals | 8.50 | 25.50 | 60.00 |

**HOLLYWOOD CONFESSIONS**
Oct, 1949 - No. 2, Dec, 1949
St. John Publishing Co.

| | | | |
|---|---|---|---|
| 1-Kubert-c/a (entire book) | 12.00 | 36.00 | 84.00 |
| 2-Kubert-c/a (entire book) (Scarce) | 18.00 | 54.00 | 125.00 |

**HOLLYWOOD DIARY**
Dec, 1949 - No. 5, July-Aug, 1950
Quality Comics Group

| | | | |
|---|---|---|---|
| 1 | 9.00 | 27.00 | 62.00 |
| 2-Photo-c | 5.70 | 17.00 | 40.00 |
| 3-5: 3,5-Photo-c | 4.50 | 14.00 | 32.00 |

**HOLLYWOOD FILM STORIES**
April, 1950 - No. 4, Oct, 1950
Feature Publications/Prize

| | | | |
|---|---|---|---|
| 1-"Fumetti" type movie comic | 9.00 | 27.00 | 62.00 |
| 2-4 | 6.00 | 18.00 | 42.00 |

**HOLLYWOOD FUNNY FOLKS** (Formerly Funny Folks; Nutsy Squirrel #61 on)
No. 27, Aug-Sept, 1950 - No. 60, July-Aug, 1954
National Periodical Publications

| | Good | Fine | N-Mint |
|---|---|---|---|
| 27 | 5.00 | 15.00 | 35.00 |
| 28-40 | 3.00 | 9.00 | 21.00 |
| 41-60 | 2.15 | 6.50 | 15.00 |

NOTE: ***Sheldon Mayer** a-27-35, 37-40, 43-46, 48-51, 53, 56, 57, 60.*

**HOLLYWOOD LOVE DOCTOR** (See Doctor Anthony King...)

**HOLLYWOOD PICTORIAL** (...Romances on cover)
No. 3, January, 1950
St. John Publishing Co.

| | | | |
|---|---|---|---|
| 3-Matt Baker-a; photo-c | 9.00 | 27.00 | 62.00 |

*(Becomes a movie magazine - Hollywood Pictorial Western with No. 4.)*

**HOLLYWOOD ROMANCES** (Formerly Brides In Love; becomes For Lovers Only #60 on)
V2#46, 11/66; #47, 10/67; #48, 11/68; V3#49, 11/69 - V3#59, 6/71
Charlton Comics

| | | | |
|---|---|---|---|
| V2#46-Rolling Stones-c/story | 1.50 | 4.50 | 10.00 |
| V2#47-V3#59: 56-"Born to Heart Break" begins | .50 | 1.50 | 3.00 |

**HOLLYWOOD SECRETS**
Nov, 1949 - No. 6, Sept, 1950
Quality Comics Group

| | | | |
|---|---|---|---|
| 1-Ward-c/a, 9pgs. | 18.00 | 54.00 | 125.00 |
| 2-Crandall-a, Ward-c/a, 9 pgs. | 11.00 | 32.00 | 75.00 |
| 3-6: All photo-c; 5-Lex Barker (Tarzan)-c | 5.00 | 15.00 | 35.00 |
| ...of Romance, I.W. Reprint #9; Kinstler-c; Ward, Crandall-a | .85 | 2.50 | 5.00 |

**HOLLYWOOD SUPERSTARS**
Nov, 1990 - Present ($2.25, color)
Epic Comics (Marvel)

| | | | |
|---|---|---|---|
| 1-($2.95, 52 pgs.)-Spiegle-c/a begins | .50 | 1.50 | 3.00 |
| 2-4 ($2.25) | .40 | 1.15 | 2.30 |

**HOLO-MAN** (See Power Record Comics)

**HOLYOKE ONE-SHOT**
1944 - No. 10, 1945 (All reprints)
Holyoke Publishing Co. (Tem Publ.)

| | | | |
|---|---|---|---|
| 1-Grit Grady (on cover only), Miss Victory, Alias X (origin)-All reprints from Captain Fearless | 6.00 | 18.00 | 42.00 |
| 2-Rusty Dugan (Corporal); Capt. Fearless (origin), Mr. Miracle (origin), app. | 6.00 | 18.00 | 42.00 |
| 3-Miss Victory-Crash #4-r; Cat Man (origin), Solar Legion by Kirby app.; Miss Victory on cover only (1945) | 13.00 | 40.00 | 90.00 |
| 4-Mr. Miracle-The Blue Streak app. | 5.50 | 16.50 | 38.00 |
| 5-U.S. Border Patrol Comics (Sgt. Dick Carter of the...), Miss Victory (story matches cover #3), Citizen Smith, & Mr. Miracle app. | 6.00 | 18.00 | 42.00 |
| 6-Capt. Fearless, Alias X, Capt. Stone (splash used as cover-#10); Diamond Jim & Rusty Dugan (splash from cover-#2) | 5.50 | 16.50 | 38.00 |
| 7-Z-2, Strong Man, Blue Streak (story matches cover-#8)-Reprints from Crash #2 | 6.50 | 19.50 | 45.00 |
| 8-Blue Streak, Strong Man (story matches cover-#7)-Crash reprints | 5.50 | 16.50 | 38.00 |
| 9-Citizen Smith, The Blue Streak, Solar Legion by Kirby & Strongman, the Perfect Human app.; reprints from Crash #4 & 5; Citizen Smith on cover only-from story in #5(1944-before #3) | 8.50 | 25.50 | 60.00 |
| 10-Captain Stone (Crash reprints); Solar Legion by S&K | 8.50 | 25.50 | 60.00 |

**HOMER COBB** (See Adventures of...)

**HOMER HOOPER**
July, 1953 - No. 4, Dec., 1953
Atlas Comics

| | Good | Fine | N-Mint |
|---|---|---|---|
| 1 | 3.50 | 10.50 | 24.00 |
| 2-4 | 2.30 | 7.00 | 16.00 |

**HOMER, THE HAPPY GHOST** (See Adventures of. . .)
3/55 - No. 22, 11/58; V2#1, 11/69 - V2#5, 7/70
Atlas(ACI/PPI/WPI)/Marvel Comics

| | | | |
|---|---|---|---|
| V1#1 | 4.50 | 14.00 | 32.00 |
| 2 | 2.30 | 7.00 | 16.00 |
| 3-10 | 1.70 | 5.00 | 12.00 |
| 11-22 | 1.50 | 4.50 | 10.00 |
| V2#1 - V2#5 (1969-70) | .70 | 2.00 | 5.00 |

**HOME RUN** (See A-1 Comics No. 89)

**HOME, SWEET HOME**
1925 (10¼xk10")
M.S. Publishing Co.

| | | | |
|---|---|---|---|
| nn-By Tuthill | 11.00 | 32.00 | 75.00 |

**HOMICIDE**
April, 1990 ($1.95, B&W)
Dark Horse Comics

| | | | |
|---|---|---|---|
| 1-Detective story | .35 | 1.00 | 2.00 |

**HONEYBEE BIRDWHISTLE AND HER PET PEPI** (Introducing. . .)
1969 (24 pgs.; B&W; slick cover)
Newspaper Enterprise Association (Giveaway)

| | | | |
|---|---|---|---|
| nn-Contains Freckles newspaper strips with a short biography of Henry Fornhals (artist) & Fred Fox (writer) of the strip | 3.50 | 10.50 | 24.00 |

**HONEYMOON** (Formerly Gay Comics)
No. 41, January, 1950
A Lover's Magazine(USA) (Marvel)

| | | | |
|---|---|---|---|
| 41-Photo-c; article by Betty Grable | 3.50 | 10.50 | 24.00 |

**HONEYMOONERS, THE** (TV)
Oct, 1986 ($1.50, color)
Lodestone Publishing

| | | | |
|---|---|---|---|
| 1-Jackie Gleason photo-c | .50 | 1.50 | 3.00 |

**HONEYMOONERS, THE** (TV)
Sept, 1987 - No. 24 ($2.00, color)
Triad Publications

| | | | |
|---|---|---|---|
| 1 | .50 | 1.50 | 3.00 |
| 2,4-8,10-12 | .35 | 1.00 | 2.00 |
| 3 ($3.50, X-Mas Special, squarebound) | .60 | 1.75 | 3.50 |
| 3-Another version w/"Collectors Edition" on-c | .70 | 2.00 | 4.00 |
| 9 ($3.95)-Jack Davis-c | .70 | 2.00 | 3.95 |
| 13-Comic book size | .40 | 1.25 | 2.50 |
| 13-Magazine size | .35 | 1.00 | 2.00 |

**HONEYMOON ROMANCE**
April, 1950 - No. 2, July, 1950 (25 cents) (digest size)
Artful Publications(Canadian)

| | | | |
|---|---|---|---|
| 1,2-(Rare) | 17.00 | 51.00 | 120.00 |

**HONEY WEST** (TV)
September, 1966 (Photo-c)
Gold Key

| | | | |
|---|---|---|---|
| 1 (10186-609) | 7.00 | 21.00 | 50.00 |

**HONG KONG PHOOEY** (Hanna-Barbera)(TV)
June, 1975 - No. 9, Nov, 1976
Charlton Comics

| | | | |
|---|---|---|---|
| 1-9 | | .40 | .80 |

**HOODED HORSEMAN, THE** (Also see Blazing West)
No. 21, 1-2/52 - No. 27, 1-2/53; No. 18, 12-1/54-55 - No. 27, 6-7/56
American Comics Group (Michel Publ.)

| | Good | Fine | N-Mint |
|---|---|---|---|
| 21(1-2/52)-Hooded Horseman, Injun Jones continues | 7.00 | 21.00 | 50.00 |
| 22 | 4.30 | 13.00 | 30.00 |
| 23-25,27(1-2/53) | 3.50 | 10.50 | 24.00 |
| 26-Origin/1st app. Cowboy Sahib by L. Starr | 4.30 | 13.00 | 30.00 |
| 18(11-12/54)(Formerly Out of the Night) | 3.50 | 10.50 | 24.00 |
| 19-Last precode (1-2/55) | 7.00 | 21.00 | 50.00 |
| 20-Origin Johnny Injun | 3.50 | 10.50 | 24.00 |
| 21-24,26,27(6-7/56) | 3.00 | 9.00 | 21.00 |
| 25-Cowboy Sahib on cover only; Hooded Horseman i.d. revealed | 3.50 | 10.50 | 24.00 |

NOTE: ***Whitney** c/a-21('52), 20-22.*

**HOODED MENACE, THE** (Also see Daring Adventures)
1951 (One Shot)
Realistic/Avon Periodicals

| | | | |
|---|---|---|---|
| nn-Based on a band of hooded outlaws in the Pacific Northwest, 1900-1906; r-/in Daring Advs. #15 | 32.00 | 95.00 | 225.00 |

**HOODS UP**
1953 (16 pgs.; 15 cents) (Eisner c/a in all)
Fram Corp. (Dist. to service station owners)

| | | | |
|---|---|---|---|
| 1-(Very Rare; only 2 known) | 36.00 | 107.00 | 250.00 |
| 2-6-(Very Rare; only 1 known of 3-4, 2 known of #2) | 36.00 | 107.00 | 250.00 |

NOTE: *Convertible Connie gives tips for service stations, selling Fram oil filters.*

**HOOT GIBSON'S WESTERN ROUNDUP** (See Western Roundup under Fox Giants)

**HOOT GIBSON WESTERN** (Formerly My Love Story)
No. 5, May, 1950 - No. 3, Sept, 1950
Fox Features Syndicate

| | | | |
|---|---|---|---|
| 5,6(#1,2): 5-Photo-c | 11.50 | 34.00 | 80.00 |
| 3-Wood-a | 14.00 | 43.00 | 100.00 |

**HOPALONG CASSIDY** (Also see Bill Boyd Western, Master Comics, Real Western Hero, Six Gun Heroes & Western Hero; Bill Boyd starred as H. Cassidy in the movies; H. Cassidy in movies, radio & TV)
Feb, 1943; No. 2, Summer, 1946 - No. 85, Jan, 1954
Fawcett Publications

| | | | |
|---|---|---|---|
| 1 (1943, 68pgs.)-H. Cassidy & his horse Topper begin (On sale 1/8/43)-Captain Marvel on-c | 133.00 | 335.00 | 800.00 |
| 2-(Sum, '46) | 43.00 | 130.00 | 300.00 |
| 3,4: 3-(Fall, '46, 52pgs. begin) | 22.00 | 65.00 | 150.00 |
| 5-"Mad Barber" story mentioned in **SOTI**, pgs. 308,309 | 20.00 | 60.00 | 140.00 |
| 6-10 | 16.00 | 48.00 | 110.00 |
| 11-19: 11,13-19-Photo-c | 11.50 | 34.00 | 80.00 |
| 20-29 (52pgs.)-Painted/photo-c | 8.50 | 25.50 | 60.00 |
| 30,31,33,34,37-39,41 (52pgs.)-Painted-c | 5.50 | 16.50 | 38.00 |
| 32,40 (36pgs.)-Painted-c | 4.50 | 14.00 | 32.00 |
| 35,42,43,45 (52pgs.)-Photo-c | 5.50 | 16.50 | 38.00 |
| 36,44,48 (36pgs.)-Photo-c | 4.50 | 14.00 | 32.00 |
| 46,47,49-51,53,54,56 (52pgs.)-Photo-c | 5.00 | 15.00 | 35.00 |
| 52,55,57-70 (36pgs.)-Photo-c | 3.70 | 11.00 | 26.00 |
| 71-84-Photo-c | 2.85 | 8.50 | 20.00 |
| 85-Last Fawcett issue; photo-c | 3.50 | 10.50 | 24.00 |

NOTE: *Line-drawn c-1-10, 12.*

| | | | |
|---|---|---|---|
| Grape Nuts Flakes giveaway (1950,9x6") | 7.00 | 21.00 | 50.00 |
| . . .& the Mad Barber (1951 Bond Bread giveaway)-7x5"; used in **SOTI**, pgs. 308,309 | 17.00 | 51.00 | 120.00 |
| . . .Meets the Brend Brothers Bandits (1951 Bond Bread giveaway, color, paper-c, 16pgs. 3½x7")-Fawcett Publ. | 6.00 | 18.00 | 42.00 |
| White Tower Giveaway (1946, 16pgs., paper-c) | 6.00 | 18.00 | 42.00 |

*The Hooded Menace nn, © AVON*

*Hoot Gibson Western #5, © FOX*

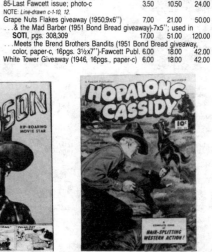

*Hopalong Cassidy #25, © FAW*

Horrific #10, © Comic Media

The Horrors #11, © STAR

Hot Rods and Racing Cars #35, © CC

**HOPALONG CASSIDY** (TV)
No. 86, Feb, 1954 - No. 135, May-June, 1959 (All-36pgs.)
National Periodical Publications

| | Good | Fine | N-Mint |
|---|---|---|---|
| 86-Photo covers continue | 14.00 | 43.00 | 100.00 |
| 87 | 8.50 | 25.50 | 60.00 |
| 88-90 | 5.70 | 17.00 | 40.00 |
| 91-99 (98 has #93 on-c & is last precode issue, 2/55) | 4.50 | 14.00 | 32.00 |
| 100 | 6.00 | 18.00 | 42.00 |
| 101-108-Last photo-c | 4.00 | 12.00 | 28.00 |
| 109-135: 124-Painted-c | 4.00 | 12.00 | 28.00 |

NOTE: ***Gil Kane** art-1956 up. **Kubert** a-123.*

**HOPE SHIP**
June-Aug, 1963
Dell Publishing Co.

| | Good | Fine | N-Mint |
|---|---|---|---|
| 1 | 1.35 | 4.00 | 8.00 |

**HOPPY THE MARVEL BUNNY** (See Fawcett's Funny Animals)
Dec, 1945 - No. 15, Sept, 1947
Fawcett Publications

| | Good | Fine | N-Mint |
|---|---|---|---|
| 1 | 14.00 | 43.00 | 100.00 |
| 2 | 7.00 | 21.00 | 50.00 |
| 3-15: 7-Xmas-c | 5.00 | 15.00 | 35.00 |
| . . . Well Known Comics (1944,8½x10½",paper-c) Bestmaid/Samuel Lowe (Printed in red or blue) | 6.75 | 20.00 | 40.00 |

**HORACE & DOTTY DRIPPLE** (Dotty Dripple No. 1-24)
No. 25, Aug, 1952 - No. 43, Oct, 1955
Harvey Publications

| | Good | Fine | N-Mint |
|---|---|---|---|
| 25-43 | .70 | 2.00 | 5.00 |

**HORIZONTAL LIEUTENANT, THE** (See Movie Classics)

**HOROBI**
1990 - No. 8, 1990 ($3.75, B&W, mature readers, 84 pgs.)
V2#1, 1990 - No. 7, 1991 ($4.25, B&W, 68 pgs.)
Viz Premiere Comics

| | Good | Fine | N-Mint |
|---|---|---|---|
| 1-8: Japanese manga | .65 | 1.90 | 3.80 |
| Part Two, #1-7 | .70 | 2.15 | 4.30 |

**HORRIFIC** (Terrific No. 14 on)
Sept, 1952 - No. 13, Sept, 1954
Artful/Comic Media/Harwell/Mystery

| | Good | Fine | N-Mint |
|---|---|---|---|
| 1 | 11.50 | 34.00 | 80.00 |
| 2 | 5.70 | 17.00 | 40.00 |
| 3-Bullet in head-c | 8.50 | 25.50 | 60.00 |
| 4,5,7,9,10 | 4.00 | 12.00 | 28.00 |
| 6-Jack The Ripper story | 4.50 | 14.00 | 32.00 |
| 8-Origin & 1st app. The Teller(E.C. parody) | 5.70 | 17.00 | 40.00 |
| 11-13: 11-Swipe/Witches Tales #6,27 | 3.15 | 9.50 | 22.00 |

NOTE: ***Don Heck** a-8; c-3-13. **Hollingsworth** a-4. **Morisi** a-8. **Palais** a-5, 8, 11.*

**HORROR FROM THE TOMB** (Mysterious Stories No. 2 on)
Sept, 1954
Premier Magazine Co.

| | Good | Fine | N-Mint |
|---|---|---|---|
| 1-Woodbridge/Torres, Check-a | 11.50 | 34.00 | 80.00 |

**HORRORS, THE**
No. 11, Jan, 1953 - No. 15, Apr, 1954
Star Publications

| | Good | Fine | N-Mint |
|---|---|---|---|
| 11-Horrors of War; Disbrow-a(2) | 7.00 | 21.00 | 50.00 |
| 12-Horrors of War; color illo in **POP** | 6.50 | 19.00 | 45.00 |
| 13-Horrors of Mystery; crime stories | 6.50 | 19.00 | 45.00 |
| 14,15-Horrors of the Underworld | 6.50 | 19.00 | 45.00 |

NOTE: *All have **L. B. Cole** covers; a-12. **Hollingsworth** a-13. **Palais** a-13r.*

**HORROR TALES** (Magazine)
V1#7, 6/69 - V6#6, 12/74; V7#1, 2/75; V7#2, 5/76 - V8#5, 1977; V9#3, 8/78; (V1-V6: 52 pgs.; V7, V8#2: 112 pgs.; V8#4 on: 68 pgs.) (No V5#3, V8#1,3)
Eerie Publications

| | Good | Fine | N-Mint |
|---|---|---|---|
| V1#7 | .85 | 2.60 | 6.00 |
| V1#8,9 | .70 | 2.00 | 4.00 |
| V2#1-6('70), V3#1-6('71) | .50 | 1.50 | 3.00 |
| V4#1-3,5-7('72) | .50 | 1.50 | 3.00 |
| V4#4-LSD story reprint/Weird V3#5 | .85 | 2.60 | 6.00 |
| V5#1,2,4,5(6/73),5(10/73),6(12/73) | .50 | 1.50 | 3.00 |
| V6#1-6('74),V7#1,2,4('76) | .50 | 1.50 | 3.00 |
| V7#3('76)-Giant issue | .50 | 1.50 | 3.00 |
| V8#2,4,5('77),V9#3(8/78, $1.50) | .50 | 1.50 | 3.00 |

NOTE: *Bondage-c-V6#1, 3, V7#2.*

**HORSE FEATHERS COMICS**
Nov, 1945 - No. 4, July, 1948 (52 pgs.)
Lev Gleason Publications

| | Good | Fine | N-Mint |
|---|---|---|---|
| 1-Wolverton's Scoop Scuttle, 2 pgs. | 10.00 | 30.00 | 70.00 |
| 2 | 4.00 | 12.00 | 28.00 |
| 3,4: 3-(5/48) | 3.00 | 9.00 | 21.00 |

**HORSEMASTERS, THE** (See 4-Color No. 1260)

**HORSE SOLDIERS, THE** (See 4-Color No. 1048)

**HORSE WITHOUT A HEAD, THE** (See Movie Comics)

**HOT DOG** (Also see Jughead's Pal . . .)
June-July, 1954 - No. 4, Dec-Jan, 1954-55
Magazine Enterprises

| | Good | Fine | N-Mint |
|---|---|---|---|
| 1(A-1 #107) | 3.00 | 9.00 | 21.00 |
| 2,3(A-1 #115),4(A-1 #136) | 1.70 | 5.00 | 12.00 |

**HOTEL DEPAREE - SUNDANCE** (See 4-Color No. 1126)

**HOT ROD AND SPEEDWAY COMICS**
Feb-Mar, 1952 - No. 5, Apr-May, 1953
Hillman Periodicals

| | Good | Fine | N-Mint |
|---|---|---|---|
| 1 | 8.00 | 24.00 | 56.00 |
| 2-Krigstein-a | 5.70 | 17.00 | 40.00 |
| 3-5 | 2.30 | 7.00 | 16.00 |

**HOT ROD COMICS** (See XMas Comics)
Nov, 1951 (no month given) - V2#7, Feb, 1953
Fawcett Publications

| | Good | Fine | N-Mint |
|---|---|---|---|
| nn (V1#1)-Powell-c/a in all | 11.00 | 32.00 | 75.00 |
| 2 (4/52) | 5.70 | 17.00 | 40.00 |
| 3-6, V2#7 | 3.50 | 10.50 | 24.00 |

**HOT ROD KING**
Fall, 1952
Ziff-Davis Publ. Co.

| | Good | Fine | N-Mint |
|---|---|---|---|
| 1-Giacoia-a; painted-c | 9.30 | 28.00 | 65.00 |

**HOT ROD RACERS** (Grand Prix No. 16 on)
Dec, 1964 - No. 15, July, 1967
Charlton Comics

| | Good | Fine | N-Mint |
|---|---|---|---|
| 1 | 1.50 | 4.50 | 10.00 |
| 2-5 | .85 | 2.60 | 6.00 |
| 6-15 | .70 | 2.00 | 4.00 |

**HOT RODS AND RACING CARS**
Nov, 1951 - No. 120, June, 1973
Charlton Comics (Motor Mag. No. 1)

| | Good | Fine | N-Mint |
|---|---|---|---|
| 1 | 7.00 | 21.00 | 50.00 |
| 2 | 3.50 | 10.50 | 24.00 |
| 3-10 | 2.30 | 7.00 | 16.00 |
| 11-20 | 1.50 | 4.50 | 10.00 |
| 21-34,36-40 | 1.00 | 3.00 | 7.00 |
| 35 (68 pgs., 6/58) | 1.50 | 4.50 | 10.00 |
| 41-60 | .70 | 2.00 | 5.00 |
| 61-80 | .50 | 1.50 | 3.00 |

| | Good | Fine | N-Mint |
|---|---|---|---|
| 81-100 | .35 | 1.00 | 2.00 |
| 101-120 | .25 | .75 | 1.50 |

**HOT SHOT CHARLIE**
1947 (Lee Elias)
Hillman Periodicals

| | Good | Fine | N-Mint |
|---|---|---|---|
| 1 | 3.15 | 9.50 | 22.00 |

**HOTSPUR**
June, 1987 - No. 3, Oct, 1987 ($1.75, color, Baxter paper)
Eclipse Comics

| | Good | Fine | N-Mint |
|---|---|---|---|
| 1-3 | .30 | .90 | 1.80 |

**HOT STUFF CREEPY CAVES**
Nov, 1974 - No. 7, Nov, 1975
Harvey Publications

| | Good | Fine | N-Mint |
|---|---|---|---|
| 1 | .55 | 1.60 | 3.20 |
| 2-5 | .25 | .80 | 1.60 |
| 6,7 | | .40 | .80 |

**HOT STUFF SIZZLERS**
July, 1960 - No. 59, March, 1974
Harvey Publications

| | Good | Fine | N-Mint |
|---|---|---|---|
| 1: 68 pgs. begin | 5.00 | 15.00 | 35.00 |
| 2-5 | 1.70 | 5.00 | 12.00 |
| 6-10 | 1.15 | 3.50 | 8.00 |
| 11-20 | .85 | 2.50 | 5.00 |
| 21-45: Last 68 pgs. | .50 | 1.50 | 3.00 |
| 46-52: All 52 pgs. | .40 | 1.20 | 2.40 |
| 53-59 | .35 | 1.00 | 2.00 |

**HOT STUFF, THE LITTLE DEVIL** (Also see Devil Kids & Harvey Hits)
10/57 - No. 141, 7/77; No. 142, 2/78 - No. 164, 8/82; No. 165, 10/86 - No. 171, 11/87; No. 172, 11/88; No. 173, Sept, 1990 - No. 177, 1/91
Harvey Publications (Illustrated Humor)

| | Good | Fine | N-Mint |
|---|---|---|---|
| 1 | 14.00 | 43.00 | 100.00 |
| 2-1st app. Stumbo the Giant | 9.00 | 27.00 | 62.00 |
| 3-5 | 6.50 | 19.00 | 45.00 |
| 6-10 | 3.15 | 9.50 | 22.00 |
| 11-20 | 1.70 | 5.00 | 12.00 |
| 21-40 | .85 | 2.60 | 6.00 |
| 41-60 | .55 | 1.60 | 3.20 |
| 61-105 | .25 | .80 | 1.60 |
| 106-112: All 52 pg. Giants | .35 | 1.00 | 2.00 |
| 113-177-Later issues $1.00-c | | .40 | .80 |
| Shoestore Giveaway('63) | .50 | 1.50 | 3.00 |

**HOT WHEELS** (TV)
Mar-Apr, 1970 - No. 6, Jan-Feb, 1971
National Periodical Publications

| | Good | Fine | N-Mint |
|---|---|---|---|
| 1,3: 3-Neal Adams-c | 2.65 | 8.00 | 18.00 |
| 2,4,5 | 1.50 | 4.50 | 10.00 |
| 6-Neal Adams-c/a | 2.85 | 8.50 | 20.00 |

NOTE: ***Toth** a-1p, 2-5; c-1p, 4, 5.*

**HOUSE OF MYSTERY** (See Brave and the Bold #93, Limited Collectors' Edition & Super DC Giant)

**HOUSE OF MYSTERY, THE** (Also see Elvira's . . .)
Dec-Jan, 1951-52 - No. 321, Oct, 1983 (No. 199-203: 52 pgs.)
National Periodical Publications/DC Comics

| | Good | Fine | N-Mint |
|---|---|---|---|
| 1 | 57.00 | 170.00 | 400.00 |
| 2 | 25.00 | 75.00 | 150.00 |
| 3 | 20.00 | 60.00 | 140.00 |
| 4,5 | 18.00 | 54.00 | 125.00 |
| 6-10 | 13.00 | 40.00 | 90.00 |
| 11-15 | 11.50 | 34.00 | 80.00 |
| 16(7/53)-25 | 7.00 | 21.00 | 50.00 |
| 26-35(2/55)-Last pre-code issue; 30-Woodish-a | 5.70 | 17.00 | 40.00 |
| 36-49 | 4.00 | 12.00 | 28.00 |
| 50-Text story of Orson Welles' War of the Worlds broadcast | 3.15 | 9.50 | 22.00 |
| 51-60 | 2.30 | 7.00 | 16.00 |
| 61,63,65,66,70,72,76,84,85-Kirby-a | 2.30 | 7.00 | 16.00 |
| 62,64,67-69,71,73-75,77-83,86-99 | 1.70 | 5.00 | 12.00 |
| 100 | 2.00 | 6.00 | 14.00 |
| 101-116: Last 10 cent issue. 109-Toth, Kubert-a | 1.70 | 5.00 | 12.00 |
| 117-119,121-130 | 1.00 | 3.00 | 7.00 |
| 120-Toth-a | 1.50 | 4.50 | 10.00 |
| 131-142 | 1.00 | 3.00 | 6.00 |
| 143-J'onn J'onzz, Manhunter begins (6/64), ends #173; story continues from Detective #326 | 6.50 | 19.00 | 45.00 |
| 144 | 3.60 | 11.00 | 25.00 |
| 145-155,157-160: 149-Toth-a. 158-Origin/lst app. Diabolu Idol-Head in J'onn J'onzz. 160-Intro Marco Xavier (Martin Manhunter) & Vulture Crime Organization; ends #173 | 2.65 | 8.00 | 18.00 |
| 156-Robby Reed begins (Origin), ends #173 | 2.85 | 8.50 | 20.00 |
| 161-173: 169-Origin/1st app. Gem Girl | 2.00 | 6.00 | 14.00 |
| 174-177,182: 174-Mystery format begins. 182-Toth-a | .70 | 2.00 | 4.00 |
| 178-Neal Adams-a; last 12 cent issue | 1.00 | 3.00 | 6.00 |
| 179-N. Adams/Orlando, Wrightson-a (1st pro work, 3 pgs.) | 1.50 | 4.50 | 10.00 |
| 180,181,183: Wrightson-a (3, 10, & 3 pgs.). 180-Kane-Wood-a(2). 183-Wood-a | .70 | 2.00 | 4.00 |
| 184-Kane/Wood, Toth-a | .50 | 1.50 | 3.00 |
| 185-Williamson/Kaluta-a; 3 pgs. Wood-a | .85 | 2.50 | 5.00 |
| 186-N. Adams-a; Wrightson-a, 10 pgs. | .85 | 2.50 | 5.00 |
| 187,190: 190-Toth-a(r) | .35 | 1.00 | 2.00 |
| 188,191,195-Wrightson-a (8, 3 & 10 pgs.). 195-Swamp creature story by Wrightson similar to Swamp Thing (10/71) | .85 | 2.50 | 5.00 |
| 189-Wood-a | .35 | 1.00 | 2.00 |
| 192-194,196-198,200-203,205-223,225-227: 194-Toth, Kirby-a; 48 pgs. begin, end #198. 207-Wrightson-a. 221-Wrightson/Kaluta-a(8 pgs.). 226-Wrightson-r; Phantom Stranger-r | .35 | 1.00 | 2.00 |
| 199-Wood, Kirby-a; 52pgs. begin, end 203 | .50 | 1.50 | 3.00 |
| 204-Wrightson-a, 9 pgs. | .50 | 1.50 | 3.00 |
| 224-N. Adams/Wrightson-a(r); begin 100 pg. issues; Phantom Stranger-r | .70 | 2.00 | 4.00 |
| 228-N. Adams inks; Wrightson-r | .50 | 1.50 | 3.00 |
| 229-321: 229-Wrightson-a(r); Toth-r; last 100 pg. issue. 230-68 pgs. 251-259, 84 pgs. 251-Wood-a | .35 | 1.00 | 2.00 |

NOTE: ***Neal Adams** a-236i; c-175-192, 197, 199, 251-254. **Aragones** a-186, 251. **Baily** a-279p. **Colan** a-202r. **Craig** a-263, 275, 295, 300. **Ditko** a-236, 247, 254, 258, 276; c-277. **Drucker** a-37. **Evans** c-218. **Giunta** a-199. **Golden** a-257, 259. **Heath** a-194r; c-203. **Howard** a-182, 187, 196, 229r, 247i, 254, 279i. **Kaluta** a-195, 200, 250r; c-200-202, 210, 212, 233, 260, 261, 263, 265, 267, 268, 273, 276, 284, 287, 288, 293-295, 300, 302, 304, 305, 309-319, 321. **Bob Kane** a-84. **Gil Kane** a-196p, 253p, 300p. **Kirby** a-194r, 199r; c-65, 76, 78, 79, 85. **Kubert** c-282, 283, 285, 286, 289-292, 297-299, 301, 303, 306-308. **Mayer** a-317p. **Meskin** a-52-144 (most), 224r, 229r; c-63, 66, 124, 127. **Mooney** a-24, 159, 160. **Moreira** a-3, 4, 20-50, 58, 59, 62, 68, 77, 79, 90, 108, 113, 123, 201r, 228; c-44, 47, 50, 54, 59, 62, 64, 68, 70, 73. **Morrow** a-192, 196, 255, 320i. **Mortimer** a-204. **Nasser** a-276. **Newton** a-259, 272. **Nino** a-204, 212, 213, 220, 224, 225, 245, 250, 252-256, 283. **Orlando** a-175(2 pgs.), 178; c-240, 258p, 262, 264p, 270p, 271, 272, 274, 275, 278, 296i. **Redondo** a-194, 195, 197, 202, 203, 207, 211, 214, 217, 219, 226, 227, 229, 235, 241, 287(layout), 302p, 303i, 308; c-229. **Reese** a-195, 200, 205i. **Rogers** a-254, 274, 277. **Roussos** a-65, 84, 224i. **Sekowsky** a-282p. **Sparling** a-203. **Starlin** a-207(2 pgs.), 282p; c-281. **Leonard Starr** a-9. **Staton** a-300p. **Sutton** a-271, 290, 291, 293, 295, 297-299, 302, 303, 306-309, 310-313i, 314. **Tuska** a-293p, 294p, 316p. **Wrightson** c-193-195, 204, 207, 209, 211, 213, 214, 217, 221, 231, 236, 255, 256.*

**HOUSE OF SECRETS** (Combined with The Unexpected after #154)
11-12/56 - No. 80, 9-10/66; No. 81, 8-9/69 - No. 140, 2-3/76;
No. 141, 8-9/76 - No. 154, 10-11/78
National Periodical Publications/DC Comics

| | Good | Fine | N-Mint |
|---|---|---|---|
| 1-Drucker-a; Moreira-c | 38.00 | 114.00 | 265.00 |
| 2-Moreira-a | 16.50 | 50.00 | 115.00 |
| 3-Kirby-c/a | 14.00 | 43.00 | 100.00 |

*The House of Mystery #1, © DC*

*The House of Mystery #164, © DC*

*House of Secrets #2, © DC*

House of Secrets #92, © DC

Howard the Duck #12, © MEG

Howdy Doody #8, © Kagran Corp.

| | Good | Fine | N-Mint |
|---|---|---|---|
| 4,8-Kirby-a | 7.00 | 21.00 | 50.00 |
| 5-7,9-11 | 5.00 | 15.00 | 35.00 |
| 12-Kirby-c/a | 6.50 | 19.00 | 45.00 |
| 13-15 | 4.00 | 12.00 | 28.00 |
| 16-20 | 3.15 | 9.50 | 22.00 |
| 21,22,24-30 | 2.65 | 8.00 | 18.00 |
| 23-Origin Mark Merlin | 3.00 | 9.00 | 21.00 |
| 31-47,49,50: Last 10 cent issue | 1.70 | 5.00 | 12.00 |
| 48-Toth-a | 2.00 | 6.00 | 14.00 |
| 51-60: 58-Origin Mark Merlin retold | 1.00 | 3.00 | 7.00 |
| 61-First Eclipso (7-8/63) and begin series | 3.60 | 11.00 | 25.00 |
| 62 | 1.70 | 5.00 | 12.00 |
| 63-67-Toth-a on Eclipso | 1.50 | 4.50 | 10.00 |
| 68-80: 73-Mark Merlin ends, Prince Ra-Man begins. 80-Eclipso, Prince Ra-Man end | .85 | 2.50 | 5.00 |
| 81-91: 81-Mystery format begins. 82-Neal Adams-c(i). 85-N. Adams-a(i). 87-Wrightson & Kaluta-a. 90-Buckler (1st pro work)/N. Adams-a | .35 | 1.00 | 2.00 |
| 92-1st app. Swamp Thing (6-7/71) by Berni Wrightson(p) w/Jeff Jones/Kaluta/Weiss ink assists (8 pgs.) | 9.30 | 28.00 | 65.00 |
| 93-100: 94-Wrightson-i. 96-Wood-a | .25 | .75 | 1.50 |
| 101-154: 140-Origin The Patchworkman | | .50 | 1.00 |

NOTE: ***Neal Adams*** *c-81, 82, 84-88, 90, 91.* ***Colan*** *a-63.* ***Ditko*** *a-139p, 148.* ***Elias*** *a-58.* ***Evans*** *a-118.* ***Finlay*** *a-7.* ***Glanzman*** *a-91.* ***Golden*** *a-151.* ***Kaluta*** *a-87, 98, 99; c-98, 99, 101, 102, 151, 154.* ***Bob Kane*** *a-18, 21.* ***G. Kane*** *a-85p.* ***Kirby*** *c-11.* ***Kubert*** *a-39.* ***Meskin*** *a-2-68 (most); c-55-60.* ***Moreira*** *a-7, 8, 102-104, 106, 108, 113, 116, 118, 121, 123, 127; c-2, 7-9.* ***Morrow*** *a-86, 89, 90; c-89, 146-148.* ***Nino*** *a-101, 103, 106, 109, 115, 117, 126, 128, 131, 147, 153.* ***Redondo*** *a-95, 99, 102, 104p, 113, 116, 134, 139, 140.* ***Reese*** *a-85.* ***Starlin*** *c-150.* ***Sutton*** *a-154.* ***Toth*** *a-63-67, 83, 93r, 94r, 96r, 98r, 123.* ***Tuska*** *a-90, 104.* ***Wrightson*** *c-92-94, 96, 100, 103, 106, 107, 135, 139.*

**HOUSE OF TERROR** (3-D)
October, 1953 (1st 3D horror comic)
St. John Publishing Co.

| | Good | Fine | N-Mint |
|---|---|---|---|
| 1-Kubert, Baker-a | 17.00 | 51.00 | 120.00 |

**HOUSE OF YANG, THE** (See Yang)
July, 1975 - No. 6, June, 1976; 1978
Charlton Comics

| | Good | Fine | N-Mint |
|---|---|---|---|
| 1 | | .50 | 1.00 |
| 2-6 | | .35 | .70 |
| Modern Comics #1,2(1978) | | .35 | .70 |

**HOUSE II: THE SECOND STORY**
1987
Marvel Comics

| | Good | Fine | N-Mint |
|---|---|---|---|
| 1-Adapts movie | .35 | 1.00 | 2.00 |

**HOWARD CHAYKIN'S AMERICAN FLAGG!** (Formerly Amer. Flagg!)
V2#1, May, 1988 - V2#12, April, 1989 ($1.75-$1.95, Baxter paper)
First Comics

| | Good | Fine | N-Mint |
|---|---|---|---|
| V2#1-5: ($1.75)-Chaykin-c(p) in all | .30 | .90 | 1.75 |
| 6-9,11,12: ($1.95) | .30 | .90 | 1.75 |
| 10-Elvis Presley photo-c | .50 | 1.50 | 3.00 |

**HOWARD THE DUCK** (See Bizarre Adventures #34, Fear, Man-Thing, & Marvel Treasury Edition)
Jan, 1976 - No. 31, May, 1979; No. 32, Jan, 1986; No. 33, Sept, 1986
Marvel Comics Group

| | Good | Fine | N-Mint |
|---|---|---|---|
| 1-Brunner-c/a; Spider-Man x-over (low distr.) | 1.15 | 3.50 | 7.00 |
| 2-Brunner-c/a (low distribution) | .25 | .75 | 1.50 |
| 3-11: 3-Buscema-a | .25 | .75 | 1.50 |
| 12-1st app. Kiss (cameo, 3/77) | .70 | 2.00 | 4.00 |
| 13-Kiss app. (1st full story) | .85 | 2.50 | 5.00 |
| 14-33: 16-Album issue; 3pgs. comics | | .50 | 1.00 |
| Annual 1(9/77, 52 pgs.) | | .50 | 1.00 |

NOTE: ***Austin*** *c-29i.* ***Bolland*** *c-33.* ***Brunner*** *a-1p, 2p; c-1, 2.* ***Buckler*** *c-3p.* ***Buscema*** *a-3p.* ***Colan*** *a(p)-4-15, 17-20, 24-27, 30, 31; c(p)-4-31, Annual 1.* ***Leialoha*** *a-1-13i; c(i)-3-5, 8-11.* ***Mayerik*** *a-22, 23, 33.* ***P. Smith*** *a-30p. Man-Thing app. in #22, 23.*

**HOWARD THE DUCK MAGAZINE**
October, 1979 - No. 9, March, 1981 (B&W)
Marvel Comics Group

| | Good | Fine | N-Mint |
|---|---|---|---|
| 1 | | .50 | 1.00 |
| 2,3,5-9: 3-Xmas issue. 7-Has poster by Byrne | | .30 | .60 |
| 4-Beatles, John Lennon, Elvis, Kiss & Devo cameos; Hitler app. | | .40 | .80 |

NOTE: ***Buscema*** *a-4p.* ***Colan*** *a-1-5p, 7-9p.* ***Davis*** *c-3.* ***Golden*** *a-1, 5p, 6p(51pgs.).* ***Rogers*** *a-7, 8.* ***Simonson*** *a-7.*

**HOWARD THE DUCK: THE MOVIE**
Dec, 1986 - No. 3, Feb, 1987 (Mini-series)
Marvel Comics Group

| | Good | Fine | N-Mint |
|---|---|---|---|
| 1-3: Movie adaptation; r/Marv. Super Special | | .40 | .80 |

**HOW BOYS AND GIRLS CAN HELP WIN THE WAR**
1942 (One Shot) (10 cents)
The Parents' Magazine Institute

| | Good | Fine | N-Mint |
|---|---|---|---|
| 1-All proceeds used to buy war bonds | 14.00 | 43.00 | 100.00 |

**HOWDY DOODY** (TV)(See Poll Parrot)
1/50 - No. 38, 7-9/56; No. 761, 1/57; No. 811, 7/57
Dell Publishing Co.

| | Good | Fine | N-Mint |
|---|---|---|---|
| 1-(Scarce)-Photo-c; 1st TV comic? | 25.00 | 75.00 | 175.00 |
| 2-Photo-c | 10.00 | 30.00 | 70.00 |
| 3-5: All photo-c | 7.00 | 21.00 | 50.00 |
| 6-Used in **SOTI**, pg. 309; painted-c begin | 6.50 | 19.00 | 45.00 |
| 7-10 | 5.70 | 17.00 | 40.00 |
| 11-20 | 4.30 | 13.00 | 30.00 |
| 21-38 | 3.50 | 10.50 | 24.00 |
| 4-Color 761,811 | 5.70 | 17.00 | 40.00 |

**HOW IT BEGAN** (See Single Series No. 15)

**HOW SANTA GOT HIS RED SUIT** (See March of Comics No. 2)

**HOW STALIN HOPES WE WILL DESTROY AMERICA**
1951 (16 pgs.) (Giveaway)
Joe Lowe Co. (Pictorial News)

| | Good | Fine | N-Mint |
|---|---|---|---|
| nn | 34.00 | 103.00 | 240.00 |

*(Prices vary widely on this book)*

**HOW THE WEST WAS WON** (See Movie Comics)

**HOW TO DRAW FOR THE COMICS**
No date (1942?) (64 pgs.; B&W & color) (10 Cents) (No ads)
Street and Smith

| | Good | Fine | N-Mint |
|---|---|---|---|
| nn-Art by Winsor McCay, George Marcoux(Supersnipe artist), Vernon Greene(The Shadow artist), Jack Binder(with biog.), Thorton Fisher, Jon Small, & Jack Farr. Has biographies of each artist | 13.00 | 40.00 | 90.00 |

**H. R. PUFNSTUF** (TV) (See March of Comics 360)
Oct, 1970 - No. 8, July, 1972
Gold Key

| | Good | Fine | N-Mint |
|---|---|---|---|
| 1 | .85 | 2.50 | 5.00 |
| 2-8 | .35 | 1.00 | 2.00 |

**HUBERT** (See 4-Color No. 251)

**HUCK & YOGI JAMBOREE** (TV)
March, 1961 (116 pgs.; $1.00) (B&W original material)
(6¼x9"; cardboard cover; high quality paper)
Dell Publishing Co.

| | Good | Fine | N-Mint |
|---|---|---|---|
| nn | 3.50 | 10.50 | 24.00 |

**HUCK & YOGI WINTER SPORTS** (See 4-Color No. 1310)

**HUCK FINN** (See The New Adventures of . . . & Power Record Comics)

**HUCKLEBERRY FINN** (See 4-Color No. 1114)

**HUCKLEBERRY HOUND** (See Dell Giant No. 31,44, Golden Picture Story Book, March of Comics No. 199,214,235, Spotlight No. 1 & Whitman Comic Books)

**HUCKLEBERRY HOUND** (TV)
No. 990, 5-7/59 - No. 43, 10/70 (Hanna-Barbera)
Dell/Gold Key No. 18 (10/62) on

| | Good | Fine | N-Mint |
|---|---|---|---|
| 4-Color 990(#1) | 4.00 | 12.00 | 28.00 |
| 4-Color 1050,1054 (12/59) | 2.65 | 8.00 | 18.00 |
| 3(1-2/60) - 7 (9-10/60) | 2.30 | 7.00 | 16.00 |
| 4-Color 1141 (10/60) | 2.30 | 7.00 | 16.00 |
| 8-10 | 2.00 | 6.00 | 14.00 |
| 11-17 (6-8/62) | 1.30 | 4.00 | 9.00 |
| 18,19 (84pgs.; 18-20 titled . . .Chuckleberry Tales) | 3.50 | 10.50 | 28.00 |
| 20-30: 20-Titled Chuckleberry Tales | 1.00 | 3.00 | 7.00 |
| 31-43: 37-reprints | .85 | 2.60 | 6.00 |
| . . .Kite Fun Book('61)-16 pgs.; 5x7¼", soft-c | 2.00 | 6.00 | 14.00 |

**HUCKLEBERRY HOUND** (TV)
Nov, 1970 - No. 8, Jan, 1972 (Hanna-Barbera)
Charlton Comics

| | Good | Fine | N-Mint |
|---|---|---|---|
| 1 | 1.00 | 3.00 | 7.00 |
| 2-8 | .70 | 2.00 | 4.00 |

**HUEY, DEWEY, & LOUIE** (See Donald Duck, 1938 for 1st app. Also see Mickey Mouse Magazine V4#2, V5#7)

**HUEY, DEWEY, & LOUIE BACK TO SCHOOL** (See Dell Giant #22,35,49 & Dell Giants)

**HUEY, DEWEY AND LOUIE JUNIOR WOODCHUCKS** (Disney)
Aug, 1966 - No. 81, 1984 (See Walt Disney's C&S #125)
Gold Key No. 1-61/Whitman No. 62 on

| | Good | Fine | N-Mint |
|---|---|---|---|
| 1 | 2.65 | 8.00 | 18.00 |
| 2,3(12/68) | 1.70 | 5.00 | 12.00 |
| 4,5(4/70)-Barks-r | 1.70 | 5.00 | 12.00 |
| 6-17-Written by Barks | 1.15 | 3.50 | 8.00 |
| 18,27-30 | .70 | 2.00 | 4.00 |
| 19-23,25-Written by Barks. 22,23,25-Barks-r | .85 | 2.50 | 5.00 |
| 24,26-Barks-r | .85 | 2.50 | 5.00 |
| 31-57,60-81: 41,70,80-Reprints | .25 | .75 | 1.50 |
| 58,59-Barks-r | .35 | 1.00 | 2.00 |

NOTE: *Barks story reprints-No. 22-26, 35, 42, 45, 51.*

**HUGGA BUNCH** (TV)
Oct, 1986 - No. 6, Aug, 1987
Star Comics (Marvel)

| | Good | Fine | N-Mint |
|---|---|---|---|
| 1-6 | | .45 | .90 |

**HULK, THE** (See The Incredible Hulk)

**HULK** (Formerly The Rampaging Hulk)
No. 10, Aug, 1978 - No. 27, June, 1981 (Magazine)($1.50, color)
Marvel Comics Group

| | Good | Fine | N-Mint |
|---|---|---|---|
| 10-27: 11-Moon Knight begins, ends 20? 23-Anti-Gay issue | | .60 | 1.20 |

NOTE: ***Alcala** a(i)-15, 17-20, 22, 24-27. **Buscema** a-23; c-26. **Chaykin** a-21-25. **Colan** a(p)-11, 19, 24-27. **Golden** a-20. **Nebres** a-16. **Sienkiewicz** a-13, 17, 20. **Simonson** a-27; c-23. Moon Knight appears in #11-13, 15, 17, 20; others?*

**HUMAN FLY**
1963 - 1964 (Reprints)
I.W. Enterprises/Super

| | Good | Fine | N-Mint |
|---|---|---|---|
| I.W. Reprint #1-Reprints Blue Beetle #44('46) | .70 | 2.00 | 4.00 |
| Super Reprint #10-R/Blue Beetle #46('47) | .70 | 2.00 | 4.00 |

**HUMAN FLY, THE**
Sept, 1977 - No. 19, Mar, 1979
Marvel Comics Group

| | Good | Fine | N-Mint |
|---|---|---|---|
| 1-Origin; Spider-Man x-over | .35 | 1.00 | 2.00 |
| 2-Ghost Rider app. | .40 | 1.25 | 2.50 |
| 3-19: 9-Daredevil x-over | | .50 | 1.00 |

NOTE: ***Austin** c-4i, 9i. **Byrne** c-9p. **Elias** a-1, 3p, 4p, 7p, 10-12p, 15p, 18p, 19p. **Layton** c-19.*

**HUMAN TORCH, THE** (Red Raven #1)(See All-Select, All Winners, Marvel Mystery, Men's Adventures, Mystic Comics (2nd series), Sub-Mariner, USA & Young Men)
No. 2, Fall, 1940 - No. 15, Spring, 1944;
No. 16, Fall, 1944 - No. 35, Mar, 1949 (Becomes Love Tales);
No. 36, April, 1954 - No. 38, Aug, 1954
Timely/Marvel Comics (TP 2,3/TCI 4-9/SePI 10/SnPC 11-25/CnPC 26-35/Atlas Comics (CPC 36-38))

| | Good | Fine | VF-NM | NM/Mint |
|---|---|---|---|---|
| 2(#1)-Intro & Origin Toro; The Falcon, The Fiery Mask, Mantor the Magician, & Microman only app.; Human Torch by Burgos, Sub-Mariner by Everett begin (origin of each in text) | 665.00 | 1665.00 | 4000.00 | 5500.00 |

(Estimated up to 190 total copies exist, 10 in NM/Mint)

| | Good | Fine | N-Mint |
|---|---|---|---|
| 3(#2)-40pg. H.T. story; H.T. & S.M. battle over who is best artist in text-Everett or Burgos | 250.00 | 625.00 | 1500.00 |
| 4(#3)-Origin The Patriot in text; last Everett Sub-Mariner; Sid Greene-a | 192.00 | 480.00 | 1150.00 |
| 5(#4)-The Patriot app; Angel x-over in Sub-Mariner (Summer, 1941) | 135.00 | 335.00 | 800.00 |
| 5-Human Torch battles Sub-Mariner (Fall,'41) | 200.00 | 500.00 | 1200.00 |
| 6,7,9 | 87.00 | 220.00 | 525.00 |
| 8-Human Torch battles Sub-Mariner; Wolverton-a, 1 pg. | 150.00 | 375.00 | 900.00 |
| 10-Human Torch battles Sub-Mariner; Wolverton-a, 1 pg. | 108.00 | 270.00 | 650.00 |
| 11-15 | 68.00 | 170.00 | 410.00 |
| 16-20: 20-Last War issue | 55.00 | 137.00 | 330.00 |
| 21-30: 23(Sum/46)-Becomes Junior Miss 24? | 48.00 | 118.00 | 285.00 |
| 31-Namora x-over in Sub-Mariner (also #30); last Toro | 39.00 | 98.00 | 235.00 |
| 32-Sungirl, Namora app.; Sungirl-c | 39.00 | 98.00 | 235.00 |
| 33-Capt. America x-over | 42.00 | 105.00 | 250.00 |
| 34-Sungirl solo | 39.00 | 98.00 | 235.00 |
| 35-Captain America & Sungirl app. (1949) | 42.00 | 105.00 | 250.00 |
| 36-38(1954)-Sub-Mariner in all | 30.00 | 75.00 | 180.00 |

NOTE: ***Burgos** c-36. **Everett** a-1-3, 27, 28, 30, 37, 38. **Powell** a-36. **Schomburg** c-1-3, 5-23. **Shores** c-27. **Mickey Spillane** text 4-6. Bondage c-2, 12, 19.*

**HUMAN TORCH, THE** (Also see Avengers West Coast, Fantastic Four, The Invaders, Saga of the Original . . . & Strange Tales #101)
Sept, 1974 - No. 8, Nov, 1975
Marvel Comics Group

| | Good | Fine | N-Mint |
|---|---|---|---|
| 1: 1-8-r/stories from Strange Tales #101-108 | .50 | 1.50 | 3.00 |
| 2-8: 1st Human Torch title since G.A. | .40 | 1.25 | 2.50 |

NOTE: *Golden Age & Silver Age Torch-r #1-8. **Ayers** r-6, 7. **Kirby/Ayers** r-1-5, 8.*

**HUMBUG** (Satire by Harvey Kurtzman)
Aug, 1957 - No. 9, May, 1958; No. 10, June, 1958; No. 11, Oct, 1958
Humbug Publications

| | Good | Fine | N-Mint |
|---|---|---|---|
| 1 | 9.00 | 27.00 | 62.00 |
| 2 | 4.30 | 13.00 | 32.00 |
| 3-9: 8-Elvis in Jailbreak Rock | 3.50 | 10.50 | 24.00 |
| 10,11-Magazine format. 10-Photo-c | 4.00 | 12.00 | 28.00 |
| Bound Volume(#1-6)-Sold by publisher | 23.00 | 70.00 | 160.00 |
| Bound Volume(#1-9) | 26.00 | 77.00 | 180.00 |

NOTE: ***Davis** a-1-11. **Elder** a-2-4, 6-9, 11. **Heath** a-2, 4-8, 10. **Jaffee** a-2, 4-9. **Kurtzman** a-11. **Wood** a-1.*

**HUMDINGER**
May-June, 1946 - V2#2, July-Aug, 1947
Novelty Press/Premium Group

| | Good | Fine | N-Mint |
|---|---|---|---|
| 1-Jerkwater Line, Mickey Starlight by Don Rico, Dink begin | 5.70 | 17.00 | 40.00 |
| 2 | 3.00 | 9.00 | 21.00 |
| 3-6, V2#1,2 | 2.30 | 7.00 | 16.00 |

*The Human Fly #1, © MEG*

*The Human Torch #33, © MEG*

*The Human Torch #1 (9/74), © MEG*

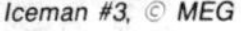
*Iceman #3,* © *MEG*

*Idaho #5,* © *DELL*

*I Loved #29,* © *FOX*

**HUMOR** (See All Humor Comics)

**HUMPHREY COMICS** (Also see Joe Palooka)
October, 1948 - No. 22, April, 1952
Harvey Publications

| | Good | Fine | N-Mint |
|---|---|---|---|
| 1-Joe Palooka's pal (r); (52 pgs.)-Powell-a | 5.70 | 17.00 | 40.00 |
| 2,3: Powell-a | 2.65 | 8.00 | 18.00 |
| 4-Boy Heroes app.; Powell-a | 3.50 | 10.50 | 24.00 |
| 5-8,10: 5,6-Powell-a. 7-Little Dot app. | 2.00 | 6.00 | 14.00 |
| 9-Origin Humphrey | 2.65 | 8.00 | 18.00 |
| 11-22 | 1.60 | 4.80 | 11.00 |

**HUNCHBACK OF NOTRE DAME, THE** (See 4-Color No. 854)

**HUNK**
August, 1961 - No. 11, 1963
Charlton Comics

| | | | |
|---|---|---|---|
| 1 | .75 | 2.25 | 4.50 |
| 2-11 | .35 | 1.10 | 2.25 |

**HUNTED** (Formerly My Love Memoirs)
No. 13, July, 1950 - No. 2, Sept, 1950
Fox Features Syndicate

| | | | |
|---|---|---|---|
| 13(#1)-Used in **SOTI**, pg. 42 & illo.-"Treating police contemptuously" (lower left); Hollingsworth bondage-c | 14.00 | 43.00 | 100.00 |
| 2 | 5.70 | 17.00 | 40.00 |

**HUNTRESS, THE** (See All-Star Comics #69, DC Super Stars #17, Infinity, Inc. #1, Sensation Comics #68 & Wonder Woman #271)
April, 1989 - No. 19, Oct, 1990 ($1.00, color, mature readers)
DC Comics

| | | | |
|---|---|---|---|
| 1-19: Staton-c/a(p) in all. 17-19-Batman-c/stories | | .50 | 1.00 |

**HURRICANE COMICS**
1945 (52 pgs.)
Cambridge House

| | | | |
|---|---|---|---|
| 1-(Humor, funny animal) | 7.00 | 21.00 | 50.00 |

**HYPER MYSTERY COMICS**
May, 1940 - No. 2, June, 1940 (68 pgs.)
Hyper Publications

| | | | |
|---|---|---|---|
| 1-Hyper, the Phenomenal begins | 61.00 | 182.00 | 425.00 |
| 2 | 45.00 | 135.00 | 315.00 |

**I AIM AT THE STARS** (See 4-Color No. 1148)

**I AM COYOTE** (See Eclipse Graphic Album Series)

**IBIS, THE INVINCIBLE** (See Fawcett Min., Mighty Midget & Whiz)
1943 (Feb) - No. 2, 1943; No. 3, Wint, 1945 - No. 6, Spring, 1948
Fawcett Publications

| | | | |
|---|---|---|---|
| 1-Origin Ibis; Raboy-c; on sale 1/2/43 | 79.00 | 235.00 | 550.00 |
| 2-Bondage-c | 39.00 | 118.00 | 275.00 |
| 3-Wolverton-a #3-6 (4 pgs. each) | 32.00 | 95.00 | 225.00 |
| 4-6: 5-Bondage-c. 6-Beck-c | 25.00 | 75.00 | 175.00 |

**ICE KING OF OZ, THE** (See First Comics Graphic Novel #13)

**ICEMAN** (Also see The Champions & X-Men #94)
Dec, 1984 - No. 4, June, 1985 (Limited series)
Marvel Comics Group

| | | | |
|---|---|---|---|
| 1,3: 3-Original X-Men x-over | .35 | 1.00 | 2.00 |
| 2,4 | .25 | .75 | 1.50 |

**IDAHO**
June-Aug, 1963 - No. 8, July-Sept, 1965
Dell Publishing Co.

| | | | |
|---|---|---|---|
| 1 | 1.15 | 3.50 | 8.00 |
| 2-8: 5-Painted-c | .75 | 2.25 | 5.00 |

**IDEAL** (. . . a Classical Comic) (2nd Series) (Love Romances No. 6?)
July, 1948 - No. 5, March, 1949 (Feature length stories)
Timely Comics

| | Good | Fine | N-Mint |
|---|---|---|---|
| 1-Antony & Cleopatra | 17.00 | 51.00 | 120.00 |
| 2-The Corpses of Dr. Sacotti | 14.00 | 43.00 | 100.00 |
| 3-Joan of Arc; used in **SOTI**, pg. 308-'Boer War' | 12.00 | 36.00 | 85.00 |
| 4-Richard the Lion-hearted; titled ". . .the World's Greatest Comics;" The Witness app. | 20.00 | 60.00 | 140.00 |
| 5-Ideal Love & Romance; photo-c | 7.00 | 21.00 | 50.00 |

**IDEAL COMICS** (1st Series) (Willie Comics No. 5 on)
Fall, 1944 - No. 4, Spring, 1946
Timely Comics (MgPC)

| | | | |
|---|---|---|---|
| 1-Super Rabbit in all | 8.50 | 25.50 | 60.00 |
| 2 | 5.70 | 17.00 | 40.00 |
| 3,4 | 5.00 | 15.00 | 35.00 |

**IDEAL LOVE & ROMANCE** (See Ideal, A Classical Comic)

**IDEAL ROMANCE** (Formerly Tender Romance)
No. 3, April, 1954 - No. 8, Feb, 1955 (Diary Confessions No. 9 on)
Key Publications

| | | | |
|---|---|---|---|
| 3 | 3.50 | 10.50 | 24.00 |
| 4-8 | 1.70 | 5.00 | 12.00 |

**I DREAM OF JEANNIE** (TV)
April, 1965 - No. 2, Dec, 1966 (Photo-c)
Dell Publishing Co.

| | | | |
|---|---|---|---|
| 1,2-Barbara Eden photo-c | 4.00 | 12.00 | 28.00 |

**IF THE DEVIL WOULD TALK**
1950; 1958 (32 pgs.; paper cover; in full color)
Roman Catholic Catechetical Guild/Impact Publ.

| | | | |
|---|---|---|---|
| nn-(Scarce)-About secularism (20-30 copies known to exist); very low distribution | 50.00 | 150.00 | 350.00 |
| 1958 Edition-(Rare)-(Impact Publ.); art & script changed to meet church criticism of earlier edition; only 6 known copies exist | 43.00 | 130.00 | 300.00 |
| Black & White version of nn edition; small size; only 4 known copies exist | 30.00 | 90.00 | 200.00 |

NOTE: *The original edition of this book was printed and killed by the Guild's board of directors. It is believed that a very limited number of copies were distributed. The 1958 version was a complete bomb with very limited, if any, circulation. In 1979, 11 original, 4 1958 reprints, and 4 B&W's surfaced from the Guild's old files in St. Paul, Minnesota.*

**ILLUSTRATED GAGS** (See Single Series No. 16)

**ILLUSTRATED LIBRARY OF. . ., AN** (See Classics Illustrated Giants)

**ILLUSTRATED STORIES OF THE OPERAS**
1943 (16 pgs.; B&W) (25 cents) (cover-B&W & red)
Baily (Bernard) Publ. Co.

| | | | |
|---|---|---|---|
| nn-(Rare)-Faust (part-r in Cisco Kid #1) | 36.00 | 107.00 | 250.00 |
| nn-(Rare)-Aida | 36.00 | 107.00 | 250.00 |
| nn-(Rare)-Carmen; Baily-a | 36.00 | 107.00 | 250.00 |
| nn-(Rare)-Rigoleito | 36.00 | 107.00 | 250.00 |

**ILLUSTRATED STORY OF ROBIN HOOD & HIS MERRY MEN, THE**
(See Classics Giveaways, 12/44)

**ILLUSTRATED TARZAN BOOK, THE** (See Tarzan Book)

**I LOVED** (Formerly Rulah; Colossal Features Magazine No. 33 on)
No. 28, July, 1949 - No. 32, Mar, 1950
Fox Features Syndicate

| | | | |
|---|---|---|---|
| 28 | 4.00 | 12.00 | 28.00 |
| 29-32 | 2.65 | 8.00 | 18.00 |

**I LOVE LUCY**
6/90 - No. 6, 1990; V2#1, 1990 - No. 6, 1991 ($2.95, B&W, mini-series)
Eternity Comics

| | | | |
|---|---|---|---|
| 1-6: Reprints 1950s comic strip; photo-c | .50 | 1.50 | 3.00 |
| Book II #1-6: Reprints comic strip; photo-c | .50 | 1.50 | 3.00 |

**I LOVE LUCY COMICS** (TV) (Also see The Lucy Show)
No. 535, Feb, 1954 - No. 35, Apr-June, 1962 (All photo-c)
Dell Publishing Co.

| | Good | Fine | N-Mint |
|---|---|---|---|
| 4-Color 535(#1) | 18.00 | 54.00 | 125.00 |
| 4-Color 559(#2, 5/54) | 13.00 | 40.00 | 90.00 |
| 3 (8-10/54) - 5 | 8.50 | 25.50 | 60.00 |
| 6-10 | 7.00 | 21.00 | 50.00 |
| 11-20 | 6.50 | 19.00 | 45.00 |
| 21-35 | 5.70 | 17.00 | 40.00 |

**I LOVE YOU**
June, 1950 (One shot)
Fawcett Publications

| | Good | Fine | N-Mint |
|---|---|---|---|
| 1-Photo-c | 6.50 | 19.00 | 45.00 |

**I LOVE YOU** (Formerly In Love)
No. 7, 9/55 - No. 121, 12/76; No. 122, 3/79 - No. 130, 5/80
Charlton Comics

| | Good | Fine | N-Mint |
|---|---|---|---|
| 7-Kirby-c, Powell-a | 4.30 | 13.00 | 30.00 |
| 8-10 | 1.50 | 4.50 | 10.00 |
| 11-16,18-20 | 1.00 | 3.00 | 7.00 |
| 17-68 pg. Giant | 1.30 | 4.00 | 9.00 |
| 21-25,27-50 | .55 | 1.65 | 4.00 |
| 26-Torres-a | 1.00 | 3.00 | 7.00 |
| 51-59 | .50 | 1.50 | 3.00 |
| 60(1/66)-Elvis Presley line drawn c/story | 7.00 | 21.00 | 50.00 |
| 61-85 | .35 | 1.00 | 2.00 |
| 86-130 | | .40 | .80 |

**I'M A COP**
1954 - No. 3, 1954?
Magazine Enterprises

| | Good | Fine | N-Mint |
|---|---|---|---|
| 1(A-1 #111)-Powell-c/a in all | 6.00 | 18.00 | 42.00 |
| 2(A-1 #126), 3(A-1 #128) | 3.15 | 9.50 | 22.00 |

**I'M DICKENS - HE'S FENSTER** (TV)
May-July, 1963 - No. 2, Aug-Oct, 1963 (Photo-c)
Dell Publishing Co.

| | Good | Fine | N-Mint |
|---|---|---|---|
| 1,2 | 2.00 | 6.00 | 14.00 |

**I MET A HANDSOME COWBOY** (See 4-Color No. 324)

**IMMORTAL DOCTOR FATE, THE**
Jan, 1985 - No. 3, Mar, 1985 ($1.25, mini-series)
DC Comics

| | Good | Fine | N-Mint |
|---|---|---|---|
| 1-3: 1-Simonson-c/a. 2-Giffen-c/a(p) | | .65 | 1.30 |

**IMPACT**
Mar-Apr, 1955 - No. 5, Nov-Dec, 1955
E. C. Comics

| | Good | Fine | N-Mint |
|---|---|---|---|
| 1 | 9.30 | 28.00 | 65.00 |
| 2 | 6.00 | 18.00 | 42.00 |
| 3-5: 4-Crandall-a | 5.30 | 16.00 | 38.00 |

NOTE: ***Crandall*** *a-1-4.* ***Davis*** *a-2-4; c-1-5.* ***Evans*** *a-1, 4, 5.* ***Ingels*** *a-in all.* ***Kamen*** *a-3.* ***Krigstein*** *a-1, 5.* ***Orlando*** *a-2, 5.*

**IMPOSSIBLE MAN SUMMER VACATION SPECTACULAR, THE**
Aug, 1990 ($2.00, 68 pgs.)
Marvel Comics

| | Good | Fine | N-Mint |
|---|---|---|---|
| 1-Spider-Man, Quasar, Dr. Strange, She-Hulk, Punisher & Dr. Doom stories; Barry Crain, Guice-a; Art Adams-c(i) | .35 | 1.00 | 2.00 |

**INCAL, THE**
Nov, 1988 - No. 3, Jan, 1989 ($9.95, adults)
Epic Comics (Marvel)

| | Good | Fine | N-Mint |
|---|---|---|---|
| 1-3: Moebius-c/a; sexual content | 1.70 | 5.00 | 10.00 |

**INCREDIBLE HULK, THE** (See Aurora, The Avengers #1, The Defenders #1, Giant-Size..., Hulk, Marvel Collectors Item Classics, Marvel Comics Presents #26, Marvel Fanfare, Marvel Treasury Edition & Power Record Comics, Rampaging Hulk)

**INCREDIBLE HULK, THE**
May, 1962 - No. 6, Mar, 1963; No. 102, Apr, 1968 - Present
Marvel Comics Group

| | Good | Fine | N-Mint | Mint |
|---|---|---|---|---|
| 1-Origin & 1st app. (skin is grey colored) | 180.00 | 540.00 | 1250.00 | 2000.00 |

(Estimated up to 1200 total copies exist, 32 in Mint)

| | Good | Fine | N-Mint |
|---|---|---|---|
| 2-1st green skinned Hulk | 72.00 | 216.00 | 500.00 |
| 3-Origin retold | 52.00 | 156.00 | 360.00 |
| 4-6: 4-Brief origin retold. 6-Intro. Teen Brigade | 46.00 | 138.00 | 320.00 |
| 102-(Formerly Tales to Astonish)-Origin retold | 16.50 | 50.00 | 115.00 |
| 103,104 | 6.50 | 19.00 | 45.00 |
| 105-108: 105-1st Missing Link | 4.00 | 12.00 | 28.00 |
| 109,110 | 2.85 | 8.50 | 20.00 |
| 111-117: 117-Last 12 cent issue | 1.70 | 5.00 | 12.00 |
| 118-125 | 1.00 | 3.00 | 7.00 |
| 126-140: 126-1st Barbara Norriss (Valkyrie). 131-1st Jim Wilson, Hulk's new sidekick. 136-1st Xeron, The Star-Slayer. 140-Written by Harlan Ellison; 1st Jarella, Hulk's love | 1.00 | 3.00 | 6.00 |
| 141-1st app. Doc Samson | .85 | 2.50 | 5.00 |
| 142-161,163-175,179: 145-(52 pgs.). 149-1st The Inheritor. 155-1st app. Shaper. 161-The Mimic dies; Beast app. 163-1st app. The Gremlin. 164-1st app. Capt. Omen & Colonel John D. Armbruster. 166-1st Zzzax. 168-1st The Harpy. 169-1st Bi-Beast. 172-X-Men cameo origin Juggernaut retold | .70 | 2.00 | 4.00 |
| 162-1st app. The Wendigo; Beast app. | .85 | 2.50 | 5.00 |
| 176-178-Warlock app. | .85 | 2.50 | 5.00 |
| 180-1st app. Wolverine (cameo on last page) | 8.50 | 25.50 | 60.00 |
| 181-Wolverine app. | 37.00 | 111.00 | 260.00 |
| 182-Wolverine cameo; 1st Crackajack Jackson | 6.50 | 19.50 | 45.00 |
| 183-199: 185-Death of Col. Armbruster | .50 | 1.50 | 3.00 |
| 200-Silver Surfer app.; anniversary issue | 2.00 | 6.00 | 12.00 |
| 201-240: 212-1st The Constrictor | .35 | 1.00 | 2.00 |
| 241-249,251-271: 271-Rocket Raccoon app. | | .60 | 1.20 |
| 250-Giant size; Silver Surfer app. | .50 | 1.50 | 3.00 |
| 272-Alpha Flight app. | .50 | 1.50 | 3.00 |
| 273-299,301-313: 278,279-Most Marvel characters app.(Wolverine in both). 279-X-Men & Alpha Flight cameos. 282-She-Hulk app. 293-F.F. app. 312-Origin Hulk | | .60 | 1.20 |
| 300-Double size | .35 | 1.00 | 2.00 |
| 314-Byrne-c/a begins, ends #319 | .85 | 2.50 | 5.00 |
| 315-319: 319-Bruce Banner & Betty Talbot wed | .35 | 1.00 | 2.00 |
| 320-323,325-329: 326-Grey vs. Green Hulk | | .60 | 1.20 |
| 324-1st app. Grey Hulk since earlier series | 1.00 | 3.00 | 6.00 |
| 330-1st McFarlane issue | 3.35 | 10.00 | 20.00 |
| 331-Grey Hulk series begins | 2.30 | 7.00 | 14.00 |
| 332-334,336-339: 336,337-X-Factor app. | 1.70 | 5.00 | 10.00 |
| 335-No McFarlane-a | .40 | 1.15 | 2.25 |
| 340-Hulk battles Wolverine by McFarlane | 4.15 | 12.50 | 25.00 |
| 341-344 | 1.00 | 3.00 | 6.00 |
| 345-($1.50, 52 pgs.) | 1.15 | 3.50 | 7.00 |
| 346-Last McFarlane issue | .85 | 2.50 | 5.00 |
| 347-349,351-358,360-380 | | .50 | 1.00 |
| 350-Double size | .35 | 1.00 | 2.00 |
| 359-Wolverine app. (illusion only) | .25 | .75 | 1.50 |
| Special 1(10/68, 68pg.)-New-a; Steranko-c | 4.30 | 13.00 | 30.00 |
| Special 2(10/69, 25 cents, 68pg.)-Origin retold | 2.85 | 8.50 | 20.00 |
| Special 3(1/71, 25 cents, 68pg.) | 1.00 | 3.00 | 6.00 |
| Annual 4 (1/72) | .70 | 2.00 | 4.00 |
| Annual 5(10/76) | .50 | 1.50 | 3.00 |
| Annual 6 (11/77) | .25 | .75 | 1.50 |
| Annual 7(8/78)-Byrne/Layton-c/a; Iceman & Angel app. | .50 | 1.50 | 3.00 |
| Annual 8-15: 8(11/79). 9(9/80). 10('81). 11(10/82)-Miller, Buckler-a(p). 12(8/83). 13(11/84). 14(12/85). 15(10/86) | .35 | 1.00 | 2.00 |

*I Love Lucy Comics #22, © L. Ball & D. Arnaz*

*The Incredible Hulk #104, © MEG*

*The Incredible Hulk #330, © MEG*

Incredible Science Fiction #32, © WMG

Indian Fighter #5, © YM

Infinity, Inc. #14, © DC

| | Good | Fine | N-Mint |
|---|---|---|---|
| Annual 16(1990, $2.00, 68 pgs.)-She-Hulk app. | .35 | 1.00 | 2.00 |
| ...Versus Quasimodo 1 (3/83, one-shot)-Based on Saturday morning cartoon | | .50 | 1.00 |

NOTE: **Adkins** *a-111-116i.* **Austin** *a(i)-350, 351, 353, 354; c-302i, 350i.* **J. Buscema** *c-202p.* **Byrne** *a-314-319p; c-314-316, 318, 319, 359.* **Colan** *c-363.* **Ditko** *a-2i, 6, 249, Annual 2r(3), 3r, 9p; c-2i, 6, 235, 249.* **Everett** *c-133i.* **Golden** *c-248, 251.* **Kane** *c(p)-193, 194, 196, 198.* **Kirby** *a-1-5, Special 2, 3p, Annual 5p; c-1-5, Annual 5.* **McFarlane** *a-330-334p, 336-339p, 340-343, 344-346p; c-330p, 340p, 341-343, 344p, 345, 346p.* **Miller** *c-258p, 261, 264, 268.* **Mooney** *a-230p, 287i, 288i.* **Powell** *a-Special 3r(2).* **Severin** *a(i)-108-110, 131-133, 141-151, 153-155; c(i)-109, 110, 132, 142, 144-155.* **Simonson** *c-283, 364-367.* **Starlin** *a-222p; c-217.* **Staton** *a(i)-187-189, 191-209.* **Tuska** *a-102i, 105i, 106i, 218p.* **Williamson** *a-310i; c-310i, 311i.* **Wrightson** *c-197.*

**INCREDIBLE HULK AND WOLVERINE, THE**
Oct, 1986 (One shot, $2.50, color)
Marvel Comics Group

| | Good | Fine | N-Mint |
|---|---|---|---|
| 1-r-/1st app. Wolverine & Incred. Hulk from Incred. Hulk #180,181; Wolverine back-up by Austin(i); Byrne-c | 1.70 | 5.00 | 10.00 |

**INCREDIBLE MR. LIMPET, THE** (See Movie Classics)

**INCREDIBLE SCIENCE FICTION** (Formerly Weird Science-Fantasy)
No. 30, July-Aug, 1955 - No. 33, Jan-Feb, 1956
E. C. Comics

| | Good | Fine | N-Mint |
|---|---|---|---|
| 30,33: 33-Story-r/W.F. No. 18 | 22.00 | 65.00 | 150.00 |
| 31-Williamson/Krenkel-a, Wood-a(2) | 26.00 | 77.00 | 180.00 |
| 32-Williamson/Krenkel-a | 26.00 | 77.00 | 180.00 |

NOTE: **Davis** *a-30, 32, 33; c-30-32.* **Krigstein** *a-in all.* **Orlando** *a-30, 32, 33("Judgement Day" reprint).* **Wood** *a-30, 31, 33; c-33.*

**INDIANA JONES** (See Further Adventures of...)

**INDIANA JONES AND THE LAST CRUSADE**
1989 - No. 4, 1989 ($1.00, color, limited series)
Marvel Comics

| | Good | Fine | N-Mint |
|---|---|---|---|
| 1-4: Movie adaptation; Williamson-i assist | | .50 | 1.00 |
| 1 (1989, $2.95, B&W mag., 80 pgs.) | .50 | 1.50 | 3.00 |

**INDIANA JONES AND THE TEMPLE OF DOOM**
Sept, 1984 - No. 3, Nov, 1984 (Movie adaptation)
Marvel Comics Group

| | Good | Fine | N-Mint |
|---|---|---|---|
| 1-3-r/Marvel Super Special; Guice-a | | .60 | 1.20 |

**INDIAN BRAVES** (Baffling Mysteries No. 5 on)
March, 1951 - No. 4, Sept, 1951
Ace Magazines

| | Good | Fine | N-Mint |
|---|---|---|---|
| 1 | 3.70 | 11.00 | 26.00 |
| 2 | 2.00 | 6.00 | 14.00 |
| 3,4 | 1.50 | 4.50 | 10.00 |
| I.W. Reprint #1 (nd) | .50 | 1.50 | 3.00 |

**INDIAN CHIEF** (White Eagle...) (Formerly The Chief)
No. 3, July-Sept, 1951 - No. 33, Jan-Mar, 1959 (All painted-c)
Dell Publishing Co.

| | Good | Fine | N-Mint |
|---|---|---|---|
| 3 | 1.70 | 5.00 | 12.00 |
| 4-11: 6-White Eagle app. | 1.15 | 3.50 | 8.00 |
| 12-1st White Eagle(10-12/53)-Not same as earlier character | 1.70 | 5.00 | 12.00 |
| 13-29 | 1.00 | 3.00 | 7.00 |
| 30-33-Buscema-a | 1.15 | 3.50 | 8.00 |

**INDIAN CHIEF** (See March of Comics No. 94, 110, 127, 140, 159, 170, 187)

**INDIAN FIGHTER, THE** (See 4-Color No. 687)

**INDIAN FIGHTER**
May, 1950 - No. 11, Jan, 1952
Youthful Magazines

| | Good | Fine | N-Mint |
|---|---|---|---|
| 1 | 4.30 | 13.00 | 30.00 |
| 2-Wildey-a/c(bondage) | 2.65 | 8.00 | 18.00 |
| 3-11: 3,4-Wildey-a | 1.70 | 5.00 | 12.00 |

NOTE: **Walter Johnson** *c-1, 3, 4, 6.* **Wildey** *a-2-4; c-2, 5.*

**INDIAN LEGENDS OF THE NIAGARA** (See American Graphics)

**INDIANS**
Spring, 1950 - No. 17, Spring, 1953
Fiction House Magazines (Wings Publ. Co.)

| | Good | Fine | N-Mint |
|---|---|---|---|
| 1-Manzar The White Indian, Long Bow & Orphan of the Storm begin | 11.50 | 34.00 | 80.00 |
| 2-Starlight begins | 5.70 | 17.00 | 40.00 |
| 3-5 | 4.50 | 14.00 | 32.00 |
| 6-10 | 3.50 | 10.50 | 24.00 |
| 11-17 | 2.85 | 8.50 | 20.00 |

**INDIANS OF THE WILD WEST**
Circa 1958? (no date) (Reprints)
I. W. Enterprises

| | Good | Fine | N-Mint |
|---|---|---|---|
| 9-Kinstler-c; Whitman-a | .50 | 1.50 | 3.00 |

**INDIANS ON THE WARPATH**
No date (Late 40s, early 50s) (132 pages)
St. John Publishing Co.

| | Good | Fine | N-Mint |
|---|---|---|---|
| nn-Matt Baker-c; contains St. John comics rebound. Many combinations possible | 16.00 | 48.00 | 110.00 |

**INDIAN TRIBES** (See Famous Indian Tribes)

**INDIAN WARRIORS** (Formerly White Rider and Super Horse)
No. 7, June, 1951 - No. 11, 1952
Star Publications

| | Good | Fine | N-Mint |
|---|---|---|---|
| 7-White Rider & Superhorse continue; L.B. Cole-c | 4.30 | 13.00 | 30.00 |
| 8-11: 11-L. B. Cole-c | 3.00 | 9.00 | 21.00 |
| 3-D 1(12/53)-L. B. Cole-c | 19.00 | 58.00 | 135.00 |
| Accepted Reprint(nn)(inside cover shows White Rider & Superhorse #11)-R-/cover/#7; origin White Rider &... L. B. Cole-c | 2.00 | 6.00 | 14.00 |
| Accepted Reprint #8 (nd); L.B. Cole-c | 2.00 | 6.00 | 14.00 |

**INDOORS-OUTDOORS** (See Wisco)

**INDOOR SPORTS**
nd (64 pgs.; 6x9"; B&W reprints; hardcover)
National Specials Co.

| | Good | Fine | N-Mint |
|---|---|---|---|
| nn-By Tad | 3.50 | 10.50 | 24.00 |

**INFERIOR FIVE, THE** (Inferior 5 #11, 12) (See Showcase #62, 63, 65)
3-4/67 - No. 10, 9-10/68; No. 11, 8-9/72 - No. 12, 10-11/72
National Periodical Publications (#1-10: 12 cents)

| | Good | Fine | N-Mint |
|---|---|---|---|
| 1-Sekowsky-a(p) | 2.85 | 8.50 | 20.00 |
| 2-Plastic Man app.; Sekowsky-a(p) | 1.50 | 4.50 | 10.00 |
| 3-10: 10-Superman x-over | 1.00 | 3.00 | 7.00 |
| 11,12-Orlando-c/a; both r-/Showcase #62,63 | 1.00 | 3.00 | 7.00 |

**INFINITY, INC.** (See All-Star Squadron #25)
Mar, 1984 - No. 53, Aug, 1988 ($1.25, Baxter paper, 36 pgs.)
DC Comics

| | Good | Fine | N-Mint |
|---|---|---|---|
| 1-Brainwave, Jr., Fury, The Huntress, Jade, Northwind, Nuklon, Obsidian, Power Girl, Silver Scarab & Star Spangled Kid begin | .50 | 1.50 | 3.00 |
| 2-5: 2-Dr. Midnite, G.A. Flash, W. Woman, Dr. Fate, Hourman, Green Lantern, Wildcat app. 5-Nudity panels | .35 | 1.00 | 2.00 |
| 6-13,38-49,51-53: 46,47-Millennium tie-ins | .25 | .80 | 1.60 |
| 14-Todd McFarlane-a (5/85, 2nd full story) | .85 | 2.50 | 5.00 |
| 15-37-McFarlane-a (20,23,24: 5 pgs. only; 33: 2 pgs.); 18-24-Crisis x-over. 21-Intro new Hourman & Dr. Midnight. 26-New Wildcat app. 31-Star-Spangled Kid becomes Skyman. 32-Green Fury becomes Green Flame. 33-Origin Obsidian | .50 | 1.50 | 3.00 |
| 50 ($2.50, 52 pgs.) | 40 | 1.25 | 2.50 |
| Annual 1,2: 1(12/85)-Crisis x-over. 2('88, $2.00) | .35 | 1.00 | 2.00 |
| Special 1 ('87, $1.50) | .25 | .75 | 1.50 |

NOTE: **Kubert** *r-4.* **McFarlane** *a-14-37p, Annual 1p; c(p)-14-19, 22, 25, 26, 31-33, 37, Annual 1.* **Newton** *a-12p, 13p(last work 4/85).* **Tuska** *a-11p. JSA app. 3-10.*

**INFORMER, THE**
April, 1954 - No. 5, Dec, 1954
Feature Television Productions

| | Good | Fine | N-Mint |
|---|---|---|---|
| 1-Sekowsky-a begins | 4.30 | 13.00 | 30.00 |
| 2 | 3.00 | 9.00 | 21.00 |
| 3-5 | 2.30 | 7.00 | 16.00 |

**IN HIS STEPS**
1973, 1977 (39, 49 cents)
Spire Christian Comics (Fleming H. Revell Co.)

| | | | |
|---|---|---|---|
| nn | | .40 | .80 |

**INHUMANOIDS, THE** (TV)
Jan, 1987 - No. 4, July, 1987
Star Comics (Marvel)

| | | | |
|---|---|---|---|
| 1-4: Based on Hasbro toys | | .50 | 1.00 |

**INHUMANS, THE** (See Amazing Adventures, Fantastic Four #45, Marvel Graphic Novel & Thor #146)
Oct, 1975 - No. 12, Aug, 1977
Marvel Comics Group

| | | | |
|---|---|---|---|
| 1 | .40 | 1.25 | 2.50 |
| 2-12: 9-Reprints | | .60 | 1.20 |
| Special 1(4/90, $1.50, 52 pgs.)-F.F. cameo | .25 | .75 | 1.50 |

NOTE: ***Buckler** c-2-4p, 5. **Gil Kane** a-5-7p; c-1p, 7p, 8p. **Kirby** a-9r. **Mooney** a-11i. **Perez** a-1-4p, 8p.*

**INKY & DINKY** (See Felix's Nephews . . .)

**IN LOVE** (I Love You No. 7 on)
Aug-Sept, 1954 - No. 6, July, 1955 ('Adult Reading' on-c)
Mainline/Charlton No. 5 (5/55)-on

| | | | |
|---|---|---|---|
| 1-Simon & Kirby-a | 9.30 | 28.00 | 65.00 |
| 2-S&K-a; book-length novel | 5.00 | 15.00 | 35.00 |
| 3,4-S&K-a. 3-Last pre-code (12-1/54-55) | 4.30 | 13.00 | 30.00 |
| 5-S&K-c only | 2.30 | 7.00 | 16.00 |
| 6-No S&K-a | 1.50 | 4.50 | 10.00 |

**IN LOVE WITH JESUS**
1952 (36 pages) (Giveaway)
Catechetical Educational Society

| | | | |
|---|---|---|---|
| nn | 2.00 | 6.00 | 14.00 |

**INSANE**
Feb, 1988 - No. 2? ($1.75, B&W)
Dark Horse Comics

| | | | |
|---|---|---|---|
| 1,2: 1-X-Men, Godzilla parodies. 2-Concrete | .30 | .90 | 1.80 |

**IN SEARCH OF THE CASTAWAYS** (See Movie Comics)

**INSIDE CRIME** (Formerly My Intimate Affair)
No. 3, July, 1950 - No. 2, Sept, 1950
Fox Features Syndicate (Hero Books)

| | | | |
|---|---|---|---|
| 3-Wood-a, 10 pgs.; L. B. Cole-c | 11.50 | 34.00 | 80.00 |
| 2-Used in **SOTI**, pg. 182,183; r-/Spook #24 | 9.30 | 28.00 | 65.00 |
| nn(no publ. listed, nd) | 3.70 | 11.00 | 26.00 |

**INSPECTOR, THE** (Also see The Pink Panther)
July, 1974 - No. 19, Feb, 1978
Gold Key

| | | | |
|---|---|---|---|
| 1 | .60 | 1.75 | 3.50 |
| 2-5 | .30 | .90 | 1.80 |
| 6-19: 11-Reprints | | .50 | 1.00 |

**INSPECTOR WADE** (See Feature Books No. 13, McKay)

**INTERFACE**
Dec, 1989 - Present ($1.95, color, adults, printed on coated paper)
Epic Comics (Marvel)

| | | | |
|---|---|---|---|
| 1-Based on ESPers; painted-c/a | .40 | 1.15 | 2.30 |
| 2-5 | .35 | 1.00 | 2.00 |
| 6-8: 6-Begin $2.25-c | .40 | 1.15 | 2.30 |

**INTERNATIONAL COMICS** (. . .Crime Patrol No. 6)
Spring, 1947 - No. 5, Nov-Dec, 1947
E. C. Comics

| | Good | Fine | N-Mint |
|---|---|---|---|
| 1 | 40.00 | 120.00 | 280.00 |
| 2 | 30.00 | 90.00 | 210.00 |
| 3-5 | 25.00 | 75.00 | 175.00 |

**INTERNATIONAL CRIME PATROL** (Formerly International Comics No. 1-5; becomes Crime Patrol No. 7 on)
No. 6, Spring, 1948
E. C. Comics

| | | | |
|---|---|---|---|
| 6-Moon Girl app. | 40.00 | 120.00 | 280.00 |

**INTERSTATE THEATRES' FUN CLUB COMICS**
Mid 1940's (10 cents on cover) (B&W cover) (Premium)
Interstate Theatres

Cover features MLJ characters looking at a copy of Top-Notch Comics, but contains an early Detective Comic on inside; many combinations possible

| | | | |
|---|---|---|---|
| | 5.35 | 16.00 | 24.00 |

**IN THE DAYS OF THE MOB** (Magazine)
Fall, 1971 (Black & White)
Hampshire Dist. Ltd. (National)

| | | | |
|---|---|---|---|
| 1-Kirby-a; has John Dillinger wanted poster inside | .70 | 2.00 | 4.00 |

**IN THE PRESENCE OF MINE ENEMIES**
1973 (35-49 cents)
Spire Christian Comics/Fleming H. Revell Co.

| | | | |
|---|---|---|---|
| nn | | .50 | 1.00 |

**INTIMATE** (Teen-Age Love No. 4 on)
December, 1957 - No. 3, May, 1958
Charlton Comics

| | | | |
|---|---|---|---|
| 1-3 | 1.00 | 3.00 | 7.00 |

**INTIMATE CONFESSIONS** (See Fox Giants)

**INTIMATE CONFESSIONS**
July-Aug, 1951 - No. 7, Aug, 1952; No. 8, Mar, 1953 (All painted-c)
Realistic Comics

| | | | |
|---|---|---|---|
| 1-Kinstler-c/a; c/Avon paperback #222 | 50.00 | 150.00 | 350.00 |
| 2 | 9.00 | 27.00 | 60.00 |
| 3-c/Avon paperback #250; Kinstler-c/a | 12.00 | 36.00 | 80.00 |
| 4-6,8: 4-c/Avon paperback #304; Kinstler-c. 6-c/Avon paperback #120. 8-c/Avon paperback #375; Kinstler-a | 9.00 | 27.00 | 60.00 |
| 7-Spanking panel | 10.00 | 30.00 | 70.00 |

**INTIMATE CONFESSIONS**
1964
I. W. Enterprises/Super Comics

| | | | |
|---|---|---|---|
| I.W. Reprint #9,10 | .70 | 2.00 | 4.00 |
| Super Reprint #12,18 | .70 | 2.00 | 4.00 |

**INTIMATE LOVE**
No. 5, 1950 - No. 28, Aug, 1954
Standard Comics

| | | | |
|---|---|---|---|
| 5 | 2.85 | 8.50 | 20.00 |
| 6-8-Severin/Elder-a | 3.50 | 10.50 | 24.00 |
| 9 | 1.50 | 4.50 | 10.00 |
| 10-Jane Russell, Robert Mitchum photo-c | 3.50 | 10.50 | 24.00 |
| 11-18,20,23,25,27,28 | 1.15 | 3.50 | 8.00 |
| 19,21,22,24,26-Toth-a | 4.00 | 12.00 | 28.00 |

NOTE: ***Celardo** a-8, 10. **Colletta** a-23. **Moreira** a-13(2). Photo-c-6, 7, 10, 12, 14, 15, 18-20, 24, 26, 27.*

**INTIMATE SECRETS OF ROMANCE**
Sept, 1953 - No. 2, April, 1954
Star Publications

| | | | |
|---|---|---|---|
| 1,2-L. B. Cole-c | 5.00 | 15.00 | 35.00 |

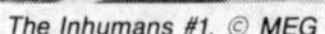
*The Inhumans #1, © MEG*

*Interface #1, © MEG*

*Intimate Love #26, ©*

*The Invaders #20, © MEG*

*Iron Fist #2, © MEG*

*Iron Man #5, © MEG*

**INTRIGUE**
January, 1955
Quality Comics Group

| | Good | Fine | N-Mint |
|---|---|---|---|
| 1-Horror; Jack Cole reprint/Web of Evil | 10.00 | 30.00 | 70.00 |

**INTRUDER**
1990 - Present ($2.95, color, 44 pgs.)
TSR, Inc.

| | Good | Fine | N-Mint |
|---|---|---|---|
| 1-8 | .50 | 1.50 | 3.00 |

**INVADERS, THE** (TV)
Oct, 1967 - No. 4, Oct, 1968 (All have photo-c)
Gold Key

| | Good | Fine | N-Mint |
|---|---|---|---|
| 1-Spiegle-a in all | 4.00 | 12.00 | 28.00 |
| 2-4 | 3.00 | 9.00 | 21.00 |

**INVADERS, THE** (Also see The Avengers #71 & Giant-Size. . .)
August, 1975 - No. 40, May, 1979; No. 41, Sept, 1979
Marvel Comics Group

| | Good | Fine | N-Mint |
|---|---|---|---|
| 1-Captain America & Bucky, Human Torch & Toro, & Sub-Mariner begin | 1.00 | 3.00 | 6.00 |
| 2-10: 2-1st app. Mailbag & Brain-Drain. 3-Battle issue; intro U-Man. 6-Liberty Legion app; intro/1st app. Union Jack; two cover prices, 25 & 30 cents. 7-Intro Baron Blood; Human Torch origin retold. 9-Origin Baron Blood. 10-G.A. Capt. America-r | .70 | 2.00 | 4.00 |
| 11-19: 11-Origin Spitfire; intro The Blue Bullet. 14-1st app. The Crusaders. 16-Re-intro The Destroyer. 17-Intro Warrior Woman. 18-Re-intro The Destroyer w/new origin. 19-Hitler-c/story | .50 | 1.50 | 3.00 |
| 20-Reprints Sub-Mariner story/Motion Picture Funnies Weekly with color added & brief write-up about MPFW | .70 | 2.00 | 4.00 |
| 21,24: Reprint Marvel Mystery #10 & 17 | .50 | 1.50 | 3.00 |
| 22,23,25-41: 22-New origin Toro. 25-All new-a begins. 28-Intro new Human Top & Golden Girl. 29-Intro Teutonic Knight. 31-Frankenstein-c/story. 32,33-Thor app. 34-Mighty Destroyer joins. 35-The Whizzer app. 41-Double-size | .35 | 1.00 | 2.00 |
| Annual 1(9/77)-Schomburg, Rico stories(r); Schomburg-c (1st for Marvel in 30 years); Avengers app.; re-intro The Shark & The Hyena | .35 | 1.00 | 2.00 |

NOTE: ***Buckler** a-5. **Everett** r-21(1940), 24, Annual 1. **Gil Kane** c(p)-13, 17, 18, 20-27. **Kirby** c(p)-3-12, 14-16, 32, 33. **Mooney** a-5i, 16, 22.*

**INVADERS FROM HOME**
1990 - No. 6, 1990 ($2.50, color, mature readers)
Piranha Press (DC)

| | Good | Fine | N-Mint |
|---|---|---|---|
| 1-6 | .40 | 1.25 | 2.50 |

**INVASION**
Holiday, 1988-'89 - No. 3, Jan, 1989 ($2.95, mini-series, 84 pgs.)
DC Comics

| | Good | Fine | N-Mint |
|---|---|---|---|
| 1-McFarlane/Russell-a | .60 | 1.75 | 3.50 |
| 2,3: 2-McFarlane/Russell-a. 3-Russell-i | .50 | 1.50 | 3.00 |

**INVINCIBLE FOUR OF KUNGFU & NINJA**
April, 1988 - No. 12?, 1990 ($2.00, color)
Leung Publications

| | Good | Fine | N-Mint |
|---|---|---|---|
| 1 ($2.75) | .45 | 1.40 | 2.75 |
| 2-12 ($2.00) | .35 | 1.00 | 2.00 |

**INVISIBLE BOY** (See Approved Comics)

**INVISIBLE MAN, THE** (See Superior Stories #1 & Supernatural Thrillers #2)

**INVISIBLE SCARLET O'NEIL** (Also see Famous Funnies #81 & Harvey Comics Hits 59)
Dec, 1950 - No. 3, April, 1951
Famous Funnies (Harvey)

| | Good | Fine | N-Mint |
|---|---|---|---|
| 1 | 9.50 | 28.00 | 65.00 |
| 2,3 | 6.50 | 19.50 | 45.00 |

**IRON CORPORAL, THE** (See Army War Heroes)
No. 23, Oct, 1985 - No. 25, Feb, 1986
Charlton Comics

| | Good | Fine | N-Mint |
|---|---|---|---|
| 23-25: Glanzman-a(r) | | .40 | .75 |

**IRON FIST** (Also see Marvel Premiere & Power Man)
Nov, 1975 - No. 15, Sept, 1977
Marvel Comics Group

| | Good | Fine | N-Mint |
|---|---|---|---|
| 1-McWilliams-a(i); Iron Man app. | 2.15 | 6.50 | 15.00 |
| 2 | 1.15 | 3.50 | 8.00 |
| 3-5 | 1.00 | 3.00 | 6.00 |
| 6-10: 8-Origin retold | .85 | 2.50 | 5.00 |
| 11-13: 12-Capt. America app. | .70 | 2.00 | 4.00 |
| 14-1st app. Saber Tooth | 4.50 | 14.00 | 32.00 |
| 15-New X-Men app., Byrne-a | 3.00 | 9.00 | 21.00 |
| 15 (35 cent edition) | 3.60 | 11.00 | 25.00 |

NOTE: ***Adkins** a-8p, 10i, 13i; c-8i. **Byrne** a-1-15p; c-8p, 15p. **G. Kane** c-4-6p.*

**IRON HORSE** (TV)
March, 1967 - No. 2, June, 1967
Dell Publishing Co.

| | Good | Fine | N-Mint |
|---|---|---|---|
| 1,2 | 1.15 | 3.50 | 8.00 |

**IRONJAW** (Also see The Barbarians)
Jan, 1975 - No. 4, July, 1975
Atlas/Seaboard Publ.

| | Good | Fine | N-Mint |
|---|---|---|---|
| 1-Neal Adams-c; Sekowsky-a(p) | .25 | .75 | 1.50 |
| 2-Neal Adams-c | | .50 | 1.00 |
| 3,4: 4-Origin | | .30 | .60 |

**IRON MAN** (Also see The Avengers #1, Giant-Size. . ., Marvel Collectors Item Classics, Marvel Double Feature, Marvel Fanfare & Tales of Suspense #39)
May, 1968 - Present
Marvel Comics Group

| | Good | Fine | N-Mint |
|---|---|---|---|
| 1-Origin; Colan-c/a(p) | 43.00 | 130.00 | 300.00 |
| 2 | 14.00 | 43.00 | 100.00 |
| 3 | 11.00 | 32.00 | 75.00 |
| 4,5 | 8.00 | 24.00 | 55.00 |
| 6-10 | 5.00 | 15.00 | 35.00 |
| 11-15: 15-Last 12 cent issue | 4.00 | 12.00 | 28.00 |
| 16-20 | 2.65 | 8.00 | 18.00 |
| 21-42: 22-Death of Janice Cord. 27-Intro Fire Brand. 33-1st app. Spymaster. 42-Last | | | |
| 43-46,48-50: 43-Intro ... man dies. 50-Prin | | | |
| 47-Origin retold; Smi | | | |
| 51-54 | | | |
| 55,56-Starlin-a; 55-St | | | |
| 57-67,69,70: 59-Fireb ... cent issue | | | |
| 68-Starlin-c; origin re | | | |
| 71-99: 76 r-/#9. 86-1s ... cent issue | | | |
| 100-Starlin-c | | | |
| 101-117: 101-Intro Dr ... 110-Origin Jack | | | |
| 118-Byrne-a(p) | | | |
| 119,120,123-128-Tony ... Sub-Mariner x-c | | | |
| 121,122,129-149: 122 | | | |
| 150-Double size | | | |
| 151-168: 152-New arr ... alcohol problem | | | |
| 169-New Iron Man ( | | | |
| 170 | | | |
| 171 | | | |

| | Good | Fine | N-Mint |
|---|---|---|---|
| 172-199: 172-Captain America x-over. 186-Intro Vibro. 190-Scarlet Witch app. 191-198-Tony Stark returns as original Iron Man. 192-Both Iron Men battle | .30 | .85 | 1.70 |
| 200-Double size ($1.25)-Tony Stark returns as new Iron Man (red & white armor) thru #230 | .70 | 2.00 | 4.00 |
| 201-224: 213-Intro new Dominic Fortune | .25 | .75 | 1.50 |
| 225-Double size ($1.25) | .90 | 2.75 | 5.50 |
| 226-243,245-249: 228-Vs. Capt. America. 231-Intro new Iron Man. 233-Antman app. 243-Tony Stark looses use of legs. 247-Hulk x-over | .25 | .75 | 1.50 |
| 244-($1.50, 52pgs.)-New Armor makes him walk | .75 | 2.20 | 4.40 |
| 250 ($1.50, 52 pgs.) | .30 | .85 | 1.70 |
| 251-268: 258-Byrne scripts begin | | .50 | 1.00 |
| Special 1(8/70)-Sub-Mariner x-over; Everett-c | 1.70 | 5.00 | 12.00 |
| Special 2(11/71) | 1.00 | 3.00 | 6.00 |
| Annual 3(6/76)-Man-Thing app. | .50 | 1.50 | 3.00 |
| Annual 5-9: 5(12/82). 6(11/83)-New Iron Man(J. Rhodes) app. 7(10/84). 8(10/86)-X-Factor app. 9(12/87) | .35 | 1.00 | 2.00 |
| Annual 10(8/89, $2.00, 68 pgs.)-Atlantis Attacks x-over; P. Smith-a; Layton/Guice-a; Sub-Mariner app. | .40 | 1.25 | 2.50 |
| Annual 11(1990, $2.00, 68 pgs.)-Origin of Mrs. Arbogast by Ditko (p&i) | .35 | 1.00 | 2.00 |
| King Size 4(8/77)-Newton-a(i) | .50 | 1.50 | 3.00 |
| Graphic Novel: Crash (1988, $12.95, Adults, 76 pgs?)-Computer generated art & color; violence & nudity | 2.15 | 6.50 | 12.95 |

NOTE: ***Austin*** *c-105i, 109-111i, 151i.* ***Byrne*** *a-118p; c-109p, 253.* ***Colan*** *a-1p, 253, Special 1p(3); c-1p.* ***Craig*** *a-1i, 2-4, 5-13i, 14, 15-19i, 24p, 25p, 26-28i; c-2-4.* ***Ditko*** *a-160p.* ***Guice*** *a-233-241p.* ***G. Kane*** *c(p)-52-54, 63, 67, 72-75, 77, 78, 88, 98.* ***Kirby*** *a-Special 1p; c-13, 80p, 90, 92-95.* ***Mooney*** *a-40i, 47i.* ***Perez*** *c-103p.* ***Simonson*** *c-Annual 8.* ***B. Smith*** *a-229, 232p, 243i; c-229, 232.* ***P. Smith*** *a-159p, 245p, Annual 10p; c-159.* ***Starlin*** *a-53p, 55p, 56p; c-55p, 160, 163.* ***Tuska*** *a-5-13p, 15-23p, 24i, 32p, 38-46p, 48-54p, 57-61p, 63-69p, 70-72p, 78p, 86-92p, 95-106p, Annual 4p.* ***Wood*** *a-Special 1i.*

**IRON MAN & SUB-MARINER**
April, 1968 (One Shot) (Pre-dates Iron Man #1)
Marvel Comics Group

| | Good | Fine | N-Mint |
|---|---|---|---|
| 1-Colan/Craig-a-Iron Man; Colan/Everett-c | 13.00 | 40.00 | 90.00 |

**IRON MARSHALL**
July, 1990 - Present ($1.75, color, plastic coated-c)
Jademan Comics

| | Good | Fine | N-Mint |
|---|---|---|---|
| 1-4: Kung-Fu stories. 1-Poster centerfold | .30 | .90 | 1.80 |

**IRON VIC** (See Comics Revue No. 3)
1940; Aug, 1947 - No. 3, 1947
United Features Syndicate/St. John Publ. Co.

| | Good | Fine | N-Mint |
|---|---|---|---|
| Single Series 22 | 16.00 | 48.00 | 110.00 |
| 2,3(St. John) | 3.00 | 9.00 | 21.00 |

**IRONWOLF** (See Weird Worlds #8)
1986 ($2.00, one shot)
DC Comics

| | Good | Fine | N-Mint |
|---|---|---|---|
| 1 | .35 | 1.00 | 2.00 |

**ISIS** (TV) (Also see Shazam)
Oct-Nov, 1976 - No. 8, Dec-Jan, 1977-78
National Periodical Publications/DC Comics

| | Good | Fine | N-Mint |
|---|---|---|---|
| 1-Wood inks | | .40 | .80 |
| 2-8: 5-Isis new look. 7-Origin | | .25 | .50 |

**ISLAND AT THE TOP OF THE WORLD** (See Walt Disney Showcase 27)

**ISLAND OF DR. MOREAU, THE** (Movie)
October, 1977 (52 pgs.)
Marvel Comics Group

| | Good | Fine | N-Mint |
|---|---|---|---|
| 1-Gil Kane-c | | .50 | 1.00 |

**I SPY** (TV)
Aug, 1966 - No. 6, Sept, 1968 (Photo-c)
Gold Key

| | Good | Fine | N-Mint |
|---|---|---|---|
| 1-Bill Cosby, Robert Culp photo covers | 5.00 | 15.00 | 35.00 |
| 2-6: 3,4-McWilliams-a | 3.00 | 9.00 | 21.00 |

**IS THIS TOMORROW?**
1947 (One Shot) (3 editions) (52 pages)
Catechetical Guild

| | Good | Fine | N-Mint |
|---|---|---|---|
| 1-Theme of communists taking over the USA; (no price on cover) Used in **POP**, pg. 102 | 10.00 | 30.00 | 70.00 |
| 1-(10 cents on cover) | 14.00 | 42.00 | 100.00 |
| 1-Has blank circle with no price on cover | 14.00 | 42.00 | 100.00 |
| Black & White advance copy titled "Confidential"-(52 pgs.)-Contains script and art edited out of the color edition, including one page of extreme violence showing mob nailing a Cardinal to a door; (only two known copies) | 43.00 | 130.00 | 300.00 |

NOTE: *The original color version first sold for 10 cents. Since sales were good, it was later printed as a giveaway. Approximately four million in total were printed. The two black and white copies listed plus two other versions as well as a full color untrimmed version surfaced in 1979 from the Guild's old files in St. Paul, Minnesota.*

**IT!** (See Astonishing Tales No. 21-24 & Supernatural Thrillers No. 1)

**IT HAPPENS IN THE BEST FAMILIES**
1920 (52 pages) (B&W Sundays)
Powers Photo Engraving Co.

| | Good | Fine | N-Mint |
|---|---|---|---|
| nn-By Briggs | 9.30 | 28.00 | 65.00 |
| Special Railroad Edition(30 cents)-r-/strips from 1914-1920 | 8.00 | 24.00 | 56.00 |

**IT REALLY HAPPENED**
1944 - No. 11, Oct, 1947
William H. Wise No. 1,2/Standard (Visual Editions)

| | Good | Fine | N-Mint |
|---|---|---|---|
| 1-Kit Carson story | 7.00 | 21.00 | 50.00 |
| 2 | 3.70 | 11.00 | 26.00 |
| 3,4,6,9 | 2.85 | 8.50 | 20.00 |
| 5-Lou Gehrig story | 5.00 | 15.00 | 35.00 |
| 7-Teddy Roosevelt story | 3.15 | 9.50 | 22.00 |
| 8-Story of Roy Rogers | 6.50 | 19.00 | 45.00 |
| 10-Honus Wagner story | 4.30 | 13.00 | 30.00 |
| 11-Baker-a | 4.50 | 14.00 | 32.00 |

NOTE: ***Guardineer*** *a-7(2), 8(2), 11.* ***Schomburg*** *c-1-7, 9-11.*

**IT RHYMES WITH LUST** (Also see Bold Stories & Candid Tales)
1950 (Digest size) (128 pages)
St. John Publishing Co.

| | Good | Fine | N-Mint |
|---|---|---|---|
| nn (Rare)-Matt Baker & Ray Osrin-a | 27.00 | 81.00 | 190.00 |

**IT'S ABOUT TIME** (TV)
January, 1967
Gold Key

| | Good | Fine | N-Mint |
|---|---|---|---|
| 1 (10195-701)-Photo-c | 2.65 | 8.00 | 18.00 |

**IT'S A DUCK'S LIFE**
Feb, 1950 - No. 11, Feb, 1952
Marvel Comics/Atlas(MMC)

| | Good | Fine | N-Mint |
|---|---|---|---|
| 1-Buck Duck, Super Rabbit begin | 6.50 | 19.00 | 45.00 |
| 2 | 3.15 | 9.50 | 22.00 |
| 3-11 | 2.00 | 6.00 | 14.00 |

**IT'S FUN TO STAY ALIVE** (Giveaway)
1948 (16 pgs.) (heavy stock paper)
National Automobile Dealers Association

| | Good | Fine | N-Mint |
|---|---|---|---|
| Featuring: Bugs Bunny, The Berrys, Dixie Dugan, Elmer, Henry, Tim Tyler, Bruce Gentry, Abbie & Slats, Joe Jinks, The Toodles, & Cokey; all art copyright 1946-48 drawn especially for this book. | 11.50 | 34.00 | 80.00 |

**IT'S GAMETIME**
Sept-Oct, 1955 - No. 4, Mar-Apr, 1956
National Periodical Publications

*It Really Happened #11, © STD*

*It's About Time #1, © United Artists*

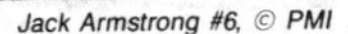
Jack Armstrong #6, © PMI

Jackie Gleason & the Honeymooners #4, © DC

Jackpot #1, © AP

| | Good | Fine | N-Mint |
|---|---|---|---|
| 1-(Scarce)-Infinity-c; Davy Crockett app. in puzzle | 32.00 | 96.00 | 225.00 |
| 2-4(Scarce): 2-Dodo & The Frog | 26.00 | 77.00 | 180.00 |

**IT'S LOVE, LOVE, LOVE**
November, 1957 - No. 2, Jan, 1958 (10 cents)
St. John Publishing Co.

| | Good | Fine | N-Mint |
|---|---|---|---|
| 1,2 | 2.15 | 6.50 | 15.00 |

**IVANHOE** (See Fawcett Movie Comics No. 20)

**IVANHOE**
July-Sept, 1963
Dell Publishing Co.

| | Good | Fine | N-Mint |
|---|---|---|---|
| 1 (12-373-309) | 2.65 | 8.00 | 18.00 |

**IWO JIMA** (See Spectacular Features Magazine)

**JACE PEARSON OF THE TEXAS RANGERS** (4-Color #396 is titled Tales of the Texas Rangers; . . .'s Tales of . . . #11-on)(See Western Roundup under Dell Giants)
No. 396, 5/52 - No. 1021, 8-10/59 (No #10) (All-Photo-c)
Dell Publishing Co.

| | Good | Fine | N-Mint |
|---|---|---|---|
| 4-Color 396 (#1) | 6.00 | 18.00 | 42.00 |
| 2(5-7/53) - 9(2-4/55) | 4.00 | 12.00 | 28.00 |
| 4-Color 648(9/55) | 4.00 | 12.00 | 28.00 |
| 11(11-2/55/56) - 14,17-20(6-8/58) | 3.00 | 9.00 | 21.00 |
| 15,16-Toth-a | 4.50 | 14.00 | 32.00 |
| 4-Color 961-Spiegle-a | 3.50 | 10.50 | 24.00 |
| 4-Color 1021 | 3.00 | 9.00 | 21.00 |

**JACK & JILL VISIT TOYTOWN WITH ELMER THE ELF**
1949 (16 pgs.) (paper cover)
Butler Brothers (Toytown Stores Giveaway)

| | Good | Fine | N-Mint |
|---|---|---|---|
| nn | 1.70 | 5.00 | 10.00 |

**JACK ARMSTRONG** (Radio)(See True Comics)
Nov, 1947 - No. 9, Sept, 1948; No. 10, Mar, 1949 - No. 13, Sept, 1949
Parents' Institute

| | Good | Fine | N-Mint |
|---|---|---|---|
| 1 | 11.50 | 34.00 | 80.00 |
| 2 | 5.70 | 17.00 | 40.00 |
| 3-5 | 4.50 | 14.00 | 32.00 |
| 6-13 | 3.70 | 11.00 | 26.00 |
| 12-Premium version(distr. in Chicago only); Free printed on upper right-c; no price (Rare) | 10.00 | 30.00 | 70.00 |

**JACK HUNTER**
July, 1987 - No. 4? ($1.25, color)
Blackthorne Publishing

| | Good | Fine | N-Mint |
|---|---|---|---|
| 1-4 | | .60 | 1.25 |

**JACKIE GLEASON** (TV) (Also see The Honeymooners)
1948 - No. 2, 1948; Sept, 1955 - No. 4, Dec, 1955?
St. John Publishing Co.

| | Good | Fine | N-Mint |
|---|---|---|---|
| 1(1948) | 39.00 | 118.00 | 275.00 |
| 2(1948) | 25.00 | 75.00 | 175.00 |
| 1(1955)(TV)-Photo-c | 29.00 | 86.00 | 200.00 |
| 2-4 | 19.00 | 58.00 | 135.00 |

**JACKIE GLEASON AND THE HONEYMOONERS** (TV)
June-July, 1956 - No. 12, Apr-May, 1958
National Periodical Publications

| | Good | Fine | N-Mint |
|---|---|---|---|
| 1 | 45.00 | 135.00 | 315.00 |
| 2 | 32.00 | 95.00 | 225.00 |
| 3-11 | 25.00 | 75.00 | 175.00 |
| 12 (Scarce) | 29.00 | 86.00 | 200.00 |

**JACKIE JOKERS** (Also see Richie Rich & . . .)
March, 1973 - No. 4, Sept, 1973
Harvey Publications

| | Good | Fine | N-Mint |
|---|---|---|---|
| 1-4: 2-President Nixon app. | | .20 | .40 |

**JACKIE ROBINSON** (Famous Plays of . . .) (Also see Negro Heroes #2 & Picture News #4)
May, 1950 - No. 6, 1952 (Baseball hero) (All photo-c)
Fawcett Publications

| | Good | Fine | N-Mint |
|---|---|---|---|
| nn | 36.00 | 107.00 | 250.00 |
| 2 | 23.00 | 70.00 | 160.00 |
| 3-6 | 20.00 | 60.00 | 140.00 |

**JACK IN THE BOX** (Formerly Yellowjacket Comics No. 1-10) (Cowboy Western Comics No. 17 on)
Feb, 1946; No. 11, Oct, 1946 - No. 16, Nov-Dec, 1947
Frank Comunale/Charlton Comics No. 11 on

| | Good | Fine | N-Mint |
|---|---|---|---|
| 1-Stitches, Marty Mouse & Nutsy McKrow | 5.70 | 17.00 | 40.00 |
| 11-Yellowjacket | 6.00 | 18.00 | 42.00 |
| 12,14,15 | 2.30 | 7.00 | 16.00 |
| 13-Wolverton-a | 10.00 | 30.00 | 70.00 |
| 16-12pg. adapt. of Silas Marner; Kiefer-a | 4.00 | 12.00 | 28.00 |

**JACK OF HEARTS** (Also see Marvel Premiere #44)
Jan, 1984 - No. 4, April, 1984 (60 cents, mini-series)
Marvel Comics Group

| | Good | Fine | N-Mint |
|---|---|---|---|
| 1-4 | | .50 | 1.00 |

**JACKPOT COMICS** (Jolly Jingles No. 10 on)
Spring, 1941 - No. 9, Spring, 1943
MLJ Magazines

| | Good | Fine | N-Mint |
|---|---|---|---|
| 1-The Black Hood, Mr. Justice, Steel Sterling & Sgt. Boyle begin; Biro-c | 125.00 | 312.00 | 750.00 |
| 2 | 52.00 | 155.00 | 365.00 |
| 3 | 43.00 | 130.00 | 300.00 |
| 4-Archie begins (on sale 12/41)-(Also see Pep Comics No. 22); Montana-c | 121.00 | 365.00 | 850.00 |
| 5-Hitler-c | 54.00 | 160.00 | 375.00 |
| 6-9: 6,7-Bondage-c | 47.00 | 140.00 | 325.00 |

**JACK Q FROST** (See Unearthly Spectaculars)

**JACK THE GIANT KILLER** (See Movie Classics)

**JACK THE GIANT KILLER** (New Advs. of . . .)
Aug-Sept, 1953
Bimfort & Co.

| | Good | Fine | N-Mint |
|---|---|---|---|
| V1#1-H. C. Kiefer-c/a | 10.00 | 30.00 | 70.00 |

**JACKY'S DIARY** (See 4-Color No. 1091)

**JADEMAN COLLECTION**
Dec, 1989 - No. 5? ($2.50, color, plastic coated-c, 68 pgs.)
Jademan Comics

| | Good | Fine | N-Mint |
|---|---|---|---|
| 1-5: 1-Wraparound-c w/fold-out poster | .40 | 1.25 | 2.50 |

**JADEMAN KUNG FU SPECIAL**
1988 ($1.50, color, 64pgs.)
Jademan Comics

| | Good | Fine | N-Mint |
|---|---|---|---|
| 1 | .25 | .75 | 1.50 |

**JAGUAR, THE** (See The Adventures of . . .)

**JAKE THRASH**
1988 - No. 3, 1988 ($2.00, color)
Aircel Publishing

| | Good | Fine | N-Mint |
|---|---|---|---|
| 1-3 | .35 | 1.00 | 2.00 |

**JAMBOREE**
Feb, 1946(no mo. given) - No. 3, April, 1946
Round Publishing Co.

| | Good | Fine | N-Mint |
|---|---|---|---|
| 1-Funny animal | 7.00 | 21.00 | 50.00 |
| 2,3 | 5.00 | 15.00 | 35.00 |

**JAMES BOND FOR YOUR EYES ONLY**
Oct, 1981 - No. 2, Nov, 1981
Marvel Comics Group

| | Good | Fine | N-Mint |
|---|---|---|---|
| 1,2-Movie adapt.; r-/Marvel Super Spec. #19 | | .30 | .60 |

**JAMES BOND: LICENCE TO KILL** (See Licence To Kill)

**JAMES BOND: PERMISSION TO DIE**
1989 - No. 3, 1990 ($3.95, color, mini-series, squarebound, 52 pgs.)
Eclipse Comics/ACME Press

| | | | |
|---|---|---|---|
| 1-3: Mike Grell-c/a/scripts in all. 3-($4.95) | .85 | 2.50 | 5.00 |

**JAM: SUPER COOL COLOR INJECTED TURBO ADVENTURE #1 FROM HELL!, THE**
May, 1988 ($2.50, 44 pgs, color)
Comico

| | | | |
|---|---|---|---|
| 1 | .40 | 1.25 | 2.50 |

**JANE ARDEN** (See Feature Funnies & Pageant of Comics)
March, 1948 - No. 2, June, 1948
St. John (United Features Syndicate)

| | | | |
|---|---|---|---|
| 1-Newspaper reprints | 10.00 | 30.00 | 70.00 |
| 2 | 6.00 | 18.00 | 42.00 |

**JANN OF THE JUNGLE** (Jungle Tales No. 1-7)
No. 8, Nov, 1955 - No. 17, June, 1957
Atlas Comics (CSI)

| | | | |
|---|---|---|---|
| 8(#1) | 10.00 | 30.00 | 70.00 |
| 9,11-15 | 5.00 | 15.00 | 35.00 |
| 10-Williamson/Colleta-c | 6.00 | 18.00 | 42.00 |
| 16,17-Williamson/Mayo-a(3), 5 pgs. each | 8.50 | 25.50 | 60.00 |

NOTE: ***Everett** c-15-17. **Heck** a-8, 15, 17. **Shores** a-8.*

**JASON & THE ARGONAUTS** (See Movie Classics)

**JAWS 2** (See Marvel Super Special, A)

**JCP FEATURES**
Feb, 1982-c; Dec, 1981-indicia ($2.00, One-shot, B&W)
J.C. Productions (Archie)

| | | | |
|---|---|---|---|
| 1-T.H.U.N.D.E.R. Agents; Black Hood by Morrow & Neal Adams | .35 | 1.00 | 2.00 |

**JEANIE COMICS** (Cowgirl Romances #28) (Formerly All Surprise)
No. 13, April, 1947 - No. 27, Oct, 1949
Marvel Comics/Atlas(CPC)

| | | | |
|---|---|---|---|
| 13-Mitzi, Willie begin | 7.00 | 21.00 | 50.00 |
| 14,15 | 4.30 | 13.00 | 30.00 |
| 16-Used in **Love and Death** by Legman; Kurtzman's "Hey Look" | 6.50 | 19.00 | 45.00 |
| 17-19,22-Kurtzman's "Hey Look," 1-3 pgs. each | 4.00 | 12.00 | 28.00 |
| 20,21,23-27 | 3.00 | 9.00 | 21.00 |

**JEEP COMICS** (Also see G.I. and Overseas Comics)
Winter, 1944 - No. 3, Mar-Apr, 1948
R. B. Leffingwell & Co.

| | | | |
|---|---|---|---|
| 1-Capt. Power, Criss Cross & Jeep & Peep (costumed) begin | 10.00 | 30.00 | 70.00 |
| 2 | 6.50 | 19.00 | 45.00 |
| 3-L. B. Cole-c | 7.00 | 21.00 | 50.00 |
| 1-29(Giveaway)-Strip reprints in all; Tarzan, Flash Gordon, Blondie, The Nebbs, Little Iodine, Red Ryder, Don Winslow, The Phantom, Johnny Hazard, Katzenjammer Kids; distr. to U.S. Armed Forces in mid 1940's | 3.35 | 10.00 | 20.00 |

**JEFF JORDAN, U.S. AGENT**
Dec, 1947 - Jan, 1948
D. S. Publishing Co.

| | | | |
|---|---|---|---|
| 1 | 5.70 | 17.00 | 40.00 |

**JEMM, SON OF SATURN**
Sept, 1984 - No. 12, Aug, 1985 (12 part maxi-series; mando paper)
DC Comics

| | Good | Fine | N-Mint |
|---|---|---|---|
| 1-12: Colan p-all; c-1-5p, 7-12p. 3-Origin | | .50 | 1.00 |

**JERRY DRUMMER** (Formerly Soldier & Marine V2No.9)
V2#10, Apr, 1957 - V3#12, Oct, 1957
Charlton Comics

| | | | |
|---|---|---|---|
| V2#10, V3#11,12 | 1.50 | 4.50 | 10.00 |

**JERRY IGER'S CLASSIC SHEENA** (Also see Sheena 3-D Special)
April, 1985 (One-shot)
Blackthorne Publishing

| | | | |
|---|---|---|---|
| 1 | .25 | .75 | 1.50 |

**JERRY IGER'S FAMOUS FEATURES**
July, 1984 (One-shot)
Pacific Comics

| | | | |
|---|---|---|---|
| 1-Unpub. Flamingo & Wonder Boy by Baker | .25 | .75 | 1.50 |

**JERRY IGER'S GOLDEN FEATURES**
1986 - No. 7? ($2.00, B&W) (All reprints)
Blackthorne Publishing

| | | | |
|---|---|---|---|
| 1-7: 2-Wonder Boy by Baker. 3-South Sea Girl & Lucky Wings by Iger; Phantom Lady. 4-Fine/Kirby-r | .35 | 1.00 | 2.00 |

**JERRY LEWIS** (See The Adventures of. . .)

**JESSE JAMES** (See 4-Color No. 757 & The Legend of. . .)

**JESSE JAMES** (See Badmen of the West & Blazing Sixguns)
8/50 - No. 9, 11/52; No. 15, 10/53 - No. 29, 8-9/56
Avon Periodicals

| | | | |
|---|---|---|---|
| 1-Kubert Alabam r-/Cowpuncher #1 | 11.00 | 33.00 | 76.00 |
| 2-Kubert-a(3) | 8.50 | 25.50 | 60.00 |
| 3-Kubert Alabam r-/Cowpuncher #2 | 7.00 | 21.00 | 50.00 |
| 4,9-No Kubert | 2.85 | 8.50 | 20.00 |
| 5,6-Kubert Jesse James-a(3); 5-Wood-a(1pg.) | 7.00 | 21.00 | 50.00 |
| 7-Kubert Jesse James-a(2) | 6.00 | 18.00 | 42.00 |
| 8-Kinstler-a(3) | 4.00 | 12.00 | 28.00 |
| 15-Kinstler r-/#3 | 2.15 | 6.50 | 15.00 |
| 16-Kinstler r-/#3 & Sheriff Bob Dixon's Chuck Wagon #1 with name changed to Sheriff Tom Wilson | 2.65 | 8.00 | 18.00 |
| 17-19,21: 17-Jesse James r-/#4; Kinstler-c idea from Kubert splash in #6. 18-Kubert Jesse James r-/#5. 19-Kubert Jesse James-r. 21-Two Jesse James r-/#4, Kinstler r-/#4 | 1.70 | 5.00 | 12.00 |
| 20-Williamson/Frazetta-a; r-Chief Vic. Apache Massacre; Kubert Jesse James r-/#6 | 8.50 | 25.50 | 60.00 |
| 22,23-No Kubert | 1.60 | 4.80 | 11.00 |
| 24-New McCarty strip by Kinstler; Kinstler-r | 1.60 | 4.80 | 11.00 |
| 25-New McCarty Jesse James strip by Kinstler; Kinstler J. James r-/#7,9 | 1.60 | 4.80 | 11.00 |
| 26,27-New McCarty J. James strip plus a Kinstler/McCann Jesse James-r | 1.60 | 4.80 | 11.00 |
| 28,29: 28-Reprints most of Red Mountain, Featuring Quantrells Raiders | 1.60 | 4.80 | 11.00 |
| Annual(nn; 1952; 25 cents)-". . .Brings Six-Gun Justice to the West" (100 pgs.)-3 earlier issues rebound; Kubert, Kinstler-a(3) | 17.00 | 51.00 | 120.00 |

NOTE: *Mostly reprints #10 on. **Fawcette** c-1, 2. **Kinstler** a-3, 4, 7-9, 15r, 16r(2), 21-27; c-3, 4, 9, 17, 18, 20-27. Painted c-5, 6.*

**JESSE JAMES**
July, 1953
Realistic Publications

| | | | |
|---|---|---|---|
| nn-Reprints Avon's #1, same-c, colors different | 5.00 | 15.00 | 35.00 |

**JEST** (Kayo No. 12) (Formerly Snap)
No. 10, 1944; No. 11, 1944
Harry 'A' Chesler

*James Bond: Permission to Die #1, © Eclipse*

*Jeanie Comics #18, © MEG*

*Jesse James #1, © AVON*

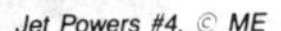
Jet Powers #4, © ME

The Jetsons #7 (Gold Key), © Hanna-Barbera

Jim Bowie #17, © CC

| | Good | Fine | N-Mint |
|---|---|---|---|
| 10-Johnny Rebel & Yankee Boy app. in text | 5.70 | 17.00 | 40.00 |
| 11-Little Nemo in Adventure Land | 6.50 | 19.00 | 45.00 |

**JESTER**
No. 10, 1945
Harry 'A' Chesler

| | | | |
|---|---|---|---|
| 10 | 5.00 | 15.00 | 35.00 |

**JESUS**
1979 (49 cents)
Spire Christian Comics (Fleming H. Revell Co.)

| | | | |
|---|---|---|---|
| nn | | .40 | .80 |

**JET** (See Jet Powers)

**JET ACES**
1952 - No. 4, 1953
Fiction House Magazines

| | | | |
|---|---|---|---|
| 1 | 6.00 | 18.00 | 42.00 |
| 2-4 | 3.50 | 10.50 | 24.00 |

**JET DREAM** (. . . & Her Stuntgirl Counterspies)
June, 1968
Gold Key

| | | | |
|---|---|---|---|
| 1 | 1.70 | 5.00 | 12.00 |

**JET FIGHTERS** (Korean War)
No. 5, Nov, 1952 - No. 7, Mar, 1953
Standard Magazines

| | | | |
|---|---|---|---|
| 5,7-Toth-a | 5.00 | 15.00 | 35.00 |
| 6-Celardo-a | 1.85 | 5.50 | 13.00 |

**JET POWER**
1963
I.W. Enterprises

| | | | |
|---|---|---|---|
| I.W. Reprint 1,2-r/Jet Powers #1,2 | 1.70 | 5.00 | 12.00 |

**JET POWERS** (American Air Forces No. 5 on)
1950 - No. 4, 1951
Magazine Enterprises

| | | | |
|---|---|---|---|
| 1(A-1 #30)-Powell-c/a begins | 17.00 | 51.00 | 120.00 |
| 2(A-1 #32) | 12.00 | 36.00 | 84.00 |
| 3(A-1 #35)-Williamson/Evans-a | 21.50 | 64.00 | 150.00 |
| 4(A-1 #38)-Williamson/Wood-a; "The Rain of Sleep" drug story | 21.50 | 64.00 | 150.00 |

**JET PUP** (See 3-D Features)

**JETSONS, THE** (TV)(See March of Comics 276,330,348, Spotlight 3)
Jan, 1963 - No. 36, Oct, 1970 (Hanna-Barbera)
Gold Key

| | | | |
|---|---|---|---|
| 1 | 13.00 | 40.00 | 90.00 |
| 2 | 8.00 | 24.00 | 55.00 |
| 3-10 | 5.70 | 17.00 | 40.00 |
| 11-20 | 4.50 | 14.00 | 32.00 |
| 21-36 | 3.60 | 11.00 | 25.00 |

**JETSONS, THE** (TV) (Hanna-Barbera)
Nov, 1970 - No. 20, Dec, 1973
Charlton Comics

| | | | |
|---|---|---|---|
| 1 | 5.00 | 15.00 | 35.00 |
| 2 | 3.00 | 9.00 | 21.00 |
| 3-10 | 2.00 | 6.00 | 14.00 |
| 11-20 | 1.50 | 4.50 | 10.00 |

**JETTA OF THE 21ST CENTURY**
No. 5, Dec, 1952 - No. 7, Apr, 1953 (Teen-age Archie type)
Standard Comics

| | | | |
|---|---|---|---|
| 5 | 8.00 | 24.00 | 56.00 |
| 6,7 | 5.00 | 15.00 | 35.00 |

**JEZEBEL JADE** (Hanna-Barbara)
Oct, 1988 - No. 3, Dec, 1988 ($2.00, color, mini-series)
Comico

| | Good | Fine | N-Mint |
|---|---|---|---|
| 1-3: Jonny Quest spin-off | .35 | 1.00 | 2.00 |

**JIGGS & MAGGIE** (See 4-Color No. 18)

**JIGGS & MAGGIE**
No. 11, 1949(Aug.) - No. 21, 2/53; No. 22, 4/53 - No. 27, 2-3/54
Standard Comics/Harvey Publications No. 22 on

| | | | |
|---|---|---|---|
| 11 | 6.50 | 19.50 | 45.00 |
| 12-15,17-21 | 3.50 | 10.50 | 24.00 |
| 16-Wood text illos. | 4.30 | 13.00 | 30.00 |
| 22-25,27: 22-24-Little Dot app. | 2.65 | 8.00 | 18.00 |
| 26-Four pgs. partially in 3-D | 10.00 | 30.00 | 70.00 |

NOTE: *Sunday page reprints by* **McManus** *loosely blended into story continuity. Based on Bringing Up Father strip. Advertised on covers as "All New."*

**JIGSAW** (Big Hero Adventures)
Sept, 1966 - No. 2, Dec, 1966 (36 pgs.)
Harvey Publications (Funday Funnies)

| | | | |
|---|---|---|---|
| 1-Origin; Crandall-a, 5pgs. | .85 | 2.60 | 6.00 |
| 2-Man From S.R.A.M. | .70 | 2.00 | 4.00 |

**JIGSAW OF DOOM** (See Complete Mystery No. 2)

**JIM BOWIE** (Formerly Danger; Black Jack No. 20 on)
No. 15, 1955? - No. 19, April, 1957
Charlton Comics

| | | | |
|---|---|---|---|
| 15 | 3.00 | 9.00 | 21.00 |
| 16-19 | 1.70 | 5.00 | 12.00 |

**JIM BOWIE** (See 4-Color No. 893,993, & Western Tales)

**JIM DANDY**
May, 1956 - No. 3, Sept, 1956 (Charles Biro)
Dandy Magazine (Lev Gleason)

| | | | |
|---|---|---|---|
| 1 | 3.15 | 9.50 | 22.00 |
| 2,3 | 1.70 | 5.00 | 12.00 |

**JIM HARDY** (Also see Sparkler & Treasury of Comics No. 2&5)
1939; 1942; 1947 - No. 2, 1947
United Features Syndicate/Spotlight Publ.

| | | | |
|---|---|---|---|
| Single Series 6 ('39) | 22.00 | 65.00 | 155.00 |
| Single Series 27('42) | 16.50 | 50.00 | 115.00 |
| 1('47)-Spotlight Publ. | 6.00 | 18.00 | 42.00 |
| 2 | 3.50 | 10.50 | 24.00 |

**JIM HARDY**
1944 (132 pages, 25 cents) (Tip Top, Sparkler-r)
Spotlight/United Features Syndicate

| | | | |
|---|---|---|---|
| (1944)-Origin Mirror Man; Triple Terror app. | 24.00 | 73.00 | 170.00 |

**JIMINY CRICKET** (See 4-Color No. 701,795,897,989, Mickey Mouse Mag. V5/3 & Walt Disney Showcase #37)

**JIMMY** (James Swinnerton)
1905 (10x15") (40 pages in color)
N. Y. American & Journal

| | | | |
|---|---|---|---|
| nn | 20.00 | 60.00 | 140.00 |

**JIMMY DURANTE** (See A-1 Comics No. 18, 20)

**JIMMY OLSEN** (See Superman's Pal . . .)

**JIMMY WAKELY** (Cowboy movie star)
Sept-Oct, 1949 - No. 18, July-Aug, 1952 (1-13: 52pgs.)
National Periodical Publications

| | | | |
|---|---|---|---|
| 1-Photo-c, 52 pgs. begin; Alex Toth-a; Kit Colby Girl Sheriff begins | 39.00 | 118.00 | 275.00 |
| 2-Toth-a | 25.00 | 75.00 | 175.00 |
| 3,6,7-Frazetta-a in all, 3 pgs. each; Toth-a in all. 7-Last photo-c? | 27.00 | 81.00 | 190.00 |

| | Good | Fine | N-Mint |
|---|---|---|---|
| 4-Frazetta-a, 3 pgs.; Kurtzman "Pot-Shot Pete," 1 pg; Toth-a | 27.00 | 81.00 | 190.00 |
| 5,8-15,18-Toth-a; 12,14-Kubert-a, 3 & 2 pgs. | 20.00 | 60.00 | 140.00 |
| 16,17 | 14.00 | 43.00 | 100.00 |

**JIM RAY'S AVIATION SKETCH BOOK**
Feb, 1946 - No. 2, May-June, 1946
Vital Publishers

1,2-Picture stories about planes and pilots 13.00 40.00 90.00

**JIM SOLAR** (See Wisco/Klarer)

**JINGLE BELLS** (See March of Comics No. 65)

**JINGLE BELLS CHRISTMAS BOOK**
1971 (20 pgs.; B&W inside; slick cover)
Montgomery Ward (Giveaway)

nn .40 .80

**JINGLE DINGLE CHRISTMAS STOCKING COMICS**
V2#1, 1951 (no date listed) (100 pgs.; giant-size)(25 cents)
Stanhall Publications (Publ.-annually)

V2#1-Foodini & Pinhead, Silly Pilly plus games & puzzles 7.00 21.00 50.00

**JINGLE JANGLE COMICS** (Also see Puzzle Fun)
Feb, 1942 - No. 42, Dec, 1949
Eastern Color Printing Co.

| | Good | Fine | N-Mint |
|---|---|---|---|
| 1-Pie-Face Prince of Old Pretzleburg, Jingle Jangle Tales by George Carlson, Hortense, & Benny Bear begin | 25.00 | 75.00 | 175.00 |
| 2,3-No Pie-Face Prince | 11.50 | 34.00 | 80.00 |
| 4-Pie-Face Prince cover | 11.50 | 34.00 | 80.00 |
| 5 | 10.00 | 30.00 | 70.00 |
| 6-10: 8-No Pie-Face Prince | 8.50 | 25.50 | 60.00 |
| 11-15 | 5.70 | 17.00 | 40.00 |
| 16-30: 17,18-No Pie-Face Prince. 30-XMas-c | 4.30 | 13.00 | 30.00 |
| 31-42: 36,42-Xmas-c | 3.00 | 9.00 | 21.00 |

NOTE: ***George Carlson** a-(2) in all except No. 2, 3, 8; c-1-6. **Carlson** 1 pg. puzzles in 9, 10, 12-15, 18, 20. **Carlson** illustrated a series of Uncle Wiggily books in 1930's.*

**JING PALS**
Feb, 1946 - No. 4, Aug?, 1946 (Funny animal)
Victory Publishing Corporation

| | Good | Fine | N-Mint |
|---|---|---|---|
| 1-Wishing Willie, Puggy Panda & Johnny Rabbit begin | 6.00 | 18.00 | 42.00 |
| 2-4 | 3.50 | 10.50 | 24.00 |

**JINKS, PIXIE, AND DIXIE** (See Whitman Comic Books)
1965 (Giveaway) (Hanna-Barbera)
Florida Power & Light

nn .70 2.00 4.00

**JOAN OF ARC** (See A-1 Comics No. 21 & Ideal a Classical Comic)

**JOAN OF ARC**
No date (28 pages)
Catechetical Guild (Topix) (Giveaway)

nn 7.00 21.00 50.00

NOTE: *Unpublished version exists which came from the Guild's files.*

**JOE COLLEGE**
Fall, 1949 - No. 2, Winter, 1950 (Teen-age humor)
Hillman Periodicals

1,2-Powell-a; 1-Briefer-a 4.00 12.00 28.00

**JOE JINKS** (See Single Series No. 12)

**JOE LOUIS** (See Fight Comics 2, Picture News 6 & True Comics 5)
Sept, 1950 - No. 2, Nov, 1950 (Photo-c) (Boxing champ)
Fawcett Publications

| | Good | Fine | N-Mint |
|---|---|---|---|
| 1-Photo-c; life story | 30.00 | 90.00 | 210.00 |
| 2-Photo-c | 20.00 | 60.00 | 140.00 |

**JOE PALOOKA**
1933 (B&W daily strip reprints) (52 pages)
Cupples & Leon Co.

| | Good | Fine | N-Mint |
|---|---|---|---|
| nn-(Scarce)-by Fisher | 50.00 | 150.00 | 350.00 |

**JOE PALOOKA** (1st Series)(Also see Big Shot, Columbia Comics & Feature Funnies)
1942 - No. 4, 1944
Columbia Comic Corp. (Publication Enterprises)

| | Good | Fine | N-Mint |
|---|---|---|---|
| 1-1st to portray American president; gov't permission required | 35.00 | 105.00 | 245.00 |
| 2 (1943)-Hitler-c | 19.00 | 58.00 | 135.00 |
| 3,4 | 13.00 | 40.00 | 90.00 |

**JOE PALOOKA** (2nd Series) (Battle Adv. #68-74; . . . Advs. #75,77-81, 83-85,87; Champ of the Comics #76,82,86,89-93) (See All-New)
Nov, 1945 - No. 118, Mar, 1961
Harvey Publications

| | Good | Fine | N-Mint |
|---|---|---|---|
| 1 | 22.00 | 65.00 | 150.00 |
| 2 | 11.00 | 32.00 | 75.00 |
| 3,4,6 | 6.50 | 19.50 | 45.00 |
| 5-Boy Explorers by S&K (7-8/46) | 9.50 | 28.00 | 65.00 |
| 7-1st Powell Flyin' Fool, ends #25 | 5.70 | 17.00 | 40.00 |
| 8-10 | 5.00 | 15.00 | 35.00 |
| 11-14,16-20: 19-Freedom Train-c | 4.00 | 12.00 | 28.00 |
| 15-Origin Humphrey; Super heroine Atoma app. by Powell | 5.00 | 15.00 | 35.00 |
| 21-30: 27-1st app. Little Max? (12/48). 30-Nude female painting | 3.00 | 9.00 | 21.00 |
| 31-61: 44-Joe Palooka marries Ann Howe | 2.30 | 7.00 | 16.00 |
| 62-S&K Boy Explorers-r | 3.00 | 9.00 | 21.00 |
| 63-80: 66,67-'commie' torture story | 1.70 | 5.00 | 12.00 |
| 81-99,101-115 | 1.50 | 4.50 | 10.00 |
| 100 | 1.75 | 5.25 | 12.00 |
| 116-S&K Boy Explorers (r) (Giant, '60) | 2.85 | 8.50 | 20.00 |
| 117,118-Giants | 2.65 | 8.00 | 18.00 |
| . . . Body Building Instruction Book (1958 Sports Toy giveaway, 16pgs., 5¼x7")-Origin | 5.00 | 15.00 | 35.00 |
| . . . Fights His Way Back (1945 Giveaway, 24 pgs.) Family Comics | 14.00 | 42.00 | 100.00 |
| . . . in Hi There! (1949 Red Cross giveaway, 12 pgs., 4¾x6") | 5.00 | 15.00 | 35.00 |
| . . . in It's All in the Family (1945 Red Cross giveaway, 16 pgs., regular size) | 6.50 | 19.50 | 45.00 |
| . . . **Visits the Lost City** (1945)(One Shot)(nn)(50 cents)-164 page continuous story strip reprint. Has biography & photo of Ham Fisher; possibly the single longest comic book story published (159 pgs.?) | 60.00 | 180.00 | 420.00 |

NOTE: ***Nostrand/Powell** a-73. **Powell** a-7, 8, 10, 12, 14, 17, 19, 26-45, 47-53, 70, 73 at least. Black Cat text stories #8, 12, 13, 19. Bondage c-50.*

**JOE YANK**
No. 5, March, 1952 - No. 16, 1954
Standard Comics (Visual Editions)

| | Good | Fine | N-Mint |
|---|---|---|---|
| 5-Celardo, Tuska-a | 2.65 | 8.00 | 18.00 |
| 6-Toth, Severin/Elder-a | 4.50 | 14.00 | 32.00 |
| 7 | 1.70 | 5.00 | 12.00 |
| 8-Toth-c | 3.00 | 9.00 | 21.00 |
| 9-16: 12-Andru-a | 1.30 | 4.00 | 9.00 |

**JOHN BOLTON'S HALLS OF HORROR**
June, 1985 - No. 2, June, 1985 ($1.75 cover, color)
Eclipse Comics

1,2-British-r; Bolton-c/a .30 .90 1.80

**JOHN CARTER OF MARS** (See 4-Color No. 375, 437, 488, The Funnies & Tarzan #207)

*Jingle Jangle Comics #1, © EAS*

*Jing Pals #1, © Victory Publ.*

*Joe Palooka #44, © HARV*

John F. Kennedy, Champion of. . . nn, © W&C

Johnny Mack Brown #8, © DELL

Johnny Thunder #1, © DC

**JOHN CARTER OF MARS**
April, 1964 - No. 3, Oct, 1964
Gold Key

Good Fine N-Mint
1(10104-404)-R/4-Color 375; Jesse Marsh-a 2.85 8.50 20.00
2(407), 3(410)-R/4-Color 437 & 488; Marsh-a 2.30 7.00 16.00

**JOHN CARTER OF MARS**
1970 (72 pgs.; paper cover; 10½x16½"; B&W)
House of Greystroke

1941-42 Sunday strip reprints; John Coleman Burroughs-a 2.65 8.00 18.00

**JOHN CARTER, WARLORD OF MARS** (Also see Weird Worlds)
June, 1977 - No. 28, Oct, 1979
Marvel Comics Group

1-Origin by Gil Kane .50 1.00
2-17,19-28: 11-Origin Dejah Thoris .30 .60
18-Miller-a(p) .35 1.00 2.00
Annuals 1-3: 1(10/77), 2(1978), 3(1979) .40 .80

NOTE: ***Austin*** *c-24i.* ***Gil Kane*** *a-1-10p; c-1p, 2p, 3, 4-9p, 10, 15p, Annual 1p.* ***Layton*** *a-17i.* ***Miller*** *c-25, 26p.* ***Nebres*** *a-2-4i, 8-16i; c(i)-6-9, 11-22, 25, Annual 1.* ***Perez*** *c-24p.* ***Simonson*** *a-15p.* ***Sutton*** *a-7i.*

**JOHN F. KENNEDY, CHAMPION OF FREEDOM**
1964 (no month) (25 cents)
Worden & Childs

nn-Photo-c 4.00 12.00 28.00

**JOHN F. KENNEDY LIFE STORY**
Aug-Oct, 1964; Nov, 1965; June, 1966 (12 cents)
Dell Publishing Co.

12-378-410 3.00 9.00 21.00
12-378-511 (reprint, 11/65) 2.00 6.00 14.00
12-378-606 (reprint, 6/66) 1.70 5.00 12.00

**JOHN FORCE** (See Magic Agent)

**JOHN HIX SCRAP BOOK, THE**
Late 1930's (no date) (68 pgs.; reg. size; 10 cents)
Eastern Color Printing Co. (McNaught Synd.)

1-Strange As It Seems (resembles Single Series books) 15.00 45.00 105.00
2-Strange As It Seems 13.00 40.00 90.00

**JOHN LAW DETECTIVE** (See Smash Comics #3)
April, 1983 ($1.50, color, Baxter paper)
Eclipse Comics

1-Three Eisner stories originally drawn in 1948 for the never published John Law No. 1; original cover pencilled in 1948 & inked in 1982 by Eisner .35 1.00 2.00

**JOHNNY APPLESEED** (See Story Hour Series)

**JOHNNY CASH** (See Hello, I'm . . .)

**JOHNNY DANGER**
1950
Toby Press

1-Photo-c; Sparling-a 8.50 25.50 60.00

**JOHNNY DANGER PRIVATE DETECTIVE**
1954 (Reprinted in Danger No. 11 (Super))
Toby Press

1-Opium den story 6.00 18.00 42.00

**JOHNNY DYNAMITE** (Formerly Dynamite No. 1-9)
No. 10, 6/55 - No. 12, 10/55 (Foreign Intrigues No. 13 on)
Charlton Comics

10-12 2.65 8.00 18.00

**JOHNNY HAZARD**
No. 5, Aug, 1948 - No. 8, May, 1949; No. 35, date?
Best Books (Standard Comics) (King Features)

Good Fine N-Mint
5-Strip reprints by Frank Robbins 8.00 24.00 56.00
6,8-Strip reprints by Frank Robbins 5.50 16.50 38.00
7-New art, not Robbins 4.00 12.00 28.00
35 4.00 12.00 28.00

**JOHNNY JASON** (. . .Teen Reporter)
Feb-Apr, 1962 - No. 2, June-Aug, 1962
Dell Publishing Co.

4-Color 1302, 2(01380-208) 1.15 3.50 8.00

**JOHNNY JINGLE'S LUCKY DAY**
1956 (16 pgs.; 7¼x5-1/8") (Giveaway) (Disney)
American Dairy Association

nn 2.35 7.00 14.00

**JOHNNY LAW, SKY RANGER**
Apr, 1955 - No. 3, Aug, 1955; No. 4, Nov, 1955
Good Comics (Lev Gleason)

1-Edmond Good-c/a 3.70 11.00 26.00
2-4 2.15 6.50 15.00

**JOHNNY MACK BROWN** (TV western star; see Western Roundup under Dell Giants)
No. 269, Mar, 1950 - No. 963, Feb, 1959 (All Photo-c)
Dell Publishing Co.

4-Color 269(#1)(3/50, 52pgs.)-Johnny Mack Brown & his horse Rebel begin; photo front/back-c begin; Marsh-a begins, ends #9 13.00 40.00 90.00
2(10-12/50, 52pgs.) 6.50 19.50 45.00
3(1-3/51, 52pgs.) 4.30 13.00 30.00
4-10 (9-11/52)(36pgs.) 3.50 10.50 24.00
4-Color 455,493,541,584,618 3.50 10.50 24.00
4-Color 645,685,722,776,834,963 3.50 10.50 24.00
4-Color 922-Manning-a 4.00 12.00 28.00

**JOHNNY NEMO**
Sept, 1985 - No. 3, Feb, 1986 (Mini-series)
Eclipse Comics

1,2 ($1.75 cover) .30 .90 1.75
3 ($2.00 cover) .35 1.00 2.00

**JOHNNY RINGO** (See 4-Color No. 1142)

**JOHNNY STARBOARD** (See Wisco)

**JOHNNY THUNDER**
Feb-Mar, 1973 - No. 3, July-Aug, 1973
National Periodical Publications

1-Johnny Thunder & Nighthawk-r begin .25 .75 1.50
2,3: 2-Trigger Twins app. .50 1.00

NOTE: ***Drucker*** *r-2, 3.* ***G. Kane*** *r-2, 3.* ***Moriera*** *r-1.* ***Toth*** *r-1, 3; c-1r, 3r. Also see All-American, All-Star Western, Flash Comics, Western Comics, World's Best & World's Finest.*

**JOHN PAUL JONES** (See Four Color No. 1007)

**JOHN STEED & EMMA PEEL** (See The Avengers, Gold Key series)

**JOHN STEELE SECRET AGENT** (Also see Freedom Agent)
December, 1964 (Freedom Agent)
Gold Key

1 1.50 4.50 10.00

**JOHN WAYNE ADVENTURE COMICS** (Movie star; See Big Tex, Oxydol-Dreft, Tim McCoy & With The Marines. . .#1)
Winter, 1949-50 - No. 31, May, 1955 (Photo-c: 1-12,17,25-on)
Toby Press

1 (36pgs.)-Photo-c begin 50.00 150.00 350.00
2 (36pgs.)-Williamson/Frazetta-a(2) 6 & 2 pgs. (one r-/Billy the Kid #1); photo back-c 41.00 125.00 290.00

| | Good | Fine | N-Mint |
|---|---|---|---|
| 3 (36pgs.)-Williamson/Frazetta-a(2), 16 pgs. total; photo back-c | 41.00 | 125.00 | 290.00 |
| 4 (52pgs.)-Williamson/Frazetta-a(2), 16 pgs. total | 41.00 | 125.00 | 290.00 |
| 5 (52pgs.)-Kurtzman-a-(Alfred "L" Newman in Potshot Pete) | 28.50 | 85.00 | 200.00 |
| 6 (52pgs.)-Williamson/Frazetta-a, 10 pgs; Kurtzman a-'Pot-Shot Pete,' 5pgs.; & "Genius Jones," 1 pg. | 39.00 | 120.00 | 275.00 |
| 7 (52pgs.)-Williamson/Frazetta-a, 10 pgs. | 32.00 | 95.00 | 225.00 |
| 8 (36pgs.)-Williamson/Frazetta-a(2), 12 & 9 pgs. | 39.00 | 120.00 | 275.00 |
| 9-11: Photo western-c | 22.00 | 65.00 | 150.00 |
| 12-Photo war-c; Kurtzman-a, 2pgs. "Genius" | 22.00 | 65.00 | 150.00 |
| 13-15: 13-Line-drawn-c begin, end #24 | 18.00 | 54.00 | 125.00 |
| 16-Williamson/Frazetta r-/Billy the Kid #1 | 20.00 | 60.00 | 140.00 |
| 17-Photo-c | 22.00 | 65.00 | 150.00 |
| 18-Williamson/Frazetta-a r-/#4 & 8, 19 pgs. | 23.00 | 70.00 | 160.00 |
| 19-24: 23-Evans-a? | 16.50 | 50.00 | 115.00 |
| 25-Photo-c return; end #31; Williamson/Frazetta-a r-/Billy the Kid #3 | 23.00 | 70.00 | 160.00 |
| 26-28,30-Photo-c | 20.00 | 60.00 | 140.00 |
| 29,31-Williamson/Frazetta-a in each, r-/#4,2 | 22.00 | 65.00 | 150.00 |

NOTE: *Williamsonish art in later issues by **Gerald McCann**.*

**JO-JO COMICS** (. . .Congo King #7-29; My Desire #30 on)
(Also see Fantastic Fears and Jungle Jo)
1945 - No. 29, July, 1949 (two No.7's; no No. 13)
Fox Feature Syndicate

| | Good | Fine | N-Mint |
|---|---|---|---|
| nn(1945)-Funny animal, humor | 6.00 | 18.00 | 42.00 |
| 2(Sum,'46)-6: Funny animal; 2-Ten pg. Electro story | 3.15 | 9.50 | 22.00 |
| 7(7/47)-Jo-Jo, Congo King begins | 30.00 | 90.00 | 210.00 |
| 7(#8) (9/47) | 23.00 | 70.00 | 160.00 |
| 8-10(#9-11): 8-Tanee begins | 19.00 | 56.00 | 130.00 |
| 11,12(#12,13),14,16: 11,16-Kamen bondage-c | 16.00 | 48.00 | 110.00 |
| 15-Cited by Dr. Wertham in 5/47 Saturday Review of Literature | 17.00 | 51.00 | 120.00 |
| 17-Kamen bondage-c | 17.00 | 51.00 | 120.00 |
| 18-20 | 16.00 | 48.00 | 110.00 |
| 21-29: 21-Hollingsworth-a(4 pgs.; 23-1 pg.) | 14.00 | 43.00 | 100.00 |

NOTE: *Many bondage-c/a by **Baker/Kamen/Feldstein/Good**. No. 7's have Princesses Gwenna, Geesa, Yolda, & Safra before settling down on Tanee.*

**JO-JOY** (Adventures of. . .)
1945 - 1953 (Christmas gift comic)
W. T. Grant Dept. Stores

| | Good | Fine | N-Mint |
|---|---|---|---|
| 1945-53 issues | 2.00 | 6.00 | 14.00 |

**JOKEBOOK COMICS DIGEST ANNUAL** (. . .Magazine No. 5 on)
Oct, 1977 - No. 13, Oct, 1983 (Digest Size)
Archie Publications

| | Good | Fine | N-Mint |
|---|---|---|---|
| 1(10/77)-Reprints; Neal Adams-a | | .60 | 1.20 |
| 2(4/78)-13 | | .60 | 1.20 |

**JOKER, THE** (See Batman, Batman: The Killing Joke, Brave & the Bold, Detective, Greatest Joker Stories & Justice League Annual #2)
May, 1975 - No. 9, Sept-Oct, 1976
National Periodical Publications

| | Good | Fine | N-Mint |
|---|---|---|---|
| 1-Two-Face app. | 3.60 | 11.00 | 25.00 |
| 2,3 | 2.00 | 6.00 | 14.00 |
| 4-6 | 1.70 | 5.00 | 12.00 |
| 7,8 | 1.30 | 4.00 | 9.00 |
| 9 | 1.50 | 4.50 | 10.00 |

**JOKER COMICS** (Adventures Into Terror No. 43 on)
April, 1942 - No. 42, August, 1950
Timely/Marvel Comics No. 36 on (TCI/CDS)

| | Good | Fine | N-Mint |
|---|---|---|---|
| 1-(Rare)-Powerhouse Pepper (1st app.) begins by Wolverton; Stuporman app. from Daring | 90.00 | 270.00 | 630.00 |
| 2-Wolverton-a; 1st app. Tessie the Typist | 38.00 | 115.00 | 265.00 |
| 3-5-Wolverton-a | 25.00 | 75.00 | 175.00 |
| 6-10-Wolverton-a | 17.00 | 51.00 | 120.00 |
| 11-20-Wolverton-a | 14.00 | 43.00 | 100.00 |
| 21,22,24-27,29,30-Wolverton cont'd. & Kurtzman's "Hey Look" in #24-27 | 11.00 | 32.00 | 75.00 |
| 23-1st "Hey Look" by Kurtzman; Wolverton-a | 13.00 | 40.00 | 90.00 |
| 28,32,34,37-41 | 2.30 | 7.00 | 16.00 |
| 31-Last Powerhouse Pepper; not in #28 | 8.50 | 25.50 | 60.00 |
| 33,35,36-Kurtzman's "Hey Look" | 3.60 | 11.00 | 25.00 |
| 42-Only app. 'Patty Pinup,' a clone of Millie the Model | 2.85 | 8.50 | 20.00 |

**JOLLY CHRISTMAS, A** (See March of Comics No. 269)

**JOLLY CHRISTMAS BOOK** (See Christmas Journey Through Space)
1951; 1954; 1955 (36 pgs.; 24 pgs.)
Promotional Publ. Co.

| | Good | Fine | N-Mint |
|---|---|---|---|
| 1951-(Woolworth giveaway)-slightly oversized; no slick cover; Marv Levy-c/a | 2.30 | 7.00 | 16.00 |
| 1954-(Hot Shoppes giveaway)-regular size-reprints 1951 issue; slick cover added; 24 pgs.; no ads | 2.30 | 7.00 | 16.00 |
| 1955-(J. M. McDonald Co. giveaway)-regular size | 1.70 | 5.00 | 12.00 |

**JOLLY COMICS**
1947
Four Star Publishing Co.

| | Good | Fine | N-Mint |
|---|---|---|---|
| 1 | 3.15 | 9.50 | 22.00 |

**JOLLY JINGLES** (Formerly Jackpot Comics)
No. 10, Sum, 1943 - No. 16, Wint, 1944/45
MLJ Magazines

| | Good | Fine | N-Mint |
|---|---|---|---|
| 10-Super Duck begins (origin & 1st app.). Woody The Woodpecker begins. (not same as Lantz character) | 20.00 | 60.00 | 140.00 |
| 11 (Fall, '43) | 9.30 | 28.00 | 65.00 |
| 12-Hitler-c | 5.70 | 17.00 | 40.00 |
| 13-16 | 5.00 | 15.00 | 35.00 |

**JONAH HEX** (See All-Star Western, Hex and Weird Western Tales)
Mar-Apr, 1977 - No. 92, Aug, 1985
National Periodical Publications/DC Comics

| | Good | Fine | N-Mint |
|---|---|---|---|
| 1 | 1.00 | 3.00 | 6.00 |
| 2-6,8-10: 9-Wrightson-c | .50 | 1.50 | 3.00 |
| 7-Explains Hex's face disfigurement | .70 | 2.00 | 4.00 |
| 11-20: 12-Starlin-c | .40 | 1.25 | 2.50 |
| 21-50: 31,32-Origin retold | .25 | .75 | 1.50 |
| 51-92: 92-Cont'd in Hex #1 | | .50 | 1.00 |

NOTE: ***Aparo** c-76p. **Ayers** a(p)-35-37, 40, 41, 44-53, 56, 58-82. **Kubert** c-43-46. **Morrow** a-90-92; c-10. **Spiegle**(Tothish) a-34, 38, 40, 49, 52. Batlash back-ups in 49, 52. El Diablo back-ups in 48, 56-60, 73-75. Scalphunter back-ups in 40, 41, 45-47.*

**JONAH HEX AND OTHER WESTERN TALES** (Blue Ribbon Digest)
Sept-Oct, 1979 - No. 3, Jan-Feb, 1980 (100 pgs.)
DC Comics

| | Good | Fine | N-Mint |
|---|---|---|---|
| 1-3: 1-Origin Scalphunter-r; painted-c. 2-Weird Western Tales-r; Neal Adams, Toth, Aragones, Gil Kane-a | | .40 | .80 |

**JONAH HEX SPECTACULAR** (See DC Special Series No. 16)

**JONESY** (Formerly Crack Western)
No. 85, Aug, 1953; No. 2, Oct, 1953 - No. 8, Oct, 1954
Comic Favorite/Quality Comics Group

| | Good | Fine | N-Mint |
|---|---|---|---|
| 85(#1)-Teen-age humor | 3.00 | 9.00 | 21.00 |
| 2 | 1.70 | 5.00 | 12.00 |
| 3-8 | 1.15 | 3.50 | 8.00 |

**JON JUAN** (Also see Great Lover Romances)
Spring, 1950

*John Wayne Adventure Comics #17, © TOBY*

*Jo-Jo Comics #12 (#13), © FOX*

*Joker Comics #15, © MEG*

Jonny Quest #5, © Hanna-Barbera

Journey Into Fear #6, © SUPR

Journey Into Mystery #123, © MEG

Toby Press

| | Good | Fine | N-Mint |
|---|---|---|---|
| 1-All Schomburg-a (signed Al Reid on-c); written by Siegel; used in **SOTI**, pg. 38 | 11.50 | 34.00 | 80.00 |

**JONNI THUNDER** (. . . A.K.A. Thunderbolt)
Feb, 1985 - No. 4, Aug, 1985 (Mini-series)
DC Comics

| | Good | Fine | N-Mint |
|---|---|---|---|
| 1-4: 1-Origin | | .45 | .90 |

**JONNY QUEST** (TV)
December, 1964 (Hanna-Barbera)
Gold Key

| | Good | Fine | N-Mint |
|---|---|---|---|
| 1 (10139-412) | 11.50 | 34.00 | 80.00 |

**JONNY QUEST** (TV)
June, 1986 - No. 31, Dec, 1988 (Hanna-Barbera)
Comico

| | Good | Fine | N-Mint |
|---|---|---|---|
| 1 | .70 | 2.00 | 4.00 |
| 2 | .45 | 1.30 | 2.60 |
| 3,5-Dave Stevens-c | .45 | 1.40 | 2.75 |
| 4,6-10 | .25 | .75 | 1.50 |
| 11-31: #15 on, $1.75. 30-Adapts TV episode | | .60 | 1.25 |
| Special 1(9/88, $1.75), 2(10/88, $1.75) | .25 | .75 | 1.50 |

NOTE: ***M. Anderson** a-9. **Mooney** a-Special 1. **Pini** a-2. **Quagmire** a-31p. **Rude** a-1; c-2i. **Sienkiewicz** c-11. **Spiegle** a-7, 12, 21; c-21. **Staton** a-2i, 11p. **Steacy** c-8. **Stevens** a-4i; c-3, 5. **Wildey** a-1, c-1, 7, 12. **Williamson** a-4i; c-4i.*

**JONNY QUEST CLASSICS** (TV)
May, 1987 - No. 3, July, 1987 ($2.00, color) (Hanna-Barbera)
Comico

| | Good | Fine | N-Mint |
|---|---|---|---|
| 1-3: Wildey-c/a; 3-Based on TV episode | .35 | 1.00 | 2.00 |

**JON SABLE, FREELANCE** (Also see Mile Grell's Sable & Sable)
6/83 - No. 56, 2/88 (#1-17, $1; #18-33, $1.25; #34-on, $1.75)
First Comics

| | Good | Fine | N-Mint |
|---|---|---|---|
| 1-Created, story/a&c by Mike Grell | .60 | 1.75 | 3.50 |
| 2-5: 3-5-Origin, parts 1-3 | .40 | 1.25 | 2.50 |
| 6-10: 6-Origin, part 4 | .35 | 1.00 | 2.00 |
| 11-20: 14-Mando paper begins | .30 | .90 | 1.80 |
| 21-33: 25-30-Shatter app. | .25 | .75 | 1.50 |
| 34-56: 34-Deluxe format begins ($1.75) | .25 | .70 | 1.40 |

NOTE: ***Aragones** a-33; c-33(part). **Grell** a-1-43; c-1-52, 53p, 54-56.*

**JOSEPH & HIS BRETHREN** (See The Living Bible)

**JOSIE** (She's . . . #1-16) (. . .& the Pussycats #45 on) (See Archie Giant Series 528, 540, 551, 562, 571, 584, 597, 610)
Feb, 1963 - No. 106, Oct, 1982
Archie Publications/Radio Comics

| | Good | Fine | N-Mint |
|---|---|---|---|
| 1 | 10.00 | 30.00 | 70.00 |
| 2 | 5.00 | 15.00 | 35.00 |
| 3-5 | 2.85 | 8.50 | 20.00 |
| 6-10 | 2.00 | 6.00 | 14.00 |
| 11-20 | 1.30 | 4.00 | 9.00 |
| 21-30: 22-Mighty Man & Mighty(Josie Girl)app. | .75 | 2.25 | 5.00 |
| 31-54 | .45 | 1.35 | 3.00 |
| 55-74(52pg. issues) | | .50 | 1.00 |
| 75-106 | | .35 | .70 |

**JOURNAL OF CRIME** (See Fox Giants)

**JOURNEY** (Also see Journey: Wardrums)
1983 - No. 14, 9/84; No. 15, 4/85 - No. 27, 7/86 (B&W)
Aardvark-Vanaheim #1-14/Fantagraphics Books #15-on

| | Good | Fine | N-Mint |
|---|---|---|---|
| 1 | 1.70 | 5.00 | 10.00 |
| 2 | 1.00 | 3.00 | 6.00 |
| 3 | .60 | 1.75 | 3.50 |
| 4-27 | .25 | .75 | 1.50 |

**JOURNEY INTO FEAR**
May, 1951 - No. 21, Sept, 1954
Superior-Dynamic Publications

| | Good | Fine | N-Mint |
|---|---|---|---|
| 1-Baker-a(2)-r | 19.00 | 58.00 | 135.00 |
| 2 | 11.50 | 34.00 | 80.00 |
| 3,4 | 9.30 | 28.00 | 65.00 |
| 5-10 | 7.00 | 21.00 | 50.00 |
| 11-14,16-21 | 6.00 | 18.00 | 42.00 |
| 15-Used in **SOTI**, pg. 389 | 7.00 | 21.00 | 50.00 |

NOTE: *Kamenish, 'headlight'-a most issues. **Robinson** a-10.*

**JOURNEY INTO MYSTERY** (1st Series) (Thor No. 126 on)
6/52 - No. 48, 8/57; No. 49, 11/58 - No. 125, 2/66
Atlas(CPS No. 1-48/AMI No. 49-68/Marvel No. 69 (6/61) on)

| | Good | Fine | N-Mint |
|---|---|---|---|
| 1 | 68.00 | 205.00 | 475.00 |
| 2 | 32.00 | 95.00 | 225.00 |
| 3,4 | 26.00 | 77.00 | 180.00 |
| 5-11 | 16.00 | 48.00 | 110.00 |
| 12-20,22: 22-Davisesque-a; last pre-code issue (2/55) | 13.00 | 40.00 | 90.00 |
| 21-Kubert-a; Tothish-a by Andru | 14.00 | 43.00 | 100.00 |
| 23-32,35-38,40: 24-Torres?-a | 7.00 | 21.00 | 50.00 |
| 33-Williamson-a | 9.30 | 28.00 | 65.00 |
| 34,39: 34-Krigstein-a. 39-Wood-a | 8.50 | 25.50 | 60.00 |
| 41-Crandall-a; Frazettaesque-a by Morrow | 6.50 | 19.00 | 45.00 |
| 42,48-Torres-a | 6.50 | 19.00 | 45.00 |
| 43,44-Williamson/Mayo-a in both | 6.50 | 19.00 | 45.00 |
| 45,47,52,53 | 5.70 | 17.00 | 40.00 |
| 46-Torres & Krigstein-a | 6.50 | 19.00 | 45.00 |
| 49-Matt Fox, Check-a | 6.50 | 19.00 | 45.00 |
| 50,54: 50-Davis-a. 54-Williamson-a | 5.70 | 17.00 | 40.00 |
| 51-Kirby/Wood-a | 5.70 | 17.00 | 40.00 |
| 55-61,63-73: 66-Return of Xemnu | 5.00 | 15.00 | 35.00 |
| 62-1st app. Xemnu (Titan) called "The Hulk" | 8.00 | 24.00 | 55.00 |
| 74-82-Fantasy content #74 on. 75-Last 10 cent issue. 80-Anti-communist propaganda story | 4.50 | 14.00 | 32.00 |

83-Origin & 1st app. The Mighty Thor by Kirby (8/62) and begin series

| | Good | Fine | N-Mint | Mint |
|---|---|---|---|---|
| | 132.00 | 396.00 | 925.00 | 1700.00 |

(Estimated up to 1500 total copies exist, 45 in Mint)

| | Good | Fine | N-Mint |
|---|---|---|---|
| 83-R-/from the Golden Record Comic Set | 7.00 | 21.00 | 50.00 |
| with the record (still sealed) | 14.00 | 43.00 | 100.00 |
| 84-2nd app. Thor | 37.00 | 111.00 | 260.00 |
| 85-1st app. Loki & Heimdall | 26.00 | 78.00 | 180.00 |
| 86-1st app. Odin | 19.30 | 58.00 | 135.00 |
| 87-89: 89-Origin Thor reprint/#83 | 16.00 | 48.00 | 110.00 |
| 90-No Kirby-a; Aunt May proto-type | 9.30 | 28.00 | 65.00 |
| 91,92,94-96-Sinnott-a | 8.00 | 24.00 | 55.00 |
| 93,97-Kirby-a; Tales of Asgard series begins #97 (origin which concludes in #99) | 11.00 | 32.00 | 75.00 |
| 98-100-Kirby/Heck-a. 98-Origin/1st app. The Human Cobra. 99-1st app. Surtur & Mr. Hyde | 8.00 | 24.00 | 55.00 |
| 101-110: 102-Intro Sif. 105-109-Ten extra pages Kirby-a in each. 107-1st app. Grey Gargoyle | 5.00 | 15.00 | 35.00 |
| 111,113,114,116-125: 119-Intro Hogun, Fandrall, Volstagg | 4.00 | 12.00 | 28.00 |
| 112-Thor Vs. Hulk; origin Loki begins; ends #113 | 8.00 | 24.00 | 55.00 |
| 115-Detailed origin Loki | 5.00 | 15.00 | 35.00 |
| Annual 1('65)-1st app. Hercules; Kirby-c/a | 10.00 | 30.00 | 70.00 |

NOTE: ***Ayers** a-14, 39. **Bailey** a-43. **Briefer** a-5, 12. **Cameron** a-35. **Check** a-17. **Colan** a-23, 81. **Ditko** a-33, 38, 50-96; c-71, 88i. **Ditko/Kirby** a-50-83. **Everett** a-20, 48; c-4-7, 9, 37, 39, 40-42, 44, 45, 47. **Forte** a-19, 35, 40. **Heath** a-4, 5, 11, 14; c-1, 11, 15, 51. **Kirby** a(p)-51, 52, 56, 57, 60, 66, 69, 72, 76, 79, 80-89, 93, 97, 98, 100(w/Heck), 101-125; c-50-82(w/Ditko), 83-152p. **Leiber/Fox** a-93, 98-102. **Maneely** c-21, 22. **Morrow** a-41, 42. **Orlando** a-30, 45, 57. **Mac Pakula** (Tothish) a-9, 35. **Powell** a-20, 27, 34. **Reinman** a-39, 87, 92, 96i. **Robinson** a-9. **Roussos** a-39. **Robert Sale** a-14. **Severin** a-27. **Sinnott** c-50. **Tuska** a-11. **Wildey** a-16.*

**JOURNEY INTO MYSTERY** (2nd Series)
Oct, 1972 - No. 19, Oct, 1975
Marvel Comics Group

| | Good | Fine | N-Mint |
|---|---|---|---|
| 1-Robert Howard adaptation; Starlin/Ploog-a | .50 | 1.50 | 3.00 |
| 2,3,5-Bloch adaptation; 5-Last new story | .35 | 1.00 | 2.00 |
| 4,6-19: 4-H. P. Lovecraft adaptation | .25 | .75 | 1.50 |

NOTE: ***N. Adams** a-2i. **Ditko** r-7, 10, 12, 14, 15, 19; c-10. **Everett** r-9, 14. **G. Kane** a-1p, 2p; c-1-3p. **Kirby** r-7, 13, 18, 19; c-7. **Mort Lawrence** r-2. **Maneely** r-3. **Orlando** r-16. **Reese** a-1, 2i. **Starlin** a-3p. **Torres** r-16. **Wildey** r-9, 14.*

**JOURNEY INTO UNKNOWN WORLDS** (Formerly Teen)
No. 36, 9/50 - No. 38, 2/51; No. 4, 4/51 - No. 59, 8/57
Atlas Comics (WFP)

| | Good | Fine | N-Mint |
|---|---|---|---|
| 36(#1)-Science fiction/weird; 'End Of The Earth' c/story | 46.00 | 138.00 | 325.00 |
| 37(#2)-Science fiction; 'When Worlds Collide' c/story; Everett-c/a; Hitler story | 33.00 | 100.00 | 230.00 |
| 38(#3)-Science fiction | 26.00 | 77.00 | 180.00 |
| 4-6,8,10-Science fiction/weird | 17.00 | 51.00 | 120.00 |
| 7-Wolverton-a-"Planet of Terror," 6 pgs; electric chair c-inset/story | 29.00 | 85.00 | 200.00 |
| 9-Giant eyeball story | 17.00 | 51.00 | 120.00 |
| 11,12-Krigstein-a | 12.00 | 36.00 | 85.00 |
| 13,16,17,20 | 8.50 | 25.50 | 60.00 |
| 14-Wolverton-a-"One of Our Graveyards Is Missing," 4 pgs; Tuska-a | 26.00 | 77.00 | 180.00 |
| 15-Wolverton-a-"They Crawl By Night," 5 pgs. | 26.00 | 77.00 | 180.00 |
| 18,19-Matt Fox-a | 11.00 | 32.00 | 75.00 |
| 21-33: 21-Decapitation-c. 24-Sci/fic story. 26-Atom bomb panel. 27-Sid Check-a. 33-Last pre-code (2/55) | 5.70 | 17.00 | 40.00 |
| 34-Kubert, Torres-a | 5.70 | 17.00 | 40.00 |
| 35-Torres-a | 5.00 | 15.00 | 35.00 |
| 36-42 | 4.30 | 13.00 | 30.00 |
| 43,44: 43-Krigstein-a. 44-Davis-a | 4.50 | 14.00 | 32.00 |
| 45,55,59-Williamson-a in all; with Mayo #55,59. Crandall-a, #55,59 | 5.70 | 17.00 | 40.00 |
| 46,47,49,52,56-58 | 3.50 | 10.50 | 24.00 |
| 48,53-Crandall-a; Check-a, #48 | 5.50 | 16.50 | 38.00 |
| 50-Davis, Crandall-a | 5.00 | 15.00 | 35.00 |
| 51-Ditko, Wood-a | 5.00 | 15.00 | 35.00 |
| 54-Torres-a | 4.00 | 12.00 | 28.00 |

NOTE: ***Ayers** a-24, 43. **Berg** a-38(#3), 43. **Lou Cameron** a-33. **Colan** a-37(#2), 6, 17, 19, 20, 23, 39. **Ditko** a-45, 51. **Evans** a-20. **Everett** a-37(#2), 11, 14, 41, 55, 56; c-11, 13, 14, 17, 22, 47, 48, 50, 53-55, 59. **Forte** a-49. **Fox** a-21i. **Heath** a-36(#1), 4, 6-8, 17, 20, 22, 36i. **Mort Lawrence** a-38, 39. **Maneely** a-7, 8, 15, 16, 22, 49; c-25, 52. **Morrow** a-48. **Orlando** a-44, 57. **Powell** a-42, 53, 54. **Reinman** a-8. **Rico** a-21. **Robert Sale** a-24, 49. **Sekowsky** a-4, 5, 9. **Severin** a-38, 51; c-38, 48i, 56. **Sinnott** a-9, 21, 24. **Tuska** a-38(#3). **Wildey** a-25, 43, 44.*

**JOURNEY OF DISCOVERY WITH MARK STEEL** (See Mark Steel)

**JOURNEY TO THE CENTER OF THE EARTH** (See 4-Color No. 1060)

**JUDE, THE FORGOTTEN SAINT**
1954 (16 pgs.; 8x11"; full color; paper cover)
Catechetical Guild Education Society

| | Good | Fine | N-Mint |
|---|---|---|---|
| nn | 1.50 | 4.50 | 10.00 |

**JUDGE COLT**
Oct, 1969 - No. 4, Sept, 1970
Gold Key

| | Good | Fine | N-Mint |
|---|---|---|---|
| 1 | .85 | 2.50 | 6.00 |
| 2-4 | .70 | 2.00 | 4.00 |

**JUDGE DREDD** (See The Law of Dredd & 2000 A.D. Monthly)
Nov, 1983 - No. 35, 1986; V2#1, Oct, 1986 - Present
Eagle Comics/IPC Magazines Ltd./Quality Comics #34-35, V2#1-37/ Fleetway #38 on

| | Good | Fine | N-Mint |
|---|---|---|---|
| 1-Bolland-c/a begins, ends #? | .85 | 2.50 | 5.00 |
| 2-35 | .35 | 1.00 | 2.00 |
| V2#1-('86)-New look begins | .35 | 1.00 | 2.00 |
| V2#2-6 | .25 | .75 | 1.50 |
| V2#7-21/22: 14-Bolland-a. 20-Begin $1.50-c | | .65 | 1.30 |
| V2#23/24-Two issue numbers in one | .25 | .75 | 1.50 |
| 25-38: 28-1st app. Megaman (super-hero) | .25 | .75 | 1.50 |
| 39-50: 39-Begin $1.75-c | .30 | .90 | 1.80 |
| Special 1 | | .70 | 1.40 |

NOTE: ***Guice** c-V2#23/24, 26, 27.*

**JUDGE DREDD'S CRIME FILE**
Aug, 1985 - No. 6, Feb, 1986 ($1.25, color, Mini-series)
Eagle Comics

| | Good | Fine | N-Mint |
|---|---|---|---|
| 1-6: 1-Byrne-a | | .65 | 1.30 |

**JUDGE DREDD'S CRIME FILE**
Aug, 1989 - Vol. 4, Oct, 1989 ($5.95, color, high quality, 52 pgs.)
Quality Comics (#1,2,4 are all dated 8/89; #3 is 9/89)

| | Good | Fine | N-Mint |
|---|---|---|---|
| Volume 1-4: Bolland-c; 4-Bolland-a | 1.00 | 3.00 | 6.00 |

**JUDGE DREDD: THE EARLY CASES**
Feb, 1986 - No. 6, July, 1986 ($1.25, Mega-series, Mando paper)
Eagle Comics

| | Good | Fine | N-Mint |
|---|---|---|---|
| 1-6: 2000 A.D.-r | | .65 | 1.30 |

**JUDGE DREDD: THE JUDGE CHILD QUEST** (Judge Child in indicia)
Aug, 1984 - No. 5, Oct, 1984 ($1.25, Limited series, Baxter paper)
Eagle Comics

| | Good | Fine | N-Mint |
|---|---|---|---|
| 1-5: 2000 A.D.-r; Bolland-c/a | | .65 | 1.30 |

**JUDGE PARKER**
Feb, 1956 - No. 2, 1956
Argo

| | Good | Fine | N-Mint |
|---|---|---|---|
| 1 | 3.15 | 9.50 | 22.00 |
| 2 | 1.70 | 5.00 | 12.00 |

**JUDO JOE**
Aug, 1953 - No. 3, Dec, 1953
Jay-Jay Corp.

| | Good | Fine | N-Mint |
|---|---|---|---|
| 1-Drug ring story | 3.70 | 11.00 | 26.00 |
| 2,3: 3-Hypo needle story | 2.30 | 7.00 | 16.00 |

**JUDOMASTER** (Gun Master No. 84-89) (Also see Crisis on Infinite Earths, Sarge Steel #6 & Special War Series)
No. 89, May-June, 1966 - No. 98, Dec, 1967 (Two No. 89's)
Charlton Comics

| | Good | Fine | N-Mint |
|---|---|---|---|
| 89-98: 91-Sarge Steel begins. 93-Intro. Tiger | 1.15 | 3.50 | 8.00 |
| 93,94,96,98(Modern Comics reprint, 1977) | | .15 | .30 |

NOTE: ***Morisi** Thunderbolt No. 90.*

**JUDY CANOVA** (Formerly My Experience) (Stage, screen, radio)
No. 23, May, 1950 - No. 3, Sept, 1950
Fox Features Syndicate

| | Good | Fine | N-Mint |
|---|---|---|---|
| 23(#1)-Wood-c,a(p)? | 10.00 | 30.00 | 70.00 |
| 24-Wood-a(p) | 10.00 | 30.00 | 70.00 |
| 3-Wood-c; Wood/Orlando-a | 11.50 | 34.00 | 80.00 |

**JUDY GARLAND** (See Famous Stars)

**JUDY JOINS THE WAVES**
1951 (For U.S. Navy)
Toby Press

| | Good | Fine | N-Mint |
|---|---|---|---|
| nn | 2.65 | 8.00 | 18.00 |

**JUGHEAD** (Formerly Archie's Pal . . .)
No. 127, Dec, 1965 - No. 352, 1987
Archie Publications

| | Good | Fine | N-Mint |
|---|---|---|---|
| 127-130 | 1.00 | 3.00 | 6.00 |
| 131,133,135-160 | .70 | 2.00 | 4.00 |

132,134: 132-Shield-c; The Fly & Black Hood app.; Shield cameo.

*Journey Into Mystery #1 (10/72), © MEG*

*Journey Into Unknown Worlds #7, © MEG*

*Judge Dredd's Crime File #1, © Quality*

Jughead's Pal Hot Dog #1, © AP

Jughead's Time Police #1, © AP

Jumbo Comics #3, © FH

| | Good | Fine | N-Mint |
|---|---|---|---|
| 134-Shield-c | 1.00 | 3.00 | 6.00 |
| 161-200 | .40 | 1.25 | 2.50 |
| 201-240 | | .60 | 1.20 |
| 241-352: 300-Anniversary issue; infinity-c | | .30 | .60 |

**JUGHEAD**
Aug, 1987 - Present (.75-$1.00)
Archie Enterprises

| | Good | Fine | N-Mint |
|---|---|---|---|
| 1-24: 4-X-Mas issue. 17-Colan-c/a | | .50 | 1.00 |

**JUGHEAD AS CAPTAIN HERO**
Oct, 1966 - No. 7, Nov, 1967
Archie Publications

| | Good | Fine | N-Mint |
|---|---|---|---|
| 1 | 3.50 | 10.50 | 24.00 |
| 2 | 2.00 | 6.00 | 14.00 |
| 3-7 | 1.15 | 3.50 | 8.00 |

**JUGHEAD JONES COMICS DIGEST, THE** (. . . Magazine No. 10-64; Jughead Jones Digest Magazine #65)
June, 1977 - Present ($1.35-$1.50, digest-size, 128 pgs.)
Archie Publications

| | Good | Fine | N-Mint |
|---|---|---|---|
| 1-Neal Adams-a; Capt. Hero-r | .70 | 2.00 | 4.00 |
| 2(9/77)-Neal Adams-a | .35 | 1.00 | 2.00 |
| 3-68: 7-Origin Jaguar-r; N. Adams-a. 13-r-/1957 Jughead's Folly | .25 | .75 | 1.50 |

**JUGHEAD'S DINER**
Apr, 1990 - Present ($1.00, color)
Archie Comics

| | Good | Fine | N-Mint |
|---|---|---|---|
| 1-6 | | .50 | 1.00 |

**JUGHEAD'S DOUBLE DIGEST** (. . . Magazine #5)
Oct, 1989 - Present ($2.25, quarterly, 256 pgs.)
Archie Comics

| | Good | Fine | N-Mint |
|---|---|---|---|
| 1-6: 2,5-Capt. Hero stories | .40 | 1.15 | 2.30 |

**JUGHEAD'S EAT-OUT COMIC BOOK MAGAZINE** (See Archie Giant Series Mag. No. 170)

**JUGHEAD'S FANTASY**
Aug, 1960 - No. 3, Dec, 1960
Archie Publications

| | Good | Fine | N-Mint |
|---|---|---|---|
| 1 | 11.50 | 34.00 | 80.00 |
| 2 | 8.50 | 25.50 | 60.00 |
| 3 | 6.50 | 19.50 | 45.00 |

**JUGHEAD'S FOLLY**
1957
Archie Publications (Close-Up)

| | Good | Fine | N-Mint |
|---|---|---|---|
| 1-Jughead a la Elvis (Rare) | 25.00 | 75.00 | 175.00 |

**JUGHEAD'S JOKES**
Aug, 1967 - No. 78, Sept, 1982
(No. 1-8, 38 on: reg. size; No. 9-23: 68 pgs.; No. 24-37: 52 pgs.)
Archie Publications

| | Good | Fine | N-Mint |
|---|---|---|---|
| 1 | 3.70 | 11.00 | 26.00 |
| 2 | 2.00 | 6.00 | 14.00 |
| 3-5 | 1.00 | 3.00 | 7.00 |
| 6-10 | .70 | 2.00 | 4.00 |
| 11-30 | .25 | .75 | 1.50 |
| 31-50 | | .45 | .90 |
| 51-78 | | .30 | .60 |

**JUGHEAD'S PAL HOT DOG** (See Laugh #14 for 1st app.)
Jan, 1990 - No. 5, Oct, 1990 ($1.00, color)
Archie Comics

| | Good | Fine | N-Mint |
|---|---|---|---|
| 1-5 | | .50 | 1.00 |

**JUGHEAD'S SOUL FOOD**
1979 (49 cents)
Spire Christian Comics (Fleming H. Revell Co.)

| | Good | Fine | N-Mint |
|---|---|---|---|
| nn | | .30 | .60 |

**JUGHEAD'S TIME POLICE**
July, 1990 - Present ($1.00, color, bi-monthly)
Archie Comics

| | Good | Fine | N-Mint |
|---|---|---|---|
| 1-5: 3-5-Colan-c/a(p) | | .50 | 1.00 |

**JUGHEAD WITH ARCHIE DIGEST** (. . . Plus Betty & Veronica & Reggie Too No. 1,2; . . . Magazine #33-?, 101-on; . . . Comics Digest Mag.)
March, 1974 - Present (Digest Size; $1.00-$1.25-$1.35-$1.50)
Archie Publications

| | Good | Fine | N-Mint |
|---|---|---|---|
| 1 | 1.15 | 3.50 | 7.00 |
| 2 | .50 | 1.50 | 3.00 |
| 3-10 | .25 | .75 | 1.50 |
| 11-20: Capt. Hero-r in #14-16; Pureheart the Powerful #18,21,22; Capt. Pureheart #17,19 | | .50 | 1.00 |
| 21-104: 29-The Shield-r. 30-The Fly-r | | .50 | 1.00 |

**JUKE BOX COMICS**
March, 1948 - No. 6, Jan, 1949
Famous Funnies

| | Good | Fine | N-Mint |
|---|---|---|---|
| 1-Toth c/a; Hollingsworth-a | 25.00 | 75.00 | 175.00 |
| 2-Transvestism story | 13.00 | 40.00 | 90.00 |
| 3-6 | 11.00 | 32.00 | 75.00 |

**JUMBO COMICS** (Created by S.M. Iger)
Sept, 1938 - No. 167, Mar, 1953 (No. 1-3: 68 pgs.; No. 4-8: 52 pgs.)
(No. 1-8 oversized-10½x14½"; black & white)
Fiction House Magazines (Real Adv. Publ. Co.)

| | Good | Fine | VF-NM | NM/Mint |
|---|---|---|---|---|
| 1-(Rare)-Sheena Queen of the Jungle by Meskin, The Hawk by Eisner, The Hunchback by Dick Briefer(ends #8) begin; 1st comic art by Jack Kirby (Count of Monte Cristo & Wilton of the West); Mickey Mouse appears (1 panel) with brief biography of Walt Disney. **Note:** Sheena was created by Iger for publication in England as a newspaper strip. The early issues of Jumbo contain Sheena strip-r | 635.00 | 1585.00 | 3800.00 | 6000.00 |

(Estimated up to 45 total copies exist, 1 in NM/Mint)

| | Good | Fine | VF-NM |
|---|---|---|---|
| 2-(Rare)-Origin Sheena. Diary of Dr. Hayward by Kirby (also #3) plus 2 other stories; contains strip from Universal Film featuring Edgar Bergen & Charlie McCarthy | 300.00 | 750.00 | 1800.00 |
| 3-Last Kirby issue | 233.00 | 585.00 | 1400.00 |
| 4-(Scarce)-Origin The Hawk by Eisner; Wilton of the West by Fine (ends #14)(1st comic work); Count of Monte Cristo by Fine (ends #15); The Diary of Dr. Hayward by Fine (cont'd. #8,9) | 233.00 | 585.00 | 1400.00 |
| 5 | 150.00 | 375.00 | 900.00 |
| 6-8-Last B&W issue. #8 was a N. Y. World's Fair Special Edition | 125.00 | 312.00 | 750.00 |
| 9-Stuart Taylor begins by Fine; Fine-c; 1st color issue(8-9/39)-8¼x10¼"(oversized in width only) | 133.00 | 335.00 | 800.00 |

| | Good | Fine | N-Mint |
|---|---|---|---|
| 10-14: 10-Regular size 68 pg. issues begin; Sheena dons new costume. 14-Lightning begins (Intro.) | 67.00 | 165.00 | 400.00 |
| 15-20 | 34.00 | 103.00 | 240.00 |
| 21-30: 22-1st Tom, Dick & Harry; origin The Hawk retold | 29.00 | 86.00 | 200.00 |
| 31-40: 35-Shows V2#11 (correct number does not appear) | 25.00 | 75.00 | 175.00 |
| 41-50 | 22.00 | 65.00 | 150.00 |
| 51-60: 52-Last Tom, Dick & Harry | 18.00 | 54.00 | 125.00 |
| 61-70: 68-Sky Girl begins, ends #130; not in #79 | 12.00 | 36.00 | 85.00 |
| 71-99: 89-ZX5 becomes a private eye. 94-Used in **Love and Death** by Legman | 11.00 | 32.00 | 75.00 |

| | Good | Fine | N-Mint |
|---|---|---|---|
| 100 | 12.00 | 36.00 | 85.00 |
| 101-110: 103-Lingerie panel | 9.30 | 28.00 | 65.00 |
| 111-140,150-158: 155-Used in **POP**, pg. 98 | 8.00 | 24.00 | 55.00 |
| 141-149-Two Sheena stories. 141-Long Bow, Indian Boy begins, ends #160 | 9.30 | 28.00 | 65.00 |
| 159-163: Space Scouts serial in all; 163-Suicide Smith app. | 8.00 | 24.00 | 55.00 |
| 164-The Star Pirate begins, ends #165 | 8.00 | 24.00 | 55.00 |
| 165-167: 165,167-Space Rangers app. | 8.00 | 24.00 | 55.00 |

NOTE: *Bondage covers, negligee panels, torture, etc. are common in this series. Hawks of the Seas, Inspector Dayton, Spies in Action, Sports Shorts, & Uncle Otto by* ***Eisner****, #1-7. Hawk by* ***Eisner****-#10-15, 114r?;* ***Eisner*** *c-1, 3-6, 12, 13, 15. 1pg. Patsy pin-ups in 92-97, 99-101. Sheena by* ***Meskin****-#1, 4; by* ***Powell****-#2, 3, 5-28;* ***Powell*** *c-14, 16, 17, 19. Sky Girl by* ***Matt Baker****-#69-78, 80-124.* ***Bailey*** *a-3-8.* ***Briefer*** *a-1-8, 10.* ***Fine*** *a-14; c-8-11.* ***Kamen*** *a-101, 105, 123, 132; c-105.* ***Bob Kane*** *a-1-8.*

**JUMPING JACKS PRESENTS THE WHIZ KIDS**
1978 (In 3-D) with glasses (4 pages)
Jumping Jacks Stores giveaway

| | Good | Fine | N-Mint |
|---|---|---|---|
| nn | | .40 | .80 |

**JUNGLE ACTION**
Oct, 1954 - No. 6, Aug, 1955
Atlas Comics (IPC)

| | Good | Fine | N-Mint |
|---|---|---|---|
| 1-Leopard Girl begins; Maneely-c/a in all | 11.50 | 34.00 | 80.00 |
| 2-(3-D effect cover) | 13.00 | 40.00 | 90.00 |
| 3-6: 3-Last precode (2/55) | 7.00 | 21.00 | 50.00 |

NOTE: ***Romita*** *a-3, 6.* ***Shores*** *a-3, 6.*

**JUNGLE ACTION** (. . .& Black Panther #18-21?)
Oct, 1972 - No. 24, Nov, 1976
Marvel Comics Group

| | Good | Fine | N-Mint |
|---|---|---|---|
| 1-Lorna, Jann-r (All reprints in 1-4) | .50 | 1.50 | 3.00 |
| 2-4 | .40 | 1.25 | 2.50 |
| 5-Black Panther begins; new stories begin | .50 | 1.50 | 3.00 |
| 6-18: 8-Origin Black Panther. 9-Contains pull-out centerfold | .35 | 1.00 | 2.00 |
| 19-24: 19-23-KKK x-over. 23-r-/#22. 24-1st Wind Eagle | .25 | .75 | 1.50 |

NOTE: ***Buckler*** *a-6-9p, 22; c-8p, 12p.* ***Buscema*** *a-5p; c-22.* ***Byrne*** *c-23.* ***Gil Kane*** *a-8p; c-2, 4, 10p, 11p, 13-17, 19, 24.* ***Kirby*** *c-18.* ***Maneely*** *r-1.* ***Russell*** *a-13i.* ***Starlin*** *c-3p.*

**JUNGLE ADVENTURES**
1963 - 1964 (Reprints)
Super Comics

| | Good | Fine | N-Mint |
|---|---|---|---|
| 10,12(Rulah), 15(Kaanga/Jungle #152) | 1.50 | 4.50 | 10.00 |
| 17(Jo-Jo) | 1.50 | 4.50 | 10.00 |
| 18-Reprints/White Princess of the Jungle #1; no Kinstler-a; origin of both White Princess & Cap'n Courage | 1.75 | 5.25 | 12.00 |

**JUNGLE ADVENTURES**
March, 1971 - No. 3, June, 1971 (25 cents, 52 pgs.)
Skywald Comics

| | Good | Fine | N-Mint |
|---|---|---|---|
| 1-Zangar origin; reprints of Jo-Jo, Blue Gorilla(origin)/White Princess #3, Kinstler-r/White Princess #2 | .70 | 2.00 | 4.00 |
| 2-Zangar, Sheena-r/Sheena #17 & Jumbo #162, Jo-Jo, origin Slave Girl Princess-r | .70 | 2.00 | 4.00 |
| 3-Zangar, Jo-Jo, White Princess-r | .70 | 2.00 | 4.00 |

**JUNGLE BOOK** (See King Louie and Mowgli, Movie Comics, Walt Disney Showcase #45 & Walt Disney's The Jungle Book)

**JUNGLE CAT** (See 4-Color No. 1136)

**JUNGLE COMICS**
1/40 - No. 157, 3/53; No. 158, Spr, 1953 - No. 163, Summer, 1954
Fiction House Magazines

| | Good | Fine | N-Mint |
|---|---|---|---|
| 1-Origin The White Panther, Kaanga, Lord of the Jungle, Tabu, Wizard of the Jungle; Wambi, the Jungle Boy, Camilla & Capt. Terry Thunder begin | 158.00 | 395.00 | 950.00 |
| 2-Fantomah, Mystery Woman of the Jungle begins | 64.00 | 193.00 | 450.00 |
| 3,4 | 54.00 | 160.00 | 375.00 |
| 5 | 43.00 | 130.00 | 300.00 |
| 6-10: 7,8-Powell-c | 37.00 | 110.00 | 255.00 |
| 11-20: 13-Tuska-c | 26.00 | 79.00 | 185.00 |
| 21-30: 25-Shows V2#1 (correct number does not appear). #27-New origin Fantomah, Daughter of the Pharoahs; Camilla dons new costume | 22.00 | 65.00 | 155.00 |
| 31-40 | 19.00 | 56.00 | 130.00 |
| 41,43-50 | 14.00 | 43.00 | 100.00 |
| 42-Kaanga by Crandall, 12 pgs. | 17.00 | 51.00 | 120.00 |
| 51-60 | 12.00 | 36.00 | 85.00 |
| 61-70 | 11.00 | 32.00 | 75.00 |
| 71-80: 79-New origin Tabu | 10.00 | 30.00 | 70.00 |
| 81-97,99,101-110 | 8.50 | 25.50 | 60.00 |
| 98-Used in **SOTI**, pg. 185 & illo-"In ordinary comic books, there are pictures within pictures for children who know how to look"; used by N.Y. Legis. Comm. | 15.00 | 45.00 | 105.00 |
| 100 | 11.00 | 32.00 | 75.00 |
| 111-163: 118-Clyde Beatty app. 135-Desert Panther begins in Terry Thunder (origin), not in #137; ends (dies) #138. 143,145-Used in **POP**, pg. 99. 152-Tiger Girl begins. 158-Sheena app. | 8.50 | 25.50 | 60.00 |
| I.W. Reprint #1,9: 9-r-/#151 | 1.00 | 3.00 | 6.00 |

NOTE: *Bondage covers, negligee panels, torture, etc. are common to this series. Camilla by* ***Fran Hopper****-#71-73, 75, 76, 78, 80-90; by* ***Baker****-#101, 103, 106, 107, 109, 111-113. Kaanga by* ***John Celardo****-#80-110; by* ***Larsen****-#71; by* ***Maurice Whitman****-#124-163. Tabu by* ***Whitman****-#93-110.* ***Astarita*** *c-46.* ***Celardo*** *a-78; c-98-100, 103, 106, 109, 112.* ***Eisner*** *c-2, 5, 6.* ***Fine*** *c-1.* ***Larsen*** *a-65, 66, 71, 72, 74, 75, 79, 83, 84, 87-90.* ***Morisi*** *a-51.*

**JUNGLE COMICS**
May, 1988 - No. 4? ($2.00, color; B&W #2 on?)
Blackthorne Publishing

| | Good | Fine | N-Mint |
|---|---|---|---|
| 1-4: 1-Dave Stevens-c. B. Jones scripts in all | .35 | 1.00 | 2.00 |

**JUNGLE GIRL** (See Lorna, . . .)

**JUNGLE GIRL** (Nyoka, Jungle Girl No. 2 on)
Fall, 1942 (One shot)(No month listed)
Fawcett Publications

| | Good | Fine | N-Mint |
|---|---|---|---|
| 1-Bondage-c; photo of Kay Aldridge who played Nyoka in movie serial app. on-c. Adaptation of the classic Republic movie serial *Perils of Nyoka*. 1st comic to devote entire contents to a movie adaptation | 54.00 | 160.00 | 375.00 |

**JUNGLE JIM** (Also see Ace Comics)
No. 11, Jan, 1949 - No. 20, Apr, 1951
Standard Comics (Best Books)

| | Good | Fine | N-Mint |
|---|---|---|---|
| 11 | 3.70 | 11.00 | 26.00 |
| 12-20 | 2.15 | 6.50 | 15.00 |

**JUNGLE JIM**
No. 490, 8/53 - No. 1020, 8-10/59 (Painted-c)
Dell Publishing Co.

| | Good | Fine | N-Mint |
|---|---|---|---|
| 4-Color 490(#1) | 2.65 | 8.00 | 18.00 |
| 4-Color 565(#2, 6/54) | 2.00 | 6.00 | 14.00 |
| 3(10-12/54)-5 | 1.70 | 5.00 | 12.00 |
| 6-19(1-3/59) | 1.50 | 4.50 | 10.00 |
| 4-Color 1020(#20) | 1.70 | 5.00 | 12.00 |

**JUNGLE JIM**
No. 5, December, 1967
King Features Syndicate

| | Good | Fine | N-Mint |
|---|---|---|---|
| 5-Reprints Dell #5; Wood-c | 1.00 | 3.00 | 7.00 |

**JUNGLE JIM** (Continued from Dell series)
No. 22, Feb, 1969 - No. 28, Feb, 1970 (No. 21 was an overseas

*Jungle Action #5 (7/73), © MEG*

*Jungle Comics #67, © FH*

*Jungle Jim #11 (Standard), © KING*

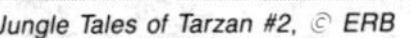
*Jungle Tales of Tarzan #2, © ERB*

*Junior Miss #31, © MEG*

*Justice Comics #10, © MEG*

edition only)
Charlton Comics

| | Good | Fine | N-Mint |
|---|---|---|---|
| 22-Dan Flagg begins; Ditko/Wood-a | 1.70 | 5.00 | 12.00 |
| 23-28: 23-Last Dan Flagg; Howard-c. 24-Jungle People begin. 27-Ditko/Howard-a. 28-Ditko-a | 1.15 | 3.50 | 8.00 |

**JUNGLE JO**
Mar, 1950 - No. 6, Mar, 1951
Fox Feature Syndicate (Hero Books)

| | | | |
|---|---|---|---|
| nn-Jo-Jo blanked out, leaving Congo King; came out after Jo-Jo #29 (intended as Jo-Jo #30?) | 14.00 | 43.00 | 100.00 |
| 1-Tangi begins; part Wood-a | 17.00 | 51.00 | 120.00 |
| 2 | 12.00 | 36.00 | 85.00 |
| 3-6 | 11.50 | 34.00 | 80.00 |

**JUNGLE LIL** (Dorothy Lamour #2 on; Also see Feat. Stories Mag.)
April, 1950
Fox Feature Syndicate (Hero Books)

| | | | |
|---|---|---|---|
| 1 | 13.00 | 40.00 | 90.00 |

**JUNGLE TALES** (Jann of the Jungle No. 8 on)
Sept, 1954 - No. 7, Sept, 1955
Atlas Comics (CSI)

| | | | |
|---|---|---|---|
| 1-Jann of the Jungle | 11.50 | 34.00 | 80.00 |
| 2-7: 3-Last precode (1/55) | 8.50 | 25.50 | 60.00 |

NOTE: *Heath c-5. Heck a-6, 7. Maneely a-2; c-1, 3. Shores a-5-7. Tuska a-2.*

**JUNGLE TALES OF TARZAN**
Dec, 1964 - No. 4, July, 1965
Charlton Comics

| | | | |
|---|---|---|---|
| 1 | 2.30 | 7.00 | 16.00 |
| 2-4 | 1.70 | 5.00 | 12.00 |

NOTE: *Giordano c-3p. Glanzman a-1-3. Montes/Bache a-4.*

**JUNGLE TERROR** (See Harvey Comics Hits No. 54)

**JUNGLE THRILLS** (Terrors of the Jungle No. 17)
No. 16, Feb, 1952; Dec, 1953; No. 7, 1954
Star Publications

| | | | |
|---|---|---|---|
| 16-Phantom Lady & Rulah story-reprint/All Top No. 15; used in **POP**, pg. 98,99; L. B. Cole-c | 17.00 | 51.00 | 120.00 |
| 3-D 1(12/53)-Jungle Lil & Jungle Jo appear; L. B. Cole-c | 22.00 | 65.00 | 155.00 |
| 7-Titled 'Picture Scope Jungle Adventures;'(1954, 36 pgs, 15 cents)-3-D effect c/stories; story & coloring book; Disbrow-a/script; L.B. Cole-c | 17.00 | 51.00 | 120.00 |

**JUNGLE TWINS, THE** (Tono & Kono)
Apr, 1972 - No. 17, Nov, 1975; No. 18, May, 1982
Gold Key/Whitman No. 18 on

| | | | |
|---|---|---|---|
| 1 | .35 | 1.00 | 2.00 |
| 2-5 | | .60 | 1.20 |
| 6-18: 18-Reprints | | .40 | .80 |

NOTE: *UFO c/story No. 13. Painted-c No. 1-17. Spiegle c-18.*

**JUNGLE WAR STORIES** (Guerrilla War No. 12 on)
July-Sept, 1962 - No. 11, Apr-June, 1965 (Painted-c)
Dell Publishing Co.

| | | | |
|---|---|---|---|
| 01-384-209 (#1) | 1.15 | 3.50 | 8.00 |
| 2-11 | .70 | 2.00 | 5.00 |

**JUNIE PROM** (Also see Dexter Comics)
Winter, 1947-48 - No. 7, Aug, 1949
Dearfield Publishing Co.

| | | | |
|---|---|---|---|
| 1-Teen-age | 5.00 | 15.00 | 35.00 |
| 2 | 2.65 | 8.00 | 18.00 |
| 3-7 | 1.70 | 5.00 | 12.00 |

**JUNIOR CARROT PATROL** (Jr. Carrot Patrol #2)
May, 1989; No. 2, Nov, 1990 ($2.00, B&W)
Dark Horse Comics

| | Good | Fine | N-Mint |
|---|---|---|---|
| 1,2-Flaming Carrot spin-off. 1-Bob Burden-c(i) | .35 | 1.00 | 2.00 |

**JUNIOR COMICS**
No. 9, Sept, 1947 - No. 16, July, 1948
Fox Feature Syndicate

| | | | |
|---|---|---|---|
| 9-Feldstein-c/a; headlights-c | 36.00 | 110.00 | 250.00 |
| 10-16-Feldstein-c/a; headlights-c on all | 31.50 | 95.00 | 220.00 |

**JUNIOR FUNNIES** (Formerly Tiny Tot Funnies No. 9)
No. 10, Aug, 1951 - No. 13, Feb, 1952
Harvey Publications (King Features Synd.)

| | | | |
|---|---|---|---|
| 10-Partial reprints in all-Blondie, Dagwood, Daisy, Henry, Popeye, Felix, Katzenjammer Kids | 1.50 | 4.50 | 10.00 |
| 11-13 | 1.20 | 3.50 | 8.00 |

**JUNIOR HOPP COMICS**
Feb, 1952 - No. 3, July, 1952
Stanmor Publ.

| | | | |
|---|---|---|---|
| 1 | 3.70 | 11.00 | 26.00 |
| 2,3: 3-Dave Berg-a | 2.00 | 6.00 | 14.00 |

**JUNIOR MEDICS OF AMERICA, THE**
1957 (15 cents)
E. R. Squire & Sons

| | | | |
|---|---|---|---|
| 1359 | 1.50 | 4.50 | 10.00 |

**JUNIOR MISS**
Winter, 1944; No. 24, April, 1947 - No. 39, Aug, 1950
Timely/Marvel Comics (CnPC)

| | | | |
|---|---|---|---|
| 1-Frank Sinatra & June Allyson life story | 9.30 | 28.00 | 65.00 |
| 24-Formerly The Human Torch #23? | 4.00 | 12.00 | 28.00 |
| 25-38 | 2.30 | 7.00 | 16.00 |
| 39-Kurtzman-a | 3.00 | 9.00 | 21.00 |

NOTE: *Painted-c 35-37. 37-all romance. 35, 36, 38-mostly teen humor.*

**JUNIOR PARTNERS** (Formerly Oral Roberts' True Stories)
No. 120, Aug, 1959 - V3#12, Dec, 1961
Oral Roberts Evangelistic Assn.

| | | | |
|---|---|---|---|
| 120(#1) | 2.00 | 6.00 | 14.00 |
| 2(9/59) | 1.50 | 4.50 | 10.00 |
| 3-12(7/60) | .85 | 2.60 | 6.00 |
| V2#1(8/60)-5(12/60) | .70 | 2.00 | 4.00 |
| V3#1(1/61)-12 | .50 | 1.50 | 3.00 |

**JUNIOR TREASURY** (See Dell Junior . . .)

**JUNIOR WOODCHUCKS** (See Huey, Dewey & Louie . . .)

**JUSTICE**
Nov, 1986 - No. 32, June, 1989
Marvel Comics Group

| | | | |
|---|---|---|---|
| 1-31: 26-32-$1.50-c | | .50 | 1.00 |
| 32-Unauthorized Joker app. | .60 | 1.75 | 3.50 |

**JUSTICE COMICS** (Tales of Justice #53 on; formerly Wacky Duck)
No. 7, Fall/47 - No. 9, 6/48; No. 4, 8/48 - No. 52, 3/55
Marvel/Atlas comics (NPP 7-9,4-19/CnPC 20-23/MjMC 24-38/Male 39-52

| | | | |
|---|---|---|---|
| 7(#1, 1947) | 8.50 | 25.50 | 60.00 |
| 8(#2)-Kurtzman-a-"Giggles 'N' Grins," (3) | 6.00 | 18.00 | 42.00 |
| 9(#3, 6/48) | 5.00 | 15.00 | 35.00 |
| 4 | 4.30 | 13.00 | 30.00 |
| 5-9: 8-Anti-Wertham editorial | 3.15 | 9.50 | 22.00 |
| 10-15-Photo-c | 3.15 | 9.50 | 22.00 |
| 16-30 | 2.65 | 8.00 | 18.00 |
| 31-40,42-47,49-52-Last precode | 2.30 | 7.00 | 16.00 |
| 41-Electrocution-c | 5.00 | 15.00 | 35.00 |
| 48-Pakula & Tuska-a | 2.15 | 6.50 | 15.00 |

NOTE: *Maneely c-44. Pakula a-43, 45, 48. Louis Ravielli a-39. Robinson a-22, 25, 41. Tuska a-48. Wildey a-52.*

**JUSTICE, INC.** (The Avenger)
May-June, 1975 - No. 4, Nov-Dec, 1975
National Periodical Publications

| | Good | Fine | N-Mint |
|---|---|---|---|
| 1-McWilliams-a, Kubert-c; origin | | .40 | .80 |
| 2-4: 2-4-Kirby-a(p), c-2,3p. 4-Kubert-c | | .25 | .50 |

NOTE: *Adapted from Kenneth Robeson novel, creator of Doc Savage.*

**JUSTICE, INC.**
1989 - #2, 1989 ($3.95, color, squarebound, mature readers, 52 pgs.)
DC Comics

| | Good | Fine | N-Mint |
|---|---|---|---|
| 1,2-Re-intro The Avenger | .70 | 2.00 | 4.00 |

**JUSTICE LEAGUE** ( . . . International #7-25; . . . America #26 on)
May, 1987 - Present (Also see Legends #6)
DC Comics

| | Good | Fine | N-Mint |
|---|---|---|---|
| 1-Batman, Green Lantern(Guy Gardner), Blue Beetle, Mr. Miracle, Capt. Marvel & Martian Manhunter begin | 1.50 | 4.50 | 9.00 |
| 2 | .90 | 2.75 | 5.50 |
| 3-Regular cover (white background) | .75 | 2.25 | 4.50 |
| 3-Limited cover (yellow background, Superman logo) | 13.00 | 40.00 | 90.00 |
| 4-Booster Gold joins | .70 | 2.00 | 4.00 |
| 5,6: 5-Origin Gray Man; Batman vs. Guy Gardner; Creeper app. | .40 | 1.25 | 2.50 |
| 7-Double size ($1.25); Capt. Marvel & Dr. Fate resign; Capt. Atom, Rocket Red join | .50 | 1.50 | 3.00 |
| 8-10: 9,10-Millennium x-over | .35 | 1.00 | 2.00 |
| 11-23: 16-Bruce Wayne-c/story | | .60 | 1.20 |
| 24-($1.50)-1st app. Justice League Europe | .25 | .75 | 1.50 |
| 25-50: 31,32-Justice League Europe x-over | | .50 | 1.00 |
| Annual 1 (9/87) | .50 | 1.50 | 3.00 |
| Annual 2 ('88)-Joker-c/story | .70 | 2.00 | 4.00 |
| Annual 3 ('89, $1.75, 68 pgs.) | .30 | .90 | 1.75 |
| Annual 4 ('90, $2.00, 68 pgs.)-Lobo story | .50 | 1.50 | 3.00 |
| Special 1 ('90, $1.50, 52 pgs.)-Giffen plots | .25 | .75 | 1.50 |
| A New Beginning Trade Paperback ($12.95, 1989)-r/1-7 | 2.15 | 6.50 | 12.95 |

NOTE: ***Austin*** *c/a-1(i).* ***Giffen*** *a-8-10; c-21p.* ***Willingham*** *a-30p, Annual 2.*

**JUSTICE LEAGUE EUROPE**
April, 1989 - Present (75 cents; $1.00 #5 on)
DC Comics

| | Good | Fine | N-Mint |
|---|---|---|---|
| 1-Giffen plots in all; breakdowns in 1-8,13-21 | .35 | 1.00 | 2.00 |
| 2-24: 7-9-Batman app. 7,8-JLA x-over. 21-Rogers-c/a(p) | | .50 | 1.00 |
| Annual 1 (1990, $2.00, 68 pgs.)-Return of the Global Guardians; Giffen plots/breakdowns | .35 | 1.00 | 2.00 |

**JUSTICE LEAGUE OF AMERICA** (See Brave & the Bold #28-30, Mystery In Space #75 & Official . . . Index)
Oct-Nov, 1960 - No. 261, Apr, 1987 (91-99,139-157: 52 pgs.)
National Periodical Publications/DC Comics

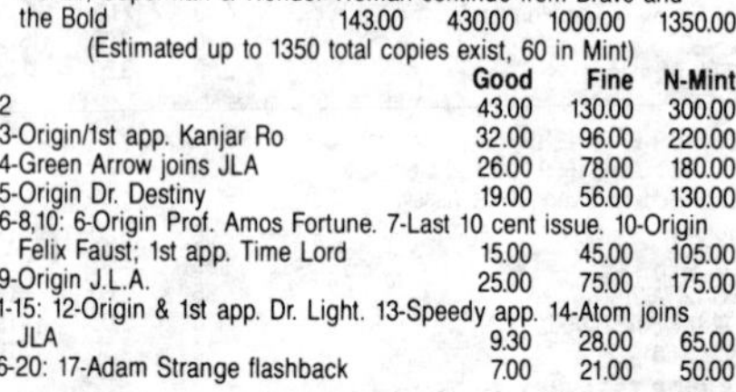

| | Good | Fine | N-Mint | Mint |
|---|---|---|---|---|
| 1-Origin Despero; Aquaman, Batman, Flash, Green Lantern, J'onn J'onzz, Superman & Wonder Woman continue from Brave and the Bold | 143.00 | 430.00 | 1000.00 | 1350.00 |

(Estimated up to 1350 total copies exist, 60 in Mint)

| | Good | Fine | N-Mint |
|---|---|---|---|
| 2 | 43.00 | 130.00 | 300.00 |
| 3-Origin/1st app. Kanjar Ro | 32.00 | 96.00 | 220.00 |
| 4-Green Arrow joins JLA | 26.00 | 78.00 | 180.00 |
| 5-Origin Dr. Destiny | 19.00 | 56.00 | 130.00 |
| 6-8,10: 6-Origin Prof. Amos Fortune. 7-Last 10 cent issue. 10-Origin Felix Faust; 1st app. Time Lord | 15.00 | 45.00 | 105.00 |
| 9-Origin J.L.A. | 25.00 | 75.00 | 175.00 |
| 11-15: 12-Origin & 1st app. Dr. Light. 13-Speedy app. 14-Atom joins JLA | 9.30 | 28.00 | 65.00 |
| 16-20: 17-Adam Strange flashback | 7.00 | 21.00 | 50.00 |
| 21,22: 21-Re-intro. of JSA (1st S.A. app. Hourman & Dr. Fate). 22-JSA x-over | 18.00 | 54.00 | 125.00 |
| 23-28: 24-Adam Strange app. 28-Robin app. | 4.30 | 13.00 | 30.00 |
| 29,30-JSA x-over; 1st Silver Age app. Starman | 5.70 | 17.00 | 40.00 |
| 31-Hawkman joins JLA, Hawkgirl cameo | 2.30 | 7.00 | 16.00 |
| 32-Intro & Origin Brain Storm | 2.00 | 6.00 | 14.00 |
| 33,35,36,40,41: 41-Intro & origin The Key | 1.70 | 5.00 | 12.00 |
| 34-Joker-c/story | 3.00 | 9.00 | 21.00 |
| 37,38-JSA x-over (1st S.A. app. Mr. Terrific) | 3.50 | 10.50 | 24.00 |
| 39-Giant G-16 | 2.85 | 8.50 | 20.00 |
| 42-45: 42-Metamorpho app. 43-Intro. Royal Flush Gang | 1.30 | 4.00 | 9.00 |
| 46-JSA x-over; 1st S.A. app. Sandman | 3.15 | 9.50 | 22.00 |
| 47-JSA x-over | 1.70 | 5.00 | 12.00 |
| 48-Giant G-29 | 1.70 | 5.00 | 12.00 |
| 49-57,59,60: 55-Intro. Earth 2 Robin | 1.15 | 3.50 | 8.00 |
| 58-Giant G-41 | 1.30 | 4.00 | 9.00 |
| 61-66,68-72: 64-Intro/origin Red Tornado. 69-Wonder Woman quits; 71-Manhunter leaves. 72-Last 12 cent issue | .85 | 2.60 | 6.00 |
| 67-Giant G-53 | 1.00 | 3.00 | 7.00 |
| 73,74,77-80: 74-Black Canary joins. 78-Re-intro Vigilante | .70 | 2.00 | 4.00 |
| 75-2nd app. Green Arrow in new costume | 1.00 | 3.00 | 6.00 |
| 76-Giant G-65 | 1.00 | 3.00 | 6.00 |
| 81-84,86-92: 83-Death of Spectre | .70 | 2.00 | 4.00 |
| 85,93-(Giant G-77,G-89; 68 pgs.) | 1.00 | 3.00 | 6.00 |
| 94-Reprints 1st Sandman story (Adv. #40) & origin/1st app. Starman (Adv. #61); Deadman x-over; N. Adams-a(4 pgs.); begin 25 cent, 52 pg. issues, ends #99 | 2.00 | 6.00 | 14.00 |
| 95-Origin Dr. Fate & Dr. Midnight reprint (More Fun #67, All-American #25) | .70 | 2.00 | 4.00 |
| 96-Origin Hourman (Adv. #48); Wildcat-r | .70 | 2.00 | 4.00 |
| 97-Origin JLA retold; Sargon, Starman-r | .70 | 2.00 | 4.00 |
| 98,99: 98-G.A. Sargon, Starman-r. 99-G.A. Sandman, Starman, Atom-r; last 52 pg. issue | .50 | 1.50 | 3.00 |
| 100-102: 102-Red Tornado dies | .85 | 2.50 | 5.00 |
| 103-106: 103-Phantom Stranger joins. 105-Elongated Man joins 106-New Red Tornado joins | .50 | 1.50 | 3.00 |
| 107,108-G.A. Uncle Sam, Black Condor, The Ray, Dollman, Phantom Lady & The Human Bomb x-over | .85 | 2.50 | 5.00 |
| 109-116: 109-Hawkman resigns. 110-116: All 100 pg. issues. 111-Shining Knight, Green Arrow-r. 112-Crimson Avenger, Vigilante, origin Starman-r | .50 | 1.50 | 3.00 |
| 117-190: 117-Hawkman rejoins. 120,121,138-Adam Strange app. 128-Wonder Woman rejoins. 129-Death of Red Tornado. 135-137-G.A. Bulletman, Bulletgirl, Spy Smasher, Mr. Scarlet, Pinky & Ibis x-over. 137-Superman battles G.A. Capt. Marvel. 139-157-(52 pgs.). 144-Origin retold; origin J'onn J'onnz. 145-Red Tornado resurrected. 158-160-(44 pgs.). 161-Zatanna joins & new costume. 171-Mr. Terrific murdered. 178-Cover similar to #1; J'onn J'onzz app. 179-Firestorm joins. 181-Gr. Arrow leaves | .35 | 1.00 | 2.00 |
| 191-199: 192,193-Real origin Red Tornado. 193-1st app. All-Star Squadron as free 16 pg. insert | .25 | .75 | 1.50 |
| 200-Anniversary issue (76pgs., $1.50); origin retold; Green Arrow rejoins | .50 | 1.50 | 3.00 |
| 201-220: 203-Intro/origin new Royal Flush Gang. 207,208-JSA, JLA, & All-Star Squadron team-up. 219,220-True origin Black Canary | .25 | .75 | 1.50 |
| 221-250 (75 cents): 228-Re-intro Martian Manhunter. 233-New JLA begins. 243-Aquaman leaves. 244,245-Crisis x-over. 250-Batman rejoins | .25 | .75 | 1.50 |
| 251-260: 253-1st time origin Despero. 258-Death of Vibe. 258-261-Legends x-over. 260-Death of Steel | | .50 | 1.00 |
| 261-Last issue | .60 | 1.75 | 3.50 |
| Annual 1(1983) | .40 | 1.25 | 2.50 |
| Annual 2(1984)-Intro new J.L.A. | .25 | .75 | 1.50 |

*Justice League #2 (6/87), © DC*

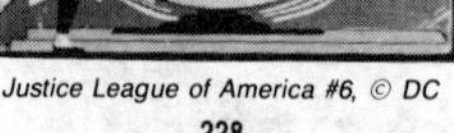

*Justice League of America #6, © DC*

*Justice League of America #96, © DC*

Justice Traps the Guilty V2#11, © PRIZE

Ka'a'nga Comics #9, © FH

Kamandi, the Last Boy on Earth #1, © DC

| | Good | Fine | N-Mint |
|---|---|---|---|
| Annual 3(1985)-Crisis x-over | .25 | .75 | 1.50 |

NOTE: ***Neal Adams*** *c-63, 66, 67, 70, 74, 79, 81, 82, 86-89, 91, 92, 94, 96-98, 138, 139.* ***Aparo*** *a-200.* ***Austin*** *a-200i.* ***Baily*** *a-96r.* ***Burnley*** *r-94, 98, 99.* ***Greene*** *a-46-61i, 64-73i, 110i(r).* ***Grell*** *c-117, 122.* ***Kaluta*** *c-154p.* ***Gil Kane*** *a-200.* ***Krigstein*** *a-96(r-Sensation #84.)* ***Kubert*** *a-200; c-72, 73.* ***Nino*** *a-228i, 230i.* ***Orlando*** *c-151i.* ***Perez*** *a-184-186p, 192-197p, 200p; c-184p, 186, 192-195, 196p, 197p, 199, 200, 201p, 202, 203-205p, 207-209, 212-215, 217, 219, 220.* ***Reinman*** *r-97.* ***Roussos*** *a-62i.* ***Sekowsky*** *a-44-63p, 110-112p(r); c-46-48p, 51p.* ***B. Smith*** *c-185i.* ***Starlin*** *c-178-180, 183, 185p.* ***Staton*** *a-244p; c-157p, 244p.* ***Toth*** *r-110.* ***Tuska*** *a-153, 228p, 241-243p. JSA x-over-55, 56, 64, 65, 73, 74, 82, 83, 91, 92, 101, 102, 107, 108, 110, 113, 115, 123, 124, 135-137, 147, 148, 159, 160, 171, 172, 183-185, 195-197, 207-209, 219, 220, 231, 232, 244.*

**JUSTICE LEAGUE QUARTERLY**
Winter, 1990-91 - Present ($2.95, 84 pgs.)
DC Comics

| | Good | Fine | N-Mint |
|---|---|---|---|
| 1 | .50 | 1.50 | 3.00 |

**JUSTICE MACHINE, THE**
June, 1981 - No. 5, Nov, 1983 ($2.00, No. 1-3, Magazine size)
Noble Comics

| | Good | Fine | N-Mint |
|---|---|---|---|
| 1-Byrne-c(p) | 2.00 | 6.00 | 12.00 |
| 2-Austin-c(i) | 1.15 | 3.50 | 7.00 |
| 3 | 1.00 | 3.00 | 6.00 |
| 4,5 | .50 | 1.50 | 3.00 |
| Annual 1 (1/84, 68 pgs.)(published by Texas Comics); 1st app. The Elementals; Golden-c(p) | 1.35 | 4.00 | 8.00 |

**JUSTICE MACHINE** (Also see The New Justice Machine)
Jan, 1987 - No. 29, May, 1989 ($1.50-1.75, color)
Comico/Innovation Publishing

| | Good | Fine | N-Mint |
|---|---|---|---|
| 1-29 | .30 | .90 | 1.75 |
| Annual 1(6/89, $2.50, 36 pgs.)-Last Comico ish. | .40 | 1.25 | 2.50 |
| Summer Spectacular 1 ('89, $2.75)-Innovation Publ.; Byrne/Gustovich cover | .45 | 1.40 | 2.75 |

**JUSTICE MACHINE, THE**
1990 - Present ($1.95-$2.25, color, mature readers, deluxe format)
Innovation Publishing

| | Good | Fine | N-Mint |
|---|---|---|---|
| 1-4: Gustovich-c/a in all | .35 | 1.00 | 2.00 |

**JUSTICE MACHINE FEATURING THE ELEMENTALS**
May, 1986 - No. 4, Aug, 1986 ($1.50, color, mini-series)
Comico

| | Good | Fine | N-Mint |
|---|---|---|---|
| 1-4 | .25 | .75 | 1.50 |

**JUSTICE TRAPS THE GUILTY** (Fargo Kid V11#3 on)
Oct-Nov, 1947 - V11#2(#92), Apr-May, 1958
Prize/Headline Publications

| | Good | Fine | N-Mint |
|---|---|---|---|
| V2#1-S&K-c/a; electrocution-c | 20.00 | 60.00 | 140.00 |
| 2-S&K-c/a | 10.00 | 30.00 | 70.00 |
| 3-5-S&K-c/a | 8.50 | 25.50 | 60.00 |
| 6-S&K-c/a; Feldstein-a | 9.30 | 28.00 | 65.00 |
| 7,9-S&K-c/a | 7.00 | 21.00 | 50.00 |
| 8,10-Krigstein-a; S&K-c. 10-S&K-a | 8.50 | 25.50 | 60.00 |
| 11,19-S&K-c | 4.00 | 12.00 | 28.00 |
| 12,14-17,20-No S&K | 2.30 | 7.00 | 16.00 |
| 13-Used in **SOTI**, pg. 110-111 | 3.50 | 10.50 | 24.00 |
| 18-S&K-c, Elder-a | 2.65 | 8.00 | 18.00 |
| 21,30-S&K-c/a | 3.00 | 9.00 | 21.00 |
| 22,23,27-S&K-c | 2.30 | 7.00 | 16.00 |
| 24-26,28,29,31-50 | 1.50 | 4.50 | 10.00 |
| 51-57,59-70 | 1.30 | 4.00 | 9.00 |
| 58-Illo. in **SOTI**, "Treating police contemptuously"(top left); text on heroin | 10.00 | 30.00 | 70.00 |
| 71-92: 76-Orlando-a | 1.30 | 4.00 | 9.00 |

NOTE: ***Bailey*** *a-12, 13.* ***Elder*** *a-8.* ***Kirby*** *a-19p.* ***Meskin*** *a-22, 27, 63, 64; c-45, 46.* ***Robinson/Meskin*** *a-5, 19.* ***Severin*** *a-8, 11p. Photo c-12, 15, 16.*

**JUST KIDS**
No. 283, 1932 (16 pages; 9½x12"; paper cover)
McLoughlin Bros.

| | Good | Fine | N-Mint |
|---|---|---|---|
| 283-Three-color text, pictures on heavy paper | 7.00 | 21.00 | 50.00 |

**JUST MARRIED**
January, 1958 - No. 114, Dec, 1976
Charlton Comics

| | Good | Fine | N-Mint |
|---|---|---|---|
| 1 | 1.70 | 5.00 | 12.00 |
| 2 | .85 | 2.60 | 6.00 |
| 3-10 | .70 | 2.00 | 4.00 |
| 11-30 | .35 | 1.00 | 2.00 |
| 31-50 | | .50 | 1.00 |
| 51-114 | | .25 | .50 |

**JUSTY**
Dec 6, 1988 - No. 9, 1989 ($1.75, B&W, bi-weekly mini-series)
Viz Comics

| | Good | Fine | N-Mint |
|---|---|---|---|
| 1-9: Japanese manga | .30 | .90 | 1.80 |

**KA'A'NGA COMICS** (. . .Jungle King)(See Jungle Comics)
Spring, 1949 - No. 20, Summer, 1954
Fiction House Magazines (Glen-Kel Publ. Co.)

| | Good | Fine | N-Mint |
|---|---|---|---|
| 1-Ka'a'nga, Lord of the Jungle begins | 27.00 | 81.00 | 190.00 |
| 2 (Wint., '49-'50) | 13.00 | 40.00 | 90.00 |
| 3,4 | 10.00 | 30.00 | 70.00 |
| 5-Camilla app. | 7.00 | 21.00 | 50.00 |
| 6-10: 7-Tuska-a. 9-Tabu, Wizard of the Jungle app. 10-Used in **POP**, pg. 99 | 5.00 | 15.00 | 35.00 |
| 11-15 | 4.00 | 12.00 | 28.00 |
| 16-Sheena app. | 4.30 | 13.00 | 30.00 |
| 17-20 | 3.50 | 10.50 | 24.00 |
| I.W. Reprint #1 (r-/#18) Kinstler-c | .70 | 2.00 | 4.00 |
| I.W. Reprint #8 (reprints #10) | .70 | 2.00 | 4.00 |

**KAMANDI, THE LAST BOY ON EARTH** (Also see Brave and the Bold No. 120 & Cancelled Comic Cavalcade)
Oct-Nov, 1972 - No. 59, Sept-Oct, 1978
National Periodical Publications/DC Comics

| | Good | Fine | N-Mint |
|---|---|---|---|
| 1-Origin | 1.15 | 3.50 | 8.00 |
| 2-10: 4-Intro. Prince Tuftan of the Tigers | .70 | 2.00 | 4.00 |
| 11-20 | .50 | 1.50 | 3.00 |
| 21-40: 29-Superman x-over. 31-Intro Pyra. 32-68 pgs.; r/origin from #1 | .35 | 1.00 | 2.00 |
| 41-59 | .25 | .80 | 1.60 |

NOTE: ***Ayers*** *a(p)-48-59 (most).* ***Kirby*** *a-1-40p; c-1-33.* ***Kubert*** *c-34-41.* ***Nasser*** *a-45p, 46p.* ***Starlin*** *a-59p; c-57, 59p.*

**KAMUI** (Legend Of. . . #2 on)
May 12, 1987 - No. 38? ($1.50, B&W, Bi-weekly)
Eclipse Comics/VIZ Comics #38 on

| | Good | Fine | N-Mint |
|---|---|---|---|
| 1-38: 1-3 have 2nd printings | .25 | .75 | 1.50 |

**KARATE KID** (See Action, Adventure, Legion of Super-Heroes, & Superboy)
Mar-Apr, 1976 - No. 15, July-Aug, 1978 (Legion spin-off)
National Periodical Publications/DC Comics

| | Good | Fine | N-Mint |
|---|---|---|---|
| 1-Meets Iris Jacobs; Estrada/Staton-a | | .40 | .80 |
| 2-15: 2-Major Disaster app. 15-Continued into Kamandi #58 | | .30 | .60 |

NOTE: ***Grell*** *c-1-4, 5p, 6p, 7, 8.* ***Staton*** *a-1-9i. Legion x-over-No. 1, 2, 4, 6, 10, 12, 13. Princess Projectra x-over-#8, 9.*

**KASCO KOMICS**
1945; No. 2, 1949 (regular size; paper cover)
Kasko Grainfeed (Giveaway)

| | Good | Fine | N-Mint |
|---|---|---|---|
| 1(1945)-Similar to Katy Keene; Bill Woggon-a; 28 pgs.; 6-7/8"x9-7/8" | 9.35 | 28.00 | 65.00 |
| 2(1949)-Woggon-a | 8.00 | 24.00 | 55.00 |

**KATHY**
September, 1949 - No. 17, Sept, 1955

Standard Comics

| | Good | Fine | N-Mint |
|---|---|---|---|
| 1-Teen-age | 3.70 | 11.00 | 26.00 |
| 2-Schomburg-c | 2.00 | 6.00 | 14.00 |
| 3-5 | 1.50 | 4.50 | 10.00 |
| 6-17: 17-Code approved | 1.00 | 3.00 | 7.00 |

**KATHY**
Oct, 1959 - No. 27, Feb, 1964
Atlas Comics/Marvel (ZPC)

| | | | |
|---|---|---|---|
| 1-Teen-age | 3.00 | 9.00 | 21.00 |
| 2 | 1.50 | 4.50 | 10.00 |
| 3-15 | .85 | 2.60 | 6.00 |
| 16-27 | .50 | 1.50 | 3.00 |

**KAT KARSON**
No date (Reprint)
I. W. Enterprises

| | | | |
|---|---|---|---|
| 1-Funny animals | .50 | 1.50 | 3.00 |

**KATY AND KEN VISIT SANTA WITH MISTER WISH**
1948 (16 pgs.; paper cover)
S. S. Kresge Co. (Giveaway)

| | | | |
|---|---|---|---|
| nn | 2.35 | 7.00 | 14.00 |

**KATY KEENE** (Also see Kasco Komics, Laugh, Pep, Suzie, & Wilbur)
1949 - No. 4, 1951; No. 5, 3/52 - No. 62, Oct, 1961
Archie Publ./Close-Up/Radio Comics

| | | | |
|---|---|---|---|
| 1-Bill Woggon-a begins | 68.00 | 205.00 | 475.00 |
| 2 | 34.00 | 100.00 | 235.00 |
| 3-5 | 29.00 | 85.00 | 200.00 |
| 6-10 | 24.00 | 72.00 | 165.00 |
| 11,13-20 | 20.00 | 60.00 | 140.00 |
| 12-(Scarce) | 22.00 | 65.00 | 155.00 |
| 21-40 | 14.00 | 43.00 | 100.00 |
| 41-62 | 11.00 | 32.00 | 75.00 |
| Annual 1('54) | 37.00 | 110.00 | 260.00 |
| Annual 2-6('55-59) | 19.00 | 57.00 | 135.00 |
| 3-D 1(1953-Large size) | 30.00 | 90.00 | 210.00 |
| Charm 1(9/58) | 17.00 | 51.00 | 120.00 |
| Glamour 1(1957) | 17.00 | 51.00 | 120.00 |
| Spectacular 1('56) | 17.00 | 51.00 | 120.00 |

**KATY KEENE COMICS DIGEST MAGAZINE**
1987 - No. 10, July, 1990 ($1.25-$1.35-$1.50, digest size, annual)
Close-Up, Inc. (Archie Ent.)

| | | | |
|---|---|---|---|
| 1-10 | | .70 | 1.35 |

**KATY KEENE FASHION BOOK MAGAZINE**
1955 - No. 13, Sum, '56 - N. 23, Wint, '58-59 (nn 3-10)
Radio Comics/Archie Publications

| | | | |
|---|---|---|---|
| 1 | 34.00 | 100.00 | 235.00 |
| 2 | 19.00 | 57.00 | 135.00 |
| 11-18: 18-Photo Bill Woggon | 15.00 | 45.00 | 105.00 |
| 19-23 | 11.50 | 34.00 | 80.00 |

**KATY KEENE HOLIDAY FUN** (See Archie Giant Series Mag. No. 7, 12)

**KATY KEENE PINUP PARADE**
1955 - No. 15, Summer, 1961 (25 cents)
Radio Comics/Archie Publications

| | | | |
|---|---|---|---|
| 1 | 34.00 | 100.00 | 235.00 |
| 2 | 19.00 | 57.00 | 135.00 |
| 3-5 | 16.50 | 50.00 | 115.00 |
| 6-10,12-14: 8-Mad parody. 10-Photo of Bill Woggon | 13.00 | 40.00 | 90.00 |
| 11-Story of how comics get CCA approved, narrated by Katy | 16.50 | 50.00 | 115.00 |
| 15(Rare)-Photo artist & family | 34.00 | 100.00 | 235.00 |

**KATY KEENE SPECIAL** (Katy Keene #7 on; also see Laugh Comics Digest)
Sept, 1983 - No. 33, 1990 (Later issues published quarterly)
Archie Enterprises

| | Good | Fine | N-Mint |
|---|---|---|---|
| 1-Woggon-r; new Woggon-c | | .50 | 1.00 |
| 2-33: 3-Woggon-r | | .30 | .60 |

**KATZENJAMMER KIDS, THE** (Also see Hans Und Fritz)
1903 (50 pgs.; 10x15¼''; in color)
New York American & Journal

(By Rudolph Dirks, strip 1st appeared in 1898)

| | | | |
|---|---|---|---|
| 1903 (Rare) | 34.00 | 103.00 | 240.00 |
| 1905-Tricks of . . . (10x15) | 24.00 | 72.00 | 165.00 |
| 1906-Stokes-10x16'', 32 pgs. in color | 24.00 | 72.00 | 165.00 |
| 1910-The Komical . . . (10x15) | 24.00 | 72.00 | 165.00 |
| 1921-Embee Dist. Co., 10x16'', 20 pgs. in color | 20.00 | 60.00 | 140.00 |

**KATZENJAMMER KIDS, THE** (See Giant Comic Album)
1945-1946; Summer, 1947 - No. 27, Feb-Mar, 1954
David McKay Publ./Standard No. 12-21(Spring/'50 - 53)/Harvey No. 22, 4/53 on

| | | | |
|---|---|---|---|
| Feature Books 30 | 10.00 | 30.00 | 70.00 |
| Feature Books 32,35('45),41,44('46) | 8.00 | 24.00 | 55.00 |
| Feature Book 37-Has photos & biog. of Harold Knerr | 9.30 | 28.00 | 65.00 |
| 1(1947) | 9.30 | 28.00 | 65.00 |
| 2 | 4.50 | 14.00 | 32.00 |
| 3-11 | 3.15 | 9.50 | 22.00 |
| 12-14(Standard) | 2.30 | 7.00 | 16.00 |
| 15-21(Standard) | 1.70 | 5.00 | 12.00 |
| 22-25,27(Harvey): 22-24-Henry app. | 1.15 | 3.50 | 8.00 |
| 26-½ in 3-D | 11.00 | 33.00 | 76.00 |

**KAYO** (Formerly Jest?)
No. 12, March, 1945
Harry 'A' Chesler

| | | | |
|---|---|---|---|
| 12-Green Knight, Capt. Glory, Little Nemo (not by McCay) | 6.00 | 18.00 | 42.00 |

**KA-ZAR** (Also see Savage Tales #6 & X-Men #10)
Aug, 1970 - No. 3, Mar, 1971 (Giant-Size, 68 pgs.)
Marvel Comics Group

| | | | |
|---|---|---|---|
| 1-Reprints earlier Ka-Zar stories; Avengers x-over in Hercules; Daredevil, X-Men app; hidden profanity-c | 1.15 | 3.50 | 8.00 |
| 2,3-Daredevil-r. 2-Ka-Zar origin, X-Men-r | 1.00 | 3.00 | 6.00 |

NOTE: ***Kirby** c/a-all. **Colan** a-1p(r). #1-Reprints X-Men #10? & Daredevil #13?*

**KA-ZAR**
Jan, 1974 - No. 20, Feb, 1977 (Regular Size)
Marvel Comics Group

| | | | |
|---|---|---|---|
| 1 | .35 | 1.00 | 2.00 |
| 2-20 | | .60 | 1.20 |

NOTE: ***Alcala** a-6i, 8i. **Brunner** c-4. **J. Buscema** a-6-10p; c-1, 5, 7. **Heath** a-12. **G. Kane** c(p)-3, 5, 8-11, 15, 20. **Kirby** c-12p. **Reinman** a-1p.*

**KA-ZAR THE SAVAGE** (See Marvel Fanfare)
Apr, 1981 - No. 34, Oct, 1984 (Regular size) (Mando paper #10 on)
Marvel Comics Group

| | | | |
|---|---|---|---|
| 1-34: 11-Origin Zabu. 12-Two versions: With & without panel missing (1600 printed with panel). 21-23,25,26-Spider-Man app. 26-Photo-c. 29-Double size; Ka-Zar & Shanna wed | | .50 | 1.00 |

NOTE: ***B. Anderson** a-1-15p, 18, 19; c-1-17, 18p, 20(back-c).*

**KEEN DETECTIVE FUNNIES** (Formerly Detective Picture Stories?)
No. 8, July, 1938 - No. 24, Sept, 1940
Centaur Publications

| | | | |
|---|---|---|---|
| V1#8-The Clock continues-r/Funny Picture Stories #1 | 92.00 | 230.00 | 550.00 |

*Katy Keene #11, © AP*

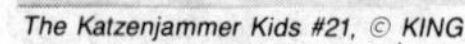
*The Katzenjammer Kids #21, © KING*

*Ka-Zar #1 (1/74), © MEG*

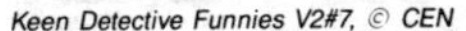
Keen Detective Funnies V2#7, © CEN

Kent Blake of the Secret Service #7, © MEG

Key Comics #2, © Consolidated Mag.

| | Good | Fine | N-Mint |
|---|---|---|---|
| 9-Tex Martin by Eisner | 48.00 | 145.00 | 335.00 |
| 10,11: 11-Dean Denton story (begins?) | 41.00 | 122.00 | 285.00 |
| V2#1,2-The Eye Sees by Frank Thomas begins; ends #23(Not in V2#3&5). 2-Jack Cole-a | 36.00 | 107.00 | 250.00 |
| 3-6,9-11: 3-TNT Todd begins. 4-Gabby Flynn begins. 5-Dean Denton story | 36.00 | 107.00 | 250.00 |
| 7-The Masked Marvel by Ben Thompson begins | 71.00 | 215.00 | 500.00 |
| 8-Nudist ranch panel w/four girls | 40.00 | 120.00 | 280.00 |
| 12(12/39)-Origin The Eye Sees by Frank Thomas; death of Masked Marvel's sidekick ZL | 48.00 | 145.00 | 335.00 |
| V3#1,2 | 41.00 | 122.00 | 285.00 |
| 18,19,21,22: 18-Bondage/torture-c | 41.00 | 122.00 | 285.00 |
| 20-Classic Eye Sees-c by Thomas | 48.00 | 145.00 | 335.00 |
| 23,24: 23-Air Man begins (intro). 24-Air Man-c | 48.00 | 145.00 | 335.00 |

NOTE: ***Burgos*** *a-V2#2.* ***Jack Cole*** *a-V2#2.* ***Eisner*** *a-V2#6r.* ***Ken Ernst*** *a-V2#4-7, 9, 10, 19, 21.* ***Everett*** *a-V2#6, 7, 9, 11, 12, 20.* ***Guardineer*** *a-V2#5, 66.* ***Gustavson*** *a-V2#4-6.* ***Simon*** *c-V3#1.*

**KEEN KOMICS**
V2#1, May, 1939 - V2#3, Nov, 1939
Centaur Publications

| | Good | Fine | N-Mint |
|---|---|---|---|
| V2#1(Large size)-Dan Hastings (s/f), The Big Top, Bob Phantom the Magician, The Mad Goddess app. | 58.00 | 145.00 | 350.00 |
| V2#2(Reg. size)-The Forbidden Idol of Machu Picchu; Cut Carson by Burgos begins | 32.00 | 95.00 | 225.00 |
| V2#3-Saddle Sniffl by Jack Cole, Circus Pays, Kings Revenge app. | 32.00 | 95.00 | 225.00 |

NOTE: ***Binder*** *a-V2#2.* ***Burgos*** *a-V2#2, 3.* ***Ken Ernst*** *a-V2#3.* ***Gustavson*** *a-V2#2.* ***Jack Cole*** *a-V2#3.*

**KEEN TEENS**
1945 - No. 6, Sept, 1947
Life's Romances Publ./Leader/Magazine Enterprises

| | Good | Fine | N-Mint |
|---|---|---|---|
| nn-14 pgs. Claire Voyant (cont'd. in other nn issue) movie photos, Dotty Dripple, Gertie O'Grady & Sissy; Van Johnson, Frank Sinatra photo-c | 11.00 | 32.00 | 75.00 |
| nn-16 pgs. Claire Voyant & 16 pgs. movie photos | 11.00 | 32.00 | 75.00 |
| 3-6: 4-Glenn Ford-c. 5-Perry Como-c | 3.70 | 11.00 | 26.00 |

**KEEPING UP WITH THE JONESES**
1920 - No. 2, 1921 (52 pgs.; 9¼x9¼"; B&W daily strip reprints)
Cupples & Leon Co.

| | Good | Fine | N-Mint |
|---|---|---|---|
| 1,2-By Pop Momand | 10.00 | 30.00 | 70.00 |

**KELLYS, THE** (Formerly Rusty Comics; Spy Cases No. 26 on)
No. 23, Jan, 1950 - No. 25, June, 1950
Marvel Comics (HPC)

| | Good | Fine | N-Mint |
|---|---|---|---|
| 23 | 6.00 | 18.00 | 42.00 |
| 24,25: 24-Margie app. | 3.50 | 10.50 | 24.00 |

**KELVIN MACE**
1986 - No. 2, 1986 ($2.00, B&W)
Vortex Publications

| | Good | Fine | N-Mint |
|---|---|---|---|
| 1,2: 1-(B&W). 2-(Color) | .70 | 2.00 | 4.00 |
| 1-2nd print (1/87, $1.75) | .30 | .85 | 1.70 |

**KEN MAYNARD WESTERN** (Movie star)(See Wow Comics, '36)
Sept, 1950 - No. 8, Feb, 1952 (All-36pgs; photo front/back-c)
Fawcett Publications

| | Good | Fine | N-Mint |
|---|---|---|---|
| 1-Ken Maynard & his horse Tarzan begin | 29.00 | 85.00 | 200.00 |
| 2 | 22.00 | 65.00 | 150.00 |
| 3-8 | 16.50 | 50.00 | 115.00 |

**KEN SHANNON** (Gabby #11) (Also see Police Comics #103)
Oct, 1951 - No. 10, 1952 (a private eye)
Quality Comics Group

| | Good | Fine | N-Mint |
|---|---|---|---|
| 1-Crandall-a | 13.00 | 40.00 | 90.00 |
| 2-Crandall c/a(2) | 10.00 | 30.00 | 70.00 |
| 3-5-Crandall-a | 7.00 | 21.00 | 50.00 |
| 6 | 4.30 | 13.00 | 30.00 |
| 7,9,10-Crandall-a | 6.50 | 19.00 | 45.00 |
| 8-Opium den drug use story | 5.50 | 16.50 | 38.00 |

NOTE: ***Jack Cole*** *a-1-9. No. 11-15 published after title change to Gabby.*

**KEN STUART**
Jan, 1949 (Sea Adventures)
Publication Enterprises

| | Good | Fine | N-Mint |
|---|---|---|---|
| 1-Frank Borth-c/a | 4.00 | 12.00 | 28.00 |

**KENT BLAKE OF THE SECRET SERVICE** (Spy)
May, 1951 - No. 14, July, 1953
Marvel/Atlas Comics(20CC)

| | Good | Fine | N-Mint |
|---|---|---|---|
| 1-Injury to eye, bondage, torture | 7.00 | 21.00 | 50.00 |
| 2-Drug use w/hypo scenes | 4.30 | 13.00 | 30.00 |
| 3-14 | 2.65 | 8.00 | 18.00 |

NOTE: ***Heath*** *c-5, 7.* ***Infantino*** *c-12.* ***Maneely*** *c-3.* ***Sinnott*** *a-2(3).*

**KERRY DRAKE**
Jan, 1956 - No. 2, March, 1956
Argo

| | Good | Fine | N-Mint |
|---|---|---|---|
| 1,2-Newspaper-r | 3.00 | 9.00 | 21.00 |

**KERRY DRAKE DETECTIVE CASES** (. . . Racket Buster No. 32,33)
(Also see Chamber of Clues & Green Hornet Comics #42-47)
1944 - No. 5, 1944; No. 6, Jan, 1948 - No. 33, Aug, 1952
Life's Romances/Compix/Magazine Ent. No.1-5/Harvey No.6 on

| | Good | Fine | N-Mint |
|---|---|---|---|
| nn(1944)(A-1 Comics)(slightly over-size) | 12.00 | 36.00 | 84.00 |
| 2 | 8.00 | 24.00 | 56.00 |
| 3-5(1944) | 6.00 | 18.00 | 42.00 |
| 6,8(1948); 8-Bondage-c | 3.50 | 10.50 | 24.00 |
| 7-Kubert-a; biog of Andriola (artist) | 4.00 | 12.00 | 28.00 |
| 9,10-Two-part marijuana story; Kerry smokes marijuana in #10 | 6.75 | 20.00 | 47.00 |
| 11-15 | 3.00 | 9.00 | 21.00 |
| 16-33 | 2.35 | 7.00 | 16.00 |
| . . . in the Case of the Sleeping City-(1951-Publishers Synd.)-16 pg. giveaway for armed forces; paper cover | 2.35 | 7.00 | 16.00 |

NOTE: ***Berg*** *a-5.* ***Powell*** *a-10-23, 28, 29.*

**KEWPIES**
Spring, 1949
Will Eisner Publications

| | Good | Fine | N-Mint |
|---|---|---|---|
| 1-Feiffer-a; Kewpie Doll ad on back cover | 29.00 | 86.00 | 200.00 |

**KEY COMICS**
Jan, 1944 - No. 5, Aug, 1946
Consolidated Magazines

| | Good | Fine | N-Mint |
|---|---|---|---|
| 1-The Key, Will-O-The-Wisp begin | 14.00 | 43.00 | 100.00 |
| 2 (3/44) | 7.00 | 21.00 | 50.00 |
| 3,4: 4-(5/46)-Origin John Quincy The Atom (begins) | 5.00 | 15.00 | 35.00 |
| 5-4pg. Faust Opera adapt; Kiefer-a; back-c advertises "Masterpieces Illustrated" by Lloyd Jacquet after he left Classic Comics (no copies of Masterpieces Ill. known) | 7.00 | 21.00 | 50.00 |

**KEY COMICS**
1951 - 1956 (32 pages) (Giveaway)
Key Clothing Co./Peterson Clothing

Contains a comic from different publishers bound with new cover. Cover changed each year. Many combinations possible. Distributed in Nebraska, Iowa, & Kansas. Contents would determine price, 40-60 percent of original.

**KEY RING COMICS**
1941 (16 pgs.; two colors) (sold 5 for 10 cents)
Dell Publishing Co.

| | Good | Fine | N-Mint |
|---|---|---|---|
| 1-Sky Hawk | 2.00 | 6.00 | 12.00 |

Good Fine N-Mint

1-Viking Carter 2.00 6.00 12.00
1-Features Sleepy Samson 2.00 6.00 12.00
1-Origin Greg Gilday r-/War Comics No. 2 2.35 7.00 14.00
1-Radior(Super hero) 2.35 7.00 14.00

NOTE: *Each book has two holes in spine to put in binder.*

**KICKERS, INC.**
Nov, 1986 - No. 12, Oct, 1987
Marvel Comics Group

1-12 .50 1.00

**KID CARROTS**
September, 1953
St. John Publishing Co.

1-Funny animal 2.30 7.00 16.00

**KID COLT OUTLAW** (Kid Colt #1-4; . . . Outlaw #5-on)(Also see All Western Winners, Best Western, Black Rider, Giant-Size. . . , Two-Gun Kid, Two-Gun Western, Western Winners, Wild Western, Wisco)
8/48 - No. 139, 3/68; No. 140, 11/69 - No. 229, 4/79
Marvel Comics(LCC) 1-16; Atlas(LMC) 17-102; Marvel 103-on

1-Kid Colt & his horse Steel begin; Two-Gun Kid app. 39.00 118.00 275.00
2 19.00 56.00 130.00
3-5: 4-Anti-Wertham editorial; Tex Taylor app. 5-Blaze Carson app. 12.00 36.00 85.00
6-8: 6-Tex Taylor app; 7-Nimo the Lion begins, ends #10 8.50 25.50 60.00
9,10 (52 pgs.) 9.30 28.00 65.00
11-Origin 10.00 30.00 70.00
12-20 6.00 18.00 42.00
21-32 5.00 15.00 35.00
33-45: Black Rider in all 3.70 11.00 26.00
46,47,49,50 3.15 9.50 22.00
48-Kubert-a 3.50 10.50 24.00
51-53,55,56 2.65 8.00 18.00
54-Williamson/Maneely-c 3.50 10.50 24.00
57-60,66: 4-pg. Williamson-a in all. 59-Reprint Rawhide Kid #79 4.00 12.00 28.00
61-63,67-78,80-86: 86-Kirby-a(r) 1.70 5.00 12.00
64,65-Crandall-a 2.30 7.00 16.00
79,87: 79-Origin retold. 87-Davis-a(r) 2.15 6.50 15.00
88,89-Williamson-a in both (4 pgs.). 89-Redrawn Matt Slade #2 2.85 8.50 20.00
90-99,101-Last 10 cent issues 1.15 3.50 8.00
100 1.50 4.50 10.00
101-120 .85 2.60 6.00
121-140: 121-Rawhide Kid x-over. 125-Two-Gun Kid x-over. 130-132-68pg. issues with one new story each; 130-Origin. 140-Reprints begin .50 1.50 3.00
141-160: 156-Giant; reprints(later issues all-r) .35 1.00 2.00
161-229: 170-Origin retold. 229-Rawhide Kid-r .40 .80
. . . Album (no date; 1950's; Atlas Comics)-132 pgs.; random binding, cardboard cover, B&W stories; contents can vary (Rare) 20.00 60.00 140.00

NOTE: ***Ayers*** *a-many.* ***Colan*** *a-52, 53; c(p)-223, 228, 229.* ***Crandall*** *a-140r, 167r.* ***Everett*** *a-137i, 225i(r).* ***Heath*** *c-34, 35, 39, 44, 46, 48, 49, 57.* ***Jack Keller*** *a-25(2), 26-68(3-4), 78, 94p, 98, 99, 108, 110, 132.* ***Kirby*** *a-86r, 93, 96, 119, 176(part); c-87, 92-95, 97, 99-112, 114-117, 121-123, 197r.* ***Maneely*** *a-12, 68, 81; c-17, 19, 40-43, 47, 52, 53, 62, 65, 68, 78, 81.* ***Morrow*** *a-173r, 216r.* ***Rico*** *a-13, 18.* ***Severin*** *c-58.* ***Shores*** *a-39, 41-43; c-4, 24.* ***Sutton*** *a-137p, 225p(r).* ***Wildey*** *a-47, 82.* ***Williamson*** *r-147, 170, 172, 216.* ***Woodbridge*** *a-64, 81. Black Rider in #33-45, 74, 86. Iron Mask in #110, 114, 121, 127. Sam Hawk in #84, 101, 111, 121, 146, 174, 181, 188.*

**KID COWBOY** (Also see Approved Comics #4)
1950 - No. 14, 1954 (painted covers)
Ziff-Davis Publ./St. John (Approved Comics)

1-Lucy Belle & Red Feather begin 5.70 17.00 40.00

Good Fine N-Mint

2-Maneely-c 3.00 9.00 21.00
3-14: 5-Berg-a. 11-Bondage-c 2.30 7.00 16.00

**KIDDIE KAPERS**
1945?(nd); Oct, 1957; 1963 - 1964
Kiddie Kapers Co., 1945/Decker Publ. (Red Top-Farrell)

1(nd, 1945-46?, 36 pgs.)-Infinity-c; funny animal 3.50 10.50 24.00
1(10/57)(Decker)-Little Bit reprints from Kiddie Karnival 1.50 4.50 10.00
Super Reprint #7, 10('63), 12, 14('63), 15,17('64), 18('64) .35 1.00 2.00

**KIDDIE KARNIVAL**
1952 (100 pgs., 25 cents) (One Shot)
Ziff-Davis Publ. Co. (Approved Comics)

nn-Rebound Little Bit #1,2 12.00 36.00 85.00

**KID ETERNITY** (Becomes Buccaneers) (See Hit Comics)
Spring, 1946 - No. 18, Nov, 1949
Quality Comics Group

1 36.00 107.00 250.00
2 18.00 54.00 125.00
3-Mac Raboy-a 19.00 58.00 135.00
4-10 10.00 30.00 70.00
11-18 6.50 19.00 45.00

**KID FROM DODGE CITY, THE**
July, 1957 - No. 2, Sept, 1957
Atlas Comics (MMC)

1 3.50 10.50 25.00
2-Everett-c 2.00 6.00 14.00

**KID FROM TEXAS, THE** (A Texas Ranger)
June, 1957 - No. 2, Aug, 1957
Atlas Comics (CSI)

1-Powell-a; Severin-c 4.00 12.00 28.00
2 2.30 7.00 16.00

**KID KOKO**
1958
I. W. Enterprises

Reprint #1,2-(r/M.E.'s Koko & Kola #4, 1947) .50 1.50 3.00

**KID KOMICS** (. . . Movie Komics No. 11)
Feb, 1943 - No. 10, Spring, 1946
Timely Comics (USA 1,2/FCI 3-10)

1-Origin Captain Wonder & sidekick Tim Mullrooney, & Subbie; intro the Sea-Going Lad, Pinto Pete, & Trixie Trouble; Knuckles & White-Wash Jones only app.; Wolverton art, 7 pgs. 138.00 345.00 825.00
2-The Young Allies, Red Hawk, & Tommy Tyme begin; last Captain Wonder & Subbie 78.00 195.00 470.00
3-The Vision & Daredevils app. 53.00 131.00 315.00
4-The Destroyer begins; Sub-Mariner app.; Red Hawk & Tommy Tyme end 46.00 115.00 275.00
5,6 35.00 88.00 210.00
7-10: The Whizzer app. 7; Destroyer not in #7,8; 10-Last Destroyer, Young Allies & Whizzer 35.00 88.00 210.00

NOTE: ***Schomburg*** *c-2-10.* ***Shores*** *c-1.*

**KID MONTANA** (Formerly Davy Crockett Frontier Fighter; The Gunfighters No. 51 on)
V2#9, Nov, 1957 - No. 50, Mar, 1965
Charlton Comics

V2#9 3.00 9.00 21.00
10 1.50 4.50 10.00
11,12,14-20 1.00 3.00 7.00

*Kid Colt Outlaw #7, © MEG*

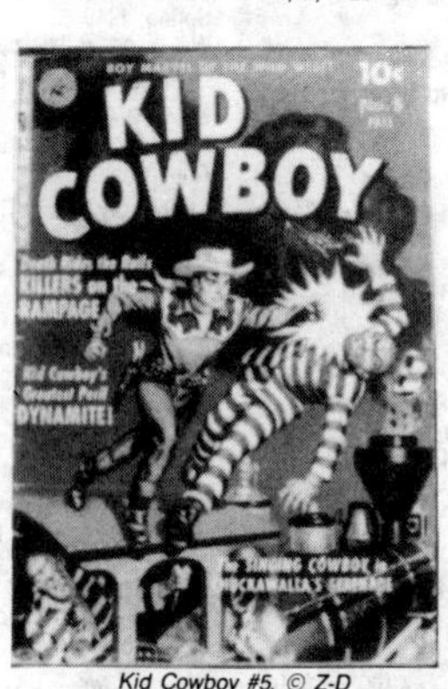

*Kid Cowboy #5, © Z-D*

*Kid Komics #3, © MEG*

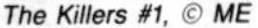
The Killers #1, © ME

King Comics #61, © KING

King Conan #1, © MEG

| | Good | Fine | N-Mint |
|---|---|---|---|
| 13-Williamson-a | 2.00 | 6.00 | 14.00 |
| 21-35 | .70 | 2.00 | 4.00 |
| 36-50 | .35 | 1.00 | 2.00 |

NOTE: *Title change to Montana Kid on cover only on No. 44; remained Kid Montana on inside.*

**KID MOVIE KOMICS** (Formerly Kid Komics; Rusty Comics #12 on)
No. 11, Summer, 1946
Timely Comics

| | | | |
|---|---|---|---|
| 11-Silly Seal & Ziggy Pig; 2 pgs. Kurtzman "Hey Look" plus 6 pg. "Pigtales" story | 13.00 | 40.00 | 90.00 |

**KIDNAPPED** (See 4-Color No. 1101 & Movie Comics)

**KIDNAP RACKET** (See Harvey Comics Hits No. 57)

**KID SLADE GUNFIGHTER** (Formerly Matt Slade...)
No. 5, Jan, 1957 - No. 8, July, 1957
Atlas Comics (SPI)

| | | | |
|---|---|---|---|
| 5-Maneely, Roth, Severin-a in all; Maneely-c | 4.00 | 12.00 | 28.00 |
| 6,8: 8-Severin-c | 2.00 | 6.00 | 14.00 |
| 7-Williamson/Mayo-a, 4 pgs. | 4.00 | 12.00 | 28.00 |

**KID ZOO COMICS**
July, 1948 (52 pgs.)
Street & Smith Publications

| | | | |
|---|---|---|---|
| 1-Funny Animal | 10.00 | 30.00 | 70.00 |

**KILLER** (...Tales By Timothy Truman)
March, 1985 ($1.75, one-shot, color, Baxter paper)
Eclipse Comics

| | | | |
|---|---|---|---|
| 1-Timothy Truman-c/a | .30 | .90 | 1.80 |

**KILLERS, THE**
1947 - No. 2, 1948 (No month)
Magazine Enterprises

| | | | |
|---|---|---|---|
| 1-Mr. Zin, the Hatchet Killer; mentioned in **SOTI**, pgs. 179,180; used by N.Y. Legis. Comm.; L. B. Cole-c | 43.00 | 130.00 | 300.00 |
| 2-(Scarce)-Hashish smoking story; "Dying, Dying, Dead" drug story; Whitney, Ingels-a; Whitney hanging-c | 43.00 | 130.00 | 300.00 |

**KILLING JOKE, THE** (See Batman: The Killing Joke)

**KILROYS, THE**
June-July, 1947 - No. 54, June-July, 1955
B&I Publ. Co. No. 1-19/American Comics Group

| | | | |
|---|---|---|---|
| 1 | 11.50 | 34.00 | 80.00 |
| 2 | 5.70 | 17.00 | 40.00 |
| 3-5: 5-Gross-a | 4.00 | 12.00 | 28.00 |
| 6-10: 8-Milt Gross's Moronica | 3.00 | 9.00 | 21.00 |
| 11-20: 14-Gross-a | 2.65 | 8.00 | 18.00 |
| 21-30 | 2.00 | 6.00 | 14.00 |
| 31-47,50-54 | 1.70 | 5.00 | 12.00 |
| 48,49-(3-D effect) | 10.00 | 30.00 | 70.00 |

**KING CLASSICS**
1977 (85 cents each) (36 pages, cardboard covers)
King Features (Printed in Spain for U.S. distr.)

1-Connecticut Yankee, 2-Last of the Mohicans, 3-Moby Dick, 4-Robin Hood, 5-Swiss Family Robinson, 6-Robinson Crusoe, 7-Treasure Island, 8-20,000 Leagues, 9-Christmas Carol, 10-Huck Finn, 11-Around the World in 80 Days, 12-Davy Crockett, 13-Don Quixote, 14-Gold Bug, 15-Ivanhoe, 16-Three Musketeers, 17-Baron Munchausen, 18-Alice in Wonderland, 19-Black Arrow, 20-Five Weeks in a Balloon, 21-Great Expectations, 22-Gulliver's Travels, 23-Prince & Pauper, 24-Lawrence of Arabia

| | | | |
|---|---|---|---|
| (Originals, 1977-78) each.... | 1.15 | 3.50 | 8.00 |
| Reprints, 1979; HRN-24) | 1.00 | 3.00 | 6.00 |

NOTE: *The first eight issues were not numbered. Issues No. 25-32 were advertised but not published. The 1977 originals have HRN 32a; the 1978 originals have HRN 32b.*

**KING COLT** (See 4-Color No. 651)

**KING COMICS** (Strip reprints)
Apr, 1936 - No. 159, Feb, 1952 (Winter on cover)
David McKay Publications/Standard No. 156-on

| | Good | Fine | VF-NM | NM/Mint |
|---|---|---|---|---|
| 1-Flash Gordon by Alex Raymond; Brick Bradford, Mandrake the Magician, Popeye & Henry begin | 367.00 | 915.00 | 2200.00 | 3600.00 |

(Estimated up to 70 total copies exist, 3 in NM/Mint)

| | Good | Fine | N-Mint |
|---|---|---|---|
| 2 | 158.00 | 395.00 | 950.00 |
| 3 | 117.00 | 290.00 | 700.00 |
| 4 | 71.00 | 215.00 | 500.00 |
| 5 | 54.00 | 160.00 | 375.00 |
| 6-10: 9-X-Mas-c | 36.00 | 107.00 | 250.00 |
| 11-20 | 29.00 | 85.00 | 200.00 |
| 21-30 | 23.00 | 70.00 | 160.00 |
| 31-40: 33-Last Segar Popeye | 20.00 | 60.00 | 140.00 |
| 41-50: 46-Little Lulu, Alvin & Tubby app. as text illos by Marge Buell 50-The Lone Ranger begins | 18.00 | 54.00 | 125.00 |
| 51-60: 52-Barney Baxter begins? | 13.00 | 40.00 | 90.00 |
| 61-The Phantom begins | 11.50 | 34.00 | 80.00 |
| 62-80: 76-Flag-c | 9.30 | 28.00 | 65.00 |
| 81-99: 82-Blondie begins? | 8.00 | 24.00 | 55.00 |
| 100 | 10.00 | 30.00 | 70.00 |
| 101-114: 114-Last Raymond issue (1 pg.); Flash Gordon by Austin Briggs begins, ends #155 | 7.00 | 21.00 | 50.00 |
| 115-145: 117-Phantom origin retold | 5.30 | 16.00 | 38.00 |
| 146,147-Prince Valiant in both | 4.00 | 12.00 | 28.00 |
| 148-155-Flash Gordon ends | 4.00 | 12.00 | 28.00 |
| 156-159 | 3.15 | 9.50 | 22.00 |

NOTE: ***Marge Buell** text illos in No. 24-46 at least.*

**KING CONAN** (Conan The King No. 20 on)
March, 1980 - No. 19, Nov, 1983 (52 pgs.)
Marvel Comics Group

| | | | |
|---|---|---|---|
| 1 | .40 | 1.25 | 2.50 |
| 2-6: 4-Death of Thoth Amon | .30 | .90 | 1.80 |
| 7-19: 7-1st Paul Smith-a, 2 pgs. (9/81) | .30 | .90 | 1.80 |

NOTE: ***Buscema** a-1-9p, 17p; c(p)-1-5, 7-9, 14, 17. **Kaluta** c-19. **Nebres** a-17i, 18, 19i. **Severin** c-18. **Simonson** c-6.*

**KING KONG** (See Movie Comics)

**KING LEONARDO & HIS SHORT SUBJECTS** (TV)
Nov-Jan, 1961-62 - No. 4, Sept, 1963
Dell Publishing Co./Gold Key

| | | | |
|---|---|---|---|
| 4-Color 1242,1278 | 5.70 | 17.00 | 40.00 |
| 01390-207(5-7/62)(Dell) | 4.50 | 14.00 | 32.00 |
| 1 (10/62) | 4.50 | 14.00 | 32.00 |
| 2-4 | 2.85 | 8.50 | 20.00 |

**KING LOUIE & MOWGLI**
May, 1968 (Disney)
Gold Key

| | | | |
|---|---|---|---|
| 1 (#10223-805)-Characters from Jungle Book | 1.50 | 4.50 | 10.00 |

**KING OF DIAMONDS** (TV)
July-Sept, 1962
Dell Publishing Co.

| | | | |
|---|---|---|---|
| 01-391-209-Photo-c | 2.00 | 6.00 | 14.00 |

**KING OF KINGS** (See 4-Color No. 1236)

**KING OF THE BAD MEN OF DEADWOOD**
1950 (See Wild Bill Hickok #16)
Avon Periodicals

| | | | |
|---|---|---|---|
| nn-Kinstler-c; Kamen/Feldstein-a r-/Cowpuncher #2 | 9.50 | 28.00 | 65.00 |

**KING OF THE ROYAL MOUNTED** (See Famous Feature Stories, Feature Books #1, Large Feature Comic #9, King Comics, Red Ryder #3 & Super Book #2, 6)

**KING OF THE ROYAL MOUNTED** (Zane Grey's)
No. 207, Dec, 1948 - No. 935, Sept-Nov, 1958

Dell Publishing Co.

| | Good | Fine | N-Mint |
|---|---|---|---|
| 4-Color 207(#1, 12/48) | 11.50 | 34.00 | 80.00 |
| 4-Color 265,283 | 8.00 | 24.00 | 56.00 |
| 4-Color 310,340 | 5.00 | 15.00 | 35.00 |
| 4-Color 363,384 | 4.00 | 12.00 | 28.00 |
| 8(6-8/52)-10 | 4.00 | 12.00 | 28.00 |
| 11-20 | 3.50 | 10.50 | 24.00 |
| 21-28(3-5/58) | 3.00 | 9.00 | 21.00 |
| 4-Color 935(9-11/58) | 3.00 | 9.00 | 21.00 |

NOTE: *4-Color No. 207, 265, 283, 310, 340, 363, 384 are all newspaper reprints with **Jim Gary** art. No. 8 on are all Dell originals. **Painted** c-No. 9-on.*

**KING RICHARD & THE CRUSADERS** (See 4-Color No. 588)

**KINGS OF THE NIGHT**
1990 - No. 2, 1990 ($2.25, color, 2 issue series)
Dark Horse Comics

| | | | |
|---|---|---|---|
| 1,2-Robert E. Howard adaptation; Bolton-c | .40 | 1.15 | 2.30 |

**KING SOLOMON'S MINES**
1951 (Movie)
Avon Periodicals

| | | | |
|---|---|---|---|
| nn(#1 on 1st page) | 20.00 | 60.00 | 140.00 |

**KISS** (See Crazy Magazine, Howard the Duck #12, 13, Marvel Comics Super Special #1, 5, Rock Fantasy Comics #10 & Rock N' Roll Comics #9)

**KISSYFUR** (TV)
1989 (Sept.) ($2.00, color, 52 pgs.)
DC Comics

| | | | |
|---|---|---|---|
| 1-Based on Saturday morning cartoon | .35 | 1.00 | 2.00 |

**KIT CARSON** (See Frontier Fighters)

**KIT CARSON** (Formerly All True Detective Cases No. 4; Fighting Davy Crockett No. 9; see Blazing Sixguns)
1950; No. 2, 8/51 - No. 3, 12/51; No. 5, 11-12/54 - No. 8, 9/55
Avon Periodicals

| | | | |
|---|---|---|---|
| nn(#1) (1950) | 6.50 | 19.50 | 45.00 |
| 2(8/51) | 3.70 | 11.00 | 26.00 |
| 3(12/51) | 3.00 | 9.00 | 21.00 |
| 5-6,8('54-'55)-Formerly All True Detective Cases (last pre-code) | 2.65 | 8.00 | 18.00 |
| 7-Kinstler-a(2) | 3.00 | 9.00 | 21.00 |
| I.W. Reprint #10('63)-Severin-c | .85 | 2.50 | 5.00 |

NOTE: ***Kinstler** c-1-3, 5-8.*

**KIT CARSON & THE BLACKFEET WARRIORS**
1953
Realistic

| | | | |
|---|---|---|---|
| nn-Reprint; Kinstler-c | 5.00 | 15.00 | 35.00 |

**KIT KARTER**
May-July, 1962
Dell Publishing Co.

| | | | |
|---|---|---|---|
| 1 | 1.15 | 3.50 | 8.00 |

**KITTY**
October, 1948
St. John Publishing Co.

| | | | |
|---|---|---|---|
| 1-Lily Renee-a | 3.50 | 10.50 | 24.00 |

**KITTY PRYDE AND WOLVERINE**
Nov, 1984 - No. 6, April, 1985 (6 issue mini-series)
Marvel Comics Group

| | | | |
|---|---|---|---|
| 1 (From X-Men) | 1.00 | 3.00 | 6.00 |
| 2-6 | .70 | 2.00 | 4.00 |

**KLARER GIVEAWAYS** (See Wisco)

**KNIGHTS OF PENDRAGON, THE**
July, 1990 - No. 6, Dec, 1990 ($1.95, color, mini-series)
Marvel Comics Ltd.

| | Good | Fine | N-Mint |
|---|---|---|---|
| 1-6: 1-Capt. Britain app. 2-Free poster inside | .35 | 1.00 | 2.00 |

**KNIGHTS OF THE ROUND TABLE** (See 4-Color No. 540)

**KNIGHTS OF THE ROUND TABLE**
No. 10, April, 1957
Pines Comics

| | | | |
|---|---|---|---|
| 10 | 1.70 | 5.00 | 12.00 |

**KNIGHTS OF THE ROUND TABLE**
Nov-Jan, 1963/64 (Painted-c)
Dell Publishing Co.

| | | | |
|---|---|---|---|
| 1 (12-397-401) | 2.30 | 7.00 | 16.00 |

**KNOCK KNOCK** (. . . Who's There?)
No. 801, 1936 (52 pages) (8x9'', B&W)
Whitman Publ./Gerona Publications

| | | | |
|---|---|---|---|
| 801-Joke book; Bob Dunn-a | 4.30 | 13.00 | 30.00 |

**KNOCKOUT ADVENTURES**
Winter, 1953-54
Fiction House Magazines

| | | | |
|---|---|---|---|
| 1-Reprints Fight Comics #53 | 6.50 | 19.00 | 45.00 |

**KNOW YOUR MASS**
No. 303, 1958 (100 Pg. Giant) (35 cents) (square binding)
Catechetical Guild

| | | | |
|---|---|---|---|
| 303-In color | 2.30 | 7.00 | 16.00 |

**KOBRA** (See DC Special Series No. 1)
Feb-Mar, 1976 - No. 7, Mar-Apr, 1977
National Periodical Publications

| | | | |
|---|---|---|---|
| 1-Art plotted by Kirby | | .40 | .80 |
| 2-7: 3-Giffen-a | | .25 | .50 |

NOTE: ***Austin** a-3i. **Buckler** a-5p; c-5p. **Kubert** c-4. **Nasser** a-6p, 7; c-7.*

**KOKEY KOALA**
May, 1952
Toby Press

| | | | |
|---|---|---|---|
| 1 | 3.50 | 10.50 | 24.00 |

**KOKO AND KOLA** (Also see Tick Tock Tales)
Fall, 1946 - No. 5, May, 1947; No. 6, 1950
Compix/Magazine Enterprises

| | | | |
|---|---|---|---|
| 1-Funny animal | 4.30 | 13.00 | 30.00 |
| 2 | 2.30 | 7.00 | 16.00 |
| 3-5,6(A-1 28) | 1.70 | 5.00 | 12.00 |

**KO KOMICS**
October, 1945
Gerona Publications

| | | | |
|---|---|---|---|
| 1-The Duke of Darkness & The Menace (hero); Kirby-c | 17.00 | 51.00 | 120.00 |

**KOMIC KARTOONS**
Fall, 1945 - No. 2, Winter, 1945
Timely Comics (EPC)

| | | | |
|---|---|---|---|
| 1,2-Andy Wolf, Bertie Mouse | 8.50 | 25.50 | 60.00 |

**KOMIK PAGES**
April, 1945 (All reprints)
Harry 'A' Chesler, Jr. (Our Army, Inc.)

| | | | |
|---|---|---|---|
| 10(#1 on inside)-Land O' Nod by Rick Yager (2 pgs.), Animal Crackers, Foxy GrandPa, Tom, Dick & Mary, Cheerio Minstrels, Red Starr plus other 1-2 pg. strips; Cole-a | 8.50 | 25.50 | 60.00 |

**KONA** (. . . Monarch of Monster Isle)
Feb-Apr, 1962 - No. 21, Jan-Mar, 1967 (Painted-c)
Dell Publishing Co.

| | | | |
|---|---|---|---|
| 4-Color 1256 (#1) | 3.50 | 10.50 | 24.00 |

*King of the Royal Mounted #25, © Zane Grey*

*Kit Carson #1, © AVON*

*Komic Kartoons #1, © MEG*

Konga #5, © CC

Korak, Son of Tarzan #23, © ERB

Krazy Komics #1 (8/48), © MEG

| | Good | Fine | N-Mint |
|---|---|---|---|
| 2-10: 4-Anak begins | 1.70 | 5.00 | 12.00 |
| 11-21 | 1.00 | 3.00 | 7.00 |

NOTE: ***Glanzman*** *a-all issues.*

**KONGA** (Fantastic Giants No. 24) (See Return of . . .)
1960; No. 2, Aug, 1961 - No. 23, Nov, 1965
Charlton Comics

| | Good | Fine | N-Mint |
|---|---|---|---|
| 1(1960)-Based on movie | 18.00 | 54.00 | 125.00 |
| 2 | 9.30 | 28.00 | 65.00 |
| 3-5 | 7.00 | 21.00 | 50.00 |
| 6-15 | 4.50 | 14.00 | 32.00 |
| 16-23 | 3.50 | 10.50 | 24.00 |

NOTE: ***Ditko*** *a-1, 3-15; c-4, 6-9.* ***Glanzman*** *a-12.* ***Montes & Bache*** *a-16-23.*

**KONGA'S REVENGE** (Formerly Return of . . .)
No. 2, Summer, 1963 - No. 3, Fall, 1964; Dec, 1968
Charlton Comics

| | Good | Fine | N-Mint |
|---|---|---|---|
| 2,3: 2-Ditko-c/a | 3.00 | 9.00 | 21.00 |
| 1('68)-Reprints Konga's Revenge #3 | 1.50 | 4.50 | 10.00 |

**KONG THE UNTAMED**
June-July, 1975 - No. 5, Feb-Mar, 1976
National Periodical Publications

| | Good | Fine | N-Mint |
|---|---|---|---|
| 1-Wrightson-c; Alcala-a | | .40 | .80 |
| 2-5: 2-Wrightson-c; 2,3-Alcala-a | | .25 | .50 |

**KOOKIE**
Feb-Apr, 1962 - No. 2, May-July, 1962
Dell Publishing Co.

| | Good | Fine | N-Mint |
|---|---|---|---|
| 1,2-Written by John Stanley; Bill Williams-a | 4.30 | 13.00 | 30.00 |

**K. O. PUNCH, THE** (Also see Lucky Fights It Through)
1948 (Educational giveaway)
E. C. Comics

| | Good | Fine | N-Mint |
|---|---|---|---|
| nn-Feldstein-splash; Kamen-a | 117.00 | 340.00 | 700.00 |

**KORAK, SON OF TARZAN** (Edgar Rice Burroughs)
Jan, 1964 - No. 45, Jan, 1972 (Painted-c No. 1-?)
Gold Key

| | Good | Fine | N-Mint |
|---|---|---|---|
| 1-Russ Manning-a | 4.00 | 12.00 | 28.00 |
| 2-11-Russ Manning-a | 2.15 | 6.50 | 15.00 |
| 12-21: 14-Jon of the Kalahari ends. 15-Mabu, Jungle Boy begins. 21-Manning-a | 1.50 | 4.50 | 10.00 |
| 22-30 | 1.00 | 3.00 | 7.00 |
| 31-45 | .70 | 2.00 | 5.00 |

NOTE: ***Warren Tufts*** *a-12, 13.*

**KORAK, SON OF TARZAN** (Tarzan Family #60 on; see Tarzan #230)
V9#46, May-June, 1972 - V12#56, Feb-Mar, 1974; No. 57, May-June, 1975 - No. 59, Sept-Oct, 1975 (Edgar Rice Burroughs)
National Periodical Publications

| | Good | Fine | N-Mint |
|---|---|---|---|
| 46-(52 pgs.)-Carson of Venus begins (origin); Pellucidar feature; Weiss-a | | .60 | 1.20 |
| 47-59: 49-Origin Korak retold. 56-Last Carson of Venus | | .40 | .80 |

NOTE: ***Kaluta*** *a-46-56. All have covers by* ***Joe Kubert. Manning*** *strip reprints-No. 57-59.* ***Frank Thorn*** *a-46-51.*

**KOREA MY HOME** (Also see Yalta to Korea)
nd (1950s)
Johnstone and Cushing

| | Good | Fine | N-Mint |
|---|---|---|---|
| nn-Anti-communist; Korean War | 15.00 | 45.00 | 105.00 |

**KORG: 70,000 B. C.** (TV)
May, 1975 - No. 9, Nov, 1976 (Hanna-Barbera)
Charlton Publications

| | Good | Fine | N-Mint |
|---|---|---|---|
| 1 | .25 | .75 | 1.50 |
| 2-9: 2-Painted-c; Byrne text illos | | .50 | 1.00 |

**KORNER KID COMICS**
1947
Four Star Publications

| | Good | Fine | N-Mint |
|---|---|---|---|
| 1 | 3.70 | 11.00 | 26.00 |

**KRAZY KAT**
1946 (Hardcover)
Holt

| | Good | Fine | N-Mint |
|---|---|---|---|
| Reprints daily & Sunday strips by Herriman | 26.00 | 78.00 | 180.00 |
| with dust jacket (Rare) . . . . | 54.00 | 162.00 | 380.00 |

**KRAZY KAT** (See Ace Comics & March of Comics No. 72, 87)

**KRAZY KAT COMICS** (. . . & Ignatz the Mouse early issues)
May-June, 1951 - F.C. #696, Apr, 1956; Jan, 1964 (None by Herriman)
Dell Publishing Co./Gold Key

| | Good | Fine | N-Mint |
|---|---|---|---|
| 1(1951) | 4.30 | 13.00 | 30.00 |
| 2-5 (#5, 8-10/52) | 3.00 | 9.00 | 21.00 |
| 4-Color 454,504 | 2.30 | 7.00 | 16.00 |
| 4-Color 548,619,696 (4/56) | 2.00 | 6.00 | 14.00 |
| 1(10098-401)(1/64-Gold Key)(TV) | 2.00 | 6.00 | 14.00 |

**KRAZY KOMICS** (1st Series) (Cindy Comics No. 27 on)
July, 1942 - No. 26, Spr, 1947 (Also see Ziggy Pig)
Timely Comics (USA No. 1-21/JPC No. 22-26)

| | Good | Fine | N-Mint |
|---|---|---|---|
| 1-Ziggy Pig & Silly Seal begins | 22.00 | 65.00 | 150.00 |
| 2 | 11.00 | 32.00 | 75.00 |
| 3-10 | 6.50 | 19.00 | 45.00 |
| 11,13,14 | 4.50 | 14.00 | 32.00 |
| 12-Timely's entire art staff drew themselves into a Creeper story | 7.00 | 21.00 | 50.00 |
| 15-(8-9/44)-Becomes Funny Tunes #16; has "Super Soldier" by Pfc. Stan Lee | 4.50 | 14.00 | 32.00 |
| 16-24,26: 16-(10-11/44) | 3.15 | 9.50 | 22.00 |
| 25-Kurtzman-a, 6 pgs. | 5.00 | 15.00 | 35.00 |

**KRAZY KOMICS** (2nd Series)
Aug, 1948 - No. 2, Nov, 1948
Timely/Marvel Comics

| | Good | Fine | N-Mint |
|---|---|---|---|
| 1-Wolverton (10 pgs.) & Kurtzman (8 pgs.)-a; Eustice Hayseed begins, Li'l Abner swipe | 22.00 | 65.00 | 150.00 |
| 2-Wolverton-a, 10 pgs.; Powerhouse Pepper cameo | 14.00 | 43.00 | 100.00 |

**KRAZY KROW** (Also see Dopey Duck, Film Funnies, Funny Frolics & Movie Tunes)
Summer, 1945 - No. 3, Wint, 1945/46
Marvel Comics (ZPC)

| | Good | Fine | N-Mint |
|---|---|---|---|
| 1 | 7.00 | 21.00 | 50.00 |
| 2,3 | 4.30 | 13.00 | 30.00 |
| I.W. Reprint #1('57), 2('58), 7 | .50 | 1.50 | 3.00 |

**KRAZYLIFE**
1945 (no month)
Fox Feature Syndicate

| | Good | Fine | N-Mint |
|---|---|---|---|
| 1-Funny animal | 6.50 | 19.00 | 45.00 |

**KREE/SKRULL WAR STARRING THE AVENGERS, THE**
Sept, 1983 - No. 2, Oct, 1983 ($2.50, 68 pgs.; Baxter paper)
Marvel Comics Group

| | Good | Fine | N-Mint |
|---|---|---|---|
| 1,2 | .40 | 1.25 | 2.50 |

NOTE: ***Neal Adams*** *p-1r, 2.* ***Buscema*** *a-1r, 2r.* ***Simonson*** *c(p)/a(p)-1.*

**KRIM-KO KOMICS**
5/18/35 - No. 6, 6/22/35; 1936 - 1939 (Giveaway) (weekly)
Krim-ko Chocolate Drink

| | Good | Fine | N-Mint |
|---|---|---|---|
| 1-(16 pgs., soft-c, Dairy giveaways)-Tom, Mary & Sparky Advs. by Russell Keaton, Jim Hawkins by Dick Moores, Mystery Island! by Rick Yager begin | 7.00 | 21.00 | 50.00 |

| | Good | Fine | N-Mint |
|---|---|---|---|
| 2-6 (6/22/35) | 4.30 | 13.00 | 30.00 |
| Lola, Secret Agent; 184 issues, 4 pg. giveaways - all original stories each.... | 1.70 | 5.00 | 12.00 |

**KROFFT SUPERSHOW** (TV)
April, 1978 - No. 6, Jan, 1979 (Photo-c: 1, 6)
Gold Key

| | | | |
|---|---|---|---|
| 1 | | .60 | 1.20 |
| 2-6 | | .35 | .70 |

**KRULL**
Nov, 1983 - No. 2, Dec, 1983 (Movie adaptation)
Marvel Comics Group

| | | | |
|---|---|---|---|
| 1,2-r/Marvel Super Spec. 1-Photo-c from movie | | .25 | .50 |

**KRYPTON CHRONICLES**
Sept, 1981 - No. 3, Nov, 1981
DC Comics

| | | | |
|---|---|---|---|
| 1-Buckler-c(p) | | .40 | .80 |
| 2,3 | | .30 | .60 |

**KULL & THE BARBARIANS** (Magazine)
May, 1975 - No. 3, Sept, 1975 (B&W) ($1.00)
Marvel Comics Group

| | | | |
|---|---|---|---|
| 1-Andru/Wood-r/Kull #1; 2 pgs. Neal Adams; Gil Kane, Severin-a | .40 | 1.25 | 2.50 |
| 2,3: 2-Red Sonja by Chaykin begins; N. Adams-i; Gil Kane-a. 3-Origin Red Sonja by Chaykin; N. Adams-a; Solomon Kane app. | .30 | .90 | 1.80 |

**KULL IN 3-D** (See Blackthorne 3-D Series #51 & 67)

**KULL THE CONQUEROR** (. . .the Destroyer #11 on; see Marvel Preview)
June, 1971 - No. 2, Sept, 1971; No. 3, July, 1972 - No. 15, Aug, 1974; No. 16, Aug, 1976 - No. 29, Oct, 1978
Marvel Comics Group

| | | | |
|---|---|---|---|
| 1-Andru/Wood-a; origin Kull | .70 | 2.00 | 4.00 |
| 2-10 | .40 | 1.25 | 2.50 |
| 11-29: 11-15-Ploog-a | .25 | .80 | 1.60 |

NOTE: *No. 1, 2, 7-9, 11 are based on Robert E. Howard stories.* ***Alcala*** *a-17p, 18-20i; c-24.* ***Ditko*** *a-12r, 15r.* ***Gil Kane*** *c-15p, 21.* ***Nebres*** *a-22i-27i; c-25i, 27i.* ***Ploog*** *c-11, 12p, 13.* ***Severin*** *a-2-9i; c-2-10i, 19.* ***Starlin*** *c-14.*

**KULL THE CONQUEROR**
Dec, 1982 - No. 2, Mar, 1983 (52 pgs., printed on Baxter paper)
Marvel Comics Group

| | | | |
|---|---|---|---|
| 1,2: 1-Buscema-a(p) | .35 | 1.00 | 2.00 |

**KULL THE CONQUEROR** (No. 9,10 titled 'Kull')
5/83 - No. 10, 6/85 (52 pgs.; $1.25-60 cents; Mando paper)
Marvel Comics Group

| | | | |
|---|---|---|---|
| V3#1-10: Buscema-a in all. 2-Sienkiewicz-c | | .50 | 1.00 |

**KUNG FU** (See Deadly Hands of..., & Master of...)

**KUNG FU FIGHTER** (See Richard Dragon...)

**LABOR IS A PARTNER**
1949 (32 pgs. in color; paper cover)
Catechetical Guild Educational Society

| | | | |
|---|---|---|---|
| nn-Anti-communism | 17.00 | 51.00 | 120.00 |
| Confidential Preview-(B&W, 8½x11", saddle stitched)-only one known copy; text varies from color version, advertises next book on secularism (If the Devil Would Talk) | 35.00 | 100.00 | 200.00 |

**LABYRINTH**
Nov, 1986 - No. 3, Jan, 1987 (Mini-series, movie adaptation)
Marvel Comics Group

| | | | |
|---|---|---|---|
| 1-3: R-/Marv. Super Spec. #40 | | .40 | .80 |

**LAD: A DOG**
1961 - No. 2, July-Sept, 1962
Dell Publishing Co.

| | Good | Fine | N-Mint |
|---|---|---|---|
| 4-Color 1303 (movie), 2 | 2.65 | 8.00 | 18.00 |

**LADY AND THE TRAMP** (See Dell Giants, 4-Color No. 629, 634, & Movie Comics)

**LADY AND THE TRAMP IN "BUTTER LATE THAN NEVER"**
1955 (16 pgs., 5x7¼", soft-c) (Walt Disney)
American Dairy Association (Premium)

| | | | |
|---|---|---|---|
| nn | 3.00 | 9.00 | 21.00 |

**LADY BOUNTIFUL**
1917 (10¼x13½"; 24 pgs.; B&W; cardboard cover)
Saalfield Publ. Co./Press Publ. Co.

| | | | |
|---|---|---|---|
| nn-By Gene Carr; 2 panels per page | 8.50 | 25.50 | 60.00 |

**LADY COP** (See First Issue Special)

**LADY FOR A NIGHT** (See Cinema Comics Herald)

**LADY LUCK** (Formerly Smash #1-85) (Also see Spirit Sections #1)
No. 86, Dec, 1949 - No. 90, Aug, 1950
Quality Comics Group

| | | | |
|---|---|---|---|
| 86(#1) | 37.00 | 110.00 | 255.00 |
| 87-90 | 29.00 | 85.00 | 200.00 |

**LAFF-A-LYMPICS** (TV)(See The Funtastic World of Hanna-Barbera)
Mar, 1978 - No. 13, Mar, 1979 (Hanna-Barbera)
Marvel Comics Group

| | | | |
|---|---|---|---|
| 1-13: Yogi Bear, Scooby Doo, Pixie & Dixie, etc. | | .30 | .60 |

**LAFFIN' GAS** (See Blackthorne 3-D Series #16)

**LAFFY-DAFFY COMICS**
Feb, 1945 - No. 2, March, 1945
Rural Home Publ. Co.

| | | | |
|---|---|---|---|
| 1,2 | 3.50 | 10.50 | 24.00 |

**LANA** (Little Lana No. 8 on)
Aug, 1948 - No. 7, Aug, 1949 (Also see Annie Oakley)
Marvel Comics (MjMC)

| | | | |
|---|---|---|---|
| 1-Rusty, Millie begin | 6.50 | 19.00 | 45.00 |
| 2-Kurtzman's "Hey Look" (1); last Rusty | 4.50 | 14.00 | 32.00 |
| 3-7: 3-Nellie begins | 2.65 | 8.00 | 18.00 |

**LANCELOT & GUINEVERE** (See Movie Classics)

**LANCELOT LINK, SECRET CHIMP** (TV)
April, 1971 - No. 8, Feb, 1973
Gold Key

| | | | |
|---|---|---|---|
| 1-Photo-c | 1.50 | 4.50 | 10.00 |
| 2-8: 2-Photo-c | .85 | 2.60 | 6.00 |

**LANCELOT STRONG** (See The Shield)

**LANCE O'CASEY** (See Mighty Midget & Whiz Comics)
Spring, 1946 - No. 3, Fall, 1946; No. 4, Summer, 1948
Fawcett Publications

| | | | |
|---|---|---|---|
| 1-Captain Marvel app. on-c | 11.00 | 32.00 | 75.00 |
| 2 | 6.00 | 18.00 | 42.00 |
| 3,4 | 5.00 | 15.00 | 35.00 |

NOTE: *The cover for the 1st issue was done in 1942 but was not published until 1946. The cover shows 68 pages but actually has only 36 pgs.*

**LANCER** (TV)(Western)
Feb, 1969 - No. 3, Sept, 1969 (All photo-c)
Gold Key

| | | | |
|---|---|---|---|
| 1 | 2.30 | 7.00 | 16.00 |
| 2,3 | 1.70 | 5.00 | 12.00 |

**LAND OF THE GIANTS** (TV)
Nov, 1968 - No. 5, Sept, 1969

*Krofft Supershow #1, © Krofft Prod.*

*Lady Luck #88, © QUA*

*Lana #7, © MEG*

*Land of the Lost Comics #7, © WMG*

*Large Feature Comic #24 (Series I), © KING*

*Larry Doby, Baseball Hero nn, © FAW*

Gold Key

| | Good | Fine | N-Mint |
|---|---|---|---|
| 1-Photo-c | 3.00 | 9.00 | 21.00 |
| 2-5: 4,5-Photo-c | 1.70 | 5.00 | 12.00 |

**LAND OF THE LOST COMICS** (Radio)
July-Aug, 1946 - No. 9, Spring, 1948
E. C. Comics

| | Good | Fine | N-Mint |
|---|---|---|---|
| 1 | 20.00 | 60.00 | 140.00 |
| 2 | 13.00 | 40.00 | 90.00 |
| 3-9 | 11.00 | 32.00 | 75.00 |

**LAND UNKNOWN, THE** (See 4-Color No. 845)

**LARAMIE** (TV)
Aug, 1960 - July, 1962 (All photo-c)
Dell Publishing Co.

| | Good | Fine | N-Mint |
|---|---|---|---|
| 4-Color 1125-Gil Kane/Heath-a | 6.00 | 18.00 | 42.00 |
| 4-Color 1223,1284 | 4.30 | 13.00 | 30.00 |
| 01-418-207 (7/62) | 4.30 | 13.00 | 30.00 |

**LAREDO** (TV)
June, 1966
Gold Key

| | Good | Fine | N-Mint |
|---|---|---|---|
| 1 (10179-606)-Photo-c | 2.00 | 6.00 | 14.00 |

**LARGE FEATURE COMIC** (Formerly called Black & White)
1939 - No. 13, 1943
Dell Publishing Co.

| | Good | Fine | N-Mint |
|---|---|---|---|
| 1 **(Series I)**-Dick Tracy Meets the Blank | 93.00 | 280.00 | 650.00 |
| 2-Terry & the Pirates (#1) | 48.00 | 145.00 | 335.00 |
| 3-Heigh-Yo Silver! The Lone Ranger (text & ill.)(76 pgs.); also exists as a Whitman #710 | 45.00 | 135.00 | 315.00 |
| 4-Dick Tracy Gets His Man | 50.00 | 150.00 | 350.00 |
| 5-Tarzan (#1) by Harold Foster (origin); reprints 1st dailies from '29 | 88.00 | 265.00 | 615.00 |
| 6-Terry & the Pirates & The Dragon Lady; reprints dailies from 1936 | 44.00 | 133.00 | 310.00 |
| 7-(Scarce)-52 pgs.; The Lone Ranger-Hi-Yo Silver the Lone Ranger to the Rescue; also exists as a Whitman #715 | 55.00 | 165.00 | 385.00 |
| 8-Dick Tracy Racket Buster | 46.00 | 140.00 | 325.00 |
| 9-King of the Royal Mounted | 22.00 | 65.00 | 154.00 |
| 10-(Scarce)-Gang Busters (No. appears on inside front cover); first slick cover | 32.00 | 95.00 | 225.00 |
| 11-Dick Tracy Foils the Mad Doc Hump | 46.00 | 140.00 | 325.00 |
| 12-Smilin' Jack | 30.00 | 90.00 | 210.00 |
| 13-Dick Tracy & Scotty | 46.00 | 140.00 | 325.00 |
| 14-Smilin' Jack | 30.00 | 90.00 | 210.00 |
| 15-Dick Tracy & the Kidnapped Princes | 46.00 | 140.00 | 325.00 |
| 16-Donald Duck-1st app. Daisy Duck on back cover (6/41-Disney) | 170.00 | 515.00 | 1200.00 |
| (Prices vary widely on this book) | | | |
| 17-Gang Busters (1941) | 20.00 | 60.00 | 140.00 |
| 18-Phantasmo | 17.00 | 51.00 | 120.00 |
| 19-Dumbo Comic Paint Book (Disney); partial-r 4-Color #17 | 114.00 | 343.00 | 800.00 |
| 20-Donald Duck Comic Paint Book (Rarer than #16) (Disney) | 230.00 | 685.00 | 1600.00 |
| (Prices vary widely on this book) | | | |
| 21,22: 21-Private Buck. 22-Nuts & Jolts | 8.00 | 24.00 | 55.00 |
| 23-The Nebbs | 10.00 | 30.00 | 70.00 |
| 24-Popeye (Thimble Theatre) ½ by Segar | 39.00 | 118.00 | 275.00 |
| 25-Smilin' Jack-1st issue to show title on-c | 30.00 | 90.00 | 210.00 |
| 26-Smitty | 17.00 | 51.00 | 120.00 |
| 27-Terry & the Pirates; Caniff-c/a | 33.00 | 100.00 | 230.00 |
| 28-Grin & Bear It | 7.00 | 21.00 | 50.00 |
| 29-Moon Mullins | 16.00 | 48.00 | 110.00 |
| 30-Tillie the Toiler | 14.00 | 43.00 | 100.00 |
| 1 **(Series II)**-Peter Rabbit by Cady; arrival date-3/27/42 | 30.00 | 90.00 | 210.00 |
| 2-Winnie Winkle (#1) | 11.50 | 34.00 | 80.00 |
| 3-Dick Tracy | 43.00 | 130.00 | 300.00 |
| 4-Tiny Tim (#1) | 22.00 | 65.00 | 155.00 |
| 5-Toots & Casper | 7.00 | 21.00 | 50.00 |
| 6-Terry & the Pirates; Caniff-a | 33.00 | 100.00 | 230.00 |
| 7-Pluto Saves the Ship (#1)(Disney) written by Carl Barks, Jack Hannah, & Nick George. (Barks' 1st comic book work) | 65.00 | 195.00 | 455.00 |
| 8-Bugs Bunny (#1)('42) | 59.00 | 175.00 | 410.00 |
| 9-Bringing Up Father | 10.00 | 30.00 | 70.00 |
| 10-Popeye (Thimble Theatre) | 34.00 | 100.00 | 230.00 |
| 11-Barney Google & Snuffy Smith | 14.00 | 42.00 | 100.00 |
| 12-Private Buck | 7.00 | 21.00 | 50.00 |
| 13-(nn)-1001 Hours Of Fun; puzzles & games; by A. W. Nugent. This book was bound as #13 with Large Feature Comics in publishers files | 7.00 | 21.00 | 50.00 |

*NOTE: The Black & White Feature Books are oversized 8½x11-3/8" comics with color covers and black and white interiors. The first nine issues all have rough, heavy stock covers and, except for #7, all have 76 pages, including covers. #7 and #10-on all have 52 pages. Beginning with #10 the covers are slick and thin and, because of their size, are difficult to handle without damaging. For this reason, they are seldom found in fine to mint condition. The paper stock, unlike Wow #1 and Capt. Marvel #1, is itself not unstable . . . just thin.*

**LARRY DOBY, BASEBALL HERO**
1950 (Cleveland Indians)
Fawcett Publications

| | Good | Fine | N-Mint |
|---|---|---|---|
| nn-Bill Ward-a; photo-c | 34.00 | 103.00 | 240.00 |

**LARRY HARMON'S LAUREL AND HARDY** (. . .Comics)
July-Aug, 1972 (Regular size)
National Periodical Publications

| | Good | Fine | N-Mint |
|---|---|---|---|
| 1 | .45 | 1.25 | 2.50 |

**LARS OF MARS**
No. 10, Apr-May, 1951 - No. 11, July-Aug, 1951 (Painted-c)
Ziff-Davis Publishing Co.

| | Good | Fine | N-Mint |
|---|---|---|---|
| 10-Origin; Anderson-a(3) in each | 32.00 | 95.00 | 225.00 |
| 11-Gene Colan-a | 27.00 | 81.00 | 190.00 |

**LARS OF MARS 3-D**
Apr, 1987 ($2.50)
Eclipse Comics

| | Good | Fine | N-Mint |
|---|---|---|---|
| 1-r-/Lars of Mars #10,11 in 3-D plus new story | .40 | 1.25 | 2.50 |
| 2-D limited edition (B&W, 100 copies) | .85 | 2.50 | 5.00 |

**LASER ERASER & PRESSBUTTON** (See Axel Pressbutton & Miracleman 9)
Nov, 1985 - No. 6, 1987 (6 issue series, color)
Eclipse Comics

| | Good | Fine | N-Mint |
|---|---|---|---|
| 1-6: 5,6-(95 cents) | | .40 | .80 |
| . . .In 3-D 1 (8/86, $2.50) | .40 | 1.25 | 2.50 |
| 2-D 1 (B&W, limited to 100 copies signed & numbered) | .40 | 1.25 | 2.50 |

**LASH LARUE WESTERN** (Movie star; king of the bullwhip)(See Six-Gun Heroes)
Sum, 1949 - No. 46, Jan, 1954 (36pgs., 1-7,9,13,16-on)
Fawcett Publications

| | Good | Fine | N-Mint |
|---|---|---|---|
| 1-Lash & his horse Black Diamond begin; photo front/back-c begin | 61.00 | 182.00 | 425.00 |
| 2(11/49) | 29.00 | 88.00 | 205.00 |
| 3-5 | 26.00 | 79.00 | 185.00 |
| 6,7,9: 6-Last photo back-c; intro. Frontier Phantom (Lash's twin brother) | 19.00 | 58.00 | 135.00 |
| 8,10 (52pgs.) | 20.00 | 60.00 | 140.00 |
| 11,12,14,15 (52pgs.) | 12.00 | 36.00 | 85.00 |

| | Good | Fine | N-Mint |
|---|---|---|---|
| 13,16-20 (36pgs.) | 11.50 | 34.00 | 80.00 |
| 21-30: 21-The Frontier Phantom app. | 10.00 | 30.00 | 70.00 |
| 31-45 | 8.50 | 25.50 | 60.00 |
| 46-Last Fawcett issue & photo-c | 9.30 | 28.00 | 65.00 |

**LASH LARUE WESTERN** (Continues from Fawcett series)
No. 47, Mar-Apr, 1954 - No. 84, June, 1961
Charlton Comics

| | | | |
|---|---|---|---|
| 47-Photo-c | 8.00 | 24.00 | 55.00 |
| 48 | 6.50 | 19.00 | 45.00 |
| 49-60 | 5.00 | 15.00 | 35.00 |
| 61-66,69,70: 52-r/#8; 53-r/#22 | 4.30 | 13.00 | 30.00 |
| 67,68-(68 pgs.). 68-Check-a | 4.50 | 14.00 | 32.00 |
| 71-83 | 2.85 | 8.50 | 20.00 |
| 84-Last issue | 3.70 | 11.00 | 26.00 |

**LASH LARUE WESTERN**
1990 ($3.50, 44 pgs.; 24 pgs. of color, 16 pgs. of B&W)
AC Comics

1-Photo covers; r/Lash #6; r/old movie posters .60 1.75 3.50

**LASSIE** (TV)(M-G-M's . . . No. 1-36)
June, 1950 - No. 70, July, 1969
Dell Publishing Co./Gold Key No. 59 (10/62) on

| | | | |
|---|---|---|---|
| 1 (52 pgs.)-Photo-c; inside lists One Shot #282 in error | 5.70 | 17.00 | 40.00 |
| 2-Painted-c begin | 3.00 | 9.00 | 21.00 |
| 3-10 | 2.30 | 7.00 | 16.00 |
| 11-19: 12-Rocky Langford (Lassie's master) marries Gerry Lawrence. 15-1st app. Timbu | 1.70 | 5.00 | 12.00 |
| 20-22-Matt Baker-a | 2.30 | 7.00 | 16.00 |
| 23-40: 33-Robinson-a. 39-1st app. Timmy as Lassie picks up her TV family | 1.15 | 3.50 | 8.00 |
| 41-70: 63-Last Timmy. 64-r-/#19. 65-Forest Ranger Corey Stuart begins, ends #69. 70-Forest Rangers Bob Ericson & Scott Turner app. (Lassie's new masters) | .85 | 2.50 | 5.00 |
| 11193(1978-Golden Press)-224 pgs.; $1.95; Baker-a(r), 92 pgs. | .55 | 1.65 | 4.00 |
| The Adventures of . . . (Red Heart Dog Food giveaway, 1949)-16 pgs, soft-c | 3.50 | 10.50 | 24.00 |
| Kite Fun Book('73)-(16 pgs.; 5x7") | 2.30 | 7.00 | 16.00 |

NOTE: *Photo c-57. (See March of Comics #210, 217, 230, 254, 266, 278, 296, 308, 324, 334, 346, 358, 370, 381, 394, 411, 432)*

**LAST AMERICAN, THE**
Dec, 1990 - No. 4, March, 1991 ($2.25, color, mini-series)
Epic Comics (Marvel)

1-4: Alan Grant scripts .40 1.15 2.30

**LAST DAYS OF THE JUSTICE SOCIETY SPECIAL**
1986 (One shot, 68 pgs.)
DC Comics

1 .50 1.50 3.00

**LAST GENERATION, THE**
1986 - No. 5, 1989 ($1.95, B&W, high quality paper)
Black Tie Studios

| | | | |
|---|---|---|---|
| 1 | .85 | 2.50 | 5.00 |
| 2 | .60 | 1.75 | 3.50 |
| 3-5 | .40 | 1.25 | 2.50 |
| Book 1 (1989, $6.95)-By Caliber Press | 1.15 | 3.50 | 7.00 |

**LAST HUNT, THE** (See 4-Color No. 678)

**LAST KISS**
1988 ($3.95, B&W, squarebound, 52 pgs.)
ACME Press (Eclipse)

1-One story adapts E.A. Poe's The Black Cat .70 2.00 4.00

**LAST OF THE COMANCHES** (See Wild Bill Hickok #28)
1953 (Movie)
Avon Periodicals

| | Good | Fine | N-Mint |
|---|---|---|---|
| nn-Kinstler-c/a, 21pgs.; Ravielli-a | 8.50 | 25.50 | 60.00 |

**LAST OF THE ERIES, THE** (See American Graphics)

**LAST OF THE FAST GUNS, THE** (See 4-Color No. 925)

**LAST OF THE MOHICANS** (See King Classics & White Rider and . . . )

**LAST OF THE VIKING HEROES, THE** (Also see Silver Star #1)
Mar, 1987 - Present ($1.50-$1.95, color)
Genesis West Comics

| | | | |
|---|---|---|---|
| 1-4: 4-Intro The Phantom Force | .40 | 1.25 | 2.50 |
| 5A-Kirby/Stevens-c | .50 | 1.50 | 3.00 |
| 5B,6 ($1.95) | .35 | 1.00 | 2.00 |
| 7-Art Adams-c | .50 | 1.50 | 3.00 |
| 8-Kirby back-c | .35 | 1.00 | 1.95 |
| Summer Special 1(1988)-Frazetta-c | .50 | 1.50 | 3.00 |
| Summer Special 2(1990, $2.50)-A TMNT app. | .40 | 1.25 | 2.50 |

NOTE: ***Art Adams** c-7. **Byrne** c-3. **Kirby** c-1p, 5p. **Perez** c-2i. **Stevens** c-5Ai.*

**LAST STARFIGHTER, THE**
Oct, 1984 - No. 3, Dec, 1984 (75 cents, movie adaptation)
Marvel Comics Group

1-3: R/Marvel Super Special; Guice-c .40 .80

**LAST TRAIN FROM GUN HILL** (See 4-Color No. 1012)

**LATEST ADVENTURES OF FOXY GRANDPA** (See Foxy Granpa)

**LATEST COMICS** (Super Duper No. 3?)
March, 1945 - No. 2
Spotlight Publ./Palace Promotions (Jubilee)

| | | | |
|---|---|---|---|
| 1-Super Duper | 6.00 | 18.00 | 42.00 |
| 2-Bee-29 (nd) | 4.30 | 13.00 | 30.00 |

**LAUGH**
June, 1987 - Present (.75-$1.00, color)
Archie Enterprises

V2#1-26: 5,19-X-Mas issues. 14-1st app. Hot Dog. 24-Re-intro Super Duck .50 1.00

**LAUGH COMICS** (Formerly Black Hood #1-19) (Laugh #226 on)
No. 20, Fall, 1946 - No. 400, 1987
Archie Publications (Close-Up)

| | | | |
|---|---|---|---|
| 20-Archie begins; Katy Keene & Taffy begin by Woggon; Suzie & Wilbur also begin | 41.00 | 122.00 | 285.00 |
| 21-25: 24-"Pipsy" by Kirby, 6 pgs. | 19.00 | 57.00 | 135.00 |
| 26-30 | 11.00 | 32.00 | 75.00 |
| 31-40 | 8.00 | 24.00 | 55.00 |
| 41-60: 41,54-Debbi by Woggon | 4.50 | 14.00 | 32.00 |
| 61-80: 67-Debbi by Woggon | 2.85 | 8.50 | 20.00 |
| 81-99 | 2.00 | 6.00 | 14.00 |
| 100 | 3.00 | 9.00 | 21.00 |
| 101-126: 125-Debbi app. | 1.35 | 4.00 | 9.00 |
| 127-144: Super-hero app. in all (see note) | 1.70 | 5.00 | 12.00 |
| 145-160: 157-Josie app. | .85 | 2.50 | 5.00 |
| 161-165,167-200 | .50 | 1.50 | 3.00 |
| 166-Beatles-c | 1.30 | 4.00 | 9.00 |
| 201-240 | .25 | .75 | 1.50 |
| 241-280 | | .40 | .80 |
| 281-400: 381-384-Katy Keene app.; by Woggon-381,382 | | .30 | .60 |

NOTE: *The Fly app. in 128, 129, 132, 134, 138, 139. Flygirl app. in 136, 137, 143. Flyman app. in 137. The Jaguar app. in 127, 130, 131, 133, 135, 140-142, 144. Josie app. in 145, 160, 164. Katy Keene app. in 20-125, 129, 130, 133. Many issues contain paper dolls.*

**LAUGH COMICS DIGEST** (. . . Magazine #23-89; Laugh Digest Magazine #90 on)
8/74; No. 2, 9/75; No. 3, 3/76 - Present (Digest-size)

*Lash LaRue Western #56, © CC*

*The Last Generation #1, © Black Tie Studios*

*Laugh Comics #20, © AP*

Law Against Crime #3, © Essenkay Publ.

Lawbreakers Suspense Stories #15, © CC

Leading Comics #4, © DC

Archie Publications (Close-Up No. 1, 3 on)

| | Good | Fine | N-Mint |
|---|---|---|---|
| 1-Neal Adams-a | .70 | 2.00 | 4.00 |
| 2,7,8,19-Neal Adams-a | .35 | 1.00 | 2.00 |
| 3-6,9-18,20-94: Later issues $1.35,$1.50-c | .25 | .75 | 1.50 |

NOTE: ***Katy Keene** in 23, 25, 27, 32-38, 40, 45-48, 50. **The Fly**-r in 19, 20. **The Jaguar**-r in 25, 27. **Mr. Justice**-r in 21. **The Web**-r in 23.*

**LAUGH COMIX** (Formerly Top Notch Laugh; Suzie No. 49 on)
No. 46, Summer, 1944 - No. 48, Winter, 1944-45
MLJ Magazines

| | Good | Fine | N-Mint |
|---|---|---|---|
| 46-Wilbur & Suzie in all | 10.00 | 30.00 | 70.00 |
| 47,48 | 7.00 | 21.00 | 50.00 |

**LAUGH-IN MAGAZINE** (TV)(Magazine)
Oct, 1968 - No. 12, Oct, 1969 (50 cents) (Satire)
Laufer Publ. Co.

| | Good | Fine | N-Mint |
|---|---|---|---|
| V1#1 | 1.30 | 4.00 | 9.00 |
| 2-12 | .70 | 2.00 | 5.00 |

**LAUREL & HARDY** (See Larry Harmon's . . . & March of Comics No. 302, 314)

**LAUREL AND HARDY** (. . .Comics)
3/49 - No. 3, 9/49; No. 26, 11/55 - No. 28, 3/56 (No #4-25)
St. John Publishing Co.

| | Good | Fine | N-Mint |
|---|---|---|---|
| 1 | 34.00 | 100.00 | 235.00 |
| 2 | 19.00 | 57.00 | 135.00 |
| 3 | 14.00 | 43.00 | 100.00 |
| 26-28 (Reprints) | 9.30 | 28.00 | 65.00 |

**LAUREL AND HARDY** (TV)
Oct, 1962 - No. 4, Sept-Nov, 1963
Dell Publishing Co.

| | Good | Fine | N-Mint |
|---|---|---|---|
| 12-423-210 (8-10/62) | 2.65 | 8.00 | 18.00 |
| 2-4 (Dell) | 2.30 | 7.00 | 16.00 |

**LAUREL AND HARDY** (Larry Harmon's)
Jan, 1967 - No. 2, Oct, 1967
Gold Key

| | Good | Fine | N-Mint |
|---|---|---|---|
| 1,2: 1-Photo back-c | 2.00 | 6.00 | 14.00 |

**LAUREL AND HARDY IN 3-D** (See Blackthorne 3-D Series #23 & 34)

**LAW AGAINST CRIME** (Law-Crime on cover)
April, 1948 - No. 3, Aug, 1948
Essenkay Publishing Co.

| | Good | Fine | N-Mint |
|---|---|---|---|
| 1-(#1-3: ½ funny animal, ½ crime)-L. B. Cole electrocution-c/a | 29.00 | 86.00 | 200.00 |
| 2-L. B. Cole-c/a | 20.00 | 60.00 | 140.00 |
| 3-L. B. Cole-c/a; used in **SOTI**, pg. 180,181 & illo-"The wish to hurt or kill couples in lovers' lanes;" reprinted in All-Famous Crime #9 | 27.00 | 81.00 | 190.00 |

**LAWBREAKERS** (. . .Suspense Stories No. 10 on)
Mar, 1951 - No. 9, Oct-Nov, 1952
Law and Order Magazines (Charlton Comics)

| | Good | Fine | N-Mint |
|---|---|---|---|
| 1 | 10.00 | 30.00 | 70.00 |
| 2 | 5.00 | 15.00 | 35.00 |
| 3,5,6,8,9 | 3.50 | 10.50 | 24.00 |
| 4-"White Death" junkie story | 5.00 | 15.00 | 35.00 |
| 7-"The Deadly Dopesters" drug story | 4.50 | 14.00 | 32.00 |

**LAWBREAKERS ALWAYS LOSE!**
Spring, 1948 - No. 10, Oct, 1949
Marvel Comics (CBS)

| | Good | Fine | N-Mint |
|---|---|---|---|
| 1-2pg. Kurtzman-a, 'Giggles 'n Grins' | 11.00 | 32.00 | 75.00 |
| 2 | 5.70 | 17.00 | 42.00 |
| 3-5: 4-Vampire story | 4.30 | 13.00 | 30.00 |
| 6(2/49)-Has editorial defense against charges of Dr. Wertham | 5.00 | 15.00 | 35.00 |
| 7-Used in **SOTI**, illo-"Comic-book philosophy" | 11.50 | 34.00 | 80.00 |

| | Good | Fine | N-Mint |
|---|---|---|---|
| 8-10: 9,10-Photo-c | 3.00 | 9.00 | 21.00 |

**LAWBREAKERS SUSPENSE STORIES** (Formerly Lawbreakers; Strange Suspense Stories No. 16 on)
No. 10, Jan, 1953 - No. 15, Nov, 1953
Capitol Stories/Charlton Comics

| | Good | Fine | N-Mint |
|---|---|---|---|
| 10 | 7.00 | 21.00 | 50.00 |
| 11 (3/53)-Severed tongues-c/story & woman negligee scene | 24.00 | 73.00 | 170.00 |
| 12-14 | 4.00 | 12.00 | 28.00 |
| 15-Acid-in-face-c/story; hands dissolved in acid story | 11.50 | 34.00 | 80.00 |

**LAW-CRIME** (See Law Against Crime)

**LAWMAN** (TV)
No. 970, Feb, 1959 - No. 11, Apr-June, 1962 (All photo-c)
Dell Publishing Co.

| | Good | Fine | N-Mint |
|---|---|---|---|
| 4-Color 970(#1) | 7.00 | 21.00 | 50.00 |
| 4-Color 1035('60) | 4.30 | 13.00 | 30.00 |
| 3(2-4/60)-Toth-a | 5.00 | 15.00 | 35.00 |
| 4-11 | 3.50 | 10.50 | 24.00 |

**LAW OF DREDD, THE** (Also see Judge Dredd)
1989 - Present ($1.50-$1.75, color)
Quality Comics/Fleetway #8 on

| | Good | Fine | N-Mint |
|---|---|---|---|
| 1-8: ($1.50)-Bolland-a in 1-6,8,10-12,14(2pg.),15 | .25 | .75 | 1.50 |
| 9-12: 9-Begin $1.75-c | .30 | .90 | 1.80 |

**LAWRENCE** (See Movie Classics)

**LEADING COMICS** (. . .Screen Comics No. 42 on)
Winter, 1941-42 - No. 41, Feb-Mar, 1950
National Periodical Publications

| | Good | Fine | N-Mint |
|---|---|---|---|
| 1-Origin The Seven Soldiers of Victory; Crimson Avenger, Green Arrow & Speedy, Shining Knight, The Vigilante, Star Spangled Kid & Stripesy begin. The Dummy (Vigilante villain) app. | 192.00 | 480.00 | 1150.00 |
| 2-Meskin-a | 68.00 | 205.00 | 475.00 |
| 3 | 54.00 | 160.00 | 375.00 |
| 4,5 | 46.00 | 140.00 | 325.00 |
| 6-10 | 39.00 | 118.00 | 275.00 |
| 11-14(Spring, 1945) | 29.00 | 86.00 | 200.00 |
| 15-(Sum,'45)-Content change to funny animal | 12.00 | 36.00 | 85.00 |
| 16-22,24-30 | 5.30 | 16.00 | 38.00 |
| 23-1st app. Peter Porkchops by Otto Feur | 12.00 | 36.00 | 85.00 |
| 31,32,34-41 | 4.00 | 12.00 | 28.00 |
| 33-(Scarce) | 6.00 | 18.00 | 42.00 |

NOTE: ***Rube Grossman**-a(Peter Porkchops)-most #15-on; c-15-41. **Post** a-23-37, 39, 41.*

**LEADING SCREEN COMICS** (Formerly Leading Comics)
No. 42, Apr-May, 1950 - No. 77, Aug-Sept, 1955
National Periodical Publications

| | Good | Fine | N-Mint |
|---|---|---|---|
| 42 | 5.00 | 15.00 | 35.00 |
| 43-77 | 3.15 | 9.50 | 22.00 |

NOTE: ***Grossman** a-most. **Mayer** a-45-48, 50, 54-57, 60, 62-74, 75(3), 76, 77.*

**LEAGUE OF CHAMPIONS, THE** (Also see The Champions)
Dec, 1990 - Present ($2.95, color, 52 pgs.)
Hero Graphics

| | Good | Fine | N-Mint |
|---|---|---|---|
| 1,2: 1-Flare app. 2-Origin Malice | .50 | 1.50 | 3.00 |

**LEATHERNECK THE MARINE** (See Mighty Midget Comics)

**LEAVE IT TO BEAVER** (TV)
No. 912, June, 1958 - May-July, 1962 (All photo-c)
Dell Publishing Co.

| | Good | Fine | N-Mint |
|---|---|---|---|
| 4-Color 912 | 14.00 | 43.00 | 100.00 |
| 4-Color 999,1103,1191,1285, 01-428-207 | 13.00 | 40.00 | 90.00 |

**LEAVE IT TO BINKY** (Binky No. 72 on) (See Showcase and Super DC Giant) (No. 1-22: 52 pgs.)
2-3/48 - #60, 10/58; #61, 6-7/68 - #71, 2-3/70 (Teen-age humor)
National Periodical Publications

| | Good | Fine | N-Mint |
|---|---|---|---|
| 1-Lucy wears Superman costume | 17.00 | 51.00 | 120.00 |
| 2 | 8.00 | 24.00 | 55.00 |
| 3-5: 5-Superman cameo | 5.70 | 17.00 | 40.00 |
| 6-10 | 4.50 | 14.00 | 32.00 |
| 11-14,16-20 | 3.60 | 11.00 | 25.00 |
| 15-Scribbly story by Mayer | 4.30 | 13.00 | 30.00 |
| 21-28,30-45: 45-Last pre-code (2/55) | 2.30 | 7.00 | 16.00 |
| 29-Used in **POP**, pg. 78 | 2.30 | 7.00 | 16.00 |
| 46-60 | 1.30 | 4.00 | 9.00 |
| 61-71 | .85 | 2.60 | 6.00 |

NOTE: ***Drucker** a-28. **Mayer** a-1, 2, 15.*

**LEE HUNTER, INDIAN FIGHTER** (See 4-Color No. 779, 904)

**LEFT-HANDED GUN, THE** (See 4-Color No. 913)

**LEGEND OF CUSTER, THE** (TV)
January, 1968
Dell Publishing Co.

| | Good | Fine | N-Mint |
|---|---|---|---|
| 1-Wayne Maunder photo-c | 1.15 | 3.50 | 8.00 |

**LEGEND OF JESSE JAMES, THE** (TV)
February, 1966
Gold Key

| | Good | Fine | N-Mint |
|---|---|---|---|
| 10172-602-Photo-c | 1.70 | 5.00 | 12.00 |

**LEGEND OF KAMUI, THE** (See Kamui)

**LEGEND OF LOBO, THE** (See Movie Comics)

**LEGEND OF WONDER WOMAN, THE**
May, 1986 - No. 4, Aug, 1986 (Mini-series)
DC Comics

| | Good | Fine | N-Mint |
|---|---|---|---|
| 1-4 | | .60 | 1.20 |

**LEGEND OF YOUNG DICK TURPIN, THE** (TV)
May, 1966 (Disney TV episode)
Gold Key

| | Good | Fine | N-Mint |
|---|---|---|---|
| 1 (10176-605)-Photo/painted-c | 1.15 | 3.50 | 8.00 |

**LEGEND OF ZELDA, THE** (Link: The Legend . . . in indicia)
1990 - Present ($1.95, color, coated-c
Valiant Comics

| | Good | Fine | N-Mint |
|---|---|---|---|
| 1-7: 4-Layton-c(i). 5,7-Layton-c | .35 | 1.00 | 2.00 |

**LEGENDS**
Nov, 1986 - No. 6, Apr, 1987 (Mini-series)
DC Comics

| | Good | Fine | N-Mint |
|---|---|---|---|
| 1-Byrne c/a(p) begins. 1st new Capt. Marvel | .35 | 1.10 | 2.20 |
| 2-5: 3-Intro new Suicide Squad; death of Blockbuster | .25 | .70 | 1.40 |
| 6-Intro/1st app. New Justice League | 1.00 | 3.00 | 6.00 |

**LEGENDS OF DANIEL BOONE, THE**
Oct-Nov, 1955 - No. 8, Dec-Jan, 1956-57
National Periodical Publications

| | Good | Fine | N-Mint |
|---|---|---|---|
| 1 (Scarce) | 27.00 | 80.00 | 185.00 |
| 2 (Scarce) | 20.00 | 60.00 | 140.00 |
| 3-8 (Scarce) | 17.00 | 51.00 | 120.00 |

**LEGENDS OF THE DARK KNIGHT** (Batman)
Nov, 1989 - Present ($1.50, color)
DC Comics

| | Good | Fine | N-Mint |
|---|---|---|---|
| 1-"The Shaman of Gotham" begins, ends #5; outer cover has four different color variations, all worth same | .85 | 2.50 | 5.00 |
| 2 | .50 | 1.50 | 3.00 |
| 3-5 | .35 | 1.00 | 2.00 |
| 6-10-"Gothic" by Grant Morrison (scripts) | .50 | 1.50 | 3.00 |
| 11-18: 11,12-Gulacy/Austin-a. 14-Catwoman app. | .25 | .75 | 1.50 |

**LEGENDS OF THE STARGRAZERS** (See Vanguard Illustrated #2)
Aug, 1989 - No. 6, 1990 ($1.95, color, mini-series, mature readers)
Innovation Publishing

| | Good | Fine | N-Mint |
|---|---|---|---|
| 1-6: 1-N. Redondo part inks | .35 | 1.00 | 2.00 |

**L.E.G.I.O.N. '89** (Becomes L.E.G.I.O.N. '90 #11-22; becomes L.E.G.I.O.N. '91 #23 on; also see Lobo)
Feb, 1989 - Present ($1.50, color)
DC Comics

| | Good | Fine | N-Mint |
|---|---|---|---|
| 1-Giffen plots/breakdowns in #1-12 | .35 | 1.00 | 2.00 |
| 2-26: 5-Lobo joins? | .25 | .75 | 1.50 |
| Annual 1 (1990, $2.95, 68 pgs.)-Superman app. | .50 | 1.50 | 3.00 |

**LEGIONNAIRES THREE**
Jan, 1986 - No. 4, May, 1986 (75 cents, mini-series)
DC comics

| | Good | Fine | N-Mint |
|---|---|---|---|
| 1-4 | | .40 | .80 |

**LEGION OF MONSTERS** (Magazine)(Also see Marvel Premiere #28 & Marvel Preview #8)
September, 1975 ($1.00, B&W, 76 pgs.)
Marvel Comics Group

| | Good | Fine | N-Mint |
|---|---|---|---|
| 1-Origin & 1st app. Legion of Monsters; Neal Adams-c; Morrow-a; origin & only app. The Manphibian | .35 | 1.00 | 2.00 |

**LEGION OF SUBSTITUTE HEROES SPECIAL**
July, 1985 (One Shot)($1.25, 52 pgs.)
DC Comics

| | Good | Fine | N-Mint |
|---|---|---|---|
| 1-Giffen-c/a(p) | | .60 | 1.25 |

**LEGION OF SUPER-HEROES** (See Action, Adventure, All New Collectors Ed., Limited Collectors Ed., Secrets of the . . ., Superboy, & Superman)
Feb, 1973 - No. 4, July-Aug, 1973
National Periodical Publications

| | Good | Fine | N-Mint |
|---|---|---|---|
| 1-Legion & Tommy Tomorrow reprints begin | 1.00 | 3.00 | 6.00 |
| 2-4: 2-Forte-r. 3-r/Adv. #340. Action #240. 4-r/Adv. #341, Action #233; Mooney-r | .70 | 2.00 | 4.00 |

**LEGION OF SUPER-HEROES, THE** (Formerly Superboy and . . .; Tales of The Legion No. 314 on)
No. 259, Jan, 1980 - No. 313, July, 1984
DC Comics

| | Good | Fine | N-Mint |
|---|---|---|---|
| 259(#1)-Superboy leaves Legion | .45 | 1.40 | 2.80 |
| 260-270: 265-Contains 28pg. insert 'Superman & the TR5-80 Computer;' Origin Tyroc; Tyroc leaves Legion | .25 | .80 | 1.60 |
| 271-284: 272-Blok joins; origin; 20pg. insert-Dial 'H' For Hero. 277-Intro Reflecto. 280-Superboy re-joins legion. 282-Origin Reflecto. 283-Origin Wildfire | | .60 | 1.20 |
| 285,286-Giffen back up story | .35 | 1.00 | 2.00 |
| 287-Giffen-a on Legion begins | .45 | 1.40 | 2.80 |
| 288-290: 290-294-Great Darkness saga | .35 | 1.00 | 2.00 |
| 291-293 | | .60 | 1.20 |
| 294-Double size (52 pgs.); Giffen-a(p) | .25 | .70 | 1.40 |
| 295-299,301-305: 297-Origin retold. 298-Free 16pg. Amethyst preview. | | .50 | 1.00 |
| 300-Double size, 64 pgs., Mando paper; c/a by almost everyone at DC | .35 | 1.00 | 2.00 |
| 306-313 (75 cent-c): 306-Brief origin Star Boy | | .35 | .70 |
| Annual 1(1982, 52 pgs.)-Giffen-c/a; 1st app./origin new Invisible Kid who joins Legion | .25 | .80 | 1.60 |
| Annual 2,3: 2(1983, 52 pgs.)-Giffen-c; Karate Kid & Princess Projectra wed & resign. 3(1984, 52 pgs.) | | .60 | 1.20 |
| . . .The Great Darkness Saga (1989, $17.95, 196 pgs.)-r/LSH #287, 290-294 & Annual #3; Giffen-c/a | 3.00 | 9.00 | 18.00 |

NOTE: ***Aparo** c-282, 283. **Austin** c-268i. **Buckler** c-273p, 274p, 276p. **Colan** a-311p.*

*Legends of the Dark Knight #6, © DC*

*L.E.G.I.O.N. '89 #5 (Lobo joins?), © DC*

*Legion of Monsters #1, © MEG*

LEGION OF SUPER-HEROES
THE GREATEST HERO OF THEM ALL


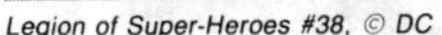

Legion of Super-Heroes #38, © DC

Liberty Comics #11, © Green Publ.

Licence To Kill nn, © Eclipse

**Ditko** a(p)-267, 268, 272, 274, 276, 281. **Giffen** a-285-313p, Annual 1p; c-287p, 288p, 289, 290p, 291p, 292, 293, 294-299p, 300, 301-313p, Annual 1p, 2p. **Perez** c-268p, 277-280, 281p. **Starlin** a-265. **Staton** a-259p, 260p, 280. **Tuska** a-308p.

**LEGION OF SUPER-HEROES**
Aug, 1984 - No. 63, Aug, 1989 ($1.25-$1.75, deluxe format)
DC Comics

| | Good | Fine | N-Mint |
|---|---|---|---|
| 1 | .35 | 1.00 | 2.00 |
| 2-10: 4-Death of Karate Kid. 5-Death of Nemesis Kid | .25 | .80 | 1.60 |
| 11-14: 12-Cosmic Boy, Lightning Lad, & Saturn Girl resign. 14-Intro new members: Tellus, Sensor Girl, Quislet | | .60 | 1.20 |
| 15-18: 15-17-Crisis tie-ins. 18-Crisis x-over | .25 | .80 | 1.60 |
| 19-25: 25-Sensor Girl i.d. revealed as Princess Projectra | | .60 | 1.20 |
| 26-36,39-44: 35-Saturn Girl rejoins. 40-$1.75 cover price begins. 42, 43-Millennium tie-ins. 44-Origin Quislet | | .55 | 1.10 |
| 37,38-Death of Superboy | 1.70 | 5.00 | 10.00 |
| 45 ($2.95, 68 pgs.) | .40 | 1.20 | 2.40 |
| 46-49,51-62 | | .55 | 1.10 |
| 50-Double size, $2.50 | .35 | 1.00 | 2.00 |
| 63-Final issue | .25 | .70 | 1.40 |
| Annual 1 (10/85, 52 pgs.)-Crisis tie-in | .30 | .90 | 1.80 |
| Annual 2 (10/86, 52 pgs.). 3 (10/87, 52 pgs.) | .25 | .80 | 1.60 |
| Annual 4(11/88, $2.50, 52 pgs.) | .35 | 1.00 | 2.00 |

NOTE: **Byrne** c-36p. **Giffen** a(p)-1, 2, 50-55, 57-63, Annual 1p, 2; c-1-5p, 54p, Annual 1. **Orlando** a-6p. **Steacy** c-45-50, Annual 3.

**LEGION OF SUPER-HEROES**
Nov, 1989 - Present ($1.75, color)
DC Comics

| | Good | Fine | N-Mint |
|---|---|---|---|
| 1-Giffen-c/a(p) & scripts in 1-14 | .40 | 1.25 | 2.50 |
| 2-16: 8-Origin. 13-Free poster by Giffen showing new costumes | .30 | .90 | 1.80 |
| Annual 1 (1990, $3.50, 68 pgs.) | .60 | 1.75 | 3.50 |

**LEMONADE KID, THE** (See Bobby Benson's B-Bar-B Riders)
1990 ($2.50, color, 28 pgs.)
AC Comics

| | Good | Fine | N-Mint |
|---|---|---|---|
| 1-Powell-c(r); Red Hawk-r by Powell; Lemonade Kid-r/Bobby Benson by Powell (2 stories) | .40 | 1.25 | 2.50 |

**LENNON SISTERS LIFE STORY, THE** (See 4-Color No. 951, 1014)

**LEONARDO** (Also see Teenage Mutant Ninja Turtles)
Dec, 1986 ($1.50, B&W, One shot)
Mirage Studios

| | Good | Fine | N-Mint |
|---|---|---|---|
| 1 | 1.35 | 4.00 | 8.00 |

**LEO THE LION**
No date (10 cents)
I. W. Enterprises

| | Good | Fine | N-Mint |
|---|---|---|---|
| 1-Reprint | .50 | 1.50 | 3.00 |

**LEROY** (Teen-age)
Nov, 1949 - No. 6, Nov, 1950
Standard Comics

| | Good | Fine | N-Mint |
|---|---|---|---|
| 1 | 3.00 | 9.00 | 21.00 |
| 2-Frazetta text illo. | 2.85 | 8.50 | 20.00 |
| 3-6: 3-Lubbers-a | 1.70 | 5.00 | 12.00 |

**LET'S PRETEND** (CBS radio)
May-June, 1950 - No. 3, Sept-Oct, 1950
D. S. Publishing Co.

| | Good | Fine | N-Mint |
|---|---|---|---|
| 1 | 7.00 | 21.00 | 50.00 |
| 2,3 | 5.00 | 15.00 | 35.00 |

**LET'S READ THE NEWSPAPER**
1974
Charlton Press

| | Good | Fine | N-Mint |
|---|---|---|---|
| nn-Features Quincy by Ted Sheares | | .30 | .60 |

**LET'S TAKE A TRIP** (TV) (CBS TV Presents)
Spring, 1958
Pines Comics

| | Good | Fine | N-Mint |
|---|---|---|---|
| 1-Marv Levy-c/a | 1.50 | 4.50 | 10.00 |

**LETTERS TO SANTA** (See March of Comics No. 228)

**LEX LUTHOR: THE UNAUTHORIZED BIOGRAPHY**
1989 ($3.95, one-shot, squarebound, 52 pgs.)
DC Comics

| | Good | Fine | N-Mint |
|---|---|---|---|
| 1-Painted-c; Clark Kent app. | .70 | 2.00 | 4.00 |

**LIBERTY COMICS** (Miss Liberty No. 1)
No. 4, 1945 - No. 15, 1946 (MLJ & other reprints)
Green Publishing Co.

| | Good | Fine | N-Mint |
|---|---|---|---|
| 4 | 9.30 | 28.00 | 65.00 |
| 5 (5/46)-The Prankster app; Starr-a | 6.50 | 19.00 | 45.00 |
| 10-Hangman & Boy Buddies app.; Suzie & Wilbur begin; reprint of Hangman #8 | 8.50 | 25.50 | 60.00 |
| 11(V2#2, 1/46)-Wilbur in women's clothes | 8.50 | 25.50 | 60.00 |
| 12-Black Hood & Suzie app. | 7.00 | 21.00 | 50.00 |
| 14,15-Patty of Airliner; Starr-a in both | 4.30 | 13.00 | 30.00 |

**LIBERTY GUARDS**
No date (1946?)
Chicago Mail Order

| | Good | Fine | N-Mint |
|---|---|---|---|
| nn-Reprints Man of War #1 with cover of Liberty Scouts #1; Gustavson-c | 18.00 | 54.00 | 125.00 |

**LIBERTY PROJECT, THE**
June, 1987 - No. 8, May, 1988 ($1.75, color, Baxter paper)
Eclipse Comics

| | Good | Fine | N-Mint |
|---|---|---|---|
| 1-8: 6-Valkyrie app. | .30 | .90 | 1.80 |

**LIBERTY SCOUTS** (See Liberty Guards & Man of War)
No. 2, June, 1941 - No. 3, Aug, 1941
Centaur Publications

| | Good | Fine | N-Mint |
|---|---|---|---|
| 2(#1)-Origin The Fire-Man, Man of War; Vapo-Man & Liberty Scouts begin; Gustavson-c/a | 82.00 | 245.00 | 575.00 |
| 3(#2)-Origin & 1st app. The Sentinel; Gustavson-c/a | 61.00 | 182.00 | 425.00 |

**LICENCE TO KILL** (James Bond 007. . .)
1989 ($7.95, color, slick paper, 52 pgs.)
Eclipse Comics

| | Good | Fine | N-Mint |
|---|---|---|---|
| nn-Movie adaptation; Timothy Dalton photo-c | 1.35 | 4.00 | 8.00 |
| Limited Hardcover ($24.95) | 4.15 | 12.50 | 25.00 |

**LIDSVILLE** (TV)
Oct, 1972 - No. 5, Oct, 1973
Gold Key

| | Good | Fine | N-Mint |
|---|---|---|---|
| 1 | 1.15 | 3.50 | 7.00 |
| 2-5 | .70 | 2.00 | 4.00 |

**LIEUTENANT, THE** (TV)
April-June, 1964
Dell Publishing Co.

| | Good | Fine | N-Mint |
|---|---|---|---|
| 1-Photo-c | 1.15 | 3.50 | 8.00 |

**LT. ROBIN CRUSOE, U.S.N.** (See Movie Comics & Walt Disney Showcase #26)

**LIFE OF CAPTAIN MARVEL, THE**
Aug, 1985 - No. 5, Dec, 1985 ($2.00 cover; Baxter paper)
Marvel Comics Group

| | Good | Fine | N-Mint |
|---|---|---|---|
| 1-5: r-/Starlin issues of Capt. Marvel | .35 | 1.00 | 2.00 |

**LIFE OF CHRIST, THE**
No. 301, 1949 (100 pages) (35 cents)
Catechetical Guild Educational Society

| | Good | Fine | N-Mint |
|---|---|---|---|
| 301-Reprints from Topix(1949)-V5#11,12 | 2.30 | 7.00 | 16.00 |

**LIFE OF CHRIST VISUALIZED**
1942 - No. 3, 1943
Standard Publishers

| | Good | Fine | N-Mint |
|---|---|---|---|
| 1-3: All came in cardboard case | 2.30 | 7.00 | 16.00 |
| With case. . . . . | 5.00 | 15.00 | 35.00 |

**LIFE OF CHRIST VISUALIZED**
1946? (48 pgs. in color)
The Standard Publ. Co.

| | | | |
|---|---|---|---|
| nn | 1.00 | 3.00 | 6.00 |

**LIFE OF ESTHER VISUALIZED**
No. 2062, 1947 (48 pgs. in color)
The Standard Publ. Co.

| | | | |
|---|---|---|---|
| 2062 | 1.00 | 3.00 | 6.00 |

**LIFE OF JOSEPH VISUALIZED**
No. 1054, 1946 (48 pgs. in color)
The Standard Publ. Co.

| | | | |
|---|---|---|---|
| 1054 | 1.00 | 3.00 | 6.00 |

**LIFE OF PAUL** (See The Living Bible)

**LIFE OF POPE JOHN PAUL II, THE**
Jan, 1983
Marvel Comics Group

| | | | |
|---|---|---|---|
| 1 | .25 | .75 | 1.50 |

**LIFE OF RILEY, THE** (See 4-Color No. 917)

**LIFE OF THE BLESSED VIRGIN**
1950 (68 pages) (square binding)
Catechetical Guild (Giveaway)

| | | | |
|---|---|---|---|
| nn-Contains "The Woman of the Promise" & "Mother of Us All" rebound | 2.30 | 7.00 | 16.00 |

**LIFE'S LIKE THAT**
1945 (68 pgs.; B&W; 25 cents)
Croyden Publ. Co.

| | | | |
|---|---|---|---|
| nn-Newspaper Sunday strip-r by Neher | 3.00 | 9.00 | 21.00 |

**LIFE'S LITTLE JOKES**
No date (1924) (52 pgs.; B&W)
M.S. Publ. Co.

| | | | |
|---|---|---|---|
| nn-By Rube Goldberg | 17.00 | 51.00 | 120.00 |

**LIFE STORIES OF AMERICAN PRESIDENTS** (See Dell Giants)

**LIFE STORY**
Apr, 1949 - V8#46, Jan, 1953; V8#47, Apr, 1953 (All have photo-c?)
Fawcett Publications

| | | | |
|---|---|---|---|
| V1#1 | 5.00 | 15.00 | 35.00 |
| 2 | 2.30 | 7.00 | 16.00 |
| 3-6 | 2.00 | 6.00 | 14.00 |
| V2#7-12 | 1.70 | 5.00 | 12.00 |
| V3#13-Wood-a | 7.00 | 21.00 | 50.00 |
| V3#14-18, V4#19-21,23,24 | 1.70 | 5.00 | 12.00 |
| V4#22-Drug use story | 2.00 | 6.00 | 14.00 |
| V5#25-30, V6#31-35 | 1.70 | 5.00 | 12.00 |
| V6#36-"I sold drugs" on-c | 2.00 | 6.00 | 14.00 |
| V7#37,40-42, V8#44,45 | 1.15 | 3.50 | 8.00 |
| V7#38, V8#43-Evans-a | 2.30 | 7.00 | 16.00 |
| V7#39-Drug Smuggling & Junkie story | 1.70 | 5.00 | 12.00 |
| V8#46,47 (Scarce) | 1.50 | 4.50 | 10.00 |

NOTE: ***Powell** a-13, 23, 24, 26, 28, 30, 32, 39.*

**LIFE WITH ARCHIE**
Sept, 1958 - Present
Archie Publications

| | Good | Fine | N-Mint |
|---|---|---|---|
| 1 | 23.00 | 70.00 | 160.00 |
| 2 | 11.50 | 34.00 | 80.00 |
| 3-5 | 8.50 | 25.50 | 60.00 |
| 6-10 | 4.00 | 12.00 | 28.00 |
| 11-20 | 2.30 | 7.00 | 16.00 |
| 21-30 | 1.70 | 5.00 | 12.00 |
| 31-41 | 1.00 | 3.00 | 7.00 |
| 42-45: 42-Pureheart begins, ends #59 | .85 | 2.60 | 6.00 |
| 46-Origin Pureheart | 1.00 | 3.00 | 7.00 |
| 47-59: 50-United Three begin: Pureheart (Archie), Superteen (Betty), Capt. Hero (Jughead). 59-Pureheart ends | .70 | 2.00 | 4.00 |
| 60-100: 60-Archie band begins | .35 | 1.00 | 2.00 |
| 101-284: 279-Intro Mustang Sally ($1.00) | | .50 | 1.00 |

**LIFE WITH MILLIE** (Formerly A Date With Millie) (Modeling With Millie No. 21 on)
No. 8, Dec, 1960 - No. 20, Dec, 1962
Atlas/Marvel Comics Group

| | | | |
|---|---|---|---|
| 8 | 3.00 | 9.00 | 21.00 |
| 9-11 | 2.15 | 6.50 | 15.00 |
| 12-20 | 1.50 | 4.50 | 10.00 |

**LIFE WITH SNARKY PARKER** (TV)
August, 1950
Fox Feature Syndicate

| | | | |
|---|---|---|---|
| 1 | 11.50 | 34.00 | 80.00 |

**LIGHT AND DARKNESS WAR, THE**
Oct, 1988 - No. 6, Dec, 1989 ($1.95, color, limited series)
Epic Comics (Marvel)

| | | | |
|---|---|---|---|
| 1-6 | .35 | 1.00 | 2.00 |

**LIGHT IN THE FOREST** (See 4-Color No. 891)

**LIGHTNING COMICS** (Formerly Sure-Fire No. 1-3)
No. 4, Dec, 1940 - No. 13(V3#1), June, 1942
Ace Magazines

| | | | |
|---|---|---|---|
| 4-Characters continue from Sure-Fire | 39.00 | 118.00 | 275.00 |
| 5,6: 6-Dr. Nemesis begins | 27.00 | 81.00 | 190.00 |
| V2#1-6: 2-"Flash Lightning" becomes "Lash. . ." | 24.00 | 72.00 | 165.00 |
| V3#1-Intro. Lightning Girl & The Sword | 24.00 | 72.00 | 165.00 |

NOTE: ***Anderson** a-V2#6. **Mooney** c-V1#6, V2#2. Bondage c-V2#6.*

**LI'L** (See Little)

**LILY OF THE ALLEY IN THE FUNNIES**
No date (1920's?) (10¼x15½"; 28 pgs. in color)
Whitman Publishers

| | | | |
|---|---|---|---|
| W936 - by T. Burke | 9.30 | 28.00 | 65.00 |

**LIMITED COLLECTORS' EDITION** (See Famous First Edition & Rudolph the Red Nosed Reindeer; becomes All-New Collectors' Edition) (#21-34,51-59: 84 pgs.; #35-41: 68 pgs.; #42-50: 60 pgs.)
C-21, Summer, 1973 - No. C-59, 1978 ($1.00) (10x13½")
National Periodical Publications/DC Comics

| | | | |
|---|---|---|---|
| nn(C-20)-Rudolph | .70 | 2.00 | 4.00 |
| C-21: Shazam (TV); Captain Marvel Jr. reprint by Raboy | .50 | 1.50 | 3.00 |
| C-22: Tarzan; complete origin reprinted from #207-210; all Kubert | .50 | 1.50 | 3.00 |
| C-23: House of Mystery; Wrightson, N. Adams, Wood, Toth, Orlando-a | .35 | 1.00 | 2.00 |
| C-24: Rudolph The Red-nosed Reindeer | .35 | 1.00 | 2.00 |
| C-25: Batman; Neal Adams-c/a | 1.00 | 3.00 | 6.00 |
| C-27: Shazam (TV) | .35 | 1.00 | 2.00 |
| C-29: Tarzan; reprints "Return of Tarzan" from #219-223 by Kubert | .50 | 1.50 | 3.00 |
| C-31: Superman; origin-r; N. Adams-a | .50 | 1.50 | 3.00 |
| C-32: Ghosts (new-a) | .35 | 1.00 | 2.00 |
| C-33: Rudolph The Red-nosed Reindeer(new-a) | .35 | 1.00 | 2.00 |

*Life Story #17, © FAW*

*Life With Archie #47, © AP*

*Lightning Comics V3#1, © ACE*

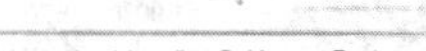
Lippy the Lion #1, © Hanna-Barbera

*Li'l Abner #89, © UFS*

*Little Al of the Secret Service #10, © Z-D*

| | Good | Fine | N-Mint |
|---|---|---|---|
| C-34: Xmas with the Super-Heroes; unpublished Angel & Ape story by Oksner & Wood | .50 | 1.50 | 3.00 |
| C-35: Shazam; cover features TV's Captain Marvel, Jackson Bostwick (TV) | .35 | 1.00 | 2.00 |
| C-36: The Bible; all new adaptation beginning with Genesis by Kubert, Redondo & Mayer | .50 | 1.50 | 3.00 |
| C-37: Batman; r-1946 Sundays | 1.00 | 3.00 | 6.00 |
| C-38: Superman; 1 pg. N. Adams; part photo-c | .35 | 1.00 | 2.00 |
| C-39: Secret Origins/Super Villains; N. Adams-a(r) | .35 | 1.00 | 2.00 |
| C-40: Dick Tracy by Gould featuring Flattop; newspaper-r from 12/21/43 - 5/17/44 | .70 | 2.00 | 4.00 |
| C-41: Super Friends; Toth-c/a | .35 | 1.00 | 2.00 |
| C-42: Rudolph | .35 | 1.00 | 2.00 |
| C-43: Christmas with the Super-Heroes; Wrightson, S&K, Neal Adams-a | .50 | 1.50 | 3.00 |
| C-44: Batman; N. Adams-r; painted-c | 1.00 | 3.00 | 6.00 |
| C-45: Secret Origins/Super Villains; Flash-r/105 | .35 | 1.00 | 2.00 |
| C-46: Justice League of America; 3 pg. Toth-a | .50 | 1.50 | 3.00 |
| C-47: Superman Salutes the Bicentennial (Tomahawk interior); 2 pgs. new-a | .25 | .75 | 1.50 |
| C-48: The Superman-Flash Race; 6 pgs. Neal Adams-a | .35 | 1.00 | 2.00 |
| C-49: Superboy & the Legion of Super-Heroes | .35 | 1.00 | 2.00 |
| C-50: Rudolph The Red-nosed Reindeer | .25 | .75 | 1.50 |
| C-51: Batman; Neal Adams-c/a | 1.00 | 3.00 | 6.00 |
| C-52: The Best of DC; Neal Adams-c/a; Toth, Kubert-a | .50 | 1.50 | 3.00 |
| C-57: Welcome Back, Kotter-r(TV)(5/78) | .25 | .75 | 1.50 |
| C-59: Batman's Strangest Cases; N. Adams, Wrightson-r; N. Adams/Wrightson-c | 1.00 | 3.00 | 6.00 |

NOTE: *All-r with exception of some special features and covers.* ***Aparo*** *a-52r; c-37.* ***Giordano*** *a-39, 45.* ***Grell*** *c-49.* ***Infantino*** *a-25, 39, 44, 45, 52.*

**LINDA** (Phantom Lady No. 5 on)
Apr-May, 1954 - No. 4, Oct-Nov, 1954
Ajax-Farrell Publ. Co.

| | | | |
|---|---|---|---|
| 1-Kamenish-a | 7.00 | 21.00 | 50.00 |
| 2-Lingerie panel | 4.65 | 14.00 | 32.00 |
| 3,4 | 4.30 | 13.00 | 30.00 |

**LINDA CARTER, STUDENT NURSE**
Sept, 1961 - No. 9, Jan, 1963
Atlas Comics (AMI)

| | | | |
|---|---|---|---|
| 1-Al Hartley-c | 2.30 | 7.00 | 16.00 |
| 2-9 | 1.50 | 4.50 | 10.00 |

**LINDA LARK**
Oct-Dec, 1961 - No. 8, Aug-Oct, 1963
Dell Publishing Co.

| | | | |
|---|---|---|---|
| 1 | 1.00 | 3.00 | 7.00 |
| 2-8 | .55 | 1.65 | 4.00 |

**LINUS, THE LIONHEARTED** (TV)
September, 1965
Gold Key

| | | | |
|---|---|---|---|
| 1 (10155-509) | 3.00 | 9.00 | 21.00 |

**LION, THE** (See Movie Comics)

**LION OF SPARTA** (See Movie Classics)

**LIPPY THE LION AND HARDY HAR HAR** (TV)
March, 1963 (Hanna-Barbera)
Gold Key

| | | | |
|---|---|---|---|
| 1 (10049-303) | 3.50 | 10.50 | 24.00 |

**LI'L ABNER** (See Comics on Parade, Sparkle, Sparkler Comics, Tip Top Comics & Tip Topper)
1939 - 1940
United Features Syndicate

| | | | |
|---|---|---|---|
| Single Series 4 ('39) | 37.00 | 110.00 | 260.00 |
| Single Series 18 ('40) (#18 on inside, #2 on cover) | 30.00 | 90.00 | 210.00 |

**LI'L ABNER** (Al Capp's) (See Oxydol-Dreft)
No. 61, Dec, 1947 - No. 97, Jan, 1955
Harvey Publ. No. 61-69 (2/49)/Toby Press No. 70 on

| | | | |
|---|---|---|---|
| 61(#1)-Wolverton & Powell-a | 17.00 | 51.00 | 120.00 |
| 62-65: 65-Powell-a | 11.00 | 32.00 | 75.00 |
| 66,67,69,70 | 9.30 | 28.00 | 65.00 |
| 68-Full length Fearless Fosdick story | 10.00 | 30.00 | 70.00 |
| 71-74,76,80 | 7.00 | 21.00 | 50.00 |
| 75,77-79,86,91-All with Kurtzman art; 91 reprints #77 | 8.50 | 25.50 | 60.00 |
| 81-85,87-90,92-94,96,97: 93-reprints #71 | 6.00 | 18.00 | 42.00 |
| 95-Full length Fearless Fosdick story | 8.50 | 25.50 | 60.00 |
| ...& the Creatures from Drop-Outer Space-nn (Job Corps giveaway; 36pgs., in color | 7.00 | 21.00 | 50.00 |
| ...Joins the Navy (1950) (Toby Press Premium) | 5.50 | 16.50 | 38.00 |
| ...by Al Capp Giveaway (Circa 1955, nd) | 6.00 | 18.00 | 42.00 |

**LI'L ABNER**
1951
Toby Press

| | | | |
|---|---|---|---|
| 1 | 11.00 | 32.00 | 75.00 |

**LI'L ABNER'S DOGPATCH** (See Al Capp's...)

**LITTLE AL OF THE F.B.I.**
No. 10, 1950 (no month) - No. 11, Apr-May, 1951
Ziff-Davis Publications (Saunders painted-c)

| | | | |
|---|---|---|---|
| 10(1950) | 6.00 | 18.00 | 42.00 |
| 11(1951) | 4.50 | 14.00 | 32.00 |

**LITTLE AL OF THE SECRET SERVICE**
No. 10, 7-8/51; No, 2, 9-10/51; No. 3, Winter, 1951
Ziff-Davis Publications (Saunders painted-c)

| | | | |
|---|---|---|---|
| 10(#1)-Spanking panel | 8.50 | 25.50 | 60.00 |
| 2,3 | 5.00 | 15.00 | 35.00 |

**LITTLE ALONZO**
1938 (B&W, 5½X8½")(Christmas giveaway)
Macy's Dept. Store

| | | | |
|---|---|---|---|
| nn-By Ferdinand the Bull's Munro Leaf | 2.85 | 8.50 | 20.00 |

**LITTLE AMBROSE**
September, 1958
Archie Publications

| | | | |
|---|---|---|---|
| 1-Bob Bolling-c | 8.50 | 25.50 | 60.00 |

**LITTLE ANGEL**
No. 5, Sept, 1954; No. 6, Sept, 1955 - No. 16, Sept, 1959
Standard (Visual Editions)/Pines

| | | | |
|---|---|---|---|
| 5 | 2.65 | 8.00 | 18.00 |
| 6-16 | 1.30 | 4.00 | 9.00 |

**LITTLE ANNIE ROONEY**
1935 (48 pgs.; B&W dailies) (25 cents)
David McKay Publications

| | | | |
|---|---|---|---|
| Book 1-Daily strip-r by Darrell McClure | 10.00 | 30.00 | 70.00 |

**LITTLE ANNIE ROONEY** (See King Comics & Treasury of Comics)
1938; Aug, 1948 - No. 3, Oct, 1948
David McKay/St. John/Standard

| | | | |
|---|---|---|---|
| Feature Books 11 (McKay, 1938) | 21.00 | 62.00 | 145.00 |
| 1 (St. John) | 7.00 | 21.00 | 50.00 |
| 2,3 | 4.00 | 12.00 | 28.00 |

**LITTLE ARCHIE** (The Adventures of... #13-on) (See Archie Giant Series #527,534,538,545,549,556,560,566,570,583,594,596,607,609,619)
1956 - No. 180, Feb, 1983 (Giants No. 3-84)
Archie Publications

| | Good | Fine | N-Mint |
|---|---|---|---|
| 1-(Scarce) | 29.00 | 86.00 | 200.00 |
| 2 | 14.00 | 43.00 | 100.00 |
| 3-5 | 9.30 | 28.00 | 65.00 |
| 6-10 | 6.00 | 18.00 | 42.00 |
| 11-20 | 3.70 | 11.00 | 26.00 |
| 21-30 | 2.30 | 7.00 | 16.00 |
| 31-40: Little Pureheart apps. #40-42,44 | 1.15 | 3.50 | 8.00 |
| 41-60: 42-Intro. The Little Archies. 59-Little Sabrina begins | .70 | 2.00 | 4.00 |
| 61-84: 84-Last Giant-Size | .35 | 1.00 | 2.00 |
| 85-100 | .25 | .75 | 1.50 |
| 101-180 | | .40 | .80 |
| ...In Animal Land 1('57) | 10.00 | 30.00 | 70.00 |
| ...In Animal Land 17(Winter, 1957-58)-19(Summer,'58)-Formerly Li'l Jinx | 4.50 | 14.00 | 32.00 |

**LITTLE ARCHIE**
Apr, 1991 - Present ($1.00, color)
Archie Comics

| | Good | Fine | N-Mint |
|---|---|---|---|
| 1,2 | | .50 | 1.00 |

**LITTLE ARCHIE CHRISTMAS SPECIAL** (See Archie Giant Series 581)

**LITTLE ARCHIE COMICS DIGEST ANNUAL** (...Magazine #5 on)
Oct, 1977 - Present (Digest-size, 128 pgs.)(Later issues $1.35-$1.50)
Archie Publications

| | Good | Fine | N-Mint |
|---|---|---|---|
| 1(10/77)-Reprints | .35 | 1.00 | 2.00 |
| 2(4/78)-Neal Adams-a | | .60 | 1.20 |
| 3(11/78)-The Fly-r by S&K; Neal Adams-a | | .60 | 1.20 |
| 4(4/79) - 46('91): 28,40,46-Christmas-c | | .60 | 1.20 |

NOTE: *Little Archie, Little Jinx, Little Jughead & Little Sabrina in most issues.*

**LITTLE ARCHIE MYSTERY**
Aug, 1963 - No. 2, Oct, 1963
Archie Publications

| | Good | Fine | N-Mint |
|---|---|---|---|
| 1 | 7.00 | 21.00 | 50.00 |
| 2 | 3.50 | 10.50 | 24.00 |

**LITTLE ASPIRIN** (See Little Lenny & Wisco)
July, 1949 - No. 3, Dec, 1949 (52 pages)
Marvel Comics (CnPC)

| | Good | Fine | N-Mint |
|---|---|---|---|
| 1-Oscar app.; Kurtzman-a, 4 pgs. | 8.00 | 24.00 | 55.00 |
| 2-Kurtzman-a, 4 pgs. | 4.30 | 13.00 | 30.00 |
| 3-No Kurtzman | 2.00 | 6.00 | 14.00 |

**LITTLE AUDREY** (Also see Playful...)
April, 1948 - No. 24, May, 1952
St. John Publ.

| | Good | Fine | N-Mint |
|---|---|---|---|
| 1-1st app. Little Audrey | 19.00 | 57.00 | 135.00 |
| 2 | 9.30 | 28.00 | 65.00 |
| 3-5 | 7.00 | 21.00 | 50.00 |
| 6-10 | 4.00 | 12.00 | 28.00 |
| 11-20 | 2.65 | 8.00 | 18.00 |
| 21-24 | 1.70 | 5.00 | 12.00 |

**LITTLE AUDREY** (See Harvey Hits #11, 19)
No. 25, Aug, 1952 - No. 53, April, 1957
Harvey Publications

| | Good | Fine | N-Mint |
|---|---|---|---|
| 25 (Paramount Pictures Famous Star) | 5.00 | 15.00 | 35.00 |
| 26-30: 26-28-Casper app. | 2.30 | 7.00 | 16.00 |
| 31-40: 32-35-Casper app. | 1.70 | 5.00 | 12.00 |
| 41-53 | 1.15 | 3.50 | 8.00 |
| ...Clubhouse 1 (9/61, 68 pg. Giant) w/reprints | 3.00 | 9.00 | 21.00 |

**LITTLE AUDREY** (...Yearbook)
1950 (260 pages) (50 cents)
St. John Publishing Co.

| | Good | Fine | N-Mint |
|---|---|---|---|
| Contains 8 complete 1949 comics rebound; Casper, Alice in Wonderland, Little Audrey, Abbott & Costello, Pinocchio, Moon Mullins, Three Stooges (from Jubilee), Little Annie Rooney app. (Rare) | 49.00 | 148.00 | 345.00 |

(Also see All Good & Treasury of Comics)

NOTE: *This book contains remaindered St. John comics; many variations possible.*

**LITTLE AUDREY & MELVIN** (Audrey &... No. 62)
May, 1962 - No. 61, Dec, 1973
Harvey Publications

| | Good | Fine | N-Mint |
|---|---|---|---|
| 1 | 5.35 | 16.00 | 32.00 |
| 2-5 | 2.75 | 8.00 | 16.00 |
| 6-10 | 1.70 | 5.00 | 10.00 |
| 11-20 | 1.00 | 3.00 | 6.00 |
| 21-40 | .70 | 2.00 | 4.00 |
| 41-50,54-61 | .50 | 1.50 | 3.00 |
| 51-53: All 52 pg. Giants | .70 | 2.00 | 4.00 |

**LITTLE AUDREY TV FUNTIME**
Sept, 1962 - No. 33, Oct, 1971 (#1-31: 68 pgs.; #32,33: 52 pgs.)
Harvey Publications

| | Good | Fine | N-Mint |
|---|---|---|---|
| 1-Richie Rich app. | 3.35 | 10.00 | 20.00 |
| 2,3: Richie Rich app. | 2.00 | 6.00 | 12.00 |
| 4,5: 5-25 & 35 cent-c issues exist | 1.70 | 5.00 | 10.00 |
| 6-10 | .85 | 2.50 | 5.00 |
| 11-20 | .70 | 2.00 | 4.00 |
| 21-33 | .50 | 1.50 | 3.00 |

**LITTLE BAD WOLF** (See 4-Color #403,473,564, Walt Disney's C&S #52, Walt Disney Showcase #21 & Wheaties)

**LITTLE BEAVER**
No. 211, Jan, 1949 - No. 870, Jan, 1958 (All painted-c)
Dell Publishing Co.

| | Good | Fine | N-Mint |
|---|---|---|---|
| 4-Color 211('49)-All Harman-a | 3.50 | 10.50 | 24.00 |
| 4-Color 267,294,332(5/51) | 2.30 | 7.00 | 16.00 |
| 3(10-12/51)-8(1-3/53) | 2.00 | 6.00 | 14.00 |
| 4-Color 483(8-10/53),529 | 2.00 | 6.00 | 14.00 |
| 4-Color 612,660,695,744,817,870 | 1.50 | 4.50 | 10.00 |

**LITTLE BIT**
March, 1949 - No. 2, 1949
Jubilee/St. John Publishing Co.

| | Good | Fine | N-Mint |
|---|---|---|---|
| 1,2 | 2.00 | 6.00 | 14.00 |

**LITTLE DOT** (See Blackthorne 3-D Series #59, Humphrey, Li'l Max, Sad Sack, and Tastee-Freez Comics)
Sept, 1953 - No. 164, April, 1976
Harvey Publications

| | Good | Fine | N-Mint |
|---|---|---|---|
| 1-Intro./1st app. Richie Rich & Little Lotta | 50.00 | 150.00 | 350.00 |
| 2-1st app. Freckles & Pee Wee (Richie Rich's poor friends) | 25.00 | 75.00 | 175.00 |
| 3 | 16.00 | 48.00 | 110.00 |
| 4 | 11.50 | 34.00 | 80.00 |
| 5-Origin dots on Little Dot's dress | 13.00 | 40.00 | 90.00 |
| 6-Richie Rich, Little Lotta, & Little Dot all on cover; 1st Richie Rich cover featured | 13.00 | 40.00 | 90.00 |
| 7-10 | 5.70 | 17.00 | 40.00 |
| 11-20 | 4.00 | 12.00 | 28.00 |
| 21-40 | 2.00 | 6.00 | 14.00 |
| 41-60 | 1.00 | 3.00 | 7.00 |
| 61-80 | .70 | 2.00 | 4.00 |
| 81-100 | .50 | 1.50 | 3.00 |
| 101-141 | .35 | 1.00 | 2.00 |
| 142-145: All 52 pg. Giants | .40 | 1.20 | 2.40 |
| 146-164 | | .50 | 1.00 |
| Shoe store giveaway 2 | 4.00 | 12.00 | 28.00 |

NOTE: *Richie Rich & Little Lotta in all.*

*Little Audrey #18, © STJ*

*Little Beaver #5, © DELL*

*Little Dot #12, © HARV*

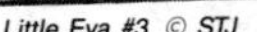

Little Eva #3, © STJ

Little Iodine #5, © DELL

Little Jack Frost #1, © AVON

**LITTLE DOT DOTLAND** (Dot Dotland No. 62, 63)
July, 1962 - No. 61, Dec, 1973
Harvey Publications

| | Good | Fine | N-Mint |
|---|---|---|---|
| 1-Richie Rich begins | 4.50 | 14.00 | 32.00 |
| 2,3 | 2.30 | 7.00 | 16.00 |
| 4,5 | 1.50 | 4.50 | 10.00 |
| 6-10 | 1.15 | 3.50 | 8.00 |
| 11-20 | .85 | 2.50 | 6.00 |
| 21-30 | .50 | 1.50 | 3.00 |
| 31-50,55-61 | .35 | 1.00 | 2.00 |
| 51-54: All 52 pg. Giants | .40 | 1.20 | 2.40 |

**LITTLE DOT'S UNCLES & AUNTS** (See Harvey Hits No. 4, 13, 24)
Oct, 1961; No. 2, Aug, 1962 - No. 52, April, 1974
Harvey Enterprises

| | | | |
|---|---|---|---|
| 1-Richie Rich begins; 68 pgs. begin | 4.50 | 14.00 | 32.00 |
| 2,3 | 2.30 | 7.00 | 16.00 |
| 4,5 | 1.50 | 4.50 | 10.00 |
| 6-10 | 1.15 | 3.50 | 8.00 |
| 11-20 | .85 | 2.50 | 6.00 |
| 21-37: Last 68 pg. issue | .50 | 1.50 | 3.00 |
| 38-52: All 52 pg. Giants | .35 | 1.00 | 2.00 |

**LITTLE EVA**
May, 1952 - No. 31, Nov, 1956
St. John Publishing Co.

| | | | |
|---|---|---|---|
| 1 | 6.50 | 19.00 | 45.00 |
| 2 | 3.00 | 9.00 | 21.00 |
| 3-5 | 2.00 | 6.00 | 14.00 |
| 6-10 | 1.30 | 4.00 | 9.00 |
| 11-31 | 1.15 | 3.50 | 8.00 |
| 3-D 1,2(10/53-11/53); 1-Infinity-c | 12.00 | 36.00 | 84.00 |
| I.W. Reprint #1-3,6-8 | .30 | .90 | 1.80 |
| Super Reprint #10,12('63),14,16,18('64) | .30 | .90 | 1.80 |

**LITTLE FIR TREE, THE**
1942 (8½x11") (12 pgs. with cover)
W. T. Grant Co. (Christmas giveaway)

nn-8 pg. Kelly-a reprint/Santa Claus Funnies not signed.
(One copy in Mint sold for $1750.00 in 1986)

**LI'L GENIUS** (Summer Fun No. 54) (See Blue Bird)
1954 - No. 52, 1/65; No. 53, 10/65; No. 54, 10/85 - No. 55, 1/86
Charlton Comics

| | | | |
|---|---|---|---|
| 1 | 3.50 | 10.50 | 24.00 |
| 2 | 1.70 | 5.00 | 12.00 |
| 3-15,19,20 | 1.30 | 4.00 | 9.00 |
| 16,17-(68 pgs.) | 1.70 | 5.00 | 12.00 |
| 18-(100 pgs., 10/58) | 2.65 | 8.00 | 18.00 |
| 21-35 | 1.00 | 3.00 | 7.00 |
| 36-53 | .70 | 2.00 | 4.00 |
| 54,55 | .25 | .75 | 1.50 |

**LI'L GHOST**
Feb, 1958 - No. 3, Mar, 1959
St. John Publishing Co./Fago No. 1 on

| | | | |
|---|---|---|---|
| 1(St. John) | 3.00 | 9.00 | 21.00 |
| 1(Fago) | 2.30 | 7.00 | 16.00 |
| 2,3 | 1.30 | 4.00 | 9.00 |

**LITTLE GIANT COMICS**
7/38 - No. 3, 10/38; No. 4, 2/39 (132 pgs.) (6¾x4½")
Centaur Publications

| | | | |
|---|---|---|---|
| 1-B&W with color-c | 29.00 | 86.00 | 200.00 |
| 2,3-B&W with color-c | 23.00 | 70.00 | 160.00 |
| 4 (6-5/8x9-3/8")(68 pgs., B&W inside) | 25.00 | 75.00 | 175.00 |

NOTE: *Gustavson* a-1. *Pinajian* a-4. *Bob Wood* a-1.

**LITTLE GIANT DETECTIVE FUNNIES**
Oct, 1938 - No. 4, Jan, 1939 (132 pgs., B&W) (6¾x4½")
Centaur Publications

| | Good | Fine | N-Mint |
|---|---|---|---|
| 1-B&W with color-c | 29.00 | 86.00 | 200.00 |
| 2,3 | 23.00 | 70.00 | 160.00 |
| 4(1/39)-B&W; color-c; 68 pgs., 6½x9½"; Eisner-r | 25.00 | 75.00 | 175.00 |

**LITTLE GIANT MOVIE FUNNIES**
Aug, 1938 - No. 2, Oct, 1938 (132 pgs., B&W) (6¾x4½")
Centaur Publications

| | | | |
|---|---|---|---|
| 1-Ed Wheelan's "Minute Movies"-r | 29.00 | 86.00 | 200.00 |
| 2-Ed Wheelan's "Minute Movies"-r | 22.00 | 65.00 | 150.00 |

**LITTLE GROUCHO** (. . .Grouchy No. 2) (See Tippy Terry)
No. 16; Feb-Mar, 1955 - No. 2, June-July, 1955
Reston Publ. Co.

| | | | |
|---|---|---|---|
| 16, 1 (2-3/55) | 3.00 | 9.00 | 21.00 |
| 2(6-7/55) | 2.00 | 6.00 | 14.00 |

**LITTLE HIAWATHA** (See 4-Color #439,787,901,988 & Walt Disney's C&S #143)

**LITTLE IKE**
April, 1953 - No. 4, Oct, 1953
St. John Publishing Co.

| | | | |
|---|---|---|---|
| 1 | 3.60 | 11.00 | 25.00 |
| 2 | 1.70 | 5.00 | 12.00 |
| 3,4 | 1.50 | 4.50 | 10.00 |

**LITTLE IODINE** (See Giant Comic Album)
No. 224, 4/49 - No. 257, 1949: 3-5/50 - No. 56, 4-6/62 (1-4: 52pgs.)
Dell Publishing Co.

| | | | |
|---|---|---|---|
| 4-Color 224-By Jimmy Hatlo | 5.00 | 15.00 | 35.00 |
| 4-Color 257 | 3.70 | 11.00 | 26.00 |
| 1(3-5/50) | 4.30 | 13.00 | 30.00 |
| 2-5 | 2.00 | 6.00 | 14.00 |
| 6-10 | 1.30 | 4.00 | 9.00 |
| 11-20 | 1.15 | 3.50 | 8.00 |
| 21-30: 27-Xmas-c | 1.00 | 3.00 | 7.00 |
| 31-40 | .70 | 2.00 | 5.00 |
| 41-56 | .45 | 1.35 | 3.00 |

**LITTLE JACK FROST**
1951
Avon Periodicals

| | | | |
|---|---|---|---|
| 1 | 3.50 | 10.50 | 24.00 |

**LI'L JINX** (Formerly Ginger?) (Little Archie in Animal Land #17)
(Also see Pep Comics #62)
No. 11(#1), Nov, 1956 - No. 16, Sept, 1957
Archie Publications

| | | | |
|---|---|---|---|
| 11 (#1) | 5.50 | 16.50 | 38.00 |
| 12-16 | 3.50 | 10.50 | 24.00 |

**LI'L JINX** (See Archie Giant Series Magazine No. 223)

**LI'L JINX CHRISTMAS BAG** (See Archie Giant Series Mag. No. 195,206,219)

**LI'L JINX GIANT LAUGH-OUT**
No. 33, Sept, 1971 - No. 43, Nov, 1973 (52 pgs.)
Archie Publications

| | | | |
|---|---|---|---|
| 33-43 | .35 | 1.00 | 2.00 |

(See Archie Giant Series Mag. No. 176,185)

**LITTLE JOE** (See 4-Color #1, Popular & Super Comics)

**LITTLE JOE**
April, 1953
St. John Publishing Co.

| | | | |
|---|---|---|---|
| 1 | 1.50 | 4.50 | 10.00 |

**LITTLE JOHNNY & THE TEDDY BEARS**
1907 (10x14") (32 pgs. in color)
Reilly & Britton Co.

| | Good | Fine | N-Mint |
|---|---|---|---|
| nn-By J. R. Bray | 19.00 | 57.00 | 132.00 |

**LI'L KIDS** (Also see Li'l Pals)
8/70 - No. 2, 10/70; No. 3, 11/71 - No. 12, 6/73
Marvel Comics Group

| | Good | Fine | N-Mint |
|---|---|---|---|
| 1 | .70 | 2.00 | 4.00 |
| 2-12: 10,11-Calvin app. | .35 | 1.00 | 2.00 |

**LITTLE KING** (See 4-Color No. 494, 597, 677)

**LITTLE KLINKER**
Nov, 1960 (20 pgs.) (slick cover)
Little Klinker Ventures (Montgomery Ward Giveaway)

| | Good | Fine | N-Mint |
|---|---|---|---|
| nn | .70 | 2.00 | 4.00 |

**LITTLE LANA** (Formerly Lana)
No. 8, Nov, 1949; No. 9, Mar, 1950
Marvel Comics (MjMC)

| | Good | Fine | N-Mint |
|---|---|---|---|
| 8,9 | 2.65 | 8.00 | 18.00 |

**LITTLE LENNY**
June, 1949 - No. 3, Nov, 1949
Marvel Comics (CDS)

| | Good | Fine | N-Mint |
|---|---|---|---|
| 1-Little Aspirin app. | 4.00 | 12.00 | 28.00 |
| 2,3 | 2.00 | 6.00 | 14.00 |

**LITTLE LIZZIE**
6/49 - No. 5, 4/50; 9/53 - No. 3, Jan, 1954
Marvel Comics (PrPl)/Atlas (OMC)

| | Good | Fine | N-Mint |
|---|---|---|---|
| 1 | 4.30 | 13.00 | 30.00 |
| 2-5 | 2.15 | 6.50 | 15.00 |
| 1 (1953, 2nd series) | 3.15 | 9.50 | 22.00 |
| 2,3 | 1.70 | 5.00 | 12.00 |

**LITTLE LOTTA** (See Harvey Hits No. 10)
11/55 - No. 110, 11/73; No. 111, 9/74 - No. 121, 5/76
Harvey Publications

| | Good | Fine | N-Mint |
|---|---|---|---|
| 1-Richie Rich (r) & Little Dot begin | 19.00 | 57.00 | 130.00 |
| 2,3 | 8.50 | 25.50 | 60.00 |
| 4,5 | 4.50 | 14.00 | 32.00 |
| 6-10 | 3.50 | 10.50 | 24.00 |
| 11-20 | 2.00 | 6.00 | 14.00 |
| 21-40 | 1.30 | 4.00 | 9.00 |
| 41-60 | .85 | 2.50 | 6.00 |
| 61-80 | .50 | 1.50 | 3.00 |
| 81-99 | .35 | 1.00 | 2.00 |
| 100-103: All 52 pg. Giants | .40 | 1.20 | 2.40 |
| 104-121 | .25 | .75 | 1.50 |

**LITTLE LOTTA FOODLAND**
9/63 - No. 14, 10/67; No. 15, 10/68 - No. 29, Oct, 1972
Harvey Publications

| | Good | Fine | N-Mint |
|---|---|---|---|
| 1: 68 pgs. begin, end #26 | 5.70 | 17.00 | 40.00 |
| 2,3 | 2.65 | 8.00 | 18.00 |
| 4,5 | 2.00 | 6.00 | 14.00 |
| 6-10 | 1.50 | 4.50 | 10.00 |
| 11-20 | 1.00 | 3.00 | 7.00 |
| 21-26 | .85 | 2.50 | 5.00 |
| 27,28: Both 52 pgs. | .70 | 2.00 | 4.00 |
| 29: 36 pgs. | .50 | 1.50 | 3.00 |

**LITTLE LULU** (Formerly Marge's...)
No. 207, Sept, 1972 - No. 268, April, 1984
Gold Key 207-257/Whitman 258 on

| | Good | Fine | N-Mint |
|---|---|---|---|
| 207,209,220-Stanley-r. 207-1st app. Henrietta | .60 | 1.75 | 3.50 |
| 208,210-219: 208-1st app. Snobbly, Wilbur's brother | .40 | 1.25 | 2.50 |
| 221-240,242-249, 250(r/166), 251-254(r/206) | .25 | .80 | 1.60 |
| 241,263,268-Stanley-r | .25 | .80 | 1.60 |
| 255-262,264-267: 256 r/212 | | .50 | 1.00 |

**LITTLE MARY MIXUP** (See Comics On Parade & Single Series #10, 26)

**LITTLE MAX COMICS** (Joe Palooka's Pal; see Joe Palooka)
Oct, 1949 - No. 73, Nov, 1961
Harvey Publications

| | Good | Fine | N-Mint |
|---|---|---|---|
| 1-Infinity-c; Little Dot begins | 8.50 | 25.50 | 60.00 |
| 2-Little Dot app. | 4.30 | 13.00 | 30.00 |
| 3-Little Dot app. | 3.00 | 9.00 | 21.00 |
| 4-10: 5-Little Dot app., 1pg. | 1.50 | 4.50 | 10.00 |
| 11-20 | 1.00 | 3.00 | 7.00 |
| 21-68,70-72: 23-Little Dot app. 38-r/20 | .75 | 2.25 | 5.00 |
| 69,73-Richie Rich app. | .85 | 2.50 | 6.00 |

**LI'L MENACE**
Dec, 1958 - No. 3, May, 1959
Fago Magazine Co.

| | Good | Fine | N-Mint |
|---|---|---|---|
| 1-Peter Rabbit app. | 3.00 | 9.00 | 21.00 |
| 2-Peter Rabbit (Vincent Fago's) | 2.00 | 6.00 | 14.00 |
| 3 | 1.50 | 4.50 | 10.00 |

**LITTLE MISS MUFFET**
No. 11, Dec, 1948 - No. 13, March, 1949
Best Books (Standard Comics)/King Features Synd.

| | Good | Fine | N-Mint |
|---|---|---|---|
| 11-Strip reprints; Fanny Cory-a | 5.00 | 15.00 | 35.00 |
| 12,13-Strip reprints; Fanny Cory-a | 3.50 | 10.50 | 24.00 |

**LITTLE MISS SUNBEAM COMICS**
June-July, 1950 - No. 4, Dec-Jan, 1950-51
Magazine Enterprises/Quality Bakers of America

| | Good | Fine | N-Mint |
|---|---|---|---|
| 1 | 6.00 | 18.00 | 42.00 |
| 2-4 | 3.00 | 9.00 | 21.00 |
| ...Advs. In Space ('55) | 2.00 | 6.00 | 14.00 |
| Bread Giveaway 1-4(Quality Bakers, 1949-50)-14 pgs. each | 1.70 | 5.00 | 12.00 |
| Bread Giveaway (1957,61; 16pgs, reg. size) | 1.30 | 4.00 | 9.00 |

**LITTLE MONSTERS, THE** (See March of Comics No. 423 & Three Stooges No. 17)
Nov, 1964 - No. 44, Feb, 1978
Gold Key

| | Good | Fine | N-Mint |
|---|---|---|---|
| 1 | 1.50 | 4.50 | 10.00 |
| 2 | .85 | 2.50 | 5.00 |
| 3-10 | .70 | 2.00 | 4.00 |
| 11-20 | .35 | 1.00 | 2.00 |
| 21-44: 20,34-39,43-reprints | | .40 | .80 |

**LITTLE MONSTERS**
1989 - No. 6, June, 1990 ($1.75, color, movie adaptation)
Now Comics

| | Good | Fine | N-Mint |
|---|---|---|---|
| 1-6: Photo-c from movie | .30 | .90 | 1.80 |

**LITTLE NEMO** (See Cocomalt, Future Comics, Help, Jest, Kayo, Punch, Red Seal, & Superworld; most by Winsor McCay Jr., son of famous artist) (Other McCay books: see Little Sammy Sneeze & Dreams of the Rarebit Fiend)

**LITTLE NEMO** (...in Slumberland)
1906, 1909 (Sunday strip reprints in color) (cardboard covers)
Doffield & Co.(1906)/Cupples & Leon Co.(1909)

| | Good | Fine | N-Mint |
|---|---|---|---|
| 1906-11x16½" in color by Winsor McCay; 30 pgs. (Very Rare) | 157.00 | 471.00 | 1100.00 |
| 1909-10x14" in color by Winsor McCay (Very Rare) | 128.00 | 385.00 | 900.00 |

**LITTLE NEMO** (...in Slumberland)
1945 (28 pgs.; 11x7¼"; B&W)
McCay Features/Nostalgia Press('69)

*Little Lenny #3, © MEG*

*Little Lotta #22, © HARV*

*Little Max Comics #2, © HARV*

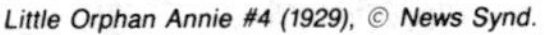

*Little Orphan Annie #4 (1929), © News Synd.*

*Little Scouts #4, © DELL*

*Li'l Willie #20, © MEG*

| | Good | Fine | N-Mint |
|---|---|---|---|
| 1905 & 1911 reprints by Winsor McCay | 4.00 | 12.00 | 28.00 |
| 1969-70 (exact reprint) | 1.50 | 4.00 | 8.00 |

**LITTLE NEMO IN SLUMBERLAND IN 3-D** (See Blackthorne 3-D Series 13)

**LITTLE ORPHAN ANNIE** (See Annie, Famous Feature Stories, Feature Books #7, Marvel Super Special, Merry Christmas..., Popular Comics, Super Book #7, 11, 23 & Super Comics)

**LITTLE ORPHAN ANNIE** (See Treasure Box of Famous Comics)
1926 - 1934 (Daily strip reprints) (7x8¾") (B&W)
Cupples & Leon Co.

(Hardcover Editions, 100 pages)

| | Good | Fine | N-Mint |
|---|---|---|---|
| 1(1926)-Little Orphan Annie | 20.00 | 60.00 | 140.00 |
| 2('27)-In the Circus | 14.00 | 42.00 | 100.00 |
| 3('28)-The Haunted House | 14.00 | 42.00 | 100.00 |
| 4('29)-Bucking the World | 14.00 | 42.00 | 100.00 |
| 5('30)-Never Say Die | 14.00 | 42.00 | 100.00 |
| 6('31)-Shipwrecked | 14.00 | 42.00 | 100.00 |
| 7('32)-A Willing Helper | 11.00 | 32.00 | 75.00 |
| 8('33)-In Cosmic City | 11.00 | 32.00 | 75.00 |
| 9('34)-Uncle Dan | 14.00 | 42.00 | 100.00 |

NOTE: *Hardcovers with dust jackets are worth 20-50 percent more; the earlier the book, the higher the percentage. Each book reprints dailies from the previous year.*

**LITTLE ORPHAN ANNIE**
No. 7, 1937 - No. 3, Sept-Nov, 1948; No. 206, Dec, 1948
David McKay Publ./Dell Publishing Co.

| | Good | Fine | N-Mint |
|---|---|---|---|
| Feature Books(McKay) 7-('37) (Rare) | 75.00 | 225.00 | 525.00 |
| 4-Color 12(1941) | 37.00 | 110.00 | 260.00 |
| 4-Color 18('43)-Flag-c | 29.00 | 86.00 | 200.00 |
| 4-Color 52('44) | 22.00 | 65.00 | 150.00 |
| 4-Color 76('45) | 17.00 | 51.00 | 120.00 |
| 4-Color 107('46) | 14.00 | 43.00 | 100.00 |
| 4-Color 152('47) | 10.00 | 30.00 | 70.00 |
| 1(3-5/48)-r/strips from 5/7/44 to 7/30/44 | 12.00 | 36.00 | 84.00 |
| 2-r/strips from 7/21/40 to 9/9/40 | 7.00 | 21.00 | 50.00 |
| 3-r/strips from 9/10/40 to 11/9/40 | 7.00 | 21.00 | 50.00 |
| 4-Color 206(12/48) | 5.70 | 17.00 | 40.00 |
| Junior Commandos Giveaway(same-c as 4-Color #18, K.K. Publ.)(Big Shoe Store); same back cover as '47 Popped Wheat giveaway; 16 pgs; flag-c; r/strips 9/7/42-10/10/42 | 14.50 | 43.50 | 100.00 |
| Popped Wheat Giveaway('47)-16 pgs. full color; reprints strips from 5/3/40 to 6/20/40 | .85 | 2.50 | 6.00 |
| Quaker Sparkies Giveaway(1940) | 6.50 | 19.50 | 45.00 |
| Quaker Sparkies Giveaway(1941, Full color, 20 pgs.); "LOA and the Rescue;" r/strips 4/13/39-6/21/39 & 7/6/39-7/17/39. "LOA and the Kidnappers;" r/strips 11/28/38-1/28/39 | 5.70 | 17.00 | 40.00 |
| Quaker Sparkies Giveaway(1942, Full color, 20 pgs.); "LOA and Mr. Gudge;" r/strips 2/13/38-3/21/38 & 4/18/37-5/30/37. "LOA and the Great Am" | 4.30 | 13.00 | 30.00 |

**LI'L PALS** (Also see Li'l Kids)
Sept, 1972 - No. 5, May, 1973
Marvel Comics Group

| | Good | Fine | N-Mint |
|---|---|---|---|
| 1-5 | | .40 | .80 |

**LI'L PAN**
No. 6, Dec-Jan, 1947 - No. 8, Apr-May, 1947
Fox Features Syndicate

| | Good | Fine | N-Mint |
|---|---|---|---|
| 6 | 3.00 | 9.00 | 21.00 |
| 7,8 | 2.00 | 6.00 | 14.00 |

**LITTLE PEOPLE** (See 4-Color #485, 573, 633, 692, 753, 809, 868, 908, 959, 1024, 1062)

**LITTLE RASCALS** (See 4-Color #674, 778, 825, 883, 936, 974, 1030, 1079, 1137, 1174, 1224, 1297)

**LI'L RASCAL TWINS** (Formerly Nature Boy)
No. 6, 1957 - No. 18, Jan, 1960
Charlton Comics

| | Good | Fine | N-Mint |
|---|---|---|---|
| 6-Li'l Genius & Tomboy in all | 2.00 | 6.00 | 14.00 |
| 7-18 | 1.00 | 3.00 | 7.00 |

**LITTLE ROQUEFORT COMICS**
June, 1952 - No. 9, Oct, 1953; No. 10, Summer, 1958
St. John Publishing Co./Pines No. 10

| | Good | Fine | N-Mint |
|---|---|---|---|
| 1 | 4.00 | 12.00 | 28.00 |
| 2 | 2.00 | 6.00 | 14.00 |
| 3-10 | 1.50 | 4.50 | 10.00 |

**LITTLE SAD SACK** (See Harvey Hits No. 73, 76, 79, 81, 83)
Oct, 1964 - No. 19, Nov, 1967
Harvey Publications

| | Good | Fine | N-Mint |
|---|---|---|---|
| 1-Richie Rich app. on cover only | 1.35 | 4.00 | 9.00 |
| 2-19 | .35 | 1.00 | 2.00 |

**LITTLE SAMMY SNEEZE**
1905 (28 pgs. in color; 11x16½")
New York Herald Co.

| | Good | Fine | N-Mint |
|---|---|---|---|
| nn-By Winsor McCay (Rare) | 157.00 | 470.00 | 1100.00 |

NOTE: *Rarely found in fine to mint condition.*

**LITTLE SCOUTS**
No. 321, Mar, 1951 - No. 587, Oct, 1954
Dell Publishing Co.

| | Good | Fine | N-Mint |
|---|---|---|---|
| 4-Color #321 (#1, 3/51) | 1.30 | 4.00 | 9.00 |
| 2(10-12/51) - 6(10-12/52) | .85 | 2.50 | 6.00 |
| 4-Color #462,506,550,587 | .85 | 2.50 | 6.00 |

**LITTLE SHOP OF HORRORS SPECIAL**
Feb, 1987 ($2.00, 68 pgs.) (Movie adaptation)
DC Comics

| | Good | Fine | N-Mint |
|---|---|---|---|
| 1-Colan-a | .35 | 1.00 | 2.00 |

**LITTLE SPUNKY**
No date (1963?) (10 cents)
I. W. Enterprises

| | Good | Fine | N-Mint |
|---|---|---|---|
| 1-Reprint | .30 | .80 | 1.60 |

**LITTLE STOOGES, THE** (The Three Stooges' Sons)
Sept, 1972 - No. 7, Mar, 1974
Gold Key

| | Good | Fine | N-Mint |
|---|---|---|---|
| 1-Norman Maurer cover/stories in all | .70 | 2.00 | 4.00 |
| 2-7 | .35 | 1.00 | 2.00 |

**LITTLEST OUTLAW** (See 4-Color #609)

**LITTLEST SNOWMAN, THE**
No. 755, 12/56; No. 864, 12/57; 12-2/1963-64
Dell Publishing Co.

| | Good | Fine | N-Mint |
|---|---|---|---|
| 4-Color #755,864, 1(1964) | 2.15 | 7.00 | 16.00 |

**LI'L TOMBOY** (Formerly Fawcett's Funny Animals)
V14#92, Oct, 1956; No. 93, Mar, 1957 - No. 107, Feb, 1960
Charlton Comics

| | Good | Fine | N-Mint |
|---|---|---|---|
| V14#92 | 1.70 | 5.00 | 12.00 |
| 93-107: 97-Atomic Bunny app. | 1.15 | 3.50 | 8.00 |

**LITTLE TREE THAT WASN'T WANTED, THE**
1960, (Color, 28 pgs.)
W. T. Grant Co. (Giveaway)

| | Good | Fine | N-Mint |
|---|---|---|---|
| nn-Christmas giveaway | .50 | 1.50 | 3.00 |

**LI'L WILLIE COMICS** (Formerly & becomes Willie Comics #22 on)
No. 20, July, 1949 - No. 21, Sept, 1949
Marvel Comics (MgPC)

| | Good | Fine | N-Mint |
|---|---|---|---|
| 20,21: 20-Little Aspirin app. | 2.30 | 7.00 | 16.00 |

**LITTLE WOMEN** (See Power Record Comics)

**LIVE IT UP**
1973, 1976 (39-49 cents)
Spire Christian Comics (Fleming H. Revell Co.)

| | Good | Fine | N-Mint |
|---|---|---|---|
| nn | | .40 | .80 |

**LIVING BIBLE, THE**
Fall, 1945 - No. 3, Spring, 1946
Living Bible Corp.

| | Good | Fine | N-Mint |
|---|---|---|---|
| 1-Life of Paul | 11.50 | 34.00 | 80.00 |
| 2-Joseph & His Brethren | 7.00 | 21.00 | 50.00 |
| 3-Chaplains At War (classic-c) | 13.00 | 40.00 | 90.00 |

NOTE: *All have **L. B. Cole** -c.*

**LOBO**
Dec, 1965; No. 2, Oct, 1966
Dell Publishing Co.

| | Good | Fine | N-Mint |
|---|---|---|---|
| 1,2 | .85 | 2.50 | 6.00 |

**LOBO** (See L.E.G.I.O.N. '89/'90 & Omega Men #3)
Nov, 1990 - No. 4, Feb, 1991 ($1.50, color, mini-series)

| | Good | Fine | N-Mint |
|---|---|---|---|
| 1-(99 cents)-Giffen plots/Breakdowns in all | .50 | 1.50 | 3.00 |
| 2-Legion '89 spin-off | .30 | .90 | 1.75 |
| 3,4 | .25 | .75 | 1.50 |

**LOCKE!**
1987 - No. 3? ($1.25, color)
Blackthorne Publishing

| | Good | Fine | N-Mint |
|---|---|---|---|
| 1-3 | | .60 | 1.25 |

**LOCO** (Magazine) (Satire)
Aug, 1958 - V1#3, Jan, 1959
Satire Publications

| | Good | Fine | N-Mint |
|---|---|---|---|
| V1#1-Chic Stone-a | 1.70 | 5.00 | 12.00 |
| V1#2,3-Severin-a, 2 pgs. Davis; 3-Heath-a | 1.15 | 3.50 | 8.00 |

**LOGAN'S RUN** (TV)
Jan, 1977 - No. 7, July, 1977
Marvel Comics Group

| | Good | Fine | N-Mint |
|---|---|---|---|
| 1 | .35 | 1.00 | 2.00 |
| 2-7 | | .60 | 1.20 |

NOTE: ***Austin** a-6i. **Gulacy** c-6. **Kane** c-7p. **Perez** a-1-5p; c-1-5p. **Sutton** a-6p, 7p.*

**LOIS LANE** (Also see Daring New Adventures of Supergirl, Showcase #9,10 & Superman's Girlfriend . . .)
Aug, 1986 - No. 2, Sept, 1986 ($1.50, 52 pgs.)
DC Comics

| | Good | Fine | N-Mint |
|---|---|---|---|
| 1,2-Morrow-c/a in each | .25 | .75 | 1.50 |

**LOLLY AND PEPPER**
No. 832, Sept, 1957 - July, 1962
Dell Publishing Co.

| | Good | Fine | N-Mint |
|---|---|---|---|
| 4-Color 832(#1) | 1.70 | 5.00 | 12.00 |
| 4-Color 940,978,1086,1206 | 1.30 | 4.00 | 9.00 |
| 01-459-207 (7/62) | 1.30 | 4.00 | 9.00 |

**LOMAX** (See Police Action)

**LONE EAGLE** (The Flame No. 5 on)
Apr-May, 1954 - No. 4, Oct-Nov, 1954
Ajax/Farrell Publications

| | Good | Fine | N-Mint |
|---|---|---|---|
| 1 | 5.00 | 15.00 | 35.00 |
| 2-4: 3-Bondage-c | 3.00 | 9.00 | 21.00 |

**LONELY HEART** (Formerly Dear Lonely Hearts; Dear Heart #15 on)
No. 9, March, 1955 - No. 14, Feb, 1956
Ajax/Farrell Publ. (Excellent Publ.)

| | Good | Fine | N-Mint |
|---|---|---|---|
| 9-Kamenesque-a; (Last precode) | 3.50 | 10.50 | 24.00 |
| 10-14 | 1.70 | 5.00 | 12.00 |

**LONE RANGER, THE** (See Ace Comics, Aurora, Dell Giants, Feature Books #21, 24(McKay), Future Comics, King Comics, Magic Comics & March of Comics #165, 174, 193, 208, 225, 238, 310, 322, 338, 350)

**LONE RANGER, THE**
No. 3, 1939 - No. 167, Feb, 1947
Dell Publishing Co.

| | Good | Fine | N-Mint |
|---|---|---|---|
| Large Feature Comic 3('39)-Heigh-Yo Silver; text with ill. by Robert Weisman; also exists as a Whitman #710 | 45.00 | 135.00 | 315.00 |
| Large Feature Comic 7('39)-Ill. by Henry Valleley; Hi-Yo Silver the Lone Ranger to the Rescue; also exists as a Whitman #715 | 55.00 | 165.00 | 385.00 |
| 4-Color 82('45) | 32.00 | 95.00 | 225.00 |
| 4-Color 98('45),118('46) | 26.00 | 77.00 | 180.00 |
| 4-Color 125('46),136('47) | 19.00 | 57.00 | 130.00 |
| 4-Color 151,167('47) | 16.00 | 48.00 | 110.00 |

**LONE RANGER, THE** (Movie, radio & TV; Clayton Moore starred as L. Ranger in the movies; No. 1-37: strip reprints)(See Dell Giants)
Jan-Feb, 1948 - No. 145, May-July, 1962
Dell Publishing Co.

| | Good | Fine | N-Mint |
|---|---|---|---|
| 1 (36pgs.)-The L. Ranger, his horse Silver, companion Tonto & his horse Scout begin | 54.00 | 160.00 | 375.00 |
| 2 (52pgs. begin, end #41) | 26.00 | 77.00 | 180.00 |
| 3-5 | 20.00 | 60.00 | 140.00 |
| 6,7,9,10 | 17.00 | 51.00 | 120.00 |
| 8-Origin retold; Indian back-c begin, end #35 | 22.00 | 65.00 | 155.00 |
| 11-20: 11-"Young Hawk" Indian boy serial begins, ends #145 | 11.50 | 34.00 | 80.00 |
| 21,22,24-31: 51-Reprint. 31-1st Mask logo | 9.30 | 28.00 | 65.00 |
| 23-Origin retold | 13.00 | 40.00 | 90.00 |
| 32-37: 32-Painted-c begin. 36-Animal photo back-c begin, end #49. 37-Last newspaper-r issue; new outfit | 7.00 | 21.00 | 50.00 |
| 38-41 (All 52pgs.) | 6.00 | 18.00 | 42.00 |
| 42-50 (36pgs.) | 5.00 | 15.00 | 35.00 |
| 51-74 (52pgs.): 71-Blank inside-c | 5.00 | 15.00 | 35.00 |
| 75-99: 76-Flag-c. 79-X-mas-c | 4.00 | 12.00 | 28.00 |
| 100 | 5.70 | 17.00 | 40.00 |
| 101-111: Last painted-c | 4.00 | 12.00 | 28.00 |
| 112-Clayton Moore photo-c begin, end #145 | 14.00 | 43.00 | 100.00 |
| 113-117 | 7.00 | 21.00 | 50.00 |
| 118-Origin Lone Ranger, Tonto, & Silver retold; Special anniversary issue | 13.00 | 40.00 | 90.00 |
| 119-145: 139-Last issue by Fran Striker | 6.50 | 19.00 | 45.00 |
| Cheerios Giveaways (1954, 16 pgs., 2½x7", soft-c) #1-"The Lone Ranger, His Mask & How He Met Tonto." #2-"The Lone Ranger & the Story of Silver" each. . . . | 6.50 | 19.00 | 45.00 |
| Doll Giveaways (Gabriel Ind.)(1973, 3¼x5")-"The Story of The L.R." & The Carson City Bank Robbery" | 1.15 | 3.50 | 8.00 |
| How the L. R. Captured Silver Book(1936)-Silvercup Bread giveaway | 34.00 | 103.00 | 240.00 |
| . . .In Milk for Big Mike(1955, Dairy Association giveaway), soft-c 5x7¼", 16 pgs. | 11.00 | 32.00 | 75.00 |
| Merita Bread giveaway('54; 16 pgs.; 5x7¼")-"How to Be a Lone Ranger Health & Safety Scout" | 11.00 | 32.00 | 75.00 |

NOTE: ***Hank Hartman** painted c(signed)-65, 66, 70, 75, 82; unsigned-64?, 67-69?, 71, 72, 73?, 74?, 76-78, 80, 81, 83-91, 92?, 93-111. **Ernest Nordli** painted c(signed)-42, 50, 52, 53, 56, 59, 60; unsigned-39-41, 44-49, 51, 54, 55, 57, 58, 61-63?*

**LONE RANGER, THE**
9/64 - No. 16, 12/69; No. 17, 11/72; No. 18, 9/74 - No. 28, 3/77
Gold Key (Reprints #13-20)

| | Good | Fine | N-Mint |
|---|---|---|---|
| 1-Retells origin | 2.85 | 8.50 | 20.00 |
| 2 | 1.50 | 4.50 | 10.00 |
| 3-10: Small Bear-r in #6-10 | 1.00 | 3.00 | 7.00 |
| 11-17: Small Bear-r in #11,12 | .85 | 2.50 | 6.00 |
| 18-28 | .55 | 1.65 | 4.00 |
| Golden West 1(30029-610)-Giant, 10/66-r/most Golden West #3-including Clayton Moore photo front/back-c | 5.70 | 17.00 | 40.00 |

*Logan's Run #1, © MEG*

*Lone Eagle #3, © AJAX*

*The Lone Ranger #6, © The Lone Ranger*

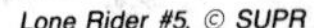
Lone Rider #5, © SUPR

Long Bow #3, © FH

Looney Tunes & Merrie. . . #9, © Warner Bros.

**LONE RANGER COMICS, THE** (10 cents)
1939(inside) (shows 1938 on-c) (68 pgs. in color; regular size)
Lone Ranger, Inc. (Ice cream mail order)

| | Good | Fine | N-Mint |
|---|---|---|---|
| nn-(Scarce)-not by Vallely | 57.00 | 171.00 | 400.00 |

**LONE RANGER'S COMPANION TONTO, THE** (TV)
No. 312, Jan, 1951 - No. 33, Nov-Jan/58-59 (All painted-c)
Dell Publishing Co.

| | | | |
|---|---|---|---|
| 4-Color 312(#1, 1951) | 10.00 | 30.00 | 70.00 |
| 2(8-10/51),3: (#2 titled 'Tonto') | 5.00 | 15.00 | 35.00 |
| 4-10 | 2.65 | 8.00 | 18.00 |
| 11-20 | 2.00 | 6.00 | 14.00 |
| 21-33 | 1.50 | 4.50 | 10.00 |

NOTE: ***Ernest Nordli*** *painted c(signed)-2, 7; unsigned-3-6, 8-11, 12?, 13, 14, 18?, 22-24? See Aurora Comic Booklets.*

**LONE RANGER'S FAMOUS HORSE HI-YO SILVER, THE** (TV)
No. 369, Jan, 1952 - No. 36, Oct-Dec, 1960 (All painted-c)
Dell Publishing Co.

| | | | |
|---|---|---|---|
| 4-Color 369(#1)-Silver's origin as told by The Lone Ranger | 6.50 | 19.00 | 45.00 |
| 4-Color 392(#2, 4/52) | 3.00 | 9.00 | 21.00 |
| 3(7-9/52)-10(4-6/52) | 1.70 | 5.00 | 12.00 |
| 11-36 | 1.30 | 4.00 | 9.00 |

**LONE RIDER** (Also see The Rider)
April, 1951 - No. 26, July, 1955 (36pgs., 3-on)
Superior Comics(Farrell Publications)

| | | | |
|---|---|---|---|
| 1 (52pgs.)-The Lone Rider & his horse Lightnin' begin; Kamenish-a begins | 8.50 | 25.50 | 60.00 |
| 2 (52pgs.)-The Golden Arrow begins (origin) | 4.30 | 13.00 | 30.00 |
| 3-6: 6-Last Golden Arrow | 3.50 | 10.50 | 24.00 |
| 7-Golden Arrow becomes Swift Arrow; origin of his shield | 4.00 | 12.00 | 28.00 |
| 8-Origin Swift Arrow | 5.00 | 15.00 | 35.00 |
| 9,10 | 2.65 | 8.00 | 18.00 |
| 11-14 | 2.30 | 7.00 | 16.00 |
| 15-Golden Arrow origin-r from #2, changing name to Swift Arrow | 2.65 | 8.00 | 18.00 |
| 16-20,22-26: 23-Apache Kid app. | 2.00 | 6.00 | 14.00 |
| 21-3-D effect-c | 6.50 | 19.00 | 45.00 |

**LONE WOLF AND CUB**
May, 1987 - Present ($1.95-$2.50-$2.95-$3.25, B&W, deluxe size)
First Comics

| | | | |
|---|---|---|---|
| 1 | 1.70 | 5.00 | 10.00 |
| 1-2nd print, 3rd print | .35 | 1.00 | 2.00 |
| 2 | .90 | 2.75 | 5.50 |
| 2-2nd print | .35 | 1.00 | 2.00 |
| 3 | .60 | 1.75 | 3.50 |
| 4-12: 6-72 pg. origin issue. 8-$2.50-c begins | .45 | 1.30 | 2.60 |
| 13-25 | .40 | 1.25 | 2.50 |
| 26-30,33 ($2.95-c) | .40 | 1.25 | 2.50 |
| 31,32,34-38,40,42 ($3.25): 40,42-Ploog-c | .55 | 1.65 | 3.25 |
| 39-($5.95, 120 pgs.)-Ploog-c | 1.00 | 3.00 | 6.00 |
| 41-($3.95, 84 pgs.)-Ploog-c | .70 | 2.00 | 4.00 |
| Deluxe Edition ($19.95; B&W) | 3.35 | 10.00 | 19.95 |

NOTE: ***Miller*** *c-1-12p; intro-1-12.* ***Sienkiewicz*** *c-13-24.* ***Matt Wagner*** *c-25-30.*

**LONG BOW** (. . .Indian Boy)(See Indians & Jumbo Comics #141)
1951 - No. 9, Wint, 1952/53
Fiction House Magazines (Real Adventures Publ.)

| | | | |
|---|---|---|---|
| 1 | 7.00 | 21.00 | 50.00 |
| 2 | 4.50 | 14.00 | 32.00 |
| 3-9 | 3.00 | 9.00 | 21.00 |

**LONG JOHN SILVER & THE PIRATES** (Formerly Terry & the Pirates)
No. 30, Aug, 1956 - No. 32, March, 1957 (TV)
Charlton Comics

| | Good | Fine | N-Mint |
|---|---|---|---|
| 30-32: Whitman-c | 3.00 | 9.00 | 21.00 |

**LONGSHOT**
Sept, 1985 - No. 6, Feb, 1986 (Limited series)
Marvel Comics Group

| | | | |
|---|---|---|---|
| 1-Arthur Adams-c/a in all | 3.70 | 11.00 | 22.00 |
| 2 | 3.00 | 9.00 | 18.00 |
| 3-5 | 2.30 | 7.00 | 14.00 |
| 6-Double size | 3.00 | 9.00 | 18.00 |
| Trade Paperback (1989, $16.95)-r/1-6 | 2.85 | 8.50 | 17.00 |

**LOONEY TUNES** (2nd Series)
April, 1975 - No. 47, July, 1984
Gold Key/Whitman

| | | | |
|---|---|---|---|
| 1 | | .50 | 1.00 |
| 2-47: Reprints: #1-4,16; 38-46(⅓r) | | .30 | .60 |

**LOONEY TUNES AND MERRIE MELODIES COMICS** ("Looney Tunes" #166 (8/55) on)
1941 - No. 246, July-Sept, 1962
Dell Publishing Co.

| | Good | Fine | VF-NM | NM/Mint |
|---|---|---|---|---|
| 1-Porky Pig, Bugs Bunny, Daffy Duck, Elmer Fudd, Mary Jane & Sniffles, Pat, Patsy and Pete begin (1st comic book app. of each). Bugs Bunny story by Win Smith (early Mickey Mouse artist) | 136.00 | 405.00 | 950.00 | 1750.00 |

(Estimated up to 170 total copies exist, 8 in NM/Mint)

| | Good | Fine | N-Mint |
|---|---|---|---|
| 2 (11/41) | 60.00 | 180.00 | 420.00 |
| 3-Kandi the Cave Kid begins by Walt Kelly; also in #4-6,8,11,15 | 54.00 | 160.00 | 375.00 |
| 4-Kelly-a | 47.00 | 140.00 | 330.00 |
| 5-Bugs Bunny The Super Rabbit app. (1st funny animal super hero?); Kelly-a | 37.00 | 110.00 | 250.00 |
| 6,8-Kelly-a | 26.00 | 77.00 | 180.00 |
| 7,9,10: 9-Painted-c. 10-Flag-c | 21.00 | 62.00 | 145.00 |
| 11,15-Kelly-a; 15-X-Mas-c | 21.00 | 62.00 | 145.00 |
| 12-14,16-19 | 17.00 | 51.00 | 120.00 |
| 20-25: Pat, Patsy & Pete by Walt Kelly in all | 17.00 | 51.00 | 120.00 |
| 26-30 | 11.50 | 34.00 | 80.00 |
| 31-40 | 8.50 | 25.50 | 60.00 |
| 41-50 | 6.00 | 18.00 | 42.00 |
| 51-60 | 4.00 | 12.00 | 28.00 |
| 61-80 | 2.65 | 8.00 | 18.00 |
| 81-99: 87-X-Mas-c | 2.00 | 6.00 | 14.00 |
| 100 | 2.15 | 7.00 | 16.00 |
| 101-120 | 1.60 | 4.80 | 11.00 |
| 121-150 | 1.30 | 4.00 | 9.00 |
| 151-200 | 1.00 | 3.00 | 7.00 |
| 201-246 | .70 | 2.00 | 5.00 |

**LOONY SPORTS** (Magazine)
Spring, 1975 (68 pages)
3-Strikes Publishing Co.

| | | | |
|---|---|---|---|
| 1-Sports satire | .25 | .80 | 1.60 |

**LOOY DOT DOPE** (See Single Series No. 13)

**LORD JIM** (See Movie Comics)

**LORDS OF THE ULTRA-REALM**
June, 1986 - No. 6, Nov, 1986 (Mini-series)
DC Comics

| | | | |
|---|---|---|---|
| 1 | .40 | 1.25 | 2.50 |
| 2-6 | .30 | .85 | 1.70 |
| Special 1(12/87, $2.25) | .40 | 1.15 | 2.30 |

**LORNA THE JUNGLE GIRL** (. . .Jungle Queen #1-5)
July, 1953 - No. 26, Aug, 1957
Atlas Comics (NPI 1/OMC 2-11/NPI 12-26)

| | Good | Fine | N-Mint |
|---|---|---|---|
| 1-Origin | 12.00 | 36.00 | 85.00 |
| 2-Intro. & 1st app. Greg Knight | 6.50 | 19.00 | 45.00 |
| 3-5 | 5.30 | 16.00 | 38.00 |
| 6-11: 11-Last pre-code (1/55) | 4.00 | 12.00 | 28.00 |
| 12-17,19-26 | 3.00 | 9.00 | 21.00 |
| 18-Williamson/Colleta-c | 4.30 | 13.00 | 30.00 |

NOTE: *Everett c-21, 23-26.* ***Heath*** *c-6, 7.* ***Maneely*** *c-12, 15.* ***Romita*** *a-20, 22.* ***Shores*** *a-16; c-13, 16.* ***Tuska*** *a-6.*

**LOSERS SPECIAL** (Also see G.I. Combat #138)
Sept, 1985 ($1.25 cover) (One Shot)(See Our Fighting Forces #123)
DC Comics

| | Good | Fine | N-Mint |
|---|---|---|---|
| 1-Capt. Storm, Gunner & Sarge; Crisis x-over | | .65 | 1.30 |

**LOST CONTINENT**
Sept?, 1990 - No. 6, 1991 ($3.50, B&W, squarebound, 60 pgs.)
Eclipse International

| | Good | Fine | N-Mint |
|---|---|---|---|
| 1-6: Japanese story translated to English | .60 | 1.75 | 3.50 |

**LOST IN SPACE** (Space Family Robinson . . ., on Space Station One)(Formerly Space Family Robinson; see Gold Key Champion)
No. 37, 10/73 - No. 54, 11/78; No. 55, 3/81 - No. 59, 5/82
Gold Key

| | Good | Fine | N-Mint |
|---|---|---|---|
| 37-48 | .40 | 1.20 | 2.40 |
| 49-59: Reprints-#49,50,55-59 | | .60 | 1.20 |

NOTE: ***Spiegle*** *a-37-59. All have painted-c.*

**LOST PLANET**
5/87 - No. 5, 2/88; No. 6, 3/89 ($1.75-$2.00, color, mini-series, Baxter)
Eclipse Comics

| | Good | Fine | N-Mint |
|---|---|---|---|
| 1,2 ($1.75)-Bo Hampton-c/a in all | .30 | .90 | 1.80 |
| 3-6 ($2.00) | .35 | 1.00 | 2.00 |

**LOST WORLD, THE** (See 4-Color #1145)

**LOST WORLDS**
No. 5, Oct, 1952 - No. 6, Dec, 1952
Standard Comics

| | Good | Fine | N-Mint |
|---|---|---|---|
| 5-"Alice in Terrorland" by Toth; J. Katz-a | 16.50 | 50.00 | 115.00 |
| 6-Toth-a | 12.00 | 36.00 | 85.00 |

**LOTS 'O' FUN COMICS**
1940's? (5 cents) (heavy stock; blue covers)
Robert Allen Co.

nn-Contents can vary; Felix, Planet Comics known; contents would determine value. Similar to Up-To-Date Comics. Remainders - re-packaged.

**LOU GEHRIG** (See The Pride of the Yankees)

**LOVE ADVENTURES** (Actual Confessions #13)
Oct, 1949; No. 2, Jan, 1950; No. 3, Feb, 1951 - No. 12, Aug, 1952
Marvel (IPS)/Atlas Comics (MPI)

| | Good | Fine | N-Mint |
|---|---|---|---|
| 1-Photo-c | 5.00 | 15.00 | 35.00 |
| 2-Powell-a; Tyrone Power, Gene Tierney photo-c | 5.00 | 15.00 | 35.00 |
| 3-8,10-12: 8-Robinson-a | 2.65 | 8.00 | 18.00 |
| 9-Everett-a | 3.00 | 9.00 | 21.00 |

**LOVE AND MARRIAGE**
March, 1952 - No. 16, Sept, 1954
Superior Comics Ltd.

| | Good | Fine | N-Mint |
|---|---|---|---|
| 1 | 5.00 | 15.00 | 35.00 |
| 2 | 2.65 | 8.00 | 18.00 |
| 3-10 | 1.70 | 5.00 | 12.00 |
| 11-16 | 1.30 | 4.00 | 9.00 |
| I.W. Reprint #1,2,8,11,14 | .25 | .80 | 1.60 |
| Super Reprint #10('63),15,17('64) | .25 | .80 | 1.60 |

NOTE: *All issues have Kamenish art.*

**LOVE AND ROCKETS**
July, 1982 - Present (B&W, adults only)
Fantagraphics Books

| | Good | Fine | N-Mint |
|---|---|---|---|
| 1-B&W-c ($2.95; small size, publ. by Hernandez Bros.)(800 printed) | 13.35 | 40.00 | 80.00 |
| 1 (Fall, '82; color-c) | 6.70 | 20.00 | 40.00 |
| 1-2nd printing | .50 | 1.50 | 3.00 |
| 2 | 2.50 | 7.50 | 15.00 |
| 2-2nd printing ($3.95, 68 pgs.) | .70 | 2.00 | 4.00 |
| 3-5 | 1.70 | 5.00 | 10.00 |
| 4-2nd printing ($3.95, 68 pgs.) | .70 | 2.00 | 4.00 |
| 6-10 | 1.00 | 3.00 | 6.00 |
| 11-15 | .40 | 1.25 | 2.50 |
| 16-33: 30($2.95, 52 pgs.). 31-on: $2.50-c | .30 | .90 | 1.80 |

**LOVE AND ROMANCE**
Sept, 1971 - No. 24, Sept, 1975
Charlton Comics

| | Good | Fine | N-Mint |
|---|---|---|---|
| 1 | | .60 | 1.20 |
| 2-24 | | .25 | .50 |

**LOVE AT FIRST SIGHT**
Oct, 1949 - No. 42, Aug, 1956 (Photo-c: 21-42)
Ace Magazines (RAR Publ. Co./Periodical House)

| | Good | Fine | N-Mint |
|---|---|---|---|
| 1-Painted-c | 5.00 | 15.00 | 35.00 |
| 2-Painted-c | 2.30 | 7.00 | 16.00 |
| 3-10: 4-Painted-c | 1.70 | 5.00 | 12.00 |
| 11-20 | 1.30 | 4.00 | 9.00 |
| 21-33: 33-Last pre-code | 1.00 | 3.00 | 7.00 |
| 34-42 | .85 | 2.50 | 6.00 |

**LOVE BUG, THE** (See Movie Comics)

**LOVE CLASSICS**
Nov, 1949 - No. 2, Feb, 1950 (Photo-c)
A Lover's Magazine/Marvel Comics

| | Good | Fine | N-Mint |
|---|---|---|---|
| 1,2: 2-Virginia Mayo photo-c; 30 pg. story 'I Was a Small Town Flirt' | 5.00 | 15.00 | 35.00 |

**LOVE CONFESSIONS**
Oct, 1949 - No. 54, Dec, 1956 (Photo-c: 6,11-18,21)
Quality Comics Group

| | Good | Fine | N-Mint |
|---|---|---|---|
| 1-Ward-c/a, 9 pgs; Gustavson-a | 14.00 | 42.00 | 100.00 |
| 2-Gustavson-a | 5.00 | 15.00 | 35.00 |
| 3 | 3.50 | 10.50 | 24.00 |
| 4-Crandall-a | 4.65 | 14.00 | 32.00 |
| 5-Ward-a, 7 pgs. | 5.50 | 16.50 | 38.00 |
| 6,7,9,11-13,15,16,18 | 1.70 | 5.00 | 12.00 |
| 8,10-Ward-a(2 stories in #10) | 4.65 | 14.00 | 32.00 |
| 14,17,19,22-Ward-a; 17-Faith Domerque photo-c | 3.85 | 11.50 | 27.00 |
| 20-Baker-a, Ward-a(2) | 4.65 | 14.00 | 32.00 |
| 21,23-28,30-38,40-42: Last precode, 4/55 | 1.15 | 3.50 | 8.00 |
| 29-Ward-a | 3.65 | 11.00 | 25.00 |
| 39-Matt Baker-a | 1.70 | 5.00 | 12.00 |
| 43,44,46-48,50-54: 47-Ward-c? | 1.00 | 3.00 | 7.00 |
| 45-Ward-a | 2.15 | 6.50 | 15.00 |
| 49-Baker-c/a | 2.65 | 8.00 | 18.00 |

**LOVE DIARY**
July, 1949 - No. 48, Oct, 1955 (Photo-c: 1-24,27,29) (52 pgs. #1-11?)
Our Publishing Co./Toytown/Patches

| | Good | Fine | N-Mint |
|---|---|---|---|
| 1-Krigstein-a | 8.00 | 24.00 | 55.00 |
| 2,3-Krigstein & Mort Leav-a in each | 5.00 | 15.00 | 35.00 |
| 4-8 | 2.00 | 6.00 | 14.00 |
| 9,10-Everett-a | 2.65 | 8.00 | 18.00 |
| 11-20: 16,20-Mort Leav-a | 1.50 | 4.50 | 10.00 |
| 21-30,32-48: 45-Leav-a. 47-Last precode(12/54) | 1.15 | 3.50 | 8.00 |
| 31-J. Buscema headlights-c | 1.50 | 4.50 | 10.00 |

**LOVE DIARY** (Diary Loves #2 on)
September, 1949

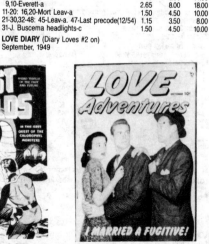

*Lorna the Jungle Girl #14, © MEG*

*Lost Worlds #5, © STD*

*Love Adventures #1, © MEG*

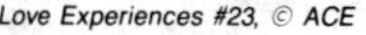

*Love Experiences #23, © ACE*

*Love Letters #18, © QUA*

*Love Problems and Advice Illus. #1, © HARV*

Quality Comics Group

| | Good | Fine | N-Mint |
|---|---|---|---|
| 1-Ward-c, 9 pgs. | 11.50 | 34.50 | 80.00 |

**LOVE DIARY**
July, 1958 - No. 102, Dec, 1976
Charlton Comics

| | Good | Fine | N-Mint |
|---|---|---|---|
| 1 | 2.65 | 8.00 | 18.00 |
| 2 | 1.30 | 4.00 | 9.00 |
| 3-5,7-10: 10-Photo-c | .85 | 2.60 | 6.00 |
| 6-Torres-a | 1.50 | 4.50 | 10.00 |
| 11-20: 20-Photo-c | .70 | 2.00 | 4.00 |
| 21-40 | .40 | 1.25 | 2.50 |
| 41-60 | .25 | .75 | 1.50 |
| 61-102 | | .25 | .50 |

**LOVE DOCTOR** (See Dr. Anthony King. . .)

**LOVE DRAMAS** (True Secrets No. 3 on?)
Oct, 1949 - No. 2, Jan, 1950
Marvel Comics (IPS)

| | Good | Fine | N-Mint |
|---|---|---|---|
| 1-Jack Kamen-a; photo-c | 7.00 | 21.00 | 50.00 |
| 2 | 4.30 | 13.00 | 30.00 |

**LOVE EXPERIENCES** (Challenge of the Unknown No. 6)
Oct, 1949 - No. 5, June, 1950; No. 6, Apr, 1951 - No. 38, June, 1956
Ace Periodicals (A.A. Wyn/Periodical House)

| | Good | Fine | N-Mint |
|---|---|---|---|
| 1-Painted-c | 4.00 | 12.00 | 28.00 |
| 2 | 2.00 | 6.00 | 14.00 |
| 3-5: 5-Painted-c | 1.50 | 4.50 | 10.00 |
| 6-10 | 1.30 | 4.00 | 9.00 |
| 11-30: 30-Last pre-code (2/55) | 1.00 | 3.00 | 7.00 |
| 31-38: 38-Indicia date-6/56; c-date-8/56 | .85 | 2.60 | 6.00 |

NOTE: ***Anne Brewster** a-15. Photo c-4, 15-35, 38.*

**LOVE JOURNAL**
No. 10, Oct, 1951 - No. 25, July, 1954
Our Publishing Co.

| | Good | Fine | N-Mint |
|---|---|---|---|
| 10 | 3.50 | 10.50 | 24.00 |
| 11-25: 19-Mort Leav-a | 1.70 | 5.00 | 12.00 |

**LOVELAND**
Nov, 1949 - No. 2, Feb, 1950 (52 pgs.)
Mutual Mag./Eye Publ. (Marvel)

| | Good | Fine | N-Mint |
|---|---|---|---|
| 1,2-Photo-c | 3.50 | 10.50 | 24.00 |

**LOVE LESSONS**
Oct, 1949 - No. 5, June, 1950
Harvey Comics/Key Publ. No. 5

| | Good | Fine | N-Mint |
|---|---|---|---|
| 1-Metallic silver-c printed over the cancelled covers of Love Letters #1; indicia title is 'Love Letters' | 4.00 | 12.00 | 28.00 |
| 2-Powell-a; photo-c | 1.70 | 5.00 | 12.00 |
| 3-5: 3-Photo-c | 1.50 | 4.50 | 10.00 |

**LOVE LETTERS** (10/49, Harvey; advertised but never published; covers were printed before cancellation and were used as the cover to Love Lessions #1)

**LOVE LETTERS** (Love Secrets No. 32 on)
11/49 - #6, 9/50; #7, 3/51 - #31, 6/53; #32, 2/54 - #51, 12/56
Quality Comics Group

| | Good | Fine | N-Mint |
|---|---|---|---|
| 1-Ward-c, Gustavson-a | 10.00 | 30.00 | 70.00 |
| 2-Ward-c, Gustavson-a | 8.50 | 25.50 | 60.00 |
| 3-Gustavson-a | 5.70 | 17.00 | 40.00 |
| 4-Ward-a, 9 pgs. | 8.50 | 25.50 | 60.00 |
| 5-8,10 | 2.00 | 6.00 | 14.00 |
| 9-One pg. Ward-"Be Popular with the Opposite Sex"; Robert Mitchum photo-c | 3.50 | 10.50 | 24.00 |
| 11-Ward-r/Broadway Romances #2 & retitled | 3.50 | 10.50 | 24.00 |
| 12-15,18-20 | 1.50 | 4.50 | 10.00 |
| 16,17-Ward-a; 16-Anthony Quinn photo-c. 17-Jane Russell photo-c | 5.00 | 15.00 | 35.00 |
| 21-29 | 1.30 | 4.00 | 9.00 |
| 30,31(6/53)-Ward-a | 2.85 | 8.50 | 20.00 |
| 32(2/54) - 39: Last precode (4/55) | 1.15 | 3.50 | 8.00 |
| 40-48 | .85 | 2.60 | 6.00 |
| 49,50-Baker-a | 2.65 | 8.00 | 18.00 |
| 51-Baker-c | 2.15 | 6.50 | 15.00 |

NOTE: *Photo-c on most 3-28.*

**LOVE LIFE**
Nov, 1951
P. L. Publishing Co.

| | Good | Fine | N-Mint |
|---|---|---|---|
| 1 | 3.00 | 9.00 | 21.00 |

**LOVELORN** (Confessions of the Lovelorn #52 on)
Aug-Sept, 1949 - No. 51, July, 1954 (No. 1-26, 52 pgs.)
American Comics Group (Michel Publ./Regis Publ.)

| | Good | Fine | N-Mint |
|---|---|---|---|
| 1 | 4.30 | 13.00 | 30.00 |
| 2 | 2.15 | 6.50 | 15.00 |
| 3-10 | 1.70 | 5.00 | 12.00 |
| 11-20,22-48: 18-Drucker-a(2pgs.). 46-Lazarus-a | 1.15 | 3.50 | 8.00 |
| 21-Prostitution story | 2.15 | 6.50 | 15.00 |
| 49-51-Has 3-D effect | 7.00 | 21.00 | 50.00 |

**LOVE MEMORIES**
1949 (no month) - No. 4, July, 1950 (All photo-c)
Fawcett Publications

| | Good | Fine | N-Mint |
|---|---|---|---|
| 1 | 4.00 | 12.00 | 28.00 |
| 2-4 | 2.30 | 7.00 | 16.00 |

**LOVE MYSTERY**
June, 1950 - No. 3, Oct, 1950 (All photo-c)
Fawcett Publications

| | Good | Fine | N-Mint |
|---|---|---|---|
| 1-George Evans-a | 10.00 | 30.00 | 70.00 |
| 2,3-Evans-a. 3-Powell-a | 7.00 | 21.00 | 50.00 |

**LOVE PROBLEMS** (See Fox Giants)

**LOVE PROBLEMS AND ADVICE ILLUSTRATED** (Becomes Romance Stories of True Love No. 45 on)
June, 1949 - No. 6, Apr, 1950; No. 7, Jan, 1951 - No. 44, Mar, 1957
McCombs/Harvey Publ./Home Comics

| | Good | Fine | N-Mint |
|---|---|---|---|
| V1#1 | 4.00 | 12.00 | 28.00 |
| 2 | 2.00 | 6.00 | 14.00 |
| 3-10 | 1.70 | 5.00 | 12.00 |
| 11-13,15-23,25-31: 31-Last pre-code (1/55) | 1.00 | 3.00 | 7.00 |
| 14,24-Rape scene | 1.15 | 3.50 | 8.00 |
| 32-37,39-44 | .70 | 2.00 | 5.00 |
| 38-S&K-c | 1.70 | 5.00 | 12.00 |

NOTE: ***Powell** a-1, 2, 7-14, 17-25, 28, 29, 33, 40, 41. #3 has True Love. . . on inside.*

**LOVE ROMANCES** (Formerly Ideal #5?)
No. 6, May, 1949 - No. 106, July, 1963
Timely/Marvel/Atlas(TCI No. 7-71/Male No. 72-106)

| | Good | Fine | N-Mint |
|---|---|---|---|
| 6-Photo-c | 4.00 | 12.00 | 28.00 |
| 7-Photo-c; Kamen-a | 3.00 | 9.00 | 21.00 |
| 8-Kubert-a; photo-c | 3.50 | 10.50 | 24.00 |
| 9-20: 9-12-Photo-c | 1.70 | 5.00 | 12.00 |
| 21,24-Krigstein-a | 3.50 | 10.50 | 24.00 |
| 22,23,25-35,37,39,40 | 1.50 | 4.50 | 10.00 |
| 36,38-Krigstein-a | 2.65 | 8.00 | 18.00 |
| 41-44,46,47: Last precode (2/55) | 1.30 | 4.00 | 9.00 |
| 45,57-Matt Baker-a | 1.70 | 5.00 | 12.00 |
| 48,50-52,54-56,58-74 | 1.00 | 3.00 | 7.00 |
| 49,53-Toth-a, 6 & ? pgs. | 2.65 | 8.00 | 18.00 |
| 75,77,82-Matt Baker-a | 1.70 | 5.00 | 12.00 |
| 76,78-81,84,86-95: Last 10 cent issue? | .85 | 2.60 | 6.00 |
| 83-Kirby-c, Severin-a | 1.70 | 5.00 | 12.00 |
| 85,96-Kirby-c/a | 2.00 | 6.00 | 14.00 |

| | Good | Fine | N-Mint |
|---|---|---|---|
| 97,100-104 | .70 | 2.00 | 5.00 |
| 98-Kirby-a(4) | 3.00 | 9.00 | 21.00 |
| 99,105,106-Kirby-a | 1.50 | 4.50 | 10.00 |

NOTE: ***Anne Brewster*** *a-67, 72.* ***Colletta*** *a-37, 40, 42, 44, 67(2); c-42, 44, 49, 80.* ***Everett*** *c-70.* ***Kirby*** *c-80, 85, 88.* ***Robinson*** *a-29.*

**LOVERS** (Formerly Blonde Phantom)
No. 23, May, 1949 - No. 86, Aug?, 1957
Marvel Comics No. 23,24/Atlas No. 25 on (ANC)

| | Good | Fine | N-Mint |
|---|---|---|---|
| 23-Photo-c | 4.30 | 13.00 | 30.00 |
| 24-Tothish plus Robinson-a; photo-c | 2.15 | 6.50 | 15.00 |
| 25,30-Kubert-a; 7, 10 pgs. | 3.00 | 9.00 | 21.00 |
| 26-29,31-36,39,40: 26-28-Photo-c | 1.50 | 4.50 | 10.00 |
| 37,38-Krigstein-a | 3.00 | 9.00 | 21.00 |
| 41-Everett-a(2) | 2.30 | 7.00 | 16.00 |
| 42,44-65: 65-Last pre-code (1/55) | 1.30 | 4.00 | 9.00 |
| 43-1pg. Frazetta ad | 1.30 | 4.00 | 9.00 |
| 66,68-86 | 1.15 | 3.50 | 8.00 |
| 67-Toth-a | 3.00 | 9.00 | 21.00 |

NOTE: ***Anne Brewster*** *a-86.* ***Colletta*** *a-54, 59, 62, 64, 69; c-64, 75.* ***Powell*** *a-27, 30.* ***Robinson*** *a-54, 56.*

**LOVERS' LANE**
Oct, 1949 - No. 41, June, 1954 (No. 1-18: 52 pgs.)
Lev Gleason Publications

| | Good | Fine | N-Mint |
|---|---|---|---|
| 1-Biro-c | 4.00 | 12.00 | 28.00 |
| 2 | 2.00 | 6.00 | 14.00 |
| 3-10 | 1.50 | 4.50 | 10.00 |
| 11-19 | 1.15 | 3.50 | 8.00 |
| 20-Frazetta 1 pg. ad | 1.30 | 4.00 | 9.00 |
| 21-38,40,41 | .85 | 2.50 | 6.00 |
| 39-Story narrated by Frank Sinatra | 2.00 | 6.00 | 14.00 |

NOTE: ***Briefer*** *a-6, 21.* ***Fuje*** *a-4, 16; c-many.* ***Guardineer*** *a-1.* ***Kinstler*** *c-41.* ***Tuska*** *a-6. Painted-c 2-18. Photo-c 19-22, 26-28.*

**LOVE SCANDALS**
Feb, 1950 - No. 5, Oct, 1950 (Photo-c #2-5) (All 52 pgs.)
Quality Comics Group

| | Good | Fine | N-Mint |
|---|---|---|---|
| 1-Ward-c/a, 9 pgs. | 11.50 | 34.00 | 80.00 |
| 2,3: 2-Gustavson-a | 4.00 | 12.00 | 28.00 |
| 4-Ward-a, 18 pgs; Gil Fox-a | 10.00 | 30.00 | 70.00 |
| 5-C. Cuidera-a; tomboy story 'I Hated Being a Woman' | 4.00 | 12.00 | 28.00 |

**LOVE SECRETS** (Formerly Love Letters #31)
No. 32, Aug, 1953 - No. 56, Dec, 1956
Quality Comics Group

| | Good | Fine | N-Mint |
|---|---|---|---|
| 32 | 3.00 | 9.00 | 21.00 |
| 33,35-39 | 1.50 | 4.50 | 10.00 |
| 34-Ward-a | 3.75 | 11.25 | 26.00 |
| 40-Matt Baker-c | 2.50 | 7.50 | 17.00 |
| 41-43: 43-Last precode (3/55) | 1.30 | 4.00 | 9.00 |
| 44,47-50,53,54 | 1.00 | 3.00 | 7.00 |
| 45,46-Ward-a. 46-Baker-a | 2.85 | 8.50 | 20.00 |
| 51,52-Ward(r). 52-r/Love Confessions #17 | 1.65 | 5.00 | 11.50 |
| 55,56-Baker-a; cover-#56 | 1.65 | 5.00 | 11.50 |

**LOVE SECRETS**
Oct, 1949 - No. 2, Jan, 1950 (52 pgs., photo-c)
Marvel Comics(IPC)

| | Good | Fine | N-Mint |
|---|---|---|---|
| 1 | 4.30 | 13.00 | 30.00 |
| 2 | 3.00 | 9.00 | 21.00 |

**LOVE STORIES**
No. 6, 1950 - No. 12, 1951
Fox Feature Syndicate

| | Good | Fine | N-Mint |
|---|---|---|---|
| 6,8-Wood-a | 9.00 | 27.00 | 62.00 |
| 7,9-12 | 3.15 | 9.50 | 22.00 |

**LOVE STORIES** (Formerly Heart Throbs)
No. 147, Nov, 1972 - No. 152, Oct-Nov, 1973
National Periodical Publications

| | Good | Fine | N-Mint |
|---|---|---|---|
| 147-152 | .35 | 1.00 | 2.00 |

**LOVE STORIES OF MARY WORTH** (See Harvey Comics Hits #55 & Mary Worth)
Sept, 1949 - No. 5, May, 1950
Harvey Publications

| | Good | Fine | N-Mint |
|---|---|---|---|
| 1-1940's newspaper reprints-#1-4 | 3.50 | 10.50 | 24.00 |
| 2 | 2.50 | 7.50 | 17.00 |
| 3-5: 3-Kamen/Baker-a? | 2.35 | 7.00 | 16.00 |

**LOVE TALES** (Formerly The Human Torch #35)
No. 36, 5/49 - No. 58, 8/52; No. 59, date? - No. 75, Sept, 1957
Marvel/Atlas Comics (ZPC No. 36-50/MMC No. 67-75)

| | Good | Fine | N-Mint |
|---|---|---|---|
| 36-Photo-c | 4.30 | 13.00 | 30.00 |
| 37 | 2.15 | 6.50 | 15.00 |
| 38-44,46-50: 40,41-Photo-c | 1.50 | 4.50 | 10.00 |
| 45-Powell-a | 1.70 | 5.00 | 12.00 |
| 51,69-Everett-a | 2.30 | 7.00 | 16.00 |
| 52-Krigstein-a | 2.65 | 8.00 | 18.00 |
| 53-60: 60-Last pre-code (2/55) | 1.15 | 3.50 | 8.00 |
| 61-68,70-75 | .85 | 2.60 | 6.00 |

**LOVE THRILLS** (See Fox Giants)

**LOVE TRAILS**
Dec, 1949 - No. 2, Mar, 1950 (52 pgs.)
A Lover's Magazine (CDS)(Marvel)

| | Good | Fine | N-Mint |
|---|---|---|---|
| 1,2: 1-Photo-c | 4.30 | 13.00 | 30.00 |

**LOWELL THOMAS' HIGH ADVENTURE** (See 4-Color #949, 1001)

**LT.** (See Lieutenant)

**LUCKY COMICS**
Jan, 1944; No. 2, Summer, 1945 - No. 5, Summer, 1946
Consolidated Magazines

| | Good | Fine | N-Mint |
|---|---|---|---|
| 1-Lucky Starr, Bobbie | 8.00 | 24.00 | 56.00 |
| 2-5 | 4.00 | 12.00 | 28.00 |

**LUCKY DUCK**
No. 5, Jan, 1953 - No. 8, Sept, 1953
Standard Comics (Literary Ent.)

| | Good | Fine | N-Mint |
|---|---|---|---|
| 5-Irving Spector-a | 3.70 | 11.00 | 26.00 |
| 6-8-Irving Spector-a | 2.65 | 8.00 | 18.00 |

**LUCKY FIGHTS IT THROUGH** (Also see The K. O. Punch)
1949 (16 pgs. in color; paper cover) (Giveaway)
Educational Comics

| | Good | Fine | N-Mint |
|---|---|---|---|
| nn-(Very Rare)-1st Kurtzman work for E. C.; V.D. prevention | 142.00 | 425.00 | 1000.00 |

(Prices vary widely on this book)

NOTE: *Subtitled "The Story of That Ignorant, Ignorant Cowboy" Prepared for Communications Materials Center, Columbia University.*

**LUCKY "7" COMICS**
1944 (No date listed)
Howard Publishers Ltd.

| | Good | Fine | N-Mint |
|---|---|---|---|
| 1-Congo Raider, Punch Powers; bondage-c | 13.00 | 40.00 | 90.00 |

**LUCKY STAR** (Western)
1950 - No. 7, 1951; No. 8, 1953 - No. 14, 1955 (5x7¼"; full color)
Nation Wide Publ. Co.

| | Good | Fine | N-Mint |
|---|---|---|---|
| 1-Jack Davis-a; 52 pgs., 5 cents | 5.70 | 17.00 | 40.00 |
| 2,3-(52 pgs.)-Davis-a | 4.00 | 12.00 | 28.00 |
| 4-7-(52 pgs.)-Davis-a | 3.50 | 10.50 | 24.00 |
| 8-14-(36 pgs.) | 2.00 | 6.00 | 14.00 |
| Given away with Lucky Star Western Wear by the Juvenile Mfg. Co. | 2.00 | 6.00 | 14.00 |

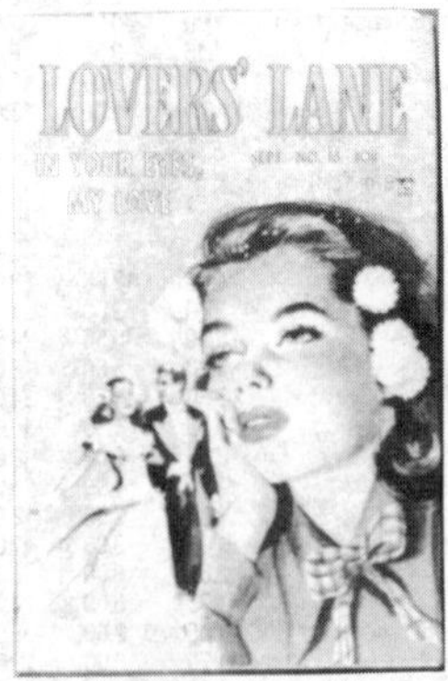

*Lovers' Lane #16, © LEV*

*Love Secrets #36, © QUA*

*Lucky Duck #6, © STD*

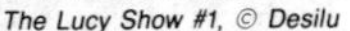
*The Lucy Show #1,* © *Desilu*

*Machine Man #4 (1978),* © *MEG*

*Mad #9,* © *WMG*

**LUCY SHOW, THE** (TV) (Also see I Love Lucy)
June, 1963 - No. 5, June, 1964 (Photo-c: 1,2)
Gold Key

| | Good | Fine | N-Mint |
|---|---|---|---|
| 1 | 6.50 | 19.00 | 45.00 |
| 2 | 4.30 | 13.00 | 30.00 |
| 3-5: Photo back-c,1,2,4,5 | 3.70 | 11.00 | 26.00 |

**LUCY, THE REAL GONE GAL** (Meet Miss Pepper #5 on)
June, 1953 - No. 4, Dec, 1953
St. John Publishing Co.

| | | | |
|---|---|---|---|
| 1-Negligee panels | 4.30 | 13.00 | 30.00 |
| 2 | 2.30 | 7.00 | 16.00 |
| 3,4: 3-Drucker-a | 2.00 | 6.00 | 14.00 |

**LUDWIG BEMELMAN'S MADELEINE & GENEVIEVE** (See 4-Color #796)

**LUDWIG VON DRAKE** (TV)(Disney)(See Walt Disney's C&S #256)
Nov-Dec, 1961 - No. 4, June-Aug, 1962
Dell Publishing Co.

| | | | |
|---|---|---|---|
| 1 | 2.00 | 6.00 | 14.00 |
| 2-4 | 1.30 | 4.00 | 9.00 |
| ...Fish Stampede (1962, Fritos giveaway)-16 pgs., 3¼x7", soft-c; also see Donald Duck & Mickey Mouse | 2.00 | 6.00 | 14.00 |

**LUGER**
Oct, 1986 - No. 3, Feb, 1987 ($1.75, color, mini-series, Baxter paper)
Eclipse Comics

| | | | |
|---|---|---|---|
| 1-3: Bruce Jones scripts; Yeates-c/a | .30 | .90 | 1.80 |

**LUKE CAGE** (See Hero for Hire)

**LUKE SHORT'S WESTERN STORIES**
No. 580, Aug, 1954 - No. 927, Aug, 1958
Dell Publishing Co.

| | | | |
|---|---|---|---|
| 4-Color 580(8/54) | 2.30 | 7.00 | 16.00 |
| 4-Color 651(9/55)-Kinstler-a | 3.00 | 9.00 | 21.00 |
| 4-Color 739,771,807,875,927 | 2.30 | 7.00 | 16.00 |
| 4-Color 848 | 3.00 | 9.00 | 21.00 |

**LUM**
1989 - No. 7? ($2.95, B&W, squarebound, 52 pgs.)
Viz Select Comics

| | | | |
|---|---|---|---|
| 1-6: Japanese manga | .50 | 1.50 | 3.00 |
| 7 ($3.25, 60 pgs.) | .55 | 1.65 | 3.30 |

**LUNATIC FRINGE, THE**
July, 1989 - No. 2, 1989 ($1.75, color, deluxe format)
Innovation Publishing

| | | | |
|---|---|---|---|
| 1,2 | .30 | .90 | 1.80 |

**LUNATICKLE** (Magazine) (Satire)
Feb, 1956 - No. 2, Apr, 1956
Whitstone Publ.

| | | | |
|---|---|---|---|
| 1,2-Kubert-a | 1.50 | 4.50 | 10.00 |

**LYNDON B. JOHNSON**
March, 1965
Dell Publishing Co.

| | | | |
|---|---|---|---|
| 12-445-503-Photo-c | 1.70 | 5.00 | 12.00 |

**M**
1990 - No. 4, 1991 ($4.95, color, 52 pgs.)
Eclipse Books

| | | | |
|---|---|---|---|
| 1-Adapts movie; contains flexi-disc ($5.95) | 1.00 | 3.00 | 6.00 |
| 2-4 | .85 | 2.50 | 5.00 |

**MACHINE MAN** (Also see 2001, A Space Odyssey)
Apr, 1978 - No. 9, Dec, 1978; No. 10, Aug, 1979 - No. 19, Feb, 1981
Marvel Comics Group

| | Good | Fine | N-Mint |
|---|---|---|---|
| 1 | .35 | 1.00 | 2.00 |
| 2-17,19: 19-Intro Jack O'Lantern | | .50 | 1.00 |
| 18-Wendigo, Alpha Flight-ties into X-Men #140 | .85 | 2.50 | 5.00 |

NOTE: ***Austin*** *c-7i, 19i.* ***Buckler*** *c-17p, 18p.* ***Byrne*** *c-14p.* ***Ditko*** *a-10-19; c-10-13, 14i, 15, 16.* ***Kirby*** *a-1-9p; c-1-5, 7-9p.* ***Layton*** *c-7i.* ***Miller*** *c-19p.* ***Simonson*** *c-6.*

**MACHINE MAN**
Oct, 1984 - No. 4, Jan, 1985 (Limited-series)
Marvel Comics Group

| | | | |
|---|---|---|---|
| 1-Barry Smith-c/a(p) in all | .25 | .75 | 1.50 |
| 2-4 | | .60 | 1.20 |

**MACKENZIE'S RAIDERS** (See 4-Color #1093)

**MACO TOYS COMIC**
1959 (36 pages; full color) (Giveaway)
Maco Toys/Charlton Comics

| | | | |
|---|---|---|---|
| 1-All military stories featuring Maco Toys | 1.00 | 3.00 | 6.00 |

**MACROSS** (Robotech: The Macross Saga #2 on)
Dec, 1984 ($1.50)
Comico

| | | | |
|---|---|---|---|
| 1 | 2.50 | 7.50 | 15.00 |

**MAD**
Oct-Nov, 1952 - Present (No. 24 on are magazine format)
(Kurtzman editor No. 1-28, Feldstein No. 29 - No. ?)
E. C. Comics

| | | | |
|---|---|---|---|
| 1-Wood, Davis, Elder start as regulars | 107.00 | 321.00 | 750.00 |
| 2-Davis-c | 47.00 | 140.00 | 325.00 |
| 3,4: 4-Reefer mention story "Flob Was a Slob" by Davis | 30.00 | 90.00 | 210.00 |
| 5-Low distribution; Elder-c | 52.00 | 155.00 | 365.00 |
| 6-11: 11-Wolverton-a | 22.00 | 65.00 | 150.00 |
| 12-15 | 20.00 | 60.00 | 140.00 |
| 16-23(5/55): 21-1st app. Alfred E. Neuman on-c in fake ad. 22-all by Elder. 23-Special cancel announcement | 15.00 | 45.00 | 105.00 |
| 24(7/55)-1st magazine issue (25 cents); Kurtzman logo & border on-c | 31.00 | 95.00 | 220.00 |
| 25-Jaffee starts as regular writer | 16.00 | 48.00 | 110.00 |
| 26,27: 27-Davis-c; Jaffee starts as story artist; new logo | 12.00 | 36.00 | 85.00 |
| 28-Elder-c; Heath back-c; last issue edited by Kurtzman; (three cover variations exist with different wording on contents banner on lower right of cover; value of each the same) | 10.00 | 30.00 | 70.00 |
| 29-Wood-c; Kamen-a; Don Martin starts as regular; Feldstein editing begins | 10.00 | 30.00 | 70.00 |
| 30-1st A. E. Neuman cover by Mingo; Crandall inside-c; last Elder-a; Bob Clarke starts as regular; Disneyland spoof | 13.00 | 40.00 | 90.00 |
| 31-Freas starts as regular; last Davis art until #99 | 8.50 | 25.50 | 60.00 |
| 32,33: 32-Orlando, Drucker, Woodbridge start as regulars; Wood back-c. 33-Orlando back-c | 8.00 | 24.00 | 55.00 |
| 34-Berg starts as regular | 7.00 | 21.00 | 50.00 |
| 35-Mingo wraparound-c; Crandall-a | 7.00 | 21.00 | 50.00 |
| 36-40 | 5.00 | 15.00 | 35.00 |
| 41-50 | 3.50 | 10.50 | 24.00 |
| 51-60: 60-Two Clarke-c; Prohias starts as reg. | 2.65 | 8.00 | 18.00 |
| 61-70: 64-Rickard starts as regular. 68-Martin-c | 2.00 | 6.00 | 14.00 |
| 71-80: 76-Aragones starts as regular | 1.70 | 5.00 | 12.00 |
| 81-90: 86-1st Fold-in. 89-One strip by Walt Kelly. 90-Frazetta back-c; Beatles app. | 1.50 | 4.50 | 10.00 |
| 91-100: 91-Jaffee starts as story artist. 99-Davis-a resumes | 1.15 | 3.50 | 8.00 |
| 101-120: 101-Infinity-c. 105-Batman TV show take-off. 106-Frazetta back-c | .85 | 2.60 | 6.00 |
| 121-140: 121-Beatles app. 122-Ronald Reagan photo inside; Drucker & Mingo-c. 128-Last Orlando. 130-Torres begins as reg. 131-Reagan photo back-c. 135,139-Davis-c | .70 | 2.00 | 4.00 |

Good Fine N-Mint

141-170: 165-Martin-c. 169-Drucker-c .40 1.25 2.50

171-200: 173,178-Davis-c. 176-Drucker-c. 182-Bob Jones starts as regular. 186-Star Trek take-off. 187-Harry North starts as regular. 196-Star Wars take-off .35 1.00 2.00

201-300: 203-Star Wars take-off. 204-Hulk TV show take-off. 208-Superman movie take-off. 286-Drucker-c. 289-Batman movie parody. 291-TMNT parody .25 .75 1.50

NOTE: ***Aragones*** *c-293.* ***Davis*** *c-178, 212, 296.* ***Drucker*** *c-286, 297, 299.* ***Jules Feiffer*** *a(r)-42.* ***Freas****-most-c and back covers-40-74.* ***Heath*** *a-14, 27.* ***Kamen*** *a-29.* ***Krigstein*** *a-12, 17, 24, 26.* ***Kurtzman*** *c-1, 3, 4, 6-10, 13, 14, 16, 18.* ***Mingo*** *c-30-37, 75-111, 171, 172, 175, 209, 211, 218.* ***John Severin*** *a-1-6, 9, 10.* ***Wolverton*** *c-11; a-11, 17, 29, 31, 36, 40, 82, 137.* ***Wood*** *a-24-45, 59; c-26, 29.* ***Woodbridge*** *a-43.*

**MAD** (See . . . Follies, . . . Special, More Trash from . . ., and The Worst from . . .)

**MAD ABOUT MILLIE** (Also see Millie the Model)
April, 1969 - No. 17, Dec, 1970
Marvel Comics Group

1-Giant issue 1.50 4.50 10.00
2-17: 16,17-r .85 2.60 6.00
Annual 1(11/71) .70 2.00 4.00

**MADAME XANADU**
July, 1981 ($1.00, no ads, 36 pgs.)
DC Comics

1-Marshall Rogers-a(25 pgs.); Kaluta-c/a(2 pgs.); pin-up of Madame Xanadu .50 1.00

**MADBALLS**
Sept, 1986 - No. 3, Nov, 1986; No. 4, June, 1987 - No. 10, June, 1988
Star Comics/Marvel Comics #9 on

1-10: Based on toys. 9-Post-a .50 1.00

**MAD FOLLIES** (Special)
1963 - No. 7, 1969
E. C. Comics

nn(1963)-Paperback book covers 9.00 27.00 62.00
2(1964)-Calendar 5.70 17.00 40.00
3(1965)-Mischief Stickers 4.30 13.00 30.00
4(1966)-Mobile; Frazetta-r/back-c Mad #90 5.00 15.00 35.00
5(1967)-Stencils 4.00 12.00 28.00
6(1968)-Mischief Stickers 2.65 8.00 18.00
7(1969)-Nasty Cards 2.65 8.00 18.00

NOTE: ***Clarke*** *c-4.* ***Frazetta*** *r-4, 6 (1 pg. ea.).* ***Mingo*** *c-1-3.* ***Orlando*** *a-5.*

**MAD HATTER, THE** (Costume Hero)
Jan-Feb, 1946; No. 2, Sept-Oct, 1946
O. W. Comics Corp.

1-Freddy the Firefly begins; Giunta-c/a 23.00 70.00 160.00
2-Has ad for E.C.'s Animal Fables #1 16.50 50.00 115.00

**MADHOUSE**
3-4/54 - No. 4, 9-10/54; 6/57 - No. 4, Dec?, 1957
Ajax/Farrell Publ. (Excellent Publ./4-Star)

1(1954) 11.00 32.00 75.00
2,3 5.70 17.00 40.00
4-Surrealistic-c 9.30 28.00 65.00
1(1957, 2nd series) 4.00 12.00 28.00
2-4 2.65 8.00 18.00

**MAD HOUSE** (Formerly Madhouse Glads; . . . Comics #104? on)
No. 95, 9/74 - No. 97, 1/75; No. 98, 8/75 - No. 130, 10/82
Red Circle Productions/Archie Publications

95,96-Horror stories through #97 .35 1.00 2.00
97-Intro. Henry Hobson; Morrow, Thorne-a .50 1.00
98-130-Satire/humor stories .50 1.00
Annual 8(1970-71)- 12(1974-75)-Formerly Madhouse Ma-ad Annual. 11-Wood-a(r) .25 .75 1.50

Good Fine N-Mint

. . . Comics Digest 1(1975-76)- 8(8/82)(. . . Mag. #5 on) .35 1.00 2.00

NOTE: ***B. Jones*** *a-96.* ***McWilliams*** *a-97.* ***Morrow*** *a-96; c-95-97.* ***Wildey*** *a-95, 96. See Archie Comics Digest #1, 13.*

**MADHOUSE GLADS** (Formerly . . . Ma-ad; Madhouse #95 on)
No. 73, May, 1970 - No. 94, Aug, 1974 (No. 78-92: 52 pgs.)
Archie Publications

73 .50 1.50 3.00
74-94 .35 1.00 2.00

**MADHOUSE MA-AD** (. . . Jokes #67-70; . . . Freak-Out #71-74)
(Formerly Archie's Madhouse) (Becomes Madhouse Glads #75 on)
No. 67, April, 1969 - No. 72, Jan, 1970
Archie Publications

67-72 .50 1.50 3.00
. . . Annual 7(1969-70)-Formerly Archie's Madhouse Annual; becomes Madhouse Annual .50 1.50 3.00

**MAD MONSTER PARTY** (See Movie Classics)

**MAD SPECIAL** (. . . Super Special)
Fall, 1970 - Present (84 - 116 pages)
E. C. Publications, Inc.

Fall 1970(#1)-Bonus-Voodoo Doll; contains 17 pgs. new material 3.50 10.50 24.00
Spring 1971(#2)-Wall Nuts; 17 pgs. new material 2.30 7.00 16.00
3-Protest Stickers 2.30 7.00 16.00
4-8: 4-Mini Posters. 5-Mad Flag. 7-Presidential candidate posters, Wild Shocking Message posters. 8-TV Guise 1.70 5.00 12.00
9(1972)-Contains Nostalgic Mad #1 (28pp) 1.50 4.50 10.00
10,11,13: 10-Nonsense Stickers (Don Martin). 11-33⅓ RPM record. 13-Sickie Stickers; 3 pgs. new Wolverton 1.50 4.50 10.00
12-Contains Nostalgic Mad #2 (36 pgs.); Davis, Wolverton-a 1.50 4.50 10.00
14-Vital Message posters & Art Depreciation paintings 1.15 3.50 8.00
15-Contains Nostalgic Mad #3 (28 pgs.) 1.50 4.50 10.00
16,17,19,20: 16-Mad-hesive Stickers. 17-Don Martin posters. 20-Martin Stickers 1.00 3.00 7.00
18-Contains Nostalgic Mad #4 (36 pgs.) 1.15 3.50 8.00
21,24-Contains Nostalgic Mad #5 (28 pgs.) & #6 (28 pgs.) 1.15 3.50 8.00
22,23,25-27,29,30: 22-Diplomas. 23-Martin Stickers. 25-Martin Posters 26-33⅓ RPM record. 27-Mad Shock-Sticks. 29-Mad Collectable-Correctables Posters. 30-The Movies .55 1.65 4.00
28-Contains Nostalgic Mad #7 (36 pgs.) .75 2.25 5.00
31,33-60 .55 1.65 4.00
32-Contains Nostalgic Mad #8 .85 2.50 6.00
61-74: 71-Batman parodies-r by Wood, Drucker .50 1.50 3.00

NOTE: *#28-30 have no number on cover.* ***Mingo*** *c-9, 11, 15, 19, 23.*

**MAGE** (The Hero Discovered . . .; also see Grendel)
Feb, 1984 (no month) - #15, Dec, 1986 ($1.50; 36 pgs; Mando paper)
Comico

1-Violence; Comico's 1st color comic 2.15 6.50 13.00
2 1.70 5.00 10.00
3-5: 3-Intro Edsel 1.00 3.00 6.00
6-Grendel begins (1st in color) 3.35 10.00 20.00
7-1st new Grendel story 1.50 4.50 9.00
8-14: 13-Grendel dies. 14-Grendel ends .70 2.00 4.00
15-$2.95, Double size w/pullout poster .85 2.50 5.00

**MAGIC AGENT** (See Forbidden Worlds & Unknown Worlds)
Jan-Feb, 1962 - No. 3, May-June, 1962
American Comics Group

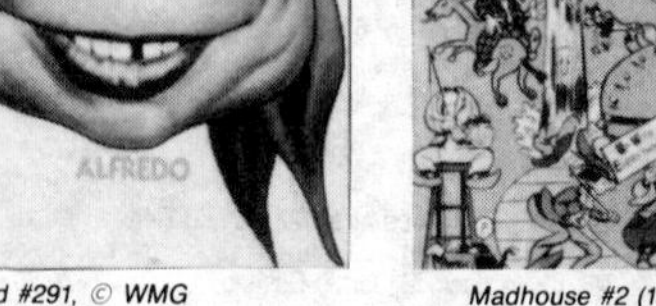

*Mad #291, © WMG*

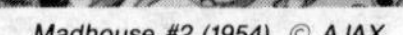

*Madhouse #2 (1954), © AJAX*

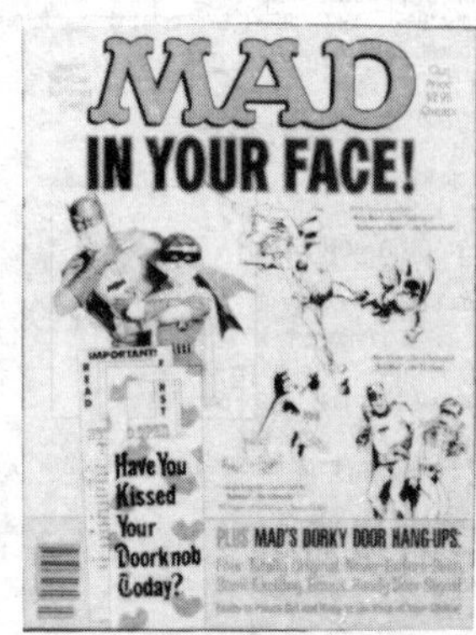


*Mad Super Special #71, © WMG*

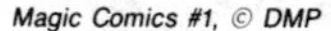
*Magic Comics #1, © DMP*

*Magnus, Robot Fighter #4, © GK*

*Malu in the Land of Adventure #1, © I.W.*

| | Good | Fine | N-Mint |
|---|---|---|---|
| 1-Origin & 1st app. John Force | 1.70 | 5.00 | 12.00 |
| 2,3 | .85 | 2.60 | 6.00 |

**MAGIC COMICS**
Aug, 1939 - No. 123, Nov-Dec, 1949
David McKay Publications

| | Good | Fine | N-Mint |
|---|---|---|---|
| 1-Mandrake the Magician, Henry, Popeye (not by Segar), Blondie, Barney Baxter, Secret Agent X-9 (not by Raymond), Bunky by Billy DeBeck & Thornton Burgess text stories illustrated by Harrison Cady begin | 117.00 | 291.00 | 700.00 |
| 2 | 47.00 | 141.00 | 330.00 |
| 3 | 36.00 | 107.00 | 250.00 |
| 4 | 30.00 | 90.00 | 210.00 |
| 5 | 24.00 | 73.00 | 170.00 |
| 6-10 | 19.00 | 58.00 | 135.00 |
| 11-16,18-20 | 16.00 | 48.00 | 110.00 |
| 17-The Lone Ranger begins | 17.00 | 51.00 | 120.00 |
| 21-30 | 11.00 | 32.00 | 75.00 |
| 31-40 | 8.50 | 25.50 | 60.00 |
| 41-50 | 7.00 | 21.00 | 50.00 |
| 51-60 | 5.30 | 16.00 | 38.00 |
| 61-70 | 4.00 | 12.00 | 28.00 |
| 71-99 | 3.15 | 9.50 | 22.00 |
| 100 | 4.00 | 12.00 | 28.00 |
| 101-106,109-123 | 2.65 | 8.00 | 18.00 |
| 107,108-Flash Gordon app; not by Raymond | 3.70 | 11.00 | 26.00 |

**MAGICA DE SPELL** (See Walt Disney Showcase #30)

**MAGIC FLUTE, THE**
1990 - No. 3, 1990 ($4.95, color, squarebound, 52 pgs.)
Eclipse Books

| | Good | Fine | N-Mint |
|---|---|---|---|
| 1-3: P. Craig Russell-c/a (Night Music #9-11) | .85 | 2.50 | 5.00 |

**MAGIC OF CHRISTMAS AT NEWBERRYS, THE**
1967 (20 pgs.; slick cover; B&W inside)
E. S. London (Giveaway)

| | Good | Fine | N-Mint |
|---|---|---|---|
| nn | .35 | 1.00 | 2.00 |

**MAGIC SWORD, THE** (See Movie Classics)

**MAGIK** (Illyana and Storm Limited Series)
Dec, 1983 - No. 4, Mar, 1984 (60 cents, mini-series)
Marvel Comics Group

| | Good | Fine | N-Mint |
|---|---|---|---|
| 1-Characters from X-Men; Inferno begins; X-Men cameo (Buscema pencils 1,2; c-1p | .40 | 1.25 | 2.50 |
| 2-4: 2-Nightcrawler app. & X-Men cameo | .35 | 1.00 | 2.00 |

**MAGILLA GORILLA** (TV)
May, 1964 - No. 10, Dec, 1968 (Hanna-Barbera)
Gold Key

| | Good | Fine | N-Mint |
|---|---|---|---|
| 1 | 3.00 | 9.00 | 21.00 |
| 2-10: 3-Vs. Yogi Bear for President | 1.50 | 4.50 | 10.00 |
| Kite Fun Book ('64, 16 pgs., 5x7¼", soft-c) | 2.00 | 6.00 | 14.00 |

**MAGILLA GORILLA** (TV)(See Spotlight #4)
Nov, 1970 - No. 5, July, 1971 (Hanna-Barbera)
Charlton Comics

| | Good | Fine | N-Mint |
|---|---|---|---|
| 1-5 | .85 | 2.60 | 6.00 |

**MAGNUS, ROBOT FIGHTER** (. . .4000 A.D.)(See Doctor Solar)
Feb, 1963 - No. 46, Jan, 1977 (Painted-covers)
Gold Key

| | Good | Fine | N-Mint |
|---|---|---|---|
| 1-Origin Magnus; Aliens series begins | 10.00 | 30.00 | 70.00 |
| 2,3 | 5.00 | 15.00 | 35.00 |
| 4-10 | 3.50 | 10.50 | 24.00 |
| 11-20 | 2.65 | 8.00 | 18.00 |
| 21,24-28: 22-Origin-r/#1. 28-Aliens ends | 1.70 | 5.00 | 12.00 |
| 22,23-12 cent and 15 cent editions exist | 1.70 | 5.00 | 12.00 |
| 29-46-Reprints | .85 | 2.60 | 6.00 |

NOTE: ***Manning** a-1-22, 29-43(r). **Spiegle** a-23, 44r.*

**MAGNUS ROBOT FIGHTER 4000 A.D.**
1990 - No. 7, 1991 ($7.95, high quality, card stock-c, 96 pgs.)
Valiant Comics

| | Good | Fine | N-Mint |
|---|---|---|---|
| 1-7: Russ Manning-r. 1-Origin-r | 1.35 | 4.00 | 8.00 |

**MAID OF THE MIST** (See American Graphics)

**MAI, THE PSYCHIC GIRL**
May 19, 1987 - No. 28, July, 1989 (Bi-weekly, $1.50, B&W, 44pgs)
Eclipse Comics

| | Good | Fine | N-Mint |
|---|---|---|---|
| 1 | .35 | 1.00 | 2.00 |
| 1,2-2nd print | | .60 | 1.20 |
| 2-10 | .25 | .75 | 1.50 |
| 11-20 | .25 | .70 | 1.40 |
| 21-28 | | .65 | 1.30 |

**MAJOR HOOPLE COMICS** (See Crackajack Funnies)
nd (Jan, 1943)
Nedor Publications

| | Good | Fine | N-Mint |
|---|---|---|---|
| 1-Mary Worth, Phantom Soldier app. by Moldoff | 18.00 | 54.00 | 125.00 |

**MAJOR INAPAK THE SPACE ACE**
1951 (20 pages) (Giveaway)
Magazine Enterprises (Inapac Foods)

| | Good | Fine | N-Mint |
|---|---|---|---|
| 1-Bob Powell-c/a | .25 | .80 | 1.60 |

NOTE: *Many warehouse copies surfaced in 1973.*

**MAJOR VICTORY COMICS** (Also see Dynamic Comics)
1944 - No. 3, Summer, 1945
H. Clay Glover/Service Publ./Harry 'A' Chesler

| | Good | Fine | N-Mint |
|---|---|---|---|
| 1-Origin Major Victory by C. Sultan (reprint from Dynamic #1); Spider Woman 1st app. | 29.00 | 86.00 | 200.00 |
| 2-Dynamic Boy app. | 18.00 | 54.00 | 125.00 |
| 3-Rocket Boy app. | 14.00 | 43.00 | 100.00 |

**MALTESE FALCON** (See Feature Books No. 48)

**MALU IN THE LAND OF ADVENTURE**
1964 (See White Princess of Jungle #2)
I. W. Enterprises

| | Good | Fine | N-Mint |
|---|---|---|---|
| 1-R/Avon's Slave Girl Comics #1; Severin-c | 3.00 | 9.00 | 21.00 |

**MAMMOTH COMICS**
1938 (84 pages) (Black & White, 8½x11½")
Whitman Publishing Co.(K. K. Publications)

| | Good | Fine | N-Mint |
|---|---|---|---|
| 1-Alley Oop, Terry & the Pirates, Dick Tracy, Little Orphan Annie, Wash Tubbs, Moon Mullins, Smilin' Jack, Tailspin Tommy & other reprints | 70.00 | 210.00 | 490.00 |

**MAMMY YOKUM & THE GREAT DOGPATCH MYSTERY**
1951 (Giveaway)
Toby Press

| | Good | Fine | N-Mint |
|---|---|---|---|
| nn-Li'l Abner | 13.00 | 40.00 | 90.00 |

**MAN-BAT** (See Batman Family, Brave & the Bold, & Detective #400)
Dec-Jan, 1975-76 - No. 2, Feb-Mar, 1976; Dec, 1984
National Periodical Publications/DC Comics

| | Good | Fine | N-Mint |
|---|---|---|---|
| 1-Ditko-a(p); Aparo-c; Batman, She-Bat app. | 1.00 | 3.00 | 6.00 |
| 2-Aparo-c | .50 | 1.50 | 3.00 |
| 1 (12/84)-N. Adams-r(3)/Det.(Vs. Batman on-c) | .70 | 2.00 | 4.00 |

**MAN COMICS**
Dec, 1949 - No. 28, Sept, 1953 (#1-6: 52 pgs.)
Marvel/Atlas Comics (NPI)

| | Good | Fine | N-Mint |
|---|---|---|---|
| 1-Tuska-a | 6.50 | 19.50 | 45.00 |
| 2-Tuska-a | 3.15 | 9.50 | 22.00 |

| | Good | Fine | N-Mint |
|---|---|---|---|
| 3-5 | 2.30 | 7.00 | 16.00 |
| 6-8 | 2.00 | 6.00 | 14.00 |
| 9-13,15: 9-Format changes to war | 1.70 | 5.00 | 12.00 |
| 14-Krenkel (3pgs.), Pakula-a | 3.00 | 9.00 | 21.00 |
| 16-21,23-28: 28-Crime issue | 1.50 | 4.50 | 10.00 |
| 22-Krigstein-a, 5 pgs. | 4.00 | 12.00 | 28.00 |

NOTE: ***Berg** a-14, 15, 19. **Colan** a-21. **Everett** a-8, 22; c-22, 25. **Heath** a-11, 17. Kubertish a-by **Bob Brown**-3. **Maneely** c-10, 11. **Robinson** a-10, 14. **Sinnott** a-22, 23. **Tuska** a-14, 23.*

**MANDRAKE THE MAGICIAN** (See Defenders Of The Earth, Feature Books #18, 19, 23, 46, 52, 55, Giant Comic Album, King Comics, Magic Comics, The Phantom #21, Tiny Tot Funnies & Wow Comics, '36)

**MANDRAKE THE MAGICIAN** (See Harvey Comics Hits #53)
Sept, 1966 - No. 10, Nov, 1967 (Also see Four Color #752)
King Comics (All 12 cents)

| | Good | Fine | N-Mint |
|---|---|---|---|
| 1-Begin S.O.S. Phantom, ends #3 | 2.15 | 6.50 | 15.00 |
| 2-5: 4-Girl Phantom app. 5-Flying Saucer-c/story. 5,6-Brick Bradford app. | 1.15 | 3.50 | 8.00 |
| 6,7,9: 7-Origin Lothar. 9-Brick Bradford app. | 1.00 | 3.00 | 7.00 |
| 8-Jeff Jones-a (4 pgs.) | 1.70 | 5.00 | 12.00 |
| 10-Rip Kirby app.; Raymond-a (14 pgs.) | 2.00 | 6.00 | 14.00 |

**MAN FROM ATLANTIS** (TV)
Feb, 1978 - No. 7, Aug, 1978
Marvel Comics Group

| | Good | Fine | N-Mint |
|---|---|---|---|
| 1-(84 pgs.; $1.00)-Sutton-a(p), Buscema-c; origin | | .30 | .60 |
| 2-7 (#1: cast photos & origin Mark Harris inside) | | .25 | .50 |

**MAN FROM PLANET X, THE**
1987 (no price; full color, probably unlicensed)
Planet X Productions

| | Good | Fine | N-Mint |
|---|---|---|---|
| 1-Reprints Fawcett Movie Comic | | .50 | 1.00 |

**MAN FROM U.N.C.L.E., THE** (TV) (Also see The Girl From . . .)
Feb, 1965 - No. 22, April, 1969 (All photo covers)
Gold Key

| | Good | Fine | N-Mint |
|---|---|---|---|
| 1 | 8.50 | 25.50 | 60.00 |
| 2-Photo back c-2-8 | 5.70 | 17.00 | 40.00 |
| 3-10: 7-Jet Dream begins (all new stories) | 3.60 | 11.00 | 25.00 |
| 11-22: 21,22-Reprint #10 & 7 | 2.85 | 8.50 | 20.00 |

**MAN FROM U.N.C.L.E., THE** (TV)
1987 - No. 11? ($1.50/$1.75, B&W)
Entertainment Publishing

| | Good | Fine | N-Mint |
|---|---|---|---|
| 1-7 ($1.50) | .25 | .75 | 1.50 |
| 8-11 ($1.75) | .30 | .90 | 1.80 |

**MAN FROM WELLS FARGO** (TV)
No. 1287, Feb-Apr, 1962 - May-July, 1962 (Photo-c)
Dell Publishing Co.

| | Good | Fine | N-Mint |
|---|---|---|---|
| 4-Color 1287, #01-495-207 | 3.70 | 11.00 | 26.00 |

**MANGLE TANGLE TALES**
1990 ($2.95, color, deluxe format)
Innovation Publishing

| | Good | Fine | N-Mint |
|---|---|---|---|
| 1-Intro by Harlan Ellison | .50 | 1.50 | 3.00 |

**MANHUNT!** (Becomes Red Fox #15 on)
Oct, 1947 - No. 14, 1953
Magazine Enterprises

| | Good | Fine | N-Mint |
|---|---|---|---|
| 1-Red Fox by L. B. Cole, Undercover Girl by Whitney, Space Ace begin; negligee panels | 21.00 | 62.00 | 145.00 |
| 2-Electrocution-c | 15.00 | 45.00 | 105.00 |
| 3-6 | 13.00 | 40.00 | 90.00 |
| 7-9: 7-Space Ace ends. 8-Trail Colt begins (intro/1st app.) by Guardineer | 11.00 | 32.00 | 75.00 |
| 10-G. Ingels-a | 11.00 | 32.00 | 75.00 |
| 11(8/48)-Frazetta-a, 7 pgs.; The Duke, Scotland Yard begin | 19.00 | 57.00 | 132.00 |
| 12 | 8.00 | 24.00 | 55.00 |
| 13(A-1 #63)-Frazetta, r-/Trail Colt #1, 7 pgs. | 17.00 | 51.00 | 120.00 |
| 14(A-1 #77)-Bondage/hypo-c; last L. B. Cole Red Fox; Ingels-a | 11.50 | 34.00 | 80.00 |

NOTE: ***Guardineer** a-1-5; c-8. **Whitney** a-2-14; c-1-6, 10. Red Fox by **L. B. Cole**-#1-14. #15 was advertised but came out as Red Fox #15. Bondage c-6.*

**MANHUNTER** (See Brave & the Bold, Detective Comics, First Issue Special, House of Mystery #143 and Justice League of America)
1984 ($2.50, 76 pgs; high quality paper)
DC Comics

| | Good | Fine | N-Mint |
|---|---|---|---|
| 1-Simonson-c/a(r)/Detective; Batman app. | .50 | 1.50 | 3.00 |

**MANHUNTER**
July, 1988 - No. 24, Apr, 1990 ($1.00, color)
DC Comics

| | Good | Fine | N-Mint |
|---|---|---|---|
| 1-24: 8,9-Flash app. 9-Invasion. 17-Batman-c/story | | .50 | 1.00 |

**MAN IN BLACK** (See Thrill-O-Rama) (Also see All New Comics, Front Page, Green Hornet #31, Strange Story & Tally-Ho Comics)
Sept, 1957 - No. 4, Mar, 1958
Harvey Publications

| | Good | Fine | N-Mint |
|---|---|---|---|
| 1-Bob Powell-c/a | 7.00 | 21.00 | 50.00 |
| 2-4: Powell-c/a | 5.00 | 15.00 | 35.00 |

**MAN IN FLIGHT** (See 4-Color #836)

**MAN IN SPACE** (See Dell Giant #27 & 4-Color #716, 954)

**MAN OF PEACE, POPE PIUS XII**
1950 (See Pope Pius XII . . . & Topix V2#8)
Catechetical Guild

| | Good | Fine | N-Mint |
|---|---|---|---|
| nn-All Powell-a | 3.00 | 9.00 | 21.00 |

**MAN OF STEEL, THE**
1986 (June) - No. 6, 1986 (75 cents, mini-series)
DC Comics

| | Good | Fine | N-Mint |
|---|---|---|---|
| 1 (silver logo)-Byrne-c/a/scripts in all; origin | | .40 | .80 |
| 1-Alternate-c for newsstand sales | .30 | .40 | .80 |
| 1-Distr. to toy stores by So Much Fun | | .40 | .80 |
| 2-6: 2-Intro. Lois Lane, Jimmy Olsen. 3-Intro/origin Magpie; Batman-c/story. 4-Intro. new Lex Luthor | | .40 | .80 |
| . . .The Complete Saga-Contains #1-6, given away in contest | .35 | 1.00 | 2.00 |
| Limited Edition, softcover | 5.00 | 15.00 | 30.00 |

**MAN OF WAR** (See Liberty Guards & Liberty Scouts)
Nov, 1941 - No. 2, Jan, 1942
Centaur Publications

| | Good | Fine | N-Mint |
|---|---|---|---|
| 1-The Fire-Man, Man of War, The Sentinel, Liberty Guards, & Vapo-Man begin; Gustavson-c/a; Flag-c | 86.00 | 257.00 | 600.00 |
| 2-Intro The Ferret; Gustavson-c/a | 72.00 | 215.00 | 500.00 |

**MAN OF WAR**
Aug, 1987 - No. 3, Feb, 1988 ($1.75, color, Baxter paper)
Eclipse Comics

| | Good | Fine | N-Mint |
|---|---|---|---|
| 1-3: Bruce Jones scripts | .30 | .90 | 1.80 |

**MAN O' MARS**
1953; 1964
Fiction House Magazines

| | Good | Fine | N-Mint |
|---|---|---|---|
| 1-Space Rangers | 18.00 | 54.00 | 125.00 |
| I.W. Reprint #1/Man O'Mars #1; Murphy Anderson-a | 3.00 | 9.00 | 21.00 |

**MANTECH ROBOT WARRIORS**
Sept, 1984 - No. 4, April, 1985 (75 cents, color)
Archie Enterprises, Inc.

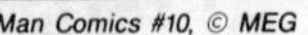
*Man Comics #10, © MEG*

*Manhunt! #9, © ME*

*Manhunter #17, © DC*

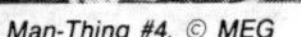
Man-Thing #4, © MEG

The Many Ghosts of Doctor Graves #2, © CC

March of Comics #35, © Roy Rogers

| | Good | Fine | N-Mint |
|---|---|---|---|
| 1-4: Ayers-c/a(p). 1-Buckler-c(i) | | .40 | .80 |

**MAN-THING** (See Fear, Giant-Size. . ., Marvel Comics Presents, Marvel Fanfare, Monsters Unleashed, Power Record Comics & Savage Tales)
Jan, 1974 - No. 22, Oct, 1975; V2#1, Nov, 1979 - V2#11, July, 1981
Marvel Comics Group

| | Good | Fine | N-Mint |
|---|---|---|---|
| 1-Howard the Duck(2nd app.) cont./Fear #19 | 1.30 | 4.00 | 9.00 |
| 2 | .70 | 2.00 | 4.00 |
| 3-1st app. original Foolkiller | .85 | 2.50 | 5.00 |
| 4-Origin Foolkiller | .35 | 1.00 | 2.00 |
| 5-11-Ploog-a | .35 | 1.00 | 2.00 |
| 12-22: 19-1st app. Scavenger. 20-Spidey cameo. 21-Origin Scavenger, Man-Thing. 22-Howard the Duck cameo | | .50 | 1.00 |
| V2#1(1979) - 11: 6-Golden-c | | .50 | 1.00 |

NOTE: ***Alcala*** *a-14.* ***Brunner*** *c-1.* ***J. Buscema*** *a-12p, 13p, 16p.* ***Gil Kane*** *c-4p, 10p, 12-20p, 21.* ***Mooney*** *a-17, 18, 19p, 20-22, V2#1-3p.* ***Ploog*** *Man-Thing-5p, 6p, 7, 8, 9-11p; c-5, 6, 8, 9, 11.* ***Sutton*** *a-13i.*

**MAN WITH THE X-RAY EYES, THE** (See X,. . . under Movie Comics)

**MANY GHOSTS OF DR. GRAVES, THE** (Doctor Graves #73 on)
5/67 - No. 60, 12/76; No. 61, 9/77 - No. 62, 10/77; No. 63, 2/78 - No. 65, 4/78; No. 66, 6/81 - No. 72, 5/82
Charlton Comics

| | Good | Fine | N-Mint |
|---|---|---|---|
| 1-Early issues 12 cent-c | .70 | 2.00 | 4.00 |
| 2-10 | .30 | 1.00 | 2.00 |
| 11-20 | .25 | .75 | 1.50 |
| 21-44,46-72: 47,49-Newton-a | | .40 | .80 |
| 45-1st Newton comic book work, 8pgs. | .35 | 1.00 | 2.00 |
| Modern Comics Reprint 12,25 ('78) | | .20 | .40 |

NOTE: ***Aparo*** *a-66r, 69r; c-66, 67.* ***Byrne*** *c-54.* ***Ditko*** *a-1, 7, 9, 11-13, 15-18, 20-22, 24, 26, 27, 35, 37, 38, 40-44, 47, 48, 51-54, 58, 60r-65r, 70, 72; c-11-13, 16-18, 22, 24, 26-35, 38, 40, 55, 58, 62-65.* ***Howard*** *a-45i; c-48.* ***Morisi*** *a-13, 14, 23, 26.* ***Newton*** *a-45, 47p, 49p; c-49, 52.* ***Sutton*** *a-42, 49; c-42.*

**MANY LOVES OF DOBIE GILLIS** (TV)
May-June, 1960 - No. 26, Oct, 1964
National Periodical Publications

| | Good | Fine | N-Mint |
|---|---|---|---|
| 1 | 14.00 | 41.00 | 95.00 |
| 2-5 | 6.50 | 19.50 | 45.00 |
| 6-10 | 5.00 | 15.00 | 35.00 |
| 11-26 | 4.00 | 12.00 | 28.00 |

**MARAUDER'S MOON** (See 4-Color #848)

**MARCH OF COMICS** (Boys' and Girls'. . .#3-353)
1946 - No. 488, Apr, 1982 (#1-4 are not numbered)
(K.K. Giveaway) (Founded by Sig Feuchtwanger)
K. K. Publications/Western Publishing Co.

Early issues were full size, 32 pages, and were printed with and without an extra cover of slick stock, just for the advertiser. The binding was stapled if the slick cover was added; otherwise, the pages were glued together at the spine. Most 1948 - 1951 issues were full size, 24 pages, pulp covers. Starting in 1952 they were half-size and 32 pages with slick covers. 1959 and later issues had only 16 pages plus covers. 1952 -1959 issues read oblong; 1960 and later issues read upright.

| | Good | Fine | N-Mint |
|---|---|---|---|
| 1(nn)(1946)-Goldilocks; Kelly back-c; 16pgs., stapled | 24.00 | 72.00 | 170.00 |
| 2(nn)(1946)-How Santa Got His Red Suit; Kelly-a(11 pgs., r-/4-Color 61)('44); 16pgs., stapled | 24.00 | 72.00 | 170.00 |
| 3(nn)(1947)-Our Gang (Walt Kelly) | 40.00 | 110.00 | 235.00 |
| 4(nn)Donald Duck by Carl Barks, "Maharajah Donald," 28 pgs.; Kelly-c? (Disney) | 500.00 | 1500.00 | 3500.00 |
| 5-Andy Panda | 14.00 | 43.00 | 100.00 |
| 6-Popular Fairy Tales; Kelly-c; Noonan-a(2) | 17.00 | 50.00 | 120.00 |
| 7-Oswald the Rabbit | 17.00 | 50.00 | 120.00 |
| 8-Mickey Mouse, 32 pgs. (Disney) | 50.00 | 150.00 | 330.00 |
| 9(nn)-The Story of the Gloomy Bunny | 8.00 | 24.00 | 56.00 |
| 10-Out of Santa's Bag | 6.75 | 20.00 | 47.00 |
| 11-Fun With Santa Claus | 5.35 | 16.00 | 37.00 |
| 12-Santa's Toys | 5.35 | 16.00 | 37.00 |
| 13-Santa's Surprise | 5.35 | 16.00 | 37.00 |
| 14-Santa's Candy Kitchen | 5.35 | 16.00 | 37.00 |
| 15-Hip-It-Ty Hop & the Big Bass Viol | 5.35 | 16.00 | 37.00 |
| 16-Woody Woodpecker (1947) | 8.50 | 25.00 | 60.00 |
| 17-Roy Rogers (1948) | 20.00 | 60.00 | 140.00 |
| 18-Popular Fairy Tales | 10.00 | 30.00 | 70.00 |
| 19-Uncle Wiggily | 7.50 | 22.50 | 52.00 |
| 20-Donald Duck by Carl Barks, "Darkest Africa," 22 pgs.; Kelly-c (Disney) | 271.00 | 815.00 | 1900.00 |
| 21-Tom and Jerry | 7.50 | 22.50 | 52.00 |
| 22-Andy Panda | 7.50 | 22.50 | 52.00 |
| 23-Raggedy Ann; Kerr-a | 12.00 | 35.00 | 84.00 |
| 24-Felix the Cat, 1932 daily strip reprints by Otto Messmer | 20.00 | 60.00 | 140.00 |
| 25-Gene Autry | 20.00 | 60.00 | 140.00 |
| 26-Our Gang; Walt Kelly | 20.00 | 60.00 | 140.00 |
| 27-Mickey Mouse; r/in M. M. #240 (Disney) | 34.00 | 100.00 | 238.00 |
| 28-Gene Autry | 20.00 | 60.00 | 140.00 |
| 29-Easter Bonnet Shop | 4.00 | 12.00 | 28.00 |
| 30-Here Comes Santa | 3.35 | 10.00 | 22.00 |
| 31-Santa's Busy Corner | 3.35 | 10.00 | 22.00 |
| 32-No book produced | | | |
| 33-A Christmas Carol | 3.35 | 10.00 | 22.00 |
| 34-Woody Woodpecker | 6.50 | 19.50 | 45.00 |
| 35-Roy Rogers (1948) | 19.00 | 57.00 | 135.00 |
| 36-Felix the Cat(1949)-by Messmer; '34 daily strip-r | 15.00 | 45.00 | 105.00 |
| 37-Popeye | 12.50 | 37.50 | 87.00 |
| 38-Oswald the Rabbit | 5.85 | 17.50 | 40.00 |
| 39-Gene Autry | 19.00 | 57.00 | 135.00 |
| 40-Andy and Woody | 5.85 | 17.50 | 40.00 |
| 41-Donald Duck by Carl Barks, "Race to the South Seas," 22 pgs.; Kelly-c; on Disney's reprint banded list | 200.00 | 600.00 | 1400.00 |
| 42-Porky Pig | 5.85 | 17.50 | 40.00 |
| 43-Henry | 3.75 | 11.00 | 26.00 |
| 44-Bugs Bunny | 5.85 | 17.50 | 40.00 |
| 45-Mickey Mouse (Disney) | 27.00 | 80.00 | 190.00 |
| 46-Tom and Jerry | 6.50 | 19.50 | 45.00 |
| 47-Roy Rogers | 17.00 | 51.00 | 120.00 |
| 48-Greetings from Santa | 2.75 | 8.00 | 19.00 |
| 49-Santa Is Here | 2.75 | 8.00 | 19.00 |
| 50-Santa Claus' Workshop (1949) | 2.75 | 8.00 | 19.00 |
| 51-Felix the Cat (1950) by Messmer | 13.00 | 40.00 | 90.00 |
| 52-Popeye | 10.00 | 30.00 | 70.00 |
| 53-Oswald the Rabbit | 5.85 | 17.50 | 40.00 |
| 54-Gene Autry | 16.00 | 48.00 | 110.00 |
| 55-Andy and Woody | 5.00 | 15.00 | 35.00 |
| 56-Donald Duck-not by Barks; Barks art on back-c (Disney) | 22.00 | 65.00 | 140.00 |
| 57-Porky Pig | 5.00 | 15.00 | 35.00 |
| 58-Henry | 3.00 | 9.00 | 21.00 |
| 59-Bugs Bunny | 5.00 | 15.00 | 35.00 |
| 60-Mickey Mouse (Disney) | 18.00 | 55.00 | 125.00 |
| 61-Tom and Jerry | 4.35 | 13.00 | 30.00 |
| 62-Roy Rogers | 16.00 | 48.00 | 110.00 |
| 63-Welcome Santa; ½-size, oblong | 2.75 | 8.00 | 19.00 |
| 64(nn)-Santa's Helpers; ½-size, oblong | 2.75 | 8.00 | 19.00 |
| 65(nn)-Jingle Bells (1950)-½-size, oblong | 2.75 | 8.00 | 19.00 |
| 66-Popeye (1951) | 9.00 | 27.00 | 62.00 |
| 67-Oswald the Rabbit | 4.00 | 12.00 | 28.00 |
| 68-Roy Rogers | 14.00 | 42.00 | 100.00 |
| 69-Donald Duck; Barks-a on back-c (Disney) | 19.00 | 57.00 | 125.00 |
| 70-Tom and Jerry | 4.00 | 12.00 | 28.00 |
| 71-Porky Pig | 4.00 | 12.00 | 28.00 |
| 72-Krazy Kat | 6.00 | 18.00 | 42.00 |

| | Good | Fine | N-Mint |
|---|---|---|---|
| 73-Roy Rogers | 12.00 | 36.00 | 84.00 |
| 74-Mickey Mouse (1951)(Disney) | 14.00 | 42.50 | 96.00 |
| 75-Bugs Bunny | 4.00 | 12.00 | 28.00 |
| 76-Andy and Woody | 4.00 | 12.00 | 28.00 |
| 77-Roy Rogers | 13.00 | 40.00 | 80.00 |
| 78-Gene Autry(1951)-Last regular size issue | 13.00 | 40.00 | 80.00 |
| 79-Andy Panda (1952)-5x7" size | 2.75 | 8.00 | 19.00 |
| 80-Popeye | 8.00 | 24.00 | 56.00 |
| 81-Oswald the Rabbit | 3.00 | 9.00 | 21.00 |
| 82-Tarzan; Lex Barker photo-c | 14.00 | 42.00 | 100.00 |
| 83-Bugs Bunny | 3.00 | 9.00 | 21.00 |
| 84-Henry | 2.35 | 7.00 | 16.00 |
| 85-Woody Woodpecker | 2.35 | 7.00 | 16.00 |
| 86-Roy Rogers | 10.00 | 30.00 | 70.00 |
| 87-Krazy Kat | 4.75 | 14.00 | 33.00 |
| 88-Tom and Jerry | 2.35 | 7.00 | 16.00 |
| 89-Porky Pig | 2.35 | 7.00 | 16.00 |
| 90-Gene Autry | 10.00 | 30.00 | 70.00 |
| 91-Roy Rogers & Santa | 10.00 | 30.00 | 70.00 |
| 92-Christmas with Santa | 2.00 | 6.00 | 14.00 |
| 93-Woody Woodpecker (1953) | 2.35 | 7.00 | 16.00 |
| 94-Indian Chief | 6.50 | 19.50 | 45.00 |
| 95-Oswald the Rabbit | 2.35 | 7.00 | 16.00 |
| 96-Popeye | 7.00 | 20.00 | 50.00 |
| 97-Bugs Bunny | 2.35 | 7.00 | 16.00 |
| 98-Tarzan; Lex Barker photo-c | 14.00 | 42.00 | 100.00 |
| 99-Porky Pig | 2.35 | 7.00 | 16.00 |
| 100-Roy Rogers | 8.00 | 24.00 | 56.00 |
| 101-Henry | 2.00 | 6.00 | 14.00 |
| 102-Tom Corbett (TV)-Painted-c | 11.50 | 34.00 | 80.00 |
| 103-Tom and Jerry | 2.00 | 6.00 | 14.00 |
| 104-Gene Autry | 8.00 | 24.00 | 56.00 |
| 105-Roy Rogers | 8.00 | 24.00 | 56.00 |
| 106-Santa's Helpers | 2.00 | 6.00 | 14.00 |
| 107-Santa's Christmas Book - not published | | | |
| 108-Fun with Santa (1953) | 2.00 | 6.00 | 14.00 |
| 109-Woody Woodpecker (1954) | 2.00 | 6.00 | 14.00 |
| 110-Indian Chief | 3.50 | 10.50 | 24.00 |
| 111-Oswald the Rabbit | 2.00 | 6.00 | 14.00 |
| 112-Henry | 1.70 | 5.00 | 12.00 |
| 113-Porky Pig | 2.00 | 6.00 | 14.00 |
| 114-Tarzan; Russ Manning-a | 14.00 | 42.00 | 100.00 |
| 115-Bugs Bunny | 2.00 | 6.00 | 14.00 |
| 116-Roy Rogers | 8.00 | 24.00 | 56.00 |
| 117-Popeye | 7.00 | 20.00 | 50.00 |
| 118-Flash Gordon-Painted-c | 10.00 | 30.00 | 70.00 |
| 119-Tom and Jerry | 2.00 | 6.00 | 14.00 |
| 120-Gene Autry | 8.00 | 24.00 | 56.00 |
| 121-Roy Rogers | 8.00 | 24.00 | 56.00 |
| 122-Santa's Surprise (1954) | 1.50 | 4.50 | 10.00 |
| 123-Santa's Christmas Book | 1.50 | 4.50 | 10.00 |
| 124-Woody Woodpecker (1955) | 1.70 | 5.00 | 12.00 |
| 125-Tarzan; Lex Barker photo-c | 13.00 | 40.00 | 90.00 |
| 126-Oswald the Rabbit | 1.70 | 5.00 | 12.00 |
| 127-Indian Chief | 3.00 | 9.00 | 21.00 |
| 128-Tom and Jerry | 1.70 | 5.00 | 12.00 |
| 129-Henry | 1.50 | 4.50 | 10.00 |
| 130-Porky Pig | 1.70 | 5.00 | 12.00 |
| 131-Roy Rogers | 8.00 | 24.00 | 56.00 |
| 132-Bugs Bunny | 1.70 | 5.00 | 12.00 |
| 133-Flash Gordon-Painted-c | 8.50 | 25.50 | 60.00 |
| 134-Popeye | 4.00 | 12.00 | 28.00 |
| 135-Gene Autry | 7.00 | 21.00 | 50.00 |
| 136-Roy Rogers | 7.00 | 21.00 | 50.00 |
| 137-Gifts from Santa | 1.35 | 4.00 | 9.00 |
| 138-Fun at Christmas (1955) | 1.35 | 4.00 | 9.00 |

| | Good | Fine | N-Mint |
|---|---|---|---|
| 139-Woody Woodpecker (1956) | 1.70 | 5.00 | 12.00 |
| 140-Indian Chief | 3.00 | 9.00 | 21.00 |
| 141-Oswald the Rabbit | 1.70 | 5.00 | 12.00 |
| 142-Flash Gordon | 8.50 | 25.50 | 60.00 |
| 143-Porky Pig | 1.70 | 5.00 | 12.00 |
| 144-Tarzan; Russ Manning-a; Painted-c | 12.00 | 36.00 | 84.00 |
| 145-Tom and Jerry | 1.70 | 5.00 | 12.00 |
| 146-Roy Rogers-Photo-c | 8.00 | 24.00 | 56.00 |
| 147-Henry | 1.35 | 4.00 | 9.00 |
| 148-Popeye | 4.00 | 12.00 | 28.00 |
| 149-Bugs Bunny | 1.70 | 5.00 | 12.00 |
| 150-Gene Autry | 7.00 | 21.00 | 50.00 |
| 151-Roy Rogers | 7.00 | 21.00 | 50.00 |
| 152-The Night Before Christmas | 1.35 | 4.00 | 9.00 |
| 153-Merry Christmas (1956) | 1.35 | 4.00 | 9.00 |
| 154-Tom and Jerry (1957) | 1.70 | 5.00 | 12.00 |
| 155-Tarzan-Photo-c | 12.00 | 36.00 | 84.00 |
| 156-Oswald the Rabbit | 1.70 | 5.00 | 12.00 |
| 157-Popeye | 3.00 | 9.00 | 21.00 |
| 158-Woody Woodpecker | 1.70 | 5.00 | 12.00 |
| 159-Indian Chief | 3.00 | 9.00 | 21.00 |
| 160-Bugs Bunny | 1.70 | 5.00 | 12.00 |
| 161-Roy Rogers | 5.70 | 17.00 | 40.00 |
| 162-Henry | 1.35 | 4.00 | 9.00 |
| 163-Rin Tin Tin (TV) | 3.50 | 10.50 | 24.00 |
| 164-Porky Pig | 1.70 | 5.00 | 12.00 |
| 165-The Lone Ranger | 6.50 | 19.50 | 45.00 |
| 166-Santa and His Reindeer | 1.35 | 4.00 | 9.00 |
| 167-Roy Rogers and Santa | 5.70 | 17.00 | 40.00 |
| 168-Santa Claus' Workshop (1957) | 1.35 | 4.00 | 9.00 |
| 169-Popeye (1958) | 3.00 | 9.00 | 21.00 |
| 170-Indian Chief | 3.00 | 9.00 | 21.00 |
| 171-Oswald the Rabbit | 1.50 | 4.50 | 10.00 |
| 172-Tarzan | 10.00 | 30.00 | 70.00 |
| 173-Tom and Jerry | 1.50 | 4.50 | 10.00 |
| 174-The Lone Ranger | 6.50 | 19.50 | 45.00 |
| 175-Porky Pig | 1.50 | 4.50 | 10.00 |
| 176-Roy Rogers | 5.50 | 16.50 | 38.00 |
| 177-Woody Woodpecker | 1.50 | 4.50 | 10.00 |
| 178-Henry | 1.35 | 4.00 | 9.00 |
| 179-Bugs Bunny | 1.50 | 4.50 | 10.00 |
| 180-Rin Tin Tin (TV) | 3.00 | 9.00 | 21.00 |
| 181-Happy Holiday | 1.20 | 3.50 | 8.00 |
| 182-Happi Tim | 1.50 | 4.50 | 10.00 |
| 183-Welcome Santa (1958) | 1.20 | 3.50 | 8.00 |
| 184-Woody Woodpecker (1959) | 1.50 | 4.50 | 10.00 |
| 185-Tarzan-Photo-c | 10.00 | 30.00 | 70.00 |
| 186-Oswald the Rabbit | 1.50 | 4.50 | 10.00 |
| 187-Indian Chief | 3.00 | 9.00 | 21.00 |
| 188-Bugs Bunny | 1.50 | 4.50 | 10.00 |
| 189-Henry | 1.20 | 3.50 | 8.00 |
| 190-Tom and Jerry | 1.50 | 4.50 | 10.00 |
| 191-Roy Rogers | 5.50 | 16.50 | 38.00 |
| 192-Porky Pig | 1.50 | 4.50 | 10.00 |
| 193-The Lone Ranger | 6.50 | 19.50 | 45.00 |
| 194-Popeye | 3.00 | 9.00 | 21.00 |
| 195-Rin Tin Tin (TV) | 3.00 | 9.00 | 21.00 |
| 196-Sears Special - not published | | | |
| 197-Santa Is Coming | 1.20 | 3.50 | 8.00 |
| 198-Santa's Helpers (1959) | 1.20 | 3.50 | 8.00 |
| 199-Huckleberry Hound (TV)(1960) | 2.65 | 8.00 | 18.00 |
| 200-Fury (TV) | 3.50 | 10.50 | 24.00 |
| 201-Bugs Bunny | 1.35 | 4.00 | 9.00 |
| 202-Space Explorer | 5.00 | 15.00 | 35.00 |
| 203-Woody Woodpecker | 1.35 | 4.00 | 9.00 |
| 204-Tarzan | 7.00 | 21.00 | 50.00 |

March of Comics #76, © Walter Lantz

March of Comics #102, © WEST

March of Comics #144, © ERB

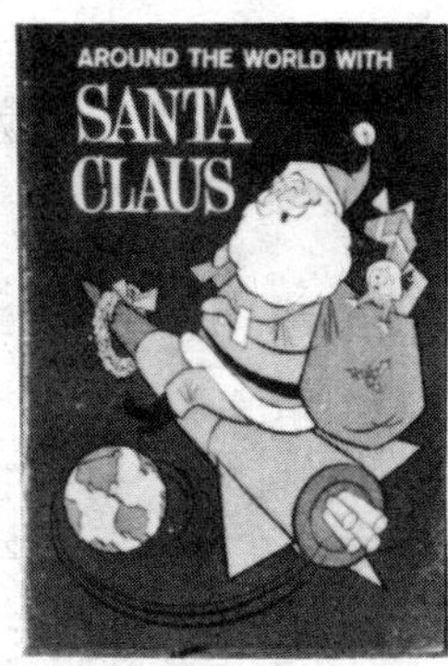

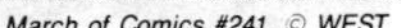
March of Comics #241, © WEST

March of Comics #296, © M.G.M.

March of Comics #315, © Warner Bros.

| | Good | Fine | N-Mint |
|---|---|---|---|
| 205-Mighty Mouse | 3.00 | 9.00 | 21.00 |
| 206-Roy Rogers-Photo-c | 5.50 | 16.50 | 38.00 |
| 207-Tom and Jerry | 1.35 | 4.00 | 9.00 |
| 208-The Lone Ranger-Clayton Moore photo-c | 10.00 | 30.00 | 70.00 |
| 209-Porky Pig | 1.35 | 4.00 | 9.00 |
| 210-Lassie (TV) | 3.00 | 9.00 | 21.00 |
| 211-Sears Special - not published | | | |
| 212-Christmas Eve | 1.20 | 3.50 | 8.00 |
| 213-Here Comes Santa (1960) | 1.20 | 3.50 | 8.00 |
| 214-Huckleberry Hound (TV)(1961) | 2.65 | 8.00 | 18.00 |
| 215-Hi Yo Silver | 4.00 | 12.00 | 28.00 |
| 216-Rocky & His Friends (TV) | 5.00 | 15.00 | 35.00 |
| 217-Lassie (TV) | 2.35 | 7.00 | 16.00 |
| 218-Porky Pig | 1.35 | 4.00 | 9.00 |
| 219-Journey to the Sun | 3.00 | 9.00 | 21.00 |
| 220-Bugs Bunny | 1.35 | 4.00 | 9.00 |
| 221-Roy and Dale-Photo-c | 5.00 | 15.00 | 35.00 |
| 222-Woody Woodpecker | 1.35 | 4.00 | 9.00 |
| 223-Tarzan | 7.00 | 21.00 | 50.00 |
| 224-Tom and Jerry | 1.35 | 4.00 | 9.00 |
| 225-The Lone Ranger | 5.00 | 15.00 | 35.00 |
| 226-Christmas Treasury (1961) | 1.20 | 3.50 | 8.00 |
| 227-Sears Special - not published? | | | |
| 228-Letters to Santa (1961) | 1.20 | 3.50 | 8.00 |
| 229-The Flintstones (TV)(1962) | 5.00 | 15.00 | 35.00 |
| 230-Lassie (TV) | 2.35 | 7.00 | 16.00 |
| 231-Bugs Bunny | 1.20 | 3.50 | 8.00 |
| 232-The Three Stooges | 6.50 | 19.50 | 45.00 |
| 233-Bullwinkle (TV) | 7.00 | 21.00 | 50.00 |
| 234-Smokey the Bear | 1.35 | 4.00 | 9.00 |
| 235-Huckleberry Hound (TV) | 2.65 | 8.00 | 18.00 |
| 236-Roy and Dale | 3.65 | 11.00 | 25.00 |
| 237-Mighty Mouse | 2.30 | 7.00 | 16.00 |
| 238-The Lone Ranger | 5.00 | 15.00 | 35.00 |
| 239-Woody Woodpecker | 1.35 | 4.00 | 9.00 |
| 240-Tarzan | 5.70 | 17.00 | 40.00 |
| 241-Santa Claus Around the World | 1.20 | 3.50 | 8.00 |
| 242-Santa's Toyland (1962) | 1.20 | 3.50 | 8.00 |
| 243-The Flintstones (TV)(1963) | 4.50 | 14.00 | 32.00 |
| 244-Mister Ed (TV)-Photo-c | 3.00 | 9.00 | 21.00 |
| 245-Bugs Bunny | 1.35 | 4.00 | 9.00 |
| 246-Popeye | 2.50 | 7.50 | 17.50 |
| 247-Mighty Mouse | 2.30 | 7.00 | 16.00 |
| 248-The Three Stooges | 6.50 | 19.50 | 45.00 |
| 249-Woody Woodpecker | 1.35 | 4.00 | 9.00 |
| 250-Roy and Dale | 3.65 | 11.00 | 25.00 |
| 251-Little Lulu & Witch Hazel | 13.50 | 41.00 | 95.00 |
| 252-Tarzan-Painted-c | 5.50 | 16.50 | 40.00 |
| 253-Yogi Bear (TV) | 3.00 | 9.00 | 21.00 |
| 254-Lassie (TV) | 2.35 | 7.00 | 16.00 |
| 255-Santa's Christmas List | 1.20 | 3.50 | 8.00 |
| 256-Christmas Party (1963) | 1.20 | 3.50 | 8.00 |
| 257-Mighty Mouse | 2.30 | 7.00 | 16.00 |
| 258-The Sword in the Stone (Disney) | 5.70 | 17.00 | 40.00 |
| 259-Bugs Bunny | 1.35 | 4.00 | 9.00 |
| 260-Mister Ed (TV) | 2.30 | 7.00 | 16.00 |
| 261-Woody Woodpecker | 1.35 | 4.00 | 9.00 |
| 262-Tarzan | 5.50 | 16.50 | 40.00 |
| 263-Donald Duck-not by Barks (Disney) | 6.00 | 18.00 | 36.00 |
| 264-Popeye | 2.50 | 7.50 | 17.50 |
| 265-Yogi Bear (TV) | 2.65 | 8.00 | 18.00 |
| 266-Lassie (TV) | 2.00 | 6.00 | 14.00 |
| 267-Little Lulu; Irving Tripp-a | 11.00 | 32.00 | 75.00 |
| 268-The Three Stooges | 5.70 | 17.00 | 40.00 |
| 269-A Jolly Christmas | 1.20 | 3.50 | 8.00 |
| 270-Santa's Little Helpers | 1.20 | 3.50 | 8.00 |

| | Good | Fine | N-Mint |
|---|---|---|---|
| 271-The Flintstones (TV)(1965) | 4.50 | 14.00 | 32.00 |
| 272-Tarzan | 5.50 | 16.50 | 40.00 |
| 273-Bugs Bunny | 1.35 | 4.00 | 9.00 |
| 274-Popeye | 2.50 | 7.50 | 17.50 |
| 275-Little Lulu-Irving Tripp-a | 9.00 | 27.00 | 62.00 |
| 276-The Jetsons (TV) | 8.00 | 24.00 | 55.00 |
| 277-Daffy Duck | 1.35 | 4.00 | 9.00 |
| 278-Lassie (TV) | 2.00 | 6.00 | 14.00 |
| 279-Yogi Bear (TV) | 2.30 | 7.00 | 16.00 |
| 280-The Three Stooges-Photo-c | 5.70 | 17.00 | 40.00 |
| 281-Tom and Jerry | 1.00 | 3.00 | 7.00 |
| 282-Mister Ed (TV) | 2.30 | 7.00 | 16.00 |
| 283-Santa's Visit | 1.20 | 3.50 | 8.00 |
| 284-Christmas Parade (1965) | 1.20 | 3.50 | 8.00 |
| 285-Astro Boy (TV) | 22.00 | 65.00 | 150.00 |
| 286-Tarzan | 5.00 | 15.00 | 35.00 |
| 287-Bugs Bunny | 1.00 | 3.00 | 7.00 |
| 288-Daffy Duck | 1.00 | 3.00 | 7.00 |
| 289-The Flintstones (TV) | 3.50 | 10.50 | 24.00 |
| 290-Mister Ed (TV)-Photo-c | 2.00 | 6.00 | 14.00 |
| 291-Yogi Bear (TV) | 2.00 | 6.00 | 14.00 |
| 292-The Three Stooges-Photo-c | 5.70 | 17.00 | 40.00 |
| 293-Little Lulu; Irving Tripp-a | 7.00 | 21.00 | 50.00 |
| 294-Popeye | 2.50 | 7.50 | 17.50 |
| 295-Tom and Jerry | .85 | 2.50 | 6.00 |
| 296-Lassie (TV)-Photo-c | 1.70 | 5.00 | 12.00 |
| 297-Christmas Bells | 1.20 | 3.50 | 8.00 |
| 298-Santa's Sleigh (1966) | 1.20 | 3.50 | 8.00 |
| 299-The Flintstones (TV)(1967) | 3.50 | 10.50 | 24.00 |
| 300-Tarzan | 5.00 | 15.00 | 35.00 |
| 301-Bugs Bunny | .85 | 2.50 | 6.00 |
| 302-Laurel and Hardy (TV)-Photo-c | 3.50 | 10.50 | 24.00 |
| 303-Daffy Duck | .70 | 2.00 | 5.00 |
| 304-The Three Stooges-Photo-c | 5.00 | 15.00 | 35.00 |
| 305-Tom and Jerry | .70 | 2.00 | 5.00 |
| 306-Daniel Boone (TV)-Fess Parker photo-c | 3.00 | 9.00 | 21.00 |
| 307-Little Lulu; Irving Tripp-a | 5.70 | 17.00 | 40.00 |
| 308-Lassie (TV)-Photo-c | 1.50 | 4.50 | 10.00 |
| 309-Yogi Bear (TV) | 1.70 | 5.00 | 12.00 |
| 310-The Lone Ranger-Clayton Moore photo-c | 10.00 | 30.00 | 70.00 |
| 311-Santa's Show | 1.00 | 3.00 | 7.00 |
| 312-Christmas Album (1967) | 1.00 | 3.00 | 7.00 |
| 313-Daffy Duck (1968) | .70 | 2.00 | 5.00 |
| 314-Laurel and Hardy (TV) | 3.00 | 9.00 | 21.00 |
| 315-Bugs Bunny | .85 | 2.50 | 6.00 |
| 316-The Three Stooges | 4.30 | 13.00 | 30.00 |
| 317-The Flintstones (TV) | 3.00 | 9.00 | 21.00 |
| 318-Tarzan | 4.65 | 13.00 | 32.00 |
| 319-Yogi Bear (TV) | 1.70 | 5.00 | 12.00 |
| 320-Space Family Robinson (TV); Spiegle-a | 7.00 | 21.00 | 50.00 |
| 321-Tom and Jerry | .70 | 2.00 | 5.00 |
| 322-The Lone Ranger | 4.35 | 13.00 | 30.00 |
| 323-Little Lulu-not Stanley | 3.50 | 10.50 | 24.00 |
| 324-Lassie (TV)-Photo-c | 1.50 | 4.50 | 10.00 |
| 325-Fun with Santa | 1.00 | 3.00 | 7.00 |
| 326-Christmas Story (1968) | 1.00 | 3.00 | 7.00 |
| 327-The Flintstones (TV)(1969) | 3.00 | 9.00 | 21.00 |
| 328-Space Family Robinson (TV); Spiegle-a | 7.00 | 21.00 | 50.00 |
| 329-Bugs Bunny | .85 | 2.50 | 6.00 |
| 330-The Jetsons (TV) | 6.50 | 19.50 | 45.00 |
| 331-Daffy Duck | .70 | 2.00 | 5.00 |
| 332-Tarzan | 3.65 | 11.00 | 25.00 |
| 333-Tom and Jerry | .70 | 2.00 | 5.00 |
| 334-Lassie (TV) | 1.15 | 3.50 | 8.00 |
| 335-Little Lulu | 3.50 | 10.50 | 24.00 |
| 336-The Three Stooges | 4.30 | 13.00 | 30.00 |

| | Good | Fine | N-Mint |
|---|---|---|---|
| 337-Yogi Bear (TV) | 1.70 | 5.00 | 12.00 |
| 338-The Lone Ranger | 4.35 | 13.00 | 30.00 |
| 339-(Was not published) | | | |
| 340-Here Comes Santa (1969) | 1.00 | 3.00 | 7.00 |
| 341-The Flintstones (TV) | 3.00 | 9.00 | 21.00 |
| 342-Tarzan | 3.65 | 11.00 | 25.00 |
| 343-Bugs Bunny | .70 | 2.00 | 5.00 |
| 344-Yogi Bear (TV) | 1.50 | 4.50 | 10.00 |
| 345-Tom and Jerry | .70 | 2.00 | 5.00 |
| 346-Lassie (TV) | 1.15 | 3.50 | 8.00 |
| 347-Daffy Duck | .70 | 2.00 | 5.00 |
| 348-The Jetsons (TV) | 5.00 | 15.00 | 35.00 |
| 349-Little Lulu-not Stanley | 3.00 | 9.00 | 21.00 |
| 350-The Lone Ranger | 3.65 | 11.00 | 25.00 |
| 351-Beep-Beep, the Road Runner (TV) | 1.35 | 4.00 | 9.00 |
| 352-Space Family Robinson (TV)-Spiegle-a | 7.00 | 21.00 | 50.00 |
| 353-Beep-Beep, the Road Runner (1971) (TV) | 1.35 | 4.00 | 9.00 |
| 354-Tarzan (1971) | 3.00 | 9.00 | 21.00 |
| 355-Little Lulu-not Stanley | 3.00 | 9.00 | 21.00 |
| 356-Scooby Doo, Where Are You? (TV) | 2.30 | 7.00 | 16.00 |
| 357-Daffy Duck & Porky Pig | .70 | 2.00 | 5.00 |
| 358-Lassie (TV) | 1.15 | 3.50 | 8.00 |
| 359-Baby Snoots | 1.35 | 4.00 | 9.00 |
| 360-H. R. Pufnstuf (TV)-Photo-c | 1.30 | 4.00 | 9.00 |
| 361-Tom and Jerry | .70 | 2.00 | 5.00 |
| 362-Smokey the Bear (TV) | .70 | 2.00 | 5.00 |
| 363-Bugs Bunny & Yosemite Sam | .70 | 2.00 | 5.00 |
| 364-The Banana Splits (TV)-Photo-c | .85 | 2.50 | 6.00 |
| 365-Tom and Jerry (1972) | .70 | 2.00 | 5.00 |
| 366-Tarzan | 3.00 | 9.00 | 21.00 |
| 367-Bugs Bunny & Porky Pig | .70 | 2.00 | 5.00 |
| 368-Scooby Doo (TV)(4/72) | 2.00 | 6.00 | 14.00 |
| 369-Little Lulu-not Stanley | 2.30 | 7.00 | 16.00 |
| 370-Lassie (TV)-Photo-c | 1.15 | 3.50 | 8.00 |
| 371-Baby Snoots | 1.00 | 3.00 | 7.00 |
| 372-Smokey the Bear (TV) | .70 | 2.00 | 5.00 |
| 373-The Three Stooges | 3.70 | 11.00 | 26.00 |
| 374-Wacky Witch | .70 | 2.00 | 5.00 |
| 375-Beep-Beep & Daffy Duck (TV) | .70 | 2.00 | 5.00 |
| 376-The Pink Panther (1972) (TV) | 1.35 | 4.00 | 9.00 |
| 377-Baby Snoots (1973) | 1.00 | 3.00 | 7.00 |
| 378-Turok, Son of Stone | 8.00 | 24.00 | 55.00 |
| 379-Heckle & Jeckle New Terrytoons (TV) | .50 | 1.50 | 3.00 |
| 380-Bugs Bunny & Yosemite Sam | .50 | 1.50 | 3.00 |
| 381-Lassie (TV) | .85 | 2.50 | 6.00 |
| 382-Scooby Doo, Where Are You? (TV) | 1.70 | 5.00 | 12.00 |
| 383-Smokey the Bear (TV) | .50 | 1.50 | 3.00 |
| 384-Pink Panther (TV) | 1.00 | 3.00 | 7.00 |
| 385-Little Lulu | 2.00 | 6.00 | 14.00 |
| 386-Wacky Witch | .50 | 1.50 | 3.00 |
| 387-Beep-Beep & Daffy Duck (TV) | .50 | 1.50 | 3.00 |
| 388-Tom and Jerry (1973) | .50 | 1.50 | 3.00 |
| 389-Little Lulu-not Stanley | 2.00 | 6.00 | 14.00 |
| 390-Pink Panther (TV) | .70 | 2.00 | 5.00 |
| 391-Scooby Doo (TV) | 1.70 | 5.00 | 12.00 |
| 392-Bugs Bunny & Yosemite Sam | .50 | 1.50 | 3.00 |
| 393-New Terrytoons (Heckle & Jeckle) (TV) | .50 | 1.50 | 3.00 |
| 394-Lassie (TV) | .70 | 2.00 | 5.00 |
| 395-Woodsy Owl | .50 | 1.50 | 3.00 |
| 396-Baby Snoots | .70 | 2.00 | 5.00 |
| 397-Beep-Beep & Daffy Duck (TV) | .50 | 1.50 | 3.00 |
| 398-Wacky Witch | .50 | 1.50 | 3.00 |
| 399-Turok, Son of Stone | 6.50 | 19.50 | 45.00 |
| 400-Tom and Jerry | .50 | 1.50 | 3.00 |
| 401-Baby Snoots (1975) (r-/No. 371) | .70 | 2.00 | 5.00 |
| 402-Daffy Duck (r-/No. 313) | .50 | 1.50 | 3.00 |

| | Good | Fine | N-Mint |
|---|---|---|---|
| 403-Bugs Bunny (r-/No. 343) | .50 | 1.50 | 3.00 |
| 404-Space Family Robinson (TV)(r-/No. 328) | 5.70 | 17.00 | 40.00 |
| 405-Cracky | .50 | 1.50 | 3.00 |
| 406-Little Lulu (r-/No. 355) | 1.70 | 5.00 | 12.00 |
| 407-Smokey the Bear (TV)(r-/No. 362) | .50 | 1.50 | 3.00 |
| 408-Turok, Son of Stone | 5.70 | 17.00 | 40.00 |
| 409-Pink Panther (TV) | .50 | 1.50 | 3.00 |
| 410-Wacky Witch | .35 | 1.00 | 2.00 |
| 411-Lassie (TV)(r-/No. 324) | .70 | 2.00 | 5.00 |
| 412-New Terrytoons (1975) (TV) | .35 | 1.00 | 2.00 |
| 413-Daffy Duck (1976)(r-/No. 331) | .35 | 1.00 | 2.00 |
| 414-Space Family Robinson (r-/No. 328) | 4.30 | 13.00 | 30.00 |
| 415-Bugs Bunny (r-/No. 329) | .35 | 1.00 | 2.00 |
| 416-Beep-Beep, the Road Runner (r-/#353)(TV) | .35 | 1.00 | 2.00 |
| 417-Little Lulu (r-/No. 323) | 1.70 | 5.00 | 12.00 |
| 418-Pink Panther (r-/No. 384) (TV) | .35 | 1.00 | 2.00 |
| 419-Baby Snoots (r-/No. 377) | .50 | 1.50 | 3.00 |
| 420-Woody Woodpecker | .35 | 1.00 | 2.00 |
| 421-Tweety & Sylvester | .35 | 1.00 | 2.00 |
| 422-Wacky Witch (r-/No. 386) | .35 | 1.00 | 2.00 |
| 423-Little Monsters | .50 | 1.50 | 3.00 |
| 424-Cracky (12/76) | .35 | 1.00 | 2.00 |
| 425-Daffy Duck | .35 | 1.00 | 2.00 |
| 426-Underdog (TV) | 1.70 | 5.00 | 12.00 |
| 427-Little Lulu (r/No. 335) | 1.15 | 3.50 | 8.00 |
| 428-Bugs Bunny | .35 | 1.00 | 2.00 |
| 429-The Pink Panther (TV) | .35 | 1.00 | 2.00 |
| 430-Beep-Beep, the Road Runner (TV) | .35 | 1.00 | 2.00 |
| 431-Baby Snoots | .50 | 1.50 | 3.00 |
| 432-Lassie (TV) | .50 | 1.50 | 3.00 |
| 433-437: 433-Tweety & Sylvester. 434-Wacky Witch. 435-New Terrytoons (TV). 436-Wacky Advs. of Cracky. 437-Daffy Duck | .35 | 1.00 | 2.00 |
| 438-Underdog (TV) | 1.70 | 5.00 | 12.00 |
| 439-Little Lulu (r/#349) | 1.15 | 3.50 | 8.00 |
| 440-442,444-446: 440-Bugs Bunny. 441-The Pink Panther (TV). 442-Beep-Beep, the Road Runner (TV). 444-Tom and Jerry. 445-Tweety and Sylvester. 446-Wacky Witch | .35 | 1.00 | 2.00 |
| 443-Baby Snoots | .50 | 1.50 | 3.00 |
| 447-Mighty Mouse | .70 | 2.00 | 4.00 |
| 448-455,457,458: 448-Cracky. 449-Pink Panther (TV). 450-Baby Snoots. 451-Tom and Jerry. 452-Bugs Bunny. 453-Popeye. 454-Woody Woodpecker. 455-Beep-Beep, the Road Runner (TV). 457-Tweety & Sylvester. 458-Wacky Witch | .35 | 1.00 | 2.00 |
| 456-Little Lulu (r/#369) | .85 | 2.50 | 6.00 |
| 459-Mighty Mouse | .70 | 2.00 | 4.00 |
| 460-466: 460-Daffy Duck. 461-The Pink Panther (TV). 462-Baby Snoots. 463-Tom and Jerry. 464-Bugs Bunny. 465-Popeye. 466-Woody Woodpecker | .35 | 1.00 | 2.00 |
| 467-Underdog (TV) | 1.50 | 3.50 | 8.00 |
| 468-Little Lulu (r/#385) | .70 | 2.00 | 4.00 |
| 469-Tweety & Sylvester | .35 | 1.00 | 2.00 |
| 470-Wacky Witch | .35 | 1.00 | 2.00 |
| 471-Mighty Mouse | .70 | 2.00 | 4.00 |
| 472-474,476-478: 472-Heckle & Jeckle(12/80). 473-Pink Panther(1/81) (TV). 474-Baby Snoots. 476-Bugs Bunny. 477-Popeye. 478-Woody Woodpecker | .35 | 1.00 | 2.00 |
| 475-Little Lulu (r/#323) | .50 | 1.50 | 3.00 |
| 479-Underdog (TV) | 1.00 | 3.00 | 7.00 |
| 480-482: 480-Tom and Jerry. 481-Tweety and Sylvester. 482-Wacky Witch | .35 | 1.00 | 2.00 |
| 483-Mighty Mouse | .70 | 2.00 | 4.00 |
| 484-Heckle & Jeckle | .35 | 1.00 | 2.00 |
| 485-487: 485-Baby Snoots. 486-The Pink Panther (TV). 487-Bugs Bunny | .35 | 1.00 | 2.00 |
| 488-Little Lulu (r/#335) | .50 | 1.50 | 3.00 |

*March of Comics #357, © Warner Bros.*

*March of Comics #393, © Viacom Int.*

*March of Comics #461, © UAC-Geoffrey*

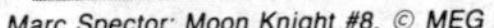
Marc Spector: Moon Knight #8, © MEG

Marge's Little Lulu #42, © WEST

Margie Comics #41, © MEG

**MARCH OF CRIME** (My Love Affair #1-6) (See Fox Giants)
No. 7, July, 1950 - No. 2, Sept, 1950; No. 3, Sept, 1951
Fox Features Syndicate

| | Good | Fine | N-Mint |
|---|---|---|---|
| 7(#1)(7/50)-Wood-a | 15.00 | 45.00 | 105.00 |
| 2(9/50)-Wood-a (exceptional) | 15.00 | 45.00 | 105.00 |
| 3(9/51) | 5.70 | 17.00 | 40.00 |

**MARCO POLO**
1962 (Movie classic)
Charlton Comics Group

| | Good | Fine | N-Mint |
|---|---|---|---|
| nn (Scarce)-Glanzman-c/a, 25pgs. | 9.00 | 27.00 | 62.00 |

**MARC SPECTOR: MOON KNIGHT** (Also see Moon Knight)
June, 1989 - Present ($1.50, color, direct sale only)
Marvel Comics

| | Good | Fine | N-Mint |
|---|---|---|---|
| 1 | .45 | 1.40 | 2.80 |
| 2-7: 4-Intro new Midnight | .25 | .75 | 1.50 |
| 8,9-Punisher app. | .85 | 2.50 | 5.00 |
| 10-18,22-26: 20-Guice-c. 21-23-Denys Cowan-c(p) | .25 | .75 | 1.50 |
| 19-21-Spider-Man & Punisher app. | .50 | 1.50 | 3.00 |

**MARGARET O'BRIEN** (See The Adventures of. . .)

**MARGE'S LITTLE LULU** (Little Lulu #207 on)
No. 74, 6/45 - No. 164, 7-9/62; No. 165, 10/62 - No. 206, 8/72
Dell Publishing Co./Gold Key #165-206

**Marjorie Henderson Buell**, born in Philadelphia, Pa., in 1904, created *Little Lulu*, a cartoon character that appeared weekly in the *Saturday Evening Post* from Feb. 23, 1935 through Dec. 30, 1944. She was not responsible for any of the comic books. **John Stanley** did pencils only on all *Little Lulu* comics through at least #135 (1959). He did pencils and inks on *Four Color* #74 & 97. **Irving Tripp** began inking stories from #1 on, and remained the comic's illustrator throughout its entire run. **Stanley** did storyboards (layouts), pencils, and scripts in all cases and inking only on covers. His word balloons were written in cursive. **Tripp** and occasionally other artists at Western Publ. in Poughkeepsie, N.Y. blew up the pencilled pages, inked the blowups, and lettered them. **Arnold Drake** did storyboards, pencils and scripts starting with #197 (1970) on, amidst reprinted issues. **Buell** sold her rights exclusively to Western Publ. in Dec., 1971. The earlier issues had to be approved by **Buell** prior to publication.

| | Good | Fine | N-Mint |
|---|---|---|---|
| 4-Color 74('45)-Intro Lulu, Tubby & Alvin | 90.00 | 270.00 | 630.00 |
| 4-Color 97(2/46) | 47.00 | 140.00 | 330.00 |
| (Above two books are all John Stanley - cover, pencils, and inks.) | | | |
| 4-Color 110('46)-1st Alvin Story Telling Time; 1st app. Willy | 33.00 | 100.00 | 230.00 |
| 4-Color 115-1st app. Boys' Clubhouse | 33.00 | 100.00 | 230.00 |
| 4-Color 120, 131: 120-1st app. Eddie | 30.00 | 90.00 | 210.00 |
| 4-Color 139('47),146,158 | 27.00 | 81.00 | 190.00 |
| 4-Color 165 (10/47)-Smokes doll hair & has wild hallucinations. 1st Tubby detective story | 27.00 | 81.00 | 190.00 |
| 1(1-2/48)-Lulu's Diary feat. begins | 56.00 | 168.00 | 390.00 |
| 2-1st app. Gloria; 1st Tubby story in a L.L. comic; 1st app. Miss Feeny | 29.00 | 87.00 | 200.00 |
| 3-5 | 25.00 | 75.00 | 175.00 |
| 6-10: 7-1st app. Annie; Xmas-c | 18.00 | 54.00 | 125.00 |
| 11-20: 19-1st app. Wilbur. 20-1st app. Mr. McNabbem | 15.00 | 45.00 | 105.00 |
| 21-30: 26-r/F.C. 110. 30-Xmas-c | 11.50 | 34.00 | 80.00 |
| 31-38,40: 35-1st Mumday story | 8.50 | 25.50 | 60.00 |
| 39-Intro. Witch Hazel in "That Awful Witch Hazel" | 10.00 | 30.00 | 70.00 |
| 41-60: 42-Xmas-c. 45-2nd Witch Hazel app. 49-Gives Stanley & others credit | 8.00 | 24.00 | 55.00 |
| 61-80: 63-1st app. Chubby (Tubby's cousin). 68-1st app. Prof. Cleff. 78-Xmas-c. 80-Intro. Little Itch (2/55) | 5.70 | 17.00 | 40.00 |
| 81-99: 90-Xmas-c | 4.00 | 12.00 | 30.00 |
| 100 | 4.60 | 14.00 | 35.00 |
| 101-130: 123-1st app. Fifi | 3.00 | 9.00 | 21.00 |
| 131-164: 135-Last Stanley-p | 2.65 | 8.00 | 18.00 |
| 165-Giant; . . . In Paris ('62) | 4.00 | 12.00 | 32.00 |
| 166-Giant; . . . Christmas Diary ('62-'63) | 4.00 | 12.00 | 32.00 |
| 167-169 | 1.70 | 5.00 | 12.00 |
| 170,172,175,176,178-196,198-200-Stanley-r. 182-1st app. Little Scarecrow Boy | 1.30 | 4.00 | 9.00 |
| 171,173,174,177,197 | .85 | 2.50 | 6.00 |
| 201,203,206-Last issue to carry Marge's name | .55 | 1.65 | 4.00 |
| 202,204,205-Stanley-r | 1.00 | 3.00 | 7.00 |
| . . . & Tubby in Japan (12 cents)(5-7/62) 01476-207 | 5.70 | 17.00 | 40.00 |
| . . . Summer Camp 1(8/67-G.K.-Giant) '57-58-r | 4.65 | 14.00 | 32.00 |
| . . . Trick 'N' Treat 1(12–)(12/62-Gold Key) | 5.00 | 15.00 | 35.00 |

NOTE: *See **Dell Giant Comics** #23, 29, 36, 42, 50, & **Dell Giants** for annuals. All Giants not by **Stanley** from L.L. on Vacation (7/54) on. **Irving Tripp** a-#1-on. Christmas c-7, 18, 30, 42, 78, 90, 126, 166, 250. Summer Camp issues #173, 177, 181, 189, 197, 201, 206.*

**MARGE'S LITTLE LULU** (See Golden Comics Digest #19, 23, 27, 29, 33, 36, 40, 43, 46 & March of Comics #251, 267, 275, 293, 307, 323, 335, 349, 355, 369, 385, 406, 417, 427, 439, 456, 468, 475, 488)

**MARGE'S TUBBY** (Little Lulu)(See Dell Giants)
No. 381, Aug, 1952 - No. 49, Dec-Feb, 1961-62
Dell Publishing Co./Gold Key

| | Good | Fine | N-Mint |
|---|---|---|---|
| 4-Color 381(#1)-Stanley script; Irving Tripp-a | 12.00 | 36.00 | 84.00 |
| 4-Color 430,444-Stanley-a | 7.00 | 21.00 | 50.00 |
| 4-Color 461 (4/53)-1st Tubby & Men From Mars story; Stanley-a | 6.50 | 19.50 | 45.00 |
| 5 (7-9/53)-Stanley-a | 5.00 | 15.00 | 35.00 |
| 6-10 | 3.50 | 10.50 | 24.00 |
| 11-20 | 2.85 | 8.50 | 20.00 |
| 21-30 | 2.35 | 7.00 | 16.00 |
| 31-49 | 2.00 | 6.00 | 14.00 |
| . . . & the Little Men From Mars No. 30020-410(10/64-G.K.)-25 cents; 68 pgs. | 5.00 | 15.00 | 40.00 |

NOTE: ***John Stanley** did all storyboards & scripts through at least #35 (1959). **Lloyd White** did all art except F.C. 381, 430, 444, 461 & #5.*

**MARGIE** (See My Little. . .)

**MARGIE** (TV)
No. 1307, Mar-May, 1962 - No. 2, July-Sept, 1962 (Photo-c)
Dell Publishing Co.

| | Good | Fine | N-Mint |
|---|---|---|---|
| 4-Color 1307(#1), 2 | 2.30 | 7.00 | 16.00 |

**MARGIE COMICS** (Formerly Comedy Comics; Reno Browne #50 on)
(Also see Cindy Comics & Teen Comics)
No. 35, Winter, 1946-47 - No. 49, Dec, 1949
Marvel Comics (ACI)

| | Good | Fine | N-Mint |
|---|---|---|---|
| 35 | 5.00 | 15.00 | 35.00 |
| 36-38,42,45,47-49 | 2.65 | 8.00 | 18.00 |
| 39,41,43(2),44,46-Kurtzman's "Hey Look" | 3.60 | 11.00 | 25.00 |
| 40-Three "Hey Looks," three "Giggles & Grins" by Kurtzman | 5.00 | 15.00 | 35.00 |

**MARINES** (See Tell It to the. . .)

**MARINES ATTACK**
Aug, 1964 - No. 9, Feb-Mar, 1966
Charlton Comics

| | Good | Fine | N-Mint |
|---|---|---|---|
| 1 | .70 | 2.00 | 4.00 |
| 2-9 | .40 | 1.25 | 2.50 |

**MARINES AT WAR** (Formerly Tales of the Marines #4)
No. 5, April, 1957 - No. 7, Aug, 1957
Atlas Comics (OPI)

| | Good | Fine | N-Mint |
|---|---|---|---|
| 5-7 | 1.30 | 4.00 | 9.00 |

NOTE: *Colan a-5. Drucker a-5. Everett a-5. Maneely a-5. Orlando a-7. Severin c-5.*

**MARINES IN ACTION**
June, 1955 - No. 14, Sept, 1957
Atlas News Co.

| | Good | Fine | N-Mint |
|---|---|---|---|
| 1-Rock Murdock, Boot Camp Brady begin | 2.65 | 8.00 | 18.00 |

| | Good | Fine | N-Mint |
|---|---|---|---|
| 2-14 | 1.50 | 4.50 | 10.00 |

NOTE: ***Berg** a-2, 8, 9, 11, 14. **Heath** c-2, 9. **Maneely** c-1. **Severin** a-4; c-7-11, 14.*

**MARINES IN BATTLE**
Aug, 1954 - No. 25, Sept, 1958
Atlas Comics (ACI No. 1-12/WPI No. 13-25)

| | Good | Fine | N-Mint |
|---|---|---|---|
| 1-Heath-c; Iron Mike McGraw by Heath; history of U.S. Marine Corps. begins | 5.00 | 15.00 | 35.00 |
| 2-Heath-c | 2.30 | 7.00 | 16.00 |
| 3-6,8-10: 4-Last precode (2/55) | 1.70 | 5.00 | 12.00 |
| 7-Kubert/Moskowitz-a (6 pgs.) | 2.65 | 8.00 | 18.00 |
| 11-16,18-22,24 | 1.50 | 4.50 | 10.00 |
| 17-Williamson-a (3 pgs.) | 3.50 | 10.50 | 24.00 |
| 23-Crandall-a; Mark Murdock app. | 2.65 | 8.00 | 18.00 |
| 25-Torres-a | 2.00 | 6.00 | 14.00 |

NOTE: ***Berg** a-22. **Drucker** a-6. **Everett** a-4, 15; c-21. **Heath** c-1, 2. **Maneely** c-24. **Orlando** a-14. **Pakula** a-6. **Powell** a-16. **Severin** c-12.*

**MARINE WAR HEROES** (Charlton Premiere #19 on)
Jan, 1964 - No. 18, Mar, 1967
Charlton Comics

| | Good | Fine | N-Mint |
|---|---|---|---|
| 1-Montes/Bache-c/a | .70 | 2.00 | 4.00 |
| 2-18: 14,18-Montes/Bache-a | .50 | 1.50 | 3.00 |

**MARK, THE** (Also see Mayhem)
Sept, 1987 - No. 6?, 1988 ($1.75, $1.95, color)
Dark Horse Comics

| | Good | Fine | N-Mint |
|---|---|---|---|
| 1,3-6 ($1.75) | .30 | .90 | 1.80 |
| 2 ($1.95) | .35 | 1.00 | 2.00 |

**MARK HAZZARD: MERC**
Nov, 1986 - No. 12, Oct, 1987 (75 cents, color)
Marvel Comics Group

| | Good | Fine | N-Mint |
|---|---|---|---|
| 1-12: Morrow-a | | .40 | .80 |
| Annual 1(11/87, $1.25) | | .60 | 1.20 |

**MARK OF ZORRO** (See 4-Color #228)

**MARKSMAN, THE** (Also see Champions)
Jan, 1988 - No. 5, 1988 ($1.95, color)
Hero Comics

| | Good | Fine | N-Mint |
|---|---|---|---|
| 1-5: 1-Rose begins. 1-3-Origin The Marksman | .35 | 1.00 | 2.00 |
| Annual 1 ('88, $2.75, 52 pgs.)-Champions app. | .45 | 1.40 | 2.80 |

**MARK STEEL**
1967, 1968, 1972 (24 pgs.) (Color)
American Iron & Steel Institute (Giveaway)

| | Good | Fine | N-Mint |
|---|---|---|---|
| 1967,1968-"Journey of Discovery with . . ."; Neal Adams art | 2.35 | 7.00 | 16.00 |
| 1972-". . . Fights Pollution;" N. Adams-a | 1.35 | 4.00 | 8.00 |

**MARK TRAIL**
Oct, 1955; No. 5, Summer, 1959
Standard Magazines (Hall Syndicate)/Fawcett Publ. No. 5

| | Good | Fine | N-Mint |
|---|---|---|---|
| 1(1955)-Sunday strip-r | 4.00 | 12.00 | 28.00 |
| 5(1959) | 2.00 | 6.00 | 14.00 |
| . . . Adventure Book of Nature 1(Summer, 1958; Pines)-100 pg. Giant; contains 78 Sunday strip-r | 5.00 | 15.00 | 35.00 |

**MARMADUKE MONK**
No date; 1963 (10 cents)
I. W. Enterprises/Super Comics

| | Good | Fine | N-Mint |
|---|---|---|---|
| 1-I.W. Reprint, 14-(Super Reprint)('63) | .35 | 1.00 | 2.00 |

**MARMADUKE MOUSE**
Spring, 1946 - No. 65, Dec, 1956 (All 52 pgs.?)
Quality Comics Group (Arnold Publ.)

| | Good | Fine | N-Mint |
|---|---|---|---|
| 1-Funny animal | 7.00 | 21.00 | 50.00 |
| 2 | 3.65 | 11.00 | 25.00 |
| 3-10 | 2.65 | 8.00 | 18.00 |
| 11-30 | 2.00 | 6.00 | 14.00 |
| 31-65 | 1.15 | 3.50 | 8.00 |
| Super Reprint #14(1963) | .50 | 1.50 | 3.00 |

**MARRIED . . . WITH CHILDREN** (TV)
June, 1990 - Present ($1.75-$1.95, color)
Now Comics

| | Good | Fine | N-Mint |
|---|---|---|---|
| 1-Based on Fox TV show | 1.00 | 3.00 | 7.00 |
| 1-2nd printing ($1.75) | .35 | 1.00 | 2.00 |
| 2-Photo-c | .85 | 2.50 | 5.00 |
| 2-2nd printing ($1.75) | .30 | .90 | 1.80 |
| 3 | .50 | 1.50 | 3.00 |
| 4-8 | .30 | .90 | 1.80 |
| 9-12: 9-Begin $1.95-c | .35 | 1.00 | 2.00 |

**MARS**
Jan, 1984 - No. 12, Jan, 1985 ($1.00, Mando paper)
First Comics

| | Good | Fine | N-Mint |
|---|---|---|---|
| 1-12: 2-The Black Flame begins. 10-Dynamo Joe begins | | .50 | 1.00 |

**MARS & BEYOND** (See 4-Color #866)

**MARSHAL LAW** (Also see Crime And Punishment: Marshall Law. . .)
Oct, 1987 - No. 6, May, 1989 ($1.95, color, adults)
Epic Comics (Marvel)

| | Good | Fine | N-Mint |
|---|---|---|---|
| 1 | .90 | 2.75 | 5.50 |
| 2 | .50 | 1.50 | 3.00 |
| 3-6 | .35 | 1.00 | 2.00 |

**M.A.R.S. PATROL TOTAL WAR** (Formerly Total War #1,2)
No. 3, Sept, 1966 - No. 10, Aug, 1969 (All-Painted-c)
Gold Key

| | Good | Fine | N-Mint |
|---|---|---|---|
| 3-Wood-a | 2.30 | 7.00 | 16.00 |
| 4-10 | 1.15 | 3.50 | 8.00 |

**MARTHA WAYNE** (See The Story of. . .)

**MARTIAN MANHUNTER**
May, 1988 - No. 4, Aug, 1988 ($1.25, color, limited series)
DC Comics

| | Good | Fine | N-Mint |
|---|---|---|---|
| 1-4: 1,4-Batman app. 2-Batman cameo | | .60 | 1.25 |

**MARTIN KANE** (Formerly My Secret Affair) (Radio-TV)(Private Eye)
No. 4, June, 1950 - No. 2, Aug, 1950
Fox Features Syndicate (Hero Books)

| | Good | Fine | N-Mint |
|---|---|---|---|
| 4(#1)-Wood-c/a(2); used in **SOTI**, pg. 160; photo back cover | 14.00 | 42.00 | 100.00 |
| 2-Orlando-a, 5pgs; Wood-a(2) | 10.00 | 30.00 | 70.00 |

**MARTY MOUSE**
No date (1958?) (10 cents)
I. W. Enterprises

| | Good | Fine | N-Mint |
|---|---|---|---|
| 1-Reprint | .50 | 1.50 | 3.00 |

**MARVEL ACTION UNIVERSE** (TV)
Jan, 1989 ($1.00, color, one-shot)
Marvel Comics

| | Good | Fine | N-Mint |
|---|---|---|---|
| 1-R/Spider-Man And His Amazing Friends | | .50 | 1.00 |

**MARVEL ADVENTURES STARRING DAREDEVIL**
Dec, 1975 - No. 6, Oct, 1976 (. . . Adventure #4 on)
Marvel Comics Group

| | Good | Fine | N-Mint |
|---|---|---|---|
| 1: 1-6-r/Daredevil 22-27 by Colan | | .40 | .80 |
| 2-6 | | .30 | .60 |

**MARVEL AND DC PRESENT** (Featuring the Uncanny X-Men and the New Teen Titans)
Nov, 1982 (One Shot, $2.00, 68 pgs., printed on Baxter paper)
Marvel Comics Group/DC Comics

| | Good | Fine | N-Mint |
|---|---|---|---|
| 1-Simonson/Austin-c/a; Perez-a(p) | 1.50 | 4.50 | 10.00 |

*Marine War Heroes #1, © CC*

*Mark Trail #1, © Hall Synd.*

*Married . . . With Children #1, © ELP Comm.*

Marvel Collectors Item Classics #14, © MEG

Marvel Comics Presents #1, © MEG

Marvel Double Feature #19, © MEG

**MARVEL BOY** (Astonishing #3 on; see Marvel Super Action #4)
Dec, 1950 - No. 2, Feb, 1951
Marvel Comics (MPC)

| | Good | Fine | N-Mint |
|---|---|---|---|
| 1-Origin Marvel Boy by Russ Heath | 35.00 | 105.00 | 245.00 |
| 2-Everett-a | 29.00 | 85.00 | 200.00 |

**MARVEL CHILLERS** (Also see Giant-Size Chillers)
Oct, 1975 - No. 7, Oct, 1976
Marvel Comics Group

| | | | |
|---|---|---|---|
| 1-Intro. Modred the Mystic; Kane-c(p) | | .50 | 1.00 |
| 2-5,7: 3-Tigra, the Were-Woman begins (origin), ends #7. Chaykin/Wrightson-c. 4-Kraven app. 7-Kirby-c, Tuska-p | | .35 | .70 |
| 6-Byrne-a(p); Buckler-c(p); Red Wolf app.(#5 also) | | .60 | 1.20 |

**MARVEL CLASSICS COMICS SERIES FEATURING...** (Also see Pendulum Illustrated Classics)
1976 - No. 36, Dec, 1978 (52 pgs., no ads)
Marvel Comics Group

| | | | |
|---|---|---|---|
| 1-Dr. Jekyll and Mr. Hyde | .50 | 1.50 | 3.00 |
| 2-27,29-36: 2-Time Machine, 3-Hunchback of Notre Dame, 4-20,000 Leagues Under the Sea, 5-Black Beauty, 6-Gulliver's Travels, 7-Tom Sawyer, 8-Moby Dick, 9-Dracula, 10-Red Badge of Courage, 11-Mysterious Island, 12-The Three Musketeers, 13-Last of the Mohicans, 14-War of the Worlds, 15-Treasure Island, 16-Ivanhoe, 17-The Count of Monte Cristo, 18-The Odyssey, 19-Robinson Crusoe, 20-Frankenstein, 21-Master of the World, 22-Food of the Gods, 23-The Moonstone, 24-She, 25-The Invisible Man, 26-The Illiad, 27-Kidnapped, 29-Prisoner of Zenda, 30-Arabian Nights, 31-First Man in the Moon, 32-White Fang, 33-The Prince and the Pauper, 34-Robin Hood, 35-Alice in Wonderland, 36-A Christmas Carol each.... | .35 | 1.00 | 2.00 |
| 28-1st M. Golden-a; The Pit and the Pendulum | 1.00 | 3.00 | 6.00 |

NOTE: ***Adkins*** *c-1i, 4i, 12i.* ***Alcala*** *a-34i; c-34.* ***Bolle*** *a-35.* ***Buscema*** *c-17p, 19p, 26p.* ***Golden*** *a-28.* ***Gil Kane*** *c-1-16p, 21p, 22p, 24p, 32p.* ***Nebres*** *a-5; c-24i.* ***Nino*** *a-2, 8, 12.* ***Redondo*** *a-1, 9. No. 1-12 were reprinted from Pendulum Illustrated Classics.*

**MARVEL COLLECTORS ITEM CLASSICS** (Marvel's Greatest #23 on)
Feb, 1965 - No. 22, Aug, 1969 (68 pgs.)
Marvel Comics Group(ATF)

| | | | |
|---|---|---|---|
| 1-Fantastic Four, Spider-Man, Thor, Hulk, Iron Man-r begin; all are 25 cent cover price | 4.50 | 14.00 | 32.00 |
| 2 (4/66) - 4 | 2.65 | 8.00 | 18.00 |
| 5-22 | 1.15 | 3.50 | 8.00 |

NOTE: *All reprints;* ***Ditko, Kirby*** *art in all.*

**MARVEL COMICS** (Marvel Mystery Comics #2 on)
October, November, 1939
Timely Comics (Funnies, Inc.)

NOTE: The first issue was originally dated October 1939. Most copies have a black circle stamped over the date (on cover and inside) with "November" printed over it. However, some copies do not have the November overprint and could have a higher value. Most No. 1's have printing defects, i.e., tilted pages which caused trimming into the panels usually on right side and bottom. Covers exist with and without gloss finish.

1-Origin Sub-Mariner by Bill Everett(1st newsstand app.); 1st 8 pgs. were produced for **Motion Picture Funnies Weekly** #1 which was probably not distributed outside of advance copies; Human Torch by Carl Burgos, Kazar the Great (1st Tarzan clone), & Jungle Terror (only app.); intro. The Angel by Gustavson, The Masked Raider (ends #12); cover by sci/fi pulp illustrator Frank R. Paul

| Good | Fine | VF-NM | NM/Mint |
|---|---|---|---|
| 5800.00 | 14,600.00 | 32,000.00 | 42,000.00 |

(Estimated up to 100 total copies exist, 5 in NM/Mint)

**MARVEL COMICS PRESENTS**
Early Sept, 1988 - Present ($1.25, color, bi-weekly)
Marvel Comics

| | Good | Fine | N-Mint |
|---|---|---|---|
| 1-Wolverine by Buscema in #1-10 | 1.00 | 3.00 | 6.00 |
| 2-5 | .50 | 1.50 | 3.00 |
| 6-10: 6-Sub-Mariner app. 10-Colossus begins | .35 | 1.00 | 2.00 |
| 11-24,26-37: 17-Cyclops begins. 19-1st app. Damage Control. 24-Havok begins. 26-Hulk begins by Rogers. 29-Quasar app. 31-Excalibur begins by Austin (i). 33-Capt. America. 37-Devil-Slayer app. | | .60 | 1.25 |
| 25-Origin & 1st app. Nth Man | .35 | 1.00 | 2.00 |
| 38-Wolverine begins by Buscema; Hulk app. | .50 | 1.50 | 3.00 |
| 39-47,51-53: 39-Spider-Man app. | .35 | 1.00 | 2.00 |
| 48-50-Wolverine & Spider-Man team-up. 48-Wasp app. 50-Silver Surfer. 50-53-Comet Man; Bill Mumy scripts | .60 | 1.75 | 3.50 |
| 54-61-Wolverine/Hulk; 54-Werewolf by Night begins; The Shroud by Ditko. 58-Iron Man by Ditko. 59-Punisher | .50 | 1.50 | 3.00 |
| 62-72: 62-Deathlok story. 62,63-Wolverine stories. 64-71-Wolverine/Ghost Rider 8 part story | .25 | .75 | 1.50 |

NOTE: ***Austin*** *a-31-37i; c-48i, 50i.* ***Buscema*** *a-1-10, 38-47; c-6.* ***Colan*** *a-37p.* ***Ditko*** *a-7p, 56p, 58.* ***Guice*** *a-62.* ***McFarlane*** *c-32.* ***Rogers*** *a-26, 46i.* ***Russell*** *c-4i.* ***Simonson*** *c-1.* ***P. Smith*** *c-34.* ***Sparling*** *a-33.* ***Williamson*** *62i.*

**MARVEL COMICS SUPER SPECIAL, A** (Marvel Super Special #5 on)
1977 - No. 41(?), Nov, 1986 (nn 7) (Magazine; $1.50)
Marvel Comics Group

| | | | |
|---|---|---|---|
| 1-Kiss, 40 pgs. comics plus photos & features; Simonson-a(p); also see Howard the Duck #12 | 6.50 | 20.00 | 45.00 |
| 2-Conan (1978) | .50 | 1.50 | 3.00 |
| 3-Close Encounters of the Third Kind (1978); Simonson-a | .35 | 1.00 | 2.00 |
| 4-The Beatles Story (1978)-Perez/Janson-a; has photos & articles | 1.35 | 4.00 | 8.00 |
| 5-Kiss (1978)-Includes poster | 3.60 | 11.00 | 25.00 |
| 6-Jaws II (1978) | .25 | .75 | 1.50 |
| 8-Battlestar Galactica-tabloid size | .35 | 1.00 | 2.00 |
| 8-Battlestar Galactica publ. in reg. magazine format; low distribution ($1.50)8½x11" | .85 | 2.50 | 5.00 |
| 9,10: 9-Conan. 10-Star-Lord | .35 | 1.00 | 2.00 |
| 11-13-Weirdworld begins #11; 25 copy special press run of each with gold seal and signed by artists (Proof quality), Spring-June, 1979 | 10.00 | 30.00 | 60.00 |
| 11-13-Weirdworld (regular issues): 11-Fold-out centerfold | .40 | 1.25 | 2.50 |
| 14-Adapts movie 'Meteor' | | .60 | 1.20 |
| 15-Star Trek with photos & pin-ups($1.50) | | .60 | 1.20 |
| 15-With $2.00 price(scarce); the price was changed at tail end of a 200,000 press run | .70 | 2.00 | 4.00 |
| 16-20 (Movie adaptations): 16-Empire Strikes Back; Williamson-a. 17-Xanadu. 18-Raiders of the Lost Ark. 19-For Your Eyes Only (James Bond). 20-Dragonslayer | .30 | .90 | 1.80 |
| 21-41 (Movie adaptations): 21-Conan. 22-Bladerunner; Williamson-a; Steranko-c. 23-Annie. 24-The Dark Crystal. 25-Rock and Rule-w/ photos; artwork is from movie. 26-Octopussy (James Bond). 27-Return of the Jedi. 28-Krull; photo-c. 29-Tarzan of the Apes (Greystoke movie). 30-Indiana Jones and the Temple of Doom. 31-The Last Star Fighter. 32-The Muppets Take Manhattan. 33-Buckaroo Bonzai. 34-Sheena. 35-Conan The Destroyer. 36-Dune. 37-2010. 38-Red Sonja. 39-Santa Claus: The Movie. 40-Labyrinth. 41-Howard The Duck | .30 | .90 | 1.80 |

NOTE: ***J. Buscema*** *a-1, 2, 9, 11-13, 18p, 21, 35, 40; c-11(part), 12.* ***Chaykin*** *a-9, 19p; c-18, 19.* ***Colan*** *a(p)-6, 10, 14.* ***Morrow*** *a-34; c-1i, 34.* ***Nebres*** *a-11.* ***Spiegle*** *a-29.* ***Stevens*** *a-27.* ***Williamson*** *a-27. #22-28 contain photos from movies.*

**MARVEL DOUBLE FEATURE**
Dec, 1973 - No. 21, Mar, 1977
Marvel Comics Group

| | | | |
|---|---|---|---|
| 1-Capt. America, Iron Man-r/T.O.S. begin | .50 | 1.50 | 3.00 |
| 2-16,20,21 | | .50 | 1.00 |
| 17-Reprints story/Iron Man & Sub-Mariner #1 | .35 | 1.00 | 2.00 |
| 18,19-Colan/Craig-r from Iron Man #1 in both | .50 | 1.50 | 3.00 |

NOTE: ***Colan*** *r-1-19p.* ***Craig*** *r-17-19i.* ***G. Kane*** *r-15p; c-15p.* ***Kirby*** *r-1-14p, 16-21p; c-17-20.*

**MARVEL FAMILY** (Also see Captain Marvel Adventures No. 18)
Dec, 1945 - No. 89, Jan, 1954
Fawcett Publications

| | Good | Fine | N-Mint |
|---|---|---|---|
| 1-Origin Captain Marvel, Captain Marvel Jr., Mary Marvel, & Uncle Marvel retold; Origin/1st app. Black Adam | 70.00 | 210.00 | 490.00 |
| 2-The 3 Lt. Marvels & Uncle Marvel app. | 35.00 | 105.00 | 245.00 |
| 3 | 25.00 | 75.00 | 175.00 |
| 4,5 | 22.00 | 65.00 | 150.00 |
| 6-10: 7-Shazam app. | 17.00 | 51.00 | 120.00 |
| 11-20 | 12.00 | 36.00 | 85.00 |
| 21-30 | 9.30 | 28.00 | 65.00 |
| 31-40 | 8.00 | 24.00 | 55.00 |
| 41-46,48-50 | 6.50 | 19.00 | 45.00 |
| 47-Flying Saucer-c/story | 8.00 | 24.00 | 55.00 |
| 51-76,79,80,82-89: 78,81-Used in **POP**, pgs. 92,93 | 5.70 | 17.00 | 40.00 |
| 77-Communist Threat-c | 8.00 | 24.00 | 55.00 |

**MARVEL FANFARE**
March, 1982 - Present ($1.25-$1.95, slick paper) (Direct Sale only)
Marvel Comics Group

| | Good | Fine | N-Mint |
|---|---|---|---|
| 1-Spider-Man/Angel team-up; 1st Paul Smith story; Daredevil app. | 1.35 | 4.00 | 8.00 |
| 2-Spider-Man, Ka-Zar, The Angel. F.F. origin retold | 1.50 | 4.50 | 9.00 |
| 3,4-X-Men & Ka-Zar | 1.00 | 3.00 | 6.00 |
| 5-Dr. Strange, Capt. America | .50 | 1.50 | 3.00 |
| 6-15: 6-Spider-Man, Scarlet Witch. 7-Incredible Hulk. 8-Dr. Strange; Wolf Boy begins. 9-Man-Thing. 10-13-Black Widow. 14-The Vision. 15-The Thing by Barry Smith, c/a | .35 | 1.00 | 1.95 |
| 16-32,34-49: 16,17-Skywolf. 18-Capt. America by Miller. 19-Cloak and Dagger. 20-Thing/Dr. Strange. 21-Thing/Dr. Strange/Hulk. 22,23-Iron Man vs. Dr. Octopus. 24-26-Weirdworld. 27-Daredevil/Spider-Man. 28-Alpha Flight. 29-Hulk. 30-Moon Knight. 31,32-Capt. America. 34-37-Warriors Three. 38-Moon Knight/Dazzler. 39-Moon Knight/Hawkeye. 40-Angel/Rogue & Storm. 41-Dr. Strange. 42-Spider-Man. 43-Sub-Mariner/Human Torch. 44-Iron Man Vs. Dr. Doom by Ken Steacy. 45-All pin-up issue by Steacy, Art Adams & others. 46-Fantastic Four. 47-Hulk. 48-She-Hulk/Vision. 49-Dr. Strange/Nick Fury | .35 | 1.00 | 1.95 |
| 33-X-Men, Wolverine app.; Punisher pin-up | .50 | 1.50 | 3.00 |
| 50,52-55: 50-X-Factor; begin $2.25-c. 52-54-Black Knight; 53-Iron Man back up. 54,55-Wolverine back ups. 55-Power Pack | .40 | 1.15 | 2.25 |
| 51-($2.95, 52 pgs.)-Silver Surfer; Fantastic Four & Capt. Marvel app.; 51,52-Colan/Williamson back-up(Dr. Strange) | .50 | 1.50 | 3.00 |

NOTE: ***Art Adams*** *c-13.* ***Austin*** *a-1i, 4i, 33i, 38i; c-8i, 33i.* ***Buscema*** *a-51p.* ***Byrne*** *a-1p, 29, 48; c-29.* ***Colan*** *a-51p.* ***Golden*** *a-1, 2, 4p, 47; c-1, 2.* ***Infantino*** *c/a(p)-8.* ***Gil Kane*** *a-8-11p.* ***Miller*** *a-18; c-1(Back-c), 18.* ***Perez*** *a-10, 11p, 12, 13p; c-10-13p.* ***Rogers*** *a-5p; c-5p.* ***Russell*** *a-5i, 6i, 8-11i, 43i; c-5i, 6.* ***Paul Smith*** *a-1p, 4p, 32; c-4p.* ***Staton*** *c/a-50(p).* ***Williamson*** *a-30i, 51i.*

**MARVEL FEATURE** (See Marvel Two-In-One)
Dec, 1971 - No. 12, Nov, 1973 (No. 1,2: 25 cents)(1-3: Quarterly)
Marvel Comics Group

| | Good | Fine | N-Mint |
|---|---|---|---|
| 1-Origin/1st app. The Defenders; Sub-Mariner, Hulk & Dr. Strange; '50s Sub-Mariner-r; Neal Adams-c | 3.60 | 11.00 | 25.00 |
| 2-G.A. 1950s Sub-Mariner-r | 1.70 | 5.00 | 12.00 |
| 3-Defender series ends | 1.70 | 5.00 | 12.00 |
| 4-Re-intro Antman(1st app. since '60s), begin series; brief origin | 1.00 | 3.00 | 7.00 |
| 5-12: 6-Wasp app. & begins team-ups. 8-Origin Antman & Wasp-r/TTA #44. 9-Iron Man app. 10-Last Antman. 11-Thing/Hulk. 12-Thing/Iron Man. 11-Origin Fantastic 4 retold | .70 | 2.00 | 4.00 |

NOTE: ***Bolle*** *a-9i.* ***Everett*** *a-1i, 3i.* ***Hartley*** *r-10.* ***Kane*** *c-3p, 7p.* ***Russell*** *a-7-10p.* ***Starlin*** *a-8, 11, 12; c-8.*

**MARVEL FEATURE** (Also see Red Sonja)
Nov, 1975 - No. 7, Nov, 1976 (Story continues in Conan #68)
Marvel Comics Group

| | Good | Fine | N-Mint |
|---|---|---|---|
| 1-Red Sonja begins (pre-dates Red Sonja #1); adapts Howard short story; Adams-r/Savage Sword of Conan #1 | .50 | 1.50 | 3.00 |
| 2-7: Thorne-c/a in #2-7. 7-Battles Conan | .25 | .75 | 1.50 |

**MARVEL FUMETTI BOOK**
April, 1984 (One shot) ($1.00 cover price)
Marvel Comics Group

| | Good | Fine | N-Mint |
|---|---|---|---|
| 1-All photos; Stan Lee photo-c | | .40 | .80 |

**MARVEL GRAPHIC NOVEL**
1982 - Present ($5.95-$6.95)
Marvel Comics Group (Epic Comics)

| | Good | Fine | N-Mint |
|---|---|---|---|
| 1-Death of Captain Marvel (1st Marvel G.N.) | 2.50 | 7.50 | 15.00 |
| 1 (2nd & 3rd Printing) | 1.00 | 3.00 | 6.00 |
| 2-Elric: The Dreaming City | 1.35 | 4.00 | 8.00 |
| 3-Dreadstar; Starlin-a, 48pgs. | 1.20 | 3.50 | 7.00 |
| 4-Origin/1st app. The New Mutants | 1.70 | 5.00 | 10.00 |
| 4-2nd Print | 1.00 | 3.00 | 5.95 |
| 5-X-Men; book-length story | 2.00 | 6.00 | 12.00 |
| 5-2nd Print | 1.00 | 3.00 | 5.95 |
| 6-18: 6-The Star Slammers. 7-Killraven. 8-Super Boxers. 9-The Futurians. 10-Heartburst. 11-Void Indigo. 12-The Dazzler. 13-Starstruck. 14-The Swords Of The Swashbucklers. 15-The Raven Banner (Asgard). 16-The Aladdin Effect. 17-Revenge Of The Living Monolith. 18-She Hulk | 1.00 | 3.00 | 6.00 |
| 19-32: 19-The Witch Queen of Acheron (Conan). 20-Greenberg the Vampire. 21-Marada The She-Wolf. 22-Amaz. Spider-Man in Hooky by Wrightson. 23-Dr. Strange. 24-Love And War (Daredevil) by Miller. 25-Alien Legion. 26-Dracula. 27-Avengers. 28-Conan The Reaver. 29-The Big Chance (Thing vs. Hulk). 30-A Sailor's Story. 31-Wolfpack. 32-Death of Groo | 1.15 | 3.50 | 7.00 |
| 32-2nd printing ($5.95) | 1.00 | 3.00 | 6.00 |
| 33,34,36,37: 33-Thor. 34-Predator & Prey (Cloak & Dagger). 36-Willow (movie adapt.). 37-Hercules | 1.15 | 3.50 | 7.00 |
| 35-Hitler's Astrologer (Shadow, $12.95, hard-c) | 2.15 | 6.50 | 13.00 |
| 35-Soft cover reprint (1990, $10.95) | 1.85 | 5.50 | 11.00 |
| 38-Silver Surfer ($14.95) | 3.00 | 8.75 | 17.50 |
| nn-Inhumans (1988, $7.95)-Williamson-i | 1.35 | 4.00 | 8.00 |
| nn-Who Framed Roger Rabbit (1989, $6.95) | 1.15 | 3.50 | 7.00 |
| nn-Roger Rabbit In The Resurrection Of Doom (1989, $8.95) | 1.50 | 4.50 | 9.00 |
| nn-Arena by Bruce Jones ($5.95) | 1.00 | 3.00 | 6.00 |

NOTE: ***Aragones*** *a-27, 32.* ***Byrne*** *c/a-18.* ***Kaluta*** *a-13, 35p; c-13.* ***Miller*** *a-24p.* ***Simonson*** *a-6; c-6.* ***Starlin*** *c/a-1,3.* ***Williamson*** *a-34.* ***Wrightson*** *c-29i.*

**MARVEL MINI-BOOKS**
1966 (50 pgs., B&W; 5/8''x7/8'') (6 different issues)
Marvel Comics Group (Smallest comics ever published)

| | Good | Fine | N-Mint |
|---|---|---|---|
| Captain America, Spider-Man, Sgt. Fury, Hulk, Thor | .50 | 1.50 | 3.00 |
| Millie the Model | .35 | 1.00 | 2.00 |

NOTE: *Each came in six diff. color covers, usually one color: Pink, yellow, green, etc.*

**MARVEL MOVIE PREMIERE** (Magazine)
Sept, 1975 (One Shot) (Black & White)
Marvel Comics Group

| | Good | Fine | N-Mint |
|---|---|---|---|
| 1-Burroughs "The Land That Time Forgot" adaptation | .35 | 1.00 | 2.00 |

**MARVEL MOVIE SHOWCASE FEATURING STAR WARS**
Nov, 1982 - No. 2, Dec, 1982 ($1.25, 68 pgs.)
Marvel Comics Group

| | Good | Fine | N-Mint |
|---|---|---|---|
| 1,2-Star Wars movie adaptation r/Star Wars #1-6 by Chaykin; 1-Reprints cover to Star Wars #1 | | .60 | 1.20 |

**MARVEL MOVIE SPOTLIGHT FEAT. RAIDERS OF THE LOST ARK**
Nov, 1982 ($1.25, 68 pgs.)
Marvel Comics Group

*Marvel Family #54, © FAW*

*Marvel Fanfare #33, © MEG*

*Marvel Feature #1 (12/71), © MEG*

*Marvel Mystery Comics #7, © MEG*

*Marvel Mystery Comics #31, © MEG*

*Marvel Premiere #14, © MEG*

| | Good | Fine | N-Mint |
|---|---|---|---|
| 1-Edited r/Raiders of the Lost Ark #1-3; Buscema-c/a(p); Movie adaptation | | .40 | .80 |

**MARVEL MYSTERY COMICS** (Formerly Marvel Comics) (Marvel Tales No. 93 on)
No. 2, Dec, 1939 - No. 92, June, 1949
Timely /Marvel Comics (TP 2-17/TCI 18-54/MCI 55-92)

| | Good | Fine | VF-NM | NM/Mint |
|---|---|---|---|---|
| 2-American Ace begins, ends #3; Human Torch (blue costume) by Burgos, Sub-Mariner by Everett continues; 2pg. origin recap of Human Torch | 817.00 | 2040.00 | 4900.00 | 6400.00 |
| (Estimated up to 100 total copies exist, 5 in NM/Mint) | | | | |

| | Good | Fine | N-Mint |
|---|---|---|---|
| 3-New logo from Marvel pulp begins | 467.00 | 1165.00 | 2800.00 |
| 4-Intro. Electro, the Marvel of the Age (ends #19), The Ferret, Mystery Detective (ends #9) | 383.00 | 960.00 | 2300.00 |

| | Good | Fine | VF-NM | NM/Mint |
|---|---|---|---|---|
| 5 (Scarce) | 567.00 | 1415.00 | 3400.00 | 4800.00 |
| (Estimated up to 75 total copies exist, 6 in NM/Mint) | | | | |

| | Good | Fine | N-Mint |
|---|---|---|---|
| 6,7 | 233.00 | 585.00 | 1400.00 |
| 8-Human Torch & Sub-Mariner battle | 300.00 | 750.00 | 1800.00 |

9-(Scarce)-Human Torch & Sub-Mariner battle

| | Good | Fine | VF-NM | NM/Mint |
|---|---|---|---|---|
| | 400.00 | 1000.00 | 2400.00 | 3200.00 |
| (Estimated up to 125 total copies exist, 7 in NM/Mint) | | | | |

| | Good | Fine | N-Mint |
|---|---|---|---|
| 10-Human Torch & Sub-Mariner battle, conclusion; Terry Vance, the Schoolboy Sleuth begins, ends #57 | 207.00 | 515.00 | 1240.00 |
| 11 | 158.00 | 395.00 | 950.00 |
| 12-Classic Kirby-c | 150.00 | 375.00 | 900.00 |
| 13-Intro. & 1st app. The Vision by S&K; Sub-Mariner dons new costume, ends #15 | 167.00 | 415.00 | 1000.00 |
| 14-16 | 107.00 | 265.00 | 640.00 |
| 17-Human Torch/Sub-Mariner team-up by Everett/Burgos; pin-up on back-c | 121.00 | 300.00 | 725.00 |
| 18 | 100.00 | 250.00 | 600.00 |
| 19-Origin Toro in text | 103.00 | 260.00 | 620.00 |
| 20-Origin The Angel in text | 98.00 | 245.00 | 585.00 |
| 21-Intro. & 1st app. The Patriot; not in #46-48; pin-up on back-c | 92.00 | 230.00 | 550.00 |
| 22-25: 23-Last Gustavson Angel; origin The Vision in text. 24-Injury-to-eye story | 77.00 | 190.00 | 460.00 |
| 26-30: 27-Ka-Zar ends; last S&K Vision who battles Satan. 28-Jimmy Jupiter in the Land of Nowhere begins, ends #48; Sub-Mariner vs. The Flying Dutchman | 70.00 | 175.00 | 420.00 |
| 31-Sub-Mariner by Everett ends, begins again #84 | 67.00 | 170.00 | 400.00 |
| 32-1st app. The Boboes | 67.00 | 170.00 | 400.00 |
| 33,35-40: 40-Zeppelin-c | 67.00 | 170.00 | 400.00 |
| 34-Everett, Burgos, Martin Goodman, Funnies, Inc. office appear in story & battles Hitler; last Burgos Human Torch | 78.00 | 195.00 | 470.00 |
| 41-43,45-48: 46-Hitler-c. 48-Last Vision; flag-c | 61.00 | 152.00 | 365.00 |
| 44-Classic Super Plane-c | 61.00 | 152.00 | 365.00 |
| 49-Origin Miss America | 78.00 | 195.00 | 470.00 |
| 50-Mary becomes Miss Patriot (origin) | 61.00 | 152.00 | 365.00 |
| 51-60: 53-Bondage-c | 57.00 | 141.00 | 340.00 |
| 61,62,64-Last German War-c | 53.00 | 160.00 | 320.00 |
| 63-Classic Hitler War-c; The Villainess Cat-Woman only app. | 57.00 | 141.00 | 340.00 |
| 65,66-Last Japanese War-c | 53.00 | 160.00 | 320.00 |
| 67-75: 74-Last Patriot. 75-Young Allies begin | 48.00 | 120.00 | 290.00 |
| 76-78: 76-Ten Chapter Miss America serial begins, ends #85 | 48.00 | 120.00 | 290.00 |
| 79-New cover format; Super Villains begin on cover; last Angel | 43.00 | 110.00 | 260.00 |
| 80-1st app. Capt. America in Marvel Comics | 58.00 | 145.00 | 350.00 |
| 81-Captain America app. | 46.00 | 115.00 | 275.00 |
| 82-Origin Namora; 1st Sub-Mariner/Namora team-up; Captain America app. | 79.00 | 200.00 | 475.00 |
| 83,85: 83-Last Young Allies. 85-Last Miss America; Blonde Phantom app. | 43.00 | 110.00 | 260.00 |
| 84-Blonde Phantom, Sub-Mariner by Everett begins; Captain America app. | 58.00 | 145.00 | 350.00 |
| 86-Blonde Phantom i.d. revealed; Captain America app.; last Bucky app. | 52.00 | 130.00 | 310.00 |
| 87-1st Capt. America/Golden Girl team-up | 57.00 | 141.00 | 340.00 |
| 88-Golden Girl, Namora, & Sun Girl (1st in Marvel Comics) x-over; Captain America, Blonde Phantom app.; last Toro | 50.00 | 125.00 | 300.00 |
| 89-1st Human Torch/Sun Girl team-up; 1st Captain America solo; Blonde Phantom app. | 52.00 | 130.00 | 310.00 |
| 90-Blonde Phantom un-masked; Captain America app. | 53.00 | 132.00 | 320.00 |
| 91-Capt. America app.; intro Venus; Blonde Phantom & Sub-Mariner end | 53.00 | 132.00 | 320.00 |
| 92-Feature story on the birth of the Human Torch and the death of Professor Horton (his creator); 1st app. The Witness in Marvel Comics; Captain America app. | 83.00 | 210.00 | 500.00 |
| (Very rare) 132 Pg. issue, B&W, 25 cents (1943-44)-printed in N. Y.; square binding, blank inside covers; has Marvel No. 33-c in color; contains 2 Capt. America & 2 Marvel Mystery Comics-r (Less than ten copies known) | 350.00 | 875.00 | 2100.00 |

NOTE: ***Crandall** a-26i. **Everett** c-7-9, 27, 84. **Schomburg** c-3-11, 13-15, 18, 19, 22-29, 33, 35, 36, 39-48, 50-57, 59, 63-66. **Shores** c-77, 82, 83. Bondage covers-3, 4, 7, 12, 28, 29, 49, 50, 52, 56, 57, 58, 59, 65. Remember Pearl Harbor issues-#30, 31.*

**MARVEL NO-PRIZE BOOK, THE**
Jan, 1983 (One Shot, Direct Sale only)
Marvel Comics Group

| | Good | Fine | N-Mint |
|---|---|---|---|
| 1-Golden-c | | .50 | 1.00 |

**MARVEL PREMIERE**
April, 1972 - No. 61, Aug, 1981 (A tryout book for new characters)
Marvel Comics Group

| | Good | Fine | N-Mint |
|---|---|---|---|
| 1-Origin Warlock (pre #1) by Gil Kane/Adkins; origin Counter-Earth | 1.50 | 4.50 | 10.00 |
| 2-Warlock ends; Kirby Yellow Claw-r | 1.00 | 3.00 | 7.00 |
| 3-Dr. Strange series begins (pre #1, 7/72), B. Smith-a(p); Smith-c? | 1.70 | 5.00 | 12.00 |
| 4-Smith/Brunner-a | 1.00 | 3.00 | 6.00 |
| 5-10: 10-Death of the Ancient One | .50 | 1.50 | 3.00 |
| 11-14: 11-Dr. Strange origin-r by Ditko. 14-Intro. God; last Dr. Strange (3/74), gets own title 3 months later | .35 | 1.00 | 2.00 |
| 15-Origin/1st app. Iron Fist (5/74), ends #25 | 1.70 | 5.00 | 12.00 |
| 16-20: Iron Fist in all. 16-Hama's 1st Marvel-a | .70 | 2.00 | 4.00 |
| 21-24,26-28: 26-Hercules. 27-Satana. 28-Legion of Monsters (Ghost Rider, Man-Thing, Morbius, Werewolf) | .50 | 1.50 | 3.00 |
| 25-1st Byrne Iron Fist(moves to own title next) | 1.15 | 3.50 | 8.00 |
| 29-49,51-56,61: 29,30-The Liberty Legion. 31-1st app. Woodgod. 32-1st app. Monark Starstalker. 33,34-1st color app. Solomon Kane. 35-Origin/1st app. 3-D Man. 38-1st Weirdworld. 41-1st Seeker 3001! 42-Tigra. 44-Jack of Hearts. 47-Origin new Ant-Man. 48-Ant-Man. 49-The Falcon(1st solo book, 8/79). 51,52-Black Panther. 54-1st Caleb Hammer. 56-1st color app. Dominic Fortune. 61-Star Lord | | .50 | 1.00 |
| 50-1st comic book app. Alice Cooper | .70 | 2.00 | 4.00 |
| 57-Dr. Who (1st U.S. app.) | .35 | 1.00 | 2.00 |
| 58-60-Dr. Who | .25 | .75 | 1.50 |

NOTE: ***N. Adams** (Crusty Bunkers) part inks-10, 12, 13. **Austin** a-50i, 56i; c-46i, 50i, 56i, 58. **Brunner** a-4i, 6p, 9-14p; c-9-14. **Byrne** a-47p, 48p. **Chaykin** a-32-34. **Giffen** a-31p, 44p; c-44. **Gil Kane** a(p)-1, 2, 15; c(p)-1, 2, 15, 16, 22-24, 27, 36, 37. **Kirby** c-26, 29-31,*

*35.* ***Layton*** *a-47i, 48i; c-47.* ***McWilliams*** *a-25i.* ***Miller*** *c-49p, 53p, 58p.* ***Nebres*** *a-44i; c-38i.* ***Nino*** *a-38i.* ***Perez*** *c/a-38p, 45p, 46p.* ***Ploog*** *a-38; c-5-7.* ***Russell*** *a-7p.* ***Simonson*** *a-60(2pgs.); c-57.* ***Starlin*** *a-8p; c-8.* ***Sutton*** *a-41, 43, 50p, 61; c-50p, 61. #57-60 published w/two different prices on-c.*

**MARVEL PRESENTS**
October, 1975 - No. 12, Aug, 1977
Marvel Comics Group

| | Good | Fine | N-Mint |
|---|---|---|---|
| 1-Origin & 1st app. Bloodstone | .50 | 1.50 | 3.00 |
| 2-Origin Bloodstone continued; Kirby-c | .35 | 1.00 | 2.00 |
| 3-Guardians of the Galaxy (1st solo book) begins, ends #12 | 1.15 | 3.50 | 8.00 |
| 4-7,9-12: 9,10-Origin Starhawk | 1.00 | 3.00 | 6.00 |
| 8-Reprints story from Silver Surfer #2 | 1.00 | 3.00 | 6.00 |

NOTE: ***Austin*** *a-6i.* ***Buscema*** *r-8p.* ***Chaykin*** *a-5.* ***Kane*** *c-1p.*

**MARVEL PREVIEW** (Magazine) (Bizarre Adventures #25 on)
Feb, 1975 - No. 24, Winter, 1980 (B&W) ($1.00)
Marvel Comics Group

| | Good | Fine | N-Mint |
|---|---|---|---|
| 1-Man Gods From Beyond the Stars; Neal Adams-a(i) & cover; Nino-a | .35 | 1.00 | 2.00 |
| 2-Origin The Punisher (see Amaz. Spider-Man 129); 1st app. Dominic Fortune; Morrow-c | 24.00 | 70.00 | 165.00 |
| 3-10: 3-Blade the Vampire Slayer. 4-Star-Lord & Sword in the Star (origins & 1st app.). 5,6-Sherlock Holmes. 7-Satana, Sword in the Star app. 8-Legion of Monsters. 9-Man-God; origin Star Hawk, ends #20. 10-Thor the Mighty; Starlin-a | .35 | 1.00 | 2.00 |
| 11-24: 11-Star-Lord; Byrne-a. 12-Haunt of Horror. 15-Star-Lord. 16-Detectives. 17-Black Mark by G. Kane. 18-Star-Lord. 19-Kull. 20-Bizarre Advs. 21-Moon Knight; Ditko-a. 22-King Arthur. 23-Bizarre Adventures; Miller-a. 24-Debut Paradox | .35 | 1.00 | 2.00 |

NOTE: ***N. Adams*** *(C. Bunkers) a-20i(r).* ***Buscema*** *a-22, 23.* ***Byrne*** *a-11.* ***Chaykin*** *c/a-20.* ***Colan*** *a-16p, 18p, 23p; c-16p.* ***Giffen*** *a-7.* ***Infantino*** *a-14.* ***Kaluta*** *a-12; c-15.* ***Miller*** *a-23.* ***Morrow*** *a-8i; c-2-4.* ***Perez*** *a-20p.* ***Ploog*** *a-8.* ***Starlin*** *c-13, 14.*

**MARVEL SAGA, THE**
Dec, 1985 - No. 25, Dec, 1987
Marvel Comics Group

| | Good | Fine | N-Mint |
|---|---|---|---|
| 1 | .35 | 1.00 | 2.00 |
| 2-25 | | .60 | 1.20 |

NOTE: ***Williamson*** *a-9i, 10i; c-10-12i, 14i, 16i.*

**MARVEL'S GREATEST COMICS** (Marvel Coll. Item Classics #1-22)
No. 23, Oct, 1969 - No. 96, Jan, 1981
Marvel Comics Group

| | Good | Fine | N-Mint |
|---|---|---|---|
| 23-30: Begin Fantastic Four-r/#30s?-116 | .50 | 1.50 | 3.00 |
| 31-34,38-96: 42-Silver Surfer-r/F.F.(others?) | .35 | 1.00 | 2.00 |
| 35-37-Silver Surfer-r/Fantastic Four #48-50 | .35 | 1.00 | 2.00 |

NOTE: *Dr. Strange, Fantastic Four, Iron Man, Watcher-#23, 24. Capt. America, Dr. Strange, Iron Man, Fantastic Four-#25-28. Fantastic Four-#38-96.* ***Buscema*** *r-85-92; c-87-92r.* ***Ditko*** *r-23-28.* ***Kirby*** *r-23-82; c-75, 77p, 80p. #81 reprints Fantastic Four #100.*

**MARVELS OF SCIENCE**
March, 1946 - No. 4, June, 1946
Charlton Comics

| | Good | Fine | N-Mint |
|---|---|---|---|
| 1-A-Bomb story | 8.50 | 25.50 | 60.00 |
| 2-4 | 5.00 | 15.00 | 35.00 |

**MARVEL SPECIAL EDITION** (Also see Special Collectors' Edition)
1975 - 1978 (84 pgs.) (Oversized)
Marvel Comics Group

| | Good | Fine | N-Mint |
|---|---|---|---|
| 1-Spider-Man(r); Ditko-a(r) | .25 | .75 | 1.50 |
| 1-Star Wars ('77); r-Star Wars #1-3 | .25 | .75 | 1.50 |
| 2-Star Wars ('78); r-Star Wars #4-6 | | .50 | 1.00 |
| 3-Star Wars ('78, 116 pgs.); r-Star Wars #1-6 | | .50 | 1.00 |
| 3-Close Encounters ('78, 56 pgs., movie) | | .50 | 1.00 |
| V2#2(Spring, 1980, $2.00, oversized)-"Star Wars: The Empire Strikes Back;" r-/Marvel Comics Super Special #16 | | .50 | 1.00 |

NOTE: ***Chaykin*** *c/a-1(1977), 2, 3.* ***Stevens*** *a-2i(r), 3i(r).*

**MARVEL SPECTACULAR**
Aug, 1973 - No. 19, Nov, 1975
Marvel Comics Group

| | Good | Fine | N-Mint |
|---|---|---|---|
| 1-Thor-r begin by Kirby | | .60 | 1.20 |
| 2-19 | | .50 | 1.00 |

**MARVEL SPOTLIGHT**
Nov, 1971 - No. 33, Apr, 1977; V2#1, July, 1979 - V2#11, Mar, 1981
Marvel Comics Group (A try-out book for new characters)

| | Good | Fine | N-Mint |
|---|---|---|---|
| 1-Origin Red Wolf (1st solo book, pre #1); Wood inks, Neal Adams-c | 1.00 | 3.00 | 7.00 |
| 2-(Giant, 52pgs.)-Venus-r by Everett; origin/1st app. Werewolf By Night (begins) by Ploog; N. Adams-c | .85 | 2.50 | 5.00 |
| 3,4: 4-Werewolf By Night ends (2/72) | .50 | 1.50 | 3.00 |
| 5-Origin/1st app. Ghost Rider (8/72) & begins | 5.00 | 15.00 | 35.00 |
| 6-8-Last Ploog issue | 2.15 | 6.50 | 15.00 |
| 9-11-Last Ghost Rider(gets own title next mo.) | 2.15 | 6.50 | 15.00 |
| 12-27,30-33: 12-The Son of Satan begins (origin), ends #24. 22-Ghost Rider app. 25-Sinbad. 26-1st app. Scarecrow. 27-Sub-Mariner. 30-The Warriors Three. 31-Nick Fury. 32-Intro/partial origin Spider-Woman(2/77); Nick Fury app. 33-Deathlok | .35 | 1.00 | 2.00 |
| 28,29: Moon Knight (28-1st solo app., 6/76) | .70 | 2.00 | 4.00 |
| V2#1-11: 1-4,8-Capt. Marvel. 5-Dragon Lord. 6,7-StarLord; origin #6. 9-11-Capt. Universe stories | | .50 | 1.00 |

NOTE: ***Austin*** *c-V2#2i, 8.* ***J. Buscema*** *c/a-30p.* ***Chaykin*** *a-31.* ***Ditko*** *a-V2#4, 5, 9-11; c-V2#4, 9-11.* ***Kane*** *c-21p, 32p.* ***Kirby*** *c-29p.* ***McWilliams*** *a-20i.* ***Miller*** *a-V2#8p; c-V2#2, 5p, 7p, 8p.* ***Mooney*** *a-8i, 10i, 14-17p, 24p, 27, 32i.* ***Nasser*** *a-33p.* ***Ploog*** *a-2-5, 6-8p; c-3-9.* ***Sutton*** *a-9-11p, V2#6, 7. #29-25 cent & 30 cent issues exist.*

**MARVEL SUPER ACTION** (Magazine)
January, 1976 (One Shot) (76 pgs.; black & white)
Marvel Comics Group

| | Good | Fine | N-Mint |
|---|---|---|---|
| 1-Origin & 2nd app. Dominic Fortune; The Punisher app., Weird World & The Huntress; Evans & Ploog-a | 12.00 | 36.00 | 85.00 |

**MARVEL SUPER ACTION**
May, 1977 - No. 37, Nov, 1981
Marvel Comics Group

| | Good | Fine | N-Mint |
|---|---|---|---|
| 1-Reprints Capt. America #100 by Kirby | .40 | 1.25 | 2.50 |
| 2,3,5-13: R/Capt. America #101,102,103-111. 11-Origin-r. 12,13-Classic Steranko-c/a(r) | .25 | .75 | 1.50 |
| 4-Marvel Boy-r(origin)/M. Boy #1 | .25 | .75 | 1.50 |
| 14-37: r-Avengers #55,56, Annual 2, others | | .50 | 1.00 |

NOTE: ***Buscema*** *a(r)-14p, 15p; c-18-20, 22, 35r-37.* ***Evans*** *a-1.* ***Everett*** *a-4.* ***Heath*** *a-4r.* ***Kirby*** *r-1-3, 5-11.* ***Ploog*** *a-1.* ***B. Smith*** *a-27r, 28r.* ***Steranko*** *a(r)-12p, 13p; c-12r, 13r.*

**MARVEL SUPER HERO CONTEST OF CHAMPIONS**
June, 1982 - No. 3, Aug, 1982 (Mini-Series)
Marvel Comics Group

| | Good | Fine | N-Mint |
|---|---|---|---|
| 1-3: Features nearly all Marvel characters currently appearing in their comics | .90 | 2.75 | 5.50 |

**MARVEL SUPER HEROES**
October, 1966 (25 cents, 68 pgs.) (1st Marvel One-shot)
Marvel Comics Group

| | Good | Fine | N-Mint |
|---|---|---|---|
| 1-r-origin Daredevil from D.D. #1; r-Avengers #2; G.A. Sub-Mariner-r/Marvel Mystery No. 8 (H. Torch app.) | 6.50 | 19.50 | 45.00 |

**MARVEL SUPER-HEROES** (Formerly Fantasy Masterpieces #1-11)
(Also see Giant-Size Super Heroes) (#12-20: 25 cents, 68 pgs.)
No. 12, 12/67 - No. 31, 11/71; No. 32, 9/72 - No. 105, 1/82
Marvel Comics Group

| | Good | Fine | N-Mint |
|---|---|---|---|
| 12-Origin & 1st app. Capt. Marvel of the Kree; G.A. Human Torch, Destroyer, Capt. America, Black Knight, Sub-Mariner-r | 7.00 | 21.00 | 50.00 |
| 13-2nd app. Capt. Marvel; G.A. Black Knight, Torch, Vision, Capt. America, Sub-Mariner-r | 3.50 | 10.50 | 24.00 |
| 14-Amazing Spider-Man (new-a, 5/68); G.A. Sub-Mariner, Torch, Mercury, Black Knight, Capt. America reprints | 5.00 | 15.00 | 35.00 |

*Marvel Presents #3, © MEG*

MARVEL COMICS GROUP
MARVEL SPOTLIGHT
THE GHOST RIDER
THE WITCH-MAN COMETH!

*Marvel Spotlight #8, © MEG*

*Marvel Super Action #1 (5/77), © MEG*

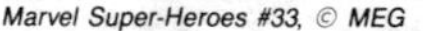
Marvel Super-Heroes #33, © MEG

Marvel Tales #1, © MEG

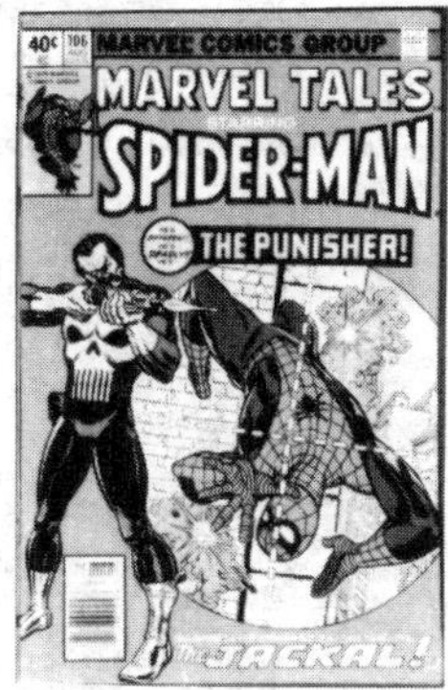

Marvel Tales #106, © MEG

Good Fine N-Mint

15-Black Bolt cameo in Medusa; G.A. Black Knight, Sub-Mariner, Black Marvel, Capt. America-r 1.15 3.50 8.00
16-Origin & 1st app. Phantom Eagle; G.A. Torch, Capt. America, Black Knight, Patriot, Sub-Mariner-r 1.15 3.50 8.00
17-Origin Black Knight; G.A. Torch, Sub-Mariner-r; reprint from All-Winners Squad #21 (cover & story) 1.15 3.50 8.00
18-Origin/1st app. Guardians of the Galaxy; G.A. Sub-Mariner, All-Winners Squad-r 2.85 8.50 20.00
19-Ka-Zar; G.A. Torch, Marvel Boy, Black Knight, Sub-Mariner-r; Smith-c(p); Tuska-a(r) 1.15 3.50 8.00
20-Doctor Doom (5/69); r/Young Men #24 w/-c 1.15 3.50 8.00
21-31: All-r issues. 31-Last Giant issue 1.15 3.50 8.00
32-105: 32-Hulk/Sub-Mariner-r begin from TTA. 56-r/origin Hulk/Inc. Hulk #102; Hulk-r begin .50 1.00

NOTE: ***Austin*** *a-104.* ***Colan*** *a(p)-12, 13, 15, 18; c-12, 13, 15, 18.* ***Everett*** *r-14i, 15i, 18, 19, 33; c-85(r). New* ***Kirby*** *c-22, 27.* ***Maneely*** *r-15, 19.* ***Severin*** *r-83-85i, 100-102; c-100-102r.* ***Starlin*** *c-47.* ***Tuska*** *a-19p. Black Knight-r by* ***Maneely*** *in 12-16, 19. Sub-Mariner-r by* ***Everett*** *in 12-20.*

**MARVEL SUPER-HEROES**
May, 1990 - Present ($2.95, 84 pgs.)
Marvel Comics

1-Moon Knight, Hercules, Black Panther, Magik, Brother Voodoo, Speedball (by Ditko) & Hellcat; Hembeck-a .60 1.75 3.50
2-4: 2-Rogue, Speedball (by Ditko), Iron man, Falcon, Tigra & Daredevil. V2#3-Retells origin Capt. America w/new facts; Blue Shield, Capt. Marvel, Speedball, Wasp; Hulk by Ditko/Rogers. 4-Spider-Man/Nick Fury, Daredevil, Speedball, Wonder Man, Spitfire & Black Knight; Byrne-c .50 1.50 3.00

**MARVEL SUPER HEROES SECRET WARS** (See Secret Wars II)
May, 1984 - No. 12, Apr, 1985 (Limited series)
Marvel Comics Group

1 .60 1.75 3.50
2-12: 6-The Wasp dies. 7-Intro. new Spider-Woman 8-Spider-Man's new costume explained. 12-($1.00, 52 pgs.) .35 1.00 2.00

**MARVEL SUPER SPECIAL** (See Marvel Comics Super. . .)

**MARVEL TAILS STARRING PETER PORKER THE SPECTACULAR SPIDER-HAM**
Nov, 1983 (One Shot)
Marvel Comics Group

1-Peter Porker, the Spectacular Spider-Ham, Captain Americat, Goose Rider, Hulk Bunny app. .25 .75 1.50

**MARVEL TALES** (Formerly Marvel Mystery #1-92)
No. 93, Aug, 1949 - No. 159, Aug, 1957
Marvel/Atlas Comics (MCI)

93 40.00 120.00 280.00
94-Everett-a 32.00 95.00 220.00
95,96,99,101,103,105 18.00 54.00 125.00
97-Sun Girl, 2 pgs; Kirbyish-a; one story used in N.Y. State Legislative document 25.00 75.00 175.00
98-Krigstein-a 19.00 56.00 130.00
100 19.00 56.00 130.00
102-Wolverton-a "The End of the World," 6 pgs. 32.00 95.00 225.00
104-Wolverton-a "Gateway to Horror," 6 pgs. 29.00 86.00 200.00
106,107-Krigstein-a. 106-Decapitation story 17.00 51.00 115.00
108-120: 118-Hypo-c/panels in End of World story. 120-Jack Katz-a 10.00 30.00 70.00
121,123-131: 128-Flying Saucer-c. 131-Last precode (2/55) 8.00 24.00 55.00
122-Kubert-a 8.50 25.50 60.00
132,133,135-141,143,145 4.50 14.00 32.00
134-Krigstein, Kubert-a; flying saucer-c 5.70 17.00 40.00
142-Krigstein-a 5.00 15.00 35.00

Good Fine N-Mint

144-Williamson/Krenkel-a, 3 pgs. 5.70 17.00 40.00
146,148-151,154,155,158 3.60 11.00 25.00
147-Ditko-a 5.00 15.00 35.00
152-Wood, Morrow-a 5.00 15.00 35.00
153-Everett End of World c/story 5.70 17.00 40.00
156-Torres-a 3.70 11.00 26.00
157,159-Krigstein-a 5.00 15.00 35.00

NOTE: ***Andru*** *a-103.* ***Briefer*** *a-118.* ***Check*** *a-147.* ***Colan*** *a-105, 107, 118, 120, 121, 127, 131.* ***Drucker*** *a-127, 135, 141, 146, 150.* ***Everett*** *a-98, 104, 106(2), 108(2), 131, 148, 151, 153, 155; c-109, 111, 114, 117, 127, 143, 147-151, 153, 155, 156.* ***Forte*** *a-125, 130.* ***Heath*** *a-110, 113, 118, 119; c-104-106, 130.* ***Gil Kane*** *a-117.* ***Lawrence*** *a-130.* ***Maneely*** *a-111, 126, 129; c-108, 116, 120, 129, 152.* ***Mooney*** *a-114.* ***Morrow*** *a-150, 152, 156.* ***Orlando*** *a-149, 151, 157.* ***Pakula*** *a-121, 144, 150, 152, 156.* ***Powell*** *a-136, 137, 150, 154.* ***Ravielli*** *a-117.* ***Rico*** *a-97, 99.* ***Romita*** *a-108.* ***Sekowsky*** *a-96-98.* ***Shores*** *a-110.* ***Sinnott*** *a-105, 116.* ***Tuska*** *a-114.* ***Whitney*** *a-107.* ***Wildey*** *a-126, 138.*

**MARVEL TALES** (. . .Annual #1,2: . . .Starring Spider-Man #123 on)
1964 - Present (No. 1-32: 72 pgs.)
Marvel Comics Group (NPP earlier issues)

1-Reprints origins of Spider-Man/Amazing Fantasy #15, Hulk/Inc. Hulk #1, Ant-Man/T.T.A. #35, Giant Man/T.T.A. #49, Iron Man/T.O.S. #39, 48, Thor/J.I.M. #83 & r/Sgt. Fury #1 22.00 65.00 150.00
2 ('65)-r-X-Men #1(origin), Avengers #1(origin), origin Dr. Strange/Strange Tales #115 & origin Hulk(Hulk #3) 8.50 25.50 60.00
3 (7/66)-Spider-Man, Strange Tales, Journey into Mystery, Tales to Astonish-r begin (r/Strange Tales #101) 3.60 11.00 25.00
4,5 1.70 5.00 12.00
6-8,10: 10-Reprints 1st Kraven/Amaz. S-M #15 1.15 3.50 8.00
9-r/Amazing Spider-Man #14 w/cover 1.50 4.50 10.00
11-32: 13-Origin Marvel Boy-r/M. Boy #1. 30-New Angel story. 32-Last 72 pg. issue .85 2.50 5.00
33-105: 75-Origin Spider-Man-r. 77-79-Drug issues-r/Spider-Man #96-98. 98-Death of Gwen Stacy-r/A. Spider-Man #121. 99-Death Green Goblin-r/A. Spider-Man #122. 100-(52 pgs.)-New Hawkeye/Two Gun Kid story. 101-105-All Spider-Man-r .50 1.00
106-1st Punisher-r/Amazing Spider-Man #129 1.30 4.00 9.00
107-133-All Spider-Man-r. 111,112-r/Spider-Man #134,135 (Punisher) .40 .80
134-136-Dr. Strange-r begin; SpM stories continue. 134-Dr. Strange r/Strange Tales #110 .40 .80
137-Origin-r Dr. Strange; shows original unprinted-c & origin Spider-Man/Amazing Fantasy #15 .70 2.00 4.00
137-Nabisco giveaway .50 1.00
138-Reprints all Amazing Spider-Man #1; begin reprints of Spider-Man with covers similar to originals .70 2.00 4.00
139-144: r/Amazing Spider-Man #2-7 .25 .75 1.50
145-199: Spider-Man-r continue w/#8 on. 150 ($1.00, 52pgs.)-r/Spider-Man Annual #14(Miller-a) & Annual 1(Kraven app.). 153-r/1st Kraven/Spider-Man #15. 187,189-Kraven-r. 191-($1.50, 68pgs.)-r/Spider-Man #96-98. 192-($1.25, 52pgs.)-r-Spider-Man #121,122. 193-Byrne-r/Marvel Team-up begin w/scripts .50 1.00
200-Double size ($1.25)-Miller-c & r/Annual #14 .65 1.30
201-208,210-221: 208-Last Byrne-r. 210,211-r/Spidey 134,135. 212,213-r/Gnt. Size Spidey 4. 214,215-r/Spidey 161,162 .40 .80
209-Reprints 1st app. The Punisher/Amazing Spider-Man #129; Punisher reprints begin, end #222 .35 1.10 2.20
222-Reprints origin Punisher/Spectacular Spider-Man #83; last Punisher reprint .40 .80
223-McFarlane-c begin, end #239 .25 .75 1.50
224-248: 233-Spider-Man/X-Men team-ups begin; r/X-Men #35. 234-r/Marvel Team-Up #4. 235,236-r/M. Team-Up Annual #1. 237, 238-r/M. Team-Up #150. 239,240-r/M. Team-Up #38,90(Beast). 242-r/M. Team-Up #89. 243-r/M. Team-Up #117(Wolverine) .50 1.00

NOTE: *All contain reprints; some have new art.* ***Austin*** *a-100i.* ***Byrne*** *a(r)-193-198p, 201-208p.* ***Ditko*** *a-1-30, 83, 100, 137-155.* ***G. Kane*** *a-71, 81, 98-101p; c-125-127p, 130p, 137-155.* ***McFarlane*** *c-223-239.* ***Mooney*** *a-63, 95-97i, 103(i).* ***Nasser*** *a-100p.* ***Nebres*** *a-242i.* ***Rogers*** *c-240, 241, 243, 244.*

**MARVEL TEAM-UP** (See Marvel Treasury Edition #18 & Official Marvel Index To. . .)
March, 1972 - No. 150, Feb, 1985
Marvel Comics Group

| | Good | Fine | N-Mint |
|---|---|---|---|

NOTE: *Spider-Man team-ups in all but Nos. 18, 23, 26, 29, 32, 35, 97, 104, 105, 137.*

1-Human Torch 5.00 15.00 35.00
2,3-H-T 1.70 5.00 12.00
4-X-Men 2.85 8.50 20.00
5-10: 5-Vision. 6-Thing. 7-Thor. 8-The Cat. 9-Iron Man. 10-H-T 1.00 3.00 6.00
11-14,16-20: 11-Inhumans. 12-Werewolf. 13-Capt. America. 14-Sub-Mariner. 16-Capt. Marvel. 17-Mr. Fantastic. 18-H-T/Hulk. 19-Ka-Zar. 20-Black Panther .85 2.50 5.00
15-Early Ghost Rider app. (11/73) 1.15 3.50 8.00
21-30: 21-Dr. Strange. 22-Hawkeye. 23-H-T/Iceman (X-Men cameo). 24-Brother Voodoo. 25-Daredevil. 26-H-T/Thor. 27-Hulk. 28-Hercules. 29-H-T/Iron Man. 30-Falcon .70 2.00 4.00
31-50: 31-Iron Fist. 32-H-T/Son of Satan. 33-Nighthawk. 34-Valkyrie. 35-H-T/Dr. Strange. 36-Frankenstein. 37-Man-Wolf. 38-Beast. 39-H-T. 40-Sons of the Tiger/H-T. 41-Scarlet Witch. 42-The Vision. 43-Dr. Doom; retells origin. 44-Moondragon. 45-Killraven. 46-Deathlok. 47-Thing. 48-Iron Man; last 25 cent issue. 49-Dr. Strange; Iron Man app. 50-Iron Man; Dr. Strange app. .50 1.50 3.00
51,52,56-58: 51-Iron Man; Dr. Strange app. 52-Capt. America. 56-Daredevil. 57-Black Widow. 58-Ghost Rider .35 1.00 2.00
53-Hulk; Woodgod & X-Men app., 1st by Byrne (1/77) 1.35 4.00 8.00
54,55,59,60: 54-Hulk; Woodgod app. 55-Warlock. 59-Yellowjacket/The Wasp. 60-The Wasp (Byrne-a in all) .85 2.50 5.00
61-70: All Byrne-a; 61-H-T. 62-Ms. Marvel. 63-Iron Fist. 64-Daughters of the Dragon. 65-Capt. Britain (1st U.S. app.). 66-Capt. Britain; 1st app. Arcade. 67-Tigra; Kraven the Hunter app. 68-Man-Thing. 69-Havok (from X-Men). 70-Thor .35 1.00 2.00
71-74,76-78,80: 71-Falcon. 72-Iron Man. 73-Daredevil. 74-Not Ready for Prime Time Players (Belushi). 76-Dr. Strange. 77-Ms. Marvel. 78-Wonder Man. 80-Dr. Strange/Clea .35 1.00 2.00
75,79: 75-Power Man. 79-Mary Jane Watson as Red Sonja. Both have Byrne-a(p) .50 1.50 3.00
81-88,90: 81-Satana. 82-Black Widow. 83-Nick Fury. 84-Shang-Chi. 85-Shang-Chi/Black Widow/Nick Fury. 86-Guardians of the Galaxy. 87-Black Panther. 88-Invisible Girl. 90-Beast .25 .75 1.50
89-Nightcrawler .35 1.00 2.00
91-99: 91-Ghost Rider. 92-Hawkeye. 93-Werewolf by Night. 94-SpM vs. The Shroud. 95-Mockingbird (intro.); Nick Fury app. 96-Howard the Duck. 97-Spider-Woman/Hulk. 98-Black Widow. 99-Machine Man .25 .75 1.50
100-(Double-size)-Fantastic Four/Storm/Black Panther; origin/1st app. Karma, one of the New Mutants; origin Storm; X-Men x-over; Miller-a/c(p); Byrne-a (on X-Men app. only) 1.00 3.00 7.00
101-116: 101-Nighthawk(Ditko-a). 102-Doc Samson. 103-Ant-Man. 104-Hulk/Ka-Zar. 105-Hulk/Powerman/Iron Fist. 106-Capt. America. 107-She-Hulk. 108-Paladin; Dazzler cameo. 109-Dazzler; Paladin app. 110-Iron Man. 111-Devil-Slayer. 112-King Kull. 113-Quasar. 114-Falcon. 115-Thor. 116-Valkyrie .50 1.00
117-Wolverine 1.15 3.50 8.00
118-149: 118-Professor X; X-Men (Wolverine) cameo. 119-Gargoyle. 120-Dominic Fortune. 121-Human Torch. 122-Man-Thing. 123-Daredevil. 124-The Beast. 125-Tigra. 126-Hulk & Powerman/Son of Satan. 127-The Watcher. 128-Capt. America; Spider-Man/Capt. America photo-c. 129-The Vision. 130-Scarlet Witch. 131-Frogman. 132-Mr. Fantastic. 133-Fantastic-4. 134-Jack of Hearts. 135-Kitty Pryde; X-Men cameo. 136-Wonder Man. 137-Aunt May/Franklin Richards. 138-Sandman. 139-Nick Fury. 140-Black Widow. 141-Daredevil; new SpM/Black Widow app.(Spidey in black costume #141-146). 142-Capt. Marvel. 143-Starfox. 144-Moon Knight. 145-Iron Man. 146-Nomad. 147-Human Torch; SpM old costume. 148-Thor. 149-Cannonball .40 .80
150-X-Men ($1.00, double-size); B. Smith-c .50 1.50 3.00
Annual 1(1976)-SpM/New X-Men (early app.) 1.30 4.00 9.00
Annuals 2-7: 2(12/79)-SpM/Hulk. 3(11/80)-Hulk/Power Man/Machine Man/Iron Fist; Miller-c(p). 4(10/81)-SpM/Daredevil/Moon Knight/Power Man/Iron Fist; brief origins of each; Miller-c; Miller scripts on Daredevil. 5(1982)-SpM/The Thing/Scarlet Witch/Dr. Strange/Quasar. 6(10/83)-SpM/New Mutants, Cloak & Dagger. 7(10/84)-Alpha Flight; Byrne-c(i) .25 .75 1.50

NOTE: ***Art Adams** c-141p. **Austin** a-79i; c-76i, 79i, 96i, 101i, 112i, 130i. **Bolle** a-9i. **Byrne** a(p)-53-55, 59-70, 75, 79, 100; c-68p, 70p, 72p, 75, 76p, 79p, 129i, 133i. **Colan** a-87p. **Ditko** a-101. **Kane** a(p)-4-6, 13, 14, 16-19, 23; c(p)-4, 13, 14, 17-19, 23, 25, 26, 32-35, 37, 41, 44, 45, 47, 53, 54. **Miller** c-95p, 99p, 102p, 106. **Mooney** a-2i, 7i, 8, 10p, 11p, 16i, 24-31p, 72, 93i, Annual 5i. **Nasser** a-89p; c-101p. **Simonson** c-99i, 148. **Paul Smith** c-131, 132. **Starlin** c-27. **Sutton** a-93p. "H-T" means Human Torch; "SpM" means Spider-Man; "S-M" means Sub-Mariner.*

**MARVEL TREASURY EDITION** ($1.50-$2.50)
Sept, 1974 - No. 28, 1981 (100 pgs.; oversized, reprints)
Marvel Comics Group

1-Spectacular Spider-Man .70 2.00 4.00
2-4: 2-Fantastic Four, Silver Surfer. 3-The Mighty Thor. 4-Conan the Barbarian; Barry Smith-c/a .40 1.25 2.50
5-14,16,17: 5-The Hulk (origin). 6-Doctor Strange. 7-Avengers. 8-Christmas stories; Spider-Man, Hulk, Nick Fury. 9-Giant; Super-hero Team-up. 10-Thor. 11-Fantastic Four. 12-Howard the Duck. 13-Giant Super-hero Holiday Grab-Bag. 14-Spider-Man. 16-Super-hero Team-up; The Defenders (origin) & Valkyrie.17-The Hulk .35 1.00 2.00
15-Conan; Barry Smith, Neal Adams-i .40 1.25 2.50
18-The Astonishing Spider-Man; Spider-Man's 1st team-ups with the X-Men, Ghost Rider & Werewolf by Night .35 1.00 2.00
19-28: 19-Conan the Barbarian. 20-Hulk. 21-Fantastic Four. 22-Spider-Man. 23-Conan. 24-Rampaging Hulk. 25-Spider-Man vs. The Hulk. 26-The Hulk; Wolverine app. 27-Spider-Man. 28-Spider-Man/Superman; (origin of each) .35 1.00 2.00

NOTE: *Reprints-2, 3, 5, 7-9, 13, 14, 16, 17. **Neal Adams** a(i)-6, 15. **Brunner** a-6, 12; c-6. **Buscema** a-15, 19, 28; c-28. **Colan** c-12p. **Ditko** a-1, 6. **Kirby** a-2, 10, 11; c-7. **B. Smith** a-4, 15, 19; c-4, 19.*

**MARVEL TREASURY OF OZ** (See MGM's Marvelous. . .)
1975 (oversized) ($1.50)
Marvel Comics Group

1-The Marvelous Land of Oz; Buscema-a .35 1.00 2.00

**MARVEL TREASURY SPECIAL** (Also see 2001: A Space Odyssey)
1974; 1976 (84 pgs.; oversized) ($1.50)
Marvel Comics Group

Vol. 1-Spider-Man, Torch, Sub-Mariner, Avengers "Giant Superhero Holiday Grab-Bag" .25 .75 1.50
Vol. 1-Capt. America's Bicentennial Battles (6/76)-Kirby-a; B. Smith inks, 11 pgs. .25 .75 1.50

**MARVEL TRIPLE ACTION** (See Giant-Size. . .)
Feb, 1972 - No. 24, Mar, 1975; No. 25, Aug, 1975 - No. 47, Apr, 1979
Marvel Comics Group

1-(25 cent giant, 52pgs.)-Dr. Doom, Silver Surfer, The Thing begin, end #4 ('66 reprints from Fantastic Four) .50 1.50 3.00
2-47: 45-r/X-Men #45. 46-r/Avengers #53(X-Men) .50 1.00

NOTE: *#5-44, 46, 47 reprint Avengers #11 thru ?. #40-r/Avengers #48(1st Black Knight). **Buscema** a(r)-35p, 36p, 38p, 39p, 41, 42, 43p, 44p, 46p, 47p. **Ditko** a-2r; c-47. **Kirby** a(r)-1-4p. **Starlin** c-7. **Tuska** a(r)-40p, 43i, 46i, 47i.*

**MARVEL TWO-IN-ONE** (. . .Featuring .... #82? on; see The Thing)
January, 1974 - No. 100, June, 1983
Marvel Comics Group

1-Thing team-ups begin; Man-Thing 1.50 4.50 10.00
2-4: 2-Sub-Mariner; last 20 cent issue. 3-Daredevil. 4-Capt. America .85 2.50 5.00

*Marvel Team-Up #1, © MEG*

*Marvel Team-Up #118, © MEG*

*Marvel Triple Action #1, © MEG*

*Marvel Two-In-One #51, © MEG*

*Mary Marvel #14, © FAW*

*Masked Ranger #5, © PG*

| | Good | Fine | N-Mint |
|---|---|---|---|
| 5-Guardians of the Galaxy | 1.30 | 4.00 | 9.00 |
| 6-Dr. Strange | 1.15 | 3.50 | 8.00 |
| 7-10: 8-Early Ghost Rider app. ('74) | .70 | 2.00 | 4.00 |
| 11-20: 17-Spider-Man. 18-Last 25 cent issue | .50 | 1.50 | 3.00 |
| 21-40: 29-2nd app. Spider-Woman. 39-Vision | .35 | 1.00 | 2.00 |
| 41,42,44-49: 42-Capt. America. 45-Capt. Marvel | | .50 | 1.00 |
| 43,50,53-55-Byrne-a. 54-Death of Deathlok | .40 | 1.25 | 2.50 |
| 51-The Beast, Nick Fury, Ms. Marvel; Miller-p | .50 | 1.50 | 3.00 |
| 52-Moon Knight app. | .35 | 1.00 | 2.00 |
| 56-82: 60-Intro. Impossible Woman. 61-63-Warlock app. 69-Guardians of the Galaxy. 76-Iceman. 80-Ghost Rider | | .40 | .80 |
| 83,84: 83-Sasquatch. 84-Alpha Flight app. | .50 | 1.50 | 3.00 |
| 85-99: 93-Jocasta dies. 96-X-Men-c & cameo | | .30 | .60 |
| 100-Double size, Byrne scripts | .25 | .75 | 1.50 |
| Annual 1(6/76, 52pgs.)-Thing/Liberty Legion | .25 | .80 | 1.60 |
| Annual 2(2/77, 52pgs.)-Thing/Spider-Man; Thanos dies; Starlin-c/a | 1.35 | 4.00 | 8.00 |
| Annual 3,4: 3(7/78, 52pgs.). 4(9/79, 52pgs.) | | .50 | 1.00 |
| Annual 5,6: 5(9/80, 52pgs.)-Hulk. 6(10/81, 52pgs.)-1st app. American Eagle | | .40 | .80 |
| Annual 7(10/82, 52pgs.)-The Thing/Champion; Sasquatch, Colossus app. | | .50 | 1.00 |

NOTE: ***Austin*** *c(i)-42, 54, 56, 58, 61, 63, 66.* ***John Buscema*** *a-30p, 45; c-30p.* ***Byrne*** *a(p)-43, 50, 53-55; c-43, 53p, 56p, 98i, 99i.* ***Gil Kane*** *a-1p, 2p; c(p)-1-3, 9, 11, 14, 28.* ***Kirby*** *c-10, 12, 19p, 20, 25, 27.* ***Mooney*** *a-18i, 38i, 90i.* ***Nasser*** *a-70p.* ***Perez*** *a(p)-56-58, 60, 64, 65; c(p)-32, 33, 42, 50-52, 54, 55, 57, 58, 61-66, 70.* ***Roussos*** *a-Annual 1i.* ***Simonson*** *c-43i; Annual 6i.* ***Starlin*** *c-6, Annual 1.* ***Tuska*** *a-6p.*

**MARVEL UNIVERSE** (See Official Handbook Of The. . .)

**MARVIN MOUSE**
September, 1957
Atlas Comics (BPC)

| | Good | Fine | N-Mint |
|---|---|---|---|
| 1-Everett-c/a; Maneely-a | 3.50 | 10.50 | 24.00 |

**MARY JANE & SNIFFLES** (See 4-Color #402, 474 & Looney Tunes)

**MARY MARVEL COMICS** (Monte Hale #29 on) (Also see Captain Marvel #18, Marvel Family, Shazam, & Wow)
Dec, 1945 - No. 28, Sept, 1948
Fawcett Publications

| | Good | Fine | N-Mint |
|---|---|---|---|
| 1-Captain Marvel intro. Mary on-c; intro/origin Georgia Sivana | 65.00 | 195.00 | 455.00 |
| 2 | 32.00 | 95.00 | 225.00 |
| 3 | 22.00 | 65.00 | 155.00 |
| 4 | 17.00 | 51.00 | 120.00 |
| 5-8: 8-Bulletgirl x-over in Mary Marvel | 14.00 | 43.00 | 100.00 |
| 9,10 | 11.00 | 32.00 | 75.00 |
| 11-20 | 8.50 | 25.50 | 60.00 |
| 21-28 | 7.00 | 21.00 | 50.00 |

**MARY POPPINS** (See Movie Comics & Walt Disney Showcase No. 17)

**MARY'S GREATEST APOSTLE** (St. Louis Grignion de Montfort)
No date (16 pages; paper cover)
Catechetical Guild (Topix) (Giveaway)

| | Good | Fine | N-Mint |
|---|---|---|---|
| nn | 1.70 | 5.00 | 12.00 |

**MARY WORTH** (See Harvey Comics Hits #55 & Love Stories of. . .)
March, 1956
Argo

| | Good | Fine | N-Mint |
|---|---|---|---|
| 1 | 3.50 | 10.50 | 24.00 |

**MASK** (TV)
Dec, 1985 - No. 4, Mar, 1986; Feb, 1987 - No. 9, Oct, 1987
DC Comics

| | Good | Fine | N-Mint |
|---|---|---|---|
| 1-(Mini-series) (Sat. morning TV show) | .35 | 1.00 | 2.00 |
| 2-4 | .25 | .70 | 1.40 |
| 1-(2nd series) | | .60 | 1.20 |
| 2-9 | | .45 | .90 |

**MASK COMICS**
Feb-Mar, 1945 - No. 2, Apr-May, 1945; No. 2, Fall, 1945
Rural Home Publications

| | Good | Fine | N-Mint |
|---|---|---|---|
| 1-Classic L. B. Cole Satan-c/a; Palais-a | 77.00 | 230.00 | 540.00 |
| 2-(Scarce)Classic L. B. Cole Satan-c; Black Rider, The Boy Magician, & The Collector app. | 43.00 | 130.00 | 300.00 |
| 2(Fall, 1945)-No publ.-same as regular #2; L. B. Cole-c | 29.00 | 86.00 | 200.00 |

**MASKED BANDIT, THE**
1952
Avon Periodicals

| | Good | Fine | N-Mint |
|---|---|---|---|
| nn-Kinstler-a | 8.50 | 25.50 | 60.00 |

**MASKED MAN, THE**
12/84 - No. 10, 4/86; No. 11, 10/87; No. 12, 4/88 ($1.75-$2.00; Baxter)
Eclipse Comics

| | Good | Fine | N-Mint |
|---|---|---|---|
| 1-Origin retold | .35 | 1.00 | 2.00 |
| 2-12: 3-Origin Aphid-Man. ($2.00; B&W #9 on) | .30 | .90 | 1.80 |

**MASKED MARVEL** (See Keen Detective Funnies)
Sept, 1940 - No. 3, Dec, 1940
Centaur Publications

| | Good | Fine | N-Mint |
|---|---|---|---|
| 1-The Masked Marvel begins | 90.00 | 270.00 | 625.00 |
| 2,3: 2-Gustavson, Tarpe Mills-a | 57.00 | 170.00 | 400.00 |

**MASKED RAIDER, THE** (Billy The Kid #9 on; Frontier Scout, Daniel Boone #10-13; also see Blue Bird)
6/55 - No. 8, 7/57; No. 14, 8/58 - No. 30, 6/61
Charlton Comics

| | Good | Fine | N-Mint |
|---|---|---|---|
| 1-Painted-c | 5.00 | 15.00 | 35.00 |
| 2 | 2.65 | 8.00 | 18.00 |
| 3-8: 8-Billy The Kid app. | 2.00 | 6.00 | 14.00 |
| 14,16-30: 22-Rocky Lane app. | 1.30 | 4.00 | 9.00 |
| 15-Williamson-a, 7 pgs. | 2.35 | 7.00 | 16.00 |

**MASKED RANGER**
April, 1954 - No. 9, Aug, 1955
Premier Magazines

| | Good | Fine | N-Mint |
|---|---|---|---|
| 1-The M. Ranger, his horse Streak, & The Crimson Avenger (origin) begin, end #9; Woodbridge/Frazetta-a | 17.00 | 51.00 | 120.00 |
| 2,3 | 4.30 | 13.00 | 30.00 |
| 4-8-All Woodbridge-a. 5-Jesse James by Woodbridge. 6-Billy The Kid by Woodbridge. 7-Wild Bill Hickok by Woodbridge. 8-Jim Bowie's Life Story | 5.70 | 17.00 | 40.00 |
| 9-Torres-a; Wyatt Earp by Woodbridge | 6.50 | 19.00 | 45.00 |

NOTE: ***Check*** *a-1.* ***Woodbridge*** *c/a-1, 4-9.*

**MASK OF DR. FU MANCHU, THE** (See Dr. Fu Manchu)
1951
Avon Periodicals

| | Good | Fine | N-Mint |
|---|---|---|---|
| 1-Sax Rohmer adapt.; Wood c/a, 26 pgs., Hollingsworth-a | 56.00 | 170.00 | 390.00 |

**MASQUE OF THE RED DEATH** (See Movie Classics)

**MASTER, THE** (Also see Young Master)
1989 - No. 2? ($1.95, B&W)
New Comics

| | Good | Fine | N-Mint |
|---|---|---|---|
| 1,2: Val Mayerik painted-c/a in all | .35 | 1.00 | 2.00 |

**MASTER COMICS** (Combined with Slam Bang Comics #7 on)
Mar, 1940 - No. 133, Apr, 1953 (No. 1-6: oversized issues)
(#1-3: 15 cents, 52pgs.; #4-6: 10 cents, 36pgs.)
Fawcett Publications

| | Good | Fine | VF-NM | NM/Mint |
|---|---|---|---|---|
| 1-Origin Master Man; The Devil's Dagger, El Carim, Master of Magic, Rick O'Say, Morton Murch, White Rajah, Shipwreck Roberts, Frontier Marshal, Streak Sloan, Mr. Clue begin (all features end #6) | 233.00 | 585.00 | 1400.00 | 2200.00 |

(Estimated up to 100 total copies exist, 4 in NM/Mint)

| | Good | Fine | N-Mint |
|---|---|---|---|
| 2 | 115.00 | 290.00 | 690.00 |
| 3-5 | 75.00 | 190.00 | 450.00 |
| 6-Last Master Man | 83.00 | 210.00 | 500.00 |

NOTE: *#1-6 rarely found in near mint to mint condition due to large-size format.*

| | Good | Fine | N-Mint |
|---|---|---|---|
| 7-(10/40)-Bulletman, Zoro, the Mystery Man (ends #22), Lee Granger, Jungle King, & Buck Jones begin; only app. The War Bird & Mark Swift & the Time Retarder | 133.00 | 335.00 | 800.00 |
| 8-The Red Gaucho (ends #13), Captain Venture (ends #22) & The Planet Princess begin | 57.00 | 170.00 | 400.00 |
| 9,10: 10-Lee Granger ends | 50.00 | 150.00 | 350.00 |
| 11-Origin Minute-Man | 117.00 | 300.00 | 700.00 |
| 12 | 57.00 | 170.00 | 400.00 |
| 13-Origin Bulletgirl | 100.00 | 250.00 | 600.00 |
| 14-16: 14-Companions Three begins, ends #31 | 50.00 | 150.00 | 350.00 |
| 17-20: 17-Raboy-a on Bulletman begins. 20-Captain Marvel cameo app. in Bulletman | 50.00 | 150.00 | 350.00 |

21-(12/41; Scarce)-Captain Marvel & Bulletman team up against Capt. Nazi; origin Capt. Marvel Jr's most famous nemesis Captain Nazi who will cause creation of Capt. Marvel Jr. in Whiz #25. Part I of trilogy origin of Capt. Marvel Jr.

| Good | Fine | VF-NM | NM/Mint |
|---|---|---|---|
| 193.00 | 580.00 | 1350.00 | 1700.00 |

(Estimated up to 110 total copies exist, 6 in NM/Mint)

22-(1/42)-Captain Marvel Jr. moves over from Whiz #25 & teams with Bulletman against Captain Nazi; part III of trilogy origin of Capt. Marvel Jr. & his 1st cover and adventure

| Good | Fine | VF-NM | NM/Mint |
|---|---|---|---|
| 165.00 | 495.00 | 1150.00 | 1500.00 |

(Estimated up to 135 total copies exist, 7 in NM/Mint)

| | Good | Fine | N-Mint |
|---|---|---|---|
| 23-Capt. Marvel Jr. c/stories begins; fights Capt. Nazi by himself | 129.00 | 385.00 | 900.00 |
| 24,25,29 | 49.00 | 148.00 | 345.00 |
| 26-28,30-Captain Marvel Jr. vs. Capt. Nazi. 30-Flag-c | 49.00 | 148.00 | 345.00 |
| 31,32: 32-Last El Carim & Buck Jones; Balbo, the Boy Magician intro. in El Carim | 35.00 | 105.00 | 245.00 |
| 33-Balbo, the Boy Magician (ends #47), Hopalong Cassidy (ends #49) begins | 35.00 | 105.00 | 245.00 |
| 34-Capt. Marvel Jr. vs. Capt. Nazi | 35.00 | 105.00 | 245.00 |
| 35 | 35.00 | 105.00 | 245.00 |
| 36-40: 40-Flag-c | 30.00 | 90.00 | 210.00 |
| 41-Bulletman, Capt. Marvel Jr. & Bulletgirl x-over in Minute-Man; only app. Crime Crusaders Club (Capt. Marvel Jr., Minute-Man, Bulletman & Bulletgirl)-only team in Fawcett Comics | 34.00 | 100.00 | 235.00 |
| 42-47,49: 47-Hitler becomes Corpl. Hitler Jr. 49-Last Minute-Man | 19.00 | 56.00 | 130.00 |
| 48-Intro. Bulletboy; Capt. Marvel cameo in Minute-Man | 23.00 | 70.00 | 160.00 |
| 50-Radar, Nyoka the Jungle Girl begin; Capt. Marvel x-over in Radar; origin Radar | 14.00 | 43.00 | 100.00 |
| 51-58 | 10.00 | 30.00 | 70.00 |
| 59-62: Nyoka serial "Terrible Tiara" in all; 61-Capt. Marvel Jr. 1st meets Uncle Marvel | 11.50 | 34.00 | 80.00 |
| 63-80 | 8.00 | 24.00 | 55.00 |
| 81-92,94-99: 88-Hopalong Cassidy begins (ends #94). 95-Tom Mix begins (ends #133) | 6.50 | 19.00 | 45.00 |
| 93-Krigstein-a | 7.00 | 21.00 | 50.00 |
| 100 | 7.00 | 21.00 | 50.00 |
| 101-106-Last Bulletman | 5.00 | 15.00 | 35.00 |
| 107-132: 132-B&W and color illos in **POP** | 4.00 | 12.00 | 28.00 |
| 133-Bill Battle app. | 5.70 | 17.00 | 40.00 |

NOTE: ***Mac Raboy** a-15-39, 40 in part, 42, 58; c-21-49, 51, 52, 54, 56, 58, 59.*

**MASTER DETECTIVE**
1964 (Reprints)
Super Comics

| | Good | Fine | N-Mint |
|---|---|---|---|
| 10,17,18: 17-Young King Cole; McWilliams-a | .40 | 1.20 | 2.40 |

**MASTER OF KUNG FU** (Formerly Special Marvel Edition; see Deadly Hands of Kung Fu, Giant-Size. . ., & Marvel Comics Presents)
No. 17, April, 1974 - No. 125, June, 1983
Marvel Comics Group

| | Good | Fine | N-Mint |
|---|---|---|---|
| 17-Starlin-a; intro Black Jack Tarr | 1.00 | 3.00 | 7.00 |
| 18-20: 19-Man-Thing app. | .50 | 1.50 | 3.00 |
| 21-23,25-30 | .35 | 1.00 | 2.00 |
| 24-Starlin, Simonson-a | .40 | 1.25 | 2.50 |
| 31-99: 33-1st Leiko Wu. 43-Last 25 cent issue | | .50 | 1.00 |
| 100,118,125-(All double size) | | .60 | 1.20 |
| 101-117,119-124: 104-Cerebus cameo | | .50 | 1.00 |
| Annual 1(4/76)-Iron Fist | | .60 | 1.20 |

NOTE: ***Austin** c-63i, 74i. **Buscema** c-44p. **Gulacy** a(p)-18-20, 22, 25, 29-31, 33-35, 38, 39, 40(p&i), 42-50; c-51, 55, 64, 67. **Gil Kane** c(p)-20, 38, 39, 42, 45, 59, 63. **Nebres** c-73i. **Starlin** a-17p; c-54. **Sutton** a-42i. #53 reprints #20.*

**MASTER OF THE WORLD** (See 4-Color #1157)

**MASTERS OF TERROR** (Magazine)
July, 1975 - No. 2, Sept, 1975 (Black & White) (All Reprints)
Marvel Comics Group

| | Good | Fine | N-Mint |
|---|---|---|---|
| 1-Brunner, Barry Smith-a; Morrow-c; Neal Adams-r(i); Starlin-a(p); Gil Kane-a | .30 | .90 | 1.80 |
| 2-Reese, Kane, Mayerik-a; Steranko-c | | .60 | 1.20 |

**MASTERS OF THE UNIVERSE**
Dec, 1982 - No. 3, Feb, 1983 (Mini-series)
DC Comics

| | Good | Fine | N-Mint |
|---|---|---|---|
| 1 | | .60 | 1.20 |
| 2,3: 2-Origin He-Man & Ceril | | .50 | 1.00 |

NOTE: ***Alcala** a-1i, 2i. **Tuska** a-1-3p; c-1-3p. #2 has 75 & 95 cent cover price.*

**MASTERS OF THE UNIVERSE** (Comic Album)
1984 (8½x11"; $2.95; 64 pgs.)
Western Publishing Co.

| | Good | Fine | N-Mint |
|---|---|---|---|
| 11362-Based on Mattel toy & cartoon | .50 | 1.50 | 2.95 |

**MASTERS OF THE UNIVERSE** (TV)
May, 1986 - No. 12, March, 1988 .75-$1.00)
Star Comics/Marvel #? on

| | Good | Fine | N-Mint |
|---|---|---|---|
| 1-12: 8-Begin $1.00-c | | .50 | 1.00 |
| . . .The Motion Picture (11/87, $2.00)-Tuska-p | .35 | 1.00 | 2.00 |

**MASTERWORKS SERIES OF GREAT COMIC BOOK ARTISTS, THE**
May, 1983 - No. 3, Dec, 1983 (Baxter paper)
Sea Gate Distributors/DC Comics

| | Good | Fine | N-Mint |
|---|---|---|---|
| 1-3: 1,2-Shining Knight by Frazetta r-/Adventure. 2-Tomahawk by Frazetta-r. 3-Wrightson-c/a(r) | .35 | 1.00 | 2.00 |

**MATT SLADE GUNFIGHTER** (Kid Slade Gunfighter #5 on?; See Western Gunfighters)
May, 1956 - No. 4, Nov, 1956
Atlas Comics (SPI)

| | Good | Fine | N-Mint |
|---|---|---|---|
| 1-Williamson/Torres-a; Maneely-c/a | 8.00 | 24.00 | 56.00 |
| 2-Williamson-a | 5.70 | 17.00 | 40.00 |
| 3,4: 4-Maneely-c | 3.00 | 9.00 | 21.00 |

NOTE: ***Maneely** a-1-4; c-1, 4. **Roth** a-2-4. **Severin** a-1-4.*

**MAUD**
1906 (32 pgs. in color; 10x15½") (cardboard covers)
Frederick A. Stokes Co.

| | Good | Fine | N-Mint |
|---|---|---|---|
| nn-By Fred Opper | 16.00 | 48.00 | 110.00 |

**MAVERICK** (TV)
No. 892, 4/58 - No. 19, 4-6/62 (All have photo-c)
Dell Publishing Co.

*Master Comics #12, © FAW*

*Master Comics #98, © FAW*

*Master of Kung Fu #125, © MEG*

Maverick #16, © Warner Bros.

The Maze Agency #1, © Comico

MD #4, © WMG

| | Good | Fine | N-Mint |
|---|---|---|---|
| 4-Color 892 (#1): James Garner/Jack Kelly photo-c begin | 8.00 | 24.00 | 55.00 |
| 4-Color 930,945,962,980,1005 (6-8/59) | 5.70 | 17.00 | 40.00 |
| 7 (10-12/59) - 14: Last Garner/Kelly-c | 4.50 | 14.00 | 32.00 |
| 15-18: Jack Kelly/Roger Moore photo-c | 4.50 | 14.00 | 32.00 |
| 19-Jack Kelly photo-c | 4.50 | 14.00 | 32.00 |

**MAVERICK MARSHAL**
Nov, 1958 - No. 7, May, 1960
Charlton Comics

| | Good | Fine | N-Mint |
|---|---|---|---|
| 1 | 1.70 | 5.00 | 12.00 |
| 2-7 | 1.00 | 3.00 | 7.00 |

**MAX BRAND** (See Silvertip)

**MAYA** (See Movie Classics)
March, 1968
Gold Key

| | Good | Fine | N-Mint |
|---|---|---|---|
| 1 (10218-803)(TV) | 1.15 | 3.50 | 8.00 |

**MAYHEM**
May, 1989 - No. 4, 1989 ($2.50, B&W, 52 pgs.)
Dark Horse Comics

| | Good | Fine | N-Mint |
|---|---|---|---|
| 1-4: 1-The Mark, The Mask & Mecha in all | .40 | 1.25 | 2.50 |

**MAZE AGENCY, THE**
Dec, 1988 - Present ($1.95-$2.50, color)
Comico/Innovation Publishing #8 on

| | Good | Fine | N-Mint |
|---|---|---|---|
| 1-6,8-15 ($1.95): 9-Ellery Queen app. | .35 | 1.00 | 2.00 |
| 7 ($2.50)-Last Comico issue | .40 | 1.25 | 2.50 |
| 16-20 ($2.50) | .40 | 1.25 | 2.50 |
| Annual 1 ('90, $2.75)-Ploog-c; Spirit tribute ish. | .45 | 1.40 | 2.80 |
| Special 1 (89?, $2.75)-Staton-p (Innovation) | .45 | 1.40 | 2.80 |

**MAZIE** (. . .& Her Friends) (See Mortie, Stevie & Tastee-Freez)
1953 - #12, 1954; #13, 12/54 - #22, 9/56; #23, 9/57 - #28, 8/58
Mazie Comics(Magazine Publ.)/Harvey Publ. No. 13-on

| | Good | Fine | N-Mint |
|---|---|---|---|
| 1-(Teen-age)-Stevie's girl friend | 2.00 | 6.00 | 14.00 |
| 2 | 1.15 | 3.50 | 8.00 |
| 3-10 | .85 | 2.60 | 6.00 |
| 11-28 | .70 | 2.00 | 4.00 |

**MAZIE**
1950 - No. 7, 1951 (5 cents) (5x7¼"-miniature)(52 pgs.)
Nation Wide Publishers

| | Good | Fine | N-Mint |
|---|---|---|---|
| 1-Teen-age | 4.00 | 12.00 | 28.00 |
| 2-7 | 2.00 | 6.00 | 14.00 |

**MAZINGER** (See First Comics Graphic Novel #17)

**'MAZING MAN**
Jan, 1986 - No. 12, Dec, 1986
DC Comics

| | Good | Fine | N-Mint |
|---|---|---|---|
| 1-12: 7,8-Hembeck-a. 12-Dark Knight part-c by Miller | | .40 | .80 |
| Special 1('87), 2(4/88), 3('90) (all $2.00, 52 pgs.) | .35 | 1.00 | 2.00 |

**McCRORY'S CHRISTMAS BOOK**
1955 (36 pgs.; slick cover)
Western Printing Co. (McCrory Stores Corp. giveaway)

| | Good | Fine | N-Mint |
|---|---|---|---|
| nn-Painted-c | 1.35 | 4.00 | 8.00 |

**McCRORY'S TOYLAND BRINGS YOU SANTA'S PRIVATE EYES**
1956 (16 pgs.)
Promotional Publ. Co. (Giveaway)

| | Good | Fine | N-Mint |
|---|---|---|---|
| nn-Has 9 pg. story plus 7 pg. toy ads | 1.00 | 3.00 | 6.00 |

**McCRORY'S WONDERFUL CHRISTMAS**
1954 (20 pgs.; slick cover)
Promotional Publ. Co. (Giveaway)

| | Good | Fine | N-Mint |
|---|---|---|---|
| nn | 1.35 | 4.00 | 8.00 |

**McHALE'S NAVY** (TV) (See Movie Classics)
May-July, 1963 - No. 3, Nov-Jan, 1963-64 (Photo-c)
Dell Publishing Co.

| | Good | Fine | N-Mint |
|---|---|---|---|
| 1 | 2.65 | 8.00 | 18.00 |
| 2,3 | 2.00 | 6.00 | 14.00 |

**McKEEVER & THE COLONEL** (TV)
Feb-Apr, 1963 - No. 3, Aug-Oct, 1963
Dell Publishing Co.

| | Good | Fine | N-Mint |
|---|---|---|---|
| 1-Photo-c | 2.65 | 8.00 | 18.00 |
| 2,3 | 2.00 | 6.00 | 14.00 |

**McLINTOCK** (See Movie Comics)

**MD**
Apr-May, 1955 - No. 5, Dec-Jan, 1955-56
E. C. Comics

| | Good | Fine | N-Mint |
|---|---|---|---|
| 1-Not approved by code | 7.00 | 21.00 | 50.00 |
| 2-5 | 5.70 | 17.00 | 40.00 |

NOTE: ***Crandall, Evans, Ingels, Orlando*** *art in all issues;* ***Craig*** *c-1-5.*

**MECHA** (Also see Mayhem)
June, 1987 - No. 6, 1988 ($1.50-$1.95, color, B&W #3 on)
Dark Horse Comics

| | Good | Fine | N-Mint |
|---|---|---|---|
| 1,2 ($1.95, color) | .35 | 1.00 | 2.00 |
| 3,4 ($1.75, B&W) | .30 | .90 | 1.80 |
| 5,6 ($1.50, B&W) | .25 | .75 | 1.50 |

**MECHANICS**
Oct, 1985 - No. 3, Dec, 1985 ($2.00 cover; adults only)
Fantagraphics Books

| | Good | Fine | N-Mint |
|---|---|---|---|
| 1-3: Love & Rockets in all | .35 | 1.00 | 2.00 |

**MEDAL FOR BOWZER, A**
No date (1948-50?)
Will Eisner Giveaway

| | Good | Fine | N-Mint |
|---|---|---|---|
| nn-Eisner-c/script | 20.00 | 60.00 | 140.00 |

**MEDAL OF HONOR COMICS**
Spring, 1946
A. S. Curtis

| | Good | Fine | N-Mint |
|---|---|---|---|
| 1-War stories | 5.30 | 16.00 | 38.00 |

**MEDIA STARR**
July, 1989 - No. 3, Sept, 1989 ($1.95, color, mini-series, 28 pgs.)
Innovation Publishing

| | Good | Fine | N-Mint |
|---|---|---|---|
| 1-3: Deluxe format | .35 | 1.00 | 2.00 |

**MEET ANGEL** (Formerly Angel & the Ape)
No. 7, Nov-Dec, 1969
National Periodical Publications

| | Good | Fine | N-Mint |
|---|---|---|---|
| 7-Wood-a(i) | 1.00 | 3.00 | 6.00 |

**MEET CORLISS ARCHER** (Radio/Movie)(My Life #4 on)
March, 1948 - No. 3, July, 1948
Fox Features Syndicate

| | Good | Fine | N-Mint |
|---|---|---|---|
| 1-(Teen-age)-Feldstein-c/a | 30.00 | 90.00 | 210.00 |
| 2-Feldstein-c only | 23.00 | 70.00 | 160.00 |
| 3-Part Feldstein-c only | 17.00 | 51.00 | 120.00 |

NOTE: *No. 1-3 used in* ***Seduction of the Innocent****, pg. 39.*

**MEET HERCULES** (See Three Stooges)

**MEET HIYA A FRIEND OF SANTA CLAUS**
1949 (18 pgs.?) (paper cover)
Julian J. Proskauer/Sundial Shoe Stores, etc. (Giveaway)

| | Good | Fine | N-Mint |
|---|---|---|---|
| nn | 3.00 | 9.00 | 21.00 |

**MEET MERTON**
Dec, 1953 - No. 4, June, 1954
Toby Press

| | Good | Fine | N-Mint |
|---|---|---|---|
| 1-(Teen-age)-Dave Berg-a | 3.00 | 9.00 | 21.00 |
| 2-Dave Berg-a | 1.70 | 5.00 | 12.00 |
| 3,4-Dave Berg-a. 3-Berg-c | 1.30 | 4.00 | 9.00 |
| I.W. Reprint #9 | | .60 | 1.20 |
| Super Reprint #11('63), 18 | | .60 | 1.20 |

**MEET MISS BLISS** (Becomes Stories Of Romance #5 on)
May, 1955 - No. 4, Nov, 1955
Atlas Comics (LMC)

| | Good | Fine | N-Mint |
|---|---|---|---|
| 1-Al Hartley-a | 4.50 | 14.00 | 32.00 |
| 2-4 | 2.65 | 8.00 | 18.00 |

**MEET MISS PEPPER** (Formerly Lucy, The Real Gone Gal)
No. 5, April, 1954 - No. 6, June, 1954
St. John Publishing Co.

| | Good | Fine | N-Mint |
|---|---|---|---|
| 5-Kubert/Maurer-a | 12.00 | 36.00 | 84.00 |
| 6-Kubert/Maurer-a; Kubert-c | 10.00 | 30.00 | 70.00 |

**MEET THE NEW POST GAZETTE SUNDAY FUNNIES**
3/12/49 (16 pgs.; paper covers) (7¼x10¼")
Commercial Comics (insert in newspaper)
Pittsburgh Post Gazette

Dick Tracy by Gould, Gasoline Alley, Terry & the Pirates, Brenda Starr, Buck Rogers by Yager, The Gumps, Peter Rabbit by Fago, Superman, Funnyman by Siegel & Shuster, The Saint, Archie, & others done especially for this book. A fine copy sold at auction in 1985 for $276.00.

Estimated value.... $150—$300

**MEGALITH** (Also see The Revengers Featuring... & Zero Patrol)
Mar, 1985 - No. 2, 1985; No. 1, 1989 - Present ($2.00, color)
Continuity Comics

| | Good | Fine | N-Mint |
|---|---|---|---|
| 1,2 (1985)-Neal Adams-a | .35 | 1.00 | 2.00 |
| 1-3: 1-('89)-Adams-c(i), Nebres-i. 3-Adams-c | .35 | 1.00 | 2.00 |

**MEGATON**
Nov, 1983; No. 2, Oct, 1985 - V2#3 (B&W, color V2#1 on)
Megaton Publ. (#3: 44 pgs.; #4: 52 pgs.)

| | Good | Fine | N-Mint |
|---|---|---|---|
| 1,2 ($2.00, 68 pgs.)-Guice-c/a(p), Gustovich-p | .35 | 1.00 | 2.00 |
| 3-8 ($1.50): 4,5-Wildman by Grass Green | .25 | .75 | 1.50 |
| V2#1-3 ($1.50, color) | .25 | .75 | 1.50 |
| Special 1 ($2.00, '87) | .35 | 1.00 | 2.00 |
| X-Mas 2 ('87) | .35 | 1.00 | 2.00 |

**MEGATON MAN** (Also see The Return Of...)
Dec, 1984 - No. 10, 1986 ($2.00, color, Baxter paper)
Kitchen Sink Enterprises

| | Good | Fine | N-Mint |
|---|---|---|---|
| 1-Silver-Age heroes parody | 1.15 | 3.50 | 6.00 |
| 1-2nd printing (1989, $2.00) | .35 | 1.00 | 2.00 |
| 2 | .45 | 1.40 | 2.80 |
| 3-10: 6-Border Worlds begins (1st app.) | .40 | 1.25 | 2.50 |
| ...Meets the Uncategorizable X+Thems 1 (4/89, $2.00, B&W) | .35 | 1.00 | 2.00 |

**MEL ALLEN SPORTS COMICS**
No. 5, Nov, 1949; No. 6, June, 1950
Standard Comics

| | Good | Fine | N-Mint |
|---|---|---|---|
| 5(#1 on inside)-Tuska-a | 8.00 | 24.00 | 56.00 |
| 6(#2) | 5.00 | 15.00 | 35.00 |

**MELVIN MONSTER** (See Peter, the Little Pest)
Apr-June, 1965 - No. 10, Oct, 1969
Dell Publishing Co.

| | Good | Fine | N-Mint |
|---|---|---|---|
| 1-By John Stanley | 8.50 | 25.50 | 60.00 |
| 2-10-All by Stanley. #10 r-/#1 | 5.70 | 17.00 | 40.00 |

**MELVIN THE MONSTER** (Dexter The Demon #7)
July, 1956 - No. 6, July, 1957
Atlas Comics (HPC)

| | Good | Fine | N-Mint |
|---|---|---|---|
| 1-Maneely-c/a | 4.30 | 13.00 | 30.00 |
| 2-6: 4-Maneely-c/a | 3.00 | 9.00 | 21.00 |

**MENACE**
March, 1953 - No. 11, May, 1954
Atlas Comics (HPC)

| | Good | Fine | N-Mint |
|---|---|---|---|
| 1-Everett-a | 16.00 | 48.00 | 110.00 |
| 2-Post-atom bomb disaster by Everett; anti-Communist propaganda/torture scenes | 10.00 | 30.00 | 70.00 |
| 3,4,6-Everett-a | 7.00 | 21.00 | 50.00 |
| 5-Origin & 1st app. The Zombie by Everett (reprinted in Tales of the Zombie #1)(7/53) | 12.00 | 36.00 | 84.00 |
| 7,8,10,11: 7-Frankenstein story. 8-End of world story. 10-H-Bomb panels | 6.50 | 19.00 | 45.00 |
| 9-Everett-a r-in Vampire Tales #1 | 7.00 | 21.00 | 50.00 |

NOTE: ***Colan*** *a-6.* ***Everett*** *a-1-6, 9; c-1-6.* ***Heath*** *a-1-8; c-10.* ***Katz*** *a-11.* ***Maneely*** *a-3, 7, 8.* ***Powell*** *a-11.* ***Romita*** *a-3, 6, 11.* ***Shelly*** *a-10.* ***Sinnott*** *a-2, 7.* ***Tuska*** *a-1, 2, 5.*

**MEN AGAINST CRIME** (Formerly Mr. Risk; Hand of Fate #8 on)
No. 3, Feb, 1951 - No. 7, Oct, 1951
Ace Magazines

| | Good | Fine | N-Mint |
|---|---|---|---|
| 3-Mr. Risk app. | 4.00 | 12.00 | 28.00 |
| 4-7: 4-Colan-a; entire book reprinted as Trapped! #4 | 2.00 | 6.00 | 14.00 |

**MEN, GUNS, & CATTLE** (See Classics Illustrated Special Issue)

**MEN IN ACTION** (Battle Brady #10 on)
April, 1952 - No. 9, Dec, 1952
Atlas Comics (IPS)

| | Good | Fine | N-Mint |
|---|---|---|---|
| 1-Berg, Pakula, Reinman-a | 4.30 | 13.00 | 30.00 |
| 2 | 2.15 | 6.50 | 15.00 |
| 3-6,8,9: 3-Heath-c/a. 6-Pakula-a | 1.70 | 5.00 | 12.00 |
| 7-Krigstein-a | 3.50 | 10.50 | 24.00 |

**MEN IN ACTION**
April, 1957 - No. 9, 1958
Ajax/Farrell Publications

| | Good | Fine | N-Mint |
|---|---|---|---|
| 1 | 3.15 | 9.50 | 22.00 |
| 2 | 1.70 | 5.00 | 12.00 |
| 3-9 | 1.30 | 4.00 | 9.00 |

**MEN INTO SPACE** (See 4-Color No. 1083)

**MEN OF BATTLE** (Also see New Men of Battle)
V1#5, March, 1943 (Hardcover)
Catechetical Guild

| | Good | Fine | N-Mint |
|---|---|---|---|
| V1#5-Topix reprints | 1.70 | 5.00 | 12.00 |

**MEN OF COURAGE**
1949
Catechetical Guild

| | Good | Fine | N-Mint |
|---|---|---|---|
| Bound Topix comics-V7#2,4,6,8,10,16,18,20 | 1.70 | 5.00 | 12.00 |

**MEN OF WAR**
August, 1977 - No. 26, March, 1980 (#9,10: 44 pgs.)
DC Comics, Inc.

| | Good | Fine | N-Mint |
|---|---|---|---|
| 1-Enemy Ace, Gravedigger (origin #1,2) begin | | .50 | 1.00 |
| 2-26: 9-Unknown Soldier app. | | .35 | .70 |

NOTE: ***Chaykin*** *a-9, 10, 12-14, 19, 20.* ***Evans*** *c-25.* ***Kubert*** *c-2-23, 24p, 26.*

**MEN'S ADVENTURES** (Formerly True Adventures)
No. 4, Aug, 1950 - No. 28, July, 1954
Marvel/Atlas Comics (CCC)

| | Good | Fine | N-Mint |
|---|---|---|---|
| 4(#1)(52 pgs.) | 8.50 | 25.50 | 60.00 |
| 5-Flying Saucer story | 5.00 | 15.00 | 35.00 |
| 6-8: 8-Sci/fic story | 3.60 | 11.00 | 25.00 |
| 9-20: All war format | 2.00 | 6.00 | 14.00 |
| 21,22,24-26: All horror format | 2.65 | 8.00 | 18.00 |
| 23-Crandall-a; Fox-a(i) | 4.00 | 12.00 | 28.00 |

*Melvin the Monster #1, © MEG*

*Menace #1, © MEG*

*Men in Action #1, © MEG*

Merry-Go-Round Comics nn (1944), © LaSalle

Metal Men #47, © DC

Metamorpho #2, © DC

| | Good | Fine | N-Mint |
|---|---|---|---|
| 27,28-Captain America, Human Torch, & Sub-Mariner app. in each | 23.00 | 70.00 | 160.00 |

NOTE: ***Berg*** *a-15, 16.* ***Burgos*** *c-27.* ***Colan*** *a-14.* ***Everett*** *a-10, 14, 22, 25, 28; c-14, 21-23.* ***Heath*** *a-8, 24; c-20.* ***Lawrence*** *a-23, 27.* ***Maneely*** *a-24.* ***Mac Pakula*** *a-15, 25.* ***Post*** *a-23.* ***Powell*** *a-27.* ***Reinman*** *a-12.* ***Robinson*** *c-19.* ***Romita*** *a-22.* ***Sinnott*** *a-21.* ***Tuska*** *a-24. Adventure-#4-8; War-#9-20; Horror-#21-26.*

**MEN WHO MOVE THE NATION**
(Giveaway) (Black & White)
Publisher unknown

| | Good | Fine | N-Mint |
|---|---|---|---|
| nn-Neal Adams-a | 2.65 | 8.00 | 18.00 |

**MEPHISTO VS. . .** (See Silver Surfer #3)
Apr, 1987 - No. 4, July, 1987 ($1.50, mini-series)
Marvel Comics Group

| | Good | Fine | N-Mint |
|---|---|---|---|
| 1-Fantastic Four; Austin-i | .35 | 1.00 | 2.00 |
| 2-4: 2-X-Factor. 3-X-Men. 4-Avengers | .25 | .80 | 1.60 |

**MERC** (See Mark Hazzard: Merc)

**MERCHANTS OF DEATH**
July, 1988 - No. 4, Nov, 1988 ($3.50, B&W/16pgs. color, 44pg. mag.)
Acme Press (Eclipse)

| | Good | Fine | N-Mint |
|---|---|---|---|
| 1-4: 4-Toth-c | .60 | 1.75 | 3.50 |

**MERLIN JONES AS THE MONKEY'S UNCLE** (See Movie Comics and The Misadventures of. . . under Movie Comics)

**MERLINREALM 3-D** (See Blackthorne 3-D Series #2)

**MERRILL'S MARAUDERS** (See Movie Classics)

**MERRY CHRISTMAS** (See A Christmas Adv., Donald Duck. . ., Dell Giant #39, & March of Comics #153)

**MERRY CHRISTMAS, A**
1948 (nn) (Giveaway)
K. K. Publications (Child Life Shoes)

| | Good | Fine | N-Mint |
|---|---|---|---|
| nn | 2.75 | 8.00 | 16.00 |

**MERRY CHRISTMAS**
1956 (7¼x5¼")
K. K. Publications (Blue Bird Shoes Giveaway)

| | Good | Fine | N-Mint |
|---|---|---|---|
| nn | 1.00 | 3.00 | 6.00 |

**MERRY CHRISTMAS FROM MICKEY MOUSE**
1939 (16 pgs.) (Color & B&W)
K. K. Publications (Shoe store giveaway)

| | Good | Fine | N-Mint |
|---|---|---|---|
| nn-Donald Duck & Pluto app.; text with art (Rare); c-reprint/Mickey Mouse Mag. V3#3 (12/37) | 75.00 | 200.00 | 450.00 |

**MERRY CHRISTMAS FROM SEARS TOYLAND**
1939 (16 pgs.) (In color)
Sears Roebuck Giveaway

| | Good | Fine | N-Mint |
|---|---|---|---|
| nn-Dick Tracy, Little Orphan Annie, The Gumps, Terry & the Pirates | 16.00 | 48.00 | 110.00 |

**MERRY COMICS**
December, 1945 (No cover price)
Carlton Publishing Co.

| | Good | Fine | N-Mint |
|---|---|---|---|
| nn-Boogeyman app. | 7.00 | 21.00 | 50.00 |

**MERRY COMICS**
1947
Four Star Publications

| | Good | Fine | N-Mint |
|---|---|---|---|
| 1 | 5.00 | 15.00 | 35.00 |

**MERRY-GO-ROUND COMICS**
1944 (132 pgs.; 25 cents); 1946; 9-10/47 - No. 2, 1948
LaSalle Publ. Co./Croyden Publ./Rotary Litho.

| | Good | Fine | N-Mint |
|---|---|---|---|
| nn(1944)(LaSalle) | 9.30 | 28.00 | 65.00 |
| 21 | 2.65 | 8.00 | 18.00 |
| 1(1946)(Croyden) | 4.30 | 13.00 | 30.00 |
| V1#1,2('47-'48; 52 pgs.)(Rotary Litho. Co. Ltd., Canada); Ken Hultgren-a | 3.00 | 9.00 | 21.00 |

**MERRY MAILMAN** (See Fawcett's Funny Animals #89)

**MERRY MOUSE** (Also see Space Comics)
June, 1953 - No. 4, Jan-Feb, 1954
Avon Periodicals

| | Good | Fine | N-Mint |
|---|---|---|---|
| 1 | 3.70 | 11.00 | 26.00 |
| 2-4 | 2.00 | 6.00 | 14.00 |

**META-4**
Feb, 1991 - Present ($2.25, color)
First Comics

| | Good | Fine | N-Mint |
|---|---|---|---|
| 1-($3.95, 52 pgs.) | .70 | 2.00 | 4.00 |
| 2-4 | .40 | 1.15 | 2.30 |

**METAL MEN** (See Brave & the Bold, DC Comics Presents, and Showcase)
4-5/63 - No. 41, 12-1/69-70; No. 42, 2-3/73 - No. 44, 7-8/73;
No. 45, 4-5/76 - No. 56, 2-3/78
National Periodical Publications/DC Comics

| | Good | Fine | N-Mint |
|---|---|---|---|
| 1 | 20.00 | 60.00 | 140.00 |
| 2 | 8.00 | 24.00 | 55.00 |
| 3-5 | 5.00 | 15.00 | 35.00 |
| 6-10 | 3.50 | 10.50 | 24.00 |
| 11-20 | 2.65 | 8.00 | 18.00 |
| 21-26,28-30 | 1.50 | 4.50 | 10.00 |
| 27-Origin Metal Men | 3.60 | 11.00 | 25.00 |
| 31-41(1968-70): 38-Last 12 cent issue | 1.50 | 4.50 | 10.00 |
| 42-44(1973)-Reprints | .70 | 2.00 | 4.00 |
| 45('76)-49-Simonson-a in all | .70 | 2.00 | 4.00 |
| 50-56: 50-Part-r. 54,55-Green Lantern x-over | .70 | 2.00 | 4.00 |

NOTE: ***Aparo*** *c-53-56.* ***Giordano*** *c-45, 46.* ***Kane*** *a-30, 31p; c-31.* ***Simonson*** *a-45-49; c-47-52.* ***Staton*** *a-50-56.*

**METAMORPHO** (See Action, Brave & the Bold, First Issue Special, & World's Finest)
July-Aug, 1965 - No. 17, Mar-Apr, 1968 (All 12 cent issues)
National Periodical Publications

| | Good | Fine | N-Mint |
|---|---|---|---|
| 1 | 7.00 | 21.00 | 50.00 |
| 2,3 | 3.15 | 9.50 | 22.00 |
| 4-6 | 2.00 | 6.00 | 14.00 |
| 7-9 | 1.30 | 4.00 | 9.00 |
| 10-Origin & 1st app. Element Girl (1-2/67) | 2.30 | 7.00 | 16.00 |
| 11-17 | 1.00 | 3.00 | 6.00 |

NOTE: ***Ramona Fraden*** *a-1-4.* ***Orlando*** *a-5, 6; c-5-9, 11.* ***Sal Trapani*** *a-7-16.*

**METEOR COMICS**
November, 1945
L. L. Baird (Croyden)

| | Good | Fine | N-Mint |
|---|---|---|---|
| 1-Captain Wizard, Impossible Man, Race Wilkins app.; origin Baldy Bean, Capt. Wizard's sidekick; Bare-breasted mermaids story | 14.00 | 42.00 | 100.00 |

**MGM'S MARVELOUS WIZARD OF OZ** (See Marvel Treasury of Oz)
November, 1975 (84 pgs.; oversize) ($1.50)
Marvel Comics Group/National Periodical Publications

| | Good | Fine | N-Mint |
|---|---|---|---|
| 1-Adaptation of MGM's movie | .70 | 2.00 | 4.00 |

**M.G.M'S MOUSE MUSKETEERS** (Formerly M.G.M.'s The Two Mouseketeers)
No. 670, Jan, 1956 - No. 1290, Mar-May, 1962
Dell Publishing Co.

| | Good | Fine | N-Mint |
|---|---|---|---|
| 4-Color 670 (#4) | 1.00 | 3.00 | 7.00 |
| 4-Color 711,728,764 | .85 | 2.50 | 6.00 |
| 8 (4-6/57) - 21 (3-5/60) | .75 | 2.25 | 5.00 |
| 4-Color 1135,1175,1290 | .85 | 2.50 | 6.00 |

**M.G.M.'S SPIKE AND TYKE**
No. 499, Sept, 1953 - No. 1266, Dec-Feb, 1961-62
Dell Publishing Co.

| | Good | Fine | N-Mint |
|---|---|---|---|
| 4-Color 499 (#1) | 1.30 | 4.00 | 9.00 |
| 4-Color 577,638 | 1.00 | 3.00 | 7.00 |
| 4(12-2/55-56)-10 | .85 | 2.50 | 6.00 |
| 11-24(12-2/60-61) | .75 | 2.25 | 5.00 |
| 4-Color 1266 | .85 | 2.50 | 6.00 |

**M.G.M.'S THE TWO MOUSKETEERS** (See 4-Color 475, 603, 642)

**MICHAELANGELO, TEENAGE MUTANT NINJA TURTLE**
1986 (One shot) ($1.50, B&W)
Mirage Studios

| | Good | Fine | N-Mint |
|---|---|---|---|
| 1 | 2.50 | 7.50 | 15.00 |
| 1-2nd printing ('89, $1.75)-Reprint plus new-a | .50 | 1.50 | 3.00 |

**MICKEY AND DONALD** (Walt Disney's. . .#3 on)
Mar, 1988 - No. 18, May, 1990 (95 cents, color)
Gladstone Publishing

| | Good | Fine | N-Mint |
|---|---|---|---|
| 1-Don Rosa-a; r-/1949 Firestone giveaway | 1.00 | 3.00 | 6.00 |
| 2 | .40 | 1.25 | 2.50 |
| 3-Infinity-c | .35 | 1.00 | 2.00 |
| 4-8: Barks-r | | .60 | 1.20 |
| 9-15: 9-r/1948 Firestone giveaway; X-Mas-c | | .50 | 1.00 |
| 16 ($1.50, 52 pgs.)-r/FC #157 | .25 | .75 | 1.50 |
| 17,18 ($1.95, 68 pgs.): 17-Barks M.M.-r/FC #79 plus Barks D.D.-r; Rosa-a; X-Mas-c. 18-Kelly-c(r); Barks-r | .35 | 1.00 | 2.00 |

NOTE: *Barks reprints in 1-15, 17, 18.* ***Kelly*** *c-13r, 14 (r/Walt Disney's C&S #58), 18r.*

**MICKEY AND DONALD IN VACATIONLAND** (See Dell Giant No. 47)

**MICKEY & THE BEANSTALK** (See Story Hour Series)

**MICKEY & THE SLEUTH** (See Walt Disney Showcase #38, 39, 42)

**MICKEY FINN** (Also see Big Shot #74 & Feature Funnies)
Nov?, 1942 - V3#2, May, 1952
Eastern Color 1-4/McNaught Synd. #5 on (Columbia)/Headline V3#2

| | Good | Fine | N-Mint |
|---|---|---|---|
| 1 | 17.00 | 51.00 | 120.00 |
| 2 | 8.50 | 25.50 | 60.00 |
| 3-Charlie Chan app. | 6.00 | 18.00 | 42.00 |
| 4 | 4.00 | 12.00 | 28.00 |
| 5-10 | 2.85 | 8.50 | 20.00 |
| 11-15(1949): 12-Sparky Watts app. | 2.30 | 7.00 | 16.00 |
| V3#1,2(1952) | 1.50 | 4.50 | 10.00 |

**MICKEY MOUSE**
1931 - No. 4, 1934 (52 pgs.; 10x9¾"; cardboard covers)
David McKay Publications

| | Good | Fine | N-Mint |
|---|---|---|---|
| 1(1931) | 93.00 | 280.00 | 650.00 |
| 2(1932) | 69.00 | 205.00 | 480.00 |
| 3(1933)-All color Sunday reprints; page #'s 5-17, 32-48 reissued in Whitman #948 | 115.00 | 345.00 | 800.00 |
| 4(1934) | 62.00 | 185.00 | 430.00 |

NOTE: *Each book reprints strips from previous year - dailies in black and white in #1, 2, 4; Sundays in color in No. 3. Later reprints exist; i.e., #2 (1934).*

**MICKEY MOUSE**
1933 (Copyright date, printing date unknown)
(30 pages; 10x8¾"; cardboard covers)
Whitman Publishing Co.

| | Good | Fine | N-Mint |
|---|---|---|---|
| 948-(1932 Sunday strips in color) | 93.00 | 280.00 | 650.00 |

NOTE: *Some copies were bound with a second front cover upside-down instead of the regular back cover; both covers have the same art, but different right and left margins. The above book is an exact, but abbreviated reissue of David McKay No. 3 but with ½-inch of border trimmed from the top and bottom.*

**MICKEY MOUSE** (See The Best of Walt Disney Comics, Cheerios giveaways, Donald and . . ., Dynabrite Comics, 40 Big Pages. . ., Gladstone Comic Album, Merry Christmas From. . ., Mickey and Donald, Walt Disney's C&S & Wheaties)

**MICKEY MOUSE** (. . .Secret Agent #107-109; Walt Disney's. . . #148-205?) (See Dell Giants for annuals)
No. 16, 1941 - No. 84, 7-9/62; No. 85, 11/62 - No. 218, 7/84; No. 219, 10/86 - No. 256, 4/90
Dell Publ. Co./Gold Key No. 85-204/Whitman No. 205-218/Gladstone No. 219 on

| | Good | Fine | VF-NM | NM/Mint |
|---|---|---|---|---|
| 4-Color 16(1941)-1st M.M. comic book-"vs. the Phantom Blot" by Gottfredson | 371.00 | 1115.00 | 2600.00 | 4500.00 |

(Estimated up to 200 total copies exist, 5 in NM/Mint)

| | Good | Fine | N-Mint |
|---|---|---|---|
| 4-Color 27(1943)-"7 Colored Terror" | 50.00 | 150.00 | 350.00 |
| 4-Color 79(1945)-By Carl Barks (1 story) | 64.00 | 193.00 | 450.00 |
| 4-Color 116(1946) | 17.00 | 51.00 | 120.00 |
| 4-Color 141,157(1947) | 16.00 | 48.00 | 110.00 |
| 4-Color 170,181,194('48) | 13.00 | 40.00 | 90.00 |
| 4-Color 214('49),231,248,261 | 10.00 | 30.00 | 70.00 |
| 4-Color 268-Reprints/WDC&S #22-24 by Gottfredson ("Surprise Visitor") | 10.00 | 30.00 | 70.00 |
| 4-Color 279,286,296 | 8.50 | 25.50 | 60.00 |
| 4-Color 304,313(#1),325(#2),334 | 5.70 | 17.00 | 40.00 |
| 4-Color 343,352,362,371,387 | 4.30 | 13.00 | 30.00 |
| 4-Color 401,411,427(10-11/52) | 3.50 | 10.50 | 24.00 |
| 4-Color 819-Mickey Mouse in Magicland | 2.00 | 6.00 | 14.00 |
| 4-Color 1057,1151,1246(1959-61)-Album | 1.70 | 5.00 | 12.00 |
| 28(12-1/52-53)-32,34 | 1.70 | 5.00 | 12.00 |
| 33-(Exists with 2 dates, 10-11/53 & 12-1/54) | 1.70 | 5.00 | 12.00 |
| 35-50 | 1.15 | 3.50 | 8.00 |
| 51-73,75-80 | .85 | 2.50 | 6.00 |
| 74-Story swipe-"The Rare Stamp Search"/4-Color 422-"The Gilded Man" | 1.15 | 3.50 | 8.00 |
| 81-99: 93,95-titled "Mickey Mouse Club Album" | .85 | 2.50 | 6.00 |
| 100-105: Reprints 4-Color 427,194,279,170,343,214 in that order | 1.00 | 3.00 | 7.00 |
| 106-120 | .75 | 2.25 | 5.00 |
| 121-130 | .70 | 2.00 | 4.00 |
| 131-146 | .50 | 1.50 | 3.00 |
| 147,148: 147-Reprints "The Phantom Fires" from WDC&S 200-202. 148-Reprints "The Mystery of Lonely Valley" from WDC&S 208-210 | .85 | 3.50 | 5.00 |
| 149-158 | .35 | 1.00 | 2.00 |
| 159-Reprints "The Sunken City" from WDC&S 205-207 | .70 | 2.00 | 4.00 |
| 160-170: 162-170-r | .35 | 1.00 | 2.00 |
| 171-178,180-199 | | .50 | 1.00 |
| 179-(52 pgs.) | | .60 | 1.20 |
| 200-218: 200-r/Four Color #371 | | .40 | .80 |
| 219-1st Gladstone issue; The Seven Ghosts serial-r begins by Gottfredson | .85 | 2.50 | 5.00 |
| 220,221 | .50 | 1.50 | 3.00 |
| 222-225: 222-Editor-in Grief strip-r | .40 | 1.25 | 2.50 |
| 226-230 | .25 | .75 | 1.50 |
| 231-243,245-254: 240-r/March of Comics #27. 245-r/F.C. #279. 250-r/F.C. #248 | | .50 | 1.00 |
| 244 (1/89, $2.95, 100 pgs.)-60th anniversary; gives history of Mickey | .60 | 1.75 | 3.50 |
| 255,256 ($1.95, 68 pgs.) | .35 | 1.00 | 2.00 |

NOTE: *Reprints #195-197, 198(⅔), 199(⅓), 200-208, 211(½), 212, 213, 215(⅓), 216-on.*

| | Good | Fine | N-Mint |
|---|---|---|---|
| Album 01-518-210(Dell), 1(10082-309)(9/63-Gold Key) | 1.00 | 3.00 | 7.00 |
| . . .& Goofy "Bicep Bungle"(1952, 16 pgs., 3¼x7") Fritos giveaway, soft-c (also see Donald Duck & Ludwig Von Drake) | 2.35 | 7.00 | 16.00 |
| . . .& Goofy Explore Business(1978) | | .40 | .80 |
| . . .& Goofy Explore Energy(1976-1978) 36 pgs.; Exxon giveaway in color; regular size | | .40 | .80 |

*Mickey and Donald #9, © The Disney Co.*

*Mickey Finn #11, © McNaught Synd.*

*Mickey Mouse #244, © The Disney Co.*

Mickey Mouse Adventures #1, © Disney Co.

Mickey Mouse Magazine V1#8, © Disney Co.

Mickey Mouse Magazine V4#3, © Disney Co.

| | Good | Fine | N-Mint |
|---|---|---|---|
| ...& Goofy Explore Energy Conservation(1976-1978)-Exxon | | .40 | .80 |
| ...& Goofy Explore The Universe of Energy(1985) 20pgs.; Exxon giveaway in color; regular size | | .40 | .80 |
| Club 1(1/64-G.K.)(TV) | 1.75 | 5.25 | 12.00 |
| Mini Comic 1(1976)(3¼x6½")-Reprints 158 | | | .15 |
| New Mickey Mouse Club Fun Book 11190 (Golden Press, $1.95; 224 pgs., 1977) | .40 | 1.20 | 2.40 |
| Surprise Party 1(30037-901, G.K.)(1/69)-40th Anniversary (see Walt Disney Showcase #47) | 2.35 | 7.00 | 16.00 |
| Surprise Party 1(1979)-r-/'69 issue | .35 | 1.00 | 2.00 |

**MICKEY MOUSE ADVENTURES**
June, 1990 - Present ($1.50, color)
Disney Comics

| | Good | Fine | N-Mint |
|---|---|---|---|
| 1-12: 1-Bradbury, Murry-r/M.M. #45,73 plus new-a. 2-Begin all new stories | .25 | .75 | 1.50 |

**MICKEY MOUSE BOOK**
1930 (4 printings, 20pgs., magazine size, paperbound)
Bibo & Lang

nn-Very first Disney book with games, cartoons & songs; only Disney book to offer the origin of Mickey (based on a story originated by 11 yr. old Bobette Bibo). First app. Mickey & Minnie Mouse. Clarabelle Cow & Horace Horsecollar app. on back cover. Walt Disney, so the story goes, named him 'Mickey Mouse' after the green color of Ireland because he ate old green cheese. The book was printed in black & green to reinforce the Irish theme.

**NOTE:** The 2nd through 4th printings have a daily Win Smith M. Mouse strip at bottom of back cover; the 1st printing is blank in this area. 1st printings are more common than all other printings combined. Most copies are missing pages 9 & 10 which contain a puzzle to be cut out. Ub Iwerks-c

| | Good | Fine | VF-NM | NM/Mint |
|---|---|---|---|---|
| 1st-4th Printings (complete) | 585.00 | 1460.00 | 3500.00 | 4500.00 |

(Estimated up to 75 total copies exist, 4 in NM/Mint)

| | Good | Fine | VF-NM |
|---|---|---|---|
| 1st-4th Printings (pgs. 9&10 cut out, but not missing) | 250.00 | 625.00 | 1500.00 |
| 1st-4th Printings (pgs. 9&10 missing) | 167.00 | 420.00 | 1000.00 |

**MICKEY MOUSE CLUB MAGAZINE** (See Walt Disney...)

**MICKEY MOUSE CLUB SPECIAL** (See The New Mickey Mouse...)

**MICKEY MOUSE COMICS DIGEST**
1986 - No. 6, 1987 (96 pgs.)
Gladstone Publishing

| | Good | Fine | N-Mint |
|---|---|---|---|
| 1-3 ($1.25) | | .60 | 1.25 |
| 4-6 ($1.50) | .25 | .75 | 1.50 |

**MICKEY MOUSE MAGAZINE**
V1#1, Jan, 1933 - V1#9, Sept, 1933 (5¼x7¼")
No. 1-3 published by Kamen-Blair (Kay Kamen, Inc.)
Walt Disney Productions

(Scarce)-Distributed by dairies and leading stores through their local theatres. First few issues had 5 cents listed on cover, later ones had no price.

| | Good | Fine | VF-NM |
|---|---|---|---|
| V1#1 | 217.00 | 600.00 | 1300.00 |
| 2-9 | 93.00 | 280.00 | 650.00 |

**MICKEY MOUSE MAGAZINE**
V1#1, Nov, 1933 - V2#12, Oct, 1935
Mills giveaways issued by different dairies
Walt Disney Productions

| | Good | Fine | N-Mint |
|---|---|---|---|
| V1#1 | 50.00 | 150.00 | 350.00 |
| 2-12: 2-X-Mas issue | 22.00 | 65.00 | 150.00 |
| V2#1-12: 2-X-Mas issue. 4-St. Valentine-c | 14.00 | 43.00 | 100.00 |

**MICKEY MOUSE MAGAZINE** (Becomes Walt Disney's Comics & Stories) (No V3#1, V4#6)
Summer, 1935 (June-Aug, indicia) - V5#12, Sept, 1940
V1#1-5, V3#11,12, V4#1-3 are 44 pgs; V2#3-100 pgs; V5#12-68 pgs; rest are 36 pgs.
K. K. Publications/Western Publishing Co.

| | Good | Fine | VF-NM | NM/Mint |
|---|---|---|---|---|
| V1#1 (Large size, 13¼x10¼"; 25 cents)-Contains puzzles, games, cels, stories and comics of Disney characters. Promotional magazine for Disney cartoon movies and paraphernalia | 500.00 | 1250.00 | 3000.00 | 4500.00 |

(Estimated up to 100 total copies exist, 3 in NM/Mint)
Note: *Some copies were autographed by the editors & given away with all early one year subscriptions.*

| | Good | Fine | VF-NM |
|---|---|---|---|
| 2 (Size change, 11½x8½"; 10/35; 10 cents)-High quality paper begins; Messmer-a | 107.00 | 320.00 | 750.00 |
| 3,4: 3-Messmer-a | 60.00 | 180.00 | 420.00 |
| 5-1st Donald Duck solo-c; last 44pg. & high quality paper issue | 65.00 | 195.00 | 455.00 |
| 6-9: 6-36 pg. issues begin; Donald becomes editor. 8-2nd Donald solo-c. 9-1st Mickey/Minnie-c | 50.00 | 150.00 | 350.00 |
| 10-12, V2#1,2: 11-1st Pluto/Mickey-c; Donald fires himself and appoints Mickey as editor | 45.00 | 135.00 | 315.00 |
| V2#3-Special 100 pg. Christmas issue (25 cents); Messmer-a; Donald becomes editor of Wise Quacks | 110.00 | 330.00 | 770.00 |
| 4-Mickey Mouse Comics & Roy Ranger (adventure strip) begin; both end V2#9; Messmer-a | 38.00 | 115.00 | 265.00 |

| | Good | Fine | N-Mint |
|---|---|---|---|
| 5-Ted True (adventure strip, ends V2#9) & Silly Symphony Comics (ends V3#3) begin | 30.00 | 90.00 | 210.00 |
| 6-9: 6-1st solo Minnie-c. 6-9-Mickey Mouse Movies cut-out in each | 30.00 | 90.00 | 210.00 |
| 10-1st full color issue; Mickey Mouse (by Gottfredson; ends V3#12) & Silly Symphony (ends V3#3) full color Sunday-r, Peter The Farm Detective (ends V5#8) & Ole Of The North (ends V3#3) begins | 43.00 | 130.00 | 300.00 |
| 11-13: 12-Hiawatha-c & feature story | 30.00 | 90.00 | 210.00 |
| V3#2-Big Bad Wolf Halloween-c | 30.00 | 90.00 | 210.00 |
| 3 (12/37)-1st app. Snow White & The Seven Dwarfs (before release of movie)(possibly 1st in print); Mickey Christmas-c | 42.00 | 125.00 | 290.00 |
| 4 (1/38)-Snow White & The Seven Dwarfs serial begins (on stands before release of movie); Ducky Symphony (ends V3#11) begins | 36.00 | 107.00 | 250.00 |
| 5-1st Snow White & Seven Dwarfs-c (St. Valentine's Day) | 36.00 | 107.00 | 250.00 |
| 6-Snow White serial ends; Lonesome Ghosts app. (2 pp.) | 30.00 | 90.00 | 210.00 |
| 7-Seven Dwarfs Easter-c | 29.00 | 86.00 | 200.00 |
| 8-10: 9-Dopey-c. 10-1st solo Goofy-c | 27.00 | 80.00 | 185.00 |
| 11,12 (44 pgs; 8 more pages color added). 11-Mickey The Sheriff serial (ends V4#3) & Donald Duck strip-r (ends V3#12) begin. Color feature on Snow White's Forest Friends | 30.00 | 90.00 | 210.00 |
| V4#1 (10/38; 44 pgs.)-Brave Little Tailor-c/feature story, nominated for Academy Award; Bobby & Chip by Otto Messmer (ends V4#2) & The Practical Pig (ends V4#2) begin | 30.00 | 90.00 | 210.00 |
| 2 (44 pgs.)-1st Huey, Dewey & Louie-c | 29.00 | 86.00 | 200.00 |
| 3 (12/38, 44 pgs.)-Ferdinand The Bull-c/feature story, Academy Award winner; Mickey Mouse & The Whalers serial begins, ends V4#12 | 30.00 | 90.00 | 210.00 |
| 4-Spotty, Mother Pluto strip-r begin, end V4#8 | 26.00 | 77.00 | 180.00 |
| 5-St. Valentine's day-c. 1st Pluto solo-c | 30.00 | 90.00 | 210.00 |
| 7 (3/39)-The Ugly Duckling-c/feature story, Academy Award winner | 30.00 | 90.00 | 210.00 |

Good Fine N-Mint

7 (4/39)-Goofy & Wilbur The Grasshopper classic-c/feature story from 1st Goofy cartoon movie; Timid Elmer begins, ends V5#5 30.00 90.00 210.00
8-Big Bad Wolf-c from Practical Pig movie poster; Practical Pig feature story 30.00 90.00 210.00
9-Donald Duck & Mickey Mouse Sunday-r begin; The Pointer feature story, nominated for Academy Award 30.00 90.00 210.00
10-Classic July 4th drum & fife-c; last Donald Sunday-r 35.00 105.00 245.00
11-1st slick-c; last over-sized issue 27.00 80.00 185.00
12 (9/39; format change, 10¼x8¼'')-1st full color, cover to cover issue. Donald's Penguin-c/feature story 34.00 100.00 235.00
V5#1-Black Pete-c; Officer Duck-c/feature story; Autograph Hound feature story; Robinson Crusoe serial begins 34.00 100.00 235.00
2-Goofy-c; 1st app. Pinocchio (cameo) 34.00 100.00 235.00
3 (12/39)-Pinocchio Christmas-c (Before movie release). 1st app. Jiminy Crickett; Pinocchio serial begins 43.00 130.00 300.00
4,5: 5-Jiminy Crickett-c; Pinocchio serial ends; Donald's Dog Laundry feature story 34.00 100.00 235.00
6-Tugboat Mickey feature story; Rip Van Winkle feature begins, ends V5#8 32.90 95.00 225.00
7-2nd Huey, Dewey & Louie-c 32.00 95.00 225.00
8-Last magazine size issue; 2nd solo Pluto-c; Figaro & Cleo feature story 32.00 95.00 225.00
9 (6/40; change to comic book size)-Jiminy Crickett feature story; Donald-c & Sunday-r begin 37.00 110.00 260.00
10-Special Independence Day issue 37.00 110.00 260.00
11-Hawaiian Holiday & Mickey's Trailor feature stories; last 36 pg. issue 37.00 110.00 260.00
12 (Format change)-The transition issue (68 pgs.) becoming a comic book. With only a title change to follow, becomes Walt Disney's Comics & Stories #1 with the next issue 143.00 430.00 1000.00
V4#1 (Giveaway) 25.00 75.00 175.00

NOTE: *Otto **Messmer**-a is in many issues of the first two-three years. The following story titles and issues have gags created by **Carl Barks:** V4#3(12/38)-'Donald's Better Self' & 'Donald's Golf Game;' V4#4(1/39)-'Donald's Lucky Day;' V4#7(3/39)-'Hockey Champ;' V4#7(4/39)-'Donald's Cousin Gus;' V4#9(6/39)-'Sea Scouts;' V4#12(9/39)-'Donald's Penguin;' V5#9(6/40)-'Donald's Vacation;' V5#10(7/40)-'Bone Trouble;' V5#12(9/40)-'Window Cleaners.'*

**MICKEY MOUSE MARCH OF COMICS**
1947 - 1951 (Giveaway)
K. K. Publications

8(1947)-32 pgs. 50.00 150.00 330.00
27(1948) 34.00 100.00 238.00
45(1949) 27.00 80.00 190.00
60(1950) 18.00 55.00 125.00
74(1951) 14.00 42.50 96.00

**MICKEY MOUSE SUMMER FUN** (See Dell Giants)

**MICKEY MOUSE'S SUMMER VACATION** (See Story Hour Series)

**MICROBOTS, THE**
December, 1971 (One Shot)
Gold Key

1 (10271-112) .85 2.50 5.00

**MICRONAUTS**
Jan, 1979 - No. 59, Aug, 1984 (Mando paper #53 on)
Marvel Comics Group

1-Intro/1st app. Baron Karza .35 1.10 2.20
2-5 .60 1.20
6-36,39-59: 7-Man-Thing app. 8-1st app. Capt. Universe. 9-1st app. Cilicia. 13-1st app. Jasmine. 15-Death of Microtron. 15-17-Fantastic Four app. 17-Death of Jasmine. 20 Ant-Man app. 21-Microverse series begins. 25-Origin Baron Karza. 25-29-Nick Fury app. 27-Death of Biotron. 34,35-Dr. Strange app. 35-Double size; origin Microverse; intro Death Squad. 40-Fantastic Four app. 57-Double size .45 .90
37-New X-Men app.; Giffen-a(p) .35 1.00 2.00
38-First direct sale .25 .80 1.60
nn-Reprints #1-3; blank UPC; diamond on top .20 .40
Annual 1(12/79)-Ditko-c/a .30 .90 1.80
Annual 2(10/80)-Ditko-c/a .50 1.00

NOTE: *#38-on distributed only through comic shops. **N. Adams** c-7i. **Chaykin** a-13-18p. **Ditko** a-39p. **Giffen** a-36p, 37p. **Golden** a-1-12p; c-2-6p, 7-23, 24p, 38, 39. **Guice** a-48-58p; c-49-58. **Gil Kane** a-38, 40-45p; c-40-45. **Layton** c-33-37. **Miller** c-31.*

**MICRONAUTS** (The New Voyages)
Oct, 1984 - No. 20, May, 1986
Marvel Comics Group

V2#1-20 .35 .70

NOTE: ***Golden** a-1; c-1, 6. **Guice** a-4p; c-2p.*

**MICRONAUTS SPECIAL EDITION**
Dec, 1983 - No. 5, Apr, 1984 ($2.00, mini-series, Baxter paper)
Marvel Comics Group

1-5: r-/original series 1-12; Guice-c(p)-all .70 1.40

**MIDGET COMICS** (Fighting Indian Stories)
Feb, 1950 - No. 2, Apr, 1950 (5-3/8''x7-3/8'')
St. John Publishng Co.

1-Matt Baker-c 5.70 17.00 40.00
2-Tex West, Cowboy Marshal 3.50 10.50 24.00

**MIDNIGHT**
April, 1957 - No. 6, June, 1958
Ajax/Farrell Publ. (Four Star Comic Corp.)

1-Reprints from Voodoo & Strange Fantasy with some changes 5.00 15.00 35.00
2-6 2.65 8.00 18.00

**MIDNIGHT MYSTERY**
Jan-Feb, 1961 - No. 7, Oct, 1961
American Comics Group

1-Sci/Fic story 3.60 11.00 25.00
2-7: 7-Gustavson-a 2.00 6.00 14.00

NOTE: ***Reinman** a-1, 3. **Whitney** a-1, 4-6; c-1-3, 5, 7.*

**MIDNIGHT TALES**
Dec, 1972 - No. 18, May, 1976
Charlton Press

V1#1 .25 .75 1.50
2-18: 11-14-Newton-a(p) .50 1.00
12,17(Modern Comics reprint, 1977) .15 .30

NOTE: ***Adkins** a-12i, 13i. **Ditko** a-12. **Howard** (Wood imitator) a-1-15, 17, 18; c-1-18. **Don Newton** a-11-14p. **Staton** a-1, 3-11, 13. **Sutton** a-3-5, 7-10.*

**MIGHTY ATOM, THE** (. . .& the Pixies #6) (Formerly The Pixies #1-5)
No. 6, 1949; Nov, 1957 - No. 6, Aug-Sept, 1958
Magazine Enterprises

6(1949-M.E.)-no month (1st Series) 2.30 7.00 16.00
1-6(2nd Series)-Pixies-r 1.00 3.00 7.00
I.W. Reprint #1(nd) .30 .90 1.80
Giveaway(1959, '63, Whitman)-Evans-a 1.35 4.00 8.00
Giveaway ('65r, '67r, '68r, '73r, '76r) .50 1.00

**MIGHTY BEAR** (Formerly Fun Comics; Mighty Ghost #4)
No. 13, Jan, 1954 - No. 14, Mar, 1954; 9/57 - No. 3, 2/58
Star Publ. No. 13,14/Ajax-Farrell (Four Star)

13,14-L. B. Cole-c 4.00 12.00 28.00
1-3('57-'58)Four Star (Ajax) 1.30 4.00 9.00

*Mickey Mouse Magazine V5#3, © Disney Co.*

*Micronauts #4, © MEG*

*Midnight Tales #1, © CC*

*Mighty Comics #41, © AP*

*The Mighty Crusaders #1, © AP*

*Mighty Mouse #1 (1946), © Viacom Int.*

**MIGHTY COMICS** (. . . Presents) (Formerly Flyman)
No. 40, Nov, 1966 - No. 50, Oct, 1967 (All 12 cent issues)
Radio Comics (Archie)

| | Good | Fine | N-Mint |
|---|---|---|---|
| 40-Web | 1.50 | 4.50 | 10.00 |
| 41-50: 41-Shield, Black Hood. 42-Black Hood. 43-Shield, Web & Black Hood. 44-Black Hood, Steel Sterling & The Shield. 45-Shield & Hangman; origin Web retold. 46-Steel Sterling, Web & Black Hood. 47-Black Hood & Mr. Justice. 48-Shield & Hangman; Wizard x-over in Shield. 49-Steel Sterling & Fox; Black Hood x-over in Steel Sterling. 50-Black Hood & Web; Inferno x-over in Web | 1.15 | 3.50 | 8.00 |

NOTE: ***Paul Reinman** a-40-50.*

**MIGHTY CRUSADERS, THE** (Also see Advs. of the Fly & Fly Man)
Nov, 1965 - No. 7, Oct, 1966 (All 12 cent issues)
Mighty Comics Group (Radio Comics)

| | Good | Fine | N-Mint |
|---|---|---|---|
| 1-Origin The Shield | 2.15 | 6.50 | 15.00 |
| 2-Origin Comet | 1.50 | 4.50 | 10.00 |
| 3-Origin Fly-Man | 1.15 | 3.50 | 8.00 |
| 4-Fireball, Inferno, Firefly, Web, Fox, Bob Phantom, Blackjack, Hangman, Zambini, Kardak, Steel Sterling, Mr. Justice, Wizard, Capt. Flag, Jaguar x-over | 1.30 | 4.00 | 9.00 |
| 5-Intro. Ultra-Men (Fox, Web, Capt. Flag) & Terrific Three (Jaguar, Mr. Justice, Steel Sterling) | 1.15 | 3.50 | 8.00 |
| 6,7: 7-Steel Sterling feature; origin Fly-Girl | 1.15 | 3.50 | 8.00 |

NOTE: ***Reinman** a-6.*

**MIGHTY CRUSADERS, THE** (All New Advs. of . . . #2)
3/83 - No. 13, 9/85 ($1.00, 36 pgs, Mando paper)
Red Circle Prod./Archie Ent. No. 6 on

| | Good | Fine | N-Mint |
|---|---|---|---|
| 1-13: 1-Origin Black Hood, The Fly, Fly Girl, The Shield, The Wizard, The Jaguar, Pvt. Strong & The Web. 2-Mister Midnight begins. 4-Darkling replaces Shield. 5-Origin Jaguar, Shield begins. 7-Untold origin Jaguar | | .45 | .90 |

NOTE: ***Buckler** a-1-3, 4i, 5p, 7p, 8i, 9i; c-1-10p.*

**MIGHTY GHOST** (Formerly Mighty Bear)
No. 4, June, 1958
Ajax/Farrell Publ.

| | Good | Fine | N-Mint |
|---|---|---|---|
| 4 | 1.15 | 3.50 | 8.00 |

**MIGHTY HERCULES, THE** (TV)
July, 1963 - No. 2, Nov, 1963
Gold Key

| | Good | Fine | N-Mint |
|---|---|---|---|
| 1,2(10072-307, 10072-311) | 3.50 | 10.50 | 24.00 |

**MIGHTY HEROES, THE** (TV) (Funny)
Mar, 1967 - No. 4, July, 1967
Dell Publishing Co.

| | Good | Fine | N-Mint |
|---|---|---|---|
| 1-1957 Heckle & Jeckle-r | .85 | 2.50 | 6.00 |
| 2-4: 4-Two 1958 Mighty Mouse-r | .60 | 1.80 | 4.00 |

**MIGHTY MARVEL WESTERN, THE**
Oct, 1968 - No. 46, Sept, 1976 (#1-14: 68 pgs.; #15,16: 52 pgs.)
Marvel Comics Group (LMC earlier issues)

| | Good | Fine | N-Mint |
|---|---|---|---|
| 1-Begin Kid Colt, Rawhide Kid, Two-Gun Kid-r | .50 | 1.50 | 3.00 |
| 2-10 | .30 | 1.00 | 2.00 |
| 11-20 | .25 | .75 | 1.50 |
| 21-46: 24-Kid Colt-r end. 25-Matt Slade-r begin. 31-Baker-r. 32-Origin-r/Ringo Kid #23; Williamson-r/Kid Slade #7. 37-Williamson, Kirby-r/Two-Gun Kid 51 | | .40 | .80 |

NOTE: ***Jack Davis** a(r)-21-24. **Keller** r-1, 22. **Kirby** a(r)-1-3, 6, 9, 12, 14, 16, 26, 29, 32, 36, 41, 43, 44; c-29. **Maneely** a(r)-22. No Matt Slade-#43.*

**MIGHTY MIDGET COMICS, THE** (Miniature)
No date; circa 1942-1943 (36 pages) (Approx. 5x4")
(Black & White & Red) (Sold 2 for 5 cents)
Samuel E. Lowe & Co.

| | Good | Fine | N-Mint |
|---|---|---|---|
| Bulletman #11(1943)-R-/cover/Bulletman #3 | 4.00 | 12.00 | 28.00 |
| Captain Marvel #11 | 4.00 | 12.00 | 28.00 |
| Captain Marvel #11 (Same as above except for full color ad on back cover; this issue was glued to cover of Captain Marvel #20 and is not found in fine-mint condition) | 4.00 | 12.00 | 28.00 |
| Captain Marvel Jr. #11 | 4.00 | 12.00 | 28.00 |
| Captain Marvel Jr. #11 (Same as above except for full color ad on back-c; this issue was glued to cover of Captain Marvel #21 and is not found in fine-mint condition) | 4.00 | 12.00 | 28.00 |
| Golden Arrow #11 | 2.65 | 8.00 | 18.00 |
| Ibis the Invincible #11(1942)-Origin; r-/cover/Ibis #1 | 4.00 | 12.00 | 28.00 |
| Spy Smasher #11(1942) | 4.00 | 12.00 | 28.00 |

NOTE: *The above books came in a box called "box full of books" and was distributed with other Samuel Lowe puzzles, paper dolls, coloring books, etc. They are not titled Mighty Midget Comics. All have a war bond seal on back cover which is otherwise blank. These books came in a "Mighty Midget" flat cardboard counter display rack.*

| | Good | Fine | N-Mint |
|---|---|---|---|
| Balbo, the Boy Magician #12 | 2.00 | 6.00 | 14.00 |
| Bulletman #12 | 3.70 | 11.00 | 26.00 |
| Commando Yank #12 | 2.65 | 8.00 | 18.00 |
| Dr. Voltz the Human Generator | 2.00 | 6.00 | 14.00 |
| Lance O'Casey #12 | 2.00 | 6.00 | 14.00 |
| Leatherneck the Marine | 2.00 | 6.00 | 14.00 |
| Minute Man #12 | 3.70 | 11.00 | 26.00 |
| Mister Q | 2.00 | 6.00 | 14.00 |
| Mr. Scarlet & Pinky #12 | 3.70 | 11.00 | 26.00 |
| Pat Wilton & His Flying Fortress | 2.00 | 6.00 | 14.00 |
| The Phantom Eagle #12 | 2.65 | 8.00 | 18.00 |
| State Trooper Stops Crime | 2.00 | 6.00 | 14.00 |
| Tornado Tom; r-/from Cyclone #1-3; origin | 2.30 | 7.00 | 16.00 |

**MIGHTY MOUSE** (See Adventures of . . ., Dell Giant #43, Giant Comics Edition, March of Comics #205, 237, 247, 257, 447, 459, 471, 483, Oxydol-Dreft, Paul Terry's, & Terry-Toons Comics)

**MIGHTY MOUSE** (1st Series)
Fall, 1946 - No. 4, Summer, 1947
Timely/Marvel Comics (20th Century Fox)

| | Good | Fine | N-Mint |
|---|---|---|---|
| 1 | 57.00 | 170.00 | 400.00 |
| 2 | 29.00 | 85.00 | 200.00 |
| 3,4 | 20.00 | 60.00 | 140.00 |

**MIGHTY MOUSE** (2nd Series) (Paul Terry's . . . #62-71)
Aug, 1947 - No. 67, 11/55; No. 68, 3/56 - No. 83, 6/59
St. John Publishing Co./Pines No. 68 (3/56) on (TV issues #72 on)

| | Good | Fine | N-Mint |
|---|---|---|---|
| 5(#1) | 19.00 | 58.00 | 135.00 |
| 6-10 | 10.00 | 30.00 | 70.00 |
| 11-19 | 5.70 | 17.00 | 40.00 |
| 20 (11/50) - 25-(52 pgs.) | 4.30 | 13.00 | 30.00 |
| 20-25-(36 pg. editions) | 4.00 | 12.00 | 28.00 |
| 26-37: 35-Flying saucer-c | 3.15 | 9.50 | 22.00 |
| 38-45-(100 pgs.) | 7.00 | 21.00 | 50.00 |
| 46-83: 62,64,67-Painted-c. 82-Infinity-c | 2.30 | 7.00 | 16.00 |
| Album 1(10/52)-100 pgs. | 14.00 | 43.00 | 100.00 |
| Album 2(11/52-St. John) - 3(12/52) (100 pgs.) | 11.50 | 34.00 | 80.00 |
| Fun Club Magazine 1(Fall, 1957-Pines, 100 pgs.) (CBS TV-Tom Terrific) | 8.00 | 24.00 | 55.00 |
| Fun Club Magazine 2-6(Winter, 1958-Pines) | 4.30 | 13.00 | 30.00 |
| 3-D 1-(1st printing-9/53)(St. John)-stiff covers | 20.00 | 60.00 | 140.00 |
| 3-D 1-(2nd printing-10/53)-slick, glossy covers, slightly smaller | 17.00 | 51.00 | 120.00 |
| 3-D 2(11/53), 3(12/53)-(St. John) | 16.00 | 48.00 | 110.00 |

**MIGHTY MOUSE** (TV)(3rd Series)(Formerly Advs. of Mighty Mouse)
No. 161, Oct, 1964 - No. 172, Oct, 1968
Gold Key/Dell Publishing Co. No. 166-on

| | Good | Fine | N-Mint |
|---|---|---|---|
| 161(10/64)-165(9/65)-(Becomes Advs. of . . . No. 166 on) | 1.70 | 5.00 | 12.00 |
| 166(3/66), 167(6/66)-172 | 1.30 | 4.00 | 9.00 |

**MIGHTY MOUSE** (TV)
1987 - No. 2, 1987 ($1.50, color)
Spotlight Comics

| | Good | Fine | N-Mint |
|---|---|---|---|
| 1,2: New stories | .25 | .75 | 1.50 |
| . . . And Friends Holiday Special (11/87, $1.75) | .30 | .90 | 1.75 |

**MIGHTY MOUSE** (TV)
Oct, 1990 - Present ($1.00, color)(Based on Saturday morning cartoon)
Marvel Comics

| | Good | Fine | N-Mint |
|---|---|---|---|
| 1-6: 1-Dark Knight-c parody. 3-Intro Bat-Bat; Byrne-c. 4,5-Crisis-c/story parodies w/Perez-c | | .50 | 1.00 |

**MIGHTY MOUSE ADVENTURES** (Adventures of . . . #2 on)
November, 1951
St. John Publishing Co.

| | Good | Fine | N-Mint |
|---|---|---|---|
| 1 | 17.00 | 51.00 | 120.00 |

**MIGHTY MOUSE ADVENTURE STORIES**
1953 (384 pgs.) (50 Cents)
St. John Publishing Co.

| | Good | Fine | N-Mint |
|---|---|---|---|
| Rebound issues | 29.00 | 86.00 | 200.00 |

**MIGHTY SAMSON** (Also see Gold Key Champion)
7/64 - #20, 11/69; #21, 8/72; #22, 12/73 - #31, 3/76; #32, 8/82
Gold Key

| | Good | Fine | N-Mint |
|---|---|---|---|
| 1-Origin; Thorne-a begins; painted c-1-31 | 1.70 | 5.00 | 12.00 |
| 2-5 | 1.15 | 3.50 | 8.00 |
| 6-10: 7-Tom Morrow begins, ends #20 | .85 | 2.60 | 6.00 |
| 11-20 | .70 | 2.00 | 5.00 |
| 21-32: 21,22,32-r | .30 | 1.00 | 2.00 |

**MIGHTY THOR** (See Thor)

**MIKE BARNETT, MAN AGAINST CRIME** (TV)
Dec, 1951 - No. 6, 1952
Fawcett Publications

| | Good | Fine | N-Mint |
|---|---|---|---|
| 1 | 6.50 | 19.00 | 45.00 |
| 2 | 3.70 | 11.00 | 26.00 |
| 3,4,6 | 3.00 | 9.00 | 21.00 |
| 5-"Market for Morphine" cover/story | 4.30 | 13.00 | 30.00 |

**MIKE GRELL'S SABLE** (Also see Jon Sable & Sable)
March, 1990 - No. 10, Dec, 1990 ($1.75, color)
First Comics

| | Good | Fine | N-Mint |
|---|---|---|---|
| 1-10: r/Jon Sable Freelance #1-10 by Grell | .30 | .90 | 1.80 |

**MIKE MIST MINUTE MIST-ERIES** (See Ms. Tree/Mike Mist in 3-D)
April, 1981 ($1.25, B&W, one-shot)
Eclipse Comics

| | Good | Fine | N-Mint |
|---|---|---|---|
| 1 | | .65 | 1.30 |

**MIKE SHAYNE PRIVATE EYE**
Nov-Jan, 1962 - No. 3, Sept-Nov, 1962
Dell Publishing Co.

| | Good | Fine | N-Mint |
|---|---|---|---|
| 1 | 1.50 | 4.50 | 10.00 |
| 2,3 | 1.15 | 3.50 | 8.00 |

**MILITARY COMICS** (Becomes Modern Comics #44 on)
Aug, 1941 - No. 43, Oct, 1945
Quality Comics Group

| | Good | Fine | VF-NM | NM/Mint |
|---|---|---|---|---|
| 1-Origin/1st app. Blackhawk by C. Cuidera (Eisner scripts); Miss America, The Death Patrol by Jack Cole (also #2-7,27-30), & The Blue Tracer by Guardineer; X of the Underground, The Yankee Eagle, Q-Boat & Shot & Shell, Archie Atkins, Loops & Banks by Bud Ernest (Bob Powell)(ends #13) begin | 333.00 | 835.00 | 2000.00 | 2500.00 |

(Estimated up to 160 total copies exist, 9 in NM/Mint)

| | Good | Fine | N-Mint |
|---|---|---|---|
| 2-Secret War News begins (by McWilliams #2-16); Cole-a | 135.00 | 410.00 | 950.00 |
| 3-Origin/1st app. Chop Chop | 107.00 | 320.00 | 750.00 |
| 4 | 93.00 | 280.00 | 650.00 |
| 5-The Sniper begins; Miss America in costume #4-7 | 75.00 | 225.00 | 525.00 |
| 6-9: 8-X of the Underground begins (ends #13). 9-The Phantom Clipper begins (ends #16) | 63.00 | 190.00 | 440.00 |
| 10-Classic Eisner-c | 67.00 | 200.00 | 470.00 |
| 11-Flag-c | 50.00 | 150.00 | 350.00 |
| 12-Blackhawk by Crandall begins, ends #22 | 67.00 | 200.00 | 470.00 |
| 13-15: 14-Private Dogtag begins (ends #83) | 45.00 | 135.00 | 315.00 |
| 16-20: 16-Blue Tracer ends. 17-P.T. Boat begins | 40.00 | 120.00 | 275.00 |
| 21-31: 22-Last Crandall Blackhawk. 27-Death Patrol revived | 36.00 | 107.00 | 250.00 |
| 32-43 | 30.00 | 90.00 | 210.00 |

NOTE: ***Berg** a-6. **J. Cole** a-1-3, 27-32. **Crandall** a-12-22; c-13-22. **Eisner** c-1, 2(part), 9, 10. **McWilliams** a-2-16. **Powell** a-1-13. **Ward** Blackhawk-30, 31(15 pgs. each); c-29, 30.*

**MILITARY WILLY**
1907 (14 pgs.; ½ in color (every other page))
(regular comic book format)(7x9½")(stapled)
J. I. Austen Co.

| | Good | Fine | N-Mint |
|---|---|---|---|
| nn-By F. R. Morgan | 14.00 | 43.00 | 100.00 |

**MILLENNIUM**
Jan, 1988 - No. 8, Feb, 1988 (nd) (Weekly mini-series)
DC Comics

| | Good | Fine | N-Mint |
|---|---|---|---|
| 1-Staton c/a(p) begins | .40 | 1.25 | 2.50 |
| 2-8 | .25 | .80 | 1.60 |

**MILLENNIUM INDEX**
Mar, 1988 - No. 2, Mar, 1988 ($2.00)
Independent Comics Group

| | Good | Fine | N-Mint |
|---|---|---|---|
| 1,2 | .35 | 1.00 | 2.00 |

**MILLIE, THE LOVABLE MONSTER**
Sept-Nov, 1962 - No. 6, Jan, 1973
Dell Publishing Co.

| | Good | Fine | N-Mint |
|---|---|---|---|
| 12-523-211, 2(8-10/63) | 1.15 | 3.50 | 8.00 |
| 3(8-10/64) | .85 | 2.50 | 6.00 |
| 4(7/72), 5(10/72), 6(1/73) | .70 | 2.00 | 4.00 |

NOTE: ***Woggon** a-3-6; c-3-6. 4 reprints 1; 5 reprints 2; 6 reprints 3.*

**MILLIE THE MODEL** (See Comedy Comics, A Date With . . ., Gay Comics, Life With . . ., Mad About . . . & Modeling With . . .)
1945 - No. 207, December, 1973
Marvel/Atlas/Marvel Comics (CnPC #1)(SPI/Male/VPI)

| | Good | Fine | N-Mint |
|---|---|---|---|
| 1-Origin | 25.00 | 75.00 | 175.00 |
| 2 (10/46)-Millie becomes The Blonde Phantom to sell Blonde Phantom perfume; a pre-Blonde Phantom app. (see All-Select #11, Fall, '46) | 14.00 | 43.00 | 100.00 |
| 3-7: 4,5- Willie app. 7-Willie smokes extra strong tobacco | 8.50 | 25.50 | 60.00 |
| 8,10-Kurtzman's "Hey Look." 8-Willie & Rusty app. | 8.50 | 25.50 | 60.00 |
| 9-Powerhouse Pepper by Wolverton, 4 pgs. | 11.50 | 34.00 | 80.00 |
| 11-Kurtzman-a, 'Giggles 'n Grins | 5.70 | 17.00 | 40.00 |
| 12,15,17-20: 12-Rusty & Hedy Devine app. | 3.60 | 11.00 | 25.00 |
| 13,14,16-Kurtzman's "Hey Look." 13-Hedy Devine app. | 4.30 | 13.00 | 30.00 |
| 21-30 | 2.65 | 8.00 | 18.00 |
| 31-60 | 1.70 | 5.00 | 12.00 |
| 61-99 | 1.15 | 3.50 | 8.00 |
| 100 | 1.70 | 5.00 | 12.00 |
| 101-190: 107-Jack Kirby app. in story. 154-New Millie begins (10/67). 192-(52 pgs.) | .50 | 1.50 | 3.00 |
| 191-207 | .35 | 1.00 | 2.00 |

*Mighty Samson #5, © WEST*

*Military Comics #3, © QUA*

*Millie the Model #24, © MEG*

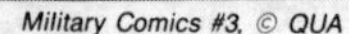

*Miracleman #9, © Eclipse*

*Miss America Magazine V7#15, © MEG*

*Miss Cairo Jones #1, © Croyden Publ.*

| | Good | Fine | N-Mint |
|---|---|---|---|
| Annual 1(1962) | 4.30 | 13.00 | 30.00 |
| Annual 2-10(1963-11/71) | 2.00 | 6.00 | 14.00 |
| Queen-Size 11(9/74), 12(1975) | .70 | 2.00 | 5.00 |

**MILLION DOLLAR DIGEST** (Also see Richie Rich. . .)
11/86 - No. 7, 11/87; No. 8, 4/88 - Present ($1.25-$1.75, digest size)
Harvey Publications

| | | | |
|---|---|---|---|
| 1-8 | | .60 | 1.25 |
| 9-20 (1991) | .30 | .90 | 1.75 |

**MILT GROSS FUNNIES** (Also see Picture News #1)
Aug, 1947 - No. 2, Sept, 1947
Milt Gross, Inc. (ACG?)

| | | | |
|---|---|---|---|
| 1,2 | 4.50 | 14.00 | 32.00 |

**MILTON THE MONSTER & FEARLESS FLY** (TV)
May, 1966
Gold Key

| | | | |
|---|---|---|---|
| 1 (10175-605) | 3.50 | 10.50 | 24.00 |

**MINUTE MAN** (See Master Comics & Mighty Midget Comics)
Summer, 1941 - No. 3, Spring, 1942
Fawcett Publications

| | | | |
|---|---|---|---|
| 1 | 72.00 | 215.00 | 500.00 |
| 2,3 | 57.00 | 170.00 | 400.00 |

**MINUTE MAN**
No date (B&W; 16 pgs.; paper cover blue & red)
Sovereign Service Station giveaway

| | | | |
|---|---|---|---|
| nn-American history | 1.00 | 3.00 | 6.00 |

**MINUTE MAN ANSWERS THE CALL, THE**
1942 (4 pages)
By M. C. Gaines (War Bonds giveaway)

| | | | |
|---|---|---|---|
| nn-Sheldon Moldoff-a | 6.00 | 18.00 | 42.00 |

**MIRACLE COMICS**
Feb, 1940 - No. 4, March, 1941
Hillman Periodicals

| | | | |
|---|---|---|---|
| 1-Sky Wizard, Master of Space, Dash Dixon, Man of Might, Dusty Doyle, Pinkie Parker, The Kid Cop, K-7, Secret Agent, The Scorpion, & Blandu, Jungle Queen begin; Masked Angel only app. | 61.00 | 182.00 | 425.00 |
| 2 | 36.00 | 107.00 | 250.00 |
| 3,4: 3-Bill Colt, the Ghost Rider begins. 4-The Veiled Prophet & Bullet Bob app. | 34.00 | 100.00 | 235.00 |

**MIRACLEMAN**
Aug, 1985 - No. 15, Nov, 1988; No. 16, Dec, 1989 - Present
($1.25-$1.75, Mando paper: 7-10; #16,17: $1.95; #18 on: $2.00)
Eclipse Comics

| | | | |
|---|---|---|---|
| 1-r-/of British Marvelman series; Alan Moore scripts in 1-16 | .35 | 1.00 | 2.00 |
| 1-Gold & Silver editions | .35 | 1.00 | 2.00 |
| 2-12: 8-Airboy preview. 9,10-Origin Miracleman. 9-Shows graphic scenes of childbirth | | .60 | 1.25 |
| 13-15 ($1.75) | .30 | .90 | 1.75 |
| 16-18 ($1.95): 16-By Alan Moore & Totleben. 17-No Moore scripts. 18-$2.00-c | .35 | 1.00 | 2.00 |
| 19-$2.50-c | .40 | 1.25 | 2.50 |
| 3-D 1 (12/85) | .40 | 1.25 | 2.50 |
| 2-D 1 ($5.00, B&W, 100 copy limited signed & numbered edition) | .40 | 1.25 | 2.50 |

**MIRACLEMAN FAMILY**
May, 1988 - No. 2, Sept, 1988 ($1.95, color, mini-series, Baxter paper)
Eclipse Comics

| | | | |
|---|---|---|---|
| 1,2: 2-Gulacy-c | .35 | 1.00 | 2.00 |

**MIRACLE OF THE WHITE STALLIONS, THE** (See Movie Comics)

**MIRACLE SQUAD, THE**
Aug, 1986 - No. 4, 1987 ($2.00, color, mini-series)
Upshot Graphics (Fantagraphics Books)

| | Good | Fine | N-Mint |
|---|---|---|---|
| 1-4 | .35 | 1.00 | 2.00 |

**MIRACLE SQUAD: BLOOD AND DUST, THE**
Jan, 1989 - No. 4, July, 1989 ($1.95, B&W, mini-series)
Apple Comics

| | | | |
|---|---|---|---|
| 1-4 | .35 | 1.00 | 2.00 |

**MISADVENTURES OF MERLIN JONES, THE** (See Movie Comics & Merlin Jones as the Monkey's Uncle under Movie Comics)

**MISCHIEVOUS MONKS OF CROCODILE ISLE, THE**
1908 (8½x11½"; 4 pgs. in color; 12 pgs.)
J. I. Austen Co., Chicago

| | | | |
|---|---|---|---|
| nn-By F. R. Morgan; reads longwise | 10.00 | 30.00 | 70.00 |

**MISS AMERICA COMICS** (Miss America Magazine #2 on; also see Blonde Phantom & Marvel Mystery Comics)
1944 (One Shot)
Marvel Comics (20CC)

| | | | |
|---|---|---|---|
| 1-2 pgs. pin-ups | 64.00 | 160.00 | 385.00 |

**MISS AMERICA MAGAZINE** (Formerly Miss America) (Miss America #51 on)
V1#2, Nov, 1944 - No. 93, Nov, 1958
Miss America Publ. Corp./Marvel/Atlas (MAP)

| | | | |
|---|---|---|---|
| V1#2: Photo-c of teenage girl in Miss America costume; Miss America, Patsy Walker (intro.) comic stories plus movie reviews & stories; intro. Buzz Baxter & Hedy Wolfe | 48.00 | 145.00 | 335.00 |
| 3,5-Miss America & Patsy Walker stories | 17.00 | 51.00 | 120.00 |
| 4-Betty Page photo-c (See Cupid #2, My Love #4); Miss America & Patsy Walker story | 25.00 | 75.00 | 175.00 |
| 6-Patsy Walker only | 4.50 | 14.00 | 32.00 |
| V2#1(4/45)-6(9/45)-Patsy Walker continues | 2.30 | 7.00 | 16.00 |
| V3#1(10/45)-6(4/46) | 2.30 | 7.00 | 16.00 |
| V4#1(5/46),2,5(9/46) | 1.85 | 5.50 | 13.00 |
| V4#3(7/46)-Liz Taylor photo-c | 4.00 | 12.00 | 28.00 |
| V4#4 (8/46; 68pgs.) | 1.85 | 5.50 | 13.00 |
| V4#6 (10/46; 92pgs.) | 1.85 | 5.50 | 13.00 |
| V5#1(11/46)-6(4/47), V6#1(5/47)-3(7/47) | 1.85 | 5.50 | 13.00 |
| V7#1(8/47)-14,16-23(6/49) | 1.50 | 4.50 | 10.00 |
| V7#15-All comics | 1.85 | 5.50 | 13.00 |
| V7#24(7/49)-Kamen-a | 1.50 | 4.50 | 10.00 |
| V7#25(8/49), 27-44(3/52), VII,nn(5/52) | 1.30 | 4.00 | 9.00 |
| V7#26(9/49)-All comics | 1.70 | 5.00 | 12.00 |
| V1,nn(7/52)-V1,nn(1/53)(#46-49) | 1.30 | 4.00 | 9.00 |
| V7#50(Spring '53), V1#51-V7?#54(7/53) | 1.15 | 3.50 | 8.00 |
| 55-93 | 1.15 | 3.50 | 8.00 |

NOTE: *Photo-c #1, V2#4, 5, V3#5, V4#3, 4, 6, V7#15, 16, 24, 26, 34, 37, 38.* ***Powell*** *a-V7#31.*

**MISS BEVERLY HILLS OF HOLLYWOOD** (See Advs. of Bob Hope)
Mar-Apr, 1949 - No. 9, July-Aug, 1950 (52 pgs.)
National Periodical Publications

| | | | |
|---|---|---|---|
| 1 (Meets Alan Ladd) | 25.00 | 75.00 | 175.00 |
| 2-William Holden photo-c | 20.00 | 60.00 | 140.00 |
| 3-5: 3,4-Part photo-c | 16.00 | 48.00 | 110.00 |
| 6,7,9 | 13.00 | 40.00 | 90.00 |
| 8-Reagan photo on-c | 19.00 | 56.00 | 130.00 |

**MISS CAIRO JONES**
1945
Croyden Publishers

| | | | |
|---|---|---|---|
| 1-Bob Oksner daily newspaper-r (1st strip story); lingerie panels | 13.00 | 40.00 | 90.00 |

**MISS FURY COMICS** (Newspaper strip reprints)
Winter, 1942-43 - No. 8, Winter, 1946
Timely Comics (NPI 1/CmPI 2/MPC 3-8)

| | Good | Fine | N-Mint |
|---|---|---|---|
| 1-Origin Miss Fury by Tarpe' Mills (68 pgs.) in costume w/pin-ups | 175.00 | 440.00 | 1050.00 |
| 2-(60 pgs.)-In costume w/pin-ups | 69.00 | 205.00 | 480.00 |
| 3-(60 pgs.)-In costume w/pin-ups; Hitler-c | 57.00 | 170.00 | 400.00 |
| 4-(52 pgs.)-In costume, 2 pgs. w/pin-ups | 47.00 | 140.00 | 325.00 |
| 5-(52 pgs.)-In costume w/pin-ups | 43.00 | 130.00 | 300.00 |
| 6-(52 pgs.)-Not in costume in inside stories, w/pin-ups | 39.00 | 115.00 | 270.00 |
| 7,8-(36 pgs.)-In costume 1 pg. each, no pin-ups | 39.00 | 115.00 | 270.00 |

NOTE: ***Schomburg** c-1, 5, 6.*

**MISSION IMPOSSIBLE** (TV)
May, 1967 - No. 4, Oct, 1968; No. 5, Oct, 1969 (All have photo-c)
Dell Publishing Co.

| | | | |
|---|---|---|---|
| 1 | 5.00 | 15.00 | 35.00 |
| 2-5: 5-reprints #1 | 3.50 | 10.50 | 24.00 |

**MISS LIBERTY** (Becomes Liberty Comics)
1945 (MLJ reprints)
Burten Publishing Co.

| | | | |
|---|---|---|---|
| 1-The Shield & Dusty, The Wizard, & Roy, the Super Boy app.; r-/Shield-Wizard #13 | 15.00 | 45.00 | 105.00 |

**MISS MELODY LANE OF BROADWAY** (See The Advs. of Bob Hope)
Feb-Mar, 1950 - No. 3, June-July, 1950 (52 pgs.)
National Periodical Publications

| | | | |
|---|---|---|---|
| 1 | 25.00 | 75.00 | 175.00 |
| 2,3 | 20.00 | 60.00 | 140.00 |

**MISS PEACH**
Oct-Dec, 1963; 1969
Dell Publishing Co.

| | | | |
|---|---|---|---|
| 1-Jack Mendelsohn-a/script | 5.70 | 17.00 | 40.00 |
| ...Tells You How to Grow(1969; 25 cents)-Mel Lazarus-a; also given away (36 pgs.) | 3.50 | 10.50 | 24.00 |

**MISS PEPPER** (See Meet Miss Pepper)

**MISS SUNBEAM** (See Little Miss...)

**MISS VICTORY** (See Captain Fearless #1,2, Holyoke One-Shot #3, Veri Best Sure Fire & Veri Best Sure Shot Comics)

**MR. & MRS.**
1922 (52 & 28 pgs.) (9x9½", cardboard-c)
Whitman Publishing Co.

| | | | |
|---|---|---|---|
| nn-By Briggs (B&W, 52pgs.) | 9.30 | 28.00 | 65.00 |
| nn-28 pgs.-(9x9½")-Sunday strips-r in color | 14.00 | 42.00 | 100.00 |

**MR. & MRS. BEANS** (See Single Series #11)

**MR. & MRS. J. EVIL SCIENTIST** (TV)(See The Flintstones)
Nov, 1963 - No. 4, Sept, 1966 (Hanna-Barbera)
Gold Key

| | | | |
|---|---|---|---|
| 1-From The Flintstones | 2.00 | 6.00 | 14.00 |
| 2-4 | 1.30 | 4.00 | 9.00 |

**MR. ANTHONY'S LOVE CLINIC** (Based on radio show)
Nov, 1949 - No. 5, Apr-May, 1950 (52 pgs.)
Hillman Periodicals

| | | | |
|---|---|---|---|
| 1-Photo-c | 5.00 | 15.00 | 35.00 |
| 2 | 3.00 | 9.00 | 21.00 |
| 3-5: 5-Photo-c | 2.65 | 8.00 | 18.00 |

**MR. BUG GOES TO TOWN** (See Cinema Comics Herald)

**MR. DISTRICT ATTORNEY** (Radio/TV)
Jan-Feb, 1948 - No. 67, Jan-Feb, 1959 (1-23: 52 pgs.)
National Periodical Publications

| | Good | Fine | N-Mint |
|---|---|---|---|
| 1 | 36.00 | 107.00 | 250.00 |
| 2 | 14.00 | 43.00 | 100.00 |
| 3-5 | 11.00 | 32.00 | 75.00 |
| 6-10 | 8.50 | 25.50 | 60.00 |
| 11-20 | 7.00 | 21.00 | 50.00 |
| 21-43: 43-Last pre-code (1-2/55) | 5.00 | 15.00 | 35.00 |
| 44-67 | 3.60 | 11.00 | 25.00 |

**MR. DISTRICT ATTORNEY** (See 4-Color #13 & The Funnies #35)

**MISTER ED, THE TALKING HORSE** (TV)
Mar-May, 1962 - No. 6, Feb, 1964 (All photo-c; photo back-c: 1-6)
Dell Publishing Co./Gold Key

| | | | |
|---|---|---|---|
| 4-Color 1295 | 6.50 | 19.00 | 45.00 |
| 1(11/62) (Gold Key)-Photo-c | 4.00 | 12.00 | 28.00 |
| 2-6-Photo-c | 2.00 | 6.00 | 14.00 |

*(See March of Comics #244, 260, 282, 290)*

**MR. MAGOO** (TV) (The Nearsighted..., ...& Gerald McBoing Boing 1954 issues; formerly Gerald McBoing-Boing And ...)
No. 6, Nov-Jan, 1953-54; 5/54 - 3-5/62; 9-11/63 - 3-5/65
Dell Publishing Co.

| | | | |
|---|---|---|---|
| 6 | 5.00 | 15.00 | 35.00 |
| 4-Color 561(5/54),602(11/54) | 5.00 | 15.00 | 35.00 |
| 4-Color 1235,1305(3-5/62) | 4.00 | 12.00 | 28.00 |
| 3(9-11/63) - 5 | 3.50 | 10.50 | 24.00 |
| 4-Color 1235(12-536-505)(3-5/65)-2nd Printing | 2.35 | 7.00 | 16.00 |

**MISTER MIRACLE** (See Brave & the Bold & Cancelled Comic Cav.)
3-4/71 - V4#18, 2-3/74; V5#19, 9/77 - V6#25, 8-9/78; 1987
National Periodical Publications/DC Comics

| | | | |
|---|---|---|---|
| 1-(#1-3 are 15 cents) | 1.00 | 3.00 | 6.00 |
| 2,3 | .60 | 1.75 | 3.50 |
| 4-8: 4-Boy Commandos-r begin; all 52 pg. giants | .70 | 2.00 | 4.00 |
| 9,10: 9-Origin Mr. Miracle | .40 | 1.25 | 2.50 |
| 11-25: 15-Intro/1st app. Shilo Norman. 18-Barda & Scott Free wed; New Gods app. | .35 | 1.00 | 2.00 |
| Special 1(1987, 52 pgs., $1.25) | .25 | .75 | 1.50 |

NOTE: ***Austin** a-19i. **Ditko** a-6r. **Golden** a-23-25p; c-25p. **Heath** a-24i, 25i; c-25i. **Kirby** a(p)/c-1-18. **Nasser** a-19i. **Rogers** a-19-22p; c-19, 20p, 21p, 22-24. **Wolverton** a-6r. 4-8 contain **Simon & Kirby** Boy Commandos reprints from Detective 82,76, Boy Commandos 1, 3 & Detective 64 in that order.*

**MISTER MIRACLE**
Jan, 1989 - Present (1.00, color)
DC Comics

| | | | |
|---|---|---|---|
| 1-Spin-off from Justice League International | .25 | .75 | 1.50 |
| 2-26: 9-Intro Maxi-Man. 22-1st new Mr. Miracle | | .50 | 1.00 |

**MR. MIRACLE** (See Capt. Fearless #1, Holyoke One-Shot #4 & Super Duck #3)

**MR. MONSTER** (Doc Stearn... #7 on; See Airboy-Mr. Monster Special, Dark Horse Presents, Super Duper Comics & Vanguard Ill. #7)
Jan, 1985 - No. 10, June, 1987 ($1.75, color, Baxter paper)
Eclipse Comics

| | | | |
|---|---|---|---|
| 1 | 1.50 | 4.50 | 9.00 |
| 2-Dave Stevens-c | .65 | 1.90 | 3.75 |
| 3-9: 3-Alan Moore scripts | .50 | 1.50 | 3.00 |
| 10-6-D issue | .30 | .90 | 1.80 |
| ...In 3-D #1 | .35 | 1.00 | 2.00 |

**MR. MONSTER**
Feb, 1988 - No. 6? ($1.75-$1.95, B&W)
Dark Horse Comics

| | | | |
|---|---|---|---|
| 1: 1,2-Origin | .40 | 1.25 | 2.50 |
| 2-6 | .35 | 1.00 | 2.00 |

**MR. MONSTER'S SUPER-DUPER SPECIAL**
May, 1986 - No. 8, July, 1987 ($1.75, color)

*Miss Melody Lane of Broadway #3, © DC*

*Mr. District Attorney #14, © DC*

*Mister Miracle #3 (1st series), © DC*

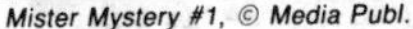
*Mister Mystery #1, © Media Publ.*

*Mister X #13, © Vortex*

*Modern Comics #54, © QUA*

Eclipse Comics

| | Good | Fine | N-Mint |
|---|---|---|---|
| 1 (5/86, $2.50)-Mr. Monster's Three Dimensional High Octane Horror #1; Kubert/Powell-r | .40 | 1.25 | 2.50 |
| 1 . . . in 2-D: 100 copies signed & #'d (B&W) | 1.00 | 3.00 | 6.00 |
| 2 (8/86) . . . High Octane Horror #1; Grandenetti, Wolverton, Evans-r | .30 | .90 | 1.80 |
| 3 (9/86) . . . True Crime #1; Cole-r | .30 | .90 | 1.80 |
| 4 (11/86) . . . True Crime #2 | .30 | .90 | 1.80 |
| 5 (1/87) . . . Hi-Voltage Super Science #1; r-/Vic Torry & His Flying Saucer #1 by Powell | .30 | .90 | 1.80 |
| 6,7: (3/87 & 5/87) . . . High Shock Schlock #1 & 2. 2-Wolverton-r | .30 | .90 | 1.80 |
| 8 (7/87) . . . Weird Tales of the Future #1; Wolverton-r | .30 | .90 | 1.80 |

**MR. MUSCLES** (Formerly Blue Beetle #18-21)
No. 22, Mar, 1956; No. 23, Aug, 1956
Charlton Comics

| | Good | Fine | N-Mint |
|---|---|---|---|
| 22,23 | 2.30 | 7.00 | 16.00 |

**MISTER MYSTERY**
Sept, 1951 - No. 19, Oct, 1954
Mr. Publ. (Media Publ.) No. 1-3/SPM Publ./Stanmore (Aragon)

| | Good | Fine | N-Mint |
|---|---|---|---|
| 1-Kurtzmanesque horror story | 23.00 | 70.00 | 160.00 |
| 2,3-Kurtzmanesque story | 15.00 | 45.00 | 105.00 |
| 4,6: Bondage-c; 6-Torture | 15.00 | 45.00 | 105.00 |
| 5,8,10 | 12.00 | 36.00 | 85.00 |
| 7-"The Brain Bats of Venus" by Wolverton; partially re-used in Weird Tales of the Future #7 | 43.00 | 130.00 | 300.00 |
| 9-Nostrand-a | 13.00 | 40.00 | 90.00 |
| 11-Wolverton "Robot Woman" story/Weird Mysteries #2, cut up, rewritten & partially redrawn | 23.00 | 70.00 | 160.00 |
| 12-Classic injury to eye-c | 35.00 | 105.00 | 245.00 |
| 13,14,17,19 | 9.30 | 28.00 | 65.00 |
| 15-"Living Dead" junkie story | 11.00 | 32.00 | 75.00 |
| 16-Bondage-c | 11.00 | 32.00 | 75.00 |
| 18-"Robot Woman" by Wolverton reprinted from Weird Mysteries #2; decapitation, bondage-c | 20.00 | 60.00 | 140.00 |

NOTE: ***Andru** c/a-1, 2p. **Bailey** c-10-19(most). Bondage c-7. Some issues have graphic dismemberment scenes.*

**MISTER Q** (See Mighty Midget Comics & Our Flag Comics #5)

**MR. RISK** (Formerly All Romances; Men Against Crime #3 on)
No. 7, Oct, 1950 - No. 2, Dec, 1950
Ace Magazines

| | Good | Fine | N-Mint |
|---|---|---|---|
| 7,2 | 2.65 | 8.00 | 18.00 |

**MR. SCARLET & PINKY** (See Mighty Midget Comics)

**MISTER UNIVERSE** (Professional wrestler)
July, 1951; No. 2, Oct, 1951 - No. 5, April, 1952
Mr. Publications Media Publ. (Stanmor, Aragon)

| | Good | Fine | N-Mint |
|---|---|---|---|
| 1 | 8.50 | 25.50 | 60.00 |
| 2-"Jungle That Time Forgot," (24 pg. story) | 5.70 | 17.00 | 40.00 |
| 3-Marijuana story | 5.70 | 17.00 | 40.00 |
| 4,5-"Goes to War" | 3.00 | 9.00 | 21.00 |

**MISTER X** (See Vortex)
6/84 - No. 14, 8/88 ($1.50-$2.25, direct sales, Coated paper, color)
V2#1, Apr, 1989 - Present ($2.00-$2.50, B&W, newsprint)
Mr. Publications/Vortex Comics

| | Good | Fine | N-Mint |
|---|---|---|---|
| 1 | 1.15 | 3.50 | 7.00 |
| 2 | .70 | 2.00 | 4.00 |
| 3-5 | .50 | 1.50 | 3.00 |
| 6-10 | .40 | 1.25 | 2.50 |
| 11-14: 13-Kaluta-c; 14-$2.25 | .35 | 1.10 | 2.25 |
| V2#1-11 (Second Coming, $2.00, B&W): 1-Four different covers. 10-Photo-c | .35 | 1.00 | 2.00 |
| V2#12-14: 12-Begin $2.50-c | .40 | 1.25 | 2.50 |
| Graphic Novel, Return of . . . ($11.95)-r/1-4 | 2.00 | 6.00 | 12.00 |
| Hardcover Limited Edition ($34.95) | 5.85 | 17.50 | 35.00 |

**MISTY**
Dec, 1985 - No. 6, May, 1986 (Mini-series)
Star Comics (Marvel)

| | Good | Fine | N-Mint |
|---|---|---|---|
| 1-6: Millie The Model's niece | | .40 | .80 |

**MITZI COMICS** (. . . Boy Friend #2 on)(See All Teen)
Spring, 1948 (One Shot)
Timely Comics

| | Good | Fine | N-Mint |
|---|---|---|---|
| 1-Kurtzman's "Hey Look" plus 3 pgs. "Giggles 'n' Grins" | 8.50 | 25.50 | 60.00 |

**MITZI'S BOY FRIEND** (Formerly Mitzi; becomes Mitzi's Romances)
No. 2, June, 1948 - No. 7, April, 1949
Marvel Comics

| | Good | Fine | N-Mint |
|---|---|---|---|
| 2 | 3.50 | 10.50 | 24.00 |
| 3-7 | 2.65 | 8.00 | 18.00 |

**MITZI'S ROMANCES** (Formerly Mitzi's Boy Friend)
No. 8, June, 1949 - No. 10, Dec, 1949
Timely/Marvel Comics

| | Good | Fine | N-Mint |
|---|---|---|---|
| 8 | 3.50 | 10.50 | 24.00 |
| 9,10: 10-Painted-c | 2.65 | 8.00 | 18.00 |

**MOBY DICK** (See Feature Presentations #6, Four Color #717, and King Classics)

**MOBY DUCK** (See Donald Duck #112 & W. D. Showcase #2,11)
Oct, 1967 - No. 11, Oct, 1970; No. 12, Jan, 1974 - No. 30, Feb, 1978
Gold Key (Disney)

| | Good | Fine | N-Mint |
|---|---|---|---|
| 1 | .85 | 2.50 | 6.00 |
| 2-5 | .70 | 2.00 | 4.00 |
| 6-11 | .35 | 1.00 | 2.00 |
| 12-30: 21,30-r | | .60 | 1.20 |

**MODEL FUN** (With Bobby Benson)
No. 3, Winter, 1954-55 - No. 5, July, 1955
Harle Publications

| | Good | Fine | N-Mint |
|---|---|---|---|
| 3-Bobby Benson | 2.85 | 8.50 | 20.00 |
| 4,5-Bobby Benson | 1.70 | 5.00 | 12.00 |

**MODELING WITH MILLIE** (Formerly Life With Millie)
No. 21, Feb, 1963 - No. 54, June, 1967
Atlas/Marvel Comics Group (Male Publ.)

| | Good | Fine | N-Mint |
|---|---|---|---|
| 21 | 2.15 | 6.50 | 15.00 |
| 22-30 | 1.50 | 4.50 | 10.00 |
| 31-54 | 1.00 | 3.00 | 7.00 |

**MODERN COMICS** (Formerly Military Comics #1-43)
No. 44, Nov, 1945 - No. 102, Oct, 1950
Quality Comics Group

| | Good | Fine | N-Mint |
|---|---|---|---|
| 44-Blackhawk continues | 30.00 | 90.00 | 210.00 |
| 45-52: 49-1st app. Fear, Lady Adventuress | 18.00 | 54.00 | 125.00 |
| 53-Torchy by Ward begins (9/46) | 23.00 | 70.00 | 160.00 |
| 54-60: 55-J. Cole-a | 16.00 | 48.00 | 110.00 |
| 61-77,79,80: 73-J. Cole-a | 14.00 | 43.00 | 100.00 |
| 78-1st app. Madame Butterfly | 16.00 | 48.00 | 110.00 |
| 81-99,101: 82,83-One pg. J. Cole-a | 14.00 | 43.00 | 100.00 |
| 100 | 14.00 | 43.00 | 100.00 |
| 102-(Scarce)-J. Cole-a; Spirit by Eisner app. | 17.00 | 51.00 | 120.00 |

NOTE: ***Crandall** Blackhawk-#46-51, 54, 56, 58-60, 64, 67-70, 73, 82, 83. **Jack Cole** a-73. **Gustavson** a-47. **Ward** Blackhawk-#52, 53, 55 (15 pgs. each). Torchy in #53-102; by **Ward** only in #53-89(9/49); by **Gil Fox** #93, 102.*

**MODERN LOVE**
June-July, 1949 - No. 8, Aug-Sept, 1950
E. C. Comics

| | Good | Fine | N-Mint |
|---|---|---|---|
| 1 | 43.00 | 130.00 | 300.00 |
| 2-Craig/Feldstein-c | 34.00 | 103.00 | 240.00 |

| | Good | Fine | N-Mint |
|---|---|---|---|
| 3-Spanking panels | 29.00 | 85.00 | 200.00 |
| 4-6 (Scarce): 4-Bra/panties panels | 41.00 | 122.00 | 285.00 |
| 7,8 | 31.00 | 92.00 | 215.00 |

NOTE: ***Feldstein** a-in most issues; c-1, 2i, 3-8. **Ingels** a-1, 2, 4-7. **Wood** a-7. (Canadian reprints known; see Table of Contents.)*

**MOD LOVE**
1967 (36 pages) (50 cents)
Western Publishing Co.

| | | | |
|---|---|---|---|
| 1 | 2.00 | 6.00 | 14.00 |

**MODNIKS, THE**
Aug, 1967 - No. 2, Aug, 1970
Gold Key

| | | | |
|---|---|---|---|
| 10206-708(#1), 2 | .85 | 2.60 | 6.00 |

**MOD SQUAD** (TV)
Jan, 1969 - No. 3, Oct, 1969 - No. 8, April, 1971
Dell Publishing Co.

| | | | |
|---|---|---|---|
| 1-Photo-c | 2.30 | 7.00 | 16.00 |
| 2-8: 2-4-Photo-c. 8-Reprints #2 | 1.50 | 4.50 | 10.00 |

**MOD WHEELS**
March, 1971 - No. 19, Jan, 1976
Gold Key

| | | | |
|---|---|---|---|
| 1 | 1.00 | 3.00 | 6.00 |
| 2-19: 11,15-Extra 16pgs. ads | .50 | 1.50 | 3.00 |

**MOE & SHMOE COMICS**
Spring, 1948 - No. 2, Summer, 1948
O. S. Publ. Co.

| | | | |
|---|---|---|---|
| 1 | 3.70 | 11.00 | 26.00 |
| 2 | 2.65 | 8.00 | 18.00 |

**MOEBIUS**
Oct, 1987 - No. 6, 1988 ($9.95, $12.95, graphic novel, adults, 8X11")
Epic Comics (Marvel)

| | | | |
|---|---|---|---|
| 1,2,4-6: (#2, 2nd printing, $9.95) | 1.70 | 5.00 | 10.00 |
| 3 (1st & 2nd printings, $12.95) | 2.15 | 6.50 | 13.00 |
| Moebius I-Signed & numbered hard-c ($45.95, Graphitti Designs, 1,500 copies)-r/1-3 | 7.70 | 23.00 | 46.00 |

**MOLLY MANTON'S ROMANCES** (Romantic Affairs #3)
Sept, 1949 - No. 2, Dec, 1949 (52 pgs.)
Marvel Comics (SePI)

| | | | |
|---|---|---|---|
| 1-Photo-c | 5.00 | 15.00 | 35.00 |
| 2-Titled "Romances of...;" photo-c | 3.50 | 10.50 | 24.00 |

**MOLLY O'DAY** (Super Sleuth)
February, 1945 (1st Avon comic)
Avon Periodicals

| | | | |
|---|---|---|---|
| 1-Molly O'Day, The Enchanted Dagger by Tuska (r-/Yankee #1), Capt'n Courage, Corporal Grant app. | 30.00 | 90.00 | 210.00 |

**MONKEES, THE** (TV)(Also see Circus Boy, Groovy, Not Brand Echh #3, Teen-Age Talk, Teen Beam & Teen Beat)
March, 1967 - No. 17, Oct, 1969 (#1-4,6,7,10 have photo-c)
Dell Publishing Co.

| | | | |
|---|---|---|---|
| 1 | 5.00 | 15.00 | 35.00 |
| 2-17: 17 reprints #1 | 2.65 | 8.00 | 18.00 |

**MONKEY & THE BEAR, THE**
Sept, 1953 - No. 3, Jan, 1954
Atlas Comics (ZPC)

| | | | |
|---|---|---|---|
| 1-Howie Post-a | 2.65 | 8.00 | 18.00 |
| 2,3 | 1.50 | 4.50 | 10.00 |

**MONKEYSHINES COMICS**
Summer, 1944 - No. 27, July, 1949
Ace Periodicals/Publishers Specialists/Current Books/Unity Publ.

| | Good | Fine | N-Mint |
|---|---|---|---|
| 1 | 4.50 | 14.00 | 32.00 |
| 2 | 2.30 | 7.00 | 16.00 |
| 3-10 | 1.70 | 5.00 | 12.00 |
| 11-27: 23,24-Fago-c/a | 1.50 | 4.50 | 10.00 |

**MONKEY SHINES OF MARSELEEN**
1909 (11½x17") (28 pages in two colors)
Cupples & Leon Co.

| | | | |
|---|---|---|---|
| nn-By Norman E. Jennett | 11.50 | 34.00 | 80.00 |

**MONKEY'S UNCLE, THE** (See Merlin Jones As... under Movie Comics)

**MONROES, THE** (TV)
April, 1967
Dell Publishing Co.

| | | | |
|---|---|---|---|
| 1-Photo-c | 1.70 | 5.00 | 12.00 |

**MONSTER**
1953 - No. 2, 1953
Fiction House Magazines

| | | | |
|---|---|---|---|
| 1-Dr. Drew by Grandenetti; reprint from Rangers Comics | 20.00 | 60.00 | 140.00 |
| 2 | 16.00 | 48.00 | 110.00 |

**MONSTER CRIME COMICS** (Also see Crime Must Stop)
October, 1952 (52 pgs., 15 cents)
Hillman Periodicals

| | | | |
|---|---|---|---|
| 1 (Scarce) | 40.00 | 120.00 | 280.00 |

**MONSTER HOWLS** (Magazine)
December, 1966 (Satire) (35 cents) (68 pgs.)
Humor-Vision

| | | | |
|---|---|---|---|
| 1 | 1.15 | 3.50 | 8.00 |

**MONSTER HUNTERS**
Aug, 1975 - No. 9, Jan, 1977; No. 10, Oct, 1977 - No. 18, Feb, 1979
Charlton Comics

| | | | |
|---|---|---|---|
| 1,2: 1-Howard-a; Newton-c. 2-Ditko-a | | .60 | 1.20 |
| 3-13,15-18 | | .40 | .80 |
| 14-Special all-Ditko issue | | .60 | 1.20 |
| 1,2(Modern Comics reprints, 1977) | | .15 | .30 |

NOTE: ***Ditko** a-2, 6, 8, 10, 13-15r, 18r; c-13-15, 18. **Howard** r-13. **Morisi** a-1. **Staton** a-1, 13. **Sutton** a-2, 4; c-2, 4. Reprints in #12-18.*

**MONSTER OF FRANKENSTEIN** (See Frankenstein)

**MONSTERS ON THE PROWL** (Chamber of Darkness #1-8)
No. 9, 2/71 - No. 27, 11/73; No. 28, 6/74 - No. 30, 10/74
Marvel Comics Group (No. 13,14: 52 pgs.)

| | | | |
|---|---|---|---|
| 9-Barry Smith inks | .35 | 1.00 | 2.00 |
| 10-30: 16-King Kull app.; Severin-c | | .50 | 1.00 |

NOTE: ***Ditko** r-5, 9, 14, 16. **Kirby** r-10-17, 21, 23, 25, 27, 28, 30; c-9, 25. **Kirby/Ditko** r-14, 17-20, 22, 24, 26, 29. **Reinman** r-5. **Marie/John Severin** a-16(Kull). 9-13, 15 contain one new story. Woodish art by **Reese**-11. King Kull created by Robert E. Howard.*

**MONSTERS UNLEASHED** (Magazine)
July, 1973 - No. 11, April, 1975; Summer, 1975 (B&W)
Marvel Comics Group

| | | | |
|---|---|---|---|
| 1 | .50 | 1.50 | 3.00 |
| 2-The Frankenstein Monster begins | .35 | 1.00 | 2.00 |
| 3,4: 3-Neal Adams-c; The Man-Thing begins (origin-r)-N. Adams-a. 4-Intro. Satana, the Devil's daughter; Krigstein-r | .35 | 1.00 | 2.00 |
| 5-7: 7-Williamson-a(r) | .35 | 1.00 | 2.00 |
| 8,10,11: 8-N. Adams-r. 10-Origin Tigra | .35 | 1.00 | 2.00 |
| 9-Wendigo app. | .50 | 1.50 | 3.00 |
| Annual 1(Summer,'75)-Kane-a | .35 | 1.00 | 2.00 |

NOTE: ***Boris** c-2, 6. **Brunner** a-2; c-11. **J. Buscema** a-2p, 4p, 5p. **Colan** a-1, 4r. **Davis** a-3r. **Everett** a-2r. **G. Kane** a-3. **Morrow** a-3; c-1. **Perez** a-8. **Ploog** a-6. **Reese** a-1, 2. **Tuska** a-3p. **Wildey** a-1r.*

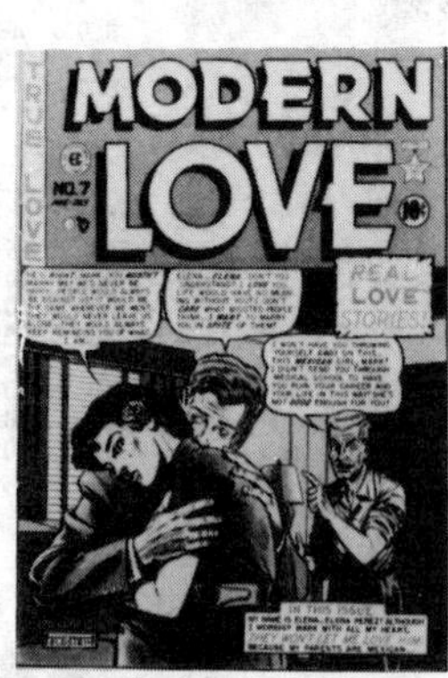

*Modern Love #7, © WMG*

*The Monkees #10, © Mayberry Prod.*

*Monkeyshines Comics #10, © ACE*

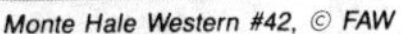
Monte Hale Western #42, © FAW

Moon Girl and the Prince #2, © WMG

Moon Knight V2#1, © MEG

**MONTANA KID, THE** (See Kid Montana)

**MONTE HALE WESTERN** (Movie star; Formerly Mary Marvel #1-28; also see Picture News #8, Real Western Hero, Six-Gun Heroes, Western Hero & XMas Comics)
No. 29, Oct, 1948 - No. 88, Jan, 1956
Fawcett Publications/Charlton No. 83 on

| | Good | Fine | N-Mint |
|---|---|---|---|
| 29-(#1, 52pgs.)-Photo-c begin, end #82; Monte Hale & his horse Pardner begin | 25.00 | 75.00 | 175.00 |
| 30-(52 pgs.)-Big Bow and Little Arrow begin, end #34; Captain Tootsie by Beck | 14.00 | 43.00 | 100.00 |
| 31-36,38-40-(52 pgs.): 34-Gabby Hayes begins, ends #80. 39-Captain Tootsie by Beck | 11.50 | 34.00 | 80.00 |
| 37,41,45,49-(36 pgs.) | 7.00 | 21.00 | 50.00 |
| 42-44,46-48,50-(52 pgs.): 47-Big Bow & Little Arrow app. | 8.00 | 24.00 | 55.00 |
| 51,52,54-56,58,59-(52 pgs.) | 6.00 | 18.00 | 42.00 |
| 53,57-(36 pgs.): 53-Slim Pickens app. | 4.50 | 14.00 | 32.00 |
| 60-81: 36pgs. #60-on. 80-Gabby Hayes ends | 4.50 | 14.00 | 32.00 |
| 82-Last Fawcett issue (6/53) | 6.50 | 19.00 | 45.00 |
| 83-1st Charlton issue (2/55); B&W photo back-c begin. Gabby Hayes returns, ends #86 | 6.50 | 19.00 | 45.00 |
| 84 (4/55) | 4.50 | 14.00 | 32.00 |
| 85-86 | 4.30 | 13.00 | 30.00 |
| 87-Wolverton-r, ½pg. | 4.50 | 14.00 | 32.00 |
| 88-Last issue | 4.50 | 14.00 | 32.00 |

NOTE: ***Gil Kane** a-33?, 34? **Rocky Lane** ½-1 pg. (Carnation ad)-38, 40, 41, 43, 44, 46, 55.*

**MONTY HALL OF THE U.S. MARINES** (See With the Marines...)
Aug, 1951 - No. 11, 1953
Toby Press

| | Good | Fine | N-Mint |
|---|---|---|---|
| 1 | 4.50 | 14.00 | 32.00 |
| 2 | 2.85 | 8.50 | 20.00 |
| 3-5 | 2.50 | 7.50 | 17.00 |
| 6-11 | 1.85 | 5.50 | 13.00 |

NOTE: *3-5 have full page pin-ups (Pin-Up Pete) by **Jack Sparling** in all.*

**MOON, A GIRL...ROMANCE, A** (Becomes Weird Fantasy #13 on; formerly Moon Girl #1-8)
No. 9, Sept-Oct, 1949 - No. 12, Mar-Apr, 1950
E. C. Comics

| | Good | Fine | N-Mint |
|---|---|---|---|
| 9-Moon Girl cameo; spanking panels | 54.00 | 160.00 | 375.00 |
| 10,11 | 41.50 | 125.00 | 290.00 |
| 12-(Scarce) | 57.00 | 170.00 | 400.00 |

NOTE: ***Feldstein, Ingels** art in all. Canadian reprints known; see Table of Contents.*

**MOON GIRL AND THE PRINCE** (#1) (Moon Girl #2-6; Moon Girl Fights Crime #7,8; becomes A Moon, A Girl, Romance #9 on)
Fall, 1947 - No. 8, Summer, 1949
E. C. Comics (Also see Happy Houlihans)

| | Good | Fine | N-Mint |
|---|---|---|---|
| 1-Origin Moon Girl | 65.00 | 200.00 | 460.00 |
| 2 | 39.00 | 115.00 | 270.00 |
| 3,4: 4-Moon Girl vs. a vampire | 33.00 | 100.00 | 230.00 |
| 5-E.C.'s 1st horror story, "Zombie Terror" | 70.00 | 210.00 | 490.00 |
| 6-8 (Scarce): 7-Origin Star (Moongirl's sidekick) | 37.00 | 110.00 | 260.00 |

NOTE: *#2 & #3 are 52 pgs., #4 on, 36 pgs. Canadian reprints known; (see Table of Contents.)*

**MOON KNIGHT** (Also see The Hulk, Marc Spector..., Marvel Preview #21, Marvel Spotlight & Werewolf by Night #32)
November, 1980 - No. 38, July, 1984 (Mando paper No. 33 on)
Marvel Comics Group

| | Good | Fine | N-Mint |
|---|---|---|---|
| 1-Origin resumed in #4; begin Sienkiewicz-c/a | .40 | 1.25 | 2.50 |
| 2-34,36-38: 4-Intro Midnight Man. 16-The Thing app. 25-Double size | | .50 | 1.00 |
| 35-($1.00, 52 pgs.)-X-men app.; F.F. cameo | .25 | .75 | 1.50 |

NOTE: ***Austin** c-27i, 31i. **Kaluta** c-36-38. **Miller** c-9, 12p, 13p, 27p. **Ploog** back c-35. **Sienkiewicz** a-1-15, 17-20, 22-26, 28-30; c-1-26, 28-30, 31p, 33, 34.*

**MOON KNIGHT**
June, 1985 - No. 6, Dec, 1985
Marvel Comics Group

| | Good | Fine | N-Mint |
|---|---|---|---|
| V2#1-6: 1-Double size; new costume. 6-Painted-c | | .50 | 1.00 |

**MOON KNIGHT SPECIAL EDITION**
Nov, 1983 - No. 3, Jan, 1984 ($2.00, mini-series, Baxter paper)
Marvel Comics Group

| | Good | Fine | N-Mint |
|---|---|---|---|
| 1-3: 1-Reprints Hulk #13,14 by Sienkiewicz | .25 | .75 | 1.50 |

**MOON MULLINS**
1927 - 1933 (52 pgs.) (daily B&W strip reprints)
Cupples & Leon Co.

| | Good | Fine | N-Mint |
|---|---|---|---|
| Series 1('27)-By Willard | 14.00 | 42.00 | 100.00 |
| Series 2('28), Series 3('29), Series 4('30) | 11.50 | 34.00 | 80.00 |
| Series 5('31), 6('32), 7('33) | 8.50 | 25.50 | 60.00 |
| Big Book 1('30)-B&W | 17.00 | 51.00 | 120.00 |

**MOON MULLINS** (See Popular, Super Book #3 & Super Comics)
1941 - 1945
Dell Publishing Co.

| | Good | Fine | N-Mint |
|---|---|---|---|
| 4-Color 14(1941) | 24.00 | 70.00 | 165.00 |
| Large Feature Comic 29(1941) | 16.00 | 48.00 | 110.00 |
| 4-Color 31(1943) | 13.00 | 40.00 | 90.00 |
| 4-Color 81(1945) | 7.00 | 21.00 | 50.00 |

**MOON MULLINS**
Dec-Jan, 1947-48 - No. 8, 1949 (52 pgs.)
Michel Publ. (American Comics Group)

| | Good | Fine | N-Mint |
|---|---|---|---|
| 1-Alternating Sunday & daily strip-r | 9.30 | 28.00 | 65.00 |
| 2 | 5.00 | 15.00 | 35.00 |
| 3-8 | 3.70 | 11.00 | 26.00 |

NOTE: ***Milt Gross** a-2-6, 8. **Willard** r-all.*

**MOON PILOT** (See 4-Color #1313)

**MOONSHADOW**
May, 1985 - No. 12, Feb, 1987 ($1.50-$1.75)(Adults only)
Epic Comics (Marvel)

| | Good | Fine | N-Mint |
|---|---|---|---|
| 1-Origin | 1.00 | 3.00 | 6.00 |
| 2-12: 11-Origin | .70 | 2.00 | 4.00 |
| Trade paperback (1987?)-reprints | 2.35 | 7.00 | 14.00 |
| Signed & numbered hard-c ($39.95, 1,200 copies)-r/1-12 | 6.70 | 20.00 | 40.00 |

**MOON-SPINNERS, THE** (See Movie Comics)

**MOONWALKER IN 3-D** (See Blackthorne 3-D Series #75)

**MOPSY** (See Pageant of Comics & TV Teens)
Feb, 1948 - No. 19, Sept, 1953
St. John Publ. Co.

| | Good | Fine | N-Mint |
|---|---|---|---|
| 1-Part-r; r-/"Some Punkins" by Neher | 11.50 | 34.00 | 80.00 |
| 2 | 5.70 | 17.00 | 40.00 |
| 3-10(1953): 8-Lingerie panels | 4.50 | 14.00 | 32.00 |
| 11-19: 19-Lingerie-c | 3.70 | 11.00 | 26.00 |

NOTE: *#1, 4-6, 8, 13, 19 have paper dolls.*

**MORE FUN COMICS** (Formerly New Fun Comics #1-6)
No. 7, Jan, 1936 - No. 127, Nov-Dec, 1947 (No. 7,9-11: paper-c)
National Periodical Publications

| | Good | Fine | VF-NM | NM/Mint |
|---|---|---|---|---|
| 7(1/36)-Oversized, paper-c; 1 pg. Kelly-a | 333.00 | 835.00 | 2000.00 | 2900.00 |

(Estimated up to 45 total copies exist, 2 in NM/Mint)

| | Good | Fine | VF-NM |
|---|---|---|---|
| 8(2/36)-Oversized (10x12"), slick-c; 1 pg. Kelly-a | 300.00 | 750.00 | 1800.00 |
| 9(3-4/36)(Very rare, 1st comic-sized issue)-Last Henri Duval by Siegel & Shuster | 300.00 | 750.00 | 1800.00 |

Good Fine VF-NM
10,11(7/36): 11-1st 'Calling All Cars' by Siegel & Shuster
192.00 480.00 1150.00
12(8/36)-Slick-c begin 167.00 417.00 1000.00
V2#1(9/36, #13) 163.00 410.00 980.00
Good Fine VF-NM NM/Mint
2(10/36, #14)-Dr. Occult in costume (Superman prototype) begins, ends #17; see The Comics Magazine
183.00 460.00 1100.00 1800.00
(Estimated up to 50 total copies exist, 3 in NM/Mint)
Good Fine VF-NM
V2#3(11/36, #15), 16(V2#4), 17(V2#5)-Cover numbering begins #16. 16-Xmas-c 121.00 300.00 725.00
18-20(V2#8, 5/37) 92.00 230.00 550.00
Good Fine N-Mint
21(V2#9)-24(V2#12, 9/37) 67.00 165.00 400.00
25(V3#1, 10/37)-27(V3#3, 12/37): 27-Xmas-c 67.00 165.00 400.00
28-30: 30-1st non-funny cover 67.00 165.00 400.00
31-35: 32-Last Dr. Occult 57.00 140.00 340.00
36-40: 36-The Masked Ranger begins, ends #41. 39-Xmas-c
53.00 130.00 315.00
41-50 47.00 115.00 280.00
51-The Spectre app. (in costume) in one panel ad at end of Buccaneer story 117.00 290.00 700.00
52-(2/40)-Origin/1st app. The Spectre (in costume splash panel only), Part 1 by Bernard Baily; last Wing Brady
Good Fine VF-NM NM/Mint
1835.00 4580.00 11,000.00 17,000.00
(Estimated up to 70 total copies exist, 3 in NM/Mint)
53-Origin The Spectre (in costume at end of story), Part 2; Capt. Desmo begins 1250.00 3125.00 7500.00 10,000.00
(Estimated up to 80 total copies exist, 4 in NM/Mint)
54-The Spectre in costume; last King Carter
467.00 1170.00 2800.00 3500.00
55-(Scarce)-Dr. Fate begins (Intro & 1st app.); last Bulldog Martin
500.00 1250.00 3000.00 4000.00
(Estimated up to 100 total copies exist, 6 in NM/Mint)
Good Fine N-Mint
56-60: 56-Congo Bill begins 205.00 510.00 1225.00
61-66: 63-Last St. Bob Neal. 64-Lance Larkin begins
150.00 375.00 900.00
67-Origin Dr. Fate; last Congo Bill & Biff Bronson
Good Fine VF-NM NM/Mint
233.00 585.00 1400.00 2000.00
(Estimated up to 105 total copies exist, 6 in NM/Mint)
68-70: 68-Clip Carson begins. 70-Last Lance Larkin
Good Fine N-Mint
125.00 312.00 750.00
71-Origin & 1st app. Johnny Quick by Mort Wysinger
Good Fine VF-NM NM/Mint
217.00 540.00 1300.00 1900.00
(Estimated up to 90 total copies exist, 6 in NM/Mint)
72-Dr. Fate's new helmet; last Sgt. Carey, Sgt. O'Malley & Captain Desmo
Good Fine N-Mint
108.00 270.00 650.00
73-Origin & 1st app. Aquaman (11/41); intro. Green Arrow & Speedy
Good Fine VF-NM NM/Mint
333.00 835.00 2000.00 3100.00
(Estimated up to 85 total copies exist, 5 in NM/Mint)
Good Fine N-Mint
74-2nd Aquaman 125.00 312.00 750.00
75-80: 76-Last Clip Carson; Johnny Quick by Meskin begins, ends #97. 80-1st small logo 108.00 270.00 650.00
81-88: 87-Last Radio Squad 77.00 190.00 460.00
89-Origin Green Arrow & Speedy Team-up 92.00 230.00 550.00
90-99: 93-Dover & Clover begin. 97-Kubert-a. 98-Last Dr. Fate
50.00 125.00 300.00

Good Fine N-Mint
100 67.00 165.00 400.00
101-Origin & 1st app. Superboy (3/44)(not by Siegel & Shuster); last Spectre issue
Good Fine VF-NM NM/Mint
317.00 790.00 1900.00 2900.00
(Estimated up to 200 total copies exist, 9 in NM/Mint)
Good Fine N-Mint
102-2nd Superboy 83.00 210.00 500.00
103-3rd Superboy 63.00 155.00 375.00
104-107: 104-1st Superboy-c. 105-Superboy-c. 107-Last J. Quick & Superboy 52.00 130.00 310.00
108-120: 108-Genius Jones begins 8.00 24.00 55.00
121-124,126: 121-123,126-Post-c 6.50 19.00 45.00
125-Superman on cover 33.00 100.00 230.00
127-(Scarce)-Post c/a 14.00 42.00 100.00

NOTE: ***All issues are scarce to rare.*** *Cover features: The Spectre-#52-55, 57-60, 62-67. Dr. Fate-#55, 56, 61, 68-76. The Green Arrow & Speedy-#77-85, 88-97, 99, 101; w/Dover & Clover-#98. Johnny Quick-#86, 87, 100. Genius Jones-#108-127.* ***Baily*** *a-45, 52-on; c-52-55, 57-60, 62-67.* ***Al Capp*** *a-45(signed Koppy).* ***Guardineer*** *c-47.* ***Kiefer*** *a-20.* ***Moldoff*** *c-51.*

**MORE SEYMOUR** (See Seymour My Son)
October, 1963
Archie Publications

1 1.50 4.50 10.00

**MORE TRASH FROM MAD** (Annual)
1958 - No. 12, 1969
E. C. Comics

nn(1958)-8 pgs. color Mad reprint from #20 10.00 30.00 70.00
2(1959)-Market Product Labels 7.00 21.00 50.00
3(1960)-Text book covers 5.70 17.00 40.00
4(1961)-Sing Along with Mad booklet 5.70 17.00 40.00
5(1962)-Window Stickers; r-/from Mad #39 3.50 10.50 24.00
6(1963)-TV Guise booklet 4.00 12.00 28.00
7(1964)-Alfred E. Neuman commemorative stamps
2.30 7.00 16.00
8(1965)-Life size poster-Alfred E. Neuman 2.30 7.00 16.00
9,10(1966-67)-Mischief Sticker 1.70 5.00 12.00
11(1968)-Campaign poster & bumper sticker 1.70 5.00 12.00
12(1969)-Pocket medals 1.70 5.00 12.00

NOTE: ***Kelly Freas*** *c-1, 2, 4.* ***Mingo*** *c-3, 5-9, 12.*

**MORGAN THE PIRATE** (See 4-Color #1227)

**MORLOCK 2001**
Feb, 1975 - No. 3, July, 1975
Atlas/Seaboard Publ.

1-(Super-hero)-Origin & 1st app. .50 1.00
2 .30 .60
3-Ditko/Wrightson-a; origin The Midnight Man & The Midnight Men
.60 1.20

**MORNINGSTAR SPECIAL**
April, 1990 ($2.50, color)
Comico

1-From The Elementals; Willingham-c/a/scripts .40 1.25 2.50

**MORTIE** (Mazie's Friend)
Dec, 1952 - No. 4, June, 1953?
Magazine Publishers

1 3.00 9.00 21.00
2-4 1.70 5.00 12.00

**MORTY MEEKLE** (See 4-Color #793)

**MOSES & THE TEN COMMANDMENTS** (See Dell Giants)

**MOTHER GOOSE** (See Christmas With Mother Goose & 4-Color #41, 59, 68, 862)

**MOTHER OF US ALL**
1950? (32 pgs.)

*More Fun Comics #56, © DC*

*More Fun Comics #104, © DC*

*Mortie #1, © Magazine Publ.*

Motion Picture Comics #104, © Republic Pic.

Movie Classics (Frankenstein), © Universal

Movie Classics (Maya), © M.G.M.

Catechetical Guild Giveaway

| | Good | Fine | N-Mint |
|---|---|---|---|
| nn | 1.15 | 3.50 | 8.00 |

**MOTHER TERESA OF CALCUTTA**
1984
Marvel Comics Group

| | Good | Fine | N-Mint |
|---|---|---|---|
| 1 | | .60 | 1.25 |

**MOTION PICTURE COMICS** (See Fawcett Movie Comics)
No. 101, 1950 - No. 114, Jan, 1953 (All-photo-c)
Fawcett Publications

| | Good | Fine | N-Mint |
|---|---|---|---|
| 101-"Vanishing Westerner"-Monte Hale (1950) | 24.00 | 73.00 | 170.00 |
| 102-"Code of the Silver Sage"-Rocky Lane (1/51) | 22.00 | 65.00 | 155.00 |
| 103-"Covered Wagon Raid"-Rocky Lane (3/51) | 22.00 | 65.00 | 155.00 |
| 104-"Vigilante Hideout"-Rocky Lane (5/51)-Book length Powell-a | 22.00 | 65.00 | 155.00 |
| 105-"Red Badge of Courage"-Audie Murphy; Bob Powell-a (7/51) | 27.00 | 81.00 | 190.00 |
| 106-"The Texas Rangers"-George Montgomery (9/51) | 21.00 | 64.00 | 150.00 |
| 107-"Frisco Tornado"-Rocky Lane (11/51) | 20.00 | 60.00 | 140.00 |
| 108-"Mask of the Avenger"-John Derek | 14.00 | 42.00 | 100.00 |
| 109-"Rough Rider of Durango"-Rocky Lane | 20.00 | 60.00 | 140.00 |
| 110-"When Worlds Collide"-George Evans-a (1951); Williamson & Evans drew themselves in story; (also see Famous Funnies No. 72-88) | 69.00 | 208.00 | 485.00 |
| 111-"The Vanishing Outpost"-Lash LaRue | 24.00 | 73.00 | 170.00 |
| 112-"Brave Warrior"-Jon Hall & Jay Silverheels | 13.00 | 40.00 | 90.00 |
| 113-"Walk East on Beacon"-George Murphy; Shaffenberger-a | 9.30 | 28.00 | 65.00 |
| 114-"Cripple Creek"-George Montgomery (1/53) | 11.00 | 32.00 | 75.00 |

**MOTION PICTURE FUNNIES WEEKLY** (Amazing Man #5 on?)
1939 (36 pgs.)(Giveaway)(Black & White)
No month given; last panel in Sub-Mariner story dated 4/39
(Also see Colossus, Green Giant & Invaders No. 20)
First Funnies, Inc.

| | Good | Fine | N-Mint |
|---|---|---|---|
| 1-Origin & 1st printed app. Sub-Mariner by Bill Everett (8 pgs.); Fred Schwab-c; reprinted in Marvel Mystery #1 with color added over the craft tint which was used to shade the black & white version; Spy Ring, American Ace (reprinted in Marvel Mystery No. 3) app. (Rare)-only seven (7) known copies, all with brown pages. | 2500.00 | 5000.00 | —— |
| Covers only to #2-4 (set) | | | 600.00 |

NOTE: The only seven known copies (with an eighth suspected) were discovered in 1974 in the estate of the deceased publisher. Covers only to issues No. 2-4 were also found which evidently were printed in advance along with #1. #1 was to be distributed only through motion picture movie houses. However, it is believed that only advanced copies were sent out and the motion picture houses not going for the idea. Possible distribution at local theaters in Boston suspected. The last panel of Sub-Mariner contains a rectangular box with "Continued Next Week" printed in it. When reprinted in Marvel Mystery, the box was left in with lettering omitted.

**MOUNTAIN MEN** (See Ben Bowie)

**MOUSE MUSKETEERS** (See M.G.M.'s . . .)

**MOUSE ON THE MOON, THE** (See Movie Classics)

**MOVIE CLASSICS**
Jan, 1963 - Dec, 1969
Dell Publishing Co.

(Before 1963, most movie adapt. were part of the 4-Color Series)

| | Good | Fine | N-Mint |
|---|---|---|---|
| Around the World Under the Sea 12-030-612 (12/66) | 1.70 | 5.00 | 12.00 |
| Bambi 3(4/56)-Disney; r-/4-Color #186 | 1.70 | 5.00 | 12.00 |
| Battle of the Bulge 12-056-606 (6/66) | 1.70 | 5.00 | 12.00 |
| Beach Blanket Bingo 12-058-509 | 5.00 | 15.00 | 35.00 |
| Bon Voyage 01-068-212 (12/62)-Disney; photo-c | 1.70 | 5.00 | 12.00 |
| Castilian, The 12-110-401 | 2.65 | 8.00 | 18.00 |
| Cat, The 12-109-612 (12/66) | 1.50 | 4.50 | 10.00 |
| Cheyenne Autumn 12-112-506 (4-6/65) | 4.30 | 13.00 | 30.00 |
| Circus World, Samuel Bronston's 12-115-411; John Wayne app. John Wayne photo-c | 7.00 | 21.00 | 50.00 |
| Countdown 12-150-710 (10/67); James Caan photo-c | 1.70 | 5.00 | 12.00 |
| Creature, The 1 (12-142-302) (12-2/62-63) | 3.50 | 10.50 | 24.00 |
| Creature, The 12-142-410 (10/64) | 1.70 | 5.00 | 12.00 |
| David Ladd's Life Story 12-173-212 (10-12/62)-Photo-c | 6.50 | 19.00 | 45.00 |
| Die, Monster, Die 12-175-603 (3/66)-Photo-c | 2.30 | 7.00 | 16.00 |
| Dirty Dozen 12-180-710 (10/67) | 3.00 | 9.00 | 21.00 |
| Dr. Who & the Daleks 12-190-612 (12/66)-Photo-c | 11.00 | 33.00 | 75.00 |
| Dracula 12-231-212 (10-12/62) | 2.30 | 7.00 | 16.00 |
| El Dorado 12-240-710 (10/67)-John Wayne; photo-c | 11.00 | 32.00 | 75.00 |
| Ensign Pulver 12-257-410 (8-10/64) | 2.00 | 6.00 | 14.00 |
| Frankenstein 12-283-305 (3-5/63) | 2.35 | 7.00 | 16.00 |
| Great Race, The 12-299-603 (3/66)-Natallie Wood, Tony Curtis photo-c | 3.00 | 9.00 | 21.00 |
| Hallelujah Trail, The 12-307-602 (2/66) (Shows 1/66 inside); Burt Lancaster, Lee Remick photo-c | 4.00 | 12.00 | 28.00 |
| Hatari 12-340-301 (1/63)-John Wayne | 6.50 | 19.00 | 45.00 |
| Horizontal Lieutenant, The 01-348-210 (10/62) | 1.70 | 5.00 | 12.00 |
| Incredible Mr. Limpet, The 12-370-408; Don Knotts photo-c | 2.30 | 7.00 | 16.00 |
| Jack the Giant Killer 12-374-301 (1/63) | 5.70 | 17.00 | 40.00 |
| Jason & the Argonauts 12-376-310 (8-10/63)-Photo-c | 6.50 | 19.00 | 45.00 |
| Lancelot & Guinevere 12-416-310 (10/63) | 5.70 | 17.00 | 40.00 |
| Lawrence 12-426-308 (8/63)-Story of Lawrence of Arabia; movie ad on back-c; not exactly like movie | 4.30 | 13.00 | 30.00 |
| Lion of Sparta 12-439-301 (1/63) | 2.00 | 6.00 | 14.00 |
| Mad Monster Party 12-460-801 (9/67) | 5.00 | 15.00 | 35.00 |
| Magic Sword, The 01-496-209 (9/62) | 3.70 | 11.00 | 26.00 |
| Masque of the Red Death 12-490-410 (8-10/64)-Vincent Price photo-c | 3.00 | 9.00 | 21.00 |
| Maya 12-495-612 (12/66)-Clint Walker part photo-c | 3.00 | 9.00 | 21.00 |
| McHale's Navy 12-500-412 (10-12/64) | 2.30 | 7.00 | 16.00 |
| Merrill's Marauders 12-510-301 (1/63)-Photo-c | 2.00 | 6.00 | 14.00 |
| Mouse on the Moon, The 12-530-312 (10/12/63)-Photo-c | 2.30 | 7.00 | 16.00 |
| Mummy, The 12-537-211 (9-11/62) 2 different back-c issues | 2.65 | 8.00 | 18.00 |
| Music Man, The 12-538-301 (1/63) | 2.00 | 6.00 | 14.00 |
| Naked Prey, The 12-545-612 (12/66)-Photo-c | 5.00 | 15.00 | 35.00 |
| Night of the Grizzly, The 12-558-612 (12/66)-Photo-c | 2.65 | 8.00 | 18.00 |
| None But the Brave 12-565-506 (4-6/65) | 4.00 | 12.00 | 28.00 |
| Operation Bikini 12-597-310 (10/63)-Photo-c | 2.65 | 8.00 | 18.00 |
| Operation Crossbow 12-590-512 (10-12/65) | 2.65 | 8.00 | 18.00 |
| Prince & the Pauper, The 01-654-207 (5-7/62)-Disney | 2.65 | 8.00 | 18.00 |
| Raven, The 12-680-309 (9/63)-Vincent Price photo-c | 3.00 | 9.00 | 21.00 |
| Ring of Bright Water 01-701-910 (10/69) (inside shows #12-701-909) | 3.00 | 9.00 | 21.00 |
| Runaway, The 12-707-412 (10-12/64) | 1.70 | 5.00 | 12.00 |
| Santa Claus Conquers the Martians #? (1964)-Photo-c | 7.00 | 21.00 | 50.00 |

| | Good | Fine | N-Mint |
|---|---|---|---|
| Santa Claus Conquers the Martians 12-725-603 (3/66, 12 cents)-Reprints 1964 issue; photo-c | 5.70 | 17.00 | 40.00 |
| Another version given away with a Golden Record, SLP 170, nn, no price (3/66) Complete with record | 11.50 | 34.00 | 80.00 |
| Six Black Horses 12-750-301 (1/63)-Photo-c | 2.30 | 7.00 | 16.00 |
| Ski Party 12-743-511 (9-11/65)-Frankie Avalon photo-c | 4.00 | 12.00 | 28.00 |
| Smoky 12-746-702 (2/67) | 1.50 | 4.50 | 10.00 |
| Sons of Katie Elder 12-748-511 (9-11/65); John Wayne app.; photo-c | 12.00 | 36.00 | 85.00 |
| Tales of Terror 12-793-302 (2/63)-Evans-a | 1.50 | 4.50 | 10.00 |
| Three Stooges Meet Hercules 01-828-208 (8/62)-Photo-c | 5.70 | 17.00 | 40.00 |
| Tomb of Ligeia 12-830-506 (4-6/65) | 1.70 | 5.00 | 12.00 |
| Treasure Island 01-845-211 (7-9/62)-Disney; r-/4-Color #624 | 1.30 | 4.00 | 9.00 |
| Twice Told Tales (Nathaniel Hawthorne) 12-840-401 (11-1/63-64); Vincent Price photo-c | 2.30 | 7.00 | 16.00 |
| Two on a Guillotine 12-850-506 (4-6/65) | 1.70 | 5.00 | 12.00 |
| Valley of Gwangi 01-880-912 (12/69) | 5.70 | 17.00 | 40.00 |
| War Gods of the Deep 12-900-509 (7-9/65) | 1.70 | 5.00 | 12.00 |
| War Wagon, The 12-533-709 (9/67); John Wayne app. | 8.50 | 25.50 | 60.00 |
| Who's Minding the Mint? 12-924-708 (8/67)-Jerry Lewis photo-c | 1.70 | 5.00 | 12.00 |
| Wolfman, The 12-922-308 (6-8/63) | 1.70 | 5.00 | 12.00 |
| Wolfman, The 1(12-922-410)(8-10/64)-2nd printing; 4-/#12-922-308 | 1.70 | 5.00 | 12.00 |
| Zulu 12-950-410 (8-10/64)-Photo-c | 7.00 | 21.00 | 50.00 |

**MOVIE COMICS** (See Cinema Comics Herald & Fawcett Movie Comics)

**MOVIE COMICS**
April, 1939 - No. 6, Sept, 1939 (Most all photo-c)
National Periodical Publications/Picture Comics

| | Good | Fine | N-Mint |
|---|---|---|---|
| 1-"Gunga Din," "Son of Frankenstein," "The Great Man Votes," "Fisherman's Wharf," & "Scouts to the Rescue part 1; Wheelan "Minute Movies" begin | 200.00 | 500.00 | 1200.00 |
| 2-"Stagecoach," "The Saint Strikes Back," "King of the Turf," "Scouts to the Rescue" part 2, "Arizona Legion" | 133.00 | 335.00 | 800.00 |
| 3-"East Side of Heaven," "Mystery in the White Room," "Four Feathers," "Mexican Rose" with Gene Autry, "Spirit of Culver," "Many Secrets," "The Mikado" | 105.00 | 260.00 | 625.00 |
| 4-"Captain Fury," Gene Autry in "Blue Montana Skies," "Streets of N.Y." with Jackie Cooper, "Oregon Trail" part 1 with Johnny Mack Brown, "Big Town Czar" with Barton MacLane, & "Star Reporter" with Warren Hull | 92.00 | 230.00 | 550.00 |
| 5-"Man in the Iron Mask," "Five Came Back," "Wolf Call," "The Girl & the Gambler," "The House of Fear," "The Family Next Door," "Oregon Trail" part 2 | 92.00 | 230.00 | 550.00 |
| 6-"The Phantom Creeps," "Chumps at Oxford," & "The Oregon Trail" part 3 | 121.00 | 300.00 | 725.00 |

NOTE: *Above books contain many original movie stills with dialogue from movie scripts. All issues are scarce.*

**MOVIE COMICS**
Dec, 1946 - No. 4, 1947
Fiction House Magazines

| | Good | Fine | N-Mint |
|---|---|---|---|
| 1-Big Town & Johnny Danger begin; Celardo-a | 29.00 | 85.00 | 200.00 |
| 2-"White Tie & Tails" with William Bendix; Mitzi of the Movies begins by Matt Baker, ends #4 | 20.00 | 60.00 | 140.00 |
| 3-Andy Hardy | 20.00 | 60.00 | 140.00 |
| 4-Mitzi In Hollywood by Matt Baker | 24.00 | 70.00 | 165.00 |

**MOVIE COMICS**
Oct, 1962 - March, 1972

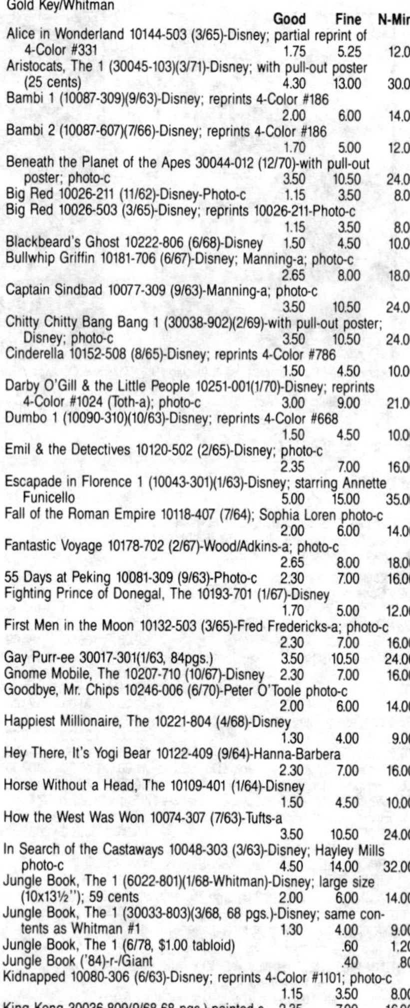
Gold Key/Whitman

| | Good | Fine | N-Mint |
|---|---|---|---|
| Alice in Wonderland 10144-503 (3/65)-Disney; partial reprint of 4-Color #331 | 1.75 | 5.25 | 12.00 |
| Aristocats, The 1 (30045-103)(3/71)-Disney; with pull-out poster (25 cents) | 4.30 | 13.00 | 30.00 |
| Bambi 1 (10087-309)(9/63)-Disney; reprints 4-Color #186 | 2.00 | 6.00 | 14.00 |
| Bambi 2 (10087-607)(7/66)-Disney; reprints 4-Color #186 | 1.70 | 5.00 | 12.00 |
| Beneath the Planet of the Apes 30044-012 (12/70)-with pull-out poster; photo-c | 3.50 | 10.50 | 24.00 |
| Big Red 10026-211 (11/62)-Disney-Photo-c | 1.15 | 3.50 | 8.00 |
| Big Red 10026-503 (3/65)-Disney; reprints 10026-211-Photo-c | 1.15 | 3.50 | 8.00 |
| Blackbeard's Ghost 10222-806 (6/68)-Disney | 1.50 | 4.50 | 10.00 |
| Bullwhip Griffin 10181-706 (6/67)-Disney; Manning-a; photo-c | 2.65 | 8.00 | 18.00 |
| Captain Sindbad 10077-309 (9/63)-Manning-a; photo-c | 3.50 | 10.50 | 24.00 |
| Chitty Chitty Bang Bang 1 (30038-902)(2/69)-with pull-out poster; Disney; photo-c | 3.50 | 10.50 | 24.00 |
| Cinderella 10152-508 (8/65)-Disney; reprints 4-Color #786 | 1.50 | 4.50 | 10.00 |
| Darby O'Gill & the Little People 10251-001(1/70)-Disney; reprints 4-Color #1024 (Toth-a); photo-c | 3.00 | 9.00 | 21.00 |
| Dumbo 1 (10090-310)(10/63)-Disney; reprints 4-Color #668 | 1.50 | 4.50 | 10.00 |
| Emil & the Detectives 10120-502 (2/65)-Disney; photo-c | 2.35 | 7.00 | 16.00 |
| Escapade in Florence 1 (10043-301)(1/63)-Disney; starring Annette Funicello | 5.00 | 15.00 | 35.00 |
| Fall of the Roman Empire 10118-407 (7/64); Sophia Loren photo-c | 2.00 | 6.00 | 14.00 |
| Fantastic Voyage 10178-702 (2/67)-Wood/Adkins-a; photo-c | 2.65 | 8.00 | 18.00 |
| 55 Days at Peking 10081-309 (9/63)-Photo-c | 2.30 | 7.00 | 16.00 |
| Fighting Prince of Donegal, The 10193-701 (1/67)-Disney | 1.70 | 5.00 | 12.00 |
| First Men in the Moon 10132-503 (3/65)-Fred Fredericks-a; photo-c | 2.30 | 7.00 | 16.00 |
| Gay Purr-ee 30017-301(1/63, 84pgs.) | 3.50 | 10.50 | 24.00 |
| Gnome Mobile, The 10207-710 (10/67)-Disney | 2.30 | 7.00 | 16.00 |
| Goodbye, Mr. Chips 10246-006 (6/70)-Peter O'Toole photo-c | 2.00 | 6.00 | 14.00 |
| Happiest Millionaire, The 10221-804 (4/68)-Disney | 1.30 | 4.00 | 9.00 |
| Hey There, It's Yogi Bear 10122-409 (9/64)-Hanna-Barbera | 2.30 | 7.00 | 16.00 |
| Horse Without a Head, The 10109-401 (1/64)-Disney | 1.50 | 4.50 | 10.00 |
| How the West Was Won 10074-307 (7/63)-Tufts-a | 3.50 | 10.50 | 24.00 |
| In Search of the Castaways 10048-303 (3/63)-Disney; Hayley Mills photo-c | 4.50 | 14.00 | 32.00 |
| Jungle Book, The 1 (6022-801)(1/68-Whitman)-Disney; large size (10x13½"); 59 cents | 2.00 | 6.00 | 14.00 |
| Jungle Book, The 1 (30033-803)(3/68, 68 pgs.)-Disney; same contents as Whitman #1 | 1.30 | 4.00 | 9.00 |
| Jungle Book, The 1 (6/78, $1.00 tabloid) | | .60 | 1.20 |
| Jungle Book ('84)-r-/Giant | | .40 | .80 |
| Kidnapped 10080-306 (6/63)-Disney; reprints 4-Color #1101; photo-c | 1.15 | 3.50 | 8.00 |
| King Kong 30036-809(9/68-68 pgs.)-painted-c | 2.35 | 7.00 | 16.00 |
| King Kong nn-Whitman Treasury($1.00,68pgs.,1968), same cover as Gold Key issue | .70 | 2.00 | 4.00 |
| King Kong 11299(#1-786, 10x13¼", 68pgs., $1.00, 1978) | | .50 | 1.00 |

*Movie Classics (Valley . . .), © DELL*

*Movie Comics #1, © FH*

*Movie Comics (King Kong), © Merian C. Cooper*

Movie Comics (Sword . . .), © The Disney Co.

Movie Love #1, © FF

Ms. Marvel #4, © MEG

| | Good | Fine | N-Mint |
|---|---|---|---|
| Lady and the Tramp 10042-301 (1/63)-Disney; r-4-Color #629 | 1.50 | 4.50 | 10.00 |
| Lady and the Tramp 1 (1967-Giant; 25 cents)-Disney; r-part of Dell #1 | 2.50 | 7.50 | 20.00 |
| Lady and the Tramp 2 (10042-203)(3/72)-Disney; r-4-Color #629 | 1.15 | 3.50 | 8.00 |
| Legend of Lobo, The 1 (10059-303)(3/63)-Disney; photo-c | 1.15 | 3.50 | 8.00 |
| Lt. Robin Crusoe, U.S.N. 10191-610 (10/66)-Disney; Dick Van Dyke photo-c | 1.50 | 4.50 | 10.00 |
| Lion, The 10035-301 (1/63)-Photo-c | 1.15 | 3.50 | 8.00 |
| Lord Jim 10156-509 (9/65)-Photo-c | 1.70 | 5.00 | 12.00 |
| Love Bug, The 10237-906 (6/69)-Disney-Buddy Hackett photo-c | 1.50 | 4.50 | 10.00 |
| Mary Poppins 10136-501 (1/65)-Disney; photo-c | 3.00 | 9.00 | 21.00 |
| Mary Poppins 30023-501 (1/65-68 pgs.)-Disney; photo-c | 4.00 | 12.00 | 28.00 |
| McLintock 10110-403 (3/64); John Wayne app.; photo-c | 11.00 | 32.00 | 75.00 |
| Merlin Jones as the Monkey's Uncle 10115-510 (10/65)-Disney; Annette Funicello front/back photo-c | 3.00 | 9.00 | 21.00 |
| Miracle of the White Stallions, The 10065-306 (6/63)-Disney | 1.70 | 5.00 | 12.00 |
| Misadventures of Merlin Jones, The 10115-405 (5/64)-Disney; Annette Funicello photo front/back-c | 3.00 | 9.00 | 21.00 |
| Moon-Spinners, The 10124-410 (10/64)-Disney; Haley Mills photo-c | 4.50 | 14.00 | 32.00 |
| Mutiny on the Bounty 1 (10040-302)(2/63)-Marlon Brando photo-c | 2.00 | 6.00 | 14.00 |
| Nikki, Wild Dog of the North 10141-412 (12/64)-Disney; reprints 4-Color #1226 | 1.15 | 3.50 | 8.00 |
| Old Yeller 10168-601 (1/66)-Disney; reprints 4-Color #869; photo-c | 1.15 | 3.50 | 8.00 |
| One Hundred & One Dalmations 1 (10247-002) (2/70)-Disney; reprints 4-Color #1183 | 1.50 | 4.50 | 10.00 |
| Peter Pan 1 (10086-309)(9/63)-Disney; reprints 4-Color #442 | 1.70 | 5.00 | 12.00 |
| Peter Pan 2 (10086-909)(9/69)-Disney; reprints 4-Color #442 | 1.15 | 3.50 | 8.00 |
| Peter Pan 1 ('83)-r/4-Color #442 | | .40 | .80 |
| P.T. 109 10123-409 (9/64)-John F. Kennedy | 3.50 | 10.50 | 24.00 |
| Rio Conchos 10143-503(3/65) | 3.00 | 9.00 | 21.00 |
| Robin Hood 10163-506 (6/65)-Disney; reprints 4-Color #413 | 1.50 | 4.50 | 10.00 |
| Shaggy Dog & the Absent-Minded Professor 30032-708 (8/67-Giant, 68 pgs.)-Disney; reprints 4-Color #985,1199 | 3.50 | 10.50 | 24.00 |
| Sleeping Beauty 1 (30042-009)(9/70)-Disney; reprints 4-Color #973; with pull-out poster | 3.50 | 10.50 | 24.00 |
| Snow White & the Seven Dwarfs 1 (10091-310)(10/63)-Disney; reprints 4-Color #382 | 1.70 | 5.00 | 12.00 |
| Snow White & the Seven Dwarfs 10091-709 (9/67)-Disney; reprints 4-Color #382 | 1.50 | 4.50 | 10.00 |
| Snow White & the Seven Dwarfs 90091-204 (2/84)-r-/4-Color #382 | | .40 | .80 |
| Son of Flubber 1 (10057-304)(4/63)-Disney; sequel to "The Absent-Minded Professor" | 1.70 | 5.00 | 12.00 |
| Summer Magic 10076-309 (9/63)-Disney; Hayley Mills photo-c; Manning-a | 5.00 | 15.00 | 35.00 |
| Swiss Family Robinson 10236-904 (4/69)-Disney; reprints 4-Color #1156; photo-c | 1.70 | 5.00 | 12.00 |
| Sword in the Stone, The 30019-402 (2/64-Giant, 84 pgs.)-Disney | 3.50 | 10.50 | 24.00 |
| That Darn Cat 10171-602 (2/66)-Disney; Hayley Mills photo-c | 4.50 | 14.00 | 32.00 |
| Those Magnificent Men in Their Flying Machines 10162-510 (10/65); photo-c | 1.70 | 5.00 | 12.00 |
| Three Stooges in Orbit 30016-211 (11/62-Giant, 32 pgs.)-All photos from movie; stiff-photo-c | 7.00 | 21.00 | 50.00 |
| Tiger Walks, A 10117-406 (6/64)-Disney; Torres, Tufts-a; photo-c | 3.00 | 9.00 | 21.00 |
| Toby Tyler 10142-502 (2/65)-Disney; reprints 4-Color #1092; photo-c | 1.50 | 4.50 | 10.00 |
| Treasure Island 1 (10200-703)(3/67)-Disney; reprints 4-Color #624; photo-c | 1.15 | 3.50 | 8.00 |
| 20,000 Leagues Under the Sea 1 (10095-312)(12/63)-Disney; reprints 4-Color #614 | 1.15 | 3.50 | 8.00 |
| Wonderful Adventures of Pinocchio, The 1 (10089-310)(10/63)-Disney; reprints 4-Color #545 | 1.15 | 3.50 | 8.00 |
| Wonderful Adventures of Pinocchio, The 10089-109 (9/71)-Disney; reprints 4-Color #545 | 1.15 | 3.50 | 8.00 |
| Wonderful World of the Brothers Grimm 1 (10008-210)(10/62) | 2.65 | 8.00 | 18.00 |
| X, the Man with the X-Ray Eyes 10083-309 (9/63)-Ray Milland photo on-c | 4.00 | 12.00 | 28.00 |
| Yellow Submarine 35000-902 (2/69-Giant, 68 pgs.)-with pull-out poster; The Beatles cartoon movie | 9.30 | 28.00 | 65.00 |

**MOVIE LOVE** (Also see Personal Love)
Feb, 1950 - No. 22, Aug, 1953
Famous Funnies

| | Good | Fine | N-Mint |
|---|---|---|---|
| 1-Dick Powell photo-c | 6.50 | 19.00 | 45.00 |
| 2 | 3.50 | 10.50 | 24.00 |
| 3-7,9 | 2.65 | 8.00 | 18.00 |
| 8-Williamson/Frazetta-a, 6 pgs. | 23.00 | 70.00 | 160.00 |
| 10-Frazetta-a, 6 pgs. | 28.00 | 85.00 | 200.00 |
| 11,12,14-16 | 2.30 | 7.00 | 16.00 |
| 13-Ronald Reagan photo-c with 1 pg. bio. | 15.00 | 45.00 | 105.00 |
| 17-One pg. Frazetta ad | 2.65 | 8.00 | 18.00 |
| 18-22 | 2.30 | 7.00 | 16.00 |

NOTE: *Each issue has a full-length movie adaptation with photo covers.*

**MOVIE THRILLERS**
1949 (Movie adaptation; photo-c)
Magazine Enterprises

| | Good | Fine | N-Mint |
|---|---|---|---|
| 1-"Rope of Sand" with Burt Lancaster | 19.00 | 57.00 | 135.00 |

**MOVIE TOWN ANIMAL ANTICS** (Formerly Animal Antics; Raccoon Kids #52 on)
No. 24, Jan-Feb, 1950 - No. 51, July-Aug, 1954
National Periodical Publications

| | Good | Fine | N-Mint |
|---|---|---|---|
| 24-Raccoon Kids continue | 5.00 | 15.00 | 35.00 |
| 25-51 | 4.00 | 12.00 | 28.00 |

NOTE: ***Sheldon Mayer** a-28-33, 35, 37-41, 43, 44, 47, 49-51.*

**MOVIE TUNES COMICS** (Formerly Animated. . .; Frankie No. 4 on)
No. 3, Fall, 1946
Marvel Comics (MgPC)

| | Good | Fine | N-Mint |
|---|---|---|---|
| 3-Super Rabbit, Krazy Krow, Silly Seal & Ziggy Pig | 5.00 | 15.00 | 35.00 |

**MOWGLI JUNGLE BOOK** (See 4-Color #487, 582, 620)

**MR.** (See Mister)

**MS. MARVEL** (Also see The Avengers #183)
Jan, 1977 - No. 23, Apr, 1979
Marvel Comics Group

| | Good | Fine | N-Mint |
|---|---|---|---|
| 1-23: 1,2-Scorpion app. 2-Origin. 5-Vision app. 18-Avengers x-over. 19-Capt. Marvel app. 20-New costume | | .50 | 1.00 |

NOTE: ***Austin** c-14i, 16i, 17i, 22i. **Buscema** a-1-3p; c(p)-2, 4, 6, 7, 15. **Infantino** a-14p, 19p. **Gil Kane** c-8. **Mooney** a-4-8p, 13p, 15-18p. **Starlin** c-12.*

**MS. MYSTIC** (Also see Captain Victory. . .)
Oct, 1982; No. 2, Feb, 1984 ($1.00, color)
Pacific Comics

Good Fine N-Mint

1-Origin; intro Erth, Ayre, Fyre & Watr; Neal Adams-c/a/script .25 .75 1.50
2 ($1.50)-N. Adams-c/a/script .25 .75 1.50

**MS. MYSTIC**
1987 - Present ($2.00, color, Baxter paper)
Continuity Comics
1-5: N. Adams-c/a; #1,2-r/Pacific #1,2 .35 1.00 2.00

**MS. TREE QUARTERLY**
Summer, 1990 - Present ($3.95, mature readers, 84 pgs.)
DC Comics
1-Midnight story; Batman text story, Grell illos .70 2.00 4.00
2,3-Midnight stories; The Butcher text stories .70 2.00 4.00

**MS. TREE'S THRILLING DETECTIVE ADVENTURES** (Ms. Tree #4 on; also see The Best of Ms. Tree) (Baxter paper #4-9)
2/83 - #9, 7/84; #10, 8/84 - #18, 5/85; #19, 6/85 - #50, 6/89
Eclipse Comics/Aardvark-Vanaheim 10-18/Renegade Press 19 on
1 .70 2.00 4.00
2-8: 2-Scythe begins .30 .90 1.80
9-Last Eclipse & last color issue .30 .90 1.80
10,11 (Aardvark-Vanaheim) 2-tone .30 .90 1.80
12-49 ($1.70; $2.00 #34 on). .30 .90 1.80
50-Contains flexi-disc ($3.95, 52 pgs.) .70 2.00 4.00
Summer Special 1(8/86) .50 1.50 3.00
. . .1950s 3-D Crime (7/87, no glasses)-Johnny Dynamite in 3-D .40 1.25 2.50
. . .Mike Mist in 3-D (8/85)-With glasses .50 1.50 3.00
NOTE: ***Miller** pin-up-1-4, 6. Johnny Dynamite-r begin #36 by **Morisi**.*

**MS. VICTORY SPECIAL** (Also see Capt. Paragon & Femforce)
Jan, 1985 (nd)
Americomics
1 .30 .85 1.70

**MUGGSY MOUSE** (Also see Tick Tock Tales)
1951 - No. 3, 1951; No. 4, 1954 - No. 5, 1954; 1963
Magazine Enterprises
1(A-1 #33) 2.30 7.00 16.00
2(A-1 #36)-Racist-c 4.30 13.00 30.00
3(A-1 #39), 4(A-1 #95), 5(A-1 #99) 1.30 4.00 9.00
Super Reprint #14(1963) .25 .80 1.60
I.W. Reprint #1,2 (nd) .25 .80 1.60

**MUGGY-DOO, BOY CAT**
July, 1953 - No. 4, Jan, 1954
Stanhall Publ.
1-Irving Spector-a 3.00 9.00 21.00
2-4 1.70 5.00 12.00
Super Reprint #12('63), 16('64) .60 1.20

**MUMMY, THE** (See Universal Presents. . . under Dell Giants & Movie Classics)

**MUNDEN'S BAR ANNUAL**
April, 1988 (52pgs.; $2.95; color)
First Comics
1-r/from Grimjack; Fish Police story .50 1.50 3.00

**MUNSTERS, THE** (TV)
Jan, 1965 - No. 16, Jan, 1968
Gold Key
1 (10134-501)-Photo-c 12.00 36.00 85.00
2 6.50 19.00 45.00
3-5: 4-Photo-c 5.70 17.00 40.00
6-16 4.50 14.00 32.00

**MUPPET BABIES, THE** (TV)(See Star Comics Magazine)
Aug, 1985 - No. 26, July, 1989 (Children's book)
Star Comics/Marvel #18 on

Good Fine N-Mint

1-13 (75 cents) .40 .80
14-26 ($1.00) .50 1.00

**MUPPETS TAKE MANHATTAN, THE**
Nov, 1984 - No. 3, Jan, 1985
Star Comics (Marvel)
1-3-Movie adapt. r-/Marvel Super Special .30 .60

**MURDER, INCORPORATED** (My Private Life #16 on)
1/48 - No. 15, 12/49; (2 No.9's); 6/50 - No. 3, 8/51
Fox Feature Syndicate
1 (1st Series) 18.00 54.00 125.00
2-Electrocution story; #1,2 have 'For Adults Only' on-c 13.00 40.00 90.00
3-7,9(4/49),10(5/49),11-15 6.50 19.00 45.00
8-Used in **SOTI**, pg. 160 9.30 28.00 65.00
9(3/49)-Possible use in **SOTI**, pg. 145; r-Blue Beetle #56('48) 7.00 21.00 50.00
5(#1, 6/50)(2nd Series)-Formerly My Desire 5.00 15.00 35.00
2(8/50)-Morisi-a 4.00 12.00 28.00
3(8/51)-Used in **POP**, pg. 81; Rico-a; lingerie-c/panels 5.00 15.00 35.00

**MURDEROUS GANGSTERS**
July, 1951; No. 2, Dec, 1951 - No. 4, June, 1952
Avon Periodicals/Realistic No. 3 on
1-Pretty Boy Floyd, Leggs Diamond; 1 pg. Wood 20.00 60.00 140.00
2-Baby-Face Nelson; 1 pg. Wood-a 12.00 36.00 85.00
3-Painted-c 10.00 30.00 70.00
4-"Murder by Needle" drug story; Mort Lawrence-a; Kinstler-c 12.00 36.00 85.00

**MURDER TALES** (Magazine)
V1#10, Nov, 1970 - V1#11, Jan, 1971 (52 pages)
World Famous Publications
V1#10-One pg. Frazetta ad .85 2.60 6.00
11-Guardineer-r; bondage-c .50 1.50 3.00

**MUSHMOUSE AND PUNKIN PUSS** (TV)
September, 1965 (Hanna-Barbera)
Gold Key
1 (10153-509) 3.50 10.50 24.00

**MUSIC MAN, THE** (See Movie Classics)

**MUTANT MISADVENTURES OF CLOAK AND DAGGER, THE** (Becomes Cloak and Dagger #14 on)
Oct, 1988 - Present (#1: $1.25; #2-on: $1.50, color)
Marvel Comics
1-8,10-20: 1-X-Factor app. 9,10-Painted-c. 12-Dr. Doom app. 14-Begin new direction .25 .75 1.50
9-($2.50, 52 pgs.)-The Avengers x-over .40 1.25 2.50
NOTE: ***Austin** a-12i; c(i)-4, 12, 13; scripts-all. **Russell** a-2i. **Williamson** a-14i, 15i; c-15i.*

**MUTANTS & MISFITS**
1987 - No. 3? ($1.95, color)
Silverline Comics (Solson)
1-3 .35 1.00 2.00

**MUTINY** (Stormy Tales of Seven Seas)
Oct, 1954 - No. 3, Feb, 1955
Aragon Magazines
1 7.00 21.00 50.00
2,3: 2-Capt. Mutiny. 3-Bondage-c 4.00 12.00 28.00

**MUTINY ON THE BOUNTY** (See Classics Illustrated #100 & Movie Comics)

**MUTT & JEFF** (. . .Cartoon, The)
1910 - No. 5, 1916 (5¾x15½") (Hardcover-B&W)

*Ms. Tree's Thrilling Det. Cases #12, © A-V*

*Murder, Incorporated #13, © FOX*

*Mutant Misadventures of C&D #12, © MEG*

My Diary #1, © MEG

My Favorite Martian #9, © Jack Cherton TV

My Girl Pearl #1, © MEG

Ball Publications

| | Good | Fine | V. Fine |
|---|---|---|---|
| 1(1910)(68 pgs., 50 cents) | 34.00 | 103.00 | 240.00 |
| 2(1911), 3(1912)(68 pgs.) | 34.00 | 103.00 | 240.00 |
| 4(1915)(68 pgs., 50 cents) (Rare) | 39.00 | 115.00 | 270.00 |
| 5(1916)(84 pages, 60 cents) (Rare) | 43.00 | 130.00 | 300.00 |

NOTE: *Mutt & Jeff first appeared in newspapers in 1908. Cover variations exist showing Mutt & Jeff reading various newspapers; i.e., The Oregon Journal, The American, and The Detroit News. Reprinting of each issue began soon after publication. No. 5 may not have been reprinted. Values listed include the reprints.*

**MUTT & JEFF**
No. 6, 1916 - No. 22, 1933? (B&W dailies) (9½x9½"; stiff-c; 52 pgs.)
Cupples & Leon Co.

| | | | |
|---|---|---|---|
| 6-22-By Bud Fisher | 20.00 | 60.00 | 140.00 |

NOTE: *Later issues are somewhat rarer.*

| | | | |
|---|---|---|---|
| nn(1920)-(Advs. of . . .) 16x11"; 20 pgs.; reprints 1919 Sunday strips | 34.00 | 103.00 | 240.00 |
| Big Book nn(1926, 144pgs., hardcovers) | 29.00 | 86.00 | 200.00 |
| w/dust jacket . . . . | 39.00 | 115.00 | 270.00 |
| Big Book 1(1928)-Thick book (hardcovers) | 29.00 | 86.00 | 200.00 |
| w/dust jacket . . . . | 39.00 | 115.00 | 270.00 |
| Big Book 2(1929)-Thick book (hardcovers) | 29.00 | 86.00 | 200.00 |
| w/dust jacket . . . . | 39.00 | 115.00 | 270.00 |

NOTE: *The Big Books contain three previous issues rebound.*

**MUTT & JEFF**
1921 (9x15")
Embee Publ. Co.

| | | | |
|---|---|---|---|
| nn-Sunday strips in color (Rare) | 57.00 | 170.00 | 400.00 |

**MUTT AND JEFF** (See All-American, All-Flash #18, Comic Cavalcade, Famous Feature Stories, The Funnies, Popular, Xmas Comics)
Summer, 1939 (nd) - No. 148, Nov, 1965
All American/National 1-103(6/58)/Dell 104(10/58)-115 (10-12/59)/ Harvey 116(2/60)-148

| | Good | Fine | N-Mint |
|---|---|---|---|
| 1(nn)-Lost Wheels | 86.00 | 257.00 | 600.00 |
| 2(nn)-Charging Bull (Summer 1940, nd; on sale 6/20/40) | 48.00 | 145.00 | 335.00 |
| 3(nn)-Bucking Broncos (Summer 1941, nd) | 34.00 | 100.00 | 235.00 |
| 4(Winter,'41), 5(Summer,'42) | 25.00 | 75.00 | 175.00 |
| 6-10 | 14.00 | 43.00 | 100.00 |
| 11-20 | 10.00 | 30.00 | 70.00 |
| 21-30 | 7.00 | 21.00 | 50.00 |
| 31-50 | 4.00 | 12.00 | 28.00 |
| 51-75-Last Fisher issue. 53-Last 52pgs. | 2.65 | 8.00 | 18.00 |
| 76-99,101-103: 76-Last precode issue(1/55) | 1.70 | 5.00 | 12.00 |
| 100 | 2.00 | 6.00 | 14.00 |
| 104-148: 117,118,120-131-Richie Rich app. | 1.00 | 3.00 | 7.00 |
| . . . Jokes 1-3(8/60-61, Harvey)-84 pgs.; Richie Rich in all; Little Dot in #2,3 | 1.70 | 5.00 | 12.00 |
| . . . New Jokes 1-4(10/63-11/65, Harvey)-68 pgs.; Richie Rich in #1-3; Stumbo in #1 | .75 | 2.25 | 5.00 |

NOTE: *Issues 1-74 by* ***Bud Fisher****. 86 on by* ***Al Smith****. Issues from 1963 on have* ***Fisher*** *reprints. Clarification: early issues signed by Fisher are mostly drawn by Smith.*

**MY BROTHERS' KEEPER**
1973 (36 pages) (35-49 cents)
Spire Christian Comics (Fleming H. Revell Co.)

| | | | |
|---|---|---|---|
| nn | | .50 | 1.00 |

**MY CONFESSIONS** (My Confession #7&8; formerly Western True Crime; A Spectacular Feature Magazine #11)
No. 7, Aug, 1949 - No. 10, Jan-Feb, 1950
Fox Feature Syndicate

| | | | |
|---|---|---|---|
| 7-Wood-a (10 pgs.) | 11.00 | 32.00 | 75.00 |
| 8-Wood-a (19 pgs.) | 8.50 | 25.50 | 60.00 |
| 9,10 | 3.70 | 11.00 | 26.00 |

**MY DATE COMICS**
July, 1947 - V1No.4, Jan, 1948 (1st Romance comic)
Hillman Periodicals

| | Good | Fine | N-Mint |
|---|---|---|---|
| 1-S&K-c/a | 14.00 | 43.00 | 100.00 |
| 2-4-S&K, Dan Barry-a | 9.30 | 28.00 | 65.00 |

**MY DESIRE** (Formerly Jo-Jo) (Murder, Inc. #5 on)
No. 30, Aug, 1949 - No. 4, April, 1950
Fox Feature Syndicate

| | | | |
|---|---|---|---|
| 30(#1) | 5.00 | 15.00 | 35.00 |
| 31 (#2), 3,4 | 3.50 | 10.50 | 24.00 |
| 31 (Canadian edition) | 2.15 | 6.50 | 15.00 |
| 32(12/49)-Wood-a | 8.50 | 25.50 | 60.00 |

**MY DIARY**
Dec, 1949 - No. 2, Mar, 1950
Marvel Comics (A Lovers Mag.)

| | | | |
|---|---|---|---|
| 1,2: 1-Photo-c | 5.00 | 15.00 | 35.00 |

**MY DOG TIGE** (Buster Brown's Dog)
1957 (Giveaway)
Buster Brown Shoes

| | | | |
|---|---|---|---|
| nn | 2.00 | 6.00 | 14.00 |

**MY EXPERIENCE** (Formerly All Top; Judy Canova #23 on)
No. 19, Sept, 1949 - No. 22, Mar, 1950
Fox Feature Syndicate

| | | | |
|---|---|---|---|
| 19-Wood-a | 11.00 | 32.00 | 75.00 |
| 20 | 3.15 | 9.50 | 22.00 |
| 21-Wood-a(2) | 11.50 | 34.00 | 80.00 |
| 22-Wood-a, 9 pgs. | 8.50 | 25.50 | 60.00 |

**MY FAVORITE MARTIAN** (TV)
1/64; No.2, 7/64 - No. 9, 10/66 (No. 1,3-9 have photo-c)
Gold Key

| | | | |
|---|---|---|---|
| 1-Russ Manning-a | 6.00 | 18.00 | 42.00 |
| 2 | 3.00 | 9.00 | 21.00 |
| 3-9 | 2.65 | 8.00 | 18.00 |

**MY FRIEND IRMA** (Radio/TV) (Formerly Western Life Romances)
No. 3, June, 1950 - No. 47, Dec, 1954; No. 48, Feb, 1955
Marvel/Atlas Comics (BFP)

| | | | |
|---|---|---|---|
| 3-52 pgs. | 6.50 | 19.00 | 45.00 |
| 4-Kurtzman-a, 10 pgs. | 7.00 | 21.00 | 50.00 |
| 5-"Egghead Doodle" by Kurtzman, 4 pgs. | 5.00 | 15.00 | 35.00 |
| 6,8-10: 9-paper dolls, 1pg; Millie app. | 3.00 | 9.00 | 21.00 |
| 7-One pg. Kurtzman | 3.50 | 10.50 | 24.00 |
| 11-23: 23-One pg. Frazetta | 2.00 | 6.00 | 14.00 |
| 24-48 | 1.30 | 4.00 | 9.00 |

**MY GIRL PEARL**
4/55 - #4, 10/55; #5, 7/57 - #6, 9/57; #7, 8/60 - #11, ?/61
Atlas Comics

| | | | |
|---|---|---|---|
| 1 | 5.00 | 15.00 | 35.00 |
| 2 | 2.30 | 7.00 | 16.00 |
| 3-6 | 1.50 | 4.50 | 10.00 |
| 7-11 | 1.00 | 3.00 | 7.00 |

**MY GREATEST ADVENTURE** (Doom Patrol #86 on)
Jan-Feb, 1955 - No. 85, Feb, 1964
National Periodical Publications

| | | | |
|---|---|---|---|
| 1-Before CCA | 53.00 | 160.00 | 370.00 |
| 2 | 24.00 | 73.00 | 170.00 |
| 3-5 | 17.00 | 51.00 | 120.00 |
| 6-10 | 11.50 | 34.00 | 80.00 |
| 11-15,19 | 8.00 | 24.00 | 55.00 |
| 16-18,20,21,28-Kirby-a; 18-Kirby-c | 7.00 | 21.00 | 50.00 |
| 22-27,29,30 | 4.30 | 13.00 | 30.00 |
| 31-40 | 3.15 | 9.50 | 22.00 |

| | Good | Fine | N-Mint |
|---|---|---|---|
| 41-57,59 | 2.00 | 6.00 | 14.00 |
| 58,60,61-Toth-a; Last 10 cent issue | 2.65 | 8.00 | 18.00 |
| 62-76,78,79 | 1.30 | 4.00 | 9.00 |
| 77-Toth-a | 1.50 | 4.50 | 10.00 |
| 80-(6/63)-Intro/origin Doom Patrol and begin series; origin Robotman, Negative Man, & Elasti-Girl | 23.00 | 70.00 | 160.00 |
| 81-85: 81,85-Toth-a | 9.30 | 28.00 | 65.00 |

NOTE: ***Anderson** a-42. **Colan** a-77. **Meskin** a-25, 26, 32, 39, 45, 50, 56, 57, 61, 64, 70, 73, 74, 76, 79; c-76. **Moreira** a-11, 17, 20, 23, 25, 27, 37, 40-43, 46, 48, 55-57, 59, 60, 62-65, 67, 69, 70. **Roussos** c/a-71-73.*

**MY GREATEST THRILLS IN BASEBALL**
Date? (16 pg. Giveaway)
Mission of California

| | Good | Fine | N-Mint |
|---|---|---|---|
| nn-By Mickey Mantle | 30.00 | 90.00 | 210.00 |

**MY GREAT LOVE**
Oct, 1949 - No. 4, Apr, 1950
Fox Feature Syndicate

| | Good | Fine | N-Mint |
|---|---|---|---|
| 1 | 5.70 | 17.00 | 40.00 |
| 2-4 | 3.15 | 9.50 | 22.00 |

**MY INTIMATE AFFAIR** (Inside Crime #3)
Mar, 1950 - No. 2, May, 1950
Fox Feature Syndicate

| | Good | Fine | N-Mint |
|---|---|---|---|
| 1 | 5.70 | 17.00 | 40.00 |
| 2 | 3.15 | 9.50 | 22.00 |

**MY LIFE** (Formerly Meet Corliss Archer)
No. 4, Sept, 1948 - No. 15, July, 1950
Fox Feature Syndicate

| | Good | Fine | N-Mint |
|---|---|---|---|
| 4-Used in **SOTI**, pg. 39; Kamen/Feldstein-a | 17.00 | 51.00 | 120.00 |
| 5-Kamen-a | 8.50 | 25.50 | 60.00 |
| 6-Kamen/Feldstein-a | 8.50 | 25.50 | 60.00 |
| 7-Wash cover | 5.00 | 15.00 | 35.00 |
| 8,9,11-15 | 3.15 | 9.50 | 22.00 |
| 10-Wood-a | 8.50 | 25.50 | 60.00 |

**MY LITTLE MARGIE** (TV)
July, 1954 - No. 54, Nov, 1964
Charlton Comics

| | Good | Fine | N-Mint |
|---|---|---|---|
| 1-Photo front/back-c | 9.30 | 28.00 | 65.00 |
| 2-Photo front/back-c | 4.50 | 14.00 | 32.00 |
| 3-7,10 | 2.65 | 8.00 | 18.00 |
| 8,9-Infinity-c | 3.00 | 9.00 | 21.00 |
| 11-13: part-photo-c (#13, 8/56) | 2.00 | 6.00 | 14.00 |
| 14-19 | 1.50 | 4.50 | 10.00 |
| 20-(100 page issue) | 3.70 | 11.00 | 26.00 |
| 21-35-Last 10 cent issue? | 1.00 | 3.00 | 7.00 |
| 36-53 | .70 | 2.00 | 5.00 |
| 54-Beatles on cover; lead story spoofs the Beatle haircut craze of the 1960's | 6.50 | 19.00 | 45.00 |

NOTE: *Doll cut-outs in 32, 33, 40, 45, 50.*

**MY LITTLE MARGIE'S BOY FRIENDS** (TV) (Freddy V2#12 on)
Aug, 1955 - No. 11, Apr?, 1958
Charlton Comics

| | Good | Fine | N-Mint |
|---|---|---|---|
| 1-Has several Archie swipes | 4.50 | 14.00 | 32.00 |
| 2 | 2.65 | 8.00 | 18.00 |
| 3-11 | 1.50 | 4.50 | 10.00 |

**MY LITTLE MARGIE'S FASHIONS** (TV)
Feb, 1959 - No. 5, Nov, 1959
Charlton Comics

| | Good | Fine | N-Mint |
|---|---|---|---|
| 1 | 4.00 | 12.00 | 28.00 |
| 2-5 | 2.15 | 6.50 | 15.00 |

**MY LOVE**
July, 1949 - No. 4, Apr, 1950 (All photo-c)
Marvel Comics (CLDS)

| | Good | Fine | N-Mint |
|---|---|---|---|
| 1 | 4.30 | 13.00 | 30.00 |
| 2,3 | 2.65 | 8.00 | 18.00 |
| 4-Betty Page photo-c (See Cupid #2, Miss. America #4) | 9.30 | 28.00 | 65.00 |

**MY LOVE**
Sept, 1969 - No. 39, Mar, 1976
Marvel Comics Group

| | Good | Fine | N-Mint |
|---|---|---|---|
| 1 | .70 | 2.00 | 4.00 |
| 2-9 | .35 | 1.00 | 2.00 |
| 10-Williamson-r/My Own Romance #71; Kirby-a | .40 | 1.25 | 2.50 |
| 11-20: 14-Morrow-c/a; Kirby/Colletta-r | | .50 | 1.00 |
| 21,22,24-39: 38,39-Reprints | | .50 | 1.00 |
| 23-Steranko-r/Our Love Story #5 | .35 | 1.00 | 2.00 |
| Special(12/71) | | .50 | 1.00 |

**MY LOVE AFFAIR** (March of Crime #7 on)
July, 1949 - No. 6, May, 1950
Fox Feature Syndicate

| | Good | Fine | N-Mint |
|---|---|---|---|
| 1 | 6.50 | 19.00 | 45.00 |
| 2 | 3.50 | 10.50 | 24.00 |
| 3-6-Wood-a | 8.50 | 25.50 | 60.00 |

**MY LOVE LIFE** (Formerly Zegra)
No. 6, June, 1949 - No. 13, Aug, 1950; No. 13, Sept, 1951
Fox Feature Syndicate

| | Good | Fine | N-Mint |
|---|---|---|---|
| 6-Kamenish-a | 7.00 | 21.00 | 50.00 |
| 7-13 | 3.50 | 10.50 | 24.00 |
| 13 (9/51) | 2.65 | 8.00 | 18.00 |

**MY LOVE MEMOIRS** (Formerly Women Outlaws; Hunted #13 on)
No. 9, Nov, 1949 - No. 12, May, 1950
Fox Feature Syndicate

| | Good | Fine | N-Mint |
|---|---|---|---|
| 9,11,12-Wood-a | 8.50 | 25.50 | 60.00 |
| 10 | 3.15 | 9.50 | 22.00 |

**MY LOVE SECRET** (Formerly Phantom Lady) (Animal Crackers #31)
No. 24, June, 1949 - No. 30, June, 1950; No. 53, 1954
Fox Feature Syndicate/M. S. Distr.

| | Good | Fine | N-Mint |
|---|---|---|---|
| 24-Kamen/Feldstein-a | 8.00 | 24.00 | 55.00 |
| 25-Possible caricature of Wood on-c? | 4.00 | 12.00 | 28.00 |
| 26,28-Wood-a | 8.50 | 25.50 | 60.00 |
| 27,29,30: 30-Photo-c | 3.15 | 9.50 | 22.00 |
| 53-(Reprint, M.S. Distr.) 1954? nd given; formerly Western Thrillers (Crimes by Women #54); photo-c | 2.00 | 6.00 | 14.00 |

**MY LOVE STORY** (Hoot Gibson Western #5 on)
Sept, 1949 - No. 4, Mar, 1950
Fox Feature Syndicate

| | Good | Fine | N-Mint |
|---|---|---|---|
| 1 | 6.00 | 18.00 | 42.00 |
| 2 | 3.50 | 10.50 | 24.00 |
| 3,4-Wood-a | 8.50 | 25.50 | 60.00 |

**MY LOVE STORY**
April, 1956 - No. 9, Aug, 1957
Atlas Comics (GPS)

| | Good | Fine | N-Mint |
|---|---|---|---|
| 1 | 3.50 | 10.50 | 24.00 |
| 2 | 1.70 | 5.00 | 12.00 |
| 3-Matt Baker-a | 3.00 | 9.00 | 21.00 |
| 4-6,8,9 | 1.50 | 4.50 | 10.00 |
| 7-Matt Baker, Toth-a | 3.00 | 9.00 | 21.00 |

NOTE: ***Colletta** a 1(2), 4(2), 5.*

**MY ONLY LOVE**
July, 1975 - No. 9, Nov, 1976
Charlton Comics

| | Good | Fine | N-Mint |
|---|---|---|---|
| 1,2,4-9 | | .50 | 1.00 |
| 3-Toth-a | .50 | 1.50 | 3.00 |

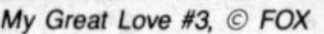
*My Great Love #3, © FOX*

*My Little Margie #33, © CC*

*My Love Secret #26, © FOX*

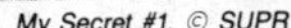
My Secret #1, © SUPR

Mysteries #6, © SUPR

Mysteries of Unexplored Worlds #22, © CC

**MY OWN ROMANCE** (Formerly My Romance; Teen-Age Romance #77 on)
No. 4, Mar, 1949 - No. 76, July, 1960
Marvel/Atlas (MjPC/RCM No. 4-59/ZPC No. 60-76)

| | Good | Fine | N-Mint |
|---|---|---|---|
| 4-Photo-c | 4.50 | 14.00 | 32.00 |
| 5-10: 5,6,8-10-Photo-c | 2.30 | 7.00 | 16.00 |
| 11-20: 14-Powell-a | 1.70 | 5.00 | 12.00 |
| 21-42: 42-Last precode (2/55) | 1.50 | 4.50 | 10.00 |
| 43-54,56-60 | 1.15 | 3.50 | 8.00 |
| 55-Toth-a | 3.00 | 9.00 | 21.00 |
| 61-70,72-76 | .85 | 2.50 | 6.00 |
| 71-Williamson-a | 3.75 | 11.25 | 26.00 |

NOTE: *Colletta a-45(2), 48, 50, 55; c-58i, 61. Everett a-25; c-58p. Morisi a-18. Orlando a-61. Romita a-36. Tuska a-10.*

**MY PAL DIZZY** (See Comic Books, Series I)

**MY PAST** (. . .Confessions) (Formerly Western Thrillers)
No. 7, Aug, 1949 - No. 11, April, 1950 (Crimes Inc. #12)
Fox Feature Syndicate

| | Good | Fine | N-Mint |
|---|---|---|---|
| 7 | 6.00 | 18.00 | 42.00 |
| 8-10 | 4.00 | 12.00 | 28.00 |
| 11-Wood-a | 8.50 | 25.50 | 60.00 |

**MY PERSONAL PROBLEM**
11/55; No. 2, 2/56; No. 3, 9/56 - No. 4, 11/56; 10/57 - No. 3, 5/58
Ajax/Farrell/Steinway Comic

| | Good | Fine | N-Mint |
|---|---|---|---|
| 1 | 3.50 | 10.50 | 24.00 |
| 2-4 | 2.00 | 6.00 | 14.00 |
| 1-3('57-'58)-Steinway | 1.50 | 4.50 | 10.00 |

**MY PRIVATE LIFE** (Formerly Murder, Inc.)
No. 16, Feb, 1950 - No. 17, April, 1950
Fox Feature Syndicate

| | Good | Fine | N-Mint |
|---|---|---|---|
| 16,17 | 4.30 | 13.00 | 30.00 |

**MYRA NORTH** (See The Comics, Crackajack Funnies, 4-Color #3 & Red Ryder)

**MY REAL LOVE**
No. 5, June, 1952
Standard Comics

| | Good | Fine | N-Mint |
|---|---|---|---|
| 5-Toth-a, 3 pgs.; Tuska, Cardy, Vern Greene-a; photo-c | 5.00 | 15.00 | 35.00 |

**MY ROMANCE** (My Own Romance #4 on)
Sept, 1948 - No. 3, Jan, 1949
Marvel Comics (RCM)

| | Good | Fine | N-Mint |
|---|---|---|---|
| 1 | 5.00 | 15.00 | 35.00 |
| 2,3: 2-Anti-Wertham editorial (11/48) | 2.65 | 8.00 | 18.00 |

**MY ROMANTIC ADVENTURES** (Formerly Romantic Adventures)
No. 68, 8/56 - No. 115, 12/60; No. 116, 7/61 - No. 138, 3/64
American Comics Group

| | Good | Fine | N-Mint |
|---|---|---|---|
| 68 | 3.00 | 9.00 | 21.00 |
| 69-85 | 1.50 | 4.50 | 10.00 |
| 86-Three pg. Williamson-a (2/58) | 2.85 | 8.50 | 20.00 |
| 87-100 | 1.00 | 3.00 | 7.00 |
| 101-138 | .70 | 2.00 | 4.00 |

NOTE: *Whitney art in most issues.*

**MY SECRET** (Our Secret #4 on)
Aug, 1949 - No. 3, Oct, 1949
Superior Comics, Ltd.

| | Good | Fine | N-Mint |
|---|---|---|---|
| 1 | 5.00 | 15.00 | 35.00 |
| 2,3 | 3.50 | 10.50 | 24.00 |

**MY SECRET AFFAIR** (Martin Kane #4)
Dec, 1949 - No. 3, April, 1950
Hero Book (Fox Feature Syndicate)

| | Good | Fine | N-Mint |
|---|---|---|---|
| 1-Harrison/Wood-a, 10 pgs. | 10.00 | 30.00 | 70.00 |
| 2-Wood-a (poor) | 6.00 | 18.00 | 42.00 |
| 3-Wood-a | 8.50 | 25.50 | 60.00 |

**MY SECRET CONFESSION**
September, 1955
Sterling Comics

| | Good | Fine | N-Mint |
|---|---|---|---|
| 1-Sekowsky-a | 2.65 | 8.00 | 18.00 |

**MY SECRET LIFE** (Formerly Western Outlaws; Romeo Tubbs #26 on)
No. 22, July, 1949 - No. 27, May, 1950
Fox Feature Syndicate

| | Good | Fine | N-Mint |
|---|---|---|---|
| 22 | 4.30 | 13.00 | 30.00 |
| 23,26-Wood-a, 6 pgs. | 8.50 | 25.50 | 60.00 |
| 24,25,27 | 3.00 | 9.00 | 21.00 |

NOTE: *The title was changed to Romeo Tubbs after #25 even though #26 & 27 did come out.*

**MY SECRET LIFE** (Formerly Young Lovers; Sue & Sally Smith #48)
No. 19, Aug, 1957 - No. 47, Sept, 1962
Charlton Comics

| | Good | Fine | N-Mint |
|---|---|---|---|
| 19 | 1.50 | 4.50 | 10.00 |
| 20-35 | .70 | 2.00 | 5.00 |
| 36-47: 44-Last 10 cent issue | .50 | 1.50 | 3.00 |

**MY SECRET MARRIAGE**
May, 1953 - No. 24, July, 1956
Superior Comics, Ltd.

| | Good | Fine | N-Mint |
|---|---|---|---|
| 1 | 4.50 | 14.00 | 32.00 |
| 2 | 2.30 | 7.00 | 16.00 |
| 3-24 | 1.50 | 4.50 | 10.00 |
| I.W. Reprint #9 | .30 | .90 | 1.80 |

NOTE: *Many issues contain Kamenish art.*

**MY SECRET ROMANCE** (A Star Presentation #3)
Jan, 1950 - No. 2, March, 1950
Hero Book (Fox Feature Syndicate)

| | Good | Fine | N-Mint |
|---|---|---|---|
| 1-Wood-a | 9.30 | 28.00 | 65.00 |
| 2-Wood-a | 8.50 | 25.50 | 60.00 |

**MY SECRET STORY** (Formerly Captain Kidd #25; Sabu #30 on)
No. 26, Oct, 1949 - No. 29, April, 1950
Fox Feature Syndicate

| | Good | Fine | N-Mint |
|---|---|---|---|
| 26 | 5.00 | 15.00 | 35.00 |
| 27-29 | 3.50 | 10.50 | 24.00 |

**MYSTERIES** (. . .Weird & Strange)
May, 1953 - No. 11, Jan, 1955
Superior/Dynamic Publ. (Randall Publ. Ltd.)

| | Good | Fine | N-Mint |
|---|---|---|---|
| 1 | 11.50 | 34.00 | 80.00 |
| 2-A-Bomb blast story | 5.70 | 17.00 | 40.00 |
| 3-9,11 | 4.30 | 13.00 | 30.00 |
| 10-Kamenish-c/a reprinted from Strange Mysteries #2; cover is from a panel in Strange Mysteries #2 | 5.00 | 15.00 | 35.00 |

**MYSTERIES OF SCOTLAND YARD** (See A-1 Comics #121)

**MYSTERIES OF UNEXPLORED WORLDS** (See Blue Bird) (Son of Vulcan V2#49 on)
Aug, 1956 No. 6, Jan, 1957; No. 7, Feb, 1958 - No. 48, Sept, 1965
Charlton Comics

| | Good | Fine | N-Mint |
|---|---|---|---|
| 1 | 14.00 | 43.00 | 100.00 |
| 2-No Ditko | 5.70 | 17.00 | 40.00 |
| 3,4,8,9-Ditko-a | 8.50 | 25.50 | 60.00 |
| 5,6-Ditko-c/a (all) | 10.00 | 30.00 | 70.00 |
| 7-(2/58, 68 pgs.); Ditko-a(4) | 10.00 | 30.00 | 70.00 |
| 10-Ditko-c/a(4) | 10.00 | 30.00 | 70.00 |
| 11-Ditko-c/a(3)-signed J. Kotdi | 10.00 | 30.00 | 70.00 |
| 12,19,21-24,26-Ditko-a | 6.50 | 19.00 | 45.00 |
| 13-18,20 | 2.00 | 6.00 | 14.00 |
| 25,27-30 | 1.50 | 4.50 | 10.00 |

| | Good | Fine | N-Mint |
|---|---|---|---|
| 31-45 | .70 | 2.00 | 5.00 |
| 46(5/65)-Son of Vulcan begins (origin) | 1.30 | 4.00 | 9.00 |
| 47,48 | .85 | 2.60 | 6.00 |

NOTE: ***Ditko** c-3-6, 10, 11, 19, 21-24.*

**MYSTERIOUS ADVENTURES**
March, 1951 - No. 24, Mar, 1955; No. 25, Aug, 1955
Story Comics

| | Good | Fine | N-Mint |
|---|---|---|---|
| 1 | 16.00 | 48.00 | 110.00 |
| 2 | 8.00 | 24.00 | 55.00 |
| 3,4,6,10 | 5.70 | 17.00 | 40.00 |
| 5-Bondage-c | 8.50 | 25.50 | 60.00 |
| 7-Daggar in eye panel | 12.00 | 36.00 | 85.00 |
| 8-Eyeball story | 10.00 | 30.00 | 70.00 |
| 9-Extreme violence | 8.00 | 24.00 | 55.00 |
| 11-13: 11(12/52)-Used in **SOTI**, pg. 84 | 11.50 | 34.00 | 80.00 |
| 14-E.C. Old Witch swipe | 7.00 | 21.00 | 50.00 |
| 15-21: 18-Used in Senate Investigative report, pgs. 5,6,; E.C. swipe/ T.F.T.C. #35. 20-Used by Wertham in the Senate hearings. 21-Bondage/beheading-c | 13.00 | 40.00 | 90.00 |
| 22-'Cinderella' parody | 7.00 | 21.00 | 50.00 |
| 23-Disbrow-a | 6.50 | 19.00 | 45.00 |
| 24,25 | 5.70 | 17.00 | 40.00 |

NOTE: *Tothish art by **Ross Andru**-#22, 23. **Bache** a-8. **Cameron** a-5-7. **Harrison** a-12. **Hollingsworth** a-3-8, 12. **Schaffenberger** a-24, 25. **Wildey** a-15, 17.*

**MYSTERIOUS ISLAND** (See 4-Color #1213)

**MYSTERIOUS ISLE**
Nov-Jan, 1963/64 (Jules Verne)
Dell Publishing Co.

| | Good | Fine | N-Mint |
|---|---|---|---|
| 1 | 1.00 | 3.00 | 7.00 |

**MYSTERIOUS STORIES** (Horror From the Tomb #1)
No. 2, Dec-Jan, 1954-1955 - No. 7, Dec, 1955
Premier Magazines

| | Good | Fine | N-Mint |
|---|---|---|---|
| 2-Woodbridge-c | 10.00 | 30.00 | 70.00 |
| 3-Woodbridge-c/a | 7.00 | 21.00 | 50.00 |
| 4-7: 5-Cinderella parody. 6-Woodbridge-c | 6.50 | 19.00 | 45.00 |

NOTE: ***Hollingsworth** a-2, 4.*

**MYSTERIOUS SUSPENSE**
October, 1968 (12 cents)
Charlton Comics

| | Good | Fine | N-Mint |
|---|---|---|---|
| 1-Return of the Question by Ditko-c/a | 2.65 | 8.00 | 18.00 |

**MYSTERIOUS TRAVELER** (See Tales of the...)

**MYSTERIOUS TRAVELER COMICS** (Radio)
Nov, 1948
Trans-World Publications

| | Good | Fine | N-Mint |
|---|---|---|---|
| 1-Powell-c/a(2); Poe adaptation, 'Tell Tale Heart' | 23.00 | 70.00 | 160.00 |

**MYSTERY COMICS**
1944 - No. 4, 1944 (No months given)
William H. Wise & Co.

| | Good | Fine | N-Mint |
|---|---|---|---|
| 1-The Magnet, The Silver Knight, Brad Spencer, Wonderman, Dick Devins, King of Futuria, & Zudo the Jungle Boy begin; Schomburg-c on all | 35.00 | 105.00 | 245.00 |
| 2-Bondage-c | 23.00 | 70.00 | 160.00 |
| 3-Lance Lewis, Space Detective begins | 20.00 | 60.00 | 140.00 |
| 4(V2#1 inside) | 20.00 | 60.00 | 140.00 |

**MYSTERY COMICS DIGEST**
March, 1972 - No. 26, Oct, 1975
Gold Key

| | Good | Fine | N-Mint |
|---|---|---|---|
| 1-Ripley's Believe It or Not; reprint of Ripley's #1 origin Ra-Ka-Tep the Mummy; Wood-a | .85 | 2.50 | 5.00 |
| 2-Boris Karloff Tales of Mystery; Wood-a; 1st app. Werewolf Count Wulfstein | .40 | 1.25 | 2.50 |
| 3-Twilight Zone (TV); Crandall, Toth & George Evans-a; 1st app. Tragg & Simbar the Lion Lord; 2 Crandall/Frazetta-a r-Twilight Zone #1 | .40 | 1.25 | 2.50 |
| 4-Ripley's Believe It or Not; 1st app. Baron Tibor, the Vampire | .35 | 1.00 | 2.00 |
| 5-Boris Karloff Tales of Mystery; 1st app. Dr. Spektor | .35 | 1.00 | 2.00 |
| 6-Twilight Zone (TV); 1st app. U.S. Marshal Reid & Sir Duane | .35 | 1.00 | 2.00 |
| 7-Ripley's Believe It or Not; origin The Lurker in the Swamp; 1st app. Duroc | | .60 | 1.20 |
| 8-Boris Karloff Tales of Mystery; McWilliams-r | | .60 | 1.20 |
| 9-Twilight Zone (TV); Williamson, Crandall, McWilliams-a; 2nd Tragg app. | .40 | 1.25 | 2.50 |
| 10,13-Ripley's Believe It or Not | | .50 | 1.00 |
| 11,14-Boris Karloff Tales of Mystery. 14-1st app. Xorkon | | .40 | .80 |
| 12,15-Twilight Zone (TV) | | .40 | .80 |
| 16,19,22,25-Ripley's Believe It or Not | | .40 | .80 |
| 17-Boris Karloff Tales of Mystery; Williamson-r | .25 | .75 | 1.50 |
| 18,21,24-Twilight Zone (TV) | | .40 | .80 |
| 20,23,26-Boris Karloff Tales of Mystery | | .40 | .80 |

NOTE: *Dr. Spektor app.-#5, 10-12, 21. Durak app.-#15. Duroc app.-#14 (later called Durak). King George 1st app.-#8.*

**MYSTERY IN SPACE**
4-5/51 - No. 110, 9/66; No. 111, 9/80 - No. 117, 3/81 (#1-3: 52 pgs.)
National Periodical Publications

| | Good | Fine | N-Mint |
|---|---|---|---|
| 1-Frazetta-a, 8 pgs.; Knights of the Galaxy begins, ends #8 | 157.00 | 470.00 | 1100.00 |
| 2 | 62.00 | 185.00 | 435.00 |
| 3 | 50.00 | 150.00 | 350.00 |
| 4,5 | 36.00 | 107.00 | 250.00 |
| 6-10: 7-Toth-a | 29.00 | 85.00 | 200.00 |
| 11-15: 13-Toth-a | 20.00 | 60.00 | 140.00 |
| 16-18,20-25: Interplanetary Insurance feature by Infantino in all. 24-Last precode issue | 17.00 | 51.00 | 120.00 |
| 19-Virgil Finlay-a | 20.00 | 60.00 | 140.00 |
| 26-40: 26-Space Cabbie begins | 12.00 | 36.00 | 85.00 |
| 41-52: 47-Space Cabbie feature ends | 10.00 | 30.00 | 70.00 |
| 53-Adam Strange begins (8/59) (1st app. in Showcase) | 65.00 | 195.00 | 460.00 |
| 54 | 25.00 | 75.00 | 175.00 |
| 55 | 16.00 | 48.00 | 110.00 |
| 56-60 | 12.00 | 36.00 | 85.00 |
| 61-71: 61-1st app. Adam Strange foe Ulthoon. 62-1st app. A.S. foe Mortan. 63-Origin Vandor. 66-Star Rovers begin. 68-Dust Devils app. 71-Last 10 cent issue | 7.00 | 21.00 | 50.00 |
| 72-74,76-80 | 5.70 | 17.00 | 40.00 |
| 75-JLA x-over in Adam Strange (5/62) | 6.50 | 19.00 | 45.00 |
| 81-86 | 3.00 | 9.00 | 21.00 |
| 87-90: 87-89-Adam Strange & Hawkman stories. 90-Adam Strange & Hawkman team-up for 1st time | 3.15 | 9.50 | 22.00 |
| 91-102: 91-End Infantino art on Adam Strange. 92-Space Ranger begins. 94,98-Adam Strange/Space Ranger team-up. 102-Adam Strange ends (no space Ranger) | 1.00 | 3.00 | 7.00 |
| 103-110: 103-Origin Ultra, the Multi-Alien; Space Ranger ends. 110-(9/66)-Last 10 cent issue | .50 | 1.50 | 3.00 |
| V17#111(9/80)-117: 117-Newton-a(3 pgs.) | | .65 | 1.30 |

NOTE: ***Anderson** a-2, 4, 8-10, 12-17, 19, 45-48, 51, 57, 61-64, 70, 76, 87-98; c-9, 10, 15-25, 87, 89, 105-108, 110. **Aparo** a-111. **Austin** a-112i. **Bolland** a-115. **Craig** a-114, 116. **Ditko** a-111, 114-116. **Drucker** a-13, 14. **Elias** a-98, 102, 103. **Golden** a-113p. **Sid Greene** a-78, 91. **Infantino** a-1-8, 11, 14-25, 27-46, 48, 49, 51, 53-91, 103, 117; c-60-86, 88, 90, 91, 105, 107. **Gil Kane** a-18, 100-102; c-52, 101. **Kubert** a-113; c-111-115. **Rogers** a-111. **Sekowsky** a-52. **Simon & Kirby** a-4(2 pgs.). **Spiegle** a-111, 114. **Starlin** c-116. **Sutton** a-112. **Tuska** a-115p, 117p.*

*Mysterious Stories #3, © PG*

*Mystery Comics #1, © WHW*

*Mystery In Space #58, © DC*

Mystery Men Comics #1, © FOX

Mystic #52, © MEG

Mystic Comics #4 (2nd series), © MEG

**MYSTERY MEN COMICS**
Aug, 1939 - No. 31, Feb, 1942
Fox Features Syndicate

| | Good | Fine | N-Mint |
|---|---|---|---|
| 1-Intro. & 1st app. The Blue Beetle, The Green Mask, Rex Dexter of Mars by Briefer, Zanzibar by Tuska, Lt. Drake, D-13-Secret Agent by Powell, Chen Chang, Wing Turner, & Captain Denny Scott | 175.00 | 440.00 | 1050.00 |
| 2 | 72.00 | 215.00 | 500.00 |
| 3 (10/39) | 61.00 | 182.00 | 425.00 |
| 4-Capt. Savage begins | 54.00 | 160.00 | 375.00 |
| 5 | 42.00 | 125.00 | 290.00 |
| 6-8 | 37.00 | 110.00 | 260.00 |
| 9-The Moth begins | 31.00 | 92.00 | 215.00 |
| 10-Wing Turner by Kirby | 31.00 | 92.00 | 215.00 |
| 11-Intro. Domino | 24.00 | 73.00 | 170.00 |
| 12,14-18 | 22.00 | 65.00 | 155.00 |
| 13-Intro. Lynx & sidekick Blackie | 24.00 | 73.00 | 170.00 |
| 19-Intro. & 1st app. Miss X (ends #21) | 24.00 | 73.00 | 170.00 |
| 20-31: 26-The Wraith begins | 20.00 | 60.00 | 140.00 |

NOTE: ***Briefer** a-1-15, 20, 24; c-9. **Cuidera** a-22. **Lou Fine** c-1-8. **Powell** a-1-15, 24. **Simon** c-10-12. **Tuska** a-1-15, 22, 24, 27. Bondage-c 1, 3, 7, 8, 25, 27-29, 31.*

**MYSTERY TALES**
March, 1952 - No. 54, Aug, 1957
Atlas Comics (20CC)

| | Good | Fine | N-Mint |
|---|---|---|---|
| 1 | 22.00 | 65.00 | 150.00 |
| 2-Krigstein-a | 11.00 | 32.00 | 75.00 |
| 3-9: 6-A-Bomb panel | 7.00 | 21.00 | 50.00 |
| 10-Story similar to 'The Assassin' from Shock SuspenStories | 8.00 | 24.00 | 55.00 |
| 11,13-17,19,20: 20-Electric chair issue | 5.30 | 16.00 | 38.00 |
| 12-Matt Fox-a | 6.50 | 19.00 | 45.00 |
| 18-Williamson-a | 6.50 | 19.00 | 45.00 |
| 21-Matt Fox-a; decapitation story | 6.00 | 18.00 | 42.00 |
| 22-Forte/Matt Fox c; a(i) | 7.00 | 21.00 | 50.00 |
| 23-26 (2/55)-Last precode issue | 4.50 | 14.00 | 32.00 |
| 27,29-32,34,35,37,38,41-43,48,49 | 3.00 | 9.00 | 21.00 |
| 28-Jack Katz-a | 3.50 | 10.50 | 24.00 |
| 33-Crandall-a | 4.30 | 13.00 | 30.00 |
| 36,39-Krigstein-a | 4.30 | 13.00 | 30.00 |
| 40,45-Ditko-a | 4.30 | 13.00 | 30.00 |
| 44,51-Williamson/Krenkel-a | 5.00 | 15.00 | 35.00 |
| 46-Williamson/Krenkel-a; Crandall text illos | 5.00 | 15.00 | 35.00 |
| 47-Crandall, Ditko, Powell-a | 4.50 | 14.00 | 32.00 |
| 50-Torres, Morrow-a | 4.30 | 13.00 | 30.00 |
| 52,53 | 2.30 | 7.00 | 16.00 |
| 54-Crandall, Check-a | 3.50 | 10.50 | 24.00 |

NOTE: ***Ayers** a-18, 49, 52. **Berg** a-17, 51. **Colan** a-1, 3, 18, 35, 43. **Everett** a-2, 29, 33, 35, 41, 43; c-8-11, 14, 38, 39, 41, 43, 44, 46, 48-51, 53. **Fass** a-16. **Forte** a-21, 22. **Matt Fox** a-12?, 21, 22; c-22. **Heath** a-3; c-3, 15, 17, 26. **Heck** a-25. **Kinstler** a-15. **Mort Lawrence** a-26, 32, 34. **Maneely** a-1, 9, 14, 22; c-12, 23, 24, 27. **Mooney** a-3, 40. **Morisi** a-43, 49, 52. **Morrow** a-50. **Pakula** a-16. **Powell** a-21, 29, 37, 38, 47. **Reinman** a-1, 14. **Robinson** a-7p, 42. **Romita** a-37. **Roussos** a-4, 44. **R.Q. Sale** a-49. **Severin** c-52. **Tuska** a-10, 12, 14. **Whitney** a-2. **Wildey** a-37.*

**MYSTERY TALES**
1964
Super Comics

| | Good | Fine | N-Mint |
|---|---|---|---|
| Super Reprint #16,17('64) | .50 | 1.50 | 3.00 |
| Super Reprint #18-Kubert-r/Strange Terrors #4 | .50 | 1.50 | 3.00 |

**MYSTIC** (3rd Series)
March, 1951 - No. 61, Aug, 1957
Marvel/Atlas Comics (CLDS 1/CSI 2-21/OMC 22-35/CSI 35-61)

| | Good | Fine | N-Mint |
|---|---|---|---|
| 1-Atom bomb panels | 22.00 | 65.00 | 150.00 |
| 2 | 12.00 | 36.00 | 85.00 |
| 3-Eyes torn out | 9.30 | 28.00 | 65.00 |
| 4-"The Devil Birds" by Wolverton, 6 pgs. | 23.00 | 70.00 | 160.00 |
| 5,7-10 | 7.00 | 21.00 | 50.00 |
| 6-"The Eye of Doom" by Wolverton, 7 pgs. | 23.00 | 70.00 | 160.00 |
| 11-20: 16-Bondage/torture c/story | 6.50 | 19.00 | 45.00 |
| 21-25,27-36-Last precode (3/55). 25-E.C. swipe. 35-Al Hartley-a | 5.00 | 15.00 | 35.00 |
| 26-Atomic War, severed head stories | 5.70 | 17.00 | 40.00 |
| 37-51,53-57,61 | 3.50 | 10.50 | 24.00 |
| 52-Wood-a; Crandall-a? | 5.70 | 17.00 | 40.00 |
| 58,59-Krigstein-a | 4.00 | 12.00 | 28.00 |
| 60-Williamson/Mayo-a, 4 pgs. | 4.30 | 13.00 | 30.00 |

NOTE: ***Andru** a-23, 25. **Ayers** a-35, 53; c-8. **Berg** a-49. **Cameron** a-49, 51. **Check** a-31, 60. **Colan** a-3, 7, 12, 21, 37. **Colletta** a-29. **Drucker** a-46, 52, 56. **Everett** a-8, 9, 17, 40, 44, 57; c-18, 21, 42, 47, 49, 51-55, 58, 59, 61. **Forte** a-35, 52. **Fox** a-24i. **Heath** a-10; c-10, 20, 22, 23, 25, 30. **Infantino** a-12. **Kane** a-8, 24p. **Jack Katz** a-31, 33. **Mort Lawrence** a-19, 37. **Maneely** a-22, 24, 58; c-15, 28, 29, 31. **Moldoff** a-29. **Morisi** a-49, 52. **Morrow** a-51. **Orlando** a-57, 61. **Pakula** a-52. **Powell** a-52, 54-56. **Robinson** a-5. **Romita** a-11, 15. **Sale** a-35, 53. **Sekowsky** a-1, 2, 4, 5. **Severin** c-56. **Tuska** a-15. **Whitney** a-33. **Wildey** a-28, 30. **Ed Win** a-20. Canadian reprints known-title 'Startling'.*

**MYSTICAL TALES**
June, 1956 - No. 8, Aug, 1957
Atlas Comics (CCC 1/EPI 2-8)

| | Good | Fine | N-Mint |
|---|---|---|---|
| 1-Everett-c/a | 12.00 | 36.00 | 85.00 |
| 2,4: 2-Berg-a | 6.00 | 18.00 | 42.00 |
| 3-Crandall-a | 7.00 | 21.00 | 50.00 |
| 5-Williamson-a, 4 pgs. | 7.00 | 21.00 | 50.00 |
| 6-Torres, Krigstein-a | 5.70 | 17.00 | 40.00 |
| 7-Bolle, Forte, Torres, Orlando-a | 5.00 | 15.00 | 35.00 |
| 8-Krigstein, Check-a | 5.70 | 17.00 | 40.00 |

NOTE: ***Everett** a-1, 7; c-1-4, 6, 7. **Orlando** a-1, 2. **Pakula** a-3. **Powell** a-1, 4.*

**MYSTIC COMICS** (1st Series)
March, 1940 - No. 10, Aug, 1942
Timely Comics (TPI 1-5/TCI 8-10)

| | Good | Fine | VF-NM | NM/Mint |
|---|---|---|---|---|
| 1-Origin The Blue Blaze, The Dynamic Man, & Flexo the Rubber Man; Zephyr Jones, 3X's & Deep Sea Demon app.; The Magician begins; c-from Spider pulp V18#1, 6/39 | 500.00 | 1250.00 | 3000.00 | 3800.00 |

(Estimated up to 110 total copies exist, 6 in NM/Mint)

| | Good | Fine | N-Mint |
|---|---|---|---|
| 2-The Invisible Man & Master Mind Excello begin; Space Rangers, Zara of the Jungle, Taxi Taylor app. | 200.00 | 500.00 | 1200.00 |
| 3-Origin Hercules, who last appears in #4 | 154.00 | 385.00 | 925.00 |
| 4-Origin The Thin Man & The Black Widow; Merzak the Mystic app.; last Flexo, Dynamic Man, Invisible Man & Blue Blaze (some issues have date sticker on cover; others have July w/August overprint in silver color); Roosevelt assassination-c | 180.00 | 450.00 | 1080.00 |
| 5-Origin The Black Marvel, The Blazing Skull, The Sub-Earth Man, Super Slave & The Terror; The Moon Man & Black Widow app. | 173.00 | 435.00 | 1040.00 |
| 6-Origin The Challenger & The Destroyer | 150.00 | 375.00 | 900.00 |
| 7-The Witness begins (origin); origin Davey & the Demon; last Black Widow; Simon & Kirby-c | 125.00 | 312.00 | 750.00 |
| 8 | 100.00 | 250.00 | 600.00 |
| 9-Gary Gaunt app.; last Black Marvel, Mystic & Blazing Skull; Hitler-c | 100.00 | 250.00 | 600.00 |
| 10-Father Time, World of Wonder, & Red Skeleton app.; last Challenger & Terror | 100.00 | 250.00 | 600.00 |

NOTE: ***Rico** a-9. **Schomburg** a-1-4; c-4. **Sekowsky** a-9. Bondage c-1, 2, 9.*

**MYSTIC COMICS** (2nd Series)
Oct, 1944 - No. 4, Winter, 1944-45
Timely Comics (ANC)

| | Good | Fine | N-Mint |
|---|---|---|---|
| 1-The Angel, The Destroyer, The Human Torch, Terry Vance the Schoolboy Sleuth, & Tommy Tyme begin | 88.00 | 220.00 | 525.00 |
| 2-Last Human Torch & Terry Vance; bondage-hypo-c | 54.00 | 135.00 | 325.00 |
| 3-Last Angel (two stories) & Tommy Tyme | 50.00 | 125.00 | 300.00 |
| 4-The Young Allies app. | 46.00 | 115.00 | 275.00 |

**MY STORY** (. . .True Romances in Pictures #5,6) (Formerly Zago)
No. 5, May, 1949 - No. 12, Aug, 1950
Hero Books (Fox Features Syndicate)

| | Good | Fine | N-Mint |
|---|---|---|---|
| 5-Kamen/Feldstein-a | 8.00 | 24.00 | 55.00 |
| 6-8,11,12: 12-Photo-c | 3.50 | 10.50 | 24.00 |
| 9,10-Wood-a | 8.50 | 25.50 | 60.00 |

**MYTHADVENTURES**
Mar, 1984 - No. 12, 1986 ($1.50-$1.75, B&W)
WaRP Graphics/Apple Comics #11, 12

| | | | |
|---|---|---|---|
| 1-11: ($1.50)-Early issues mag. size | .25 | .75 | 1.50 |
| 12 ($1.75) | .30 | .90 | 1.80 |

**MYTH CONCEPTIONS**
Nov, 1987 - No. 8, Jan, 1989 ($1.75/$1.95, B&W)
Apple Comics

| | | | |
|---|---|---|---|
| 1-3 ($1.75) | .30 | .90 | 1.80 |
| 4-8 ($1.95) | .35 | 1.00 | 2.00 |

**MY TRUE LOVE** (Formerly Western Killers #64; Frank Buck #70 on)
No. 65, July, 1949 - No. 69, March, 1950
Fox Features Syndicate

| | | | |
|---|---|---|---|
| 65 | 5.00 | 15.00 | 35.00 |
| 66-69: 69-Morisi-a | 3.50 | 10.50 | 24.00 |

**NAKED PREY, THE** (See Movie Classics)

**'NAM, THE** (See Savage Tales #1, 2nd series)
Dec, 1986 - Present
Marvel Comics Group

| | | | |
|---|---|---|---|
| 1-Golden a(p)/c begins, ends #13 | 1.85 | 5.50 | 11.00 |
| 1 (2nd printing) | .50 | 1.50 | 3.00 |
| 2 | 1.15 | 3.50 | 7.00 |
| 3,4 | .85 | 2.50 | 5.00 |
| 5-7 | .60 | 1.75 | 3.50 |
| 8-10 | .35 | 1.00 | 2.00 |
| 11-20: 12-Severin-a | .25 | .75 | 1.50 |
| 21-55: 25-begin $1.50-c. 32-Death R. Kennedy. 52,53-Frank Castle (The Punisher) app. | | .60 | 1.20 |
| Trade Paperback 1-r/1-4 | .75 | 2.25 | 4.50 |
| Trade Paperback 2-r/5-8 | 1.10 | 3.25 | 6.50 |

**'NAM MAGAZINE, THE**
August, 1988 - No. 10, May, 1989 ($2.00, B&W, 52 pgs.)
Marvel Comics

| | | | |
|---|---|---|---|
| 1-10: Each issue reprints two of the comic | .35 | 1.00 | 2.00 |

**NAMORA** (See Marvel Mystery & Sub-Mariner Comics)
Fall, 1948 - No. 3, Dec, 1948
Marvel Comics (PrPI)

| | | | |
|---|---|---|---|
| 1-Sub-Mariner x-over in Namora; Everett, Rico-a | 81.00 | 245.00 | 485.00 |
| 2-The Blonde Phantom & Sub-Mariner story; Everett-a | 67.00 | 200.00 | 400.00 |
| 3-(Scarce)-Sub-Mariner app.; Everett-a | 60.00 | 150.00 | 360.00 |

**NAMOR, THE SUB-MARINER** (See Prince Namor & Sub-Mariner)
Apr, 1990 - Present ($1.00, color)
Marvel Comics

| | | | |
|---|---|---|---|
| 1-Byrne-c/a/scripts in all | .25 | .75 | 1.50 |
| 2-14: 5-Iron Man app. | | .50 | 1.00 |

**NANCY AND SLUGGO** (See Comics On Parade & Sparkle Comics)
No. 16, 1949 - No. 23, 1954
United Features Syndicate

| | | | |
|---|---|---|---|
| 16(#1) | 3.70 | 11.00 | 26.00 |
| 17-23 | 2.15 | 6.50 | 15.00 |

**NANCY & SLUGGO** (Nancy #146-173; formerly Sparkler Comics)
No. 121, Apr, 1955 - No. 192, Oct, 1963
St. John/Dell #146-187/Gold Key #188 on

| | Good | Fine | N-Mint |
|---|---|---|---|
| 121(4/55)(St. John) | 3.15 | 9.50 | 22.00 |
| 122-145(7/57)(St. John) | 2.15 | 6.50 | 15.00 |
| 146(9/57)-Peanuts begins, ends #192 (Dell) | 2.30 | 7.00 | 16.00 |
| 147-161 (Dell) | 1.60 | 4.80 | 11.00 |
| 162-165,177-180-John Stanley-a | 3.70 | 11.00 | 26.00 |
| 166-176-Oona & Her Haunted House series; Stanley-a | 4.00 | 12.00 | 28.00 |
| 181-187(3-5/62)(Dell) | 1.50 | 4.50 | 10.00 |
| 188(10/62)-192 (Gold Key) | 1.50 | 4.50 | 10.00 |
| 4-Color 1034(9-11/59)-Summer Camp | 1.70 | 5.00 | 12.00 |

(See Dell Giant #34, 45 & Dell Giants)

**NANNY AND THE PROFESSOR** (TV)
Aug, 1970 - No. 2, Oct, 1970 (Photo-c)
Dell Publishing Co.

| | | | |
|---|---|---|---|
| 1(01-546-008), 2 | 2.65 | 8.00 | 18.00 |

**NAPOLEON** (See 4-Color No. 526)

**NAPOLEON & SAMANTHA** (See Walt Disney Showcase No. 10)

**NAPOLEON & UNCLE ELBY** (See Clifford McBride's. . .)
July, 1942 (68 pages) (One Shot)
Eastern Color Printing Co.

| | | | |
|---|---|---|---|
| 1 | 16.00 | 48.00 | 110.00 |
| 1945-American Book-Strafford Press (128 pgs.) (8x10½''-B&W reprints; hardcover) | 8.50 | 25.50 | 60.00 |

**NATHANIEL DUSK**
Feb, 1984 - No. 4, May, 1984 ($1.25, mini-series; Baxter paper)
DC Comics (Direct Sale only)

| | | | |
|---|---|---|---|
| 1-4: 1-Intro/origin; Gene Colan-c/a in all | | .65 | 1.30 |

**NATHANIEL DUSK II**
Oct, 1985 - No. 4, Jan, 1986 ($2.00, mini-series; Baxter paper)
DC Comics

| | | | |
|---|---|---|---|
| 1-4: Gene Colan-c/a in all | .35 | 1.00 | 2.00 |

**NATIONAL COMICS**
July, 1940 - No. 75, Nov, 1949
Quality Comics Group

| | | | |
|---|---|---|---|
| 1-Uncle Sam begins; Origin sidekick Buddy by Eisner; origin Wonder Boy & Kid Dixon; Merlin the Magician (ends #45); Cyclone, Kid Patrol, Sally O'Neil Policewoman, Pen Miller (ends #22), Prop Powers (ends #26), & Paul Bunyan (ends #22) begin | 178.00 | 535.00 | 1250.00 |
| 2 | 86.00 | 255.00 | 600.00 |
| 3-Last Eisner Uncle Sam | 67.00 | 200.00 | 465.00 |
| 4-Last Cyclone | 48.00 | 145.00 | 335.00 |
| 5-(11/40)-Quicksilver begins (3rd w/lightning speed?); origin Uncle Sam; bondage-c | 61.00 | 182.00 | 425.00 |
| 6-11: 8-Jack & Jill begins (ends #22). 9-Flag-c | 45.00 | 135.00 | 315.00 |
| 12 | 34.00 | 100.00 | 235.00 |
| 13-16-Lou Fine-a | 42.00 | 125.00 | 290.00 |
| 17,19-22 | 30.00 | 90.00 | 210.00 |
| 18-(12/41)-Shows orientals attacking Pearl Harbor; on stands one month before actual event | 37.00 | 110.00 | 255.00 |
| 23-The Unknown & Destroyer 171 begin | 34.00 | 100.00 | 235.00 |
| 24-26,28,30: 26-Wonder Boy ends | 24.00 | 71.00 | 165.00 |
| 27-G-2 the Unknown begins (ends #46) | 24.00 | 71.00 | 165.00 |
| 29-Origin The Unknown | 24.00 | 71.00 | 165.00 |
| 31-33: 33-Chic Carter begins (ends #47) | 21.00 | 62.00 | 145.00 |
| 34-40: 35-Last Kid Patrol. 39-Hitler-c | 12.00 | 36.00 | 85.00 |
| 41-50: 42-The Barker begins (1st app?). 48-Origin The Whistler | 9.30 | 28.00 | 65.00 |
| 51-Sally O'Neil by Ward, 8 pgs. (12/45) | 12.00 | 36.00 | 85.00 |
| 52-60 | 7.00 | 21.00 | 50.00 |

My Story #12, © FOX

Namor the Sub-Mariner #1, © MEG

National Comics #3, © QUA

*National Velvet #12-556-210, © M.G.M.*

*Navy Combat #11, © MEG*

*Negro Heroes #2, © PMI*

| | Good | Fine | N-Mint |
|---|---|---|---|
| 61-67: 67-Format change; Quicksilver app. | 5.00 | 15.00 | 35.00 |
| 68-75: The Barker ends | 3.50 | 10.50 | 24.00 |

NOTE: ***Cole*** *Quicksilver-13; Barker-43; c-43, 46, 47, 49, 50, 51.* ***Crandall*** *Uncle Sam-11-13 (with* ***Fine****), 25, 26; c-24-26, 30-33, 43.* ***Crandall*** *Paul Bunyan-10-13.* ***Fine*** *Uncle Sam-13 (w/****Crandall****), 17, 18; c-1-14, 16, 18, 21.* ***Guardineer*** *Quicksilver-27.* ***Gustavson*** *Quicksilver -14-26.* ***McWilliams*** *a-23-28, 55, 57. Uncle Sam-c #1-41.*

**NATIONAL CRUMB, THE** (Magazine-Size)
August, 1975 (52 pages) (Satire)
Mayfair Publications

| | Good | Fine | N-Mint |
|---|---|---|---|
| 1 | .70 | 2.00 | 4.00 |

**NATIONAL VELVET** (TV)
May-July, 1961 - No. 2, March, 1963 (All photo-c)
Dell Publishing Co./Gold Key

| | Good | Fine | N-Mint |
|---|---|---|---|
| 4-Color 1195 | 2.65 | 8.00 | 18.00 |
| 4-Color 1312 | 2.30 | 7.00 | 16.00 |
| 01-556-207, 12-556-210 (Dell) | 2.00 | 6.00 | 14.00 |
| 1(12/62), 2(3/63) (Gold Key) | 2.00 | 6.00 | 14.00 |

**NATION OF SNITCHES**
1990 ($4.95, color, 52 pgs.)
Piranha Press (DC)

| | Good | Fine | N-Mint |
|---|---|---|---|
| nn | .85 | 2.50 | 5.00 |

**NATURE BOY** (Formerly Danny Blaze; Li'l Rascal Twins #6 on)
No. 3, March, 1956 - No. 5, Feb, 1957
Charlton Comics

| | Good | Fine | N-Mint |
|---|---|---|---|
| 3-Origin; Blue Beetle story; Buscema-c/a | 12.00 | 36.00 | 84.00 |
| 4,5 | 9.30 | 28.00 | 65.00 |

NOTE: ***John Buscema*** *a-3, 4p, 5; c-3.* ***Powell*** *a-4.*

**NATURE OF THINGS** (See 4-Color No. 727, 842)

**NAUSICAA OF THE VALLEY OF WIND**
1988 - No. 7, 1989; 1989 - No. 4, 1990 ($2.50-$2.95, B&W, 68 pgs.)
Viz Comics

| | Good | Fine | N-Mint |
|---|---|---|---|
| Book 1-7: ($2.50) 1-Contains Moebius poster | .40 | 1.25 | 2.50 |
| Part II, Book 1-3 ($2.95) | .50 | 1.50 | 3.00 |
| Part II, Book 4 ($3.25) | .55 | 1.65 | 3.30 |

**NAVY ACTION** (Sailor Sweeney #12-14)
Aug, 1954 - No. 11, Apr, 1956; No. 15, 1/57 - No. 18, 8/57
Atlas Comics (CDS)

| | Good | Fine | N-Mint |
|---|---|---|---|
| 1-Powell-a | 4.50 | 14.00 | 32.00 |
| 2-Lawrence-a | 2.30 | 7.00 | 16.00 |
| 3-11: 4-Last precode (2/55) | 1.50 | 4.50 | 10.00 |
| 15-18 | 1.00 | 3.00 | 7.00 |

NOTE: ***Berg*** *a-9.* ***Colan*** *a-8.* ***Drucker*** *a-7, 17.* ***Everett*** *a-3, 7, 16; c-16, 17.* ***Heath*** *c-2, 6.* ***Maneely*** *a-8, 18; c-1, 9, 11.* ***Pakula*** *a-2, 3, 9.* ***Reinman*** *a-17.*

**NAVY COMBAT**
June, 1955 - No. 20, Oct, 1958
Atlas Comics (MPI)

| | Good | Fine | N-Mint |
|---|---|---|---|
| 1-Torpedo Taylor begins by Don Heck | 4.50 | 14.00 | 32.00 |
| 2 | 2.30 | 7.00 | 16.00 |
| 3-10 | 1.70 | 5.00 | 12.00 |
| 11,13,15,16,18-20 | 1.30 | 4.00 | 9.00 |
| 12-Crandall-a | 2.65 | 8.00 | 18.00 |
| 14-Torres-a | 2.30 | 7.00 | 16.00 |
| 17-Williamson-a, 4 pgs. | 2.75 | 8.00 | 18.00 |

NOTE: ***Berg*** *a-10, 11.* ***Drucker*** *a-7, 11.* ***Everett*** *a-3, 20; c-8 & 9 w/****Tuska****, 10, 13-16.* ***Maneely*** *c-1, 11.* ***Pakula*** *a-7.* ***Powell*** *a-20.*

**NAVY HEROES**
1945
Almanac Publishing Co.

| | Good | Fine | N-Mint |
|---|---|---|---|
| 1-Heavy in propaganda | 4.50 | 14.00 | 32.00 |

**NAVY: HISTORY & TRADITION**
1958 - 1961 (nn) (Giveaway)
Stokes Walesby Co./Dept. of Navy

| | Good | Fine | N-Mint |
|---|---|---|---|
| 1772-1778, 1778-1782, 1782-1817, 1817-1865, 1865-1936, 1940-1945 | 2.65 | 8.00 | 18.00 |
| 1861: Naval Actions of the Civil War: 1865 | 2.65 | 8.00 | 18.00 |

**NAVY PATROL**
May, 1955 - No. 4, Nov, 1955
Key Publications

| | Good | Fine | N-Mint |
|---|---|---|---|
| 1 | 2.30 | 7.00 | 16.00 |
| 2-4 | 1.15 | 3.50 | 8.00 |

**NAVY TALES**
Jan, 1957 - No. 4, July, 1957
Atlas Comics (CDS)

| | Good | Fine | N-Mint |
|---|---|---|---|
| 1-Everett-c; Berg, Powell-a | 4.30 | 13.00 | 30.00 |
| 2-Williamson/Mayo-a, 5 pgs; Crandall-a | 3.70 | 11.00 | 26.00 |
| 3,4-Reinman-a; Severin-c. 4-Colan, Crandall, Sinnott-a | 3.00 | 9.00 | 21.00 |

**NAVY TASK FORCE**
Feb, 1954 - No. 8, April, 1956
Stanmor Publications/Aragon Mag. No. 4-8

| | Good | Fine | N-Mint |
|---|---|---|---|
| 1 | 3.00 | 9.00 | 21.00 |
| 2 | 1.50 | 4.50 | 10.00 |
| 3-8: #8-r/Navy Patrol #1 | 1.00 | 3.00 | 7.00 |

**NAVY WAR HEROES**
Jan, 1964 - No. 7, Mar-Apr, 1965
Charlton Comics

| | Good | Fine | N-Mint |
|---|---|---|---|
| 1 | .70 | 2.00 | 4.00 |
| 2-7 | .35 | 1.00 | 2.00 |

**NAZA** (Stone Age Warrior)
Nov-Jan, 1963/64 - No. 9, March, 1966
Dell Publishing Co.

| | Good | Fine | N-Mint |
|---|---|---|---|
| 1 (12-555-401)-Painted-c | 1.15 | 3.50 | 8.00 |
| 2-9: 2-4-Painted-c | .85 | 2.60 | 6.00 |

**NAZZ, THE**
1990 - No. 4, 1991 ($4.95, color, mature readers, 52 pgs.)
DC Comics

| | Good | Fine | N-Mint |
|---|---|---|---|
| 1-4 | .85 | 2.50 | 5.00 |

**NEBBS, THE**
1928 (Daily B&W strip reprints; 52 pages)
Cupples & Leon Co.

| | Good | Fine | N-Mint |
|---|---|---|---|
| nn-By Sol Hess; Carlson-a | 8.50 | 25.50 | 60.00 |

**NEBBS, THE** (Also see Crackajack Funnies)
1941; 1945
Dell Publishing Co./Croydon Publishing Co.

| | Good | Fine | N-Mint |
|---|---|---|---|
| Large Feature Comic 23(1941) | 10.00 | 30.00 | 70.00 |
| 1(1945, 36 pgs.)-Reprints | 5.70 | 17.00 | 40.00 |

**NECROMANCER: THE GRAPHIC NOVEL**
1989 ($9.95, color)
Epic Comics (Marvel)

| | Good | Fine | N-Mint |
|---|---|---|---|
| nn | 1.70 | 5.00 | 10.00 |

**NEGRO** (See All-Negro)

**NEGRO HEROES** (Calling All Girls, Real Heroes, & True Comics-r)
Spring, 1947 - No. 2, Summer, 1948
Parents' Magazine Institute

| | Good | Fine | N-Mint |
|---|---|---|---|
| 1 | 30.00 | 90.00 | 210.00 |
| 2-Jackie Robinson story | 34.00 | 103.00 | 240.00 |

**NEGRO ROMANCE** (Negro Romances #4)
June, 1950 - No. 3, Oct, 1950 (All photo-c)
Fawcett Publications

| | Good | Fine | N-Mint |
|---|---|---|---|
| 1-Evans-a | 65.00 | 195.00 | 455.00 |

| | Good | Fine | N-Mint |
|---|---|---|---|
| 2,3 | 50.00 | 150.00 | 350.00 |

**NEGRO ROMANCES** (Formerly Negro Romance)
No. 4, May, 1955 (Romantic Secrets #5 on)
Charlton Comics

| | | | |
|---|---|---|---|
| 4-Reprints Fawcett #2 | 37.00 | 110.00 | 260.00 |

**NEIL THE HORSE** (See Charlton Bullseye #2)
2/83 - No. 10, 12/84; No. 11, 4/85 - Present? (B&W)
Aardvark-Vanaheim #1-10/Renegade Press #11 on

| | | | |
|---|---|---|---|
| 1 ($1.40) | .60 | 1.75 | 3.50 |
| 1-2nd print | .25 | .75 | 1.50 |
| 2 | .40 | 1.25 | 2.50 |
| 3-13: 13-Double size.; 11,13-w/paperdolls | .35 | 1.00 | 2.00 |
| 14,15-Double size ($3.00). 15 is a flip book(2-c) | .50 | 1.50 | 3.00 |

**NELLIE THE NURSE** (Also see Gay Comics)
1945 - No. 36, Oct, 1952; 1957
Marvel/Atlas Comics (SPI/LMC)

| | | | |
|---|---|---|---|
| 1 | 12.00 | 36.00 | 85.00 |
| 2 | 6.00 | 18.00 | 42.00 |
| 3,4 | 4.50 | 14.00 | 32.00 |
| 5-Kurtzman's "Hey Look"(3); Georgie app. | 5.70 | 17.00 | 40.00 |
| 6-8,10: 7,8-Georgie app. 10-Millie app. | 3.50 | 10.50 | 24.00 |
| 9-Wolverton-a (1 pg.); Mille the Model app. | 4.00 | 12.00 | 28.00 |
| 11,14-16,18-Kurtzman's "Hey Look" | 4.50 | 14.00 | 32.00 |
| 12-"Giggles 'n' Grins" by Kurtzman | 3.50 | 10.50 | 24.00 |
| 13,17,19,20: 17-Annie Oakley app. | 3.00 | 9.00 | 21.00 |
| 21-27,29,30 | 2.65 | 8.00 | 18.00 |
| 28-Kurtzman's Rusty reprint | 3.00 | 9.00 | 21.00 |
| 31-36: 36-Post-c | 2.00 | 6.00 | 14.00 |
| 1('57)-Leading Mag. (Atlas)-Everett-a, 20pgs. | 2.00 | 6.00 | 14.00 |

**NELLIE THE NURSE** (See 4-Color No. 1304)

**NEMESIS THE WARLOCK** (Also see Spellbinders)
Sept, 1984 - No. 7, Mar, 1985 (Limited series; 36 pgs.)
Eagle Comics (Baxter paper)

| | | | |
|---|---|---|---|
| 1-7: 2000 A.D. reprints | .25 | .75 | 1.50 |

**NEMESIS THE WARLOCK**
1989 - Present ($1.95, B&W)
Quality Comics/Fleetway Quality #2 on

| | | | |
|---|---|---|---|
| 1-10 | .35 | 1.00 | 2.00 |

**NEUTRO**
January, 1967
Dell Publishing Co.

| | | | |
|---|---|---|---|
| 1-Jack Sparling-c/a (super hero) | 1.00 | 3.00 | 7.00 |

**NEVADA** (See Zane Grey's Stories of the West #1)

**NEVER AGAIN** (War stories; becomes Soldier & Marine V2#9)
Aug, 1955 - No. 2, Oct?, 1955; No. 8, July, 1956 (No #3-7)
Charlton Comics

| | | | |
|---|---|---|---|
| 1 | 3.50 | 10.50 | 24.00 |
| 2 (Becomes Fightin' Air Force #3), 8(Formerly Foxhole?) | 1.70 | 5.00 | 12.00 |

**NEW ADVENTURE COMICS** (Formerly New Comics; becomes Adventure Comics #32 on)
V1#12, Jan, 1937 - No. 31, Oct, 1938
National Periodical Publications

| | Good | Fine | VF-NM |
|---|---|---|---|
| V1#12-Federal Men by Siegel & Shuster continues; Jor-L mentioned | 154.00 | 385.00 | 925.00 |
| V2#1(2/37, #13), V2#2 (#14) | 113.00 | 285.00 | 680.00 |

| | Good | Fine | N-Mint |
|---|---|---|---|
| 15(V2#3)-20(V2#8): 15-1st Adventure logo. 16-1st Shuster-c; 1st non-funny cover. 17-Nadir, Master of Magic begins, ends #30 | 113.00 | 285.00 | 680.00 |
| 21(V2#9),22(V2#10, 2/37): 22-X-Mas-c | 92.00 | 230.00 | 550.00 |
| 23-31 | 75.00 | 190.00 | 450.00 |

**NEW ADVENTURE OF WALT DISNEY'S SNOW WHITE AND THE SEVEN DWARFS, A** (See Snow White Bendix Giveaway)

**NEW ADVENTURES OF CHARLIE CHAN, THE** (TV)
May-June, 1958 - No. 6, Mar-Apr, 1959
National Periodical Publications

| | | | |
|---|---|---|---|
| 1 (Scarce)-Gil Kane/Sid Greene-a in all | 29.00 | 86.00 | 200.00 |
| 2 (Scarce) | 18.00 | 54.00 | 125.00 |
| 3-6 (Scarce) | 14.00 | 43.00 | 100.00 |

**NEW ADVENTURES OF HUCK FINN, THE** (TV)
December, 1968 (Hanna-Barbera)
Gold Key

| | | | |
|---|---|---|---|
| 1-"The Curse of Thut;" part photo-c | 1.30 | 4.00 | 9.00 |

**NEW ADVENTURES OF PETER PAN** (Disney)
1953 (36 pgs.; 5x7¼") (Admiral giveaway)
Western Publishing Co.

| | | | |
|---|---|---|---|
| nn | 4.65 | 14.00 | 32.00 |

**NEW ADVENTURES OF PINOCCHIO** (TV)
Oct-Dec, 1962 - No. 3, Sept-Nov, 1963
Dell Publishing Co.

| | | | |
|---|---|---|---|
| 12-562-212(#1) | 5.00 | 15.00 | 35.00 |
| 2,3 | 4.00 | 12.00 | 28.00 |

**NEW ADVENTURES OF ROBIN HOOD** (See Robin Hood)

**NEW ADVENTURES OF SHERLOCK HOLMES** (See 4-Color #1169, 1245)

**NEW ADVENTURES OF SUPERBOY, THE** (Also see Superboy)
Jan, 1980 - No. 54, June, 1984
DC Comics

| | | | |
|---|---|---|---|
| 1 | | .65 | 1.30 |
| 2-5 | | .50 | 1.00 |
| 6-49,51-54: 7-Has extra story "The Computers That Saved Metropolis" by Starlin (Radio Shack giveaway w/indicia) 11-Superboy gets new power. 14-Lex Luthor app. 15-Superboy gets new parents. 28-Dial "H" For Hero begins, ends #49. 45-47-1st app. Sunburst. 48-Begin 75 cent-c | | .40 | .80 |
| 50 ($1.25, 52 pgs.)-Legion app. | | .65 | 1.30 |

NOTE: ***Buckler** a-9p; c-36p. **Giffen** a-50; c-50. 40i. **Gil Kane** c-32p, 33p, 35, 39, 41-49. **Miller** c-51. **Starlin** a-7. Krypto back-ups in 17, 22. Superbaby in 11, 14, 19, 24.*

**NEW ADVS. OF THE PHANTOM BLOT, THE** (See The Phantom Blot)

**NEW AMERICA**
Nov, 1987 - No. 4, Feb, 1988 ($1.75, color, Baxter paper)
Eclipse Comics

| | | | |
|---|---|---|---|
| 1-4-Scout mini-series | .30 | .90 | 1.80 |

**NEW ARCHIES, THE** (TV)
Oct, 1987 - No. 22, May, 1990 (75 cents)
Archie Comic Publications

| | | | |
|---|---|---|---|
| 1-16: 3-Xmas issue | | .40 | .80 |
| 17-22 (.95-$1.00): 21-Xmas issue | | .50 | 1.00 |

**NEW ARCHIES DIGEST** (TV)(. . .Comics Digest Magazine #4? on)
1988 - Present ($1.35-$1.50, digest size, quarterly)(. . .Digest Mag. #11)
Archie Comics

| | | | |
|---|---|---|---|
| 1-11: 6-Begin $1.50-c | .25 | .75 | 1.50 |

**NEW BOOK OF COMICS** (Also see Big Book Of Fun)
1937; No. 2, Spring, 1938 (100 pgs. each) (Reprints)
National Periodical Publ.

1(Rare)-1st regular size comic annual; 2nd DC annual; contains r-/ New Comics #1-4 & More Fun #9; r-Federal Men (8pgs.), Henri Duval (1pg.), & Dr. Occult in costume (1pg.) by Siegel & Shuster;

*Neil the Horse #15, © Renegade Press*

*New Adventure Comics #30, © DC*

*The New Adventures of Charlie Chan #1, © DC*

New Comics #11, © DC

New Funnies #67, © DELL

The New Gods #2 (4-5/71), © DC

Good Fine VF-NM NM/Mint
Moldoff, Sheldon Mayer (15pgs.)-a 433.00 1085.00 2600.00 3600.00
(Estimated up to 50 total copies exist, 2 in NM/Mint)
2-Contains r-/More Fun #15 & 16; r-/Dr. Occult in costume (a Superman proto-type), & Calling All Cars (4pgs.) by Siegel & Shuster
Good Fine N-Mint
250.00 625.00 1500.00

**NEW COMICS** (New Adventure #12 on)
12/35 - No. 11, 12/36 (No. 1-6: paper cover) (No. 1-5: 84 pgs.)
National Periodical Publ.
Good Fine VF-NM NM/Mint
V1#1-Billy the Kid, Sagebrush 'n' Cactus, Jibby Jones, Needles, The Vikings, Sir Loin of Beef, Now-When I Was a Boy, & other 1-2 pg. strips; 2 pgs. Kelly art(1st)-(Gulliver's Travels); Sheldon Mayer-a(1st) 533.00 1335.00 3200.00 4500.00
(Estimated up to 50 total copies exist, 2 in NM/Mint)
2-Federal Men by Siegel & Shuster begins (Also see The Comics Magazine #2); Sheldon Mayer, Kelly-a (Rare)
Good Fine VF-NM
285.00 710.00 1700.00
3-6: 3,4-Sheldon Mayer-a which continues in The Comics Magazine #1. 5-Kiefer-a 167.00 415.00 1000.00
7-11: 11-Christmas-c 133.00 335.00 800.00
NOTE: *#1-6 rarely occur in mint condition.*

**NEW DEFENDERS** (See Defenders)

**NEW DNAGENTS, THE** (Formerly DNAgents)
V2#1, Oct, 1985 - V2#17, Mar, 1987 (Whole #s 25-40; Mando paper)
Eclipse Comics
Good Fine N-Mint
V2#1-12: 1-Origin recap. 7-Begin 95 cent-c. 9,10-Airboy preview .50 1.00
13-17 ($1.25-c) .60 1.20
3-D 1 (1/86, $2.25) .40 1.15 2.30
2-D 1 (1/86)-Limited ed. (100 copies) .85 2.50 5.00

**NEW FUN COMICS** (More Fun #7 on; see Big Book of Fun Comics)
Feb, 1935 - No. 6, Oct, 1935 (10x15", No. 1-4,6: slick covers)
(No. 1-5: 36 pgs; 68 pgs. No. 6-on)
National Periodical Publications
Good Fine V. Fine VF-NM
V1#1 (1st DC comic); 1st app. Oswald The Rabbit. Jack Woods (cowboy) begins 1335.00 3335.00 8000.00 15,000.00
(Estimated up to 24 total copies exist, 1 in VF/NM)
Good Fine V.Fine
2(3/35)-(Very Rare) 917.00 2300.00 5500.00
3-5(8/35): 5-Soft-c 417.00 1040.00 2500.00
6(10/35)-1st Dr. Occult (Superman proto-type) by Siegel & Shuster (Leger & Reughts); last "New Fun" title. "New Comics #1 begins in Dec. which is reason for title change to More Fun; Henri Duval (ends #9) by Siegel & Shuster begins; paper-c
500.00 1250.00 3000.00

**NEW FUNNIES** (The Funnies #1-64; Walter Lantz. . .#109 on; New TV. . . #259, 260, 272, 273; TV Funnies #261-271)
No. 65, July, 1942 - No. 288, Mar-Apr, 1962
Dell Publishing Co.
Good Fine N-Mint
65(#1)-Andy Panda in a world of real people, Raggedy Ann & Andy, Oswald the Rabbit (with Woody Woodpecker x-overs), Li'l Eight Ball & Peter Rabbit begin 42.00 125.00 290.00
66-70: 67-Billy & Bonnie Bee by Frank Thomas & Felix The Cat begin. 69-2pg. Kelly-a; The Brownies begin (not by Kelly)
19.00 58.00 135.00
71-75: 72-Kelly illos. 75-Brownies by Kelly? 12.00 36.00 85.00
76-Andy Panda (Carl Barks & Pabian-a); Woody Woodpecker x-over in Oswald ends 57.00 171.00 400.00
77,78: 78-Andy Panda in a world with real people ends
12.00 36.00 85.00
79-81 8.50 25.50 60.00

Good Fine N-Mint
82-Brownies by Kelly begins; Homer Pigeon begins
10.00 30.00 70.00
83-85-Brownies by Kelly in ea. 83-X-mas-c. 85-Woody Woodpecker, 1pg. strip begins 10.00 30.00 70.00
86-90: 87-Woody Woodpecker stories begin 5.00 15.00 35.00
91-99 3.15 9.50 22.00
100 (6/45) 3.70 11.00 26.00
101-110 2.15 6.50 15.00
111-120: 119-X-mas-c 1.60 4.80 11.00
121-150: 143-X-mas-c 1.15 3.50 8.00
151-200: 155-X-mas-c. 168-X-mas-c, 182-Origin & 1st app. Knothead & Splinter. 191-X-mas-c .85 2.50 6.00
201-240 .70 2.00 5.00
241-288: 270,271-Walter Lantz c-app. 281-1st story swipe/WDC&S #100 .60 1.80 4.00
NOTE: *Early issues written by* ***John Stanley***.

**NEW GODS, THE** (New Gods #12 on)(See Adventure #459, First Issue Special & Super-Team Family)
2-3/71 - V2#11, 10-11/72; V3#12, 7/77 - V3#19, 7-8/78
National Periodical Publications/DC Comics
1-Intro/1st app. Orion (#1-3 are 15 cents) 1.50 4.50 10.00
2-11: 2-Darkseid app. 4-Origin Manhunter-r. 5,7,8-Young Gods feature. 7-Origin Orion. 9-1st app. Bug .85 2.50 5.00
12-19: 12-New costume Orion .25 .75 1.50
NOTE: *#4-9(25 cents, 52 pgs.) contain Manhunter-r by* ***Simon & Kirby*** *from Adventure #73, 74, 75, 76, 77, 78 with covers in that order.* ***Adkins*** *i-12-14, 17-19.* ***Kirby*** *c/a-1-11p.* ***Newton*** *p-12-14, 16-19.* ***Starlin*** *c-17.* ***Staton*** *c-19p.*

**NEW GODS, THE**
May, 1984 - No. 6, Nov,1984 ($2.00, direct sale; Baxter paper)
DC Comics
1-New Kirby-c begin; r-/New Gods #1&2 .35 1.00 2.00
2-6: 6-Original art by Kirby .35 1.00 2.00

**NEW GODS**
Feb, 1989 - Present ($1.50, color)
DC Comics
1-Russell-i .35 1.00 2.00
2-18: 2-4-Starlin scripts. 17-Darkseid app. .25 .75 1.50

**NEW GUARDIANS, THE**
Sept, 1988 - No. 12, Sept, 1989 ($1.25, color)
DC Comics
1-($2.00, 52 pgs.)-Staton-c/a in #1-9 .35 1.00 2.00
2-12 .60 1.25

**NEW HEROIC** (See Heroic)

**NEW HUMANS, THE** (See The Ex-Mutants)
Dec, 1987 - No. 15, 1989 ($1.95, B&W)
Eternity Comics
1-15: 1-Origin .30 .90 1.80
Annual 1 (1988, $2.95, B&W) .50 1.50 3.00

**NEW JUSTICE MACHINE, THE** (Also see The Justice Machine)
1989 - No. 3, 1989 ($1.95, color, mini-series)
Innovation Publishing
1-3 .35 1.00 2.00

**NEW KIDS ON THE BLOCK, THE** (Also see Richie Rich and. . .)
Dec, 1990 - Present ($1.25, color)
Harvey Comics
1-5 .65 1.30
. . .Backstage Pass 1(12/90, $1.25) - 5 .65 1.30
. . .Chillin' 1(12/90, $1.25) - 5: 1-Photo-c .65 1.30
. . .Comics Tour '90/91 1(12/90, $1.25) - 5 .65 1.30
. . .Hanging Tough 1(2/91, $1.25) - 3 .65 1.30
. . .Live 1(2/91, $1.25) - 3 .65 1.30

Good Fine N-Mint

...Magic Summer Tour 1(Fall/90, $1.25, one-shot) .65 1.30

...Step By Step 1(Fall/90, $1.25, one-shot) .65 1.30

...Valentine Girl 1(Fall/90, $1.25, one-shot)-Photo-c .65 1.30

**NEWLYWEDS**

1907; 1917 (cardboard covers)

Saalfield Publ. Co.

...& Their Baby' by McManus; Saaalfield, 1907, 13x10," 52pgs. daily strips in full color 30.00 90.00 210.00

...& Their Baby's Comic Pictures, The, by McManus, Saalfield, 1917, 14x10," 22pgs, oblong, cardboard-c, reprints 'Newlyweds' (Baby Snookums stips) mainly from 1916; blue cover; says for painting & crayoning, but some pages in color. (Scarce) 24.00 73.00 170.00

**NEW MEN OF BATTLE, THE**

1949 (nn) (Carboard covers)

Catechetical Guild

nn(V8#1-3,5,6)-192pgs.; contains 5 issues of Topix rebound 2.00 6.00 14.00

nn(V8#7-V8#11)-160pgs.; 5 issues of Topix 2.00 6.00 14.00

**NEW MUTANTS, THE** (See Marvel Graphic Novel #4 for 1st app.)

March, 1983 - No. 100, April, 1991

Marvel Comics Group

1 1.30 4.00 8.00

2,3 .70 2.00 4.00

2-Limited test cover (75 cents) 10.00 30.00 60.00

4-10: 10-1st app. Magma .50 1.50 3.00

11-20: 13-Kitty Pryde app. 18-Intro. Warlock .40 1.25 2.50

21-Double size; new Warlock origin .50 1.50 3.00

22-30: 23-25-Cloak & Dagger app. .40 1.25 2.50

31-58: 50-Double size. 58-Contains pull-out mutant registration form .35 1.00 2.00

59-Fall of The Mutants begins, ends #61 .60 1.75 3.50

60-Double size, $1.25 .40 1.25 2.50

61-Fall of The Mutants ends .35 1.00 2.00

62,64-72,74-85,88,89: 68-Intro Spyder. 76-X-Factor & X-Terminator app. .50 1.00

63-X-Men & Wolverine app.; begin $1.00-c .50 1.50 3.00

73-($1.50, 52 pgs.) .35 1.00 2.00

86-McFarlane-c(i) swiped from Ditko splash pg. .40 1.25 2.50

87-1st app. Cable 1.00 3.00 6.00

90,91: 90-New costumes. 90,91-Sabertooth app. .40 1.25 2.50

92-94,98,99: 94-Wolverine app. .50 1.00

95-97-X-Tinction Agenda x-over .35 1.00 2.00

100-($1.50, 52 pgs.)-1st app. X-Force .25 .75 1.50

Annual 1 (1984) .85 2.50 5.00

Annual 2 (10/86; $1.25) .35 1.00 2.00

Annual 3(9/87, $1.25) .25 .75 1.50

Annual 4('88, $1.75)-Evolutionary War x-over .60 1.75 3.50

Annual 5('89, $2.00, 68 pgs.)-Atlantis Attacks .35 1.00 2.00

Annual 6(;90, $2.00, 68 pgs.)-1st new costumes .35 1.00 2.00

Special 1-Special Edition ('85, 68 pgs.)-ties in with X-Men Alpha Flight mini-series; Art Adams/Austin-a 1.00 3.00 6.00

Summer Special 1(Sum/90, $2.95, 84 pgs.) .50 1.50 3.00

NOTE: ***Art Adams** c-38, 39. **Austin** c-57i. **Byrne** c/a-75p. **McFarlane** c-85-89i, 93i. **Russell** a-48i. **Sienkiewicz** c/a-18-31, 35-38i. **Simonson** c-11p. **B. Smith** c-36, 40-48. **Williamson** a(i)-69, 71-73, 78-80, 82, 83; c-69, 72, 73, 78i.*

**NEW PEOPLE, THE** (TV)

Jan, 1970 - No. 2, May, 1970

Dell Publishing Co.

1,2 1.15 3.50 8.00

**NEW ROMANCES**

No. 5, May, 1951 - No. 21, Apr?, 1954

Standard Comics

Good Fine N-Mint

5 4.50 14.00 32.00

6-9: 6-Barbara Bel Geddes, Richard Basehart "Fourteen Hours" 2.30 7.00 16.00

10,14,16,17-Toth-a 5.00 15.00 35.00

11-Toth-a; Liz Taylor, Montgomery Cliff photo-c 6.00 19.00 45.00

12,13,15,18-21 1.50 4.50 10.00

NOTE: ***Celardo** a-9. **Moreira** a-6. **Tuska** a-7, 20. Photo c-6-16.*

**NEW STATESMEN, THE**

1989 - No. 5, 1990 ($3.95, color, mini-series, mature readers, 52 pgs.)

Fleetway Publications (Quality Comics)

1-5: Futuristic; squarebound; 3-Photo-c .70 2.00 4.00

**NEWSTRALIA**

July, 1989 - Present ($1.75, color, deluxe format; #3 on: $2.25, B&W)

Innovation Publishing

1-2: Timothy Truman-c/a; Gustovich-i .35 1.00 2.00

3-5 ($2.25-c, B&W) .40 1.15 2.30

**NEW TALENT SHOWCASE** (Talent Showcase No. 16 on)

Jan, 1984 - No. 19, Oct, 1985 (Direct sales only)

DC Comics

1-10: Features new strips & artists .35 .70

11-19 ($1.25): 18-Williamson-c(i) .65 1.30

**NEW TEEN TITANS, THE** (See DC Comics Presents 26, Marvel and DC Present & Teen Titans; Tales of the Teen Titans #41 on)

November, 1980 - No. 40, March, 1984

DC Comics

1-Robin, Kid Flash, Wonder Girl, The Changeling, Starfire, The Raven, Cyborg begin; partial origin 1.50 4.50 9.00

2 1.00 3.00 6.00

3-Origin Starfire; Intro The Fearsome 5 .70 2.00 4.00

4-Origin continues; J.L.A. app. .70 2.00 4.00

5-10: 6-Origin Raven. 7-Cyborg origin. 8-Origin Kid Flash retold. 10-Origin Changeling retold .50 1.50 3.00

11-20: 13-Return of Madame Rouge & Capt. Zahl; Robotman revived. 14-Return of Mento; origin Doom Patrol. 15-Death of Madame Rouge & Capt. Zahl; intro. new Brotherhood of Evil 16-1st app. Capt. Carrot (free 16 pg. preview). 18-Return of Starfire. 19-Hawkman teams-up .25 .75 1.50

21-30: 21-Intro Night Force in free 16 pg. insert; intro Brother Blood. 23-1st app. Vigilante (not in costume), & Blackfire. 24-Omega Men app. 25-Omega Men cameo; free 16 pg. preview Masters of the Universe. 26-1st Terra. 27-Free 16 pg. preview Atari Force. 29-The New Brotherhood of Evil & Speedy app. 30-Terra joins the Titans .60 1.20

31-38,40: 38-Origin Wonder Girl .40 .75

39-Last Dick Grayson as Robin; Kid Flash quits .35 1.00 2.00

Annual 1(11/82)-Omega Men app. .25 .70 1.40

Annual 2(9/83)-1st app. Vigilante in costume .45 .90

Annual 3(1984)-Death of Terra .45 .90

nn(11/83-Keebler Co. Giveaway)-In cooperation with "The President's Drug Awareness Campaign" .60 1.20

nn-(re-issue of above on Mando paper for direct sales market); American Soft Drink Ind. version; I.B.M. Corp. version .50 1.00

NOTE: ***Perez** a-1-4p, 6-34p, 37-40p, Annual 1p, 2p; c-1-12, 13-17p, 18-21, 22p, 23p, 24-37, 38, 39(painted), 40, Annual 1, 2.*

**NEW TEEN TITANS, THE** (The New Titans #50 on)

Aug, 1984 - No. 49, Nov, 1988 ($1.25-$1.75; deluxe format)

DC Comics

1-New storyline; Perez-c/a begins .75 2.25 4.50

2,3: 2-Re-intro Lilith .45 1.40 2.80

4-10: 5-Death of Trigon. 7-9-Origin Lilith. 8-Intro Kole. 10-Kole joins .30 .90 1.80

*The New Mutants #10, © MEG*

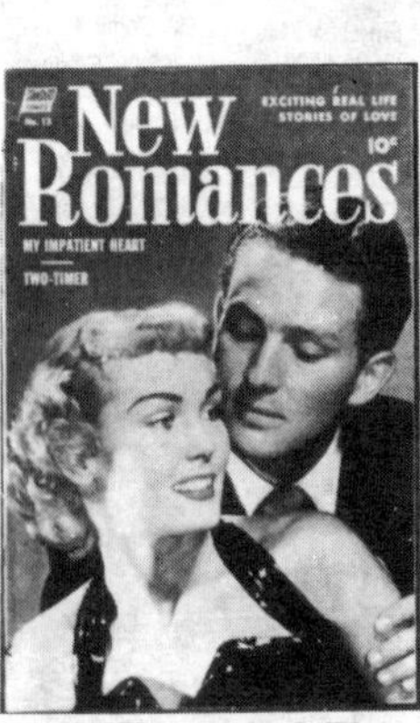


*New Romances #13, © STD*

*The New Teen Titans #7 (5/81), © DC*

*The New Titans #61, © DC*

*The New Warriors #1, © MEG*

*New York World's Fair 1940, © DC*

| | Good | Fine | N-Mint |
|---|---|---|---|
| 11-19: 13,14-Crisis x-over | | .60 | 1.20 |
| 20-Robin (Jason Todd) joins; original T.T. return | .35 | 1.00 | 2.00 |
| 21-49: 37-Begin $1.75-c. 38-Infinity, Inc. x-over. 47-Origin all Titans. 48-1st app. Red Star | .25 | .70 | 1.40 |
| Annual 1 (9/85)-Intro. Vanguard | .35 | 1.00 | 2.00 |
| Annual 2 (8/86; $2.50): Byrne c/a(p); origin Brother Blood; intro new Dr. Light | .40 | 1.25 | 2.50 |
| Annual 3 (11/87)-Intro. Danny Chase | .35 | 1.00 | 2.00 |
| Annual 4 ('88, $2.50)-Perez-c | .40 | 1.15 | 2.30 |

NOTE: *Orlando c-33p.* ***Perez*** *a-1-5; c-1-6, 19-23, 43.* ***Steacy*** *c-47.*

**NEW TERRYTOONS** (TV)
6-8/60 - No. 8, 3-5/62; 10/62 - No. 54, 1/79
Dell Publishing Co./Gold Key

| | Good | Fine | N-Mint |
|---|---|---|---|
| 1('60-Dell)-Deputy Dawg, Dinky Duck & Hashimoto San begin | 2.00 | 6.00 | 14.00 |
| 2-8('62) | 1.15 | 3.50 | 8.00 |
| 1(30010-210)(10/62-Gold Key, 84 pgs.)-Heckle & Jeckle begins | 3.50 | 10.50 | 28.00 |
| 2(30010-301)-84 pgs. | 2.75 | 8.25 | 22.00 |
| 3-10 | .85 | 2.50 | 6.00 |
| 11-20 | .60 | 1.75 | 3.50 |
| 21-30 | .25 | .75 | 1.50 |
| 31-54 | | .40 | .80 |

NOTE: *Reprints: #4-12, 38, 40, 47. (See March of Comics #379, 393, 412, 435)*

**NEW TESTAMENT STORIES VISUALIZED**
1946 - 1947
Standard Publishing Co.

"New Testament Heroes—Acts of Apostles Visualized, Book I"
"New Testament Heroes—Acts of Apostles Visualized, Book II"
"Parables Jesus Told" Set.... 10.00 30.00 60.00

NOTE: *All three are contained in a cardboard case, illustrated on front and info about the set.*

**NEW TITANS, THE** (Formerly The New Teen Titans)
No. 50, Dec, 1988 - Present ($1.75, color)
DC Comics

| | Good | Fine | N-Mint |
|---|---|---|---|
| 50-Perez-c/a begins; new origin Wonder Girl | .75 | 2.25 | 4.50 |
| 51-59: 50-55-Painted-c. 55-Nightwing (Dick Grayson) forces Danny Chase to resign; Batman app. in flashback | .40 | 1.25 | 2.50 |
| 60-A Lonely Place of Dying Part 2 continues from Batman #440; new Robin tie-in | 1.10 | 3.25 | 6.50 |
| 61-A Lonely Place of Dying Part 4 | .70 | 2.00 | 4.00 |
| 62-75: 65-Timothy Drake (Robin) app. 71 (44 pgs.)-10th anniversary issue | .30 | .90 | 1.75 |
| Annual 5,6 (1989, 1990, $3.50, 68 pgs.) | .60 | 1.75 | 3.50 |

NOTE: ***Perez*** *a-50-55p, 57-60p, 61(layouts); c-50-61, 62-67i, Annual 5i; co-plots-66.*

**NEW TV FUNNIES** (See New Funnies)

**NEW WARRIORS, THE** (See Thor #411,412)
July, 1990 - Present ($1.00, color)
Marvel Comics

| | Good | Fine | N-Mint |
|---|---|---|---|
| 1-Williamson-i | .85 | 2.50 | 5.00 |
| 2-Williamson-c/a(i) | .50 | 1.50 | 3.00 |
| 3-7: 3-Guice-c(i) | .25 | .75 | 1.50 |
| 8,9-Punisher app. | .35 | 1.00 | 2.00 |
| 10-12 | | .50 | 1.00 |

**NEW WAVE, THE**
6/10/86 - No. 13, 3/87 (#1-8: bi-weekly, 20 pgs.; #9-13: monthly)
Eclipse Comics

| | Good | Fine | N-Mint |
|---|---|---|---|
| 1-8 (50 cents): 1-Origin, concludes #5. 6-Origin Megabyte. 8,9-The Heap returns | | .25 | .50 |
| 9-13 ($1.50) | .25 | .75 | 1.50 |
| ...Versus the Volunteers 3-D #1,2(4/87) | .40 | 1.25 | 2.50 |

**NEW WORLD** (See Comic Books, series I)

**NEW YORK GIANTS** (See Thrilling True Story of the Baseball Giants)

**NEW YORK STATE JOINT LEGISLATIVE COMMITTEE TO STUDY THE PUBLICATION OF COMICS, THE**
1951, 1955
N.Y. State Legislative Document

This document was referenced by Wertham for **Seduction of the Innocent**. Contains numerous repros from comics showing violence, sadism, torture, and sex.
1955 version (196p, No. 37, 2/23/55)-Sold for $180 in 1986.

**NEW YORK WORLD'S FAIR**
1939, 1940 (100pgs.; cardboard covers) (DC's 4th & 5th annuals)
National Periodical Publ.

| | Good | Fine | VF-NM | NM/Mint |
|---|---|---|---|---|
| 1939-Scoop Scanlon, Superman (blonde haired Superman on-c), Sandman, Zatara, Slam Bradley, Ginger Snap by Bob Kane begin; 1st published app. The Sandman (see Adventure #40 for his 1st drawn story) | 500.00 | 1250.00 | 3000.00 | 4000.00 |
| (Estimated up to 110 total copies exist, 4 in NM/Mint) | | | | |
| 1940-Batman, Hourman, Johnny Thunderbolt app.; Superman, Batman & Robin-c | 315.00 | 790.00 | 1900.00 | 2500.00 |

NOTE: The 1939 edition was published 4/30/39, the day the fair opened, at 25 cents, and was first sold only at the fair. Since all other comics were 10 cents, it didn't sell. Remaining copies were advertised beginning in the August issues of most DC comics for 25 cents, but soon the price was dropped to 15 cents. Everyone that sent a quarter throught the mail for it received a free Superman #2 to make up the dime difference. 15 cent stickers were placed over the 25 cent price. Four variations on the 15 cent stickers are known. The 1940 edition was priced at 15 cents.

**NEW YORK: YEAR ZERO**
July?, 1988 - No. 4, Oct, 1988 ($2.00, B&W, mini-series)
Eclipse Comics

| | Good | Fine | N-Mint |
|---|---|---|---|
| 1-4 | .35 | 1.00 | 2.00 |

**NEXT MAN**
Mar, 1985 - No. 5, Oct, 1985 ($1.50, color; Baxter paper)
Comico

| | Good | Fine | N-Mint |
|---|---|---|---|
| 1-5 | .25 | .75 | 1.50 |

**NEXT NEXUS, THE**
Jan, 1989 - No. 4, April, 1989 ($1.95, mini-series, color, Baxter)
First Comics

| | Good | Fine | N-Mint |
|---|---|---|---|
| 1-4: By Baron & Rude | .35 | 1.00 | 2.00 |

**NEXUS** (See First Comics Graphic Novel #4, 19 & The Next Nexus)
June, 1981 - No. 6, Mar, 1984; No. 7, Apr, 1985 - Present
(Direct sale only, 36 pgs.; V2#1('83)-printed on Baxter paper
Capital Comics/First Comics No. 7 on

| | Good | Fine | N-Mint |
|---|---|---|---|
| 1-B&W version; magazine size | 3.50 | 10.00 | 20.00 |
| 1-B&W 1981 limited edition; 500 copies printed and signed; same as above except this version has a 2-pg. poster & a pencil sketch on paperboard by Rude | 5.00 | 15.00 | 30.00 |
| 2-B&W, magazine size | 1.70 | 5.00 | 10.00 |
| 3-B&W, magazine size; contains 33⅓ rpm record ($2.95 price) | 1.00 | 3.00 | 6.00 |
| V2#1-Color version | .60 | 1.75 | 3.50 |
| 2-49,51-72: 2-Nexus' origin begins | .35 | 1.00 | 2.00 |
| 50 ($3.50, 52 pgs.) | .60 | 1.75 | 3.50 |
| 73-80: 73-Begin $2.25-c | .40 | 1.15 | 2.30 |

NOTE: ***Bissette*** *c-29.* ***Rude*** *c-3(B&W), V2#1-22, 24-27, 33-36, 39-42, 45-48, 50, 58-60; a-1-3, V2#1-7, 8-16p, 18-22p, 24-27p, 33-36p, 39-42p, 45-48p, 50, 58, 59p, 60.* ***Paul Smith*** *a-37, 38, 43, 44, 51-55p; c-37, 38, 43, 44, 51-55.*

**NEXUS FILES**
1989 ($4.50, color/16 pgs. B&W, One-shot, squarebound, 52 pgs.)
First Comics

| | Good | Fine | N-Mint |
|---|---|---|---|
| 1-New Rude-a; info on Nexus | .75 | 2.25 | 4.50 |

**NEXUS LEGENDS**
May, 1989 - No. 23, Mar, 1991 ($1.50, color, Baxter paper)
First Comics

| | Good | Fine | N-Mint |
|---|---|---|---|
| 1-23: R/1-3(Capital) & early First Comics issues w/new Rude covers #1-6,9,10 | .25 | .75 | 1.50 |

**NICKEL COMICS**
1938 (Pocket size - 7½x5½")(132 pgs.)
Dell Publishing Co.

| | Good | Fine | N-Mint |
|---|---|---|---|
| 1-"Bobby & Chip" by Otto Messmer, Felix the Cat artist. Contains some English reprints | 27.00 | 80.00 | 185.00 |

**NICKEL COMICS**
May, 1940 - No. 8, Aug, 1940 (36 pgs.; Bi-Weekly; 5 cents)
Fawcett Publications

| | Good | Fine | N-Mint |
|---|---|---|---|
| 1-Origin/1st app. Bulletman | 110.00 | 330.00 | 770.00 |
| 2 | 50.00 | 150.00 | 350.00 |
| 3 | 43.00 | 130.00 | 300.00 |
| 4-The Red Gaucho begins | 39.00 | 115.00 | 270.00 |
| 5-7 | 34.00 | 102.00 | 240.00 |
| 8-World's Fair-c; Bulletman moved to Master Comics #7 in Oct. | 34.00 | 102.00 | 240.00 |

NOTE: ***Beck** c-5-8. **Jack Binder** c-1-4. Bondage c-5.*

**NICK FURY, AGENT OF SHIELD** (See Marv. Spotlight #31 & Shield)
6/68 - No. 15, 11/69; No. 16, 11/70 - No. 18, 3/71
Marvel Comics Group

| | Good | Fine | N-Mint |
|---|---|---|---|
| 1 | 4.30 | 13.00 | 30.00 |
| 2-4: 4-Origin retold | 2.30 | 7.00 | 16.00 |
| 5-Classic-c | 2.85 | 8.50 | 20.00 |
| 6,7 | 1.50 | 4.50 | 10.00 |
| 8-11,13: 9-Hate Monger begins (ends #11). 11-Smith-c. 13-Last 12 cent issue | .85 | 2.50 | 5.00 |
| 12-Smith-c/a | 1.00 | 3.00 | 6.00 |
| 14 | .50 | 1.50 | 3.00 |
| 15-(15 cents)-1st app. Bullseye (11/69) | 1.70 | 5.00 | 12.00 |
| 16-18-(25 cents, 52 pgs.)-r/Str. Tales #135-143 | .30 | .90 | 1.80 |

NOTE: ***Adkins** a-3i. **Craig** a-10i. **Sid Greene** a-12i. **Kirby** a-16-18r. **Springer** a-4, 6, 7, 8p, 9, 10p, 11; c-8, 9. **Steranko** a(p)-1-3, 5; c-1-7.*

**NICK FURY AGENT OF SHIELD** (Also see Strange Tales #135)
Dec, 1983 - No. 2, Jan, 1984 ($2.00, Baxter paper, 52 pgs.)
Marvel Comics Group

| | Good | Fine | N-Mint |
|---|---|---|---|
| 1,2-r/Nick Fury #1-4; new Steranko-c | .35 | 1.00 | 2.00 |

**NICK FURY, AGENT OF S.H.I.E.L.D.**
Sept, 1989 - Present ($1.50, color)
Marvel Comics

| | Good | Fine | N-Mint |
|---|---|---|---|
| V2#1-22: 13-Return of The Yelow Claw | .25 | .75 | 1.50 |

**NICK FURY VS. SHIELD**
June, 1988 - No. 6, Dec, 1988 ($3.50, 52pgs, color, deluxe format)
Marvel Comics

| | Good | Fine | N-Mint |
|---|---|---|---|
| 1-Steranko-c | 1.85 | 5.50 | 11.00 |
| 2 | 2.35 | 7.00 | 14.00 |
| 3 | 1.00 | 3.00 | 6.00 |
| 4-6 | .60 | 1.75 | 3.50 |

**NICK HALIDAY**
May, 1956
Argo

| | Good | Fine | N-Mint |
|---|---|---|---|
| 1-Daily & Sunday strip-r by Petree | 4.00 | 12.00 | 28.00 |

**NIGHT AND THE ENEMY** (Graphic Novel)
1988 (8½x11") (color; 80pgs.; $11.95)
Comico

| | Good | Fine | N-Mint |
|---|---|---|---|
| 1-Harlan Ellison scripts/Ken Steacy-c/a; r/Epic Illustrated & new-a (1st and 2nd printings) | 2.00 | 6.00 | 12.00 |
| 1-Limited edition ($39.95) | 7.00 | 20.00 | 39.95 |

**NIGHT BEFORE CHRISTMAS, THE** (See March of Comics No. 152)

**NIGHTBREED** (See Clive Barker's Nightbreed)

**NIGHTCRAWLER**
Nov, 1985 - No. 4, Feb, 1986 (Mini-series from X-Men)
Marvel Comics Group

| | Good | Fine | N-Mint |
|---|---|---|---|
| 1-Cockrum-c/a | .50 | 1.50 | 3.00 |
| 2-4 | .35 | 1.00 | 2.00 |

**NIGHT FORCE, THE** (See New Teen Titans #21)
Aug, 1982, No. 14, Sept, 1983 (60 cents)
DC Comics

| | Good | Fine | N-Mint |
|---|---|---|---|
| 1-14: 13-Origin The Baron. 14-Nudity panels | | .30 | .60 |

NOTE: ***Colan** c/a-1-14p. **Giordano** c-1i, 2i, 4i, 5i, 7i, 12i.*

**NIGHTINGALE, THE**
1948 (14 pgs., 7¼x10¼", ½B&W) (10 cents)
Henry H. Stansbury Once-Upon-A-Time Press, Inc.

(Very Rare)-Low distribution; distributed to Westchester County & Bronx, N.Y. only; used in **Seduction of the Innocent**, pf. 312,313 as the 1st and only "good" comic book ever published. Ill. by Dong Kingman; 1,500 words of text, printed on high quality paper & no word balloons. Copyright registered 10/22/48, distributed week of 12/5/48. (By Hans Christian Andersen) Estimated value ........ $135

**NIGHTMARE**
Summer, 1952 - No. 2, Fall, 1952; No. 3,4, 1953 (Painted-c)
Ziff-Davis (Approved Comics)/St. John No. 3,4

| | Good | Fine | N-Mint |
|---|---|---|---|
| 1-1pg. Kinstler-a; Tuska-a(2) | 19.00 | 58.00 | 135.00 |
| 2-Kinstler-a-Poe's "Pit & the Pendulum" | 13.00 | 40.00 | 90.00 |
| 3-Kinstler-a | 11.50 | 34.00 | 80.00 |
| 4 | 9.30 | 28.00 | 65.00 |

**NIGHTMARE** (Weird Horrors #1-9) (Amazing Ghost Stories #14 on)
No. 10, Dec, 1953 - No. 13, Aug, 1954
St. John Publishing Co.

| | Good | Fine | N-Mint |
|---|---|---|---|
| 10-Reprints Ziff-Davis Weird Thrillers #2 w/new Kubert-c plus 2 pgs. Kinstler-a; Anderson, Colan & Toth-a | 20.00 | 60.00 | 140.00 |
| 11-Krigstein-a; Poe adapt., "Hop Frog" | 14.00 | 43.00 | 100.00 |
| 12-Kubert bondage-c; adaptation of Poe's "The Black Cat;" Cannibalism story | 11.50 | 34.00 | 80.00 |
| 13-Reprints Z-D Weird Thrillers #3 with new cover; Powell-a(2), Tuska-a; Baker-c | 7.00 | 21.00 | 50.00 |

**NIGHTMARE** (Magazine)
Dec, 1970 - No. 23, Feb, 1975 (B&W, 68 pages)
Skywald Publishing Corp.

| | Good | Fine | N-Mint |
|---|---|---|---|
| 1-Everett-a | 1.15 | 3.50 | 8.00 |
| 2-5: 4-Decapitation story | .85 | 2.50 | 5.00 |
| 6-Kaluta-a; Jeff Jones photo & interview | .85 | 2.50 | 5.00 |
| 7,9,10 | .70 | 2.00 | 4.00 |
| 8-Features E. C. movie "Tales From the Crypt;" reprints some E.C. comics panels | 1.30 | 4.00 | 9.00 |
| 11-23: 12-Excessive gore, severed heads. 20-Severed head-c. 21-(1974 Summer Special)-Kaluta-a. 22-Tomb of Horror issue. 23-(1975 Winter Special) | .40 | 1.25 | 2.50 |
| Annual 1(1972)-B. Jones-a | .60 | 1.80 | 3.50 |
| Winter Special 1(1973) | .60 | 1.80 | 3.50 |
| Yearbook-nn(1974) | .60 | 1.80 | 3.50 |

NOTE: ***Adkins** a-5. **Boris** c-2, 3, 5 (#4 is not by Boris). **Byrne** a-20p. **Everett** a-4, 5. **Jeff Jones** a-6, 21r(Psycho #6); c-6. **Katz** a-5. **Reese** a-4, 5. **Wildey** a-5, 6, 21, '74 Yearbook. **Wrightson** a-9.*

**NIGHTMARE** (Alex Nino's)
1989 ($1.95, color)
Innovation Publishing

| | Good | Fine | N-Mint |
|---|---|---|---|
| 1-Alex Nino-a | .35 | 1.00 | 2.00 |

**NIGHTMARE & CASPER** (See Harvey Hits #71) (Casper & Nightmare #6 on)(See Casper The Friendly Ghost #19)
Aug, 1963 - No. 5, Aug, 1964 (25 cents)
Harvey Publications

| | Good | Fine | N-Mint |
|---|---|---|---|
| 1-All reprints? | 5.35 | 16.00 | 32.00 |
| 2-5: All reprints? | 2.35 | 7.00 | 14.00 |

**NIGHTMARE ON ELM STREET** (Magazine)
Oct, 1989 - No. 2, Dec, 1989 ($2.25, B&W, movie adaptation)

*Nickel Comics #1, © FAW*

*Nick Fury, Agent of Shield #8 (1/69), © MEG*

*Nightmare #1, © Z-D*

Night of Mystery #1, © AVON

Northwest Mounties #2, © STJ

Not Brand Echh #8, © MEG

Marvel Comics — Good / Fine / N-Mint

1,2: Origin Freddy Krueger; Buckler/Alcala-a .40 1.15 2.30

**NIGHTMARES** (See Do You Believe in Nightmares)

**NIGHTMARES**
May, 1985 - No. 2, May, 1985 ($1.75, color, Baxter paper)
Eclipse Comics

1,2 .30 .90 1.80

**NIGHTMASK**
Nov, 1986 - No. 12, Oct, 1987
Marvel Comics Group

1-12 .40 .80

**NIGHT MASTER**
Feb, 1987 ($1.50, B&W, 28 pgs.)
Silverwolf Comics

1-Tim Vigil-c/a .70 2.00 4.00

**NIGHT MUSIC** (See Eclipse Graphic Album Series, The Magic Flute)
Dec, 1984 - No. 7, Feb, 1988 ($1.75, color, Baxter paper)
Eclipse Comics

1-7: 3-Russell's Jungle Book adapt. 4,5-Pelleas And Melisande (double titled). 6-Salome' (double titled). 7-Red Dog #1 .30 .90 1.80

**NIGHT NURSE**
Nov, 1972 - No. 4, May, 1973
Marvel Comics Group

1-4 .40 .80

**NIGHT OF MYSTERY**
1953 (no month) (One Shot)
Avon Periodicals

nn-1pg. Kinstler-a, Hollingsworth-c 16.00 48.00 110.00

**NIGHT OF THE GRIZZLY, THE** (See Movie Classics)

**NIGHT RIDER**
Oct, 1974 - No. 6, Aug, 1975
Marvel Comics Group

1: 1-6 reprint Ghost Rider #1-6 (#1-origin) .60 1.20
2-6 .40 .80

**NIGHTVEIL** (See Femforce)
Nov, 1984 - No. 7, 1985 ($1.75, color)
Americomics/AC Comics

1 .50 1.50 3.00
2-7 .35 1.00 2.00
...'s Cauldron Of Horror 1 (1989, $2.50, B&W)-Kubert, Powell, Wood-r plus new Nightveil story .40 1.25 2.50
...'s Cauldron Of Horror 2 (1990, $2.95, B&W, 44 pgs.)-Pre-code horror-r by Kubert & Powell .50 1.50 3.00
Special 1 ('88, $1.95)-Kaluta-c .35 1.00 2.00

**NIGHTWINGS** (See DC Science Fiction Graphic Novel)

**NIKKI, WILD DOG OF THE NORTH** (See 4-Color 1226 & Movie Comics)

**1984** (Magazine) (1994 #11 on)
June, 1978 - No. 10, Jan, 1980 ($1.50)
Warren Publishing Co.

1-Nino-a in all .50 1.50 3.00
2-10 .30 .90 1.80

NOTE: ***Alacla** a-1-3, 5i. **Corben** a-1-8; c-1, 2. **Thorne** a-7-10. **Wood** a-1, 2, 5i.*

**1994** (Formerly 1984) (Magazine)
No. 11, Feb, 1980 - No. 29, Feb, 1983
Warren Publishing Co.

11-29: 27-The Warhawks return .35 1.00 2.00

NOTE: ***Corben** c-26. **Nino** a-11-19, 20(2), 21, 25, 26, 28; c-21. **Redondo** c-20. **Thorne** a-11-14, 17-21, 25, 26, 28, 29.*

**NINTENDO COMICS SYSTEM**
1990 - Present ($4.95, color, card stock-c, 68 pgs.)
Valiant Comics — Good / Fine / N-Mint

1-3: 3-Layton-c (features 8 stories each) .85 2.50 5.00

**NIPPY'S POP**
1917 (Sunday strip reprints-B&W) (10½x13½")
The Saalfield Publishing Co.

nn-32 pages 8.00 24.00 56.00

**NOAH'S ARK**
1973 (35-49 Cents)
Spire Christian Comics/Fleming H. Revell Co.

nn-By Al Hartley .40 .80

**NOID IN 3-D, THE** (See Blackthorne 3-D Series #74 & 80)

**NOMAD** (See Captain America #180)
Nov, 1990 - No. 4, Feb, 1991 ($1.50, color)
Marvel Comics

1-4: 1,4-Captain America app. .25 .75 1.50

**NOMAN** (See Thunder Agents)
Nov, 1966 - No. 2, March, 1967 (25 cents, 68 pgs.)
Tower Comics

1-Wood/Williamson-c; Lightning begins; Dynamo cameo; Kane-a(p) 3.60 11.00 25.00
2-Wood-c only; Dynamo x-over; Whitney-a-#1,2 2.15 6.50 15.00

**NONE BUT THE BRAVE** (See Movie Classics)

**NOODNIK COMICS** (See Pinky the Egghead)
1953; No. 2, Feb, 1954 - No. 5, Aug, 1954
Comic Media/Mystery/Biltmore

3-D(1953-Comic Media)(#1) 23.00 70.00 160.00
2-5 2.65 8.00 18.00

**NORMALMAN**
Jan, 1984 - No. 12, Dec, 1985 ($1.70-$2.00, color)
Aardvark-Vanaheim/Renegade Press

1-5 ($1.70)-Jim Valentino-c/a in all .30 .85 1.70
6-12 ($2.00): 10-Cerebus cameo .35 1.00 2.00
3-D 1(Annual, 1986, $2.25) .40 1.15 2.30
...The Novel (Published by Slave Labor Graphics)($12.95)-R/all issues 2.15 6.50 12.95

**NORTH AVENUE IRREGULARS** (See Walt Disney Showcase #49)

**NORTH TO ALASKA** (See 4-Color No. 1155)

**NORTHWEST MOUNTIES** (Also see Approved Comics #12)
Oct, 1948 - No. 4, July, 1949
Jubilee Publications/St. John

1-Rose of the Yukon by Matt Baker; Walter Johnson-a; Lubbers-c 18.00 54.00 125.00
2-Baker-a; Lubbers-c. Ventrilo app. 13.00 40.00 90.00
3-Bondage-c, Baker-a; Sky Chief, K-9 app. 13.50 41.00 95.00
4-Baker-c, 2 pgs.; Blue Monk app. 13.50 41.00 95.00

**NO SLEEP 'TIL DAWN** (See 4-Color #831)

**NOT BRAND ECHH** (Brand Echh #1-4; See Crazy, 1973)
Aug, 1967 - No. 13, May, 1969 (No. 9-13: 25 cents, 68 pages)
Marvel Comics Group (LMC)

1: 1-8 are 12 cent issues 2.65 8.00 18.00
2-4: 3-Origin Thor, Hulk & Capt. America; Monkees, Alfred E. Neuman cameo. 4-X-Men app. 1.50 4.50 10.00
5-8: 5-Origin/intro. Forbush Man. 7-Origin Fantastical-4 & Stupor-man. 8-Beatles cameo; X-Men satire 1.50 4.50 10.00
9-13-All Giants. 9-Beatles cameo. 10-All-r; The Old Witch, Crypt Keeper & Vault Keeper cameos. 12,13-Beatles cameo, Avengers

| | Good | Fine | N-Mint |
|---|---|---|---|
| satire #12 | 1.50 | 4.50 | 10.00 |

NOTE: ***Colan** a-4p, 5p, 8p. **Everett** a-1i. **Kirby** a(p)-1, 3, 5-7, 10; c-1. **Severin** a-1; c-3, 7, 8. **Sutton** a-4, 5i, 7i, 8; c-5. Archie satire in #9. Avengers satire in #8.*

**NOTHING CAN STOP THE JUGGERNAUT**
1989 ($3.95, color)
Marvel Comics

| | Good | Fine | N-Mint |
|---|---|---|---|
| 1-r/Amazing Spider-Man #229 & 230 | .70 | 2.00 | 4.00 |

**NO TIME FOR SERGEANTS** (TV)
No. 914, July, 1958; Feb-Apr, 1965 - No. 3, Aug-Oct, 1965
Dell Publishing Co.

| | Good | Fine | N-Mint |
|---|---|---|---|
| 4-Color 914 (Movie)-Toth-a | 6.00 | 18.00 | 42.00 |
| 1(2-4/65)-3 (TV): Photo-c | 2.30 | 7.00 | 16.00 |

**NOVA** (The Man Called. . .No. 22-25)
Sept, 1976 - No. 25, May, 1979
Marvel Comics Group

| | Good | Fine | N-Mint |
|---|---|---|---|
| 1-Origin/1st app. Nova | .50 | 1.50 | 3.00 |
| 2-25: 4-Thor x-over. 13-Intro Crime-Buster. 14-Last 30 cent issue. 18-Yellow Claw app. | | .60 | 1.20 |

NOTE: ***Austin** c-21i, 23i. **John Buscema** a(p)-1-3, 8, 21; c-1p, 2, 15. **Infantino** a(p)-15-20, 22-25; c-17-20, 21p, 23p, 24p. **Kirby** c-4p, 5, 7. **Nebres** c-25i. **Simonson** a-23i.*

**NOW AGE ILLUSTRATED** (See Pendulum Illustrated Classics)

**NTH MAN THE ULTIMATE NINJA** (See Marvel Comics Presents 25)
Aug, 1989 - No. 16, Sept, 1990 ($1.00, color)
Marvel Comics

| | Good | Fine | N-Mint |
|---|---|---|---|
| 1-Ninja mercenary | .25 | .80 | 1.60 |
| 2-16: 10-on title is just "Nth Man" | | .50 | 1.00 |

**NUCLEUS** (Also see Cerebus)
May, 1979 ($1.50, B&W, adult fanzine)
Heiro-Graphic Publications

| | Good | Fine | N-Mint |
|---|---|---|---|
| 1-Contains "Demonhorn" by Dave Sim, 1st app. of Cerebus The Aardvark, 4 pg. story | 4.30 | 13.00 | 30.00 |

**NUKLA**
Oct-Dec, 1965 - No. 4, Sept, 1966
Dell Publishing Co.

| | Good | Fine | N-Mint |
|---|---|---|---|
| 1-Origin Nukla (super hero) | 1.70 | 5.00 | 12.00 |
| 2,3 | 1.00 | 3.00 | 7.00 |
| 4-Ditko-a, c(p) | 1.15 | 3.50 | 8.00 |

**NURSE BETSY CRANE** (Formerly Teen Secret Diary)
V2#12, Aug, 1961 - V2#27, Mar, 1964 (See Soap Opera Romances)
Charlton Comics

| | Good | Fine | N-Mint |
|---|---|---|---|
| V2#12-27 | .35 | 1.00 | 2.00 |

**NURSE HELEN GRANT** (See The Romances of. . .)

**NURSE LINDA LARK** (See Linda Lark)

**NURSERY RHYMES**
No. 2, 1950 - No. 10, July-Aug, 1951 (Painted-c)
Ziff-Davis Publ. Co. (Approved Comics)

| | Good | Fine | N-Mint |
|---|---|---|---|
| 2 | 8.00 | 24.00 | 55.00 |
| 3-10: 10-Howie Post-a | 5.00 | 15.00 | 35.00 |

**NURSES, THE** (TV)
April, 1963 - No. 3, Oct, 1963 (Photo-c: #1,2)
Gold Key

| | Good | Fine | N-Mint |
|---|---|---|---|
| 1 | 1.50 | 4.50 | 10.00 |
| 2,3 | .85 | 2.50 | 6.00 |

**NUTS!** (Satire)
March, 1954 - No. 5, Nov, 1954
Premiere Comics Group

| | Good | Fine | N-Mint |
|---|---|---|---|
| 1-Hollingsworth-a | 10.00 | 30.00 | 70.00 |
| 2,4,5: 5-Capt. Marvel parody | 7.00 | 21.00 | 50.00 |
| 3-Drug "reefers" mentioned | 8.00 | 24.00 | 50.00 |

**NUTS** (Magazine) (Satire)
Feb, 1958 - No. 2, April, 1958
Health Knowledge

| | Good | Fine | N-Mint |
|---|---|---|---|
| 1 | 2.85 | 8.50 | 20.00 |
| 2 | 2.00 | 6.00 | 14.00 |

**NUTS & JOLTS** (See Large Feature Comic #22)

**NUTSY SQUIRREL** (Formerly Hollywood Funny Folks)
(Also see Comic Cavalcade)
#61, 9-10/54 - #69, 1-2/56; #70, 8-9/56 - #71, 10-11/56; #72, 11/57
National Periodical Publications

| | Good | Fine | N-Mint |
|---|---|---|---|
| 61-Mayer-a; Grossman-a in all | 4.00 | 12.00 | 28.00 |
| 62-72: Mayer a-62,65,67-72 | 2.65 | 8.00 | 18.00 |

**NUTTY COMICS**
Winter, 1946 (Funny animal)
Fawcett Publications

| | Good | Fine | N-Mint |
|---|---|---|---|
| 1-Capt. Kidd story; 1pg. Wolverton-a | 7.00 | 21.00 | 50.00 |

**NUTTY COMICS**
1945 - No. 8, June-July, 1947
Home Comics (Harvey Publications)

| | Good | Fine | N-Mint |
|---|---|---|---|
| nn-Helpful Hank, Bozo Bear & others | 3.00 | 9.00 | 21.00 |
| 2-4 | 2.00 | 6.00 | 14.00 |
| 5-8: 5-Rags Rabbit begins(1st app.); infinity-c | 1.50 | 4.50 | 10.00 |

**NUTTY LIFE**
No. 2, Summer, 1946
Fox Features Syndicate

| | Good | Fine | N-Mint |
|---|---|---|---|
| 2 | 4.00 | 12.00 | 28.00 |

**NYOKA, THE JUNGLE GIRL** (Formerly Jungle Girl; see The Further Adventures of. . ., Master Comics #50 & XMas Comics)
No. 2, Winter, 1945 - No. 77, June, 1953 (Movie serial)
Fawcett Publications

| | Good | Fine | N-Mint |
|---|---|---|---|
| 2 | 34.00 | 103.00 | 240.00 |
| 3 | 19.00 | 57.00 | 135.00 |
| 4,5 | 16.00 | 48.00 | 110.00 |
| 6-10 | 11.50 | 34.00 | 80.00 |
| 11,13,14,16-18-Krigstein-a | 11.50 | 34.00 | 80.00 |
| 12,15,19,20 | 9.30 | 28.00 | 65.00 |
| 21-30: 25-Clayton Moore photo-c? | 5.70 | 17.00 | 40.00 |
| 31-40 | 4.30 | 13.00 | 30.00 |
| 41-50 | 3.15 | 9.50 | 22.00 |
| 51-60 | 2.30 | 7.00 | 16.00 |
| 61-77 | 1.70 | 5.00 | 12.00 |

NOTE: *Photo-c from movies 25, 27, 28, 30-70. Bondage c-4, 5, 7, 8, 14, 24.*

**NYOKA, THE JUNGLE GIRL** (Formerly Zoo Funnies; Space Adventures #23 on)
No. 14, Nov, 1955 - No. 22, Nov, 1957
Charlton Comics

| | Good | Fine | N-Mint |
|---|---|---|---|
| 14 | 3.50 | 10.50 | 24.00 |
| 15-22 | 2.30 | 7.00 | 16.00 |

**OAK ISLAND ADVENTURE**
1990 ($5.95, color, graphic novel, 68 pgs.)
Disney Comics

| | Good | Fine | N-Mint |
|---|---|---|---|
| nn-Donald Duck, nephews & Scrooge McDuck | 1.00 | 3.00 | 6.00 |

**OAKLAND PRESS FUNNYBOOK, THE**
9/17/78 - 4/13/80 (16 pgs.) (Weekly)
Full color in comic book form; changes to tabloid size 4/20/80-on
The Oakland Press

Contains Tarzan by Manning, Marmaduke, Bugs Bunny, etc. (low distribution); 9/23/79 - 4/13/80 contain Buck Rogers by Gray Morrow

*Nova #4, © MEG*

*Nutsy Squirrel #66, © DC*

*Nyoka, the Jungle Girl #5, © FAW*

The Official Hawkman Index #1, © DC

Official True Crime Cases #25, © MEG

O.G. Whiz #1, © WEST

| | Good | Fine | N-Mint |
|---|---|---|---|
| & Jim Lawrence | .25 | .80 | 1.60 |

**OAKY DOAKS**
July, 1942 (One Shot)
Eastern Color Printing Co.

| | Good | Fine | N-Mint |
|---|---|---|---|
| 1 | 16.00 | 48.00 | 110.00 |

**OBIE**
1953 (6 cents)
Store Comics

| | Good | Fine | N-Mint |
|---|---|---|---|
| 1 | .70 | 2.00 | 4.00 |

**OBNOXIO THE CLOWN**
April, 1983 (One Shot) (Character from Crazy Magazine)
Marvel Comics Group

| | Good | Fine | N-Mint |
|---|---|---|---|
| 1-Vs. the X-Men | | .30 | .60 |

**OCCULT FILES OF DR. SPEKTOR, THE**
Apr, 1973 - No. 24, Feb, 1977; No. 25, May, 1982 (Painted-c #1-24)
Gold Key/Whitman No. 25

| | Good | Fine | N-Mint |
|---|---|---|---|
| 1-1st app. Lakota; Baron Tibor begins | .85 | 2.60 | 6.00 |
| 2-5 | .50 | 1.50 | 3.00 |
| 6-10 | .40 | 1.25 | 2.50 |
| 11-25: 11-1st app. Spektor as Werewolf. 14-Dr. Solar app. 25-Reprints | .25 | .75 | 1.50 |
| 9(Modern Comics reprint, 1977) | | .15 | .30 |

NOTE: *Also see Dan Curtis, Golden Comics Digest 33, Gold Key Spotlight, Mystery Comics Digest 5, & Spine Tingling Tales.*

**ODELL'S ADVENTURES IN 3-D** (See Adventures in 3-D)

**OFFICIAL CRISIS ON INFINITE EARTHS INDEX, THE**
March, 1986 ($1.75, color)
Independent Comics Group (Eclipse)

| | Good | Fine | N-Mint |
|---|---|---|---|
| 1 | .30 | .90 | 1.80 |

**OFFICIAL CRISIS ON INFINITE EARTHS CROSSOVER INDEX, THE**
July, 1986 ($1.75, color)
Independent Comics Group (Eclipse)

| | Good | Fine | N-Mint |
|---|---|---|---|
| 1 | .30 | .90 | 1.80 |

**OFFICIAL DOOM PATROL INDEX, THE**
Feb, 1986 - No. 2, Mar, 1986 ($1.50, color, 2 part series)
Independent Comics Group (Eclipse)

| | Good | Fine | N-Mint |
|---|---|---|---|
| 1,2 | .25 | .75 | 1.50 |

**OFFICIAL HANDBOOK OF THE CONAN UNIVERSE** (See Handbook . . .)

**OFFICIAL HANDBOOK OF THE MARVEL UNIVERSE, THE**
Jan, 1983 - No. 15, May, 1984
Marvel Comics Group

| | Good | Fine | N-Mint |
|---|---|---|---|
| 1-Lists Marvel heroes & villains (letter A) | 1.00 | 3.00 | 6.00 |
| 2 (B-C) | .85 | 2.50 | 5.00 |
| 3-5: 3-(C-D). 4-(D-G). 5-(H-J) | .70 | 2.00 | 4.00 |
| 6-9: 6-(K-L). 7-(M). 8-(N-P); Punisher-c. 9-(Q-S) | .50 | 1.50 | 3.00 |
| 10-15: 10-(S). 11-(S-U). 12-(V-Z); Wolverine-c. 13,14-Book of the Dead. 15-Weaponry catalogue | .40 | 1.25 | 2.50 |

NOTE: ***Byrne** c/a(p)-1-14; c-13-15p. **Grell** a-9. **Layton** a-2, 5, 7. **Miller** a-2, 3. **Nebres** a-3, 4, 8. **Simonson** a-11. **Paul Smith** a-1-3, 6, 7, 9, 10, 12. **Starlin** a-7. **Steranko** a-8p.*

**OFFICIAL HANDBOOK OF THE MARVEL UNIVERSE, THE**
Dec, 1985 - No. 20, April?, 1987 ($1.50 cover; maxi-series)
Marvel Comics Group

| | Good | Fine | N-Mint |
|---|---|---|---|
| V2#1-Byrne-c | .70 | 2.00 | 4.00 |
| 2-5: 2,3-Byrne-c | .50 | 1.50 | 3.00 |
| 6-10 | .40 | 1.25 | 2.50 |
| 11-20 | .35 | 1.00 | 2.00 |
| Trade paperback Vol. 1-9 | 1.15 | 3.50 | 7.00 |

**OFFICIAL HANDBOOK OF THE MARVEL UNIVERSE, THE**
July, 1989 - No. 8, Mid-Dec, 1990 ($1.50, color, mini-series, 52 pgs.)
Marvel Comics

| | Good | Fine | N-Mint |
|---|---|---|---|
| V3#1-8: 1-McFarlane-a(2 pgs.) | .25 | .75 | 1.50 |

**OFFICIAL HAWKMAN INDEX, THE**
Nov, 1986 - No. 2, Dec, 1986 ($2.00)
Independent Comics Group

| | Good | Fine | N-Mint |
|---|---|---|---|
| 1,2 | .35 | 1.00 | 2.00 |

**OFFICIAL JUSTICE LEAGUE OF AMERICA INDEX, THE**
April, 1986 - No. 8, Mar, 1987 ($2.00, Baxter)
Independent Comics Group (Eclipse)

| | Good | Fine | N-Mint |
|---|---|---|---|
| 1-8 | .35 | 1.00 | 2.00 |

**OFFICIAL LEGION OF SUPER-HEROES INDEX, THE**
Dec, 1986 - No. 5, 1987 ($2.00, color)(No Official in title #2 on)
Independent Comics Group (Eclipse)

| | Good | Fine | N-Mint |
|---|---|---|---|
| 1-5: 4-Mooney-c | .35 | 1.00 | 2.00 |

**OFFICIAL MARVEL INDEX TO MARVEL TEAM-UP**
Jan, 1986 - No. 6?, 1986 ($1.25, color)
Marvel Comics Group

| | Good | Fine | N-Mint |
|---|---|---|---|
| 1-6 | | .65 | 1.30 |

**OFFICIAL MARVEL INDEX TO THE AMAZING SPIDER-MAN**
Apr, 1985 - No. 9, Dec, 1985 ($1.25, color)
Marvel Comics Group

| | Good | Fine | N-Mint |
|---|---|---|---|
| 1 ($1.00-c) | .40 | 1.25 | 2.50 |
| 2-9: 5,6,8,9-Punisher-c | .35 | 1.00 | 2.00 |

**OFFICIAL MARVEL INDEX TO THE AVENGERS, THE**
June, 1987 - No. 7, Oct, 1988 ($2.95, color, squarebound, 52 pgs.)
Marvel Comics Group

| | Good | Fine | N-Mint |
|---|---|---|---|
| V5#1-7: All have wraparound-c | .50 | 1.50 | 3.00 |

**OFFICIAL MARVEL INDEX TO THE FANTASTIC FOUR**
Dec, 1985 - No. 5, 1986 ($1.25, color)
Marvel Comics Group

| | Good | Fine | N-Mint |
|---|---|---|---|
| 1-5: 1-Byrne-c | .25 | .75 | 1.50 |

**OFFICIAL MARVEL INDEX TO THE X-MEN, THE**
May, 1987 - No. 8, 1988? ($2.95, color, squarebound, 52 pgs.)
Marvel Comics Group

| | Good | Fine | N-Mint |
|---|---|---|---|
| V4#1-8: All have wraparound-c | .50 | 1.50 | 3.00 |

**OFFICIAL SOUPY SALES COMIC** (See Soupy Sales)

**OFFICIAL TEEN TITANS INDEX, THE**
Aug, 1985 - No. 5, 1986 ($1.50, color)
Independent Comics Group (Eclipse)

| | Good | Fine | N-Mint |
|---|---|---|---|
| 1-5 | .25 | .75 | 1.50 |

**OFFICIAL TRUE CRIME CASES** (Formerly Sub-Mariner #23; All-True Crime Cases #26 on)
No. 24, Fall, 1947 - No. 25, Winter, 1947-48
Marvel Comics (OCI)

| | Good | Fine | N-Mint |
|---|---|---|---|
| 24(#1)-Burgos-a; Syd Shores-c | 8.50 | 25.50 | 60.00 |
| 25-Kurtzman's "Hey Look" | 7.00 | 21.00 | 50.00 |

**OF SUCH IS THE KINGDOM**
1955 (36 pgs., 15 cents)
George A. Pflaum

| | Good | Fine | N-Mint |
|---|---|---|---|
| nn-R-/1951 Treasure Chest | 1.15 | 3.50 | 8.00 |

**O.G. WHIZ** (See Gold Key Spotlight #10)
2/71 - No. 6, 5/72; No. 7, 5/78 - No. 11, 1/79 (No. 7: 52 pgs.)
Gold Key

| | Good | Fine | N-Mint |
|---|---|---|---|
| 1,2-John Stanley scripts | 5.00 | 15.00 | 35.00 |
| 3-6(1972) | 2.00 | 6.00 | 14.00 |
| 7-11('78-'79)-Part-r: 9-Tubby app. | .60 | 1.75 | 3.50 |

**OH, BROTHER!** (Teen Comedy)
Jan, 1953 - No. 5, Oct, 1953

Stanhall Publ.

| | Good | Fine | N-Mint |
|---|---|---|---|
| 1-By Bill Williams | 2.65 | 8.00 | 18.00 |
| 2-5 | 1.50 | 4.50 | 10.00 |

**OH SKIN-NAY!**
1913 (8½x13")
P.F. Volland & Co.

| | | | |
|---|---|---|---|
| nn-The Days Of Real Sport by Briggs | 11.50 | 34.00 | 80.00 |

**OH SUSANNA** (See 4-Color #1105)

**OKAY COMICS**
July, 1940
United Features Syndicate

| | | | |
|---|---|---|---|
| 1-Captain & the Kids & Hawkshaw the Detective reprints | 22.00 | 65.00 | 150.00 |

**OK COMICS**
July, 1940 - No. 2, Oct, 1940
United Features Syndicate

| | | | |
|---|---|---|---|
| 1-Little Giant, Phantom Knight, Sunset Smith, & The Teller Twins begin | 35.00 | 105.00 | 245.00 |
| 2 (Rare)-Origin Mister Mist | 30.00 | 90.00 | 210.00 |

**OKLAHOMA KID**
June, 1957 - No. 4, 1958
Ajax/Farrell Publ.

| | | | |
|---|---|---|---|
| 1 | 4.00 | 12.00 | 28.00 |
| 2-4 | 2.00 | 6.00 | 14.00 |

**OKLAHOMAN, THE** (See 4-Color #820)

**OLD GLORY COMICS**
1944 (Giveaway)
Chesapeake & Ohio Railway

| | | | |
|---|---|---|---|
| nn-Capt. Fearless reprint | 2.35 | 7.00 | 16.00 |

**OLD IRONSIDES** (See 4-Color #874)

**OLD YELLER** (See 4-Color #869, Movie Comics, and Walt Disney Showcase #25)

**OMAC** (One Man Army, . . . Corps. #4 on; also see Warlord)
Sept-Oct, 1974 - No. 8, Nov-Dec, 1975
National Periodical Publications

| | | | |
|---|---|---|---|
| 1-Origin | .35 | 1.00 | 2.00 |
| 2-8: 8-2pg. Neal Adams ad | .25 | .75 | 1.50 |

NOTE: ***Kirby*** *a-1-8p; c-1-7p.* ***Kubert*** *c-8. See Kamandi #59 & Cancelled Comic Caval.*

**OMAHA THE CAT DANCER**
1984 (no month) - No. 2, 1984 ($1.60-$1.75, B&W, adults)
SteelDragon Press

| | | | |
|---|---|---|---|
| 1-Preview ($1.60) | 1.70 | 5.00 | 10.00 |
| 1-Regular 1 | 1.15 | 3.50 | 7.00 |
| 1-2nd print | .35 | 1.00 | 2.00 |
| 2-($1.75-c) | .85 | 2.50 | 5.00 |

**OMAHA THE CAT DANCER**
184 - Present ($2.00, B&W, adults)
Kitchen Sink Press

| | | | |
|---|---|---|---|
| 1-Reprints SteelDragon #1 | 1.15 | 3.50 | 7.00 |
| 1-2nd printing ($2.50) | .50 | 1.50 | 3.00 |
| 2-Reprints SteelDragon #2 | .50 | 1.50 | 3.00 |
| 2-2nd printing | .35 | 1.00 | 2.00 |
| 3,4 | .50 | 1.50 | 3.00 |
| 3,4-2nd printings | .35 | 1.00 | 2.00 |
| 5-13 | .35 | 1.00 | 2.00 |
| 14-Begin $2.50-c? | .40 | 1.25 | 2.50 |

NOTE: *Issues 1 thru 13 have been reprinted with $2.50 cover price. 3rd prints exist?*

**O'MALLEY AND THE ALLEY CATS**
April, 1971 - No. 9, Jan, 1974 (Disney)
Gold Key

| | Good | Fine | N-Mint |
|---|---|---|---|
| 1 | 1.50 | 4.50 | 10.00 |
| 2-9 | .85 | 2.60 | 6.00 |

**OMEGA ELITE**
1987 ($1.25, color)
Blackthorne Publishing

| | | | |
|---|---|---|---|
| 1-Starlin-c | | .60 | 1.25 |

**OMEGA MEN, THE** (See Green Lantern #141)
Dec, 1982 - No. 38, May, 1986 ($1.00-$1.50; Baxter paper)
DC Comics

| | | | |
|---|---|---|---|
| 1 | .25 | .75 | 1.50 |
| 2,4,6-8,11-18,21-38: 2-Origin Broot. 7-Origin The Citadel. 26,27-Alan Moore scripts. 30-Intro new Primus. 31-Crisis x-over. 34,35-Teen Titans x-over. 37-Lobo cameo | | .50 | 1.00 |
| 3-1st app. Lobo (cameo, 2 pgs.)(2/83) | 1.50 | 4.50 | 10.00 |
| 5,9-2nd & 3rd app. Lobo (cameo, 2 pgs. each) | 1.00 | 3.00 | 6.00 |
| 10-1st full Lobo story | 1.50 | 4.50 | 10.00 |
| 19-Lobo cameo | .50 | 1.50 | 3.00 |
| 20-2nd full Lobo story | 1.00 | 3.00 | 6.00 |
| Annual 1(11/84, 52 pgs.), 2(11/85) | .25 | .75 | 1.50 |

NOTE: ***Giffen*** *c/a-1-6p.* ***Morrow*** *a-24r.* ***Nino*** *c/a-16, 21.*

**OMEGA THE UNKNOWN**
March, 1976 - No. 10, Oct, 1977
Marvel Comics Group

| | | | |
|---|---|---|---|
| 1 | .25 | .75 | 1.50 |
| 2-7,10: 2-Hulk app. 3-Electro app. | | .50 | 1.00 |
| 8-1st app. 2nd Foolkiller (Greg Salinger), small cameos only | .85 | 2.50 | 5.00 |
| 9-1st full app. Foolkiller | 1.15 | 3.50 | 7.00 |

NOTE: ***Kane*** *c(p)-3, 5, 8, 9.* ***Mooney*** *a-1-3, 4p, 5, 6p, 7, 8i, 9, 10.*

**OMEN**
1989 - Present? ($2.00, B&W, adults)
Northstar Publishing

| | | | |
|---|---|---|---|
| 1-Tim Vigil-c/a in all | 1.00 | 3.00 | 6.00 |
| 1-2nd printing | .40 | 1.25 | 2.50 |
| 2,3 | .50 | 1.50 | 3.00 |

**OMNI MEN**
1987 - No. 3? ($1.25, color)
Blackthorne Publishing

| | | | |
|---|---|---|---|
| 1-3 | | .60 | 1.25 |

**ONE, THE**
July, 1985 - No. 6, Feb, 1986 (Mini-series; adults only)
Epic Comics (Marvel)

| | | | |
|---|---|---|---|
| 1-Post nuclear holocaust super-hero | .25 | .75 | 1.50 |
| 2-6: 2-Intro. The Other | .25 | .75 | 1.50 |

**ONE-ARM SWORDSMAN, THE**
1987 - No. 12?, 1990 ($2.75-$1.80, color, 52 pgs.)
Victory Prod./Lueng's Publications #4 on

| | | | |
|---|---|---|---|
| 1-3 ($2.75) | .45 | 1.40 | 2.80 |
| 4-12: 4-6-$1.80-c. 7-12-$2.00-c | .30 | .90 | 1.80 |

**ONE HUNDRED AND ONE DALMATIANS** (See 4-Color #1183, Movie Comics, and Walt Disney Showcase #9,51)

**100 PAGES OF COMICS**
1937 (Stiff covers; square binding)
Dell Publishing Co.

| | | | |
|---|---|---|---|
| 101(Found on back cover)-Alley Oop, Wash Tubbs, Capt. Easy, Og Son of Fire, Apple Mary, Tom Mix, Dan Dunn, Tailspin Tommy, Doctor Doom | 60.00 | 180.00 | 420.00 |

**100 PAGE SUPER SPECTACULAR** (See DC 100 Page . . .)

**$1,000,000 DUCK** (See Walt Disney Showcase #5)

*Omaha the Cat Dancer #2, © SteelDragon*

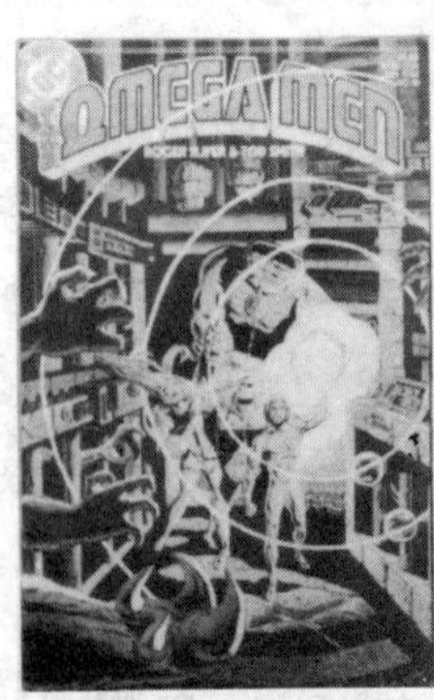

*The Omega Men #10, © DC*

*Omega the Unknown #8, © MEG*

Orbit #1, © Eclipse

The Original Astro Boy #5, © NBC

Oscar Comics #5, © MEG

**ONE MILLION YEARS AGO** (Tor #2 on)
September, 1953
St. John Publishing Co.

| | Good | Fine | N-Mint |
|---|---|---|---|
| 1-Origin; Kubert-c/a | 13.00 | 40.00 | 90.00 |

**ONE SHOT** (See 4-Color. . .)

**1001 HOURS OF FUN** (See Large Feature Comic #13)

**ON STAGE** (See 4-Color #1336)

**ON THE AIR**
1947 (Giveaway) (paper cover)
NBC Network Comic

| | | | |
|---|---|---|---|
| nn-(Rare) | 11.00 | 32.00 | 75.00 |

**ON THE DOUBLE** (See 4-Color #1232)

**ON THE LINKS**
December, 1926 (48 pages) (9x10")
Associated Feature Service

| | | | |
|---|---|---|---|
| nn-Daily strip-r | 9.00 | 27.00 | 62.00 |

**ON THE ROAD WITH ANDRAE CROUCH**
1973, 1977 (39 cents)
Spire Christian Comics (Fleming H. Revell)

| | | | |
|---|---|---|---|
| nn | | .50 | 1.00 |

**ON THE SPOT** (Pretty Boy Floyd. . .)
Fall, 1948
Fawcett Publications

| | | | |
|---|---|---|---|
| nn-Pretty Boy Floyd photo on-c; bondage-c | 14.00 | 43.00 | 100.00 |

**OPEN SPACE**
Mid-Dec, 1989 - No. 4, Aug, 1990 ($4.95, color, bi-monthly, 68 pgs.)
Marvel Comics

| | | | |
|---|---|---|---|
| 1-4: 1-Bill Wray-a; Freas-c | .85 | 2.50 | 5.00 |

**OPERATION BIKINI** (See Movie Classics)

**OPERATION BUCHAREST** (See The Crusaders)

**OPERATION CROSSBOW** (See Movie Classics)

**OPERATION PERIL**
Oct-Nov, 1950 - No. 16, Apr-May, 1953 (52 pgs.: #1-5)
American Comics Group (Michel Publ.)

| | | | |
|---|---|---|---|
| 1-Time Travelers, Danny Danger (by Leonard Starr) & Typhoon Tyler (by Ogden Whitney) begin | 13.00 | 40.00 | 90.00 |
| 2 | 8.00 | 24.00 | 55.00 |
| 3-5: 3-Horror story. 5-Sci/fi story | 7.00 | 21.00 | 50.00 |
| 6-12-Last Time Travelers | 5.70 | 17.00 | 40.00 |
| 13-16: All war format | 2.30 | 7.00 | 16.00 |

NOTE: *Starr a-2, 5. Whitney a-1, 2, 5-10, 12; c-1, 3, 5, 8, 9.*

**ORAL ROBERTS' TRUE STORIES** (Junior Partners #120 on)
1956 (no month) - No. 119, 7/59 (15 cents)(No #102: 25 cents)
TelePix Publ. (Oral Roberts' Evangelistic Assoc./Healing Waters)

| | | | |
|---|---|---|---|
| V1#1(1956)-(Not code approved)-"The Miracle Touch" | 8.50 | 25.50 | 60.00 |
| 102-(only issue approved by code)(10/56) | 4.30 | 13.00 | 30.00 |
| 103-119: 115-(114 on inside) | 2.65 | 8.00 | 18.00 |

NOTE: *Also see Happiness & Healing For You.*

**ORANGE BIRD, THE**
No date (1980) (36 pgs.; in color; slick cover)
Walt Disney Educational Media Co.

| | | | |
|---|---|---|---|
| nn-Included with educational kit on foods | | .30 | .60 |

**ORBIT**
1990 - Present ($4.95, color, squarebound, 52 pgs.)
Eclipse Books

| | | | |
|---|---|---|---|
| 1-3: Reprints from Isaac Asimov's Science Fiction Magazine; 1-Dave Stevens-c, Bolton-a. 3-Bolton-c/a, Yeates-a | .85 | 2.50 | 5.00 |

**ORIENTAL HEROES**
Aug, 1988 - Present ($1.50-$1.95, color, 68 pgs.)
Jademan Comics

| | Good | Fine | N-Mint |
|---|---|---|---|
| 1-9 ($1.50) | .25 | .75 | 1.50 |
| 10-26 ($1.95) | .35 | 1.00 | 2.00 |

**ORIGINAL ASTRO BOY, THE** (See Astro Boy)
Sept, 1987 - No. 19, 1989 ($1.50 - $1.75, color)
Now Comics

| | | | |
|---|---|---|---|
| 1-All have Ken Steacy painted-c/a | .50 | 1.50 | 3.00 |
| 2,3: 3-Begin $1.75-c | .35 | 1.00 | 2.00 |
| 4-19 | .25 | .75 | 1.50 |

**ORIGINAL BLACK CAT, THE**
Oct. 6, 1988 - Present ($2.00, color)
Recollections

| | | | |
|---|---|---|---|
| 1-3: Elias-r; 1-Bondage-c. 2-M. Anderson-c | .35 | 1.00 | 2.00 |

**ORIGINAL DICK TRACY, THE**
Sept, 1990 - Present ($1.95, color, bi-monthly, 68 pgs.)($2.00 #3 on)
Gladstone Publishing

| | | | |
|---|---|---|---|
| 1-4: 1-Vs. Pruneface. 2-& the Evil Influence | .35 | 1.00 | 2.00 |

NOTE: *#1 reprints strips 7/16/43 - 9/30/43; #2 reprints strips 12/1/46 - 2/2/47; #3 reprints 8/31/46 - 11/14/46; #4 reprints 9/17/45 - 12/23/45.*

**ORIGINAL E-MAN AND MICHAEL MAUSER, THE**
Oct, 1985 - No. 7, April, 1986 ($1.75 cover; Baxter paper)
First Comics

| | | | |
|---|---|---|---|
| 1-Has r-/Charlton's E-Man, Vengeance Squad | .35 | 1.00 | 2.00 |
| 2-6: 2-Shows #4 in indicia by mistake | .30 | .90 | 1.80 |
| 7 ($2.00; 44 pgs.)-Staton-a | .35 | 1.00 | 2.00 |

**ORIGINAL NEXUS GRAPHIC NOVEL** (See First Comics Graphic Novel #19)

**ORIGINAL SHIELD, THE**
April, 1984 - No. 4, Oct, 1984
Archie Enterprises, Inc.

| | | | |
|---|---|---|---|
| 1-4: 1,2-Origin Shield; Ayers p-1-4, Nebres c-1,2 | | .35 | .70 |

**ORIGINAL SWAMP THING SAGA, THE** (See DC Spec. Series #2, 14, 17, 20)

**OSCAR COMICS** (Formerly Funny Tunes; Awful. . .#11 & 12)
(Also see Cindy Comics)
No. 24, Spring, 1947 - No. 10, Apr, 1949; No. 13, Oct, 1949
Marvel Comics

| | | | |
|---|---|---|---|
| 24(#1, Spring, 1947) | 5.00 | 15.00 | 35.00 |
| 25(#2, Sum, '47)-Wolverton-a plus Kurtzman's "Hey Look" | 7.00 | 21.00 | 50.00 |
| 3-9,13: 8-Margie app. | 3.50 | 10.50 | 24.00 |
| 10-Kurtzman's "Hey Look" | 4.50 | 14.00 | 32.00 |

**OSWALD THE RABBIT** (Also see New Fun Comics #1)
No. 21, 1943 - No. 1268, 12-2/61-62 (Walter Lantz)
Dell Publishing Co.

| | | | |
|---|---|---|---|
| 4-Color 21(1943) | 24.00 | 73.00 | 170.00 |
| 4-Color 39(1943) | 17.00 | 51.00 | 120.00 |
| 4-Color 67(1944) | 11.50 | 34.00 | 80.00 |
| 4-Color 102(1946)-Kelly-a, 1 pg. | 10.00 | 30.00 | 70.00 |
| 4-Color 143,183 | 5.00 | 15.00 | 35.00 |
| 4-Color 225,273 | 3.00 | 9.00 | 21.00 |
| 4-Color 315,388 | 2.00 | 6.00 | 14.00 |
| 4-Color 458,507,549,593 | 1.30 | 4.00 | 9.00 |
| 4-Color 623,697,792,894,979,1268 | .85 | 2.50 | 6.00 |

**OSWALD THE RABBIT** (See The Funnies, March of Comics #7, 38, 53, 67, 81, 95, 111, 126, 141, 156, 171, 186, New Funnies & Super Book #8, 20)

**OUR ARMY AT WAR** (Sgt. Rock #302 on; Also see Army At War)
Aug, 1952 - No. 301, Feb, 1977
National Periodical Publications

| | | | |
|---|---|---|---|
| 1 | 50.00 | 150.00 | 350.00 |

| | Good | Fine | N-Mint |
|---|---|---|---|
| 2 | 24.00 | 70.00 | 165.00 |
| 3,4: 4-Krigstein-a | 22.00 | 65.00 | 150.00 |
| 5-7 | 14.00 | 43.00 | 100.00 |
| 8-11,14-Krigstein-a | 14.00 | 43.00 | 100.00 |
| 12,15-20 | 10.00 | 30.00 | 70.00 |
| 13-Krigstein c/a; flag-c | 16.00 | 48.00 | 110.00 |
| 21-31: Last precode (2/55) | 7.00 | 21.00 | 50.00 |
| 32-40 | 5.70 | 17.00 | 40.00 |
| 41-60 | 5.00 | 15.00 | 35.00 |
| 61-70 | 3.50 | 10.50 | 24.00 |
| 71-80 | 2.65 | 8.00 | 18.00 |
| 81-1st Sgt. Rock app. by Andru & Esposito in Easy Co. story | 52.00 | 154.00 | 360.00 |
| 82-Sgt. Rock cameo in Easy Co. story (6 panels) | 14.00 | 40.00 | 95.00 |
| 83-1st Kubert Sgt. Rock (6/59) | 16.00 | 50.00 | 115.00 |
| 84,86-90 | 5.70 | 17.00 | 40.00 |
| 85-Origin & 1st app. Ice Cream Soldier | 6.50 | 19.50 | 45.00 |
| 91-All Sgt. Rock issue | 13.00 | 40.00 | 90.00 |
| 92-100: 92-1st app. Bulldozer. 95-1st app. Zack | 3.60 | 11.00 | 25.00 |
| 101-120: 101-1st app. Buster. 111-1st app. Wee Willie & Sunny. 113-1st app. Jackie Johnson. 118-Sunny dies. 120-1st app. Wildman | 1.50 | 4.50 | 10.00 |
| 121-127,129-150: 126-1st app. Canary. 139-1st app. Little Sure Shot | 1.15 | 3.50 | 8.00 |
| 128-Training & origin Sgt. Rock | 5.00 | 15.00 | 35.00 |
| 151-Intro. Enemy Ace by Kubert | 4.00 | 12.00 | 28.00 |
| 152,154-157,159-163,165-170: 155-Enemy Ace story. 157-2 pg. pin-up. 162,163-Viking Prince x-over in Sgt. Rock | 1.00 | 3.00 | 6.00 |
| 153-2nd app. Enemy Ace | 2.85 | 8.50 | 20.00 |
| 158-Origin & 1st app. Iron Major(1965), formerly Iron Captain | 1.15 | 3.50 | 8.00 |
| 164-Giant G-19 | 1.15 | 3.50 | 8.00 |
| 171-176,178-181 | .70 | 2.00 | 4.00 |
| 177-(80 pg. Giant G-32) | 1.00 | 3.00 | 6.00 |
| 182,183,186-Neal Adams-a. 186-Origin retold | 1.15 | 3.50 | 7.00 |
| 184,185,187-189,191-199: 184-Wee Willie dies. 189-Intro. The Teen-age Underground Fighters of Unit 3 | .50 | 1.50 | 3.00 |
| 190-(80 pg. Giant G-44) | .70 | 2.00 | 4.00 |
| 200-12 pg. Rock story told in verse; Evans-a | .50 | 1.50 | 3.00 |
| 201-Krigstein-r/No. 14 | .50 | 1.50 | 3.00 |
| 202,206-215 | .35 | 1.00 | 2.00 |
| 203-(80 pg. Giant G-56)-All-r, no Sgt. Rock | .40 | 1.25 | 2.50 |
| 204,205-All reprints; no Sgt. Rock | .35 | 1.00 | 2.00 |
| 216,229-(80 pg. Giants G-68, G-80) | .40 | 1.25 | 2.50 |
| 217-228,230-239,241,243-301: 249-Wood-a | .35 | 1.00 | 2.00 |
| 240-Neal Adams-a | .40 | 1.25 | 2.50 |
| 242-(50 cent issue DC-9)-Kubert-c | .40 | 1.25 | 2.50 |

NOTE: ***Alcala*** *a-251.* ***Drucker*** *a-27, 67, 68, 79, 82, 83, 96, 164, 177, 203, 212, 243r, 244, 269r, 275r, 280r.* ***Evans*** *a-165-175, 200, 266, 269, 270, 274, 276, 278, 280.* ***Glanzman*** *a-218, 220, 222, 223, 225, 227, 230-232, 238, 240, 241, 244, 247, 248, 256-259, 261, 265-267, 271, 282, 283, 298.* ***Grell*** *a-287.* ***Heath*** *a-50, & most 176-271.* ***Kubert*** *a-38, 59, 67, 68 & most issues from 83-165.* ***Maurer*** *a-233, 237, 239, 240, 280, 284, 288, 290, 291, 295.* ***Severin*** *a-252, 265, 267, 269r, 272.* ***Toth*** *a-235, 241, 254.* ***Wildey*** *a-283-285, 287p.*

## OUR FIGHTING FORCES

Oct-Nov, 1954 - No. 181, Sept-Oct, 1978
National Periodical Publications/DC Comics

| | Good | Fine | N-Mint |
|---|---|---|---|
| 1-Grandenetti-c/a | 34.00 | 103.00 | 240.00 |
| 2 | 17.00 | 50.00 | 115.00 |
| 3-Kubert-c; last precode (3/55) | 14.00 | 43.00 | 100.00 |
| 4,5 | 11.00 | 32.00 | 75.00 |
| 6-9 | 9.30 | 28.00 | 65.00 |
| 10-Wood-a | 11.50 | 34.00 | 80.00 |
| 11-20 | 7.00 | 21.00 | 50.00 |
| 21-30 | 4.30 | 13.00 | 30.00 |
| 31-40 | 3.70 | 11.00 | 26.00 |
| 41-44: 41-Unknown Soldier tryout | 3.00 | 9.00 | 21.00 |
| 45-Gunner & Sarge begin (ends #94) | 11.00 | 32.00 | 75.00 |
| 46-50 | 2.65 | 8.00 | 18.00 |
| 51-64: 64-Last 10 cent issue | 1.50 | 4.50 | 10.00 |
| 65-90 | .85 | 2.50 | 5.00 |
| 91-100: 95-Devil-Dog begins, ends 98. 99-Capt. Hunter begins, ends #106 | .50 | 1.50 | 3.00 |
| 101-122: 106-Hunters Hellcats begin. 116-Mlle. Marie app. 121-Intro. Heller | .50 | 1.50 | 3.00 |
| 123-181: 123-Losers (Capt. Storm, Gunner/Sarge, Johnny Cloud) begin. 134,146-Toth-a | .50 | 1.50 | 3.00 |

NOTE: ***N. Adams*** *c-147.* ***Drucker*** *a-28, 37, 39, 42-44, 49, 53, 133r.* ***Evans*** *a-149, 164-174, 177-181.* ***Glanzman*** *a-125-128, 132, 134, 138-141, 143, 144.* ***Heath*** *a-2, 16, 18, 28, 41, 44, 49, 114, 135-138r; c-51.* ***Kirby*** *a-151-162p; c-152-159.* ***Kubert*** *c/a in many issues.* ***Maurer*** *a-135.* ***Redondo*** *a-166.* ***Severin*** *a-123-130, 131i, 132-150.*

## OUR FIGHTING MEN IN ACTION (See Men In Action)

## OUR FLAG COMICS

Aug, 1941 - No. 5, April, 1942
Ace Magazines

| | Good | Fine | N-Mint |
|---|---|---|---|
| 1-Captain Victory, The Unknown Soldier (intro.) & The Three Cheers begin | 100.00 | 300.00 | 700.00 |
| 2-Origin The Flag (patriotic hero); 1st app? | 50.00 | 150.00 | 350.00 |
| 3-5: 5-Intro & 1st app. Mr. Risk | 43.00 | 130.00 | 300.00 |

NOTE: ***Anderson*** *a-1, 4.* ***Mooney*** *a-1, 2; c-2.*

## OUR GANG COMICS (With Tom & Jerry #39-59; becomes Tom & Jerry #60 on; based on film characters)

Sept-Oct, 1942 - No. 59, June, 1949
Dell Publishing Co.

| | Good | Fine | N-Mint |
|---|---|---|---|
| 1-Our Gang & Barney Bear by Kelly, Tom & Jerry, Pete Smith, Flip & Dip, The Milky Way begin | 60.00 | 180.00 | 420.00 |
| 2 | 27.00 | 81.00 | 190.00 |
| 3-5: 3-Benny Burro begins | 18.00 | 54.00 | 125.00 |
| 6-Bumbazine & Albert only app. by Kelly | 31.00 | 92.00 | 220.00 |
| 7-No Kelly story | 14.00 | 42.00 | 100.00 |
| 8-Benny Burro begins by Barks | 31.00 | 92.00 | 215.00 |
| 9-Barks-a(2): Benny Burro & Happy Hound; no Kelly story | 25.00 | 75.00 | 175.00 |
| 10-Benny Burro by Barks | 20.00 | 60.00 | 140.00 |
| 11-1st Barney Bear & Benny Burro by Barks; Happy Hound by Barks | 20.00 | 60.00 | 140.00 |
| 12-20 | 12.00 | 36.00 | 84.00 |
| 21-30: 30-Christmas-c | 9.00 | 27.00 | 63.00 |
| 31-36-Last Barks issue | 6.50 | 19.50 | 45.00 |
| 37-40 | 2.65 | 8.00 | 18.00 |
| 41-50 | 2.00 | 6.00 | 14.00 |
| 51-57 | 1.70 | 5.00 | 12.00 |
| 58,59-No Kelly art or Our Gang stories | 1.50 | 4.50 | 10.00 |

NOTE: ***Barks*** *art in part only.* ***Barks*** *did not write Barney Bear stories #30-34. (See March of Comics #3,26). Early issues have photo back-c.*

## OUR LADY OF FATIMA

3/11/55 (15 cents) (36 pages)
Catechetical Guild Educational Society

| | Good | Fine | N-Mint |
|---|---|---|---|
| 395 | 1.70 | 5.00 | 12.00 |

## OUR LOVE (True Secrets #3 on)

Sept, 1949 - No. 2, Jan, 1950
Marvel Comics (SPC)

| | Good | Fine | N-Mint |
|---|---|---|---|
| 1-Photo-c | 5.00 | 15.00 | 35.00 |
| 2-Photo-c | 2.65 | 8.00 | 18.00 |

## OUR LOVE STORY

Oct, 1969 - No. 38, Feb, 1976
Marvel Comics Group

| | Good | Fine | N-Mint |
|---|---|---|---|
| 1 | .70 | 2.00 | 5.00 |
| 2-4,6-13: 2,9-J. Buscema-a | .50 | 1.50 | 3.00 |

*Our Army At War #62, © DC*

*Our Fighting Forces #156, © DC*

*Our Gang Comics #30, © M.G.M.*

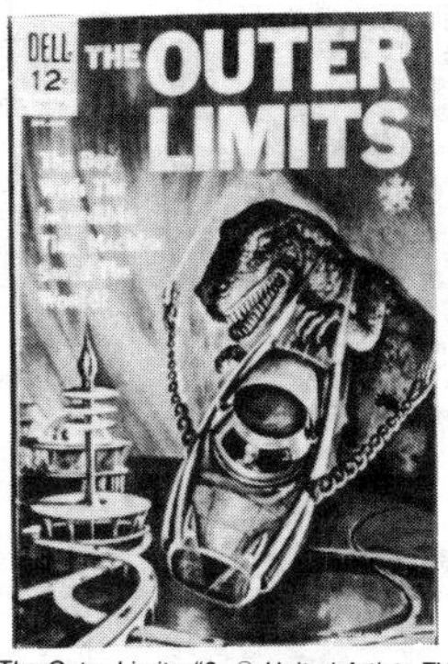

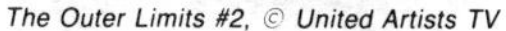
The Outer Limits #2, © United Artists TV

The Outlaws #14, © STAR

Out of the Night #2, © ACG

| | Good | Fine | N-Mint |
|---|---|---|---|
| 5-Steranko-a | 1.50 | 4.50 | 10.00 |
| 14-New story by Gary Fredrich & Tarpe' Mills | .55 | 1.65 | 4.00 |
| 15-38 | | .40 | .80 |

**OUR MISS BROOKS** (See 4-Color #751)

**OUR SECRET** (Formerly My Secret)
No. 4, Dec, 1949 - No. 8, Jun, 1950
Superior Comics Ltd.

| | Good | Fine | N-Mint |
|---|---|---|---|
| 4-Kamen-a; spanking scene | 5.00 | 15.00 | 35.00 |
| 5,6,8 | 3.50 | 10.50 | 24.00 |
| 7-Contains 9 pg. story intended for unpublished Ellery Queen #5 | 4.00 | 12.00 | 28.00 |

**OUTBURSTS OF EVERETT TRUE**
1921 (32 pages) (B&W)
Saalfield Publ. Co.

| | Good | Fine | N-Mint |
|---|---|---|---|
| 1907 (2-panel strips reprint) | 10.00 | 30.00 | 70.00 |

**OUTCASTS**
Oct, 1987 - No. 12, Sept, 1988 ($1.75, mini-series, color)
DC Comics

| | Good | Fine | N-Mint |
|---|---|---|---|
| 1-12 | .30 | .90 | 1.80 |

**OUTER LIMITS, THE** (TV)
Jan-Mar, 1964 - No. 18, Oct, 1969 (All painted-c)
Dell Publishing Co.

| | Good | Fine | N-Mint |
|---|---|---|---|
| 1 | 4.00 | 12.00 | 28.00 |
| 2 | 2.00 | 6.00 | 14.00 |
| 3-10 | 1.50 | 4.50 | 10.00 |
| 11-18: 17 reprints #1. 18-r-#2 | 1.15 | 3.50 | 8.00 |

**OUTER SPACE** (Formerly This Magazine Is Haunted, 2nd Series)
No. 17, May, 1958 - No. 25, Dec, 1959; Nov, 1968
Charlton Comics

| | Good | Fine | N-Mint |
|---|---|---|---|
| 17-Williamson/Wood style art; not by them (Sid Check?) | 5.00 | 15.00 | 35.00 |
| 18-20-Ditko-a | 7.00 | 21.00 | 50.00 |
| 21-25: 21-Ditko-c | 3.50 | 10.50 | 24.00 |
| V2#1(11/68)-Ditko-a, Boyette-c | 1.30 | 4.00 | 9.00 |

**OUTLANDERS**
Dec, 1988 - Present ($2.00-$2.25-$2.50, B&W, 44 pgs.)
Dark Horse Comics

| | Good | Fine | N-Mint |
|---|---|---|---|
| 1-7: Japanese Sci-fi manga | .35 | 1.00 | 2.00 |
| 8-21 ($2.25) | .40 | 1.15 | 2.30 |
| 22-25 ($2.50-c) | .40 | 1.25 | 2.50 |

**OUTLAW** (See Return of the . . .)

**OUTLAW FIGHTERS**
Aug, 1954 - No. 5, April, 1955
Atlas Comics (IPC)

| | Good | Fine | N-Mint |
|---|---|---|---|
| 1-Tuska-a | 5.00 | 15.00 | 35.00 |
| 2-5: 5-Heath-c/a, 7pgs. | 3.00 | 9.00 | 21.00 |

NOTE: *Heath c/a-5.* ***Maneely*** *c-2.* ***Pakula*** *a-2.* ***Reinman*** *a-2.* ***Tuska*** *a-1, 2.*

**OUTLAW KID, THE** (1st Series; see Wild Western)
Sept, 1954 - No. 19, Sept, 1957
Atlas Comics (CCC No. 1-11/EPI No. 12-29)

| | Good | Fine | N-Mint |
|---|---|---|---|
| 1-Origin; The Outlaw Kid & his horse Thunder begin; Black Rider app. | 10.00 | 30.00 | 70.00 |
| 2-Black Rider app. | 5.00 | 15.00 | 35.00 |
| 3-Woodbridge/Williamson-a | 5.00 | 15.00 | 35.00 |
| 4-7,9 | 3.50 | 10.50 | 24.00 |
| 8-Williamson/Woodbridge-a, 4 pgs. | 4.30 | 13.00 | 30.00 |
| 10-Williamson-a | 4.30 | 13.00 | 30.00 |
| 11-17,19 | 2.30 | 7.00 | 16.00 |
| 18-Williamson-a | 4.00 | 12.00 | 28.00 |

NOTE: ***Berg*** *a-4, 7, 13.* ***Maneely*** *c-1-3, 5-8, 11, 12, 18.* ***Pakula*** *a-3.* ***Severin*** *c-10.* ***Shores*** *a-1.* ***Wildey*** *a-1(3), 2-8, 10-18; c-4.*

**OUTLAW KID, THE** (2nd Series)
Aug, 1970 - No. 30, Oct, 1975
Marvel Comics Group

| | Good | Fine | N-Mint |
|---|---|---|---|
| 1,2-Reprints; 1-Orlando-r, Wildey-r(3) | .50 | 1.50 | 3.00 |
| 3,9-Williamson-a(r) | .25 | .75 | 1.50 |
| 4-8: 8-Crandall-r | | .50 | 1.00 |
| 10-30: 10-Origin; new-a in #10-16. 27-Origin r-/#10 | | .35 | .70 |

NOTE: ***Ayers*** *a-10, 27r.* ***Berg*** *a-7, 25r.* ***Gil Kane*** *c-10, 11, 15, 27r, 28.* ***Roussos*** *a-10i, 27i(r).* ***Severin*** *c-1, 9, 20.* ***Wildey*** *r-1, 3, 6, 7, 9, 19-22, 25, 26.* ***Williamson*** *a-28r.* ***Woodbridge*** *a(p)-9r.*

**OUTLAWS**
Feb-Mar, 1948 - No. 9, June-July, 1949
D. S. Publishing Co.

| | Good | Fine | N-Mint |
|---|---|---|---|
| 1 | 12.00 | 36.00 | 85.00 |
| 2-Ingels-a | 12.00 | 36.00 | 85.00 |
| 3,5,6: 3-Not Frazetta. 6-McWilliams-a | 5.00 | 15.00 | 35.00 |
| 4-Orlando-a | 6.50 | 19.00 | 45.00 |
| 7,8-Ingels-a in each | 9.30 | 28.00 | 65.00 |
| 9-(Scarce)-Frazetta-a, 7 pgs. | 27.00 | 81.00 | 190.00 |

NOTE: *Another #3 was printed in Canada with* ***Frazetta*** *art "Prairie Jinx," 7 pgs.*

**OUTLAWS, THE** (Formerly Western Crime Cases?)
No. 10, May, 1952 - No. 13, Sept, 1953; No. 14, April, 1954
Star Publishing Co.

| | Good | Fine | N-Mint |
|---|---|---|---|
| 10-L. B. Cole-c | 4.00 | 12.00 | 28.00 |
| 11-14-L. B. Cole-c. 14-Kamen, Feldstein-a | 3.00 | 9.00 | 21.00 |

**OUTLAWS OF THE WEST** (Formerly Cody of the Pony Express #10)
No. 11, 7/57 - No. 81, 5/70; No. 82, 7/79 - No. 88, 4/80
Charlton Comics

| | Good | Fine | N-Mint |
|---|---|---|---|
| 11 | 3.70 | 11.00 | 26.00 |
| 12,13,15-17,19,20 | 1.70 | 5.00 | 12.00 |
| 14-(68 pgs., 2/58) | 2.30 | 7.00 | 16.00 |
| 18-Ditko-a | 4.50 | 14.00 | 32.00 |
| 21-30 | 1.00 | 3.00 | 7.00 |
| 31-50 | .70 | 2.00 | 4.00 |
| 51-70: 54-Kid Montana app. 64-Captain Doom begins (1st app.) | .30 | 1.00 | 2.00 |
| 71-81: 73-Origin & 1st app. The Sharp Shooter, last app. #74. 75-Last Capt. Doom. 80,81-Ditko-a | | .60 | 1.20 |
| 82-88 | | .35 | .70 |
| 64,79(Modern Comics-r, 1977, '78) | | .15 | .30 |

**OUTLAWS OF THE WILD WEST**
1952 (132 pages) (25 cents)
Avon Periodicals

| | Good | Fine | N-Mint |
|---|---|---|---|
| 1-Wood back-c; Kubert-a (3 Jesse James-r) | 17.00 | 51.00 | 120.00 |

**OUT OF SANTA'S BAG** (See March of Comics #10)

**OUT OF THE NIGHT** (The Hooded Horseman #18 on)
Feb-Mar, 1952 - No. 17, Oct-Nov, 1954
American Comics Group (Creston/Scope)

| | Good | Fine | N-Mint |
|---|---|---|---|
| 1-Williamson/LeDoux-a, 9 pgs | 25.00 | 75.00 | 175.00 |
| 2-Williamson-a, 5 pgs. | 21.00 | 62.00 | 145.00 |
| 3,5-10: 9-Sci/Fic story | 7.00 | 21.00 | 50.00 |
| 4-Williamson-a, 7 pgs. | 19.00 | 57.00 | 135.00 |
| 11,12,14-16 | 5.00 | 15.00 | 35.00 |
| 13-Nostrand-a; lingerie panels | 5.70 | 17.00 | 40.00 |
| 17-E.C. Wood swipe; lingerie panels | 5.70 | 17.00 | 40.00 |

NOTE: ***Landau*** *a-14, 16, 17.* ***Shelly*** *a-12.*

**OUT OF THE PAST A CLUE TO THE FUTURE**
1946? (16 pages) (paper cover)
E. C. Comics (Public Affairs Comm.)

| | Good | Fine | N-Mint |
|---|---|---|---|
| nn-Based on public affairs pamphlet-"What Foreign Trade Means to You" | 11.50 | 34.00 | 80.00 |

**OUT OF THE SHADOWS**
No. 5, July, 1952 - No. 14, Aug, 1954
Standard Comics/Visual Editions

| | Good | Fine | N-Mint |
|---|---|---|---|
| 5-Toth-p; Moreira, Tuska-a | 11.50 | 34.00 | 80.00 |
| 6-Toth/Celardo-a; Katz-a(2) | 10.00 | 30.00 | 70.00 |
| 7-Jack Katz-a(2) | 6.50 | 19.00 | 45.00 |
| 8,10: 10-Sekowsky-a | 4.30 | 13.00 | 30.00 |
| 9-Crandall-a(2) | 6.00 | 18.00 | 42.00 |
| 11-Toth-a, 2 pgs.; Katz-a | 5.30 | 16.00 | 38.00 |
| 12-Toth/Peppe-a(2); Katz-a | 10.00 | 30.00 | 70.00 |
| 13-Cannabalism story; Sekowsky-a | 6.50 | 19.00 | 45.00 |
| 14-Toth-a | 7.00 | 21.00 | 50.00 |

**OUT OF THIS WORLD**
June, 1950 (One Shot)
Avon Periodicals

| | Good | Fine | N-Mint |
|---|---|---|---|
| 1-Kubert-a(2) (one reprint/Eerie #1-'47) plus Crom the Barbarian by Giunta (origin); Fawcette-c | 37.00 | 110.00 | 260.00 |

**OUT OF THIS WORLD**
Aug, 1956 - No. 16, Dec, 1959
Charlton Comics

| | Good | Fine | N-Mint |
|---|---|---|---|
| 1 | 8.00 | 24.00 | 55.00 |
| 2 | 4.00 | 12.00 | 28.00 |
| 3-6-Ditko-a(4) each | 11.00 | 32.00 | 75.00 |
| 7-(2/58, 15 cents, 68 pgs.)-Ditko-c/a(4) | 11.00 | 32.00 | 75.00 |
| 8-(5/58, 15 cents, 68 pgs.)-Ditko-a(2) | 8.50 | 25.50 | 60.00 |
| 9-12,16-Ditko-a | 7.00 | 21.00 | 50.00 |
| 13-15 | 2.30 | 7.00 | 16.00 |

NOTE: ***Ditko*** *c-3-7, 11, 12, 16.* ***Reinman*** *a-10.*

**OUT OUR WAY WITH WORRY WART** (See 4-Color No. 680)

**OUTPOSTS**
June, 1987 - No. 4? ($1.25, color)
Blackthorne Publishing

| | Good | Fine | N-Mint |
|---|---|---|---|
| 1-4: 1-Kaluta-c(p) | | .60 | 1.20 |

**OUTSIDERS, THE** (Also see Adventures of . . . & Batman & the . . .)
Nov, 1985 - No. 28, Feb, 1988
DC Comics

| | Good | Fine | N-Mint |
|---|---|---|---|
| 1 | .25 | .75 | 1.50 |
| 2-28: 18-26-Batman returns. 21-Intro. Strike Force Kobra. 22-E.C. parody; Orlando-a. 21-1st app. Clayface IV. 25-Atomic Knight app. 27,28-Millennium tie-ins | | .50 | 1.00 |
| Annual 1 (12/86; $2.50) | .35 | 1.00 | 2.00 |
| Special 1 (7/87, $1.50) | .25 | .75 | 1.50 |

**OUTSTANDING AMERICAN WAR HEROES**
1944 (16 pgs.) (paper cover)
The Parents' Institute

| | Good | Fine | N-Mint |
|---|---|---|---|
| nn-Reprints from True Comics | 2.30 | 7.00 | 16.00 |

**OVERSEAS COMICS** (Also see G.I. & Jeep Comics)
1944 (7¼x10¼"; 16 pgs. in color)
Giveaway (Distributed to U.S. armed forces)

| | Good | Fine | N-Mint |
|---|---|---|---|
| 23-65-Bringing Up Father, Popeye, Joe Palooka, Dick Tracy, Superman, Gasoline Alley, Buz Sawyer, Li'l Abner, Blondie, Terry & the Pirates, Out Our Way | 3.00 | 9.00 | 21.00 |

**OWL, THE**
April, 1967; No. 2, April, 1968
Gold Key

| | Good | Fine | N-Mint |
|---|---|---|---|
| 1,2-Written by Jerry Siegel | 1.50 | 4.50 | 10.00 |

**OXYDOL-DREFT**
1950 (Set of 6 pocket-size giveaways; distributed through the mail as a set) (Scarce)
Oxydol-Dreft

| | Good | Fine | N-Mint |
|---|---|---|---|
| 1-3: 1-Li'l Abner. 2-Daisy Mae. 3-Shmoo | 8.00 | 24.00 | 55.00 |
| 4-John Wayne; Williamson/Frazetta-c from John Wayne #3 | 10.00 | 30.00 | 70.00 |
| 5-Archie | 6.00 | 18.00 | 42.00 |
| 6-Terrytoons Mighty Mouse | 4.00 | 12.00 | 28.00 |

NOTE: *Set is worth more with original envelope.*

**OZ** (See First Comics Graphic Novel, Marvel Treaury Of Oz & MGM's Marvelous . . .)

**OZARK IKE**
Feb, 1948; Nov, 1948 - No. 24, Dec, 1951; No. 25, Sept, 1952
Dell Publishing Co./Standard Comics B11 on

| | Good | Fine | N-Mint |
|---|---|---|---|
| 4-Color 180(1948-Dell) | 5.75 | 17.25 | 40.00 |
| B11, B12, 13-15 | 4.35 | 13.00 | 30.00 |
| 16-25 | 3.50 | 10.50 | 24.00 |

**OZ-WONDERLAND WARS, THE**
Jan, 1986 - No. 3, March, 1986 (mini-series)
DC Comics

| | Good | Fine | N-Mint |
|---|---|---|---|
| 1-3 | .35 | 1.00 | 2.00 |

**OZZIE & BABS** (TV Teens #14 on)
Dec, 1947 - No. 13, Fall, 1949
Fawcett Publications

| | Good | Fine | N-Mint |
|---|---|---|---|
| 1-Teen-age | 4.50 | 14.00 | 32.00 |
| 2 | 2.30 | 7.00 | 16.00 |
| 3-13 | 1.70 | 5.00 | 12.00 |

**OZZIE & HARRIET** (See The Adventures of . . .)

**PACIFIC COMICS GRAPHIC NOVEL**
Sept, 1984
Pacific Comics

| | Good | Fine | N-Mint |
|---|---|---|---|
| 1-The Seven Samuroid; Brunner-a | 1.00 | 3.00 | 6.00 |

**PACIFIC PRESENTS**
Oct, 1982 - No. 2, Apr, 1983; No. 3, Mar, 1984 - No. 4, June, 1984
Pacific Comics

| | Good | Fine | N-Mint |
|---|---|---|---|
| 1-The Rocketeer app.; Stevens-c/a | 1.00 | 3.00 | 6.00 |
| 2-The Rocketeer app.; nudity; Stevens-c/a | .75 | 2.25 | 4.50 |
| 3,4: 3-1st app. Vanity | .35 | 1.00 | 2.00 |

NOTE: ***Conrad*** *a-3, 4; c-3.* ***Ditko*** *a-1-3.* ***Dave Stevens*** *c/a-1, 2.*

**PADRE OF THE POOR**
nd (Giveaway) (16 pgs.; paper cover)
Catechetical Guild

| | Good | Fine | N-Mint |
|---|---|---|---|
| nn | 1.50 | 4.50 | 10.00 |

**PAGEANT OF COMICS** (See Jane Arden & Mopsy)
Sept, 1947 - No. 2, Oct, 1947
Archer St. John

| | Good | Fine | N-Mint |
|---|---|---|---|
| 1-Mopsy strip-r | 5.00 | 15.00 | 35.00 |
| 2-Jane Arden strip-r | 5.00 | 15.00 | 35.00 |

**PANCHO VILLA**
1950
Avon Periodicals

| | Good | Fine | N-Mint |
|---|---|---|---|
| nn-Kinstler-c | 13.00 | 40.00 | 90.00 |

**PANHANDLE PETE AND JENNIFER** (TV)
July, 1951 - No. 3, Nov, 1951
J. Charles Laue Publishing Co.

| | Good | Fine | N-Mint |
|---|---|---|---|
| 1 | 4.00 | 12.00 | 28.00 |
| 2,3 | 2.65 | 8.00 | 18.00 |

**PANIC** (Companion to Mad)
Feb-Mar, 1954 - No. 12, Dec-Jan, 1955-56
E. C. Comics (Tiny Tot Comics)

| | Good | Fine | N-Mint |
|---|---|---|---|
| 1-Used in Senate Investigation hearings; Elder draws entire E. C. staff | 9.30 | 28.00 | 65.00 |
| 2 | 7.00 | 21.00 | 50.00 |

*The Outsiders #18, © DC*

*Ozzie & Babs #1, © FAW*

*Panic #1, © WMG*

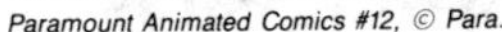
Paramount Animated Comics #12, © Para.

Pat Boone #1, © DC

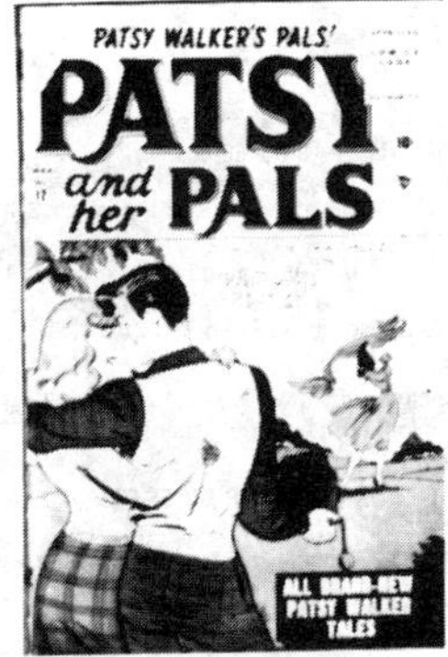

Patsy & Her Pals #12, © MEG

| | Good | Fine | N-Mint |
|---|---|---|---|
| 3,4: 3-Senate Subcommittee parody; Davis draws Gaines, Feldstein & Kelly, 1 pg.; Old King Cole smokes marijuana. 4-Infinity-c | 4.50 | 14.00 | 32.00 |
| 5-11 | 4.30 | 13.00 | 30.00 |
| 12 (Low distribution; many thousands were destroyed) | 5.00 | 15.00 | 35.00 |

NOTE: ***Davis** a-1-12; c-12. **Elder** a-1-12. **Feldstein** c-1-3, 5. **Kamen** a-1. **Orlando** a-1-9. **Wolverton** c-4, panel-3. **Wood** a-2-9, 11, 12.*

**PANIC** (Magazine) (Satire)
July, 1958 - No. 6, July, 1959; V2#10, Dec, 1965 - V2#12, 1966
Panic Publications

| | | | |
|---|---|---|---|
| 1 | 3.00 | 9.00 | 21.00 |
| 2-6 | 1.70 | 5.00 | 12.00 |
| V2#10-12: Reprints earlier issues | .85 | 2.60 | 6.00 |

NOTE: ***Davis** a-3(2 pgs.), 4, 5, 10; c-10. **Elder** a-5. **Powell** a-V2#10, 11. **Torres** a-1-5. **Tuska** a-V2#11.*

**PARADAX** (Also see Strange Days)
1986 (One shot)
Eclipse Comics

| | | | |
|---|---|---|---|
| 1 | .35 | 1.00 | 2.00 |

**PARADAX**
April, 1987 - No. 2, August, 1987 ($1.75, color, mature readers)
Vortex Comics

| | | | |
|---|---|---|---|
| 1,2-nudity, adult language | .30 | .90 | 1.80 |

**PARADE** (See Hanna-Barbera . . .)

**PARADE COMICS** (Frisky Animals on Parade #2 on)
Sept, 1957
Ajax/Farrell Publ. (World Famous Publ.)

| | | | |
|---|---|---|---|
| 1 | 1.70 | 5.00 | 12.00 |

NOTE: *Cover title: Frisky Animals on Parade.*

**PARADE OF PLEASURE**
1954 (192 pgs.) (Hardback book)
Derric Verschoyle Ltd., London, England

| | | | |
|---|---|---|---|
| By Geoffrey Wagner. Contains section devoted to the censorship of American comic books with illustrations in color and black and white. (Also see **Seduction of the Innocent** ). Distributed in USA by Library Publishers, N. Y. | 30.00 | 90.00 | 210.00 |
| with dust jacket . . . . | 55.00 | 165.00 | 385.00 |

**PARAMOUNT ANIMATED COMICS** (See Harvey Comics Hits #60,62)
Feb, 1953 - No. 22, July, 1956
Harvey Publications

| | | | |
|---|---|---|---|
| 1-Baby Huey, Herman & Katnip, Buzzy the Crow begin | 10.00 | 30.00 | 70.00 |
| 2 | 6.00 | 18.00 | 42.00 |
| 3-6 | 5.00 | 15.00 | 35.00 |
| 7-Baby Huey becomes permanent cover feature; cover title becomes Baby Huey with #9 | 11.00 | 32.00 | 75.00 |
| 8-10: 9-Infinity-c | 4.00 | 12.00 | 28.00 |
| 11-22 | 2.65 | 8.50 | 18.00 |

**PARENT TRAP, THE** (See 4-Color #1210)

**PAROLE BREAKERS**
Dec, 1951 - No. 3, July, 1952
Avon Periodicals/Realistic #2 on

| | | | |
|---|---|---|---|
| 1(#2 on inside)-c-/Avon paperback #283 | 18.00 | 54.00 | 125.00 |
| 2-Kubert-a; c-/Avon paperback #114 | 13.00 | 40.00 | 90.00 |
| 3-Kinstler-c | 11.50 | 34.00 | 80.00 |

**PARTRIDGE FAMILY, THE** (TV)
March, 1971 - No. 21, Dec, 1973
Charlton Comics

| | Good | Fine | N-Mint |
|---|---|---|---|
| 1 | 1.30 | 4.00 | 9.00 |
| 2-4,6-21 | .70 | 2.00 | 5.00 |
| 5-Partridge Family Summer Special (52 pgs.); The Shadow, Lone Ranger, Charlie McCarthy, Flash Gordon, Hopalong Cassidy, Gene Autry & others app. | 1.70 | 5.00 | 12.00 |

**PASSION, THE**
No. 394, 1955
Catechetical Guild

| | | | |
|---|---|---|---|
| 394 | 1.70 | 5.00 | 12.00 |

**PAT BOONE** (TV)(Also see Superman's Girlfriend Lois Lane #9)
Sept-Oct, 1959 - No. 5, May-Jun, 1960
National Periodical Publications

| | | | |
|---|---|---|---|
| 1-Photo-c | 20.00 | 60.00 | 140.00 |
| 2-5: 4-Previews 'Journey To The Center Of The Earth'. 2,5-Photo-c | 14.00 | 41.00 | 95.00 |

**PATCHES**
Mar-Apr, 1945 - No. 11, Nov, 1947
Rural Home/Patches Publ. (Orbit)

| | | | |
|---|---|---|---|
| 1-L. B. Cole-c | 11.50 | 34.00 | 80.00 |
| 2 | 5.70 | 17.00 | 40.00 |
| 3-8,10,11: 5-Danny Kaye-c/story; L.B. Cole-c. 7-Hopalong Cassidy-c/story. 10-Jack Carson (radio) c/story; Leav-c. 11-Red Skelton story | 4.50 | 14.00 | 32.00 |
| 9-Leav/Krigstein-a, 16 pgs. | 5.00 | 15.00 | 35.00 |

**PATHWAYS TO FANTASY**
July, 1984
Pacific Comics

| | | | |
|---|---|---|---|
| 1-Barry Smith-c/a; Jeff Jones-a (4 pgs.) | .25 | .75 | 1.50 |

**PATORUZU** (See Adventures of . . .)

**PATSY & HEDY** (Also see Hedy Wolfe)
Feb, 1952 - No. 110, Feb, 1967
Atlas Comics/Marvel (GPI/Male)

| | | | |
|---|---|---|---|
| 1-Patsy Walker & Hedy Wolfe | 6.50 | 19.00 | 45.00 |
| 2 | 3.15 | 9.50 | 22.00 |
| 3-10 | 2.65 | 8.00 | 18.00 |
| 11-20 | 1.70 | 5.00 | 12.00 |
| 21-40 | 1.30 | 4.00 | 9.00 |
| 41-60 | .85 | 2.60 | 6.00 |
| 61-110: 88-Lingerie panel | .50 | 1.50 | 3.00 |
| Annual 1('63) | 2.30 | 7.00 | 16.00 |

**PATSY & HER PALS**
May, 1953 - No. 29, Aug, 1957
Atlas Comics (PPI)

| | | | |
|---|---|---|---|
| 1-Patsy Walker | 5.30 | 16.00 | 38.00 |
| 2 | 2.65 | 8.00 | 18.00 |
| 3-10 | 2.00 | 6.00 | 14.00 |
| 11-29: 24-Everett-c | 1.50 | 4.50 | 10.00 |

**PATSY WALKER** (See All Teen, A Date With Patsy, Girls' Life, Miss America Magazine, Patsy & Hedy, Patsy & Her Pals & Teen Comics)
1945 (no month) - No. 124, Dec, 1965
Marvel/Atlas Comics (BPC)

| | | | |
|---|---|---|---|
| 1 | 22.00 | 65.00 | 150.00 |
| 2 | 10.00 | 30.00 | 70.00 |
| 3-10: 5-Injury-to-eye-c | 6.50 | 19.00 | 45.00 |
| 11,12,15,16,18 | 4.30 | 13.00 | 30.00 |
| 13,14,17,19-22-Kurtzman's "Hey Look" | 5.30 | 16.00 | 38.00 |
| 23,24 | 3.15 | 9.50 | 22.00 |
| 25-Rusty by Kurtzman; painted-c | 5.30 | 16.00 | 38.00 |
| 26-29,31: 26-31: 52 pgs. | 2.65 | 8.00 | 18.00 |
| 30(52 pgs.)-Egghead Doodle by Kurtzman, 1pg. | 4.00 | 12.00 | 28.00 |
| 32-57: Last precode (3/55) | 1.70 | 5.00 | 12.00 |

| | Good | Fine | N-Mint |
|---|---|---|---|
| 58-80 | 1.00 | 3.00 | 7.00 |
| 81-99: 92,98-Millie x-over | .70 | 2.00 | 5.00 |
| 100 | .85 | 2.60 | 6.00 |
| 101-124 | .40 | 1.25 | 2.50 |
| Fashion Parade 1('66)-68 pgs. | 2.30 | 7.00 | 16.00 |

*NOTE: Painted c-25-28. Anti-Wertham editorial in #21. Georgie app. in #8, 11. Millie app. in #10, 92, 98. Mitzi app. in #11. Rusty app. in #12, 25. Willie app. in #12.* ***Al Jaffee*** *c-57, 58.*

**PAT THE BRAT** (Adventures of Pipsqueak #34 on)
June, 1953; Summer, 1955 - No. 4, 5/56; No. 15, 7/56 - No. 33, 7/59
Archie Publications (Radio)

| | Good | Fine | N-Mint |
|---|---|---|---|
| nn(6/53) | 7.00 | 21.00 | 50.00 |
| 1(Summer, 1955) | 4.50 | 14.00 | 32.00 |
| 2-4-(5/56) (#5-14 not published) | 2.65 | 8.00 | 18.00 |
| 15-(7/56)-33 | 1.30 | 4.00 | 9.00 |

**PAT THE BRAT COMICS DIGEST MAGAZINE**
October, 1980
Archie Publications

| | Good | Fine | N-Mint |
|---|---|---|---|
| 1 | | .50 | 1.00 |

**PATTY POWERS** (Formerly Della Vision #3)
No. 4, Oct, 1955 - No. 7, Oct, 1956
Atlas Comics

| | Good | Fine | N-Mint |
|---|---|---|---|
| 4 | 3.00 | 9.00 | 21.00 |
| 5-7 | 1.70 | 5.00 | 12.00 |

**PAT WILTON** (See Mighty Midget Comics)

**PAUL**
1978 (49 cents)
Spire Christian Comics (Fleming H. Revell Co.)

| | Good | Fine | N-Mint |
|---|---|---|---|
| nn | | .40 | .80 |

**PAULINE PERIL** (See The Close Shaves of. . .)

**PAUL REVERE'S RIDE** (See 4-Color #822 & Walt Disney Showcase #34)

**PAUL TERRY'S ADVENTURES OF MIGHTY MOUSE** (See Adventures of. . .)

**PAUL TERRY'S COMICS** (Formerly Terry-Toons Comics; becomes Adventures of Mighty Mouse No. 126 on)
No. 85, Mar, 1951 - No. 125, May, 1955
St. John Publishing Co.

| | Good | Fine | N-Mint |
|---|---|---|---|
| 85,86-Same as Terry-Toons #85, & 86 with only a title change; published at same time? | 4.50 | 14.00 | 32.00 |
| 87-99: 89-Mighty Mouse begins, ends #125 | 3.00 | 9.00 | 21.00 |
| 100 | 3.60 | 11.00 | 25.00 |
| 101-104,107-125: 121,122,125-Painted-c | 2.65 | 8.00 | 18.00 |
| 105,106-Giant Comics Edition, 100pgs. (9/53 & ?) | 8.00 | 24.00 | 55.00 |

**PAUL TERRY'S HOW TO DRAW FUNNY CARTOONS**
1940's (14 pages) (Black & White)
Terrytoons, Inc. (Giveaway)

| | Good | Fine | N-Mint |
|---|---|---|---|
| nn-Heckle & Jeckle, Mighty Mouse, etc. | 7.00 | 21.00 | 50.00 |

**PAUL TERRY'S MIGHTY MOUSE** (See Mighty Mouse)

**PAUL TERRY'S MIGHTY MOUSE ADVENTURE STORIES**
1953 (384 pgs.) (50 cents) (cardboard covers)
St. John Publishing Co.

| | Good | Fine | N-Mint |
|---|---|---|---|
| nn | 36.00 | 107.00 | 250.00 |

**PAWNEE BILL**
Feb, 1951 - No. 3, July, 1951
Story Comics

| | Good | Fine | N-Mint |
|---|---|---|---|
| 1-Bat Masterson, Wyatt Earp app. | 5.00 | 15.00 | 35.00 |
| 2,3: 3-Origin Golden Warrior; Cameron-a | 2.65 | 8.00 | 18.00 |

**PAY-OFF** (This Is the. . ., . . .Crime, . . .Detective Stories)
July-Aug, 1948 - No. 5, Mar-Apr, 1949 (52 pages)
D. S. Publishing Co.

| | Good | Fine | N-Mint |
|---|---|---|---|
| 1 | 7.00 | 21.00 | 50.00 |
| 2 | 4.00 | 12.00 | 28.00 |
| 3-5 | 3.15 | 9.50 | 22.00 |

**PEACEMAKER, THE** (Also see Fightin' 5)
Mar, 1967 - No. 5, Nov, 1967
Charlton Comics

| | Good | Fine | N-Mint |
|---|---|---|---|
| 1-Fightin' Five begins | .85 | 2.60 | 6.00 |
| 2,3,5 | .70 | 2.00 | 4.00 |
| 4-Origin The Peacemaker | .85 | 2.60 | 6.00 |
| 1,2(Modern Comics reprint, 1978) | | .15 | .30 |

**PEACEMAKER** (Also see Crisis On Infinite Earths)
Jan, 1988 - No. 4, April, 1988 ($1.25, mini-series)
DC Comics

| | Good | Fine | N-Mint |
|---|---|---|---|
| 1-4 | | .65 | 1.30 |

**PEANUTS** (Charlie Brown) (See Fritzi Ritz, Nancy & Sluggo, Tip Top, Tip Topper & United Comics)
No. 878, 2/58 - No. 13, 5-7/62; 5/63 - No. 4, 2/64
Dell Publishing Co./Gold Key

| | Good | Fine | N-Mint |
|---|---|---|---|
| 4-Color 878(#1) | 7.00 | 21.00 | 50.00 |
| 4-Color 969,1015('59) | 5.70 | 17.00 | 40.00 |
| 4(2-4/60) | 4.00 | 12.00 | 28.00 |
| 5-13 | 2.65 | 8.00 | 18.00 |
| 1(Gold Key, 5/63) | 3.50 | 10.50 | 24.00 |
| 2-4 | 2.30 | 7.00 | 16.00 |
| 1(1953-54)-Reprints United Features' Strange As It Seems, Willie, Ferdnand | 5.00 | 15.00 | 35.00 |

**PEBBLES & BAMM BAMM** (TV)
Jan, 1972 - No. 36, Dec, 1976 (Hanna-Barbera)
Charlton Comics

| | Good | Fine | N-Mint |
|---|---|---|---|
| 1 | 1.70 | 5.00 | 12.00 |
| 2-10 | .85 | 2.60 | 6.00 |
| 11-36 | .70 | 2.00 | 5.00 |

**PEBBLES FLINTSTONE** (TV)
Sept, 1963 (Hanna-Barbera)
Gold Key

| | Good | Fine | N-Mint |
|---|---|---|---|
| 1 (10088-309) | 4.00 | 12.00 | 28.00 |

**PECKS BAD BOY**
1906 - 1908 (Strip reprints) (11¼x15¾")
Thompson of Chicago (by Walt McDougal)

| | Good | Fine | N-Mint |
|---|---|---|---|
| . . .& Cousin Cynthia(1907)-In color | 20.00 | 60.00 | 140.00 |
| . . .& His Chums(1908)-Hardcover; in full color; 16 pgs. | 20.00 | 60.00 | 140.00 |
| Advs. of. . .And His Country Cousins (1906)-In color, 18 pgs., oblong | 20.00 | 60.00 | 140.00 |
| Advs. of. . .in Pictures(1908)-In color; Stanton & Van V. Liet Co. | 20.00 | 60.00 | 140.00 |

**PEDRO** (Also see Romeo Tubbs)
No. 18, June, 1950 - No. 2, Aug, 1950?
Fox Features Syndicate

| | Good | Fine | N-Mint |
|---|---|---|---|
| 18(#1)-Wood-c/a(p) | 12.00 | 36.00 | 85.00 |
| 2-Wood-a? | 9.30 | 28.00 | 65.00 |

**PEE-WEE PIXIES** (See The Pixies)

**PELLEAS AND MELISANDE** (See Night Music #4, 5)

**PENALTY** (See Crime Must Pay the. . .)

**PENDULUM ILLUSTRATED BIOGRAPHIES**
1979 (B&W)
Pendulum Press

*Paul Terry's Comics #107, © Viacom Int.*

*Pawnee Bill #1, © Story Comics*

*Pebbles Flintstone #1, © Hanna-Barbera*

Penny #6, © AVON

Pep Comics #12, © AP

The Perfect Crime #2, © Cross Publ.

19-355x-George Washington/Thomas Jefferson, 19-3495-Charles Lindbergh/Amelia Earhart, 19-3509-Harry Houdini/Walt Disney, 19-3517-Davy Crockett/Daniel Boone-Redondo-a, 19-3525-Elvis Presley/Beatles, 19-3533-Benjamin Franklin/Martin Luther King Jr, 19-3541-Abraham Lincoln/Franklin D. Roosevelt, 19-3568-Marie Curie/Albert Einstein-Redondo-a, 19-3576-Thomas Edison/Alexander Graham Bell-Redondo-a, 19-3584-Vince Lombardi/Pele, 19-3592-Babe Ruth/Jackie Robinson, 19-3606-Jim Thorpe/Althea Gibson

Softback 1.50
Hardback 4.50

NOTE: *Above books still available from publisher.*

**PENDULUM ILLUSTRATED CLASSICS** (Now Age Illustrated)
1973 - 1978 (62pp, B&W, 5-3/8x8") (Also see Marvel Classics)
Pendulum Press

64-100x(1973)-Dracula-Redondo art, 64-131x-The Invisible Man-Nino art, 64-0968-Dr Jekyll and Mr Hyde-Redondo art, 64-1005-Black Beauty, 64-1010-Call of the Wild, 64-1020-Frankenstein, 64-1025-Hucklebury Finn, 64-1030-Moby Dick-Nino-a, 64-1040-Red Badge of Courage, 64-1045-The Time Machine-Nino-a, 64-1050-Tom Sawyer, 64-1055-Twenty Thousand Leagues Under the Sea, 64-1069-Treasure Island, 64-1328 (1974)-Kidnapped, 64-1336-Three Musketeers-Nino art, 64-1344-A Tale of Two Cities, 64-1352-Journey to the Center of the Earth, 64-1360-The War of the Worlds-Nino-a, 64-1379-The Greatest Advs of Sherlock Holmes-Redondo art, 64-1387-Mysterious Island, 64-1395-Hunchback of Notre Dame, 64-1409-Helen Keller-story of my life, 64-1417-Scarlet Letter, 64-1425-Gulliver's Travels, 64-2618(1977)-Around the World in Eighty Days, 64-2626-Captains Courageous, 64-2634-Connecticut Yankee, 64-2642-The Hound of the Baskervilles, 64-2650-The House of Seven Gables, 64-2669-Jane Eyre, 64-2677-The Last of the Mohicans, 64-2685-The Best of O'Henry, 64-2693-The Best of Poe-Redondo-a, 64-2707-Two Years Before the Mast, 64-2715-White Fang, 64-2723-Wuthering Heights, 64-3126(1978)-Ben Hur-Redondo art, 64-3134-A Christmas Carol, 64-3142-The Food of the Gods, 64-3150-Ivanhoe, 64-3169-The Man in the Iron Mask, 64-3177-The Prince and the Pauper, 64-3185-The Prisoner of Zenda, 64-3193-The Return of the Native, 64-3207-Robinson Crusoe, 64-3215-The Scarlet Pimpernel, 64-3223-The Sea Wolf, 64-3231-The Swiss Family Robinson, 64-3851-Billy Budd, 64-386x-Crime and Punishment, 64-3878-Don Quixote, 64-3886-Great Expectations, 64-3894-Heidi, 64-3908-The Iliad, 64-3916-Lord Jim, 64-3924-The Mutiny on Board H.M.S. Bounty, 64-3932-The Odyssey, 64-3940-Oliver Twist, 64-3959-Pride and Prejudice, 64-3967-The Turn of the Screw

Softback 1.45
Hardback 4.50

NOTE: *All of the above books can be ordered from the publisher; some were reprinted as Marvel Classic Comics #1-12. In 1972 there was another brief series of 12 titles which contained Classics Ill. artwork. They were entitled* ***Now Age Books Illustrated****, but can be easily distinguished from later series by the small Classics Illustrated logo at the top of the front cover. The format is the same as the later series. The 48 pg. C.I. art was stretched out to make 62 pgs. After Twin Circle Publ. terminated the Classics Ill. series in 1971, they made a one year contract with Pendulum Press to print these twelve titles of C.I. art. Pendulum was unhappy with the contract, and at the end of 1972 began their own art series, utilizing the talents of the Filipino artist group. One detail which makes this rather confusing is that when they redid the art in 1973, they gave it the same identifying no. as the 1972 series. All 12 of the 1972 C.I. editions have new covers, taken from internal art panels. In spite of their recent age, all of the 1972 C.I. series are very rare. Mint copies would fetch at least $50. Here is a list of the 1972 series, with C.I. title no. counterpart:*

64-1005 (CI#60-A2) 64-1010 (CI#91) 64-1015 (CI-Jr #503) 64-1020 (CI#26) 64-1025 (CI#19-A2) 64-1030 (CI#5-A2) 64-1035 (CI#169) 64-1040 (CI#98) 64-1045 (CI#133) 64-1050 (CI#50-A2) 64-1055 (CI#47) 64-1060 (CI-Jr#535)PS6

**PENDULUM ILLUSTRATED ORIGINALS**
1979 (in color)
Pendulum Press

| | Good | Fine | N-Mint |
|---|---|---|---|
| 94-4254-Solarman: The Beginning | .25 | .80 | 1.60 |

**PENNY**
1947 - No. 6, Sept-Oct, 1949 (Newspaper reprints)
Avon Comics

| | | | |
|---|---|---|---|
| 1-Photo & biography of creator | 5.50 | 16.50 | 38.00 |
| 2-5 | 2.85 | 8.50 | 20.00 |
| 6-Perry Como photo on-c | 3.50 | 10.50 | 24.00 |

**PEP COMICS** (See Archie Giant Series Mag. #576, 589, 601, 614)
Jan, 1940 - No. 411?, 1987 **Good Fine VF-NM NM/Mint**
MLJ Magazines/Archie Publications No. 56 (3/46) on

1-Intro. The Shield by Irving Novick (1st patriotic hero); origin The Comet by Jack Cole, The Queen of Diamonds & Kayo Ward; The Rocket, The Press Guardian (The Falcon #1 only), Sergeant Boyle, Fu Chang, & Bentley of Scotland Yard
233.00 585.00 1400.00 1900.00

(Estimated up to 150 total copies exist, 7 in NM/Mint)

| | Good | Fine | N-Mint |
|---|---|---|---|
| 2-Origin The Rocket | 77.00 | 230.00 | 540.00 |
| 3 | 62.00 | 185.00 | 435.00 |
| 4-Wizard cameo | 54.00 | 160.00 | 375.00 |
| 5-Wizard cameo in Shield story | 54.00 | 160.00 | 375.00 |
| 6-10: 8-Last Cole Comet; no Cole-a in #6,7 | 39.00 | 116.00 | 270.00 |
| 11-Dusty, Shield's sidekick begins; last Press Guardian, Fu Chang | 40.00 | 120.00 | 280.00 |
| 12-Origin Fireball; last Rocket & Queen of Diamonds | 54.00 | 160.00 | 375.00 |
| 13-15 | 37.00 | 110.00 | 255.00 |
| 16-Origin Madam Satan; blood drainage-c | 54.00 | 163.00 | 380.00 |
| 17-Origin The Hangman; death of The Comet | 110.00 | 330.00 | 775.00 |
| 18-20-Last Fireball | 36.00 | 107.00 | 250.00 |
| 21-Last Madam Satan | 36.00 | 107.00 | 250.00 |

22-Intro. & 1st app. Archie, Betty, & Jughead(12/41); (also see Jackpot)

| Good | Fine | VF-NM | NM/Mint |
|---|---|---|---|
| 235.00 | 705.00 | 1650.00 | 2700.00 |

(Estimated up to 150 total copies exist, 7 in NM/Mint)

| | Good | Fine | N-Mint |
|---|---|---|---|
| 23 | 63.00 | 190.00 | 440.00 |
| 24,25 | 53.00 | 160.00 | 370.00 |
| 26-1st app. Veronica Lodge | 64.00 | 193.00 | 450.00 |
| 27-30: 30-Capt. Commando begins | 42.00 | 125.00 | 295.00 |
| 31-35: 34-Bondage/Hypo-c | 34.00 | 100.00 | 235.00 |
| 36-1st Archie-c | 54.00 | 160.00 | 375.00 |
| 37-40 | 25.00 | 75.00 | 175.00 |
| 41-50: 41-Archie-c begin. 47-Last Hangman issue; infinity-c. 48-Black Hood begins (5/44); ends #51,59,60 | 19.00 | 56.00 | 130.00 |
| 51-60: 52-Suzie begins. 56-Last Capt. Commando. 59-Black Hood not in costume; spanking & lingerie panels; Archie dresses as his aunt; Suzie ends. 60-Katy Keene begins, ends #154 | 13.00 | 40.00 | 90.00 |
| 61-65-Last Shield. 62-1st app. Li'l Jinx | 9.30 | 28.00 | 65.00 |
| 66-80: 66-G-Man Club becomes Archie Club (2/48) | 6.50 | 19.50 | 45.00 |
| 81-99 | 4.35 | 13.00 | 30.00 |
| 100 | 5.00 | 15.00 | 35.00 |
| 101-130 | 2.00 | 6.00 | 14.00 |
| 131-149 | 1.00 | 3.00 | 7.00 |
| 150-160-Super-heroes app. in each (see note). 150 (10/61?)-2nd or 3rd app. The Jaguar? 157-Li'l Jinx story | 1.15 | 3.50 | 8.00 |
| 161-167,169-200 | .35 | 1.00 | 2.50 |
| 168-Jaguar app. | .85 | 2.60 | 6.00 |
| 201-260 | .25 | .75 | 1.50 |
| 261-411: 383-Marvelous Maureen begins (Sci/fi). 393-Thunderbunny begins | | .35 | .70 |

NOTE: ***Biro*** *a-2, 4, 5.* ***Jack Cole*** *a-1-5, 8.* ***Fuje*** *a-39, 45, 47.* ***Meskin*** *a-2, 4, 5, 11(2).* ***Novick*** *c-1-10, 20, 22, 23, 25.* ***Schomburg*** *c-38.* ***Bob Wood*** *a-2, 4-6, 11. The Fly app. in 151, 154, 160. Flygirl app. in 153, 155, 156, 158. Jaguar app. in 150, 152, 157, 159, 168. Katy Keene by* ***Bill Woggon*** *in many later issues. Bondage c-7, 12, 13, 15, 18, 21, 31, 32.*

**PEPE** (See 4-Color #1194)

**PERCY & FERDIE**
1921 (52 pages) (B&W dailies, 10x10", cardboard-c)
Cupples & Leon Co.

| | | | |
|---|---|---|---|
| nn-By H. A. MacGill | 8.00 | 24.00 | 56.00 |

**PERFECT CRIME, THE**
Oct, 1949 - No. 33, May, 1953 (#2-12, 52 pgs.)
Cross Publications

| | | | |
|---|---|---|---|
| 1-Powell-a(2) | 9.30 | 28.00 | 65.00 |
| 2 (4/50) | 5.70 | 17.00 | 40.00 |
| 3-10: 7-Steve Duncan begins, ends #30 | 4.50 | 14.00 | 32.00 |
| 11-Used in **SOTI**, pg. 159 | 6.00 | 18.00 | 42.00 |

| | Good | Fine | N-Mint |
|---|---|---|---|
| 12-14 | 3.00 | 9.00 | 21.00 |
| 15-"The Most Terrible Menace"-2 pg. drug editorial | 3.85 | 11.50 | 27.00 |
| 16,17,19-25,27-29,31-33 | 2.30 | 7.00 | 16.00 |
| 18-Drug cover, heroin drug propaganda story, plus 2 pg. drug editorial | 9.30 | 28.00 | 65.00 |
| 26-Drug-c with hypodermic; drug propaganda story | 11.00 | 32.00 | 75.00 |
| 30-Strangulation cover | 8.50 | 25.50 | 60.00 |

NOTE: *Powell a-No. 1, 2, 4.* ***Wildey*** *a-1, 5. Bondage c-11.*

**PERFECT LOVE**
#10, 8-9/51 (cover date; 5-6/51 indicia date); #2, 10-11/51 - #10, 12/53
Ziff-Davis(Approved Comics)/St. John No. 9 on

| | | | |
|---|---|---|---|
| 10(#1)(8-9/51) | 7.00 | 21.00 | 50.00 |
| 2(10-11/51) | 4.30 | 13.00 | 30.00 |
| 3,5-7: 3-Painted-c. 5-Photo-c | 3.15 | 9.50 | 22.00 |
| 4,8 (Fall, '52)-Kinstler-a; last Z-D issue | 3.50 | 10.50 | 24.00 |
| 9,10 (10/53, 12/53, St. John): 9-Kinstler painted-c. 10-Photo-c | 3.00 | 9.00 | 21.00 |

**PERRI** (See 4-Color #847)

**PERRY MASON** (See Feature Books #49, 50)

**PERRY MASON MYSTERY MAGAZINE** (TV)
June-Aug, 1964 - No. 2, Oct-Dec, 1964
Dell Publishing Co.

| | | | |
|---|---|---|---|
| 1,2: 2-Raymond Burr photo-c | 2.00 | 6.00 | 14.00 |

**PERSONAL LOVE** (Also see Movie Love)
Jan, 1950 - No. 33, June, 1955
Famous Funnies

| | | | |
|---|---|---|---|
| 1 | 7.00 | 21.00 | 50.00 |
| 2 | 3.70 | 11.00 | 26.00 |
| 3-7,10 | 3.15 | 9.50 | 22.00 |
| 8,9-Kinstler-a | 3.70 | 11.00 | 26.00 |
| 11-Toth-a | 5.70 | 17.00 | 40.00 |
| 12,16,17-One pg. Frazetta each | 3.50 | 10.50 | 24.00 |
| 13-15,18-23 | 2.65 | 8.00 | 18.00 |
| 24,25,27,28-Frazetta-a in all-8,7,8&6 pgs. | 23.00 | 70.00 | 160.00 |
| 26,29-31,33: 31-Last pre-code (2/55) | 2.00 | 6.00 | 14.00 |
| 32-Classic Frazetta-a, 8 pgs.; Kirk Douglas/Bella Darvi photo-c | 39.00 | 116.00 | 270.00 |

NOTE: *All have photo-c.* ***Everett*** *a-5, 9, 10, 24.*

**PERSONAL LOVE** (Going Steady V3#3 on)
V1#1, Sept, 1957 - V3#2, Nov-Dec, 1959
Prize Publ. (Headline)

| | | | |
|---|---|---|---|
| V1#1 | 3.00 | 9.00 | 21.00 |
| 2 | 1.70 | 5.00 | 12.00 |
| 3-6(7-8/58) | 1.50 | 4.50 | 10.00 |
| V2#1(9-10/58)-V2#6(7-8/59) | 1.15 | 3.50 | 8.00 |
| V3#1-Wood/Orlando-a | 2.00 | 6.00 | 14.00 |
| 2 | 1.00 | 3.00 | 7.00 |

**PETER COTTONTAIL**
Jan, 1954; Feb, 1954 - No. 2, Mar, 1954
Key Publications

| | | | |
|---|---|---|---|
| 1(1/54)-Not 3-D | 4.00 | 12.00 | 28.00 |
| 1(2/54)-(3-D); written by Bruce Hamilton | 14.00 | 42.00 | 100.00 |
| 2-Reprints 3-D #1 but not in 3-D | 3.00 | 9.00 | 21.00 |

**PETER GUNN** (See 4-Color #1087)

**PETER PAN** (See 4-Color #442,446,926, Movie Classics & Comics, New Adventures of . . . & Walt Disney Showcase #36)

**PETER PANDA**
Aug-Sept, 1953 - No. 31, Aug-Sept, 1958
National Periodical Publications

| | Good | Fine | N-Mint |
|---|---|---|---|
| 1-Grossman-c/a in all | 19.00 | 58.00 | 135.00 |
| 2 | 8.50 | 25.50 | 60.00 |
| 3-10 | 5.70 | 17.00 | 40.00 |
| 11-31 | 2.85 | 8.50 | 20.00 |

**PETER PAN TREASURE CHEST** (See Dell Giants)

**PETER PARKER** (See The Spectacular Spider-Man)

**PETER PAT** (See Single Series #8)

**PETER PAUL'S 4 IN 1 JUMBO COMIC BOOK**
No date (1953)
Capitol Stories

| | | | |
|---|---|---|---|
| 1-Contains 4 comics bound; Space Adventures, Space Western, Crime & Justice, Racket Squad in Action | 20.00 | 60.00 | 140.00 |

**PETER PENNY AND HIS MAGIC DOLLAR**
1947 (16 pgs.; paper cover; regular size)
American Bankers Association, N. Y. (Giveaway)

| | | | |
|---|---|---|---|
| nn-(Scarce)-Used in **SOTI**, pg. 310, 311 | 8.50 | 25.50 | 60.00 |
| Another version (7¼x11")-redrawn, 16 pgs., paper-c | 5.70 | 17.00 | 40.00 |

**PETER PIG**
No. 5, May, 1953 - No. 6, Aug, 1953
Standard Comics

| | | | |
|---|---|---|---|
| 5,6 | 1.70 | 5.00 | 12.00 |

**PETER PORKCHOPS** (See Leading Comics #23)
11-12/49 - No. 61, 9-11/59; No. 62, 10-12/60 (1-5: 52 pgs.)
National Periodical Publications

| | | | |
|---|---|---|---|
| 1 | 19.00 | 58.00 | 135.00 |
| 2 | 9.30 | 28.00 | 65.00 |
| 3-10 | 6.50 | 19.00 | 45.00 |
| 11-30 | 4.50 | 14.00 | 32.00 |
| 31-62 | 2.85 | 8.50 | 20.00 |

NOTE: ***Otto Feur*** *a-all.* ***Sheldon Mayer*** *a-30-38, 40-44, 46-52, 61.*

**PETER PORKER, THE SPECTACULAR SPIDER-HAM**
May, 1985 - No. 17, Sept, 1987 (Also see Marvel Tails)
Star Comics (Marvel)

| | | | |
|---|---|---|---|
| 1 | .35 | 1.00 | 2.00 |
| 2-17: 13-Halloween issue | | .50 | 1.00 |

**PETER POTAMUS** (TV)
January, 1965 (Hanna-Barbera)
Gold Key

| | | | |
|---|---|---|---|
| 1 | 2.65 | 8.00 | 18.00 |

**PETER RABBIT** (See Large Feature Comic #1, New Funnies #65 & Space Comics)

**PETER RABBIT**
1922 - 1923 (9¼x6¼") (paper cover)
John H. Eggers Co. The House of Little Books Publishers

| | | | |
|---|---|---|---|
| B1-B4-(Rare)-(Set of 4 books which came in a cardboard box)-Each book reprints ½ of a Sunday page per page and contains 8 B&W and 2 color pages; by Harrison Cady each. . . . | 20.00 | 60.00 | 140.00 |

**PETER RABBIT** (Adventures of . . . ; New Advs. of . . . later issues)
1947 - No. 34, Aug-Sept, 1956
Avon Periodicals

| | | | |
|---|---|---|---|
| 1(1947)-Reprints 1943-44 Sunday strips; contains a biography & drawing of Cady | 23.00 | 70.00 | 160.00 |
| 2 (4/48) | 18.00 | 54.00 | 125.00 |
| 3 ('48) - 6(7/49)-Last Cady issue | 16.50 | 50.00 | 115.00 |
| 7-10(1950-8/51) | 3.00 | 9.00 | 21.00 |
| 11(11/51)-34('56)-Avon's character | 1.85 | 5.50 | 13.00 |
| . . . Easter Parade (132 pgs.; 1952) | 10.00 | 30.00 | 70.00 |

. . . Jumbo Book(1954-Giant Size, 25 cents)-6 pgs. Jesse James by

Personal Love #1, © FF

Peter Porkchops #5, © DC

Peter Rabbit #2, © AVON

Peter Wheat #18, © Bakers Associates

*The Phantom #17 (Gold Key), © KING*

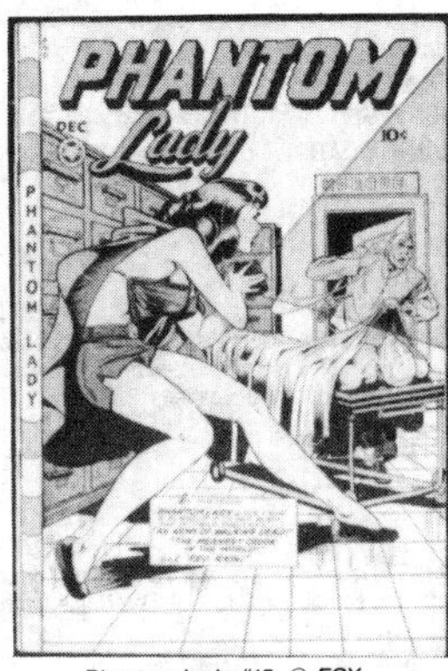


*Phantom Lady #15, © FOX*

| | Good | Fine | N-Mint |
|---|---|---|---|
| Kinstler | 15.00 | 45.00 | 105.00 |

**PETER RABBIT**
1958
Fago Magazine Co.

| | Good | Fine | N-Mint |
|---|---|---|---|
| 1 | 3.50 | 10.50 | 24.00 |

**PETER RABBIT 3-D**
April, 1990 ($2.95, with glasses; sealed in plastic bag)
Eternity Comics

| | Good | Fine | N-Mint |
|---|---|---|---|
| 1-By Harrison Cady (reprints) | .50 | 1.50 | 3.00 |

**PETER, THE LITTLE PEST** (#4 titled Petey)
Nov, 1969 - No. 4, May, 1970
Marvel Comics Group

| | Good | Fine | N-Mint |
|---|---|---|---|
| 1 | .70 | 2.00 | 4.00 |
| 2-4-Reprints Dexter the Demon & Melvin the Monster | .50 | 1.50 | 3.00 |

**PETER WHEAT** (The Adventures of . . .)
1948 - 1956? (16 pgs. in color) (paper covers)
Bakers Associates Giveaway

| | Good | Fine | N-Mint |
|---|---|---|---|
| nn(No.1)-States on last page, end of 1st Adventure of . . .; Kelly-a | 22.00 | 65.00 | 140.00 |
| nn(4 issues)-Kelly-a | 17.00 | 50.00 | 100.00 |
| 6-10-All Kelly-a | 12.00 | 36.00 | 72.00 |
| 11-20-All Kelly-a | 10.00 | 30.00 | 60.00 |
| 21-35-All Kelly-a | 8.00 | 24.00 | 48.00 |
| 36-66 | 5.00 | 15.00 | 30.00 |
| . . . Artist's Workbook ('54, digest size) | 4.50 | 13.50 | 27.00 |
| . . . Four-In-One Fun Pack (Vol. 2, '54), oblong, comics w/puzzles | 5.00 | 15.00 | 30.00 |
| . . . Fun Book ('52, 32pgs., paper-c, B&W & color, 8¼"x10¾"), contains cut-outs, puzzles, games, magic & pages to color | 7.00 | 21.00 | 50.00 |

NOTE: ***Al Hubbard** art #36 on; written by Del Connell.*

**PETER WHEAT NEWS**
1948 - No. 30, 1950 (4 pgs. in color)
Bakers Associates

| | Good | Fine | N-Mint |
|---|---|---|---|
| Vol. 1-All have 2 pgs. Peter Wheat by Kelly | 20.00 | 60.00 | 140.00 |
| 2-10 | 13.00 | 40.00 | 80.00 |
| 11-20 | 6.75 | 20.00 | 40.00 |
| 21-30 | 4.00 | 12.00 | 24.00 |

NOTE: *Early issues have no date & Kelly art.*

**PETE'S DRAGON** (See Walt Disney Showcase #43)

**PETE THE PANIC**
November, 1955
Stanmor Publications

| | Good | Fine | N-Mint |
|---|---|---|---|
| nn-Code approved | 1.30 | 4.00 | 9.00 |

**PETEY** (See Peter, the Little Pest)

**PETTICOAT JUNCTION** (TV)
Oct-Dec, 1964 - No. 5, Oct-Dec, 1965 (All have photo-c)
Dell Publishing Co.

| | Good | Fine | N-Mint |
|---|---|---|---|
| 1 | 4.00 | 12.00 | 28.00 |
| 2-5 | 2.30 | 7.00 | 16.00 |

**PETUNIA** (See 4-Color #463)

**PHANTASMO** (See Large Feature Comic #18)

**PHANTOM, THE**
1939 - 1949
David McKay Publishing Co.

| | Good | Fine | N-Mint |
|---|---|---|---|
| Feature Books 20 | 43.00 | 130.00 | 300.00 |
| Feature Books 22 | 36.00 | 107.00 | 250.00 |
| Feature Books 39 | 29.00 | 85.00 | 200.00 |
| Feature Books 53,56,57 | 22.00 | 65.00 | 150.00 |

**PHANTOM, THE** (See Ace Comics, Defenders Of The Earth, Eat Right to Work and Win, Future Comics, Harvey Comics Hits #51,56, Harvey Hits #1, 6, 12, 15, 26, 36, 44, 48 & King Comics)

**PHANTOM, THE** (nn 29-Published overseas only) (Also see Comics Reading Library)
Nov, 1962 - No. 17, July, 1966; No. 18, Sept, 1966 - No. 28, Dec, 1967; No. 30, Feb, 1969 - No. 74, Jan, 1977
Gold Key (#1-17)/King (#18-28)/Charlton (#30 on)

| | Good | Fine | N-Mint |
|---|---|---|---|
| 1-Manning-a | 5.70 | 17.00 | 40.00 |
| 2-King, Queen & Jack begins, ends #11 | 2.85 | 8.50 | 20.00 |
| 3-10 | 2.00 | 6.00 | 14.00 |
| 11-17: 12-Track Hunter begins | 1.50 | 4.50 | 10.00 |
| 18-Flash Gordon begins; Wood-a | 1.70 | 5.00 | 12.00 |
| 19,20-Flash Gordon ends (both by Gil Kane) | 1.30 | 4.00 | 9.00 |
| 21-24,26,27: 21-Mandrake begins. 20,24-Girl Phantom app. 26-Brick Bradford app. | 1.15 | 3.50 | 8.00 |
| 25-Jeff Jones-a(4 pgs.); 1 pg. Williamson ad | 1.30 | 4.00 | 9.00 |
| 28(nn)-Brick Bradford app. | 1.00 | 3.00 | 7.00 |
| 30-40: 36,39-Ditko-a | .70 | 2.00 | 5.00 |
| 41-66: 46-Intro. The Piranha. 62-Bolle-c | .50 | 1.50 | 3.00 |
| 67-71,73-Newton-c/a; 67-Origin retold | .35 | 1.00 | 2.00 |
| 72 | .25 | .75 | 1.50 |
| 74-Newton Flag-c; Newton-a | .35 | 1.00 | 2.00 |

NOTE: ***Aparo** a-31-34, 36-38; c-31-38, 60, 61. Painted c-1-17.*

**PHANTOM, THE**
May, 1988 - No. 4, Aug, 1988 ($1.25, color)
DC Comics

| | Good | Fine | N-Mint |
|---|---|---|---|
| 1-Orlando-c/a in all | .35 | 1.00 | 2.00 |
| 2-4 | .25 | .75 | 1.50 |

**PHANTOM, THE**
Mar, 1989 - No. 13, Mar, 1990 ($1.50, color)
DC Comics

| | Good | Fine | N-Mint |
|---|---|---|---|
| 1-Brief origin | .35 | 1.00 | 2.00 |
| 2-13 | .25 | .75 | 1.50 |

**PHANTOM BLOT, THE** (#1 titled New Adventures of . . .)
Oct, 1964 - No. 7, Nov, 1966 (Disney)
Gold Key

| | Good | Fine | N-Mint |
|---|---|---|---|
| 1 (Meets The Beagle Boys) | 2.00 | 6.00 | 14.00 |
| 2-1st Super Goof | 1.50 | 4.50 | 10.00 |
| 3-7 | 1.15 | 3.50 | 8.00 |

**PHANTOM EAGLE** (See Mighty Midget, Marvel Super Heroes #16 & Wow #6)

**PHANTOM LADY** (1st Series) (My Love Secret #24 on) (Also see All Top, Daring Advs., Freedom Fighters, Jungle Thrills, & Wonder Boy)
No. 13, Aug, 1947 - No. 23 April, 1949
Fox Features Syndicate

| | Good | Fine | N-Mint |
|---|---|---|---|
| 13(#1)-Phantom Lady by Matt Baker begins; The Blue Beetle app. | 121.00 | 365.00 | 850.00 |
| 14(#2) | 79.00 | 235.00 | 550.00 |
| 15-P.L. injected with experimental drug | 63.00 | 190.00 | 440.00 |
| 16-Negligee-c, panels | 63.00 | 190.00 | 440.00 |
| 17-Classic bondage cover; used in **SOTI**, illo-"Sexual stimulation by combining 'headlights' with the sadist's dream of tying up a woman" | 154.00 | 460.00 | 1075.00 |
| 18,19 | 57.00 | 171.00 | 400.00 |
| 20-23: 23-Bondage-c | 49.00 | 146.00 | 340.00 |

NOTE: ***Matt Baker** a-in all; c-13, 15-21. **Kamen** a-22, 23.*

**PHANTOM LADY** (2nd Series) (See Terrific Comics) (Formerly Linda)
V1#5, Dec-Jan, 1954/1955 - No. 4, June, 1955
Ajax/Farrell Publ.

| | Good | Fine | N-Mint |
|---|---|---|---|
| V1#5(#1)-by Matt Baker | 33.00 | 100.00 | 230.00 |

| | Good | Fine | N-Mint |
|---|---|---|---|
| V1#2-Last pre-code | 26.00 | 77.00 | 180.00 |
| 3,4-Red Rocket | 22.00 | 65.00 | 150.00 |

**PHANTOM PLANET, THE** (See 4-Color No. 1234)

**PHANTOM STRANGER, THE** (1st Series)(See Saga of Swamp Thing)
Aug-Sept, 1952 - No. 6, June-July, 1953
National Periodical Publications

| | | | |
|---|---|---|---|
| 1 (Scarce) | 65.00 | 195.00 | 455.00 |
| 2 (Scarce) | 50.00 | 150.00 | 350.00 |
| 3-6 (Scarce) | 40.00 | 120.00 | 280.00 |

**PHANTOM STRANGER, THE** (2nd Series) (See Showcase #80)
May-June, 1969 - No. 41, Feb-Mar, 1976
National Periodical Publications

| | | | |
|---|---|---|---|
| 1-Only 12 cent issue | 3.15 | 9.50 | 22.00 |
| 2,3: 2-? are 15 cents | 1.50 | 4.50 | 10.00 |
| 4-Neal Adams-a | 1.70 | 5.00 | 12.00 |
| 5-10 | 1.00 | 3.00 | 6.00 |
| 11-20 | .50 | 1.50 | 3.00 |
| 21-41: 22-Dark Circle begins. 23-Spawn of Frankenstein begins by Kaluta; series ends #30. 31-The Black Orchid begins. 39-41-Deadman app. | .35 | 1.00 | 2.00 |

NOTE: ***N. Adams*** *a-4; c-3-19.* ***Aparo*** *a-7-26; c-20-24, 33-41.* ***B. Bailey*** *a-27-30.* ***DeZuniga*** *a-14-16, 19-22, 31, 34.* ***Grell*** *a-33.* ***Kaluta*** *a-23-25; c-26.* ***Meskin*** *r-15, 16, 18.* ***Redondo*** *a-32, 35, 36.* ***Sparling*** *a-20.* ***Starr*** *a-17r.* ***Toth*** *a-15r. Black Orchid by* ***Carrilo****-38-41. Dr. 13 solo in-13, 18, 20. Frankenstein by* ***Kaluta****-23-25; by* ***Baily****-27-30. No Black Orchid-33, 34, 37.*

**PHANTOM STRANGER** (See Justice League of America #103)
Oct, 1987 - No. 4, Jan, 1988 (75 cents, color, mini-series)
DC Comics

| | | | |
|---|---|---|---|
| 1-Mignola/Russell-c/a in all | .25 | .75 | 1.50 |
| 2-4 | | .50 | 1.00 |

**PHANTOM WITCH DOCTOR** (Also see Durango Kid #8 & Eerie #8)
1952
Avon Periodicals

| | | | |
|---|---|---|---|
| 1-Kinstler-c/a (7 pgs.) | 22.00 | 65.00 | 150.00 |

**PHANTOM ZONE, THE** (See Adventure #283 & Superboy #100, 104)
January, 1982 - No. 4, April, 1982
DC Comics

| | | | |
|---|---|---|---|
| 1-Superman app. in all | | .50 | 1.00 |
| 2-4: Batman, Gr. Lantern app. | | .60 | 1.25 |

NOTE: ***Colan*** *a-1-4p; c-1-4p.* ***Giordano*** *c-1-4i.*

**PHAZE**
Apr, 1988 - No. 2, Oct, 1988 ($2.25, color)
Eclipse Comics

| | | | |
|---|---|---|---|
| 1,2: 2-Gulacy painted-c | .35 | 1.10 | 2.25 |

**PHIL RIZZUTO** (Baseball Hero)(See Sport Thrills, Accepted reprint)
1951 (New York Yankees)
Fawcett Publications

| | | | |
|---|---|---|---|
| nn-Photo-c | 30.00 | 90.00 | 210.00 |

**PHOENIX**
Jan, 1975 - No. 4, Oct, 1975
Atlas/Seaboard Publ.

| | | | |
|---|---|---|---|
| 1-Origin | | .30 | .60 |
| 2-4: 3-Origin & only app. The Dark Avenger. 4-New origin/costume The Protector (formerly Phoenix) | | .25 | .50 |

NOTE: ***Infantino*** *appears in #1, 2.* ***Austin*** *a-3i.* ***Thorne*** *c-3.*

**PHOENIX** (. . .The Untold Story)
April, 1984 ($2.00, One shot)
Marvel Comics Group

| | | | |
|---|---|---|---|
| 1-Byrne/Austin-r/X-Men 137 with original unpublished ending | 1.35 | 4.00 | 8.00 |

**PICNIC PARTY** (See Dell Giants)

**PICTORIAL CONFESSIONS** (Pictorial Romances #4 on)
Sept, 1949 - No. 3, Dec, 1949
St. John Publishing Co.

| | Good | Fine | N-Mint |
|---|---|---|---|
| 1-Baker-c/a(3) | 12.00 | 36.00 | 84.00 |
| 2-Baker-a; photo-c | 6.00 | 18.00 | 42.00 |
| 3-Kubert, Baker-a; part Kubert-c | 8.50 | 25.50 | 60.00 |

**PICTORIAL LOVE STORIES** (Formerly Tim McCoy)
No. 22, Oct, 1949 - No. 26, July, 1950
Charlton Comics

| | | | |
|---|---|---|---|
| 22-26-"Me-Dan Cupid" in all | 6.00 | 18.00 | 42.00 |

**PICTORIAL LOVE STORIES**
October, 1952
St. John Publishing Co.

| | | | |
|---|---|---|---|
| 1-Baker-c/a | 10.00 | 30.00 | 70.00 |

**PICTORIAL ROMANCES** (Formerly Pictorial Confessions)
No. 4, Jan, 1950; No. 5, Jan, 1951 - No. 24, Mar, 1954
St. John Publishing Co.

| | | | |
|---|---|---|---|
| 4-All Baker | 11.00 | 32.00 | 75.00 |
| 5,10-All Matt Baker issues | 8.00 | 24.00 | 55.00 |
| 6-9,12,13,15,16-Baker-c, 2-3 stories | 5.30 | 16.00 | 38.00 |
| 11-Baker-c/a(3); Kubert-a | 6.00 | 18.00 | 42.00 |
| 14,21-24-Baker-c/a each | 4.00 | 12.00 | 28.00 |
| 17-20(7/53)-100 pgs. each; Baker-c/a | 11.00 | 32.00 | 75.00 |

NOTE: ***Matt Baker*** *art in most issues.* ***Estrada*** *a-19(2).*

**PICTURE NEWS**
Jan, 1946 - No. 10, Jan-Feb, 1947
Lafayette Street Corp.

| | | | |
|---|---|---|---|
| 1-Milt Gross begins, ends No. 6; 4 pg. Kirby-a; A-Bomb-c/story | 16.00 | 48.00 | 110.00 |
| 2-Atomic explosion panels; Frank Sinatra, Perry Como stories | 6.50 | 19.00 | 45.00 |
| 3-Atomic explosion panels; Frank Sinatra, June Allyson stories | 5.70 | 17.00 | 40.00 |
| 4-Atomic explosion panels; "Caesar and Cleopatra" movie adaptation; Jackie Robinson story | 6.50 | 19.00 | 45.00 |
| 5-7: 5-Hank Greenberg story. 6-Joe Louis c/story | 3.60 | 11.00 | 25.00 |
| 8-Monte Hale story(9-10/46; 1st?) | 5.70 | 17.00 | 40.00 |
| 9-A-Bomb story; "Crooked Mile" movie adaptation; Joe DiMaggio story | 6.50 | 19.00 | 45.00 |
| 10-A-Bomb story; Krigstein, Gross-a | 5.70 | 17.00 | 40.00 |

**PICTURE PARADE** (Picture Progress #5 on)
Sept, 1953 - V1#4, Dec, 1953 (28 pages)
Gilberton Company (Also see A Christmas Adventure)

| | | | |
|---|---|---|---|
| V1#1-Andy's Atomic Adventures-A-bomb blast-c; (Teachers version distributed to schools exists) | 7.00 | 21.00 | 50.00 |
| 2-Around the World with the United Nations | 5.00 | 15.00 | 35.00 |
| 3-Adventures of the Lost One(The Amer. Indian), 4-A Christmas Adventure (r-under same title in '69) | 5.00 | 15.00 | 35.00 |

**PICTURE PROGRESS** (Formerly Picture Parade)
V1#5, Jan, 1954 - V3#2, Oct, 1955 (28-36 pgs.)
Gilberton Corp.

| | | | |
|---|---|---|---|
| V1#5-News in Review 1953, 6-The Birth of America, 7-The Four Seasons, 8-Paul Revere's Ride, 9-The Hawaiian Islands(5/54), V2#1-The Story of Flight(9/54), 2-Vote for Crazy River(The Meaning of Elections), 3-Louis Pasteur, 4-The Star Spangled Banner, 5-News in Review 1954, 6-Alaska: The Great Land, 7-Life in the Circus, 8-The Time of the Cave Man, 9-Summer Fun(5/55) each.... | 2.65 | 8.00 | 18.00 |

V3#1-The Man Who Discovered America, 2-The Lewis & Clark Ex-

*The Phantom Stranger #2 (7-8/69), © DC*

*Phil Rizzuto nn, © FAW*

*Picture News #4, © Lafayette Street Corp.*

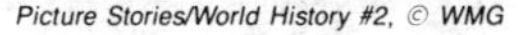
Picture Stories/World History #2, © WMG

Pin-Up Pete #1, © TOBY

Pioneer West Romances #4, © FH

| | Good | Fine | N-Mint |
|---|---|---|---|
| pedition each.... | 2.65 | 8.00 | 18.00 |

**PICTURE SCOPE JUNGLE ADVENTURES** (See Jungle Thrills)

**PICTURE STORIES FROM AMERICAN HISTORY**
1945 - No. 4, 1947 (#1,2: 10 cents, 56 pgs.; #3: 15 cents, 52pgs.)
National/All-American/E. C. Comics

| | Good | Fine | N-Mint |
|---|---|---|---|
| 1 | 10.00 | 30.00 | 70.00 |
| 2-4 | 6.50 | 19.00 | 45.00 |

**PICTURE STORIES FROM SCIENCE**
Spring, 1947 - No. 2, Fall, 1947
E.C. Comics

| | Good | Fine | N-Mint |
|---|---|---|---|
| 1,2 | 10.00 | 30.00 | 70.00 |

**PICTURE STORIES FROM THE BIBLE**
Fall, 1942-3 & 1944-46
National/All-American/E.C. Comics

| | Good | Fine | N-Mint |
|---|---|---|---|
| 1-4('42-Fall,'43)-Old Testament (DC) | 9.30 | 28.00 | 65.00 |
| Complete Old Testament Edition, 232pgs.(12/43-DC);-1st printing; contains #1-4. 2nd & 3rd printings exists | 12.00 | 36.00 | 85.00 |
| Complete Old Testament Edition (1945-publ. by Bible Pictures Ltd.)-232 pgs., hardbound, in color with dust jacket | 12.00 | 36.00 | 85.00 |

NOTE: *Both Old and New Testaments published in England by Bible Pictures Ltd. in hardback, 1943, in color, 376 pages, and were also published by Scarf Press in 1979 (Old Test., $9.95) and in 1980 (New Test., $7.95)*

| | Good | Fine | N-Mint |
|---|---|---|---|
| 1-3(New Test.; 1944-46, DC)-52pgs. ea. | 7.00 | 21.00 | 50.00 |
| The Complete Life of Christ Edition (1945)-96pgs.; contains #1&2 of the New Testament Edition | 10.00 | 30.00 | 70.00 |
| 1,2(Old Testament-r in comic book form)(E.C., 1946; 52pgs.) | 7.00 | 21.00 | 50.00 |
| 1-3(New Testament-r in comic book form)(E.C., 1946; 52pgs.) | 7.00 | 21.00 | 50.00 |
| Complete New Testament Edition (1946-E.C.)-144 pgs.; contains #1-3 | 10.00 | 30.00 | 70.00 |

NOTE: *Another British series entitled* ***The Bible Illustrated*** *from 1947 has recently been discovered, with the same internal artwork. This eight edition series (5-OT, 3-NT) is of particular interest to Classics Ill. collectors because it exactly copied the C.I. logo format. The British publisher was Thorpe & Porter, who in 1951 began publishing the British Classics Ill. series. All editions of The Bible Ill. have new British painted covers. While this market is still new, and not all editions have as yet been found, current market value is about the same as the first U.S. editions of Picture Stories From The Bible.*

**PICTURE STORIES FROM WORLD HISTORY**
Spring, 1947 - No. 2, Summer, 1947 (52,48 pgs.)
E.C. Comics

| | Good | Fine | N-Mint |
|---|---|---|---|
| 1,2 | 11.00 | 32.00 | 75.00 |

**PINEAPPLE ARMY**
Dec. 6, 1988 - No. 10, 1989 ($1.75, B&W, bi-weekly mini-series)
Viz Comics

| | Good | Fine | N-Mint |
|---|---|---|---|
| 1-10: Japanese manga | .30 | .90 | 1.80 |

**PINHEAD & FOODINI** (TV)(Also see Foodini)
July, 1951 - No. 4, Jan, 1952
Fawcett Publications

| | Good | Fine | N-Mint |
|---|---|---|---|
| 1-Photo-c; 52 pgs. | 8.50 | 25.50 | 60.00 |
| 2-Photo-c | 5.70 | 17.00 | 40.00 |
| 3,4: 3-Photo-c | 4.30 | 13.00 | 30.00 |

**PINK LAFFIN**
1922 (9x12")(strip-r)
Whitman Publishing Co.

| | Good | Fine | N-Mint |
|---|---|---|---|
| ...the Lighter Side of Life, ...He Tells 'Em, ...and His Family, ...Knockouts; Ray Gleason-a (All rare) each... | 10.00 | 30.00 | 70.00 |

**PINK PANTHER, THE** (TV)
April, 1971 - No. 87, 1984
Gold Key

| | Good | Fine | N-Mint |
|---|---|---|---|
| 1-The Inspector begins | 1.20 | 3.50 | 8.00 |
| 2-10 | .70 | 2.00 | 4.00 |
| 11-30: Warren Tufts-a #16-on | .40 | 1.20 | 2.50 |
| 31-60 | .25 | .75 | 1.50 |
| 61-87 | | .50 | 1.00 |
| Kite Fun Book(1972)-16pgs. | .70 | 2.00 | 4.00 |
| Mini-comic No. 1(1976)(3¼x6½") | | .50 | 1.00 |

NOTE: *Pink Panther began as a movie cartoon. (See Golden Comics Digest #38, 45 and March of Comics #376, 384, 390, 409, 418, 429, 441, 449, 461, 473, 486); #37, 72, 80-85 contain reprints.*

**PINKY LEE** (See Adventures of...)

**PINKY THE EGGHEAD**
1963 (Reprints from Noodnik)
I.W./Super Comics

| | Good | Fine | N-Mint |
|---|---|---|---|
| I.W. Reprint #1,2(nd) | | .60 | 1.20 |
| Super Reprint #14 | | .60 | 1.20 |

**PINOCCHIO** (See 4-Color #92, 252, 545, 1203, Mickey Mouse Mag. V5#3, Movie Comics under Wonderful Advs. of..., New Advs. of..., Thrilling Comics #2, Walt Disney Showcase, Walt Disney's..., Wonderful Advs. of..., & World's Greatest Stories #2)

**PINOCCHIO**
1940 (10 pages; linen-like paper)
Montgomery Ward Co. (Giveaway)

| | Good | Fine | N-Mint |
|---|---|---|---|
| nn | 12.00 | 36.00 | 84.00 |

**PINOCCHIO AND THE EMPEROR OF THE NIGHT**
Mar, 1988 (52 pgs., $1.25)
Marvel Comics

| | Good | Fine | N-Mint |
|---|---|---|---|
| 1-Adapts film | | .65 | 1.30 |

**PINOCCHIO LEARNS ABOUT KITES** (Also see Brer Rabbit & Donald Duck) (Disney)
1954 (8 pages) (Premium)
Pacific Gas & Electric Co./Florida Power & Light

| | Good | Fine | N-Mint |
|---|---|---|---|
| nn | 20.00 | 60.00 | 130.00 |

**PIN-UP PETE** (Also see Great Lover Romances & Monty Hall...)
1952
Toby Press

| | Good | Fine | N-Mint |
|---|---|---|---|
| 1-Jack Sparling pin-ups | 9.00 | 27.00 | 62.00 |

**PIONEER MARSHAL** (See Fawcett Movie Comics)

**PIONEER PICTURE STORIES**
Dec, 1941 - No. 9, Dec, 1943
Street & Smith Publications

| | Good | Fine | N-Mint |
|---|---|---|---|
| 1 | 12.00 | 36.00 | 85.00 |
| 2 | 7.00 | 21.00 | 50.00 |
| 3-9 | 5.30 | 16.00 | 38.00 |

**PIONEER WEST ROMANCES** (Firehair #1,2,7-11)
No. 3, Spring, 1950 - No. 6, Winter, 1950-51
Fiction House Magazines

| | Good | Fine | N-Mint |
|---|---|---|---|
| 3-(52 pgs.)-Firehair continues | 9.30 | 28.00 | 65.00 |
| 4-6 | 7.00 | 21.00 | 50.00 |

**PIPSQUEAK** (See The Adventures of...)

**PIRACY**
Oct-Nov, 1954 - No. 7, Oct-Nov, 1955
E. C. Comics

| | Good | Fine | N-Mint |
|---|---|---|---|
| 1-Williamson/Torres-a | 14.00 | 43.00 | 100.00 |
| 2-Williamson/Torres-a | 11.00 | 32.00 | 75.00 |
| 3-7 | 8.50 | 25.50 | 60.00 |

NOTE: ***Crandall*** *a-in all; c-2-4.* ***Davis*** *a-1, 2, 6.* ***Evans*** *a-3-7; c-7.* ***Ingels*** *a-3-7.* ***Krigstein*** *a-3-5, 7; c-5, 6.* ***Wood*** *a-1, 2; c-1.*

**PIRANA** (See Thrill-O-Rama #2, 3)

**PIRATE CORPS, THE**
1987 - No. 5, 1988 ($1.95, color #3 on)
Eternity Comics/Slave Labor Graphics

| | Good | Fine | N-Mint |
|---|---|---|---|
| 1-5 | .35 | 1.00 | 2.00 |
| Special 1 ('89, $1.95, B&W)-Slave Labor publ. | .35 | 1.00 | 2.00 |

**PIRATE OF THE GULF, THE** (See Superior Stories #2)

**PIRATES COMICS**
Feb-Mar, 1950 - No. 4, Aug-Sept, 1950 (All 52 pgs.)
Hillman Periodicals

| | Good | Fine | N-Mint |
|---|---|---|---|
| 1 | 10.00 | 30.00 | 70.00 |
| 2-Dave Berg-a | 5.70 | 17.00 | 40.00 |
| 3,4-Berg-a | 4.30 | 13.00 | 30.00 |

**P.I.'S: MICHAEL MAUSER AND MS. TREE, THE**
Jan, 1985 - No. 3, May, 1985 ($1.25, color, mini-series)
First Comics

| | Good | Fine | N-Mint |
|---|---|---|---|
| 1-3: Staton-c/a(p) | | .65 | 1.30 |

**PITT, THE** (Also see The Draft & The War)
Mar, 1988 (one shot, $3.25, 52 pgs.)
Marvel Comics

| | Good | Fine | N-Mint |
|---|---|---|---|
| 1-Ties into Starbrand, D.P. 7 | .70 | 2.00 | 4.00 |

**PIUS XII MAN OF PEACE**
No date (12 pgs.; 5½x8½") (B&W)
Catechetical Guild Giveaway

| | Good | Fine | N-Mint |
|---|---|---|---|
| nn | 3.00 | 9.00 | 21.00 |

**PIXIE & DIXIE & MR. JINKS** (TV)(See Jinks, Pixie, and Dixie & Whitman Comic Books)
July-Sept, 1960 - Feb, 1963 (Hanna-Barbera)
Dell Publishing Co./Gold Key

| | Good | Fine | N-Mint |
|---|---|---|---|
| 4-Color 1112 | 3.50 | 10.50 | 24.00 |
| 4-Color 1196,1264 | 2.30 | 7.00 | 16.00 |
| 01-631-207 (Dell) | 2.00 | 6.00 | 14.00 |
| 1(2/63-Gold Key) | 2.00 | 6.00 | 14.00 |

**PIXIE PUZZLE ROCKET TO ADVENTURELAND**
November, 1952
Avon Periodicals

| | Good | Fine | N-Mint |
|---|---|---|---|
| 1 | 6.00 | 18.00 | 42.00 |

**PIXIES, THE** (Advs. of...) (The Mighty Atom and ...#6 on)
Winter, 1946 - No. 4, Fall?, 1947; No. 5, 1948
Magazine Enterprises

| | Good | Fine | N-Mint |
|---|---|---|---|
| 1-Mighty Atom | 3.50 | 10.50 | 24.00 |
| 2-5-Mighty Atom | 1.70 | 5.00 | 12.00 |
| I.W. Reprint #1(1958), 8-(Pee-Wee Pixies), 10-I.W. on cover, Super on inside | .50 | 1.50 | 3.00 |

**P. J. WARLOCK**
Nov, 1986 - No. 3, March, 1987 ($2.00, B&W)
Eclipse Comics

| | Good | Fine | N-Mint |
|---|---|---|---|
| 1-3-Funny animal | .35 | 1.00 | 2.00 |

**PLANET COMICS**
1/40 - No. 62, 9/49; No. 63, Wint, 1949-50; No. 64, Spring, 1950; No. 65, 1951(nd); No. 66-68, 1952(nd); No. 69, Wint, 1952-53; No. 70-72, 1953(nd); No. 73, Winter, 1953-54
Fiction House Magazines

| | Good | Fine | VF-NM | NM/Mint |
|---|---|---|---|---|
| 1-Origin Auro, Lord of Jupiter; Flint Baker & The Red Comet begin; Eisner/Fine-c | 500.00 | 1250.00 | 3000.00 | 4000.00 |

(Estimated up to 160 total copies exist, 10 in NM/Mint)

| | Good | Fine | N-Mint |
|---|---|---|---|
| 2-(Scarce) | 233.00 | 585.00 | 1400.00 |
| 3-Eisner-c | 192.00 | 480.00 | 1150.00 |
| 4-Gale Allen and the Girl Squadron begins | 167.00 | 415.00 | 1000.00 |
| 5,6-(Scarce) | 150.00 | 375.00 | 900.00 |
| 7-12: 12-The Star Pirate begins | 107.00 | 320.00 | 750.00 |
| 13-14: 13-Reff Ryan begins | 82.00 | 245.00 | 575.00 |
| 15-(Scarce)-Mars, God of War begins | 86.00 | 257.00 | 600.00 |
| 16-20,22 | 79.00 | 235.00 | 550.00 |
| 21-The Lost World & Hunt Bowman begin | 82.00 | 245.00 | 575.00 |
| 23-26: 26-The Space Rangers begin | 79.00 | 235.00 | 505.00 |
| 27-30 | 57.00 | 170.00 | 400.00 |
| 31-35: 33-Origin Star Pirates Wonder Boots, reprinted in #52. 35-Mysta of the Moon begins | 49.00 | 145.00 | 340.00 |
| 36-45: 41-New origin of "Auro, Lord of Jupiter." 42-Last Gale Allen. 43-Futura begins | 43.00 | 130.00 | 300.00 |
| 46-60: 53-Used in **SOTI**, pg. 32 | 32.00 | 95.00 | 220.00 |
| 61-64 | 22.00 | 65.00 | 150.00 |
| 65-68,70: 65-70-All partial-r of earlier issues | 22.00 | 65.00 | 150.00 |
| 69-Used in **POP**, pgs. 101,102 | 22.00 | 65.00 | 150.00 |
| 71-73-No series stories | 17.00 | 51.00 | 120.00 |
| I.W. Reprint #1(nd)-r-/#70; c-from Attack on Planet Mars | 3.50 | 10.50 | 24.00 |
| I.W. Reprint #8 (r-/#72), 9-r-/#73 | 3.50 | 10.50 | 24.00 |

NOTE: ***Anderson*** *a-33-38, 40-51 (Star Pirate).* ***Matt Baker*** *a-53-59 (Mysta of the Moon).* ***Celardo*** *c-12.* ***Elias*** *c-70.* ***Evans*** *a-50-64 (Lost World).* ***Fine*** *c-2, 5.* ***Ingels*** *a-24-31, 56-61 (Auro, Lord of Jupiter).* ***Lubbers*** *c-40, 41.* ***Renee*** *a-40 (Lost World); c-33, 35, 39.* ***Tuska*** *a-30 (Star Pirate).* ***M. Whitman*** *a-51, 52 (Mysta of the Moon), 54-56 (Star Pirate).* ***Starr*** *a-59. 53-Bondage-c.*

**PLANET COMICS**
1988 - No. 3? (2.00, color; B&W #3)
Blackthorne Publishing

| | Good | Fine | N-Mint |
|---|---|---|---|
| 1-3: New stories. 1-Dave Stevens-c | .35 | 1.00 | 2.00 |

**PLANET OF THE APES** (Magazine) (Also see Adventures on the... & Power Record Comics)
Aug, 1974 - No. 29, Feb, 1977 (B&W) (Based on movies)
Marvel Comics Group

| | Good | Fine | N-Mint |
|---|---|---|---|
| 1-Ploog-a | .40 | 1.25 | 2.50 |
| 2-Ploog-a | .35 | 1.00 | 2.00 |
| 3-10 | .25 | .70 | 1.40 |
| 11-20 | | .50 | 1.00 |
| 21-29 | | .40 | .80 |

NOTE: ***Alcala*** *a-7-11, 17-22, 24.* ***Ploog*** *a-1-8, 11, 13, 14, 19.* ***Sutton*** *a-11, 12, 15, 17, 19, 20, 23, 24, 29.* ***Tuska*** *a-1-6.*

**PLANET OF THE APES**
Apr, 1990 - Present ($2.50, B&W)
Adventure Comics

| | Good | Fine | N-Mint |
|---|---|---|---|
| 1-New movie tie-in; comes w/outer-c(3 colors) | .50 | 1.50 | 3.00 |
| 1-Limited serial numbered edition ($5.00) | 1.00 | 3.00 | 6.00 |
| 1-2nd printing (no outer-c) | .40 | 1.25 | 2.50 |
| 2-8 | .40 | 1.25 | 2.50 |

**PLANET OF VAMPIRES**
Feb, 1975 - No. 3, July, 1975
Seaboard Publications (Atlas)

| | Good | Fine | N-Mint |
|---|---|---|---|
| 1-Neal Adams-c(i); 1st Broderick c/a(p) | | .40 | .80 |
| 2,3: 2-Neal Adams-c. 3-Heath-c/a | | .30 | .60 |

**PLANET TERRY**
April, 1985 - No. 12, March, 1986 (Children's comic)
Star Comics/Marvel

| | Good | Fine | N-Mint |
|---|---|---|---|
| 1-12 | | .35 | .70 |

**PLASTIC FORKS**
1990 - No. 5, 1990 ($4.95, color, adults, limited series, 68 pgs.)
Epic Comics (Marvel)

| | Good | Fine | N-Mint |
|---|---|---|---|
| Book 1-5: Squarebound | .85 | 2.50 | 5.00 |

**PLASTIC MAN** (Also see Police Comics & Smash Comics #17)
Sum, 1943 - No. 64, Nov, 1956
Vital Publ. No. 1,2/Quality Comics No. 3 on

*Pirates Comics #1, © HILL*

*Planet Comics #15, © FH*

*Planet of the Apes #1 (Adv.), © 20th Cent. Fox*

Plastic Man #7 (1940s), © QUA

Plastic Man #9 (3-4/68), © DC

Police Action #4 (1954), © MEG

| | Good | Fine | N-Mint |
|---|---|---|---|
| nn(#1)-'In The Game of Death;' Jack Cole-c/a begins; ends-#64? | 143.00 | 430.00 | 1000.00 |
| nn(#2, 2/44)-'The Gay Nineties Nightmare' | 84.00 | 250.00 | 585.00 |
| 3 (Spr, '46) | 55.00 | 165.00 | 385.00 |
| 4 (Sum, '46) | 47.00 | 140.00 | 325.00 |
| 5 (Aut, '46) | 40.00 | 120.00 | 280.00 |
| 6-10 | 29.00 | 88.00 | 205.00 |
| 11-20 | 25.00 | 75.00 | 175.00 |
| 21-30: 26-Last non-r issue? | 21.00 | 62.00 | 145.00 |
| 31-40: 40-Used in **POP**, pg. 91 | 15.00 | 45.00 | 105.00 |
| 41-64: 53-Last precode issue | 12.00 | 36.00 | 85.00 |
| Super Reprint 11('63, r-/#16), 16 (r-#21, Cole-a), 18('64-Spirit app. by Eisner/Police #95) | 2.30 | 7.00 | 16.00 |

NOTE: ***Cole** r-44, 49, 56, 58, 59 at least.*

**PLASTIC MAN** (See DC Special #15)
11-12/66 - No. 10, 5-6/68; V4#11, 2-3/76 - No. 20, 10-11/77
National Periodical Publications/DC Comics

| | Good | Fine | N-Mint |
|---|---|---|---|
| 1-Gil Kane-c/a; 12 cent issues begin | 2.85 | 8.50 | 20.00 |
| 2-5: 4-Infantino-c; Mortimer-a | 1.50 | 4.50 | 10.00 |
| 6-10('68): 10-Sparling-a; last 12 cent issue | .85 | 2.60 | 6.00 |
| V4#11('76)-20: 11-20-Fraden-p. 17-Origin retold | .25 | .75 | 1.50 |

**PLASTIC MAN**
Nov, 1988 - No. 4, Feb, 1989 ($1.00, mini-series)
DC Comics

| | Good | Fine | N-Mint |
|---|---|---|---|
| 1-4: 1-Origin; Woozy Winks app | | .50 | 1.00 |

**PLAYFUL LITTLE AUDREY** (TV)(Also see Little Audrey #25)
6/57 - No. 110, 11/73; No. 111, 8/74 - No. 121, 4/76
Harvey Publications

| | Good | Fine | N-Mint |
|---|---|---|---|
| 1 | 11.50 | 34.50 | 80.00 |
| 2 | 5.70 | 17.00 | 40.00 |
| 3-5 | 5.00 | 15.00 | 35.00 |
| 6-10 | 3.35 | 10.00 | 23.00 |
| 11-20 | 1.70 | 5.00 | 12.00 |
| 21-40 | 1.35 | 4.00 | 9.00 |
| 41-60 | .85 | 2.50 | 5.00 |
| 61-80 | .50 | 1.50 | 3.00 |
| 81-99 | .40 | 1.25 | 2.50 |
| 100: 52 pg. Giant | .70 | 2.00 | 4.00 |
| 101-103: 52 pg. Giants | .50 | 1.50 | 3.00 |
| 104-121 | .35 | 1.00 | 2.00 |

**PLAYFUL LITTLE AUDREY IN 3-D** (See Blackthorne 3-D Series #66)

**PLOP!**
Sept-Oct, 1973 - No. 24, Nov-Dec, 1976
National Periodical Publications

| | Good | Fine | N-Mint |
|---|---|---|---|
| 1-20: Sergio Aragones-a. 1,5-Wrightson-a | .50 | 1.50 | 3.00 |
| 21,22,24 (52 pgs.) | .70 | 2.00 | 4.00 |
| 23-No Aragones-a (52 pgs.) | .25 | .75 | 1.50 |

NOTE: ***Alcala** a-1-3. **Anderson** a-5. **Aragones** a-1-22, 24. **Ditko** a-16p. **Evans** a-1. **Mayer** a-1. **Orlando** a-21, 22; c-21. **Sekowsky** a-5, 6p. **Toth** a-11. **Wolverton** r-4, 22, 23(1 pg.); c(r)-1-12, 14, 17, 18. **Wood** a-14, 16i, 18-24; c-13, 15, 16, 19.*

**PLUTO** (See Cheerios Premiums, Four Color #537, Mickey Mouse Magazine, Walt Disney Showcase #4,7,13,20,23,33 & Wheaties)
No. 7, 1942; No. 429, 10/52 - No. 1248, 11-1/61-62 (Walt Disney)
Dell Publishing Co.

| | Good | Fine | N-Mint |
|---|---|---|---|
| Large Feature Comic 7(1942) | 65.00 | 195.00 | 455.00 |
| 4-Color 429,509 | 3.50 | 10.50 | 24.00 |
| 4-Color 595,654 | 2.30 | 7.00 | 16.00 |
| 4-Color 736,853,941,1039,1143,1248 | 1.70 | 5.00 | 12.00 |

**POCAHONTAS**
1941 - No. 2, 1942
Pocahontas Fuel Company

| | Good | Fine | N-Mint |
|---|---|---|---|
| nn(#1), 2 | 5.00 | 15.00 | 35.00 |

**POCKET COMICS** (Also see Double Up)
Aug, 1941 - No. 4, Jan, 1942 (Pocket size; 100 pgs.)
Harvey Publications (1st Harvey comic)

| | Good | Fine | N-Mint |
|---|---|---|---|
| 1-Origin The Black Cat, Cadet Blakey the Spirit of '76, The Red Blazer, The Phantom, Sphinx, & The Zebra; Phantom Ranger, British Agent #99, Spin Hawkins, Satan, Lord of Evil begin | 45.00 | 135.00 | 315.00 |
| 2 | 30.00 | 90.00 | 210.00 |
| 3,4 | 22.00 | 65.00 | 154.00 |

**POGO PARADE** (See Dell Giants)

**POGO POSSUM** (Also see Animal Comics & Special Delivery)
No. 105, 4/46 - No. 148, 5/47; 10-12/49 - No. 16, 4-6/54
Dell Publishing Co.

| | Good | Fine | N-Mint |
|---|---|---|---|
| 4-Color 105(1946)-Kelly-c/a | 60.00 | 180.00 | 420.00 |
| 4-Color 148-Kelly-c/a | 50.00 | 150.00 | 350.00 |
| 1-(10-12/49)-Kelly-c/a in all | 48.00 | 145.00 | 335.00 |
| 2 | 25.00 | 75.00 | 175.00 |
| 3-5 | 19.00 | 57.00 | 130.00 |
| 6-10: 10-Infinity-c | 16.00 | 48.00 | 110.00 |
| 11-16: 11-X-mas-c | 13.00 | 40.00 | 90.00 |

NOTE: *#1-4, 9-13: 52 pgs.; #5-8, 14-16: 36 pgs.*

**POINT BLANK**
May, 1989 - No. 2, 1989 ($2.95, B&W, magazine)
Acme Press (Eclipse)

| | Good | Fine | N-Mint |
|---|---|---|---|
| 1,2-European-r | .50 | 1.50 | 3.00 |

**POLICE ACADEMY** (TV)
Nov, 1989 - No. 6, Feb, 1990 ($1.00, color)
Marvel Comics

| | Good | Fine | N-Mint |
|---|---|---|---|
| 1-6: Based on TV cartoon; Post-c/a(p) in all | | .50 | 1.00 |

**POLICE ACTION**
Jan, 1954 - No. 7, Nov, 1954
Atlas News Co.

| | Good | Fine | N-Mint |
|---|---|---|---|
| 1-Violent-a by Robert Q. Sale | 6.50 | 19.00 | 45.00 |
| 2 | 3.15 | 9.50 | 22.00 |
| 3-7: 7-Powell-a | 2.65 | 8.00 | 18.00 |

NOTE: ***Ayers** a-4, 5. **Colan** a-1. **Forte** a-1, 2. **Mort Lawrence** a-5. **Maneely** a-3; c-1, 5. **Reinman** a-6, 7.*

**POLICE ACTION**
Feb, 1975 - No. 3, June, 1975
Atlas/Seaboard Publ.

| | Good | Fine | N-Mint |
|---|---|---|---|
| 1-Lomax, N.Y.P.D., Luke Malone begin; McWilliams-a; bondage-c | | .40 | .80 |
| 2,3: 2-Origin Luke Malone, Manhunter | | .30 | .60 |

NOTE: ***Ploog** art in all. **Sekowsky/McWilliams** a-1-3. **Thorne** c-3.*

**POLICE AGAINST CRIME**
April, 1954 - No. 9, Aug, 1955
Premiere Magazines

| | Good | Fine | N-Mint |
|---|---|---|---|
| 1-Disbrow-a; extreme violence - man's face slashed with knife; Hollingsworth-a | 8.00 | 24.00 | 55.00 |
| 2-Hollingsworth-a | 4.30 | 13.00 | 30.00 |
| 3-9 | 3.00 | 9.00 | 21.00 |

**POLICE BADGE #479** (Formerly Spy Thrillers #1-4)
No. 5, Sept, 1955
Atlas Comics (PrPl)

| | Good | Fine | N-Mint |
|---|---|---|---|
| 5-Maneely-c | 2.65 | 8.00 | 18.00 |

**POLICE CASE BOOK** (See Giant Comics Editions)

**POLICE CASES** (See Authentic . . . & Record Book of . . .)

**POLICE COMICS**
Aug, 1941 - No. 127, Oct, 1953
Quality Comics Group (Comic Magazines)

| | Good | Fine | N-Mint |
|---|---|---|---|
| 1-Origin Plastic Man (1st app.) by Jack Cole, The Human Bomb by Gustavson, & No. 711; intro. Chic Carter by Eisner, The Firebrand by Reed Crandall, The Mouthpiece, Phantom Lady, & The Sword; r-in DC Special #15 | 350.00 | 875.00 | 2100.00 |
| 2-Plastic Man smuggles opium | 143.00 | 430.00 | 1000.00 |
| 3 | 115.00 | 343.00 | 800.00 |
| 4 | 100.00 | 300.00 | 700.00 |
| 5-Plastic Man forced to smoke marijuana | 100.00 | 300.00 | 700.00 |
| 6,7 | 90.00 | 270.00 | 630.00 |
| 8-Manhunter begins (origin) | 105.00 | 315.00 | 735.00 |
| 9,10 | 82.00 | 245.00 | 575.00 |
| 11-The Spirit strip reprints begin by Eisner(Origin-strip #1) | 134.00 | 400.00 | 935.00 |
| 12-Intro. Ebony | 86.00 | 257.00 | 600.00 |
| 13-Intro. Woozy Winks; last Firebrand | 86.00 | 257.00 | 600.00 |
| 14-19: 15-Last No. 711; Destiny begins | 56.00 | 167.00 | 390.00 |
| 20-The Raven x-over in Phantom Lady; features Jack Cole himself | 56.00 | 167.00 | 390.00 |
| 21,22-Raven & Spider Widow x-over in Phantom Lady #21; cameo in Phantom Lady #22 | 43.00 | 130.00 | 300.00 |
| 23-30: 23-Last Phantom Lady. 24-26-Flatfoot Burns by Kurtzman in all | 37.00 | 110.00 | 260.00 |
| 31-41-Last Spirit-r by Eisner | 27.00 | 80.00 | 185.00 |
| 42,43-Spirit-r by Eisner/Fine | 23.00 | 70.00 | 160.00 |
| 44-Fine Spirit-r begin, end #88,90,92 | 19.00 | 58.00 | 135.00 |
| 45-50-(#50 on-c, #49 on inside)(1/46) | 19.00 | 58.00 | 135.00 |
| 51-60: 58-Last Human Bomb | 15.00 | 45.00 | 105.00 |
| 61-88: 63-(Some issues have #65 printed on cover, but #63 on inside) Kurtzman-a, 6pgs. | 13.00 | 40.00 | 90.00 |
| 89,91,93-No Spirit | 11.50 | 34.00 | 80.00 |
| 90,92-Spirit by Fine | 13.00 | 40.00 | 90.00 |
| 94-99,101,102: Spirit by Eisner in all; 101-Last Manhunter. 102-Last Spirit & Plastic Man by Jack Cole | 17.00 | 51.00 | 120.00 |
| 100 | 20.00 | 60.00 | 140.00 |
| 103-Content change to crime - Ken Shannon begins (1st app.) | 9.30 | 28.00 | 65.00 |
| 104-111,114-127-Crandall-a most issues | 6.50 | 19.00 | 45.00 |
| 112-Crandall-a | 6.50 | 19.00 | 45.00 |
| 113-Crandall-c/a(2), 9 pgs. each | 7.00 | 21.00 | 50.00 |

NOTE: *Most Spirit stories signed by **Eisner** are not by him; all are reprints. **Cole** c-17, 19-21, 24-26, 28-31, 36-38, 40-42, 45-48, 65-68, 69, 73, 75. **Crandall** Firebrand-1-8. Spirit by **Eisner** 1-41, 94-102; by **Eisner/Fine**-42, 43; by **Fine**-44-88, 90, 92. 103, 109, Bondage c-103, 109, 125.*

**POLICE LINE-UP**
Aug, 1951 - No. 4, July, 1952 (Painted-c)
Realistic Comics/Avon Periodicals

| | Good | Fine | N-Mint |
|---|---|---|---|
| 1-Wood-a, 1 pg. plus part-c; spanking panel-r/Saint #5 | 17.00 | 51.00 | 115.00 |
| 2-Classic story "The Religious Murder Cult," drugs, perversion r-/Saint #5; c-/Avon paperback #329 | 14.00 | 43.00 | 100.00 |
| 3-Kubert-a(r)/part-c, Kinstler-a | 9.30 | 28.00 | 65.00 |
| 4-Kinstler-a | 9.30 | 28.00 | 65.00 |

**POLICE THRILLS**
1954
Ajax/Farrell Publications

| | Good | Fine | N-Mint |
|---|---|---|---|
| 1 | 4.00 | 12.00 | 28.00 |

**POLICE TRAP** (Public Defender In Action #7 on)
8-9/54 - No. 4, 2-3/55; No. 5, 7/55 - No. 6, 9/55
Mainline No. 1-4/Charlton No. 5,6

| | Good | Fine | N-Mint |
|---|---|---|---|
| 1-S&K covers-all issues | 8.50 | 25.50 | 60.00 |
| 2-4 | 5.00 | 15.00 | 35.00 |
| 5,6-S&K-c/a | 8.00 | 24.00 | 55.00 |

**POLICE TRAP**
No. 11, 1963; No. 16-18, 1964
Super Comics

| | Good | Fine | N-Mint |
|---|---|---|---|
| Reprint #11,16-18 | .50 | 1.50 | 3.00 |

**POLL PARROT**
Poll Parrot Shoe Store/International Shoe
1950 - No. 4, 1951; No. 2, 1959 - No. 16, 1962
K. K. Publications (Giveaway)

| | Good | Fine | N-Mint |
|---|---|---|---|
| 1 ('50)-Howdy Doody; small size | 2.65 | 8.00 | 18.00 |
| 2-4('51)-Howdy Doody | 1.70 | 5.00 | 12.00 |
| 2('59)-16('62): 2-The Secret of Crumbley Castle. 5-Bandit Busters. 7-The Make-Believe Mummy. 8-Mixed Up Mission('60). 10-The Frightful Flight. 11-Showdown at Sunup. 12-Maniac at Mubu Island. 13-. . .and the Runaway Genie. 14-Bully for You. 15-Trapped In Tall Timber. 16-. . .& the Rajah's Ruby('62) | .50 | 1.50 | 3.00 |

**POLLY & HER PALS** (See Comic Monthly #1)

**POLLYANNA** (See 4-Color #1129)

**POLLY PIGTAILS** (Girls' Fun & Fashion Magazine #44 on)
Jan, 1946 - V4#43, Oct-Nov, 1949
Parents' Magazine Institute/Polly Pigtails

| | Good | Fine | N-Mint |
|---|---|---|---|
| 1-Infinity-c; photo-c | 5.50 | 16.50 | 38.00 |
| 2 | 2.65 | 8.00 | 18.00 |
| 3-5 | 2.00 | 6.00 | 14.00 |
| 6-10: 7-Photo-c | 1.50 | 4.50 | 10.00 |
| 11-30: 22-Photo-c | 1.15 | 3.50 | 8.00 |
| 31-43 | 1.00 | 3.00 | 7.00 |

**PONY EXPRESS** (See Four Color #942)

**PONYTAIL**
7-9/62 - No. 12, 10-12/65; No. 13, 11/69 - No. 20, 1/71
Dell Publishing Co./Charlton No. 13 on

| | Good | Fine | N-Mint |
|---|---|---|---|
| 12-641-209(#1) | .75 | 2.25 | 5.00 |
| 2-12 | .50 | 1.50 | 3.00 |
| 13-20 | .35 | 1.00 | 2.00 |

**POP COMICS** (7 cents)
1955 (36 pgs.; 5x7"; in color)
Modern Store Publ.

| | Good | Fine | N-Mint |
|---|---|---|---|
| 1-Funny animal | .50 | 1.50 | 3.00 |

**POPEYE** (See Comic Album #7,11,15, Comics Reading Libraries, Eat Right to Work and Win, Giant Comic Album, King Comics, Magic Comics, March of Comics #37, 52, 66, 80, 96, 117, 134, 148, 157, 169, 194, 246, 264, 274, 294, 453, 465, 477 & Wow Comics, 1st series)

**POPEYE** (See Thimble Theatre)
1935 (25 cents; 52 pgs.; B&W) (By Segar)
David McKay Publications

| | Good | Fine | N-Mint |
|---|---|---|---|
| 1-Daily strip serial reprints-"The Gold Mine Thieves" | 49.00 | 146.00 | 340.00 |
| 2-Daily strip-r | 41.00 | 122.00 | 285.00 |

NOTE: *Popeye first entered Thimble Theatre in 1929.*

**POPEYE**
1937 - 1939 (All by Segar)
David McKay Publications

| | Good | Fine | N-Mint |
|---|---|---|---|
| Feature Books nn (100 pgs.) (Very Rare) | 500.00 | 1400.00 | 3000.00 |
| Feature Books 2 (52 pgs.) | 54.00 | 160.00 | 375.00 |
| Feature Books 3 (100 pgs.)-r-/nn issue with a new-c | 46.00 | 139.00 | 325.00 |
| Feature Books 5,10 (76 pgs.) | 39.00 | 118.00 | 275.00 |
| Feature Books 14 (76 pgs.) (Scarce) | 54.00 | 160.00 | 375.00 |

**POPEYE** (Strip reprints through 4-Color #70)
1941 - 1947; #1, 2-4/48 - #65, 7-9/62; #66, 10/62 - #80, 5/66; #81, 8/66 - #92, 12/67; #94, 2/69 - #138, 1/77; #139, 5/78 - #171, 7/84 (no #93,160,161)
Dell #1-65/Gold Key #66-80/King #81-92/Charlton #94-138/Gold Key

*Police Comics #29, © QUA*

*Police Line-Up #2, © AVON*

*Polly Pigtails #1, © PMI*

Popeye #50, © KING

Popular Comics #53, © DELL

Popular Comics #109, © DELL

#139-155/Whitman #156 on — Good / Fine / N-Mint

Large Feat. Comic 24('41)-½ by Segar 39.00 118.00 275.00
4-Color 25('41)-by Segar 43.00 129.00 300.00
Large Feature Comic 10('43) 34.00 100.00 235.00
4-Color 17('43)-by Segar 36.00 107.00 250.00
4-Color 26('43)-by Segar 34.00 100.00 235.00
4-Color 43('44) 23.00 70.00 160.00
4-Color 70('45)-Title: . . .& Wimpy 19.00 58.00 135.00
4-Color 113('46-original strips begin),127,145('47),168 10.00 30.00 70.00
1(2-4/48)(Dell) 24.00 71.00 165.00
2 12.00 36.00 85.00
3-10 10.00 30.00 70.00
11-20 8.00 24.00 55.00
21-40 5.70 17.00 40.00
41-45,47-50 4.00 12.00 28.00
46-Origin Swee' Pee 5.70 17.00 40.00
51-60 3.15 9.50 22.00
61-65 (Last Dell issue) 2.65 8.00 18.00
66,67-Both 84 pgs. (Gold Key) 4.00 12.00 32.00
68-80 2.00 6.00 14.00
81-92,94-100 1.15 3.50 8.00
101-130 .85 2.60 6.00
131-159,162-171: 144-50th Anniversary issue .55 1.65 4.00

NOTE: *Reprints-#145, 147, 149, 151, 153, 155, 157, 163-68(⅓), 170.*

Bold Detergent giveaway (Same as regular issue #94) .35 1.00 2.00
. . .Kite Fun Book ('77, 5x7¼", 16p., soft-c) 1.00 3.00 7.00

**POPEYE**
1972 - 1974 (36 pgs. in color)
Charlton (King Features) (Giveaway)

E-1 to E-15 (Educational comics) .25 .75 1.50
nn-Popeye Gettin' Better Grades-4 pgs. used as intro. to above giveaways (in color) .25 .75 1.50

**POPEYE CARTOON BOOK**
1934 (40 pgs. with cover)(8½x13")(cardboard covers)
The Saalfield Publ. Co.

2095-(Rare)-1933 strip reprints in color by Segar; each page contains a vertical half of a Sunday strip, so the continuity reads row by row completely across each double page spread. If each page is read by itself, the continuity makes no sense. Each double page spread reprints one complete Sunday page (from 1933) 85.00 255.00 595.00
12 Page Version 50.00 150.00 350.00

**POPEYE SPECIAL**
Summer, 1987 - No. 2, Sept, 1988 ($1.75-$2.00, color)
Ocean Comics

1-Origin ($1.75) .30 .90 1.80
2 ($2.00) .35 1.00 2.00

**POPPLES** (TV, movie)
Dec, 1986 - No. 5, Aug, 1987
Star Comics (Marvel)

1-3-Based on toys .35 .70
4,5 ($1.00) .50 1.00

**POPPO OF THE POPCORN THEATRE**
10/29/55 - No. 13, 1956 (published weekly)
Fuller Publishing Co. (Publishers Weekly)

1 3.00 9.00 21.00
2-5 1.70 5.00 12.00
6-13 1.15 3.50 8.00

NOTE: *By* ***Charles Biro***. *10 cent cover, given away by supermarkets such as IGA.*

**POP-POP COMICS**
No date (Circa 1945) (52 pgs.)
R. B. Leffingwell Co. — Good / Fine / N-Mint

1-Funny animal 4.50 14.00 32.00

**POPSICLE PETE FUN BOOK** (See All-American Comics #6)
1947, 1948
Joe Lowe Corp.

nn-36 pgs. in color; Sammy 'n' Claras, The King Who Couldn't Sleep & Popsicle Pete stories, games, cut-outs; has ad, pg. 20, to order Classics Ill. by sending wrappers 5.00 15.00 35.00
Adventure Book ('48) 3.70 11.00 26.00

**POPULAR COMICS**
Feb, 1936 - No. 145, July-Sept, 1948
Dell Publishing Co. — Good / Fine / VF-NM / NM/Mint

1-Dick Tracy (1st comic book app.), Little Orphan Annie, Terry & the Pirates, Gasoline Alley, Don Winslow, Harold Teen, Little Joe, Skippy, Moon Mullins, Mutt & Jeff, Tailspin Tommy, Smitty, Smokey Stover, Winnie Winkle & The Gumps begin (all strip-r) 183.00 460.00 1100.00 2000.00
(Estimated up to 90 total copies exist, 4 in NM/Mint)

Good / Fine / VF-NM

2 77.00 231.00 540.00
3 60.00 180.00 420.00
4,5: 5-Tom Mix begins 47.00 141.00 330.00
6-10: 8,9-Scribbly, Reglar Fellers app. 39.00 116.00 270.00

Good / Fine / N-Mint

11-20: 12-Xmas-c 30.00 90.00 210.00
21-27-Last Terry & the Pirates, Little Orphan Annie, & Dick Tracy 22.00 65.00 150.00
28-37: 28-Gene Autry app. 31,32-Tim McCoy app. 35-Christmas-c; Tex Ritter app. 18.00 54.00 125.00
38-43-Tarzan in text only. 38-Gang Busters (radio) & Zane Grey's Tex Thorne begins? 43-1st non-funny-c? 21.00 62.00 145.00
44,45: 45-Tarzan-c 14.00 43.00 100.00
46-Origin Martan, the Marvel Man 19.00 57.00 135.00
47-50 13.00 40.00 90.00
51-Origin The Voice (The Invisible Detective) strip begins 14.00 43.00 100.00
52-59: 55-End of World story 11.50 34.00 80.00
60-Origin Professor Supermind and Son 12.00 36.00 85.00
61-71: 63-Smilin' Jack begins 10.00 30.00 70.00
72-The Owl & Terry & the Pirates begin; Smokey Stover reprints begin 16.00 48.00 110.00
73-75 12.00 36.00 85.00
76-78-Capt. Midnight in all 14.00 43.00 100.00
79-85-Last Owl 11.00 32.00 75.00
86-99: 98-Felix the Cat, Smokey Stover-r begin 8.50 25.50 60.00
100 10.00 30.00 70.00
101-130: 114-Last Dick Tracy-r? 5.30 16.00 38.00
131-145: 142-Last Terry & the Pirates 4.50 14.00 32.00

**POPULAR FAIRY TALES** (See March of Comics #6, 18)

**POPULAR ROMANCE**
No. 5, Dec, 1949 - No. 29, July, 1954
Better-Standard Publications

5 3.70 11.00 26.00
6-9: 7-Palais-a; lingerie panels 2.30 7.00 16.00
10-Wood-a, 2 pgs. 3.65 11.00 25.00
11,12,14-16,18-21,28,29 1.70 5.00 12.00
13,17-Severin/Elder-a, 3&8 pgs. 2.30 7.00 16.00
22-27-Toth-a 5.00 15.00 35.00

NOTE: *All have photo-c.* ***Tuska*** *art in most issues.*

**POPULAR TEEN-AGERS** (Secrets of Love) (Formerly School Day Romances)
No. 5, Sept, 1950 - No. 23, Nov, 1954
Star Publications

5-Toni Gay, Honey Bunn, etc.; L. B. Cole-c 11.00 32.00 75.00

| | Good | Fine | N-Mint |
|---|---|---|---|
| 6-8 (7/51)-Toni Gay, Honey Bunn, etc.; all have L. B. Cole-c; 6-Negligee panels | 9.30 | 28.00 | 65.00 |
| 9-(. . .Romances; 1st romance issue, 10/51) | 4.30 | 13.00 | 30.00 |
| 10-(. . .Secrets of Love) | 4.30 | 13.00 | 30.00 |
| 11,16,18,19,22,23 | 3.50 | 10.50 | 24.00 |
| 12,13,17,20,21-Disbrow-a | 4.00 | 12.00 | 28.00 |
| 14-Harrison/Wood-a; 2 spanking scenes | 11.50 | 34.50 | 80.00 |
| 15-Wood?, Disbrow-a | 8.00 | 24.00 | 55.00 |
| Accepted Reprint 5,6 (nd); L.B. Cole-c | 2.00 | 6.00 | 14.00 |

NOTE: *All have* ***L. B. Cole*** *covers.*

**PORE LI'L MOSE**
1902 (30 pgs.; 10½x15"; in full color)
New York Herald Publ. by Grand Union Tea
Cupples & Leon Co.

| | Good | Fine | N-Mint |
|---|---|---|---|
| nn-By R. F. Outcault; 1 pg. strips about early Negroes | 43.00 | 130.00 | 300.00 |

**PORKY PIG** (See Bugs Bunny &. . ., March of Comics #42, 57, 71, 89, 99, 113, 130, 143, 164, 175, 192, 209, 218, 367, and Super Book #6, 18, 30)

**PORKY PIG** (. . .& Bugs Bunny #40-69)
No. 16, 1942 - No. 81, Mar-Apr, 1962; Jan, 1965 - No. 109, July, 1984
Dell Publishing Co./Gold Key No. 1-93/Whitman No. 94 on

| | Good | Fine | N-Mint |
|---|---|---|---|
| 4-Color 16(#1, 1942) | 40.00 | 120.00 | 280.00 |
| 4-Color 48(1944)-Carl Barks-a | 70.00 | 210.00 | 490.00 |
| 4-Color 78(1945) | 16.00 | 48.00 | 110.00 |
| 4-Color 112(7/46) | 8.50 | 25.50 | 60.00 |
| 4-Color 156,182,191('49) | 6.50 | 19.50 | 45.00 |
| 4-Color 226,241('49),260,271,277,284,295 | 4.30 | 13.00 | 30.00 |
| 4-Color 303,311,322,330 | 3.00 | 9.00 | 21.00 |
| 4-Color 342,351,360,370,385,399,410,426 | 2.30 | 7.00 | 16.00 |
| 25 (11-12/52)-30 | 1.30 | 4.00 | 9.00 |
| 31-50 | .70 | 2.00 | 4.50 |
| 51-81(3-4/62) | .45 | 1.35 | 3.00 |
| 1(1/65-Gold Key)(2nd Series) | .75 | 2.25 | 5.00 |
| 2,4,5-R/4-Color 226,284 & 271 in that order | .45 | 1.35 | 3.00 |
| 3,6-10 | .35 | 1.00 | 2.00 |
| 11-50 | | .50 | 1.00 |
| 51-109 | | .30 | .60 |
| Kite Fun Book (1960, 16pgs., 5x7¼", soft-c) | 2.00 | 6.00 | 12.00 |

NOTE: *Reprints-#1-8, 9-35(⅔); 36-46, 58, 67, 69-74, 76, 78, 102-109(⅓-½).*

**PORKY'S BOOK OF TRICKS**
1942 (48 pages) (8½x5½")
K. K. Publications (Giveaway)

| | Good | Fine | N-Mint |
|---|---|---|---|
| nn-7 pg. comic story, text stories, plus games & puzzles | 25.00 | 75.00 | 175.00 |

**PORTIA PRINZ OF THE GLAMAZONS**
Dec, 1986 - No. 6, Oct, 1987 ($2.00, B&W, Baxter paper)
Eclipse Comics

| | Good | Fine | N-Mint |
|---|---|---|---|
| 1-6 | .35 | 1.00 | 2.00 |

**POST GAZETTE** (See Meet the New. . .)

**POWDER RIVER RUSTLERS** (See Fawcett Movie Comics)

**POWER COMICS**
1944 - No. 4, 1945
Holyoke Publ. Co./Narrative Publ.

| | Good | Fine | N-Mint |
|---|---|---|---|
| 1-L. B. Cole-c | 23.00 | 70.00 | 160.00 |
| 2-4: 2-Hitler, Hirohito-c. 3?-Dr. Mephisto begins. 3,4-L. B. Cole-c; Miss Espionage app. each | 20.00 | 60.00 | 140.00 |

**POWER COMICS**
1977 - No. 5, Dec, 1977 (B&W)
Power Comics Co.

| | Good | Fine | N-Mint |
|---|---|---|---|
| 1-"A Boy And His Aardvark" by Dave Sim; first Dave Sim aardvark (not Cerebus) | 2.50 | 7.50 | 15.00 |
| 1-Reprint (3/77, black-c) | 1.00 | 3.00 | 6.00 |
| 2-Cobalt Blue by Gustovich | 1.70 | 5.00 | 10.00 |
| 3-5: 3-Nightwitch. 4-Northern Light. 5-Bluebird | .35 | 1.00 | 2.00 |

**POWER COMICS**
Mar, 1988 - No. 4, Sept, 1988 ($2.00, B&W, mini-series)
Eclipse Comics (Acme Press)

| | Good | Fine | N-Mint |
|---|---|---|---|
| 1-4: Bolland, Gibbons-r in all | .35 | 1.00 | 2.00 |

**POWER FACTOR**
May, 1987 - No. 3, 1987? ($1.95, color)
Wonder Color Comics

| | Good | Fine | N-Mint |
|---|---|---|---|
| 1-3: Super team. 2-Infantino-c | .35 | 1.00 | 2.00 |

**POWER FACTOR**
Oct, 1990 - Present ($1.95, color)($2.25 #2 on)
Innovation Publishing

| | Good | Fine | N-Mint |
|---|---|---|---|
| 1-Reprints 1st story plus new-a | .35 | 1.00 | 2.00 |
| 2,3: 2-r/2nd story plus new-a. 3-Infantino-a | .40 | 1.15 | 2.30 |

**POWER GIRL** (See Infinity, Inc. & Showcase #97-99)
June, 1988 - No. 4, Sept, 1988 ($1.00, mini-series)
DC Comics

| | Good | Fine | N-Mint |
|---|---|---|---|
| 1-4 | | .50 | 1.00 |

**POWERHOUSE PEPPER COMICS** (See Gay Comics, Joker Comics & Tessie the Typist)
No. 1, 1943; No. 2, May, 1948 - No. 5, Nov, 1948
Marvel Comics (20CC)

| | Good | Fine | N-Mint |
|---|---|---|---|
| 1-(60 pgs.)-Wolverton-c/a in all | 63.00 | 190.00 | 440.00 |
| 2 | 39.00 | 116.00 | 270.00 |
| 3,4 | 36.00 | 107.00 | 250.00 |
| 5-(Scarce) | 43.00 | 130.00 | 300.00 |

**POWER LINE**
May, 1988 - No. 8, Sept, 1989 ($1.25, $1.50 #4 on, color)
Epic Comics (Marvel)

| | Good | Fine | N-Mint |
|---|---|---|---|
| 1-3: 2-Williamson-i; 3-Austin-i, Dr. Zero app. | | .60 | 1.25 |
| 4-8: 4-7-Morrow-a. 8-Williamson-i | .25 | .75 | 1.50 |

**POWER LORDS**
Dec, 1983 - No. 3, Feb, 1984 (Mini-series, Mando paper)
DC Comics

| | Good | Fine | N-Mint |
|---|---|---|---|
| 1-3-Based on Revell toys | | .40 | .80 |

**POWER MAN** (Formerly Hero for Hire; . . .& Iron Fist #68 on; see Giant-Size. . .)
No. 17, Feb, 1974 - No. 125, Sept, 1986
Marvel Comics Group

| | Good | Fine | N-Mint |
|---|---|---|---|
| 17-Luke Cage continues; Iron Man app. | .85 | 2.60 | 6.00 |
| 18-20: 18-Last 20 cent issue | .70 | 2.00 | 4.00 |
| 21-31: 31-Part Neal Adams-i. 34-Last 25 cents | .35 | 1.00 | 2.00 |
| 32-47: 36-r/Hero For Hire #12. 45-Starlin-c | | .50 | 1.00 |
| 48-Byrne-a; Powerman/Iron Fist 1st meet | .50 | 1.50 | 3.00 |
| 49,50-Byrne-a(p); 50-Iron Fist joins Cage | .50 | 1.50 | 3.00 |
| 51-56,58-60: 58-Intro El Aguila | | .40 | .80 |
| 57-Early New X-Men app. | .85 | 2.50 | 5.00 |
| 61-65,67-83,85-125: 75-Double size. 77-Daredevil app. 87-Moon Knight app. 90-Unus app. 109-The Reaper app. 100-Double size; origin K'un L'un. 125-Double size | | .40 | .80 |
| 66,84-2nd & 3rd Sabretooth app. | .60 | 1.75 | 3.50 |
| Annual 1(1976)-Punisher cameo in flashback | .50 | 1.50 | 3.00 |

NOTE: ***Austin*** *c-102i.* ***Byrne*** *a-48-50; c-102, 104, 106, 107, 112-116.* ***Kane*** *c(p)-24, 25, 28, 48.* ***Miller*** *a-68, 76(2pgs.); c-66-68, 70-74, 80i.* ***Mooney*** *a-38i, 53i, 55i.* ***Nebres*** *a-76p.* ***Nino*** *a-42i, 43i.* ***Perez*** *a-27.* ***B. Smith*** *a-47i.* ***Tuska*** *a(p)-17, 20, 24, 26, 28, 29, 36, 47. Painted c-75, 100.*

**POWER OF STRONGMAN, THE** (Also see Strongman)
1989 ($2.95, color)

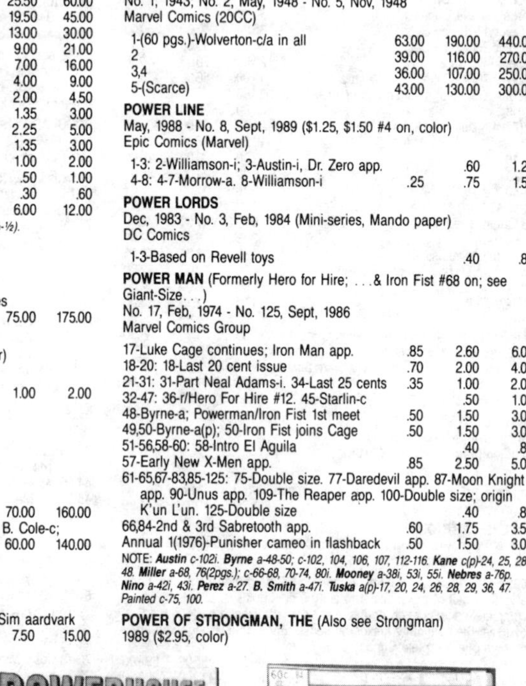

*Popular Teen-Agers #8, © STAR*

*Powerhouse Pepper #2, © MEG*

*Power Man #84, © MEG*

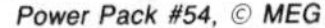
Power Pack #54, © MEG

The Pride of the Yankees nn, © ME

The Prisoner #2, © ITC Entertainment

AC Comics

| | Good | Fine | N-Mint |
|---|---|---|---|
| 1-Powell G.A.-r | .50 | 1.50 | 3.00 |

**POWER OF THE ATOM** (See Secret Origins #29)
Aug, 1988 - No. 18, Nov, 1989 ($1.00, color)
DC Comics

| | Good | Fine | N-Mint |
|---|---|---|---|
| 1-18: 6-Chronos returns; Byrne-p. 9-JLI app. | | .50 | 1.00 |

**POWER PACHYDERMS**
Sept, 1989 ($1.25, color, one-shot)
Marvel Comics

| | Good | Fine | N-Mint |
|---|---|---|---|
| 1-Elephant super-heroes | | .65 | 1.30 |

**POWER PACK**
Aug, 1984 - No. 62, Feb, 1991
Marvel Comics Group

| | Good | Fine | N-Mint |
|---|---|---|---|
| 1-($1.00, 52 pgs.) | .70 | 2.00 | 4.00 |
| 2-5 | .45 | 1.35 | 2.70 |
| 6-8-Cloak & Dagger app. 6-Spider-man app. | .35 | 1.00 | 2.00 |
| 9-18 | .25 | .75 | 1.50 |
| 19-Dbl. size; Cloak & Dagger, Wolverine app. | 1.15 | 3.50 | 8.00 |
| 20-24 | | .60 | 1.25 |
| 25-Double size | .30 | .90 | 1.80 |
| 26-Begin direct sale; Cloak & Dagger app. | | .60 | 1.25 |
| 27-Mutant massacre; Wolverine app. | 1.30 | 4.00 | 9.00 |
| 28-43: 42-1st Inferno tie-in | | .60 | 1.25 |
| 44,45,47-49,51-62: 44-Begin $1.50-c | .25 | .75 | 1.50 |
| 46-Punisher app. | .70 | 2.00 | 4.00 |
| 50-Double size ($1.95) | .35 | 1.00 | 2.00 |

NOTE: ***Austin** scripts-53.* ***Morrow** a-51.* ***Spiegle** a-55i.* ***Williamson** a-50i, 52i.*

**POWER RECORD COMICS**
1974 - 1978 ($1.49, 7X10" comics, 20 pgs. with 45 R.P.M. record)
Marvel Comics/Power Records

PR10-Spider-Man-r/from #124,125; Man-Wolf app. PR11-Hulk-r. PR12-Captain America-r/#168. PR13-Fantastic Four-r/#126. PR14-Frankenstein-Ploog-r/#1. PR15-Tomb of Dracula-Colan-r/#2. PR16-Man-Thing-Ploog-r/#5. PR17-Werewolf By Night-Ploog-r/Marvel Spotlight #2. PR18-Planet of the Apes-r. PR19-Escape From the Planet of the Apes-r. PR20-Beneath the Planet of the Apes-r. PR21-Battle for the Planet of the Apes-r. PR24-Spider-Man II-New-a begins. PR25-Star Trek "Passage to Moauv." PR26-Star Trek "Crier in Emptiness." PR27-Batman "Stacked Cards;" N. Adams-a(p). PR28-Superman "Alien Creatures." PR29-Space: 1999 "Breakaway." PR30-Batman; N. Adams-r/Det.(7 pgs.). PR31-Conan-N. Adams-r/#116. PR32-Space: 1999 "Return to the Beginning." PR33-Superman-G.A. origin, Buckler-a(p). PR34-Superman. PR35-Wonder Woman-Buckler-a(p). PR36-Holo-Man. PR37-Robin Hood. PR39-Huckleberry Finn. PR40-Davy Crockett. PR41-Robinson Crusoe. PR42-20,000 Leagues Under the Sea. PR47-Little Women

| | Good | Fine | N-Mint |
|---|---|---|---|
| With record; each... | .85 | 2.50 | 5.00 |

**POW MAGAZINE** (Bob Sproul's) (Satire Magazine)
Aug, 1966 - No. 3, Feb, 1967 (30 cents)
Humor-Vision

| | Good | Fine | N-Mint |
|---|---|---|---|
| 1-3: 2-Jones-a. 3-Wrightson-a | 1.50 | 4.50 | 10.00 |

**PREDATOR** (Also see Aliens Vs. Predator & Dark Horse Presents)
May, 1989 - No. 4, 1990 ($2.25, color, mini-series)
Dark Horse Comics

| | Good | Fine | N-Mint |
|---|---|---|---|
| 1-Based on movie | 3.00 | 9.00 | 18.00 |
| 1-2nd printing | 1.00 | 3.00 | 6.00 |
| 2 | 1.70 | 5.00 | 10.00 |
| 3 | 1.30 | 4.00 | 8.00 |
| 4 | .85 | 2.50 | 5.00 |
| Trade paperback (1990, $12.95)-r/1-4 | 2.15 | 6.50 | 13.00 |

**PREHISTORIC WORLD** (See Classics Illustsrated Special Issue)

**PREMIERE** (See Charlton Premiere)

**PRESTO KID, THE** (See Red Mask)

**PRETTY BOY FLOYD** (See On the Spot)

**PREZ** (See Cancelled Comic Cavalcade & Supergirl #10)
Aug-Sept, 1973 - No. 4, Feb-Mar, 1974
National Periodical Publications

| | Good | Fine | N-Mint |
|---|---|---|---|
| 1-4: 1-Origin; Joe Simon scripts | | .40 | .80 |

**PRICE, THE** (See Eclipse Graphic Album Series)

**PRIDE AND THE PASSION, THE** (See 4-Color #824)

**PRIDE OF THE YANKEES, THE** (See Real Heroes & Sport Comics)
1949 (The Life of Lou Gehrig)
Magazine Enterprises

| | Good | Fine | N-Mint |
|---|---|---|---|
| nn-Photo-c; Ogden Whitney-a | 35.00 | 105.00 | 245.00 |

**PRIMAL MAN** (See The Crusaders)

**PRIMER** (Comico...)
Oct, 1982 - No. 6, Feb, 1984 (B&W)
Comico

| | Good | Fine | N-Mint |
|---|---|---|---|
| 1 (52 pgs.) | .85 | 2.50 | 5.00 |
| 2-1st app. Grendel & Argent by Wagner | 7.50 | 22.50 | 45.00 |
| 3-5 | .60 | 1.75 | 3.50 |
| 6-Intro & 1st app. Evangeline | 1.70 | 5.00 | 10.00 |

**PRIMUS** (TV)
Feb, 1972 - No. 7, Oct, 1972
Charlton Comics

| | Good | Fine | N-Mint |
|---|---|---|---|
| 1-5,7-Staton-a in all | .50 | 1.50 | 3.00 |
| 6-Drug propaganda story | .50 | 1.50 | 3.00 |

**PRINCE & THE PAUPER, THE** (See Movie Classics)

**PRINCE NAMOR, THE SUB-MARINER** (Also see Namor ...)
Sept, 1984 - No. 4, Dec, 1984 (Mini-series)
Marvel Comics Group

| | Good | Fine | N-Mint |
|---|---|---|---|
| 1 | .30 | .90 | 1.80 |
| 2-4 | | .60 | 1.20 |

**PRINCE NIGHTMARE**
1987 ($2.95, color, 68 pgs.)
Aaaargh! Associated Artists

| | Good | Fine | N-Mint |
|---|---|---|---|
| Book 1 | .50 | 1.50 | 3.00 |

**PRINCE VALIANT** (See Ace Comics, Comics Reading Libraries, Feature Books #26, McKay, and 4-Color #567, 650, 699, 719, 788, 849, 900)

**PRIORITY WHITE HEAT**
1986 - No. 2, 1986 ($1.75, color, mini-series)
AC Comics

| | Good | Fine | N-Mint |
|---|---|---|---|
| 1,2-Bill Black-a | .30 | .90 | 1.80 |

**PRISCILLA'S POP** (See 4-Color #569,630,704,799)

**PRISON BARS** (See Behind...)

**PRISON BREAK!**
1951 (Sept) - No. 5, Sept, 1952
Avon Periodicals/Realistic No. 3 on

| | Good | Fine | N-Mint |
|---|---|---|---|
| 1-Wood-c & 1 pg.; has r-/Saint #7 retitled Michael Strong Private Eye | 19.00 | 56.00 | 130.00 |
| 2-Wood-c/Kubert-a plus 2 pgs. Wood-a | 13.00 | 40.00 | 90.00 |
| 3-Orlando, Check-a; c-/Avon paperback 179 | 11.00 | 32.00 | 78.00 |
| 4,5: Kinstler-c. 5-Infantino-a | 10.00 | 30.00 | 70.00 |

**PRISONER, THE** (TV)
1988 - No. 4, Jan, 1989 ($3.50, mini-series, squarebound)
DC Comics

| | Good | Fine | N-Mint |
|---|---|---|---|
| 1-Book A | .75 | 2.25 | 4.50 |
| 2-4: Book B-D | .60 | 1.75 | 3.50 |
| Graphic Novel (1990, $19.95)-r/1-4 | 3.35 | 10.00 | 20.00 |

**PRISON RIOT**
1952
Avon Periodicals

| | Good | Fine | N-Mint |
|---|---|---|---|
| 1-Marijuana Murders-1 pg. text; Kinstler-c | 13.00 | 40.00 | 90.00 |

**PRISON TO PRAISE**
1974 (35 cents)
Logos International

| | Good | Fine | N-Mint |
|---|---|---|---|
| nn-True Story of Merlin R. Carothers | | .30 | .60 |

**PRIVATE BUCK** (See Large Feature Comic #12 & 21)

**PRIVATEERS**
Aug, 1987 - No. 2, 1987 ($1.50, color)
Vanguard Graphics

| | Good | Fine | N-Mint |
|---|---|---|---|
| 1,2 | .25 | .75 | 1.50 |

**PRIVATE EYE** (Cover title: Rocky Jordan. . . #6-8)
Jan, 1951 - No. 8, March, 1952
Atlas Comics (MCI)

| | Good | Fine | N-Mint |
|---|---|---|---|
| 1-Cover title: Crime Cases. . . #1-5 | 7.00 | 21.00 | 50.00 |
| 2,3-Tuska c/a(3) | 4.30 | 13.00 | 30.00 |
| 4-8 | 3.50 | 10.50 | 24.00 |

NOTE: ***Henkel** a-6(3), 7; c-7. **Sinnott** a-6.*

**PRIVATE EYE** (See Mike Shayne. . .)

**PRIVATE SECRETARY**
Dec-Feb, 1962-63 - No. 2, Mar-May, 1963
Dell Publishing Co.

| | Good | Fine | N-Mint |
|---|---|---|---|
| 1,2 | 1.00 | 3.00 | 7.00 |

**PRIVATE STRONG** (See The Double Life of. . .)

**PRIZE COMICS** (. . .Western #69 on) (Also see Treasure Comics)
March, 1940 - No. 68, Feb-Mar, 1948
Prize Publications

| | Good | Fine | N-Mint |
|---|---|---|---|
| 1-Origin Power Nelson, The Futureman & Jupiter, Master Magician; Ted O'Neil, Secret Agent M-11, Jaxon of the Jungle, Bucky Brady & Storm Curtis begin | 84.00 | 250.00 | 585.00 |
| 2-The Black Owl begins | 41.00 | 122.00 | 285.00 |
| 3,4 | 34.00 | 100.00 | 235.00 |
| 5,6: Dr. Dekkar, Master of Monsters app. in each | 30.00 | 90.00 | 210.00 |
| 7-(Scarce)-Black Owl by S&K; origin/1st app. Dr. Frost & Frankenstein; The Green Lama, Capt. Gallant, The Great Voodini & Twist Turner begin; Kirby-c | 68.00 | 205.00 | 475.00 |
| 8,9-Black Owl & Ted O'Neil by S&K | 35.00 | 105.00 | 245.00 |
| 10-12,14-20: 11-Origin Bulldog Denny. 16-Spike Mason begins | 30.00 | 90.00 | 210.00 |
| 13-Yank & Doodle begin (origin) | 36.00 | 107.00 | 250.00 |
| 21-24 | 20.00 | 60.00 | 140.00 |
| 25-30 | 13.00 | 40.00 | 90.00 |
| 31-33 | 10.00 | 30.00 | 70.00 |
| 34-Origin Airmale, Yank & Doodle; The Black Owl joins army, Yank & Doodle's father assumes Black Owl's role | 11.50 | 34.00 | 80.00 |
| 35-40: 35-Flying Fist & Bingo begin. 37-Intro. Stampy, Airmale's sidekick; Hitler-c | 8.50 | 25.50 | 60.00 |
| 41-50: 45-Yank & Doodle learn Black Owl's I.D. (their father). 48-Prince Ra begins | 6.50 | 19.00 | 45.00 |
| 51-62,64-68: 53-Transvestism story. 55-No Frankenstein. 64-Black Owl retires. 65,66-Frankenstein-c by Briefer | 5.70 | 17.00 | 40.00 |
| 63-Simon & Kirby c/a | 8.00 | 24.00 | 55.00 |

NOTE: ***Briefer** a 7-on; c-65, 66. **J. Binder** a-16; c-22, 26, 29. **Guardineer** a-62. **Kiefer** c-62.*

**PRIZE COMICS WESTERN** (Formerly Prize Comics #1-68)
No. 69(V7#2), Apr-May, 1948 - No. 119, Nov-Dec, 1956
Prize Publications (Feature) (No. 69-84: 52 pgs.)

| | Good | Fine | N-Mint |
|---|---|---|---|
| 69(V7#2) | 8.00 | 24.00 | 55.00 |
| 70-75 | 5.30 | 16.00 | 38.00 |
| 76-Randolph Scott photo-c; "Canadian Pacific" movie adaptation | 8.00 | 24.00 | 55.00 |
| 77-Photo-c; Severin, Mart Bailey-a; "Streets of Laredo" movie adapt. | 6.50 | 19.00 | 45.00 |
| 78-Photo-c; Kurtzman-a, 10 pgs.; Severin, Mart Bailey-a; "Bullet Code," & "Roughshod" movie adapt. | 9.30 | 28.00 | 65.00 |
| 79-Photo-c; Kurtzman-a, 8 pgs.; Severin & Elder, Severin, Mart Bailey-a; "Stage To Chino" movie adapt. | 9.30 | 28.00 | 65.00 |
| 80,81-Photo-c; Severin/Elder-a(2) | 6.50 | 19.00 | 45.00 |
| 82-Photo-c; 1st app. The Preacher by Mart Bailey; Severin/Elder-a(3) | 6.50 | 19.00 | 45.00 |
| 83,84 | 5.00 | 15.00 | 35.00 |
| 85-American Eagle by John Severin begins (1-2/50) | 13.00 | 40.00 | 90.00 |
| 86,92,95,101-105 | 5.70 | 17.00 | 40.00 |
| 87-91,93,94,96-99,110,111-Severin/Elder a(2-3) each | 6.50 | 19.00 | 45.00 |
| 100 | 8.00 | 24.00 | 55.00 |
| 106-108,112 | 4.00 | 12.00 | 28.00 |
| 109-Severin/Williamson-a | 6.50 | 19.00 | 45.00 |
| 113-Williamson/Severin-a(2)/Frazetta? | 7.00 | 21.00 | 50.00 |
| 114-119: Drifter series in all; by Mort Meskin #114-118 | 3.00 | 9.00 | 21.00 |

NOTE: ***Fass** a-81. **Severin & Elder** c-84, 88, 92, 94-96, 98. **Severin** a-72, 75, 77-79, 83-86, 96, 97, 100-105; c-most 85-109. **Simon & Kirby** c-75, 83.*

**PRIZE MYSTERY**
May, 1955 - No. 3, Sept, 1955
Key Publications

| | Good | Fine | N-Mint |
|---|---|---|---|
| 1 | 3.50 | 10.50 | 24.00 |
| 2,3 | 2.65 | 8.00 | 18.00 |

**PROFESSIONAL FOOTBALL** (See Charlton Sport Library)

**PROFESSOR COFFIN**
No. 19, Oct, 1985 - No. 21, Feb, 1986
Charlton Comics

| | Good | Fine | N-Mint |
|---|---|---|---|
| 19-21: Wayne Howard-a(r) | | .40 | .80 |

**PROFESSOR OM**
May, 1990 - No. 2, 1990 ($2.50, color, mini-series)
Innovation Publishing

| | Good | Fine | N-Mint |
|---|---|---|---|
| 1,2-East Meets West spin-off | .40 | 1.25 | 2.50 |

**PROJECT: HERO**
Aug, 1987 ($1.50, color)
Vanguard Graphics (Canadian)

| | Good | Fine | N-Mint |
|---|---|---|---|
| 1 | .25 | .75 | 1.50 |

**PROWLER** (Also see Revenge of the. . .)
July, 1987 - No. 4, Oct, 1987 ($1.75, color)
Eclipse Comics

| | Good | Fine | N-Mint |
|---|---|---|---|
| 1-4: 3,4-Origin | .30 | .90 | 1.80 |

**PROWLER IN "WHITE ZOMBIE", THE**
Oct, 1988 ($2.00, B&W, Baxter paper)
Eclipse Comics

| | Good | Fine | N-Mint |
|---|---|---|---|
| 1-Adapts Bela Lugosi movie White Zombie | .35 | 1.00 | 2.00 |

**PSI-FORCE**
Nov, 1986 - No. 32, June, 1989 (.75-$1.25-$1.50, color)
Marvel Comics Group

| | Good | Fine | N-Mint |
|---|---|---|---|
| 1-32: 11-13-Williamson-i | | .65 | 1.30 |
| Annual 1 (10/87) | | .65 | 1.30 |

**PSI-JUDGE ANDERSON**
1989 - Present ($1.95, B&W)
Fleetway Publications (Quality)

| | Good | Fine | N-Mint |
|---|---|---|---|
| 1-10 | .35 | 1.00 | 2.00 |

**PSYCHO** (Magazine)
Jan, 1971 - No. 24, Mar, 1975 (68 pgs.; B&W) (no No.22?)
Skywald Publishing Corp.

| | Good | Fine | N-Mint |
|---|---|---|---|
| 1-All reprints | .85 | 2.50 | 6.00 |

*Prize Comics #37, © PRIZE*

*Prize Comics Western #119, © PRIZE*

*Prize Mystery #2, © Key Publ.*

*Psychoanalysis #3, © WMG*

*Punch Comics #15, © CHES*

*Punisher #29, © MEG*

| | Good | Fine | N-Mint |
|---|---|---|---|
| 2-Origin & 1st app. The Heap, & Frankenstein series by Adkins | .70 | 2.00 | 4.00 |
| 3-24: 13-Cannabalism. 18-Injury to eye-c. 20-Severed Head-c. 24-1975 Winter Special | .40 | 1.25 | 2.50 |
| Annual 1('72) | .60 | 1.75 | 3.50 |
| Fall Special('74)-Reese, Wildey-a(r) | .40 | 1.25 | 2.50 |
| Yearbook(1974-nn) | .40 | 1.25 | 2.50 |

NOTE: ***Boris*** *c-3, 5.* ***Buckler*** *a-4, 5.* ***Everett*** *a-3-6.* ***Jeff Jones*** *a-6, 7, 9; c-12.* ***Kaluta*** *a-13.* ***Katz/Buckler*** *a-3.* ***Morrow*** *a-1.* ***Reese*** *a-5.* ***Sutton*** *a-3.* ***Wildey*** *a-5.*

**PSYCHOANALYSIS**
Mar-Apr, 1955 - No. 4, Sept-Oct, 1955
E. C. Comics

| | Good | Fine | N-Mint |
|---|---|---|---|
| 1-All Kamen-c/a; not approved by code | 8.50 | 25.50 | 60.00 |
| 2-4-Kamen-c/a in all | 6.50 | 19.00 | 45.00 |

**PSYCHOBLAST**
Nov, 1987 - No. 9, July, 1988 ($1.75, color)
First Comics

| | Good | Fine | N-Mint |
|---|---|---|---|
| 1-9 | .30 | .90 | 1.80 |

**P.T. 109** (See Movie Comics)

**PUBLIC DEFENDER IN ACTION** (Formerly Police Trap)
No. 7, Mar, 1956 - No. 12, Oct, 1957
Charlton Comics

| | Good | Fine | N-Mint |
|---|---|---|---|
| 7 | 3.70 | 11.00 | 26.00 |
| 8-12 | 2.30 | 7.00 | 16.00 |

**PUBLIC ENEMIES**
1948 - No. 9, June-July, 1949
D. S. Publishing Co.

| | Good | Fine | N-Mint |
|---|---|---|---|
| 1 | 8.50 | 25.50 | 60.00 |
| 2-Used in **SOTI**, pg. 95 | 9.30 | 28.00 | 65.00 |
| 3-5: 5-Arrival date of 10/1/48 | 5.00 | 15.00 | 35.00 |
| 6,8,9 | 4.30 | 13.00 | 30.00 |
| 7-McWilliams-a; injury to eye panel | 5.70 | 17.00 | 40.00 |

**PUDGY PIG**
Sept, 1958 - No. 2, Nov, 1958
Charlton Comics

| | Good | Fine | N-Mint |
|---|---|---|---|
| 1,2 | 1.15 | 3.50 | 8.00 |

**PUMA BLUES**
1986 - No. 26?, 1990 ($1.70-$1.75, B&W)
Aardvark One International/Mirage Studios #21 on

| | Good | Fine | N-Mint |
|---|---|---|---|
| 1-19,21-26: 1-1st & 2nd printings. 25,26-$1.75-c | .30 | .85 | 1.70 |
| 20 ($2.25)-By Alan Moore, Miller, Grell, others | .40 | 1.15 | 2.30 |
| Trade Paperback (12/88, $14.95) | 2.50 | 7.50 | 14.95 |

**PUNCH & JUDY COMICS**
1944; No. 2, Fall, 1944 - V3#2, 12/47; V3#3, 6/51 - V3#9, 12/51
Hillman Periodicals

| | Good | Fine | N-Mint |
|---|---|---|---|
| V1#1-(60 pgs.) | 8.50 | 25.50 | 60.00 |
| 2 | 4.30 | 13.00 | 30.00 |
| 3-12(7/46) | 2.85 | 8.50 | 20.00 |
| V2#1,3-9 | 2.00 | 6.00 | 14.00 |
| V2#2,10-12, V3#1-Kirby-a(2) each | 8.50 | 25.50 | 60.00 |
| V3#2-Kirby-a | 8.00 | 24.00 | 55.00 |
| 3-9 | 1.70 | 5.00 | 12.00 |

**PUNCH COMICS**
12/41; #2, 2/42; #9, 7/44 - #19, 10/46; #20, 7/47 - #23, 1/48
Harry 'A' Chesler

| | Good | Fine | N-Mint |
|---|---|---|---|
| 1-Mr. E, The Sky Chief, Hale the Magician, Kitty Kelly begin | 50.00 | 150.00 | 350.00 |
| 2-Captain Glory app. | 25.00 | 75.00 | 175.00 |
| 9-Rocketman & Rocket Girl & The Master Key begin | 17.00 | 51.00 | 115.00 |
| 10-Sky Chief app.; J. Cole-a; Master Key r-/Scoop #3 | 13.00 | 40.00 | 90.00 |
| 11-Origin Master Key-r/Scoop #1; Sky Chief, Little Nemo app.; Jack Cole-a; Fineish art by Sultan | 13.00 | 40.00 | 90.00 |
| 12-Rocket Boy & Capt. Glory app; Skull-c | 11.50 | 34.00 | 80.00 |
| 13-17,19: 13-Cover has list of 4 Chesler artists' names on tombstone | 11.00 | 32.00 | 75.00 |
| 18-Bondage-c; hypodermic panels | 13.00 | 40.00 | 90.00 |
| 20-Unique cover with bare-breasted women | 22.00 | 65.00 | 150.00 |
| 21-Hypo needle story | 11.50 | 34.00 | 80.00 |
| 22,23-Little Nemo-not by McCay | 9.30 | 28.00 | 65.00 |

**PUNCHY AND THE BLACK CROW**
No. 10, Oct, 1985 - No. 12, Feb, 1986
Charlton Comics

| | Good | Fine | N-Mint |
|---|---|---|---|
| 10-12: Al Fago funny animal-r | | .40 | .80 |

**PUNISHER** (See Amazing Spider-Man #129, Captain America #241, Classic Punisher, Daredevil #182-184, 257, Daredevil and the..., Marc Spector #8 & 9, Marvel Preview #2, Marvel Super Action, Marvel Tales, Power Pack #46, Spectacular Spider-Man #81-83, 140, 141, 143 & new Strange Tales #13 & 14)

**PUNISHER**
Jan, 1986 - No. 5, May, 1986 (Mini-series)
Marvel Comics Group

| | Good | Fine | N-Mint |
|---|---|---|---|
| 1-Double size | 6.50 | 19.00 | 45.00 |
| 2 | 3.50 | 10.50 | 24.00 |
| 3-Has 2 cover prices, 75 & 95(w/UPC) cents | 2.00 | 6.00 | 12.00 |
| 4,5 | 1.70 | 5.00 | 10.00 |
| Trade Paperback-r/1-5 (1988) | 1.70 | 5.00 | 10.00 |

**PUNISHER**
July, 1987 - Present
Marvel Comics Group

| | Good | Fine | N-Mint |
|---|---|---|---|
| V2#1 | 3.70 | 11.00 | 22.00 |
| 2 | 2.35 | 7.00 | 14.00 |
| 3-5 | 1.30 | 4.00 | 8.00 |
| 6-8 | 1.15 | 3.50 | 7.00 |
| 9 | 1.70 | 5.00 | 10.00 |
| 10-Daredevil app. | 3.35 | 10.00 | 20.00 |
| 11-15: 13-18-Kingpin app. | 1.15 | 3.50 | 7.00 |
| 16-20 | .85 | 2.50 | 5.00 |
| 21-24,26-30: 24-1st app. Shadowmasters | .50 | 1.50 | 3.00 |
| 25-Double size ($1.50)-Shadowmasters app. | .70 | 2.00 | 4.00 |
| 31-40 | .25 | .75 | 1.50 |
| 41-48 | | .65 | 1.25 |
| Annual 1(8/88)-Evolutionary War app. | 1.70 | 5.00 | 10.00 |
| Annual 2('89, $2.00, 68 pgs.)-Atlantis Attacks x-over; Moon Knight app. | .85 | 2.50 | 5.00 |
| Annual 3(1990, $2.00, 68 pgs.) | .50 | 1.50 | 3.00 |
| ...and Wolverine in African Saga nn (1989, 52 pgs.)-Reprints Punisher War Journal #6 & 7 | 1.00 | 3.00 | 6.00 |
| ...Movie Special 1(6/90, $5.95, 68 pgs.) | 1.00 | 3.00 | 6.00 |
| ...: No Escape nn (1990, $4.95, 52 pgs.)-New-a | .85 | 2.50 | 5.00 |
| ...The Prize nn (1990, $4.95, 68 pgs.)-New-a | .85 | 2.50 | 5.00 |

NOTE: ***Heath*** *a-26, 27.* ***Williamson*** *a-25i.*

**PUNISHER ARMORY, THE**
July, 1990 ($1.50, one-shot)
Marvel Comics

| | Good | Fine | N-Mint |
|---|---|---|---|
| 1-Reprints weapons pgs. from War Journal | .40 | 1.25 | 2.50 |

**PUNISHER MAGAZINE, THE**
Oct, 1989 - No. 16, 1990 ($2.25, B&W, Magazine, 52 pgs.)
Marvel Comics

| | Good | Fine | N-Mint |
|---|---|---|---|
| 1-3: 1-r/Punisher #1('86). 2,3-r/Punisher 2-5 | .40 | 1.15 | 2.25 |
| 4-16: 4-7-r/Punisher V2#1-8. 4-Chiodo-c. 14-r/Punisher War Journal #1,2. 16-r/Punisher War Journal #3,8 | .40 | 1.15 | 2.25 |

**PUNISHER MOVIE COMIC**
Nov, 1989 - No. 3, Dec, 1989 ($1.00, color, mini-series)
Marvel Comics

| | Good | Fine | N-Mint |
|---|---|---|---|
| 1-3: Movie adaptation | | .50 | 1.00 |
| 1 (1989, $4.95, squarebound)-contains #1-3 | .85 | 2.50 | 5.00 |

**PUNISHER WAR JOURNAL, THE**
Nov, 1988 - Present ($1.50, color)
Marvel Comics

| | Good | Fine | N-Mint |
|---|---|---|---|
| 1-Origin The Punisher; Matt Murdock cameo | 2.50 | 7.50 | 15.00 |
| 2-Daredevil x-over | 1.70 | 5.00 | 10.00 |
| 3-5: 3-Daredevil x-over | 1.30 | 4.00 | 8.00 |
| 6-Two part Wolverine story begins | 2.50 | 7.50 | 15.00 |
| 7-Wolverine story ends | 1.30 | 4.00 | 8.00 |
| 8-10 | .85 | 2.50 | 5.00 |
| 11-13 | .50 | 1.50 | 3.00 |
| 14-20: 13-15-Heath-i. 14,15-Spider-Man x-over | .35 | 1.00 | 2.00 |
| 21-30: 23-Begin $1.75-c | .30 | .90 | 1.80 |

**PUPPET COMICS**
Spring, 1946 - No. 2, Summer, 1946
George W. Dougherty Co.

| | Good | Fine | N-Mint |
|---|---|---|---|
| 1,2-Funny animal | 4.00 | 12.00 | 28.00 |

**PUPPETOONS** (See George Pal's . . .)

**PURE OIL COMICS** (Also see Salerno Carnival of Comics, 24 Pages of Comics, & Vicks Comics)
Late 1930's (24 pgs.; regular size) (paper cover)
Pure Oil Giveaway

| | Good | Fine | N-Mint |
|---|---|---|---|
| nn-Contains 1-2 pg. strips; i.e., Hairbreadth Harry, Skyroads, Buck Rogers by Calkins & Yager, Olly of the Movies, Napoleon, S'Matter Pop, etc. | 25.00 | 75.00 | 175.00 |
| Also a 16 pg. 1938 giveaway w/Buck Rogers | 20.00 | 60.00 | 140.00 |

**PURPLE CLAW, THE** (Also see Tales of Horror)
Jan, 1953 - No. 3, May, 1953
Minoan Publishing Co./Toby Press

| | Good | Fine | N-Mint |
|---|---|---|---|
| 1-Origin | 11.50 | 34.00 | 80.00 |
| 2,3: 1-3 r-in Tales of Horror #9-11 | 7.00 | 21.00 | 50.00 |
| I.W. Reprint #8-Reprints #1 | .80 | 2.40 | 4.80 |

**PUSSYCAT** (Magazine)
Oct, 1968 (B&W reprints from Men's magazines)
Marvel Comics Group

| | Good | Fine | N-Mint |
|---|---|---|---|
| 1-(Scarce)-Ward, Everett, Wood-a; Everett-c | 13.00 | 40.00 | 90.00 |

**PUZZLE FUN COMICS** (Also see Jingle Jangle)
Spring, 1946 - No. 2, Summer, 1946 (52 pgs.)
George W. Dougherty Co.

| | Good | Fine | N-Mint |
|---|---|---|---|
| 1(1946)-Gustavson-a | 10.00 | 30.00 | 70.00 |
| 2 | 7.00 | 21.00 | 50.00 |

NOTE: *#1 & 2('46) each contain a* ***George Carlson*** *cover plus a 6 pg. story "Alec in Fumbleland;" also many puzzles in each.*

**QUADRANT**
1983 - No. 7, 1986 (B&W, nudity, adult)
Quadrant Publications

| | Good | Fine | N-Mint |
|---|---|---|---|
| 1-Peter Hsu-c/a in all | 7.50 | 15.00 | 30.00 |
| 2 | 1.35 | 4.00 | 8.00 |
| 3 | 1.00 | 3.00 | 6.00 |
| 4 | .70 | 2.00 | 4.00 |
| 5 | .50 | 1.50 | 3.00 |
| 6,7: 8-Exist? | .35 | 1.00 | 2.00 |

**QUAKER OATS** (Also see Cap'n Crunch)
1965 (Giveaway) (2½x5½") (16 pages)
Quaker Oats Co.

| | Good | Fine | N-Mint |
|---|---|---|---|
| "Plenty of Glutton," "Lava Come-Back," "Kite Tale," "A Witch in Time" | | .50 | 1.00 |

**QUASAR** (See Avengers #302 & Marvel Team-Up #113)
Oct, 1989 - Present ($1.00, color) (Direct sale #17 on)
Marvel Comics

| | Good | Fine | N-Mint |
|---|---|---|---|
| 1-Origin; formerly Marvel Boy | .25 | .75 | 1.50 |
| 2-5: 3-Human Torch app. | | .60 | 1.20 |
| 6-15,17-22: 6-Venom app. 7-Cosmic Spidey app. 11-Excalibur x-over. 14-McFarlane-c | | .60 | 1.00 |
| 16 ($1.50, 52 pgs.) | .25 | .75 | 1.50 |

**QUEEN OF THE WEST, DALE EVANS** (TV)(See Western Roundup under Dell Giants)
No. 479, 7/53 - No. 22, 1-3/59 (All photo-c; photo back c-4-8, 15)
Dell Publishing Co.

| | Good | Fine | N-Mint |
|---|---|---|---|
| 4-Color 479(#1, '53) | 8.00 | 24.00 | 55.00 |
| 4-Color 528(#2, '54) | 5.70 | 17.00 | 40.00 |
| 3(4-6/54)-Toth-a | 6.50 | 19.00 | 45.00 |
| 4-Toth, Manning-a | 6.50 | 19.00 | 45.00 |
| 5-10-Manning-a. 5-Marsh-a | 4.30 | 13.00 | 30.00 |
| 11,19,21-No Manning 21-Tufts-a | 3.50 | 10.50 | 24.00 |
| 12-18,20,22-Manning-a | 4.00 | 12.00 | 28.00 |

**QUENTIN DURWARD** (See 4-Color #672)

**QUESTAR ILLUSTRATED SCIENCE FICTION CLASSICS**
1977 (224 pgs.) ($1.95)
Golden Press

| | Good | Fine | N-Mint |
|---|---|---|---|
| 11197-Stories by Asimov, Sturgeon, Silverberg & Niven; Starstream-r | .50 | 1.50 | 3.00 |

**QUESTION, THE** (See Americomics, Blue Beetle (1967), Charlton Bullseye & Mysterious Suspense)

**QUESTION, THE** (Also see Crisis on Infinite Earths)
Feb, 1987 - No. 36, Mar, 1990 ($1.50-$1.75, color, mature readers)
DC Comics

| | Good | Fine | N-Mint |
|---|---|---|---|
| 1-Sienkiewicz painted-c | .60 | 1.75 | 3.50 |
| 2-5 | .40 | 1.25 | 2.50 |
| 6-36: 8-Intro. The Mikado. 16-Begin $1.75-c | .35 | 1.00 | 2.00 |
| Annual 1(9/88)-Sienkiewicz-c(i) | .45 | 1.40 | 2.75 |
| Annual 2('89, $3.50, 68 pgs.)-Green Arrow app. | .60 | 1.75 | 3.50 |

NOTE: ***Denys Cowan*** *a-1-25, 27-36; c-2-25i, 27-36i.* ***Sienkiewicz*** *c-1, 2-19i, 21-23i.*

**QUESTION QUARTERLY, THE**
Autumn, 1990 - Present ($2.50, color, 52 pgs.)
DC Comics

| | Good | Fine | N-Mint |
|---|---|---|---|
| 1,2-Denys Cowan-c/a | .40 | 1.25 | 2.50 |

**QUESTPROBE**
8/84; No. 2, 1/85; No. 3, 11/85 - No. 4, 12/85 (Limited series)
Marvel Comics Group

| | Good | Fine | N-Mint |
|---|---|---|---|
| 1-4: 1-The Hulk app. by Romita | | .40 | .80 |

**QUICK-DRAW McGRAW** (TV) (Hanna-Barbera)
No. 1040, 12-2/59-60 - No. 11, 7-9/62; No. 12, 11/62; No. 13, 2/63; No. 14, 4/63; No. 15, 6/69
Dell Publishing Co./Gold Key No. 12 on

| | Good | Fine | N-Mint |
|---|---|---|---|
| 4-Color 1040(#1) | 4.30 | 13.00 | 30.00 |
| 2(4-6/60)-6 | 3.00 | 9.00 | 21.00 |
| 7-11 | 2.00 | 6.00 | 14.00 |
| 12,13-Title change to . . . Fun-Type Roundup (84 pgs.) | 4.00 | 12.00 | 32.00 |
| 14,15 | 1.70 | 5.00 | 12.00 |

(See Whitman Comic Books)

**QUICK-DRAW McGRAW** (TV)(See Spotlight #2)
Nov, 1970 - No. 8, Jan, 1972 (Hanna-Barbera)
Charlton Comics

| | Good | Fine | N-Mint |
|---|---|---|---|
| 1 | 1.50 | 4.50 | 10.00 |
| 2-8 | .85 | 2.60 | 6.00 |

*Punisher War Journal #14, © MEG*

*The Question #3, © DC*

*Quick Draw McGraw #3, © Hanna-Barbera*

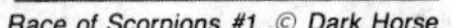
Race of Scorpions #1, © Dark Horse

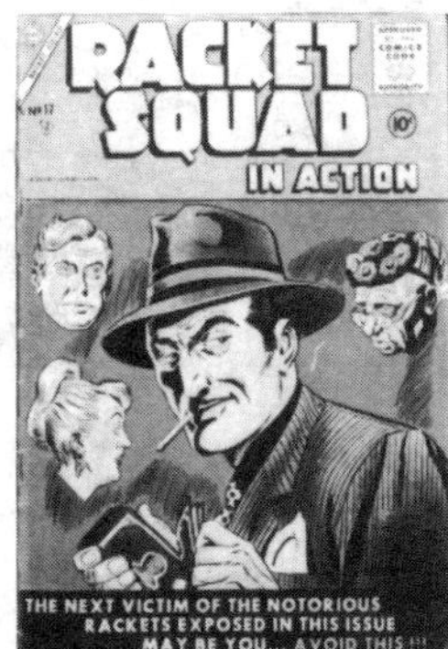

Racket Squad in Action #17, © CC

Raggedy Ann and Andy #35, © DELL

**QUICK-TRIGGER WESTERN** (. . . Action #12; Cowboy Action #5-11)
No. 12, May, 1956 - No. 19, Sept, 1957
Atlas Comics (ACI No. 12/WPI No. 13-19)

| | Good | Fine | N-Mint |
|---|---|---|---|
| 12-Baker-a | 5.00 | 15.00 | 35.00 |
| 13-Williamson-a, 5 pgs. | 5.70 | 17.00 | 40.00 |
| 14-Everett, Crandall, Torres-a; Heath-c | 5.00 | 15.00 | 35.00 |
| 15-Torres, Crandall-a | 4.00 | 12.00 | 28.00 |
| 16-Orlando, Kirby-a | 3.50 | 10.50 | 24.00 |
| 17,18: 17-Crandall-a. 18-Baker-a | 3.50 | 10.50 | 24.00 |
| 19 | 2.15 | 6.50 | 15.00 |

NOTE: ***Colan** a-16. **Maneely** a-15, 17; c-15, 18. **Morrow** a-18. **Powell** a-14. **Severin** c-12, 13, 16, 17, 19. **Shores** a-16. **Tuska** a-17.*

**QUINCY** (See Comics Reading Libraries)

**RACCOON KIDS, THE** (Formerly Movietown Animal Antics)
No. 52, Sept-Oct, 1954 - No. 64, Nov, 1957
National Periodical Publications (Arleigh No. 63,64)

| | Good | Fine | N-Mint |
|---|---|---|---|
| 52-Doodles Duck by Mayer | 5.00 | 15.00 | 35.00 |
| 53-64: 53-62-Doodles Duck by Mayer | 3.50 | 10.50 | 24.00 |

**RACE FOR THE MOON**
March, 1958 - No. 3, Nov, 1958
Harvey Publications

| | Good | Fine | N-Mint |
|---|---|---|---|
| 1-Powell-a(5); ½-pg. S&K-a; c-redrawn from Galaxy Science Fiction pulp (5/53) | 6.50 | 19.00 | 45.00 |
| 2-Kirby/Williamson-c(r)/a(3) | 15.00 | 45.00 | 105.00 |
| 3-Kirby/Williamson-c/a(4) | 16.00 | 48.00 | 110.00 |

**RACE OF SCORPIONS**
1990 - Present ($4.50-$4.95, color, 52 pgs.)
Dark Horse Comics

| | Good | Fine | N-Mint |
|---|---|---|---|
| 1-r/stories from Dark Horse Presents 23-27 | .75 | 2.25 | 4.50 |
| 2-Begin $4.95-c; r/Dark Horse Presents | .85 | 2.50 | 5.00 |

**RACER-X**
8/88 - No. 11, 8/89; V2#1, 9/89 - V2#10, 1990 ($1.75, color)
Now Comics

| | Good | Fine | N-Mint |
|---|---|---|---|
| 0-Deluxe ($3.50) | .60 | 1.75 | 3.50 |
| 1 (9/88) - 11, V2#1-10 | .30 | .90 | 1.80 |

**RACKET SQUAD IN ACTION**
May-June, 1952 - No. 29, March, 1958
Capitol Stories/Charlton Comics

| | Good | Fine | N-Mint |
|---|---|---|---|
| 1 | 10.00 | 30.00 | 70.00 |
| 2-4 | 4.30 | 13.00 | 30.00 |
| 5-Dr. Neff, Ghost Breaker app; headlights-c | 6.00 | 18.00 | 42.00 |
| 6-Dr. Neff, Ghost Breaker app. | 4.00 | 12.00 | 28.00 |
| 7-10: 10-Explosion-c | 3.15 | 9.50 | 22.00 |
| 11-Ditko-c/a | 11.00 | 32.00 | 75.00 |
| 12-Ditko explosion-c (classic); Shuster-a(2) | 20.00 | 60.00 | 140.00 |
| 13-Shuster-c(p)/a; acid in woman's face | 4.30 | 13.00 | 30.00 |
| 14-"Shakedown"-marijuana story | 5.00 | 15.00 | 35.00 |
| 15-28 | 2.65 | 8.00 | 18.00 |
| 29-(68 pgs.)(15 cents) | 3.15 | 9.50 | 22.00 |

**RADIANT LOVE** (Formerly Daring Love #1)
No. 2, Dec, 1953 - No. 6, Aug, 1954
Gilmor Magazines

| | Good | Fine | N-Mint |
|---|---|---|---|
| 2 | 3.00 | 9.00 | 21.00 |
| 3-6 | 2.00 | 6.00 | 14.00 |

**RAGAMUFFINS**
Jan, 1985 ($1.75, One Shot)
Eclipse Comics

| | Good | Fine | N-Mint |
|---|---|---|---|
| 1-Eclipse Magazine-r, w/color | .30 | .90 | 1.80 |

**RAGGEDY ANN AND ANDY** (See Dell Giants, March of Comics #23 & New Funnies)
No. 5, 1942 - No. 533, 2/54; 10-12/64 - No. 4, 3/66
Dell Publishing Co.

| | Good | Fine | N-Mint |
|---|---|---|---|
| 4-Color 5(1942) | 37.00 | 110.00 | 255.00 |
| 4-Color 23(1943) | 27.00 | 80.00 | 185.00 |
| 4-Color 45(1943) | 22.00 | 65.00 | 155.00 |
| 4-Color 72(1945) | 18.00 | 54.00 | 125.00 |
| 1(6/46)-Billy & Bonnie Bee by Frank Thomas | 18.00 | 54.00 | 125.00 |
| 2,3: 3-Egbert Elephant by Dan Noonan begins | 9.30 | 28.00 | 65.00 |
| 4-Kelly-a, 16 pgs. | 10.00 | 30.00 | 70.00 |
| 5-10: 7-Little Black Sambo, Black Mumbo & Black Jumbo only app; Christmas-c | 7.00 | 21.00 | 50.00 |
| 11-20 | 5.70 | 17.00 | 40.00 |
| 21-Alice In Wonderland cover/story | 5.70 | 17.00 | 40.00 |
| 22-27,29-39(8/49), 4-Color 262(1/50) | 4.00 | 12.00 | 28.00 |
| 28-Kelly-c | 4.30 | 13.00 | 30.00 |
| 4-Color 306,354,380,452,533 | 3.00 | 9.00 | 21.00 |
| 1(10-12/64-Dell) | 1.15 | 3.50 | 8.00 |
| 2,3(10-12/65), 4(3/66) | .75 | 2.25 | 5.00 |

NOTE: ***Kelly** art ("Animal Mother Goose")-#1-34, 36, 37; c-28. Peterkin Pottle by **John Stanley** in 32-38.*

**RAGGEDY ANN AND ANDY**
Dec, 1971 - No. 6, Sept, 1973
Gold Key

| | Good | Fine | N-Mint |
|---|---|---|---|
| 1 | .70 | 2.00 | 4.00 |
| 2-6 | .35 | 1.00 | 2.00 |

**RAGGEDY ANN & THE CAMEL WITH THE WRINKLED KNEES** (See Dell Jr. Treasury #8)

**RAGMAN** (See Batman Family #20, Brave & The Bold #196 & Cancelled Comic Cavalcade)
Aug-Sept, 1976 - No. 5, June-July, 1977
National Periodical Publications/DC Comics No. 5

| | Good | Fine | N-Mint |
|---|---|---|---|
| 1-Origin | | .40 | .80 |
| 2-5: 2-Origin ends; Kubert-c. 4-Drug use story | | .30 | .60 |

NOTE: ***Kubert** a-4, 5; c-1-5. **Redondo** studios a-1-4.*

**RAGS RABBIT** (See Harvey Hits #2, Harvey Wiseguys & Tastee Freez)
No. 11, June, 1951 - No. 18, March, 1954
Harvey Publications

| | Good | Fine | N-Mint |
|---|---|---|---|
| 11-(See Nutty Comics #5 for 1st app.) | 1.50 | 4.50 | 10.00 |
| 12-18 | 1.00 | 3.00 | 7.00 |

**RAIDERS OF THE LOST ARK**
Sept, 1981 - No. 3, Nov, 1981 (Movie adaptation)
Marvel Comics Group

| | Good | Fine | N-Mint |
|---|---|---|---|
| 1-r/Marvel Comics Super Special #18 | | .40 | .80 |
| 2,3 | | .30 | .60 |

NOTE: ***Buscema** a(p)-1-3; c(p)-1. **Simonson** a-2i, 3i.*

**RAINBOW BRITE AND THE STAR STEALER**
1985
DC Comics

| | Good | Fine | N-Mint |
|---|---|---|---|
| nn-Movie adaptation | | .40 | .80 |

**RALPH KINER, HOME RUN KING**
1950 (Pittsburgh Pirates)
Fawcett Publications

| | Good | Fine | N-Mint |
|---|---|---|---|
| nn-Photo-c | 27.00 | 80.00 | 185.00 |

**RALPH SNART ADVENTURES**
June, 1986 - V2#9, 1987; V3#1, Sept, 1988 - Present ($1.25, B&W)
Now Comics

| | Good | Fine | N-Mint |
|---|---|---|---|
| 1 ($1.00) | .60 | 1.75 | 3.50 |
| 2,3 | .40 | 1.25 | 2.50 |
| V2#1 (11/86)-Origin Rodent Ralph | .35 | 1.00 | 2.00 |
| V2#2-9 | .25 | .75 | 1.50 |
| V3#1 (9/88, $1.75, begin color series) | .35 | 1.00 | 2.00 |

| | Good | Fine | N-Mint |
|---|---|---|---|
| V3#2-23,25-28: 16-Halloween issue | .30 | .90 | 1.80 |
| V3#24: 3-D Special with glasses ($2.50) | .40 | 1.25 | 2.50 |
| V3#29-31: 29-Begin $1.95-c | .35 | 1.00 | 2.00 |
| Book 1 | 1.35 | 4.00 | 8.00 |

**RAMAR OF THE JUNGLE** (TV)
1954 (no month); No. 2, Sept, 1955 - No. 5, Sept, 1956
Toby Press No. 1/Charlton No. 2 on

| | Good | Fine | N-Mint |
|---|---|---|---|
| 1-Jon Hall photo-c | 7.00 | 21.00 | 50.00 |
| 2-5 | 5.70 | 17.00 | 40.00 |

**RAMBO IN 3-D** (See Blackthorne 3-D Series #49)

**RAMPAGING HULK** (The Hulk #10 on; see Marvel Treasury Edition)
Jan, 1977 - No. 9, June, 1978 ($1.00, B&W magazine)
Marvel Comics Group

| | Good | Fine | N-Mint |
|---|---|---|---|
| 1-Bloodstone featured | .50 | 1.50 | 3.00 |
| 2-Old X-Men app; origin old & new X-Men in text w/Rogers illos | .85 | 2.50 | 5.00 |
| 3-9: 9-Shanna the She-Devil story | .35 | .75 | 1.50 |

NOTE: ***Alcala** a-1-3i, 5i, 8i. **Buscema** a-1. **Giffen** a-4. **Nino** a-4i. **Simonson** a-1-3p. **Starlin** a-4(w/**Nino**), 7; c-4, 5, 7.*

**RANGE BUSTERS**
Sept, 1950 - No. 8, 1951
Fox Features Syndicate

| | Good | Fine | N-Mint |
|---|---|---|---|
| 1 | 8.00 | 24.00 | 55.00 |
| 2 | 4.50 | 14.00 | 32.00 |
| 3-8 | 4.00 | 12.00 | 28.00 |

**RANGE BUSTERS** (Formerly Cowboy Love?; Wyatt Earp, Frontier Marshall #11 on)
No. 8, May, 1955 - No. 10, Sept, 1955
Charlton Comics

| | Good | Fine | N-Mint |
|---|---|---|---|
| 8 | 3.70 | 11.00 | 26.00 |
| 9,10 | 2.00 | 6.00 | 14.00 |

**RANGELAND LOVE**
Dec, 1949 - No. 2, Mar, 1950
Atlas Comics (CDS)

| | Good | Fine | N-Mint |
|---|---|---|---|
| 1,2-Photo-c | 5.70 | 17.00 | 40.00 |

**RANGER, THE** (See 4-Color #255)

**RANGE RIDER** (See The Flying A's . . .)

**RANGE RIDER, THE** (See 4-Color #404)

**RANGE ROMANCES**
Dec, 1949 - No. 5, Aug, 1950 (#5: 52 pgs.)
Comic Magazines (Quality Comics)

| | Good | Fine | N-Mint |
|---|---|---|---|
| 1-Gustavson-c/a | 12.00 | 36.00 | 85.00 |
| 2-Crandall-c/a; "spanking" scene | 14.00 | 43.00 | 100.00 |
| 3-Crandall, Gustavson-a; photo-c | 10.00 | 30.00 | 70.00 |
| 4-Crandall-a; photo-c | 8.00 | 24.00 | 55.00 |
| 5-Gustavson-a; Crandall-a(p); photo-c | 8.50 | 25.50 | 60.00 |

**RANGERS COMICS** (. . .of Freedom #1-7)
10/41 - No. 67, 10/52; No. 68, Fall, 1952; No. 69, Winter, 1952-53
Fiction House Magazines (Flying stories)

| | Good | Fine | N-Mint |
|---|---|---|---|
| 1-Intro. Ranger Girl & The Rangers of Freedom; ends #7, cover app. only-#5 | 100.00 | 250.00 | 600.00 |
| 2 | 40.00 | 120.00 | 280.00 |
| 3 | 34.00 | 100.00 | 235.00 |
| 4,5 | 29.00 | 85.00 | 200.00 |
| 6-10: 8-U.S. Rangers begin | 24.00 | 71.00 | 165.00 |
| 11,12-Commando Rangers app. | 22.00 | 65.00 | 150.00 |
| 13-Commando Ranger begins-not same as Commando Rangers | 22.00 | 65.00 | 150.00 |
| 14-20 | 16.00 | 48.00 | 110.00 |
| 21-Intro/origin Firehair (begins) | 21.00 | 62.00 | 145.00 |
| 22-30: 23-Kazanda begins, ends #28. 28-Tiger Man begins (origin). 30-Crusoe Island begins, ends #40 | 14.00 | 43.00 | 100.00 |
| 31-40: 33-Hypodermic panels | 12.00 | 36.00 | 84.00 |
| 41-46 | 9.30 | 28.00 | 65.00 |
| 47-56-"Eisnerish" Dr. Drew by Grandenetti | 10.00 | 30.00 | 70.00 |
| 57-60-Straight Dr. Drew by Grandenetti | 8.00 | 24.00 | 55.00 |
| 61,62,64-66: 64-Suicide Smith begins | 7.00 | 21.00 | 50.00 |
| 63-Used in **POP**, pgs. 85, 99 | 7.00 | 21.00 | 50.00 |
| 67-69: 67-Space Rangers begin, end #69 | 7.00 | 21.00 | 50.00 |

NOTE: *Bondage, discipline covers, lingerie panels are common. **Baker** a-36-38. **John Celardo** a-36-39. **Lee Elias** a-21-28. **Evans** a-19, 38-45, 47, 52. **Ingels** a-13-16. **Larsen** a-34. **Bob Lubbers** a-30-38, 40, 42-44; c-40, 42, 44. **Moreira** a-43-45. **Tuska** a-16, 17, 19, 22. **Zolne** c-1-17.*

**RANGO** (TV)
August, 1967
Dell Publishing Co.

| | Good | Fine | N-Mint |
|---|---|---|---|
| 1-Tim Conway photo-c | 1.75 | 5.25 | 12.00 |

**RAPHAEL** (See Teenage Mutant Ninja Turtles)
1985 (One shot, $1.50, B&W)
Mirage Studios

| | Good | Fine | N-Mint |
|---|---|---|---|
| 1 | 2.15 | 6.50 | 13.00 |
| 1-2nd print. (11/87)-New-c & 8pgs.-a | 1.00 | 3.00 | 6.00 |

**RATFINK** (See Frantic & Zany)
October, 1964
Canrom, Inc.

| | Good | Fine | N-Mint |
|---|---|---|---|
| 1-Woodbridge-a | 2.30 | 7.00 | 16.00 |

**RAT PATROL, THE** (TV)
March, 1967 - No. 5, Nov, 1967; No. 6, Oct, 1969
Dell Publishing Co.

| | Good | Fine | N-Mint |
|---|---|---|---|
| 1-Christopher George photo-c | 4.00 | 12.00 | 28.00 |
| 2 | 3.00 | 9.00 | 21.00 |
| 3-6: 3-6-Photo-c | 2.30 | 7.00 | 16.00 |

**RAVEN, THE** (See Movie Classics)

**RAVENS AND RAINBOWS**
Dec, 1983 (Baxter paper)(Reprints fanzine work in color)
Pacific Comics

| | Good | Fine | N-Mint |
|---|---|---|---|
| 1-Jeff Jones-c/a(r); nudity scenes | .25 | .75 | 1.50 |

**RAWHIDE** (TV)
Sept-Nov, 1959 - June-Aug, 1962; July, 1963 - No. 2, Jan, 1964
Dell Publishing Co./Gold Key

| | Good | Fine | N-Mint |
|---|---|---|---|
| 4-Color 1028 | 17.00 | 51.00 | 120.00 |
| 4-Color 1097,1160,1202,1261,1269 | 13.00 | 40.00 | 90.00 |
| 01-684-208(8/62-Dell) | 11.50 | 34.00 | 80.00 |
| 1(10071-307, G.K.), 2 | 9.30 | 28.00 | 65.00 |

NOTE: *All have Clint Eastwood photo-c. **Tufts** a-1028.*

**RAWHIDE KID**
3/55 - No. 16, 9/57; No. 17, 8/60 - No. 151, 5/79
Atlas/Marvel Comics (CnPC No. 1-16/AMI No. 17-30)

| | Good | Fine | N-Mint |
|---|---|---|---|
| 1-Rawhide Kid, his horse Apache & sidekick Randy begin; Wyatt Earp app. | 29.00 | 86.00 | 200.00 |
| 2 | 13.00 | 40.00 | 90.00 |
| 3-5 | 8.00 | 24.00 | 55.00 |
| 6-10: 7-Williamson-a, 4pgs. | 5.70 | 17.00 | 40.00 |
| 11-16: 16-Torres-a | 4.30 | 13.00 | 30.00 |
| 17-Origin by Jack Kirby | 7.00 | 21.00 | 50.00 |
| 18-22,24-30 | 3.15 | 9.50 | 22.00 |
| 23-Origin retold by Jack Kirby | 5.70 | 17.00 | 40.00 |
| 31,32,36-44: 40-Two-Gun Kid x-over. 42-1st Larry Lieber issue | 2.65 | 8.00 | 18.00 |
| 33-35-Davis-a. 35-Intro & death of The Raven | 3.00 | 9.00 | 21.00 |
| 45,46: 45-Origin retold. 46-Toth-a | 3.00 | 9.00 | 21.00 |

*Rangers Comics #5, © FH*

*The Rat Patrol #4, © Mirisch-Rich TV Prod.*

*Rawhide #2, © CBS*

Real Clue Crime Stories V2#9, © HILL

Real Fact Comics #2, © DC

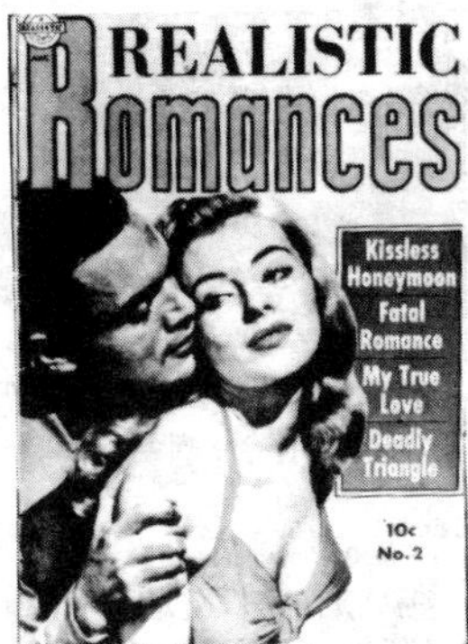

Realistic Romances #2, © REAL

| | Good | Fine | N-Mint |
|---|---|---|---|
| 47-70: 50-Kid Colt x-over. 64-Kid Colt story. 66-Two-Gun Kid story. 67-Kid Colt story | 1.30 | 4.00 | 9.00 |
| 71-86: 79-Williamson-a(r). 86-Origin-r; Williamson-a r-/Ringo Kid #13 (4 pgs.) | .70 | 2.00 | 5.00 |
| 87-99,101-151: 115-Last new story | .50 | 1.50 | 3.00 |
| 100-Origin retold & expanded | .70 | 2.00 | 4.00 |
| Special 1(9/71)-All Kirby/Ayers reprints | .50 | 1.50 | 3.00 |

NOTE: ***Ayers** a-13, 14, 16. **Colan** a-5, 35, 37; c-145p, 148p, 149p. **Davis** a-125r. **Everett** a-54i, 65, 66, 88, 96i, 148i(r). **Gulacy** c-147. **Heath** c-4. **G. Kane** c-101, 144. **Keller** a-5, 144r. **Kirby** a-17-32, 34, 42, 43, 84, 86, 92, 109r, 112r, 137r, Spec. 1; c-17-35, 37, 40, 41, 43-47, 137r. **Maneely** c-1, 2, 5, 14. **Morisi** a-13. **Roussos** r-146i, 147i, 149-151i. **Severin** a-16; c-8, 13. **Torres** a-99r. **Tuska** a-14. **Wildey** r-146-151(Outlaw Kid). **Williamson** a-79r, 86r, 95r, 111r.*

**RAWHIDE KID**
Aug, 1985 - No. 4, Nov, 1985 (Mini-series)
Marvel Comics Group

| | Good | Fine | N-Mint |
|---|---|---|---|
| 1-4 | | .50 | 1.00 |

**REAGAN'S RAIDERS**
Aug, 1986 - No. 3, 1987 (no month) ($1.95, B&W)
Solson Publications

| | Good | Fine | N-Mint |
|---|---|---|---|
| 1-3-Ayers-a | .35 | 1.00 | 2.00 |

**REAL ADVENTURE COMICS** (Action Adventure #2 on)
April, 1955
Gillmor Magazines

| | Good | Fine | N-Mint |
|---|---|---|---|
| 1 | 1.70 | 5.00 | 12.00 |

**REAL CLUE CRIME STORIES** (Formerly Clue Comics)
V2#4, June, 1947 - V8#3, May, 1953
Hillman Periodicals

| | Good | Fine | N-Mint |
|---|---|---|---|
| V2#4(#1)-S&K c/a(3); Dan Barry-a | 16.00 | 48.00 | 110.00 |
| 5-7-S&K c/a(3-4); 7-Iron Lady app. | 13.00 | 40.00 | 90.00 |
| 8-12 | 3.00 | 9.00 | 21.00 |
| V3#1-8,10-12, V4#1-3,5-8,11,12 | 2.30 | 7.00 | 16.00 |
| V3#9-Used in **SOTI**, pg. 102 | 5.00 | 15.00 | 35.00 |
| V4#4-S&K-a | 4.00 | 12.00 | 28.00 |
| V4#9,10-Krigstein-a | 4.00 | 12.00 | 28.00 |
| V5#1-5,7,8,10,12 | 1.70 | 5.00 | 12.00 |
| 6,9,11-Krigstein-a | 3.50 | 10.50 | 24.00 |
| V6#1-5,8,9,11 | 1.50 | 4.50 | 10.00 |
| 6,7,10,12-Krigstein-a. 10-Bondage-c | 3.00 | 9.00 | 21.00 |
| V7#1-3,5-11, V8#1-3: V7#6-1 pg. Frazetta ad | 1.50 | 4.50 | 10.00 |
| 4,12-Krigstein-a | 3.50 | 10.50 | 24.00 |

NOTE: ***Barry** a-9, 10; c-V2#8. **Briefer** a-V6#6. **Fuje** a- V2#7(2), 8, 11. **Infantino** a-V2#8; c-V2#11. **Lawrence** a-V3#8, V5#7. **Powell** a-V4#11, 12. V5#4, 5, 7 are 68 pgs.*

**REAL EXPERIENCES** (Formerly Tiny Tessie)
No. 25, January, 1950
Atlas Comics (20CC)

| | Good | Fine | N-Mint |
|---|---|---|---|
| 25 | 2.00 | 6.00 | 14.00 |

**REAL FACT COMICS**
Mar-Apr, 1946 - No. 21, July-Aug, 1949
National Periodical Publications

| | Good | Fine | N-Mint |
|---|---|---|---|
| 1-S&K-a; Harry Houdini story; Just Imagine begins (not by Finlay) | 26.00 | 77.00 | 180.00 |
| 2-S&K-a; Rin-Tin-Tin story | 17.00 | 51.00 | 115.00 |
| 3-H.G. Wells, Lon Chaney story | 9.30 | 28.00 | 65.00 |
| 4-Virgil Finlay-a on 'Just Imagine' begins, ends #12 (2 pgs. each); Jimmy Stewart story | 13.50 | 40.00 | 95.00 |
| 5-Batman/Robin-c; 5pg. story about creation of Batman & Robin; Tom Mix story | 81.00 | 242.00 | 565.00 |
| 6-Origin & 1st app. Tommy Tomorrow by Finlay; Flag-c; 1st writing by Harlan Ellison (letter column, non-professional); 1st man to reach Mars story | 55.00 | 165.00 | 385.00 |
| 7-(No. 6 on inside)-Roussos-a | 7.00 | 21.00 | 50.00 |
| 8-2nd app. Tommy Tomorrow by Finlay | 29.00 | 86.00 | 200.00 |
| 9-S&K-a; Glenn Miller story | 12.00 | 36.00 | 85.00 |
| 10-Vigilante by Meskin; 4 pg. Finlay s/f story | 11.50 | 34.00 | 80.00 |
| 11,12: 11-Kinstler-a | 7.00 | 21.00 | 50.00 |
| 13-Dale Evans and Tommy Tomorrow cover/stories | 26.00 | 77.00 | 180.00 |
| 14,17,18: 14-Will Rogers story | 6.50 | 19.00 | 45.00 |
| 15-Nuclear Explosion part-c | 7.00 | 21.00 | 50.00 |
| 16-Tommy Tomorrow app.; 1st Planeteers? | 24.00 | 71.00 | 165.00 |
| 19-Sir Arthur Conan Doyle story | 6.50 | 19.00 | 45.00 |
| 20-Kubert-a, 4 pgs; Daniel Boone story | 10.00 | 30.00 | 70.00 |
| 21-Kubert-a, 2 pgs; Kit Carson story | 6.50 | 19.00 | 45.00 |

NOTE: ***Roussos** a-1-4.*

**REAL FUN OF DRIVING!!, THE**
1965, 1967 (Regular size)
Chrysler Corp.

| | Good | Fine | N-Mint |
|---|---|---|---|
| nn-Shaffenberger-a, 12pgs. | .85 | 2.50 | 5.00 |

**REAL FUNNIES**
Jan, 1943 - No. 3, June, 1943
Nedor Publishing Co.

| | Good | Fine | N-Mint |
|---|---|---|---|
| 1-Funny animal, humor; Black Terrier app. (clone of The Black Terror) | 13.00 | 40.00 | 90.00 |
| 2,3 | 7.00 | 21.00 | 50.00 |

**REAL GHOSTBUSTERS, THE** (Also see Slimer)
Aug, 1988 - Present ($1.75, color)
Now Comics

| | Good | Fine | N-Mint |
|---|---|---|---|
| 1-Based on Ghostbusters movie | .45 | 1.40 | 2.80 |
| 2-32: 30-Begin $1.95-c | .35 | 1.00 | 2.00 |

**REAL HEROES COMICS**
Sept, 1941 - No. 16, Oct, 1946
Parents' Magazine Institute

| | Good | Fine | N-Mint |
|---|---|---|---|
| 1-Roosevelt c/story | 14.00 | 43.00 | 100.00 |
| 2 | 5.70 | 17.00 | 40.00 |
| 3-5,7-10 | 4.00 | 12.00 | 28.00 |
| 6-Lou Gehrig c/story | 7.00 | 21.00 | 50.00 |
| 11-16: 13-Kiefer-a | 2.65 | 8.00 | 18.00 |

**REAL HIT**
1944 (Savings Bond premium)
Fox Features Publications

| | Good | Fine | N-Mint |
|---|---|---|---|
| 1-Blue Beetle-r | 8.50 | 25.50 | 60.00 |

NOTE: *Two versions exist, with and without covers. The coverless version has the title, No. 1 and price printed at top of splash page.*

**REALISTIC ROMANCES**
July-Aug, 1951 - No. 17, Aug-Sept, 1954 (no No. 9-14)
Realistic Comics/Avon Periodicals

| | Good | Fine | N-Mint |
|---|---|---|---|
| 1-Kinstler-a; c-/Avon paperback #211 | 10.00 | 30.00 | 70.00 |
| 2 | 4.50 | 14.00 | 32.00 |
| 3,4 | 3.60 | 11.00 | 25.00 |
| 5,8-Kinstler-a | 4.00 | 12.00 | 28.00 |
| 6-c-/Diversey Prize Novels #6; Kinstler-a | 4.50 | 14.00 | 32.00 |
| 7-Evans-a?; c-/Avon paperback #360 | 4.50 | 14.00 | 32.00 |
| 15,17 | 3.00 | 9.00 | 21.00 |
| 16-Kinstler marijuana story-r/Romantic Love #6 | 5.00 | 15.00 | 35.00 |
| I.W. Reprint #1,8,9 | .30 | .90 | 1.80 |

NOTE: ***Astarita** a-2-4, 7, 8.*

**REAL LIFE COMICS**
Sept, 1941 - No. 59, Sept, 1952
Nedor/Better/Standard Publ./Pictorial Magazine No. 13

| | Good | Fine | N-Mint |
|---|---|---|---|
| 1-Uncle Sam c/story | 15.00 | 45.00 | 105.00 |
| 2 | 7.00 | 21.00 | 50.00 |
| 3-Hitler cover | 11.00 | 32.00 | 75.00 |
| 4,5: 4-Story of American flag "Old Glory" | 4.50 | 14.00 | 32.00 |

| | Good | Fine | N-Mint |
|---|---|---|---|
| 6-10 | 3.70 | 11.00 | 26.00 |
| 11-20: 17-Albert Einstein story | 2.85 | 8.50 | 20.00 |
| 21-23,25,26,28-30: 29-A-Bomb story | 2.30 | 7.00 | 16.00 |
| 24-Story of Baseball | 4.30 | 13.00 | 30.00 |
| 27-Schomburg A-Bomb-c; story of A-Bomb | 4.50 | 14.00 | 32.00 |
| 31-33,35,36,42-44,48,49 | 1.70 | 5.00 | 12.00 |
| 34,37-41,45-47: 34-Jimmy Stewart story. 37-Story of motion pictures; Bing Crosby story. 38-Jane Froman story. 39-"1,000,000 A.D." sty. 40-Bob Feller sty. 41-Jimmie Foxx sty; "Home Run" Baker sty. 45-Story of Olympic games; Burl Ives story. 46-Douglas Fairbanks Jr. & Sr. story. 47-George Gershwin story | 2.30 | 7.00 | 16.00 |
| 50-Frazetta-a, 5 pgs. | 11.50 | 34.00 | 80.00 |
| 51-Jules Verne "Journey to the Moon" by Evans | 6.00 | 18.00 | 42.00 |
| 52-Frazetta-a, 4 pgs.; Severin/Elder-a(2); Evans-a | 12.00 | 36.00 | 84.00 |
| 53-57-Severin/Elder-a | 3.70 | 11.00 | 26.00 |
| 58-Severin/Elder-a(2) | 4.30 | 13.00 | 30.00 |
| 59-1pg. Frazetta; Severin/Elder-a | 3.70 | 11.00 | 26.00 |

NOTE: *Some issues had two titles.* ***Guardineer*** *a-40(2), 44.* ***Schomburg*** *c-1, 2, 4, 5, 7, 11, 13-21, 23, 24, 26, 28, 30-32, 34-40, 42, 44-47. Photo-c 5, 6.*

**REAL LIFE SECRETS** (Real Secrets #2 on)
Sept, 1949 (One shot)
Ace Periodicals

| | Good | Fine | N-Mint |
|---|---|---|---|
| 1-Painted-c | 3.50 | 10.50 | 24.00 |

**REAL LIFE STORY OF FESS PARKER** (Magazine)
1955
Dell Publishing Co.

| | Good | Fine | N-Mint |
|---|---|---|---|
| 1 | 5.70 | 17.00 | 40.00 |

**REAL LIFE TALES OF SUSPENSE** (See Suspense)

**REAL LOVE** (Formerly Hap Hazard)
No. 25, April, 1949 - No. 76, Nov, 1956
Ace Periodicals (A. A. Wyn)

| | Good | Fine | N-Mint |
|---|---|---|---|
| 25 | 4.30 | 13.00 | 30.00 |
| 26 | 2.15 | 6.50 | 15.00 |
| 27-L. B. Cole-a | 3.50 | 10.50 | 24.00 |
| 28-35 | 1.50 | 4.50 | 10.00 |
| 36-66: 66-Last pre-code (2/55) | 1.30 | 4.00 | 9.00 |
| 67-76 | .85 | 2.60 | 6.00 |

NOTE: *Photo-c No. 50-76. Painted-c No. 46.*

**REALM, THE**
Feb, 1986 - No. 20? ($1.50-$1.95, B&W)
Arrow Comics/WeeBee Comics #13/Caliber Press #14 on

| | Good | Fine | N-Mint |
|---|---|---|---|
| 1 | 1.00 | 3.00 | 6.00 |
| 2 | .35 | 1.00 | 2.00 |
| 3,5-16: 13-Begin $1.95-c | | .65 | 1.30 |
| 4-1st app. Deadworld | 3.35 | 10.00 | 20.00 |
| 17-20: 17-Begin $2.50-c | .40 | 1.25 | 2.50 |
| Book 1 ($4.95, B&W) | .85 | 2.50 | 4.95 |

**REAL McCOYS, THE** (TV)
No. 1071, 1-3/60 - 5-7/1962 (Photo-c)
Dell Publishing Co.

| | Good | Fine | N-Mint |
|---|---|---|---|
| 4-Color 1071,1134-Toth-a in both | 8.00 | 24.00 | 55.00 |
| 4-Color 1193,1265 | 6.50 | 19.00 | 45.00 |
| 01-689-207 (5-7/62) | 5.70 | 17.00 | 40.00 |

**REAL SCREEN COMICS** (#1 titled Real Screen Funnies; TV Screen Cartoons #129-138)
Spring, 1945 - No. 128, May-June, 1959 (#1-40: 52 pgs.)
National Periodical Publications

| | Good | Fine | N-Mint |
|---|---|---|---|
| 1-The Fox & the Crow, Flippity & Flop, Tito & His Burro begin | 61.00 | 182.00 | 425.00 |
| 2 | 29.00 | 86.00 | 200.00 |
| 3-5 | 16.00 | 48.00 | 110.00 |
| 6-10 (2-3/47) | 11.00 | 32.00 | 75.00 |
| 11-20 (10-11/48): 13-The Crow x-over in Flippity & Flop | 8.50 | 25.50 | 60.00 |
| 21-30 (6-7/50) | 6.50 | 19.00 | 45.00 |
| 31-50 | 4.00 | 12.00 | 28.00 |
| 51-99 | 2.85 | 8.50 | 20.00 |
| 100 | 4.00 | 12.00 | 28.00 |
| 101-128 | 2.15 | 6.50 | 15.00 |

**REAL SECRETS** (Formerly Real Life Secrets)
No. 2, Nov, 1950 - No. 5, May, 1950
Ace Periodicals

| | Good | Fine | N-Mint |
|---|---|---|---|
| 2 | 3.50 | 10.50 | 24.00 |
| 3-5: 3-Photo-c | 1.70 | 5.00 | 12.00 |

**REAL SPORTS COMICS** (All Sports Comics #2 on)
Oct-Nov, 1948 (52 pgs.)
Hillman Periodicals

| | Good | Fine | N-Mint |
|---|---|---|---|
| 1-Powell-a (12 pgs.) | 17.00 | 51.00 | 120.00 |

**REAL WAR STORIES**
July, 1987; 2nd printing, Feb, 1988 ($2.00, color, 52 pgs.)
Eclipse Comics

| | Good | Fine | N-Mint |
|---|---|---|---|
| 1-Bolland, Bissette, Totleben-a (1st, 2nd prints) | .35 | 1.00 | 2.00 |

**REAL WESTERN HERO** (Formerly Wow #1-69; becomes Western Hero #76 on)
No. 70, Sept, 1948 - No. 75, Feb, 1949 (All 52 pgs.)
Fawcett Publications

| | Good | Fine | N-Mint |
|---|---|---|---|
| 70(#1)-Tom Mix, Monte Hale, Hopalong Cassidy, Young Falcon begin | 21.00 | 62.00 | 145.00 |
| 71-Gabby Hayes begins; Captain Tootsie by Beck | 13.00 | 40.00 | 90.00 |
| 72-75: 72-Captain Tootsie by Beck. 75-Big Bow and Little Arrow app. | 13.00 | 40.00 | 90.00 |

NOTE: *Painted/photo c-70-73; painted c-74, 75.*

**REAL WEST ROMANCES**
4-5/49 - V1#6, 3/50; V2#1, Apr-May, 1950 (All 52 pgs. & photo-c)
Crestwood Publishing Co./Prize Publ.

| | Good | Fine | N-Mint |
|---|---|---|---|
| V1#1-S&K-a(p) | 9.30 | 28.00 | 65.00 |
| 2-Spanking panel | 8.50 | 25.50 | 60.00 |
| 3-Kirby-a(p) only | 4.30 | 13.00 | 30.00 |
| 4-S&K-a; Whip Wilson, Reno Browne photo-c | 8.00 | 24.00 | 55.00 |
| 5-Audie Murphy, Gale Storm photo-c; S&K-a | 6.00 | 18.00 | 42.00 |
| 6-S&K-a | 5.70 | 17.00 | 40.00 |
| V2#1-Kirby-a(p) | 4.00 | 12.00 | 28.00 |

NOTE: ***Meskin*** *a-V1#5.* ***Severin & Elder*** *a-V1#3-6, V2#1.* ***Leonard Starr*** *a-1-3. Photo-c V1#1-5, V2#1.*

**REAP THE WILD WIND** (See Cinema Comics Herald)

**REBEL, THE** (See 4-Color #1076, 1138, 1207, 1262)

**RECORD BOOK OF FAMOUS POLICE CASES**
1949 (132 pages) (25 cents)
St. John Publishing Co.

| | Good | Fine | N-Mint |
|---|---|---|---|
| nn-Kubert-a(3) r-/Son of Sinbad; Baker-c | 20.00 | 60.00 | 140.00 |

**RED ARROW**
May-June, 1951 - No. 3, Oct, 1951
P. L. Publishing Co.

| | Good | Fine | N-Mint |
|---|---|---|---|
| 1 | 4.30 | 13.00 | 30.00 |
| 2,3 | 3.00 | 9.00 | 21.00 |

**RED BALL COMIC BOOK**
1947 (Red Ball Shoes giveaway)

*The Realm #4, © Arrow Comics*

*Real Screen Comics #7, © DC*

*Real West Romances V2#1, © PRIZE*

Red Circle Sorcery #8, © AP

Red Dragon Comics #5 (1/43), © S&S

Red Mask #43, © ME

Parents' Magazine Institute — Good / Fine / N-Mint
nn-Reprints from True Comics 1.50 4.50 10.00

**RED BAND COMICS**
Feb, 1945 - No. 4, May, 1945
Enwil Associates
1 12.00 36.00 84.00
2-Origin Bogeyman & Santanas 10.00 30.00 70.00
3,4-Captain Wizard app. in both; each has identical contents/cover 8.50 25.50 60.00

**RED CIRCLE COMICS**
Jan, 1945 - No. 4, April, 1945
Rural Home Publications (Enwil)
1-The Prankster & Red Riot begin 12.00 36.00 85.00
2-Starr-a; The Judge (costumed hero) app. 9.00 27.00 62.00
3,4-Starr-c/a. 3-The Prankster not in costume 6.50 19.00 45.00
4-(dated 4/45)-Leftover covers to #4 were later restapled over early 1950s coverless comics. Variations in the coverless comics used are endless; Woman Outlaws, Dorothy Lamour, Crime Does Not Pay, Sabu, Diary Loves, Love Confessions & Young Love V3#3 known 5.70 17.00 40.00

**RED CIRCLE SORCERY** (Chilling Adventures in Sorcery #1-5)
No. 6, Apr, 1974 - No. 11, Feb, 1975
Red Circle Productions (Archie)
6-11: 8-Only app. The Cobra. 10-Wood-a .40 .80
NOTE: *Chaykin a-6, 10.* ***B. Jones*** *a-7(w/****Wrightson, Kaluta, J. Jones****).* ***McWilliams*** *a-10(2 & 3 pgs.).* ***Mooney*** *a-11p.* ***Morrow*** *a-6, 8, 11i; c-6-11.* ***Thorne*** *a-8, 10.* ***Toth*** *a-8, 9.*

**RED DOG** (See Night Music #7)

**RED DRAGON COMICS** (1st Series) (Formerly Trail Blazers; see Super Magician V5#7, 8)
No. 5, Jan, 1943 - No. 9, Jan, 1944
Street & Smith Publications
5-Origin Red Rover, the Crimson Crimebuster; Rex King, Man of Adventure, Captain Jack Commando, & The Minute Man begin; text origin Red Dragon; Binder-c 40.00 120.00 280.00
6-Origin The Black Crusader & Red Dragon (3/43) 30.00 90.00 210.00
7,8: 8-The Red Knight app. 22.00 65.00 155.00
9-Origin Chuck Magnon, Immortal Man 22.00 65.00 155.00

**RED DRAGON COMICS** (2nd Series)(See Super Magician V2#8)
Nov, 1947 - No. 6, Jan, 1949; No. 7, July, 1949
Street & Smith Publications
1-Red Dragon begins; Elliman, Nigel app.; Ed Cartier-c/a 41.00 122.00 285.00
2-Cartier-c 32.00 95.00 220.00
3-1st app. Dr. Neff by Powell; Elliman, Nigel app. 25.00 75.00 175.00
4-Cartier c/a 35.00 105.00 245.00
5-7 19.00 57.00 135.00
NOTE: ***Maneely*** *a-5, 7.* ***Powell*** *a-2-7; c-3, 5, 7.*

**REDDY GOOSE**
No #, 1958?; No. 2, Jan, 1959 - No. 16, July, 1962 (Giveaway)
International Shoe Co. (Western Printing)
nn,2-16 .50 1.50 3.00

**REDDY KILOWATT** (5 cents) (Also see Story of Edison)
1946 - No. 2, 1947; 1956 - 1960 (no month) (16 pgs.; paper cover)
Educational Comics (E. C.)
nn-Reddy Made Magic (1946, 5 cents) 12.00 35.00 70.00
nn-Reddy Made Magic (1958) 5.35 16.00 32.00
2-Edison, the Man Who Changed the World (¾" smaller than #1) (1947, 5 cents) 12.00 35.00 70.00
...Comic Book 2 (1954)-"Light's Diamond Jubilee" 6.75 20.00 40.00

Good / Fine / N-Mint
...Comic Book 2 (1958)-"Wizard of Light," 16 pgs. 5.35 16.00 32.00
...Comic Book 3 (1956)-"The Space Kite," 8 pgs.; Orlando story; regular size 5.35 16.00 32.00
...Comic Book 3 (1960)-"The Space Kite," 8 pgs.; Orlando story; regular size 4.75 14.00 28.00
NOTE: *Several copies surfaced in 1979.*

**REDDY MADE MAGIC**
1956, 1958 (16 pages) (paper cover)
Educational Comics (E. C.)
1-Reddy Kilowatt-r (splash panel changed) 8.00 24.00 48.00
1 (1958 edition) 5.00 15.00 30.00

**RED EAGLE** (See Feature Books #16, McKay)

**REDEYE** (See Comics Reading Libraries)

**RED FOX** (Formerly Manhunt! #1-14; also see Extra Comics)
No. 15, 1954
Magazine Enterprises
15(A-1 #108)-Undercover Girl story; L.B. Cole-c/a (Red Fox); r-from Manhunt; Powell-a 9.00 27.00 62.00

**REDFOX**
Jan, 1986 - No. 20? ($1.75-$2.00, B&W)
Harrier Comics/Valkyrie Press #11 on
1 .70 2.00 4.00
1-2nd print .25 .75 1.50
2 .40 1.25 2.50
3 .35 1.00 2.00
4 .25 .75 1.50
5-20: 7-Bolton painted-c. 11-Begin $2.00-c? .65 1.30

**RED GOOSE COMIC SELECTIONS** (See Comic Selections)

**RED HAWK** (See A-1 Comics #90, Bobby Benson's... #14-16 & Straight Arrow #2)

**RED HEAT IN 3-D** See Blackthorne 3-D Series #45)

**RED ICEBERG, THE**
1960 (10 cents) (16 pgs.) (Communist propaganda)
Impact Publ. (Catechetical Guild)
nn-(Rare)-'We The People'-back-c 37.00 110.00 240.00
2nd version-'Impact Press'-back-c 43.00 130.00 280.00
NOTE: *This book was the Guild's last anti-communist propaganda book and had very limited circulation. 3 - 4 copies surfaced in 1979 from the defunct publisher's files. Other copies do turn up.*

**RED MASK** (Formerly Tim Holt; see Best Comics, Blazing Six-Guns)
No. 42, 6-7/1954 - No. 53, 5/56; No. 54, 9/57
Magazine Enterprises No. 42-53/Sussex No. 54 (M.E. on-c)
42-Ghost Rider by Ayers continues, ends #50; Black Phantom continues; 3-D effect c/stories begin 11.50 34.00 80.00
43-3-D effect-c/stories 9.30 28.00 65.00
44-50: 47-Last pre-code. 3-D effect stories only. 50-Last Ghost Rider 8.50 25.50 60.00
51-The Presto Kid begins by Ayers (1st app.); Presto Kid-c begins, ends #54; last 3-D effect story 8.50 25.50 60.00
52-Origin The Presto Kid 8.50 25.50 60.00
53,54-Last Black Phantom 6.50 19.00 45.00
I.W. Reprint #1 (r-/#52). 2 (nd, r/#51 w/diff.-c). 3, 8 (nd; Kinstler-c) .80 2.40 4.80
NOTE: ***Ayers*** *art on Ghost Rider & Presto Kid.* ***Bolle*** *art in all (Red Mask); c-43, 44, 49.* ***Guardineer*** *a-52.* ***Black Phantom*** *in #42-44, 47-50, 53, 54.*

**REDMASK OF THE RIO GRANDE**
1990 ($2.50, color, 28 pgs.)(Has photos of movie posters)
AC Comics
1-Bolle-c/a(r); photo inside-c .40 1.25 2.50

**RED MOUNTAIN FEATURING QUANTRELL'S RAIDERS**
1952 (Movie) (Also see Jesse James #28)
Avon Periodicals

| | Good | Fine | N-Mint |
|---|---|---|---|
| nn-Alan Ladd; Kinstler c/a | 14.00 | 42.00 | 100.00 |

**"RED" RABBIT COMICS**
Jan, 1947 - No. 22, Aug-Sept, 1951
Dearfield Comic/J. Charles Laue Publ. Co.

| | | | |
|---|---|---|---|
| 1 | 5.70 | 17.00 | 40.00 |
| 2 | 3.00 | 9.00 | 21.00 |
| 3-10 | 2.30 | 7.00 | 16.00 |
| 11-22: 18-Flying Saucer-c (1/51) | 1.70 | 5.00 | 12.00 |

**RED RAVEN COMICS** (Human Torch #2 on)
August, 1940 (Also see Sub-Mariner #26, 2nd series)
Timely Comics

| | Good | Fine | VF-NM | NM/Mint |
|---|---|---|---|---|
| 1-Origin Red Raven; Comet Pierce & Mercury by Kirby, The Human Top & The Eternal Brain; intro. Magar, the Mystic & only app.; Kirby-c | 583.00 | 1460.00 | 3500.00 | 4500.00 |

(Estimated up to 135 total copies exist, 6 in NM/Mint)

**RED RYDER COMICS** (Hi Spot #2)(Movies, radio)
(Also see Crackajack Funnies)
9/40; No. 3, 8/41 - No. 5, 12/41; No. 6, 4/42 - No. 151, 4-6/57
Hawley Publ. No. 1-5/Dell Publishing Co.(K.K.) No. 6 on

| | Good | Fine | N-Mint |
|---|---|---|---|
| 1-Red Ryder, his horse Thunder, Little Beaver & his horse Papoose strip reprints begin by Fred Harman; 1st meeting of Red & Little Beaver; Harman line-drawn-c #1-85 | 89.00 | 265.00 | 620.00 |
| 3-(Scarce)-Alley Oop, King of the Royal Mtd., Capt. Easy, Freckles & His Friends, Myra North & Dan Dunn strip-r begin | 54.00 | 163.00 | 380.00 |
| 4,5 | 30.00 | 90.00 | 210.00 |
| 6-1st Dell issue | 30.00 | 90.00 | 210.00 |
| 7-10 | 24.00 | 71.00 | 165.00 |
| 11-20 | 17.00 | 51.00 | 120.00 |
| 21-32-Last Alley Oop, Dan Dunn, Capt. Easy, Freckles | 11.00 | 32.00 | 75.00 |
| 33-40 (52 pgs.) | 7.00 | 21.00 | 50.00 |
| 41 (52 pgs.)-Rocky Lane photo back-c; photo back-c begin, end #57 | 8.00 | 24.00 | 55.00 |
| 42-46 (52 pgs.): 46-Last Red Ryder strip-r | 6.00 | 18.00 | 42.00 |
| 47-53 (52 pgs.): 47-New stories on Red Ryder begin | 4.50 | 14.00 | 32.00 |
| 54-57 (36 pgs.) | 3.70 | 11.00 | 26.00 |
| 58-73 (36 pgs.): 73-Last King of the Royal Mtd; strip-r by Jim Gary | 3.50 | 10.50 | 24.00 |
| 74-85,93 (52 pgs.)-Harman line-drawn-c | 3.70 | 11.00 | 26.00 |
| 86-92 (52 pgs.)-Harman painted-c | 3.70 | 11.00 | 26.00 |
| 94-96 (36 pgs.)-Harman painted-c | 2.65 | 8.00 | 18.00 |
| 97,98,107,108 (36 pgs.)-Harman line-drawn-c | 2.65 | 8.00 | 18.00 |
| 99,101-106 (36 pgs.)-Jim Bannon Photo-c | 2.65 | 8.00 | 18.00 |
| 100 (36 pgs.)-Bannon photo-c | 3.00 | 9.00 | 21.00 |
| 109-118 (52 pgs.)-Harman line-drawn-c | 2.00 | 6.00 | 14.00 |
| 119-129 (52 pgs.): 119-Painted-c begin, not by Harman, end #151 | 1.70 | 5.00 | 12.00 |
| 130-144 (#130 on have 36 pgs.) | 1.50 | 4.50 | 10.00 |
| 145-148: 145-Title change to Red Ryder Ranch Magazine with photos | 1.30 | 4.00 | 9.00 |
| 149-151: 149-Title changed to Red Ryder Ranch Comics | 1.30 | 4.00 | 9.00 |
| 4-Color 916 (7/58) | 1.70 | 5.00 | 12.00 |
| Buster Brown Shoes Giveaway (1941, 32pgs., color, soft-c) | 19.00 | 57.00 | 132.00 |
| Red Ryder Super Book Of Comics 10 (1944; paper-c; 32 pgs.; blank back-c)-Magic Morro app. | 19.00 | 57.00 | 132.00 |
| Red Ryder Victory Patrol-nn(1944, 32 pgs.)-r-/#43,44; comic has a paper-c & is stapled inside a triple cardboard fold-out-c; contains membership card, decoder, map of R.R. home range, etc. Herky app. (Langendorf Bread giveaway; sub-titled 'Super Book of Comics') | 40.00 | 120.00 | 280.00 |
| Wells Lamont Corp. giveaway (1950)-16 pgs. in color; regular size; paper-c; 1941-r | 17.00 | 52.00 | 120.00 |

NOTE: ***Fred Harman** a-1-99; c-1-98, 107-118. Don Red Barry, Allan Rocky Lane, Wild Bill Elliott & Jim Bannon starred as Red Ryder in the movies. Robert Blake starred as Little Beaver.*

**RED RYDER PAINT BOOK**
1941 (148 pages) (8½x11½")
Whitman Publishing Co.

| | | | |
|---|---|---|---|
| nn-Reprints 1940 daily strips | 14.00 | 42.00 | 100.00 |

**RED SEAL COMICS**
No. 14, 10/45 - No. 18, 10/46; No. 19, 6/47 - No. 22, 12/47
Harry 'A' Chesler/Superior Publ. No. 19 on

| | | | |
|---|---|---|---|
| 14-The Black Dwarf begins; Little Nemo app; bondage/hypo-c; Tuska-a | 22.00 | 65.00 | 155.00 |
| 15-Torture story | 17.00 | 51.00 | 120.00 |
| 16-Used in **SOTI**, pg. 181, illo-"Outside the forbidden pages of de Sade, you find draining a girl's blood only in children's comics;" drug club story r-later in Crime Reporter #1; Veiled Avenger & Barry Kuda app; Tuska-a | 24.00 | 71.00 | 165.00 |
| 17-Lady Satan, Yankee Girl & Sky Chief app; Tuska-a | 14.00 | 43.00 | 100.00 |
| 18,20-Lady Satan & Sky Chief app. | 14.00 | 43.00 | 100.00 |
| 19-No Black Dwarf-on cover only; Zor, El Tigre app. | 11.50 | 34.00 | 80.00 |
| 21-Lady Satan & Black Dwarf app. | 11.50 | 34.00 | 80.00 |
| 22-Zor, Rocketman app. (68 pgs.) | 11.50 | 34.00 | 80.00 |

**REDSKIN** (Famous Western Badmen #13 on)
Sept, 1950 - No. 12, Oct, 1952
Youthful Magazines

| | | | |
|---|---|---|---|
| 1 | 5.70 | 17.00 | 40.00 |
| 2 | 3.50 | 10.50 | 24.00 |
| 3-12: 6,12-Bondage-c | 2.65 | 8.00 | 18.00 |

**RED SONJA** (Also see Blackthorne 3-D Series #53, Conan #23, Kull & The Barbarians, Marvel Feature & Savage Sword Of Conan #1)
1/77 - No. 15, 5/79; V1#1, 2/83 - V2#2, 3/83; V3#1, 8/83 - V3#4, 2/84; V3#5, 1/85 - V3#13, 1986
Marvel Comics Group

| | | | |
|---|---|---|---|
| 1-Created by Robert E. Howard | .50 | 1.50 | 3.00 |
| 2-5 | .35 | 1.00 | 2.00 |
| 6-15, V1#1,2 | | 50 | 1.00 |
| V3#1-4 ($1.00, 52 pgs.) | | .60 | 1.20 |
| 5-13 (65-75 cents) | | .50 | 1.00 |

NOTE: ***Brunner** c-12-14. **J. Buscema** a(p)-12, 13, 15; c-V#1. **Nebres** a-V3#3i(part). **N. Redondo** a-8i, V3#2i, 3i. **Simonson** a-V3#1. **Thorne** c/a-1-11.*

**RED SONJA: THE MOVIE**
Nov, 1985 - No. 2, Dec, 1985 (Limited-series)
Marvel Comics Group

| | | | |
|---|---|---|---|
| 1,2-Movie adapt-r/Marvel Super Spec. #38 | | .40 | .80 |

**RED TORNADO** (See Justice League of America #64)
July, 1985 - No. 4, Oct, 1985 (Mini-series)
DC Comics

| | | | |
|---|---|---|---|
| 1-4: 1-3-Superman cameos. 1,3-Batman cameos | | .50 | 1.00 |

**RED WARRIOR**
Jan, 1951 - No. 6, Dec, 1951
Marvel/Atlas Comics (TCI)

| | | | |
|---|---|---|---|
| 1-Tuska-a | 7.00 | 21.00 | 50.00 |
| 2-Tuska-c | 4.50 | 14.00 | 32.00 |
| 3-6: 4-Origin White Wing, his horse | 3.15 | 9.50 | 22.00 |

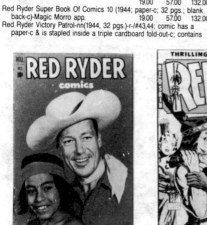

*Red Ryder Comics #99, © DELL*

*Redskin #6, © YM*

*Red Warrior #2, © MEG*

Reid Fleming V2#3, © Eclipse

Remember Pearl Harbor nn, © S&S

Reptilicus #1, © CC

**RED WOLF** (See Avengers #80 & Marvel Spotlight #1)
May, 1972 - No. 9, Sept, 1973
Marvel Comics Group

| | Good | Fine | N-Mint |
|---|---|---|---|
| 1-Gil Kane/Severin-c; Shores-a (#2 also) | | .40 | .80 |
| 2-9: 2-Kane-c. 9-Origin sidekick, Lobo (wolf) | | .30 | .60 |

**REESE'S PIECES**
Oct, 1985 - No. 2, Oct, 1985 ($1.75, color, Baxter)
Eclipse Comics

| | Good | Fine | N-Mint |
|---|---|---|---|
| 1,2-B&W-r in color | .30 | .90 | 1.80 |

**REFORM SCHOOL GIRL!**
1951
Realistic Comics

| | Good | Fine | N-Mint |
|---|---|---|---|
| nn-Used in **SOTI**, pg. 358, & cover ill. with caption "Comic books are supposed to be like fairy tales" | 71.00 | 215.00 | 500.00 |
| (Prices vary widely on this book) | | | |

NOTE: *The cover and title originated from a digest-sized book published by Diversey Publishing Co. of Chicago in 1948. The original book "House of Fury," Doubleday, came out in 1941. The girl's real name which appears on the cover of the digest and comic is Marty Collins, Canadian model and ice skating star who posed for this special color photograph for the Diversey novel.*

**REGENTS ILLUSTRATED CLASSICS**
1981 (Plus more recent reprintings)
(48 pgs., b&w-a with 14 pages of teaching helps)
Prentice Hall Regents, Englewood Cliffs, NJ 07632

NOTE: This series contains Classics Ill. art, and was produced from the same illegal source as **Cassette Books**. But when Twin Circle sued to stop the sale of the Cassette Books, they decided to permit this series to continue. This series was produced as a teaching aid. The 20 title series is divided into four levels based upon number of basic words used therein. There is also a teacher's manual for each level. All of the titles are still available from the publisher for about $5 each retail. The number to call for mail order purchases is (201)767-5937. Almost all of the issues have new covers taken from some interior art panel. Here is a list of the series by Regents ident. no. and the Classics Ill. counterpart.

16770(Cl#24-A2) 18333(Cl#3-A2) 21668(Cl#13-A2) 32224(Cl#21) 33051(Cl#26) 35788(Cl#84) 37153(Cl#16) 44460(Cl#19-A2) 44808(Cl#18-A2) 52395(Cl#4-A2) 58627(Cl#5-A2) 60067(Cl#30) 68405(Cl#23-A1) 70302(Cl#29) 78192(Cl#7-A2) 78193(Cl#10-A2) 79679(Cl#85) 92046(Cl#1-A2) 93062(Cl#64) 93512(Cl#25)

**REGGIE** (Formerly Archie's Rival . . .; Reggie & Me #19 on)
No. 15, Sept, 1963 - No. 18, Nov, 1965
Archie Publications

| | Good | Fine | N-Mint |
|---|---|---|---|
| 15(9/63), 16(10/64) | 5.00 | 15.00 | 35.00 |
| 17(8/65), 18(11/65) | 5.00 | 15.00 | 35.00 |

NOTE: *Cover title No. 15 & 16 is Archie's Rival Reggie.*

**REGGIE AND ME** (Formerly Reggie)
No. 19, Aug, 1966 - No. 126, Sept, 1980 (No. 50-68: 52 pgs.)
Archie Publications

| | Good | Fine | N-Mint |
|---|---|---|---|
| 19-Evilheart app. | 2.00 | 6.00 | 14.00 |
| 20-23-Evilheart app.; with Pureheart #22 | 1.15 | 3.50 | 8.00 |
| 24-40 | .40 | 1.25 | 2.50 |
| 41-60 | | .50 | 1.00 |
| 61-126 | | .30 | .60 |

**REGGIE'S JOKES** (See Reggie's Wise Guy Jokes)

**REGGIE'S WISE GUY JOKES**
Aug, 1968 - No. 60, Jan, 1982 (#5 on are Giants)
Archie Publications

| | Good | Fine | N-Mint |
|---|---|---|---|
| 1 | 1.70 | 5.00 | 12.00 |
| 2-4 | .70 | 2.00 | 5.00 |
| 5-10 | .35 | 1.00 | 2.00 |
| 11-28 | | .40 | .80 |
| 29-60 | | .25 | .50 |

**REGISTERED NURSE**
Summer, 1963
Charlton Comics

| | Good | Fine | N-Mint |
|---|---|---|---|
| 1-R/Nurse Betsy Crane & Cynthia Doyle | .35 | 1.00 | 2.00 |

**REG'LAR FELLERS** (See All-American Comics, Popular Comics & Treasure Box of Famous Comics)
1921 - 1929
Cupples & Leon Co./MS Publishng Co.

| | Good | Fine | N-Mint |
|---|---|---|---|
| 1(1921)-52 pgs. B&W dailies (Cupples & Leon, 10x10") | 11.50 | 34.00 | 80.00 |
| 1925, 48 pgs. B&W dailies (MS Publ.) | 11.50 | 34.00 | 80.00 |
| Softcover (1929, nn, 36 pgs.) | 11.50 | 34.00 | 80.00 |
| Hardcover (1929)-B&W reprints, 96 pgs. | 12.00 | 36.00 | 85.00 |

**REG'LAR FELLERS**
No. 5, Nov, 1947 - No. 6, Mar, 1948
Visual Editions (Standard)

| | Good | Fine | N-Mint |
|---|---|---|---|
| 5,6 | 4.00 | 12.00 | 28.00 |

**REG'LAR FELLERS HEROIC** (See Heroic Comics)

**REID FLEMING, WORLD'S TOUGHEST MILKMAN**
8/86; V2#1, 12/86 - V2#3, 12/88; V2#4, 11/89; V2#5, 11/90 (B&W)
Eclipse Comics

| | Good | Fine | N-Mint |
|---|---|---|---|
| 1 (3rd print, large size, 8/86, $2.50) | 1.00 | 3.00 | 6.00 |
| 1-4th & 5th printings ($2.50) | .40 | 1.25 | 2.50 |
| V2#1 (10/86, regular size, $2.00) | .50 | 1.50 | 3.00 |
| 1-2nd print, 3rd print ($2.00, 2/89) | .40 | 1.25 | 2.50 |
| 2-4 ($2.00) | .40 | 1.25 | 2.50 |
| V2#2-2nd & 3rd printings ($2.00) | .35 | 1.00 | 2.00 |
| V2#4-2nd printing ($2.00) | .35 | 1.00 | 2.00 |
| V2#5 ($2.00) | .35 | 1.00 | 2.00 |

**RELUCTANT DRAGON, THE** (See 4-Color #13)

**REMEMBER PEARL HARBOR**
1942 (68 pages) (Illustrated story of the battle)
Street & Smith Publications

| | Good | Fine | N-Mint |
|---|---|---|---|
| nn-Uncle Sam-c; Jack Binder-a | 25.00 | 75.00 | 175.00 |

**RENO BROWNE, HOLLYWOOD'S GREATEST COWGIRL** (Formerly Margie Comics; Apache Kid #53 on)
No. 50, April, 1950 - No. 52, Sept, 1950 (52 pgs.)
Marvel Comics (MPC)

| | Good | Fine | N-Mint |
|---|---|---|---|
| 50-Photo-c | 13.00 | 40.00 | 90.00 |
| 51,52: 51-Photo-c | 11.50 | 34.00 | 80.00 |

**REPTILICUS** (Reptisaurus #3 on)
Aug, 1961 - No. 2, Oct, 1961
Charlton Comics

| | Good | Fine | N-Mint |
|---|---|---|---|
| 1 (Movie) | 7.00 | 21.00 | 50.00 |
| 2 | 5.00 | 15.00 | 35.00 |

**REPTISAURUS** (Reptilicus #1,2)
Jan, 1962 - No. 8, Dec, 1962; Summer, 1963
Charlton Comics

| | Good | Fine | N-Mint |
|---|---|---|---|
| V2#3-8: 8-Montes/Bache-c/a | 2.65 | 8.00 | 18.00 |
| Special Edition 1 (Summer, 1963) | 2.65 | 8.00 | 18.00 |

**RESCUERS, THE** (See Walt Disney Showcase #40)

**RESTLESS GUN** (See 4-Color #934, 986, 1045, 1089, 1146)

**RETURN FROM WITCH MOUNTAIN** (See Walt Disney Showcase #44)

**RETURN OF GORGO, THE** (Formerly Gorgo's Revenge)
No. 2, Aug, 1963 - No. 3, Fall, 1964
Charlton Comics

| | Good | Fine | N-Mint |
|---|---|---|---|
| 2,3-Ditko-a, c-#3; based on M.G.M. movie | 4.00 | 12.00 | 28.00 |

**RETURN OF KONGA, THE** (Konga's Revenge #2 on)
1962
Charlton Comics

| | Good | Fine | N-Mint |
|---|---|---|---|
| nn | 4.00 | 12.00 | 28.00 |

**RETURN OF MEGATON MAN** (Also see Megaton Man)
July, 1988 - No. 3, 1988? ($2.00, color, mini-series)

Kitchen Sink Press

| | Good | Fine | N-Mint |
|---|---|---|---|
| 1-3: Simpson-c/a | .35 | 1.00 | 2.00 |

**RETURN OF THE OUTLAW**
Feb, 1953 - No. 11, 1955
Toby Press (Minoan)

| | Good | Fine | N-Mint |
|---|---|---|---|
| 1-Billy the Kid | 4.30 | 13.00 | 30.00 |
| 2 | 2.30 | 7.00 | 16.00 |
| 3-11 | 1.70 | 5.00 | 12.00 |

**REVEALING LOVE STORIES** (See Fox Giants)

**REVEALING ROMANCES**
Sept, 1949 - No. 6, Aug, 1950
Ace Magazines

| | Good | Fine | N-Mint |
|---|---|---|---|
| 1 | 3.70 | 11.00 | 26.00 |
| 2 | 1.70 | 5.00 | 12.00 |
| 3-6 | 1.30 | 4.00 | 9.00 |

**REVENGE OF THE PROWLER** (Also see The Prowler)
Feb, 1988 - No. 4, June, 1988 ($1.75/$1.95, color)
Eclipse Comics

| | Good | Fine | N-Mint |
|---|---|---|---|
| 1,3,4: 1-$1.75-c. 3,4-$1.95-c | .35 | 1.00 | 2.00 |
| 2 ($2.50)-Contains flexidisc | .40 | 1.25 | 2.50 |

**REVENGERS FEATURING MEGALITH** (Also see Megalith)
Sept, 1985; 1987 - Present ($2.00, color, Baxter)
Continuity Comics

| | Good | Fine | N-Mint |
|---|---|---|---|
| 1 (1985)-Origin; Neal Adams-c/a, scripts | .35 | 1.00 | 2.00 |
| 1 (1987, newsstand) - 5 | .35 | 1.00 | 2.00 |

**REX ALLEN COMICS** (Movie star)(Also see 4-Color #877 & Western Roundup under Dell Giants)
No. 316, Feb, 1951 - No. 31, Dec-Feb, 1958-59 (All-photo-c)
Dell Publishing Co.

| | Good | Fine | N-Mint |
|---|---|---|---|
| 4-Color 316(#1)(52 pgs.)-Rex Allen & his horse Koko begin; Marsh-a | 12.00 | 36.00 | 85.00 |
| 2 (9-11/51, 36 pgs.) | 6.00 | 18.00 | 42.00 |
| 3-10 | 4.65 | 14.00 | 32.00 |
| 11-20 | 3.70 | 11.00 | 26.00 |
| 21-23,25-31 | 3.50 | 10.50 | 24.00 |
| 24-Toth-a | 4.30 | 13.00 | 30.00 |

NOTE: ***Manning** a-20, 27-30. Photo back-c F.C. 316, 2-12, 20, 21.*

**REX DEXTER OF MARS** (See Mystery Men Comics)
Fall, 1940
Fox Features Syndicate

| | Good | Fine | N-Mint |
|---|---|---|---|
| 1-Rex Dexter, Patty O'Day, & Zanzibar (Tuska-a) app.; Briefer-c/a | 90.00 | 270.00 | 625.00 |

**REX HART** (Formerly Blaze Carson; Whip Wilson #9 on)
No. 6, Aug, 1949 - No. 8, Feb, 1950 (All photo-c)
Timely/Marvel Comics (USA)

| | Good | Fine | N-Mint |
|---|---|---|---|
| 6-Rex Hart & his horse Warrior begin; Black Rider app; Captain Tootsie by Beck | 11.50 | 34.00 | 80.00 |
| 7,8: 18pg. Thriller in each. 8-Blaze the Wonder Collie app. in text | 8.50 | 25.50 | 60.00 |

**REX MORGAN, M.D.** (Also see Harvey Comics Library)
Dec, 1955 - No. 3, 1956
Argo Publ.

| | Good | Fine | N-Mint |
|---|---|---|---|
| 1-Reprints Rex Morgan daily newspaper strips & daily panel-r of "These Women" by D'Alessio & "Timeout" by Jeff Keate | 5.70 | 17.00 | 40.00 |
| 2,3 | 3.70 | 11.00 | 26.00 |

**REX THE WONDER DOG** (See The Adventures of...)

**RHUBARB, THE MILLIONAIRE CAT** (See 4-Color #423, 466, 563)

**RIBIT!**
Jan, 1989 - No. 4, April?, 1989 ($1.95, color, mini-series)
Comico

| | Good | Fine | N-Mint |
|---|---|---|---|
| 1-4: Created, written & art by Frank Thorne | .35 | 1.00 | 2.00 |

**RIBTICKLER** (Also see Fox Giants)
1945 - No. 9, Aug, 1947; 1957; 1959
Fox Feature Synd./Green Publ. (1957)/Norlen (1959)

| | Good | Fine | N-Mint |
|---|---|---|---|
| 1 | 5.70 | 17.00 | 40.00 |
| 2 | 2.85 | 8.50 | 20.00 |
| 3-9: 3,7-Cosmo Cat app. | 2.00 | 6.00 | 14.00 |
| 3,7,8 (Green Publ.-1957) | 1.15 | 3.50 | 8.00 |
| 3,7,8 (Norlen Mag.-1959) | 1.15 | 3.50 | 8.00 |

**RICHARD DRAGON, KUNG-FU FIGHTER** (See Brave & the Bold)
Apr-May, 1975 - No. 18, Nov-Dec, 1977
National Periodical Publications/DC Comics

| | Good | Fine | N-Mint |
|---|---|---|---|
| 1,2: 2-Starlin-a(p). 3-Kirby-c/a(p) | | .50 | 1.00 |
| 3-18: 4-8-Wood inks (1-4 are based on novel) | | .40 | .80 |

**RICHARD THE LION-HEARTED** (See Ideal a Classical Comic)

**RICHIE RICH** (See Harvey Collectors Comics, Harvey Hits, Little Dot, Little Lotta, Little Sad Sack, Million Dollar Digest, Mutt & Jeff, Super Richie, and 3-D Dolly)

**RICHIE RICH** (...the Poor Little Rich Boy) (See Harvey Hits #3, 9)
Nov, 1960 - #218, Oct, 1982; #219, Oct, 1986 - #254, Jan, 1991
Harvey Publications

| | Good | Fine | N-Mint |
|---|---|---|---|
| 1-(See Little Dot for 1st app.) | 90.00 | 250.00 | 440.00 |
| 2 | 40.00 | 100.00 | 180.00 |
| 3-5 | 20.00 | 60.00 | 120.00 |
| 6-10: 8-Christmas-c | 12.50 | 37.50 | 75.00 |
| 11-20 | 5.35 | 16.00 | 32.00 |
| 21-40 | 3.00 | 9.00 | 18.00 |
| 41-60 | 2.00 | 6.00 | 12.00 |
| 61-80: 65-1st app. Dollar the Dog | 1.20 | 3.50 | 7.00 |
| 81-100 | .70 | 2.00 | 4.00 |
| 101-111,117-120 | .50 | 1.50 | 3.00 |
| 112-116: All 52 pg. Giants | .60 | 1.80 | 3.60 |
| 121-140 | .40 | 1.25 | 2.50 |
| 141-160: 145-Infinity-c | .35 | 1.00 | 2.00 |
| 161-180 | .25 | .75 | 1.50 |
| 181-254 | | .50 | 1.00 |

**RICHIE RICH AND...**
Oct, 1987 - Present?
Harvey Comics

| | Good | Fine | N-Mint |
|---|---|---|---|
| 1 (75 cents)-Diff. characters app. each issue | | .40 | .75 |
| 2-10 ($1.00) | | .50 | 1.00 |

**RICHIE RICH AND BILLY BELLHOPS**
October, 1977 (One Shot) (52pgs.)
Harvey Publications

| | Good | Fine | N-Mint |
|---|---|---|---|
| 1 | .50 | 1.50 | 3.00 |

**RICHIE RICH AND CADBURY**
10/77; No. 2, 9/78 - No. 23, 7/82; No. 24, 7/90 - Present (1-10: 52pgs.)
Harvey Publications

| | Good | Fine | N-Mint |
|---|---|---|---|
| 1 | .70 | 2.00 | 4.00 |
| 2-5 | .35 | 1.00 | 2.00 |
| 6-28: 24-Begin $1.00-c | | .50 | 1.00 |

**RICHIE RICH AND CASPER** (Also see Blackthorne 3-D Series #32)
Aug, 1974 - No. 45, Sept, 1982
Harvey Publications

| | Good | Fine | N-Mint |
|---|---|---|---|
| 1 | 1.15 | 3.50 | 7.00 |
| 2-5 | .50 | 1.50 | 3.00 |
| 6-10: 10-Xmas-c | .35 | 1.00 | 2.00 |
| 11-20 | | .50 | 1.00 |
| 21-40: 22-Xmas-c | | .40 | .80 |
| 41-45 | | .30 | .60 |

*Rex Allen Comics #19, © DELL*

*Ribtickler #2, © FOX*

*Richie Rich #8, © HARV*

**RICHIE RICH AND DOLLAR THE DOG** (See Richie Rich #65)
Sept, 1977 - No. 24, Aug, 1982 (#1-10: 52pgs.)
Harvey Publications

| | Good | Fine | N-Mint |
|---|---|---|---|
| 1 | .70 | 2.00 | 4.00 |
| 2-10 | .35 | 1.00 | 2.00 |
| 11-24 | | .50 | 1.00 |

**RICHIE RICH AND DOT**
October, 1974 (One Shot)
Harvey Publications

| | Good | Fine | N-Mint |
|---|---|---|---|
| 1 | 1.00 | 3.00 | 6.00 |

**RICHIE RICH AND GLORIA**
Sept, 1977 - No. 25, Sept, 1982 (#1-11: 52pgs.)
Harvey Publications

| | Good | Fine | N-Mint |
|---|---|---|---|
| 1 | .70 | 2.00 | 4.00 |
| 2-5 | .35 | 1.00 | 2.00 |
| 6-25 | | .40 | .80 |

**RICHIE RICH AND HIS GIRLFRIENDS**
April, 1979 - No. 16, Dec, 1982
Harvey Publications

| | Good | Fine | N-Mint |
|---|---|---|---|
| 1: 52 pg. Giant | .50 | 1.50 | 3.00 |
| 2: 52 pg. Giant | .40 | 1.20 | 2.40 |
| 3-10 | .35 | 1.00 | 2.00 |
| 11-16 | | .40 | .80 |

**RICHIE RICH AND HIS MEAN COUSIN REGGIE**
April, 1979 - No. 3, 1980 (50 cents) (#1,2: 52pgs.)
Harvey Publications

| | Good | Fine | N-Mint |
|---|---|---|---|
| 1 | .35 | 1.00 | 2.00 |
| 2-3: (#4 was advertised, but never released) | .25 | .75 | 1.50 |

**RICHIE RICH AND JACKIE JOKERS**
Nov, 1973 - No. 48, Dec, 1982
Harvey Publications

| | Good | Fine | N-Mint |
|---|---|---|---|
| 1: 52 pg. Giant | 1.70 | 5.00 | 10.00 |
| 2,3: 52 pg. Giants | 1.00 | 3.00 | 6.00 |
| 4,5 | .85 | 2.50 | 5.00 |
| 6-10 | .50 | 1.50 | 3.00 |
| 11-20 | .35 | 1.00 | 2.00 |
| 21-40 | | .50 | 1.00 |
| 41-48 | | .40 | .80 |

**RICHIE RICH AND PROFESSOR KEENBEAN**
Sept, 1990 - Present ($1.00, color)
Harvey Comics

| | Good | Fine | N-Mint |
|---|---|---|---|
| 1-4 | | .50 | 1.00 |

**RICHIE RICH & THE NEW KIDS ON THE BLOCK**
Feb, 1991 - Present ($1.25, color)
Harvey Comics

| | Good | Fine | N-Mint |
|---|---|---|---|
| 1-3 | | .65 | 1.30 |

**RICHIE RICH AND TIMMY TIME**
Sept, 1977 (50 Cents) (One Shot) (52 pages)
Harvey Publications

| | Good | Fine | N-Mint |
|---|---|---|---|
| 1 | .50 | 1.50 | 3.00 |

**RICHIE RICH BANK BOOKS**
Oct, 1972 - No. 59, Sept, 1982
Harvey Publications

| | Good | Fine | N-Mint |
|---|---|---|---|
| 1 | 2.65 | 8.00 | 16.00 |
| 2-5 | 1.00 | 3.00 | 6.00 |
| 6-10 | .70 | 2.00 | 4.00 |
| 11-20 | .50 | 1.50 | 3.00 |
| 21-30 | .35 | 1.00 | 2.00 |
| 31-40 | | .50 | 1.00 |
| 41-59 | | .40 | .80 |

**RICHIE RICH BEST OF THE YEARS**
Oct, 1977 - No. 6, June, 1980 (Digest) (128 pages)
Harvey Publications

| | Good | Fine | N-Mint |
|---|---|---|---|
| 1(10/77)-Reprints, #2(10/78)-Reprints, #3(6/79-75 cents) | .35 | 1.00 | 2.00 |
| 4-6(11/79-6/80-95 cents) | | .50 | 1.00 |

**RICHIE RICH BILLIONS**
Oct, 1974 - No. 48, Oct, 1982 (#1-33: 52pgs.)
Harvey Publications

| | Good | Fine | N-Mint |
|---|---|---|---|
| 1 | 1.70 | 5.00 | 10.00 |
| 2-5 | .85 | 2.50 | 5.00 |
| 6-10 | .70 | 2.00 | 4.00 |
| 11-20 | .35 | 1.00 | 2.00 |
| 21-33 (Last 52 pgs.) | | .50 | 1.00 |
| 34-48 | | .40 | .80 |

**RICHIE RICH CASH**
Sept, 1974 - No. 47, Aug, 1982
Harvey Publications

| | Good | Fine | N-Mint |
|---|---|---|---|
| 1 | 1.70 | 5.00 | 10.00 |
| 2-5 | .85 | 2.50 | 5.00 |
| 6-10 | .50 | 1.50 | 3.00 |
| 11-20 | .35 | 1.00 | 2.00 |
| 21-30 | | .50 | 1.00 |
| 31-47 | | .40 | .80 |

**RICHIE RICH, CASPER & WENDY NATIONAL LEAGUE**
June, 1976 (52 pages)
Harvey Publications

| | Good | Fine | N-Mint |
|---|---|---|---|
| 1 | .50 | 1.50 | 3.00 |

**RICHIE RICH COLLECTORS COMICS** (See Harvey Collectors Comics)

**RICHIE RICH DIAMONDS**
Aug, 1972 - No. 59, Aug, 1982 (#1, 23-45: 52pgs.)
Harvey Publications

| | Good | Fine | N-Mint |
|---|---|---|---|
| 1: 52 pg. Giant | 2.65 | 8.00 | 16.00 |
| 2-5 | 1.00 | 3.00 | 6.00 |
| 6-10 | .70 | 2.00 | 4.00 |
| 11-22 | .50 | 1.50 | 3.00 |
| 23-30 | .35 | 1.00 | 2.00 |
| 31-45: 39-Origin Little Dot | | .50 | 1.00 |
| 46-50 | | .40 | .80 |
| 51-59 | | .30 | .60 |

**RICHIE RICH DIGEST**
Oct, 1986 - Present ($1.25-$1.75, digest-size)
Harvey Publications

| | Good | Fine | N-Mint |
|---|---|---|---|
| 1-28 | .25 | .75 | 1.50 |

**RICHIE RICH DIGEST STORIES** (. . . Magazine #?-on)
Oct, 1977 - No. 17, Oct, 1982 (Digest) (132 pages) (75-95 cents)
Harvey Publications

| | Good | Fine | N-Mint |
|---|---|---|---|
| 1-Reprints | .25 | .80 | 1.60 |
| 2-17: 4-Infinity-c | | .40 | .80 |

**RICHIE RICH DIGEST WINNERS**
Dec, 1977 - No. 16, Sept, 1982 (Digest) (132 pages) (75-95 Cents)
Harvey Publications

| | Good | Fine | N-Mint |
|---|---|---|---|
| 1 | .25 | .80 | 1.60 |
| 2-16 | | .40 | .80 |

**RICHIE RICH DOLLARS & CENTS**
Aug, 1963 - No. 109, Aug, 1982 (#1-43: 68 pgs.; 44-60, 71-94: 52pgs.)
Harvey Publications

| | Good | Fine | N-Mint |
|---|---|---|---|
| 1: (#1-64 are all reprint issues) | 8.00 | 24.00 | 56.00 |
| 2 | 4.00 | 12.00 | 24.00 |
| 3-5: 5-r/1st app. of R.R. from Little Dot #1 | 2.35 | 7.00 | 14.00 |
| 6-10 | 1.70 | 5.00 | 10.00 |
| 11-20 | 1.35 | 4.00 | 8.00 |
| 21-30 | .85 | 2.50 | 5.00 |
| 31-43: Last 68 pg. issue | .50 | 1.50 | 3.00 |
| 44-60: All 52 pgs. | .40 | 1.20 | 2.40 |
| 61-70 | .35 | 1.00 | 2.00 |
| 71-94: All 52 pgs. | | .50 | 1.00 |
| 95-109: 100-Anniversary issue | | .40 | .80 |

**RICHIE RICH FORTUNES**
Sept, 1971 - No. 63, July, 1982 (#1-15: 52pgs.)
Harvey Publications

| | Good | Fine | N-Mint |
|---|---|---|---|
| 1 | 2.35 | 7.00 | 16.00 |
| 2-5 | 1.15 | 3.50 | 7.00 |
| 6-10 | .85 | 2.50 | 5.00 |
| 11-15: Last 52 pg. Giant | .70 | 2.00 | 4.00 |
| 16-30 | .35 | 1.00 | 2.00 |
| 31-40 | | .50 | 1.00 |
| 41-63 | | .40 | .80 |

**RICHIE RICH GEMS**
Sept, 1974 - No. 43, Sept, 1982
Harvey Publications

| | Good | Fine | N-Mint |
|---|---|---|---|
| 1 | 1.70 | 5.00 | 10.00 |
| 2-5 | .85 | 2.50 | 5.00 |
| 6-10 | .50 | 1.50 | 3.00 |
| 11-20 | .35 | 1.00 | 2.00 |
| 21-30 | | .50 | 1.00 |
| 31-43 | | .40 | .80 |

**RICHIE RICH GOLD AND SILVER**
Sept, 1975 - No. 42, Oct, 1982 (#1-27: 52pgs.)
Harvey Publications

| | Good | Fine | N-Mint |
|---|---|---|---|
| 1 | 1.35 | 4.00 | 8.00 |
| 2-5 | .70 | 2.00 | 4.00 |
| 6-10 | .35 | 1.00 | 2.00 |
| 11-27 | | .50 | 1.00 |
| 28-42 | | .40 | .80 |

**RICHIE RICH GOLD NUGGETS DIGEST**
Feb, 1991 - Present ($1.75, color, digest size)
Harvey Comics

| | Good | Fine | N-Mint |
|---|---|---|---|
| 1 | .30 | .90 | 1.75 |

**RICHIE RICH HOLIDAY DIGEST MAGAZINE** (. . . Digest #4)
Jan, 1980 - #3, Jan, 1982; #4, 3/88 - Present (Published annually)
Harvey Publications

| | Good | Fine | N-Mint |
|---|---|---|---|
| 1-3: All X-Mas-c | | .50 | 1.00 |
| 4-(3/88, $1.25), 5-(2/89, $1.75) | | .60 | 1.25 |

**RICHIE RICH INVENTIONS**
Oct, 1977 - No. 26, Oct, 1982 (#1-11: 52pgs.)

Harvey Publications

| | Good | Fine | N-Mint |
|---|---|---|---|
| 1 | .70 | 2.00 | 4.00 |
| 2-5 | .35 | 1.00 | 2.00 |
| 6-11 | | .50 | 1.00 |
| 12-26 | | .40 | .80 |

**RICHIE RICH JACKPOTS**
Oct, 1972 - No. 58, Aug, 1982 (#41-43: 52pgs.)
Harvey Publications

| | Good | Fine | N-Mint |
|---|---|---|---|
| 1 | 2.65 | 8.00 | 16.00 |
| 2-5 | 1.00 | 3.00 | 6.00 |
| 6-10 | .70 | 2.00 | 4.00 |
| 11-20 | .35 | 1.00 | 2.00 |
| 21-30 | .25 | .75 | 1.50 |
| 31-40,44-50 | | .50 | 1.00 |
| 41-43 (52 pgs.) | | .60 | 1.20 |
| 51-58 | | .40 | .80 |

**RICHIE RICH MILLION DOLLAR DIGEST** (. . .Magazine #?-on)(Also see Million Dollar Digest)
October, 1980 - No. 10, Oct, 1982
Harvey Publications

| | Good | Fine | N-Mint |
|---|---|---|---|
| 1-10 | | .50 | 1.00 |

**RICHIE RICH MILLIONS**
9/61; #2, 9/62 - #113, 10/82 (#1-48: 68 pgs.; 49-64, 85-97: 52 pgs.)
Harvey Publications

| | Good | Fine | N-Mint |
|---|---|---|---|
| 1: (#1-5 are all reprint issues) | 10.00 | 30.00 | 70.00 |
| 2 | 5.00 | 15.00 | 35.00 |
| 3-10: (All other giants are new & reprints) | 3.35 | 10.00 | 23.00 |
| 11-20 | 1.70 | 5.00 | 12.00 |
| 21-30 | 1.00 | 3.00 | 6.00 |
| 31-48: Last 68 pg. Giant | .75 | 2.30 | 4.60 |
| 49-64: 52 pg. Giants | .50 | 1.50 | 3.00 |
| 65-74 | .35 | 1.00 | 2.00 |
| 75-94: 52 pg. Giants | .40 | 1.20 | 2.40 |
| 95-100 | | .50 | 1.00 |
| 101-113 | | .40 | .80 |

**RICHIE RICH MONEY WORLD**
Sept, 1972 - No. 59, Sept, 1982
Harvey Publications

| | Good | Fine | N-Mint |
|---|---|---|---|
| 1: 52 pg. Giant | 2.65 | 8.00 | 16.00 |
| 2-5 | 1.00 | 3.00 | 6.00 |
| 6-10: 9,10-Richie Rich mistakenly named Little Lotta on covers | .50 | 1.50 | 3.00 |
| 11-20 | .35 | 1.10 | 2.20 |
| 21-30 | .25 | .75 | 1.50 |
| 31-50 | | .50 | 1.00 |
| 51-59 | | .40 | .80 |
| . . .Digest 1 (2/91, $1.75) | .30 | .90 | 1.80 |

**RICHIE RICH PROFITS**
Oct, 1974 - No. 47, Sept, 1982
Harvey Publications

| | Good | Fine | N-Mint |
|---|---|---|---|
| 1 | 2.00 | 6.00 | 12.00 |
| 2-5 | 1.00 | 3.00 | 6.00 |
| 6-10 | .50 | 1.50 | 3.00 |
| 11-20 | .35 | 1.00 | 2.00 |
| 21-30 | | .50 | 1.00 |
| 31-47 | | .40 | .80 |

**RICHIE RICH RELICS**
Jan, 1988 - No. 5?, Aug, 1989 (All reprints, .75-$1.00)
Harvey Comics

| | Good | Fine | N-Mint |
|---|---|---|---|
| 1-5 | | .50 | 1.00 |

**RICHIE RICH RICHES**
July, 1972 - No. 59, Aug, 1982 (#1, 2, 41-45: 52pgs.)
Harvey Publications

| | Good | Fine | N-Mint |
|---|---|---|---|
| 1: 52 pg. Giant | 2.00 | 6.00 | 12.00 |
| 2: 52 pg. Giant | 1.15 | 3.50 | 7.00 |
| 3-5 | 1.00 | 3.00 | 6.00 |
| 6-10 | .50 | 1.50 | 3.00 |
| 11-20 | .35 | 1.00 | 2.00 |
| 21-40 | | .50 | 1.00 |
| 41-45: 52 pg. Giants | | .60 | 1.20 |
| 46-59 | | .40 | .80 |

**RICHIE RICH SUCCESS STORIES**
Nov, 1964 - No. 105, Sept, 1982 (#1-38: 68pgs., 39-55, 67-90: 52pgs.)
Harvey Publications

| | Good | Fine | N-Mint |
|---|---|---|---|
| 1 | 8.00 | 24.00 | 56.00 |
| 2-5 | 3.00 | 9.00 | 21.00 |
| 6-10 | 2.00 | 6.00 | 12.00 |
| 11-30: 27-1st Penny Van Dough (8/69) | 1.00 | 3.00 | 6.00 |
| 31-38: Last 68 pg. Giant | .85 | 2.50 | 5.00 |
| 39-55: 52 pgs. | .50 | 1.50 | 3.00 |
| 56-66 | .35 | 1.00 | 2.00 |
| 67-90: 52 pgs. (Early issues are reprints) | | .60 | 1.20 |
| 91-105 | | .40 | .80 |

**RICHIE RICH TREASURE CHEST DIGEST** (. . .Magazine #3)
Apr, 1982 - No. 3, Aug, 1982 (95 Cents, Digest Magazine)
Harvey Publications

| | Good | Fine | N-Mint |
|---|---|---|---|
| 1-3 | | .50 | 1.00 |

**RICHIE RICH VACATIONS DIGEST**
11/77; No. 2, 10/78 - No. 7, 10/81; No. 8, 8/82 (Digest, 132 pgs.)
Harvey Publications

| | Good | Fine | N-Mint |
|---|---|---|---|
| 1-Reprints | .25 | .80 | 1.60 |
| 2-8 | | .50 | 1.00 |

**RICHIE RICH VAULTS OF MYSTERY**
Nov, 1974 - No. 47, Sept, 1982
Harvey Publications

| | Good | Fine | N-Mint |
|---|---|---|---|
| 1 | 1.50 | 4.50 | 9.00 |
| 2-10 | .70 | 2.00 | 4.00 |
| 11-20 | .35 | 1.00 | 2.00 |
| 21-30 | .25 | .75 | 1.50 |
| 31-47 | | .40 | .80 |

**RICHIE RICH ZILLIONZ**
Oct, 1976 - No. 33, Sept, 1982 (#1-4: 68pgs.; #5-18: 52pgs.)
Harvey Publications

| | Good | Fine | N-Mint |
|---|---|---|---|
| 1 | 1.35 | 4.00 | 8.00 |
| 2-4: Last 68 pg. Giant | .70 | 2.00 | 4.00 |
| 5-10 | .35 | 1.00 | 2.00 |
| 11-18: Last 52 pg. Giant | | .50 | 1.00 |
| 19-33 | | .40 | .80 |

**RICK GEARY'S WONDERS AND ODDITIES**
Dec, 1988 ($2.00, B&W, one-shot)
Dark Horse Comics

| | Good | Fine | N-Mint |
|---|---|---|---|
| 1 | .35 | 1.00 | 2.00 |

**RICKY**
No. 5, September, 1953
Standard Comics (Visual Editions)

| | Good | Fine | N-Mint |
|---|---|---|---|
| 5 | 1.70 | 5.00 | 12.00 |

**RICKY NELSON** (TV)(See Sweethearts V2#42)
No. 956, Dec, 1958 - No. 1192, June, 1961 (All photo-c)
Dell Publishing Co.

| | Good | Fine | N-Mint |
|---|---|---|---|
| 4-Color 956,998 | 14.00 | 43.00 | 100.00 |
| 4-Color 1115,1192-Manning-a | 14.00 | 43.00 | 100.00 |

**RIDER, THE** (Frontier Trail #6)
March, 1957 - No. 5, 1958

*Richie Rich Millions #45, © HARV*

*Richie Rich Success Stories #17, © HARV*

*Ricky Nelson #998, © Ozzie Nelson*

The Rifleman #5, © Four Star

The Ringo Kid Western #1, © MEG

Ripley's Believe It or Not! #1, © HARV

Ajax/Farrell Publ. (Four Star Comic Corp.)

| | Good | Fine | N-Mint |
|---|---|---|---|
| 1-Swift Arrow, Lone Rider begin | 4.00 | 12.00 | 28.00 |
| 2-5 | 2.15 | 6.50 | 15.00 |

**RIFLEMAN, THE** (TV)
No. 1009, 7-9/59 - No. 12, 7-9/62; No. 13, 11/62 - No. 20, 10/64
Dell Publ. Co./Gold Key No. 13 on

| | | | |
|---|---|---|---|
| 4-Color 1009 (#1) | 10.00 | 30.00 | 70.00 |
| 2 (1-3/60) | 7.00 | 21.00 | 50.00 |
| 3-Toth-a, 4 pgs. | 8.50 | 25.50 | 60.00 |
| 4,5,7-10 | 5.70 | 17.00 | 40.00 |
| 6-Toth-a, 4pgs. | 7.00 | 21.00 | 50.00 |
| 11-20 | 5.00 | 15.00 | 35.00 |

NOTE: *Warren Tufts a-2-9. All have Chuck Connors photo-c. Photo back-c, #13-15.*

**RIMA, THE JUNGLE GIRL**
Apr-May, 1974 - No. 7, Apr-May, 1975
National Periodical Publications

| | | | |
|---|---|---|---|
| 1-Origin, part 1 | .25 | .75 | 1.50 |
| 2-4-Origin, part 2,3,&4 | | .50 | 1.00 |
| 5-7: 7-Origin & only app. Space Marshal | | .35 | .70 |

NOTE: ***Kubert** c-1-7. **Nino** a-1-5. **Redondo** a-1-6.*

**RING OF BRIGHT WATER** (See Movie Classics)

**RING OF THE NIBELUNG, THE**
1989 - No. 4, 1990 ($4.95, squarebound, mature readers, 52 pgs.)
DC Comics

| | | | |
|---|---|---|---|
| 1-4: Adapts novel; G. Kane-c/a; nudity | .85 | 2.50 | 5.00 |

**RINGO KID, THE** (2nd Series)
Jan, 1970 - No. 23, Nov, 1973; No. 24, Nov, 1975 - No. 30, Nov, 1976
Marvel Comics Group

| | | | |
|---|---|---|---|
| 1-Williamson-a r-from #10, 1956 | | .60 | 1.20 |
| 2-30: 13-Wildey-r. 20-Williamson-r/#1 | | .40 | .80 |

**RINGO KID WESTERN, THE** (1st Series)(See Wild Western & Western Trails)
Aug, 1954 - No. 21, Sept, 1957
Atlas Comics (HPC)/Marvel Comics

| | | | |
|---|---|---|---|
| 1-Origin; The Ringo Kid begins | 11.00 | 32.00 | 75.00 |
| 2-Black Rider app.; origin/1st app. Ringo's Horse Arab | 5.70 | 17.00 | 40.00 |
| 3-5 | 3.60 | 11.00 | 25.00 |
| 6-8-Severin-a(3) each | 4.30 | 13.00 | 30.00 |
| 9,11,12,14-21: 12-Orlando-a, 4pgs. | 2.65 | 8.00 | 18.00 |
| 10,13-Williamson-a, 4 pgs. | 4.50 | 14.00 | 32.00 |

NOTE: ***Berg** a-8. **Maneely** a-1-5, 15, 16, 18, 20, 21; c-1-6, 8, 13, 15, 16, 18, 20. **J. Severin** c-10, 11. **Sinnott** a-1. **Wildey** a-16-18.*

**RIN TIN TIN** (See March of Comics #163,180,195)

**RIN TIN TIN** (TV) (. . & Rusty #21 on; see Western Roundup under Dell Giants)
Nov, 1952 - No. 38, May-July, 1961; Nov, 1963 (All Photo-c)
Dell Publishing Co./Gold Key

| | | | |
|---|---|---|---|
| 4-Color 434 (#1) | 6.00 | 18.00 | 42.00 |
| 4-Color 476,523 | 4.30 | 13.00 | 30.00 |
| 4(3-5/54)-10 | 3.50 | 10.50 | 24.00 |
| 11-20 | 2.65 | 8.00 | 18.00 |
| 21-38 | 2.30 | 7.00 | 16.00 |
| . . . & Rusty 1 (11/63-Gold Key) | 2.30 | 7.00 | 16.00 |

**RIO**
June, 1987 ($8.95, color, 64 pgs.)
Comico

| | | | |
|---|---|---|---|
| 1-Wildey-c/a | 1.50 | 4.50 | 9.00 |

**RIO BRAVO** (See 4-Color #1018)

**RIO CONCHOS** (See Movie Comics)

**RIOT** (Satire)
Apr, 1954 - No. 3, Aug, 1954; No. 4, Feb, 1956 - No. 6, June, 1956
Atlas Comics (ACI No. 1-5/WPI No. 6)

| | Good | Fine | N-Mint |
|---|---|---|---|
| 1-Russ Heath-a | 9.30 | 28.00 | 65.00 |
| 2-Li'l Abner satire by Post | 7.00 | 21.00 | 50.00 |
| 3-Last precode (8/54) | 5.70 | 17.00 | 40.00 |
| 4-Infinity-c; Marilyn Monroe "7 Year Itch" movie satire; Mad Rip-off ads | 8.50 | 25.50 | 60.00 |
| 5-Marilyn Monroe, John Wayne parody; part photo-c | 9.30 | 28.00 | 65.00 |
| 6-Lorna of the Jungle satire by Everett; Dennis the Menace satire cover/story | 5.70 | 17.00 | 40.00 |

NOTE: ***Berg** a-3. **Burgos** c-1, 2. **Colan** a-1. **Everett** a-1, 4, 6. **Heath** a-1. **Maneely** a-1, 2, 4-6; c-3, 4, 6. **Post** a-1-4. **Reinman** a-2. **Severin** a-4-6.*

**R.I.P.**
1990 - Present ($2.95, color, 44 pgs.)
TSR, Inc.

| | | | |
|---|---|---|---|
| 1-8-Based on TSR game | .50 | 1.50 | 3.00 |

**RIPCORD** (See 4-Color #1294)

**RIP HUNTER TIME MASTER** (See Showcase #20, 21, 25, 26)
Mar-Apr, 1961 - No. 29, Nov-Dec, 1965 (Also see Time Masters)
National Periodical Publications

| | | | |
|---|---|---|---|
| 1 | 24.00 | 70.00 | 165.00 |
| 2 | 12.00 | 36.00 | 85.00 |
| 3-5: 5-Last 10 cent issue | 7.00 | 21.00 | 50.00 |
| 6,7-Toth-a in each | 6.50 | 19.00 | 45.00 |
| 8-15 | 4.50 | 14.00 | 32.00 |
| 16-20 | 3.70 | 11.00 | 26.00 |
| 21-29: 29-G. Kane-c | 3.00 | 9.00 | 21.00 |

**RIP IN TIME** (Also see Teenage Mutant Ninja Turtles #5-7)
Aug, 1986 - No. 5, 1987 ($1.50, B&W)
Fantagor Press

| | | | |
|---|---|---|---|
| 1-5: Corben-c/a in all | .25 | .75 | 1.50 |

**RIP KIRBY** (See Feature Books #51, 54, Harvey Comics Hits #57, & Street Comix)

**RIPLEY'S BELIEVE IT OR NOT!**
Sept, 1953 - No. 4, March, 1954
Harvey Publications

| | | | |
|---|---|---|---|
| 1-Powell-a | 5.70 | 17.00 | 40.00 |
| 2-4 | 3.00 | 9.00 | 21.00 |
| J. C. Penney giveaway (1948) | 4.00 | 12.00 | 28.00 |

**RIPLEY'S BELIEVE IT OR NOT!** (Formerly . . .True War Stories)
No. 4, April, 1967 - No. 94, Feb, 1980
Gold Key

| | | | |
|---|---|---|---|
| 4-Photo-c; McWilliams-a | 2.00 | 6.00 | 14.00 |
| 5-Subtitled "True War Stories;" Evans-a | 1.30 | 4.00 | 9.00 |
| 6-10: 6-McWilliams-a. 10-Evans-a(2) | 1.30 | 4.00 | 9.00 |
| 11-20: 15-Evans-a | .85 | 2.60 | 6.00 |
| 21-30 | .70 | 2.00 | 4.00 |
| 31-38,40-60 | .40 | 1.25 | 2.50 |
| 39-Crandall-a | .50 | 1.50 | 3.00 |
| 61-94: 74,77-83 (52 pgs.) | .25 | .75 | 1.50 |
| Story Digest Mag. 1(6/70)-4¾x6½" | .70 | 2.00 | 4.00 |

NOTE: ***Evanish** art by **Luiz Dominguez** #22-25, 27, 30, 31, 40. **Jeff Jones** a-5(2 pgs.). **McWilliams** a-65, 70, 89. **Orlando** a-8. **Sparling** c-68. Reprints-74, 77-84, 87 (part); 91, 93 (all). **Williamson, Wood** a-80r/#1.*

**RIPLEY'S BELIEVE IT OR NOT!** (See Ace Comics, All-American Comics, Mystery Comics Digest #1, 4, 7, 10, 13, 16, 19, 22, 25)

**RIPLEY'S BELIEVE IT OR NOT TRUE GHOST STORIES** (Becomes . . .True War Stories) (See Dan Curtis)
June, 1965 - No. 2, Oct, 1966
Gold Key

| | | | |
|---|---|---|---|
| 1-Williamson, Wood & Evans-a; photo-c | 3.00 | 9.00 | 21.00 |

| | Good | Fine | N-Mint |
|---|---|---|---|
| 2-Orlando, McWilliams-a; photo-c | 1.70 | 5.00 | 12.00 |
| Mini-Comic 1(1976-3¼x6½") | | .30 | .60 |
| 11186(1977)-Golden Press; 224 pgs. ($1.95)-Reprints | .50 | 1.50 | 3.00 |
| 11401(3/79)-Golden Press; 96 pgs. ($1.00)-Reprints | | .60 | 1.20 |

**RIPLEY'S BELIEVE IT OR NOT TRUE WAR STORIES** (Formerly ...True Ghost Stories; becomes Ripley's Believe It or Not #4 on)
Nov, 1966
Gold Key

| | Good | Fine | N-Mint |
|---|---|---|---|
| 1(#3)-Williamson-a | 2.00 | 6.00 | 14.00 |

**RIPLEY'S BELIEVE IT OR NOT! TRUE WEIRD**
June, 1966 - No. 2, Aug, 1966 (B&W Magazine)
Ripley Enterprises

| | Good | Fine | N-Mint |
|---|---|---|---|
| 1,2-Comic stories & text | .50 | 1.50 | 3.00 |

**RIVERDALE HIGH**
Aug, 1990 - Present ($1.00, color, bi-monthly)
Archie Comics

| | Good | Fine | N-Mint |
|---|---|---|---|
| 1-4 | | .50 | 1.00 |

**RIVETS** (See 4-Color #518)

**RIVETS** (A dog)
Jan, 1956 - No. 3, May, 1956
Argo Publ.

| | Good | Fine | N-Mint |
|---|---|---|---|
| 1-Reprints Sunday & daily newspaper strips | 3.00 | 9.00 | 21.00 |
| 2,3 | 1.70 | 5.00 | 12.00 |

**ROACHMILL** (1st series)
Dec, 1986 - No. 6, Oct, 1987 ($1.75, B&W)
Blackthorne Publishing

| | Good | Fine | N-Mint |
|---|---|---|---|
| 1 | 1.00 | 3.00 | 6.00 |
| 2-6 | .70 | 2.00 | 4.00 |

**ROACHMILL** (2nd series)
May, 1988 - Present ($1.75-$1.95, B&W)
Dark Horse Comics

| | Good | Fine | N-Mint |
|---|---|---|---|
| 1 | .70 | 2.00 | 4.00 |
| 2-10: 9-Begin $1.95-c | .40 | 1.25 | 2.50 |
| 11,12 | .30 | .90 | 1.75 |

**ROAD RUNNER** (See Beep Beep, the...)

**ROBERT E. HOWARD'S CONAN THE BARBARIAN**
1983 (No month) ($2.50, printed on Baxter paper, 68 pgs.)
Marvel Comics Group

| | Good | Fine | N-Mint |
|---|---|---|---|
| 1-r-/Savage Tales No. 2,3 by Smith; c-r/Conan No. 21 by Smith | .45 | 1.25 | 2.50 |

**ROBIN** (See Aurora, Detective Comics #38, New Teen Titans, Star Spangled Comics #65 & Teen Titans)

**ROBIN**
Jan, 1991 - No. 5, May, 1991 ($1.00, color, mini-series)
DC Comics

| | Good | Fine | N-Mint |
|---|---|---|---|
| 1-Free poster by N. Adams; Bolland-c on all | 1.70 | 5.00 | 10.00 |
| 1-2nd printing (without poster) | .35 | 1.00 | 2.00 |
| 2 | .50 | 1.50 | 3.00 |
| 3-5 | | .50 | 1.00 |

**ROBIN HOOD** (See The Advs. of..., Brave and the Bold, Four Color #413, 669, King Classics, Movie Comics & Power Record Comics)

**ROBIN HOOD** (...& His Merry Men, The Illustrated Story of...) (See Classic Comics #7 & Classics Giveaways, 12/44)

**ROBIN HOOD** (New Adventures of...)
1952 (36 pages) (5x7¼")
Walt Disney Productions (Flour giveaways)

| | Good | Fine | N-Mint |
|---|---|---|---|
| "New Adventures of Robin Hood," "Ghosts of Waylea Castle," & "The Miller's Ransom" each.... | 1.70 | 5.00 | 12.00 |

**ROBIN HOOD** (Adventures of... #7, 8)
No. 52, Nov, 1955 - No. 6, June, 1957
Magazine Enterprises (Sussex Publ. Co.)

| | Good | Fine | N-Mint |
|---|---|---|---|
| 52 (#1)-Origin Robin Hood & Sir Gallant of the Round Table | 5.70 | 17.00 | 40.00 |
| 53, 3-6 | 4.00 | 12.00 | 28.00 |
| I.W. Reprint #1,2 (r-#4), 9 (r-#52)(1963) | .50 | 1.50 | 3.00 |
| Super Reprint #10 (r-#53?), 11,15 (r-#5), 17('64) | .50 | 1.50 | 3.00 |

NOTE: *Bolle a-in all; c-52. Powell a-6.*

**ROBIN HOOD** (Not Disney)
May-July, 1963 (One shot)
Dell Publishing Co.

| | Good | Fine | N-Mint |
|---|---|---|---|
| 1 | 1.15 | 3.50 | 8.00 |

**ROBIN HOOD**
1973 (Disney) (8½x11"; cardboard covers) ($1.50, 52 pages)
Western Publishing Co.

| | Good | Fine | N-Mint |
|---|---|---|---|
| 96151-"Robin Hood," based on movie, 96152-"The Mystery of Sherwood Forest," 96153-"In King Richard's Service," 96154-"The Wizard's Ring" each.... | .70 | 2.00 | 4.00 |

**ROBIN HOOD AND HIS MERRY MEN** (Formerly Danger & Adv.)
No. 28, April, 1956 - No. 38, Aug, 1958
Charlton Comics

| | Good | Fine | N-Mint |
|---|---|---|---|
| 28 | 3.15 | 9.50 | 22.00 |
| 29-37 | 1.70 | 5.00 | 12.00 |
| 38-Ditko-a (5 pgs.) | 5.00 | 15.00 | 35.00 |

**ROBIN HOOD'S FRONTIER DAYS** (...Western Tales)
No date (Circa 1955) 20 pages, slick-c (Seven issues?)
Shoe Store Giveaway (Robin Hood Stores)

| | Good | Fine | N-Mint |
|---|---|---|---|
| nn | 2.65 | 8.00 | 18.00 |
| nn-Issues with Crandall-a | 4.00 | 12.00 | 28.00 |

**ROBIN HOOD TALES** (Published by National Periodical #7 on)
Feb, 1956 - No. 6, Nov-Dec, 1956
Quality Comics Group (Comic Magazines)

| | Good | Fine | N-Mint |
|---|---|---|---|
| 1 | 5.30 | 16.00 | 38.00 |
| 2-5-Matt Baker-a | 6.00 | 18.00 | 42.00 |
| 6 | 3.00 | 9.00 | 21.00 |
| Frontier Days giveaway (1956) | 2.65 | 8.00 | 18.00 |

**ROBIN HOOD TALES** (Continued from Quality series)
No. 7, Jan-Feb, 1957 - No. 14, Mar-Apr, 1958
National Periodical Publications

| | Good | Fine | N-Mint |
|---|---|---|---|
| 7 | 13.00 | 40.00 | 90.00 |
| 8-14 | 11.00 | 32.00 | 75.00 |

**ROBINSON CRUSOE** (See King Classics & Power Record Comics)
Nov-Jan, 1963-64
Dell Publishing Co.

| | Good | Fine | N-Mint |
|---|---|---|---|
| 1 | 1.00 | 3.00 | 7.00 |

**ROBOCOP**
Oct, 1987 ($2.00, B&W, magazine, one-shot)
Marvel Comics

| | Good | Fine | N-Mint |
|---|---|---|---|
| 1-Movie adaptation | .35 | 1.00 | 2.00 |

**ROBOCOP**
March, 1990 - Present ($1.50, color)
Marvel Comics

| | Good | Fine | N-Mint |
|---|---|---|---|
| 1-Based on movie | 1.70 | 5.00 | 10.00 |
| 2 | .85 | 2.50 | 5.00 |
| 3-6 | .40 | 1.25 | 2.50 |
| 7-14 | .25 | .75 | 1.50 |
| nn (7/90, $4.95, color, 52 pgs.)-r/B&W magazine in color; adapts 1st movie | .85 | 2.50 | 5.00 |

*Rivets #1, © Argo Publ.*

*Robin Hood and His Merry Men #29, © CC*

*Robocop #1 (3/89), © Orion Pictures*

*Robotech: The New Generation #9, © Comico*

*The Rocketeer Special Edition #1, © Eclipse*

*Rocket Ship X #1, © FOX*

**ROBOCOP 2**
Aug, 1990 ($2.25, B&W, magazine, 68 pgs.)
Marvel Comics

| | Good | Fine | N-Mint |
|---|---|---|---|
| 1-Adapts movie sequel | .40 | 1.25 | 2.50 |

**ROBOCOP 2**
Aug, 1990; Late Aug, 1990 - #3, Late Sept, 1990 ($1.00, mini-series)
Marvel Comics

| | Good | Fine | N-Mint |
|---|---|---|---|
| nn-(8/90, $4.95, color, 68 pgs.)-Same contents as B&W magazine | .85 | 2.50 | 5.00 |
| 1 | .35 | 1.00 | 2.00 |
| 2,3: 1-3 reprint no number issue. 2-Guice-c(i) | | .75 | 1.50 |

**ROBO-HUNTER** (Also see Sam Slade...)
April, 1984 - No. 6, 1984 ($1.00, color)
Eagle Comics

| | Good | Fine | N-Mint |
|---|---|---|---|
| 1-6-2000 A.D.-r | | .50 | 1.00 |

**R.O.B.O.T. BATTALION 2050**
March, 1988 ($2.00, B&W, one-shot)
Eclipse Comics

| | Good | Fine | N-Mint |
|---|---|---|---|
| 1 | .35 | 1.00 | 2.00 |

**ROBOT COMICS**
June, 1987 (One shot, $2.00, B&W)
Renegade Press

| | Good | Fine | N-Mint |
|---|---|---|---|
| 0-Bob Burden story/art | .35 | 1.10 | 2.20 |

**ROBOTECH DEFENDERS**
Mar, 1985 - No. 2, Apr, 1985 (Mini-series)
DC Comics

| | Good | Fine | N-Mint |
|---|---|---|---|
| 1,2 | .35 | 1.00 | 2.00 |

**ROBOTECH IN 3-D**
Aug, 1987 ($2.50)
Comico

| | Good | Fine | N-Mint |
|---|---|---|---|
| 1-Adapts TV show; Steacy painted-c | .40 | 1.25 | 2.50 |

**ROBOTECH MASTERS** (TV)
July, 1985 - No. 23, Apr, 1988 ($1.50, color)
Comico

| | Good | Fine | N-Mint |
|---|---|---|---|
| 1 | .60 | 1.75 | 3.50 |
| 2,3 | .40 | 1.25 | 2.50 |
| 4-23: 23-$1.75-c | .35 | 1.00 | 2.00 |

**ROBOTECH SPECIAL**
May, 1988 ($2.50, color, one shot, 44pgs.)
Comico

| | Good | Fine | N-Mint |
|---|---|---|---|
| 1-Ken Steacy wraparound-c; part photo-c | .40 | 1.25 | 2.50 |

**ROBOTECH THE GRAPHIC NOVEL**
Aug, 1986 ($5.95, 8½x11", 52 pgs.)
Comico

| | Good | Fine | N-Mint |
|---|---|---|---|
| 1-Origin SDF-1; intro T.R. Edwards; Ken Steacy c/a; 2nd printing also exists (12/86) | 1.00 | 3.00 | 6.00 |

**ROBOTECH: THE MACROSS SAGA** (TV)(Formerly Macross)
No. 2, Feb, 1985 - No. 36, Feb, 1989 ($1.50, color)
Comico

| | Good | Fine | N-Mint |
|---|---|---|---|
| 2 | .85 | 2.50 | 5.00 |
| 3-5 | .50 | 1.50 | 3.00 |
| 6,7 | .40 | 1.25 | 2.50 |
| 8-25: 12,17-Ken Steacy painted-c | .35 | 1.00 | 2.00 |
| 26-36: 26-34-$1.75. 35,36-$1.95-c | .30 | .90 | 1.75 |

**ROBOTECH: THE NEW GENERATION** (TV)
July, 1985 - No. 25, July, 1988 ($1.50, color)
Comico

| | Good | Fine | N-Mint |
|---|---|---|---|
| 1 | .50 | 1.50 | 3.00 |
| 2-4 | .40 | 1.25 | 2.50 |
| 5-25: 9,13-Ken Steacy painted-c. 22-25 ($1.75) | .35 | 1.00 | 2.00 |

**ROBOTIX**
Feb, 1986 (75 cents, one shot)
Marvel Comics Group

| | Good | Fine | N-Mint |
|---|---|---|---|
| 1-Based on toy | | .40 | .80 |

**ROBOTMEN OF THE LOST PLANET** (Also see Space Thrillers)
1952 (Also see Strange Worlds #19)
Avon Periodicals

| | Good | Fine | N-Mint |
|---|---|---|---|
| 1-Kinstler-a (3 pgs.) | 57.00 | 171.00 | 400.00 |

**ROB ROY** (See 4-Color #544)

**ROCK AND ROLLO** (Formerly TV Teens)
V2#14, Oct, 1957 - No. 19, Sept, 1958
Charlton Comics

| | Good | Fine | N-Mint |
|---|---|---|---|
| V2#14-19 | 1.15 | 3.50 | 8.00 |

**ROCKET COMICS**
Mar, 1940 - No. 3, May, 1940
Hillman Periodicals

| | Good | Fine | N-Mint |
|---|---|---|---|
| 1-Rocket Riley, Red Roberts the Electro Man (origin), The Phantom Ranger, The Steel Shark, The Defender, Buzzard Barnes, Lefty Larson, & Man With a Thousand Faces begin | 79.00 | 235.00 | 550.00 |
| 2,3 | 50.00 | 150.00 | 350.00 |

**ROCKETEER, THE** (See Eclipse Graphic Album Series, Pacific Presents & Starslayer #2)

**ROCKETEER ADVENTURE MAGAZINE, THE**
July, 1988 - Present ($2.00, color)
Comico

| | Good | Fine | N-Mint |
|---|---|---|---|
| 1-Dave Stevens-c/a in all; Kaluta back-up-a | .70 | 2.00 | 4.00 |
| 2 ($2.75) | .50 | 1.50 | 3.00 |

**ROCKETEER SPECIAL EDITION, THE**
Nov, 1984 ($1.50, color, Baxter paper)
Eclipse Comics

| | Good | Fine | N-Mint |
|---|---|---|---|
| 1-Stevens-c/a; Kaluta back-c; pin-ups inside | 1.15 | 3.50 | 7.00 |

**ROCKET KELLY** (See The Bouncer & Green Mask #10)
1944; Fall, 1945 - No. 5, Oct-Nov, 1946
Fox Feature Syndicate

| | Good | Fine | N-Mint |
|---|---|---|---|
| nn (1944) | 11.50 | 34.00 | 80.00 |
| 1 | 11.50 | 34.00 | 80.00 |
| 2-The Puppeteer app. (costumed hero) | 8.00 | 24.00 | 55.00 |
| 3-5: 5-(#5 on cover, #4 inside) | 6.50 | 19.00 | 45.00 |

**ROCKETMAN** (Strange Fantasy #2 on)
June, 1952 (Also see Hello Pal & Scoop Comics)
Ajax/Farrell Publications

| | Good | Fine | N-Mint |
|---|---|---|---|
| 1-Rocketman & Cosmo | 16.00 | 48.00 | 110.00 |

**ROCKET RACCOON**
May, 1985 - No. 4, Aug, 1985 (Mini-series)
Marvel Comics Group

| | Good | Fine | N-Mint |
|---|---|---|---|
| 1-4 | .25 | .75 | 1.50 |

**ROCKETS AND RANGE RIDERS**
May, 1957 (16 pages, soft-c) (Giveaway)
Richfield Oil Corp.

| | Good | Fine | N-Mint |
|---|---|---|---|
| nn-Toth-a | 11.50 | 34.00 | 80.00 |

**ROCKET SHIP X**
September, 1951; 1952
Fox Features Syndicate

| | Good | Fine | N-Mint |
|---|---|---|---|
| 1 | 37.00 | 110.00 | 255.00 |
| 1952 (nn, nd, no publ.)-Edited '51-c | 24.00 | 71.00 | 165.00 |

**ROCKET TO ADVENTURE LAND** (See Pixie Puzzle. . .)

**ROCKET TO THE MOON**
1951
Avon Periodicals

| | Good | Fine | N-Mint |
|---|---|---|---|
| nn-Orlando-c/a; adapts Otis Aldebert Kline's "Maza of the Moon" | 60.00 | 180.00 | 420.00 |

**ROCK FANTASY COMICS**
Dec, 1989 - Present ($2.25-$3.00, B&W)(No cover price)
Rock Fantasy Comics

| | | | |
|---|---|---|---|
| 1-Pink Floyd part I | .70 | 2.00 | 4.00 |
| 1-2nd printings ($3.00-c) | .50 | 1.50 | 3.00 |
| 2,3: 2-Rolling Stones #1. 4-Led Zeppelin #1 | .40 | 1.15 | 2.30 |
| 2,3: 2nd printings ($3.00-c, 1/90 & 2/90) | .50 | 1.50 | 3.00 |
| 4-Stevie Nicks — Not published | | | |
| 5-Monstrosities of Rock #1; photo back-c | .40 | 1.25 | 2.50 |
| 5-2nd printing ($3.00, 3/90 indicia, 2/90-c | .50 | 1.50 | 3.00 |
| 6-11: 6-Guns n' Roses #1 (1st & 2nd prints, 3/90)-Begin $3.00-c. 7-Sex Pistols #1. 8-Alice Cooper — Not published. 9-Van Halen #1; photo back-c. 10-Kiss #1; photo back-c. 11-Jimi Hendrix #1; wrap-around-c | .50 | 1.50 | 3.00 |

**ROCK HAPPENING** (Harvey Pop Comics:. . .)(See Bunny)
Sept, 1969 - No. 2, Nov, 1969
Harvey Publications

| | | | |
|---|---|---|---|
| 1,2: Featuring Bunny | 1.15 | 3.50 | 8.00 |

**ROCK N' ROLL COMICS**
June, 1989 - Present ($1.50-$1.95, B&W; color #15 on)
Revolutionary Comics

| | | | |
|---|---|---|---|
| 1-Guns N' Roses | 1.70 | 5.00 | 10.00 |
| 1-2nd thru 6th printings | .25 | .75 | 1.50 |
| 1-7th printing (Full color w/new-c/a; $1.95) | .35 | 1.00 | 2.00 |
| 2-Metallica | .85 | 2.50 | 5.00 |
| 2-2nd thru 6th printings | .25 | .75 | 1.50 |
| 3-Bon Jovi (no reprints) | .40 | 1.25 | 2.50 |
| 4-22: 4-Motley Crue(2 printings). 5-Def Leppard(2 printings). 6-Rolling Stones(4 printings). 7-The Who(3 printings). 8-Skid Row; not published. 9-Kiss(3 printings; new back-c on 3rd). 10-Warrant/Whitesnake(2 printings). 11-Aerosmith(2 printings). 12-New Kids on the Block(2 printings). 12-3rd printing; rewritten & titled NKOTB Hate Book. 13-Led Zeppelin. 14-Sex Pistols. 15-Poison; 1st color issue. 16-Van Halen. 17-Madonna. 18-Alice Cooper. 19-Public Enemy/2 Live Crew. 20-Queensryche/Tesla. 21-? 22-AC/DC ($2.50-c) | .35 | 1.00 | 2.00 |

NOTE: *Most issues were reprinted except for #3. Later reprints are in color. #8 was not released.*

**ROCKY AND HIS FIENDISH FRIENDS** (TV)(Bullwinkle)
Oct, 1962 - No. 5, Sept, 1963 (Jay Ward)
Gold Key

| | | | |
|---|---|---|---|
| 1 (84 pgs., 25 cents) | 10.00 | 30.00 | 80.00 |
| 2,3 (84 pgs., 25 cents) | 8.00 | 24.00 | 65.00 |
| 4,5 (Regular size, 12 cents) | 5.70 | 17.00 | 40.00 |
| Kite Fun Book ('63, 16p, soft-c, 5x7¼") | 7.00 | 21.00 | 50.00 |
| Kite Fun Book ('70, 16p, soft-c, 5x7¼") | 5.00 | 15.00 | 35.00 |

**ROCKY AND HIS FRIENDS** (See 4-Color #1128, 1152, 1166, 1208, 1275, 1311 and March of Comics #216)

**ROCKY HORROR PICTURE SHOW THE COMIC BOOK, THE**
July, 1990 - No. 3, 1990 ($2.95, color, mini-series, 52 pgs.)(Photo-c #1)
Caliber Press

| | | | |
|---|---|---|---|
| 1-Adapts cult film plus photos, etc. | .85 | 2.50 | 5.00 |
| 1-2nd printing | .50 | 1.50 | 3.00 |
| 2,3 | .60 | 1.75 | 3.50 |

**ROCKY JONES SPACE RANGER** (See Space Adventures #15-18)

**ROCKY JORDAN PRIVATE EYE** (See Private Eye)

**ROCKY LANE WESTERN** (Allan Rocky Lane starred in Republic movies & TV (for a short time as Allan Lane, Red Ryder & Rocky Lane) (See Black Jack Fawcett Movie Comics, Motion Picture Comics & Six Gun Heroes)
May, 1949 - No. 87, Nov, 1959
Fawcett Publications/Charlton No. 56 on

| | Good | Fine | N-Mint |
|---|---|---|---|
| 1 (36 pgs.)-Rocky, his stallion Black Jack, & Slim Pickens begin; photo-c begin, end #57; photo back-c | 49.00 | 145.00 | 340.00 |
| 2 (36 pgs.)-Last photo back-c | 18.00 | 54.00 | 125.00 |
| 3-5 (52 pgs.): 4-Captain Tootsie by Beck | 14.00 | 43.00 | 100.00 |
| 6,10 (36 pgs.) | 11.00 | 32.00 | 75.00 |
| 7-9 (52 pgs.) | 12.00 | 36.00 | 85.00 |
| 11-13,15-17 (52 pgs.): 15-Black Jack's Hitching Post begins, ends #25 | 9.30 | 28.00 | 65.00 |
| 14,18 (36 pgs.) | 8.00 | 24.00 | 55.00 |
| 19-21,23,24 (52 pgs.): 20-Last Slim Pickens. 21-Dee Dickens begins, ends #55,57,65-68 | 8.00 | 24.00 | 55.00 |
| 22,25-28,30 (36 pgs. begin) | 7.00 | 21.00 | 50.00 |
| 29-Classic complete novel "The Land of Missing Men,"-hidden land of ancient temple ruins (r-in #65) | 8.50 | 25.50 | 60.00 |
| 31-40 | 6.50 | 19.00 | 45.00 |
| 41-54 | 5.30 | 16.00 | 38.00 |
| 55-Last Fawcett issue (1/54) | 5.70 | 17.00 | 40.00 |
| 56-1st Charlton issue (2/54)-Photo-c | 7.00 | 21.00 | 50.00 |
| 57,60-Photo-c | 5.00 | 15.00 | 35.00 |
| 58,59,61-64: 59-61-Young Falcon app. 64-Slim Pickens app. | 3.70 | 11.00 | 26.00 |
| 65-R-/#29, "The Land of Missing Men" | 4.00 | 12.00 | 28.00 |
| 66-68: Reprints #30,31,32 | 3.00 | 9.00 | 21.00 |
| 69-78,80-86 | 3.00 | 9.00 | 21.00 |
| 79-Giant Edition, 68 pgs. | 4.00 | 12.00 | 28.00 |
| 87-Last issue | 3.70 | 11.00 | 26.00 |

NOTE: ***Complete novels*** *in #10, 14, 18, 22, 25, 30-32, 36, 38, 39, 49.* ***Captain Tootsie*** *in #4, 12, 20.* ***Big Bow and Little Arrow*** *in #11, 28, 63.* ***Black Jack's Hitching Post*** *in #15-25, 64, 73.*

**ROCKY LANE WESTERN**
1989 - Present? ($2.50, B&W, one-shot?)
AC Comics

| | | | |
|---|---|---|---|
| 1-Photo covers; Giordano reprints | .40 | 1.25 | 2.50 |

**ROD CAMERON WESTERN** (Movie star)
Feb, 1950 - No. 20, April, 1953
Fawcett Publications

| | | | |
|---|---|---|---|
| 1-Rod Cameron, his horse War Paint, & Sam The Sheriff begin; photo front/back-c begin | 35.00 | 105.00 | 245.00 |
| 2 | 17.00 | 51.00 | 120.00 |
| 3-Novel length story "The Mystery of the Seven Cities of Cibola" | 14.00 | 43.00 | 100.00 |
| 4-10: 9-Last photo back-c | 11.50 | 34.00 | 80.00 |
| 11-19 | 10.00 | 30.00 | 70.00 |
| 20-Last issue & photo-c | 11.00 | 32.00 | 75.00 |

NOTE: ***Novel length stories*** *in No. 1-8, 12-14.*

**RODEO RYAN** (See A-1 Comics #8)

**ROGER BEAN, R. G.** (Regular Guy)
1915 - No. 5, 1917 (34 pgs.; B&W; 4¾x16"; cardboard covers)
(No. 1 & 4 bound on side, No. 3 bound at top)
The Indiana News Co.

| | | | |
|---|---|---|---|
| 1-By Chic Jackson (48 pgs.) | 9.00 | 27.00 | 62.00 |
| 2-5 | 6.50 | 19.00 | 45.00 |

**ROGER DODGER** (Also in Exciting Comics #57 on)
No. 5, Aug, 1952
Standard Comics

| | | | |
|---|---|---|---|
| 5-Teen-age | 1.70 | 5.00 | 12.00 |

*Rocket to the Moon nn, © AVON*

*Rock Fantasy Comics #1, © Rock Fantasy*

*Rocky Lane Western #15, © FAW*

Roger Rabbit #1, © The Disney Co.

Rogue Trooper #10, © Quality

Romantic Adventures #20, © ACG

**ROGER RABBIT** (Also see Marvel Graphic Novel)
June, 1990 - Present ($1.50, color)
Disney Comics

| | Good | Fine | N-Mint |
|---|---|---|---|
| 1-All new stories | .50 | 1.50 | 3.00 |
| 2,3 | .30 | 1.00 | 2.00 |
| 4-12 | .25 | .75 | 1.50 |

**ROG 2000**
June, 1982 ($2.95)
Pacific Comics

| | Good | Fine | N-Mint |
|---|---|---|---|
| nn-Byrne-c/a(r) | .50 | 1.50 | 3.00 |

**ROG 2000**
1987 - No. 2, 1987 ($2.00, color, mini-series)
Fantagraphics Books

| | Good | Fine | N-Mint |
|---|---|---|---|
| 1,2-Byrne-r | .35 | 1.00 | 2.00 |

**ROGUE TROOPER**
Oct, 1986 - Present ($1.25-$1.50, color)
Quality Comics/Fleetway Quality #38 on

| | Good | Fine | N-Mint |
|---|---|---|---|
| 1-19: ($1.25) 6-Double size | | .60 | 1.25 |
| 20,21/22,23/24-38 ($1.50): 21/22,25-27-Guice-c | .25 | .75 | 1.50 |
| 39-46 ($1.75) | .30 | .90 | 1.80 |

**ROLY POLY COMIC BOOK**
1944 - No. 15, 1946 (MLJ reprints)
Green Publishing Co.

| | Good | Fine | N-Mint |
|---|---|---|---|
| 1-Red Rube & Steel Sterling begin | 14.00 | 43.00 | 100.00 |
| 6-The Blue Circle & The Steel Fist app. | 7.00 | 21.00 | 50.00 |
| 10-Origin Red Rube retold; Steel Sterling story (Zip #41) | 8.00 | 24.00 | 55.00 |
| 11,12,14: 11,14-The Black Hood app. | 7.00 | 21.00 | 50.00 |
| 15-The Blue Circle & The Steel Fist app.; cover exact swipe from Fox Blue Beetle #1 | 18.00 | 54.00 | 125.00 |

**ROM**
December, 1979 - No. 75, Feb, 1986
Marvel Comics Group

| | Good | Fine | N-Mint |
|---|---|---|---|
| 1-Based on a Parker Bros. toy; origin | .40 | 1.25 | 2.50 |
| 2-5 | | .60 | 1.20 |
| 6-16: 13-Saga of the Space Knights begins | | .50 | 1.00 |
| 17,18-X-Men app. | .40 | 1.25 | 2.50 |
| 19-24,26-30: 19-X-Men cameo. 24-F.F. cameo; Skrulls, Nova & The New Champions app. 26,27-Galactus app. | | .45 | .90 |
| 25-Double size | | .60 | 1.20 |
| 31-49: 31,32-Brother of Evil Mutants app. 32-X-Men cameo. 34,35-Sub-Mariner app. 41,42-Dr. Strange app. | | .40 | .80 |
| 50-Double size | | .50 | 1.00 |
| 51-55,58-75: 58,59-Ant-Man app. 65-West Coast Avengers & Beta Ray Bill app. 65,66-X-Men app. | | .40 | .80 |
| 56,57-Alpha Flight app. | | .60 | 1.20 |
| Annual 1,4: 1(1982, 52 pgs.). 4(1985, 52 pgs.) | | .60 | 1.20 |
| Annual 2,3: 2(1983, 52 pgs.). 3(1984, 52 pgs.) | | .50 | 1.00 |

NOTE: ***Austin*** *c-3i, 18i, 61i.* ***Byrne*** *a-74i; c-56, 57, 74.* ***Ditko*** *a-59-75p.* ***Golden*** *c-7-12, 19.* ***Guice*** *a-61i; c-55, 58, 60p, 70p.* ***Layton*** *a-59i, 72i; c-15, 59i, 69.* ***Miller*** *c-3p, 17p, 18p.* ***Russell*** *a(i)-64, 65, 67, 69, 71, 75; c-64, 65i, 66, 71, 75.* ***Severin*** *c-41p.* ***Sienkiewicz*** *c-46, 47, 52-54, 68, 71p, Annual 2.* ***P. Smith*** *c-59p.* ***Starlin*** *c-67.*

**ROMANCE** (See True Stories of...)

**ROMANCE AND CONFESSION STORIES** (See Giant Comics Ed.)
No date (1949) (100pgs.)
St. John Publishing Co.

| | Good | Fine | N-Mint |
|---|---|---|---|
| 1-Baker-c/a; remaindered St. John love comics | 22.00 | 65.00 | 150.00 |

**ROMANCE DIARY**
December, 1949 - No. 2, March, 1950
Marvel Comics (CDS)(CLDS)

| | Good | Fine | N-Mint |
|---|---|---|---|
| 1,2 | 5.00 | 15.00 | 35.00 |

**ROMANCE OF FLYING, THE** (See Feature Books #33)

**ROMANCES OF MOLLY MANTON** (See Molly Manton)

**ROMANCES OF NURSE HELEN GRANT, THE**
August, 1957
Atlas Comics (VPI)

| | Good | Fine | N-Mint |
|---|---|---|---|
| 1 | 2.00 | 6.00 | 14.00 |

**ROMANCES OF THE WEST**
Nov, 1949 - No. 2, Mar, 1950 (52 pgs.)
Marvel Comics (SPC)

| | Good | Fine | N-Mint |
|---|---|---|---|
| 1-Movie photo of Calamity Jane/Sam Bass | 9.30 | 28.00 | 65.00 |
| 2 | 6.50 | 19.00 | 45.00 |

**ROMANCE STORIES OF TRUE LOVE** (Formerly Love Problems & Advice)
No. 45, 5/57 - No. 50, 3/58; No. 51, 9/58 - No. 52, 11/58
Harvey Publications

| | Good | Fine | N-Mint |
|---|---|---|---|
| 45-51: 45,46,48-50-Powell-a | 1.30 | 4.00 | 9.00 |
| 52-Matt Baker-a | 2.65 | 8.00 | 18.00 |

**ROMANCE TALES**
No. 7, Oct, 1949 - No. 9, March, 1950 (7,8: photo-c)
Marvel Comics (CDS)

| | Good | Fine | N-Mint |
|---|---|---|---|
| 7 | 4.30 | 13.00 | 30.00 |
| 8,9: 8-Everett-a | 3.15 | 9.50 | 22.00 |

**ROMANCE TRAIL**
July-Aug, 1949 - No. 6, May-June, 1950
National Periodical Publications

| | Good | Fine | N-Mint |
|---|---|---|---|
| 1-Kinstler, Toth-a; Jimmy Wakely photo-c | 22.00 | 65.00 | 150.00 |
| 2-Kinstler-a; photo-c | 11.00 | 32.00 | 75.00 |
| 3-Photo-c; Kinstler, Toth-a | 11.00 | 32.00 | 75.00 |
| 4-Photo-c; Toth-a | 8.50 | 25.50 | 60.00 |
| 5,6: 5-Photo-c | 8.00 | 24.00 | 55.00 |

**ROMAN HOLIDAYS, THE** (TV)
Feb, 1973 - No. 4, Nov, 1973 (Hanna-Barbera)
Gold Key

| | Good | Fine | N-Mint |
|---|---|---|---|
| 1 | 1.35 | 4.00 | 8.00 |
| 2-4 | 1.00 | 3.00 | 6.00 |

**ROMANTIC ADVENTURES** (My... #49-67, covers only)
Mar-Apr, 1949 - No. 67, July, 1956 (Becomes My... No. 68 on)
American Comics Group (B&I Publ. Co.)

| | Good | Fine | N-Mint |
|---|---|---|---|
| 1 | 6.50 | 19.00 | 45.00 |
| 2 | 3.50 | 10.50 | 24.00 |
| 3-10 | 2.00 | 6.00 | 14.00 |
| 11-20 (4/52) | 1.50 | 4.50 | 10.00 |
| 21-46,48-52: 52-Last Pre-code (2/55) | 1.00 | 3.00 | 7.00 |
| 47-3-D effect | 3.15 | 9.50 | 22.00 |
| 53-67 | .85 | 2.60 | 6.00 |

NOTE: *#1-23, 52 pgs.* ***Shelly*** *a-40.* ***Whitney*** *c/art in many issues.*

**ROMANTIC AFFAIRS** (Formerly Molly Manton's Romances #2)
No. 3, March, 1950
Marvel Comics (Select Publications)

| | Good | Fine | N-Mint |
|---|---|---|---|
| 3-Photo-c from Molly Manton's Romances #2 | 2.65 | 8.00 | 18.00 |

**ROMANTIC CONFESSIONS**
Oct, 1949 - V3#1, April-May, 1953
Hillman Periodicals

| | Good | Fine | N-Mint |
|---|---|---|---|
| V1#1-McWilliams-a | 5.70 | 17.00 | 40.00 |
| 2-Briefer-a; negligee panels | 3.50 | 10.50 | 24.00 |
| 3-12 | 2.15 | 6.50 | 15.00 |
| V2#1,2,4-8,10-12: 2-McWilliams-a | 1.70 | 5.00 | 12.00 |
| 3-Krigstein-a | 4.00 | 12.00 | 28.00 |
| 9-One pg. Frazetta ad | 1.70 | 5.00 | 12.00 |
| V3#1 | 1.50 | 4.50 | 10.00 |

**ROMANTIC HEARTS**
Mar, 1951 - No. 10, Oct, 1952; July, 1953 - No. 12, July, 1955
Story Comics/Master/Merit Pubs.

| | Good | Fine | N-Mint |
|---|---|---|---|
| 1(3/51) (1st Series) | 5.00 | 15.00 | 35.00 |
| 2 | 2.65 | 8.00 | 18.00 |
| 3-10 | 2.00 | 6.00 | 14.00 |
| 1(7/53) (2nd Series) | 3.00 | 9.00 | 21.00 |
| 2 | 1.70 | 5.00 | 12.00 |
| 3-12 | 1.30 | 4.00 | 9.00 |

**ROMANTIC LOVE**
9-10/49 - #3, 1-2/50; #4, 2-3/51 - #13, 10/52; #20, 3-4/54 - #23, 9-10/54
Avon Periodicals/Realistic (No #14-19)

| | Good | Fine | N-Mint |
|---|---|---|---|
| 1-c-/Avon paperback #252 | 11.50 | 34.00 | 80.00 |
| 2-5: 3-c-/paperback Novel Library #12. 4-c-/paperback Diversey Prize Novel #5. 5-c-/paperback Novel Library #34 | 5.70 | 17.00 | 40.00 |
| 6-"Thrill Crazy"-marijuana story; c-/Avon paperback #207; Kinstler-a | 8.00 | 24.00 | 55.00 |
| 7,8: 8-Astarita-a(2) | 5.00 | 15.00 | 35.00 |
| 9-12: 9-c-/paperback Novel Library #41; Kinstler-a. 10-c-/Avon paperback #212. 11-c-/paperback Novel Library #17; Kinstler-a. 12-c-/paperback Novel Library #13 | 5.70 | 17.00 | 40.00 |
| 13,21,22: 22-Kinstler-c | 5.00 | 15.00 | 35.00 |
| 20-Kinstler-c/a | 5.00 | 15.00 | 35.00 |
| 23-Kinstler-c | 4.00 | 12.00 | 28.00 |
| nn(1-3/53)(Realistic-r) | 3.00 | 9.00 | 21.00 |

NOTE: ***Astarita*** *a-7, 10, 11, 21. Painted c-7, 9, 10, 11.*

**ROMANTIC LOVE**
No. 4, June, 1950
Quality Comics Group

| | Good | Fine | N-Mint |
|---|---|---|---|
| 4 (6/50)(Exist?) | 2.65 | 8.00 | 18.00 |
| I.W. Reprint #2,3,8 | | .60 | 1.20 |

**ROMANTIC MARRIAGE** (Cinderella Love #25 on)
#1-3 (1950, no months); #4, 5-6/51 - #17, 9/52; #18, 9/53 - #24, 9/54
Ziff-Davis/St. John No. 18 on (#1-8: 52 pgs.)

| | Good | Fine | N-Mint |
|---|---|---|---|
| 1-Photo-c | 8.00 | 24.00 | 55.00 |
| 2-Painted-c | 4.30 | 13.00 | 30.00 |
| 3-9: 3,4,8,9-Painted-c; 5-7-Photo-c | 3.15 | 9.50 | 22.00 |
| 10-Unusual format; front-c is a painted-c; back-c is a photo-c complete with logo, price, etc. | 5.70 | 17.00 | 40.00 |
| 11-17 (9/52; last Z-D issue): 13-Photo-c | 2.85 | 8.50 | 20.00 |
| 18-22,24: 20-Photo-c | 2.85 | 8.50 | 20.00 |
| 23-Baker-c | 3.15 | 9.50 | 22.00 |

**ROMANTIC PICTURE NOVELETTES**
1946
Magazine Enterprises

| | Good | Fine | N-Mint |
|---|---|---|---|
| 1-Mary Worth-r | 7.00 | 21.00 | 50.00 |

**ROMANTIC SECRETS** (Becomes Time For Love)
Sept, 1949 - No. 39, 4/53; No. 5, 10/55 - No. 52, 11/64 (#1-5: photo-c)
Fawcett/Charlton Comics No. 5 (10/55) on

| | Good | Fine | N-Mint |
|---|---|---|---|
| 1 | 5.70 | 17.00 | 40.00 |
| 2,3 | 2.85 | 8.50 | 20.00 |
| 4,9-Evans-a | 4.00 | 12.00 | 28.00 |
| 5-8,10 | 2.00 | 6.00 | 14.00 |
| 11-23 | 1.70 | 5.00 | 12.00 |
| 24-Evans-a | 3.00 | 9.00 | 21.00 |
| 25-39 | 1.30 | 4.00 | 9.00 |
| 5 (Charlton, 2nd series)(10/55, formerly Negro Romances #4) | 2.65 | 8.00 | 18.00 |
| 6-10 | 1.30 | 4.00 | 9.00 |
| 11-20 | .70 | 2.00 | 4.00 |
| 21-35: Last 10 cent issue? | .50 | 1.50 | 3.00 |
| 36-52('64) | .25 | .75 | 1.50 |

NOTE: ***Bailey*** *a-20.* ***Powell*** *a(1st series)-5, 7, 10, 12, 16, 17, 20, 26, 29, 33, 34, 36, 37.*

***Sekowsky*** *a-26. Photo c(1st series)-1-5, 16, 25, 27, 33.*

**ROMANTIC STORY** (Cowboy Love #28 on)
11/49 - #22, Sum, 1953; #23, 5/54 - #27, 12/54; #28, 8/55 - #130, 11/73
Fawcett/Charlton Comics No. 23 on

| | Good | Fine | N-Mint |
|---|---|---|---|
| 1-Photo-c begin, end #22,24 | 7.00 | 21.00 | 50.00 |
| 2 | 3.15 | 9.50 | 22.00 |
| 3-5 | 2.65 | 8.00 | 18.00 |
| 6-14 | 2.30 | 7.00 | 16.00 |
| 15-Evans-a | 3.50 | 10.50 | 24.00 |
| 16-22(Sum, '53; last Fawcett issue). 21-Toth-a? | 1.70 | 5.00 | 12.00 |
| 23-39: 26,29-Wood swipes | 1.70 | 5.00 | 12.00 |
| 40-(100 pgs.) | 3.50 | 10.50 | 24.00 |
| 41-50 | 1.15 | 3.50 | 8.00 |
| 51-80: 57-Hypo needle story | .70 | 2.00 | 4.00 |
| 81-100 | .35 | 1.00 | 2.00 |
| 101-130 | | .50 | 1.00 |

NOTE: ***Powell*** *a-7, 8, 16, 20, 30.*

**ROMANTIC THRILLS** (See Fox Giants)

**ROMANTIC WESTERN**
Winter, 1949 - No. 3, June, 1950 (All Photo-c)
Fawcett Publications

| | Good | Fine | N-Mint |
|---|---|---|---|
| 1 | 8.50 | 25.50 | 60.00 |
| 2-Williamson, McWilliams-a | 10.00 | 30.00 | 70.00 |
| 3 | 5.70 | 17.00 | 40.00 |

**ROMEO TUBBS** (Formerly My Secret Life)
No. 26, 5/50 - No. 28, 7/50; No. 1, 1950; No. 27, 12/52
Fox Feature Syndicate/Green Publ. Co. No. 27

| | Good | Fine | N-Mint |
|---|---|---|---|
| 26-Teen-age | 5.70 | 17.00 | 40.00 |
| 27-Contains Pedro on inside; Wood-a | 8.50 | 25.50 | 60.00 |
| 28, 1 | 4.30 | 13.00 | 30.00 |

**RONALD McDONALD** (TV)
Sept, 1970 - No. 4, March, 1971
Charlton Press (King Features Synd.)

| | Good | Fine | N-Mint |
|---|---|---|---|
| 1 | .35 | 1.00 | 2.00 |
| 2-4 | | .50 | 1.00 |

**RONIN**
July, 1983 - No. 6, Apr, 1984 ($2.50, mini-series, 52 pgs.)
DC Comics

| | Good | Fine | N-Mint |
|---|---|---|---|
| 1-Miller script, c/a in all | 1.00 | 3.00 | 6.00 |
| 2 | .85 | 2.50 | 5.00 |
| 3-5 | .70 | 2.00 | 4.00 |
| 6-Scarcer | 1.35 | 4.00 | 8.00 |
| Trade paperback (1987, $12.95)-Reprints 1-6 | 2.50 | 7.50 | 15.00 |

**ROOK** (See Eerie Magazine & Warren Presents: The Rook)
November, 1979 - No. 14, April, 1982
Warren Publications

| | Good | Fine | N-Mint |
|---|---|---|---|
| 1-Nino-a | | .40 | .80 |
| 2-14: 3,4-Toth-a | | .30 | .60 |

**ROOKIE COP** (Formerly Crime and Justice?)
No. 27, Nov, 1955 - No. 33, Aug, 1957
Charlton Comics

| | Good | Fine | N-Mint |
|---|---|---|---|
| 27 | 3.70 | 11.00 | 26.00 |
| 28-33 | 2.00 | 6.00 | 14.00 |

**ROOM 222** (TV)
Jan, 1970; No. 2, May, 1970 - No. 4, Jan, 1971
Dell Publishing Co.

| | Good | Fine | N-Mint |
|---|---|---|---|
| 1-4: 2,4-Photo-c. 3-Marijuana story. 4 r-/#1 | 3.00 | 9.00 | 21.00 |

**ROOTIE KAZOOTIE** (TV)(See 3-D-ell)
No. 415, Aug, 1952 - No. 6, Oct-Dec, 1954
Dell Publishing Co.

| | Good | Fine | N-Mint |
|---|---|---|---|
| 4-Color 415 (#1) | 5.00 | 15.00 | 35.00 |

*Romantic Picture Novelettes #1, © ME*

*Romeo Tubbs #27, © Green Publ.*

*Room 222 #2, © 20th Century Fox*

Roundup #5, © DS

Roy Rogers Comics #37, © Roy Rogers

Rugged Action #4, © MEG

| | Good | Fine | N-Mint |
|---|---|---|---|
| 4-Color 459,502 | 4.00 | 12.00 | 28.00 |
| 4(4-6/54)-6 | 4.00 | 12.00 | 28.00 |

**ROOTS OF THE SWAMPTHING**
July, 1986 - No. 5, Nov, 1986 ($2.00, Baxter paper, 52 pgs.)
DC Comics

| | Good | Fine | N-Mint |
|---|---|---|---|
| 1-5: R/Swamp Thing #1-10 by Wrightson & House of Myst.-r; 1-new Wrightson-c(2-5-r). 4-Batman-c/story-r/S.T. #7 | .40 | 1.25 | 2.50 |

**ROUND THE WORLD GIFT**
No date (mid 1940's) (4 pages)
National War Fund (Giveaway)

| | Good | Fine | N-Mint |
|---|---|---|---|
| nn | 10.00 | 30.00 | 70.00 |

**ROUNDUP** (Western Crime)
July-Aug, 1948 - No. 5, Mar-Apr, 1949 (52 pgs.)
D. S. Publishing Co.

| | Good | Fine | N-Mint |
|---|---|---|---|
| 1-Ingels-a? | 8.50 | 25.50 | 60.00 |
| 2-Marijuana drug mention story | 7.00 | 21.00 | 50.00 |
| 3-5 | 5.00 | 15.00 | 35.00 |

**ROYAL ROY**
May, 1985 - No. 6, Mar, 1986 (Children's book)
Star Comics (Marvel)

| | Good | Fine | N-Mint |
|---|---|---|---|
| 1-6 | | .35 | .70 |

**ROY CAMPANELLA, BASEBALL HERO**
1950
Fawcett Publications

| | Good | Fine | N-Mint |
|---|---|---|---|
| nn-Photo-c | 29.00 | 85.00 | 200.00 |

**ROY ROGERS** (See March of Comics #17, 35, 47, 62, 68, 73, 77, 86, 91, 100, 105, 116, 121, 131, 136, 146, 151, 161, 167, 176, 191, 206, 221, 236, 250)

**ROY ROGERS AND TRIGGER**
April, 1967
Gold Key

| | Good | Fine | N-Mint |
|---|---|---|---|
| 1-Photo-c; reprints | 2.65 | 8.00 | 18.00 |

**ROY ROGERS COMICS** (See Western Roundup under Dell Giants)
No. 38, 4/44 - No. 177, 12/47 (#38-166: 52 pgs.)
Dell Publishing Co.

| | Good | Fine | N-Mint |
|---|---|---|---|
| 4-Color 38 (1944)-49pg. story; photo front/back-c on all 4-Color issues | 55.00 | 165.00 | 385.00 |
| 4-Color 63 (1945)-Color photos inside-c | 37.00 | 110.00 | 250.00 |
| 4-Color 86,95 (1945) | 29.00 | 85.00 | 200.00 |
| 4-Color 109 (1946) | 22.00 | 65.00 | 150.00 |
| 4-Color 117,124,137,144 | 16.00 | 48.00 | 110.00 |
| 4-Color 153,160,166: 166-48pg. story | 12.00 | 36.00 | 85.00 |
| 4-Color 177 (36 pgs.)-32pg. story | 12.00 | 36.00 | 85.00 |

**ROY ROGERS COMICS** (. . . & Trigger #92(8/55)-on)(Roy starred in Republic movies, radio & TV) (Singing cowboy) (Also see Dale Evans, It Really Happened #8, Queen of the West . . ., & Roy Rogers' Trigger)
Jan, 1948 - No. 145, Sept-Oct, 1961 (#1-19: 36 pgs.)
Dell Publishing Co.

| | Good | Fine | N-Mint |
|---|---|---|---|
| 1-Roy, his horse Trigger, & Chuck Wagon Charley's Tales begin; photo-c begin, end #145 | 47.00 | 140.00 | 325.00 |
| 2 | 22.00 | 65.00 | 150.00 |
| 3-5 | 17.00 | 51.00 | 120.00 |
| 6-10 | 12.00 | 36.00 | 85.00 |
| 11-19: 19-. . . Charley's Tales ends | 8.50 | 25.50 | 60.00 |
| 20 (52 pgs.)-Trigger feature begins, ends #46 | 8.50 | 25.50 | 60.00 |
| 21-30 (52 pgs.) | 7.00 | 21.00 | 50.00 |
| 31-46 (52 pgs.): 37-X-mas-c | 5.30 | 16.00 | 38.00 |
| 47-56 (36 pgs.): 47-Chuck Wagon Charley's Tales returns, ends #133 49-X-mas-c. 55-Last photo back-c | 4.30 | 13.00 | 30.00 |
| 57 (52 pgs.)-Heroin drug propaganda story | 5.00 | 15.00 | 35.00 |
| 58-70 (52 pgs.): 61-X-mas-c | 3.70 | 11.00 | 26.00 |
| 71-80 (52 pgs.): 73-X-mas-c | 3.15 | 9.50 | 22.00 |
| 81-91 (36 pgs. #81-on): 85-X-mas-c | 2.65 | 8.00 | 18.00 |
| 92-99,101-110,112-118: 92-Title changed to Roy Rogers and Trigger (8/55) | 2.65 | 8.00 | 18.00 |
| 100-Trigger feature returns, ends #133? | 4.00 | 12.00 | 28.00 |
| 111,119-124-Toth-a | 4.35 | 13.00 | 30.00 |
| 125-131 | 3.00 | 9.00 | 21.00 |
| 132-144-Manning-a. 144-Dale Evans featured | 3.50 | 10.50 | 24.00 |
| 145-Last issue | 4.30 | 13.00 | 30.00 |
| . . . & the Man From Dodge City (Dodge giveaway, 16 pgs., 1954)-Frontier, Inc. (5x7¼") | 10.00 | 30.00 | 70.00 |
| Official Roy Rogers Riders Club Comics (1952; 16 pgs., reg. size, paper-c) | 11.00 | 32.00 | 75.00 |

NOTE: *Buscema a-2 each-74-108. **Manning** a-123, 124, 132-144. **Marsh** a-110. Photo back-c No. 1-9, 11-35, 38-55.*

**ROY ROGERS' TRIGGER** (TV)
No. 329, May, 1951 - No. 17, June-Aug, 1955
Dell Publishing Co.

| | Good | Fine | N-Mint |
|---|---|---|---|
| 4-Color 329 (#1)-Painted-c | 8.00 | 24.00 | 55.00 |
| 2 (9-11/51)-Photo-c | 5.00 | 15.00 | 35.00 |
| 3-5: 3-Painted-c begin, end #17 | 2.00 | 6.00 | 14.00 |
| 6-17 | 1.30 | 4.00 | 9.00 |

**ROY ROGERS WESTERN CLASSICS**
1989 - Present ($2.95-$3.95, 44 pgs.; 24 pgs. in color, 16 pgs. B&W)
AC Comics

| | Good | Fine | N-Mint |
|---|---|---|---|
| 1-Dale Evans-r by Manning, Gabby Hayes-r & Buscema-r; photo covers and interior photos of Roy & Dale | .50 | 1.50 | 3.00 |
| 2-Buscema-r(3); photo-c & B&W photos inside | .50 | 1.50 | 3.00 |
| 3-($3.95)-Dale Evans-r by Manning, Trigger-r by Buscema plus other Buscema-r; photo-c | .70 | 2.00 | 4.00 |

**RUDOLPH, THE RED NOSED REINDEER** (See Limited Collectors' Edition #20, 24, 33, 42, 50)

**RUDOLPH, THE RED NOSED REINDEER**
1939 (2,400,000 copies printed); Dec, 1951
Montgomery Ward (Giveaway)

| | Good | Fine | N-Mint |
|---|---|---|---|
| Paper cover - 1st app. in print; written by Robert May; ill. by Denver Gillen | 8.35 | 25.00 | 50.00 |
| Hardcover version | 11.50 | 34.00 | 80.00 |
| 1951 version (Has 1939 date)-36 pgs., illos in three colors; red-c | 3.00 | 9.00 | 21.00 |

**RUDOLPH, THE RED-NOSED REINDEER**
1950 - No. 13?, Winter, 1962-63 (Issues are not numbered)
National Periodical Publications

| | Good | Fine | N-Mint |
|---|---|---|---|
| 1950 issue; Grossman-c/a begins | 5.70 | 17.00 | 40.00 |
| 1951-54 issues (4 total) | 4.00 | 12.00 | 28.00 |
| 1955-62 issues (8 total) | 2.00 | 6.00 | 14.00 |

NOTE: *The 1962-63 issue is 84 pages. 13 total issues published.*

**RUFF AND REDDY** (TV)
No. 937, 9/58 - No. 12, 1-3/62 (Hanna-Barbera)(#9 on: 15 cents)
Dell Publishing Co.

| | Good | Fine | N-Mint |
|---|---|---|---|
| 4-Color 937(#1)(1st Hanna-Barbera comic book) | 3.50 | 10.50 | 24.00 |
| 4-Color 981,1038 | 2.30 | 7.00 | 16.00 |
| 4(1-3/60)-12: 8-Last 10 cent issue | 1.70 | 5.00 | 12.00 |

**RUGGED ACTION** (Strange Stories of Suspense #5 on)
Dec, 1954 - No. 4, June, 1955
Atlas Comics (CSI)

| | Good | Fine | N-Mint |
|---|---|---|---|
| 1 | 4.30 | 13.00 | 30.00 |
| 2-4: 2-Last precode (2/55) | 2.65 | 8.00 | 18.00 |

NOTE: ***Ayers** a-2, 3. **Maneely** c-2, 3. **Severin** a-2.*

**RULAH JUNGLE GODDESS** (Formerly Zoot; I Loved #28 on) (Also see All Top Comics & Terrors of the Jungle)

No. 17, Aug, 1948 - No. 27, June, 1949
Fox Features Syndicate

| | Good | Fine | N-Mint |
|---|---|---|---|
| 17 | 35.00 | 105.00 | 245.00 |
| 18-Classic girl-fight interior splash | 29.00 | 86.00 | 200.00 |
| 19,20 | 27.00 | 80.00 | 185.00 |
| 21-Used in **SOTI**, pg. 388,389 | 29.00 | 86.00 | 200.00 |
| 22-Used in **SOTI**, pg. 22,23 | 27.00 | 80.00 | 185.00 |
| 23-27 | 19.00 | 57.00 | 130.00 |

NOTE: *Kamen c-17-19, 21, 22.*

**RUMIC WORLD**
1989 - No. 2, 1989 ($3.25, B&W, 60 pgs.)($3.50, 68 pgs. #2 on)
Viz Select Comics

| | Good | Fine | N-Mint |
|---|---|---|---|
| 1,2: Japanese manga | .55 | 1.65 | 3.25 |

**RUNAWAY, THE** (See Movie Classics)

**RUN BABY RUN**
1974 (39 cents)
Logos International

| | Good | Fine | N-Mint |
|---|---|---|---|
| nn-By Tony Tallarico from Nicky Cruz's book | | .30 | .60 |

**RUN, BUDDY, RUN** (TV)
June, 1967 (Photo-c)
Gold Key

| | Good | Fine | N-Mint |
|---|---|---|---|
| 1 (10204-706) | 1.50 | 4.50 | 10.00 |

**RUST**
7/87 - No. 15, 1988; V2#1, 2/89 - No. 7, 1989 ($1.50-$1.75, color)
Now Comics

| | Good | Fine | N-Mint |
|---|---|---|---|
| 1-3 ($1.50) | .25 | .75 | 1.50 |
| 4-15, V2#1-7 ($1.75) | .30 | .90 | 1.80 |

**RUSTY, BOY DETECTIVE**
Mar-April, 1955 - No. 5, Nov, 1955
Good Comics/Lev Gleason

| | Good | Fine | N-Mint |
|---|---|---|---|
| 1-Bob Wood, Carl Hubbell-a begins | 3.50 | 10.50 | 24.00 |
| 2-5 | 2.00 | 6.00 | 14.00 |

**RUSTY COMICS** (Formerly Kid Movie Comics; Rusty and Her Family #21, 22; The Kelleys #23 on; see Millie The Model)
No. 12, Apr, 1947 - No. 22, Sept, 1949
Marvel Comics (HPC)

| | Good | Fine | N-Mint |
|---|---|---|---|
| 12-Mitzi app. | 7.00 | 21.00 | 50.00 |
| 13 | 4.00 | 12.00 | 28.00 |
| 14-Wolverton's Powerhouse Pepper (4 pgs.) plus Kurtzman's "Hey Look" | 7.00 | 21.00 | 50.00 |
| 15-17-Kurtzman's "Hey Look" | 6.00 | 18.00 | 42.00 |
| 18,19 | 2.85 | 8.50 | 20.00 |
| 20-Kurtzman, 5 pgs. | 6.00 | 18.00 | 42.00 |
| 21,22-Kurtzman, 17 & 22 pgs. | 10.00 | 30.00 | 70.00 |

**RUSTY DUGAN** (See Holyoke One-Shot #2)

**RUSTY RILEY** (See 4-Color #418, 451, 486, 554)

**SAARI** (The Jungle Goddess)
November, 1951
P. L. Publishing Co.

| | Good | Fine | N-Mint |
|---|---|---|---|
| 1 | 19.00 | 57.00 | 130.00 |

**SABLE** (Formerly Jon Sable, Freelance; also see Mike Grell's Sable)
Mar, 1988 - No. 27, May, 1990 ($1.75-$1.95, color)
First Comics

| | Good | Fine | N-Mint |
|---|---|---|---|
| 1-27: 10-Begin $1.95-c. 23-25-Tim Vigil-c | .30 | .90 | 1.80 |

**SABOTAGE** (See The Crusaders)

**SABRE** (See Eclipse Graphic Album Series)
Aug, 1982 - No. 14, Aug, 1985; (Color, Baxter paper #4 on)
Eclipse Comics

| | Good | Fine | N-Mint |
|---|---|---|---|
| 1-($1.00)-Sabre & Morrigan Tales begin | | .50 | 1.00 |
| 2-14: 4-6-Origin Incredible Seven | | .50 | 1.00 |

NOTE: *Colan c-11p.* ***Gulacy*** *c/a-1, 2. Later issues are $1.75 & $2.00 cover price.*

**SABRINA'S CHRISTMAS MAGIC** (See Archie Giant Series Magazine #196, 207, 220, 231, 243, 455, 467, 479, 491, 503, 515)

**SABRINA, THE TEEN-AGE WITCH** (TV)(See Archie Giant Series #544, Archie's Madhouse, Archie's TV. . ., Chilling Advs. In Sorcery)
April, 1971 - No. 77, Jan, 1983 (Giants No. 1-17)
Archie Publications

| | Good | Fine | N-Mint |
|---|---|---|---|
| 1 | 2.65 | 8.00 | 18.00 |
| 2 | 1.30 | 4.00 | 9.00 |
| 3-5: 3,4-Archie's Group x-over | .70 | 2.00 | 4.00 |
| 6-10 | .50 | 1.50 | 3.00 |
| 11-20 | | .75 | 1.50 |
| 21-77 | | .35 | .70 |

**SABU, "ELEPHANT BOY"** (Movie; formerly My Secret Story)
No. 30, June, 1950 - No. 2, Aug, 1950
Fox Features Syndicate

| | Good | Fine | N-Mint |
|---|---|---|---|
| 30(#1)-Wood-a; photo-c | 11.00 | 32.00 | 75.00 |
| 2-Photo-c; Kamen-a | 7.00 | 21.00 | 50.00 |

**SACRAMENTS, THE**
October, 1955 (25 cents)
Catechetical Guild Educational Society

| | Good | Fine | N-Mint |
|---|---|---|---|
| 304 | 2.00 | 6.00 | 12.00 |

**SACRED AND THE PROFANE, THE** (See Eclipse Graphic Album Series #9 & Epic Illustrated #20)

**SAD CASE OF WAITING ROOM WILLIE, THE**
1950? (nd) (14 pgs. in color; paper covers; regular size)
American Visuals Corp. (For Baltimore Medical Society)

| | Good | Fine | N-Mint |
|---|---|---|---|
| nn-By Will Eisner (Rare) | 30.00 | 90.00 | 210.00 |

**SADDLE JUSTICE** (Happy Houlihans #1,2; Saddle Romances #9 on)
No. 3, Spring, 1948 - No. 8, Sept-Oct, 1949
E. C. Comics

| | Good | Fine | N-Mint |
|---|---|---|---|
| 3-The 1st E.C. by Bill Gaines to break away from M. C. Gaines' old Educational Comics format. Craig, Feldstein, H. C. Kiefer, & Stan Asch-a. Mentioned in **Love and Death** | 30.00 | 90.00 | 210.00 |
| 4-1st Graham Ingels-a for E.C. | 30.00 | 90.00 | 210.00 |
| 5-8-Ingels-a in all | 27.00 | 81.00 | 190.00 |

NOTE: ***Craig*** *and* ***Feldstein*** *art in most issues. Canadian reprints known; see Table of Contents.* ***Craig*** *c-3, 4.* ***Ingels*** *c-5-8.*

**SADDLE ROMANCES** (Saddle Justice #3-8; Weird Science #12 on)
No. 9, Nov-Dec, 1949 - No. 11, Mar-Apr, 1950
E. C. Comics

| | Good | Fine | N-Mint |
|---|---|---|---|
| 9-Ingels-c/a | 34.00 | 100.00 | 235.00 |
| 10-Wood's 1st work at E. C.; Ingels-a | 36.00 | 107.00 | 250.00 |
| 11-Ingels-a | 34.00 | 100.00 | 235.00 |

NOTE: *Canadian reprints known; see Table of Contents.* ***Feldstein*** *c-10.*

**SADIE SACK** (See Harvey Hits #93)

**SAD SACK AND THE SARGE**
Sept, 1957 - No. 155, June, 1982
Harvey Publications

| | Good | Fine | N-Mint |
|---|---|---|---|
| 1 | 5.00 | 15.00 | 35.00 |
| 2 | 2.00 | 6.00 | 14.00 |
| 3-10 | 1.70 | 5.00 | 12.00 |
| 11-20 | 1.00 | 3.00 | 6.00 |
| 21-50 | .40 | 1.20 | 2.40 |
| 51-90,97-100 | | .50 | 1.00 |
| 91-96: All 52 pg. Giants | | .60 | 1.20 |
| 101-155 | | .25 | .50 |

**SAD SACK COMICS** (See Harvey Collector's Comics #16, Little Sad Sack, Tastee Freez Comics #4 & True Comics #55)

*Rulah Jungle Goddess #21, © FOX*

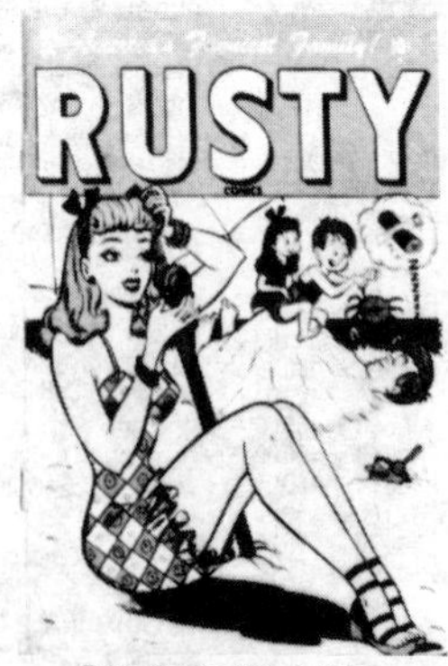

*Rusty Comics #14, © MEG*

*Saddle Romances #10, © WMG*

Sad Sack Comics #1, © HARV

The Saga of Ra's Al Ghul #3, © DC

The Saga of Swamp Thing #37, © DC

Sept, 1949 - No. 287, Oct, 1982
Harvey Publications

| | Good | Fine | N-Mint |
|---|---|---|---|
| 1-Infinity-c; Little Dot begins (1st app.); civilian issues begin, end #21 | 22.00 | 65.00 | 150.00 |
| 2-Flying Fool by Powell | 10.00 | 30.00 | 70.00 |
| 3 | 5.70 | 17.00 | 40.00 |
| 4-10 | 3.50 | 10.50 | 24.00 |
| 11-21 | 2.35 | 7.00 | 16.00 |
| 22-("Back In The Army Again" on covers #22-36). "The Specialist" story about Sad Sack's return to Army | 1.35 | 4.00 | 8.00 |
| 23-50 | .85 | 2.50 | 5.00 |
| 51-100 | .50 | 1.50 | 3.00 |
| 101-150 | .25 | .75 | 1.50 |
| 151-222 | | .40 | .80 |
| 223-228 (25 cent Giants, 52 pgs.) | .25 | .75 | 1.50 |
| 229-287: 286,287 had limited distribution | | .40 | .80 |
| 3-D 1 (1/54-titled "Harvey 3-D Hits") | 11.50 | 34.00 | 80.00 |
| Armed Forces Complimentary copies, HD #1-40 ('57-'62) | .70 | 2.00 | 4.00 |

NOTE: *The **Sad Sack Comics** comic book was a spin-off from a Sunday Newspaper strip launched through John Wheeler's Bell Syndicate. The previous Sunday page and the first 21 comics depicted the Sad Sack in civvies. Unpopularity caused the Sunday page to be discontinued in the early '50s. Meanwhile Sad Sack returned to the Army, by popular demand, in issue No. 22, remaining there ever since. Incidentally, relatively few of the first 21 issues were ever collected and remain scarce due to this.*

**SAD SACK FUN AROUND THE WORLD**
1974 (no month)
Harvey Publications

| | Good | Fine | N-Mint |
|---|---|---|---|
| 1-About Great Britain | | .40 | .80 |

**SAD SACK GOES HOME**
1951 (16 pgs. in color)
Harvey Publications

| | Good | Fine | N-Mint |
|---|---|---|---|
| nn-by George Baker | 3.50 | 10.50 | 24.00 |

**SAD SACK IN 3-D** (See Blackthorne 3-D Series #49)

**SAD SACK LAUGH SPECIAL**
Winter, 1958-59 - No. 93, Feb, 1977 (#1-60: 68 pgs.; #61-76: 52 pgs.)
Harvey Publications

| | Good | Fine | N-Mint |
|---|---|---|---|
| 1 | 3.50 | 10.50 | 24.00 |
| 2 | 1.70 | 5.00 | 12.00 |
| 3-10 | 1.35 | 4.00 | 8.00 |
| 11-30 | .70 | 2.00 | 4.00 |
| 31-60: Last 68 pg. Giant | .40 | 1.20 | 2.40 |
| 61-76: 52 pg. issues | .35 | 1.00 | 2.00 |
| 77-93 | | .50 | 1.00 |

**SAD SACK NAVY, GOBS 'N' GALS**
Aug, 1972 - No. 8, Oct, 1973
Harvey Publications

| | Good | Fine | N-Mint |
|---|---|---|---|
| 1: 52 pg. Giant | | .50 | 1.00 |
| 2-8 | | .30 | .60 |

**SAD SACK'S ARMY LIFE** (See Harvey Hits #8, 17, 22, 28, 32, 39, 43, 47, 51, 55, 58, 61, 64, 67, 70)

**SAD SACK'S ARMY LIFE** (. . . Parade #1-57, . . . Today #58 on)
Oct, 1963 - No. 60, Nov, 1975; No. 61, May, 1976
Harvey Publications

| | Good | Fine | N-Mint |
|---|---|---|---|
| 1: 68 pg. issues begin | 2.00 | 6.00 | 14.00 |
| 2-10 | 1.00 | 3.00 | 6.00 |
| 11-20 | .40 | 1.20 | 2.40 |
| 21-34: Last 68 pg. issue | .35 | 1.00 | 2.00 |
| 35-51: All 52 pgs. | | .50 | 1.00 |
| 52-61 | | .30 | .60 |

**SAD SACK'S FUNNY FRIENDS** (See Harvey Hits #75)
Dec, 1955 - No. 75, Oct, 1969
Harvey Publications

| | Good | Fine | N-Mint |
|---|---|---|---|
| 1 | 3.50 | 10.50 | 24.00 |
| 2-10 | 1.70 | 5.00 | 10.00 |
| 11-20 | .85 | 2.50 | 5.00 |
| 21-30 | .40 | 1.20 | 2.40 |
| 31-75 | | .50 | 1.00 |

**SAD SACK'S MUTTSY** (See Harvey Hits #74, 77, 80, 82, 84, 87, 89, 92, 96, 99, 102, 105, 108, 111, 113, 115, 117, 119, 121)

**SAD SACK USA** (. . .Vacation #8)
Nov, 1972 - No. 7, Nov, 1973; No. 8, Oct, 1974
Harvey Publications

| | Good | Fine | N-Mint |
|---|---|---|---|
| 1 | | .50 | 1.00 |
| 2-8 | | .25 | .50 |

**SAD SACK WITH SARGE & SADIE**
Sept, 1972 - No. 8, Nov, 1973
Harvey Publications

| | Good | Fine | N-Mint |
|---|---|---|---|
| 1: 52 pg. Giant | | .50 | 1.00 |
| 2-8 | | .25 | .50 |

**SAD SAD SACK WORLD**
Oct, 1964 - No. 46, Dec, 1973 (#1-31: 68 pgs.; #32-38: 52 pgs.)
Harvey Publications

| | Good | Fine | N-Mint |
|---|---|---|---|
| 1 | .85 | 2.50 | 6.00 |
| 2-10 | .40 | 1.20 | 2.40 |
| 11-31: Last 68 pg. issue | .35 | 1.00 | 2.00 |
| 32-38: All 52 pgs. | .25 | .75 | 1.50 |
| 39-46 | | .50 | 1.00 |

**SAGA OF BIG RED, THE**
Sept, 1976 ($1.25) (In color)
Omaha World-Herald

| | Good | Fine | N-Mint |
|---|---|---|---|
| nn-by Win Mumma; story of the Nebraska Cornhuskers (sports) | .25 | .80 | 1.60 |

**SAGA OF CRYSTAR, CRYSTAL WARRIOR, THE**
May, 1983 - No. 11, Feb, 1985
Marvel Comics Group

| | Good | Fine | N-Mint |
|---|---|---|---|
| 1-($2.00; Baxter paper)-Remco toy tie-in | .35 | 1.00 | 2.00 |
| 2-5,7-11: 3-Dr. Strange app. 7-9,11-Golden-c. 10,11($1.00). 11-Alpha Flight app. | | .50 | 1.00 |
| 6-Nightcrawler app.; Golden-c | .25 | .75 | 1.50 |

**SAGA OF RA'S AL GHUL, THE** (See Batman #232)
Jan, 1988 - No. 4, Apr, 1988 ($2.50, color, mini-series)
DC Comics

| | Good | Fine | N-Mint |
|---|---|---|---|
| 1-Batman reprints; Neal Adams-a(r) in all | .75 | 2.25 | 4.50 |
| 2-4: 4-New N. Adams/Nebres-c | .65 | 1.90 | 3.75 |

**SAGA OF SWAMP THING, THE** (Swamp Thing #39-41,46 on)
May, 1982 - Present (Later issues for mature readers; #86 on: $1.50)
DC Comics

| | Good | Fine | N-Mint |
|---|---|---|---|
| 1-Origin retold; Phantom Stranger series begins; ends #13; movie adaptation; Yeates-c/a begins | .25 | .75 | 1.50 |
| 2-15: 2-Photo-c from movie | | .50 | 1.00 |
| 16-19: Bissette-a. 13-Last Yeates-a | .35 | 1.00 | 2.00 |
| 20-1st Alan Moore issue | 3.15 | 9.50 | 22.00 |
| 21-New origin | 2.85 | 8.50 | 20.00 |
| 22-25: 24-JLA x-over; Last Yeates-c | 1.30 | 4.00 | 8.00 |
| 26-30 | .90 | 2.75 | 5.50 |
| 31-33: 33-Reprints 1st app./H.O.M. #92 | .50 | 1.50 | 3.00 |
| 34 | 1.50 | 4.50 | 9.00 |
| 35,36 | .35 | 1.10 | 2.25 |
| 37-1st app. John Constantine, apps. thru #40 | 1.25 | 3.75 | 7.50 |
| 38-40: John Constantine app. | .70 | 2.00 | 4.00 |
| 41-45: 44-Batman cameo | .30 | .90 | 1.75 |
| 46-51: 46-Crisis x-over; Batman cameo & John Constantine app. 50-($1.25, 52 pgs.)-Deadman, Dr. Fate, Demon | .25 | .75 | 1.50 |

| | Good | Fine | N-Mint |
|---|---|---|---|
| 52-Arkham Asylum-c/story; Joker-c/cameo | .50 | 1.50 | 3.00 |
| 53-($1.25, 52 pgs.)-Arkham Asylum; Batman-c/story | .70 | 2.00 | 4.00 |
| 54-64: 58-Spectre preview. 64-Last Moore issue | | .60 | 1.25 |
| 65-99,101-106: 65-Direct only begins. 79-Superman-c/story. 85-Jonah Hex app. | .25 | .75 | 1.50 |
| 100 ($2.50, 52 pgs.) | .40 | 1.25 | 2.50 |
| Annual 1(11/82)-Movie Adaptation | | .50 | 1.00 |
| Annual 2(1/85)-Alan Moore scripts, Bissette-a(p) | .50 | 1.50 | 3.00 |
| Annual 3(10/87, $2.00) | .35 | 1.00 | 2.00 |
| Annual 4(10/88)-Batman-c/story | .50 | 1.50 | 3.00 |
| Annual 5('89, $2.95, 68 pgs.)-Batman cameo; re-intro Brother Power, 1st app. since 1968 | .50 | 1.50 | 3.00 |
| Saga of the Swamp Thing (1987, $10.95)-reprints #21-27 | 1.85 | 5.50 | 11.00 |
| 2nd printing (1989, $12.95) | 2.15 | 6.50 | 13.00 |
| ...Love and Death (1990, $17.95)-r/#28-34 & Annual #2; Totleben painted-c | 3.00 | 9.00 | 18.00 |

NOTE: ***Bissette** a(p)-16-19, 21-27, 29, 30, 34-36, 39-42, 44, 46, 50, 64; c-17i, 24-32p, 35-37p, 40p, 44p, 46-50p, 51-56, 57i, 58, 61, 62, 63p. **Kaluta** c/a-74. **Spiegle** a-1-3, 6. **Sutton** a-98p. **Totleben** a(i)-10, 16-27, 29, 31, 34-40, 42, 44, 46, 48, 50, 53, 55i; c-25-32i, 33, 35-40i, 42i, 44i, 46-50i, 53, 55i, 59p, 64, 65, 68, 73, 76, 80, 82, 84, 89, 91-100, Annual 4, 5. **Williamson** 86i. **Wrightson** a-18i(r), 33r; c-57p.*

**SAGA OF THE ORIGINAL HUMAN TORCH** (See Avengers W.C.)
Apr, 1990 - No. 4, July, 1990 ($1.50, color, limited series)
Marvel Comics

| | | | |
|---|---|---|---|
| 1-4: Buckler-c/a(p); 1-Origin. 3-Hitler-c | .25 | .75 | 1.50 |

**SAGA OF THE SUB-MARINER, THE**
Nov, 1988 - No. 12, Oct, 1989 ($1.25-$1.50 #9 on, limited series)
Marvel Comics

| | | | |
|---|---|---|---|
| 1-12: Buckler-c/a. 9-Original X-Men app. | .25 | .75 | 1.50 |

**SAILOR ON THE SEA OF FATE** (See First Comics Graphic Novel #11)

**SAILOR SWEENEY** (Navy Action #1-11, 15 on)
No. 12, July, 1956 - No. 14, Nov, 1956
Atlas Comics (CDS)

| | | | |
|---|---|---|---|
| 12-14: 12-Shores-a. 13-Severin-c | 3.00 | 9.00 | 21.00 |

**SAINT, THE**( Also see Movie Comics(DC) #2 & Silver Streak #18)
Aug, 1947 - No. 12, Mar, 1952
Avon Periodicals

| | | | |
|---|---|---|---|
| 1-Kamen bondage-c/a | 31.00 | 92.00 | 215.00 |
| 2 | 17.00 | 51.00 | 115.00 |
| 3,4: 4-Lingerie panels | 13.00 | 40.00 | 90.00 |
| 5-Spanking panel | 20.00 | 60.00 | 140.00 |
| 6-Miss Fury app., 14 pgs. | 22.00 | 65.00 | 155.00 |
| 7-c-/Avon paperback #118 | 12.00 | 36.00 | 85.00 |
| 8,9(12/50): Saint strip-r in #8-12; 9-Kinstler-c | 10.00 | 30.00 | 70.00 |
| 10-Wood-a, 1 pg; c-/Avon paperback #289 | 10.00 | 30.00 | 70.00 |
| 11 | 7.00 | 21.00 | 50.00 |
| 12-c-/Avon paperback #123 | 9.30 | 28.00 | 65.00 |

NOTE: *Lucky Dale, Girl Detective in #1,2,4,6. **Hollingsworth** a-4, 6. Painted-c 8,10,11.*

**ST. GEORGE**
June, 1988 - No. 8, Oct, 1989 ($1.25-$1.50, color)
Epic Comics (Marvel)

| | | | |
|---|---|---|---|
| 1-8: 1-Sienkiewicz-c. 3-Begin $1.50-c | .25 | .75 | 1.50 |

**ST. SWITHIN'S DAY**
Apr, 1990 ($2.50, color, one-shot)
Trident Comics

| | | | |
|---|---|---|---|
| 1 | .40 | 1.25 | 2.50 |

**SALERNO CARNIVAL OF COMICS** (Also see Pure Oil Comics, 24 Pages of Comics, & Vicks Comics)
Late 1930s (16 pgs.) (paper cover) (Giveaway)
Salerno Cookie Co.

| | Good | Fine | N-Mint |
|---|---|---|---|
| nn-Color reprints of Calkins' Buck Rogers & Skyroads, plus other strips from Famous Funnies | 25.00 | 75.00 | 175.00 |

**SALIMBA IN 3-D** (See Blackthorne 3-D Series #6 & 9)

**SALOME'** (See Night Music #6)

**SAM AND MAX, FREELANCE POLICE SPECIAL**
1987 ($1.75, B&W); Jan, 1989 ($2.75, color, 44 pgs.)
Fishwrap Productions/Comico

| | | | |
|---|---|---|---|
| 1 ($1.75, B&W)-Fishwrap | .30 | .90 | 1.80 |
| 1 ($2.75, color)-Comico | .45 | 1.40 | 2.80 |

**SAM HILL PRIVATE EYE**
1950 - No. 7, 1951
Close-Up (Archie)

| | | | |
|---|---|---|---|
| 1 | 6.50 | 19.00 | 45.00 |
| 2 | 3.70 | 11.00 | 26.00 |
| 3-7 | 3.00 | 9.00 | 21.00 |

**SAM SLADE ROBOHUNTER** (Also see Robo-Hunter)
Oct, 1986 - No. 31, 1989 ($1.25-$1.50, color)
Quality Comics

| | | | |
|---|---|---|---|
| 1-19 ($1.25) | | .65 | 1.30 |
| 20,21/22,23/24,25-31 ($1.50): 26,27-Guice-c | .25 | .75 | 1.50 |

**SAMSON** (1st Series) (Capt. Aero #7 on; see Big 3 Comics)
Fall, 1940 - No. 6, Sept, 1941 (See Fantastic Comics)
Fox Features Syndicate

| | | | |
|---|---|---|---|
| 1-Powell-a, signed 'Rensie;' Wing Turner by Tuska app; Fine-c? | 65.00 | 195.00 | 455.00 |
| 2-Dr. Fung by Powell; Fine-c? | 32.00 | 95.00 | 220.00 |
| 3-Navy Jones app.; Simon-c | 25.00 | 75.00 | 175.00 |
| 4-Yarko the Great, Master Magician by Eisner begins; Fine-c? | 22.00 | 65.00 | 150.00 |
| 5,6: 6-Origin The Topper | 20.00 | 60.00 | 140.00 |

**SAMSON** (2nd Series) (Formerly Fantastic Comics #10, 11)
No. 12, April, 1955 - No. 14, Aug, 1955
Ajax/Farrell Publications (Four Star)

| | | | |
|---|---|---|---|
| 12-Wonder Boy | 11.00 | 32.00 | 75.00 |
| 13,14: 13-Wonder Boy, Rocket Man | 7.00 | 21.00 | 50.00 |

**SAMSON** (See Mighty Samson)

**SAMSON & DELILAH** (See A Spectacular Feature Magazine)

**SAMUEL BRONSTON'S CIRCUS WORLD** (See Circus World under Movie Comics)

**SAMURAI** (Also see Eclipse Graphic Album Series #14)

**SAMUREE**
May, 1987 - Present ($2.00, color, Baxter)
Continuity Comics

| | | | |
|---|---|---|---|
| 1-8 | .35 | 1.00 | 2.00 |

**SANDMAN, THE** (See Adventure Comics #40 & World's Finest #3)
Winter, 1974; No. 2, Apr-May, 1975 - No. 6, Dec-Jan, 1975-76
National Periodical Publications

| | | | |
|---|---|---|---|
| 1-Kirby-a; Joe Simon scripts | .85 | 2.50 | 5.00 |
| 2-6: 6-Kirby/Wood-c/a | .50 | 1.50 | 3.00 |

NOTE: ***Kirby** a-1p, 4-6p; c-1-5, 6p.*

**SANDMAN**
Jan, 1989 - Present ($1.50, color, mature readers)
DC Comics

| | | | |
|---|---|---|---|
| 1 ($2.00, 52 pgs.) | 2.50 | 7.50 | 15.00 |
| 2 | 1.70 | 5.00 | 10.00 |
| 3-5: 3-John Constantine app. | 1.30 | 4.00 | 8.00 |
| 6-8: 8-Regular ed. has Jeanette Kahn publishorial & American Cancer Society ad w/no indicia on inside front-c | 1.00 | 3.00 | 6.00 |

*The Saint #11, © AVON*

*Samson #2, © FOX*

*The Sandman #1 (1974), © DC*

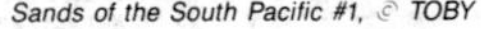
Sands of the South Pacific #1, © TOBY

Santa Claus Funnies #61, © DELL

Santa's Christ. Time Stories, © Prem. Sales

| | Good | Fine | N-Mint |
|---|---|---|---|
| 8-Limited ed. (600+ copies?); has Karen Berger editorial and next issue teaser (has indicia) | 10.00 | 30.00 | 60.00 |
| 9-14: 14-($2.50, 52 pgs.) | .70 | 2.00 | 4.00 |
| 15-20: 16-Photo-c | .35 | 1.00 | 2.00 |
| 21-26 | .25 | .75 | 1.50 |
| Trade paperback (1990, $12.95, 296 pgs.)-r/8-16 | 2.15 | 6.50 | 13.00 |

**SANDS OF THE SOUTH PACIFIC**
January, 1953
Toby Press

| | | | |
|---|---|---|---|
| 1 | 10.00 | 30.00 | 70.00 |

**SANTA AND HIS REINDEER** (See March of Comics #166)

**SANTA AND POLLYANNA PLAY THE GLAD GAME**
Aug, 1960 (16 pages) (Disney giveaway)
Sales Promotion

| | | | |
|---|---|---|---|
| nn | 1.15 | 3.50 | 8.00 |

**SANTA AND THE ANGEL** (See Dell Junior Treasury #7 & 4-Color #259)

**SANTA & THE BUCCANEERS**
1959
Promotional Publ. Co. (Giveaway)

| | | | |
|---|---|---|---|
| nn-Reprints 1952 Santa & the Pirates | .70 | 2.00 | 4.00 |

**SANTA & THE CHRISTMAS CHICKADEE**
1974 (20 pgs.)
Murphy's (Giveaway)

| | | | |
|---|---|---|---|
| nn | .35 | 1.00 | 2.00 |

**SANTA & THE PIRATES**
1952
Promotional Publ. Co. (Giveaway)

| | | | |
|---|---|---|---|
| nn-Marv Levy-c/a | .85 | 2.60 | 6.00 |

**SANTA AT THE ZOO** (See 4-Color #259)

**SANTA CLAUS AROUND THE WORLD** (See March of Comics #241)

**SANTA CLAUS CONQUERS THE MARTIANS** (See Movie Classics)

**SANTA CLAUS FUNNIES**
nd; 1940 (Color & B&W; 8x10''; 12pgs., heavy paper)
W. T. Grant Co./Whitman Publishing (Giveaway)

| | | | |
|---|---|---|---|
| nn-(2 versions) | 6.75 | 20.00 | 40.00 |

**SANTA CLAUS FUNNIES** (Also see Dell Giants)
Dec?, 1942 - No. 1274, Dec, 1961
Dell Publishing Co.

| | | | |
|---|---|---|---|
| nn(#1)(1942)-Kelly-a | 30.00 | 90.00 | 210.00 |
| 2(12/43)-Kelly-a | 20.00 | 60.00 | 140.00 |
| 4-Color 61(1944)-Kelly-a | 22.00 | 65.00 | 150.00 |
| 4-Color 91(1945)-Kelly-a | 16.00 | 48.00 | 110.00 |
| 4-Color 128('46),175('47)-Kelly-a | 12.00 | 36.00 | 84.00 |
| 4-Color 205,254-Kelly-a | 11.00 | 32.00 | 76.00 |
| 4-Color 302,361 | 2.30 | 7.00 | 16.00 |
| 4-Color 525,607,666,756,867 | 1.70 | 5.00 | 12.00 |
| 4-Color 958,1063,1154,1274 | 1.50 | 4.50 | 10.00 |

NOTE: *Most issues contain only one **Kelly** story.*

**SANTA CLAUS PARADE**
1951; No. 2, Dec, 1952; No. 3, Jan, 1955 (25 cents)
Ziff-Davis (Approved Comics)/St. John Publishing Co.

| | | | |
|---|---|---|---|
| nn(1951-Ziff-Davis)-116 pgs. (Xmas Special 1,2) | 10.00 | 30.00 | 70.00 |
| 2(12/52-Ziff-Davis)-100 pgs.; Dave Berg-a | 8.00 | 24.00 | 55.00 |
| V1#3(1/55-St. John)-100 pgs. | 7.00 | 21.00 | 50.00 |

**SANTA CLAUS' WORKSHOP** (See March of Comics #50, 168)

**SANTA IS COMING** (See March of Comics #197)

**SANTA IS HERE** (See March of Comics #49)

**SANTA ON THE JOLLY ROGER**
1965
Promotional Publ. Co. (Giveaway)

| | Good | Fine | N-Mint |
|---|---|---|---|
| nn-Marv Levy-c/a | .70 | 2.00 | 4.00 |

**SANTA! SANTA!**
1974 (20 pgs.)
R. Jackson (Montgomery Ward giveaway)

| | | | |
|---|---|---|---|
| nn | | .50 | 1.00 |

**SANTA'S BUSY CORNER** (See March of Comics #31)

**SANTA'S CANDY KITCHEN** (See March of Comics #14)

**SANTA'S CHRISTMAS BOOK** (See March of Comics #123)

**SANTA'S CHRISTMAS COMICS**
December, 1952 (100 pages)
Standard Comics (Best Books)

| | | | |
|---|---|---|---|
| nn-Supermouse, Dizzy Duck, Happy Rabbit, etc. | 7.00 | 21.00 | 50.00 |

**SANTA'S CHRISTMAS COMIC VARIETY SHOW**
1943 (24 pages)
Sears Roebuck & Co.

| | | | |
|---|---|---|---|
| Contains puzzles & new comics of Dick Tracy, Little Orphan Annie, Moon Mullins, Terry & the Pirates, etc. | 10.00 | 30.00 | 70.00 |

**SANTA'S CHRISTMAS LIST** (See March of Comics #255)

**SANTA'S CHRISTMAS TIME STORIES**
nd (late 1940s) (16 pgs.; paper cover)
Premium Sales, Inc. (Giveaway)

| | | | |
|---|---|---|---|
| nn | 2.00 | 6.00 | 12.00 |

**SANTA'S CIRCUS**
1964 (half-size)
Promotional Publ. Co. (Giveaway)

| | | | |
|---|---|---|---|
| nn-Marv Levy-c/a | .70 | 2.00 | 4.00 |

**SANTA'S FUN BOOK**
1951, 1952 (regular size, 16 pages, paper-c)
Promotional Publ. Co. (Murphy's giveaway)

| | | | |
|---|---|---|---|
| nn | 1.70 | 5.00 | 10.00 |

**SANTA'S GIFT BOOK**
No date (16 pgs.)
No Publisher

| | | | |
|---|---|---|---|
| nn-Puzzles, games only | 1.00 | 3.00 | 6.00 |

**SANTA'S HELPERS** (See March of Comics #64, 106, 198)

**SANTA'S LITTLE HELPERS** (See March of Comics #270)

**SANTA'S NEW STORY BOOK**
1949 (16 pgs.; paper cover)
Wallace Hamilton Campbell (Giveaway)

| | | | |
|---|---|---|---|
| nn | 3.00 | 9.00 | 18.00 |

**SANTA'S REAL STORY BOOK**
1948, 1952 (16 pgs.)
Wallace Hamilton Campbell/W. W. Orris (Giveaway)

| | | | |
|---|---|---|---|
| nn | 2.35 | 7.00 | 14.00 |

**SANTA'S RIDE**
1959
W. T. Grant Co. (Giveaway)

| | | | |
|---|---|---|---|
| nn | 1.35 | 4.00 | 8.00 |

**SANTA'S RODEO**
1964 (half-size)
Promotional Publ. Co. (Giveaway)

| | | | |
|---|---|---|---|
| nn-Marv Levy-a | .70 | 2.00 | 4.00 |

**SANTA'S SECRETS**
1951, 1952? (16 pgs.; paper cover)
Sam B. Anson Christmas giveaway

| | Good | Fine | N-Mint |
|---|---|---|---|
| nn | 2.00 | 6.00 | 12.00 |

**SANTA'S SHOW** (See March of Comics #311)

**SANTA'S SLEIGH** (See March of Comics #298)

**SANTA'S STORIES**
1953 (regular size; paper cover)
K. K. Publications (Klines Dept. Store)

| | Good | Fine | N-Mint |
|---|---|---|---|
| nn-Kelly-a | 12.00 | 36.00 | 84.00 |
| nn-Another version (1953, glossy-c, half-size, 7¼X5¼")-Kelly-a | 8.50 | 25.50 | 60.00 |

**SANTA'S SURPRISE** (See March of Comics #13)

**SANTA'S SURPRISE**
1947 (36 pgs.; slick cover)
K. K. Publications (Giveaway)

| | Good | Fine | N-Mint |
|---|---|---|---|
| nn | 2.75 | 8.00 | 16.00 |

**SANTA'S TINKER TOTS**
1958
Charlton Comics

| | Good | Fine | N-Mint |
|---|---|---|---|
| 1-Based on "The Tinker Tots Keep Christmas" | 1.30 | 4.00 | 9.00 |

**SANTA'S TOYLAND** (See March of Comics #242)

**SANTA'S TOYS** (See March of Comics #12)

**SANTA'S TOYTOWN FUN BOOK**
1952, 1953?
Promotional Publ. Co. (Giveaway)

| | Good | Fine | N-Mint |
|---|---|---|---|
| nn-Marv Levy-c | 1.00 | 3.00 | 6.00 |

**SANTA'S VISIT** (See March of Comics #283)

**SANTIAGO** (See 4-Color #723)

**SARGE SNORKEL** (Beetle Bailey)
Oct, 1973 - No. 17, Dec, 1976
Charlton Comics

| | Good | Fine | N-Mint |
|---|---|---|---|
| 1 | .35 | 1.00 | 2.00 |
| 2-17 | | .40 | .80 |

**SARGE STEEL** (Becomes Secret Agent #9 on; see Judomaster)
Dec, 1964 - No. 8, Mar-Apr, 1966
Charlton Comics

| | Good | Fine | N-Mint |
|---|---|---|---|
| 1-Origin | .85 | 2.60 | 6.00 |
| 2-8: 6-Judo Master app. (2nd app?) | .50 | 1.50 | 3.00 |

**SAVAGE COMBAT TALES**
Feb, 1975 - No. 3, July, 1975
Atlas/Seaboard Publ.

| | Good | Fine | N-Mint |
|---|---|---|---|
| 1-3: 1-Sgt. Stryker's Death Squad begins (origin). 2-Only app. Warhawk | | .30 | .60 |

NOTE: ***McWilliams** a-1-3; c-1. **Sparling** a-1, 3. **Toth** a-2.*

**SAVAGE HENRY**
Jan, 1987 - Present ($1.75-$2.00, B&W, mature readers)
Vortex Comics

| | Good | Fine | N-Mint |
|---|---|---|---|
| 1-9 ($1.75) | .30 | .90 | 1.80 |
| 10-15 ($2.00) | .35 | 1.00 | 2.00 |
| 16-Begin $2.50-c | .40 | 1.25 | 2.50 |

**SAVAGE RAIDS OF GERONIMO** (See Geronimo #4)

**SAVAGE RANGE** (See 4-Color #807)

**SAVAGE SHE-HULK, THE** (See The Avengers, Marvel Graphic Novel #18 & The Sensational She-Hulk)
Feb, 1980 - No. 25, Feb, 1982
Marvel Comics Group

| | Good | Fine | N-Mint |
|---|---|---|---|
| 1-Origin & 1st app. She-Hulk | .70 | 2.00 | 4.00 |
| 2-10 | .35 | 1.00 | 2.00 |
| 11-25: 25-(52 pgs.) | .25 | .75 | 1.50 |

NOTE: ***Austin** a-25i; c-23i-25i. **J. Buscema** a-1p; c-1, 2p. **Golden** c-8-11.*

**SAVAGE SWORD OF CONAN, THE** (. . .The Barbarian #? on)
Aug, 1974 - Present (B&W magazine)(Mature readers)
Marvel Comics Group

| | Good | Fine | N-Mint |
|---|---|---|---|
| 1-Smith-r; J. Buscema/N. Adams/Krenkel-a; origin Blackmark by Gil Kane (part 1) & Red Sonja (3rd app.) | 6.50 | 19.50 | 45.00 |
| 2-Neal Adams-c; Chaykin/N. Adams-a | 2.85 | 8.50 | 20.00 |
| 3-Severin/B. Smith-a; N. Adams-a | 1.70 | 5.00 | 10.00 |
| 4-N. Adams/Kane-a(r) | 1.50 | 4.50 | 9.00 |
| 5-10: 5-Jeff Jones frontispiece (r) | 1.35 | 4.00 | 8.00 |
| 11-20 | 1.15 | 3.50 | 7.00 |
| 21-50 | 1.00 | 3.00 | 6.00 |
| 51-100: 63-Toth frontispiece. 70-Article on movie. 83-Red Sonja-r by Neal Adams from #1 | .70 | 2.00 | 4.00 |
| 101-176: 163-Begin $2.25-c. 169-King Kull story. 171-Soloman Kane by Williamson (i). 172-Red Sonja story | .50 | 1.50 | 3.00 |
| 177-184: 179-Red Sonja app. | .40 | 1.15 | 2.30 |
| Special 1('75, B&W)-B. Smith-r/Conan #10,13 | 1.00 | 3.00 | 6.00 |

NOTE: ***N. Adams** a-14p, 60, 83p(r). **Alcala** a-2 ,4, 7, 12, 15-20, 23, 24, 28, 59, 67, 69, 75, 76i, 80i, 82i, 83i, 89. **Austin** a-78i. **Boris** c-1, 4, 5, 7, 9, 10, 12, 15. **Brunner** a-30; c-8, 30. **Buscema** a-1-5, 7, 10-12, 15-24, 26-28, 31, 32, 36-43, 45, 47-58p, 60-67p, 70, 71-74p, 76-81p, 87-96p, 98, 99-101p; c-40. **Corben** a-4, 16, 29. **Finlay** a-16. **Golden** a-98, 101; c-150. **Kaluta** a-11, 18; c-3, 91, 93. **Gil Kane** a-2, 3, 8, 13r, 29, 47, 64, 65, 67, 85p, 86p. **Krenkel** a-9, 11, 14, 16, 24. **Morrow** a-7. **Nebres** a-93i, 101i, 107, 114. **Newton** a-6. **Nino** c/a-6. **Redondo** c-48, 50, 52, 56, 57, 85i, 90, 96i. **Severin** a-Special 1. **Simonson** a-7, 8, 12, 15-17. **Barry Smith** a-7, 16, 24, 82r, Special 1r. **Starlin** c-26. **Toth** a-64. **Williamson** a-162i, 171i. No. 8 & 10 contain a Robert E. Howard Conan adaptation.*

**SAVAGE TALES** (Magazine) (B&W)
May, 1971; No. 2, 10/73; No. 3, 2/74 - No. 12, Summer, 1975
Marvel Comics Group

| | Good | Fine | N-Mint |
|---|---|---|---|
| 1-Origin/1st app. The Man-Thing by Morrow; Conan the Barbarian by Barry Smith, Femizons by Romita begin; Ka-Zar app. | 8.50 | 22.50 | 60.00 |
| 2-B. Smith, Brunner, Morrow, Williamson, Wrightson-a (reprint/Creatures on the Loose #10); King Kull app. | 4.30 | 13.00 | 30.00 |
| 3-B. Smith, Brunner, Steranko, Williamson-a | 2.50 | 7.50 | 17.00 |
| 4,5-N. Adams-c; last Conan (Smith-r/#4) plus Kane/N. Adams-a. 5-Brak the Barbarian begins, ends #8 | 1.60 | 4.80 | 11.00 |
| 6-8: 6-Ka-Zar begins; Williamson-r; N. Adams-c. 7-N. Adams-i. 8-Shanna, the She-Devil app. thru #10; Williamson-r | .70 | 2.00 | 4.00 |
| 9,11 | .50 | 1.50 | 3.00 |
| 10-Neal Adams-a(i), Williamson-r | .70 | 2.00 | 4.00 |
| . . .Featuring Ka-Zar Annual 1(Summer'75, B&W)(#12 on inside)-Ka-Zar origin by G. Kane; B. Smith-r/Astonish. Tales | .70 | 2.00 | 4.00 |

NOTE: ***Boris** c-7, 10. **Buscema** a-5r, 6p, 8p; c-2. **Fabian** c-8. **Golden** a-1, 4; c-1. **Heath** a-10p, 11p. **Kaluta** c-9. **Maneely** a-2r. **Morrow** a-1, 2, 7, Annual 1. **Reese** a-2. **Severin** a-1-4, 7. **Starlin** a-5. Robert E. Howard adaptations-1-4.*

**SAVAGE TALES** (Magazine size)
Nov, 1985 - No. 9, Mar, 1987 ($1.50, B&W, mature readers)
Marvel Comics Group

| | Good | Fine | N-Mint |
|---|---|---|---|
| 1-1st app. The Nam; Golden-a | 1.35 | 4.00 | 8.00 |
| 2-9: 4-2nd Nam story; Golden-a in all | .25 | .75 | 1.50 |

**SCAMP** (Walt Disney)(See Walt Disney's Comics & Stories #204)
No. 703, 5/56 - No. 1204, 8-10/61; 11/67 - No. 45, 1/79
Dell Publishing Co./Gold Key

| | Good | Fine | N-Mint |
|---|---|---|---|
| 4-Color 703(No. 1) | 1.70 | 5.00 | 12.00 |
| 4-Color 777,806('57),833 | 1.15 | 3.50 | 8.00 |
| 5(3-5/58)-10(6-8/59) | .85 | 2.50 | 6.00 |
| 11-16(12-2/60-61) | .70 | 2.00 | 5.00 |
| 4-Color 1204(1961) | .85 | 2.50 | 6.00 |
| 1(12/67-Gold Key)-Reprints begin | .55 | 1.65 | 4.00 |

*Savage Henry #1, © Vortex*

*The Savage She-Hulk #4, © MEG*

*The Savage Sword of Conan #1, © MEG*

Tops in Teen Age Stories
school-day ROMANCES

*School Day Romances #2, © STAR*

*Science Comics #1, © FOX*

*The Score #1, © DC*

| | Good | Fine | N-Mint |
|---|---|---|---|
| 2(3/69)-10 | .35 | 1.00 | 2.00 |
| 11-20 | .25 | .75 | 1.50 |
| 21-45 | | .40 | .80 |

NOTE: *New stories-#20(in part), 22-25, 27, 29-31, 34, 36-40, 42-45. New covers-#11, 12, 14, 15, 17-25, 27, 29-31, 34, 36-38.*

**SCAR FACE** (See The Crusaders)

**SCARECROW OF ROMNEY MARSH, THE** (See W.D. Showcase #53)
April, 1964 - No. 3, Oct, 1965 (Disney TV Show)
Gold Key

| | Good | Fine | N-Mint |
|---|---|---|---|
| 10112-404 (#1) | 2.65 | 8.00 | 18.00 |
| 2,3 | 1.70 | 5.00 | 12.00 |

**SCARLET O'NEIL** (See Harvey Comics Hits #59 & Invisible. . .)

**SCARY TALES**
8/75 - #9, 1/77; #10, 9/77 - #20, 6/79; #21, 8/80 - #46, 10/84
Charlton Comics

| | Good | Fine | N-Mint |
|---|---|---|---|
| 1-Origin/1st app. Countess Von Bludd, not in #2 | | .40 | .80 |
| 2-11 | | .30 | .60 |
| 12-36,39,46-All reprints | | .30 | .60 |
| 37,38,40-45-New-a. 38-Mr. Jigsaw app. | | .30 | .60 |
| 1(Modern Comics reprint, 1977) | | .15 | .30 |

NOTE: ***Adkins** a-31i; c-31i. **Ditko** a-3, 5, 7, 8(2), 11, 12, 14-16r, 18(3)r, 19r, 21r, 30r, 32, 39r; c-5, 11, 14, 18, 30, 32. **Newton** a-31p; c-31p. **Powell** a-18r. **Staton** a-1(2 pgs.), 4, 20r; c-1, 20. **Sutton** a-9; c-4, 9.*

**SCAVENGERS**
Feb, 1988 - No. 14, 1989 ($1.25-$1.50, color)
Quality Comics

| | Good | Fine | N-Mint |
|---|---|---|---|
| 1-7 ($1.25) | | .60 | 1.25 |
| 8-14: ($1.50) 9-13-Guice-c | .25 | .75 | 1.50 |

**SCHOOL DAY ROMANCES** (. . .of Teen-Agers #4) (Popular Teen-Agers #5 on)
Nov-Dec, 1949 - No. 4, May-June, 1950
Star Publications

| | Good | Fine | N-Mint |
|---|---|---|---|
| 1-Tony Gayle (later Gay), Gingersnapp | 9.30 | 28.00 | 65.00 |
| 2,3: 3-Photo-c | 5.00 | 15.00 | 35.00 |
| 4-Ronald Reagan photo-c/L.B. Cole-c | 13.00 | 40.00 | 90.00 |

NOTE: *All have **L. B. Cole** covers.*

**SCHWINN BICYCLE BOOK** (. . .Bike Thrills, 1959)
1949; 1952; 1959 (10 cents)
Schwinn Bicycle Co.

| | Good | Fine | N-Mint |
|---|---|---|---|
| 1949 | 2.65 | 8.00 | 18.00 |
| 1952-Believe It or Not type facts; comic format; 36 pgs. | 1.30 | 4.00 | 9.00 |
| 1959 | 1.00 | 3.00 | 7.00 |

**SCIENCE COMICS** (1st Series)
Feb, 1940 - No. 8, Sept, 1940
Fox Features Syndicate

| | Good | Fine | N-Mint |
|---|---|---|---|
| 1-Origin Dynamo (called Electro in #1), The Eagle (1st app.), & Navy Jones; Marga, The Panther Woman (1st app.), Cosmic Carson & Perisphere Payne, Dr. Doom begin; bondage/hypo-c | 143.00 | 430.00 | 1000.00 |
| 2 | 72.00 | 215.00 | 500.00 |
| 3,4: 4-Kirby-a | 57.00 | 170.00 | 400.00 |
| 5-8 | 40.00 | 120.00 | 280.00 |

NOTE: *Cosmic Carson by **Tuska**-#1-3; by **Kirby**-#4. **Lou Fine** c-1-3 only.*

**SCIENCE COMICS** (2nd Series)
January, 1946 - No. 5, 1946
Humor Publications (Ace Magazines?)

| | Good | Fine | N-Mint |
|---|---|---|---|
| 1-Palais-c/a in No. 1-3; A-Bomb-c | 5.70 | 17.00 | 40.00 |
| 2 | 2.85 | 8.50 | 20.00 |
| 3-Feldstein-a, 6 pgs. | 7.00 | 21.00 | 50.00 |
| 4,5 | 2.65 | 8.00 | 18.00 |

**SCIENCE COMICS**
May, 1947 (8 pgs. in color)
Ziff-Davis Publ. Co.

| | Good | Fine | N-Mint |
|---|---|---|---|
| nn-Could be ordered by mail for 10 cents; like the nn Amazing Advs. (1950)-used to test the market | 24.00 | 73.00 | 170.00 |

**SCIENCE COMICS**
March, 1951
Export Publication Ent., Toronto, Canada
Distr. in U.S. by Kable News Co.

| | Good | Fine | N-Mint |
|---|---|---|---|
| 1-Science Adventure stories plus some true science features | 2.65 | 8.00 | 18.00 |

**SCIENCE FICTION SPACE ADVENTURES** (See Space Adventures)

**SCOOBY DOO** (. . .Where are you? #1-16,26; . . .Mystery Comics #17-25,27 on) (TV) (See March Of Comics #356,368,382,391)
March, 1970 - No. 30, Feb, 1975 (Hanna-Barbera)
Gold Key

| | Good | Fine | N-Mint |
|---|---|---|---|
| 1 | 2.85 | 8.50 | 20.00 |
| 2-5 | 1.50 | 4.50 | 10.00 |
| 6-10 | 1.00 | 3.00 | 7.00 |
| 11-20: 11-Tufts-a | .70 | 2.00 | 5.00 |
| 21-30 | .50 | 1.50 | 3.00 |

**SCOOBY DOO** (TV)
April, 1975 - No. 11, Dec, 1976 (Hanna Barbera)
Charlton Comics

| | Good | Fine | N-Mint |
|---|---|---|---|
| 1 | 1.15 | 3.50 | 8.00 |
| 2-5 | .70 | 2.00 | 4.00 |
| 6-11 | .50 | 1.50 | 3.00 |

**SCOOBY-DOO** (TV)
Oct, 1977 - No. 9, Feb, 1979 (Hanna-Barbera)
Marvel Comics Group

| | Good | Fine | N-Mint |
|---|---|---|---|
| 1-Dyno-Mutt begins | .40 | 1.25 | 2.50 |
| 2-9 | | .50 | 1.00 |

**SCOOP COMICS**
November, 1941 - No. 8, 1946
Harry 'A' Chesler (Holyoke)

| | Good | Fine | N-Mint |
|---|---|---|---|
| 1-Intro. Rocketman & Rocketgirl; origin The Master Key; Dan Hastings begins; Charles Sultan-c/a | 43.00 | 130.00 | 300.00 |
| 2-Rocket Boy app; Injury to eye story (Same as Spotlight #3) | 25.00 | 75.00 | 175.00 |
| 3-Injury to eye story-r from #2; Rocket Boy | 20.00 | 60.00 | 140.00 |
| 4-8 | 14.00 | 43.00 | 100.00 |

**SCOOTER** (See Swing With. . .)

**SCOOTER COMICS**
April, 1946
Rucker Publ. Ltd. (Canadian)

| | Good | Fine | N-Mint |
|---|---|---|---|
| 1-Teen-age/funny animal | 3.70 | 11.00 | 26.00 |

**SCORE, THE**
1989 - No. 4, 1990 ($4.95, color, squarebound, adults, 52 pgs.)
Piranha Press (DC Comics)

| | Good | Fine | N-Mint |
|---|---|---|---|
| Book One - Four: Mark Badger painted-c/a | .85 | 2.50 | 5.00 |

**SCORPION**
Feb, 1975 - No. 3, July, 1975
Atlas/Seaboard Publ.

| | Good | Fine | N-Mint |
|---|---|---|---|
| 1-Intro.; bondage-c by Chaykin | | .40 | .80 |
| 2,3: 2-Wrightson, Kaluta, Simonson-a(i) | | .30 | .60 |

NOTE: ***Chaykin** a-1, 2; c-1. **Mooney** a-3i.*

**SCORPIO ROSE**
Jan, 1983; No. 2, Oct, 1983 ($1.25, color, Baxter paper)
Eclipse Comics

| | Good | Fine | N-Mint |
|---|---|---|---|
| 1,2: 1-Dr. Orient back-up story begins. 2-Origin | | .65 | 1.30 |

NOTE: ***Rogers** c/a-1. 2.*

**SCOTLAND YARD** (Inspector Farnsworth of . . .) (Texas Rangers in Action #5 on?)
June, 1955 - No. 4, March, 1956
Charlton Comics Group

| | Good | Fine | N-Mint |
|---|---|---|---|
| 1-Tothish-a | 6.50 | 19.00 | 45.00 |
| 2-4: 2-Tothish-a | 3.70 | 11.00 | 26.00 |

**SCOUT** (See Eclipse Graphic Album #16, New America & Swords of Texas)(Becomes Scout: War Shaman)
Dec, 1985 - No. 24, Oct, 1987 ($1.75, color, Baxter)(#9,10: $1.25)
Eclipse Comics

| | Good | Fine | N-Mint |
|---|---|---|---|
| 1-8,11,12: 11-Monday: The Eliminator begins | .30 | .90 | 1.80 |
| 9,10 ($1.25): 9-Airboy preview. 10-Bissette-a | | .65 | 1.25 |
| 13-15,17,18,20-24 ($1.75): 15-Swords of Texas | .30 | .90 | 1.80 |
| 16-Scout 3-D Special ($2.50) | .40 | 1.25 | 2.50 |
| 16-Scout 2-D Limited Edition | .40 | 1.25 | 2.50 |
| 19-Contains Flexidisk ($2.50) | .40 | 1.25 | 2.50 |
| . . . Handbook 1 (8/87, $1.75, B&W) | .30 | .90 | 1.80 |

**SCOUT: WAR SHAMAN** (Formerly Scout)
March, 1988 - No. 16, Dec, 1989 ($1.95, color)
Eclipse Comics

| | Good | Fine | N-Mint |
|---|---|---|---|
| 1-16 | .35 | 1.00 | 2.00 |

**SCREAM** (. . . Comics) (Andy Comics #20 on)
Fall, 1944 - No. 19, April, 1948
Humor Publications/Current Books(Ace Magazines)

| | Good | Fine | N-Mint |
|---|---|---|---|
| 1 | 6.50 | 19.00 | 45.00 |
| 2 | 3.15 | 9.50 | 22.00 |
| 3-15: 11-Racist humor (Indians) | 2.65 | 8.00 | 18.00 |
| 16-Intro. Lily-Belle | 2.65 | 8.00 | 18.00 |
| 17,19 | 2.30 | 7.00 | 16.00 |
| 18-Hypo needle story | 3.70 | 11.00 | 26.00 |

**SCREAM** (Magazine)
Aug, 1973 - No. 11, Feb, 1975 (68 pgs.) (B&W)
Skywald Publishing Corp.

| | Good | Fine | N-Mint |
|---|---|---|---|
| 1 | .70 | 2.00 | 4.00 |
| 2-5: 2-Origin Lady Satan. 3 (12/73)-#3 found on pg. 22 | .35 | 1.00 | 2.00 |
| 6-11: 6-Origin The Victims. 9-Severed head-c | .25 | .75 | 1.50 |

**SCRIBBLY** (See All-American Comics, Buzzy, The Funnies, Leave It To Binky & Popular Comics)
8-9/48 - No. 13, 8-9/50; No. 14, 10-11/51 - No. 15, 12-1/51-52
National Periodical Publications

| | Good | Fine | N-Mint |
|---|---|---|---|
| 1-Sheldon Mayer-a in all; 52pgs. begin | 55.00 | 165.00 | 385.00 |
| 2 | 35.00 | 105.00 | 245.00 |
| 3-5 | 29.00 | 86.00 | 200.00 |
| 6-10 | 20.00 | 60.00 | 140.00 |
| 11-15: 13-Last 52 pgs. | 16.00 | 48.00 | 110.00 |

**SEA DEVILS** (See DC Special #10,19, DC Super-Stars #14,17, Limited Collectors' Edition #39,45, & Showcase #27-29)
Sept-Oct, 1961 - No. 35, May-June, 1967
National Periodical Publications

| | Good | Fine | N-Mint |
|---|---|---|---|
| 1 | 26.00 | 78.00 | 180.00 |
| 2-Last 10 cent issue | 10.00 | 30.00 | 70.00 |
| 3-5: 3-Begin 12 cent issues thru #35 | 5.70 | 17.00 | 40.00 |
| 6-10 | 3.60 | 11.00 | 25.00 |
| 11,12,14-20 | 2.65 | 8.00 | 18.00 |
| 13-Kubert, Colan-a | 2.85 | 8.50 | 20.00 |
| 21,23-35 | 1.70 | 5.00 | 12.00 |
| 22-Intro. International Sea Devils; origin & 1st app. Capt. X & Man Fish | 1.70 | 5.00 | 12.00 |

NOTE: ***Heath** a-1-10; c-1-10, 14-16. **Moldoff** a-16i.*

**SEADRAGON** (Also see The Epsilon Wave)
May, 1986 - No. 8, 1987 ($1.75, color)
Elite Comics

| | Good | Fine | N-Mint |
|---|---|---|---|
| 1-8: 1-First & second printings exist | .30 | .90 | 1.80 |

**SEA HOUND, THE** (Capt. Silver's Log Of The . . .)
1945 (no month) - No. 4, Jan-Feb, 1946
Avon Periodicals

| | Good | Fine | N-Mint |
|---|---|---|---|
| nn | 6.50 | 19.00 | 45.00 |
| 2-4 (#2, 9-10/45) | 4.50 | 14.00 | 32.00 |

**SEA HOUND, THE** (Radio)
No. 3, July, 1949 - No. 4, Sept, 1949
Capt. Silver Syndicate

| | Good | Fine | N-Mint |
|---|---|---|---|
| 3,4 | 3.70 | 11.00 | 26.00 |

**SEA HUNT** (TV)
No. 928, 8/58 - No. 1041, 10-12/59; No. 4, 1-3/60 - No. 13, 4-6/62
Dell Publishing Co. (All have Lloyd Bridges photo-c)

| | Good | Fine | N-Mint |
|---|---|---|---|
| 4-Color 928(#1) | 6.50 | 19.00 | 45.00 |
| 4-Color 994(#2), 4-13: Manning-a #4-6,8-11,13 | 5.00 | 15.00 | 35.00 |
| 4-Color 1041(#3)-Toth-a | 7.00 | 21.00 | 50.00 |

**SEARCH FOR LOVE**
Feb-Mar, 1950 - No. 2, Apr-May, 1950 (52 pgs.)
American Comics Group

| | Good | Fine | N-Mint |
|---|---|---|---|
| 1 | 4.50 | 14.00 | 32.00 |
| 2,3(6-7/50): 3-Exist? | 2.65 | 8.00 | 18.00 |

**SEARCHERS** (See 4-Color #709)

**SEARS** (See Merry Christmas From . . .)

**SEASON'S GREETINGS**
1935 (6¼x5¼") (32 pgs. in color)
Hallmark (King Features)

Cover features Mickey Mouse, Popeye, Jiggs & Skippy. "The Night Before Christmas" told one panel per page, each panel by a famous artist featuring their character. Art by Alex Raymond, Gottfredson, Swinnerton, Segar, Chic Young, Milt Gross, Sullivan (Messmer), Herriman, McManus, Percy Crosby & others (22 artists in all)
Estimated value. . . . $200.00 — $400.00

**SECRET AGENT** (Formerly Sarge Steel)
V2#9, Oct, 1966; V2#10, Oct, 1967
Charlton Comics

| | Good | Fine | N-Mint |
|---|---|---|---|
| V2#9-Sarge Steel part-r begins | .70 | 2.00 | 4.00 |
| 10-Tiffany Sinn, CIA app. (from Career Girl Romances #39); Aparo-a | .50 | 1.50 | 3.00 |

**SECRET AGENT** (TV)
Nov, 1966 - No. 2, Jan, 1968
Gold Key

| | Good | Fine | N-Mint |
|---|---|---|---|
| 1,2-Photo-c | 3.00 | 9.00 | 21.00 |

**SECRET AGENT X-9** (See Flash Gordon #4 by King)
1934 (Book 1: 84 pgs.; Book 2: 124 pgs.) (8x7½")
David McKay Publications

| | Good | Fine | N-Mint |
|---|---|---|---|
| Book 1-Contains reprints of the first 13 weeks of the strip by Alex Raymond; complete except for 2 dailies | 38.00 | 115.00 | 265.00 |
| Book 2-Contains reprints immediately following contents of Book 1, for 20 weeks by Alex Raymond; complete except for two dailies. Note: Raymond mis-dated the last five strips from 6/34, and while the dating sequence is confusing, the continuity is correct | 32.00 | 95.00 | 225.00 |

**SECRET AGENT X-9** (See Feature Books #8 & Magic Comics)

**SECRET AGENT Z-2** (See Holyoke One-Shot No. 7)

**SECRET DIARY OF EERIE ADVENTURES**
1953 (One Shot) (25 cent giant; 100 pgs.)

*Scotland Yard #1, © CC*

*Sea Devils #6, © DC*

*Secret Agent #1 (GK), © Independent TV*

Secret Hearts #8, © DC

Secret Mysteries #16, © Ribage

Secret Origins #13, © DC

Avon Periodicals

| | Good | Fine | N-Mint |
|---|---|---|---|
| nn-(Rare) Kubert-a; Hollingsworth-c; Sid Check back-c | 86.00 | 257.00 | 600.00 |

**SECRET HEARTS**
9-10/49 - No. 6, 7-8/50; No. 7, 12-1/51-52 - No. 153, 7/71
(No. 1-6: photo-c; all 52 pgs.)
National Periodical Publications (Beverly)(Arleigh No. 50-113)

| | Good | Fine | N-Mint |
|---|---|---|---|
| 1-Photo-c begin, end #6 | 20.00 | 60.00 | 140.00 |
| 2-Toth-a | 10.00 | 30.00 | 70.00 |
| 3,6 (1950) | 8.00 | 24.00 | 55.00 |
| 4,5-Toth-a | 10.00 | 30.00 | 70.00 |
| 7(12-1/51-52) (Rare) | 10.00 | 30.00 | 70.00 |
| 8-10 (1952) | 5.00 | 15.00 | 35.00 |
| 11-20 | 4.00 | 12.00 | 28.00 |
| 21-26: 26-Last precode (2-3/55) | 3.15 | 9.50 | 22.00 |
| 27-40 | 2.30 | 7.00 | 16.00 |
| 41-50 | 1.70 | 5.00 | 12.00 |
| 51-60 | 1.15 | 3.50 | 8.00 |
| 61-75: Last 10 cent issue | .85 | 2.60 | 6.00 |
| 76-109 | .70 | 2.00 | 4.00 |
| 110-"Reach for Happiness" serial begins, ends #138 | .50 | 1.50 | 3.00 |
| 111-119,121-126,128-133,135-138 | | .75 | 1.50 |
| 120,134-Neal Adams-c | .50 | 1.50 | 3.00 |
| 127 (4/68)-Beatles cameo | .50 | 1.50 | 3.00 |
| 139,140 | | .75 | 1.50 |
| 141,142-"20 Miles to Heartbreak," Chapter 2 & 3 (See Young Love for Chapter 1 & 4); Toth, Colletta-a | | .50 | 1.00 |
| 143-148,150-153: 144-Morrow-a. 153-Kirby-i | | .35 | .70 |
| 149-Toth-a | | .50 | 1.00 |

**SECRET ISLAND OF OZ, THE** (See First Comics Graphic Novel)

**SECRET LOVE** (See Fox Giants & Sinister House of. . .)

**SECRET LOVE**
12/55 - No. 3, 8/56; 4/57 - No. 5, 2/58; No. 6, 6/58
Ajax-Farrell/Four Star Comic Corp. No. 2 on

| | Good | Fine | N-Mint |
|---|---|---|---|
| 1(12/55-Ajax, 1st series) | 3.00 | 9.00 | 21.00 |
| 2,3 | 1.70 | 5.00 | 12.00 |
| 1(4/57-Ajax, 2nd series) | 2.30 | 7.00 | 16.00 |
| 2-6: 5-Bakerish-a | 1.50 | 4.50 | 10.00 |

**SECRET LOVES**
Nov, 1949 - No. 6, Sept, 1950 (#5: photo-c)
Comic Magazines/Quality Comics Group

| | Good | Fine | N-Mint |
|---|---|---|---|
| 1-Ward-c | 10.00 | 30.00 | 70.00 |
| 2-Ward-c | 8.50 | 25.50 | 60.00 |
| 3-Crandall-a | 6.00 | 18.00 | 42.00 |
| 4,6 | 3.50 | 10.50 | 24.00 |
| 5-Suggestive art-"Boom Town Babe" | 5.00 | 15.00 | 35.00 |

**SECRET LOVE STORIES** (See Fox Giants)

**SECRET MISSIONS**
February, 1950
St. John Publishing Co.

| | Good | Fine | N-Mint |
|---|---|---|---|
| 1-Kubert-c | 9.30 | 28.00 | 65.00 |

**SECRET MYSTERIES** (Formerly Crime Mysteries & Crime Smashers)
No. 16, Nov, 1954 - No. 19, July, 1955
Ribage/Merit Publications No. 17 on

| | Good | Fine | N-Mint |
|---|---|---|---|
| 16-Horror, Palais-a | 6.50 | 19.00 | 45.00 |
| 17-19-Horror; #17-mis-dated 3/54? | 4.50 | 14.00 | 32.00 |

**SECRET ORIGINS** (See 80 Page Giant #8)
Aug-Oct, 1961 (Annual) (Reprints)
National Periodical Publications

| | Good | Fine | N-Mint |
|---|---|---|---|
| 1('61)-Origin Adam Strange (Showcase #17), Green Lantern (G.L. #1), Challangers (partial/Showcase #6, 6 pgs. Kirby-a). J'onn J'onzz (Det. #225), The Flash (Showcase #4). Green Arrow (1pg. text). Superman-Batman team (W. Finest #94). Wonder Woman (Wonder Woman #105) | 19.00 | 58.00 | 135.00 |

**SECRET ORIGINS**
Feb-Mar, 1973 - No. 6, Jan-Feb, 1974; No. 7, Oct-Nov, 1974
National Periodical Publications (All origin reprints)

| | Good | Fine | N-Mint |
|---|---|---|---|
| 1-Superman(Action #1, 1st time since G.A.), Batman(Batman #33), Ghost(Flash #88), The Flash(Showcase #4) | 1.00 | 3.00 | 7.00 |
| 2-4: 2-Green Lantern(Showcase #22), The Atom(Showcase #34), & Supergirl(Action #252). 3-Wonder Woman(W.W. #1), Wildcat(Sensation #1). 4-Vigilante(Action #42) by Meskin, Kid Eternity(Hit #25) | .50 | 1.50 | 3.00 |
| 5-7: 5-The Spectre(More Fun?). 6-Blackhawk(Military #1) & Legion of Super-Heroes(Adv?). 7-Robin(Detective #38), Aquaman(More Fun #73?) | .40 | 1.25 | 2.50 |

NOTE: ***Colan*** *c-5p.* ***Infantino*** *a-1.* ***Kane*** *a-2.* ***Kubert*** *a-1.*

**SECRET ORIGINS**
4/86 - No. 50, 8/90 (All origins)(52 pgs. #6 on)(#27 on: $1.50)
DC Comics

| | Good | Fine | N-Mint |
|---|---|---|---|
| 1-Origin Superman | .60 | 1.75 | 3.50 |
| 2-Blue Beetle | .50 | 1.50 | 3.00 |
| 3-5: 3-Shazam. 4-Firestorm. 5-Crimson Avenger/Shadow/Doll Man | .40 | 1.25 | 2.50 |
| 6-G.A. Batman | .70 | 2.00 | 4.00 |
| 7-10: 7-Green Lantern(Guy Gardner)/G.A. Sandman. 8-Doll Man. 9-G.A. Flash/Skyman. 10-Phantom Stranger w/Alan Moore scripts; Legends spin-off | .40 | 1.15 | 2.25 |
| 11,12,14-26: 11-G.A. Hawkman/Power Girl. 12-Challs of Unknown/G.A. Fury. 14-Suicide Squad; Legends spin-off. 15-Spectre/Deadman. 16-G.A. Hourman/Warlord. 17-Adam Strange/Dr. Occult. 18-G.A. Gr. Lantern/The Creeper. 19-Uncle Sam/The Guardian. 20-Batgirl/G.A. Dr. Mid-Nite. 21-Jonah Hex/Black Condor. 22-Manhunters. 23-Floronic Man/Guardians of the Universe. 24-Blue Devil/Dr. Fate. 25-LSH/Atom. 26-Black Lightning/Miss America | .35 | 1.00 | 2.00 |
| 13-Origin Nightwing; Johnny Thunder app. | .70 | 2.00 | 4.00 |
| 27-38,40-44: 27-Zatara/Zatanna. 28-Midnight/Nightshade. 29-Power of the Atom/Mr. America. 30-Plastic Man/Elongated Man. 31-JSA. 32-JLA. 33-35-JLI. 36-Green Lantern/Poison Ivy. 37-Legion Of Substitute Heroes/Doctor Light. 38-Green Arrow/Speedy; Grell scripts. 40-All Ape issue. 41-Rogues Gallery of Flash. 42-Phantom Girl/Grim Ghost. 43-Original Hawk & Dove/Cave Carson/Chris KL-99. 44-Batman app.; story based on Det. #40 | .30 | .90 | 1.80 |
| 39-Animal Man-c/story; Batman app. | .70 | 2.00 | 4.00 |
| 45-49: 45-Blackhawk/El Diablo. 46-JLA/LSH/New Titans. 47-LSH. 48-Ambush Bug/Stanley & His Monster/Rex the Wonder Dog/Trigger Twins. 49-Newsboy Legion/Silent Knight/brief origin Bouncing Boy | .25 | .75 | 1.50 |
| 50-($3.95, 100 pgs.)-Batman & Robin in text, Flash of Two Worlds, Johnny Thunder, Dolphin, Black Canary & Space Museum | .70 | 2.00 | 4.00 |
| Annual 1 (8/87)-Capt. Comet/Doom Patrol | .35 | 1.00 | 2.00 |
| Annual 2 ('88, $2.00)-Origin Flash II & Flash III | .35 | 1.00 | 2.00 |
| Annual 3 ('89, $2.95, 84 pgs.)-Teen Titans; 1st app. new Flamebird who replaces original Bat-Girl | .50 | 1.50 | 3.00 |
| Special 1 (10/89, $2.00)-Batman villains: Penguin, Riddler, & Two-Face; Bolland-c | .40 | 1.25 | 2.50 |

NOTE: ***Art Adams*** *a-33i(part).* ***M. Anderson*** *8, 19, 21; c-19(part).* ***Bolland*** *c-7.* ***Byrne*** *c/a-Annual 1.* ***Colan*** *a-5p.* ***Forte*** *a-37.* ***Giffen*** *a-18p, 44p, 48.* ***Kaluta*** *c-39.* ***Gil Kane*** *a-2, 28; c-2p.* ***Kirby*** *c-19(part).* ***Mayer*** *a-29.* ***Morrow*** *a-21.* ***Orlando*** *a-10.* ***Perez*** *a-50i; c-Annual 3.* ***Rogers*** *a-6p.* ***Russell*** *a-27p.* ***Steacy*** *a-35.* ***Staton*** *a-36, 50p.* ***Tuska*** *a-4p, 9p.*

**SECRET ORIGINS OF SUPER-HEROES** (See DC Special Series #10,19)

**SECRET ORIGINS OF THE WORLD'S GREATEST SUPER-HEROES**
1989 ($4.95, squarebound, 148 pgs.)

DC Comics

| | Good | Fine | N-Mint |
|---|---|---|---|
| nn-r/origins of Superman by Byrne, Flash by Infantino/Anderson, Green Lantern, Martian Manhunter by Steacy & JLA; all new origin The Batman; Bolland-c | 1.00 | 3.00 | 6.00 |

**SECRET ROMANCE**
Oct, 1968 - No. 41, Nov, 1976; No. 42, Mar, 1979 - No. 48, Feb, 1980
Charlton Comics

| | | | |
|---|---|---|---|
| 1-Begin 12 cent issues, ends ? | .60 | 1.75 | 3.50 |
| 2-10: 9-Reese-a | .30 | 1.00 | 2.00 |
| 11-48 | | .35 | .70 |

NOTE: *Beyond the Stars app.-No. 9, 11, 12, 14.*

**SECRET ROMANCES**
April 1951 - No. 27, July, 1955
Superior Publications Ltd.

| | | | |
|---|---|---|---|
| 1 | 6.00 | 18.00 | 42.00 |
| 2 | 3.50 | 10.50 | 24.00 |
| 3-10 | 2.85 | 8.50 | 20.00 |
| 11-13,15-18,20-27 | 2.00 | 6.00 | 14.00 |
| 14,19-Lingerie panels | 2.85 | 8.50 | 20.00 |

**SECRET SERVICE** (See Kent Blake of the . . .)

**SECRET SIX** (See Action Comics Weekly)
Apr-May, 1968 - No. 7, Apr-May, 1969 (12 cents)
National Periodical Publications

| | | | |
|---|---|---|---|
| 1-Origin | 2.65 | 8.00 | 18.00 |
| 2-7 | 1.50 | 4.50 | 10.00 |

**SECRET SOCIETY OF SUPER-VILLAINS**
May-June, 1976 - No. 15, June-July, 1978
National Periodical Publications/DC Comics

| | | | |
|---|---|---|---|
| 1-Origin; JLA cameo & Capt. Cold app. | | .75 | 1.50 |
| 2-5: 2-Re-intro/origin Capt. Comet; Gr. Lantern x-over. 5-Green Lantern, Hawkman x-over; Darkseid app. | | .40 | .80 |
| 6-15: 9,10-Creeper x-over. 11-Capt. Comet; Orlando-i. 15-G.A. Atom, Dr. Midnite, & JSA app. | | .35 | .70 |

**SECRET SOCIETY OF SUPER-VILLAINS SPECIAL** (See DC Special Series #6)

**SECRETS OF HAUNTED HOUSE**
4-5/75 - #5, 12-1/75-76; #6, 6-7/77 - #14, 10-11/78; #15, 8/79 - #46, 3/82
National Periodical Publications/DC Comics

| | | | |
|---|---|---|---|
| 1 | | .50 | 1.00 |
| 2-46: 31-Mr. E series begins, ends #41 | | .25 | .50 |

NOTE: ***Bissette** a-46. **Buckler** c-32-40p. **Ditko** a-9, 12, 41, 45. **Golden** a-10. **Howard** a-13i. **Kaluta** c-8, 10, 11, 14, 16, 29. **Kubert** c-41, 42. **Sheldon Mayer** a-43p. **McWilliams** a-35. **Nasser** a-24. **Newton** a-30p. **Nino** a-1, 13, 19. **Orlando** c-13, 30, 43, 45i. **N. Redondo** a-4, 5, 29. **Rogers** c-26. **Spiegle** a-31-41. **Wrightson** c-5, 44.*

**SECRETS OF HAUNTED HOUSE SPECIAL** (See DC Special Series #12)

**SECRETS OF LIFE** (See 4-Color #749)

**SECRETS OF LOVE** (See Popular Teen-Agers . . .)

**SECRETS OF LOVE AND MARRIAGE**
V2#1, Aug, 1956 - V2#25, June, 1961
Charlton Comics

| | | | |
|---|---|---|---|
| V2#1 | 1.70 | 5.00 | 12.00 |
| V2#2-6 | 1.00 | 3.00 | 7.00 |
| V2#7-9(All 68 pgs.) | .70 | 2.00 | 5.00 |
| 10-25 | .70 | 2.00 | 4.00 |

**SECRETS OF MAGIC** (See Wisco)

**SECRETS OF SINISTER HOUSE** (Sinister H. of Secret Love #1-4)
No. 5, June-July, 1972 - No. 18, June-July, 1974
National Periodical Publications

| | | | |
|---|---|---|---|
| 5-9: 7-Redondo-a | | .50 | 1.00 |
| 10-Neal Adams-a(i) | .50 | 1.50 | 3.00 |

| | Good | Fine | N-Mint |
|---|---|---|---|
| 11-18: 17-Barry-a | | .35 | .70 |

NOTE: ***Alcala** a-6, 13, 14. **Kaluta** c-6, 7. **Nino** a-8, 11-13. Ambrose Bierce adapt.-#14.*

**SECRETS OF THE LEGION OF SUPER-HEROES**
Jan, 1981 - No. 3, March, 1981 (Mini-series)
DC Comics

| | | | |
|---|---|---|---|
| 1-Origin of the Legion | | .50 | 1.00 |
| 2,3: 2-Retells origins of Brainiac 5, Shrinking Violet, Sun-Boy, Bouncing Boy, Ultra-Boy, Matter-Eater Lad, Mon-El, Karate Kid, & Dream Girl | | .40 | .80 |

**SECRETS OF TRUE LOVE**
February, 1958
St. John Publishing Co.

| | | | |
|---|---|---|---|
| 1 | 1.70 | 5.00 | 12.00 |

**SECRETS OF YOUNG BRIDES**
No. 5, Sept, 1957 - No. 44, Oct, 1964; July, 1975 - No. 9, Nov, 1976
Charlton Comics

| | | | |
|---|---|---|---|
| 5 | 1.70 | 5.00 | 12.00 |
| 6-10: 8-Negligee panel | .85 | 2.60 | 6.00 |
| 11-20 | .70 | 2.00 | 5.00 |
| 21-30: Last 10 cent issue? | .70 | 2.00 | 4.00 |
| 31-44 | .35 | 1.00 | 2.00 |
| 1-9 (2nd series) | | .30 | .60 |

**SECRET SQUIRREL** (TV)
October, 1966 (Hanna-Barbera)
Gold Key

| | | | |
|---|---|---|---|
| 1 | 3.00 | 9.00 | 21.00 |
| Kite Fun Book (1966, 16p, 5x7¼", soft-c)-PG&E & Southern California Edison editions (SCE has Reddy Kilowatt x-over) | 3.00 | 9.00 | 21.00 |

**SECRET STORY ROMANCES** (Becomes True Tales of Love)
Nov, 1953 - No. 21, Mar, 1956
Atlas Comics (TCI)

| | | | |
|---|---|---|---|
| 1-Everett-a | 4.50 | 14.00 | 32.00 |
| 2 | 2.30 | 7.00 | 16.00 |
| 3-11: 11-Last pre-code (2/55) | 1.70 | 5.00 | 12.00 |
| 12-21 | 1.50 | 4.50 | 10.00 |

NOTE: ***Colletta** a-10, 14, 15, 17, 21; c-10, 14, 17.*

**SECRET VOICE, THE** (See Great American Comics Presents . . .)

**SECRET WARS II** (Also see Marvel Super Heroes . . .)
July, 1985 - No. 9, Mar, 1986 (maxi-series)
Marvel Comics Group

| | | | |
|---|---|---|---|
| 1-Byrne/Austin-c | .30 | .90 | 1.80 |
| 2-9: 9-Double sized (75 cents) | | .65 | 1.30 |

**SECTAURS**
June, 1985 - No. 10?, 1986 (75 cents, color)
Marvel Comics Group

| | | | |
|---|---|---|---|
| 1-10: Based on Coleco Toys | | .40 | .80 |
| 1-Coleco giveaway; diff-c | | .40 | .80 |

**SEDUCTION OF THE INNOCENT** (Also see N. Y. State Joint Legis. Committee to Study . . .)
1953, 1954 (399 pages) (Hardback)
Rinehart & Co., Inc., N. Y. (Also printed in Canada by Clarke, Irwin & Co. Ltd., Toronto)

Written by Dr. Fredric Wertham

| | | | |
|---|---|---|---|
| (1st Version)-with bibliographical note intact (several copies got out before the comic publishers forced the removal of this page) | | 70.00 | 150.00 |
| with dust jacket . . . . | | 150.00 | 300.00 |
| (2nd Version)-without bibliographical note | | 42.00 | 90.00 |
| with dust jacket . . . . | | 65.00 | 140.00 |

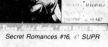

*Secret Romances #16, © SUPR*

*Secrets of the L.S.H. #1, © DC*

*Secret Story Romances #15, © MEG*

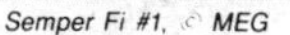
Semper Fi #1, © MEG

Sensation Comics #1, © DC

Sensation Mystery #115, © DC

| | Good | Fine | N-Mint |
|---|---|---|---|
| (3rd Version)-Published in England by Kennikat Press, 1954, 399pp. has bibliographical page | | 30.00 | 60.00 |
| 1972 r-/of 3rd version; 400pgs w/bibliography page; Kennikat Press | | 12.00 | 24.00 |

NOTE: *Material from this book appeared in the November, 1953(Vol.70, pp50-53,214) issue of the* ***Ladies' Home Journal*** *under the title "What Parents Don't Know About Comic Books." With the release of this book, Dr. Wertham reveals seven years of research attempting to link juvenile delinquency to comic books. Many illustrations showing excessive violence, sex, sadism, and torture are shown. This book was used at the Kefauver Senate hearings which led to the Comics Code Authority. Because of the influence this book had on the comic industry and the collector's interest in it, we feel this listing is justified. Also see* ***Parade of Pleasure.***

**SEDUCTION OF THE INNOCENT!**
Nov, 1985 - No. 6, April, 1986 ($1.75, color)
Eclipse Comics

| | Good | Fine | N-Mint |
|---|---|---|---|
| 1-6: Double listed under cover title #7 on | .30 | .90 | 1.80 |
| ...3-D 1(10/85; $2.25 cover)-Contains unpub. Advs. Into Darkness #15 (pre-code) (36 pgs.); Dave Stevens-c | .40 | 1.15 | 2.30 |
| 2-D 1 (100 copy limited signed & numbered edition)(B&W) | .85 | 2.50 | 5.00 |
| ...3-D 2 (4/86)-Baker, Toth-r; Wrightson-c | .40 | 1.25 | 2.50 |
| 2-D 2 (100 copy limited signed & numbered edition)(B&W) | .85 | 2.50 | 5.00 |

**SELECT DETECTIVE**
Aug-Sept, 1948 - No. 3, Dec-Jan, 1948-49
D. S. Publishing Co.

| | Good | Fine | N-Mint |
|---|---|---|---|
| 1-Matt Baker-a | 9.30 | 28.00 | 65.00 |
| 2-Baker, McWilliams-a | 6.50 | 19.00 | 45.00 |
| 3 | 5.00 | 15.00 | 35.00 |

**SEMPER FI** (Tales of the Marine Corps)
Dec, 1988 - No. 9, Aug, 1989 (75 cents, color)
Marvel Comics

| | Good | Fine | N-Mint |
|---|---|---|---|
| 1-9: Severin-c/a, Glanzman back-up-a in all | | .40 | .80 |

**SENSATIONAL POLICE CASES** (Becomes Captain Steve Savage, 2nd series)
1952; 1954 - No. 4, 1954
Avon Periodicals

| | Good | Fine | N-Mint |
|---|---|---|---|
| nn-100 pg. issue (1952, 25 cents)-Kubert & Kinstler-a | 19.00 | 58.00 | 135.00 |
| 1 (1954) | 7.00 | 21.00 | 50.00 |
| 2,3: 2-Kirbyish-a | 5.00 | 15.00 | 35.00 |
| 4-Reprint/Saint #5 | 5.00 | 15.00 | 35.00 |

**SENSATIONAL POLICE CASES**
No date (1963?)
I. W. Enterprises

| | Good | Fine | N-Mint |
|---|---|---|---|
| Reprint #5-Reprints Prison Break #5(1952-Avon); Infantino-a | 1.00 | 3.00 | 7.00 |

**SENSATIONAL SHE-HULK, THE** (Also see Savage She-Hulk)
May, 1989 - Present ($1.50, color, deluxe format) (She-Hulk #21 on)
Marvel Comics

| | Good | Fine | N-Mint |
|---|---|---|---|
| 1-Byrne-c/a(p)/scripts begin, end #8 | .35 | 1.00 | 2.00 |
| 2-8: 4-Reintro G.A. Blonde Phantom | .30 | .90 | 1.75 |
| 9-26: 14-17-Howard the Duck app. 21-23-Return of the Blonde Phantom. 22-All Winners Squad app. | .25 | .75 | 1.50 |

**SENSATIONAL SHE-HULK IN CEREMONY, THE**
1989 - No. 2, 1989 ($3.95, squarebound, 52 pgs.)
Marvel Comics

| | Good | Fine | N-Mint |
|---|---|---|---|
| nn-Part 1, nn-Part 2 | .70 | 2.00 | 4.00 |

**SENSATIONAL SPIDER-MAN**
April, 1989 ($5.95, color, squarebound, 80 pgs.)
Marvel Comics

| | Good | Fine | N-Mint |
|---|---|---|---|
| 1-r/Amaz. Spider-Man Annual #14,15 by Miller and Annual #8 by Kirby/Ditko | 1.00 | 3.00 | 6.00 |

**SENSATION COMICS** (Sensation Mystery #110 on)
Jan, 1942 - No. 109, May-June, 1952
National Periodical Publ./All-American

| | Good | Fine | VF-NM | NM/Mint |
|---|---|---|---|---|
| 1-Origin Mr. Terrific, Wildcat, The Gay Ghost, & Little Boy Blue; Wonder Woman(cont'd from All Star #8), The Black Pirate begin; intro. Justice & Fair Play Club | 417.00 | 1040.00 | 2500.00 | 3600.00 |

(Estimated up to 150 total copies exist, 7 in NM/Mint)

1-Reprint, Oversize 13½"x10." **WARNING:** This comic is an exact duplicate reprint of the original except for its size. DC published it in 1974 with a second cover titling it as a Famous First Edition. There have been many reported cases of the outer cover being removed and the interior sold as the original edition. The reprint with the new outer cover removed is practically worthless.

| | Good | Fine | N-Mint |
|---|---|---|---|
| 2 | 150.00 | 450.00 | 1050.00 |
| 3-W. Woman gets secretary's job | 87.00 | 260.00 | 610.00 |
| 4-1st app. Stretch Skinner in Wildcat | 79.00 | 235.00 | 550.00 |
| 5-Intro. Justin, Black Pirate's son | 59.00 | 175.00 | 410.00 |
| 6-Origin/1st app. Wonder Woman's magic lasso | 52.00 | 155.00 | 360.00 |
| 7-10 | 48.00 | 145.00 | 335.00 |
| 11-20: 13-Hitler, Tojo, Mussolini-c | 41.00 | 122.00 | 285.00 |
| 21-30 | 30.00 | 90.00 | 210.00 |
| 31-33 | 23.00 | 70.00 | 160.00 |
| 34-Sargon, the Sorcerer begins, ends #36; begins again #52 | 23.00 | 70.00 | 160.00 |
| 35-40: 38-Xmas-c | 19.00 | 57.00 | 135.00 |
| 41-50: 43-The Whip app. | 16.00 | 48.00 | 110.00 |
| 51-60: 51-Last Black Pirate. 56,57-Sargon by Kubert | 14.00 | 43.00 | 100.00 |
| 61-80: 63-Last Mr. Terrific. 65,66-Wildcat by Kubert. 68-Origin Huntress | 14.00 | 43.00 | 100.00 |
| 81-Used in **SOTI**, pg. 33,34; Krigstein-a | 16.00 | 48.00 | 110.00 |
| 82-90: 83-Last Sargon. 86-The Atom app. 90-Last Wildcat | 11.50 | 34.00 | 80.00 |
| 91-Streak begins by Alex Toth | 11.50 | 34.00 | 80.00 |
| 92,93: 92-Toth-a, 2 pgs. | 11.00 | 32.00 | 75.00 |
| 94-1st all girl issue | 13.00 | 40.00 | 90.00 |
| 95-99,101-106: Wonder Woman ends. 99-1st app. Astra, Girl of the Future, ends 106. 105-Last 52 pgs. | 13.00 | 40.00 | 90.00 |
| 100 | 18.00 | 54.00 | 125.00 |
| 107-(Scarce)-1st mystery issue; Toth-a | 24.00 | 70.00 | 165.00 |
| 108-(Scarce)-Johnny Peril by Toth(p) | 21.00 | 62.00 | 145.00 |
| 109-(Scarce)-Johnny Peril by Toth(p) | 24.00 | 70.00 | 165.00 |

NOTE: ***Krigstein*** *a-(Wildcat)-81, 83, 84.* ***Moldoff*** *Black Pirate-1-25; Black Pirate not in 34-36, 43-48. Wonder Woman by* ***H. G. Peter,*** *all issues except #8, 17-19, 21.* ***Toth*** *a-91, 98.*

**SENSATION MYSTERY** (Formerly Sensation #1-109)
No. 110, July-Aug, 1952 - No. 116, July-Aug, 1953
National Periodical Publications

| | Good | Fine | N-Mint |
|---|---|---|---|
| 110-Johnny Peril continues | 13.00 | 40.00 | 90.00 |
| 111-116-Johnny Peril in all | 12.00 | 36.00 | 85.00 |

NOTE: ***Colan*** *a-114p.* ***Giunta*** *a-112.* ***G. Kane*** *c-112, 113, 115.*

**SENSEI**
Aug, 1989 - No. 4, Dec, 1989 ($2.75, color, mini-series, deluxe)
First Comics

| | Good | Fine | N-Mint |
|---|---|---|---|
| 1-4: 1-Mayerik painted-c | .45 | 1.40 | 2.80 |

**SENTINELS OF JUSTICE, THE** (See Americomics & Captain Paragon & ...)

**SERAPHIM**
May, 1990 ($2.50, color, adults, 28 pgs.)
Innovation Publishing

| | Good | Fine | N-Mint |
|---|---|---|---|
| 1 | .40 | 1.25 | 2.50 |

**SERGEANT BARNEY BARKER** (G. I. Tales #4 on)
Aug, 1956 - No. 3, Dec, 1956
Atlas Comics (MCI)

| | Good | Fine | N-Mint |
|---|---|---|---|
| 1-Severin-a(4) | 8.00 | 24.00 | 55.00 |
| 2,3-Severin-a(4) | 5.00 | 15.00 | 35.00 |

**SERGEANT BILKO** (Phil Silvers) (TV)
May-June, 1957 - No. 18, Mar-Apr, 1960
National Periodical Publications

| | Good | Fine | N-Mint |
|---|---|---|---|
| 1 | 22.00 | 65.00 | 150.00 |
| 2 | 14.00 | 43.00 | 100.00 |
| 3-5 | 12.00 | 36.00 | 85.00 |
| 6-18: 11,12,15,17-Photo-c | 10.00 | 30.00 | 70.00 |

**SGT. BILKO'S PVT. DOBERMAN** (TV)
June-July, 1958 - No. 11, Feb-Mar, 1960
National Periodical Publications

| | Good | Fine | N-Mint |
|---|---|---|---|
| 1 | 16.00 | 48.00 | 110.00 |
| 2 | 10.00 | 30.00 | 70.00 |
| 3-5: 5-Photo-c | 8.00 | 24.00 | 55.00 |
| 6-11: 6,9-Photo-c | 5.70 | 17.00 | 40.00 |

**SGT. DICK CARTER OF THE U.S. BORDER PATROL** (See Holyoke One-Shot)

**SGT. FURY** (& His Howling Commandos)(See Special Marvel Ed.)
May, 1963 - No. 167, Dec, 1981
Marvel Comics Group (BPC earlier issues)

| | Good | Fine | N-Mint |
|---|---|---|---|
| 1-1st app. Sgt. Nick Fury; Kirby/Ayers-c/a | 36.00 | 107.00 | 250.00 |
| 2-Kirby-a | 13.00 | 40.00 | 90.00 |
| 3-5: 3-Reed Richards x-over. 4-Death of Junior Juniper. 5-1st Baron Strucker app.; Kirby-a | 8.50 | 25.50 | 60.00 |
| 6-10: 8-Baron Zemo, 1st Percival Pinkerton app. 10-1st app. Capt. Savage (the Skipper) | 6.50 | 19.00 | 45.00 |
| 11,12,14-20: 14-1st Blitz Squad. 18-Death of Pamela Hawley | 3.15 | 9.50 | 22.00 |
| 13-Captain America & Bucky app.(12/64); 1st Capt. America x-over outside The Avengers; Kirby-a | 9.30 | 28.00 | 65.00 |
| 21-30: 25-Red Skull app. 27-1st app. Eric Koenig; origin Fury's eye patch | 1.70 | 5.00 | 12.00 |
| 31-50: 34-Origin Howling Commandos. 35-Eric Koenig joins Howlers. 43-Bob Hope, Glen Miller app. 44-Flashback-Howlers 1st mission | 1.30 | 4.00 | 9.00 |
| 51-100: 64-Capt. Savage & Raiders x-over. 76-Fury's Father app. in WWI story. 98-Deadly Dozen x-over. 100-Captain America, Fantastic Four cameos; Stan Lee, Martin Goodman & others app. | .70 | 2.00 | 5.00 |
| 101-167: 101-Origin retold. 167-reprints #1 | .55 | 1.65 | 3.30 |
| Annual 1('65, 25 cents, 72pgs.)-r/#4,5 & new-a | 4.30 | 13.00 | 30.00 |
| Special 2('66) | 1.50 | 4.50 | 10.00 |
| Special 3('67) | 1.15 | 3.50 | 8.00 |
| Special 4('68) | 1.00 | 3.00 | 7.00 |
| Special 5-7('69-11/71) | .70 | 2.00 | 5.00 |

NOTE: ***Ditko*** *a-15i.* ***Gil Kane*** *c-37, 96.* ***Kirby*** *a-1-8, 13p, 167p(r). Special 5; c-1-20, 25, 167p.* ***Severin*** *a-44-46, 48, 162, 164; inks-4, 6, 49-79; c-4i, 5, 6, 44, 46, 110, 149i, 155i, 162-166.* ***Sutton*** *a-57p. Reprints in #80, 82, 85, 87, 89, 91, 93, 95, 99, 101, 103, 105, 107, 109, 111, 145.*

**SGT. FURY AND HIS HOWLING DEFENDERS** (See The Defenders)

**SERGEANT PRESTON OF THE YUKON** (TV)
No. 344, Aug, 1951 - No. 29, Nov-Jan, 1958-59
Dell Publishing Co.

| | Good | Fine | N-Mint |
|---|---|---|---|
| 4-Color 344(#1)-Sergeant Preston & his dog Yukon King begin; painted-c begin, end #18 | 6.50 | 19.00 | 45.00 |
| 4-Color 373,397,419('52) | 4.00 | 12.00 | 28.00 |
| 5(11-1/52-53)-10(2-4/54) | 3.00 | 9.00 | 21.00 |
| 11,12,14-17 | 2.30 | 7.00 | 16.00 |
| 13-Origin Sgt. Preston | 3.00 | 9.00 | 21.00 |
| 18-Origin Yukon King; last painted-c | 3.00 | 9.00 | 21.00 |
| 19-29: All photo-c | 3.50 | 10.50 | 24.00 |

**SERGEANT PRESTON OF THE YUKON**
1956 (4 comic booklets) (Soft-c, 16p, 7x2½" & 5x2½")
Giveaways with Quaker Cereals

| | Good | Fine | N-Mint |
|---|---|---|---|
| "How He Found Yukon King, The Case That Made Him A Sergeant, How Yukon King Saved Him From The Wolves, How He Became A Mountie" each... | 4.00 | 12.00 | 28.00 |

**SGT. ROCK** (Formerly Our Army at War; see Brave & the Bold #52)
No. 302, March, 1977 - No. 422, July, 1988
National Periodical Publications/DC Comics

| | Good | Fine | N-Mint |
|---|---|---|---|
| 302 | .85 | 2.60 | 6.00 |
| 303-320: 318-Reprints | .70 | 2.00 | 4.00 |
| 321-350 | .50 | 1.50 | 3.00 |
| 351-422: 422-1st Joe, Adam, Andy Kubert-a team | .25 | .75 | 1.50 |
| Annual 2-4: 2(9/82), 3(8/83), 4(8/84) | .35 | 1.00 | 2.00 |

NOTE: ***Estrada*** *a-322, 327, 331, 336, 337, 341, 342i.* ***Glanzman*** *a-384, 421.* ***Kubert*** *a-302, 303, 305r, 306, 328, 351, 356, 368, 373, 422; c-317, 318r, 319-323, 325-333-on, Annual 2, 3.* ***Spiegle*** *a-382, Annual 2, 3.* ***Thorne*** *a-384.* ***Toth*** *a-385r.*

**SGT. ROCK SPECIAL** (Also see DC Special Series #3)
Oct, 1988 - Present ($2.00, color, quarterly, 52 pgs.)
DC Comics

| | Good | Fine | N-Mint |
|---|---|---|---|
| 1-8,10: All reprints; 5-r/1st Sgt. Rock/Our Army At War #81. 7-Tomahawk-r by Thorne. 10-All Rock issue | .35 | 1.00 | 2.00 |
| 9-Enemy Ace-r by Kubert | .40 | 1.25 | 2.50 |

NOTE: ***Neal Adams*** *r-1, 8.* ***Chaykin*** *r-3, 9(2pg.); c-3.* ***Drucker*** *r-6.* ***Heath*** *r-5, 9, 10.* ***Krigstein*** *r-4, 8.* ***Kubert*** *r-1-10; c-1p, 2, 8.* ***Miller*** *r-6p.* ***Severin*** *r-3, 6, 10.* ***Simonson*** *r-2, 4; c-4.* ***Thorne*** *r-7.* ***Toth*** *r-2, 8.* ***Wood*** *r-4.*

**SGT. ROCK SPECTACULAR** (See DC Special Series #13)

**SGT. ROCK'S PRIZE BATTLE TALES** (See DC Special Series #18)
Winter, 1964 (One Shot) (Giant - 80 pgs.)(See 80 Page Giant #7)
National Periodical Publications

| | Good | Fine | N-Mint |
|---|---|---|---|
| 1-Kubert, Heath-r; new Kubert-c | 4.30 | 13.00 | 30.00 |

**SGT. STRYKER'S DEATH SQUAD** (See Savage Combat Tales)

**SERGIO ARAGONES' GROO THE WANDERER** (Also see Groo...)
March, 1985 - Present
Epic Comics (Marvel)

| | Good | Fine | N-Mint |
|---|---|---|---|
| 1-Aragones-c/a in all | 2.65 | 8.00 | 18.00 |
| 2 | 1.70 | 5.00 | 12.00 |
| 3-5 | 1.50 | 4.50 | 9.00 |
| 6-10 | 1.15 | 3.50 | 7.00 |
| 11-20 | .85 | 2.50 | 5.00 |
| 21-26 | .60 | 1.75 | 3.50 |
| 27-35-($1.00-c) | .50 | 1.50 | 3.00 |
| 36-48 ($1.50-c) | .35 | 1.00 | 2.00 |
| 49,51-76 ($1.00-c) | | .50 | 1.00 |
| 50-($1.50, double size) | .25 | .75 | 1.50 |

**SEVEN BLOCK**
1990 ($4.50, color, one-shot, 52 pgs.)
Epic Comics (Marvel)

| | Good | Fine | N-Mint |
|---|---|---|---|
| 1 | .75 | 2.25 | 4.50 |

**SEVEN DEAD MEN** (See Complete Mystery #1)

**SEVEN DWARFS** (See 4-Color #227, 382)

**SEVEN SEAS COMICS**
Apr, 1946 - No. 6, 1947 (no month)
Universal Phoenix Features/Leader No. 6

| | Good | Fine | N-Mint |
|---|---|---|---|
| 1-South Sea Girl by Matt Baker, Capt. Cutlass begin; Tugboat Tessie by Baker app. | 32.00 | 95.00 | 225.00 |
| 2 | 27.00 | 81.00 | 190.00 |
| 3-6: 3-Six pg. Feldstein-a | 25.00 | 75.00 | 175.00 |

NOTE: ***Baker*** *a-1-6; c-3-6.*

*Sgt. Fury #2, © MEG*

*Sergio Aragones' Groo... #62, © MEG*

*Seven Seas Comics #6, © Leader Publ.*

The Shadow #1 (10-11/73), © Conde Nast

Shadow Comics V1#1, © Conde Nast Publ.

Shadowmasters #4, © MEG

**1776** (See Charlton Classic Library)

**7TH VOYAGE OF SINBAD, THE** (See 4-Color #944)

**77 SUNSET STRIP** (TV)
No. 1066, 1-3/60 - No. 2, 2/63 (All photo-c)
Dell Publ. Co./Gold Key

| | Good | Fine | N-Mint |
|---|---|---|---|
| 4-Color 1066-Toth-a | 8.00 | 24.00 | 55.00 |
| 4-Color 1106,1159-Toth-a | 6.50 | 19.00 | 45.00 |
| 4-Color 1211,1263,1291, 01-742-209(7-9/62)-Manning-a in all | 5.30 | 16.00 | 38.00 |
| 1(11/62-G.K.), 2-Manning-a in each | 5.00 | 15.00 | 35.00 |

**77TH BENGAL LANCERS, THE** (See 4-Color #791)

**SEYMOUR, MY SON** (See More Seymour)
September, 1963
Archie Publications (Radio Comics)

| | Good | Fine | N-Mint |
|---|---|---|---|
| 1 | 3.00 | 9.00 | 21.00 |

**SHADE, THE CHANGING MAN** (See Cancelled Comic Cavalcade)
June-July, 1977 - No. 8, Aug-Sept, 1978 (Also see Suicide Squad #16)
National Periodical Publications/DC Comics

| | Good | Fine | N-Mint |
|---|---|---|---|
| 1-Ditko-c/a in all | .50 | 1.50 | 3.00 |
| 2-8 | .35 | 1.00 | 2.00 |

**SHADE, THE CHANGING MAN** (2nd series)
July, 1990 - Present ($1.50, color, mature readers)
DC Comics

| | Good | Fine | N-Mint |
|---|---|---|---|
| 1-($2.50, 52 pgs.) | .40 | 1.25 | 2.50 |
| 2-10 | .25 | .75 | 1.50 |

**SHADOW, THE**
Aug, 1964 - No. 8, Sept, 1965 (All 12 cents)
Archie Comics (Radio Comics)

| | Good | Fine | N-Mint |
|---|---|---|---|
| 1 | 2.85 | 8.50 | 20.00 |
| 2-8-The Fly app. in some issues | 1.70 | 5.00 | 12.00 |

**SHADOW, THE**
Oct-Nov, 1973 - No. 12, Aug-Sept, 1975
National Periodical Publications

| | Good | Fine | N-Mint |
|---|---|---|---|
| 1-Kaluta-a begins | 1.70 | 5.00 | 12.00 |
| 2 | 1.00 | 3.00 | 7.00 |
| 3-Kaluta/Wrightson-a | 1.15 | 3.50 | 8.00 |
| 4,6-Kaluta-a ends | .70 | 2.00 | 5.00 |
| 5,7-12: 11-The Avenger (pulp character) x-over | .50 | 1.50 | 3.00 |

NOTE: ***Craig*** *a-10.* ***Cruz*** *a-10-12.* ***Kaluta*** *a-1, 2, 3p, 4, 6; c-1-4, 6, 10-12.* ***Kubert*** *c-9.* ***Robbins*** *a-5, 7-9; c-5, 7, 8.*

**SHADOW, THE**
May, 1986 - No. 4, Aug, 1986 (Mini-series, mature readers)
DC Comics

| | Good | Fine | N-Mint |
|---|---|---|---|
| 1-Chaykin-a in all | 1.15 | 3.50 | 7.00 |
| 2-4 | .75 | 2.25 | 4.50 |
| . . .Blood & Judgement (1987, $12.95)-r/Shadow #1-4, 1986 | 2.35 | 7.00 | 14.00 |

**SHADOW, THE** (Also see Marvel Graphic Novel #35)
Aug, 1987 - No. 19, Jan, 1989 ($1.50, mature readers)
DC Comics

| | Good | Fine | N-Mint |
|---|---|---|---|
| 1 | .50 | 1.50 | 3.00 |
| 2-19: 7-Rogers-c/a. 13-Death of Shadow. 18-E.C.-c swipe | .35 | 1.00 | 2.00 |
| Annual 1 (12/87, $2.25)-Orlando-a | .40 | 1.25 | 2.50 |
| Annual 2 (12/88, $2.50) | .40 | 1.25 | 2.50 |

**SHADOW COMICS** (Pulp, radio)
March, 1940 - V9#5, Aug, 1949
Street & Smith Publications

NOTE: *The Shadow first appeared in Fame & Fortune Magazine, 1929, began on radio the same year, and was featured in pulps beginning in 1931. The early covers of this series were reprinted from the pulp covers.*

| | Good | Fine | N-Mint |
|---|---|---|---|
| V1#1-Shadow, Doc Savage, Bill Barnes, Nick Carter, Frank Merriwell, Iron Munro, the Astonishing Man begin | 200.00 | 500.00 | 1200.00 |
| 2-The Avenger begins, ends #6; Capt. Fury only app. | 72.00 | 215.00 | 500.00 |
| 3(nn-5/40)-Norgil the Magician app. | 57.00 | 171.00 | 400.00 |
| 4,5: 4-The Three Musketeers begins, ends #8. 5-Doc Savage ends | 50.00 | 150.00 | 350.00 |
| 6,8,9: 9-Norgil the Magician app. | 40.00 | 120.00 | 280.00 |
| 7-Origin & 1st app. Hooded Wasp & Wasplet; series ends V3#8 | 45.00 | 135.00 | 315.00 |
| 10-Origin The Iron Ghost, ends #11; The Dead End Kids begins, ends #14 | 40.00 | 120.00 | 280.00 |
| 11-Origin The Hooded Wasp & Wasplet retold | 40.00 | 120.00 | 280.00 |
| 12-Dead End Kids app. | 34.00 | 103.00 | 240.00 |
| V2#1,2(11/41): 2-Dead End Kids story | 30.00 | 90.00 | 210.00 |
| 3-Origin & 1st app. Supersnipe; series begins; Little Nemo story | 40.00 | 120.00 | 280.00 |
| 4,5: 4-Little Nemo story | 29.00 | 85.00 | 200.00 |
| 6-9: 6-Blackstone the Magician app. | 26.00 | 77.00 | 180.00 |
| 10-12: 10-Supersnipe app. | 26.00 | 77.00 | 180.00 |
| V3#1-12: 10-Doc Savage begins, not in V5#5, V6#10-12, V8#4 | 23.00 | 70.00 | 160.00 |
| V4#1-12 | 21.00 | 62.00 | 145.00 |
| V5#1-12 | 19.00 | 58.00 | 135.00 |
| V6#1-11: 9-Intro. Shadow, Jr. | 18.00 | 54.00 | 125.00 |
| 12-Powell-c/a; atom bomb panels | 19.00 | 58.00 | 135.00 |
| V7#1,2,5,7-9,12: 2,5-Shadow, Jr. app.; Powell-a | 19.00 | 58.00 | 135.00 |
| 3,6,11-Powell-c/a | 21.00 | 62.00 | 145.00 |
| 4-Powell-c/a; Atom bomb panels | 23.00 | 70.00 | 160.00 |
| 10(1/48)-Flying Saucer issue; Powell-c/a (2nd of this theme; see The Spirit 9/28/47) | 27.00 | 80.00 | 185.00 |
| V8#1-12-Powell-a | 21.00 | 62.00 | 145.00 |
| V9#1,5-Powell-a | 19.00 | 58.00 | 135.00 |
| 2-4-Powell-c/a | 21.00 | 62.00 | 145.00 |

NOTE: ***Powell*** *art in most issues beginning V6#12.*

**SHADOWLINE SAGA: CRITICAL MASS, A** Graphic novel)
Jan, 1990 - No. 7, July, 1990 ($4.95, limited series, 68 pgs.)
Epic Comics (Marvel) (#1 shows Jan, 1989 by mistake)

| | Good | Fine | N-Mint |
|---|---|---|---|
| 1-6: Dr. Zero, Powerline, St. George | .85 | 2.50 | 5.00 |
| 7-(5.95, 84 pgs.)-Morrow-a; Williamson-c(i) | 1.00 | 3.00 | 6.00 |

NOTE: ***Bolton*** *c-3.* ***Morrow*** *a-1, 3, 4, 6.* ***Sienkiewicz*** *a-1; c-5.* ***Spiegle*** *a-4.*

**SHADOWMASTERS** (See Punisher #24)
10/89 - No. 4, 1/90 ($3.95, squarebound, limited series, 52pgs.)
Marvel Comics

| | Good | Fine | N-Mint |
|---|---|---|---|
| 1-4: 1,4-Heath-i; story cont'd from Punisher | .70 | 2.00 | 4.00 |

**SHADOW OF THE BATMAN**
Dec, 1985 - No. 5, Apr, 1986 ($1.75 cover; mini-series)
DC Comics

| | Good | Fine | N-Mint |
|---|---|---|---|
| 1-Detective-r (all have wraparound-c) | 1.85 | 5.50 | 11.00 |
| 2,3,5 | 1.15 | 3.50 | 7.00 |
| 4-Joker-c/story | 1.70 | 5.00 | 10.00 |

NOTE: ***Austin*** *a(new)-2i, 3i; r-2-4i.* ***Rogers*** *a(new)-1, 2p, 3p, 4, 5; r-1-5p; c-1-5.*

**SHADOW PLAY** (Tales of the Supernatural)
June, 1982
Whitman Publications

| | Good | Fine | N-Mint |
|---|---|---|---|
| 1-Painted-c | | .30 | .60 |

**SHADOWS FROM BEYOND** (Formerly Unusual Tales)
V2#50, October, 1966
Charlton Comics

| | Good | Fine | N-Mint |
|---|---|---|---|
| V2#50-Ditko-c | .75 | 2.25 | 4.50 |

**SHADOW STRIKES!, THE**
Sept, 1989 - Present ($1.75, color)
DC Comics

| | Good | Fine | N-Mint |
|---|---|---|---|
| 1-10: 5,6-Doc Savage x-over | .30 | .90 | 1.80 |
| Annual 1('89, $3.50, 68pgs.)-Spiegle-a; Kaluta-c | .60 | 1.75 | 3.50 |

**SHADOW WAR OF HAWKMAN**
May, 1985 - No. 4, Aug, 1985 (Mini-series)
DC Comics

| | Good | Fine | N-Mint |
|---|---|---|---|
| 1-4: Alcala inks | | .50 | 1.00 |

**SHAGGY DOG & THE ABSENT-MINDED PROFESSOR** (See 4-Color #985, Movie Comics & Walt Disney Showcase #46)

**SHANNA, THE SHE-DEVIL** (See Savage Tales #8)
Dec, 1972 - No. 5, Aug, 1973
Marvel Comics Group

| | Good | Fine | N-Mint |
|---|---|---|---|
| 1-Steranko-c; Tuska-a(p) | | .60 | 1.20 |
| 2-5: 2-Steranko-c | | .40 | .80 |

**SHARK FIGHTERS, THE** (See 4-Color No. 762)

**SHARP COMICS** (Slightly large size)
Winter, 1945-46 - V1#2, Spring, 1946 (52 pgs.)
H. C. Blackerby

| | Good | Fine | N-Mint |
|---|---|---|---|
| V1#1-Origin Dick Royce Planetarian | 17.00 | 51.00 | 120.00 |
| 2-Origin The Pioneer; Michael Morgan, Dick Royce, Sir Gallagher, Planetarian, Steve Hagen, Weeny and Pop app. | 13.00 | 40.00 | 90.00 |

**SHARPY FOX** (See Comic Capers & Funny Frolics)
1958; 1963
I. W. Enterprises/Super Comics

| | Good | Fine | N-Mint |
|---|---|---|---|
| 1,2-I.W. Reprint (1958) | .35 | 1.00 | 2.00 |
| 14-Super Reprint (1963) | .35 | 1.00 | 2.00 |

**SHATTER** (See Jon Sable #25-30)
June, 1985 ($1.75, one-shot, color, Baxter paper)
First Comics

| | Good | Fine | N-Mint |
|---|---|---|---|
| 1-1st computer-generated artwork in a comic book (1st & 2nd printings) | .30 | .90 | 1.80 |

NOTE: *1st printings have the number "1" included in the row of numbers at the bottom of the indicia.*

**SHATTER**
Dec, 1985 - No. 14, April, 1988 ($1.75 cover; deluxe paper)
First Comics

| | Good | Fine | N-Mint |
|---|---|---|---|
| 1-14: Computer-generated art and lettering | .30 | .90 | 1.80 |

**SHAZAM** (See Giant Comics to Color & Limited Collectors' Edition)

**SHAZAM!** (TV)(See World's Finest #253)
Feb, 1973 - No. 35, May-June, 1978
National Periodical Publications/DC Comics

| | Good | Fine | N-Mint |
|---|---|---|---|
| 1-1st revival of original Captain Marvel since G.A. (origin retold), by Beck; Capt. Marvel Jr. & Mary Marvel x-over | .35 | 1.00 | 2.00 |
| 2-35: 2,6-Infinity photo-c; re-intro Mr. Mind & Tawney. 4-Origin retold. 5-Capt. Marvel Jr. origin retold. 8-(100 pgs.)-r/Capt. Marvel Jr. by Raboy; origin/C.M. #80; origin Mary Marvel/C.M. #18. 10-Last C.C. Beck issue. 11-Shaffenberger-a begins. 12-17-(All 100 pgs.). 15-Lex Luthor x-over. 25-1st app. Isis. 30-1st DC app. 3 Lt. Marvels. 31-1st DC app. Minuteman. 34-Origin Capt. Nazi & Capt. Marvel Jr. retold | | .60 | 1.20 |

NOTE: *Reprints in #1-8, 10, 12-17, 21-24.* ***Beck*** *a-1-10, 12-17r, 21-24r; c-1, 3-9.* ***Nasser*** *c-35p.* ***Newton*** *a-35p.* ***Rayboy*** *a-5r, 8r, 17r.* ***Shaffenberger*** *a-11, 14-20, 25, 26, 27p, 28, 29-31p, 33i, 35i; c-20, 22, 23, 25, 26i, 27i, 28-33.*

**SHAZAM: THE NEW BEGINNING**
Apr, 1987 - No. 4, July, 1987 (Mini-series; Legends spin-off)
DC Comics

| | Good | Fine | N-Mint |
|---|---|---|---|
| 1-New origin Captain Marvel; Marvel Family cameos | .25 | .75 | 1.50 |
| 2-4: Sivana & Black Adam app. | | .60 | 1.20 |

**SHEA THEATRE COMICS**
No date (1940's) (32 pgs.)
Shea Theatre

| | Good | Fine | N-Mint |
|---|---|---|---|
| nn-Contains Rocket Comics; MLJ cover in mono color | 5.00 | 15.00 | 35.00 |

**SHEENA**
Dec, 1984 - No. 2, Feb, 1985 (Limited series, movie adaptation)
Marvel Comics Group

| | Good | Fine | N-Mint |
|---|---|---|---|
| 1,2-r-/Marvel Comics Super Special #34 | | .40 | .80 |

**SHEENA, QUEEN OF THE JUNGLE** (See Jerry Iger's Classic . . ., Jumbo Comics, & 3-D Sheena)
Spring, 1942; No. 2, Wint, 1942-43; No. 3, Spring, 1943; No. 4, Fall, 1948; No. 5, Sum, 1949; No. 6, Spring, 1950; No. 7-10, 1950(nd); No. 11, Spring, 1951 - No. 18, Winter, 1952-53 (#1,2: 68 pgs.)
Fiction House Magazines

| | Good | Fine | N-Mint |
|---|---|---|---|
| 1-Sheena begins | 118.00 | 355.00 | 825.00 |
| 2 (Winter, 1942/43) | 61.00 | 182.00 | 425.00 |
| 3 (Spring, 1943) | 40.00 | 120.00 | 280.00 |
| 4, 5 (Fall, 1948 - Sum., '49) | 25.00 | 75.00 | 175.00 |
| 6,7 (Spring, '50 - '50, 52 pgs.) | 22.00 | 65.00 | 150.00 |
| 8-10('50, 36 pgs.) | 19.00 | 57.00 | 130.00 |
| 11-18: 18-Used in **POP**, pg. 98 | 16.00 | 48.00 | 110.00 |
| I.W. Reprint #9-Reprints #17 | 2.50 | 7.50 | 15.00 |

**SHEENA 3-D** (Also see Blackthorne 3-D Series #1)
Jan, 1985 ($2.00)
Eclipse Comics

| | Good | Fine | N-Mint |
|---|---|---|---|
| 1-Dave Stevens-c | .50 | 1.50 | 3.00 |

**SHE-HULK** (See The Savage She-Hulk & The Sensational She-Hulk)

**SHERIFF BOB DIXON'S CHUCK WAGON** (TV)
November, 1950 (See Wild Bill Hickok #22)
Avon Periodicals

| | Good | Fine | N-Mint |
|---|---|---|---|
| 1-Kinstler-c/a(3) | 7.00 | 21.00 | 50.00 |

**SHERIFF OF COCHISE, THE**
1957 (16 pages) (TV Show)
Mobil Giveaway

| | Good | Fine | N-Mint |
|---|---|---|---|
| nn-Shaffenberger-a | 1.15 | 3.50 | 8.00 |

**SHERIFF OF TOMBSTONE**
Nov, 1958 - No. 17, Sept, 1961
Charlton Comics

| | Good | Fine | N-Mint |
|---|---|---|---|
| V1#1-Williamson/Severin-c | 4.00 | 12.00 | 28.00 |
| 2 | 2.30 | 7.00 | 16.00 |
| 3-17 | 1.30 | 4.00 | 9.00 |

**SHERLOCK HOLMES** (See Cases of . . ., 4-Color #1169,1245, Marvel Preview & Spectacular Stories)

**SHERLOCK HOLMES** (All New Baffling Adventures of . . .)
Oct, 1955 - No. 2, Mar, 1956 (Young Eagle #3 on?)
Charlton Comics

| | Good | Fine | N-Mint |
|---|---|---|---|
| 1-Dr. Neff, Ghost Breaker app. | 24.00 | 71.00 | 165.00 |
| 2 | 21.00 | 62.00 | 145.00 |

**SHERLOCK HOLMES** (Also see The Joker)
Sept-Oct, 1975
National Periodical Publications

| | Good | Fine | N-Mint |
|---|---|---|---|
| 1-Cruz-a; Simonson-c | | .50 | 1.00 |

**SHERRY THE SHOWGIRL** (Showgirls #4)
July, 1956 - No. 3, Dec, 1956; No. 5, Apr, 1957 - No. 7, Aug, 1957
Atlas Comics

| | Good | Fine | N-Mint |
|---|---|---|---|
| 1 | 4.50 | 14.00 | 32.00 |

*Shazam! #4, © DC*

*Sheena, Queen of the Jungle #4, © FH*

*Sherlock Holmes #2, © CC*

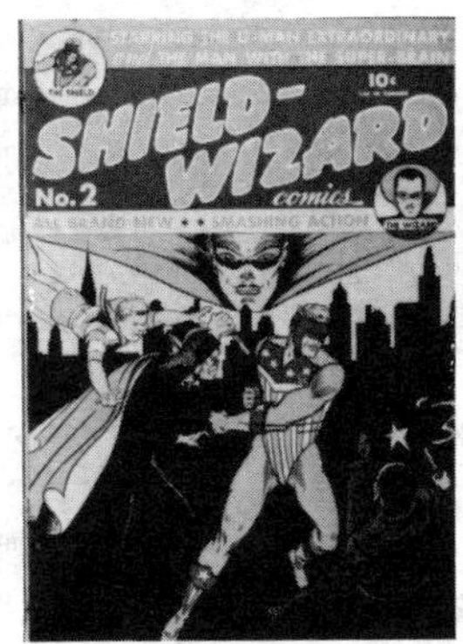

Shield Wizard Comics #2, © AP

Shocking Mystery Cases #55, © STAR

Shogun Warriors #1, © MEG

| | Good | Fine | N-Mint |
|---|---|---|---|
| 2 | 2.85 | 8.50 | 20.00 |
| 3,5-7 | 2.15 | 6.50 | 15.00 |

**SHIELD** (Nick Fury & His Agents of . . .) (Also see Nick Fury)
Feb, 1973 - No. 5, Oct, 1973 (All 20 cents)
Marvel Comics Group

| | Good | Fine | N-Mint |
|---|---|---|---|
| 1-Steranko-c | .70 | 2.00 | 4.00 |
| 2-Steranko flag-c | .35 | 1.00 | 2.00 |
| 3-5: 1-5 all contain-r from Strange Tales #146-155. 3-5-are cover-r; 3-Kirby/Steranko-c(r). 4-Steranko-c(r) | .35 | 1.00 | 2.00 |

NOTE: ***Buscema** a-3p(r). **Kirby** layouts 1-5; c-3 (w/**Steranko**). **Steranko** a-3r, 4r(2).*

**SHIELD, THE** (Becomes Shield-Steel Sterling #3; #1 titled 'Lancelot Strong;' also see Advs. of the Fly, Double Life of Private Strong, Fly Man, Mighty Comics, The Mighty Crusaders & The Original . . .)
June, 1983 - No. 2, Aug, 1983
Archie Enterprises, Inc.

| | Good | Fine | N-Mint |
|---|---|---|---|
| 1,2: Steel Sterling app. | | .45 | .90 |

**SHIELD-STEEL STERLING** (Formerly The Shield)
No. 3, Dec, 1983 (Becomes Steel Sterling No. 4)
Archie Enterprises, Inc.

| | Good | Fine | N-Mint |
|---|---|---|---|
| 3-Nino-a | | .45 | .90 |

**SHIELD WIZARD COMICS** (Also see Pep & Top-Notch Comics)
Summer, 1940 - No. 13, Spring, 1944
MLJ Magazines

| | Good | Fine | N-Mint |
|---|---|---|---|
| 1-(V1#5 on inside)-Origin The Shield by Irving Novick & The Wizard by Ed Ashe, Jr; Flag-c | 136.00 | 407.00 | 950.00 |
| 2-Origin The Shield retold; intro. Wizard's sidekick, Roy | 62.00 | 185.00 | 435.00 |
| 3,4 | 42.00 | 125.00 | 290.00 |
| 5-Dusty, the Boy Detective begins | 37.00 | 110.00 | 255.00 |
| 6-8: 6-Roy the Super Boy begins | 32.00 | 95.00 | 225.00 |
| 9-13: 13-Bondage-c | 27.00 | 81.00 | 190.00 |

**SHIP AHOY**
November, 1944 (52 pgs.)
Spotlight Publishers

| | Good | Fine | N-Mint |
|---|---|---|---|
| 1-L. B. Cole-c | 6.50 | 19.00 | 45.00 |

**SHMOO** (See Al Capp's . . . & Washable Jones & . . .)

**SHOCK** (Magazine)
(Reprints from horror comics) (Black & White)
May, 1969 - V3#4, Sept, 1971
Stanley Publications

| | Good | Fine | N-Mint |
|---|---|---|---|
| V1#1-Cover-r/Weird Tales of the Future #7 by Bernard Baily | 1.50 | 4.50 | 10.00 |
| 2-Wolverton-r/Weird Mysteries 5; r-Weird Mysteries #7 used in **SOTI**; cover r-/Weird Chills #1 | 1.30 | 4.00 | 9.00 |
| 3,5,6 | .70 | 2.00 | 5.00 |
| 4-Harrison/Williamson-r/Forbid. Worlds #6 | 1.00 | 3.00 | 7.00 |
| V2#2, V1#8, V2#4-6, V3#1-4 | .70 | 2.00 | 5.00 |

NOTE: ***Disbrow** r-V2#4; bondage c-V1#4, V2#6, V3#1.*

**SHOCK DETECTIVE CASES** (Formerly Crime Fighting Detective)
(Becomes Spook Detective Cases No. 22)
No. 20, Sept, 1952 - No. 21, Nov, 1952
Star Publications

| | Good | Fine | N-Mint |
|---|---|---|---|
| 20,21-L.B. Cole-c | 5.00 | 15.00 | 35.00 |

NOTE: ***Palais** a-20. No. 21-Fox-r.*

**SHOCK ILLUSTRATED** (Magazine format)
Sept-Oct, 1955 - No. 3, Spring, 1956 (Adult Entertainment on-c #1,2)
E. C. Comics

| | Good | Fine | N-Mint |
|---|---|---|---|
| 1-All by Kamen; drugs, prostitution, wife swapping | 3.50 | 10.50 | 24.00 |
| 2-Williamson-a redrawn from Crime SuspenStories #13 plus Ingels, Crandall, & Evans | 4.00 | 12.00 | 28.00 |
| 3-Only 100 known copies bound & given away at E.C. office; Crandall, Evans-a | 100.00 | 300.00 | 700.00 |

(Prices vary widely on this book)

**SHOCKING MYSTERY CASES** (Formerly Thrilling Crime Cases)
No. 50, Sept, 1952 - No. 60, Oct, 1954
Star Publications

| | Good | Fine | N-Mint |
|---|---|---|---|
| 50-Disbrow "Frankenstein" story | 13.00 | 40.00 | 90.00 |
| 51-Disbrow-a | 6.50 | 19.00 | 45.00 |
| 52-55,57-60 | 5.30 | 16.00 | 38.00 |
| 56-Drug use story | 6.00 | 18.00 | 42.00 |

NOTE: ***L. B. Cole** covers on all; a-60(2 pgs.). **Hollingsworth** a-52. **Morisi** a-55.*

**SHOCKING TALES DIGEST MAGAZINE**
Oct, 1981 (95 cents)
Harvey Publications

| | Good | Fine | N-Mint |
|---|---|---|---|
| 1-1957-58-r; Powell, Kirby, Nostrand-a | | .50 | 1.00 |

**SHOCK SUSPENSTORIES**
Feb-Mar, 1952 - No. 18, Dec-Jan, 1954-55
E. C. Comics

| | Good | Fine | N-Mint |
|---|---|---|---|
| 1-Classic Feldstein electrocution-c; Ray Bradbury adaptation | 50.00 | 150.00 | 350.00 |
| 2 | 30.00 | 90.00 | 210.00 |
| 3 | 21.00 | 62.00 | 145.00 |
| 4-Used in **SOTI**, pg. 387,388 | 21.00 | 62.00 | 145.00 |
| 5-Hanging-c | 19.00 | 58.00 | 135.00 |
| 6,7: 6-Classic bondage-c. 7-Classic face melting-c | 24.00 | 73.00 | 170.00 |
| 8-Williamson-a | 21.00 | 62.00 | 145.00 |
| 9-11: 9-Injury to eye panel. 10-Junkie story | 17.00 | 51.00 | 115.00 |
| 12-"The Monkey"-classic junkie cover/story; drug propaganda issue | 20.00 | 60.00 | 140.00 |
| 13-Frazetta's only solo story for E.C., 7 pgs. | 24.00 | 73.00 | 170.00 |
| 14-Used in Senate Investigation hearings | 13.00 | 40.00 | 90.00 |
| 15-Used in 1954 Reader's Digest article, "For the Kiddies to Read" | 13.00 | 40.00 | 90.00 |
| 16-"Red Dupe" editorial; rape story | 12.00 | 36.00 | 85.00 |
| 17,18 | 12.00 | 36.00 | 85.00 |

NOTE: ***Craig** a-11; c-11. **Crandall** a-9-13, 15-18. **Davis** a-1-5. **Evans** a-7, 8, 14-18; c-16-18. **Feldstein** c-1, 7-9, 12. **Ingels** a-1, 2, 6. **Kamen** a-in all; c-10. **Krigstein** a-14, 18. **Orlando** a-1, 3-7, 9, 10, 12, 16, 17. **Wood** a-2-15; c-2-6, 14.*

**SHOGUN WARRIORS**
Feb, 1979 - No. 20, Sept, 1980 (Based on Mattel toys)
Marvel Comics Group

| | Good | Fine | N-Mint |
|---|---|---|---|
| 1-Raydeen, Combatra, & Dangard Ace begin | .40 | 1.25 | 2.50 |
| 2-10 | .35 | 1.00 | 2.00 |
| 11-20: 11-Austin-c. 12-Simonson-c | .25 | .75 | 1.50 |

**SHOOK UP** (Magazine) (Satire)
November, 1958
Dodsworth Publ. Co.

| | Good | Fine | N-Mint |
|---|---|---|---|
| V1#1 | 1.00 | 3.00 | 7.00 |

**SHORT RIBS** (See 4-Color #1333)

**SHORT STORY COMICS** (See Hello Pal, . . .)

**SHORTY SHINER**
June, 1956 - No. 3, Oct, 1956
Dandy Magazine (Charles Biro)

| | Good | Fine | N-Mint |
|---|---|---|---|
| 1 | 2.65 | 8.00 | 18.00 |
| 2,3 | 1.70 | 5.00 | 12.00 |

**SHOTGUN SLADE** (See 4-Color #1111)

**SHOWCASE** (See Cancelled Comic Cavalcade & New Talent . . .)
3-4/56 - No. 93, 9/70; No. 94, 8-9/77 - No. 104, 9/78
National Periodical Publications/DC Comics

| | Good | Fine | N-Mint |
|---|---|---|---|
| 1-Fire Fighters | 80.00 | 235.00 | 550.00 |
| 2-King of the Wild; Kubert-a (animal stories) | 29.00 | 86.00 | 200.00 |
| 3-The Frogmen | 25.00 | 75.00 | 175.00 |

4-Origin/1st app. The Flash (1st DC Silver Age hero, Sept-Oct, 1956) & The Turtle; Kubert-a; reprinted in Secret Origins #1 ('61 & '73)

| Good | Fine | VF-NM | NM/Mint |
|---|---|---|---|
| 400.00 | 1600.00 | 4000.00 | 8000.00 |

(Estimated up to 470 total copies exist, 9 in NM/Mint)

| | Good | Fine | N-Mint |
|---|---|---|---|
| 5-Manhunters | 36.00 | 107.00 | 250.00 |
| 6-Origin/1st app. Challengers of the Unknown by Kirby, partly r-/in Secret Origins #1 & Challengers #64,65 (1st DC Silver Age super-hero team) | 100.00 | 300.00 | 700.00 |
| 7-Challengers of the Unknown by Kirby r-in/Challengers of the Unknown #75 | 54.00 | 160.00 | 375.00 |

| | Good | Fine | VF-NM | NM/Mint |
|---|---|---|---|---|
| 8-The Flash; intro/origin Capt. Cold | 200.00 | 600.00 | 1400.00 | 2200.00 |

(Estimated up to 790 total copies exist, 20 in NM/Mint)

| | Good | Fine | N-Mint |
|---|---|---|---|
| 9,10-Lois Lane. 9-(Pre-#1, 7-8/57). 10-Jor-el cameo | 71.00 | 215.00 | 500.00 |
| 11,12-Challengers of the Unknown by Kirby | 40.00 | 118.00 | 275.00 |
| 13-The Flash; origin Mr. Element | 117.00 | 350.00 | 820.00 |
| 14-The Flash; origin Dr. Alchemy, former Mr. Element | 117.00 | 350.00 | 820.00 |
| 15-Space Ranger (1st app., 7-8/58) | 29.00 | 86.00 | 200.00 |
| 16-Space Ranger | 20.00 | 60.00 | 140.00 |
| 17-Adventures on Other Worlds; origin/1st app. Adam Strange (11-12/58) | 61.00 | 185.00 | 430.00 |
| 18-Adventures on Other Worlds(A. Strange) | 34.00 | 103.00 | 240.00 |
| 19-Adam Strange | 34.00 | 103.00 | 240.00 |
| 20-Origin & 1st app. Rip Hunter (5-6/59); Moriera-a | 31.00 | 95.00 | 220.00 |
| 21-Rip Hunter; Sekowsky-c/a | 14.00 | 43.00 | 100.00 |

| | Good | Fine | N-Mint | Mint |
|---|---|---|---|---|
| 22-Origin & 1st app. Silver Age Green Lantern by Gil Kane (9-10/59); reprinted in Secret Origins #2 | 150.00 | 450.00 | 1050.00 | 2000.00 |

(Estimated up to 650 total copies exist, 25 in mint)

| | Good | Fine | N-Mint |
|---|---|---|---|
| 23,24-Green Lantern. 23-Nuclear explosion-c | 57.00 | 171.00 | 400.00 |
| 25,26-Rip Hunter by Kubert | 11.00 | 32.00 | 75.00 |
| 27-1st app. Sea Devils (7-8/60); Heath-c/a | 29.00 | 86.00 | 200.00 |
| 28,29-Sea Devils; Heath-c/a | 17.00 | 51.00 | 120.00 |
| 30-Origin Silver Age Aquaman (see Adventure #260 for 1st app.) | 27.00 | 81.00 | 190.00 |
| 31-33-Aquaman | 10.00 | 30.00 | 70.00 |
| 34-Origin & 1st app. Silver Age Atom by Kane & Anderson (9-10/61); reprinted in Secret Origins #2 | 64.00 | 195.00 | 450.00 |
| 35-The Atom by Gil Kane; last 10 cent issue | 22.00 | 65.00 | 150.00 |
| 36-The Atom by Gil Kane (1-2/61-62) | 14.00 | 43.00 | 100.00 |
| 37-1st app. Metal Men (3-4/62) | 29.00 | 86.00 | 200.00 |
| 38-40-Metal Men | 11.50 | 34.00 | 80.00 |
| 41,42-Tommy Tomorrow (parts 1&2). 42-Origin | 4.00 | 12.00 | 28.00 |
| 43-Dr. No (James Bond); Nodel-a; originally published as British Classics Illustrated #158A, and as #6 in a European Detective series, all with a diff. painted-c. This Showcase #43 version is actually censored, deleting all racial skin color, and dialogue thought to be racially demeaning (1st DC Silver Age movie adaptation)(based on Ian Fleming novel & movie) | 25.00 | 75.00 | 175.00 |
| 44-Tommy Tomorrow | 2.65 | 8.00 | 18.00 |
| 45-Sgt. Rock; origin retold; Heath-c | 7.00 | 21.00 | 50.00 |
| 46,47-Tommy Tomorrow | 1.50 | 4.50 | 10.00 |
| 48,49-Cave Carson | 1.50 | 4.50 | 10.00 |
| 50,51-I Spy (Danger Trail-r by Infantino), King Farady story (#50 is not a reprint) | 1.50 | 4.50 | 10.00 |
| 52-Cave Carson | 1.50 | 4.50 | 10.00 |
| 53,54-G.I. Joe; Heath-a | 1.50 | 4.50 | 10.00 |
| 55-Dr. Fate & Hourman. (3-4/65)-G.A. Green Lantern app. (early Silver Age app.)(pre-dates Gr. Lantern #40) | 2.85 | 8.50 | 20.00 |
| 56-Dr. Fate & Hourman | 1.50 | 4.50 | 10.00 |
| 57,58-Enemy Ace by Kubert | 3.15 | 9.50 | 22.00 |
| 59-Teen Titans (3rd app., 11-12/65) | 5.70 | 17.00 | 40.00 |
| 60-1st Silver Age app. The Spectre; Anderson-a (1-2/66); origin in text | 8.00 | 24.00 | 55.00 |
| 61,64-The Spectre by Anderson | 2.85 | 8.50 | 20.00 |
| 62-Origin & 1st app. Inferior Five (5-6/66) | 3.60 | 11.00 | 25.00 |
| 63,65-Inferior Five | 1.70 | 5.00 | 12.00 |
| 66,67-B'wana Beast | .70 | 2.00 | 5.00 |
| 68,69,71-Maniaks | .70 | 2.00 | 5.00 |
| 70-Binky | .70 | 2.00 | 5.00 |
| 72-Top Gun (Johnny Thunder-r)-Toth-a | .70 | 2.00 | 5.00 |
| 73-Origin/1st app. Creeper; Ditko-c/a (3-4/67) | 4.00 | 12.00 | 28.00 |
| 74-Intro/1st app. Anthro; Post-c/a (5-6/67) | 2.65 | 8.00 | 18.00 |
| 75-Origin/1st app. Hawk & the Dove; Ditko-c/a | 4.30 | 13.00 | 30.00 |
| 76-1st app. Bat Lash (9-10/67) | 1.30 | 4.00 | 9.00 |
| 77-1st app. Angel & The Ape | 2.00 | 6.00 | 14.00 |
| 78-Jonny Double | .70 | 2.00 | 4.00 |
| 79-Dolphin; Aqualad origin-r | .85 | 2.60 | 6.00 |
| 80-Phantom Stranger-r; Neal Adams-c | .85 | 2.60 | 6.00 |
| 81-Windy & Willy | .70 | 2.00 | 4.00 |
| 82-1st app. Nightmaster by Grandenetti & Giordano; Kubert-c | 3.15 | 9.50 | 22.00 |
| 83,84-Nightmaster by Wrightson w/Jones/Kaluta ink assist in each; Kubert-c. 84-Origin retold | 3.15 | 9.50 | 22.00 |
| 85-87-Firehair; Kubert-a | .85 | 2.60 | 6.00 |
| 88-90-Jason's Quest: 90-Manhunter 2070 app. | .50 | 1.50 | 3.00 |
| 91-93-Manhunter 2070; origin-92 | .50 | 1.50 | 3.00 |
| 94-Intro/origin new Doom Patrol & Robotman | .70 | 2.00 | 4.00 |
| 95,96-The Doom Patrol. 95-Origin Celsius | .35 | 1.00 | 2.00 |
| 97-99-Power Girl; origin-97,98; JSA cameos | .35 | 1.00 | 2.00 |
| 100-(52 pgs.)-Most Showcase characters feat. | .35 | 1.00 | 2.00 |
| 101-103-Hawkman; Adam Strange x-over | .35 | 1.00 | 2.00 |
| 104-(52 pgs.)-O.S.S. Spies at War | .35 | 1.00 | 2.00 |

NOTE: ***Anderson*** *a-22-24i, 34-36i, 55, 56, 60, 61, 64, 101-103i; c-50i, 51i, 55, 56, 60, 61, 64.* ***Aparo*** *c-94-96.* ***Estrada*** *a-104.* ***Infantino*** *c/a-4, 8, 13, 14; c-50p, 51p.* ***Gil Kane*** *a-22-24p, 34-36p; c-17-19, 22-24, 31, 34-36.* ***Kirby*** *c-6, 7, 11, 12.* ***Kubert*** *a-2, 4i, 25, 26, 45, 53, 54, 72; c-25, 26, 53, 54, 57, 58, 82-87, 101-104.* ***Orlando*** *a-62p, 63p, 97i; c-62, 63, 97i.* ***Sekowsky*** *a-65p.* ***Sparling*** *a-78.* ***Staton*** *a-94, 95-99p, 100; c-97-100p.*

**SHOWGIRLS** (Formerly Sherry the Showgirl #3)
No. 4, 2/57; June, 1957 - No. 2, Aug, 1957
Atlas Comics (MPC No. 2)

| | Good | Fine | N-Mint |
|---|---|---|---|
| 4 | 3.15 | 9.50 | 22.00 |
| 1-Millie, Sherry, Chili, Pearl & Hazel begin | 5.00 | 15.00 | 35.00 |
| 2 | 3.15 | 9.50 | 22.00 |

**SHROUD OF MYSTERY**
June, 1982
Whitman Publications

| | Good | Fine | N-Mint |
|---|---|---|---|
| 1 | | .30 | .60 |

**SICK** (Magazine) (Satire)
Aug, 1960 - No. 140?, 1980?
Feature Publ./Headline Publ./Crestwood Publ. Co./Hewfred Publ./Pyramid Comm./Charlton Publ. No. 109 (4/76) on

| | Good | Fine | N-Mint |
|---|---|---|---|
| V1#1-Torres-a | 9.30 | 28.00 | 65.00 |
| 2-5-Torres-a in all | 4.50 | 14.00 | 32.00 |
| 6 | 2.85 | 8.50 | 20.00 |
| V2#1-8(#7-14) | 2.15 | 6.50 | 15.00 |
| V3#1-8(#15-22) | 1.70 | 5.00 | 12.00 |
| V4#1-5(#23-27) | 1.30 | 4.00 | 9.00 |
| 28-40 | .85 | 2.60 | 6.00 |

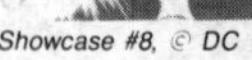
*Showcase #8, © DC*

*Showcase #22, © DC*

*Showcase #82, © DC*

Silver Star #1, © Pacific Comics

Silver Streak Comics #5, © LEV

The Silver Surfer #2 (10/68), © MEG

| | Good | Fine | N-Mint |
|---|---|---|---|
| 41-140: 45 has #44 on-c & #45 on inside | .50 | 1.50 | 3.00 |
| Annual 1969, 1970, 1971 | 1.15 | 3.50 | 8.00 |
| Annual 2-4('80) | .60 | 1.75 | 3.50 |
| Special 2 ('78) | .35 | 1.00 | 2.00 |

NOTE: ***Davis*** *c/a in most issues of #16-27, 30-32, 34, 35.* ***Powell*** *a-2, 8-11, 14, 16, 41-43.* ***Simon*** *a-1-3, 10, 41, 42.* ***Torres*** *a-9-11, V2#7, V4#2, V6#1-3.* ***Tuska*** *a-14, 41-43. Civil War Blackouts-23, 24.*

**SIDESHOW**
1949 (One Shot)
Avon Periodicals

| | | | |
|---|---|---|---|
| 1-(Rare)-Similar to Bachelor's Diary | 16.00 | 48.00 | 110.00 |

**SIEGEL AND SHUSTER: DATELINE 1930s**
Nov, 1984 - No. 2, Sept, 1985 (Baxter paper #1; $1.50-$1.75)
Eclipse Comics

| | | | |
|---|---|---|---|
| 1-Unpubbed samples of strips from 1935; includes 'Interplanetary Police;' Shuster-c | .25 | .75 | 1.50 |
| 2 ($1.75, B&W)-Unpubbed strips; Shuster-c | .30 | .90 | 1.80 |

**SILENT INVASION, THE**
April, 1986 - No. 12, March, 1988 ($1.70/$2.00, B&W)
Renegade Press

| | | | |
|---|---|---|---|
| 1-UFO sightings of '50s | .60 | 1.75 | 3.50 |
| 2 | .50 | 1.50 | 3.00 |
| 3-12 | .40 | 1.25 | 2.50 |
| Book 1-Reprints | 1.35 | 4.00 | 7.95 |

**SILK HAT HARRY'S DIVORCE SUIT**
1912 (5¾x15½") (B&W)
M. A. Donoghue & Co.

| | | | |
|---|---|---|---|
| Newspaper reprints by Tad (Thomas Dorgan) | 10.00 | 30.00 | 70.00 |

**SILLY PILLY** (See Frank Luther's . . .)

**SILLY SYMPHONIES** (See Dell Giants)

**SILLY TUNES**
Fall, 1945 - No. 7, June, 1947
Timely Comics

| | | | |
|---|---|---|---|
| 1-Silly Seal, Ziggy Pig begin | 8.00 | 24.00 | 55.00 |
| 2 | 4.00 | 12.00 | 28.00 |
| 3-7 | 3.00 | 9.00 | 21.00 |

**SILVER** (See Lone Ranger's Famous Horse . . .)

**SILVERBACK**
1989 - No. 3, 1990 ($2.50, color, mini-series, adults)
Comico

| | | | |
|---|---|---|---|
| 1-3: Character from Grendel; Matt Wagner-a | .40 | 1.25 | 2.50 |

**SILVERBLADE**
Sept, 1987 - No. 12, Sept, 1988
DC Comics

| | | | |
|---|---|---|---|
| 1-12: Colan-c/a(p) in all | .25 | .75 | 1.50 |

**SILVERHAWKS**
Aug, 1987 - No. 6, June, 1988 ($1.00)
Star Comics/Marvel #6

| | | | |
|---|---|---|---|
| 1-6 | | .50 | 1.00 |

**SILVERHEELS** (See Eclipse Graphic Album #12)
Dec, 1983 - No. 3, May, 1984 ($1.50, color)
Pacific Comics

| | | | |
|---|---|---|---|
| 1-3 | .25 | .75 | 1.50 |

**SILVER KID WESTERN**
Oct, 1954 - No. 5, 1955
Key/Stanmor Publications

| | | | |
|---|---|---|---|
| 1 | 4.00 | 12.00 | 28.00 |
| 2 | 2.15 | 6.50 | 15.00 |

| | Good | Fine | N-Mint |
|---|---|---|---|
| 3-5 | 1.70 | 5.00 | 12.00 |
| I.W. Reprint #1,2 | .50 | 1.50 | 3.00 |

**SILVER STAR**
Feb, 1983 - No. 6, Jan, 1984 ($1.00, color)
Pacific Comics

| | | | |
|---|---|---|---|
| 1-6: 1-1st app. Last of the Viking Heroes | | .50 | 1.00 |

NOTE: ***Kirby*** *a-1-5p; c-1-5p.*

**SILVER STREAK COMICS** (Crime Does Not Pay #22 on)
Dec, 1939 - May, 1942; 1946 (Silver logo-#1-5)
Your Guide Publs. No. 1-7/New Friday Publs. No. 8-17/Comic House Publ./Newsbook Publ.

| | Good | Fine | VF-NM | NM/Mint |
|---|---|---|---|---|
| 1-(Scarce)-Intro The Claw by Cole (r-/in Daredevil #21), Red Reeves, Boy Magician, & Captain Fearless; The Wasp, Mister Midnight begin; Spirit Man app. Silver metallic-c begin, end #5 | 400.00 | 1000.00 | 2400.00 | 3100.00 |

(Estimated up to 100 total copies exist, 6 in NM/Mint)

| | Good | Fine | N-Mint |
|---|---|---|---|
| 2-The Claw by Cole; Simon c/a | 157.00 | 470.00 | 1100.00 |
| 3-1st app. & origin Silver Streak (2nd with lightning speed); Dickie Dean the Boy Inventor, Lance Hale, Ace Powers, Bill Wayne, & The Planet Patrol begin | 135.00 | 405.00 | 945.00 |
| 4-Sky Wolf begins; Silver Streak by Jack Cole (new costume); 1st app. Jackie, Lance Hale's sidekick | 71.00 | 215.00 | 500.00 |
| 5-Jack Cole c/a(2) | 82.00 | 245.00 | 575.00 |

6-(Scarce)-Origin & 1st app. Daredevil (blue & yellow costume) by Jack Binder; The Claw returns; classic Cole Claw-c

| | Good | Fine | VF-NM | NM/Mint |
|---|---|---|---|---|
| 6 | 285.00 | 857.00 | 2000.00 | 2700.00 |
| 7-Claw vs. Daredevil (new costume-blue & red) by Jack Cole & 3 other Cole stories (38 pgs.) | 193.00 | 580.00 | 1350.00 | 1800.00 |

(#6, 7-Estimated up to 120 total copies of each exist, 7-10 in NM/Mint)

8-Claw vs. Daredevil by Cole; last Cole Silver Streak

| | Good | Fine | N-Mint |
|---|---|---|---|
| 8 | 110.00 | 330.00 | 775.00 |
| 9-Claw vs. Daredevil by Cole | 82.00 | 245.00 | 575.00 |
| 10-Origin Captain Battle; Claw vs. Daredevil by Cole | 75.00 | 225.00 | 525.00 |
| 11-Intro. Mercury by Bob Wood, Silver Streak's sidekick; conclusion Claw vs. Daredevil by Rico; in 'Presto Martin,' 2nd pg., newspaper says 'Roussos does it again' | 52.00 | 154.00 | 360.00 |
| 12-14: 13-Origin Thun-Dohr | 43.00 | 130.00 | 300.00 |
| 15-17-Last Daredevil issue | 40.00 | 120.00 | 280.00 |
| 18-The Saint begins; by Leslie Charteris (See Movie Comics #2, DC) | 34.00 | 100.00 | 235.00 |
| 19-21(1942): 20,21 have Wolverton's Scoop Scuttle | 22.00 | 64.00 | 150.00 |
| 22,24(1946)-Reprints | 13.00 | 40.00 | 90.00 |
| 23-Reprints?; bondage-c | 13.00 | 40.00 | 90.00 |
| nn(11/46)(Newsbook Publ.)-R-/S.S. story from #4-7 plus 2 Captain Fearless stories, all in color; bondage/torture-c | 24.00 | 70.00 | 170.00 |

NOTE: ***Binder*** *c-3, 4, 13-15, 17.* ***Jack Cole*** *a-(Daredevil)-#6-10, (Dickie Dean)-#3-10, (Pirate Prince)-#7, (Silver Streak)-#4-8, nn; c-5 (Silver Streak), 6-8 (Daredevil).* ***Everett*** *Red Reed begins #20.* ***Guardineer*** *a-#8-13.* ***Don Rico*** *a-11-17 (Daredevil); c-11, 12, 16.* ***Simon*** *a-3 (Silver Streak).* ***Bob Wood*** *a-9 (Silver Streak); c-9, 10. Claw c-#1, 2, 6-8.*

**SILVER SURFER** (See Fantastic Four, Fantasy Masterpieces V2#1, Marvel Graphic Novel, Marvel Presents #8, Marvel's Greatest Comics & Tales To Astonish)

**SILVER SURFER, THE**
Aug, 1968 - No. 18, Sept, 1970; June, 1982 (No. 1-7: 68 pgs.)
Marvel Comics Group

| | | | |
|---|---|---|---|
| 1-Origin by John Buscema (p); Watcher begins (origin), ends #7 | 25.00 | 75.00 | 175.00 |
| 2 | 8.00 | 24.00 | 55.00 |
| 3-1st app. Mephisto | 6.50 | 19.00 | 45.00 |
| 4-Low distribution; Thor app. | 16.00 | 48.00 | 110.00 |

| | Good | Fine | N-Mint |
|---|---|---|---|
| 5-7-Last giant size. 5-The Stranger app. 6-Brunner inks. 7-Brunner-c | 5.00 | 15.00 | 35.00 |
| 8-10,14: 14-Spider-Man x-over | 3.60 | 11.00 | 25.00 |
| 11-13,15-18: 18-Kirby-c/a | 2.30 | 7.00 | 16.00 |
| V2#1 (6/82, 52 pgs.)-Byrne-c/a | 1.00 | 3.00 | 6.00 |

NOTE: ***Adkins*** *a-8-15i.* ***Brunner*** *a-6i.* ***J. Buscema*** *a-1-17p.* ***Colan*** *a-1-3p.* ***Reinman*** *a-1-4i.*

**SILVER SURFER, THE** (See Marvel Graphic Novel #38)
July, 1987 - Present
Marvel Comics Group

| | Good | Fine | N-Mint |
|---|---|---|---|
| 1-Double size ($1.25) | .75 | 2.25 | 4.50 |
| 2 | .50 | 1.50 | 3.00 |
| 3-10 | .35 | 1.00 | 2.00 |
| 11-20 | .25 | .75 | 1.50 |
| 21-24,26-30,32-48: 34-Starlin scripts begin. 34,35-Thanos returns. 36-Capt. Marvel, Warlock app. 38-Thanos app. | | .50 | 1.00 |
| 25,31 ($1.50, 52 pgs.): 25-Skrulls app. | .30 | .90 | 1.80 |
| Annual 1 (8/88, $1.75)-Evolutionary War app. | .40 | 1.25 | 2.50 |
| Annual 2 ('89, $2.00, 68 pgs.)-Atlantis Attacks | .35 | 1.00 | 2.00 |
| Annual 3 ('90, $2.00, 68 pgs.) | .35 | 1.00 | 2.00 |

NOTE: ***Marshall Rogers*** *a-1-10, 12, 19; c-1-12.*

**SILVER SURFER, THE**
Dec, 1988 - No. 2, Jan, 1989 ($1.00, limited series)
Epic Comics (Marvel)

| | Good | Fine | N-Mint |
|---|---|---|---|
| 1,2: By Stan Lee & Moebius | .35 | 1.00 | 2.00 |

**SILVERTIP** (Max Brand)
No. 491, Aug, 1953 - No. 898, May, 1958
Dell Publishing Co.

| | Good | Fine | N-Mint |
|---|---|---|---|
| 4-Color 491 | 4.00 | 12.00 | 28.00 |
| 4-Color 572,608,637,667,731,789,898-Kinstler-a; all painted-c | 3.50 | 10.50 | 24.00 |
| 4-Color 835 | 2.65 | 8.00 | 18.00 |

**SINBAD, JR** (TV Cartoon)
Sept-Nov, 1965 - No. 3, May, 1966
Dell Publishing Co.

| | Good | Fine | N-Mint |
|---|---|---|---|
| 1 | 1.70 | 5.00 | 12.00 |
| 2,3 | 1.00 | 3.00 | 7.00 |

**SINDBAD** (See Movie Comics: Capt. Sindbad, and Fantastic Voyages of Sindbad)

**SINGING GUNS** (See Fawcett Movie Comics)

**SINGLE SERIES** (Comics on Parade #30 on)(Also see John Hix . . .)
1938 - No. 28, 1942 (All 68 pgs.)
United Features Syndicate

| | Good | Fine | N-Mint |
|---|---|---|---|
| 1-Captain and the Kids (#1) | 43.00 | 130.00 | 300.00 |
| 2-Broncho Bill (1939) (#1) | 26.00 | 77.00 | 180.00 |
| 3-Ella Cinders (1939) | 24.00 | 71.00 | 165.00 |
| 4-Li'l Abner (1939) (#1) | 37.00 | 110.00 | 260.00 |
| 5-Fritzi Ritz (#1) | 16.00 | 48.00 | 110.00 |
| 6-Jim Hardy by Dick Moores (#1) | 22.00 | 65.00 | 155.00 |
| 7-Frankie Doodle | 16.00 | 48.00 | 110.00 |
| 8-Peter Pat (On sale 7/14/39) | 16.00 | 48.00 | 110.00 |
| 9-Strange As It Seems | 16.00 | 48.00 | 110.00 |
| 10-Little Mary Mixup | 16.00 | 48.00 | 110.00 |
| 11-Mr. and Mrs. Beans | 16.00 | 48.00 | 110.00 |
| 12-Joe Jinks | 14.00 | 43.00 | 100.00 |
| 13-Looy Dot Dope | 13.00 | 40.00 | 90.00 |
| 14-Billy Make Believe | 13.00 | 40.00 | 90.00 |
| 15-How It Began (1939) | 16.00 | 48.00 | 110.00 |
| 16-Illustrated Gags (1940)-Has ad for Captain and the Kids #1 reprint listed below | 8.50 | 25.50 | 60.00 |
| 17-Danny Dingle | 11.50 | 34.00 | 80.00 |
| 18-Li'l Abner (#2 on-c) | 30.00 | 90.00 | 210.00 |
| 19-Broncho Bill (#2 on-c) | 22.00 | 65.00 | 150.00 |
| 20-Tarzan by Hal Foster | 79.00 | 235.00 | 550.00 |
| 21-Ella Cinders (#2 on-c; on sale 3/19/40) | 20.00 | 60.00 | 140.00 |
| 22-Iron Vic | 16.00 | 48.00 | 110.00 |
| 23-Tailspin Tommy by Hal Forrest (#1) | 19.00 | 58.00 | 135.00 |
| 24-Alice in Wonderland (#1) | 24.00 | 71.00 | 165.00 |
| 25-Abbie and Slats | 20.00 | 60.00 | 140.00 |
| 26-Little Mary Mixup (#2 on-c, 1940) | 16.00 | 48.00 | 110.00 |
| 27-Jim Hardy by Dick Moores (1942) | 17.00 | 51.00 | 115.00 |
| 28-Ella Cinders and Abbie and Slats (1942) | 18.00 | 54.00 | 125.00 |
| 1-Captain and the Kids (1939 reprint)-2nd Edition | 24.00 | 73.00 | 170.00 |
| 1-Fritzi Ritz (1939 reprint)-2nd edition | 13.00 | 40.00 | 90.00 |

NOTE: *Some issues given away at the 1939-40 New York World's Fair (#6).*

**SINISTER HOUSE OF SECRET LOVE, THE** (Secrets of Sinister House No. 5 on)
Oct-Nov, 1971 - No. 4, Apr-May, 1972
National Periodical Publications

| | Good | Fine | N-Mint |
|---|---|---|---|
| 1 | | .60 | 1.20 |
| 2-4: 2-Jeff Jones-c. 3-Toth-a, 36 pgs. | | .40 | .80 |

**SIR LANCELOT** (See 4-Color #606, 775)

**SIR WALTER RALEIGH** (See 4-Color #644)

**SISTERHOOD OF STEEL** (See Eclipse Graphic Album #13)
Dec, 1984 - No. 8, Feb, 1986 ($1.50; Baxter paper) (Adults only)
Epic Comics (Marvel)

| | Good | Fine | N-Mint |
|---|---|---|---|
| 1-(Women mercenaries) | .35 | 1.10 | 2.20 |
| 2-8 | .30 | .90 | 1.80 |

**6 BLACK HORSES** (See Movie Classics)

**SIX FROM SIRIUS**
July, 1984 - No. 4, Oct, 1984 ($1.50, mini-series)
Epic Comics (Marvel)

| | Good | Fine | N-Mint |
|---|---|---|---|
| 1-Gulacy-c/a in all | .35 | 1.00 | 2.00 |
| 2-4 | .30 | .90 | 1.80 |

**SIX FROM SIRIUS II**
Feb, 1986 - No. 4, May, 1986 ($1.50, color, Adults only)
Epic Comics (Marvel)

| | Good | Fine | N-Mint |
|---|---|---|---|
| 1-4 | .25 | .75 | 1.50 |

**SIX-GUN HEROES**
March, 1950 - No. 23, Nov, 1953 (Photo-c #1-23)
Fawcett Publications

| | Good | Fine | N-Mint |
|---|---|---|---|
| 1-Rocky Lane, Hopalong Cassidy, Smiley Burnette begin | 30.00 | 90.00 | 210.00 |
| 2 | 17.00 | 50.00 | 115.00 |
| 3-5 | 12.00 | 36.00 | 85.00 |
| 6-15: 6-Lash LaRue begins | 9.30 | 28.00 | 65.00 |
| 16-22: 17-Last Smiley Burnette. 18-Monte Hale begins | 8.00 | 24.00 | 55.00 |
| 23-Last Fawcett issue | 8.50 | 25.50 | 60.00 |

NOTE: *Hopalong Cassidy photo c-1-3. Monte Hale photo c-18. Rocky Lane photo c-4, 5, 7, 9, 11, 13, 15, 17, 20, 21, 23. Lash LaRue photo c-6, 8, 10, 12, 14, 16, 19, 22.*

**SIX-GUN HEROES** (Continued from Fawcett; Gunmasters #84 on)
No. 24, Jan, 1954 - No. 83, Mar-Apr, 1965 (All Vol. 4)(See Blue Bird)
Charlton Comics

| | Good | Fine | N-Mint |
|---|---|---|---|
| 24-Lash LaRue, Hopalong Cassidy, Rocky Lane & Tex Ritter begin; photo-c | 8.00 | 24.00 | 55.00 |
| 25 | 4.50 | 14.00 | 32.00 |
| 26-30: 26-Rod Cameron story. 28-Tom Mix begins? | 4.00 | 12.00 | 28.00 |
| 31-40 | 3.00 | 9.00 | 21.00 |
| 41-46,48,50 | 2.65 | 8.00 | 18.00 |
| 47-Williamson-a, 2 pgs; Torres-a | 3.50 | 10.50 | 24.00 |
| 49-Williamson-a, 5 pgs. | 3.50 | 10.50 | 24.00 |

*The Silver Surfer #34, © MEG*

*Single Series #2, © UFS*

*Six-Gun Heroes #19, © FAW*

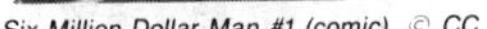
Six Million Dollar Man #1 (comic), © CC

Skyrocket nn, © CHES

Slam Bang Comics #1, © FAW

| | Good | Fine | N-Mint |
|---|---|---|---|
| 51-60: 58-Gunmaster app. | 1.70 | 5.00 | 12.00 |
| 61-70: 62-Origin, Gunmaster | 1.30 | 4.00 | 9.00 |
| 71-83: 76-Gunmaster begins | .85 | 2.60 | 6.00 |

**SIXGUN RANCH** (See 4-Color #580)

**SIX-GUN WESTERN**
Jan, 1957 - No. 4, July, 1957
Atlas Comics (CDS)

| | Good | Fine | N-Mint |
|---|---|---|---|
| 1-Crandall-a; two Williamson text illos | 8.00 | 24.00 | 55.00 |
| 2,3-Williamson-a in both | 6.50 | 19.00 | 45.00 |
| 4-Woodbridge-a | 3.15 | 9.50 | 22.00 |

NOTE: ***Ayers** a-2, 3. **Maneely** c-2, 3. **Orlando** a-2. **Pakula** a-2. **Powell** a-3. **Romita** a-1, 4. **Severin** c-1, 4. **Shores** a-2.*

**SIX MILLION DOLLAR MAN** (TV)(Magazine)
June, 1976 - No. 7, Nov, 1977 (B&W)
Charlton Comics

| | Good | Fine | N-Mint |
|---|---|---|---|
| 1-Neal Adams-c/a | .50 | 1.50 | 3.00 |
| 2-N. Adams-c | .25 | .80 | 1.60 |
| 3-7: 3-N. Adams part inks | | .60 | 1.20 |

**SIX MILLION DOLLAR MAN, THE** (TV)
6/76 - No. 4, 1/77; No. 5, 10/77; No. 6, 2/78 - No. 9, 6/78
Charlton Comics

| | Good | Fine | N-Mint |
|---|---|---|---|
| 1-Staton-c/a; Lee Majors photo on-c | .25 | .80 | 1.60 |
| 2-Neal Adams-c; Staton-a | | .50 | 1.00 |
| 3-9 | | .30 | .60 |

**SKATEMAN**
Nov, 1983 (One Shot) (Baxter paper)
Pacific Comics

| | Good | Fine | N-Mint |
|---|---|---|---|
| 1-Neal Adams-c/a | .25 | .75 | 1.50 |

**SKATING SKILLS**
1957 (36 & 12 pages; 5x7", two versions) (10 cents)
Custom Comics, Inc./Chicago Roller Skates

| | Good | Fine | N-Mint |
|---|---|---|---|
| nn-Resembles old ACG cover plus interior art | .70 | 2.00 | 4.00 |

**SKEEZIX** (Also see Gasoline Alley)
1925 - 1928 (Strip reprints) (soft covers) (pictures & text)
Reilly & Lee Co.

| | Good | Fine | N-Mint |
|---|---|---|---|
| . . .and Uncle Walt (1924)-Origin | 10.00 | 30.00 | 70.00 |
| . . .and Pal (1925) | 7.00 | 21.00 | 50.00 |
| . . .at the Circus (1926) | 7.00 | 21.00 | 50.00 |
| . . .& Uncle Walt (1927) | 7.00 | 21.00 | 50.00 |
| . . .Out West (1928) | 7.00 | 21.00 | 50.00 |
| Hardback Editions. . . | 11.50 | 34.00 | 80.00 |

**SKELETON HAND** (. . .In Secrets of the Supernatural)
Sept-Oct, 1952 - No. 6, July-Aug, 1953
American Comics Group (B&M Dist. Co.)

| | Good | Fine | N-Mint |
|---|---|---|---|
| 1 | 15.00 | 45.00 | 105.00 |
| 2 | 9.30 | 28.00 | 65.00 |
| 3-6 | 8.00 | 24.00 | 55.00 |

**SKI PARTY** (See Movie Classics)

**SKIPPY**
Circa 1920s (10X8," 16 pgs., color/B&W cartoons)
No publisher listed

| | Good | Fine | N-Mint |
|---|---|---|---|
| nn-By Percy Crosby | 65.00 | 200.00 | 450.00 |

**SKIPPY'S OWN BOOK OF COMICS** (See Popular Comics)
1934 (52 pages) (Giveaway)(Strip reprints)
No publisher listed

| | Good | Fine | VF-NM | NM/Mint |
|---|---|---|---|---|
| nn-(Rare)-By Percy Crosby | 300.00 | 750.00 | 1800.00 | 2500.00 |

(Estimated up to 50 total copies exist, 4 in NM/Mint)

Published by Max C. Gaines for Phillip's Dental Magnesia to be advertised on the Skippy Radio Show and given away with the purchase of a tube of Phillip's Tooth Paste. This is the first four-color comic book of reprints about one character.

**SKREEMER**
May, 1989 - No. 6, Oct, 1989 ($2.00, color, mini-series, adults)
DC Comics

| | Good | Fine | N-Mint |
|---|---|---|---|
| 1-6: Contains graphic violence | .35 | 1.00 | 2.00 |

**SKULL, THE SLAYER**
August, 1975 - No. 8, Nov, 1976
Marvel Comics Group

| | Good | Fine | N-Mint |
|---|---|---|---|
| 1-Origin; Gil Kane-c | | .50 | 1.00 |
| 2-8: 2-Gil Kane-c. 8-Kirby-c | | .35 | .70 |

**SKY BLAZERS** (Radio)
Sept, 1940 - No. 2, Nov, 1940
Hawley Publications

| | Good | Fine | N-Mint |
|---|---|---|---|
| 1-Sky Pirates, Ace Archer, Flying Aces begin | 22.00 | 65.00 | 150.00 |
| 2 | 17.00 | 51.00 | 120.00 |

**SKY KING "RUNAWAY TRAIN"** (TV)
1964 (16 pages) (regular size)
National Biscuit Co.

| | Good | Fine | N-Mint |
|---|---|---|---|
| nn | 1.50 | 4.50 | 10.00 |

**SKYMAN** (See Big Shot Comics & Sparky Watts)
Fall?, 1941 - No. 2, 1941; No. 3, 1948 - No. 4, 1948
Columbia Comics Group

| | Good | Fine | N-Mint |
|---|---|---|---|
| 1-Origin Skyman, The Face, Sparky Watts app.; Whitney-a; 3rd story r-/Big Shot #1 | 39.00 | 118.00 | 275.00 |
| 2 (1941)-Yankee Doodle | 22.00 | 65.00 | 155.00 |
| 3,4 (1948) | 13.00 | 40.00 | 90.00 |

**SKY PILOT**
No. 10, 1950(nd) - No. 11, Apr-May, 1951 (Saunders painted-c)
Ziff-Davis Publ. Co.

| | Good | Fine | N-Mint |
|---|---|---|---|
| 10,11-Frank Borth-a | 5.00 | 15.00 | 35.00 |

**SKY RANGER** (See Johnny Law. . .)

**SKYROCKET**
1944
Harry 'A' Chesler

| | Good | Fine | N-Mint |
|---|---|---|---|
| nn-Alias the Dragon, Dr. Vampire, Skyrocket app. | 11.50 | 34.00 | 80.00 |

**SKY SHERIFF** (Breeze Lawson. . .) (Also see Exposed)
Summer, 1948
D. S. Publishing Co.

| | Good | Fine | N-Mint |
|---|---|---|---|
| 1-Edmond Good-a | 5.30 | 16.00 | 38.00 |

**SKY WOLF** (Also see Airboy)
Mar, 1988 - No. 3, Oct, 1988 ($1.75-$1.95, color, mini series)
Eclipse Comics

| | Good | Fine | N-Mint |
|---|---|---|---|
| 1,2 ($1.75) | .30 | .90 | 1.80 |
| 3 ($1.95) | .35 | 1.00 | 2.00 |

**SLAINE, THE BERSERKER** (Slaine the King #21 on)
July, 1987 - No. 28, 1989 ($1.25; $1.50 #13 on, color)
Quality Comics

| | Good | Fine | N-Mint |
|---|---|---|---|
| 1-12 ($1.25) | | .65 | 1.30 |
| 13,14/15,16/17,18-28 | .25 | .75 | 1.50 |

**SLAM BANG COMICS** (Western Desperado #8)
March, 1940 - No. 7, Sept, 1940 (Combined with Master Comics #7)
Fawcett Publications

| | Good | Fine | N-Mint |
|---|---|---|---|
| 1-Diamond Jack, Mark Swift & The Time Retarder, Lee Granger, Jungle King begin | 65.00 | 195.00 | 455.00 |
| 2 | 30.00 | 90.00 | 210.00 |
| 3-Classic-c | 40.00 | 120.00 | 280.00 |
| 4-7: 7-Bondage-c | 25.00 | 75.00 | 175.00 |

**SLAM BANG COMICS**
No. 9, No date

| | Good | Fine | N-Mint |
|---|---|---|---|
| Post Cereal Giveaway | | | |
| 9-Dynamic Man, Echo, Mr. E, Yankee Boy app. | 2.00 | 6.00 | 14.00 |

**SLAPSTICK COMICS**
nd (1946?) (36 pages)
Comic Magazines Distributors

| | | | |
|---|---|---|---|
| nn-Firetop feature; Post-a(2) | 9.00 | 27.00 | 62.00 |

**SLASH-D DOUBLECROSS**
1950 (132 pgs.) (pocket size)
St. John Publishing Co.

| | | | |
|---|---|---|---|
| nn-Western comics | 8.50 | 25.50 | 60.00 |

**SLASH MARAUD**
Nov, 1987 - No. 6, April, 1988 ($1.75, mini-series)
DC Comics

| | | | |
|---|---|---|---|
| 1-6 | .35 | 1.00 | 2.00 |

**SLAUGHTERMAN** (See Primer #1 for 1st app.)
Feb, 1983 - No. 2, 1983 ($1.50, B&W)
Comico

| | | | |
|---|---|---|---|
| 1,2 | .25 | .75 | 1.50 |

**SLAVE GIRL COMICS** (See Malu . . . & White Princess of/Jungle #2)
Feb, 1949 - No. 2, Apr, 1949 (52 pgs.)
Avon Periodicals/Eternity Comics

| | | | |
|---|---|---|---|
| 1-Larsen-c/a | 50.00 | 150.00 | 350.00 |
| 2-Larsen-a | 35.00 | 105.00 | 245.00 |
| 1 (3/89, $2.25, B&W, 44 pgs., Eternity)-r/#1 | .40 | 1.15 | 2.30 |

**SLEDGE HAMMER** (TV)
Feb, 1988 - No. 2, Mar, 1988 ($1.00, color)
Marvel Comics

| | | | |
|---|---|---|---|
| 1,2 | | .50 | 1.00 |

**SLEEPING BEAUTY** (See Dell Giants, 4-Color #973, 984 & Movie Comics)

**SLEEZE BROTHERS, THE**
Aug, 1989 - Jan, 1990 ($1.75, color, mature readers, direct sale only)
Epic Comics (Marvel)

| | | | |
|---|---|---|---|
| 1-6: Private eyes; 4-6-(9/89-11/89 indicia dates) | .30 | .90 | 1.80 |

**SLICK CHICK COMICS**
1947(nd) - No. 3, 1947(nd)
Leader Enterprises

| | | | |
|---|---|---|---|
| 1 | 5.50 | 16.50 | 38.00 |
| 2,3 | 3.70 | 11.00 | 26.00 |

**SLIMER** (TV) (Also see The Real Ghostbusters)
1989 - Present ($1.75, color)
Now Comics

| | | | |
|---|---|---|---|
| 1-15: Based on animated TV cartoon | .30 | .90 | 1.80 |

**SLIM MORGAN** (See Wisco)

**SLUGGER** (Of the Little Wise Guys)
April, 1956
Lev Gleason Publications

| | | | |
|---|---|---|---|
| 1-Biro-c | 2.30 | 7.00 | 16.00 |

**SMASH COMICS** (Lady Luck #86 on)
Aug, 1939 - No. 85, Oct, 1949
Quality Comics Group

| | Good | Fine | N-Mint |
|---|---|---|---|
| 1-Origin Hugh Hazard & His Iron Man, Bozo the Robot, Espionage, Starring Black X by Eisner, & Invisible Justice; Chic Carter & Wings Wendall begin | 79.00 | 235.00 | 550.00 |
| 2-The Lone Star Rider app; Invisible Hood gains power of invisibility | 36.00 | 107.00 | 250.00 |
| 3-Captain Cook & John Law begin | 24.00 | 73.00 | 170.00 |
| 4,5: 4-Flash Fulton begins | 22.00 | 65.00 | 155.00 |
| 6-12: 12-One pg. Fine-a | 18.00 | 54.00 | 125.00 |
| 13-Magno begins; last Eisner issue; The Ray app. in full page ad; The Purple Trio begins | 18.00 | 54.00 | 125.00 |
| 14-Intro. The Ray by Lou Fine & others | 110.00 | 330.00 | 770.00 |
| 15,16 | 55.00 | 165.00 | 385.00 |
| 17-Wun Cloo becomes plastic super-hero by Jack Cole (9-months before Plastic Man) | 55.00 | 165.00 | 385.00 |
| 18-Midnight by Jack Cole begins (origin) | 65.00 | 195.00 | 455.00 |
| 19-22: Last Fine Ray; The Jester begins-#22 | 38.00 | 115.00 | 265.00 |
| 23,24: 24-The Sword app.; last Chic Carter; Wings Wendall dons new costume #24,25 | 32.00 | 95.00 | 225.00 |
| 25-Origin Wildfire | 38.00 | 115.00 | 265.00 |
| 26-30: 28-Midnight-c begin | 29.00 | 85.00 | 200.00 |
| 31,32,34: Ray by Rudy Palais; also #33 | 22.00 | 65.00 | 150.00 |
| 33-Origin The Marksman | 27.00 | 80.00 | 185.00 |
| 35-37 | 22.00 | 65.00 | 150.00 |
| 38-The Yankee Eagle begins; last Midnight by Jack Cole | 22.00 | 65.00 | 150.00 |
| 39,40-Last Ray issue | 17.00 | 51.00 | 120.00 |
| 41,43-50 | 8.00 | 24.00 | 55.00 |
| 42-Lady Luck begins by Klaus Nordling | 9.50 | 28.50 | 65.00 |
| 51-60 | 6.50 | 19.00 | 45.00 |
| 61-70 | 5.30 | 16.00 | 38.00 |
| 71-85 | 5.00 | 15.00 | 35.00 |

NOTE: *Cole a-17-38, 68, 69, 72, 73, 78, 80, 83, 85; c-38, 60-62, 69, 75, 80.* ***Crandall*** *a-(Ray)-23-29, 35-38; c-36, 39, 40, 43, 44, 46.* ***Fine*** *a(Ray)-14, 15, 16(w/****Tuska****), 17-22.* ***Fuje*** *Ray-30.* ***Gil Fox*** *a-6-7, 9, 11-13.* ***Guardineer*** *a-(The Marksman)-39-?, 49, 52.* ***Gustavson*** *a-4-7, 9, 11-13 (The Jester)-22-46; (Magno)-13-21; (Midnight)-39(****Cole*** *inks), 49, 52, 63-65.* ***Kotzky*** *a-(Espionage)-33-38; c-45, 47.* ***Nordling*** *a-49, 52, 63-65.* ***Powell*** *a-11, 12, (Abdul the Arab)-13-24.*

**SMASH HIT SPORTS COMICS**
V2#1, Jan, 1949
Essankay Publications

| | | | |
|---|---|---|---|
| V2#1-L.B. Cole-c/a | 8.50 | 25.50 | 60.00 |

**S'MATTER POP?**
1917 (44 pgs.; B&W; 10x14''; cardboard covers)
Saalfield Publ. Co.

| | | | |
|---|---|---|---|
| nn-By Charlie Payne; ½ in full color; pages printed on one side | 9.30 | 28.00 | 65.00 |

**SMILE COMICS** (Also see Gay Comics, Tickle, & Whee)
1955 (52 pages; 5x7¼'') (7 cents)
Modern Store Publ.

| | | | |
|---|---|---|---|
| 1 | .50 | 1.50 | 3.00 |

**SMILEY BURNETTE WESTERN** (See Six-Gun Heroes)
March, 1950 - No. 4, Oct, 1950 (All photo-c)
Fawcett Publications

| | | | |
|---|---|---|---|
| 1 | 20.00 | 60.00 | 140.00 |
| 2-4 | 13.00 | 40.00 | 90.00 |

**SMILIN' JACK** (See Famous Feature Stories, Popular Comics, Super Book #1, 2, 7, 19 & Super Comics)
No. 5, 1940 - No. 8, Oct-Dec, 1949
Dell Publishing Co.

| | | | |
|---|---|---|---|
| 4-Color 5 | 45.00 | 135.00 | 315.00 |
| 4-Color 10 (1940) | 43.00 | 130.00 | 300.00 |
| Large Feature Comic 12,14,25 (1941) | 30.00 | 90.00 | 210.00 |
| 4-Color 4 (1942) | 34.00 | 103.00 | 240.00 |
| 4-Color 14 (1943) | 27.00 | 81.00 | 190.00 |
| 4-Color 36,58 (1943-44) | 16.00 | 48.00 | 110.00 |
| 4-Color 80 (1945) | 12.00 | 36.00 | 85.00 |
| 4-Color 149 (1947) | 8.50 | 25.50 | 60.00 |
| 1 (1-3/48) | 8.50 | 25.50 | 60.00 |
| 2 | 4.65 | 14.00 | 32.00 |
| 3-8 (10-12/49) | 3.50 | 10.50 | 24.00 |

*Slave Girl Comics #2, © AVON*

*Smash Comics #1, © QUA*

*Smiley Burnette Western #1, © FAW*

Smitty #7, © N.Y. News Synd.

Snooper and Blabber #1, © Hanna-Barbera

A NEW ADVENTURE of WALT DISNEY'S
Snow White and the Seven Dwarfs

Snow White & the 7 Dwarfs (1952), © Disney

| | Good | Fine | N-Mint |
|---|---|---|---|
| Popped Wheat Giveaway(1947)-1938 reprints; 16 pgs. in full color | .80 | 2.40 | 4.80 |
| Shoe Store Giveaway-1938 reprints; 16 pgs. | 2.65 | 8.00 | 18.00 |
| Sparked Wheat Giveaway(1942)-16 pgs. in full color | 2.30 | 7.00 | 16.00 |

**SMILING SPOOK SPUNKY** (See Spunky)

**SMITTY** (See Treasure Box of Famous Comics)
1928 - 1933 (B&W newspaper strip reprints)
(cardboard covers; 9½x9½", 52 pgs.; 7x8¼", 36 pgs.)
Cupples & Leon Co.

| | Good | Fine | N-Mint |
|---|---|---|---|
| 1928-(96pgs. 7x8¾") | 11.00 | 32.00 | 75.00 |
| 1928-(Softcover, 36pgs., nn) | 12.00 | 36.00 | 84.00 |
| 1929-At the Ball Game, 1930-The Flying Office Boy, 1931-The Jockey, 1932-In the North Woods....each.... | 8.50 | 25.50 | 60.00 |
| 1933-At Military School | 8.50 | 25.50 | 60.00 |
| Mid-1930s issue (reprint of 1928 Treasure Box issue)-36 pgs.; 7x8¾" | 7.00 | 21.00 | 50.00 |
| Hardback Editions (100 pgs., 7x8¼") with dust jacket each.... | 14.00 | 42.00 | 100.00 |

**SMITTY** (See Popular Comics, Super Book #2,4 & Super Comics)
No. 11, 1940 - No. 7, Aug-Oct, 1949; Apr, 1958
Dell Publishing Co.

| | Good | Fine | N-Mint |
|---|---|---|---|
| 4-Color 11 (1940) | 26.00 | 77.00 | 180.00 |
| Large Feature Comic 26 (1941) | 17.00 | 51.00 | 120.00 |
| 4-Color 6 (1942) | 14.00 | 43.00 | 100.00 |
| 4-Color 32 (1943) | 11.50 | 34.00 | 80.00 |
| 4-Color 65 (1945) | 9.30 | 28.00 | 65.00 |
| 4-Color 99 (1946) | 8.00 | 24.00 | 55.00 |
| 4-Color 138 (1947) | 6.50 | 19.50 | 45.00 |
| 1 (11-1/47-48) | 6.50 | 19.50 | 45.00 |
| 2 | 3.50 | 10.50 | 24.00 |
| 3 (8-10/48), 4 (1949) | 2.30 | 7.00 | 16.00 |
| 5-7, 4-Color 909 (4/58) | 1.70 | 5.00 | 12.00 |

**SMOKEY BEAR** (TV) (See March Of Comics #362, 372, 383, 407)
Feb, 1970 - No. 13, Mar, 1973
Gold Key

| | Good | Fine | N-Mint |
|---|---|---|---|
| 1 | .70 | 2.00 | 4.00 |
| 2-13 | .40 | 1.25 | 2.50 |

**SMOKEY STOVER** (See Popular Comics, Super Book #5,17,29 & Super Comics)
No. 7, 1942 - No. 827, Aug, 1957
Dell Publishing Co.

| | Good | Fine | N-Mint |
|---|---|---|---|
| 4-Color 7 (1942)-Reprints | 24.00 | 70.00 | 165.00 |
| 4-Color 35 (1943) | 12.00 | 36.00 | 84.00 |
| 4-Color 64 (1944) | 9.30 | 28.00 | 65.00 |
| 4-Color 229 (1949) | 3.00 | 9.00 | 21.00 |
| 4-Color 730,827 | 1.70 | 5.00 | 12.00 |
| General Motors giveaway (1953) | 3.00 | 9.00 | 21.00 |
| National Fire Protection giveaway('53 & '54)-16 pgs., paper-c | 3.00 | 9.00 | 21.00 |

**SMOKEY THE BEAR** (See Forest Fire for 1st app.)
No. 653, 10/55 - No. 1214, 8/61 (See March of Comics #234)
Dell Publishing Co.

| | Good | Fine | N-Mint |
|---|---|---|---|
| 4-Color 653 (#1) | 3.00 | 9.00 | 21.00 |
| 4-Color 708,754,818,932 | 2.00 | 6.00 | 14.00 |
| 4-Color 1016,1119,1214 | 1.50 | 4.50 | 10.00 |
| True Story of..., The('59)-U.S. Forest Service giveaway-Publ. by Western Printing Co. (reprinted in '64 & '69)-Reprints 1st 16 pgs. of 4-Color 932 | .85 | 2.50 | 6.00 |

**SMOKY** (See Movie Classics)

**SMURFS** (TV)
1982 (Dec) - No. 3, 1983
Marvel Comics Group

| | Good | Fine | N-Mint |
|---|---|---|---|
| 1-3 | | .30 | .60 |
| ...Treasury Edition 1(64pgs.)-r/#1-3 | .40 | 1.25 | 2.50 |

**SNAFU** (Magazine)
Nov, 1955 - V2#2, Mar, 1956 (B&W)
Atlas Comics (RCM)

| | Good | Fine | N-Mint |
|---|---|---|---|
| V1#1-Heath/Severin-a | 5.00 | 15.00 | 35.00 |
| V2#1,2-Severin-a | 3.50 | 10.50 | 24.00 |

**SNAGGLEPUSS** (TV)(See Spotlight #4)
Oct, 1962 - No. 4, Sept, 1963 (Hanna-Barbera)
Gold Key

| | Good | Fine | N-Mint |
|---|---|---|---|
| 1 | 3.50 | 10.50 | 24.00 |
| 2-4 | 2.30 | 7.00 | 16.00 |

**SNAP** (Becomes Jest #10,11)
No. 9, 1944
Harry 'A' Chesler

| | Good | Fine | N-Mint |
|---|---|---|---|
| 9-Manhunter, The Voice | 6.50 | 19.00 | 45.00 |

**SNAPPY COMICS**
1945
Cima Publ. Co. (Prize Publ.)

| | Good | Fine | N-Mint |
|---|---|---|---|
| 1-Airmale app; 9pg. Sorcerer's Apprentice adapt; Kiefer-a | 7.00 | 21.00 | 50.00 |

**SNARKY PARKER** (See Life With...)

**SNIFFY THE PUP**
No. 5, Nov, 1949 - No. 18, Sept, 1953
Standard Publications (Animated Cartoons)

| | Good | Fine | N-Mint |
|---|---|---|---|
| 5-Two Frazetta text illos | 4.00 | 12.00 | 28.00 |
| 6-10 | 1.50 | 4.50 | 10.00 |
| 11-18 | 1.00 | 3.00 | 7.00 |

**SNOOPER AND BLABBER DETECTIVES** (TV)
Nov, 1962 - No. 3, May, 1963 (Hanna-Barbera)
Gold Key

| | Good | Fine | N-Mint |
|---|---|---|---|
| 1 (See Whitman Comic Books) | 3.50 | 10.50 | 24.00 |
| 2,3 | 2.30 | 7.00 | 16.00 |

**SNOW FOR CHRISTMAS**
1957 (16 pages) (Giveaway)
W. T. Grant Co.

| | Good | Fine | N-Mint |
|---|---|---|---|
| nn | 1.50 | 4.50 | 10.00 |

**SNOW WHITE** (See Christmas With..., 4-Color #49,227,382, Mickey Mouse Mag., & Movie Comics)

**SNOW WHITE AND THE SEVEN DWARFS**
1952 (32 pgs.; 5x7¼", soft-c) (Disney)
Bendix Washing Machines

| | Good | Fine | N-Mint |
|---|---|---|---|
| nn | 5.00 | 15.00 | 35.00 |

**SNOW WHITE AND THE SEVEN DWARFS**
April, 1982 (60 cent cover price)
Whitman Publications

| | Good | Fine | N-Mint |
|---|---|---|---|
| nn-r/4-Color #49 | | .30 | .60 |

**SNOW WHITE AND THE 7 DWARFS IN "MILKY WAY"**
1955 (16 pgs., 5x7¼", soft-c) (Disney premium)
American Dairy Association

| | Good | Fine | N-Mint |
|---|---|---|---|
| nn | 5.00 | 15.00 | 35.00 |

**SNOW WHITE AND THE SEVEN DWARFS**
1957 (small size)
Promotional Publ. Co.

| | Good | Fine | N-Mint |
|---|---|---|---|
| nn | 2.75 | 8.00 | 19.00 |

**SNOW WHITE AND THE SEVEN DWARFS**
1958 (16 pgs, 5x7¼", soft-c) (Disney premium)
Western Printing Co.

| | Good | Fine | N-Mint |
|---|---|---|---|
| nn-"Mystery of the Missing Magic" | 3.50 | 10.50 | 24.00 |

**SOAP OPERA LOVE**
Feb, 1983 - No. 3, June, 1983
Charlton Comics

| | Good | Fine | N-Mint |
|---|---|---|---|
| 1-3 | | .25 | .50 |

**SOAP OPERA ROMANCES**
July, 1982 - No. 5, March, 1983
Charlton Comics

| | Good | Fine | N-Mint |
|---|---|---|---|
| 1-5-Nurse Betsy Crane-r | | .25 | .50 |

**SOJOURN** ($1.50)
Sept, 1977 - No. 2, 1978 (Full tabloid size) (Color & B&W)
White Cliffs Publ. Co.

| | Good | Fine | N-Mint |
|---|---|---|---|
| 1-Tor by Kubert, Eagle by Severin, E. V. Race, Private Investigator by Doug Wildey, T. C. Mars by S. Aragones begin plus other strips | .25 | .80 | 1.60 |
| 2 | .25 | .80 | 1.60 |

**SOLARMAN**
Jan, 1989; No. 2, May, 1990 ($1.00, color)
Marvel Comics

| | Good | Fine | N-Mint |
|---|---|---|---|
| 1,2 | | .50 | 1.00 |

**SOLDIER & MARINE COMICS** (Fightin' Army #16 on)
No. 11, Dec, 1954 - No. 15, Aug, 1955; V2#9, Dec, 1956
Charlton Comics (Toby Press of Conn. V1#11)

| | Good | Fine | N-Mint |
|---|---|---|---|
| V1#11 (12/54)-Bob Powell-a | 1.50 | 4.50 | 10.00 |
| V1#12(2/55)-15 | .85 | 2.60 | 6.00 |
| V2#9(Formerly Never Again; Jerry Drummer V2#10 on) | .85 | 2.60 | 6.00 |

**SOLDIER COMICS**
Jan, 1952 - No. 11, Sept, 1953
Fawcett Publications

| | Good | Fine | N-Mint |
|---|---|---|---|
| 1 | 4.00 | 12.00 | 28.00 |
| 2 | 2.15 | 6.50 | 15.00 |
| 3-5 | 1.70 | 5.00 | 12.00 |
| 6-11: 8-Illo. in **POP** | 1.30 | 4.00 | 9.00 |

**SOLDIERS OF FORTUNE**
Feb-Mar, 1951 - No. 13, Feb-Mar, 1953
American Comics Group (Creston Publ. Corp.)

| | Good | Fine | N-Mint |
|---|---|---|---|
| 1-Capt. Crossbones by Shelly, Ace Carter, Lance Larson begin | 10.00 | 30.00 | 70.00 |
| 2 | 6.00 | 18.00 | 42.00 |
| 3-10: 6-Bondage-c | 4.50 | 14.00 | 32.00 |
| 11-13 (War format) | 1.70 | 5.00 | 12.00 |

NOTE: ***Shelly*** *a-1-3, 5.* ***Whitney*** *a-6, 8-11, 13; c-1-3, 5, 6.*

**SOLDIERS OF FREEDOM**
1987 - No. 2? ($1.75, color)
Americomics

| | Good | Fine | N-Mint |
|---|---|---|---|
| 1,2 | .30 | .90 | 1.80 |

**SOLO AVENGERS** (Becomes Avengers Spotlight #21 on)
Dec, 1987 - No. 20, July, 1989 (75 cents-$1.00)
Marvel Comics

| | Good | Fine | N-Mint |
|---|---|---|---|
| 1 | .35 | 1.10 | 2.20 |
| 2-5 | .25 | .70 | 1.40 |
| 6-20: 11-Intro Bobcat | | .50 | 1.00 |

**SOLO EX-MUTANTS** (Also see Ex-Mutants)
Jan, 1988 - No. 6, 1988 ($1.95, B&W)
Eternity Comics

| | Good | Fine | N-Mint |
|---|---|---|---|
| 1-6 | .35 | 1.00 | 2.00 |

**SOLOMON AND SHEBA** (See 4-Color #1070)

**SOLOMON KANE** (Also see Blackthorne 3-D Series #60)
Sept, 1985 - No. 6, July, 1986 (Mini-series)(Also see Marvel Premiere)
Marvel Comics Group

| | Good | Fine | N-Mint |
|---|---|---|---|
| 1-Double-size | | .50 | 1.00 |
| 2-6: 3-6-Williamson-a(i) | | .40 | .80 |

**SOMERSET HOLMES** (See Eclipse Graphic Album Series)
9/83 - No. 4, 4/84; No. 5, 11/84 - No. 6, 12/84 ($1.50; Baxter)
Pacific Comics/Eclipse Comics No. 5, 6

| | Good | Fine | N-Mint |
|---|---|---|---|
| 1-B. Anderson-c/a; Cliff Hanger by Williamson begins, ends #6 | .40 | 1.25 | 2.50 |
| 2-6 | .35 | 1.00 | 2.00 |

**SONG OF THE SOUTH** (See Brer Rabbit & 4-Color #693)

**SONIC DISRUPTORS**
Dec, 1987 - No. 7, July, 1988 ($1.75, limited series, mature readers)
DC Comics

| | Good | Fine | N-Mint |
|---|---|---|---|
| 1-7 | .30 | .90 | 1.80 |

**SON OF AMBUSH BUG** (Also see Ambush Bug)
July, 1986 - No. 6, Dec, 1986 (75 cents, color)
DC Comics

| | Good | Fine | N-Mint |
|---|---|---|---|
| 1-6: Giffen-c/a(p) in all | | .40 | .80 |

**SON OF BLACK BEAUTY** (See 4-Color #510,566)

**SON OF FLUBBER** (See Movie Comics)

**SON OF MUTANT WORLD**
1990 - No. 5, 1990? ($2.00, color, bi-monthly)
Fantagor Press

| | Good | Fine | N-Mint |
|---|---|---|---|
| 1-3: By Jan Strnad & Richard Corben (c/a) | .35 | 1.00 | 2.00 |
| 4,5-($1.75, B&W) | .30 | .90 | 1.80 |

**SON OF SATAN** (Also see Marvel Spotlight #12)
Dec, 1975 - No. 8, Feb, 1977
Marvel Comics Group

| | Good | Fine | N-Mint |
|---|---|---|---|
| 1-Mooney-a; Kane-c(p), Starlin splash(p) | | .40 | .80 |
| 2-8: 2-Origin The Possessor. 8-Heath-a | | .25 | .50 |

**SON OF SINBAD** (Also see Abbott & Costello & Daring Adventures)
February, 1950
St. John Publishing Co.

| | Good | Fine | N-Mint |
|---|---|---|---|
| 1-Kubert-c/a | 26.00 | 78.00 | 180.00 |

**SON OF TOMAHAWK** (See Tomahawk)

**SON OF VULCAN** (Mysteries of Unexplored Worlds #1-48; Thunderbolt, V3#51 on)
V2#49, Nov, 1965 - V2#50, Jan, 1966
Charlton Comics

| | Good | Fine | N-Mint |
|---|---|---|---|
| V2#49,50 | 1.00 | 3.00 | 7.00 |

**SONS OF KATIE ELDER** (See Movie Classics)

**SORCERY** (See Chilling Adventures in . . . & Red Circle . . .)

**SORORITY SECRETS**
July, 1954
Toby Press

| | Good | Fine | N-Mint |
|---|---|---|---|
| 1 | 3.00 | 9.00 | 21.00 |

**SOULQUEST** (See Against Blackshard 3-D)
April, 1989 ($3.95, color, squarebound, 52 pgs.)
Innovation Publishing

| | Good | Fine | N-Mint |
|---|---|---|---|
| 1-Blackshard app. | .70 | 2.00 | 4.00 |

**SOUPY SALES COMIC BOOK** (TV)(The Official . . .)
1965
Archie Publications

| | Good | Fine | N-Mint |
|---|---|---|---|
| 1 | 6.50 | 19.00 | 45.00 |

*Soldier Comics #7, © FAW*

*Son of Mutant World #1, © Fantagor*

*Son of Vulcan V2#49, © CC*

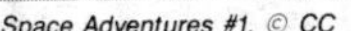
Space Adventures #1, © CC

Space Family Robinson #2, © WEST

Space Kat-ets #1, © Power Publ.

**SOUTHERN KNIGHTS, THE** (Formerly Crusaders No. 1)
No. 2, 1983 - No. 7, 9/84; No. 8, 1984 - Present ($1.75, B&W)
Guild Publ./Fictioneer Books(Comics Interview) No. 8 on

| | Good | Fine | N-Mint |
|---|---|---|---|
| 2-Magazine size | 1.35 | 4.00 | 8.00 |
| 3 | .75 | 2.25 | 4.50 |
| 4,5 | .60 | 1.80 | 3.60 |
| 6-10 | .50 | 1.50 | 3.00 |
| 11-15 | .40 | 1.25 | 2.50 |
| 16-33: 28-Begin $1.95-c | .35 | 1.00 | 2.00 |
| 34-Christmas issue ($2.25) | .40 | 1.15 | 2.25 |
| Dread Halloween Special 1 (1988) | .35 | 1.10 | 2.25 |
| Special 1 (Spring, 1989, $2.25) | .35 | 1.10 | 2.25 |
| Graphic Novels #1-4 ($4.95) | .85 | 2.50 | 5.00 |

**SPACE ACE** (Also see Manhunt!)
No. 5, 1952
Magazine Enterprises

| | Good | Fine | N-Mint |
|---|---|---|---|
| 5(A-1 #61)-Guardineer-a | 19.00 | 56.00 | 130.00 |

**SPACE ACTION**
June, 1952 - No. 3, Oct, 1952
Ace Magazines (Junior Books)

| | Good | Fine | N-Mint |
|---|---|---|---|
| 1 | 30.00 | 90.00 | 210.00 |
| 2,3 | 24.00 | 71.00 | 165.00 |

**SPACE ADVENTURES** (War At Sea #22 on)
7/52 - No. 21, 8/56; No. 23, 5/58 - No. 59, 11/64; V3#60, 10/67; V1#2, 7/68 - V1#8, 7/69; No. 9, 5/78 - No. 13, 3/79
Capitol Stories/Charlton Comics

| | Good | Fine | N-Mint |
|---|---|---|---|
| 1 | 17.00 | 51.00 | 120.00 |
| 2 | 8.50 | 25.50 | 60.00 |
| 3-5 | 6.50 | 19.00 | 45.00 |
| 6-9: 7-Sex change story | 5.70 | 17.00 | 40.00 |
| 10,11-Ditko-c/a; 11-Two Ditko stories | 19.00 | 57.00 | 130.00 |
| 12-Ditko-c (classic) | 22.00 | 65.00 | 150.00 |
| 13-(Fox-r, 10-11/54); Blue Beetle story | 6.50 | 19.00 | 45.00 |
| 14-Blue Beetle story (Fox-r, 12-1/54-55, last pre-code) | 5.30 | 16.00 | 38.00 |
| 15,17,18-Rocky Jones app.(TV); 15-Part photo-c | 6.50 | 19.00 | 45.00 |
| 16-Krigstein-a; Rockey Jones app. | 10.00 | 30.00 | 70.00 |
| 19 | 4.50 | 14.00 | 32.00 |
| 20-Reprints Fawcett's "Destination Moon" | 12.00 | 36.00 | 85.00 |
| 21-(8/56) (no #22)(Becomes War At Sea) | 5.70 | 17.00 | 40.00 |
| 23-(5/58; formerly Nyoka, The Jungle Girl)-Reprints Fawcett's "Destination Moon" | 10.00 | 30.00 | 70.00 |
| 24,25,31,32-Ditko-a | 7.00 | 21.00 | 50.00 |
| 26,27-Ditko-a(4) each | 9.00 | 27.00 | 62.00 |
| 28-30 | 2.65 | 8.00 | 18.00 |
| 33-Origin/1st app. Captain Atom by Ditko (3/60) | 19.00 | 58.00 | 135.00 |
| 34-40,42-All Captain Atom by Ditko | 8.00 | 24.00 | 55.00 |
| 41-59: 44,45-Mercury Man in each | 1.00 | 3.00 | 7.00 |
| V3#60(#1, 10/67)-Origin Paul Mann & The Saucers From the Future | 1.15 | 3.50 | 8.00 |
| 2-8('68-'69)-2,5,6,8-Ditko-a; 2,4-Aparo-c/a | .70 | 2.00 | 4.00 |
| 9-13('78-'79)-Capt. Atom-r/Space Adventures by Ditko; 9-Reprints origin/1st app. from #33 | | .50 | 1.00 |

NOTE: ***Aparo** a-V3#60. c-V3#8. **Ditko** c-12, 31-42. **Shuster** a-11.*

**SPACE BUSTERS**
Spring/52 - No. 3, Fall/52 (Painted covers by Norman Saunders)
Ziff-Davis Publ. Co.

| | Good | Fine | N-Mint |
|---|---|---|---|
| 1-Krigstein-a(3) | 36.00 | 107.00 | 250.00 |
| 2,3: 2-Kinstler-a(2pgs.); Krigstein-a(3) | 29.00 | 86.00 | 200.00 |

NOTE: ***Anderson** a-2. Bondage c-2.*

**SPACE CADET** (See Tom Corbett, . . .)

**SPACE COMICS** (Formerly Funny Tunes)
No. 4, Mar-Apr, 1954 - No. 5, May-June, 1954
Avon Periodicals

| | Good | Fine | N-Mint |
|---|---|---|---|
| 4,5-Space Mouse, Peter Rabbit, Super Pup, & Merry Mouse app. | 2.65 | 8.00 | 18.00 |
| I.W. Reprint #8 (nd)-Space Mouse-r | .50 | 1.50 | 3.00 |

**SPACED**
1982 - No. 13, 1988 ($1.50, B&W, quarterly)
Anthony Smith Publ. #1,2/Unbridled Ambition/Eclipse Comics #10 on

| | Good | Fine | N-Mint |
|---|---|---|---|
| 1 | 5.00 | 15.00 | 30.00 |
| 2 | 3.70 | 10.00 | 20.00 |
| 3,4 | 1.70 | 5.00 | 10.00 |
| 5,6 | .70 | 2.00 | 4.00 |
| 7-13 | .25 | .75 | 1.50 |
| Special Edition (1983, Mimeo) | 1.30 | 4.00 | 8.00 |

**SPACE DETECTIVE**
July, 1951 - No. 4, July, 1952
Avon Periodicals

| | Good | Fine | N-Mint |
|---|---|---|---|
| 1-Rod Hathway, Space Det. begins, ends #4; Wood-c/a(3)-23 pgs.; "Opium Smugglers of Venus" drug story; Lucky Dale-r/Saint #4 | 65.00 | 195.00 | 455.00 |
| 2-Tales from the Shadow Squad story; Wood/Orlando-c; Wood inside layouts | 32.00 | 95.00 | 225.00 |
| 3-Kinstler-c | 20.00 | 60.00 | 140.00 |
| 4-Kinstler-a | 20.00 | 60.00 | 140.00 |
| I.W. Reprint #1(Reprints #2), 8(Reprints cover #1 & part Famous Funnies #191) | 1.50 | 4.50 | 10.00 |
| I.W. Reprint #9 | 1.50 | 4.50 | 10.00 |

**SPACE EXPLORER** (See March of Comics #202)

**SPACE FAMILY ROBINSON** (TV)(. . . Lost in Space #15-36)(Becomes Lost in Space #37 on)
Dec, 1962 - No. 36, Oct, 1969 (All painted covers)
Gold Key

| | Good | Fine | N-Mint |
|---|---|---|---|
| 1-(low distr.); Spiegle-a in all | 10.00 | 30.00 | 70.00 |
| 2(3/63)-Family becomes lost in space | 5.00 | 15.00 | 35.00 |
| 3-10: 6-Captain Venture begins | 2.65 | 8.00 | 18.00 |
| 11-20 | 1.70 | 5.00 | 12.00 |
| 21-36 | 1.15 | 3.50 | 8.00 |

**SPACE FAMILY ROBINSON** (See March of Comics #320, 328, 352, 404, 414)

**SPACE GHOST** (TV) (Also see Golden Comics Digest #2 & Hanna Barbera Super TV Heroes #3-7)
March, 1967 (Hanna-Barbera) (TV debut was 9/10/66)
Gold Key

| | Good | Fine | N-Mint |
|---|---|---|---|
| 1 (10199-703)-Spiegle-a | 14.00 | 43.00 | 100.00 |

**SPACE GHOST** (TV) (Graphic Novel)
Dec, 1987 (One Shot) (52pgs.; deluxe format; $3.50)(Hanna-Barbera)
Comico

| | Good | Fine | N-Mint |
|---|---|---|---|
| 1-Steve Rude-c/a(p) | .85 | 2.50 | 5.00 |

**SPACE GIANTS, THE**
1979 (One shot, $1.00, B&W, TV)
FBN Publications

| | Good | Fine | N-Mint |
|---|---|---|---|
| 1-Based on Japanese TV series | 1.50 | 4.50 | 10.00 |

**SPACEHAWK** (See Epic Illustrated, Target Comics & 3-D Zone #18)
1989 - No. 2, 1989; No. 3, 1990 ($2.00, B&W)
Dark Horse Comics

| | Good | Fine | N-Mint |
|---|---|---|---|
| 1-3-Wolverton-c/a(r) plus new stories by others | .35 | 1.00 | 2.00 |

**SPACE KAT-ETS** (in 3-D)
Dec, 1953 (25 cents)
Power Publishing Co.

| | Good | Fine | N-Mint |
|---|---|---|---|
| 1 | 22.00 | 65.00 | 155.00 |

**SPACEMAN** (Speed Carter. . .)
Sept, 1953 - No. 6, July, 1954
Atlas Comics (CnPC)

| | Good | Fine | N-Mint |
|---|---|---|---|
| 1 | 26.00 | 77.00 | 180.00 |
| 2 | 17.00 | 51.00 | 120.00 |
| 3-6: 4-A-Bomb-c | 14.00 | 43.00 | 100.00 |

NOTE: ***Everett** c-1, 3.* ***Maneely** a-1-6?; c-6.* ***Tuska** a-5(3).*

**SPACE MAN**
No. 1253, 1-3/62 - No. 8, 3-5/64; No. 9, 7/72 - No. 10, 10/72
Dell Publishing Co.

| | | | |
|---|---|---|---|
| 4-Color 1253 (#1)(1-3/62) | 4.00 | 12.00 | 28.00 |
| 2,3 | 2.00 | 6.00 | 14.00 |
| 4-8 | 1.30 | 4.00 | 9.00 |
| 9-Reprints #1253 | .50 | 1.50 | 3.00 |
| 10-Reprints #2 | .40 | 1.25 | 2.50 |

**SPACE MOUSE** (Also see Space Comics)
April, 1953 - No. 5, Apr-May, 1954
Avon Periodicals

| | | | |
|---|---|---|---|
| 1 | 4.00 | 12.00 | 28.00 |
| 2 | 2.65 | 8.00 | 18.00 |
| 3-5 | 1.70 | 5.00 | 12.00 |

**SPACE MOUSE** (Walter Lantz. . .#1; see Comic Album #17)
No. 1132, Aug-Oct, 1960 - No. 5, Nov, 1963 (Walter Lantz)
Dell Publishing Co./Gold Key

| | | | |
|---|---|---|---|
| 4-Color 1132,1244 | 1.70 | 5.00 | 12.00 |
| 1(11/62)(G.K.) | 1.70 | 5.00 | 12.00 |
| 2-5 | 1.15 | 3.50 | 8.00 |

**SPACE MYSTERIES**
1964 (Reprints)
I.W. Enterprises

| | | | |
|---|---|---|---|
| 1-r-/Journey Into Unknown Worlds #4 w/new-c | .50 | 1.50 | 3.00 |
| 8,9 | .50 | 1.50 | 3.00 |

**SPACE: 1999** (TV) (Also see Power Record Comics)
Nov, 1975 - No. 7, Nov, 1976
Charlton Comics

| | | | |
|---|---|---|---|
| 1-Staton-c/a; origin Moonbase Alpha | .50 | 1.50 | 3.00 |
| 2,7: 2-Staton-a | .35 | 1.00 | 2.00 |
| 3-6: All Byrne-a; c-5 | .70 | 2.00 | 4.00 |

**SPACE: 1999** (TV)(Magazine)
Nov, 1975 - No. 8, Nov, 1976 (B&W) (#7 shows #6 on inside)
Charlton Comics

| | | | |
|---|---|---|---|
| 1-Origin Moonbase Alpha; Morrow-c/a | .50 | 1.50 | 3.00 |
| 2,3-Morrow-c/a | .30 | .90 | 1.80 |
| 4-8: 4-6-Morrow-c. 5,8-Morrow-a | .25 | .80 | 1.60 |

**SPACE PATROL** (TV)
Summer/52 - No. 2, Oct-Nov/52 (Painted-c by Norman Saunders)
Ziff-Davis Publishing Co. (Approved Comics)

| | | | |
|---|---|---|---|
| 1-Krigstein-a | 42.00 | 125.00 | 290.00 |
| 2-Krigstein-a(3) | 35.00 | 105.00 | 245.00 |
| . . .'s Special Mission (8 pgs., B&W, Giveaway) | 50.00 | 150.00 | 300.00 |

**SPACE PIRATES** (See Archie Giant Series #533)

**SPACE SQUADRON** (Becomes Space Worlds #6)
June, 1951 - No. 5, Feb, 1952
Marvel/Atlas Comics (ACI)

| | | | |
|---|---|---|---|
| 1 | 27.00 | 81.00 | 190.00 |
| 2 | 22.00 | 65.00 | 150.00 |
| 3-5 | 17.00 | 51.00 | 120.00 |

**SPACE THRILLERS**
1954 (Giant) (25 cents)
Avon Periodicals

| | Good | Fine | N-Mint |
|---|---|---|---|
| nn-(Scarce)-Robotmen of the Lost Planet; contains 3 rebound comics of The Saint & Strange Worlds. Contents could vary | 68.00 | 205.00 | 475.00 |

**SPACE TRIP TO THE MOON** (See Space Adventures #23)

**SPACE WAR** (Fightin' Five #28 on)
Oct, 1959 - No. 27, Mar, 1964; No. 28, Mar, 1978 - No. 34, 3/79
Charlton Comics

| | | | |
|---|---|---|---|
| V1#1 | 8.00 | 24.00 | 55.00 |
| 2,3 | 3.15 | 9.50 | 22.00 |
| 4-6,8,10-Ditko-c/a | 8.50 | 25.50 | 60.00 |
| 7,9,11-15: Last 10 cent issue? | 2.00 | 6.00 | 14.00 |
| 16-27 | 1.50 | 4.50 | 10.00 |
| 28,29,33,34-Ditko-c/a(r) | 2.65 | 8.00 | 18.00 |
| 30-Ditko-c/a(r); Staton, Sutton/Wood-a | 2.85 | 8.50 | 20.00 |
| 31-Ditko-c/a; atom-blast-c | 2.85 | 8.50 | 20.00 |
| 32-r-/Charlton Premiere V2#2; Sutton-a | .30 | .90 | 1.80 |

**SPACE WESTERN** (Formerly Cowboy Western Comics; becomes Cowboy Western Comics #46 on)
No. 40, Oct, 1952 - No. 45, Aug, 1953
Charlton Comics (Capitol Stories)

| | | | |
|---|---|---|---|
| 40-Intro Spurs Jackson & His Space Vigilantes; flying saucer story | 25.00 | 75.00 | 175.00 |
| 41,43-45: 41-Flying saucer-c | 19.00 | 57.00 | 135.00 |
| 42-Atom bomb explosion-c | 21.00 | 62.00 | 145.00 |

**SPACE WORLDS** (Formerly Space Squadron #1-5)
No. 6, April, 1952
Atlas Comics (Male)

| | | | |
|---|---|---|---|
| 6 | 13.00 | 40.00 | 90.00 |

**SPANKY & ALFALFA & THE LITTLE RASCALS** (See The Little Rascals)

**SPANNER'S GALAXY**
Dec, 1984 - No. 6, May, 1985 (Mini-series)
DC Comics

| | | | |
|---|---|---|---|
| 1-6: Mandrake-c/a in all. 2-Intro sidekick Gadg | | .50 | 1.00 |

**SPARKIE, RADIO PIXIE** (Radio)(Becomes Big Jon & Sparkie #4)
Winter, 1951 - No. 3, July-Aug, 1952 (Painted-c)(Sparkie #2,3; #1?)
Ziff-Davis Publ. Co.

| | | | |
|---|---|---|---|
| 1-Based on children's radio program | 10.00 | 30.00 | 70.00 |
| 2,3: 3-Big Jon and Sparkie on-c only | 8.00 | 24.00 | 55.00 |

**SPARKLE COMICS**
Oct-Nov, 1948 - No. 33, Dec-Jan, 1953-54
United Features Syndicate

| | | | |
|---|---|---|---|
| 1-Li'l Abner, Nancy, Captain & the Kids, Ella Cinders (52 pgs.) | 6.50 | 19.50 | 45.00 |
| 2 | 3.50 | 10.50 | 24.00 |
| 3-10 | 2.30 | 7.00 | 16.00 |
| 11-20 | 1.70 | 5.00 | 12.00 |
| 21-33 | 1.15 | 3.50 | 8.00 |

**SPARKLE PLENTY** (See 4-Color #215 & Harvey Comics Library #2)

**SPARKLER COMICS** (1st Series)
July, 1940 - No. 2, 1940
United Feature Comic Group

| | | | |
|---|---|---|---|
| 1-Jim Hardy | 20.00 | 60.00 | 140.00 |
| 2-Frankie Doodle | 13.00 | 40.00 | 90.00 |

**SPARKLER COMICS** (2nd Series)(Nancy & Sluggo #121 on)(Cover title becomes Nancy and Sluggo #101? on)
July, 1941 - No. 120, Jan, 1955
United Features Syndicate

1-Origin Sparkman; Tarzan (by Hogarth in all issues), Captain & the Kids, Ella Cinders, Danny Dingle, Dynamite Dunn, Nancy, Abbie

*Space Squadron #5, © MEG*

*Space War #8, © CC*

*Space Worlds #6, © MEG*

Sparkler Comics #1 (7/41), © UFS

Special Edition #4, © DC

Special Marvel Edition #15, © MEG

| | Good | Fine | N-Mint |
|---|---|---|---|
| & Slats, Frankie Doodle, Broncho Bill begin; Sparkman c-#1-12 | 79.00 | 235.00 | 550.00 |
| 2 | 35.00 | 105.00 | 245.00 |
| 3,4 | 30.00 | 90.00 | 210.00 |
| 5-10: 9-Sparkman's new costume | 25.00 | 75.00 | 175.00 |
| 11-13,15-20: 12-Sparkman new costume-color change. 19-1st Race Riley | 21.00 | 62.00 | 145.00 |
| 14-Tarzan-c by Hogarth | 24.00 | 71.00 | 165.00 |
| 21-24,26,27,29,30: 22-Race Riley & the Commandos strips begin, ends #44 | 16.00 | 48.00 | 110.00 |
| 25,28,31,34,37,39-Tarzan-c by Hogarth | 20.00 | 60.00 | 140.00 |
| 32,33,35,36,38,40 | 9.30 | 28.00 | 65.00 |
| 41,43,45,46,48,49 | 6.50 | 19.00 | 45.00 |
| 42,44,47,50-Tarzan-c | 12.00 | 36.00 | 85.00 |
| 51,52,54-70: 57-Li'l Abner begins (not in #58); Fearless Fosdick app.-#58 | 4.50 | 14.00 | 32.00 |
| 53-Tarzan-c by Hogarth | 11.00 | 32.00 | 75.00 |
| 71-80 | 3.70 | 11.00 | 26.00 |
| 81,82,84-90: 85-Li'l Abner ends. 86-Lingerie panels | 2.85 | 8.50 | 20.00 |
| 83-Tarzan-c | 5.00 | 15.00 | 35.00 |
| 91-96,98-99 | 2.65 | 8.00 | 18.00 |
| 97-Origin Casey Ruggles by Warren Tufts | 5.70 | 17.00 | 40.00 |
| 100 | 3.60 | 11.00 | 25.00 |
| 101-107,109-112,114-120 | 2.00 | 6.00 | 14.00 |
| 108,113-Toth-a | 5.70 | 17.00 | 40.00 |

**SPARKLING LOVE**
June, 1950; 1953
Avon Periodicals/Realistic (1953)

| | Good | Fine | N-Mint |
|---|---|---|---|
| 1(Avon)-Kubert-a; photo-c | 11.50 | 34.00 | 80.00 |
| nn(1953)-Reprint; Kubert-a | 5.00 | 15.00 | 35.00 |

**SPARKLING STARS**
June, 1944 - No. 33, March, 1948
Holyoke Publishing Co.

| | Good | Fine | N-Mint |
|---|---|---|---|
| 1-Hell's Angels, FBI, Boxie Weaver & Ali Baba begin | 8.00 | 24.00 | 55.00 |
| 2 | 4.50 | 14.00 | 32.00 |
| 3-Actual FBI case photos & war photos | 3.15 | 9.50 | 22.00 |
| 4-10: 7-X-mas-c | 2.65 | 8.00 | 18.00 |
| 11-19: 13-Origin/1st app. Jungo the Man-Beast | 2.30 | 7.00 | 16.00 |
| 20-Intro Fangs the Wolf Boy | 2.65 | 8.00 | 18.00 |
| 21-29,32,33: 29-Bondage-c | 2.30 | 7.00 | 16.00 |
| 31-Spanking panel; Sid Greene-a | 2.65 | 8.00 | 18.00 |

**SPARK MAN** (See Sparkler Comics)
1945 (One Shot) (36 pages)
Frances M. McQueeny

| | Good | Fine | N-Mint |
|---|---|---|---|
| 1-Origin Spark Man; female torture story; cover redrawn from Sparkler No. 1 | 14.00 | 43.00 | 100.00 |

**SPARKY WATTS** (Also see Columbia Comics)
Nov?, 1942 - No. 10, 1949
Columbia Comic Corp.

| | Good | Fine | N-Mint |
|---|---|---|---|
| 1(1942)-Skyman & The Face app; Hitler-c | 18.00 | 54.00 | 125.00 |
| 2(1943) | 8.00 | 24.00 | 55.00 |
| 3(1944) | 7.00 | 21.00 | 50.00 |
| 4(1944)-Origin | 6.50 | 19.00 | 45.00 |
| 5(1947)-Skyman app. | 5.00 | 15.00 | 35.00 |
| 6('47),7,8('48),9,10('49): 8-Surrealistic-c | 3.15 | 9.50 | 22.00 |

**SPARTACUS** (See 4-Color #1139)

**SPECIAL AGENT** (Steve Saunders. . .)(Also see True Comics #68)
Dec, 1947 - No. 8, Sept, 1949
Parents' Magazine Institute (Commended Comics No. 2)

| | Good | Fine | N-Mint |
|---|---|---|---|
| 1-J. Edgar Hoover photo-c | 5.00 | 15.00 | 35.00 |
| 2 | 2.65 | 8.00 | 18.00 |
| 3-8 | 2.00 | 6.00 | 14.00 |

**SPECIAL COLLECTORS' EDITION**
Dec, 1975 (No month given) (10¼x13½")
Marvel Comics Group

| | Good | Fine | N-Mint |
|---|---|---|---|
| 1-Kung Fu, Iron Fist & Sons of the Tiger | .30 | .90 | 1.80 |

**SPECIAL COMICS** (Hangman #2 on)
Winter, 1941-42
MLJ Magazines

| | Good | Fine | N-Mint |
|---|---|---|---|
| 1-Origin The Boy Buddies (Shield & Wizard x-over); death of The Comet; origin The Hangman retold | 100.00 | 300.00 | 700.00 |

**SPECIAL DELIVERY**
1951 (32 pgs.; B&W)
Post Hall Synd. (Giveaway)

nn-Origin of Pogo, Swamp, etc.; 2 pg. biog. on Walt Kelly
(One copy sold in 1980 for $150.00)

**SPECIAL EDITION** (See Gorgo and Reptisaurus)

**SPECIAL EDITION** (U. S. Navy Giveaways)
1944 - 1945 (Regular comic format with wording simplified, 52pgs.)
National Periodical Publications

| | Good | Fine | N-Mint |
|---|---|---|---|
| 1-Action (1944)-reprints Action #80 | 70.00 | 210.00 | 490.00 |
| 2-Action (1944)-reprints Action #81 | 70.00 | 210.00 | 490.00 |
| 3-Superman (1944)-reprints Superman #33 | 70.00 | 210.00 | 490.00 |
| 4-Detective (1944)-reprints Detective #97 | 75.00 | 225.00 | 525.00 |
| 5-Superman (1945)-reprints Superman #34 | 70.00 | 210.00 | 490.00 |
| 6-Action (1945)-reprints Action #84 | 70.00 | 210.00 | 490.00 |

**SPECIAL EDITION COMICS**
1940 (August) (One Shot, 68pgs.)
Fawcett Publications

| | Good | Fine | VF-NM | NM/Mint |
|---|---|---|---|---|
| 1-1st book devoted entirely to Captain Marvel; C.C. Beck-c/a; only app. of Capt. Marvel with belt buckle; Capt. Marvel appears with button-down flap, 1st story (came out before Captain Marvel #1) | 300.00 | 900.00 | 2100.00 | 3000.00 |

(Estimated up to 150 total copies exist, 7 in NM/Mint)

NOTE: *Prices vary widely on this book. Since this book is all Captain Marvel stories, it is actually a pre-Captain Marvel #1. There is speculation that this book almost became **Captain Marvel** #1. After **Special Edition** was published, there was an editor change at Fawcett. The new editor commissioned Kirby to do a nn **Captain Marvel** book early in 1941. This book was followed by a 2nd book several months later. This 2nd book was advertised as a #3 (making Special Edition the #1, & the nn issue the #2). However, the 2nd book did come out as a #2.*

**SPECIAL EDITION X-MEN**
Feb, 1983 (One Shot) (Baxter paper, $2.00)
Marvel Comics Group

| | Good | Fine | N-Mint |
|---|---|---|---|
| 1-R/Giant-Size X-Men #1 plus one new story | 1.35 | 4.00 | 8.00 |

**SPECIAL MARVEL EDITION** (Master of Kung Fu #17 on)
Jan, 1971 - No. 16, Feb, 1974
Marvel Comics Group

| | Good | Fine | N-Mint |
|---|---|---|---|
| 1-Thor-r by Kirby; 68 pgs. | .50 | 1.50 | 3.00 |
| 2-4: Thor-r by Kirby; 68 pg. Giant | .40 | 1.25 | 2.50 |
| 5-14: Sgt. Fury-r; 11-Reprints Sgt. Fury #13 (Captain America app.) | .35 | 1.00 | 2.00 |
| 15-Master of Kung Fu begins (1st app.); Starlin-a; origin & 1st app. Nayland Smith & Dr. Petric | 1.70 | 5.00 | 12.00 |
| 16-1st app. Midnight; Starlin-a | 1.00 | 3.00 | 7.00 |

**SPECIAL MISSIONS** (See G.I. Joe. . .)

**SPECIAL WAR SERIES** (Attack V4#3 on?)
Aug, 1965 - No. 4, Nov, 1965
Charlton Comics

| | Good | Fine | N-Mint |
|---|---|---|---|
| V4#1-D-Day (Also see D-Day listing) | .70 | 2.00 | 4.00 |
| 2-Attack! | .50 | 1.50 | 3.00 |

| | Good | Fine | N-Mint |
|---|---|---|---|
| 3-War & Attack (Also see War & Attack) | .50 | 1.50 | 3.00 |
| 4-Judomaster (Intro/1st app.) | 1.70 | 5.00 | 12.00 |

**SPECTACULAR ADVENTURES** (See Adventures)

**SPECTACULAR FEATURE MAGAZINE, A** (Formerly My Confessions) (Spectacular Features Magazine #12)
No. 11, April, 1950
Fox Feature Syndicate

| | | | |
|---|---|---|---|
| 11 (#1)-Samson & Delilah | 13.00 | 40.00 | 90.00 |

**SPECTACULAR FEATURES MAGAZINE** (Formerly A Spectacular Feature Magazine)
No. 12, June, 1950 - No. 3, Aug, 1950
Fox Feature Syndicate

| | | | |
|---|---|---|---|
| 12 (#2)-Iwo Jima; photo flag-c | 13.00 | 40.00 | 90.00 |
| 3-True Crime Cases | 9.30 | 28.00 | 65.00 |

**SPECTACULAR SPIDER-MAN, THE** (See Marvel Special Edition and Marvel Treasury Edition)

**SPECTACULAR SPIDER-MAN, THE** (Magazine)
July, 1968 - No. 2, Nov, 1968 (35 cents)
Marvel Comics Group

| | | | |
|---|---|---|---|
| 1-(Black & White) | 4.30 | 13.00 | 30.00 |
| 2-(Color)-Green Goblin-c & app. | 8.00 | 24.00 | 55.00 |

**SPECTACULAR SPIDER-MAN, THE** (Peter Parker. . .#54-132,134)
Dec, 1976 - Present
Marvel Comics Group

| | | | |
|---|---|---|---|
| 1-Origin retold; Tarantula app. | 5.00 | 15.00 | 35.00 |
| 2-Kraven the Hunter app. | 2.00 | 6.00 | 14.00 |
| 3-5: 4-Vulture app. | 1.50 | 4.50 | 10.00 |
| 6-10: 6-8-Morbius app. 9,10-White Tiger app. | 1.00 | 3.00 | 6.00 |
| 11-20: 17,18-Champions x-over | .85 | 2.50 | 5.00 |
| 21,24-26: 21-Scorpion app. 26-Daredevil app. | .70 | 2.00 | 4.00 |
| 22,23-Moon Knight app. | 1.00 | 3.00 | 6.00 |
| 27-Miller's 1st art on Daredevil (7/79); also see Captain America #235 | 2.15 | 6.50 | 15.00 |
| 28-Miller Daredevil (p) | 1.70 | 5.00 | 12.00 |
| 29-57,59: 33-Origin Iguana. 38-Morbius app. | .50 | 1.50 | 3.00 |
| 58-Byrne-a(p) | .70 | 2.00 | 4.00 |
| 60-Double size; origin retold with new facts revealed | .50 | 1.50 | 3.00 |
| 61-63,65-68,71-74: 65-Kraven the Hunter app. | .35 | 1.00 | 2.00 |
| 64-1st app. Cloak & Dagger (3/82) | 1.70 | 5.00 | 12.00 |
| 69,70-Cloak & Dagger app. | 1.15 | 3.50 | 7.00 |
| 75-Double size | .40 | 1.25 | 2.50 |
| 76-80: 79-Punisher cameo | .35 | 1.00 | 2.00 |
| 81,82-Punisher, Cloak & Dagger app. | 1.50 | 4.50 | 10.00 |
| 83-Origin Punisher retold | 1.70 | 5.00 | 12.00 |
| 84-99: 90-Spider-man's new black costume, last panel(ties w/Amaz. Spider-Man #252). 94-96-Cloak & dagger app. 98-Intro The Spot | .35 | 1.00 | 2.00 |
| 100-Double size | .70 | 2.00 | 4.00 |
| 101-130: 107-Death of Jean DeWolff. 111-Secret Wars II tie-in. 128-Black Cat new costume. 130-Hobgoblin app. | .35 | 1.00 | 2.00 |
| 131-Six part Kraven tie-in | 1.00 | 3.00 | 6.00 |
| 132-Kraven tie-in | .85 | 2.50 | 5.00 |
| 133-139: 139-Origin Tombstone | .35 | 1.00 | 2.00 |
| 140-Punisher cameo app. | .50 | 1.50 | 3.00 |
| 141-Punisher app. | 1.00 | 3.00 | 6.00 |
| 142,143-Punisher app. | .70 | 2.00 | 4.00 |
| 144-157: 147-Hobgoblin app. 151-Tombstone returns. | .35 | 1.00 | 2.00 |
| 158-Spider-Man gets new powers (1st Cosmic Spidey, continued in Web of Spider-Man #59) | .50 | 1.50 | 3.00 |
| 159-176: 161-163-Hobgoblin app. 168-170-Avengers x-over. 169-1st app. The Outlaws | | .50 | 1.00 |
| Annuals 1-7: 1(1979). 2(1980)-Origin/1st app. Rapier. 3(1981)-Last Manwolf. 4(1984). 5(1985). 6(1985). 7(1987) | .50 | 1.50 | 3.00 |
| Annual 8 ('88, $1.75)-Evolutionary War x-over | .70 | 2.00 | 4.00 |
| Annual 9 ('89, $2.00, 68 pgs.)-Atlantis Attacks | .50 | 1.50 | 3.00 |
| Annual 10 ('90, $2.00, 68 pgs.)-McFarlane-a | .40 | 1.25 | 2.50 |

NOTE: *Austin c-21i. **Byrne** c(p)-17, 43, 58, 101, 102. **Giffen** a-120p. **Miller** c-46p, 48p, 50, 51p, 52p, 54p, 55, 56p, 57, 60. **Mooney** a-7i, 11i, 21p, 23p, 25p, 26p, 29-34p, 36p, 37p, 39i, 41, 42i, 49p, 50i, 51i, 53p, 54-57i, 59-66i, 68i, 71i, 73-79i, 81-83i, 85i, 87-99i, 102i, 125p, Annual 1i, 2p. **Nasser** c-37p. **Perez** c-10. **Simonson** c-54i.*

**SPECTACULAR STORIES MAGAZINE** (Formerly A Star Presentation)
No. 4, July, 1950 - No. 3, Sept, 1950
Fox Feature Sydicate (Hero Books)

| | | | |
|---|---|---|---|
| 4-Sherlock Holmes | 19.00 | 58.00 | 135.00 |
| 3-The St. Valentine's Day Massacre | 11.50 | 34.00 | 80.00 |

**SPECTRE, THE** (See Adventure Comics 431, More Fun & Showcase)
Nov-Dec, 1967 - No. 10, May-June, 1969 (All 12 cents)
National Periodical Publications

| | | | |
|---|---|---|---|
| 1-Anderson-c/a | 4.30 | 13.00 | 30.00 |
| 2-5-Neal Adams-c/a; 3-Wildcat x-over | 2.85 | 8.50 | 20.00 |
| 6-8,10: 6-8-Anderson inks. 7-Hourman app. | 1.30 | 4.00 | 9.00 |
| 9-Wrightson-a | 1.50 | 4.50 | 10.00 |

**SPECTRE, THE** (See Saga of Swamp Thing #58 & Wrath of the. . .)
Apr, 1987 - No. 31, Oct, 1989 ($1.00, new format)
DC Comics

| | | | |
|---|---|---|---|
| 1-Colan-a(p) begins | .40 | 1.25 | 2.50 |
| 2-10: 9-Nudity panels | .25 | .75 | 1.50 |
| 11-31: 10-Batman cameo. 10,11-Millennium tie-ins | | .60 | 1.25 |
| Annual 1 (1988, $2.00)-Deadman app. | .35 | 1.00 | 2.00 |

NOTE: ***Art Adams** c-Annual #1. **Colan** a-1-6p. **Kaluta** c-1-3. **Morrow** a-9-15.*

**SPEEDBALL** (See Amazing Spider-Man Annual #12)
Sept, 1988(10/88-inside) - No. 11, July, 1989 (75 cents, color)
Marvel Comics

| | | | |
|---|---|---|---|
| 1-11: Ditko/Guice a-1-4, c-1; Ditko c-5,9 | | .40 | .80 |

**SPEED BUGGY** (TV)(Also see Fun-In #12,15)
July, 1975 - No. 9, Nov, 1976 (Hanna-Barbera)
Charlton Comics

| | | | |
|---|---|---|---|
| 1-9 | | .25 | .50 |

**SPEED CARTER SPACEMAN** (See Spaceman)

**SPEED COMICS** (New Speed)(Also see Double Up)
10/39 - No. 11, 8/40; No. 12, 3/41 - No. 44, 1-2/47 (No. 14-16: pocket size, 100 pgs.)
Brookwood Publ./Speed Publ./Harvey Publications No. 14 on

| | | | |
|---|---|---|---|
| 1-Origin Shock Gibson; Ted Parrish, the Man with 1000 Faces begins; Powell-a | 86.00 | 257.00 | 600.00 |
| 2-Powell-a | 43.00 | 130.00 | 300.00 |
| 3 | 26.00 | 77.00 | 180.00 |
| 4-Powell-a? | 22.00 | 65.00 | 155.00 |
| 5 | 21.00 | 62.00 | 145.00 |
| 6-11: 7-Mars Mason begins, ends #11 | 18.00 | 54.00 | 125.00 |
| 12 (3/41; shows #11 in indicia)-The Wasp begins; Major Colt app. (Capt. Colt #12) | 22.00 | 65.00 | 155.00 |
| 13-Intro. Captain Freedom & Young Defenders; Girl Commandos, Pat Parker, War Nurse begins; Major Colt app. | 27.00 | 80.00 | 185.00 |
| 14-16 (100 pg. pocket size, 1941): 14-2nd Harvey comic (See Pocket). 15-Pat Parker dons costume, last in costume #23; no Girl Commandos | 20.00 | 60.00 | 140.00 |
| 17-Black Cat begins (origin), r-/Pocket #1; not in #40,41 | 35.00 | 105.00 | 245.00 |
| 18-20 | 18.00 | 54.00 | 125.00 |
| 21,22,25-30: 26-Flag-c | 16.00 | 48.00 | 110.00 |
| 23-Origin Girl Commandos | 23.00 | 70.00 | 160.00 |
| 24-Pat Parker team-up with Girl Commandos | 16.00 | 48.00 | 110.00 |

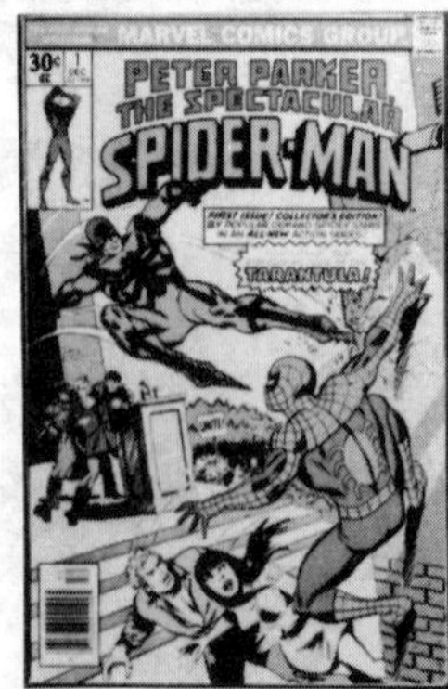

*The Spectacular Spider-Man #1, © MEG*

*The Spectre #3 (3-4/68), © DC*

*Speed Comics #6, © HARV*

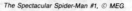

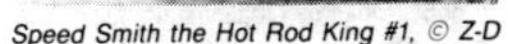
Speed Smith the Hot Rod King #1, © Z-D

Spellbound #13, © MEG

Spider-Man #1 (silver unbagged), © MEG

| | Good | Fine | N-Mint |
|---|---|---|---|
| 31-44: 38-Flag-c | 13.00 | 40.00 | 90.00 |

NOTE: **Briefer** a-6, 7. **Kubert** a-7-11(Mars Mason), 37, 38, 42-44. **Powell** a-1, 2, 4-7, 28, 31, 44. **Schomburg** c-31-36. **Tuska** a-3, 6, 7. Bondage c-18, 35.

**SPEED DEMONS** (Formerly Frank Merriwell at Yale #1-4?; Submarine Attack #11 on)
No. 5, Feb, 1957 - No. 10, 1958
Charlton Comics

| | | | |
|---|---|---|---|
| 5-10 | .70 | 2.00 | 5.00 |

**SPEED RACER** (See Dai Kamikaze! & Racer-X)
July, 1987 - Present (#1-3: $1.50, 4 on: $1.75; color)
Now Comics

| | | | |
|---|---|---|---|
| 1 | .60 | 1.75 | 3.50 |
| 1-2nd printing | .25 | .75 | 1.50 |
| 2-10 | .35 | 1.00 | 2.00 |
| 11-40 | .30 | .90 | 1.75 |
| 41,42: 41-Begin $1.95-c | .35 | 1.00 | 2.00 |
| Special 1 (3/88, $2.00)-Origin Mach 5 | .35 | 1.00 | 2.00 |
| Special 2 ('88, $3.50) | .60 | 1.75 | 3.50 |

NOTE: **Steacy** c-3, 4, 11-14, Special #1.

**SPEED SMITH THE HOT ROD KING**
Spring, 1952
Ziff-Davis Publishing Co.

| | | | |
|---|---|---|---|
| 1-Saunders painted-c | 9.00 | 27.00 | 62.00 |

**SPEEDY GONZALES** (See 4-Color #1084)

**SPEEDY RABBIT** (See Television Puppet Show)
nd (1953); 1963
Realistic/I. W. Enterprises/Super Comics

| | | | |
|---|---|---|---|
| nn (1953)-Realistic Reprint? | 1.00 | 3.00 | 7.00 |
| I.W. Reprint #1 (2 versions w/diff. c/stories exist) | .25 | .80 | 1.60 |
| Super Reprint #14(1963) | .25 | .80 | 1.60 |

**SPELLBINDERS**
Dec, 1986 - No. 12, Jan, 1988 ($1.25, color)
Quality Comics

| | | | |
|---|---|---|---|
| 1-12: Nemesis The Warlock, Amadeus Wolf | | .65 | 1.30 |

**SPELLBOUND** (See The Crusaders)

**SPELLBOUND** (Tales to Hold You... #1, Stories to Hold You...)
Mar, 1952 - #23, June, 1954; #24, Oct, 1955 - #34, June, 1957
Atlas Comics (ACI 1-15/Male 16-23/BPC 24-34)

| | | | |
|---|---|---|---|
| 1 | 20.00 | 60.00 | 140.00 |
| 2-Edgar A. Poe app. | 11.00 | 32.00 | 75.00 |
| 3-5: 3-Whitney-a; cannibalism story | 8.50 | 25.50 | 60.00 |
| 6-Krigstein-a | 8.50 | 25.50 | 60.00 |
| 7-10: 8-Ayers-a | 6.50 | 19.00 | 45.00 |
| 11-16,18-20: 14-Ed Win-a | 5.00 | 15.00 | 35.00 |
| 17-Krigstein-a | 6.00 | 18.00 | 42.00 |
| 21-23-Last precode (6/54) | 4.30 | 13.00 | 30.00 |
| 24-28,30,31,34: 25-Orlando-a | 2.85 | 8.50 | 20.00 |
| 29-Ditko-a | 4.30 | 13.00 | 30.00 |
| 32,33-Torres-a | 4.30 | 13.00 | 30.00 |

NOTE: **Colan** a-17. **Everett** a-2, 5, 7, 10, 16, 28, 31; c-2, 8, 9, 14, 17-19, 28, 30. **Forte/Fox** a-16. **Heath** a-2, 4, 8-10, 12, 14, 16; c-3, 4, 12, 16, 20, 21. **Infantino** a-15. **Maneely** a-7, 14, 27; c-10, 24, 31. **Mooney** a-5, 13, 18. **Mac Pakula** a-22, 32. **Post** a-8. **Powell** a-19, 20, 32. **Robinson** a-1. **Romita** a-24, 26, 27. **Severin** c-29. **Sinnott** a-8, 16.

**SPELLBOUND**
Jan, 1988 - No. 6, Apr, 1988 ($1.50, bi-weekly; Baxter paper)
Marvel Comics

| | | | |
|---|---|---|---|
| 1-5 | .25 | .75 | 1.50 |
| 6 ($2.25, 52 pgs.) | .35 | 1.10 | 2.25 |

**SPELLJAMMER** (Also see TSR Worlds Comics Annual)
Sept, 1990 - Present ($1.75, color)
DC Comics

| | Good | Fine | N-Mint |
|---|---|---|---|
| 1-6: Based on TSR game; sci/fi | .30 | .90 | 1.80 |

**SPENCER SPOOK** (Formerly Giggle Comics; see Advs. of...)
No. 100, Mar-Apr, 1955 - No. 101, May-June, 1955
American Comics Group

| | | | |
|---|---|---|---|
| 100,101 | 2.15 | 6.50 | 15.00 |

**SPIDER-MAN** (See Amazing..., Giant-Size..., Marvel Tales, Marvel Team-Up, Spectacular..., Spidey Super Stories, & Web Of...)

**SPIDER-MAN**
Aug, 1990 - Present ($1.75, color)
Marvel Comics

| | | | |
|---|---|---|---|
| 1-Silver edition, direct sale only (unbagged) | 1.70 | 4.00 | 8.00 |
| 1-Silver bagged edition; direct sale, no price on comic, but $2.00 on plastic bag (still sealed) | 3.35 | 10.00 | 20.00 |
| 1-Regular edition w/Spidey face in UPC area (unbagged); green-c | .85 | 2.50 | 5.00 |
| 1-Regular bagged edition w/Spidey face in UPC area (price is for still sealed only); green cover | 2.50 | 7.50 | 15.00 |
| 1-Newsstand bagged w/UPC code (sealed) | .85 | 2.50 | 5.00 |
| 1-Gold edition, 2nd printing (unbagged) | 1.00 | 3.00 | 6.00 |
| 2-McFarlane-c/a/scripts continue | .70 | 2.00 | 4.00 |
| 3 | .50 | 1.50 | 3.00 |
| 4,5 | .35 | 1.00 | 2.00 |
| 6-10: 6,7-Ghost Rider & Hobgoblin app. 8-Wolverine app. | .30 | .90 | 1.75 |

**SPIDER-MAN AND DAREDEVIL**
March, 1984 (One-Shot; $2.00; deluxe paper)
Marvel Comics Group

| | | | |
|---|---|---|---|
| 1-r-/Spectacular Spider-Man #26-28 by Miller | .50 | 1.50 | 3.00 |

**SPIDER-MAN AND HIS AMAZING FRIENDS**
Dec, 1981 (One shot) (See Marvel Action Universe)
Marvel Comics Group

| | | | |
|---|---|---|---|
| 1-Adapted from TV cartoon show; Green Goblin app.; Spiegle-a(p); 1st Spidey, Firestar, Iceman team-up | .25 | .75 | 1.50 |

**SPIDER-MAN COMICS MAGAZINE**
Jan, 1987 - No. 13, 1988 ($1.50, Digest-size)
Marvel Comics Group

| | | | |
|---|---|---|---|
| 1-13-Reprints | .25 | .75 | 1.50 |

**SPIDER-MAN GRAPHIC NOVEL**
Summer, 1987 ($5.95)
Marvel Comics

| | | | |
|---|---|---|---|
| 1-Kingpin app. | 1.00 | 3.00 | 5.95 |

**SPIDER-MAN VS. VENOM**
1990 ($8.95, trade paperback)
Marvel Comics

| | | | |
|---|---|---|---|
| nn-r/Amazing Spider-Man #300,315-317 w/new McFarlane-c | 1.50 | 4.50 | 9.00 |

**SPIDER-MAN VS. WOLVERINE**
Feb, 1987 (One-shot); V2#1, 1990 (Both have 68 pgs.)
Marvel Comics Group

| | | | |
|---|---|---|---|
| 1-Williamson-c(i); intro Charlemagne | 2.00 | 6.00 | 12.00 |
| V2#1 (1990, $4.95)-Reprints #1 (2/87) | .85 | 2.50 | 5.00 |

**SPIDER-WOMAN** (Also see The Avengers #240, Marvel Spotlight #32 & Marvel Two-In-One #29)
April, 1978 - No. 50, June, 1983 (New logo #47 on)
Marvel Comics Group

| | | | |
|---|---|---|---|
| 1-New origin & mask added | .40 | 1.25 | 2.50 |
| 2-36,39-50: 6,19-Werewolf by Night app. 20,28,29-Spider-Man app. 46-Kingpin app. 49-Tigra app. 50-Double size; photo-c; death of Spider-Woman | .25 | .75 | 1.50 |

Good Fine N-Mint

37,38-New X-Men x-over; 37-1st Siryn; origin retold; photo-c .40 1.25 2.50

NOTE: ***Austin** a-37i. **Byrne** c-26p. **Layton** c-19. **Miller** c-32p.*

**SPIDEY SUPER STORIES** (Spider-Man)
Oct, 1974 - No. 57, Mar, 1982 (35 cents) (no ads)
Marvel/Children's TV Workshop

1-(Stories simplified) .30 .60
2-57: 2-Kraven. 6-Iceman. 45-Silver Surfer .25 .50

**SPIKE AND TYKE** (See M.G.M.'s . . .)

**SPIN & MARTY** (TV) (Walt Disney's)(See W. Disney Showcase #32)
No. 714, June, 1956 - No. 1082, Mar-May, 1960 (All photo-c)
Dell Publishing Co. (Mickey Mouse Club)

4-Color 714 4.50 14.00 32.00
4-Color 767,808 4.00 12.00 28.00
4-Color 826-Annette Funicello photo-c 10.00 30.00 70.00
5(3-5/58) - 9(6-8/59) 4.00 12.00 28.00
4-Color 1026,1082 4.00 12.00 28.00

**SPINE-TINGLING TALES** (Doctor Spektor Presents . . .)
May, 1975 - No. 4, Jan, 1976
Gold Key

1-4: 1-1st Tragg r-/Mystery Comics Digest #3. 2-Origin Ra-Ka-Tep r-/Mystery Comics Digest #1; Dr. Spektor #12. 3-All Durak issue; (r). 4-Baron Tibor's 1st app. r-/Mystery Comics Digest #4 .40 .80

**SPIRAL PATH, THE**
7/86 - No. 2, 7/86 ($1.75, Baxter paper, color, mini-series)
Eclipse Comics

1,2 .30 .90 1.80

**SPIRAL ZONE**
Feb, 1988 - No. 4, May, 1988 ($1.00, mini-series)
DC Comics

1-4-Based on Tonka toys .50 1.00

**SPIRIT, THE** (Weekly Comic Book)
6/2/40 - 10/5/52 (16 pgs.; 8 pgs.) (no cover) (in color)
(Distributed through various newspapers and other sources)
Will Eisner

*NOTE: **Eisner** script, pencils/inks for the most part from 6/2/40-4/26/42; a few stories assisted by Jack Cole, Fine, Powell and Kotsky.*

6/2/40(#1)-Origin/1st app. The Spirit; reprinted in Police #11; Lady Luck (Brenda Banks)(1st app.) by Chuck Mazoujian & Mr. Mystic (1st. app.) by S. R. (Bob) Powell begin 60.00 180.00 420.00
6/9/40(#2) 26.00 78.00 180.00
6/16/40(#3)-Black Queen app. in Spirit 17.00 51.00 110.00
6/23/40(#4)-Mr. Mystic receives magical necklace 13.00 40.00 90.00
6/30/40(#5) 13.00 40.00 90.00
7/7/40(#6)-Black Queen app. in Spirit 13.00 40.00 90.00
7/14/40(#7)-8/4/40(#10) 10.00 30.50 70.00
8/11/40-9/22/40 9.00 27.00 62.00
9/29/40-Ellen drops engagement with Homer Creep 8.00 24.00 56.00
10/6/40-11/3/40 8.00 24.00 56.00
11/10/40-The Black Queen app. 8.00 24.00 56.00
11/17/40, 11/24/40 8.00 24.00 56.00
12/1/40-Ellen spanking by Spirit on cover & inside; Eisner-1st 3 pgs., J. Cole rest 11.50 34.00 80.00
12/8/40-3/9/41 5.70 17.00 40.00
3/16/41-Intro. & 1st app. Silk Satin 10.00 30.00 70.00
3/23/41-6/1/41: 5/11/41-Last Lady Luck by Mazoujian; 5/18/41-Lady Luck by Nick Viscardi begins, ends 2/22/42 5.70 17.00 40.00

Good Fine N-Mint

6/8/41-2nd app. Satin; Spirit learns Satin is also a British agent 8.50 25.50 60.00
6/15/41-1st app. Twilight 7.00 21.00 50.00
6/22/41-Hitler app. in Spirit 5.00 15.00 35.00
6/29/41-1/25/42,2/8/42 5.00 15.00 35.00
2/1/42-1st app. Duchess 7.00 21.00 50.00
2/15/42-4/26/42-Lady Luck by Klaus Nordling begins 3/1/42 5.00 15.00 35.00
5/3/42-8/16/42-Eisner/Fine/Quality staff assists on Spirit 4.00 12.00 24.00
8/23/42-Satin cover splash; Spirit by Eisner/Fine although signed by Fine 8.00 24.00 56.00
8/30/42,9/27/42-10/11/42,10/25/42-11/8/42-Eisner/Fine/Quality staff assists on Spirit 4.00 12.00 24.00
9/6/42-9/20/42,10/18/42-Fine/Belfi art on Spirit; scripts by Manly Wade Wellman 2.75 8.00 16.00
11/15/42-12/6/42,12/20/42,12/27/42,1/17/43-4/18/43,5/9/43-8/8/43-Wellman/Woolfolk scripts, Fine pencils, Quality staff inks 2.75 8.00 16.00
12/13/42,1/3/43,1/10/43,4/25/43,5/2/43-Eisner scripts/layouts; Fine pencils, Quality staff inks 3.35 10.00 20.00
8/15/43-Eisner script/layout; pencils/inks by Quality staff; Jack Cole-a 2.00 6.00 12.00
8/22/43-12/12/43-Wellman/Woolfolk scripts, Fine pencils, Quality staff inks; Mr. Mystic by Guardineer-10/10/43-10/24/43 2.00 6.00 12.00
12/19/43-8/13/44-Wellman/Woolfolk/Jack Cole scripts; Cole, Fine & Robin King-a; Last Mr. Mystic-5/14/44 1.70 5.00 10.00
8/22/44-12/16/45-Wellman/Woolfolk scripts; Fine art with unknown staff assists 1.70 5.00 10.00

*NOTE: Scripts/layouts by Eisner, or Eisner/Nordling, Eisner/Mercer or Spranger/Eisner; inks by Eisner or Eisner/Spranger in issues 12/23/45-2/2/47.*

12/23/45-1/6/46 4.00 12.00 28.00
1/13/46-Origin Spirit retold 6.00 18.00 42.00
1/20/46-1st postwar Satin app. 5.70 17.00 40.00
1/27/46-3/10/46: 3/3/46-Last Lady Luck by Nordling 4.00 12.00 28.00
3/17/46-Intro. & 1st app. Nylon 5.70 17.00 40.00
3/24/46,3/31/46,4/14/46 4.00 12.00 28.00
4/7/46-2nd app. Nylon 5.00 15.00 35.00
4/21/46-Intro. & 1st app. Mr. Carrion & His Pet Buzzard Julia 6.50 19.50 45.00
4/28/46-5/12/46,5/26/46-6/30/46: Lady Luck by Fred Schwab in issues 5/5/46-11/3/46 4.00 12.00 28.00
5/19/46-2nd app. Mr. Carrion 5.00 15.00 35.00
7/7/46-Intro. & 1st app. Dulcet Tone & Skinny 6.00 18.00 42.00
7/14/46-9/29/46 4.00 12.00 28.00
10/6/46-Intro. & 1st app. P'Gell 7.00 21.00 50.00
10/13/46-11/3/46,11/16/46-11/24/46 4.00 12.00 28.00
11/10/46-2nd app. P'Gell 5.00 15.00 35.00
12/1/46-3rd app. P'Gell 4.65 14.00 32.00
12/8/46-2/2/47 3.70 11.00 26.00

*NOTE: Scripts, pencils/inks by Eisner except where noted in issues 2/9/47-12/19/48.*

2/9/47-7/6/47: 6/8/47-Eisner self satire 3.70 11.00 26.00
7/13/47-"Hansel & Gretel" fairy tales 5.70 17.00 40.00
7/20/47-Li'L Abner, Daddy Warbucks, Dick Tracy, Fearless Fosdick parody; A-Bomb blast-c 5.70 17.00 40.00
7/27/47-9/14/47 3.70 11.00 26.00
9/21/47-Pearl Harbor flashback 3.70 11.00 26.00
9/28/47-1st mention of Flying Saucers in comics-3 months after 1st sighting in Idaho on 6/25/47 8.00 24.00 56.00
10/5/47-"Cinderella" fairy tales 5.70 17.00 40.00
10/12/47-11/30/47 3.70 11.00 26.00
12/7/47-Intro. & 1st app. Powder Pouf 6.00 18.00 42.00
12/14/47-12/28/47 3.70 11.00 26.00

*Spider-Woman #50, © MEG*

*Spin & Marty #7, © The Disney Co.*

*The Spirit, 9/8/40, © Will Eisner*

The Spirit, 2/12/50, © Will Eisner

The Spirit #20 (Quality), © Will Eisner

The Spirit #5 (Fiction House), © Will Eisner

| | Good | Fine | N-Mint |
|---|---|---|---|
| 1/4/48-2nd app. Powder Pouf | 5.00 | 15.00 | 35.00 |
| 1/11/48-1st app. Sparrow Fallon; Powder Pouf app. | 5.00 | 15.00 | 35.00 |
| 1/18/48-He-Man ad cover; satire issue | 5.00 | 15.00 | 35.00 |
| 1/25/48-Intro. & 1st app. Castanet | 5.70 | 17.00 | 40.00 |
| 2/1/48-2nd app. Castanet | 4.00 | 12.00 | 28.00 |
| 2/8/48-3/7/48 | 3.70 | 11.00 | 26.00 |
| 3/14/48-Only app. Kretchma | 4.00 | 12.00 | 28.00 |
| 3/21/48,3/28/48,4/11/48-4/25/48 | 3.70 | 11.00 | 26.00 |
| 4/4/48-Only app. Wild Rice | 4.00 | 12.00 | 28.00 |
| 5/2/48-2nd app. Sparrow | 3.70 | 11.00 | 26.00 |
| 5/9/48-6/27/48,7/11/48,7/18/48: 6/13/48-Television issue | 3.70 | 11.00 | 26.00 |
| 7/4/48-Spirit by Andre Le Blanc | 2.75 | 8.00 | 16.00 |
| 7/25/48-Ambrose Bierce's "The Thing" adaptation classic by Eisner/Grandenetti | 8.00 | 24.00 | 56.00 |
| 8/1/48-8/15/48,8/29/48-9/12/48 | 3.70 | 11.00 | 26.00 |
| 8/22/48-Poe's "Fall of the House of Usher" classic by Eisner/Grandenetti | 8.00 | 24.00 | 56.00 |
| 9/19/48-Only app. Lorelei | 4.30 | 13.00 | 30.00 |
| 9/26/48-10/31/48 | 3.70 | 11.00 | 26.00 |
| 11/7/48-Only app. Plaster of Paris | 5.00 | 15.00 | 35.00 |
| 11/14/48-12/19/48 | 3.70 | 11.00 | 26.00 |

NOTE: *Scripts by Eisner or Feiffer or Eisner/Feiffer or Nordling. Art by Eisner with backgrounds by Eisner, Grandenetti, Le Blanc, Stallman, Nordling, Dixon and/or others in issues 12/26/48-4/1/51 except where noted.*

| | Good | Fine | N-Mint |
|---|---|---|---|
| 12/26/48-Reprints some covers of 1948 with flashbacks | 3.70 | 11.00 | 26.00 |
| 1/2/49-1/16/49 | 3.70 | 11.00 | 26.00 |
| 1/23/49,1/30/49-1st & 2nd app. Thorne | 6.75 | 20.00 | 35.00 |
| 2/6/49-8/14/49 | 3.70 | 11.00 | 26.00 |
| 8/21/49,8/28/49-1st & 2nd app. Monica Veto | 6.75 | 20.00 | 35.00 |
| 9/4/49,9/11/49 | 3.70 | 11.00 | 26.00 |
| 9/18/49-Love comic cover; has gag love comic ads on inside | 7.35 | 22.00 | 38.00 |
| 9/25/49-Only app. Ice | 4.65 | 14.00 | 32.00 |
| 10/2/49,10/9/49-Autumn News appears & dies in 10/9 issue | 4.65 | 14.00 | 32.00 |
| 10/16/49-11/27/49,12/18/49,12/25/49 | 3.70 | 11.00 | 26.00 |
| 12/4/49,12/11/49-1st & 2nd app. Flaxen | 4.30 | 13.00 | 30.00 |
| 1/1/50-Flashbacks to all of the Spirit girls-Thorne, Ellen, Satin, & Monica | 6.50 | 19.50 | 45.00 |
| 1/8/50-Intro. & 1st app. Sand Saref | 9.00 | 27.00 | 62.00 |
| 1/15/50-2nd app. Saref | 6.50 | 19.50 | 45.00 |
| 1/22/50-2/5/50 | 3.70 | 11.00 | 26.00 |
| 2/12/50-Roller Derby issue | 4.00 | 12.00 | 28.00 |
| 2/19/50-Half Dead Mr. Lox - Classic horror | 4.65 | 14.00 | 32.00 |
| 2/26/50-4/23/50,5/14/50,5/28/50,7/23/50-9/3/50 | 3.70 | 11.00 | 26.00 |
| 4/30/50-Script/art by Le Blanc with Eisner framing | 1.70 | 5.00 | 10.00 |
| 5/7/50,6/4/50-7/16/50-Abe Kanegson-a | 1.70 | 5.00 | 10.00 |
| 5/21/50-Script by Feiffer/Eisner, art by Blaisdell, Eisner framing | 1.70 | 5.00 | 10.00 |
| 9/10/50-P'Gell returns | 5.00 | 15.00 | 35.00 |
| 9/17/50-1/7/51 | 3.70 | 11.00 | 26.00 |
| 1/14/51-Life Magazine cover; brief biography of Comm. Dolan, Sand Saref, Silk Satin, P'Gell, Sammy & Willum, Darling O'Shea, & Mr. Carrion & His Pet Buzzard Julia, with pin-ups by Eisner | 4.65 | 14.00 | 32.00 |
| 1/21/51,2/4/51-4/1/51 | 3.70 | 11.00 | 26.00 |
| 1/28/51-"The Meanest Man in the World" classic by Eisner | 4.65 | 14.00 | 32.00 |
| 4/8/51-7/29/51,8/12/51-Last Eisner issue | 3.70 | 11.00 | 26.00 |
| 8/5/51,8/19/51-7/20/52-Not Eisner | 1.70 | 5.00 | 10.00 |
| 7/27/52-(Rare)-Denny Colt in Outer Space by Wally Wood; 7 pg. S/F story of E.C. vintage | 40.00 | 120.00 | 280.00 |

| | Good | Fine | N-Mint |
|---|---|---|---|
| 8/3/52-(Rare)-"Mission...The Moon" by Wood | 40.00 | 120.00 | 280.00 |
| 8/10/52-(Rare)-"A DP On The Moon" by Wood | 40.00 | 120.00 | 280.00 |
| 8/17/52-(Rare)-"Heart" by Wood/Eisner | 42.00 | 125.00 | 240.00 |
| 8/24/52-(Rare)-"Rescue" by Wood | 40.00 | 120.00 | 280.00 |
| 8/31/52-(Rare)-"The Last Man" by Wood | 40.00 | 120.00 | 280.00 |
| 9/7/52-(Rare)-"The Man in The Moon" by Wood | 40.00 | 120.00 | 280.00 |
| 9/14/52-(Rare)-Eisner/Wenzel-a | 8.00 | 24.00 | 56.00 |
| 9/21/52-(Rare)-"Denny Colt, Alias The Spirit/Space Report" by Eisner/Wenzel | 14.00 | 42.00 | 100.00 |
| 9/28/52-(Rare)-"Return From The Moon" by Wood | 40.00 | 120.00 | 280.00 |
| 10/5/52-(Rare)-"The Last Story" by Eisner | 14.00 | 42.00 | 100.00 |

Large Tabloid pages from 1946 on (Eisner) - Price 30 percent over listed prices.

NOTE: *Spirit sections came out in both large and small format. Some newspapers went to the 8-pg. format months before others. Some printed the pages so they cannot be folded into a small comic book section; these are worth less. (Also see Three Comics & Spiritman).*

**SPIRIT, THE** (Section)
January 9, 1966
N. Y. Sunday Herald Tribune

| | Good | Fine | N-Mint |
|---|---|---|---|
| New 5-pg. Spirit story by Eisner; 2 pg. article on super-heroes; 2 pgs. color strips (BC, Miss Peach, Peanuts, Wizard of Id) | 13.00 | 40.00 | 80.00 |

**SPIRIT, THE** (1st Series)(Also see Police Comics #11)
1944 - No. 22, Aug, 1950
Quality Comics Group (Vital)

| | Good | Fine | N-Mint |
|---|---|---|---|
| nn(#1)-"Wanted Dead or Alive" | 43.00 | 130.00 | 300.00 |
| nn(#2)-"Crime Doesn't Pay" | 27.00 | 81.00 | 190.00 |
| nn(#3)-"Murder Runs Wild" | 21.00 | 62.00 | 145.00 |
| 4,5 | 15.00 | 45.00 | 105.00 |
| 6-10 | 14.00 | 41.00 | 95.00 |
| 11 | 12.00 | 36.00 | 85.00 |
| 12-17-Eisner-c | 22.00 | 65.00 | 150.00 |
| 18-21-Strip-r by Eisner; Eisner-c | 30.00 | 90.00 | 210.00 |
| 22-Used by N.Y. Legis. Comm; Classic Eisner-c | 46.00 | 137.00 | 320.00 |
| Super Reprint #11-r-/Quality Spirit #19 by Eisner | 1.35 | 4.00 | 8.00 |
| Super Reprint #12-r-/Quality Spirit #17 by Fine | 1.00 | 3.00 | 6.00 |

**SPIRIT, THE** (2nd Series)
Spring, 1952 - No. 5, 1954
Fiction House Magazines

| | Good | Fine | N-Mint |
|---|---|---|---|
| 1-Not Eisner | 21.00 | 62.00 | 145.00 |
| 2-Eisner-c/a(2) | 23.00 | 70.00 | 160.00 |
| 3-Eisner/Grandenetti-c | 15.00 | 45.00 | 105.00 |
| 4-Eisner/Grandenetti-c; Eisner-a | 19.00 | 57.00 | 130.00 |
| 5-Eisner-c/a(4) | 24.00 | 71.00 | 165.00 |

**SPIRIT, THE**
Oct, 1966 - No. 2, Mar, 1967 (Giant Size, 25 cents, 68 pgs.)
Harvey Publications

| | Good | Fine | N-Mint |
|---|---|---|---|
| 1-Eisner-r plus 9 new pgs.(Origin Denny Colt, Take 3, plus 2 filler pages) | 4.00 | 12.00 | 24.00 |
| 2-Eisner-r plus 9 new pgs.(Origin of the Octopus) | 4.00 | 12.00 | 24.00 |

**SPIRIT, THE** (Underground)
Jan, 1973 - No. 2, Sept, 1973 (Black & White)
Kitchen Sink Enterprises (Krupp Comics)

| | Good | Fine | N-Mint |
|---|---|---|---|
| 1-New Eisner-c, 4 pgs. new Eisner-a plus-r (titled Crime Convention) | 1.00 | 3.00 | 6.00 |

| | Good | Fine | N-Mint |
|---|---|---|---|
| 2-New Eisner-c, 4 pgs. new Eisner-a plus-r(titled Meets P'Gell) | 1.35 | 4.00 | 8.00 |

**SPIRIT, THE** (Magazine)
4/74 - No. 16, 10/76; No. 17, Winter, 1977 - No. 41, 6/83 (B&W w/color)
Warren Publ. Co./Krupp Comic Works No. 17 on

| | Good | Fine | N-Mint |
|---|---|---|---|
| 1-Eisner-r begin | .80 | 2.40 | 4.80 |
| 2-5 | .50 | 1.50 | 3.00 |
| 6-9,11-16: 7-All Ebony issue. 8-Female Foes issue. 12-X-Mas issue. 16-Giant Summer Special ($1.50) | .40 | 1.20 | 2.40 |
| 10-Giant Summer Special ($1.50)-Origin | .45 | 1.40 | 2.80 |
| 17,18(8/78) | | .60 | 1.20 |
| 19-21-New Eisner-a plus Wood #20,21 | | .60 | 1.20 |
| 22,23-Wood-r | | .60 | 1.20 |
| 24-35: 28-r-last story (10/5/52) | | .60 | 1.20 |
| 36-Begin Spirit Section-r; r-1st story (6/2/40) in color; new Eisner-c/a (18 pgs.)($2.95) | .50 | 1.50 | 3.00 |
| 37-41: 37-r-2nd story in color plus 18 pgs. new Eisner-a. 38-41: r-3rd through 6th story in color | .50 | 1.50 | 3.00 |
| Special 1('75)-All Eisner-a | .30 | .90 | 1.80 |

NOTE: *Covers pencilled/inked by* **Eisner** *only #1-9,12-16; painted by Eisner & Ken Kelly #10 & 11; painted by Eisner #17-up; one color story reprinted in #1-10.* **Austin** *a-30i.* **Byrne** *a-30p.* **Miller** *a-30p.*

**SPIRIT, THE**
Oct, 1983 - Present (Baxter paper) ($2.00)
Kitchen Sink Enterprises

| | Good | Fine | N-Mint |
|---|---|---|---|
| 1-4: 1-Origin-r/12/23/45 Spirit Section. 2-r/sections 1/20/46-2/10/46. 3-r/2/17/46-3/10/46. 4-r/3/17/46-4/7/46 | .70 | 2.00 | 4.00 |
| 5-11 ($2.95 cover): 11-Last color issue | .50 | 1.50 | 3.00 |
| 12-78 ($1.95-$2.00, B&W): 54-r/section 2/19/50 | .35 | 1.00 | 2.00 |
| ...In 3-D #1 (11/85)-Eisner-r; new Eisner-c | .35 | 1.00 | 2.00 |

**SPIRITMAN** (Also see Three Comics)
No date (1944) (10 cents)
(Triangle Sales Co. ad on back cover)
No publisher listed

| | Good | Fine | N-Mint |
|---|---|---|---|
| 1-Three 16pg. Spirit sections bound together, (1944, 48 pgs., 10 cents) | 12.00 | 35.00 | 84.00 |
| 2-Two Spirit sections (3/26/44, 4/2/44) bound together; by Lou Fine | 9.20 | 27.50 | 64.00 |

**SPIRIT WORLD** (Magazine)
Fall, 1971 (Black & White)
National Periodical Publications

| | Good | Fine | N-Mint |
|---|---|---|---|
| 1-Kirby-a; Neal Adams-c | .70 | 2.00 | 4.00 |

**SPITFIRE**
No. 132, 1944 (Aug) - No. 133, 1945 (Female undercover agent)
Malverne Herald (Elliot)(J. R. Mahon)

| | Good | Fine | N-Mint |
|---|---|---|---|
| 132,133: Both have Classics Gift Box ads on b/c with checklist to #20 | 9.00 | 27.00 | 62.00 |

**SPITFIRE AND THE TROUBLESHOOTERS**
Oct, 1986 - No. 9, June, 1987 (Codename: Spitfire #10 on)
Marvel Comics Group

| | Good | Fine | N-Mint |
|---|---|---|---|
| 1-3,5-9 | | .50 | 1.00 |
| 4-McFarlane-a(p) | .25 | .75 | 1.50 |

**SPITFIRE COMICS** (Also see Double Up)
Aug, 1941 - No. 2, Oct, 1941 (Pocket size; 100 pgs.)
Harvey Publications

| | Good | Fine | N-Mint |
|---|---|---|---|
| 1-Origin The Clown, The Fly-Man, The Spitfire & The Magician From Bagdad | 30.00 | 90.00 | 210.00 |
| 2 | 25.00 | 75.00 | 175.00 |

**SPOOF!**
Oct, 1970; No. 2, Nov, 1972 - No. 5, May, 1973
Marvel Comics Group

| | Good | Fine | N-Mint |
|---|---|---|---|
| 1-Infinity-c | | .50 | 1.00 |
| 2-5: 5-Beatles-c | | .35 | .70 |

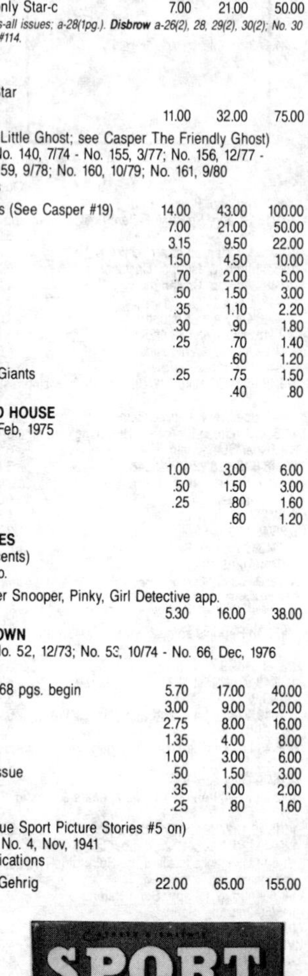

**SPOOK** (Formerly Shock Detective Cases)
No. 22, Jan, 1953 - No. 30, Oct, 1954
Star Publications

| | Good | Fine | N-Mint |
|---|---|---|---|
| 22-Sgt. Spook-r; acid in face story; hanging-c | 9.30 | 28.00 | 65.00 |
| 23,25,27: 27-Two Sgt. Spook-r | 6.50 | 19.00 | 45.00 |
| 24-Used in **SOTI**, pg. 182,183-r/Inside Crime #2; Transvestism story | 8.50 | 25.50 | 60.00 |
| 26-Disbrow-a | 7.00 | 21.00 | 50.00 |
| 28,29-Rulah app. 29-Jo-Jo app. | 7.00 | 21.00 | 50.00 |
| 30-Disbrow-c/a(2); only Star-c | 7.00 | 21.00 | 50.00 |

NOTE: **L. B. Cole** *covers-all issues; a-28(1pg.).* **Disbrow** *a-26(2), 28, 29(2), 30(2); No. 30 r-/Blue Bolt Weird Tales #114.*

**SPOOK COMICS**
1946
Baily Publications/Star

| | Good | Fine | N-Mint |
|---|---|---|---|
| 1-Mr. Lucifer app. | 11.00 | 32.00 | 75.00 |

**SPOOKY** (The Tuff Little Ghost; see Casper The Friendly Ghost)
11/55 - 139, 11/73; No. 140, 7/74 - No. 155, 3/77; No. 156, 12/77 - No. 158, 4/78; No. 159, 9/78; No. 160, 10/79; No. 161, 9/80
Harvey Publications

| | Good | Fine | N-Mint |
|---|---|---|---|
| 1-Nightmare begins (See Casper #19) | 14.00 | 43.00 | 100.00 |
| 2 | 7.00 | 21.00 | 50.00 |
| 3-10(1956-57) | 3.15 | 9.50 | 22.00 |
| 11-20(1957-58) | 1.50 | 4.50 | 10.00 |
| 21-40(1958-59) | .70 | 2.00 | 5.00 |
| 41-60 | .50 | 1.50 | 3.00 |
| 61-80 | .35 | 1.10 | 2.20 |
| 81-100 | .30 | .90 | 1.80 |
| 101-120 | .25 | .70 | 1.40 |
| 121-126,133-140 | | .60 | 1.20 |
| 127-132: All 52 pg. Giants | .25 | .75 | 1.50 |
| 141-161 | | .40 | .80 |

**SPOOKY HAUNTED HOUSE**
Oct, 1972 - No. 15, Feb, 1975
Harvey Publications

| | Good | Fine | N-Mint |
|---|---|---|---|
| 1 | 1.00 | 3.00 | 6.00 |
| 2-5 | .50 | 1.50 | 3.00 |
| 6-10 | .25 | .80 | 1.60 |
| 11-15 | | .60 | 1.20 |

**SPOOKY MYSTERIES**
No date (1946) (10 cents)
Your Guide Publ. Co.

| | Good | Fine | N-Mint |
|---|---|---|---|
| 1-Mr. Spooky, Super Snooper, Pinky, Girl Detective app. | 5.30 | 16.00 | 38.00 |

**SPOOKY SPOOKTOWN**
9/61; No. 2, 9/62 - No. 52, 12/73; No. 53, 10/74 - No. 66, Dec, 1976
Harvey Publications

| | Good | Fine | N-Mint |
|---|---|---|---|
| 1-Casper, Spooky; 68 pgs. begin | 5.70 | 17.00 | 40.00 |
| 2 | 3.00 | 9.00 | 20.00 |
| 3-5 | 2.75 | 8.00 | 16.00 |
| 6-10 | 1.35 | 4.00 | 8.00 |
| 11-20 | 1.00 | 3.00 | 6.00 |
| 21-39: Last 68 pg. issue | .50 | 1.50 | 3.00 |
| 40-45: All 52 pgs. | .35 | 1.00 | 2.00 |
| 46-66 | .25 | .80 | 1.60 |

**SPORT COMICS** (True Sport Picture Stories #5 on)
Oct, 1940(No mo.) - No. 4, Nov, 1941
Street & Smith Publications

| | Good | Fine | N-Mint |
|---|---|---|---|
| 1-Life story of Lou Gehrig | 22.00 | 65.00 | 155.00 |

Spook #26, © STAR

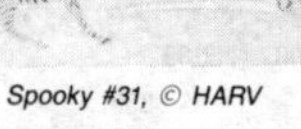
Spooky #31, © HARV

Sport Comics #1, © S&S

*Sports Action #5, © MEG*

*Spy-Hunters #7, © ACG*

*Spy Smasher #8, © FAW*

| | Good | Fine | N-Mint |
|---|---|---|---|
| 2 | 11.50 | 34.00 | 80.00 |
| 3,4 | 10.00 | 30.00 | 70.00 |

**SPORT LIBRARY** (See Charlton Sport Library)

**SPORTS ACTION** (Formerly Sport Stars)
No. 2, Feb, 1950 - No. 14, Sept, 1952
Marvel/Atlas Comics (ACI No. 2,3/SAI No. 4-14)

| | Good | Fine | N-Mint |
|---|---|---|---|
| 2-Powell painted-c; George Gipp life story | 10.00 | 30.00 | 70.00 |
| 3-Everett-a | 7.00 | 21.00 | 50.00 |
| 4-11,14: Weiss-a. 9,10-Maneely-c | 6.50 | 19.00 | 45.00 |
| 12-Everett-c | 7.00 | 21.00 | 50.00 |
| 13-Krigstein-a | 7.00 | 21.00 | 50.00 |

NOTE: *Title may have changed after No. 3, to Crime Must Lose No. 4 on, due to publisher change.*

**SPORTS HALL OF SHAME IN 3-D** (See Blackthorne 3-D Series #72)

**SPORT STARS**
Feb-Mar, 1946 - No. 4, Aug-Sept, 1946 (½ comic, ½ photo magazine)
Parents' Magazine Institute (Sport Stars)

| | Good | Fine | N-Mint |
|---|---|---|---|
| 1-"How Tarzan Got That Way" story of Johnny Weissmuller | 16.00 | 48.00 | 110.00 |
| 2-Baseball greats | 11.00 | 32.00 | 75.00 |
| 3,4 | 8.00 | 24.00 | 55.00 |

**SPORT STARS** (Becomes Sports Action #2 on)
Nov, 1949 (52 pgs.)
Marvel Comics (ACI)

| | Good | Fine | N-Mint |
|---|---|---|---|
| 1-Knute Rockne; painted-c | 16.00 | 48.00 | 110.00 |

**SPORT THRILLS** (Formerly Dick Cole)
No. 11, Nov, 1950 - No. 15, Nov, 1951
Star Publications

| | Good | Fine | N-Mint |
|---|---|---|---|
| 11-Dick Cole app; Ted Williams & Ty Cobb life stories | 7.00 | 21.00 | 50.00 |
| 12-L. B. Cole c/a | 5.00 | 15.00 | 35.00 |
| 13-15-All L. B. Cole-c; 13-Dick Cole app. | 5.00 | 15.00 | 35.00 |
| Accepted Reprint #11 (#15 on-c, nd); L.B. Cole-c | 2.00 | 6.00 | 14.00 |
| Accepted Reprint #12 (nd); L.B. Cole-c; Joe DiMaggio & Phil Rizzuto life stories | 2.00 | 6.00 | 14.00 |

**SPOTLIGHT** (TV)
Sept, 1978 - No. 4, Mar, 1979 (Hanna-Barbera)
Marvel Comics Group

| | Good | Fine | N-Mint |
|---|---|---|---|
| 1-Huckleberry Hound, Yogi Bear; Shaw-a. 2-Quick Draw McGraw, Augie Doggie, Snooper & Blabber. 3-The Jetsons, Yakky Doodle, 4-Magilla Gorilla, Snagglepuss | | .30 | .60 |

**SPOTLIGHT COMICS**
Nov, 1944 - No. 3, 1945
Harry 'A' Chesler (Our Army, Inc.)

| | Good | Fine | N-Mint |
|---|---|---|---|
| 1-The Black Dwarf, The Veiled Avenger, & Barry Kuda begin; Tuska-c | 24.00 | 71.00 | 165.00 |
| 2 | 19.00 | 58.00 | 135.00 |
| 3-Injury to eye story(Same as Scoop #3) | 22.00 | 65.00 | 150.00 |

**SPOTTY THE PUP** (Becomes Super Pup No. 4)
(Also see Television Puppet Show)
No. 2, Oct-Nov, 1953 - No. 3, Dec-Jan, 1953-54
Avon Periodicals/Realistic Comics

| | Good | Fine | N-Mint |
|---|---|---|---|
| 2,3 | 1.70 | 5.00 | 12.00 |
| nn (1953, Realistic-r) | 1.00 | 3.00 | 7.00 |

**SPUNKY** (. . .Junior Cowboy)(. . .Comics #2 on)
April, 1949 - No. 7, Nov, 1951
Standard Comics

| | Good | Fine | N-Mint |
|---|---|---|---|
| 1,2-Text illos by Frazetta | 4.00 | 12.00 | 28.00 |
| 3-7 | 2.00 | 6.00 | 14.00 |

**SPUNKY THE SMILING SPOOK**
Aug, 1957 - No. 4, May, 1958
Ajax/Farrell (World Famous Comics/Four Star Comic Corp.)

| | Good | Fine | N-Mint |
|---|---|---|---|
| 1-Reprints from Frisky Fables | 2.65 | 8.00 | 18.00 |
| 2-4 | 1.70 | 5.00 | 12.00 |

**SPY AND COUNTERSPY** (Spy Hunters #3 on)
Aug-Sept, 1949 - No. 2, Oct-Nov, 1949 (52 pgs.)
American Comics Group

| | Good | Fine | N-Mint |
|---|---|---|---|
| 1-Origin, 1st app. Jonathan Kent, Counterspy | 8.00 | 24.00 | 55.00 |
| 2 | 5.70 | 17.00 | 40.00 |

**SPY CASES** (Formerly The Kellys)
No. 26, Sept, 1950 - No. 19, Oct, 1953
Marvel/Atlas Comics (Hercules Publ.)

| | Good | Fine | N-Mint |
|---|---|---|---|
| 26 (#1) | 7.00 | 21.00 | 50.00 |
| 27,28(2/51): 27-Everett-a; bondage-c | 5.00 | 15.00 | 35.00 |
| 4(4/51) - 7,9,10: 7-Tuska-a | 2.85 | 8.50 | 20.00 |
| 8-A-Bomb-c/story; Maneely-a | 4.00 | 12.00 | 28.00 |
| 11-19: 11-14-War format | 2.65 | 8.00 | 18.00 |

**SPY FIGHTERS**
March, 1951 - No. 15, July, 1953
Marvel/Atlas Comics (CSI)

| | Good | Fine | N-Mint |
|---|---|---|---|
| 1 | 8.00 | 24.00 | 55.00 |
| 2-Tuska-a | 4.00 | 12.00 | 28.00 |
| 3-13 | 2.85 | 8.50 | 20.00 |
| 14,15-Pakula-a(3), Ed Win-a | 3.15 | 9.50 | 22.00 |

**SPY-HUNTERS** (Formerly Spy & Counterspy)
No. 3, Dec-Jan, 1949-50 - No. 24, June-July, 1953 (#3-11: 52 pgs.)
American Comics Group

| | Good | Fine | N-Mint |
|---|---|---|---|
| 3-Jonathan Kent continues, ends #10 | 8.00 | 24.00 | 55.00 |
| 4-10: 4,8,10-Starr-a | 4.50 | 14.00 | 32.00 |
| 11-15,17-22,24: 18-War-c begin. 21-War-c/stories begin | 2.85 | 8.50 | 20.00 |
| 16-Williamson-a (9 pgs.) | 6.50 | 19.00 | 45.00 |
| 23-Graphic torture, injury to eye panel | 7.00 | 21.00 | 50.00 |

NOTE: ***Whitney** a-many issues; c-7, 8, 10-12, 16.*

**SPYMAN** (Top Secret Adventures on cover)
Sept, 1966 - No. 3, Feb, 1967 (12 cents)
Harvey Publications (Illustrated Humor)

| | Good | Fine | N-Mint |
|---|---|---|---|
| 1-Steranko-a(p)-1st pro work; 1pg. Neal Adams ad; Tuska-c/a, Crandall-a(i) | 1.70 | 5.00 | 12.00 |
| 2,3: Simon-c. 2-Steranko-a(p) | .85 | 2.60 | 6.00 |

**SPY SMASHER** (See Mighty Midget, Whiz & XMas Comics)
Fall, 1941 - No. 11, Feb, 1943 (Also see Crime Smasher)
Fawcett Publications

| | Good | Fine | N-Mint |
|---|---|---|---|
| 1-Spy Smasher begins; silver metallic-c | 130.00 | 390.00 | 910.00 |
| 2-Raboy-c | 65.00 | 195.00 | 455.00 |
| 3,4: 3-Bondage-c | 55.00 | 165.00 | 385.00 |
| 5-7: Raboy-a; 6-Raboy-c/a. 7-Part photo-c | 47.00 | 140.00 | 325.00 |
| 8-11: 9-Hitler, Tojo, Mussolini-c. 10-Hitler-c | 40.00 | 120.00 | 280.00 |
| Well Known Comics (1944, 12 pgs., 8½x10½", paper-c, glued binding, printed in green; Bestmaid/Samuel Lowe giveaway | 15.00 | 45.00 | 90.00 |

**SPY THRILLERS** (Police Badge No. 479 #5)
Nov, 1954 - No. 4, May, 1955
Atlas Comics (PrPI)

| | Good | Fine | N-Mint |
|---|---|---|---|
| 1 | 6.00 | 18.00 | 42.00 |
| 2-Last precode (1/55) | 3.60 | 11.00 | 25.00 |
| 3,4 | 2.65 | 8.00 | 18.00 |

**SQUADRON SUPREME**
Sept, 1985 - No. 12, Aug, 1986 (Maxi-series)
Marvel Comics Group

| | Good | Fine | N-Mint |
|---|---|---|---|
| 1 | .30 | .90 | 1.80 |
| 2-11 | | .50 | 1.00 |
| 12-Double size ($1.25) | .25 | .75 | 1.50 |

**SQUALOR**
Dec, 1989 - No. 4, Aug, 1990 ($2.75, color, mini-series)
First Comics

| | Good | Fine | N-Mint |
|---|---|---|---|
| 1-4: Sutton-a | .45 | 1.40 | 2.80 |

**SQUEEKS**
Oct, 1953 - No. 5, June, 1954
Lev Gleason Publications

| | Good | Fine | N-Mint |
|---|---|---|---|
| 1-Funny animal; Biro-c | 3.50 | 10.50 | 24.00 |
| 2-Biro-c | 1.70 | 5.00 | 12.00 |
| 3-5: 3-Biro-c | 1.50 | 4.50 | 10.00 |

**STAINLESS STEEL RAT**
Oct, 1985 - No. 6, Mar, 1986 (Limited-series, color)
Eagle Comics

| | Good | Fine | N-Mint |
|---|---|---|---|
| 1 (52 pgs.; $2.25 cover) | .35 | 1.10 | 2.20 |
| 2-6 (36 pgs.) | .25 | .75 | 1.50 |

**STALKER**
June-July, 1975 - No. 4, Dec-Jan, 1975-76
National Periodical Publications

| | Good | Fine | N-Mint |
|---|---|---|---|
| 1-Origin & 1st app; Ditko/Wood-c/a | .25 | .75 | 1.50 |
| 2-4-Ditko/Wood-c/a | | .50 | 1.00 |

**STALKERS**
Apr, 1990 - Present ($1.50, color)
Epic Comics (Marvel)

| | Good | Fine | N-Mint |
|---|---|---|---|
| 1-12: 1-Chadwick-c. 4-6,8,9-Mayerik-a | .25 | .75 | 1.50 |

**STAMP COMICS** (Stamps... on-c; Thrilling Advs. In...#8)
Oct, 1951 - No. 7, Oct, 1952 (No. 1: 15 cents)
Youthful Magazines/Stamp Comics, Inc.

| | Good | Fine | N-Mint |
|---|---|---|---|
| 1('Stamps' on indicia No. 1) | 14.00 | 43.00 | 100.00 |
| 2 | 8.00 | 24.00 | 55.00 |
| 3-6: 3,4-Kiefer, Wildey-a | 6.50 | 19.00 | 45.00 |
| 7-Roy Krenkel, 4 pgs. | 10.00 | 30.00 | 70.00 |

NOTE: *Promotes stamp collecting; gives stories behind various commemorative stamps. No. 2, 10 cents printed over 15 cents c-price.* ***Kiefer*** *a-1-7.* ***Kirkel*** *a-1-6.* ***Napoli*** *a-2-7.* ***Palais*** *a-2-4, 7.*

**STANLEY & HIS MONSTER** (Formerly The Fox & the Crow)
No. 109, Apr-May, 1968 - No. 112, Oct-Nov, 1968
National Periodical Publications

| | Good | Fine | N-Mint |
|---|---|---|---|
| 109-112 | 1.00 | 3.00 | 7.00 |

**STAR BLAZERS**
Apr, 1987 - No. 4, July, 1987 ($1.75, color, mini-series)
Comico

| | Good | Fine | N-Mint |
|---|---|---|---|
| 1-4 | .30 | .90 | 1.80 |

**STAR BLAZERS**
1989 - No. 5, 1989 ($1.95-$2.50, color, mini-series)
Comico

| | Good | Fine | N-Mint |
|---|---|---|---|
| 1,2 ($1.95)-Steacy wraparound painted-c on all | .35 | 1.00 | 2.00 |
| 2-5 ($2.50) | .40 | 1.25 | 2.50 |

**STAR BRAND**
Oct, 1986 - No. 19, May, 1989 (.75-$1.50 #17 on, color)
Marvel Comics Group

| | Good | Fine | N-Mint |
|---|---|---|---|
| 1-19: 14-Begin $1.25-c. 16-19-Byrne-c/a/scripts | | .50 | 1.00 |
| Annual 1 (10/87) | | .65 | 1.30 |

NOTE: ***Williamson*** *a(i)-1-6; c-(i)-1, 3, 4, 10.*

**STAR COMICS**
Feb, 1937 - V2#7 (No. 23), Aug, 1939 (#1-6: large size)
Ultem Publ. (Harry 'A' Chesler)/Centaur Publications

| | Good | Fine | N-Mint |
|---|---|---|---|
| V1#1-Dan Hastings (s/f) begins | 76.00 | 230.00 | 535.00 |
| 2 | 37.00 | 110.00 | 260.00 |
| 3-6 (#6, 9/37): 5-Little Nemo | 32.00 | 95.00 | 225.00 |
| 7-9: 8-Severed head centerspread; Impy & Little Nemo by Winsor McCay Jr, Popeye app. by Bob Wood; Mickey Mouse-c app. | 30.00 | 90.00 | 210.00 |
| 10 (1st Centaur; 3/38)-Impy by Winsor McCay Jr; Don Marlow by Guardineer begins | 46.00 | 137.00 | 320.00 |
| 11-1st Jack Cole comic-a, 1 pg. (4/38) | 30.00 | 90.00 | 210.00 |
| 12-15: 12-Riders of the Golden West begins; Little Nemo app. 15-Speed Silvers by Gustavson & The Last Pirate by Burgos begins | 29.00 | 85.00 | 200.00 |
| 16 (12/38)-The Phantom Rider begins, ends V2#6 | 29.00 | 85.00 | 200.00 |
| V2#1(#17, 2/39) | 29.00 | 85.00 | 200.00 |
| 2-7(#18-23): 2-Diana Deane by Tarpe Mills app. 3-Drama of Hollywood by Mills begins. 7-Jungle Queen app. | 26.00 | 77.00 | 180.00 |

NOTE: ***Biro*** *c-9, 10.* ***Burgos*** *a-15, 16, V2#1-7.* ***Ken Ernst*** *a-10, 12, 14.* ***Gill Fox*** *c-V2#2.* ***Guardineer*** *a-6, 8-14.* ***Gustavson*** *a-13-16, V2#1-7.* ***Tarpe Mills*** *a-15, V2#1-7.* ***Bob Wood*** *a-10, 12, 13; c-8.*

**STAR COMICS MAGAZINE**
Dec, 1986 - No. 13, 1988 ($1.50, Digest-size)
Star Comics (Marvel)

| | Good | Fine | N-Mint |
|---|---|---|---|
| 1-13: Heathcliff, Muppet Babies, Ewoks, Carebears, Top Dog, Alf, Flintstone Kids app. | .25 | .75 | 1.50 |

**STAR FEATURE COMICS**
1963
I. W. Enterprises

| | Good | Fine | N-Mint |
|---|---|---|---|
| Reprint #9-Stunt-Man Stetson app. | .50 | 1.50 | 3.00 |

**STARFIRE** (See New Teen Titans & Teen Titans)
Aug-Sept, 1976 - No. 8, Oct-Nov, 1977
National Periodical Publications/DC Comics

| | Good | Fine | N-Mint |
|---|---|---|---|
| 1-Origin (CCA stamp fell off cover art; so it **was** approved by code) | | .50 | 1.00 |
| 2-8 | | .30 | .60 |

**STAR HUNTERS** (See DC Super Stars #16)
Oct-Nov, 1977 - No. 7, Oct-Nov, 1978
National Periodical Publications/DC Comics

| | Good | Fine | N-Mint |
|---|---|---|---|
| 1-7: 1-Newton-a(p). 7-Giant | | .30 | .60 |

NOTE: ***Buckler*** *a-4-7p; c-1-7p.* ***Layton*** *a-1-5i; c-1-6i.* ***Nasser*** *a-3p.* ***Sutton*** *a-6i.*

**STARK TERROR** (Magazine)
Dec, 1970 - No. 5, Aug, 1971 (52 pages) (B&W)
Stanley Publications

| | Good | Fine | N-Mint |
|---|---|---|---|
| 1-Bondage, torture-c | 1.30 | 4.00 | 9.00 |
| 2-4 (Gillmor/Aragon-r) | .85 | 2.25 | 5.00 |
| 5 (ACG-r) | .70 | 2.00 | 4.00 |

**STARLET O'HARA IN HOLLYWOOD** (Teen-age) (Also see Cookie)
Dec, 1948 - No. 4, Sept, 1949
Standard Comics

| | Good | Fine | N-Mint |
|---|---|---|---|
| 1-Owen Fitzgerald-a in all | 9.30 | 28.00 | 65.00 |
| 2 | 6.50 | 19.00 | 45.00 |
| 3,4 | 5.00 | 15.00 | 35.00 |

**STAR-LORD THE SPECIAL EDITION** (Also see Marvel Comics Super Special #10, Marvel Premiere & Preview & Marvel Spotlight V2#6,7)
Feb, 1982 (One Shot) (Direct sale, 1st Baxter paper comic)
Marvel Comics Group

| | Good | Fine | N-Mint |
|---|---|---|---|
| 1-Byrne/Austin-a; Austin-c, Golden-a(p); 8 pgs. of new-a; Dr. Who story | .70 | 2.00 | 4.00 |

**STARMAN** (See Adventure #467, Brave & the Bold, First Issue Special, Justice League & Showcase)

*Stalker #3, © DC*

*Star Comics #1, © CHES*

*Starlet O'Hara in Hollywood #1, © STD*

Star Ranger Funnies #1, © CEN

Starslayer #18, © First Comics

Star Spangled Comics #1, © DC

Oct, 1988 - Present ($1.00, color)
DC Comics

| | Good | Fine | N-Mint |
|---|---|---|---|
| 1-32: 1-Origin. 4-Intro The Power Elite. 9,10-Batman app. 14-Superman app. 17-Power Girl app. 26,27-G.A. Starman app. | | .50 | 1.00 |

**STARMASTERS**
Mar, 1984 (Color)
Americomics

| | Good | Fine | N-Mint |
|---|---|---|---|
| 1-The Women of W.O.S.P. & Breed begin | .25 | .75 | 1.50 |

**STAR PRESENTATION, A** (Formerly My Secret Romance #1,2; Spectacular Stories #4 on) (Also see This Is Suspense)
No. 3, May, 1950
Fox Features Syndicate (Hero Books)

| | Good | Fine | N-Mint |
|---|---|---|---|
| 3-Dr. Jekyll & Mr. Hyde by Wood & Harrison (reprinted in Startling Terror Tales #10); 'The Repulsing Dwarf' by Wood; Wood-c | 30.00 | 90.00 | 210.00 |

**STAR QUEST COMIX** (Warren Presents... on cover)
October, 1978
Warren Publications

| | Good | Fine | N-Mint |
|---|---|---|---|
| 1 | | .50 | 1.00 |

**STAR RAIDERS** (See DC Graphic Novel #1)

**STAR RANGER** (Cowboy Comics #13 on)
Feb, 1937 - No. 12, May, 1938 (Large size: No. 1-6)
Ultem Publ./Centaur Publications

| | Good | Fine | N-Mint |
|---|---|---|---|
| 1-(1st Western comic)-Ace & Deuce, Air Plunder; Flessel-a | 86.00 | 257.00 | 600.00 |
| 2 | 39.00 | 118.00 | 275.00 |
| 3-6 | 35.00 | 105.00 | 245.00 |
| 7-9: 8-Christmas-c | 30.00 | 90.00 | 210.00 |
| V2#10 (1st Centaur; 3/38) | 45.00 | 135.00 | 315.00 |
| 11,12 | 35.00 | 105.00 | 245.00 |

NOTE: *J. Cole a-10, 12; c-12.* ***Ken Ernst*** *a-11.* ***Gill Fox*** *a-8(illo), 9, 10.* ***Guardineer*** *a-1, 3, 6, 7, 8(illos), 9, 10, 12.* ***Gustavson*** *a-8-10, 12.* ***Bob Wood*** *a-8-10.*

**STAR RANGER FUNNIES** (Formerly Cowboy Comics)
V1#15, Oct, 1938 - V2#5, Oct, 1939
Centaur Publications

| | Good | Fine | N-Mint |
|---|---|---|---|
| V1#15-Eisner, Gustavson-a | 50.00 | 150.00 | 350.00 |
| V2#1 (1/39) | 37.00 | 110.00 | 255.00 |
| 2-5: 2-Night Hawk by Gustavson. 4-Kit Carson app. | 30.00 | 90.00 | 210.00 |

NOTE: ***Jack Cole*** *a-V2#1, 3; c-V2#1.* ***Guardineer*** *a-V2#3.* ***Gustavson*** *a-V2#2.* ***Pinajian*** *c/a-V2#5.*

**STAR REACH CLASSICS**
Mar, 1984 - No. 6, Aug, 1984 ($1.50; color; Baxter paper)
Eclipse Comics

| | Good | Fine | N-Mint |
|---|---|---|---|
| 1-6: Neal Adams-r/Star Reach #1 | .25 | .75 | 1.50 |

NOTE: ***Brunner*** *c/a-4r.* ***Nino*** *a-3r.* ***Russell*** *c/a-3r.*

**STARR FLAGG, UNDERCOVER GIRL** (See Undercover...)

**STARRIORS**
Aug, 1984 - No. 4, Feb, 1985 (Limited-series)
Marvel Comics Group

| | Good | Fine | N-Mint |
|---|---|---|---|
| 1-Based on Tomy Toy robots | | .60 | 1.20 |
| 2-4 | | .50 | 1.00 |

**STARS AND STRIPES COMICS**
No. 2, May, 1941 - No. 6, Dec, 1941
Centaur Publications

| | Good | Fine | N-Mint |
|---|---|---|---|
| 2(#1)-The Shark, The Iron Skull, Aman, The Amazing Man, Mighty Man, Minimidget begin; The Voice & Dash Dartwell, the Human Meteor, Reef Kinkaid app.; Gustavson Flag-c | 112.00 | 335.00 | 780.00 |
| 3-Origin Dr. Synthe; The Black Panther app. | 75.00 | 225.00 | 525.00 |
| 4-Origin/1st app. The Stars and Stripes; injury to eye-c | 63.00 | 190.00 | 440.00 |
| 5(#5 on cover & inside) | 47.00 | 140.00 | 330.00 |
| 5(#6)-(#5 on cover, #6 on inside) | 47.00 | 140.00 | 330.00 |

NOTE: ***Gustavson*** *c/a-3.* ***Myron Strauss*** *c-5.*

**STARSLAYER**
Sept, 1981 - No. 6, Apr, 1983; No. 7, Aug, 1983 - No. 34, Nov, 1985
Pacific Comics/First Comics No. 7 on

| | Good | Fine | N-Mint |
|---|---|---|---|
| 1-Origin; excessive blood & gore | .50 | 1.50 | 3.00 |
| 2-Intro & origin the Rocketeer by Dave Stevens | 1.70 | 7.00 | 10.00 |
| 3-Rocketeer continues | 1.00 | 3.00 | 6.00 |
| 4 | .35 | 1.00 | 2.00 |
| 5-2nd app. Groo the Wanderer by Aragones | 1.25 | 3.75 | 7.50 |
| 6,7: 7-Grell-a ends | .35 | 1.00 | 2.00 |
| 8-34: 10-1st app. Grimjack (11/83, ends #17). 18-Starslayer meets Grimjack; 20-The Black Flame begins(1st app.), ends #33. 27-Book length Black Flame story | | .50 | 1.00 |

NOTE: ***Grell*** *a-1-7; c-1-8.* ***Sutton*** *a-17p, 20-22p, 24-27p, 29-33p.*

**STAR SPANGLED COMICS** (...War Stories #131 on)
Oct, 1941 - No. 130, July, 1952
National Periodical Publications

| | Good | Fine | N-Mint |
|---|---|---|---|
| 1-Origin Tarantula; Captain X of the R.A.F., Star Spangled Kid (see Action #40) & Armstrong of the Army begin | 175.00 | 440.00 | 1050.00 |
| 2 | 80.00 | 200.00 | 480.00 |
| 3-5 | 43.00 | 130.00 | 300.00 |
| 6-Last Armstrong of the Army | 30.00 | 90.00 | 210.00 |

7-Origin/1st app. The Guardian by S&K, & Robotman by Paul Cassidy; The Newsboy Legion & TNT begin; last Captain X

| Good | Fine | VF-NM | NM/Mint |
|---|---|---|---|
| 217.00 | 540.00 | 1300.00 | 1800.00 |

(Estimated up to 100 total copies exist, 5 in NM/Mint)

| | Good | Fine | N-Mint |
|---|---|---|---|
| 8-Origin TNT & Dan the Dyna-Mite | 93.00 | 280.00 | 650.00 |
| 9,10 | 79.00 | 235.00 | 550.00 |
| 11-17 | 65.00 | 195.00 | 455.00 |
| 18-Origin Star Spangled Kid | 80.00 | 240.00 | 560.00 |
| 19-Last Tarantula | 65.00 | 195.00 | 455.00 |
| 20-Liberty Belle begins | 65.00 | 195.00 | 455.00 |
| 21-29-Last S&K issue; 23-Last TNT. 25-Robotman by Jimmy Thompson begins | 50.00 | 150.00 | 350.00 |
| 30-40: 31-S&K-c | 23.00 | 70.00 | 160.00 |
| 41-50 | 20.00 | 60.00 | 140.00 |
| 51-64: Last Newsboy Legion & The Guardian; last Liberty Belle? #53 by S&K | 20.00 | 60.00 | 140.00 |
| 65-Robin begins with cover app. (2/47); Batman cameo in 1 panel; Robin-c begin, end #95 | 47.00 | 140.00 | 325.00 |
| 66-Batman cameo in Robin story | 25.00 | 75.00 | 175.00 |
| 67,68,70-80 | 22.00 | 65.00 | 150.00 |
| 69-Origin/1st app. Tomahawk by F. Ray | 30.00 | 90.00 | 210.00 |
| 81-Origin Merry, Girl of 1000 Gimmicks in Star Spangled Kid story | 19.00 | 56.00 | 130.00 |
| 82,85: 82-Last Robotman? | 19.00 | 56.00 | 130.00 |
| 83-Tomahawk enters the lost valley, a land of dinosaurs; Capt. Compass begins, ends #130 | 19.00 | 56.00 | 130.00 |
| 84,87 (Rare): 87-Batman cameo in Robin | 22.00 | 65.00 | 155.00 |
| 86-Batman cameo in Robin story; last Star Spangled Kid | 22.00 | 65.00 | 150.00 |
| 88(1/49)-94: Batman-c/stories in all. 91-Federal Men begin, end #93. 94-Manhunters Around the World begin, end #121 | 24.00 | 70.00 | 165.00 |
| 95-Batman story; last Robin-c | 19.00 | 56.00 | 130.00 |

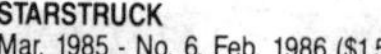

| | Good | Fine | N-Mint |
|---|---|---|---|
| 96,98-Batman cameo in Robin stories. 96-1st Tomahawk-c | 16.00 | 48.00 | 110.00 |
| 97,99 | 14.00 | 43.00 | 100.00 |
| 100 | 19.00 | 58.00 | 135.00 |
| 101-109,118,119,121 | 11.50 | 34.00 | 80.00 |
| 110,111,120-Batman cameo in Robin stories. 120-Last 52 pgs. | 14.00 | 43.00 | 100.00 |
| 112-Batman & Robin story | 16.00 | 48.00 | 110.00 |
| 113-Frazetta-a (10 pgs.) | 26.50 | 80.00 | 185.00 |
| 114-Retells Robin's origin (3/51); Batman & Robin story | 19.00 | 58.00 | 135.00 |
| 115,117-Batman app. in Robin stories | 13.00 | 40.00 | 90.00 |
| 116-Flag-c | 12.00 | 36.00 | 85.00 |
| 122-(11/51)-Ghost Breaker-c/stories begin (origin), ends #130 | 12.00 | 36.00 | 85.00 |
| 123-126,128,129 | 8.50 | 25.50 | 60.00 |
| 127-Batman cameo | 10.00 | 30.00 | 70.00 |
| 130-Batman cameo in Robin story | 12.00 | 36.00 | 85.00 |

NOTE: *Most all issues after #29 signed by **Simon & Kirby** are **not** by them.*

**STAR SPANGLED WAR STORIES** (Star Spangled Comics #1-130; The Unknown Soldier #205 on) (See Showcase)
No. 131, 8/52 - No. 133, 10/52; No. 3, 11/52 - No. 204, 2-3/77
National Periodical Publications

| | Good | Fine | N-Mint |
|---|---|---|---|
| 131(#1) | 29.00 | 86.00 | 200.00 |
| 132 | 18.00 | 54.00 | 125.00 |
| 133-Used in **POP**, Pg. 94 | 18.00 | 54.00 | 125.00 |
| 3-5: 4-Devil Dog Dugan app. | 13.00 | 40.00 | 90.00 |
| 6-Evans-a | 11.00 | 32.00 | 75.00 |
| 7-10 | 8.50 | 25.50 | 60.00 |
| 11-20 | 7.00 | 21.00 | 50.00 |
| 21-30: Last precode (2/55) | 5.70 | 17.00 | 40.00 |
| 31-33,35-40 | 4.30 | 13.00 | 30.00 |
| 34-Krigstein-a | 5.70 | 17.00 | 40.00 |
| 41-50 | 3.60 | 11.00 | 25.00 |
| 51-83: 67-Easy Co. story w/out Sgt. Rock | 2.85 | 8.50 | 20.00 |
| 84-Origin Mlle. Marie | 5.70 | 17.00 | 40.00 |
| 85-89-Mlle. Marie in all | 3.60 | 11.00 | 25.00 |
| 90-1st dinosaur issue (4-5/60) | 14.00 | 43.00 | 100.00 |
| 91-No dinosaur story | 2.85 | 8.50 | 20.00 |
| 92-100: 92-2nd dinosaur issue, begin series | 5.70 | 17.00 | 40.00 |
| 101-133,135-137-Last dinosaur story; Heath Birdman-#129,131 | 4.30 | 13.00 | 30.00 |
| 134-Neal Adams-a | 5.00 | 15.00 | 35.00 |
| 138-Enemy Ace begins by Joe Kubert | 2.15 | 6.50 | 15.00 |
| 139-143,145: 145-Last 12 cent issue (6-7/69) | 2.65 | 8.00 | 8.00 |
| 144-Neal Adams & Kubert-a | 1.50 | 4.50 | 10.00 |
| 146-148,152,153,155: 149,150-Viking Prince by Kubert | .85 | 2.60 | 6.00 |
| 149,150-Viking Prince by Kubert | 1.00 | 3.00 | 7.00 |
| 151-1st Unknown Soldier (6-7/70) | 1.50 | 4.50 | 10.00 |
| 154-Origin Unknown Soldier | 1.15 | 3.50 | 8.00 |
| 156-1st Battle Album | .70 | 2.00 | 4.00 |
| 157-161-Last Enemy Ace | .50 | 1.50 | 3.00 |
| 162-204: 181-183-Enemy Ace vs. Balloon Buster serial app. | | .50 | 1.00 |

NOTE: ***Drucker** a-59, 61, 64, 66, 67, 73-84. **Estrada** a-149. **John Giunta** a-72. **Glanzman** a-167, 171, 172, 174. **Heath** a-122, 132, 133; c-67, 122, 132-134. **Kaluta** a-197i; c-167. **G. Kane** a-169. **Kubert** a-6-163(most later issues), 200. **Maurer** a-160, 165. **Severin** a-65. **S&K** c-7-31, 33, 34, 37, 40. **Simonson** a-170, 172, 174, 180. **Sutton** a-168. **Thorne** a-183. **Toth** a-164. **Wildey** a-161. Suicide Squad in 110, 116-118, 120, 121, 127.*

**STARSTREAM** (Adventures in Science Fiction)(See Questar Illustr.)
1976 (68 pgs.; cardboard covers) (79 cents)
Whitman/Western Publishing Co.

| | Good | Fine | N-Mint |
|---|---|---|---|
| 1-Bolle-a | .25 | .80 | 1.60 |
| 2-4-McWilliams & Bolle-a | | .60 | 1.20 |

**STARSTRUCK**
Mar, 1985 - No. 6, Feb, 1986 ($1.50; adults only)
Epic Comics (Marvel)

| | Good | Fine | N-Mint |
|---|---|---|---|
| 1-6: Kaluta-c/a; nudity & strong language | .25 | .75 | 1.50 |

**STARSTRUCK**
Aug, 1990 - No. 4, 1990 ($2.95, B&W, mini-series, 52 pgs.)
Dark Horse Comics

| | Good | Fine | N-Mint |
|---|---|---|---|
| 1-3: Kaluta-r/Epic series plus new-c/a | .50 | 1.50 | 3.00 |
| 4-($4.95, 68 pgs.)-Reprints & new-a (12 pgs.) | .85 | 2.50 | 5.00 |

**STAR STUDDED**
1945 (25 cents; 132 pgs.); 1945 (196 pgs.)
Cambridge House/Superior Publishers

| | Good | Fine | N-Mint |
|---|---|---|---|
| 1-Captain Combat by Giunta, Ghost Woman, Commandette, & Red Rogue app. | 13.00 | 40.00 | 90.00 |
| nn-The Cadet, Edison Bell, Hoot Gibson, Jungle Lil (196 pgs.); copies vary - Blue Beetle in some | 11.00 | 32.00 | 75.00 |

**STAR TEAM**
1977 (20 pgs.) (6½x5")
Marvel Comics Group (Ideal Toy Giveaway)

| | Good | Fine | N-Mint |
|---|---|---|---|
| nn | | .15 | .30 |

**STARTLING COMICS**
June, 1940 - No. 53, May, 1948
Better Publications (Nedor)

| | Good | Fine | N-Mint |
|---|---|---|---|
| 1-Origin Captain Future-Man Of Tomorrow, Mystico (By Eisner/Fine), The Wonder Man; The Masked Rider begins; drug use story | 77.00 | 230.00 | 540.00 |
| 2 | 32.00 | 95.00 | 220.00 |
| 3 | 24.00 | 73.00 | 170.00 |
| 4 | 19.00 | 57.00 | 130.00 |
| 5-9 | 14.00 | 43.00 | 100.00 |
| 10-The Fighting Yank begins (origin/1st app.) | 61.00 | 182.00 | 425.00 |
| 11-15: 12-Hitler, Hirohito, Mussolini-c | 18.00 | 54.00 | 125.00 |
| 16-Origin The Four Comrades; not in #32,35 | 21.00 | 62.00 | 145.00 |
| 17-Last Masked Rider & Mystico | 13.00 | 40.00 | 90.00 |
| 18-Pyroman begins (origin) | 35.00 | 105.00 | 245.00 |
| 19 | 14.00 | 43.00 | 100.00 |
| 20-The Oracle begins; not in #26,28,33,34 | 14.00 | 43.00 | 100.00 |
| 21-Origin The Ape, Oracle's enemy | 13.00 | 40.00 | 90.00 |
| 22-33 | 11.50 | 34.00 | 80.00 |
| 34-Origin The Scarab & only app. | 13.00 | 40.00 | 90.00 |
| 35-Hypodermic syringe attacks Fighting Yank in drug story | 13.00 | 40.00 | 90.00 |
| 36-43: 36-Last Four Comrades. 38-Bondage/torture-c. 40-Last Capt. Future & Oracle. 41-Front Page Peggy begins; A-Bomb-c. 43-Last Pyroman | 11.50 | 34.00 | 80.00 |
| 44-Lance Lewis, Space Detective begins; Ingels-c | 20.00 | 60.00 | 140.00 |
| 45-Tygra begins (Intro/origin) | 20.00 | 60.00 | 140.00 |
| 46-Ingels-c/a | 20.00 | 60.00 | 140.00 |
| 47-53: 49-Last Fighting Yank. 50,51-Sea-Eagle app. | 14.00 | 43.00 | 100.00 |

NOTE: ***Ingels** c-44, 46(wash). **Schomburg (Xela)** c-21-43; 47-53 (airbrush). **Tuska** c-45? Bondage c-16, 21, 37, 46-49.*

**STARTLING TERROR TALES**
No. 10, May, 1952 - No. 14, Feb, 1953; No. 4, Apr, 1953 - No. 11, 1954
Star Publications

| | Good | Fine | N-Mint |
|---|---|---|---|
| 10-(1st Series)-Wood/Harrison-a (r-A Star Presentation #3) Disbrow/Cole-c | 24.00 | 70.00 | 165.00 |
| 11-L. B. Cole Spider-c; r-Fox's "A Feature Presentation" #5 | 12.00 | 36.00 | 85.00 |
| 12,14 | 4.50 | 14.00 | 32.00 |
| 13-Jo-Jo-r; Disbrow-a | 5.00 | 15.00 | 35.00 |
| 4-7,9,11('53-54) (2nd Series) | 4.00 | 12.00 | 28.00 |

*Star Spangled Comics #122, © DC*

*Star Spangled War Stories #18, © DC*

*Startling Comics #50, © BP*

Star Trek #1 (10/89), © Paramount

Star Trek: Next Gener. #2 (3/88), © Paramount

Star Wars #4, © Lucasfilms

| | Good | Fine | N-Mint |
|---|---|---|---|
| 8-Spanking scene; Palais-a(r) | 5.70 | 17.00 | 40.00 |
| 10-Disbrow-a | 4.50 | 14.00 | 32.00 |

NOTE: ***L. B. Cole** covers-all issues. **Palais** a-V2#11r.*

**STAR TREK** (TV) (See Dan Curtis, Dynabrite Comics & Power Record Comics)
7/67; No. 2, 6/68; No. 3, 12/68; No. 4, 6/69 - No. 61, 3/79
Gold Key

| | Good | Fine | N-Mint |
|---|---|---|---|
| 1-Photo-c begin, end #9 | 29.00 | 86.00 | 200.00 |
| 2-5 | 14.00 | 43.00 | 100.00 |
| 6-9 | 10.00 | 30.00 | 70.00 |
| 10-20 | 6.50 | 19.00 | 45.00 |
| 21-30 | 4.00 | 12.00 | 28.00 |
| 31-40 | 2.30 | 7.00 | 16.00 |
| 41-61: 52-Drug propaganda story | 1.70 | 5.00 | 12.00 |
| ...the Enterprise Logs nn(8/76)-Golden Press, ($1.95, 224 pgs.)-Reprints #1-8 plus 7 pgs. by McWilliams (#11185) | 1.30 | 4.00 | 9.00 |
| ...the Enterprise Logs Vol.2('76)-Reprints #9-17 (#11187) | 1.15 | 3.50 | 8.00 |
| ...the Enterprise Logs Vol.3('77)-Reprints #18-26 (#11188); McWilliams-a (4 pgs.) | 1.00 | 3.00 | 7.00 |
| Star Trek Vol.4(Winter'77)-Reprints #27,28,30-34,36,38 (#11189) plus 3 pgs. new art | 1.00 | 3.00 | 7.00 |

NOTE: ***McWilliams** a-38, 40-44, 46-61. #29 reprints #1; #35 reprints #4; #37 reprints #5; #45 reprints #7. The tabloids all have photo covers and blank inside covers. Painted covers #10-44, 46-59.*

**STAR TREK**
April, 1980 - No. 18, Feb, 1982
Marvel Comics Group

| | Good | Fine | N-Mint |
|---|---|---|---|
| 1-r/Marvel Super Special; movie adapt. | .70 | 2.00 | 4.00 |
| 2-18: 5-Miller-c | .40 | 1.25 | 2.50 |

NOTE: ***Austin** c-18i. **Buscema** a-13. **Gil Kane** a-15. **Nasser** c/a-7. **Simonson** c-17.*

**STAR TREK** (Also see Who's Who In Star Trek)
Feb, 1984 - No. 56, Nov, 1988 (Mando paper, 75 cents)
DC Comics

| | Good | Fine | N-Mint |
|---|---|---|---|
| 1-Sutton-a(p) begin | 1.30 | 4.00 | 8.00 |
| 2-5 | .85 | 2.50 | 5.00 |
| 6-10: 7-Origin Saavik | .70 | 2.00 | 4.00 |
| 11-20 | .40 | 1.25 | 2.50 |
| 21-32 | .35 | 1.00 | 2.00 |
| 33-($1.25, 52 pgs.)-20th anniversary issue | .50 | 1.50 | 3.00 |
| 34-49: 37-Painted-c. 49-Begin $1.00-c | .25 | .75 | 1.50 |
| 50-($1.50, 52 pgs.) | .40 | 1.25 | 2.50 |
| 51-56 | | .50 | 1.00 |
| Annual 1-3: 1(1985). 2(1986). 3(1988, $1.50) | .40 | 1.25 | 2.50 |

NOTE: ***Morrow** a-28, 35, 36, 56. **Orlando** c-8i. **Perez** c-1-3. **Spiegle** a-19. **Starlin** c-24, 25. **Sutton** a-1-6p, 8-18p, 20-27p, 29p, 31-34p, 39-52p, 55p; c-4-6p, 8-22p, 46p.*

**STAR TREK**
Oct, 1989 - Present ($1.50, color)
DC Comics

| | Good | Fine | N-Mint |
|---|---|---|---|
| 1-Capt. Kirk and crew | .50 | 1.50 | 3.00 |
| 2,3 | .35 | 1.00 | 2.00 |
| 4-18: 10-12-The Trial of James T. Kirk | .25 | .75 | 1.50 |
| Annual 1 (1990, $2.95, 68 pgs.)-Morrow-a | .50 | 1.50 | 3.00 |

**STAR TREK MOVIE SPECIAL**
June, 1984 - No. 2, 1987 ($1.50, 68pgs); 1989 ($2.00, 52 pgs.)
DC Comics

| | Good | Fine | N-Mint |
|---|---|---|---|
| 1-Adapts Star Trek III; Sutton-p (64 pgs.) | .25 | .75 | 1.50 |
| 2-Adapts Star Trek IV; Sutton-a (64 pgs.) | .25 | .75 | 1.50 |
| 1 (1989)-Adapts Star Trek V; painted-c | .35 | 1.00 | 2.00 |

**STAR TREK: THE NEXT GENERATION** (TV)
Feb, 1988 - No. 6, July, 1988 (Mini series, based on TV show)
DC Comics

| | Good | Fine | N-Mint |
|---|---|---|---|
| 1 (52 pgs.)-Sienkiewicz painted-c | 1.00 | 3.00 | 6.00 |
| 2-6 ($1.00) | .70 | 2.00 | 4.00 |

**STAR TREK: THE NEXT GENERATION** (TV)
Oct, 1989 - Present ($1.50, color)
DC Comics

| | Good | Fine | N-Mint |
|---|---|---|---|
| 1-Capt. Picard and crew from TV show | .70 | 2.00 | 4.00 |
| 2,3 | .40 | 1.25 | 2.50 |
| 4-10 | .35 | 1.00 | 2.00 |
| 11-18 | .25 | .75 | 1.50 |
| Annual 1 (1990, $2.95, 68 pgs.) | .50 | 1.50 | 3.00 |

**STAR WARS** (Movie) (See Contemporary Motivators, The Droids, The Ewoks, Marvel Movie Showcase & Marvel Special Edition)
July, 1977 - No. 107, Sept, 1986
Marvel Comics Group

| | Good | Fine | N-Mint |
|---|---|---|---|
| 1-(Regular 30 cent edition)-Price in square w/UPC code | 2.50 | 7.50 | 15.00 |
| 1-(35 cent cover; limited distribution - 1500 copies?)- Price in square w/UPC code (see note below) | 46.50 | 140.00 | 325.00 |
| 2-4: 4-Battle with Darth Vader | .85 | 2.50 | 5.00 |
| 5-10: 6-Dave Stevens inks | .50 | 1.50 | 3.00 |
| 11-20 | .35 | 1.00 | 2.00 |
| 21-38 | .25 | .75 | 1.50 |
| 39-44-The Empire Strikes Back-r by Al Williamson in all | .35 | 1.00 | 2.00 |
| 45-107: 92,100-($1.00, 52 pgs.) | | .50 | 1.00 |
| 1-9-Reprints; has "reprint" in upper lefthand corner of cover or on inside or price and number inside a diamond with no date or UPC on cover; 30 cents and 35 cents issues published | | .25 | .50 |
| Annual 1 (12/79) | .35 | 1.00 | 2.00 |
| Annual 2 (11/82), 3(12/83) | | .60 | 1.20 |

NOTE: *The rare 35 cent edition has the cover price in a square box, and the UPC box in the lower left hand corner has the UPC code lines running through it. **Austin** c-11-15i, 21i, 38; c-12-15i, 21i. **Byrne** c-13p. **Chaykin** a-1-10p; c-1. **Golden** c/a-38. **Miller** c-47p. **Nebres** c/a-Annual 2i. **Sienkiewicz** c-92i, 98. **Simonson** a-16p, 49p, 51-63p, 65p, 66p; c-16, 49-51, 52p, 53-62, Annual 1. **Williamson** a-39-44p, 50p, 98; c-39, 40, 41-44p. Painted c-81, 87, 92, 95, 98, 100, 105.*

**STAR WARS IN 3-D** (See Blackthorne 3-D Series #30, 47, 48)

**STAR WARS: RETURN OF THE JEDI**
Oct, 1983 - No. 4, Jan, 1984 (Mini-series, movie adaptation)
Marvel Comics Group

| | Good | Fine | N-Mint |
|---|---|---|---|
| 1-4-Williamson-a(p) in all | | .50 | 1.00 |
| Oversized issue ('83; 10¾x8¼"; 68 pgs.; cardboard-c)-Reprints above 4 issues | .50 | 1.50 | 2.95 |

**STATIC** (Also see Ditko's World)
No. 11, Oct, 1985 - No. 12, Dec, 1985
Charlton Comics

| | Good | Fine | N-Mint |
|---|---|---|---|
| 11,12-Ditko-c/a | | .40 | .80 |

**STEEL CLAW, THE**
Dec, 1986 - No. 4, Mar, 1987 (.75-$1.50, color, mini-series)
Quality Comics

| | Good | Fine | N-Mint |
|---|---|---|---|
| 1-3 (75 cents) | | .40 | .80 |
| 4 ($1.50) | .25 | .75 | 1.50 |

**STEELGRIP STARKEY**
July, 1986 - No. 6, June, 1987 ($1.50, mini-series, Baxter paper)
Epic Comics (Marvel)

| | Good | Fine | N-Mint |
|---|---|---|---|
| 1-6 | .25 | .75 | 1.50 |

**STEEL STERLING** (Formerly Shield-Steel Sterling; see Blue Ribbon, Jackpot, Mighty Comics, Mighty Crusaders, Roly Poly & Zip Comics)
No. 4, Jan, 1984 - No. 7, July, 1984
Archie Enterprises, Inc.

| | Good | Fine | N-Mint |
|---|---|---|---|
| 4-7: 6-McWilliams-a | | .40 | .80 |

**STEEL, THE INDESTRUCTIBLE MAN** (See All-Star Squadron #8)
March, 1978 - No. 5, Oct-Nov, 1978
DC Comics

| | Good | Fine | N-Mint |
|---|---|---|---|
| 1 | | .30 | .60 |
| 2-5: 5-Giant | | .25 | .50 |

**STEELTOWN ROCKERS**
Apr, 1990 - No. 6, Sept, 1990 ($1.00, color, mini-series)
Marvel Comics

| | Good | Fine | N-Mint |
|---|---|---|---|
| 1-6: Small town teenagers form own rock band | | .50 | 1.00 |

**STEVE CANYON** (See 4-Color #519, 578, 641, 737, 804, 939, 1033, and Harvey Comics Hits #52)

**STEVE CANYON**
1959 (96 pgs.; no text; 6¾x9"; hardcover)(B&W inside)
Grosset & Dunlap

| | Good | Fine | N-Mint |
|---|---|---|---|
| 100100-Reprints 2 stories from strip (1953, 1957) | 3.00 | 9.00 | 21.00 |
| 100100 (softcover edition) | 2.50 | 7.50 | 17.00 |

**STEVE CANYON COMICS**
Feb, 1948 - No. 6, Dec, 1948 (Strip reprints) (No. 4,5: 52pgs.)
Harvey Publications

| | Good | Fine | N-Mint |
|---|---|---|---|
| 1-Origin; has biog of Milton Caniff; Powell-a, 2pgs.; Caniff-a | 15.00 | 45.00 | 105.00 |
| 2-Caniff, Powell-a | 11.00 | 32.00 | 75.00 |
| 3-6: Caniff, Powell-a in all. 6-Intro Madame Lynx | 9.30 | 28.00 | 65.00 |
| Dept. Store giveaway #3(6/48, 36pp) | 9.30 | 28.00 | 65.00 |
| . . .'s Secret Mission (1951, 16 pgs., Armed Forces giveaway); Caniff-a | 8.50 | 25.50 | 60.00 |
| Strictly for the Smart Birds-16 pgs., 1951; Information Comics Div. (Harvey) Premium | 8.00 | 24.00 | 56.00 |

**STEVE CANYON IN 3-D**
June, 1986 (One shot, $2.25)
Kitchen Sink Press

| | Good | Fine | N-Mint |
|---|---|---|---|
| 1-Contains unpublished story from 1954 | .40 | 1.15 | 2.30 |

**STEVE DONOVAN, WESTERN MARSHAL** (TV)
No. 675, Feb, 1956 - No. 880, Feb, 1958 (All photo-c)
Dell Publishing Co.

| | Good | Fine | N-Mint |
|---|---|---|---|
| 4-Color 675-Kinstler-a | 5.00 | 15.00 | 35.00 |
| 4-Color 768-Kinstler-a | 4.00 | 12.00 | 28.00 |
| 4-Color 880 | 2.65 | 8.00 | 18.00 |

**STEVE ROPER**
April, 1948 - No. 5, Dec, 1948
Famous Funnies

| | Good | Fine | N-Mint |
|---|---|---|---|
| 1-Contains 1944 daily newspaper-r | 6.00 | 18.00 | 42.00 |
| 2 | 3.00 | 9.00 | 21.00 |
| 3-5 | 2.65 | 8.00 | 18.00 |

**STEVE SAUNDERS SPECIAL AGENT** (See Special Agent)

**STEVE SAVAGE** (See Captain. . .)

**STEVE ZODIAC & THE FIRE BALL XL-5** (TV)
January, 1964
Gold Key

| | Good | Fine | N-Mint |
|---|---|---|---|
| 1 (10108-401) | 4.50 | 14.00 | 32.00 |

**STEVIE** (Also see Mazie & Mortie)
Nov, 1952 - No. 6, April, 1954
Mazie (Magazine Publ.)

| | Good | Fine | N-Mint |
|---|---|---|---|
| 1 | 2.65 | 8.00 | 18.00 |
| 2-6 | 1.50 | 4.50 | 10.00 |

**STEVIE MAZIE'S BOY FRIEND** (See Harvey Hits #5)

**STEWART THE RAT** (See Eclipse Graphic Album Series)

**ST. GEORGE** (See listing under Saint. . .)

**STIGG'S INFERNO**
1985 - No. 7, Mar, 1987 ($2.00, B&W)
Vortex Publs./Eclipse Comics #6 on

| | Good | Fine | N-Mint |
|---|---|---|---|
| 1 ($1.95) | .70 | 2.00 | 4.00 |
| 2-4 | .50 | 1.50 | 3.00 |
| 5-7 | .35 | 1.00 | 2.00 |
| Graphic Album ('88, $6.95, B&W, 100pgs.)-r | 1.15 | 3.50 | 7.00 |

**STONEY BURKE** (TV)
June-Aug, 1963 - No. 2, Sept-Nov, 1963
Dell Publishing Co.

| | Good | Fine | N-Mint |
|---|---|---|---|
| 1,2 | 1.15 | 3.50 | 8.00 |

**STONY CRAIG**
1946 (No #)
Pentagon Publishing Co.

| | Good | Fine | N-Mint |
|---|---|---|---|
| nn-Reprints Bell Syndicate's "Sgt. Stony Craig" newspaper strips | 4.00 | 12.00 | 28.00 |

**STORIES BY FAMOUS AUTHORS ILLUSTRATED** (Fast Fiction #1-5)
No. 6, Aug, 1950 - No. 13, March, 1951
Seaboard Publ./Famous Authors Ill.

| | Good | Fine | N-Mint |
|---|---|---|---|
| 1-Scarlet Pimpernel-Baroness Orczy | 18.00 | 54.00 | 125.00 |
| 2-Capt. Blood-Raphael Sabatini | 18.00 | 54.00 | 125.00 |
| 3-She, by Haggard | 23.00 | 70.00 | 160.00 |
| 4-The 39 Steps-John Buchan | 11.50 | 34.00 | 80.00 |
| 5-Beau Geste-P. C. Wren | 12.00 | 36.00 | 85.00 |

NOTE: *The above five issues are exact reprints of Fast Fiction #1-5 except for the title change and new Kiefer covers on #1 and 2. The above 5 issues were released before Famous Authors #6.*

| | Good | Fine | N-Mint |
|---|---|---|---|
| 6-Macbeth, by Shakespeare; Kiefer art (8/50); used in **SOTI**, pg. 22,143. Kiefer-c; 36p | 14.00 | 43.00 | 100.00 |
| 7-The Window; Kiefer-c/a; 52p | 11.50 | 34.00 | 80.00 |
| 8-Hamlet, by Shakespeare; Kiefer-c/a; 36p | 14.00 | 43.00 | 100.00 |
| 9-Nicholas Nickleby, by Dickens; G. Schrotter-a; 52p | 12.00 | 36.00 | 85.00 |
| 10-Romeo & Juliet, by Shakespeare; Kiefer-c/a; 36p | 12.00 | 36.00 | 85.00 |
| 11-Ben-Hur; Schrotter-a; 52p | 13.00 | 40.00 | 90.00 |
| 12-La Svengali; Schrotter-a; 36p | 13.00 | 40.00 | 90.00 |
| 13-Scaramouche; Kiefer-c/a; 36p | 13.00 | 40.00 | 90.00 |

NOTE: Artwork was prepared/advertised for #14, *The Red Badge Of Courage*. Gilberton bought out Famous Authors, Ltd. and used that story as C.I. #98. Famous Authors, Ltd. then published the Classics Junior series. The Famous Authors titles were published as part of the regular Classics Ill. Series in Brazil starting in 1952.

**STORIES OF CHRISTMAS**
1942 (32 pages; paper cover) (Giveaway)
K. K. Publications

| | Good | Fine | N-Mint |
|---|---|---|---|
| nn-Adaptation of "A Christmas Carol;" Kelly story-"The Fir Tree;" Infinity-c | 40.00 | 100.00 | 200.00 |

**STORIES OF ROMANCE** (Formerly Meet Miss Bliss)
No. 5, Mar, 1956 - No. 13, Aug, 1957
Atlas Comics (LMC)

| | Good | Fine | N-Mint |
|---|---|---|---|
| 5-Baker-a? | 3.00 | 9.00 | 21.00 |
| 6-13 | 1.30 | 4.00 | 9.00 |

NOTE: ***Ann Brewster** a-13. **Colletta** a-9(2); c-5.*

**STORMWATCHER**
April, 1989 - No. 4, Dec, 1989 ($2.00, B&W, mini-series)
Eclipse Comics (Acme Press)

| | Good | Fine | N-Mint |
|---|---|---|---|
| 1-4 | .35 | 1.00 | 2.00 |

**STORMY** (See 4-Color #537)

**STORY HOUR SERIES** (Disney)
1948, 1949; 1951-1953 (36 pgs., paper-c) (4½x6¼")
Given away with subscription to Walt Disney's Comics & Stories

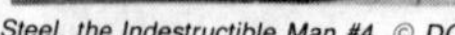

*Steel, the Indestructible Man #4, © DC*

*Stories By Famous Authors Ill. #11, © FMI*

*Stormwatcher #1, © Eclipse Comics*

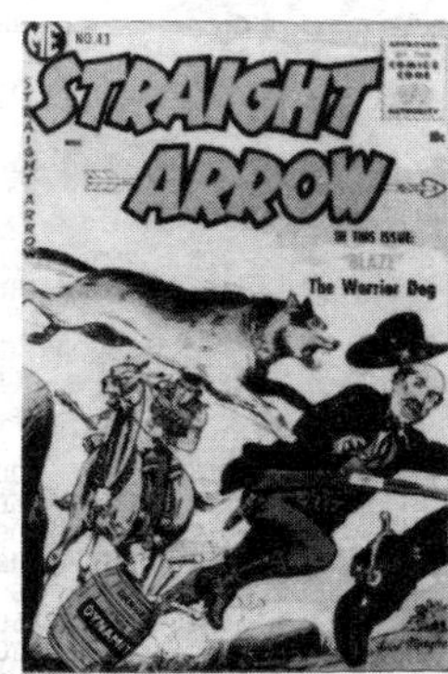

*Straight Arrow #43, © ME*

*Strange Adventures #14, © DC*

*Strange Adventures #150, © DC*

Whitman Publishing Co.

| | Good | Fine | N-Mint |
|---|---|---|---|
| nn(1948)-Mickey Mouse and Boy Thursday | 5.70 | 17.00 | 40.00 |
| nn(1948)-Mickey Mouse Miracle Maker | 5.70 | 17.00 | 40.00 |
| nn(1948)-Minnie Mouse and Antique Chair | 5.70 | 17.00 | 40.00 |
| nn(1949)-The Three Orphan Kittens(B&W & color) | 2.65 | 8.00 | 18.00 |
| nn(1949)-Danny-The Little Black Lamb | 2.65 | 8.00 | 18.00 |
| 800-Donald Duck in "Bringing Up the Boys;" 1948 | 8.50 | 25.50 | 60.00 |
| 1953 edition | 4.50 | 14.00 | 32.00 |
| 801-Mickey Mouse's Summer Vacation; 1948 | 4.50 | 14.00 | 32.00 |
| 1951, 1952 edition | 2.30 | 7.00 | 16.00 |
| 802-Bugs Bunny's Adventures; 1948 | 3.50 | 10.50 | 24.00 |
| 803-Bongo; 1948 | 3.00 | 9.00 | 21.00 |
| 804-Mickey and the Beanstalk; 1948 | 3.70 | 11.00 | 26.00 |
| 805-15-Andy Panda and His Friends; 1949 | 3.50 | 10.50 | 24.00 |
| 806-15-Tom and Jerry; 1949 | 3.50 | 10.50 | 24.00 |
| 808-15-Johnny Appleseed; 1949 | 3.00 | 9.00 | 21.00 |

1948, 1949 Hard Cover Edition of each . . . $2.00 - $3.00 more.

**STORY OF EDISON, THE**
1956 (16 pgs.) (Reddy Killowatt)
Educational Comics

| | | | |
|---|---|---|---|
| nn-Reprint of Reddy Kilowatt #2(1947) | 4.75 | 14.00 | 30.00 |

**STORY OF HARRY S. TRUMAN, THE**
1948 (16 pgs.) (in color, regular size)(Soft-c)
Democratic National Committee (Giveaway)

| | | | |
|---|---|---|---|
| nn-Gives biography on career of Truman; used in **SOTI**, pg. 311 | 10.00 | 30.00 | 70.00 |

**STORY OF JESUS** (See Classics Illustrated Special Issue)

**STORY OF MANKIND, THE** (See 4-Color #851)

**STORY OF MARTHA WAYNE, THE**
April, 1956
Argo Publ.

| | | | |
|---|---|---|---|
| 1-Newspaper-r | 2.00 | 6.00 | 14.00 |

**STORY OF RUTH, THE** (See 4-Color #1144)

**STORY OF THE COMMANDOS, THE** (Combined Operations)
1943 (68 pgs.; B&W) (15 cents)
Long Island Independent (Distr. by Gilberton)

| | | | |
|---|---|---|---|
| nn-All text (no comics); photos & illustrations; ad for Classic Comics on back cover (Rare) | 13.00 | 40.00 | 90.00 |

**STORY OF THE GLOOMY BUNNY, THE** (See March of Comics #9)

**STRAIGHT ARROW** (Radio)(See Best of the West & Great Western)
Feb-Mar, 1950 - No. 55, Mar, 1956 (All 36 pgs.)
Magazine Enterprises

| | Good | Fine | N-Mint |
|---|---|---|---|
| 1-Straight Arrow (alias Steve Adams) & his palomino Fury begin; 1st mention of Sundown Valley & the Secret Cave; Whitney-a | 21.50 | 64.00 | 150.00 |
| 2-Red Hawk begins (1st app?) by Powell (Origin), ends #55 | 10.00 | 30.00 | 70.00 |
| 3-Frazetta-c | 14.00 | 42.00 | 100.00 |
| 4,5: 4-Secret Cave-c | 6.00 | 18.00 | 42.00 |
| 6-10 | 4.65 | 14.00 | 32.00 |
| 11-Classic story "The Valley of Time," with an ancient civilization made of gold | 5.00 | 15.00 | 35.00 |
| 12-19 | 3.50 | 10.50 | 24.00 |
| 20-Origin Straight Arrow's Shield | 5.00 | 15.00 | 35.00 |
| 21-Origin Fury | 5.70 | 17.00 | 40.00 |
| 22-Frazetta-c | 10.00 | 30.00 | 70.00 |
| 23,25-30: 25-Secret Cave-c. 28-Red Hawk meets The Vikings | 3.00 | 9.00 | 21.00 |
| 24-Classic story "The Dragons of Doom!" with prehistoric pteradactyls | 4.65 | 14.00 | 32.00 |
| 31-38 | 2.65 | 8.00 | 18.00 |
| 39-Classic story "The Canyon Beast," with a dinosaur egg hatching a Tyranosaurus Rex | 3.50 | 10.50 | 24.00 |
| 40-Classic story "Secret of The Spanish Specters," with Conquistadors' lost treasure | 3.50 | 10.50 | 24.00 |
| 41,42,44-54: 45-Secret Cave-c | 2.15 | 6.50 | 15.00 |
| 43-Intro & 1st app. Blaze, Straight Arrow's Warrior dog | 2.65 | 8.00 | 18.00 |
| 55-Last issue | 3.00 | 9.00 | 21.00 |

NOTE: ***Fred Meagher** a 1-55; c-1, 2, 4-21, 23-55. **Powell** a 2-55. Many issues advertise the radio premiums associated with Straight Arrow.*

**STRAIGHT ARROW'S FURY** (See A-1 Comics #119)

**STRANGE**
March, 1957 - No. 6, May, 1958
Ajax-Farrell Publ. (Four Star Comic Corp.)

| | | | |
|---|---|---|---|
| 1 | 7.00 | 21.00 | 50.00 |
| 2 | 3.60 | 11.00 | 25.00 |
| 3-6 | 2.65 | 8.00 | 18.00 |

**STRANGE ADVENTURES**
Aug-Sept, 1950 - No. 244, Oct-Nov, 1973 (No. 1-12: 52 pgs.)
National Periodical Publications

| | | | |
|---|---|---|---|
| 1-Adaptation of "Destination Moon;" Kris KL-99 & Darwin Jones begin; photo-c | 130.00 | 390.00 | 910.00 |
| 2 | 59.00 | 175.00 | 410.00 |
| 3,4 | 39.00 | 116.00 | 270.00 |
| 5-8,10: 7-Origin Kris KL-99 | 34.00 | 100.00 | 240.00 |
| 9-Captain Comet begins (6/51, Intro/origin) | 93.00 | 280.00 | 650.00 |
| 11,14,15 | 30.00 | 90.00 | 210.00 |
| 12,13,17,18-Toth-a | 32.00 | 95.00 | 220.00 |
| 16,19,20 | 21.00 | 62.00 | 145.00 |
| 21-30 | 18.00 | 54.00 | 125.00 |
| 31,34-38 | 16.00 | 48.00 | 110.00 |
| 32,33-Krigstein-a | 17.00 | 51.00 | 120.00 |
| 39-Ill. in **SOTI**-"Treating police contemptuously" (top right) | 23.00 | 70.00 | 160.00 |
| 40-49-Last Capt. Comet; not in 45,47,48 | 14.00 | 41.00 | 95.00 |
| 50-53-Last precode issue (2/55) | 10.00 | 30.00 | 70.00 |
| 54-70 | 5.70 | 17.00 | 40.00 |
| 71-99 | 4.30 | 13.00 | 30.00 |
| 100 | 6.50 | 19.00 | 45.00 |
| 101-110: 104-Space Museum begins by Sekowsky | 3.15 | 9.50 | 22.00 |
| 111-116: 114-Star Hawkins begins, ends #185; Heath-a in Wood E.C. style | 2.85 | 8.50 | 20.00 |
| 117-Origin/1st app. Atomic Knights & begins (6/60) | 20.00 | 60.00 | 140.00 |
| 118-120 | 5.70 | 17.00 | 40.00 |
| 121-134: 124-Origin Faceless Creature. 134-Last 10 cent issue | 3.60 | 11.00 | 25.00 |
| 135-160: 159-Star Rovers app.; G. Kane/Anderson-a. 160-Last Atomic Knights | 2.15 | 6.50 | 15.00 |
| 161-179: 161-Last Space Museum. 163-Star Rovers app. 170-Infinity-c. 177-Origin Immortal Man | .85 | 2.60 | 6.00 |
| 180-Origin/1st app. Animal Man | 26.00 | 77.00 | 180.00 |
| 181-183,185-189,191-194,196-200,202-204: 187-Origin The Enchantress | .70 | 2.00 | 5.00 |
| 184-2nd app. Animal Man | 14.00 | 43.00 | 100.00 |
| 190-1st app. Animal Man in costume | 17.00 | 51.00 | 120.00 |
| 195-1st full length Animal Man story | 10.00 | 30.00 | 70.00 |
| 201-Last Animal Man; 2nd full length story | 5.00 | 15.00 | 35.00 |
| 205-Intro/origin Deadman by Infantino (10/67) | 5.70 | 17.00 | 40.00 |
| 206-Neal Adams-a begins | 3.15 | 9.50 | 22.00 |
| 207-210 | 2.15 | 6.50 | 15.00 |

| | Good | Fine | N-Mint |
|---|---|---|---|
| 211-216: 211-Space Museum-r. 216-Last Deadman | 1.70 | 5.00 | 12.00 |
| 217-230: 217-Adam Strange & Atomic Knights-r begin. 218-Last 12 cent issue? 222-New Adam Strange story by Kane/Anderson. 226-236-(68-52 pgs.) | .50 | 1.50 | 3.00 |
| 231-244: 231-Last Atomic Knights-r | .25 | .75 | 1.50 |

NOTE: ***Neal Adams*** *a-206-216; c-207-216, 228, 235.* ***Anderson*** *a-8-52, 94, 96, 97, 99, 115, 117, 119-163, 217r, 218r, 222-225r, 222, 226, 242i(r); c/r-157i, 190i, 217-224, 228-231, 233, 235-239, 241-243.* ***Ditko*** *a-188, 189.* ***Drucker*** *a-42, 43, 45.* ***Elias*** *a-212.* ***Finlay*** *a-2, 3, 6, 7, 210r, 229r.* ***Giunta*** *a-237r.* ***Infantino*** *a-10-101, 106-151, 154, 157-163, 180, 190, 218-221r, 223-244p(r); c(r)-190p, 197, 199-211, 218-221, 223-244.* ***Kaluta*** *c-238, 240.* ***Gil Kane*** *a-8-116, 124, 125, 130, 138, 146-157, 173-186, 204r, 222r, 227-231r; c-154p, 157p.* ***Kubert*** *a-55(2 pgs.), 226; c-219, 220, 225-227, 232, 234.* ***Moriera*** *c-71.* ***Morrow*** *c-230.* ***Powell*** *a-4.* ***Mike Sekowsky*** *a-71p, 97-162p, 217p(r), 218p(r); c-206, 217-219r.* ***Simon & Kirby*** *a-2r (2 pg. )* ***Sparling*** *a-201.* ***Toth*** *a-8, 12, 13, 17-19.* ***Wood*** *a-154i. Atomic Knights reprints by* ***Anderson*** *in 119-221. Chris KL99 in 1-3, 5, 7, 9, 11, 15. Capt. Comet covers-9-14, 17-19, 24, 26, 27, 32-44.*

**STRANGE AS IT SEEMS** (See Famous Funnies-A Carnival of Comics, Feature Funnies #1, The John Hix Scrap Book & Peanuts)

**STRANGE AS IT SEEMS**
1932 (64 pgs.; B&W; square binding)
Blue-Star Publishing Co.

| | Good | Fine | N-Mint |
|---|---|---|---|
| 1-Newspaper-r | 13.00 | 40.00 | 90.00 |

NOTE: *Published with and without No. 1 and price on cover.*

| | Good | Fine | N-Mint |
|---|---|---|---|
| Ex-Lax giveaway(1936,24pgs,5x7'',B&W)-McNaught Synd. | 2.00 | 6.00 | 14.00 |

**STRANGE AS IT SEEMS**
1939
United Features Syndicate

| | Good | Fine | N-Mint |
|---|---|---|---|
| Single Series 9, 1, 2 | 16.00 | 48.00 | 110.00 |

**STRANGE CONFESSIONS**
Jan-Mar, 1952 - No. 4, Fall, 1952
Ziff-Davis Publ. Co. (Approved)

| | Good | Fine | N-Mint |
|---|---|---|---|
| 1(Scarce)-Photo-c; Kinstler-a | 22.00 | 65.00 | 155.00 |
| 2(Scarce) | 14.00 | 43.00 | 100.00 |
| 3(Scarce)-#3 on-c, #2 on inside; Reformatory girl story; photo-c | 14.00 | 43.00 | 100.00 |
| 4(Scarce)-Reformatory girl story | 14.00 | 43.00 | 100.00 |

**STRANGE DAYS**
Oct, 1984 - No. 3, Apr, 1985 ($1.75, color, Baxter paper)
Eclipse Comics

| | Good | Fine | N-Mint |
|---|---|---|---|
| 1-3-Freakwave & Johnny Nemo & Paradax from Vanguard Ill.; nudity, violence, strong language | .30 | .90 | 1.80 |

**STRANGE FANTASY** (Formerly Rocketman)
Aug, 1952 - No. 14, Oct-Nov, 1954
Ajax-Farrell

| | Good | Fine | N-Mint |
|---|---|---|---|
| 2(#1, 8/52)-Jungle Princess story; Kamenish-a; r-/Ellery Queen #1 | 10.00 | 30.00 | 70.00 |
| 2(10/52)-No Black Cat or Rulah; Bakerish, Kamenish-a; hypo/meat-hook-c | 9.30 | 28.00 | 65.00 |
| 3-Rulah story, called Pulah | 9.30 | 28.00 | 65.00 |
| 4-Rocket Man app. | 7.00 | 21.00 | 50.00 |
| 5,6,8,10,12,14 | 5.70 | 17.00 | 40.00 |
| 7-Madam Satan/Slave story | 7.00 | 21.00 | 50.00 |
| 9(w/Black Cat), 9(w/Boy's Ranch; S&K-a)(A rebinding of Harvey enteriors; not publ. by Ajax) | 8.00 | 24.00 | 55.00 |
| 9-Regular issue | 5.70 | 17.00 | 40.00 |
| 11-Jungle story | 6.50 | 19.00 | 45.00 |
| 13-Bondage-c; Rulah (Kolah) story | 8.50 | 25.50 | 60.00 |

**STRANGE GALAXY** (Magazine)
V1#8, Feb, 1971 - No. 11, Aug, 1971 (B&W)
Eerie Publications

| | Good | Fine | N-Mint |
|---|---|---|---|
| V1#8-Cover-r/from Fantastic V19#3 (2/70) (a pulp) | 1.15 | 3.50 | 8.00 |
| 9-11 | .70 | 2.00 | 5.00 |

**STRANGE JOURNEY**
Sept, 1957 - No. 4, June, 1958 (Farrell reprints)
America's Best (Steinway Publ.) (Ajax/Farrell)

| | Good | Fine | N-Mint |
|---|---|---|---|
| 1 | 7.00 | 21.00 | 50.00 |
| 2-4 | 4.00 | 12.00 | 28.00 |

**STRANGE LOVE** (See Fox Giants)

**STRANGE MYSTERIES**
Sept, 1951 - No. 21, Jan, 1955
Superior/Dynamic Publications

| | Good | Fine | N-Mint |
|---|---|---|---|
| 1-Kamenish-a begins | 20.00 | 60.00 | 140.00 |
| 2 | 11.00 | 32.00 | 75.00 |
| 3-5 | 8.00 | 24.00 | 55.00 |
| 6-8 | 7.00 | 21.00 | 50.00 |
| 9-Bondage 3-D effect-c | 9.30 | 28.00 | 65.00 |
| 10-Used in **SOTI**, pg. 181 | 6.50 | 19.00 | 45.00 |
| 11-18 | 5.00 | 15.00 | 35.00 |
| 19-r-/Journey Into Fear #1; cover is a splash from one story; Baker-r(2) | 7.00 | 21.00 | 50.00 |
| 20,21-Reprints; 20-r-/#1 with new-c | 4.30 | 13.00 | 30.00 |

**STRANGE MYSTERIES**
1963 - 1964
I. W. Enterprises/Super Comics

| | Good | Fine | N-Mint |
|---|---|---|---|
| I.W. Reprint #9; Rulah-r | .85 | 2.60 | 6.00 |
| Super Reprint #10-12,15-17('63-'64): #12-reprints Tales of Horror #5 (3/53) less-c. #15,16-reprints The Dead Who Walk | .70 | 2.00 | 5.00 |
| Super Reprint #18-R-/Witchcraft #1; Kubert-a | .85 | 2.60 | 6.00 |

**STRANGE PLANETS**
1958; 1963-64
I. W. Enterprises/Super Comics

| | Good | Fine | N-Mint |
|---|---|---|---|
| I.W. Reprint #1(nd)-E. C. Incred. S/F #30 plus-c/Strange Worlds #3 | 5.00 | 15.00 | 35.00 |
| I.W. Reprint #8 | 2.30 | 7.00 | 16.00 |
| I.W. Reprint #9-Orlando/Wood-a (Strange Worlds #4); c-from Flying Saucers #1 | 7.00 | 21.00 | 50.00 |
| Super Reprint #10-22 pg. Wood-a from Space Detective #1; c-/Attack on Planet Mars | 6.50 | 19.50 | 45.00 |
| Super Reprint #11-25 pg. Wood-a from An Earthman on Venus | 10.00 | 30.00 | 70.00 |
| Super Reprint #12-Orlando-a from Rocket to the Moon | 6.50 | 19.50 | 45.00 |
| Super Reprint #15-Reprints Atlas stories; Heath, Colan-a | 1.70 | 5.00 | 12.00 |
| Super Reprint #16-Avon's Strange Worlds #6; Kinstler, Check-a | 2.65 | 8.00 | 18.00 |
| Super Reprint #17 | 1.35 | 4.00 | 9.00 |
| Super Reprint #18-Reprints Daring Adventures; Space Busters, Explorer Joe, The Son of Robin Hood; Krigstein-a | 2.00 | 6.00 | 14.00 |

**STRANGE SPORTS STORIES** (See Brave & the Bold, DC Special, and DC Super Stars #10)
Sept-Oct, 1973 - No. 6, July-Aug, 1974
National Periodical Publications

| | Good | Fine | N-Mint |
|---|---|---|---|
| 1 | | .50 | 1.00 |
| 2-6: 3-Swan/Anderson-a | | .35 | .70 |

**STRANGE STORIES FROM ANOTHER WORLD** (Unknown World #1)
No. 2, Aug, 1952 - No. 5, Feb, 1953
Fawcett Publications

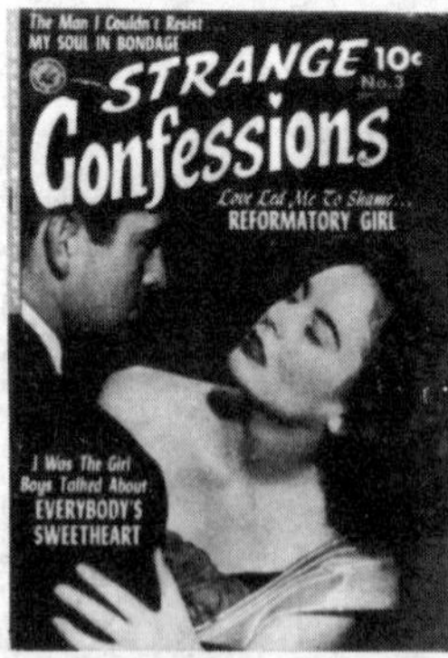

*Strange Confessions #3, © Z-D*

*Strange Journey #2, © AJAX*

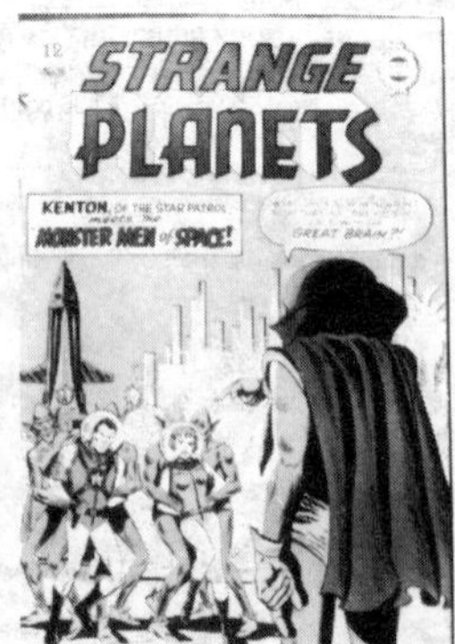

*Strange Planets #16, © Super*

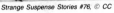

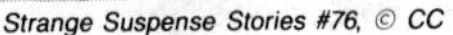
Strange Suspense Stories #76, © CC

Strange Tales #111, © MEG

Strange Tales #167, © MEG

| | Good | Fine | N-Mint |
|---|---|---|---|
| 2-Saunders painted-c | 17.00 | 51.00 | 120.00 |
| 3-5-Saunders painted-c | 13.00 | 40.00 | 90.00 |

**STRANGE STORIES OF SUSPENSE** (Rugged Action #1-4)
No. 5, Oct, 1955 - No. 16, Aug, 1957
Atlas Comics (CSI)

| | Good | Fine | N-Mint |
|---|---|---|---|
| 5(#1) | 10.00 | 30.00 | 70.00 |
| 6,9 | 6.00 | 18.00 | 42.00 |
| 7-E. C. swipe cover/Vault of Horror #32 | 6.50 | 19.00 | 45.00 |
| 8-Williamson/Mayo-a; Pakula-a | 7.00 | 21.00 | 50.00 |
| 10-Crandall, Torres, Meskin-a | 7.00 | 21.00 | 50.00 |
| 11 | 3.60 | 11.00 | 25.00 |
| 12-Torres, Pakula-a | 4.30 | 13.00 | 30.00 |
| 13-E.C. art swipes | 3.60 | 11.00 | 25.00 |
| 14-Williamson-a | 5.00 | 15.00 | 35.00 |
| 15-Krigstein-a | 4.50 | 14.00 | 32.00 |
| 16-Fox, Powell-a | 5.00 | 15.00 | 35.00 |

NOTE: ***Everett** a-6, 7, 13; c-9, 11-14. **Heath** a-5. **Maneely** c-5. **Morrow** a-13. **Powell** a-8. **Severin** c-7. **Wildey** a-14.*

**STRANGE STORY** (Also see Front Page)
June-July, 1946 (52 pages)
Harvey Publications

| | Good | Fine | N-Mint |
|---|---|---|---|
| 1-The Man in Black Called Fate by Powell | 11.50 | 34.00 | 80.00 |

**STRANGE SUSPENSE STORIES** (Lawbreakers Suspense Stories #10-15; This Is Suspense #23-26; Captain Atom V1#78 on)
6/52 - No. 5, 2/53; No. 16, 1/54 - No. 22, 11/54; No. 27, 10/55 - No. 77, 10/65; V3#1, 10/67 - V1#9, 9/69
Fawcett Publications/Charlton Comics No. 16 on

| | Good | Fine | N-Mint |
|---|---|---|---|
| 1-(Fawcett)-Powell, Sekowsky-a | 25.00 | 75.00 | 175.00 |
| 2-George Evans horror story | 17.00 | 51.00 | 120.00 |
| 3-5 (2/53)-George Evans horror stories | 14.00 | 43.00 | 100.00 |
| 16(1-2/54) | 7.00 | 21.00 | 50.00 |
| 17,21 | 5.70 | 17.00 | 40.00 |
| 18-E.C. swipe/HOF 7; Ditko-c/a(2) | 12.00 | 36.00 | 85.00 |
| 19-Ditko electric chair-c; Ditko-a | 14.00 | 43.00 | 100.00 |
| 20-Ditko-c/a(2) | 12.00 | 36.00 | 85.00 |
| 22(11/54)-Ditko-c, Shuster-a; last pre-code issue; becomes This Is Suspense | 10.00 | 30.00 | 70.00 |
| 27(10/55)-(Formerly This Is Suspense #26) | 2.30 | 7.00 | 16.00 |
| 28-30,38 | 2.15 | 6.50 | 15.00 |
| 31-33,35,37,40,51-Ditko-c/a(2-3 each) | 7.00 | 21.00 | 50.00 |
| 34-Story of ruthless business man, Wm. B. Gaines; Ditko-c/a | 10.00 | 30.00 | 70.00 |
| 36-(68 pgs.); Ditko-a(4) | 8.00 | 24.00 | 55.00 |
| 39,41,52,53-Ditko-a | 5.70 | 17.00 | 40.00 |
| 42-44,46,49,54-60 | 1.70 | 5.00 | 12.00 |
| 45,47,48,50-Ditko-c/a | 4.50 | 14.00 | 32.00 |
| 61-74 | .70 | 2.00 | 4.00 |
| 75(6/65)-Reprints origin/1st app. Captain Atom by Ditko from Space Adventures #33 (75-77: 12 cent issues) | 8.50 | 25.50 | 60.00 |
| 76,77-Captain Atom-r by Ditko/Space Advs. | 3.50 | 10.50 | 24.00 |
| V3#1(10/67)-4: All 12 cent issues | 1.15 | 3.50 | 8.00 |
| V1#2-9: 2-Ditko-a, atom bomb-c (all 12 cents) | .70 | 2.00 | 4.00 |

NOTE: ***Alascia** a-19. **Aparo** a-V3#1, 2. **Bailey** a-1-3; c-5. **Evans** c-4. **Montes/Bache** c-66. **Powell** a-4. **Shuster** a-19, 21.*

**STRANGE TALES** (Becomes Doctor Strange #169 on)
June, 1951 - #168, May, 1968; #169, Sept, 1973 - #188, Nov, 1976
Atlas (CCPC #1-67/ZPC #68-79/VPI #80-85)/Marvel #86(7/61) on

| | Good | Fine | N-Mint |
|---|---|---|---|
| 1 | 90.00 | 270.00 | 630.00 |
| 2 | 42.00 | 125.00 | 290.00 |
| 3,5: 3-Atom bomb panels | 31.00 | 92.00 | 215.00 |
| 4-"The Evil Eye," cosmic eyeball story | 33.00 | 100.00 | 230.00 |
| 6-9 | 22.00 | 64.00 | 150.00 |
| 10-Krigstein-a | 23.00 | 70.00 | 160.00 |
| 11-14,16-20 | 11.50 | 34.00 | 80.00 |
| 15-Krigstein-a | 12.00 | 36.00 | 85.00 |
| 21,23-27,29-32,34-Last precode issue(2/55): 27-Atom bomb panels | 9.30 | 28.00 | 65.00 |
| 22-Krigstein, Forte/Fox-a | 10.00 | 30.00 | 70.00 |
| 28-Jack Katz story used in Senate Investigation report, pgs. 7 & 169 | 10.00 | 30.00 | 70.00 |
| 33-Davis-a | 9.30 | 28.00 | 65.00 |
| 35-41,43,44 | 6.50 | 19.00 | 45.00 |
| 42,45,59,61-Krigstein-a; #61 (2/58) | 7.00 | 21.00 | 50.00 |
| 46-52,54,55,57,60: 60 (8/57) | 5.70 | 17.00 | 40.00 |
| 53-Torres, Crandall-a | 7.00 | 21.00 | 50.00 |
| 56-Crandall-a | 6.00 | 18.00 | 42.00 |
| 58,64-Williamson-a in each, with Mayo-#58 | 7.00 | 21.00 | 50.00 |
| 62-Torres-a | 5.70 | 17.00 | 40.00 |
| 63,65 | 5.30 | 16.00 | 38.00 |
| 66-Crandall-a | 5.70 | 17.00 | 40.00 |
| 67-80-Ditko/Kirby-a. 79-Dr. Strange proto-type app. | 5.00 | 15.00 | 35.00 |
| 81-92-Last 10 cent issue. Ditko/Kirby-a | 4.50 | 14.00 | 32.00 |
| 93-96,98-100-Kirby-a | 4.30 | 13.00 | 30.00 |
| 97-Aunt May & Uncle Ben prototype by Ditko, 3 months before Amaz. Fantasy #15. Kirby-a | 7.00 | 21.00 | 50.00 |
| 101-Human Torch begins by Kirby (10/62) | 47.00 | 140.00 | 325.00 |
| 102 | 18.00 | 54.00 | 125.00 |
| 103-105 | 15.00 | 45.00 | 105.00 |
| 106,108,109 | 10.00 | 30.00 | 70.00 |
| 107-Human Torch/Sub-Mariner battle | 13.00 | 40.00 | 90.00 |
| 110-(7/63)-Intro Doctor Strange, Ancient One & Wong by Ditko | 40.00 | 120.00 | 280.00 |
| 111-2nd Dr. Strange | 10.00 | 30.00 | 70.00 |
| 112,113 | 6.50 | 19.00 | 45.00 |
| 114-Acrobat disguised as Captain America, 1st app. since the G.A.; intro. & 1st app. Victoria Bentley; 3rd Dr. Strange app. & begin series (11/63) | 14.00 | 41.00 | 95.00 |
| 115-Origin Dr. Strange; Spider-Man & Sandman (Spidey villain) app. (early Spider-Man x-over, 12/63) | 20.00 | 60.00 | 140.00 |
| 116-120: 116-Human Torch battles The Thing; 1st Thing x-over. 120-1st Iceman x-over (from X-Men) | 5.00 | 15.00 | 35.00 |
| 121-129,131-134: Thing/Torch team-up in all; 123-1st Thor x-over. 126-Intro Clea. 134-Last H. Torch; Wood-a(i) | 2.85 | 8.50 | 20.00 |
| 130-The Beatles cameo | 3.60 | 11.00 | 25.00 |
| 135-Origin/1st app. Nick Fury, Agent of Shield by Kirby (8/65); series begins, ends #168 | 5.00 | 15.00 | 35.00 |
| 136-147,149: 146-Last Ditko Dr. Strange who is in consecutive stories since #113 | 2.00 | 6.00 | 14.00 |
| 148-Origin Ancient One | 2.30 | 7.00 | 16.00 |
| 150(11/66)-John Buscema's 1st work at Marvel | 2.00 | 6.00 | 14.00 |
| 151-1st Marvel work by Steranko (w/Kirby) | 2.30 | 7.00 | 16.00 |
| 152,153-Kirby/Steranko-a | 2.00 | 6.00 | 14.00 |
| 154-158-Steranko-a/script | 2.00 | 6.00 | 14.00 |
| 159-Origin Nick Fury; Intro Val; Captain America app; Steranko-a | 2.30 | 7.00 | 16.00 |
| 160-162-Steranko-a/scripts; Capt. America app. | 2.00 | 6.00 | 14.00 |
| 163-166,168-Steranko-a(p). 168-Last Nick Fury | 2.00 | 6.00 | 14.00 |
| 167-Steranko pen/script; classic flag-c | 2.65 | 8.00 | 18.00 |
| 169-177: 169,170-Brother Voodoo origin in each; series ends #173. 174-Origin Golem. 177-Brunner-c | .35 | 1.00 | 2.00 |
| 178-Warlock by Starlin with covers; origin Warlock & Him; Starlin scripts in 178-181 | 1.50 | 4.50 | 10.00 |
| 179-181-Warlock by Starlin with covers. 179-Intro/1st app. Pip the Troll. 180-Intro Gamora | .85 | 2.60 | 6.00 |
| 182-188 | | .50 | 1.00 |
| Annual 1(1962)-Reprints from Strange Tales #73,76,78, Tales of Suspense #7,9, Tales to Astonish #1,6,7, & Journey Into Mystery #53, 55,59 | 24.00 | 71.00 | 165.00 |

Good Fine N-Mint

Annual 2(7/63)-r-/from Strange Tales #67, Strange Worlds (Atlas) #1-3, World of Fantasy #16; new Human Torch vs. Spider-Man story by Kirby/Ditko (1st Spidey x-over); Kirby-c 29.00 86.00 200.00

NOTE: ***Briefer** a-17. **Burgos** a-123p. **J. Buscema** a-174p. **Colan** a-11, 20, 53, 169-173p, 188p. **Davis** c-71. **Ditko** a-46, 50, 67-122, 123-125p, 126-146, 175r, 182-188r; c-33, 51, 93, 115, 121, 146. **Everett** a-4, 21, 40-42, 73, 147-152, 164i; c-8, 10, 11, 13, 24, 45, 49-54, 56, 58, 60, 61, 63, 148, 150, 152, 158i. **Forte** a-27, 43, 50, 53, 54, 60. **Heath** c-20. **Kamen** a-45. **G. Kane** c-170-173, 182p. **Kirby** Human Torch-101-105, 108, 109, 114, 120; Nick Fury-135p, 141-143p; (Layouts)-135-153; other **Kirby** a-67-100p; c-68-70, 72-92, 94, 95, 101-114, 116-123, 125-130, 132-135, 136p, 138-145, 147, 149, 151p. **Lawrence** a-29. **Leiber/Fox** a-110, 111, 113. **Maneely** a-3, 42; c-33. **Moldoff** a-20. **Mooney** a-174i. **Morisi** a-53. **Morrow** a-54. **Orlando** a-41, 44, 46, 49, 52. **Powell** a-42, 44, 49, 54, 130-134p; c-131p. **Reinman** a-50, 74, 88, 91, 95, 104, 106, 112i, 124-127i. **Robinson** a-17. **Sekowski** a-3, 11. **Starlin** a-178, 179, 180p, 181p; c-178-180, 181p. **Steranko** a-151-161, 162-168p; c-151i, 153, 155, 157, 159, 161, 163, 165, 167. **Tuska** a-14, 166p. **Wildey** a-42. **Woodbridge** a-59. Fantastic Four cameos in #101-134. Jack Katz app.-26.*

**STRANGE TALES**
Apr, 1987 - No. 19, Oct, 1988
Marvel Comics Group

V2#1 .50 1.00
2-12,15-19: 5,7-Defenders app. 18-X-Factor app. .40 .80
13,14-Punisher app. .25 .75 1.50

NOTE: ***Austin** c-10, 12i, 13i. **Williamson** a-3i. Painted c-9.*

**STRANGE TALES OF THE UNUSUAL**
Dec, 1955 - No. 11, Aug, 1957
Atlas Comics (ACI No. 1-4/WPI No. 5-11)

1-Powell-a 13.00 40.00 90.00
2 6.50 19.00 45.00
3-Williamson-a, 4 pgs. 7.00 21.00 50.00
4,6,8,11 4.00 12.00 28.00
5-Crandall, Ditko-a 6.50 19.00 45.00
7,9: 7-Kirby, Orlando-a. 9-Krigstein-a 5.00 15.00 35.00
10-Torres, Morrow-a 4.30 13.00 30.00

NOTE: ***Baily** a-6. **Everett** a-2, 6; c-6, 9, 11. **Heck** a-1. **Maneely** c-1. **Orlando** a-7. **Pakula** a-10. **Romita** a-1.*

**STRANGE TERRORS**
June, 1952 - No. 7, Mar, 1953
St. John Publishing Co.

1-Bondage-c; Zombies spelled Zoombies on-c; Fineesque-a 16.00 48.00 110.00
2 8.50 25.50 60.00
3-Kubert-a; painted-c 11.50 34.00 80.00
4-Kubert-a(reprinted in Mystery Tales #18); Ekgren-c; Fineesque-a; Jerry Iger caricature 18.00 54.00 125.00
5-Kubert-a; painted-c 11.50 34.00 80.00
6-Giant, 100 pgs.(1/53); bondage-c 16.00 48.00 110.00
7-Giant, 100 pgs.; Kubert-c/a 18.50 56.00 130.00

NOTE: ***Cameron** a-6, 7. **Morisi** a-6.*

**STRANGE WORLD OF YOUR DREAMS**
Aug, 1952 - No. 4, Jan-Feb, 1953
Prize Publications

1-Simon & Kirby-a 26.00 77.00 180.00
2,3-Simon & Kirby-a. 2-Meskin-a 19.00 57.00 135.00
4-S&K-c; Meskin-a 16.00 48.00 110.00

**STRANGE WORLDS** (#18 continued from Avon's Eerie #1-17)
11/50 - No. 9, 11/52; No. 18, 10-11/54 - No. 22, 9-10/55 (No #11-17)
Avon Periodicals

1-Kenton of the Star Patrol by Kubert (r-/Eerie #1-'47); Crom the Barbarian by John Giunta 41.00 122.00 285.00
2-Wood-a; Crom the Barbarian by Giunta; Dara of the Vikings app.; used in **SOTI**, pg. 112; injury to eye panel 36.00 107.00 250.00
3-Wood/Orlando-a(Kenton), Wood/Williamson/Frazetta/Krenkel/Orlando-a (7 pgs.); Malu Slave Girl Princess app.; Kinstler-c 73.00 220.00 510.00
4-Wood-c/a (Kenton); Orlando-a; origin The Enchanted Daggar; Sultan-a 34.00 103.00 240.00
5-Orlando/Wood-a (Kenton); Wood-c 29.00 86.00 200.00
6-Kinstler-a(2); Orlando/Wood-c; Check-a 19.00 57.00 130.00
7-Kinstler, Fawcette & Becker/Alascia-a 14.00 43.00 100.00
8-Kubert, Kinstler, Hollingsworth & Lazarus-a; Lazarus-c 16.00 48.00 110.00
9-Kinstler, Fawcette, Alascia-a 14.00 43.00 100.00
18-(Formerly Eerie #17)-R/"Attack on Planet Mars" by Kubert 14.00 43.00 100.00
19-R/Avon's "Robotmen of the Lost Planet" 14.00 43.00 100.00
20-War stories; Wood-c(r)/U.S. Paratroops #1 3.65 11.00 25.00
21,22-War stories 3.35 10.00 23.00
I.W. Reprint #5-Kinstler-a(r)/Avon's #9 1.35 4.00 8.00

**STRANGE WORLDS**
Dec, 1958 - No. 5, Aug, 1959
Marvel Comics (MPI No. 1,2/Male No. 3,5)

1-Kirby & Ditko-a; flying saucer issue 22.00 65.00 150.00
2-Ditko-c/a 13.00 40.00 90.00
3-Kirby-a(2) 11.00 32.00 75.00
4-Williamson-a 11.00 32.00 75.00
5-Ditko-a 9.30 28.00 65.00

NOTE: ***Buscema** a-3. **Ditko** a-1-5; c-2. **Kirby** a-1, 3; c-1, 3-5.*

**STRAWBERRY SHORTCAKE**
June, 1985 - No. 7, April, 1986 (Children's comic)
Star Comics (Marvel)

1-7: Howie Post-a .35 .70

**STRAY TOASTERS**
Jan, 1988 - No. 4, April, 1989 ($3.50, squarebound, color, mini-series)
Epic Comics (Marvel)

1-4: Sienkiewicz story & art .60 1.75 3.50

**STREET COMIX** (50 cents)
1973 (36 pgs.; B&W) (20,000 print run)
Street Enterprises/King Features

1-Rip Kirby .40 .80
2-Flash Gordon .60 1.20

**STREETFIGHTER**
Aug, 1986 - No. 4, Spr, 1987 ($1.75, color, mini-series)
Ocean Comics

1-4: 2-Origin begins .30 .90 1.80

**STREET POET RAY**
Spring, 1989; 1990 - Present ($2.95, B&W, squarebound, bi-monthly)
Blackthorne Publ./Marvel Comics

1 (Blackthorne, $2.00) .35 1.00 2.00
1-4 (Marvel, $2.95, thick-c & paper) .50 1.50 3.00

**STRICTLY PRIVATE**
July, 1942 (#1 on sale 6/15/42)
Eastern Color Printing Co.

1,2 12.00 36.00 85.00

**STRIKE!**
Aug, 1987 - No. 6, Jan, 1988 ($1.75, color)
Eclipse Comics

1-6 .30 .90 1.80
...Vs. Sgt. Strike Special 1 (5/88, $1.95) .35 1.00 2.00

**STRIKEFORCE: MORITURI**
Dec, 1986 - No. 31, July, 1989
Marvel Comics Group

1-12,14: 14-Williamson-i .50 1.00
13-Double size .25 .75 1.50
15-23 ($1.00-$1.25) .60 1.25
24-31 ($1.50): 25-Heath-c .25 .75 1.50

*Strange Tales Annual #2, © MEG*

*Strange Terrors #7, © STJ*

*Strange Worlds #2 (2/59), © MEG*

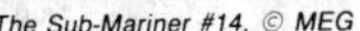

The Sub-Mariner #14, © MEG

Sub-Mariner Comics #21, © MEG

Sugar & Spike #1, © DC

**STRIKEFORCE MORITURI: ELECTRIC UNDERTOW**
Dec, 1989 - No. 5, Mar, 1990 ($3.95, color, mini-series, 52 pgs.)
Marvel Comics

| | Good | Fine | N-Mint |
|---|---|---|---|
| 1-5: Squarebound | .70 | 2.00 | 4.00 |

**STRONG MAN** (Also see Complimentary Comics & Power of . . .)
Mar-Apr, 1955 - No. 4, Sept-Oct, 1955
Magazine Enterprises

| | | | |
|---|---|---|---|
| 1(A-1 #130)-Powell-c/a | 10.00 | 30.00 | 70.00 |
| 2-4: (A-1 #132,134,139)-Powell-a. 2-Powell-c | 9.00 | 27.00 | 62.00 |

**STRONTIUM DOG**
Dec, 1985 - No. 4, Mar, 1986 ($1.25, mutie series)
Eagle Comics

| | | | |
|---|---|---|---|
| 1-4 | | .65 | 1.30 |
| Special 1 ('86)-Moore scripts | .25 | .75 | 1.50 |

**STRONTIUM DOG**
July, 1987 - No. 29, 1989 ($1.25-$1.50, color)
Quality Comics

| | | | |
|---|---|---|---|
| 1-12 ($1.25) | | .65 | 1.30 |
| 13,14/15,16-29 ($1.50): 13,18,20-Guice-c | .25 | .75 | 1.50 |

**STUMBO THE GIANT** (See Harvey Hits #49, 54, 57, 60, 63, 66, 69, 72, 78, 88 & Hot Stuff #2)

**STUMBO TINYTOWN**
Oct, 1963 - No. 13, Nov, 1966
Harvey Publications

| | | | |
|---|---|---|---|
| 1 | 10.00 | 30.00 | 70.00 |
| 2 | 5.00 | 15.00 | 35.00 |
| 3-5 | 3.50 | 10.50 | 24.00 |
| 6-13 | 2.65 | 8.00 | 18.00 |

**STUNTMAN COMICS** (Also see Thrills Of Tomorrow)
Apr-May, 1946 - No. 2, June-July, 1946; No. 3, Oct-Nov, 1946
Harvey Publications

| | | | |
|---|---|---|---|
| 1-Origin Stuntman by S&K reprinted in Black Cat #9 | 60.00 | 180.00 | 420.00 |
| 2-S&K-a | 39.00 | 115.00 | 270.00 |

3-Small size (5½x8½"; B&W; 32 pgs.); distributed to mail subscribers only; S&K-a; Kid Adonis by S&K reprinted in Green Hornet #37 Estimated value. . . $250.00-$400.00
(Also see All-New #15, Boy Explorers #2, Flash Gordon #5 & Thrills of Tomorrow)

**SUBMARINE ATTACK** (Formerly Speed Demons)
No. 11, May, 1958 - No. 54, Feb-Mar, 1966
Charlton Comics

| | | | |
|---|---|---|---|
| 11 | 1.15 | 3.50 | 8.00 |
| 12-20 | .70 | 2.00 | 5.00 |
| 21-54 | .50 | 1.50 | 3.00 |

NOTE: *Glanzman c/a-25. **Montes/Bache** a-38, 40, 41.*

**SUB-MARINER** (See All-Select, All-Winners, Blonde Phantom, Daring, The Defenders, Fantastic Four #4, Human Torch, The Invaders, Iron Man & . . ., Marvel Mystery, Marvel Spotlight #27, Men's Adventures, Motion Picture Funnies Weekly, Namora, Namor, The. . ., Prince Namor, The Sub-Mariner, Saga Of The. . ., Tales to Astonish #70 & 2nd series, USA & Young Men)

**SUB-MARINER, THE** (2nd Series)(Sub-Mariner #31 on)
May, 1968 - No. 72, Sept, 1974 (No. 43: 52 pgs.)
Marvel Comics Group

| | Good | Fine | N-Mint |
|---|---|---|---|
| 1-Origin Sub-Mariner | 13.00 | 40.00 | 90.00 |
| 2-Triton app. | 4.30 | 13.00 | 30.00 |
| 3-10: 5-1st Tiger Shark. 7-Photo-c. 9-1st app. Serpent Crown (origin in #10 & 12) | 2.15 | 6.50 | 15.00 |
| 11-13 | 1.30 | 4.00 | 9.00 |
| 14-Sub-Mariner vs. G.A. Human Torch; death of Toro | 2.85 | 8.50 | 20.00 |
| 15-20: 19-1st Sting Ray | 1.00 | 3.00 | 7.00 |
| 21-40: 37-Death of Lady Dorma. 35-Ties into 1st Defenders story; 38-Origin | .70 | 2.00 | 5.00 |
| 41-72: 44,45-Sub-Mariner vs. H. Torch. 50-1st app. Nita, Namor's niece. 61-Last artwork by Everett; 1st 4 pgs. completed by Mortimer; pgs. 5-20 by Mooney. 62-1st Tales of Atlantis, ends #66 | .50 | 1.50 | 3.00 |
| Special 1(1/71), Special 2(1/72)-Everett-a | .70 | 2.00 | 4.00 |

NOTE: ***Bolle** a-67i. **Buscema** a(p)-1-8, 20, 24. **Colan** a-10p, 11p, 40p, 43p, 46-49p, Spec. 1p, 2; c(p)-10, 11, 40. **Craig** a-17, 19-23i. **Everett** a-45r, 50-55, 57, 58, 59-61(plot), 63(plot); c-47, 48i, 55, 57-59i, 61, Spec. 2. **G. Kane** c(p)-42-52, 58, 66, 70, 71. **Mooney** a-24i, 25i, 32-35i, 39i, 42i, 44i, 45i, 60i, 61i, 65p, 66p, 68i. **Severin** c/a-38i. **Starlin** c-59p. **Tuska** a-41p, 42p, 69-71p. **Wrightson** a-36i.*

**SUB-MARINER COMICS** (1st Series) (The Sub-Mariner #1,2,33-42)
(Official True Crime Cases #24 on; Amazing Mysteries #32 on; Best Love #33 on)
Spring, 1941 - No. 23, Sum, '47; No. 24, Wint, '47 - No. 31, 4/49; No. 32, 7/49; No. 33, 4/54 - No. 42, 10/55
Timely/Marvel Comics (TCI 1-7/SePI 8/MPI 9-32/Atlas Comics (CCC 33-42))

| | Good | Fine | VF-NM | NM/Mint |
|---|---|---|---|---|
| 1-The Sub-Mariner by Everett & The Angel begin | 533.00 | 1335.00 | 3200.00 | 4200.00 |

(Estimated up to 190 total copies exist, 8 in NM/Mint)

| | Good | Fine | N-Mint |
|---|---|---|---|
| 2-Everett-a | 242.00 | 605.00 | 1450.00 |
| 3-Churchill assassination-c; 40 pg. Sub-Mariner story | 167.00 | 415.00 | 1000.00 |
| 4-Everett-a, 40 pgs.; 1 pg. Wolverton-a | 158.00 | 395.00 | 950.00 |
| 5 | 112.00 | 280.00 | 675.00 |
| 6-10: 9-Wolverton-a, 3 pgs.; flag-c | 83.00 | 210.00 | 500.00 |
| 11-15 | 58.00 | 146.00 | 350.00 |
| 16-20 | 52.00 | 130.00 | 310.00 |
| 21-Last Angel; Everett-a | 39.00 | 100.00 | 235.00 |
| 22-Young Allies app. | 39.00 | 100.00 | 235.00 |
| 23-The Human Torch, Namora x-over | 39.00 | 100.00 | 235.00 |
| 24-Namora x-over | 39.00 | 100.00 | 235.00 |
| 25-The Blonde Phantom begins, ends No. 31; Kurtzman-a; Namora x-over | 50.00 | 125.00 | 300.00 |
| 26,27 | 44.00 | 110.00 | 265.00 |
| 28-Namora cover; Everett-a | 44.00 | 110.00 | 265.00 |
| 29-31 (4/49): 29-The Human Torch app. 31-Capt. America app. | 44.00 | 110.00 | 265.00 |
| 32 (7/49, Scarce)-Origin Sub-Mariner | 67.00 | 167.00 | 400.00 |
| 33 (4/54)-Origin Sub-Mariner; The Human Torch app.; Namora x-over in Sub-Mariner #33-42 | 39.00 | 100.00 | 235.00 |
| 34,35-Human Torch in each | 28.00 | 70.00 | 165.00 |
| 36,37,39-41: 36,39-41-Namora app. | 28.00 | 70.00 | 165.00 |
| 38-Origin Sub-Mariner's wings; Namora app. Last pre-code (2/55) | 36.00 | 90.00 | 215.00 |
| 42-Last issue | 32.00 | 80.00 | 190.00 |

NOTE: *Angel by **Gustavson**-#1. **Everett** a-1-4, 22-24, 26-42; c-32, 33, 40. **Maneely** a-38; c-37, 39-41. **Rico** c-27, 28, 30. **Schomburg** c-1-4, 6, 8-18, 20. **Sekowsky** c-24, 25. **Shores** c-21-23, 38. Bondage c-13, 22, 24, 25, 34.*

**SUE & SALLY SMITH** (Formerly My Secret Life)
V2#48, Nov, 1962 - No. 54, Nov, 1963 (Flying Nurses)
Charlton Comics

| | | | |
|---|---|---|---|
| V2#48 | .50 | 1.50 | 3.00 |
| 49-54 | .35 | 1.00 | 2.00 |

**SUGAR & SPIKE** (Also see The Best of DC)
Apr-May, 1956 - No. 98, Oct-Nov, 1971
National Periodical Publications

| | | | |
|---|---|---|---|
| 1 (Scarce) | 68.00 | 205.00 | 475.00 |
| 2 | 34.00 | 100.00 | 235.00 |
| 3-5 | 30.00 | 90.00 | 210.00 |
| 6-10 | 19.00 | 58.00 | 135.00 |
| 11-20 | 14.00 | 43.00 | 100.00 |
| 21-29,31-40: 26-XMas-c | 8.00 | 24.00 | 55.00 |

| | Good | Fine | N-Mint |
|---|---|---|---|
| 30-Scribbly x-over | 9.30 | 28.00 | 65.00 |
| 41-60 | 3.70 | 11.00 | 26.00 |
| 61-80: 72-Origin & 1st app. Bernie the Brain | 2.65 | 8.00 | 18.00 |
| 81-98: 85-(68 pgs.); r-#72. #96-(68 pgs.). #97,98-(52 pgs.) | 2.00 | 6.00 | 14.00 |

NOTE: *All written and drawn by* ***Sheldon Mayer.***

**SUGAR BEAR**
No date, circa 1975? (16 pages) (2½x4½")
Post Cereal Giveaway

| | Good | Fine | N-Mint |
|---|---|---|---|
| "The Almost Take Over of the Post Office," "The Race Across the Atlantic," "The Zoo Goes Wild" each... | | .40 | .80 |

**SUGAR BOWL COMICS** (Teen-age)
May, 1948 - No. 5, Jan, 1949
Famous Funnies

| | Good | Fine | N-Mint |
|---|---|---|---|
| 1-Toth-c/a | 8.50 | 25.50 | 60.00 |
| 2,4,5 | 2.65 | 8.00 | 18.00 |
| 3-Toth-a | 5.70 | 17.00 | 40.00 |

**SUGARFOOT** (See 4-Color #907, 992, 1059, 1098, 1147, 1209)

**SUICIDE SQUAD** (See Brave & the Bold, Doom Patrol & Suicide Squad Spec., Legends #3 & note under Star Spangled War Stories)
May, 1987 - Present (Direct sale only #32 on)
DC Comics

| | Good | Fine | N-Mint |
|---|---|---|---|
| 1-44: 9-Millennium x-over. 10-Batman-c/story. 13-JLI app.(Batman). 16-Re-intro Shade The Changing Man. 40-43-"The Phoenix Gambit" Batman storyline. 40-Free Batman/Suicide Squad poster | | .50 | 1.00 |
| Annual 1 (1988, $1.50)-Manhunter x-over | .25 | .75 | 1.50 |

**SUMMER FUN** (See Dell Giants)

**SUMMER FUN** (Formerly Li'l Genius; Holiday Surprise #55)
No. 54, Oct, 1966 (Giant)
Charlton Comics

| | Good | Fine | N-Mint |
|---|---|---|---|
| 54 | .50 | 1.50 | 3.00 |

**SUMMER LOVE** (Formerly Brides in Love?)
V2#46, Oct, 1965; V2#47, Oct, 1966; V2#48, Nov, 1968
Charlton Comics

| | Good | Fine | N-Mint |
|---|---|---|---|
| V2#46-Beatles-c/story | 3.50 | 10.50 | 24.00 |
| 47-Beatles story | 3.50 | 10.50 | 24.00 |
| 48 | .50 | 1.50 | 3.00 |

**SUMMER MAGIC** (See Movie Comics)

**SUNDANCE** (See 4-Color #1126)

**SUNDANCE KID** (Also see Blazing Six-Guns)
June, 1971 - No. 3, Sept, 1971 (52 pages)
Skywald Publications

| | Good | Fine | N-Mint |
|---|---|---|---|
| 1-Durango Kid; Two Kirby Bullseye-r | .25 | .75 | 1.50 |
| 2-Swift Arrow, Durango Kid, Bullseye by S&K; Meskin plus 1 pg. origin | | .50 | 1.00 |
| 3-Durango Kid, Billy the Kid, Red Hawk-r | | .35 | .70 |

**SUNDAY FUNNIES**
1950
Harvey Publications

| | Good | Fine | N-Mint |
|---|---|---|---|
| 1 | 1.70 | 5.00 | 12.00 |

**SUN DEVILS**
July, 1984 - No. 12, June, 1985 ($1.25, 12-issue series)
DC Comics

| | Good | Fine | N-Mint |
|---|---|---|---|
| 1-12: 6-Death of Sun Devil | | .60 | 1.25 |

**SUN FUN KOMIKS**
1939 (15 cents; black, white & red)
Sun Publications

| | Good | Fine | N-Mint |
|---|---|---|---|
| 1-Satire on comics | 14.00 | 43.00 | 100.00 |

**SUN GIRL** (See The Human Torch & Marvel Mystery Comics #88)
Aug, 1948 - No. 3, Dec, 1948
Marvel Comics (CCC)

| | Good | Fine | N-Mint |
|---|---|---|---|
| 1-Sun Girl begins; Miss America app. | 67.00 | 167.00 | 400.00 |
| 2,3: 2-The Blonde Phantom begins | 50.00 | 125.00 | 300.00 |

**SUNNY, AMERICA'S SWEETHEART**
No. 11, Dec, 1947 - No. 14, June, 1948
Fox Features Syndicate

| | Good | Fine | N-Mint |
|---|---|---|---|
| 11-Feldstein-c/a | 30.00 | 90.00 | 210.00 |
| 12-14-Feldstein-c/a; 14-Lingerie panels | 26.00 | 77.00 | 180.00 |
| I.W. Reprint #8-Feldstein-a; r-Fox issue | 5.00 | 15.00 | 35.00 |

**SUN-RUNNERS** (Also see Tales of the...)
2/84 - No. 3, 5/84; No. 4, 11/84 - No. 6, 1986 (Baxter paper)
Pacific Comics/Eclipse Comics/Amazing Comics

| | Good | Fine | N-Mint |
|---|---|---|---|
| 1-6: P. Smith-a in some | .25 | .80 | 1.60 |
| Christmas Special 1 (1987, $1.95)-By Amazing | .35 | 1.00 | 2.00 |

**SUNSET CARSON** (Also see Cowboy Western)
Feb, 1951 - No. 4, Aug, 1951
Charlton Comics

| | Good | Fine | N-Mint |
|---|---|---|---|
| 1-Photo/retouched-c (Scarce, all issues) | 66.00 | 197.00 | 460.00 |
| 2 | 45.00 | 135.00 | 310.00 |
| 3,4 | 34.00 | 100.00 | 235.00 |

**SUPER ANIMALS PRESENTS PIDGY & THE MAGIC GLASSES**
Dec, 1953
Star Publications

| | Good | Fine | N-Mint |
|---|---|---|---|
| 3-D 1-L. B. Cole-c | 26.00 | 77.00 | 180.00 |

**SUPER BOOK OF COMICS**
nd (1943?) (32 pgs., soft-c) (Pan-Am/Gilmore Oil/Kelloggs premiums)
Western Publishing Co.

| | Good | Fine | N-Mint |
|---|---|---|---|
| nn-Dick Tracy (Gilmore)-Magic Morro app. | 30.00 | 90.00 | 210.00 |
| 1-Dick Tracy & The Smuggling Ring; Stratosphere Jim app. (Rare) (Pan-Am) | 26.00 | 78.00 | 180.00 |
| 1-Smilin' Jack, Magic Morro (Pan-Am) | 5.00 | 15.00 | 35.00 |
| 2-Smilin' Jack, Stratosphere Jim (Pan-Am) | 5.00 | 15.00 | 35.00 |
| 2-Smitty, Magic Morro (Pan-Am) | 5.00 | 15.00 | 35.00 |
| 3-Captain Midnight, Magic Morro (Pan-Am) | 9.00 | 27.00 | 62.00 |
| 3-Moon Mullins? | 4.00 | 12.00 | 28.00 |
| 4-Red Ryder, Magic Morro (Pan-Am) | 4.00 | 12.00 | 28.00 |
| 4-Smitty, Stratosphere Jim (Pan-Am) | 5.00 | 15.00 | 35.00 |
| 5-Don Winslow, Magic Morro (Gilmore) | 4.00 | 12.00 | 28.00 |
| 5-Don Winslow, Stratosphere Jim (Pan-Am) | 4.00 | 12.00 | 28.00 |
| 5-Terry & the Pirates | 9.00 | 27.00 | 62.00 |
| 6-Don Winslow, Stratosphere Jim (Pan-Am)-McWilliams-a | 5.00 | 15.00 | 35.00 |
| 6-King of the Royal Mounted, Magic Morro (Pan-Am) | 5.00 | 15.00 | 35.00 |
| 7-Dick Tracy, Magic Morro (Pan-Am) | 10.00 | 30.00 | 70.00 |
| 7-Little Orphan Annie | 5.00 | 15.00 | 35.00 |
| 8-Dick Tracy, Stratosphere Jim (Pan-Am) | 10.00 | 30.00 | 70.00 |
| 8-Dan Dunn, Magic Morro (Pan-Am) | 5.00 | 15.00 | 35.00 |
| 9-Terry & the Pirates, Magic Morro (Pan-Am) | 8.00 | 24.00 | 56.00 |
| 10-Red Ryder, Magic Morro (Pan-Am) | 4.00 | 12.00 | 28.00 |

**SUPER-BOOK OF COMICS**
(Omar Bread & Hancock Oil Co. giveaways)
1944 - No. 30, 1947 (Omar); 1947 - 1948 (Hancock) (16 pgs.)
Western Publishing Co.

Note: The Hancock issues are all exact reprints of the earlier Omar issues. The issue numbers were removed in some of the reprints.

| | Good | Fine | N-Mint |
|---|---|---|---|
| 1-Dick Tracy (Omar, 1944) | 16.00 | 48.00 | 110.00 |
| 1-Dick Tracy (Hancock, 1947) | 12.00 | 36.00 | 84.00 |
| 2-Bugs Bunny (Omar, 1944) | 3.50 | 10.50 | 24.00 |
| 2-Bugs Bunny (Hancock, 1947) | 2.65 | 8.00 | 18.00 |

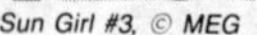
*Sun Girl #3, © MEG*

*Sunset Carson #2, © CC*

*Super Book of Comics #4, © N.Y. News Synd.*

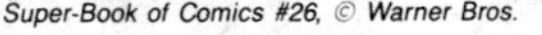
Super-Book of Comics #26, © Warner Bros.

Superboy #7, © DC

Superboy #68, © DC

| | Good | Fine | N-Mint |
|---|---|---|---|
| 3-Terry & the Pirates (Omar, 1944) | 8.00 | 24.00 | 56.00 |
| 3-Terry & the Pirates (Hancock, 1947) | 6.00 | 18.00 | 42.00 |
| 4-Andy Panda (Omar, 1944) | 3.50 | 10.50 | 24.00 |
| 4-Andy Panda (Hancock, 1947) | 2.65 | 8.00 | 18.00 |
| 5-Smokey Stover (Omar, 1945) | 2.65 | 8.00 | 18.00 |
| 5-Smokey Stover (Hancock, 1947) | 1.70 | 5.00 | 12.00 |
| 6-Porky Pig (Omar, 1945) | 3.50 | 10.50 | 24.00 |
| 6-Porky Pig (Hancock, 1947) | 2.65 | 8.00 | 18.00 |
| 7-Smilin' Jack (Omar, 1945) | 3.50 | 10.50 | 24.00 |
| 7-Smilin' Jack (Hancock, 1947) | 2.65 | 8.00 | 18.00 |
| 8-Oswald the Rabbit (Omar, 1945) | 2.65 | 8.00 | 18.00 |
| 8-Oswald the Rabbit (Hancock, 1947) | 1.70 | 5.00 | 12.00 |
| 9-Alley Oop (Omar, 1945) | 8.50 | 25.50 | 60.00 |
| 9-Alley Oop (Hancock, 1947) | 7.00 | 21.00 | 50.00 |
| 10-Elmer Fudd (Omar, 1945) | 2.65 | 8.00 | 18.00 |
| 10-Elmer Fudd (Hancock, 1947) | 1.70 | 5.00 | 12.00 |
| 11-Little Orphan Annie (Omar, 1945) | 4.35 | 13.00 | 30.00 |
| 11-Little Orphan Annie (Hancock, 1947) | 3.00 | 9.00 | 21.00 |
| 12-Woody Woodpecker (Omar, 1945) | 2.65 | 8.00 | 18.00 |
| 12-Woody Woodpecker (Hancock, 1947) | 1.70 | 5.00 | 12.00 |
| 13-Dick Tracy (Omar, 1945) | 9.00 | 27.00 | 62.00 |
| 13-Dick Tracy (Hancock, 1947) | 7.00 | 21.00 | 50.00 |
| 14-Bugs Bunny (Omar, 1945) | 2.65 | 8.00 | 18.00 |
| 14-Bugs Bunny (Hancock, 1947) | 1.70 | 5.00 | 12.00 |
| 15-Andy Panda (Omar, 1945) | 2.30 | 7.00 | 16.00 |
| 15-Andy Panda (Hancock, 1947) | 1.70 | 5.00 | 12.00 |
| 16-Terry & the Pirates (Omar, 1945) | 7.00 | 21.00 | 50.00 |
| 16-Terry & the Pirates (Hancock, 1947) | 5.00 | 15.00 | 35.00 |
| 17-Smokey Stover (Omar, 1946) | 2.65 | 8.00 | 18.00 |
| 17-Smokey Stover (Hancock, 1948?) | 1.70 | 5.00 | 12.00 |
| 18-Porky Pig (Omar, 1946) | 2.30 | 7.00 | 16.00 |
| 18-Porky Pig (Hancock, 1948?) | 1.70 | 5.00 | 12.00 |
| 19-Smilin' Jack (Omar, 1946) | 2.65 | 8.00 | 18.00 |
| nn-Smilin' Jack (Hancock, 1948) | 1.70 | 5.00 | 12.00 |
| 20-Oswald the Rabbit (Omar, 1946) | 2.30 | 7.00 | 16.00 |
| nn-Oswald the Rabbit (Hancock, 1948) | 1.70 | 5.00 | 12.00 |
| 21-Gasoline Alley (Omar, 1946) | 4.00 | 12.00 | 28.00 |
| nn-Gasoline Alley (Hancock, 1948) | 3.00 | 9.00 | 21.00 |
| 22-Elmer Fudd (Omar, 1946) | 2.30 | 7.00 | 16.00 |
| nn-Elmer Fudd (Hancock, 1948) | 1.70 | 5.00 | 12.00 |
| 23-Little Orphan Annie (Omar, 1946) | 3.50 | 10.50 | 24.00 |
| nn-Little Orphan Annie (Hancock, 1948) | 2.65 | 8.00 | 18.00 |
| 24-Woody Woodpecker (Omar, 1946) | 2.30 | 7.00 | 16.00 |
| nn-Woody Woodpecker (Hancock, 1948) | 1.70 | 5.00 | 12.00 |
| 25-Dick Tracy (Omar, 1946) | 7.00 | 21.00 | 50.00 |
| nn-Dick Tracy (Hancock, 1948) | 5.00 | 15.00 | 35.00 |
| 26-Bugs Bunny (Omar, 1946)) | 2.30 | 7.00 | 16.00 |
| nn-Bugs Bunny (Hancock, 1948) | 1.70 | 5.00 | 12.00 |
| 27-Andy Panda (Omar, 1946) | 2.30 | 7.00 | 16.00 |
| 27-Andy Panda (Hancock, 1948) | 1.70 | 5.00 | 12.00 |
| 28-Terry & the Pirates (Omar, 1946) | 7.00 | 21.00 | 50.00 |
| 28-Terry & the Pirates (Hancock, 1948) | 5.00 | 15.00 | 35.00 |
| 29-Smokey Stover (Omar, 1947) | 2.30 | 7.00 | 16.00 |
| 29-Smokey Stover (Hancock, 1948) | 1.70 | 5.00 | 12.00 |
| 30-Porky Pig (Omar, 1947) | 2.30 | 7.00 | 16.00 |
| 30-Porky Pig (Hancock, 1948) | 1.70 | 5.00 | 12.00 |
| nn-Bugs Bunny (Hancock, 1948)-Does not match any Omar book | 1.70 | 5.00 | 12.00 |

**SUPERBOY** (See Adventure, Aurora, DC Comics Presents, DC 100 Page Super Spect. #15, DC Super Stars, 80 Page Giant #10, More Fun, The New Advs. of . . . & Superman Family #191)

**SUPERBOY** (. . . & the Legion of Super-Heroes with #231)
(Becomes The Legion of Super-Heroes No. 259 on)
Mar-Apr, 1949 - No. 258, Dec, 1979 (#1-16: 52 pgs.)
National Periodical Publications/DC Comics

| | Good | Fine | VF-NM | NM/Mint |
|---|---|---|---|---|
| 1-Superman cover | 271.00 | 815.00 | 1900.00 | 2600.00 |
| (Estimated up to 275 total copies exist, 15 in NM/Mint) | | | | |

| | Good | Fine | N-Mint |
|---|---|---|---|
| 2-Used in **SOTI**, pg. 35-36,226 | 101.00 | 305.00 | 710.00 |
| 3 | 74.00 | 220.00 | 515.00 |
| 4,5: 5-Pre-Supergirl tryout | 62.00 | 185.00 | 435.00 |
| 6-10: 8-1st Superbaby. 10-1st app. Lana Lang | 45.00 | 135.00 | 315.00 |
| 11-15 | 34.00 | 100.00 | 235.00 |
| 16-20 | 24.00 | 70.00 | 165.00 |
| 21-26,28-30 | 18.00 | 54.00 | 125.00 |
| 27-Low distribution | 19.00 | 56.00 | 130.00 |
| 31-38: 38-Last pre-code issue | 13.00 | 40.00 | 90.00 |
| 39-48,50 (7/56) | 10.00 | 30.00 | 70.00 |
| 49 (6/56)-1st app. Metallo (Jor-El's robot) | 11.50 | 34.00 | 80.00 |
| 51-60: 55-Spanking-c | 7.00 | 21.00 | 50.00 |
| 61-67 | 5.70 | 17.00 | 40.00 |
| 68-Origin/1st app. original Bizarro (10-11/58) | 22.00 | 64.00 | 150.00 |
| 69-77,79: 75-Spanking-c. 76-1st Supermonkey. 77-Pre-Pete Ross tryout | 5.00 | 15.00 | 35.00 |
| 78-Origin Mr. Mxyzptlk & Superboy's costume | 8.50 | 25.50 | 60.00 |
| 80-1st meeting Superboy/Supergirl (4/60) | 5.00 | 15.00 | 35.00 |
| 81-85,87,88: 82-1st Bizarro Krypto. 83-Origin & 1st app. Kryptonite Kid | 3.60 | 11.00 | 25.00 |
| 86(1/61)-4th Legion app; Intro Pete Ross | 9.30 | 28.00 | 65.00 |
| 89(6/61)-Mon-el 1st app. | 14.00 | 43.00 | 100.00 |
| 90-92: 90-Pete Ross learns Superboy's I.D. 92-Last 10 cent issue | 3.15 | 9.50 | 22.00 |
| 93(12/61)-10th Legion app; Chameleon Boy app. | 3.50 | 10.50 | 24.00 |
| 94-97,99 | 1.70 | 5.00 | 12.00 |
| 98(7/62)-18th Legion app; Origin & intro. Ultra Boy; Pete Ross joins Legion | 2.85 | 8.50 | 20.00 |
| 100(10/62)-Ultra Boy app; 1st app. Phantom Zone villains, Dr. Xadu & Erndine. 2 pg. map of Krypton; origin Superboy retold; r-cover of Superman #1; Pete Ross joins Legion | 12.00 | 36.00 | 85.00 |
| 101-120: 104-Origin Phantom Zone. 115-Atomic bomb-c. 117-Legion app. | 1.15 | 3.50 | 8.00 |
| 121-128: 124(10/65)-1st app. Insect Queen (Lana Lang). 125-Legion cameo. 126-Origin Krypto the Super Dog retold with new facts | .70 | 2.00 | 4.00 |
| 129 (80-pg. Giant G-22)-Reprints origin Mon-el | .85 | 2.60 | 6.00 |
| 130-137,139,140: 131-Legion statues cameo in Dog Legionnaires story. 132-1st app. Supremo | .50 | 1.50 | 3.00 |
| 138 (80-pg. Giant G-35) | .85 | 2.60 | 6.00 |
| 141-146,148-155,157-164,166-173,175,176: 145-Superboy's parents regain their youth. 172,173,176-Legion app.; 172-Origin Yango (Super Ape) | .35 | 1.00 | 2.00 |
| 147(6/68)-Giant G-47; origin Saturn Girl, Lightning Lad, Cosmic Boy; origin Legion of Super-Pets-r/Adv. 293? | .85 | 2.60 | 6.00 |
| 156,165,174 (Giants G-59,71,83) | .70 | 2.00 | 4.00 |
| 177-184,186,187 (All 52 pgs.): 184-Origin Dial H for Hero-r | | .50 | 1.00 |
| 185-DC 100 Pg. Super Spectacular #12; Legion-c/story; Teen Titans, Kid Eternity, Star Spangled Kid-r | .25 | .75 | 1.50 |
| 188-196: 188-Origin Karkan. 191-Origin Sunboy retold; Legion app. 193-Chameleon Boy & Shrinking Violet get new costumes. 195-1st app. Erg/Wildfire; Phantom Girl gets new costume. 196-Last Superboy solo story | | .50 | 1.00 |
| 197-Legion series begins; Lightning Lad's new costume | .75 | 2.25 | 4.50 |
| 198,199: 198-Element Lad & Princess Projectra get new costumes | .35 | 1.00 | 2.00 |
| 200-Bouncing Boy & Duo Damsel marry; Jonn' Jonzz' cameo | .75 | 2.25 | 4.50 |
| 201,204,206,207,209: 201-Re-intro Erg as Wildfire. 204-Supergirl | | | |

| | Good | Fine | N-Mint |
|---|---|---|---|
| resigns from Legion. 206-Ferro Lad & Invisible Kid app. 209-Karate Kid new costume | .35 | 1.00 | 2.00 |
| 202,205-(100 pgs.): 202-Light Lass gets new costume | .45 | 1.25 | 2.50 |
| 203-Invisible Kid dies | .50 | 1.50 | 3.00 |
| 208-(68 pgs.) | .45 | 1.25 | 2.50 |
| 210-Origin Karate Kid | .45 | 1.25 | 2.50 |
| 211-220: 212-Matter-Eater Lad resigns. 216-1st app. Tyroc who joins Legion in #218 | .30 | .90 | 1.80 |
| 221-249: 226-Intro. Dawnstar. 228-Death of Chemical King. 240-Origin Dawnstar. 242-(52pgs.). 243-Legion of Substitute Heroes app. 243-245-(44pgs.) | | .60 | 1.20 |
| 250-258: 253-Intro Blok. 257-Return of Bouncing Boy & Duo Damsel by Ditko | | .50 | 1.00 |
| Annual 1(Sum/64, 84 pgs.)-Origin Krypto-r | 7.00 | 21.00 | 50.00 |
| ...Spectacular 1(1980, Giant)-Distr. through comic stores; mostly-r | | .50 | 1.00 |

NOTE: ***Neal Adams*** *c-143, 145, 146, 148-155, 157-161, 163, 164, 166-168, 172, 173, 175, 176, 178.* ***M. Anderson*** *a-245i.* ***Ditko*** *a-257p.* ***Grell*** *a-202i, 203-219, 220-224p, 235p; c-207-232, 235, 236p, 237, 239p, 240p, 243p, 246, 258.* ***Nasser*** *a(p)-222, 225, 226, 230, 231, 233, 236.* ***Simonson*** *a-237p.* ***Starlin*** *a(p)-239, 250, 251; c-238.* ***Staton*** *a-227p, 243-249p, 252-258p; c-247-251p.* ***Tuska*** *a-172, 173, 176, 183, 235p.* ***Wood*** *inks-152-155, 157-161. Legion app.-172, 173, 176, 177, 183, 184, 188, 190, 191, 193, 195.*

**SUPERBOY** (TV)
Feb, 1990 - Present ($1.00, color)
DC Comics

| | Good | Fine | N-Mint |
|---|---|---|---|
| 1-15: Mooney-a(p) in 1-8; 1-Photo-c from TV show. 8-Bizarro-c/story; Arthur Adams-a(i). 9,10-Swan-p | | .50 | 1.00 |

**SUPER BRAT**
January, 1954 - No. 4, July, 1954
Toby Press

| | Good | Fine | N-Mint |
|---|---|---|---|
| 1 (1954) | 2.00 | 6.00 | 14.00 |
| 2-4: 4-Li'l Teevy by Mel Lazarus | 1.00 | 3.00 | 7.00 |
| I.W. Reprint #1,2,3,7,8('58) | | .40 | .80 |
| I.W. (Super) Reprint #10('63) | | .40 | .80 |

**SUPERCAR** (TV)
Nov, 1962 - No. 4, Aug, 1963 (All painted covers)
Gold Key

| | Good | Fine | N-Mint |
|---|---|---|---|
| 1 | 4.30 | 13.00 | 30.00 |
| 2-4 | 3.00 | 9.00 | 21.00 |

**SUPER CAT** (Formerly Frisky Animals; also see Animal Crackers)
No. 56, Nov, 1953 - No. 58, May, 1954; Sept, 1957 - No. 4, May, 1958
Star Publications #56-58/Ajax/Farrell Publ. (Four Star Comic Corp.)

| | Good | Fine | N-Mint |
|---|---|---|---|
| 56-58-L.B. Cole-c on all | 5.70 | 17.00 | 40.00 |
| 1('57-Ajax) | 2.30 | 7.00 | 16.00 |
| 2-4 | 1.59 | 4.50 | 10.00 |

**SUPER CIRCUS** (TV)
January, 1951 - No. 5, 1951 (Mary Hartline)
Cross Publishing Co.

| | Good | Fine | N-Mint |
|---|---|---|---|
| 1-Cast photos on-c | 4.30 | 13.00 | 30.00 |
| 2-Cast photos on-c | 3.00 | 9.00 | 21.00 |
| 3-5 | 2.30 | 7.00 | 16.00 |

**SUPER CIRCUS** (TV)
No. 542, March, 1954 - No. 694, Mar, 1956 (Feat. Mary Hartline)
Dell Publishing Co.

| | Good | Fine | N-Mint |
|---|---|---|---|
| 4-Color 542,592,694: Mary Hartline photo-c | 3.00 | 9.00 | 21.00 |

**SUPER COMICS**
May, 1938 - No. 121, Feb-Mar, 1949
Dell Publishing Co.

| | Good | Fine | N-Mint |
|---|---|---|---|
| 1-Terry & The Pirates, The Gumps, Dick Tracy, Little Orphan Annie, Gasoline Alley, Little Joe, Smilin' Jack, Smokey Stover, Smitty, Tiny Tim, Moon Mullins, Harold Teen, Winnie Winkle begin | 111.00 | 277.00 | 665.00 |
| 2 | 46.00 | 140.00 | 325.00 |
| 3 | 41.00 | 125.00 | 290.00 |
| 4,5 | 32.00 | 95.00 | 225.00 |
| 6-10 | 26.00 | 79.00 | 185.00 |
| 11-20 | 21.00 | 62.00 | 145.00 |
| 21-29: 21-Magic Morro begins (Origin, 2/40). 22-Ken Ernst-c | 18.00 | 54.00 | 125.00 |
| 30-"Sea Hawk" movie adaptation-c/story with Errol Flynn | 18.00 | 54.00 | 125.00 |
| 31-40 | 14.00 | 43.00 | 100.00 |
| 41-50: 43-Terry & The Pirates ends | 11.50 | 34.00 | 80.00 |
| 51-60 | 8.50 | 25.50 | 60.00 |
| 61-70: 65-Brenda Starr-r begin? 67-X-mas-c | 7.00 | 21.00 | 50.00 |
| 71-80 | 6.00 | 19.00 | 45.00 |
| 81-99 | 5.00 | 15.00 | 35.00 |
| 100 | 6.00 | 19.00 | 45.00 |
| 101-115-Last Dick Tracy (moves to own title) | 4.00 | 12.00 | 28.00 |
| 116,118-All Smokey Stover | 3.15 | 9.50 | 22.00 |
| 117-All Gasoline Alley | 3.15 | 9.50 | 22.00 |
| 119-121-Terry & The Pirates app. in all | 3.15 | 9.50 | 22.00 |

**SUPER COPS, THE**
July, 1974 (One Shot)
Red Circle Productions (Archie)

| | Good | Fine | N-Mint |
|---|---|---|---|
| 1-Morrow-c/a | | .30 | .60 |

**SUPER COPS**
Sept, 1990 - Present ($1.75-$1.95, color)
Now Comics

| | Good | Fine | N-Mint |
|---|---|---|---|
| 1-($2.75, 52 pgs.)-Dave Dorman painted-c | .45 | 1.40 | 2.80 |
| 1-2nd printing ($2.75) | .45 | 1.40 | 2.80 |
| 2-5 | .30 | .90 | 1.80 |
| 6-8: 6-Begin $1.95-c | .35 | 1.00 | 2.00 |

**SUPER CRACKED** (See Cracked)

**SUPER DC GIANT** (25-50 cents, all 68-52 pg. Giants)
No. 13, 9-10/70 - No. 26, 7-8/71; V3#27, Summer, 1976 (No #1-12)
National Periodical Publications

| | Good | Fine | N-Mint |
|---|---|---|---|
| S-13-Binky | .35 | 1.00 | 2.00 |
| S-14-Top Guns of the West; Kubert-c; Trigger Twins, Johnny Thunder, Wyoming Kid-r; Moreira-r (9-10/70) | .35 | 1.00 | 2.00 |
| S-15-Western Comics; Kubert-c; Pow Wow Smith, Vigilante, Buffalo Bill-r; new Gil Kane-a (9-10/70) | .50 | 1.50 | 3.00 |
| S-16-Best of the Brave & the Bold; Batman-r & Metamorpho origin-r from Brave & the Bold | .50 | 1.50 | 3.00 |
| S-17-Love 1970 | .25 | .75 | 1.50 |
| S-18-Three Mouseketeers; Dizzy Dog, Doodles Duck, Bo Bunny-r; Sheldon Mayer-a | .35 | 1.00 | 2.00 |
| S-19-Jerry Lewis; no Neal Adams-a | .35 | 1.00 | 2.00 |
| S-20-House of Mystery; N. Adams-c; Kirby-r(3) | .35 | 1.00 | 2.00 |
| S-21-Love 1971 | | .50 | 1.00 |
| S-22-Top Guns of the West | .25 | .75 | 1.50 |
| S-23-The Unexpected | | .50 | 1.00 |
| S-24-Supergirl | | .50 | 1.00 |
| S-25-Challengers of the Unknown; all Kirby/Wood-r | .35 | 1.00 | 2.00 |
| S-26-Aquaman (1971) | .35 | 1.00 | 2.00 |
| 27-Strange Flying Saucers Adventures (Sum, '76) | | .50 | 1.00 |

NOTE: ***Sid Greene*** *r-27p(2),* ***Heath*** *r-27.* ***G. Kane*** *a-14r(2), 15, 27r(p).* ***Kubert*** *r-16.*

**SUPER-DOOPER COMICS**
1946 - No. 8, 1946 (10 cents)(32 pages)(paper cover)
Able Manufacturing Co.

| | Good | Fine | N-Mint |
|---|---|---|---|
| 1-The Clock, Gangbuster app. | 7.00 | 21.00 | 50.00 |
| 2 | 3.50 | 10.50 | 24.00 |

*Superboy #1 (2/90), © DC*

*Super Circus #1, © Cross Publ.*

*Super Comics #22, © DELL*

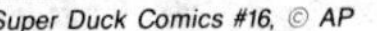
Super Duck Comics #16, © AP

Super Funnies #3, © SUPR

Super-Heroes Versus Super-Villains #1, © AP

| | Good | Fine | N-Mint |
|---|---|---|---|
| 3,4,6 | 2.65 | 8.00 | 18.00 |
| 5,7-Capt. Freedom & Shock Gibson | 4.00 | 12.00 | 28.00 |
| 8-Shock Gibson, Sam Hill | 4.00 | 12.00 | 28.00 |

**SUPER DUCK COMICS** (The Cockeyed Wonder) (See Jolly Jingles)
Fall, 1944 - No. 94, Dec, 1960 (Also see Laugh #24)
MLJ Mag. No. 1-4(9/45)/Close-Up No. 5 on (Archie)

| | | | |
|---|---|---|---|
| 1-Origin | 22.00 | 65.00 | 150.00 |
| 2 | 9.30 | 28.00 | 65.00 |
| 3-5: 3-1st Mr. Monster | 7.00 | 21.00 | 50.00 |
| 6-10 | 5.00 | 15.00 | 35.00 |
| 11-20 | 3.15 | 9.50 | 22.00 |
| 21,23-40 | 2.65 | 8.00 | 18.00 |
| 22-Used in **SOTI**, pg. 35,307,308 | 3.50 | 10.50 | 24.00 |
| 41-60 | 1.70 | 5.00 | 12.00 |
| 61-94 | 1.30 | 4.00 | 9.00 |

**SUPER DUPER**
No. 5, 1941 - No. 11, 1941
Harvey Publications

| | | | |
|---|---|---|---|
| 5-Captain Freedom & Shock Gibson app. | 14.00 | 43.00 | 100.00 |
| 8,11 | 7.00 | 21.00 | 50.00 |

**SUPER DUPER COMICS** (Formerly Latest Comics?)
No. 3, May-June, 1947
F. E. Howard Publ.

| | | | |
|---|---|---|---|
| 3-Mr. Monster app. | 4.00 | 12.00 | 28.00 |

**SUPER FRIENDS** (TV) (Also see Best of DC & Limited Coll. Ed.)
Nov, 1976 - No. 47, Aug, 1981
National Periodical Publications/DC Comics

| | | | |
|---|---|---|---|
| 1-Superman, Batman, Wonder Woman, Aquaman, Atom, Robin, Wendy, Marvin & Wonder Dog begin | | .40 | .80 |
| 2-47: 7-1st app. Wonder Twins, & The Seraph. 8-1st app. Jack O'Lantern. 9-1st app. Icemaiden. 13-1st app. Dr. Mist. 14-Origin Wonder Twins. 25-1st app. Fire & Green Fury. 31-Black Orchid app. 36,43-Plastic Man app. 47-Origin Fire & Green Fury | | .35 | .70 |
| ...Special 1 (1981, giveaway, no ads, no code or price)-r/Super Friends #19 & 36 | | .30 | .60 |

NOTE: ***Estrada** a-1p, 2p. **Orlando** a-1p. **Staton** a-43, 45.*

**SUPER FUN**
January, 1956 (By A.W. Nugent)
Gillmor Magazines

| | | | |
|---|---|---|---|
| 1-Comics, puzzles, cut-outs | 1.50 | 4.50 | 10.00 |

**SUPER FUNNIES** (...Western Funnies #3,4)
Dec, 1953 - No. 4, June, 1954
Superior Comics Publishers Ltd. (Canada)

| | | | |
|---|---|---|---|
| 1-(3-D)-Dopey Duck; make your own 3-D glasses cut-out inside front-c; did not come w/glasses | 27.00 | 80.00 | 185.00 |
| 2-Horror & crime satire | 3.50 | 10.50 | 24.00 |
| 3-Geronimo, Billy The Kid app. | 2.30 | 7.00 | 16.00 |
| 4-(Western-Phantom Ranger) | 2.30 | 7.00 | 16.00 |

**SUPERGEAR COMICS**
1976 (4 pages in color) (slick paper)
Jacobs Corp. (Giveaway)

| | | | |
|---|---|---|---|
| nn-(Rare)-Superman, Lois Lane; Steve Lombard app. (500 copies printed, over half destroyed?) | 1.00 | 3.00 | 6.00 |

**SUPERGIRL** (See Action, Adventure, Brave & the Bold, Crisis on Infinite Earths #7, Daring New Advs. of..., Super DC Giant, Superman Family, & Super-Team Family)

**SUPERGIRL**
Nov, 1972 - No. 9, Dec-Jan, 1973-74; No. 10, Sept-Oct, 1974
National Periodical Publications

| | | | |
|---|---|---|---|
| 1-Zatanna begins; ends #5 | | .60 | 1.20 |
| 2-10: 5-Zatanna origin-r. 8-JLA x-over; Batman cameo | | .40 | .80 |

NOTE: *Zatanna in #1-5, 7(Guest); Prez app. in #10.*

**SUPERGIRL** (Formerly Daring New Adventures of...)
No. 14, Dec, 1983 - No. 23, Sept, 1984
DC Comics

| | Good | Fine | N-Mint |
|---|---|---|---|
| 14,15,17-23: 20-JLA & New Teen Titans app. | | .40 | .80 |
| 16-Ambush Bug app. | | .60 | 1.20 |
| ... Movie Special (1985)-Adapts movie | | .60 | 1.20 |
| Giveaway ('84, '86 Baxter, nn)(American Honda/U.S. Dept. Transportation)-Torres-c/a | | .60 | 1.20 |

**SUPER GOOF** (Walt Disney) (See Dynabrite & The Phantom Blot)
Oct, 1965 - No. 74, 1982
Gold Key No. 1-57/Whitman No. 58 on

| | | | |
|---|---|---|---|
| 1 | 1.15 | 3.50 | 8.00 |
| 2-10 | .55 | 1.65 | 4.00 |
| 11-20 | .45 | 1.35 | 3.00 |
| 21-30 | .35 | 1.00 | 2.00 |
| 31-50 | | .50 | 1.00 |
| 51-74 | | .30 | .60 |

NOTE: *Reprints in #16, 24, 28, 29, 37, 38, 43, 45, 46, 54(½), 56-58, 65(½), 72(r-#2).*

**SUPER GREEN BERET** (Tod Holton...)
April, 1967 - No. 2, June, 1967 (68 pages)
Lightning Comics (Milson Publ. Co.)

| | | | |
|---|---|---|---|
| 1,2 | 1.15 | 3.50 | 8.00 |

**SUPER HEROES** (See Giant-Size... & Marvel...)

**SUPER HEROES**
Jan, 1967 - No. 4, June, 1967
Dell Publishing Co.

| | | | |
|---|---|---|---|
| 1-Origin & 1st app. Fab 4 | 1.50 | 4.50 | 10.00 |
| 2-4 | 1.00 | 3.00 | 7.00 |

**SUPER-HEROES BATTLE SUPER-GORILLAS** (See DC Special #16)
Winter, 1976 (One Shot, 52 pgs.)
National Periodical Publications

| | | | |
|---|---|---|---|
| 1-Superman, Batman, Flash stories; Infantino-a(p); all reprints | | .35 | .70 |

**SUPER HEROES PUZZLES AND GAMES**
1979 (32 pgs.) (regular size)
General Mills Giveaway (Marvel Comics Group)

| | | | |
|---|---|---|---|
| nn-Four 2-pg. origin stories of Spider-Man, Captain America, The Hulk, & Spider-Woman | .50 | 1.50 | 3.00 |

**SUPER HEROES VERSUS SUPER VILLAINS**
July, 1966 (no month given)(68 pgs.)
Archie Publications (Radio Comics)

| | | | |
|---|---|---|---|
| 1-Flyman, Black Hood, The Web, Shield-r; Reinman-a | 2.30 | 7.00 | 16.00 |

**SUPERICHIE** (Formerly Super Richie)
No. 5, Oct, 1976 - No. 18, Jan, 1979
Harvey Publications

| | | | |
|---|---|---|---|
| 5-18: All 52 pg. Giants | | .25 | .50 |

**SUPERIOR STORIES**
May-June, 1955 - No. 4, Nov-Dec, 1955
Nesbit Publishing Co.

| | | | |
|---|---|---|---|
| 1-Invisible Man app. | 8.00 | 24.00 | 55.00 |
| 2-The Pirate of the Gulf by J.H. Ingrahams | 4.00 | 12.00 | 28.00 |
| 3-Wreck of the Grosvenor | 4.00 | 12.00 | 28.00 |
| 4-O'Henry's "The Texas Rangers" | 4.50 | 14.00 | 32.00 |

NOTE: ***Morisi** c/a in all.*

**SUPER MAGIC** (Super Magician Comics #2 on)
May, 1941
Street & Smith Publications

V1#1-Blackstone the Magician app.; origin & 1st app. Rex King (Black

Good Fine N-Mint

Fury); not Eisner-c 42.00 125.00 290.00

**SUPER MAGICIAN COMICS** (Super Magic #1)
No. 2, Sept, 1941 - V5#8, Feb-Mar, 1947
Street & Smith Publications

V1#2-Rex King, Man of Adventure app. 17.00 51.00 120.00
3-Tao-Anwar, Boy Magician begins 10.00 30.00 70.00
4-Origin Transo 9.30 28.00 65.00
5-7,9-12: 8-Abbott & Costello story. 11-Supersnipe app. 9.30 28.00 65.00
8-Abbott & Costello story 11.00 32.00 75.00
V2#1-The Shadow app. 14.00 43.00 100.00
2-12: 5-Origin Tigerman. 8-Red Dragon begins 5.00 15.00 35.00
V3#1-12: 5-Origin Mr. Twilight 5.00 15.00 35.00
V4#1-12: 11-Nigel Elliman begins 4.30 13.00 30.00
V5#1-6 4.30 13.00 30.00
7,8-Red Dragon by Cartier 13.00 40.00 90.00

**SUPERMAN** (See Action Comics, Advs. of. . ., All-New Coll. Ed., All-Star Comics, Best of DC, Brave & the Bold, Cosmic Odyssey, DC Comics Presents, Heroes Against Hunger, Krypton Chronicles, Limited Coll. Ed., Man of Steel, Phantom Zone, Power Record Comics, Special Edition, Super Friends, Taylor's Christmas Tabloid, Three-Dimension Advs., World Of Krypton, World Of Metropolis, World Of Smallville & World's Finest Comics)

**SUPERMAN** (Becomes Adventures Of. . .#424 on)
Summer, 1939 - No. 423, Sept, 1986
National Periodical Publications/DC Comics

Good Fine VF-NM NM/Mint

1(nn)-1st four Action stories reprinted; origin Superman by Siegel & Shuster; has a new 2 pg. origin plus 4 pgs. omitted in Action story 4,300.00 11,800.00 28,000.00 47,000.00
(Estimated up to 190 total copies exist, 3 in NM/Mint)

1-Reprint, Oversize 13½"x10." **WARNING:** This comic is an exact duplicate reprint of the original except for its size. DC published it in 1978 with a second cover titling it as a Famous First Edition. There have been many reported cases of the outer cover being removed and the interior sold as the original edition. The reprint with the new outer cover removed is practically worthless.

Good Fine N-Mint

2-All daily strip-r 600.00 1500.00 3600.00
3-2nd story-r from Action #5; 3rd story-r from Action #6 450.00 1125.00 2700.00
4-1st mention of Daily Planet? (Spr/40)-Also see Action #23. 1st Luthor story in this title 350.00 875.00 2100.00
5 258.00 645.00 1550.00
6,7: 7-1st Perry White? 200.00 500.00 1200.00
8-10: 10-1st bald Luthor 158.00 395.00 950.00
11-13,15: 13-Jimmy Olsen app. 119.00 300.00 715.00
14-Patriotic Shield-c by Fred Ray 142.00 355.00 850.00
16-20: 17-Hitler, Hirohito-c 100.00 250.00 600.00
21-23,25 79.00 200.00 475.00
24-Flag-c 92.00 230.00 550.00
26-29: 28-Lois Lane Girl Reporter series begins, ends #40,42 72.00 180.00 430.00
28-Overseas edition for Armed Forces; same as reg. #28 72.00 180.00 430.00
30-Origin & 1st app. Mr. Mxyztplk (pronounced "Mix-it-plk"); name later became Mxyzptlk ("Mix-yez-pit-l-ick"); the character was inspired by a combination of the name of Al Capp's Joe Blyfstyk (the little man with the black cloud over his head) & the devilish antics of Bugs Bunny 100.00 300.00 700.00
31-40: 33-(3-4/45)-3rd app. Mxyztplk 54.00 160.00 375.00
41-50: 45-Lois Lane as Superwoman (see Action #60 for 1st app.) 40.00 120.00 280.00
51,52 32.00 95.00 225.00
53-Origin Superman retold 79.00 235.00 550.00
54,56-60 33.00 100.00 230.00
55-Used in **SOTI**, pg. 33 36.00 107.00 250.00
61-Origin Superman retold; origin Green Kryptonite (1st Kryptonite story) 59.00 175.00 410.00
62-65,67-70: 62-Orson Welles app. 65-1st Krypton Foes: Mala, K120, & U-Ban 33.00 100.00 230.00
66-2nd Superbaby story 33.00 100.00 230.00
71-75: 75-Some have #74 on-c 30.00 90.00 210.00
72-Giveaway(9-10/51)-(Rare)-Price blackened out; came with banner wrapped around book 38.00 115.00 265.00
76-Batman x-over; Superman & Batman learn each other's I.D. 79.00 235.00 550.00
77-80: 78-Last 52 pgs. 27.00 80.00 185.00
81-Used in **POP**, pg. 88 27.00 80.00 185.00
82-90 24.00 73.00 170.00
91-95: 95-Last precode issue 23.00 70.00 160.00
96-99 19.00 58.00 135.00
100 (9-10/55) 67.00 200.00 460.00
101-110 16.00 48.00 110.00
111-120 14.00 41.00 95.00
121-130: 123-Pre-Supergirl tryout. 127-Origin/1st app. Titano. 128-Red Kryptonite used (4/59). 129-Intro/origin Lori Lemaris, The Mermaid 11.50 34.00 80.00
131-139: 139-Lori Lemaris app. 8.50 25.50 60.00
140-1st Blue Kryptonite & Bizarro Supergirl; origin Bizarro Jr. #1 8.50 25.50 60.00
141-145,148: 142-2nd Batman x-over 5.70 17.00 40.00
146-Superman's life story 7.00 21.00 50.00
147(8/61)-7th Legion app; 1st app. Legion of Super-Villains; 1st app. Adult Legion 9.30 28.00 65.00
149(11/61)-9th Legion app. (cameo); last 10 cent issue 8.00 24.00 55.00
150-162: 152(4/62)-15th Legion app. 155(8/62)-19th Legion app; Lightning Man & Cosmic Man, & Adult Legion app. 156,162-Legion app. 157-Gold Kryptonite used (see Adv. 299); Mon-el app.; Lightning Lad cameo (11/62). 158-1st app. Flamebird & Nightwing & Nor-Kan of Kandor. 161-1st told death of Ma and Pa Kent 3.60 11.00 25.00
163-166,168-180: 166-XMas-c. 168-All Luthor issue. 169-Last Sally Selwyn. 172,173-Legion cameos. 174-Super-Mxyzptlk; Bizarro app. 2.65 8.00 18.00
167-New origin Brainiac & Brainiac 5; intro Tixarla (Later Luthor's wife) 5.00 15.00 35.00
181,182,184-186,188-192,194-196,198-200: 181-1st 2965 story/series 189-Origin/destruction of Krypton II. 199-1st Superman/Flash race (8/67) 1.50 4.50 10.00
183,187,193,197 (Giants G-18,G-23,G-31,G-36) 1.70 5.00 12.00
201,203-206,208-211,213-216,218-221,223-226,228-231,234-238: 213-Brainiac-5 app. 1.00 3.00 7.00
202 (80-pg. Giant G-42)-All Bizarro issue 1.30 4.00 9.00
207,212,217,222,227,239 (Giants G-48,G-54,G-60,G-66,G-72,G-84): 207-Legion app.; 30th anniversary Superman 1.30 4.00 9.00
232(Giant, G-78)-All Krypton issue 1.30 4.00 9.00
233-2nd app. Morgan Edge, Clark Kent switch from newspaper reporter to TV newscaster 1.00 3.00 7.00
240-Kaluta-a .70 2.00 4.00
241-244 (52 pgs.). 243-G.A.-r/#38 .50 1.50 3.00
245-DC 100 Pg. Super Spectacular #7; Air Wave, Kid Eternity, Hawkman-r; Atom-r/Atom #3 .70 2.00 4.00
246-248,250,251,253 (All 52 pgs.): 246-G.A.-r/#40. 248-World of Krypton story. 251-G.A.-r/#45. 253-Finlay-a, 2pgs., G.A.-r/#13 .35 1.00 2.00
249,254-Neal Adams-a. 249-(52 pgs.); origin & 1st app. Terra-Man by Neal Adams (inks) 1.00 3.00 6.00
252-DC 100 Pg. Super Spectacular #13; Ray, Black Condor, Hawkman-r; Starman-r/Adv. #67; Dr. Fate & Spectre-r/More Fun #57; N. Adams-c .85 2.50 5.00
255-263: 263-Photo-c .25 .75 1.50
264-1st app. Steve Lombard .35 1.00 2.00

*Super Magician Comics V5#7, © S&S*

*Superman #4, © DC*

*Superman #76, © DC*

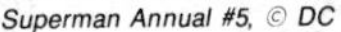
Superman Annual #5, © DC

Superman #9 (9/87), © DC

Superman Record Comic, © DC

| | Good | Fine | N-Mint |
|---|---|---|---|
| 265-271,273-277,279-283,285-299: 276-Intro Capt. Thunder. 289-Photo-c. 292-Origin Lex Luthor retold | .25 | .75 | 1.50 |
| 272,278,284-All 100 pgs. G.A.-r in all | .35 | 1.00 | 2.00 |
| 300-Retells origin | .70 | 2.00 | 4.00 |
| 301-399: 301,320-Solomon Grundy app. 323-Intro. Atomic Skull. 327-329-(44 pgs.). 330-More facts revealed about I. D. 338-The bottled city of Kandor enlarged. 344-Frankenstein & Dracula app. 353-Brief origin. 354,355,357-Superman 2020 stories (354-Debut Superman III). 356-World of Krypton story (also #360,367,375). 372-Superman 2021 story. 376-Free 16 pg. preview Daring New Advs. of Supergirl. 377-Free 16 pg. preview Masters of the Univ. | .25 | .75 | 1.50 |
| 400 (10/84, $1.50, 68 pgs.)-Many top artists featured; Chaykin painted cover, Miller back-c | .50 | 1.50 | 3.00 |
| 401-410,412-422: 405-Super-Batman story. 408-Nuclear Holocaust-c/story. 414,415-Crisis x-over. 422-Horror-c | .25 | .75 | 1.50 |
| 411-Special Julius Schwartz tribute issue | .25 | .75 | 1.50 |
| 423-Alan Moore scripts; Perez-a(i) | 1.00 | 3.00 | 7.00 |
| Annual 1(10/60, 84 pgs.)-Reprints 1st Supergirl story/Action #252; r-/Lois Lane #1 (1st Silver Age DC annual) | 32.00 | 95.00 | 225.00 |
| Annual 2(1960)-Brainiac, Titano, Metallo, Bizarro origin-r | 19.00 | 58.00 | 135.00 |
| Annual 3(1961) | 14.00 | 43.00 | 100.00 |
| Annual 4(1961)-11th Legion app; 1st Legion origins-text & pictures | 12.00 | 36.00 | 85.00 |
| Annual 5(Sum, '62)-All Krypton issue | 8.50 | 25.50 | 60.00 |
| Annual 6(Wint, '62-'63)-Legion-r/Adv. #247 | 7.00 | 21.00 | 50.00 |
| Annual 7(Sum/'63)-Origin-r/Superman-Batman team/Adv. 275; r-1955 Superman dailies | 5.70 | 17.00 | 40.00 |
| Annual 8(Wint, '63-'64)-All origins issue | 4.30 | 13.00 | 30.00 |
| Annual 9(8/64)-Superman/Batman team-up | 4.30 | 13.00 | 30.00 |
| Annuals 9-12: 9(9/83)-Toth/Austin-a. 10(11/84, $1.25)-M. Anderson inks. 11(9/85)-Moore scripts. 12(8/86) | .50 | 1.50 | 3.00 |
| Special 1(3/83)-G. Kane-c/a; contains German-r | .50 | 1.50 | 3.00 |
| Special 2(3/84, 48pgs.), 3(4/85, $1.25) | .50 | 1.50 | 3.00 |
| The Amazing World of Superman "Official Metropolis Edition" ($2.00; 1973, 14x10½")-Origin retold | 1.35 | 4.00 | 8.00 |
| Kelloggs Giveaway-(⅔ normal size, 1954)-r-two stories/Superman #55 | 30.00 | 90.00 | 200.00 |
| ...Meets the Quik Bunny ('87, Nestles Quik premium, 36 pgs.) | | .50 | 1.00 |
| ...Movie Special-(9/83)-Adaptation of Superman III; other versions exist with store logos on bottom ⅓ of-c | | .50 | 1.00 |
| Pizza Hut Premium(12/77)-Exact-r of #97,113 | .25 | .75 | 1.50 |
| Radio Shack Giveaway-36pgs. (7/80) 'The Computers That Saved Metropolis;' Starlin/Giordano-a; advertising insert in Action 509, New Advs. of Superboy 7, Legion of Super-Heroes 265, & House of Mystery 282. (All comics were 64 pgs.) Cover of inserts printed on newsprint. Giveaway contains 4 extra pgs. of Radio Shack advertising that inserts do not | .25 | .75 | 1.50 |
| Radio Shack Giveaway-(7/81) 'Victory by Computer' | .25 | .75 | 1.50 |
| Radio Shack Giveaway-(7/82) 'Computer Masters of Metropolis' | | .50 | 1.00 |
| 11195(2/79,224pp,$1.95)-Golden Press | .40 | 1.20 | 2.40 |

NOTE: ***N. Adams*** *a-249i, 254p; c-204-208, 210, 212-215, 219, 231, 233-237, 240-243, 249-252, 254, 263, 307, 308, 313, 314, 317.* ***Adkins*** *a-323i.* ***Austin*** *c-368i.* ***Wayne Boring*** *art-late 1940's to early 1960's.* ***Buckler*** *a-352p, 363p, 364p, 369p; c(p)-324-327, 356, 363, 368, 369, 373, 376, 378.* ***Burnley*** *a-252r.* ***Fine*** *a-252r.* ***Gil Kane*** *a-272r, 367, 372, 375, Special 2; c-374p, 375p, 377, 381, 382, 384-390, 392, Annual 9.* ***Kubert*** *c-216.* ***Morrow*** *a-238.* ***Perez*** *c-364p.* ***Starlin*** *c-355.* ***Staton*** *a-354i, 355i.* ***Williamson*** *a-408-410i, 412i, 416i; c-408i, 409i.* ***Wrightson*** *a-416.*

**SUPERMAN** (2nd series)
Jan, 1987 - Present (.75-$1.00, bi-weekly #19-?)
DC Comics

| | Good | Fine | N-Mint |
|---|---|---|---|
| 1-Byrne-c/a begins; intro Metallo | .35 | 1.00 | 2.00 |
| 2-8,10: 3-Legends x-over. 7-Origin/1st app. Rampage. 8-Legion app. | | .60 | 1.20 |
| 9-Joker-c | .50 | 1.50 | 3.00 |
| 11-49: 11-1st app. Mr. Mxyzptlk. 12-Lori Lemaris revived. 13-1st app. Toyman. 13,14-Millennium x-over. 20-Doom Patrol app.; Supergirl revived in cameo. 28-Steranko-c(p). 31-Mr. Mxyzptlk app. 37-Kirby-c(p); Newsboy Legion app. 44-"Dark Knight Over Metropolis" part 1; Batman story. 45-Free extra 8 pgs. | | .40 | .80 |
| 50-($1.50, 52 pgs.)-Clark Kent proposes to Lois | 1.35 | 4.00 | 8.00 |
| Annual 1 (8/87)-No Byrne-a | .25 | .75 | 1.50 |
| Annual 2 ('88)-Byrne-a; Newsboy Legion | .25 | .75 | 1.50 |

**SUPERMAN & THE GREAT CLEVELAND FIRE** (Giveaway)
1948 (4 pages, no cover)(Hospital Fund)
National Periodical Publications

| | Good | Fine | N-Mint |
|---|---|---|---|
| nn-In full color | 43.00 | 130.00 | 300.00 |

**SUPERMAN FAMILY, THE** (Formerly Superman's Pal Jimmy Olsen)
No. 164, Apr-May, 1974 - No. 222, Sept, 1982
National Periodical Publications/DC Comics

| | Good | Fine | N-Mint |
|---|---|---|---|
| 164-Jimmy Olsen, Supergirl, Lois Lane begin | .25 | .75 | 1.50 |
| 165-176 (100-68 pgs.) | | .60 | 1.20 |
| 177-181 (52 pgs.) | | .50 | 1.00 |
| 182-$1.00 issues begin; Marshall Rogers-a; Krypto begins, ends #192 | .35 | 1.00 | 2.00 |
| 183-193,195-222: 183-Nightwing-Flamebird begins, ends #194. 189-Brainiac 5, Mon-el app. 191-Superboy begins, ends #198. 200-Book length story. 211-Earth II Batman & Catwoman marry | | .50 | 1.00 |
| 194-Rogers-a | .35 | 1.00 | 2.00 |

NOTE: ***N. Adams*** *c-182-185.* ***Anderson*** *a-186i.* ***Buckler*** *c(p)-190, 191, 209, 210, 215, 217, 220.* ***Jones*** *a-191-193.* ***Gil Kane*** *c-221p, 222p.* ***Mortimer*** *a-191-193p, 199p, 201-222p.* ***Orlando*** *a-186i, 187i.* ***Rogers*** *a-182, 194.* ***Staton*** *a-191-194, 196p.* ***Tuska*** *a-203p, 207-209p.*

**SUPERMAN IV MOVIE SPECIAL**
1987 ($2.00, color, one-shot)
DC Comics

| | Good | Fine | N-Mint |
|---|---|---|---|
| 1-Movie adaptation; Heck-a | .35 | 1.00 | 2.00 |

**SUPERMAN** (Miniature)
1942; 1955 - 1956 (3 issues; no #'s; 32 pgs.)
The pages are numbered in the 1st issue: 1-32; 2nd: 1A-32A, and 3rd: 1B-32B
National Periodical Publications

| | Good | Fine | N-Mint |
|---|---|---|---|
| No date-Py-Co-Pay Tooth Powder giveaway (8 pgs.; circa 1942) | 49.00 | 145.00 | 340.00 |
| 1-The Superman Time Capsule (Kellogg's Sugar Smacks)(1955) | 24.00 | 70.00 | 165.00 |
| 1A-Duel in Space | 19.00 | 58.00 | 135.00 |
| 1B-The Super Show of Metropolis (also #1-32, no B) | 19.00 | 58.00 | 135.00 |

NOTE: *Numbering variations exist. Each title could have any combination-#1, 1A, or 1B.*

**SUPERMAN RECORD COMIC**
1966 (Golden Records)
National Periodical Publications

| | Good | Fine | N-Mint |
|---|---|---|---|
| (with record)-Record reads origin of Superman from comic; came with iron-on patch, decoder, membership card & button; comic r-/Superman 125, 146 | 4.65 | 14.00 | 32.00 |
| Comic only | 2.00 | 6.00 | 14.00 |

**SUPERMAN'S BUDDY** (Costume Comic)
1954 (4 pgs.) (One Shot) (Came in box w/costume; slick-paper/c)
National Periodical Publications

| | Good | Fine | N-Mint |
|---|---|---|---|
| 1-(Rare)-w/box & costume | 65.00 | 195.00 | 455.00 |
| Comic only | 35.00 | 105.00 | 245.00 |

## SUPERMAN'S CHRISTMAS ADVENTURE

1940, 1944 (16 pgs.) (Giveaway)
Distr. by Nehi drinks, Bailey Store, Ivey-Keith Co., Kennedy's Boys Shop, Macy's Store, Boston Store
National Periodical Publications

| | Good | Fine | N-Mint |
|---|---|---|---|
| 1(1940)-by Burnley | 75.00 | 225.00 | 525.00 |
| nn(1944) | 60.00 | 180.00 | 420.00 |

**SUPERMAN SCRAPBOOK** (Has blank pages; contains no comics)

**SUPERMAN'S GIRLFRIEND LOIS LANE** (See Action Comics #1, 80 Page Giant #3,14, Lois Lane, Showcase #9,10, Superman #28 & Superman Family)

## SUPERMAN'S GIRLFRIEND LOIS LANE

Mar-Apr, 1958 - No. 136, Jan-Feb, 1974; No. 137, Sept-Oct, 1974
National Periodical Publications

| | Good | Fine | N-Mint |
|---|---|---|---|
| 1 | 64.00 | 193.00 | 450.00 |
| 2 | 27.00 | 80.00 | 185.00 |
| 3-Spanking panel | 19.00 | 58.00 | 135.00 |
| 4,5 | 16.00 | 48.00 | 110.00 |
| 6-10: 9-Pat Boone app. | 11.00 | 32.00 | 75.00 |
| 11-20: 14-Supergirl x-over | 6.50 | 19.00 | 45.00 |
| 21-29: 23-1st app. Lena Thorul, Lex Luthor's sister. 29-Aquaman, Batman, Green Arrow cameo; last 10 cent issue | 4.00 | 12.00 | 28.00 |
| 30-32,34-49: 47-Legion app. | 1.50 | 4.50 | 10.00 |
| 33(5/62)-Mon-el app. | 2.00 | 6.00 | 14.00 |
| 50(7/64)-Triplicate Girl, Phantom Girl & Shrinking Violet app. | 1.50 | 4.50 | 10.00 |
| 51-55,57-67,69: 59-Jor-el app.; Batman back-up story | .50 | 1.50 | 3.00 |
| 56-Saturn Girl app. | .85 | 2.50 | 5.00 |
| 68-(Giant G-26) | 1.00 | 3.00 | 7.00 |
| 70-Penguin & Catwoman app. (1st S.A. Catwoman, 11/66); Batman & Robin cameo | 2.85 | 8.50 | 20.00 |
| 71-76,78: 74-1st Bizarro Flash; JLA cameo | .50 | 1.50 | 3.00 |
| 77-(Giant G-39) | .70 | 2.00 | 4.00 |
| 79-Neal Adams-c begin, end #95,108 | .35 | 1.00 | 2.00 |
| 80-85,87-94: 89-Batman x-over; all N. Adams-c | .35 | 1.00 | 2.00 |
| 86-(Giant G-51)-Neal Adams-c | .70 | 2.00 | 4.00 |
| 95-(Giant G-63)-Wonder Woman x-over; N. Adams-c | .70 | 2.00 | 4.00 |
| 96-103,105-111: 105-Origin/1st app. The Rose & the Thorn. 108-Neal Adams-c. 111-Morrow-a | .35 | 1.00 | 2.00 |
| 104,113-(Giants G-75,87) | .70 | 2.00 | 4.00 |
| 112,114-123 (52 pgs.): 122-G.A.-r/Superman #30. 123-G.A. Batman-r | .35 | 1.00 | 2.00 |
| 124-137: 130-Last Rose & the Thorn. 132-New Zatanna story. 136-Wonder Woman x-over | .35 | 1.00 | 2.00 |
| Annual 1(Sum,'62) | 6.50 | 19.00 | 45.00 |
| Annual 2(Sum,'63) | 3.60 | 11.00 | 25.00 |

NOTE: ***Buckler** a-117-121p. **Curt Swan** a-1-50(most).*

## SUPERMAN'S PAL JIMMY OLSEN (Superman Family #164 on)

(See Action Comics #6 for 1st app. & 80 Page Giant)
Sept-Oct, 1954 - No. 163, Feb-Mar, 1974
National Periodical Publications

| | Good | Fine | N-Mint |
|---|---|---|---|
| 1 | 97.00 | 291.00 | 680.00 |
| 2 | 42.00 | 125.00 | 290.00 |
| 3-Last pre-code issue | 27.00 | 80.00 | 185.00 |
| 4,5 | 19.00 | 56.00 | 130.00 |
| 6-10 | 14.00 | 43.00 | 100.00 |
| 11-20 | 9.30 | 28.00 | 65.00 |
| 21-30: 29-1st app. Krypto in Jimmy Olsen | 5.00 | 15.00 | 35.00 |
| 31-40: 31-Origin Elastic Lad. 33-One pg. biography of Jack Larson (TV Jimmy Olsen). 36-Intro Lucy Lane. 37-2nd app. Elastic Lad; 1st cover app. | 3.15 | 9.50 | 22.00 |
| 41-50: 41-1st J.O. Robot. 48-Intro/origin Superman Emergency Squad | 2.15 | 6.50 | 15.00 |
| 51-56: 56-Last 10 cent issue | 1.30 | 4.00 | 9.00 |
| 57-62,64-70: 57-Olsen marries Supergirl. 62-Mon-el & Elastic Lad app. but not as Legionnaires. 70-Element Lad app. | .70 | 2.00 | 5.00 |
| 63(9/62)-Legion of Super-Villains app. | .85 | 2.50 | 6.00 |
| 71,74,75,78,80-84,86,89,90: 86-J.O. Robot becomes Congorilla | .50 | 1.50 | 3.00 |
| 72(10/63)-Legion app; Elastic Lad (Olsen) joins | .70 | 2.00 | 5.00 |
| 73-Ultra Boy app. | .70 | 2.00 | 5.00 |
| 76,85-Legion app. | .70 | 2.00 | 5.00 |
| 77-Olsen with Colossal Boy's powers & costume; origin Titano retold | .50 | 1.50 | 3.00 |
| 79(9/64)-Titled The Red-headed Beatle of 1000 B.C. | .50 | 1.50 | 3.00 |
| 87-Legion of Super-Villains app. | .70 | 2.00 | 5.00 |
| 88-Star Boy app. | .50 | 1.50 | 3.00 |
| 91-94,96-99,101-103,105-110: 99-Olsen w/powers & costumes of Lightning Lad, Sun Boy & Star Boy. 106-Legion app. 110-Infinity-c | .35 | 1.00 | 2.00 |
| 95,104 (Giants G-25,G-38) | .85 | 2.60 | 6.00 |
| 100-Legion cameo | .50 | 1.50 | 3.00 |
| 111,112,114-121,123-130,132 | .35 | 1.00 | 2.00 |
| 113,122,131 (Giants G-50,G-62,G-74) | .35 | 1.00 | 2.00 |
| 133-Re-intro Newsboy Legion & begins by Kirby | .50 | 1.50 | 3.00 |
| 134-163: 134-1st app. Darkseid (cameo) & Morgan Edge. 135-G.A. Guardian app. 136-Origin new Guardian. 139-Last 15 cent issue. 140-(Giant G-86). 141-Newsboy Legion reprints by S&K begin (52 pg. issues begin). 149,150-G.A. Plastic Man reprint in both; last 52 pg. issue. 150-Newsboy Legion app. | .35 | 1.00 | 2.00 |

NOTE: *Issues #141-148 contain **Simon & Kirby** Newsboy Legion reprints from Star Spangled #7, 8, 9, 10, 11, 12, 13, 14 in that order. **N. Adams** c-109-112, 115, 117, 118, 120, 121, 132, 134-136, 147, 148. **Kirby** a-133-139p, 141-148p; c-133, 139, 145p. **Kirby/N. Adams** c-137, 138, 141-144, 146.*

## SUPERMAN SPECTACULAR (Also see DC Special Series #5)

1982 (Magazine size)(Square binding)
DC Comics

| | Good | Fine | N-Mint |
|---|---|---|---|
| 1 | .35 | 1.00 | 2.00 |

## SUPERMAN: THE EARTH STEALERS

1988 (one-shot, $2.95, 52pgs, prestige format)
DC Comics

| | Good | Fine | N-Mint |
|---|---|---|---|
| 1-Byrne scripts; painted-c | .60 | 1.75 | 3.50 |
| 1-2nd printing | .50 | 1.50 | 2.95 |

## SUPERMAN: THE SECRET YEARS

Feb, 1985 - No. 4, May, 1985 (Mini-series)
DC Comics

| | Good | Fine | N-Mint |
|---|---|---|---|
| 1-Miller-c on all | .25 | .75 | 1.50 |
| 2-4 | | .50 | 1.00 |

**SUPERMAN 3-D** (See Three-Dimension Adventures)

## SUPERMAN-TIM (Becomes Tim)

Aug, 1942 - May, 1950 (½-size) (B&W Giveaway w/2 color covers)
Superman-Tim Stores/National Periodical Publications

| | Good | Fine | N-Mint |
|---|---|---|---|
| 8/42, 2/43, 3/43, 6/43, 8/43, 9/43, 3/44, 2/45, 11/49 issues-Two pg. Superman illos in each | 9.30 | 28.00 | 65.00 |
| 10/43, 12/43, 2/44, 4/44-1/45, 3/45, 4/45, 4/46, 6/46, 8/46 issues-no Superman | 7.00 | 21.00 | 50.00 |
| 9/46-1st stamp album issue (worth more if complete with Superman stamps) | 8.00 | 24.00 | 55.00 |
| 10/46-1st Superman story | 16.00 | 48.00 | 110.00 |
| 11/46, 12/46, 1/47, 2/47, 3/47, 4/47, 5/47-8/47 issues-Superman story in each | 16.00 | 48.00 | 110.00 |
| 9/47-Stamp album issue & Superman story | 17.00 | 51.00 | 120.00 |
| 10/47, 11/47, 12/47-Superman stories | 16.00 | 48.00 | 110.00 |

1/48, 2/48, 6/48, 8/48, 10/48, 11/48, 2/49-10/49, 12/49-5/50 issues-no

*Superman's Girlfriend Lois Lane #70, © DC*

*Superman's Pal Jimmy Olsen #26, © DC*

*Superman-Tim 8/48, © DC*

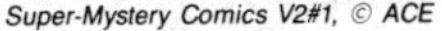
Super-Mystery Comics V2#1, © ACE

Supernatural Thrillers #1, © MEG

Supersnipe Comics V2#12, © S&S

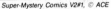

| | Good | Fine | N-Mint |
|---|---|---|---|
| Superman | 6.50 | 19.00 | 45.00 |
| 9/48-Stamp album issue | 7.00 | 21.00 | 50.00 |

NOTE: *16 pgs. through 9/47; 8 pgs. 10/47 on? The stamp album issues (3) may contain Superman stamps that were made to glue in these books. Books with the stamps included would be worth more, and the value would depend upon completeness of the album. There is no stamp album in the 9/49 issue.*

**SUPERMAN VS. THE AMAZING SPIDER-MAN** (Also see Marvel Treasury Edition No. 28)
April, 1976 (100 pgs.) ($2.00) (Over-sized)
National Periodical Publications/Marvel Comics Group

| | Good | Fine | N-Mint |
|---|---|---|---|
| 1 | .85 | 2.60 | 6.00 |
| 1-2nd printing; 5000 numbered copies signed by Stan Lee & Carmine Infantino on front cover & sold through mail | 1.70 | 5.00 | 12.00 |

**SUPERMAN WORKBOOK**
1945 (One Shot) (68 pgs; reprints) (B&W)
National Periodical Publ./Juvenile Group Foundation

| | Good | Fine | N-Mint |
|---|---|---|---|
| nn-Cover-r/Superman #14 | 71.00 | 215.00 | 500.00 |

**SUPER MARIO BROS.**
1990 - Present ($1.95, color, slick-c)
Valiant Comics

| | Good | Fine | N-Mint |
|---|---|---|---|
| 1-7: 1-Wildman-a. 7-Layton-c | .35 | 1.00 | 2.00 |
| Special Edition 1 (1990, $1.95)-Wildman-a | .35 | 1.00 | 2.00 |

**SUPERMOUSE** (. . .the Big Cheese; see Coo Coo Comics)
Dec, 1948 - No. 34, Sept, 1955; No. 35, Apr, 1956 - No. 45, Fall, 1958
Standard Comics/Pines No. 35 on (Literary Ent.)

| | Good | Fine | N-Mint |
|---|---|---|---|
| 1-Frazetta text illos (3) | 17.00 | 51.00 | 120.00 |
| 2-Frazetta text illos | 9.30 | 28.00 | 65.00 |
| 3,5,6-Text illos by Frazetta in all | 7.00 | 21.00 | 50.00 |
| 4-Two pg. text illos by Frazetta | 8.00 | 24.00 | 55.00 |
| 7-10 | 2.65 | 8.00 | 18.00 |
| 11-20: 13-Racist humor (Indians) | 2.00 | 6.00 | 14.00 |
| 21-45 | 1.30 | 4.00 | 9.00 |
| 1-Summer Holiday issue (Summer,'56-Pines)-100 pgs. | 5.70 | 17.00 | 40.00 |
| 2-Giant Summer issue (Summer,'58-Pines)-100 pgs. | 4.50 | 14.00 | 32.00 |

**SUPER-MYSTERY COMICS**
July, 1940 - V8#6, July, 1949
Ace Magazines (Periodical House)

| | Good | Fine | N-Mint |
|---|---|---|---|
| V1#1-Magno, the Magnetic Man & Vulcan begin | 79.00 | 235.00 | 550.00 |
| 2 | 38.00 | 115.00 | 265.00 |
| 3-The Black Spider begins | 30.00 | 90.00 | 210.00 |
| 4-Origin Davy | 27.00 | 81.00 | 190.00 |
| 5-Intro. The Clown; begin series | 27.00 | 81.00 | 190.00 |
| 6(2/41) | 23.00 | 70.00 | 160.00 |
| V2#1(4/41)-Origin Buckskin | 23.00 | 70.00 | 160.00 |
| 2-6(2/42) | 21.00 | 62.00 | 145.00 |
| V3#1(4/42),2: 1-Vulcan & Black Ace begin | 19.00 | 56.00 | 130.00 |
| 3-Intro. The Lancer; Dr. Nemesis & The Sword begin; Kurtzman-c/a(2) (Mr. Risk & Paul Revere Jr.) | 25.00 | 75.00 | 175.00 |
| 4-Kurtzman-a | 21.00 | 62.00 | 145.00 |
| 5-Kurtzman-a(2); L.B. Cole-a; Mr. Risk app. | 22.00 | 65.00 | 150.00 |
| 6(10/43)-Mr. Risk app.; Kurtzman's Paul Revere Jr.; L.B. Cole-a | 22.00 | 65.00 | 150.00 |
| V4#1(1/44)-L.B. Cole-a | 16.00 | 48.00 | 110.00 |
| 2-6(4/45): 2,5,6-Mr. Risk app. | 12.00 | 36.00 | 85.00 |
| V5#1(7/45)-6 | 10.00 | 30.00 | 70.00 |
| V6#1-6: 3-Torture story. 4-Last Magno. Mr. Risk app. in #2,4-6 | 8.50 | 25.50 | 60.00 |
| V7#1-6, V8#1-4,6 | 8.50 | 25.50 | 60.00 |
| V8#5-Meskin, Tuska, Sid Greene-a | 10.00 | 30.00 | 70.00 |

NOTE: ***Sid Greene** a-V7#4. **Mooney** c-V1#5, 6, V2#1-6. **Palais** c/a-V5#3,4. Bondage c-V2#5, 6, V3#2, 5.*

**SUPERNATURAL THRILLERS**
Dec, 1972 - No. 6, Nov, 1973; No. 7, July, 1974 - No. 15, Oct, 1975
Marvel Comics Group

| | Good | Fine | N-Mint |
|---|---|---|---|
| 1-3: 1-It!-Sturgeon adaptation. 2-The Invisible Man. 3-The Valley of the Worm | | .50 | 1.00 |
| 4-15: 4-Dr. Jekyll & Mr. Hyde. 5-The Living Mummy. 6-The Headless Horseman. 7-The Living Mummy begins | | .35 | .70 |

NOTE: ***Brunner** c-11. **Buckler** a-5p. **Ditko** a-8r, 9r. **G. Kane** a-3p; c-3, 9p, 15p. **Mayerik** a-2p, 7, 8, 9p, 10p, 11. **McWilliams** a-14i. **Mortimer** a-4. **Steranko** c-1, 2. **Sutton** a-15. **Tuska** a-6p. Robert E. Howard story-#3.*

**SUPER POWERS**
7/84 - No. 5, 11/84; 9/85 - No. 6, 2/86; 9/86 - No. 4, 12/86
DC Comics

| | Good | Fine | N-Mint |
|---|---|---|---|
| 1 (7/84, 1st series)-Joker/Penguin-c/story; Batman app.; Kirby-c | | .60 | 1.20 |
| 2-5: 5-Kirby-c/a | | .45 | .90 |
| 1 (9/85, 2nd series)-Kirby-c/a in all; Capt. Marvel & Firestorm join; Batman cameo | | .50 | 1.00 |
| 2-6: 4-Batman cameo. 5,6-Batman app. | | .45 | .90 |
| 1-4 (1986, 3rd series): 1-Cyborg joins; 1st app. Samurai from Super Friends TV show. 1-4-Batman cameos | | .40 | .80 |

**SUPER PUP** (Formerly Spotty The Pup) (See Space Comics)
No. 4, Mar-Apr, 1954 - No. 5, 1954
Avon Periodicals

| | Good | Fine | N-Mint |
|---|---|---|---|
| 4,5 | 1.70 | 5.00 | 12.00 |

**SUPER RABBIT** (See All Surprise, Animated Movie Tunes, Comedy Comics, Comic Capers, Ideal Comics, It's A Duck's Life, Movie Tunes & Wisco)
Fall, 1944 - No. 14, Nov, 1948
Timely Comics (CmPI)

| | Good | Fine | N-Mint |
|---|---|---|---|
| 1-Hitler-c | 37.00 | 110.00 | 255.00 |
| 2 | 18.00 | 54.00 | 125.00 |
| 3-5 | 10.00 | 30.00 | 70.00 |
| 6-Origin | 10.00 | 30.00 | 70.00 |
| 7-10; 9-Infinity-c | 6.00 | 18.00 | 42.00 |
| 11-Kurtzman's "Hey Look" | 7.00 | 21.00 | 50.00 |
| 12-14 | 5.00 | 15.00 | 35.00 |
| I.W. Reprint #1,2('58),7,10('63) | .70 | 2.00 | 4.00 |

**SUPER RICHIE** (Superichie #5 on)
Sept, 1975 - No. 4, Mar, 1976 (All 52 pg. Giants)
Harvey Publications

| | Good | Fine | N-Mint |
|---|---|---|---|
| 1 | .35 | 1.00 | 2.00 |
| 2-4 | | .50 | 1.00 |

**SUPERSNIPE COMICS** (Formerly Army & Navy #1-5)
V1#6, Oct, 1942 - V5#1, Aug-Sept, 1949 (See Shadow Comics V2#3)
Street & Smith Publications

| | Good | Fine | N-Mint |
|---|---|---|---|
| V1#6-Rex King Man of Adventure(costumed hero) by Jack Binder begins; Supersnipe by George Marcoux continues from Army & Navy #5; Bill Ward-a | 39.00 | 115.00 | 270.00 |
| 7,8,10-12: 8-Hitler, Tojo, Mussolini-c. 11-Little Nemo app. | 21.00 | 62.00 | 145.00 |
| 9-Doc Savage x-over in Supersnipe; Hitler-c | 25.00 | 75.00 | 175.00 |
| V2#1-12: 1-Huck Finn by Clare Dwiggins begins, ends V3#5 | 14.00 | 43.00 | 100.00 |
| V3#1-12: 8-Bobby Crusoe by Dwiggins begins, ends V3#12. 9-Xmas-c | 11.00 | 32.00 | 75.00 |
| V4#1-12, V5#1: V4#10-Xmas-c | 8.00 | 24.00 | 55.00 |

NOTE: *Doc Savage app. in some issues.*

**SUPERSPOOK** (Formerly Frisky Animals on Parade)
No. 4, June, 1958
Ajax/Farrell Publications

| | Good | Fine | N-Mint |
|---|---|---|---|
| 4 | 2.00 | 6.00 | 14.00 |

**SUPER SPY** (See Wham Comics)
Oct, 1940 - No. 2, Nov, 1940 (Reprints)
Centaur Publications

| | Good | Fine | N-Mint |
|---|---|---|---|
| 1-Origin The Sparkler | 75.00 | 225.00 | 525.00 |
| 2-The Inner Circle, Dean Denton, Tim Blain, The Drew Ghost, The Night Hawk by Gustavson, & S.S. Swanson by Glanz app. | 53.00 | 160.00 | 370.00 |

**SUPER STAR HOLIDAY SPECIAL** (See DC Special Series #21)

**SUPER-TEAM FAMILY**
10-11/75 - No. 15, 3-4/78 (#1-4: 68 pgs.; #5 on: 52 pgs.)
National Periodical Publications/DC Comics

| | Good | Fine | N-Mint |
|---|---|---|---|
| 1-Reprints by Neal Adams & Kane/Wood | | .50 | 1.00 |
| 2-15: 4-7-Reprints; 4-G.A. JSA-r & Superman/Batman/Robin-r from World's Finest. 8-15-New stories; Challengers of the Unknown in #8-10 | | .35 | .70 |

NOTE: ***Neal Adams** r-1-3. **Brunner** c-3. **Buckler** c-8p. **Estrada** a-2. **Tuska** a-7r. **Wood** a-1i(r), 3.*

**SUPER TV HEROES** (See Hanna-Barbera . . .)

**SUPER-VILLAIN CLASSICS**
May, 1983 (One Shot)
Marvel Comics Group

| | Good | Fine | N-Mint |
|---|---|---|---|
| 1-"Galactus the Origin" | | .50 | 1.00 |

**SUPER-VILLAIN TEAM-UP** (See Fantastic Four #6 & Giant-Size . . .)
8/75 - No. 14, 10/77; No. 15, 11/78; No. 16, 5/79; No. 17, 6/80
Marvel Comics Group

| | Good | Fine | N-Mint |
|---|---|---|---|
| 1-Sub-Mariner & Dr. Doom begin, end #10 | .60 | 1.75 | 3.50 |
| 2-17: 5-1st Shroud. 6-F.F., Shroud app. 7-Origin The Shroud. 9-The Avengers app. 11-15-Dr. Doom & Red Skull app. | .35 | 1.00 | 2.00 |

NOTE: ***Buckler** c-4p, 5p, 7p. **Buscema** c-1. **Byrne/Austin** c-14. **Evans** a-1p, 3p. **Everett** a-1p. **Giffen** a-8p, 13p; c-13p. **Kane** c-2p, 9p. **Mooney** a-4i. **Starlin** c-6. **Tuska** a-1p, 15p(r). **Wood** a-15p(r).*

**SUPER WESTERN COMICS** (Also see Buffalo Bill)
Aug, 1950 - No. 4, Mar, 1951
Youthful Magazines

| | Good | Fine | N-Mint |
|---|---|---|---|
| 1-Buffalo Bill begins; Calamity Jane app; Powell-c/a | 4.50 | 14.00 | 32.00 |
| 2-4 | 2.65 | 8.00 | 18.00 |

**SUPER WESTERN FUNNIES** (See Super Funnies)

**SUPERWORLD COMICS**
April, 1940 - No. 3, Aug, 1940 (All have 68 pgs.)
Hugo Gernsback (Komos Publ.)

| | Good | Fine | N-Mint |
|---|---|---|---|
| 1-Origin Hip Knox, Super Hypnotist; Mitey Powers & Buzz Allen, the Invisible Avenger, Little Nemo begin; cover by Frank R. Paul | 143.00 | 430.00 | 1000.00 |
| 2-Marvo 1,2 Go+, the Super Boy of the Year 2680 | 97.00 | 290.00 | 680.00 |
| 3 | 76.00 | 230.00 | 535.00 |

**SURE-FIRE COMICS** (Lightning Comics #4 on)
June, 1940 - No. 4, Oct, 1940 (Two No. 3's)
Ace Magazines

| | Good | Fine | N-Mint |
|---|---|---|---|
| V1#1-Origin Flash Lightning; X-The Phantom Fed, Ace McCoy, Buck Steele, Marvo the Magician, The Raven, Whiz Wilson (Time Traveler) begin | 67.00 | 200.00 | 465.00 |
| 2 | 40.00 | 120.00 | 280.00 |
| 3(9/40) | 34.00 | 100.00 | 235.00 |
| 3(#4)(10/40)-nn on-c, #3 on inside | 34.00 | 100.00 | 235.00 |

**SURF 'N' WHEELS**
Nov, 1969 - No. 6, Sept, 1970
Charlton Comics

| | Good | Fine | N-Mint |
|---|---|---|---|
| 1 | .50 | 1.50 | 3.00 |
| 2-6 | .35 | 1.00 | 2.00 |

**SURGE**
July, 1984 - No. 4, Jan, 1985 ($1.50, mini-series, Baxter paper)
Eclipse Comics

| | Good | Fine | N-Mint |
|---|---|---|---|
| 1-4-Ties into DNAgents series | .25 | .75 | 1.50 |

**SURPRISE ADVENTURES** (Formerly Tormented)
No. 3, Mar, 1955 - No. 5, July, 1955
Sterling Comic Group

| | Good | Fine | N-Mint |
|---|---|---|---|
| 3-5: 3,5-Sekowsky-a | 2.00 | 6.00 | 14.00 |

**SUSIE Q. SMITH** (See Four Color #323, 377, 453, 553)

**SUSPENSE** (Radio/TV; Real Life Tales of . . . #1-4) (Amazing Detective Cases #3 on?)
Dec, 1949 - No. 29, Apr, 1953 (#1-8,17-23: 52 pgs.)
Marvel/Atlas Comics (CnPC No. 1-10/BFP No. 11-29)

| | Good | Fine | N-Mint |
|---|---|---|---|
| 1-Powell-a; Peter Lorre, Sidney Greenstreet photo-c from Hammett's 'The Maltese Falcon' | 22.00 | 65.00 | 150.00 |
| 2-Crime stories; Gale Storm & Dennis O'Keefe photo-c | 11.00 | 32.00 | 75.00 |
| 3-Change to horror | 11.00 | 32.00 | 75.00 |
| 4,7-10 | 7.00 | 21.00 | 50.00 |
| 5-Krigstein, Tuska, Everett-a | 8.50 | 25.50 | 60.00 |
| 6-Tuska, Everett, Morisi-a | 8.00 | 24.00 | 55.00 |
| 11-17,19,20: 14-Hypo-c; A-Bomb panels | 6.00 | 18.00 | 42.00 |
| 18,22-Krigstein-a | 7.00 | 21.00 | 50.00 |
| 21,23,26-29 | 4.50 | 14.00 | 32.00 |
| 24-Tuska-a | 5.00 | 15.00 | 35.00 |
| 25-Electric chair-c/story | 7.00 | 21.00 | 50.00 |

NOTE: ***Ayers** a-20. **Briefer** a-5, 7, 27. **Colan** a-8(2), 9. **Everett** a-5, 6(2), 19, 23, 28; c-21-23, 26. **Fuje** a-29. **Heath** a-5, 6, 8, 10, 12, 14; c-14, 19, 24. **Maneely** a-24, 28, 29; c-10, 15. **Mooney** a-24, 28. **Morisi** a-6. **Palais** a-10. **Rico** a-7-9. **Robinson** a-29. **Romita** a-20(2), 25. **Sekowsky** a-11, 13, 14. **Sinnott** a-23, 25. **Tuska** a-5, 6, 12; c-12. **Whitney** a-15, 16, 22. **Ed Win** a-27.*

**SUSPENSE COMICS**
Dec, 1943 - No. 12, Dec?, 1946
Continental Magazines

| | Good | Fine | N-Mint |
|---|---|---|---|
| 1-The Grey Mask begins; bondage/torture-c; L. B. Cole-a, 7pgs. | 47.00 | 140.00 | 325.00 |
| 2-Intro. The Mask; Rico, Giunta, L. B. Cole-a, 7pgs. | 27.00 | 81.00 | 190.00 |
| 3-L.B. Cole-a; Schomburg-c | 27.00 | 81.00 | 190.00 |
| 4-6: 5-Schomburg-c | 24.00 | 73.00 | 170.00 |
| 7,9,10 | 23.00 | 70.00 | 160.00 |
| 8-Classic L. B. Cole spider-c | 50.00 | 150.00 | 350.00 |
| 11-Classic Devil-c | 36.00 | 107.00 | 250.00 |
| 12-Reprints cover to #7 | 23.00 | 70.00 | 160.00 |

NOTE: ***L. B. Cole** c-6-12. **Larsen** a-11. **Palais** a-10, 11. Bondage c-1, 3, 4.*

**SUSPENSE DETECTIVE**
June, 1952 - No. 5, Mar, 1953
Fawcett Publications

| | Good | Fine | N-Mint |
|---|---|---|---|
| 1-Evans-a (11 pgs); Baily-c/a | 14.00 | 43.00 | 100.00 |
| 2-Evans-a (10 pgs.) | 8.50 | 25.50 | 60.00 |
| 3,5 | 6.50 | 19.00 | 45.00 |
| 4-Bondage-c | 7.00 | 21.00 | 50.00 |

NOTE: ***Baily** a-4, 5. **Sekowsky** a-2, 4, 5; c-5.*

**SUSPENSE STORIES** (See Strange Suspense Stories)

**SUZIE COMICS** (Formerly Laugh Comix; see Laugh Comics, Liberty Comics #10, Pep Comics & Top-Notch Comics #28)
No. 49, Spring, 1945 - No. 100, Aug, 1954
Close-Up No. 49,50/MLJ Mag./Archie No. 51 on

*Superworld Comics #1, © Hugo Gernsback*

*Suspense #18, © MEG*

*Suspense Detective #1, © FAW*

*Swamp Thing #10, © DC*

*Sweethearts #112, © FAW*

*Sweet Sixteen #1, © PMI*

| | Good | Fine | N-Mint |
|---|---|---|---|
| 49-Ginger begins | 13.00 | 40.00 | 90.00 |
| 50-55: 54-Transvestism story | 9.30 | 28.00 | 65.00 |
| 56-Katy Keene begins by Woggon | 8.50 | 25.50 | 60.00 |
| 57-65 | 6.00 | 18.00 | 42.00 |
| 66-80 | 5.30 | 16.00 | 38.00 |
| 81-100: 88-Used in **POP**, pgs. 76,77; Bill Woggon draws himself in story. 100-Last Katy Keene | 4.50 | 14.00 | 32.00 |

NOTE: *Katy Keene app. in 53-82, 85-100.*

**SWAMP FOX, THE** (See 4-Color #1179 & Walt Disney Presents #2)

**SWAMP FOX, THE**
1960 (14 pgs, small size) (Canada Dry Premiums)
Walt Disney Productions

Titles: (A)-Tory Masquerade, (B)-Rindau Rampage, (C)-Turnabout Tactics; each came in paper sleeve, books 1,2 & 3;

| | Good | Fine | N-Mint |
|---|---|---|---|
| Set with sleeves | 3.50 | 10.50 | 24.00 |
| Comic only | 1.00 | 3.00 | 6.00 |

**SWAMP THING** (See Brave & the Bold, Challengers of the Unknown #82, DC Comics Presents #8 & 85, DC Special Series #2, 14, 17, 20, House of Secrets #92, Roots of the . . ., & The Saga of . . .)

**SWAMP THING**
Oct-Nov, 1972 - No. 24, Aug-Sept, 1976
National Periodical Publications/DC Comics

| | Good | Fine | N-Mint |
|---|---|---|---|
| 1-Wrightson-c/a begins | 3.60 | 11.00 | 25.00 |
| 2 | 1.70 | 5.00 | 12.00 |
| 3-Intro. Patchworkman | 1.15 | 3.50 | 8.00 |
| 4-6,8-10: 10-Last Wrightson issue | .85 | 2.60 | 6.00 |
| 7-Batman-c/story | 1.30 | 4.00 | 9.00 |
| 11-24-Redondo-a; 23-Swamp Thing reverts back to Dr. Holland | .25 | .75 | 1.50 |

NOTE: ***J. Jones*** *a-9i(assist).* ***Kaluta*** *a-9i.* ***Redondo*** *c-12-19, 21. Wrightson issues (#1-10) reprinted in DC Special Series #2, 14, 17, 20 & Roots of the Swampthing.*

**SWAT MALONE**
Sept, 1955
Swat Malone Enterprises

| | Good | Fine | N-Mint |
|---|---|---|---|
| V1#1-Hy Fleishman-a | 4.50 | 14.00 | 32.00 |

**SWEENEY** (Formerly Buz Sawyer)
No. 4, 6, 1949 - No. 5, 10, 1949
Standard Comics

| | Good | Fine | N-Mint |
|---|---|---|---|
| 4,5-Crane-a #5 | 4.00 | 12.00 | 28.00 |

**SWEE'PEA** (See 4-Color #219)

**SWEETHEART DIARY** (Cynthia Doyle #66-on)
Wint, 1949; #2, Spr, 1950; #3, 6/50 - #5, 10/50; #6, 1951(nd); #7, 9/51 - #14, 1/53; #32, 10/55; #33, 4/56 - #65, 8/62 (#1-14: photo-c)
Fawcett Publications/Charlton Comics No. 33 on

| | Good | Fine | N-Mint |
|---|---|---|---|
| 1 | 7.00 | 21.00 | 50.00 |
| 2 | 4.00 | 12.00 | 28.00 |
| 3,4-Wood-a | 9.00 | 27.00 | 62.00 |
| 5-10: 8-Bailey-a | 3.00 | 9.00 | 21.00 |
| 11-14-Last Fawcett issue | 1.70 | 5.00 | 12.00 |
| 32 (10/55; 1st Charlton issue)(Formerly Cowboy Love #31) | 1.70 | 5.00 | 12.00 |
| 34-40 | 1.00 | 3.00 | 7.00 |
| 41-60 | .70 | 2.00 | 4.00 |
| 61-65 | .35 | 1.00 | 2.00 |

**SWEETHEARTS** (Formerly Captain Midnight)
#68, 10/48 - #121, 5/53; #122, 3/54; V2#23, 5/54 - #137, 12/73
Fawcett Publications/Charlton No. 122 on

| | Good | Fine | N-Mint |
|---|---|---|---|
| 68-Robert Mitchum photo-c | 7.00 | 21.00 | 50.00 |
| 69-80 | 2.65 | 8.00 | 18.00 |
| 81-84,86-93,95-99 | 1.85 | 5.50 | 13.00 |
| 85,94,103,105,110,117-George Evans-a | 3.00 | 9.00 | 21.00 |
| 100 | 2.30 | 7.00 | 16.00 |
| 101,107-Powell-a | 2.00 | 6.00 | 14.00 |
| 102,104,106,108,109,112-116,118,121 | 1.30 | 4.00 | 9.00 |
| 111-1 pg. Ronald Reagan biography | 3.70 | 11.00 | 26.00 |
| 119-Marilyn Monroe photo-c; also appears in story; part Wood-a | 13.00 | 40.00 | 90.00 |
| 120-Atom Bomb story | 4.50 | 14.00 | 32.00 |
| 122-(1st Charlton? 3/54)-Marijuana story | 2.65 | 8.00 | 18.00 |
| V2#23 (5/54)-28: 28-Last precode issue (2/55) | 1.15 | 3.50 | 8.00 |
| 29-39,41,43-45,47-50 | .85 | 2.60 | 6.00 |
| 40-Photo-c; Tommy Sands story | 1.30 | 4.00 | 9.00 |
| 42-Ricky Nelson photo-c/story | 2.30 | 7.00 | 16.00 |
| 46-Jimmy Rodgers photo-c/story | 1.15 | 3.50 | 8.00 |
| 51-60 | .85 | 2.60 | 6.00 |
| 61-80 | .70 | 2.00 | 4.00 |
| 81-100 | .35 | 1.00 | 2.00 |
| 101-110 | .25 | .75 | 1.50 |
| 111-137 | | .40 | .80 |

NOTE: *Photo c-68-121(Fawcett), 40, 42, 46(Charlton).*

**SWEETHEART SCANDALS** (See Fox Giants)

**SWEETIE PIE** (See 4-Color #1185, 1241)

**SWEETIE PIE**
Dec, 1955 - No. 15, Fall, 1957
Ajax-Farrell/Pines (Literary Ent.)

| | Good | Fine | N-Mint |
|---|---|---|---|
| 1-By Nadine Seltzer | 2.65 | 8.00 | 18.00 |
| 2 (5/56; last Ajax?) | 1.50 | 4.50 | 10.00 |
| 3-15 (#3-10, exist?) | 1.00 | 3.00 | 7.00 |

**SWEET LOVE**
Sept, 1949 - No. 5, May, 1950
Home Comics (Harvey)

| | Good | Fine | N-Mint |
|---|---|---|---|
| 1-Photo-c | 3.00 | 9.00 | 21.00 |
| 2-Photo-c | 1.70 | 5.00 | 12.00 |
| 3,4: 3-Powell-a; 4-Photo-c | 1.50 | 4.50 | 10.00 |
| 5-Kamen, Powell-a; photo-c | 3.00 | 9.00 | 21.00 |

**SWEET ROMANCE**
October, 1968
Charlton Comics

| | Good | Fine | N-Mint |
|---|---|---|---|
| 1 | .35 | 1.00 | 2.00 |

**SWEET SIXTEEN**
Aug-Sept, 1946 - No. 13, Jan, 1948
Parents' Magazine Institute

| | Good | Fine | N-Mint |
|---|---|---|---|
| 1-Van Johnson's life story; Dorothy Dare, Queen of Hollywood Stunt Artists begins (in all issues); part photo-c | 6.50 | 19.00 | 45.00 |
| 2-Jane Powell, Roddy McDowall "Holiday in Mexico" photo-c | 4.00 | 12.00 | 28.00 |
| 3-6,8-11: 6-Dick Haymes story | 2.85 | 8.50 | 20.00 |
| 7-Ronald Reagan's life story | 11.00 | 32.00 | 75.00 |
| 12-Bob Cummings, Vic Damone story | 3.70 | 11.00 | 26.00 |
| 13-Robert Mitchum's life story | 4.30 | 13.00 | 30.00 |

**SWIFT ARROW** (Also see Lone Rider & The Rider)
Feb-Mar, 1954 - No. 5, Oct-Nov, 1954; Apr, 1957 - No. 3, Sept, 1957
Ajax/Farrell Publications

| | Good | Fine | N-Mint |
|---|---|---|---|
| 1(1954) (1st Series) | 5.70 | 17.00 | 40.00 |
| 2 | 2.85 | 8.50 | 20.00 |
| 3-5: 5-Lone Rider story | 2.30 | 7.00 | 16.00 |
| 1 (2nd Series) (Swift Arrow's Gunfighters #4) | 2.30 | 7.00 | 16.00 |
| 2,3: 2-Lone Rider begins | 2.00 | 6.00 | 14.00 |

**SWIFT ARROW'S GUNFIGHTERS** (Formerly Swift Arrow)
No. 4, Nov, 1957
Ajax/Farrell Publ. (Four Star Comic Corp.)

| | Good | Fine | N-Mint |
|---|---|---|---|
| 4 | 2.30 | 7.00 | 16.00 |

**SWING WITH SCOOTER**
June-July, 1966 - No. 35, Aug-Sept, 1971; No. 36, Oct-Nov, 1972
National Periodical Publications

| | Good | Fine | N-Mint |
|---|---|---|---|
| 1 | 1.50 | 4.50 | 10.00 |
| 2-10 | .85 | 2.60 | 6.00 |
| 11-20 | .60 | 1.75 | 3.50 |
| 21-36: 33-Interview with David Cassidy. 34-Interview with Ron Ely (Doc Savage) | .50 | 1.50 | 3.00 |

NOTE: ***Orlando** a-1-11; c-1-11, 13. #20, 33, 34: 68 pgs.; #35: 52 pgs.*

**SWISS FAMILY ROBINSON** (See 4-Color #1156, King Classics & Movie Comics)

**SWORD & THE DRAGON, THE** (See 4-Color #1118)

**SWORD & THE ROSE, THE** (See 4-Color #505, 682)

**SWORD IN THE STONE, THE** (See March of Comics #258 & Movie Comics)

**SWORD OF LANCELOT** (See Movie Comics)

**SWORD OF SORCERY**
Feb-Mar, 1973 - No. 5, Nov-Dec, 1973
National Periodical Publications

| | Good | Fine | N-Mint |
|---|---|---|---|
| 1-Leiber Fafhrd & The Grey Mouser; Neal Adams (Crusty Bunkers) inks; also #2; Kaluta-c | .35 | 1.00 | 2.00 |
| 2-Wrightson-c(i); Neal Adams-a(i) | .25 | .75 | 1.50 |
| 3-5: 5-Starlin-a(p); Conan cameo | | .60 | 1.20 |

NOTE: ***Chaykin** a-1p, 2-4; c-2p, 3-5. **Kaluta** a-3i. **Simonson** a-1i, 3p, 4, 5p; c-5.*

**SWORD OF THE ATOM**
Sept, 1983 - No. 4, Dec, 1983 (Mini-series)
DC Comics

| | Good | Fine | N-Mint |
|---|---|---|---|
| 1-4: Kane-c/a in all | | .50 | 1.00 |
| Special 1(7/84), 2(7/85): Kane-c/a each | | .65 | 1.30 |
| Special 3(6/88, $1.50) | | .65 | 1.30 |

**SWORDS OF TEXAS** (See Scout #15)
Oct, 1987 - No. 4, Jan, 1988 ($1.75, color, Baxter paper)
Eclipse Comics

| | Good | Fine | N-Mint |
|---|---|---|---|
| 1-4: Scout app. | .30 | .90 | 1.80 |

**SWORDS OF THE SWASHBUCKLERS** (See Marvel Graphic Novel)
May, 1985 - No. 12, June,1987 ($1.50; Mature readers)
Epic Comics (Marvel)

| | Good | Fine | N-Mint |
|---|---|---|---|
| 1-12-Butch Guice-c/a cont'd from Marvel G. N. | .25 | .80 | 1.60 |

**SYPHONS**
July, 1986 - No. 7, 1987 ($1.50-$1.75, color)
Now Comics

| | Good | Fine | N-Mint |
|---|---|---|---|
| 1-7 | .25 | .75 | 1.50 |

**TAFFY COMICS**
Mar-Apr, 1945 - No. 12, 1948
Rural Home/Orbit Publ.

| | Good | Fine | N-Mint |
|---|---|---|---|
| 1-L.B. Cole-c; origin of Wiggles The Wonderworm plus 7 chapter WWII funny animal adventures | 7.00 | 21.00 | 50.00 |
| 2-L.B. Cole-c | 4.50 | 14.00 | 32.00 |
| 3,4,6-12: 6-Perry Como-c/story. 7-Duke Ellington, 2pgs. | 3.50 | 10.50 | 24.00 |
| 5-L.B. Cole-c; Van Johnson story | 4.00 | 12.00 | 28.00 |

**TAILGUNNER JO**
Sept, 1988 - No. 6, Jan, 1989 ($1.25, color)
DC Comics

| | Good | Fine | N-Mint |
|---|---|---|---|
| 1-6 | | .60 | 1.25 |

**TAILSPIN**
November, 1944
Spotlight Publishers

| | Good | Fine | N-Mint |
|---|---|---|---|
| nn-Firebird app.; L.B. Cole-c | 8.50 | 25.50 | 60.00 |

**TAILSPIN TOMMY STORY & PICTURE BOOK**
No. 266, 1931? (nd) (Color stip reprints; 10½x10")
McLoughlin Bros.

| | Good | Fine | N-Mint |
|---|---|---|---|
| 266-By Forrest | 16.00 | 48.00 | 110.00 |

**TAILSPIN TOMMY** (Also see Famous Feature Stories & The Funnies)
1932 (100 pages)(hardcover)
Cupples & Leon Co.

| | Good | Fine | N-Mint |
|---|---|---|---|
| nn-(Rare)-B&W strip reprints from 1930 by Hal Forrest & Glenn Claffin | 19.00 | 57.00 | 130.00 |

**TAILSPIN TOMMY** (Also see Popular Comics)
1940; 1946
United Features Syndicate/Service Publ. Co.

| | Good | Fine | N-Mint |
|---|---|---|---|
| Single Series 23('40) | 19.00 | 58.00 | 130.00 |
| Best Seller (nd, '46)-Service Publ. Co. | 9.30 | 28.00 | 65.00 |

**TALENT SHOWCASE** (See New Talent Showcase)

**TALES CALCULATED TO DRIVE YOU BATS**
Nov, 1961 - No. 7, Nov, 1962; 1966 (Satire)
Archie Publications

| | Good | Fine | N-Mint |
|---|---|---|---|
| 1-Only 10 cent issue; has cut-out Werewolf mask (price includes mask) | 4.50 | 14.00 | 32.00 |
| 2-Begin 12 cent issues | 2.30 | 7.00 | 16.00 |
| 3-6 | 1.70 | 5.00 | 12.00 |
| 7-Storyline change | 1.15 | 3.50 | 8.00 |
| 1('66)-25 cents | 1.30 | 4.00 | 9.00 |

**TALES FROM THE CRYPT** (Formerly The Crypt Of Terror; see Three Dimensional . . .)
No. 20, Oct-Nov, 1950 - No. 46, Feb-Mar, 1955
E.C. Comics

| | Good | Fine | N-Mint |
|---|---|---|---|
| 20 | 68.00 | 205.00 | 480.00 |
| 21-Kurtzman-r/Haunt of Fear #15(#1) | 56.00 | 170.00 | 395.00 |
| 22-Moon Girl costume at costume party, one panel | 45.00 | 135.00 | 315.00 |
| 23-25 | 34.00 | 100.00 | 235.00 |
| 26-30 | 27.00 | 81.00 | 190.00 |
| 31-Williamson-a(1st at E.C.); B&W and color illos. in **POP**; Kamen draws himself, Gaines & Feldstein; Ingels, Craig & Davis draw themselves in his story | 31.00 | 92.00 | 215.00 |
| 32,35-39 | 22.00 | 65.00 | 150.00 |
| 33-Origin The Crypt Keeper | 38.00 | 115.00 | 265.00 |
| 34-Used in **POP**, pg. 83; lingerie panels | 22.00 | 65.00 | 150.00 |
| 40-Used in Senate hearings & in Hartford Cournat anti-comics editorials-1954 | 22.00 | 65.00 | 150.00 |
| 41-45: 45-2pgs. showing E.C. staff | 20.00 | 60.00 | 140.00 |
| 46-Low distribution; pre-advertised cover for unpublished 4th horror title 'Crypt of Terror' used on this book | 25.00 | 75.00 | 175.00 |

NOTE: ***Craig** a-20, 22-24; c-20. **Crandall** a-38, 44. **Davis** a-24-46; c-29-46. **Elder** a-37, 38. **Evans** a-32-34, 36, 40, 41, 43, 46. **Feldstein** a-20-23; c-21-25, 28. **Ingels** a-in all. **Kamen** a-20, 22, 25, 27-31, 33-36, 39, 41-45. **Krigstein** a-40, 42, 45. **Kurtzman** a-21. **Orlando** a-27-30, 35, 37, 39, 41-45. **Wood** a-21, 24, 25; c-26, 27. Canadian reprints known; see Table of Contents.*

**TALES FROM THE CRYPT** (Magazine)
No. 10, July, 1968 (35 cents)(B&W)
Eerie Publications

| | Good | Fine | N-Mint |
|---|---|---|---|
| 10-Contains Farrell reprints from 1950s | .85 | 2.60 | 6.00 |

**TALES FROM THE CRYPT**
July, 1990 - Present ($1.95, color, 68 pgs.)(#4 on: $2.00)
Gladstone Publishing

| | Good | Fine | N-Mint |
|---|---|---|---|
| 1-r/TFTC #33 & Crime S.S. #17; Davis-c(r) | .60 | 1.75 | 3.50 |
| 2-Davis-c(r) | .40 | 1.25 | 2.50 |
| 3-5: 3-Davis-c(r). 4-Craig-c(r) | .35 | 1.00 | 2.00 |

**TALES FROM THE GREAT BOOK**
Feb, 1955 - No. 4, Jan, 1956
Famous Funnies

| | Good | Fine | N-Mint |
|---|---|---|---|
| 1-Story of Samson | 3.70 | 11.00 | 26.00 |

*Tales Calculated to Drive You Bats #1, © AP*

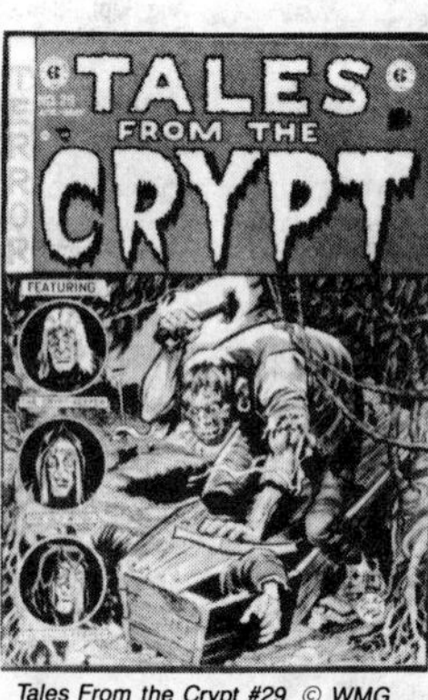

*Tales From the Crypt #29, © WMG*

*Tales From the Crypt #1 (7/90), © WMG*

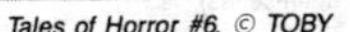

Tales of Horror #6, © TOBY

Tales of Suspense #39, © MEG

Tales of Suspense #74, © MEG

| | Good | Fine | N-Mint |
|---|---|---|---|
| 2-4-Lehti-a in all | 2.00 | 6.00 | 14.00 |

**TALES FROM THE HEART OF AFRICA** (The Temporary Natives)
Aug, 1990 - Present ($3.95, color, 52 pgs.)
Epic Comics (Marvel)

| | Good | Fine | N-Mint |
|---|---|---|---|
| 1 | .70 | 2.00 | 4.00 |

**TALES FROM THE TOMB**
Oct, 1962 - No. 2, Dec, 1962
Dell Publishing Co.

| | Good | Fine | N-Mint |
|---|---|---|---|
| 1(02-810-210)(25 cent Giant)-All stories written by John Stanley | 2.65 | 8.00 | 18.00 |
| 2 | 1.70 | 5.00 | 12.00 |

**TALES FROM THE TOMB** (Magazine)
V1#6, July, 1969 - V7#1, Feb, 1975 (52 pgs.)
Eerie Publications

| | Good | Fine | N-Mint |
|---|---|---|---|
| V1#6-8 | 1.50 | 4.50 | 10.00 |
| V2#1-3,5,6: 6-Rulah-r | .85 | 2.60 | 6.00 |
| 4-LSD story-r/Weird V3#5 | .85 | 2.50 | 6.00 |
| V3#1-Rulah-r | .85 | 2.60 | 6.00 |
| 2-6('70),V4#1-5('72),V5#1-6('73),V6#1-6('74),V7#1('75) | .70 | 2.00 | 4.00 |

**TALES OF ASGARD**
Oct, 1968 (25 cents, 68 pages); Feb, 1984 ($1.25, 52 pgs.)
Marvel Comics Group

| | Good | Fine | N-Mint |
|---|---|---|---|
| 1-Thor r-/from Journey into Mystery #97-106; new Kirby-c | 2.30 | 7.00 | 16.00 |
| V2#1 (2/84)-Thor-r; Simonson-c | | .50 | 1.00 |

**TALES OF DEMON DICK & BUNKER BILL**
1934 (78 pgs; 5x10½''; B&W)(hardcover)
Whitman Publishing Co.

| | Good | Fine | N-Mint |
|---|---|---|---|
| 793-By Dick Spencer | 10.00 | 30.00 | 70.00 |

**TALES OF EVIL**
Feb, 1975 - No. 3, July, 1975
Atlas/Seaboard Publ.

| | Good | Fine | N-Mint |
|---|---|---|---|
| 1-3: 2-Intro. The Bog Beast; Sparling-a. 3-Origin The Man-Monster; Buckler-a(p) | | .30 | .60 |

NOTE: ***Grandenetti** a-1, 2. **Lieber** c-1. **Sekowsky** a-1. **Sutton** a-2. **Thorne** c-2.*

**TALES OF GHOST CASTLE**
May-June, 1975 - No. 3, Sept-Oct, 1975
National Periodical Publications

| | Good | Fine | N-Mint |
|---|---|---|---|
| 1-3: 1,3-Redondo-a. 2-Nino-a | | .35 | .70 |

**TALES OF G.I. JOE**
Jan, 1988 - No. 14, 1989 (Color)
Marvel Comics

| | Good | Fine | N-Mint |
|---|---|---|---|
| 1 ($2.25, 52 pgs.) | .35 | 1.00 | 2.00 |
| 2-14 ($1.50): 1-14-r/G.I. Joe #1-14 | .25 | .75 | 1.50 |

**TALES OF HORROR**
June, 1952 - No. 13, Oct, 1954
Toby Press/Minoan Publ. Corp.

| | Good | Fine | N-Mint |
|---|---|---|---|
| 1 | 13.00 | 40.00 | 90.00 |
| 2-Torture scenes | 9.30 | 28.00 | 65.00 |
| 3-8,13 | 5.70 | 17.00 | 40.00 |
| 9-11-Reprints Purple Claw #1-3 | 6.50 | 19.00 | 45.00 |
| 12-Myron Fass-c/a; torture scenes | 7.00 | 21.00 | 50.00 |

NOTE: ***Andru** a-5. **Bailey** a-5. **Myron Fass** a-2, 3, 12; c-1-3, 12. **Hollingsworth** a-2. **Sparling** a-6, 9; c-9.*

**TALES OF JUSTICE**
No. 53, May, 1955 - No. 67, Aug, 1957
Atlas Comics(MjMC No. 53-66/Male No. 67)

| | Good | Fine | N-Mint |
|---|---|---|---|
| 53 | 6.50 | 19.00 | 45.00 |
| 54-57 | 3.60 | 11.00 | 25.00 |
| 58,59-Krigstein-a | 4.50 | 14.00 | 32.00 |
| 60-63,65 | 2.30 | 7.00 | 16.00 |
| 64,67-Crandall-a | 3.60 | 11.00 | 25.00 |
| 66-Torres, Orlando-a | 3.60 | 11.00 | 25.00 |

NOTE: ***Everett** a-53, 60. **Orlando** a-65, 66. **Powell** a-54. **Severin** c-58, 60, 65.*

**TALES OF SUSPENSE** (Captain America #100 on)
Jan, 1959 - No. 99, March, 1968
Atlas (WPI No. 1,2/Male No. 3-12/VPI No. 13-18)/Marvel No. 19 on

| | Good | Fine | N-Mint |
|---|---|---|---|
| 1-Williamson-a, 5 pgs. | 55.00 | 165.00 | 385.00 |
| 2,3 | 25.00 | 75.00 | 175.00 |
| 4-Williamson-a, 4 pgs; Kirby/Everett c/a | 26.00 | 77.00 | 180.00 |
| 5-10 | 16.00 | 48.00 | 110.00 |
| 11,13-15,17-20: 14-Intro. Colossus | 11.00 | 32.00 | 75.00 |
| 12-Crandall-a | 11.50 | 34.00 | 80.00 |
| 16-1st Metallo (Iron Man prototype) | 12.00 | 36.00 | 85.00 |
| 21-25: 25-Last 10 cent issue | 8.00 | 24.00 | 55.00 |
| 26-38: 32-Sazzik The Sorcerer app. (Dr. Strange prototype) | 5.70 | 17.00 | 40.00 |

| | Good | Fine | N-Mint | Mint |
|---|---|---|---|---|
| 39 (3/63)-Origin/1st app. Iron Man & begin series; 1st Iron Man story has Kirby layouts | 115.00 | 460.00 | 1150.00 | 2100.00 |

(Estimated up to 2100 total copies exist, 55 in Mint)

| | Good | Fine | N-Mint |
|---|---|---|---|
| 40-Iron Man in new armor | 79.00 | 235.00 | 550.00 |
| 41 | 43.00 | 130.00 | 300.00 |
| 42-45: 45-Intro. & 1st app. Happy & Pepper | 18.00 | 54.00 | 125.00 |
| 46,47 | 10.00 | 30.00 | 70.00 |
| 48-New Iron Man armor | 12.00 | 36.90 | 85.00 |
| 49-X-Men x-over (same date as X-Men #3, 1/64); 1st Tales of the Watcher back-up story | 8.00 | 24.00 | 55.00 |
| 50,51: 50-1st app. Mandarin | 6.50 | 19.00 | 45.00 |
| 52-1st app. The Black Widow (4/64) | 9.30 | 28.00 | 65.00 |
| 53-Origin & 2nd app. The Watcher (5/64); 2nd Black Widow app. | 7.00 | 21.00 | 50.00 |
| 54-56 | 4.30 | 13.00 | 30.00 |
| 57-Origin/1st app. Hawkeye (9/64) | 11.00 | 32.00 | 75.00 |
| 58-Captain America battles Iron Man (10/64)-Classic-c; 2nd Kraven app. | 12.00 | 36.00 | 85.00 |
| 59-Iron Man plus Captain America double feature begins (11/64); 1st S.A. Captain America solo story; intro Jarvis, Avenger's butler; classic-c | 16.00 | 48.00 | 110.00 |
| 60 | 5.70 | 17.00 | 40.00 |
| 61,62,64: 62-Origin Mandarin (2/65) | 4.50 | 14.00 | 32.00 |
| 63-1st Silver Age origin Captain America(3/65) | 10.00 | 30.00 | 70.00 |
| 65-1st Silver-Age Red Skull (6/65) | 6.50 | 19.00 | 45.00 |
| 66-Origin Red Skull | 6.50 | 19.00 | 45.00 |
| 67-98: 69-1st app. Titanium Man. 75-1st app. Agent 13 later named Sharon Carter. 76-Intro Batroc & Sharon Carter, Agent 13 of Shield. 79-1st app. Cosmic Cube. 92-1st Nick Fury x-over (as Agent of Shield, 8/67). 94-Intro Modok. 95-Capt. America's i.d. revealed | 2.85 | 8.50 | 20.00 |
| 99-Becomes Captain America with #100 | 2.85 | 8.50 | 20.00 |

NOTE: ***Colan** a-39, 73-99p; c(p)-73, 75, 77, 79, 81, 83, 85-87, 89, 91, 93, 95, 97, 99. **Craig** a-99i. **Crandall** a-12. **Davis** a-38. **Ditko/Kirby** art in most issues #1-15, 17-49. **Everett** a-8. **Forte** a-5, 9. **Heath** a-10. **Gil Kane** a-88p, 89-91; c-88, 89-91p. **Kirby** a(p)-40, 41, 43, 59-75, 77-86, 92-99; layouts-69-75, 77; c(p)-29-56, 58-72, 74, 76, 78, 80, 82, 84, 86, 92, 94, 96, 98. **Leiber/Fox** a-42, 43, 45, 51. **Reinman** a-26, 44i, 49i, 52i, 53i. **Tuska** a-58, 70-74. **Wood** c/a-71i.*

**TALES OF SWORD & SORCERY** (See Dagar)

**TALES OF TERROR**
1952 (no month)
Toby Press Publications

| | Good | Fine | N-Mint |
|---|---|---|---|
| 1-Fawcette-c; Ravielli-a | 6.50 | 19.00 | 45.00 |

NOTE: *This title was cancelled due to similarity to the E.C. title.*

**TALES OF TERROR** (See Movie Classics)

**TALES OF TERROR** (Magazine)
Summer, 1964
Eerie Publications

| | Good | Fine | N-Mint |
|---|---|---|---|
| 1 | 2.15 | 6.50 | 15.00 |

**TALES OF TERROR**
July, 1985 - No. 13, July, 1987 ($2.00, Baxter paper, mature readers)
Eclipse Comics

| | | | |
|---|---|---|---|
| 1: 1-8-($1.75-c) | .40 | 1.25 | 2.50 |
| 2-13: 7-Bissette scripts. 12-Vampire story | .35 | 1.00 | 2.00 |

NOTE: ***Bolton** a-7, 9, 12; painted c-9, 11, 12. **Chiodo** painted c-7. **Morrow** a-3.*

**TALES OF TERROR ANNUAL**
1951 - No. 3, 1953 (25 cents) (132 pgs.)
E.C. Comics

| | Good | Fine | VF-NM | NM/Mint |
|---|---|---|---|---|
| nn(1951)(Scarce)-Feldstein infinity-c | 230.00 | 685.00 | 1600.00 | 2600.00 |

(Estimated up to 85 total copies exist, 6 in NM/Mint)

| | Good | Fine | N-Mint |
|---|---|---|---|
| 2(1952)-Feldstein-c | 107.00 | 320.00 | 750.00 |
| 3(1953) | 79.00 | 235.00 | 550.00 |

NOTE: No. 1 contains three horror and one science fiction comic which came out in 1950. No. 2 contains a horror, crime, and science fiction book which generally had cover dates in 1951, and No. 3 had horror, crime, and shock books that generally appeared in 1952. All E.C. annuals contain four complete books that did not sell on the stands which were rebound in the annual format, minus the covers, and sold from the E.C. office and on the stands in key cities. The contents of each annual may vary in the same year.

**TALES OF TERROR ILLUSTRATED** (See Terror Illustrated)

**TALES OF TEXAS JOHN SLAUGHTER** (See 4-Color #997)

**TALES OF THE BEANWORLD**
Feb, 1985 - Present ($1.50/$2.00, B&W)
Beanworld Press/Eclipse Comics

| | | | |
|---|---|---|---|
| 1 | 1.70 | 5.00 | 10.00 |
| 2 | .70 | 2.00 | 4.00 |
| 3-17 | .35 | 1.00 | 2.00 |

**TALES OF THE GREEN BERET**
Jan, 1967 - No. 5, Oct, 1969
Dell Publishing Co.

| | | | |
|---|---|---|---|
| 1 | 1.30 | 4.00 | 9.00 |
| 2-5: 5 reprints #1 | .85 | 2.60 | 6.00 |

NOTE: ***Glanzman** a 1-4, 5r.*

**TALES OF THE GREEN HORNET**
Sept, 1990 - No. 2, Oct?, 1990 ($1.75, color, mini-series)
Now Comics

| | | | |
|---|---|---|---|
| 1-Painted-c/a; 1960s Green Hornet & Kato | .40 | 1.25 | 2.50 |
| 2-Painted-c/a | .35 | 1.00 | 2.00 |

**TALES OF THE GREEN LANTERN CORPS** (See Green Lantern 107)
May, 1981 - No. 3, July, 1981
DC Comics

| | | | |
|---|---|---|---|
| 1-Origin of G.L. & the Guardians; Staton-a(p) | | .50 | 1.00 |
| 2,3-Staton-a(p) | | .40 | .80 |
| Annual 1 (1/85)-Gil Kane-c/a | | .65 | 1.30 |

**TALES OF THE INVISIBLE SCARLET O'NEIL** (See Harvey Comics Hits #59)

**TALES OF THE KILLERS** (Magazine)
V1#10, Dec, 1970 - V1#11, Feb, 1971 (B&W, 52pgs.)
World Famous Periodicals

| | | | |
|---|---|---|---|
| V1#10-One pg. Frazetta | 1.50 | 4.50 | 10.00 |
| 11 | .70 | 2.00 | 5.00 |

**TALES OF THE LEGION** (. . . of Super-Heroes #332 on; formerly The Legion of Super-Heroes)
No. 314, Aug, 1984 - No. 354, Dec, 1987 (75 cents; 353,354: $1.00-c)
DC Comics

| | Good | Fine | N-Mint |
|---|---|---|---|
| 314-320: 314-Origin The White Witch | | .50 | 1.00 |
| 321-354: r-/Legion of S.H. (Baxter series) | | .50 | 1.00 |
| Annual 4 (1986), 5 (1987) | | .60 | 1.20 |

**TALES OF THE MARINES** (Formerly Devil-Dog Dugan #1-3)
No. 4, Feb, 1957 (Marines At War #5 on)
Atlas Comics (OPI)

| | | | |
|---|---|---|---|
| 4-Powell-a | 1.70 | 5.00 | 12.00 |

**TALES OF THE MYSTERIOUS TRAVELER** (See Mysterious . . .)
Aug, 1956 - No. 13, June, 1959; V2#14, Oct, 1985 - No. 15, Dec, 1985
Charlton Comics

| | | | |
|---|---|---|---|
| 1-No Ditko-a | 17.00 | 51.00 | 120.00 |
| 2-Ditko-a(1) | 14.00 | 40.00 | 95.00 |
| 3-Ditko-c/a(1) | 12.00 | 36.00 | 85.00 |
| 4-6-Ditko-c/a(3-4 stories each) | 19.00 | 56.00 | 130.00 |
| 7-9-Ditko-a(1-2 each) | 12.00 | 36.00 | 85.00 |
| 10,11-Ditko-c/a(3-4 each) | 15.00 | 45.00 | 105.00 |
| 12,13 | 5.30 | 16.00 | 38.00 |
| V2#14,15 (1985)-Ditko-c/a | | .40 | .80 |

**TALES OF THE NEW TEEN TITANS**
June, 1982 - No. 4, Sept, 1982 (Mini-series)
DC Comics

| | | | |
|---|---|---|---|
| 1-Origin Cyborg-book length story; Perez-c/a | .35 | 1.00 | 2.00 |
| 2-4: 2-Origin Raven. 3-Origin Changeling. 4-Origin Starfire; all issues contain Perez-c/a(p) | .25 | .75 | 1.50 |

**TALES OF THE PONY EXPRESS** (See 4-Color #829, 942)

**TALES OF THE SUN RUNNERS**
V2#1, July, 1986 - V2#3, 1986? ($1.50, color)
Sirius Comics/Amazing Comics No. 3

| | | | |
|---|---|---|---|
| V2#1 | .25 | .75 | 1.50 |
| V2#2,3 ($1.95) | .35 | 1.00 | 2.00 |
| Christmas Special 1(12/86) | .25 | .75 | 1.50 |

**TALES OF THE TEENAGE MUTANT NINJA TURTLES**
May, 1987 - No. 7, Apr, 1989 (B&W, $1.50)(See Teenage Mutant . . .)
Mirage Studios

| | | | |
|---|---|---|---|
| 1 | 1.10 | 3.25 | 6.50 |
| 2-7: Title merges w/Teenage Mutant Ninja . . . | .60 | 1.75 | 3.50 |

**TALES OF THE TEEN TITANS** (Formerly The New Teen Titans)
No. 41, April, 1984 - No. 91, July, 1988 (75 cents)
DC Comics

| | | | |
|---|---|---|---|
| 41-43,45-59: 43-1st app. Terminator. 46-Aqualad & Aquagirl join. 50-Double size. 53-Intro Azreal. 56-Intro Jinx. 57-Neutron app. 59-r/DC Comics Presents #26 | | .40 | .80 |
| 44-Dick Grayson becomes Nightwing (3rd to be Nightwing) & joins Titans; Jericho joins also; origin Terminator | .85 | 2.50 | 5.00 |
| 60-91: r/New Teen Titans Baxter series. 68-B. Smith-c. 70-Origin Kole. #83-91 are $1.00 cover | | .40 | .80 |
| Annual 3('84; $1.25)-Death of Terra | | .60 | 1.20 |
| Annual 4(11/86, reprints), 5('87) | | .60 | 1.20 |

**TALES OF THE TEXAS RANGERS** (See Jace Pearson . . .)

**TALES OF THE UNEXPECTED** (The Unexpected #105 on)(See Super DC Giant)
Feb-Mar, 1956 - No. 104, Dec-Jan, 1967-68
National Periodical Publications

| | | | |
|---|---|---|---|
| 1 | 43.00 | 130.00 | 300.00 |
| 2 | 19.00 | 56.00 | 130.00 |
| 3-5 | 11.50 | 34.00 | 80.00 |
| 6-10 | 8.50 | 25.50 | 60.00 |
| 11,14 | 5.00 | 15.00 | 35.00 |
| 12,13,15-18,21-24: All have Kirby-a. 16-Character named 'Thor' with a magic hammer (not like later Thor) | 5.70 | 17.00 | 40.00 |

*Tales of Terror Annual #1, © WMG*

*Tales of the Mysterious Traveler #8, © CC*

*Tales of the Teenage Mutant . . . #1, © Mirage*

Tales of the Unexpected #78, © DC

Tales to Astonish #35, © MEG

Tales to Astonish #63, © MEG

| | Good | Fine | N-Mint |
|---|---|---|---|
| 19,20,25-39 | 3.60 | 11.00 | 25.00 |
| 40-Space Ranger begins (8/59), ends #82 (1st app. in Showcase #15) | 24.00 | 71.00 | 165.00 |
| 41 | 5.70 | 17.00 | 40.00 |
| 42-50 | 4.30 | 13.00 | 30.00 |
| 51-67: 67-Last 10 cent issue | 3.15 | 9.50 | 22.00 |
| 68-82: 82-Last Space Ranger | 1.70 | 5.00 | 12.00 |
| 83-100: 91-1st Automan (also in #94,97) | 1.15 | 3.50 | 8.00 |
| 101-104 | .85 | 2.60 | 6.00 |

NOTE: ***Neal Adams** c-104. **Anderson** a-50. **Brown** a-50-82(Space Ranger). **Cameron** c/a-24. **Heath** a-31, 49. **Bob Kane** a-24, 48. **Kirby** a-12, 13, 15-18, 21-24; c-18, 22. **Meskin** a-15, 18, 26, 27, 35, 66. **Moreira** a-16, 39, 38, 44, 62; c-38.*

**TALES OF THE WEST** (See 3-D...)

**TALES OF THE WIZARD OF OZ** (See 4-Color #1308)

**TALES OF THE ZOMBIE** (Magazine)
Aug, 1973 - No. 10, Mar, 1975 (75 cents)(B&W)
Marvel Comics Group

| | Good | Fine | N-Mint |
|---|---|---|---|
| V1#1-Reprint/Menace #5; origin | 1.50 | 4.50 | 10.00 |
| 2,3: 2-Everett biography & memorial | .85 | 2.60 | 6.00 |
| V2#1(#4)-Photos & text of James Bond movie "Live & Let Die" | .70 | 2.00 | 5.00 |
| 5-10: 8-Kaluta-a | .70 | 2.00 | 5.00 |
| Annual 1(Summer,'75)(#11)-B&W; Everett, Buscema-a | .70 | 2.00 | 5.00 |

NOTE: ***Alcala** a-7-9. **Boris** c-1-4. **Colan** a-2r, 6. **Heath** a-5r. **Reese** a-2. **Tuska** a-2r.*

**TALES OF THUNDER**
March, 1985
Deluxe Comics

| | Good | Fine | N-Mint |
|---|---|---|---|
| 1-Dynamo, Iron Maiden & Menthor app.; Giffen-a | .35 | 1.00 | 2.00 |

**TALES OF VOODOO** (Magazine)
V1#11, Nov, 1968 - V7#6, Nov, 1974
Eerie Publications

| | Good | Fine | N-Mint |
|---|---|---|---|
| V1#11 | 1.70 | 5.00 | 12.00 |
| V2#1(3/69)-V2#4(9/69) | .85 | 2.60 | 6.00 |
| V3#1-6('70): 4-'Claws of the Cat' redrawn from Climax #1 | .70 | 2.00 | 5.00 |
| V4#1-6('71), V5#1-6('72), V6#1-6('73), V7#1-6('74) | .70 | 2.00 | 5.00 |
| Annual 1 | .75 | 2.25 | 5.25 |

NOTE: *Bondage-c-V1#10, V2#4, V3#4.*

**TALES OF WELLS FARGO** (See 4-Color #876, 968, 1023,1075, 1113, 1167, 1215, & Western Roundup under Dell Giants)

**TALESPIN LIMITED SERIES** (See Disney's...)

**TALES TO ASTONISH** (Becomes The Incredible Hulk #102 on)
Jan, 1959 - No. 101, March, 1968
Atlas (MAP No. 1/ZPC No. 2-14/VPI No. 15-21/Marvel No. 22 on

| | Good | Fine | N-Mint |
|---|---|---|---|
| 1-Jack Davis-a | 55.00 | 165.00 | 385.00 |
| 2-Ditko-c | 25.00 | 75.00 | 175.00 |
| 3-5: 5-Williamson-a (4 pgs.) | 19.00 | 58.00 | 135.00 |
| 6-10 | 16.00 | 48.00 | 110.00 |
| 11-20 | 9.30 | 28.00 | 65.00 |
| 21-26,28-34 | 5.70 | 17.00 | 40.00 |

27-1st Antman app. (1/62); last 10 cent issue

| Good | Fine | N-Mint | Mint |
|---|---|---|---|
| 129.00 | 385.00 | 900.00 | 1600.00 |

(Estimated up to 1600 total copies exist, 50 in Mint)

| | Good | Fine | N-Mint |
|---|---|---|---|
| 35-(9/62)-2nd app. Antman, 1st in costume; begin series | 90.00 | 270.00 | 630.00 |
| 36 | 40.00 | 120.00 | 280.00 |
| 37-40 | 19.00 | 58.00 | 135.00 |
| 41-43 | 11.50 | 34.00 | 80.00 |
| 44-Origin & 1st app. The Wasp (6/63) | 13.00 | 40.00 | 90.00 |
| 45-48: 46-1st Crimson Dynamo | 8.00 | 24.00 | 55.00 |
| 49-Antman becomes Giant Man | 11.50 | 34.00 | 80.00 |
| 50-56,58: 50-Origin/1st app. Human Top. 52-Origin/1st app. Black Knight (2/64) | 4.30 | 13.00 | 30.00 |
| 57-Early Spider-Man app. (7/64) | 7.00 | 21.00 | 50.00 |
| 59-Giant Man vs. Hulk feature story | 8.50 | 25.50 | 60.00 |
| 60-Giant Man/Hulk double feature begins | 11.50 | 34.00 | 80.00 |
| 61-69: 62-1st app./origin The Leader; new Wasp costume. 65-New Giant Man costume. 68-New Human Top costume. 69-Last Giant Man | 4.30 | 13.00 | 30.00 |
| 70-Sub-Mariner & Incredible Hulk begins | 6.50 | 19.00 | 45.00 |
| 71-81,83-91,94-99,101: 90-1st app. The Abomination | 3.15 | 9.50 | 22.00 |
| 82-1st Iron Man x-over (outside The Avengers) | 4.30 | 13.00 | 30.00 |
| 92,93-1st Silver Surfer x-over (outside of F.F., 7/67 & 8/67) | 4.30 | 13.00 | 30.00 |
| 100-Hulk battles Sub-Mariner | 4.30 | 13.00 | 30.00 |

NOTE: ***Berg** a-1. **Burgos** a-62-64p. **Buscema** a-85-87p. **Colan** a(p)-70-76, 78-82, 84, 85, 101; c(p)-71-76, 78, 80, 82, 84, 86, 88, 90. **Ditko** a-most issues-1-48, 50i, 60-67. **Everett** a-78, 79i, 80-84, 85-90i, 94i, 95, 96; c(i)-79-81, 83, 86, 88. **Forte** a-6. **Kane** a-76, 88-91; c-89, 91. **Kirby** a(p)-1-34(most), 35-40, 44, 49-51, 68-70, 82, 83; layouts-71-84; c(p)-1-48, 50-70, 72, 73, 75, 77, 78, 79, 81, 85, 90. **Leiber/Fox** a-47, 48, 50, 51. **Powell** a-65-69p, 73, 74. **Reinman** a-6, 36, 45, 46, 54i, 56-60i.*

**TALES TO ASTONISH** (2nd Series)
Dec, 1979 - No. 14, Jan, 1981
Marvel Comics Group

| | Good | Fine | N-Mint |
|---|---|---|---|
| V1#1-Reprints Sub-Mariner #1 by Buscema | | .40 | .80 |
| 2-14: Reprints Sub-Mariner #2-14 | | .35 | .70 |

**TALES TO HOLD YOU SPELLBOUND** (See Spellbound)

**TALKING KOMICS**
1957 (20 pages) (Slick covers)
Belda Record & Publ. Co.

| | Good | Fine | N-Mint |
|---|---|---|---|
| Each comic contained a record that followed the story - much like the Golden Record sets. Known titles: Chirpy Cricket, Lonesome Octopus, Sleepy Santa, Grumpy Shark, Flying Turtle, Happy Grasshopper with records... | .85 | 2.60 | 6.00 |

**TALLY-HO COMICS**
December, 1944
Swappers Quarterly (Baily Publ. Co.)

| | Good | Fine | N-Mint |
|---|---|---|---|
| nn-Frazetta's 1st work as Giunta's assistant; Man in Black horror story; violence; Giunta-c | 22.00 | 65.00 | 150.00 |

**TALOS OF THE WILDERNESS SEA**
Aug, 1987 ($2.00, color, One Shot)
DC Comics

| | Good | Fine | N-Mint |
|---|---|---|---|
| 1 | .35 | 1.00 | 2.00 |

**TALULLAH** (See Comic Books Series I)

**TAMMY, TELL ME TRUE** (See 4-Color #1233)

**TAPPING THE VEIN** (Clive Barker's ...)
1989 - Present ($6.95, color, adults, squarebound, 68 pgs.)
Eclipse Comics

| | Good | Fine | N-Mint |
|---|---|---|---|
| Book 1-4: 1-Russell-a, Bolton-c. 2-Bolton-a | 1.15 | 3.50 | 7.00 |

**TARANTULA** (See Weird Suspense)

**TARGET: AIRBOY**
Mar, 1988 ($1.95, color)
Eclipse Comics

| | Good | Fine | N-Mint |
|---|---|---|---|
| 1 | .35 | 1.00 | 2.00 |

**TARGET COMICS** (...Western Romances #106 on)
Feb, 1940 - V10#3 (#105), Aug-Sept, 1949
Funnies, Inc./Novelty Publications/Star Publications

| | Good | Fine | N-Mint |
|---|---|---|---|
| V1#1-Origin & 1st app. Manowar, The White Streak by Burgos, & Bulls-Eye Bill by Everett; City Editor (ends #5), High Grass Twins by Jack Cole(ends #4), T-Men by Joe Simon(ends #9), Rip Rory (ends #4), Fantastic Feature Films by Tarpe Mills (ends #39, & Calling 2-R(ends #14) begin; Marijuana use story | 182.00 | 550.00 | 1275.00 |
| 2 | 86.00 | 257.00 | 600.00 |
| 3,4 | 61.00 | 182.00 | 425.00 |
| 5-Origin The White Streak in text; Space Hawk by Wolverton begins (See Blue Bolt & Circus) | 143.00 | 430.00 | 1000.00 |
| 6-The Chameleon by Everett begins; White Streak origin cont'd. in text | 81.00 | 242.00 | 565.00 |
| 7-Wolverton Spacehawk-c (Scarce) | 186.00 | 557.00 | 1300.00 |
| 8,9,12 | 59.00 | 175.00 | 410.00 |
| 10-Intro. & 1st app. The Target; Kirby-c | 84.00 | 250.00 | 585.00 |
| 11-Origin The Target & The Targeteers | 80.00 | 240.00 | 560.00 |
| V2#1-Target by Bob Wood; flag-c | 43.00 | 130.00 | 300.00 |
| 2-10-part Treasure Island serial begins; Harold Delay-a; reprinted in Catholic Comics V3#1-10 (See Key Comics #5) | 41.00 | 122.00 | 285.00 |
| 3-5: 4-Kit Carter, The Cadet begins | 30.00 | 90.00 | 210.00 |
| 6-9:Red Seal with White Streak in 6-10 | 30.00 | 90.00 | 210.00 |
| 10-Classic-c | 36.00 | 107.00 | 250.00 |
| 11,12: 12-10-part Last of the Mohicans serial begins; Delay-a | 30.00 | 90.00 | 210.00 |
| V3#1-10-Last Wolverton issue. 8-Flag-c; 6-part Gulliver Travels serial begins; Delay-a | 30.00 | 90.00 | 210.00 |
| 11,12 | 5.30 | 16.00 | 38.00 |
| V4#1-5,7-12 | 3.15 | 9.50 | 22.00 |
| 6-Targetoons by Wolverton, 1 pg. | 3.15 | 9.50 | 22.00 |
| V5#1-8 | 2.65 | 8.00 | 18.00 |
| V6#1-10, V7#1-12 | 2.30 | 7.00 | 16.00 |
| V8#1,3-5,8,9,11,12 | 2.00 | 6.00 | 14.00 |
| 2,6,7-Krigstein-a | 2.65 | 8.00 | 18.00 |
| 10-L.B. Cole-c | 5.30 | 16.00 | 38.00 |
| V9#1,3,6,8,10,12, V10#2-L.B. Cole-c | 5.30 | 16.00 | 38.00 |
| V9#2,4,5,7,9,11, V10#1,3 | 2.00 | 6.00 | 14.00 |

NOTE: ***Jack Cole** a-1-8. **Everett** a-1-9. **Tarpe Mills** a-1-4, 6, 8, 11, V3#1. **Rico** a-V7#4, 10, V8#5, 6, V9#3. **Simon** a-1, 2.*

**TARGET: THE CORRUPTORS** (TV)
No. 1306, Mar-May, 1962 - No. 3, Oct-Dec, 1962 (All Photo-c)
Dell Publishing Co.

| | Good | Fine | N-Mint |
|---|---|---|---|
| 4-Color 1306(#1), #2,3 | 2.30 | 7.00 | 16.00 |

**TARGET WESTERN ROMANCES** (Formerly Target Comics)
No. 106, Oct-Nov, 1949 - No. 107, Dec-Jan, 1949-50
Star Publications

| | Good | Fine | N-Mint |
|---|---|---|---|
| 106-Silhouette nudity panel; L.B. Cole-c | 13.00 | 40.00 | 90.00 |
| 107-L.B. Cole-c; lingerie panels | 10.00 | 30.00 | 70.00 |

**TARGITT**
March, 1975 - No. 3, July, 1975
Atlas/Seaboard Publ.

| | Good | Fine | N-Mint |
|---|---|---|---|
| 1-Origin; Nostrand-a in all | | .30 | .60 |
| 2,3: 2-1st in costume | | .25 | .50 |

**TARZAN** (See Aurora, Comics on Parade, Crackajack, DC 100-Page Super Spec., Famous Feat. Stories 1, Golden Comics Digest #4,9, Jeep Comics 1-29, Jungle Tales of...., Limited Coll. Edition, Popular, Sparkler, Sport Stars 1, Tip Top & Top Comics)

**TARZAN**
No. 5, 1939 - No. 161, Aug, 1947
Dell Publishing Co./United Features Syndicate

| | Good | Fine | N-Mint |
|---|---|---|---|
| Large Feature Comic 5('39)-(Scarce)-By Hal Foster; r-1st dailies from 1929 | 88.00 | 265.00 | 615.00 |
| Single Series 20(:40)-By Hal Foster | 79.00 | 235.00 | 550.00 |
| 4-Color 134(2/47)-Marsh-a | 45.00 | 135.00 | 315.00 |
| 4-Color 161(8/47)-Marsh-a | 40.00 | 120.00 | 280.00 |

**TARZAN** (. . .of the Apes #138 on)
1-2/48 - No. 131, 7-8/62; No. 132, 11/62 - No. 206, 2/72
Dell Publishing Co./Gold Key No. 132 on

| | Good | Fine | N-Mint |
|---|---|---|---|
| 1-Jesse Marsh-a begins | 79.00 | 235.00 | 550.00 |
| 2 | 47.00 | 140.00 | 325.00 |
| 3-5 | 34.00 | 103.00 | 240.00 |
| 6-10: 6-1st Tantor the Elephant. 7-1st Valley of the Monsters | 27.00 | 81.00 | 190.00 |
| 11-15: 11-Two Against the Jungle begins, ends #24. 13-Lex Barker photo-c begin | 23.00 | 70.00 | 160.00 |
| 16-20 | 17.00 | 51.00 | 120.00 |
| 21-24,26-30 | 13.00 | 40.00 | 90.00 |
| 25-1st "Brothers of the Spear" episode; series ends #156,160,161, 196-206 | 16.00 | 48.00 | 110.00 |
| 31-40 | 8.00 | 24.00 | 55.00 |
| 41-54: Last Barker photo-c | 6.50 | 19.00 | 45.00 |
| 55-60: 56-Eight pg. Boy story | 5.00 | 15.00 | 35.00 |
| 61,62,64-70 | 4.00 | 12.00 | 28.00 |
| 63-Two Tarzan stories, 1 by Manning | 4.30 | 13.00 | 30.00 |
| 71-79 | 3.15 | 9.50 | 22.00 |
| 80-99: 80-Gordon Scott photo-c begin | 3.50 | 10.50 | 24.00 |
| 100 | 4.30 | 13.00 | 30.00 |
| 101-109 | 2.85 | 8.50 | 20.00 |
| 110 (Scarce)-Last photo-c | 3.15 | 9.50 | 22.00 |
| 111-120 | 2.30 | 7.00 | 16.00 |
| 121-131: Last Dell issue | 1.70 | 5.00 | 12.00 |
| 132-154: 132-1st Gold Key issue | 1.50 | 4.50 | 10.00 |
| 155-Origin Tarzan | 1.70 | 5.00 | 12.00 |
| 156-161: 157-Banlu, Dog of the Arande begins, ends #159, 195. 169-Leopard Girl app. | 1.00 | 3.00 | 7.00 |
| 162,165,168,171 (TV)-Ron Ely photo covers | 1.30 | 4.00 | 9.00 |
| 163,164,166-167,169-170: 169-Leopard Girl app. | .85 | 2.60 | 6.00 |
| 172-199,201-206: 178-Tarzan origin r-/#155; Leopard Girl app, also in #179,190-193 | .70 | 2.00 | 5.00 |
| 200 (Scarce) | .85 | 2.60 | 6.00 |
| Story Digest 1(6/70)-G.K. | .85 | 2.60 | 6.00 |

NOTE: *#162, 165, 168, 171 are TV issues. #1-153 all have **Marsh** art on Tarzan. #154-161, 163, 164, 166, 167, 172-177 all have **Manning** art on Tarzan. #178, 202 have **Manning** Tarzan reprints. No "Brothers of the Spear" in #1-24, 157-159, 162-195. #39-126, 128-156 all have **Russ Manning** art on "Brothers of the Spear." #196-201, 203-205 all have **Manning** B.O.T.S. reprints; #25-38, 127 all have **Jesse Marsh** art on B.O.T.S. #206 has a **Marsh** B.O.T.S. reprint. **Doug Wildey** art-#179-187. Many issues have front and back photo covers.*

**TARZAN** (Continuation of Gold Key series)
No. 207, April, 1972 - No. 258, Feb, 1977
National Periodical Publications

| | Good | Fine | N-Mint |
|---|---|---|---|
| 207-Origin Tarzan by Joe Kubert, part 1; John Carter begins (origin); 52 pg. issues thru #209 | .70 | 2.00 | 4.00 |
| 208-210: Origin, parts 2-4. 209-Last John Carter. 210-Kubert-a | .35 | 1.00 | 2.00 |
| 211-Hogarth, Kubert-a | .25 | .75 | 1.50 |
| 212-214: Adaptations from "Jungle Tales of Tarzan." 213-Beyond the Farthest Star begins, ends #218 | .25 | .75 | 1.50 |
| 215-218,224,225-All by Kubert. 215-part Foster-r | .25 | .75 | 1.50 |
| 219-223: "The Return of Tarzan" by Kubert | .25 | .75 | 1.50 |
| 226-229: 226-Manning-a | .25 | .75 | 1.50 |
| 230-100 pgs.; Kubert, Kaluta-a(p); Korak begins, ends #234; Carson of Venus app. | .35 | 1.00 | 2.00 |
| 231-234: Adapts "Tarzan and the Lion Man;" all 100 pgs.; Rex, the Wonder Dog r-#232, 233 | .25 | .75 | 1.50 |
| 235-Last Kubert issue; 100 pgs. | .25 | .75 | 1.50 |
| 236-258: 238-(68 pgs.). 240-243 adapts "Tarzan & the Castaways." 250-256 adapts "Tarzan the Untamed." 252,253-r/#213 | .25 | .75 | 1.50 |

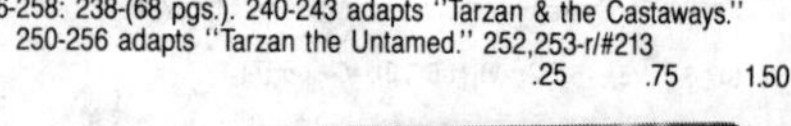

*Target Comics V2#10, © NOVP*

*Tarzan #5, © ERB*

*Tarzan #95, © ERB*

*Tarzan, Lord of the Jungle #1, © ERB*

*Team America #11, © MEG*

*Teen-Age Brides #1, © HARV*

| | Good | Fine | N-Mint |
|---|---|---|---|
| Comic Digest 1(Fall,'72)(DC)-50 cents; 160 pgs.; digest size; Kubert-c, Manning-a | .50 | 1.50 | 3.00 |

NOTE: ***Anderson*** *a-207, 209, 217, 218.* ***Chaykin*** *a-216.* ***Finlay*** *a(r)-212.* ***Foster*** *strip-r #207-209, 211, 212, 221.* ***Heath*** *a-230i.* ***G. Kane*** *a-232p, 233p.* ***Kubert*** *a-207-225, 227-235, 257r, 258r; c-207-249, 253.* ***Lopez*** *a-250-550p; c-250p, 251, 252, 254.* ***Manning*** *strip-r 230-235, 238.* ***Morrow*** *a-208.* ***Nino*** *a-231-234.* ***Sparling*** *a-230.* ***Starr*** *a-233r.*

**TARZAN**
June, 1977 - No. 29, Oct, 1979
Marvel Comics Group

| | Good | Fine | N-Mint |
|---|---|---|---|
| 1 | | .35 | .70 |
| 2-29: 2-Origin by John Buscema | | .25 | .50 |
| Annual 1 (1977) | | .35 | .70 |
| Annual 2 (1978), Annual 3 (1979) | | .25 | .50 |

NOTE: ***N. Adams*** *c-11i, 12i.* ***Alcala*** *a-9i, 10i; c-8i, 9i.* ***Buckler*** *c-25-27p, Annual 3p.* ***John Buscema*** *a-1-3, 4-18p, Annual 1; c-1-7, 8p, 9p, 10, 11p, 12p, 13, 14-19p, 21p, 22, 23p, 24p, 28p, Annual 1.* ***Mooney*** *a-22i.* ***Nebres*** *a-22i.* ***Russell*** *a-29i.*

**TARZAN BOOK** (The Illustrated. . .)
1929 (80 pages)(7x9")
Grosset & Dunlap

| | Good | Fine | N-Mint |
|---|---|---|---|
| 1(Rare)-Contains 1st B&W Tarzan newspaper comics from 1929. Cloth reinforced spine & dust jacket (50 cents); Foster-c | | | |
| with dust jacket. . . | 50.00 | 150.00 | 350.00 |
| without dust jacket. . . | 22.00 | 65.00 | 154.00 |
| 2nd Printing(1934)-76 pgs.; 25 cents; 4 Foster pages dropped; paper spine, circle in lower right cover with 25 cents price. The 25 cents is barely visible on some copies | 15.00 | 45.00 | 105.00 |
| 1967-House of Greystoke reprint-7x10", using the complete 300 illustrations/text from the 1929 edition minus the original indicia, foreword, etc. Initial version bound in gold paper & sold for $5. Officially titled **Burroughs Biblophile #2**. A very few additional copies were bound in heavier blue paper. | | | |
| Gold binding. . . | 2.65 | 8.00 | 18.00 |
| Blue binding. . . | 3.50 | 10.50 | 24.00 |

**TARZAN FAMILY, THE** (Formerly Korak, Son of Tarzan)
No. 60, Nov-Dec, 1975 - No. 66, Nov-Dec, 1976
(No. 60-62: 68 pgs.; No. 63 on: 52 pgs.)
National Periodical Publications

| | Good | Fine | N-Mint |
|---|---|---|---|
| 60-66: 60-Korak begins; Kaluta-r | | .40 | .80 |

NOTE: *Carson of Venus-r 60-65. New John Carter-62-64, 65r, 66r. New Korak-60-66. Pellucidar feature-66.* ***Foster*** *strip r-60(9/4/32-10/16/32), 62(6/29/32-7/31/32), 63(10/11/31-12/13/31).* ***Kaluta*** *Carson of Venus-60-65.* ***Kubert*** *a-61, 64; c-60-64.* ***Manning*** *strip-r 60-62, 64.* ***Morrow*** *a-66r.*

**TARZAN KING OF THE JUNGLE** (See Dell Giant #37,51)

**TARZAN, LORD OF THE JUNGLE**
Sept, 1965 (Giant)(soft paper cover)(25 cents)
Gold Key

| | Good | Fine | N-Mint |
|---|---|---|---|
| 1-Marsh-r | 3.50 | 10.50 | 24.00 |

**TARZAN MARCH OF COMICS** (See March of Comics #82, 98, 114, 125, 144, 155, 172, 185, 204, 223, 240, 252, 262, 272, 286, 300, 332, 342, 354, 366)

**TARZAN OF THE APES**
1934? (Hardcover, 68 pgs., 4X12")
Metropolitan Newspaper Service

| | Good | Fine | N-Mint |
|---|---|---|---|
| 1-Strip reprints | 11.50 | 34.00 | 80.00 |

**TARZAN OF THE APES**
July, 1984 - No. 2, Aug, 1984 (Movie adaptation)
Marvel Comics Group

| | Good | Fine | N-Mint |
|---|---|---|---|
| 1,2: Origin-r/Marvel Super Spec. | | .30 | .60 |

**TARZAN OF THE APES TO COLOR**
No. 988, 1933 (24 pages)(10¾x15¼")(Coloring book)
Saalfield Publishing Co.

| | Good | Fine | N-Mint |
|---|---|---|---|
| 988-(Very Rare)-Contains 1929 daily-r with some new art by Hal Foster. Two panels blown up large on each page; 25 percent in color; believed to be the only time these panels ever appeared in color | 82.00 | 245.00 | 575.00 |

**TARZAN'S JUNGLE ANNUAL** (See Dell Giants)

**TARZAN'S JUNGLE WORLD** (See Dell Giant #25)

**TASMANIAN DEVIL & HIS TASTY FRIENDS**
November, 1962
Gold Key

| | Good | Fine | N-Mint |
|---|---|---|---|
| 1-Bugs Bunny & Elmer Fudd x-over | 4.00 | 12.00 | 28.00 |

**TASTEE-FREEZ COMICS**
1957 (36 pages)(10 cents)(6 different issues)
Harvey Comics

| | Good | Fine | N-Mint |
|---|---|---|---|
| 1,3: 1-Little Dot. 3-Casper | 3.35 | 10.00 | 23.00 |
| 2,4,5: 2-Rags Rabbit. 4-Sad Sack. 5-Mazie | 2.00 | 6.00 | 14.00 |
| 6-Dick Tracy | 4.00 | 12.00 | 28.00 |

**TAYLOR'S CHRISTMAS TABLOID**
Mid 1930s, Cleveland, Ohio
Dept. Store Giveaway (Tabloid size; in color)

nn-(Very Rare)-Among the earliest pro work of Siegel & Shuster; one full color page called "The Battle in the Stratosphere," with a pre-Superman look; Shuster art thoughout. (Only 1 known copy)
Estimated value. . . $1000.00

**TEAM AMERICA** (See Captain America #269)
June, 1982 - No. 12, May, 1983
Marvel Comics Group

| | Good | Fine | N-Mint |
|---|---|---|---|
| 1-Origin; Ideal Toy motorcycle characters | | .40 | .80 |
| 2-12: 9-Iron man. 11-Ghost Rider. 12-Dbl. size | | .30 | .60 |

**TEAM YANKEE**
Jan, 1989 - No. 6, Feb, 1989 ($1.95, weekly limited series, color)
First Comics

| | Good | Fine | N-Mint |
|---|---|---|---|
| 1-6 | .35 | 1.00 | 2.00 |

**TEDDY ROOSEVELT & HIS ROUGH RIDERS** (See Real Heroes #1)
1950
Avon Periodicals

| | Good | Fine | N-Mint |
|---|---|---|---|
| 1-Kinstler-c; Palais-a; Flag-c | 10.00 | 30.00 | 70.00 |

**TEDDY ROOSEVELT ROUGH RIDER** (See Battlefield #22 & Classics Illustrated Special Issue)

**TEE AND VEE CROSLEY IN TELEVISION LAND COMICS**
(Also see Crosley's House of Fun)
1951 (52 pgs.; 8x11"; paper cover; in color)
Crosley Division, Avco Mfg. Corp. (Giveaway)

| | Good | Fine | N-Mint |
|---|---|---|---|
| Many stories, puzzles, cut-outs, games, etc. | 3.00 | 9.00 | 21.00 |

**TEENA**
No. 11, 1948 - No. 15, 1948; No. 20, Aug, 1949 - No. 22, Oct, 1950
Magazine Enterprises/Standard Comics No. 20 on

| | Good | Fine | N-Mint |
|---|---|---|---|
| A-1 #11-Teen-age | 3.00 | 9.00 | 21.00 |
| A-1 #12, 15 | 2.30 | 7.00 | 16.00 |
| 20-22 (Standard) | 1.30 | 4.00 | 9.00 |

**TEEN-AGE BRIDES** (True Bride's Experiences #8 on)
Aug, 1953 - No. 7, Aug, 1954
Harvey/Home Comics

| | Good | Fine | N-Mint |
|---|---|---|---|
| 1-Powell-a | 2.65 | 8.00 | 18.00 |
| 2-Powell-a | 1.70 | 5.00 | 12.00 |
| 3-7: 3,6-Powell-a | 1.50 | 4.50 | 10.00 |

**TEEN-AGE CONFESSIONS** (See Teen Confessions)

**TEEN-AGE CONFIDENTIAL CONFESSIONS**
July, 1960 - No. 22, 1964
Charlton Comics

| | Good | Fine | N-Mint |
|---|---|---|---|
| 1 | 1.15 | 3.50 | 8.00 |

| | Good | Fine | N-Mint |
|---|---|---|---|
| 2-10 | .70 | 2.00 | 4.00 |
| 11-22 | .40 | 1.25 | 2.50 |

**TEEN-AGE DIARY SECRETS** (Formerly Blue Ribbon Comics; becomes Diary Secrets #10 on)
No. 4, 9/49; nn (#5), 9/49 - No. 7, 11/49; No. 8, 2/50; No. 9, 8/50
St. John Publishing Co.

| | Good | Fine | N-Mint |
|---|---|---|---|
| 4(9/49)-oversized; part mag., part comic | 11.00 | 32.00 | 75.00 |
| nn(#5),6,8: 8-Photo-c; Baker-a(2-3) in each | 7.00 | 21.00 | 50.00 |
| 7,9-Digest size | 9.30 | 28.00 | 65.00 |

**TEEN-AGE DOPE SLAVES** (See Harvey Comics Library #1)

**TEENAGE HOTRODDERS** (Top Eliminator #25 on; see Blue Bird)
April, 1963 - No. 24, July, 1967
Charlton Comics

| | Good | Fine | N-Mint |
|---|---|---|---|
| 1 | 1.15 | 3.50 | 8.00 |
| 2-10 | .70 | 2.00 | 4.00 |
| 11-24 | .50 | 1.50 | 3.00 |

**TEEN-AGE LOVE** (See Fox Giants)

**TEEN-AGE LOVE** (Formerly Intimate)
V2#4, July, 1958 - No. 96, Dec, 1973
Charlton Comics

| | Good | Fine | N-Mint |
|---|---|---|---|
| V2#4 | 1.50 | 4.50 | 10.00 |
| 5-9 | .75 | 2.25 | 5.00 |
| 10(9/59)-20 | .70 | 2.00 | 4.00 |
| 21-35 | .50 | 1.50 | 3.00 |
| 36-70 | .25 | .75 | 1.50 |
| 71-96: 61&62-Jonnie Love begins (origin) | | .30 | .60 |

**TEENAGE MUTANT NINJA TURTLES** (Also see Anything Goes, Donatello, First Comics Graphic Novel, Grimjack #26, Leonardo, Michaelangelo, Raphael & Tales Of The. . .)
1984 - Present ($1.50-$1.75, B&W; all 44-52 pgs.)
Mirage Studios

| | Good | Fine | N-Mint |
|---|---|---|---|
| 1-1st printing (3000 copies)-Only printing to have ad for Gobbledygook #1 & 2 | 54.00 | 163.00 | 325.00 |
| 1-2nd printing (6/84)(15,000 copies) | 12.50 | 37.50 | 75.00 |
| 1-3rd printing (2/85)(36,000 copies) | 5.80 | 17.50 | 35.00 |
| 1-4th printing, new-c (50,000 copies) | 3.35 | 10.00 | 20.00 |
| 1-5th printing, new-c (8/88-c, 11/88 inside) | .70 | 2.00 | 4.00 |
| 1-Counterfeit. **Note:** Most counterfeit copies have a ½ inch wide white streak or scratch marks across the center of back cover. Black part of cover is a bluish black instead of a deep black. Inside paper is very white & inside cover is bright white. These counterfeit the 1st printings. | | | |
| 2-1st printing (15,000 copies) | 17.00 | 50.00 | 100.00 |
| 2-2nd printing | 2.50 | 7.50 | 15.00 |
| 2-3rd printing; new Corben-c/a (2/85) | 1.00 | 3.00 | 6.00 |
| 2-Counterfeit with glossy cover stock. | | | |
| 3-1st printing | 7.50 | 22.50 | 45.00 |
| 3-Variant, 500 copies, given away in NYC. Has 'Laird's Photo' in white rather than light blue | 14.00 | 42.50 | 85.00 |
| 3-2nd printing; contains new back-up story | 1.00 | 3.00 | 6.00 |
| 4-1st printing | 4.15 | 12.50 | 25.00 |
| 4-2nd printing (5/87) | .70 | 2.00 | 4.00 |
| 5-1st printing; Fugitoid begins, ends #7 | 3.00 | 9.00 | 18.00 |
| 5-2nd printing (11/87) | .70 | 2.00 | 4.00 |
| 6-1st printing (4/87-c, 5/87 inside) | 2.50 | 7.50 | 15.00 |
| 6-2nd printing | .50 | 1.50 | 3.00 |
| 7-4pg. Corben color insert; 1st color TMNT | 2.50 | 7.50 | 15.00 |
| 7-2nd printing (1/89) | .50 | 1.50 | 3.00 |
| 8-Cerebus guest stars | 1.70 | 5.00 | 10.00 |
| 9,10: 9 (9/86)-Rip In Time by Corben | 1.15 | 3.50 | 7.00 |
| 11-15 | .85 | 2.50 | 5.00 |
| 16-18: 18-Mark Bode'-a | .70 | 2.00 | 4.00 |
| 18-2nd printing ($2.25, color, 44 pgs.)-New-c | .40 | 1.15 | 2.30 |
| 19-30: 19-Begin $1.75-c. 24-26-Veitch-c/a | .35 | 1.00 | 2.00 |
| Book 1,2($1.50, B&W): 2-Corben-c | .25 | .75 | 1.50 |

**TEENAGE MUTANT NINJA TURTLES** (The Movie)
Summer, 1990 ($5.95, B&W, squarebound, 68 pgs.)
Mirage Studios/Archie Comics

| | Good | Fine | N-Mint |
|---|---|---|---|
| nn-($5.95)-Adapts live action movie | 1.00 | 3.00 | 6.00 |
| 1-($4.95, color)-Prestige format, direct sale | .85 | 2.50 | 5.00 |
| 1-($2.50, color)-Newsstand edition | .40 | 1.25 | 2.50 |

**TEENAGE MUTANT NINJA TURTLES ADVENTURES** (TV)
8/88 - No. 3, 12/88; 3/89 - Present ($1.00, color)
Archie Comics

| | Good | Fine | N-Mint |
|---|---|---|---|
| 1-Adapts TV cartoon; not by Eastman/Laird | .85 | 2.50 | 5.00 |
| 2,3 (Mini-series) | .50 | 1.50 | 3.00 |
| 1 (2nd on going series) | .50 | 1.50 | 3.00 |
| 2-5: 5-Begins original stories not based on TV | .35 | 1.00 | 2.00 |
| 6-18: 14-Donald Simpson-a(p) | | .60 | 1.20 |
| 1-11: 2nd printings | | .50 | 1.00 |
| nn ($2.50, Spring, 1991, 68 pgs.)-(Meet Archie) | .40 | 1.25 | 2.50 |

NOTE: *There are 2nd printings of #1-11 w/B&W inside covers. Originals are color.*

**TEEN-AGE ROMANCE** (Formerly My Own Romance)
No. 77, Sept, 1960 - No. 86, March, 1962
Marvel Comics (ZPC)

| | Good | Fine | N-Mint |
|---|---|---|---|
| 77-86 | .85 | 2.60 | 6.00 |

**TEEN-AGE ROMANCES**
Jan, 1949 - No. 45, Dec, 1955
St. John Publ. co. (Approved Comics)

| | Good | Fine | N-Mint |
|---|---|---|---|
| 1-Baker-c/a(1) | 16.00 | 48.00 | 110.00 |
| 2-Baker-c/a | 9.30 | 28.00 | 65.00 |
| 3-Baker-c/a(3); spanking panel | 10.00 | 30.00 | 70.00 |
| 4,5,7,8-Photo-c; Baker-a(2-3) each | 7.00 | 21.00 | 50.00 |
| 6-Slightly large size; photo-c; part magazine; Baker-a (10/49) | 7.00 | 21.00 | 50.00 |
| 9-Baker-c/a; Kubert-a | 10.00 | 30.00 | 70.00 |
| 10-12,20-Baker-c/a(2-3) each | 6.50 | 19.00 | 45.00 |
| 13-19,21,22-Complete issues by Baker | 10.00 | 30.00 | 70.00 |
| 23-25-Baker-c/a(2-3) each | 5.30 | 16.00 | 38.00 |
| 26,27,33,34,36-42-Last Precode, 3/55; Baker-a. 38-Suggestive-c | 3.70 | 11.00 | 26.00 |
| 28-30-No Baker-a | 2.00 | 6.00 | 14.00 |
| 31-Baker-c | 2.30 | 7.00 | 16.00 |
| 32-Baker-c/a, 1pg. | 2.30 | 7.00 | 16.00 |
| 35-Baker-c/a, 16pgs. | 3.65 | 11.00 | 25.00 |
| 43-45-Baker-a | 2.65 | 8.00 | 18.00 |

**TEEN-AGE TALK**
1964
I.W. Enterprises

| | Good | Fine | N-Mint |
|---|---|---|---|
| Reprint #1-Monkees photo-c | 1.00 | 3.00 | 6.00 |
| Reprint #5,8,9 | .25 | .80 | 1.60 |

**TEEN-AGE TEMPTATIONS** (Going Steady #10 on)(See True Love Pic.)
Oct, 1952 - No. 9, Aug, 1954
St. John Publishing co.

| | Good | Fine | N-Mint |
|---|---|---|---|
| 1-Baker-c/a; has story "Reform School Girl" by Estrada | 17.00 | 51.00 | 120.00 |
| 2-Baker-c | 5.70 | 17.00 | 40.00 |
| 3-7,9-Baker-c/a | 9.30 | 28.00 | 65.00 |
| 8-Teenagers smoke reefers; Baker-c/a | 10.00 | 30.00 | 70.00 |

NOTE: ***Estrada** a-1, 4, 5.*

**TEEN BEAM** (Formerly Teen Beat #1)
No. 2, Jan-Feb, 1968
National Periodical Publications

*Teen-Age Diary Secrets #6, © STJ*

*Teenage Mutant Ninja Turtles #7, © Mirage*

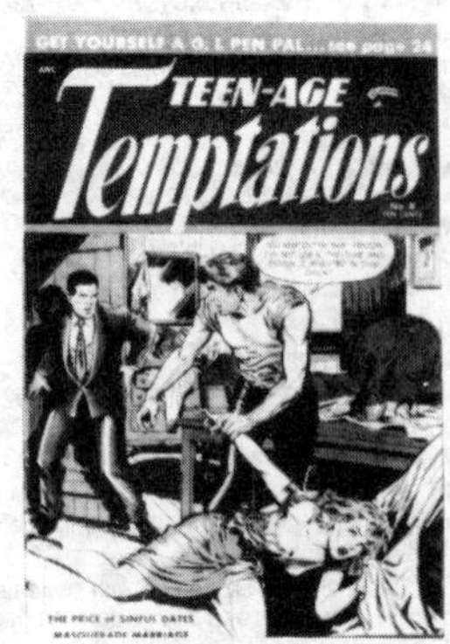

*Teen-Age Temptations #8, © STJ*

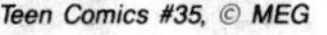
Teen Comics #35, © MEG

Teen Titans #6, © DC

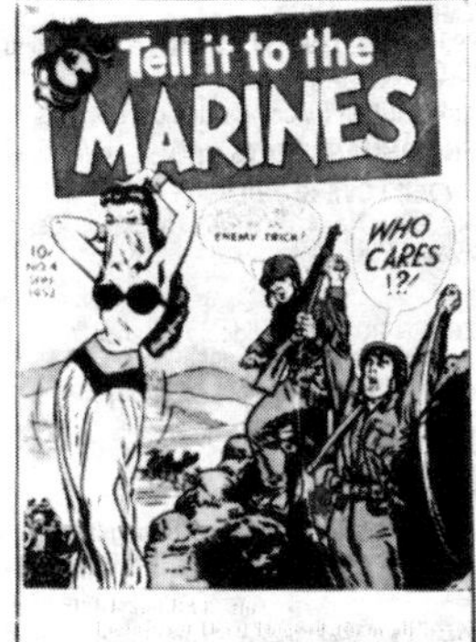

Tell It to the Marines #4, © TOBY

**Good Fine N-Mint**

2-Orlando, Drucker-a(r); Monkees photo-c 1.50 4.50 10.00

**TEEN BEAT** (Becomes Teen Beam #2)
Nov-Dec, 1967
National Periodical Publications

1-Photos & text only; Monkees photo-c 1.70 5.00 12.00

**TEEN COMICS** (Formerly All Teen; Journey Into Unknown Worlds #36 on)
No. 21, April, 1947 - No. 35, May, 1950
Marvel comics (WFP)

21-Kurtzman's "Hey Look;" Patsy Walker, Cindy, Georgie, Margie app. 5.00 15.00 35.00
22,23,25,27,29,31-35 3.00 9.00 21.00
24,26,28,30-Kurtzman's "Hey Look" 4.50 14.00 32.00

**TEEN CONFESSIONS**
Aug, 1959 - No. 97, Nov, 1976
Charlton Comics

1 3.50 10.50 24.00
2 1.70 5.00 12.00
3-10 1.15 3.50 8.00
11-30 .70 2.00 4.00
31-Beatles-c 3.50 10.50 24.00
32-36,38-55 .35 1.00 2.00
37 (1/66)-Beatles Fan Club story; Beatles-c 3.50 10.50 24.00
56-97: 89,90-Newton-c .35 .70

**TEENIE WEENIES, THE**
No. 10, 1950 - No. 11, 1951 (Newspaper reprints)
Ziff-Davis Publishing Co.

10,11 7.00 21.00 50.00

**TEEN-IN** (Tippy Teen)
Summer, 1968 - No. 4, Fall, 1969
Tower Comics

nn(#1, Summer,'68), nn(#2, Spring,'69),3,4 .85 2.60 6.00

**TEEN LIFE** (Formerly Young Life)
No. 3, Winter, 1945 - No. 5, Fall, 1945
New Age/Quality Comics Group

3-June Allyson photo-c 4.00 12.00 28.00
4-Duke Ellington story 2.65 8.00 18.00
5-Van Johnson, Woody Herman & Jackie Robinson articles 4.00 12.00 28.00

**TEEN ROMANCES**
1964
Super Comics

10,11,15-17-Reprints .40 .80

**TEEN SECRET DIARY** (Nurse Betsy Crane #12 on)
Oct, 1959 - No. 11, June, 1961; No. 1, 1972
Charlton Comics

1 1.70 5.00 12.00
2 .85 2.60 6.00
3-11 .70 2.00 4.00
1 (1972) .50 1.00

**TEEN TALK** (See Teen)

**TEEN TITANS** (See Brave & the Bold, DC Super-Stars #1, Marvel & DC Present, New Teen Titans, Official . . . Index and Showcase)
1-2/66 - No. 43, 1-2/73; No. 44, 11/76 - No. 53, 2/78
National Periodical Publications/DC Comics

1-Titans join Peace Corps; Batman, Flash, Aquaman, Wonder Woman cameos 15.00 45.00 105.00
2 7.00 21.00 50.00
3-5: 4-Speedy app. 3.60 11.00 25.00

**Good Fine N-Mint**

6-10: 6-Doom Patrol app. 2.65 8.00 18.00
11-19: 11-Speedy app. 18-1st app. Starfire (11-12/68). 19-Wood-i; Speedy begins as regular 2.00 6.00 14.00
20-22: All Neal Adams-a. 21-Hawk & Dove app. 22-Origin Wonder Girl 2.15 6.50 15.00
23-30: 23-Wonder Girl dons new costume. 25-Flash, Aquaman, Batman, Green Arrow, Green Lantern, Superman, & Hawk & Dove guests; 1st app. Lilith who joins T.T. West in #50. 29-Hawk & Dove & Ocean Master app. 30-Aquagirl app. 1.15 3.50 8.00
31-43: 31-Hawk & Dove app. 36,37-Superboy-r. 38-Green Arrow/ Speedy-r; Aquaman/Aqualad story. 39-Hawk & Dove-r. (36-39: 52 pgs.) 1.00 3.00 6.00
44,45,47,49,51,52: 44-Mal becomes the Guardian .70 2.00 4.00
46-Joker's daughter begins 1.35 4.00 9.00
48-Intro Bumblebee; Joker's daughter becomes Harlequin 1.35 4.00 9.00
50-1st revival original Bat-Girl; intro. Teen Titans West 1.00 3.00 7.00
53-Origin retold .85 2.50 5.00

NOTE: ***Aparo** a-36. **Buckler** c-46-53. **Kane** a(p)-19, 22-24, 39r. **Tuska** a(p)-31, 36, 38, 39.*

**TEEN TITANS SPOTLIGHT**
Aug, 1986 - No. 21, Apr, 1988
DC Comics

1 .25 .75 1.50
2-21: 7-Guice's 1st work at DC. 14-Nightwing; Batman app. 15-Austin-c(i). 18,19-Millennium x-over. 21-($1.00-c)-Original Teen Titans; Spiegle-a .50 1.00

NOTE: ***Guice** a-7p, 8p; c-7, 8. **Orlando** c/a-11p. **Perez** c-1, 17i, 19. **Sienkiewicz** c-10.*

**TEEPEE TIM** (Formerly Ha Ha Comics)
No. 100, Feb-Mar, 1955 - No. 102, June-July, 1955
American Comics Group

100-102 1.15 3.50 8.00

**TEGRA JUNGLE EMPRESS** (Zegra Jungle Empress #2 on)
August, 1948
Fox Features Syndicate

1-Blue Beetle, Rocket Kelly app.; used in **SOTI**, pg. 31 22.00 65.00 150.00

**TELEVISION** (See TV)

**TELEVISION COMICS**
No. 5, Feb, 1950 - No. 8, Nov, 1950
Standard Comics (Animated Cartoons)

5-1st app. Willy Nilly 3.00 9.00 21.00
6-8: 6 has #2 on inside 2.00 6.00 14.00

**TELEVISION PUPPET SHOW**
1950 - No. 2, Nov, 1950
Avon Periodicals

1,2: Speedy Rabbit, Spotty The Pup 7.00 21.00 50.00

**TELEVISION TEENS MOPSY** (See TV Teens)

**TELL IT TO THE MARINES**
Mar, 1952 - No. 15, July, 1955
Toby Press Publications

1-Lover O'Leary and His Liberty Belles (with Pin-ups), ends #6 6.50 19.00 45.00
2-Madame Cobra app. c/story 4.30 13.00 30.00
3-5 3.15 9.50 22.00
6-12,14,15: 7-9,14,15-Photo-c 2.00 6.00 14.00
13-John Wayne photo-c 3.50 10.50 24.00
I.W. Reprint #1,9 .30 .90 1.80
Super Reprint #16('64) .30 .90 1.80

**TEMPUS FUGITIVE**
1990 - No. 4, 1990 ($4.95, color, squarebound, 52 pgs.)
DC Comics

| | Good | Fine | N-Mint |
|---|---|---|---|
| Book 1-4: Ken Steacy painted-c/a & scripts | .85 | 2.50 | 5.00 |

**TEN COMMANDMENTS** (See Moses & the. . .and Classics Illustrated Special)

**TENDER LOVE STORIES**
Feb, 1971 - No. 4, July, 1971 (All 52pgs.)(25 cents)
Skywald Publ. Corp.

| | | | |
|---|---|---|---|
| 1-4 | .35 | 1.00 | 2.00 |

**TENDER ROMANCE** (Ideal Romance #3 on)
Dec, 1953 - No. 2, Feb, 1954
Key Publications (Gilmour Magazines)

| | | | |
|---|---|---|---|
| 1-Headlight & lingerie panels | 6.50 | 19.00 | 45.00 |
| 2 | 3.00 | 9.00 | 21.00 |

**TENNESSEE JED** (Radio)
nd (1945) (16 pgs.; paper cover; regular size; giveaway)
Fox Syndicate? (Wm. C. Popper & Co.)

| | | | |
|---|---|---|---|
| nn | 8.50 | 25.50 | 60.00 |

**TENNIS** (. . .For Speed, Stamina, Strength, Skill)
1956 (16 pgs.; soft cover; 10 cents)
Tennis Educational Foundation

| | | | |
|---|---|---|---|
| Book 1-Endorsed by Gene Tunney, Ralph Kiner, etc. showing how tennis has helped them | 2.30 | 7.00 | 16.00 |

**TENSE SUSPENSE**
Dec, 1958 - No. 2, Feb, 1959
Fago Publications

| | | | |
|---|---|---|---|
| 1,2 | 2.65 | 8.00 | 18.00 |

**TEN STORY LOVE** (Formerly a pulp magazine with same title)
V29#3, June-July, 1951 - V36#5(#209), Sept, 1956 (#3-6: 52 pgs.)
Ace Periodicals

| | | | |
|---|---|---|---|
| V29#3(#177)-Part comic, part text | 3.70 | 11.00 | 26.00 |
| 4-6(1/52) | 1.70 | 5.00 | 12.00 |
| V30#1(3/52)-6(1/53) | 1.30 | 4.00 | 9.00 |
| V31#1(2/53),V32#2(4/53)-6(12/53) | 1.00 | 3.00 | 7.00 |
| V33#1(1/54)-3(5#54, #195), V34#4(7/54, #196)-6(10/54, #198) | 1.00 | 3.00 | 7.00 |
| V35#1(12/54, #199)-3(4/55, #201)-Last precode | .85 | 2.60 | 6.00 |
| V35#4-6(9/55, #201-204), V36#1(11/55, #205)-3, 5(9/56, #209) | .70 | 2.00 | 5.00 |
| V36#4-L.B. Cole-a | 1.30 | 4.00 | 9.00 |

**TEN WHO DARED** (See 4-Color #1178)

**TERMINATOR, THE**
Sept, 1988 - No. 17, 1989 ($1.75, color, Baxter paper)
Now Comics

| | | | |
|---|---|---|---|
| 1-Based on movie | 3.00 | 9.00 | 18.00 |
| 2 | 1.70 | 5.00 | 10.00 |
| 3-5 | 1.00 | 3.00 | 6.00 |
| 6-10 | .70 | 2.00 | 4.00 |
| 11,13-17 | .40 | 1.25 | 2.50 |
| 12 ($1.75, 52pgs.)-Intro. John Connor | .50 | 1.50 | 3.00 |

**TERMINATOR, THE**
Aug, 1990 - No. 4, Nov, 1990 ($2.50, color, mini-series)
Dark Horse Comics

| | | | |
|---|---|---|---|
| 1-Set 39 years later than the movie | .50 | 1.50 | 3.00 |
| 2-4 | .40 | 1.25 | 2.50 |

**TERMINATOR: ALL MY FUTURES PAST, THE**
V3#1, Aug, 1990 - V3#2, Sept, 1990 ($1.75, color, mini-series)
Now Comics

| | | | |
|---|---|---|---|
| V3#1,2 | .30 | .90 | 1.80 |

**TERMINATOR: THE BURNING EARTH, THE**
V2#1, Mar, 1990 - V2#5, July, 1990 ($1.75, color, mini-series)
Now Comics

| | Good | Fine | N-Mint |
|---|---|---|---|
| V2#1 | 1.00 | 3.00 | 6.00 |
| 2 | .70 | 2.00 | 4.00 |
| 3-5 | .40 | 1.25 | 2.50 |
| Trade paperback ($9.95)-Reprints V2#1-5 | 1.70 | 5.00 | 10.00 |

**TERRAFORMERS**
April, 1987 - No. 2?, 1987 ($1.95, color)
Wonder Color Comics

| | | | |
|---|---|---|---|
| 1,2-Kelley Jones-a | .35 | 1.00 | 2.00 |

**TERRANAUTS**
Aug, 1986 - No. 2, 1986? ($1.75, color)
Fantasy General Comics

| | | | |
|---|---|---|---|
| 1,2 | .30 | .90 | 1.80 |

**TERRIFIC COMICS**
Jan, 1944 - No. 6, Nov, 1944
Continental Magazines

| | | | |
|---|---|---|---|
| 1-Kid Terrific; opium story | 40.00 | 120.00 | 280.00 |
| 2-The Boomerang by L.B. Cole & Ed Wheelan's "Comics" McCormick, called the world's #1 comic book fan begins; Schomburg-c | 35.00 | 105.00 | 245.00 |
| 3,4: 3-Diana becomes Boomerang's costumed aide | 30.00 | 90.00 | 210.00 |
| 5-The Reckoner begins; Boomerang & Diana by L.B. Cole; Schomburg bondage-c | 35.00 | 105.00 | 245.00 |
| 6-L.B. Cole-c/a | 35.00 | 105.00 | 245.00 |

NOTE: ***L.B. Cole** a-1, 2(2), 3-6. **Fuje** a-5, 6. **Rico** a-2.*

**TERRIFIC COMICS** (Formerly Horrific; Wonder Boy #17 on)
No. 14, Dec, 1954; No. 16, Mar, 1955 (No #15)
Mystery Publ.(Comic Media)/(Ajax/Farrell)

| | | | |
|---|---|---|---|
| 14-Art swipe/Advs. into the Unknown #37; injury-to-eye-c; page-2, panel 5 swiped from Phantom Stranger #4; surrealistic Palais-a; Human Cross story | 7.00 | 21.00 | 50.00 |
| 16-Wonder Boy app. (precode) | 5.70 | 17.00 | 40.00 |

**TERRIFYING TALES**
No. 11, Jan, 1953 - No. 15, Apr, 1954
Star Publications

| | | | |
|---|---|---|---|
| 11-Used in **POP**, pgs. 99,100; all Jo-Jo-r | 19.00 | 57.00 | 130.00 |
| 12-All Jo-Jo-r; L.B. Cole splash | 14.00 | 43.00 | 100.00 |
| 13-All Rulah-r; classic devil-c | 20.00 | 60.00 | 140.00 |
| 14-All Rulah reprints | 14.00 | 43.00 | 100.00 |
| 15-Rulah, Zago-r; used in **SOTI**-r/Rulah #22 | 14.00 | 43.00 | 100.00 |

NOTE: *All issues have **L.B. Cole** covers; bondage covers-No. 12-14.*

**TERROR ILLUSTRATED** (Adult Tales of. . .)
Nov-Dec, 1955 - No. 2, Spring, 1956 (Magazine, 25 cents)
E.C. Comics

| | | | |
|---|---|---|---|
| 1-Adult Entertainment on-c | 7.00 | 21.00 | 50.00 |
| 2 | 6.00 | 18.00 | 42.00 |

NOTE: ***Craig, Evans, Ingels, Orlando** art in each. **Crandall** c-1, 2.*

**TERRORS OF THE JUNGLE** (Formerly Jungle Thrills)
No. 17, May, 1952 - No. 10, Sept, 1954
Star Publications

| | | | |
|---|---|---|---|
| 17-Reprints Rulah #21, used in **SOTI**; L.B. Cole bondage-c | 18.00 | 54.00 | 125.00 |
| 18-Jo-Jo-r | 11.50 | 34.00 | 80.00 |
| 19,20(1952)-Jo-Jo-r; Disbrow-a | 10.00 | 30.00 | 70.00 |
| 21-Jungle Jo, Tangi-r; used in **POP**, pg. 100 & color illos. | 12.00 | 36.00 | 85.00 |
| 4,6,7-Disbrow-a | 10.00 | 30.00 | 70.00 |
| 5,8,10: All Disbrow-a. 5-Jo-Jo-r. 8-Rulah, Jo-Jo-r. 10-Rulah-r | 10.00 | 30.00 | 70.00 |

*Tempus Fugitive #1, © DC*

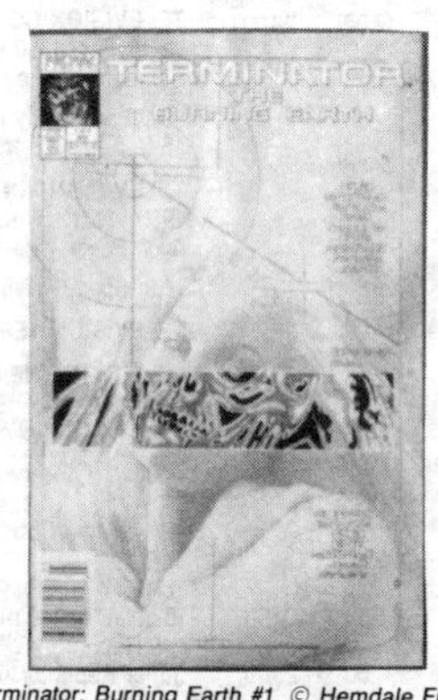

*Terminator: Burning Earth #1, © Hemdale Film*

*Terrors of the Jungle #8, © STAR*

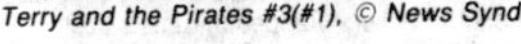
Terry and the Pirates #3(#1), © News Synd.

Terry-Toons Comics #2 (11/42), © Paul Terry

The Texan #6, © STJ

| | Good | Fine | N-Mint |
|---|---|---|---|
| 9-Jo-Jo-r; Disbrow-a; Tangi by Orlando | 10.00 | 30.00 | 70.00 |

NOTE: *L.B. Cole c-all; bondage c-17, 19, 21, 5, 7.*

**TERROR TALES** (See Beware Terror Tales)

**TERROR TALES** (Magazine)
V1#7, 1969 - V6#6, Dec, 1974; V7#1, Apr, 1976 - V10, 1979?
(V1-V6: 52 pgs.; V7 on: 68 pgs.)
Eerie Publications

| | Good | Fine | N-Mint |
|---|---|---|---|
| V1#7 | 1.50 | 4.50 | 10.00 |
| V1#8-11('69): 9-Bondage-c | .85 | 2.60 | 6.00 |
| V2#1-6('70), V3#1-6('71), V4#1-7('72), V5#1-6('73), V6#1-6('74) | .70 | 2.00 | 4.00 |
| V7#1,4(no V7#2), V8#1-3('77), V9, V10 | .70 | 2.00 | 4.00 |
| V7#3-LSD story-r/Weird V3#5 | .70 | 2.00 | 4.00 |

**TERRY AND THE PIRATES** (See Famous Feature Stories, Merry Christmas From Sears Toyland, Popular Comics, Super Book #3,5,9,16,28, & Super Comics)

**TERRY AND THE PIRATES**
1939 - 1953 (By Milton Caniff)
Dell Publishing Co.

| | Good | Fine | N-Mint |
|---|---|---|---|
| Large Feature Comic 2('39) | 48.00 | 145.00 | 335.00 |
| Large Feature Comic 6('39)-1936 dailies | 44.00 | 133.00 | 285.00 |
| 4-Color 9(1940) | 48.00 | 145.00 | 335.00 |
| Large Feature Comic 27('41), 6('42) | 33.00 | 100.00 | 230.00 |
| 4-Color 44('43) | 29.00 | 85.00 | 200.00 |
| 4-Color 101('45) | 19.00 | 57.00 | 130.00 |
| Buster Brown Shoes giveaway(1938)-32 pgs.; in color | 20.00 | 60.00 | 140.00 |
| Canada Dry Premiums-Books #1-3(1953-Harvey)-36 pgs.; 2x5" | 5.00 | 15.00 | 35.00 |
| Family Album(1942) | 10.00 | 30.00 | 70.00 |
| Gambles Giveaway ('38)-16 pgs. | 4.35 | 13.00 | 26.00 |
| Gillmore Giveaway('38)-24 pgs. | 5.00 | 15.00 | 30.00 |
| Popped Wheat Giveaway('38)-Reprints in full color; Caniff-a | .85 | 2.50 | 5.00 |
| Shoe Store giveaway (Weatherbird)('38, 16 pgs., soft-c)(2-diff.) | 4.60 | 14.00 | 32.00 |
| Sparked Wheat Giveaway('42)-16 pgs. in color | 4.60 | 14.00 | 32.00 |

**TERRY AND THE PIRATES**
1941 (16 pgs.; regular size)
Libby's Radio Premium

| | Good | Fine | N-Mint |
|---|---|---|---|
| "Adventure of the Ruby of Genghis Khan" - Each pg. is a puzzle that must be completed to read the story | 10.00 | 30.00 | 70.00 |

**TERRY AND THE PIRATES** (Formerly Boy Explorers; Long John Silver & the Pirates #30 on) (Daily strip-r) (Two #26's)
No. 3, 4/47 - No. 26, 4/51; No. 26, 6/55 - No. 28, 10/55
Harvey Publications/Charlton No. 26-28

| | Good | Fine | N-Mint |
|---|---|---|---|
| 3(#1)-Boy Explorers by S&K; Terry & the Pirates begin by Caniff | 22.00 | 65.00 | 150.00 |
| 4-S&K Boy Explorers | 14.00 | 43.00 | 100.00 |
| 5-10 | 7.00 | 21.00 | 50.00 |
| 11-Man in Black app. by Powell | 7.00 | 21.00 | 50.00 |
| 12-20: 16-Girl threatened with red hot poker | 5.35 | 16.00 | 37.00 |
| 21-26(4/51)-Last Caniff issue | 4.75 | 14.00 | 33.00 |
| 26-28('55)(Formerly This Is Suspense)-Not by Caniff | 3.70 | 11.00 | 26.00 |

NOTE: *Powell a (Tommy Tween)-5-10, 12, 14; 15-17(½-2 pgs.).*

**TERRY BEARS COMICS** (TerryToons, The... #4)
June, 1952 - No. 3, Oct, 1952
St. John Publishing Co.

| | Good | Fine | N-Mint |
|---|---|---|---|
| 1 | 2.00 | 6.00 | 14.00 |
| 2,3 | 1.70 | 5.00 | 12.00 |

**TERRY-TOONS COMICS** (1st Series) (Becomes Paul Terry's Comics #85 on; later issues titled "Paul Terry's...) (See Giant Comics Ed.)
Oct, 1942 - No. 86, May, 1951 (Two #60s exist)
Timely/Marvel No. 1-60 (8/47)(Becomes Best Western No. 58 on?, Marvel)/St. John No. 60 (9/47) on

| | Good | Fine | N-Mint |
|---|---|---|---|
| 1 (Scarce)-Features characters that 1st app. on movie screen; Gandy Goose begins | 57.00 | 170.00 | 400.00 |
| 2 | 29.00 | 85.00 | 200.00 |
| 3-5 | 17.00 | 51.00 | 120.00 |
| 6-10: 7-Hitler, Hirohito, Mussolini-c | 11.50 | 34.00 | 80.00 |
| 11-20 | 8.00 | 24.00 | 55.00 |
| 21-37 | 5.00 | 15.00 | 35.00 |
| 38-Mighty Mouse begins (1st app., 11/45) | 43.00 | 130.00 | 300.00 |
| 39-2nd Mighty Mouse app. | 14.00 | 43.00 | 100.00 |
| 40-49: 43-Infinity-c | 6.50 | 19.00 | 45.00 |
| 50-1st app. Heckle & Jeckle | 14.00 | 43.00 | 100.00 |
| 51-60(8/47): 55-Infinity-c. 60(9/47)-Atomic explosion panel | 4.50 | 14.00 | 32.00 |
| 61-84 | 3.00 | 9.00 | 21.00 |
| 85,86-Same book as Paul Terry's Comics #85,86 with only a title change; published at same time? | 3.00 | 9.00 | 21.00 |

**TERRY-TOONS COMICS** (2nd Series)
June, 1952 - No. 9, Nov, 1953
St. John Publishing Co./Pines

| | Good | Fine | N-Mint |
|---|---|---|---|
| 1 | 5.70 | 17.00 | 40.00 |
| 2 | 3.00 | 9.00 | 21.00 |
| 3-9 | 2.65 | 8.00 | 18.00 |
| Giant Summer Fun Book 101,102(Summer,'57-Summer,'58)(TV, Tom Terrific app.) | 3.50 | 10.50 | 24.00 |

**TERRYTOONS, THE TERRY BEARS** (Formerly Terry Bears)
No. 4, Summer, 1958
Pines Comics

| | Good | Fine | N-Mint |
|---|---|---|---|
| 4 | 1.70 | 5.00 | 12.00 |

**TESSIE THE TYPIST** (Tiny Tessie #24; see Comedy Comics, Gay & Joker Comics)
Summer, 1944 - No. 23, Aug, 1949
Timely/Marvel Comics (20CC)

| | Good | Fine | N-Mint |
|---|---|---|---|
| 1-Doc Rockblock & others by Wolverton | 25.00 | 75.00 | 175.00 |
| 2-Wolverton's Powerhouse Pepper | 14.00 | 43.00 | 100.00 |
| 3-No Wolverton | 4.50 | 14.00 | 32.00 |
| 4,5,7,8-Wolverton-a | 9.30 | 28.00 | 65.00 |
| 6-Kurtzman's "Hey Look," 2 pgs. Wolverton | 10.00 | 30.00 | 70.00 |
| 9-Wolverton's Powerhouse Pepper (8 pgs.) & 1 pg. Kurtzman's "Hey Look" | 12.00 | 36.00 | 85.00 |
| 10-Wolverton's Powerhouse Pepper (4 pgs.) | 11.00 | 32.00 | 75.00 |
| 11-Wolverton's Powerhouse Pepper (8 pgs.) | 12.00 | 36.00 | 85.00 |
| 12-Wolverton's Powerhouse Pepper (4 pgs.) & 1 pg. Kurtzman's "Hey Look" | 11.00 | 32.00 | 75.00 |
| 13-Wolverton's Powerhouse Pepper (4 pgs.) | 10.00 | 30.00 | 70.00 |
| 14-Wolverton's Dr. Whackyhack (1 pg.); 1½ pgs. Kurtzman's "Hey Look" | 7.00 | 21.00 | 50.00 |
| 15-Kurtzman's "Hey Look" (3 pgs.) & 3 pgs. Giggles 'n' Grins | 7.00 | 21.00 | 50.00 |
| 16-18-Kurtzman's "Hey Look" (?, 2 & 1 pg.) | 4.30 | 13.00 | 30.00 |
| 19-Annie Oakley story (8 pgs.) | 3.00 | 9.00 | 21.00 |
| 20-23: 20-Anti-Wertham editorial (2/49) | 2.30 | 7.00 | 16.00 |

NOTE: *Lana app.-21. Millie The Model app.-13, 15, 17, 21. Rusty app.-10, 11, 13, 15, 17.*

**TEXAN, THE** (Fightin' Marines #15 on; Fightin' Texan #16 on)
Aug, 1948 - No. 15, Oct, 1951
St. John Publishing Co.

| | Good | Fine | N-Mint |
|---|---|---|---|
| 1-Buckskin Belle | 8.00 | 24.00 | 55.00 |
| 2 | 4.00 | 12.00 | 28.00 |
| 3,5,10: 10-Oversized issue | 3.15 | 9.50 | 22.00 |
| 4,7,15-Baker-c/a | 6.50 | 19.00 | 45.00 |
| 6,9-Baker-c | 4.00 | 12.00 | 28.00 |
| 8,11,13,14-Baker-c/a(2-3) each | 6.50 | 19.00 | 45.00 |

| | Good | Fine | N-Mint |
|---|---|---|---|
| 12-All Matt Baker; Peyote story | 8.50 | 25.50 | 60.00 |

NOTE: ***Matt Baker** c-6-15. **Larsen** a-6, 8. **Tuska** a-1, 2, 8.*

**TEXAN, THE** (See 4-Color #1027, 1096)

**TEXAS JOHN SLAUGHTER** (See 4-Color #997, 1181 & W. Disney Presents #2)

**TEXAS KID** (See Two-Gun Western, Wild Western)
Jan, 1951 - No. 10, July, 1952
Marvel/Atlas Comics (LMC)

| | Good | Fine | N-Mint |
|---|---|---|---|
| 1-Origin; Texas Kid (alias Lance Temple) & his horse Thunder begin; Tuska-a | 8.50 | 25.50 | 60.00 |
| 2 | 4.30 | 13.00 | 30.00 |
| 3-10 | 3.50 | 10.50 | 24.00 |

NOTE: ***Maneely** a-1-4; c-1, 3, 5-10.*

**TEXAS RANGERS, THE** (See Jace Pearson of . . . ans Superior Stories #4)

**TEXAS RANGERS IN ACTION** (Formerly Captain Gallant or Scotland Yard?) (See Blue Bird Comics)
No. 5, July, 1956 - No. 79, Aug, 1970
Charlton Comics

| | Good | Fine | N-Mint |
|---|---|---|---|
| 5 | 3.50 | 19.50 | 24.00 |
| 6-10 | 1.70 | 5.00 | 12.00 |
| 11-Williamson-a(5,5,&8 pgs.); Torres-a | 4.35 | 13.00 | 30.00 |
| 12,14-20 | 1.15 | 3.50 | 8.00 |
| 13-Williamson-a, 5 pgs; Torres-a | 3.50 | 10.50 | 24.00 |
| 21-30: 30-Last 10 cent issue? | .85 | 2.60 | 6.00 |
| 31-59 | .70 | 2.00 | 4.00 |
| 60-Rileys Rangers begin | .35 | 1.00 | 2.00 |
| 61-70: 65-1st app. The Man Called Loco, origin-#67 | .25 | .75 | 1.50 |
| 71-79 | | .50 | 1.00 |
| 76(Modern Comics-r, 1977) | | .15 | .30 |

**TEXAS SLIM** (See A-1 Comics #2-8,10)

**TEX DAWSON, GUN-SLINGER** (Gunslinger #2 on)
January, 1973 (Also see Western Kid, 1st series)
Marvel Comics Group

| | Good | Fine | N-Mint |
|---|---|---|---|
| 1-Steranko-c; Williamson-a(r); Tex Dawson-r | | .60 | 1.20 |

**TEX FARNUM** (See Wisco)

**TEX FARRELL**
Mar-Apr, 1948
D. S. Publishing Co.

| | Good | Fine | N-Mint |
|---|---|---|---|
| 1-Tex Farrell & his horse Lightning; Shelly-c | 6.50 | 19.00 | 45.00 |

**TEX GRANGER** (Formerly Calling All Boys; see True Comics)
No. 18, June, 1948 - No. 24, Sept, 1949
Parents' Magazine Institute/Commended

| | Good | Fine | N-Mint |
|---|---|---|---|
| 18-Tex Granger & his horse Bullet begin | 5.00 | 15.00 | 35.00 |
| 19 | 3.60 | 11.00 | 25.00 |
| 20-24: 22-Wild Bill Hickok story | 2.85 | 8.50 | 20.00 |

**TEX MORGAN** (See Blaze Carson and Wild Western)
Aug, 1948 - No. 9, Feb, 1950
Marvel Comics (CCC)

| | Good | Fine | N-Mint |
|---|---|---|---|
| 1-Tex Morgan, his horse Lightning & sidekick Lobo begin | 11.50 | 34.00 | 80.00 |
| 2 | 8.50 | 25.50 | 60.00 |
| 3-6: 4-Arizona Annie app. | 5.70 | 17.00 | 40.00 |
| 7-9: All photo-c. 7-Captain Tootsie by Beck. 8-18pg. story "The Terror of Rimrock Valley;" Diablo app. | 8.00 | 24.00 | 55.00 |

NOTE: ***Tex Taylor** app.-6, 7, 9.*

**TEX RITTER WESTERN** (Movie star; singing cowboy; see Six-Gun Heroes and Western Hero)
Oct, 1950 - No. 46, May, 1959 (Photo-c: 1-21)
Fawcett No. 1-20 (1/54)/Charlton No. 21 on

| | Good | Fine | N-Mint |
|---|---|---|---|
| 1-Tex Ritter, his stallion White Flash & dog Fury begin; photo front/back-c begin | 33.00 | 100.00 | 230.00 |
| 2 | 18.00 | 54.00 | 125.00 |
| 3-5: 5-Last photo back-c | 14.00 | 43.00 | 100.00 |
| 6-10 | 12.00 | 36.00 | 85.00 |
| 11-19 | 8.00 | 24.00 | 55.00 |
| 20-Last Fawcett issue (1/54) | 9.30 | 28.00 | 65.00 |
| 21-1st Charlton issue; photo-c (3/54) | 9.30 | 28.00 | 65.00 |
| 22-B&W photo back-c begin, end #32 | 5.00 | 15.00 | 35.00 |
| 23-30: 23-25-Young Falcon app. | 3.70 | 11.00 | 26.00 |
| 31-38,40-45 | 3.15 | 9.50 | 22.00 |
| 39-Williamson-a; Whitman-c (1/58) | 4.35 | 13.00 | 30.00 |
| 46-Last issue | 3.50 | 10.50 | 24.00 |

**TEX TAYLOR** (See Blaze Carson, Kid Colt, Tex Morgan, Wild West, Wild Western, & Wisco)
Sept, 1948 - No. 9, March, 1950
Marvel Comics (HPC)

| | Good | Fine | N-Mint |
|---|---|---|---|
| 1-Tex Taylor & his horse Fury begin | 12.00 | 36.00 | 85.00 |
| 2 | 8.00 | 24.00 | 55.00 |
| 3 | 7.00 | 21.00 | 50.00 |
| 4-6: All photo-c. 4-Anti-Wertham editorial. 5,6-Blaze Carson app. | 8.00 | 24.00 | 55.00 |
| 7-Photo-c; 18pg. Movie-Length Thriller "Trapped in Time's Lost Land!" with sabre toothed tigers, dinosaurs; Diablo app. | 9.30 | 28.00 | 65.00 |
| 8-Photo-c; 18pg. Movie-Length Thriller "The Mystery of Devil-Tree Plateau!" with dwarf horses, dwarf people & a lost miniature Inca type village; Diablo app. | 9.30 | 28.00 | 65.00 |
| 9-Photo-c; 18pg. Movie-Length Thriller "Guns Along the Border!" Captain Tootsie by Schreiber; Nimo The Mountain Lion app. | 9.30 | 28.00 | 65.00 |

**THANE OF BAGARTH** (Also see Hercules, 1967 series)
No. 24, Oct, 1985 - No. 25, Dec, 1985
Charlton Comics

| | Good | Fine | N-Mint |
|---|---|---|---|
| 24,25 | | .40 | .80 |

**THANOS QUEST, THE** (See Silver Surfer #34)
1990 - No. 2, 1990 ($4.95, color, squarebound, 52 pgs.)
Marvel Comics

| | Good | Fine | N-Mint |
|---|---|---|---|
| 1,2-Starlin scripts & covers | .85 | 2.50 | 5.00 |

**THAT DARN CAT** (See Movie Comics & Walt Disney Showcase #19)

**THAT'S MY POP! GOES NUTS FOR FAIR**
1939 (76 pages) (B&W)
Bystander Press

| | Good | Fine | N-Mint |
|---|---|---|---|
| nn-by Milt Gross | 9.30 | 28.00 | 65.00 |

**THAT THE WORLD MAY BELIEVE**
No date (16 pgs.) (Graymoor Friars distr.)
Catechetical Guild Giveaway

| | Good | Fine | N-Mint |
|---|---|---|---|
| nn | 1.15 | 3.50 | 8.00 |

**THAT WILKIN BOY** (Meet Bingo. . .)
Jan, 1969 - No. 52, Oct, 1982
Archie Publications

| | Good | Fine | N-Mint |
|---|---|---|---|
| 1 | 1.35 | 4.00 | 8.00 |
| 2-10 | .70 | 2.00 | 4.00 |
| 11-26 (last Giant issue) | .35 | 1.00 | 2.00 |
| 27-52 | | .50 | 1.00 |

**T.H.E. CAT** (TV)
Mar, 1967 - No. 4, Oct, 1967 (All have photo-c)
Dell Publishing Co.

| | Good | Fine | N-Mint |
|---|---|---|---|
| 1 | 1.70 | 5.00 | 12.00 |
| 2-4 | 1.15 | 3.50 | 8.00 |

*Texas Rangers in Action #30, © CC*

*Tex Ritter Western #6, © FAW*

*Tex Taylor #5, © MEG*

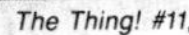
The Thing! #11, © CC

This Is War #9, © STD

This Magazine Is Haunted #16, © CC

**THERE'S A NEW WORLD COMING**
1973 (35-49 Cents)
Spire Christian Comics/Fleming H. Revell Co.

| | Good | Fine | N-Mint |
|---|---|---|---|
| nn | | .50 | 1.00 |

**THEY ALL KISSED THE BRIDE** (See Cinema Comics Herald)

**THEY RING THE BELL**
1946
Fox Feature Syndicate

| | Good | Fine | N-Mint |
|---|---|---|---|
| 1 | 7.00 | 21.00 | 50.00 |

**THIEF OF BAGHDAD** (See 4-Color #1229)

**THIMBLE THEATRE STARRING POPEYE**
1931 - No. 2, 1932 (52 pgs.; 25 cents; B&W)
Sonnet Publishing Co.

| | Good | Fine | N-Mint |
|---|---|---|---|
| 1-Daily strip serial-r in both by Segar | 57.00 | 171.00 | 400.00 |
| 2 | 50.00 | 150.00 | 350.00 |

NOTE: *Probably the first Popeye reprint book. Popeye first entered Thimble Theatre in 1929.*

**THIMK** (Magazine) (Satire)
May, 1958 - No. 6, May, 1959
Counterpoint

| | Good | Fine | N-Mint |
|---|---|---|---|
| 1 | 3.00 | 9.00 | 21.00 |
| 2-6 | 1.70 | 5.00 | 12.00 |

**THING!, THE** (Blue Beetle #18 on)
Feb, 1952 - No. 17, Nov, 1954
Song Hits No. 1,2/Capitol Stories/Charlton

| | Good | Fine | N-Mint |
|---|---|---|---|
| 1 | 29.00 | 85.00 | 200.00 |
| 2,3 | 21.00 | 62.00 | 145.00 |
| 4-6,8,10: 5-Severed head-c; headlights | 14.00 | 43.00 | 100.00 |
| 7-Injury to eye-c & inside panel. E.C. swipes from Vault of Horror #28 | 29.00 | 85.00 | 200.00 |
| 9-Used in **SOTI**, pg. 388 & illo-"Stomping on the face is a form of brutality which modern children learn early" | 32.00 | 95.00 | 220.00 |
| 11-Necronomicon story; Hansel & Gretel parody; Injury-to-eye panel; Check-a | 25.00 | 75.00 | 175.00 |
| 12-"Cinderella" parody; Ditko-c/a; lingerie panels | 37.00 | 110.00 | 260.00 |
| 13,15-Ditko c/a(3 & 5); 13-Ditko E.C. swipe/Haunt of Fear #15(#1)-"House of Horror" | 37.00 | 110.00 | 260.00 |
| 14-Extreme violence/torture; Rumpelstiltskin story; Ditko-c/a(4) | 37.00 | 110.00 | 260.00 |
| 16-Injury to eye panel | 19.00 | 58.00 | 135.00 |
| 17-Ditko-c; classic parody-"Through the Looking Glass;" Powell-a(r) | 30.00 | 90.00 | 210.00 |

NOTE: *Excessive violence, severed heads, injury to eye are common No. 5 on.*

**THING, THE** (See Fantastic Four, Marvel Fanfare, Marvel Feature #11, 12, Marvel Two-In-One)
July, 1983 - No. 36, June, 1986
Marvel Comics Group

| | Good | Fine | N-Mint |
|---|---|---|---|
| 1-Life story of Ben Grimm; Byrne scripts begin | .25 | .75 | 1.50 |
| 2-36: 5-Spider-Man, She-Hulk app. | | .50 | 1.00 |

NOTE: ***Byrne** a-2i, 7; c-1, 7, 36i; scripts-1-13, 19-22. **Sienkiewicz** c-13i.*

**THIRD WORLD WAR**
1990 - No. 6, 1991 ($2.50, color, high quality, thick-c)
Fleetway Publications (Quality)

| | Good | Fine | N-Mint |
|---|---|---|---|
| 1-6 | .40 | 1.25 | 2.50 |

**THIRTEEN** (. . .Going on 18)
11-1/61-62 - No. 25, 12/67; No. 26, 7/69 - No. 29, 1/71
Dell Publishing Co.

| | Good | Fine | N-Mint |
|---|---|---|---|
| 1 | 3.50 | 10.50 | 24.00 |
| 2-10 | 2.65 | 8.00 | 18.00 |
| 11-29: 26-29-r | 2.00 | 6.00 | 14.00 |

NOTE: ***John Stanley** script-No. 3-29; art?*

**13: ASSASSIN**
1990 - Present ($2.95, color, 44 pgs.)
TSR, Inc.

| | Good | Fine | N-Mint |
|---|---|---|---|
| 1-8: Agent 13; Alcala-a(i) | .50 | 1.50 | 3.00 |

**THIRTY SECONDS OVER TOKYO** (Also see Guadacanal Diary)
1943 (Movie) (Also see American Library)
David McKay Co.

| | Good | Fine | N-Mint |
|---|---|---|---|
| nn-(B&W, text & pictures) | 22.00 | 65.00 | 150.00 |

**THIS IS SUSPENSE!** (Formerly Strange Suspense Stories; Strange Suspense Stories #27 on)
No. 23, Feb, 1955 - No. 26, Aug, 1955
Charlton Comics

| | Good | Fine | N-Mint |
|---|---|---|---|
| 23-Wood-a(r)/A Star Presentation #3-"Dr. Jekyll & Mr. Hyde" | 12.00 | 36.00 | 85.00 |
| 24-Evans-a | 5.70 | 17.00 | 40.00 |
| 25,26 | 3.60 | 11.00 | 25.00 |

**THIS IS THE PAYOFF** (See Pay-Off)

**THIS IS WAR**
No. 5, July, 1952 - No. 9, May, 1953
Standard Comics

| | Good | Fine | N-Mint |
|---|---|---|---|
| 5-Toth-a | 6.50 | 19.00 | 45.00 |
| 6,9-Toth-a | 5.00 | 15.00 | 35.00 |
| 7,8 | 1.50 | 4.50 | 10.00 |

**THIS IS YOUR LIFE, DONALD DUCK** (See 4-Color #1109)

**THIS MAGAZINE IS CRAZY** (Crazy V3#3 on)
V3#2, July, 1957 (68 pgs.) (25 cents) (Satire)
Charlton Publ. (Humor Magazines)

| | Good | Fine | N-Mint |
|---|---|---|---|
| V3#2 | 1.30 | 4.00 | 9.00 |

**THIS MAGAZINE IS HAUNTED** (Danger and Adventure #22 on)
Oct, 1951 - No. 14, 12/53; No. 15, 2/54 - V3#21, Nov, 1954
Fawcett Publications/Charlton No. 15(2/54) on

| | Good | Fine | N-Mint |
|---|---|---|---|
| 1-Evans-a(i?) | 20.00 | 60.00 | 140.00 |
| 2,5-Evans-a | 14.00 | 43.00 | 100.00 |
| 3,4 | 7.00 | 21.00 | 50.00 |
| 6-9,11,12 | 5.70 | 17.00 | 40.00 |
| 10-Severed head-c | 9.30 | 28.00 | 65.00 |
| 13-Severed head-c/story | 8.50 | 25.50 | 60.00 |
| 14,17-Ditko-c/a(3&4). 17-Blood drainage story | 16.00 | 48.00 | 110.00 |
| 15,20 | 5.00 | 15.00 | 35.00 |
| 16,19-Ditko-c. 19-Injury-to-eye panel; story r-/#1 | 11.00 | 32.00 | 75.00 |
| 18-Ditko-c/a; E.C. swipe/Haunt of Fear 5; injury-to-eye panel | 14.00 | 40.00 | 95.00 |
| 21-Ditko-c, Evans-a | 10.00 | 30.00 | 70.00 |

NOTE: ***Bailey** a-1, 3, 4, 21r/#1. **Powell** a-3-5, 11, 12, 17. **Shuster** a-18-20.*

**THIS MAGAZINE IS HAUNTED** (2nd Series) (Formerly Zaza the Mystic; Outer Space #17 on)
V2#12, July, 1957 - V2#16, April, 1958
Charlton Comics

| | Good | Fine | N-Mint |
|---|---|---|---|
| V2#12-14-Ditko-c/a in all | 13.00 | 40.00 | 90.00 |
| 15-No Ditko-c/a | 2.00 | 6.00 | 14.00 |
| 16-Ditko-a | 8.00 | 24.00 | 55.00 |

**THIS MAGAZINE IS WILD** (See Wild)

**THIS WAS YOUR LIFE** (Religious)
1964 (3½x5½") (40 pgs.) (Black, white & red)
Jack T. Chick Publ.

| | Good | Fine | N-Mint |
|---|---|---|---|
| nn | | .40 | .80 |
| Another version (5x2¾", 26pgs.) | | .60 | 1.20 |

**THOR** (See Avengers #1, Giant-Size. . ., Marvel Collectors Item Classics, Marvel Graphic Novel 33, Marvel Preview, Marvel Spectacular, Marvel Treasury Edition, Special Marvel Edition & Tales of Asgard)

**THOR** (Formerly Journey Into Mystery)(The Mighty Thor #? on)
March, 1966 - Present
Marvel Comics Group

| | Good | Fine | N-Mint |
|---|---|---|---|
| 126 | 8.50 | 25.50 | 60.00 |
| 127-133,135-140 | 3.60 | 11.00 | 25.00 |
| 134-Intro High Evolutionary | 5.00 | 15.00 | 35.00 |
| 141-157,159,160: 146-Inhumans begin, end #151. 146,147-Origin The Inhumans. 148,149-Origin Black Bolt in each; 149-Origin Medusa, Crystal, Maximus, Gorgon, Kornak | 2.65 | 8.00 | 18.00 |
| 158-Origin-r/#83; 158,159-Origin Dr. Blake | 6.50 | 19.00 | 45.00 |
| 161,163,164,167,170-179-Last Kirby issue | 1.70 | 5.00 | 12.00 |
| 162,168,169-Origin Galactus | 3.00 | 9.00 | 21.00 |
| 165,166-Warlock (Him) app. | 1.50 | 4.50 | 10.00 |
| 180,181-Neal Adams-a | 1.30 | 4.00 | 9.00 |
| 182-192,194-200 | .70 | 2.00 | 4.00 |
| 193-(52 pgs.); Silver Surfer x-over | 2.85 | 8.50 | 20.00 |
| 201-299: 225-Intro. Firelord. 271-Iron Man x-over. 274-Death of Balder the Brave. 294-Origin Asgard & Odin | .35 | 1.00 | 2.00 |
| 300-End of Asgard; origin of Odin & The Destroyer | .50 | 1.50 | 3.00 |
| 301-336: 316-Iron Man x-over | .25 | .75 | 1.50 |
| 337-Simonson-c/a begins, ends #382; Beta Ray Bill becomes new Thor | 1.15 | 3.50 | 7.00 |
| 338 | .50 | 1.50 | 3.00 |
| 339,340: 340-Donald Blake returns as Thor | .25 | .75 | 1.50 |
| 341-373,375-381,383: 373-X-Factor tie-in | | .50 | 1.00 |
| 374-Mutant massacre; X-Factor app. | 1.15 | 3.50 | 7.00 |
| 382-($1.25)-Anniversary issue; last Simonson-a | .35 | 1.00 | 2.00 |
| 384-Intro. new Thor | .35 | 1.00 | 2.00 |
| 385-399,401-411,413-432: 395-Intro Earth Force. 411-New Warriors cameo. 427,428-Excalibur app. 429-Ghost Rider app. | .50 | | 1.00 |
| 400-($1.75, 68 pgs.)-Origin Loki | .40 | 1.25 | 2.50 |
| 412-Intro New Warriors (Marvel Boy, Kid Nova, Namorita, Night Thrasher, Firestar & Speedball) | 1.00 | 3.00 | 6.00 |
| Special 2(9/66)-See Journey Into Mystery for 1st annual | 3.60 | 11.00 | 25.00 |
| King Size Special 3(1/71) | .85 | 2.60 | 6.00 |
| Special 4(12/71) | .85 | 2.60 | 6.00 |
| Annual 5,7,8: 5(11/76). 7(1978). 8(1979) | .70 | 2.00 | 5.00 |
| Annual 6 (10/77)-Guardians of the Galaxy app. | .70 | 2.00 | 5.00 |
| Annual 9-12: 9(1981). 10(1982). 11(1983). 12(1984) | .50 | 1.50 | 3.00 |
| Annual 13(1985) | .35 | 1.00 | 2.00 |
| Annual 14(1989, $2.00, 68 pgs.)-Atlantis Attacks | .35 | 1.00 | 2.00 |
| Annual 15(1990, $2.00, 68 pgs.) | .35 | 1.00 | 2.00 |

NOTE: ***Neal Adams** a-180,181; c-179-181. **Austin** a-342i, 346i; c-312i. **Buscema** a(p)-178, 182-213, 215-226, 231-238, 241-253, 254r, 256-259, 272-278, 283-285, 370, Annual 6, 8; c(p)-175, 182-196, 198-200, 202-204, 206, 211, 212, 215, 219, 221, 226, 256, 259, 261, 262, 272-278, 283, 289, 370, Annual 6. **Everett** a(i)-143, 170-175; c(i)-171, 172, 174, 176, 241. **Gil Kane** a-318p; c(p)-201, 205, 207-210, 216, 220, 222, 223, 231, 233-240, 242, 243, 318. **Kirby** a(p)-126-177, 179, 194, 254r; c(p)-126-169, 171-174, 176-178, 249-253, 255, 257, 258, Annual 5, Special 1-4. **Mooney** a(i)-201, 204, 214-216, 218, 322i, 324i, 325i, 327i. **Sienkiewicz** c-332, 333, 335. **Simonson** a-260-271p, 337-354, 357-367, 380, 382, Annual 7p; c-260, 263-271, 337-355, 357-369, 371, 373-382, Annual 7. **Starlin** c-213.*

**THOSE ANNOYING POST BROS.**
Jan, 1985 - Present ($1.75-$2.00, B&W)
Vortex Comics

| | Good | Fine | N-Mint |
|---|---|---|---|
| 1-14 ($1.75); 15-$2.00-c | .30 | .90 | 1.80 |
| 16-20 ($2.50) | .40 | 1.25 | 2.50 |

**THOSE MAGNIFICENT MEN IN THEIR FLYING MACHINES** (See Movie Comics)

**THREE CABALLEROS** (See 4-Color #71)

**THREE CHIPMUNKS, THE** (See 4-Color #1042)

**THREE COMICS** (Also see Spiritman)
1944 (10 cents, 48pgs.) (2 different covers exist)
The Penny King Co.

| | Good | Fine | N-Mint |
|---|---|---|---|
| 1,3,4-Lady Luck, Mr. Mystic, The Spirit app. (3 Spirit sections bound together)-Lou Fine-a | 14.00 | 43.00 | 100.00 |

NOTE: *No. 1 contains Spirit Sections 4/9/44 - 4/23/44, and No. 4 is also from 4/44.*

**3-D** (NOTE: The prices of all the 3-D comics listed include glasses. Deduct 40-50 percent if glasses are missing, and reduce slightly if glasses are loose.)

**3-D ACTION**
Jan, 1954 (Oversized) (15 cents)(2 pairs glasses included)
Atlas Comics (ACI)

| | Good | Fine | N-Mint |
|---|---|---|---|
| 1-Battle Brady | 27.00 | 80.00 | 185.00 |

**3-D ADVENTURE COMICS**
Aug, 1986 (One shot)
Stats, Etc.

| | Good | Fine | N-Mint |
|---|---|---|---|
| 1-Promo material | .25 | .75 | 1.50 |

**3-D ALIEN TERROR**
June, 1986 ($2.50)
Eclipse Comics

| | Good | Fine | N-Mint |
|---|---|---|---|
| 1-Old Witch, Crypt-Keeper, Vault Keeper cameo; Morrow, John Pound-a, Yeates-c | .40 | 1.25 | 2.50 |
| . . .in 2-D: 100 copies signed & numbered (B&W) | .85 | 2.50 | 5.00 |

**3-D ANIMAL FUN** (See Animal Fun)

**3-D BATMAN**
1953, Reprinted in 1966
National Periodical Publications

| | Good | Fine | N-Mint |
|---|---|---|---|
| 1953-Reprints Batman #42 & 48; Tommy Tomorrow app. (25 cents) | 79.00 | 235.00 | 550.00 |
| 1966-Tommy Tomorrow app. | 25.00 | 75.00 | 175.00 |

**3-D CIRCUS**
1953 (25 cents)
Fiction House Magazines (Real Adventures Publ.)

| | Good | Fine | N-Mint |
|---|---|---|---|
| 1 | 27.00 | 80.00 | 185.00 |

**3-D COMICS** (See Mighty Mouse and Tor)

**3-D DOLLY**
December, 1953 (2 pairs glasses included)
Harvey Publications

| | Good | Fine | N-Mint |
|---|---|---|---|
| 1-Richie Rich story redrawn from his 1st app. in Little Dot #1 | 13.00 | 40.00 | 90.00 |

**3-D-ELL**
1953 - No. 3, 1953 (3-D comics) (25 cents)
Dell Publishing Co.

| | Good | Fine | N-Mint |
|---|---|---|---|
| 1,2-Rootie Kazootie | 27.00 | 81.00 | 190.00 |
| 3-Flukey Luke | 24.00 | 73.00 | 170.00 |

**3-D EXOTIC BEAUTIES**
Nov, 1990 ($2.95, 28 pgs.)
The 3-D Zone

| | Good | Fine | N-Mint |
|---|---|---|---|
| 1-L.B. Cole-c | .50 | 1.50 | 3.00 |

**3-D FEATURES PRESENT JET PUP**
Oct-Dec, 1953
Dimensions Public

| | Good | Fine | N-Mint |
|---|---|---|---|
| 1-Irving Spector-a(2) | 26.00 | 77.00 | 180.00 |

**3-D FUNNY MOVIES**
1953 (25 cents)
Comic Media

| | Good | Fine | N-Mint |
|---|---|---|---|
| 1-Bugsey Bear & Paddy Pelican | 25.00 | 75.00 | 175.00 |

**3-D HEROES** (See Blackthorne 3-D Series #3)

*Thor #412, © MEG*

*Those Annoying Post Bros. #3, © Vortex*

*3-D Funny Movies #1, © Comic Media*

*Three Dimensional E.C. Classics #1, © WMG*

*The 3-D Zone #11, © Ray Zone*

*Three Stooges #2 (5/49), © Norman Maurer*

**THREE-DIMENSION ADVENTURES** (Superman)
1953 (Large size)
National Periodical Publications

| | Good | Fine | N-Mint |
|---|---|---|---|
| nn-Origin Superman (new art) | 83.00 | 250.00 | 580.00 |

**THREE DIMENSIONAL ALIEN WORLDS** (See Alien Worlds)
July, 1984 (One-Shot)(1st Ray Zone 3-D book)
Pacific Comics

| | | | |
|---|---|---|---|
| 1-Bolton/Stevens-a; Art Adams 1st published-a | .85 | 2.50 | 5.00 |

**THREE DIMENSIONAL DNAGENTS** (See New DNAgents)

**THREE DIMENSIONAL E. C. CLASSICS** (Three Dimensional Tales From the Crypt No. 2)
Spring, 1954 (Prices include glasses; came with 2 pairs)
E. C. Comics

| | | | |
|---|---|---|---|
| 1-Stories by Wood (Mad #3), Krigstein (W.S. #7), Evans (F.C. #13), & Ingels (CSS #5); Kurtzman-c | 47.00 | 140.00 | 330.00 |

NOTE: *Stories redrawn to 3-D format. Original stories not necessarily by artists listed. CSS: Crime SuspenStories; F.C.: Frontline Combat; W.S.: Weird Science.*

**THREE DIMENSIONAL TALES FROM THE CRYPT** (Formerly Three Dimensional E. C. Classics)(Cover title: . . . From the Crypt of Terror)
No. 2, Spring, 1954 (Prices include glasses; came with 2 pair)
E. C. Comics

| | | | |
|---|---|---|---|
| 2-Davis (TFTC #25), Elder (VOH #14), Craig (TFTC #24), & Orlando (TFTC #22) stories; Feldstein-c | 51.00 | 154.00 | 360.00 |

NOTE: *Stories redrawn to 3-D format. Original stories not necessarily by artists listed. TFTC: Tales From the Crypt; VOH: Vault of Horror.*

**3-D LOVE**
December, 1953 (25 cents)
Steriographic Publ. (Mikeross Publ.)

| | | | |
|---|---|---|---|
| 1 | 25.00 | 75.00 | 175.00 |

**3-D NOODNICK** (See Noodnick)

**3-D ROMANCE**
January, 1954 (25 cents)
Steriographic Publ. (Mikeross Publ.)

| | | | |
|---|---|---|---|
| 1 | 25.00 | 75.00 | 175.00 |

**3-D SHEENA, JUNGLE QUEEN** (Also see Sheena 3-D)
1953
Fiction House Magazines

| | | | |
|---|---|---|---|
| 1 | 40.00 | 120.00 | 280.00 |

**3-D SUBSTANCE**
July, 1990 ($2.95, 28 pgs.)
The 3-D Zone

| | | | |
|---|---|---|---|
| 1-Ditko-c/a(r) | .50 | 1.50 | 3.00 |

**3-D TALES OF THE WEST**
Jan, 1954 (Oversized) (15 cents)(2 pair glasses included)
Atlas Comics (CPS)

| | | | |
|---|---|---|---|
| 1 (3-D) | 27.00 | 81.00 | 190.00 |

**3-D THREE STOOGES** (Also see Three Stooges)
Sept, 1986 - No. 2, Nov, 1986; No. 3, Oct, 1987; No. 4, 1989 ($2.50)
Eclipse Comics

| | | | |
|---|---|---|---|
| 1-3 (10/87)-Maurer-r | .40 | 1.25 | 2.50 |
| 4 ('89, $3.50)-Reprints "Three Missing Links" | .60 | 1.75 | 3.50 |
| 1-3 (2-D) | .85 | 2.50 | 5.00 |

**3-D WHACK** (See Whack)

**3-D ZONE, THE**
Feb, 1987 - No. 20, 1989 ($2.50)
The 3-D Zone(Renegade Press)/Ray Zone

| | Good | Fine | N-Mint |
|---|---|---|---|
| 1-10: 1-r-/A Star Presentation, 2-Wolverton-r, 3-Picture Scope Jungle Advs., 4-Electric Fear, 5-Krazy Kat-r, 6-Ratfink, 7-Hollywood 3-D; Jayne Mansfield photo-c, 8-High Seas 3-D, 9-Redmask-r, 10-Jet 3-D; Powell & Williamson-r | .40 | 1.25 | 2.50 |
| 11-20: 11-Danse Macabre; Matt Fox c/a(r). 12-3-D Presidents. 13-Flash 13-Gordon. 14-Tyranostar. 15-3-Dementia Comics; Kurtzman-c, Kubert, Maurer-a. 16-Space Vixens; Dave Stevens-c/a. 17-Thrilling Love. 18-Spacehawk; Wolverton-r. 19-Cracked Classics. 20-Commander Battle and His Atomic Submarine | .40 | 1.25 | 2.50 |

NOTE: ***Davis** r-19. **Ditko** r-19. **Elder** r-19. **Everett** r-19. **Feldstein** r-17. **Frazetta** r-17. **Heath** r-19. **Kamen** r-17. **Severin** r-19. **Ward** r-17, 19. **Wolverton** r-2, 18, 19. **Wood** r-1, 17. Photo c-12.*

**3 FUNMAKERS, THE**
1908 (64 pgs.) (10x15")
Stokes and Company

| | | | |
|---|---|---|---|
| nn-Maude, Katzenjammer Kids, Happy Hooligan (1904-06 Sunday strip reprints in color) | 30.00 | 90.00 | 210.00 |

**3 LITTLE PIGS** (See 4-Color #218)

**3 LITTLE PIGS, THE** (See Walt Disney Showcase #15 & 21)
May, 1964; No. 2, Sept, 1968 (Walt Disney)
Gold Key

| | | | |
|---|---|---|---|
| 1-Reprints 4-Color #218 | 1.00 | 3.00 | 7.00 |
| 2 | .75 | 2.25 | 5.00 |

**THREE MOUSEKETEERS, THE** (1st Series)
3-4/56 - No. 24, 9-10/59; No. 25, 8-9/60 - No. 26, 10-12/60
National Periodical Publications

| | | | |
|---|---|---|---|
| 1 | 10.00 | 30.00 | 70.00 |
| 2 | 5.00 | 15.00 | 35.00 |
| 3-10 | 3.50 | 10.50 | 24.00 |
| 11-26 | 2.65 | 8.00 | 18.00 |

NOTE: ***Rube Grossman** a-1-26. **Sheldon Mayer** a-1-8; c-1, 3, 4, 6, 7.*

**THREE MOUSEKETEERS, THE** (2nd Series) (See Super DC Giant)
May-June, 1970 - No. 7, May-June, 1971 (#5-7: 68 pgs.)
National Periodical Publications

| | | | |
|---|---|---|---|
| 1-Mayer-a | .50 | 1.50 | 3.00 |
| 2-7-Mayer-a | .35 | 1.00 | 2.00 |

**THREE NURSES** (Formerly Confidential Diary; Career Girl Romances #24 on)
V3#18, May, 1963 - V3#23, Mar, 1964
Charlton Comics

| | | | |
|---|---|---|---|
| V3#18-23 | .40 | 1.25 | 2.50 |

**THREE RASCALS**
1958; 1963
I. W. Enterprises

| | | | |
|---|---|---|---|
| I.W. Reprint #1 (Says Super Comics on inside)-(M.E.'s Clubhouse Rascals), #2('58) | .25 | .80 | 1.60 |
| 10('63)-Reprints #1 | .25 | .80 | 1.60 |

**THREE RING COMICS**
March, 1945
Spotlight Publishers

| | | | |
|---|---|---|---|
| 1 | 5.00 | 15.00 | 35.00 |

**THREE ROCKETEERS** (See Blast-Off)

**THREE STOOGES** (See Comic Album #18, The Little Stooges, March of Comics #232, 248, 268, 280, 292, 304, 316, 336, 373, Movie Classics & Comics & 3-D Three Stooges)

**THREE STOOGES**
Feb, 1949 - No. 2, May, 1949; Sept, 1953 - No. 7, Oct, 1954
Jubilee No. 1,2/St. John No. 1 (9/53) on

| | | | |
|---|---|---|---|
| 1-(Scarce, 1949)-Kubert-a; infinity-c | 57.00 | 170.00 | 400.00 |
| 2-(Scarce)-Kubert, Maurer-a | 43.00 | 130.00 | 300.00 |
| 1(9/53)-Hollywood Stunt Girl by Kubert, 7 pgs. | 38.00 | 115.00 | 265.00 |
| 2(3-D, 10/53)-Stunt Girl story by Kubert | 27.00 | 81.00 | 190.00 |

| | Good | Fine | N-Mint |
|---|---|---|---|
| 3(3-D, 11/53) | 24.00 | 73.00 | 170.00 |
| 4(3/54)-7(10/54) | 18.00 | 54.00 | 125.00 |

NOTE: *All issues have* ***Kubert-Maurer*** *art.* ***Maurer*** *c-1, 2('49), 1('53).*

**THREE STOOGES**
No. 1043, Oct-Dec, 1959 - No. 55, June, 1972
Dell Publishing Co./Gold Key No. 10 (10/62) on

| | Good | Fine | N-Mint |
|---|---|---|---|
| 4-Color 1043 (#1) | 8.50 | 25.50 | 60.00 |
| 4-Color 1078,1127,1170,1187 | 5.70 | 17.00 | 40.00 |
| 6(9-11/61) - 10: 6-Professor Putter begins; ends #16 | 4.30 | 13.00 | 30.00 |
| 11-14,16-20: 17-The Little Monsters begin (5/64)(1st app.?) | 4.00 | 12.00 | 28.00 |
| 15-Go Around the World in a Daze (movie scenes) | 4.50 | 14.00 | 32.00 |
| 21,23-30 | 3.00 | 9.00 | 21.00 |
| 22-Movie scenes/'The Outlaws Is Coming' | 4.30 | 13.00 | 30.00 |
| 31-55 | 2.30 | 7.00 | 16.00 |

NOTE: *All Four Colors, 6-50, 52-55 have photo-c.*

**3 WORLDS OF GULLIVER** (See 4-Color #1158)

**THRILL COMICS** (See Flash Comics, Fawcett)

**THRILLER**
Nov, 1983 - No. 12, Nov, 1984 ($1.25; Baxter paper)
DC Comics

| | Good | Fine | N-Mint |
|---|---|---|---|
| 1-9,11,12: 1-Intro Seven Seconds. 2-Origin. 5,6-Elvis satire | | .65 | 1.30 |
| 10-($2.00) | .35 | 1.00 | 2.00 |

**THRILLING ADVENTURES IN STAMPS COMICS**
V1#8, Jan, 1953 (25 cents) (100 pages) (Formerly Stamp Comics)
Stamp Comics, Inc. (Very Rare)

| | Good | Fine | N-Mint |
|---|---|---|---|
| V1#8-Harrison, Wildey, Kiefer, Napoli-a | 32.00 | 95.00 | 225.00 |

**THRILLING ADVENTURE STORIES** (See Tigerman)
Feb, 1975 - No. 2, July-Aug, 1975 (B&W) (68 pgs.)
Atlas/Seaboard Publ.

| | Good | Fine | N-Mint |
|---|---|---|---|
| 1,2: 1-Tigerman, Kromag the Killer begin; Heath, Thorne-a. 2-Heath, Toth, Severin, Simonson-a; Neal Adams-c | .40 | 1.20 | 2.40 |

**THRILLING COMICS**
Feb, 1940 - No. 80, April, 1951
Better Publ./Nedor/Standard Comics

| | Good | Fine | N-Mint |
|---|---|---|---|
| 1-Origin Doc Strange (37 pgs.); Nickie Norton of the Secret Service begins | 68.00 | 205.00 | 475.00 |
| 2-The Rio Kid, The Woman in Red, Pinocchio begins | 30.00 | 90.00 | 210.00 |
| 3-The Ghost & Lone Eagle begin | 27.00 | 81.00 | 190.00 |
| 4-10 | 18.00 | 54.00 | 125.00 |
| 11-18,20 | 14.00 | 41.00 | 95.00 |
| 19-Origin The American Crusader, ends #39,41 | 19.50 | 58.00 | 135.00 |
| 21-30: 24-Intro. Mike, Doc Strange's sidekick. 29-Last Rio Kid | 12.00 | 36.00 | 85.00 |
| 31-40: 36-Commando Cubs begin | 10.00 | 30.00 | 70.00 |
| 41,44-Hittler-c | 10.00 | 30.00 | 70.00 |
| 42,43,45-52: 52-The Ghost ends | 8.00 | 24.00 | 55.00 |
| 53-The Phantom Detective begins; The Cavalier app.; no Commando Cubs | 8.00 | 24.00 | 55.00 |
| 54-The Cavalier app.; no Commando Cubs | 8.00 | 24.00 | 55.00 |
| 55-Lone Eagle ends | 8.00 | 24.00 | 55.00 |
| 56-Princess Pantha begins | 16.00 | 48.00 | 110.00 |
| 57-60 | 13.00 | 40.00 | 90.00 |
| 61-66: 61-Ingels-a; The Lone Eagle app. 65-Last Phantom Detective & Commando Cubs. 66-Frazetta text illo | 13.00 | 40.00 | 90.00 |
| 67,70-73: Frazetta-a(5-7 pgs.) in each. 72-Sea Eagle app. | 18.00 | 54.00 | 125.00 |
| 68,69-Frazetta-a(2), 8 & 6 pgs.; 9 & 7 pgs. | 19.00 | 57.00 | 132.00 |
| 74-Last Princess Pantha; Tara app. Buck Ranger, Cowboy Detective begins | 7.00 | 21.00 | 50.00 |
| 75-78: 75-Western format begins | 4.00 | 12.00 | 28.00 |
| 79-Krigstein-a | 5.30 | 16.00 | 38.00 |
| 80-Severin & Elder, Celardo, Moreira-a | 5.30 | 16.00 | 38.00 |

NOTE: *Bondage c-5, 9, 13, 20, 22, 27-30, 38, 41, 52, 54, 70.* ***Kinstler*** *a-45, 48.* ***Leo Morey*** *a-7.* ***Schomburg (Xela)*** *c-7, 11-18, 36-71 (airbrush 62-71).* ***Tuska*** *a-63. Woman in Red not in #19, 23, 31-33, 39-45. No. 72 exists as a Canadian reprint with no Frazetta story.*

**THRILLING CRIME CASES** (Shocking Mystery Cases #50 on)
No. 41, June-July, 1950 - No. 49, 1952
Star Publications

| | Good | Fine | N-Mint |
|---|---|---|---|
| 41 | 6.50 | 19.00 | 45.00 |
| 42-44-Chameleon story-Fox-r | 5.00 | 15.00 | 35.00 |
| 45-48: 47-Used in **POP**, pg. 84 | 4.30 | 13.00 | 30.00 |
| 49-Classic L. B. Cole-c | 12.00 | 36.00 | 85.00 |

NOTE: ***L. B. Cole*** *c-all; a-43p, 45p, 46p, 49(2pgs.).* ***Disbrow*** *a-48.* ***Hollingsworth*** *a-48.*

**THRILLING ROMANCES**
No. 5, Dec, 1949 - No. 26, June, 1954
Standard Comics

| | Good | Fine | N-Mint |
|---|---|---|---|
| 5 | 4.00 | 12.00 | 28.00 |
| 6,8 | 2.00 | 6.00 | 14.00 |
| 7-Severin/Elder-a, 7 pgs. | 3.50 | 10.50 | 24.00 |
| 9,10-Severin/Elder-a | 2.65 | 8.00 | 18.00 |
| 11,14-21,26: 15-Tony Martin/Janet Leigh photo-c | 1.30 | 4.00 | 9.00 |
| 12-Wood-a, 2 pgs.; photo-c | 4.50 | 14.00 | 32.00 |
| 13-Severin-a | 2.30 | 7.00 | 16.00 |
| 22-25-Toth-a | 4.00 | 12.00 | 28.00 |

NOTE: *All photo-c.* ***Celardo*** *a-9, 16.* ***Colletta*** *a-23, 24(2).* ***Tuska*** *a-9.*

**THRILLING SCIENCE TALES**
1989 - Present ($3.50, ⅔ color, 52 pgs.)
AC Comics

| | Good | Fine | N-Mint |
|---|---|---|---|
| 1-r/Bob Colt #6(saucer); Frazetta, Guardineer (Space Ace), Wood, Krenkel, Orlando, Williamson-r; Kaluta-c | .60 | 1.75 | 3.50 |
| 2-Capt. Video-r by Evans, Capt. Science-r by Wood, Star Pirate-r by Whitman & Mysta of the Moon-r by Moreira | .60 | 1.75 | 3.50 |

**THRILLING TRUE STORY OF THE BASEBALL. . . .**
1952 (Photo-c, each)
Fawcett Publications

| | Good | Fine | N-Mint |
|---|---|---|---|
| . . .Giants-photo-c; has Willie Mays rookie photo-biography | 36.00 | 107.00 | 250.00 |
| . . .Yankees-photo-c | 32.00 | 95.00 | 225.00 |

**THRILLOGY**
Jan, 1984 (One-shot, color)
Pacific Comics

| | Good | Fine | N-Mint |
|---|---|---|---|
| 1-Conrad-c/a | | .50 | 1.00 |

**THRILL-O-RAMA**
Oct, 1965 - No. 3, Dec, 1966
Harvey Publications (Fun Films)

| | Good | Fine | N-Mint |
|---|---|---|---|
| 1-Fate (Man in Black) by Powell app.; Doug Wildey-a; Simon-c; Williamson-a (5 pgs.) | 1.00 | 3.00 | 7.00 |
| 2-Pirana begins; Williamson 2 pgs.; Fate (Man in Black) app.; Tuska/Simon-c | 1.00 | 3.00 | 7.00 |
| 3-Fate (Man in Black) app.; Sparling-c | .70 | 2.00 | 4.00 |

**THRILLS OF TOMORROW** (Formerly Tomb of Terror)
No. 17, Oct, 1954 - No. 20, April, 1955
Harvey Publications

| | Good | Fine | N-Mint |
|---|---|---|---|
| 17-Powell-a (horror); r/Witches Tales #7 | 3.00 | 9.00 | 21.00 |
| 18-Powell-a (horror); r/Tomb of Terror #1 | 2.30 | 7.00 | 16.00 |

19,20-Stuntman by S&K (r/from Stuntman #1 & 2); 19 has origin & is

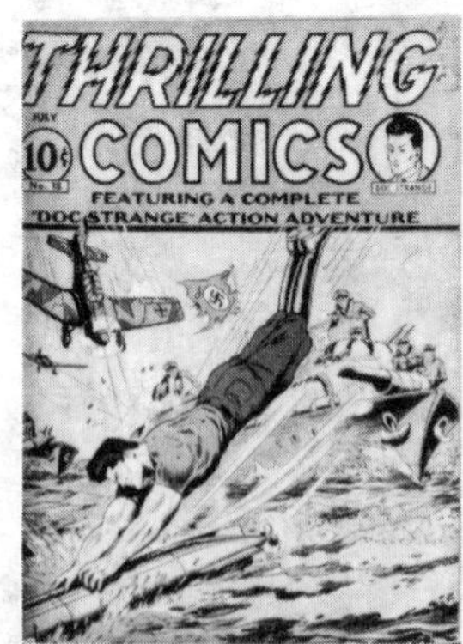

*Thrilling Comics #18, © STD*

*Thrilling Romances #15, © STD*

*Thrill-O-Rama #1, © HARV*

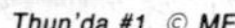
Thun'da #1, © ME

Thunder Agents #4, © TC

Tick Tock Tales #1, © ME

| | Good | Fine | N-Mint |
|---|---|---|---|
| last pre-code (2/55) | 13.50 | 40.50 | 95.00 |

NOTE: ***Palais** a-17.*

**THROBBING LOVE** (See Fox Giants)

**THROUGH GATES OF SPLENDOR**
1973, 1974 (36 pages) (39-49 cents)
Spire Christian Comics (Fleming H. Revell Co.)

| | Good | Fine | N-Mint |
|---|---|---|---|
| nn | | .40 | .80 |

**THUMPER** (See 4-Color #19 & 243)

**THUN'DA** (. . .King of the Congo)
1952 - No. 6, 1953
Magazine Enterprises

| | Good | Fine | N-Mint |
|---|---|---|---|
| 1(A-1 #47)-Origin; Frazetta c/a; only comic done entirely by Frazetta; All Thun'da stories, no Cave Girl | 83.00 | 250.00 | 580.00 |
| 2(A-1 #56)-Powell-c/a begins, ends #6; Intro/1st app. Cave Girl in filler strip (also app. in 3-6) | 12.00 | 36.00 | 84.00 |
| 3(A-1 #73), 4(A-1 #78) | 9.00 | 27.00 | 62.00 |
| 5(A-1 #83), 6(A-1 #86) | 8.00 | 24.00 | 56.00 |

**THUN'DA TALES** (See Frank Frazetta's. . .)

**THUNDER AGENTS** (See Dynamo, Noman & Tales Of Thunder)
11/65 - No. 17, 12/67; No. 18, 9/68, No. 19, 11/68, No. 20, 11/69
(No. 1-16: 68 pgs.; No. 17 on: 52 pgs.)(All are 25 cents)
Tower Comics

| | Good | Fine | N-Mint |
|---|---|---|---|
| 1-Origin & 1st app. Dynamo, Noman, Menthor, & The Thunder Squad; 1st app. The Iron Maiden | 8.00 | 24.00 | 55.00 |
| 2-Death of Egghead | 4.30 | 13.00 | 30.00 |
| 3-5: 4-Guy Gilbert becomes Lightning who joins Thunder Squad; Iron Maiden app. | 3.15 | 9.50 | 22.00 |
| 6-10: 7-Death of Menthor. 8-Origin & 1st app. The Raven | 2.00 | 6.00 | 14.00 |
| 11-15: 13-Undersea Agent app.; no Raven story | 1.30 | 4.00 | 9.00 |
| 16-19 | 1.00 | 3.00 | 7.00 |
| 20-Special Collectors Edition; all reprints | .70 | 2.00 | 4.00 |

NOTE: ***Crandall** a-1, 4p, 5p, 18, 20r; c-18. **Ditko** a-6, 7p, 12p, 13, 14p, 16, 18. **Kane** a-1, 5p, 6p, 14, 16p; c-14, 15. **Tuska** a-1p, 7, 8, 10, 13-17, 19. **Whitney** a-9p, 10, 13, 15, 17, 18; c-17. **Wood** a-1-11, 15(w/**Ditko**-12, 18), (inks-#9, 13, 14, 16, 17), 19i, 20r; c-1-8, 9i, 10-13(#10 w/**Williamson**(p)), 16.*

**T.H.U.N.D.E.R. AGENTS** (See Blue Ribbon Comics, Hall of Fame Featuring the. . ., JCP Features & Wally Wood's. . .)
May, 1983 - No. 2, Jan, 1984
JC Comics (Archie Publications)

| | Good | Fine | N-Mint |
|---|---|---|---|
| 1,2-New material | .35 | 1.00 | 2.00 |

**THUNDER BIRDS** (See Cinema Comics Herald)

**THUNDERBOLT** (See The Atomic. . .)

**THUNDERBOLT** (Peter Cannon. . .; see Crisis on Infinite Earths)
Jan, 1966; No. 51, Mar-Apr, 1966 - No. 60, Nov, 1967
Charlton Comics

| | Good | Fine | N-Mint |
|---|---|---|---|
| 1-Origin | 1.00 | 3.00 | 7.00 |
| 51-(Formerly Son of Vulcan #50) | .70 | 2.00 | 4.00 |
| 52-60: 54-Sentinels begin. 59-Last Thunderbolt & Sentinels. 60-Prankster app. | .50 | 1.50 | 3.00 |
| Modern Comics-r. 57,58('77) | | .15 | .30 |

NOTE: ***Aparo** a-60. **Morisi** a-1, 51-56, 58; c-1, 51-56, 58, 59.*

**THUNDERBUNNY** (Also see Blue Ribbon Comics #13, Charlton Bullseye & Pep Comics #393)
Jan, 1984 (Direct sale only)
Red Circle Comics

| | Good | Fine | N-Mint |
|---|---|---|---|
| 1-Origin | | .60 | 1.20 |

**THUNDERCATS** (TV)
Dec, 1985 - No. 24, June, 1988 (75 cents)
Star Comics/Marvel #22 on

| | Good | Fine | N-Mint |
|---|---|---|---|
| 1-Mooney c/a begins | | .40 | .80 |
| 2-11: 2-(65 & 75 cent cover exists) | | .40 | .80 |
| 12-24: 12-Begin $1.00-c; 18,20-Williamson-i. 23-Williamson-c(i) | | .50 | 1.00 |

**THUNDER MOUNTAIN** (See 4-Color #246)

**TICK, THE**
June, 1988 - Present ($1.75-$1.95-$2.25; B&W, over-sized)
New England Comics Press

| | Good | Fine | N-Mint |
|---|---|---|---|
| Special Edition 1-1st comic book app. serially numbered & limited to 5000 copies | 5.00 | 15.00 | 30.00 |
| Special Edition 2-Serially numbered and limited to 3000 copies | 4.15 | 12.50 | 25.00 |
| 1-Reprints Special Ed. 1 w/minor changes | 4.15 | 12.50 | 25.00 |
| 1-2nd printing | .50 | 1.50 | 3.00 |
| 1-3rd printing ($1.95, 6/89) | .35 | 1.00 | 2.00 |
| 1-4th printing ($2.25) | .40 | 1.15 | 2.25 |
| 2-Reprints Special Ed. 2 w/minor changes | 2.50 | 7.50 | 15.00 |
| 2-2nd printing ($1.95) | .50 | 1.50 | 3.00 |
| 2-3rd & 4th printings ($2.25) | .40 | 1.15 | 2.25 |
| 3-5 ($1.95) | .70 | 2.00 | 4.00 |
| 3-2nd & 3rd printings ($2.25) | .40 | 1.15 | 2.25 |
| 4-2nd printing ($2.25) | .40 | 1.15 | 2.25 |
| 6-8 ($2.25): 5-1st app. Paul the Samurai | .40 | 1.15 | 2.30 |
| 8-Variant with no logo, price, issue number | 1.35 | 4.00 | 8.00 |
| 9/10-($4.25, 60 pgs.)-Two issues in one | .70 | 2.15 | 4.30 |

**TICKLE COMICS** (Also see Gay, Smile, & Whee Comics)
1955 (52 pages) (5x7¼") (7 cents)
Modern Store Publ.

| | Good | Fine | N-Mint |
|---|---|---|---|
| 1 | .40 | 1.20 | 2.40 |

**TICK TOCK TALES**
1/46 - No. 26, 3/48; No. 27, 11-12/51
Magazine Enterprises

| | Good | Fine | N-Mint |
|---|---|---|---|
| 1-Koko & Kola begin | 5.70 | 17.00 | 40.00 |
| 2 | 3.00 | 9.00 | 21.00 |
| 3-10 | 2.30 | 7.00 | 16.00 |
| 11-27: 19-Flag-c. 23-Muggsy Mouse, The Pixies & Tom-Tom The Jungle Boy app. | 1.50 | 4.50 | 10.00 |

**TIGER** (Also see Comics Reading Libraries)
March, 1970 - No. 6, Jan, 1971 (15 cents)
Charlton Press (King Features)

| | Good | Fine | N-Mint |
|---|---|---|---|
| 1 | .35 | 1.00 | 2.00 |
| 2-6 | | .50 | 1.00 |

**TIGER BOY** (See Unearthly Spectaculars)

**TIGER GIRL**
September, 1968
Gold Key

| | Good | Fine | N-Mint |
|---|---|---|---|
| 1 (10227-809) | 2.00 | 6.00 | 14.00 |

NOTE: ***Sparling** c/a; written by Jerry Siegel.*

**TIGERMAN** (Also see Thrilling Adventure Stories)
April, 1975 - No. 3, Sept, 1975
Seaboard Periodicals (Atlas)

| | Good | Fine | N-Mint |
|---|---|---|---|
| 1 | | .40 | .80 |
| 2,3-Ditko-p in each | | .30 | .60 |

**TIGER WALKS, A** (See Movie Comics)

**TILLIE THE TOILER**
1925 - No. 8, 1933 (52 pgs.) (B&W daily strip reprints)
Cupples & Leon Co.

| | Good | Fine | N-Mint |
|---|---|---|---|
| nn (#1) | 11.50 | 34.00 | 80.00 |
| 2-8 | 7.00 | 21.00 | 50.00 |

NOTE: *First strip appearance was January, 1921.*

**TILLIE THE TOILER** (See Comic Monthly)
No. 15, 1941 - No. 237, July, 1949
Dell Publishing Co.

| | Good | Fine | N-Mint |
|---|---|---|---|
| 4-Color 15(1941) | 24.00 | 70.00 | 165.00 |
| Large Feature Comic 30(1941) | 14.00 | 43.00 | 100.00 |
| 4-Color 8(1942) | 14.00 | 43.00 | 100.00 |
| 4-Color 22(1943) | 11.00 | 32.00 | 75.00 |
| 4-Color 55(1944) | 8.50 | 25.50 | 60.00 |
| 4-Color 89(1945) | 8.00 | 24.00 | 55.00 |
| 4-Color 106('45),132('46) | 6.50 | 19.00 | 45.00 |
| 4-Color 150,176,184 | 5.00 | 15.00 | 35.00 |
| 4-Color 195,213,237 | 3.70 | 11.00 | 26.00 |

**TILLY AND TED-TINKERTOTLAND**
1945 (Giveaway) (20 pgs.)
W. T. Grant Co.

nn-Christmas comic 2.65 8.00 18.00

**TIM** (Formerly Superman-Tim; becomes Gene Autry-Tim)
June, 1950 - Oct, 1950 (Half-size, B&W)
Tim Stores

4 issues; 6/50, 9/50, 10/50 known 3.00 9.00 21.00

**TIME BANDITS**
Feb, 1982 (One shot)
Marvel Comics Group

1-Movie adaptation .50 1.00

**TIME BEAVERS** (See First Comics Graphic Novel #2)

**TIME FOR LOVE** (Formerly Romantic Secrets)
V2#53, Oct, 1966; Oct, 1967 - No. 47, May, 1976
Charlton Comics

V2#53(10/66), 1(10/67), 2(12/67)-20 .35 1.00 2.00
21-47 .40 .80

**TIMELESS TOPIX** (See Topix)

**TIME MACHINE, THE** (See 4-Color #1085)

**TIME MASTERS**
Feb, 1990 - No. 8, Sept, 1990 ($1.75, mini-series)
DC Comics

1-8: New Rip Hunter series. 5-Cave Carson, Viking Prince app. 6-Dr. Fate app. .30 .90 1.80

**TIMESPIRITS**
Jan, 1985 - No. 8, Mar, 1986 ($1.50, Baxter paper; adults only)
Epic Comics (Marvel)

1-8: 4-Williamson-a .25 .75 1.50

**TIME TO RUN**
1973 (39, 49 cents)
Spire Christian Comics (Fleming H. Revell Co.)

nn-by Al Hartley (from Billy Graham movie) .40 .80

**TIME TUNNEL, THE** (TV)
Feb, 1967 - No. 2, July, 1967
Gold Key

1,2-Photo back-c 3.00 9.00 21.00

**TIME TWISTERS**
Sept, 1987 - No. 21, 1989 ($1.25-$1.50, color)
Quality Comics

1-10: Alan Moore scripts in 1-4, 6-9,14(2pg.) .60 1.25
11-21 ($1.50): 14-Bolland-a(2pg.). 15,16-Guice-c .25 .75 1.50

**TIME 2: THE EPIPHANY** (See First Comics Graphic Novel #9)

**TIME WARP** (See The Unexpected #210)
Oct-Nov, 1979 - No. 5, June-July, 1980 ($1.00, 68 pgs.)
DC Comics, Inc.

| | Good | Fine | N-Mint |
|---|---|---|---|
| 1 | | .40 | .80 |
| 2-5 | | .30 | .60 |

NOTE: *Aparo a-1. Buckler a-1p. Chaykin a-2. Ditko a-1-4. Kaluta c-1-5. G. Kane a-2. Nasser a-4. Newton a-1-5p. Orlando a-2. Sutton a-1-3.*

**TIME WARRIORS THE BEGINNING**
1986 (Aug) - No. 2, 1986? ($1.50, color)
Fantasy General Comics

1,2-Alpha Track/Skellon Empire .25 .75 1.50

**TIM HOLT** (Movie star) (Becomes Red Mask #42 on; also see Crack Western #72, & Great Western)
1948 - No. 41, April-May, 1954 (All 36 pgs.)
Magazine Enterprises

| | Good | Fine | N-Mint |
|---|---|---|---|
| 1-(A-1 #14)-Photo-c begin, end No. 18, 29; Tim Holt, His horse Lightning & sidekick Chito begin | 38.00 | 115.00 | 265.00 |
| 2-(A-1 #17)(9-10/48) | 24.00 | 71.00 | 165.00 |
| 3-(A-1 #19)-Photo back-c | 16.00 | 48.00 | 110.00 |
| 4(1-2/49),5: 5-Photo back-c | 12.00 | 36.00 | 85.00 |
| 6-1st app. The Calico Kid (alias Rex Fury), his horse Ebony & Sidekick Sing-Song (begin series); photo back-c | 14.00 | 41.00 | 95.00 |
| 7-10: 7-Calico Kid by Ayers. 8-Calico Kid by Guardineer (r-/in Great Western 10). 9-Map of Tim's Home Range | 10.00 | 30.00 | 70.00 |
| 11-The Calico Kid becomes The Ghost Rider (Origin & 1st app.) by Dick Ayers (r-/in Great Western 8); his horse Spectre & sidekick Sing-Song begin series | 27.00 | 81.00 | 185.00 |
| 12-16,18-Last photo-c | 7.00 | 21.00 | 50.00 |
| 17-Frazetta Ghost Rider-c | 25.00 | 75.00 | 175.00 |
| 19,22,24: 19-Last Tim Holt-c; Bolle line-drawn-c begin | 5.70 | 17.00 | 40.00 |
| 20-Tim Holt becomes Redmask (Origin); begin series; Redmask-c #20-on | 9.50 | 28.50 | 65.00 |
| 21-Frazetta Ghost Rider/Redmask-c | 21.50 | 65.00 | 150.00 |
| 23-Frazetta Redmask-c | 17.00 | 51.00 | 120.00 |
| 25-1st app. Black Phantom | 11.00 | 32.00 | 75.00 |
| 26-30: 28-Wild Bill Hickok, Bat Masterson team up with Redmask. 29-B&W photo-c | 5.00 | 15.00 | 35.00 |
| 31-33-Ghost Rider ends | 4.50 | 14.00 | 32.00 |
| 34-Tales of the Ghost Rider begins (horror)-Classic "The Flower Women" & "Hard Boiled Harry!" | 5.70 | 17.00 | 40.00 |
| 35-Last Tales of the Ghost Rider | 5.00 | 15.00 | 35.00 |
| 36-The Ghost Rider returns, ends #41; liquid hallucinogenic drug story | 5.70 | 17.00 | 40.00 |
| 37-Ghost Rider classic "To Touch Is to Die!," about Inca treasure | 5.70 | 17.00 | 40.00 |
| 38-The Black Phantom begins (not in #39); classic Ghost Rider "The Phantom Guns of Feather Gap!" | 5.70 | 17.00 | 40.00 |
| 39-41: All 3-D effect c/stories | 8.50 | 25.50 | 60.00 |

NOTE: *Dick Ayers a-7, 9-41. Bolle a-1-41; c-19, 20, 22, 24-28, 30-41.*

**TIM IN SPACE** (Formerly Gene Autry Tim; becomes Tim Tomorrow)
1950 (½-size giveaway) (B&W)
Tim Stores

nn 1.70 5.00 12.00

**TIM McCOY** (Formerly Zoo Funnies; Pictorial Love Stories #22 on)
No. 16, Oct, 1948 - No. 21, Aug-Sept, 1949 (Western Movie Stories)
Charlton Comics

16-John Wayne, Montgomery Clift app. in 'Red River;' photo back-c 20.00 60.00 140.00
17-21: 17-Rod Cameron guest stars 16.00 48.00 110.00

**TIM McCOY, POLICE CAR 17**
No. 674, 1934 (32 pgs.) (11x14¾") (B&W) (Like Feature Books)
Whitman Publishing Co.

674-1933 movie ill. 13.00 40.00 90.00

**TIMMY** (See 4-Color #715, 823, 923, 1022)

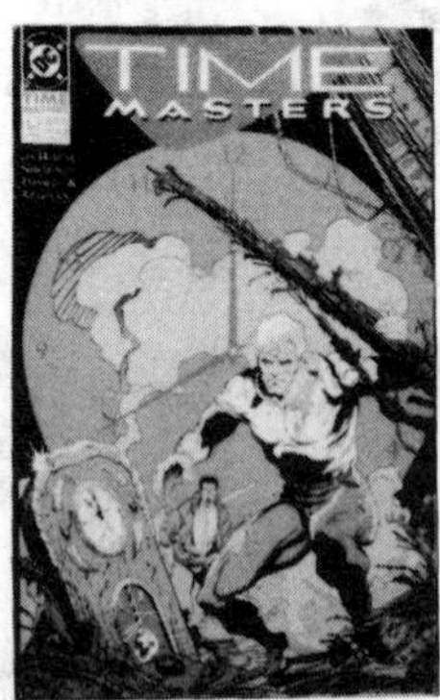

*Time Masters #1, © DC*

*Time Warp #2, © DC*

*Tim Holt #12, © ME*

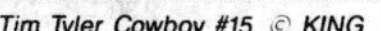
Tim Tyler Cowboy #15, © KING

Tiny Tot Comics #2, © WMG

Tip Top Comics #4, © UFS

**TIMMY THE TIMID GHOST** (Formerly Win-A-Prize?; see Blue Bird)
No. 3, 2/56 - No. 44, 10/64; No. 45, 9/66; 10/67 - No. 23, 7/71; V4#24, 9/85 - No. 26, 1/86
Charlton Comics

| | Good | Fine | N-Mint |
|---|---|---|---|
| 3(1956) (1st Series) | 3.00 | 9.00 | 21.00 |
| 4,5 | 1.50 | 4.50 | 10.00 |
| 6-10 | .70 | 2.00 | 5.00 |
| 11,12(4/58,10/58)(100pgs.) | 2.00 | 6.00 | 14.00 |
| 13-20 | .70 | 2.00 | 5.00 |
| 21-45('66) | .35 | 1.00 | 2.00 |
| 1(10/67, 2nd series) | .35 | 1.00 | 2.00 |
| 2-23 | | .60 | 1.20 |
| 24-26 (1985-86): Fago-r | | .40 | .80 |

**TIM TOMORROW** (Formerly Tim In Space)
8/51, 9/51, 10/51, Christmas, 1951 (5x7¾")
Tim Stores

| | | | |
|---|---|---|---|
| nn-Prof. Fumble & Captain Kit Comet in all | 1.50 | 4.50 | 10.00 |

**TIM TYLER** (See Harvey Comics Hits #54)

**TIM TYLER** (Also see Comics Reading Libraries)
1942
Better Publications

| | | | |
|---|---|---|---|
| 1 | 6.50 | 19.00 | 45.00 |

**TIM TYLER COWBOY**
No. 11, Nov, 1948 - No. 18, 1950
Standard Comics (King Features Synd.)

| | | | |
|---|---|---|---|
| 11 | 4.00 | 12.00 | 28.00 |
| 12-18 | 2.65 | 8.00 | 18.00 |

**TINKER BELL** (See 4-Color #896, 982, & Walt Disney Showcase #37)

**TINY FOLKS FUNNIES** (See 4-Color #60)

**TINY TESSIE** (Tessie #1-23; Real Experiences #25)
No. 24, Oct, 1949
Marvel Comics (20CC)

| | | | |
|---|---|---|---|
| 24 | 2.65 | 8.00 | 18.00 |

**TINY TIM** (Also see Super Comics)
No. 4, 1941 - No. 235, July, 1949
Dell Publishing Co.

| | | | |
|---|---|---|---|
| Large Feature Comic 4('41) | 22.00 | 65.00 | 155.00 |
| 4-Color 20(1941) | 23.00 | 70.00 | 160.00 |
| 4-Color 42(1943) | 12.00 | 36.00 | 85.00 |
| 4-Color 235 | 3.70 | 11.00 | 26.00 |

**TINY TOT COMICS**
Mar, 1946 - No. 10, Nov-Dec, 1947 (For younger readers)
E. C. Comics

| | | | |
|---|---|---|---|
| 1(nn) (52 pgs.) | 17.00 | 50.00 | 115.00 |
| 2 (5/46, 52 pgs.) | 11.50 | 34.00 | 80.00 |
| 3-10: 10-Christmas-c | 10.00 | 30.00 | 70.00 |

**TINY TOT FUNNIES** (Formerly Family Funnies)
No. 9, June, 1951 (Becomes Junior Funnies)
Harvey Publ. (King Features Synd.)

| | | | |
|---|---|---|---|
| 9-Flash Gordon, Mandrake | 3.00 | 9.00 | 21.00 |

**TINY TOTS COMICS**
1943 (Not reprints)
Dell Publishing Co.

| | | | |
|---|---|---|---|
| 1-Kelly-a(2); fairy tales | 30.00 | 90.00 | 210.00 |

**TIPPY & CAP STUBBS** (See 4-Color #210, 242 & Popular Comics)

**TIPPY'S FRIENDS GO-GO & ANIMAL**
July, 1966 - No. 15, Oct, 1969 (25 cents)
Tower Comics

| | Good | Fine | N-Mint |
|---|---|---|---|
| 1 | 1.30 | 4.00 | 9.00 |
| 2-7,9-15: 12-15 titled "Tippy's Friend Go-Go" | .85 | 2.60 | 6.00 |
| 8-Beatles app. on front/back-c | 3.50 | 10.50 | 24.00 |

**TIPPY TEEN** (See Vicki)
Nov, 1965 - No. 27, Feb, 1970 (25 cents)
Tower Comics

| | | | |
|---|---|---|---|
| 1 | 1.00 | 3.00 | 7.00 |
| 2-27: 5-1pg. Beatles pin-up. 16-Twiggy photo-c | .70 | 2.00 | 4.00 |
| Special Collectors' Editions('69-nn)(25 cents) | .70 | 2.00 | 4.00 |

**TIPPY TERRY**
1963
Super/I. W. Enterprises

| | | | |
|---|---|---|---|
| Super Reprint #14('63)-Little Grouchy reprints | | .60 | 1.20 |
| I.W. Reprint #1 (nd) | | .60 | 1.20 |

**TIP TOP COMICS**
4/36 - No. 210, 1957; No. 211, 11-1/57-58 - No. 225, 5-7/61
United Features #1-187/St. John #188-210/Dell Publishing Co. #211 on

| | Good | Fine | VF-NM | NM/Mint |
|---|---|---|---|---|
| 1-Tarzan by Hal Foster, Li'l Abner, Broncho Bill, Fritzi Ritz, Ella Cinders, Capt. & The Kids begin; strip-r (1st comic book app. of each) | 195.00 | 490.00 | 1175.00 | 2200.00 |

(Estimated up to 80 total copies exist, 4 in NM/Mint)

| | Good | Fine | VF-NM |
|---|---|---|---|
| 2 | 90.00 | 225.00 | 540.00 |
| 3 | 61.00 | 182.00 | 425.00 |
| 4 | 46.00 | 137.00 | 320.00 |
| 5-10: 7-Photo & biography of Edgar Rice Burroughs. 8-Christmas-c | 36.00 | 107.00 | 250.00 |

| | Good | Fine | N-Mint |
|---|---|---|---|
| 11-20: 20-Christmas-c | 27.00 | 81.00 | 190.00 |
| 21-40: 36-Kurtzman panel (1st published comic work) | 24.00 | 70.00 | 165.00 |
| 41-Has 1st Tarzan Sunday | 24.00 | 70.00 | 165.00 |
| 42-50: 43-Mort Walker panel | 20.00 | 60.00 | 140.00 |
| 51-53 | 17.00 | 51.00 | 120.00 |
| 54-Origin Mirror Man & Triple Terror, also featured on cover | 22.00 | 65.00 | 150.00 |
| 55,56,58,60: Last Tarzan by Foster | 14.00 | 43.00 | 100.00 |
| 57,59,61,62-Tarzan by Hogarth | 19.00 | 57.00 | 130.00 |
| 63-80: 65,67-70,72-74,77,78-No Tarzan | 9.30 | 28.00 | 65.00 |
| 81-90 | 8.50 | 25.50 | 60.00 |
| 91-99 | 6.00 | 18.00 | 42.00 |
| 100 | 7.00 | 21.00 | 50.00 |
| 101-140: 110-Gordo story. 111-Li'l Abner app. 118, 132-No Tarzan | 4.00 | 12.00 | 28.00 |
| 141-170: 145,151-Gordo stories. 157-Last Li'l Abner; lingerie panels | 2.85 | 8.50 | 20.00 |
| 171-188-Tarzan reprints by B. Lubbers in all. #177?-Peanuts by Schulz begins; no Peanuts in #178,179,181-183 | 3.15 | 9.50 | 22.00 |
| 189-225 | 1.85 | 5.50 | 13.00 |

Bound Volumes (Very Rare) sold at 1939 World's Fair; bound by publ. in pictorial comic boards. (Also see Comics on Parade)

| | | | |
|---|---|---|---|
| Bound issues 1-12 | 171.00 | 515.00 | 1200.00 |
| Bound issues 13-24 | 115.00 | 345.00 | 800.00 |
| Bound issues 25-36 | 93.00 | 280.00 | 650.00 |

NOTE: *Tarzan covers-#3, 9, 11, 13, 16, 18, 21, 24, 27, 30, 32-34, 36, 37, 39, 41, 43, 45, 47, 50, 52 (all worth 10-20 percent more). Tarzan by* ***Foster****-#1-40, 44-50; by* ***Rex Maxon****-#41-43; by* ***Byrne Hogarth****-#57, 59, 62.*

**TIP TOPPER COMICS**
Oct-Nov, 1949 - No. 28, 1954
United Features Syndicate

| | | | |
|---|---|---|---|
| 1-Li'l Abner, Abbie & Slats | 4.30 | 13.00 | 30.00 |
| 2 | 2.65 | 8.00 | 18.00 |
| 3-5: 5-Fearless Fosdick app. | 2.15 | 6.50 | 15.00 |
| 6-10: 6-Fearless Fosdick app. | 1.70 | 5.00 | 12.00 |

| | Good | Fine | N-Mint |
|---|---|---|---|
| 11-25: 17-22,24,26-Peanuts app. (2 pgs.) | 1.50 | 4.50 | 10.00 |
| 26-28-Twin Earths | 3.50 | 10.50 | 24.00 |

NOTE: *Many lingerie panels in Fritzi Ritz stories.*

**T-MAN**
Sept, 1951 - No. 38, Dec, 1956
Quality Comics Group

| | Good | Fine | N-Mint |
|---|---|---|---|
| 1-Jack Cole-a | 14.00 | 43.00 | 100.00 |
| 2-Crandall-c | 8.50 | 25.50 | 60.00 |
| 3,6-8: All Crandall-c | 7.00 | 21.00 | 50.00 |
| 4,5-Crandall-c/a each | 8.00 | 24.00 | 55.00 |
| 9,10-Crandall-c | 5.70 | 17.00 | 40.00 |
| 11-Used in **POP**, pg. 95 & color illo. | 4.30 | 13.00 | 30.00 |
| 12-19,21,22,24,26: 24-Last pre-code (4/55) | 2.85 | 8.50 | 20.00 |
| 20,23-H-Bomb explosion-c/stories | 6.00 | 18.00 | 42.00 |
| 25-All Crandall-a | 5.00 | 15.00 | 35.00 |
| 27-38 | 2.30 | 7.00 | 16.00 |

NOTE: *Anti-communist stories are common. Bondage c-15.*

**TNT COMICS**
Feb, 1946 (36 pgs.)
Charles Publishing Co.

| | Good | Fine | N-Mint |
|---|---|---|---|
| 1-Yellowjacket app. | 10.00 | 30.00 | 70.00 |

**TOBY TYLER** (See 4-Color #1092 and Movie Comics)

**TODAY'S BRIDES**
Nov, 1955; No. 2, Feb, 1956; No. 3, Sept, 1956; No. 4, Nov, 1956
Ajax/Farrell Publishing Co.

| | Good | Fine | N-Mint |
|---|---|---|---|
| 1 | 3.50 | 10.50 | 24.00 |
| 2-4 | 1.70 | 5.00 | 12.00 |

**TODAY'S ROMANCE**
No. 5, March, 1952 - No. 8, Sept, 1952
Standard Comics

| | Good | Fine | N-Mint |
|---|---|---|---|
| 5 | 3.00 | 9.00 | 21.00 |
| 6-Toth-a | 4.00 | 12.00 | 28.00 |
| 7,8 | 1.50 | 4.50 | 10.00 |

**TO DIE FOR IN 3-D** (See Blackthorne 3-D Series #64)

**TOKA** (Jungle King)
Aug-Oct, 1964 - No. 10, Jan, 1967 (Painted-c #1,2)
Dell Publishing Co.

| | Good | Fine | N-Mint |
|---|---|---|---|
| 1 | 1.00 | 3.00 | 7.00 |
| 2 | .70 | 2.00 | 4.00 |
| 3-10 | .50 | 1.50 | 3.00 |

**TOMAHAWK** (Son of. . . on-c of #131-140; see Star Spangled Comics #69 & World's Finest Comics #65)
Sept-Oct, 1950 - No. 140, May-June, 1972
National Periodical Publications

| | Good | Fine | N-Mint |
|---|---|---|---|
| 1-Tomahawk begins by F. Ray | 54.00 | 160.00 | 375.00 |
| 2-Frazetta/Williamson-a, 4 pgs. | 27.00 | 81.00 | 190.00 |
| 3-5 | 16.00 | 48.00 | 110.00 |
| 6-10: 7-Last 52 pgs. | 12.00 | 36.00 | 85.00 |
| 11-20 | 8.00 | 24.00 | 55.00 |
| 21-27,30: Last precode (2/55) | 6.00 | 18.00 | 42.00 |
| 28-1st app. Lord Shilling (arch-foe) | 8.00 | 24.00 | 55.00 |
| 29-Frazetta-r/Jimmy Wakely #3 (3 pgs.) | 12.00 | 36.00 | 84.00 |
| 31-40 | 5.00 | 15.00 | 35.00 |
| 41-50 | 3.50 | 10.50 | 24.00 |
| 51-56,58-60 | 2.65 | 8.00 | 18.00 |
| 57-Frazetta-r/Jimmy Wakely #6 (3 pgs.) | 6.50 | 19.50 | 45.00 |
| 61-77: 77-Last 10 cent issue | 1.70 | 5.00 | 12.00 |
| 78-85: 81-1st app. Miss Liberty. 83-Origin Tomahawk's Rangers | 1.00 | 3.00 | 7.00 |
| 86-100: 96-Origin/1st app. The Hood, alias Lady Shilling | .70 | 2.00 | 4.00 |
| 101-110: 107-Origin/1st app. Thunder-Man | .50 | 1.50 | 3.00 |
| 111-130,132-138,140 | .35 | 1.00 | 2.00 |
| 131-Frazetta-r/Jimmy Wakely #7 (3 pgs.); origin Firehair retold | .40 | 1.25 | 2.50 |
| 139-Frazetta-r/Star Spangled #113 | .25 | .75 | 1.50 |

NOTE: ***Neal Adams** c-116-119, 121, 123-130. Firehair by **Kubert**-131-134, 136. **Maurer** a-138. **Severin** a-135.*

**TOM AND JERRY** (See Comic Album #4, 8, 12, Dell Giant #21, Dell Giants, Four Color #193, Golden Comics Digest #1, 5, 8, 13, 15, 18, 22, 25, 28, 35, & March of Comics #21, 46, 61, 70, 88, 103, 119, 128, 145, 154, 173, 190, 207, 224, 281, 295, 305, 321, 333, 345, 361, 365, 388, 400, 444, 451, 463, 480)

**TOM AND JERRY** (. . .Comics, early issues) (M.G.M.)
(Formerly Our Gang No. 1-59) (See Dell Giants for annuals)
No. 193, 6/48; No. 60, 7/49 - No. 212, 7-9/62; No. 213, 11/62 - No. 291, 2/75; No. 292, 3/77 - No. 342, 5/82 - No. 344, 1982?
Dell Publishing Co./Gold Key No. 213-327/Whitman No. 328 on

| | Good | Fine | N-Mint |
|---|---|---|---|
| 4-Color 193 (#1)-Titled "M.G.M. Presents. . ." | 9.00 | 27.00 | 62.00 |
| 60 | 4.50 | 14.00 | 32.00 |
| 61 | 3.70 | 11.00 | 26.00 |
| 62-70: 66-X-mas-c | 2.85 | 8.50 | 20.00 |
| 71-80: 77-X-mas-c | 2.30 | 7.00 | 16.00 |
| 81-99: 90-X-mas-c | 2.00 | 6.00 | 14.00 |
| 100 | 2.30 | 7.00 | 16.00 |
| 101-120 | 1.50 | 4.50 | 10.00 |
| 121-140: 126-X-mas-c | 1.15 | 3.50 | 8.00 |
| 141-160 | .85 | 2.60 | 6.00 |
| 161-200 | .70 | 2.00 | 5.00 |
| 201-212(7-9/62)(Last Dell issue) | .70 | 2.00 | 4.00 |
| 213,214-(84 pgs.)-titled ". . .Funhouse" | 1.75 | 5.25 | 14.00 |
| 215-240: 215-titled ". . .Funhouse" | .45 | 1.35 | 3.00 |
| 241-270 | .35 | 1.00 | 2.00 |
| 271-300: 286 "Tom & Jerry" | .25 | .75 | 1.50 |
| 301-344 | | .40 | .80 |
| Mouse From T.R.A.P. 1(7/66)-Giant, G. K. | 1.75 | 5.25 | 14.00 |
| Summer Fun 1(7/67, 68pgs.)(Gold Key)-R-/Barks' Droopy/Summer Fun #1 | 1.75 | 5.25 | 14.00 |
| . . .Kite Fun Book (1958, 5x7¼", 16pgs.) | 1.50 | 4.50 | 12.00 |

NOTE: *#60-87, 98-121, 268, 277, 289, 302 are 52 pages. Reprints-#225, 241, 245, 247, 252, 254, 266, 268, 270, 292-327, 329-342, 344.*

**TOMB OF DARKNESS** (Formerly Beware)
No. 9, July, 1974 - No. 23, Nov, 1976
Marvel Comics Group

| | Good | Fine | N-Mint |
|---|---|---|---|
| 9-23: 15,19-Ditko-r. 17-Woodbridge-r/Astonishing #62. 20-Everett Venus r-/Venus #19. 23-Everett-a(r) | | .40 | .80 |

**TOMB OF DRACULA** (See Giant-Size Dracula, Dracula Lives & Power Record Comics)
April, 1972 - No. 70, Aug, 1979
Marvel Comics Group

| | Good | Fine | N-Mint |
|---|---|---|---|
| 1-Colan-p in all | 2.15 | 6.50 | 15.00 |
| 2-10: 3-Intro. Dr. Rachel Van Helsing & Inspector Chelm. 10-1st app. Blade the Vampire Slayer | 1.00 | 3.00 | 7.00 |
| 11-20: 12-Brunner-c(p). 13-Origin Blade | .70 | 2.00 | 4.00 |
| 21-70: 50-Silver Surfer app. 70-Double size | .35 | 1.00 | 2.00 |

NOTE: ***N. Adams** c-1, 6. **Colan** a-1-70p; c(p)-8, 38-42, 44-56, 58-70. **Wrightson** c-43.*

**TOMB OF DRACULA** (Magazine)
Nov, 1979 - No. 6, Sept, 1980 (B&W)
Marvel Comics Group

| | Good | Fine | N-Mint |
|---|---|---|---|
| 1,4-6 | | .60 | 1.20 |
| 2,3: 2-Ditko-a (36 pgs.). 3-Miller-a(2 pg. sketch) | .35 | 1.00 | 2.00 |

NOTE: ***Buscema** a-4p, 5p. **Chaykin** c-5, 6. **Colan** a(p)-1, 3-6. **Miller** a-3.*

**TOMB OF LIGEIA** (See Movie Classics)

**TOMB OF TERROR** (Thrills of Tomorrow #17 on)
June, 1952 - No. 16, July, 1954

*T-Man #20, © QUA*

*Tomahawk #7, © DC*

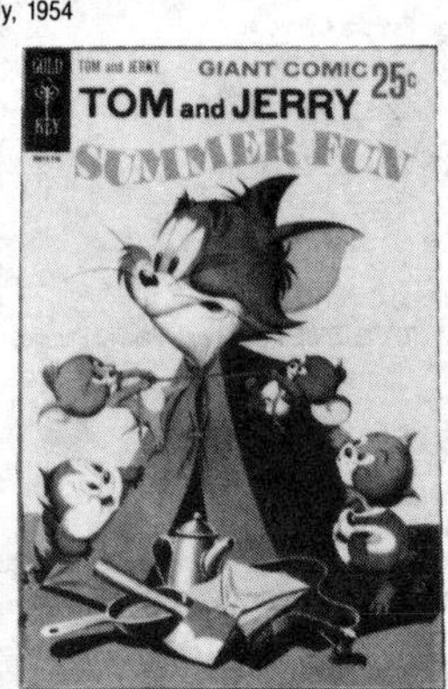

*Tom and Jerry Summer Fun #1, © M.G.M.*

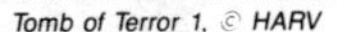
*Tomb of Terror 1, © HARV*

*Tom Mix Western #7, © FAW*

*Tommy of the Big Top #12, © KING*

Harvey Publications

| | Good | Fine | N-Mint |
|---|---|---|---|
| 1 | 8.00 | 24.00 | 55.00 |
| 2 | 5.00 | 15.00 | 35.00 |
| 3-Bondage-c; atomic disaster story | 6.00 | 18.00 | 42.00 |
| 4-12: 4-Heart ripped out. 8-12-Nostrand-a | 5.00 | 15.00 | 35.00 |
| 13,14-Special S/F issues. 14-Check-a | 8.00 | 24.00 | 55.00 |
| 15-S/F issue; c-shows head exploding | 11.00 | 32.00 | 75.00 |
| 16-Special S/F issue; Nostrand-a | 8.00 | 24.00 | 55.00 |

NOTE: ***Kremer** a-1, 7; c-1. **Nostrand** a-8-12, 15r 16. **Palais** a-2, 3, 5-7. **Powell** a-1, 3, 5, 9-16. **Sparling** a-12, 13, 15.*

**TOMBSTONE TERRITORY** (See 4-Color #1123)

**TOM CAT** (Formerly Bo; Atom The Cat #9 on)
No. 4, Apr, 1956 - No. 8, July, 1957
Charlton Comics

| | Good | Fine | N-Mint |
|---|---|---|---|
| 4-Al Fago-c/a | 2.00 | 6.00 | 14.00 |
| 5-8 | 1.30 | 4.00 | 9.00 |

**TOM CORBETT, SPACE CADET** (TV)
No. 378, Jan-Feb, 1952 - No. 11, Sept-Nov, 1954 (All painted covers)
Dell Publishing Co.

| | Good | Fine | N-Mint |
|---|---|---|---|
| 4-Color 378 (#1)-McWilliams-a | 8.50 | 25.50 | 60.00 |
| 4-Color 400,421-McWilliams-a | 6.50 | 19.00 | 45.00 |
| 4(11-1/53) - 11 | 4.00 | 12.00 | 28.00 |

**TOM CORBETT SPACE CADET** (See March of Comics #102)

**TOM CORBETT SPACE CADET** (TV)
V2#1, May-June, 1955 - V2#3, Sept-Oct, 1955
Prize Publications

| | Good | Fine | N-Mint |
|---|---|---|---|
| V2#1 | 11.50 | 34.00 | 80.00 |
| 2,3: 3-Meskin-c | 10.00 | 30.00 | 70.00 |

**TOM, DICK & HARRIET** (See Gold Key Spotlight)

**TOM LANDRY AND THE DALLAS COWBOYS**
1973 (35-49 cents)
Spire Christian Comics/Fleming H. Revell Co.

| | Good | Fine | N-Mint |
|---|---|---|---|
| nn | .25 | .75 | 1.50 |

**TOM MIX** (. . .Commandos Comics #10-12)
Sept, 1940 - No. 12, Nov, 1942 (36 pages); 1983 (One-shot)
Given away for two Ralston box-tops; in cereal box, 1983
Ralston-Purina Co.

| | Good | Fine | N-Mint |
|---|---|---|---|
| 1-Origin (life) Tom Mix; Fred Meagher-a | 85.00 | 257.00 | 600.00 |
| 2 | 45.00 | 135.00 | 315.00 |
| 3-9 | 38.00 | 115.00 | 265.00 |
| 10-12: 10-Origin Tom Mix Commando Unit; Speed O'Dare begins. 12-Sci/fi-c | 30.00 | 90.00 | 210.00 |
| 1983-'Taking of Grizzly Grebb,' Toth-a; 16 pg. miniature | 1.00 | 3.00 | 6.00 |

**TOM MIX WESTERN** (Movie, radio star) (Also see The Comics, Crackajack Funnies, Master Comics, 100 Pages Of Comics, Popular Comics, Real Western Hero, Six Gun Heroes, Western Hero & XMas Comics)
Jan, 1948 - No. 61, May, 1953 (1-17: 52 pgs.)
Fawcett Publications

| | Good | Fine | N-Mint |
|---|---|---|---|
| 1 (Photo-c, 52 pgs.)-Tom Mix & his horse Tony begin; Tumbleweed Jr begins, ends #52,54,55 | 50.00 | 150.00 | 350.00 |
| 2 (Photo-c) | 26.00 | 77.00 | 180.00 |
| 3-5 (Painted/photo-c): 5-Billy the Kid & Oscar app. | 21.00 | 62.00 | 145.00 |
| 6,7 (Painted/photo-c) | 17.00 | 51.00 | 120.00 |
| 8-Kinstler tempera-c | 17.00 | 51.00 | 120.00 |
| 9,10 (Painted/photo-c)-Used in **SOTI**, pgs. 323-325 | 16.00 | 48.00 | 110.00 |
| 11-Kinstler oil-c | 14.00 | 43.00 | 100.00 |
| 12 (Painted/photo-c) | 12.00 | 36.00 | 85.00 |
| 13-17 (Painted-c, 52 pgs.) | 12.00 | 36.00 | 85.00 |
| 18,22 (Painted-c, 36 pgs.) | 10.00 | 30.00 | 70.00 |
| 19 (Photo-c, 52 pgs.) | 12.00 | 36.00 | 85.00 |
| 20,21,23 (Painted-c, 52 pgs.) | 10.00 | 30.00 | 70.00 |
| 24,25,27-29 (52 pgs.): 24-Photo-c begin, end #61. 29-Slim Pickens app. | 10.00 | 30.00 | 70.00 |
| 26,30 (36 pgs.) | 9.30 | 28.00 | 65.00 |
| 31-33,35-37,39,40,42 (52 pgs.): 39-Red Eagle app. | 8.50 | 25.50 | 60.00 |
| 34,38 (36 pgs. begin) | 7.00 | 21.00 | 50.00 |
| 41,43-60 | 5.00 | 15.00 | 35.00 |
| 61-Last issue | 6.00 | 18.00 | 42.00 |

NOTE: *Photo-c from 1930s Tom Mix movies (he died in 1940). Many issues contain ads for Tom Mix, Rocky Lane, Space Patrol and other premiums. **Captain Tootsie** by C.C. Beck in No. 6-11, 20.*

**TOM MIX WESTERN**
1988 - Present ($2.95, B&W w/16 pgs. color, 44 pgs.)
AC Comics

| | Good | Fine | N-Mint |
|---|---|---|---|
| 1-Tom Mix-r/Master #124,128,131,102 plus Billy the Kid-r by Severin; photo front/back-c | .50 | 1.50 | 3.00 |
| 2-($2.50, B&W)-Gabby Hayes-r; photo covers | .40 | 1.25 | 2.50 |

**TOMMY OF THE BIG TOP**
No. 10, Sept, 1948 - No. 12, Mar, 1949
King Features Syndicate/Standard Comics

| | Good | Fine | N-Mint |
|---|---|---|---|
| 10-By John Lehti | 3.00 | 9.00 | 21.00 |
| 11,12 | 1.70 | 5.00 | 12.00 |

**TOMORROW KNIGHTS**
June, 1990 - Present ($1.50, color)(Painted-c #1,2)
Epic Comics (Marvel)

| | Good | Fine | N-Mint |
|---|---|---|---|
| 1-($1.95, 52 pgs.)-Sci/fi | .35 | 1.00 | 2.00 |
| 2-4 | .25 | .75 | 1.50 |

**TOM SAWYER** (See Adventures of . . . & Famous Stories)

**TOM SAWYER & HUCK FINN**
1925 (52 pgs.) (10¾x10") (stiff covers)
Stoll & Edwards Co.

| | Good | Fine | N-Mint |
|---|---|---|---|
| nn-By Dwiggins; reprints 1923, 1924 Sunday strips in color | 11.50 | 34.00 | 80.00 |

**TOM SAWYER COMICS**
1951? (paper cover)
Giveaway

| | Good | Fine | N-Mint |
|---|---|---|---|
| nn-Contains a coverless Hopalong Cassidy from 1951; other combinations possible | 1.00 | 3.00 | 6.00 |

**TOM SKINNER-UP FROM HARLEM** (See Up From Harlem)

**TOM TERRIFIC!** (TV)(See Mighty Mouse Fun Club Mag. #1)
Summer, 1957 - No. 6, Fall, 1958
Pines Comics (Paul Terry)

| | Good | Fine | N-Mint |
|---|---|---|---|
| 1 | 8.50 | 25.50 | 60.00 |
| 2-6 | 6.50 | 19.50 | 45.00 |

**TOM THUMB** (See 4-Color #972)

**TOM-TOM, THE JUNGLE BOY** (See Tick Tock Tales)
1947 - No. 3, 1947; Nov, 1957 - No. 3, Mar, 1958
Magazine Enterprises

| | Good | Fine | N-Mint |
|---|---|---|---|
| 1-Funny animal | 4.00 | 12.00 | 28.00 |
| 2,3(1947) | 2.65 | 8.00 | 18.00 |
| . . . & Itchi the Monk 1(11/57) - 3(3/58) | 1.15 | 3.50 | 8.00 |
| I.W. Reprint No. 1,2,8,10 | | .40 | .80 |

**TONKA** (See 4-Color #966)

**TONTO** (See The Lone Ranger's Companion . . .)

**TONY TRENT** (The Face #1,2)
No. 3, 1948 - No. 4, 1949

Big Shot/Columbia Comics Group

| | Good | Fine | N-Mint |
|---|---|---|---|
| 3,4: 3-The Face app. by Mart Bailey | 6.00 | 18.00 | 42.00 |

**TOODLE TWINS, THE**
Jan-Feb, 1951 - No. 10, July-Aug, 1951; Mar, 1956 (Newspaper-r)
Ziff-Davis (Approved Comics)/Argo

| | Good | Fine | N-Mint |
|---|---|---|---|
| 1 | 4.30 | 13.00 | 30.00 |
| 2 | 2.85 | 8.50 | 20.00 |
| 3-9 | 2.65 | 8.00 | 18.00 |
| 10-Painted-c, some newspaper-r | 2.65 | 8.00 | 18.00 |
| 1(Argo, 3/56) | 2.30 | 7.00 | 16.00 |

**TOONERVILLE TROLLEY**
1921 (Daily strip reprints) (B&W) (52 pgs.)
Cupples & Leon Co.

| | Good | Fine | N-Mint |
|---|---|---|---|
| 1-By Fontaine Fox | 16.00 | 48.00 | 110.00 |

**TOOTS & CASPER** (See Large Feature Comic #5)

**TOP ADVENTURE COMICS**
1964 (Reprints)
I. W. Enterprises

| | Good | Fine | N-Mint |
|---|---|---|---|
| 1-Reprints Explorer Joe #2; Krigstein-a | .70 | 2.00 | 4.00 |
| 2-Black Dwarf | .80 | 2.40 | 4.80 |

**TOP CAT** (TV) (Hanna-Barbera)
12-2/61-62 - No. 3, 6-8/62; No. 4, 10/62 - No. 31, 9/70
Dell Publishing Co./Gold Key No. 4 on

| | Good | Fine | N-Mint |
|---|---|---|---|
| 1 | 2.85 | 8.50 | 20.00 |
| 2-5 | 1.70 | 5.00 | 12.00 |
| 6-10 | 1.30 | 4.00 | 9.00 |
| 11-20 | .85 | 2.50 | 6.00 |
| 21-31: 21,24,25,29-Reprints | .60 | 1.80 | 4.00 |
| Kite Fun Book (1963, 16pgs., 5x7¼'', soft-c) | 1.15 | 3.50 | 8.00 |

**TOP CAT** (TV) (Hanna-Barbera)(See TV Stars #4)
Nov, 1970 - No. 20, Nov, 1973
Charlton Comics

| | Good | Fine | N-Mint |
|---|---|---|---|
| 1 | 1.00 | 3.00 | 7.00 |
| 2-10 | .60 | 1.75 | 3.50 |
| 11-20 | .35 | 1.00 | 2.00 |

NOTE: *#8 (1/72) went on sale late in 1972 between #14 and #15 with the 1/73 issues.*

**TOP COMICS**
July, 1967 (All rebound issues)
K. K. Publications/Gold Key

| | Good | Fine | N-Mint |
|---|---|---|---|
| nn-The Gnome-Mobile (Disney-movie) | .50 | 1.50 | 3.00 |
| 1-Beagle Boys (#7), Bugs Bunny, Chip 'n' Dale, Daffy Duck (#50), Flipper, Huckleberry Hound, Huey, Dewey & Louie, Junior Woodchucks, Lassie, The Little Monsters (#71), Moby Duck, Porky Pig (has Gold Key label - says Top Comics on inside), Scamp, Super Goof, Tarzan of the Apes (#169), Three Stooges (#35), Tom & Jerry, Top Cat (#21), Tweety & Sylvester (#7), Walt Disney C&S (#322), Woody Woodpecker, Yogi Bear, Zorro known; each character given own book | .30 | .90 | 1.80 |
| 1-Uncle Scrooge (#70) | 1.00 | 3.00 | 6.00 |
| 1-Donald Duck (not Barks), Mickey Mouse | .70 | 2.00 | 4.00 |
| 1-Flintstones | 1.70 | 5.00 | 12.00 |
| 1-The Jetsons | 2.00 | 6.00 | 14.00 |
| 2-Bugs Bunny, Daffy Duck, Donald Duck (not Barks), Mickey Mouse (#114), Porky Pig, Super Goof, Three Stooges, Tom & Jerry, Tweety & Sylvester, Uncle Scrooge (#71)-Barks-c, Walt Disney's C&S (r-/#325), Woody Woodpecker, Yogi Bear (#30), Zorro (r-#8; Toth-a) | .30 | .90 | 1.80 |
| 2-Snow White & 7 Dwarfs(6/67)(1944-r) | .80 | 2.40 | 4.80 |
| 3-Donald Duck | .50 | 1.50 | 3.00 |
| 3-Uncle Scrooge (#72) | 1.00 | 3.00 | 6.00 |
| 3,4-The Flintstones | 1.50 | 4.50 | 10.00 |
| 3-Mickey Mouse (r-/#115), Tom & Jerry, Woody Woodpecker, Yogi Bear | .35 | 1.00 | 2.00 |
| 4-Mickey Mouse, Woody Woodpecker | .35 | 1.00 | 2.00 |

NOTE: *Each book in this series is identical to its counterpart except for cover, and came out at same time. The number in parentheses is the original issue it contains.*

**TOP DETECTIVE COMICS**
1964 (Reprints)
I. W. Enterprises

| | Good | Fine | N-Mint |
|---|---|---|---|
| 9-Young King Cole & Dr. Drew (not Grandenetti) | .40 | 1.20 | 2.40 |

**TOP DOG** (See Star Comics Magazine)
Apr, 1985 - No. 14, June, 1987 (Children's book)
Star Comics (Marvel)

| | Good | Fine | N-Mint |
|---|---|---|---|
| 1-13 (75 cents) | | .35 | .70 |
| 14 ($1.00) | | .50 | 1.00 |

**TOP ELIMINATOR** (Formerly Teenage Hotrodders; Drag 'n' Wheels #30 on)
No. 25, Sept, 1967 - No. 29, July, 1968
Charlton Comics

| | Good | Fine | N-Mint |
|---|---|---|---|
| 25-29 | .35 | 1.00 | 2.00 |

**TOP FLIGHT COMICS**
1947; July, 1949
Four Star Publications/St. John Publishing Co.

| | Good | Fine | N-Mint |
|---|---|---|---|
| 1(1947) | 4.00 | 12.00 | 28.00 |
| 1(7/49, St. John)-Hector the Inspector | 3.00 | 9.00 | 21.00 |

**TOP GUN** (See 4-Color #927 & Showcase #72)

**TOP GUNS OF THE WEST** (See Super DC Giant)

**TOPIX** (. . .Comics) (Timeless Topix-early issues) (Also see Men of Battle, Men of Courage & Treasure Chest)(V1-V5#1,V7#1-20-paper-c)
11/42 - V10#15, 1/28/52 (Weekly - later issues)
Catechetical Guild Educational Society

| | Good | Fine | N-Mint |
|---|---|---|---|
| V1#1(8pgs.,8x11'') | 7.00 | 21.00 | 42.00 |
| 2,3(8pgs.,8x11'') | 4.00 | 12.00 | 24.00 |
| 4-8(16pgs.,8x11'') | 2.70 | 8.00 | 16.00 |
| V2#1-10(16pgs.,8x11''): V2#8-Pope Pius XII | 2.70 | 8.00 | 16.00 |
| V3#1-10(16pgs.,8x11'') | 2.15 | 6.50 | 13.00 |
| V4#1-10 | 2.15 | 6.50 | 13.00 |
| V5#1(10/46,52pgs.)-9,12-15(12/47)-#13 shows V5#4 | 1.15 | 3.50 | 7.00 |
| 10,11-Life of Christ editions | 2.35 | 7.00 | 14.00 |
| V6#1-14 | .70 | 2.00 | 4.00 |
| V7#1(9/1/48)-20(6/15/49), 32pgs. | .70 | 2.00 | 4.00 |
| V8#1(9/19/49)-3,5-11,13-30(5/15/50) | .70 | 2.00 | 4.00 |
| 4-Dagwood Splits the Atom(10/10/49)-Magazine format | 1.35 | 4.00 | 8.00 |
| 12-Ingels-a | 2.75 | 8.00 | 16.00 |
| V9#1(9/25/50)-11,13-30(5/14/51) | .50 | 1.50 | 3.00 |
| 12-Special 36pg. Xmas issue, text illos format | .85 | 2.50 | 5.00 |
| V10#1(10/1/51)-15: 14-Hollingsworth-a | .50 | 1.50 | 3.00 |

**TOP JUNGLE COMICS**
1964 (Reprint)
I. W. Enterprises

| | Good | Fine | N-Mint |
|---|---|---|---|
| 1(nd)-Reprints White Princess of the Jungle #3, minus cover | .80 | 2.40 | 4.80 |

**TOP LOVE STORIES** (Formerly Gasoline Alley #2)
No. 3, 5/51 - No. 19, 3/54
Star Publications

| | Good | Fine | N-Mint |
|---|---|---|---|
| 3(#1) | 5.00 | 15.00 | 35.00 |
| 4,5,7-9 | 4.00 | 12.00 | 28.00 |
| 6-Wood-a | 8.00 | 24.00 | 55.00 |

*Top Adventure Comics #2, © I.W.*

*Top Cat #1, © Hanna-Barbera*

*Top Love Stories #7, © STAR*

Top-Notch Comics #19, © AP

Top Spot Comics #1, © Top Spot

Tor #4, © STJ

| | Good | Fine | N-Mint |
|---|---|---|---|
| 10-16,18,19-Disbrow-a | 4.00 | 12.00 | 28.00 |
| 17-Wood art (Fox-r) | 5.30 | 16.00 | 38.00 |

NOTE: *All have* ***L. B. Cole*** *covers.*

**TOP-NOTCH COMICS** (. . . Laugh #28-45; Laugh Comix #46 on)
Dec, 1939 - No. 45, June, 1944
MLJ Magazines

| | Good | Fine | N-Mint |
|---|---|---|---|
| 1-Origin The Wizard; Kardak the Mystic Magician, Swift of the Secret Service (ends #3), Air Patrol, The Westpointer, Manhunters (by J. Cole), Mystic (ends #2) & Scott Rand (ends #3) begin | 107.00 | 321.00 | 750.00 |
| 2-Dick Storm (ends #8), Stacy Knight M.D. (ends #4) begin; Jack Cole-a | 52.00 | 155.00 | 365.00 |
| 3-Bob Phantom, Scott Rand on Mars begin; J. Cole-a | 41.00 | 122.00 | 285.00 |
| 4-Origin/1st app. Streak Chandler on Mars; Moore of the Mounted only app.; J. Cole-a | 35.00 | 105.00 | 245.00 |
| 5-Flag-c; origin/1st app. Galahad; Shanghai Sheridan begins (ends #8); Shield cameo | 30.00 | 90.00 | 210.00 |
| 6-Meskin-a | 26.00 | 77.00 | 180.00 |
| 7-The Shield x-over in Wizard; The Wizard dons new costume | 38.00 | 115.00 | 265.00 |
| 8-Origin The Firefly & Roy, the Super Boy | 43.00 | 130.00 | 300.00 |
| 9-Origin & 1st app. The Black Hood; Fran Frazier begins | 107.00 | 320.00 | 750.00 |
| 10 | 44.00 | 132.00 | 310.00 |
| 11-20 | 29.00 | 86.00 | 200.00 |
| 21-30: 23,24-No Wizard, Roy app. in each. 25-Last Bob Phantom, Roy app. 26-Roy app. 27-Last Firefly. 28-Suzie begins. 29-Last Kardak | 23.00 | 70.00 | 160.00 |
| 31-44: 33-Dotty & Ditto by Woggon begins. 44-Black Hood series ends | 13.00 | 40.00 | 90.00 |
| 45-Last issue | 8.00 | 24.00 | 55.00 |

NOTE: ***J. Binder*** *a-1-3.* ***Meskin*** *a-2, 3, 6, 15.* ***Woggon*** *a-33-40, 42. Bondage c-17, 19. Black Hood also appeared on radio in 1944.*

**TOPPER & NEIL** (See 4-Color #859)

**TOPPS COMICS**
1947
Four Star Publications

| | Good | Fine | N-Mint |
|---|---|---|---|
| 1-L. B. Cole-c | 5.00 | 15.00 | 35.00 |

**TOPS**
July, 1949 - No. 2, Sept, 1949 (68 pgs, 25 cents) (10¼x13¼")
(Large size-magazine format; for the adult reader)
Tops Magazine, Inc. (Lev Gleason)

| | Good | Fine | N-Mint |
|---|---|---|---|
| 1 (Rare)-Story by Dashiell Hammett; Crandall/Lubbers, Tuska, Dan Barry, Fuje-a; Biro painted-c | 62.00 | 185.00 | 435.00 |
| 2 (Rare)-Crandall/Lubbers, Biro, Kida, Fuje, Guardineer-a | 54.00 | 160.00 | 375.00 |

**TOPS COMICS** (See Tops in Humor)
1944 (Small size, 32 pgs.) (7¼x5")
Consolidated Book (Lev Gleason)

| | Good | Fine | N-Mint |
|---|---|---|---|
| 2001-The Jack of Spades | 10.00 | 30.00 | 70.00 |
| 2002-Rip Raider | 5.00 | 15.00 | 35.00 |
| 2003-Red Birch (gag cartoons) | 1.00 | 3.00 | 7.00 |

**TOPS COMICS**
1944 (132 pages) (10 cents)
Consolidated Book Publishers

| | Good | Fine | N-Mint |
|---|---|---|---|
| nn(Color-c, inside in red shade & some in full color)-Ace Kelly by Rick Yager, Black Orchid, Don on the Farm, Dinky Dinkerton (Rare) | 16.00 | 48.00 | 110.00 |

NOTE: *This book is printed in such a way that when the staple is removed, the strips on the left side of the book correspond with the same strips on the right side. Therefore, if strips are removed from the book, each strip can be folded into a complete comic section of its own.*

**TOP SECRET**
January, 1952
Hillman Publ.

| | Good | Fine | N-Mint |
|---|---|---|---|
| 1 | 9.30 | 28.00 | 65.00 |

**TOP SECRET ADVENTURES** (See Spyman)

**TOP SECRETS** (. . . of the F.B.I.)
Nov, 1947 - No. 10, July-Aug, 1949
Street & Smith Publications

| | Good | Fine | N-Mint |
|---|---|---|---|
| 1-Powell-c/a | 13.00 | 40.00 | 90.00 |
| 2-Powell-c/a | 10.00 | 30.00 | 70.00 |
| 3-6,8-10-Powell-a | 9.30 | 28.00 | 65.00 |
| 7-Used in **SOTI**, pg. 90 & illo.-"How to hurt people;" used by N.Y. Legis. Comm.; Powell-c/a | 13.00 | 40.00 | 90.00 |

NOTE: ***Powell*** *c-1-3, 5-10.*

**TOPS IN ADVENTURE**
Fall, 1952 (25 cents, 132 pages)
Ziff-Davis Publishing Co.

| | Good | Fine | N-Mint |
|---|---|---|---|
| 1-Crusader from Mars, The Hawk, Football Thrills, He-Man; Powell-a; painted-c | 25.00 | 75.00 | 175.00 |

**TOPS IN HUMOR** (See Tops Comics?)
1944 (Small size) (7¼x5")
Consolidated Book Publ. (Lev Gleason)

| | Good | Fine | N-Mint |
|---|---|---|---|
| 2001(#1)-Origin The Jack of Spades, Ace Kelly by Rick Yager, Black Orchid (female crime fighter) app. | 11.00 | 32.00 | 75.00 |
| 2 | 5.70 | 17.00 | 40.00 |

**TOP SPOT COMICS**
1945
Top Spot Publ. Co.

| | Good | Fine | N-Mint |
|---|---|---|---|
| 1-The Menace, Duke of Darkness app. | 11.00 | 32.00 | 75.00 |

**TOPSY-TURVY**
April, 1945
R. B. Leffingwell Publ.

| | Good | Fine | N-Mint |
|---|---|---|---|
| 1-1st app. Cookie | 4.00 | 12.00 | 28.00 |

**TOR** (Formerly One Million Years Ago)
No. 2, Oct, 1953; No. 3, May, 1954 - No. 5, Oct, 1954
St. John Publishing Co.

| | Good | Fine | N-Mint |
|---|---|---|---|
| 3-D 2(10/53)-Kubert-a | 9.30 | 28.00 | 65.00 |
| 3-D 2(10/53)-Oversized, otherwise same contents | 8.00 | 24.00 | 55.00 |
| 3-D 2(11/53)-Kubert-a | 8.00 | 24.00 | 55.00 |
| 3-5-Kubert-a; 3-Danny Dreams by Toth | 9.30 | 28.00 | 65.00 |

NOTE: *The two October 3-D's have same contents and* ***Powell*** *art; the November issue is titled 3-D Comics.*

**TOR** (See Sojourn)
May-June, 1975 - No. 6, Mar-Apr, 1976
National Periodical Publications

| | Good | Fine | N-Mint |
|---|---|---|---|
| 1-New origin by Kubert | | .30 | .60 |
| 2-6: 2-Origin-r/St. John #1 | | .25 | .50 |

NOTE: ***Kubert*** *a-1, 2-6r; c-1-6.* ***Toth*** *a(p)-3r.*

**TOR** (3-D)
July, 1986 - No. 2, Aug, 1987 ($2.50)
Eclipse Comics

| | Good | Fine | N-Mint |
|---|---|---|---|
| 1,2: 1-r/One Million Years Ago. 2-r/Tor 3-D #2 | .40 | 1.25 | 2.50 |
| 2-D 1,2-Limited signed & numbered editions | .40 | 1.25 | 2.50 |

**TORCHY** (. . . Blonde Bombshell) (See Dollman, Military, & Modern)
Nov, 1949 - No. 6, Sept, 1950
Quality Comics Group

| | Good | Fine | N-Mint |
|---|---|---|---|
| 1-Bill Ward-c, Gil Fox-a | 75.00 | 225.00 | 525.00 |
| 2,3-Fox-c/a | 32.00 | 95.00 | 225.00 |
| 4-Fox-c/a(3), Ward-a, 9pgs. | 42.00 | 125.00 | 295.00 |

| | Good | Fine | N-Mint |
|---|---|---|---|
| 5,6-Ward-c/a, 9 pgs; Fox-a(3) each | 52.00 | 155.00 | 365.00 |
| Super Reprint #16('64)-R-/#4 with new-c | 6.00 | 18.00 | 36.00 |

**TO RIVERDALE AND BACK AGAIN** (Archie Comics Presents. . .)
1990 ($2.50, 68 pgs.)
Archie Comics

| | Good | Fine | N-Mint |
|---|---|---|---|
| nn-Byrne-c, Colan-a(p); adapts NBC TV movie | .40 | 1.25 | 2.50 |

**TORMENTED, THE** (Surprise Adventures #3 on)
July, 1954 - No. 2, Sept, 1954
Sterling Comics

| | Good | Fine | N-Mint |
|---|---|---|---|
| 1,2 | 6.00 | 18.00 | 42.00 |

**TORNADO TOM** (See Mighty Midget Comics)

**TOTAL ECLIPSE**
May, 1988 - No. 5, Apr, 1989 ($3.95, color, deluxe size, 52 pgs.)
Eclipse Comics

| | Good | Fine | N-Mint |
|---|---|---|---|
| Book 1-5: 3-Intro/1st app. new Black Terror | .70 | 2.00 | 4.00 |

**TOTAL ECLIPSE: THE SERAPHIM OBJECTIVE**
Nov, 1988 ($1.95, color, one-shot, Baxter paper)
Eclipse Comics

| | Good | Fine | N-Mint |
|---|---|---|---|
| 1-Airboy, Valkyrie, The Heap app. | .35 | 1.00 | 2.00 |

**TOTAL RECALL**
1990 ($2.95, color, 68 pgs., movie adaptation)
DC Comics

| | Good | Fine | N-Mint |
|---|---|---|---|
| 1-Arnold Scwarzenegger photo-c | .50 | 1.50 | 3.00 |

**TOTAL WAR** (M.A.R.S. Patrol #3 on)
July, 1965 - No. 2, Oct, 1965 (Painted covers)
Gold Key

| | Good | Fine | N-Mint |
|---|---|---|---|
| 1,2-Wood-a in each | 2.00 | 6.00 | 14.00 |

**TOUGH KID SQUAD COMICS**
March, 1942
Timely Comics (TCI)

| | Good | Fine | VF-NM | NM/Mint |
|---|---|---|---|---|
| 1-(Scarce)-Origin The Human Top & The Tough Kid Squad; The Flying Flame app. | 350.00 | 875.00 | 2100.00 | 2800.00 |

(Estimated up to 100 total copies exist, 6 in NM/Mint)

**TOWER OF SHADOWS** (Creatures on the Loose #10 on)
Sept, 1969 - No. 9, Jan, 1971
Marvel Comics Group

| | Good | Fine | N-Mint |
|---|---|---|---|
| 1-Steranko, Craig-a | .85 | 2.60 | 6.00 |
| 2,4: 2-Neal Adams-a. 4-Kirby/Everett-c | .50 | 1.50 | 3.00 |
| 3-Barry Smith, Tuska-a | .70 | 2.00 | 4.00 |
| 5,7-B. Smith(p), Wood-a (Wood draws himself-1st pg., 1st panel-#5) | .70 | 2.00 | 4.00 |
| 6,8: Wood-a; 8-Wrightson-c | .50 | 1.50 | 3.00 |
| 9-Wrightson-c; Roy Thomas app. | .35 | 1.00 | 2.00 |
| Special 1(12/71)-Neal Adams-a | .50 | 1.50 | 3.00 |

NOTE: ***J. Buscema** a-1p, 2p. **Colan** a-3p, 6p. **J. Craig** a-1. **Ditko** a-6, 8, 9r, Special 1. **Everett** a-9(i)r; c-5i. **Kirby** a-9(p)r. **Severin** c-5p, 6. **Steranko** a-1. **Tuska** a-3. **Wood** a-5-8. Issues 1-9 contain new stories with some pre-Marvel age reprints in 6-9. H. P. Lovecraft adaptation-9.*

**TOWN & COUNTRY**
May, 1940
Publisher?

| | Good | Fine | N-Mint |
|---|---|---|---|
| nn-Origin The Falcon | 24.00 | 73.00 | 170.00 |

**TOWN THAT FORGOT SANTA, THE**
1961 (24 pages) (Giveaway)
W. T. Grant Co.

| | Good | Fine | N-Mint |
|---|---|---|---|
| nn | 1.35 | 4.00 | 9.00 |

**TOYBOY**
Oct, 1986 - Present ($2.00, color, Baxter paper)
Continuity Comics

| | Good | Fine | N-Mint |
|---|---|---|---|
| 1-7: 1,2-N. Adams-c. 1-Adams-a. 1,2-Nebres-i | .35 | 1.00 | 2.00 |

**TOYLAND COMICS**
Jan, 1947 - No. 4, July?, 1947
Fiction House Magazines

| | Good | Fine | N-Mint |
|---|---|---|---|
| 1 | 11.00 | 32.00 | 75.00 |
| 2-4: 3-Tuska-a | 6.50 | 19.00 | 45.00 |
| 148 pg. issue | 12.00 | 36.00 | 85.00 |

NOTE: *All above contain strips by **Al Walker**.*

**TOY TOWN COMICS**
1945 - No. 7, May, 1947
Toytown/Orbit Publ./B. Antin/Swapper Quarterly

| | Good | Fine | N-Mint |
|---|---|---|---|
| 1-Mertie Mouse; L. B. Cole-c/a | 10.00 | 30.00 | 70.00 |
| 2-L. B. Cole-a | 5.70 | 17.00 | 40.00 |
| 3-7-L. B. Cole-a | 4.50 | 14.00 | 32.00 |

**TRAGG AND THE SKY GODS** (See Gold Key Spotlight, Mystery Comics Digest #3,9 & Spine Tingling Tales) (Painted-c #3-8)
June, 1975 - No. 8, Feb, 1977; No. 9, May, 1982
Gold Key/Whitman No. 9

| | Good | Fine | N-Mint |
|---|---|---|---|
| 1-Origin | | .60 | 1.20 |
| 2-9: 4-Sabre-Fang app. 8-Ostellon app.; 9-r #1 | | .40 | .80 |

NOTE: ***Santos** a-1, 2, 9r; c-3-7. **Spiegel** a-3-8.*

**TRAIL BLAZERS** (Red Dragon #5 on)
1941 - No. 4, 1942
Street & Smith Publications

| | Good | Fine | N-Mint |
|---|---|---|---|
| 1-True stories of American heroes | 16.00 | 48.00 | 110.00 |
| 2 | 10.00 | 30.00 | 70.00 |
| 3,4 | 8.50 | 25.50 | 60.00 |

**TRAIL COLT** (Also see Extra Comics & Manhunt!)
1949 - No. 2, 1949
Magazine Enterprises

| | Good | Fine | N-Mint |
|---|---|---|---|
| nn(A-1 #24)-7 pg. Frazetta-a r-in Manhunt #13; Undercover Girl app.; The Red Fox by L. B. Cole; Ingels-c; Whitney-a (Scarce) | 29.00 | 85.00 | 200.00 |
| 2(A-1 #26)-Undercover Girl; Ingels-c; L. B. Cole-a, 6pgs. | 23.00 | 70.00 | 160.00 |

**TRANSFORMERS, THE** (TV)(Also see G.I. Joe and. . .)
Sept, 1984 - Present (.75-$1.00)
Marvel Comics Group

| | Good | Fine | N-Mint |
|---|---|---|---|
| 1-Based on Hasbro toys | .60 | 1.75 | 3.50 |
| 2,3 | .35 | 1.00 | 2.00 |
| 4-10,75: 75-($1.50, 52 pgs.) | .25 | .75 | 1.50 |
| 11-74,76: 21-Intro Aerialbots. 54-Intro Micromasters | | .50 | 1.00 |

NOTE: *Second and third printings of all issues exist and are worth less than originals. Was originally planned as a four issue mini-series. **Wrightson** a-64i(4 pgs.).*

**TRANSFORMERS COMICS MAGAZINE, THE**
Oct, 1986 - No. 11, 1988 ($1.50, Digest-size)
Marvel Comics Group

| | Good | Fine | N-Mint |
|---|---|---|---|
| 1-11 | .25 | .75 | 1.50 |

**TRANSFORMERS: HEADMASTERS, THE**
July, 1987 - No. 4, Jan, 1988 (Mini-series)
Marvel Comics Group

| | Good | Fine | N-Mint |
|---|---|---|---|
| 1-4 | .25 | .75 | 1.50 |

**TRANSFORMERS IN 3-D** See Blackthorne 3-D Series #25, 29, 37)

**TRANSFORMERS, THE MOVIE**
Dec, 1986 - No. 3, Feb, 1987 (Mini-series)
Marvel Comics Group

| | Good | Fine | N-Mint |
|---|---|---|---|
| 1-3: Adapts animated movie | | .50 | 1.00 |

**TRANSFORMERS UNIVERSE, THE**
Dec, 1986 - No. 4, March, 1987 ($1.25, mini-series)

*Total Eclipse #1, © Eclipse Comics*

*Tower of Shadows #1, © MEG*

*The Transformers #1, © MEG*

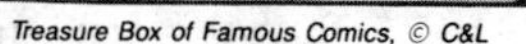
Treasure Box of Famous Comics, © C&L

Treasure Comics #1, © PRIZE

Treasury of Comics #5, © UFS

Marvel Comics Group

| | Good | Fine | N-Mint |
|---|---|---|---|
| 1-4: A guide to all characters | .25 | .75 | 1.50 |

**TRAPPED**
1951 (Giveaway) (16 pages) (soft cover)
Harvey Publications (Columbia University Press)

| | Good | Fine | N-Mint |
|---|---|---|---|
| nn-Drug education comic (30,000 printed?) distributed to schools. Mentioned in **SOTI**, pgs. 256,350 | 2.00 | 6.00 | 12.00 |

NOTE: *Many copies surfaced in 1979 causing a setback in price; beware of trimmed edges, because many copies have a brittle edge.*

**TRAPPED!**
Oct, 1954 - No. 5, June?, 1955
Periodical House Magazines (Ace)

| | Good | Fine | N-Mint |
|---|---|---|---|
| 1 (All reprints) | 4.30 | 13.00 | 30.00 |
| 2-5: 4-r/Men Against Crime #4 in its entirety | 2.65 | 8.00 | 18.00 |

NOTE: ***Colan** a-1, 4. **Sekowsky** a-1.*

**TRAVELS OF HAPPY HOOLIGAN, THE**
1906 (10¼"x15¾", 32 pgs., cardboard covers)
Frederick A. Stokes Co.

| | Good | Fine | N-Mint |
|---|---|---|---|
| nn-Contains reprints from 1905 | 24.00 | 71.00 | 165.00 |

**TRAVELS OF JAIMIE McPHEETERS, THE** (TV)
December, 1963
Gold Key

| | Good | Fine | N-Mint |
|---|---|---|---|
| 1-Kurt Russell | 2.00 | 6.00 | 14.00 |

**TREASURE BOX OF FAMOUS COMICS**
Mid 1930's (36 pgs.) (6-7/8"x8½") (paper covers)
Cupples & Leon Co.

| | Good | Fine | N-Mint |
|---|---|---|---|
| Box plus 5 titles: Reg'lar Fellers(1928), Little Orphan Annie(1926), Smitty(1928), Harold Teen(1931), How D. Tracy & D. Tracy Jr. Caught The Racketeers (1933) (These are abbreviated versions of hardcover editions) (Set).... | 71.00 | 215.00 | 500.00 |

NOTE: *Dates shown are copyright dates; all books actually came out in 1934 or later.*

**TREASURE CHEST** (Catholic Guild; also see Topix)
3/12/46 - V27#8, July, 1972 (Educational comics)
George A. Pflaum (not publ. during Summer)

| | Good | Fine | N-Mint |
|---|---|---|---|
| V1#1 | 7.00 | 21.00 | 50.00 |
| 2-6 (5/21/46): 5-Dr. Styx app. by Baily | 3.00 | 9.00 | 21.00 |
| V2#1-20 (9/3/46-5/27/47) | 1.50 | 4.50 | 10.00 |
| V3#1-5,7-20 (1st slick cover) | 1.50 | 4.50 | 10.00 |
| V3#6-Jules Verne's "Voyage to the Moon" | 3.35 | 10.00 | 22.00 |
| V4#1-20 (9/9/48-5/31/49) | 1.35 | 4.00 | 8.00 |
| V5#1-20 (9/6/49-5/31/50) | 1.00 | 3.00 | 6.00 |
| V6#1-20 (9/14/50-5/31/51) | 1.00 | 3.00 | 6.00 |
| V7#1-20 (9/13/51-6/5/52) | .70 | 2.00 | 4.00 |
| V8#1-20 (9/11/52-6/4/53) | .70 | 2.00 | 4.00 |
| V9#1-20 ('53-'54) | .50 | 1.50 | 3.00 |
| V10#1-20 ('54-'55) | .50 | 1.50 | 3.00 |
| V11('55-'56), V12('56-'57) | .50 | 1.50 | 3.00 |
| V13#1,3-5,7,9-V17#1 ('57-'63) | .35 | 1.00 | 2.00 |
| V13#2,6,8-Ingels-a | 2.00 | 6.00 | 14.00 |
| V17#2-'This Godless Communism' series begins(not in odd numbered issues); Cover shows hammer & sickle over Statue of Liberty; 8pg. Crandall-a of family life under communism | 9.00 | 27.00 | 62.00 |
| V17#3,5,7,9,11,13,15,17,19 | .25 | .80 | 1.60 |
| V17#4,6,14-'This Godless Communism' stories | 6.00 | 18.00 | 42.00 |
| V17#8-Shows red octopus encompassing Earth, firing squad; 8pg. Crandall-a | 6.50 | 19.50 | 45.00 |
| V17#10-'This Godless Communism'-how Stalin came to power, part I; Crandall-a | 6.00 | 18.00 | 42.00 |
| V17#12-Stalin in WWII, forced labor, death by exhaustion; Crandall-a | 6.00 | 18.00 | 42.00 |
| V17#16-Kruschev takes over; de-Stalinization | 6.00 | 18.00 | 42.00 |
| V17#18-Kruschev's control; murder of revolters, brainwash, space race by Crandall | 6.00 | 18.00 | 42.00 |
| V17#20-End of series; Kruschev-people are puppets, firing squads hammer & sickle over Statue of Liberty, snake around communist manifesto by Crandall | 6.00 | 18.00 | 42.00 |
| V18#1-20, V19#11-20, V20#1-20('64-'65): V18#11-Crandall draws himself & 13 other artists on cover | | .40 | .80 |
| V18#5-'What About Red China?'-describes how communists took over China | 2.75 | 8.00 | 16.00 |
| V19#1-10-'Red Victim' anti-communist series in all | 2.75 | 8.00 | 16.00 |
| V21-V25('65-'70)-(two V24#5's 11/7/68 & 11/21/68) (no V24#6) | | .30 | .60 |
| V26, V27#1-8 (V26,27-68 pgs.) | | .30 | .60 |
| Summer Edition V1#1-6('66), V2#1-6('67) | | .20 | .40 |

NOTE: ***Anderson** a-V18#13. **Borth** a-V7#10-19 (serial), V8#8-17 (serial), V9#1-10 (serial), V13#2, 6, 11, V14-V25 (except V22#1-3, 11-13), Summer Ed. V1#3-6. **Crandall** a-V16#7, 9, 12, 14, 16-18, 20; V17#1, 2, 4-6, 10, 12, 14, 16-18, 20; V18#1, 2, 3(2pg.), 7, 9-20; V19#4, 11, 13, 16, 19, 20; V20#1, 2, 4, 6, 8-10, 12, 14-16, 18, 20; V21#1-5, 8-11, 13, 16-18; V22#3, 7, 9-11, 14; V23#3, 6, 9, 16, 18; V24#7, 8, 10, 13, 16; V25#8, 16; V27#1-7r, 8r(2 pg.), Summer Ed. V1#3-5, V2#3; c-V16#7, V18#2(part), 7, 11, V19#4, 19, 20, V20#15, V21#5, 9, V22#3, 7, 9, 11, V23#9, 16, V24#13, 16, V25#8, Summer Ed. V1#2 (back c-V1#2-5). **Powell** a-V10#11. V19#11, 15, V10#13, V13#6, 8 all have wraparound covers. All the above Crandall issues should be priced by condition from $4-8.00 in mint unless already priced.*

**TREASURE CHEST OF THE WORLD'S BEST COMICS**
1945 (500 pgs.) (hardcover)
Superior, Toronto, Canada

| | Good | Fine | N-Mint |
|---|---|---|---|
| Contains Blue Beetle, Captain Combat, John Wayne, Dynamic Man, Nemo, Li'l Abner; contents can vary - represents random binding of extra books; Capt. America on-c | 47.00 | 140.00 | 330.00 |

**TREASURE COMICS**
No date (1943) (324 pgs.; cardboard covers) (50 cents)
Prize Publications? (no publisher listed)

| | Good | Fine | N-Mint |
|---|---|---|---|
| 1-(Rare)-Contains Prize Comics #7-11 from 1942 (blank inside-c) | 136.00 | 407.00 | 950.00 |

**TREASURE COMICS**
June-July, 1945 - No. 12, Fall, 1947
Prize Publications (American Boys' Comics)

| | Good | Fine | N-Mint |
|---|---|---|---|
| 1-Paul Bunyan & Marco Polo begin; Highwayman & Carrot Topp only app.; Kiefer-a | 11.50 | 34.00 | 80.00 |
| 2-Arabian Knight, Gorilla King, Dr. Styx begin | 6.00 | 18.00 | 42.00 |
| 3,4,9,12: 9-Kiefer-a | 4.00 | 12.00 | 28.00 |
| 5-Marco Polo-c; Kirby a(p); Krigstein-a | 8.50 | 25.50 | 60.00 |
| 6,11-Krigstein-a; 11-Krigstein-c | 7.00 | 21.00 | 50.00 |
| 7,8-Frazetta-a, 5 pgs. each | 22.00 | 65.00 | 154.00 |
| 10-Kirby-c/a | 11.50 | 34.00 | 80.00 |

NOTE: ***Barry** a-9, 11. **Roussos** a-11.*

**TREASURE ISLAND** (See 4-Color #624, King Classics, & Movie Classics & Movie Comics)

**TREASURY OF COMICS**
1947; No. 2, July, 1947 - No. 4, Sept, 1947; No. 5, Jan, 1948
St. John Publishing Co.

| | Good | Fine | N-Mint |
|---|---|---|---|
| nn(#1)-Abbie 'n' Slats (nn on-c, #1 on inside) | 9.30 | 28.00 | 65.00 |
| 2-Jim Hardy | 6.50 | 19.00 | 45.00 |
| 3-Bill Bumlin | 4.50 | 14.00 | 32.00 |
| 4-Abbie 'n' Slats | 5.70 | 17.00 | 40.00 |
| 5-Jim Hardy Comics #1 | 5.70 | 17.00 | 40.00 |

**TREASURY OF COMICS**
Mar, 1948 - No. 5, 1948 (Reg. size); 1948-1950 (Over 500 pgs., $1.00)
St. John Publishing Co.

| | Good | Fine | N-Mint |
|---|---|---|---|
| 1 | 11.50 | 34.00 | 80.00 |
| 2(#2 on-c, #1 on inside) | 7.00 | 21.00 | 50.00 |
| 3-5 | 6.00 | 18.00 | 42.00 |

1-(1948, 500 pgs., hard-c)-Abbie & Slats, Abbott & Costello, Casper,

| | Good | Fine | N-Mint |
|---|---|---|---|
| Little Annie Rooney, Little Audrey, Jim Hardy, Ella Cinders (16 books bound together) (Rare) | 90.00 | 270.00 | 630.00 |
| 1(1949, 500pgs.)-Same format as above | 90.00 | 270.00 | 630.00 |
| 1(1950, 500pgs.)-Same format as above; different-c; (Also see Little Audrey Yearbook) (Rare) | 90.00 | 270.00 | 630.00 |

**TREASURY OF DOGS, A** (See Dell Giants)

**TREASURY OF HORSES, A** (See Dell Giants)

**TREKKER** (See Dark Horse Presents #6)
May, 1987 - No. 9?, 1988 ($1.50, B&W)
Dark Horse Comics

| | Good | Fine | N-Mint |
|---|---|---|---|
| 1-9: Sci/Fi stories | .25 | .75 | 1.50 |
| Color Special 1 (1989, $2.95, 52 pgs.) | .50 | 1.50 | 3.00 |
| . . . Collection ($5.95, B&W) | 1.00 | 3.00 | 6.00 |

**TRIALS OF LULU AND LEANDER, THE**
1906 (32 pgs. in color) (10x16")
William A. Stokes Co.

| | Good | Fine | N-Mint |
|---|---|---|---|
| nn-By F. M. Howarth | 16.00 | 48.00 | 110.00 |

**TRIGGER** (See Roy Rogers. . .)

**TRIGGER TWINS**
Mar-Apr, 1973 (One Shot)
National Periodical Publications

| | Good | Fine | N-Mint |
|---|---|---|---|
| 1-Trigger Twins & Pow Wow Smith-r/All-Star Western #94,103 & Western Comics #81; Infantino-r(p) | | .40 | .80 |

**TRIPLE GIANT COMICS** (See Archie All-Star Specials under Archie Comics)

**TRIPLE THREAT**
Winter, 1945
Special Action/Holyoke/Gerona Publ.

| | Good | Fine | N-Mint |
|---|---|---|---|
| 1-Duke of Darkness, King O'Leary | 7.00 | 21.00 | 50.00 |

**TRIP WITH SANTA ON CHRISTMAS EVE, A**
No date (early 50's) (16 pgs.; full color; paper cover)
Rockford Dry Goods Co. (Giveaway)

| | Good | Fine | N-Mint |
|---|---|---|---|
| nn | 2.00 | 6.00 | 12.00 |

**TROLLORDS**
2/86 - No. 15, 1988; V2#1, 11/88 - V2#4, 1989 (1-15: $1.50, B&W)
Tru Studios/Comico V2#1 - on

| | Good | Fine | N-Mint |
|---|---|---|---|
| 1-1st & 2nd printings | .25 | .75 | 1.50 |
| 2-15: 6-Christmas issue; silver logo | .25 | .75 | 1.50 |
| V2#1-($1.75, color, Comico) | .30 | .90 | 1.80 |
| V2#2,3-($1.95, color) | .35 | 1.00 | 2.00 |
| 4-($2.50, color) | .40 | 1.25 | 2.50 |
| Special 1($1.75, 2/87, color)-Jerry's Big Fun Bk. | .30 | .90 | 1.80 |

**TROLLORDS: DEATH AND KISSES**
July, 1989 - No. 6, 1990 ($2.25, B&W, mini-series)
Apple Comics

| | Good | Fine | N-Mint |
|---|---|---|---|
| 1-6: 1-"The Big Batman Movie Parody" | .40 | 1.15 | 2.30 |

**TROUBLE SHOOTERS, THE** (See 4-Color #1108)

**TROUBLE WITH GIRLS, THE**
Aug, 1987 - No. 14, 1988; V2#1, Feb, 1989 - Present ($1.95, B&W)
Malibu Comics/Eternity Comics #7-14/Comico V2#1-4/Eternity #5 on

| | Good | Fine | N-Mint |
|---|---|---|---|
| 1-14 ($1.95, B&W) | .35 | 1.00 | 2.00 |
| V2#1-4 ($1.95, color, Comico) | .35 | 1.00 | 2.00 |
| 5-10 ($1.95, B&W, Eternity) | .35 | 1.00 | 2.00 |
| Annual 1 ($2.95, '88) | .50 | 1.50 | 3.00 |
| Graphic Novel 1 (7/88, $6.95, B&W)-r/1-3 | 1.15 | 3.50 | 7.00 |
| Graphic Novel 2 (1989, $7.95, B&W)-r/4-6 | 1.35 | 4.00 | 8.00 |

**TRUE ADVENTURES** (Formerly True Western)(Men's Advs. #4 on)
No. 3, May, 1950 (52 pgs.)
Marvel Comics (CCC)

| | Good | Fine | N-Mint |
|---|---|---|---|
| 3-Powell, Sekowsky-a | 7.00 | 21.00 | 50.00 |

**TRUE ANIMAL PICTURE STORIES**
Winter, 1947 - No. 2, Spr-Summer, 1947
True Comics Press

| | Good | Fine | N-Mint |
|---|---|---|---|
| 1,2 | 4.00 | 12.00 | 28.00 |

**TRUE AVIATION PICTURE STORIES** (Becomes Aviation Adventures & Model Building #16 on)
1942 - No. 15, Sept-Oct, 1946
Parents' Magazine Institute

| | Good | Fine | N-Mint |
|---|---|---|---|
| 1-(#1 & 2 titled . . . Aviation Comics Digest)(not digest size) | 8.00 | 24.00 | 56.00 |
| 2 | 4.00 | 12.00 | 28.00 |
| 3-14 | 3.50 | 10.50 | 24.00 |
| 15-(titled "True Aviation Adventures & Model Building") | 2.65 | 8.00 | 18.00 |

**TRUE BRIDE'S EXPERIENCES** (Formerly Teen-Age Brides)
(True Bride-To-Be Romances No. 17 on)
No. 8, Oct, 1954 - No. 16, Feb, 1956
True Love (Harvey Publications)

| | Good | Fine | N-Mint |
|---|---|---|---|
| 8 | 2.00 | 6.00 | 14.00 |
| 9,10: 10-Last pre-code (2/55) | 1.50 | 4.50 | 10.00 |
| 11-15 | 1.15 | 3.50 | 8.00 |
| 16-Spanking issue | 3.50 | 10.50 | 24.00 |

NOTE: ***Powell** a-8-10, 12, 13.*

**TRUE BRIDE-TO-BE ROMANCES** (Formerly True Bride's Exp.)
No. 17, Apr, 1956 - No. 30, Nov, 1958
Home Comics/True Love (Harvey)

| | Good | Fine | N-Mint |
|---|---|---|---|
| 17-S&K-c, Powell-a | 2.65 | 8.00 | 18.00 |
| 18-20,22,25-28,30 | 1.30 | 4.00 | 9.00 |
| 21,23,24-Powell-a | 1.50 | 4.50 | 10.00 |
| 29-Powell-a; 1 pg. Baker-a | 1.50 | 4.50 | 10.00 |

**TRUE COMICS** (Also see Outstanding American War Heroes)
April, 1941 - No. 84, Aug, 1950
True Comics/Parents' Magazine Press

| | Good | Fine | N-Mint |
|---|---|---|---|
| 1-Marathon run story | 16.00 | 48.00 | 110.00 |
| 2-Everett-a | 8.00 | 24.00 | 55.00 |
| 3-Basebasll Hall of Fame story | 8.50 | 25.50 | 60.00 |
| 4,5: 4-Story of American flag "Old Glory." 5-Life story of Joe Louis | 6.50 | 19.00 | 45.00 |
| 6-Baseball World Series story | 7.00 | 21.00 | 50.00 |
| 7-10 | 4.50 | 14.00 | 32.00 |
| 11-17,18-20: 13-Harry Houdini story. 14-Charlie McCarthy story. 15-Flag-c; Bob Feller story. 18-Story of America begins, ends #26 | 3.70 | 11.00 | 26.00 |
| 17-Brooklyn Dodgers story | 4.30 | 13.00 | 30.00 |
| 21-30 | 3.50 | 10.50 | 24.00 |
| 31-Red Grange story | 2.85 | 8.50 | 20.00 |
| 32-45: 39-FDR story | 2.30 | 7.00 | 16.00 |
| 46-George Gershwin story | 2.30 | 7.00 | 16.00 |
| 47-Atomic bomb issue | 4.30 | 13.00 | 30.00 |
| 48-66: 55(12/46)-1st app. Sad Sack by Baker, ½ pg. 58-Jim Jeffries (boxer) story; Harry Houdini story. 59-Bob Hope story. 66-Will Rogers story | 1.70 | 5.00 | 12.00 |
| 67-1st oversized issue (12/47); Steve Saunders, Special Agent begins | 2.65 | 8.00 | 18.00 |
| 68-72,74-79: 69-Jack Benny story. 71-Joe DiMaggio story. 78-Stan Musial story | 1.50 | 4.50 | 10.00 |
| 73-Walt Disney's life story | 2.35 | 7.00 | 16.00 |
| 80-84 (Scarce)-All distr. to subscribers through mail only; paper-c; 81-Red Grange story | 14.30 | 43.00 | 100.00 |

(Prices vary widely on these books)

NOTE: ***Bob Kane** a-7. **Palais** a-80. **Powell** c/a-80. #80-84 have soft covers and combin-*

*Trollords: Death and Kisses #1, © Apple*

*True Adventures #3, © MEG*

*True Comics #58, © PMI*

True Complete Mystery #8, © MEG

True Life Secrets #6, © CC

True Stories of Romance #1, © FAW

*ed with Tex Granger, Jack Armstrong, and Calling All Kids. #68-78 featured true FBI adventures.*

**TRUE COMICS AND ADVENTURE STORIES**
1965 (Giant) (25 cents)
Parents' Magazine Institute

| | Good | Fine | N-Mint |
|---|---|---|---|
| 1,2-Fighting Hero of Viet Nam; LBJ on-c | .70 | 2.00 | 4.50 |

**TRUE COMPLETE MYSTERY** (Formerly Complete Mystery)
No. 5, April, 1949 - No. 8, Oct, 1949
Marvel Comics (PrPI)

| | | | |
|---|---|---|---|
| 5 | 10.00 | 30.00 | 70.00 |
| 6-8: 6,8-Photo-c | 8.00 | 24.00 | 55.00 |

**TRUE CONFIDENCES**
1949 (Fall) - No. 4, June, 1950 (All photo-c)
Fawcett Publications

| | | | |
|---|---|---|---|
| 1-Has ad for Fawcett Love Adventures #1, but publ. as Love Memoirs #1 as Marvel publ. the title first | 7.00 | 21.00 | 50.00 |
| 2-4: 4-Powell-a | 3.60 | 11.00 | 25.00 |

**TRUE CRIME CASES**
1944 (100 pgs.)
St. John Publishing Co.

| | | | |
|---|---|---|---|
| 1944 | 22.00 | 65.00 | 150.00 |

**TRUE CRIME COMICS** (Also see Complete Book of . . .)
No. 2, May, 1947; No. 3, July-Aug, 1948 - No. 6, June-July, 1949; V2#1, Aug-Sept, 1949 (52 pgs.)
Magazine Village

| | | | |
|---|---|---|---|
| 2-Jack Cole-c/a; used in **SOTI**, pg. 81,82 plus illo.-"A sample of the injury-to-eye motif" & illo.-"Dragging living people to death;" used in **POP**, pg. 105; "Murder, Morphine and Me" classic drug propaganda story used by N.Y. Legis. Comm. | 75.00 | 225.00 | 525.00 |
| 3-Classic Cole-c/a; drug story with hypo, opium den & withdrawing addict | 52.00 | 155.00 | 365.00 |
| 4-Jack Cole-c/a; c-taken from a story panel in #3; r-(2) **SOTI** & **POP** stories/#2 | 45.00 | 135.00 | 315.00 |
| 5-Jack Cole-c; Marijuana racket story | 24.00 | 73.00 | 170.00 |
| 6 | 11.50 | 34.00 | 80.00 |
| V2#1-Used in **SOTI**, pgs. 81,82 & illo.-"Dragging living people to death;" Toth, Wood (3 pgs.), Roussos-a; Cole-r from #2 | 35.00 | 105.00 | 245.00 |

*NOTE: V2#1 was reprinted in Canada as V2#9 (12/49); same cover & contents minus Wood-a.*

**TRUE GHOST STORIES** (See Ripley's . . .)

**TRUE LIFE ROMANCES** ( . . . Romance on cover)
Dec, 1955 - No. 3, Aug, 1956
Ajax/Farrell Publications

| | | | |
|---|---|---|---|
| 1 | 4.30 | 13.00 | 30.00 |
| 2 | 2.15 | 6.50 | 15.00 |
| 3-Disbrow-a | 3.00 | 9.00 | 21.00 |

**TRUE LIFE SECRETS**
Mar-April, 1951 - No. 28, Sept, 1955; No. 29, Jan, 1956
Romantic Love Stories/Charlton

| | | | |
|---|---|---|---|
| 1 | 5.70 | 17.00 | 40.00 |
| 2 | 3.00 | 9.00 | 21.00 |
| 3-19 | 2.30 | 7.00 | 16.00 |
| 20-29: 25-Last precode(3/55) | 1.70 | 5.00 | 12.00 |

**TRUE LIFE TALES**
No. 8, Oct, 1949 - No. 2, Jan, 1950
Marvel Comics (CCC)

| | | | |
|---|---|---|---|
| 8(10/49), 2(1/50)-Photo-c | 4.00 | 12.00 | 28.00 |

**TRUE LOVE**
Jan, 1986 - No. 2, Jan, 1986 ($2.00, color, Baxter paper)
Eclipse Comics

| | Good | Fine | N-Mint |
|---|---|---|---|
| 1,2-Love stories-r from pre-code Standard Comics; Toth-a(p) in both; 1-Dave Stevens-c. 2-Mayo-a | .35 | 1.00 | 2.00 |

**TRUE LOVE CONFESSIONS**
May, 1954 - No. 11, Jan, 1956
Premier Magazines

| | | | |
|---|---|---|---|
| 1-Marijuana story | 5.00 | 15.00 | 35.00 |
| 2 | 2.30 | 7.00 | 16.00 |
| 3-11 | 1.70 | 5.00 | 12.00 |

**TRUE LOVE PICTORIAL**
1952 - No. 11, Aug, 1954
St. John Publishing Co.

| | | | |
|---|---|---|---|
| 1 | 7.00 | 21.00 | 50.00 |
| 2 | 3.50 | 10.50 | 24.00 |
| 3-5(All 100 pgs.): 5-Formerly Teen-Age Temptations (4/53); Kubert-a in #3,5; Baker-a in #3-5 | 16.00 | 48.00 | 110.00 |
| 6,7-Baker-c/a | 6.50 | 19.00 | 45.00 |
| 8,10,11-Baker-c/a | 5.70 | 17.00 | 40.00 |
| 9-Baker-c | 4.50 | 14.00 | 32.00 |

**TRUE MOVIE AND TELEVISION** (Part magazine)
Aug, 1950 - No. 3, Nov, 1950; No. 4, Mar, 1951 (52 pgs.) (10 cents)
Toby Press

| | | | |
|---|---|---|---|
| 1-Liz Taylor photo-c; Gene Autry, Shirley Temple, Li'l Abner app. | 22.00 | 65.00 | 155.00 |
| 2-Frazetta John Wayne illo | 14.00 | 43.00 | 100.00 |
| 3-June Allyson photo-c; Montgomery Cliff, Esther Williams, Andrews Sisters app; Li'l Abner featured | 14.00 | 43.00 | 100.00 |
| 4 | 4.30 | 13.00 | 30.00 |

*NOTE: 16 pages in color, rest movie material in black & white.*

**TRUE SECRETS** (Formerly Our Love)
No. 3, Mar, 1950; No. 4, Feb, 1951 - No. 40, Sept, 1956
Marvel (IPS)/Atlas Comics (MPI)

| | | | |
|---|---|---|---|
| 3 (52 pgs.) | 5.00 | 15.00 | 35.00 |
| 4,5,7-10 | 2.30 | 7.00 | 16.00 |
| 6,22-Everett-a | 3.00 | 9.00 | 21.00 |
| 11-20 | 1.70 | 5.00 | 12.00 |
| 21,23-28: 28-Last pre-code (2/55) | 1.30 | 4.00 | 9.00 |
| 29-40: 24-Colletta-c. 34,36-Colletta-a | 1.15 | 3.50 | 8.00 |

**TRUE SPORT PICTURE STORIES** (Formerly Sport Comics)
V1#5, Feb, 1942 - V5#2, July-Aug, 1949
Street & Smith Publications

| | | | |
|---|---|---|---|
| V1#5 | 13.00 | 40.00 | 90.00 |
| 6-12 (1942-43) | 7.00 | 21.00 | 50.00 |
| V2#1-12 (1944-45) | 6.50 | 19.00 | 45.00 |
| V3#1-12 (1946-47) | 5.00 | 15.00 | 35.00 |
| V4#1-12 (1948-49), V5#1,2 | 4.00 | 12.00 | 28.00 |

*NOTE: **Powell** a-V3#10, V4#1-4, 6-8, 10-12; V5#1, 2; c-V4#5-7, 9, 10.*

**TRUE STORIES OF ROMANCE**
Jan, 1950 - No. 3, May, 1950 (All photo-c)
Fawcett Publications

| | | | |
|---|---|---|---|
| 1 | 5.00 | 15.00 | 35.00 |
| 2,3 | 3.00 | 9.00 | 21.00 |

**TRUE STORY OF JESSE JAMES, THE** (See 4-Color #757)

**TRUE SWEETHEART SECRETS**
5/50; No. 2, 7/50; No. 3, 1951(nd); No. 4, 9/51 - No. 11, 1/53
Fawcett Publications (All photo-c)

| | | | |
|---|---|---|---|
| 1-Photo-c; Debbie Reynolds? | 5.70 | 17.00 | 40.00 |
| 2-Wood-a, 11 pgs. | 9.30 | 28.00 | 65.00 |
| 3-11: 4,5-Powell-a | 3.00 | 9.00 | 21.00 |

**TRUE TALES OF LOVE** (Formerly Secret Story Romances)
No. 22, April, 1956 - No. 31, Sept, 1957

Atlas Comics (TCI)

| | Good | Fine | N-Mint |
|---|---|---|---|
| 22 | 2.65 | 8.00 | 18.00 |
| 23-31-Colletta-a in most | 1.30 | 4.00 | 9.00 |

**TRUE TALES OF ROMANCE**
No. 4, June, 1950
Fawcett Publications

| | Good | Fine | N-Mint |
|---|---|---|---|
| 4 | 3.50 | 10.50 | 24.00 |

**TRUE 3-D**
Dec, 1953 - No. 2, Feb, 1954
Harvey Publications

| | Good | Fine | N-Mint |
|---|---|---|---|
| 1-Nostrand, Powell-a | 5.70 | 17.00 | 40.00 |
| 2-Powell-a | 10.00 | 30.00 | 70.00 |

NOTE: *Many copies of #1 surfaced in 1984.*

**TRUE-TO-LIFE ROMANCES** (Formerly Guns Against Gangsters)
#8, 11-12/49; #9, 1-2/50; #3, 4/50 - #5, 9/50; #6, 1/51 - #23, 10/54
Star Publications

| | Good | Fine | N-Mint |
|---|---|---|---|
| 8 (#1, 1949) | 7.00 | 21.00 | 50.00 |
| 9,3-10: 3-Janet Leigh/Glenn Ford photo on-c | 5.70 | 17.00 | 40.00 |
| 11,22,23 | 5.00 | 15.00 | 35.00 |
| 12-14,17-21-Disbrow-a | 6.00 | 18.00 | 42.00 |
| 15,16-Wood & Disbrow-a in each | 9.30 | 28.00 | 65.00 |

NOTE: ***Kamen** a-13. **Kamen/Feldstein** a-14. All have **L.B. Cole** covers.*

**TRUE WAR EXPERIENCES**
Aug, 1952 - No. 4, Dec, 1952
Harvey Publications

| | Good | Fine | N-Mint |
|---|---|---|---|
| 1 | 3.00 | 9.00 | 21.00 |
| 2-4 | 1.70 | 5.00 | 12.00 |

**TRUE WAR ROMANCES**
Sept, 1952 - No. 21, June, 1955
Quality Comics Group

| | Good | Fine | N-Mint |
|---|---|---|---|
| 1-Photo-c | 5.70 | 17.00 | 40.00 |
| 2 | 3.00 | 9.00 | 21.00 |
| 3-10: 9-Whitney-a | 2.30 | 7.00 | 16.00 |
| 11-21: 20-Last precode (4/55). 14-Whitney-a | 1.70 | 5.00 | 12.00 |

**TRUE WAR STORIES** (See Ripley's. . .)

**TRUE WESTERN** (True Adventures #3)
Dec, 1949 - No. 2, March, 1950
Marvel Comics (MMC)

| | Good | Fine | N-Mint |
|---|---|---|---|
| 1-Photo-c; Billy The Kid story | 8.50 | 25.50 | 60.00 |
| 2: Alan Ladd photo-c | 10.00 | 30.00 | 70.00 |

**TRUE WEST ROMANCE**
No. 21, 1952
Quality Comics Group

| | Good | Fine | N-Mint |
|---|---|---|---|
| 21 (Exist?) | 2.65 | 8.00 | 18.00 |

**TRUMP** (Magazine format)
Jan, 1957 - No. 2, Mar, 1957 (50 cents)
HMH Publishing Co.

| | Good | Fine | N-Mint |
|---|---|---|---|
| 1-Harvey Kurtzman satire | 11.00 | 32.00 | 75.00 |
| 2-Harvey Kurtzman satire | 9.30 | 28.00 | 65.00 |

NOTE: ***Davis, Elder, Heath, Jaffee** art-#1,2; **Wood** a-1. Article by Mel Brooks in #2.*

**TRUMPETS WEST** (See 4-Color #875)

**TRUTH ABOUT CRIME** (See Fox Giants)

**TRUTH ABOUT MOTHER GOOSE** (See 4-Color #862)

**TRUTH BEHIND THE TRIAL OF CARDINAL MINDSZENTY, THE** (See Cardinal Mindszenty)

**TRUTHFUL LOVE** (Formerly Youthful Love)
No. 2, July, 1950
Youthful Magazines

| | Good | Fine | N-Mint |
|---|---|---|---|
| 2-Ingrid Bergman's true life story | 3.00 | 9.00 | 21.00 |

**TRY-OUT WINNER BOOK**
Mar, 1988
Marvel Comics

| | Good | Fine | N-Mint |
|---|---|---|---|
| 1-Spider-Man vs. Doc. Octopus | | .60 | 1.25 |

**TSR WORLDS** (. . .Annual on cover only)
1990 - Present ($3.95, color, 84 pgs.) (Published annually)
DC Comics

| | Good | Fine | N-Mint |
|---|---|---|---|
| 1-Advanced D&D, Forgotten Realms, Dragonlance & 1st app. Spelljammer | .70 | 2.00 | 4.00 |

**TUBBY** (See Marge's. . .)

**TUFF GHOSTS STARRING SPOOKY**
July, 1962 - No. 39, Nov, 1970; No. 40, Sept, 1971 - No. 43, Oct, 1972
Harvey Publications

| | Good | Fine | N-Mint |
|---|---|---|---|
| 1 | 4.00 | 12.00 | 24.00 |
| 2-5 | 2.00 | 6.00 | 12.00 |
| 6-10 | 1.35 | 4.00 | 8.00 |
| 11-20 | .70 | 2.00 | 4.00 |
| 21-30 | .50 | 1.50 | 3.00 |
| 31-39,43 | | .50 | 1.00 |
| 40-42: 52 pg. Giants | | .60 | 1.20 |

**TUFFY**
No. 5, July, 1949 - No. 9, Oct, 1950
Standard Comics

| | Good | Fine | N-Mint |
|---|---|---|---|
| 5-All by Sid Hoff | 2.65 | 8.00 | 18.00 |
| 6-9 | 1.15 | 3.50 | 8.00 |

**TUFFY TURTLE**
No date
I. W. Enterprises

| | Good | Fine | N-Mint |
|---|---|---|---|
| 1-Reprint | .25 | .80 | 1.60 |

**TUROK, SON OF STONE** (See Dan Curtis, Golden Comics Digest #31, and March of Comics #378, 399, 408)
No. 596, 12/54 - No. 29, 9/62; No. 30, 12/62 - No. 91, 7/74; No. 92, 9/74 - No. 125, 1/80; No. 126, 3/81 - No. 130, 4/82
Dell Publ. Co. No. 1-29/Gold Key No. 30-91/Gold Key or Whitman No. 92-125/Whitman No. 126 on

| | Good | Fine | N-Mint |
|---|---|---|---|
| 4-Color 596 (12/54)(#1)-1st app./origin Turok & Andar | 27.00 | 81.00 | 190.00 |
| 4-Color 656 (10/55)(#2)-1st mention of Lanok | 19.00 | 58.00 | 135.00 |
| 3(3-5/56)-5 | 14.00 | 41.00 | 95.00 |
| 6-10 | 9.00 | 27.00 | 62.00 |
| 11-20: 17-Prehistoric pygmies | 4.50 | 14.00 | 32.00 |
| 21-30: 30-Back-c pin-ups begin. 30-33-Painted back-c pin-ups | 2.65 | 8.00 | 18.00 |
| 31-50 | 1.50 | 4.50 | 10.00 |
| 51-60: 58-Flying Saucer c/story | .85 | 2.60 | 6.00 |
| 61-83: 62-12 & 15 cent-c. 63-Only line drawn-c | .50 | 1.50 | 3.00 |
| 84-Origin & 1st app. Hutec | .35 | 1.00 | 2.00 |
| 85-130: 114,115-(52 pgs.) | | .50 | 1.00 |
| Giant 1(30031-611) (11/66) | 4.50 | 13.50 | 36.00 |

NOTE: *Most painted-c; line-drawn #63 & 130. **Alberto Gioletti** painted-c No. 30-129. **Sparling** a-117-120, 122, 124, 126, 129, 130. Reprints-#36, 54, 57, 75, 112, 114(⅓), 115(⅓), 118, 125, 127(⅓), 128, 129(⅓), 130(⅓), Giant 1.*

**TURTLE SOUP**
Sept, 1987 ($2.00, B&W, one shot, 76 pgs.)
Mirage Studios

| | Good | Fine | N-Mint |
|---|---|---|---|
| 1-Featuring Teenage Mutant Ninja Turtles | .85 | 2.50 | 5.00 |

**TV CASPER & COMPANY**
Aug, 1963 - No. 46, April, 1974 (25 cent Giants)
Harvey Publications

| | Good | Fine | N-Mint |
|---|---|---|---|
| 1: 68 pg. Giants begin | 4.30 | 13.00 | 30.00 |
| 2-5 | 2.00 | 6.00 | 14.00 |

True 3-D #1, © HARV

True-To-Life Romances #20, © STAR

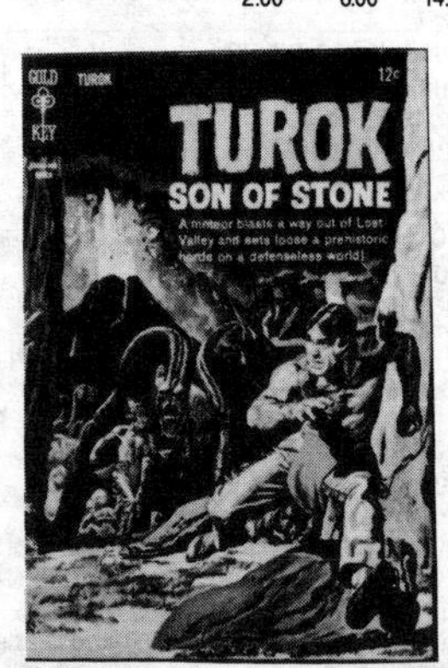

Turok, Son of Stone #44, © DELL

TV Stars #1, © Hanna-Barbera

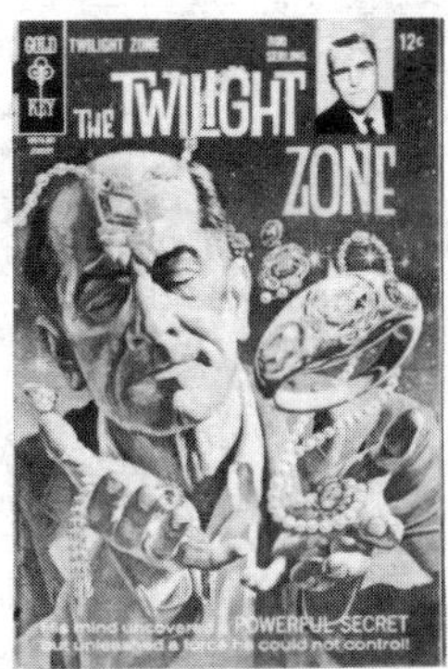

The Twilight Zone #24, © Cayuga Prod.

Twinkle Comics #1, © Spotlight Publ.

| | Good | Fine | N-Mint |
|---|---|---|---|
| 6-10 | 1.35 | 4.00 | 8.00 |
| 11-20 | .70 | 2.00 | 4.00 |
| 21-31: Last 68 pg. issue | .50 | 1.50 | 3.00 |
| 32-46: All 52 pgs. | | .50 | 1.00 |

NOTE: *Many issues contain reprints.*

**TV FUNDAY FUNNIES** (See Famous TV . . .)

**TV FUNNIES** (See New Funnies)

**TV FUNTIME** (See Little Audrey)

**TV LAUGHOUT** (See Archie's . . .)

**TV SCREEN CARTOONS** (Formerly Real Screen)
No. 129, July-Aug, 1959 - No. 138, Jan-Feb, 1961
National Periodical Publications

| | Good | Fine | N-Mint |
|---|---|---|---|
| 129-138 (Scarce) | 3.00 | 9.00 | 21.00 |

**TV STARS** (TV)(Hanna-Barbera)
Aug, 1978 - No. 4, Feb, 1979
Marvel Comics Group

| | Good | Fine | N-Mint |
|---|---|---|---|
| 1-Great Grape Ape app. | .60 | 1.75 | 3.50 |
| 2,4: 4-Top Cat app. | | .60 | 1.20 |
| 3-Toth-c/a; Dave Stevens inks | .60 | 1.75 | 3.50 |

**TV TEENS** (Formerly Ozzie & Babs; Rock and Rollo #14 on)
V1#14, Feb, 1954 - V2#13, July, 1956
Charlton Comics

| | Good | Fine | N-Mint |
|---|---|---|---|
| V1#14-Ozzie & Babs | 3.50 | 10.50 | 24.00 |
| 15 | 1.85 | 5.50 | 13.00 |
| V2#3(6/54) - 7-Don Winslow | 2.15 | 6.50 | 15.00 |
| 8(7/55)-13-Mopsy | 1.85 | 5.50 | 13.00 |

**TWEETY AND SYLVESTER** (1st Series)
No. 406, June, 1952 - No. 37, June-Aug, 1962
Dell Publishing Co.

| | Good | Fine | N-Mint |
|---|---|---|---|
| 4-Color 406 (#1) | 2.00 | 6.00 | 14.00 |
| 4-Color 489,524 | 1.15 | 3.50 | 8.00 |
| 4 (3-5/54) - 20 | .85 | 2.50 | 6.00 |
| 21-37 | .55 | 1.65 | 4.00 |

(See March of Comics #421, 433, 445, 457, 469, 481)

**TWEETY AND SYLVESTER** (2nd Series)
Nov, 1963; No. 2, Nov, 1965 - No. 121, July, 1984
Gold Key No. 1-102/Whitman No. 103 on

| | Good | Fine | N-Mint |
|---|---|---|---|
| 1 | .85 | 2.50 | 6.00 |
| 2-10 | .45 | 1.35 | 3.00 |
| 11-30 | .25 | .75 | 1.50 |
| 31-70 | | .50 | 1.00 |
| 71-121: 99,119-r(⅓) | | .30 | .60 |
| Kite Fun Book (1965, 16pgs., 5x7¼", soft-c)-PG&E; Southern California Edison version w/Reddy Kilowatt app. | .70 | 2.00 | 4.00 |
| Mini Comic No. 1(1976)-3¼x6½" | | .30 | .60 |

**12 O'CLOCK HIGH** (TV)
Jan-Mar, 1965 - No. 2, Apr-June, 1965 (Photo-c)
Dell Publishing Co.

| | Good | Fine | N-Mint |
|---|---|---|---|
| 1,2 | 2.65 | 8.00 | 18.00 |

**24 PAGES OF COMICS** (No title) (Also see Pure Oil Comics, Salerno Carnival of Comics, & Vicks Comics)
Late 1930s
Giveaway by various outlets including Sears

| | Good | Fine | N-Mint |
|---|---|---|---|
| nn-Contains strip reprints-Buck Rogers, Napoleon, Sky Roads, War on Crime | 20.00 | 60.00 | 140.00 |

**20,000 LEAGUES UNDER THE SEA** (See 4-Color #614, King Classics, Movie Comics & Power Record Comics)

**TWICE TOLD TALES** (See Movie Classics)

**TWILIGHT AVENGER, THE**
July, 1986 - No. 2, 1987 ($1.75, color, mini-series)
Elite Comics

| | Good | Fine | N-Mint |
|---|---|---|---|
| 1,2 | .30 | .90 | 1.80 |

**TWILIGHT MAN**
June, 1989 - No. 4, Sept, 1989 ($2.75, color, mini-series)
First Publishing

| | Good | Fine | N-Mint |
|---|---|---|---|
| 1-4 | .45 | 1.40 | 2.80 |

**TWILIGHT ZONE, THE** (TV) (See Dan Curtis)
No. 1173, 3-5/61 - No. 91, 4/79; No. 92, 5/82
Dell Publishing Co./Gold Key/Whitman No. 92

| | Good | Fine | N-Mint |
|---|---|---|---|
| 4-Color 1173-Crandall/Evans-c/a | 7.00 | 21.00 | 50.00 |
| 4-Color 1288-Crandall/Evans-c/a | 5.70 | 17.00 | 40.00 |
| 01-860-207 (5-7/62-Dell, 15 cents) | 4.50 | 14.00 | 32.00 |
| 12-860-210 on-c; 01-860-210 on inside(8-10/62-Dell)-Evans-c/a; Crandall/Frazetta-a(2) | 4.50 | 14.00 | 32.00 |
| 1(11/62-Gold Key)-Crandall/Frazetta-a(10 & 11 pgs.); Evans-a | 4.00 | 12.00 | 28.00 |
| 2 | 2.00 | 6.00 | 14.00 |
| 3,4,9-Toth-a, 11,10 & 15 pgs. | 2.30 | 7.00 | 16.00 |
| 5-8,10,11 | 1.70 | 5.00 | 12.00 |
| 12,13,15: 12-Williamson-a. 13-Williamson/Crandall-a. 15-Crandall-a | 2.00 | 6.00 | 14.00 |
| 14-Williamson/Orlando/Crandall/Torres-a | 2.30 | 7.00 | 16.00 |
| 16-20 | 1.30 | 4.00 | 9.00 |
| 21-Crandall-a(r) | .85 | 2.60 | 6.00 |
| 22-27: 25-Evans/Crandall-a(r). 26-Crandall, Evans-a(r). 27-Evans-r(2) | .60 | 1.80 | 4.00 |
| 28-32: 32-Evans-a(r) | .35 | 1.00 | 2.00 |
| 33-42,44-50,52-70 | .25 | .75 | 1.50 |
| 43,51: 43-Crandall-a. 51-Williamson-a | .30 | .90 | 1.80 |
| 71-92: 71-Reprint. 83,84-(52 pgs.) | | .50 | 1.00 |
| Mini Comic #1(1976-3¼x6½") | | .30 | .60 |

NOTE: ***Bolle*** *a-13(w/**McWilliams**), 50, 57, 59.* ***McWilliams*** *a-59.* ***Orlando*** *a-19, 20, 22, 23.* ***Sekowsky*** *a-3. (See Mystery Comics Digest 3, 6, 9, 12, 15, 18, 21, 24). Reprints-26(⅓), 71, 73, 79, 83, 84, 86, 92. Painted-c 1-91.*

**TWILIGHT ZONE, THE** (TV)
Nov, 1990 - Present ($1.75-$1.95, color)
Now Comics

| | Good | Fine | N-Mint |
|---|---|---|---|
| 1-($2.95, 52 pgs.)-Neal Adams-a, Sienkiewicz-c | .85 | 2.50 | 5.00 |
| 2 | .60 | 1.75 | 3.50 |
| 3,4: 4-1.95-c | .50 | 1.50 | 3.00 |
| 5,6: 5-Begin $2.25-c | .40 | 1.15 | 2.30 |

**TWINKLE COMICS**
May, 1945
Spotlight Publishers

| | Good | Fine | N-Mint |
|---|---|---|---|
| 1 | 8.50 | 25.50 | 60.00 |

**TWIST, THE**
July-September, 1962
Dell Publishing Co.

| | Good | Fine | N-Mint |
|---|---|---|---|
| 01-864-209-Painted-c | 3.00 | 9.00 | 21.00 |

**TWISTED TALES** (See Eclipse Graphic Album Series #15)
11/82 - No. 8, 5/84; No. 9, 11/84; No. 10, 12/84 (Baxter paper)
Pacific Comics/Independent Comics Group (Eclipse) #9, 10

| | Good | Fine | N-Mint |
|---|---|---|---|
| 1-B. Jones/Corben-c; nudity/Violence in all | .60 | 1.75 | 3.50 |
| 2-10 | .35 | 1.00 | 2.00 |

NOTE: ***Alcala*** *a-1.* ***Bolton*** *painted c-4, 6, 7; a-7.* ***Conrad*** *a-1.* ***Corben*** *a-1, 3, 5; c-1i, 3, 5.* ***Guice*** *a-8.* ***Morrow*** *a-10.* ***Ploog*** *a-2.* ***Wildey*** *a-3.* ***Wrightson*** *a(Painted)-10; c-2.*

**TWISTED TALES IN 3-D** (See Blackthorne 3-D Series #7)

**TWISTED TALES OF BRUCE JONES, THE**
Feb, 1986 - No. 4, Mar, 1986 ($1.75, Baxter paper)
Eclipse Comics

| | Good | Fine | N-Mint |
|---|---|---|---|
| 1-4 | .30 | .90 | 1.80 |

**TWO BIT THE WACKY WOODPECKER** (See Wacky. . .)
1951 - No. 3, May, 1953
Toby Press

| | | | |
|---|---|---|---|
| 1 | 3.00 | 9.00 | 21.00 |
| 2,3 | 1.50 | 4.50 | 10.00 |

**TWO FACES OF COMMUNISM** (Also see Double Talk)
1961 (36 pgs.; paper cover) (Giveaway)
Christian Anti-Communism Crusade, Houston, Texas

| | | | |
|---|---|---|---|
| nn | 10.00 | 30.00 | 70.00 |

**TWO-FISTED TALES** (Formerly Haunt of Fear #15-17)
No. 18, Nov-Dec, 1950 - No. 41, Feb-Mar, 1955
E. C. Comics

| | | | |
|---|---|---|---|
| 18(#1)-Kurtzman-c | 70.00 | 210.00 | 490.00 |
| 19-Kurtzman-c | 51.00 | 152.00 | 355.00 |
| 20-Kurtzman-c | 30.00 | 90.00 | 210.00 |
| 21,22-Kurtzman-c | 22.00 | 65.00 | 155.00 |
| 23-25-Kurtzman-c | 17.00 | 51.00 | 115.00 |
| 26-35: 33-"Atom Bomb" by Wood | 12.00 | 36.00 | 85.00 |
| 36-41 | 8.00 | 24.00 | 55.00 |
| Two-Fisted Annual, 1952 | 63.00 | 190.00 | 440.00 |
| Two-Fisted Annual, 1953 | 47.00 | 140.00 | 325.00 |

NOTE: **Berg** *a-29.* **Craig** *a-18, 19, 32.* **Crandall** *a-35, 36.* **Davis** *a-20-36, 40; c-30, 34, 35, 41, Annual 2.* **Evans** *a-34, 40, 41; c-40.* **Feldstein** *a-18.* **Krigstein** *a-41.* **Kubert** *a-32, 33.* **Kurtzman** *a-18-25; c-18-29, 31, Annual 1.* **Severin** *a-26, 28, 29, 31, 34-41 (No. 37-39 are all-Severin issues); c-36-39.* **Severin/Elder** *a-19-29, 31, 33, 36.* **Wood** *a-18-28, 30-35, 41; c-32, 33. Special issues: #26 (ChanJin Reservoir), 31 (Civil War), 35 (Civil War). Canadian reprints known; see Table of Contents.*

**TWO-GUN KID** (Also see All Western Winners, Best Western, Black Rider, Blaze Carson, Kid Colt, Western Winners, Wild West, & Wild Western)
3/48(No mo.) - No. 10, 11/49; No. 11, 12/53 - No. 59, 4/61; No. 60, 11/62 - No. 92, 3/68; No. 93, 7/70 - No. 136, 4/77
Marvel/Atlas (MCI No. 1-10/HPC No. 11-59/Marvel No. 60 on)

| | | | |
|---|---|---|---|
| 1-Two-Gun Kid & his horse Cyclone begin; The Sheriff begins | 40.00 | 120.00 | 280.00 |
| 2 | 18.00 | 54.00 | 125.00 |
| 3,4: 3-Annie Oakley app. | 13.00 | 40.00 | 90.00 |
| 5-Pre-Black Rider app. (Wint. 48/49); Spanking panel. Anti-Wertham editorial (1st?) | 16.00 | 48.00 | 110.00 |
| 6-10(11/49): 9-Black Rider app. | 10.00 | 30.00 | 70.00 |
| 11(12/53)-Black Rider app.; explains how Kid Colt became an outlaw | 8.50 | 25.50 | 60.00 |
| 12-Black Rider app. | 8.50 | 25.50 | 60.00 |
| 13-20: 13-1st to have Atlas globe on-c | 6.00 | 18.00 | 42.00 |
| 21-24,26-29 | 4.50 | 14.00 | 32.00 |
| 25,30-Williamson-a in both, 5 & 4 pgs. | 5.70 | 17.00 | 40.00 |
| 31-33,35,37-40 | 3.60 | 11.00 | 25.00 |
| 34-Crandall-a | 4.00 | 12.00 | 28.00 |
| 36,41,42,48-Origin in all | 4.00 | 12.00 | 28.00 |
| 43,44,47 | 2.65 | 8.00 | 18.00 |
| 45,46-Davis-a | 3.60 | 11.00 | 25.00 |
| 49,50,52,55,57-Severin-a(2) in each | 2.65 | 8.00 | 18.00 |
| 51-Williamson-a, 5pgs. | 3.50 | 10.50 | 24.00 |
| 53,54,56,59: 59-Last 10 cent issue (4/61) | 1.50 | 4.50 | 10.00 |
| 58,60-New origin | 1.50 | 4.50 | 10.00 |
| 61-80: 64-Intro. Boom-Boom | .70 | 2.00 | 5.00 |
| 81-92: 92-Last new story; last 12 cent issue | .35 | 1.00 | 2.00 |
| 93-100,102-136 | | .50 | 1.00 |
| 101-Origin retold/#58 | | .60 | 1.20 |

NOTE: **Ayers** *a-26, 27.* **Davis** *c-45-47.* **Everett** *a-82, 91.* **Fuje** *a-13.* **Heath** *a-3(2), 4(3), 5(2), 7; c-13, 21, 23.* **Keller** *a-16, 19, 28.* **Kirby** *a-54, 55, 57-62, 75-77, 90, 95, 101, 119, 120, 129; c-10, 52, 54-65, 67-72, 74-76, 116.* **Maneely** *a-20; c-11, 12, 16, 19, 20, 25-28, 49.* **Powell** *a-38, 102, 104.* **Severin** *a-9, 29, 51; c-9, 99.* **Shores** *c-5.* **Tuska** *a-11, 12.* **Whitney** *a-87, 89-91, 98-113, 124, 129; c-87, 89, 91, 113.* **Wildey** *a-21.* **Williamson** *a-110r. Kid Colt in #13, 14, 16-21.*

**TWO GUN WESTERN** (1st Series) (Casey Crime Photographer #1-4)
No. 5, Nov, 1950 - No. 14, June, 1952
Marvel/Atlas Comics (MPC)

| | Good | Fine | N-Mint |
|---|---|---|---|
| 5-The Apache Kid (Intro & origin) & his horse Nightwind begin by Buscema | 11.00 | 32.00 | 75.00 |
| 6-10: 8-Kid Colt, The Texas Kid & his horse Thunder begin? | 6.50 | 19.00 | 45.00 |
| 11-14: 13-Black Rider app. | 5.00 | 15.00 | 35.00 |

NOTE: **Maneely** *a-6, 7, 9; c-6, 11-13.* **Romita** *a-8.* **Wildey** *a-8.*

**2-GUN WESTERN** (2nd Series) (Formerly Billy Buckskin; Two-Gun Western #5 on)
No. 4, May, 1956
Atlas Comics (MgPC)

| | | | |
|---|---|---|---|
| 4-Apache Kid; Ditko-a | 7.00 | 21.00 | 50.00 |

**TWO-GUN WESTERN** (Formerly 2-Gun Western)
No. 5, July, 1956 - No. 12, Sept, 1957
Atlas Comics (MgPC)

| | | | |
|---|---|---|---|
| 5-Apache Kid, Kid Colt Outlaw, Doc Holiday begin; Black Rider app. | 5.70 | 17.00 | 40.00 |
| 6,7,10 | 3.00 | 9.00 | 21.00 |
| 8,12-Crandall-a | 4.30 | 13.00 | 30.00 |
| 9,11-Williamson-a in both, 5 pgs. each | 4.50 | 14.00 | 32.00 |

NOTE: **Ayers** *a-9.* **Everett** *c-12.* **Kirby** *a-12.* **Maneely** *a-6, 8, 12; c-5, 6, 8.* **Morrow** *a-9, 10.* **Powell** *a-7, 11.* **Severin** *c-10.*

**TWO MOUSEKETEERS, THE** (See 4-Color #475, 603, 642 under M.G.M.'s. . .; becomes M.G.M.'s Mouse Musketeers)

**TWO ON A GUILLOTINE** (See Movie Classics)

**2000 A.D. MONTHLY/PRESENTS** (. . .Showcase #25 on)
4/85 - #6, 9/85; 4/86 - #54, 1990 ($1.25-$1.50, color, Mando paper)
Eagle Comics/Quality Comics No. 5 on

| | | | |
|---|---|---|---|
| 1-6 ($1.25): 1-4-r/British series featuring Judge Dredd; Alan Moore scripts begin | | .65 | 1.30 |
| 1-25 ($1.25)-Reprints from British 2000 AD | | .65 | 1.30 |
| 26,27/28,29/30,31-44: 27/28,29/30,31-Guice-c | .25 | .75 | 1.50 |
| 45-54: 45-Begin $1.75-c | .30 | .90 | 1.80 |

**2001: A SPACE ODYSSEY** (Marvel Treasury Special)
Oct, 1976 (One Shot) (Over-sized)
Marvel Comics Group

| | | | |
|---|---|---|---|
| 1-Based on movie; Kirby, Giacoia-a | .35 | 1.00 | 2.00 |

**2001, A SPACE ODYSSEY**
Dec, 1976 - No. 10, Sept, 1977 (Regular size)
Marvel Comics Group

| | | | |
|---|---|---|---|
| 1-Based on movie; Kirby-c/a in all | .25 | .75 | 1.50 |
| 2-10: 8-Origin/1st app. Machine Man (called Mr. Machine) | | .50 | 1.00 |
| Howard Johnson giveaway(1968, 8pp); 6pg. movie adaptation, 2pg. games, puzzles | | .25 | .50 |

**2001 NIGHTS**
1990 - #10, 1991 ($3.75, B&W limited series, mature readers, 84 pgs.)
Viz Premiere Comics

| | | | |
|---|---|---|---|
| 1-5: Japanese sci-fi. 1-Wraparound-c | .65 | 1.90 | 3.80 |
| 6-10: 6-Begin $4.25-c | .70 | 2.15 | 4.30 |

**2010**
Apr, 1985 - No. 2, May, 1985
Marvel Comics Group

| | | | |
|---|---|---|---|
| 1,2-r/Marvel Super Special; movie adapt. | | .40 | .80 |

**UFO & ALIEN COMIX**
Jan, 1978 (One Shot)
Warren Publishing Co.

| | | | |
|---|---|---|---|
| nn-Toth, Severin-a(r) | .25 | .80 | 1.60 |

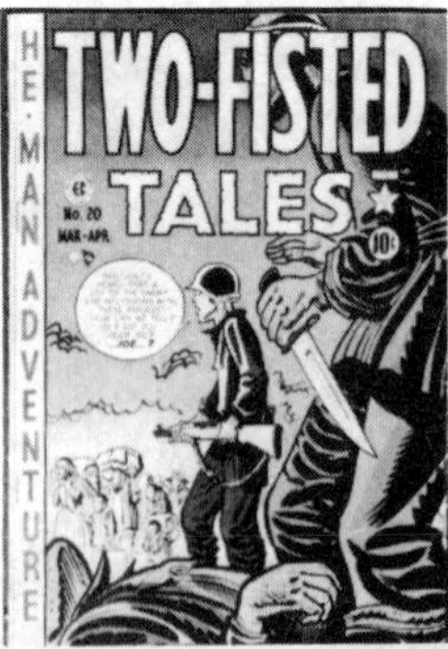

*Two-Fisted Tales #20, © WMG*

*Two Gun Western #12 (1st series), © MEG*

*2001, A Space Odyssey #1 (12/76), © MEG*

Uncanny Tales #7 (4/53), © MEG

Uncle Charlie's Fables #2, © LEV

Uncle Sam Quarterly #3, © QUA

**UFO & OUTER SPACE** (Formerly UFO Flying Saucers)
No. 14, June, 1978 - No. 25, Feb, 1980 (All painted covers)
Gold Key

| | Good | Fine | N-Mint |
|---|---|---|---|
| 14-Reprints UFO Flying Saucers #3 | .35 | 1.00 | 2.00 |
| 15,16-Reprints | | .60 | 1.20 |
| 17-20-New material | .25 | .75 | 1.50 |
| 21-25: 23-McWilliams-a. 24-3 pg.-r. 25-Reprints UFO Flying Saucers #2 w/cover | | .50 | 1.00 |

**UFO ENCOUNTERS**
May, 1978 (228 pages) ($1.95)
Western Publishing Co.

| | Good | Fine | N-Mint |
|---|---|---|---|
| 11192-Reprints UFO Flying Saucers | .70 | 2.00 | 4.00 |
| 11404-Vol.1 (128 pgs.)-See UFO Mysteries for Vol.2 | .35 | 1.00 | 2.00 |

**UFO FLYING SAUCERS** (UFO & Outer Space #14 on)
Oct, 1968 - No. 13, Jan, 1977 (No. 2 on, 36 pgs.)
Gold Key

| | Good | Fine | N-Mint |
|---|---|---|---|
| 1(30035-810) (68 pgs.) | 1.15 | 3.50 | 8.00 |
| 2(11/70), 3(11/72), 4(11/74) | 1.00 | 3.00 | 6.00 |
| 5(2/75)-13: Bolle-a No. 4 on | .70 | 2.00 | 4.00 |

**UFO MYSTERIES**
1978 (96 pages) ($1.00) (Reprints)
Western Publishing Co.

| | Good | Fine | N-Mint |
|---|---|---|---|
| 11400($1.00, 96 pgs.) | .25 | .75 | 1.50 |
| 11404(Vol.2)-Cont'd from UFO Encounters, pgs. 129-224 | .25 | .75 | 1.50 |

**ULTRA KLUTZ**
1981; 6/86 - #27, 1/89; #28, 4/90 - Present ($1.50, B&W; #18-22: $1.75)
Onward Comics

| | Good | Fine | N-Mint |
|---|---|---|---|
| 1 (1981)-re-released after 2nd #1 | .25 | .75 | 1.50 |
| 1 (6/86) | .35 | 1.00 | 2.00 |
| 2-22 | .25 | .75 | 1.50 |
| 23-31: ($2.00). 27-Photo back-c | .35 | 1.00 | 2.00 |

**UNBIRTHDAY PARTY WITH ALICE IN WONDERLAND** (See 4-Color #341)

**UNCANNY TALES**
June, 1952 - No. 56, Sept, 1957
Atlas Comics (PrPl/PPI)

| | Good | Fine | N-Mint |
|---|---|---|---|
| 1-Heath-a | 25.00 | 75.00 | 175.00 |
| 2 | 13.00 | 40.00 | 90.00 |
| 3-5 | 11.00 | 32.00 | 75.00 |
| 6-Wolvertonish-a by Matt Fox | 11.00 | 32.00 | 75.00 |
| 7-10: 8-Tothish-a. 9-Crandall-a | 9.30 | 28.00 | 65.00 |
| 11-20: 17-Atom bomb panels; anti-communist story. 19-Krenkel-a | 7.00 | 21.00 | 50.00 |
| 21-27: 25-Nostrand-a? | 6.00 | 18.00 | 42.00 |
| 28-Last precode issue (1/55); Kubert-a; #1-28 contain 2-3 sci/fic stories each | 7.00 | 21.00 | 50.00 |
| 29-41,43-49,52 | 2.85 | 8.50 | 20.00 |
| 42,54,56-Krigstein-a | 4.50 | 14.00 | 32.00 |
| 50,53,55-Torres-a | 3.70 | 11.00 | 26.00 |
| 51,57-Williamson-a (#57, exist?) | 4.50 | 14.00 | 32.00 |

NOTE: ***Andru*** *a-15, 27.* ***Ayers*** *a-22.* ***Bailey*** *a-51.* ***Briefer*** *a-19, 20.* ***Cameron*** *a-47.* ***Colan*** *a-11, 16, 17, 52.* ***Drucker*** *a-37, 42, 45.* ***Everett*** *a-2, 7, 12, 32, 36, 39, 47, 48; c-7, 11, 17, 39, 41, 50, 52, 53.* ***Fass*** *a-9, 10, 15, 24.* ***Forte*** *a-18, 27, 34, 52.* ***Heath*** *a-13, 14; c-10.* ***Keller*** *a-3.* ***Lawrence*** *a-14, 17, 19, 23, 27, 28, 35.* ***Maneely*** *a-4, 8, 10, 16, 29, 35; c-2, 22, 26, 33, 38.* ***Moldoff*** *a-23.* ***Morisi*** *a-48, 52.* ***Morrow*** *a-46, 51.* ***Orlando*** *a-49, 50, 53.* ***Powell*** *a-12, 18, 34, 36, 38, 43, 50, 53, 56.* ***Robinson*** *a-3, 13.* ***Reinman*** *a-12.* ***Romita*** *a-10.* ***Roussos*** *a-8.* ***Sale*** *a-47.* ***Sekowsky*** *a-25.* ***Sinnott*** *a-15, 52.* ***Tothish****-a by* ***Andru****-27.* ***Wildey*** *a-22, 48.*

**UNCANNY TALES**
Dec, 1973 - No. 12, Oct, 1975
Marvel Comics Group

| | Good | Fine | N-Mint |
|---|---|---|---|
| 1-Crandall-a(r-'50s #9) | | .50 | 1.00 |
| 2-12 | | .40 | .80 |

NOTE: ***Ditko*** *reprints-#4, 6-8, 10-12.*

**UNCANNY X-MEN, THE** (See X-Men)

**UNCANNY X-MEN AND THE NEW TEEN TITANS** (See Marvel and DC Present)

**UNCANNY X-MEN AT THE STATE FAIR OF TEXAS, THE**
1983 (36 pgs.)(One-Shot)
Marvel Comics Group

| | Good | Fine | N-Mint |
|---|---|---|---|
| nn | 1.70 | 5.00 | 10.00 |

**UNCANNY X-MEN IN DAYS OF FUTURE PAST, THE**
1989 ($3.95, color, squarebound, 52 pgs.)
Marvel Comics

| | Good | Fine | N-Mint |
|---|---|---|---|
| nn-Byrne/Austin-r (2 stories); Guice-c(p) | .70 | 2.00 | 4.00 |

**UNCENSORED MOUSE, THE**
1989 - No. 2, 1989 ($1.95, B&W)(Came sealed in plastic bag)
Eternity Comics

| | Good | Fine | N-Mint |
|---|---|---|---|
| 1-Early Gottfredson strip-r in each | 1.15 | 3.50 | 7.00 |
| 2-Both contain racial stereotyping & violence | 1.70 | 5.00 | 10.00 |

NOTE: *Both issues contain unauthorized reprints. Series was cancelled.*

**UNCLE CHARLIE'S FABLES**
Jan, 1952 - No. 5, Sept, 1952
Lev Gleason Publications

| | Good | Fine | N-Mint |
|---|---|---|---|
| 1-Norman Maurer-a; has Biro's picture | 4.50 | 14.00 | 32.00 |
| 2-Fuje-a; Biro photo; Biro painted-c | 3.50 | 10.50 | 24.00 |
| 3-5: 4-Biro-c | 2.65 | 8.00 | 18.00 |

**UNCLE DONALD & HIS NEPHEWS DUDE RANCH** (See Dell Giant #52)

**UNCLE DONALD & HIS NEPHEWS FAMILY FUN** (See Dell Giant #38)

**UNCLE JOE'S FUNNIES**
1938 (B&W)
Centaur Publications

| | Good | Fine | N-Mint |
|---|---|---|---|
| 1-Games/puzzles, some interior art; Bill Everett-c | 24.00 | 71.00 | 165.00 |

**UNCLE MILTY** (TV)
Dec, 1950 - No. 4, July, 1951 (52 pgs.)
Victoria Publications/True Cross

| | Good | Fine | N-Mint |
|---|---|---|---|
| 1-Milton Berle | 23.00 | 70.00 | 160.00 |
| 2 | 12.00 | 36.00 | 85.00 |
| 3,4 | 11.00 | 32.00 | 75.00 |

**UNCLE REMUS & HIS TALES OF BRER RABBIT** (See 4-Color #129, 208, 693)

**UNCLE SAM QUARTERLY** (Blackhawk #9 on)(See Freedom Fighters)
Autumn, 1941 - No. 8, Fall, 1943 (Also see National Comics)
Quality Comics Group

| | Good | Fine | N-Mint |
|---|---|---|---|
| 1-Origin Uncle Sam; Fine/Eisner-c, chapter headings, 2 pgs. by Eisner. (2 versions: dark cover, no price; light cover with price); Jack Cole-a | 120.00 | 360.00 | 840.00 |
| 2-Cameos by The Ray, Black Condor, Quicksilver, The Red Bee, Alias the Spider, Hercules & Neon the Unknown; Eisner, Fine-c/a | 57.00 | 170.00 | 400.00 |
| 3-Tuska-c/a | 43.00 | 130.00 | 300.00 |
| 4 | 36.00 | 107.00 | 250.00 |
| 5-8 | 30.00 | 90.00 | 210.00 |

NOTE: ***Kotzky*** *or* ***Tuska*** *a-4-8.*

**UNCLE SAM'S CHRISTMAS STORY**
1958
Promotional Publ. Co. (Giveaway)

| | Good | Fine | N-Mint |
|---|---|---|---|
| nn-Reprints 1956 Christmas USA | 1.30 | 4.00 | 9.00 |

**UNCLE SCROOGE** (Disney)(See Dell Giants 33,55, Dynabrite, Four Color #178, Gladstone Comic Album & Walt Disney's C&S #98)
No. 386, 3/52 - No. 39, 8-10/62; No. 40, 12/62 - No. 209, 1984; No. 210, 10/86 - No. 242, 4/90; No. 243, 5/90 - Present
Dell #1-39/Gold Key #40-173/Whitman #174-209/Gladstone #210-242/ Disney Comics #243 on

| | Good | Fine | N-Mint |
|---|---|---|---|
| 4-Color 386(#1)-in "Only a Poor Old Man" by Carl Barks; r-in Uncle Scrooge & Donald Duck #1('65) & The Best of Walt Disney Comics (1974) | 60.00 | 180.00 | 450.00 |
| 4-Color 456(#2)-in "Back to the Klondike" by Carl Barks; r-in Best of U.S. & D.D. #1('66) & Gladstone C.A. #4 | 29.00 | 86.00 | 215.00 |
| 4-Color 495(No.3)-r-in #105 | 26.00 | 77.00 | 190.00 |
| 4(12-2/53-54)-r-Gladstone Comic Album #11 | 20.00 | 60.00 | 150.00 |
| 5-r-in Gladstone Spec. #2 & W.D. Digest #1 | 16.00 | 48.00 | 120.00 |
| 6-r-in U.S. #106,165,233 & Best of U.S. & D.D. #1('66) | 15.00 | 45.00 | 115.00 |
| 7-The Seven Cities of Cibola by Barks; r-in #217 & Best of D.D. & U.S. #2('67) | 11.50 | 34.00 | 85.00 |
| 8-10: 8-r-in #111,222. 9-r-in #104,214. 10-r-in #67 | 9.30 | 28.00 | 70.00 |
| 11-20: 11-r-in #237. 17-r-in #215. 19-r-in Gladstone C.A. #1. 20-r-in #213 | 8.00 | 24.00 | 60.00 |
| 21-30: 26-r-in #211 | 6.50 | 19.50 | 50.00 |
| 31-40: 34-r-in #228 | 5.50 | 16.50 | 42.00 |
| 41-50 | 4.00 | 12.00 | 32.00 |
| 51-60 | 3.70 | 11.00 | 28.00 |
| 61-66,68-70: 70-Last Barks issue with original story | 2.85 | 8.50 | 22.00 |
| 67,72,73-Barks-r | 1.85 | 5.50 | 14.00 |
| 71-Written by Barks only | 1.85 | 5.50 | 14.00 |
| 74-One pg. Barks-r | 1.15 | 3.50 | 9.00 |
| 75-81,83-Not by Barks | 1.15 | 3.50 | 9.00 |
| 82,84-Barks-r begin | 1.15 | 3.50 | 9.00 |
| 85-100 | 1.00 | 3.00 | 7.00 |
| 101-110 | .85 | 2.50 | 6.00 |
| 111-120 | .70 | 2.00 | 5.00 |
| 121-141,143-152,154-157 | .60 | 1.75 | 4.00 |
| 142-Reprints 4-Color #456 with-c | .70 | 2.00 | 5.00 |
| 153,158,162-164,166,168-170,178,180: No Barks | .25 | .75 | 2.00 |
| 159-160,165,167,172-176-Barks-a | .25 | .75 | 2.00 |
| 161(r-#14), 171(r-#11), 177(r-#16), 179(r-#9), 183(r-#6)-Barks-r | .25 | .75 | 2.00 |
| 181(r-4-Color #495), 195(r-4-Color #386) | .25 | .70 | 1.50 |
| 182,186,191-194,197-202,204-206: No Barks | | .50 | 1.00 |
| 184,185,187,188-Barks-a | | .50 | 1.00 |
| 189(r-#5), 190(r-#4), 196(r-#13), 203(r-#12), 207(r-#93,92), 208(r-U.S. #18), 209(r-U.S. #21)-Barks-r | | .60 | 1.20 |
| 210-1st Gladstone issue; r-WDC&S #134 (1st Beagle Boys) | .85 | 2.50 | 5.00 |
| 211-218: 217-R-U.S. #7(Seven Cities of Cibola) | .40 | 1.25 | 2.50 |
| 219-Son Of The Sun by Rosa | 1.70 | 5.00 | 10.00 |
| 220-Don Rosa story/a | .50 | 1.50 | 3.00 |
| 221-230: 224-Rosa-c/a. 226,227-Rosa-a | .25 | .75 | 1.50 |
| 231-240: 235-Rosa story/art | | .50 | 1.00 |
| 241-($1.95, 68 pgs.)-Rosa finishes over Barks-r | .35 | 1.00 | 2.00 |
| 242-($1.95, 68 pgs.)-Barks-r; Rosa-a(1 pg.) | .35 | 1.00 | 2.00 |
| 243-249,251-254($1.50)-Disney Comics; new-a begins | .25 | .75 | 1.50 |
| 250-($2.25, 52 pgs.)-Barks-r; wraparound-c | .40 | 1.15 | 2.30 |
| Uncle Scrooge & Money(G.K.)-Barks-r/from WDC&S #130 (3/67) | 4.00 | 12.00 | 24.00 |
| Mini Comic #1(1976)(3¼x6½")-R-/U.S. #115; Barks-c | | | .20 |

NOTE: ***Barks*** *c-4-Color 386, 456, 495, #4-37, 39, 40, 43-71.* ***Barks*** *r-210-218, 220-223, 224(2pg.), 225-234, 236-242, 250, 251; c(r)-210, 212, 221, 228, 229, 232, 233.* ***Rosa*** *a-219, 220, 224, 226, 227, 235; c-219, 224, 231; scripts-219, 220, 224, 235.*

**UNCLE SCROOGE ADVENTURES** (Walt Disney's. . .#4 on)
Nov, 1987 - No. 21, May, 1990
Gladstone Publishing

| | Good | Fine | N-Mint |
|---|---|---|---|
| 1-Barks-r begin | .70 | 2.00 | 4.00 |
| 2-5: 5-Rosa-c/a | .25 | .75 | 1.50 |
| 6-19: 9,14-Rosa-a. 10-r/U.S. #18(all Barks) | | .50 | 1.00 |
| 20,21 ($1.95, 68 pgs.) 20-Rosa-c/a. 21-Rosa-a | .35 | 1.00 | 2.00 |

NOTE: ***Barks*** *r-1-4, 6-8, 10-13, 15-21; c(r)-15, 16, 17, 21.* ***Rosa*** *a-5, 9, 14, 20, 21; c-5, 13, 14, 17(finishes), 20; scripts-5, 9, 14.*

**UNCLE SCROOGE & DONALD DUCK**
June, 1965 (25 cents) (Paper cover)
Gold Key

| | Good | Fine | N-Mint |
|---|---|---|---|
| 1-Reprint of 4-Color #386(#1) & lead story from 4-Color #29 | 8.35 | 25.00 | 50.00 |

**UNCLE SCROOGE COMICS DIGEST**
Dec, 1986 - No. 5, Aug, 1987 ($1.25, Digest-size)
Gladstone Publishing

| | Good | Fine | N-Mint |
|---|---|---|---|
| 1-5 | | .60 | 1.25 |

**UNCLE SCROOGE GOES TO DISNEYLAND** (See Dell Giants)
Aug, 1985 ($2.50)
Gladstone Publishing Ltd.

| | Good | Fine | N-Mint |
|---|---|---|---|
| 1-Reprints Dell Giant w/new-c by Mel Crawford, based on old cover | .40 | 1.25 | 2.50 |
| . . .Comics Digest 1 ($1.50, digest size) | .25 | .75 | 1.50 |

**UNCLE WIGGILY** (See 4-Color #179, 221, 276, 320, 349, 391, 428, 503, 543, & March of Comics #19)

**UNDERCOVER GIRL** (Starr Flagg) (See Extra Comics & Manhunt!)
No. 5, 1952 - No. 7, 1954
Magazine Enterprises

| | Good | Fine | N-Mint |
|---|---|---|---|
| 5(#1)(A-1 #62)-Fallon of the F.B.I. in all | 22.00 | 65.00 | 155.00 |
| 6(A-1 #98), 7(A-1 #118)-All have Starr Flagg | 20.00 | 60.00 | 140.00 |

NOTE: ***Powell*** *c-6, 7.* ***Whitney*** *a-5-7.*

**UNDERDOG** (TV) (See March of Comics 426, 438, 467, 479)
July, 1970 - No. 10, Jan, 1972; Mar, 1975 - No. 23, Feb, 1979
Charlton Comics/Gold Key

| | Good | Fine | N-Mint |
|---|---|---|---|
| 1 (1st series) | 3.00 | 9.00 | 21.00 |
| 2-10 | 1.15 | 3.50 | 8.00 |
| 1 (Gold Key)(2nd series) | 1.70 | 5.00 | 12.00 |
| 2-10 | .70 | 2.00 | 5.00 |
| 11-23: 13-1st app. Shack of Solitude | .60 | 1.80 | 4.00 |
| Kite Fun Book('74)-5x7"; 16 pgs. | .70 | 2.00 | 5.00 |

**UNDERDOG**
1987 - No. 3?, 1987 ($1.50, color)
Spotlight Comics

| | Good | Fine | N-Mint |
|---|---|---|---|
| 1-3 | .25 | .75 | 1.50 |

**UNDERDOG IN 3-D** (See Blackthorne 3-D Series #43)

**UNDERSEA AGENT**
Jan, 1966 - No. 6, Mar, 1967 (25 cents, 68 pages)
Tower Comics

| | Good | Fine | N-Mint |
|---|---|---|---|
| 1-Davy Jones, Undersea Agent begins | 2.30 | 7.00 | 16.00 |
| 2-6: 2-Jones gains magnetic powers. 5-Origin & 1st app. of Merman. 6-Kane?/Wood-c(r) | 1.50 | 4.50 | 10.00 |

NOTE: ***Gil Kane*** *a-3-6; c-4, 5.* ***Moldoff*** *a-2i.*

**UNDERSEA FIGHTING COMMANDOS** (See Fighting Undersea. . .)
May, 1952 - No. 5, Jan, 1953; 1964
Avon Periodicals

| | Good | Fine | N-Mint |
|---|---|---|---|
| 1-Ravielli-c | 4.30 | 13.00 | 30.00 |
| 2 | 2.65 | 8.00 | 18.00 |
| 3-5 | 2.30 | 7.00 | 16.00 |
| I.W. Reprint #1,2('64): 2-Severin-c | .85 | 2.00 | 4.00 |

*Uncle Scrooge #65, © The Disney Co.*

*Undercover Girl #5, © ME*

*Undersea Agent #5, © TC*

*The Underworld Story nn, © AVON*

*The Unexpected #107, © DC*

*United States Fighting Air Force #9, © SUPR*

**UNDERWATER CITY, THE** (See 4-Color #1328)

**UNDERWORLD** (True Crime Stories)
Feb-Mar, 1948 - No. 9, June-July, 1949 (52 pgs.)
D. S. Publishing Co.

| | Good | Fine | N-Mint |
|---|---|---|---|
| 1-Moldoff-c; excessive violence | 17.00 | 51.00 | 120.00 |
| 2-Moldoff-c; Ma Barker story used in **SOTI**, pg. 95; female electrocution panel; lingerie art | 19.00 | 57.00 | 130.00 |
| 3-McWilliams-c/a; extreme violence, mutilation | 14.00 | 43.00 | 100.00 |
| 4-Used in **Love and Death** by Legman; Ingels-a | 11.00 | 32.00 | 75.00 |
| 5-Ingels-a | 8.00 | 24.00 | 55.00 |
| 6-9: 8-Ravielli-a | 6.00 | 18.00 | 42.00 |

**UNDERWORLD**
Dec, 1987 - No. 4, Mar, 1988 ($1.00, mini-series, adults)
DC Comics

| | Good | Fine | N-Mint |
|---|---|---|---|
| 1-4 | | .50 | 1.00 |

**UNDERWORLD CRIME**
June, 1952 - No. 9, Oct, 1953
Fawcett Publications

| | Good | Fine | N-Mint |
|---|---|---|---|
| 1 | 13.00 | 40.00 | 90.00 |
| 2 | 7.00 | 21.00 | 50.00 |
| 3-6,8,9 (8,9-exist?) | 6.50 | 19.00 | 45.00 |
| 7-Bondage/torture-c | 11.50 | 34.00 | 80.00 |

**UNDERWORLD STORY, THE**
1950 (Movie)
Avon Periodicals

| | Good | Fine | N-Mint |
|---|---|---|---|
| nn-(Scarce)-Ravielli-c | 13.00 | 40.00 | 90.00 |

**UNEARTHLY SPECTACULARS**
Oct, 1965 - No. 3, Mar, 1967 (#1: 12 cents; #2,3: 25 cent giants)
Harvey Publications

| | Good | Fine | N-Mint |
|---|---|---|---|
| 1-Tiger Boy; Simon-c | .70 | 2.00 | 4.00 |
| 2-Jack Q. Frost, Tiger Boy & Three Rocketeers app.; Williamson, Wood, Kane-a; r-1 story/Thrill-O-Rama #2 | 1.70 | 5.00 | 12.00 |
| 3-Jack Q. Frost app.; Williamson/Crandall-a; r-from Alarming Advs. No. 1, 1962 | 1.70 | 5.00 | 12.00 |

NOTE: ***Crandall** a-3r. **G. Kane** a-2. **Orlando** a-3. **Simon, Sparling, Wood** c-2. **Simon/Kirby** a-3r. **Torres** a-1?. **Wildey** a-1(3). **Williamson** a-2, 3r. **Wood** a-2(2).*

**UNEXPECTED, THE** (Formerly Tales of the...)
No. 105, Feb-Mar, 1968 - No. 222, May, 1982
National Periodical Publications/DC Comics

| | Good | Fine | N-Mint |
|---|---|---|---|
| 105-Begin 12 cent cover price, ends ? | .85 | 2.60 | 6.00 |
| 106-115,117,118,120,122-127 | .70 | 2.00 | 4.00 |
| 116,119,121,128-Wrightson-a | .70 | 2.00 | 5.00 |
| 129-162: 132-136-(52 pgs.). 157-162-(100 pgs.) | .35 | 1.00 | 2.00 |
| 163-188: 187,188-(44 pgs.) | | .50 | 1.00 |
| 189,190,192-195 ($1.00, 68 pgs.): 189 on are combined with House of Secrets & The Witching Hour | | .60 | 1.20 |
| 191-Rogers-a(p) ($1.00, 68 pgs.) | .25 | .75 | 1.50 |
| 196-221: 200-Return of Johhny Peril by Tuska. 205-213-Johnny Peril app. 210-Time Warp story | | .40 | .80 |

NOTE: ***Neal Adams** c-110, 112-118, 121, 124. **J. Craig** a-195. **Ditko** a-189, 221p, 222p; c-222. **Drucker** a-107r. **Giffen** a-219, 222. **Kaluta** c-203, 212. **Kirby** a-127r, 162. **Kubert** c-204, 214-216, 219-221. **Mayer** a-217p, 220, 221p. **Moldoff** a-136r. **Moreira** a-133. **Mortimer** a-212p. **Newton** a-204p. **Orlando** a-202; c-191. **Perez** a-217p. **Redondo** a-155, 195. **Reese** a-145. **Sparling** a-107, 205-209p, 212p. **Spiegle** a-217. **Starlin** c-198. **Toth** a-126r, 127r. **Tuska** a-132, 134, 136, 139, 152, 180, 200p. **Wildey** a-193. **Wood** a-122i, 133i, 137i, 138i. **Wrightson** a-161r(2 pgs.). Johnny Peril in #106-117, 200, 205-213.*

**UNEXPECTED ANNUAL, THE** (See DC Special Series #4)

**UNIDENTIFIED FLYING ODDBALL** (See Walt Disney Showcase #52)

**UNITED COMICS** (Formerly Fritzi Ritz #7)
Aug, 1940; No. 8, 1950 - No. 26, Jan-Feb, 1953
United Features Syndicate

| | Good | Fine | N-Mint |
|---|---|---|---|
| 1(68 pgs.)-Fritzi Ritz & Phil Fumble | 13.00 | 40.00 | 90.00 |
| 8-Fritzi Ritz, Abbie & Slats | 2.30 | 7.00 | 16.00 |
| 9-26: 20-Strange As It Seems; Russell Patterson Cheesecake-a. 22, 25-Peanuts app. | 2.00 | 6.00 | 14.00 |

NOTE: *Abbie & Slats reprinted from Tip Top.*

**UNITED NATIONS, THE** (See Classics Illustrated Special Issue)

**UNITED STATES AIR FORCE PRESENTS: THE HIDDEN CREW**
1964 (36 pages) (full color)
U.S. Air Force

| | Good | Fine | N-Mint |
|---|---|---|---|
| nn-Shaffenberger-a | .50 | 1.50 | 3.00 |

**UNITED STATES FIGHTING AIR FORCE**
Sept, 1952 - No. 29, Oct, 1956
Superior Comics Ltd.

| | Good | Fine | N-Mint |
|---|---|---|---|
| 1 | 4.00 | 12.00 | 28.00 |
| 2 | 2.00 | 6.00 | 14.00 |
| 3-10 | 1.15 | 3.50 | 8.00 |
| 11-29 | 1.00 | 3.00 | 7.00 |
| I.W. Reprint #1,9(nd) | .35 | 1.10 | 2.20 |

**UNITED STATES MARINES**
1943 - No. 4, 1944; No. 5, 1952 - No. 11, 1953
William H. Wise/Life's Romances Publ. Co./Magazine Enterprises No. 5-8/Toby Press No. 7-11

| | Good | Fine | N-Mint |
|---|---|---|---|
| nn-Mart Bailey-a | 4.50 | 14.00 | 32.00 |
| 2-Bailey-a | 3.50 | 10.50 | 24.00 |
| 3,4 | 2.85 | 8.50 | 20.00 |
| 5(A-1 #55), 6(A-1 #60), 7(A-1 #68), 8(A-1 #72) | 2.65 | 8.00 | 18.00 |
| 7-11 (Toby) | 1.15 | 3.50 | 8.00 |

NOTE: ***Powell** a-5-7.*

**UNIVERSAL PRESENTS DRACULA** (See Dell Giants)

**UNKEPT PROMISE**
1949 (24 pages)
Legion of Truth (Giveaway)

| | Good | Fine | N-Mint |
|---|---|---|---|
| nn-Anti-alcohol | 5.00 | 15.00 | 35.00 |

**UNKNOWN MAN, THE**
1951 (Movie)
Avon Periodicals

| | Good | Fine | N-Mint |
|---|---|---|---|
| nn-Kinstler-c | 14.00 | 43.00 | 100.00 |

**UNKNOWN SOLDIER** (Formerly Star-Spangled War Stories)
No. 205, Apr-May, 1977 - No. 268, Oct, 1982
National Periodical Publications/DC Comics

| | Good | Fine | N-Mint |
|---|---|---|---|
| 205-268: 219-221-(44 pgs.). 248,249-Origin. 251-Enemy Ace begins. 268-Death of Unknown Soldier | | .30 | .60 |

NOTE: ***Evans** a-265-267; c-235. **Kubert** c-Most. **Miller** a-219p. **Severin** a-251-253, 260, 261, 265-267. **Simonson** a-254-256. **Spiegle** a-258, 259, 262-264.*

**UNKNOWN SOLDIER, THE** (Also see Brave & the Bold #146)
Winter, 1988-'89 - No. 12, Dec, 1989 ($1.50, maxi-series, adults)
DC Comics

| | Good | Fine | N-Mint |
|---|---|---|---|
| 1-12: 8-Begin $1.75-c | .25 | .75 | 1.50 |

**UNKNOWN WORLD** (Strange Stories From Another World #2 on)
June, 1952
Fawcett Publications

| | Good | Fine | N-Mint |
|---|---|---|---|
| 1-Norman Saunders painted-c | 16.00 | 48.00 | 110.00 |

**UNKNOWN WORLDS** (See Journey Into...)

**UNKNOWN WORLDS**
Aug, 1960 - No. 57, Aug, 1967
American Comics Group/Best Synd. Features

| | Good | Fine | N-Mint |
|---|---|---|---|
| 1 | 7.00 | 21.00 | 50.00 |
| 2-5: 2-Dinosaur-c/story | 3.60 | 11.00 | 25.00 |
| 6-11: 9-Dinosaur-c/story. 11-Last 10 cent issue | 2.30 | 7.00 | 16.00 |

| | Good | Fine | N-Mint |
|---|---|---|---|
| 12-19: 12-Begin 12 cent issues?; ends #57 | 1.70 | 5.00 | 12.00 |
| 20-Herbie cameo (12-1/62-63) | 2.00 | 6.00 | 14.00 |
| 21-35 | 1.50 | 4.50 | 10.00 |
| 36-"The People vs. Hendricks" by Craig; most popular ACG story ever | 1.70 | 5.00 | 12.00 |
| 37-46 | 1.00 | 3.00 | 7.00 |
| 47-Williamson-a r-from Adventures Into the Unknown #96, 3 pgs.; Craig-a | 1.15 | 3.50 | 8.00 |
| 48-57 | .70 | 2.00 | 5.00 |

NOTE: ***Ditko** a-49, 50p, 54. **Forte** a-3, 6, 11. **Landau** a-56(2). **Reinman** a-3, 9, 13, 20, 22, 23, 36, 38, 54. **Whitney** c/a-most issues. John Force, Magic Agent app.-No. 35, 36, 48, 50, 52, 54, 56.*

**UNKNOWN WORLDS OF FRANK BRUNNER**
Aug, 1985 - No. 2, Aug, 1985 ($1.75 cover)
Eclipse Comics

| | Good | Fine | N-Mint |
|---|---|---|---|
| 1,2-B&W-r in color | .30 | .90 | 1.80 |

**UNKNOWN WORLDS OF SCIENCE FICTION**
Jan, 1975 - No. 6, Nov, 1975; 1976 (B&W Magazine) ($1.00)
Marvel Comics Group

| | Good | Fine | N-Mint |
|---|---|---|---|
| 1-Williamson/Krenkel/Torres/Frazetta r-/Witzend #1, Neal Adams-r/ Phase 1; Brunner & Kaluta-r; Freas/Romita-c | .50 | 1.50 | 3.00 |
| 2-6 | .40 | 1.20 | 2.40 |
| Special 1(1976,100 pgs.)-Newton painted-c | .40 | 1.20 | 2.40 |

NOTE: ***Brunner** a-2; c-4, 6. **Buscema** a-Special 1p. **Chaykin** a-5. **Colan** a(p)-1, 3, 5, 6. **Corben** a-4. **Kaluta** a-2; c-2. **Morrow** a-3, 5. **Nino** a-3, 6, Special 1. **Perez** a-2, 3. **N. Redondo** a-Special 1.*

**UNSANE**
No. 15, June, 1954
Star Publications

| | Good | Fine | N-Mint |
|---|---|---|---|
| 15-Disbrow-a(2); L. B. Cole-c | 13.00 | 40.00 | 90.00 |

**UNSEEN, THE**
No. 5, 1952 - No. 15, July, 1954
Visual Editions/Standard Comics

| | Good | Fine | N-Mint |
|---|---|---|---|
| 5-Toth-a | 10.00 | 30.00 | 70.00 |
| 6,7,9,10-Jack Katz-a | 7.00 | 21.00 | 50.00 |
| 8,11,13,14 | 4.50 | 14.00 | 32.00 |
| 12,15-Toth-a. 12-Tuska-a | 8.00 | 24.00 | 55.00 |

NOTE: ***Fawcette** a-13, 14. **Sekowsky** a-7, 8(2), 10, 13.*

**UNTAMED LOVE** (Also see Frank Frazetta's Untamed Love)
Jan, 1950 - No. 5, Sept, 1950
Quality Comics Group (Comic Magazines)

| | Good | Fine | N-Mint |
|---|---|---|---|
| 1-Ward-c, Gustavson-a | 12.00 | 36.00 | 85.00 |
| 2,4: 2-Photo-c | 7.00 | 21.00 | 50.00 |
| 3,5-Gustavson-a | 8.00 | 24.00 | 55.00 |

**UNTOLD LEGEND OF THE BATMAN, THE**
July, 1980 - No. 3, Sept, 1980 (Mini-series)
DC Comics

| | Good | Fine | N-Mint |
|---|---|---|---|
| 1-Origin; Joker-c; Byrne's 1st work at DC | .70 | 2.00 | 4.00 |
| 2,3 | .50 | 1.50 | 3.00 |
| 1-3: Batman cereal premiums (28 pgs., 6X9"); 1st & 2nd printings known | | .50 | 1.00 |

NOTE: ***Aparo** a-1i, 2, 3. **Byrne** a-1p.*

**UNTOUCHABLES, THE** (TV)
No. 1237, 10-12/61 - No. 4, 8-10/62 (All have Robert Stack photo-c)
Dell Publishing Co.

| | Good | Fine | N-Mint |
|---|---|---|---|
| 4-Color 1237,1286 | 6.50 | 19.00 | 45.00 |
| 01-879-207, 12-879-210(01879-210 on inside) | 5.00 | 15.00 | 35.00 |
| Topps Bubblegum premiums-2½x4½", 8 pgs. (3 different issues) "The Organization, Jamaica Ginger, The Otto Frick Story (drug), 3000 Suspects, The Antidote, Mexican Stakeout, Little Egypt, Purple Gang, Bugs Moran Story, & Lily Dallas Story" | 1.70 | 5.00 | 12.00 |

**UNUSUAL TALES** (Blue Beetle & Shadow From Beyond #50 on)
Nov, 1955 - No. 49, Mar-Apr, 1965
Charlton Comics

| | Good | Fine | N-Mint |
|---|---|---|---|
| 1 | 8.50 | 25.50 | 60.00 |
| 2 | 3.60 | 11.00 | 25.00 |
| 3-5 | 2.65 | 8.00 | 18.00 |
| 6-8-Ditko-c/a | 9.30 | 28.00 | 65.00 |
| 9-Ditko-c/a, 20 pgs. | 10.00 | 30.00 | 70.00 |
| 10-Ditko-c/a(4) | 11.50 | 34.00 | 80.00 |
| 11-(3/58, 68 pgs.)-Ditko-a(4) | 11.50 | 34.00 | 80.00 |
| 12,14-Ditko-a | 6.50 | 19.00 | 45.00 |
| 13,16-20 | 1.70 | 5.00 | 12.00 |
| 15-Ditko-c/a | 7.00 | 21.00 | 50.00 |
| 21,24,28 | 1.15 | 3.50 | 8.00 |
| 22,25-27,29-Ditko-a | 4.30 | 13.00 | 30.00 |
| 23-Ditko-c | 1.70 | 5.00 | 12.00 |
| 30-49 | .85 | 2.60 | 6.00 |

NOTE: ***Colan** a-11. **Ditko** c-22, 23, 25-27, 31(part).*

**UP FROM HARLEM** (Tom Skinner. . .)
1973 (35-49 Cents)
Spire Christian Comics (Fleming H. Revell Co.)

| | Good | Fine | N-Mint |
|---|---|---|---|
| nn | | .50 | 1.00 |

**UP-TO-DATE COMICS**
No date (1938) (36 pgs.; B&W cover) (10 cents)
King Features Syndicate

| | Good | Fine | N-Mint |
|---|---|---|---|
| nn-Popeye & Henry cover; The Phantom, Jungle Jim & Flash Gordon by Raymond, The Katzenjammer Kids, Curley Harper & others | 17.00 | 51.00 | 120.00 |

(Variations to above contents exist.)

**UP YOUR NOSE AND OUT YOUR EAR** (Magazine)
April, 1972 - No. 2, June, 1972 (52 pgs.) (Satire)
Klevart Enterprises

| | Good | Fine | N-Mint |
|---|---|---|---|
| V1#1,2 | .30 | .90 | 1.80 |

**USA COMICS**
Aug, 1941 - No. 17, Fall, 1945
Timely Comics (USA)

| | Good | Fine | VF-NM | NM/Mint |
|---|---|---|---|---|
| 1-Origin Major Liberty (called Mr. Liberty #1), Rockman by Wolverton, & The Whizzer by Avison; The Defender with sidekick Rusty & Jack Frost begin; The Young Avenger only app.; S&K-c plus 1 pg. art | 383.00 | 960.00 | 2300.00 | 3000.00 |

(Estimated up to 145 total copies exist, 7 in NM/Mint)

| | Good | Fine | N-Mint |
|---|---|---|---|
| 2-Origin Captain Terror & The Vagabond; last Wolverton Rockman | 200.00 | 500.00 | 1200.00 |
| 3-No Whizzer | 154.00 | 385.00 | 925.00 |
| 4-Last Rockman, Major Liberty, Defender, Jack Frost, & Capt. Terror; Corporal Dix app. | 129.00 | 323.00 | 775.00 |
| 5-Origin American Avenger & Roko the Amazing; The Blue Blade, The Black Widow & Victory Boys, Gypo the Gypsy Giant & Hills of Horror only app.; Sergeant Dix begins; no Whizzer. Hitler-c | 106.00 | 265.00 | 635.00 |
| 6-Captain America, The Destroyer, Jap Buster Johnson, Jeep Jones begin; Terror Squad only app. | 125.00 | 312.00 | 750.00 |
| 7-Captain Daring, Disk-Eyes the Detective by Wolverton app.; origin & only app. Marvel Boy; Secret Stamp begins; no Whizzer, Sergeant Dix | 108.00 | 270.00 | 650.00 |
| 8-10: 9-Last Secret Stamp. 10-The Thunderbird only app. | 73.00 | 181.00 | 435.00 |
| 11,12: 11-No Jeep Jones | 61.00 | 152.00 | 365.00 |
| 13-17: 13-No Whizzer; Jeep Jones ends. 15-No Destroyer; Jap Buster Johnson ends | 46.00 | 115.00 | 275.00 |

NOTE: ***Schomburg** c-6-10, 12, 13, 15-17. **Shores** c-11.*

**U.S. AGENT** (See Jeff Jordan. . .)

*Unsane #15, © STAR*

*Unusual Tales #9, © CC*

*USA Comics #7, © MEG*

*USA Is Ready #1, © DELL*

*U.S. Tank Commandos #1, © AVON*

*Valor #1, © WMG*

**USAGI YOJIMBO** (See Albedo & Doomsday Squad #3)
July, 1987 - Present ($2.00, B&W)
Fantagraphics Books

| | Good | Fine | N-Mint |
|---|---|---|---|
| 1 | .70 | 2.00 | 4.00 |
| 1-2nd print | .35 | 1.00 | 2.00 |
| 2-9,11-26: 11-Aragones-a | .35 | 1.00 | 2.00 |
| 10-Leonardo app. (TMNT) | .70 | 2.00 | 4.00 |
| Color Special 1 (11/89, $2.95, 68 pgs.)-new & r | .50 | 1.50 | 3.00 |
| Summer Special 1 (1986, B&W, $2.75)-r/early Albedo issues | 2.00 | 6.00 | 12.00 |

**U.S. AIR FORCE COMICS** (Army Attack #38 on)
Oct, 1958 - No. 37, Mar-Apr, 1965
Charlton Comics

| | Good | Fine | N-Mint |
|---|---|---|---|
| 1 | 1.70 | 5.00 | 12.00 |
| 2 | .85 | 2.60 | 6.00 |
| 3-10 | .70 | 2.00 | 4.00 |
| 11-20 | .50 | 1.50 | 3.00 |
| 21-37 | .35 | 1.00 | 2.00 |

NOTE: *Glanzman c/a-9, 10, 12. Montes/Bache a-33.*

**USA IS READY**
1941 (68 pgs.) (One Shot)
Dell Publishing Co.

| | Good | Fine | N-Mint |
|---|---|---|---|
| 1-War propaganda | 22.00 | 65.00 | 150.00 |

**U.S. BORDER PATROL COMICS** (Sgt. Dick Carter of the...) (See Holyoke One Shot)

**U.S. FIGHTING MEN**
1963 - 1964 (Reprints)
Super Comics

| | Good | Fine | N-Mint |
|---|---|---|---|
| 10-Avon's With the U.S. Paratroops | .50 | 1.50 | 3.00 |
| 11,12,15-18 | .25 | .80 | 1.60 |

**U.S. JONES** (Also see Wonderworld Comics #28)
Nov, 1941 - No. 2, Jan, 1942
Fox Features Syndicate

| | Good | Fine | N-Mint |
|---|---|---|---|
| 1-U.S. Jones & The Topper begin | 60.00 | 180.00 | 420.00 |
| 2 | 45.00 | 135.00 | 315.00 |

**U.S. MARINES**
Fall, 1964 (One shot, 12 cents)
Charlton Comics

| | Good | Fine | N-Mint |
|---|---|---|---|
| 1 | .50 | 1.50 | 3.00 |

**U.S. MARINES IN ACTION!**
Aug, 1952 - No. 3, Dec, 1952
Avon Periodicals

| | Good | Fine | N-Mint |
|---|---|---|---|
| 1-Louis Ravielli-c/a | 3.60 | 11.00 | 25.00 |
| 2,3: 3-Kinstler-c | 2.00 | 6.00 | 14.00 |

**U.S. 1**
May, 1983 - No. 12, Oct, 1984 (7,8: painted-c)
Marvel Comics Group

| | Good | Fine | N-Mint |
|---|---|---|---|
| 1 | | .30 | .60 |
| 2-12: 5-7,9,10,12-Michael Golden-c | | .25 | .50 |

**U.S. PARATROOPS** (See With the...)

**U.S. PARATROOPS**
1964?
I. W. Enterprises

| | Good | Fine | N-Mint |
|---|---|---|---|
| 1,8: 1-Wood-c r-/With the... #1. 8-Kinstler-c | .50 | 1.50 | 3.00 |

**U.S. TANK COMMANDOS**
June, 1952 - No. 4, March, 1953
Avon Periodicals

| | Good | Fine | N-Mint |
|---|---|---|---|
| 1-Kinstler-c | 3.75 | 11.25 | 26.00 |
| 2-4: 2-Kinstler-c | 2.15 | 6.50 | 15.00 |
| I.W. Reprint #1,8 | .35 | 1.10 | 2.20 |

NOTE: *Kinstler a-3, 4, I.W. #1; c-1-4, I.W. #1, 8.*

**"V"** (TV)
Feb, 1985 - No. 18, July, 1986
DC Comics

| | Good | Fine | N-Mint |
|---|---|---|---|
| 1-Based on TV movie & series (Sci/Fi) | .25 | .75 | 1.50 |
| 2-18: 17,18-Denys Cowan-c/a | | .45 | .90 |

**VACATION COMICS** (See A-1 Comics #16)

**VACATION DIGEST**
Sept, 1987 ($1.25, digest size)
Harvey Comics

| | Good | Fine | N-Mint |
|---|---|---|---|
| 1 | | .60 | 1.25 |

**VACATION IN DISNEYLAND** (Also see Dell Giants)
Aug-Oct, 1959; May, 1965 (Walt Disney)
Dell Publishing Co./Gold Key (1965)

| | Good | Fine | N-Mint |
|---|---|---|---|
| 4-Color 1025-Barks-a | 6.00 | 18.00 | 42.00 |
| 1(30024-508)(G.K., 5/65)-Reprints Dell Giant #30 & cover to #1('58) | 1.50 | 4.50 | 12.00 |

**VACATION PARADE** (See Dell Giants)

**VALKYRIE** (See Airboy)
May, 1987 - No. 3, July, 1987 ($1.75, color, mini-series)
Eclipse Comics

| | Good | Fine | N-Mint |
|---|---|---|---|
| 1-3: 2-Holly becomes new Black Angel | .40 | 1.25 | 2.50 |

**VALKYRIE!**
July, 1988 - No. 3, Sept, 1988 ($1.95, color, mini-series)
Eclipse Comics

| | Good | Fine | N-Mint |
|---|---|---|---|
| 1-3 | .35 | 1.00 | 2.00 |

**VALLEY OF THE DINOSAURS** (TV)
April, 1975 - No. 11, Dec, 1976 (Hanna-Barbara)
Charlton Comics

| | Good | Fine | N-Mint |
|---|---|---|---|
| 1 | | .50 | 1.00 |
| 2-11 | | .40 | .80 |

**VALLEY OF GWANGI** (See Movie Classics)

**VALOR**
Mar-Apr, 1955 - No. 5, Nov-Dec, 1955
E. C. Comics

| | Good | Fine | N-Mint |
|---|---|---|---|
| 1-Williamson/Torres-a; Wood-c/a | 18.00 | 54.00 | 125.00 |
| 2-Williamson-c/a; Wood-a | 16.00 | 48.00 | 110.00 |
| 3,4: 3-Williamson, Crandall-a. 4-Wood-c | 11.00 | 32.00 | 75.00 |
| 5-Wood-c/a; Williamson/Evans-a | 9.30 | 28.00 | 65.00 |

NOTE: *Crandall a-3, 4. Ingels a-1, 2, 4, 5. Krigstein a-1-5. Orlando a-3, 4; c-3. Wood a-1, 2, 5; c-1, 4, 5.*

**VALOR THUNDERSTAR AND HIS FIREFLIES**
Dec, 1986 ($1.50, color)
Now Comics

| | Good | Fine | N-Mint |
|---|---|---|---|
| 1-Ordway-c(p) | .25 | .75 | 1.50 |

**VAMPIRE LESTAT, THE**
Jan, 1990 - No. 12 ($2.50, painted color, mini-series)
Innovation Publishing

| | Good | Fine | N-Mint |
|---|---|---|---|
| 1-Adapts novel; Bolton painted-c on all | 2.00 | 6.00 | 12.00 |
| 1-3: 2nd printings | .50 | 1.50 | 3.00 |
| 2 | 1.70 | 4.00 | 8.00 |
| 3-5 | .70 | 2.00 | 4.00 |
| 6-10 | .50 | 1.50 | 3.00 |

**VAMPIRELLA** (Magazine)(See Warren Presents)
Sept, 1969 - No. 112, Feb, 1983; No. 113, Jan, 1988? (B&W)
Warren Publishing Co./Harris Publications #113

| | Good | Fine | N-Mint |
|---|---|---|---|
| 1-Intro. Vampirella | 13.00 | 40.00 | 90.00 |
| 2-Amazonia series begins, ends #12 | 5.00 | 15.00 | 35.00 |
| 3 (Low distribution) | 15.00 | 45.00 | 105.00 |

| | Good | Fine | N-Mint |
|---|---|---|---|
| 4-7 | 4.00 | 12.00 | 28.00 |
| 8-Vampi begins by Tom Sutton as serious strip (early issues-gag line) | 3.60 | 11.00 | 25.00 |
| 9-Barry Smith-a | 4.00 | 12.00 | 28.00 |
| 10-No Vampi story | 2.00 | 6.00 | 14.00 |
| 11-15: 11-Origin, 1st app. Pendragon. 12-Vampi by Gonzales begins | 2.65 | 8.00 | 18.00 |
| 16-18,20-25: 17-Tomb of the Gods begins, ends #22 | 1.50 | 4.50 | 10.00 |
| 19 (1973 Annual) | 1.70 | 5.00 | 12.00 |
| 26,28-36,38-40: 30-on contain some color; intro. Pantha. 31-Origin Luana, the Beast Girl. 33-Pantha ends | 1.00 | 3.00 | 7.00 |
| 27 (1974 Annual) | 1.30 | 4.00 | 9.00 |
| 37 (1975 Annual) | 1.15 | 3.50 | 8.00 |
| 41-45,47-50: 50-Spirit cameo | .70 | 2.00 | 4.00 |
| 46-Origin retold | .75 | 2.25 | 4.50 |
| 51-99: 93-Cassandra St. Knight begins, ends #103; new Pantha series begins, ends 108 | .40 | 1.25 | 2.50 |
| 100 (96pg. r-special)-Origin retold | .50 | 1.50 | 3.00 |
| 101-112: 108-Torpedo series by Toth begins | .35 | 1.00 | 2.00 |
| 113 (1988) | .25 | .75 | 1.50 |
| Annual 1('72)-New origin Vampirella by Gonzales; reprints by Neal Adams (from #1), Wood (from #9) | 10.00 | 30.00 | 70.00 |
| Special 1 ('77; large-square bound) | 1.00 | 3.00 | 7.00 |

NOTE: ***Neal Adams** a-1, 10p, 19p. **Alcala** a-90, 93i. **Bode'/Todd** c-3. **Bode'/Jones** c-4. **Boris** c-9. **Brunner** a-10. **Corben** a-30, 31, 33, 54. **Crandall** a-1, 19. **Frazetta** c-1, 5, 7, 11, 31. **Jones** a-5, 9, 12, 27, 32, 33(2pg.), 34, 50i, 83r. **Nino** a-59i, 61i, 67, 76, 85, 90. **Ploog** a-14. **Barry Smith** a-9. **Sutton** a-11. **Toth** a-90i, 108, 110. **Wood** a-9, 10, 12, 19, 27; c-9. **Wrightson** a-33(w/Jones), 63. All reprint issues-37, 74, 83, 87, 91, 105, 107, 109, 111. Annuals from 1973 on are included in regular numbering. Later annuals are same format as regular issues.*

**VAMPIRE TALES** (Magazine)
Aug, 1973 - No. 11, June, 1975 (B&W) (75 cents)
Marvel Comics Group

| | Good | Fine | N-Mint |
|---|---|---|---|
| 1-Morbius, the Living Vampire begins by Pablo Marcos | .50 | 1.50 | 3.00 |
| 2-Intro. Satana; Steranko-r | .35 | 1.00 | 2.00 |
| 3-11: 3-Satana app. 5-Origin Morbius. 6-1st Lilith app. 8-Blade app. (see Tomb of Dracula) | .25 | .75 | 1.50 |
| Annual 1(10/75)-Heath-r/#9 | .35 | 1.00 | 2.00 |

NOTE: ***Alcala** a-6, 8, 9i. **Boris** c-4, 6. **Chaykin** a-7. **Everett** a-1r. **Gulacy** a-7p. **Heath** a-9. **Infantino** a-3r. **Gil Kane** a-4, 5r.*

**VANGUARD ILLUSTRATED**
Nov, 1983 - No. 11, Oct, 1984 (Color, Baxter paper)
Pacific Comics

| | Good | Fine | N-Mint |
|---|---|---|---|
| 1-6,8-11: 1-Nudity scenes. 2-1st app. Stargrazers | .25 | .75 | 1.50 |
| 7-1st app. Mr. Monster | 1.15 | 3.50 | 7.00 |

NOTE: ***Evans** a-7. **Kaluta** c-5, 7p. **Perez** a-6; c-6. **Rude** a-3-5; c-4. **Williamson** c-3.*

**VANITY** (See Pacific Presents #3)
Jun, 1984 - No. 2, Aug, 1984 ($1.50, color)
Pacific Comics

| | Good | Fine | N-Mint |
|---|---|---|---|
| 1,2-Origin | .25 | .75 | 1.50 |

**VARIETY COMICS**
1944 - No. 2, 1945; No. 3, 1946 - No. 5, 1946?
Rural Home Publications/Croyden Publ. Co.

| | Good | Fine | N-Mint |
|---|---|---|---|
| 1-Origin Captain Valiant | 9.00 | 27.00 | 62.00 |
| 2-Captain Valiant | 4.50 | 14.00 | 32.00 |
| 3(1946-Croyden)-Captain Valiant | 4.00 | 12.00 | 28.00 |
| 4,5 | 3.15 | 9.50 | 22.00 |

**VARIETY COMICS** (See Fox Giants)

**VARSITY**
1945
Parents' Magazine Institute

| | Good | Fine | N-Mint |
|---|---|---|---|
| 1 | 3.00 | 9.00 | 21.00 |

**VAUDEVILLE AND OTHER THINGS**
1900 (10½x13") (in color) (18+ pgs.)
Isaac H. Blandiard Co.

| | Good | Fine | N-Mint |
|---|---|---|---|
| nn-By Bunny | 22.00 | 65.00 | 150.00 |

**VAULT OF EVIL**
Feb, 1973 - No. 23, Nov, 1975
Marvel Comics Group

| | Good | Fine | N-Mint |
|---|---|---|---|
| 1 (1950s reprints begin) | | .50 | 1.00 |
| 2-23: 3,4-Brunner-c | | .35 | .70 |

NOTE: ***Ditko** a-14r, 15r, 20-22r. **Drucker** a-10r(Mystic #52), 13r(Uncanny Tales #42). **Everett** a-11r(Menace #2), 13r(Menace #4); c-10. **Heath** a-5r. **Krigstein** a-20r(Uncanny Tales #54). **Reinman** r-1. **Tuska** a-6r.*

**VAULT OF HORROR** (War Against Crime #1-11)
No. 12, Apr-May, 1950 - No. 40, Dec-Jan, 1954-55
E. C. Comics

| | Good | Fine | N-Mint |
|---|---|---|---|
| 12 | 150.00 | 450.00 | 1050.00 |
| 13-Morphine story | 64.00 | 193.00 | 450.00 |
| 14 | 56.00 | 167.00 | 390.00 |
| 15 | 47.00 | 141.00 | 330.00 |
| 16 | 36.00 | 107.00 | 250.00 |
| 17-19 | 27.00 | 81.00 | 190.00 |
| 20-25: 23-Used in **POP**, pg. 84 | 21.00 | 62.00 | 145.00 |
| 26-B&W & color illos in **POP** | 21.00 | 62.00 | 145.00 |
| 27-35: 35-X-Mas-c | 16.00 | 48.00 | 110.00 |
| 36-"Pipe Dream"-classic opium addict story by Krigstein; "Twin Bill" cited in articles by T.E. Murphy, Wertham | 16.00 | 48.00 | 110.00 |
| 37-Williamson-a | 16.00 | 48.00 | 110.00 |
| 38-39: 39-Bondage-c | 13.00 | 40.00 | 90.00 |
| 40-Low distribution | 16.00 | 48.00 | 110.00 |

NOTE: ***Craig** art in all but No. 13 & 33; c-12-40. **Crandall** a-33, 34, 39. **Davis** a-17-38. **Evans** a-27, 28, 30, 32, 33. **Feldstein** a-12-16. **Ingels** a-13-20, 22-40. **Kamen** a-15-22, 25, 29, 35. **Krigstein** a-36, 38-40. **Kurtzman** a-12, 13. **Orlando** a-24, 31, 40. **Wood** a-12-14.*

**VAULT OF HORROR, THE**
Aug, 1990 - Present ($1.95, color, 68 pgs.)(#4 on: $2.00)
Gladstone Publishing

| | Good | Fine | N-Mint |
|---|---|---|---|
| 1-Craig-c(r); reprints | .40 | 1.25 | 2.50 |
| 2-5: 2,4-Craig-c(r). 3-Ingels-c(r) | .35 | 1.00 | 2.00 |

**V. . .-COMICS** (Morse code for "V" - 3 dots, 1 dash)
Jan, 1942 - No. 2, Mar-Apr, 1942
Fox Features Syndicate

| | Good | Fine | N-Mint |
|---|---|---|---|
| 1-Origin V-Man & the Boys; The Banshee & The Black Fury, The Queen of Evil, & V-Agents begin | 59.00 | 178.00 | 415.00 |
| 2-Bondage/torture-c | 47.00 | 141.00 | 330.00 |

**VECTOR**
1986 - No. 4, 1986? ($1.50; 1st color comic by Now Comics)
Now Comics

| | Good | Fine | N-Mint |
|---|---|---|---|
| 1-4: Computer-generated art | .25 | .70 | 1.40 |

**VEGAS KNIGHTS**
1989 ($1.95, color)
Pioneer Comics

| | Good | Fine | N-Mint |
|---|---|---|---|
| 1 | .35 | 1.00 | 2.00 |

**VENGEANCE SQUAD**
July, 1975 - No. 6, May, 1976
Charlton Comics

| | Good | Fine | N-Mint |
|---|---|---|---|
| 1-Mike Mauser, Private eye begins by Staton | | .50 | 1.00 |
| 2-6: Morisi-a in all | | .35 | .70 |
| 5,6(Modern Comics-r, 1977) | | .15 | .30 |

**VENTURE**
Aug, 1986 - No. 3, 1986? ($1.75, color)
AC Comics (Americomics)

*Vampirella #19, © WP*

*Vault of Horror #17, © WMG*

*Vengeance Squad #1, © CC*

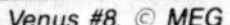
Venus #8, © MEG

Vicky #4 (12/48), © ACE

Victory Comics #2, © HILL

| | Good | Fine | N-Mint |
|---|---|---|---|
| 1-3: 1-3-Bolt. 1-Astron. 2-Femforce. 3-Fazers | .30 | .90 | 1.80 |

**VENUS** (See Marvel Spotlight #2 & Weird Wonder Tales)
August, 1948 - No. 19, April, 1952 (Also see Marvel Mystery #91)
Marvel/Atlas Comics (CMC 1-9/LCC 10-19)

| | | | |
|---|---|---|---|
| 1-Venus & Hedy Devine begin; Kurtzman's "Hey Look" | 46.00 | 139.00 | 325.00 |
| 2 | 27.00 | 81.00 | 190.00 |
| 3,5 | 24.00 | 71.00 | 165.00 |
| 4-Kurtzman's "Hey Look" | 25.00 | 75.00 | 175.00 |
| 6-9: 6-Loki app. 7,8-Painted-c | 22.00 | 65.00 | 155.00 |
| 10-S/F-horror issues begin (7/50) | 24.00 | 71.00 | 165.00 |
| 11-S/F end of the world(11/50) | 29.00 | 86.00 | 200.00 |
| 12 | 22.00 | 65.00 | 150.00 |
| 13-19-Venus by Everett, 2-3 stories each; covers-#13,15-19; 14-Everett part cover (Venus) | 32.00 | 95.00 | 220.00 |

NOTE: *Bondage c-17. **Colan** a-12.*

**VERI BEST SURE FIRE COMICS**
No date (circa 1945) (Reprints Holyoke One-Shots)
Holyoke Publishing Co.

| | | | |
|---|---|---|---|
| 1-Captain Aero, Alias X, Miss Victory, Commandos of the Devil Dogs, Red Cross, Hammerhead Hawley, Capt. Aero's Sky Scouts, Flagman app. | 14.00 | 43.00 | 100.00 |

**VERI BEST SURE SHOT COMICS**
No date (circa 1945) (Reprints Holyoke One-Shots)
Holyoke Publishing Co.

| | | | |
|---|---|---|---|
| 1-Capt. Aero, Miss Victory by Quinlan, Alias X, The Red Cross, Flagman, Commandos of the Devil Dogs, Hammerhead Hawley, Capt. Aero's Sky Scouts | 14.00 | 43.00 | 100.00 |

**VERONICA** (Also see Archie's Girls, Betty &...)
April, 1989 - Present (75 & 95 cents, color)
Archie Comics

| | | | |
|---|---|---|---|
| 1,2 (75 cents) | | .40 | .80 |
| 3-14 (.95-$1.00) | | .50 | 1.00 |

**VERONICA'S SUMMER SPECIAL** (See Archie Giant Series Magazine #615)

**VERY BEST OF DENNIS THE MENACE, THE**
July, 1979 - No. 2, Apr, 1980 (132 pgs., Digest, 95 cents, $1.00)
Fawcett Publications

| | | | |
|---|---|---|---|
| 1,2-Reprints | | .50 | 1.00 |

**VERY BEST OF DENNIS THE MENACE, THE**
April, 1982 - No. 3, Aug, 1982 (Digest Size) ($1.25)
Marvel Comics Group

| | | | |
|---|---|---|---|
| 1-3-Reprints | | .65 | 1.25 |

NOTE: ***Hank Ketcham** c-all. A few thousand of #1 & 2 were printed with DC emblem.*

**V FOR VENDETTA**
Sept, 1988 - No. 10, May, 1989 ($2.00, maxi-series, mature readers)
DC Comics

| | | | |
|---|---|---|---|
| 1-Alan Moore scripts in all | .75 | 2.25 | 4.50 |
| 2-5 | .40 | 1.25 | 2.50 |
| 6-10 | .35 | 1.00 | 2.00 |
| Trade paperback (1990, $14.95)-Reprints #1-10 | 2.50 | 7.50 | 15.00 |

**VIC AND BLOOD**
Oct, 1987 - No. 2, 1988 ($2.00, B&W)
Mad Dog Graphics

| | | | |
|---|---|---|---|
| 1,2-Harlan Ellison adaptation; Corben-a | .35 | 1.00 | 2.00 |

**VIC BRIDGES FAZERS SKETCHBOOK AND FACT FILE**
Nov, 1986 ($1.75, color)
AC Comics

| | | | |
|---|---|---|---|
| 1 | .30 | .90 | 1.80 |

**VIC FLINT** (Crime Buster...)(See Authentic Police Cases #10-14 & Fugitives From Justice #2)
August, 1948 - No. 5, April, 1949 (Newspaper reprints; NEA Service)
St. John Publishing Co.

| | Good | Fine | N-Mint |
|---|---|---|---|
| 1 | 6.00 | 18.00 | 42.00 |
| 2 | 3.70 | 11.00 | 26.00 |
| 3-5 | 3.00 | 9.00 | 21.00 |

**VIC FLINT**
Feb, 1956 - No. 2, May, 1956 (Newspaper reprints)
Argo Publ.

| | | | |
|---|---|---|---|
| 1,2 | 3.15 | 9.50 | 22.00 |

**VIC JORDAN** (Also see Big Shot Comics #32)
April, 1945
Civil Service Publ.

| | | | |
|---|---|---|---|
| 1-1944 daily newspaper-r | 6.50 | 19.00 | 45.00 |

**VICKI** (Humor)
Feb, 1975 - No. 4, July, 1975 (No. 1,2: 68 pgs.)
Atlas/Seaboard Publ.

| | | | |
|---|---|---|---|
| 1-Reprints Tippy Teen | .50 | 1.50 | 3.00 |
| 2-4 | .30 | .80 | 1.60 |

**VICKI VALENTINE** (...Summer Special #1)
July, 1985 - No. 4, July, 1986 ($1.70 cover; B&W)
Renegade Press

| | | | |
|---|---|---|---|
| 1-4: Woggon, Rausch-a; all have paper dolls. 2-Christmas issue | .30 | .85 | 1.70 |

**VICKS COMICS** (Also see Pure Oil Comics, Salerno Carnival of Comics, & 24 Pages of Comics)
nd (circa 1938) (68 pgs. in color) (Giveaway)
Eastern Color Printing Co. (Vicks Chemical Co.)

| | | | |
|---|---|---|---|
| nn-Famous Funnies-r (before #40). Contains 5 pgs. Buck Rogers (4 pgs. from F.F. #15, & 1 pg. from #16) Joe Palooka, Napoleon, etc. app. | 55.00 | 165.00 | 385.00 |
| nn-16 loose, untrimmed page giveaway; paper-c; r-/Famous Funnies #14; Buck Rogers, Joe Palooka app. | 20.00 | 60.00 | 140.00 |

**VICKY**
Oct, 1948 - No. 5, June, 1949
Ace Magazine

| | | | |
|---|---|---|---|
| nn(10/48) | 3.00 | 9.00 | 21.00 |
| 4(12/48), nn(2/49), 4(4/49), 5(6/49) | 2.30 | 7.00 | 16.00 |

**VIC TORRY & HIS FLYING SAUCER** (Also see Mr. Monster's...#5)
1950 (One Shot)
Fawcett Publications

| | | | |
|---|---|---|---|
| nn-Book-length saucer story by Powell; photo/painted-c | 30.00 | 90.00 | 210.00 |

**VICTORY COMICS**
Aug, 1941 - No. 4, Dec, 1941
Hillman Periodicals

| | | | |
|---|---|---|---|
| 1-The Conqueror by Bill Everett, The Crusader, & Bomber Burns begin; Conqueror's origin in text; Everett-c; #1 by Funnies, Inc. | 95.00 | 290.00 | 675.00 |
| 2-Everett-c/a | 54.00 | 160.00 | 375.00 |
| 3,4 | 38.00 | 115.00 | 265.00 |

**VIC VERITY MAGAZINE**
1945 - No. 7, Sept, 1946 (A comic book)
Vic Verity Publications

| | | | |
|---|---|---|---|
| 1-C. C. Beck-c/a | 8.50 | 25.50 | 60.00 |
| 2 | 4.50 | 14.00 | 32.00 |
| 3-7: 6-Beck-a. 7-Beck-c | 4.00 | 12.00 | 28.00 |

**VIDEO JACK**
Nov, 1987 - No. 6, Nov, 1988 ($1.25, color)

Epic Comics (Marvel)

| | Good | Fine | N-Mint |
|---|---|---|---|
| 1-6: 6-Neal Adams, Wrightson, others-a | | .65 | 1.30 |

**VIETNAM JOURNAL**
Nov, 1987 - No. 11, July, 1989 ($1.75/$1.95, B&W)
Apple Comics

| | Good | Fine | N-Mint |
|---|---|---|---|
| 1-Don Lomax-c/a/scripts in all | .70 | 2.00 | 4.00 |
| 1-2nd print | .35 | 1.00 | 2.00 |
| 2 | .40 | 1.25 | 2.50 |
| 3-11: 11-$2.25-c | .35 | 1.00 | 2.00 |
| . . . : Indian Country Vol. 1 (1990, $12.95)-r/1-4 plus one new story | 2.15 | 6.50 | 13.00 |

**VIGILANTE, THE** (Also see Action Comics #42, Justice League of America, Leading Comics, New Teen Titans & World's Finest #244)
Oct, 1983 - No. 50, Feb, 1988 ($1.25; Baxter paper)
DC Comics

| | Good | Fine | N-Mint |
|---|---|---|---|
| 1-Origin | .85 | 2.50 | 5.00 |
| 2 | .50 | 1.50 | 3.00 |
| 3-10: 3-Cyborg app. 4-1st app. The Exterminator; Newton-a(p). 6,7-Origin | .35 | 1.00 | 2.00 |
| 11-50: 17,18-Alan Moore scripts. 20,21-Nightwing app. 35-Origin Mad Bomber. 47-Batman-c/story. 50-Ken Steacy painted-c | .30 | .90 | 1.75 |
| Annual 1 (1985) | .40 | 1.25 | 2.50 |
| Annual 2 (1986) | .35 | 1.10 | 2.25 |

**VIGILANTES, THE** (See 4-Color #839)

**VIKINGS, THE** (See 4-Color #910)

**VILLAINS AND VIGILANTES**
Dec, 1986 - No. 4, May, 1987 ($1.50-$1.75, color, mini-series, Baxter)
Eclipse Comics

| | Good | Fine | N-Mint |
|---|---|---|---|
| 1-4: Based on role-playing game. 2-4-$1.75-c | .30 | .90 | 1.75 |

**VIRGINIAN, THE** (TV)
June, 1963
Gold Key

| | Good | Fine | N-Mint |
|---|---|---|---|
| 1(10060-306)-Part photo-c | 2.30 | 7.00 | 16.00 |

**VISION AND THE SCARLET WITCH, THE** (See Marvel Fanfare)
Nov, 1982 - No. 4, Feb, 1983 (Mini-series)
Marvel Comics Group

| | Good | Fine | N-Mint |
|---|---|---|---|
| 1 | .30 | .90 | 1.75 |
| 2-4: 2-Nuklo & Future Man app. | | .60 | 1.25 |

**VISION AND THE SCARLET WITCH, THE**
Oct, 1985 - No. 12, Sept, 1986 (maxi-series)
Marvel Comics Group

| | Good | Fine | N-Mint |
|---|---|---|---|
| V2#1-Origin; 1st app. in Avengers #57 | .30 | .90 | 1.75 |
| 2-5: 2-West Coast Avengers x-over | .25 | .75 | 1.50 |
| 6-12 | | .60 | 1.25 |

**VISIONARIES**
Nov, 1987 - No. 6, Sept, 1988
Star Comics/Marvel #3 on

| | Good | Fine | N-Mint |
|---|---|---|---|
| 1 | .25 | .75 | 1.50 |
| 2-6 | | .50 | 1.00 |

**VISIONS**
1979 - No. 5, 1983 (B&W, fanzine)
Vision Publications

| | Good | Fine | N-Mint |
|---|---|---|---|
| 1-Flaming Carrot begins | 20.00 | 60.00 | 120.00 |
| 2 | 5.85 | 17.50 | 35.00 |
| 3 | 2.50 | 7.50 | 15.00 |
| 4-Flaming Carrot-c & info. | 3.35 | 10.00 | 20.00 |
| 5-1 pg. Flaming Carrot | 1.70 | 5.00 | 10.00 |

NOTE: *After #4, Visions became an annual publication of The Atlanta Fantasy Fair.*

**VOID INDIGO** (Also see Marvel Graphic Novel)
Nov, 1984 - No. 2, Mar, 1985 ($1.50, Baxter paper)
Epic Comics (Marvel)

| | Good | Fine | N-Mint |
|---|---|---|---|
| 1,2-Cont. from Marvel G.N.; sex, violence | .25 | .75 | 1.50 |

**VOLTRON** (TV)
1985 - No. 3, 1985 (75 cents, color, limited series)
Modern Publishing

| | Good | Fine | N-Mint |
|---|---|---|---|
| 1-3: Ayers-a in all | | .40 | .80 |

**VOODA** (Jungle Princess) (Formerly Voodoo)
No. 20, April, 1955 - No. 22, Aug, 1955
Ajax-Farrell (Four Star Publications)

| | Good | Fine | N-Mint |
|---|---|---|---|
| 20-Baker-c/a; Baker-r/Seven Seas #4 | 11.00 | 32.00 | 75.00 |
| 21,22-Baker-a plus Kamen/Baker story, Kimbo Boy of Jungle, & Baker-c (p) in all | 9.30 | 28.00 | 65.00 |

**VOODOO** (Vooda #20 on)
May, 1952 - No. 19, Jan-Feb, 1955
Ajax-Farrell (Four Star Publ.)

| | Good | Fine | N-Mint |
|---|---|---|---|
| 1-South Sea Girl-r by Baker | 20.00 | 60.00 | 140.00 |
| 2-Rulah story-r plus South Sea Girl from Seven Seas #2 by Baker (name changed from Alani to El'nee) | 16.00 | 48.00 | 110.00 |
| 3-Bakerish-a; man stabbed in face | 11.50 | 34.00 | 80.00 |
| 4,8-Baker-r. 8-Severed head panels | 11.50 | 34.00 | 80.00 |
| 5-7,9,10: 5-Nazi flaying alive. 6-Severed head panels | 9.00 | 27.00 | 62.00 |
| 11-14,16-18: 14-Zombies take over America. 17-Electric chair panels | 7.00 | 21.00 | 50.00 |
| 15-Opium drug story-r/Ellery Queen #3 | 8.00 | 24.00 | 55.00 |
| 19-Bondage-c; Baker-a(2)(r) | 11.00 | 32.00 | 75.00 |
| Annual 1(1952)(25 cents); Baker-a | 29.00 | 85.00 | 200.00 |

**VOODOO** (See Tales of. . .)

**VORTEX**
Nov, 1982 - No. 15, 1988(No month) ($1.50-$1.75, B&W)
Vortex Publs.

| | Good | Fine | N-Mint |
|---|---|---|---|
| 1 ($1.95)-Peter Hsu-a; Ken Steacy-c; nudity | 2.85 | 8.50 | 20.00 |
| 2-1st app. Mister X (on-c only) | 1.25 | 3.75 | 7.50 |
| 3 | 1.00 | 3.00 | 6.00 |
| 4-8 | .50 | 1.50 | 3.00 |
| 9-15 | .35 | 1.00 | 2.00 |

**VOYAGE TO THE BOTTOM OF THE SEA** (TV)
No. 1230, Sept-Nov, 1961; Dec, 1964 - #16, Apr, 1970 (Painted covers)
Dell Publishing Co./Gold Key

| | Good | Fine | N-Mint |
|---|---|---|---|
| 4-Color 1230(Movie-1961) | 4.50 | 14.00 | 32.00 |
| 10133-412(#1, 12/64)(Gold Key) | 3.00 | 9.00 | 21.00 |
| 2(7/65) - 5: Photo back-c, 1-5 | 2.00 | 6.00 | 14.00 |
| 6-14 | 1.50 | 4.50 | 10.00 |
| 15,16-Reprints | .85 | 2.60 | 6.00 |

**VOYAGE TO THE DEEP**
Sept-Nov, 1962 - No. 4, Nov-Jan, 1964 (Painted-c)
Dell Publishing Co.

| | Good | Fine | N-Mint |
|---|---|---|---|
| 1 | 2.65 | 8.00 | 18.00 |
| 2-4 | 1.50 | 4.50 | 10.00 |

**WACKY ADVENTURES OF CRACKY** (Also see Gold Key Spotlight)
Dec, 1972 - No. 12, Sept, 1975
Gold Key

| | Good | Fine | N-Mint |
|---|---|---|---|
| 1 | .70 | 2.00 | 4.00 |
| 2 | .35 | 1.00 | 2.00 |
| 3-12 | | .50 | 1.00 |

(See March of Comics #405, 424, 436, 448)

**WACKY DUCK** (Formerly Dopey Duck?; Justice Comics #7 on)
No. 3, Fall, 1946 - No. 6, Summer, 1947; 8/48 - No. 2, 10/48
Marvel Comics (NPP)

*The Vigilante #20, © DC*

*Vooda #22, © AJAX*

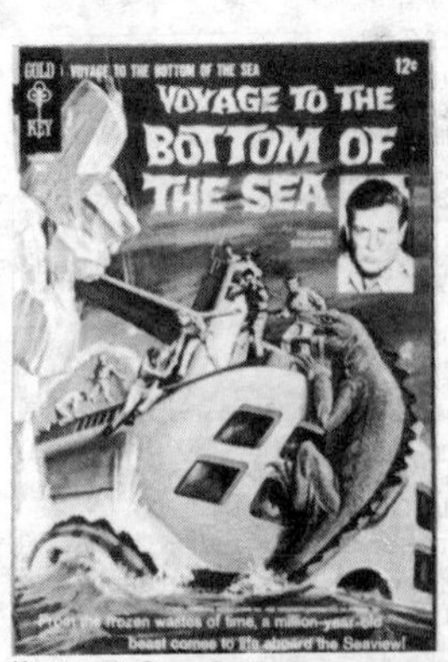

*Voyage to the Bottom/Sea #8, © 20th Cen. Fox*

*Wagon Train #10, © Revue Prod.*

*Walt Disney Presents #6, © The Disney Co.*

*Walt Disney's Comics & Stories #2, © Disney*

| | Good | Fine | N-Mint |
|---|---|---|---|
| 3 | 7.00 | 21.00 | 50.00 |
| 4-Infinity-c | 10.00 | 30.00 | 70.00 |
| 5,6('46-47) | 5.70 | 17.00 | 40.00 |
| 1,2(1948) | 4.00 | 12.00 | 28.00 |
| I.W. Reprint #1,2,7('58) | .30 | .90 | 1.80 |
| Super Reprint #10(I.W. on-c, Super-inside) | .30 | .90 | 1.80 |

**WACKY QUACKY** (See Wisco)

**WACKY RACES** (TV)
Aug, 1969 - No. 7, Apr, 1972 (Hanna-Barbera)
Gold Key

| | Good | Fine | N-Mint |
|---|---|---|---|
| 1 | 1.50 | 4.50 | 10.00 |
| 2-7 | .85 | 2.50 | 6.00 |

**WACKY SQUIRREL** (Also see Dark Horse Presents)
Oct, 1987 - No. 4, 1988 ($1.75, B&W)
Dark Horse Comics

| | Good | Fine | N-Mint |
|---|---|---|---|
| 1-4: 4-Superman parody | .30 | .90 | 1.80 |
| Halloween Adventure Special 1 (1987, $2.00) | .35 | 1.00 | 2.00 |
| Summer Fun Special 1 (1988, $2.00) | .35 | 1.00 | 2.00 |

**WACKY WITCH** (Also see Gold Key Spotlight)
March, 1971 - No. 21, Dec, 1975
Gold Key

| | Good | Fine | N-Mint |
|---|---|---|---|
| 1 | 1.00 | 3.00 | 6.00 |
| 2 | .60 | 1.75 | 3.50 |
| 3-21 | .35 | 1.00 | 2.00 |

(See March of Comics #374, 398, 410, 422, 434, 446, 458, 470, 482)

**WACKY WOODPECKER** (See Two Bit . . .)
1958; 1963
I. W. Enterprises/Super Comics

| | Good | Fine | N-Mint |
|---|---|---|---|
| I.W. Reprint #1,2,7(nd-r-/Two Bit . . .) | .30 | .90 | 1.80 |
| Super Reprint #10('63) | .30 | .90 | 1.80 |

**WAGON TRAIN** (1st Series) (TV) (See Western Roundup under Dell Giants)
No. 895, Mar, 1958 - No. 13, Apr-June, 1962 (All photo-c)
Dell Publishing Co.

| | Good | Fine | N-Mint |
|---|---|---|---|
| 4-Color 895 (#1) | 5.70 | 17.00 | 40.00 |
| 4-Color 971,1019 | 3.70 | 11.00 | 26.00 |
| 4(1-3/60),6-13 | 3.00 | 9.00 | 21.00 |
| 5-Toth-a | 4.00 | 12.00 | 28.00 |

**WAGON TRAIN** (2nd Series)(TV)
Jan, 1964 - No. 4, Oct, 1964 (All photo-c)
Gold Key

| | Good | Fine | N-Mint |
|---|---|---|---|
| 1 | 3.00 | 9.00 | 21.00 |
| 2-4: 3,4-Tufts-a | 2.00 | 6.00 | 14.00 |

**WAITING ROOM WILLIE** (See Sad Case of . . .)

**WALLY** (Teen-age)
Dec, 1962 - No. 4, Sept, 1963
Gold Key

| | Good | Fine | N-Mint |
|---|---|---|---|
| 1 | 1.30 | 4.00 | 9.00 |
| 2-4 | .75 | 2.25 | 5.00 |

**WALLY THE WIZARD**
Apr, 1985 - No. 12, Mar, 1986 (Children's comic)
Star Comics (Marvel)

| | Good | Fine | N-Mint |
|---|---|---|---|
| 1-12: Bob Bolling a-1,3; c-1,9,11,12 | | .35 | .70 |

**WALLY WOOD'S T.H.U.N.D.E.R. AGENTS** (See Thunder Agents)
Nov, 1984 - No. 5, Oct, 1986 ($2.00, 52 pgs.)
Deluxe Comics

| | Good | Fine | N-Mint |
|---|---|---|---|
| 1-5: 5-Jerry Ordway-c/a in Wood style | .35 | 1.00 | 2.00 |

NOTE: *Giffen a-1p, 2p. Perez a-1p, 2.*

**WALT DISNEY CHRISTMAS PARADE** (Also see Christmas Parade)
Winter, 1977 (224 pgs.) (cardboard covers, $1.95)
Whitman Publishing Co. (Golden Press)

| | Good | Fine | N-Mint |
|---|---|---|---|
| 11191-Barks-a r-/Christmas in Disneyland #1, Dell Christmas Parade #9, Dell Giant #53 | .40 | 1.20 | 2.40 |

**WALT DISNEY COMICS DIGEST**
June, 1968 - No. 57, Feb, 1976 (50 cents) (Digest size)
Gold Key

| | Good | Fine | N-Mint |
|---|---|---|---|
| 1-Reprints Uncle Scrooge #5; 192 pgs. | 3.00 | 9.00 | 21.00 |
| 2-4-Barks-r | 1.70 | 5.00 | 12.00 |
| 5-Daisy Duck by Barks (8 pgs.); last published story by Barks (art only) plus 21 pg. Scrooge-r by Barks | 2.00 | 6.00 | 14.00 |
| 6-13-All Barks-r | 1.00 | 3.00 | 6.00 |
| 14,15 | .70 | 2.00 | 4.00 |
| 16-Reprints Donald Duck #26 by Barks | 1.35 | 4.00 | 8.00 |
| 17-20-Barks-r | .80 | 2.40 | 4.80 |
| 21-31,33,35-37-Barks-r; 24-Toth Zorro | .70 | 2.00 | 4.00 |
| 32 | .50 | 1.50 | 3.00 |
| 34-Reprints 4-Color #318 | 1.35 | 4.00 | 8.00 |
| 38-Reprints Christmas in Disneyland #1 | 1.00 | 3.00 | 6.00 |
| 39-Two Barks-r/WDC&S #272, 4-Color #1073 plus Toth Zorro-r | .80 | 2.40 | 4.80 |
| 40-Mickey Mouse-r by Gottfredson | .50 | 1.50 | 3.00 |
| 41,45,47-49 | .30 | .90 | 1.80 |
| 42,43-Barks-r | .50 | 1.50 | 3.00 |
| 44-(Has Gold Key emblem, 50 cents)-Reprints 1st story of 4-Color 29,256,275,282 | 2.00 | 6.00 | 14.00 |
| 44-Republished in 1976 by Whitman; not identical to original; a bit smaller, blank back-c, 69 cent-c | 1.00 | 3.00 | 6.00 |
| 46,50,52-Barks-r. 52-Barks-r/WDC&S #161,132 | .50 | 1.50 | 3.00 |
| 51-Reprints 4-Color #71 | .80 | 2.40 | 4.80 |
| 53-55: 53-Reprints Dell Giant #30. 54-Reprints Donald Duck Beach Party #2. 55-Reprints Dell Giant #49 | .25 | .80 | 1.60 |
| 56-Reprint/Uncle Scrooge #32 (Barks) plus another Barks story | .50 | 1.50 | 3.00 |
| 57-Reprint/Mickey Mouse Almanac('57) & two Barks stories | .50 | 1.50 | 3.00 |

NOTE: *#1-10, 196 pgs.; #11-41, 164 pgs.; #42 on, 132 pgs. Old issues were being reprinted & distributed by Whitman in 1976.*

**WALT DISNEY PRESENTS** (TV)
No. 997, June-Aug, 1959 - No. 6, Dec-Feb, 1960-61 (All photo-c)
Dell Publishing Co.

| | Good | Fine | N-Mint |
|---|---|---|---|
| 4-Color 997 (#1) | 3.00 | 9.00 | 21.00 |
| 2(12-2/60)-The Swamp Fox(origin), Elfego Baca, Texas John Slaughter (Disney TV Show) begin | 2.00 | 6.00 | 14.00 |
| 3-6 | 2.00 | 6.00 | 14.00 |

**WALT DISNEY'S CHRISTMAS PARADE** (Also see Christmas Parade)
Winter, 1988; No. 2, Winter, 1989 ($2.95, 100 pgs.)
Gladstone Publishing

| | Good | Fine | N-Mint |
|---|---|---|---|
| 1,2: 1-Barks-r/painted-c. 2-Barks-r | .50 | 1.50 | 3.00 |

**WALT DISNEY'S COMICS AND STORIES** (Cont. of Mickey Mouse Magazine) (#1-30 contain Donald Duck newspaper reprints)
(Titled 'Comics And Stories' #264 on)
10/40 - #263, 8/62; #264, 10/62 - #510, 1984; #511, 10/86 - Present
Dell Publishing Co./Gold Key #264-473/Whitman #474-510/Gladstone #511-547(4/90)/Disney Comics #548(5/90) on

**NOTE:** The whole number can always be found at the bottom of the title page in the lower left-hand or right hand panel.

| | Good | Fine | VF-NM | NM/Mint |
|---|---|---|---|---|
| 1(V1#1-c; V2#1-indicia)-Donald Duck strip-r by Al Taliaferro & Gottfredson's Mickey Mouse begin | 370.00 | 1480.00 | 3800.00 | 5100.00 |

(Estimated up to 245 total copies exist, 12 in NM/Mint)

| | Good | Fine | N-Mint |
|---|---|---|---|
| 2 | 220.00 | 660.00 | 1850.00 |

| | Good | Fine | N-Mint |
|---|---|---|---|
| 3 | 107.00 | 320.00 | 775.00 |
| 4-X-mas-c | 77.00 | 231.00 | 575.00 |
| 4-Special promotional, complimentary issue; cover same except one corner was blanked out & boxed in to identify the giveaway (not a paste-over). This special pressing was probably sent out to former subscribers to Mickey Mouse Mag. whose subscriptions had expired. (Very rare-5 known copies) | 115.00 | 345.00 | 840.00 |
| 5 | 64.00 | 190.00 | 470.00 |
| 6-10 | 50.00 | 150.00 | 370.00 |
| 11-14 | 43.00 | 130.00 | 315.00 |
| 15-17: 15-The 3 Little Kittens (17 pgs.). 16-The 3 Little Pigs (29 pgs.); X-mas-c. 17-The Ugly Duckling (4 pgs.) | 38.00 | 115.00 | 285.00 |
| 18-21 | 30.00 | 90.00 | 235.00 |
| 22-30: 22-Flag-c | 27.00 | 80.00 | 200.00 |
| 31-Donald Duck by Carl Barks begins; see Four Color #9 for first Barks Donald Duck | 157.00 | 470.00 | 1150.00 |
| 32-Barks-a | 90.00 | 270.00 | 650.00 |
| 33-Barks-a (infinity-c) | 64.00 | 190.00 | 470.00 |
| 34-Gremlins by Walt Kelly begin, end #41; Barks-a | 52.00 | 156.00 | 385.00 |
| 35,36-Barks-a | 45.00 | 135.00 | 335.00 |
| 37-Donald Duck by Jack Hannah | 21.00 | 64.00 | 160.00 |
| 38-40-Barks-a. 39-Christmas-c. 40-Gremlins by Kelly | 32.00 | 95.00 | 235.00 |
| 41-50-Barks-a; 41-Gremlins by Kelly | 26.00 | 77.00 | 190.00 |
| 51-60-Barks-a; 51-Christmas-c. 52-Li'l Bad Wolf begins, ends #203 (not in #55). 58-Kelly flag-c | 19.00 | 58.00 | 140.00 |
| 61-70: Barks-a. 61-Dumbo story. 63,64-Pinocchio stories. 63-c-swipe from New Funnies #94. 64-X-mas-c. 65-Pluto story. 66-Infinity-c. 67,68-M. Mouse Sunday-r by Bill Wright | 16.00 | 48.00 | 115.00 |
| 71-80: Barks-a. 75-77-Brer Rabbit stories, no Mickey Mouse. 76-X-Mas-c | 11.50 | 34.00 | 80.00 |
| 81-87,89,90: Barks-a. 82-84-Bongo stories. 86-90-Goofy & Agnes app. 89-Chip 'n' Dale story | 9.50 | 28.50 | 65.00 |
| 88-1st app. Gladstone Gander by Barks | 11.50 | 34.00 | 80.00 |
| 91-97,99: Barks-a. 95-1st WDC&S Barks-c. 96-No Mickey Mouse; Little Toot begins, ends #97. 99-X-Mas-c | 7.50 | 22.50 | 52.00 |
| 98-1st Uncle Scrooge app. in WDC&S | 16.00 | 48.00 | 110.00 |
| 100-Barks-a | 8.50 | 25.50 | 60.00 |
| 101-106,108-110-Barks-a | 6.50 | 19.50 | 45.00 |
| 107-Barks-a; Taliaferro-c. Donald acquires super powers | 6.50 | 19.50 | 45.00 |
| 111,114,117-All Barks | 5.00 | 15.00 | 35.00 |
| 112-Drug (ether) issue (Donald Duck) | 5.50 | 16.50 | 38.00 |
| 113,115,116,118-123: Not by Barks. 116-Dumbo x-over. 121-Grandma Duck begins, ends #168; not in #135,142,146,155 | 2.15 | 6.50 | 15.00 |
| 124,126-130-All Barks. 124-X-Mas-c | 4.35 | 13.00 | 30.00 |
| 125-1st app. Junior Woodchucks; Barks-a | 7.00 | 21.00 | 50.00 |
| 131,133,135-139-All Barks | 4.35 | 13.00 | 30.00 |
| 132-Barks-a(2) (D. Duck & Grandma Duck) | 5.15 | 15.50 | 36.00 |
| 134-Intro. & 1st app. The Beagle Boys | 8.50 | 25.50 | 60.00 |
| 140-1st app. Gyro Gearloose by Barks | 8.50 | 25.50 | 60.00 |
| 141-150-All Barks. 143-Little Hiawatha begins, ends #151,159 | 2.65 | 8.00 | 18.00 |
| 151-170-All Barks | 2.35 | 7.00 | 16.00 |
| 171-200-All Barks | 2.00 | 6.00 | 14.00 |
| 201-240: All Barks. 204-Chip 'n' Dale & Scamp begin | 1.70 | 5.00 | 12.00 |
| 241-283: Barks-a. 241-Dumbo x-over. 247-Gyro Gearloose begins, ends #274. 256-Ludwig Von Drake begins, ends #274 | 1.50 | 4.50 | 9.00 |
| 284,285,287,290,295,296,309-311-Not by Barks | .85 | 2.50 | 5.00 |
| 286,288,289,291-294,297,298,308-All Barks stories; 293-Grandma Duck's Farm Friends. 297-Gyro Gearloose. 298-Daisy Duck's Diary-r | 1.35 | 4.00 | 8.00 |
| 299-307-All contain early Barks-r (#43-117). 305-Gyro Gearloose | 1.50 | 4.50 | 9.00 |
| 312-Last Barks issue with original story | 1.35 | 4.00 | 8.00 |
| 313-315,317-327,329-334,336-341 | .70 | 2.00 | 4.00 |
| 316-Last issue published during life of Walt Disney | .70 | 2.00 | 4.00 |
| 328,335,342-350-Barks-r | .85 | 2.50 | 5.00 |
| 351-360-w/posters inside; Barks reprints (2 versions of each with & without posters)-without posters. . . | .75 | 2.25 | 4.50 |
| 351-360-With posters | 1.15 | 3.50 | 8.00 |
| 361-400-Barks-r | .75 | 2.25 | 4.50 |
| 401-429-Barks-r. 410-Annette Funicello photo-c | .50 | 1.50 | 3.00 |
| 430,433,437,438,441,444,445,466,506-No Barks | | .35 | .70 |
| 431,432,434-436,439,440,442,443-Barks-r | .25 | .75 | 1.50 |
| 446-465,467-505,507-510: All Barks-r. 494-r/WDC&S #98 (1st Uncle Scrooge) | | .50 | 1.00 |
| 511-Wuzzles by Disney studio | .85 | 2.50 | 5.00 |
| 512 | .50 | 1.50 | 3.00 |
| 513-520: 518-Infinity-c | .30 | .90 | 1.80 |
| 521-540: 522-r/1st app. Huey, Dewey & Louie from D. Duck Sunday page. 535-546-Barks-r | .25 | .75 | 1.50 |
| 541-545: (All $1.50, 52 pgs.) | .25 | .75 | 1.50 |
| 546,547-($1.95, 68 pgs.): 546-Kelly-r. 547-Rosa-a | .35 | 1.00 | 2.00 |
| 548,549,551-560 ($1.50): 548-New-a. 549-Barks-r begin | .25 | .75 | 1.50 |
| 550 ($2.25, 52 pgs.)-Donald Duck by Barks; previously only printed in The Netherlands (1st time in U.S.) | .40 | 1.15 | 2.30 |

NOTE: *(#1-38, 68 pgs.; #39-42, 60 pgs.; #43-57, 61-134, 143-168, 446, 447, 52 pgs.; #58-60, 135-142, 169-540, 36 pgs.)*

NOTE: ***Barks** art in all issues #31 on, except where noted; c-95, 96, 104, 108, 109, 130-172, 174-178, 183, 198-200, 204, 206-209, 212-216, 218, 220, 226, 228-233, 235-238, 240-243, 247, 250, 253, 256, 260, 261, 276-283, 288-292, 295-298, 301, 303, 304, 306, 307, 309, 310, 313-316, 319, 321, 322, 324, 326, 328, 329, 331, 332, 334, 341, 342, 350, 351, 540(never before published), 546r. **Kelly** r-546, 547; covers(most)-34-94, 97-103, 105, 106, 110-123, 537r, 538r, 541r, 543r, 544r. Walt Disney's Comics & Stories featured Mickey Mouse serials which were in practically every issue from #1 through #394. The titles of the serials, along with the issues they are in, are listed in previous editions of this price guide. **Floyd Gottfredson** Mickey Mouse serials in issues #1-61, 63-74, 77-92 plus "Mickey Mouse in a Warplant" (3 pgs.), and "Pluto Catches a Nazi Spy" (4 pgs.) in #62; "Mystery Next Door," #93; "Sunken Treasure," #94; "Aunt Marissa," #95; "Gangland," #98; "Thanksgiving Dinner," #99; and "The Talking Dog," #100. Mickey Mouse by **Paul Murry** #152 on except 155-57 (**Dick Moore**), 327-29 (**Tony Strobl**), 348-50 (**Jack Manning**). **Don Rosa** story/a-523, 524, 526, 528, 531, 547. **Al Taliaferro** Silly Symphonies in #5-"Three Little Pigs;" #13-"Birds of a Feather;" #14-"The Boarding School Mystery;" #15-"Cookieland" and "Three Little Kittens;" #16-"Three Little Pigs;" #17-"The Ugly Duckling" and "The Robber Kitten;" #19-"Penguin Isle;" and "Bucky Bug" in #20-23, 25, 26, 28 (one continuous story from 1932-34; first 2 pgs. not Taliaferro).*

**WALT DISNEY'S COMICS & STORIES**
1943 (36 pgs.) (Dept. store Xmas giveaway)
Walt Disney Productions

| | Good | Fine | N-Mint |
|---|---|---|---|
| nn | 45.00 | 135.00 | 300.00 |

**WALT DISNEY'S COMICS & STORIES**
Mid 1940's ('45-48), 1952 (4 pgs. in color) (slick paper)
Dell Publishing Co.(Special Xmas offer)

| | Good | Fine | N-Mint |
|---|---|---|---|
| 1940's version - subscription form for WDC&S - (Reprints two different WDC&S covers with subscription forms printed on inside covers) | 8.50 | 25.50 | 60.00 |
| 1952 version | 5.00 | 15.00 | 35.00 |

**WALT DISNEY'S COMICS DIGEST**
Dec, 1986 - No. 7, Sept, 1987
Gladstone Publishing

| | Good | Fine | N-Mint |
|---|---|---|---|
| 1-7 | | .60 | 1.25 |

**WALT DISNEY SHOWCASE**
Oct, 1970 - No. 54, Jan, 1980 (No. 44-48: 68pgs., 49-54: 52pgs.)
Gold Key

| | Good | Fine | N-Mint |
|---|---|---|---|
| 1-Boatniks (Movie)-Photo-c | 1.00 | 3.00 | 6.00 |
| 2-Moby Duck | .50 | 1.50 | 3.00 |

Walt Disney's Comics & Stories #13, © Disney

Walt Disney's Comics & Stories #58, © Disney

Walt Disney's Comics & Stories #512, © Disney

*Walt Kelly's Springtime Tales #1, © Eclipse*

*Wambi, Jungle Boy #2, © FH*

*Wanderers #2, © DC*

| | Good | Fine | N-Mint |
|---|---|---|---|
| 3,4,7: 3-Bongo & Lumpjaw-r. 4,7-Pluto-r | .35 | 1.00 | 2.00 |
| 5-$1,000,000 Duck (Movie)-Photo-c | .70 | 2.00 | 4.00 |
| 6-Bedknobs & Broomsticks (Movie) | .70 | 2.00 | 4.00 |
| 8-Daisy & Donald | .35 | 1.00 | 2.00 |
| 9-101 Dalmatians (cartoon feature); r/F.C. #1183 | .50 | 1.50 | 3.00 |
| 10-Napoleon & Samantha (Movie)-Photo-c | .70 | 2.00 | 4.00 |
| 11-Moby Duck-r | .25 | .75 | 1.50 |
| 12-Dumbo-r/Four Color #668 | .35 | 1.00 | 2.00 |
| 13-Pluto-r | .30 | .90 | 1.80 |
| 14-World's Greatest Athlete (Movie)-Photo-c | .70 | 2.00 | 4.00 |
| 15-3 Little Pigs-r | .25 | .75 | 1.50 |
| 16-Aristocats (cartoon feature); r/Aristocats #1 | .70 | 2.00 | 4.00 |
| 17-Mary Poppins; r/M.P. #10136-501-Photo-c | .70 | 2.00 | 4.00 |
| 18-Gyro Gearloose; Barks-r/F.C. #1047,1184 | .70 | 2.00 | 4.00 |
| 19-That Darn Cat; r/That Darn Cat #10171-602-Hayley Mills photo-c | .50 | 1.50 | 3.00 |
| 20,23-Pluto-r | .25 | .75 | 1.50 |
| 21-Li'l Bad Wolf & The Three Little Pigs | .30 | .90 | 1.80 |
| 22-Unbirthday Party with Alice in Wonderland; r/Four Color #341 | .50 | 1.50 | 3.00 |
| 24-26: 24-Herbie Rides Again (Movie); sequel to "The Love Bug;" photo-c. 25-Old Yeller (Movie); r/F.C. #869; Photo-c. 26-Lt. Robin Crusoe USN (Movie); r/Lt. Robin Crusoe USN #10191-601; photo-c | .35 | 1.00 | 2.00 |
| 27-Island at the Top of the World (Movie)-Photo-c | .40 | 1.25 | 2.50 |
| 28-Brer Rabbit, Bucky Bug-r/WDC&S #58 | .25 | .75 | 1.50 |
| 29-Escape to Witch Mountain (Movie)-Photo-c | .50 | 1.50 | 3.00 |
| 30-Magica De Spell; Barks-r/Uncle Scrooge #36 & WDC&S #258 | 1.00 | 3.00 | 6.00 |
| 31-Bambi (cartoon feature); r/Four Color #186 | .50 | 1.50 | 3.00 |
| 32-Spin & Marty-r/F.C. #1026; Mickey Mouse Club (TV)-Photo-c | .70 | 2.00 | 4.00 |
| 33-39: 33-Pluto-r/F.C. #1143. 34-Paul Revere's Ride with Johnny Tremain (TV); r/F.C. #822. 35-Goofy-r/F.C. #952. 36-Peter Pan-r/F.C. #442. 37-Tinker Bell & Jiminy Cricket-r/F.C. #982,989. 38,39-Mickey & the Sleuth, Parts 1 & 2 | .25 | .75 | 1.50 |
| 40-The Rescuers (cartoon feature) | .40 | .90 | 1.80 |
| 41-Herbie Goes to Monte Carlo (Movie); sequel to "Herbie Rides Again;" photo-c | .35 | 1.00 | 2.00 |
| 42-Mickey & the Sleuth | .25 | .75 | 1.50 |
| 43-Pete's Dragon (Movie)-Photo-c | .70 | 2.00 | 4.00 |
| 44-Return From Witch Mountain (new) & In Search of the Castaways-r (Movies)-Photo-c; 68 pg. giants begin | .50 | 1.50 | 3.00 |
| 45-The Jungle Book (Movie); r/#30033-803 | .50 | 1.50 | 3.00 |
| 46-The Cat From Outer Space (Movie)(new), & The Shaggy Dog (Movie)-r/F.C. #985; photo-c | .50 | 1.50 | 3.00 |
| 47-Mickey Mouse Surprise Party-r | .50 | 1.50 | 3.00 |
| 48-The Wonderful Advs. of Pinocchio-r/F.C. #1203; last 68 pg. issue | .50 | 1.50 | 3.00 |
| 49-54: 49-North Avenue Irregulars (Movie); Zorro-r/Zorro #11; 52 pgs. begin; photo-c. 50-Bedknobs & Broomsticks-r/#6; Mooncussers-r/World of Adv. #1; photo-c. 51-101 Dalmatians-r. 52-Unidentified Flying Oddball (Movie); r-/Picnic Party #8; photo-c. 53-The Scarecrow-r (TV). 54-The Black Hole (Movie)-Photo-c | .25 | .75 | 1.50 |

**WALT DISNEY'S MAGAZINE** (TV)(Formerly Walt Disney's Mickey Mouse Club Magazine) (50 cents) (Bi-monthly)
V2#4, June, 1957 - V4#6, Oct, 1959
Western Publishing Co.

| | Good | Fine | N-Mint |
|---|---|---|---|
| V2#4-Stories & articles on the Mouseketeers, Zorro, & Goofy and other Disney characters & people | 4.00 | 12.00 | 28.00 |
| V2#5, V2#6(10/57) | 3.50 | 10.50 | 24.00 |
| V3#1(12/57), V3#3-6(10/58) | 2.30 | 7.00 | 16.00 |
| V3#2-Annette Funicello photo-c | 5.70 | 17.00 | 40.00 |
| V4#1(12/58) - V4#2-4,6(10/59) | 2.30 | 7.00 | 16.00 |
| V4#5-Annette Funicello photo-c | 5.00 | 15.00 | 35.00 |

NOTE: *V2#4-V3#6 were 11½x8½", 48 pgs.; V4#1 on were 10x8", 52 pgs. (Peak circulation of 400,000).*

**WALT DISNEY'S MERRY CHRISTMAS** (See Dell Giant #39)

**WALT DISNEY'S MICKEY MOUSE CLUB MAGAZINE** (TV)(Becomes Walt Disney's Magazine) (Quarterly)
Winter, 1956 - V2#3, April, 1957 (11½x8½") (48 pgs.)
Western Publishing Co.

| | Good | Fine | N-Mint |
|---|---|---|---|
| V1#1 | 10.00 | 30.00 | 70.00 |
| 2-4 | 5.00 | 15.00 | 35.00 |
| V2#1-3 | 4.00 | 12.00 | 28.00 |
| Annual(1956)-Two different issues; ($1.50-Whitman); 120 pgs., cardboard covers, 11¾x8¾"; reprints | 10.00 | 30.00 | 70.00 |
| Annual(1957)-Same as above | 7.00 | 21.00 | 50.00 |

**WALT DISNEY'S PINOCCHIO SPECIAL**
Spring, 1990 ($1.00, color)
Gladstone Publishing

| | Good | Fine | N-Mint |
|---|---|---|---|
| 1-50th anniversary edition; Kelly-r/F.C. #92 | | .50 | 1.00 |

**WALT DISNEY'S THE JUNGLE BOOK**
1990 ($5.95, color, graphic novel, 68 pgs.)
W. D. Publications (Disney Comics)

| | Good | Fine | N-Mint |
|---|---|---|---|
| nn-Movie adaptation; movie rereleased in 1990 | 1.00 | 3.00 | 6.00 |
| nn-($2.95, 68 pgs.)-Comic edition; wraparound-c | .50 | 1.50 | 3.00 |

**WALT DISNEY'S WHEATIES PREMIUMS** (See Wheaties)

**WALTER LANTZ ANDY PANDA** (Also see Andy Panda)
Aug, 1973 - No. 23, Jan, 1978 (Walter Lantz)
Gold Key

| | Good | Fine | N-Mint |
|---|---|---|---|
| 1-Reprints | .35 | 1.00 | 2.00 |
| 2-10-All reprints | | .40 | .80 |
| 11-23: 15,17-19,22-Reprints | | .15 | .30 |

**WALT KELLY'S. . .**
Dec, 1987; April, 1988 ($1.75-$2.50, color, Baxter)
Eclipse Comics

| | Good | Fine | N-Mint |
|---|---|---|---|
| . . .Christmas Classics 1 ('87, $1.75)-Kelly-r/Peter Wheat & Santa Claus Funnies | .30 | .90 | 1.75 |
| . . .Springtime Tales 1 (4/88, $2.50)-Kelly-r | .40 | 1.25 | 2.50 |

**WALT SCOTT'S CHRISTMAS STORIES** (See 4-Color #959, 1062)

**WAMBI, JUNGLE BOY** (See Jungle Comics)
Spring, 1942; No. 2, Wint, 1942-43; No. 3, Spring, 1943; No. 4, Fall, 1948; No. 5, Sum, 1949; No. 6, Spring, 1950; No. 7-10, 1950(nd); No. 11, Spring, 1951 - No. 18, Winter, 1952-53 (#1-3: 68 pgs.)
Fiction House Magazines

| | Good | Fine | N-Mint |
|---|---|---|---|
| 1-Wambi, the Jungle Boy begins | 34.00 | 100.00 | 235.00 |
| 2 (1942)-Kiefer-c | 17.00 | 51.00 | 120.00 |
| 3 (1943)-Kiefer-c/a | 12.00 | 36.00 | 85.00 |
| 4 (1948)-Origin in text | 8.00 | 24.00 | 55.00 |
| 5 (Fall, '49, 36pgs.)-Kiefer-c/a | 7.00 | 21.00 | 50.00 |
| 6-10: 7-52 pgs. | 5.70 | 17.00 | 40.00 |
| 11-18 | 4.00 | 12.00 | 28.00 |
| I.W. Reprint #8('64)-R-/#12 with new-c | 1.00 | 3.00 | 6.00 |

**WANDERERS** (See Adventure Comics #375, 376)
June, 1988 - No. 13, April, 1989 ($1.25, color)
DC Comics

| | Good | Fine | N-Mint |
|---|---|---|---|
| 1-13: Legion spin-off. 1,2-Steacy-c. 3-Legion app. | | .65 | 1.30 |

**WANTED COMICS**
No. 9, Sept-Oct, 1947 - No. 53, April, 1953 (#9-33: 52 pgs.)
Toytown Publications/Patches/Orbit Publ.

| | Good | Fine | N-Mint |
|---|---|---|---|
| 9 | 7.00 | 21.00 | 50.00 |
| 10,11: 10-Giunta-a; radio's Mr. D. A. app. | 4.00 | 12.00 | 28.00 |

| | Good | Fine | N-Mint |
|---|---|---|---|
| 12-Used in **SOTI**, pg. 277 | 4.30 | 13.00 | 30.00 |
| 13-Heroin drug propaganda story | 4.00 | 12.00 | 28.00 |
| 14-Marijuana drug mention story, 2 pgs. | 2.65 | 8.00 | 18.00 |
| 15-17,19,20 | 2.30 | 7.00 | 16.00 |
| 18-Marijuana story, 'Satan's Cigarettes'; r-in #45 & retitled | 10.00 | 30.00 | 70.00 |
| 21-Krigstein-a | 3.00 | 9.00 | 21.00 |
| 22-Extreme violence | 3.00 | 9.00 | 21.00 |
| 23,25-34,36-38,40-44,46-48,53 | 1.50 | 4.50 | 10.00 |
| 24-Krigstein-a; 'The Dope King,' marijuana mention story | 3.00 | 9.00 | 21.00 |
| 35-Used in **SOTI**, pg. 160 | 3.00 | 9.00 | 21.00 |
| 39-Drug propaganda sty "The Horror Weed" | 5.50 | 16.50 | 38.00 |
| 45-Marijuana story from #18 | 3.00 | 9.00 | 21.00 |
| 49-Has unstable pink-c that fades easily; rare in mint condition | 1.70 | 5.00 | 12.00 |
| 50-Has unstable pink-c like #49; surrealist-c by Buscema; horror stories | 4.00 | 12.00 | 28.00 |
| 51-"Holiday of Horror"-junkie story; drug-c | 3.00 | 9.00 | 21.00 |
| 52-Classic "Cult of Killers" opium use story | 3.00 | 9.00 | 21.00 |

NOTE: ***Buscema** c-50, 51. **Lawrence** and **Leav** c/a most issues. **Syd Shores** c/a-48.*

**WANTED: DEAD OR ALIVE** (See 4-Color #1102,1164)

**WANTED, THE WORLD'S MOST DANGEROUS VILLAINS**
July-Aug, 1972 - No. 9, Aug-Sept, 1973 (All reprints)
National Periodical Publications (See DC Special)

| | Good | Fine | N-Mint |
|---|---|---|---|
| 1-Batman, Green Lantern (story r-from G.L. #1), & Green Arrow | .50 | 1.50 | 3.00 |
| 2-Batman/Joker/Penguin-c/story r-from Batman #25; plus Flash story r-from Flash #121 | .70 | 2.00 | 4.00 |
| 3-9: 3-Dr. Fate, Hawkman(r/Flash #100), & Vigilante. 4-Gr. Lantern & Kid Eternity. 5-Dollman/Green Lantern. 6-Burnley Starman; Wildcat/Sargon. 7-Johnny Quick/Hawkman/Hourman by Baily. 8-Dr. Fate/Flash(r/Flash #114). 9-S&K Sandman/Superman | .25 | .75 | 1.50 |

NOTE: ***Kane** r-1, 5. **Kubert** r-3i, 6, 7. **Meskin** r-3, 7. **Reinman** r-4, 6.*

**WAR**
July, 1975 - No. 9, Nov, 1976; No. 10, Sept, 1978 - No. 49?, 1984
Charlton Comics

| | Good | Fine | N-Mint |
|---|---|---|---|
| 1-49: 47-r | | .15 | .30 |
| 7,9(Modern Comics-r, 1977) | | .15 | .30 |

**WAR, THE**
1989 - No. 4, 1990 ($3.50, color, squarebound, 52 pgs.)
Marvel Comics

| | Good | Fine | N-Mint |
|---|---|---|---|
| 1-4: Sequel to The Draft & The Pitt | .60 | 1.75 | 3.50 |

**WAR ACTION**
April, 1952 - No. 14, June, 1953
Atlas Comics (CPS)

| | Good | Fine | N-Mint |
|---|---|---|---|
| 1 | 6.50 | 19.00 | 45.00 |
| 2 | 3.00 | 9.00 | 21.00 |
| 3-10,14: 7-Pakula-a | 2.00 | 6.00 | 14.00 |
| 11-13-Krigstein-a | 4.00 | 12.00 | 28.00 |

NOTE: ***Heath** a-1; c-7, 14. **Keller** a-6. **Maneely** a-1. **Tuska** a-2, 8.*

**WAR ADVENTURES**
Jan, 1952 - No. 13, Feb, 1953
Atlas Comics (HPC)

| | Good | Fine | N-Mint |
|---|---|---|---|
| 1-Tuska-a | 5.70 | 17.00 | 40.00 |
| 2 | 2.65 | 8.00 | 18.00 |
| 3-7,9-13 | 2.00 | 6.00 | 14.00 |
| 8-Krigstein-a | 4.00 | 12.00 | 28.00 |

NOTE: ***Heath** a-5; c-4, 5, 9, 13. **Pakula** a-3. **Robinson** a-3; c-10.*

**WAR ADVENTURES ON THE BATTLEFIELD** (See Battlefield)

**WAR AGAINST CRIME!** (Vault of Horror #12 on)
Spring, 1948 - No. 11, Feb-Mar, 1950
E. C. Comics

| | Good | Fine | N-Mint |
|---|---|---|---|
| 1 | 45.00 | 135.00 | 315.00 |
| 2,3 | 25.00 | 75.00 | 175.00 |
| 4-9 | 24.00 | 70.00 | 165.00 |
| 10-1st Vault Keeper app. | 82.00 | 245.00 | 575.00 |
| 11-2nd Vault Keeper app. | 60.00 | 180.00 | 420.00 |

NOTE: *All have **Johnny Craig** covers. **Feldstein** a-4, 7-9. **Ingels** a-1, 2, 8.*

**WAR AND ATTACK** (Also see Special War Series #3)
Fall, 1964; V2#54, June, 1966 - V2#63, Dec, 1967
Charlton Comics

| | Good | Fine | N-Mint |
|---|---|---|---|
| 1-Wood-a | 1.00 | 3.00 | 7.00 |
| V2#54(6/66)-#63 (Formerly Fightin' Air Force) | .50 | 1.50 | 3.00 |

NOTE: ***Montes/Bache** a-55, 56, 60, 63.*

**WAR AT SEA** (Formerly Space Adventures)
No. 22, Nov, 1957 - No. 42, June, 1961
Charlton Comics

| | Good | Fine | N-Mint |
|---|---|---|---|
| 22 | 1.50 | 4.00 | 10.00 |
| 23-30 | .70 | 2.00 | 5.00 |
| 31-42 | .50 | 1.50 | 3.00 |

**WAR BATTLES**
Feb, 1952 - No. 9, Dec, 1953
Harvey Publications

| | Good | Fine | N-Mint |
|---|---|---|---|
| 1-Powell-a | 3.00 | 9.00 | 21.00 |
| 2-Powell-a | 1.70 | 5.00 | 12.00 |
| 3-5,7-9: 3,7-Powell-a | 1.50 | 4.50 | 10.00 |
| 6-Nostrand-a | 2.65 | 8.00 | 18.00 |

**WAR BIRDS**
1952(nd) - No. 3, Winter, 1952-53
Fiction House Magazines

| | Good | Fine | N-Mint |
|---|---|---|---|
| 1 | 6.00 | 19.00 | 45.00 |
| 2,3 | 3.60 | 11.00 | 25.00 |

**WAR COMBAT** (Combat Casey #6 on)
March, 1952 - No. 5, Nov, 1952
Atlas Comics (LBI 1/SAI 2-5)

| | Good | Fine | N-Mint |
|---|---|---|---|
| 1 | 4.50 | 14.00 | 32.00 |
| 2 | 2.30 | 7.00 | 16.00 |
| 3-5 | 1.70 | 5.00 | 12.00 |

NOTE: ***Berg** a-2, 4, 5. **Henkel** a-5. **Maneely** a-1, 4; c-3.*

**WAR COMICS** (War Stories #5 on)(See Key Ring Comics)
May, 1940 (No mo. given) - No. 4, 1941(nd)
Dell Publishing Co.

| | Good | Fine | N-Mint |
|---|---|---|---|
| 1-Sikandur the Robot Master, Sky Hawk, Scoop Mason, War Correspondent begin | 26.00 | 77.00 | 180.00 |
| 2-Origin Greg Gilday | 13.00 | 40.00 | 90.00 |
| 3-Joan becomes Greg Gilday's aide | 9.00 | 27.00 | 62.00 |
| 4-Origin Night Devils | 10.00 | 30.00 | 70.00 |

**WAR COMICS**
Dec, 1950 - No. 49, Sept, 1957
Marvel/Atlas (USA No. 1-41/JPI No. 42-49)

| | Good | Fine | N-Mint |
|---|---|---|---|
| 1 | 8.00 | 24.00 | 55.00 |
| 2 | 4.00 | 12.00 | 28.00 |
| 3-10 | 3.00 | 9.00 | 21.00 |
| 11-20 | 1.70 | 5.00 | 12.00 |
| 21,23-32: Last precode (2/55). 26-Valley Forge story | 1.50 | 4.50 | 10.00 |
| 22-Krigstein-a | 3.70 | 11.00 | 26.00 |
| 33-37,39-42,44,45,47,48 | 1.50 | 4.50 | 10.00 |
| 38-Kubert/Moskowitz-a | 2.65 | 8.00 | 18.00 |
| 43,49-Torres-a. 43-Davis E.C. swipe | 2.30 | 7.00 | 16.00 |
| 46-Crandall-a | 2.65 | 8.00 | 18.00 |

*Wanted Comics #52, © Toytown Publ.*

*War Adventures #6, © MEG*

*War Comics #4 (6/51), © MEG*

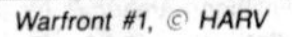
Warfront #1, © HARV

War Heroes #6, © ACE

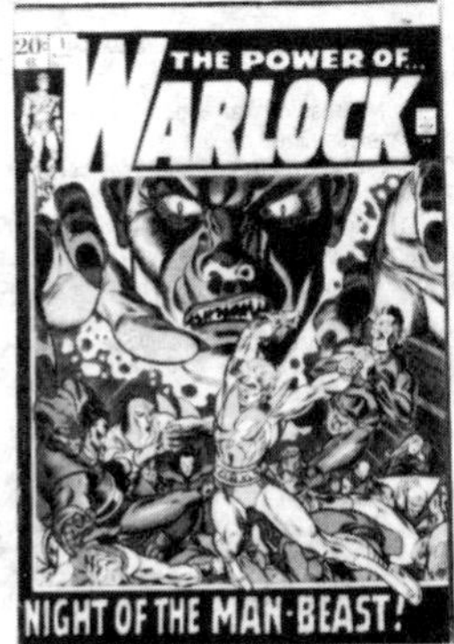

Warlock #1 (8/72), © MEG

NOTE: ***Colan*** *a-4, 48, 49.* ***Drucker*** *a-37, 43, 48.* ***Everett*** *a-17.* ***Heath*** *a-7-9, 19; c-11, 26, 29-31.* ***G. Kane*** *a-19.* ***Maneely*** *c-37.* ***Orlando*** *a-42, 48.* ***Pakula*** *a-26.* ***Reinman*** *a-26.* ***Robinson*** *a-15; c-13.* ***Severin*** *a-26; c-48.*

**WAR DOGS OF THE U.S. ARMY**
1952
Avon Periodicals

| | Good | Fine | N-Mint |
|---|---|---|---|
| 1-Kinstler-c/a | 6.50 | 19.00 | 45.00 |

**WARFRONT**
9/51 - #35, 11/58; #36, 10/65; #37, 9/66 - #38, 12/66; #39, 2/67
Harvey Publications

| | Good | Fine | N-Mint |
|---|---|---|---|
| 1 | 4.00 | 12.00 | 28.00 |
| 2 | 2.00 | 6.00 | 14.00 |
| 3-10 | 1.50 | 4.50 | 10.00 |
| 11,12,14,16-20 | 1.00 | 3.00 | 7.00 |
| 13,15,22-Nostrand-a | 3.00 | 9.00 | 21.00 |
| 21,23-27,29,31-33,35 | .85 | 2.60 | 6.00 |
| 28,30,34-Kirby-c | 1.70 | 5.00 | 12.00 |
| 36-Dynamite Joe begins, ends #39; Williamson-a | 1.35 | 4.00 | 9.00 |
| 37-Wood-a, 17pgs. | 1.35 | 4.00 | 9.00 |
| 38,39-Wood-a, 2-3 pgs.; Lone Tiger app. | .85 | 2.50 | 6.00 |

NOTE: ***Powell*** *a-1-6, 9-11, 14, 17, 20, 23, 25-28, 30, 31, 34, 36.* ***Powell/Nostrand*** *a-12, 13, 15.* ***Simon*** *c-36?, 38.*

**WAR FURY**
Sept, 1952 - No. 4, March, 1953
Comic Media/Harwell (Allen Hardy Associates)

| | Good | Fine | N-Mint |
|---|---|---|---|
| 1-Heck-c/a in all; Bullet hole in forehead-c | 3.50 | 10.50 | 24.00 |
| 2-4: 4-Morisi-a | 1.70 | 5.00 | 12.00 |

**WAR GODS OF THE DEEP** (See Movie Classics)

**WARHAWKS**
1990 - Present ($2.95, color, 44 pgs.)
TSR, Inc.

| | Good | Fine | N-Mint |
|---|---|---|---|
| 1-8-Based on TSR game | .50 | 1.50 | 3.00 |

**WAR HEROES** (See Marine War Heroes)

**WAR HEROES**
7-9/42 (no month); No. 2, 10-12/42 - No. 10, 10-12/44; No. 11, 3/45
Dell Publishing Co.

| | Good | Fine | N-Mint |
|---|---|---|---|
| 1 | 11.00 | 32.00 | 75.00 |
| 2 | 5.70 | 17.00 | 40.00 |
| 3,5: 3-Pro-Russian back-c | 4.00 | 12.00 | 28.00 |
| 4-Disney's Gremlins app. | 10.00 | 30.00 | 70.00 |
| 6-11: 6-Tothish-a by Discount | 3.50 | 10.50 | 24.00 |

NOTE: *No. 1 was to be released in July, but was delayed.* ***Cameron*** *a-6.*

**WAR HEROES**
May, 1952 - No. 8, April, 1953
Ace Magazines

| | Good | Fine | N-Mint |
|---|---|---|---|
| 1 | 3.50 | 10.50 | 24.00 |
| 2-Lou Cameron-a | 1.70 | 5.00 | 12.00 |
| 3-8: 6-8-Cameron-a | 1.50 | 4.50 | 10.00 |

**WAR HEROES** (Also see Blue Bird Comics)
Feb, 1963 - No. 27, Nov, 1967
Charlton Comics

| | Good | Fine | N-Mint |
|---|---|---|---|
| 1 | .85 | 2.60 | 6.00 |
| 2-10: 2-John F. Kennedy story | .50 | 1.50 | 3.00 |
| 11-27: 27-1st Devils Brigade by Glanzman | .25 | .75 | 1.50 |

NOTE: ***Montes/Bache*** *a-3-7, 21, 25, 27; c-3-7.*

**WAR IS HELL**
Jan, 1973 - No. 15, Oct, 1975
Marvel Comics Group

| | Good | Fine | N-Mint |
|---|---|---|---|
| 1-Williamson-a(r), 5 pgs.; Ayers-a | | .50 | 1.00 |
| 2-15: 2-9-All reprints | | .35 | .70 |

NOTE: ***Bolle*** *a-3r.* ***Powell*** *a-1.* ***Woodbridge*** *a-1. Sgt. Fury reprints-7, 8.*

**WARLOCK** (The Power of. . .)(See Marvel Premiere & Strange Tales)
Aug, 1972 - No. 8, Oct, 1973; No. 9, Oct, 1975 - No. 15, Nov, 1976
Marvel Comics Group

| | Good | Fine | N-Mint |
|---|---|---|---|
| 1-Origin by Kane | 1.00 | 3.00 | 7.00 |
| 2,3 | .70 | 2.00 | 4.00 |
| 4-8: 4-Death of Eddie Roberts | .60 | 1.75 | 3.50 |
| 9-15-Starlin-c/a in all. 9-New costume. 10-Origin Thanos & Gamora. 14-Origin Star Thief | .50 | 1.50 | 3.00 |

NOTE: ***Buscema*** *a-2p; c-8p.* ***G. Kane*** *a-1p, 3-5p; c-1p, 2, 3, 4p, 5p, 7p.* ***Starlin*** *a-9-14p, 15; c-12p, 13-15.* ***Sutton*** *a-1-8i.*

**WARLOCK** (. . .Special Edition on-c)
Dec, 1982 - No. 6, May, 1983 ($2.00, 52 pgs.) (slick paper)
Marvel Comics Group

| | Good | Fine | N-Mint |
|---|---|---|---|
| 1-6: 1-Warlock r-/Str. Tales #178-180. 2-Warlock r-/Str. Tales #180,181 & Warlock #9. 3-r/Warlock #10-12. 4-r/Warlock #12-15. 5-r/Warlock #15 (Starlin-r in all) | .35 | 1.00 | 2.00 |
| Special Edition #1(12/83) | .35 | 1.00 | 2.00 |

NOTE: ***Byrne*** *a-5r.* ***Starlin*** *a-1-6r; c-1-4. Direct sale only.*

**WARLOCK 5**
11/86 - No, 22, 5/89; V2#1, June, 1989 - V2#5?, 1989 ($1.70, B&W)
Aircel Publishing

| | Good | Fine | N-Mint |
|---|---|---|---|
| 1-All issues by Barry Blair | 1.00 | 2.95 | 5.90 |
| 2 | .70 | 2.05 | 4.10 |
| 3 | 1.30 | 3.85 | 7.70 |
| 4-6: 5-Green Cyborg on-c. 6-Misnumbered; Blue Girl on-c | 1.00 | 2.95 | 5.90 |
| 7-9 | .85 | 2.50 | 5.00 |
| 10,11 | .55 | 1.60 | 3.20 |
| 12-22: 18-Begin $1.95-c | .30 | .90 | 1.80 |
| V2#1-5 ($2.00, B&W) | .30 | .90 | 1.80 |
| Compilation 1-r/#1-5 (1988, $5.95) | .90 | 2.75 | 5.40 |
| Compilation 2-r/#6-9 ($5.95) | .90 | 2.75 | 5.40 |

**WARLORD** (See 1st Issue Special)
1-2/76; No.2, 3-4/76; No.3, 10-11/76 - No. 133, Wint, 1988-89
National Periodical Publications/DC Comics #123 on

| | Good | Fine | N-Mint |
|---|---|---|---|
| 1-Story cont'd. from First Issue Special #8 | 2.50 | 7.50 | 15.00 |
| 2-Intro. Machiste | 1.35 | 4.00 | 8.00 |
| 3-5 | .85 | 2.50 | 5.00 |
| 6-10: 6-Intro Mariah. 7-Origin Machiste. 9-Dons new costume | .70 | 2.00 | 4.00 |
| 11-20: 11-Origin-r. 12-Intro Aton. 15-Tara returns; Warlord has son | .50 | 1.50 | 3.00 |
| 21-40: 27-New facts about origin. 28-1st app. Wizard World. 32-Intro Shakira. 37,38-Origin Omac by Starlin. 38-Intro Jennifer Morgan, Warlord's daughter. 39-Omac ends. 40-Warlord gets new costume | .35 | 1.00 | 2.00 |
| 41-47,49-52: 42-47-Omac back-up series. 49-Claw The Unconquered app. 50-Death of Aton. 51-r-/No.1 | | .50 | 1.00 |
| 48-(52pgs.)-1st app. Arak; contains free 16pg. Arak Son of Thunder; Claw The Unconquered app. | .35 | 1.00 | 2.00 |
| 53-99,101-122: 55-Arion Lord of Atlantis begins, ends #62. 63-The Barren Earth begins; free 16pg. Masters of the Universe preview. 91-Origin w/new facts. 114,115-Legends x-over | | .50 | 1.00 |
| 100-Double size ($1.25) | | .50 | 1.00 |
| 123-133: 125-Death of Tara. 133-($1.50, 52 pgs.) | | .50 | 1.00 |
| Remco Toy Giveaway (2¾x4") | | .50 | 1.00 |
| Annual 1(1982)-Grell-c, a(p) | .35 | 1.00 | 2.00 |
| Annual 2(1983) | | .50 | 1.00 |
| Annual 3(1984), 4(1985), 5(1986), 6(1987) | | .50 | 1.00 |

NOTE: ***Grell*** *a-1-15, 16-50p, 51r, 52p, 59p, Annual 1p; c-1-70, 100-104, 112, 116, 117, Annual 1, 5.* ***Wayne Howard*** *a-64i.* ***Starlin*** *a-37-39p.*

**WARLORDS** (See DC Graphic Novel #2)

## WARP
March, 1983 - No. 19, Feb, 1985 ($1.00-$1.25, Mando paper)
First Comics

| | Good | Fine | N-Mint |
|---|---|---|---|
| 1-Sargon-Mistress of War app. | .30 | .90 | 1.80 |
| 2-5: 2-Faceless Ones begins | | .65 | 1.30 |
| 6-10: 10-New Warp advs., & Outrider begin | | .50 | 1.00 |
| 11-19 | | .45 | .90 |
| Special 1-3: 1(7/83, 36 pgs.)-Origin Chaos-Prince of Madness; origin of Warp Universe begins, ends #3. 2(1/84)-Lord Cumulus vs. Sargon Mistress of War ($1.00). 3(6/84)-Chaos-Prince of Madness | | .50 | 1.00 |

NOTE: ***Brunner** a-1-9p; c-1-9. **Chaykin** a(p)-Special 1; c-Special 1. **Ditko** a-2-4. **Staton** a-1i. No. 1-9 are adapted from the Warp plays.*

## WARPATH
Nov, 1954 - No. 3, April, 1955
Key Publications/Stanmor

| | Good | Fine | N-Mint |
|---|---|---|---|
| 1 | 4.00 | 12.00 | 28.00 |
| 2,3 | 2.30 | 7.00 | 16.00 |

## WARP GRAPHICS ANNUAL
Dec, 1985; 1988 ($2.50 cover)
WaRP Graphics

| | Good | Fine | N-Mint |
|---|---|---|---|
| 1-Elfquest, Blood of the Innocent, Thunderbunny & Mythadventures app. | .40 | 1.25 | 2.50 |
| 1 ('88) | .40 | 1.25 | 2.50 |

## WARREN PRESENTS
Jan, 1979 - No. 14, Nov, 1981
Warren Publications

| | Good | Fine | N-Mint |
|---|---|---|---|
| 1-14-Eerie, Creepy, & Vampirella-r | | .50 | 1.00 |
| . . .The Rook 1 (5/79)-r/Eerie #82-85 | | .50 | 1.00 |

## WAR REPORT
Sept, 1952 - No. 5, May, 1953
Ajax/Farrell Publications (Excellent Publ.)

| | Good | Fine | N-Mint |
|---|---|---|---|
| 1 | 3.50 | 10.50 | 24.00 |
| 2 | 1.70 | 5.00 | 12.00 |
| 3,5 | 1.50 | 4.50 | 10.00 |
| 4-Used in **POP**, pg. 94 | 1.50 | 4.50 | 10.00 |

## WARRIOR COMICS
1945 (1930s DC reprints)
H.C. Blackerby

| | Good | Fine | N-Mint |
|---|---|---|---|
| 1-Wing Brady, The Iron Man, Mark Markon | 6.50 | 19.00 | 45.00 |

## WARRIORS
1987 - No. 7, 1988 ($1.95, B&W)
Adventure Publications

| | Good | Fine | N-Mint |
|---|---|---|---|
| 1-Hsu painted-c | .50 | 1.50 | 3.00 |
| 2-7 | .35 | 1.00 | 2.00 |

## WAR ROMANCES (See True. . .)

## WAR SHIPS
1942 (36 pgs.)(Similar to Large Feature Comics)
Dell Publishing Co.

| | Good | Fine | N-Mint |
|---|---|---|---|
| nn-Cover by McWilliams; contains photos & drawings of U.S. war ships | 8.00 | 24.00 | 55.00 |

## WAR STORIES (Formerly War Comics)
No. 5, 1942(nd) - No. 8, Feb-Apr, 1943
Dell Publishing Co.

| | Good | Fine | N-Mint |
|---|---|---|---|
| 5-Origin The Whistler | 11.50 | 34.00 | 80.00 |
| 6-8: 6-8-Night Devils app. | 8.50 | 25.50 | 60.00 |

## WAR STORIES (Korea)
Sept, 1952 - No. 5, May, 1953
Ajax/Farrell Publications (Excellent Publ.)

| | Good | Fine | N-Mint |
|---|---|---|---|
| 1 | 3.70 | 11.00 | 26.00 |
| 2 | 1.70 | 5.00 | 12.00 |
| 3-5 | 1.50 | 4.50 | 10.00 |

## WAR STORIES (See Star Spangled. . .)

## WART AND THE WIZARD
Feb, 1964 (Walt Disney)
Gold Key

| | Good | Fine | N-Mint |
|---|---|---|---|
| 1 (10102-402) | 1.75 | 5.25 | 12.00 |

## WARTIME ROMANCES
July, 1951 - No. 18, Nov, 1953
St. John Publishing co.

| | Good | Fine | N-Mint |
|---|---|---|---|
| 1-All Baker-a | 12.00 | 36.00 | 85.00 |
| 2-All Baker-a | 7.00 | 21.00 | 50.00 |
| 3,4-All Baker-a | 6.50 | 19.00 | 45.00 |
| 5-8-Baker-c/a(2-3) each | 5.70 | 17.00 | 40.00 |
| 9-12,16,18-Baker-c/a each | 4.30 | 13.00 | 30.00 |
| 13-15,17-Baker-c only | 3.15 | 9.50 | 22.00 |

## WAR VICTORY ADVENTURES (#1 titled War Victory Comics)
Summer, 1942 - No. 3, Winter, 1943-44 (5 cents)
U.S. Treasury Dept./War Victory/Harvey Publ.

| | Good | Fine | N-Mint |
|---|---|---|---|
| 1-(Promotion of Savings Bonds)-Featuring America's greatest comic art by top syndicated cartoonists; Blondie, Joe Palooka, Green Hornet, Dick Tracy, Superman, Gumps, etc.; (36 pgs.); All profits contributed to U.S.O. | 21.00 | 62.00 | 145.00 |
| 2-Powell-a | 11.00 | 32.00 | 75.00 |
| 3-Capt. Red Cross (cover & text only); Powell-a | 8.50 | 25.50 | 60.00 |

## WAR WAGON, THE (See Movie Classics)

## WAR WINGS
October, 1968
Charlton Comics

| | Good | Fine | N-Mint |
|---|---|---|---|
| 1 | .35 | 1.00 | 2.00 |

## WARWORLD!
Feb, 1989 ($1.75, B&W, One-shot)
Dark Horse Comics

| | Good | Fine | N-Mint |
|---|---|---|---|
| 1-Gary Davis sci/fi art in Moebius style | .30 | .90 | 1.80 |

## WASHABLE JONES & SHMOO
June, 1953
Harvey Publications

| | Good | Fine | N-Mint |
|---|---|---|---|
| 1 | 11.50 | 34.00 | 80.00 |

## WASH TUBBS (See The Comics, Crackajack Funnies & 4-Color #11, 28, 53)

## WASTELAND
Dec, 1987 - No. 18, May, 1989 ($1.75-$2.00 #13 on, color, adults)
DC Comics

| | Good | Fine | N-Mint |
|---|---|---|---|
| 1-5(4/88), 5(5/88), 6(5/88)-18: 13,15-Orlando-a | .30 | .90 | 1.80 |

## WATCHMEN
Sept, 1986 - No. 12, Oct, 1987 (12 issue maxi-series)
DC Comics

| | Good | Fine | N-Mint |
|---|---|---|---|
| 1-Alan Moore scripts in all | 1.10 | 3.25 | 6.50 |
| 2,3 | .75 | 2.25 | 4.50 |
| 4-10 | .60 | 1.75 | 3.50 |
| 11,12 | .50 | 1.50 | 3.00 |
| Trade paperback ('87, $14.95) | 2.65 | 8.00 | 16.00 |
| Hardcover (SF Book Club, $15) | 4.15 | 12.50 | 25.00 |
| Hardcover (Limited, Graphitti Designs, $50) | 10.00 | 30.00 | 60.00 |
| DC Portfolio (24 plate, $20) | 4.15 | 12.50 | 25.00 |

## WATCH OUT FOR BIG TALK
1950
Giveaway

| | Good | Fine | N-Mint |
|---|---|---|---|
| nn-Dan Barry-a (about crooked politicians) | 2.35 | 7.00 | 16.00 |

War Stories #6, © DELL

Wartime Romances #1, © STJ

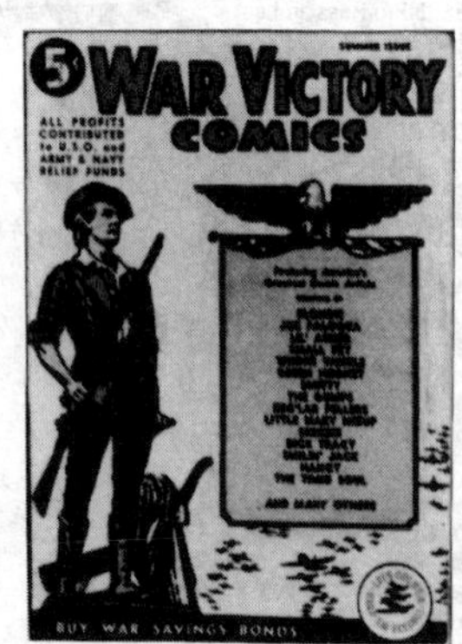

War Victory Comics #1, © HARV

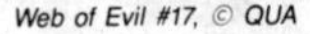
Web of Evil #17, © QUA

Web of Mystery #1, © ACE

The Web of Spider-Man #31, © MEG

**WATER BIRDS AND THE OLYMPIC ELK** (See 4-Color #700)

**WAXWORK IN 3-D** (See Blackthorne 3-D Series #55)

**WEASEL PATROL SPECIAL, THE** (Also see Fusion #17)
April, 1989 ($2.00, B&W, one-shot)
Eclipse Comics

| | Good | Fine | N-Mint |
|---|---|---|---|
| 1-Funny animal | .35 | 1.00 | 2.00 |

**WEATHER-BIRD** (See Comics From . . ., Dick Tracy, Free Comics to You . . . & Terry and the Pirates)
1958 - No. 16, July, 1962 (Shoe store giveaway)
International Shoe Co./Western Printing Co.

| | Good | Fine | N-Mint |
|---|---|---|---|
| 1 | .70 | 2.00 | 4.00 |
| 2-16 | .45 | 1.25 | 2.50 |

NOTE: *The numbers are located in the lower bottom panel, pg. 1. All feature a character called Weather-Bird.*

**WEATHER BIRD COMICS** (See Comics From Weather Bird)
1957 (Giveaway)
Weather Bird Shoes

nn-Contains a comic bound with new cover. Several combinations possible; contents determines price (40 - 60 percent of contents).

**WEB OF EVIL**
Nov, 1952 - No. 21, Dec, 1954
Comic Magazines/Quality Comics Group

| | Good | Fine | N-Mint |
|---|---|---|---|
| 1-Used in **SOTI**, pg. 388. Jack Cole-a; morphine use story | 20.00 | 60.00 | 140.00 |
| 2,3-Jack Cole-a | 12.00 | 36.00 | 85.00 |
| 4,6,7-Jack Cole-c/a | 12.00 | 36.00 | 85.00 |
| 5-Electrocution-c; Jack Cole-c/a | 16.00 | 48.00 | 110.00 |
| 8-11-Jack Cole-a | 9.30 | 28.00 | 65.00 |
| 12,13,15,16,19-21 | 4.50 | 14.00 | 32.00 |
| 14-Part Crandall-c; Old Witch swipe | 5.30 | 16.00 | 38.00 |
| 17-Opium drug propaganda story | 4.50 | 14.00 | 32.00 |
| 18-Acid-in-face story | 6.00 | 18.00 | 42.00 |

NOTE: ***Jack Cole** a(2 each)-2, 6, 8, 9. **Ravielli** a-13.*

**WEB OF HORROR** (Magazine)
Dec, 1969 - No. 3, Apr, 1970
Major Magazines

| | Good | Fine | N-Mint |
|---|---|---|---|
| 1-Jeff Jones painted-c; Wrightson-a | 3.00 | 9.00 | 18.00 |
| 2-Jones painted-c; Wrightson-a(2), Kaluta-a | 2.00 | 6.00 | 12.00 |
| 3-Wrightson-c; Brunner, Kaluta, Bruce Jones, Wrightson-a | 2.00 | 6.00 | 12.00 |

**WEB OF MYSTERY**
Feb, 1951 - No. 29, Sept, 1955
Ace Magazines (A. A. Wyn)

| | Good | Fine | N-Mint |
|---|---|---|---|
| 1 | 16.00 | 48.00 | 110.00 |
| 2-Bakerish-a | 9.30 | 28.00 | 65.00 |
| 3-10 | 8.00 | 24.00 | 55.00 |
| 11-18,20-26: 12-John Chilly's 1st cover art. 13-Surrealistic-c. 20-r/The Beyond #1 | 6.50 | 19.00 | 45.00 |
| 19-Reprints Challenge of the Unknown #6 used in N.Y. Legislative Committee | 6.50 | 19.00 | 45.00 |
| 27-Bakerish-a(r-/The Beyond #2); last pre-code issue | 5.70 | 17.00 | 40.00 |
| 28,29: 28-All-r | 3.70 | 11.00 | 26.00 |

NOTE: *This series was to appear as "Creepy Stories," but title was changed before publication.* ***Cameron** a-6, 8, 12, 13, 17-20, 22, 24, 25, 27; c-8, 13, 17. **Colan** a-4. **Palais** a-28r. **Sekowsky** a-1-3, 7, 8, 11, 14, 21, 29. **Tothish** a-by **Bill Discount** #16. #29-all-r, 19-28-partial-r.*

**WEB OF SPIDER-MAN, THE**
Apr, 1985 - Present
Marvel Comics Group

| | Good | Fine | N-Mint |
|---|---|---|---|
| 1-Painted-c (3rd app. black costume?) | 2.00 | 6.00 | 12.00 |
| 2,3 | .85 | 2.50 | 5.00 |
| 4-8: 7-Hulk x-over; Wolverine splash | .70 | 2.00 | 4.00 |
| 9-13: 10-Dominic Fortune guest stars; painted-c | .60 | 1.75 | 3.50 |
| 14-28: 19-Intro Humbug & Solo | .50 | 1.50 | 3.00 |
| 29-Wolverine app. | 1.50 | 4.50 | 9.00 |
| 30-Origin The Rose & Hobgoblin; Punisher & Wolverine cameo in flashback | 1.15 | 3.50 | 7.00 |
| 31-Six part Kraven storyline | 1.15 | 3.50 | 7.00 |
| 32-Kraven storyline continues | 1.15 | 3.50 | 7.00 |
| 33,34 | .25 | .75 | 1.50 |
| 35-49: 38-Hobgoblin app.; begin $1.00-c. 48-Hobgoblin, Kingpin app. | | .60 | 1.20 |
| 50-($1.50, 52 pgs.) | .35 | 1.00 | 2.00 |
| 51-58 | | .55 | 1.10 |
| 59-Cosmic Spidey cont./Spect. Spider-Man | .50 | 1.50 | 3.00 |
| 60-76: 67-Green Goblin app. 69,70-Hulk x-over | | .50 | 1.00 |
| Annual 1 (9/85) | .45 | 1.30 | 2.60 |
| Annual 2 (9/86)-New Mutants; Art Adams-a | 1.15 | 3.50 | 7.00 |
| Annual 3 (10/87) | .35 | 1.10 | 2.20 |
| Annual 4 (10/88, $1.75)-Evolutionary War x-over | .55 | 1.65 | 3.30 |
| Annual 5 (1989, $2.00, 68pgs.)-Atlantis Attacks; Captain Universe by Ditko (p) & Silver Sable stories; F.F. app. | .35 | 1.10 | 2.20 |
| Annual 6 ('90, $2.00, 68pgs.)-Punisher back-up plus Capt. Universe by Ditko; G. Kane-a | .35 | 1.00 | 2.00 |

**WEDDING BELLS**
Feb, 1954 - No. 19, Nov, 1956
Quality Comics Group

| | Good | Fine | N-Mint |
|---|---|---|---|
| 1-Whitney-a | 6.50 | 19.00 | 45.00 |
| 2 | 3.00 | 9.00 | 21.00 |
| 3-9: 8-Last precode (4/55) | 2.00 | 6.00 | 14.00 |
| 10-Ward-a, 9 pgs. | 6.85 | 20.50 | 48.00 |
| 11-14,17 | 1.50 | 4.50 | 10.00 |
| 15-Baker-c | 2.00 | 6.00 | 14.00 |
| 16-Baker-c/a | 3.15 | 9.50 | 22.00 |
| 18,19-Baker-a each | 2.65 | 8.00 | 18.00 |

**WEEKENDER, THE**
V1#4, 1945 - V2#1, 1946 (52 pages)
Rucker Publ. Co.

| | Good | Fine | N-Mint |
|---|---|---|---|
| V1#4(1945) | 10.00 | 30.00 | 70.00 |
| V2#1-36 pgs. comics, 16 in newspaper format with photos; partial Dynamic Comics reprints; 4 pgs. of cels from the Disney film Pinocchio; Little Nemo story by Winsor McCay, Jr.; Jack Cole-a | 12.00 | 36.00 | 85.00 |

**WEEKLY COMIC MAGAZINE**
May 12, 1940 (16 pgs.) (Full Color) (Others exist without super-heroes)
Fox Publications

(1st Version)-8 pg. Blue Beetle story, 7 pg. Patty O'Day story; two copies known to exist. Estimated value. . . . $500.00

(2nd Version)-7 two-pg. adventures of Blue Beetle, Patty O'Day, Yarko, Dr. Fung, Green Mask, Spark Stevens, & Rex Dexter; one copy known to exist Estimated value. . . . $400.00

Discovered with business papers, letters and exploitation material promoting **Weekly Comic Magazine** for use by newspapers in the same manner of **The Spirit** weeklies. Interesting note: these are dated three weeks before the first **Spirit** comic. Letters indicate that samples may have been sent to a few newspapers. These sections were actually 15½x22" pages which will fold down to an approximate 8x10" comic booklet. Other various comic sections were found with the above, but were more like the Sunday comic sections in format.

**WEIRD** (Magazine)
V1#10, 1/66 - V8#6, 12/74; V9#1, 1/75 - V10#3, 1977
(V1-V8: 52 pgs.; V9 on: 68 pgs.)
Eerie Publications

| | Good | Fine | N-Mint |
|---|---|---|---|
| V1#10(#1)-Intro. Morris the Caretaker of Weird (ends V2#10); Burgos-a | 1.50 | 4.50 | 10.00 |
| 11,12 | .70 | 2.00 | 5.00 |

Good Fine N-Mint

V2#1-4(10/67), V3#1(1/68), V2#6(4/68)-V2#7,9,10(12/68), V3#1(2/69)-V3#4 .70 2.00 5.00
V2#8-r/Ditko's 1st story/Fantastic Fears #5 1.00 3.00 7.00
5(12/69)-Rulah reprint; "Rulah" changed to "Pulah;" LSD story reprinted in Horror Tales V4#4, Tales From the Tomb V2#4, & Terror Tales V7#3 .70 2.00 5.00
V4#1-6('70), V5#1-6('71), V6#1-7('72), V7#1-7('73), V8#1-6('74), V9#1-4 (1/75-'76)(no V9#1), V10#1-3('77) .70 2.00 5.00

**WEIRD, THE**
Apr, 1988 - No. 4, July, 1988 ($1.50, color, mini-series)
DC Comics

1-Wrightson-c/a in all .40 1.25 2.50
2-4 .35 1.00 2.00

**WEIRD ADVENTURES**
May-June, 1951 - No. 3, Sept-Oct, 1951
P. L. Publishing Co. (Canada)

1-"The She-Wolf Killer" by Matt Baker, 6 pgs. 15.00 45.00 105.00
2-Bondage/hypodermic panel 11.50 34.00 80.00
3-Male bondage/torture-c; severed head story 10.00 30.00 70.00

**WEIRD ADVENTURES**
No. 10, July-Aug, 1951
Ziff-Davis Publishing Co.

10-Painted-c 13.00 40.00 90.00

**WEIRD CHILLS**
July, 1954 - No. 3, Nov, 1954
Key Publications

1-Wolverton-a r-/Weird Mysteries No. 4; blood transfusion-c by Baily 25.00 75.00 175.00
2-Extremely violent injury to eye-c 24.00 73.00 170.00
3-Bondage E.C. swipe-c 13.00 40.00 90.00

**WEIRD COMICS**
April, 1940 - No. 20, Jan, 1942
Fox Features Syndicate

1-The Birdman, Thor, God of Thunder (ends #5), The Sorceress of Zoom, Blast Bennett, Typhon, Voodoo Man, & Dr. Mortal begin; Fine bondage-c 118.00 355.00 825.00
2-Lou Fine-c 57.00 171.00 400.00
3,4: 3-Simon-c. 4-Torture-c 40.00 120.00 280.00
5-Intro. Dart & sidekick Ace (ends #20); bondage/hypo-c 43.00 130.00 300.00
6,7-Dynamite Thor app. in each 39.00 118.00 275.00
8-Dynamo, the Eagle (1st app.) & sidekick Buddy & Marga, the Panther Woman begin 39.00 118.00 275.00
9 32.00 95.00 225.00
10-Navy Jones app. 32.00 95.00 225.00
11-16: 16-Flag-c 26.00 77.00 180.00
17-Origin The Black Rider 26.00 77.00 180.00
18-20: 20-Origin The Rapier; Swoop Curtis app; Churchill, Hitler-c 26.00 77.00 180.00

**WEIRD FANTASY** (Formerly A Moon, A Girl, Romance; becomes Weird Science-Fantasy #23 on)
No. 13, May-June, 1950 - No. 22, Nov-Dec, 1953
E. C. Comics

13(#1) (1950) 93.00 280.00 650.00
14-Necronomicon story; atomic explosion-c 51.00 152.00 355.00
15,16: 16-Used in **SOTI**, pg. 144 42.00 125.00 290.00
17 (1951) 35.00 105.00 245.00
6-10 26.00 77.00 180.00
11-13 (1952) 19.00 58.00 135.00
14-Frazetta/Williamson(1st team-up at E.C.)/Krenkel-a, 7 pgs.; Orlando draws E.C. staff 34.00 100.00 235.00

Good Fine N-Mint

15-Williamson/Evans-a(3), 4,3,&7 pgs. 22.00 65.00 150.00
16-19-Williamson/Krenkel-a in all. 18-Williamson/Feldstein-c 19.00 58.00 135.00
20-Frazetta/Williamson-a, 7 pgs. 22.00 65.00 150.00
21-Frazetta/Williamson-c & Williamson/Krenkel-a 34.00 100.00 235.00
22-Bradbury adaptation 14.00 43.00 100.00

NOTE: ***Crandall** a-22. **Elder** a-17. **Feldstein** a-13(#1)-8; c-13(#1)-18 (#18 w/**Williamson**), 20. **Kamen** a-13(#1)-16, 18-22. **Krigstein** a-22. **Kurtzman** a-13(#1)-17(#5), 6. **Orlando** a-9-22 (2 stories in #16); c-19, 22. **Severin/Elder** a-18-21. **Wood** a-13(#1)-14, 17(2 stories ea. in #10-13). Canadian reprints exist; see Table of Contents.*

**WEIRD HORRORS** (Nightmare #10 on)
June, 1952 - No. 9, Oct, 1953
St. John Publishing Co.

1-Tuska-a 16.00 48.00 110.00
2,3: 3-Hashish story 8.00 24.00 55.00
4,5 7.00 21.00 50.00
6-Ekgren-c 14.00 43.00 100.00
7-Ekgren-c; Kubert, Cameron-a 16.00 48.00 110.00
8,9-Kubert-c/a 11.00 32.00 75.00

NOTE: ***Cameron** a-7, 9. **Finesque** a-1-5. **Morisi** a-3. Bondage c-8.*

**WEIRD MYSTERIES**
Oct, 1952 - No. 12, Sept, 1954
Gillmore Publications

1-Partial Wolverton-c swiped from splash page "Flight to the Future" in Weird Tales of the Future #2; "Eternity" has an Ingels swipe 23.00 70.00 160.00
2-"Robot Woman" by Wolverton; Bernard Baily-c-reprinted in Mister Mystery #18; acid in face panel 41.00 122.00 285.00
3,6: Both have decapitation-c 14.00 43.00 100.00
4-"The Man Who Never Smiled" (3 pgs.) by Wolverton; B. Baily skull-c 32.00 95.00 225.00
5-Wolverton story "Swamp Monster," 6 pgs. 36.00 107.00 250.00
7-Used in **SOTI**, illo-"Indeed" & illo-"Sex and blood" 24.00 73.00 170.00
8-Wolverton-c panel reprint/No. 5; used in a 1954 Readers Digest anti-comics article by T. E. Murphy entitled "For the Kiddies to Read" 14.00 43.00 100.00
9-Excessive violence, gore & torture 13.00 40.00 90.00
10-Silhouetted nudity panel 11.50 34.00 80.00
11,12 8.50 25.50 60.00

NOTE: ***Baily** c-2-8, 10-12.*

**WEIRD MYSTERIES** (Magazine)
Mar-Apr, 1959 (68 pages) (35 cents) (B&W)
Pastime Publications

1-Torres-a; E. C. swipe from Tales From the Crypt #46 by Tuska-"The Ragman" 2.65 8.00 18.00

**WEIRD MYSTERY TALES** (See DC 100 Page Super Spectacular)

**WEIRD MYSTERY TALES** (See Cancelled Comic Cavalcade)
Jul-Aug, 1972 - No. 24, Nov, 1975
National Periodical Publications

1-Kirby-a .50 1.00
2-24 .20 .40

NOTE: ***Alcala** a-5, 10, 13, 14. **Aparo** c-4. **Bolle** a-8. **Howard** a-4. **Kaluta** a-24; c-1. **G. Kane** a-10. **Kirby** a-1, 2p, 3p. **Nino** a-5, 6, 9, 13, 16, 21. **Redondo** a-9. **Starlin** a-3, 4. **Wood** a-23. **Wrightson** c-21.*

**WEIRD ROMANCE**
Feb, 1988 ($2.00, B&W)
Eclipse Comics

1-Lou Cameron-r(2) .35 1.00 2.00

*Weird Comics #10, © FOX*

*Weird Fantasy #16 (#4), © WMG*

*Weird Horrors #9, © STJ*

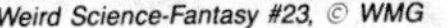
Weird Science-Fantasy #23, © WMG

Weird Tales of the Future #8, © Aragon

Weird Thrillers #2, © Z-D

**WEIRD SCIENCE** (Formerly Saddle Romances) (Becomes Weird Science-Fantasy #23 on)
No. 12, May-June, 1950 - No. 22, Nov-Dec, 1953
E. C. Comics

| | Good | Fine | N-Mint |
|---|---|---|---|
| 12(#1) (1950) | 97.00 | 290.00 | 675.00 |
| 13 | 54.00 | 163.00 | 380.00 |
| 14,15 (1950) | 49.00 | 145.00 | 340.00 |
| 5-10: 5-Atomic explosion-c | 30.00 | 90.00 | 210.00 |
| 11-14 (1952) | 19.00 | 58.00 | 135.00 |
| 15-18-Williamson/Krenkel-a in each; 15-Williamson-a. 17-Used in **POP**, pgs. 81,82 | 22.00 | 65.00 | 155.00 |
| 19,20-Williamson/Frazetta-a, 7 pgs each. 19-Used in **SOTI**, illo-"A young girl on her wedding night stabs her sleeping husband to death with a hatpin. . ." | 30.00 | 90.00 | 210.00 |
| 21-Williamson/Frazetta-a, 6 pgs.; Wood draws E.C. staff; Gaines & Feldstein app. in story | 30.00 | 90.00 | 210.00 |
| 22-Williamson/Frazetta/Krenkel-a, 8 pgs.; Wood draws himself in his story - last pg. & panel | 30.00 | 90.00 | 210.00 |

NOTE: *__Elder__ a-14, 19. __Evans__ a-22. __Feldstein__ a-12(#1)-8; c-12(#1)-8, 11. __Ingels__ a-15. __Kamen__ a-12(#1)-13, 15-18, 20, 21. __Kurtzman__ a-12(#1)-7. __Orlando__ a-10-22. __Wood__ a-12(#1), 13(#2), 5-22 (#9, 10, 12, 13 all have 2 __Wood__ stories); c-9, 10, 12-22. Canadian reprints exist; see Table of Contents.*

**WEIRD SCIENCE**
Sept, 1990 - Present ($1.95, color, 68 pgs.)(#3 on: $2.00)
Gladstone Publishing

| | Good | Fine | N-Mint |
|---|---|---|---|
| 1-Wood-c(r); all reprints in each | .40 | 1.25 | 2.50 |
| 2-5: 2-4-Wood-c(r) | .35 | 1.00 | 2.00 |

**WEIRD SCIENCE-FANTASY** (Formerly Weird Science & Weird Fantasy) (Becomes Incredible Science Fiction #30)
No. 23 Mar, 1954 - No. 29, May-June, 1955
E. C. Comics

| | Good | Fine | N-Mint |
|---|---|---|---|
| 23-Williamson & Wood-a | 22.00 | 65.00 | 150.00 |
| 24-Williamson & Wood-a; Harlan Ellison's 1st professional story, 'Upheaval!,' later adapted into a short story as 'Mealtime,' and then into a TV episode of Voyage to the Bottom of the Sea as 'The Price of Doom' | 22.00 | 65.00 | 150.00 |
| 25-Williamson-c; Williamson/Torres/Krenkel-a plus Wood-a | 26.00 | 77.00 | 180.00 |
| 26-Flying Saucer Report; Wood, Crandall, Orlando-a | 21.00 | 62.00 | 145.00 |
| 27 | 22.00 | 65.00 | 150.00 |
| 28-Williamson/Krenkel/Torres-a; Wood-a | 24.00 | 73.00 | 170.00 |
| 29-Frazetta-c; Williamson/Krenkel & Wood-a | 44.00 | 133.00 | 310.00 |

NOTE: *__Crandall__ a-26, 27, 29. __Evans__ a-26. __Feldstein__ c-24, 26, 28. __Kamen__ a-27, 28. __Krigstein__ a-23-25. __Orlando__ a-in all. __Wood__ a-in all; c-23, 27.*

**WEIRD SCIENCE-FANTASY ANNUAL**
1952, 1953 (Sold thru the E. C. office & on the stands in some major cities) (25 cents, 132 pgs.)
E. C. Comics

| | Good | Fine | N-Mint |
|---|---|---|---|
| 1952-Feldstein-c | 115.00 | 345.00 | 800.00 |
| 1953 | 69.00 | 210.00 | 485.00 |

NOTE: *The 1952 annual contains books cover-dated in 1951 & 1952, and the 1953 annual from 1952 & 1953. Contents of each annual may vary in same year.*

**WEIRD SUSPENSE**
Feb, 1975 - No. 3, July, 1975
Atlas/Seaboard Publ.

| | Good | Fine | N-Mint |
|---|---|---|---|
| 1-3: 1-Tarantula begins. 3-Buckler-c | | .30 | .60 |

**WEIRD SUSPENSE STORIES** (Canadian reprint of Crime SuspenStories #1-3; see Table of Contents)

**WEIRD TALES OF THE FUTURE**
March, 1952 - No. 8, July, 1953
S.P.M. Publ. No. 1-4/Aragon Publ. No. 5-8

| | Good | Fine | N-Mint |
|---|---|---|---|
| 1-Andru-a(2) | 29.00 | 85.00 | 200.00 |
| 2,3-Wolverton-c/a(3) each. 2-"Jumpin Jupiter" satire by Wolverton begins, ends #5 | 50.00 | 150.00 | 350.00 |
| 4-"Jumpin Jupiter" satire by Wolverton; partial Wolverton-c | 27.00 | 80.00 | 185.00 |
| 5-Wolverton-c/a(2) | 50.00 | 150.00 | 350.00 |
| 6-Bernard Baily-c | 15.00 | 45.00 | 105.00 |
| 7-"The Mind Movers" from the art to Wolverton's "Brain Bats of Venus" from Mr. Mystery #7 which was cut apart, pasted up, partially redrawn, and rewritten by Harry Kantor, the editor; Bernard Baily-c | 27.00 | 80.00 | 185.00 |
| 8-Reprints Weird Mysteries #1(10/52) minus cover; gory cover showing heart ripped out | 15.00 | 45.00 | 105.00 |

**WEIRD TALES OF THE MACABRE** (Magazine)
Jan, 1975 - No. 2, Mar, 1975 (B&W) (75 cents)
Atlas/Seaboard Publ.

| | Good | Fine | N-Mint |
|---|---|---|---|
| 1-Jeff Jones painted-c | .35 | 1.00 | 2.00 |
| 2-Boris Vallejo painted-c, Severin-a | .25 | .80 | 1.60 |

**WEIRD TERROR** (Also see Horrific)
Sept, 1952 - No. 13, Sept, 1954
Allen Hardy Associates (Comic Media)

| | Good | Fine | N-Mint |
|---|---|---|---|
| 1-"Portrait of Death," adapted from Lovecraft's "Pickman's Model;" lingerie panels, Hitler story | 14.00 | 43.00 | 100.00 |
| 2-Text on Marquis DeSade, Torture, Demonology, & St. Elmo's Fire | 8.50 | 25.50 | 60.00 |
| 3-Extreme violence, whipping, torture; article on sin eating, dowsing | 7.00 | 21.00 | 50.00 |
| 4-Dismemberment, decapitation, article on human flesh for sale, Devil, whipping | 11.00 | 32.00 | 75.00 |
| 5-Article on body snatching, mutilation; cannibalism story | 7.00 | 21.00 | 50.00 |
| 6-Dismemberment, decapitation, man hit by lightning | 11.00 | 32.00 | 75.00 |
| 7,9,10 | 7.00 | 21.00 | 50.00 |
| 8-Decapitation story; Ambrose Bierce adapt. | 9.30 | 28.00 | 65.00 |
| 11-End of the world story with atomic blast panels; Tothish-a by Bill Discount | 9.30 | 28.00 | 65.00 |
| 12-Discount-a | 5.70 | 17.00 | 40.00 |
| 13-Severed head panels | 6.50 | 19.00 | 45.00 |

NOTE: *__Don Heck__ c/a-most issues. __Landau__ a-6. __Morisi__ a-2-5, 7, 9, 12. __Palais__ a-1, 5, 6, 8(2), 10, 12. __Powell__ a-10. __Ravielli__ a-11, 20.*

**WEIRD THRILLERS**
Sept-Oct, 1951 - No. 5, Oct-Nov, 1952 (#2-4: painted-c)
Ziff-Davis Publ. Co. (Approved Comics)

| | Good | Fine | N-Mint |
|---|---|---|---|
| 1-Rondo Hatton photo-c | 20.00 | 60.00 | 140.00 |
| 2-Toth, Anderson, Colan-a | 15.00 | 45.00 | 105.00 |
| 3-Two Powell, Tuska-a | 11.50 | 34.00 | 80.00 |
| 4-Kubert, Tuska-a | 13.00 | 40.00 | 90.00 |
| 5-Powell-a | 11.50 | 34.00 | 80.00 |

NOTE: *__Anderson__ a-2. __Roussos__ a-4. #2, 3 reprinted in Nightmare #10 & 13; #4, 5 r-/in Amazing Ghost Stories #16 & #15.*

**WEIRD WAR TALES**
Sept-Oct, 1971 - No. 124, June, 1983
National Periodical Publications/DC Comics

| | Good | Fine | N-Mint |
|---|---|---|---|
| 1 | .35 | 1.00 | 2.00 |
| 2-7,9,10: 5,6,10-Toth-a. 7-Krigstein-a | | .50 | 1.00 |
| 8-Neal Adams-c/a(i) | .35 | 1.00 | 2.00 |
| 11-50: 36-Crandall, Kubert r-/No.2 | | .30 | .60 |
| 51-63,65-67,69-124: 67-69-(44 pgs.). 69-Sci-Fic issue. 93-Intro/origin Creature Commandos. 101-Intro/origin G.I. Robot. 111-Creature Commandos & G.I. Robot team-ups begin | | .25 | .50 |
| 64,68-Miller-a | | .40 | .80 |

NOTE: *__Austin__ a-51i, 52i. __Bailey__ a-21, 33. __Chaykin__ a-82. __Crandall__ a-2, 36r. __Ditko__ a-46p, 49p, 95, 99, 104-106. __Drucker__ a-2, 3. __Evans__ a-17, 22, 35, 46, 74; c-73, 74, 82, 83, 85. __Giffen__ a-124p. __Grell__ a-67. __Heath__ a-3, 59. __Howard__ a-53i. __Kaluta__ c-12. __Gil Kane__ c-115, 116, 118. __Kubert__ a-1-4, 7, 36r, 68, 69; c-51, 60, 62-69, 72, 75-81, 84, 86-88, 90-96, 100, 103,*

*104, 106, 107, 123, 124.* ***Lopez*** *a-108.* ***Maurer*** *a-5.* ***Meskin*** *a-4r.* ***Morrow*** *c-54.* ***Newton*** *a-82p, 122p.* ***Redondo*** *a-10, 13, 30, 38, 42, 52.* ***Rogers*** *a-51p, 52p.* ***Sekowsky*** *a-75p.* ***Simonson*** *a-10, 72.* ***Sparling*** *a-86p.* ***Spiegle*** *a-96, 97, 107, 109-112.* ***Starlin*** *c-89.* ***Staton*** *a-106p; c-108p.* ***Sutton*** *a-66, 87, 91, 92, 103.* ***Tuska*** *a-103p, 122p.*

**WEIRD WESTERN TALES** (Formerly All-Star Western)
No. 12, June-July, 1972 - No. 70, Aug, 1980 (No. 12: 52 pgs.)
National Periodical Publications/DC Comics

| | Good | Fine | N-Mint |
|---|---|---|---|
| 12-Bat Lash, Pow Wow Smith reprints; El Diablo by Neal Adams/ Wrightson | .50 | 1.50 | 3.00 |
| 13,15-Neal Adams-a. 15-N. Adams-c | .50 | 1.50 | 3.00 |
| 14,29: 14-Toth-a. 29-Origin Jonah Hex | .25 | .75 | 1.50 |
| 16-28,30-70: 39-Origin/1st app. Scalphunter | | .35 | .70 |

NOTE: ***Evans*** *inks-39-48; c-39i, 40, 47.* ***G. Kane*** *a-15.* ***Kubert*** *c-12, 33.* ***Starlin*** *c-44, 45.* ***Wildey*** *a-26. 48 & 49 are 44 pages.*

**WEIRD WONDER TALES**
Dec, 1973 - No. 22, May, 1977
Marvel Comics Group

| | Good | Fine | N-Mint |
|---|---|---|---|
| 1-Wolverton-r/Mystic #6 (Eye of Doom) | | .50 | 1.00 |
| 2-22: 16-18-Venus r-by Everett/Venus #19,18 & 17. 19-22-Dr. Druid (Droom)-r | | .30 | .60 |

NOTE: *All 1950s & early 1960s reprints.* ***Check*** *r-1.* ***Colan*** *r-17.* ***Ditko*** *r-4, 5, 10-13, 19-21.* ***Drucker*** *r-12, 20.* ***Everett*** *r-3(Spellbound #16), 6(Astonishing #10), 9(Adv. Into Mystery #5).* ***Kirby*** *r-6, 11, 13, 16-22; c-17, 19, 20.* ***Krigstein*** *r-19.* ***Kubert*** *r-22.* ***Maneely*** *r-8.* ***Mooney*** *r-7p.* ***Powell*** *r-3, 7.* ***Torres*** *r-7.* ***Wildey*** *r-2, 7.*

**WEIRD WORLDS** (See Adventures Into. . .)

**WEIRD WORLDS** (Magazine)
V1#10(12/70), V2#1(2/71) - No. 4, Aug, 1971 (52 pgs.)
Eerie Publications

| | Good | Fine | N-Mint |
|---|---|---|---|
| V1#10 | .85 | 2.60 | 6.00 |
| V2#1-4 | .70 | 2.00 | 4.00 |

**WEIRD WORLDS**
Aug-Sept, 1972 - No. 9, Jan-Feb, 1974; No. 10, Oct-Nov, 1974
National Periodical Publications

| | Good | Fine | N-Mint |
|---|---|---|---|
| 1-Edgar Rice Burrough's John Carter Warlord of Mars & David Innes begin (1st Marvel app.); Kubert-c | .35 | 1.00 | 2.00 |
| 2-7: 7-Last John Carter | | .50 | 1.00 |
| 8-10: 8-Iron Wolf begins by Chaykin (1st app?) | | .40 | .80 |

NOTE: ***Neal Adams*** *a-2i, 3i. John Carter by* ***Anderson****-No. 1-3.* ***Chaykin*** *c-7, 8.* ***Kaluta*** *a-4; c-4-6, 10.* ***Orlando*** *a-4i; c-2-4.* ***Wrightson*** *a-2i.*

**WELCOME BACK, KOTTER** (TV) (See Limited Collectors' Ed. #57)
Nov, 1976 - No. 10, Mar-Apr, 1978
National Periodical Publications/DC Comics

| | Good | Fine | N-Mint |
|---|---|---|---|
| 1-Sparling-a(p) | | .50 | 1.00 |
| 2-10: 3-Estrada-a | | .35 | .70 |

**WELCOME SANTA** (See March of Comics #63,183)

**WELLS FARGO** (See Tales of. . .)

**WENDY DIGEST**
Oct, 1990 - No. 2, Nov, 1990 ($1.75, digest size)
Harvey Comics

| | Good | Fine | N-Mint |
|---|---|---|---|
| 1,2 | .30 | .90 | 1.80 |

**WENDY IN 3-D** (See Blackthorne 3-D Series #70)

**WENDY PARKER COMICS**
July, 1953 - No. 8, July, 1954
Atlas Comics (OMC)

| | Good | Fine | N-Mint |
|---|---|---|---|
| 1 | 4.30 | 13.00 | 30.00 |
| 2 | 2.30 | 7.00 | 16.00 |
| 3-8 | 1.70 | 5.00 | 12.00 |

**WENDY, THE GOOD LITTLE WITCH** (TV)
8/60 - #82, 11/73; #83, 8/74 - #93, 4/76; #94, 9/90 - #97, 12/90
Harvey Publications

| | Good | Fine | N-Mint |
|---|---|---|---|
| 1-Casper the Ghost begins | 8.35 | 25.00 | 50.00 |
| 2 | 4.00 | 12.00 | 24.00 |
| 3-5 | 3.35 | 10.00 | 20.00 |
| 6-10 | 2.50 | 7.50 | 15.00 |
| 11-20 | 1.70 | 5.00 | 10.00 |
| 21-30 | .85 | 2.50 | 5.00 |
| 31-50 | .50 | 1.50 | 3.00 |
| 51-69 | .40 | 1.20 | 2.40 |
| 70-74: All 52 pg. Giants | .50 | 1.50 | 3.00 |
| 75-93 | .25 | .75 | 1.50 |
| 94-97 (1990, $1.00-c) | | .50 | 1.00 |

*(See Casper the Friendly Ghost #20 & Harvey Hits #7, 16, 21, 23, 27, 30, 33)*

**WENDY WITCH WORLD**
10/61; No. 2, 9/62 - No. 52, 12/73; No. 53, 9/74
Harvey Publications

| | Good | Fine | N-Mint |
|---|---|---|---|
| 1: 68 pg. Giants begin | 5.35 | 16.00 | 32.00 |
| 2-5 | 2.75 | 8.00 | 16.00 |
| 6-10 | 1.70 | 5.00 | 10.00 |
| 11-20 | 1.00 | 3.00 | 6.00 |
| 21-30 | .50 | 1.50 | 3.00 |
| 31-39: Last 68 pg. issue | .35 | 1.00 | 2.00 |
| 40-45: 52 pg. issues | .25 | .75 | 1.50 |
| 46-53 | | .60 | 1.20 |

**WEREWOLF** (Super Hero)
Dec, 1966 - No. 3, April, 1967
Dell Publishing Co.

| | Good | Fine | N-Mint |
|---|---|---|---|
| 1 | .50 | 1.50 | 3.00 |
| 2,3 | .25 | .75 | 1.50 |

**WEREWOLF BY NIGHT** (See Giant-Size. . ., Marvel Spotlight #2-4 & Power Record Comics)
Sept, 1972 - No. 43, Mar, 1977
Marvel Comics Group

| | Good | Fine | N-Mint |
|---|---|---|---|
| 1-Ploog-a-cont'd. from Marvel Spotlight #4 | 1.00 | 3.00 | 7.00 |
| 2-31: 15-New origin Werewolf | .25 | .75 | 1.50 |
| 32-Origin & 1st app. Moon Knight | 2.65 | 8.00 | 18.00 |
| 33-2nd app. Moon Knight | 1.30 | 4.00 | 9.00 |
| 34-36,38-43: 35-Starlin/Wrightson-c | .25 | .75 | 1.50 |
| 37-Moon Knight app; part Wrightson-c | 1.15 | 3.50 | 8.00 |

NOTE: ***Bolle*** *a-6i.* ***G. Kane*** *a-11p, 12p; c-21, 22, 24-30, 34p.* ***Mooney*** *a-7i.* ***Ploog*** *1-4p, 5, 6p, 7p, 13-16p; c-5-8, 13-16.* ***Reinman*** *a-8i.* ***Sutton*** *a(i)-9, 11, 16, 35.*

**WEREWOLF IN 3-D** (See Blackthorne 3-D Series #61)

**WEREWOLVES & VAMPIRES** (Magazine)
1962 (One Shot)
Charlton Comics

| | Good | Fine | N-Mint |
|---|---|---|---|
| 1 | 3.60 | 11.00 | 25.00 |

**WEST COAST AVENGERS**
Sept, 1984 - No. 4, Dec, 1984 (Mini-series; Mando paper)
Marvel Comics Group

| | Good | Fine | N-Mint |
|---|---|---|---|
| 1-Hawkeye, Iron Man, Mockingbird, Tigra | 1.15 | 3.50 | 7.00 |
| 2-4 | .75 | 2.25 | 4.50 |

**WEST COAST AVENGERS** (Becomes Avengers West Coast #48 on)
Oct, 1985 - No. 47, Aug, 1989 (On-going series)
Marvel Comics Group

| | Good | Fine | N-Mint |
|---|---|---|---|
| V2#1 | 1.00 | 3.00 | 6.00 |
| 2,3 | .70 | 2.00 | 4.00 |
| 4-6 | .50 | 1.50 | 3.00 |
| 7-10 | .40 | 1.25 | 2.50 |
| 11-20 | .35 | 1.10 | 2.20 |
| 21-30 | .25 | .75 | 1.50 |
| 31-41 | | .60 | 1.20 |
| 42-Byrne-a(p)/scripts begin | .35 | 1.10 | 2.20 |

*Weird Worlds #1, © ERB*

*Wendy, the Good Little Witch #4, © Paramount*

*Werewolf by Night #13, © MEG*

Western Adventures Comics #1, © ACE

Western Comics #8, © DC

Western Fighters #6, © HILL

Good / Fine / N-Mint

43-47: 46,46-Byrne-c. 46-1st app. Great Lakes Avengers — .55 1.10
Annual 1 (10/86) — .35 1.10 2.20
Annual 2 (9/87) — .35 1.00 2.00
Annual 3 (10/88, $1.75)-Evolutionary War app. — .45 1.40 2.80
Annual V2#4 ('89, $2.00, 68 pgs.)-Atlantis Attacks; Byrne/Austin-a — .35 1.10 2.20
Annual V2#5 ('90, $2.00, 68 pgs.) — .35 1.00 2.00

**WESTERN ACTION**
No. 7, 1964
I. W. Enterprises

7-Reprint — .30 .90 1.80

**WESTERN ACTION**
February, 1975
Atlas/Seaboard Publ.

1-Kid Cody by Wildey & The Comanche Kid stories; intro. The Renegade — .30 .60

**WESTERN ACTION THRILLERS**
April, 1937 (100 pages)(Square binding)
Dell Publishers

1-Buffalo Bill, The Texas Kid, Laramie Joe, Two-Gun Thompson, & Wild West Bill app. — 43.00 130.00 300.00

**WESTERN ADVENTURES COMICS** (Western Love Trails #7 on)
Oct, 1948 - No. 6, Aug, 1949
Ace Magazines

nn(#1)-Sheriff Sal, The Cross-Draw Kid, Sam Bass begin — 11.00 32.00 75.00
nn(#2)(12/48) — 5.70 17.00 40.00
nn(#3)(2/49)-Used in **SOTI**, pgs. 30,31 — 6.50 19.00 45.00
4-6 — 4.50 14.00 32.00

**WESTERN BANDITS**
1952 (Painted-c)
Avon Periodicals

1-Butch Cassidy, The Daltons by Larsen; Kinstler-a; c-part r-/paperback Avon Western Novel #1 — 8.50 25.50 60.00

**WESTERN BANDIT TRAILS** (See Approved Comics)
Jan, 1949 - No. 3, July, 1949
St. John Publishing Co.

1-Tuska-a; Baker-c; Blue Monk, Ventrilo app. — 11.00 32.00 75.00
2-Baker-c — 7.00 21.00 50.00
3-Baker-c/a, Tuska-a — 8.50 25.50 60.00

**WESTERN COMICS** (See Super DC Giant #15)
Jan-Feb, 1948 - No. 85, Jan-Feb, 1961 (1-27: 52pgs.)
National Periodical Publications

1-The Wyoming Kid & his horse Racer, The Vigilante (Meskin-a), The Cowboy Marshal, Rodeo Rick begin — 36.00 107.00 250.00
2 — 20.00 60.00 140.00
3,4-Last Vigilante — 16.00 48.00 110.00
5-Nighthawk & his horse Nightwind begin (not in #6); Captain Tootsie by Beck — 14.00 43.00 100.00
6,7,9,10 — 11.00 32.00 75.00
8-Origin Wyoming Kid; 2pg. pin-ups of rodeo queens — 14.00 43.00 100.00
11-20 — 8.50 25.50 60.00
21-40: 27-Last 52 pgs. — 6.00 18.00 42.00
41-49: Last precode (2/55). 43-Pow Wow Smith begins, ends #85 — 5.00 15.00 35.00
50-60 — 5.00 15.00 35.00
61-85-Last Wyoming Kid. 77-Origin Matt Savage Trail Boss. 82-1st app. Fleetfoot, Pow Wow's girlfriend — 3.00 9.00 21.00

NOTE: ***G. Kane, Infantino*** *art in most.* ***Meskin*** *a-1-4.* ***Moreira*** *a-35, 37, 39.* ***Post*** *a-3-5.*

**WESTERN CRIME BUSTERS**
Sept, 1950 - No. 10, Mar-Apr, 1952
Trojan Magazines

Good / Fine / N-Mint

1-Six-Gun Smith, Wilma West, K-Bar-Kate, & Fighting Bob Dale begin; headlight-a — 13.00 40.00 90.00
2 — 8.00 24.00 55.00
3-5: 3-Myron Fass-c — 7.00 21.00 50.00
6-Wood-a — 20.00 60.00 140.00
7-Six-Gun Smith by Wood — 20.00 60.00 140.00
8 — 6.50 19.00 45.00
9-Tex Gordon & Wilma West by Wood; Lariat Lucy app. — 20.00 60.00 140.00
10-Wood-a — 19.00 56.00 130.00

**WESTERN CRIME CASES** (The Outlaws #10 on?)
No. 9, Dec, 1951
Star Publications

9-White Rider & Super Horse; L. B. Cole-c — 3.60 11.00 25.00

**WESTERN DESPERADO COMICS** (Formerly Slam Bang Comics)
No. 8, 1940 (Oct.?)
Fawcett Publications

8-(Rare) — 35.00 105.00 245.00

**WESTERNER, THE** (Wild Bill Pecos)
No. 14, June, 1948 - No. 41, Dec, 1951 (#14-31: 52 pgs.)
"Wanted" Comic Group/Toytown/Patches

14 — 5.70 17.00 40.00
15-17,19-21: 19-Meskin-a — 2.85 8.50 20.00
18,22-25-Krigstein-a — 4.50 14.00 32.00
26(4/50)-Origin & 1st app. Calamity Kate, series ends #32; Krigstein-a — 5.70 17.00 40.00
27-Krigstein-a(2) — 6.50 19.00 45.00
28-41: 33-Quest app. 37-Lobo, the Wolf Boy begins — 2.00 6.00 14.00

NOTE: ***Mort Lawrence*** *c-19, 27.* ***Leav*** *c-14, 31.* ***Syd Shores*** *c-35, 40.*

**WESTERNER, THE**
1964
Super Comics

Super Reprint #15,16(Crack West. #65), 17 — .25 .75 1.50

**WESTERN FIGHTERS**
Apr-May, 1948 - V4#7, Mar-Apr, 1953 (#1-V3#2: 52 pgs.)
Hillman Periodicals/Star Publ.

V1#1-Simon & Kirby-c — 14.00 43.00 100.00
2-Kirby-a(p)? — 5.00 15.00 35.00
3-Fuje-c — 4.00 12.00 28.00
4-Krigstein, Ingels, Fuje-a — 5.00 15.00 35.00
5,6,8,9,12 — 3.15 9.50 22.00
7,10-Krigstein-a — 5.00 15.00 35.00
11-Williamson/Frazetta-a — 16.00 48.00 110.00
V2#1-Krigstein-a — 5.00 15.00 35.00
2-12: 4-Berg-a — 2.00 6.00 14.00
V3#1-11 — 1.70 5.00 12.00
12-Krigstein-a — 4.30 13.00 30.00
V4#1,4-7 — 1.70 5.00 12.00
2,3-Krigstein-a — 4.00 12.00 28.00
3-D 1(12/53, Star Publ.)-L. B. Cole-c — 20.00 60.00 140.00

NOTE: ***Kinstlerish*** *a-V2#6, 8, 9, 12; V3#2, 5-7, 11, 12; V4#1(plus cover).* ***McWilliams*** *a-11.* ***Powell*** *a-V2#2.* ***Reinman*** *a-1-11.* ***Rowich*** *c-6i.*

**WESTERN FRONTIER**
Apr-May, 1951 - No. 7, 1952
P. L. Publishers

1 — 5.00 15.00 35.00
2 — 3.00 9.00 21.00
3-7 — 2.15 6.50 15.00

**WESTERN GUNFIGHTERS** (1st Series) (Apache Kid #11-19)
No. 20, June, 1956 - No. 27, Aug, 1957
Atlas Comics (CPS)

| | Good | Fine | N-Mint |
|---|---|---|---|
| 20 | 5.00 | 15.00 | 35.00 |
| 21,25-27 | 3.00 | 9.00 | 21.00 |
| 22-Wood & Powell-a | 8.50 | 25.50 | 60.00 |
| 23-Williamson-a | 5.70 | 17.00 | 40.00 |
| 24-Toth-a | 5.00 | 15.00 | 35.00 |

NOTE: ***Colan** a-27. **Heath** a-25. **Maneely** a-25; c-22, 23, 25. **Pakula** a-23. **Severin** c-27. **Woodbridge** a-27.*

**WESTERN GUNFIGHTERS** (2nd Series)
Aug, 1970 - No. 33, Nov, 1975 (#1-6: 25 cents, 68 pgs.; #7: 52 pgs.)
Marvel Comics Group

| | Good | Fine | N-Mint |
|---|---|---|---|
| 1-Ghost Rider begins; Fort Rango, Renegades & Gunhawk app. | .35 | 1.00 | 2.00 |
| 2-33: 2-Origin Nightwind (Apache Kid's horse). 7-Origin Ghost Rider retold. 10-Origin Black Rider. 12-Origin Matt Slade | | .50 | 1.00 |

NOTE: ***Baker** r-2, 3. **Colan** r-2. **Drucker** r-3. **Everett** a-6i. **G. Kane** c-29, 31. **Kirby** a-1p(r), 10, 11. **Kubert** r-2. **Maneely** r-2, 10. **Morrow** r-29. **Severin** c-10. **Barry Smith** a-4. **Steranko** c-14. **Sutton** a-1, 2i, 3, 4. **Torres** r-26('57). **Wildey** r-8, 9. **Williamson** r-2, 18. **Woodbridge** r-27('57). Renegades in #4, 5; Ghost Rider-#1-7.*

**WESTERN HEARTS**
Dec, 1949 - No. 10, Mar, 1952
Standard Comics

| | Good | Fine | N-Mint |
|---|---|---|---|
| 1-Severin-a; Whip Wilson & Reno Browne photo-c | 8.50 | 25.50 | 60.00 |
| 2-Williamson/Frazetta-a, 2 pgs; photo-c | 12.00 | 36.00 | 85.00 |
| 3 | 3.60 | 11.00 | 25.00 |
| 4-7,10-Severin & Elder, Al Carreno-a. 5,6-Photo-c | 3.60 | 11.00 | 25.00 |
| 8-Randolph Scott/Janis Carter photo-c from 'Santa Fe;' Severin & Elder-a | 4.50 | 14.00 | 32.00 |
| 9-Whip Wilson & Reno Browne photo-c; Severin & Elder-a | 5.00 | 15.00 | 35.00 |

**WESTERN HERO** (Wow Comics #1-69; Real Western Hero #70-75)
No. 76, Mar, 1949 - No. 112, Mar, 1952
Fawcett Publications

| | Good | Fine | N-Mint |
|---|---|---|---|
| 76(#1, 52 pgs.)-Tom Mix, Hopalong Cassidy, Monte Hale, Gabby Hayes, Young Falcon (ends #78,80), & Big Bow and Little Arrow (ends #102,105) begin; painted-c begin | 17.00 | 51.00 | 120.00 |
| 77 (52 pgs.) | 11.50 | 34.00 | 80.00 |
| 78,80-82 (52 pgs.): 81-Capt. Tootsie by Beck | 11.50 | 34.00 | 80.00 |
| 79,83 (36 pgs.): 83-Last painted-c | 8.50 | 25.50 | 60.00 |
| 84-86,88-90 (52 pgs.): 84-Photo-c begin, end #112. 86-Last Hopalong Cassidy | 9.30 | 28.00 | 65.00 |
| 87,91,95,99 (36 pgs.): 87-Bill Boyd begins, ends #95 | 8.00 | 24.00 | 55.00 |
| 92-94,96-98,101 (52 pgs.): 96-Tex Ritter begins. 101-Red Eagle app. | 8.50 | 25.50 | 60.00 |
| 100 (52 pgs.) | 9.30 | 28.00 | 65.00 |
| 102-111 (36pgs. begin) | 8.00 | 24.00 | 55.00 |
| 112-Last issue | 8.50 | 25.50 | 60.00 |

NOTE: *½-1 pg. Rocky Lane (Carnation) in 80-83, 86, 88, 97.*

**WESTERN KID** (1st Series)
Dec, 1954 - No. 17, Aug, 1957
Atlas Comics (CPC)

| | Good | Fine | N-Mint |
|---|---|---|---|
| 1-Origin; The Western Kid (Tex Dawson), his stallion Whirlwind & dog Lightning begin | 8.50 | 25.50 | 60.00 |
| 2 (2/55)-Last pre-code | 4.00 | 12.00 | 28.00 |
| 3-8 | 3.15 | 9.50 | 22.00 |
| 9,10-Williamson-a in both, 4 pgs. each | 4.30 | 13.00 | 30.00 |
| 11-17 | 2.30 | 7.00 | 16.00 |

NOTE: ***Ayers** a-6, 7. **Maneely** c-2-7, 10, 14. **Romita** a-1-17; c-1, 12. **Severin** c-17.*

**WESTERN KID, THE** (2nd Series)
Dec, 1971 - No. 5, Aug, 1972
Marvel Comics Group

| | Good | Fine | N-Mint |
|---|---|---|---|
| 1-Reprints; Romita-c/a(3) | | .50 | 1.00 |
| 2,4,5: 2-Romita-a; Severin-c. 4-Everett-r | | .50 | 1.00 |
| 3-Williamson-r | | .50 | 1.00 |

**WESTERN KILLERS**
No. 60, 1948 - No. 64, May, 1949; No. 6, July, 1949
Fox Features Syndicate

| | Good | Fine | N-Mint |
|---|---|---|---|
| nn(nd, F&J Trading Co.)-Range Busters | 7.00 | 21.00 | 50.00 |
| 60 (#1, 9/48)-Extreme violence; lingerie panel | 10.00 | 30.00 | 70.00 |
| 61-64, 6: 61-Jack Cole-a | 6.50 | 19.00 | 45.00 |

**WESTERN LIFE ROMANCES** (My Friend Irma #3?)
Dec, 1949 - No. 2, Mar, 1950 (52 pgs.)
Marvel Comics (IPP)

| | Good | Fine | N-Mint |
|---|---|---|---|
| 1-Whip Wilson & Reno Browne photo-c | 7.00 | 21.00 | 50.00 |
| 2-Spanking scene | 5.70 | 17.00 | 40.00 |

**WESTERN LOVE**
July-Aug, 1949 - No. 5, Mar-Apr, 1950 (All photo-c & 52 pgs.)
Prize Publications

| | Good | Fine | N-Mint |
|---|---|---|---|
| 1-S&K-a; Randolph Scott "Canadian Pacific" photo-c (see Prize Comics #76) | 11.00 | 32.00 | 75.00 |
| 2,5-S&K-a: 2-Whip Wilson & Reno Browne photo-c | 8.50 | 25.50 | 60.00 |
| 3,4 | 5.70 | 17.00 | 40.00 |

NOTE: ***Meskin & Severin/Elder** a-2-5.*

**WESTERN LOVE TRAILS** (Formerly Western Adventures)
No. 7, Nov, 1949 - No. 9, Mar, 1950
Ace Magazines (A. A. Wyn)

| | Good | Fine | N-Mint |
|---|---|---|---|
| 7 | 5.70 | 17.00 | 40.00 |
| 8,9 | 4.00 | 12.00 | 28.00 |

**WESTERN MARSHAL** (See Steve Donovan. . . & Ernest Haycox's 4-Color 534, 591, 613, 640 [based on Haycox's "Trailtown"])

**WESTERN OUTLAWS** (My Secret Life #22 on)
No. 17, Sept, 1948 - No. 21, May, 1949
Fox Features Syndicate

| | Good | Fine | N-Mint |
|---|---|---|---|
| 17-Kamen-a; Iger shop-a in all; 1 pg. 'Death and the Devil Pills' r-in Ghostly Weird #122 | 11.50 | 34.00 | 80.00 |
| 18-21 | 7.00 | 21.00 | 50.00 |

**WESTERN OUTLAWS**
Feb, 1954 - No. 21, Aug, 1957
Atlas Comics (ACI No. 1-14/WPI No. 15-21)

| | Good | Fine | N-Mint |
|---|---|---|---|
| 1-Heath, Powell-a; Maneely hanging-c | 8.50 | 25.50 | 60.00 |
| 2 | 4.00 | 12.00 | 28.00 |
| 3-10: 7-Violent-a by R.Q. Sale | 3.15 | 9.50 | 22.00 |
| 11,14-Williamson-a in both, 6 pgs. each | 4.50 | 14.00 | 32.00 |
| 12,18,20,21: Severin covers | 2.65 | 8.00 | 18.00 |
| 13-Baker-a | 3.00 | 9.00 | 21.00 |
| 15-Torres-a | 3.60 | 11.00 | 25.00 |
| 16-Williamson text illo | 2.30 | 7.00 | 16.00 |
| 17-Crandall-a, Williamson text illo | 3.50 | 10.50 | 24.00 |
| 19-Crandall-a | 2.85 | 8.50 | 20.00 |

NOTE: ***Ayers** a-7, 10, 18, 20. **Bolle** a-21. **Colan** a-5, 17. **Everett** a-9, 10. **Heath** a-1; c-3, 4, 8, 16. **Kubert** a-9p. **Maneely** a-13, 16, 17; c-5, 7, 9, 10, 12, 13. **Morisi** a-18. **Powell** a-3, 16. **Romita** a-7, 13. **Severin** a-8, 16; c-17, 18, 20, 21. **Tuska** a-6, 15.*

**WESTERN OUTLAWS & SHERIFFS** (Formerly Best Western)
No. 60, Dec, 1949 - No. 73, June, 1952
Marvel/Atlas Comics (IPC)

| | Good | Fine | N-Mint |
|---|---|---|---|
| 60 (52 pgs.) | 8.50 | 25.50 | 60.00 |
| 61-65: 61-Photo-c | 6.50 | 19.00 | 45.00 |
| 66,68-73: 66-Story contains 5 hangings | 4.00 | 12.00 | 28.00 |
| 67-Cannibalism story | 5.70 | 17.00 | 40.00 |

*Western Kid #5 (1st series), © MEG*

*Western Love #3, © PRIZE*

*Western Outlaws #17, © FOX*

*Western Thrillers #3 (1/55), © MEG*

*Western Winners #7, © MEG*

*What If. . . ? #3, © MEG*

NOTE: ***Maneely*** *a-62, 67; c-62, 69, 70, 73.* ***Robinson*** *a-68.* ***Sinnott*** *a-70.* ***Tuska*** *a-69, 70.*

**WESTERN PICTURE STORIES** (1st Western comic)
Feb, 1937 - No. 4, June, 1937
Comics Magazine Company

| | Good | Fine | N-Mint |
|---|---|---|---|
| 1-Will Eisner-a | 92.00 | 275.00 | 645.00 |
| 2-Will Eisner-a | 57.00 | 171.00 | 400.00 |
| 3,4: 3-Eisner-a | 45.00 | 135.00 | 315.00 |

**WESTERN PICTURE STORIES** (See Giant Comics Edition #6, 11)

**WESTERN ROMANCES** (See Target. . .)

**WESTERN ROUGH RIDERS**
Nov, 1954 - No. 4, May, 1955
Gillmor Magazines No. 1,4 (Stanmor Publications)

| | Good | Fine | N-Mint |
|---|---|---|---|
| 1 | 3.60 | 11.00 | 25.00 |
| 2-4 | 2.15 | 6.50 | 15.00 |

**WESTERN ROUNDUP** (See Dell Giants & Fox Giants)

**WESTERN TALES** (Formerly Witches. . .)
No. 31, Oct, 1955 - No. 33, July-Sept, 1956
Harvey Publications

| | Good | Fine | N-Mint |
|---|---|---|---|
| 31,32-All S&K-a; Davy Crockett app. in each | 7.00 | 21.00 | 50.00 |
| 33-S&K-a; Jim Bowie app. | 7.00 | 21.00 | 50.00 |

NOTE: *#32 & 33 contain Boy's Ranch reprints.*

**WESTERN TALES OF BLACK RIDER** (Formerly Black Rider; Gunsmoke Western #32 on)
No. 28, May, 1955 - No. 31, Nov, 1955
Atlas Comics (CPS)

| | Good | Fine | N-Mint |
|---|---|---|---|
| 28 (#1): The Spider (a villain) dies | 7.00 | 21.00 | 50.00 |
| 29-31 | 5.00 | 15.00 | 35.00 |

NOTE: ***Lawrence*** *a-30.* ***Maneely*** *c-28-30.* ***Severin*** *a-28.* ***Shores*** *c-31.*

**WESTERN TEAM-UP**
November, 1973
Marvel Comics Group

| | Good | Fine | N-Mint |
|---|---|---|---|
| 1-Origin & 1st app. The Dakota Kid; Rawhide Kid-r; Gunsmoke Kid-r by Jack Davis | | .40 | .80 |

**WESTERN THRILLERS** (My Past Confessions #7 on)
Aug, 1948 - No. 6, June, 1949; No. 52, 1954?
Fox Features Syndicate/M.S. Distr. No. 52

| | Good | Fine | N-Mint |
|---|---|---|---|
| 1-"Velvet Rose"-Kamenish-a; "Two-Gun Sal," "Striker Sisters" (all women outlaws issue) | 22.00 | 65.00 | 150.00 |
| 2 | 7.00 | 21.00 | 50.00 |
| 3,6: 3-Tuska-a, Heath-c | 5.70 | 17.00 | 40.00 |
| 4,5-Bakerish-a; 5-Butch Cassidy app. | 8.00 | 24.00 | 55.00 |
| 52-(Reprint, M.S. Dist.)-1954? No date given (Becomes My Love Secret #53) | 2.65 | 8.00 | 18.00 |

**WESTERN THRILLERS** (Cowboy Action #5 on)
Nov, 1954 - No. 4, Feb, 1955 (All-r/ Western Outlaws & Sheriffs)
Atlas Comics (ACI)

| | Good | Fine | N-Mint |
|---|---|---|---|
| 1-Severin-c? | 7.00 | 21.00 | 50.00 |
| 2-4 | 3.70 | 11.00 | 26.00 |

NOTE: ***Heath*** *c-3.* ***Maneely*** *a-1; c-2.* ***Powell*** *a-4.* ***Robinson*** *a-4.* ***Romita*** *c-4.* ***Tuska*** *a-2.*

**WESTERN TRAILS**
May, 1957 - No. 2, July, 1957
Atlas Comics (SAI)

| | Good | Fine | N-Mint |
|---|---|---|---|
| 1-Ringo Kid app.; Severin-c | 4.30 | 13.00 | 30.00 |
| 2-Severin-c | 3.00 | 9.00 | 21.00 |

NOTE: ***Bolle*** *a-1, 2.* ***Maneely*** *a-1, 2.* ***Severin*** *c-1, 2.*

**WESTERN TRUE CRIME** (Becomes My Confessions)
No. 15, Aug, 1948 - No. 6, June, 1949
Fox Features Syndicate

| | Good | Fine | N-Mint |
|---|---|---|---|
| 15(#1)-Kamenish-a | 11.50 | 34.00 | 80.00 |
| 16(#2)-Kamenish-a; headlight panels, violence | 7.00 | 21.00 | 50.00 |
| 3,5,6 | 4.30 | 13.00 | 30.00 |
| 4-Johnny Craig-a | 11.00 | 32.00 | 75.00 |

**WESTERN WINNERS** (Formerly All-West. Winners; Black Rider #8)
No. 5, June, 1949 - No. 7, Dec, 1949
Marvel Comics (CDS)

| | Good | Fine | N-Mint |
|---|---|---|---|
| 5-Two-Gun Kid, Kid Colt, Black Rider | 14.00 | 43.00 | 100.00 |
| 6-Two-Gun Kid, Black Rider, Heath Kid Colt story; Captain Tootsie by C.C. Beck | 12.00 | 36.00 | 85.00 |
| 7-Randolph Scott Photo-c w/true stories about the West | 12.00 | 36.00 | 85.00 |

**WEST OF THE PECOS** (See 4-Color #222)

**WESTWARD HO, THE WAGONS** (See 4-Color #738)

**WHACK** (Satire)
Oct, 1953 - No. 3, May, 1954
St. John Publishing Co.

| | Good | Fine | N-Mint |
|---|---|---|---|
| 1-(3-D)-Kubert-a; Maurer-c | 18.00 | 54.00 | 125.00 |
| 2,3-Kubert-a in each; 3-Maurer-c | 8.00 | 24.00 | 55.00 |

**WHACKY** (See Wacky)

**WHAM COMICS** (See Super Spy)
Nov, 1940 - No. 2, Dec, 1940
Centaur Publications

| | Good | Fine | N-Mint |
|---|---|---|---|
| 1-The Sparkler, The Phantom Rider, Craig Carter and the Magic Ring Detector, Copper Slug, Speed Silvers by Gustavson, Speed Centaur & Jon Linton (s/f) begin | 76.00 | 230.00 | 535.00 |
| 2-Origin Blue Fire & Solarman; The Buzzard app. | 57.00 | 171.00 | 400.00 |

**WHAM-O GIANT COMICS** (98 cents)
April, 1967 (Newspaper size) (One Shot) (Full Color)
Wham-O Mfg. Co. (Six issue subscription was advertised)

| | Good | Fine | N-Mint |
|---|---|---|---|
| 1-Radian & Goody Bumpkin by Wood; 1 pg. Stanley-a; Fine, Tufts-a; flying saucer reports; wraparound-c | 2.85 | 8.50 | 20.00 |

**WHAT DO YOU KNOW ABOUT THIS COMICS SEAL OF APPROVAL?**
nd (1955) (4pgs.; color; slick paper-c)
No publisher listed (DC Comics Giveaway)

| | Good | Fine | N-Mint |
|---|---|---|---|
| nn-(Rare) | 45.00 | 135.00 | 315.00 |

**WHAT IF. . .?** (1st series)
Feb, 1977 - No. 47, Oct, 1985; June, 1988 (All 52 pgs.)
Marvel Comics Group

| | Good | Fine | N-Mint |
|---|---|---|---|
| 1-Brief origin Spider-Man, Fantastic Four | 1.70 | 5.00 | 12.00 |
| 2-Origin The Hulk retold | 1.00 | 3.00 | 7.00 |
| 3-5 | .85 | 2.50 | 5.00 |
| 6-10: 9-Origins Venus, Marvel Boy, Human Robot, 3-D Man | .70 | 2.00 | 4.00 |
| 11,12 | .50 | 1.50 | 3.00 |
| 13-Conan app. | .85 | 2.50 | 5.00 |
| 14-26,29,30: 22-Origin Dr. Doom retold | .40 | 1.25 | 2.50 |
| 27-X-Men app.; Miller-c | 1.15 | 3.50 | 8.00 |
| 28-Daredevil by Miller | 1.10 | 3.30 | 6.60 |
| 31-X-Men app.; death of Hulk, Wolverine & Magneto | 1.30 | 4.00 | 9.00 |
| 32-47: 32,36-Byrne-a. 34-Marvel crew each draw themselves. 35-What if Elektra had lived?; Miller/Austin-a. 37-Old X-Men & Silver Surfer app. | .30 | .85 | 1.70 |
| Special 1 ($1.50, 6/88)-Iron Man, F.F., Thor app. | .35 | 1.00 | 2.00 |

NOTE: ***Austin*** *a-27p, 32i, 34, 35i; c-35i, 36i.* ***J. Buscema*** *a-13p, 15p; c-10, 13p, 23p.* ***Byrne*** *a-32i, 36; c-36p.* ***Colan*** *a-21p; c-17p, 18p, 21p.* ***Ditko*** *a-35, Special 1.* ***Golden*** *c-29, 40, 42.* ***Guice*** *a-40p.* ***Gil Kane*** *a-3p, 24p; c(p)-2-4, 7, 8.* ***Kirby*** *a-11p; c-9p, 11p.* ***Layton*** *a-32i, 33i; c-30, 32p, 33i, 34.* ***Miller*** *a-28p, 32i, 35p; c-27, 28p.* ***Mooney*** *a-8i, 30i.* ***Perez*** *a-15p.* ***Simonson*** *a-15p, 32i.* ***Starlin*** *a-32i.* ***Stevens*** *a-16i.* ***Sutton*** *a-2i, 18p, 28.* ***Tuska*** *a-5p.*

**WHAT IF. . .?** (2nd series)
July, 1989 - Present ($1.25 color)
Marvel Comics

| | Good | Fine | N-Mint |
|---|---|---|---|
| V2#1-. . .The Avengers Had Lost the Evol. War | .50 | 1.50 | 3.00 |
| 2-5: 2-Daredevil, Punisher app. | .25 | .70 | 1.40 |
| 6-X-Men app. | .40 | 1.25 | 2.50 |
| 7-Wolverine app. | .35 | 1.00 | 2.00 |
| 8-12: 9,12-X-Men. 10-Punisher. 11-F.F. | .25 | .75 | 1.50 |
| 13-22: 13-Prof. X. 14-Capt. Marvel; Austin-c. 15-F.F. 16-Conan/Wolverine; Red Sonja app. 17-Spider-Man/Kraven. 18-F.F. 19-Vision. 20,21-Spider-Man. 22-Silver Surfer; Austin-i | | .60 | 1.25 |

**WHAT'S BEHIND THESE HEADLINES**
1948 (16 pgs.)
William C. Popper Co.

| | Good | Fine | N-Mint |
|---|---|---|---|
| nn-Comic insert-"The Plot to Steal the World" | 1.50 | 4.50 | 10.00 |

**WHAT THE-?!**
Aug, 1988 - Present ($1.25-$1.50, semi-annually #5 on)
Marvel Comics

| | Good | Fine | N-Mint |
|---|---|---|---|
| 1-All contain parodies | .35 | 1.00 | 2.00 |
| 2,4,5: 5-Punisher/Wolverine parody | .25 | .75 | 1.50 |
| 3-X-Men parody; Todd McFarlane-a | .50 | 1.50 | 3.00 |
| 6 ($1.00)-Acts of Vengeance (Punisher, Wolverine & Alpha Flight)-Byrne/Austin-a | | .50 | 1.00 |
| 7-10 ($1.25): 7-Avengers vs. Justice League parody; Patsy Walker story. 9-Wolverine. 10-Byrne-c/a | | .60 | 1.25 |

NOTE: ***Byrne** a-6, 10; c-6-8, 10. **Austin** a-6i. **McFarlane** a-3.*

**WHEATIES** (Premiums) (32 titles)
1950 & 1951 (32 pages) (pocket size)
Walt Disney Productions

(Set A-1 to A-8, 1950)
A-1 Mickey Mouse & the Disappearing Island, A-2 Grandma Duck, Homespun Detective, A-3 Donald Duck & the Haunted Jewels, A-4 Donald Duck & the Giant Ape, A-5 Mickey Mouse, Roving Reporter, A-6 Li'l Bad Wolf, Forest Ranger, A-7 Goofy, Tightrope Acrobat, A-8 Pluto & the Bogus Money each.... 2.00 6.00 12.00

(Set B-1 to B-8, 1950)
B-1 Mickey Mouse & the Pharoah's Curse, B-2 Pluto, Canine Cowpoke, B-3 Donald Duck & the Buccaneers, B-4 Mickey Mouse & the Mystery Sea Monster, B-5 Li'l Bad Wolf in the Hollow Tree Hideout, B-6 Donald Duck, Trail Blazer, B-7 Goofy & the Gangsters, B-8 Donald Duck, Klondike Kid each.... 1.70 5.00 10.00

(Set C-1 to C-8, 1951)
C-1 Donald Duck & the Inca Idol, C-2 Mickey Mouse & the Magic Mountain, C-3 Li'l Bad Wolf, Fire Fighter, C-4 Gus & Jaq Save the Ship, C-5 Donald Duck in the Lost Lakes, C-6 Mickey Mouse & the Stagecoach Bandits, C-7 Goofy, Big Game Hunter, C-8 Donald Duck Deep-Sea Diver each.... 1.70 5.00 10.00

(Set D-1 to D-8, 1951)
D-1 Donald Duck in Indian Country, D-2 Mickey Mouse and the Abandoned Mine, D-3 Pluto & the Mysterious Package, D-4 Bre'r Rabbit's Sunken Treasure, D-5 Donald Duck, Mighty Mystic, D-6 Mickey Mouse & the Medicine Man, D-7 Li'l Bad Wolf and the Secret of the Woods, D-8 Minnie Mouse, Girl Explorer
each.... 1.70 5.00 10.00

NOTE: *Some copies lack the Wheaties ad.*

**WHEE COMICS** (Also see Gay, Smile & Tickle Comics)
1955 (52 pgs.) (5x7¼") (7 cents)
Modern Store Publications

| | Good | Fine | N-Mint |
|---|---|---|---|
| 1-Funny animal | .40 | 1.20 | 2.40 |

**WHEELIE AND THE CHOPPER BUNCH** (TV)
July, 1975 - No. 7, July, 1976 (Hanna-Barbera)
Charlton Comics

| | Good | Fine | N-Mint |
|---|---|---|---|
| 1,2-Byrne-a (see Flintstones for 1st art) | .85 | 2.50 | 5.00 |

| | Good | Fine | N-Mint |
|---|---|---|---|
| 3-7-Staton-a | .40 | 1.25 | 2.50 |

**WHEN KNIGHTHOOD WAS IN FLOWER** (See 4-Color #505, 682)

**WHEN SCHOOL IS OUT** (See Wisco)

**WHERE CREATURES ROAM**
July, 1970 - No. 8, Sept, 1971
Marvel Comics Group

| | Good | Fine | N-Mint |
|---|---|---|---|
| 1-Kirby/Ayers-r | | .50 | 1.00 |
| 2-8-Kirby-r | | .35 | .70 |

NOTE: ***Ditko** r-1, 2, 4, 6, 7. All contain pre super-hero reprints.*

**WHERE MONSTERS DWELL**
Jan, 1970 - No. 38, Oct, 1975
Marvel Comics Group

| | Good | Fine | N-Mint |
|---|---|---|---|
| 1-Kirby/Ditko-r; all contain pre super-hero-r | | .60 | 1.20 |
| 2-10,12: 4-Crandall-a(r). 12-Giant issue | | .40 | .80 |
| 11,13-37: 18,20-Starlin-c | | .30 | .60 |
| 38-Williamson-r/World of Suspense #3 | | .40 | .80 |

NOTE: ***Ditko** a(r)-4, 8, 10, 12, 17-19, 23-25, 37. **Reinman** a-4r. **Severin** c-15.*

**WHERE'S HUDDLES?** (TV) (See Fun-In #9)
Jan, 1971 - No. 3, Dec, 1971 (Hanna-Barbera)
Gold Key

| | Good | Fine | N-Mint |
|---|---|---|---|
| 1 | .85 | 2.50 | 5.00 |
| 2,3: 3-r-most #1 | .50 | 1.50 | 3.00 |

**WHIP WILSON** (Movie star) (Formerly Rex Hart; Gunhawk #12 on; see Western Hearts, Western Life Romances, Western Love)
No. 9, April, 1950 - No. 11, Sept, 1950 (#9,10: 52pgs.; #11: 36pgs.)
Marvel Comics

| | Good | Fine | N-Mint |
|---|---|---|---|
| 9-Photo-c; Whip Wilson & his horse Bullet begin; origin Bullet; issue #23 listed on splash page; cover changed to #9 | 23.00 | 70.00 | 160.00 |
| 10,11-Photo-c | 19.00 | 56.00 | 130.00 |
| I.W. Reprint #1('64)-Kinstler-c; r-Marvel #11 | 1.15 | 3.50 | 8.00 |

**WHIRLWIND COMICS** (Also see Cyclone Comics)
June, 1940 - No. 3, Sept, 1940
Nita Publication

| | Good | Fine | N-Mint |
|---|---|---|---|
| 1-Cyclone begins (origin) | 47.00 | 140.00 | 325.00 |
| 2,3 | 30.00 | 90.00 | 210.00 |

**WHIRLYBIRDS** (See 4-Color #1124, 1216)

**WHISPER** (Female Ninja)
Dec, 1983 - No. 2, 1984 ($1.75, color, Baxter paper)
Capital Comics

| | Good | Fine | N-Mint |
|---|---|---|---|
| 1-Origin; Golden-c | 1.35 | 4.00 | 8.00 |
| 2 | .50 | 1.50 | 3.00 |

**WHISPER** (Also see First Adventures)
June, 1986 - No. 37, June, 1990 ($1.25, $1.75, $1.95, color, Baxter)
First Comics

| | Good | Fine | N-Mint |
|---|---|---|---|
| V2#1-Begin $1.25 cover price | .50 | 1.50 | 3.00 |
| 2 | .35 | 1.00 | 2.00 |
| 3-9: 9-Last $1.25 issue | | .65 | 1.30 |
| 10-16 ($1.75) | .30 | .90 | 1.80 |
| 17-37 ($1.95) | .35 | 1.00 | 2.00 |
| Special 1 (11/85, First Comics) | .40 | 1.25 | 2.50 |

**WHITE CHIEF OF THE PAWNEE INDIANS**
1951
Avon Periodicals

| | Good | Fine | N-Mint |
|---|---|---|---|
| nn-Kit West app.; Kinstler-c | 7.00 | 21.00 | 50.00 |

**WHITE EAGLE INDIAN CHIEF** (See Indian Chief)

**WHITE INDIAN**
No. 11, July, 1953 - No. 15, 1954
Magazine Enterprises

*What If. . .? V2#16, © MEG*

*What The-?! #6, © MEG*

*Whisper V2#2, © First Comics*

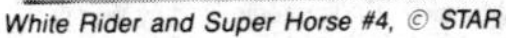
*White Rider and Super Horse #4, © STAR*

*Whiz Comics #3, © FAW*

*Whodunit #1, © DS*

**Good Fine N-Mint**

11(A-1 94), 12(A-1 101), 13(A-1 104)-Frazetta-r(Dan Brand) in all from Durango Kid. 11-Powell-c 16.00 48.00 110.00

14(A-1 117), 15(A-1 135)-Check-a; Torres-a-#15 6.50 19.50 45.00

NOTE: *#11 contains reprints from Durango Kid #1-4; #12 from #5, 9, 10, 11; #13 from #7, 12, 13, 16. #14 & 15 contain all new stories.*

**WHITE PRINCESS OF THE JUNGLE** (Also see Jungle Adventures & Top Jungle Comics)
July, 1951 - No. 5, Nov, 1952
Avon Periodicals

1-Origin of White Princess (Taanda) & Capt'n Courage (r); Kinstler-c 23.00 70.00 160.00

2-Reprints origin of Malu, Slave Girl Princess from Avon's Slave Girl Comics #1 w/Malu changed to Zora; Kinstler-c/a(2) 17.00 51.00 120.00

3-Origin Blue Gorilla; Kinstler-c/a 13.00 40.00 90.00

4-Jack Barnum, White Hunter app.; r-/Sheena #9 11.00 32.00 75.00

5-Blue Gorilla by Kinstler 11.00 32.00 75.00

**WHITE RIDER AND SUPER HORSE** (Indian Warriors #7 on; also see Blue Bolt #1, Four Most & Western Crime Cases)
Dec, 1950 - No. 6, Mar, 1951
Novelty-Star Publications/Accepted Publ.

1 6.00 18.00 42.00

2,3 3.50 10.50 24.00

4-6-Adapts "The Last of the Mohicans" 4.00 12.00 28.00

Accepted Reprint #5(r/#5),6 (nd); L.B. Cole-c 2.30 7.00 16.00

NOTE: *All have **L. B. Cole** covers.*

**WHITE WILDERNESS** (See 4-Color #943)

**WHITMAN COMIC BOOKS**
1962 (136 pgs.; 7¾x5¾"; hardcover) (B&W)
Whitman Publishing Co.

1-7: 1-Yogi Bear. 2-Huckleberry Hound. 3-Mr. Jinks and Pixie & Dixie. 4-The Flintstones. 5-Augie Doggie & Loopy de Loop. 6-Snooper & Blabber Fearless Detectives/Quick Draw McGraw of the Wild West. 7-Bugs Bunny-(r)-/from #47,51,53,54 & 55 each.... .50 1.50 3.00

8-Donald Duck-reprints most of WDC&S #209-213. Includes 5 Barks stories, 1 complete Mickey Mouse serial & 1 Mickey Mouse serial missing the 1st episode 7.75 22.00 44.00

NOTE: *Hanna-Barbera #1-6(TV), original stories. Dell reprints-#7, 8.*

**WHIZ COMICS** (Formerly Flash Comics & Thrill Comics #1)
No. 2, Feb, 1940 - No. 155, June, 1953
Fawcett Publications

**Good Fine VF-NM NM/Mint**

1-(nn on cover, #2 inside)-Origin & 1st newsstand app. Captain Marvel (formerly Captain Thunder) by C. C. Beck (created by Bill Parker), Spy Smasher, Golden Arrow, Ibis the Invincible, Dan Dare, Scoop Smith, Sivana, & Lance O'Casey begin 3,800.00 10,600.00 23,000.00 32,000.00
(Estimated up to 135 total copies exist, 4 in NM/Mint)
(The only Mint copy sold in 1990 for $74,000 cash/trade)

1-Reprint, oversize 13½"x10". **WARNING:** This comic is an exact duplicate reprint of the original except for its size. DC published it in 1974 with a second cover titling it as a Famous First Edition. There have been many reported cases of the outer cover being removed and the interior sold as the original edition. The reprint with the new outer cover removed is practically worthless.

**Good Fine N-Mint**

2-(nn on cover, #3 inside); cover to Flash #1 redrawn, pg. 12, panel 4; Spy Smasher reveals I.D. to Eve 315.00 942.00 2200.00

3-(#3 on cover, #4 inside)-1st app. Beautia 195.00 590.00 1370.00

4-(#4 on cover, #5 inside) 160.00 480.00 1125.00

5-Captain Marvel wears button-down flap on splash page only 120.00 360.00 840.00

6-10: 7-Dr. Voodoo begins (by Raboy-#9-22) 98.00 295.00 685.00

11-14 64.00 193.00 450.00

**Good Fine N-Mint**

15-Origin Sivana; Dr. Voodoo by Raboy 82.00 245.00 575.00

16-18-Spy Smasher battles Captain Marvel 82.00 245.00 575.00

19,20 45.00 135.00 315.00

21-Origin & 1st app. Lt. Marvels 47.00 141.00 330.00

22-24: 23-Only Dr. Voodoo by Tuska 37.00 110.00 260.00

25-(12/41)-Captain Nazi jumps from Master Comics #21 to take on Capt. Marvel solo after being beaten by Capt. Marvel/Bulletman team, causing the creation of Capt. Marvel Jr.; 1st app./origin of Capt. Marvel Jr. (part II of trilogy origin); Captain Marvel sends Jr. back to Master #22 to aid Bulletman against Capt. Nazi; origin Old Shazam in text 115.00 345.00 800.00

26-30 32.00 95.00 225.00

31,32: 32-1st app. The Trolls 25.00 75.00 175.00

33-Spy Smasher, Captain Marvel x-over on cover and inside 29.00 86.00 200.00

34,36-40: 37-The Trolls app. by Swayze 21.00 62.00 145.00

35-Captain Marvel & Spy Smasher-c 24.00 70.00 165.00

41-50: 43-Spy Smasher, Ibis, Golden Arrow x-over in Capt. Marvel. 44-Flag-c. 47-Origin recap (1 pg.) 13.00 40.00 90.00

51-60: 52-Capt. Marvel x-over in Ibis. 57-Spy Smasher, Golden Arrow, Ibis cameo 11.00 32.00 75.00

61-70 9.30 28.00 65.00

71,77-80 7.00 21.00 50.00

72-76-Two Captain Marvel stories in each; 76-Spy Smasher becomes Crime Smasher 8.00 24.00 55.00

81-99: 86-Captain Marvel battles Sivana Family. 91-Infinity-c 7.00 21.00 50.00

100 10.00 30.00 70.00

101,103-105 5.70 17.00 40.00

102-Commando Yank app. 5.70 17.00 40.00

106-Bulletman app. 5.70 17.00 40.00

107-141,143-152: 107-White House photo-c. 108-Brooklyn Bridge photo-c. 112-photo-c. 139-Infinity-c 5.00 15.00 35.00

142-Used in **POP**, pg. 89 5.00 15.00 35.00

153-155-(Scarce) 10.00 30.00 70.00

Wheaties Giveaway(1946, Miniature)-6½x8¼", 32 pgs.; all copies were taped at each corner to a box of Wheaties and are never found in fine or mint condition; "Capt. Marvel & the Water Thieves," plus Golden Arrow, Ibis stories 14.00 43.00 100.00

NOTE: ***Krigstein** Golden Arrow-No. 75, 78, 91, 95, 96, 98-100. **Marcus Swayze** a-37, 38, 59; c-38. **Wolverton** ½ pg. "Culture Corner"-No. 65-68, 70-85, 87-96, 98-100, 102-109, 112-121, 123, 125, 126, 128-131, 133, 134, 136, 142, 143, 146.*

**WHODUNIT**
Aug-Sept, 1948 - No. 3, Dec-Jan, 1948-49 (#1: 52 pgs.)
D.S. Publishing Co.

1-Baker-a, 7pgs. 8.00 24.00 55.00

2,3 4.50 14.00 32.00

**WHODUNNIT?**
June, 1986 - No. 3, April, 1987 ($2.00, color)
Eclipse Comics

1-3: Spiegle-a. 2-Gulacy-c .35 1.00 2.00

**WHO FRAMED ROGER RABBIT** (See Marvel Graphic Novel)

**WHO IS NEXT?**
No. 5, January, 1953
Standard Comics

5-Toth, Sekowsky, Andru-a 10.00 30.00 70.00

**WHO'S MINDING THE MINT?** (See Movie Classics)

**WHO'S WHO IN STAR TREK**
March, 1987 - No. 2, April, 1987
DC Comics

1,2-Chaykin-c; 1-3 pgs.-a by most DC artists .85 2.50 5.00

**WHO'S WHO IN THE LEGION OF SUPER-HEROES**
Apr, 1987 - No. 7, Nov, 1988 ($1.25, color index)
DC Comics

| | Good | Fine | N-Mint |
|---|---|---|---|
| 1-7 | | .65 | 1.30 |

**WHO'S WHO: THE DEFINITIVE DIRECTORY OF THE DC UNIVERSE**
Mar, 1985 - No. 26, Apr, 1987 (26 issue maxi-series, no ads)
DC Comics

| | Good | Fine | N-Mint |
|---|---|---|---|
| 1-DC heroes from A-Z | .35 | 1.00 | 2.00 |
| 2-26: All have 1-2 pgs.-a by most DC artists | | .60 | 1.20 |

**WHO'S WHO UPDATE '87**
Aug, 1987 - No. 5, Dec, 1987 ($1.25, color)
DC Comics

| | Good | Fine | N-Mint |
|---|---|---|---|
| 1-5: contains art by most DC artists | .25 | .75 | 1.50 |

**WHO'S WHO UPDATE '88**
Aug, 1988 - No. 4, Nov, 1988 ($1.25)
DC Comics

| | Good | Fine | N-Mint |
|---|---|---|---|
| 1-4: Contains art by most DC artists | | .60 | 1.25 |

**WILBUR COMICS** (Teen-age) (Also see Laugh Comics, Laugh Comix, Liberty Comics #10 & Zip Comics)
Sum', 1944 - No. 87, 11/59; No. 88, 9/63; No. 89, 10/64; No. 90, 10/65 (No. 1-46: 52 pgs.)
MLJ Magazines/Archie Publ. No. 8, Spring, 1946 on

| | Good | Fine | N-Mint |
|---|---|---|---|
| 1 | 27.00 | 80.00 | 185.00 |
| 2(Fall,'44) | 13.00 | 40.00 | 90.00 |
| 3,4(Wint,'44-'45; Spr,'45) | 11.00 | 32.00 | 75.00 |
| 5-1st app. Katy Keene (Sum, 1945) & begin series; Wilbur story same as Archie story in Archie #1 except that Wilbur replaces Archie | 43.00 | 130.00 | 300.00 |
| 6-10(Fall,'46) | 10.00 | 30.00 | 70.00 |
| 11-20 | 5.70 | 17.00 | 40.00 |
| 21-30(1949) | 4.00 | 12.00 | 28.00 |
| 31-50 | 2.30 | 7.00 | 16.00 |
| 51-70 | 1.50 | 4.50 | 10.00 |
| 71-90: 88-Last 10 cent issue (9/63) | .85 | 2.60 | 6.00 |

NOTE: *Katy Keene in No. 5-56, 58-69.*

**WILD**
Feb, 1954 - No. 5, Aug, 1954
Atlas Comics (IPC)

| | Good | Fine | N-Mint |
|---|---|---|---|
| 1 | 8.50 | 25.50 | 60.00 |
| 2 | 5.00 | 15.00 | 35.00 |
| 3-5 | 4.30 | 13.00 | 30.00 |

NOTE: ***Berg** a-5; c-4. **Burgos** c-3. **Colan** a-4. **Everett** a-1-3. **Heath** a-2, 3, 5. **Maneely** a-1-3, 5; c-1, 5. **Post** a-2, 5. **Ed Win** a-1, 3.*

**WILD** (This Magazine Is. . .) (Magazine)
Jan, 1968 - No. 3, 1968 (52 pgs.) (Satire)
Dell Publishing Co.

| | Good | Fine | N-Mint |
|---|---|---|---|
| 1-3 | .85 | 2.60 | 6.00 |

**WILD ANIMALS**
Dec, 1982 ($1.00, color) (One-Shot)
Pacific Comics

| | Good | Fine | N-Mint |
|---|---|---|---|
| 1-Funny animal; Sergio Aragones-a; Shaw-c/a | | .50 | 1.00 |

**WILD BILL ELLIOTT** (Also see Western Roundup under Dell Giants)
No. 278, 5/50 - No. 643, 7/55 (No #11,12) (All photo-c)
Dell Publishing Co.

| | Good | Fine | N-Mint |
|---|---|---|---|
| 4-Color 278(#1, 52pgs.)-Titled "Bill Elliott;" Bill & his horse Stormy begin; photo front/back-c begin | 11.50 | 34.00 | 80.00 |
| 2 (11/50), 3 (52 pgs.) | 5.70 | 17.00 | 40.00 |
| 4-10(10-12/52) | 4.50 | 14.00 | 32.00 |
| 4-Color 472(6/53),520(12/53)-Last photo back-c | 4.50 | 14.00 | 32.00 |
| 13(4-6/54) - 17(4-6/55) | 3.70 | 11.00 | 26.00 |
| 4-Color 643 (7/55) | 3.70 | 11.00 | 26.00 |

**WILD BILL HICKOK** (Also see Blazing Sixguns)
Sept-Oct, 1949 - No. 28, May-June, 1956
Avon Periodicals

| | Good | Fine | N-Mint |
|---|---|---|---|
| 1-Ingels-c | 11.50 | 34.00 | 80.00 |
| 2-Painted-c; Kit West app. | 5.70 | 17.00 | 40.00 |
| 3,5-Painted-c | 3.00 | 9.00 | 21.00 |
| 4-Painted-c by Howard Winfield | 3.00 | 9.00 | 21.00 |
| 6-10,12: 8-10-Painted-c. 9-Ingels-a? | 3.00 | 9.00 | 21.00 |
| 11,14-Kinstler-c/a | 3.65 | 11.00 | 25.00 |
| 13,15,17,18,20,23: 20-Kit West by Larsen | 2.15 | 6.50 | 15.00 |
| 16-Kamen-a; r-3 stories/King of the Badmen of Deadwood | 3.00 | 9.00 | 21.00 |
| 19-Meskin-a | 2.15 | 6.50 | 15.00 |
| 21-Reprints 2 stories/Chief Crazy Horse | 2.15 | 6.50 | 15.00 |
| 22-Kinstler-a; r-/Sheriff Bob Dixon's. . . | 2.15 | 6.50 | 15.00 |
| 24-27-Kinstler-c/a(r) | 2.85 | 8.50 | 20.00 |
| 28-Kinstler-c/a (new); r-/Last of the Comanches | 2.85 | 8.50 | 20.00 |
| I.W. Reprint #1-Kinstler-c | .50 | 1.50 | 3.00 |
| Super Reprint #10-12 | .50 | 1.50 | 3.00 |

NOTE: *#23, 25 contain numerous editing deletions in both art and script due to code. **Kinstler** c-6, 7, 11-14, 17, 18, 20-22, 24-28. **Howard Larsen** a-1, 2(3), 4(4), 5(3), 7(3), 9(3), 11(4), 12(4), 17, 18, 20, 21(2), 22, 24(3), 26. **Meskin** a-7. **Reinman** a-17.*

**WILD BILL HICKOK & JINGLES** (TV)(Formerly Cowboy Western)
No. 68, March, 1958 - No. 76?, 1960 (Also see Blue Bird)
Charlton Comics

| | Good | Fine | N-Mint |
|---|---|---|---|
| 68,69-Williamson-a | 4.00 | 12.00 | 28.00 |
| 70-Two pgs. Williamson-a | 2.30 | 7.00 | 16.00 |
| 71-76 (#75,76, exist?) | 1.30 | 4.00 | 9.00 |

**WILD BILL PECOS** (See The Westerner)

**WILD BOY OF THE CONGO** (Also see Approved Comics)
No. 10, Feb-Mar, 1951 - No. 15, June, 1955
Ziff-Davis No. 10-12,4-6/St. John No. 7? on

| | Good | Fine | N-Mint |
|---|---|---|---|
| 10(#1)(2-3/51)-Origin; bondage-c by Saunders; used in **SOTI**, pg. 189 | 9.30 | 28.00 | 65.00 |
| 11(4-5/51),12(8-9/51)-Norman Saunders-c | 5.00 | 15.00 | 35.00 |
| 4(10-11/51)-Saunders bondage-c | 5.00 | 15.00 | 35.00 |
| 5(Winter,'51)-Saunders-c | 4.00 | 12.00 | 28.00 |
| 6,8,9(10/53),10: 6-Saunders-c | 4.00 | 12.00 | 28.00 |
| 7(8-9/52)-Baker-c; Kinstler-a | 4.50 | 14.00 | 32.00 |
| 11-13-Baker-c(St. John) | 4.50 | 14.00 | 32.00 |
| 14(4/55)-Baker-c; r-#12('51) | 4.50 | 14.00 | 32.00 |
| 15(6/55) | 3.00 | 9.00 | 21.00 |

**WILD CARDS**
Sept, 1990 - No. 4, Dec, 1990 ($4.50, color, mini-series, 52 pgs.)
Epic Comics (Marvel)

| | Good | Fine | N-Mint |
|---|---|---|---|
| 1-4: 1-Rogers-a. 1,2-Guice-a | .75 | 2.25 | 4.50 |

**WILD DOG**
Sept, 1987 - No. 4, Dec, 1987 (75 cents, mini-series)
DC Comics

| | Good | Fine | N-Mint |
|---|---|---|---|
| 1-4 | | .40 | .80 |
| Special 1 (1989, $2.50, 52 pgs.) | .40 | 1.25 | 2.50 |

**WILD FRONTIER** (Cheyenne Kid #8 on)
Oct, 1955 - No. 7, April, 1957
Charlton Comics

| | Good | Fine | N-Mint |
|---|---|---|---|
| 1-Davy Crockett | 3.50 | 10.50 | 24.00 |
| 2-6-Davy Crockett in all | 1.70 | 5.00 | 12.00 |
| 7-Origin Cheyenne Kid | 1.70 | 5.00 | 12.00 |

**WILD KINGDOM** (TV)
1965 (Giveaway) (regular size) (16 pgs., slick-c)
Western Printing Co.

| | Good | Fine | N-Mint |
|---|---|---|---|
| nn-Mutual of Omaha's. . . | 1.00 | 3.00 | 7.00 |

*Wilbur Comics #2, © AP*

*Wild Bill Elliott #8, © DELL*

*Wild Boy of the Congo #4, © Z-D*

*Wild Western #6, © MEG*

*Willie Comics #15, © MEG*

*Willie the Penguin #3, © STD*

**WILD WEST** (Wild Western #3 on)
Spring, 1948 - No. 2, July, 1948
Marvel Comics (WFP)

| | Good | Fine | N-Mint |
|---|---|---|---|
| 1-Two-Gun Kid, Arizona Annie, & Tex Taylor begin; Shores-c | 11.50 | 34.00 | 80.00 |
| 2-Captain Tootsie by Beck; Shores-c | 10.00 | 30.00 | 70.00 |

**WILD WEST** (Black Fury #1-57)
V2#58, November, 1966
Charlton Comics

| | Good | Fine | N-Mint |
|---|---|---|---|
| V2#58 | | .60 | 1.20 |

**WILD WESTERN** (Wild West #1,2)
No. 3, 9/48 - No. 57, 9/57 (3-11: 52pgs; 12-on: 36pgs)
Marvel/Atlas Comics (WFP)

| | Good | Fine | N-Mint |
|---|---|---|---|
| 3(#1)-Tex Morgan begins; Two-Gun Kid, Tex Taylor, & Arizona Annie continue from Wild West | 13.00 | 40.00 | 90.00 |
| 4-Last Arizona Annie; Captain Tootsie by Beck; Kid Colt app. | 9.30 | 28.00 | 65.00 |
| 5-2nd app. Black Rider (1/49); Blaze Carson, Captain Tootsie by Beck app. | 10.00 | 30.00 | 70.00 |
| 6-8: 6-Blaze Carson app; anti-Wertham editorial | 7.00 | 21.00 | 50.00 |
| 9-Photo-c; Black Rider begins, ends #19 | 8.00 | 24.00 | 55.00 |
| 10-Charles Starrett photo-c | 10.00 | 30.00 | 70.00 |
| 11-(Last 52 pg. issue) | 6.50 | 19.00 | 45.00 |
| 12-14,16-19: All Black Rider-c/stories. 12-14-The Prairie Kid & his horse Fury app. | 5.00 | 15.00 | 35.00 |
| 15-Red Larabee, Gunhawk (Origin), his horse Blaze, & Apache Kid begin, end #22; Black Rider-c/story | 6.50 | 19.00 | 45.00 |
| 20-29: 20-Kid Colt-c begin | 4.50 | 14.00 | 32.00 |
| 30-Katz-a | 5.00 | 15.00 | 35.00 |
| 31-40 | 3.15 | 9.50 | 22.00 |
| 41-47,49-51,53,57 | 2.15 | 6.50 | 15.00 |
| 48-Williamson/Torres-a (4 pgs); Drucker-a | 4.30 | 13.00 | 30.00 |
| 52-Crandall-a | 3.70 | 11.00 | 26.00 |
| 54,55-Williamson-a in both (5 & 4 pgs.), #54 with Mayo plus 2 text illos | 4.00 | 12.00 | 28.00 |
| 56-Baker-a? | 2.30 | 7.00 | 16.00 |

NOTE: ***Annie Oakley** in #46, 47. **Apache Kid** in #15-22, 39. **Arizona Kid** in #21, 23. **Arrowhead** in #34-39. **Black Rider** in #5, 9-19, 33-44. **Fighting Texan** in #17. **Kid Colt** in #4-6, 9-11, 20-47, 52, 54-56. **Outlaw Kid** in #43. **Red Hawkins** in #13, 14. **Ringo Kid** in #26, 39, 41, 43, 44, 46, 47, 50, 52-56. **Tex Morgan** in #3, 4, 6, 9, 11. **Tex Taylor** in #3-6, 9, 11. **Texas Kid** in #23-25. **Two-Gun Kid** in #3-6, 9, 11, 12, 33-39, 41. **Wyatt Earp** in #47. **Ayers** a-41. **Berg** a-26; c-24. **Colan** a-49. **Forte** a-28, 30. **Heath** a-4, 5, 8; c-34, 44. **Keller** a-24, 26, 29-40, 44-46, 52. **Maneely** a-10, 12, 15, 16, 28, 35, 38, 40, 41, 43-45; c-18-22, 33, 35, 36, 38, 39, 41, 45. **Morisi** a-23, 52. **Pakula** a-52. **Powell** a-51. **Severin** a-46, 47. **Shores** a-3, 5, 30, 31, 33, 35, 36, 38, 41; c-4, 5. **Sinnott** a-34-39. **Wildey** a-43. Bondage c-19.*

**WILD WESTERN ACTION** (Also see The Bravados)
March, 1971 - No. 3, June, 1971 (Reprints, 25 cents, 52 pgs.)
Skywald Publishing Corp.

| | Good | Fine | N-Mint |
|---|---|---|---|
| 1-Durango Kid, Straight Arrow; with all references to "Straight" in story relettered to "Swift;" Bravados begin | .25 | .75 | 1.50 |
| 2-Billy Nevada, Durango Kid | | .50 | 1.00 |
| 3-Red Mask, Durango Kid | | .50 | 1.00 |

**WILD WESTERN ROUNDUP**
Oct, 1957; 1960-'61
Red Top/Decker Publications/I. W. Enterprises

| | Good | Fine | N-Mint |
|---|---|---|---|
| 1(1957)-Kid Cowboy-r | 1.30 | 4.00 | 9.00 |
| I.W. Reprint #1('60-61) | .35 | 1.00 | 2.00 |

**WILD WEST RODEO**
1953 (15 cents)
Star Publications

| | Good | Fine | N-Mint |
|---|---|---|---|
| 1-A comic book coloring book with regular full color cover & B&W inside | 2.65 | 8.00 | 18.00 |

**WILD WILD WEST, THE** (TV)
June, 1966 - No. 7, Oct, 1969
Gold Key

| | Good | Fine | N-Mint |
|---|---|---|---|
| 1,2-McWilliams-a | 5.00 | 15.00 | 35.00 |
| 3-7 | 4.00 | 12.00 | 28.00 |

**WILD, WILD WEST, THE** (TV)
Oct, 1990 - No. 4, Jan?, 1991 ($2.95, color, mini-series)
Millennium Publications

| | Good | Fine | N-Mint |
|---|---|---|---|
| 1-4-Based on TV show | .50 | 1.50 | 3.00 |

**WILKIN BOY** (See That...)

**WILLIE COMICS** (Formerly Ideal #1-4; Crime Cases #24 on; Li'l Willie #20 & 21) (See Gay Comics, Laugh, Millie The Model & Wisco)
#5, Fall, 1946 - #19, 4/49; #22, 1/50 - #23, 5/50 (No #20 & 21)
Marvel Comics (MgPC)

| | Good | Fine | N-Mint |
|---|---|---|---|
| 5(#1)-George, Margie, Nellie The Nurse & Willie begin | 6.00 | 18.00 | 42.00 |
| 6,8,9 | 3.00 | 9.00 | 21.00 |
| 7(1),10,11-Kurtzman's "Hey Look" | 4.30 | 13.00 | 30.00 |
| 12,14-18,22,23 | 2.30 | 7.00 | 16.00 |
| 13,19-Kurtzman's "Hey Look" | 3.70 | 11.00 | 26.00 |

NOTE: *Cindy app. in #17. Jeanie app. in #17. Little Lizzie app. in #22.*

**WILLIE MAYS** (See The Amazing...)

**WILLIE THE PENGUIN**
April, 1951 - No. 6, April, 1952
Standard Comics

| | Good | Fine | N-Mint |
|---|---|---|---|
| 1 | 2.65 | 8.00 | 18.00 |
| 2-6 | 1.50 | 4.50 | 10.00 |

**WILLIE THE WISE-GUY** (Also see Cartoon Kids)
Sept, 1957
Atlas Comics (NPP)

| | Good | Fine | N-Mint |
|---|---|---|---|
| 1-Kida, Maneely-a | 2.65 | 8.00 | 18.00 |

**WILLIE WESTINGHOUSE EDISON SMITH THE BOY INVENTOR**
1906 (36 pgs. in color) (10x16")
William A. Stokes Co.

| | Good | Fine | N-Mint |
|---|---|---|---|
| nn-By Frank Crane | 20.00 | 60.00 | 140.00 |

**WILLOW**
Aug, 1988 - No. 3, Oct, 1988 ($1.00, color)
Marvel Comics

| | Good | Fine | N-Mint |
|---|---|---|---|
| 1-3-R/Marvel Graphic Novel #36 (movie adapt.) | | .50 | 1.00 |

**WILL ROGERS WESTERN** (See Blazing & True Comics #66)
No. 5, June, 1950 - No. 2, Aug, 1950
Fox Features Syndicate

| | Good | Fine | N-Mint |
|---|---|---|---|
| 5,2: Photo-c | 11.50 | 34.00 | 80.00 |

**WILL-YUM** (See 4-Color #676, 765, 902)

**WIN A PRIZE COMICS** (Timmy The Timid Ghost #3 on?)
Feb, 1955 - No. 2, Apr, 1955
Charlton Comics

| | Good | Fine | N-Mint |
|---|---|---|---|
| V1#1-S&K-a; Poe adapt; E.C. War swipe | 25.00 | 75.00 | 175.00 |
| 2-S&K-a | 18.00 | 54.00 | 125.00 |

**WINDY & WILLY**
May-June, 1969 - No. 4, Nov-Dec, 1969
National Periodical Publications

| | Good | Fine | N-Mint |
|---|---|---|---|
| 1-4: r-/Dobie Gillis with some art changes | .35 | 1.00 | 2.00 |

**WINGS COMICS**
9/40 - No. 109, 9/49; No. 110, Wint, 1949-50; No. 111, Spring, 1950; No. 112, 1950(nd); No. 113 - No. 115, 1950(nd); No. 116, 1952(nd); No. 117, Fall, 1952 - No. 122, Wint, 1953-54; No. 123 - No. 124, 1954(nd)
Fiction House Magazines

1-Skull Squad, Clipper Kirk, Suicide Smith, Jane Martin, War Nurse,

| | Good | Fine | N-Mint |
|---|---|---|---|
| Phantom Falcons, Greasemonkey Griffin, Parachute Patrol & Powder Burns begin | 79.00 | 235.00 | 550.00 |
| 2 | 40.00 | 120.00 | 280.00 |
| 3-5 | 29.00 | 85.00 | 200.00 |
| 6-10 | 25.00 | 75.00 | 175.00 |
| 11-15 | 22.00 | 65.00 | 150.00 |
| 16-Origin Captain Wings | 24.00 | 71.00 | 165.00 |
| 17-20 | 16.00 | 48.00 | 110.00 |
| 21-30 | 14.00 | 43.00 | 100.00 |
| 31-40 | 11.50 | 34.00 | 80.00 |
| 41-50 | 9.30 | 28.00 | 65.00 |
| 51-60: 60-Last Skull Squad | 8.00 | 24.00 | 55.00 |
| 61-67: 66-Ghost Patrol begins (becomes Ghost Squadron #71 on) | 8.00 | 24.00 | 55.00 |
| 68,69: 68-Clipper Kirk becomes The Phantom Falcon-origin, Part 1; part 2 in #69 | 8.00 | 24.00 | 55.00 |
| 70-72: 70-1st app. The Phantom Falcon in costume, origin-Part 3; Capt. Wings battles Col. Kamikaze in all | 6.00 | 19.00 | 45.00 |
| 73-99 | 6.00 | 19.00 | 45.00 |
| 100 | 7.00 | 21.00 | 50.00 |
| 101-124: 111-Last Jane Martin. 112-Flying Saucer-c/story. 115-Used in **POP**, pg. 89 | 5.00 | 15.00 | 35.00 |

*NOTE: Bondage covers are common. Captain Wings battles Sky Hag-#75, 76; . . . Mr. Atlantis-#85-92; . . . Mr. Pupin(Red Agent)-#98-103. Capt. Wings by **Elias**-#52-64; by **Lubbers**-#29-32, 70-103; by **Renee**-#33-46. **Evans** a-85-103, 108(Jane Martin). **Larsen** a-52, 59, 64, 73-77. Jane Martin by **Fran Hopper**-#68-84; Suicide Smith by **John Celardo**-#76-103; by **Hollingsworth**-#105-109; Ghost Squadron by **Maurice Whitman**-#72-77, 82-110; Skull Squad by **M. Baker**-#52-60; Clipper Kirk by **Baker**-#60, 61. **Elias** c-61-69. **Fawcette** c-6, 7, 10, 11, 17, 19, 24-27, 30, 32. **Lubbers** c-75-109. **Tuska** a-5.*

**WINGS OF THE EAGLES, THE** (See 4-Color #790)

**WINKY DINK** (Adventures of. . .)
No. 75, March, 1957 (One Shot)
Pines Comics

| | Good | Fine | N-Mint |
|---|---|---|---|
| 75-Marv Levy-c/a | 2.00 | 6.00 | 14.00 |

**WINKY DINK** (See 4-Color #663)

**WINNIE-THE-POOH** (Also see Dynabrite Comics)
January, 1977 - No. 33, 1984 (Walt Disney)
(Winnie-The-Pooh began as Edward Bear in 1926 by Milne)
Gold Key No. 1-17/Whitman No. 18 on

| | Good | Fine | N-Mint |
|---|---|---|---|
| 1-New art | .25 | .75 | 1.50 |
| 2-4,6-11 | | .40 | .80 |
| 5,12-33-New material | | .35 | .70 |

**WINNIE WINKLE**
1930 - No. 4, 1933 (52 pgs.) (B&W daily strip reprints)
Cupples & Leon Co.

| | Good | Fine | N-Mint |
|---|---|---|---|
| 1 | 10.00 | 30.00 | 70.00 |
| 2-4 | 7.00 | 21.00 | 50.00 |

**WINNIE WINKLE** (See Popular Comics & Super Comics)
1941 - No. 7, Sept-Nov, 1949
Dell Publishing Co.

| | Good | Fine | N-Mint |
|---|---|---|---|
| Large Feature Comic 2('41) | 11.50 | 34.00 | 80.00 |
| 4-Color 94('45) | 9.30 | 28.00 | 65.00 |
| 4-Color 174 | 5.00 | 15.00 | 35.00 |
| 1(3-5/48)-Contains daily & Sunday newspaper-r from 1939-1941 | 4.00 | 12.00 | 28.00 |
| 2 (6-8/48) | 2.65 | 8.00 | 18.00 |
| 3-7 | 1.70 | 5.00 | 12.00 |

**WINTERWORLD**
Sept, 1987 - No. 3, Mar, 1988 ($1.75, color, mini-series)
Eclipse Comics

| | Good | Fine | N-Mint |
|---|---|---|---|
| 1-3 | .30 | .90 | 1.80 |

**WISCO/KLARER COMIC BOOK** (Miniature)
1948 - 1964 (24 pgs.) (3½x6¾")
Given away by Wisco "99" Service Stations, Carnation Malted Milk, Klarer Health Wieners, Fleers Dubble Bubble Gum, Rodeo All-Meat Wieners, Perfect Potato Chips, & others; see ad in Tom Mix #21
Marvel Comics/Vital Publications/Fawcett Publications

| | Good | Fine | N-Mint |
|---|---|---|---|
| Blackstone & the Gold Medal Mystery(1948) | 2.65 | 8.00 | 18.00 |
| Blackstone "Solves the Sealed Vault Mystery"(1950) | 2.65 | 8.00 | 18.00 |
| Blaze Carson in "The Sheriff Shoots It Out"(1950) | 2.65 | 8.00 | 18.00 |
| Captain Marvel & Billy's Big Game (r-/Capt. Marvel Adv. #76) | 24.00 | 70.00 | 155.00 |
| (Prices vary widely on this book) | | | |
| China Boy in "A Trip to the Zoo" #10 | .85 | 2.50 | 5.00 |
| Indoors-Outdoors Game Book | .85 | 2.50 | 5.00 |
| Jim Solar Space Sheriff in "Battle for Mars," "Between Two Worlds," "Conquers Outer Space," "The Creatures on the Comet," "Defeats the Moon Missile Men," "Encounter Creatures on Comet," "Meet the Jupiter Jumpers," "Meets the Man From Mars," "On Traffic Duty," "Outlaws of the Spaceways," "Pirates of the Planet X," "Protects Space Lanes," "Raiders From the Sun," "Ring Around Saturn," "Robots of Rhea," "The Sky Ruby," "Spacetts of the Sky," "Spidermen of Venus," "Trouble on Mercury" | 2.35 | 7.00 | 16.00 |
| Johnny Starboard & the Underseas Pirates('48) | .70 | 2.00 | 4.00 |
| Kid Colt in "He Lived by His Guns"('50) | 3.00 | 9.00 | 21.00 |
| Little Aspirin as "Crook Catcher" #2('50) | .60 | 1.80 | 3.60 |
| Little Aspirin in "Naughty But Nice" #6(1950) | .60 | 1.80 | 3.60 |
| Return of the Black Phantom (not M.E. character)(Roy Dare) | 1.00 | 3.00 | 6.00 |
| Secrets of Magic | 1.00 | 3.00 | 6.00 |
| Slim Morgan "Brings Justice to Mesa City" #3 | 1.30 | 4.00 | 9.00 |
| Super Rabbit(1950)-Cuts Red Tape, Stops Crime Wave! | 1.20 | 3.50 | 8.00 |
| Tex Farnum, Frontiersman(1948) | 1.50 | 4.50 | 10.00 |
| Tex Taylor in "Draw or Die, Cowpoke!"('50) | 2.65 | 8.00 | 18.00 |
| Tex Taylor in "An Exciting Adventure at the Gold Mine"('50) | 2.35 | 7.00 | 16.00 |
| Wacky Quacky in "All-Aboard" | .50 | 1.50 | 3.00 |
| When School Is Out | .50 | 1.50 | 3.00 |
| Willie in a "Comic-Comic Book Fall" #1 | .50 | 1.50 | 3.00 |
| Wonder Duck "An Adventure at the Rodeo of the Fearless Quacker!" (1950) | .50 | 1.50 | 3.00 |
| Rare uncut version of three; includes Capt. Marvel, Tex Farnum, Black Phantom — Estimated value. . . | | | $300.00 |

**WISE GUYS** (See Harvey. . .)

**WISE LITTLE HEN, THE**
1934 (48 pgs.); 1935; 1937 (Story book)
David McKay Publ./Whitman

| | Good | Fine | N-Mint |
|---|---|---|---|
| nn-2nd book app. Donald Duck; Donald app. on cover with Wise Little Hen & Practical Pig; painted cover; same artist as the B&W's from Silly Symphony Cartoon, The Wise Little Hen (1934) (McKay) | 35.00 | 105.00 | 245.00 |
| 1935 Edition with dust jacket; 44 pgs. with color, 8¾x9¾" (Whitman) | 26.00 | 77.00 | 180.00 |
| 888(1937)-9½x13", 12 pgs. (Whitman) Donald Duck app. | 16.00 | 48.00 | 110.00 |

**WITCHCRAFT** (See Strange Mysteries, Super Reprint #18)
Mar-Apr, 1952 - No. 6, Mar, 1953
Avon Periodicals

| | Good | Fine | N-Mint |
|---|---|---|---|
| 1-Kubert-a; 1pg. Check-a | 29.00 | 85.00 | 200.00 |
| 2-Kubert & Check-a | 17.00 | 51.00 | 120.00 |
| 3,6: 3-Kinstler, Lawrence-a | 12.00 | 36.00 | 85.00 |

*Wings Comics #57, © FH*

*Winnie Winkle #4, © DELL*

*Witchcraft #1, © AVON*

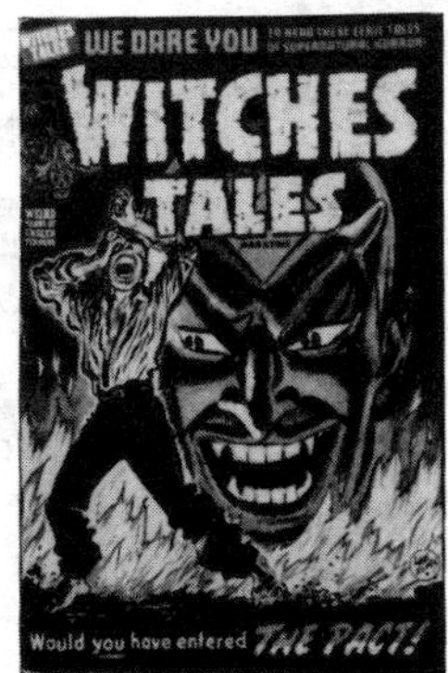


*Witches Tales #19, © HARV*

*Witty Comics #1, © I.H. Rubin*

*Wolverine Saga #1, © MEG*

| | Good | Fine | N-Mint |
|---|---|---|---|
| 4-People cooked alive c/story | 13.00 | 40.00 | 90.00 |
| 5-Kelly Freas-c | 19.00 | 57.00 | 130.00 |

NOTE: ***Hollingsworth*** *a-4-6; c-4, 6.*

**WITCHES TALES** (Witches Western Tales #29,30)
Jan, 1951 - No. 28, Dec, 1954 (date misprinted as 4/55)
Witches Tales/Harvey Publications

| | Good | Fine | N-Mint |
|---|---|---|---|
| 1-1pg. Powell-a | 14.00 | 43.00 | 100.00 |
| 2-Eye injury panel | 6.00 | 18.00 | 42.00 |
| 3-7,9,10 | 4.30 | 13.00 | 30.00 |
| 8-Eye injury panels | 5.00 | 15.00 | 35.00 |
| 11-13,15,16: 12-Acid in face story | 3.70 | 11.00 | 26.00 |
| 14,17-Powell/Nostrand-a. 17-Atomic disaster story | 5.00 | 15.00 | 35.00 |
| 18-Nostrand-a; E.C. swipe/Shock S.S. | 5.00 | 15.00 | 35.00 |
| 19-Nostrand-a; E.C. swipe/"Glutton" | 5.00 | 15.00 | 35.00 |
| 20-24-Nostrand-a. 21-E.C. swipe; rape story. 23-Wood E.C. swipes/ Two-Fisted Tales #34 | 5.00 | 15.00 | 35.00 |
| 25-Nostrand-a; E.C. swipe/Mad Barber | 5.00 | 15.00 | 35.00 |
| 26-28: 27-r-/#6 with diff.-c. 28-r-/#8 with diff.-c | 2.65 | 8.00 | 18.00 |

NOTE: ***Check*** *a-24.* ***Kremer*** *a-18; c-25.* ***Nostrand*** *a-17-25; 14, 17(w/****Powell****).* ***Palais*** *a-1, 2, 4(2), 5(2), 7-9, 12, 14, 15, 17.* ***Powell*** *a-3-7, 10, 11, 19-27. Bondage-c 1, 3, 5, 6, 8, 9.*

**WITCHES TALES** (Magazine)
V1#7, July, 1969 - V7#1, Feb, 1975 (52 pgs.) (B&W)
Eerie Publications

| | Good | Fine | N-Mint |
|---|---|---|---|
| V1#7(7/69) - 9(11/69) | 1.15 | 3.50 | 8.00 |
| V2#1-6('70), V3#1-6('71) | .70 | 2.00 | 5.00 |
| V4#1-6('72), V5#1-6('73), V6#1-6('74), V7#1 | .70 | 2.00 | 5.00 |

NOTE: *Ajax/Farrell reprints in early issues.*

**WITCHES' WESTERN TALES** (Formerly Witches Tales) (Western Tales #31 on)
No. 29, Feb, 1955 - No. 30, April, 1955
Harvey Publications

| | Good | Fine | N-Mint |
|---|---|---|---|
| 29,30-S&K-r/from Boys' Ranch including-c. 29-Last pre-code | 8.50 | 25.50 | 60.00 |

**WITCHING HOUR** (The . . . later issues)
Feb-Mar, 1969 - No. 85, Oct, 1978
National Periodical Publications/DC Comics

| | Good | Fine | N-Mint |
|---|---|---|---|
| 1-Toth plus Neal Adams-a, 3 pgs. | .85 | 2.60 | 6.00 |
| 2,6: 2-Toth-a | .50 | 1.50 | 3.00 |
| 3,5-Wrightson-a; Toth-p. 3-Last 12 cent issue | .60 | 1.75 | 3.50 |
| 4,7,9-12: Toth-a in all | .35 | 1.00 | 2.00 |
| 8-Toth, Neal Adams-a | .50 | 1.50 | 3.00 |
| 13-Neal Adams-c/a, 2pgs. | .35 | 1.00 | 2.00 |
| 14-Williamson/Garzon, Jones-a; N. Adams-c | .35 | 1.00 | 2.00 |
| 15-20 | | .60 | 1.20 |
| 21-85: 38-(100 pgs.). 84-(44 pgs.) | | .35 | .70 |

NOTE: *Combined with The Unexpected with No. 189.* ***Neal Adams*** *c-7-11, 13, 14.* ***Alcala*** *a-24, 27, 33, 41, 43.* ***Anderson*** *a-9, 38.* ***Cardy*** *c-4, 5.* ***Kaluta*** *a-7.* ***Kane*** *a-12p.* ***Morrow*** *a-10, 13, 15, 16.* ***Nino*** *a-31, 40, 45, 47.* ***Redondo*** *a-20, 23, 24, 34, 65; c-53.* ***Reese*** *a-23.* ***Toth*** *a-1-5, 6-12, 38r.* ***Tuska*** *a-11, 12.* ***Wood*** *a-12i, 15.*

**WITH THE MARINES ON THE BATTLEFRONTS OF THE WORLD**
1953 (no month) - No. 2, March, 1954 (Photo covers)
Toby Press

| | Good | Fine | N-Mint |
|---|---|---|---|
| 1-John Wayne story | 14.00 | 43.00 | 100.00 |
| 2-Monty Hall in #1,2 | 2.65 | 8.00 | 18.00 |

**WITH THE U.S. PARATROOPS BEHIND ENEMY LINES** (Also see U.S. Paratroops . . .; #2-5 titled U.S. Paratroops . . .)
1951 - No. 6, Dec, 1952
Avon Periodicals

| | Good | Fine | N-Mint |
|---|---|---|---|
| 1-Wood-c & inside-c | 9.30 | 28.00 | 65.00 |
| 2 | 5.00 | 15.00 | 35.00 |
| 3-6 | 4.00 | 12.00 | 28.00 |

NOTE: ***Kinstler*** *a-2, 5, 6; c-2, 4, 5.*

**WITNESS, THE** (Also see Amazing Mysteries, Captain America #71, Ideal #4, Marvel Mystery #92 & Mystic #7)
Sept, 1948
Marvel Comics (MjMe)

| | Good | Fine | N-Mint |
|---|---|---|---|
| 1(Scarce)-No Everett-c | 50.00 | 150.00 | 350.00 |

**WITTY COMICS**
1945 - No. 7, 1945
Irwin H. Rubin Publ./Chicago Nite Life News No. 2

| | Good | Fine | N-Mint |
|---|---|---|---|
| 1-The Pioneer, Junior Patrol | 6.50 | 19.00 | 45.00 |
| 2-The Pioneer, Junior Patrol | 4.00 | 12.00 | 28.00 |
| 3-7-Skyhawk | 3.00 | 9.00 | 21.00 |

**WIZARD OF FOURTH STREET, THE**
Dec, 1987 - No. 2, 1988 ($1.75, B&W, mini-series)
Dark Horse Comics

| | Good | Fine | N-Mint |
|---|---|---|---|
| 1,2: Adapts novel by S/F author Simon Hawke | .30 | .90 | 1.80 |

**WIZARD OF OZ** (See Classics Illustrated Jr. 535, Dell Jr. Treasury No. 5, First Comics Graphic Novel, 4-Color No. 1308, Marvelous . . ., & Marvel Treasury of Oz)

**WOLF GAL** (See Al Capp's . . .)

**WOLFMAN, THE** (See Movie Classics)

**WOLFPACK**
Feb, 1988 ($7.95); Aug, 1988 - No. 12, July, 1989 (Limited series)
Marvel Comics

| | Good | Fine | N-Mint |
|---|---|---|---|
| 1-1st app./origin (Marvel Graphic Novel #31) | 1.35 | 4.00 | 8.00 |
| 1-12 | | .40 | .80 |

**WOLVERINE** (See Alpha Flight, Daredevil #196, 249, Havok & . . ., Incredible Hulk #180, Incredible Hulk & . . ., Kitty Pryde And . . ., Marvel Comics Presents, Power Pack, Punisher Vs. . ., Spider-Man vs. . . & X-Men #94)

**WOLVERINE**
Sept, 1982 - No. 4, Dec, 1982 (Mini-series)
Marvel Comics Group

| | Good | Fine | N-Mint |
|---|---|---|---|
| 1-Frank Miller-c/a(p) in all | 3.00 | 9.00 | 18.00 |
| 2,3 | 2.00 | 6.00 | 12.00 |
| 4 | 2.50 | 7.50 | 15.00 |

**WOLVERINE**
Nov, 1988 - Present ($1.50-$1.75, color, Baxter paper)
Marvel Comics

| | Good | Fine | N-Mint |
|---|---|---|---|
| 1-Buscema a-1-16, c-1-10; Williamson i-1,4-8 | 2.50 | 7.50 | 15.00 |
| 2 | 1.35 | 4.00 | 8.00 |
| 3-5 | 1.00 | 3.00 | 6.00 |
| 6-9: 6-McFarlane back-c. 7,8-Hulk app. | .85 | 2.50 | 5.00 |
| 10-1st battle with Sabertooth (before Claws) | 2.00 | 6.00 | 12.00 |
| 11-16: 11-New costume | .50 | 1.50 | 3.00 |
| 17-20: 17-Byrne-c/a(p) begins | .35 | 1.00 | 2.00 |
| 21-25 | .25 | .75 | 1.50 |
| 26-38: 26-Begin $1.75-c? | .30 | .90 | 1.80 |

NOTE: ***Austin*** *c-3i.* ***Buscema*** *25, 27p.* ***Byrne*** *a-17-22p, 23; c-17-22, 23p.* ***Colan*** *a-24.*

**WOLVERINE BATTLES THE INCREDIBLE HULK**
1989 ($4.95, squarebound, 52 pgs.)
Marvel Comics

| | Good | Fine | N-Mint |
|---|---|---|---|
| nn-r/Incredible Hulk #180,181 | 1.15 | 3.50 | 7.00 |

**WOLVERINE SAGA**
Mid-Sept, 1989 - No. 4, Dec, 1989 ($3.95, color, mini-series, 52 pgs.)
Marvel Comics

| | Good | Fine | N-Mint |
|---|---|---|---|
| 1-Gives history; Austin-c(i) | .85 | 2.50 | 5.00 |
| 2-4: 4-Kaluta-c | .70 | 2.00 | 4.00 |

**WOLVERINE: THE JUNGLE ADVENTURE**
1990 ($4.50, color, squarebound)
Marvel Comics

| | Good | Fine | N-Mint |
|---|---|---|---|
| nn-Simonson scripts; Mignola-c/a(p) | .75 | 2.25 | 4.50 |

**WOMAN OF THE PROMISE, THE**
1950 (General Distr.) (32 pgs.) (paper cover)
Catechetical Guild

| | Good | Fine | N-Mint |
|---|---|---|---|
| nn | 2.15 | 6.50 | 15.00 |

**WOMEN IN LOVE** (A Feature Presentation #5)
Aug, 1949 - No. 4, Feb, 1950
Fox Features Synd./Hero Books

| | | | |
|---|---|---|---|
| 1 | 11.00 | 32.00 | 76.00 |
| 2-Kamen/Feldstein-c | 8.50 | 25.50 | 60.00 |
| 3 | 5.70 | 17.00 | 40.00 |
| 4-Wood-a | 8.00 | 24.00 | 56.00 |

**WOMEN IN LOVE**
Winter, 1952 (100 pgs.)
Ziff-Davis Publishing Co.

| | | | |
|---|---|---|---|
| nn-Kinstler-a (Scarce) | 24.00 | 73.00 | 170.00 |

**WOMEN OUTLAWS** (My Love Memories #9 on)(Also see Red Circle)
July, 1948 - No. 8, Sept, 1949
Fox Features Syndicate

| | | | |
|---|---|---|---|
| 1-Used in **SOTI**, illo-"Giving children an image of American womanhood"; negligee panels | 27.00 | 81.00 | 190.00 |
| 2-Spanking panel | 23.00 | 70.00 | 160.00 |
| 3-Kamen-a | 20.00 | 60.00 | 140.00 |
| 4-8 | 14.00 | 42.00 | 100.00 |
| nn(nd)-Contains Cody of the Pony Express; same cover as #7 | 11.00 | 32.00 | 75.00 |

**WOMEN TO LOVE**
No date (1953)
Realistic

| | | | |
|---|---|---|---|
| nn-(Scarce)-Reprints Complete Romance #1; c-/Avon paperback #165 | 20.00 | 60.00 | 140.00 |

**WONDER BOY** (Formerly Terrific Comics) (See Blue Bolt, Bomber Comics & Samson)
No. 17, May, 1955 - No. 18, July, 1955
Ajax/Farrell Publ.

| | | | |
|---|---|---|---|
| 17-Phantom Lady app. Bakerish-c/a | 13.00 | 40.00 | 90.00 |
| 18-Phantom Lady app. | 12.00 | 36.00 | 85.00 |

NOTE: *Phantom Lady not by Matt Baker.*

**WONDER COMICS** (Wonderworld #3 on)
May, 1939 - No. 2, June, 1939
Fox Features Syndicate

| | Good | Fine | VF-NM | NM/Mint |
|---|---|---|---|---|
| 1-(Scarce)-Wonder Man only app. by Will Eisner; Dr. Fung (by Powell), K-51 begins; Bob Kane-a; Eisner-c | 383.00 | 960.00 | 2300.00 | 3200.00 |

(Estimated up to 70 total copies exist, 3 in NM/Mint)

| | Good | Fine | N-Mint |
|---|---|---|---|
| 2-(Scarce)-Yarko the Great, Master Magician by Eisner begins; 'Spark' Stevens by Bob Kane, Patty O'Day, Tex Mason app. Lou Fine's 1st-c; Fine-a (2 pgs.) | 217.00 | 540.00 | 1300.00 |

**WONDER COMICS**
May, 1944 - No. 20, Oct, 1948
Great/Nedor/Better Publications

| | | | |
|---|---|---|---|
| 1-The Grim Reaper & Spectro, the Mind Reader begin; Hitler/Hirohito bondage-c | 36.00 | 107.00 | 250.00 |
| 2-Origin The Grim Reaper; Super Sleuths begin, end #8,17 | 22.00 | 65.00 | 150.00 |
| 3-5 | 19.00 | 56.00 | 130.00 |
| 6-10: 6-Flag-c. 8-Last Spectro. 9-Wonderman begins | 16.00 | 48.00 | 110.00 |
| 11-14-Dick Devens, King of Futuria begins #11, ends #14 | 19.00 | 56.00 | 130.00 |
| 15-Tara begins (origin), ends #20 | 21.00 | 62.00 | 145.00 |

| | Good | Fine | N-Mint |
|---|---|---|---|
| 16,18: 16-Spectro app.; last Grim Reaper. 18-The Silver Knight begins | 18.00 | 54.00 | 125.00 |
| 17-Wonderman with Frazetta panels; Jill Trent with all Frazetta inks | 20.00 | 60.00 | 140.00 |
| 19-Frazetta panels | 19.00 | 56.00 | 130.00 |
| 20-Most of Silver Knight by Frazetta | 23.00 | 70.00 | 160.00 |

NOTE: *Ingels c-11, 12.* ***Schomburg (Xela)*** *c-1-10; (airbrush)-13-20. Bondage c-12, 13, 15.*

**WONDER DUCK** (See Wisco)
Sept, 1949 - No. 3, Mar, 1950
Marvel Comics (CDS)

| | | | |
|---|---|---|---|
| 1 | 5.70 | 17.00 | 40.00 |
| 2,3 | 3.60 | 11.00 | 25.00 |

**WONDERFUL ADVENTURES OF PINOCCHIO, THE** (See Movie Comics & Walt Disney Showcase #48)
No. 3, April, 1982 (Walt Disney)
Whitman Publishing Co.

| | | | |
|---|---|---|---|
| 3-(Cont. of Movie Comics?); r-/FC #92 | | .30 | .60 |

**WONDERFUL WORLD OF DUCKS** (See Golden Picture Story Book)
1975
Colgate Palmolive Co.

| | | | |
|---|---|---|---|
| 1-Mostly-r | | .30 | .60 |

**WONDERFUL WORLD OF THE BROTHERS GRIMM** (See Movie Comics)

**WONDERLAND COMICS**
Summer, 1945 - No. 9, Feb-Mar, 1947
Feature Publications/Prize

| | | | |
|---|---|---|---|
| 1 | 5.00 | 15.00 | 35.00 |
| 2-Howard Post-c/a(2) | 2.65 | 8.00 | 18.00 |
| 3-9: 4-Post-c | 2.00 | 6.00 | 14.00 |

**WONDER MAN** (See The Avengers #9 & 151)
Mar, 1986 ($1.25, color, One-Shot, 52 pgs.)
Marvel Comics Group

| | | | |
|---|---|---|---|
| 1 | | .65 | 1.30 |

**WONDERS OF ALADDIN, THE** (See 4-Color #1255)

**WONDER WOMAN** (See Adventure Comics #459, All-Star Comics, Brave & the Bold, DC Comics Presents, Justice League of America, Legend of. . ., Power Record Comics, Sensation Comics, Super Friends and World's Finest Comics #244)

**WONDER WOMAN**
Summer, 1942 - No. 329, Feb, 1986
National Periodical Publications/All-American Publ./DC Comics

| | Good | Fine | VF-NM | NM/Mint |
|---|---|---|---|---|
| 1-Origin Wonder Woman retold (see All-Star #8); r-/in Famous First Edition; H. G. Peter-a begins | 417.00 | 1040.00 | 2500.00 | 3500.00 |

(Estimated up to 150 total copies exist, 8 in NM/Mint)

| | Good | Fine | N-Mint |
|---|---|---|---|
| 2-Origin & 1st app. Mars; Duke of Deception app. | 115.00 | 345.00 | 800.00 |
| 3 | 82.00 | 245.00 | 575.00 |
| 4,5: 5-1st Dr. Psycho app. | 60.00 | 180.00 | 420.00 |
| 6-10: 6-1st Cheetah app. | 47.00 | 140.00 | 330.00 |
| 11-20 | 36.00 | 107.00 | 250.00 |
| 21-30 | 27.00 | 81.00 | 190.00 |
| 31-40 | 20.00 | 60.00 | 140.00 |
| 41-44,46-48 | 16.00 | 48.00 | 110.00 |
| 45-Origin retold | 27.00 | 81.00 | 190.00 |
| 49-Used in **SOTI**, pgs. 234,236; Last 52 pg. issue | 16.00 | 48.00 | 110.00 |
| 50-(44 pgs.)-Used in **POP**, pg. 97 | 14.00 | 43.00 | 100.00 |
| 51-60 | 11.00 | 32.00 | 75.00 |
| 61-72: 62-Origin of W.W. i.d. 64-Story about 3-D movies. 70-1st Angle Man app. 72-Last pre-code | 9.30 | 28.00 | 65.00 |

*Women Outlaws #4, © FOX*

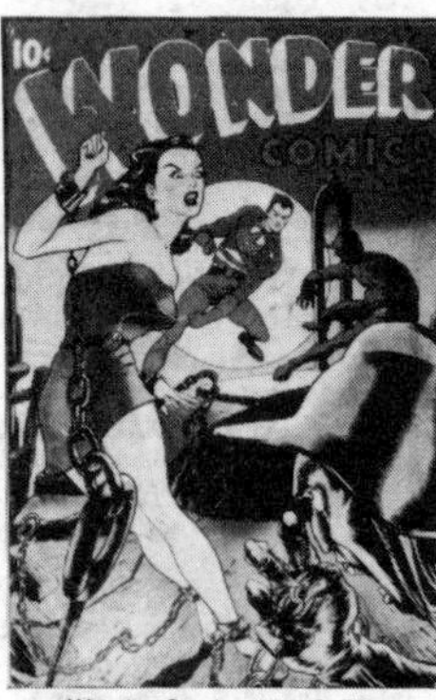

*Wonder Comics #12, © BP*

*Wonder Woman #31, © DC*

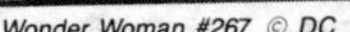
Wonder Woman #267, © DC

Wonderworld Comics #11, © FOX

Woody Woodpecker F. C. #188, © W. Lantz

| | Good | Fine | N-Mint |
|---|---|---|---|
| 73-90: 80-Origin The Invisible Plane. 89-Flying saucer-c/story | 7.00 | 21.00 | 50.00 |
| 91-94,96-99: 97-Last H. G. Peter-a. 98-Origin W.W. i.d. with new facts | 5.00 | 15.00 | 35.00 |
| 95-A-Bomb-c | 5.70 | 17.00 | 40.00 |
| 100 | 6.50 | 19.00 | 45.00 |
| 101-104,106-110: 107-1st advs. of Wonder Girl; 1st Merboy; tells how Wonder Woman won her costume | 4.30 | 13.00 | 30.00 |
| 105-(Scarce)-Wonder Woman's secret origin; W. Woman appears as a girl (not Wonder Girl) | 11.50 | 34.00 | 80.00 |
| 111-120 | 2.65 | 8.00 | 18.00 |
| 121-126: 122-1st app. Wonder Tot. 124-1st app. Wonder Woman Family. 126-Last 10 cent issue | 1.50 | 4.50 | 10.00 |
| 127-130: 128-Origin The Invisible Plane retold | 1.30 | 4.00 | 9.00 |
| 131-150: 132-Flying saucer-c | .85 | 2.60 | 6.00 |
| 151-158,160-170 (1967) | .70 | 2.00 | 5.00 |
| 159-Origin retold | .85 | 2.60 | 6.00 |
| 171-178 | .60 | 1.75 | 3.50 |
| 179-195: 179-Wears no costume to issue #203. 180-Death of Steve Trevor. 195-Wood inks? | .45 | 1.25 | 2.50 |
| 196 (52 pgs.)-Origin r-/All-Star 8 | .50 | 1.50 | 3.00 |
| 197,198 (52 pgs.)-Reprints | .50 | 1.50 | 3.00 |
| 199,200 (5-6/72)-Jeff Jones-c; 52 pgs. | .85 | 2.50 | 5.00 |
| 201-210: 204-Return to old costume; death of I Ching. 202-Fafhrd & The Grey Mouser debut | | .60 | 1.20 |
| 211-240: 211,214-(100 pgs.), 217-(68 pgs.). 220-N. Adams assist. 223-Steve Trevor revived as Steve Howard & learns W.W.'s I.D. 228-Both W. Women team up & new World War II stories begin, end #243. 237-Origin retold | | .50 | 1.00 |
| 241-266,269-280,284-286: 241-Intro Bouncer. 247-249-(44 pgs.). 248-Steve Trevor Howard dies. 249-Hawkgirl app. 250-Origin/1st app. Orana, the new W. Woman. 251-Orana dies. 269-Last Wood a(i) for DC? (7/80). 271-Huntress & 3rd Life of Steve Trevor begin | | .50 | 1.00 |
| 267,268-Re-intro Animal Man (5/80 & 6/80) | 2.85 | 8.50 | 20.00 |
| 281-283: Joker covers & stories | .50 | 1.50 | 3.00 |
| 287-New Teen Titans x-over | .25 | .75 | 1.50 |
| 288-299,301-328: 288-New costume & logo. 291-293-Three part epic with Super-Heroines | | .50 | 1.00 |
| 300-($1.50, 76 pgs.)-Anniversary issue; Giffen-a; New Teen Titans, JLA & G.A. Wonder Woman app. | .25 | .75 | 1.50 |
| 329-Double size | .25 | .75 | 1.50 |
| Pizza Hut Giveaways (12/77)-Reprints #60, 62 | | .40 | .80 |

NOTE: *Colan a-288-305p; c-288-290p.* ***Giffen*** *a-300p.* ***Grell*** *c-217.* ***Kaluta*** *c-297.* ***Gil Kane*** *c-294p. 303-305, 307, 312, 314.* ***Miller*** *c-298p.* ***Morrow*** *c-233.* ***Nasser*** *a-232p; c-231p, 232p.* ***Perez*** *c-283p, 284p.* ***Spiegle*** *a-312.* ***Staton*** *a(p)-241, 271-287, 289, 290, 294-299; c(p)-241, 245, 246. Huntress app. 271-290, 294-299, 301-321.*

**WONDER WOMAN**
Feb, 1987 - Present
DC Comics

| | Good | Fine | N-Mint |
|---|---|---|---|
| 1-New origin; Perez-c/a begins | .50 | 1.50 | 3.00 |
| 2-20: 8-Origin Cheetah. 12,13-Millennium x-over. 18,26-Free 16 pg. story | | .65 | 1.30 |
| 21-49,51-54: 24-Last Perez-a; c/scripts continue | | .50 | 1.00 |
| 50-($1.50, 52 pgs.)-New Titans, Justice League | .25 | .75 | 1.50 |
| Annual 1 ('88, $1.50)-Art Adams-a(p&i) | .25 | .75 | 1.50 |
| Annual 2 ('89, $2.00, 68 pgs.)-All women artists issue; Perez-c(i) | .35 | 1.00 | 2.00 |

**WONDER WOMAN SPECTACULAR** (See DC Special Series #9)

**WONDER WORKER OF PERU**
No date (16 pgs.) (B&W) (5x7")
Catechetical Guild (Giveaway)

| | Good | Fine | N-Mint |
|---|---|---|---|
| nn | 1.70 | 5.00 | 10.00 |

**WONDERWORLD COMICS** (Formerly Wonder Comics)
No. 3, July, 1939 - No. 33, Jan, 1942
Fox Features Syndicate

| | Good | Fine | N-Mint |
|---|---|---|---|
| 3-Intro The Flame by Fine; Dr. Fung (Powell-a), K-51 (Powell-a?), & Yarko the Great, Master Magician (Eisner-a) continues; Eisner/Fine-c | 150.00 | 375.00 | 900.00 |
| 4 | 59.00 | 175.00 | 410.00 |
| 5-10 | 54.00 | 160.00 | 375.00 |
| 11-Origin The Flame | 63.00 | 190.00 | 440.00 |
| 12-20: 13-Dr. Fung ends | 34.00 | 100.00 | 235.00 |
| 21-Origin The Black Lion & Cub | 30.00 | 90.00 | 210.00 |
| 22-27: 22,25-Dr. Fung app. | 23.00 | 70.00 | 160.00 |
| 28-1st app/origin U.S. Jones; Lu-Nar, the Moon Man begins | 29.00 | 85.00 | 200.00 |
| 29,31-33: 32-Hitler-c | 18.00 | 54.00 | 125.00 |
| 30-Origin Flame Girl | 34.00 | 100.00 | 235.00 |

NOTE: *Yarko by* ***Eisner****-No. 3-11.* ***Eisner*** *text illos-3.* ***Lou Fine*** *a-3-11; c-3-13, 15; text illos-4.* ***Nordling*** *a-4-14.* ***Powell*** *a-3-12.* ***Tuska*** *a-5-9. Bondage-c 14, 15, 28, 31, 32.*

**WOODSY OWL** (See March of Comics #395)
Nov, 1973 - No. 10, Feb, 1976
Gold Key

| | Good | Fine | N-Mint |
|---|---|---|---|
| 1 | .35 | 1.00 | 2.00 |
| 2-10 | | .50 | 1.00 |

**WOODY WOODPECKER** (Walter Lantz . . . #73 on?)(See Dell Giants for annuals) (Also see The Funnies, Jolly Jingles & New Funnies)
No. 169, 10/47 - No. 72, 5-7/62; No. 73, 10/62 - No. 201, 4/84 (nn 192)
Dell Publishing Co./Gold Key No. 73-187/Whitman No. 188 on

| | Good | Fine | N-Mint |
|---|---|---|---|
| 4-Color 169-Drug turns Woody into a Mr. Hyde | 8.50 | 25.50 | 60.00 |
| 4-Color 188 | 5.70 | 17.00 | 40.00 |
| 4-Color 202,232,249,264,288 | 3.50 | 10.50 | 24.00 |
| 4-Color 305,336,350 | 2.30 | 7.00 | 16.00 |
| 4-Color 364,374,390,405,416,431('52) | 1.70 | 5.00 | 12.00 |
| 16 (12-1/52-53) - 30('55) | 1.15 | 3.50 | 8.00 |
| 31-50 | .75 | 2.25 | 5.00 |
| 51-72 (Last Dell) | .55 | 1.65 | 4.00 |
| 73-75 (Giants, 84 pgs., Gold Key) | 1.75 | 5.25 | 14.00 |
| 76-80 | .50 | 1.50 | 3.00 |
| 81-100 | .35 | 1.00 | 2.00 |
| 101-120 | | .60 | 1.20 |
| 121-191,193-201 (No #192) | | .40 | .80 |
| Christmas Parade 1(11/68-Giant)(G.K.) | 1.70 | 5.00 | 12.00 |
| Clover Stamp-Newspaper Boy Contest('56)-9 pg. story-(Giveaway) | .85 | 2.50 | 6.00 |
| In Chevrolet Wonderland(1954-Giveaway)(Western Publ.)-20 pgs., full story line; Chilly Willy app. | 3.00 | 9.00 | 21.00 |
| Kite Fun Book (1956, 5x7¼", 16p, soft-c) | 4.00 | 12.00 | 28.00 |
| Meets Scotty McTape(1953-Scotch Tape giveaway)-16 pgs., full size | 2.30 | 7.00 | 16.00 |
| Summer Fun 1(6/66-G.K.)(84 pgs.) | 2.25 | 6.75 | 18.00 |

NOTE: *15 cent editions exist. Reprints-No. 92, 102, 103, 105, 106, 124, 125, 152, 153, 157, 162, 165, 194(⅓)-200(⅓).*

**WOODY WOODPECKER** (See Comic Album #5,9,13, Dell Giant #24, 40, 54, Dell Giants, The Funnies, Golden Comics Digest #1, 3, 5, 8, 15, 16, 20, 24, 32, 37, 44, March of Comics #16, 34, 85, 93, 109, 124, 139, 158, 177, 184, 203, 222, 239, 249, 261, 420, 454, 466, 478, New Funnies & Super Book #12, 24)

**WOOLWORTH'S CHRISTMAS STORY BOOK**
1952 - 1954 (16 pgs., paper-c) (See Jolly Christmas Book)
Promotional Publ. Co.(Western Printing Co.)

| | Good | Fine | N-Mint |
|---|---|---|---|
| nn | 2.00 | 6.00 | 14.00 |

NOTE: *1952 issue-**Marv Levy** c/a.*

**WOOLWORTH'S HAPPY TIME CHRISTMAS BOOK**
1952 (Christmas giveaway, 36 pgs.)
F. W. Woolworth Co.(Whitman Publ. Co.)

| | Good | Fine | N-Mint |
|---|---|---|---|
| nn | 2.00 | 6.00 | 14.00 |

**WORLD AROUND US, THE** (Illustrated Story of...)
Sept, 1958 - No. 36, Oct, 1961 (25 cents)
Gilberton Publishers (Classics Illustrated)

| | Good | Fine | N-Mint |
|---|---|---|---|
| 1-Dogs | 2.65 | 8.00 | 18.00 |
| 2-4: 2-Indians; Crandall-a. 3-Horses; L. B. Cole-c. 4-Railroads | 2.30 | 7.00 | 16.00 |
| 5-Space; Ingels-a | 3.50 | 10.50 | 24.00 |
| 6-The F.B.I.; Disbrow, Evans, Ingels-a | 3.00 | 9.00 | 21.00 |
| 7-Pirates; Disbrow, Ingels-a | 3.50 | 10.50 | 24.00 |
| 8-Flight; Evans, Ingels, Crandall-a | 3.50 | 10.50 | 24.00 |
| 9-Army; Disbrow, Ingels, Orlando-a | 3.00 | 9.00 | 21.00 |
| 10-13: 10-Navy; Disbrow, Kinstler-a. 11-Marine Corps. 12-Coast Guard. 13-Air Force; L.B. Cole-c | 2.30 | 7.00 | 16.00 |
| 14-French Revolution; Crandall, Evans-a | 3.70 | 11.00 | 26.00 |
| 15-Prehistoric Animals; Al Williamson-a, 6 & 10 pgs. plus Morrow-a | 4.00 | 12.00 | 28.00 |
| 16-18: 16-Crusades. 17-Festivals; Evans, Crandall-a. 18-Great Scientists; Crandall, Evans, Torres, Williamson, Morrow-a | 3.50 | 10.50 | 24.00 |
| 19-Jungle; Crandall, Williamson, Morrow-a | 4.50 | 14.00 | 32.00 |
| 20-Communications; Crandall, Evans-a | 4.50 | 14.00 | 32.00 |
| 21-American Presidents | 3.50 | 10.50 | 24.00 |
| 22-Boating; Morrow-a | 2.30 | 7.00 | 16.00 |
| 23-Great Explorers; Crandall, Evans-a | 2.65 | 8.00 | 18.00 |
| 24-Ghosts; Morrow, Evans-a | 3.50 | 10.50 | 24.00 |
| 25-Magic; Evans, Morrow-a | 3.50 | 10.50 | 24.00 |
| 26-The Civil War | 4.00 | 12.00 | 28.00 |
| 27-Mountains (High Advs.); Crandall/Evans, Morrow, Torres-a | 3.00 | 9.00 | 21.00 |
| 28-Whaling; Crandall, Evans, Morrow, Torres, Wildey-a; L.B. Cole-c | 2.65 | 8.00 | 18.00 |
| 29-Vikings; Crandall, Evans, Torres, Morrow-a | 3.00 | 9.00 | 21.00 |
| 30-Undersea Adventure; Crandall/Evans, Kirby-a | 4.00 | 12.00 | 28.00 |
| 31-Hunting; Crandall/Evans, Ingels, Kinstler, Kirby-a | 3.50 | 10.50 | 24.00 |
| 32,33: 32-For Gold & Glory; Morrow, Kirby, Crandall, Evans-a. 33-Famous Teens; Torres, Crandall, Evans-a | 3.00 | 9.00 | 21.00 |
| 34-36: 34-Fishing; Crandall/Evans, Ingels-a. 35-Spies; Kirby, Morrow, Evans-a. 36-Fight for Life (Medicine); Kirby-a | 2.65 | 8.00 | 18.00 |

NOTE: See Classics Illustrated Special Edition. Another *World Around Us* issue entitled *The Sea* had been prepared in 1962 but was never published in the U.S. It was published in the British/European *World Around Us* series. Those series then continued with seven additional WAU titles not in the U.S. series.

**WORLD FAMOUS HEROES MAGAZINE**
Oct, 1941 - No. 4, Apr, 1942 (a comic book)
Comic Corp. of America (Centaur)

| | Good | Fine | N-Mint |
|---|---|---|---|
| 1-Gustavson-c; Lubbers, Glanzman-a; Davy Crockett story; Flag-c | 43.00 | 130.00 | 300.00 |
| 2-Lou Gehrig life story; Lubbers-a | 23.00 | 70.00 | 160.00 |
| 3,4-Lubbers-a; 4-Wild Bill Hickok app. | 20.00 | 60.00 | 140.00 |

**WORLD FAMOUS STORIES**
1945
Croyden Publishers

| | Good | Fine | N-Mint |
|---|---|---|---|
| 1-Ali Baba, Hansel & Gretel, Rip Van Winkle, Mid-Summer Night's Dream | 6.00 | 18.00 | 42.00 |

**WORLD IS HIS PARISH, THE**
1953 (15 cents)
George A. Pflaum

| | Good | Fine | N-Mint |
|---|---|---|---|
| nn-The story of Pope Pius XII | 3.50 | 10.50 | 22.00 |

**WORLD OF ADVENTURE** (Walt Disney's...)(TV)
April, 1963 - No. 3, Oct, 1963 (All 12 cents)
Gold Key

| | Good | Fine | N-Mint |
|---|---|---|---|
| 1-3-Disney TV characters; Savage Sam, Johnny Shiloh, Capt. Nemo, The Mooncussers | .75 | 2.25 | 5.00 |

**WORLD OF ARCHIE, THE** (See Archie Giant Series Mag. #148, 151, 156, 160, 165, 171, 177, 182, 188, 193, 200, 208, 213, 225, 232, 237, 244, 249, 456, 461, 468, 473, 480, 485, 492, 497, 504, 509, 516, 521, 532, 543, 554, 565, 574, 587, 599, 612)

**WORLD OF FANTASY**
May, 1956 - No. 19, Aug, 1959
Atlas Comics (CPC No. 1-15/ZPC No. 16-19)

| | Good | Fine | N-Mint |
|---|---|---|---|
| 1 | 11.50 | 34.00 | 80.00 |
| 2-Williamson-a, 4 pgs. | 8.50 | 25.50 | 60.00 |
| 3-Sid Check, Roussos-a | 5.70 | 17.00 | 40.00 |
| 4-7 | 4.30 | 13.00 | 30.00 |
| 8-Matt Fox, Orlando, Berg-a | 6.50 | 19.00 | 45.00 |
| 9-Krigstein-a | 5.00 | 15.00 | 35.00 |
| 10,12-15: 12-Everett-c | 3.60 | 11.00 | 25.00 |
| 11-Torres-a | 4.30 | 13.00 | 30.00 |
| 16-Williamson-a, 4 pgs.; Ditko, Kirby-a | 5.70 | 17.00 | 40.00 |
| 17-19-Ditko, Kirby-a | 5.00 | 15.00 | 35.00 |

NOTE: ***Ayers*** *a-3.* ***Berg*** *a-5, 6, 8.* ***Check*** *a-3.* ***Ditko*** *a-17, 19.* ***Everett*** *c-4-7, 9, 13.* ***Kirby*** *c-15, 17-19.* ***Krigstein*** *a-9.* ***Maneely*** *c-14.* ***Morrow*** *a-7, 8, 14.* ***Orlando*** *a-8, 13, 14.* ***Powell*** *a-4, 6.* ***Sale*** *a-3.*

**WORLD OF GIANT COMICS, THE** (See Archie All-Star Specials under Archie Comics)

**WORLD OF GINGER FOX, THE** (Also see Ginger Fox)
Nov, 1986 ($6.95, 68 pgs, mature readers, 8½ x 11")
Comico

| | Good | Fine | N-Mint |
|---|---|---|---|
| Graphic Novel ($6.95) | 1.15 | 3.50 | 7.00 |
| Hardcover ($27.95) | 4.70 | 14.00 | 28.00 |

**WORLD OF JUGHEAD, THE** (See Archie Giant Series Mag. #9, 14, 19, 24, 30, 136, 143, 149, 152, 157, 161, 166, 172, 178, 183, 189, 194, 202, 209, 215, 227, 233, 239, 245, 251, 457, 463, 469, 475, 481, 487, 493, 499, 505, 511, 517, 523, 531, 542, 553, 564, 577, 590, 602)

**WORLD OF KRYPTON, THE** (World of...#3; see Superman #248)
7/79 - No. 3, 9/79; 12/87 - No. 4, 3/88 (Both are mini-series)
DC Comics, Inc.

| | Good | Fine | N-Mint |
|---|---|---|---|
| 1 ('79, 40 cents)-Jor-El marries Lara | | .35 | .70 |
| 2,3: 3-Baby Superman sent to Earth; Krypton explodes; Mon-el app. | | .35 | .70 |
| 1-4 (75 cents)-Byrne scripts; Byrne/Simonson-c | | .50 | 1.00 |

**WORLD OF METROPOLIS, THE**
Aug, 1988 - No. 4, July, 1988 ($1.00, mini-series)
DC Comics

| | Good | Fine | N-Mint |
|---|---|---|---|
| 1-4: Byrne scripts | | .50 | 1.00 |

**WORLD OF MYSTERY**
June, 1956 - No. 7, July, 1957
Atlas Comics (GPI)

| | Good | Fine | N-Mint |
|---|---|---|---|
| 1-Torres, Orlando-a | 11.00 | 32.00 | 75.00 |
| 2-Woodish-a | 3.60 | 11.00 | 25.00 |
| 3-Torres, Davis, Ditko-a | 5.70 | 17.00 | 40.00 |
| 4-Pakula, Powell-a; Ditko-c | 6.50 | 19.00 | 45.00 |
| 5,7: 5-Orlando-a | 3.60 | 11.00 | 25.00 |
| 6-Williamson/Mayo-a, 4 pgs.; Ditko-a; Crandall text illo | 6.50 | 19.00 | 45.00 |

NOTE: ***Colan*** *a-7.* ***Everett*** *c-1-3.* ***Romita*** *a-2.* ***Severin*** *c/a-7.*

**WORLD OF SMALLVILLE**
Apr, 1988 - No. 4, July, 1988 (75 cents, color, mini-series)
DC Comics

| | Good | Fine | N-Mint |
|---|---|---|---|
| 1-4: Byrne scripts | | .50 | 1.00 |

**WORLD OF SUSPENSE**
April, 1956 - No. 8, July, 1957
Atlas News Co.

*The World Around Us #15, © GIL*

*World Famous Heroes Magazine #1, © CEN*

*World of Fantasy #8, © MEG*

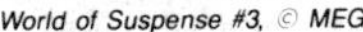
World of Suspense #3, © MEG

World's Finest Comics #5, © DC

World's Finest Comics #113, © DC

| | Good | Fine | N-Mint |
|---|---|---|---|
| 1-Orlando-a | 11.00 | 32.00 | 75.00 |
| 2-Ditko-a | 5.70 | 17.00 | 40.00 |
| 3,7-Williamson-a in both, 4 pgs. each; #7-with Mayo | 6.00 | 18.00 | 42.00 |
| 4-6,8 | 3.60 | 11.00 | 25.00 |

NOTE: *Berg a-6. Ditko a-2. Everett a-1, 5; c-6. Heck a-5. Orlando a-5. Powell a-6. Reinman a-4. Roussos a-6.*

**WORLD OF WHEELS** (Formerly Dragstrip Hotrodders)
No. 17, Oct, 1967 - No. 32, June, 1970
Charlton Comics

| | | | |
|---|---|---|---|
| 17-20-Features Ken King | .35 | 1.00 | 2.00 |
| 21-32-Features Ken King | .25 | .75 | 1.50 |
| Modern Comics Reprint 23('78) | | .15 | .30 |

**WORLD OF WOOD**
1986 - No. 4, 1987?; No. 5, Feb, 1989 ($1.75, color, mini-series)
Eclipse Comics

| | | | |
|---|---|---|---|
| 1-4: 1-Dave Stevens-c. 2-Wood/Stevens-c | .30 | .90 | 1.80 |
| 5 ($2.00, B&W)-r/Avon's Flying Saucers | .35 | 1.00 | 2.00 |

**WORLD'S BEST COMICS** (World's Finest Comics #2 on)
Spring, 1941 (Cardboard-c)(DC's 6th annual format comic)
National Periodical Publications (100 pgs.)

| | Good | Fine | VF-NM | NM/Mint |
|---|---|---|---|---|
| 1-The Batman, Superman, Crimson Avenger, Johnny Thunder, The King, Young Dr. Davis, Zatara, Lando, Man of Magic, & Red, White & Blue begin; Superman, Batman & Robin covers begin (inside-c blank) | 500.00 | 1250.00 | 3000.00 | 4000.00 |

(Estimated up to 185 total copies exist, 6 in NM/Mint)

**WORLDS BEYOND** (Worlds of Fear #2 on)
Nov, 1951
Fawcett Publications

| | Good | Fine | N-Mint |
|---|---|---|---|
| 1-Powell, Bailey-a | 14.00 | 43.00 | 100.00 |

**WORLD'S FAIR COMICS** (See New York. . . )

**WORLD'S FINEST**
1990 - No. 3, 1990 ($3.95, squarebound, mini-series, 52 pgs.)
DC Comics

| | | | |
|---|---|---|---|
| 1-3: Batman & Superman team-up against The Joker and Lex Luthor. 2,3-Joker/Luthor painted-c by Steve Rude | .75 | 2.25 | 4.50 |

**WORLD'S FINEST COMICS** (Formerly World's Best Comics #1)
No. 2, Sum, 1941 - No. 323, Jan, 1986 (early issues have 100 pgs.)
National Periodical Publ./DC Comics (#1-17 have cardboard covers)

| | Good | Fine | N-Mint |
|---|---|---|---|
| 2 (100 pgs.)-Superman, Batman & Robin covers continue | 225.00 | 562.00 | 1350.00 |
| 3-The Sandman begins; last Johnny Thunder; origin & 1st app. The Scarecrow | 192.00 | 480.00 | 1150.00 |
| 4-Hop Harrigan app.; last Young Dr. Davis | 133.00 | 335.00 | 800.00 |
| 5-Intro. TNT & Dan the Dyna-Mite; last King & Crimson Avenger | 133.00 | 335.00 | 800.00 |
| 6-Star Spangled Kid begins; Aquaman app.; S&K Sandman with Sandy in new costume begins, ends #7 | 107.00 | 270.00 | 640.00 |
| 7-Green Arrow begins; last Lando, King, & Red, White & Blue; S&K art | 107.00 | 270.00 | 640.00 |
| 8-Boy Commandos begin | 96.00 | 240.00 | 575.00 |
| 9-Batman cameo in Star Spangled Kid; S&K-a; last 100pg. issue; Hitler, Mussolini, Tojo-c | 83.00 | 210.00 | 500.00 |
| 10-S&K-a | 83.00 | 210.00 | 500.00 |
| 11-17-Last cardboard cover issue | 75.00 | 190.00 | 450.00 |
| 18-20: 18-Paper covers begin; last Star Spangled Kid | 67.00 | 167.00 | 400.00 |
| 21-30: 30-Johnny Peril app. | 48.00 | 120.00 | 285.00 |
| 31-40: 33-35-Tomahawk app. | 41.00 | 102.00 | 245.00 |
| 41-50: 41-Boy Commandos end. 42-Wyoming Kid begins, ends #63. 43-Full Steam Foley begins, ends #48. 48-Last square binding. 49-Tom Sparks, Boy Inventor begins | 32.00 | 80.00 | 190.00 |
| 51-60: 51-Zatara ends. 59-Manhunters Around the World begins, ends #62 | 32.00 | 80.00 | 190.00 |
| 61-64: 63-Capt. Compass app. | 28.00 | 70.00 | 165.00 |
| 65-Origin Superman; Tomahawk begins, ends #101 | 35.00 | 88.00 | 210.00 |
| 66-70-(15 cent issues)(Scarce)-Last 68 pg. issue | 26.00 | 77.00 | 180.00 |
| 71-(10 cent issue)(Scarce)-Superman & Batman begin as team | 32.00 | 95.00 | 220.00 |
| 72,73-(10 cent issues)(Scarce) | 24.00 | 70.00 | 165.00 |
| 74-80: 74-Last pre-code issue | 13.00 | 40.00 | 90.00 |
| 81-90: 88-1st Joker/Luthor team-up. 90-Batwoman's 1st app. in World's Finest | 8.50 | 25.50 | 60.00 |
| 91-93,95-99: 96-99-Kirby Green Arrow | 5.70 | 17.00 | 40.00 |
| 94-Origin Superman/Batman team retold | 26.00 | 77.00 | 180.00 |
| 100 (3/59) | 14.00 | 41.00 | 95.00 |
| 101-121: 102-Tommy Tomorrow begins, ends. #124. 113-Intro. Miss Arrowette in Green Arrow; 1st Bat-Mite/Mr. Mxyzptlk team-up. 121-Last 10 cent issue | 4.30 | 13.00 | 30.00 |
| 122-128,130-142: 123-2nd Bat-Mite/Mr. Mxyzptlk team-up. 125-Aquaman begins, ends #139. 135-Last Dick Sprang story. 140-Last Green Arrow. 142-Origin The Composite Superman (villain); Legion app. | 2.15 | 6.50 | 15.00 |
| 129-Joker-c/story | 3.60 | 11.00 | 25.00 |
| 143-150: 143-1st Mailbag | 1.30 | 4.00 | 9.00 |
| 151-155,157-160 | 1.00 | 3.00 | 7.00 |
| 156-1st Bizarro Batman; Joker-c/story | 5.00 | 15.00 | 35.00 |
| 161,170 (80-Pg. Giants G-28,G-40) | 1.30 | 4.00 | 9.00 |
| 162-165,167-169,171-174: 168,172-Adult Legion app. | .70 | 2.00 | 5.00 |
| 166-Joker-c/story | 1.30 | 4.00 | 9.00 |
| 175,176-Neal Adams-a; both r-J'onn J'onzz origin/Detective #225,226 | .85 | 2.60 | 6.00 |
| 177-Joker-c/story | .85 | 2.60 | 6.00 |
| 178,180-187,189-196,198-204: 182-Silent Knight-r/Brave & Bold #6. 186-Johnny Quick-r. 187-Green Arrow origin-r/Adv. #256. 190-193-Robin-r. 198,199-3rd Superman/Flash race | .50 | 1.50 | 3.00 |
| 179,188,197 (80-Pg. Giant G-52,G-64,G-76) | .70 | 2.00 | 4.00 |
| 205-6 pgs. Shining Knight by Frazetta/Adv. #153; 52 pgs.; Teen Titans x-over | .35 | 1.00 | 2.00 |
| 206 (80-Pg. Giant G-88) | .35 | 1.00 | 2.00 |
| 207-248: 207-212-(52 pgs.). 215-Intro. Batman Jr. & Superman Jr. 217-Metamorpho begins, ends #220; Batman/Superman team-ups begin. 223-228-(100 pgs.). 223-N. Adams-r. 223-Deadman origin. 226-N. Adams S&K, Toth-r; Manhunter part origin-r/Detective #225,226. 229-r/origin Superman-Batman team. 244-Green Arrow, Black Canary, Wonder Woman, Vigilante begin; $1.00, 84 pg. issues begin. 246-Death of Stuff in Vigilante; origin Vigilante retold. 248-Last Vigilante | .25 | .75 | 1.50 |
| 249-The Creeper begins by Ditko, ends #255 | .70 | 2.00 | 4.00 |
| 250-299: 250-The Creeper origin retold by Ditko. 252-Last 84 pg. issue. 253-Capt. Marvel begins; 68 pgs. begin, end #265. 255-Last Creeper. 256-Hawkman begins. 257-Black Lightning begins. 266-282-(52 pgs.). 267-Challengers of the Unknown app. 268-Capt. Marvel Jr. origin retold. 271-Origin Superman/Batman team retold. 274-Zatanna begins. 279,280-Capt. Marvel Jr. & Kid Eternity learn they are brothers. 284-Legion app. 298-Begin 75 cent-c | .25 | .75 | 1.50 |
| 300-($1.25, 52pgs.)-Justice League of America, New Teen Titans & The Outsiders app.; Perez-a(3 pgs.) | .35 | 1.00 | 2.00 |
| 301-323: 304-Origin Null and Void. 309,319-Free 16 pg. story in each (309-Flash Force 2000, 319-Mask preview) | .25 | .75 | 1.50 |
| Giveaway (c. 1944-45, 8 pgs., in color, paper-c)-Johnny Everyman-r/World's Finest | 11.50 | 34.00 | 80.00 |

NOTE: *Neal Adams a-230r; c-174-176, 178-180, 182, 183, 185, 186, 199-205, 208-211.*

244-246, 258. **Austin** a-244-246i. **Burnley** a-8, 10; c-7-9, 12. **Colan** a-274p, 297, 299. **Ditko** a-249-255. **Giffen** c-284p. **G. Kane** a-38, 174r, 282, 283; c-281, 282, 289. **Kirby** a-187. **Kubert** Zatara-40-44. **Miller** c-285p. **Morrow** a-245-248. **Nasser** a(p)-244-246, 259, 260. **Newton** a-253-281p. **Orlando** a-224r. **Perez** a-300i; c-271, 276, 277p, 278p. **Robinson** a-2, 9, 13-15; c-2-4, 6. **Rogers** a-259p. **Roussos** a-212r. **Simonson** c-291. **Spiegle** a-275-278, 284. **Staton** a-262p, 273p. **Toth** a-228r. **Tuska** a-230r, 250p, 252p, 254p, 257p, 283p, 284p, 308p.

*(Also see 80 Page Giant #15)*

**WORLD'S FINEST COMICS DIGEST** (See DC Special Series #23)

**WORLD'S GREATEST ATHLETE** (See Walt Disney Showcase #14)

**WORLD'S GREATEST SONGS**
Sept, 1954
Atlas Comics (Male)

| | Good | Fine | N-Mint |
|---|---|---|---|
| 1-(Scarce) Heath & Harry Anderson-a; Eddie Fisher life story | 16.00 | 48.00 | 110.00 |

**WORLD'S GREATEST STORIES**
Jan, 1949 - No. 2, May, 1949
Jubilee Publications

| | | | |
|---|---|---|---|
| 1-Alice in Wonderland | 13.00 | 40.00 | 90.00 |
| 2-Pinocchio | 11.50 | 34.00 | 80.00 |

**WORLD'S GREATEST SUPER HEROES**
1977 (3¾x3¾") (24 pgs. in color) (Giveaway)
DC Comics (Nutra Comics) (Child Vitamins, Inc.)

| | | | |
|---|---|---|---|
| nn-Batman & Robin app.; health tips | .25 | .75 | 1.50 |

**WORLDS OF FEAR** (Formerly Worlds Beyond #1)
V1#2, Jan, 1952 - V2#10, June, 1953
Fawcett Publications

| | | | |
|---|---|---|---|
| V1#2 | 12.00 | 36.00 | 85.00 |
| 3-Evans-a | 9.30 | 28.00 | 65.00 |
| 4-6(9/52) | 8.50 | 25.50 | 60.00 |
| V2#7-9 | 7.00 | 21.00 | 50.00 |
| 10-Saunders Painted-c; man with no eyes surrounded by eyeballs-c | 14.00 | 43.00 | 100.00 |

NOTE: **Powell** a-2, 4, 5. **Sekowsky** a-4, 5.

**WORLDS UNKNOWN**
May, 1973 - No. 8, Aug, 1974
Marvel Comics Group

| | | |
|---|---|---|
| 1-R-/from Astonishing #54; Torres, Reese-a | .50 | 1.00 |
| 2-8 | .35 | .70 |

NOTE: **Adkins/Mooney** a-5. **Buscema** c/a-4p. **W. Howard** c/a-3i. **Kane** a(p)-1,2; c(p)-5, 6, 8. **Sutton** a-2. **Tuska** a(p)-7, 8; c-7p. No. 7, 8 has Golden Voyage of Sinbad movie adaptation.

**WORLD WAR STORIES**
Apr-June, 1965 - No. 3, Dec, 1965
Dell Publishing Co.

| | | | |
|---|---|---|---|
| 1-Glanzman-a in all | 1.70 | 5.00 | 12.00 |
| 2,3 | 1.00 | 3.00 | 7.00 |

**WORLD WAR II** (See Classics Illustrated Special Issue)

**WORLD WAR III**
Mar, 1953 - No. 2, May, 1953
Ace Periodicals

| | | | |
|---|---|---|---|
| 1-(Scarce)-Atomic bomb-c | 33.00 | 100.00 | 230.00 |
| 2-Used in **POP**, pg. 78 & B&W & color illos. | 27.00 | 80.00 | 185.00 |

**WORLD WITHOUT END**
1990 - No. 6, 1991 ($2.50, mini-series, mature readers)
DC Comics

| | | | |
|---|---|---|---|
| 1-6: Horror/fantasy | .40 | 1.25 | 2.50 |

**WORST FROM MAD, THE** (Annual)
1958 - No. 12, 1969 (Each annual cover is reprinted from the cover of the Mad issues being reprinted)
E. C. Comics

| | Good | Fine | N-Mint |
|---|---|---|---|
| nn(1958)-Bonus; record labels & travel stickers; 1st Mad annual; r-/Mad #29-34 | 13.00 | 40.00 | 90.00 |
| 2(1959)-Bonus is small 33⅓ rpm record entitled "Meet the Staff of Mad;" r-/Mad #35-40 | 18.00 | 54.00 | 125.00 |
| 3(1960)-20"x30" campaign poster "Alfred E. Neuman for President;" r-/Mad #41-46 | 10.00 | 30.00 | 70.00 |
| 4(1961)-Sunday comics section; r-/Mad #47-54 | 10.00 | 30.00 | 70.00 |
| 5(1962)-Has 33⅓ record; r-/Mad #55-62 | 14.00 | 43.00 | 100.00 |
| 6(1963)-Has 33⅓ record; r-/Mad #63-70 | 16.00 | 48.00 | 110.00 |
| 7(1964)-Mad protest signs; r-/Mad #71-76 | 6.50 | 19.00 | 45.00 |
| 8(1965)-Build a Mad Zeppelin | 7.00 | 21.00 | 50.00 |
| 9(1966)-33⅓ rpm record | 11.00 | 32.00 | 75.00 |
| 10(1967)-Mad bumper sticker | 3.70 | 11.00 | 26.00 |
| 11(1968)-Mad cover window stickers | 3.70 | 11.00 | 26.00 |
| 12(1969)-Mad picture postcards; Orlando-a | 3.70 | 11.00 | 26.00 |

NOTE: *Covers:* **Bob Clarke**-#8. **Mingo**-#7, 9-12.

**WOTALIFE COMICS**
No. 3, Aug-Sept, 1946 - No. 12, July, 1947; 1959
Fox Features Syndicate/Norlen Mag.

| | | | |
|---|---|---|---|
| 3-Cosmo Cat | 4.30 | 13.00 | 30.00 |
| 4-12-Cosmo Cat | 2.65 | 8.00 | 18.00 |
| 1('59-Norlen)-Atomic Rabbit, Atomic Mouse | 2.15 | 6.50 | 15.00 |

**WOTALIFE COMICS**
1957 - No. 5, 1957
Green Publications

| | | | |
|---|---|---|---|
| 1 | 1.70 | 5.00 | 12.00 |
| 2-5 | 1.30 | 4.00 | 9.00 |

**WOW COMICS**
July, 1936 - No. 4, Nov, 1936 (52 pgs., magazine size)
Henle Publishing Co.

| | | | |
|---|---|---|---|
| 1-Fu Manchu; Eisner-a; Briefer-c | 183.00 | 460.00 | 1100.00 |
| 2-Ken Maynard, Fu Manchu, Popeye by Segar; Eisner-a | 117.00 | 290.00 | 700.00 |
| 3-Eisner-c/a(3); Popeye by Segar, Fu Manchu, Hiram Hick by Bob Kane, Space Limited app. | 117.00 | 290.00 | 700.00 |
| 4-Flash Gordon by Raymond, Mandrake, Popeye by Segar, Tillie The Toiler, Fu Manchu, Hiram Hick by Bob Kane; Eisner-a(3), Briefer-c | 150.00 | 375.00 | 900.00 |

**WOW COMICS** (Real Western Hero #70 on)(See XMas Comics)
Winter, 1940-41; No. 2, Summer, 1941 - No. 69, Fall, 1948
Fawcett Publications

| | Good | Fine | VF-NM | NM/Mint |
|---|---|---|---|---|
| nn(#1)-Origin Mr. Scarlet by S&K; Atom Blake, Boy Wizard, Jim Dolan, & Rick O'Shay begin; Diamond Jack, The White Rajah, & Shipwreck Roberts, only app.; the cover was printed on unstable paper stock and is rarely found in fine or mint condition; blank inside-c; bondage-c by Beck | 650.00 | 1950.00 | 5200.00 | 6000.00 |

(Estimated up to 110 total copies exist, 3 in NM/Mint)

| | Good | Fine | N-Mint |
|---|---|---|---|
| 2 (Scarce)-The Hunchback begins | 75.00 | 225.00 | 525.00 |
| 3 (Fall, 1941) | 46.00 | 137.00 | 320.00 |
| 4-Origin Pinky | 50.00 | 150.00 | 350.00 |
| 5 | 36.00 | 107.00 | 250.00 |
| 6-Origin The Phantom Eagle; Commando Yank begins | 30.00 | 90.00 | 210.00 |
| 7,8,10: 10-Swayze-c/a on Mary Marvel | 27.00 | 81.00 | 190.00 |
| 9 (1/6/43)-Capt. Marvel, Capt. Marvel Jr., Shazam app.; Scarlet & Pinky x-over; Mary Marvel c/stories begin (cameo #9) | 50.00 | 150.00 | 350.00 |
| 11-17,19,20: 15-Flag-c | 18.00 | 54.00 | 125.00 |
| 18-1st app. Uncle Marvel (10/43); infinity-c | 22.00 | 65.00 | 150.00 |
| 21-30: 28-Pinky x-over in Mary Marvel | 11.00 | 32.00 | 75.00 |
| 31-40: 32-68-Phantom Eagle by Swayze | 7.00 | 21.00 | 50.00 |
| 41-50 | 5.70 | 17.00 | 40.00 |

*Worlds of Fear #6, © FAW*

*Worlds Unknown #1, © MEG*

*Wow Comics #1, © FAW*

Wyatt Earp #25, © MEG

X-Factor #50, © MEG

X-Mas Comics #7 (12/52), © FAW

| | Good | Fine | N-Mint |
|---|---|---|---|
| 51-58: Last Mary Marvel | 5.00 | 15.00 | 35.00 |
| 59-69: 59-Ozzie begins. 62-Flying Saucer gag-c (1/48). 65-69-Tom Mix stories | 4.30 | 13.00 | 30.00 |

**WRATH OF THE SPECTRE, THE**
May, 1988 - No. 4, Aug, 1988 ($2.50, color, mini-series)
DC Comics

1-4: Aparo-r/Adventure #431-440 .40 1.25 2.50

**WRECK OF GROSVENOR** (See Superior Stories #3)

**WRINGLE WRANGLE** (See 4-Color #821)

**WULF THE BARBARIAN**
Feb, 1975 - No. 4, Sept, 1975
Atlas/Seaboard Publ.

1-Origin .40 .80
2-4: 2-Intro. Berithe the Swordswoman; Neal Adams, Wood, Reese-a assists .30 .60

**WYATT EARP** (Hugh O'Brian Famous Marshal)
No. 860, Nov, 1957 - No. 13, Dec-Feb, 1960-61 (Photo-c)
Dell Publishing Co.

4-Color 860 (#1)-Manning-a 8.00 24.00 55.00
4-Color 890,921(6/58)-All Manning-a 4.50 14.00 32.00
4 (9-11/58) - 12-Manning-a 3.70 11.00 26.00
13-Toth-a 4.50 14.00 32.00

**WYATT EARP**
Nov, 1955 - #29, June, 1960; #30, Oct, 1972 - #34, June, 1973
Atlas Comics/Marvel No. 23 on (IPC)

1 8.50 25.50 60.00
2-Williamson-a, 4 pgs. 5.70 17.00 40.00
3-6,8-11: 3-Black Bart app. 8-Wild Bill Hickok app. 3.60 11.00 25.00
7,12-Williamson-a, 4pgs. ea.; #12 with Mayo 4.50 14.00 32.00
13-19: 17-1st app. Wyatt's deputy, Grizzly Grant 3.00 9.00 21.00
20-Torres-a 3.50 10.50 24.00
21-Davis-c 2.65 8.00 18.00
22-24,26-29: 22-Ringo Kid app. 23-Kid From Texas app. 29-Last 10 cent issue 1.70 5.00 12.00
25-Davis-a 2.00 6.00 14.00
30-Williamson-r ('72) .50 1.00
31,33,34-Reprints .25 .50
32-Torres-a(r) .30 .60

NOTE: ***Ayers** a-8, 17. **Everett** c-6. **Kirby** c-25, 29. **Maneely** a-1; c-1, 3, 4, 8, 12, 17, 20. **Maurer** a-3(4), 4(4), 8(4). **Severin** a-4, 10; c-10, 14. **Wildey** a-5, 17, 24, 28.*

**WYATT EARP FRONTIER MARSHAL** (Formerly Range Busters)
No. 12, Jan, 1956 - No. 72, Dec, 1967 (Also see Blue Bird)
Charlton Comics

12 2.65 8.00 18.00
13-19 1.30 4.00 9.00
20-Williamson-a(4), 8,5,5,& 7 pgs.; 68 pgs. 5.50 16.50 38.00
21-30 .85 2.60 6.00
31-50: 31-Crandall-r .70 2.00 4.00
51-72 .35 1.00 2.00

**XANADU COLOR SPECIAL**
Dec, 1988 ($2.00, color, one-shot)
Eclipse Comics

1-Reprints Xanadu from Thoughts & Images .35 1.00 2.00

**XENON**
Dec. 1, 1987 - No. 23, Nov. 1, 1988 ($1.50, bi-weekly, B&W)
Eclipse Comics

1-23 .25 .75 1.50

**XENOZOIC TALES** (Also see Cadillacs & Dinosaurs)
Feb, 1987 - Present ($2.00, B&W)
Kitchen Sink Press

| | Good | Fine | N-Mint |
|---|---|---|---|
| 1-11: 1-2nd printing exists (1/89) | .35 | 1.00 | 2.00 |

**X-FACTOR** (Also see The Avengers #263 & Fantastic Four #286)
Feb, 1986 - Present
Marvel Comics Group

1-($1.25, 52 pgs)-Story recaps 1st app. from Avengers #263; original X-Men app.; Layton/Guice-a 1.35 4.00 8.00
2,3 .85 2.50 5.00
4,5 .75 2.25 4.50
6-10 .60 1.75 3.50
11-20 .50 1.50 3.00
21-23 .40 1.25 2.50
24-26: Fall Of The Mutants. 26-New outfits .70 2.00 4.00
27-30 .35 1.00 2.00
31-37,39-49: 35-Origin Cyclops .25 .75 1.50
38,50-Double size ($1.50) .35 1.00 2.00
51-59,63-65: 52,53-Sabertooth app. 54-Intro Crimson .50 1.00
60-62-X-Tinction Agenda x-over. 62-Jim Lee-c .35 1.00 2.00
Annual 1 (10/86), 2 (10/87) .40 1.25 2.50
Annual 3 ('88, $1.75)-Evolutionary War app. .50 1.50 3.00
Annual 4 ('89, $2.00, 68 pgs.)-Atlantis Attacks; Byrne/Simonson-a, Byrne-c .40 1.25 2.50
Annual 5 ('90, $2.00, 68 pgs.)-F.F., New Mutants x-over .35 1.00 2.00
. . .Prisoner of Love nn (1990, $4.95, 52 pgs.)-Starlin scripts; Guice-a .85 2.50 5.00

NOTE: ***Art Adams** a-41p, 42p. **Buckler** a-50p. **McFarlane** c-50i. **Paul Smith** a-44-48; c-43. **Simsonson** c/a-10, 11, 13-15, 17-19, 21, 23-31, 38.*

**XMAS COMICS**
12?/1941 - No. 2, 12?/1942 (324 pgs.) (50 cents)
No. 3, 12?/1943 - No. 7, 12?/1947 (132 pgs.)
Fawcett Publications

| | Good | Fine | VF-NM | NM/Mint |
|---|---|---|---|---|
| 1-Contains Whiz #21, Capt. Marvel #3, Bulletman #2, Wow #3, & Master #18; Raboy back-c. Not rebound, remaindered comics printed at same time as originals | 135.00 | 410.00 | 950.00 | 1400.00 |

(Estimated up to 110 total copies exist, 5 in NM/Mint)

| | Good | Fine | N-Mint |
|---|---|---|---|
| 2-Capt. Marvel, Bulletman, Spy Smasher | 68.00 | 205.00 | 475.00 |
| 3-7-Funny animals | 20.00 | 60.00 | 140.00 |

**XMAS COMICS**
No. 4, Dec, 1949 - No. 7, Dec, 1952 (196 pgs.)
Fawcett Publications

4-Contains Whiz, Master, Tom Mix, Captain Marvel, Nyoka, Capt. Video, Bob Colt, Monte Hale, Hot Rod Comics, & Battle Stories. Not rebound, remaindered comics—printed at the same time as originals 29.00 85.00 200.00
5-7-Same as above 25.00 75.00 175.00

**XMAS FUNNIES**
No date (paper cover) (36 pgs.?)
Kinney Shoes (Giveaway)

Contains 1933 color strip-r; Mutt & Jeff, etc. 10.00 30.00 70.00

**X-MEN, THE** (See Amazing Adventures, Capt. America #172, Classic X-Men, Giant-Size. . ., Heroes For Hope. . ., Kitty Pryde &. . ., Marvel & DC Present, Marvel Fanfare, Marvel Graphic Novel, Marvel Team-up, Marvel Triple Action, Nightcrawler, Official Marvel Index To. . ., Special Edition. . ., The Uncanny. . ., X-Factor & X-Terminators)

**X-MEN, THE** (X-Men #94-141; The Uncanny X-Men #142 on)
Sept, 1963 - Present
Marvel Comics Group

| | Good | Fine | N-Mint | Mint |
|---|---|---|---|---|
| 1-Origin/1st app. X-Men; 1st app. Magneto | 140.00 | 530.00 | 1260.00 | 1900.00 |

(Estimated up to 1900 total copies exist, 60 in Mint)

| | Good | Fine | N-Mint |
|---|---|---|---|
| 2-1st app. The Vanisher | 60.00 | 180.00 | 420.00 |
| 3-1st app. The Blob | 31.00 | 95.00 | 220.00 |
| 4-1st Quick Silver & Scarlet Witch & Brotherhood of the Evil Mutants | 27.00 | 80.00 | 185.00 |
| 5 | 21.00 | 62.00 | 145.00 |
| 6-10: 6-Sub-Mariner app. 8-1st Unus the Untouchable. 9-Early Avengers app. 10-1st S.A. app. Ka-Zar | 16.00 | 48.00 | 110.00 |
| 11,13-15: 11-1st app. The Stranger. 14-1st app. Sentinels. 15-Origin Beast | 10.00 | 30.00 | 70.00 |
| 12-Origin Prof. X | 13.00 | 40.00 | 90.00 |
| 16-20: 19-1st app. The Mimic | 7.00 | 21.00 | 50.00 |
| 21-27,29,30: 27-Re-enter The Mimic (r-in #75) | 5.70 | 17.00 | 40.00 |
| 28-1st app. The Banshee (r-in #76) | 6.50 | 19.00 | 45.00 |
| 31-34,36,37,39,40: 39-New costumes | 4.00 | 12.00 | 28.00 |
| 35-Spider-Man x-over (8/67)(r-in #83) | 6.50 | 19.00 | 45.00 |
| 38-Origins of the X-Men series begins, ends #57 | 5.00 | 15.00 | 35.00 |
| 41-49: 42-Death of Prof. X (Changeling disguised as). 44-Red Raven app. (G.A.). 49-Steranko-c; 1st Polaris | 3.15 | 9.50 | 22.00 |
| 50,51-Steranko-c/a | 4.00 | 12.00 | 28.00 |
| 52 | 2.65 | 8.00 | 18.00 |
| 53-Barry Smith-c/a (1st comic book work) | 4.00 | 12.00 | 28.00 |
| 54,55-B. Smith-c. 54-1st app. Alex Summers | 3.15 | 9.50 | 22.00 |
| 56-63,65-Neal Adams-a(p). 56-Intro Havoc without costume. 65-Return of Professor X. 58-1st app. Havoil | 4.30 | 13.00 | 30.00 |
| 64-1st Sunfire app. | 3.15 | 9.50 | 22.00 |
| 66-Last new story w/original X-Men | 2.15 | 6.50 | 15.00 |
| 67-70,72: All 52 pgs. 67-Reprints begin, end #93 | 1.85 | 5.50 | 13.00 |
| 71,73-93: 73-86 r-#25-38 w/new-c. 87-93 r-#39-45 with-c | 1.70 | 5.00 | 12.00 |
| 94(8/75)-New X-Men begin (See Giant-Size X-Men for 1st app.); Colossus, Nightcrawler, Thunderbird, Storm, Wolverine, & Banshee join; Angel, Marvel Girl, & Iceman resign | 20.00 | 60.00 | 140.00 |
| 95-Death Thunderbird | 5.70 | 17.00 | 40.00 |
| 96-99 (regular 25 cent cover) | 4.00 | 12.00 | 28.00 |
| 98,99 (30 cent cover) | 4.50 | 14.00 | 32.00 |
| 100-Old vs. New X-Men; part origin Phoenix | 4.30 | 13.00 | 30.00 |
| 101-Phoenix origin concludes | 4.00 | 12.00 | 28.00 |
| 102-107: 102-Origin Storm. 104-Intro. Star Jammers. 106-Old vs. New X-Men | 1.85 | 5.50 | 13.00 |
| 108-Byrne-a begins (See Marvel Team-Up 53) | 4.35 | 13.00 | 30.00 |
| 109-1st Vindicator | 3.70 | 11.00 | 25.00 |
| 110,111: 110-Phoenix joins | 2.15 | 6.50 | 15.00 |
| 112-119: 117-Origin Professor X | 1.70 | 5.00 | 12.00 |
| 120-1st Alpha Flight (cameo), story line begins | 4.00 | 12.00 | 28.00 |
| 121-1st Alpha Flight (full story) | 4.35 | 13.00 | 30.00 |
| 122-128: 124-Colossus becomes Proletarian | 1.85 | 5.50 | 11.00 |
| 129-Intro Kitty Pryde | 2.15 | 6.50 | 13.00 |
| 130-1st app. The Dazzler by Byrne | 2.35 | 7.00 | 14.00 |
| 131-135: 131-Dazzler app. 133-Wolverine app. 134-Phoenix becomes Dark Phoenix | 1.70 | 5.00 | 10.00 |
| 136,138: 138-Dazzler app.; Cyclops leaves | 1.45 | 4.25 | 8.50 |
| 137-Giant; death of Phoenix | 1.85 | 5.50 | 11.00 |
| 139-Alpha Flight app.; Kitty Pryde joins; new costume for Wolverine | 2.50 | 7.50 | 15.00 |
| 140-Alpha Flight app. | 3.00 | 9.00 | 18.00 |
| 141-Intro Future X-Men & The New Brotherhood of Evil Mutants; death of Frank Richards | 1.75 | 5.25 | 10.50 |
| 142,143: 142-Deaths of Wolverine, Storm & Colossus. 143-Last Byrne issue | 1.05 | 3.15 | 6.30 |
| 144-150: 144-Man-Thing app. 145-Old X-Men app. 148-Spider-Woman, Dazzler app. 150-Double size | .90 | 2.65 | 5.30 |
| 151-157,159-161,163,164: 161-Origin Magneto. 163-Origin Binary. 164-1st app. Binary as Carol Danvers | .60 | 1.85 | 3.70 |
| 158-1st app. Rogue in X-Men (See Avengers Annual #10) | | | |

| | Good | Fine | N-Mint |
|---|---|---|---|
| | .70 | 2.10 | 4.20 |
| 162-Wolverine solo story | .85 | 2.50 | 5.00 |
| 165-Paul Smith-a begins | .90 | 2.65 | 5.30 |
| 166-Double size; Paul Smith-a | .70 | 2.10 | 4.20 |
| 167-170: 167-New Mutants x-over. 168-1st app. Madelyne Pryor in X-Men (See Avengers Annual #10) | .55 | 1.60 | 3.20 |
| 171-Rogue joins X-Men; Simonson-c/a | 1.00 | 3.00 | 6.00 |
| 172-174: 172,173-Two part Wolverine solo story. 173-Two cover variations, blue & black. 174-Phoenix cameo | .55 | 1.60 | 3.20 |
| 175-Double size; anniversary issue; Phoenix returns. Last Paul Smith-c/a | .70 | 2.00 | 4.00 |
| 176-185: 181-Sunfire app. 182-Rogue solo story | .45 | 1.30 | 2.60 |
| 186-Double-size; Barry Smith/Austin-a | .60 | 1.75 | 3.50 |
| 187-192,194-199: 190,191-Spider-Man & Avengers x-over. 195-Power Pack x-over | .40 | 1.25 | 2.50 |
| 193-Double size; 100th app. New X-Men | .70 | 2.00 | 4.00 |
| 200-Double size | 1.00 | 3.00 | 6.00 |
| 201-209: 204-Nightcrawler solo story. 207-Wolverine/Phoenix story | .70 | 2.00 | 4.00 |
| 210-213-Mutant Massacre. 212-Wolverine vs. Sabertooth | 2.15 | 6.50 | 15.00 |
| 214-224: 219-Havok joins | .50 | 1.50 | 3.00 |
| 225-227: Fall Of The Mutants. 226-Double size | 1.00 | 3.00 | 7.00 |
| 228-241: 229-$1.00 begin | .40 | 1.25 | 2.50 |
| 242-Double size, X-Factor app., Inferno tie-in | .50 | 1.50 | 3.00 |
| 243-247,249-252 | .25 | .75 | 1.50 |
| 248-1st Jim Lee art on X-Men | 1.70 | 5.00 | 10.00 |
| 253-All new X-men begin | .35 | 1.00 | 2.00 |
| 254-269,273-276: 258-Wolverine solo story. 268-Capt. America, Black Widow & Wolverine team-up | | .50 | 1.00 |
| 270-272-X-Tinction Agenda x-over | .35 | 1.00 | 2.00 |
| Special 1(12/70)-Kirby-c/a; origin The Stranger | 3.60 | 11.00 | 25.00 |
| Special 2(11/71) | 3.60 | 11.00 | 25.00 |
| Annual 3(1979)-New story | 1.30 | 4.00 | 9.00 |
| Annual 4(1980)-Dr. Strange app. | 1.00 | 3.00 | 6.00 |
| Annual 5(1981) | .70 | 2.10 | 4.25 |
| Annual 6(1982) | .50 | 1.50 | 3.00 |
| Annual 7(1983), 8(1984) | .40 | 1.25 | 2.50 |
| Annual 9(1985)-New Mutants; Art Adams-a | 1.50 | 4.50 | 10.00 |
| Annual 10(1986)-Art Adams-a | 1.50 | 4.50 | 10.00 |
| Annual 11(1987) | .35 | 1.00 | 2.00 |
| Annual 12(1988, $1.75)-Evolutionary War app. | .50 | 1.50 | 3.00 |
| Annual 13(1989, $2.00, 68 pgs.)-Atlantis Attacks | .35 | 1.00 | 2.00 |
| Annual 14(1990, $2.00, 68 pgs.)Fantastic Four, New Mutants & X-Factor x-over; Arthur Adams-a(p) | .35 | 1.00 | 2.00 |

NOTE: ***Art Adams*** *a-Annual 9, 10p, 12p, 14p; c-218p.* ***Neal Adams*** *a-56-63p, 65p; c-56-63.* ***Adkins*** *c-34.* ***Austin*** *a-108i, 109i, 111-117i, 119-143i, 186i, 204i, 228i, Annual 3i, 7i, 9i, 13; c-109-111i, 114-122i, 123, 124-141i, 142, 143, 196i, 204i, 228i, Annual 3i.* ***J. Buscema*** *c-42, 43p, 45p.* ***Byrne*** *a(p)-108, 109, 111-143; c(p)-113-116, 127, 129, 131-141.* ***Ditko*** *r-86, 90.* ***Everett*** *c-73.* ***Golden*** *a-Annual 7p.* ***Guice*** *a-216p, 217p.* ***G. Kane*** *c(p)-33, 74-76, 79, 80, 94, 95.* ***Kirby*** *a(p)-1-17 (#12-17, 24, 27-29, 32, 67r-layouts); c(p)-1-22, 25, 26, 30, 31, 35.* ***Layton*** *a-105i; c-112i, 113i.* ***Perez*** *a-Annual 3p; c(p)-112, 128, Annual 3.* ***Roussos*** *a-84i.* ***Simonson*** *a-171p; c-171, 217.* ***B. Smith*** *a-53, 186p, 198p, 205, 214; c-53-55, 186p, 198, 205, 212, 216.* ***Paul Smith*** *a-165-170p, 172-175p; c-165-170, 172-175.* ***Sparling*** *a-78p.* ***Steranko*** *a-50p, 51p; c-49-51.* ***Sutton*** *a-106i.* ***Toth*** *a-12p, 67p(r).* ***Tuska*** *a-40-42i, 44-46p, 88i(r); c-39-41, 77p, 78p.* ***Williamson*** *a-202i, 203i, 211i; c-202i, 203i, 206i.* ***Wood*** *c-14i.*

**X-MEN/ALPHA FLIGHT**
Jan, 1986 - No. 2, Jan, 1986 ($1.50, mini-series)
Marvel Comics Group

| | Good | Fine | N-Mint |
|---|---|---|---|
| 1,2: 1-Intro The Berserkers; Paul Smith-a | .60 | 1.75 | 3.50 |

**X-MEN AND THE MICRONAUTS, THE**
Jan, 1984 - No. 4, April, 1984 (Mini-series)
Marvel Comics Group

| | Good | Fine | N-Mint |
|---|---|---|---|
| 1-4: Guice-c/a(p) in all | .25 | .75 | 1.50 |

**X-MEN CLASSIC** (Formerly Classic X-Men)
No. 46, Apr, 1990 - Present ($1.25, color)

*The X-Men #12, © MEG*

*The X-Men #49, © MEG*

*The Uncanny X-Men #171, © MEG*

X-Men Vs. the Avengers #2, © MEG

The Yardbirds #1, © Z-D

Yellowjacket Comics #4, © F. Comunale

Marvel Comics

| | Good | Fine | N-Mint |
|---|---|---|---|
| 46-54: Reprints from X-Men. 54-($1.25, 52 pgs.) | | .60 | 1.25 |

**X-MEN CLASSICS** (Also see Classic X-Men)
Dec, 1983 - No. 3, Feb, 1984 ($2.00; Baxter paper)
Marvel Comics Group

| | Good | Fine | N-Mint |
|---|---|---|---|
| 1-3: X-Men-r by Neal Adams | .50 | 1.50 | 3.00 |

**X-MEN SPOTLIGHT ON . . . STARJAMMERS**
1990 - No. 2, 1990 ($4.50, squarebound, 52 pgs.)
Marvel Comics

| | Good | Fine | N-Mint |
|---|---|---|---|
| 1,2-Cockrum/Albrecht-a | .75 | 2.25 | 4.50 |

**X-MEN VS. THE AVENGERS**
Apr, 1987 - No. 4, July, 1987 ($1.50, mini-series, Baxter paper)
Marvel Comics Group

| | Good | Fine | N-Mint |
|---|---|---|---|
| 1 | .60 | 1.75 | 3.50 |
| 2-4 | .40 | 1.25 | 2.50 |

**X-TERMINATORS**
Oct, 1988 - No. 4, Jan, 1989 ($1.00, color, mini-series)
Marvel Comics

| | Good | Fine | N-Mint |
|---|---|---|---|
| 1-X-Men/X-Factor tie-in; Williamson-i | .50 | 1.50 | 3.00 |
| 2 | .30 | .90 | 1.75 |
| 3,4 | | .60 | 1.25 |

**X, THE MAN WITH THE X-RAY EYES** (See Movie Comics)

**X-VENTURE**
July, 1947 - No. 2, Nov, 1947 (Super heroes)
Victory Magazines Corp.

| | Good | Fine | N-Mint |
|---|---|---|---|
| 1-Atom Wizard, Mystery Shadow, Lester Trumble begin | 30.00 | 90.00 | 210.00 |
| 2 | 20.00 | 60.00 | 140.00 |

**XYR** (See Eclipse Graphic Album series #21)

**YAK YAK** (See 4-Color #1186, 1348)

**YAKKY DOODLE & CHOPPER** (TV) (Also see Spotlight #3)
Dec, 1962 (Hanna-Barbera)
Gold Key

| | Good | Fine | N-Mint |
|---|---|---|---|
| 1 | 2.35 | 7.00 | 16.00 |

**YALTA TO KOREA** (Also see Korea My Home)
1952 (8 pgs.) (Giveaway) (paper cover)
M. Phillip Corp. (Republican National Committee)

| | Good | Fine | N-Mint |
|---|---|---|---|
| nn-Anti-communist propaganda book | 15.00 | 45.00 | 90.00 |

**YANG** (See House of Yang)
Nov, 1973 - No. 13, May, 1976; V14#14, Sept, 1985 - No. 17, Jan, 1986
Charlton Comics

| | Good | Fine | N-Mint |
|---|---|---|---|
| 1-Origin | | .60 | 1.20 |
| 2-13(1976) | | .40 | .80 |
| 14-17(1986) | | .40 | .80 |
| 3,10,11(Modern Comics-r, 1977) | | .15 | .30 |

**YANKEE COMICS**
Sept, 1941 - No. 4, Mar, 1942
Harry 'A' Chesler

| | Good | Fine | N-Mint |
|---|---|---|---|
| 1-Origin The Echo, The Enchanted Dagger, Yankee Doodle Jones, The Firebrand, & The Scarlet Sentry; Black Satan app. | 45.00 | 135.00 | 315.00 |
| 2-Origin Johnny Rebel; Major Victory app.; Barry Kuda begins | 27.00 | 81.00 | 190.00 |
| 3,4 | 23.00 | 70.00 | 160.00 |
| 4 (nd, '40s; 7¼x5", 68pgs, distr. to the service)-Foxy Grandpa, Tom, Dick & Harry, Impy, Ace & Deuce, Dot & Dash, Ima Slooth by Jack Cole (Remington Morse publ.) | 1.70 | 5.00 | 12.00 |

**YANKS IN BATTLE**
Sept, 1956 - No. 4, Dec, 1956
Quality Comics Group

| | Good | Fine | N-Mint |
|---|---|---|---|
| 1 | 3.00 | 9.00 | 21.00 |
| 2-4 | 1.70 | 5.00 | 12.00 |

**YANKS IN BATTLE**
1963
I. W. Enterprises

| | Good | Fine | N-Mint |
|---|---|---|---|
| Reprint #3 | .25 | .75 | 1.50 |

**YARDBIRDS, THE** (G. I. Joe's Sidekicks)
Summer, 1952
Ziff-Davis Publishing Co.

| | Good | Fine | N-Mint |
|---|---|---|---|
| 1-By Bob Oskner | 4.00 | 12.00 | 28.00 |

**YARNS OF YELLOWSTONE**
1972 (36 pages) (50 cents)
World Color Press

| | Good | Fine | N-Mint |
|---|---|---|---|
| nn-Illustrated by Bill Chapman | .50 | 1.50 | 3.00 |

**YELLOW CLAW** (Also see Giant Size Master of Kung Fu)
Oct, 1956 - No. 4, April, 1957
Atlas Comics (MjMC)

| | Good | Fine | N-Mint |
|---|---|---|---|
| 1-Origin by Joe Maneely | 35.00 | 105.00 | 245.00 |
| 2-Kirby-a | 26.00 | 77.00 | 180.00 |
| 3,4-Kirby-a; 4-Kirby/Severin-a | 24.00 | 70.00 | 165.00 |

NOTE: ***Everett*** *c-3.* ***Maneely*** *c-1.* ***Reinman*** *a-2i, 3.* ***Severin*** *c-2, 4.*

**YELLOWJACKET COMICS** (Jack in the Box #11 on)(See TNT Comics)
Sept, 1944 - No. 10, June, 1946
E. Levy/Frank Comunale/Charlton

| | Good | Fine | N-Mint |
|---|---|---|---|
| 1-Origin Yellowjacket; Diana, the Huntress begins | 20.00 | 60.00 | 140.00 |
| 2 | 11.50 | 34.00 | 80.00 |
| 3,5 | 10.00 | 30.00 | 70.00 |
| 4-Poe's 'Fall Of The House Of Usher' adaptation; Palais-a | 11.50 | 34.00 | 80.00 |
| 6-10: 7-10-Have stories narrated by old witch in 'Tales of Terror' | 9.30 | 28.00 | 65.00 |

**YELLOWSTONE KELLY** (See 4-Color #1056)

**YELLOW SUBMARINE** (See Movie Comics)

**YIN FEI THE CHINESE NINJA**
1988 - No. 12?, 1990 ($1.80-$2.00, color, 52 pgs.)
Leung's Publications

| | Good | Fine | N-Mint |
|---|---|---|---|
| 1-6 ($1.80) | .30 | .90 | 1.80 |
| 7-12 ($2.00) | .35 | 1.00 | 2.00 |

**YOGI BEAR** (TV) (Hanna-Barbera)
No. 1067, 12-2/59-60 - No. 9, 7-9/62; No. 10, 10/62 - No. 42, 10/70
Dell Publishing Co./Gold Key No. 10 on

| | Good | Fine | N-Mint |
|---|---|---|---|
| 4-Color 1067 (#1) | 5.00 | 15.00 | 35.00 |
| 4-Color 1104,1162 (5-7/61) | 3.50 | 10.50 | 24.00 |
| 4(8-9/61) - 6(12-1/61-62) | 2.65 | 8.00 | 18.00 |
| 4-Color 1271(11/61), 1349(1/62) | 2.65 | 8.00 | 18.00 |
| 7(2-3/62) - 9(7-9/62)-Last Dell | 2.30 | 7.00 | 16.00 |
| 10(10/62-G.K.), 11(1/63)-titled "Yogi Bear Jellystone Jollies"-80 pgs.; 11-Xmas-c | 2.50 | 7.50 | 20.00 |
| 12(4/63), 14-20 | 1.70 | 5.00 | 12.00 |
| 13(7/63)-Surprise Party, 68 pgs. | 2.50 | 7.50 | 20.00 |
| 21-30 | 1.00 | 3.00 | 7.00 |
| 31-42 | .60 | 1.80 | 4.00 |
| . . . Kite Fun Book('62, 16 pgs., soft-c) | 1.50 | 3.50 | 8.00 |

**YOGI BEAR** (See Dell Giant #41, March of Comics #253, 265, 279, 291, 309, 319, 337, 344, Movie Comics under "Hey There It's. . ." & Whitman Comic Books)

**YOGI BEAR** (TV)
Nov, 1970 - No. 35, Jan, 1976 (Hanna-Barbera)
Charlton Comics

| | Good | Fine | N-Mint |
|---|---|---|---|
| 1 | 1.00 | 3.00 | 7.00 |
| 2-6,8-35: 28-31-partial-r | .70 | 2.00 | 4.00 |
| 7-Summer Fun (Giant); 52 pgs. | .70 | 2.00 | 4.00 |

**YOGI BEAR** (TV)(See The Flintstones, 3rd series & Spotlight #1)
Nov, 1977 - No. 9, Mar, 1979 (Hanna-Barbera)
Marvel Comics Group

| | Good | Fine | N-Mint |
|---|---|---|---|
| 1-Flintstones begin | | .40 | .80 |
| 2-9 | | .20 | .40 |

**YOGI BEAR'S EASTER PARADE** (See The Funtastic World of Hanna-Barbera #2)

**YOGI BERRA** (Baseball hero)
1951 (Yankee catcher)
Fawcett Publications

| | Good | Fine | N-Mint |
|---|---|---|---|
| nn-Photo-c | 34.00 | 100.00 | 235.00 |

**YOSEMITE SAM** (. . .& Bugs Bunny)
Dec, 1970 - No. 81, Feb, 1984
Gold Key/Whitman

| | Good | Fine | N-Mint |
|---|---|---|---|
| 1 | .70 | 2.00 | 5.00 |
| 2-10 | .40 | 1.25 | 2.50 |
| 11-30 | | .60 | 1.20 |
| 31-81: 81-r(1/3) | | .30 | .60 |

*(See March of Comics #363, 380, 392)*

**YOUNG ALLIES COMICS** (All-Winners #21; see Kid Komics #2)
Summer, 1941 - No. 20, Oct, 1946
Timely Comics (USA 1-7/NPI 8,9/YAI 10-20)

| | Good | Fine | VF-NM | NM/Mint |
|---|---|---|---|---|
| 1-Origin/1st app. The Young Allies; 1st meeting of Captain America & Human Torch; Red Skull app.; S&K-c/splash; Hitler-c | 283.00 | 710.00 | 1700.00 | 2400.00 |

(Estimated up to 165 total copies exist, 9 in NM/Mint)

| | Good | Fine | N-Mint |
|---|---|---|---|
| 2-Captain America & Human Torch app.; Simon & Kirby-c | 129.00 | 323.00 | 775.00 |
| 3-Fathertime, Captain America & Human Torch app. | 100.00 | 250.00 | 600.00 |
| 4-The Vagabond & Red Skull, Capt. America, Human Torch app. | 104.00 | 260.00 | 625.00 |
| 5-Captain America & Human Torch app. | 57.00 | 140.00 | 340.00 |
| 6-10: 9-Hitler, Tojo, Mussolini-c. 10-Origin Tommy Tyme & Clock of Ages; ends #19 | 44.00 | 110.00 | 265.00 |
| 11-20: 12-Classic decapitation story | 35.00 | 88.00 | 210.00 |

NOTE: ***Schomburg** c-5-13, 15, 17-19.*

**YOUNG ALL-STARS**
June, 1987 - No. 31, Nov, 1989 ($1.00, deluxe format, color)
DC Comics

| | Good | Fine | N-Mint |
|---|---|---|---|
| 1-1st app. Iron Munro & The Flying Fox | .70 | 2.00 | 4.00 |
| 2,3 | .35 | 1.00 | 2.00 |
| 4-31: 7-18-$1.25. 8,9-Millennium tie-ins. 19-23-$1.50. 24-Begin $1.75-c | .30 | .90 | 1.75 |
| Annual 1 (1988, $2.00) | .35 | 1.00 | 2.00 |

**YOUNG BRIDES**
Sept-Oct, 1952 - No. 30, Nov-Dec, 1956 (Photo-c: 1-3)
Feature/Prize Publications

| | Good | Fine | N-Mint |
|---|---|---|---|
| V1#1-Simon & Kirby-a | 8.50 | 25.50 | 60.00 |
| 2-S&K-a | 4.50 | 14.00 | 32.00 |
| 3-6-S&K-a | 4.00 | 12.00 | 28.00 |
| V2#1,3-7,10-12 (#7-18)-S&K-a | 3.00 | 9.00 | 21.00 |
| 2,8,9-No S&K-a | 1.50 | 4.50 | 10.00 |
| V3#1-3(#19-21)-Last precode (3-4/55) | 1.15 | 3.50 | 8.00 |
| 4,6(#22,24), V4#1,3(#25,27) | 1.00 | 3.00 | 7.00 |
| V3#5(#23)-Meskin-c | 1.50 | 4.50 | 10.00 |
| V4#2(#26)-All S&K issue | 3.00 | 9.00 | 21.00 |
| V4#4(#28)-S&K-a, V4#5,6(#29,30) | 2.00 | 6.00 | 14.00 |

**YOUNG DR. MASTERS** (See The Adventures of Young Dr. Masters)

**YOUNG DOCTORS, THE**
January, 1963 - No. 6, Nov, 1963
Charlton Comics

| | Good | Fine | N-Mint |
|---|---|---|---|
| V1#1 | .50 | 1.50 | 3.00 |
| 2-6 | .25 | .75 | 1.50 |

**YOUNG EAGLE**
12/50 - No. 10, 6/52; No. 3, 7/56 - No. 5, 4/57 (Photo-c: 1-10)
Fawcett Publications/Charlton

| | Good | Fine | N-Mint |
|---|---|---|---|
| 1 | 10.00 | 30.00 | 70.00 |
| 2 | 5.00 | 15.00 | 35.00 |
| 3-9 | 4.00 | 12.00 | 28.00 |
| 10-Origin Thunder, Young Eagle's Horse | 3.00 | 9.00 | 21.00 |
| 3-5(Charlton)-Formerly Sherlock Holmes? | 1.70 | 5.00 | 12.00 |

**YOUNG HEARTS**
Nov, 1949 - No. 2, Feb, 1950
Marvel Comics (SPC)

| | Good | Fine | N-Mint |
|---|---|---|---|
| 1-Photo-c | 4.50 | 14.00 | 32.00 |
| 2 | 2.65 | 8.00 | 18.00 |

**YOUNG HEARTS IN LOVE**
1964
Super Comics

| | Good | Fine | N-Mint |
|---|---|---|---|
| 17,18: 17-r/Young Love V5#6 (4-5/62) | .25 | .75 | 1.50 |

**YOUNG HEROES** (Formerly Forbidden Worlds #34)
No. 35, Feb-Mar, 1955 - No. 37, June-July, 1955
American Comics Group (Titan)

| | Good | Fine | N-Mint |
|---|---|---|---|
| 35-37-Frontier Scout | 2.65 | 8.00 | 18.00 |

**YOUNG KING COLE** (Becomes Criminals on the Run)
Fall, 1945 - V3#12, July, 1948
Premium Group/Novelty Press

| | Good | Fine | N-Mint |
|---|---|---|---|
| V1#1-Toni Gayle begins | 10.00 | 30.00 | 70.00 |
| 2 | 5.70 | 17.00 | 40.00 |
| 3-6 | 4.30 | 13.00 | 30.00 |
| V2#1-7(7/47) | 3.50 | 10.50 | 24.00 |
| V3#1,3-6,12: 5-McWilliams-c/a | 2.65 | 8.00 | 18.00 |
| 2-L.B. Cole-a | 3.50 | 10.50 | 24.00 |
| 7-L.B. Cole-c/a | 5.00 | 15.00 | 35.00 |
| 8-11-L.B. Cole-c | 4.50 | 14.00 | 32.00 |

**YOUNG LAWYERS, THE** (TV)
Jan, 1971 - No. 2, April, 1971
Dell Publishing co.

| | Good | Fine | N-Mint |
|---|---|---|---|
| 1,2 | 1.15 | 3.50 | 8.00 |

**YOUNG LIFE** (Teen Life #3 on)
Spring, 1945 - No. 2, Summer, 1945
New Age Publ./Quality Comics Group

| | Good | Fine | N-Mint |
|---|---|---|---|
| 1-Skip Homeier, Louis Prima stories | 4.50 | 14.00 | 32.00 |
| 2-Frank Sinatra c/story | 3.70 | 11.00 | 26.00 |

**YOUNG LOVE**
2-3/49 - No. 73, 12-1/56-57; V3#5, 2-3/60 - V7#1, 6-7/63
Prize(Feature)Publ.(Crestwood)

| | Good | Fine | N-Mint |
|---|---|---|---|
| V1#1-S&K-c/a(2) | 14.00 | 43.00 | 100.00 |
| 2-Photo-c begin; S&K-a | 7.00 | 21.00 | 50.00 |
| 3-S&K-a | 5.00 | 15.00 | 35.00 |
| 4-5-Minor S&K-a | 3.00 | 9.00 | 21.00 |
| V2#1(#7)-S&K-a | 5.00 | 15.00 | 35.00 |
| 2-5(#8-11)-Minor S&K-a | 2.30 | 7.00 | 16.00 |
| 6,8(#12,14)-S&K-c only | 3.00 | 9.00 | 21.00 |
| 7,9-12(#13,15-18)-S&K-c/a | 5.00 | 15.00 | 35.00 |

*Young Allies Comics #1, © MEG*

*Young Eagle #4, © FAW*

*Young King Cole V2#3, © NOVP*

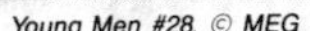
Young Men #28, © MEG

Young Romance Comics #65, © PRIZE

Your United States, © Lloyd Jaquet Studios

| | Good | Fine | N-Mint |
|---|---|---|---|
| V3#1-4(#19-22)-S&K-c/a | 3.00 | 9.00 | 21.00 |
| 5-7,9-12(#23-25,27-30)-Photo-c resume; S&K-a | 2.30 | 7.00 | 16.00 |
| 8(#26)-No S&K-a | 1.70 | 5.00 | 12.00 |
| V4#1,6(#31,36)-S&K-a | 2.30 | 7.00 | 16.00 |
| 2-5,7-12(#32-35,37-42)-Minor S&K-a | 2.00 | 6.00 | 14.00 |
| V5#1-12(#43-54), V6#1-9(#55-63)-Last precode; S&K-a-some | 1.50 | 4.50 | 10.00 |
| V6#10-12(#64-66) | 1.15 | 3.50 | 8.00 |
| V7#1-7(#67-73) | .85 | 2.60 | 6.00 |
| V3#5(2-3/60),6(4-5/60)(Formerly All For Love) | .70 | 2.00 | 4.00 |
| V4#1(6-7/60)-6(4-5/61) | .60 | 1.75 | 3.50 |
| V5#1(6-7/61)-6(4-5/62) | .60 | 1.75 | 3.50 |
| V6#1(6-7/62)-6(4-5/63), V7#1 | .40 | 1.25 | 2.50 |

NOTE: ***Meskin*** *a-27.* ***Powell*** *a-V4#6.* ***Severin/Elder*** *a-V1#3.* ***S&K*** *art not in #53, 57, 58, 61, 63-65. Photo c-V3#5-V5#11.*

**YOUNG LOVE**
#39, 9-10/63 - #120, Wint./75-76; #121, 10/76 - #126, 7/77
National Periodical Publ.(Arleigh Publ. Corp #49-60)/DC Comics

| | Good | Fine | N-Mint |
|---|---|---|---|
| 39 | 1.00 | 3.00 | 7.00 |
| 40-50 | .75 | 2.25 | 4.50 |
| 51-70: 64-Simon & Kirby-a | .50 | 1.50 | 3.00 |
| 71,72,74-77,80 | .35 | 1.00 | 2.00 |
| 73,78,79-Toth-a | .25 | .75 | 1.50 |
| 81-126: 107-114 (100 pgs.). 122-Orlando-a. 122-124-Toth-r | | .40 | .80 |

**YOUNG LOVER ROMANCES** (Formerly & becomes Great Lover. . .)
No. 4, June, 1952 - No. 5, Aug, 1952
Toby Press

| | Good | Fine | N-Mint |
|---|---|---|---|
| 4,5-Photo-c | 2.00 | 6.00 | 14.00 |

**YOUNG LOVERS** (My Secret Life #19 on)(Formerly Brenda Starr?)
No. 16, July, 1956 - No. 18, May, 1957
Charlton Comics

| | Good | Fine | N-Mint |
|---|---|---|---|
| 16,17('56) | 1.50 | 4.50 | 10.00 |
| 18-Elvis Presley picture-c, text story (biography) | 22.00 | 65.00 | 155.00 |

**YOUNG MARRIAGE**
June, 1950
Fawcett Publications

| | Good | Fine | N-Mint |
|---|---|---|---|
| 1-Powell-a; photo-c | 5.00 | 15.00 | 35.00 |

**YOUNG MASTER** (Also see The Master)
Nov, 1987 - No. 9, 1989 ($1.75, B&W)
New Comics Group

| | Good | Fine | N-Mint |
|---|---|---|---|
| 1-9: Val Mayerik-c/a | .30 | .90 | 1.80 |

**YOUNG MEN** (Formerly Cowboy Romances)(. . .on the Battlefield #12-20(4/53); . . .In Action #21)
No. 4, 6/50 - No. 11, 10/51; No.12, 12/51 - No. 28, 6/54
Marvel/Atlas Comics (IPC)

| | Good | Fine | N-Mint |
|---|---|---|---|
| 4-(52 pgs.) | 6.50 | 19.00 | 45.00 |
| 5-11 | 3.60 | 11.00 | 25.00 |
| 12-23: 15-Colan, Pakula-a | 3.00 | 9.00 | 21.00 |
| 24-Origin Captain America, Human Torch, & Sub-Mariner which are revived thru #28. Red Skull app. | 36.00 | 107.00 | 250.00 |
| 25-28: 25-Romita-c/a | 27.00 | 81.00 | 185.00 |

NOTE: ***Berg*** *a-7, 17, 20; c-17.* ***Colan*** *a-15. Human Torch by* ***Burgos***-*#25, 27, 28. Sub-Mariner by* ***Everett***-*#24-28.* ***Everett*** *a-18-20.* ***Heath*** *a-13, 14.* ***Maneely*** *c-12, 15.*

**YOUNG REBELS, THE** (TV)
January, 1971
Dell Publishing Co.

| | Good | Fine | N-Mint |
|---|---|---|---|
| 1-Photo-c | 1.00 | 3.00 | 6.00 |

**YOUNG ROMANCE COMICS** (The 1st romance comic)
Sept-Oct, 1947 - V16#4, June-July, 1963 (#1-33: 52 pgs.)
Prize/Headline (Feature Publ.)

| | Good | Fine | N-Mint |
|---|---|---|---|
| V1#1-S&K-c/a(2) | 16.00 | 48.00 | 110.00 |
| 2-S&K-c/a(2-3) | 8.50 | 25.50 | 60.00 |
| 3-6-S&K-c/a(2-3) each | 7.00 | 21.00 | 50.00 |
| V2#1-6(#7-12)-S&K-c/a(2-3) each | 6.00 | 18.00 | 42.00 |
| V3#1-3(#13-15): V3#1-Photo-c begin; S&K-a | 3.50 | 10.50 | 24.00 |
| 4-12(#16-24)-Photo-c; S&K-a | 3.50 | 10.50 | 24.00 |
| V4#1-11(#25-35)-S&K-a | 3.00 | 9.00 | 21.00 |
| 12(#36)-S&K, Toth-a | 5.00 | 15.00 | 35.00 |
| V5#1-12(#37-48), V6#4-12(#52-60)-S&K-a | 3.00 | 9.00 | 21.00 |
| V6#1-3(#49-51)-No S&K-a | 2.00 | 6.00 | 14.00 |
| V7#1-11(#61-71)-S&K-a in most | 2.65 | 8.00 | 18.00 |
| V7#12(#72), V8#1-3(#73-75)-Last precode (12-1/54-55)-No S&K-a | 1.30 | 4.00 | 9.00 |
| V8#4(#76, 4-5/55), 5(#77)-No S&K-a | 1.15 | 3.50 | 8.00 |
| V8#6-8(#78-80, 12-1/55-56)-S&K-a | 1.70 | 5.00 | 12.00 |
| V9#3,5,6(#81, 2-3/56, 83,84)-S&K-a | 1.50 | 4.50 | 10.00 |
| 4, V10#1(#82,85)-All S&K-a | 2.00 | 6.00 | 14.00 |
| V10#2-6(#86-90, 10-11/57)-S&K-a | 1.50 | 4.50 | 10.00 |
| V11#1,2,5,6(#91,92,95,96)-S&K-a | 1.50 | 4.50 | 10.00 |
| 3,4(#93,94), V12#2,4,5(#98,100,101)-No S&K | 1.00 | 3.00 | 7.00 |
| V12#1,3,6(#97,99,102)-S&K-a | 1.50 | 4.50 | 10.00 |
| V13#1(#103)-S&K, Powell-a | 1.70 | 5.00 | 12.00 |
| 2-6(#104-108) | .70 | 2.00 | 4.00 |
| V14#1-6, V15#1-6, V16#1-4(#109-124) | .50 | 1.50 | 3.00 |

NOTE: ***Meskin*** *a-16, 24(2), 47.* ***Robinson/Meskin*** *a-6.* ***Leonard Starr*** *a-11. Photo c-13-32, 34-65.*

**YOUNG ROMANCE COMICS** (Continued from Prize series)
No. 125, Aug-Sept, 1963 - No. 208, Nov-Dec, 1975
National Periodical Publ.(Arleigh Publ. Corp. No. 127)

| | Good | Fine | N-Mint |
|---|---|---|---|
| 125 | 1.00 | 3.00 | 7.00 |
| 126-162: 154-Neal Adams-c | .70 | 2.00 | 4.00 |
| 163,164-Toth-a | .35 | 1.00 | 2.00 |
| 165-196: 170-Michell from Young Love ends; Lily Martin, the Swinger begins | | .50 | 1.00 |
| 197 (100 pgs.)-208 | | .50 | 1.00 |

**YOUR DREAMS** (See Strange World of. . .)

**YOUR TRIP TO NEWSPAPERLAND**
June, 1955 (12 pgs.; 14x11½")
Philadelphia Evening Bulletin (Printed by Harvey Press)

| | Good | Fine | N-Mint |
|---|---|---|---|
| nn-Joe Palooka takes kids on tour through newspaper | 3.00 | 9.00 | 21.00 |

**YOUR UNITED STATES**
1946
Lloyd Jacquet Studios

| | Good | Fine | N-Mint |
|---|---|---|---|
| nn-Used in **SOTI**, pg. 309,310; Sid Greene-a | 13.00 | 40.00 | 90.00 |

**YOUTHFUL HEARTS** (Daring Confessions #4 on)
May, 1952 - No. 3, Sept, 1952
Youthful Magazines

| | Good | Fine | N-Mint |
|---|---|---|---|
| 1-"Monkey on Her Back" swipes E.C. drug story from Shock SuspenStories #12; Doug Wildey-a in all | 11.50 | 34.00 | 80.00 |
| 2,3 | 7.00 | 21.00 | 50.00 |

**YOUTHFUL LOVE** (Truthful Love #2)
May, 1950
Youthful Magazines

| | Good | Fine | N-Mint |
|---|---|---|---|
| 1 | 4.30 | 13.00 | 30.00 |

**YOUTHFUL ROMANCES**
8-9/49 - No. 5, 4/50; No. 6, 2/51; No. 7, 5/51 - #14, 10/52; #15, 1/53 - #18, 7/53; #5, 9/53 - #8, 5/54
Pix-Parade #1-14/Ribage #15 on

| | Good | Fine | N-Mint |
|---|---|---|---|
| 1-(1st series)-Titled Youthful Love-Romances | 10.00 | 30.00 | 70.00 |
| 2 | 6.50 | 19.00 | 45.00 |
| 3-5 | 5.00 | 15.00 | 35.00 |
| 6,7,9-14(10/52, Pix-Parade; becomes Daring Love #15); 7-Tony Martin photo on-c | 3.50 | 10.50 | 24.00 |
| 8-Wood-c | 10.00 | 30.00 | 70.00 |
| 15-18 (Ribage) | 3.00 | 9.00 | 21.00 |
| 5(9/53, Ribage) | 2.30 | 7.00 | 16.00 |
| 6,7(#7, 2/54), 8(5/54) | 2.00 | 6.00 | 14.00 |

**YUPPIES FROM HELL**
1989 ($2.95, B&W, one-shot, direct sale only, 52 pgs.)
Marvel Comics

| | Good | Fine | N-Mint |
|---|---|---|---|
| 1-Satire | .50 | 1.50 | 3.00 |

**ZAGO, JUNGLE PRINCE** (My Story #5 on)
Sept, 1948 - No. 4, March, 1949
Fox Features Syndicate

| | Good | Fine | N-Mint |
|---|---|---|---|
| 1-Blue Beetle app.-partial r-/Atomic #4 (Toni Luck) | 19.00 | 58.00 | 135.00 |
| 2,3-Kamen-a | 14.00 | 43.00 | 100.00 |
| 4-Baker-c | 13.00 | 40.00 | 90.00 |

**ZANE GREY'S STORIES OF THE WEST**
No. 197, 9/48 - No. 996, 5-7/59; 11/64 (All painted-c)
Dell Publishing Co./Gold Key 11/64

| | Good | Fine | N-Mint |
|---|---|---|---|
| 4-Color 197(#1)(9/48) | 7.00 | 21.00 | 50.00 |
| 4-Color 222,230,236('49) | 5.00 | 15.00 | 35.00 |
| 4-Color 246,255,270,301,314,333,346 | 3.70 | 11.00 | 26.00 |
| 4-Color 357,372,395,412,433,449,467,484 | 3.00 | 9.00 | 21.00 |
| 4-Color 511-Kinstler-a | 3.50 | 10.50 | 24.00 |
| 4-Color 532,555,583,604,616,632(5/55) | 3.00 | 9.00 | 21.00 |
| 27(9-11/55) - 39(9-11/58) | 2.30 | 7.00 | 16.00 |
| 4-Color 996(5-7/59) | 2.30 | 7.00 | 16.00 |
| 10131-411-(11/64-G.K.)-Nevada; r-4-Color #996 | 1.30 | 4.00 | 9.00 |

**ZANY** (Magazine)(Satire)(See Frantic & Ratfink)
Sept, 1958 - No. 4, May, 1959
Candor Publ. Co.

| | Good | Fine | N-Mint |
|---|---|---|---|
| 1-Bill Everett-c | 4.00 | 12.00 | 28.00 |
| 2-4 | 2.00 | 6.00 | 14.00 |

**ZATANNA SPECIAL** (See Adventure Comics #413, Justice League of America #161, Supergirl #1 & World's Finest Comics #274)
1987 ($2.00, One shot)
DC Comics

| | Good | Fine | N-Mint |
|---|---|---|---|
| 1 | .35 | 1.00 | 2.00 |

**ZAZA, THE MYSTIC** (Formerly Charlie Chan; This Magazine Is Haunted V2#12 on)
No. 10, April, 1956 - No. 11, Sept, 1956
Charlton Comics

| | Good | Fine | N-Mint |
|---|---|---|---|
| 10,11 | 4.30 | 13.00 | 30.00 |

**ZEGRA JUNGLE EMPRESS** (Formerly Tegra)(My Love Life #6 on)
No. 2, Oct, 1948 - No. 5, April, 1949
Fox Features Syndicate

| | Good | Fine | N-Mint |
|---|---|---|---|
| 2 | 23.00 | 70.00 | 160.00 |
| 3-5 | 16.00 | 48.00 | 110.00 |

**ZERO PATROL, THE**
Nov, 1984 - No. 2; 1987 - No. 5, 1989? ($2.00, color)
Continuity Comics

| | Good | Fine | N-Mint |
|---|---|---|---|
| 1,2: Neal Adams-c/a; Megalith begins | .35 | 1.00 | 2.00 |
| 1-5 (#1,2-reprints above, 1987) | .35 | 1.00 | 2.00 |

**ZERO TOLERANCE**
Oct, 1990 - No. 4, Jan, 1991 ($2.25, color, limited series)
First Comics

| | Good | Fine | N-Mint |
|---|---|---|---|
| 1-Tim Vigil-c/a(p) (his 1st color mini-series) | .45 | 1.40 | 2.80 |
| 2-4: Vigil-c/a(p) | .40 | 1.15 | 2.30 |

**ZIGGY PIG-SILLY SEAL COMICS** (See Animated Movie-Tunes, Comic Capers, Krazy Komics & Silly Tunes)
Fall, 1944 - No. 6, Fall, 1946
Timely Comics (CmPL)

| | Good | Fine | N-Mint |
|---|---|---|---|
| 1-Vs. the Japs | 9.30 | 28.00 | 65.00 |
| 2 | 4.50 | 14.00 | 32.00 |
| 3-5 | 4.00 | 12.00 | 28.00 |
| 6-Infinity-c | 5.70 | 17.00 | 40.00 |
| I.W. Reprint #1('58)-r/Krazy Komics | .50 | 1.50 | 3.00 |
| I.W. Reprint #2,7,8 | .25 | .75 | 1.50 |

**ZIP COMICS**
Feb, 1940 - No. 47, Summer, 1944
MLJ Magazines

| | Good | Fine | N-Mint |
|---|---|---|---|
| 1-Origin Kalathar the Giant Man, The Scarlet Avenger, & Steel Sterling; Mr. Satan, Nevada Jones & Zambini, the Miracle Man, War Eagle, Captain Valor begins | 125.00 | 312.00 | 750.00 |
| 2 | 54.00 | 160.00 | 375.00 |
| 3 | 42.00 | 125.00 | 290.00 |
| 4,5 | 36.00 | 107.00 | 250.00 |
| 6-9: 9-Last Kalathar & Mr. Satan | 31.00 | 92.00 | 215.00 |
| 10-Inferno, the Flame Breather begins, ends #13 | 29.00 | 85.00 | 200.00 |
| 11,12: 11-Inferno without costume | 27.00 | 80.00 | 185.00 |
| 13-17,19: 17-Last Scarlet Avenger | 27.00 | 80.00 | 185.00 |
| 18-Wilbur begins (1st app.) | 29.00 | 85.00 | 200.00 |
| 20-Origin Black Jack (1st app.) | 40.00 | 120.00 | 280.00 |
| 21-26: 25-Last Nevada Jones. 26-Black Witch begins; last Captain Valor | 26.00 | 77.00 | 180.00 |
| 27-Intro. Web | 40.00 | 120.00 | 280.00 |
| 28-Origin Web | 40.00 | 120.00 | 280.00 |
| 29,30 | 22.00 | 65.00 | 150.00 |
| 31-38: 34-1st Applejack app. 35-Last Zambini, Black Jack. 38-Last Web issue | 16.00 | 48.00 | 110.00 |
| 39-Red Rube begins (origin, 8/43) | 16.00 | 48.00 | 110.00 |
| 40-47: 45-Wilbur ends | 11.50 | 34.00 | 80.00 |

NOTE: ***Biro*** *a-5, 9, 17; c-4-7, 9, 11, 12, 14, 17.* ***Meskin*** *a-1-3, 5-7, 9, 10, 12, 13, 15, 16 at least.* ***Novick*** *c-19, 20, 24, 25, 31. Bondage c-8, 9, 33, 34.*

**ZIP-JET** (Hero)
Feb, 1953 - No. 2, Apr-May, 1953
St. John Publishing Co.

| | Good | Fine | N-Mint |
|---|---|---|---|
| 1,2-Rocketman-r from Punch Comics; #1-c from splash in Punch #10 | 19.00 | 57.00 | 135.00 |

**ZIPPY THE CHIMP** (CBS TV Presents. . .)
No. 50, March, 1957 - No. 51, Aug, 1957
Pines (Literary Ent.)

| | Good | Fine | N-Mint |
|---|---|---|---|
| 50,51 | 2.00 | 6.00 | 14.00 |

**ZODY, THE MOD ROB**
July, 1970
Gold Key

| | Good | Fine | N-Mint |
|---|---|---|---|
| 1 | .70 | 2.00 | 4.00 |

**ZONE**
1990 ($1.95, B&W)
Dark Horse Comics

| | Good | Fine | N-Mint |
|---|---|---|---|
| 1-Character from Dark Horse Presents | .35 | 1.00 | 2.00 |

**ZOO ANIMALS**
No. 8, 1954 (36 pages; 15 cents)
Star Publications

| | Good | Fine | N-Mint |
|---|---|---|---|
| 8-(B&W for coloring) | 2.00 | 6.00 | 14.00 |

*Zago, Jungle Prince #3, © FOX*

*Zero Tolerance #1, © First Comics*

*Zip Comics #9, © AP*

*Zoo Funnies #8 (1950s), © CC*

*Zorro #10 (Dell), © The Disney Co.*

*Zot! #12, © Eclipse Comics*

**ZOO FUNNIES** (Tim McCoy #16 on)
Nov, 1945 - No. 15, 1947
Charlton Comics/Children Comics Publ.

| | Good | Fine | N-Mint |
|---|---|---|---|
| 101(#1)(1945; 1st Charlton comic book?)-Funny animal; Al Fago-c | 7.00 | 21.00 | 50.00 |
| 2(12/45, 52 pgs.) | 3.60 | 11.00 | 25.00 |
| 3-5 | 2.65 | 8.00 | 18.00 |
| 6-15: 8-Diana the Huntress app. | 2.00 | 6.00 | 14.00 |

**ZOO FUNNIES** (Becomes Nyoka, The Jungle Girl #14 on?)
July, 1953 - No. 13, Sept, 1955; Dec, 1984
Capitol Stories/Charlton Comics

| | Good | Fine | N-Mint |
|---|---|---|---|
| 1-1st app.? Timothy The Ghost; Fago-c/a | 4.00 | 12.00 | 28.00 |
| 2 | 2.30 | 7.00 | 16.00 |
| 3-7 (8/46) | 1.70 | 5.00 | 12.00 |
| 8-13-Nyoka app. | 3.70 | 11.00 | 26.00 |
| 1('84) | | .40 | .80 |

**ZOONIVERSE**
8/86 - No. 6, 6/87 ($1.25-$1.75, color, mini-series, Mando paper)
Eclipse Comics

| | Good | Fine | N-Mint |
|---|---|---|---|
| 1-5 ($1.25) | | .65 | 1.30 |
| 6 ($1.75) | .30 | .90 | 1.80 |

**ZOO PARADE** (See 4-Color #662)

**ZOOM COMICS**
December, 1945 (One Shot)
Carlton Publishing Co.

| | Good | Fine | N-Mint |
|---|---|---|---|
| nn-Dr. Mercy, Satannas, from Red Band Comics; Capt. Milksop origin retold | 20.00 | 60.00 | 140.00 |

**ZOOT** (Rulah Jungle Goddess #17 on)
nd (1946) - No. 16, July, 1948 (Two #13s & 14s)
Fox Features Syndicate

| | Good | Fine | N-Mint |
|---|---|---|---|
| nn-Funny animal only | 9.30 | 28.00 | 65.00 |
| 2-The Jaguar app. | 8.00 | 24.00 | 55.00 |
| 3(Fall,'46) - 6-Funny animals & teen-age | 4.30 | 13.00 | 30.00 |
| 7-Rulah, Jungle Goddess begins (6/47); origin & 1st app. | 36.00 | 107.00 | 250.00 |
| 8-10 | 27.00 | 80.00 | 185.00 |
| 11-Kamen bondage-c | 29.00 | 85.00 | 200.00 |
| 12-Injury-to-eye panels | 17.00 | 51.00 | 120.00 |
| 13(2/48) | 17.00 | 51.00 | 120.00 |
| 14(3/48)-Used in **SOTI**, pg. 104, "One picture showing a girl nailed by her wrists to trees with blood flowing from the wounds, might be taken straight from an ill. ed. of the Marquis deSade" | 22.00 | 65.00 | 150.00 |
| 13(4/48), 14(5/48) | 17.00 | 51.00 | 120.00 |
| 15,16 | 17.00 | 51.00 | 120.00 |

**ZORRO** (Walt Disney with #882)(TV)(See Eclipse Graphic Album)
May, 1949 - No. 15, Sept-Nov, 1961 (Photo-c 882 on)
Dell Publishing Co.

| | Good | Fine | N-Mint |
|---|---|---|---|
| 4-Color 228 | 18.00 | 54.00 | 125.00 |
| 4-Color 425,497,574,617,732 | 10.00 | 30.00 | 70.00 |
| 4-Color 538-Kinstler-a | 11.00 | 32.00 | 75.00 |
| 4-Color 882-Photo-c begin; Toth-a | 8.50 | 25.50 | 60.00 |
| 4-Color 920,933,960,976-Toth-a in all | 8.50 | 25.50 | 60.00 |
| 4-Color 1003('59) | 7.00 | 21.00 | 50.00 |
| 4-Color 1037-Annette Funicello photo-c | 9.30 | 28.00 | 65.00 |
| 8(12-2/59-60) | 4.50 | 14.00 | 32.00 |
| 9,12-Toth-a | 5.70 | 17.00 | 40.00 |
| 10,11,13-15-Last photo-c | 3.60 | 11.00 | 25.00 |

NOTE: ***Warren Tufts** a-4-Color 1037, 8, 9, 13.*

**ZORRO** (Walt Disney)(TV)
Jan, 1966 - No. 9, March, 1968 (All photo-c)
Gold Key

| | Good | Fine | N-Mint |
|---|---|---|---|
| 1-Toth-a | 4.00 | 12.00 | 28.00 |
| 2,4,5,7-9-Toth-a | 2.85 | 8.50 | 20.00 |
| 3,6-Tufts-a | 2.30 | 7.00 | 16.00 |

NOTE: *#1-9 are reprinted from Dell issues. **Tufts** a-3, 4. #3-r/#12-c & #8 inside; #4-r/#9-c & insides; #6-r/#11(all); #7-r/#14-c.*

**ZORRO** (TV)
Dec, 1990 - No. 6, May, 1991 ($1.00, color, limited series)
Marvel Comics

| | Good | Fine | N-Mint |
|---|---|---|---|
| 1-6: Based on TV show on Family Channel | | .50 | 1.00 |

**ZOT!** (Also see Adventures of Zot)
4/84 - No. 10, 7/85; No. 11, 1/87 - Present ($1.50, Baxter paper)
Eclipse Comics

| | Good | Fine | N-Mint |
|---|---|---|---|
| 1 | 1.00 | 3.00 | 6.00 |
| 2,3 | .50 | 1.50 | 3.00 |
| 4-10: 4-Origin. 10-Last color issue | .35 | 1.00 | 2.00 |
| 11-33: 11-Begin $2.00-c, B&W issues | .35 | 1.00 | 2.00 |

**Z-2 COMICS** (Secret Agent . . .)(See Holyoke One-Shot #7)

**ZULU** (See Movie Classics)

Comics Buyer's Guide...
COMICS BUYER'S GUIDE
Where the world of comics turns every week

# WE PAY MORE

***Always have, always will***

☎ (317) 293-2551

**NATIONAL COMIC & COIN COLLECTIBLES**

**President: John K. Snyder, Jr.**

**BUYING PRE-1965 COMICS ONLY**

**Box 34404**

**Indianapolis, Indiana 46234**

**☎ (317) 293-2551**

CBG
Customer Service
Award - 1990

CBG
Customer Service
Award - 1990

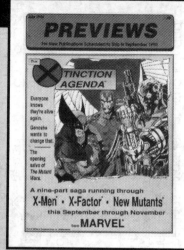

"THE OBVIOUS CHOICE"
OTHER SIDE OF THE TRACKS COMIC STORE
4th ANNUAL Going out of BUSINESS SALE
SEWER HIGH COMICS ALL MINT
US POST
JOE NY EVE
BATMAN
ACTION COMICS
AMAZING FANTASY
MARVEL MYSTERY
SUPERMAN
SPIDER MAN
GREEN LANTERN
FLASH
MAD
DONALD DUCK
FANTASTIC FOUR
CLASSICS
ALL-STAR COMICS
DETECTIVE COMICS
X-MEN
CAPTAIN AMERICA
SHADOW COMICS
ACTION COMICS
BATMAN
X MEN
HULK
WIERD FANTASY
WIERD SCIENCE
FLASH
TOMORROW'S TREASURE
These books are so incredibly HOT HOT HOT HOT
JUNK COMIC
YUCK COMICS
FOO FUN
NEVER BUY COMICS
50% OFF
FLIM FLAM the COMIC MAN
SINCE 1972
TOMORROW'S TREASURES
We specialize in
GOLDEN AGE • SILVER AGE • DC • TIMELY • EC
DISNEY • EARLY MARVEL • (1933-1969)
Mail Order Service Guaranteed / Send Want Lists / Comic Collections Wanted
Send to: RICHARD MUCHIN P.O. BOX 925 COMMACK, NY 11725
Phone: (516) 543-7574

"I SEE SOMETHING VERY BIG
IN YOUR FUTURE..."
TROPIC
comics
GLKKK...

# THE GREATEST STORIES EVER TOLD SERIES

Reprinting some of the most popular and memorable stories from the vast DC Universe.

## HARDCOVER EDITIONS

**THE GREATEST FLASH STORIES EVER TOLD**
288 pages . . . . . . . . . . . . . $29.95

**THE GREATEST 1950s STORIES EVER TOLD**
288 pages . . . . . . . . . . . . . $29.95

**THE GREATEST GOLDEN AGE STORIES EVER TOLD**
288 pages . . . . . . . . . . . . . $24.95

**THE GREATEST TEAM-UP STORIES EVER TOLD**
288 pages . . . . . . . . . . . . . $24.95

## SOFTCOVER EDITIONS

**THE GREATEST BATMAN STORIES EVER TOLD**
352 pages . . . . . . . . . . . . . $15.95

**THE GREATEST JOKER STORIES EVER TOLD**
288 pages . . . . . . . . . . . . . $14.95

**THE GREATEST SUPERMAN STORIES EVER TOLD**
336 pages . . . . . . . . . . . . . $15.95

**THE GREATEST TEAM-UP STORIES EVER TOLD**
288 pages . . . . . . . . . . . . . $14.95

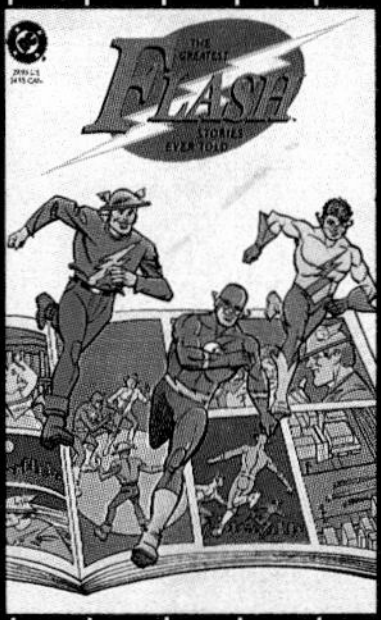


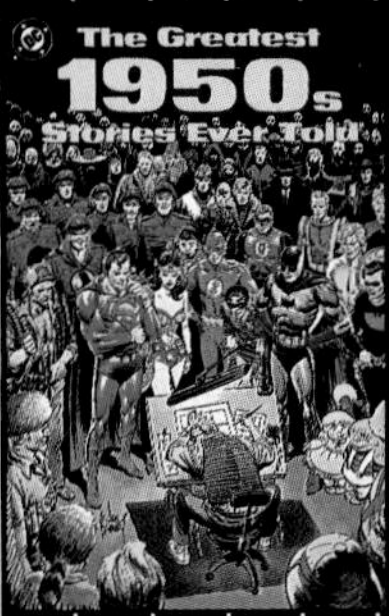


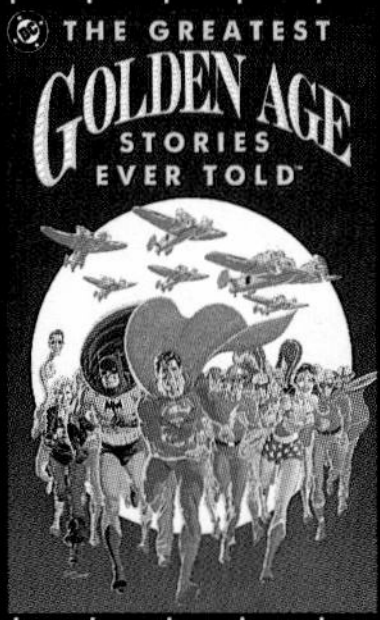


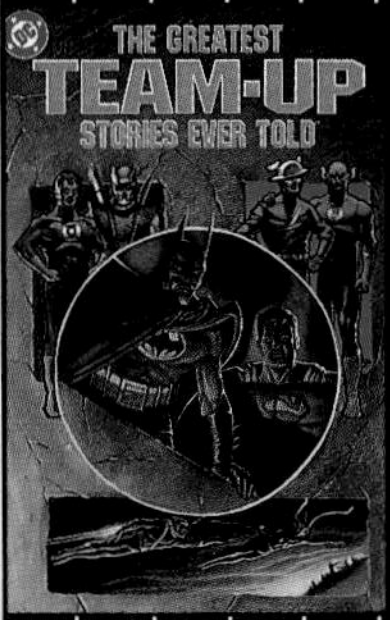


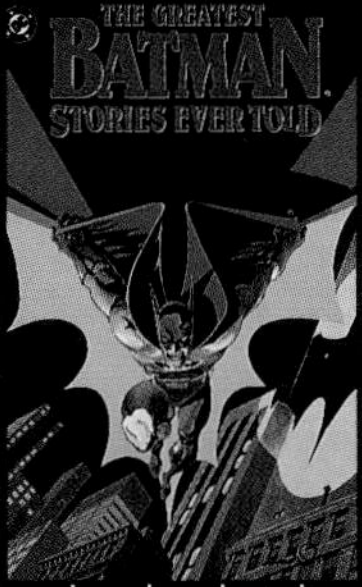


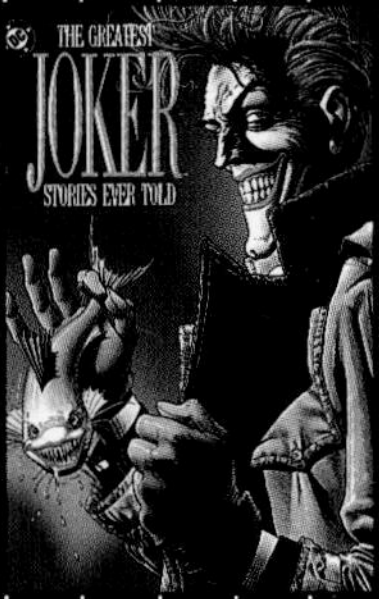


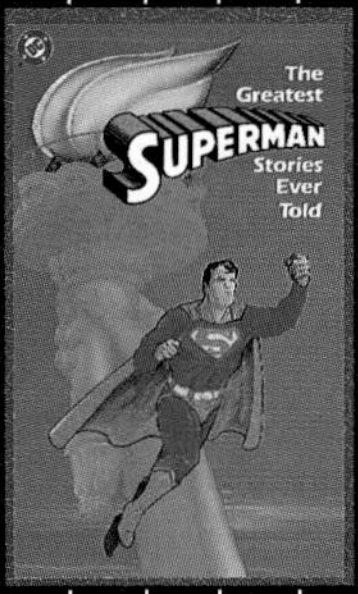


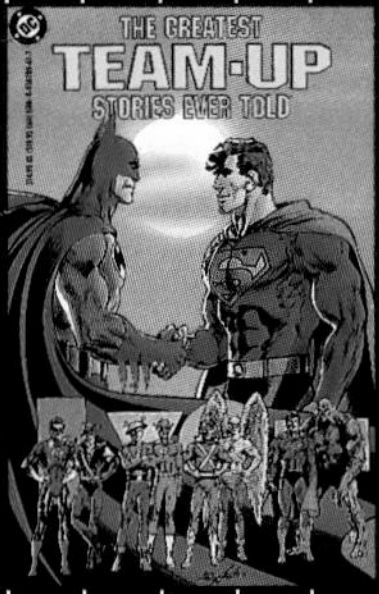

JOIN THE PARADE TO. . .

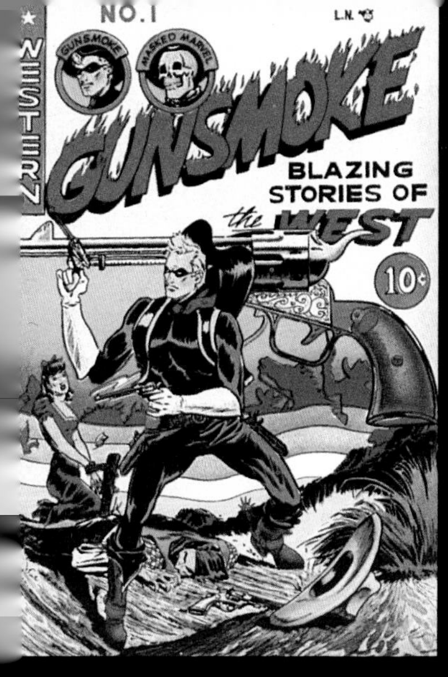


Gunsmoke #1, 1949, © YM. Ingels cover art.

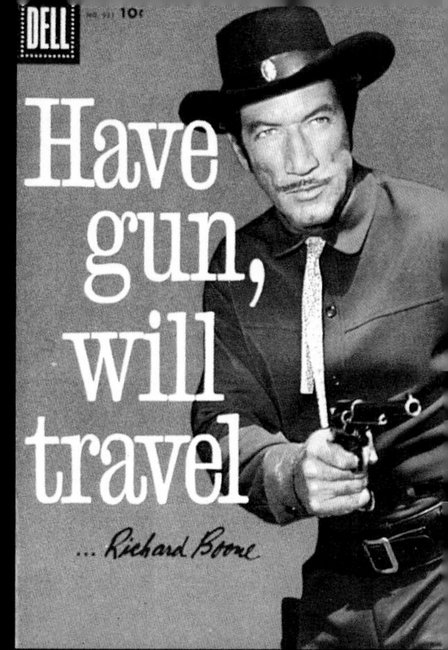


**Have Gun, Will Travel** #931 (#1), 1958, © Columbia Broadcasting System.

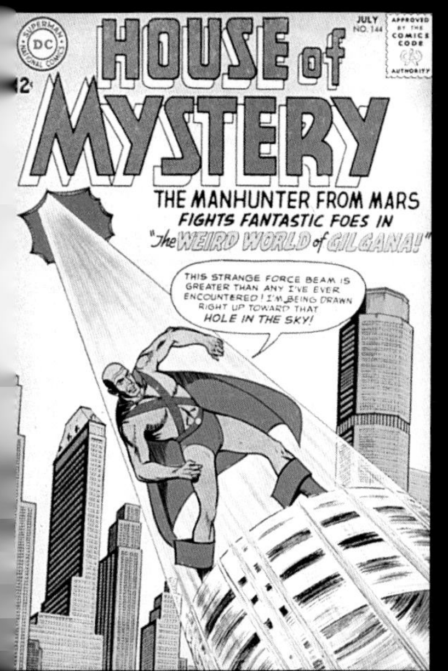


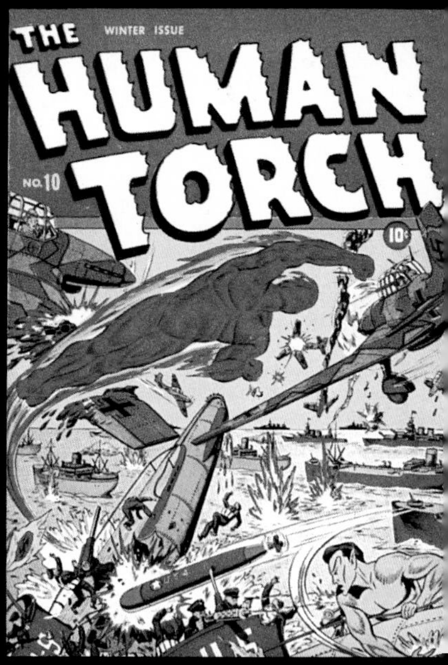

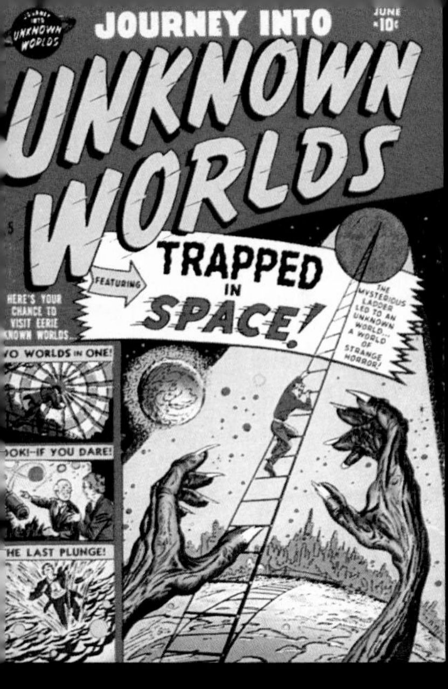


Journey Into Unknown Worlds #5, 1951, © MCG.

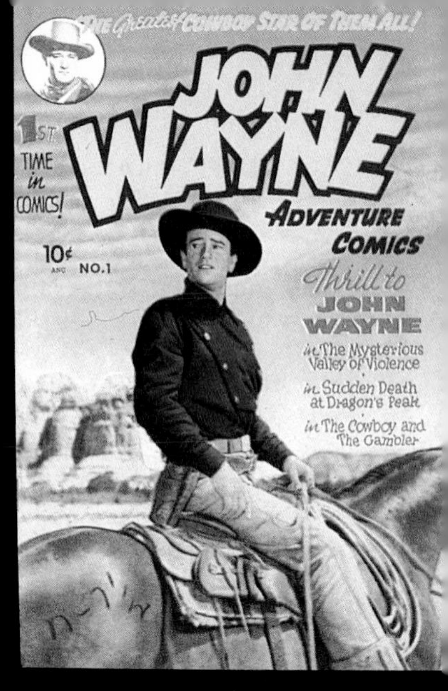


John Wayne Adventure Comics #1, 1949, © TOBY. First comic book app.

Key Comics #5, 1946, © Consolidated

King Comics #5, 1936, © KING

**The Lone Rider** #1, 1951, © SUPR.

**Marvel Mystery Comics** #40, 1943, © MCG. Schomburg Zeppelin cover.

**Metal Men** #1, 1963, © DC.

Military Comics #5, 1941, © QUA.

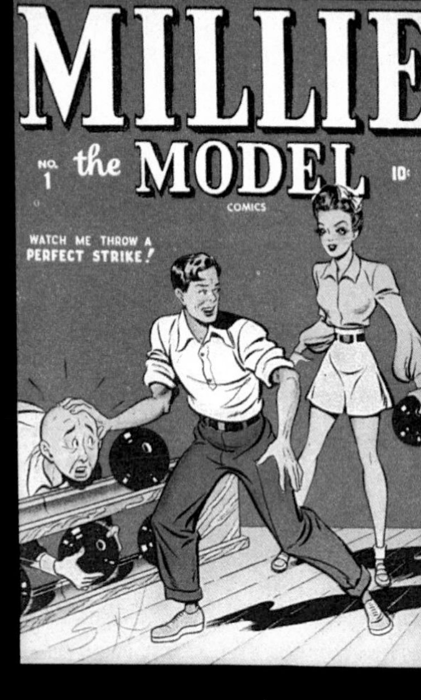


Millie The Model #1, 1945, © MCG.

More Fun Comics #71, 1941, © DC.

**Rangers Comics** #13, 1943, © FH.

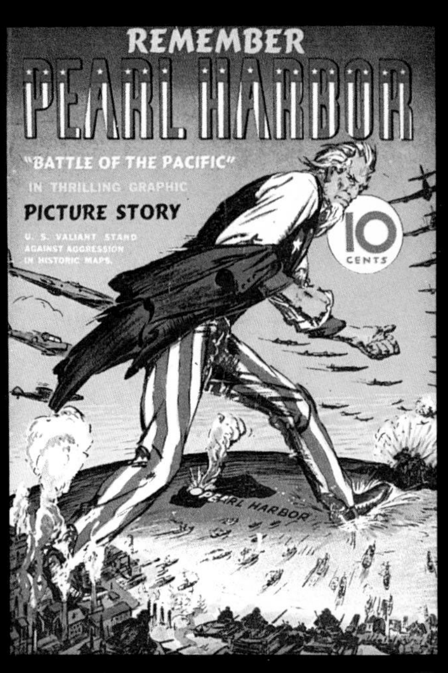


**Remember Pearl Harbor** nn, 1942, © S&S.

**Rin-Tin-Tin** #434 (#1), 1952, © Lee Duncan. Based on TV series.

**Rip Hunter Time Master** #1, 1961, © DC.

**Roy Rogers** Four Color #38, 1944, © Roy Rogers. 1st photo cover western comic.

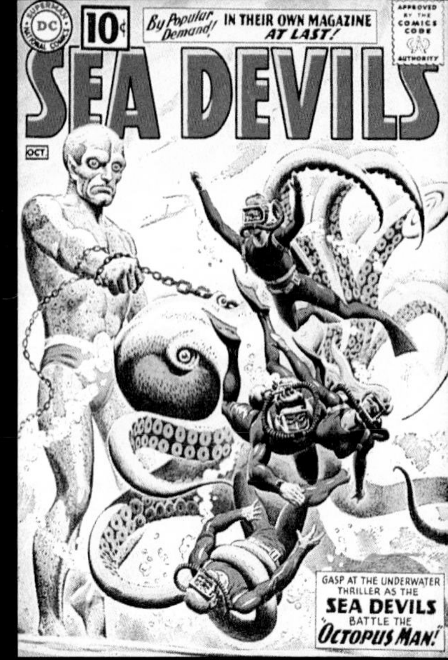


**Sea Devils** #1, 1961, © DC.

**Sensation Comics** #103, 1951, © DC.

**Showcase** #13, 1958, © DC. Third Flash comic book.

MEANWHILE, IN THE BACK STOCKROOM...
HEE! HEE!
UT!
Fox & Crow
Mutt and Jeff
Sea Devils
MORE FUN
ALL STAR
FLASH
ALL FLASH
DCs
SILVER AND
GOLDEN AGE
ACTION
ADVENTURE
GREEN LANT.
ALL AMERICAN
COMIC CAVAL.
BATMAN
DETECTIVE
WORLD'S FINEST

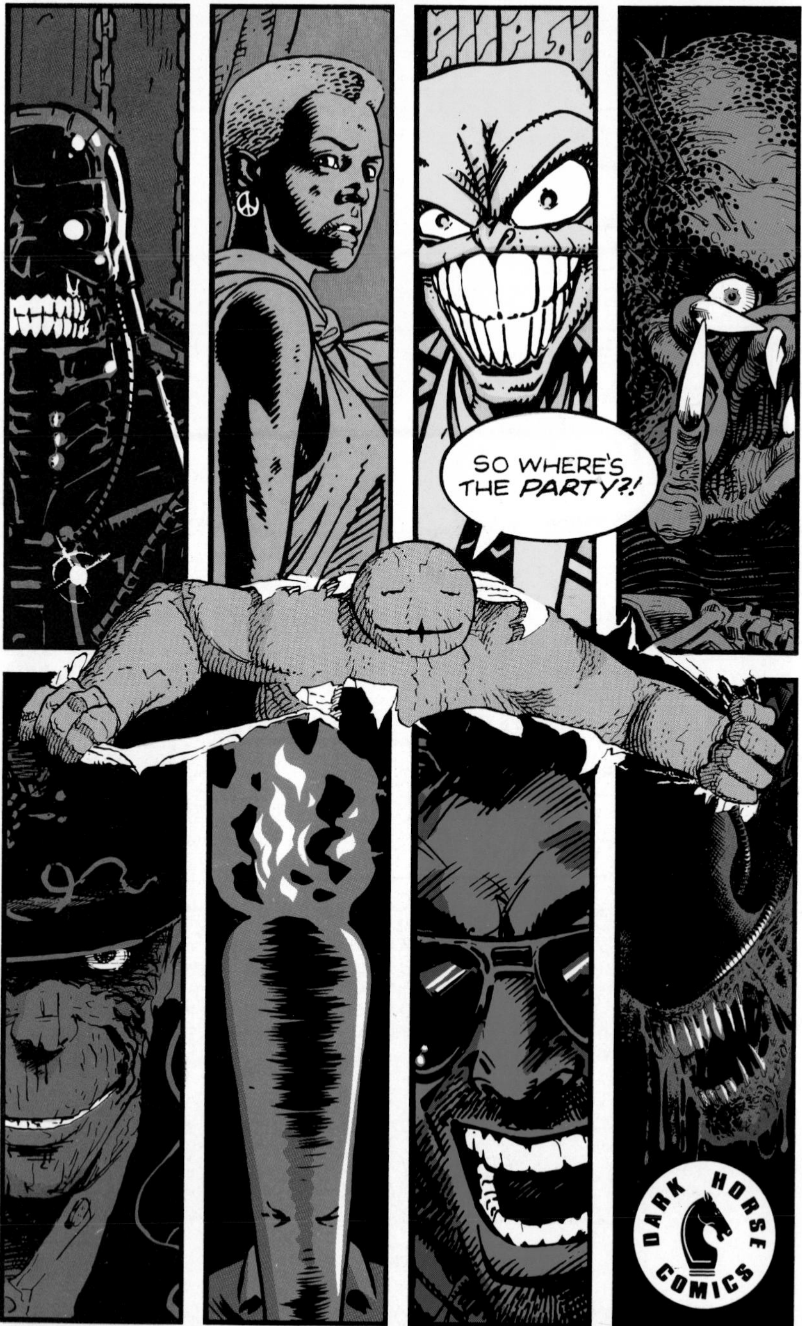
SO WHERE'S THE PARTY?!
DARK HORSE COMICS

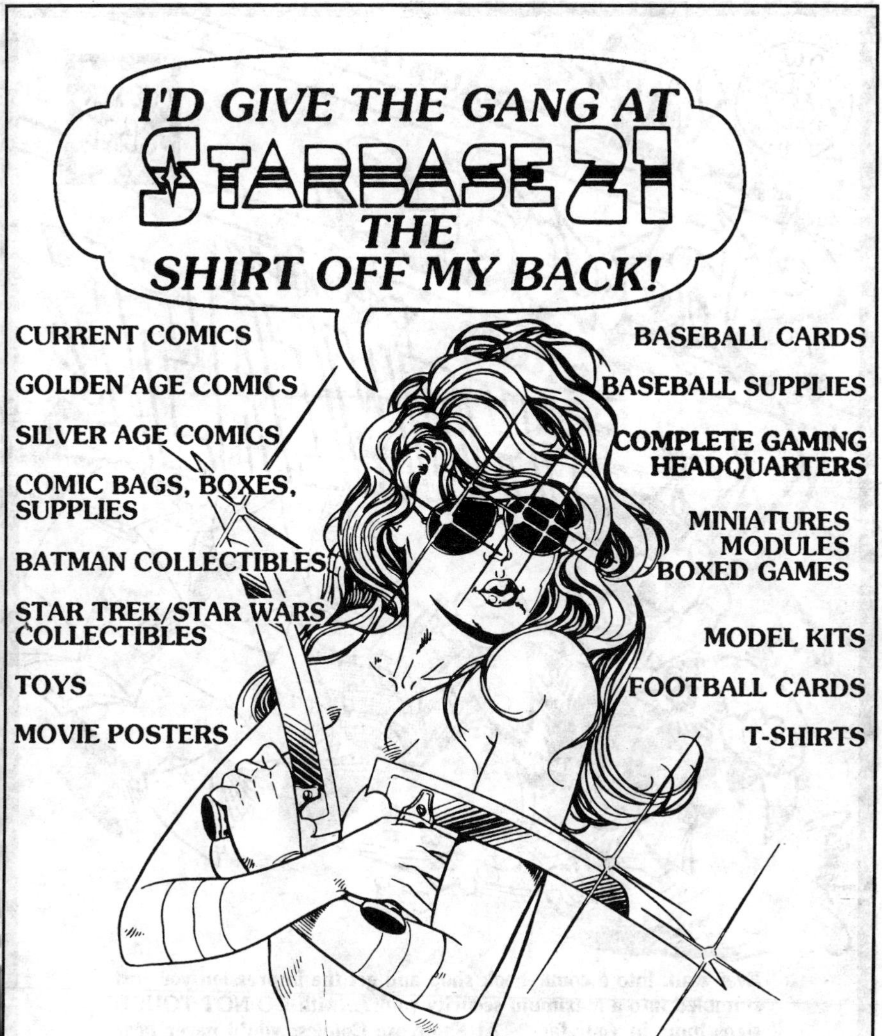

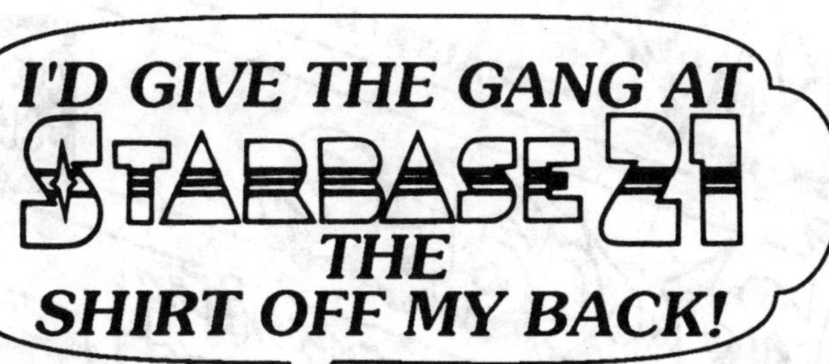

I'D GIVE THE GANG AT STARBASE 21 THE SHIRT OFF MY BACK!
CURRENT COMICS
GOLDEN AGE COMICS
SILVER AGE COMICS
COMIC BAGS, BOXES, SUPPLIES
BATMAN COLLECTIBLES
STAR TREK/STAR WARS COLLECTIBLES
TOYS
MOVIE POSTERS
BASEBALL CARDS
BASEBALL SUPPLIES
COMPLETE GAMING HEADQUARTERS
MINIATURES
MODULES
BOXED GAMES
MODEL KITS
FOOTBALL CARDS
T-SHIRTS
© TM R. A. JONES
OKLAHOMA'S LARGEST COMIC STORE!
STARBASE 21
2130 S. SHERIDAN RD.
TULSA, OK 74129 (918) 838-3388
Send 50¢ for current catalog. All inquiries answered.

HIGH
QUALITY
COMICS
*OVER 200,000 COMICS FOR COLLECTORS
*THOUSANDS OF HOT SILVER AGE COMICS
IN HIGH TO MEDIUM GRADES
* A HUGE INVENTORY OF RECENT ('75-'90)
COMICS
* BUYING - SELLING - TRADING ! !
* SEND $ 1.00 FOR OUR GIANT CATALOG
*SEND YOUR WANT LIST W/S.A.S.E. FOR
REPLIES
*BUYING COLLECTIONS - LARGE & SMALL
OLD & NEW
PAYING TOP PRICES ! ! ! !
WRITE OR CALL:
(619) 943-0367
HIGH QUALITY
COMICS
1106 2nd St.
SUITE 110
ENCINITAS, CA
92024

# ED KALB

## 1353 S. Los Alamos, Mesa, AZ 85204

*"SERVING COLLECTORS WORLDWIDE SINCE 1967"*

**HOW TO ORDER** - Simply list on any sheet of paper what you would like. Add $2.25 for postage. Print your name and address clearly. Payment with order please. All orders are securely packaged and sent out promptly. Quality material and fast dependable service are guaranteed. All items listed are returnable for refund or exchange - no explanation necessary.

**CONDITION** - Fine to Mint. 90% Near Mint to Mint. We send the best quality on hand - we're **looking for satisfied customers**.

Alternate choices are greatly appreciated, but not a must. Your alternate selections are used **only** when your first choice is out of stock. Refunds are sent when an item is out of stock. Please note if you prefer credit vouchers.

**POSTAGE** - Please add $2.25 to all orders to help with postage. All orders are insured. Overseas customers are appreciated. Overseas please add extra for postage and specify air or surface delivery. All unused postage (overseas) shall be reimbursed.

**10% discount** - To qualify for your 10% discount simply include a list of alternate choices that equal or exceed the value of your original order. All items qualify for discount except those with value of $15.00 or more. Deduct your 10% discount before adding postage (see postage). All prices are per item. All items listed are original First Printings. This ad will be honored thru March 31, 1992 (Note: This is a Mail Order only business).

***-FAST SAME DAY SERVICE ON ALL YOUR ORDERS AND INQUIRIES-***

The following is a sample listing of our inventory. For our complete sales catalog please send $1.00. Catalog will be mailed free with any order.

**ACTION COMICS**
367-376,393-413 . . 4.00
414-450 . . . . . . . . 2.50
451-599 . . . . . . . . 1.50

**ACTION COMICS WEEKLY**
601-649,up . . . . . 2.00

**ADVENTURE COMICS**
362-380 . . . . . . . . 5.00
381-441,459-466 . . 4.00
442-458 . . . . . . . . 2.00
467-490 . . . . . . . . 1.50

**ALL STAR**
58 . . . . . . . . . . . 4.00
59-74 . . . . . . . . . 2.50

**ALL STAR SQUADRON**
1,25,26,47,50 . . . . 4.00
2-24 . . . . . . . . . . 2.00
27-67 . . . . . . . . . 1.50

**ALPHA FLIGHT**
1 . . . . . . . . . . . . 5.00
2-12 . . . . . . . . . . 2.00
13,17,34,52,53 . . . 3.00
14-90, up . . . . . . . 1.50

**AMAZING ADVENTURES**
(1970)
1,5-8,18 . . . . . . . 6.00
2-17 . . . . . . . . . . 4.50
19-39 . . . . . . . . . 2.00

**ANIMAL MAN**
15-up . . . . . . . . . 2.00

**ASTONISHING TALES**
(1970)
1-24 . . . . . . . . . . 4.50
26-36 . . . . . . . . . 2.50

**THE AVENGERS**
113-138 . . . . . . . . 4.50
139-150 . . . . . . . . 4.00
151-163,167-180 . . 2.50
164-166 . . . . . . . . 4.50
181-191,200 . . . . . 3.00
192-199,201-250 . . 1.50
251-325,up . . . . . . 1.00
Annual 8-20, up . . 2.50

**AVENGERS SPOTLIGHT**
21-up . . . . . . . . . 1.00

**AVENGERS WEST COAST**
48-up . . . . . . . . . 1.00

**BATMAN**
401-403,411-416,
421-425 . . . . . . . . 2.00
405-410 . . . . . . . . 4.00
427,428 . . . . . . . 20.00
429 . . . . . . . . . . . 8.00
430-436 . . . . . . . . 3.00
437-460, up . . . . . 1.50

**BATMAN & THE OUTSIDERS**, 1 . . . . . . 4.00
2-32 . . . . . . . . . . 1.50

**BIG LITTLE BOOKS**
. . . . . . . . please write

**BLAZING COMBAT**
(magazine)
2-4 . . . . . . . . . . . 7.50

**CAPTAIN AMERICA**
120-139 . . . . . . . . 6.00
140-149 . . . . . . . . 5.00
150-159 . . . . . . . . 4.50
160-171,176-180 . . 2.50
172-175 . . . . . . . . 6.00
181-240 . . . . . . . . 2.00
242-246,256-331 . . 1.50
247-255 . . . . . . . . 3.00
332-334 . . . . . . . . 4.00
335-339 . . . . . . . . 2.00
340-380, up . . . . . 1.00
Annual 3-7,9-up . . 2.50

**CAPTAIN MARVEL**
(1968)
3-16,18-24 . . . . . . 5.00
17 . . . . . . . . . . . 7.50
25 . . . . . . . . . . 12.00
26-34,36 . . . . . . . 4.00
35,37-62 . . . . . . . 2.00

**CHALLENGERS OF THE UNKNOWN**
40-47,49-60 . . . . . 6.00
61-73 . . . . . . . . . 5.00

**CHAMPIONS** (1975)
1,17 . . . . . . . . . . 5.00
2-16 . . . . . . . . . . 2.50

**CLASSICS ILLUSTRATED**
. . . . . . . . please write

**CONAN THE BARBARIAN**
1 . . . . . . . . . . . 65.00
2 . . . . . . . . . . . 25.00
3 . . . . . . . . . . . 30.00
4,5 . . . . . . . . . . 20.00
12,13,16 . . . . . . 10.00
6-11,14,15,23 . . . 15.00
17-22,24,25 . . . . . 7.50
26-29,37 . . . . . . . 5.00
30-36,38-50 . . . . . 4.50
51-69 . . . . . . . . . 3.00
70-100 . . . . . . . . . 2.00
101-150 . . . . . . . . 1.50
151-240, up . . . . . 1.00
King Size/Annual
1 . . . . . . . . . . . . 8.00
2-13, up . . . . . . . 2.50
Giant-Size 1-5 . . . . 5.00

**CONAN THE KING/KING CONAN**
1 . . . . . . . . . . . . 5.00
2-65, up . . . . . . . 2.00

**CREEPY** (mag.)
1 . . . . . . . . . . . 15.00
2-17,19 . . . . . . . . 7.50
20,23-28,30,31,33,35
. . . . . . . . . . . . . 5.00
81-145 . . . . . . . . . 3.00

**CRISIS ON INFINITE EARTHS**, 1-12 . . . 2.50

**DAREDEVIL**
101-109 . . . . . . . . 3.50
110-119 . . . . . . . . 2.50
120-157 . . . . . . . . 2.00
165-167,171-181 . . 4.00
226,227,241,248,249,
252,257,259,260 . . 4.00
228-290, up . . . . . 1.00

**DAZZLER**
1,2,38 . . . . . . . . . 4.00
3-37,39-42 . . . . . . 1.50

**DELL COMICS**
. . . . . . . . please write

**DC COMICS PRESENTS**
1,13,41,44,72 . . . . 4.00
2-12,14-25,27-40 . . 2.00
26 . . . . . . . . . . 15.00
42,43,45-71,73-97 . 1.50

**DEFENDERS** (1972)
1 . . . . . . . . . . . 25.00
2-10 . . . . . . . . . . 6.00
11-19 . . . . . . . . . 4.00
20-29 . . . . . . . . . 3.00
30-54 . . . . . . . . . 2.00
55-151 . . . . . . . . . 1.50
100,125,150,152 . . 2.50
Giant Size 1-5 . . . . 4.50
Annual 1 . . . . . . . 3.00

**DETECTIVE**
484-499,501-525 . . 2.50
527-573 . . . . . . . . 2.50
579-597,599 . . . . . 2.00
598 . . . . . . . . . . . 7.50
600 . . . . . . . . . . . 4.00
601-625, up . . . . . 1.50

**DOC SAVAGE** (1972)
1-8, Giant 1 . . . . . 3.00

**DOC SAVAGE**-Bantam Paperbacks/Pulps
. . . . . . . . please write

**DOCTOR SOLAR**
(Gold Key)
2-31 . . . . . . . . . . 4.50

**DOCTOR STRANGE**
(1974), 1 . . . . . . 10.00
2-9 . . . . . . . . . . . 4.00
10-39 . . . . . . . . . 2.00
40-81 . . . . . . . . . 1.50

**DOOM PATROL** (1987)
1 . . . . . . . . . . . . 4.00
2-18 . . . . . . . . . . 1.50

**EERIE** (Magazine)
2,4-8,10-12 . . . . . 7.50
14-29,32,33,37 . . . 5.00
82-139 . . . . . . . . . 3.00

**ELEKTRA ASSASSIN**
1-8 . . . . . . . . . . . 2.50

**ELEKTRA SAGA**
1-4 . . . . . . . . . . . 4.00

**EXCALIBUR**
1 One shot . . . . . . 8.00
1 . . . . . . . . . . . . 6.00
2-5 . . . . . . . . . . . 3.50
6-30, up . . . . . . . 1.75

**FANTASTIC FOUR**
104-111,113-120 . . 5.50
121-123 . . . . . . . . 8.00
124-138 . . . . . . . . 4.50
139-150 . . . . . . . . 4.00
151-159 . . . . . . . . 2.50
160-200 . . . . . . . . 2.00
201-231 . . . . . . . . 1.50
232-250 . . . . . . . . 2.00
251-269 . . . . . . . . 1.50
270-349, up . . . . . 1.00
Annual 4 . . . . . . 15.00
7-9 . . . . . . . . . . . 6.00
12-24 . . . . . . . . . 2.50
Vs. X-Men . . . . . . 2.50

**FANTASY MASTERPIECES** (1966)
2-11 . . . . . . . . . . 6.00

**FIRESTAR**
1-4 . . . . . . . . . . . 2.00

**FLASH**
220-239 . . . . . . . . 4.00
240-276 . . . . . . . . 2.00
277-350 . . . . . . . . 1.50

**FLASH** (1987)
1 . . . . . . . . . . . . 7.50
2-10 . . . . . . . . . . 2.00
11-up . . . . . . . . . 1.00

**FLASH GORDON**
(Gold Key/Whitman)
19-37 . . . . . . . . . 4.00

**FOREVER PEOPLE**
(1971)
1 . . . . . . . . . . . . 7.50
2-11 . . . . . . . . . . 4.50

**FURY OF FIRESTORM**
1 . . . . . . . . . . . . 4.00
2-90, up . . . . . . . 1.00

**GARGOYLE**
1-4 . . . . . . . . . . . 2.00

**GHOST RIDER**
1 . . . . . . . . . . . 18.00
2-10,20 . . . . . . . . 5.00
11-19 . . . . . . . . . 4.00
21-81 . . . . . . . . . 2.00

**GHOST RIDER** (1990)
1 . . . . . . . . . . . . 6.00
2-4 . . . . . . . . . . . 3.00
5,6 . . . . . . . . . . . 4.00
7-up . . . . . . . . . . 1.50

**G-8 AND HIS BATTLE ACES**
1 . . . . . . . . . . . 15.00

**G.I. JOE**
1 . . . . . . . . . . . 20.00
2 . . . . . . . . . . . 30.00
3-12 . . . . . . . . . . 8.00
13-27 . . . . . . . . . 6.00
28-50 . . . . . . . . . 2.00
51-99, up . . . . . . . 1.00

**GODZILLA** (1977)
1 . . . . . . . . . . . . 4.50
2-24 . . . . . . . . . . 2.00

**GOLD KEY COMICS**
. . . . . . . . please write

**GREEN ARROW** ('88)
2-35, up . . . . . . . 1.50

**GREEN LANTERN**
77-89 . . . . . . . . 12.00
90-150 . . . . . . . . . 2.00
151-224 . . . . . . . . 1.00

**HAWKEYE** (1983)
1-4 . . . . . . . . . . . 2.00

**HOWARD THE DUCK**
1 . . . . . . . . . . . . 9.00
2 . . . . . . . . . . . . 4.00
3-19 . . . . . . . . . . 3.00
20-33 . . . . . . . . . 2.00

**ICEMAN**, 1-4 . . . . 2.50

**INFINITY INC.**
1,14,50 . . . . . . . . 4.00
2-13,15-49,51-53 . 2.00

**INCREDIBLE HULK**
123-141 . . . . . . . . 6.00
142-162,172,176-178,
200 . . . . . . . . . . . 4.50
163-171,173-175 . . 3.00
179,183-199,201-219
. . . . . . . . . . . . . 2.00
180-182 . . . . . . . write
220-260 . . . . . . . . 1.50
261-313,315-323,325
-329,347-385, up . . 1.00
Special/Annual 3,5-16,
up . . . . . . . . . . . 2.50

**INVADERS** (1975)
1 . . . . . . . . . . . . 7.50
2-9 . . . . . . . . . . . 3.00
10-41 . . . . . . . . . 2.00
Annual 1, . . . . . . . 4.00

**IRON FIST**
1 . . . . . . . . . . . . 7.50
2-13 . . . . . . . . . . 3.00

**IRON MAN**
72-79 . . . . . . . . . 4.00
80-99 . . . . . . . . . 3.00
101-128 . . . . . . . . 2.50
129-168 . . . . . . . . 1.50
169,170,200 . . . . . 4.00
171-199,201-224 . . 1.00

## Ed Kalb, page 2 (For Sale)

233-260, up .... 1.00
Annual/King Size
4-12, up .... 2.50
**JIMMY OLSEN**
91-94,96-98,101-103,
105 .... 4.50
107-112,114-121,123-
130,132-150 .... 4.00
151-163 .... 2.50
**JUSTICE**, 1-45,up 1.50
**JUSTICE LEAGUE OF AMERICA**
117-160 .... 2.50
161-200 .... 2.00
201-261 .... 1.50
**JUSTICE LEAGUE** (1987), 1 .... 8.00
2 .... 6.00
3 .... 4.00
4-10 .... 2.50
11-45, up .... 1.00
**KITTY PRYDE & WOLVERINE**
1-6 .... 3.00
**KORAK** (Gold Key)
12-45 .... 4.00
**LEGENDS OF THE DARK KNIGHT**
1 .... 4.00
2-4 .... 2.50
5-up .... 1.50
**LEGION OF SUPER-HEROES**, 259,285-290,
294,300 .... 3.00
260-284 .... 2.00
291-293,295-299,301-
313 .... 1.50
314-354 .... 1.00
**LEGION OF SUPER HEROES** (1984)
1, 45,50,63 .... 4.00
2-36,39-44,46-49,51-
62, .... 2.00
**LOIS LANE**
51-67,69-76 .... 5.00
78-85,87-94,96-103,
105-112,114-123 .. 4.50
124-137 .... 2.50
**LOONEY TUNES**
.... please write
**MAD** (Magazine)
101-117 .... 6.00
119-150 .... 4.00
**MAGIC** 1-4 .... 2.00
**MAN OF STEEL**
1-6 .... 2.00
**MARVEL CLASSICS**
1-36 .... 2.00
**MARVEL COMICS PRESENTS** 1-2 ... 4.00
3-65, up .... 1.25
**MARVEL FANFARE**
1,2 .... 6.00
3,4 .... 4.00
5-60, up .... 1.50
**MARVEL PREMIERE**
1-4,15,25 .... 6.00
5-14,16-24 .... 4.00
26-61 .... 2.00
**MARVEL PRESENTS** (1975) 1,2 .... 2.50
3-12 .... 3.00
**MARVEL SPOTLIGHT** (1971), 1-4,28,29 .. 5.00
6-11 .... 6.50
12-27,30-33 .... 2.00
**MARVEL TALES**
4-10 .... 6.00
11-33 .... 4.50
34-100 .... 1.50
**MARVEL TEAM UP**
2,3,5-10 .... 6.00
4 .... 10.00
11-19 .... 4.50
20-29 .... 3.00
30-52,54-70,75,79 2.50
53 .... 7.50
71-74,76-78,80-88,90-
116 .... 1.50
89,100,117,150 .. 4.00
118-149 .... 1.50
Annual 1 .... 10.00
2-7 .... 2.50

**MARVEL TWO IN ONE**
1 .... 10.00
2-10 .... 4.00
11-100 .... 1.50
Annual 1,3-7 .... 2.50
2 .... 6.00
**MARVEL UNIVERSE** (1983), 1-15 .... 2.50
**MARVEL UNIVERSE** (1985), 1-20 .... 2.50
**MASTER OF KUNG FU**
15 .... 15.00
16-29 .... 4.00
30-39 .... 3.00
40-50 .... 2.50
51-125 .... 1.50
**MEPHISTO VS FOUR HEROES**, 1-4 .... 2.50
**MICRONAUTS** (1979)
1,37,38 .... 4.00
2-36,39-59 .... 1.50
**MIGHTY MARVEL WESTERN**, 1-14 .... 4.00
**MISTER MIRACLE** (1971), 1 .... 7.50
2-8 .... 4.50
9-25 .... 3.00
**MONSTER TIMES**
all issues .... 4.00
**MOON KNIGHT** (1980)
1 .... 5.00
2-38 .... 1.50
**MOVIE COMICS**
.... please write
**MS. MARVEL** 1 .. 5.00
2-23 .... 2.00
**NEW GODS** (1971)
1 .... 7.50
2-11 .... 4.50
12-19 .... 3.00
**NEW MUTANTS**
1 .... 6.00
2-17 .... 2.50
18-50,85-up .... 1.50
51-84 .... 1.00
Annual 1-5, up .... 2.50
**NEW TEEN TITANS**
1 .... 15.00
2-4 .... 6.00
5-10 .... 4.00
11-29 .... 2.00
30-91 .... 1.50
**NICK FURY VS SHIELD**, 1 .... 15.00
2 .... 8.00
3-6 .... 3.50
**NIGHTCRAWLER**
1-4 .... 2.50
**NOT BRAND ECHH**
1-8 .... 6.00
**NOVA**, 1 .... 5.00
2-25 .... 2.00
**OMEGA MEN** (1982)
1 .... 4.00
2,4-38 .... 2.00
**PHANTOM STR/GER** (1969) 2,3,5-19 ... 4.50
20-41 .... 2.00
**PHOENIX** (1984)
1 .... 6.00
**POWERMAN (Hero For Hire/Iron Fist)**
1 .... 7.50
2-10 .... 4.00
11-39 .... 2.50
40-50 .... 2.00
51-56,58-125 .... 1.00
57 .... 6.00
**POWER PACK**
1,19,27,46 .... 4.00
2-18,20-26,28-50, up
.... 1.50
**PUNISHER** (1987)
1 .... 8.00
2-8 .... 6.00
11-17 .... 4.50
18-29 .... 2.00
30-up .... 1.50
**PUNISHER WAR JOURNAL**
1,6 .... 7.50

2 .... 5.00
3-5,7-10 .... 4.50
11-25, up .... 2.00
**QUESTION**, 1 .... 4.00
2-36, Annual 1,2 .2.00
**RAGMAN** 1-5 .... 2.50
**RAWHIDE KID**
52-89 .... 3.00
**ROM**
1,17,18 .... 4.50
2-16,19-75 .... 1.50
**SAVAGE SWORD OF CONAN** (mag)
1 .... 25.00
2-5 .... 15.00
6-10 .... 12.00
11-19 .... 6.00
20-69 .... 4.00
70-119 .... 3.00
120-180, up .... 2.50
**SECRET ORIGINS** (1986), 1 .... 4.00
2-50, up .... 1.50
**SECRET WARS I**
1-3 .... 4.00
4-12 .... 2.50
**SECRET WARS II**
1-9 .... 2.00
**SGT. FURY**
40-61 .... 4.00
84-101 .... 3.00
**SHADOW** (1973)
1 .... 5.00
2-12 .... 4.00
**SHADOW** (1986)
1-4 .... 4.00
**SHADOW** (1987)
1 .... 4.00
2-19,Annual 1,2 .. 2.00
**SHADOW** Paperbacks
.... please write
**SHAZAM!** (1973)
1-7,9-11,18-35 .... 2.00
**SHE HULK** (1980)
1 .... 4.00
2-25 .... 1.50
1-up (1989) .... 1.50
**SILVER SURFER** ('87)
1 .... 4.00
2-40, up .... 1.50
**SOLO AVENGERS**
1 .... 4.00
2-20 .... 1.00
**SPECTACULAR SPIDER-MAN**
(Peter Parker)1 .. 25.00
2 .... 8.00
3-10 .... 4.50
11-26 .... 4.00
27,28,64 .... 10.00
29-39 .... 2.50
40-63,65-68, .... 2.00
71-80,84-99 .... 1.50
69,70,100 .... 4.50
81-83 .... 6.00
101-130,133-139 .. 1.00
131,132,140-143,158-
160 .... 4.00
144-157,161-up ... 1.00
Annual 1 .... 5.00
2-9, up .... 2.50
**SPECTRE** (1987)
1 .... 4.00
2-31, Annual 1 ... 1.50
**SPIDER-MAN** (Amaz.)
147-160 .... 4.50
163-179 .... 3.00
180-237,240-251 .. 2.50
252,253,284,285,289,
293,294 .... 5.00
254-283,286-288,290-
292,295-297 .... 2.00
326-332 .... 2.50
333-up .... 1.50
Annual 16-24,up .. 2.50
**SPIDER-MAN** (1990)
1 regular .... 3.00
1 silver .... 4.00
2 .... 2.50
3-up .... 2.00
silver bagged ... 20.00
regular bagged .. 10.00

**SPIDER-WOMAN**
1,37,38,50 .... 4.00
2-36,39-49 .... 1.50
**SQUADRON SUPREME**, 1-12 .. 1.50
**STAR WARS**
1 (30¢) .... 6.00
2-10 .... 4.00
11-44 .... 2.50
45-107 .... 1.50
**STRANGE ADVENTURES**
207-216 .... 7.50
**SUB-MARINER** (1968)
15-29,34,35 .... 5.00
30-33,36-39 .... 4.50
40-72 .... 2.50
**SUPERBOY**
119-128 .... 6.00
130-140 .... 5.00
141-210 .... 4.00
211-258 .... 2.00
80/100 pg. giants on
above .... 8.00
**SUPERGIRL** (1972)
1-10 .... 3.00
**SUPERMAN**
201-254 .... 4.00
255-299 .... 2.00
301-399,401-422 .. 1.50
424-465, up .... 1.00
**SUPERMAN** (1987)
1,9 .... 4.00
2-8,10-49,51-up ... 1.00
**SUPERMAN FAMILY**
164-176 .... 4.00
177-222 .... 2.50
**SUPERTEAM FAMILY**
164-176 .... 4.00
177-222 .... 2.50
**SUPER VILLAIN TEAM UP**, 1 .... 6.00
2-17 .... 2.50
**SWAMP THING** ('72)
1 .... 10.00
2-10 .... 4.50
11-24 .... 3.00
**SWAMP THING** ('82)
1,16-19 .... 3.00
2-15 .... 2.00
20,21 .... 15.00
22-25 .... 6.00
26-30 .... 4.00
31-40 .... 2.50
41-95, up .... 1.50
**TARZAN** (Gold Key)
170-206 .... 4.00
**TARZAN** (DC)
207-211,230-235 .. 4.00
212-229,236-258 .. 2.00
**THE THING** 1 .... 4.00
2-36 .... 1.50
**THOR**
190-192,194-199 .. 3.00
201-239 .... 2.00
240-336,338-352 .. 1.50
337 .... 5.00
353-430, up .... 1.00
Special/Annual
8-15, up .... 2.50
**TOMB OF DRACULA**
2-10 .... 4.50
11-69 .... 2.00
**TV COMICS**
.... please write
**VIGILANTE** 1 .... 4.00
2-50, Annual1,2 .. 2.00
**VISION AND THE SCARLET WITCH**
1-4 (1982) .... 2.50
1-12 (1985) .... 2.00
**WALT DISNEY COMICS**
.... please write
**WANTED, THE WORLDS MOST DANGEROUS VILLIANS**
1-9 .... 4.50
**WARLOCK** (1972)
1 .... 6.00
2-15 .... 4.00
**WARLORD** 1 ... 12.00

2 .... 6.00
3-20 .... 4.50
21-40 .... 2.50
41-60 .... 1.50
61-133 .... 1.00
Annual 1-6 .... 2.50
**WATCHMEN**
1-12 .... 3.00
**WEB OF SPIDER-MAN**
1 .... 7.50
2,3 .... 4.00
4-10 .... 2.50
11-20 .... 2.00
21-28,30 .... 1.50
33-70, up .... 1.00
Annual 1-5, up .. 2.50
**WEIRD TALES** (pulps)
.... please write
**WEST COAST AVENGERS**
1-4 (1984) .... 3.00
1 (1985) .... 6.00
2-10 .... 2.50
11-47 .... 1.00
Annual 1-4 .... 2.50
**WHAT IF?** (1977)
1 .... 7.50
2-13,27,28 .... 4.50
14-26,29,30,32-47
.... 2.50
**WHAT IF?** (1988)
1-20, up .... 1.50
**WOLVERINE** (1982)
1 .... 14.00
2-4 .... 12.00
**WOLVERINE** (1987)
1 .... 7.50
2-5 .... 4.00
6-10 .... 3.00
11-30, up .... 2.00
**WONDER WOMAN**
170-200 .... 6.00
201-214 .... 4.50
215-239 .... 2.00
240-299,301-328 .. 1.50
**WONDER WOMAN** ('87) 1 .... 4.00
2-10 .... 1.50
11-50, up .... 1.00
**WORLD'S FINEST**
180-187,189-196,198-
212,223-228 .... 4.50
213-222 .... 2.50
229-243 .... 2.00
244-282,300 .... 2.50
283-299,301-323 .. 1.50
**X-FACTOR** 1 .... 6.00
2,3 .... 4.00
4-10 .... 2.50
11-23 .... 1.50
24-26 .... 3.00
27-60, up .... 1.00
Annual 1-5, up ... 2.50
**X-MEN**
96-99,102,108-111,120,
121 .... 20.00
100,101 .... 30.00
103-107 .... 14.00
112-119,130,137,139,
140 .... 12.00
122-129,131-136,138,
141,142 .... 8.50
143-170 .... 4.00
172-199,201-209 .. 2.50
214-224 .... 2.00
225-227 .... 4.00
228-275, up .... 1.50
Special/Annual 5-8,
11-15 .... 2.50
9,10 .... 4.50
**X-MEN AND ALPHA FLIGHT**, 1,2 .... 3.00
**X-MEN AND THE MICRONAUTS**
1-4 .... 2.00
**X-MEN VS THE AVENGERS**
1-4 .... 2.50

# NATIONAL SURVEY

## Purpose: to determine the feasibility of a computerized collector's marketplace to be organized Spring of this year.

The technology to offer collectors and dealers a computerized "electronic adzine" which can be accessed with **NO** long distance telephone charges and **NO** hourly connect charges is now available. Imagine: unlimited connect time for FREE! You would simply dial a local phone number (over 800 cities in USA and CANADA) and connect to our service - then you could spend as long as you like searching for issues for your collection, corresponding with "electronic pen pals", reading online market reports and articles, asking questions, posting buy, sell and trade notices(pre-screened dealers only), and all the other things that make collecting so enjoyable. You could even make online purchases from our pre-screened dealers or post your wantlist for dealers to search.

This technology is available, but is there enough demand for it? That is the purpose of this survey.

## BENEFITS OF COMPUTERIZED TRADING:

### For National Mail-Order Dealers:

- Instant response. Your lists are posted immediately - you can begin receiving orders the same day you post your list.
- Affordable advertising. No per page cost. Dealers will pay one low monthly fee for unlimited advertising.
- Have the ability to post literally their entire inventory for online access. Upload and download from your disk!
- Reach serious collectors - for less than the cost of maintaining and mailing catalogs. Collectors subscribing to this service will be serious and aggressive - willing to use the newest technologies in order to achieve an extra advantage. These are the people with whom you will want to do business.

### For Store Owners:

- Instantly replace those hot sellers by ordering online. We will be discussing online re-orders with the major Distributors. Communicate with other store owners nation-wide!
- Post "wanted to buy" notices to help your customers locate items that you do not have available
- Sell overstock or items for which you have no local market

### For Collectors:

- Imagine a daily electronic convention - and that is what you will have with Collectors Online
- Electronic pen pals
- Post your wantlist
- Online articles and discussions - the latest news from Marvel and DC, how to grade, timely information
- Online market reports and experts - ask the experts!
- Best of all - search our pre-screened dealers lists for items for your collection. We will allow only dealers which pass a comprehensive screening process. Our goal will be to make this service a safe haven for collectors. We will protect collectors from unscrupulous dealers by allowing only top-notch dealers to place "for sale" lists.
- Online auctions

## COSTS:

__Collectors:__ $10 or less monthly (tentative), no long distance, no hourly connect charges. How much do you spend each month calling mail-order dealers long distance?

__Store Owners:__ $15 - $25 monthly (tentative) , no long distance, no hourly connect charges

__National Mail-Order Dealers:__ ? Not determined as yet. What would it be worth to you to be able to maintain your entire inventory, online, available to a large group of serious buyers? PLEASE INQUIRE!

# PLEASE RESPOND IMMEDIATELY

## Computer-Linked Marketplace Survey (use add'tl sheets if desired)

Name:
Address:
City/State/Zip
Telephone:

Please circle one:
Collector
Store Owner
National Mail-Order Dealer

Computer Type:
Will you have a modem soon?
If you are a collector, what would you most like to see in an electronic service?

How often would you use the service?

Would the monthly cost mentioned above be within your budget, considering that there would be no long distance or access time charges?

**COMPLETE AND RETURN TO:**

***COLLECTORS ONLINE • P.O. Box 2512 • Chattanooga, TN 37409***

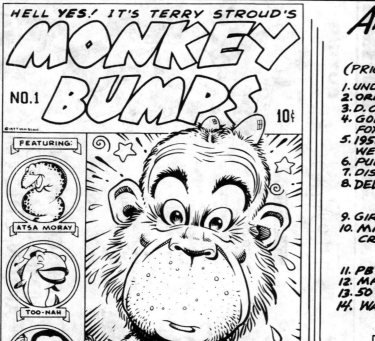

# HI DE HO COMICS & FANTASY

Buying & Selling Comic Books, Baseball Cards,
Underground Comix, Posters, Science Fiction & Fantasy

64 Windward Ave.
Venice, Calif. 90291
(213) 399-6206

525 Santa Monica Blvd
Santa Monica, Calif. 90401
(213) 394-2820 or 451-0463

Games • T-Shirts • Books • Original Art

Baseball Cards •

COMICS

Buy & Trade •

1630 SUPERIOR AVE.
COSTA MESA, CA 92627
(714) 631-3933

220 PIER AVE.
SANTA MONICA, CA 90405
(213) 396-7005

In Western New York People call,
**"THE COLLECTOR"**

Pulps, Golden and Silver Age, Gum Cards, VHS., Posters, Toys, Fanzines, Figures, Paperbacks, MONSTERS-HORROR-SCI FI-FANTASY Items dating back to 1861, thru. today. Overstock Sales Liquidator

**DON'T SPEND MORE, DON'T SELL LESS**
— Buy'n, Sell'n, Trade'n, Apprais'n —
WE WILL BUY WHOLE COLLECTIONS-
NOT JUST THE BEST PART
Write for **Newest Catalog** $2.00
125 Winspear, Buffalo, NY, 14214
Call for consultation
(716) 831-9272

# 20 - 30 % OFF EVERYTHING!

Newsletter that's not full of publisher hype, but honest opinions of what's good and what's not.

Fast, Accurate, Dependable & Friendly Service.

For full details see our full page ad.
(consult advertisers directory)

GOLDEN
APPLE

old & new comics
t-shirts ∘ toys
role-playing games
comic & cartoon related
merchandise
GEM
GEM Comics
156 N York Rd
Elmhurst, IL 60126
708/833-8787
COMICS

RELAX
WITH MARVEL® COMICS!
DON'T GET HUNG UP!
• NEW COMIC BOOKS FROM ALL COMPANIES AIR FREIGHTED IN ON THURSDAY AT 4:00 p.m.
• TEN (10%) PERCENT DISCOUNT ON CASH PURCHASES OVER $10.00 ON NEW COMICS ALWAYS
Copyright © 1990 Marvel Entertainment Group, Inc.
AVENGERS
AKIRA
WOLVERINE
QUASAR
Fantastic Four
★ FULL SUBSCRIPTION SERVICE
FOR NEW COMIC BOOKS, MAGAZINES
IN PERSON OR VIA MAIL
© Copyright 1988 Gustaveson
25 Years Experience
NINTH NEBULA
COMIC BOOK STORE
Franchises Available
Hours: Tues., Wed. 1-5
Thurs. 1-10, Fri. 12-6, Sat. 1-5
Other Hours Call
Information Hot Line Phone # For
Weekly Air Arrivals Of New Comics!
(818) 509-2901
11517 Burbank Blvd.
North Hollywood
Southern California 91601
Wanted Old 10¢
Silver Age Comics
CASH FOR OLD COMICS
BUY/SELL
GOLDEN &
SILVER AGE
COMICS
TM & © 1989 Marvel Entertainment Group, Inc. All rights reserved.
NINTH NEBULA
COMIC BOOK STORE

COMFILER-C

COMIC BOOK DATABASE & REPORT GENERATOR

POWERFUL MENU DRIVEN SYSTEM & EASY TO USE

DISPLAY & PRINT COLLECTION, INVESTMENT MARGIN AND WANT/BUY LISTS

SEARCH BY TITLE, ARTIST OR SPECIAL CHARACTER

PROGRAM AND REPORTS CUSTOMIZED WITH YOUR NAME OR BUSINESS

$35.00 + $5.00 S/H, CA RESIDENTS ADD 6.75% SALES TAX

***SIMAS PUBLISHING***

4195 CHINO HILLS PKWY. SUITE E-128, CHINO HILLS CA 91709

IBM™ COMPATIBLE WITH 640K OF RAM & 1 DOUBLE SIDED FLOPPY PLUS HARD DISK
SPECIFY DISK SIZE (3.5" - 720K OR 5.25" - 360K)

CHECK OR MONEY ORDER ONLY - ALLOW 3-4 WEEKS FOR DELIVERY

## 30% - 40% DISCOUNT ON NEW COMICS !!

**Let AT YOUR SERVICE SUBSCRIPTIONS be your one-stop mail order shop for all of your comic book & trading card needs! We offer:**

- 30 % discount on ALL new comics- Marvel, DC, as well as those hard to find Independent titles.
- Complimentary monthly Previews magazine & newsletter, along with an easy to use order form.
- Back Issues at competitive prices - Silver Age as well as the recent Hot Titles !.
- Expertly packed shipments to guarantee MINT condition of your order.
- Weekly, Bi-weekly or Monthly shipping available at a one low, flat rate of $3.50 per shipment.
- **40% discount on new comics when you join the At Your Service Investment Club !**
- A full line of preservation supplies at a discount.
- Trading cards, T-shirts, posters, gaming supplies & figurines, etc. - all at less than retail price.
- Friendly, Reliable and PERSONALIZED service.

new comics back issues games etc.

DON'T YOU DESERVE THE BEST? WE THINK YOU DO, SO CALL US TODAY!
Once you become a regular **AT YOUR SERVICE SUBSCRIPTIONS** customer, you will enjoy:

- Being able to use your Mastercard or Visa to purchase your comics.
- Phone calls returned within 24 hours, if we happen to be out..
- Excellent service, great savings, and best of all - No Hassles !

To be among the hundreds who have joined one of North Texas' fastest growing mail order services, call or write today and we will send you our free ordering packet ... all from your buddies at **AT YOUR SERVICE SUBSCRIPTIONS**

And don't forget to mention you saw this ad in Overstreet Price Guide # 21 !

AT YOUR
SERVICE SUBSCRIPTIONS
P.O. BOX 867434 PLANO, TEXAS 75086

Phone (214) 964-0766

1,000,000
COMIX

# GOOD GRIEF!

## It's Their 40th Anniversary!

*The Official® Price Guide to Peanuts® Collectibles* is the *first* guide ever to *Peanuts®* paraphernalia!

Experts and *Peanuts®* lovers FREDDI MARGOLIN and ANDREA PODLEY feature the wide range of collectibles of the lovable *Peanuts®* gang!

From advertising to Hallmark cards to music boxes to toys, and a special foreword by Charles M. Schulz!

## JOIN THE *PEANUTS®* GANG AND BUY THIS BOOK!

**HOUSE OF COLLECTIBLES**
**201 East 50th Street**
**New York, New York 10022**

Please send me *The Official® Price Guide to Peanuts® Collectibles,* 1st Ed. . . . 0-876-37809-2 . . . $9.95. I am enclosing $________________ (add $2.00 for the first book and 50¢ for each additional book to cover postage and handling). Send check or money order—no cash or C.O.D.'s, please. Prices and numbers are subject to change without notice.

Name ________________________________________

Address ______________________________________

City ________________ State _________ Zip Code _________

*Allow at least 4 weeks for delivery.*

100
100
100
100
EXCALIBUR
COMICS, CARDS & GAMES
2811 State Line Ave.
Texarkana, TX 75503
(903) 792-5767
9066 Mansfield Rd.
Shreveport, LA 71118
(318) 686-7076
★New Comics Weekly
★Golden Age
★Silver Age
★Big Little Books
★Toys
★Sports Cards
★Posters
★Role Playing Games
★War Games
★Star Trek Collectibles
★Star Wars Collectibles
★Collecting Supplies
FREE
Write to our Texas Store for either our Comics Catalog or our Star Trek/Star Wars Catalog.
FREE
FRANKLIN
ONE HUNDRED DOLLARS

THE TICK © + TM 1991 BEN EDLUND APES + RAD MAX © 1991 NEC

NEW ENGLAND
COMICS
NEC TAMPA!

# BIGGEST DISCOUNTS ON NEW COMICS

| | |
|---|---|
| **$1 - $50** | **32%** |
| **$50 - $100** | **37%** |
| **$100 - $500** | **40%** |
| **$500 up** | **42%** |

Discounts apply to retail prices on complete line of comics, B & W's, undergrounds, graphic novels, & more.

**FLAT SHIPPING CHARGE**

| | |
|---|---|
| $3.50 | Monthly |
| $7.00 | Bi-weekly |
| $14.00 | Weekly |

Send for monthly catalogue:

**DAVE'S COMICS**
1240 Harvard
Salt Lake City, UT 84105

# COMICS BY MAIL

MARVELS 1962-1970 ALWAYS IN STOCK

*Phone Credit Cards Accepted*
*Books Shipped Immediately!*

**SPARKLE CITY COMICS**
P.O. Box 67 Sewell, NJ 08080
Toll Free 800-284-6555 To Buy Comics
609-881-1174 For Free Catalog Info

## To keep up with the latest price trends in the comic book market...

# ORDER
# OVERSTREET'S PRICE UPDATE

Published bi-monthly between June & February

**Featuring:**

★ The Latest Price Reports From Across The Country.
★ Illustrated Throughout.
★ Full Color Cover.
★ "What's Hot & What's Not" Reports.

Release dates in June, August, October, December and February.

Send $3.95 plus $1.00 for airmail postage for the latest Update.

Or order all five issues for $22.00.

**SEND TO:**

**OVERSTREET PUBLICATIONS, INC.**
**780 Hunt Cliff Dr. NW**
**Cleveland, TN 37311**

LeaF®
PHIL.A
G. DUFNER

PHILIP M. LEVINE AND SONS
RARE AND ESOTERIC BOOKS
P.O. BOX 246, THREE BRIDGES, N.J. 08887
(908) 788-0532
SEND US ALL OF YOUR
OLD COMIC BOOKS TODAY
We will make you an immediate cash offer. If we don't buy your books, we will pay the postage both ways. We are always buying and selling comics, giveaway comics, big little books, paperbacks, true crime paperbacks, Seduction of the Innocent and related censorship material, radio premiums, early crime magazines, "Cardboard Age" comics, antediluvian comics, pulps, Catechetical Guild comics and related material, Golden Age comics, Silver Age comics, old toys, and old Japanese toys. We do not publish a selling list. Send us your want lists.
YOU CAN COME AND SEE US
AT ALL NEW YORK AREA
"CREATION" COMIC SHOWS.
Don't forget to send us your books. We have been buying and selling comic books for 31 years.
CATALOG
SUPER DAVID SUPER JEFFREY
JIM BALENT

# CLASSIFIED ADVERTISING

FREE COMIC CATALOG of over 10,000 silver & golden age comic books. James Haack, Box 650, Milwaukee, WI 53201. Strict grading, prompt service.

COMIC BOOKS WANTED 1933-1968
DC, TIMELY, FAWCETTS, QUALITY, MLJ, MARVELS, FICTION HOUSE, EC, DISNEY, HORROR, WESTERNS, AND TV/MOVIE. PAYING 50% TO 150%. (313) 533-2731, HARLEY YEE, PO BOX 19578, DETROIT, MI 48219-0578

COMIC SOFTWARE!
Organize your comics with COMIC BOOK II.
(see full page ad in front of guide)
Send $36.95 to: Data Loggers, PO Box 434
Burlington, IA 52601

Selling my pre-'62 "10¢" comics! Uncle Scrooge, D. Duck, C&S, Supermans, ½-size-March of Comics. List: Tom Sheridan 845 5th San Rafael CA 94901

ORIGINAL ART WANTED: HIGHEST PRICES PAID FOR QUALITY PIECES. TOP WANTS: GOLDEN AND SILVER AGE COVERS, SPLASHES, AND GOOD INTERIORS. ALSO LOOKING FOR ADAMS, WRIGHTSON, SMITH, TOTH, GOLDEN, AND MANY OTHERS. SCOTT DUNBIER 212-666-0982 OR (FAX) 212-662-8732

COLLECTOR CARDS Comic Book Indexing System shows what you need, have & their conditions. One card per title, 3X5 pocket-sized, easy instructions. Satisfaction guaranteed, our 18th year. 50/$1.75, 100/$3.00, 200/$5.50, 400/$10.50, 600/$14.75, 800/$18.00, postage & handling 1¢ per card ($4.00 maximum). SASE for quantity discounts or sample. VISIONS, Box 28283-091, Tempe, AZ 85285-8283.

QUALITY COMICS at reasonable prices. We specialize in Hi grade SILVER and select Gold, hot books. Send for free catalog. Buy-Sell-Trade. PAYING 150% GUIDE for Flash 175, Superman 199, W. Finest 198-9. ALL SELECT COMICS, c/o Mike Richards, Box 455, Dorchester, MA 02122. (617) 436-7995

Super Power, Secret War figures, Star Trek & Star Wars toys etc. Send want list to: T&U, 5460 Brandt Pike, Huber Hts., OH 45424. 513-233-6535.

Buying: Character watches & clocks (pre-1975), Marx playsets, Character board games (pre-1972), Tin robots & Space toys, Radio & Cereal premiums (1920's-1970's), David Welch, RR2 Box 233, Murphysboro, IL 62966

SEND TO: E.K. WONG, 4282 10th Ave., Port Alberni, BC

ROCKETRY COLLECTABLES: world's largest selection. Out-of-production model rocketry, plastic kits, memorabilia, literature, plans. Catalog $1. ACME ROCKET COMPANY, Box 28283-091, Tempe, AZ 85285.

WANTED! Anything by or about HOWARD CHAYKIN, especially obscure and unusual material and not just comic books. Also wanted: syndicated work by FRAZETTA, and live tapes and printed collectibles relating to RANDY CALIFORNIA/SPIRIT. Write me: TIM BARNES, 103 Tredworth Road, Gloucester, Glos. GL1 4QU ENGLAND. Third Glorious Year!

FREE Comic Catalogue. LOW PRICES. Golden-Silver Age, Marvels, DCs, Disneys, All Kinds. I like to TRADE too. Money Back Guarantee. SPECIAL BONUS WITH PURCHASE. Send an EXTRA 1st Class Stamp to: DAVE YARUSS, 7916 BLUE LAKE DR., SAN DIEGO, CALIF. 92119. WANTED: Disney Animation Art.

COMICS-Thousands of Marvels, DCs & others, late 70s to present! Many Superhero role playing games available as well! For list, send stamp to: A. Christians, 75 Wynford Heights Cres. Apt #1507, Don Mills, Ont. Canada M3C 3H9

PEZ! PEZ! PEZ! Paying over $150 for certain items (premiums, ads, dispensers, anything) DAVID WELCH, RR2 BOX 233, Murphysboro, IL 62966

SPECIAL SALE!!! KEY/HOT ISSUES, TOP ARTISTS!! MARVEL, DC, DISNEY, GOLD, SILVER, MORE!! ALL BARGAIN PRICED AS LOW AS 10¢ EACH!! TRADES (FOR COMICS, GAMES, CARDS ETC.) WELCOMED!!! SEND $2 + SASE FOR CATALOG #11 TODAY!!! HM LEVY, BOX 197-S, EAST MEADOW, NY 11554.

Japanese video & Manga available
Send SASE (long) for catalog
T&U, 5460 Brandt Pike, Dayton OH 45424
513-233-6535

NEWER COMICS at 50% O.P.G. (GA 75% & up). Send a SASE plus 25¢ per list. Request lists desired. Comic Book • BLB • N.P.Comic strip • Pulp • Paperbacks • Movie/TV Items • Old LIFE, LOOK, POST, Misc. Magazines. Above also bought. GLENN'S BOOKS, 3500 Manila Dr., Westerville OH 43081

PAYING $1800+ for Aurora Godzilla Go-Cart model kit; also buying Aurora Comic, monster, TV & Sci-Fi kits; D. Welch, RR2 BOX233, Murphysboro IL 62966

COLLECTOR'S CLASSIFIED, BOX 347A, HOLBROOK, MASS. 02343. ADVERTISE COMICS, CARDS, COINS, STAMPS, ALL COLLECTIBLES. 4 ISSUES (USA) $1.00. SAMPLE 25¢. FREE SUBSCRIBER ADS. PUBLISHED MONTHLY SINCE 1975.

The axmen will cut U a deal. We BUY/SELL. 201-79-AXMEN. COMICBOOK HOTLINE, INC., P.O. BOX 8230, NORTH BERGEN, NJ 07047 SASE FOR LISTS.

FIGURES (PVC). Comic/Cartoon Stars. Free Saleslist. Wholesale too. Mr. A.H.M. Kohne, Bosschestraat I80, NL-2587 HJ Den Haag, Holland.

## COLLECTIBLE INVESTMENT AGENT
## AKA GARY CODDINGTON

### BUYING • SELLING • TRADING • CONSIGNMENT

I have been a devoted serious collector of Comics, Toys and Comic Art for over three decades. I have bought and sold at auctions, conventions, shows and exhibits. I now hope to help and advise my fellow collectors and also investors in the marketplace to find that one unique collectible, that toy collector's ultimate dream, or the art collector's No. 1 acquisition!

### MY SERVICE IS NOT FOR EVERYBODY!!!

Only for the: Completist, Connoisseur, Conditionist, Perfectionist, Hard-core or "One of a Kind" Collector or Investor.

This is a HOBBY for you and me not a BUSINESS, so I am hoping to use my knowledge gained through experience to work for the most serious, advanced and discriminating Collectors and Investors!

Specializing in: Rare Golden and Silver Age Comics, Comic Book Page Art, Dailies, Sundays, Animations Cels from all major studios and Comic Character Paintings, Comic Character Toys and related memorabilia!

**Gary Coddington**
**(818) 791-1621**

P.O. Box 5064
Pasadena, Calif. 91117

# WANTED BY COLLECTOR:

**Memorabilia**

™ **Collectables**

**1933 - 1980**

©DC Comics Inc. 1940

**All domestic and foreign Toys, Games, Buttons, Rings, Watches, Puzzles, Statues, Original Art, Paper Items, Premiums, Coloring Books and any other rare, unusual or unique items pertaining to SUPERMAN!**

**Other comic character toys and comics bought also!!**

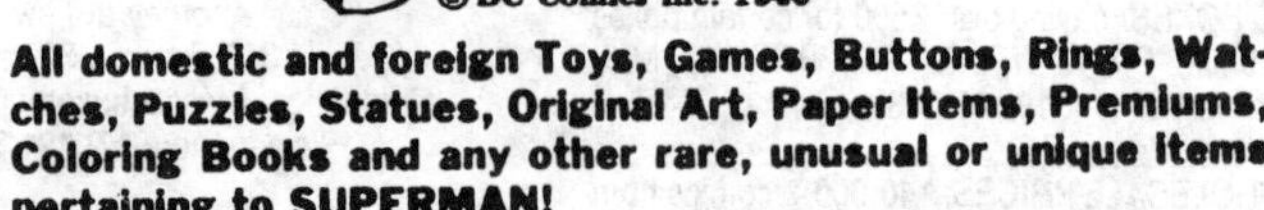

**The Overstreet Price Guide Superman Advisor** • **Gary Coddington P.O. Box 5064 Pasadena, CA 91117** • **World's Foremost Superman Collector & Authority**

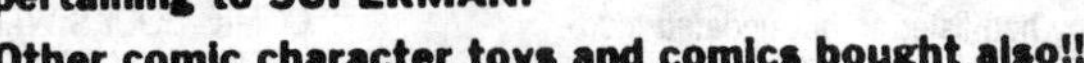

**Original Artwork Wanted**

**Representative works of comic art unrelated to Superman also wanted! From A to Z — Horror, Science Fiction, Humor, Adventure, Good Girl, Animal, Super Hero. All professional artist work wanted.**

***LONG BEACH BOOKS***